FROMMER'S

COMPREHENSIVE TRAVEL GUIDE

U.S.A.

4ᵀᴴ EDITION

by Edouard De Blaye
Edited by Nicole De Blaye
Assisted by Ted Brewer

MACMILLAN • USA

Macmillan Travel

A Prentice Hall Macmillan Company
15 Columbus Circle
New York, NY 10023

Original French edition copyright © 1988 by Edouard De Blaye

English translation copyright © 1989, 1991, 1993, 1995 by Simon & Schuster Inc.
Introduction copyright © 1989, 1991, 1993, 1995 by Simon & Schuster Inc.

Translation by Maxwell R.D. Vos

ISBN 0-671-88502-2
ISSN 0899-2797

Design by Levavi & Levavi, Inc.
Maps by Geografix, Ortelius

Special Sales: Bulk purchases (10+ copies) of Frommer's Travel Guides are available to
corporations at special discounts. The Special Sales Department can produce custom
editions to be used as premiums and/or for sales promotion to suit individual needs.
Existing editions can be produced with custom cover imprints such as corporate logos. For
more information write to: Special Sales, Prentice Hall, 15 Columbus Circle, New York,
NY 10023.

Manufactured in the United States of America

CONTENTS

Maps

WHAT THE SYMBOLS MEAN

HOTELS

 Modest but acceptable, with a good price-to-quality ratio.

 A quality establishment, but with shortcomings in service or comfort.

 Worth a detour.

 Exceptional comfort or service, among the best in the U.S. Try to fit it into your trip.

One of the dozen best hotels in the country. Don't miss it.

RESTAURANTS

Modest but acceptable, with a good price-to-quality ratio.

A quality establishment, but with shortcomings in service or cuisine.

 Worth a detour.

 Exceptional standard in service or cuisine, among the best in the U.S. Try to fit it into your trip.

One of the dozen best restaurants in the country. Don't miss it.

BUILDINGS, MUSEUMS, OR NATURAL FEATURES

Interesting and worth a visit or at least a look.

Remarkable and should be seen.

A building, museum, or natural feature that should not be missed.

Unique of its kind, and worth a journey in itself.

CITIES OR AREAS

Interesting and worth a visit.

Remarkable and should be seen.

A city or area that should not be missed.

Exceptionally interesting, and worth a journey in itself.

OF SPECIAL INTEREST

Highly recommended as an unusual and worthwhile experience, of very special interest.

ABBREVIATIONS

Abbreviations in Hotel, Restaurant, and Attractions Listings

A/C	air-conditioned	min.	minutes
adj.	adjoining	M	moderate (price range)
AE	American Express (credit card)	Mon–Fri	Monday through Friday
apt(s)	apartment(s)	Mon–Sat	Monday through Saturday
B	budget (price range)		
CB	Carte Blanche (credit card)	nr.	near
DC	Diners Club (credit card)	rest(s).	restaurant(s)
dwntwn	downtown	resv.	reservations
E	expensive (price range)	rm(s)	room(s)
gar.	garage	r.t.	round trip
grdn(s)	garden(s)	svce	service
hols.	holidays	w.	with
hr.	hour(s)	V	VISA (credit card)
hrdrsr	hairdresser	VE	very expensive (price range)
I	inexpensive (price range)	vic.	vicinity
J&T	jacket and tie required	wknd(s)	weekend(s)
Jkt.	jacket required	ZIP	ZIP Code
MC	MasterCard (credit card)		

Abbreviations on the Road

Ave.	Avenue	NW	northwest
Blvd.	Boulevard	Pkwy.	Parkway
Dr.	Drive	Pl	place
E.	east	Rd.	Road
Expwy.	Expressway	r.t.	round-trip
Fwy.	Freeway	S.	south
Hwy.	Highway	SE	southeast
km	kilometers	SW	southwest
mi.	miles	Sq.	Square
N.	north	Tpke.	Turnpike
NE	northeast	W.	West

Hotel Rate and Restaurant Price Codes

VE	very expensive	I	inexpensive
E	expensive	B	budget
M	moderate		

INVITATION TO THE READERS

In researching this book, the authors have come across many wonderful establishments, the best of which are included here. Many of you will also come across appealing hotels, inns, restaurants, guesthouses, shops, and attractions. Please don't keep them to yourself. Share your experiences, especially if you want to comment on places that have been included in this edition that have changed for the worse. You can address your letters to:

Nicole De Blaye
Frommer's U.S.A.
c/o Macmillan Travel
15 Columbus Circle
New York, NY 10023

A DISCLAIMER

Readers are advised that prices fluctuate in the course of time, and travel information changes under the impact of the varied and volatile factors that affect the travel industry. Neither the author nor the publisher can be held responsible for the experiences of readers while traveling. Readers are invited to write to the publisher with ideas, comments, and suggestions for future editions.

SAFETY ADVISORY

Whenever you're traveling in an unfamiliar city or country, stay alert. Be aware of your immediate surroundings. Wear a moneybelt and keep a close eye on your possessions. Be particularly careful with cameras, purses, and wallets, all favorite targets of thieves and pickpockets.

INTRODUCTION

□ □ □

Any traveler in the United States will find the very vastness of the country—some 3,628,062 sq. mi. (9,396,681km²)—impressive, even a trifle intimidating. Within this huge area, the 50 states of the Union, including Alaska, separated from the other 48 by about 500 mi. (305km), and Hawaii, 2,500 mi. (1,525km) offshore in the Pacific, offer the traveler a bewildering range of options: from the semitropical Everglades to San Francisco Bay, from the Native American reservations of Arizona to the villages of New England, from the arid landscape of Nevada to the deep woods of Vermont, from the Great Plains of the Dakotas to the beaches of California, from the volcanoes of Hawaii to the glaciers of Alaska, from the deserts of New Mexico to the sprawling megalopolis of Boswash (the conurbation that stretches from Boston through New York, Philadelphia, and Baltimore to Washington along the northeastern corridor).

Choice of diversions is equally limitless. You can hunt big game or fish for salmon; run the Colorado River rapids on a rubber raft; follow the trail of the pioneers in a covered wagon; see the Indianapolis 500, the world's most dangerous automobile race; or watch a rocket launching from Cape Canaveral. You can explore America in an RV, a real home on wheels, or if you can afford it, spend a dream vacation at a super-luxury California spa/resort. You can discover the ski resorts of the Rockies or the Sierra Nevada, encounter the future at EPCOT and good ole Mickey at Walt Disney World, and wonder at some of the world's great natural marvels—from the Grand Canyon to Death Valley, from Niagara Falls to the geysers of Yellowstone National Park. And then of course there are America's wondrous cities—New York, Los Angeles, Chicago, San Francisco, Washington, New Orleans—all repositories of great art, culture, and architecture, providing some of the premier urban experiences of the world.

For Americans setting out to get to know their own country, the options may indeed seem endless—for the foreign visitor they can be overwhelming—so let's try to make some sense out of this welter of options.

WHERE & WHEN

The United States can be divided into eight great tourist regions.

THE NORTHEAST & MID-ATLANTIC: From the Canadian frontier to the Potomac and from the shores of Maine to Niagara Falls, its principal regions are New England, with its slightly old-fashioned charm, and Boswash, sheltering 50 million people along the Boston–Washington corridor. American History with a capital *H* is evident everywhere, from Philadelphia's Independence Park to Boston's Freedom Trail, from New York's Federal Hall to Washington's Capitol Hill. See the chapters on Boston, Cape Cod, New York, Niagara Falls, the Atlantic Coast, Philadelphia, Pittsburgh, Baltimore, and Washington.

Best Time to Visit: Cities in the spring and fall, beaches in summer. Fall foliage colors are at their peak in Vermont in late September, and move south to New York state by mid-October. Winter skiing begins in late November.

THE SOUTH: From Washington, D.C., along the Atlantic coast to Florida and west to Louisiana and Arkansas, this is the homeland of the great plantations of the legendary *Gone with the Wind* era. Traces of this Old South exist in the historic cities of Alexandria, Williamsburg, Charleston, and Savannah, and in the plantation country along the Mississippi River in Louisiana and Mississippi. This region has given birth to much that is original in American culture—jazz (from

New Orleans), the blues (from Memphis), and country music (from Nashville). Today the romance of Rhett Butler's and Scarlett O'Hara's South has been replaced by the progressive New South represented by such cosmopolitan cities as Atlanta, New Orleans, and Miami. See the chapters on Charleston, Savannah, Atlanta, Nashville, Memphis, New Orleans, Florida's East Coast, Tampa/St. Petersburg, Orlando, and Miami/Miami Beach.

Best Time to Visit: Spring, fall, and winter; summers tend to be hot and humid with temperatures averaging 80°–90°F (26.6°–32.2°C) in Florida and along the Gulf Coast.

THE MIDWEST: From North Dakota to the Great Lakes and from Missouri to Kansas, this region is often called the Heartland of America, where the plains stretch to a vast horizon and where grain and cattle have been, and still are, king. Although few tourists go there, many of its cities—St. Louis, Kansas City, Minneapolis, and above all, Chicago—are well worth seeing. See the chapters on Detroit, Cleveland, Cincinnati, Chicago, Milwaukee, Minneapolis/St. Paul, Indianapolis, St. Louis, and Kansas City.

Best Time to Visit: Spring and fall; winters are harsh (20°F/−6.6°C, and lower in the northernmost states); scorching summer temperatures can rise above 100°F (38°C) on the plains.

THE MOUNTAIN STATES: Montana, Wyoming, Idaho, Colorado, and Utah—a spectacular scenic playground, this is one of the country's most beautiful and dramatic regions. Colorado and Utah with their dozens of national parks and awesome landscapes are worth a trip in themselves. City highlights include Salt Lake City, the terminus of the great Mormon trek overland, and Denver, a thoroughly modern city that has not entirely shaken off its earlier heritage as a wild and wooly frontier town. Great summer hiking and winter skiing. See the chapters on Denver, the Rocky Mountains, Salt Lake City, Utah National Parks, Yellowstone National Park, and the Black Hills and Mount Rushmore.

Best Time to Visit: Year round. Summers are sunny and moderately hot, except in desert areas where the thermometer can register 110°F (44°C) plus. Spring and fall are temperate, although temperatures can drop mightily at night.

THE SOUTHWEST: From Texas to Arizona, including the adjoining states of New Mexico and Oklahoma, a land of tawny, rust-colored deserts and lunar landscapes, of splendid canyons and Native American reservations, it also boasts archeological remains from the dawn of civilization. Fascinating culturally and historically, especially for those in search of the Old West. See the chapters on Dallas/Fort Worth, Houston, Albuquerque, San Antonio, Santa Fe, Navajoland, the Grand Canyon, Phoenix, and Tucson.

Best Time to Visit: Fall, winter, and spring, before the temperatures rise.

THE NORTHWEST: The beautiful countrysides of Oregon and Washington —rugged coastline, mountain peaks, lakes, rivers, rich farmland, and burgeoning wine country—are attracting more visitors every year. Two major cities, Portland and Seattle, are also attracting more and more people to their livable cosmopolitan environments. See the chapters on Portland, Seattle, and the Pacific Coast.

Best Time to Visit: Summer and fall—least rainfall in July.

THE WEST: The Pacific Coast of California along with Nevada. California, America's experimental social laboratory, sets the pace for the rest of the country, exporting its technology, lifestyle, and social trends, fads, and fashions to the other 49 states. An eclectic mix of European, Asian, and Latin American cultures, movie stars and millionaires, computer age technology, alternative lifestyle devotees, natural wonders, and fine wineries. And then, of course, there's glitter gulch Las Vegas in nearby Nevada. See the chapters on Las Vegas, Death Valley,

Reno, San Francisco, Sequoia National Park, Yosemite National Park, Los Angeles, San Diego, and the California Coast.

Best Time to Visit: Anytime except in the rainy early spring.

ALASKA & HAWAII: While not a region per se, the states of Alaska and Hawaii are major destinations for both Americans and foreign visitors. See the chapters on Anchorage and Alaska, and Honolulu and the Hawaiian Islands.

Best Time to Visit: Spring and summer for Alaska, year round for Hawaii.

Average Temperatures, in ° Fahrenheit, for Representative Cities

	Jan	Feb	Mar	Apr	May	June	July	Aug	Sept	Oct	Nov	Dec
Anchorage	23	25	28	35	46	57	62	58	48	39	33	28
Atlanta	44	47	52	62	70	76	80	82	71	62	52	44
Chicago	25	27	35	48	57	68	73	71	64	55	41	30
Dallas	44	48	55	64	73	80	86	86	77	66	55	48
Denver	30	32	37	48	58	66	73	71	62	51	39	32
Kansas City	30	33	44	55	66	73	80	78	69	59	44	33
Las Vegas	44	50	57	66	73	86	93	91	82	68	57	48
Los Angeles	55	55	57	59	62	66	68	69	68	62	51	55
Miami	68	68	71	73	77	80	82	82	80	78	71	69
Minneapolis	13	15	30	44	57	66	73	69	62	50	33	19
New York	30	30	39	48	60	69	77	75	66	55	44	33
San Francisco	50	51	53	55	55	59	59	60	62	60	57	51
Washington, D.C.	37	39	44	55	66	73	78	77	69	59	48	39

The daily newspaper *USA Today,* on sale in all large cities, carries a daily weather map, detailed and in color, as well as forecasts for the whole U.S. Its "weather hotline" (900/370-8728) tells you the temperatures and weather forecasts for about 490 cities in the U.S. and abroad.

SPECIAL VACATION IDEAS

NATIONAL PARKS & FORESTS: Scattered throughout the United States are 50 national parks—well over 30 million acres (12.15 million ha) of land that has been set aside for the specific preservation of the landscape and its wildlife. Among the most popular are: Acadia (Maine), Glacier (Montana), Grand Canyon (Arizona), Grand Teton (Wyoming), Great Smoky Mountain (Tennessee and North Carolina), Hawaii Volcanoes (Hawaii), Mammoth Cave (Kentucky), Mount Rainier (Washington), Olympic (Washington), Rocky Mountain (Colorado), Sequoia/Kings Canyon (California), Shenandoah (Virginia), Yellowstone (Wyoming, Montana, and Idaho), Yosemite (California), and Zion (Utah).

Camping facilities, ranging from primitive campsites to rustic cabins, are usually open from late spring to early fall (year round at some parks). Rates are reasonable, and because of the parks' popularity, it's wise to reserve ahead.

For more information, refer to *The National Park Guide* by Michael Frome (Prentice Hall Travel) or his *America's Favorite National Parks 1989* (Prentice Hall Travel), or contact the **National Park Service,** U.S. Dept. of the Interior, P.O. Box 37127, Washington, DC 20013-7127 (202/619-7222).

The national forests are less well known and usually less crowded. For a complete list, contact the **National Forest Service,** U.S. Department of Agriculture, P.O. Box 96090, Washington, DC 20019-6090 (202/205-8333).

STATE PARKS: Most states also maintain state parks, often with some type of camping facilities. Again, at the more popular parks you'll need to reserve ahead —for example, in New York to camp on the Long Island shoreline at Hither Hills State Park in Montauk, you have to enter a lottery at the beginning of the year. Although this is unusual, reservations are wise to avoid disappointment.

For **information about state parks,** contact each state's tourism organization. See the Appendix.

THEME PARKS: Almost every state worth its name has a theme park of some sort. They run the gamut from Sea World to Opryland and include, of course, the stars, Walt Disney World and Disneyland. If you're planning a trip to either of the last two, pick up copies of *The Unofficial Guide to Disney World and EPCOT* by Bob Sehlinger and John Finley (Prentice Hall) and *The Unofficial Guide to Disneyland* by Bob Sehlinger (Prentice Hall). Both are vital planning aides.

Just for the record, here are the top-drawing amusement and theme parks: Walt Disney World Disney/MGM Studios, and EPCOT center (Lake Buena Vista, Fla.); Disneyland (Anaheim, Calif.); Universal Studios (Universal City, Calif.); Knott's Berry Farm (Buena Vista, Calif.); Busch Gardens (Tampa, Fla.; also in Williamsburg, Va.); Universal Studios Florida (Orlando, Fla.); Sea World of Florida (Orlando, Fla.; also in San Diego, Calif.; Aurora, Ohio; and San Antonio, Texas); Six Flags Great Adventure (Jackson, N.J.; also in Arlington, Texas; Atlanta, Ga.; St. Louis, Mo.; Gurnee, Ill.; and Valencia, Calif.); Cedar Point (Sandusky, Ohio); Kings Island (Cincinnati, Ohio); Opryland USA (Nashville, Tenn.); Marriott's Great America (Santa Clara, Calif.); AstroWorld (Houston, Texas); and Hersheypark, the granddaddy of them all (Hershey, Penna.).

For a list of amusement parks, contact the **International Association of Amusement Parks and Attractions,** 1448 Duke St., Alexandria, VA 22302 (703/836-4800).

AMERICA'S ZOOS: Scattered across the continent are more than 750 licensed zoos. Some, such as the Bronx Zoo in New York City and the San Diego Zoo, have gained an international reputation for designs that provide natural habitats for most species. Others, like the Gladys Porter Zoo in Brownsville, Texas, have as their primary goal the preservation of endangered species and often breed animals in order to return them to the wild.

For any lover of animals and devotee of zoos, the following are all well worth a visit. Most have an admission fee, and almost all have a last admittance time no less than half an hour before the official closing time.

Arizona: Arizona-Sonora Desert Museum and Biological Park, 2021 N. Kinney Rd., Tucson (602/883-1380); Phoenix Zoo, 5810 E. Van Buren, Phoenix (602/273-1341).

California: San Diego Zoo, 2900 Zoo Dr., San Diego (619/234-3153); Los Angeles Zoo, 5333 Zoo Dr., Griffith Park, Los Angeles (213/666-4090).

District of Columbia: National Zoo, 3001 Connecticut Ave. NW, Washington (202/673-4800).

Florida: Miami Metrozoo, 12400 SW 152nd St., Miami (305/251-0401).

Georgia: Zoo Atlanta, 800 Cherokee Ave. SE, Atlanta (404/624-5678).

Louisiana: Audubon Zoo, 6500 Magazine St., New Orleans (504/861-2537).

Missouri: St. Louis Zoo, Forest Park, St. Louis (314/781-0900).

New York: Bronx Zoo, Bronx River Pkwy. at Fordham Rd., Bronx (718/367-1010); Central Park Zoo, Fifth Ave. and 64th St., New York (212/861-6030).

Texas: Gladys Porter Zoo, 500 Ringgold St., Brownsville (210/546-7187); Dallas Zoo, 621 Clarendon, Dallas (214/946-5154).

Washington: Woodland Park Zoo, 5500 Phinny Ave. N., Seattle (206/684-4800).
Wisconsin: Milwaukee County Zoo, 10001 W. Bluemound Rd., Milwaukee (414/771-3040).

ATTENDING A SPECIAL EVENT: Festivals abound throughout the United States with special events ranging from maple sugar festivals, cherry blossom festivals, winter carnivals, crafts fairs, ethnic celebrations, antiques fairs, flea markets—everything from Mardi Gras to Oktoberfest—as well as block-buster cultural events like the Spoleto Festival in Charleston or Tanglewood in Massachusetts. In each chapter you'll find major special events highlighted, but for a full list, contact any state's tourist organization (see the list in the Appendix). Inquire well in advance. Some events draw large audiences.

VISITING NATIONAL MONUMENTS: These are monuments that recall the great moments of American history—places like Gettysburg, Penn.; Custer Battlefield, Mont.; the Alamo, Texas; and Minute Man National Historical Park, Mass. For information, contact the **National Park Foundation,** 1101 17th St. NW, Suite 1102, Washington, DC 20036 (202/785-4500). A good resource is *The Complete Guide to America's National Parks* (Prentice Hall Press).

ACTIVE VACATIONS: For up-to-date information about specialty travel in general, obtain a copy of *Specialty Travel Index,* a biyearly magazine, either from your travel agent, your library, or by subscription from Specialty Travel Index, 305 San Anselmo Ave., Suite 217, San Anselmo, CA 94960 (415/459-4900). Cost is $8 for one year.
　　Here's a very brief resource list to stimulate ideas:
　　Ballooning: Contact the **Balloon Federation of America,** P.O. Box 400, Indianola, IA 50125 (515/961-8809).
　　Bicycling: *Bicycle USA,* published nine times a year, puts out an issue called *Tourfinder,* which lists tour operators around the U.S. It's available to the public for $6. Contact Bicycle USA, 190 W. Ostend, Suite 120, Baltimore, MD 21230-3755 (410/539-3399).
　　Birdwatching: Contact the **National Audubon Society** Headquarters, 700 Broadway, New York, NY 10023 (212/979-3000).
　　Camping and Hiking: Contact the **Sierra Club,** Outing Department, 730 Polk St., San Francisco, CA 94109 (415/776-2211).
　　Skiing: The **U.S. Ski Association,** P.O. Box 100, Park City, UT 84060 (801/649-9090).
　　Spelunking: The **National Speleological Society,** Cave Ave., Huntsville, AL 35810 (205/852-1300), can put you in touch with fellow enthusiasts.
　　Tennis: Contact the **U.S. Tennis Association,** 70 W. Red Oak Lane, White Plains, NY 10604 (914/696-7000).
　　Wilderness Trips: The major source is the **Sierra Club** (see address above), which organizes wilderness treks to various forests and parks. Other organizations include: **Appalachian Mountain Club,** 5 Joy St., Boston, MA 02108 (617/523-0636), with single annual membership at $40 and family membership at $65; **American Wildlands,** 7500 E. Arapahoe Rd., Suite 305, Englewood, CO 80112 (303/773-1804); **American Forests,** P.O. Box 2000, Washington, DC 20013 (202/667-3300; toll free 800/368-5748); **Nature Expeditions International,** P.O. Box 11496, Eugene, OR 97440 (503/484-6529); and **Yosemite Institute,** P.O. Box 487, Yosemite, CA 95389 (209/372-9300).

TRAVEL FOR PARTICULAR GROUPS

FOR STUDENTS: Pay attention to discounts given with a high school or college ID, or with an International Student Identity Card (ISIC), which is available from the **Council on International Educational Exchange (CIEE),** 205 E. 42nd

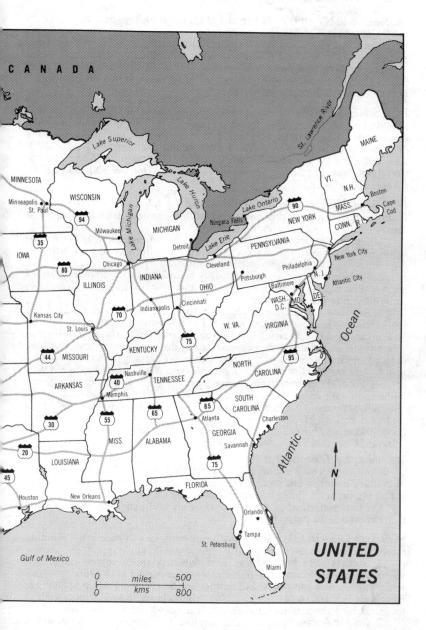

CANADA

MINNESOTA

Minneapolis
St. Paul

Lake Superior

WISCONSIN

Milwaukee

Lake Michigan

MICHIGAN

Lake Huron

Detroit

MAINE

VT.
N.H.

Boston
Cape
Cod

MASS.

Lake Ontario

NEW YORK

CONN. R.I.

Niagara Falls

Lake Erie

PENNSYLVANIA

New York City

Cleveland

Philadelphia

N.J.

IOWA

Chicago

ILLINOIS

INDIANA

OHIO

Pittsburgh

Baltimore

Atlantic City

Kansas City

Indianapolis

Cincinnati

WASH.
D.C.

MD.
DEL.

St. Louis

MISSOURI

KENTUCKY

W. VA.

VIRGINIA

Ocean

Nashville

TENNESSEE

NORTH
CAROLINA

ARKANSAS

Memphis

SOUTH
CAROLINA

Atlanta

Charleston

MISS.

ALABAMA

GEORGIA

Savannah

Atlantic

LOUISIANA

Houston

New Orleans

FLORIDA

Orlando

Tampa

St. Petersburg

Miami

Gulf of Mexico

UNITED
STATES

N

0   miles   500
0   kms   800

St. Lawrence River

94

35

80

70

44

40

55

30

20

45

90

95

75

85

65

75

St., New York, NY 10017 (212/661-1414), and 530 Bush St., San Francisco, CA 94108 (415/421-3473).

Youth travel tour operators include: **Contiki Holidays,** 300 Plaza Alicante, Suite 900, Garden Grove, CA 92640 (toll free 800/466-0610), for ages 18–35; and **Green Tortoise Adventure Travel,** P.O. Box 24459, San Francisco, CA 94124 (415/821-0803), which offers true "roughing-it" travel experiences nationwide at an all-inclusive $20 per day.

FOR SINGLES: The only way to avoid the extra cost of the single supplement is to find someone to share those "doubles" rates. The following organizations specialize in matching up individuals for this purpose (most charge modest monthly or annual membership fees): **Travel Companion Exchange,** P.O. Box 833, Amityville, NY 11701 (516/454-0673 or 516/454-0880); and **Saga International Holidays,** 122 Berkley St., Boston, MA 02116 (toll free 800/343-0273), for ages 60 and over.

FOR FAMILIES: Careful planning makes all the difference between a successful enjoyable vacation and one that ends with exhausted, irritable parents and cranky kids. Here are just a few hints to help:

1. Get the kids involved. Let them, if they're old enough, write to the tourist offices for information and color brochures. Give them a map on which they can outline the route; let them help decide the itinerary.

2. Packing. Although your home may be toddler-proof, accommodations are not. Bring portable gates for stairways and other off-limits areas, and also some blank plugs to cover outlets.

3. En route. Carry a few simple games to relieve boredom in the car. A few snacks will also help and will save money. In some states it's mandatory for children under age 2 to have an infant's car seat; you may want to bring your own on a fly-drive trip. Check Amtrak for special family discounts; the airlines, too, have reduced airfares for those under 17; both let under-2s travel free.

4. Accommodations. Children under a certain age usually stay free in their parents' room. Look for establishments that have pools and other recreational facilities. Reserve equipment such as cribs and playpens in advance.

5. Resources. What to do with the kids this year: *Traveling with Children in the U.S.A.* by Leila Hadley (Morrow), *Travel with Children* by Maureen Wheeler (Lonely Planet), *How to Take Trips with Your Kids* by Joan and Sanford Portnoy (Harvard Common Press), and the Frommer Family Guides.

Traveling by Train or Bus

On Amtrak, children under 2 travel free. Children 2–12 travel for half fare. Also don't forget to ask about special family fares and promotions, as well as package rates that include accommodations and a car.

On Greyhound, when accompanied by an adult, children under 5 travel free; children 5–11 pay half fare.

FOR THE DISABLED: Standards of accessibility vary so widely that planning is crucial. Here are a few helpful hints:

1. Accessibility Information. Unfortunately there are few centralized sources. Two of the best are the Travel Information Service (215/456-9600), offering information only over the telephone; and SATH, 347 Fifth Ave., Suite 16, New York, NY 10016 (212/447-7284), which charges $3 ($45 membership) for researching and mailing information on any given travel destination.

2. Golden Access Passport. This admits a disabled person and companion into a national park, forest, or wildlife refuge at no charge. At some sites a 50% discount on camping and other facilities is also given. For information, call the National Park Service (202/619-7222).

3. Tour Packagers. Fewer and fewer tours are arranged for within America as travelers choose to go by their own means. Two recommended packagers with U.S. tours are: Evergreen Travel Service, 4114 198th St. SW, Lynnwood, WA

98036 (206/776-1184); and Accessible Journeys, 35 W. Sellers Ave., Ridley Park, PA 19078 (toll free 800/846-4537).
   4. Book Resources. *Access to the World: A Travel Guide for the Handicapped* by Louise Weiss (H. Holt & Co.) and *Travel for the Disabled: A Handbook of Travel Resources & 400 Worldwide Access Guides* by Helen Hecker (Twin Peaks Press).

Traveling by Bus and Train

   A companion can accompany a disabled person at no charge aboard Greyhound. This is available only to disabled people who have a letter from their doctor certifying that they are handicapped and who cannot negotiate the bus steps alone.
   Amtrak has a standard handicapped person's fare of at least 25% off regular fare. Amtrak also provides wheelchair-accessible sleeping accommodations in both eastern and western trains. Although pets are not allowed, guide dogs are permissible and travel free of charge. Notify your reservation agent for the lowest fare and authorization for any special needs.

FOR SENIORS: For the fastest-growing travel group, there's a lot available:
   1. Discounts. To find them, there's one major resource: *The Discount Guide for Travelers Over Fifty-Five* by Caroline and Walter Weinz (E.P. Dutton). The only other way to find them is to ask for them everywhere—at cinemas, theaters, museums, hotels, restaurants, attractions, and on local transit.
   2. Information Sources. The **American Association of Retired Persons (AARP),** 601 E. St. NW, Washington, DC 20049 (202/434-2277); **Mature Outlook,** 6001 N. Clark St., Chicago, IL 60660 (toll free 800/336-6330); and the **National Council of Senior Citizens,** 1331 F St. NW, Washington, DC 20004 (202/347-8800).
   3. Tour and Other Specialists. Fascinating, reasonably priced learning vacations are offered by **Elderhostel, Inc.,** 75 Federal St., Boston, MA 02110 (617/426-7788); the **AARP Travel Service,** 3200 E. Carson St., Lakewood, CA 90245 (toll free 800/424-3410); **Saga International Holidays,** 122 Berkley St., Boston, MA 02116 (617/262-2262; toll free 800/343-0273); and **Grand Circle Travel, Inc.,** 347 Congress St., Boston, MA 02210 (617/350-7500). The last two concentrate on foreign destinations.
   4. Book Resources. *Travel Easy: The Practical Guide for People Over 50* by Rosalind Massow (AARP).

RECOMMENDED TOURING ITINERARIES: It's relatively easy to take in the sights of widely separated regions by flying to a major transportation hub and renting a car with unlimited mileage. Below you will find suggestions for touring itineraries lasting from one week to one month, covering the main tourist areas of the United States. Note that the cheapest available rates for rental cars and motor homes are currently offered in California (for the West Coast) and Florida (for the East Coast). For the Northeast, choose Boston over Washington as your home base, and avoid New York, which has the highest car-rental rates in the whole country.
   For detailed descriptions of touring areas listed in the itineraries table, consult the chapters corresponding to the names marked with an asterisk (see the index).

Region	Cities or Tourist Areas	Length of Stay (in days)	Miles	Via Highway No.
		If you only have a week . . .		
Arizona	1. Phoenix*	2	—	
	2. Navajoland* & Monument Valley	2	395	I-17, U.S. 89, U.S. 160, U.S. 163

	3. Grand Canyon*	2	173	U.S. 160, U.S. 89, Ariz. 64
	4. return to Phoenix	1	218	U.S. 180, I-17
			786	
S. Dakota	1. Rapid City	1	—	
	2. Badlands Nat'l Park	2	70	I-90, S. Dak. 240
	3. Mt. Rushmore*	1	86	S. Dak. 44, U.S. 16
	4. Devil's Tower Nat'l Monument	1	153	U.S. 85, I-90, U.S. 14
	5. Spearfish	1	84	U.S. 14, I-90
	6. return to Rapid City	1	53	I-90
			446	
East Coast	1. Boston*	2	—	
	2. Cape Cod* & Martha's Vineyard or Nantucket	3	89	Mass. 3, U.S. 6
	3. Newport, R.I.	1	86	U.S. 6, R.I. 24, R.I. 138
	4. return to Boston	1	68	R.I. 138, R.I. 24, Mass. 24
			243	
East Coast	1. Boston*	2	—	
	2. Salem & Gloucester	2	37	Mass. 1A, Mass. 128
	3. Portland, Maine	1	91	Mass. 128, Mass. 133, Mass. 1A, I-95
	4. Portsmouth, N.H.	1	50	I-95
	5. return to Boston	1	55	I-95
			233	
East Coast	1. Washington*	3	—	
	2. Annapolis	1	28	U.S. 50
	3. Chincoteague	1	113	U.S. 50, U.S. 13, Va. 175
	4. Williamsburg	1	176	U.S. 13, I-64, Va. 31
	5. return to Washington	1	205	U.S. 60, I-64, I-95
			522	
Florida	1. Orlando*, and Disney World	3	—	
	2. West Palm Beach	1	161	Fla. Tpke.
	3. Fort Lauderdale	1	42	U.S. 1
	4. Miami*	2	25	U.S. 1
			228	
Great Lakes	1. Chicago*	2		
	2. Milwaukee*	1	87	I-94
	3. Sault Ste. Marie	1	398	U.S. 43, U.S. 41, U.S. 2, I-75
	4. Mackinaw City	1	56	I-75
	5. Holland	1	284	U.S. 31
	6. return to Chicago	1	140	U.S. 31, I-94
			965	
Rockies	1. Denver*	1	—	
	2. Colorado Springs	1	76	I-25
	3. Canon City	1	44	Colo. 115, U.S. 50

	4. Gunnison	1	121	U.S. 50
	5. Glenwood Springs	1	173	U.S. 50, Colo. 92, Colo. 133, Colo. 82
	6. Dillon	1	91	I-70
	7. return to Denver	1	76	I-70
			581	
Rockies	1. Denver*	1	—	
	2. Great Sand Dunes & Alamosa	1	239	I-25, U.S. 160
	3. Santa Fe*	2	140	U.S. 285
	4. Durango and Mesa Verde	2	215	U.S. 84, U.S. 160
	5. return to Denver	1	390	U.S. 160, I-25
			984	
West	1. Los Angeles*	2	—	
	2. Las Vegas*	2	272	I-15
	3. Palm Springs	1	309	I-15, I-10, Calif. 111
	4. San Diego*	2	133	Calif. 111, Calif. 74, Calif. 79, I-15
			714	
West	1. San Francisco*	2	—	
	2. Sacramento	1	86	I-80
	3. Reno	1	136	I-80
	4. Lake Tahoe*	2	56	U.S. 395, U.S. 50
	5. return to San Francisco	1	204	U.S. 50, I-80
			482	

If you have two weeks or more . . .

Florida & Georgia	1. Atlanta*	2	—	
	2. Savannah*	2	256	I-75, I-16
	3. St. Augustine	1	175	I-95, U.S. 1
	4. Orlando* & Disney World	3	200	I-95, I-4
	5. Palm Beach	1	146	I-95, U.S. 1
	6. Miami*	2	75	I-95, U.S. 1
	7. Sarasota	1	212	U.S. 41
	8. St. Petersburg*	1	51	U.S. 41, I-275
	9. Tallahassee	1	256	U.S. 19, U.S. 27
	10. return to Atlanta	1	268	U.S. 319, I-75
			1,628	
Florida & Louisiana	1. Atlanta*	2	—	
	2. Great Smoky Mountains	2	231	U.S. 19, U.S. 441
	3. Nashville*	2	225	U.S. 441, I-40
	4. Memphis*	2	200	I-40
	5. Vicksburg	1	231	I-55, I-20
	6. New Orleans*	4	250	U.S. 61, I-10
	7. Montgomery	1	312	I-10, I-65
	8. return to Atlanta	1	168	I-85
			1,617	
Arizona & the Grand Canyon	1. Phoenix*	3	—	
	2. Grand Canyon*	2	218	I-17, U.S. 180
	3. Las Vegas*	2	290	Ariz. 64, I-40, U.S. 93
	4. Zion National Park	2	162	I-15, Utah 9

	5. Monument Valley	2	256	Utah 9, U.S. 89, Ariz. 98, U.S. 160, U.S. 163
	6. Canyon de Chelly	2	112	U.S. 163, U.S. 160, U.S. 191
	7. Native American Pueblos	1	81	U.S. 191, Ariz. 264
	8. return to Phoenix	1	281	Ariz. 264, U.S. 89, I-17
			1,375	
California	1. Los Angeles*	3	—	
	2. Death Valley*	2	306	I-15, Calif. 127
	3. Sequoia Nat'l Park*	1	362	Calif. 190
	4. Yosemite Nat'l Park*	2	177	Calif. 190, Calif. 178, Calif. 65, Calif. 198
	5. San Francisco*	3	210	Calif. 198, Calif. 180, Calif. 41
	6. California Coast*	3	487	Calif. 120, I-205, I-580
	7. return to Los Angeles	1	126	U.S. 101, Calif. 1
			1,668	
California & Navajoland	1. Denver*	2	—	
	2. Mesa Verde Nat'l Park	2	416	I-25, U.S. 160
	3. Monument Valley	2	158	U.S. 160, U.S. 163
	4. Canyon de Chelly	2	112	U.S. 163, U.S. 160, U.S. 191
	5. Santa Fe*	3	287	U.S. 191, Ariz. 264, I-40, I-25
	6. Durango	1	215	U.S. 84, N. Mex. 96, N. Mex. 44, U.S. 550
	7. Colorado Springs	2	316	U.S. 160, I-25
	8. return to Denver	1	66	I-25
			1,573	
Colorado & Yellowstone	1. Denver*	2	—	
	2. Dinosaur Nat'l Park	1	303	I-70, Colo. 13, Colo. 64, U.S. 40
	3. Salt Lake City*	3	200	U.S. 40, I-80
	4. Jackson, Wyo.	1	301	I-15, U.S. 26
	5. Yellowstone Nat'l Park*	4	79	U.S. 89
	6. Casper	1	293	U.S. 20, Wyo. 120, U.S. 20
	7. Rocky Mountain Nat'l Park	2	275	I-25, U.S. 34
	8. return to Denver	1	70	U.S. 34, U.S. 36
			1,521	
Texas & Louisiana	1. Dallas*	3	—	
	2. Austin	1	192	I-35
	3. San Antonio*	2	80	I-35
	4. Houston*	3	196	I-10
	5. Baton Rouge	1	281	I-10
	6. New Orleans*	3	81	I-10
	7. Vicksburg	1	253	I-10, U.S. 61
	8. return to Dallas	1	362	I-20
			1,445	

If you have three weeks or more . . .

East Coast &	1. Boston*	2	—
the South	2. New York*	2	212 I-95
	3. Philadelphia*	2	100 I-278, I-95
	4. Washington*	2	134 I-95
	5. Williamsburg	1	160 I-395, I-95, I-64
	6. Roanoke	1	221 I-64, I-81
	7. Great Smoky Mountains	1	303 I-81, U.S. 441
	8. Atlanta*	2	231 U.S. 441, U.S. 19
	9. Charleston*	2	306 I-20, U.S. 78, I-26
	10. Raleigh	1	261 U.S. 52, I-95, U.S. 70
	11. Virginia Beach	1	184 U.S. 64, I-95, U.S. 58
	12. Assateague Island	1	106 U.S. 60, U.S. 13,
			Va. 175
	13. Atlantic City	1	145 Va. 175, U.S. 13,
		+Ferry	U.S. 113, U.S. 9,
			Garden St. Pkwy.
	14. New York*	1	128 I-95, I-278
	15. return to Boston	1	<u>212</u> I-95
			2,706

California &	1. San Francisco*	4	—
Nevada	2. Sacramento	1	93 I-80
	3. Reno*	2	137 U.S. 50, U.S. 395, I-80
	4. Death Valley*	2	380 Nev. 50, U.S. 95,
			Nev. 267
	5. Zion Park & Bryce Canyon	3	381 Calif. 190, Calif. 127,
			Nev. 373, U.S. 95,
			I-15, Utah 9
	6. Grand Canyon	2	312 U.S. 89, Ariz. 64
	7. Las Vegas*	2	290 Ariz. 64, I-40, U.S. 93
	8. Los Angeles*	3	282 I-15, I-10
	9. return to San Francisco	2	<u>487</u> Calif. 1, U.S. 101
			2,365

California	1. Los Angeles*	3	—
& Grand	2. San Diego*	2	125 Calif. 1, I-5
Canyon	3. Phoenix*	2	356 I-8, Ariz. 85
	4. Grand Canyon*	2	218 I-17, U.S. 180
	5. Las Vegas*	2	290 Ariz. 64, I-40, U.S. 93
	6. Death Valley*	2	143 U.S. 95, Nev. 373,
			Calif. 190
	7. Sequoia Nat'l Park*	1	362 Calif. 190, Calif. 178,
			Calif. 65, Calif. 198
	8. Yosemite Nat'l Park*	2	177 Calif. 180, Calif. 41
	9. San Francisco*	3	210 Calif. 120, I-205,
			I-580, I-80
	10. return to Los Angeles	2	<u>487</u> U.S. 101, Calif. 1
			2,371

Utah,	1. Las Vegas*	2	—
Arizona,	2. Zion Park & Bryce	3	243 I-15, Utah 9, U.S. 89,
& Nevada	Canyon		Utah 12
	3. Salt Lake City*	2	262 Utah 12, U.S. 89,
			I-15
	4. Canyonlands & Arches Park	3	243 I-15, U.S. 6, U.S. 191

5. Mesa Verde Park	2	150	U.S. 191, U.S. 666, U.S. 160
6. Monument Valley	2	158	U.S. 160, U.S. 163
7. Canyon de Chelley	1	112	U.S. 163, U.S. 160, U.S. 191
8. Indian Pueblos	1	81	U.S. 191, Ariz. 264
9. Glen Canyon	2	141	Ariz. 264, U.S. 89
10. Grand Canyon*	2	137	U.S. 89, Ariz. 64
11. return to Las Vegas	1	290	Ariz. 64, I-40, U.S. 93
		1,840	

If you have a month or more . . .

Colorado,	1. Denver*	3	—	
Yellowstone,	2. Rocky Mountain Nat'l Park	1	70	U.S. 36, U.S. 34
the Pacific	3. Casper	1	275	U.S. 34, I-25
Northwest,	4. Yellowstone Nat'l Park*	3	293	U.S. 20, Wyo. 120, U.S. 20
& California	5. Butte	1	212	U.S. 89, I-90
	6. Spokane	1	315	I-90
	7. Seattle*	2	293	U.S. 2, Wash. 174, Wash. 155, U.S. 2, Wash. 522
	8. Pacific Coast*	2	468	Ferry + U.S. 101, U.S. 30
	9. Portland*	2	—	—
	10. Medford & Jacksonville	1	250	I-5
	11. Sacramento	2	341	I-5
	12. San Francisco*	3	93	I-80
	13. Yosemite Nat'l Park*	2	210	I-580, I-205, Calif. 120, Calif. 41
	14. Death Valley*	2	321	Calif. 41, Calif. 120, U.S. 395, Calif. 190
	15. Las Vegas*	1	143	Calif. 190, Nev. 373, U.S. 95
	16. Zion Park & Bryce Canyon	2	243	I-15, Utah 9, U.S. 89, Utah 12
	17. Grand Junction	1	337	Utah 12, U.S. 89, I-70
	18. return to Denver	1	259	I-70
			4,124	

BEFORE YOU LEAVE HOME

SOURCES OF INFORMATION: Begin planning as far in advance as possible, especially if you will travel during peak seasons. Every state has a central tourist information office and a series of regional offices; most cities also have convention and tourist bureaus; both will provide a lot of information. For a complete listing of state tourist organizations, see the Appendix; for city bureaus, see each city chapter under "Tourist Information."

You can also contact the **International Association of Convention and Visitors Bureaus,** P.O. Box 6690, Champaign, IL 61826-6690 (217/359-8881).

USING A TRAVEL AGENT: To use a travel agent successfully you need to find a good one, and you need to know where you want to go and what you want to do, so that you're free to go over the details with the agent, modifying your plans to incorporate his or her professional advice. Ask for personal recommendations among your friends, or contact the **American Society of Travel Agents (ASTA),** 1101 King St., Alexandria, VA 22314 (703/739-2782), whose members have been in business a minimum of three years; or the **Institute of Certified Travel Agents,** 148 Linden St. (P.O. Box 812059), Wellesley, MA 02181 (617/237-0280), whose certification means that the agent has taken an 18-month training course sponsored by the institute.

If your main interest is saving money on airfares, to really make good use of your travel agent, keep asking for the lowest fare and request the agent to check out the many ways that can be used to find the lowest price—flying to a destination in two or more segments to take advantage of discounts on particular highly competitive or infrequently flown routes, traveling on certain days of the week, etc. If the agent is not willing to do this, you need to find one who will, although you may be charged a modest additional fee for these services.

WHAT & HOW TO PACK: Just some brief hints:

1. Leave at home clothes that need to be ironed before each wearing, unless you're staying at a deluxe resort/hotel. Pack coordinated separates so that you can vary your outfits easily.

2. Pack a pair of comfortable shoes.

3. Travel light, even if you're driving—lugging heavy bags in and out of the trunk is tedious. Two small, light bags are better than one heavy, large one.

4. If you're flying, pack one carry-on bag with toiletries and other necessities, in case checked luggage gets lost. Airlines are strictly enforcing the limit of two carry-on bags; both must fit under the seat (about 9 × 14 × 22 in.; 25 × 35 × 92cm) or in an overhead bin (10 × 14 × 36 in.; 23 × 35 × 56cm).

5. Pack an extra folding bag for shopping finds.

INSURANCE: If you're taking a prepaid package tour, cruise, or charter flight, you may want to take out a special traveler's insurance for a specific trip that covers baggage loss, cancellation/trip interruption, and medical emergencies. Always check the fine print for exclusions from coverage, limits, and restricted definitions of whatever sort. Be sure that the policy is adequate to cover nondiscounted airfares and unexpected hotel expenses, if you do have to interrupt your trip for any emergency reason. Such policies are obtainable from an insurance broker or travel agent. Whatever you do, before you leave home, check:

1. Your homeowner's insurance; if it doesn't cover off-premises theft and loss you may want to purchase a floater to protect you during your vacation.

2. Your health insurance, for any pretreatment emergency requirements— hotline numbers, etc. Most standard health-insurance policies will cover you while on vacation.

3. Your auto insurance, for full coverage—accident insurance for medical expenses, injury to other passengers in your car, and loss of pay if you're injured; liability for injury you cause to another person or property; comprehensive and collision; and uninsured-motorist protection if you're involved in an accident with an uninsured driver of another car.

4. Your personal insurance, because if it doesn't cover you for injury or death when flying, you may want to amend your policy. Although your plane ticket price automatically includes airline-liability insurance, the limits are set by individual state laws and each claim is hard fought and consequently costly. Some credit- and charge-card companies automatically provide flight insurance if your ticket is charged to that account—American Express, for example.

A TRAVEL-PLANNING CHECKLIST: Here's a quick list of things to take care of in advance and at the very last minute:

In Advance

1. Leave with a friend or neighbor a house key, your auto-registration number, and a trip itinerary (including, if possible, names of specific accommodations where you'll be staying).

2. Write or call state and local tourist boards along your route and at your destination for information on attractions, special events, and special weather conditions (remember the vagaries of weather when packing).

3. Have your car checked and serviced. Fluid levels and tire pressures should be up to capacity, oil and oil filter clean, and ignition system tuned.

4. Prepare an emergency road kit, including basic tools, flares, flashlight, a duplicate set of car keys (to be kept with you); check the jack and spare tire.

5. Carry an adequate supply of any prescription drugs and medications you require, and take along a copy of important prescriptions, in case of loss. Have extras for other important personal items, such as a pair of glasses and contact lenses. Carry a first-aid kit in your car.

6. Store valuables at home in a safe place. You may want to rent a safe-deposit box for silverware and jewelry, or register major appliances (stereo, television) with the police (check your homeowner's insurance for theft coverage).

7. Check important documents and their expiration dates: driver's license, credit cards, auto-insurance policy, auto registration, auto club membership card.

8. Purchase traveler's checks and record the check numbers in two places, keeping both lists separate from the checks.

9. Install automatic timers on a few lights in your home, or arrange for a friend to turn various lights on and off during your absence.

10. Discontinue deliveries, such as mail and newspapers. Have someone check periodically for unexpected deliveries, pamphlets, or circulars, which tend to pile up at the door, sending a message to thieves that no one is home.

11. Arrange for yardwork at regular times.

At Departure

1. Disconnect electrical appliances, lower the thermostat, and turn off gas jets, including the hot-water heater. Set automatic timers on lights.

2. Make sure traveler's checks and important documents get packed.

3. Make a final check of all doors and windows as you're leaving the house.

4. And finally, check your travel documents, making sure that the destinations printed on your airline tickets are correct. Also, if you're flying, reconfirm your flight (even though that's not required for domestic flights).

GETTING AROUND

BY CAR: Although it may not be the least expensive way to go unless you're traveling with family or friends, it's certainly the most flexible.

Driving Your Own Car

PRETRIP PREPARATIONS Inspect your car thoroughly before setting out on a long trip. The best time to do this is when the engine and tires are cool. Run through the following:

1. Check all lights—headlights, tail lights, parking lights, license-plate lights, and hazard lights. Test the brake lights, backup lights, and turn signals.

2. Make sure the horn, seatbelts, and windshield wipers are functioning properly.

3. Inspect the tires carefully and replace any tire that's cut, shows sidewall bulges, or has bald patches on its tread. Also replace any tire whose tread depth is worn to ¹⁄₁₆th in. (1mm) or less. Check for uneven wear. If there's any sign of this, take the car for wheel alignment. While the tires are cool, check the tire pressure and inflate to correct pressure. Don't forget to fill the spare.

4. With the engine off and the vehicle on a level surface, check all fluid levels: the oil level should be between "add" and "full" on the dipstick; top up the engine coolant (a 50/50 mixture of antifreeze and water) to the appropriate level, as marked on the plastic reservoir; check the power-steering and automatic-transmission fluid levels according to the instructions in the owner's manual. Fill the windshield washer bottle and test the system.

5. Check the battery. Make sure it's clean and dry. Top up the electrolyte (water) level, if necessary. It should be half an inch (about 1.25cm) above the vertical plates in the battery. Replace the battery if the case is cracked or leaking. Also replace any battery cables that have damaged strands. Clean corroded battery and cable connections, and tighten any loose cable clamps on the battery posts.

6. Inspect the drive belts and replace any that are cracked, frayed, glazed, or contaminated by grease or oil. Press the belt with your thumb midway between the pulleys. The belt needs tightening if it depresses more than half an inch (about 1.25cm).

7. Squeeze the radiator and heater hoses. If they feel brittle or spongy, replace them. With the engine running, check for any leaks in the cooling system.

8. After inspection, road-test the car, checking to see if it pulls to the left or right on a straight road. If it does, it may need a front-end alignment. Also test the brakes. If the brake pedal feels spongy, have the brakes checked by a professional.

9. Before you leave, check that the following documents are still valid: vehicle registration, safety-inspection sticker, auto insurance, auto-club membership, and driver's license.

MAPS There are several good road atlases: *The Mobil Road Atlas & Trip Planning Guide* (Prentice Hall); *The Rand McNally Road Atlas & Vacation Guide* is also very popular. Many auto clubs also supply maps to members (see below).

PACING Don't drive more than 300 or 400 miles a day. Stop every two hours or so, and try to phone and make reservations for the night by midafternoon to avoid a wearying search at the end of an exhausting day's drive.

LEGAL ISSUES Watch the speed limit, which in most states is 55 mph. The higher speed limit of 65 mph voted by Congress in 1987 is essentially restricted to the highways of some 20 states in the South, West, and Northwest, in particular, Arizona, Arkansas, California, Colorado, Missouri, Nevada, New Mexico, North Dakota, Oklahoma, South Dakota, Texas, Utah, and Wyoming. But since other states may have the higher 65-mph speed limit, be sure to check roadside postings carefully every time you cross a state line.

Buckle up! Seatbelts for driver and front-seat passengers are mandatory in all but a few states. Seatbelts must be worn by all passengers in California, Hawaii, Montana, Nevada, Oregon, South Carolina, Washington, and Wisconsin. Note also that in all fifty states and in Washington, D.C., children under 4 must be in a child's seat or be buckled up. Check with the Department of Public Safety in the appropriate state for more information.

AUTO CLUBS Join one of the auto clubs. They will supply maps, recommended routes, guidebooks, accident and bail-bond insurance, and, most important of all, emergency road service. The leader, with 850 offices and 28 million members, is the **American Automobile Association (AAA),** with national headquarters at 1000 AAA Dr., Heathrow, FL 32746 (toll free 800/222-4357). Check telephone book for local offices. Membership for both U.S. citizens and foreign visitors ranges from $17 to $75, depending on which particular local office you join. AAA also has a 24-hr. emergency toll-free number: 800/336-4357.

Other recommended auto clubs include the **Allstate Motor Club,** P.O. Box 3093, Arlington Heights, IL 60006 (toll free 800/323-6282); and the **Amoco Motor Club,** P.O. Box 9014, Des Moines, IA 50368 (toll free 800/334-3300).

A NOTE FOR FOREIGN VISITORS The AAA can provide you with an *International Driving Permit* validating your driving license. Members of some foreign auto clubs that have reciprocal arrangements with AAA enjoy AAA's services at no charge.

Auto Rentals

To rent a car you need a major credit card or you'll have to leave a sizeable cash deposit ($100 or more for each day). Though the minimum rental age is usually 25, some regional agencies will rent to those between 21 and 24 for an additional fee.

SHOP AROUND Rates vary from company to company, from location to location (airport vs. downtown, Florida vs. New York City). In addition, companies offer unlimited-mileage options vs. per-mile charges and also special discounts on weekends. So it pays to shop around. Use the major companies' toll-free 800 numbers to do this. Other variable costs include drop-off charges if you're picking up the car in one city and leaving it in another; the cost of daily collision damage and personal accident insurance (some credit-card companies cover collision if you charge the rental on your card). And always return your car with a full tank —the rental companies charge excessive prices for gasoline.

THE COMPANIES The majors are: **Hertz** (toll free 800/654-3131), **Avis** (toll free 800/331-1212), **National** (toll free 800/227-7368), **Budget** (toll free 800/527-0700), **Dollar** (toll free 800/800-4000), and **Thrifty** (toll free 800/367-2277). Also check the smaller local companies and **Rent a Wreck** (toll free 800/535-1391), if there is one in a particular city.

BY RECREATIONAL VEHICLE (RV): Accommodating four to six people,

these vehicles are ideal for long family trips. Air-conditioned, and equipped with showers, refrigerators, and a full kitchen, they're also comfortable. Throughout the U.S., campsites have hookups for electricity, water, and sewage disposal.

Book Resources

The *RV Park and Campground Directories*—one national book and two smaller editions covering the eastern U.S. and Canada and the western U.S. and Canada (Prentice Hall Travel)—contain thousands of listings in easy-to-read chart format that are cross-referenced to maps, as well as establishments that sell and service RVs. The AAA also publishes regional campground directories.

Renting an RV

Check the *Yellow Pages* under "Recreational Vehicles—Renting & Leasing." Major companies include **Cruise America** (toll free 800/327-7799), **Travelhome Vacations** (toll free 800/663-7848), and **Go Vacations, Inc.** (toll free 800/487-4652).

For information, contact the **Recreation Vehicle Dealer's Association,** 3930 University Dr., Fairfax, VA 22030 (703/591-7130). The RVDA publishes *Rental Ventures,* a directory of rental agencies, for a small charge.

BY AIR: Since deregulation in 1987, shopping the airlines has become increas-

ingly complex and travel by air increasingly irksome as airlines delay and often cancel flights without warning.

Shop Around

Use the toll-free lines to call all the airlines that go to your destination. Always ask the agent for the lowest fare as opposed to a particular fare, such as an APEX (an advance-purchase fare). This way you're asking them to search for the cheapest ticket to your destination. Once you've located it and made a reservation, still check a day or so before your departure to see if there has been a fare change since you booked—you'll be due a refund if it has decreased, but no extra charge if it has increased—because airlines, as the departure date draws nearer, will make more seats available for discounting if the flight is not being booked. So it really is worth calling almost daily up to the departure time to see if any discounts have opened up.

The Regular Fare Structure

At the top there's **first class.** You're paying for larger seats, more leg room, superior service and meals. In **business class,** the next step down, you get a little extra leg room and some extra little services, including free drinks. A **coach** or **economy** fare puts you in cramped seating, and ensures typical airline food and service. For all three classes you can book at the last moment, you incur no cancellation penalties, and your round-trip ticket will be good for a year, longer if you renew it.

Discount Fares

Referred to variously as Excursion, Super Saver, or Advance Purchase (APEX), these offer savings as much as 35%–45% of the regular fare—but they do have strings attached. Usually they must be booked anywhere from a week to a month in advance; they carry penalties for changing either the date of departure or return, and also for cancellation.

To find these discount fares, check your local newspaper advertisements. Among them, sometimes you'll find promotions for specified destinations or for age groups such as senior citizens. Discounts can be quite substantial, 50% or more.

Other money-savers are: flying off-season (mid-Jan through Mar and Oct through mid-Dec, except Thanksgiving weekend); off-hour flights (10am–3pm and after-8pm departures); day-of-the-week reductions (usually Tuesday, Wednesday, Thursday, or Saturday when traffic is lightest); and routing with stops or connections ("direct" means stops but no change of plane; "nonstop" means exactly that).

Be aware, too, that you may be able to save a lot of money by splitting your trip into segments and taking advantage of particularly low fares on a given segment. For example, a travel agent looking for the lowest fare from Pittsburgh to Portland, Oregon, might see only an American Airlines fare of $505 each way, but if the agent "digs" he or she may find that you can fly from Pittsburgh to Denver and then from Denver to Portland for a total of only $320—a great savings. It's worth checking alternative routings either through an agent or by calling the airlines constantly and asking them, "Isn't there anything cheaper?"

Anyone requiring only a one-way fare should always look into the comparable price of a round-trip SuperSaver or other discount ticket. Sometimes it's simply cheaper to take the round-trip ticket and throw away the return half (better yet, you can sell it to someone). Anomalies like this can always be found.

Airline Passes, Charters, and Tour Packages

Often airlines will offer special passes for particular groups—such as senior citizens or youths. For example, in the past some major airlines have offered a pass to 62-year-olds-plus, good for one year's unlimited flying anywhere within their system.

Frequent-flyer plans can cut costs dramatically. Bonus points accumulate every time you fly, and recently the airlines have been offering triple-mileage bonuses. Estimates are that the public currently has billions of dollars' worth of free flying miles!

Often you can take advantage of an all-inclusive tour package that will deliver a very low airfare, and possibly some extra discounts on car rentals, accommodations, and sightseeing. These are most often offered in Florida and the Southwest. Remember that although you don't have to use the whole package, you may still save money by purchasing it.

Notes and Special Airfares for Foreign Visitors

There are about six "major" airlines (although several are owned by the same corporate parent), half a dozen somewhat smaller "nationals," and some two dozen local commuter carriers, offering day and night service at more than 1,000 airports. Taking the plane in the U.S.A. has become almost as simple as taking the subway or a cab. Some lines, like Delta's or USAir's New York–Washington and New York–Boston shuttles, require no reservations.

SPECIAL AIRFARES Foreign visitors can take advantage of the special promotional airfares that have been discussed above, but from time to time they can also obtain special passes *before they leave home* that allow unlimited flying anywhere on the airline's network for a stated time period, usually 21 days, one month, three months, etc. These passes usually carry restrictions—blackout days of the week; holidays, etc.; no backtracking; and so on. In the recent past none has been available, but it's well worth your while to check before leaving home for any that may have come on the market.

SMOKING By federal law, smoking has been banned on all flights within the U.S.

Some Easy Flying Hints

Use the secondary airports if you can—Midway instead of O'Hare in Chicago, Dulles instead of National in Washington, D.C., Newark instead of LaGuardia or Kennedy in New York.

Allow plenty of time between connecting flights; unless you have to, don't book the last flight of the day since you'll be stuck overnight if you miss it or are "bumped." To protect themselves against people who reserve seats and don't show up, the airlines do overbook their planes. If everyone shows up, obviously something has to give. The airlines, however, must abide by certain rules in resolving the situation. If the airlines can arrange alternative flights that arrive within one hour of the originally scheduled flight, then it doesn't have to pay compensation of any sort. If the delay is longer, compensation is mandatory. Airlines usually offer ticket vouchers. If you're bumped, find out immediately what the airline will do to make your enforced delay more comfortable—meal vouchers, overnight accommodations, etc. Speak to a supervisor if a reservations clerk cannot give you a good answer. If you have connecting flights, make sure that those airlines are informed.

For a booklet entitled "Fly Rights" that discusses passengers' rights, send $1 to the Superintendent of Documents, U.S. Government Printing Office, Washington, DC 20402 (202/783-3238).

If you have any complaints about the airlines—regarding lost baggage, bumping, or anything else—inform the Office of Consumer Affairs, U.S. Department of Transportation, 400 7th St. SW, Room 10405, Washington DC 20590 (202/366-2220).

BY TRAIN: Although the savings over air travel can be negligible, going by train is a comfortable option if you have the time. It takes 49 hours by train from Chicago to San Francisco, 28 hours from New York to New Orleans, and 33 hours from Seattle to Los Angeles. On some routes—Washington to New York, for example—you're better off taking the Metroliner than the airplane. Total travel time by train will be about the same or less.

Amtrak services more than 500 cities, in all states except Maine, Oklahoma, South Dakota, Hawaii, and Alaska. Facilities along the Boswash corridor and on long-distance lines west of the Mississippi are good, but a bit uneven elsewhere. Some of these trains boast panoramic cars from which you can admire the landscape—they include the *California Zephyr* (Chicago–San Francisco), the *Coast Starlight* (Seattle–Los Angeles), the *Southwest Chief* (Chicago–Los Angeles), the *Desert Wind* (Chicago–Salt Lake City–Los Angeles), the *Empire Builder* (Chicago–Seattle), and the *Sunset Limited* (New Orleans–Los Angeles). Long-distance trains have full dining and lounge cars; on others there's usually a snack bar and lounge.

Seat Types and Fares

Reclining day-coach seats are allocated on both a first-come/first-served basis and a reservation basis, depending on the train. The most economical for overnight is a reclining coach seat with a pull-up leg rest—pillows and blankets are provided as well.

Sleeping compartments vary in eastern and western trains. East of the Mississippi River, a single traveler can reserve a roomette, which consists of one lounge seat, which is stowed away when the bed is pulled down from the wall, a private toilet, and a closet. Or two travelers can reserve a bedroom with two lounge or bench seats, two berths, and toilet facilities. On trains running west of the Mississippi River, two options are available. There's an economy room, with two lounge seats by day and two berths by night; or a deluxe bedroom, with showers and private toilet facilities. The price of sleeping accommodations is added on to the coach fare and includes three meals daily in the dining car.

Railpasses and Special Fares

All Aboard America passes can be purchased in the U.S. and allow unlimited travel within one of Amtrak's regional divisions for 45 days, with two stopovers allowed in addition to your final destination. One-region travel is currently priced at $179 for coach accommodations (they can be upgraded). A three-region (total country) ticket costs $259. Be sure to check regular fares to compare, since the savings on such a pass are proportionate to the distance traveled.

Amtrak also offers substantial discounts for families and the handicapped.

The Auto Train

Running between Lorton, Va. (just south of Washington, D.C.), and Sanford, Fla. (just north of Orlando), this nonstop train will transport you *and* your car. Coach accommodations, dinner with wine, and a continental breakfast are provided. The Auto Train leaves daily at 4:30pm (at both ends) and takes approximately 18 hours. Fares vary substantially from season to season. A low-season one-way fare for an adult and a car in 1994 was $175. Sleeping accommodations are available for an extra charge.

Amtrak Tours, Information, and Bookings

Get a copy of Amtrak's National Timetable from any Amtrak station, from ticket agents, or by contacting Amtrak, 60 Massachusetts Ave. NW, Washington, DC 20002 (toll free 800/USA-RAIL).

The reservations system is computerized; tickets can be purchased at stations and sales offices, from travel agents, or aboard the train (for a small added fee). Some major stations now also have self-service machines that dispense reserved tickets (you must have booked by telephone and have an assigned reservation number).

Amtrak offers some 75 tour packages throughout the U.S. For information, pick up the booklet "Amtrak's America" at train stations or travel agencies, or call the toll-free number above and request a copy.

Notes for Foreign Visitors

International visitors can also buy a **USA Railpass,** good for 15 or 30 days of unlimited travel on Amtrak. The pass is available through many overseas travel agents, and is usually purchased outside the United States, although with a foreign passport, you can also buy the passes at Amtrak offices in San Francisco, Los Angeles, Chicago, New York, Miami, Boston, and Washington, D.C. Prices in 1994 for a 15-day pass are $208 off-peak, $308 peak; a 30-day pass costs $309 off-peak, $389 peak. Reservations are generally required for train travel, and should be made for each part of your trip as early as possible.

Visitors should also be aware of the limitations of long-distance rail travel in the U.S. With a few notable exceptions (for instance, the Northeast Corridor line between Boston and Washington, D.C.), service is rarely up to European standards: delays are common, routes are limited and infrequently served, and fares are rarely significantly lower than discount airfares. Thus, cross-country train travel should be approached with caution.

BY BUS: The least expensive way to travel, but often the most time-consuming (New York to Chicago takes 17 hours). Greyhound reaches more than 8,000 cities and towns. Coaches are air-conditioned in summer (bring a sweater) and heated in winter, and long-distance buses have toilets. Rest and meal stops are made about every four hours—best to bring your own snacks, though.

For longer trips, book an express or nonstop bus. Also, plan to arrive at your destination in daylight; some bus terminals are located in unsavory neighborhoods.

Always ask about promotional fares. For extensive travel, Greyhound's **Ameripass** is a real bargain, priced in 1994 at $250 for 7 days, $350 for 15 days, and $450 for 30 days, with optional extensions for $10 per day (do it before the pass expires). The Ameripass may be purchased at any Greyhound bus terminal.

No reservations are necessary, but you should arrive at least a half hour before departure time. Greyhound also offers reasonably priced package tours.

For Information

Contact the **Greyhound Bus Company,** P.O. Box 660362, Dallas, TX 75266 (toll free 800/231-2222), or check the telephone directory for the local number.

Notes for Foreign Visitors

Greyhound's **International Ameripass** gives unlimited travel within the U.S. and Canada. For 7 days of travel, the cost is $135; for 15 days, $199; for 30 days, $270. The pass can be purchased in New York, San Francisco, and Los Angeles. It can also be purchased from International Greyhound in Europe. Designed mainly for students, the pass is basically available to any foreigner with a passport.

HITCHHIKING: Although hitching a ride is not advised, people still do it. As a general rule it's forbidden on major highways and on limited-access roads (Interstates, freeways, expressways, and turnpikes). Women should never hitchhike alone.

The best way to find a ride is by contacting a ride-line group: their telephone numbers can easily be obtained on any college campus, and the only cost is a few dollars' membership fee and a share of the gas costs.

Hitchhiking is either illegal or severely restricted in most states. Contact the highway patrol in the appropriate state to find out if solicitation of rides is tolerated.

GROUP TOURS/PACKAGES: These fly/drive, rail/drive, fully escorted, and various other types of tours save time and effort—and often money. Before booking though, you should:

1. Check to see if the tour operator is reliable. You can be pretty sure of this if the operator is a member of USTOA (United States Tour Operators Association), 211 E. 51st St., Suite 12B, New York, NY 10022 (212/750-7371), which requires for membership a minimum three years in business and hefty professional liability insurance. Also, check with your local Better Business Bureau.

2. Read the fine print. Make sure you know exactly what the overall price includes and what it doesn't; what the cancellation penalties are; and whether or not the company is free to cancel if not enough people sign up or to change the prices before departure.

DISCOUNT TRAVEL

The travel industry is so large and diverse that, like any other retail industry, there are an increasing number of professional discounters as well as newsletters and other information sources that clue you in on the latest travel discounts and bargains, from airfares to hotels and tour packages.

NEWSLETTERS: The following are reputable and useful:
Consumer Reports Travel Letter, Subscription Department, P.O. Box 53029, Boulder, CO 80322 (303/447-9330; toll free 800/525-0643): Particularly useful for airfare discounts. A monthly, the subscription is $22.
Travel Smart, 40 Beechdale Rd., Dobbs Ferry, NY 10522 (914/693-8300): One of the oldest in the business. Published 12 times a year; subscription is $44.

LAST-MINUTE TRAVEL CLUBS & OTHER DISCOUNTERS: The first category purchases the excess inventory of travel suppliers and then sells it off at a discount to its membership. Members are given a toll-free hotline to call to obtain the latest offerings; occasionally, too, they receive newssheets detailing future offerings. Among such organizations are:
Discount Travel International, 114 Forrest Ave., Narberth, PA 19072 (215/668-7184): Annual membership is $45.
Last Minute Travel Club, 1249 Boylston St., Boston, MA 02215 (617/267-9800): No membership fees.
Moment's Notice, 425 Madison Ave., New York, NY 10017 (212/486-0503): Annual fee is $45, which covers spouse and family.
Stand Buys Ltd. and Travelers Advantage, CUC Travel Services, 3033 S. Parker Rd., Suite 900, Aurora, CO 80014 (toll free 800/848-8402): Annual fee is $49.
Worldwide Discount Travel Club, 1674 Meridian Ave., Miami Beach, FL 33139 (305/534-2082): Family membership is $50; individual, $40.
Encore Marketing International, 4501 Forbes Blvd., Lanham, MD 20706 (301/459-8020; toll free 800/444-9800), operates three specialty discounting organizations: Short Notice (annual membership is $36) gives you access to last-minute discounts on tour packages and organized trips; Encore (annual membership is $49) provides additional free nights at hotels and discounts on car rentals and airfares; Villas of the World ($60 for one year) delivers 20%- to 25%-per-night discounts on villa, resort, and hotel accommodations.
Travel Avenue (formerly **McTravel**), 10 S. Riverside Plaza, Suite 1404, Chicago, IL 60606 (312/876-1116; toll free 800/333-3335), is one of the better-known organizations in this area.

WHERE TO STAY

HOTELS & MOTELS: For the last word in decor and facilities like health clubs or spas, there are the major players like Hilton, Hyatt, Ritz Carlton, Sheraton, Westin. In big cities, especially New York, Washington, Los Angeles, and Chicago, expect to pay $200 and up a night. Elsewhere, expect to pay $90–$120 double in a two-star establishment, $120–$160 in three- and most four-stars, and $160 and up in a few deluxe, four-star hotels. (*Money-Saving Hint:* Always ask about weekend packages, corporate rates, and any other special promotions being offered.)

Below the leaders are a host of motel chains offering comfortable rooms with full facilities at moderate prices. Sure they're standardized, but at least you know what to expect. Among them are Best Western, Holiday Inn, Howard Johnson, La Quinta Motor Inns, Ramada Inns, Rodeway Inns, Travelodge, and Vagabond. Doubles range from $60 to $90. (*Money-Saving Hint:* Again, ask about weekend packages and other discount rates. Use their toll-free numbers, listed in the Appendix.)

Even more standardized, often located on the outskirts of cities and with limited facilities (sometimes without a restaurant) are the budget motel chains. Color TV and telephone, though, tend to be standard. Look for Days Inns,

Econo Lodges, Friendship Inns, Motel 6, Red Roof Inns, Holiday Inns' Hampton Inns, and Marriott's Fairfield Inns. Doubles range between $30 and $60.

INNS: Staying at a country inn is extremely popular across the whole country, although perhaps the greatest number of inns are in the Northeast, the South, and California. Many of these accommodations are historic homes that once served as stagecoach stops or were mansions for the wealthy. Usually they have a distinctive ambience, antique or other noteworthy furnishings, and a personality that reflects the style and interests of the innkeepers. By definition, an inn should have a restaurant; otherwise, technically it's only a bed-and-breakfast establishment, but sometimes the definitions blur. Many inns often lack TV and room phone—the whole atmosphere is usually one of quiet relaxation, peace and quiet, and personal charm. Inns and children don't usually mix—kids may find them boring. The price tag can be high—from $80 and up, depending on the character and style of the particular inn.

How to Locate Them

Consult one of the many books available. In my opinion, the best among the many series is *Marilyn Wood's Wonderful Weekends* (Prentice Hall Travel), which contains full descriptions of several hundred inns in the states surrounding New York City—Connecticut, Rhode Island, Massachusetts, Vermont, Pennsylvania, New York, New Jersey, and Delaware.

BED-&-BREAKFAST: These establishments are increasingly popular and also increasingly sophisticated. Some are beautifully renovated historic homes and breakfasts are lavish; others are simply homes and breakfast is taken with the family. Both types are very personal and a great way to meet the locals.

How to Locate Them

Check with local tourist offices for locations in a specific area, as well as local newspapers. Book resources include *Frommer's Bed & Breakfast North America* (Prentice Hall Travel), which among other things lists all the bed-and-breakfast registries that you can contact to locate pre-inspected B&Bs. The *West Coast Bed & Breakfast Guide* and the *East Coast Bed & Breakfast Guide* (both Prentice Hall Travel) describe and picture in four-color the prime B&B places.

YOUTH HOSTELS, Ys & UNIVERSITY ACCOMMODATIONS: There are more than 230 youth hostels across the country that are open to members of any age. Annual membership is $10 for those age 17 and under, $25 for ages 18–54, and $15 for ages 55 and over. Nightly charges in rural hostels are in the $8–$10 range; in urban and resort areas, $10–$20. Sleeping accommodations are usually in small single-sex dorms, although some hostels have private and family accommodations. Cooking and laundry facilities are available.

For more information, contact **American Youth Hostels, Inc.,** National Administrative Offices, 733 15th St. NW, Suite 840, Washington, DC 20005 (202/783-6161).

A Note on Accommodation Rates

Rooms rates in this book are coded as follows: **VE,** Very Expensive ($180 and up); **E,** Expensive ($130–$180); **M,** Moderate ($80–$130); **I,** Inexpensive ($50–$80); **B,** Budget (up to $50).

A Note on Restaurant Prices

In this book, restaurant prices, per person, excluding drinks and service charges, are coded as follows: **VE,** Very Expensive ($60 and up); **E,** Expensive ($40–$60); **M,** Moderate ($25–$40); **I,** Inexpensive ($15–$25); **B,** Budget (up to $15).

The 40 or so YMCA (Young Men's Christian Association) and YWCA (Young Women's Christian Association) hostels are clustered in the bigger cities, charging $15–$20 a night without bath or $30–$40 with bath (you'll pay a little more in the major cities). Generally they are clean and well equipped (pools, health clubs), with private rooms. Because of their popularity you should arrive early to secure a room.

During the summer many campus accommodations are open to travelers. Accommodations are usually very comfortable and low priced. For more information, contact the **Council on International Educational Exchange (CIEE)**, 205 E. 42nd St., New York, NY 10017 (212/661-1414), and ask for their publication *Where to Stay USA,* which is co-published with Prentice Hall and also available in bookstores.

CAMPING: There's an excellent network of 8,000 public and 8,000 private campgrounds across the U.S., many with sites fully equipped with water, electricity, sewer connections, barbecues, showers, general store, and often with a swimming pool and other recreational facilities. For a family tent site the fee is $15–$20 per night, $18–$30 for a motor home or cabin. Send $3 to **Kampgrounds of America (KOA)**, P.O. Box 30558, Billings, MT 59114 (406/248-7444), for a list of some 650 KOA campgrounds.

Book Resources: *RV Park & Campground Directories* (Prentice Hall Press); *Camp USA* (Prentice Hall Travel). The AAA also publishes regional campground directories.

TIPS ON HAPPY STAYS: Make reservations, particularly in peak tourist seasons and in large cities where conventions and other special events may block out accommodations. Small inns and bed-and-breakfasts also require advance bookings, particularly on weekends.

If you expect to arrive late, ask for "guaranteed late arrival"—that way your room will be held. When you book, make sure you understand the rate categories: European Plan (EP) is room only; Continental Plan (CP), room and Continental breakfast; Modified American Plan (MAP), room, full breakfast, and dinner; American Plan (AP), room, breakfast, lunch, and dinner. Don't forget to include local and state taxes in the total price.

A NOTE ON TAXES   In considering how much you want to pay for your accommodations, be sure to take into account the sales tax and/or occupancy tax levied by many states and localities throughout the country. These two taxes, taken together, could add almost 25% to the cost of your accommodations. (See the table of sample tax rates in the next chapter, "For the Foreign Visitor.")

FOOD & DRINK

The United States, this great melting pot of cultures, offers many cuisines to choose from: At one end of the spectrum are four-star restaurants serving "nouvelle cuisine"; at the other end, little Greek *tavernas,* Mexican *cantinas,* and Thai restaurants with unbeatable prices. From the authentic New York "deli" to Chinese restaurants better than any in Asia, the U.S. has them all.

CUISINE OF THE NORTHEAST: The whole Northeast, and especially New England, prominently features seafood, beginning with the typical Boston dish, *clam chowder,* a thick shellfish soup. Other respected specialties are *Boston baked beans* (salt pork, beans, onions, and molasses baked slowly in a clay crockpot), and *Yankee pot roast* (beef braised with onions, tomatoes, carrots, and celery). Cape Cod (*Chatham, Wellfleet, Cotuit*) and Long Island (*Blue Point*) are famous for their oysters. Chesapeake Bay, south of Baltimore, is well known for its blue crabs, scallops, and *Pocomoke oysters.* Chesapeake Bay crabs are the base for Maryland's great specialty, *crab cakes,* little crabmeat patties, breaded and sautéed.

The best *lobsters* come from Maine, the northernmost state of New England. They are the heart of a dish of Native American origin, the *clam bake*, which involves digging a hole in the sand at the bottom of which raw fish, clams, and lobsters are laid on a bed of red-hot stones and allowed to cook under a tarpaulin or a layer of branches.

Besides its shellfish, Long Island, to the east of New York City, is famous for its *Long Island ducklings*. Vermont, near the Canadian border, is the birthplace of *cheddar cheese soup* and the principal producer of *maple syrup*, traditionally served with pancakes and waffles. New England offers two desserts drawn from the cookbooks of the earliest settlers: sweet *pumpkin pie*, and *Indian pudding*, made from cornmeal and molasses and generally topped with whipped cream.

Other northeastern specialties include: *clam fritters* (Maine and Rhode Island); *codfish balls* (New England); *crab Imperial*, crabmeat baked in a white-wine sauce (from Maryland); *hoagie* or submarine, an enormous hero sandwich made with ham, salami, provolone, onions, tomatoes, lettuce, and fresh pepper, all doused in olive oil (a Philadelphia classic); *lobster pie*, a flaky pastry crust filled with lobster in white sauce (Maine); *Manhattan clam chowder*, a New York City variation on Boston clam chowder, with tomatoes, green pepper, carrots, and celery instead of milk and potatoes; *New England boiled dinner*, a local version of the classic French pot-au-feu; *New York cheesecake*, served plain or with pineapple or strawberry topping; *oyster pie*, a country pie from Pennsylvania filled with oysters and mushrooms in a light white sauce; *pepper pot*, a thick, highly seasoned tripe soup (from Pennsylvania); *Philadelphia cheese steak*, a sandwich made from thin slices of steak covered in fried onions and melted cheese; *red flannel hash*, made of corned beef, potatoes, and red beets cooked in a frying pan over a low flame, the New England treatment for leftovers; *shad roe*, rolled in bacon, broiled, and served on toast (a springtime specialty in Maryland); *shoofly pie*, a Pennsylvania-Dutch open tart with a filling of brown sugar and molasses; *snail salad*, cut into thin slices and served in a tart marinade (Rhode Island); *succotash*, a dish of Native American origin consisting of sweet-corn kernels and lima beans cooked in milk over a low flame (Massachusetts and Rhode Island).

CUISINE OF THE SOUTH: Although much more venturesome than that of New England, the cuisine of the South also draws heavily on the excellent seafood of the Atlantic and the Gulf of Mexico: oysters, scallops, *soft-shell crabs* (eaten with their shells), *stone crabs* (of Florida), shrimp, sea bass, swordfish, etc. Rice figures in many meat and fish dishes, notably *Hopping John* (rice, bacon, and red beans), *Limping Susan* (rice, bacon, and gumbo), or *dirty rice* (rice, vegetables, and chopped chicken liver).

But the two famous dishes of the region are still *southern fried chicken*, crisp on the outside and moist on the inside, and *Virginia ham* (the best comes from Smithfield, near Norfolk), which Queen Victoria consumed in such quantity that she ordered 20 a month. Smoked for six weeks over a hickory-wood fire, from which it derives its delicate amber color, it's served baked with honey, wine, apricots, or pineapple—a real treat.

Another great regional dish is *spareribs*, related to *soul food*, which was the cuisine of the slave quarters in the plantations of the Old South. It was a simple but delicious style of cooking based on ingredients spurned by whites, such as pigs' trotters, tripe, or catfish stewed with bacon, and accompanied by such poor man's vegetables as turnips, dandelion greens, collards, and kale.

Spoon bread, the typical cornbread of the South, is served so soaked in molasses and butter that it can only be eaten with a spoon—hence the name. Florida citrus fruits (oranges, lemons, limes, grapefruit) are not the least important of the South's dependable delicacies, witness such classics as *orange bread pudding, orange baked custard*, or the most famous of all, *key lime pie*. Another famous southern dessert, *pecan pie*, is very sweet and on the heavy side. Students of liquid refreshment should take care to try a *mint julep* on a hot summer's day: bourbon (or cognac), fresh mint, and sugar poured over crushed ice.

Other southern specialties include: *Brunswick stew,* of pork and vegetables, usually served with a barbecue (Georgia and Alabama); *burgoo,* originally a ragoût of game, now a lamb-and-vegetable stew (Kentucky); *Carpetbagger steak,* stuffed with oysters (a favorite in Georgia, and also found in Louisiana); *chess pie,* made of sugared cream in a chessboard pattern (Kentucky, Tennessee, Virginia); *cobbler,* a fruit pie with a thick crust (Kentucky, Tennessee); *conch chowder,* thick soup made with conch, salt pork, and tomatoes (Florida); *fried pie,* batter turnovers filled with fruit, usually apples or peaches (Arkansas, Louisiana); *greens,* turnip-tops, collards, or mustard greens cooked slowly with a ham bone, a traditional African American dish; *hominy grits,* thick corn gruel (Virginia); *hushpuppies,* fried balls of cornmeal; *peanut soup,* celery-and-carrot soup with peanut butter, sour cream, and chopped peanuts (Virginia and Georgia); *picadillo,* chopped pork, onion, and olives, highly spiced and served with rice and beans (of Cuban origin, now a Florida classic); and *red rice,* cooked with tomatoes and ham (very popular in Savannah).

CREOLE CUISINE: Créole and Cajun cooking are a very successful synthesis of several strains—French, Spanish, African, and Caribbean. The interaction produces deftly seasoned delicacies exemplified by the two best-known dishes: *gumbo,* a thick okra-and-vegetable soup to which may be added a choice of sausage, chicken, shrimp, crab, and fish, the whole seasoned with gumbo filé (powdered sassafras leaves); and *jambalaya,* a kind of New World paella made with rice, tomatoes, shrimp or crayfish, oysters, sausage, and chicken.

Also worth looking for are *shrimp remoulade* New Orleans style, *oysters Benedict* (fried oysters wrapped in bacon and covered with hollandaise sauce), *oysters Bienville* (baked, with mushrooms, shrimp, and white-wine sauce), *oysters Casino* (baked and served under a layer of bacon with cocktail sauce), *oysters Rockefeller* (baked with spinach, au gratin, and flavored with Pernod), the *crayfish* (or *crawfish*) that abound in Louisiana's "bayous," and two delicious fish from the Gulf of Mexico, *pompano,* usually served "en papillote" (cooked in paper), and *red snapper.* Rice, fish, and shellfish figure in many Créole main dishes.

Contrary to expectation, *pig's ears,* a New Orleans favorite, have nothing to do with pigs or ears; they're horns of batter filled with cream. Other desserts are the famous *bananas Foster* (caramelized bananas with a dash of rum served with vanilla ice cream), *sweet-potato pudding, beignets* (square sugar doughnuts) eaten with the traditional *café au lait* (made with chicory), as served in the morning at the Café du Monde in New Orleans, and *pain perdu,* an old French country recipe (stale bread soaked in milk, eggs, brandy, and lemon juice, and fried in butter). And don't miss paying your respects to *café brûlot* (black coffee with cognac flambé, lemon peel, cloves, cinnamon) and spices: "black as night, soft as love, and hot as hell," in the words of the poet.

Other Créole specialties include: *blackened redfish,* filets of red snapper broiled over a high flame till the outside is blackened, a very typical Cajun dish; *boudin,* pork-and-rice sausage, highly spiced (*boudin rouge* is seasoned blood-and-lard sausage); *Calas cakes,* little fried rice cakes flavored with cinnamon or orange-flower water (a standard New Orleans dessert); *crab Imperial, New Orleans style,* crabmeat, red pepper, and green onions, covered in a spicy mayonnaise and glazed in the oven (not to be confused with crab Imperial, Maryland style); *filet mignon debris,* a medium filet mignon covered in a rich brown sauce made with burgundy, cognac, and crisp little pieces of leftover roast beef, the debris of the name (a New Orleans specialty); *muffuletta,* the great Créole sandwich, served on a round roll and made with salami, mortadella, provolone, and ham, garnished with olives; *poor boy* (or *po'boy*), a New Orleans–style hero of roast beef, ham, or sausage.

MIDWESTERN CUISINE: This country of wide-open spaces and great herds of cattle is not distinguished for the originality of its cuisine, in spite of a flow of immigrants from Germany, Italy, and Scandinavia. The always-dependable dishes are *meat and potatoes* or *freshwater fish* from the region's lakes and rivers. The reputation of such restaurants as Morton's in Chicago, the Golden Ox in Kansas City, and the Iowa Beef Steak House in Des Moines—to name only a few—rests on their red meats: *T-bone steak, sirloin* or *New York steak, rib-eye* or *Delmonico steak, porterhouse steak* or *chateaubriand, tournedos, filet mignon, top loin* or *shell steak,* etc., usually served with *french fries* or *baked potatoes,* of which the best are made from Idaho potatoes. (Idaho is "the Potato State.")

Other midwestern specialties are: *barbecued ribs,* spareribs brushed with barbecue sauce and cooked over an open fire of wood or charcoal until glazed (they have made the name of such restaurants as Carsons, in Skokie, Illinois); *deep-dish pizza,* which originated in Chicago, a pizza with a very thick, soft crust baked in a casserole; *five-way chili,* made with beans, spaghetti, chopped beef, onions, and cheese (comes from Cincinnati and should not be confused with Tex-Mex chili); *pan-fried chicken* (a specialty in Indiana, Missouri, and Ohio); *pasties* are turnovers filled with meat (Michigan); *sour-cream raisin pie,* a thick, creamy, raisin-filled cake covered in meringue (Indiana, Minnesota, and Wisconsin); *persimmon pudding,* made with the flavorful small native fruit (Indiana); and *toasted ravioli,* a specialty of St. Louis, is fried meat-filled ravioli.

SOUTHWESTERN CUISINE: Better known as Tex-Mex, this is essentially an adaptation of Mexican dishes (and particularly their explosive chili sauces) for the North American palate. Among the best-known dishes from this region north of the Rio Grande are *chili con carne* (chopped beef with red beans, minced onions, cumin or paprika, tomatoes, and chili); *tortillas* (flat cornmeal cakes used instead of bread); *frijoles refritos* (boiled beans mashed, seasoned with chili, and refried in a pan; traditional cowboy fare); *enchiladas* (tortillas stuffed with meat, beans, or cheese and baked in the oven); *tamales* (patties of chopped meat, cornmeal, and chili powder, steamed in a cornhusk); and *barbecue* (beef or pork brushed with a special spicy sauce and cooked over a wood or charcoal fire; usually eaten with corn on the cob). To wash it all down there's nothing better than a few generously proportioned *margaritas* (tequila and lime juice, served over crushed ice in a frosted glass whose rim has been dipped in salt).

Other southwestern specialties include: *carne adobada,* pork marinated in a chili sauce; *chicken-fried steak,* thin slices of steak floured and sautéed, a cowboy tradition; *chiles rellenos,* green peppers stuffed with meat or cheese, brushed with egg and fried; *hot links,* spicy Texan sausages broiled over a barbecue; *jerky,* air-dried beef (Oklahoma, Texas); *menudo,* tripe-and-cornmeal stew (New Mexico, Texas); *Rocky Mountain oysters,* fried bull's (although usually lamb's) testicles, a Colorado specialty; *sopaipilla,* fried honey-dipped bread served hot (Arizona, New Mexico).

WESTERN & NORTHWESTERN CUISINE: Geography and climate have endowed the Pacific coast, and particularly California, with an abundance of fine foodstuffs. *Dungeness crabs,* superb salmon (*chinook, king, coho, sockeye*), *Dolly Varden trout, Rex* and *Petrale* sole, halibut, tuna, anchovy, *geoduck clams* (great shellfish whose meat weighs up to 15 lb./6.8kg, served sliced and grilled as steak or chopped in tasty soup; a Washington state specialty), *razor clams,* turtles, oysters (*Olympia, Petit Points, Pigeon Points, Quilcene, Tamales Bay, Drakes Bay, Yakima Bay,* and others), and above all the delectable—but now strictly protected—*abalone* are its glories of seafood.

There are so many fruits and vegetables that it's hard to choose: *figs* in the San Joaquin Valley, *tomatoes* in the Sacramento Valley, *vineyards* in the Sonoma and Napa Valleys, *avocados* in the San Diego Valley, *dates* in the Coachella Valley, *lettuce* and *melons* in Imperial Valley, are among the best in the country.

Two unexpected discoveries in the region: crusty, tasty, yeasty *sourdough bread* (the best is from San Francisco), and *chop suey,* a stew or stir-fry of meat, bean sprouts, mushrooms, and celery, served with rice, country fare of the Chinese workers who helped to build the first California railroads. Lovers of Chinese food can choose among thousands of Cantonese, Mandarin, Hunan, or Szechuan restaurants.

Other western specialties include: *artichoke soup* (from California); *barbecued salmon,* fresh marinated salmon cooked over hot coals or a wood fire (the great northwestern specialty); *Caesar salad,* romaine lettuce, chopped hard-boiled egg, toast croutons, anchovies, and Parmesan cheese; *cioppino,* seafood stew seasoned with spices, herbs, and fresh tomatoes; *crab* (or *shrimp*) *Louie,* salad made with lettuce, hard-boiled egg, crabmeat, and mayonnaise blended with chili sauce (found all along the Pacific coast); and *Hangtown Fry,* scrambled eggs with oysters (California, Washington).

FOR FURTHER READING

To attempt to present an overview of U.S. history, economics, politics, and culture in the space permitted in this introduction seems folly indeed. Instead, we have chosen to compile this selective booklist. Readers can pick and choose from the following titles in the areas that interest them. All should be available in public libraries.

Economic, Political, and Social History

Acuno, Rodolfo. *Occupied America: A History of Chicanos* (2nd ed.).

Algren, Nelson. *Chicago: City on the Make.*

Bailyn, Bernard. *The Ideological Origins of the American Revolution.*

Beard, Charles M. *An Economic Interpretation of the Constitution of the United States.*

Becker, Carl L. *The Declaration of Independence: A Study of the History of Political Ideas.*

Birmingham, Stephen. *America's Secret Aristocracy.*

Boorstin, Daniel J. *The Exploring Spirit: America and the World, Then and Now.*

——————. *The Americans* (3 vols.).

Brandon, William. *The Last American: The Indian in American Culture.*

Bridenbaugh, Carl, and Jessica Bridenbaugh. *Rebels and Gentlemen: Philadelphia in the Age of Franklin.*

Brown, Dee. *Bury My Heart at Wounded Knee: An Indian History of the American West.*

Burns, James MacGregor. *The Vineyard of Liberty.*

Catton, Bruce, and the American Heritage Editors. *American Heritage Picture History of the Civil War.*

Chen, Jack. *The Chinese of America.*

Commager, Henry Steele, ed. *The American Destiny.*

Connell, Evan. *Son of Morning Star: Custer and the Little Big Horn.*

Cooke, Alistair. *The Americans: Fifty Talks on Our Life and Times.*

Dangerfield, George. *Awakening of American Nationalism, 1815–1828.*

De Voto, Bernard. *Course of Empire.*

Du Plessix Gray, Francine. *Hawaii, the Sugar-Coated Fortress.*

Fitzgerald, Frances. *Fire in the Lake: The Vietnamese and the Americans in Vietnam.*

Franklin, John Hope, and Alfred Moss. *From Slavery to Freedom: A History of Negro America.*

Galbraith, John Kenneth. *The Great Crash of 1929.*

Garreau, Joel. *The Nine Nations of North America.*

Genovese, Eugene D. *The Political Economy of Slavery: Studies in Economy and Society of the Slave South.*

Goldman, Eric. *Rendezvous with Destiny: A History of Modern American Reform.*
Goldman, Eric F. *The Crucial Decade and After: America, 1945–1960.*
Handlin, Oscar. *The Uprooted* (rev. ed.).
Hellman, Lillian. *Scoundrel Time.*
Hofstadter, Richard. *The Age of Reform: From Bryan to F.D.R.*
————. *The American Political Tradition and the Men Who Made It.*
Howe, Irving. *World of Our Fathers.*
Inge, M. Thomas, ed. *Handbook of American Popular Culture.*
Jordan, Winthrop D. *White Over Black: American Attitudes Toward the Negro, 1550–1812.*
Lewis, David L. *When Harlem Was in Vogue.*
Lewis, Oscar. *La Vida: A Puerto Rican Family in the Culture of Poverty.*
Liebling, A. J. *Back Where I Come From.*
Marquis, Arnold. *Guide to America's Indians: Ceremonials, Reservations, and Museums.*
McPhee, John. *Coming into the Country.*
McPherson, James. *Battle Cry of Freedom.*
Mencken, H. L. *The American Language.*
Morison, Samuel Eliot. *The Growth of the American Republic.*
Parish, Peter J. *The American Civil War.*
Parrington, Vernon L. *Main Currents in American Thought.*
Rose, Al. *Storyville, New Orleans.*
Schlesinger, Arthur M., Jr. *The Age of Jackson.*
————. *The Rise of the City.*
Shannon, William V. *The American Irish.*
Terkel, Studs. *American Dreams: Lost and Found.*
————. *Division Street: America.*
Trudgill, Peter. *Coping with America* (2nd ed.).
Turner, Frederick J. *The Frontier in American History.*
Whitman, Walt. *Democratic Vistas and Other Papers.*
Williams, Juan. *Eyes on the Prize: America's Civil Rights Years, 1954–1965.*
Wilson, Edmund, and Joseph Mitchell. *Apologies to the Iroquois: With a Study of the Mohawks on High Street.*
Wilson, Robert A., and Bill Hosokawa. *East to America: A History of Japanese in the United States.*
Woodward, Bob, and Carl Bernstein. *All the President's Men.*
Woodward, C. Vann. *The Origins of the New South, 1877–1913.*
Zinn, Howard. *The Twentieth Century: A People's History.*

Art, Architecture, Photography, and Film

Adams, Ansel. *Classic Images.*
Agee, James. *Agee on Film.*
Baigell, Matthew. *Dictionary of American Art.*
Barnouw, Erik. *Tube of Plenty: The Evolution of American Television* (rev. ed.).
Everson, William. *American Silent Film.*
Goldberger, Paul. *The City Observed: New York. A Guide to the Architecture of Manhattan.*
Highwater, Jamake. *Song from the Earth: American Indian Painting.*
Jacobs, Jane. *The Death and Life of Great American Cities.*
Jacobs, Lewis. *The Rise of the American Film.*
Kael, Pauline. *Deeper into the Movies.*
Kidder-Smith, G. E. *The Architecture of the United States.*
Larkin, Oliver W. *Art and Life in America.*
Mumford, Lewis. *The Culture of Cities.*
Novotny, Ann. *Alice's World: The Life and Photography of an American Original: Alice Austin, 1866–1952.*

Rifkind, Carole. *A Field Guide to American Architecture.*
Rose, Barbara. *American Art Since 1900* (rev. and expanded ed.).
Sklar, Robert. *Movie-Made America: A Cultural History of American Movies.*
Steichen, Edward. *Steichen: A Life in Photography.*
Trachtenberg, Allan. *America and Lewis Hine.*

Fiction, Poetry, Theater, and Travel

Adams, Henry. *The Education of Henry Adams.*
Baldwin, James. *Go Tell It on the Mountain.*
Bellow, Saul. *The Adventures of Augie March.*
Brooks, Van Wyck. *The Flowering of New England, 1815–65.*
Cather, Willa. *O Pioneers.*
Chandler, Raymond. *The Raymond Chandler Omnibus.*
Cooper, James Fenimore. *The Last of the Mohicans.*
—————. *The Deerslayer.*
Crane, Stephen. *The Red Badge of Courage.*
Dickens, Charles. *American Notes.*
Dickinson, Emily. *Collected Poems of Emily Dickinson.*
Dos Passos, John. *USA.*
Dreiser, Theodore. *Sister Carrie.*
Ehrlich, Eugene, and Gorton Carruth. *The Oxford Illustrated Literary Guide to the United States.*
Ellison, Ralph. *The Invisible Man.*
Faulkner, William. *The Sound and the Fury.*
—————. *Absalom! Absalom!*
Fitzgerald, F. Scott. *The Great Gatsby.*
Hammett, Dashiell. *The Maltese Falcon.*
Harte, Bret. *The Outcasts of Poker Flat.*
Hawthorne, Nathaniel. *The Scarlet Letter.*
Hemingway, Ernest. *In Our Time.*
Irving, Washington. *Diedrich Knickerbocker's A History of New York.*
James, Henry. *The American Scene.*
—————. *The Bostonians.*
Kerouac, Jack. *On the Road.*
Kingston, Maxine Hong. *The Woman Warrior.*
London, Jack. *Call of the Wild.*
MacDonald, Ross. *The Underground Man.*
Mailer, Norman. *The Deer Park.*
Melville, Herman. *Bartleby the Scrivener.*
Michener, James A. *Hawaii.*
Mitchell, Margaret. *Gone with the Wind.*
Moon, William Least Heat. *Blue Highways: A Journey into America.*
Morris, Jan. *Manhattan '45.*
Mukherjee, Bharati. *Darkness.*
Nabokov, Vladimir. *Lolita.*
Naipaul, V. S. *A Turn in the South.*
Norris, Frank. *McTeague: A Story of San Francisco.*
Raban, Jonathan. *Old Glory: An American Voyage.*
Reeves, Richard. *American Journey: Traveling with Tocqueville in Search of Democracy in America.*
Roth, Philip. *Portnoy's Complaint.*
Runyon, Damon. *Guys and Dolls.*
Sinclair, Upton. *The Jungle.*
Steffens, Lincoln. *The Shame of Cities.*
Stein, Gertrude. *The Making of Americans.*
Steinbeck, John. *The Grapes of Wrath.*
—————. *Travels with Charley in Search of America.*

Stevenson, Robert Louis. *Travels in Hawaii.*
Twain, Mark. *The Adventures of Huckleberry Finn.*
——————. *Roughing It.*
Updike, John. *Rabbit Run.*
Walker, Alice. *The Color Purple.*
Warren, Robert Penn. *All the King's Men.*
Wharton, Edith. *The Age of Innocence.*
White, E. B. *Here Is New York.*
White, Edmund. *States of Desire: Travels in Gay America.*
Whitman, Walt. *Leaves of Grass.*
Wilder, Thornton. *Our Town.*
Williams, Tennessee. *Cat on a Hot Tin Roof.*
Wilson, Edmund. *Patriotic Gore: Studies in the Literature of the American Civil War.*
Wolfe, Thomas. *Look Homeward, Angel.*
Wolfe, Tom. *The Bonfire of the Vanities.*
Wright, Richard. *Native Son.*

Biography

Amory, Cleveland. *The Proper Bostonians.*
Baker, Russell. *Growing Up.*
Burns, James MacGregor. *Roosevelt: The Lion and the Fox.*
Dillard, Annie. *An American Childhood.*
Flexner, James Thomas. *Washington: The Indispensable Man.*
Goodwin, Doris Kearns. *Lyndon Johnson and the American Dream.*
Hecht, Ben. *Child of the Century.*
Link, Arthur S. *Woodrow Wilson and the Progressive Era, 1910–1917.*
McCullough, David. *Mornings on Horseback.*
Miller, Merle. *Plain Speaking: An Oral Biography of Harry S Truman.*
Morris, Edmund. *The Rise of Theodore Roosevelt.*
Padover, Saul. *Jefferson.*
Sandburg, Carl. *Abraham Lincoln: The Prairie Years and the War Years.*
Schlesinger, Arthur M., Jr. *A Thousand Days.*
Van Doren, Carl C. *Benjamin Franklin.*
Vidal, Gore. *Lincoln.*
Williams, T. Harry. *Huey Long.*

FOR THE
FOREIGN VISITOR

□ □ □

Although American fads and fashions have spread across Europe and other parts of the world so that America may seem like familiar territory before your arrival, there are still many peculiarities and uniquely American situations that any foreign visitor will encounter. This chapter is meant to clue you in on what they are. International visitors should also read the Introduction carefully.

PREPARING FOR YOUR TRIP

DOCUMENT REGULATIONS: Canadian citizens may enter the U.S. without visas; they need only proof of residence.

British, Dutch, French, German, Italian, Japanese, Swedish, and Swiss citizens traveling on valid national (or EC) passports do not need a visa for holiday or business travel in the U.S. of 90 days or less if they hold round-trip or return tickets and if they enter the U.S. on an airline or cruise line that participates in the no-visa travel program.

(Note that citizens of these visa-exempt countries who first enter the U.S. may then visit Mexico, Canada, Bermuda, and/or the Caribbean islands and then reenter the U.S., by any mode of transportation, without needing a visa. Further information is available from any U.S. embassy or consulate.)

Citizens of countries other than those above require:

□ a valid **passport,** with an expiration date at least six months later than the scheduled end of the visit to the U.S.; and
□ a **tourist visa,** available without charge from the nearest U.S. consulate; the traveler must submit a completed application form (either in person or by mail) with a passport photograph attached.

Usually you will be given your visa at once, or within 24 hours at most; try to avoid the summer rush in June–Aug. If applying by mail, enclose a large stamped, self-addressed envelope, and expect an average wait of two weeks. Visa application forms are also available at airline offices or from leading travel agents as well as from U.S. consulates. The U.S. tourist visa (visa B-2) is theoretically valid for a year, and for any number of entries, but the U.S. consulate that gives you the tourist visa will determine the length of stay for a multiple- or single-entry visa. However, there is some latitude here, and especially if you can give the address of a relative, friend, or business connection living in the U.S. (useful, too, for car rental, passage through Customs, etc.), you have an excellent chance of getting a longer permit if you want one.

MEDICAL REQUIREMENTS: No inoculations are needed to enter the U.S. unless you are coming from areas known to be suffering from epidemics, especially of cholera or yellow fever. Applicants for immigrants' visas (and only they) must undergo a screening test for AIDS under a law passed in 1987.

If you have a disease requiring treatment with medications containing controlled drugs, carry a valid, signed prescription from your physician to allay any suspicions that you are smuggling drugs. Ditto for syringes.

TRAVEL INSURANCE (BAGGAGE, HEALTH & LOSS): All such insurance is voluntary in the U.S.; however, given the very high cost of medical care, I cannot too strongly advise every traveler to arrange for appropriate coverage before setting out. There are specialized insurance companies that will, for a relatively low premium, cover:

- □ loss or theft of your baggage;
- □ trip-cancellation costs;
- □ guarantee of bail in case you are sued;
- □ sickness or injury costs (medical, surgical, and hospital);
- □ costs of an accident, repatriation, or death.

Such packages (for example, "Europe Assistance" in Europe) are sold by automobile clubs at attractive rates, as well as by banks and travel agencies.

GETTING TO THE U.S.

Travelers from overseas can take advantage of the **APEX (Advance Purchase Excursion) fares** offered by all the major U.S. and European carriers. Aside from these, attractive values are offered by **Icelandair** on flights from Luxembourg to New York or Orlando; by **Virgin Atlantic** from London to New York/Newark or Miami; and by **Tower Air** from Paris to New York.

Some large airlines (for example, TWA, American, Northwest, United, and Delta) offer travelers on their transatlantic or transpacific flights special discount tickets under the name **Visit USA,** allowing travel between any U.S. destinations at minimum rates. They are not on sale in the U.S., and must therefore be purchased before you leave your foreign point of departure. This system is the best way of seeing the U.S. at low cost. You should obtain information well in advance from your travel agent or the office of the airline concerned, since the conditions attached to these discount tickets can be changed without advance notice.

GETTING AROUND

For information on transportation around the U.S., see the "Notes for Foreign Visitors" sections in the Introduction under the modes of transportation.

FAST FACTS FOR THE FOREIGN TRAVELER

ACCOMMODATIONS: See the Introduction.

AUTOMOBILE ORGANIZATIONS: See "Getting Around" "By Car," in the Introduction.

BUSINESS HOURS: Public and private **offices** are usually open 9am–5pm Mon–Fri, except in Hawaii and parts of California (7:30 or 8am–4pm).

Banking hours are generally 9am–3pm Mon–Fri, but in some cases until 6pm on Fri, and sometimes also on Sat morning.

Post offices are open 8am–5:30 or 6pm Mon–Fri and 8am–noon on Sat.

Store hours are 9:30 or 10am–5:30 or 6pm Mon–Sat, though often until 9pm one or two evenings a week. Shopping centers, drugstores, and supermarkets are open 9am–9pm six days a week (seven days, and even in some cases 24 hours, in certain large cities).

Museum hours vary widely. The norm for big cities is 10am–5pm six days a week (closing day is usually Mon). Some art museums stay open until 9pm one or, rarely, two evenings a week.

CLIMATE: Any season is a good time for travel in the U.S.—provided you understand how to juggle climates and distances! Summer is hot and humid in the

East and the Southeast from New York to Louisiana. From Texas to California it can be scorching—95°F (35°C) in the shade is not unusual. On the other hand, it's a delightful time to visit the Northwest and the Rockies. Winter is severe across the North and a good deal of the Central Tier—the mercury often goes down to 10°–15°F (−12° to −9.5°C) in Chicago and Denver—but very agreeable in Florida and California. From coast to coast, the best seasons for travel are spring and (even more) fall, which can be very mild during the "Indian Summer." See the table of average temperatures for representative cities in the Introduction.

CURRENCY & EXCHANGE: The U.S. monetary system has a decimal base: one **dollar** ($1) = 100 **cents** (100¢).

The commonest **bills** (all green) are the $1 ("a buck"), $5, $10, and $20 denominations. There are also $2 (seldom encountered), $50, and $100 bills (the two latter are not welcome when paying for small purchases).

There are six denominations of **coins:** 1¢ (one cent, or "penny"); 5¢ (five cents, or "nickel"); 10¢ (ten cents, or "dime"); 25¢ (twenty-five cents, or "quarter"); 50¢ (fifty cents, or "half dollar"); and the rare $1 piece.

You will find currency exchange services in major airports with international service. Elsewhere they may be hard to come by. In New York, a very reliable source is **Thomas Cook Currency Services, Inc.** They sell commission-free foreign and U.S. traveler's checks, drafts, and wire transfers. They maintain several offices in New York City (one is at 630 Fifth Ave., tel. 212/757-6915), at the JFK International Arrivals Terminal (718/656-8444), and at La Guardia in the Delta terminal (718/533-0784).

Traveler's Checks and Credit Cards

Traveler's checks denominated in *dollars* are accepted without demur at most hotels, motels, restaurants, and large stores. But as any experienced traveler knows, the best place to change traveler's checks is at a bank.

However, the method of payment most widely used is the **credit or charge card**: VISA (BarclayCard in Britain, Chargex in Canada), MasterCard (EuroCard in Europe, Access in Britain, Diamond in Japan, etc.), American Express, Diners Club, and Carte Blanche, in descending order of acceptance. You can save yourself trouble by using "plastic money," rather than cash or traveler's checks, in most hotels, motels, restaurants, and retail stores. You must have a credit card to rent a car at most rental agencies. It can also be used as proof of identity (often carrying more weight than a passport), or as a "cash card," enabling you to draw money from banks that accept them.

CUSTOMS & IMMIGRATION: Every adult visitor may bring in, free of duty: 1 liter of wine or hard liquor; 200 cigarettes or 100 cigars (but *no* cigars from Cuba) or 3 lb. (1.35kg) of smoking tobacco; $400 worth of gifts. These exemptions are offered to travelers who spend at least 72 hours in the U.S. and who have not claimed them within the preceding six months. It is altogether forbidden to bring into the country foodstuffs (particularly fruit and cooked meats) and plants (vegetables, seeds, tropical plants, etc.). Foreign tourists may bring in or take out up to $10,000 in U.S. or foreign currency with no formalities; larger sums must be declared to Customs on entering or leaving.

The visitor arriving by air, no matter what the port of entry—New York, Boston, Miami, Honolulu, Los Angeles, or the rest—should cultivate patience and resignation before setting foot on U.S. soil. The U.S. Customs and Immigration Services are among the slowest and most suspicious on earth. On some days, especially summer weekends, you may wait to have your passport stamped at Miami or New York's John F. Kennedy Airport for nearly two hours, sometimes three hours. The situation is just as bad at other major international airports. Add the time it takes to clear Customs and you'll see that you should make very generous allowance for delay in planning connections between international and domestic flights—an average of at least two to three hours.

In contrast, for the traveler arriving by car or by rail from Canada, the border-crossing formalities have been streamlined to the vanishing point. And for the traveler by air from Canada, Bermuda, and some points in the Caribbean, you can go through Customs and Immigration at the point of *departure*, which is much quicker and less painful.

DRINKING LAWS: As with marriage and divorce, every state, and sometimes every county and community, has its own laws governing the sale of liquor. The only federal regulation (based on a judgment of the U.S. Supreme Court on June 23, 1987) restricts the consumption of liquor in public places anywhere in the country to persons aged 21 or over (states not respecting this rule may be penalized by a withdrawal of federal highway funds).

Hours of operation for liquor stores, as well as for bars and nightclubs, are strictly limited in certain states; in most, establishments selling liquor are closed Sunday and public holidays. In Alabama, Maine, New Hampshire, Ohio, Oregon, Pennsylvania, Utah, and Vermont, liquor may be sold by the bottle only in state-owned outlets.

Not all restaurants are licensed to serve beer, wine, or hard liquor, though you may generally bring your drink with you. As far as possible, restaurants not having beverage licenses are noted as such in this book.

DRIVING: Americans drive on the right. Traffic laws may differ from state to state, so consult the local tourist office or your car-rental agency. Also see "Driving" under "Safety," below.

ELECTRIC CURRENT: U.S. wall outlets give power at 110–115 volts A.C., 60 cycles, compared to 220 volts A.C., 50 cycles, in most of Europe. Besides a 110-volt transformer, small appliances of non-American manufacture, such as hairdryers or shavers, will require a plug adapter with two flat, parallel pins.

EMBASSIES & CONSULATES: All embassies are located in the national capital, Washington, D.C.; some consulates are located in major cities, and most nations have a mission to the United Nations in New York City.

Listed here are the embassies and consulates of the major English-speaking countries—Australia, Canada, Ireland, New Zealand, and the United Kingdom. If you are from another country, you can get the telephone number of your embassy by calling "information" in Washington, D.C. (202/555-1212).

AUSTRALIA Embassy: 1601 Massachusetts Ave. NW, Washington, DC 20036 (202/797-3000). **Consulates: Honolulu**—1000 Bishop St., Penthouse, HI 96813 (808/524-5050). **Houston**—3 Post Oak Central A.H., 1990 Post Oak Rd., Suite 800, TX 77056 (713/629-9140). **Los Angeles**—611 N. Larchmont Blvd., CA 90004 (213/469-4300). **New York**—International Building, 630 Fifth Ave., NY 10111 (212/245-4000). **San Francisco**—1 Bush St., CA 94104 (415/362-6160).

CANADA Embassy: 501 Pennsylvania Ave. NW, Washington, DC 20001 (202/682-1740). **Consulates: Atlanta**—One CNN Center, Suite 400 South Tower, GA 30303 (404/577-6810). **Boston**—3 Copley Pl., Suite 400, MA 02116 (617/262-3760). **Buffalo**—One Marine Midland Center, Suite 3550, NY 14203 (716/852-1247). **Chicago**—180 N. Stetson St., Suite 2400, IL 60604 (312/616-1800). **Dallas**—St. Paul Place, 750 N. St. Paul, Suite 1700, TX 75201 (214/922-9806). **Detroit**—600 Renaissance Center, Suite 1100, MI 48243 (313/567-2340). **Los Angeles**—300 S. Grand Ave., 10th Floor, CA 90071 (213/687-7432). **Minneapolis**—701 Fourth Ave. South, MN 55415

(612/333-4641). **New York**—1251 Ave. of the Americas, NY 10020 (212/596-1600). **Seattle**—412 Plaza 600, Sixth and Stewart, WA 98101 (206/443-1777).

IRELAND **Embassy:** 2234 Massachusetts Ave. NW, Washington, DC 20008 (202/462-3939). **Consulates: Boston**—Chase Bldg., 535 Boylston St., MA 02116 (617/267-9330). **Chicago**—400 N. Michigan Ave., IL 60611 (312/337-1868). **New York**—345 Park Ave., NY 10514-0037 (212/319-2555). **San Francisco**—655 Montgomery St., Suite 930, CA 94111 (415/392-4214).

NEW ZEALAND **Embassy:** 37 Observatory Circle NW, Washington, DC 20008 (202/328-4800). **Consulates: Los Angeles**—Tishman Bldg., 10960 Wilshire Blvd., Suite 1530, Westwood, CA 90024 (310/477-8241).

UNITED KINGDOM **Embassy:** 3100 Massachusetts Ave. NW, Washington, DC 20008 (202/462-1340). **Consulates: Atlanta**—245 Peachtree Center Ave., Suite 2700, GA 30303 (404/524-8823). **Boston**—60 Atlantic Ave., MA 02210 (617/248-9555). **Chicago**—33 N. Dearborn St., IL 60602 (312/346-1810). **Dallas**—2730 Stemmons Freeway, TX 75207 (214/637-3600). **Houston**—1100 Milam Bldg., TX 77002 (713/659-6270). **Los Angeles**—3701 Wilshire Blvd., Suite 312, CA 90010 (310/385-7381). **Miami**—1001 S. Bay Shore Dr., Suite 2110, FL 33131 (305/374-1522). **New York**—845 Third Ave., NY 10022 (212/752-8400).

EMERGENCIES: In all major cities you can call the police, an ambulance, or the fire brigade through the single emergency telephone number **911.** Another useful way of reporting an emergency is to call the telephone-company operator by dialing **0** (zero, *not* the letter "O"). Outside major cities, call the county sheriff or the fire brigade at the number you'll find in the local telephone book.

If you encounter such travelers' problems as sickness, accident, or lost or stolen baggage, it will pay you to call **Travelers' Aid,** an organization that specializes in helping distressed travelers, whether American or foreign. Check the local telephone book for the nearest office, or dial 0 (zero) and ask the telephone operator.

FAX: See "Telephone, Telegraph, Fax, Telex" below.

HOLIDAYS: On the following legal national holidays, banks, government offices, post offices, and many stores, restaurants, and museums are closed: January 1 (New Year's Day); Third Monday in January (Martin Luther King Day); Third Monday in February (Presidents Day, Washington's Birthday); Last Monday in May (Memorial Day); July 4 (Independence Day); First Monday in September (Labor Day); Second Monday in October (Columbus Day); November 11 (Veteran's Day/Armistice Day); Last Thursday in November (Thanksgiving Day); December 25 (Christmas Day). Also celebrated in some cities and states are the following: February 12 (in the North) (Lincoln's Birthday); March 17 (St. Patrick's Day); April 19 (Patriot's Day).

In addition, many states and cities have their own special holidays.

Finally, the Tuesday following the first Monday in November is Election Day, and is a legal holiday in presidential-election years.

INFORMATION: See the opening of each chapter and the Appendix for a list of state tourism information offices.

LEGAL AID: The foreign tourist, unless positively identified as a member of the Mafia or of a drug ring, will probably never become involved with the American legal system. If you are pulled up for a minor infraction (for example, of the highway code, such as speeding), never attempt to pay the fine directly to a police officer; you may wind up arrested on the much more serious charge of attempted bribery. Pay fines by mail, or directly into the hands of the clerk of the court. If accused of a more serious offense, it is wise to say and do nothing before consulting a lawyer. Under U.S. law, an arrested person is allowed one telephone call to a party of his choice. Call your embassy or consulate.

MAIL: If you want your mail to follow you on your vacation, you need only fill out a change-of-address card at any post office. The post office will also hold your mail for up to one month. If you aren't sure of your address, your mail can be sent to you, in your name, **c/o General Delivery** at the main post office of the city or region where you expect to be. The addressee must pick it up in person, and produce proof of identity (driver's license, credit card, passport, etc.).

Generally to be found at intersections, mailboxes are blue with a red-and-white stripe, and carry the inscription U.S. MAIL. If your mail is addressed to a U.S. destination, don't forget to add the five-figure postal code or ZIP (Zone Improvement Plan) Code, after the two-letter abbreviation of the state to which the mail is addressed (CA for California, MA for Massachusetts, NY for New York, and so on).

MEASUREMENTS: While most of the rest of the world is on the metric system, for nonscientific purposes the United States still adheres to its own units of measurement. See the Appendix for tables that will help you with conversions, for both standard metric measurements and clothing and shoe sizes.

MEDICAL EMERGENCIES: See "Emergencies," above.

NEWSPAPERS AND MAGAZINES: With a few exceptions, such as the *New York Times, USA Today,* the *Wall Street Journal,* and the *Christian Science Monitor,* daily newspapers in the U.S. are local, not national. Most large cities have at least two daily papers, of which the most important, after those mentioned above, are the *Washington Post,* the *Chicago Tribune,* and the *Los Angeles Times.* These papers are much larger than the great dailies of Europe or Australia; their Sunday editions can weigh six to seven pounds (2.75–3.2kg).

There are also innumerable newsweeklies like *Newsweek, Time, U.S. News & World Report,* and specialized periodicals, such as the monthly magazines each devoted to a single city—*New York* magazine (weekly), *Chicago* magazine, *Los Angeles* magazine, *The Washingtonian*—ideal starting points for your voyage of discovery into the city concerned.

The airmail editions of foreign newspapers and magazines are on sale only belatedly, and only at the airports and international bookstores in the largest U.S. cities.

POST: See "Mail," above.

RADIO & TELEVISION: Audiovisual media, with coast-to-coast networks—ABC, CBS, NBC, and FOX—along with the Public Broadcasting System (PBS) and the cable network CNN, play a major part in American life. In the big cities, televiewers have a choice of about a dozen channels (including the UHF channels), most of them transmitting 24 hours a day, without counting the pay-TV channels showing recent movies or sports events. In smaller communities the choice may be limited to four TV channels (there are 1,200 in the entire country), and a half dozen local radio stations (there are 6,500 in all), each broadcasting a particular kind of music—classical, country, jazz, pop, gospel—punctuated by news broadcasts and frequent commercials.

SAFETY:

GENERAL While tourist areas are generally safe, crime is on the increase everywhere, and U.S. urban areas tend to be less safe than those in Europe or Japan.

Visitors should always stay alert. This is particularly true of large U.S. cities. It is wise to ask the city or area's tourist office if you are in doubt about which neighborhoods are safe. Avoid deserted areas, especially at night. Don't go into any city park at night unless there is an occasion that attracts crowds—for example, New York City's concerts in the parks. Generally speaking, you can feel safe in areas where there are many people, and many open establishments.

Avoid carrying valuables with you on the street, and don't display expensive cameras or electronic equipment. Hold on to your pocketbook, and place your billfold in an inside pocket. In restaurants, theaters, and other public places, keep your possessions in sight.

Remember also that hotels are open to the public, and in a large hotel, security may not be able to screen everyone entering. Always lock your room door; don't assume that once inside your hotel you are automatically safe and need no longer be aware of your surroundings.

In general, the U.S. is safer than most other countries, particularly in rural areas, but there are "danger zones" in the big cities, pinpointed in this guide, which should be approached only with extreme caution.

As a general rule, isolated areas such as gardens and parking lots should be avoided after dark. Elevators and public-transport systems in off-hours, particularly between 10pm and 6am, are also potential crime scenes. You should drive through decaying neighborhoods with your car doors locked and the windows closed. Never carry on your person valuables like jewelry or large sums of cash; traveler's checks are much safer.

You may wish to contact the local tourist information bureau in your destination before you arrive. They may be able to provide you with a safety brochure.

DRIVING Safety while driving is particularly important. Question your rental agency about personal safety, or ask for a traveler safety tips brochure when you pick up your car. Obtain written directions, or a map with the route marked in red, from the agency showing how to get to your destination. And, if possible, arrive and depart during daylight hours.

Recently more and more crime has involved cars and drivers. If you drive off a highway into a doubtful neighborhood, leave the area as quickly as possible. If you have an accident, even on the highway, stay in your car with the doors locked until you assess the situation, or until the police arrive. If you are bumped from behind on the street or are involved in a minor accident with no injuries and the situation appears to be suspicious, motion to the other driver to follow you. *Never* get out of your car in such situations. You can also keep a premade sign in your car which reads: "**PLEASE FOLLOW THIS VEHICLE TO REPORT THE ACCIDENT.**" Show the sign to the other driver and go directly to the nearest police precinct, well-lighted service station, or all-night store.

If you see someone on the road who indicates a need for help, do not stop. Take note of the location, drive on to a well-lighted area, and telephone the police by dialing 911.

TAXES: In the U.S. there is no VAT (Value-Added Tax), or other indirect tax at a national level. Every state, and each city in it, has the right to levy its own local tax on all purchases, including hotel and restaurant checks, airline tickets, etc. It is automatically added to the price of certain services such as public transportation, cab fares, phone calls, and gasoline. It varies from 4% to 10% depending on the state and city, so when you're making major purchases such as photographic equipment, clothing, or high-fidelity components, it can be a significant part of the cost.

Each locality also has the right to levy its own separate tax on hotel occupancy. Since this tax is in addition to any general sales tax, taken together these two taxes can add a considerable amount to the basic cost of your accommodations.

The table below shows the rate of sales tax and hotel tax for certain major cities:

City	Sales Tax	Hotel Tax
Atlanta	6.00%	13.00%
Boston	5.00%	9.70%
Chicago	8.75%	14.90%
Dallas	8.25%	11.00%
Denver	7.30%	11.80%
Los Angeles	8.25%	14.00%
Miami	6.50%	12.50%
New Orleans	9.00%	11.00%
New York	8.25%	14.25%
Philadelphia	6.00%	13.00%
San Francisco	8.50%	12.00%
Washington, D.C.	6.50%	11.00%

TELEPHONE, TELEGRAPH, FAX, TELEX: The telephone system in the U.S. is run by private corporations, so rates, especially for long-distance service, can vary widely—even on calls made from public telephones. Local calls in the U.S. usually cost 25 cents.

Generally, hotel surcharges on long-distance and local calls are astronomical. You are usually better off using a public pay telephone, which you will find clearly marked in most public buildings and private establishments as well as on the street. Outside metropolitan areas, public telephones are more difficult to find. Stores and gas stations are your best bet.

For **long-distance or international calls,** stock up with a supply of quarters; the pay phone will instruct you when, and in what quantity, you should put them into the slot. For direct overseas calls, first dial 011, followed by the country code (Australia, 61; New Zealand, 64; United Kingdom, 44; and so on), and then by the city code and the number of the person you wish to call. For Canada and long-distance calls in the U.S., dial 1 followed by the area code and number you want.

Before calling from a hotel room, always ask the hotel phone operator if there are any telephone surcharges. These are best avoided by using a public phone, calling collect, or using a telephone charge card.

For **reversed-charge or collect calls,** and for **person-to-person calls,** dial 0 (zero, *not* the letter "O") followed by the area code and number you want; an operator will then come on the line, and you should specify that you are calling collect, or person-to-person, or both. If your operator-assisted call is international, ask for the overseas operator.

For local **directory assistance** ("information"), dial 411; for **long-distance information,** dial 1, then the appropriate area code and 555-1212.

Faxing facilities are offered by most hotels and are widespread; they are found in photocopying shops and mailing and packing establishments (such as Mailbox) and even in some supermarket grocery stores.

Like the telephone system, **telegraph and telex** services are provided by private corporations like ITT, MCI, and above all, Western Union, the most important. You can bring your telegram in to the nearest Western Union office (there are hundreds across the country), or dictate it over the phone (a toll-free call, 800/325-6000). You can also telegraph money, or have it telegraphed to you, very quickly over the Western Union system.

TELEPHONE DIRECTORY: See "Yellow Pages," below.

TIME: The U.S. is divided into four **time zones** (six, if Alaska and Hawaii are included). From east to west, these are: eastern standard time (EST), central standard time (CST), mountain standard time (MST), Pacific standard time (PST), Alaska standard time (AST), and Hawaii standard time (HST). Always keep changing time zones in mind if you're traveling (or even telephoning) long distances in the U.S. For example, noon in New York City (EST) is 11am in Chicago (CST), 10am in Denver (MST), 9am in Los Angeles (PST), 8am in Anchorage (AST), and 7am in Honolulu (HST).

Daylight saving time is in effect from the last Sunday in April through the last Saturday in Oct (actually, the change is made at 2am on Sun) except in Arizona, Hawaii, part of Indiana, and Puerto Rico. Daylight saving time moves the clock one hour ahead of standard time.

TIPPING: This is part of the American way of life, on the principle that you must expect to pay for any service you get. Here are some rules of thumb:

Bartenders: 10%–15%.
Bellhops: at least 50¢ per piece; $2–$3 for a lot of baggage.
Cab drivers: 15% of the fare (20% in large cities).
Cafeterias, fast-food restaurants: no tip.
Chambermaids: $1 a day; more in big-city hotels.
Cinemas, movies, theaters: no tip.
Checkroom attendants (restaurants): $1 a garment. (Theater checkrooms usually have a fixed charge—no tip is necessary.)
Doormen (hotels or restaurants): not obligatory, but $1 at top hotels.
Gas-station attendants: no tip.
Hairdressers: 15%–20%.
Parking-lot attendant: $1.
Redcaps (airport and railroad station): at least 50¢ per piece; $2–$3 for a lot of baggage.
Restaurants, nightclubs: 15%–20% of the check.
Sleeping-car porters: $2–$3 per night to your attendant.

TOILETS: Foreign visitors often complain that public toilets are hard to find in most U.S. cities. True, there are none on the streets, but the visitor can usually find one in a bar, restaurant, hotel, museum, department store, or service station —and it will probably be clean (although the last-mentioned sometimes leave much to be desired). Note, however, a growing practice in some restaurants and bars of displaying a notice that "toilets are for the use of patrons only." You can ignore this sign, or better yet, avoid arguments by paying for a cup of coffee or soft drink, which will qualify you as a patron. The cleanliness of toilets at railroad stations and bus depots may be more open to question, and some public places are equipped with pay toilets, which require you to insert one or more 10¢ coins (dimes) into a slot on the door before it will open.

YELLOW PAGES: There are two kinds of telephone directory available to you. The general directory is the so-called **White Pages,** in which private and business subscribers are listed in alphabetical order. The inside front cover lists the emergency number for police, fire, and ambulance, and other vital numbers (like the Coast Guard, poison-control center, crime-victims hotline, etc.). The first few pages are devoted to community service numbers, including a guide to long-distance and international calling, complete with country codes and area codes.

The second directory, printed on yellow paper (thus its name, *Yellow Pages*), lists all local services, businesses, and industries by type of activity, with an index at the back. The listings cover not only such obvious items as automobile repairs by make of car, or drugstores (pharmacies), often by geographical location, but also restaurants by type of cuisine and geographical location, bookstores by special subject and/or language, places of worship by religious denomination, and other information that the tourist might otherwise not readily find. The *Yellow Pages* also include city plans or detailed area maps, often showing postal ZIP Codes and public transportation routes.

PART ONE

THE NORTHEAST AND MID-ATLANTIC

CHAPTER 1

BOSTON

□ □ □

Cradle of American puritanism and the largest city in New England, Boston has played a starring role in U.S. history since the 17th century. In 1630 a group of 800 English colonists led by governor-to-be John Winthrop landed at **Charlestown,** on the north shore of the Charles River. During the following months the settlers acquired the south shore and moved there, on what is now **Beacon Hill.** They established a village of fishermen, craftsmen, and fur traders (commerce with the Native Americans flourished for a long time) known originally as **Tremont** because of its three hills. But the new arrivals, being loyal subjects of His Majesty, quickly renamed the town Boston, after their small Lincolnshire birthplace. Boston was the scene of the 1770 revolt against British rule (the Boston Massacre), which snowballed into the 1773 Boston Tea Party. And nearby **Lexington, Concord,** and **Bunker Hill** became the theater two years later for the first major battles against British colonialism. After its 1776 liberation by George Washington, Boston grew and prospered, quickly becoming the third-largest American city, with a population of 93,000 in 1840, 360,000 in 1890, and more than 500,000 in 1914. After World War I the city passed through almost four decades of eclipse, suffering economic setbacks and political and racial conflicts. The city lost a third of its inhabitants during this troubled time.

In the early 1960s, the capital of Massachusetts initiated an exemplary urban-renewal plan. Witness the **Government Center,** with its futurist architecture; the sweeping gray-green silhouette of the **John Hancock Tower,** designed by I. M. Pei (62 stories: 790 ft./243m); as well as the new business district near the harbor. Boston's renaissance coincided, not accidentally, with the presidency of one of the city's most illustrious sons, John Fitzgerald Kennedy, the first Roman Catholic president in the country's history.

With the possible exception of New York, Boston has produced more noteworthy politicians, writers, and intellectuals than any other U.S. city: from Paul Revere to Ralph Waldo Emerson, from John Hancock to John Adams, from Benjamin Franklin to Samuel Morse (inventor of the telegraph), and from Henry Wadsworth Longfellow to architect Louis Sullivan and actor Jack Lemmon. Boston also prides itself on the first American newspaper, the *Boston Newsletter,* published by postmaster John Campbell from 1704 to 1776.

Taking pride, as it understandably does, in its glorious history, Boston is the most European of American cities. If you follow the red arrows of the **Freedom Trail** along the small, winding downtown streets, you'll encounter all the landmarks of Boston life over 350 years: the venerable **Boston Common,** the country's first public park (1634); charming **Faneuil Hall,** known as "the cradle of American liberty"; the one-time British governor's mansion (**Old State House**); the elegant patrician homes of **Beacon Hill;** and the old red-brick houses of the **North End,** a once-seedy area now the heart of picturesque Little Italy, with Italian food stores, cafés, and restaurants. Some old Boston buildings, like the **Paul Revere House** (1677), are among the oldest still standing in the country. Important waves of immigrants (mostly Roman Catholic)—especially Irish, but also Italian, Polish, and more recently, Puerto Rican—have transformed this sanctuary of American puritanism into a vast, expanding industrial center (navy yards, electronics, machine tools, clothing), a port city, and a very active university town: one Bostonian in six is a student. Home of two of the world's most prestigious universities—**Harvard,** which recently celebrated its 350th anniversary, and the **Massachusetts Institute of Technology (MIT)**—a world-renowned symphony orchestra, countless museums, libraries, and more, Boston is, not surprisingly, still referred to as "the Athens of North America."

Since the 1988 opening of the unsightly **J. B. Hynes Veterans Memorial Convention Center,** Boston has joined the list of leading convention cities in the U.S., with 14,000 hotel rooms and nine million visitors a year.

BASIC FACTS: Capital of the state of Massachusetts. Area code: 617. Time zone: eastern. ZIP Code (of central post office): 02109. Founded: 1630. Approximate population: city, 570,000; metropolitan area, 4,180,000. Seventh-largest metropolitan area in the U.S.

CLIMATE: Except for a brief and sunny spring, Boston's climate is less than ideal. Summer is heavy with humidity (mean July temperature, 72°F/22°C), and winter is freezing and snow-covered (mean Jan temperature, 29°F/−2°C). Outside of spring, the best time to visit Boston is during the chilly but clear days of autumn.

DISTANCES: Chicago, 965 mi. (1,545km); Montréal, 318 mi. (508km); New York, 209 mi. (335km); Niagara Falls, 480 mi. (768km); Washington, 431 mi. (690km).

ARRIVAL & TRANSIT INFORMATION

AIRPORT: Logan International Airport (BOS): 3 mi. (5km) east. Information: 973-5500. Ranks worst in on-time arrivals among major U.S. airports.

DOMESTIC AIRLINES: American (toll free 800/433-7300), Continental (toll free 800/525-0280), Delta (toll free 800/221-1212), Northwest (toll free 800/225-2525), United (toll free 800/241-6522), USAir (toll free 800/428-4322), and USAir Shuttle (toll free 800/247-8786).

FOREIGN CARRIERS: Aer Lingus (toll free 800/223-6537), Air Canada (toll free 800/776-3000), British Airways (toll free 800/247-9297), Lufthansa (toll free 800/645-3880), and Swissair (toll free 800/221-4750).

CITY LINK: Cab fare to city center, about $18; time, 20–25 min. Bus: Airways Transportation Co. (toll free 800/235-6426); leaves every 30 min.; serves major downtown hotels; fare, $8; time, 25–30 min. There is a not-too-convenient downtown connection by subway (MBTA Blue Line). Taxi Boat: Airport Water Shuttle (328-0600) motorboat service to two downtown quays, Long Wharf and Rowes Wharf; time, 7 min.; leaves every 15 min.; fare, $7. Unless you're planning some East Coast excursions, the proximity of the airport and the compact layout of downtown Boston may make car rental superfluous. There's also a good public transportation system that combines bus and subway (MBTA) (722-3200).

CAR RENTAL (at the airport unless otherwise indicated): Avis (toll free 800/331-1212), Budget (toll free 800/527-0700), Dollar (toll free 800/800-4000), Hertz (toll free 800/654-3131), National (toll free 800/227-7368), Thrifty, 125 Bremen St., East Boston (toll free 800/367-2277). For downtown locations, consult the local phone directory.

LIMOUSINE SERVICES: Carey Limousine (623-8700), Dav El Limousine (toll free 800/922-0343), Fifth Avenue Limousine (286-1590).

TAXIS: Taxis are hard to find and expensive. They may be hailed on the street, but priority response goes to waiting lines at the major hotels and phone orders. Major companies: Boston Cab (536-5010), Checker Cab (536-7000), Red Cab (734-5000), and Yellow Cab (876-5000).

TRAIN: Amtrak, South Station, Atlantic Ave. and Summer St. (482-3660).

INTERCITY BUSES: Greyhound, 10 St. James Ave. (423-5810).

INFORMATION & TOURS

TOURIST INFORMATION: Greater Boston Convention & Visitors Bureau, Prudential Plaza, 800 Boylston St., MA 02199 (617/536-4100; toll free 800/888-5515).
    Visitor Information Center, 146 Tremont St. at Boston Common (617/426-3115).
    National Park Visitor Center, 15 State St. (617/242-5642).

GUIDED TOURS: Bay State Cruises (harbor cruise), 67 Long Wharf (617/723-7800): mid-May to late October. Also high-speed catamaran service to Martha's Vineyard (June–Sept).
    Boston by Foot (guided walking tours), 77 N. Washington St. (617/367-2345): daily, May–Oct.
    Clipper Cruise Lines (boat). (See "Guided Tours" in the chapter on Baltimore.)
    Gray Line of Boston (bus), 275 Tremont St. (617/426-8805): guided tours of the city and environs. Serves the major hotels.
    Old Town Trolley (bus), 329 W. 2nd St. (617/269-7150): 100-min. tours of historic Boston in a turn-of-the-century streetcar replica.

SIGHTS, ATTRACTIONS & ACTIVITIES

ADVENTURE TOURS: The New England Aquarium (Central Wharf) organizes daily **whale-watching boat trips** May–Oct. Cost, $24; resv. needed (973-5281).

ARCHITECTURAL HIGHLIGHTS: ⚓ **Government Center,** City Hall Plaza: Complex of ultramodern administrative buildings including **City Hall,** a commanding brick-and-concrete structure humorously nicknamed "the Aztec Tomb" by Bostonians, and the **J. F. Kennedy Federal Building,** designed by I. M. Pei. Worth a look.
    John Hancock Tower, Copley Sq. (247-1977): New England's tallest building, a striking 60-story skyscraper in steel and glass by I. M. Pei, 740 ft. (243m) tall. (See "Panoramas," below.) Open daily. Worth seeing.
    Massachusetts Institute of Technology (MIT), Massachusetts Ave. at Memorial Dr., Cambridge: The country's (and perhaps the world's) most prestigious university of science and technology, MIT is home to 9,000 students who make up a veritable breeding ground of future academics and Nobel prize winners (nine Nobel laureates currently teach at

MIT). The many interesting buildings on the 127-acre campus include I. M. Pei's **Green Building** (Pei was a student at MIT) and the chapel designed by Eero Saarinen. Open Mon–Fri. **Information Center:** 77 Massachusetts Ave. (253-4795). An absolute must-see.

    🔔 **Prudential Tower,** 800 Boylston St. (236-3318): This modern, 752-ft. (229m) skyscraper offers a very lovely panorama from the **Skywalk** on the 50th floor (see "Panoramas," below). Open daily.

CHURCHES/SYNAGOGUES: 🔆🔔 King's Chapel, Tremont St. and School

St. (523-1749): Boston's first Episcopalian church. The present building, on the site of an Anglican chapel dating from 1686, was erected in 1754. A favorite of British sovereigns, the church has received many royal gifts: the communion plate is from George III, the pulpit from James II, and the red velvet cushions from Queen Anne. See it. Open Tues–Sun.

    🔔🔔 **Old North Church,** 193 Salem St. (523-6676): One of the prettiest and the most history-laden of Boston's churches. The two lanterns hanging in this church's bell tower on the night of April 18, 1775, warned Bostonians of the British offensive against Concord and Lexington (an episode immortalized in the words of Longfellow, "One if by land, two if by sea"). Very beautiful interior decoration. Not to be missed. Open daily.

    🔔 **Park Street Church,** 1 Park St. (523-3383): One of Boston's most famous churches (1809) was a powder magazine during the War of 1812. William Lloyd Garrison here delivered the first public speech against slavery (1829), and the hymn "America" was first sung here (July 4, 1831). See it. Open daily.

    🔔 **Trinity Church,** Copley Sq. (536-0944): Romanesque Episcopalian church completed in 1877. Henry Hobson Richardson's interesting architecture was inspired by Spain's Salamanca cathedral. Sumptuous interior. Absolutely worth a look. Open daily.

HISTORIC BUILDINGS: 🔔 U.S.S. Constitution & Museum, Constitution

Rd., Charlestown (426-1812): The renowned frigate launched in 1797, undefeated in 42 engagements at sea, is nicknamed *Old Ironsides.* In dry-dock until the spring of 1996, the ship is open daily.

    🔔🔔 **Faneuil Hall,** Merchant's Row (951-2556): Former indoor market (1742), beautifully restored. Scene of the first public meetings protesting British rule, thus the nickname "Cradle of Liberty." The place offers many historic sights, including relics from the **Ancient & Honorable Artillery Company,** the country's oldest military school (1638). Attracts 10 million visitors each year. Not to be missed. Open daily.

    🔔 **Granary Burying Ground,** Tremont St. at Bromfield St.: Boston's oldest cemetery (1660), with the graves of Samuel Adams, John Hancock, Paul Revere, Benjamin Franklin's parents, and the five casualties of the Boston Massacre (see "Monuments," below). Worth a visit. Open daily.

    🔔 **Harrison Gray Otis House,** 141 Cambridge St. (227-3956): Beautiful Federal-style mansion designed in 1796 by Charles Bulfinch. Currently headquarters for the Society for the Preservation of New England Antiquities. Six museum rooms have been restored to reflect the taste and decoration of Boston during the 1800s. Worth a visit. Guided tours Tues–Sat.

    🔔🔔 **Harvard University,** around Harvard Sq., Cambridge: Temple of secular learning, Harvard (17,000 students) is the country's oldest (1636) and most famous university. Attended by the cultural and political elite (from poet Henry Longfellow to Pres. John F. Kennedy), its ivy-covered buildings have become the symbol of the East Coast's Ivy League, whose members include Columbia, Harvard, Princeton, and Yale. Among the university's many interesting modern buildings are the **Graduate Center,** designed by Wal-

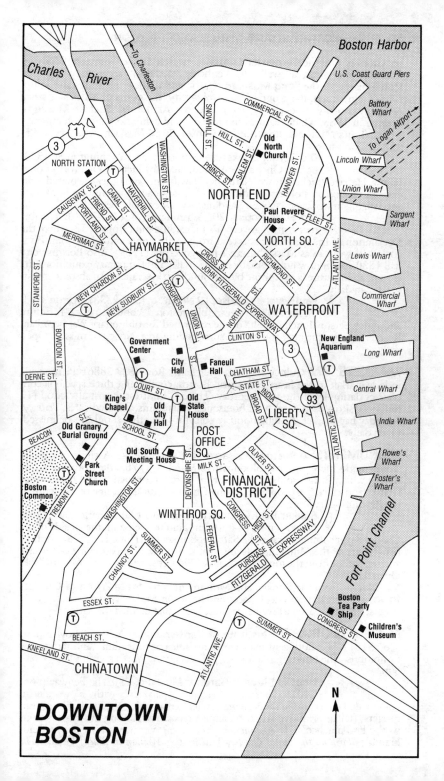

DOWNTOWN BOSTON

ter Gropius, and the **Carpenter Center,** conceived by Le Corbusier. Many remarkable museums, as well: the **Peabody Museum** (archeology and pre-Columbian art), the **Fogg Museum** (classic and modern paintings and sculptures, Chinese art), the group of four **University Museums of Natural History** (zoology, botany, mineralogy, etc.), and the **Arthur M. Sackler Museum,** opened in 1985, which features modern art and exhibitions of contemporary works. Tours Mon–Sat. **Information Center:** 1350 Massachusetts Ave. (495-1573). Don't miss it.

    Old Corner Bookstore, School St. and Washington St. (523-6658): Once a library frequented by Henry Wadsworth Longfellow, Harriet Beecher Stowe, Nathaniel Hawthorne, and other celebrated writers, one of Boston's oldest buildings (1712) is today an interesting bookstore specializing in works on New England history. Open daily. See it.

    Old State House, 206 Washington St. (720-3290): The former British governor's mansion dating from 1713, where the Declaration of Independence was read from the balcony, and where John Hancock was sworn in as Massachusetts's first governor (1789). Also Boston's city hall 1830–41, it now houses many historic relics and temporary exhibitions. Its elegant architecture is overborne by surrounding skyscrapers. An absolute must-see. Open daily.

    Paul Revere's House, 19 North Sq. (523-2338): Boston's oldest (1677) house, carefully restored, contains period furniture and much personal memorabilia of the renowned Revolutionary War hero Paul Revere. Picturesque little square and surrounding area. Not to be missed. Open daily.

MARKETS: ☀☖☖ **Quincy Market,** Merchants Row (523-3886): Picturesque indoor market in the heart of historic Boston comprising three spacious concourses dating from the 19th century. The city's hottest tourist attraction (12 million visitors each year) with boutiques, restaurants, terraced cafés, Friday/Saturday hay market. A tremendously colorful scene that shouldn't be missed. Open daily.

MONUMENTS: ☖ **Boston Massacre Site,** 30 State St.: A circle of cobblestones marks the site of the "bloodbath of March 5, 1770," the historic episode during which British soldiers, stoned by the crowd, opened fire on the demonstrators and killed five people, including Crispus Attucks, the first black victim of the Revolutionary War.

    Bunker Hill Monument, Monument Sq., Charlestown (252-5641): This 214-ft. (67m) granite obelisk on the far side of the Charles River commemorates the Battle of Bunker Hill (June 17, 1775), the baptism by fire of the Minutemen facing British troops. Fine panorama of the city and the harbor from the top of the obelisk (294 steps; no elevator). Worth a look. Open daily.

    Not far from the Bunker Hill Monument is the **State Prison of Charlestown,** where anarchists Nicola Sacco and Bartolomeo Vanzetti were executed on August 23, 1927, after a seven-year court battle that divided the nation.

MUSEUMS OF ART: ☖ **Institute of Contemporary Art,** 955 Boylston St. (266-5151): Has 20th-century art plus notable concerts, films, and temporary exhibitions. The building is a former police station. Worth a visit. Open Wed–Sun.

    ☀☖☖☖ **Isabella Stewart Gardner Museum,** 280 The Fenway (566-1401): Startling baroque "palazzo" with a wonderful colonnaded courtyard in the Venetian style. Remarkable collection of European masters, Italian primitive art, and Flemish tapestries. Among the most famous works: Fra Angelico's *The Assumption of the Virgin,* Vermeer's *The Concert,* Rembrandt's *Storm on the Sea of Galilee,* Tintoretto's *Woman in Black,* Titian's *The*

Rape of Europa, Matisse's *Terrace in St. Tropez,* and Degas's *Madame Gaujelin.*
Boston's loveliest museum. (Unfortunately some of these paintings were stolen
in the Mar 1990 break-in and have not yet been recovered.) Concerts Sat and Sun
(734-1359). Open Tues–Sun in summer; Wed–Sun the rest of the year. Not to
be missed.

☀☖☖☖ **Museum of Fine Arts,** 465 Huntington Ave. (267-9300):
Hundreds of masterworks from Rembrandt to Morris Louis
and from Monet to Gauguin (see especially his famous painting *Who are we?*
Where do we come from? Where are we going?). Among its other notable works: a
Greek head of Aphrodite from the 4th century B.C., Van der Weyden's *St. Luke
Painting the Virgin,* El Greco's *Portrait of Brother Paravicino,* Renoir's *Dance at
Bougival,* Cézanne's *Turn in the Road,* van Gogh's *House at Auvers,* and Jackson
Pollock's *Number Ten.* Very fine collections of Asian and Egyptian art. The West
Wing was designed by I. M. Pei. Don't miss it. Open Tues–Sun.

☖ **Public Library,** 666 Boylston St. (536-5400): Rich public library (more than three million volumes). Italian Renaissance
architecture by Charles McKim. Noteworthy bronze doors by Daniel Chester
French and remarkable interior decoration. Open Mon–Sat.

MUSEUMS OF SCIENCE & HISTORY: ☖ Boston African American His-
toric Site, 46 Joy St. (742-1854): Built by free African American Bostonians in
1806, the African Meeting House is the oldest standing African American
church building in North America. Museum open Tues–Fri.

☖ **Boston Tea Party Ship & Museum,** Congress St. Bridge (338-
1773): The spot where the revolt against the British began
(1773). Life-size replica of the British sailing ship *The Beaver,* whose cargo of
100,000 pounds of tea was dumped overboard by protesting Bostonians. Historic exhibition and, of course, tea is served. Not to be missed. Open daily.

☖ **Bunker Hill Pavilion,** 55 Constitution Rd., Charlestown (241-
7575): Neighbor of the frigate *Constitution* (see "Historic
Buildings," above) and the Bunker Hill Monument (see "Monuments," above),
this specially conceived hall offers a multimedia show that reproduces the Battle
of Bunker Hill on 14 movie screens and seven soundtracks. Hear Israel Putnam's
immortal words, "Don't fire until you see the whites of their eyes." Worth a look.
Open daily.

☖ **Children's Museum,** 300 Congress St. (426-8855): One of
the most famous children's museums in the U.S. Interactive
exhibits encourage kids of all ages to toy with hand-on displays. Open daily
(closed Mon off-season).

☖ **Computer Museum,** Museum Wharf, 300 Congress St. (423-
6758): From the good old UNIVAC 1 of the 1950s to the massive AN/FSQ-7, the biggest computer in the world (175 tons), this museum offers a complete panorama of the history of data processing. Demonstrations of
state-of-the-art technology. Marvelous. Open daily in summer; Tues–Sun the
rest of the year.

☖☖ **John F. Kennedy Library & Museum,** University of Massachusetts, Columbia Point Campus, 5 mi. (8km) SE on I-93
(929-4523): The life of the 35th president in movies, documents, and photographs in a very effective futurist setting designed by I. M. Pei. Very lovely view
of the skyline and the ocean. Open daily.

☖ **John F. Kennedy National Historic Site,** 83 Beals St., Brookline (566-7937): The birthplace of the president on the outskirts of Boston. JFK lived in the house 1917–21. Period furniture and Kennedy
family memorabilia. Simple and moving. See it. Open daily.

☖☖ **Museum of Science & Hayden Planetarium,** Science Park
(723-2500): Large, ultramodern science museum devoted to
technology and natural history, including a life-size dinosaur replica. The interesting medical section has a giant model of the human heart. Boasts the largest

Omnimax 360° film screen in the world (73 ft./22m in diameter; 84 speakers). For science and astronomy buffs. Open Tues–Sun.

    New England Aquarium, Central Wharf (973-5200): Huge, four-story glass aquarium with more than 7,000 fish and marine creatures of all kinds, from sea lions to sharks. Worth a visit. Open daily. (See also "Adventure Tours," above.)

    Old South Meeting House, Washington St. and Milk St. (482-6439): Built in 1729 on the site of an earlier house of worship where Benjamin Franklin was baptized in 1706, this red-brick building, once a religious and public meeting center, is today home to the historical museum of the city. This was also the starting point of Bostonians (some disguised as Native Americans) who took part in the Boston Tea Party (see above). A definite must-see. Open Mon–Sat.

    State House, Beacon St. (727-3676): The gold-domed Massachusetts legislative building, designed by Charles Bulfinch (1795). Its unique historical archives contain notably the passenger list of the *Mayflower* and the original Massachusetts Constitution of 1780, the country's first written constitution. Very lovely Hall of Flags. Not to be missed. Open daily.

PANORAMAS: **Bunker Hill Monument** (see "Monuments," above).

    John Hancock Observatory, 200 Clarendon St. (247-1977): Splendid panorama of the city and harbor from the 60th floor of the John Hancock Tower. Absolutely worth a look. Open daily until 11pm.

    Prudential Tower, 800 Boylston St. (236-2318): The observation platform on the 50th floor affords a 360° panorama of the city that's almost as impressive as the view from the John Hancock Observatory. Worth a look. Open daily until 11pm.

PARKS & GARDENS: **Arnold Arboretum,** Arborway, Jamaica Plain (524-1717): This very lovely 265-acre park was designed by Frederick Law Olmsted, the renowned landscape architect. It contains more than 6,000 kinds of trees and shrubs, and offers floral exhibits year round. 25 min. from dwntwn.

    Boston Common, Tremont St., Park St., and Beacon St. (954-2096): The first of the country's large public parks (1634), it encompasses 48 acres of trees, lawns, and shrubbery in the heart of Boston. Once a training ground for the redcoats, it is much enjoyed by amblers and soapbox orators, but should be avoided after nightfall. The Bostonian gathering point for all great occasions, the Common was the site of Pope John Paul II's outdoor mass before 200,000 people (1979). The adjacent **Public Garden** has a lake for boating in summer and skating in winter.

    Mount Auburn Cemetery, 580 Mt. Auburn St., Cambridge (547-7105): The country's oldest garden cemetery, this flower-filled park overlooking the Charles contains the graves of such notables as Henry Wadsworth Longfellow, Justice Oliver Wendell Holmes, and Mary Baker Eddy, founder of the Christian Science Church. Worth a detour. Open daily.

PERFORMING ARTS: For a daily listing of all shows and cultural events, consult the entertainment pages of the daily papers *Boston Globe* (morning), *Boston Herald* (morning), and *Christian Science Monitor* (morning); the weekly *Boston Phoenix;* and the monthly magazine *Boston*. **Bostix,** a kiosk in Faneuil Hall Marketplace, Faneuil Hall Sq. (423-4454), sells half-price tickets for all shows on the day of performance. Cash only.

    Charles Playhouse Theatre, 74 Warrenton St. (426-6912): Drama, comedy, modern theater.

    Emerson Majestic Theatre, 219 Tremont St. (451-2345): Opera, concerts, ballet. Home of the Boston Lyric Opera (artistic director: Sarah Caldwell).

Hatch Shell, Esplanade, Memorial Dr. (727-9548): Open-air Boston Pops Orchestra concerts and Boston Ballet Company performances. Summer only.

Huntington Theater Co., 264 Huntington Ave. (266-0800): Classical and modern theater, at Boston University. Solid artistic reputation.

Loeb Drama Center, 64 Brattle St., Cambridge (547-8300): Home of the American Repertory Theater, offering classical and modern works.

Next Move Theatre, 1 Boylston Pl. (423-5572): Experimental theater.

Shubert Theatre, 265 Tremont St. (426-4520): Broadway shows (often previews). Year round.

Symphony Hall, 301 Massachusetts Ave. (266-1492): Home of the celebrated Boston Symphony Orchestra, one of the country's "big six" orchestras (principal conductor: Seiji Ozawa); Sept–Apr. Also the home of the Boston Pops Orchestra (principal conductor: John Williams); May–July.

Tower Auditorium, 621 Huntington Ave. (277-4274): Concerts, Off-Broadway theater, ballet.

Wang Center for the Performing Arts, 270 Tremont St. (482-9393): Home of the Boston Ballet Company.

Wilbur Theatre, 246 Tremont St. (423-4008): Modern theater, Broadway shows. Year round.

SHOPPING: The Coop, 1 Federal St. at Harvard Sq., Cambridge: The world's biggest student-oriented store: from textbooks to blue jeans, from posters to backpacks, and from records to the latest in microcomputers. A classic since 1882.

Copley Place, 100 Huntington Ave.: Gigantic shopping center with a futurist look (interior gardens, huge waterfalls), plus dozens of luxury boutiques, from Neiman-Marcus to Gucci and Vuitton to Tiffany's. Spectacular.

☼ **Filene's,** 426 Washington St.: A real landmark. In the famous basement of this crowded store are Boston's best deals on cut-rate clothing—in a hurly-burly atmosphere. Many other interesting stores close by, along Washington St. and Summer St.

Newbury Street: Boston's chic shopping street, with fashionable boutiques, art galleries, famous food stores. Worth a look.

Tower Records, Massachusetts Ave. and Newbury St.: The biggest and most up-to-date record and video store in the U.S. (more than 40,000 sq. ft./ 3,730m²). Impressive. Close to Symphony Hall.

SPECIAL EVENTS: For the exact schedule of events below, consult the **Greater Boston Convention & Tourist Bureau** (see "Tourist Information," above).

Patriots Day Celebration (mid-Apr): Parades, celebrations, and the Boston Marathon, a local tradition since 1896.

Esplanade Concerts (first two weeks of July): Free open-air concerts by the world-famous Boston Pops Orchestra at the Hatch Memorial Shell (on the banks of the Charles River). Don't miss it.

Harborfest (July): A celebration of Boston's history and harbor. Fireworks, concerts, regattas.

Head of the Charles River Regatta (last Sun in Oct): Boat races on the Charles, a classic of the Boston season. The largest such event in the U.S.

Harvard-Yale Football Game (Nov): When the great rivals Harvard and Yale clash, the famous match-up guarantees excitement and a great atmosphere. The game is played in Cambridge and New Haven, alternating every year.

SPORTS: Boston has four professional teams:

Baseball (Apr–Oct): Red Sox, Fenway Park (267-1700).

Basketball (Oct to late Apr): Celtics, Boston Garden (526-6050).

Football (Sept–Dec): New England Patriots, Foxboro Stadium (toll free 800/543-1776).

Ice Hockey (Oct–Apr): Bruins, Boston Garden (227-3206).

Horse Racing
Suffolk Downs, on Mass. 1A, East Boston (568-3320), year round.

STROLLS: ☀︎🔺 **Freedom Trail:** This red-arrow-marked circuit begins at Beacon St. and Park St. and winds for 2½ mi. (4km) through 16 colonial and Revolutionary-era sites. National Park Service rangers offer free 90-min. tours. Its **Visitor Center,** where a short film is shown, is at 15 State St. (242-5642). Don't miss it.

☀︎ 🔔 **Beacon Hill,** around Mt. Vernon St.: Boston's aristocratic neighborhood, with old gas lamps, cobblestone streets, lovely private homes with elegant facades and carefully polished brass nameplates. A whiff of nostalgia. An absolute must-see (especially, gorgeous **Louisburg Square**).

🔔 **North End,** bordered by Commercial St. and John F. Fitzgerald Expwy.: Surrounded by warehouses and the docks of Boston's old harbor, this picturesque area composed of small, narrow streets with red-brick houses has become the local *Little Italy* over the years. Numerous agreeable restaurants, bars, and food stores contribute to a colorful atmosphere (especially during religious festivals). From Commercial St. or Atlantic Ave., you can enjoy an unobstructed view of the port and its maritime traffic.

THEME PARKS: See **Old Sturbridge Village,** in "Farther Afield," below.

WINTER SPORTS RESORTS: Nashova Valley (26 mi./42km NW on I95, Mass. 2, Mass. 119, and Power Rd.; 508/692-3033): Eight lifts, open Dec–Mar.

Pat's Peak (100 mi./160km NW on I93, I89, N.H. 202, and N.H. 114; 603/428-3245): Seven lifts, open Dec–Mar.

Temple Mountain (87 mi./139km NW on Mass. 2, Mass. 12, U.S. 202, and N.H. 101; 603/924-6949): Four lifts, open Dec–Apr.**Wachusett Mountain** (58 mi./93km NW on Mass. 2 and Mass. 140 (toll free 800/754-1234): Five lifts, open Dec–Mar.

ACCOMMODATIONS
Personal Favorites (in order of preference)
♟♟♟♟ **Ritz Carlton Hotel** (dwntwn), 15 Arlington St., MA 02117 (617/536-5700; toll free 800/241-3333). 326 rms, A/C, color TV, in-rm movies. AE, CB, DC, MC, V. Gar. $20, sauna, two rests. (including the Ritz Carlton Dining Room), two bars, 24-hr. rm svce, hrdrsr, boutiques, concierge, free crib. *Note:* "The" grand palace of Boston since 1927 and one of the 12 best hotels in the country, across from the Public Garden. Elegant, refined decor, irreproachable comfort w. period furniture. Ultra-polished svce. Renowned bar and rests. (the Ritz Café is the "in" place for working breakfasts). VIP floor. Recently received a $25-million facelift. A symbol of Boston's graciousness and elegance. **VE**

☀︎♟♟♟♟ **The Bostonian** (dwntwn), Faneuil Hall Marketplace, MA 02109 (617/523-3600; toll free, see Preferred). 155 rms. A/C, cable color TV. AE, CB, DC, MC, V. Valet gar. $18, rest. (The Seasons), bar, 24-hr. rm svce, free crib. *Note:* The hotel's modern red-brick architecture is perfectly integrated into the Old Boston setting. Inside is an elegant four-story glass atrium and cramped but comfortable rms with exposed beams and fireplaces (some w. balconies). Intimate, sophisticated atmosphere and impeccable svce, plus an excellent rest. (The Seasons). The best location in Boston, across from Faneuil Hall and Quincy Market. **VE**

♟♟♟ **The Charles Hotel** (vic.), 1 Bennett St. (at Eliot St.), MA 02138 (617/864-1200; toll free 800/882-1818). 296 rms, A/C, color TV, in-rm movies. AE, CB, DC, MC, V. Valet gar. $20, pool, health club, sauna, two rests. (including Rarities), bar, 24-hr. rm svce, nightclub, boutiques, hrdrsr, concierge. *Note:* This relatively new luxury hotel in the European manner is very near the Harvard campus, and has become a favorite roost for passing VIPs from Jack Nicholson to corporate tycoons. The elegant red-brick building commands a view of the Charles River and the Boston skyline. Comfortable, agreeably furnished rms, exemplary svce, rest. of quality—and the best jazz joint in greater Boston. 15 min. from dwntwn. **VE**

☀️ 🏛️ 🏛️ 🏛️ **Omni Parker House** (dwntwn), 60 School St., MA 02107 (617/227-8600; toll free, see Omni). 535 rms. A/C, color TV in-rm movies. AE, CB, DC, MC, V. Gar. $22, health club, sauna, three rests. (including The Last Hurrah), coffee shop, three bars, rm svce, disco, hrdrsr, boutiques, free crib. *Note:* In this venerable (dates from 1855), history-laden palace in the heart of Boston, Charles Dickens stayed, Ho Chi Minh was a bellboy, and the Kennedys were a familiar sight. Marble, woodwork, and Oriental rugs abound. The rms are outdated but comfortable and the atmosphere calm and distinguished. Polished reception and svce. Good rests. **VE**

🏛️ 🏛️ **Boston Park Plaza Hotel and Towers** (dwntwn), 64 Arlington St., MA 02117 (617/426-2000; toll free 800/225-2008). 976 rms, A/C, color TV, in-rm movies. AE, CB, DC, MC, V. Gar. $12, health club, rest. (Fox & Hounds), coffee shop, bars, 24-hr. rm svce, hrdrsr, boutiques, free crib. *Note:* Massive, aging palace near the Common w. slightly faded interior decoration but comfortable rms. Svce so-so, and the group and convention clientele is somewhat obtrusive. Very good location. **E–VE**

🏛️ 🏛️ **Howard Johnson–57 Park Plaza Hotel** (dwntwn), 200 Stuart St., MA 02116 (617/482-1800; toll free, see Howard Johnson's). 352 rms, A/C, color TV, in-rm movies. AE, CB, DC, MC, V. Free parking, pool, sauna, rest. (57 Restaurant), bar, rm svce, disco, hrdrsr, free crib. *Note:* Rather ordinary modern architecture, but a very good location just off the Common. Functional rms w. balconies and a satisfactory rest. Fair svce. Business clientele. VIP suites on the 23rd floor. Movie theaters. **M–E**

🏛️ **Chandler Inn** (nr. dwntwn), 26 Chandler St., MA 02116 (617/482-3450; toll free 800/842-3450). 56 rms, A/C, color TV. AE, CB, DC, MC, V. Parking $12, bar. *Note:* Small, modest, and inviting hotel, 5 min. from dwntwn. Free breakfast. Recently renovated. Very good value for those on a budget. **M**

🏛️ **Quality Hotel Tremont House** (formerly the Bradford Hotel) (dwntwn), 275 Tremont St., MA 02116 (617/426-1400; toll free, see Choice). 288 rms, A/C, color TV, in-rm movies. AE, CB, DC, MC, V. Parking $15, rest. bar, rm svce, disco. *Note:* Oldish but well-maintained hotel in the theater district. Regular clientele. Recently renovated. A good overall value. **M–E**

🏛️ **Susse Chalet Inn** (vic.), 900 Morrissey Blvd., MA 02122 (617/287-9200; toll free 800/258-1980). 105 rms, A/C, color TV, in-rm movies. AE, CB, DC, MC, V. Free parking, pool, adjacent coffee shop, crib $3. *Note:* Inviting modern motel 15 min. from dwntwn on the Southeast Expwy. Close to the University of Massachusetts and the Kennedy Library. Good basic accommodations. Free continental breakfast. Resv. recommended in summer. Excellent value. **I**

Other Accommodations (from top bracket to budget)

☀️ 🏛️ 🏛️ 🏛️ **Boston Harbor Hotel** (dwntwn), 70 Rowes Wharf (on Atlantic Ave.), MA 02110 (617/439-7000; toll free, see Preferred). 230 rms, A/C, color TV, in-rm movies. AE, CB, DC, MC, V. Valet gar. $20, pool, health club, sauna, rest. (Rowes Wharf), bar, 24-hr. rm svce, nightclub, boutiques, concierge, free crib. *Note:* This most distinctive and luxurious of Boston's dwntwn hotels, uncompromisingly postmodern in appearance, towers above the bustle of Boston Harbor from its 16 floors. Elegant decoration and furnishing; spacious, ultra-comfortable rms with minibars, remote-control TVs, and private balconies (the best overlooking the water). Svce of the highest order. Direct water-taxi link with airport (7 min.). Big-business clientele. **VE**

ଅ ଅ ଅ ଅ **Four Seasons** (dwntwn), 200 Boylston St., MA 02116 (617/ 338-4400; toll free, see Four Seasons). 301 rms, A/C, color TV, in-rm movies. AE, CB, DC, MC, V. Valet gar. $20, pool, health club, sauna, two rests. (including Aujourd'hui), two bars, 24-hr. rm svce, nightclub, concierge, free crib. *Note:* Opened in 1985, this elegant, modern 15-story hotel overlooking the Public Garden is a favorite of financial-industry executives. Spacious, comfortable rms w. minibars (the most pleasant have a view of the park). The decor complements the hotel's period furniture and unassuming modernism. Personalized svce of great distinction. Excellent nouvelle cuisine rest. One of Boston's finest. **VE**

ଅ ଅ ଅ ଅ **Westin Hotel** (nr. dwntwn), 10 Huntington Ave., MA 02116 (617/262-9600; toll free, see Westin). 848 rms, A/C, color TV, in-rm movies. AE, CB, DC, MC, V. Parking $15, pool, health club, sauna, three rests. (including Ten Huntington), coffee shop, three bars, 24-hr. rm svce, nightclub, boutiques, concierge, free crib. *Note:* New 36-story building that towers over Copley Place Shopping Center. Spectacular lobby w. waterfalls and interior gardens. Ultramodern comfort w. vast, well-equipped rms (those on the top floors have a very lovely view of the city). Efficient, diligent svce. Frequented by VIPs and businesspeople. Very good location. **VE**

☼ ଅ ଅ ଅ **Copley Plaza Hotel** (dwntwn), 138 St. James Ave. (at Copley Sq.), MA 02116 (617/267-5300; toll free 800/826-7539). 371 rms, A/C, color TV, in-rm movies. AE, CB, DC, MC, V. Valet parking $20, two rests. (including Café Plaza), two bars, 24-hr. rm svce, boutiques, hrdrsr, concierge, free crib. *Note:* Along with the Ritz Carlton, this 1912 dowager can lay claim to the title of Queen Mother of Boston's hotels. Its 75th anniversary was celebrated with a comprehensive restoration designed to restore its former splendor. Svce and comfort above reproach; works of art and period furniture. Distinguished reception; excellently located nr. the Prudential Center and the smart stores of Newbury St. Guests are mostly regulars. **VE**

ଅ ଅ ଅ **Royal Sonesta** (vic.), 5 Cambridge Pkwy., Cambridge, MA 02142 (617/491-3600; toll free 800/766-3782). 430 rms. A/C, color TV, in-rm movies. AE, CB, DC, MC, V. Free parking, two pools, health club, two rests. (including Davio's), two bars, rm svce, nightclub, hrdrsr, concierge, free crib. *Note:* Large postmodern convention hotel, recently enlarged. Irreproachable comfort and facilities. The interior is adorned w. numerous original works of contemporary art, from Roy Lichtenstein to Buckminster Fuller. Spacious rms with minibars. VIP floors. Excellent svce and a very lovely view of Boston from the opposite side of the Charles River. Business clientele. Convenient to M.I.T., 20 min. from dwntwn. **E–VE**

ଅ ଅ **The Colonnade** (nr. dwntwn), 120 Huntington Ave., MA 02116 (617/424-7000; toll free 800/962-3030). 298 rms, A/C, color TV. AE, CB, DC, MC, V. Valet gar. $12, pool, health club, rest. (Café Promenade), bar, 24-hr. rm svce, concierge, free crib. *Note:* Contemporary-style hotel next to Copley Place, offering European ambience and an efficient but unobtrusive personal svce. Large, comfortable rms w. minibars and computer hookups. Good value overall. **E–VE**

ଅ ଅ **Holiday Inn Government Center** (dwntwn), 5 Blossom St., MA 02114 (617/742-7630; toll free, see Holiday Inns). 300 rms, A/C, color TV, in-rm movies. AE, CB, DC, MC, V. Parking $9, pool, rest. (Lobster Trap), coffee shop, bar, rm svce, disco, boutiques, free crib. *Note:* Functional, modern 15-story tower à la Holiday Inn but more inviting than usual. Comfortable rms, group clientele. Quite close to City Hall. Overlooks the Charles River. Interesting wknd packages. **E–VE**

ଅ ଅ **Lenox Hotel** (dwntwn), 710 Boylston St. (at Exeter St.), MA 02116 (617/536-5300; toll free 800/225-7676). 222 rms, A/C, color TV, in-rm movies. AE, CB, DC, MC, V. Parking $14, two rests. (including Lenox Pub & Grill), two bars, rm svce, hrdrsr. *Note:* Elegant luxury in a small turn-of-the-century hotel at the heart of Back Bay. Traditional comfort and furnishings; rms (some w. fireplaces) decorated in American Colonial or French Provincial. Thoughtful, friendly svce. Diamond Jim's is an agreeable piano bar. Good value overall. **E–VE**

Harvard Manor House (vic.), 110 Mount Auburn St., Cambridge, MA 02138 (617/864-5200; toll free 800/458-5886). 72 rms, A/C, color TV, in-rm movies. AE, DC, MC, V. Parking $8, coffee shop, free crib. *Note:* 1950s-style motel in the heart of Cambridge–Harvard Square. Minutes walk to Harvard University, 15 min. from downtown. **M**

Midtown Hotel (nr. dwntwn), 220 Huntington Ave., MA 02115 (617/262-1000; toll free 800/343-1177). 160 rms, A/C, color TV. AE, CB, DC, MC, V. Free parking, pool, rest., bar, rm svce. *Note:* Relatively modern motel across from the Prudential Tower. Spacious, comfortable rms. The svce fluctuates. Interesting wknd packages. **M**

Susse Chalet (vic.), 800 Morrissey Blvd., MA 02122 (617/287-9100; toll free 800/258-1980). 177 rms, A/C, color TV. AE, MC, V. Free parking, pool, adjacent coffee shop, crib $3. *Note:* Relatively old but well-maintained motel 15 min. from dwntwn on the Southeast Expwy. Inviting rms. Close to the University of Massachusetts and the Kennedy Library. Ideal if you're driving through. Free Continental breakfast. Very good value. **I**

Airport Accommodations

Hilton Logan Airport (vic.), 75 Service Rd., Logan Airport, MA 02128 (617/569-9300; toll free, see Hilton). 542 rms, A/C, color TV, in-rm movies. AE, CB, DC, MC, V. Free parking, pool, rest. (Appleton's), coffee shop, bar, rm svce, disco, free crib. *Note:* This entirely renovated convention hotel offers comfortable, well-soundproofed rms w. private balconies and cheerful svce. Business clientele. 25 min. from dwntwn. Free airport limo 24 hrs. **E–VE**

YMCAs/Youth Hostels

Boston International Hostel (nr. dwntwn), 12 Hemenway St., MA 02115 (617/536-9455). 220 beds. Youth hostel, 10 min. from dwntwn. Coffee shop.

YMCA Boston (nr. dwntwn), 316 Huntington Ave., MA 02115 (617/536-7800). 300 rms, pool, health club, rest. Men and women.

RESTAURANTS

Personal Favorites (in order of preference)

Jasper's (dwntwn), 240 Commercial St. (523-1126). A/C. Dinner only, Tues–Sat; closed hols. AE, CB, DC, MC, V. Jkt. *Specialties:* cod cakes, cape scallops w. wasabi and julienne of ginger, pan-roasted lobster w. herbs, boiled dinner, applewood-smoked pork loin, grilled salmon trout w. ragoût of white beans, sun-dried tomatoes, artichoke hearts and penne, bread-and-butter pudding w. raspberries. The menu changes regularly. Long, expensive wine list. *Note:* Jasper White's original talent commands reverence among the great American young chefs. Chubby, bearded White combines brilliantly subtle, urbane gloss w. hearty, regional cookery. Based on New England foodstuffs, its modern and inventive cuisine includes some of the best seafood dishes in town. Minimalist setting w. gray-painted bricks and bold artwork. Efficient, flawless svce. Resv. a must. One of the 12 best rests. in the country. *American.* **E**

Biba (dwntwn), 272 Boylston St. (426-7878). A/C. Lunch Mon–Fri; dinner Mon–Sat; closed hols. CB, MC, V. Jkt. *Specialties:* ash-baked potato w. osetra caviar, lobster w. whisky butter, calves' brains w. crisp-fried capers, roast wild boar, crème brûlée, soft brownies w. mocha sauce. Interesting, fairly priced wine list. *Note:* Eclectic cuisine w. Asian and Indian influences by the very talented chef Lydia Shire. This distinguished rest. in the new Heritage Building across from the Public Garden quickly became Boston's "in" place. The interior is rather startling Hollywood Mexican, the svce a touch lackadaisical. Highly recommended in spite of the incongruous setting; successful enough that resv. should be made some days ahead. *American*. **M–E**

🍷🍷🍷 **Olives** (vic.), 10 City Square, Charlestown (242-1999). A/C.
🍷🍷 Dinner only, Tues–Sun; closed holidays. AE, MC, V. Jkt. *Specialties:* tuna carpaccio w. mesclun greens and capers; tortelli of butternut squash w. brown butter, sage, and Parmesan; spit-roasted, herb-and-garlic-basted chicken; falling chocolate cake. *Note:* This relative newcomer to the Boston gastronomic scene has built its reputation on the refined but fairly priced Mediterranean cuisine of chef Todd English. Olives offers a subdued decor w. ocher walls, antique sconces, and a fragrant wood-burning oven. Friendly, smiling svce. Olives unfortunately doesn't take resv. and the wait could be lengthy, especially on Saturday night. *Mediterranean*. **I–M**

☀🍷🍷 **Locke Ober Café** (dwntwn), 3 Winter Place (542-1340).
🍷🍷 A/C. Lunch/dinner daily; closed hols. AE, CB, DC, MC, V. J&T. *Specialties:* lobster Savannah, duckling bigarade, sole bonne femme, oysters Rockefeller, filet Mirabeau, steak tartare, Nesselrode sundae, Indian pudding. *Note:* The most famous eating place in Boston. Since 1875 this venerable institution has retained its Victorian woodwork and its old-world club atmosphere. The only break with tradition: Women are now admitted to the mezzanine, or most elegant, dining room. Cuisine and svce exemplary on all counts. Resv. advised. A favorite of Boston society (especially the late President Kennedy). *Continental/American*. **I–M**

🍷🍷 **Anthony's Pier 4** (dwntwn), 140 Northern Ave. (423-6363).
🍷🍷 A/C. Lunch/dinner daily; closed Dec 25. AE, CB, DC, MC, V. Jkt. *Specialties:* clam chowder, fish chowder, lobster, and remarkable seafood of all kinds, fresh and reasonably priced. Good wine list. *Note:* Criticized by purists for its "eating factory" appearance, Anthony's Pier 4 is, according to a *Boston Globe* poll, the favorite restaurant of Bostonians. Not surprisingly, it's often jampacked despite the imposing dimensions of the windowed dining rm. Generous portions, diligent svce, and an agreeable view of the harbor. Rather amusing marine bric-a-brac decor, very noisy atmosphere. No dinner resv., unfortunately. Valet parking. *Seafood*. **I–M**

🍷 **Daddy-O's Bohemian Cafe** (vic.), 134 Hampshire St., Cambridge (354-8371). A/C. Dinner only, Tues–Sun; closed Thanksgiving, Dec 24 and 25. MC, V. Jkt. *Specialties:* mussel fritters, macaroni and cheese, grilled pork chops and potato latkes, charred steak, grilled chicken breast w. garlic gravy, sweet potato–pecan pie. Seasonal menu. Affordable, well-chosen wines. *Note:* A fun way to spend an evening. If the name doesn't hook you, then the jazzy decor—complete with two stuffed beatniks reading Ferlinghetti and playing bongos—will. The "Daddy-O Patio," with its flower-and-herb garden, attracts a crowd in the summer. Live jazz every Sunday night. No resv. *American*. **I**

☀🍷 **Ye Olde Union Oyster House** (dwntwn), 41 Union St. (227-2750). A/C. Lunch/dinner daily; closed Thanksgiving, Dec 25. AE, CB, DC, MC, V. *Specialties:* clam chowder, oysters, coquilles St-Jacques, lobster. *Note:* Boston's oldest oyster bar (1826) in a more-than-three-centuries-old little one-story house is a tourist favorite. Superb raw bar on the mezzanine. Charming period decor. Cheerful svce. Resv. are useless. *Seafood*. **I**

Other Restaurants (from top bracket to budget)

🍷🍷🍷 **L'Espalier** (nr. dwntwn), 30 Gloucester St. (262-3023). A/C.
🍷🍷 Dinner only, Mon–Sat; closed hols. AE, CB, DC, MC, V. J&T. *Specialties:* Saffroned mussel soup, grilled quail salad w. oranges, lobster-truffle ravioli, veal sautéed in honey and lemon, pigeon mousse in pastry shell, grilled bass w. soy-and-lemon sauce, filet of beef bordelaise w. green peppercorns, excellent desserts, and a rich wine list. The menu changes regularly. *Note:* The

temple of Boston nouvelle cuisine since Dodin Bouffant moved to New York, it offers light, inspired cuisine from chef Frank McClelland at painful prices. Pretty, antique decor in an elegant, Edwardian three-story house. Very lovely floral arrangements. Exemplary svce. Trendy clientele. Resv. a must. Valet parking $5. *French/Continental.* **E–VE**

🍸🍸🍸 **Anago Bistro** (vic.), 798 Main St., Cambridge (876-8444).
🍽🍽 Lunch Tues–Fri; dinner Tues–Sat. AE, MC, V. Jkt. *Specialties:* celery-root-and-leek bisque w. apples; grilled portobello mushrooms and asparagus w. sweet red pepper oil; linguine w. artichoke ragoût, tomato, black and green olives, and fresh herbs; baked vegetable casserole w. grilled flatbread and goat cheese; herb-roasted chicken w. crimini mushrooms. Wine a bargain. *Note:* Named one of the best new rests. in the U.S. in 1993 by *Bon Appetit* magazine, Anago worthily succeeded 798 Main St., the previous rest. of the same locale where present co-owner and chef Bob Calderone landed his first job cooking. Calderone combines Italian cuisine with New England staples. *Mediterranean.* **M**

🍸🍸🍸 **Hamersley's Bistro** (dwntwn), 553 Tremont St. (267-6068).
🍽🍽 A/C. Dinner only, nightly; closed Dec 25. AE, MC, V. Jkt. *Specialties:* grilled wild mushrooms on toasted garlic country bread; boned leg of lamb stuffed w. kale, olives, and roasted sweet peppers; roast chicken w. garlic and lemon; oven-roasted skate w. grapefruit and mint; warm pear tart w. burnt caramel and crème fraîche; souffléed lemon custard. Decently priced wine list. *Note:* Gordon Hamersley's country cooking is one of the gastronomic joys of Boston, and has been voted the best bistro cuisine in the city by the readers of *Boston* magazine. The slick look of the old place has given way to a new and warmer setting with earth tones. The friendly reception, the relaxed and efficient svce, and the young, fashionable crowd make this a place that no visitor to Boston should miss. Resv. a must. *American.* **M**

🍸🍸🍸 **Michela's** (vic.), 1 Athenaeum St., Cambridge (225-2121).
🍽🍽 A/C. Lunch Mon–Fri; dinner Mon–Sat; closed hols. AE, CB, DC, MC, V. Jkt. *Specialties:* zuppa di fagioli (white-bean soup), risotto of wild mushrooms, aquacotta porcini broth w. tallegio cheese and poached egg; pizza w. 5 cheeses and truffle oil, roasted fresh salt cod wrapped in pancetta, roasted Long Island duck w. duck liver crostini, excellent homemade desserts. Menu changes twice a year. Good list of Italian and California wines. *Note:* Occupying the ground floor of an attractively redesigned printers'-ink plant, Michela's gives a new twist to Italian *nuova cucina.* Michela Larson gracefully interweaves the recipes of her native Italy with Spanish, Portuguese, and—since the arrival of her chef Jody Adams—even American traditions. Novel "patio" look with colored wall-paintings; noisy. The adjoining Michela's Café offers excellent value. Locally popular. *Italian/American.* **M**

🍸🍸 **Suntory** (dwntwn), 212 Stuart St. (338-2111). A/C. Lunch
🍽🍽 Mon–Sat; dinner nightly. AE, CB, DC, MC, V. Jkt. *Specialties:* sushi, shabu-shabu, tempura, teppanyaki, yakitori. *Note:* Experts consider this the best Japanese rest. in Boston. It's one of a dozen luxury rests. around the world (including one in Chicago and one in Honolulu) owned by the renowned Japanese brewer Suntory. Sober, elegant Oriental decor. The customer has a choice between the sushi bar and the upstairs dining rms, specializing in different types of Japanese cuisine. Resv. advised. *Japanese.* **I–M**

🍸🍸 **Legal Seafoods** (dwntwn), 100 Huntington Ave. (266-
🍽🍽 7775). A/C. Lunch/dinner daily; closed Thanksgiving, Dec 25. AE, CB, DC, MC, V. *Specialties:* huge variety of seafood that's baked, steamed, fried, or grilled to perfection; clam chowder, smoked hake pâté cioppino, mussels au gratin. *Note:* One of the country's best seafood restaurants in a vast, modern, and luminous setting of big picture windows, and a dining rm spread over several levels. Legal Seafoods is at once a rest. chain and a retail fish store, and the more than 50 tons of fresh seafood it sells each week are its best recommendation. No resv. Inevitable waits. Other locations: 43 Boylston St., Newton (426-4444); and Kendall Sq., Cambridge (864-3400). *Seafood.* **B–I**

♀ **Mi-Vami** (vic.), 14-A Pleasant St., Brookline (277-0272).
♗ Lunch Sat; nightly dinner. No credit cards. *Specialties:* eggplant
puree; peppers, eggplant, and cabbage stuffed w. beef, onions, and rice; chicken
schnitzel; sautéed chicken liver and onions. *Note:* Authentic Middle Eastern
food; some of the best you'll find in Boston. One of the few places to serve real
Turkish coffee. Bring your own alcohol. *Middle Eastern.* **I**

♀ **Felicia's** (dwntwn), 145A Richmond St. (second floor) (523-
♗ 9885). A/C. Dinner only, nightly; closed Easter, Thanksgiv-
ing, Dec 25. AE, MC, V. Jkt. *Specialties:* fresh homemade pasta, shrimp Toscano,
chicken w. verdicchio, seafood cannelloni, veal Margarita. *Note:* Wholly authentic Italian trattoria with charming period decor and diligent, courteous svce. Locally popular for more than 30 years. No resv., unfortunately. *Italian.* **I**

☼♀ **Jimmy's Harborside** (nr. dwntwn), 242 Northern Ave., on
♗ the waterfront (423-1000). A/C. Lunch/dinner Mon–Sat;
closed Dec 24, 25. AE, CB, DC, MC, V. *Specialties:* clam chowder, shrimp
Charles, oysters Rockefeller, excellent seafood. Good American wine list. *Note:*
The best clam chowder in all Boston. Remarkable seafood at reasonable prices
and a very lovely view of the harbor (especially from the second floor). Locally
very popular for more than half a century. Very efficient svce. One disappointment: Jimmy's closes relatively early (9:30pm). Resv. advised. Valet parking.
Seafood. **I**

☼♀ **The Last Hurrah Bar and Grill** (dwntwn), in the Omni Parker
♗ House (see "Accommodations," above) (227-8600). A/C.
Lunch/dinner daily (until midnight). AE, CB, DC, MC, V. Jkt. *Specialties:* Boston scrod (haddock), clam chowder, prime rib, daily specials. *Note:* A favorite
hangout of Boston journalists and politicians in the basement of the venerable
Parker House Hotel. Pleasant atmosphere, especially at lunch (the orchestra is a
bit obtrusive in the evening). Pretty, retro decor w. a mahogany bar and Tiffany
lamps. Resv. advised. *American.* **I**

♀ **Chau Chow** (dwntwn), 52 Beach St. (426-6266). A/C.
♗ Breakfast/lunch/dinner daily (until 4am). No credit cards.
Specialties: baby clams in black-bean sauce, crab w. ginger and scallion, chow
foon, soyed whole duck. No alcoholic beverages. *Note:* The best rest. in Boston
after midnight and simply the best, period, in Boston's tiny Chinatown. The decor is resolutely humble, but the seafood dishes are excellent and attractively
priced. *Chinese.* **I**

♀ **No Name** (dwntwn), 15½ Fish Pier (338-7539). A/C.
♗ Lunch/dinner Mon–Sat (until 10pm). No credit cards. *Spe-
cialties:* clam chowder, grilled fish, fried clams. *Note:* On the pier itself, this seafood rest. w. rather spartan decor is one of the most popular in Boston. The
seagulls and the ship horns add to the local color. The cuisine is as simple as the
decor, but the seafood is the highest quality. Efficient svce and an excellent value.
A Boston classic since 1917. *Seafood.* **B–I**

Cafeterias/Fast Food

☼ **Elsie's** (vic.), 71 Mt. Auburn St., Cambridge (354-8781).
☼ Lunch/dinner daily. No credit cards. *Note:* Entire generations
of Harvard students have sung the praises (and continue to do so) of Elsie's huge
sandwiches. A "must" for all (preferably famished) visitors.

Museum of Fine Arts Cafeteria (nr. dwntwn), 465 Huntington Ave.
(267-9300). Lunch only, Tues–Sun. *Note:* Excellent cafeteria cuisine.

BARS & NIGHTCLUBS

☼ **Bull & Finch Pub** (dwntwn), in the Hampshire House, 84
☼ Beacon St. (227-9605). Very lively pub (especially on week-
ends) and by far the most popular bar in Boston. Was the model for the television
show "Cheers." Trendy restaurant on the second floor. Rather pleasant retro
decor.

Catch a Rising Star (dwntwn), Charles Playhouse, 76 Warrenton St. (426-3737). The best comedy club in town. Also live music. Open nightly.

Harper's Ferry (vic.), 158 Brighton Ave., Allston (254-9743). Blues bar that hosts local and national acts. Well known, but never crowded in this spacious venue. Open nightly.

The Middle East Restaurant (vic.), 472 Massachusetts Ave., Cambridge (472-9181). Jazz, rock, and international music to be heard in this hippest of clubs in Boston. Open nightly.

RegattaBar (vic.), in the Charles Hotel (see "Accommodations," above) (876-7777). Upscale jazz club near Harvard Sq. in Cambridge. All the big names from Paquito D'Rivera to Sonny Rollins to Tommy Flanagan. Call for performance dates and times. The best jazz music in the Boston area.

The Ritz Bar (dwntwn), in the Ritz Carlton Hotel (see "Accommodations," above) (536-5700). Open daily. Classy, very British bar. "High society" describes the decor, the svce, and the prices.

Ryles (vic.), Inman Sq., Cambridge (876-9330). Live jazz, pop, and blues with the biggest stars. Locally popular.

Venus de Milo (nr. dwntwn), 11 Lansdowne St., Kenmore Sq. (421-9595). Stylish place, glitzy and hip w. great music and a sophisticated, multicultural crowd.

Zanzibar (dwntwn), 1 Boylston Place (451-1955). Hot pop-music dance club with jungle motif decor. Open Wed–Sat.

NEARBY EXCURSIONS

CONCORD (20 mi./32km NW on Mass. 2): Known as "the cradle of the Republic," this charming historic New England town owes its name to the treaty, or concord, signed with the Native Americans soon after it was settled in 1635. A bloody confrontation at the North Bridge between British troops and the Minutemen on April 19, 1775, set the Revolutionary War in full motion. There are many historical landmark houses and museums here, including the **Old Manse**, Monument St. (open Thurs–Mon), **Orchard House**, 399 Lexington Rd. (open daily), **Concord Antiquarium Museum**, 200 Lexington Rd. (508/369-9609; open daily); and **Concord Art Association**, 37 Lexington Rd. (508/369-2578; open Tues–Sun). Many famous writers are buried in the **Sleepy Hollow Cemetery** on Bedford St., including Ralph Waldo Emerson and Nathaniel Hawthorne. Well worth the trip. Makes a good joint excursion with Lexington (see below).

GLOUCESTER (35 mi./56km NE on U.S. 1 and Mass. 128): Old fishing village with narrow, picturesque streets and very lovely beaches and cliffs nearby. Don't miss the **Hammond Castle Museum**, 80 Hesperus Ave. (508/283-7673; open daily). Built in the late 1920s by inventor John Hayes Hammond in the image of a medieval castle, the museum is dramatically situated on the Atlantic Ocean and houses its collection of Roman, medieval and Renaissance art as well as an 8,200-pipe organ.

LEXINGTON (12 mi./19km NW on Mass. 2): With Concord, another hallmark town of the Revolutionary War. There are a number of historic structures and relics here, including the **Hancock-Clarke House**, 36 Hancock St. (617/861-0928; open daily), where Paul Revere sounded warning for the Minutemen; **Buckman Tavern**, 1 Bedford St. (617/861-0928; open daily), on the site of the battle against the British (April 19, 1775); and **Munroe Tavern**, 1332 Massachusetts Ave. (617/862-1703; open daily), which served as a hospital for British troops. Worth a side trip.

LINCOLN (18 mi./29km NW on Mass. 2 and 126): See the **Gropius House,** 68 Baker Bridge Rd. (617/227-3956). The Walter Gropius family residence and the first of his designs realized in this country, this house's unadorned lines were considered avant-garde at the time of its construction (1937). Original Bauhaus furniture. Open Fri–Sun. A "must" for architecture lovers. A recommended joint excursion with Concord (see above).

LOWELL (25 mi./40km NW on Mass. 3): Resting on the banks of the Merrimack River, this once-handicraft hamlet was transformed into the nation's center for the mechanized production of cotton cloth. **Lowell National Historic Park** (508/970-5000) gives tours of restored mills and an impressive canal system. **Whistler House Museum of Art** (508/452-7641) has a collection of 19th- and early-20th-century art. Annual folk festival during the last weekend in July.

MARBLEHEAD (17 mi./27km NE on Mass. 1A): On a large Massachusetts Bay promontory, this former fishing port was founded in 1629 by British sailors from Cornwall and has since become a well-known summer resort. Numerous interesting colonial houses. Don't miss the **town hall,** on Washington Sq. (617/631-0528; open daily), and its famous painting, *Spirit of '76.* Very popular boat races on summer wknds.

PLYMOUTH (39 mi./65km SE on Mass. 3): A name known to every American. The first permanent British colony of New England was founded on December 21, 1620, by the Pilgrims of the *Mayflower.* (For more details, see the chapter on the Atlantic Coast.)

PORTSMOUTH (55 mi./88km NE on I-95): With its old waterfront neighborhood known as **Strawbery Banke,** this former New Hampshire capital of British colonial times offers one of the most handsome groups of historic buildings in the country. (For more details, see the chapter on the Atlantic Coast.)

ROCKPORT (38 mi./61km NE on U.S. 1, Mass. 128, and Mass. 127): Charming little port that has become a haven for artists. See especially the famous **Paper House,** 52 Pigeon Hill St. (508/546-2629; open daily July–Aug, rest of the year by appointment)—a baroque monument to the glory of the newspaper. A recommended combined excursion w. Gloucester (see above).

ROUTE 128 (at the I-95N and I-95S fork): Along 26 mi. (42km), this Boston beltway encompasses the largest complex of science and space research laboratories in the country. Some 700 firms, including all the giants of the electronics industry (General Electric, Honeywell, Raytheon, Wang, Digital, Geodyne, etc.), are represented, as well as NASA and U.S. Army research centers. Overall, some 50,000 scholars, engineers, and technicians make the famous Rte. 128 one of the most highly concentrated centers of brain power in the world. Also known as the "Silicon Valley of the East Coast."

SALEM (16 mi./26km NE on Mass. 1A): First capital of Massachusetts (1626–30) and scene of the infamous witch trials of 1692 (described in Arthur Miller's famous play *The Crucible*), which ended only after the hanging of 19 victims of religious fanaticism. Lovely old houses carefully preserved in the harbor area **(Maritime National Historic Site)** and around Chestnut St., notably. Many remarkable museums including the **House of the Seven Gables,** 54 Turner St. (open daily), dating from 1668, which inspired Nathaniel Hawthorne's famous novel; **Witch House,** 310½ Essex St.

(open daily), where the "witches" were interrogated; the **Peabody Museum,** E. Indian Sq. (open daily), and its rich naval collections; and the **Witch Museum,** 19½ Washington Sq. (open daily), which offers a detailed re-creation of a witch trial. The **Information Center,** 174 Derby St. (617/745-1470), offers relatively complete brochures and written material. An excursion not to be missed.

            SAUGUS (8 mi./13km NE on U.S. 1): Cradle of the American iron and steel industry, Saugus was the site of the continent's first foundry (1646). Don't miss the **Iron Works National Historic Site,** 224 Central St. (617/233-0050), a minutely detailed replica of the period's first smelting furnaces with forging demonstrations. Open daily, Apr–Oct. Worth the detour.

FARTHER AFIELD

            CAPE COD (202 mi./323km r.t. on Mass. 3S and U.S. 6E): A virtual island, this sandy, 60-mile-long (97km) area is where the Pilgrims of the *Mayflower* landed in 1620. Charming old fishing villages and beautiful seascapes. The two neighboring islands—**Martha's Vineyard** and **Nantucket**—are favorite vacation spots of well-to-do New Yorkers and Bostonians, offering fishing, sailing, and a temperate summer climate. (For more details, see the chapter on Cape Cod.) An excursion not to be missed.

            OLD STURBRIDGE VILLAGE (65 mi./104km SW on the Massachusetts Tpke., I-84, and U.S. 20) (508/347-3362): Faithful rendition of a rural New England town of the 1830s, with more than 40 old houses, stalls, workshops, and people in period dress. Interesting slice of history. Also, a nearby car museum, the **Sturbridge Automuseum,** 2 mi. (4km) west on U.S. 20. Worth a visit. Open daily Apr–Oct, Tues–Sun the rest of the year.

      Heading back to Boston, turn off at **Webster** (via Mass. 131 and 197), a small industrial town on the edge of the largest natural body of water in Massachusetts. Renamed **Lake Webster** for convenience sake, the lake's official name is actually **Lake Chargoggagoggmanchauggagoggchaubunagungamaug,** a term which, in the Nipmuc dialect, means "you fish on your side, I fish on my side, no one fishes in the middle." In addition to having the longest and most complicated name in U.S. geography, the lake is also a fishing paradise, with trout, perch, and pike. Worth going out of your way for.

Where to Stay En Route

IN STURBRIDGE The **Publick House Inn,** Mass. 131, Sturbridge, MA 01566 (508/347-3313). 17 rms. A charming little colonial inn dating from 1771 with a very satisfactory restaurant.**M**

            THE BERKSHIRES (336 mi./538km r.t. on I-90W and U.S. 20N to Pittsfield): With its undulating landscapes, dense forests, and dozens of lakes and charming old New England villages, the Berkshires region is a favorite vacation haven in all seasons: in winter for cross-country skiing; in summer for its music and theater festivals (the Tanglewood Music Festival, the Williamstown Theater Festival, and the Berkshire Theater Festival are among the most popular in the country); and from mid-Sept to late Oct, for the sumptuous colors of its autumn leaves.

Crossing through the Berkshires from the Vermont border to southern Connecticut, U.S. 7 allows a complete picture of the area and its most remarkable locales: **Lenox,** the picturesque town celebrated by Nathaniel Hawthorne (*Tanglewood Tales*), has been the backdrop each summer for half a century for the **Tanglewood Music Festival** (late June to late Aug) with the Boston Symphony Orchestra (for information, call 413/637-1940).

Pittsfield offers, among other attractions, the **Berkshire Museum,** 39 South St., with its collection of European paintings (Rubens, van Dyck, etc.); **Arrowhead,** 780 Holmes Rd., the residence-museum where Herman Melville wrote *Moby-Dick;* and the very lovely Shaker village of **Hancock** (5 mi./8km west on U.S. 20) (413/443-0188), a religious community founded in 1790 where some 20 period buildings still stand. A visit not to be missed.

Stockbridge, a magnificent little summer community that seems to come straight out of an old picture book, has attracted many artists (sculptor Daniel Chester French, painter Norman Rockwell, author Norman Mailer, etc.) and is home to the renowned **Berkshire Theater Festival** (late June to Sept; for information, call 413/298-5576). Two stops not to be missed: the **Norman Rockwell Museum,** on Main St. (413/298-3822), and the **studio of Daniel Chester French,** on Mass. 183.

Williamstown, another charming little village typical of the Berkshires with its old houses in pastel tones, has a very beautiful art museum with rich impressionist collections, the **Sterling and Francine Clark Institute,** 225 South St. Home of venerable **Williams College** (est. 1793) and of the **Williamstown Theater Festival** (late June to late Aug), which offers modern and classical theater with famous actors. (For information, call 413/597-3400.)

A visit to the Berkshires is not to be missed for all lovers of art and culture. For regional tourist information, contact the **Berkshire Hills Visitors Bureau,** Berkshire Commons South, Pittsfield, MA 01201 (toll free 800/237-5747).

Where to Stay En Route

IN LENOX ☼ ⚑⚑ **Apple Tree,** 224 West St., Lenox, MA 01240 (413/637-1477). 33 rms. Century-old inn amid lovely gardens. **M–E**

IN PITTSFIELD ⚑⚑ **Hilton Inn,** Berkshire Common and West St., Pittsfield, MA 01201 (413/499-2000). 175 rms. Modern comfort. **M**
⚑ **Heart of the Berkshires,** 970 W. Housatonic, Pittsfield, MA 01201 (413/443-1255). 16 rms. Small, functional motel. **I**

IN SOUTH LEE ☼⚑ **Merrell Tavern Inn,** Main St. at Mass. 102, South Lee, MA 01260 (413/243-1794). 9 rms. Charming historic inn built around 1794. **I–M**

IN STOCKBRIDGE ☼⚑⚑⚑ **Red Lion Inn,** Main St. at U.S. 7, Stockbridge, MA 01262 (413/298-5545). 100 rms. Charming inn dating from 1773. **I–E**

IN WILLIAMSTOWN ⚑⚑⚑ **Orchards,** 222 Adams Rd., Williamstown, MA 01267 (413/458-9611). 49 rms. Elegant old-English–style inn. **E**

🔭 VERMONT & THE NEW HAMPSHIRE MOUNTAINS

(568 mi./908km r.t. from Boston via I-93N, N.H. 106N, U.S. 3N, N.H. 25E, N.H. 16N, U.S. 302W, N.H. 10S, U.S. 4W, U.S. 7S, Vt. 9E, N.H. 9E, N.H. 101E, U.S. 3S, Mass. 128W, and Mass. 2E): This trip, requiring at least three or four days and taking you through some of the most beautiful wooded country in the U.S., is suitable for all seasons: the long winter snows, the lovely New England spring, the radiant summer, or the splendid autumn that sets the forests of New Hampshire's **White Mountains** and Vermont's **Green Mountains** ablaze with color.

Leaving Boston northward along I-93, you soon come to your first stop, **Concord,** the capital of New Hampshire. See the 1819 **State House,** on Main St.

(603/271-2154; open Mon–Fri), with its hall of flags and its characteristic dome. If you enjoy handcrafts you'll certainly want to visit the ⚱ **Concord Arts and Crafts Center,** 36 N. Main St. (open Mon–Sat).

Farther north on N.H. 106 you'll come to ⚱ **Canterbury Shaker Village,** on Shaker Rd. off N.H. 106 (603/783-9511), open Tues–Sat from mid-May through Oct. Founded in 1792 and today one of the only two active Shaker villages remaining in the U.S., it can still show half a dozen of its original buildings and a little museum illustrating the unusual Shaker lifestyle.

The next stop is ❋ **Laconia,** a popular summer resort in the heart of the "lakes region" (one of the lakes is New Hampshire's largest, Lake Winnipesaukee). Continue north to ❋ **White Mountain National Forest,** a wooded tract of 741,000 acres (300,000ha) whose highest peak, ⚌⚌ **Mount Washington,** rises to 6,288 ft. (1,917m). A road reached from **Glen House** on N.H. 16, and a **cog railway** whose terminus is a little north of Crawford House on U.S. 302 (603/846-5404), will take you to the top of Mt. Washington from the end of May till Oct, and give you a breathtaking view. Many winter-sports resorts and spectacular gorges are nearby: **Crawford Notch, Dixville Notch, Franconia Notch, Pinkham Notch,** etc.

A very lovely scenic drive, the ⚱ **Kancamagus Highway** (N.H. 112) crosses the White Mountains from side to side. On your way, don't fail to visit the lovely resort of ⚱ **Bretton Woods,** famous as the scene of a 1944 international monetary conference that fixed the price of gold at $35 per ounce and created the International Bank for Reconstruction and Development (World Bank).

Regaining the right bank of the Connecticut River at **Woodsville,** your route stays on it for about 50 mi. (80km) on beautiful, scenic N.H. 10, passing the historic little town of ❋ **Hanover,** the home of famous Dartmouth College, founded in 1796. ❋⚱ **Woodstock,** the next stop, with its charming old houses, is one of Vermont's best-known ski resorts. Continuing toward the Green Mountains and **Sherburne Pass,** you'll come to **Rutland** and its renowned marble quarries; at the ⚱ **Vermont Marble Exhibit,** 61 Main St. (802/459-3311), open daily from late May through Oct, see how marble is quarried and then turned into works of art.

Manchester, the next stop, has been a popular summer and winter resort for more than a century. The ❋⚱ **Equinox Skyline Drive,** a mountain road rising as high as 3,835 ft. (1,169m), will give you a magnificent view of the endless woodlands of the **Green Mountain National Forest;** it can be reached from U.S. 7, 6 mi. (9km) south of Manchester. Road open May–Oct; difficult in rainy or foggy weather. Don't miss it. There's a very popular classical-music festival every summer at the **Southern Vermont Art Center,** West Rd.; call 802/362-1405 for programs and schedules.

The trip ends at ❋ **Bennington,** where in 1777, in one of the decisive engagements of the War of Independence, Ethan Allen's "Green Mountain Boys" held off the British under General Burgoyne. Lovely old Colonial houses at ⚱ **Old Bennington,** and a remarkable **city museum** on W. Main St. (802/447-1571; open daily, Mar–Nov), with paintings by the American primitive, Grandma Moses. Don't miss it.

Finally, back to Boston across the Appalachian foothills, following various scenic highways: Vt. 9, N.H. 9, and N.H. 101. A spectacular excursion for lovers of unspoiled nature.

Where to Stay En Route

IN BENNINGTON, VT. 🍴 **Vermonter,** Vt. 9W, Bennington, VT 05201 (802/442-2529). 32 rms and cottages. Comfortable, well-run little motel on a lake with sand beach. Closed Mar–Apr. I

IN BETHLEHEM, N.H. ❋🍴🍴 **Wayside Inn,** U.S. 302, Bethlehem, NH 03574 (603/869-3364). 36 rms. Inviting old mansion (1825) on the Ammonoosuc River. Originally the homestead of Pres. Franklin Pierce's family. Open Dec–Oct. I

IN BRETTON WOODS, N.H. ☀☖☖ **Mount Washington,** U.S. 302, Bretton Woods, NH 03575 (603/278-1000). 216 rms. Charming old Edwardian-style hotel against a splendid mountain backdrop. **E–VE** (Modified American Plan).

IN CONWAY, N.H. ☀☖☖ **Merrill Farm,** N.H. 16, Conway, NH 03818 (603/447-3866). 43 rms. Picturesque riverside country inn whose oldest parts date from 1780. Open May–Oct. **M–E**

IN WOODSTOCK, VT. ☖☖☖ **Woodstock Inn and Resort,** Village Green, Woodstock, VT 05091 (802/457-1100). 146 rms. Luxurious resort hotel with a clear view over the town. **VE**

☀☖☖ **Kedron Valley,** Vt. 106, South Woodstock, VT 05071 (802/457-1473). 29 rms. Charming old inn built in 1840 and prettily restored. Closed Apr. **M–E**

Where to Eat En Route

IN MENDON, VT. ☀☖☖ **Countryman's Pleasure,** Townline Rd. (802/773-7141). Dinner only, Tues–Sat. Poached salmon, rack of lamb. Century-old Colonial-style house; open-air dining in good weather. **I–M**

IN NORTH CONWAY, N.H. ☀☖☖ **Scottish Lion,** on U.S. 302 (603/356-6381). Lunch/dinner daily. 1872 country inn; Scottish-inspired food. **I**

CHAPTER 2

CAPE COD

□ □ □

With Martha's Vineyard and Nantucket ⚑

It was in **Provincetown** Bay, at the northern end of Cape Cod, that on November 19, 1620, the 101 Pilgrim Fathers disembarked from the *Mayflower* and set foot for the first time on American soil. The long, sandy promontory, for years a region of simple fishing villages, has undergone a profound change since the beginning of the 20th century: It is now one of the most sought-after and select resort areas in the country. The peninsula of Cape Cod, shaped strangely like a lobster's claw, is a 70-mile stretch of sand dunes, pine forests, immaculate beaches discreetly hidden from the highway, nature reserves such as the **Cape Cod National Seashore** and **Monomoy National Wildlife Refuge** (once a haunt of pirates), and spruce little towns of old houses and unobtrusive newer estates such as **Brewster, Chatham, Falmouth, Harwich, Orleans, Sandwich,** and **Yarmouth.**

Much of the political and financial establishment of New York and Boston, led by the Kennedy family, has taken to summering at the Cape or on one of the two delightful islands nearby, **Martha's Vineyard** and **Nantucket.** The price of this success is that the "sold out" notices go up all along the Cape seashore in July and August, particularly over weekends. The best times to go are spring and, even better, fall; the favorite amusements (besides idling or strolling on the 275 mi./440km of fine sand beaches) are sailing, surfing, and above all deep-sea fishing. There are more than a dozen species of big-game fish in these waters, including a highly prized variety of giant tuna.

BASIC FACTS: State of Massachusetts. Area code: 508. Time zone: eastern. First colonized: 1637 (Sandwich), 1639 (Hyannis-Yarmouth), 1642 (Martha's Vineyard). Approximate population: 175,000 year round; 450,000 in July–Aug.

CLIMATE: Although the city of Boston is quite close, Cape Cod enjoys a much less extreme climate due to the sea breezes in summer (mean temperature in July 71°F/22°C) and the Gulf Stream in winter (mean temperature in Jan 38°F/4°C). Spring and fall offer enjoyable temperatures and plenty of sunshine.

DISTANCES: Boston, 55 mi. (89km); New York, 270 mi. (432km).

ARRIVAL & TRANSIT INFORMATION

AIRPORTS: Hyannis-Barnstable Municipal Airport (HYA), 1 mi. (1.6km) north of Hyannis. Cab, $17. Information: 775-2020.

Martha's Vineyard Airport (MVY), 6 mi. (9.6km) west of Edgartown. Cab, $15. Information: 693-7022.
Nantucket Memorial Airport (ACK), 3 mi. (5km) south. Cab, $10. Information: 228-1700.

AIRLINES: Delta Connection (toll free 800/221-1212), Hyannis and Nantucket to Boston; Continental Express (toll free 800/525-0280), Hyannis, Martha's Vineyard, and Nantucket to Boston and New York.

BUS OR CAR RENTAL? Given the distances involved, the only ways of seeing Cape Cod are by bus or a rental car. Greyhound buses provide direct connections between Hyannis or Woods Hole (from which the ferry leaves for the islands) and Boston or New York. Bonanza Bus Lines offers several buses a day from either New York or Boston to Hyannis. Plymouth and Brockton have a service between Boston and Provincetown. For service completely within Cape Cod try Sea Lines.

CAR RENTAL: Avis, Hyannis-Barnstable Airport (toll free 800/331-1212); Budget, on Mass. 132, Hyannis (toll free 800/527-0700); Hertz, Hyannis-Barnstable Airport (toll free 800/654-3131); National, on Mass. 132, Hyannis (toll free 800/227-7368); Thrifty, on Mass. 132, Hyannis (toll free 800/367-2277).

TRAIN: Nearest Amtrak station: 100 Gaspee St., Providence, R.I. (401/727-7382). From May to Sept there is regular svce (6 hr.) between New York and Hyannis; for information, call toll free 800/872-7245. Also between Boston (Braintree T Station) and Hyannis, May–Oct; for information, call 617/482-3660.

INTERCITY BUSES: Bonanza (617/720-4110; toll free 800/556-3815); **Plymouth and Brockton** (508/775-5524); **Sea Line** (508/385-8311; toll free 800/352-7155).

FERRY: Boston–Nantucket or Provincetown, Bay State Spray Cruises (June–Sept). 3 hr. by catamaran. 20 Long Wharf, Boston (617/723-7800).
Falmouth–Martha's Vineyard, from the end of May to mid-Oct, on the *Island Queen* (548-4800).
Hyannis–Martha's Vineyard and Nantucket, Hy-Line (May–Dec), Pier 1, Ocean St. Dock (778-2600).
Provincetown–Boston, Bay State Cruises Company, Inc. (June–Sept), Town Wharf (617/723-7800).
Woods Hole–Martha's Vineyard and Nantucket (year round), Steamship Authority (540-2022).

INFORMATION & TOURS

TOURIST INFORMATION: Cape Cod Chamber of Commerce, U.S. 6 and Mass. 132, Hyannis, MA 02061 (508/362-3225); **Martha's Vineyard Chamber of Commerce,** Beach Rd., Vineyard Haven, MA 02568 (508/693-0085); **Nantucket Island Chamber of Commerce,** Main St., Nantucket, MA 02554 (508/228-1700); **Provincetown Chamber of Commerce,** 307 Commercial St., Provincetown, MA 02657 (508/487-3424).

GUIDED TOURS: Hy-Line, Pier 1, Ocean St. Dock, Hyannis (778-2600): Boat excursions, summer only.
Cape Cod & Hyannis Railroad, 252 Main St., Hyannis (771-3788): Entertaining round trip between Hyannis and Woods Hole in a little steam train. Daily May–Oct.

Island Tours, Straight Wharf Boat Basin, Nantucket (228-0334): 75-min. bus tours of the island. Daily May–Oct.

Portuguese Princess, Town Wharf, Provincetown (487-2651; toll free 800/442-3188): 3½-hr. narrated whale-watch boat excursion. Daily Apr–Nov.

Whale Watcher cruises, Barnstable Harbor (362-6088): Narrated 4-hr. whale-watching excursion. Twice daily from early Apr to late Oct. Resv. required.

SIGHTS, ATTRACTIONS & ACTIVITIES

CAPE COD NATIONAL SEASHORE (26 mi./41km NE of Hyannis along U.S. 6): A 44,000-acre nature reserve along the shore, offering beautiful seascapes including dramatic white ocean beaches, dunes, woodlands, and marshes. Established in 1961 by President Kennedy to protect the less-developed areas of the Cape from commercialism, the area preserves notable examples of typical Cape Cod architecture. There are **Visitor Centers** at Provincetown and at Eastham (508/349-3785). Worth going out of your way for.

MARTHA'S VINEYARD & NANTUCKET (respectively 5 mi./8km and 30 mi./48km off Woods Hole): These islands, home to a very active whaling community in the 18th century, have now become fashionable summer resorts with a wealth of attractions for holidaymakers. They have many charming small villages with beautiful old houses, the climate is generally temperate, and there are ferries all year from Woods Hole. Martha's Vineyard is also a naturalist's paradise. Both are worth visiting. Off Martha's Vineyard lies the half-wild little island of **Chappaquiddick.**

MONOMOY NATIONAL WILDLIFE REFUGE (3 mi./5km, off Chatham): Designated a wilderness area by the federal government in 1970, Monomoy Island attracts tens of thousands of migrating birds to its dunes (late May to Nov). Access by boat only from Chatham. For further information: Refuge manager, Morris Island, Chatham, MA 02633 (508/945-0594).

PROVINCETOWN (50 mi./80km NE of Hyannis along U.S. 6): The first landfall for the Pilgrims (see the introduction to this chapter). A picturesque little port at the tip of Cape Cod, whose waters attracted at the turn of the century a large colony of Portuguese fishermen, still plying their trade today. Today the town is an artists' colony and hosts a large gay community. A 247-ft. (77m) granite tower with a splendid view over the Cape, and a little historical museum commemorate the landing of the Pilgrims. An absolute must-see.

YARMOUTH (4 mi./6km north of Hyannis by Willow Rd.): One of the oldest (1639) villages on the Cape, with an authentic New England atmosphere. Not to be missed.

MUSEUMS: At Brewster, the **Drummer Boy Museum,** 2½ mi. (4km) west on Mass. 6A (896-3823), is housed in a converted windmill built in 1750; devoted to Revolutionary history. Worth the detour. Open daily from the end of May to the end of Oct only.

At Hyannis, the **John F. Kennedy Hyannis Museum,** Old Town Hall, 397 Main St. (775-2201), exhibits over 50 candid photographs depicting the president's life on Cape Cod from the age of 17 until his death. Open daily Jan–Oct; closed Sun and Mon in Nov–Dec.

At Nantucket, the ☖ **Whaling Museum,** Broad St. (228-1736), depicts the life of the Nantucket whalers that inspired Herman Melville to write *Moby-Dick.* Fascinating. Open daily in summer, wknds the rest of the year.

At Provincetown, the ☖ **Historical Museum** and **Pilgrim Monument,** Monument Hill (487-1310), give the history of the *Mayflower* and the Pilgrims. Open daily.

At Sandwich, ☖ **Heritage Plantation,** Grove St. and Pine St. (888-3300), is a small historical museum housed, as its name suggests, in a 19th-century plantation house. It has a fine collection of classic cars, including a fabulous 1931 Duesenberg that belonged to Gary Cooper. Don't miss it. Open daily from late May to late Oct; closed the rest of the year.

SPECIAL EVENTS: For the exact schedule of events below, consult the appropriate chamber of commerce (see above under "Information & Tours").

Daffodil Weekend (Nantucket; last wknd in Apr): Classic-car parade.

Academy Playhouse (Orleans; late June through Aug): Theater festival with comedy, drama, and musicals. For information, call 255-1963.

Blessing of the Fleet (Provincetown; late June): Lively and colorful.

Antiques Fair (Hyannis; Feb): More than 30 exhibitors.

Striped Bass & Bluefish Derby (Martha's Vineyard; Sept–Oct): Annual deep-sea fishing tournament which attracts some 2,000 contestants.

ACCOMMODATIONS

Personal Favorites (in order of preference)

☼☖♙♙♙ **Jared Coffin House,** 29 Broad St., Nantucket, MA 02554 (508/228-2400). 58 rms, color TV (in most). AE, CB, DC, MC, V. Free parking, rest. (Jared's) bar, rm svce, free crib. *Note:* Old private house artistically restored, to which five adjoining buildings, dating from 1720 to 1870, have been added after an elegant job of renovation. Comfortable rms w. period furniture, each decorated in a different style. Romantic atmosphere, beautiful gardens, exemplary svce and reception. Very acceptable rest. Resv. required. Open year round. **M–E**

♙♙♙ **New Seabury Resort,** Great Neck Rd., New Seabury, MA 02649 (508/477-9111; toll free 800/999-9033). 368 rms (some w. kitchenettes), A/C, color TV, in-rm movies. AE, CB, DC, MC, V. Free parking, private beach, health club, sauna, two golf courses, 16 tennis courts, boating, rest., bar, rm svce, nightclub, free crib. *Note:* Resort complex offering both comfort and luxury, standing in its own 1,900+ acres, with 5 mi. (8km) of private beach. Individual villas or spacious rms w. patios. Efficient svce but so-so rest. Sailboats available to guests; very comprehensive sports facilities. Resv. advised, well in advance. Open year round. **E–VE**

☼☖♙♙ **Bramble Inn,** Mass. 6A, Brewster, MA 02631 (508/896-7644). 12 rms, A/C. AE, CB, DC, MC, V. Free parking, rest. *Note:* Charmingly restored buildings dating from 1793 to 1861. The rms are furnished w. antiques and Persian rugs; excellent rest. Reception w. a smile. Dinner served daily from late May to late Sept; Thurs–Sat the rest of the time. Open Apr–Dec. **M**

☼☖♙♙ **Charlotte Inn,** 27 S. Summer St., Edgartown, Martha's Vineyard, MA 02539 (508/627-4751). 24 rms, color TV in some. AE, MC, V. Free parking, rest. (L'Etoile), antiques shop, free breakfast. *Note:* The best in Martha's Vineyard, with both style and refinement; five delightful houses from the 1820s lovingly restored. Rms elegant and comfortable, w. antique furniture and private patios. Well-regarded rest.; reception and svce w. a smile. A few steps from the harbor. **E–VE**

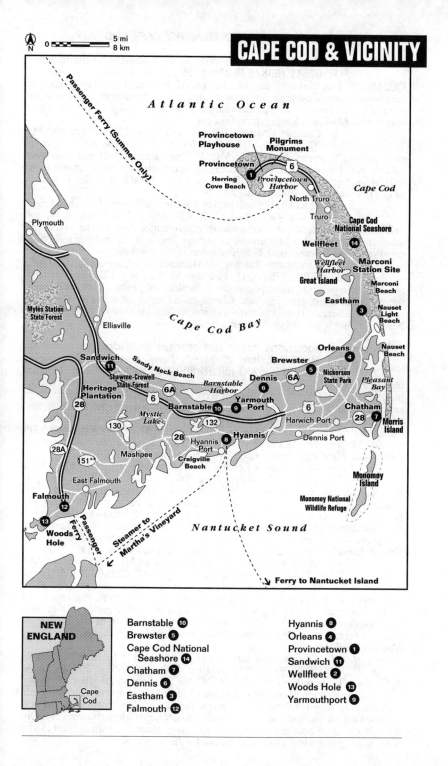

CAPE COD & VICINITY

0 — 5 mi
  — 8 km

Atlantic Ocean

Passenger Ferry (Summer Only)

Provincetown
Playhouse
Pilgrims
Monument
Provincetown
Herring
Cove Beach
Provincetown
Harbor
6
1

Plymouth

North Truro

Truro

Cape Cod

Cape Cod
National Seashore

Wellfleet
14

*Wellfleet
Harbor*

Marconi
Station Site

Great Island

Marconi
Beach

Eastham
3

Nauset
Light
Beach

Myles Station
State Forest

Ellisville

Cape Cod Bay

Orleans
4

Nauset
Beach

Brewster
5

Sandwich
11

Sandy Neck Beach

Shawme-Crowell
State Forest

Heritage
Plantation
28

6A

*Barnstable
Harbor*

Dennis
6

6A

Nickerson
State Park

*Pleasant
Bay*

Barnstable
10

Yarmouth
Port
9

6

Chatham
28 **7**

Morris
Island

6

Harwich Port

*Mystic
Lake*

130

132

28

Hyannis
8

Dennis Port

Hyannis
Port

Mashpee

151**

Craigville
Beach

28A

East Falmouth

Monomoy
Island

Monomoy National
Wildlife Refuge

Falmouth
12

13

Woods
Hole

Passenger Ferry

Steamer to Martha's Vineyard

Nantucket Sound

Ferry to Nantucket Island

NEW
ENGLAND

Cape
Cod

Barnstable **10**
Brewster **5**
Cape Cod National
  Seashore **14**
Chatham **7**
Dennis **6**
Eastham **3**
Falmouth **12**

Hyannis **8**
Orleans **4**
Provincetown **1**
Sandwich **11**
Wellfleet **2**
Woods Hole **13**
Yarmouthport **9**

☖ ☖ **Coonamessett Inn,** Jones Rd. (at Gifford St.), Falmouth, MA ☖ 02541 (508/548-2300). 26 rms, A/C, color TV. AE, CB, DC, MC, V. Free parking, rest., bar, free breakfast. *Note:* Typical small country farmhouse, Cape Cod style, in its own fine gardens beautifully situated at the edge of a lake. Interior arrangements at once lavish and cozy. Good rest. Open year round. **M–E,** but lower rates off-season.

☖ **Captain Gosnold Village,** 230 Gosnold St., Hyannis, MA ☖ 02601 (508/775-9111). 54 rms and studios half w. kitchenettes, color TV, in-rm movies. AE, MC, V. Free parking, pool, gardens. *Note:* Likable motel near the beach, w. friendly reception and svce. Inviting rms w. refrigerators. Very pleasant gardens. Free airport limo. Ideal for families. Good value out of season. Open year round. **M**

☖ **Earl of Sandwich Motor Manor,** Old Kings Hwy. (Mass. 6A), ☖ E. Sandwich, MA 02537 (508/888-1415). 24 rms, A/C, color TV. AE, CB, DC, MC, V. Free parking, nearby coffee shop, free breakfast, crib $5. *Note:* Comfortable little motel in vaguely Tudor style; friendly reception; good value; open year round. **I–M,** but lower rates off-season.

☖ **Americana Holiday,** 99 Main St., West Yarmouth, MA 02673 ☖ (508/775-5511). 154 rms, A/C, color TV, in-rm movies. MC, V. Free parking, three pools, sauna, health club, bicycles, putting green, nearby coffee shop, crib $5. *Note:* Classic motel style, modest but well maintained, w. utilitarian comforts. Family clientele. Good overall value. Open Mar–Nov. **I–M,** but lower rates off-season.

Other Accommodations (from top bracket to budget)

☖ ☖ ☖ **Nantucket Inn,** 27 Macy's Lane, Nantucket, MA 02554 ☖ ☖ ☖ (508/228-6900; toll free 800/321-8484). 100 rms, A/C, cable color TV. AE, CB, DC, MC, V. Free parking, two pools, two tennis courts, health club, rest. (Windsong), bar, rm svce, nightclub. *Note:* A newcomer to the ranks of the area's deluxe hotels. Modern architecture gives the effect of an island rising out of an attractive garden. All the rms are commodious and comfortable minisuites furnished in period style. Svce of the highest order. Caters to VIPs and conferences. Free bus service to the beach and dwntwn Nantucket; time, 5 min. A fine place; open year round. **E–VE,** but lower rates off-season.

☖ ☖ ☖ **Tara Hyannis Resort,** 35 Scudder Ave., Hyannis, MA 02601 ☖ ☖ ☖ (508/775-7775; toll free 800/843-8272). 225 rms, A/C, cable color TV. AE, CB, DC, MC, V. Free parking, two pools, golf, tennis court, health club, saunas, rest. (Silver Shell), coffee shop, bar, rm svce, nightclub, hrdrsr, cinema, concierge, free crib. *Note:* A comfortable, luxurious modern hotel, 5 min. from the beach, surrounded by more than 50 acres of gardens. Very comprehensive sports facilities. Spacious rms w. patios or balconies. Good svce. Group clientele. Open year round. **E–VE,** but lower rates off-season.

☖ ☖ **Wequassett Inn,** Pleasant Bay Rd., Mass. 28, Chatham, MA ☖ ☖ 02633 (508/432-5400; toll free 800/225-7125). 104 rms, cable color TV. AE, MC, V. Valet parking, rest., rm svce, heated pool, poolside svce, tennis court, exercise equipment, gardens, free crib. *Note:* A grand resort well utilizing its 23 acres right on the bay. Rms w. private patios or balconies overlooking the water. Inn offers a nice array of activities, from windsurfing to deep-sea fishing to whale-watching. Private beach and lovely garden. Open early May to Oct. **E–VE**

☀ ☖ ☖ **Queen Anne Inn,** 70 Queen Anne Rd., Chatham, MA 02633 ☖ ☖ (508/945-0394; toll free 800/545-4667). 30 rms, most A/C, color TV in public rms. AE, CB, DC, MC, V. Free parking, pool, boating, rest., bar, rm svce, free crib. *Note:* Gracious Victorian house very near the beach; enormous antique-furnished rms (some with balconies and fireplaces), the best overlooking garden and bay. A warm welcome here; also admirable cooking. Observation trips by boat offered during whale migrations. This small hotel can be warmly recommended. Open year round. **E–VE**

Sheraton–Ocean Park Inn, U.S. 6, Eastham, MA 02642 (508/255-5000; toll free, see Sheraton). 107 rms, A/C, cable color TV. AE, CB, DC, MC, V. Free parking, two pools, tennis court, health club, sauna, rest., bar, rm svce, disco, crib $5. *Note:* Congenial hotel at the entrance to Cape Cod National Seashore. Comfortable rms, good sports facilities, efficient svce. Good value out of season. Interesting full American Plan rates. Open year round. **M–E,** but lower rates off-season.

Bradford Gardens, 178 Bradford St., Provincetown, MA 02657 (508/487-1616). 18 rms (doubles only, 10 w. kitchenettes), color TV. AE, MC, V. Free parking. *Note:* Two elegant cottages dating from 1820, w. comfortable rms, patios, and balconies. No bar, no rest., but coffee shop nearby. Open from Apr to the end of Nov. Near beach. **M–E,** but lower rates off-season.

Daggett House, 59 N. Water St., Edgartown (Martha's Vineyard), MA 02539 (508/627-4600). 26 rms, cable color TV in lounge. MC, V. Free parking. *Note:* Inviting rms in a charming 17th-century house and two adjoining cottages; atmosphere very characteristic of New England. Beautiful gardens; no bar, no rest., but free breakfast. Private beach. Open year round. **M–E,** but lower rates off-season.

Green Harbor, Shore Rd., East Falmouth, MA 02536 (508/548-4747). 40 rms (doubles only, 17 w. kitchen), A/C, color TV. AE, CB, DC, MC, V. Free parking, pool, beach. Boats available to guests. *Note:* Small, quiet, comfortable motel ideal for families. No bar, no rest. Open May–Nov. **I–M,** but lower rates off-season.

Lewis Bay Marina, 53 South St., Hyannisport, MA 02601 (508/775-6633). 63 rms (doubles only), A/C, color TV. AE, CB, DC, MC, V. Free parking, pool, rest., bar. *Note:* Typical motel nr. the terminal of the Nantucket ferry, looking out over the harbor and marina. Run-of-the-mill comfort, affable svce, good overall value. Open year round. **I–M**

Hampton Inn Hyannis, Iyanough Rd., Hyannis, MA 02601 (508/771-4804; toll free 800/426-7866). 104 rms, A/C, cable color TV. AE, MC, V. Free parking, free breakfast, pool, sauna. Adjoining coffee shop, gardens. *Note:* Congenial, well-run motel 5 min. from Hyannis airport. Huge, comfortable rms, some w. kitchenettes. Good-natured svce. Attractive family packages. Very good overall value. Open year round. **I–M**

YMCAs/Youth Hostels

Hy Land Hostel, 465 Falmouth Rd., Hyannis, MA 02601 (508/775-2970): 50 beds; family rms available. Resv. recommended. Open June–Sept.

Little America Hostel, N. Pamet Rd., Truro, MA 02666 (508/349-3889): 48 bunks. Resv. recommended. Open June–Sept.

RESTAURANTS

Personal Favorites (in order of preference)

Chillingsworth Restaurant, 2449 Main St., Brewster (896-3640). A/C. Lunch Tues–Sat late May to Dec; dinner Tues–Sun late June to mid-Sept, wknds only in spring and fall; brunch Sun. AE, CB, DC, MC, V. Jkt. *Specialties:* magret de canard with figs, broiled shrimp in sauce chinois, escalope of salmon with asparagus, lobster w. basil and cognac cream, grilled pheasant w. raspberry sauce. Menu changes regularly. Rather sparse wine list. *Note:* French-inspired cuisine in an enchanting colonial house almost three centuries old amid wonderful gardens. Handsome Louis XV decor. Polished reception and svce. The Cape's premier restaurant. Resv. a must. *French/Continental.* **M–E** (prix fixe).

21 Federal, 21 Federal St., Nantucket (228-2121). Lunch/dinner daily; brunch Sun; closed Oct–Mar. AE, MC, V. *Specialties:* lobster ravioli w. chanterelles, sautéed Muscovy duck w. figs and port, catch of the day, luscious homemade desserts. *Note:* Housed in a charming 1847 Greek Revival building, it's "the" place to see and be seen; offers innovative modern American food and efficient, friendly svce. A truly remarkable place. Resv. advisable. *American/Seafood.* **I–M**

> 🍷🍽 **Chanticleer,** 9 New St., Siasconset (Nantucket Is.) (257-6231). Lunch/dinner Thurs–Tues; closed Nov to early May. MC, V. Jkt. *Specialties:* scallops with truffles, bass with sorrel, quail w. brandy, roast rack of lamb w. herbs, fruit sherbets. Fine wine list. *Note:* An oasis for those who love to eat, wholly French and under the masterly direction of the admirable chef, J. Charles Berruet. Engaging, urbane decor and atmosphere, but painful prices; one of the best rests. on the island. Resv. advised. *French.* **M–E**

> 🍷🍽 **L'Etoile,** in the Charlotte Inn (see "Accommodations," above), 27 S. Summer St., Edgartown, Martha's Vineyard (627-4751). Dinner nightly during summer; brunch Sun.; closed Jan to mid-Feb. AE, MC, V. Jkt. *Specialties:* lobster w. cognac and cream, rack of lamb w. red wine and garlic, sautéed scallops w. wild mushrooms, rabbit salad. Fine wine list. *Note:* This hotel rest., very busy during the season, is one of the most elegant and highly regarded on the island. Refined French-inspired cuisine with a menu that changes regularly. Attractive Victorian setting amid lovely gardens, irreproachable svce, resv. a must. *French/Continental.* **E** (prix fixe).

> 🍷🍽 **The Paddock,** W. Main St. at W. End Rotary, Hyannis (775-7677). A/C. Lunch/dinner daily, mid-Apr to mid-Nov; closed the rest of the year. AE, CB, DC, MC, V. Jkt. *Specialties:* coq au vin, rack of lamb, roast duckling, lobster, scampi. *Note:* A fashionable place, done up in the purest Victorian idiom. Cuisine very worthy, but devoid of imagination. Open-air terrace for fine days. Excellent svce, resv. a must, valet parking. *Continental/Seafood.* **I–M**

> ☀️🍷🍽 **Cap'n Linnell House,** Skaket Rd., Orleans (255-3400). Dinner nightly, brunch Sun; closed Dec 25. AE, CB, DC, MC, V. *Specialties:* scallops, tournedos, chicken Provençal, Mandarin duck. *Note:* Modest, inviting sea captain's home from the 1850s. Rather elaborate cooking. Open-air dining in summer; live jazz in season. Very popular locally, so resv. advised. *Continental/Seafood.* **I–M**

Other Restaurants (from top bracket to budget)

> ☀️🍷🍽 **Abbicci** (formerly Cranberry Moose), 43 Main St. (Mass. 6A), Yarmouth Port (362-3501). Lunch/dinner daily; brunch Sun; closed Tues mid-Oct to mid-May. AE, CB, DC, MC, V. Jkt. *Specialties:* rack of lamb w. pistachio crust, Mediterranean seafood stew. The menu changes periodically. *Note:* One of the Cape's more interesting rests. in a quaint 200-year-old inn. Creative French and Italian cuisine. Resv. advised. *Mediterranean.* **M–E**

> 🍷🍽 **The Regatta of Cotuit,** 4631 Falmouth Rd., Cotuit (428-5715). Dinner only, nightly; brunch Sun; closed Tues mid-Nov to mid-May. AE, MC, V. *Specialties:* wild mushroom strudel, lamb en chemise, grilled shrimp w. a three-mustard sauce. Menu changes regularly. *Note:* Martin Murphy's creative dishes have made this a locally popular restaurant. Charming 1790s house w. Early American decor and many antiques. *French/Continental.* **M**

> ☀️🍷🍽 **Daniel Webster Inn,** 149 Main St., Sandwich (888-3622). A/C. Breakfast/lunch/dinner daily. AE, CB, DC, MC, V. Jkt. *Specialties:* fish and shellfish of the day, veal Oscar, prime beef, sautéed scallops, roast duckling. Fine wine list. *Note:* Decent but unimaginative cooking. Magnificently reconstructed interior of an 18th-century tavern. Excellent svce. Very popular locally, so resv. are advised. Beautiful English-style gardens. *Steak/Seafood.* **I–M**

> 🍷🍽 **Scargo Café,** 799 Mass. 6A, Dennis (385-8200). Lunch/dinner daily. MC, V. *Specialties:* pasta dishes, chicken wildcat, scrod bonne femme, grapenut custard. *Note:* A longtime local favorite situated

across from the Cape Playhouse. Somewhere between home-style and gourmet cuisine. Fairly priced. *Continental/American.* **I–M**

🍸 **Nauset Beach Club,** 222 Main St., East Orleans (255-8547).
A/C. Dinner daily May–Oct, open Tues–Sat, Nov–Apr. AE, CB, MC, DC, V. *Specialties:* Spiedini (Italian flat bread) sautéed with capers and olives; saltimbocca (scalloped veal) layered w. cheese, spinach, and prosciutto; cranberry-orange cobbler w. ginger ice cream. *Note:* Cozy interior w. a wood-burning stove in which crespelle is baked. Great wine list at fair prices. *Northern Italian.* **I–M**

☀️🍸🍸 **Bishop Terrace,** 118 Main St., West Harwich (432-0253).
A/C. Lunch/dinner daily; brunch Sun. MC, V. Jkt. *Specialties:* stuffed lobster, roast duckling, ribs of beef, swordfish steak. *Note:* Pleasant glassed-in terrace in an inviting 250-year-old colonial house. Classic, appetizing fare; friendly svce. Resv. advised. Valet parking. Dancing wknds. *Continental/ Seafood.* **I**

🍸🍸 **Coonamessett Inn,** in the hotel of the same name (see "Accommodations," above), Jones Rd. at Gifford St., Falmouth (548-2300). A/C. Breakfast/lunch/dinner daily; brunch Sun. AE, CB, DC, MC, V. Jkt. *Specialties:* fresh lobster and fish of the day. *Note:* Impressive dining rm w. lake view and a cathedral ceiling. Built in 1796. Cooking and svce both urbane. Resv. advised; a fine place. Dancing in summer. Very good value. *Seafood.* **I**

🍸 **Captain's Chair,** 166 Bay View St., Hyannis (775-5000).
A/C. Lunch Mon–Fri; dinner nightly; closed Mon in winter, Thanksgiving, Dec 25. AE, CB, DC, MC, V. *Specialties:* fish of the day, sautéed scallops, roast beef, duck à l'orange. *Note:* Country setting with a fine view of the bay. Piano bar. Unfussy, unaffected cooking and svce. *Steak/Seafood.* **B–I**

🍸 **Kelley St. Cafe,** Kelley St., Edgartown (Martha's Vineyard) (627-4394). A/C. Breakfast/lunch/dinner Mon–Sat; brunch Sun. Closed Dec 25. AE, DC, MC, V. *Specialties:* fish of the day, steak, some very acceptable French dishes. *Note:* Pleasant, friendly inn dating from 1742. Food worthy but no more than that; svce assiduous. A short distance from the Chappaquiddick ferry. *Continental/American/Seafood.* **B–I**

🍸 **Landfall,** 2 Luscombe Ave., Woods Hole (548-1758). Lunch/ dinner daily; closed from the end of Sept to mid-June. AE, CB, DC, MC, V. *Specialties:* sandwiches (at lunch), broiled swordfish, baked lobster, catch of the day. *Note:* This likable fish-and-seafood restaurant stands right on the docks and offers a very fine view of the harbor. Appropriate 100% maritime decor. Friendly svce, good value. *American.* **B–I**

🍸 **The Marshside,** 28 Bridge St., East Dennis (385-4010). Breakfast/lunch/dinner daily. AE, MC, V. *Specialties:* lobster salad roll, meatloaf, chicken pot pie, seafood stew, coconut cream pie. *Note:* A comfortable place bypassed by tourists, serving hearty daily specials at attractive prices. Casual atmosphere. *American.* **B–I**

BARS & NIGHTCLUBS

Atlantic Connection, 124 Circuit Ave., Oak Bluffs, Martha's Vineyard (693-7129). The Vineyard club of choice. DJ dancing, jazz, big-name dance bands. Open Thurs–Sun, summer only.

Fiddlebee's, 72 North St., Hyannis (771-6032). Live classic rock music. Open nightly, summer only.

Muse, 44 Atlantic Ave., Nantucket (228-6873). Rock, reggae, and ska bands. Also DJ dancing. Open nightly, Mar to late Dec.

Surf Club, 315A Commercial St., Provincetown (487-1367). The Provincetown jug band, now in its 25th season. Pop and rock music live seven nights a week. Open summer only.

Woodshed, Mass. 6A, Brewster (896-7771). Boisterous summer club with live music in a rustic, informal setting. Open nightly, summer only.

NEARBY EXCURSIONS

🔭🔭 **NEWPORT** (60 mi./96km SW of Sagamore Bridge via U.S. 6, Mass. 124, and R.I. 138): American yachting capital (see Chapter 5 on the Atlantic Coast).

🔭🔭 **PLYMOUTH** (12 mi./19km NW of Sagamore Bridge on Mass. 3): Pretty little port that has come down in history because of its connection with the epic of the *Mayflower* (see Chapter 5 on the Atlantic Coast for details about the Plymouth Plantation reconstruction and the *Mayflower II*). Not to be missed.

CHAPTER 3

NEW YORK

□ □ □

New York has about 200 skyscrapers, around whose feet swirl crowds of all nations, colors, and tongues. But it is not—repeat, *not*—America. New York is everything and the opposite of everything: a unique melting pot of races, cultures, and religions. Any adjective you can conceive can be applied to this symbol of the New World, visited each year by 19 million tourists (including 3½ million foreigners), all singing the same chorus: "I love New York!"

It was a little more than 4½ centuries ago, in 1524, that Giovanni da Verrazano, a Florentine navigator in the service of King François I of France, dropped anchor—the first European to do so—in the bay of what was to become the most exciting, the most electric, and the most neurotic city of our times, the city that the architect Le Corbusier described as "a magnificent catastrophe on an enormous scale." In 1609 a British navigator employed by the Dutch East India Company, Henry Hudson, sailed up the river that bears his name, as far as Albany, now the capital of New York State, 155 mi. (250km) north of the river's mouth, thereby giving the Dutch their claim to the region. And 17 years later, in 1626, Peter Minnewit (or Minuit, as it is more commonly spelled), the first governor-general of New Netherland, purchased the island of Manhattan, 12½ mi. (20km) long and 2½ mi. (4km) wide at its widest point, from the Algonquin Indians for the moderate amount of 60 florins ($24), paid in cloth, glass beads, and other trinkets. He had his 200 Batavian and Walloon colonists build the fort of Nieuw Amsterdam on the site of what is now **Wall Street.**

Over the next half century the British, asserting a prior claim based on the explorations of John Cabot in 1497–98, pushed steadily toward New Amsterdam from the north and northeast. By 1664 the town's position was so untenable that when a British fleet sailed into the bay, the Dutch governor, Peter Stuyvesant, surrendered without a fight. New Netherland was given by King Charles II of England to his brother, the Duke of York (later the ill-fated King James II), and divided into the twin colonies of New York, named in honor of its new patron, and New Jersey. It was briefly recaptured and held by the Dutch in 1673–74, but otherwise remained British until the Revolution.

When it was designated the first official capital of the young United States in 1784, the city already boasted 33,000 inhabitants, and it has never stopped growing. In 1898 the original city on Manhattan Island was swelled by the accession of four more boroughs, **Brooklyn, Queens, the Bronx,** and **Staten Island,** each with its own style, ethnic mix, and individual character. Indeed, few of the world's great cities present as wide a gamut of characteristics as New York.

Where can more striking contrasts be found than between the trendsetters haunting the fashionable stores on Madison Ave. or Fifth Ave. and the homeless who sleep curled in corners at nearby Grand Central Terminal? Or between the twin 1,350-ft. (412m), 110-story towers of the World Trade Center or the luxury apartment houses of the Upper East Side or Battery Park City, and the wretched slums of Harlem, of "Loisaida" (a phonetic rendering by Hispanics of "Lower East Side"), or Fort Apache, the most disreputable neighborhood in the Bronx? If temples of haute cuisine like Lutèce, Le Cirque, and Le Bernardin are called "restaurants" in New York, how can the greasy spoons of the Bowery or the

South Bronx bear the same name? What can the trendy lovers of opera and classical music who flock to Lincoln Center and the gaudy crowds of Greenwich Village, Chinatown, or La Marqueta, the popular marketplace for Puerto Rican foods, have in common? There's no obvious link except that "the Big Apple" (New York's nickname, which came from New Orleans jazz musicians who during the 1920s saw New York as a succulent fruit to bite into) simply *is* all these things at once—a giant melting pot for more than seven million human beings, of whom a quarter were born in foreign lands.

The mixture of races is reflected in a mixture of tongues, which has in turn engendered a flourishing foreign-language press. New York boasts no fewer than three daily papers in Chinese, along with others in Spanish, Italian, Polish, German, Korean, Greek, and Russian.

The sheer size of New York is at the root of most of its problems—pollution, unemployment, the crime rate, the traffic snarls, the homeless, the lack of coherent city planning—and sometimes even calls into question its ability to survive. The Big Apple nearly went broke in the 1970s. But although the city lost 400,000 jobs during those dark days, it experienced a kind of economic, architectural, and cultural renaissance in the 1980s. In a skyline that changes like a kaleidoscope, old surfaces of stone or brick gave way to arrogant facades of steel, glass, and concrete: New York, "the upright city," reached for the sky to express its super-abundance of energy. The former massive exodus toward distant suburbs suddenly reversed itself, causing an unprecedented real-estate boom in Manhattan and restoring to the city its almost-forfeited title as the world's financial and cultural torchbearer. In the 1990s trouble has again appeared; no doubt the next few years will see many changes.

Not content with being the country's literary and artistic capital, New York is also its greatest port, through which 30,000 ships pass every year; its biggest stock market (Wall Street handles more than 70% of all the country's financial transactions); its biggest convention city (almost 10,000 trade shows and conventions annually); the center for its communications and media businesses; its biggest industrial city; and—for good measure—the nation's busiest international airport. Of the 500 largest corporations in America, 118 have their headquarters here; more than 1,800 foreign corporations, including at least 250 banks, maintain branches or representatives' offices here. The revenues of New York businesses, at some $350 billion annually, exceed the gross national product of such countries as Brazil and Canada, and represent one-tenth of the GNP of the United States.

Obviously the tourist can't hope to see all this in two or three days. You should set aside at least a week for any kind of worthwhile overview of the modern Babylon, this enormous, jovial city which boasts no fewer than 250 theaters, 500 art galleries, and more than 150 museums devoted to every form of human self-expression, no matter how far-fetched. As the publicity leaflets of the New York Visitors Bureau proudly proclaim, "You name it, and New York has a museum for it."

The city's numberless shops, boutiques, and department stores, its thousands of restaurants, its bars, its jazz dives, and its nightclubs warrant a visit all by themselves. Not to mention the famous "sidewalks of New York," for this is a city where life is often to be seen out on the street—even when it takes the form of potholes and piles of garbage.

Here are some of the scenes that make Manhattan "the world's greatest show":

□ A walk up Avenue of the Americas (Sixth Ave.), through the high-rises of Rockefeller Center;

□ The sight of the MetLife building astride Park Ave., the most affluent residential street in the city;

□ A bird's-eye view, from a helicopter, of Manhattan's 200 or so skyscrapers, of which a full third are of recent construction;

☐ A ride around Central Park in a horse-drawn cab (for those who enjoy tourist picture postcards);

☐ A trip on the Staten Island Ferry, which gives you the best view of the city; for backdrop you'll have the Statue of Liberty, which celebrated its 100th birthday with appropriate festivities in 1986;

☐ The modern-day bohemian picture of Washington Square, with its roller skaters, chess players, and buskers;

☐ The very "in" art galleries and wild and crazy fashion boutiques of Soho;

☐ The magic panorama of New York by night from the top of the Empire State Building;

☐ The Visitors' Gallery at the New York Stock Exchange, with the crowd of shouting, gesticulating brokers below;

☐ The faces of "intellectuals," straight out of a Woody Allen movie, to be seen thronging the counterculture shrines and avant-garde galleries of Soho and Tribeca;

☐ The screaming neon signs and Asian-bazaar atmosphere of Times Square.

As the writer John Dos Passos used to say, "If you can be bored in New York, you're in sorry shape."

Manhattan is laid out in a grid system (dating from 1811), with streets running from east to west and numbered from 1 to 220, and avenues running from south to north and numbered from 1 to 12, with three of the most famous—Lexington, Park, and Madison—sandwiched between Third Ave. and Fifth Ave. Broadway is the only major deviation from the grid pattern: it slants across the city from west (in the north) to east (in the south). In Lower Manhattan, in Greenwich Village and below Houston (or "Zero") St., the oldest section of the city, most streets are named rather than numbered, and the grid system of midtown is practically nonexistent. Fifth Ave. is the boundary between the east and west sides, and all midtown and uptown street addresses are numbered according to their distance from it. For New Yorkers, "uptown" means north of where you are, "downtown" means south, and "crosstown" refers to anywhere east or west of your location: This is crucial when asking for directions.

Some 12,000 "Yellow Cabs," 4,000 buses, and 250 mi. (400km) of subway lines (carrying nearly four million riders every working day) serve Manhattan and the adjoining boroughs. Aside from a few notoriously tough neighborhoods such as the north end of Harlem between 125th St. and 155th St., New York is no more unsafe for tourists than any other great city. In spite of the persistent legend to the contrary, FBI figures rank New York 10th among U.S. cities in terms of homicides (30.9 a year per 100,000 inhabitants), far behind Washington, New Orleans, Atlanta, Detroit, or St. Louis. Sensible caution should still be exercised: Don't walk alone after dark in Central Park, in the East Village and the Lower East Side (below 14th St. between First Ave. and the East River), or around Times Square after midnight. And keep alert in the subway late at night.

There are about 17,000 restaurants, cafeterias, and fast-food outlets in New York, and more than 70,000 hotel rooms in all categories. But demand exceeds supply, so reserve your hotel room (unless you're in search of adventure, avoid New York hotels charging less than $80 a night). It's a good idea to make reservations, too, at any restaurant with two or more stars.

New York has dozens of tourist agencies that run conducted tours of the city; some of these are mentioned under "Guided Tours," below. But the fun way to see the Big Apple is to set out through its streets on foot, without any very precise destination in mind. It's by rubbing shoulders with the nine million people of all sorts and sizes who live here that you'll capture the real flavor of the city. Manhattan's big attraction is not the Statue of Liberty or even its incredible skyline, but the endless ebb and flow of the nameless multitudes in "the city that never sleeps."

You'd need a good-sized phone book to list all the famous people who were born in one or another of New York's five boroughs. President Theodore Roosevelt was born here; so were physicist J. Robert Oppenheimer, 19th-century railroad tycoon Cornelius Vanderbilt, and Jonas Salk, inventor of the polio vaccine. You can add publisher DeWitt Wallace, founder of *Reader's Digest;* playwrights Arthur Miller, Eugene O'Neill, and Neil Simon, and violinist Yehudi Menuhin. Then there's choreographer Jerome Robbins and composers George Gershwin and Aaron Copland, sculptor George Segal, designer Louis Comfort Tiffany, and singers Harry Belafonte and Barbra Streisand. How about movie directors Stanley Kubrick, Martin Scorsese, and Woody Allen; actresses Mae West, Lauren Bacall, Rita Hayworth, and Jane Fonda; actors Groucho Marx, Humphrey Bogart, Danny Kaye, Mickey Rooney, Burt Lancaster, Walter Matthau, Tony Perkins, Robert De Niro, Alan Alda, and Al Pacino? To say nothing of writers Washington Irving, Henry James, J. D. Salinger, Henry Miller, James Baldwin, Irwin Shaw, Robert Ludlum, Mario Puzo, James Michener, Harold Robbins, and Herman Wouk, and tennis player John McEnroe. Want more? Let's close with a list of famous jazzmen: Benny Carter, Sonny Rollins, Buddy Rich, Bud Powell, Artie Shaw, Fats Waller, and Gerry Mulligan.

BASIC FACTS: State of New York. Area codes: 212 (Manhattan), 718 (the Bronx, Queens, Brooklyn, Staten Island), 917 (citywide for beepers and cellular phones), 516 (Long Island). Time zone: eastern. Manhattan ZIP Codes: 10001–10040. Founded: 1615. Approximate population: city, 7,360,000; metropolitan area, 8,560,000. Largest city and largest metropolitan area in the U.S. The "New York/Northeastern New Jersey Standard Consolidated Area," lying in a 50-mi. (80km) radius around Manhattan and taking in parts of New Jersey and Connecticut, has a population of more than 18 million.

CLIMATE: Its climate is one of New York's principal drawbacks. Aside from a few weeks of agreeable weather in spring (mid-Apr to mid-May) and fall (mid-Sept to mid-Oct) the rest of the year swings between sweating and shivering weather. Summer is usually hot and muggy, with an average temperature of 77°F (25°C) in July, but high humidity. Luckily, all public buildings, stores, hotels, and restaurants are heated and air-conditioned, but watch out for the rise—or fall—in temperature when you leave. Winter is often severe, with temperatures dropping to 10°F (−15°C), particularly when the icy winds out of the north whistle down the glass-and-steel canyons of Manhattan's avenues. There's no rainy season, but it rains intermittently year round (except in winter, when it snows). It's wise to bring raincoats and umbrellas in spring and fall.

DISTANCES: Boston, 209 mi. (335km); Chicago, 806 mi. (1,290km); Dallas, 1,550 mi. (2,480km); Denver, 1,768 mi. (2,830km); Detroit, 634 mi. (1,015km); Los Angeles, 2,790 mi. (4,465km); Miami, 1,309 mi. (2,095km); Montréal, 378 mi. (605km); New Orleans, 1,335 mi. (2,136km); Niagara Falls, 410 mi. (656km); Philadelphia, 100 mi. (160km); Washington, D.C., 234 mi. (375km).

ARRIVAL & TRANSIT INFORMATION

AIRPORTS: The three New York airports, served by 106 airlines, collectively handle the world's heaviest passenger traffic: nearly 80 million travelers a year.
   John F. Kennedy International Airport (JFK), in Queens, 15 mi. (24km) SE of Manhattan (718/656-4520).

La Guardia Airport (LGA), in Queens, 8 mi. (13km) NE of Manhattan (718/476-5000).

Newark International Airport (EWR), in Newark, N.J., 16 mi. (25km) SW of Manhattan (201/961-2000).

U.S. AIRLINES: American (toll free 800/433-7300), America West (toll free 800/247-5962), Continental (toll free 800/525-0280), Delta (toll free 800/221-1212), Northwest (toll free 800/225-2525), TWA (toll free 800/221-2000), United (toll free 800/241-6522), USAir (toll free 800/428-4322), and USAir Shuttle (toll free 800/247-8786).

FOREIGN CARRIERS: Aer Lingus (toll free 800/557-1110), Air Canada (toll free 800/776-3000), Air France (toll free 800/237-2747), British Airways (toll free 800/247-9297), Icelandair (toll free 800/223-5500), Japan Air Lines (toll free 800/525-3663), KLM (toll free 800/777-5553), Lufthansa (toll free 800/645-3880), S.A.S. (toll free 800/221-2350), Swissair (toll free 800/221-4750), and Virgin Atlantic (toll free 800/862-8621).

CITY LINK: There is comparatively easy access between all three of the metropolitan airports and Manhattan.

John F. Kennedy International

Cab fare to mid-Manhattan, about $40; time, about 1 hr; more at peak traffic periods. Traffic can be nightmarish at rush hours.

Bus: Carey Transportation (718/632-0500) departs every 30 min. for Grand Central Terminal and the Port Authority Bus Terminal, with intermediate stops at selected midtown hotels. Fare, $11; time, 1 to 1½ hr.

Gray Line Air Shuttle (212/757-6840) provides door-to-door service to/from Manhattan hotels. Fare, $16.

La Guardia

Cab fare from La Guardia to midtown Manhattan, about $35; time, about 40 min; more at rush hour.

Bus: Carey Transportation (718/632-0500) departs every 20–30 min., serving Grand Central Terminal and the Port Authority Bus Terminal, with intermediate stops at selected hotels. Fare, $8.50; time, 1–1¼ hr.

Gray Line Air Shuttle (212/757-6840) provides door-to-door service to/from Manhattan hotels. Fare, $13.

Newark International

Cab fare from Newark to midtown Manhattan, about $35–$40; time, about 45 min.

Bus: Gray Line Air Shuttle (212/757-6840) provides door-to-door service to/from Manhattan hotels. Fare, $18.

New Jersey Transit (201/762-5100) departs every 15 min. for the Port Authority Bus Terminal. Fare, $7; time, 30 min.

CAR RENTAL (all serving the three New York airports as well as operating out of the in-town locations listed): Avis, 10 Manhattan offices (toll free 800/331-1212); Budget, nine Manhattan offices (toll free 800/527-0700); Dollar, two Manhattan offices (toll free 800/800-4000); Hertz, 10 Manhattan offices (toll free 800/654-3131); National, nine Manhattan offices (toll free 800/227-7368); and Thrifty, two Manhattan offices (toll free 800/367-2277).

LIMOUSINE SERVICES: Allstar Limousine Service (718/784-7766), Carey Limousine (599-1122), Fifth Avenue Limo (718/392-1070), London Towncars (988-9700), and Scripps Edward Limousine (371-2460).

TAXIS: New York City has two kinds of taxis, both licensed and regulated by a city agency: metered cabs and unmetered ("gypsy") cabs. The tourist unfamiliar with New York is advised to stick to metered cabs where the fare is as shown on the meter. For trips to (or even more, back from) one of the outer boroughs (except the airports), a metered cab may be hard to find; in that case it may be advisable to telephone a local unmetered cab company or "car service," taking care to agree beforehand on the fare.

Easily recognized because they're painted yellow, metered cabs may be hailed on the street, or taken from the waiting lines outside the major hotels; some may also be called by phone: **Utoc** (713/361-7270). Many of the drivers are recent immigrants, ill-acquainted with the topography of New York and even with the English language. A tip equivalent to 20% of the meter fare is expected. To report lost property, call 840-4734; complaints, 221-8294.

PUBLIC TRANSPORTATION: Car-rental rates in New York are among the highest in the nation; parking lots and garages are crowded and very expensive; fines for illegal parking are hard to avoid. Taxis (abundant and fairly expensive), buses, and subways are the best means of getting around Manhattan. The subway is noisy, dirty, and aging, but it runs around the clock (late-evening and night trips should be avoided) and is much the quickest and cheapest way of traveling; the fare is $1.25 regardless of how far you ride. You'll need exact change or a token on New York City buses, where the fare is the same; tokens only (purchased when you enter the station) on the subway. Trains run either local or express, and provide very complete service in Manhattan and the outer boroughs. For information, call the New York Transit Authority (718/330-1234).

TRAIN: Amtrak trains no longer service historic Grand Central Terminal, Park Ave. and E. 42nd St., which today handles only commuter lines heading north of New York City. All Amtrak trains now arrive at and depart from **Pennsylvania Station,** Eighth Ave. and W. 31st St. (582-6875). For reservations on the Metroliner (fast train to Philadelphia, Baltimore, and Washington) *only,* call toll free 800/523-8720.

And there's also the **Rockefeller Center Ticket Office,** 12 W. 51st St. (582-6875).

INTERCITY BUSES: Greyhound, Port Authority Bus Terminal, Eighth Ave. and W. 42nd St. (971-6363 or 730-7460).

MANHATTAN AREAS & NEIGHBORHOODS

Manhattan—a Native American word meaning "the island of hills"—is a mosaic of neighborhoods, each of which is pretty much a separate village with its own distinct character. The island does indeed constitute a huge multiracial, socially diverse patchwork, with the boundaries between the patches sharply drawn.

Note: Given the size of Manhattan, the different hotels, restaurants, buildings, museums, etc., referred to below are classified by these areas or neighborhoods. From south to north, Manhattan's principal neighborhoods are:

LOWER MANHATTAN (WALL ST. & THE FINANCIAL DISTRICT)

(around Wall St. and Broad St., from City Hall to the Battery): Here you'll find the banks, the financial institutions, and the New York Stock Exchange. Wall Street takes its name from the wooden palisade built in 1653 by Gov. Peter Stuyvesant to protect Nieuw Amsterdam against incursions by the English and

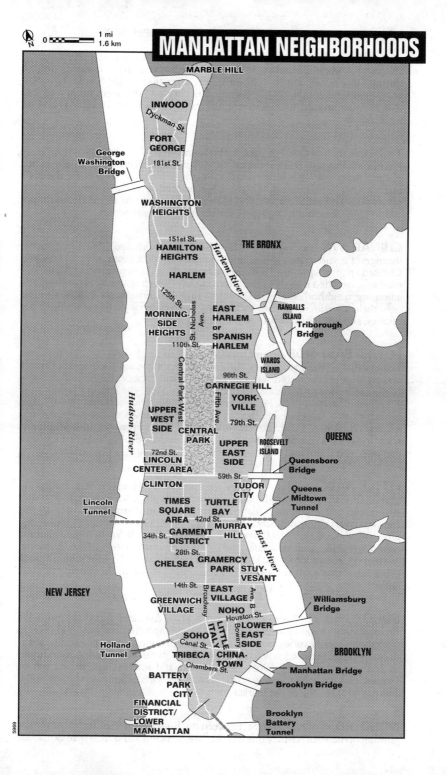

the local tribes. This district, whose narrow streets are fenced in by skyscrapers, is the historic heart of Manhattan. Like most business districts it's at its liveliest during office hours, but such major tourist attractions as the South Street Seaport, apartment complexes like Battery Park City, and the stores and restaurants that grow up around them keep the streets fairly busy in the evenings and on weekends too.

TRIBECA (below Canal St. to City Hall, and west of W. Broadway): An acronym of "*TRI*angle *BE*low *CA*nal St." This neighborhood, originally called "Lower Broadway," has succeeded Soho as the fashionable hangout for the city's intelligentsia. Real-estate speculation has reached fever pitch here; run-down warehouses and old abandoned workshops are giving way to trendy boutiques and to lofts where big-name artists and actors make their homes.

CHINATOWN (around lower Mott, Bayard, and Pell Sts.): The first Chinese immigrant is said to have moved into a small, closetlike room here in 1865, and Chinatown grew up around him almost by accident. An ever-growing Asian population is crowded into this Far Eastern enclave, which is rapidly expanding into adjoining neighborhoods. Less colorful than San Francisco's Chinatown but nonetheless picturesque, with its lanterns, dragon carvings, pagoda-topped pay phones, and jumble of stores and restaurants.

LOWER EAST SIDE (from Canal St. north to E. Houston St. and from the Bowery east to the East River): An area that once housed thousands of newly arrived immigrants in cold-water tenements, it still provides the homes for many of the city's poorest residents. In one of its local areas, the **Bowery** (around the Bowery and Delancey St.), Peter Stuyvesant, last governor of Nieuw Amsterdam, built himself a farm outside the city wall; it was known as *de bouwerij,* which means "farm" in old Dutch. A century ago this was the theater and red-light district. Today it is a run-down neighborhood full of drug dealers and homeless people. Here you'll also find Orchard St., famous for discount famous-name clothes.

LITTLE ITALY (around Mulberry St. south of E. Houston St.): Butted up against Chinatown (and today being progressively absorbed into it), this former stronghold of Neapolitan, Calabrian, and Sicilian immigrants has been all but forsaken by its original inhabitants. Of the 800,000 New Yorkers of Italian origin, only about 5,000–10,000 still live in Little Italy. It has become an ethnic tourist attraction, featuring cafés, the aroma of espresso, statues of the Madonna, restaurants, and groceries tricked out in the Italian national colors, with religious processions that look as though they come straight out of the movie *The Godfather.*

SOHO (*SO*uth of *HO*uston St. between Sixth Ave. and Broadway, with W. Broadway as its main thoroughfare): Just 20 years ago this neighborhood of huge workshops and factories built in the mid-19th century was practically abandoned, in spite of the acknowledged splendor of its cast-iron facades. Soho began its recovery in the early 1960s, when artists and intellectuals, driven out of Greenwich Village by spiraling rents, invaded the lofts of Soho—which are now also priced at the top of the market.

NOHO (*NO*rth of *HO*uston St. between the Bowery and Broadway): At the beginning of the 19th century this was the "swell" neighborhood, where Cornelius

Vanderbilt, the Croesus of the day, chose to live. Now it's full of loft apartments, electronics, and microcomputer stores, and the Public Theater—a doggedly trendy, up-and-coming part of town.

GREENWICH VILLAGE (around Washington Sq. at the lower end of Fifth Ave., from slightly below Houston St. north to W. 14th St. and from Broadway west to the Hudson River): It began as a real village of farmers, settled by the first English colonists out among the fields and the woods. New Yorkers still call it the Village, but by the 19th century it had already become an artists' and writers' colony and has numbered among its inhabitants Edgar Allan Poe, Henry James, John Dos Passos, and e.e. cummings. With its narrow streets, little brick houses, small shops, and taverns, the Village was long regarded as New York's literary and bohemian center. Now the upper middle class and the tourists have taken over, but the neighborhood is still picturesque. Stay away on summer weekends because of the crowds.

EAST VILLAGE (around Tompkins Sq. Park, from E. Houston St. north to E. 14th St. and from the Bowery east to the East River): This neighborhood, north of the Lower East Side, is where new cultural movements and schools of avant-garde art ("graffiti art," "real art," "street art") are born. The influx of young, creative people have made it one of the most lively, newsworthy parts of the city. Many art galleries. As you proceed farther east past First Ave. to Aves. A, B, C, and D, the area becomes progressively blighted and progressively dangerous, especially at night.

CHELSEA (around Chelsea Park at Eighth, Ninth, and Tenth Aves., from W. 14th to W. 30th Sts. and from Fifth Ave. to the Hudson River): Forty years ago this was largely a district of Hispanic immigrants, as witness the many Spanish-language store signs still to be seen on 14th Street. Now Chelsea has become typical of New York's "mixed bag" neighborhoods, where old New Yorkers live cheek by jowl with new arrivals, where run-down, grimy brick buildings and old, elegant brownstones stand shoulder to shoulder with modern high-rises.

GRAMERCY PARK (around Gramercy Park at Lexington Ave. and 20th St., from E. 14th to E. 30th Sts. and from Fifth Ave. east): Includes both the high-rise apartments of **Stuyvesant Town** (east of First Ave. between E. 14th and E. 19th Sts.) and the elegant town houses around Gramercy Park itself, as well as the office towers along lower Third Ave. and Park Ave. South and the huge hospitals between First Ave. and the East River in the E. 20s.

MIDTOWN (from 30th to 59th Sts., river to river): Takes in the whole center of Manhattan, south of Central Park. From the frantic bustle of the **Garment District** (Sixth and Seventh Aves. between 30th and 39th Sts.), where fabrics and ready-to-wear clothing are manufactured, to the permanent Big Top of **Broadway and the Theater District** (from Sixth to Eighth Aves. between W. 43rd and W. 53rd Sts.), the heart of America's show business, with more than 50 theaters and music halls and dozens of cinemas, their lights blazing through the crush of nighttime idlers (not a safe district after midnight); from the magical reflections off the glass facades of the **Rockefeller Center** high-rises to the porno movie houses and the drug and sex industry of **Times Square** (soon, it is hoped, to fall before a giant urban-renewal project), by way of the big new office buildings of **Murray Hill** (between Third and Madison Aves. south of E. 42nd St.) and the little island of tranquility of 1920s-style fantasy of **Tudor City** (around First Ave. between E. 38th and E. 44th Sts.), where a cluster of apartment houses, in an unusual Neo-Tudor idiom, stands on a huge elevated platform overlooking the East River and the "glass palace" of the U.N. (many diplomats and U.N. officials live here)—midtown is a microcosm of the city itself.

UPPER WEST SIDE (from Central Park to the Hudson River between W. 60th and W. 125th sts.): At the end of the 19th century this was an upscale "WASP" neighborhood, the chicest in Manhattan. At the end of the 1930s it started a long process of deterioration, which was only halted in the 1970s. Now it has become fashionable again, attracting a young, well-to-do, trendy crowd that has made the area along Columbus Ave. from W. 65th to W. 86th sts. into a sort of smart new version of Greenwich Village. It includes the huge **Lincoln Center for the Performing Arts** complex, and at its northern extremity, the **Morningside Heights** neighborhood with Columbia University and the Cathedral of St. John the Divine.

UPPER EAST SIDE (from Fifth Ave. to the East River between E. 59th and E. 96th sts.): The gilt-edged ghetto of New York's upper classes, symbolized by the uniformed chauffeurs and their long limousines gliding silently down Park Ave., and by the luxurious apartment houses that run the length of East End Ave. The only lighter note to be found in this money-oriented universe is provided by the little restaurants and singles bars of First and Second aves.

"EL BARRIO" (East Harlem around Lexington and Fifth aves. between E. 105th and E. 125th Sts.): *Barrio* is the Spanish for "neighborhood," and this is the Puerto Rican neighborhood, its heart the renowned Marqueta, the colorful covered market with its swirling crowds and hundreds of stalls. It's a Hispanic enclave in the heart of Harlem.

HARLEM (between Central Park North, or 110th St., and 155th St.): Originally named Nieuw Haarlem after the town in the Netherlands, and founded as a community for Dutch settlers in 1658 by Gov. Peter Stuyvesant, Harlem was, in the latter part of the 19th century, one of the most elegant residential districts in Manhattan, as witness the imposing upper-class houses of Convent Ave., Sugar Hill, Mount Morris Park West, and Strivers' Row. The first African Americans arrived around 1910, and with the coming of the first jazz bands at the famous Cotton Club, the Savoy Ballroom, and the Apollo Theater, Harlem became for a while the center of New York's nightlife. Today its community of 300,000 African Americans makes it the symbol of Black America. However, the real-estate speculators are slowly moving in on behalf of their yuppie clients. Several museums and some distinguished turn-of-the-century architecture merit your attention, but stay away from the high-risk areas such as Lenox Ave. around W. 125th St. and Eighth Ave. around W. 116th St.

UPPER MANHATTAN (WASHINGTON HEIGHTS) (north of 155th St.): Most of this area is taken up by middle-class apartment buildings, but the George Washington Bridge and its bus station are at 177th St., and at the northern tip of Manhattan is Fort Tryon Park and the Cloisters.

INFORMATION & TOURS

Note: All telephone numbers are in the 212 area code, unless otherwise indicated.

TOURIST INFORMATION: The **New York Convention and Visitors Bureau** (midtown), 2 Columbus Circle, NY 10019 (397-8222).

Information Desk (midtown), in the lobby at 30 Rockefeller Plaza (698-2950). Pick up a pamphlet for a self-guided tour.

GUIDED TOURS: Adventure on a Shoestring (walking tours) (midtown), 300 W. 53rd St. (265-2663): Conducted walking tours of Chinatown, Greenwich Village, and other picturesque neighborhoods. For lovers of the unexpected.
   Circle Line (boat) (midtown), Pier 83, W. 43rd St. at the Hudson River (563-3200): Around Manhattan Island by boat; a spectacular three-hour ride. Daily mid-Mar to mid-Nov.
   Gray Line Tours (bus) (midtown), 900 Eighth Ave. at W. 54th St. (397-2620): 24 different guided tours of the city and surroundings.
   Harlem Renaissance Tours (bus) (midtown), 900 Eighth Ave. at the Gray Line terminal (722-9534): Tours, including a Sunday gospel one.
   Harlem Spirituals (bus) (midtown), (302-2594): Guided tours of Harlem, including its museums, ethnic restaurants, jazz clubs, and even gospel singing in a Baptist church (Sun only). Tours leave daily from the Short Line Tours Terminal, 166 W. 46th St. Resv. advised.
   Manhattan Trolley (bus) (Lower Manhattan), 210 Front St. (677-7269): 90-min. shuttle tour across Lower Manhattan in a replica of a turn-of-the-century streetcar, making stops at South Street Seaport, Battery Park, the World Trade Center, Chinatown, Little Italy, etc. Pass gives riders unlimited boarding rights between 11am and 5pm Sun–Sun.
   New York Big Apple Tours (bus) (midtown), 209 E. 94th St. (410-4190): Conducted tours of Manhattan with multilingual guides—French, German, Italian, Spanish, etc. For foreign visitors.
   New York Helicopter (helicopter) (midtown), E. 34th St. Heliport, at the East River (683-4575): Flights over Manhattan and the Statue of Liberty. Unforgettable. Fare: $49–$119, depending on duration of flight.

SIGHTS, ATTRACTIONS & ACTIVITIES

ARCHITECTURAL HIGHLIGHTS: ☖ **The Beresford** (Upper West Side), 211 Central Park West at W. 81st St.: Luxury apartment building dating from 1929, designed by architect Emery Roth. With its ocher sandstone facade, rococo carvings, and three unusual towers, this designated historic landmark has been, and still is, home to many celebrities such as violinist Isaac Stern, tennis star John McEnroe, and TV newscaster Peter Jennings.
   ☼☖ **Dakota Apartments** (Upper West Side), 1 W. 72nd St. at Central Park West: Perhaps the most famous address in New York. A strange blend of English Victorian and German Neo-Gothic, this 1884 structure by Henry Hardenbergh was New York's first luxury apartment building. Among its present residents are Lauren Bacall; John Lennon, who also lived here, was assassinated outside the entrance, and the building was a setting for the movie *Rosemary's Baby*.
   ☼☖ **Federal Reserve Bank** (Lower Manhattan), 33 Liberty St. (720-6130): The world's largest hoard of gold—900,000 ingots worth $114 billion—slumbers in the armored vaults here, 80 ft. (24m) underground and protected by a steel door weighing 90 tons. Visits, by appointment only, Mon–Fri; no still or movie cameras permitted.
   ☼☖☖ **Jacob K. Javits Convention Center** (midtown), 11th Ave. and W. 35th St. (216-2000): Designed by the great I. M. Pei, this futuristic convention center, largest of its kind in the Western world, has an immense facade of glass made up of more than 16,000 individual panes, supported by a web of metal girders; the design was inspired by London's famous Crystal Palace, and will delight all lovers of contemporary architecture. Opened in April 1986 at a cost of more than $500 million.

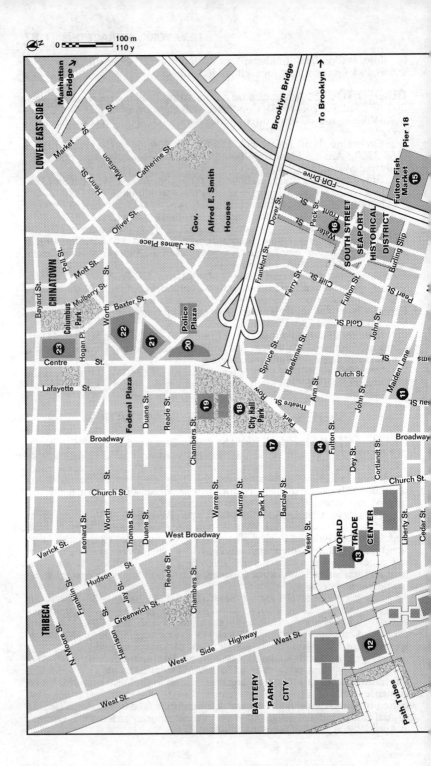

LOWER MANHATTAN

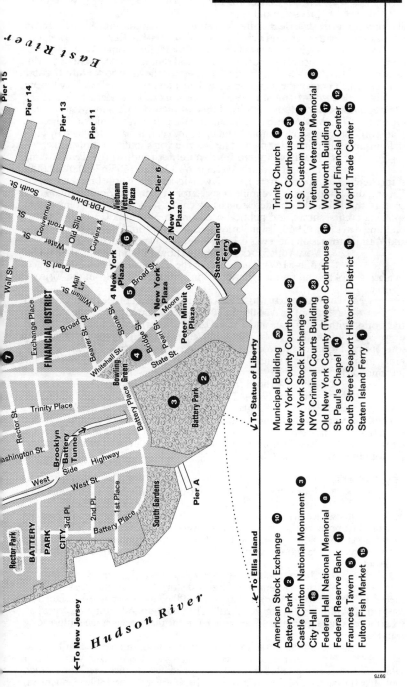

Trinity Church 9
U.S. Courthouse 21
U.S. Custom House 4
Vietnam Veterans Memorial 6
Woolworth Building 17
World Financial Center 12
World Trade Center 13

Municipal Building 20
New York County Courthouse 22
New York Stock Exchange 7
NYC Criminal Courts Building 23
Old New York County (Tweed) Courthouse 19
St. Paul's Chapel 14
South Street Seaport Historical District 16
Staten Island Ferry 1

American Stock Exchange 10
Battery Park 2
Castle Clinton National Monument 3
City Hall 18
Federal Hall National Memorial 8
Federal Reserve Bank 11
Fraunces Tavern 5
Fulton Fish Market 15

←To Statue of Liberty

←To Ellis Island

←To New Jersey

Hudson River

East River

5975

☀☊☊ **Lincoln Center for the Performing Arts** (Upper West Side), Broadway and W. 64th St. (877-1800): This renowned cultural center comprises five elegant, modernist theaters and concert halls arranged in a harmonious pattern around a central plaza. **Avery Fisher Hall** (1962), designed by Max Abramovitz, is the home of the New York Philharmonic; **Alice Tully Hall,** home of the Chamber Music Society, and the adjoining **Juilliard School of Music** are by Pietro Belluschi; Philip Johnson designed the **New York State Theater** (1964), which houses the New York City Ballet and the New York City Opera; the **Vivian Beaumont Theater** (1965) is the work of Eero Saarinen, while the **Metropolitan Opera House** (1966), home of the world-famous Metropolitan Opera (or "The Met"), with its Chagall murals, is from the hand of Wallace K. Harrison. The very lovely marble fountain in the central plaza, designed by Philip Johnson, is illuminated at night. This is a visit you should certainly make.

☊ **Madison Square Garden Center** (midtown), 4 Pennsylvania Plaza, at Seventh Ave. and W. 32nd St. (465-6741): A 20,000-seat covered stadium (the Arena), which with its adjoining little brother, the Felt Forum, draws more than five million spectators a year to various events. For a century this hall and its predecessors has been the scene of the most important sporting events, shows, and political occasions in New York City. The present building dates from 1968. Penn Station (trains to Boston, Miami, New Orleans, and Washington) is on the levels below Madison Square Garden.

☀☊ **New York Stock Exchange** (Lower Manhattan), 20 Broad St. (656-5167): The center of the U.S. financial community; gesticulating brokers and frantic agitation. Don't miss the show from the Visitors' Gallery.

☊ **Radio City Music Hall** (midtown), Ave. of the Americas (Sixth Ave.) at W. 50th St. (247-4777): The largest movie theater in the world, with 6,000 seats and a stage 144 ft. (44m) across and 65 ft. (20m) deep. Splendid art deco lobby with giant chandeliers in crystal weighing two tons apiece. Home of the world-renowned precision-dancing Rockettes; draws more than eight million visitors a year. Guided tours daily (call 246-4600 for information).

☀☊ **United Nations** (midtown), First Ave. between E. 42nd and E. 48th Sts. (963-1234): Designed by Le Corbusier and Oscar Niemeyer, the 39-story, 1952 glass tower of Babel overlooks the East River. Guided tours daily; you should see it, preferably between early Sept and mid-Dec when the General Assembly is in session and the flags of the 181 member nations (at last count), ranked in alphabetical order, are flown in front of the complex. For tour information, call 963-4440.

Skyscrapers

☀☊ **Sony Building** (midtown) (formerly the AT&T building), 550 Madison Ave. at E. 56th St.: Its salmon-colored granite facade, popular Renaissance-inspired arcade, and the pediment drawn from a Chippendale breakfront make this building by the well-known duo Philip Johnson and John Burgee one of the most innovative of postmodern high-rises. In the lobby is a deliberately old-fashioned statue of Mercury and a glass-covered pedestrian walkway.

☊ **Chase Manhattan Bank Building** (Lower Manhattan), 1 Chase Manhattan Plaza: 60 stories of steel and glass—one of the world's largest bank buildings (about 15,000 people work here), designed by the firm of Skidmore, Owings & Merrill. The underground vault is protected by six armored doors weighing 45 tons each. On the plaza is a strange sculpture by Jean Dubuffet.

☀☊☊ **Chrysler Building** (midtown), 405 Lexington Ave. at E. 42nd St.: Art deco masterpiece designed by William Van Alen in 1930; 77 stories rising 1,048 ft. (319m), capped by a stainless-steel spire which looks like the jawbone of a swordfish. Superb lobby with remarkable wood inlays,

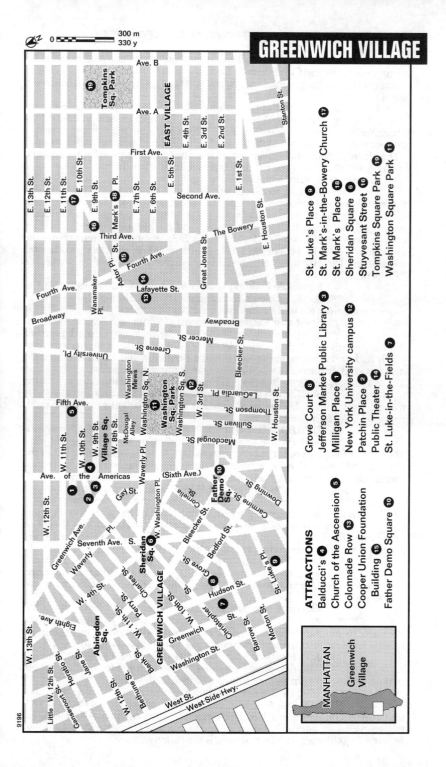

GREENWICH VILLAGE

ATTRACTIONS

Balducci's **4**
Church of the Ascension **5**
Colonnade Row **13**
Cooper Union Foundation
Building **15**
Father Demo Square **10**

Grove Court **8**
Jefferson Market Public Library **3**
Milligan Place **1**
New York University campus **12**
Patchin Place **2**
Public Theater **14**
St. Luke-in-the-Fields **7**

St. Luke's Place **9**
St. Mark's-in-the-Bowery Church **17**
St. Mark's Place **18**
Sheridan Square **6**
Stuyvesant Street **16**
Tompkins Square Park **19**
Washington Square Park **11**

MANHATTAN

Greenwich Village

9196

African marble, and modernist wall paintings. You'll be able to admire the architecture while visiting **Con Edison's Conservation Center,** an interesting little energy exhibit on the ground floor. Nearly 9,000 people come to work here every day. Open Tues–Sat.

☼ ◬ **Citicorp Center** (midtown), Lexington Ave. and E. 54th St.: An unusual modern (1978) 79-story building designed by Hugh Stubbins, with a roofline angled to receive and store solar energy. It stands on four massive columns so tall that the second floor is 14 stories above ground. "The Market" is an enticing, very popular atrium-garden with cafés, restaurants, shops, bookstores, and even a church. Free concerts at lunchtime.

☼ ◬ **Empire State Building** (midtown), 34th St. and Fifth Ave.: Built in 1929–31 on the site of the original Waldorf Hotel, this world-famous skyscraper, designed by Shreve, Lamb and Harmon, was long the tallest building in the world (today it's third-tallest) and the quintessential symbol of New York. Its construction required 60,000 tons of steel; it is solid enough that when, on a foggy day in 1945, a B-25 bomber flew straight into the 79th floor—and 14 people were killed—the building sustained no damage whatsoever. The 102 floors are served by 73 elevators. For further details, see "Panoramas," below.

◬ **Equitable Building** (Lower Manhattan), 120 Broadway at Cedar St.: One of the earliest (1915) high-rises in the city; its monumental mass led to the adoption of the city's first zoning law.

◬ **Equitable Center** (midtown), 787 Seventh Ave. at W. 52nd St.: Impressive new high-rise by architect Edward Larrabee Barnes, proudly wearing its name in letters of gold across the front. At street level you'll find two outstanding restaurants: Le Bernardin and Palio. Has brought new class and distinction to the Broadway area; not to be missed.

◬ **Flatiron Building** (Gramercy Park), 175 Fifth Ave. at E. 23rd St.: The first true office skyscraper built in New York (1903). Its name derives from its 22-floor height and its dramatic triangular form. The architect was D. W. Burnham.

◬ **Ford Foundation Building** (midtown), 320 E. 42nd St.: Beautiful 1967 glass-and-brick building by Kevin Roche and John Dinkeloo; headquarters of the Ford Foundation, which sponsors research in the physical and social sciences. A splendid tree-planted lobby serves as an indoor garden, the first of its kind in Manhattan.

☼ ◬◬ **IBM Building** (midtown), 590 Madison Ave. at E. 56th St.: Edward Larrabee Barnes designed this 40-floor tower of polished green granite and green glass; the head office of the giant international computer company is one of New York's loveliest modern skyscrapers. There's an unexpected tropical greenhouse with giant reeds and a Japanese garden on the ground floor. Interesting temporary art exhibitions.

◬ **Lever House** (midtown), 390 Park Ave. at E. 54th St.: This elegant 24-story building by Gordon Bunshaft of Skidmore, Owings & Merrill, dating from 1952, is one of the earliest all-glass curtain-wall buildings.

☼ ◬◬ **Marriott Marquis Hotel** (midtown), 1535 Broadway at W. 45th St.: Impressive 52-story high-rise designed by John Portman; its looming mass dominates Times Sq. It's one of the most comprehensive hotel facilities in the world; note the 46-floor glass-walled lobby.

◬ **J. P. Morgan & Co. Tower** (Lower Manhattan), 60 Wall St.: This new giant by architect Kevin Roche rears its 47-story bulk of pure postmodernism far above its downtown neighbors.

☼ ◬◬ **MetLife Building** (midtown) (formerly the Pan Am building), 200 Park Ave. at E. 45th St.: The masterpiece of the great Walter Gropius, completed in 1963. This elegant 59-story octagon, 810 ft. (247m) tall, atop Grand Central Terminal, is one of the world's biggest office buildings, housing 25,000 workers. The best view is the Park Ave. view.

☀️🔔🔔 **Park Avenue Tower** (midtown), 65 E. 55th St.: One of Manhattan's most flamboyant buildings, with its astonishing marble and granite lobby, pyramidal cap, and ever-changing surface colors—pink to chestnut to metallic gray. It's half *Star Wars,* half art deco, and all the work of the prolific Chicago architect Helmut Jahn.

🔔 **Philip Morris Building** (midtown), Park Ave. at E. 42nd St.: This ultramodern high-rise, headquarters of a cigarette conglomerate, is principally noteworthy for the annex of the **Whitney Museum** on its ground floor, with sculptures by Calder, Segal, Claes Oldenburg, Nevelson, etc., standing in an indoor garden open to the public.

☀️🔔🔔 **Rockefeller Center** (midtown), between Fifth and Sixth Aves. from W. 48th to W. 52nd Sts.: A breathtaking forest of skyscrapers, 21 in all, built during the early 1930s in the heart of Manhattan. Among the best-known and most often visited are the 70-story **General Electric Building** (formerly the RCA Building), where NBC has its TV studios, with a restaurant (the **Rainbow Room**) on the 65th floor; **Radio City Music Hall** (see "Architectural Highlights," above); the 51-floor **McGraw-Hill Building;** the **Exxon Building** (54 floors); and the **Time-Life Building** (48 floors). Also terraced gardens, an open-air ice-skating rink (in winter), an underground shopping mall, restaurants, cafés, etc. In 1989 Japan's Mitsubishi Estates Co. acquired a controlling interest in Rockefeller Center for $846 million.

☀️🔔 **Seagram Building** (midtown), 375 Park Ave. at E. 52nd St.: Lovely skyscraper of steel and bronze-tinted glass, a 1958 work of Ludwig Mies van der Rohe and the crowning achievement of the International School. The splendid interior decor was designed by Philip Johnson around works by Picasso, Chagall, Rodin, and others.

☀️🔔 **Trump Tower** (midtown), 725 Fifth Ave. between 56th and 57th Sts.: This 68-story tower with a profusion of gilding and pink marble had cost a mere $150 million by the time it was completed in 1983. The six-floor lobby, with an unbelievable indoor waterfall 82 ft. (25m) high, is tenanted by some of the world's most upscale boutiques: Charles Jourdan, Cartier, Galeries Lafayette, etc. The quintessence of nouveau riche ostentation.

🔔 **Waldorf-Astoria Hotel** (midtown), 301 Park Ave. at E. 50th St.: When it was opened in 1931, this imposing structure with its 47 floors and 1,410 rooms was described as "the largest and most luxurious hotel in the world." It has retained, through several facelifts, some vestiges of its original glory, such as its magnificent art deco lobby and its unique ballroom, the Starlight Roof, whose roof really does open to the stars.

☀️🔔 **Woolworth Building** (Lower Manhattan), 233 Broadway at Barclay St.: A curious Gothic Revival skyscraper originally described as a "cathedral of commerce." It was the world's tallest building from its construction in 1913 until the completion of the Chrysler Building in 1930. Rising 60 floors and 792 ft. (241m), it is the work of the great Cass Gilbert. Wonderful entrance hall with delightful stone gargoyle carvings and gold-leaf mosaics; the building's tower is modeled after the campanile of St. Mark's Basilica in Venice.

🔔🔔 **World Financial Center** (Lower Manhattan), bordered by West, Vesey, and Liberty Sts. and the Hudson River: Part of the Battery Park City complex (see "Strolls," below), architect Cesar Pelli's grouping of four austerely geometrical futurist towers is one of the most ambitious developments Manhattan has seen in the past decade. The four innovative glass-and-granite towers are headquarters to such financial giants as American Express, Merrill Lynch, and Dow Jones. The magnificent **Winter Garden** is a giant glasshouse with palms and other tropical vegetation; there are also marble-floored plazas and terraces overlooking the river, as well as fashionable cafés and restaurants.

☀️🔔🔔 **World Trade Center** (Lower Manhattan), bordered by West, Church, Vesey, and Liberty Sts.: Twin shimmering silver tow-

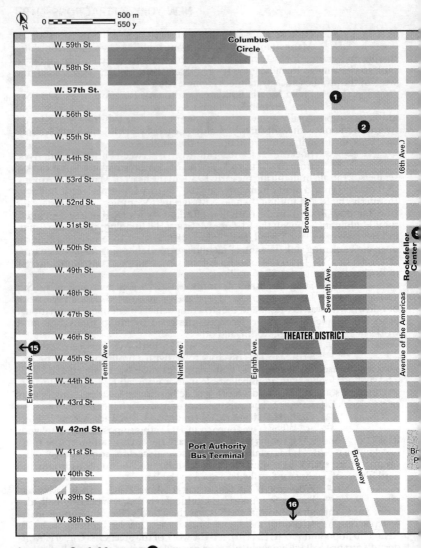

American Craft Museum **4**
Carnegie Hall **1**
Chrysler Building **14**
City Center Theater **2**
Citycorp Center **11**
Empire State Building **17**
IBM Building **7**
Intrepid-Sea-Air-Space Museum **15**
Lever House **9**

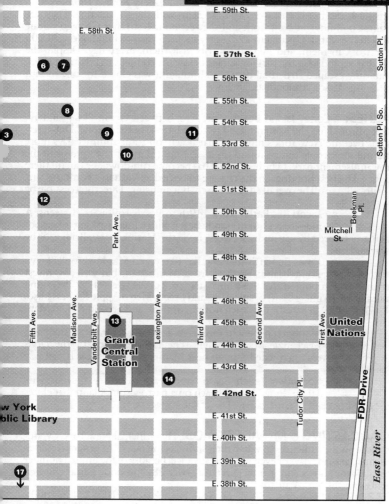

ers, designed by architects Minoru Yamasaki and Emery Roth, 110 floors high and rising 1,350 ft. (411m)—1,710 ft. (521m) with the TV antenna. These are the tallest buildings in New York and the second-tallest (after Chicago's Sears Tower) in the world. Opened in 1977, they took 15 years to build. Now 70,000 people work in them, and 80,000 tourists visit them, every day. Despite the bomb that exploded in the parking garage below the complex in February 1993, the building escaped structural damage, although it was closed for one month after the attack. See "Panoramas," below.

BEACHES: 🏖 **Coney Island Beach,** Surf Ave. between Ocean Pkwy. and W. 37th St., Brooklyn: The Konijn Eiland (Rabbit Island) of the original Dutch settlers has become New York's most popular beach; on some summer days more than a million people can be found on its 3.2 mi. (5km) of fine sand or in the nearby amusement park. (The boardwalk has become run-down; be careful there at night.) The best hot dogs in the city are to be had at **Nathan's Famous,** Surf and Stillwell Aves. The overall effect is kitsch, but amusing. Directly accessible by subway.

🏖 **Jacob Riis Park,** Beach 149th to Beach 169th Sts., Queens: A mile-long (1.6km) sandy beach with a huge parking lot; a spot particularly favored by gay nudists. Access is via the Marine Pkwy. Bridge, or by subway and bus.

☼🏖 **Jones Beach State Park,** Bay Pkwy. and Meadowbrook Pkwy., Long Island: Farthest from Manhattan, but also the nicest beach in the metropolitan area. It's a huge state park of 2,413 acres (977ha) along the ocean, with 6 mi. (10km) of splendid sand beach. Metro Apple Express buses (718/788-8000) depart for the beach from E. 56th St. and Second Ave. in Manhattan.

🏖 **Manhattan Beach,** Ocean Ave. between Oriental Blvd. and Mackenzie St., Brooklyn: The favorite beach of the city's young, it's relatively uncrowded though near Manhattan. Accessible by subway and bus.

🏖 **Rockaway Beach,** Beach 1st to Beach 149th Sts., Queens: Fine 10-mi.-long (16km) beach on a narrow spit of land that closes off the southern end of Jamaica Bay. Direct subway access.

BROADCASTING & MOVIE STUDIOS: The principal New York TV studios allow public audiences to watch their shows being taped. In general, reservations must be made days or even weeks in advance, because of the limited number of seats. Some shows admit only spectators over 18, and none admit children under 6 months old. Write to:

ABC Guest Relations, 38A W. 66th St., New York, NY 10023 (456-1000).

CBS Ticket Bureau, 524 W. 57th St., New York, NY 10019 (887-3537).

NBC Ticket Information, 30 Rockefeller Plaza, New York, NY 10112 (664-3055). NBC also offers conducted tours of its studios Mon–Sat (664-7174).

The **New York Convention and Visitors Bureau,** 2 Columbus Circle (397-8222), usually has some free same-day tickets for TV shows; out-of-town or foreign visitors are given priority.

CHURCHES/SYNAGOGUES: 🏛 **Church of the Ascension** (Greenwich Village), 36 Fifth Ave. at 10th St. (254-8620): Designed by Richard Upjohn; the first church (1841) built in New York in the Gothic Revival style then popular in England. Extensively restored in 1885–89 under the direction of Stanford White. Very fine mural of the Ascension, and stained-glass windows, by John La Farge. Carvings of angels by Louis Saint-Gaudens. Open daily.

☼🏛 **Cathedral of St. John the Divine** (Upper West Side), Amsterdam Ave. at W. 112th St. (316-7540): Largest Gothic cathedral in the world, 601 ft. (183m) long, 124 ft. (38m) wide, and capable of seating 10,000 people; the great rose (west) window is 40 ft. (12m) across. The work of Ralph Adams Cram, it was begun in 1892. The transept and twin towers were never completed, though work has been resumed in the last 10 years.

☀️🔔 **St. Patrick's Cathedral** (midtown), Fifth Ave. and 50th St. (753-2261): Roman Catholic cathedral, built in 1858–74. A fine, flamboyant example of Gothic by James Renwick, somewhat overshadowed by the surrounding high-rises despite its 330-ft. (100m) spires. Very rich interior. The seat of New York's Catholic archdiocese. Open daily.

☀️🔔 **St. Paul's Chapel** (Lower Manhattan), Broadway and Fulton St. (602-0874): The oldest (1766) church in the city, designed by Thomas McBean; George Washington had his private pew in the north aisle; Jefferson and Cornwallis were other famous parishioners. The elegant Georgian design is reminiscent of London's St. Martin-in-the-Fields. Open daily.

☀️🔔 **Temple Emanu-El** (Upper East Side), Fifth Ave. and 65th St. (744-1400): The largest synagogue in the country, with 2,500 seats, built in 1929 in majestic Romano-Byzantine style. Open daily.

☀️🔔 **Trinity Church** (Lower Manhattan), Broadway and Wall St. (602-0872): Dwarfed today by the surrounding skyscrapers of the financial district, the steeple of this church was, when it was built in 1846 on the site of two earlier churches, the tallest structure in New York. Its churchyard is the oldest in the city (1681); in it may be found the tombs of Robert Fulton, inventor of the steamboat, and Alexander Hamilton. A favorite place for lunchtime picnics among Wall Street workers. Undergoing renovation. Open daily.

HISTORIC BUILDINGS & STRUCTURES: ☀️🔔 Brooklyn Bridge (Lower Manhattan), between City Hall Park, Manhattan, and Cadman Plaza, Brooklyn: The first (1883) steel-cable suspension bridge in the world, designed by engineer Johann August Roebling. A triumph of technical skill with its two piers resting on hydraulic caissons, this magnificent structure also offers an impressive view of Manhattan. A sight not to be missed.

🔔 **Carnegie Hall** (midtown), 154 W. 57th St. at Seventh Ave. (247-7800): One of New York's two famous concert halls, the other being Avery Fisher Hall at Lincoln Center. The 1891 inaugural concert in this lovely 2,700-seat auditorium was conducted by Tchaikovsky himself. In 1986 it reopened after a $50-million renovation had restored all its former splendor, but some feel its outstanding acoustics have been somewhat compromised. For concert schedules, consult the entertainment pages of the daily papers.

🔔 **City Hall** (Lower Manhattan), Broadway at Murray St. (566-5200): An elegant Renaissance-style 1811 building of marble and brown sandstone. Not open to the public.

🔔 **Columbia University** (Upper West Side), Broadway and W. 116th St. (854-2845): Founded in 1754 as King's College, this is one of the oldest and most respected of American universities—a member, along with Harvard, Yale, Princeton, and others, of the famous Ivy League. Its campus, attended by 19,000 students, has 60 buildings, of which the most interesting are Low Memorial Library, whose Palladian style is reminiscent of the Pantheon in Rome; University Hall; the Sherman Fairchild Center for the Life Sciences; and Butler Library, which contains five million books. Conducted tours of the campus Mon–Fri.

🔔 **Dyckman House** (Upper Manhattan), 4881 Broadway at 204th St. (304-9422): The only 18th-century Dutch Colonial house still standing in modern Manhattan. Built by William Dyckman in 1782, it's decorated and furnished in a style typical of the wealthy farmers of the period. Open Tues–Sun.

☀️🔔 **Ellis Island** (Lower Manhattan), Upper Bay off Battery Park: Reopened early in 1990 after six years (and more than $150 million) of rehabilitation work, this impressive cluster of brick and red sandstone buildings is mute witness to some of the most moving episodes in American history. From 1892 to 1954, 17 million immigrants from all parts of the world shuffled through these great echoing halls, now splendidly restored, before trying their luck on U.S. soil. Now a living Museum of Immigration (even the original graffiti have been scrupulously preserved on the walls of the Great Hall, the dormitories, and the baggage room), Ellis Island illustrates four centuries of immigration into the U.S. with original documents, maps, photographs, old passports, personal mementos, etc. Fascinating. Open daily; ferry from Battery Park (for ferry information, call 269-5755).

☀️🔔 **Federal Hall National Memorial** (Lower Manhattan), 26 Wall St. (264-8711): As steeped in history as any building in Manhattan. The first City Hall was built here in 1699; here the Stamp Act imposed by the British in 1765 was rejected by the colonists; here the British made their headquarters during the War of Independence; here George Washington delivered his inaugural address as first president of the U.S. in 1789; here the first Congress met in 1789–90. The present building, in the Doric style, dates from 1842. J. Q. A. Ward's statue of Washington dominates the facade. Open Mon–Fri.

🔔 **Gracie Mansion** (Upper East Side), East End Ave. at E. 88th St. (570-4751): Pretty country house in the Federal style, built in 1799 by a wealthy merchant, Archibald Gracie; now the official residence of the mayor of New York. Visits by appointment Wed.

☀️🔔🔔 **Grand Central Terminal** (midtown), E. 42nd St. and Lexington Ave: Busiest railroad station in the world. This magnificent example of the beaux arts style, dating from 1912, is a kind of underground cathedral, and is a designated historic landmark. The central hall has a lovely ceiling. The flood of humanity that descends on the station at rush hours (150,000 commuters daily) must be seen to be believed. Guided tours on Wed. Call 935-3960 for information.

☀️🔔 **Theodore Roosevelt Birthplace National Historic Shrine** (Gramercy Park), 28 E. 20th St. (260-1616): Birthplace of the 26th president, the much-loved "Teddy" Roosevelt, with his furniture and personal memorabilia. He lived here from 1858 to 1872. The original house burned to the ground; the present replica dates from 1923. Regular classical concerts and temporary exhibitions. Open Wed–Sun.

☀️🔔 **Yeshiva University** (Upper Manhattan), 500 W. 185th St. (960-5390): The oldest (1886) and largest (7,000 students) Jewish university in America. Interesting buildings both Oriental in feeling—with Byzantine domes, like Tanenbaum Hall—or modern like the Science Center; museum devoted to Jewish history, architecture, and art, with particularly interesting models of synagogues from the 3rd to the 19th century. Open Tues, Wed, Thurs, and Sun during the academic year.

MARKETS: 🔔 **Antiques Fair & Flea Market** (midtown), Ave. of the Americas between W. 24th and W. 26th Sts. (243-5343): Picturesque open-air flea market held every Sat and Sun (weather permitting) for more than a dozen years. Opens 6am. You'll find everything from fine art and real collector's pieces to junk. Well worth a visit. Open year round.

🔔 **Canal West Flea Market** (Soho) 370 Canal St. at W. Broadway: Lively flea market with lots of bargains. Open Sat–Sun throughout the year from 7am on.

🔔 **Essex Street Market** (Lower East Side), Essex St. between Broome and Stanton Sts.: Built in 1938 by then-mayor Fiorello La Guardia, this enormous covered market, the city's largest, is worth visiting not only for its many stalls overflowing with all kinds of foodstuffs, but for the variety of languages you'll hear—Yiddish, Spanish, Greek, Italian, Polish, Vietnamese, and many more. Open daily except Jewish holidays.

☼☪ **Fulton Fish Market** (Lower Manhattan), at South and Fulton Sts.: Adjacent to the South Street Seaport Museum (see "Museums of Science and History," below), this fish market, in existence since 1869 though the present building dates only from 1907, is one of the most important on the East Coast. Atmosphere and local color guaranteed, from 3am on, seven days a week.

☼☪ **La Marqueta** (El Barrio), Park Ave. between E. 110th and E. 116th Sts.: Puerto Rican covered market displaying all the exotic fruit, vegetables, seeds, spices, smoked meats, and fish from that Caribbean island. One of the most colorful places in New York.

☪ **Paddy's Market** (midtown), Ninth Ave. between W. 37th and W. 42nd Sts.: Once the stronghold of Greek and Italian grocers and produce merchants, this has become a kind of U.N. of the food business, displaying products of all nations. Its annual International Food Festival takes place in May, and is much appreciated by New Yorkers.

MONUMENTS: ☪ General Grant National Memorial (Upper West Side), Riverside Dr. and W. 122nd St.: Tomb of Gen. Ulysses S. Grant, commander of the Union armies during the Civil War and 18th president of the U.S., and his wife. The marble-and-granite memorial is derivative of the mausoleum of Halicarnassus, one of the seven wonders of the ancient world, and is beautifully situated on a height overlooking the Hudson. The surrounding park should be avoided after dark. Open Wed–Sun.

☼☪☪ **Statue of Liberty National Monument,** Liberty Island, in New York Harbor (363-3200): Probably the most famous statue in the world. Affectionately known as "Miss Liberty," or "The Green Lady," this colossal work of French sculptor Frédéric-Auguste Bartholdi and French engineer Gustave Eiffel is 152 ft. (46m) tall (305 ft./93m including its base), and consists of 300 plates of copper fitted around a steel armature; the whole weighs 225 tons (200,000kg). A gift from the people of France to the people of the United States, since she was unveiled in 1886 *Liberty Enlightening the World* has become a symbol of the U.S., and once again opened to the public after a two-year rehabilitation project for the centennial in 1986. An elevator takes you to the statue's feet, and you then climb a spiral staircase of 168 steps to the top, where 40 people can enter the head (without crowding) and enjoy the magnificent view it affords of New York. There's an interesting little museum of immigration in the statue's base. A must for every visitor, but bear in mind that in summer, when 12,000 tourists make the trip every day, you may have to wait a couple of hours. Access by ferry from Battery Park at the southern tip of Manhattan (call 269-5755 for ferry information). Open daily.

☪ **Washington Arch** (Greenwich Village), Washington Sq. at the foot of Fifth Ave.: An 86-ft. (26m) triumphal arch by Stanford White, erected in 1892–95 to mark the centennial of George Washington's election to the presidency. The surrounding park is the heart of Greenwich Village.

MUSEUMS OF ART: ☪ American Craft Museum (midtown), 40 W. 53rd St. (956-3535): The youngest (1987) of the city's art museums is entirely devoted to handcrafts in wood, metal, fabric, ceramics, etc. There are hundreds of objects on display, from an art deco rocking chair to blown glass. This triumph of the unusual occupies the ground floor of a 30-story high-rise opposite the Museum of Modern Art (see below). Open Tues–Sun.

☼☪☪ **Brooklyn Museum,** 200 Eastern Pkwy. at Washington Ave., Brooklyn (718/638-5000): One of the country's most richly stocked and innovative museums, best known for its fine Egyptian collection and its primitive art, particularly from North America, Africa, and Polynesia; also offers interesting special exhibitions. Among the major works on display are *Pa-*

lazzo Dogale in Venice by Monet, *Mlle Fiocre* by Degas, *The Lady in Red* by Thomas Anshutz, and 12 bas-reliefs from the palace of the Assyrian king Assurbanipal at Nimrud. A new display area houses one of the world's largest collections of sculpture by Auguste Rodin. Open Wed–Sun. Directly accessible by subway.

☼☙☙ **The Cloisters** (Upper Manhattan), Fort Tryon Park at Fort Washington Ave. and 193rd St. (923-3700): Medieval French and Spanish cloisters acquired at the turn of the century by the millionaire art patron John D. Rockefeller, and transported stone by stone to the U.S. from the monasteries of St. Michael de Cuxa, Saint-Guilhem-le-Désert, and Bonnefont-en-Comminges, as well as others. Admirable collection of medieval art including the famous series of 15th-century "Unicorn Tapestries," and the almost equally famous Mérode Altarpiece painted around 1425. Lovely gardens overlooking the Hudson make up a magnificent whole, which you mustn't miss. One of the most beautiful museums in the city. Open Tues–Sun.

☙☙ **Cooper-Hewitt Museum** (Upper East Side), 2 E. 91st St. at Fifth Ave. (860-6868): In what was once the sumptuous private house of the Carnegie family, this museum, entirely devoted to the decorative arts, displays a rich collection of furniture, ceramics, old fabrics (including a silken bonnet and mittens from China that are more than 2,000 years old), wallpaper, bronzes, architectural drawings, etc., as well as interesting temporary exhibitions. Open Tues–Sun.

☙ **El Museo del Barrio** (Upper East Side), 1230 Fifth Ave. at E. 104th St. (831-7272): Exhibitions of painting, sculpture, and photography by Latin American artists, in the heart of the Puerto Rican quarter ("El Barrio") of New York. Also public concerts, movies, plays, etc. Fascinating. Open Wed–Sun.

☙ **Forbes Galleries** (Greenwich Village), 62 Fifth Ave. at 12th St. (620-2389): A highly eclectic private museum belonging to the late publisher and businessman Malcolm Forbes. It includes the world's largest collection of Fabergé Easter eggs, some old paintings, 500 ship models, and an army of 12,000 lead toy soldiers. Unexpected. Open Tues–Sat.

☼☙☙ **Frick Collection** (Upper East Side), 1 E. 70th St. at Fifth Ave. (288-0700): European masters (Velázquez, Vermeer, Gainsborough, Boucher, Van Eyck, and many others of equal stature) and fine furniture displayed in a lovely little Renaissance-style palace designed by architect Thomas Hastings for the Pittsburgh steel magnate Henry Clay Frick. Delightful covered courtyard. Among the most famous paintings on exhibition: *Man in a Red Hat* by Titian, *Self-Portrait* by Rembrandt, *Portrait of Philip IV* by Velázquez, and Holbein the Younger portraits *Sir Thomas More* and *Thomas Cromwell*. Perhaps New York's most exquisite museum. Open Tues–Sun.

☼☙☙☙ **Solomon R. Guggenheim Museum** (Upper East Side), 1071 Fifth Ave. at E. 89th St. (727-6200): One of the world's most beautiful and original museum buildings, truly a work of art in its own right, designed in 1959 by Frank Lloyd Wright, the greatest American architect, in the form of an inverted spiral supposedly inspired by the legendary Tower of Babel. Splendid collection of impressionist and modern painting and sculpture by Kandinsky, Paul Klee, Delaunay, Picasso, Rauschenberg—but also by Renoir, Cézanne, van Gogh, Manet, and the like. In all, some 5,000 paintings, sculptures, and drawings including such acknowledged masterpieces as Kandinsky's *Blue Mountain*, Picasso's *Moulin de la Galette*, Jackson Pollock's *Ocean Greyness*, Chagall's *Green Violinist*, and *The Watchmaker* by Paul Cézanne. Has recently reopened after a two-year, $40-million complete remodeling, including the construction of a 10-story annex with new galleries. You should plan not to leave New York without coming to the Guggenheim. Open Tues–Sun.

☙ **International Center of Photography** (Upper East Side), Fifth Ave. at E. 94th St. (860-1777): The only museum in New York entirely devoted to photography. Temporary exhibitions and a permanent collection by the greatest masters of the lens: Robert Capa, Henri Cartier-

Bresson, Ernst Haas, David Seymour, Marc Riboud, Ken Heyman, Edward Weston, and Ansel Adams. A larger (and friendlier) annex to the museum was opened in September 1989 at 1133 Ave. of the Americas at W. 43rd St. (768-4680). Fascinating. Open Tues–Sun.

&& **Isamu Noguchi Garden Museum,** 32–37 Vernon Blvd. at 33rd Rd., Long Island City, Queens (718/204-7088): Very beautiful museum and sculpture garden with more than 250 works by the famous American sculptor Isamu Noguchi, who died in 1988. Open Wed and Sat Apr–Nov.

☼&&& **Metropolitan Museum of Art** (Upper East Side), Fifth Ave. at 82nd St. (535-7710): Familiarly known to New Yorkers as "the Met," this cultural colossus is the world's largest art museum—more than three million objects are displayed in 236 galleries plus a very fine Rooftop Sculpture Garden with a clear view of the Manhattan skyline. The presentation is admirable: From Egyptian temples to Gauguin and from medieval art to Jackson Pollock, the Met offers you a complete panorama of mankind's artistic evolution over the last 5,000 years. You should take care to see the new Lila Acheson Wallace Wing, devoted to 20th-century art. Among the world-famous works of art you will see are Giovanni Pisano's *Head of King David,* the *Mezzetin* of Antoine Watteau, Rembrandt's *Aristotle Contemplating the Bust of Homer,* Vermeer's *Woman at a Window,* an *Annunciation* by Hans Memling and another by Botticelli, a *Crucifixion* by Jan van Eyck, *The Harvest* by Pieter Breughel the Elder, Ingres's *Princesse de Broglie,* Gauguin's *Ia Orana Maria,* Picasso's *Portrait of Gertrude Stein,* Georgia O'Keeffe's *Cow's Skull, Red, White, and Blue,* and *Autumn Rhythm* by Jackson Pollock. Five million people visit the museum every year; you should allow at least two full days for it. In itself it's worth the trip to New York. Open Tues–Sun.

& **The New Museum** (SoHo), 583 Broadway (219-1222): New York's only museum featuring exclusively contemporary art, emerging artists or lesser-known works of established artists. Located in the landmark Astor Bldg. Open Wed–Sun.

☼&&& **Museum of Modern Art (MOMA)** (midtown), 11 W. 53rd St. (708-9480): From impressionism to cubism, from expressionism to abstract art, MOMA's collection of 100,000 priceless works covers the spectrum from Dalí to Monet, from Bacon to Chagall, and from Andy Warhol to de Kooning and Mark Rothko. Recently modernized, and enlarged by the construction of an adjoining 52-story tower designed by Cesar Pelli with an enormous glassed-in atrium, MOMA also boasts a superb garden court with modern sculpture by Lipchitz, Rodin (*The Burghers of Calais*), Picasso, Nevelson, Henry Moore, Reginald Butler, and others. With its 5,000 visitors a day, this is one of the most popular museums in the country. Its most cherished canvas, Picasso's *Guernica,* was returned to Spain in 1981, but you can still admire the same artist's famous *Demoiselles d'Avignon,* along with such other masterpieces as van Gogh's *Starry Night,* Matisse's *The Dance,* Douanier Rousseau's *Sleeping Gypsy,* the waterlily triptych by Monet, Edward Hopper's *House by the Railroad,* and *Christina's World* by Andrew Wyeth. This museum alone could justify the trip to New York. Open Thur–Tues.

& **Studio Museum in Harlem** (Harlem), 144 W. 125th St. (864-4500): This little-known museum in the heart of Harlem has interesting temporary exhibitions of the work of black artists, both American and Third World. Open Wed–Sun.

☼&& **Whitney Museum of American Art** (Upper East Side), 945 Madison Ave. at E. 75th St. (570-3676): Founded in 1930 by sculptor Gertrude Vanderbilt Whitney, this remarkable museum displays the most representative works by contemporary American artists, from Georgia O'Keeffe and Louise Nevelson to Edward Hopper and George Segal. The odd granite-and-concrete building in the shape of a truncated Aztec pyramid dates from 1954, and is the work of Marcel Breuer. Major exhibits: *Circus* by Calder,

Early Sunday Morning by Edward Hopper, *Dempsey and Firpo* by George Bellows, Charles Demuth's *My Egypt*, and Jackson Pollock's *Number 27*. Don't miss it. Open Tues–Sun. The museum has an annex in the Philip Morris Building (see "Skyscrapers," above).

MUSEUMS OF SCIENCE & HISTORY: ※☆ American Museum of the Moving Image/AMMI, 35th Ave. at 36th St., Queens (718/784-0077): The nation's first public museum wholly devoted to chronicling the history of cinema, television, and video art. This $15-million shrine to the motion picture, inaugurated in Sept 1988, is part of the old Astoria Studios, once Paramount Pictures' production center for silent films. The 60,000-item collection includes vintage movie cameras and television sets, old posters, photographs, souvenirs, costumes of movie and TV stars, and three theaters where visitors can see films or TV serials rarely seen. A must for movie buffs. Open Tues–Sun.

※☆ **American Numismatic Society** (Upper Manhattan), Audubon Terrace, Broadway at 155th St. (234-3130): The largest numismatic library in the world, and one of the greatest collections ever assembled of coins, medals, and decorations, including rare Chinese, Greek, and Roman gold coins. A collector's paradise. Open Tues–Sun.

☆ **AT&T Infoquest** (midtown), 550 Madison Ave. at E. 56th St. (605-5555): Four-level exhibition space devoted to communications and information technology. The visitor programs an "access card" with his or her first name, which is then displayed in lights on a "Gateway to the Information Age," and serves as a key to the 40 interactive exhibits. Fascinating. Open Tues–Sun.

☆ **Children's Museum of Manhattan** (Upper West Side), 212 W. 83rd St. (721-1234): Opened in 1989, this technologically sophisticated four-story museum has about 60 exhibition areas, including a fully functioning TV studio, a 20-ft. (6m) domed theater called the Brainatarium, and hands-on exhibits. A must for children and adults alike. Open Mon, Wed, Fri, Sat–Sun.

※☆ **Fraunces Tavern Museum** (Lower Manhattan), 54 Pearl St. (425-1778): This picturesque tavern in dull-brown brick is as faithful a replica as can be made of the original structure, dating from 1719, which was razed by two successive fires in 1837 and 1852; it belonged to Samuel Fraunces (the name is a corruption of "Français," French), a black man from the Antilles who became steward to George Washington. It was here that Washington gave a farewell banquet for his generals before temporarily leaving New York for Philadelphia in 1783. Museum, with historical collection, open Mon–Fri. On the ground floor is a very acceptable restaurant with incomparable American Colonial atmosphere; breakfast/lunch/dinner Mon–Fri.

※☆☆ **Hayden Planetarium** (Upper West Side), Central Park West at W. 81st St. (769-5920): This famous planetarium, and its comprehensive museum of the history of astronomy, form an integral part of the Musuem of Natural History (see below). You'll be interested in a 30-ton meteorite found in Greenland in 1897, a reproduction of the solar system, and an exact representation of the moon's surface. For ardent amateur astronomers. Exciting. Open daily.

※☆ ***Intrepid* Sea-Air-Space Museum** (midtown), Pier 86 at W. 46th St. (245-0072): The famous World War II and Vietnam War aircraft carrier, 890 ft. (270m) long, now converted into a floating museum with aircraft, helicopters, ballistic missiles, and space capsules. Interesting audio-visual show. Impressive. Open Wed–Sun.

※☆ **Jewish Museum** (Upper East Side), 1109 Fifth Ave. at E. 92nd St. (860-1888): Housed in the Warburg Mansion, a French Gothic château-style building, the world's largest Jewish museum illustrates the history of Judaism by means of painting, sculpture, manuscripts, cere-

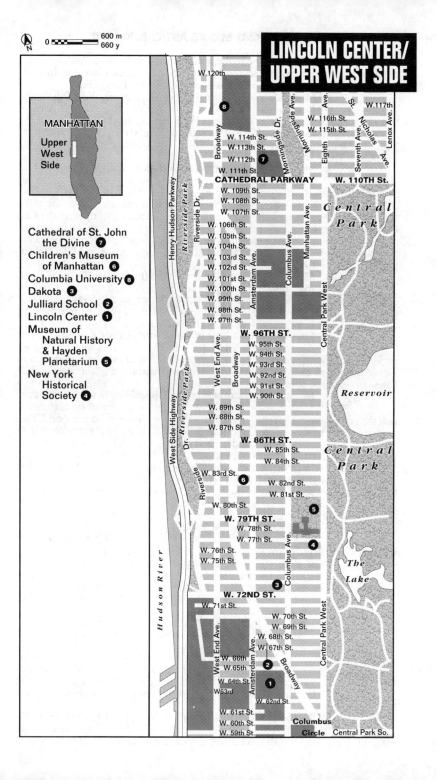

LINCOLN CENTER/ UPPER WEST SIDE

MANHATTAN

Upper
West
Side

Cathedral of St. John the Divine ⑦
Children's Museum of Manhattan ⑥
Columbia University ⑧
Dakota ③
Julliard School ②
Lincoln Center ①
Museum of Natural History & Hayden Planetarium ⑤
New York Historical Society ④

0 — 600 m
— 660 y

W.120th
W.117th
W. 116th St.
W. 115th St.
W. 114th St.
W.113th St.
W.112th
W.111th St.
CATHEDRAL PARKWAY
W. 109th St.
W. 108th St.
W. 107th St.
W. 106th St.
W. 105th St.
W. 104th St.
W. 103rd St.
W. 102nd St.
W. 101st St.
W. 100th St.
W. 99th St.
W. 98th St.
W. 97th St.
W. 96TH ST.
W. 95th St.
W. 94th St.
W. 93rd St.
W. 92nd St.
W. 91st St.
W. 90th St.
W. 89th St.
W. 88th St.
W. 87th St.
W. 86TH ST.
W. 85th St.
W. 84th St.
W. 83rd St.
W. 82nd St.
W. 81st St.
W. 80th St.
W. 79TH ST.
W. 78th St.
W. 77th St.
W. 76th St.
W. 75th St.
W. 72ND ST.
W. 71st St.
W. 70th St.
W. 69th St.
W. 68th St.
W. 67th St.
W. 66th
W.65th
W. 64th St.
W63rd
W. 62nd St.
W. 61st St.
W. 60th St.
W. 59th St.

W. 110TH St.
W. 117th

Broadway
Morningside Dr.
Eighth Ave.
Seventh Ave.
St. Nicholas Ave.
Lenox Ave.
Manhattan Ave.
Columbus Ave.
Amsterdam Ave.
Central Park West
West End Ave.
Broadway
Riverside Dr.
Henry Hudson Parkway
West Side Highway
Dr. Riverside Park
Riverside Park
Riverside

Central Park

Reservoir

Central Park

The Lake

Columbus Circle   Central Park So.

Hudson River

monial objects, etc. Samuel Friedenberg numismatic collection. Take care to see the beautiful composition by sculptor George Segal entitled *Holocaust*. In 1991 the museum began a $15-million expansion. Open Sun, Tues–Thurs.

Morris-Jumel Mansion (Upper Manhattan), W. 160th St. and Edgecombe Ave. (923-8008): With its four-column portico, this elegant 1765 Georgian mansion was Washington's headquarters before the battle of Harlem Heights in 1776. This is the only surviving pre-Revolutionary house in Manhattan. Very fine old furniture. For lovers of glimpses from the past. Open Tues–Sun.

Museum of the American Indian (Lower Manhattan), Old U.S. Custom House, State St. at Bowling Green: Long accommodated in a badly run-down building in Upper Manhattan, this fabulous collection—the world's largest—of Native American artifacts is now part of the new National Museum of the American Indian scheduled to open at the Old U.S. Custom House in October 1994. The rest of the collection, which contains more than a million items, gleaned from the Artic Circle to the tip of Tierra del Fuego, will be housed in a brand-new Smithsonian museum on the Mall in Washington, D.C., by 1999.

Museum of Television and Radio (midtown), 25 W. 52nd St. (621-6600): In a brand-new building is an enormous archive of tapes on which are stored more than 25,000 TV programs, 15,000 radio programs, and 10,000 commercials made during the last 70 years, from which the visitor may select favorites for replay. Open Tues–Sat.

Museum of the City of New York (Upper East Side), Fifth Ave. and E. 103rd St. (534-1672): New York history in models, dioramas, paintings, prints, toys, old furniture, etc., from the foundation of New Amsterdam in the 17th century. Multimedia show on "the Big Apple." Fascinating. Open Tues–Sun.

Museum of Natural History (Upper West Side), Central Park West at W. 79th St. (769-5100): Some 34 million objects enrich the collection of this, the largest natural-history museum in the world. Particularly important zoology and anthropology sections, with every animal in creation, including dinosaurs and a 98-ft. (30m) blue whale. Many dioramas showing the habitats of the people and animals of America, Asia, Africa, and the Pacific. Gallery of meteorites and minerals. Enormous collection of fossils. One of the world's largest assemblages of gemstones, including some unique and valuable specimens. Movies shown on the giant "Naturemax" screen. Dazzling new permanent-exhibition hall retracing the 12,000-year cultural history of the peoples of the Andean highlands and Amazon basin. Open daily.

New-York Historical Society (Upper West Side), 170 Central Park West at 77th St. (873-3400): An indispensable complement to the Museum of the City of New York (see above), with a very rich collection of American decorative art (Tiffany lamps, silverware, toys), and in particular 433 of the 435 famous original watercolors by John James Audubon of the *Birds of America*. History of transportation in New York. The library has more than four million manuscripts, prints, photos, engravings, and rare books relating to New York. Open Tues–Sun.

New York Public Library (midtown), Fifth Ave. and 42nd St. (340-0849 or 869-8089): Imposing Italian Renaissance structure, guarded by two enormous stone lions and housing the second-largest public library in the country, after the Library of Congress in Washington: 30 million works, paintings, posters, etc. Among the rarities: a letter from Christopher Columbus dated 1493, and a rough draft of the Declaration of Independence in the handwriting of Thomas Jefferson. Very interesting temporary exhibitions. Open Mon–Sat.

Pierpont Morgan Library (midtown), 29 E. 36th St. (685-0610): This magnificent library, assembled by financier and art patron J. Pierpont Morgan, specializes in valuable manuscripts and rare books.

Since 1906 it has been housed in a sumptuous Renaissance palazzo by McKim, Mead & White, opened to the public in 1924. It has, among its other treasures, three Gutenberg Bibles, the 15th-century illuminated *Book of Hours* of Catherine of Cleves, 9th-century Coptic manuscripts, the oldest-known edition of Boccaccio's *Decameron* (1473), and autograph letters by Shakespeare, Byron, Shelley, Dickens, etc. Its temporary exhibitions are wonderful. Open Tues–Sun.

    Police Academy Museum (Gramercy Park), 235 E. 20th St. (477-9753): This fascinating museum, part of the New York City Policy Academy, houses crime-fighting artifacts including Al Capone's machine gun, real contraband, counterfeit money, unusual weapons, badges, and uniforms dating from 1845 to the present day. Open Mon–Fri.

    Queens Museum, Flushing Meadow–Corona Park, Grand Central Pkwy. and Roosevelt Ave., Queens (718/592-5555): Since 1972 this museum has occupied the former New York City building of the 1964 World's Fair. Halfway between Kennedy and La Guardia airports, it's worth a side trip because of its extraordinary 9,000-sq.-ft. scale model of New York. Open Tues–Sun.

    South Street Seaport Museum (Lower Manhattan), 207 Front St. (669-9400): The historic port district of old New York converted into an open-air museum, with carefully restored 19th-century houses, pubs, restaurants, shops, a covered market, and street musicians. Along its piers are moored old ships such as the very fine four-master *Peking* (1911), the Ambrose lightship (1907), the three-master *Wavertree* (1885), and the schooner *Lettie G. Howard* (1893). In addition, a maritime museum (207 Water St.) houses ship models, navigational instruments, tools, and fish-market artifacts. The setting is admittedly touristy, but lively and colorful; it could have come straight out of an old picture book. Stay away Thurs and Fri evenings when the horde of Wall St. brokers comes out to play. Open daily.

NIGHTTIME ENTERTAINMENT: No city in the world offers a gamut of nighttime diversions equal to New York's. Leaving aside its dozens of theaters, concert halls, and opera houses, including the prestigious Met and Carnegie Hall, the visitor may find it hard to choose among several hundred bars, discos, comedy clubs, jazz dives, dance halls, and nightclubs—ranging from smart to sleazy. When it comes, specifically, to nightclubs, bars, and discos, the problem is to pick the "in" places; on the New York scene, discos, in particular, can be born, flourish, and die in less than a year. Some safe bets will be found listed under "Bars and Nightclubs," below.

    For lovers of theater and musicals, no visit to New York can be complete without at least one evening on Broadway, "the greatest show on earth." The 38 theaters around Times Sq. generally present high-grade entertainment, from Shakespeare to Arthur Miller and from Neil Simon to the latest musicals. Elsewhere in the city, more than 200 Off- and Off-Off-Broadway houses are home to avant-garde plays or comedy clubs which may become tomorrow's big hits. Most of New York's theaters may be old and uncomfortable, but with 10 million playgoers a year the "Sold Out" signs are often up, so tickets should be obtained well in advance. You can use a ticket broker, or charge tickets on your credit card through Telecharge (239-6200) or Ticketmaster (307-4100). **TKTS,** in Times Sq. at 49th St. (midtown) or 2 World Trade Center (Lower Manhattan), sells tickets at half price. The drawback is that they're available only on the day of the performance and there are often long waiting lines. Matinee tickets from noon on, and evening tickets from 3pm. Cash only. Open daily. Finally, in the big hotels, the concierge may be induced by the suggestive rustle of $10 bills to unearth the ticket(s) that you've been told are not to be had. For other information, see "Performing Arts," below.

OUTDOOR ART & PLAZAS: The streets and squares of New York boast many important works of art, including an amusing 40-ft. (12m) fiberglass composition by Jean Dubuffet entitled *Group of Four Trees,* in the Chase Manhattan Plaza in Lower Manhattan. In front of Lincoln Center (Upper West Side) are *Reclining Figure,* a monumental bronze by British sculptor Henry Moore, and *The Ticket Window* by Alexander Calder. Other noteworthy pieces include *The Alamo,* an enormous cubic structure by Tony Rosenthal on Astor Place (Noho); *Shadows and Flags,* a group of seven abstracts in black-painted steel by Louise Nevelson at Liberty and William Sts. (Lower Manhattan); *Red Cube,* a 24-ft.-high (7m) steel sculpture balanced on point by Isamu Noguchi at 140 Broadway (Lower Manhattan); a strange mobile globe in bronze by the German Fritz Koenig in the World Trade Center Plaza (Lower Manhattan); and a giant Jacques Lipchitz outside the Law School at Columbia University, Broadway and 116th St. (Morningside Heights). In a more classical vein are the monumental 45-ft. (14m) *Atlas Bearing the Heavens* and the famous *Prometheus* by Paul Manship in gilt bronze dominating the lower plaza of Rockefeller Center (midtown).

PANORAMAS: ☼🜨**Brooklyn Bridge** (Lower Manhattan), between City Hall Park in Manhattan and Cadman Plaza, Brooklyn: The city's oldest (1883) suspension bridge; a beautiful piece of functional architecture in steel, whose pedestrian walkway affords a superb view of downtown Manhattan.

☼🜨🜨 **Brooklyn Heights Esplanade,** Columbia Heights between Remsen and Orange Sts., Brooklyn: Smart residential neighborhood on a hill overlooking the East River. Writer Truman Capote used to live here; Norman Mailer is a current resident. Splendid view of the skyline and the southern tip of Manhattan from the promenade that runs above the Brooklyn-Queens Expwy.

☼🜨🜨🜨 **Empire State Building** (midtown), 34th St. and Fifth Ave. (736-3100): Probably the world's most famous skyscraper, particularly to *King Kong* fans. Its 102 stories add up to a height of 1,250 ft. (381m), its TV transmitting antenna adds another 223 ft. (68m). There are two observation platforms, one in the open air on the 86th floor, the other closed and glassed in on the 102nd floor. On a clear day you can see more than 60 mi. (100km) over four states. New York's most astonishing view, especially by night, attracting two million visitors a year. Open daily until 11:30pm. For more details, see "Architectural Highlights: Skyscrapers," above.

🜨 **Roosevelt Island Aerial Tramway** (Upper East Side), Second Ave. at E. 60th St. (832-4555): Running 200 ft. (60m) above the East River, parallel to the Queensboro Bridge, this cable car connecting Manhattan and Roosevelt Island gives you a fine view of the East Side skyline. Runs every 15 min., daily.

☼🜨🜨 **Staten Island Ferry** (Lower Manhattan), Ferry Terminal, Peter Minuit Plaza (806-6940 or 718/727-2508): New York's most spectacular view. The ferry links the southern tip of Manhattan to Staten Island, and passes near the Statue of Liberty. It runs daily around the clock, leaving every 15 min. in rush hours, once an hour late at night. The trip takes about 25 min. each way. An experience not to be passed up.

☼🜨🜨 **Statue of Liberty,** Liberty Island, in New York Harbor (363-3200): Reached by an elevator and a spiral staircase (trying), and 12 stories high, the statue's head offers a splendid view of New York and the bay through the windows in the crown. Advisable only for those in good physical condition. Open daily; accessible by ferry from Battery Park (call 269-5755 for boat schedules).

☼🜨🜨 **World Trade Center** (Lower Manhattan), at West, Church, Vesey, and Liberty Sts. (466-7397): These twin towers, 1,350 ft. (411m) tall—1,710 ft. (521m) with the TV antenna—took the championship away from the Empire State Building, but were themselves defeated by the 1,454-ft. (443m) Sears Tower in Chicago. Unique panorama of New York from the Observation Deck on the 107th floor, or the open terrace on the 110th floor of the No. 2 tower. Open daily until 9:30pm. Target of a terrorist bomb in 1993, the building has fortunately suffered no structural damage. For more information, see "Architectural Highlights: Skyscrapers," above.

PARKS & GARDENS: ☼⚓ **Battery Park** (Lower Manhattan), Battery Place and State St.: Standing at the tip of Manhattan Island, with a magnificent view of New York Bay and the Statue of Liberty, this park marks the spot where Giovanni da Verrazano is supposed to have made his first landfall in 1524. The lowering bulk of **Castle Clinton,** a fort built in 1811 to defend the city against British warships, was an immigrant-processing center from 1855 to 1890. At the water's edge are the terminals for the Statue of Liberty, Ellis Island, and Staten Island ferries. For those who like to take souvenir photographs, a stroll around here is definitely indicated.

⚓ **Bowling Green** (Lower Manhattan), Battery Place and Broadway: According to legend, this is where Peter Minuit bought Manhattan from the Indians. There is still lawn bowling here as there was in Dutch Colonial days—the distant ancestor of present-day American 10-pin bowling.

☼⚓⚓ **Brooklyn Botanic Gardens,** 1000 Washington Ave. off Eastern Pkwy., Brooklyn (718/622-4433): On a 50-acre (20.5ha) site tucked between Olmsted and Vaux's masterly **Prospect Park** and the Brooklyn Museum you'll find azaleas and rhododendrons, lilacs, wisteria, one of the country's most beautiful rose gardens, a Japanese water garden, an unspoiled tract of New York woodland, a lovely grove of cherry trees, and more. The greenhouses reopened in 1988 after a two-year expansion project; they house, among other attractions, an unequaled collection of bonsai (Japanese miniature trees). The gardens are scrupulously maintained—no graffiti or litter—and it's hard to believe you're in the city. Combine this with a visit to the adjoining Brooklyn Museum (see "Museums of Art," above) for a day's escape.

☼⚓ **Central Park,** between Fifth Ave. and Central Park West from 59th to 110th Sts.: This magnificent park, covering 840 acres (340ha) in the center of the city (twice the size of the principality of Monaco) is Manhattan's lung; it was designed by Frederick Law Olmsted and Calvert Vaux, fathers of American landscape architecture. Much frequented by New York joggers and cyclists. Pleasantly undulating, and stitched together by more than 30 mi. (50km) of surfaced roads, footpaths, and riding trails, it also has several lakes (on some of which boating is available), a herb garden, a small zoo with a special children's zoo, an ice-skating rink, a carousel, and other attractions. Many tourists take a daytime ride through the park in a horse-drawn carriage, but the park is less safe at night; avoid it after dark unless you're attending one of the many festivals and free concerts in summer.

☼⚓ **Fort Tryon Park** (Upper Manhattan), between Riverside Dr. and Broadway from W. 192nd to Dyckman Sts.: A gift of the Rockefeller family to the city, this park occupies the site of the old Fort Washington, which played an important role during the War of Independence. There's a splendid view of the Hudson flowing below. Lovely terraced flower gardens. Don't miss it. In the middle of the park stands the Cloisters (see "Museums of Art," above). Strolls should not be taken after dark.

⚓ **Gramercy Park,** Lexington Ave. between E. 20th and E. 21st Sts.: In the middle of a square lined with fine century-old buildings stands this quiet, green oasis in mid-Manhattan, the last private square in New York. Only residents, and guests at the Gramercy Park Hotel on the square, have access to it.

⚓ **Inwood Hill Park** (Upper Manhattan), bounded by the Hudson River and Harlem River, Dyckman St., and Payson Ave.: 434 acres (176ha) of hilly woods along the river, centuries-old trees, and lawns much appreciated by picnickers, at the northern tip of Manhattan. Here once stood the village of Shorakkopoch, consisting in part of cave dwellings belonging to the Algonquins who, in 1626, sold Manhattan Island to Peter Minuit for a mess of pottage.

☼ 🐚🐚 **New York Botanical Gardens,** 200th St. and Southern Blvd., The Bronx (718/817-8705): This splendid 250-acre (102.5ha) tract of greenery has everything: the only first-growth timber still standing within the city limits; acres of tree-studded lawns; beautiful flowerbeds; the tremendous, recently renovated Enid Haupt Conservatory with its stunning seasonal flower shows; a rushing country stream, beside which stands an 18th-century snuff mill where you can have a snack. Less elegant and intimate than the Brooklyn gardens, but more spacious. Free, unless you bring your car (parking $4).

☼ 🐚 **Washington Square** (Greenwich Village), Fifth Ave. at Waverly Place: A square whose triumphal arch (by Stanford White) is dedicated to George Washington, in the heart of Greenwich Village. Here was once the burial ground for African American slaves and executed criminals. Today jam sessions, roller skaters, artists, buskers, and sidewalk orators of every kind may be found here; a lively, colorful place, though overwhelmed by tourists.

☼ 🐚 **Woodlawn Cemetery,** Jerome Ave. at E. 233rd St., The Bronx (718/652-2100): Huge landscaped cemetery with 250,000 graves, some sumptuous crypts, and beautiful gardens, now a designated bird sanctuary. Among the illustrious dead here are writer Herman Melville (*Moby-Dick*), Duke Ellington, newspaperman and publisher Joseph Pulitzer (founder of the prizes that bear his name), 19th-century railroad magnate Jay Gould, five-and-dime king Frank W. Woolworth, and the great New York City mayor Fiorello La Guardia. Open daily.

PERFORMING ARTS: For daily listings of the innumerable shows and cultural events in New York, consult the entertainment pages of the **daily papers** *New York Times, New York Newsday,* or *Daily News* (morning) and *New York Post* (morning and evening), as well as the weeklies *The Village Voice, New York* magazine, and *The New Yorker,* or call **New York City On Stage** (768-1818) for current theater schedules.

Alice Tully Hall (Upper West Side), Lincoln Center, 140 W. 65th St. (875-5000): Recitals, chamber concerts, movies.

American Place Theater (midtown), 111 W. 46th St. (840-3074): Off-Broadway theater.

Apollo Theater (Harlem), 253 W. 125th St. (749-5838): Harlem's great popular theater, made famous by Duke Ellington, Count Basie, Billie Holiday, and others. The Amateur Night provides a preview of the stars of the future, and the chance to be a part of the toughest, funniest audience in town. Go by cab and use caution in the neighborhood.

Astor Place (Noho), 434 Lafayette St. (254-4370): Musicals, Off-Broadway theater.

Avery Fisher Hall (Upper West Side), Lincoln Center, 140 W. 65th St. (875-5030): Home of the New York Philharmonic, one of the world's great orchestras (principal conductor: Kurt Masur).

Booth Theatre (midtown), 222 W. 45th St. (239-6200): Contemporary theater.

Broadhurst Theater (midtown), 235 W. 44th St. (239-6200): Contemporary theater.

Broadway Theater (midtown), 1681 Broadway at W. 52nd St. (239-6200): Musicals.

Brooklyn Academy of Music, 30 Lafayette St., Brooklyn (718/636-4100): Concerts, contemporary theater, opera, dance, experimental performances.

Brooks Atkinson Theater (midtown), 256 W. 47th St. (719-4099): Contemporary theater.

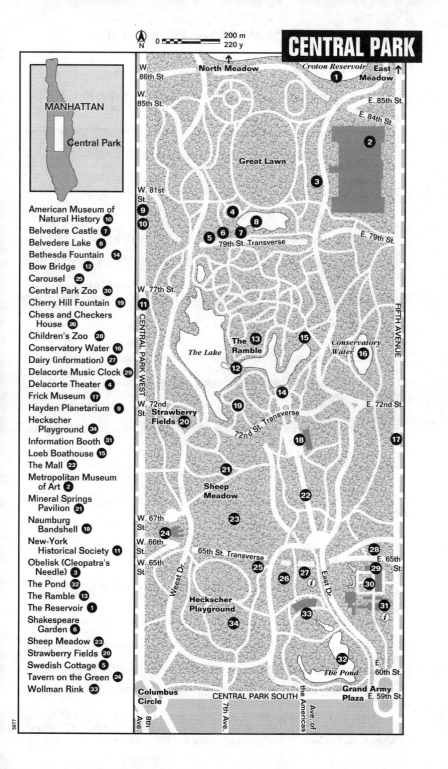

CENTRAL PARK

MANHATTAN

Central Park

American Museum of
  Natural History **10**
Belvedere Castle **7**
Belvedere Lake **8**
Bethesda Fountain **14**
Bow Bridge **12**
Carousel **25**
Central Park Zoo **30**
Cherry Hill Fountain **19**
Chess and Checkers
  House **26**
Children's Zoo **28**
Conservatory Water **16**
Dairy (information) **27**
Delacorte Music Clock **29**
Delacorte Theater **4**
Frick Museum **17**
Hayden Planetarium **9**
Heckscher
  Playground **34**
Information Booth **31**
Loeb Boathouse **15**
The Mall **22**
Metropolitan Museum
  of Art **2**
Mineral Springs
  Pavilion **21**
Naumburg
  Bandshell **18**
New-York
  Historical Society **11**
Obelisk (Cleopatra's
  Needle) **3**
The Pond **32**
The Ramble **13**
The Reservoir **1**
Shakespeare
  Garden **6**
Sheep Meadow **23**
Strawberry Fields **20**
Swedish Cottage **5**
Tavern on the Green **24**
Wollman Rink **33**

0   200 m
     220 y

North Meadow

Croton Reservoir

East
Meadow

W. 86th St.
W. 85th St.
E. 85th St.
E. 84th St.

Great Lawn

W. 81st St.

E. 79th St.
79th St. Transverse

W. 77th St.

CENTRAL PARK WEST

FIFTH AVENUE

The Lake

The Ramble

Conservatory
Water

W. 72nd St.
Strawberry
Fields

72nd St. Transverse
E. 72nd St.

Sheep
Meadow

W. 67th St.
W. 66th St.
65th St. Transverse
W. 65th St.

West Dr.

East Dr.

E. 65th St.

Heckscher
Playground

The Pond

E. 60th St.

Columbus
Circle

CENTRAL PARK SOUTH

Grand Army
Plaza
E. 59th St.

8th Ave.
7th Ave.
Ave. of the Americas

5977

Carnegie Hall (midtown), 154 W. 57th St. (247-7800): Concerts, recitals.

Cherry Lane Theater (Greenwich Village), 38 Commerce St. (989-2020): The oldest Off Broadway theater.

Circle in the Square (Greenwich Village), 159 Bleecker St. (254-6330): Musicals, Off-Broadway theater. Another Off-Broadway theater with the same name is in midtown: 1633 Broadway (307-2700).

Circle Repertory Company (Greenwich Village), Seventh Ave. at W. 4th St. (505-6010): Off-Broadway theater.

City Center Theater (midtown), 131 W. 55th St. (581-7907): Ballet, modern dance, theater.

Delacorte Theater (Upper West Side), W. 81st St. in Central Park (861-7277): Open-air theater; the New York Shakespeare Festival is staged here every summer.

Douglas Fairbanks Theater (midtown), 432 W. 42nd St. (239-4321): Musicals, recitals.

Ethel Barrymore Theater (midtown), 243 W. 47th St. (239-6200): Contemporary theater.

Eugene O'Neill Theater (midtown), 230 W. 49th St. (840-0300): Contemporary theater.

Gershwin Theater (midtown), 222 W. 51st St. (586-6510): Musicals.

Guggenheim Bandshell (Upper West Side), Lincoln Center, 140 W. 65th St. (875-5000): Open-air concerts.

Helen Hayes Theater (midtown), 240 W. 44th St. (944-9450): Contemporary theater.

Imperial Theater (midtown), 249 W. 45th St. (239-6200): Musicals.

Joyce Theater (Chelsea), 175 Eighth Ave. at W. 19th St. (242-0800): Modern dance, ballet.

John Houseman Theater (midtown), 450 W. 42nd St. (967-9077): Contemporary theater.

The Kitchen (Chelsea), 512 W. 19th St. (255-5793): Experimental events, performance artists.

La Mama Experimental Theater Club (East Village), 74 E. 4th St. (475-7710): Avant-garde theater.

Lamb's Theater (midtown), 130 W. 44th St. (997-1780): Contemporary theater.

Longacre Theater (midtown), 220 W. 48th St. (239-6200): Musicals.

Majestic Theater (midtown), 245 W. 44th St. (239-6200): Musicals.

Manhattan Theater Club (midtown) 131 W. 55th St. (581-7907): Off-Broadway theater.

Marquis Theater (midtown), 1535 Broadway at 46th St. (382-0100): Musicals.

Martin Beck Theater (midtown), 302 W. 45th St. (840-0300): Musicals.

Merkin Concert Hall (Upper West Side), 129 W. 67th St. (362-8719): Concerts, recitals.

Metropolitan Opera House (Upper West Side), Lincoln Center, 140 W. 65th St. (362-6000): Home of the New York Metropolitan Opera (artistic director: James Levine).

Minskoff Theater (midtown), 200 W. 45th St. (869-0550): Musicals, revues.

Mitzi E. Newhouse Theater (Upper West Side), Lincoln Center, 140 W. 65th St. (875-5000): Concerts, recitals, musicals.

Nederlander Theater (midtown), 208 W. 41st St. (921-8000): Contemporary theater.

Neil Simon Theater (midtown), 250 W. 52nd St. (757-8646): Contemporary theater.

New York State Theater (Upper West Side), Lincoln Center, 140 W. 65th St. (870-5570): Home of the New York City Opera (director: Christopher Keene) and the New York City Ballet (director: Peter Martins).

Playwrights Horizon (midtown), 416 W. 42nd St. (564-1235): Off-Broadway theater.

Plymouth Theater (midtown), 236 W. 45th St. (239-6200): Contemporary theater.

Promenade Theater (Upper West Side), 2162 Broadway at W. 76th St. (580-1313): Off-Broadway theater.

Provincetown Playhouse (Greenwich Village), 133 MacDougal St. (477-5048): One of the best-known Off Broadway theaters.

Joseph Papp Public Theater (Noho), 425 Lafayette St. (598-7150): Very popular; Off-Broadway and classical theater.

Richard Rodgers Theater (midtown), 226 W. 46th St. (221-1211): Contemporary theater.

Roundabout Theater (midtown), 1530 Broadway (869-8400): Contemporary theater.

Royale Theater (midtown), 45th Street W. of Broadway: (239-6200): Contemporary theater.

St. James Theater (midtown), 246 W. 44th St. (398-0280): Musicals.

Shubert Theater (midtown), 225 W. 44th St. (239-6200): Musicals.

Sullivan St. Playhouse (Greenwich Village), 181 Sullivan St. (674-3838): Off-Broadway theater. The musical *The Fantasticks* has run here since 1960—a world record.

Theater Four (midtown), 424 W. 55th St. (757-3900): Contemporary theater.

Vivian Beaumont Theater (Upper West Side), Lincoln Center, 140 W. 65th St. (875-5000): Musicals, light opera.

Walter Kerr Theater (midtown), 219 W. 48th St.: Musicals, modern theater.

Westside Arts Theater (midtown), 407 W. 43rd St. (315-2244): Contemporary theater.

Winter Garden Theater (midtown), 1634 Broadway at W. 51st St. (239-6200): Operetta, musicals.

WPA Theater (Chelsea), 519 W. 23rd St. (206-0523): Off-Broadway theater.

SHOPPING: In spite of high state and local sales taxes (8.25%), New York maintains its reputation as the "shopping capital of the world" for at least three reasons: (1) the tremendous range of choice in a city with almost 200,000 shops, stores, and merchants of all kinds; (2) the generally attractive level of prices; (3) the clustering of certain kinds of stores in certain neighborhoods, making the shopper's task easier. Note, also, that if you have your purchases shipped to an address outside New York State, you should not be charged the 8.25% sales tax. If you can't find what you want through these listings, consult the *Yellow Pages.*

Shopping Areas

The concentrations of various kinds of retailers in New York is roughly as follows:

Antiques Dealers and Art Galleries: Second Ave. between E. 47th and E. 57th Sts.; Madison Ave. between E. 57th and E. 80th Sts.; Greenwich Village; Soho.

Cameras, Photography, Electronics: W. 32nd to W. 34th Sts. between Sixth and Seventh Aves.; Essex St. (Lower East Side); W. 45th to W. 47th Sts. between Fifth and Sixth Aves.

Cookware: The Bowery from Houston to E. 3rd Sts.

Fabrics: W. 35th to W. 41st Sts. between Fifth and Eighth Aves.; Broadway between Canal and 8th Sts.

Flowers: W. 28th St. and Sixth Ave.

Furs: W. 26th to W. 30th Sts. between Broadway and Sixth Ave.

Jewels and Diamonds: W. 47th St. between Fifth and Sixth Aves. ("Diamond Row"); Fifth Ave. between 42nd and 59th Sts.

Lamps and Lighting Fixtures: The Bowery between Delancey and Grand Sts.

TV/Stereo Equipment: Canal St.; W. 45th St.; Leonard, Warren, and Chambers Sts. between Broadway and Greenwich St. (Tribeca).

Some Recommended Establishments

ANTIQUES DEALERS **Manhattan Art and Antiques Center** (midtown), 1050 Second Ave. at E. 56th St., comprising more than 100 antiques dealers and art galleries on three levels; **Place des Antiquaires** (midtown), 125 E. 57th St., an elegant gallery-mall with 70 dealers in art and antiques.

BOOKS In addition to the independent bookstores, the nationwide chains are well represented: **Barnes and Noble** (Chelsea and Upper West Side), 128 Fifth Ave. at 18th St.; **B. Dalton Booksellers** (midtown), 666 Fifth Ave.; **Doubleday** (midtown), 673 Fifth Ave. at 53rd St.; **Strand** (East Village), Broadway at 12th St., with two million secondhand books; and **Waldenbooks** (midtown), 931 Lexington Ave.

DEPARTMENT STORES **Bergdorf Goodman** (midtown), 715 Fifth Ave. at 57th St.; **Bloomingdales** (midtown), 1000 Third Ave. at E. 59th St., New York's chicest, to see and be seen; ❊ **Macy's** (midtown), W. 34th St. and Broadway, largest store in the world, with 400,000 items, 150,000 customers per day; **Saks Fifth Ave.** (midtown), 611 Fifth Ave. at 50th St., with very yuppie customers; **Lord & Taylor** (midtown), 424 Fifth Ave. at 34th St.

FOOD **Balducci's** (Greenwich Village), 424 Ave. of the Americas (Sixth Ave.) at W. 9th St.; **Dean & DeLuca** (Soho), 560 Broadway; **Fairway Market** (Upper West Side), 2127 Broadway at W. 74th St.; **Sherry-Lehmann** (Upper East Side), 679 Madison Ave. at E. 61st St., New York's most famous wine store; **Zabar's** (Upper West Side), 2245 Broadway at W. 80th St., the biggest food store in the country, offering an unbelievable range of choice, which is best visited like a museum.

GADGETS AND GIFTS **Hammacher Schlemmer** (midtown), 147 E. 57th St., with every kind of gift idea for the home, including the silliest (and the most expensive).

MICROCOMPUTERS AND VIDEO GAMES **Penta Computer** (midtown), 885 Sixth Ave.; **Computer Factory** (Upper East Side), 480 Lexington Ave. at E. 72nd St.; **47th St. Photo** (midtown), 115 W. 45th St.

MILITARY SURPLUS, T-SHIRTS, LOW-PRICED CLOTHING **Canal Jean Co.** (Soho), 504 Broadway at Spring St.; **Hudson's** (East Village), Third Ave. at E. 13th St.; **Urban Outfitters** (Noho), 628 Broadway between Houston and Bleecker Sts.

OUTLET AND THRIFT STORES **Curaçao Export Ltd** (midtown), 20 W. 57th St., 4th floor; **Job Lot** (Lower Manhattan), 140 Church St. at Warren St.; **Romano** (midtown), 12th Ave. and W. 45th St.

PHOTOGRAPHIC EQUIPMENT **47th St. Photo** (midtown), 67 W. 47th St.; **Olden Camera** (midtown), 1265 Broadway; **Willoughby's** (midtown), 110 W. 32nd St.

POSTERS **L'Affiche Galerie** (Soho), 145 Spring St., for modern art posters; **Jerry Ohlinger** (Greenwich Village), 242 W. 14th St., for movie posters; **The Old Print Shop** (Gramercy Park), 150 Lexington Ave. at E. 29th St., for old art posters; **Triton Gallery** (midtown), 323 W. 45th St., for theater posters.

RECORDS **Disc-O-Mart** (midtown), Lexington Ave. and E. 58th St.; **Sam Goody's** (midtown), 1290 Sixth Ave. at W. 53rd St.; **Tower Records** (Noho), 692 Broadway at E. 4th St., with one of the country's largest selections, 400,000 records in all; **J & R Music World** (Lower Manhattan), 23 Park Row; **Triton** (Greenwich Village), 247 Bleecker St.

SPORTING GOODS **Herman's** (midtown), 135 W. 42nd St. or 845 Third Ave. at 51st St.; **Paragon** (Gramercy Park), 871 Broadway at E. 17th St.

STEREO AND ELECTRONIC EQUIPMENT **6th Ave. Electronics City** (midtown), 1024 Sixth Ave.; **Grand Central Radio** (midtown), 155 E. 45th St., with equipment for European voltages; **Harvey Electronics** (midtown), 2 W. 45th St. at Fifth Ave., with equipment for any voltage you need; **Rabson's** (midtown), 119 W. 57th St., also with equipment for European and other foreign voltages; **Uncle Steve** (Chinatown), 343 Canal St., with unbeatable prices.

TOYS ☀ **F. A. O. Schwarz** (midtown), Fifth Ave. at 58th St., the world's biggest toyshop; **Macy's** (midtown), W. 34th St. and Broadway.

SPECIAL EVENTS: For the exact schedule of events below, consult the **New York Convention and Visitors Bureau** (see "Tourist Information" under "Information and Tours," above).

Chinese New Year (Jan–Feb): Ten days of gargantuan banquets, processions, fireworks, and the dragon parade through the streets of Chinatown. Colorful. For information, call the Chinese Cultural Center (373-1800).

St. Patrick's Day Parade (Mar 17): On this feast day of the Irish, the sons and daughters of Erin parade up Fifth Ave. from 44th to 86th Sts. One of the most popular parades in the U.S. More than 150,000 revelers.

Easter Parade (Easter Sunday): Parade on Fifth Ave. near St. Patrick's Cathedral; more a fashion show than a religious occasion.

Washington Sq. Art Show (last weekend in May/first in June; last weekend in Aug/first in Sept): Transforms the sidewalks of Washington Sq. and the surrounding streets into a huge open-air art gallery, where hundreds of artists and craftspeople exhibit their work.

Festa di San Antonio/Feast of St. Anthony of Padua (mid-June): An Italian street "festa" dedicated to the food of the motherland. In Little Italy—a spring must.

Lesbian and Gay Pride Day Parade (last Sunday in June): Since 1970, a yearly procession along Fifth Ave. of all New York's homosexual groups, with more than 100,000 marchers. Colorful.

JVC Jazz Festival (late June to early July): Two weeks of concerts and club appearances around the city, with the biggest names in jazz. For information, call 496-9000.

Shakespeare in the Park (June–Sept): Free open-air performances of Shakespeare and other great plays at the Delacorte Theater in Central Park.

Harbor Festival (July 1–4): Naval review and parade of boats in the harbor.

San Paolino Festival (mid-July): Spectacular procession of the "Giglio," a four-story tower borne on men's backs through the streets of Williamsburg; the biggest Italian religious festival in Brooklyn.

U.S. Open (late Aug to early Sept): Tennis championships at the USTA National Tennis Center, Flushing Meadows Park, Queens.

Greenwich Village Jazz Festival (late Aug to early Sept): The leading jazz performers play for 10 days in a dozen clubs in the Village.

Caribbean Festival (Labor Day weekend): Starting on Thurs with nightly music performances representing different parts of the Caribbean—including reggae, steel band, and calypso—this colorful celebration culminates in an exuberant parade on Labor Day. Spicy food, dancing in the streets—the closest thing to Mardi Gras in New York. Takes place on Eastern Pkwy. in Brooklyn.

San Gennaro Festival (10 days in Sept): The feast of the patron saint of Naples, and of New York's Little Italy. Pizza and chianti at every street corner in Little Italy. Plenty of atmosphere.

Columbus Day Parade (2nd Mon in Oct.): Spectacular parade on Fifth Ave., commemorating the discovery of America by Christopher Columbus—the great Italian-American occasion. On the previous day there's an equally spectacular procession of the Latin American communities—the **Hispanic-American Day Parade.**

New York City Marathon (late Oct to early Nov): 20,000 marathoners compete along a course from the Staten Island end of the Verrazano-Narrows Bridge through Brooklyn, Queens, and the southern Bronx, and into Manhattan to the finish line in Central Park. One of the world's biggest marathons.

Macy's Thanksgiving Day Parade (fourth Thurs in Nov): The prettiest parade of the year, with tens of thousands of participants, bands, floats, and giant balloons in procession down Broadway. You might call it New York's Carnival.

Times Sq. New Year's Eve (Dec 31): If you want to wish yourself a Happy New Year, you have to be in Times Sq. for the 12 strokes of midnight. A must for New Yorkers since 1904.

SPORTS: New York boasts eight major-league teams in four professional sports: **Baseball** (Apr–Oct): Mets, Shea Stadium, Queens (718/507-8499); Yankees, Yankee Stadium, Bronx (718/293-6000).

Basketball (Oct–Apr): Knicks, Madison Sq. Garden, midtown (564-4400); New Jersey Nets, Byrne Meadowlands Arena, E. Rutherford, N.J. (201/935-3900).

Football (Sept–Dec): Giants, Giants Stadium, E. Rutherford, N.J. (201/935-8222); Jets, Giants Stadium, E. Rutherford, N.J. (201/935-8500).

Ice Hockey (Sept–Apr): Islanders, Nassau Coliseum, Hempstead, Long Island (516/794-4100); Rangers, Madison Sq. Garden, midtown (563-8300).

Horse Racing

Aqueduct Race Track, Rockaway Blvd., Ozone Park, Queens (718/641-4700), with racing Jan–May and Oct–Dec.

Belmont Park Race Track, Cross Island Pkwy., Elmont, Queens (718/641-4700), with racing May–July and Sept–Oct.

Meadowlands Racetrack, at the Meadowlands, E. Rutherford, N.J. (201/935-8500), with trotters Jan–Aug and thoroughbred racing Sept–Dec.

Yonkers Raceway, Central Ave. and Yonkers Ave., Yonkers (914/968-4200), with racing Mar to mid-Apr, June to mid-July, Sept–Oct, and Dec.

STROLLS: ⚓ **Battery Park City** (Lower Manhattan), along West St. between Battery Place and Chambers St.: New residential complex on land reclaimed from the Hudson at the southern tip of Manhattan. The fill was excavated from the site of the nearby World Trade Center. Pleasant walkway along the river, and a splendid tropical garden in an enormous glass-roofed atrium 128 ft. (40m) high (the Winter Garden at World Financial Center) with a stunning view of the Hudson River and several shops and cafés.

    Chinatown, around lower Mott, Bayard, and Pell Sts.: Picturesque Chinese district next door to Little Italy. Countless stalls, groceries, restaurants, and stores with souvenirs (often made in Japan or Korea). Uncommonly gaudy and crowded, especially on Mott St., Chinatown's main drag. Interesting little museum of Chinese culture, religion, and art at 8 Mott St. (964-1542), open daily. A stroll you shouldn't miss.

    Columbus Ave. (Upper West Side), around Lincoln Center: Long overlooked by well-to-do New Yorkers, this neighborhood regained its lost youth a couple of decades ago, and now attracts yuppies, artists, and intellectuals. Many trendy boutiques, fashionable restaurants, outdoor cafés. The style is well-heeled fashionable crossed with screwy. Amusing.

    Diamond Row (midtown), W. 47th St. between Fifth and Sixth Aves.: The New York diamond-merchants' street, where a polyglot crowd of dealers haggles in all languages—from Flemish to Yiddish—over 80% of all the precious stones bought and sold in the U.S. Take a look at all the diamonds and rubies glittering in the display windows.

    Fifth Ave. (midtown), between E. 48th and E. 59th Sts.: The stores here are a *Who's Who* of international high fashion: Bergdorf Goodman, Cartier, Tiffany, Van Cleef & Arpels, Saks Fifth Avenue, Valentino, Gucci, Ted Lapidus. For well-lined bank accounts.

    Greenwich Village, around Washington Sq.: New York's traditional bohemian quarter, with old houses and narrow streets. Many inviting cafés, bars, and little restaurants. Bookstores, galleries, dress shops, antiques dealers, jazz clubs, and souvenir stores are all there to tempt the idler. The people are an amusing intellectual-hippy mix, with lots of tourists and young African American rappers, but you'll find junkies here too. Although it appeals blatantly to the tourist trade, it's worth a visit.

    Harlem, between Central Park North (110th St.) and W. 155th St.: "The black capital of America," with several interesting museums, the Apollo Theater, and some lovely 19th-century houses, particularly along Striver's Row (139th St. between Seventh and Eighth aves.). Don't walk alone after dark; the rate of death by violence is, according to police statistics, twice as high in Harlem as in the rest of Manhattan.

    Little Italy, around Mulberry St.: With its typically Italian grocery stores, cafés, bars, *trattorie,* and funeral parlors, this is a postcard Italy of chianti, pizza, and espresso—but it's slowly being swallowed by its neighbor, Chinatown. Guaranteed local color, especially on such saints' days as San Antonio (mid-June) or San Gennaro (mid-Sept). Worth the detour.

    Soho, around W. Broadway south of Houston St.: The artists' quarter, with art galleries, far-out boutiques, and trendy restaurants. Many lofts—former commercial or light-industrial space converted into artists' studios or luxury apartments for yuppies. Lovely old cast-iron facades around Broome and Greene Sts.

    Times Square and the Theater District (midtown), Broadway between W. 42nd and W. 52nd Sts.: Dozens of theaters and movie houses with their neon signs flashing, but also porno houses and the headquarters of the retail drug traffic. Currently in the midst of a vast urban-renewal project. Fascinating—but imprudent alone after midnight.

THEME PARKS: **Coney Island Astroland Park,** W. 10th St. between Surf Ave. and the Boardwalk, Brooklyn (718/372-0275). The granddaddy of American amusement parks, born 1884. Numerous attractions, including the famous 60-year-old giant roller-coaster *Cyclone,* a spectacular Ferris wheel, and a Parachute Jump tower, all historical landmarks. Kitsch but picturesque. Overrun by New Yorkers on summer weekends. Open weekends only, Apr and May; daily,

June to mid-Sept; weekends only to mid-Oct; closed the rest of the year. Reached directly by subway from Manhattan.

    Six Flags Great Adventure, in Jackson, N.J., 60 mi. (96km) SW on the N.J. Tpke., I-195E, and N.J. 537S (201/928-1821): Enormous 1,700-acre (688ha) theme park with more than 100 attractions—carousels and giant roller-coasters including the terrifying "Great American Scream Machine" (173 ft./53m high; 68 m.p.h.), as well as a safari zoo with 1,200 wild animals that you can see from your car. Variety and other shows. Open daily, Apr–Sept; weekends only to late Oct; closed the rest of the year.

WINTER SPORTS RESORTS: Although most New York skiers prefer the slopes of the Adirondacks (see "Farther Afield," below), there are some very acceptable resorts nearer the city, notably the following in the Catskills:

    Bellayre Mountain, 154 mi. (246km) NW on I-87N and N.Y. 28W (914/254-5600): 7 lifts. Open Dec–Mar. For snow conditions, call toll free 800/942-6904.

    Holiday Mountain, 101 mi. (162km) NW along I-87N and N.Y. 17W (914/796-3161): 9 lifts. Open Dec–Mar.

    Hunter Mountain Ski Bowl, 155 mi. (248km) NW on I-87N and N.Y. 23A (518/263-4223): 16 lifts. Open Nov–Apr.

    Ski Windham, 178 mi. (285km) NW on I-87 N and N.Y. 23 (518/734-4300): 7 lifts. Open Nov–Mar.

ZOOS: **Bronx Zoo**, Fordham Rd. and Bronx River Pkwy., Bronx (718/367-1010): One of the top 10 zoos in the U.S., with 3,600 creatures of 700 different species on 265 acres (107ha). Although the overall layout of a zoo dating from 1899 has to be somewhat antiquated, this one has some interesting reconstructions of natural habitats: "Wild Asia," "Jungle World," "World of Darkness" for nocturnal animals, etc. The "World of Birds" is a splendid collection of tropical birds. Visit by monorail or safari train. Open daily.

    New York Aquarium, Boardwalk and W. 8th St., Coney Island, Brooklyn (718/265-3474): Very well-stocked aquarium where you can see 200 species of marine creatures, from the giant octopus to the shark and from the beluga whale to the electric eel. Shows by trained sea creatures. Reached by subway directly from Manhattan: F or D trains to W. 8th St. Worth the trip. Open daily.

    Staten Island Zoo, Barrett Park, 614 Broadway, W. New Brighton, Staten Island (718/442-3100): Best known for its reptiles, this interesting little zoo exhibits animals as strange as they are rarely seen, including 32 varieties of rattlesnake (the world's largest collection), scorpions, alligators, crocodiles, and other reptiles and amphibians. Fascinating. Open daily.

ACCOMMODATIONS

Personal Favorites (in order of preference)

    Carlyle (Upper East Side), Madison Ave. at E. 76th St., NY 10021 (212/744-1600). 500 rms, A/C, color TV, in-rm movies. AE, CB, DC, MC, V. Gar. $24, health club, two rests. (including Carlyle Restaurant), bar, 24-hr. rm svce, nightclub, concierge. *Note:* Splendid and refined, w. rms for servants and luxury kennels, the Carlyle is the most elegant and chic hotel in New York, favored by the Kennedy family and former President Reagan, among others. Spacious and luxuriously inviting rms w. minibars and VCRs. Exemplary, personalized svce. Discreet, plush ambience. Perfection—at a price. Good rest., ideal for lunch. Very popular piano bar (Café Carlyle). 80% of the rms are rented by the year. Luxury, calm, and voluptuousness. Probably the best hotel in the U.S. **VE**

♟♟♟♟ **St. Regis Sheraton** (midtown), 2 E. 55th St. (at Fifth Ave.),
♟♟♟♟ NY 10022 (212/753-4500; toll free, see Sheraton). 363 rms,
A/C, color TV, in-rm movies. AE, CB, DC, MC, V. Valet gar. $35, health club,
sauna, rest. (Lespinasse), two bars (including the famous King Cole Bar), 24-hr.
rm svce, nightclub, hrdrsr, boutiques, concierge. *Note:* Reopened in 1991 after a
$100-million restoration, this Beaux Arts landmark built by John Jacob Astor in
1904 boasts some of the city's most luxurious and expensive (w. single rms starting at $350) accommodations. The oversize guest rms feature Louis XV–style
furnishings, 12-foot ceilings, and luxurious gray marble bathrooms. Packing and
unpacking butler svce for each floor. Quiet, distinguished atmosphere. Unusually polished svce. A sentimental favorite of New Yorkers. **VE**

♟♟♟♟ **Plaza Athénée** (Upper East Side), 37 E. 64th St., NY 10021
♟♟♟♟ (212/734-9100; toll free 800/225-5843). 199 rms, A/C,
color TV, in-rm movies. AE, CB, DC, MC, V. Valet gar. $38, rest. (La Regence),
bar, 24-hr. rm svce, free crib, concierge. *Note:* This newcomer on the New York
hotel scene is an outpost of the luxurious and very exclusive Paris hotel of the
same name. Same refined elegance, same intimate, protected atmosphere. Remarkably comfortable rms and suites w. Louis XVI furniture and refrigerators,
some w. private terraces, solariums, and dining rms. Flawless personalized svce.
Remarkable rest. w. sumptuous turn-of-the-century decor. Lots of class, but
pricey; one duplex suite goes for $2,500 a night. Belongs to Britain's Trusthouse
Forte hotel chain. Draws VIPs and leaders of the financial community. **VE**

♟♟♟ **Holiday Inn Crowne Plaza** (midtown), W. 49th St. and Broad-
♟♟♟ way, NY 10019 (212/977-4000; toll free, see Holiday Inns).
770 rms, A/C, color TV, in-rm movies. AE, CB, DC, MC, V. Valet gar. $28,
pool, health club, sauna, two rests. (including Broadway Grill), two bars, rm
svce. *Note:* Futuristic 46-floor tower of crystal opened in 1989—a splendid piece
of modern architecture from the drawing-board of Alan Lapidus. Elegant, civilized interiors; spacious, well-laid-out rms; and exemplary standards of comfort.
Good physical-fitness facilities for a New York City hotel; ultra-professional svce.
Rms on the six highest floors, w. spectacular views, are reserved for VIPs. Conveniently located on Broadway at the heart of the theater district. Business and
package-tour clientele. **VE**

☼♟♟♟ **Waldorf-Astoria** (midtown), 301 Park Ave. (at E. 49th St.),
♟♟♟ NY 10022 (212/355-3000; toll free, see Hilton). 1,410 rms,
A/C, color TV, in-rm movies. AE, CB, DC, MC, V. Valet gar. $32, five rests.
(including Bull & Bear), three bars, 24-hr. rm svce, nightclub, hrdrsr, boutiques,
free crib, concierge. *Note:* A landmark since 1931; everybody of any importance
on the planet has stayed in this immense rococo caravanserai. The art deco lobby
is superb, and the Starlight Roof is the only ballroom in New York whose roof
opens to the stars. The rms have been entirely redecorated and refurnished at a
cost of $150 million. Very good rm svce; inadequate reception. Excellent loca-
tion. A favorite w. foreigners, since the help speaks 37 languages. Luxurious VIP
suites in the adjoining Waldorf Towers. Interesting wknd packages. President
Bush occupies the Presidential Suite when he's in town. **VE**

♟♟ **Doral Tuscany Hotel** (midtown), 120 E. 39th St., NY 10016
♟♟ (212/686-1600; toll free 800/223-5823). 120 rms, A/C,
color TV, in-rm movies. AE, CB, DC, MC, V. Gar. $35, rest., bar, rm svce, night-
club, free crib. *Note:* Remarkable reception and atmosphere in one of New York's
best small hotels. Spacious, elegant rms w. refrigerators and VCRs. Faultless
comfort; polished svce. Regular clientele. A favorite w. those in-the-know, half a
block from Park Ave. Good rest. (Time and Again). Interesting wknd discounts.
VE

☼♟♟ **Algonquin** (midtown), 59 W. 44th St., NY 10036 (212/840-
♟♟ 6800). 188 rms, A/C, color TV. AE, CB, DC, MC, V. Gar.
$25, rest., bar, rm svce, drugstore, crib free. *Note:* Turn-of-the-century hotel pop-
ular w. distinguished writers and theater-goers, since it's a stone's throw from
Broadway. Authentic 1900 decor. Reception and svce attentive. The rms are co-

zily old-fashioned. The Blue Bar is famous; the after-theater buffet is fashionable but so-so. There's a slight aura of the past, for those who hanker for the bohemian 1930s when Dorothy Parker, James Thurber, and others met at the "Algonquin Round Table." Sir John Gielgud and Lord Olivier have been among the hotel's patrons. Designated historic landmark. Recently rehabilitated to restore its pristine splendor. **E–VE**

Gramercy Park Hotel (Gramercy Park), 2 Lexington Ave. (at E. 21st St.), NY 10010 (212/475-4320; toll free 800/221-4083). 507 rms, A/C, color TV. AE, CB, DC, MC, V. Parking adj., rest., bar, rm svce. *Note:* Quiet, agreeable 1920s hotel far from Manhattan's bustle. Courteous reception and svce. Comfortably renovated. Regular clientele w. many Europeans. Relaxed, inviting atmosphere. The best rms overlook Gramercy Park. Very acceptable rest. A good place to stay. **E**

Best Western Milford Plaza (midtown), 270 W. 45th St., NY 10036 (212/869-3600; toll free, see Best Western). 1,310 rms, A/C, color TV, in-rm movies. AE, CB, DC, MC, V. Gar. $12, rest., bar, rm svce, nightclub. *Note:* The old Royal Manhattan renovated and improved. Rms small and functional at best; most have refrigerators. Many package tours and airline crews come here from abroad. The only plus: accommodation and show-ticket packages at very attractive prices ("Show Time New York"). In the heart of the Broadway theater district—not a safe neighborhood after midnight. **M–E**

Pickwick Arms (midtown), 230 E. 51st St., NY 10022 (212/355-0300; toll free 800/742-5945). 400 rms, A/C, cable color TV. AE, CB, DC, MC, V. No private parking. Roof grdn, rest., coffee shop, bar, rm svce. *Note:* An excellent buy for the budget traveler, in the heart of the fashionable East Side. Clean but minuscule rms, recently renovated (some without private bath). Some studios w. kitchenette. Functional level of comfort; friendly, multilingual svce (many foreign guests). Resv. advisable well in advance. Conveniently located near the U.N. Very good overall value. **I–M**

Other Hotels (from top bracket to budget)

Four Seasons (midtown), 57 E. 57th St. (between Park and Madison Aves.), NY 10022 (212/758-5700; toll free, see Four Seasons). 367 rms, A/C, color TV, in-rm movies. AE, CB, DC, MC, V. Valet gar. $30, rest. (Fifty Seven Fifty Seven), bar, 24-hr. rm svce, hrdrsr, boutiques, health club, free crib, concierge. *Note:* Opened in 1993 and built for $360 million, this is New York's tallest hotel at 52 stories, rising 682 ft. (211m) above the ground. The building, designed by I. M Pei, is clad in French limestone (the same limestone used in Pei's addition to the Louvre in Paris). With ceilings more than 10 ft. (3m) high, rms are elegantly comfortable, featuring bathtubs that fill in one min. and bedside switches that operate window blinds. Rates begin at $325 and run as high as $3,000 a night for the two-rm presidential suite, which occupies the entire top floor. **VE**

Sherry Netherland (Upper East Side), 781 Fifth Ave. (at 59th St.), NY 10022 (212/355-2800). 370 rms, A/C, color TV, in-rm movies. AE. Gar. $30, rest. (Harry Cipriani), bar, rm svce, nightclub, hrdrsr, crib $10. *Note:* Quiet and distinguished, with one of New York's best locations, facing Central Park and a stone's throw from the smart Fifth Ave. stores. The building is slightly kitsch Gothic Revival, but the rms and suites are very elegant, some w. balconies or terraces. Many clients rent by the year. Exceptionally polished svce; renowned Italian rest. The only grand hotel in New York that accepts only one charge card. **VE**

Essex House Nikko (midtown), 160 Central Park South, NY 10019 (212/247-0300; toll free 800/645-5687). 591 rms, A/C, color TV, in-rm movies. AE, CB, DC, MC, V. Valet gar. $30, health club, business center, three rests. (including Les Célébrités), bar, 24-hr. rm svce, concierge. *Note:* Elegant 40-story art deco hotel overlooking Central Park. Underwent a $100-million renovation in 1993 to enhance its image as the North

American flagship of Nikko hotels, a chain that has earned a reputation for svce excellence worldwide. Large, beautifully appointed rms, many w. spectacular views of Central Park. Excellent French rest. Gracious, diligent svce. Business and Japanese clientele. **VE**

♔♔♔ **Drake Swissôtel** (midtown), 440 Park Ave. (at E. 56th St.), NY 10022 (212/421-0900; toll free 800/637-9477). 640 rms, A/C, color TV, in-rm movies. AE, CB, DC, MC, V. Valet gar. $24, two rests. (including Lafayette), bar, 24-hr. rm svce, nightclub, free crib, concierge. *Note:* Since it was bought by Swiss interests this venerable, and indeed somewhat decrepit, pile has been restored to its former luster by a multi-million-dollar facelift. Its spacious peach-and-ivory rms w. marble bathrooms and refrigerators, exemplary svce, and excellent rest. (Lafayette) supervised by the great French chef Louis Outhier, combine to make it one of the best places to stay on Park Ave. Free morning limo to Wall St. Draws many business travelers from Europe. **VE**

♔♔♔ **Helmsley Palace Hotel** (midtown), 455 Madison Ave. (at E. 49th St.), NY 10022 (212/888-7000; toll free 800/221-4982). 1,050 rms, A/C, color TV, in-rm movies. AE, CB, DC, MC, V. Gar. $46, two rests. (including the Trianon), two bars, 24-hr. rm svce, nightclub, hrdrsr, boutiques, free crib, concierge. *Note:* Extravagant grand hotel deluxe, built at a cost of $100 million. The attempt to integrate the modern 51-story glass tower w. an 1882 Renaissance Revival house, the Villard Mansion, doesn't come off. The opulence is often strident but the comfort and rm svce are incomparable. Opposite St. Patrick's Cathedral. One triplex suite rents for $2,500 a night plus taxes and svce. Very successful since its 1980 opening. **VE**

♔♔♔ **Helmsley Park Lane** (midtown), 36 Central Park South, NY 10019 (212/371-4000; toll free 800/221-4982). 640 rms, A/C, color TV, in-rm movies. AE, CB, DC, MC, V. Gar. $42, rest., bar, 24-hr. rm svce, nightclub, hrdrsr, free crib. *Note:* 46 floors of glass and steel overlooking Central Park. Huge, very comfortable rms w. refrigerators, the best w. park views. Big business clientele. Rm svce on the surly side. The Park Room is a so-so rest. Multilingual help. **VE**

♔♔♔ **Hilton and Towers at Rockefeller Center** (midtown), 1335 Ave. of the Americas (at W. 54th St.), NY 10019 (212/586-7000; toll free, see Hilton). 2,117 rms, A/C, color TV, in-rm movies. AE, CB, DC, MC, V. Valet gar. $30, health club, rest. (Grill 53), coffee shop, three bars, 24-hr. rm svce, disco, hrdrsr, free crib. *Note:* Huge 46-floor tourist mill. Modern, functional rms, some very small. Public areas and rests. crowded and noisy. Svce often overburdened. The Hilton and Towers has been revamped to the tune of $80 million w. a three-level convention area connected to the hotel by a glass-enclosed bridge. Excellent location. Draws American and Japanese business travelers. Interesting wknd discounts. VIP suites in the Executive Tower from the 39th to the 44th floor. Business center. The city's largest hotel. **VE**

♔♔♔ **Marriott Marquis** (midtown), 1535 Broadway (at W. 44th St.), NY 10036 (212/398-1900; toll free, see Marriott). 2,022 rms, color TV, in-rm movies. AE, CB, DC, MC, V. Valet gar. $28, health club, sauna, three rests. (including The View revolving rest. on the top floor), coffee shop, four bars, 24-hr. rm svce, theater, boutiques, concierge. *Note:* One of the most eye-catching hotels in New York: an ultramodern 52-story high-rise by architect John Portman. The glass-walled lobby is 46 floors high, w. fountains, indoor grdns, and glass-walled elevators. Exceptionally spacious, comfortable rms, w. unobstructed views of Manhattan from the top two floors. Impersonal but efficient svce. As in all Marriotts, the rests, are mediocre. Overlooks Times Sq. and the theater district. Two VIP floors. Well-equipped business center. **VE**

♔♔♔ **Millenium Hotel** (Lower Manhattan), 55 Church St., NY 10007 (212/693-2001; toll free 800/835-2220). 561 rms, A/C, color TV, in-rm movies. AE, DC, MC, V. Valet gar. $30, pool, health club, sauna, two rests., bar, 24-hr. rm svce, concierge. *Note:* A brand new, sleek, 58-story black glass tower located in the heart of Wall Street. Geared primarily to business travelers, the rms are classy and spacious w. two-line phones, voice mail, and fax and computer connections. Spectacular views of Manhattan and the harbor. Ultraprofessional svce. Free limo uptown. Comprehensive business center. **VE**

♀♀♀ **The Pierre** (Upper East Side), 2 E. 61st St. (at Fifth Ave.), NY
🛏🛏🛏 10021 (212/838-8000; toll free, see Four Seasons). 206 rms, A/C, color TV, in-rm movies. AE, CB, DC, MC, V. Gar. $28, rest. (Café Pierre), bar, rm svce, nightclub, hrdrsr, boutiques, free crib, concierge. *Note:* The Pierre long enjoyed a reputation as New York's best hotel, but doesn't deserve it today. Plush but depressing interior decoration; svce sometimes defective. Wonderfully situated opposite Central Park. So-so rest. Thronged w. aristocratic and/or wealthy Europeans. Along w. the Stanhope, one of New York's most expensive hotels. **VE**

♀♀♀ **New York Renaissance** (formerly the Ramada; midtown), 2
🛏🛏🛏 Times Sq., NY 10036 (212/765-7676). 305 rms, A/C, color TV, in-rm movies, VCR. AE, CB, DC, MC, V. Valet parking $28, health club, business center, rest., two bars, 24-hr. rm svce, boutiques, concierge. *Note:* A brand-new sleek black 25-story tower constructed at the epicenter of neon glitter on Times Sq. Spectacular exterior glass elevators. Huge, elegant rms w. fax machines and minibars. Special svces include a butler and valet on each floor. Flawless, personalized svce. Corporate clientele. In the heart of the theater district. **VE**

♀♀♀ **Rihga Royal Hotel** (midtown), 151 W. 54th St. (at Seventh
🛏🛏🛏 Ave.), NY 10019 (212/307-5000; toll free 800/937-5454). 500 suites, A/C, color TV, in-rm movies. AE, CB, DC, MC, V. Gar. $25, pool, health club, rest. (Halcyon), bar, 24-hr. rm svce, concierge. *Note:* The 54-story Rihga Royal opened in May 1990 in the heart of the new West Side. Every rm is a one- or two-bedroom luxury suite w. contemporary furnishings and marble bath. Each suite offers three phones (two lines each), a refrigerator and icemaker, two TVs, a VCR, and computer/fax outlets. Flawless, polished svce. Very complete amenities. Big business clientele. **VE**

♀♀♀ **The Royalton** (midtown), 44 W. 44th St. (at Ave. of the
🛏🛏🛏 Americas), NY 10036 (212/869-4400). 157 rms, A/C, color TV, in-rm movies. AE, CB, DC, MC, V. Valet gar. $26, rest. (44), bar, 24-hr. rm svce, concierge. *Note:* A 90-year-old Neo-Georgian limestone building turned into a haven for well-traveled sophisticates by superstar of French design Philippe Starck. Reopened in October 1988 after 18 months and more than $40-million renovation program. Spacious suitelike rms w. minimalist decor in beige shades, startling contemporary furniture and stainless-steel bathrooms (some rms w. working fireplaces). Spectacular columned lobby that stretches from W. 43rd to W. 44th Sts. Faultless svce. The 44 Restaurant is notable. **VE**

♀♀♀ **The Stanhope** (Upper East Side), 995 Fifth Ave. (at 81st St.),
🛏🛏🛏 NY 10028 (212/288-5800; toll free, see Preferred). 132 rms (of which 106 are suites), A/C, color TV, in-rm movies. AE, CB, DC, MC, V. No private parking; rest. (Stanhope Dining Room), bar, rm svce, nightclub, free crib, concierge. *Note:* On elegant Fifth Ave. opposite the Metropolitan Museum of Art, this small, intimate, ultra-luxurious hotel was elegantly restored in the tradition of the grand hotels of Europe in 1986 at a cost of $26 million. Its discreet, refined decorative scheme weds Louis XVI furniture, Baccarat crystal chandeliers, impressionist paintings, cream-colored leather and silk. Free Chanel toiletries in every bathroom. Extremely polished svce. A sidewalk café fronting the hotel serves drinks and light meals during warm months. The rest. is of the highest order, but the prices are even higher than that. Among the most expensive hotels in town, where single rooms start at $275 a night and the most lavish suite reaches $4,000 a night. **VE**

♀♀♀ **United Nations Plaza–Park Hyatt** (midtown), 1 U.N. Plaza
🛏🛏🛏 (at E. 44th St.), NY 10017 (212/355-3400; toll free, see Hyatt). 444 rms, A/C, color TV, in-rm movies. AE, CB, DC, MC, V. Valet gar. $26, pool, health club, sauna, tennis court, rest. (Ambassador Grill), bar, rm

svce, free crib. *Note:* The hotel begins on the 28th floor of an ultramodern 40-story glass tower by architect Kevin Roche. Pool and tennis court in the sky. Comfortable, inviting rms w. refrigerators, all w. superb view of New York. Efficient svce. Overlooks the East River and the U.N. building. Good French rest. Clientele of diplomats and big-business travelers; free morning Wall St. limo. A favorite w. those in-the-know. **VE**

Vista International New York (Lower Manhattan), 3 World Trade Center, NY 10048 (212/938-9100; toll free, see Hilton). 820 rms, A/C, color TV, in-rm movies. AE, CB, DC, MC, V. Gar. $24, pool, health club, sauna, tennis court, squash, two rests. (including the American Harvest), two bars, rm svce, concierge. *Note:* The only hotel of quality in the Wall St. district. Ultramodern and comfortable; very inviting rms w. minibars, some w. Statue of Liberty views. Comprehensive physical-fitness facilities. Business clientele. Good rest. specializing in modern American cuisine (The American Harvest). The area is not really suitable for tourists. **VE**

Dorset (midtown), 30 W. 54th St., NY 10019 (212/247-7300; toll free 800/227-2348). 210 rms, A/C, color TV, in-rm movies. AE, CB, DC, MC, V. Gar. $22, rest., coffee shop, bar, rm svce, free crib. *Note:* Discreet, charming, polished small hotel a stone's throw from the Museum of Modern Art and the smart Fifth Ave. stores. Inviting, comfortable rms, the best overlooking the interior court. Attentive service. Coffee shop very popular w. TV and show-business people at lunchtime. A fine place. **E–VE**

The Kimberly (midtown), 145 E. 50th St., NY 10022 (212/755-0400; toll free 800/683-0400). 192 suites, A/C, color TV, in-rm movies. AE, DC, MC, V. Pay parking available, rest. (Paradis Barcelona), rm svce, 24-hr. concierge. *Note:* New and luxurious suite hotel in the heart of Manhattan's east side. The one- and two-bedroom suites feature French country-style furnishings, fully equipped kitchens, and marble baths. Good Spanish rest. Complimentary passes to adjoining health club and pool. Impeccable svce. Some standard and double rms in the annex. **E–VE**

Mayflower (Upper West Side), 15 Central Park West, NY 10023 (212/265-0060; toll free 800/223-4164). 577 rms, A/C, color TV. AE, CB, DC, MC, V. Pay parking available; rest. (The Conservatory), bar, rm svce, free crib. *Note:* The favorite place to stay for theater-goers, music lovers, and opera buffs; Lincoln Center is a few minutes' walk. Decor and furnishings completely renovated; spacious, comfortable rms w. refrigerators (ask for one overlooking Central Park). Cordial, efficient svce; pleasant but expensive rest. Interesting wknd discounts. Free shuttle to/from the Jacob K. Javits Convention Center. **E–VE**

Radisson Empire (Upper West Side), W. 63rd St. and Broadway, NY 10023 (212/265-7400; toll free, see Radisson). 405 rms, A/C, cable color TV. AE, CB, DC, MC, V. Parking $16, health club w. sauna, rest., coffee shop, bar, 24-hr. rm svce, free crib. *Note:* Pleasant, comfortable hotel a stone's throw from Lincoln Center. Recently underwent a major ($20-million) facelift. Very adequate rest. (Empire Grill). Efficient svce. A fine place; try to reserve well ahead. **E–VE**

Roosevelt (midtown), Madison Ave. at E. 45th St., NY 10017 (212/661-9600; toll free 800/223-1870). 1,070 rms, A/C, color TV, in-rm movies. AE, CB, DC, MC, V. Valet gar. $24, two rests. (including Crawdaddy's), two bars, rm svce, hrdrsr. *Note:* One of the best locations in the city, in the heart of the midtown business district, opposite Grand Central Terminal and three blocks from the airport limo for Kennedy and La Guardia airports. Massive, unattractive building, but renovated, comfortable interior. Good Créole rest. popular at lunchtime. Svce a little undependable. Business clientele. **E–VE**

Roger Smith Hotel (midtown), 501 Lexington Ave. (at E. 47th St.), NY 10017 (212/755-1400; toll free 800/445-0277). 183 rms, A/C, color TV. AE, CB, DC, MC, V. Public parking adjacent;

rest. (Nibbles), bar, free crib. *Note:* Older, elegant small hotel in the heart of midtown. Spacious, comfortable rms done in pastel shades, all w. refrigerators and some w. kitchenettes and fireplaces. Free Continental breakfast. Good svce; central location. Currently undergoing renovation. **E**

Wyndham (midtown), 42 W. 58th St., NY 10019 (212/753-3500). 189 rms, A/C, cable color TV. AE, CB, DC, MC, V. Parking lot adj. (fee), rest. (closed wknds), bar. *Note:* Charming, intimate hotel in the European manner, much frequented by literary and theatrical folk, with the "feel" of a venerable London club. Spacious, cozily comfortable rms and svce of the highest order (but no rm svce). One of the few remaining New York hotels w. elevator operators. Well located a block from Central Park and the smart stores on Fifth Ave. Make resv. well ahead. A fine place. **M–E**

Comfort Inn Murray Hill (midtown), 42 W. 35th St., NY 10001 (212/947-0200; toll free, see Choice). 118 rms, A/C, color TV, in-rm movies. AE, CB, DC, MC, V. No private parking; rest. (Myong Dong), bar, free crib. *Note:* Completely renovated at a cost of $4.5 million, this once run-down small hotel now offers you modern, functional rms. Svce undependable. Business clientele. Free Continental breakfast. Acceptable Korean rest. A couple of blocks from the Garment District and the Empire State Building. **M–E**

Days Inn New York (midtown), 440 W. 57th St., NY 10019 (212/581-8100; toll free, see Days Inn). 603 rms, A/C, color TV, in-rm movies. AE, CB, DC, MC, V. Gar. $7, open-air pool (in summer), rest., bar, rm svce. *Note:* The most attractive things about this reasonably modern motel (consisting of an 18- and an 11-floor tower), are its location near Lincoln Center and its rooftop pool in summer. Functionally comfortable; svce undependable. Caters to groups and conventions (special rates). **M–E**

Ramada Inn (midtown), 790 Eighth Ave. (at W. 49th St.), NY 10019 (212/581-7000; toll free, see Ramada Inns). 366 rms, A/C, color TV, in-rm movies. AE, CB, DC, MC, V. Gar. $7.75, pool, rest., bar, valet svce, free crib. *Note:* Typical convention and package-tour hotel. Rms quite large and functionally comfortable. Reception and svce undependable. Well located near the theater district. Rooftop swimming pool (open in summer). **M–E**

Edison (midtown), 228 W. 47th St., NY 10036 (212/840-5000; toll free 800/223-1900). 930 rms, A/C, color TV. AE, CB, DC, MC, V. Gar. $15, rest., coffee shop, two bars, free crib. *Note:* Massive, antiquated 50-year-old hotel; deplorable svce but functionally comfortable. Recently renovated. Clientele largely of groups and Europeans. Smack in the middle of the theater district. Cafeteria (Polish Tea Room) much frequented by theater people. **M–E**

Gorham (midtown), 136 W. 55th St., NY 10019 (212/245-1800; toll free 800/735-0710). 120 rms, A/C, color TV. AE, CB, DC, MC, V. Parking adj. $20; rest., bar, rm svce, free crib, concierge. *Note:* One of the best of New York's charming small hotels. Spacious, comfortable rms w. kitchenettes and refrigerators. Pleasing reception and svce. Good overall value. Ideal for families and budget travelers. **M–E**

Salisbury (midtown), 123 W. 57th St., NY 10019 (212/246-1300; toll free 800/223-0680). 320 rms, A/C, color TV. AE, CB, DC, MC, V. No private parking; rest. (Terrace Café), rm svce, free crib. *Note:* Opposite Carnegie Hall, this charming, scrupulously clean old hotel is run by the Calvary Baptist Church; hence no alcoholic beverages are served in rest. Vast, comfortable rms, most w. refrigerators; friendly reception and svce. Caters mostly to musicians and theater-goers. Good value. **M–E**

Chatwal Inn (Gramercy Park), 429 Park Ave. South (at E. 29th St.), NY 10016 (212/532-4860; toll free 800/826-4667). 113 rms, A/C, cable color TV. AE, CB, DC, MC, V. Parking $20, coffee shop. *Note:* Built in the early 1980s, this modern hotel off the beaten tourist path is one of New York's best buys. Its reasonable rates and proximity to the Garment District attract textile and clothing executives. Inviting, comfortable suites and rms; good svce; free Continental breakfast; good overall value. **M**

Wellington (midtown), W. 55th St. and Seventh Ave., NY 10019 (212/247-3900; toll free 800/652-1212). 800 rms, A/C, color TV. AE, CB, DC, MC, V. Gar. $19, rest., coffee shop, bar. *Note:* Slightly cramped rms, some w. kitchenettes, recently renovated. Very acceptable standard of comfort. Attracts musicians (Carnegie Hall is two blocks away) and groups. Good value overall. **M**

Wentworth (midtown), 59 W. 46th St., NY 10036 (212/719-2300; toll free 800/223-1900). 245 rms, A/C, cable color TV. AE, CB, DC, MC, V. No private parking; coffee shop, rm svce. *Note:* Near as it is to the Garment District, this is a favorite hotel for out-of-town buyers. Aging and functionally comfortable, it offers good value. Clean, renovated rms; efficient svce. **M**

The Franklin (Upper East Side), 164 E. 87th St., NY 10128 (212/369-1000; toll free 800/600-8787). 46 rms, A/C, color TV, in-rm movies. AE, MC, V. Free parking, complimentary continental breakfast, free crib. *Note:* Stylish hotel w. rms that are small (100 sq. ft./31 sq. m) but pleasing. **M**, but cheaper off-season.

Excelsior (Upper West Side), 45 W. 81st St., NY 10024 (212/362-9200; toll free 800/368-4575). 150 rms, A/C, color TV. AE, MC, V. Nearby parking, coffee shop, valet svce. *Note:* Older family-style hotel a block from Central Park and the Hayden Planetarium. Rms w. kitchenettes. Very acceptable comfort level. The rms on the uppermost floors have a fine view of the city. Pleasant and safe neighborhood; good value. **I–M**

Herald Square (midtown), 19 W. 31st St., NY 10001 (212/279-4017; toll free 800/727-1888). 114 rms, A/C, cable color TV. AE, MC, V. *Note:* Housed in the 1893 former home of *Life* magazine, this freshly spruced-up inn offers immaculate, comfortable quarters. Ideal for budget-minded visitors. Near the Empire State Building and Macy's. **I–M**

President Hotel (midtown), 234 W. 48th St., NY 10036 (212/246-8800; toll free 800/826-4667). 400 rms, A/C, cable color TV. AE, DC, MC, V. Pay parking available; rest., bar. *Note:* Clean budget hotel near the theater district. Rms a little confining but comfortable. Friendly staff. **I–M**

Washington Square Hotel (Greenwich Village), 103 Waverly Place, NY 10011 (212/777-9515; toll free 800/222-0418). 180 rms, A/C, color TV. MC, V. Pay parking available, coffee shop. *Note:* An old, informal hotel in the heart of historic Greenwich Village. Spotless, refurbished rms at very low rates. Many overseas guests. Good overall value. **I–M**

Malibu Studios Hotel (Upper West Side), 2688 Broadway, NY 10023 (212/222-2954; toll free 800/647-2227). 150 rms, A/C and TV in some rms. No credit cards. Street parking. *Note:* Rather spare hotel offering clean rms with private or shared baths at basement prices. Many European students bunk here. Reserve well in advance. **B–I**

Airport Accommodations

Holiday Inn JFK, 144–02 135th Ave., Jamaica (Queens), NY 11436 (718/659-0200; toll free, see Holiday Inns). 370 rms, A/C, color TV, in-rm movies. AE, CB, DC, MC, V. Free parking, pool, health club, sauna, rest. (Claudine's), bar, rm svce, nightclub, free crib. *Note:* New 12-story building; the first hotel built near JFK in 20 years. Comfort and facilities above the Holiday Inn average. Rms perfectly soundproofed, spacious, and well designed. Efficient svce. Free airport limo. Caters to groups and business travelers; ideal for a stopover between flights. **E–VE**

La Guardia Inn (formerly the Holiday Inn), 100–15 Ditmars Blvd., East Elmhurst (Queens), NY 11369 (718/898-1225). 224 rms, A/C, color TV, in-rm movies. AE, CB, DC, MC, V. Free parking, pool, rest., bar, rm svce, free crib. *Note:* Typical airport motel 3 min. from La Guardia. Completely renovated rms w. refrigerators. Airport limo. Svce so-so. **M–E**

YMCA/Youth Hostels

McBurney YMCA (midtown), 206 W. 24th St., NY 10011 (212/741-9226). 270 rms. Men only. Limited standard of comfort. Health club.

New York International Youth Hostel (Upper West Side), 891 Amsterdam Ave. (at W. 103rd St.), NY 10025 (212/932-2300). 480-bed youth hostel in a historic-landmark building. Freshly renovated. Outdoor grdns. Coffee shop.

Vanderbilt YMCA (midtown), 224 E. 47th St., NY 10017 (212/755-2410). 392 rms. Men, women, and families. Good facilities (pool, health club), coffee shop. The most comfortable and inviting YMCA in New York. Down the road from the U.N.

West Side YMCA (Upper West Side), 5 W. 63rd St., NY 10023 (212/787-4400). 525 rms. Men, a limited number of women. Pool, health club, coffee shop. A stone's throw from Lincoln Center.

RESTAURANTS

Personal Favorites (in order of preference)

♟♟♟♟ **Lutèce** (midtown), 249 E. 50th St. (752-2225). A/C. Lunch Tues–Fri, dinner Mon–Sat; closed Aug until Labor Day. AE, CB, DC, MC, V. J&T. *Specialties:* sweetbreads in white wine w. capers, scallops sautéed w. truffles, roast back of rabbit w. homemade noodles, filet of sturgeon w. Chambertin sauce and julienned celery root, filets de St. Pierre (John Dory) w. fresh mint, navarin of lobster w. Pernod, filet mignon in pastry shell, chicken w. tarragon, bitter-chocolate mousse, tarte tatin. Menu changes regularly. Very fine wine list, balanced and clear (there are 20,000 bottles in the cellar). *Note:* A shrine for French *grande cuisine;* for three decades Lutèce has earned the title of New York's best rest. Under the direction of André Soltner, from Alsace, the menu is progressively enriched and refined. Pretty winter garden on the ground floor; elegant little rms, recently renovated, upstairs. Flawless reception and svce. Resv. a must, many days or even weeks ahead. Former President Reagan's special favorite is the filet of salmon w. mustard. One of the country's 12 finest rests. *French.* **E** (lunch), **VE** (dinner).

♟♟♟♟ **Le Bernardin** (midtown), 155 W. 51st St. (489-1515). A/C. Lunch Mon–Fri, dinner Mon–Sat; closed hols. AE, CB, DC, MC, V. J&T. *Specialties:* lobster vichyssoise, monkfish w. cabbage; cod salad w. juniper, basil, and truffle oil; scallop salad w. cream and juice of truffles; slice of salmon w. julienne of fennel; poached halibut w. warm herbed vinaigrette; filet of black bass in scallion-ginger nage; carpaccio of tuna. Menu changed regularly. Good wine list at reasonable prices. *Note:* This remarkable seafood rest., housed in the dazzling Equitable Center, has established itself since 1986 in a place of honor on the New York gastronomic scene. The credit goes to its owner, Gilbert Le Coze, whose former rest. in Paris rated a coveted two stars from Michelin, and its talented chef Eric Ripert. The exceptional quality of the seafood, minimally cooked, and a particular talent for refined simplicity explain its unprecedented popularity (it almost requires a miracle to get a dinner resv.). Elegant London club interior w. Danish teak woodwork, bluish-gray tones, and rather hackneyed maritime paintings. Maguy Le Coze, Gilbert's sister, has taken over the restaurant since his unfortunate death in July 1994. Resv. absolutely essential. One of the best rests. in the country. *Seafood.* **E** (lunch, prix fixe), **VE** (dinner, prix fixe).

♟♟♟ **Bouley** (Tribeca), 165 Duane St. at Hudson St. (608-3852). A/C. Lunch Mon–Fri, dinner Mon–Sat; closed hols. AE, DC, MC, V. J&T. *Specialties:* duck liver with roasted onions and balsamic vinegar, sea scallops w. verjuice sauce and purée of celery root, roast squab w. sweet onions and red cabbage, langoustine tails w. red Sancerre sauce, roast chicken w. cèpes, pot-au-feu of pheasant w. foie gras, fig millefeuille w. coconut ice cream.

Menu changes regularly. Long list of French wines at discouraging prices. *Note:* Young American chef David Bouley, who studied in Switzerland and France with such grand masters as Bocuse, Girardet, and Vergé, cooks with wonderful delicacy and balance, using the finest in local produce. Decorated like a flower-filled inn in Provence. The svce is a trifle offhand; patrons are a Wall St. crowd at lunch and fashionable New York at dinner. Resv. a must. A memorable place. *French.* **E–VE**

🍷🍷🍷 **Remi** (midtown), 145 W. 53rd St. (581-4242). A/C. Lunch Mon–Fri, dinner nightly, closed hols. AE, CB, DC, MC, V. *Specialties:* prosciutto w. truffle oil, ravioli w. tuna and ginger in light tomato sauce, sautéed scallops w. white beans, quail wrapped in bacon, fegato Veneziana, lemon-raspberry soufflé. Remarkable wine list and the largest grappa selection in America (45). *Note:* This reincarnation of the old Upper East Side Little Remi features a stunning, huge space w. a larger-than-life pastel fantasy mural of Venice. And for a very good reason: Chef co-owner Francesco Antonucci is Venetian, and the refined, zesty fare pays homage to his hometown. The prices are assertive but not cutthroat like many other upscale Italian rests. Polished, attentive svce. Big business clientele. Resv. should be made far ahead. *Italian.* **E**

🍷🍷🍷 **JoJo** (Upper East Side), 160 E. 64th St. (223-5656). A/C. Lunch Mon–Fri, dinner Mon–Sat. AE, CB, DC, MC, V. *Specialties:* shrimp in spiced carrot juice, ravioli of rabbit w. vegetables and tomato oil, duck breast w. truffle juice, warm chocolate cake w. vanilla ice cream. Fine French regional wine list fairly priced. *Note:* Elected "Restaurant of the Year 1991" by *Esquire* magazine, this graceless two-story eatery offers upscale bistro fare at bargain prices, given the quality of the food and the soaring imagination of the gallic chef, Jean-Georges (JoJo) Vongerichten. Two minuses: the noisy atmosphere and the elbow-to-elbow setting. Somewhat overburdened svce. Resv. a must, far ahead. The hottest spot in town. *French.* **M**

🍷🍷🍷 **Gotham Bar and Grill** (Greenwich Village), 12 E. 12th St., nr. Fifth Ave. (620-4020). A/C. Lunch Mon–Fri, dinner nightly; closed hols. AE, CB, DC, MC, V. J&T. *Specialties:* grilled squab w. roasted garlic, pancetta, and ratatouille; smoked duck breast w. apricot-cherry chutney; grilled saddle of rabbit; pumpkin tart. The menu changes seasonally. Good wine list at fair prices. *Note:* Bright and young French-trained chef Alfred Portale offers a vibrant and innovative cuisine of clear Mediterranean inspiration. Spacious and strikingly designed multilevel dining rm w. a pink marble bar. Attentive but not obtrusive svce. One of the best places in town for true food lovers. Resv. highly advised. *American.* **E**

🔆🍷 **Oyster Bar and Restaurant** (midtown), in Grand Central Terminal at E. 42nd St. and Vanderbilt Ave. (490-6650). A/C. Lunch/dinner Mon–Fri; closed hols. AE, CB, DC, MC, V. Jkt. *Specialties:* every kind of oyster and clam on the half shell, broiled fish and shellfish, clam chowder, bouillabaisse, Florida stone crab (in season), pan-roasted shellfish, cheesecake. Good list of California wines. *Note:* A vast, tile cavern on the lower level of Grand Central Terminal. Usually crowded and noisy, particularly at lunch, but still one of the best selections of fish and shellfish in the entire country, at prices that are reasonable given the quality of the food. Svce sometimes distracted. Resv. advised (ask for a table in the cozy "Saloon"). A New York landmark since 1913. *Seafood.* **M**

🔆🍷 **Palm** (midtown), 837 Second Ave. at E. 45th St. (687-2953). A/C. Lunch Mon–Fri, dinner Mon–Sat (until midnight); closed hols. AE, CB, DC, MC, V. Jkt. *Specialties:* shrimp sautéed w. herbs, clams Posillipo, steak tartare, steak, prime cuts, lamb chops, Maine lobster, cheesecake. *Note:* A living legend for six decades among those who like solid food. Superb steaks, enormous lobsters, and some passable Italian dishes. The portions are gargantuan. The caricatures on the walls are amusing, but the place is very noisy, bustling, and resolutely macho. Svce efficient but brusque. The annex across the avenue (Palm Too) is less picturesque, but the meat is of the same high quality. Resv. accepted for lunch only. *Steak/Seafood.* **M–E**

🍸🍸 **Hatsuhana** (midtown), 17 E. 48th St. (355-3345). A/C.
Lunch Mon–Fri, dinner Mon–Sat; closed hols. AE, CB, DC,
MC, V. Jkt. *Specialties:* natto, squid w. sea urchin roe, sushi, chawan mushi,
sashimi, tempura. *Note:* Purists maintain that here you'll find the widest choice of
the best sushi in all New York. Modern, comfortably furnished setting w. dining
rms on two levels, and sushi bars behind which the artist-chefs, past masters in
the preparation and presentation of their 35 varieties of raw fish, go about their
business. Generally crowded, especially at lunch. Svce overburdened. Mostly
Japanese clientele; resv. advised. Also at 237 Park Ave. (661-3400). *Japanese.*
M–E

🍸🍸 **Rosa Mexicano** (midtown), 1063 First Ave. at E. 58th St.
(753-7407). A/C. Dinner only, nightly (until midnight). AE,
CB, DC, MC, V. *Specialties:* taquitos, guacamole, carnitas, chiles en mogada,
snapper w. coriander, shell steak w. sautéed chilis poblanos, budín azteca. Excellent margaritas. *Note:* A worthy representative of Mexico, this likeable, fashionable rest. will give you, as it were, a foretaste of exotic vacations. The food is
completely authentic, the atmosphere congenial, the bar inviting though
crowded, and the rustic decor executed in a beautiful shade of pink. Efficient,
smiling svce. Resv. a must. A fine place. *Mexican.* **M**

🍸 **Carmine's** (Upper West Side), 2450 Broadway at 91st St.
(362-2200). A/C. Lunch Sun, dinner nightly; closed Thanks-
giving, Dec 25. AE. *Specialties:* fried calamari, antipasto salad, linguine w. clam
sauce, veal Milanese. Skimpy wine list, mediocre desserts. *Note:* Retro-chic, big,
loud "trattoria" serving old-time southern Italian fare in gargantuan portions
and family-style atmosphere. Friendly waiters, but slow kitchen. Perpetually
overcrowded: The rest. serves 400 people a night. The wait is lengthy, up to 45
min. (no resv. accepted for parties smaller than six). *Italian/American.* **M**

☀🍸 **Frank's** (Greenwich Village), 431 W. 14th St. (243-1349).
A/C. Lunch Mon–Fri, dinner Mon–Sat. AE, CB, DC, MC,
V. *Specialties:* tagliarini puttanesca (pasta w. capers, olives, and anchovies), tripe
Florentine, rack of lamb, steak, roast beef, veal cutlets, broiled kidney. *Note:* A
stone's throw from Gansevoort Market, headquarters of the city's wholesale
meat business, this stronghold of meat eating makes a point of opening its doors
at 2am to feed breakfast to the neighborhood butchers. Sturdy portions, and
prime meat as you'd expect, all at very attractive prices. The long mahogany bar,
lazy ceiling fans, and sawdusted floor contribute to a friendly, unpretentious setting. Efficient svce. A Manhattan landmark since 1912. *Steak.* **I–M**

Other Restaurants (from top bracket to budget)

🍸🍸🍸 **Lespinasse** (midtown), in the St. Regis Sheraton (see "Accommodations" above) (339-6719). A/C. Lunch/dinner daily.
AE, CB, DC, MC, V. J&T. *Specialties:* sautéed foie gras w. lentil salad and quince,
ragoût of squab w. rice-flour crêpe, roast rack of lamb w. carrot emulsion,
steamed black bass w. kaffir lime; baked apple. Strong wine list but highly priced.
Note: Old-world gold-leafed dining room w. soaring ceilings and classical murals
in the newly renovated St. Regis Hotel. Ethereal, eclectic, and visually striking
cuisine by master chef Gray Kunz, trained in Switzerland (at the world-famous
Girardet) and in Asia. Slightly stuffy atmosphere. Svce polished and prompt.
Resv. should be made no less than two or three days ahead. *Continental.* **E**
(lunch), **VE** (dinner).

🍸🍸 **An American Place** (midtown), 2 Park Ave. at E. 32nd St.
(684-2122). A/C. Lunch Mon–Fri, dinner Mon–Sat; closed
hols. AE, CB, DC, MC, V. J&T. *Specialties:* grilled-vegetable terrine w. baked
goat cheese, terrine of smoked fish w. three caviars, sautéed lobster w. chives,
charred Black Angus steak marinated in beer w. caramelized onions, roast salmon in cider vinegar, broiled chicken w. fettuccine and wild mushrooms, double
chocolate pudding, warm banana betty. Very fine list of American wines at reasonable prices. The menu changes regularly. *Note:* Modern American cuisine ad-

mirable in its elegance and simplicity. Chef Larry Forgione, a virtuoso of short cooking times and light sauces, uses American products exclusively (even the caviar). Fashionable art deco interior; svce usually faultless. Resv. a must. *American.* **E–VE**

    Aureole (Upper East Side), 34 E. 61st St. (319-1660). A/C. Lunch Mon–Fri, dinner Mon–Sat; closed hols. AE, CB, DC, MC, V. Jkt. *Specialties:* sea-scallop "sandwich," butternut squash soup w. cheese ravioli, grilled lobster and scallops w. lobster consommé in artichoke bulb, seared quail w. foie gras polenta and chanterelles, filet mignon of Savoyarde w. stuffed morels, timbale of praline mousse. Good wine list, short but decently priced. *Note:* After several years of intensive experience at the well-known River Café, distinguished chef Charles Palmer has made this elegant spot one of Manhattan's most fashionable addresses. The cuisine is contemporary, sophisticated, and decorative; the two-level setting is luminously decorated in shades of cream. Efficient, friendly svce. Resv. a must, but not always honored. *American.* **E–VE**

    Chanterelle (Tribeca), 2 Harrison St. at Hudson St. (966-6960). A/C. Lunch/dinner, Tues–Sat; closed hols. and July 1–15. AE, DC, MC, V. J&T. *Specialties:* grilled seafood sausage, crabmeat ravioli, rack of lamb w. thyme and mustard, Muscovy duck w. sherry vinegar and wild mushrooms, rhubarb tart w. scallops and shad roe, braised rabbit w. cream-and-herb sauce, red snapper w. red-wine butter sauce, poached pears in sauternes sabayon, orange-flavored chocolate torte. *Note:* In 1989 this rest., worthy of three stars in any French gastronomic guidebook, moved from its original cramped quarters in Soho to a setting scarcely larger (16 tables) but agreeably renovated on the ground floor of the old Mercantile Exchange in the heart of Tribeca. Chef David Waltuck continues to offer ambitious, inspired food, the quintessence of French nouvelle cuisine American style. Efficient but rather casual svce. You'll need to make your resv. far in advance; a splendid place with prices to match. *French.* **E–VE**

    Daniel (Upper East Side), 20 E. 76th St. (288-0033). A/C. Lunch/dinner Mon–Sat; closed hols. AE, DC, MC, V. Jkt. *Specialties:* poached foie gras w. morels and cranberry beans; Vidalia onion stuffed w. Swiss chard; herb ravioli w. tomato coulis; swordfish wrapped in eggplant; crayfish-and-quail casserole w. wild mushrooms, asparagus, and chervil; poached cod w. pesto broth; warm chocolate soufflé w. pistachio ice cream. *Note:* A premier chef of Le Cirque fame, Daniel Boulud opened this rest. w. a clientele that instantaneously bombarded the telephone lines, vying for resv. Boulud is heralded for his style and finesse, which is presented now in this casual and comfortable setting. Ultra-professional svce. Resv. a must. Of course, prices reflect quality, and quality is of the highest degree. *French.* **E** (lunch), **VE** (dinner)

    Les Célébrités (midtown), in the Essex House (see "Accommodations," above) (484-5113). A/C. Dinner only, Tues–Sat; closed hols. AE, DC, MC, V. J&T. *Specialties:* caramel pasta w. truffled cream; shrimp w. saffron risotto; wild-mushroom gnocchi glazed w. chicken jus; alicuit of duck legs and magret; smoked salmon and cod in potato cake; squab w. garlic confit, rosemary-roasted artichokes, and truffled polenta; lavish but mediocre desserts. Good wine list w. some acceptably priced bottles. *Note:* A pinnacle of fine dining. If the Lalique and gold leaf in the 56-seat dining room that cost $5 million to renovate don't capture your attention, then the dishes, just as ornate and relatively comparable in price, will. Chef Christian Delouvier gives everything that comes out of the kitchen his mark of precision and creativity. Resv. a must. *French.* **E–VE**

    San Domenico (midtown), 240 Central Park S. (265-5959). A/C. Lunch Mon–Fri, dinner Mon–Sat; closed hols. AE, CB, DC, MC, V. J&T. *Specialties:* frog legs in herb broth; agnolotti stuffed w. duck liver; risotto w. butter, parmigiano, and beef glaze; lobster w. cannellini beans and rosemary; roast squab w. soft polenta; great desserts. The menu changes regularly. Exquisite choice of wines at prices to match. *Note:* One of the finest examples of *nuova cucina* in the U.S. Owner Tony May painstakingly searches out the best of elements that go into Theo Shoenegger's creations. The dishes harbor a complexity of tastes in presentations of simple design. Listed as having one of the five best dinners in America by *Esquire* magazine. Resv. a must. *Italian.* **E**

♛♛♛ **Shun Lee Palace** (midtown), 155 E. 55th St. (371-8844). A/C. Lunch/dinner daily; closed Thanksgiving. AE, CB, DC, MC, V. Jkt. *Specialties:* hot-and-sour soup, Szechuan lobster, smoked duckling w. scallion pancakes, crispy whole sea bass w. Hunan sauce, frog legs w. broccoli, jellyfish w. hot mustard, carp w. ginger and shallots. So-so desserts. *Note:* Purists might find cause for regret in the slight over-Americanization of Michael Tong's cuisine in this excellent Chinese rest., but the result is still delectable. There are Szechuan, Hunan, and Mandarin dishes, more elaborate at dinner than at lunch. Elegant, intimate Far Eastern setting; discreet but efficient svce. *Chinese.* **E**

♛♛♛ **Mitsukoshi** (midtown), 461 Park Ave. at E. 57th St. (935-6444). A/C. Lunch/dinner Mon–Fri; closed hols. AE, CB, DC, MC, V. Jkt. *Specialties:* sushi, sashimi, sukiyaki, shabu-shabu, tempura, beef negimaki, broiled fish, kaiseki (formal Japanese dinner of seven or nine courses), ginger ice cream. *Note:* Of the many Japanese rests. in Manhattan, this offers the greatest luxury and refinement. For lovers of raw fish there is an immense choice of sushi; the prices are also on the raw side. You may eat either at a Western-style table or in the quieter, more elegant tatami rms. Service w. a smile from kimono'd waitresses—unfortunately, a little hectic during the lunch-hour rush. Much favored by New York's Japanese business community; resv. advised. *Japanese.* **M–E**

☼♛♛♛ **River Café**, 1 Water St., Brooklyn (718/522-5200). A/C. Lunch/dinner daily, brunch Sun. AE, CB, DC, MC, V. Jkt./ J&T. *Specialties:* sautéed oysters w. endives and artichokes, snails in puff pastry, Black Angus steak w. bourbon sauce, broiled pheasant w. risotto of wild mushrooms, lamb cutlets w. charlotte of eggplant, braised sea bass w. morel mushrooms and tomatoes, mignon of veal w. pears, chocolate terrine, raspberry cheesecake. Exceptional wine list, particularly the California section. Menu changes regularly. *Note:* By day, and even more by night, one of the most fabulous sights New York has to offer. From a charming barge moored below the Brooklyn Bridge, you can see at a glance the distant Statue of Liberty and the skyscrapers of dwntwn Manhattan. The rest. serves a sophisticated, contemporary American cuisine using only U.S. raw materials, including the caviar and the olive oil. Ultra-professional svce; resv. essential many days ahead. Ask for a table near the bay window or, in summer, on the terrace. A must for tourists, but also draws many bankers from nearby Wall St. at lunchtime. *American.* **M** (lunch), **E** (dinner).

♛♛ **Vong** (midtown), 200 E. 54th St. (486-9592). A/C. Lunch Mon–Fri, dinner Mon–Sat; closed hols. AE, DC, MC, V. *Specialties:* shrimp sate w. cucumber-and-peanut relish, sautéed foie gras w. ginger and mango, lobster-and-turnip salad w. honey-ginger vinaigrette, raw tuna and vegetables wrapped in rice paper, grilled beef in ginger broth, spiced codfish w. curried artichoke, soft-center chocolate cake. Good selection of beers. *Note:* Jean-Georges Vongerichten of JoJo (see above) showcases his unique talent of perfectly uniting French and Thai cuisine in a manner that astounds taste buds. The decor is seductively Asian—from the curving pearwood walls to the collage of Thai money, train tickets, and newspaper clippings, to the Oriental tunics worn by the servers. Svce is helpful and well-versed. Resv. a must. *Thai/French.* **M–E**

♛♛ **Fu's** (Upper East Side), 1395 Second Ave., between 72nd and 73rd Sts. (517-9670). A/C. Lunch/dinner daily (until midnight), brunch Sat–Sun. AE, CB, MC, V. *Specialties:* fried half-moon dumplings, honey baby spareribs, soft-shell crab w. black-bean sauce, crispy fried sea bass, Peking duck. *Note:* Unlike the clattering, neon-and-Formica eating places in Chinatown, this is an elegant, accommodating Chinese rest. where the setting is matched by light and attractive food from the major regional cuisines. Svce friendly and helpful. A fine place. Resv. advised, considering its success. *Chinese.* **M–E**

🍸 **Manhattan Ocean Club** (midtown), 57 W. 58th St. (371-7777). A/C. Lunch Mon–Fri, dinner nightly; closed Thanksgiving, Dec 25. AE, CB, DC, MC, V. Jkt. *Specialties:* tuna w. latke potatoes and salsa verde; baked oysters w. morel cream; artichoke w. club-smoked salmon and chervil; grilled swordfish w. curry, cream of lentils, and crisp onions; tuna seared w. grapefruit; 2½- and 4-lb. (1.1–1.8kg) lobsters; chocolate "bag" w. white chocolate mousse and raspberry sauce. Well-thought-out wine list at reasonable prices. *Note:* With Picasso ceramics on the walls, Mediterranean-style pillars, diffused lighting, and a pastel color scheme, this rest. will make you dream of travel. Huge selection of absolutely fresh, beautifully prepared fish and seafood. Elegant atmosphere, polished svce. Resv. recommended; a fashionable spot. *Seafood.* **M–E**

🍸 **Arizona 206** (Upper East Side), 206 E. 60th St. (838-0440). A/C. Lunch Mon–Sat, dinner nightly; closed Dec. 25 and Jan 1. *Specialties:* black bean terrine w. yellow pear tomatoes, goat cheese, and chorizo; skate w. corn-mushroom salsa and caper berries; grilled salmon w. red chili syrup; charred venison loin w. picadillo huckleberries and caramelized parsnip; cajeta-banana sundae. Well-chosen American wines. *Note:* Combining Southwestern flavors w. an urban sophistication, chef David Walzog, who got his training in Southwestern cuisine from Mark Miller at the Red Sage in Washington, D.C., tempts the palate w. creatively strewn combinations of flavors and textures. Southwestern decor seems a bit overbearing. But annoyance fades once the food is on the table. Resv. highly advised. If you don't get in, you can go to the additional cheaper café serving American-style tapas that are made in the same kitchen. *American.* **M–E**

☀🍸 **Smith & Wollensky** (midtown), 201 E. 49th St. at Third Ave. (753-1530). A/C. Lunch Mon–Fri, dinner nightly; closed Jan 1 and Dec 25. AE, CB, DC, MC, V. Jkt. *Specialties:* crabmeat cocktail, 16-oz. (455g) steak, T-bone, filet mignon au poivre, veal cutlet, 4- to 5-lb. (1.8–2.3kg) lobster, broiled fish of the day, chocolate-mousse cake. Exceptional wine list, one of the best in New York. *Note:* In a huge two-story turn-of-the-century building, this typical New York steakhouse serves man-sized portions of choice red meat to a following of devotees. Its wine list, especially the California cabernet sauvignons, is also praiseworthy. Warm, efficient svce; a fine place in spite of prices on the high side. Resv. recommended. *Steak/seafood.* **M–E**

🍸 **Tribeca Grill** (Tribeca), 375 Greenwich St. at Franklin St. (941-3900). A/C. Lunch Mon–Fri, dinner nightly, brunch Sun. AE, DC, MC, V. *Specialties:* lobster consommé w. favas and scallops, tomato porridge w. sausage bread, squab w. endive and lentils vinaigrette, smoked barbecued duck w. bok choy, calves' liver steak on onion marmalade, catch of the day, glazed lemon tart on poppyseed crust. Menu changes regularly. Excellent house wines. *Note:* An upbeat celebrity-owned rest. Besides the managing partner, Drew Nieporent, proprietor of the nearby three-star rest. Montrachet, the other investors are Robert De Niro, Bill Murray, Christopher Walken, Sean Penn, and Mikhail Baryshnikov. This old warehouse w. exposed brick walls and brightly painted heating pipes offers good American bistro fare in a comfortable space. Generally overcrowded and noisy. The place to see and be seen. Resv. a must. *American.* **M–E**

🍸 **Le Chantilly** (midtown), 106 E. 57th St. (751-2931). A/C. Lunch Mon–Sat, dinner nightly; closed hols. AE, DC, MC, V. *Specialties:* crab ravioli w. lemongrass-and-kaffir lime broth; quail risotto; al dente fettuccine w. sweet peas, chervil, and smoked salmon; seared red snapper w. compote of tomato and chives; minced fresh lobster w. fried leeks; rabbit w. a terrarium of fennel, rosemary, marjoram, and thyme; blackberry tart; good sorbets. Decent list of pricey wines. *Note:* An established French rest. that has changed w. the times. From the deft hand of American chef David Ruggerio come some spruced-up traditional dishes as well as some great innovative ones. Soft lighting w. enough comfortable space make this a romantic setting. Svce is ultra-professional. Resv. suggested. *French.* **M–E**

� **Chin Chin** (midtown), 216 E. 49th St. (888-4555). A/C. Lunch Mon–Fri, dinner nightly. AE, DC, MC, V. Jkt. *Specialties:* velvet corn soup, steamed pork dumplings w. fresh ginger, tea-smoked duck, Grand Marnier prawns, clams w. black-bean sauce, lobster Cantonese, crispy sea bass w. spicy sauce, Szechuan prawns, homemade fresh fruit sherbets. *Note:* Named for its proprietors Jimmy and Wally Chin, this rest. also styles itself "Restaurant chinois," bearing witness to the Western influence evident in its kitchen. Traditional Chinese dishes w. a dash of nouvelle cuisine. Elegant modern Oriental setting (especially the downstairs rm w. its handsome Chinese ceramics); highly professional waiters in tuxedos. Popular, so book ahead. *Chinese.* **M**

� **Dawat** (midtown), 210 E. 58th St. (355-7555). A/C. Lunch Mon–Sat, dinner nightly. AE, DC, MC, V. *Specialties:* bhaja, lentil soup, baghari jhinga (shrimp in garlic and curry leaves), salmon in coriander chutney, tandoori chicken, parsi fish, tamarind-spiked eggplant, rice pudding. Good wine selection. *Note:* The flavors of India mingle artfully (sometimes w. fire) thanks to the culinary skills of Madhur Jaffrey, the Indian actress turned cookbook author who supervises Dawat's kitchen. Stylish peach and blue-green setting. Soothing svce, sometimes inattentive. Nevertheless Manhattan's most attractive Indian rest. Resv. advised. *Indian.* **M**

☀� **Gage & Tollner**, 372 Fulton St., Brooklyn (718/875-5181). A/C. Lunch Mon–Fri, dinner nightly; closed hols. and Sun July–Aug. AE, CB, DC, MC, V. Jkt. *Specialties:* she-crab soup, seafood gumbo, pan-fried oysters, catch of the day, English mixed grill (mutton chops w. veal kidney and sausages), chicken cooked in parchment, pan-fried quail w. spoon bread, lamb chops, hazelnut cheesecake. Huge selection of beer. *Note:* A handsome haven of authentic American cooking since 1879; the wall-mounted gas jets (recently wired for electricity) and the paneling are of the period. So, it might seem, are the waiters, proudly wearing their long-service stripes on their sleeves. Absolutely fresh seafood and wonderful meat as well. A designated landmark. Worth the 30-min. drive across the East River. *American.* **M**

� **Solera** (midtown), 216 E. 53rd St. (644-1166). A/C. Lunch Mon–Fri, dinner Mon–Sat (until midnight). AE, DC, MC, V. *Specialties:* superb tapas, gazpacho, fried calamares w. basil mayonnaise, grilled shrimp in herbs, paella, braised duck in sherry and olives, perfectly cooked fish dishes, crema Catalana. Good selection of finos, amontilliados, and olorosos sherries (the name *Solera* refers to the traditional process of blending used to produce sherry). *Note:* The new shrine of Iberian cuisine in Manhattan, courtesy of chef Dominick Cerrone, a graduate of famed Le Bernardin. Cheerful Mediterranean setting w. colored tiles, terra-cotta floors, and a sunny patio room. Helpful, diligent svce. Resv. strongly advisable at this fashionable spot. *Spanish.* **M**

� **Docks Oyster Bar & Seafood Grill** (midtown), 633 Third Ave. at 40th St. (986-8080). A/C. Lunch Mon–Fri, dinner nightly; brunch Sun. AE, CB, DC, MC, V. Jkt. *Specialties:* Oysters on the half shell, clam chowder, crabcakes, grilled swordfish and red snapper, seafood brochette, fried seafood platter, steamed lobster, clams. This restaurant has a good wine selection fairly priced. *Note:* Lively art deco brasserie with piscatorial artwork and tall windows facing the avenue. The seafood is as fresh as it can be and cooked to absolute perfection. Sharp, efficient svce. An excellent place. Resv. necessary. *Seafood.* **M**

� **Periyali** (Chelsea), 35 W. 20th St. at Fifth Ave. (463-7890). A/C. Lunch Mon–Fri, dinner Mon–Sat; closed hols. AE, DC, MC, V. Jkt. *Specialties:* fried calamari, tiropita (cheese pie), herbed shish kebab, kouneli stifado (ragoût of rabbit), baked sea bass w. tomato and white-wine sauce, garides Periylai (grilled shrimp w. herbs and lemon), sautéed chicken livers w. lentils, moussaka, Greek pastry. Good selection of little-known Greek wines. *Note:* Generally held to be the best place in New York for those who like their Greek cooking contemporary and (surprise, surprise) amazingly light. Warm Mediterranean setting w. dark woodwork and whitewashed walls hung with antique pots and pans. Friendly, smiling svce. A fine place, locally very popular; resv. a must. *Greek.* **M**

☼♀ **Peter Luger,** 178 Broadway, Brooklyn (718/387-7400). A/C. Lunch/dinner daily. No credit cards. Jkt. *Specialties:* shrimp cocktail, steak, roast beef, creamed spinach, cheesecake, chocolate mousse. Rickety wine list. *Note:* Since 1887 this venerable, vaguely Germanic tavern has been serving the best T-bone and porterhouse steaks in the city on its scrubbed wooden tables. The svce is rough. You should eat here, though the surrounding streets are not inviting after dark. 30 min. from midtown. Resv. advised. *Steak.* **M**

♀ **Russian Tea Room** (midtown), 150 W. 57th St. (265-0947). A/C. Lunch/dinner daily (till 12:30am). AE, CB, DC, MC, V. Jkt. *Specialties:* borscht, caviar w. blinis, zakuski, Kiev cutlet, lamb steak, Caucasian shashlik, pirozhki, broiled salmon w. lemon butter. The desserts and wine list are unworthy of a good rest. *Note:* The rest. is sandwiched between skyscrapers, the clientele is well-heeled, the decor is Christmas-tree primitive—and the place is crowded seven days a week. The Russian food is satisfactory but pricey. You may see such stars of stage, screen, and concert hall as Woody Allen, Dustin Hoffman, and Isaac Stern. Svce so-so. A place to see and be seen. Resv. advised. Was a setting for the movie *Tootsie. East European.* **M**

♀♀ **Becco** (midtown), 335 W. 46th St. (397-7597). A/C. Lunch/dinner Mon–Sat; closed hols. AE, CB, DC, MC, V. *Specialties:* pastas of the day, osso bucco, swordfish w. balsamic vinegar-and-caper sauce, spit-roasted suckling pig, salmon w. mustard sauce, chocolate zabaglione cake. List of regional Italian wines at decent prices. *Note:* One of the more notable openings of 1993 and now a favorite for a pretheater dinner. Exposed beams, wood floors, and Italian farmhouse furnishings make for a casual dining experience in this upbeat, sometimes loud setting. Interesting antipasto menu. Friendly svce. *Italian.* **I–M**

♀♀ **Christer's** (midtown), 145 W. 55th St. (974-7224). A/C. Lunch Mon–Fri, dinner Mon–Sat; closed hols. AE, DC, MC, V. *Specialties:* smorgasbord sampler, dill pancakes, salmon soup, ginger-glazed salmon, brazed lamb shank w. winter vegetables, fricassée of monkfish, lingonberry bread pudding. *Note:* A cozy environment decked w. raw wood and enhanced by a large fireplace. The well-executed Scandinavian haute cuisine combined w. the log-cabin feel of the dining room transport you to the snowy backcountry of Scandinavia. Chef/owner Christer Larsson, formerly the executive chef at the famous Aquavit, creates a truly exotic dining experience without breaking your wallet. Resv. a must. *Scandinavian.* **I–M**

♀♀ **Odeon** (Tribeca), 145 W. Broadway (233-0507). A/C. Lunch Mon–Sat, dinner nightly (until 2:30am), brunch Sun. AE, DC, MC, V. Jkt. *Specialties:* sea mussels w. cilantro-ginger-garlic broth, grilled leeks w. goat cheese, grilled mahimahi w. soy vinaigrette, loin of lamb w. cumin, steak au poivre, banana cream pie. Good wine list. *Note:* Successful bistro fare in a stylishly threadbare setting of vinyl and linoleum. Trendy clientele from punk to banker; congenial but noisy atmosphere, especially at night. Efficient, smiling, long-aproned servers. A godsend if you are up late in Tribeca. Resv. advised. *French.* **I–M**

♀♀ **One Fifth Avenue** (Greenwich Village), 1 Fifth Ave. at 8th St. (529-1515). A/C. Lunch/dinner Mon–Sat, brunch Sun; closed hols. AE, DC, MC, V. *Specialties:* clams w. frisée salad, house-smoked whitefish, black-bean chile, rigatoni w. shrimp and ginger, rabbit-and-wild-mushroom enchilada, grilled tuna in tomato-black olive vinaigrette, scallops w. sea urchin roe, chocolate box w. frozen espresso mousse. Menu changes periodically. *Note:* Since being overtaken by the group that established Gotham Bar and Grill and Mesa Grill, this venture has become a huge success, drawing in those who have heard of its creative cuisine at very reasonable, sometimes budget-standard, prices. Somewhat uncomfortable decor that's decked w. mirrors. Knowledgeable and helpful svce. Resv. a must. *American.* **I–M**

🍸🍸 **Chikubu** (midtown), 12 E. 44th St. (818-0715). A/C. Lunch Mon–Fri, dinner Mon–Sat; closed Jan 1. AE, DC. *Specialties:* sushi, sashimi, soba (noodles in soy sauce), yosenabe (fish-and-cabbage soup), tonkatsu (pan-fried pork chops), shioyaki (fish broiled whole), nabe (stews), kamemeshi (a Japanese risotto), pumpkin pudding. *Note:* With its contemporary decor in light wood and tones of pearl-gray, this rest. is a favorite of Manhattan's Japanese community, though so far it has largely escaped the attention of tourists. Chikubu's specialty is Kyoto cuisine, noted for its slow-cooked dishes and stews. Relatively quiet for a Japanese rest. An excellent place to eat; resv. advisable. *Japanese.* **I–M**

🍸🍸 **Nusantara** (midtown), 219 E. 44th St. between Second and Third Aves. (983-1919). A/C. Lunch Mon–Fri, dinner Mon–Sat. AE. *Specialties:* nasi goreng (fried rice) w. saté (broiled meat or fish), rijstaffel (rice accompanied by 20 or so assorted side dishes), squid stuffed w. mousse of fish, broiled red snapper in chili sauce, lamb curry w. cumin, coconut tart, krakatau (flambéed pineapple). *Note:* Seekers after the exotic will not be disappointed by this new, luxurious Indonesian rest., whose cuisine is as original as its lovely decor w. woodwork, carved chairs, and a giant dragon's head at the entrance. Considerate, efficient svce. An excellent place to eat, particularly in the light of its moderate prices. Resv. advisable. *Indonesian.* **I–M**

☼🍸 **Bridge Café** (Lower Manhattan), 279 Water St. (227-3344). A/C. Lunch Mon–Fri, dinner nightly, brunch Sun. AE, DC. *Specialties:* soft-shell crab (in season), corn fritters, duck w. green peppercorns, sautéed salmon, braised lamb shank w. lentils, and chocolate indulgence. *Note:* This early 19th-century seamen's tavern, now a lunchtime meeting place for yuppies, is often graced by Edward I. Koch, the former mayor of New York, as well as a clutch of Wall St. bankers. The cuisine is uneven, w. good and bad appearing side by side. Pleasant atmosphere; good-mannered but muddle-headed svce. A fashionable place in the shadow of the Brooklyn Bridge. No resv., and sometimes a long wait. *American.* **I–M**

🍸 **Gallagher's Steak House** (midtown), 228 W. 52nd St. (245-5336). A/C. Lunch/dinner daily (until midnight). AE, CB, DC, MC, V. Jkt. *Specialties:* oysters on the half shell, steak, roast beef, lamb chops, steak-and-kidney pie, brains w. hazelnut butter, lobster, broiled catch of the day. Very good cheesecake. *Note:* Long considered one of New York's best steakhouses, the fabled Gallagher's has lost some of its luster in the course of half a century. Its meats, still displayed for your inspection in a large glass-walled aging box as you come in, are as good as ever, but there are weaknesses in the kitchen, and the svce is less professional than it used to be. Unchanged are the gallery of yellowing photos of entertainers and early sports greats on the walls, and the elderly barmen working behind the oval bar in the middle of the room. Resv. advised. *Steak.* **I–M**

🍸 **Mi Cocina** (Greenwich Village), 57 Jane St. at Hudson St. (627-8273). A/C. Lunch Thurs–Fri, dinner nightly, brunch Sun. AE, CB, DC, MC, V. *Specialties:* guacamole, tamales of pork and Swiss chard, empanaditas, pasta fresca con salmon, fajitas of skirt steak, pollo in mixiote, almond flan. Skimpy wine list. *Note:* A pretty rose-and-yellow dining room offering upscale Mexican food by inventive owner-chef José Hurtado-Prud'homme. Svce is prompt and affable, even when the rm becomes overcrowded. A Mexican outpost w. grace and style. Resv. advised. *Mexican.* **I–M**

♓ **Nanni** (midtown), 146 E. 46th St. (697-4161). A/C. Lunch
Mon–Fri, dinner Mon–Sat; closed hols. AE, CB, DC, MC, V.
Jkt. *Specialties:* fettuccine alla Nanni, fresh homemade pasta, chicken ortolana,
sea bass alla marecchiara, veal cutlet milanese, game (in season). *Note:* Colorful
little *trattoria.* Intimate setting pleasantly renovated; praiseworthy food especially pastas. Quick, efficient svce. Often noisy and crowded. Resv. advised. A very
good place. *Italian.* I–M

♓ **The Nice Restaurant** (Chinatown), 35 E. Broadway (406-
9510). A/C. Lunch/dinner daily. AE. *Specialties:* spring rolls
w. shrimp, chopped squab in lettuce leaf, fried prawns, roast suckling pig, lac-
quered duck, salted chicken, melon-and-coconut soup. *Note:* Huge (ask to be
seated upstairs) and frantic though it is, this is one of Chinatown's best. Truly
outstanding Cantonese food; unusually (for a Chinese rest.) efficient svce. The
elaborate decor might be described as glittery Hong Kong Revival. Popular
enough that resv. are advised. *Chinese.* I–M

♓ **Le Taxi** (midtown), 37 E. 60th St. (832-5500). A/C. Lunch/
dinner Mon–Sat, brunch Sun; closed hols. AE, DC, MC, V.
Specialties: pheasant terrine, saucisson en croute, céleri rémoulade, steak,
crumbed lamb, cod w. brandade, monkfish w. lobster sauce, braised sweetbreads,
tarte tatin. *Note:* A lively bistro atmosphere where pretty people are seen amid the
brass sconces and turn-of-the-century posters. Weak appetizers but very satisfying entrées. Resv. advised. *French.* I–M

♓♓ **Japonica** (Greenwich Village), 90 University Place at E. 12th
St. (243-7752). A/C. Lunch/dinner daily. AE. *Specialties:* avocado Japonica, gyoza, kyoage, nabeyaki udon, negimaki, sushi, sashimi. *Note:*
This small, pretty, unpretentious rest. is well known for the ultra-fresh quality of
its sushi and sashimi. Svce is swift and courteous; the decor above the sushi bar
changes to reflect the seasons. Expect to wait if you arrive after 7:30pm, particularly on wknds. *Japanese.* I

☼♓♓ **Sylvia's** (Harlem), 328 Lenox Ave. at W. 126th St. (996-
0660). A/C. Breakfast Mon–Sat, lunch/dinner daily, brunch
w. music live on Sun. No credit cards. *Specialties:* smothered steak, stewed chick-
en w. dumplings, fried chicken, turnips and collard greens, barbecued spareribs,
butter beans w. ham bone, sweet-potato pie. *Note:* Sylvia Woods's rest. in the
heart of Harlem has been an institution for more than 20 years. The flavors and
spices of her cuisine are as savory and colorful as the Deep South where she was
born. The decor is unobtrusive and the neighborhood not inviting; you should
come and go by cab. But the atmosphere is warm and the svce congenial. The
clientele is made up mostly of regulars and local politicians, w. a sprinkling of
celebrities and tourists who come, in increasing numbers, to discover Harlem
and Sylvia's food. A fine place. *American.* I

♓ **Abyssinia** (Soho), 35 Grand St. (226-5959). A/C. Dinner
nightly, brunch Sat–Sun. AE. *Specialties:* kitfo (raw chopped
beef seasoned w. spiced butter and topped w. hot chili powder), ye'beg tibs (lamb
w. tomato, onion fried w. rosemary, and black pepper), doro wot (chicken marinated in hot Berber sauce, served w. boiled egg), shuro (purée of chickpeas, tomatoes, onions, garlic, and other herbs), chocolate-chip cake, pear-and-almond
tart. *Note:* A mecca for a young crowd who come here for the great-value cuisine
eaten sans tableware, using the large, round injera bread as plate and scoop. You
sit on wooden stools at low, round, woven basket tables in two small rms decorated w. authentic Ethiopian artifacts too. Fun and different. Brief wine and beer
selection. *Ethiopian.* I

♓ **Acme Bar & Grill** (Noho), 9 Great Jones St. (420-1934). A/C.
Lunch/dinner daily; closed Thanksgiving and Dec 25. AE,
CB, DC, MC, V. *Specialties:* golden fried oysters, jambalaya, chicken fried steak,
fish grilled over pecan wood, grilled chicken. *Note:* A no-frills, American-diner
ambience at this big, bright, cheerful meeting place for neighborhood loft dwell-

ers and visiting gentry in Noho. Renowned for its jukebox and the shelf of hot sauces that runs the length of the rest. From "Cajun Power Garlic Sauce" (Louisiana) to "Acme Almost Flammable Hot Sauce of Chile Habanero" (Mexico) or the fearsome "Pepper Creek Farms Jalapeño TNT" (Texas). No resv. accepted. *American/Cajun.* **I**

    ♀ **Cabana Carioca** (midtown), 123 W. 45th St. (581-8088). A/C. Lunch/dinner daily; closed hols. AE, CB, DC, MC, V. *Specialties:* caldo verde (vegetable soup), feijoada (the Brazilian national dish — stewed beef, sausage, and black beans), shrimp Paulista (cooked in white wine), mixed grill, broiled pork chops w. rice and black beans, steak. Excellent caipirinhas (a punch made w. lime juice and cachaça, a high-octane Brazilian spirit). *Note:* The unchallenged shrine of Brazilian cooking, Cabana Carioca is one of the most pleasing and authentic ethnic rests. in Manhattan. Its enormous helpings and diminutive prices keep the regulars coming back in crowds, and draw every Brazilian passing through town. Funky tropical atmosphere and decor. *Brazilian.* **I**

    ♀ **Lou G. Siegel's** (midtown), 209 W. 38th St. (921-4433). A/C. Lunch Sun–Fri, dinner Sun–Thurs; closed Jewish hols. AE, CB, DC, MC, V. *Specialties:* brisket, roast beef, broiled veal cutlets, gefilte fish, stuffed cabbage, goulash, chopped liver. *Note:* Authentic Jewish food since 1917: From pastrami to roast beef and from matzoh balls to pastry, everything is scrupulously kosher. At both lunch and dinner it's packed w. workers from the nearby Garment District. Friendly, efficient svce. Depressing decor. Styles itself "the world's most famous kosher rest." *Continental.* **I**

    ♀ **Turkish Kitchen** (Gramercy Park), 386 Third Ave. (679-1810). A/C. Dinner only, nightly; closed hols. AE, MC, V. *Specialties:* bean-and-carrot stew; mussels stuffed w. pine nuts, currents, and rice; phyllo scrolls stuffed w. feta; wood-grilled shish kebabs; almond pudding. Menu changes daily. *Note:* The color red prevails in this rest. serving excellent Turkish fare that ranges from the exotic (such as the hot yogurt soup) to favorite standbys (the kebabs). Diligent, friendly svce. Resv. recommended. *Turkish.* **B–I**

    ♀ **Mo's Caribbean Bar and Grille** (Upper East Side), 1454 Second Ave. at 76th St. (650-0561). A/C. Lunch/brunch Sat–Sun, dinner nightly (until 2am); closed hols. AE, DC, MC, V. *Specialties:* Cuban black-bean soup, shrimp-and-lobster salad, conch fritters, jerked chicken, curried chicken, jerked pork chops, chocolate mousse mud cake. Huge drink menu. *Note:* Despite the loud Caribbean kitschy decor (that includes the drinks) and the seven TVs, the snappy meals grab your attention. Generous portions at a bargain. Plenty of house concoctions or simply good Jamaican beer to wash it all down. *Caribbean.* **B–I**

    ♀ **Blue Ribbon** (Soho), 97 Sullivan St. (274-0404). A/C. Dinner only, Tues–Sun (until 4am); closed hols. AE, MC, V. *Specialties:* pu-pu platter, paella, marrow w. oxtail marmalade, cheese fondue, banana split. *Note:* The perfect answer to a late-night (or early-morning) hunger in Soho. The menu's variety is enough to satisfy just about any craving, no matter how strange it gets. Serves a stunning three-tiered shellfish platter. No resvs. *Continental.* **B–I**

    ♀ **Bayamo** (Noho), 704 Broadway near E. 4th St. (475-5151). A/C. Lunch/dinner daily; closed Thanksgiving and Dec 25. AE, CB, DC, MC, V. *Specialties:* ropa vieja (traditional Cuban beef stew), picadillo de camarones (spicy shrimp minced w. cheese, tortilla, and guacamole), chicken w. ginger, pan-fried lo mein noodles. *Note:* Named for a Cuban village where Chinese settlers had immigrated in the early 1900s, this busy two-level rest. is in the heart of the action along lower Broadway. The rm is dominated by a huge papier-mâché red pepper simulating the boats of the Chinese immigrants to Cuba, and the brilliant wall frescoes are interesting to contemplate while you sip one of the house special margaritas or Foster's beer. Curious combination of Chinese-Latino cuisine. Stick to the simpler dishes. Good for a snack or a full dinner. *Cuban/Chinese.* **B–I**

☼♀ **Hard Rock Café** (midtown), 221 W. 57th St. (459-9320).
A/C. Lunch/dinner daily (until 3am). AE, MC, V. *Specialties:*
pig sandwich (roast pork), hamburgers, salads, ice-cream sundaes. *Note:* A pretty
faithful copy of London's famous establishment of the same name, this funky
landmark of rock 'n' roll serves excellent hamburgers and sandwiches, and praiseworthy desserts. Far-out decor w. a 45-ft. (14m) bar in the shape of a guitar, and
the rear half of an elderly 1959 Cadillac Biarritz cemented into the facade. Very
high-level sound system. Very popular w. the New York young; serves 1,800–
2,500 customers a day. No resv. Also a crowded rock joint. *American.* **B–I**

♀ **Kinh Do** (Tribeca), 19 Ave. of the Americas, near Walker St.
(219-3181). A/C. Lunch/dinner daily. AE, DC, MC, V. *Spe-*
cialties: spring rolls, tom bo nuong (thinly sliced beef and shrimp in a sweet peanut marinade rolled in rice paper), bo nuong sa (marinated beef cubes w.
lemongrass), chicken in sweet-hot broth. *Note:* One of the best new Asian spots
dwntwn. Authentic Vietnamese fare (most of the patrons are also Vietnamese).
Clean and colorful setting. Friendly staff. Very good value overall. *Vietnamese.*
B–I

♀ **Oriental Pearl** (Chinatown), 103–105 Mott St. at Canal St.
(219-8388). A/C. Breakfast/lunch/dinner daily. MC, V.
Specialties: dim sum, spareribs w. black-bean sauce, deep-fried shrimp w. walnuts,
braised goose and taro-root casserole, scallops w. black-pepper sauce, nondescript desserts. *Note:* Sprawling 500-seat Chinese palace complete w. ceramic
statues, dragons w. flashing eyes, and colored lights. Superior Chinese food fairly
priced. The svce is prompt. *Chinese.* **B–I**

☼♀ **Carnegie Delicatessen** (midtown), 854 Seventh Ave. at W.
55th St. (757-2245). A/C. Breakfast/lunch/dinner daily
(until 4am). No credit cards. *Specialties:* chicken soup w. matzoh balls, corned
beef, brisket, pastrami, roast beef, smoked herring and salmon, cheese blintzes,
Jewish specialties; excellent cheesecake. *Note:* Generally acknowledged to be
New York's best deli, the place is overrun at lunchtime. Gigantic sandwiches, remarkable desserts. The ideal place to eat on the run, before or after a show. A
lively local institution since 1935; part of Woody Allen's movie *Broadway Danny*
Rose was shot here. No resv. Beer but no liquor. *American.* **B**

♀ **Veselka** (East Village), 144 Second Ave. at E. 9th St. (228-
9682). A/C. Open daily around the clock. No credit cards.
Specialties: mushroom-barley soup, asparagus-and-mushroom crêpe, cheese
blintzes, pierogi. *Note:* Small, homey coffee shop (Veselka means "rainbow" in
Ukrainian) serving down-to-earth, unpretentious food at unbeatable prices. *East*
European. **B**

Other Well-Known Restaurants

Le Cirque (Upper East Side), 58 E. 65th St. (794-9292). Lunch/dinner
Mon–Sat. AE, CB, DC. Trend-setting rest. whose patrons range from Richard
Nixon and Fiat chairman Giovanni Agnelli to Liza Minelli and the Greek ship-
owner Livanos. Sky-high prices and fussy fare. President Reagan also occasionally
honored the place w. his presence. **E** (lunch), **VE** (dinner)

Rainbow Room (midtown), 30 Rockefeller Plaza (632-5000). Dinner Tues
–Sun, brunch Sat–Sun. AE. On the 65th floor of the General Electric Building
(formerly the RCA Building), this dazzling recently remodeled art deco rest. is
so New York City, it offers a splendid view of the lighted skyline and nostalgic
dining and dancing. Prices are predictably steep. **E–VE**

Four Seasons (midtown), 99 E. 52nd St. (754-9494). Lunch Mon–Fri,
dinner Mon–Sat. AE, CB, DC, MC, V. The "Pool Room" w. its enormous skylight and marble pool is a triumph of elegant modern design. The wine list is
exhaustive. A favorite of New York's publishing community in particular. Super-
expensive. Designated an official New York City landmark in 1989. **E–VE**

Café des Artistes (Upper West Side), 1 W. 67th St. (877-3500). Lunch
Mon–Fri, dinner nightly, brunch Sat–Sun. AE, DC, MC, V. The plush Central

European atmosphere and the exquisite painted murals are what draw regulars to this festive rest. The food is not as consistently pleasing as the setting. **E**

Tavern on the Green (Upper West Side), Central Park West at W. 67th St. (873-3200). Lunch Mon–Fri, dinner nightly, brunch Sat–Sun. AE, DC, MC, V. The food and svce. are at best uneven; it's worth visiting for the dazzling Crystal Room setting on the edge of Central Park, glorious by day in sunshine and snow. Sheer New York. **E**

"21" Club (midtown), 21 W. 52nd St. (582-7200). Lunch Mon–Fri, dinner Mon–Sat. AE, CB, DC, MC, V. Movers and shakers make this old speakeasy, recently renovated their "club" for socializing and deal making. The food is only one of the issues—the "21" burger is $25. **E**

Windows on the World (the Restaurant) (Lower Manhattan), 1 World Trade Center (938-1111). After the bombing of the World Trade Center in 1993 this rest., the highest skyscraper rest. in the world (107 floors above the sidewalk), closed for renovation with plans to reopen in the spring of 1995. Call the rest. for information. **E**

Cafeterias/Specialty Spots/Fast Food

☀ **Broadway Diner** (midtown), 1726 Broadway at W. 55th St. (765-0909). Breakfast/lunch/dinner daily (7am–11pm). Corned-beef hash w. poached eggs, hamburgers, very good sandwiches, and broiled chicken in an *American Graffiti*–style luncheonette, all Formica, chromium, and stainless steel. For 1940s enthusiasts.

Hamburger Harry's (Lower Manhattan), 157 Chambers St. (267-4446). Lunch/dinner daily (until 10pm). Some 16 kinds of hamburgers (connoisseurs call them the best in New York) and mesquite-grilled chicken sandwiches, a stone's throw from the World Trade Center.

John's Pizzeria (Greenwich Village), 278 Bleeker St. (243-1680). Lunch/dinner daily. No credit cards. The best classic brick-oven pizzas in town: good crisp crust and just enough cheese (54 options). Usually crowded and noisy. Other location: 408 E. 64th St. (Upper East Side) (935-2895).

Katz's Delicatessen (Lower East Side), 205 E. Houston St. at Ludlow St. (254-2246). Breakfast/lunch/dinner daily. No credit cards. A living relic founded in 1888. Gigantic sandwiches of brisket, corned beef, tongue, roast beef, etc.

☀ **Museum of Modern Art Garden Café** (midtown), 11 W. 53rd St. (708-9400). Lunch Thurs–Tues. The tourists' favorite: big bay windows w. unobstructed view of the Sculpture Garden. Crowded out at lunch. Praiseworthy food.

Nathan's Famous (midtown), 1482 Broadway at W. 43rd St. (382-0620). Open daily (7am–3am). New York's best hot dogs, excellent french fries and sandwiches, but so-so burgers. Three other locations in Manhattan and Brooklyn, besides the famous original at Coney Island (see "Nearby Excursions," below).

Zip City Brewery (Chelsea), 3 W. 18th St. (366-6333). A/C. Open daily (until 4am). AE, CB, DC, MC, V. Two-level bar dominated by the copper brewing kettles in the center of the room. Excellent hamburgers that go superbly w. any of their flavorful beers. Very busy and noisy after work.

Where to Eat What in New York

American: Acme Bar & Grill (p. 133), An American Place (p. 126), Arizona 206 (p. 129), Aureole (p. 127), Bridge Café (p. 132), Carmine's (p. 126), Carnegie Delicatessen (p. 135), Gage & Tollner (p. 130), Gotham Bar and Grill (p. 125), Hard Rock Café (p. 135), One Fifth Avenue (p. 131), River Café (p. 128), Sylvia's (p. 133), Tribeca Grill (p. 129), "21" (p. 136)

Brazilian: Cabana Carioca (p. 134)

Cajun: Acme Bar & Grill (p. 133)

Caribbean: Mo's Caribbean Bar & Grille (p. 134)

Chinese: Chin Chin (p. 130), Fu's (p. 128), The Nice Restaurant (p. 133), Oriental Pearl (p. 135), Shun Lee Palace (p. 128)

Continental: Blue Ribbon (p. 134), Café des Artistes (p. 135), Four Seasons (p. 135), Lespinasse (p. 126), Lou G. Siegel's (p. 133), Rainbow Room (p. 135), Tavern on the Green (p. 136), Windows on the World Restaurant (p. 136)

Cuban-Chinese: Bayamo (p. 134)

East European: Russian Tea Room (p. 131), Veselka (p. 135)

Ethiopian: Abyssinia (p. 133)

Fast Food/Specialty Spots/Cafeterias: Broadway Diner (p. 136), Hamburger Harry's (p. 136), John's Pizzeria (p. 136), Katz's Delicatessen (p. 136), Museum of Modern Art Garden Café (p. 136), Nathan's Famous (p. 136), Zip City Brewery (p. 136)

French: Bouley (p. 124), Les Célébrités (p. 127), Chanterelle (p. 127), Le Chantilly (p. 129), Le Cirque (p. 135), Daniel (p. 127), JoJo (p. 125), Lutèce (p. 124), Odéon (p. 131), Le Taxi (p. 133), Vong (p. 128)

Greek: Periyali (p. 130)

Indian: Dawat (p. 130)

Indonesian: Nusantara (p. 132)

Italian: Becco (p. 131), Carmine's (p. 126), Nanni (p. 133), Remi (p. 125), San Domenico (p. 127)

Japanese: Chikubu (p. 132), Hatsuhana (p. 126), Japonica (p. 133), Mitsukoshi (p. 128)

Mexican: Mi Cocina (p. 132), Rosa Mexicano (p. 126)

Scandinavian: Christer's (p. 131)

Seafood: Le Bernardin (p. 124), Docks Oyster Bar & Seafood Grill (p. 130), Manhattan Ocean Club (p. 129), Oyster Bar and Restaurant (p. 125), Palm (p. 125), Smith & Wollensky (p. 129)

Spanish: Solera (p. 130)

Steak: Christ Cella (p. 000), Frank's (p. 126), Gallagher's Steak House (p. 132), Palm (p. 125), Peter Luger (p. 131), Smith & Wollensky (p. 129)

Thai: Vong (p. 128)

Turkish: Turkish Kitchen (p. 134)

Vietnamese: Kinh Do (p. 135)

BARS & NIGHTCLUBS

BARS/PUBS: The Ballroom (Chelsea), 253 W. 28th St. (244-3005). An unusual nightspot which contrives to be simultaneously a cabaret, comedy club, Off Off Broadway theater, commendable rest., and excellent "tapas" bar, serving the highly esteemed Spanish hors d'oeuvres. Open Tues.–Sun.

Café Carlyle (Upper East Side), in the Hotel Carlyle (see "Accommodations," above) (744-1600). Preppy piano bar, enlivened for the last two decades by the talented Bobby Short. Also a rest. Open nightly.

Café Skylight (midtown), in the Novotel (see "Accommodations," above) (315-0100). On a terrace on the seventh floor of the Novotel, this wine bar has a panoramic view of Broadway and Times Sq. Large selection by the glass or the bottle. Excellent sandwiches, cheeses, and pâtés to accompany the wine. Spectacular view after dark. Open nightly till 1am.

Chumley's (Greenwich Village), 86 Bedford St. (675-4449). The entrance is unmarked—a reminder that this was originally a speakeasy. Sawdust on the floor, fire burning in winter. The bar area is small and decorated with book jackets, reminders of the original denizens. A Greenwich Village literary landmark. Good burgers. Open nightly until midnight.

Clarke's (midtown), 915 Third Ave. at E. 56th St. (759-1650). Only the uninitiated refer to this old-time Irish bar by its full name, P.J. Clarke's. Hearty masculine atmosphere. So-so rest. Crowded at night. Open nightly till 4am.

Landmark Tavern (midtown), 626 11th Ave. at W. 46th St. (757-8595). A/C. AE, MC, V. Victorian-style bar built in 1868 w. tin ceiling, tile floor, and pot-belly stove. Good Irish-style food too, available at lunch and dinner. Open daily from noon to midnight.

Lion's Head Ltd. (Greenwich Village), 59 Christopher St. nr. Seventh Ave. (929-0670). Likable, relaxed bar; very Greenwich Village. Also a restaurant. Open nightly until 4am.

McSorley's Old Ale House (East Village), 15 E. 7th St. (473-9148). Classic alehouse serving beer. Young, student crowd along w. locals from the Ukrainian neighborhood. Historic atmosphere—one of Brendan Behan's haunts. The corned-beef sandwiches are also famous. Open daily 11am–4am.

    ☼ **White Horse Tavern** (Greenwich Village), 560 Hudson St. (243-9260). One of Manhattan's oldest literary cafés (1880), once the favorite of Dylan Thomas and Norman Mailer. Now a mostly student and tourist clientele; excellent hamburgers, Open daily noon–3am.

COUNTRY & WESTERN MUSIC: Lone Star Roadhouse (midtown), 240 W. 52nd St. (245-2950). Since its illustrious ancestor, the Lone Star Café, closed in 1989, this has become New York City's shrine to country music, attracting all the big stars. Pleasant bar; acceptable Tex-Mex rest. Open daily.

O'Lunney's (midtown), 12 W. 44th St. (840-6688). Another place for country music lovers, *Urban Cowboy* style, with bluegrass as well on Sun. Also a passable rest. Open Mon–Sat.

DISCO/ROCK: ☼ **Au Bar** (midtown), 41 E. 58th St. (308-9455). Intimate, very upscale bar-rest. modeled on a smart London club. Dance floor, elegant dining rm, library (!), and smoking rm. A world away from the ear-splitting modern disco. Thronged by well-brought-up yuppies. Open Tues–Sun.

Blondie's (Upper West Side), 2180 Broadway at 77th St. (362-4360). Live R&B and rock bands. Open nightly.

China Club (Upper West Side), 2130 Broadway at W. 75th St. (877-1166). One of the most amusing "in" discos in the city. The decor, Far Eastern crossed with art deco, is bizarre. Frequented by New York celebrities and entertainers. Open nightly.

Le Bar Bat (Upper West Side), 311 W. 57th St. (307-7228). Wildly funky bat cave; looks like an overcrowded bordello in a Far Eastern country at war. The DJ is equally delirious, tossing off every sound you've ever heard since the Charleston. Happily, the near-Vietnamese food is better than expected. Open daily at lunch and dinner.

Limelight (Chelsea), 660 Ave. of the Americas at W. 20th St. (807-7850). This enormous disco, in an old Gothic church, holds 1,400 people on three floors. The bar is in the adjoining chapel. Very "in" atmosphere. Open nightly.

Nell's (Greenwich Village), 246 W. 14th St. (675-1567). Very trendy semi-private nightclub which draws New York's artistic and literary crowd. Sumptuously venerable Victorian decor; background music ranges from modern jazz to Dvorak. For with-it intellectuals. Open nightly.

    ☼ **Palladium** (East Village), 126 E. 14th St. (473-7171). World's biggest disco, 320,000 sq. ft. (30,000m^2) on seven floors. The famous architect Arato Isozaki did the interior, where 3,500 people can be comfortable. Far out. Open Wed–Sat.

Ritz (midtown), 254 W. 54th St. (541-8900). Old movie house now a rendezvous for rockers. Ear-splitting audio. Lavish neo-deco decor. Very with-it atmosphere. Open nightly.

    ☼ **Roseland** (midtown), 239 W. 52nd St. (247-0200). Enormous 1930s dance hall. Super-kitsch in a very populist way; some evenings you can count 3,000 dancers. Guaranteed atmosphere; patriotic decor with huge star-spangled banner. A sight to be seen. Open Thurs–Sun.

S.O.B. (Sounds of Brazil) (Greenwich Village), 204 Varick St. at W. Houston St. (243-4940). Fashionable super-disco; Latin rhythms to an American beat. One of the "hottest" places in town. Open Tues–Sun.

Tatou (midtown), 151 E. 53rd St. (753-1144). Chic and trendy, with an ornate decor. Monday night variety showcase.
The Tunnel (Chelsea), 220 12th Ave. at W. 27th St. (695-7292). Giant disco in an old dockside railroad terminal. Entirely revamped decor. Open nightly.
Wetlands Preserve (Tribeca), 161 Hudson St. (966-4225). Two-story earthy bar and music space spectacular that caters to the no-nukes/save-the-rain forest crowd. Good reggae, blues, rock, folk; live music nightly.

COMEDY CLUBS: **Caroline's Comedy Club** (midtown), 1626 Broadway (757-4100): Leading club, whose acts are often seen on cable TV. A sophisticated venue for the hottest names in comedy.
The Comic Strip (Upper East Side), 1568 2nd Ave. at 81st St. (861-9386): A showcase club w. cutting-edge quality comedians. Open nightly.
Improvisation (The Original) (midtown), 358 W. 44th St. (765-8268). The oldest (1963) of New York's comedy clubs, which has showcased such future superstars as Richard Pryor, Joe Piscopo, and Robin Williams. Casual ambience and decor w. no affectations. Open nightly.

JAZZ: The magic **Jazzline** telephone number (479-7888) gives current programs for all the jazz clubs.
Blue Note (Greenwich Village), 131 W. 3rd St. (475-8592). The biggest stars of the day. Rest. as well. Open nightly.
Bottom Line (Greenwich Village), 15 W. 4th St. (228-7880). Jazz, rock, blues. Switched-on clientele. Resv. a must.
Bradley's (Greenwich Village), 70 University Place at W. 11th St. (228-6440). Very good modern jazz in an elegant dark-paneled setting. Also acceptable rest. Usually crowded; resv. a must. Open daily.
Fat Tuesday's (Gramercy Park), Third Ave. and E. 17th St. (533-7902). Modern and traditional jazz; rest. as well. Open nightly.
Manny's Car Wash (Upper East Side), 1558 Third Ave. at 87th St. (369-2583). An unlikely name for the shrine of the Chicago-style blues. A popular pit stop for musicians passing through town. Open nightly.
Michael's Pub (midtown), 211 E. 55th St. (758-2272). New Orleans jazz; rest. Every now and then Woody Allen still turns up on a Mon evening to play clarinet. Open Mon–Sat.
Sweet Basil (Greenwich Village), 88 Seventh Ave. South (242-1785). Modern jazz; several stars appear regularly, including Art Blakey and the Jazz Messengers. Pretty rustic decor; likable atmosphere. Open nightly.
Village Vanguard (Greenwich Village), 178 Seventh Ave. (255-4037). The jazz shrine of New York City since 1935; probably the world's most famous jazz club. All the biggest names in jazz put in an appearance here. Generally crowded. Open nightly.
Zanzibar & Grill (midtown), 550 Third Ave. at E. 36th St. (779-0606). New jazz club and rest. w. live music daily. The setting is a kind of tropical art deco.

NEARBY EXCURSIONS

⚓ **CONEY ISLAND** (Surf Ave., Brooklyn; 718/266-1234): Beach somewhat run-down, crowded in summer (see "Beaches," above). Kitsch but entertaining amusement park (see "Theme Parks," above). Famous aquarium (see the New York Aquarium under "Zoos," above), and New York's best hot dogs at Nathan's Famous, 1315 Surf Ave. at Stillwell Ave. (718/946-2202). In a word, don't miss it, but avoid the summer weekend crush, and be alert at night.

☼☖ **STATEN ISLAND** (10 mi./16km SW via the Brooklyn-Battery Tunnel, I-278, and the Verrazano-Narrows Bridge, or via ferry from Battery Park, in Lower Manhattan): Facing Manhattan across New York Bay, this small island, only 14 by 8 mi. (22 by 12km), still retains a rural touch with its many parks, old villages, and rolling hills that invite you to a stroll.

You should certainly see **Richmondtown Restoration,** 441 Clarke Ave. at Arthur Kill Rd. (718/351-1617), a museum village with 30 or so carefully restored buildings from the 17th to the 19th century, including the Voorlezer's House, the country's oldest standing elementary school, built around 1690.

Not far away is the curious **Jacques Marchais Center of Tibetan Art,** 338 Lighthouse Ave. (718/987-3478), open Wed–Sun afternoons Apr–Nov; by appointment the rest of the year. This interesting museum of Buddhist art stands in its own fine Oriental garden.

The **Snug Harbor Cultural Center,** 1000 Richmond Terrace (718/448-2500), open daily, is a cultural and creative-arts center in what used to be a sailors' retirement home dating from the early 19th century. Interesting Greek Revival and Victorian buildings, art museum, fine sculpture garden, and 80-acre (39ha) park.

An oasis of peace and calm within New York's city limits, 30 min. from Manhattan by the Staten Island Ferry.

☼☖☖ **VERRAZANO-NARROWS BRIDGE** (9 mi/15km SW via the Brooklyn-Battery Tunnel and I-278): The bridge connecting Brooklyn to Staten Island was designed by Othmar Ammann, an architect of Swiss origin. It's the world's third-longest suspension bridge, with a total length of 13,700 ft. (4,176m); the central span is 4,260 ft. (1,299m) long. The twin towers are 70 stories high; there are two decks, each with six lanes. Opened in 1964, it cost $305 million. More than 50 million vehicles cross it every year. A truly riveting sight. **Fort Wadsworth,** at the Staten Island approach to the bridge, has a fine view of New York Bay.

FARTHER AFIELD

☼☖☖ **THE HUDSON VALLEY** (229 mi./366km r.t. via U.S. 9N, N.Y. 9A, U.S. 9N, N.Y. 199W, N.Y. 28N/S and N.Y. 375N/S, I-87S, U.S. 9W, Palisades Interstate Pkwy., and the George Washington Bridge): A car trip along a very lovely valley, which reminds seasoned travelers of the Rhine. Next to Manhattan this may be richer in historical associations than any other part of New York State. Leave Manhattan on U.S. 9, the northward extension of Broadway, and begin the tour with a visit to ☖ **Philipse Manor Hall State Historic Site,** Warburton Ave. and Dock St., Yonkers (914/965-4027) (open Wed, Thurs, and Sun). Built in 1682, this was the home of a family of noble loyalists from England. Superb Georgian-style interior decoration. Not far is the **Hudson River Museum,** 511 Warburton Ave. (914/963-4550), open Wed–Sun, where exhibits bearing on the art and history of the Hudson Valley are housed in an imposing 19th-century home.

Tarrytown, 11 mi. (17km) north, was founded in the 17th century by the Dutch, and made famous by Washington Irving, whose house, ☖ **Sunnyside,** W. Sunnyside Lane (914/631-8200), is open Wed–Mon. Many other fine old homes have been restored at the expense of the Rockefeller family. They include **Lyndhurst,** 635 S. Broadway (914/631-0046), open Tues–Sun Apr–Oct, Sat–Sun the rest of the year, a splendid 1838 Gothic Revival estate overlooking the river; and ☖☖ **Philipsburg Manor,** on U.S. 9, Kingsland Point Park (914/631-7766), open Wed–Sun Apr–Dec, a beautiful 1683 manor house, still with its old mill, where a very popular classical-music festival is held every summer. Near here, see the old Dutch church built in 1685 and the charming little **Sleepy Hol-**

low cemetery (Broadway and Pierson), with the graves of Washington Irving, Andrew Carnegie, and William Rockefeller.

U.S. 9 continues northward through **Ossining,** with the famous **Sing Sing Federal Penitentiary** (no visitors), on its way to **Croton-on-Hudson** and the lovely ⚑ **Van Cortlandt Manor,** Croton Point Ave. (914/631-8200), open Wed –Mon Apr–Dec, dating from the War of Independence and built on the old post road to Albany; fine 18th-century garden. Between Garrison and Cold Spring, on a height of land overlooking the river, see ⚑ **Boscobel,** built in 1805 in the Federal style by wealthy landowner States Morris Dyckman, with its beautiful orangery.

North another 23 mi (36km) is **Poughkeepsie,** home of **Vassar College** (914/437-7000), long the most famous women's college in the country, co-ed since 1969; its campus on Raymond Ave. is worth a look.

On to **Hyde Park,** birthplace of Franklin D. Roosevelt; visit the ☀⚑⚑ **Roosevelt-Vanderbilt National Historic Sites,** on U.S. 9 (914/229-9115), open daily May–Oct, Thurs–Mon Nov–Apr. You'll see the house where the 32nd president was born; his tomb, and that of his wife, Eleanor, are in the rose garden. There's a museum, a library with Roosevelt's private papers, and the sumptuous mansion of the railroad magnate Frederick Vanderbilt, built in 1898 to the Beaux Arts design of McKim, Mead and White. Don't miss it.

A little off U.S. 9 at **Staatsburg,** the ⚑ **Mills Mansion Historic Site** (914/ 889-8851), a magnificent 65-room 1895 classical revival building by Stanford White, certainly deserves a visit. Elegant Louis XV and Louis XVI furniture. Open Wed–Sun Apr–Oct and last three weeks of Dec.

☀⚑ **Rhinebeck,** a little distance north, has two claims to fame: the oldest inn in the country (see the Beekman Arms, under "Where to Stay," below), and a wonderful collection of early aircraft at the **Old Rhinebeck Aerodrome,** Stone Church Rd. (914/758-8610). Weekend air shows mid-June to Oct; museum open daily mid-May to mid-Oct. Then take the opposite bank of the Hudson River on to ☀⚑ **Woodstock,** at the foot of the Catskills. This agreeable little summer resort and artists' colony is famous for its chamber-music festival (started in 1916), and also as the scene (August 15–17, 1969) of the legendary rock festival that was attended by almost half a million people and that in a sense marked the end of the '60s.

Head back to Manhattan via ☀ **Kingston,** founded by the Dutch in 1652 and the first capital of New York State before it was burned by the British. Many interesting buildings including the ⚑ **Senate House Historic Site** of 1676 at 312 Fair St. (914/338-2786), open Wed–Sun.

George Washington made his headquarters in ☀ **Newburgh,** 34 mi. (55km) south, from Apr 1782 to Aug 1783 during the War of Independence, and it was from here that he made the official announcement of the end of hostilities. You may visit the site at 84 Liberty St. (914/562-1195), Wed–Sun Apr–Dec (wknds only, Jan–Mar). Also see the **New Windsor Cantonment Site,** Temple Hill Rd. (914/561-1765), open Wed–Sun from mid-Apr through Oct, the last encampment of the Continental Army. Interesting museum. Don't miss this page of history.

On your way to West Point, make a detour along N.Y. 32 to the ☀ **Storm King Art Center,** Old Pleasant Hill Rd. in Mountainville (914/534-3115), open daily Apr to mid-Nov, a fine museum of modern art in a superb 350-acre (142ha) park adorned with monumental sculpture by such artists as Isamu Noguchi, Alexander Calder, and Louise Nevelson. Don't miss it.

☀⚑⚑ **West Point,** home of the U.S. Military Academy, founded in 1802, turns out 4,000 cadets a year. **Fort Putnam** (1779), dominating the campus, the **Cadet Chapel,** and the **West Point Museum** are all worth visiting. At the **Information Center,** at Thayer Gate (914/ 938-2638), you can obtain dates and times of parades Apr–May and Sept–Oct. Don't miss it.

☀ **Bear Mountain State Park,** just south of West Point, is a lovely wooded park of some 5,000 acres (2,000ha) overlooking the Hudson. **Perkins Memorial Drive,** a scenic highway, will take you to the top of Bear Mountain and give you a splendid view across the valley. If you like flea markets you should stop at ☀⚓ **Nyack** (where painter Edward Hopper was born) to see its **Arts & Crafts & Antiques,** with almost 100 art galleries, handcraft shops, and antiques dealers (914/358-8443), open Tues–Sun.

Finally, back to Manhattan by the Palisades Interstate Pkwy. and the George Washington Bridge; allow two to three days for this exciting tour.

Where to Stay En Route

The following hotels, motels, and inns are recommended as suitable places for a stopover.

IN BEAR MOUNTAIN STATE PARK The ▯ **Bear Mountain Inn,** U.S. 9W, Bear Mountain, NY 10911 (914/786-2731). 60 rms. Small rustic motel inside the park. **I–M**

HYDE PARK The ▯ **Roosevelt Inn,** 38 Albany Post Rd., Hyde Park, NY 12538 (914/229-2443). 25 rms. Modest but very well-run motel w. modern comforts. Open Mar–Dec. **I**

LAKE MOHONK/NEW PALTZ The ☀ ▯▯▯ **Mohonk Mountain House,** N.Y. 299, New Paltz, NY 12561 (914/255-1000; toll free 800/772-6646). 277 rms, some without bath. Flamboyant castle-hotel dating from 1869; the Victorian structure is a designated historic landmark. Resv. strongly advised at all times, and as far in advance as possible during the summer. **E–VE** (American Plan).

NEWBURGH The ▯▯ **Days Inn,** 845 Union Ave., Newburgh, NY 12550 (914/564-7550). 88 rms. Small, comfortable hotel overlooking Washington Lake. **I–M**

RHINEBECK The ☀ ▯▯ **Beekman Arms,** Beekman Sq., Rhinebeck, NY 12572 (914/876-7077). 50 rms. The oldest inn (1766) in the country; period decor and atmosphere but modern standards of comfort. **I–M**

WEST POINT The ☀ ▯ **Hotel Thayer,** S. Entry (off N.Y. 218), U.S. Military Academy, West Point, NY 10996 (914/446-4731). 197 rms. Venerable old hotel on the academy campus looking out on the Hudson. **I–M**

Where to Eat En Route

The following restaurants and inns are suitable places for a meal, if you're following the above itinerary.

GARRISON The ☀▯▯ **Bird and Bottle Inn,** Old Albany Post Rd. (914/424-3000). Lunch/dinner Wed–Sun. Authentic Revolutionary-period tavern attractively restored. French-inspired cuisine of refinement. **M**

HYDE PARK The ▯▯▯ **Escoffier Room,** on U.S. 9, 3 mi. (5km) north of town (914/471-6608). Lunch/dinner Tues–Sat. This is the dining rm of the Culinary Institute of America, where the country's future culinary greats are trained. Very carefully prepared French-inspired cuisine. Resv. a must. **M–E**

POUGHKEEPSIE The ☀▯▯ **Le Pavilion,** 230 Salt Point Tpke. (914/473-2525). Lunch Tues–Fri, dinner Mon–Sat. Charming inn in a 200-year-old building. Excellent Continental cooking. **I–M**

RHINEBECK The ☀☂☂ **Beekman 1766,** Beekman Sq. (914/871-1766). Lunch/ dinner daily. This is the oldest inn (1766) in the country; period decor and atmosphere. Contemporary cuisine supervised by Larry Forgione (of An American Place in Manhattan). **M–E**

STORMVILLE ☂☂☂ **Harrald's,** N.Y. 52 (914/878-6595). Dinner only, Wed–Sat. One of the finest rests. on the East Coast; with refined Continental cuisine and exemplary svce. **E** (prix fixe).

☖☖ **LONG ISLAND** (244 mi./390km r.t. by the Queens-Midtown Tunnel, Long Island Expwy., N.Y. 25A, N.Y. 106N, N.Y. 25A West, N.Y. 25W, ferry from Greenport to Shelter Island, N.Y. 1145, N.Y. 27W, N.Y. 27E, Robert Moses Pkwy. South, Ocean Pkwy. West, Loop Pkwy., the beaches at Long Beach, Atlantic Beach, Rockaway Beach, Flatbush Ave., the Belt Pkwy., the Brooklyn-Queens Expwy., and the Brooklyn-Battery Tunnel): White-sand beaches, dozens of little museums, old homes that recall the island's past, and picturesque fishing harbors, all just two or three hours' drive from the center of New York. Long Island has always been the favorite country retreat of celebrities, including Pres. Theodore Roosevelt; Albert Einstein (who worked out his General Theory of Relativity between two sailing trips); painters Willem de Kooning and Jackson Pollock; sculptor Isamu Noguchi; writers James Fenimore Cooper, John Steinbeck, Saul Bellow, Truman Capote, Edward Albee, and Kurt Vonnegut; and many others.

Leaving Manhattan to the east via the Queens-Midtown Tunnel and the Long Island Expwy. (I-495), stop first at **Great Neck,** home of the ☖ **U.S. Merchant Marine Academy** with its 1,000 students, at King's Point Rd. (516/773-5000), open daily; parades of midshipmen are on Sat in spring and fall.

Another 15 mi. (24km) east is ☀ **Oyster Bay,** a busy pleasure-boat harbor at the head of a long, narrow bay. See the ☖ **Raynham Hall Museum,** 20 W. Main St. (516/922-6808), open Tues–Sun. This old farmhouse, which was bought by Samuel Townsend in 1738, has been scrupulously restored; it played an important part in the War of Independence, particularly as the headquarters of the "Queens Rangers." ☀☖ **Sagamore Hill Historic Site,** 304 Cove Neck Rd. (516/922-4447), open daily, was the Summer White House from 1901 to 1909, and the final home of Theodore Roosevelt, who died in 1919. Authentic furnishings and many personal memorabilia of "Teddy." It's only a short distance to the ☖ **Theodore Roosevelt Memorial Sanctuary,** E. Main St. at Cove Rd., open daily, tomb of the 26th president in an 11-acre (4ha) park that is also a sea-bird sanctuary (516/922-3200).

On to the interesting ☖ **Whaling Museum,** commemorating a trade that once flourished on these shores, at **Cold Spring Harbor,** on Main St. (516/367-3418), open Tues–Sun. At nearby **Huntington,** lovers of poetry will be sure to pay their respects at the ☖ **birthplace of Walt Whitman** at 246 Old Walt Whitman Rd. (516/427-5240), with a museum and library devoted to the famous poet, open Tues–Sun.

Continuing eastward, don't fail to visit ☀☖☖ **"Eagles Nest,"** Little Neck Rd. in **Centerport** (516/854-5555), open Tues–Sun, a lovely house belonging to the Vanderbilt family, which stands in a 43-acre (17ha) park looking out over **Northport Bay.** It's now the home of the **Vanderbilt Museum,** with its natural-history collection. N.Y. 25A now passes part of **Sunken Meadow State Park,** a well-laid-out recreation area with huge sand beach and golf course, on its way to ☀ **Stony Brook,** a delightful seaside village founded in 1655 by settlers from Boston, which seems to have changed very little since colonial times. Several old houses and a remarkable group of small museums of art and history, ☖☖ **The Museums at Stony Brook,** Main St. at N.Y. 25A (516/751-0066), open Wed–Sun. Don't miss them—particularly the unique collection of 250 horse-drawn vehicles, coaches, and carriages. The road now passes through **Port Jefferson,** terminal of the ferry for Bridgeport, Conn., and rejoins N.Y. 25, passing through **Riverhead** (interesting **Suffolk County Historical Museum,** 300 W. Main St.; open Mon–Sat) on its way to **Greenport** and the ferry.

☀☖ **Sag Harbor,** at the head of Gardiners Bay, was once one of the most important whaling ports in the world; it inspired James Fenimore Cooper to write several stories about sailors and the sea. Besides the little streets lined with charming small houses, you should see the **Custom House,** on Garden St., a late 18th-century building that also served as the post office, and the **Whaling and Historic Museum,** Garden and Main Sts. (516/725-0770), open daily mid-May to Oct.

At **East Hampton,** founded in 1648 and also once a prosperous whaling port, the fishermen have by now given way to artists and wealthy summer so-journers. In and around the town are many 19th-century windmills, including one at 14 James Lane (516/324-0713), open daily Apr–Dec and by appointment the rest of the year; this is the ☖ **birthplace of John Howard Payne** (1791–1852), who wrote the words of "Home, Sweet Home." On to the east, and after a look at the **Town Marine Museum** in **Amagansett** on Bluff Rd. (516/267-6544), open Tues–Sun in summer (by appointment the rest of the year), with its delightful ship models, you reach ☀ **Montauk,** at the eastern tip of the island, a busy and picturesque fishing port (swordfish, tuna). Its miles of deserted beach, and the facilities for leasing sailboats, make it a very appealing resort. From ☖ **Montauk Point State Park,** with its 1795 lighthouse built on the orders of George Washington, you'll have a splendid view of the ocean. The Okeanos Ocean Research Foundation offers **whale-watching cruises** daily May–Sept, from Viking Dock, Montauk (516/728-4522).

On your way back to the city along N.Y. 27W, stop at ☖ **Southampton,** one of the island's two oldest towns (1640). With its many Colonial houses, it is to-day an elegant beach resort noted for its luxurious homes and fashionable shops. See the **Old Halsey Homestead** (1648), the oldest wooden house in all New York State, on S. Main St. (516/283-1612), open Tues–Sun from mid-June to mid-Sept. Return to Manhattan via N.Y. 27W as far as **Bay Shore,** where the Robert Moses Pkwy. leads off on the left to the long beach at **Jones Beach State Park,** very popular with New Yorkers during the summer. In the last stage of the trip you follow a succession of coastal highways between **Long Beach** and **Brooklyn.** On the way, lovers of lonelier beaches can explore **Fire Island National Seashore,** a thin belt of pine-planted sand dunes 31 mi. (50km) long abounding in fish and wildlife; it can be reached at either end of the park by bridge, or by ferry from Sayville or Bay Shore.

A very full two- to three-day trip.

Where to Stay En Route

The following hotels, motels, and inns are recommended as suitable places for a stopover.

EAST HAMPTON The ☀ ☘☘ **1770 House–Philip Taylor,** 143 Main St., East Hampton, NY 11937 (516/324-1770). 8 rms. Charming old inn dating from 1770, elegantly and comfortably furnished. **M–E**

EAST NORWICH The ☘☘ **East Norwich Inn,** jct. N.Y. 25A and N.Y. 106, East Norwich, NY 11732 (516/922-1500). 72 rms. Modern, very comfortable motel; acceptable rest. **M–E**

GREENPORT The ☘☘ **Sound View Inn,** North Rd., Greenport, NY 11944 (516/477-1910). 48 rms. Comfortable motel w. private beach. **M–E**

MONTAUK The ☘☘☘☘ **Montauk Yacht Club Resort Marina,** Star Island, Montauk, NY 11954 (516/668-3100). 107 rms. One of the most comfortable hotel-marinas on the eastern seaboard. **VE**

SHELTER ISLAND   The 🛎🛎 **Pridwin,** Shore Rd., Shelter Island, NY 11964 (516/749-0476). 40 rms. Comfortable motel on its own beach. Open May–Oct. **M–E**

SOUTHAMPTON   The 🛎🛎 **Cold Spring Bay,** N.Y. 27, Southampton, NY 11968 (516/283-7600). 64 rms. Inviting motel on Peconic Bay. **M**
   🛎 **Shinnecock,** 240 Montauk Hwy., Southampton, NY 11968 (516/283-2406). 30 rms. Functional motel a stone's throw from the beach. Open daily Apr–Dec, weekends only rest of the year. **M**

Where to Eat En Route

   The following inns and restaurants are suitable places for a meal, if you're following the above itinerary.

BAYVILLE   🍴🍴 **Steve's Pier 1,** 33 Bayville Ave. (516/628-2153). Lunch/dinner daily. Continental rest. on Long Island Sound. Excellent value. **I**

COLD SPRING HARBOR   The 🍴🍴 **Inn on the Harbor,** 105 Harbor Rd. (516/367-3166). Lunch/dinner daily. Good, reasonably priced continental rest. in a charming inn dating from 1680 with view of the harbor. **I–M**

EAST HAMPTON   The 🍴🍴 **Maidstone Arms,** 207 Main St. (516/324-5006). Breakfast/lunch/dinner daily. Pleasant French country inn setting, praiseworthy Continental cuisine. **I–M**

ISLAND PARK   🍴🍴🍴 **Coyote Grill,** 105 Waterview Rd. (516/889-8009). Lunch/dinner daily in the summer; closed Mon and Tues rest of the year. Southwestern-style gourmet *cocina* by chef Brendan Walsh (creator of Arizona 206 in Manhattan). Trendy clientele. Call two weeks ahead to book a wknd dinner. **M–E**

MONTAUK   The 🍴🍴 **Blue Marlin,** Edgemere and Flamingo Sts. (516/668-9880). Lunch/dinner Wed–Mon; closed Jan–Mar. Good seafood rest. in a pretty Early American setting. Good value. **I–M**

SHELTER ISLAND   🍴 **Cook,** 15 Grand Ave. at North Ferry (516/749-2005). Lunch/dinner Wed–Mon; closed Nov–May. Good fish rest. in an early 19th-century building. **B–I**

STONY BROOK   The 🍴🍴🍴 **Three Village Inn,** 150 Main St. (516/751-0555). Breakfast/lunch/dinner daily. 1785 Colonial inn with very good country food. A great place. **M**

🔭   **FINGER LAKES** (785 mi./1,256km r.t. via the George Washington Bridge, Palisades Interstate Pkwy., U.S. 6W, N.Y. 17N, I-81N, N.Y. 175W, U.S. 20W, N.Y. 89S, N.Y. 79W, N.Y. 14N, U.S. 20W,

N.Y. 21S, N.Y. 53S, N.Y. 54S, N.Y. 17E, I-81S, I-84E, N.Y. 235, I-80N, I-95N, and the George Washington Bridge): With its 11 lakes extended like fingers (the Iroquois legend says that God wanted to leave his handprint on the most beautiful place in his creation), its vineyards with about 40 growers, its green hills, gorges, and waterfalls, the Finger Lakes region draws more than half a million holidaymakers a year. As well as its beautiful landscapes, this quietly charming countryside offers a foothold in history, as the birthplace of some of the ideas and institutions that have helped to shape America: the abolition of slavery (Auburn), women's rights (Seneca Falls), and the Mormon church (Palmyra).

Head NE out of Manhattan by the George Washington Bridge, the Palisades Interstate Pkwy., and N.Y. 17 (also known as the Southern Tier Expwy.) on to I-81. Your first stop will be at ☀ **Syracuse,** capital of the lakes district, 270 mi. (430km) NE of New York, famed for its parks and its museums. Make a point of seeing the **Everson Museum of Art,** 401 Harrison St. (315/474-6064), open Tues–Sun, the first museum designed by I. M. Pei, with a fine collection of American painting and ceramics; the **Erie Canal Museum,** Erie Blvd. and Montgomery St. (315/471-0593), open daily, with exhibits on the construction of the historic canal; and ⚓ **Onondaga Lake Park,** Onondaga Lake Pkwy. (315/451-7275), where you'll find an interesting zoo, the **Salt Museum** (open daily May–Oct), as well as a faithful reconstruction of **Fort Ste. Marie Among the Iroquois,** the first camp set up here by the French in the 17th century.

After a stop at the delightful tourist town of **Skaneateles,** on the northern shore of the lake of the same name, go on to **Auburn** at the tip of **Owasco Lake,** a site occupied by Native Americans since the 11th century. In the 19th century it had two famous residents: William H. Seward, the secretary of state who bought Alaska from the Russians for a trifling consideration (see "Introducing Alaska" in Chapter 57 on Anchorage), and Harriet Tubman, a former slave whose influence and determination were instrumental in bringing about abolition; she saved more than 300 fleeing black slaves through her network of secret helpers, the Underground Railroad. The ⚓ **Tubman House** at 180 South St. (315/252-2081), now a museum, may be visited by appointment only.

Some 16 miles (25km) farther west, ☀ **Seneca Falls** is a place of pilgrimage for American feminists; here, in 1848, was held the first Convention for Women's Rights. The ⚓ **National Women's Hall of Fame,** 76 Fall St. (315/568-2936), open daily May–Oct, Wed–Sun the rest of the year, commemorates two centuries of the struggle for equal rights, and pays tribute to such past leaders as Amelia Earhart, Mary Harris (Mother Jones), Mary Cassatt, Abigail Adams, Helen Hayes, and Marian Anderson.

The route now runs along the left shore of **Cayuga Lake,** 40 mi. (64km) long, and after a stop to admire **Taughannock Falls,** higher than Niagara (215 ft./65m), you'll arrive in **Ithaca,** home of renowned ☀ **Cornell University** with 18,000 students. Visit the campus in its magnificent natural setting with two gorges formed by glacial runoff that cut through the campus and plummet about 100 ft. at their steepest point. The ⚓ **Herbert F. Johnson Museum,** Central Ave. (607/255-6464), open Tues–Sun, is an interesting art museum. Another must-see is the new ⚓⚓ **Performing Arts Center** and its innovative architecture designed by James Stirling and Michael Wilford.

Going on to the west, you come next to ⚓⚓ **Watkins Glen,** at the southern tip of beautiful **Seneca Lake,** the deepest in the region (630 ft./192m). Best known for its race track and **racing-car museum,** at 110 N. Franklin St. (607/535-4202), open Thurs–Sun afternoon June–Aug (by appointment the rest of the year), the town is scored across by the impressive glens that give it its name.

Now drive northward along the whole length of Seneca Lake as far as **Geneva;** if you enjoy fishing you'll want to know that summer visitors call it "the fisherman's paradise." ☀ **Canandaigua** is a little summer resort 17 mi. (27km) farther west at the tip of the lake of the same name; stop at the **Sonnenberg Gardens,** a lovely 50-acre (20ha) landscaped park on N.Y. 21N, open daily May–Oct; also see the ⚓ **Granger Homestead,** 295 N. Main St. (716/394-1472), the splendidly restored 1816 house of Gideon Granger, postmaster general under Presidents Jefferson and Madison. Complete with period furniture and a collection of horse-drawn carriages. Open Tues–Sat in May, Sept, and Oct; Tues–Sun June–Aug; closed rest of the year.

History buffs are advised to turn aside to **Palmyra,** 16 mi. (25km) north, where in 1820 the prophet Joseph Smith had the vision of the angel Moroni that led him to found the Mormon religion. See his childhood home, now a museum, on Stafford Rd., open daily; also **Hill Cumorah,** the hill where the prophet is said to have found the golden plates from which the Book of Mormon was translated. Visitor Center on N.Y. 21 (315/597-5851), open daily.

Head on past Lake Canandaigua to 🏚 **Hammondsport,** New York State's largest wine-growing center; the first vines were brought here from Germany and Switzerland in 1829. Many vineyards give conducted tours of their storehouses, among them **Bully Hill Vineyards,** Bully Hill Rd. via N.Y. 54A (607/868-3610), open daily May–Oct (Sat only, the rest of the year); and **Taylor Wineries,** on Pleasant Valley Rd. via N.Y. 54 (607/569-6111), open daily May–Oct (Mon–Sat the rest of the year), with the largest and finest cellars in the region. Two other places you won't want to miss here: the **Wine Museum of Greyton H. Taylor,** with everything about vines and wine, on G. H. Taylor Memorial Dr. via N.Y. 54A (607/569-6111), open daily Mon–Sat; and the **Glenn H. Curtiss Museum,** birthplace of one of the great early figures of aviation, now a historical museum, at Lake and Main Sts. (607/569-2160), open daily year round. Hammondsport shouldn't be bypassed.

Next stop is 🏚 **Corning,** the world's glass capital, where the giant 200-in. (5m) mirror of the Mount Palomar telescope was cast. Don't miss the **Corning Glass Center,** Centerway (607/974-8271), open daily, with its fascinating museum containing a unique collection of 23,000 glass objects, some of them 3,500 years old. Also interesting is the 🏚 **Rockwell Museum,** Denison Pkwy. and Cedar St. (607/937-5386), specializing in western art with pictures by Remington, Russell, Bierstadt, etc., and also displaying the very fine glass collection of Baron Steuben. Open daily.

At the end of the tour lies ☀ **Elmira,** famous as Mark Twain's favorite vacation spot; the author of *Huckleberry Finn,* who came here regularly for 20 years, is buried in **Woodlawn Cemetery** on Walnut St. You should also see his 🏚 writing study on the campus of **Elmira College,** Park Place (607/735-1800), open daily in summer, by appointment the rest of the year.

Back to Manhattan by way of **Binghamton,** an industrial city at the confluence of the Chenango River and Susquehanna River; the **Roberson Center for the Arts and Sciences,** 30 Front St. (607/772-0660), open Tues–Sun, has interesting collections of art and historical material. Then through the foothills of the **Pocono Mountains.**

A trip of at least four to five days, ideal for nature lovers.

Where to Stay En Route

The following hotels, motels, and inns are recommended as suitable places for a stopover.

GENEVA ☀🛎🛎 **Geneva on the Lake,** 1001 Lochland Rd., Geneva, NY 14456 (315/789-7190). 29 suites. Lovely old villa overlooking Lake Seneca; period furniture and romantic atmosphere. **E–VE**

☀🍷🍷 **Belhurst Castle,** Lochland Rd., Geneva, NY 14456 (315/781-0201). 13 rms. A small castle in the Romanesque style built on the shores of Lake Seneca in 1885 w. decor and furniture of the period. **M–E**

HIMROD The 🛎 **Rainbow Cove,** on N.Y. 14, Himrod, NY 14842 (607/243-7535). Inviting, likable small motel on Lake Seneca. Very good value. Closed Nov to mid-Apr. ∎

SKANEATELES The ☀ ¶¶ **Sherwood Inn,** 26 W. Genesee St., Skaneateles, NY 13152 (315/685-3405). 18 rms. Charming 1807 inn w. rest. on Lake Skaneateles. Good value. **I–M**

Where to Eat En Route

The restaurants and inns that follow are suitable places for a meal, if you're following the above itinerary.

ELMIRA HEIGHTS ☀♈♈♈ **Pierce's 1894,** 228 Oakwood Ave. (607/734-2022). Dinner only, Tues–Sun. Cuisine of a very high order in a lovely Victorian rest., run by the Pierce family since 1894. **I–M**

GENEVA The ☀♈♈ **Belhurst Castle,** on N.Y. 14 (315/781-0201). Impeccably prepared and served Continental cuisine in this small castle in the Romanesque style built on the shores of Lake Seneca in 1885 w. decor and furniture of the period; terrace on fine days. **I–M**

ITHACA ☀♈♈♈ **L'Auberge du Cochon Rouge,** 1152 Danby Rd. (607/273-3464). Dinner only, nightly. Some of the best food in the region—magnificent, refined French cuisine. Elegant old farmhouse w. duck pond. **I–M**

♈ **Turback's,** 919 Elmira Rd. (607/272-6484). Dinner nightly, brunch Sun. Luxurious Victorian manor; very skilled continental cuisine. **I**

SKANEATELES The ☀♈♈ **Sherwood Inn,** 26 W. Genesee St. (315/685-3405). Charming 1807 inn on Lake Skaneateles w. lake-view rest. and flawless traditional hotel cuisine. **I**

SYRACUSE ♈♈♈ **Pascale Wine Bar and Restaurant,** 304 Hawley Ave. (315/471-3040). Lunch Mon–Fri, dinner Mon–Sat. Wonderful French food at painless prices, and an elegant Victorian setting, account for the success of this very good rest. **I–M**

TRUMANSBURG The ♈♈ **Taughannock Farms Inn,** on N.Y. 89 (607/387-7711). Dinner nightly, brunch Sun. In this old farmhouse overlooking Cayuga Lake and Taughannock Park, you'll be served excellent family cooking at reasonable prices. Very good value. **I–M**

🏕🏕🏕 **ADIRONDACK PARK** (806 mi./1,290km r.t. via the Saw Mill River Pkwy., Taconic State Pkwy., I-90W, U.S. 4N, N.Y. 29W, I-87N, N.Y. 9N, N.Y. 22N, N.Y. 86W, N.Y. 30S, N.Y. 8W, I-90E, N.Y. 28S, N.Y. 80E, I-90E, I-87S, Palisades Interstate Pkwy. South, and the George Washington Bridge): There are places steeped in history like Lake George, Saratoga, and Ticonderoga, but also, and just as important, there are 2,800 lakes, 1,200 mi. (1,920km) of rivers, thousands of miles of brooks and streams, 42 mountains more than 4,000 ft. (1,200m) high, deep forests, peaks crowned with snow in winter, dozens of campgrounds, 750 mi. (1,200km) of marked trails. Plus a **Visitor Center** situated on N.Y. 30 in Paul Smith's, N.Y., about 15 mi. (24km) north of Saranac Lake, open daily year round. The Adirondacks (from the Iroquois name for the Algonquin, "Ha-de-ron-dah," or "skin-eaters"), are a paradise for lovers of unspoiled nature.

Leaving Manhattan northward along the Henry Hudson, Saw Mill River, and Taconic State Pkwys., make your first stop 155 mi. (248km) from Manhattan at ☀ **Albany,** the capital of New York State. Visit the **State Capitol,** a fine 1898 French Renaissance-style building on State St. (518/474-2418), open daily, and the **State University** on its beautiful campus at Washington and Western

Aves. (518/442-5571), open Mon–Fri. Also, take time to admire **Empire State Plaza,** one of the most successful complexes of modern architecture in the country, comprising a dozen striking structures devoted to administrative or cultural uses, including the **Performing Arts Center** (familiarly known as "the egg" on account of its shape), the 44-story **Corning Tower Building,** with an observation platform at the top, and the fascinating ♨♨**New York State Museum** (518/474-5877), open daily. There are a number of ♨ architecturally interesting old buildings you should see, including the 1761 **Schuyler Mansion** at 32 Catherine St.; the 1798 **Ten Broeck Mansion,** 9 Ten Broeck St., open Wed–Sun; and **Historic Cherry Hill,** dating from 1787, at 523½ Pearl St., open Tues–Sun.

Then on to ☀♨♨**Saratoga National Historical Park,** where in engagements on September 19 and October 7, 1777, American forces under the command of Gen. Horatio Gates inflicted a decisive defeat on Gen. John Burgoyne's British army, as a result of which France decided to make common cause with the Americans. Visitor center-museum (518/664-9821) open daily, and a marked road around the battlefield. Not far away is **Saratoga Springs,** whose renowned hot springs, two racecourses, and a polo ground attract every year a crown of racegoers—not to mention lovers of classical music and ballet: the ☀**Saratoga Performing Arts Center,** S. Broadway (518/587-3330), is open June–Sept. Also see the very unusual ♨**Petrified Sea Gardens,** 3 mi. (5km) west on N.Y. 29 (518/584-7102), open daily late May through Sept, with its fossils of prehistoric plants.

Glens Falls, which owes its name to the falls on the Hudson south of the town, has a beautiful art museum, the **Hyde Collection** at 161 Warren St. (518/792-1761), open afternoons Tues–Sun, with many paintings by such masters as Rembrandt, Rubens, and Picasso. Between mid-July and Aug it's also the scene of the very popular ♨ **Lake George Opera Festival** (for information, call 518/793-3858).

Continue on I-87N to ☀♨ **Lake George,** a pretty little resort town at the southern end of the lake of the same name. **Fort William Henry Museum,** Canada St., open daily May–Oct, is an exact replica of a British fort built in 1755. The **Lake George Steamboat Co.,** Beach Rd. (518/668-5777), offers one- to four-hour lake cruises, May–Oct.

Follow the lovely N.Y. 9N, which traces the shore of Lake George for almost 35 mi. (56km), to ☀♨♨**Ticonderoga,** another summer resort with historic interest. For almost two centuries it was the storm-center of countless battles and bloody engagements among Native Americans, French, British, Canadians, and Americans, witness the history of **Fort Ticonderoga,** built by the French in 1755 under the name of Fort Carillon and destroyed by the British in 1777, after it had been occupied by Ethan Allen and his Green Mountain Boys in the early morning of May 10, 1775. Now restored to its original condition and converted to a military museum, it should be visited by all history buffs; you'll find it on N.Y. 74 (518/585-2821), open daily mid-May to mid-Oct.

Next comes a 50-mi. (80km) scenic drive on N.Y. 9N and N.Y. 22N along the great and magnificent ☀**Lake Champlain** as far as ☀♨**Ausable Chasm,** 200-ft. (60m) gorges carved by the Ausable River and spilling into Lake Champlain in a series of torrential falls. Continuing westward, you come upon spectacular gorges (like the **High Falls Gorge,** near **Wilmington,** on N.Y. 86), before you reach ☀♨♨**Lake Placid,** the famous resort town where the Winter Olympics have been held twice: in 1932 and 1980. With the 5,344-ft. (1,629m) crest of New York State's highest mountain, Mount Marcy, looming in the background, Lake Placid draws a full house of tourists in winter and summer alike.

Leaving Lake Placid, the route touches, like gems on a long necklace, many of the countless lakes and resort areas of the Adirondacks: **Saranac Lake, Tupper Lake, Long Lake, Blue Mountain Lake**—where you should be sure to visit the splendid ♨ **Adirondack Museum,** devoted to the history of the region, on N.Y. 30 (518/352-7311), open daily mid-May to mid-Oct—before reaching ☀♨♨

Utica, a small industrial city on the Mohawk River distinguished by possessing one of the finest art museums in the entire state, the **Munson-Williams-Proctor Institute,** 310 Genesee St. (315/797-0000), open Tues–Sun. Works of Picasso, Jackson Pollock, Kandinsky, Paul Klee, and Thomas Cole, and sculptures by Calder and Henry Moore among others.

Last stop is ※🏠 **Cooperstown,** on Otsego Lake, a town dear to all American sports fans because it was here, in 1839, that Gen. Abner Doubleday devised the game of baseball; that's why it is now the site of the ※ **National Baseball Hall of Fame and Museum,** Main St. (607/547-7200), open daily, devoted to the history of the national sport and its greatest players—attendance tops 300,000 each year. Also see the **Farmer's Museum,** N.Y. 80N (607/547-2533), open daily May–Oct, illustrative of rural life in the 19th century; and **Fenimore House,** on N.Y. 80N (607/547-2533), open daily May–Dec, a lovely museum of American folklore dedicated to the writer James Fenimore Cooper, whose father founded the town in 1786.

Then back to Manhattan on I-90 and I-87. This trip, to which you should devote at least five days, can easily be combined with the tour of the Hudson Valley, since both follow the same highways for part of their routes (see "Hudson Valley," above).

Where to Stay En Route

The following hotels, motels, and inns are recommended as suitable places for a stopover.

BLUE MOUNTAIN LAKE ¶ **Hemlock Hall,** N.Y. 30, Blue Mountain Lake, NY 12812 (518/352-7706). 23 rms. Inviting little country motel on a lake. Closed Oct 15–May 15. **M** (Modified American Plan).

BOLTON LANDING The ※ ¶¶¶¶ **Sagamore Omni Hotel,** N.Y. 9N, Bolton Landing, NY 12814 (518/644-9400; toll free, see Omni). 350 rms. Wonderful Victorian palace, built in 1883 and now a designated historic landmark. Wonderfully situated on Lake George. Elegant and distinguished. Open year round. **VE** (Modified American Plan).

COOPERSTOWN The ※ ¶¶¶ **Otesaga Hotel,** Lake St., Cooperstown, NY 13326 (607/547-9931). 135 rms. Elegant, luxuriously furnished grand hotel in the Georgian style on Otsego Lake. Closed late Oct through Apr. **E–VE**
    ¶ **Lake View Motel,** 6 mi. (10km) north on N.Y. 80, Cooperstown, NY 13326 (607/547-9740). 14 rms. Small, engaging hotel w. direct access to the lake. Closed Nov–Mar. **I–M**

LAKE GEORGE ¶¶ **Dunham's Bay Lodge,** N.Y. 9N, Lake George, NY 12845 (518/656-9242). 44 rms. Modern, comfortable motel on Lake George. Closed Oct 15–May 15. **M–E**
    ¶¶ **Tahoe Beach Club,** N.Y. 9N, Lake George, NY 12845 (518/668-5711). 73 rms. Large, modern motel-marina on the lake. Closed from the end of Oct to mid-Apr. **I–M**

LAKE PLACID The ※ ¶¶¶ **Mirror Lake Inn,** 35 Mirror Lake Dr., Lake Placid, NY 12946 (518/523-2544). 140 rms. Luxury motel w. elegant Colonial interior on the lake. Rebuilt after a fire. Open year round. **M–E**
    ¶ **Town & Country,** 67 Saranac Ave., Lake Placid, NY 12946 (518/523-9268). 24 rms. Small motel w. attractive rms and balconies. Café nearby. **I–M**

LONG LAKE The ¶ **Shamrock Motel,** N.Y. 30, Long Lake, NY 12847 (518/624-3861). 17 rms and cottages. Rustic but comfortable lakeside motel. Closed Oct–May. **I**

SARANAC LAKE The ✻ 🍷🍷 **Hotel Saranac,** 101 Main St., Saranac Lake, NY 12983 (518/891-2200). 92 rms. Venerable hotel built in the '20s, now run w. masterly touch by the pupils of the hotel school at Paul Smith's College. Open year round. **I–M**

SARATOGA SPRINGS 🍷🍷🍷 **Sheraton** (formerly the Ramada Renaissance), 534 Broadway, Saratoga Springs, NY 12866 (518/584-4000; toll free, see Sheraton). 265 rms. Airy brick-with-copper exterior and contemporary comfort and equipment. Open year round. **M–E**

🌣🍷🍷 **Adelphi Hotel,** 365 Broadway, Saratoga Springs, NY 12866 (518/587-4688). 60 rms. A Victorian caravansary where musicians can occasionally be heard in impromptu performances. Pleasantly renovated several years ago. Closed Nov–May. **M–E**

Where to Eat En Route

The following restaurants and inns are suitable places for a meal, if you're following the above itinerary.

ALBANY 🌣🍷🍷 **Jack's Oyster House,** 42 State St. (518/465-8854). Lunch/ dinner daily. One of the city's oldest rests., passed from father to son since 1913. Excellent Continental food. **M**

GLENMONT The 🍷🍷 **Stone Ends Restaurant,** U.S. 9W, 4 mi. (6.5km) S of Albany (518/465-3178). Dinner only, Mon–Sat. Excellent contemporary American cuisine in a rustic mountain-chalet setting. **I–M**

LAKE GEORGE The 🍷 **Trolley Steak and Seafood,** Canada St. (518/668-3165). Lunch/dinner daily; closed Nov to mid-May. Appealing steakhouse w. very attractive prices. Terrace in summer. **B–I**

LAKE PLACID The 🍷 **Alpine Cellar,** Wilmington Rd. (518/523-2180). Dinner only, nightly; closed Apr to mid-May and Nov to mid-Dec. Bavarian setting and atmosphere. Very laudable German food. **I–M**

SARATOGA SPRINGS The ✻🍷🍷 **Spring Water Inn,** 139 Union Ave. (518/584-6440). Dinner Tues–Sun; also lunch July–Aug. A coaching inn dating from 1872, as does the decor. Praiseworthy continental cuisine. **M**

🌣🍷🍷 **Ye Olde Wishing Well,** U.S. 9, 4 mi. (6.5km) N of town (518/584-7640). Dinner nightly, brunch Sun; closed Mon Sept–June. A favorite of track regulars in a stagecoach stop from 1823 w. fireplaces and antiques. The cuisine is haute and hearty. **M**

UTICA 🍷🍷 **Café Metro,** 606 Huntington St. (315/735-0900). Lunch Tues–Fri, dinner Tues–Sat. Elegant rest. serving continental cuisine, in a 1920s building that once housed a bank. **I–M**

CHAPTER 4

NIAGARA FALLS 👯

□ □ □

Although of modest size (35 mi./55km long), the Niagara River ("thundering waters" in the Iroquois language) has the most famous, the most visited, and the most photographed falls in the world. Formed during the last glacial period 30,000–50,000 years ago, the falls, located midway between Lake Erie and Lake Ontario (which differ 324 ft./99m in water level), offer visitors a fabulous spectacle. Viewing the roaring waters of the **Horseshoe Falls** and the **American Falls** hurtling down from as high as 184 ft. (56m) is an awesome experience, especially from the Canadian side of the river—or better yet, on board the *Maid of the Mist* amid the swirling waters near the base of the falls.

Legend has it that the French explorer Jacques Cartier, in 1535, was the first "paleface" to be dazzled by the falls. Their "official discovery" 78 years later is credited to another Frenchman, Samuel de Champlain. Defining the border between New York State and the Canadian province of Ontario, the falls have become over the years one of the top tourist attractions in the United States—(15 million visitors each year). Despite Oscar Wilde's celebrated witticism—"the wedding trip brings two disappointments, the second being Niagara Falls"—tens of thousands of newlyweds have made Niagara Falls the country's honeymoon capital since 1806. This pleasant tradition will no doubt endure for some time to come; while the falls recede about 11.8 inches (30cm) every year, it will take at least 125,000 years before they reach Lake Erie and totally disappear!

Although the falls were formally given parkland status by the state of New York in 1885, the chemical and metallurgical industries, heavy consumers of electricity (the power station built below the falls is one of the most powerful in the United States), pollute and disfigure the American side. Also distressing to the eye is the scene on the Canadian side of the falls, which has been gradually transformed into a giant amusement park of dismaying vulgarity. But in spite of these ecological affronts, the falls remain an incredible living spectacle, even in winter when the water is frozen. Maximum rate of flow is approximately 740,000 gallons (7,000m³) per second.

BASIC FACTS: State of New York. Area codes: U.S. side, 716; Canadian side, 905. ZIP Code: 14302. Time zone: eastern. First discovery by a European, 1535?/1613. Settled: 1806. Approximate population of Niagara Falls: American side, 72,000; Canadian side, 70,000.

CLIMATE: Summer temperatures are relatively high, averaging 77° F (25° C) in July and Aug, but much more tolerable and a lot less humid than in New York City. Spring and autumn, both quite brief, are sunny but chilly. Winters—from the end of Oct to the end of Apr—are glacial, to the point where the falls themselves are frozen.

DISTANCES: Boston, 480 mi. (768km); Cleveland, 200 mi. (320km); Montréal, 421 mi. (674km); New York, 395 mi. (634km); Toronto, 145 mi. (232km); Washington, 425 mi. (680km).

ARRIVAL & TRANSIT INFORMATION

AIRPORT: Buffalo International Airport (BUF): 22 mi. (35km) SE.

AIRLINES: American (toll free 800/433-7300), Continental (toll free 800/525-0280), Delta (toll free 800/221-1212), Northwest (toll free 800/225-2525), United (toll free 800/241-6522), and USAir (toll free 800/428-4322).

CITY LINK: The **cab** fare from Buffalo Airport to Niagara Falls is about $25–$30; time, 35–40 min.

BUS Airport Shuttle (toll free 800/551-9369), departing 8am and 11am, serves the major hotels of Niagara Falls; fare, $14.50 (American side) or $15.75 (Canadian side); time, 50–60 min.

There is ample bus service in the Niagara Falls/border area (Metro Transit System: 716/285-9319); renting a car with unlimited mileage is thus not necessary unless you're planning an excursion to outlying places.

CAR RENTAL (at the Buffalo International Airport unless otherwise indicated): Avis (toll free 800/331-1212); Budget (toll free 800/527-0700); Dollar (toll free 800/800-4000); Hertz (toll free 800/654-3131); National (toll free 800/227-7368); Thrifty, 4646 Genesee St., Buffalo (toll free 800/367-2277).

LIMOUSINE SERVICES: Buffalo Limousine (716/835-4997), Carey Limousine (toll free 800/336-4646).

TAXIS: Although in theory you can hail a taxi on the street, the best way is to telephone **La Salle Cab Co.** (284-8833) or **United Cab** (285-9331).

TRAIN: Amtrak Station, 27th St. and Lockport Rd., Niagara Falls, N.Y. (toll free 800/872-7245). Area unsafe at night.

INTERCITY BUSES: Greyhound has bus stations on both sides of the border: **in the U.S.** at 4th and Niagara Sts., Niagara Falls (716/282-1331); and **in Canada** at 6761 Oakes Dr., Niagara Falls (905/734-8535).

INFORMATION & TOURS

TOURIST INFORMATION: The **Niagara Falls Convention & Visitors Bureau** (U.S.), 345 3rd St., Suite 101, Niagara Falls, NY 14303 (716/285-2400; toll free 800/338-7890).
Niagara Falls Visitor & Convention Bureau (Canada), 5433 Victoria Dr., Suite 202, Niagara Falls, ON L2G 3L1 (905/356-6061).

GUIDED TOURS (AMERICAN SIDE): Gray Lines Tours (bus) (716/694-3600): Guided tour of both sides of the falls and surrounding areas, serving major hotels.
Maid of the Mist (boat), Prospect Tower (716/284-4233): Boat tour to the foot of the falls through clouds of foam and spray; passengers are furnished with rain slickers. This is an unforgettable experience, not to be missed. Daily May–Oct.
Niagara Viewmobile, Prospect Point (716/278-1730): Tour by open-air shuttle system along the falls. Daily mid-May to mid-Oct.
Rainbow Helicopter Tours (helicopter), 454 Main St. (716/284-2800): Tour of the falls by air, lasting 6–7 min.; $35 per person. Impressive.

GUIDED TOURS (CANADIAN SIDE): Double Deck Tours (bus), 3957 Bossert Rd. (905/295-3051): Tour along the falls in an English double-decker bus. Pleasantly quaint.

Gray Line Tours (bus), 4555 Erie Ave. (905/357-2133).

Maid of the Mist (boat), Niagara River Pkwy. (905/358-5781): Boat tour to the foot of the falls through clouds of foam and spray; rain slickers furnished. An unforgettable experience, not to be missed. Daily May–Oct.

Niagara Helicopters (helicopter), 3731 Victoria Ave. (905/357-5672): Scenic helicopter flights over the falls. Year round, daily: 9am until sunset.

SIGHTS, ATTRACTIONS & ACTIVITIES— AMERICAN SIDE

THE FALLS: ※&& **American Falls,** between the east bank and Goat Island, 1,082 ft. (330m) wide, 184 ft. (56m) high. More headlong than the Canadian falls. Best viewing is in the morning from Prospect Point.

※&& **Cave of the Winds,** at the foot of Goat Island (716/278-1770): Underground grotto at the foot of the American Falls. Spectacular observation point. Access is by elevator and then by tunnel. Wooden footbridges allow you to venture within a few feet of **Bridal Veil Falls** (slickers and rubber boots provided). Open daily, mid-May to mid-Oct. Don't miss this!

MUSEUMS: & **Aquarium of Niagara Falls,** 701 Whirlpool St. (716/285-3575): From piranhas and sharks to dolphins and electric eels, more than 2,000 aquatic creatures from the world over can be seen here. The aquarium is of modern design and surrounded by beautiful gardens graced with outdoor sculpture. Worth seeing. Open daily.

& **Native American Center for the Living Arts ("The Turtle"),** 25 Rainbow Mall (716/284-2427): Curiously designed in the shape of a tortoise shell. Inside you'll find temporary art exhibitions, Native American crafts boutiques, a restaurant, etc. Open daily in summer, Tues–Sun the rest of the year.

※& **Schoellkopf Geological Museum,** Prospect Park (716/278-1780): Features the geological history of the falls. Interesting as much for its spiral design as for its collection of minerals tracing the evolution of the falls area over 500 million years. Lovely view of the Niagara River gorge. Open daily in summer, Wed–Sun the rest of the year.

PANORAMAS: ※&& **Goat Island,** in the Niagara River between the American and Canadian sides: Offers a striking view of the Horseshoe Falls from **Terrapin Point,** located at the extreme SW tip of the island. You'll enjoy an equally fantastic vista of the American Falls, and especially the Bridal Veil Falls, from tiny **Luna Island,** reached by footbridge from the extreme NW point of Goat Island.

※&& **Prospect Point Observation Tower,** Prospect Park (716/278-1770): A 282-ft. (86m) tower with a long footbridge over the void offering a magnificent scenic view of the American Falls. The *Maid of the Mist* tour boat leaves from the foot of the tower; see "Guided Tours (American Side)," above. Open daily.

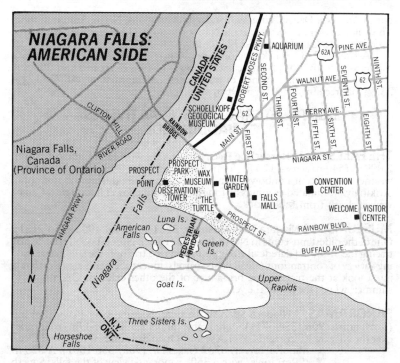

PARKS & GARDENS: ☼🏛 **Goat Island,** in the Niagara River between the American and Canadian sides: Auto and footbridges permit access to this little island planted squarely in the middle of the roaring Niagara River. Visitors will enjoy both splendid viewing and the chance for a pleasant stroll among the island's trees and flowers. It was here, in times past, that local Native American tribes practiced human sacrifice and buried their chiefs.

🏛 **Prospect Park,** Prospect Point: Great Lakes Garden w. kinetic water sculptures. In the visitor center, check out *Niagara Wonders,* a wide-screen, special-effect-filled look at the falls, shown daily on the hour (for information, call 278-1796).

🏛 **Wintergarden,** Rainbow Blvd. (716/285-8007): Immense seven-story greenhouse of ultramodern design. More than 7,000 plants and tropical trees flourish within the futuristic decor created by overhead walkways, glass elevators, waterfalls, and lagoons. Very pleasant atmosphere. Open daily.

SPECIAL EVENTS: Intertribal Pow-Wow (mid-May): Festival of Native American art and culture with hundreds of participants from all the tribes of

North America. Dances, singing, handcraft exhibitions, Native American food. This colorful event takes place at the Native American Center for the Living Arts, American side. Call 716/284-2427 for information.

Artpark, 7 mi. (11km) north on Robert Moses Pkwy. (June–Sept): Modern-art festival displaying current, original works of art in a vast 200-acre (80ha) park setting. Jazz, dance, opera, theater. For information, call 716/745-3377; toll free 800/659-7275. Open daily.

SIGHTS, ATTRACTIONS & ACTIVITIES— CANADIAN SIDE

THE FALLS: ☀️🔺🔺 **Horseshoe Falls,** between the west bank and Goat Island, 2,099 ft. (640m) across, 176 ft. (54m) high. The most spectacular falls; in sunny weather magnificent rainbows form above it, especially during the afternoon. Strikingly illuminated evenings by four-billion-candlepower floodlights. Can be viewed clearly from **Table Rock.**

MUSEUMS: ☀️🔺 **Niagara Falls Museum,** 5651 River Rd. (905/356-2151): One of the oldest museums in North America (1827). Note especially the display tracing the history of daredevil attempts to survive a trip over the falls in an amazing variety of contraptions (small boats, barrels, inner tubes). It's also worth taking a look at the picturesque bric-a-brac of the other exhibits. Open daily in summer; wknds the rest of the year.

PANORAMAS: 🔺 **Niagara Spanish Aerocar,** Niagara River Pkwy., 3½ mi. (5km) north (905/354-5711): Aerial cable car; its 1,800-ft. (549m) route goes over the Niagara River rapids. Worth seeing. Open daily mid-April to mid-Oct.

🔺 **Minolta Tower,** 6732 Oakes Dr. (905/356-1501): A 325-ft. (99m) tower with a 360° panoramic view of the falls. Superb observation point. Open daily.

☀️🔺🔺 **Skylon Tower,** 5200 Robinson St. (905/356-2651): Soaring to 518 ft. (158m), the tower offers unobstructed viewing and the most beautiful bird's-eye view of both the American and the Canadian Falls. The revolving restaurant at the top of the tower is mediocre, but don't miss the views! Open daily.

☀️🔺🔺🔺 **Table Rock,** Queen Victoria Park, Niagara River Pkwy. (905/358-3268): Awesome viewing from this observation platform located 25 ft. (8m) above the river's surface at the base of the Canadian Falls (slickers and rubber boots are furnished). Open daily.

PARKS & GARDENS: 🔺 **Queen Victoria Park,** Niagara River Pkwy.: A lovely English garden with flower-planted slopes stretching along the Niagara River. Splendid panoramic view of the American and Horseshoe Falls.

SHOPPING: **Maple Leaf Village,** 5685 Falls Ave. (905/374-4444): Both an amusement park and a giant shopping center. An additional feature is the 350-ft. (107m) Kodak observation tower. Shops, food stalls, restaurant. Open daily.

Skylon Centre, 5200 Robinson St. (905/356-2651): Shops, restaurants, a museum of automatons, and the adjacent **Imax Theatre,** an astonishing pyramidal movie house with a giant screen six stories tall. Worth a look. A stone's throw from the falls. Open daily.

THEME PARKS: 🔺 **Marineland,** 7657 Portage Rd., 1 mi. (1.6km) south of the falls (905/356-9565): Modern zoo with performing animal shows, from bears to killer whales. Amusement park with gigantic roller coaster. Open daily year round.

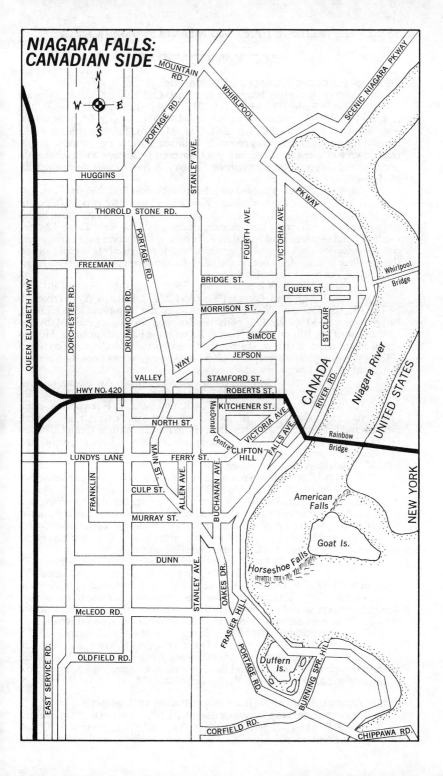

ACCOMMODATIONS

Personal Favorites (in order of preference)

ᗺ ᗺ ᗺ **Radisson Niagara** (dwntwn), Old Falls at 3rd St., Niagara Falls, NY 14303 (716/285-3361; toll free, see Radisson). 396 rms, A/C, color TV, in-rm movies. AE, CB, DC, MC, V. Gar. $5, pool, sauna, rest., bar, rm svce, nightclub, free crib. *Note:* Modern, functional hotel in the heart of the dwntwn area. Very complete facilities; spacious rms, some w. refrigerators; very efficient svce; pleasant pool. Favored by groups and convention-goers (direct access to the Convention Center). A 5-min. walk from the falls. **M–E,** but lower rates off-season.

ᗺ ᗺ ᗺ **Oakes Inn** (dwntwn), 6546 Buchanan Ave., Niagara Falls, ON L2G 3W2, Canada (905/356-4514). 167 rms, A/C, color TV, in-rm movies. AE, CB, DC, MC, V. Free parking, two pools, sauna, health club, miniature golf, rest., bar, rm svce, disco, crib $10. *Note:* Large 12-story modern hotel overlooking Horseshoe Falls on one of the best sites in the entire city. Observation deck on top. Large, comfortable rms (the best—especially on the top three floors—look out on the falls). Cheerful reception and svce. A fine place. **M–E,** but lower rates off-season.

ᗺ ᗺ **Michael's Inn** (dwntwn), 5599 River Rd., Niagara Falls, ON L2E 3H3, Canada (905/354-2727). 130 rms, A/C, cable color TV. AE, CB, DC, MC, V. Free parking, sauna, rest. (Embers Open Hearth), bar, rm svce, crib $10. *Note:* One of the best locations in Niagara Falls. Many rms have a view of the falls or of the Niagara River; some have refrigerators. Honeymoon Suites rather kitsch w. heart-shaped tubs for two. Modern and comfortable. Courteous, pleasant reception. Good steakhouse. Across from the Rainbow Bridge. **M–E,** but lower rates off-season.

ᗺ ᗺ **Ramada Inn** (nr. dwntwn), 401 Buffalo Ave., Niagara Falls, NY 14303 (716/285-2541; toll free, see Ramada Inns). 195 rms, A/C, color TV, in-rm movies. AE, CB, DC, MC, V. Free parking, pool, bike rental, rest. (Circle), bar, rm svce, disco, free crib. *Note:* A classic motel, modern and comfortable, a few steps away from the Convention Center. The terrace overlooks the Niagara River. Spacious rms w. balconies. Very acceptable rest. Frequented by groups and conventioneers. Good value. A 5-min. walk from the falls. **M–E,** but lower rates off-season.

ᗺ ᗺ **Days Inn** (dwntwn), 201 Rainbow Blvd., Niagara Falls, NY 14303 (716/285-9321; toll free, see Days Inn). 220 rms, A/C, color TV. AE, CB, DC, MC, V. Free parking, rest., bar, rm svce, disco, crib $3. *Note:* Antiquated but well-maintained hotel w. views of the falls from the upper floors. Spacious rms, some w. refrigerators. Friendly reception and service. Favored by groups and organized tours. Two minutes' walk from the base of the falls. Good value overall. **I–M,** but lower rates off-season.

ᗺ **Cascade Inn** (dwntwn), 5305 Murray St., Niagara Falls, ON L2G 2J3, Canada (905/354-2796). 67 rms, A/C, color TV, in-rm movies. AE, CB, DC, MC, V. Free parking, rest. (breakfast only), bar, rm svce, free crib. *Note:* Pleasant little motel open year round, close to the Skylon Tower. Comfortable and well maintained. Some rms have balconies and a view of the falls. Three minutes by foot from the falls. **M,** but lower rates off-season.

ᗺ **Budget Host Motel** (dwntwn), 219 4th St., Niagara Falls, NY 14303 (716/282-1734). 57 rms, A/C, color TV. AE, CB, DC, MC, V. Free parking, 24-hr. coffee shop adj., valet svce, crib $4. *Note:* Small modern motel very nr. the falls and the Convention Center. Huge, comfortable rms; friendly reception and svce. Very good value. **I–M**

Other Accommodations (from top bracket to budget)

ᗺ ᗺ ᗺ **Sheraton Fallsview** (dwntwn), 6755 Oakes Dr., Niagara Falls, ON L2G 3W7, Canada (905/374-1077). 295 rms, A/C, color TV, in-rm movies. AE, CB, DC, MC, V. Free parking, pool, sauna, health club, jogging track, two rests. (including Fallsview Dining Room), bar, rm svce, disco, free crib. *Note:* Brand-new 20-story hotel offering unobstructed views of the falls. Oversize, comfortable rms and suites. Efficient, attentive svce. The best location in town. **M–E,** but lower rates off-season.

♀♀ **Best Western Falls View** (nr. dwntwn), 5551 Murray Hill St.,
Niagara Falls, ON L2G 2J4, Canada (416/356-0551; toll free, see Best Western). 280 rms, A/C, color TV, in-rm movies. AE, CB, DC, MC, V. Free parking, two pools, saunas, rest. (Coach Room), coffee shop, bar, rm svce, free crib. *Note:* Huge functional six-story motel close to the falls. Comfortable rms w. private balconies or patios and refrigerators (some rather cramped). Good svce. Ideal for families. The Skylon Tower is close by. **M–E,** but lower rates off-season.

♀♀ **Holiday Inn Downtown** (dwntwn), 114 Buffalo Ave., Niagara
Falls, NY 14303 (716/285-2521; toll free, see Holiday Inns). 194 rms, A/C, color TV, in-rm movies. AE, CB, DC, MC, V. Free parking, pool, health club, sauna, holidome (indoor recreation center), rest., bar, rm svce, disco. *Note:* Typical Holiday Inn, 2-min. walk from the falls. Functional comfort. Good facilities. Clientele of groups and organized tours. Rates seem high for a plain motel. Excellent location for visiting the falls. **M–E,** but lower rates off-season.

♀♀ **Inn at the Falls** (formerly the Radisson; dwntwn), 240 Rain-
bow Blvd., Niagara Falls, NY 14301 (716/282-1212). 217 rms, A/C, color TV, in-rm movies. AE, CB, DC, MC, V. Free parking, pool, rest. (Wintergarden), coffee shop, bar, rm svce, disco, hrdrsr, boutiques. *Note:* Big new motel adjacent to the Wintergarden. Welcoming, comfortable rooms. Very acceptable rest. Good svce. Frequented by business travelers and groups (very close to the Convention Center). 3 min. on foot to the falls. **M–E,** but lower rates off-season.

♀ **Quality Inn Rainbow Bridge** (dwntwn), 443 Main St., Niaga-
ra Falls, NY 14301 (716/284-8801; toll free, see Choice). 166 rms, A/C, color TV, in-rm movies. AE, CB, DC, MC, V. Free parking, pool, rest., bar, valet svce, disco, crib $8. *Note:* A comfortable motel, recently renovated. Middling rest. Clientele mainly groups and organized tours. 5-min. walk from the falls. Good value overall. Right in the middle of dwntwn. **M,** but lower rates off-season.

♀ **Ameri-Cana Resort** (nr. dwntwn), 8444 Lundy's Lane, Niag-
ara Falls, ON L2H 1H4, Canada (416/356-8444; toll free 800/263-3508). 120 rms, A/C, color TV, in-rm movies. AE, MC, V. Free parking, pool, two tennis courts, rest. (V.I.P.), coffee shop, bar, disco, free crib. *Note:* Classic type of motel, but very well maintained and surrounded by 25 acres (10ha) of lawns and gardens. It's 15 min. by car to the falls; there's also free shuttle svce during the summer. Spacious, comfortable rms. The rest. is adequate. Ideal for families. Generally a group clientele. Good value. **I–M,** but lower rates off-season.

♀ **Lincoln Motor Inn** (nr. dwntwn), 6417 Main St. (Portage
Rd.), Niagara Falls, ON L2G 5Y3, Canada (905/356-1748). 60 rms, A/C, color TV, in-rm movies. AE, MC, V. Free parking, pool, rest. (Traveller's Delight), bar, crib $5. *Note:* Comfortable, well-kept little motel 5 min. by car from the falls. The rms are spacious; the rest. is adequate. Friendly reception. Good value. **I–M,** but lower rates off-season.

Hotels in the Vicinity

♀♀♀ **Holiday Inn Conference Center** (vic.), 100 Whitehaven Rd.
(at E. River), Grand Island, NY 14072 (716/773-1111; toll free, see Holiday Inns). 262 rms, A/C, color TV, in-rm movies. AE, CB, DC, MC, V. Free parking, two pools, health club, sauna, golf, two tennis courts, putting green, marina, fishing, cross-country skiing in winter, rest., coffee shop, bar, rm svce, disco, free crib. *Note:* Large, modern, comfortable six-story motel on the

banks of the Niagara River. Ideal for physical-fitness buffs. Pleasant rms w. balconies (renovated in 1990); good svce. Holiday Inn style, only better. Groups and conventioneers make up much of the clientele. It's 15-min. driving distance from the falls or from Buffalo Airport. **M–E,** but lower rates off-season.

YMCAs/Youth Hostels
Niagara Falls HI/AYH Hostel (nr. dwntwn), 1101 Ferry Ave. (at Memorial Pkwy.), Niagara Falls, N.Y. 14301 (716/282-3700): Youth hostel with 44 beds. Close to the falls.

Niagara Falls International Hostel (vic.), 4699 Zimmerman Ave., Niagara Falls, ON L2E 3M7 Canada (905/357-0770). 58 beds. Comfortable Tudorstyle building.

RESTAURANTS

Personal Favorites (in order of preference)

💯 **Rinderlin's** (vic.), 24 Burger St., Welland, Ont. (905/735-4411). Lunch Tues–Fri, dinner Tues–Sat; closed Dec 25. AE, MC, V. Jkt. *Specialties:* French cream of leek soup, veal w. cream of sage, Dover sole w. lemon-and-butter sauce, venison, white chocolate mousse torte w. raspberry sauce. *Note:* Served within an 1850s Victorian house, Emile Rinderlin's traditional French cuisine has been lauded as some of the best in Ontario. A nice array of Canadian wine. *French.* **I–M**

💯 **Victoria Park** (dwntwn), Niagara Pkwy., Queen Victoria Park, Niagara Falls, Ont. (905/356-2217). Lunch/dinner daily; closed mid-Oct to mid-May. AE, MC, V. *Specialties:* fresh salmon, roast beef, homemade pastry. *Note:* Venerable Victorian-style rest. w. open terrace facing the park and the falls. Pleasant gardens. Rather pretentious cuisine. Excellent svce. *Continental.* **I**

💯 **The Happy Wanderer** (dwntwn), 6405 Stanley Ave., Niagara Falls, Ont. (905/354-9825). A/C. Lunch/dinner daily; closed hols. AE, DC, MC, V. *Specialties:* Wiener schnitzel, sauerbraten, rouladen, schweinebraten. *Note:* Typical Bavarian-style chalet 2 min. from the falls. Rather kitschy interior decor. A classic of its kind for over 20 years. The German cuisine is hearty and the servings generous. *German.* **I**

💯 **Embers Open Hearth** (dwntwn), in Michael's Inn (see "Accommodations," above) (905/354-2727). A/C. Breakfast/lunch/dinner daily; closed Dec 25. AE, CB, DC, MC, V. *Specialties:* steak, prime rib, roast chicken, roast piglet. *Note:* Excellent broiled meats and spitted fowl, prepared while you watch, are the main attractions of this rest. Highly regarded by Niagara Falls residents. Honest, unimaginative cuisine. Diligent svce, good value. *Steak/American.* **I**

💯 **Arterial Restaurant** (dwntwn), 314 Niagara St., nr. 4th St., Niagara Falls, N.Y. (716/282-9459). A/C. Lunch/dinner daily (until 2am). MC, V. *Specialties:* hamburger, steak, seafood. *Note:* Nondescript setting but good burgers and chicken wings w. "napkins of distinction." A few steps from the Convention Center. *American.* **B**

Other Restaurants (from top bracket to budget)

💯 **Clarkson House** (vic.), 810 Center St., Lewiston, N.Y. (716/754-4544). A/C. Dinner only, Tues–Sun; closed Dec 25. AE, MC, V. Jkt. *Specialties:* char-broiled steak, lamb chops, Maine lobster, roast beef. Good homemade desserts. *Note:* Old inn dating from the 19th century and retaining the elegant decor of that era. The cooking, however, is uneven. 10 min. from Niagara Falls. Resv. desirable. *Steak.* **I–M**

💯 **Red Coach Inn** (dwntwn), 2 Buffalo Ave., Niagara Falls, N.Y. (716/252-1459). A/C. Lunch/dinner daily; closed Dec 25. AE, MC, V. Jkt. *Specialties:* trout meunière, roast duck, roast beef, veal boursin, chicken alouette. Good wine list. *Note:* Very pleasant decor in the style of an old English inn. During the summer, diners on the outdoor terrace enjoy a view of the Niagara River rapids. The cooking is respectable, the svce efficient. Resv. recommended. Heavily patronized by tourists. *Continental/American.* I

    ♀ **Queenston Heights** (vic.), 6 mi. (9.5km) north on Niagara Pkwy., Niagara Falls, Ont. (905/262-4274). A/C. AE, MC, V. Lunch/dinner daily, brunch Sun; closed 25. *Specialties:* ribs, roast beef, roast pork, leg of lamb, quail, rabbit stew. *Note:* Lovely view of the Niagara River from the glassed-in terrace. Tudor decor, w. a pleasant patio for summer dining. The cooking is estimable and the svce friendly. A 10-min. drive from the falls. Resv. advised. *Continental.* I

    ♀ **Suisha Gardens** (dwntwn), 5705 Falls Ave., Niagara Falls, Ont. (905/357-2660). A/C. Lunch daily during the summer, dinner nightly year round; closed Dec 25. AE, CB, DC, MC, V. Jkt. *Specialties:* tempura, sukiyaki, teriyaki. *Note:* Located on the second floor of the Maple Leaf Village Shopping Center, Suisha is the only Japanese restaurant in Niagara Falls worthy of the name. The cuisine is 100% authentic, the decor all-purpose Oriental. The cooks show off their dexterity w. the chopping knife right in front of your eyes. Resv. advised during the summer and on wknds. *Japanese.* I

    ♀ **Riverside Inn** (vic.), 115 South Water St., Lewiston (716/ 754-8206). A/C. Lunch Mon–Sat, dinner daily, brunch Sun. AE, CB, DC, MC, V. *Specialties:* slow-roasted prime rib, fresh fish, aged steaks, lobster. *Note:* A lively rest. w. a distinguished wine list at fair prices. The deck, set on the river, has an amazing view of the Niagara Gorge. 10 minutes from dwntwn Niagara. *Steak/Seafood.* I

    ☼♀ **Table Rock Restaurant** (dwntwn), Queen Victoria Park, Niagara Falls, Ont. (905/354-3631). A/C. Breakfast/lunch/dinner daily; closed Dec 25. AE, MC, V. *Specialties:* hamburger, steak, seafood, Canadian dishes. *Note:* The only rest. situated right at the brink of the Horseshoe Falls. Entirely renovated in 1991. Uninspired food, but breathtaking view of the falls and upper rapids. *American.* B–I

    ♀ **Alps Chalet** (nr. dwntwn), 1555 Military Rd., Niagara Falls, N.Y. (716/297-8990). A/C. Lunch/dinner Tues–Sun (until 2am). AE, CB, DC, MC, V. *Specialties:* roast beef, Greek dishes, lobster, baklava. *Note:* Some good Greek-inspired dishes in a rest. whose decor suggests a mountain chalet. The quality of the cooking doesn't seem to suffer much from this curious mix of styles. *American/Greek.* B–I

    ♀ **Carlos O'Brian's** (dwntwn), 5645 Victoria Ave., Niagara Falls, Ont. (905/357-1283). A/C. Lunch/dinner daily (until midnight); closed Mon Nov to late March and Dec 25. AE, DC, MC, V. *Specialties:* steak, prime rib, catch of the day, shellfish. *Note:* Pleasant tavern w. inviting rustic decor. Good broiled prime cuts and fish dishes. Relaxed atmosphere, friendly svce. Popular w. the locals. Resv. suggested wknds. *Steak/Seafood.* B–I

    ♀ **Como Restaurant** (nr. dwntwn), 2220 Pine Ave., Niagara Falls, N.Y. (716/285-9341). A/C. Lunch/dinner daily (until midnight); closed Dec 25. AE, MC, V. *Specialties:* homemade pasta, Italian dishes, steaks, sandwiches. *Note:* Both a deli and an Italian rest., this establishment run by the same family since 1927 has become a local institution. You'll enjoy good, honest Italian-American cooking in a pleasant, relaxed atmosphere. Excellent value. 8 min. from dwntwn. *Italian/American.* B–I

    ♀ **John's Flaming Hearth** (nr. dwntwn), 1965 Military Rd., Niagara Falls, N.Y. (716/297-1414). A/C. Lunch/dinner daily. AE, DC, MC, V. *Specialties:* steak, surf and turf (steak and lobster), catch of the day, pumpkin ice-cream pie. *Note:* Enormous rest. 10 min. from the falls. A true local institution. The USSR's Premier Kosygin ate here during his visit to the States in 1967. Good value. Usually crowded and noisy. Pleasant atmosphere. *Steak/Seafood.* B–I

In the Vicinity

☀☿♈ **Schimschack's** (vic.), 2943 Upper Mountain Rd., Pekin, N.Y. (716/731-4111). A/C. Dinner nightly, brunch Sun; closed Mon–Tues Dec–Apr, also Dec 24–25. AE, CB, DC, MC, V. Jkt. *Specialties:* Florida stone crab (in season), charcoal-broiled baby back ribs, steak, catch of the day, peanut-butter pie. *Note:* Located on the heights overlooking Lake Ontario—on a clear day you can see Toronto—this rest. offers excellent country cooking. Colonial-style decor w. a terraced dining room. Legend holds that Marilyn Monroe first met Joe Di Maggio here during the filming of the movie *Niagara.* Good svce. Definitely worth the 20-min. drive from Niagara Falls (via N.Y. 104, N.Y. 31, and N.Y. 429). *Steak/Seafood.* **I–M**

NEARBY EXCURSIONS IN NEW YORK STATE

☀♨♙ **OLD FORT NIAGARA** (14 mi./22km north on Robert Moses Pkwy.) (716/745-7611): French military fortress dating from 1726; its well-preserved fortifications tower above Lake Ontario. Occupies the site of an earlier fortress built in 1679. Numerous artillery pieces from bygone eras are on display in the fort **museum,** and in summer there are military parades featuring soldiers in period uniforms. Fort Niagara played an important role in the War of 1812. Worth a side trip. Open daily year round.

♙ **GRAND ISLAND** (6 mi./9km south on I-190): Very popular summer vacation spot. Numerous parks, campsites, and picnic areas dot this 7½- by 5½-mi. (12-by 9km) island located in the middle of the Niagara River upstream from the falls. Amusement park—**Fantasy Island,** 2400 Grand Island Blvd. (716/773-7591)—open daily in summer.

☀♙ **NIAGARA POWER PROJECT** (5 mi./8km north via Lewiston Rd./N.Y. 104) (716/285-3211): Inaugurated in 1963, this is one of the most powerful hydroelectric power stations in the U.S.; with a continuous output of 2.5 million kilowatts per hour, it can more than meet all the electricity needs of a city the size of Chicago. There's an arresting panoramic view of the river gorge from the **observation platform,** and an interesting model of the power station in the **Visitor Center.** Open daily.

NEARBY EXCURSIONS IN CANADA

☀♙ **FORT GEORGE** (14 mi./23km north on the Niagara River Pkwy.) (905/468-3938): Constructed in 1796, this imposing fortress, sheltered behind massive ramparts, was formerly the principal British stronghold along the Canadian frontier. Consists of 12 restored buildings. Particularly active during the War of 1812. Open daily mid-May through Oct; visit by appointment during the rest of the year.

☀♨♙ **NIAGARA-ON-THE-LAKE** (14 mi./22km north on the Niagara River Pkwy.): Formerly the capital of Upper Canada, this picturesque town founded in 1776 is one of the region's main tourist attractions. Built on a lovely site along Lake Ontario, the town contains dozens of carefully restored old houses (the town was put to the torch in 1813 during the second British-American war). Charming Edwardian-vintage ambience.

The **Shaw Festival Theatre** is very popular in the summer. For information, call 905/468-2172.

Where to Stay and Eat

Two 19th-century inns are highly recommended:

☀♦♙♙ **Pillar & Post Inn,** King and John Sts., Niagara-on-the-Lake, ON L0S 1J0 (905/468-2123). 91 rms. Also a good rest. **E**

♙♙ **Prince of Wales,** 6 Picton St., Niagara-on-the-Lake, ON L0S 1J0 (905/468-3246): 104 rms. Also a very decent rest. **M–E**

🔔 **WHIRLPOOL RAPIDS** (2 mi./3.5km north on the Niagara River Pkwy.): Very lovely view of the Niagara River's rapids and whirlpools. Should be seen.

CHAPTER 5

THE ATLANTIC COAST ♟♟

☐ ☐ ☐

From the Canadian Border to New York City

The Atlantic seaboard, for a stretch of some 900 mi. (1,400km) between the border with the Canadian province of New Brunswick and New York City, is at once the historic cradle of the United States, the theater of its seafaring destiny, and an eye-opening testimony to its diverse countrysides and landscapes.

The rocky, jagged shores of **Maine;** the gentle, eye-pleasing sands of **Long Island Sound** or the dunes of **Cape Cod;** the little fishing ports and pleasure harbors of New England with their innumerable churches and old brick or pastel-washed frame houses, such as **Bar Harbor, Mystic, Gloucester,** and **New Bedford,** are a wonderful background to the giant megalopolis of Boston and New York. The stark Canadian winters and blizzards of **Acadia National Park** will help take your mind off New York's hot, sticky summers. And the futurist highrises of Boston and New York must share your attention with some of the oldest buildings in this country, some of them going back more than 300 years. For it was along this coast, which you can drive from end to end in a matter of hours, that America first saw the light. From **Plymouth,** where the Pilgrims landed, the earliest permanent settlements in the northern U.S. are strung out like beads on a necklace: **Hartford** (1623), **New York** (1626), **Salem** (1626), **Boston** (1630), **Cambridge** (1630), **Portland** (1631), **Newburyport** (1635), **Providence** (1636), **New Haven** (1638), **Hyannis** (1639), and so on. The Atlantic seaboard between New York and Boston is, to this day, that part of the country most thickly populated by immigrants from the Old World and their descendants.

Besides these cities and history-laden harbor towns, there is much to attract lovers of the seashore, from the endless beaches of Massachusetts to the dozens of islands, big and little, scattered along the coast—including **Monhegan Island,** offshore from Maine, where according to some historians the Viking Leif Ericson made landfall around the year 1000, almost 500 years before Christopher Columbus "discovered" America. Big-game fishermen can indulge their passion at **Martha's Vineyard, Marblehead,** and **Nantucket Island,** all three also fashionable resorts. Art enthusiasts will not fail to visit such museum towns as **Portsmouth** and above all **Newport,** with its dream mansions; Newport, long the scene of the America's Cup races, is also well known for its regattas (see Chapter 1 on Boston, Chapter 2 on Cape Cod, and Chapter 3 on New York).

BASIC FACTS: States of Maine, New Hampshire, Massachusetts, Rhode Island, Connecticut, and New York. Area codes: 207 (Maine), 603 (New Hampshire), 617 and 508 (Massachusetts), 401 (Rhode Island), 203 (Connecticut), and 212, 718, 917, 914, and 516 (New York). Time zone: eastern. Distance as the crow flies from New York City to the Canadian border at Calais, Maine: 810 mi. (1,300km).

CLIMATE: With the cold Labrador Current washing its entire coastline, the climate of the New England littoral tends to extremes. Harsh and snowy—indeed, in the case of Maine or New Hampshire, downright icy—winters (Jan mean temperature, 21°F/−6°C) are followed by a short, temperate spring and a summer that's rarely too hot but often very humid, particularly in the coastal strip from New York City to Cape Cod (avg. temperature for July, 69°F/21°C). By far the best time to visit the Atlantic coast is the fall, with its crisp, dry days (about 59°F/15°C), to say nothing of the glorious coloring of the leaves during the "Indian summer." Except in late summer and fall, bring your umbrella.

ARRIVAL & TRANSIT INFORMATION

AIRPORTS: The **Bangor** International Airport (BGR), 2 mi. (3.5km) NW.
   Boston: Logan International Airport (BOS) (see Chapter 1 on Boston).
   Hartford: Bradley International Airport (BDL), 11 mi. (17km) north.
   New York: John F. Kennedy International Airport (JFK), La Guardia Airport (LGA), and Newark International Airport (EWR) (see Chapter 3 on New York).
   Portland: International Jet Port (PWM), 2 mi. (3km) west.
   Providence: T. F. Green State Airport (PVD), 7 mi. (11km) south.

U.S. & FOREIGN AIRLINES: Hartford: Air Canada (toll free 800/776-3000), American (toll free 800/433-7300), Continental (toll free 800/525-0280), Delta (toll free 800/221-1212), TWA (toll free 800/221-2000), United (toll free 800/241-6522), and USAir (toll free 800/428-4322).
   Providence: American (toll free 800/433-7300), Continental (toll free 800/525-0280), United (toll free 800/241-6522), and USAir (toll free 800/428-4322).
   Boston, Cape Cod, New York: See Chapters 1, 2, and 3.

BUS OR CAR RENTAL? The Greyhound Bus Company has excellent service along the entire coast from New York to the Canadian border. However, the innumerable opportunities for side trips in the area strongly suggest renting a car or mobile home with unlimited mileage. (But don't do it in New York, where the rates are among the highest in the country.)

CAR RENTAL: See Chapters 1, 2, and 3 on Boston, Cape Cod, and New York. For rentals elsewhere, consult the local telephone directory.

TRAIN: Amtrak (toll free 800/872-7245) has stations on Union Place in **Hartford,** Conn.; Union Ave. in **New Haven,** Conn.; and at 100 Gaspee St. in **Providence,** R.I.
   For the terminal in **Boston,** see Chapter 1; for the terminal in **New York,** see Chapter 3.

INTERCITY BUSES: The **Greyhound Bus Co.** has terminals or stops at 158 Main St., **Bangor,** Me. (207/945-3000); 1 Union Place, **Hartford,** Conn. (203/522-9267); 45 George St., **New Haven,** Conn. (203/772-2470); 950 Congress St., **Portland,** Me. (207/772-6587); and 9 Congress St., **Portsmouth,** N.H. (603/436-0163).

For the terminal in **Boston,** see Chapter 1; for the terminal in Cape Cod, see Chapter 2; for the terminal in **New York,** see Chapter 3.

INFORMATION, TOURS & ADVENTURES

TOURIST INFORMATION: You'll find a flood of tourist information available from both state-government and local sources. On the road, feel free to stop at the local chambers of commerce or convention and visitors bureaus for on-the-spot assistance and information.

State-Government Sources

Connecticut Department of Economic Development, 865 Brook St., Rocky Hill, CT 06067 (203/258-4200; toll free 800/282-6863).

Maine Publicity Bureau, 325 B Water St., Hallowell, ME 04347 (207/623-0363).

Massachusetts Office of Travel & Tourism, 100 Cambridge St., Boston, MA 02202 (617/727-3203; toll free 800/632-8038).

New Hampshire Hospitality Association, 4 Park St. (P.O. Box 1175), Concord, NH 03301 (603/228-9585).

Rhode Island Tourist Promotion Division, 7 Jackson Walkway, Providence, RI 02903 (401/277-2601).

Local Sources

Augusta Office of Tourism, 189 State St., Augusta, ME 04333 (207/289-5710).

Bangor Chamber of Commerce, 519 Main St. (P.O. Box 1443), Bangor, ME 04401 (207/947-0307).

Bar Harbor Chamber of Commerce, 93 Cottage St. (P.O. Box 158), Bar Harbor, ME 04609 (207/288-5103).

New Bedford–Bristol County Convention and Visitors Bureau, 70 N. 2nd St. (P.O. Box 976), New Bedford, MA 02741 (508/997-1250).

New Haven Convention and Visitors Bureau, 900 Chapel St., New Haven, CT 06510 (203/787-8822).

Newport Convention and Visitors Bureau, 23 America's Cup Ave. South, Long Wharf Mall, Newport, RI 02840 (401/849-8048).

Portland Chamber of Commerce, 145 Middle St., Portland, ME 04101 (207/772-5800).

Portsmouth Chamber of Commerce, P.O. Box 239, Portsmouth, NH 03801 (603/436-1118).

Providence Convention and Visitors Bureau, 30 Exchange Terrace, Providence, RI 02903 (401/274-1636).

GUIDED TOURS: In addition to the information below, see also Chapters 1 and 2 on Boston and Cape Cod. For all other locations, see the local *Yellow Pages* under "Sightseeing."

Newport, R.I.

Viking Tours (bus), 23 America's Cup Ave. (401/847-6921): Guided bus tour of the city and surroundings, year round. Serves the principal hotels.

Viking Queen (boat), Goat Island Marina, Washington St. (401/847-6921): One-hour trip on Newport Bay and Rhode Island Sound, allowing you a view from offshore of the mansions of bygone millionaires. Daily May to mid-Oct.

Portland, Me.

Casco Bay Lines (boat), Custom House Wharf, 56 Commercial St. (207/774-7871): Scenic-cruises around Portland Harbor and lovely Casco Bay with its 136 islands. Daily year round.

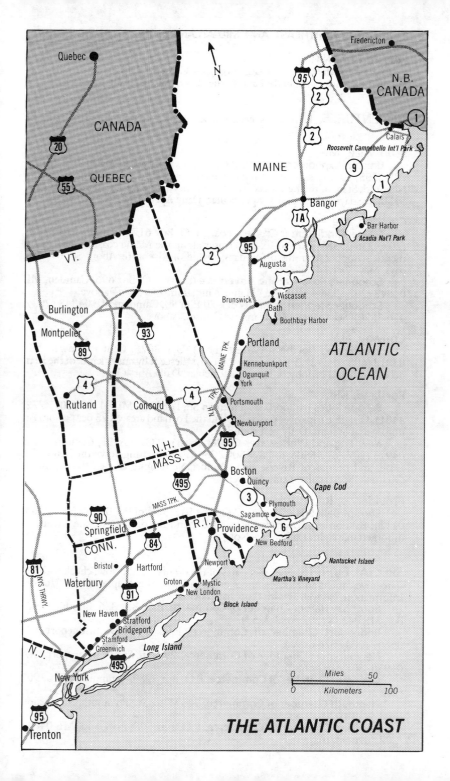

THE ATLANTIC COAST

Portsmouth, N.H.
　　Portsmouth Harbor Cruises (boat), 64 Ceres St., Old Harbor (603/436-8084): Boat trips in the harbor and to the Isles of Shoals. Daily June–Oct.

ADVENTURES: Here are special cruises/trips available along the Atlantic coast.

Brunswick, Me.
　　Unicorn Expeditions (boat), P.O. Box T, Brunswick, ME 04011 (207/725-2255): One to six days rafting down the upper Hudson and Moose River in New York State or the Kennebec River and Penobscot River in Maine. Two days, $180; five days, $545 approx. Spectacular. Daily Apr–Oct.

Camden, Me.
　　Maine Windjammer Cruises (boat), P.O. Box 617, Camden, ME 04843 (207/236-2938): Two- to six-day cruises along the Maine coast aboard an authentic schooner from the olden days; a whiff of adventure. About $600 for six days. May–Oct.
　　Schooners *Roseway* and *Adventure* (boat), P.O. Box 696, Camden, ME 04843 (207/236-4449): See "Maine Windjammer Cruises," above.
　　Schooner *Stephen Taber* (boat), 70 Elm St., Camden, ME 04843 (207/236-3520): See "Maine Windjammer Cruises," above.

Conway, N.H.
　　Saco Bound Northern Waters (boat), U.S. 302E, Center Conway, NH 03813 (603/447-2177): One to several days' descent by raft or kayak of the Kennebec River and Penobscot River. Spectacular. Daily Apr–Oct.

Portland, Me.
　　Balloon Rides (balloon), 17 Freeman St., Portland, ME 04103 (207/772-4401): Dirigible trips over Casco Bay and the Portland area; $125 per person. An unforgettable sight. Daily year round.
　　New England Whitewater Center (boat), P.O. Box 21, Caratunk, ME 04925 (207/672-5506; toll free 800/766-7238): Rafting down the Kennebec, Dead, and Penobscot Rivers, with comfortable lodging at the Sterling Inn at Caratunk. Spectacular. Daily Apr–Oct.

Providence, R.I.
　　Stumpf Balloons (balloon), P.O. Box 913, Bristol, RI 02809 (401/253-0111): Balloon trips over Narragansett Bay and the coast of Rhode Island; an unforgettable sight. Daily May–Nov.

SPECIAL EVENTS: For exact dates of the events listed below, check with the state-government and local sources listed earlier in this chapter under "Tourist Information," as well as with those listed below:
　　Boothbay Harbor Chamber of Commerce, P.O. Box 356, Boothbay Harbor, ME 04538 (207/633-2353).
　　Bridgeport Chamber of Commerce, P.O. Box 999, Bridgeport, CT 06601 (203/576-8491).
　　Newburyport Chamber of Commerce, 29 State St., Newburyport, MA 01950 (508/462-6680).
　　Ogunquit Chamber of Commerce, P.O. Box 2289, Ogunquit, ME 03907 (207/646-2939).
　　Plymouth Chamber of Commerce, 225 Water St., Plymouth, MA 02360 (508/830-1620).
　　Rockland Chamber of Commerce, P.O. Box 508, Rockland, ME 04841 (207/596-0376).

Bar Harbor, Me.
Art Exhibit (third wknds of July and Aug): Work by local artists.

Boothbay Harbor, Me.
Windjammer Days (late June): Review of old schooners in the bay; very picturesque. Parade, concert.

Bridgeport, Conn.
Barnum Festival (late June to early July): Parades, concerts, and art exhibitions bearing on the history of the circus. The 10-day event includes a drum corps competition, circus, rodeo, etc.

Camden, Me.
Camden Amphitheatre (July–Aug): Outdoor theater; musical and theatrical performances (Atlantic Ave.; call 207/236-4404 for information).

Newburyport, Mass.
Yankee Homecoming (late July to early Aug): Boat races, parades, food festival.

New Haven, Conn.
Powder House Day (first Sat of May): Pageant showing the capture of the arsenal during the Revolutionary War.

Newport, R.I.
Music Festival (two weeks in mid-July): Chamber-music concerts in the mansions of 19th-century millionaires; call 401/846-1133 for information.
Jazz Festival (mid-Aug): With all the big stars. Fort Adams State Park.
Wooden Boat Show and Classic Yacht Regatta (mid-Aug): Annual yachting competition, very popular with sailboat buffs.

Ogunquit, Me.
Ogunquit Playhouse (late June to Labor Day): Plays of high quality and musicals; call 207/646-5511 for information.

Plymouth, Mass.
Thanksgiving Week (Nov): Commemorating the first celebration of Thanksgiving by the Pilgrims.

Portland, Me.
New Year's Eve Portland (Dec 31): Shows, parades, fireworks, concerts.

Portsmouth, N.H.
Jazz Festival (late June to early July): Jazz concerts on the historic Portsmouth waterfront; call 603/436-7678 for information.

Providence, R.I.
House and garden tours of privately owned Colonial, Federal, and Victorian homes. Costumed guides and candlelight tours, first wknd of June.

Rockland, Me.
Maine Lobster Festival (first wknd of Aug): Three days of joyous gluttony devoted to that most illustrious denizen of Maine's waters—the lobster. Also wooden crate race in Penobscot Bay and parade.

A NORTH TO SOUTH ITINERARY
The section of this guide devoted to the Atlantic coast has been organized as an itinerary, starting at Calais, Me., and ending in New York City, a distance of almost 900 miles (1,440km). You may choose not to drive the whole distance; key towns such as Bangor, Portland, Boston, Portsmouth, Providence, Hartford, and New York are linked by air, bus, and train, while car rentals are available

everywhere. In that case, you may select from the following travel plan the parts that appeal to you most.

Distances Down the Atlantic Coast

From	To	Distance
Calais, Me.	Roosevelt/Campobello	53 mi. (84km)
Roosevelt/Campobello	Bar Harbor	110 mi. (176km)
Bar Harbor	Camden	78 mi. (125km)
Camden	Pemaquid Point	48 mi. (77km)
Pemaquid Point	Wiscasset	22 mi. (35km)
Wiscasset	Boothbay Harbor	12 mi. (19km)
Boothbay Harbor	Bath	22 mi. (36km)
Bath	Brunswick	10 mi. (16km)
Brunswick	Portland	26 mi. (44km)
Portland	Kennebunkport	30 mi. (45km)
Kennebunkport	Ogunquit	11 mi. (18km)
Ogunquit	York	7 mi. (11km)
York	Portsmouth, N.H.	6 mi. (10km)
Portsmouth, N.H.	Newburyport, Mass.	21 mi. (33km)
Newburyport, Mass.	Boston area (Gloucester, Marblehead, Rockport, Salem)	28–72 mi. (45–115km)
Boston area	Quincy	9 mi. (15km)
Quincy	Hull	15 mi. (24km)
Hull	Plymouth	32 mi. (51km)
Plymouth	Sagamore	18 mi. (29km)
Sagamore	New Bedford	30 mi. (48km)
New Bedford	Providence, R.I.	29 mi. (46km)
Providence, R.I.	Bristol	14 mi. (23km)
Bristol	Portsmouth	6 mi. (9km)
Portsmouth	Newport	10 mi. (16km)
Newport	Narragansett Pier	17 mi. (27km)
Narragansett Pier	Mystic, Conn.	30 mi. (48km)
Mystic, Conn.	Groton	6 mi. (10km)
Groton	New London	2 mi. (3km)
New London	Hartford	44 mi. (71km)
Hartford	New Haven	40 mi. (64km)
New Haven	Stratford	12 mi. (19km)
Stratford	Bridgeport	3 mi. (5km)
Bridgeport	Stamford	20 mi. (32km)
Stamford	Greenwich	7 mi. (11km)
Greenwich	Rye Brook, N.Y.	6 mi. (9km)
Rye Brook, N.Y.	New York City	22 mi. (36km)

☼☆⚲ **CALAIS:** Small market town on the Canadian border. Some 15 mi. (25km) south, a marker at the side of U.S. 1 marks the 45th parallel and tells you that you're precisely halfway between the Equator and the North Pole. Still on this stretch of U.S. 1, opposite Red Beach, the **St. Croix Island International Historic Site** marks the place of the first attempted European settlement on the Atlantic coast north of Florida, in 1604 by French explorer Samuel de Champlain and 78 of his companions. The park is not open to the public.

☼☆⚲ **ROOSEVELT CAMPOBELLO INTERNATIONAL PARK** (at Lubec): Campobello Island, at the mouth of the St. Croix River, is jointly owned by the U.S. and Canada, and marks the border between the two countries. It was here that Franklin D. Roosevelt had his summer home, where he contracted polio. The Visitor Center, with movies of the life and career of the 32nd president of the U.S., is on Me. 189 (506/752-2922), open daily from Memorial Day to the end of Oct.

BAR HARBOR: Charming old fishing village on **Mount Desert Island,** a site explored by the French at the beginning of the 17th century. Much favored by vacationers for the last 100 years because of the neighboring **Acadia National Park** (see below). The town, almost entirely rebuilt after a blaze in 1947, boasts dozens of hotels and restaurants in all price ranges. Boats may be hired for big-game fishing. A car-ferry, the *Bluenose,* connects Bar Harbor to Yarmouth, Nova Scotia, in Canada, in six hours daily from mid-June through Sept: Ferry Terminal (207/288-3395).

ACADIA NATIONAL PARK: Discovered in 1604 by French explorer Samuel de Champlain, and part of French Acadia until 1713, the site of Acadia National Park is a perfect representation on a small scale of all the natural beauties of the Maine seaboard. On its 64 sq. mi. (168km²) of splendid landscapes, the only large national park in the Northeast finds room for jagged coastlines, pine forests, little fishing villages, deep blue lakes, steep cliffs, clear streams, storm-beaten granite islands, and mountains: **Cadillac Mountain,** at 1,530 ft. (466m), is the highest on the Atlantic coast of the U.S.

The **Loop Road,** a 33-mi. (55km) scenic drive, takes you along the shore of the park's largest island, with fine views of its fjords (particularly **Somes Sound**) and its lakes; you should follow it in a clockwise direction, beginning from the **Visitors Center** at Hulls Cove on Me. 3, about 3 mi. (5km) NW of Bar Harbor. The **Abbe Museum of Indian Artifacts,** on Me. 3 at Sieur de Monts Springs (207/288-3519), open daily mid-May to mid-Oct, displays some interesting Native American material evidencing that Mount Desert Island has been inhabited since the Stone Age.

There is year-round ferry service between the mainland harbors and the little islands scattered offshore like **Isle-au-Haut, Little Cranberry Island,** and **Great Cranberry Island.** Many campsites, beaches with facilities, and 120 mi. (193km) of trails.

Opened in 1919, Acadia National Park is ranked second among national parks in the number of its visitors (4.5 million a year). For information, contact the Superintendent, Acadia National Park, P.O. Box 177, Bar Harbor, ME 04609 (207/288-3338). A nature lover's dream; don't miss it. Portions of the park are open year round. (For weather forecast, call 207/667-8910.)

Where to Stay

Bayview Hotel & Inn, 111 Eden St., Bar Harbor, ME 04609 (207/288-5861; toll free 800/356-3585). 38 rms, A/C, cable color TV. AE, CB, DC, MC, V. Free parking, pool, rest., bar, valet service, disco in season. *Note:* Elegant Georgian-style mansion standing in a fine garden. Spacious, tastefully decorated rms, period furniture, private patios, and open fireplaces. Excellent svce. Great charm and great quality. Open year round. **E–VE**

Atlantic Oakes, Eden St. at Me. 3, Bar Harbor, ME 04609 (207/288-5801; toll free 800/336-2463). 109 rms, cable color TV (no A/C). MC, V. Free parking, pool, marina, five tennis courts, nearby coffee shop, free breakfast, free crib. *Note:* Friendly, comfortable motel adjoining the *Bluenose* ferry terminal. Huge, inviting rms, all w. ocean view. Private marina; grdn. Affable reception. Open year round. **M–E,** but lower rates off-season.

Edenbrook, 96 Eden St., Bar Harbor, ME 04609 (207/288-4975). 45 rms, cable color TV (no A/C). AE, MC, V. Free parking, cafe adj., crib $5. *Note:* Modest but well-kept motel near the ferry pier.

Some very good rms w. bay view in the newest upper building. Good value overall. Closed late Oct to late May. **I–M**

Where to Eat

🍷🍷 **Bar Harbor Inn,** 7 Newport Dr. (207/288-3351). Breakfast/ lunch/dinner daily, brunch Sun; closed mid-Nov to Mar. AE, MC, V. *Specialties:* stuffed mushrooms, broiled lobster, medallion of lamb in marsala, catch of the day. Good wine list. *Note:* Charming 19th-century inn overlooking the bay. Conventional but elegant cooking; efficient svce. Distinguished background music. A very good place; resv. advisable. *Continental/Seafood.* **I–M**

🍷 **Miguel's,** 51 Rodick St. (207/288-5117). Dinner only, nightly; closed Dec–Mar. AE, MC, V. *Specialties:* quesadillas, tostadas, fajitas, combination plates, own pastries. *Note:* Delicious Mexican food in an authentic southwestern setting complete w. tiled floors and Mexican artifacts. Casual atmosphere. Locally popular. Friendly svce. *Mexican.* **B–I**

IN NEARBY HANCOCK ☼🍷🍷 **Le Domaine,** U.S. 1, 18 mi. (30km) north of Bar Harbor (207/422-3916). Dinner only, nightly; closed Dec–Apr. AE, MC, V. *Specialties:* magret of duck w. cherries, rabbit w. prunes, catch of the day broiled w. fennel, sautéed sweetbreads, calves' liver dijonnaise, émincé of beef w. aioli. *Note:* The cooking of Nicole Purslow and the decor of this enchanting little country inn, w. its huge fireplace and open-hearth grill, smell sweetly of France. All the vegetables and herbs come from her own garden. Applauded by tourists for more than four decades. Le Domaine also offers seven very comfortable guest rms. *French.* **M**

IN NEARBY SEAL HARBOR 🍷 **Jordan Pond House,** Park Loop Rd., 2 mi. (3.2km) north of Seal Harbor (207/276-3316). Lunch/dinner daily; closed Nov–May. AE, DC, MC, V. Jkt. *Specialties:* steak, broiled lobster, broiled chicken, homemade ice cream. *Note:* Charming rest. in a little farmhouse more than a century old, on the grounds of Acadia National Park, which was generously donated to the National Park Service in 1945 by John D. Rockefeller, Jr. Painstaking but unimaginative cuisine; open-air dining on fine days. Good value. *American.* **I**

☼🙙🙙 **CAMDEN:** In its splendid natural setting where the mountains plunge steeply into Penobscot Bay, with its mosaic of little islands, this town is particularly lively in summer, with many productions at the **Camden Amphitheatre,** on Atlantic Ave. (207/236-4404). From here many sailboats offer three- to six-day cruises along the Maine coast (see "Adventures," above). You should stop here.

Where to Stay

🛏🛏 **Lord Camden Inn,** 24 Main St., Camden, ME 04843 (207/ 236-4325; toll free 800/336-4325). 31 rms (some w. A/C), cable color TV. AE, MC, V. On-street parking, rest. opposite; free breakfast. *Note:* Charming historical inn on the waterfront. Elegantly appointed rms, many w. balconies and harbor view. Courteous svce. Open year round. **M–E**

IN NEARBY LINCOLNVILLE 🛏 **Mt. Battie,** U.S. 1, Lincolnville Beach, ME 04849 (207/236-3870). 21 rms, A/C, color TV. AE, MC, V. Free parking, nearby coffee shop, free morning coffee. *Note:* Attractive budget motel, functionally comfortable. Great ocean view. Good value. Closed late Oct to early May. **I–M**

IN NEARBY ROCKPORT 🛏🛏🛏 **Samoset,** 220 Warrenton St., Rockport, ME 04856 (207/594-2511). 150 rms, A/C, cable color TV. AE, CB, DC, MC, V. Free parking, two pools, health club, saunas, tennis court, golf course, marina, boats, rest. (Marcel's), bar, valet svce, disco, free crib, concierge. *Note:* Luxurious resort complex, modern and comfortable, overlooking Penobscot Bay. Spacious, comfortable rms w. private patios (most w. ocean view), in small buildings scattered around 230 acres (93ha) of green grdns and woods. Elegant rest.; attentive svce. A fine place. Interesting vacation packages. Open year round. **M–E,** but lower rates off-season.

IN NEARBY ROCKLAND 🍴 **Navigator Motor Inn,** 520 Main St., Rockland, ME 04841 (207/594-2131). 62 rms, A/C, cable color TV. AE, MC, V. Free parking, rest., bar, rm svce. *Note:* Typical but inviting motel on the ocean, opposite the ferry terminal. Comfortable rms w. balconies and refrigerators, some w. kitchenettes. Efficient svce. Good overall value. **I–M,** but lower rates off-season.

Where to Eat

🍷 **Peter Ott's,** 16 Bayview St. (207/236-4032). Dinner only, nightly; closed Jan 1, Dec 25, and Mon mid-Sept to mid-May. AE, DC, MC, V. *Specialties:* local seafood, Black Angus beef. *Note:* Pleasant contemporary cuisine. Inviting, rustic setting. On-street parking. Resv. advised in season. *American.* **I–M**

IN NEARBY SEARSPORT 🍷 **Nickerson Tavern,** on U.S. 1 (207/548-2220). A/C. Dinner only, nightly June–Sep, closed Mon–Wed mid-Sept to Memorial Day. *Specialties:* baked brie, roasted duckling w. chutney, scallops, sea bass, catch of the day, cappuccino cheesecake. *Note:* A very popular rest. in this area. A rustic atmosphere in every sense of the word, as it is housed in an old sea captain's house built in 1738. Resv. strongly advised. *American.* **I–M**

IN NEARBY LINCOLNVILLE 🍷 **Lobster Pound,** on U.S. 1 (207/789-5550). A/C. Lunch/dinner daily; closed Nov–Apr. AE, CB, DC, MC, V. *Specialties:* lobster, catch of the day, roast turkey, steak, fried clams, good desserts. *Note:* As the name implies, the specialty is lobster, in a ragoût, broiled, or steamed; shellfish lovers can go to town here. Dining rm overlooking Penobscot Bay, or eat in the open on the wharf. Efficient, smiling svce; a local landmark for over 30 years. *American.* **I–M**

IN NEARBY ROCKPORT 🍷 **The Helm,** U.S. 1 (207/236-4337). A/C. Lunch/ dinner Tues–Sun; closed mid-Oct to early Apr. MC, V. *Specialties:* onion soup, steak au poivre, catch of the day, shellfish. *Note:* Locally popular little rest. serving good *cuisine bourgeoise* of French inspiration, and tasty homemade desserts. Friendly svce.; good value. *French/American.* **I**

IN NEARBY ROCKLAND 🍷 **Marcel's,** in the Samoset (see "Where to Stay," above) (207/594-0774). A/C. Breakfast/lunch/dinner daily. AE, CB, DC, MC, V. Jkt. *Specialties:* Maine lobster, highest-quality prime cuts and fish. *Note:* Elegant rest. w. view of Penobscot Bay and the ocean; classic grand-hotel food, impeccably prepared and served (by tuxedoed waiters). Pianist at dinner. Valet parking. Resv. advised. *Continental.* **I–M**

☀🏛 **PEMAQUID POINT:** Situated at the end of a long peninsula jutting into the Atlantic, this was the site of the first permanent settlement in Maine (1625). Near Pemaquid Beach, **Fort William Henry** was constructed in 1692 by the British, then captured and destroyed by the French four years later. Reconstructed on the original foundation, the fort contains an interesting museum (207/677-2423) and historical relics. Open daily Memorial Day–Labor Day.

☀☆♨ **WISCASSET:** Tucked into the side of a hill at the mouth of the Sheepscot River, this enchanting little harbor, long the home of shipping tycoons and sea captains, is now an artists' and writers' colony. Louis-Philippe, king of France, landed here when he went into exile in the U.S.

Charming early 19th-century houses along Main St. The **Musical Wonder House,** 16-18 High St. (207/882-7163), open daily June to mid-Oct, is an interesting museum of old music boxes and other automata. See also the picturesque **Lincoln County Museum and Old Jail,** built in 1811, the first penitentiary in the state, on Federal St. (207/882-6817), open daily July to Labor Day, by appointment the rest of the year. Should positively be seen.

♨ **BOOTHBAY HARBOR:** With its old jetties and neat little houses, it gives you an engaging, representative picture of the seaports of Maine. A well-known regatta, **Windjammer Days,** is held in July.

Where to Stay

♙♙ **Brown's Wharf Inn,** 107 Atlantic Ave., Boothbay Harbor, ME 04538 (207/633-5440; toll free 800/334-8110). 70 rms (some w. A/C), color TV. Free parking, boat, fishing, rest. (Brown Bros.), bar, free crib. *Note:* Nicely appointed motel overlooking the harbor. All rms have balconies and views of the marina. Dockage. Good rest. Efficient svce. Closed Nov to early Apr. **I–M**

IN NEARBY SOUTHPORT ♙♙ **Ocean Gate Motor Inn,** Me. 27, Southport, ME 04576 (207/633-3321). 72 rms, color TV (no A/C). AE, CB, DC, MC, V. Free parking, pool, tennis court, marina, boats, rest. (open May–Oct), bar, valet svce, crib $5. *Note:* Inviting, comfortable motel on the ocean. Agreeable rms w. offshore or harbor view, some w. private porches; also cottages for two to six people. Reception and svce w. a smile. 85 acres (34ha) of pretty woods and grdns. A fine place. Closed Dec–May. **I–M** but lower rates off-season.

Where to Eat

☀♈♈ **Brown Bros.,** Atlantic Ave. (207/633-5440). A/C. Breakfast/dinner daily; closed late Sept to mid-June. AE, CB, DC, MC, V. *Specialties:* lobster, catch of the day. *Note:* Picturesque rest. in an 18th-century salt shed overlooking the water; the menu emphasizes local seafood. In the hands of the same family for almost half a century. Relaxed atmosphere; good value. No lunch served. *Seafood.* **B–I**

♨ **BATH:** Harbor town on the Kennebec River, with fine old houses and famous shipyards from which more than 4,000 vessels have been launched since the beginning of the 18th century. See the splendid **Maine Maritime Museum,** 243 Washington St. (207/443-1316), open daily (closed Dec 25). Its exhibits cover three centuries of shipbuilding. Worth the side trip.

☀♨ **BRUNSWICK:** This historic little port, dating from 1628, has wonderful old houses the whole length of Park Row and Federal St. Among them is the 1806 **Stowe House,** 63 Federal St. (207/725-5543), where Harriet Beecher Stowe wrote *Uncle Tom's Cabin.* See also **Bowdoin College,** founded in 1794, whose alumni include the writers Nathaniel Hawthorne and Henry Wadsworth Longfellow; the 14th president of the U.S., Franklin Pierce; and the first man to reach the North Pole, Adm. Robert Peary.

The campus and its museums at Maine and College Sts. (207/725-3275) may be visited Tues–Sun year round.

    🔔 **FREEPORT:** Dubbed "the birthplace of Maine." The documents granting Maine independence from Massachusetts, and eventually its statehood, were signed by legislators in 1820 at the historic **Jameson Tavern,** 115 Main St. Today Freeport is best known as a factory-outlet capital w. over 100 dwntwn stores; the most famous of all, **L. L. Bean,** on Main St., is open 24 hrs. daily, 365 days a year.

    ☀️👓 **PORTLAND:** The most important fishing port north of Boston, on beautiful **Casco Bay,** whose 136 islands attract many summer vacationers. The **Portland Historic Trail** through the streets of the old port town takes you to several historic 18th-century homes, including **Tate House,** 1270 Westbrook St. (207/774-9781), open Tues–Sun mid-June to mid-Sept; and the **Wadsworth-Longfellow House,** birthplace of the poet, 487 Congress St. (207/772-1807), open Tues–Sat June to mid-Oct.

And don't overlook the **Portland Museum of Art,** 7 Congress Sq. (207/775-6148), open Tues–Sun, where you'll find choice works by such American artists as Andrew Wyeth, Winslow Homer, and John Marin.

Four mi. (6.5km) south on Me. 77, the **Portland Headlight** at Cape Elizabeth, dating from 1791 and built by order of George Washington, is the oldest lighthouse in the U.S. still in service. Worth seeing.

Don't miss trips on Casco Bay (see above under "Guided Tours"). A car-ferry, the *Scotia Prince,* links Portland to Yarmouth, Nova Scotia (Canada), in 11 hr., daily mid-May to Oct, from the International Terminal (207/775-5616).

Where to Stay

    🛏️🛏️ **Sonesta Hotel–Portland,** 157 High St., Portland, ME 04101 (207/775-5411; toll free 800/766-3782). 200 rms, A/C, cable color TV. AE, CB, DC, MC, V. Gar. free, health club, sauna, two rests., two bars (including a rooftop lounge overlooking Casco Bay), rm svce, disco, free crib. *Note:* Portland's "grande dame," w. all New England charm. Comfortable rms, the best offering a beautiful view of Portland harbor. Flawless reception and svce. Centrally located in dwntwn Portland; free airport limo. **M–E**

    🛏️🛏️ **Ramada Inn,** 1230 Congress St., Portland, ME 04102 (207/774-5611). 149 rms, A/C, cable color TV. AE, CB, DC, MC, V. Free parking, pool, sauna, rest., bar, rm svce, disco, free crib. *Note:* Large, comfortable motel midway between the airport and dwntwn. Huge, functional rms; comprehensive facilities. Impersonal but efficient svce. Free limos to airport and dwntwn. Business clientele. Open year round. **I–M**

Where to Eat

    🍸🍸 **Café Always,** 47 Middle St. (774-9399). A/C. Dinner only, Tues–Sat; closed hols. MC, V. *Specialties:* crostini w. eggplant purée, mozzarella and roasted red peppers; lobster w. Thai curry-coconut sauce; chocolate roulade w. ricotta. The menu changes daily. *Note:* Sophisticated little rest. (35 seats) serving an inventive bistro fare. Beautiful exotic-flower arrangements and contemporary pale-yellow setting. Polished svce; successful enough that resv. are advisable. *American.* **I**

    🍸 **The Roma,** 769 Congress St. (773-9873). A/C. Lunch Mon–Fri, dinner Mon–Sat (nightly July–Sept); closed Dec 25. AE, MC, V. *Specialties:* mushroom caps stuffed w. crabmeat, Caesar salad, veal saltimbocca, seafood linguini, chocolate-walnut cheesecake. *Note:* A rest. w. a 60-year tradition. Housed in a Victorian brick mansion classically decorated. A great value. Resv. advised. *Italian/American.* **I**

    🍸 **Lyceum Bar and Grill,** 43 Church St. (508/745-7665). A/C. Lunch/dinner daily, brunch Sun; closed Thanksgiving and Dec 25. AE, MC, V. *Specialties:* marinated portobello mushrooms, homemade pasta, fresh fish, chocolate-raspberry truffle cake. *Note:* Health-conscious dishes served in a building with an illustrious history. Emerson and Thoreau lectured here. Alexander Graham Bell first demonstrated long-distance telephone conversation here. *Continental.* I

KENNEBUNKPORT: Well-known beach resort with an interesting streetcar museum displaying 200 vehicles from all periods and places, from horse-drawn trams to cable cars: **Seashore Trolley Museum,** Log Cabin Rd. (207/967-2712), open daily, mid-June to early Sept; call ahead the rest of the year. Worth going out of your way for. Former President George Bush's summer home, an 11-acre (4.5ha) family compound known as **Walker's Point** on Ocean Ave., is built on a rocky promontory overlooking the Maine coast.

Where to Stay

The Colony, Ocean Ave. and Kings Rd., Kennebunkport, ME 04046 (207/967-3331; toll free 800/552-2363). 139 rms, color TV (no A/C). AE, MC, V. Free parking, pool, tennis court, putting green, private beach, rest., bar, rm svce, disco, cinema, crib $5. *Note:* Charming old 1920s-style hotel w. direct access to beach. Lovely gardens. Elegant, comfortable rms; faultless svce. One of the best places to stay on the coast. Closed mid-Sept to mid-June. **E–VE** (American Plan).

Clarion Nonantum Resort, Ocean Ave., Kennebunkport, ME 06046 (207/967-4050; toll free, see Choice). 125 rms, some w. A/C, cable color TV. AE, MC, V. Free parking, pool, boats, rest., bar, rm svce. *Note:* Pleasant old hotel on the Kennebunk River. Accommodated part of the White House staff when President Bush was in town. Functional comfort; the best rms overlook the river. 5 min. on foot from beach. Good value overall. Closed Nov to mid-May. **M–E,** but lower rates off-season.

OGUNQUIT: The jagged, rocky shores of Maine here yield to sandy beaches; this is another delightful fishing port, as much for its setting as for the high quality of its lobsters. In summer, an important artists' colony exhibits in the Shore Rd. galleries. Beautiful fine-sand beach, 3 mi. (5km) long, ideal for surfing. Worth seeing.

Where to Stay

Terrace by the Sea, 11 Wharf Lane, Ogunquit, ME 03907 (207/646-3232). 60 rms, A/C, cable color TV. No credit cards. Free parking, pool, tennis court, beach, free breakfast. *Note:* Typical motel w. direct beach access. Comfortable rms w. balconies and refrigerators. Efficient svce. Closed Nov–May. **M–E,** but lower rates off-season.

Where to Eat

Arrow's Restaurant and Bar, Berwick Rd., 1½ mi. W of dwntwn Ogunquit (207/361-1100). A/C. Dinner only, nightly; closed mid-Oct to Apr. AE, MC, V. *Specialties:* crab cake w. gazpacho relish and lime-butter sauce; Thai pork bundles w. cucumber sauce; halibut w. eggplant, polenta, and parsley pesto; steamed lobster w. julienned vegetables and coconut green-curry sauce. The menu changes regularly. *Note:* One of the most interesting culinary experiences in the northern Atlantic coast region. Superb American nouvelle cuisine by chef-owners Clark Frasier and Mark Gaier in a renovated 18th-century farmhouse complete w. creaky plank floors, lots of period furniture, and big windows looking over the manicured grdns. Efficient, competent svce. Resv. a must. *American.* **M–E**

YORK: A picturesque anachronism, York could be taken for a small fragment of the Colonial period that has escaped the burden of the years. Many historic buildings, dating from 1720 to 1760, along York

St. and Lindsay Rd.: the **Old Gaol,** whose cells were in use until the 1860s; the **Old School House** (1755); **Jefferd's Tavern** (1759); **First Parish Congregational Church** (1747); the **Elizabeth Perkins House** (1730); etc. All may be visited daily June–Sept.

Busy **York Harbor** provides the economic underpinnings for this little piece of a bygone era, with many charter companies offering trips on the ocean and deep-sea fishing parties.

PORTSMOUTH: Founded in 1630, the same year as Boston, the former capital of New Hampshire allows you to immerse yourself in 17th- and 18th-century America, and is a must for history lovers. In the Old Harbor neighborhood, **Strawbery Banke,** at Hancock and Marcy Sts. (603/433-1100), you can see three dozen craftsman's shops and old houses, built between 1695 and the end of the 19th century and carefully restored; open to visitors daily May–Oct; signposted pedestrian trail.

See also some fine upscale homes such as the **John Paul Jones House,** once the home of the famous naval commander, at 43 Middle St. (603/436-8420), open Mon–Sat mid-May to mid-Oct; the **John Langdon House,** which George Washington termed "the handsomest house in Portsmouth," 143 Pleasant St. (603/436-3205), open Wed–Sun June to mid-Oct; or the **Wentworth-Coolidge Mansion,** one of the oldest in the city (1695), on Little Harbor Rd. (603/436-6607), open daily mid-June to Labor Day.

Fort Constitution, on the site of a post built in 1632 that had its moment of glory during the War of Independence, is also worth a side trip; the present structure, imposing in granite, dates from 1808. Go 4 mi. (6.5km) east on N.H. 1B to New Castle, open daily mid-June to mid-Sept; wknds only from mid-May to mid-June and mid-Sept to mid-Oct.

Where to Stay

Sheraton, 250 Market St., Portsmouth, NH 03801 (603/431-2300; toll free, see Sheraton). 175 rms, A/C, color TV, in-rm movies. AE, CB, DC, MC, V. Free parking, pool, health club, rest., bar, rm svce, disco, free crib. *Note:* Sleek, modern, glass-and-brick hotel overlooking the harbor; 5 min. from the Strawbery Banke historic district. Spacious rms; efficient svce; business clientele. Open year round. **M–E**

Where to Eat

Metro, 20 High St. (603/436-0521). A/C. Lunch Mon–Fri, dinner Mon–Sat; closed hols. AE, MC, V. *Specialties:* smoked salmon pancetta; veal medallions w. mushrooms, marsala, and mozzarella; chicken baked w. spinach and feta; Grand Marnier chocolate torte. *Note:* A solid rest. that's been in the family since the 1920s. Interesting stained-glass windows. Resv. advised. *Continental.* **I**

NEWBURYPORT: The main thoroughfare of this harbor town with its three-centuries-old shipyards, **High Street** is a journey 200 years back through time. A living museum of American Federalist architecture, High St. displays rows of big, square, three-story houses, built around 1800 by rich shipowners or long-haul sea captains in an architectural idiom reminiscent of nearby Salem. Newburyport, at the mouth of the Merrimack River, is also renowned as the birthplace of the U.S. Coast Guard in 1790. Worth going out of your way for.

BOSTON, GLOUCESTER, MARBLEHEAD, ROCKPORT, SALEM:
See Chapter 1 on Boston.

QUINCY: An important industrial town founded in 1625, this Boston suburb is the home of the famous Adams family of statesmen and patriots, whose origin can be traced back to 1636 in the colony's earliest days. Among their number is John Adams, second president of the U.S., and his son, John Quincy Adams, sixth president. See the **John and John Quincy Adams Birthplaces,** two 17th-century saltbox houses at 133 and 141 Franklin St. (617/773-1177), open daily mid-Apr to mid-Nov; also the **Adams National Historic Site,** 135 Adams St. (same phone number and visiting days as the preceding), built in 1731, acquired by John Adams in 1787 and retained in the family until 1946, still with its original fixtures and furniture. The tombs of the two presidents are not far away, in the **United First Parish Church** (the only church in the country with crypts of *two* presidents), 1306 Hancock St. (617/773-1290), open Mon–Sat mid-May to Labor Day, by appointment the rest of the year. John Hancock, the first signer of the Declaration of Independence, was also a native of Quincy.

HULL: At the tip of **Nantasket Peninsula,** Hull boasts the oldest lighthouse in the country, the **Boston Light (Little Brewster Island).** The original, built in 1716, was destroyed 60 years later by the British when they were forced to evacuate Little Brewster Island; the present lighthouse, dating from 1783, is worth seeing.

PLYMOUTH: It was on these desolate, windswept shores that on December 21, 1620, after an Atlantic crossing that lasted 66 days, the *Mayflower* cast anchor in the lee of **Plymouth Rock,** with its passenger list of 101 men, women, and children known as the "Pilgrims." That first winter was terrible. Half the colonists perished, and were buried in secret, at night, on **Cole's Hill** so that the Wampanoag tribe should not be able to determine how few were the survivors. All the same, but for these Native Americans and their gifts of food, there might well have been no survivors.

Plymouth, affectionately referred to as "America's Hometown," was the first permanent British settlement north of Virginia, and to this day it looks like something from an old book of prints. The precious relics of the first settlers are carefully arranged in the **Pilgrim Hall Museum,** 75 Court St. (508/746-1620), open daily. There are many old houses around Water and Summer Sts., including the oldest in the city, the **Richard Sparrow House** (508/747-1240), built in 1640 at 42 Summer St.

The *Mayflower II* is a full-size replica of its illustrious namesake, and like it, built in England. Having crossed the Atlantic in 1957, the *Mayflower II* is now at State Pier. The ship may be visited daily Apr–Nov.

See also on Water St. **Plymouth Rock** itself, now sheltered behind a Greek Revival columned portico in granite; this is the exact spot where the Pilgrims made their landfall. The Rock, which weighs about 6 tons (5,450kg), attracts a million tourists a year.

Three mi. (5km) south along Mass. 3A, the museum-village of **Plimoth Plantation** is a faithful reconstruction of the life of the original colonists in the 1620s, with costumed staff and a re-created Wampanoag tribal encampment. It attracts more than 400,000 visitors each year. Find it on Mass. 3A (508/746-1622), open daily Apr–Nov. Plymouth is an absolute must.

Where to Stay

Sheraton Inn Plymouth at Village Landing, 180 Water St., Plymouth, MA 02360 (508/747-4900; toll free, see Sheraton). 175 rms, A/C, cable color TV. AE, CB, DC, MC, V. Free parking, pool, health club, sauna, rest., bar, rm svce, nightclub, concierge, crib $10. *Note:* Big vacation motel on the Plymouth waterfront. Spacious, very comfortable rms, some w. balconies, the best overlooking the ocean. Acceptable rest. Good svce. A stone's throw from Plymouth's principal tourist attractions. Open year round. **M**

Cold Spring, 188 Court St., Plymouth, MA 02360 (508/746-2222). 31 rms, A/C, color TV. AE, MC, V. Free parking, nearby coffee shop, free breakfast, crib $5. *Note:* Smart little motel in a typical

New England building; functionally comfortable. Friendly reception. Good value. Closed Dec to mid-Mar. **I**

SAGAMORE: The access port for **Cape Cod,** at the junction of U.S. 6 and Mass. 3. There are charming old fishing towns and splendid seascapes the whole 60-mi. (100km) length of Cape Cod, while the nearby islands of **Martha's Vineyard** and **Nantucket** are the favorite country retreat for well-off Bostonians and New Yorkers. Fishing, sailing, and a temperate climate in summer. For more details on the peninsula, see Chapter 2 on Cape Cod.

NEW BEDFORD: Although by now partly given over to textile production, New Bedford has retained intact its seafaring traditions and its very large fishing fleet. The port, which is home to some 10,000 sailors, including a Portuguese colony that goes back almost to the town's foundation in 1640, was the world's largest whaling port in the 19th century, and inspired Herman Melville to write *Moby-Dick.* Readers of that great work will find fascinating new viewpoints opened to them, probably more than at any of the region's other museums devoted to man and the sea, at the superb **New Bedford Whaling Museum,** 18 Johnny Cake Hill (508/997-0046), open daily. Be sure also to see the lovely old houses of the **County Street Historic District,** which once belonged to wealthy merchants and whaler captains.

Car-ferry service in summer between New Bedford and the island of Martha's Vineyard: **Cape Island Express Lines,** 1494 E. Rodney French Blvd. (508/997-1688), daily mid-May to Sept.

PROVIDENCE: Sheltered at the head of the enormous **Narragansett Bay,** the capital of Rhode Island was christened "[Divine] Providence" by its founder, Roger Williams, a religious leader of British origin who in 1636 took refuge here from the dogmatic intolerance of the Salem puritans. The rich historical inheritance of this liberal, hardworking, business-oriented city is reflected in its ※ **old neighborhoods,** of which Kennedy Plaza and Benefit St. are the finest examples.

Built at the beginning of the 20th century, the **Rhode Island State House,** on Smith St. (401/277-2311), open daily, with its imposing dome of white Georgia marble, fittingly sets off the downtown office high-rises. In it you may see the charter originally granted by King Charles II in 1663 to the new Rhode Island colony. Dating from 1762, the **Old State House,** 150 Benefit St. (401/277-2678), open Mon–Fri, is still dear to Rhode Islanders because it was here that the Declaration of Independence was originally signed on May 4, 1776— two full months before it was ratified by the original 13 colonies in Philadelphia.

The splendid Georgian **John Brown House** (1786), 52 Power St. (401/331-8575), open Tues–Sun, was described by John Quincy Adams as "the most magnificent mansion in the continent," and very definitely deserves a visit. Nearby, see the ※ **First Baptist Church in America,** 75 N. Main St. (401/454-3418), open daily, the oldest Baptist church in the country, founded by Roger Williams in 1638; the present building, a very fine work by architect Joseph Brown, dates from 1775.

While you're here, in the adjoining suburb of **Pawtucket** you should see the extremely interesting ※ **Slater Mill Historic Site** (1793), often termed "the cradle of American industry." Its mill and its antique machines give you a vivid picture of America at the beginning of the Industrial Revolution in the very early 19th century. See it at Roosevelt Ave. and Main St. (401/725-8638), open daily from Memorial Day to Labor Day, wknds only the rest of the year.

Where to Eat

Al Forno, 577 S. Main St. (401/273-9760). A/C. Dinner only, Tues–Sat; closed hols. AE, MC, V. *Specialties:* baked clams w. tomato sauce, fresh homemade pasta and pizza, hot sausage roasted w.

vegetables, roasted fresh fish, fresh fruit tarts. Menu changes regularly. *Note:* Handsome decor of brick walls and bamboo blinds. The light, inventive cuisine of George Germon and his wife, Johanne, is worth going out of your way for. One negative: Al Forno accepts no reservations, so—small as it is and successful as it is—you may have a long wait, but it's worth it. *American/Italian.* **I**

Bluepoint Oyster Bar & Restaurant, 99 N. Main St. (401/272-6145). A/C. Dinner only, nightly. AE, MC, V. *Specialties:* fresh oysters on the half-shell w. grilled sausages, scrod w. rhubarb sauce and wild mushrooms, spaghettini w. scampi, Dover sole charcoaled w. rosemary, sautéed haddock w. sun-dried tomatoes, capers, and pine nuts. The menu changes regularly. Remarkable wine list fairly priced. *Note:* "The" place in the Providence area for seafood. Casual, friendly atmosphere. Very good value overall. *Seafood.* **I–M**

BRISTOL: A busy port in the 19th century (in 1800–10 it was fourth in importance in the nation), Bristol can show you a rich gamut of Colonial houses, particularly along **Hope Street,** as well as some charming small museums. Among the latter, on Tower Rd., 1 mi. (1.6km) east along Metacom Ave. (401/253-8388), you'll find the **Haffenreffer Museum of Anthropology,** open Tues–Sun June–Aug, wknds only the rest of the year. It has a remarkable collection in the areas of Inuit, Native American, and Polynesian culture.

PORTSMOUTH: The **Green Animals Topiary Gardens** on R.I. 114 (401/683-1267), open daily May–Sept (wknds only in Oct; closed the rest of the year), is one of the most original examples of the landscape gardener's art on the eastern seaboard, dating from 1880. Dozens of shrubs and bushes trimmed into the shape of giant animals: elephant, lion, giraffe, antelope, etc. Very beautiful rose garden. Well worth the side trip.

NEWPORT: America's yachting capital; in the bay off this famous Rhode Island resort the America's Cup races were held every four years for more than a century (1870–1983). It was this engaging little city, steeped in history, that in 1657 welcomed the first Quaker settlers from Europe and only a year later the first 15 Jewish families (from Holland) to come to the New World.

In the latter part of the 19th century Newport became the favorite summer home of New York millionaires such as the Astors, Belmonts, Vanderbilts, Stuyvesants, and McAllisters. It still preserves from its glory days some splendid residences, worthy of Scott Fitzgerald's *The Great Gatsby:* **Marble House,** on Bellevue Ave., modeled after Versailles, and **The Breakers,** a 70-room palace on Ochre Point Ave., both belonging to the Vanderbilt family; **Rosecliff,** with its huge ballroom, on Bellevue Ave.; and again on Bellevue Ave. such fantasy estates as the Victorian **Château-Sur-Mer, The Elms** (a copy of the old château at Asnières near Paris), the Gothic Revival **Kingscote,** and so on. All these houses are open daily Apr–Oct; call 401/847-1000 for information.

Among the town's other notable buildings are **Hammersmith Farm** on Ocean Dr., where John and Jackie Kennedy were married; the **Redwood Library,** at 50 Bellevue Ave. (401/847-0292), open daily, believed to be the oldest library in the U.S. still in operation (1748); and the **Touro Synagogue,** 85 Touro St. (401/847-4794), open Sun–Fri from late June to Labor Day (Sun only, the rest of the year), an architectural treasure which, dating from 1763, is the oldest synagogue in the continental U.S.

Tennis fans won't want to miss the remarkable museum at the **International Tennis Hall of Fame,** Newport Casino, 194 Bellevue Ave. (401/849-3990), open daily (closed hols.), devoted to the glories of that great game.

The world-famous **Jazz Festival** has returned to Newport after many years in eclipse, and again draws crowds in Aug of each year, as does the chamber-music festival in mid-July.

Where to Stay

♟♟♟ **Doubletree Hotel,** Goat Island (causeway from Washington St.), Newport, RI 02840 (401/849-2600; toll free 800/528-0444). 253 rms, A/C, color TV. AE, CB, DC, MC, V. Free parking, two pools, health club, tennis court, marina, rest., coffee shop, bars, rm svce, disco, hrdrsr, free crib. *Note:* Luxurious convention hotel on a little island in dwntwn Newport, w. its own marina and heliport. Spacious, well-laid-out rms w. private balconies or patios. Very good svce. VIP floor. Caters to big-business people and well-heeled vacationers. Open year round. **E–VE**

♟♟ **Newport Harbor Hotel,** 49 America's Cup Ave., Newport, RI 02840 (401/847-9000; toll free 800/777-1700). 133 rms, A/C, color TV. AE, CB, DC, MC, V. Free parking, pool, sauna, rest., bar, rm svce, free crib. *Note:* Very comfortable hotel-marina overlooking the harbor and the bay w. spectacular views. Huge, inviting rms w. balconies. Flawless svce. Excellent dwntwn location a stone's throw from Newport's main tourist attractions. Open year round. **M–E**

Where to Eat

☼♟♟♟ **White Horse Tavern,** Marlborough and Farewell Sts. (401/849-3600). A/C. Lunch Wed–Mon, dinner daily, brunch Sun; closed Dec 24 and 25. AE, CB, DC, MC, V. Jkt. *Specialties:* rack of lamb, beef Wellington, ratatouille w. five kinds of mushrooms, roast duck, steak Diane. Good wine list. *Note:* Gracious Colonial inn in one of the oldest (1673) buildings in New England. Slightly affected continental cuisine; svce of a very high order. Resv. advised. *Continental.* **M–E**

⚓ **NARRAGANSETT PIER:** Among New England's most magnificent beaches. Don't miss the **Point Judith Lighthouse** at the south entrance to Narragansett Bay in heavy weather, when the enormous waves breaking over the rocky promontory offer mute testimony of past shipwrecks.

☼⚓ **BLOCK ISLAND:** Sighted in 1524 by Verrazano, the discoverer of New York, this picturesque little island, 12 mi. (19km) out to sea from **Point Judith,** temperate in summer and winter alike, was a pirate stronghold as late as 1815. A treeless moor with many little ponds, a sanctuary for seabirds, and a paradise for fishermen (tuna, swordfish, sea bass, etc.), the island has some fine cliffs at **Mohegan Bluffs,** and strange black-sand beaches.

At a favorite vacation resort in summer, it's reached by the **ferries** of the Interstate Navigation Co. from New London, Conn. (daily mid-June to Labor Day), from Providence and Newport, R.I. (daily late June to Labor Day), and from Point Judith, R.I. (daily year round). For information, call 203/442-9553 in Connecticut, 401/789-4613 in Rhode Island.

☼⚓⚓ **MYSTIC:** This old whaling port, founded in 1654 and built athwart the Mystic River, has the country's finest maritime museum, **Mystic Seaport.** This is a fascinating reconstruction of a 19th-century seaport, with old houses, crafts workshops, sailing boats anchored at the docks, and staff in period costume. Allow at least three to four hours for your visit. On Conn. 27 (203/572-0711), open daily year round.

Where to Stay

♟♟ **Inn at Mystic,** U.S. 1 and Conn. 27, Mystic, CT 06355 (203/536-9604; toll free 800/237-2415). 67 rms, A/C, cable color TV. AE, MC, V. Free parking, pool, tennis court, boats, rest. (Flood Tide), bar, rm svce, crib $10. *Note:* Colonial Revival inn surrounded by beautiful grdns. Inviting rms w. fireplaces and whirlpool baths, some w. private balconies or patios.

Very good svce; agreeable setting overlooking Long Island Sound. Open year round. **E,** but lower rates off-season.

　　　🍸 **Days Inn,** 26 Michelle Lane, Mystic, CT 06355 (203/572-
　　　🛏 0574; toll free, see Days Inn). 122 rms, A/C, cable color TV. AE, CB, DC, MC, V. Free parking, pool, coffee shop, free crib. *Note:* Typical modern motel nr. Mystic Seaport. Functionally comfortable rms; reception and svce w. a smile. Good value overall. Open year round. **I–M**

Where to Eat

　　　🍸🍸 **Flood Tide,** in the Inn at Mystic (see "Where to Stay," above) (203/536-8140). A/C. Breakfast/lunch/dinner daily. AE, DC, MC, V. *Specialties:* duck w. peaches, Maine lobster, roast rack of lamb, shrimp-and-artichoke Provençal, beef Wellington, Caesar salad. *Note:* On a hill overlooking Mystic Harbor, this quiet, comfortable hotel rest. serves carefully prepared classic food. Attentive, polished svce. Resv. highly advisable. *Continental/American.* **I–M**

　　　☀ **GROTON:** Important naval base where the first diesel-
　　　　 powered submarine was built in 1912, and the first nuclear-powered submarine, U.S.S. *Nautilus,* in 1975. The *Nautilus* is now a floating museum, at Crystal Lake Rd. at Conn. 12 (203/449-3174), open Tues–Sun; closed one week in Mar, June, Sept, and Dec.

　　　🔔 **NEW LONDON:** Old seaport at the mouth of the Thames
　　　　 River (whence its name), since 1876 home of the **U.S. Coast Guard Academy,** on I-95, Exit 83 (203/444-8270). The Visitor Center and museum are open daily May–Oct, Mon–Fri the rest of the year; cadet parades on Fri in spring and fall.

Opposite the base, the **Lyman Allyn Museum,** 625 Williams St. (203/443-2545), open Tues–Sun, is rich in classical art and antiquities, 18th- and 19th-century American furniture, and enchanting old dolls and dollhouses. Downtown, on Huntington St., see **Whale Oil Row** with its early 19th-century classical revival shipowners' homes.

Ferry connection with Orient Point, at the NE tip of Long Island, N.Y.: 2 Ferry St. (203/443-5281), daily year round.

Where to Eat

IN NEARBY ESSEX ☀🍸 **Griswold Inn,** 36 Main St. (203/767-1776). A/C. Lunch/dinner daily; closed Dec 24–25. AE, DC, MC, V. *Specialties:* filet of beef w. fried oysters and sauce béarnaise, roast beef, broiled haddock, seafood of the day, meat pie, homemade sausages. *Note:* Founded in 1776, this delightful inn w. its historic decor is well worth a visit, as much for the inimitable atmosphere as for the quality of its praiseworthy, flavorful food. Superb old bar. Youthful, smiling svce. Resv. advised. A fine place. *American.* **I**

　　　☀ **HARTFORD:** The world's insurance capital, where no fewer
　　　　 than 35 corporate headquarters buildings reach proudly for the sky, Hartford, founded by Dutch settlers in 1623, presents a happy mix of old and modern architecture. With their futuristic towers and their dozens of stores, boutiques, and restaurants, **Constitution Plaza** and the **Civic Center,** both in the heart of downtown, are among the most remarkable achievements of urban renewal in the country.

Lovers of the grand antique would sooner visit the 1796 **Old State House,** by Charles Bulfinch, where there's a fine portrait of George Washington by Gilbert Stuart. It's at 800 Main St. (203/522-6766), open daily. Or there's the 1782 **Butler-McCook Homestead,** with its ornate interior, at 396 Main St. (203/522-1806), open Tues–Thurs and Sun, mid-May to mid-Oct.

Book-lovers will want to see the gaudy Victorian home where Mark Twain wrote part of *Huckleberry Finn* and *Tom Sawyer* (and the adjoining cottage, once the home of Harriet Beecher Stowe, who wrote *Uncle Tom's Cabin*): **Nook Farm,** Farmington Ave. and Forest St. (203/525-9317), open daily June–Aug, Tues–Sun the rest of the year.

Another absolute must is the ☀☖☖ **Wadsworth Atheneum,** 600 Main St. (203/247-9111), open Tues–Sun, one of the oldest and richest art museums in America, with several hundred major works by artists both European (Caravaggio, Zurbarán, Rembrandt, Goya, Picasso, Monet, Gauguin) and American (Church, Sargent, Whistler, Wyeth, Calder).

Hartford prides itself on possessing the oldest continuously published daily paper in the country, the *Hartford Courant,* which was founded in 1764 and became a daily in 1837. Hartford is the birthplace of Noah Webster, author of the first American dictionary (1828). Hartford is also the heart of the firearms industry in the United States. Along the Connecticut River Valley (nicknamed "Gun Valley"), where the modern system of manufacturing firearms was invented in the 1800s, are such famous gun companies as Colt Industries, Remington, Smith & Wesson, and Winchester.

Where to Stay

🏛🏛🏛 **Sheraton Hotel,** 315 Trumbull St., CT 06103 (203/728-5151; toll free, see Sheraton). 400 rms, A/C, color TV, in-rm movies. AE, CB, DC, MC, V. Gar. $9, pool, health club, sauna, rest., bar, 24-hr. rm svce, disco, free crib. *Note:* Modern 22-floor hotel adjacent to Civic Center Plaza and its shops. Elegant furnishings; comfortable and well-equipped rms. Good physical-fitness facilities. Efficient svce; acceptable rest. Business clientele. Located right in middle of dwntwn. Open year round. **M–E**

🏛🏛 **Ramada Inn–Capitol Hill,** 440 Asylum St., Hartford, CT 06103 (203/246-6591; toll free, see Ramada Inns). 96 rms. A/C, color TV. AE, CB, DC, MC, V. Free parking, rest., bar, valet svce. *Note:* Elderly hotel recently renovated; functionally comfortable. Undependable svce. Very centrally located. Good value overall. Open year round. **M**

Where to Eat

🍸🍸 **Gaetano's,** 1 Civic Center Plaza (203/249-1629). A/C. Lunch Mon–Fri, dinner Mon–Sat; closed hols. AE, DC, MC, V. *Specialties:* grilled portobello mushrooms w. gorgonzola cream sauce and roasted red peppers; veal stuffed w. mushrooms, fontina cheese, pine nuts, and creamy polenta; sautéed shrimp served over cappellini pasta w. mascarpone cheese; white flourless chocolate cheesecake w. fresh strawberries. *Note:* Inventive cooking and exquisite range of ingredients. Impressive international wine list. The window-encased dining room overlooks downtown Hartford from the third floor of the Civic Center. Resv. advised, especially on nights of events. *Italian.* **I**

☀☖☖ **NEW HAVEN:** Although only 75 mi. (120km) from New York, New Haven is a typical New England port, on whose stones 350 years of history (it was founded in 1638) have left their mark.

As Harvard has done for Cambridge, so rival ☖☖ **Yale University** has raised New Haven to a place of eminence in science and learning. Founded in 1701 at **Brandford** and moved to New Haven in 1716, the university owes its name to a bygone patron of letters, Elihu Yale. On the old campus with its charming ivied buildings, mostly English Gothic Revival or Romanesque, see the **Peabody Museum of Natural History,** with its spectacular collection of prehistoric animals, at 170 Whitney Ave. (203/432-5050), open daily. Be sure to glance at the splendid **Art and Architecture Building,** York and Chapel Sts., a groundbreaking 1963 masterpiece from the drawing board of architect Carl Rudolph. The **Sterling Memorial and Beinecke Libraries,** Wall and High Sts. (203/432-2977), open daily, house between them more than three million works, including such rarities as a Gutenberg Bible, the Yale archives, and an unparalleled collection of playing cards. Louis I. Kahn's 1976 **Center for British Art and Studies,** 1080 Chapel St. (203/432-2800), open Tues–Sun, houses the most important public collection outside Great Britain of that country's art, including works by Hogarth, Constable, Turner, and many others. You should take a **guided tour of the campus,** given daily; apply to the University Information Office, Phelps Gateway, 344 College St. (203/432-2300).

On **The Green,** a 16-acre (6ha) park contemporary with the city, see ☖ **three lovely churches** of Georgian design from 1813–14. Al Capp, the creator of "Li'l Abner," was born in New Haven. The **Long Wharf Theater** is one of the country's most important theaters. For information, call 787-4282.

Where to Stay

🛏🛏 **Park Plaza and Conference Center,** 155 Temple St., New Haven, CT 06510 (203/772-1700). 300 rms, A/C, color TV. AE, CB, DC, MC, V. Gar. $2.35, pool, rest. (Top of the Park), bar, rm svce, disco, crib $10. *Note:* Modern 19-story building overlooking dwntwn and the Yale campus; rest. w. panorama on top floor. Spacious, comfortable rms. Good svce on balance. Business clientele; open year round. **M**

Where to Eat

🍷 **Delmonaco's,** 232 Wooster St. (203/865-1109). A/C. Lunch Mon–Fri, dinner Mon–Sat; closed hols. AE, CB, DC, MC, V. *Specialties:* spaghetti alla carbonara, fresh homemade pasta, sautéed scallops, veal cutlet milanese. *Note:* Large, noisy *trattoria* serving straightforward, tasty Italian food. Likeable atmosphere; very efficient svce. Good value. *Italian.* **I**

☖ **STRATFORD:** In 1955 Stratford acknowledged the destiny inseparable from its name and paid tribute to Shakespeare with the **Shakespeare Theater State Park.** Intended to be an important classical theater, it has faded in recent years. For information call 1850 Elm St., Stratford, CT 06497 (203/381-9518).

☖ **BRIDGEPORT:** An important industrial town on Long Island Sound, which is best known as the longtime winter home of the famous Barnum Circus, "The Greatest Show on Earth." Its principal attraction, a 28-in. (70cm) dwarf known as "General Tom Thumb," was himself a Bridgeport native; his tomb, with life-size effigy, is in Mountain Grove Cemetery, North Ave. and Dewey St. See the ☖ **Barnum Museum,** reopened in 1989 following a $7.5-million renovation, 820 Main St. (203/331-9881), open Tues –Sun, with many personal memorabilia of the circus's founder, P. T. Barnum, and of Gen. Tom Thumb. There's a **Barnum Festival,** with parades, concerts, and exhibitions of circus art, every year in late June or early July.

Daily year-round **car-ferry service** between Bridgeport and Port Jefferson, Long Island, N.Y., from Union Sq. Dock (203/367-3043).

☖ **STAMFORD:** Both a residential suburb of New York and— by latest count—home to 24 of the Fortune 500 largest corporations, Stamford also has many scientific laboratories and research centers.

See the astonishing 1958 **First Presbyterian Church** by Wallace Harrison in the shape of a giant fish; 1101 Bedford St. (203/324-9522), open daily.

Where to Eat

IN NEARBY SOUTH NORWALK 🍷🍷 **Pasta Nostra,** 116 Washington St. (203/854-9700). A/C. Lunch Tues–Fri, dinner Thurs–Sat; closed hols. MC, V. *Specialties:* squash-filled tortellini in brown butter, red-pepper linguine in asparagus sauce and rolled scamorza, skewered stuffed swordfish. The menu changes regularly. Well-stocked Italian wine list fairly priced. *Note:* Unpretentious *trattoria* and pasta store w. an all-white minimalist decor and plain, flavorsome Italian food (remarkable homemade pastas). Quick, efficient svce. Resv. advised. *Italian.* **I–M**

※ **GREENWICH:** A smart suburb for well-to-do New Yorkers, with a very New England vintage charm. Among its most remarkable and historic buildings are the 1685 **Bush-Holley House,** 39 Strickland Rd. (203/869-6899), open Tues–Fri, housing many works of art and pieces of antique furniture; and the 1690 **Putnam Cottage,** where Gen. Israel Putnam, a Revolutionary hero, was detained by, and escaped from, the British in 1779; it's at 243 E. Putnam Ave. (203/869-9697), open Mon, Wed, and Fri, or by appointment. Worth seeing.

Where to Eat

※♈♈♈ **Bertrand,** 253 Greenwich Ave. (203/661-4459). A/C. Lunch Mon–Fri, dinner Mon–Sat. AE, DC, MC, V. Jkt. *Specialties:* seafood in puff pastry w. leeks and basil, salmon marinated w. aniseed, confit of duck w. chanterelle mushrooms, red snapper braised in white wine, sautéed breast of chicken w. cream of basil, very good desserts. Large wine list. *Note:* Chef Christian Bertrand was once the associate of André Soltner at New York's Lutèce (see Chapter 3 on New York). That tells you all you need to know about the quality and delicacy of the food. The decor, running to Roman arches, vaulted ceilings, and a glassed lobby, is on the elaborate side. Polished svce; resv. a must. Has quickly established itself as one of the best rests. in the New York area. *French.* **E**

CHAPTER 6

PHILADELPHIA 🔦🔦

□ □ □

With Atlantic City and the Pennsylvania Dutch Country

There is no properly brought-up U.S. citizen who doesn't know that Philadelphia is "the cradle of our nation." Here the Declaration of Independence was drawn up and adopted; here the Constitution, the cornerstone of the American government, was approved; here George Washington presided, for the eight years 1790–97, over the new nation. Philadelphia can also claim the country's first bank, its first daily newspaper, its first hospital, its first stock exchange, its first zoo, its first mint, and its first school for African American children.

In the 18th century London was the only English-speaking city in the world larger than Philadelphia, and from so illustrious a past the American city has retained a sense of history, and a love of old buildings. Not far from the spot on the Delaware River where Englishman William Penn (who gave his name to the state of Pennsylvania) led the first Quaker settlers ashore in 1682 may still be found some of the country's best-known public buildings: **Independence Hall** with its famous **Liberty Bell; Congress Hall,** the Old City Hall; the **Jacob Graff House,** where Thomas Jefferson drafted the Declaration of Independence; **Carpenters' Hall,** where the first Continental Congress was held; **Franklin Court,** where stood the home of Benjamin Franklin, one of Philadelphia's most illustrious citizens; the house of **Betsy Ross,** who sewed together the first American flag. For the bicentennials of the Declaration of Independence (1976) and the Constitution (1987), much restoration and rehabilitation was done in **Independence National Park,** known as "America's most historic square mile."

Some of the nearby side streets with their pretty little red-brick houses, such as **Elfreth's Alley,** the oldest street in the U.S., are strangely reminiscent of 18th-century London. Art galleries, antiques shops, and above all, restaurants elbow each other in these little streets near Independence Mall. Philadelphia, which once had little enough to offer the gourmet, has become a place of pilgrimage; in the last dozen years more than 500 new restaurants, some of the highest order, have opened their doors here.

Lovers of the picturesque will make a point of visiting **Little Italy,** the domain of *Rocky,* of little family-owned *trattorie,* and open-air markets. To the north of the city, **Germantown,** founded by Mennonite settlers in the 17th century, is another interesting ethnic enclave; around Germantown Ave., a Native American trail in pre-Colonial days, there are many very lovely old homes.

Philadelphia (in classical Greek, "the city of brotherly love") is a thriving center of industry and commerce, with strong representation in health care, publishing, pharmaceuticals, petrochemicals, and electronics. Handling more than 38 million tons of cargo annually, it's also one of the world's largest river ports. In spite of uncertainties in municipal politics, dozens of corporations have moved their head offices here, attracted by Philadelphia's strategic position halfway between New York and Washington, its abundant labor supply, its rich cultural life—and a booming real-estate market. U.S. 202, on the city's northern periphery, fills the role of the local Silicon Valley, as does the more famous "Route 128" in Boston.

"Philly," as its citizens affectionately call it, takes pride in a long-standing tradition of intellectual and artistic activity: It boasts no fewer than 1,400 churches, synagogues, and other places of worship; 90 museums; eight universities, including the renowned **University of Pennsylvania** and **Temple University;** and a world-famous symphony orchestra. In spite of its size, it's still a city on a human scale, watched over by the statue of William Penn, perched 548 ft. (167m) in the air atop the astonishing City Hall.

According to FBI figures, Philadelphia's crime rate (32 homicides per 100,000 inhabitants) is the lowest of the nation's largest cities. But the 1985 bombing by the police of a house inhabited by members of the African American cult Move, which killed 11 people and incinerated 60 adjacent rowhouses, has not yet been forgotten.

Famous children of "Philly" include movie directors Sidney Lumet and Arthur Penn; painter Thomas Eakins, painter-photographer Man Ray; sculptor Alexander Calder; the late Princess Grace of Monaco (Grace Kelly); comedians W. C. Fields and Bill Cosby; actor Richard Gere; contralto Marian Anderson, singer Patti LaBelle; jazzmen Rex Stewart, Benny Golson, Stan Getz, and Sam Wooding; and anthropologist Margaret Mead.

BASIC FACTS: State of Pennsylvania. Area code: 215. Time zone: eastern. ZIP Code: 19014. Founded: 1682. Approximate population: city, 1,580,000; metropolitan area, 5,890,000. Fifth-largest metropolitan area in the country.

CLIMATE: Spring and fall, usually sunny and cool, are the best times for a visit, but the climate of the Atlantic seaboard is unpredictable at best, so bring an umbrella and a raincoat. Winter is cold, though the temperature rarely drops below 23°F (−5°C), and the Jan average is 35°F (2°C). The weather is hot and sticky from June to Sept, with July averaging 78°F (25°C).

DISTANCES: Baltimore, 94 mi. (150km); Niagara Falls, 385 mi. (623km); New York, 100 mi. (160km); Pittsburgh, 308 mi. (498km); Washington, 134 mi. (215km).

ARRIVAL & TRANSIT INFORMATION

AIRPORT: Philadelphia International Airport (PHL), 7 mi. (11km) SW, is a very up-to-date terminal. Call 215/492-3181 for information.

U.S. AIRLINES: American (toll free 800/433-7300), Continental (toll free 800/525-0280), Delta (toll free 800/221-1212), Northwest (toll free 800/225-2525), TWA (toll free 800/221-2000), United (toll free 800/241-6522), and USAir (toll free 800/428-4322).

FOREIGN AIRLINES: British Airways (toll free 800/247-9297) and Swissair (toll free 800/221-4750).

CITY LINK: The **cab** fare from the airport to dwntwn is about $22; time, about 20–30 min. Express train from the airport to dwntwn, the **SEPTA Airport Line,**

leaves every 30 min.; serves the 30th St., 16th St., and Market St. East stations dwntwn; fare, $4.75–$5.50; time, 25 min.

Taxis are expensive and reliable, but the **public transportation** system (bus, subway, and streetcar) is efficient and cheap (though to be avoided at night). For information, call SEPTA (580-7800). Subway fare: $1.50.

The dwntwn area is small enough that you shouldn't need to rent a car, unless you're planning trips to Atlantic City or Pennsylvania Dutch Country.

CAR RENTAL (at the airport unless otherwise indicated): Avis (toll free 800/331-1212); Budget (toll free 800/527-0700); Dollar (toll free 800/800-4000); Hertz (toll free 800/654-3131); National (toll free 800/227-7368); and Thrifty, 70th St. and Holstein Ave. (toll free 800/367-2277). For dwntwn locations, consult the local telephone directory.

LIMOUSINE SERVICES: Carey Limousine (492-8402), Dav-El Livery (334-7900), and King Limousine (toll free 800/245-5460).

TAXIS: Abundant during daylight hours; may be hailed in the street, or taken from the waiting lines at the major hotels or the downtown cab stands. After 5pm it's better to phone: **Quaker City Cab** (728-8000), **United Cab Assoc.** (238-9500), or **Yellow Cab** (922-8400).

TRAIN: Amtrak Station, 30th and Market Sts. There's a ticket office at 4 Penn Center (toll free 800/872-7245); for information and reservations for the Metroliner, call 824-1600.

INTERCITY BUSES: Greyhound, 1001 Filbert St. (toll free 800/231-2222).

INFORMATION & TOURS

TOURIST INFORMATION: The **Philadelphia Convention and Visitors Bureau,** 1515 Market St., Suite 2020, PA 19102 (636-1666; toll free 800/537-7676).

Visitors Center, 16th St. and John F. Kennedy Blvd. (636-1666), open daily year round.

For a **recorded message** with a current listing of shows and cultural events, call 337-7777 ext. 2540.

GUIDED TOURS: Audio Walk and Tour, Norman Rockwell Museum, 6th and Sansom Sts. (925-1234): Rent a "Walkman" with prerecorded cassettes and visit the Historic District on foot. Open daily year round.

Centipede Tours, 1315 Walnut St. (735-3123): A 90-min. Walk through the Historic District with Colonial-costumed guides. Original and instructive. Mid-May to mid-Oct on Wed, Fri, and Sat in good weather. Resv. advised.

Foundation for Architecture, 1 Penn Center (569-3187): 1–2-hr. guided tours of themes such as City Hall area, Penn's Squares, neighborhoods, Art Deco, and "Littlest Streets." Regular tours mid-Apr to mid-Nov. Call for schedule.

Historical Tours, 923 Christian St. (923-0355): Tour of the Italian Market by a historical scholar who will provide you with the facts on the area's early organized crime, immigrants' Settlement House, Irish ghettos, and nativist riots. Daily year round.

Penn's Landing Trolley, Christopher Columbus Blvd. and Dock or Spruce Sts. (627-0807): Round-trip rides along the historic waterfront aboard antique streetcars. Sat–Sun Apr–Nov and Thurs–Sun, July–Aug.

Philadelphia Carriage Co. (carriage), 500 N. 13th St. (922-6840): Carriage trip around the city center, leaving from the Carriage Stand in front of the Liberty Bell Pavilion. Daily Feb–Dec, weather permitting.

SIGHTS, ATTRACTIONS & ACTIVITIES

ARCHITECTURAL HIGHLIGHTS: ⚓ **Boat House Row,** Kelly Dr., in Fairmount Park: Picturesque Victorian boathouses along the Schuylkill River, used by the many local rowing clubs. Afternoon regattas throughout the summer (for information on times, call 686-2176). Should be seen.

🔆🔔👓 **City Hall,** Broad and Market Sts. (686-9074): John McArthur designed this flamboyant 1894 building in French-Renaissance style. The 548-ft (167m) tower is crowned by a bronze statue of William Penn. With 750 rooms, it's the biggest City Hall in the country, and took 20 years to build. Open daily; guided tours Mon–Fri by appointment.

🔔 **One Liberty Place,** 1 Liberty Place: This 61-story office building, whose conical crest recalls New York's famous Chrysler Building, was designed by Chicago architect Helmut Jahn and opened in 1987. At 816 ft. (248m), or 955 ft. (290m) with its needle, it was the first building to violate the hallowed limit of 548 ft. (167m)—the height of William Penn's hat on the City Hall statue—above which no building in Philadelphia had previously been allowed to rise. Nearby false-twin tower, **Two Liberty Place,** completed in 1990, at 58 stories stands slightly shorter than its predecessor.

🔆🔔 **U.S. Mint,** 5th and Arch Sts. (597-7350): The world's largest, producing 25,000 coins a minute. Visitors' gallery and display of old coins and medals in the Rittenhouse Room. Interesting. Open daily in summer, Mon–Fri the rest of the year.

CHURCHES/SYNAGOGUES: 🔆👓 **Christ Church,** 2nd St. between Market and Arch Sts. (922-1695): A handsome 1754 Colonial church, once attended by George Washington, Benjamin Franklin, and other historic figures. In the churchyard and the neighboring cemetery at 5th and Arch Sts. are buried seven signers of the Declaration of Independence, including Franklin. Open daily.

🔆🔔 **Gloria Dei Church,** Delaware and Washington Sts. (389-1513): The oldest place of worship in Pennsylvania (1700). Called "Old Swedes' Church" because many of the first Scandinavian settlers worshiped here. Open daily.

🔔 **Old St. Mary's Church,** 252 S. 4th St., between Locust and Spruce Sts. (923-7930): Built in 1763 as the city's original Roman Catholic cathedral. The tomb of Commodore John Barry, "Father of the U.S. Navy," is behind the church. Open daily.

🔔 **St. George's United Methodist Church,** 235 N. 4th St. (925-7788): The oldest (1769) Methodist church in the country; the first African American Methodist minister was ordained here in 1799. An interesting Colonial building; see the chalice that belonged to John Wesley, the English theologian who founded the Methodist church. Open daily.

HISTORIC BUILDINGS: The largest group of historic buildings are in Independence National Historic Park, but others are scattered around town.

Independence National Historic Park

Called "America's most historic square mile." For information on all the buildings listed below, phone 597-8974. Park **Visitor Center:** 3rd and Chestnut Sts.

Carpenters' Hall, 320 Chestnut St. (925-0167): The 1770 Hall of the Carpenters' Guild; the First Continental Congress met here in 1774. Museum. Open Tues–Sun.

City Tavern, 2nd and Walnut Sts. (923-6059): A careful reconstruction of a famous Revolutionary tavern, once described by Pres. John Adams as "the most elegant tavern in America." Here, two centuries ago, the Founding Fathers dined while framing the Constitution. Today it has become an appealing (and successful) restaurant with lunch/dinner daily.

Congress Hall, 6th and Chestnut Sts.: Adjoining Independence Hall, this 1789 building housed the meetings of the first Congress of the United States from 1790 to 1800, while the Capitol in Washington was under construction. The reelection of George Washington to the presidency in 1793, and the election of John Adams in 1797, took place here. You can see the chambers of the House of Representatives (first floor) and the Senate (second floor). Open daily.

First Bank of the U.S., 3rd St. between Walnut and Chestnut Sts.: The oldest American bank, founded in 1791 by Alexander Hamilton. Closed to visitors.

Franklin Court, Market St. between 3rd and 4th Sts.: Group of old buildings conceived and designed by Benjamin Franklin. His house, where he died in 1790, was destroyed by fire in 1812. An underground museum is devoted to this genial inventor and statesman. Open daily.

Independence Hall, Chestnut St. between 5th and 6th Sts. (627-1776): With its rounded bell tower, four-faced clock, and elegant Georgian facade in ocher brick, Independence Hall is one of the most historically meaningful public buildings in the U.S. The Declaration of Independence was signed here on July 4, 1776, and the Constitution was adopted here in 1787. In the former assembly hall, now renovated, you can see several pieces of historic furniture, including Washington's armchair. Independence Hall, open daily, is worth the trip all by itself.

Jacob Graff House, 701 Market St. at 7th St.: A 1975 reconstruction of the house where Thomas Jefferson was living in 1776 while he worked on the text of the Declaration of Independence. The two rooms he occupied have been carefully re-created. A short film is shown on this historic episode. Open daily.

Liberty Bell Pavilion, Independence Mall between Market and Chestnut Sts.: The bell here, which once was perched on the tower of Independence Hall, was the first to be rung after the first public reading of the Declaration of Independence on July 8, 1776. Bearing on its side the engraved inscription (Leviticus 10:25) "Proclaim liberty throughout all the land unto all the inhabitants thereof," the bell was cracked in 1835 and has not sounded since 1846. This symbol of Liberty is now housed in a glass structure built in 1976 in the center of the mall. A must—on no account to be missed—for every visitor to Philadelphia.

Old City Hall, 5th and Chestnut Sts.: In spite of its name this building was never City Hall; it was the first seat of the U.S. Supreme Court from 1791 to 1800. Museum devoted to life in 18th-century Philadelphia. Interesting. Open daily.

Todd House, 4th and Walnut Sts.: Handsome middle-class home dating from 1785, where Dolley Payne Todd lived before she married Pres. James Madison and became first lady. Interesting reconstruction of life in a middle-class Quaker family of the period. Open daily.

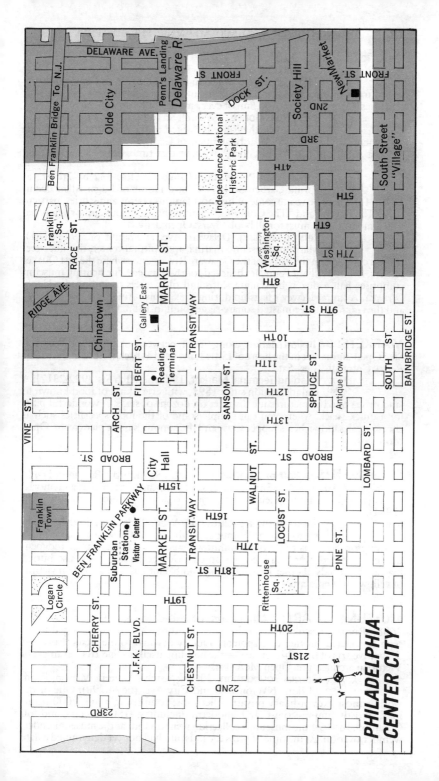

PHILADELPHIA CENTER CITY

Historic Buildings Outside the Park

☀️🌙☖ **"A Man Full of Trouble" Tavern,** 127–129 Spruce St. (744-2470). Picturesque tavern built in 1759 and splendidly restored to its original condition. Furniture and handcrafts of the 17th and 18th centuries. Open on the second Sun of every month or by appointment.

☀️🌙☖ **Betsy Ross House,** 239 Arch St. (627-5343): Pretty little Colonial house that once belonged to the seamstress Betsy Ross, and where (so the story goes), at the request of George Washington, she sewed the first American flag ("Old Glory," with, at that time, only 13 stars). Open daily.

☀️🌙☖ **Edgar Allan Poe National Historic Site,** 532 N. 7th St., at Spring Garden St. (597-8780): Home of Edgar Allan Poe in 1843–44, where he wrote some of his most famous poems and stories, particularly "The Raven" and "The Gold Bug". This is the illustrious author's only national memorial. A must for all book lovers. Open daily.

☀️🌙☖ **Penn's Landing,** Delaware Ave. at Walnut St. (923-8181): Maritime museum, marina, and cultural center, this huge recreation complex on the banks of the Delaware River stands where the first Quaker settlers, led by William Penn, are believed to have landed. The floating museum comprises half a dozen big sailing ships and old vessels including the U.S.S. *Olympia*, Admiral Dewey's flagship during the Spanish-American War of 1898, and the *Gazela*, a three-masted square-rigger built in 1883. Open daily.

MARKETS: ☀️☖ **Italian Market,** along 9th St. between Christian and Wharton Sts.: Open-air market in the heart of Little Italy; used as background in the movie *Rocky.* Colorful. Tues–Sat.

☀️🌙☖ **Reading Terminal Market,** 12th and Arch Sts. (922-2317): A real institution since 1893, with every kind of food known to land or sea piled in picturesque disorder on dozens of stalls. A wonderful place for a quick snack, where you can sample some of the local specialties such as cheese-steak sandwiches, snapper soup, and the famous Bassett's ice cream. Open Mon–Sat.

MONUMENTS: ☖ *Bolt of Lightning,* Franklin Sq. near the Benjamin Franklin Bridge: A 102-ft.-tall (33m) stainless-steel sculpture designed as a memorial to Benjamin Franklin by celebrated American-Japanese sculptor Isamu Noguchi (1984).

☀️🌙☖ **Tomb of the Revolutionary War's Unknown Soldier,** Washington Sq. at Walnut and 6th Sts.: In the west sector of huge Washington Sq., this tomb of an unknown soldier from the War of Independence is watched over by a life-size statue of George Washington. Also buried here are hundreds of other Revolutionary combatants, as well as civilian victims of yellow-fever epidemics.

MUSEUMS OF ART: ☖ **Athenaeum of Philadelphia,** 219 S. 6th St. (925-2688): Paintings, sculpture, and Empire furniture which once belonged to Joseph Bonaparte, brother of Napoleon. Library devoted to the architecture and decorative arts of the 19th century—the building itself is a fine 1847 example of Victorian architecture. Open Mon–Fri.

☀️🌙☖☖ **Barnes Foundation,** 300 N. Latch's Lane in Merion, 7 mi. (12km) NW on I-76 and City Ave. (667-0290): One of the world's most extraordinary private collections, comprising a full 1,000 paintings, mostly impressionist and modern, including 150 Renoirs and 60 Cézannes. In 1994 the museum's collection went on tour as the museum underwent renovation. At the time of press the museum had not yet determined a date for its reopening, planned for sometime in 1995. Call the museum for information on its new schedule.

☼☖ **Norman Rockwell Museum,** 6th and Sansom Sts. (922-4345): Works on display from the 60-year career of this famous painter and illustrator include drawings, paintings, posters, lithographs, etc., with a faithful reconstruction of his studio. Open daily.

☼☖☖ **Pennsylvania Academy of the Fine Arts,** Broad and Cherry Sts. (972-7600): Founded in 1805 and now installed in an elegant Victorian building, this is the oldest academy of fine arts in the country. The museum has a fine collection of American painting from the 18th century to the present day, with works by Charles Willson Peale, Benjamin West, Thomas Eakins, Thomas Sully, etc. Open Tues–Sun.

☖ **Pennsylvania Convention Center,** 1101 Arch St. (418-4700): An eclectic and impressive collection of paintings, photographs, sculptures, and crafts from over 50 local artists. Tours of the convention center's collection are given Mon–Thurs by appointment only for free.

☼☖☖☖ **Philadelphia Museum of Art,** 26th St. and Benjamin Franklin Pkwy. (763-8100): Rising majestically at the end of Ben Franklin Pkwy., this is one of the greatest, as well as one of the largest, art museums in America, housing nearly 500,000 paintings, sculptures, drawings, watercolors, prints, and other works of art. Imposing Greco-Roman building whose monumental staircase figured in the movie *Rocky.* Superb collections of medieval art, Oriental art, and European painting (particularly works by Marcel Duchamp). Among the most famous works on display: *Christ on the Cross and the Virgin and St. John* by Roger van der Weyden, Giovanni di Paolo's *Miracle of St. Nicolas of Tolentino,* Charles Willson Peale's *The Staircase Group,* Marcel Duchamp's *Nude Descending a Staircase,* van Gogh's *Sunflowers,* Cézanne's *The Large Bathers,* Fernand Léger's *The City, Woman and Child Driving* by Mary Cassatt, and *Three Musicians* by Picasso. An absolute must for art lovers. Open Tues–Sun.

☼☖ **Rodin Museum,** 22nd St. and Benjamin Franklin Pkwy. (787-5476): The largest collection of Rodin sculptures, drawings, and watercolors outside France, including versions of *The Thinker, The Gates of Hell,* and *The Burghers of Calais.* Open Tues–Sun.

MUSEUMS OF SCIENCE & HISTORY: ☼☖ Academy of Natural Sciences Museum, 19th St. and Benjamin Franklin Pkwy. (299-1000): Many prehistoric animals, including a dozen dinosaurs; a panorama of the animal kingdom throughout the world, in facsimiles of its natural habitats; Egyptian mummies; an enormous selection of precious stones and minerals. Open daily.

☖ **Afro-American Historical and Cultural Museum,** 7th and Arch Sts. (574-0380): The first American museum entirely devoted to African American art and culture in Africa and the U.S.; also a history of racial discrimination. Open Tues–Sun.

☖ **Army-Navy Museum,** Chestnut St. between 3rd and 4th Sts. (597-7128): In a building **(Pemberton House)** that is a facsimile of the home of a wealthy Quaker merchant of the Colonial period, this museum recapitulates the history of the U.S. Army and Navy during the War of Independence. Open daily.

☖ **Atwater Kent Museum,** The History Museum of Philadelphia, 15 S. 7th St. (922-3031): A fascinating collection of over 40,000 objects that characterize the material culture of the city's 300-year history. Exhibits on Colonial, Revolutionary, and industrial urban archeology. Open Tues–Sat.

☖ **Civil War Library and Museum,** 1805 Pine St. (735-8196): With 12,000 different books and documents, this is one of the richest Civil War libraries in the country. Unique collection of period weapons, uniforms, flags, and other memorabilia. A must for all history buffs. Open Mon–Fri; Sat–Sun by appointment only.

Fireman's Hall Museum, 149 N. 2nd St. (923-1438): Unique collection of material relating to firefighting in the 18th and 19th centuries, the largest of its kind in the country. Housed in an 1876 fire station. Open Tues–Sat.

Franklin Institute Science Museum, 20th St. and Benjamin Franklin Pkwy. (448-1200): One of the country's most complete and up-to-date science museums. Everything on nuclear fission and fusion, computers, astronomy, space flight, and aviation. A giant human heart 20 ft. (6m) high demonstrates the circulation of the blood. The **Futures Center,** a $72-million wing opened in 1990, takes visitors on a thoughtful journey into the near and distant future through technology exhibits, including experimental high-speed trains, robotized lunar mining and other chores, and undersea gardening. Also home of the highly regarded **Fels Planetarium.** Fine view of the city. Open daily.

Historical Society of Pennsylvania, 1300 Locust St. (732-6201): Interesting small history museum with some important Colonial objects, from William Penn's furniture to Martha Washington's cookbook. Open Tues–Sat.

Marine Corps Memorial Museum, Chestnut St. between 3rd and 4th Sts. (597-8974): On the site of **New Hall,** built in 1791 by the Carpenters' Guild, this relatively new museum commemorates the birth and early days of the U.S. Marine Corps. For military-history enthusiasts. Open daily.

Mummers Museum, 2nd St. and Washington Ave. (336-3050): The "Mummers" parade—eight hours of spectacle and music along Broad St. on Jan 1 (see "Special Events," below). The museum has memorabilia, costumes, videotapes, and sound recordings of past parades. Free concerts Tues evenings May–Oct. Open Tues–Sun.

National Museum of American Jewish History, 55 N. 5th St. (923-3811): Bears witness to the contributions that America's Jewish communities have made to the arts, the sciences, and society since 1654. Memorabilia of famous Philadelphians, including Haym Salomon, the financier of the War of Independence. There is a synagogue attached to the museum. Open Sun–Thurs.

Philadelphia Maritime Museum, Penn's Landing, Delaware Ave. and Walnut St. (925-5439): Moving into the space that formerly housed the Port of History Museum, this maritime museum reopens in the spring of 1995 with a permanent exhibition of artifacts and audio and visual displays depicting the history of maritime activity in Philadelphia and with a collection of small crafts and engines. Call the museum for its schedule.

Please Touch Museum, 210 N. 21st St. (963-0667): Unusual museum for children under 7. In an inviting, colorful setting, the young visitors are encouraged to participate directly in educational experiences relating to art, technology, and natural science. Fascinating for young and old alike. Open Tues–Sun.

University Museum, 33rd and Spruce Sts. (898-4000): One of the finest museums of archeology and anthropology in the world. From Egyptian mummies to Inuit and Polynesian art, and from African masks to Roman, Chinese, and Mayan antiquities, you'll find here a complete panorama of the ancient cultures of five continents. Open Tues–Sun (but closed Sun in summer).

OUTDOOR ART & PLAZAS: More than 200 modern sculptures embellish the greensward and avenues of **Fairmount Park.** Notable among them are the *Swann Memorial Fountain* by Alexander Calder (a native Philadelphian), *Washington Monument* by Rudolf Siemering, *Cowboy* by Frederic Remington, *Spirit of Enterprise* by Jacques Lipchitz, *Playing Angels* by Carl Milles, *Love* by Robert Indiana, and *Stone Age in America* by John Boyle.

Other remarkable modern sculptures are Claes Oldenburg's giant *Clothespin* in chromed steel, 45 ft. (13m) high, standing like a challenge in front of **City Hall** at 15th and Market Sts., and *Bolt of Lightning* by Isamu Noguchi (see "Monuments," above).

PANORAMAS: ⚜ **City Hall,** Broad and Market Sts. (686-9074): Fine view of dwntwn Philadelphia and the Delaware Valley from the top of the observation deck at 548 ft. (167m). Open Mon–Fri.

PARKS & GARDENS: ☼⚜ **Fairmount Park,** NW of the city on both sides of the Schuylkill River: 8,900 acres (3,600ha) of woods, lawns, and lovely gardens, designed by the famous landscape architect Frederick Law Olmsted, one of the two creators of Central Park in New York. The "lung" of Philadelphia, with more than 100 mi. (160km) of paths for cycling and jogging. Many carefully restored Colonial houses, including the Georgian **Mount Pleasant Mansion** (1761) and the 1798 **Strawberry Mansion,** a blend of the Federal and Greek Revival styles. Open-air symphony concerts in summer at **Robin Hood Dell.** Highly regarded zoo (see below). For information, call 685-0000.

☼⚜ **Independence Mall,** bounded by 5th and 6th Sts. between Race and Walnut Sts.: Shady, flower-planted promenade with lawns and fountains, in the heart of historic Philadelphia. The glass pavilion housing the Liberty Bell stands in the middle of the mall.

⚜ **Laurel Hill Cemetery,** Randolph Dr.: Adjoining Fairmount Park and overlooking the Schuylkill River, this landscaped cemetery offers an unbelievably rich selection of funerary art, from Victorian crypts with marble angels and lions, to a replica of the Egyptian temple of Philae and giant obelisks in the style of the Washington Monument. The bronze statue of a goddess by Alexander Calder should also be seen. Open daily.

⚜ **Pennsylvania Horticultural Society,** 325 Walnut St. (625-8250): The oldest horticultural society in the country, founded in 1765. Its garden contains flowers, plants, and shrubs typical of that period. Open Mon–Fri.

PERFORMING ARTS: For a daily listing of all shows and cultural events, consult the entertainment pages of the daily papers *Philadelphia Inquirer* (morning) and *Philadelphia Daily News* (morning), and of the monthly *Philadelphia* magazine. **Upstages,** a ticket booth in the Philadelphia Visitors Center, 16th and John F. Kennedy Blvd. (567-0670), sells tickets to most music, theater, dance, film, and museum events. Open daily.

☼ **Academy of Music,** Broad and Locust Sts. (893-1930): A fine classical revival building dating from 1847; home of the Philadelphia Orchestra (principal conductor: Wolfgang Sawallisch), the Opera Company of Philadelphia (director: Robert Driver), and the Pennsylvania Ballet (artistic director: Christopher D'Amboise). Also big-name recitals.

Annenberg Center, University of Pennsylvania, 3680 Walnut St. (898-6791): Modern and classical theater, children's theater, musicals. Home of the Philadelphia Drama Guild.

Forrest Theater, 1114 Walnut St. (923-1515): Broadway and Off-Broadway hits, musicals.

Mann Music Center, George's Hill, W. Fairmount Park (567-0707): Concerts by the Philadelphia Orchestra, June–Aug. Big-name recitals.

Plays and Players Theatre, 1714 Delancey St. (592-8333): Modern and classical theater; home of the Philadelphia Company.

Robin Hood Dell East, 33rd and Dauphin Sts., Fairmount Park (477-8810): Pop, jazz, gospel music concerts (summer only).

Merriam Theater (formerly the Schubert), Broad and Locust Sts. (732-5997): Ballet performances by the Pennsylvania Ballet and other dance and theater companies.

Society Hill Playhouse, 507 S. 8th St. (923-0210): Modern theater, Off-Broadway shows.

The Spectrum, Broad St. and Pattison Ave. (336-3600): Concerts by leading pop and rock stars.

☀ **Walnut Street Theater,** 9th and Walnut Sts. (574-3550): One of the oldest theaters (1809) in the country. Comedy, drama, experimental theater, modern dance. Home of the Concerto Soloist Chamber Orchestra (director: Marc Mostovoy).

SHOPPING: ⚱ **Antique Row,** Pine St. from 9th to 12th Sts.: Philadelphia's haven for antiques buffs. The three-block area comprises dozens of stores and curio shops appealing to collectors.

The Bourse, 5th St. between Market and Chestnut Sts. (625-0300): More than 50 boutiques, shops, and restaurants in a handsomely restored Victorian-style building, once the home of the Philadelphia Stock Exchange. Opposite the Liberty Bell Pavilion. Open daily.

The Gallery, 9th and Market Sts. (925-7162): The biggest enclosed mall in the city, with 250 stores, boutiques, and restaurants under one roof, with indoor gardens, fountains, and glass-walled elevators. Spectacular. Open daily.

☀ **Jewelers' Row,** 7th and Sansom Sts.: The diamond and jewelry district, with more than 300 stores—Philadelphia's answer to New York's W. 47th St. A sight not to be missed.

John Wanamaker, 13th and Market Sts. (422-2000): The most famous department store in Philadelphia, truly a city within the city, with a splendid nine-story rococo-columned main hall, post office, and free organ recitals at 11:15am and 5:15pm. Open daily.

The Shops at Liberty Place, Two Liberty Place, 16th and Chestnut Sts. (851-9055): A spectacular 58-story skyscraper housing an assortment of upscale retail shops and a 700-car underground parking garage. Products range from the recognized to the uncharted. Open daily.

SPECIAL EVENTS: For the exact schedule of events listed below, consult the **Philadelphia Convention and Visitors Bureau** (see "Tourist Information," above).

☀ **Mummers Parade** (Jan 1): Big costumed parade, with bands and floats, down Broad St.; eight hours of colorful carnival. 20,000 marchers in ornate costumes. A solidly entrenched tradition since 1901.

☀ **Devon Horse Show** (nine days in late May to early June), 22 mi. (35km) NW on U.S. 30 in Devon: One of the biggest horse shows in the country, with more than 1,200 horses competing. Harness races. Spectacular. For information on schedules, call 688-1312.

Elfreth's Alley Fête Day (first wknd in June): Tour of the charming old houses on Elfreth's Alley (see "Strolls," below), with colonially costumed guides. Don't miss it.

Mellon Jazz Festival (late June): More than 40 concerts, many of them free. Features the greatest soloists.

Freedom Week (late June to July 4): A week of festivities celebrating Independence, with processions, fireworks, fountain festival, nighttime Mummers Parade. Shouldn't be missed.

Thanksgiving Day Parade (Thanksgiving Day): Parade of giant floats through the dwntwn streets.

Army-Navy Football Game (last Sat in Nov or first Sat in Dec): A football classic, held at Veterans Stadium.

SPORTS: Philadelphia has four professional teams:
Baseball (Apr–Oct): Phillies, Veterans Stadium (463-1000).
Basketball (Oct–Apr): 76ers, Spectrum Sports Arena (336-3600).

Football (Aug–Dec): Eagles, Veterans Stadium (463-5500).
Ice Hockey (Oct–Apr): Flyers, Spectrum Sports Arena (336-3600).
Horse Racing
Garden State Park, N.J. 70 in Cherry Hill (609/488-8400): Thorough-bred racing from mid-Feb to mid-June; harness racing Aug–Dec.
Philadelphia Park, Street Rd., Bensalem (639-9000): Flat racing June–Feb.

STROLLS: ⚓ **Chinatown,** bounded by Franklin Sq. and 11th St. from Arch to Vine Sts.: With more than 15,000 people, this is one of the most important Chinese districts in America's great cities. There are no fewer than 80 restaurants and an interesting cultural center at 125 N. 10th St. (923-6767), with visits by appointment.

☀⚖⚓ **Elfreth's Alley,** north of Arch St. between Front and 2nd Sts.: Narrow cobbled lane dating from the late 1690s; probably the oldest street in the country. Still has around 30 original craftsmen's and sailors' houses, the oldest from 1728. There's a museum, with period furnishing and equipment, in **Elfreth's House,** no. 126 (574-0560), open daily.

⚓ **Head House Square,** 2nd and Pine Sts.: Head House is an old hall built in 1775, surrounded by old buildings, boutiques, art galleries, restaurants, and the New Market Shopping Center. Concerts in summer. Very lively atmosphere.

⚓ **Rittenhouse Square,** 18th and Walnut Sts.: One of the city's most elegant residential neighborhoods, a mixture of upscale 19th-century houses and luxurious modern apartment buildings, with a shady square in the middle where in spring and summer there are flower shows, concerts, and art exhibitions. Worth a look.

☀⚖⚓ **Society Hill Area,** bounded by Front, Walnut, 7th, and Lombard Sts.: So called after the Free Society of Traders founded by William Penn. Many celebrated figures of the Revolutionary period once lived here. Their houses, now scrupulously restored, add to the charm of the neighborhood, which with its tree-lined streets and little red-brick houses is straight out of the 18th century.

☀⚓ **South Philly,** bounded by Front and 20th Sts., Washington Ave., and South St.: Colorful working-class neighborhood which became widely known through the movie *Rocky*. There are many cafés and family *trattorie* around the **Italian Market,** making this local **Little Italy** a must for visitors.

THEME PARKS: ⚓ **Sesame Place,** 100 Sesame Rd. in Langhorne, 22 mi. (35km) NE on I-95 (757-1100): Amusement park for small children, based on the TV program "Sesame Street" and its characters. More than 100 games and other attractions. The kingdom of the moppets. Open daily May to early Sept, Sat–Sun from Labor Day to mid-Oct; closed the rest of the year.

⚓ **Six Flags Great Adventure,** at Jackson, N.J., 56 mi. (90km) NE via I-95, Pennsylvania Tpke. Connection, New Jersey Tpke. north, I-195E, and N.J. 537S (908/928-1821): Huge 1,700-acre (688ha) theme park, with a hundred attractions including carousels, one of the world's fastest roller coasters (68mph), and a drive-through safari-zoo with 2,000 wild animals (you stay in your car). Shows and vaudeville. Open daily May–Sept, wknds only to late Oct; closed the rest of the year.

WINTER SPORTS RESORTS: ⚓ **Doe Mountain,** near Hereford, 58 mi. (92km) along U.S. 76W, U.S. 422W, and Penna. 100N (682-7109): Seven lifts; open Dec to mid-Mar.

⚓ **Spring Mountain Ski Area,** near Limerick, 36 mi (57km) via U.S. 76W, U.S. 422W, and Penna. 29N (287-7900): Four lifts; open mid-Dec to mid-Mar.

ZOOS: ※ẞ **Zoological Garden,** Fairmount Park, 34th St. and Girard Ave. (243-1100): Opened in 1874, this is the oldest zoo in the U.S. More than 1,600 animals; important collections of reptiles and primates. Children's zoo. Monorail tour. Open daily.

ACCOMMODATIONS

Personal Favorites (in order of preference)

ẞẞẞẞ **Four Seasons** (dwntwn), 1 Logan Sq., PA 19103 (215/963-1500; toll free, see Four Seasons). 371 rms, A/C, color TV, in-rm movies. AE, CB, DC, MC, V. Valet gar. $19, pool, health club, sauna, two rests. (including the Fountain), bar, 24-hr. rm svce, concierge. *Note:* The most distinguished place to stay in Philadelphia; eight-floor modern building adj. an office high-rise from which it's separated by a lovely landscaped courtyard and grdn w. fountains. Spacious, ultra-comfortable rms decorated in Federal style, w. minibars (some w. balconies). Excellent svce. Sophisticated rest. Very well located a stone's throw from the museum district. Big business clientele. Interesting wknd discounts. **VE**

※ẞẞẞẞ **Hotel Atop the Bellevue** (dwntwn), 1415 Chancellor Court (at Broad and Walnut Sts.), PA 19102 (215/893-1776; toll free, see Preferred). 173 rms, A/C, color TV, in-rm movies. AE, CB, DC, MC, V. Valet gar. $16, pool, health club, sauna, squash courts, jogging track, massage, two rests., coffee shop, bar, 24-hr. rms svce, boutiques, concierge. *Note:* Occupying the top seven floors of the venerable Bellevue Building, a designated turn-of-the-century landmark, this super-deluxe hotel reopened in 1989 after 18 months (and $100 million) of renovation. Spacious rms w. every imaginable convenience (VCRs, minibars, marble bathrooms w. TV and telephone). Period furnishings. Magnificent seven-story atrium–winter garden. Absolutely first-class physical-fitness facilities; personalized svce; rest. open to hotel guests only. Quality with elegance; VIP clientele. **VE**

ẞẞẞ **Ritz Carlton** (dwntwn), 17th and Chestnut Sts. (at Liberty Place), PA 19103 (215/536-1600; toll free 800/241-3333). 290 rms, A/C, color TV, in-rm movies. AE, CB, DC, MC, V. Valet gar. $18, health club, sauna, two rests. (including The Dining Room), piano bar, 24-hr. rm svce, concierge. *Note:* Philadelphia's newest luxury hotel, adjacent to the Shops at Liberty Place in the heart of center city's business district. Beautifully appointed rms and suites, w. marble baths, in-rm svce cabinets, and minibars. Polished, efficient svce. Two VIP floors w. private lounge and concierge. Big business clientele. **VE**

ẞẞ **Embassy Suites Hotel Center City** (formerly Radisson) (dwntwn), Benjamin Franklin Pkwy. at 18th St., PA 19103 (215/963-2222; toll free 800/362-2779). 285 suites, A/C, color TV, in-rm movies. AE, CB, DC, MC, V. Gar. $14, rest. (T. G. I. Friday), bar, rm svce, free crib, concierge. *Note:* Large 28-floor cylindrical tower, a block or two from Logan Circle and the museum district. Has only suites, spacious, w. terraces, microwave ovens, and refrigerators. Ideal for long stays and/or business travelers (fully equipped business center). Physical-fitness facilities. Caters mostly to groups and conventions. **E–VE**

ẞẞ **Comfort Inn Penn's Landing** (dwntwn), 100 N. Delaware Ave., PA 19107 (215/627-7900; toll free, see Choice). 185 rms, A/C, color TV, in-rm movies. AE, CB, DC, MC, V. Free parking, rest. adj., bar, rm svce, free breakfast. *Note:* New 10-story motel on the banks of the Delaware River. Functional, comfortable rms overlooking river or city. Friendly reception and svce. Ideal for visiting Independence Mall and its historic monuments. Very good overall value. **I–M**

ẞ **Days Inn–Brooklawn** (vic.), 801 Rte. 130, Brooklawn, NJ 08030 (609/456-6688; toll free, see Days Inns). 116 rms, A/C, color TV, in-rm movies. AE, DC, MC, V. Free parking, pool, rests. nearby, crib $5. *Note:* Brand-new motel, 15 min. by car from dwntwn Philadelphia by the Walt Whitman Bridge. Comfortable, serviceable rms (some w. refrigerators). Ideal if you're driving. Good value. **I**

Other Accommodations (from top bracket to budget)

♀♀♀ **Omni Independence Park** (dwntwn), 401 Chestnut St., PA 19106 (215/925-0000; toll free, see Omni). 155 rms, A/C, color TV, in-rm movies. AE, CB, DC, MC, V. Valet parking $14, pool, health club, sauna, rest. (Azalea), bar, 24-hr. rm svce, free crib, concierge. *Note:* Brand-new luxury grand hotel located in the heart of Independence Historical Park. All the comfort, elegance, and refinement of a European-style hotel. Spacious guest rms and suites overlooking Independence Park. The rest. features contemporary American cuisine. State-of-the-art business equipment. Very efficient svce. Superb location. **VE**

♀♀♀ **Wyndham Franklin Plaza** (dwntwn), 2 Franklin Plaza, PA 19103 (215/448-2000; toll free 800/822-4200). 761 rms, A/C, color TV, in-rm movies. AE, CB, DC, MC, V. Valet gar. $14, pool, health club, tennis court, sauna, two rests. (including the Terrace), coffee shop, two bars, rm svce, nightclub, hrdrsr, drugstore, free crib. *Note:* Large, ultramodern convention hotel w. 26 floors, Philadelphia's biggest. Functional, comfortable rms w. refrigerators; impersonal but efficient svce; very good physical-fitness facilities. Caters mostly to groups and business travelers. Halfway between City Hall and the museum district. **E–VE**

♀♀♀ **Doubletree Towers** (formerly the Hilton) (dwntwn), Broad and Locust Sts., PA 19107 (215/893-1600; toll free 800/222-8733). 428 rms, A/C, color TV, in-rm movies. AE, CB, DC, MC, V. Valet gar. $15, pool, health club, sauna, squash courts, rest. (Café Académie), bar, rm svce, concierge, crib free. *Note:* Ultramodern 25-story tower in the heart of dwntwn. Inviting, spacious, very comfortable rms, some w. refrigerator. Spectacular four-story atrium. Excellent svce; mediocre rest.; VIP floor. Since the financial district is right next door many business travelers stay here. **E–VE,** but lower rates off-season.

☼♀♀♀ **The Warwick** (dwntwn), 17th and Locust Sts., PA 19103 (215/735-6000; toll free 800/523-4210). 180 rms, A/C, color TV, in-rm movies. AE, CB, DC, MC, V. Valet gar. $12, rest. (1701 Café), bar, rm svce, disco, hrdrsr, drugstore, free crib, concierge. *Note:* Elegant, intimate little hotel dating from the '20s. Lobby sumptuously decorated w. rare rugs and period pieces. Spacious, inviting rms; top-notch rest. Polished svce. Conveniently located very near Rittenhouse Sq. and the business district. Clientele of wealthy businesspeople. Has both charm and distinction; offers interesting wknd discounts. **E**

♀♀♀ **Penn Tower Hotel** (formerly the Hilton; nr. dwntwn), Civic Center Blvd. at 34th St., PA 19104 (215/387-8333; toll free 800/356-7366). 225 rms, A/C, color TV, in-rm movies. AE, CB, DC, MC, V. Gar. $10, pool, health club, rest., bar, rm svce. *Note:* Large, very modern hotel on the University of Pennsylvania campus, w. completely renovated interior. Inviting, comfortable atmosphere; efficient svce. VIP floor. With the Civic Center and the Convention Hall nearby, attracts mostly groups and conventions. **M–E**

♀♀ **Holiday Inn Independence Mall** (dwntwn), 4th and Arch Sts., PA 19106 (215/923-8660; toll free, see Holiday Inns). 364 rms, A/C, color TV, in-rm movies. AE, CB, DC, MC, V. Gar. $8, rooftop pool, rest. (Benjamin's), coffee shop, bar, rm svce, disco, free crib. *Note:* Large, comfortable, very well-run motel; rms and facilities recently modernized. Pool open in summer only. One of the best locations for visiting the Historic District. Group and tourist clientele. A better class of Holiday Inn. **M–E**

☼♀♀ **Ramada Suites–Convention Center** (formerly Quality Inn) (dwntwn), 1010 Race St., PA 19016 (215/922-1730; toll free, see Choice). 96 suites, A/C, color TV. AE, CB, DC, MC, V. Free gar., free continental breakfast. *Note:* Unusual all-suites hotel in the heart of Chinatown, in a building that used to be a rocking-chair factory—Victorian rococo, now pleasingly restored. Spacious, comfortable suites w. kitchenettes; good svce. Well situated, near City Hall and the picturesque Reading Terminal Market. **I–M**

♀♀ Ramada Inn Center City (formerly the Franklin Motor Inn; **♌♌** nr. dwntwn), 501 N. 22nd St., PA 19130 (215/568-8300); toll free, see Ramada). 280 rms, A/C, color TV, in-rm movies. AE, CB, DC, MC, V. Free parking, pool, rest., coffee shop, bar, rm svce. *Note:* Recently renovated motel in the museum district. Comfortable rms, though some are on the small side; good svce. Good value on balance. 10 min. from dwntwn. **I–M**

♀♀ Landmark Inn Motor Lodge (vic.), NJ 73 and 38, Cherry Hill, **♌♌** NJ 08052 (609/235-6400; toll free 800/635-5917). 163 rms, A/C, cable and color TV, in-rm movies. AE, CB, DC, MC, V. Free valet parking, pool, health club, sauna, rest., bar, disco, rm svce, free crib, refrigerators. *Note:* Friendly, modern motel 15 min. from dwntwn by the Ben Franklin Bridge. Comfortable accommodations; good equipment. Reception w. a smile. Very good value. Ideal if you're driving. **I**

♀ Days Inn–Roosevelt (nr. dwntwn), 4200 Roosevelt Blvd. at **♌** U.S. 1, PA 19124 (215/289-9200; toll free, see Days Inns). 115 rms, A/C, color and cable TV, AE, MC, V. Free parking, complimentary breakfast. *Note:* Motel north of the city. Functionally comfortable. Great if you're driving; 15 min. from dwntwn. **I**

♀ Roosevelt Motor Inn (vic.), 7600 Roosevelt Blvd., PA 19152 **♌** (215/338-7600). 101 rms, A/C, color TV. AE, MC, V. Free parking, rest., bar. *Note:* Typical, well-run motel w. acceptable comforts and facilities. Ideal if you're driving; 25 min. from dwntwn. **I**

Airport Accommodations

♀♀ Holiday Inn–Airport (vic.), 45 Industrial Hwy., Essington, **♌♌** PA 19029 (215/521-2400; toll free, see Holiday Inns). 306 rms, A/C, color TV, in-rm movies. AE, CB, DC, MC, V. Free parking, pool, rest., coffee shop, bar, rm svce, disco, free crib. *Note:* Large, modern, six-story motel in true Holiday Inn style, 5 min. from the airport. Comfortable, well-soundproofed rms; free airport limo. Business clientele. **M**

YMCAs/Youth Hostels

☼ Chamounix Mansion (nr. dwntwn), Chamounix Dr., Fairmount Park (215/878-3676). Inviting youth hostel in a renovated 19th-century farmhouse. Dormitories (50 beds). Closed at Christmas.

International House (nr. dwntwn), 3701 Chestnut St. (215/387-5125). If you're on a tight budget, this is the best place in town (though reserved for students only). Nr. U. of Pennsylvania; acceptable rest.

RESTAURANTS

Personal Favorites (in order of preference)

♀♀♀ The Fountain (dwntwn), in the Four Seasons (see "Accommodations," above) (963-1500). A/C. Breakfast/lunch/dinner daily. AE, CB, DC, MC, V. Jkt. *Specialties:* linguine w. shrimp and cream of saffron, cold tomato soup w. coriander, red snapper w. three caviars, grilled salmon, roast pheasant w. cabbage and walnuts, sautéed veal chops, chocolate mousse cake. Very fine wine list, particularly strong on half bottles; low-calorie menu available. *Note:* The most acclaimed among Philadelphia's top-notch rests. Dazzling international food w. a French accent. Facing enhanced competition, the Fountain just keeps getting better. Luxurious, expensive decor featuring wood paneling, Italian marble floors covered in Oriental rugs, and magnificent flower arrangements. Beautiful view of Logan Sq. and the fountain for which the rest. is named. Ultra-polished svce. The fashionable place for entertaining. Resv. a must. *Continental.* **M–E**

⚱⚱⚱ **Jack's Firehouse** (nr. dwntwn), 2130 Fairmount Ave. (232-
⚱⚱⚱ 9000). A/C. Lunch/dinner daily, brunch Sun; closed hols.
AE, DC, MC, V. *Specialties:* corn chowder w. shiitake and crabmeat, venison w. roasted-beechnut sauce, tenderloin of pork on potato cakes w. sage sauce, grilled bass w. Georgia salsa, bison w. Jack Daniel sauce, wild-rice pudding. Menu changes daily. *Note:* Dubbed by some food critics as "haute hillbilly," the cuisine of Jack McDavid is an unorthodox but attractive amalgam of classical French technique and Pennsylvania country cooking. Converted landmark firehouse complete w. brass pole and original wood-slat walls. Friendly, cheerful svce. Resv. a must, given its success. *American.* **M–E**

⚱⚱⚱ **Susanna Foo** (dwntwn), 1512 Walnut St. (545-2666). A/C.
⚱⚱⚱ Lunch Mon–Fri, dinner Mon–Sat; closed hols. AE, MC. J&T. *Specialties:* smoked-duck salad w. endive and mango, curried-chicken dumplings w. grilled eggplant salad, salmon w. lemon-grass, sweetbreads w. Kung Pao sauce, sautéed quail w. shiitake and ginger, fried honey banana w. almond and warm coconut sauce. Menu changes regularly. Good list of French and California wines. *Note:* The most interesting Far Eastern rest. in greater Philadelphia. Chef Susanna Foo, who arrived here from her native China in 1979, serves up a wholly original merger of different traditions and tastes: Chinese, French, Mexican, and Californian. Rather chilly modern decor; courteous and attentive svce. You shouldn't miss this great dining experience. Resv. strongly advised. *Chinese.* **I–M**

☼⚱⚱ **The Garden** (dwntwn), 1617 Spruce St. (546-4455). A/C.
☼⚱⚱ Lunch Tues–Fri, dinner Mon–Sat; closed hols. AE, CB, DC,
MC, V. Jkt. *Specialties:* carpaccio, pasta primavera, oysters on the half shell, mussels and clams w. chives, roast chicken w. cognac, aged prime beef, broiled breaded Dover sole, raspberry and chocolate cake. Rather skimpy wine list. *Note:* With its open-air garden, yellow umbrellas, and centuries-old trees surrounded by old Georgian houses, this dwntwn rest. offers you the loveliest setting you could ask for on a fine day. The five indoor dining rms are no less delightful. Excellent, unaffected bistro food; the meat is especially noteworthy. Friendly, smiling svce. Locally popular; resv. advised. *Continental/ American.* **M**

⚱ **DiNardo's Famous Crabs** (dwntwn), 312 Race St. (925-
⚱ 5115). A/C. Lunch Mon–Sat, dinner nightly; closed hols.
AE, CB, DC, MC, V. *Specialties:* clams, oysters on the half shell, steamed Louisiana crabs, steamed mussels, stuffed flounder and shrimp, fresh broiled fish. *Note:* As its name implies, this venerable Philadelphia institution is renowned for delicious steamed hard-shell crabs and other equally fine seafood, plus the DiNardo family's secret sauce recipes. Definitely a "don't dress" place. *Seafood.* **I**

☼⚱ **The City Tavern** (dwntwn), 2nd and Walnut Sts. (923-6059).
☼⚱ A/C. Lunch/dinner daily; closed Jan 1, Dec 25. AE, MC, V.
Jkt. *Specialties:* salmagundi salad, chicken w. cider, roast beef, catch of the day, Indian pudding. *Note:* This famous Revolutionary War tavern, rebuilt in 1974, perfectly recaptures the feeling of the 1770s, when John Adams described it as "the most elegant tavern in America." Period-costumed waitresses and a harpist at dinner. Unpretentious, praiseworthy food based on old recipes. Resv. advised. A must for history buffs. *American.* **I–M**

⚱ **Down Home Grill** (nr. dwntwn), 1800 Spring Garden St.
⚱ (557-7510). A/C. Break/lunch/dinner daily; closed hols.
AE. *Specialties:* sawmill gravy and biscuits, jambalaya, ham and smoked Monterey Jack cheese on black bread, Cajun pizzas, pork chops w. apples, rice noodles w. chicken and curry. *Note:* The best deal in Philadelphia. Jack McDavid (see Jack's Firehouse) serves up honest, irresistible meals that give Southern cooking a renewed respectability. Named one of the best new rests. of 1993 by *Bon Appétit* magazine. All entrées are under $10. *American.* **B**

Other Restaurants (from top bracket to budget)

🍷🍷🍷🍷 **Le Bec Fin** (dwntwn), 1523 Walnut St. (567-1000). A/C. Lunch Mon–Fri, dinner Mon–Sat (two sittings, at 6 and 9pm); closed hols. and mid-Aug to early Sept. AE, CB, DC, MC, V. J&T. *Specialties:* scallops sautéed w. sugar peas; squab w. cream sauce, thyme, and garlic; medaillons of veal w. morel mushrooms; oysters in millefeuille pastry shell; veal kidneys moutardier; civet of lobster. Remarkable desserts; large wine list. Menu changed seasonally. *Note:* One of the most honorable exponents of French haute cuisine in the country, chef George Perrier, from Lyons, works wonders at his stoves; his dishes and sauces are marvels of delicacy and balance. Elegant, flower-decked setting w. only 14 tables, so that resv. must be made well ahead for Fri and Sat evenings. Big business clientele and celebrities passing through. Flawless svce. *French.* **M** (lunch), **VE** (dinner, prix fixe).

🍷🍷🍷 **Ciboulette** (dwntwn), in Hotel Atop the Bellevue (see "Accommodations" above) (790-1210). A/C. Lunch Mon–Fri, dinner nightly. A/C. AE, CB, DC, MC, V. Jkt. *Specialties:* warm eggplant terrine, sautéed foie gras on a bed of vegetables and shallots, roast duckling w. honey-and-ginger glaze, roasted salmon w. genevoise sauce, roast saddle of lamb w. zucchini tart and goat cheese, terrine of bitter chocolate covered w. pear coulis, crème brûlée. Rather wimpy wine list. *Note:* The Provençal-inspired French cooking of young chef Bruce Lim is wonderfully elegant and balanced. The decor is luxuriously rococo; the svce, highly professional. The four-dish tasting menu is a bargain at $45. At a rest. so successful, and so small (40 seats), resv. are a must—but so is the rest. itself for all lovers of good food. *French.* **M (E** for tasting menu).

🍷🍷 **Bookbinder's Seafood House** (dwntwn), 215 S. 15th St. (545-1137). A/C. Lunch Mon–Fri, dinner nightly; closed Sun July–Aug, Thanksgiving, Dec 25. AE, CB, DC, MC, V. J&T. *Specialties:* oysters on the half shell, snapper (snapping turtle) soup, mussels in red sauce, Florida stone crabs in season, crab Imperial, fried squid, lobster Coleman, filet of flounder stuffed w. crabmeat. Weak on wines and desserts. *Note:* "Booky's," as Philadelphians call it, has been a landmark for half a century (by the way, don't confuse it with its nr. namesake, Old Original Bookbinders, a typical tourist rest. in the heart of the Historic District), and has belonged to four generations of the Bookbinder family. Dependable but unimaginative food; traditional seafaring decor w. the inevitable fishing trophies stuffed and mounted on the walls. Popular for business lunches; often crowded and noisy. Svce on the curt side. Resv. advised. *Seafood.* **M**

🍷🍷 **Friday, Saturday, Sunday** (nr. dwntwn), 261 S. 21st St. (546-4232). A/C. Lunch Mon–Fri, dinner nightly. AE, DC, MC, V. *Specialties:* wild-mushroom soup, artichoke-heart casserole w. fresh mozzarella, poached salmon w. sorrel, duck w. sun-dried cherries and port sauce, rack of lamb, Cornish hen Normandie stuffed w. apples and walnuts. *Note:* Elegant, romantic little bistro w. a pleasant bar upstairs. The daily menu, scrawled on a chalkboard, is contemporary American. Trendy clientele; friendly, hardworking svce; a very good place. *American.* **I–M**

🍷🍷 **Marabella's** (dwntwn), 1420 Locust St. (545-1845). A/C. Lunch/dinner daily; closed hols. AE, MC, V. Jkt. *Specialties:* fresh homemade pasta, gourmet pizzas, catch of the day, broiled chicken and veal chops, chocolate and raspberry cake. *Note:* This new-age *trattoria* is warm and colorful; its fresh homemade pasta (particularly the outstanding tortellini with goat cheese) are excellent, as are the attractively priced broiled (over mesquite) specialties. The decor is bold and brassy, and the place is usually noisy, but the svce is quick and efficient. Locally very popular; resv. recommended. *Italian.* **I–M**

🍷🍷 **Sansom Street Oyster House** (dwntwn), 1516 Sansom St. (567-7683). A/C. Lunch/dinner Mon–Sat; closed hols. AE, CB, DC, MC, V. *Specialties:* oysters and clams, broiled fish of the day, crab Imperial. *Note:* Likable seafood bistro where the decor is unpretentious but the seafood is remarkably fresh. Locally popular; often noisy. Setting recently refurbished. No resv., so sometimes a long wait. *Seafood.* I–M

    ♈ **White Dog Café** (nr. dwntwn), 3420 Sansom St. (386-9224). A/C. Lunch/dinner daily, brunch Sat–Sun; closed hols. AE, DC, MC, V. *Specialties:* calamari in masa chile crust, mustard-baked salmon, grilled leg of lamb, pan-fried trout, filet mignon w. fettuccine and Gorgonzola cream sauce. Good wines by the glass. *Note:* A local favorite for wholesome yet classy food. Bohemian-style decor and stylish but fun atmosphere. Resv. advised. *American.* I–M

    ♈ **Zocalo** (nr dwntwn), 3600 Lancaster Ave. (895-0139). A/C. Lunch Mon–Fri, dinner nightly; closed hols. AE, MC, V. *Specialties:* shrimp in adobo, guacamole, chicken mole, carne asada tampiqueña, grilled lamb chops. *Note:* Upscale Mexican rest. featuring traditional regional recipes along w. *nueva cocina*—style dishes. Clean-lined and casual w. outdoor dining in summer. Good margaritas and attentive svce. *Mexican.* I

    ♈ **Moriarty's** (dwntwn), 1116 Walnut St. (627-7676). A/C. Lunch/dinner daily (until 2am). AE, DC, MC, V. *Specialties:* Buffalo wings, hamburgers, steak, seafood, Mexican dishes. *Note:* Voted best Buffalo wings in Philadelphia. A very popular place w. the dwntwn crowd, especially after work. 14 beers on draft. *American.* B–I.

    ♈ **Famous 4th St. Delicatessen** (dwntwn), 4th and Bainbridge Sts. (922-3274). A/C. Breakfast/lunch daily (7am–6pm, until 4pm Sun); closed Jewish hols. AE. *Specialties:* corned-beef sandwiches, pastrami, kugel, whitefish, lox, chocolate-chip cookies, milkshakes. *Note:* This New York–style deli is a favorite of those in-the-know. The decor and svce are without pretension or affectation, boasting collections of old telephones and old milk cartons. Generous servings; very popular locally. Has been in the same family for more than 60 years. *American.* B

    ♈ **Jim's Steaks** (dwntwn), 400 South St., at 4th St. (928-1911). A/C. Lunch/dinner daily (until 1am). No credit cards. *Specialties:* cheese steak, hoagies. *Note:* Undisputed master of these two local specialties. Hoagies are giant hero sandwiches of ham, provolone, and salami; cheese steaks are thin slices of steak broiled w. onion, green pepper, tomato sauce, and cheese, all served on a crusty loaf of Italian bread. Both are real Philadelphia institutions. You can eat them here in a superb art deco setting—black-and-white tiles and sparkling chrome. Generally crowded at lunch. *American.* B

    ♈ **Melrose Diner** (nr. dwntwn), 1501 Snyder Ave., at Broad St. (467-6644). A/C. Breakfast/lunch/dinner 24 hr. daily. No credit cards. *Specialties:* chicken soup, scrapple (leftover pork, sliced and fried up w. buckwheat meal or cornmeal), hamburgers, pork chops, apple pie. *Note:* A South Philly favorite for more than half a century. Praiseworthy plain food served w. a smile in generous portions. Crowded at all hours of day and night. A real landmark. *American.* B

In the Vicinity

    ♈ **Joe's,** 450 S. 7th St., at Laurel St., in Reading, 60 mi. (96km) NW on I-76 and U.S. 422 (373-6794). A/C. Dinner only, Tues–Sat; closed hols. AE, CB, DC, MC, V. Jkt. *Specialties:* wild-mushroom soup, mushrooms in pastry shell, morels Marie stuffed w. mousse of pheasant, shiitake w. pepper and burgundy sauce, duck in black-bean sauce w. fresh mushrooms, squab stuffed w. mushrooms. Good homemade desserts. *Note:* One of Pennsylvania's best, and certainly one of its most original, rests. Owner Jack Czarnecki, an expert who picks his own wild mushrooms in the surrounding woodlands, knows them all and blends their different flavors to perfection; his food is delicate and inspired. The rest., which has been in the Czarnecki family since 1916, is well worth the 1¼-hr. trip from Philadelphia by car. Resv. a must. *Continental.* M

🍷 **Restaurant Taquet** (vic.), 139 E. Lancaster Ave., Wayne (687-5005). A/C. Lunch Mon–Sat, dinner nightly, Sun brunch; closed hols. AE, DC, MC, V. Jkt. *Specialties:* black bean soup w. cream of garlic, mosaique of fish carpaccio, paupiette of sole w. salmon mousse in dill sauce, sautéed quail w. madère sauce and barley, chocolate-and-almond layer cake mingled w. Italian coffee. Menu changes regularly. *Note:* The best recent addition to a tough host of competing Philadelphia rests. Jean-François Taquet, an inductee to the prestigious *Maîtres Cuisiniers de France,* has gathered much attention for the solidity of his craft. Housed in an old Victorian hotel elegantly renovated. *French.* **I–M**

Cafeterias/Fast Food
Marathon Grill (dwntwn), 1818 Market St. (561-1818). A/C. Breakfast/lunch/dinner daily (7am–8pm). AE, MC, V. *Specialties:* char-grilled sirloin burgers, grilled chicken, filet mignon sandwiches, Caesar salad, hot and cold pasta salads. *Note:* A favorite place among city dwellers to grab a fast bite to eat. Good salads.

BARS & NIGHTCLUBS
Blue Moon Jazz Club (dwntwn), 4th St. between Market and Chestnut Sts. (413-2272). Slick jazz scene featuring well-known musicians. Open nightly.

Chestnut Cabaret (dwntwn), 3801 Chestnut St. (382-1201). Trendy dance club and concert hall presenting rock, jazz, reggae, and blues to a mostly twenty-something crowd. Open Tues–Sat.

Circa (dwntwn), 1518 Walnut St. (545-6800). Huge mahogany bar serving 12 draft beers, sure to draw a yuppy crowd. Open Mon–Sat.

Comedy Cabaret (dwntwn), 126 Chestnut St. (625-5653). Famous comedy club above the Middle East Restaurant. A landmark on the Philadelphia scene.

Dobb's (nr. dwntwn), 304 South St., between 3rd and 4th Sts. (928-1943). Live rock Tues–Sun. Also a mixed-menu rest.

Downey's (dwntwn), 526 Front St., at South St. (625-9500). Irish pub favored by local sports figures; dance floor. Also praiseworthy rest. Usually crowded. Open nightly.

Funny Bone (dwntwn), 221 South St. (440-9670). One of the local high places of improvisation, featuring the biggest stars in that sky.

Katmandu (nr. dwntwn), Pier 25, at Delaware Ave. (629-1101). A South Seas island getaway, complete w. palm trees, white-sand beaches, and exotic cocktails. Unmatched waterfront vistas. Entertainment nightly; also rest.

Magnolia (dwntwn), 1602 Locust St. (546-4180). This popular bar draws a business-suited crowd of singles. Live music Tues and Wed.

Ortlieb's Jazz House (dwntwn), 847 N. 3rd St. (922-1035). Jazz Tues–Sun.

Zanzibar Blue (dwntwn), 301-305 S. 11th St. (829-0300). Upscale jazz club w. attractive rest. serving Mediterranean fare. Housed in a historic landmark building. Sophisticated atmosphere. Open nightly.

NEARBY EXCURSIONS

CAMDEN (1 mi./2km east by the Benjamin Franklin Bridge): This little New Jersey city, founded in 1681 and now an industrial suburb of Philadelphia, boasts the new ☼🏛 **New Jersey State Aquarium,** 1 Riverside Dr. (609/365-3300), just across the river from Philadelphia. This 760,000-gallon open ocean tank affords visitors fish-eye views of the sharks, rays, and other fin fellows. Spectacular 18- by 24-foot window on the "edge of the Abyss." Open daily. Direct access from Penn's Landing by ferry (Riverbus).

Also in Camden is the 🏛 **house of Walt Whitman,** singer of the "American Dream," where he spent the last eight years of his life, at 330 Mickle Blvd. (609/

964-5383), open Wed–Sun. You'll find the original furniture, books, and personal memorabilia of the "Good Gray Poet." His tomb is in Harleigh Cemetery, Heddon Ave. and Vesper Blvd.

☼ **DOYLESTOWN** (28 mi./44km north on Penna. 611): Seat of picturesque Bucks County, country retreat of many artists, writers, and theatrical people. Be sure to see the ⌂ **home of Pearl Buck,** the novelist and Nobel laureate, at 520 Dublin Rd., Hilltown Township (249-0100), open Tues–Sun Mar–Sept. It was here that she wrote her most famous novel, *The Good Earth,* which won the Pulitzer prize in 1932.

While you're here, don't miss the cavernous ⌂ **Mercer Museum** and its famous collection of old Americana at Pine and E. Ashland Sts. (345-0210), open daily.

☼♟♟ **GERMANTOWN** (7 mi./11km north on Broad St. and Germantown Ave.): Settled toward the end of the 17th century by Mennonite immigrants from the Rhineland in Germany, this old village, now a residential neighborhood, has dozens of old houses that are designated historic monuments. Its main thoroughfare, **Germantown Avenue,** is an old Native American trail, which is itself a National Historic Landmark.

Among the most interesting buildings (all open to the public Tues–Sun Apr–Dec) are: **Cliveden,** a 1767 Georgian house at 6401 Germantown Ave.; George Washington's summer residence at 5442 Germantown Ave., the 1773 **Deshler-Morris House;** the **Germantown Historical Society Complex,** comprising several museums in houses built between 1745 and 1798, at 5503 Germantown Ave. (844-0514); the 1744 **Grumblethorpe House,** at 5267 Germantown Ave.; **Stenton,** at 18th St. and Windrim Ave., constructed in 1730, which was Washington's headquarters during the Battle of Germantown; **Upsala,** 6430 Germantown Ave., a 1798 gem of Federal architecture; and the town's oldest house, the 1690 **Wyck** at 6026 Germantown Ave. (848-1690).

☼♟♟ **LONGWOOD GARDENS** (at Kennett Sq., 31 mi./49km SW on I-95S, U.S. 322N, and U.S. 1S): Magnificent 350-acre (140ha) park, once the property of Pierre S. DuPont, where something is in bloom almost any time of year; there are tropical greenhouses, lush Italian gardens, an arboretum, an orchid house, and pools covered with giant water lilies. Concerts and shows in summer. Open daily; call 388-6741 for information. Well worth the trip.

On the way see ☼ **Brandywine Battlefield,** on U.S. 1 near Chadds Ford (459-3342), where the colonists sustained a defeat at the hands of the British in 1777. Visitor Center; Washington's and Lafayette's headquarters. Open Tues–Sun.

Another place you shouldn't miss is the ☼♟♟ **Brandywine River Museum,** on U.S. 1 in Chadds Ford (388-2700), open daily, housed in a century-old mill. Contains Andrew Wyeth's private collection of his own works; those of his father, the famous illustrator N. C. Wyeth; and paintings by his father's teacher, Howard Pyle, and many other American artists.

☼⌂ **NEW HOPE** (46 mi./73km NE on I-95N and Penna. 32): Charming 300-year-old village on the banks of the Delaware River, which has long proved irresistible to artists and writers. Many old houses, boutiques, art galleries, and inns. Apr–Nov you can take a picturesque trip in a **mule-drawn barge** along the Old Delaware Canal; apply on New St. (862-2842).

On the way, visit ☼ **Washington Crossing State Park,** on either side of the

Delaware River at the exact spot where Washington and 2,400 of his men crossed it in a snowstorm on the night of December 25, 1776, on his way to capture the town of Trenton by surprise. This brilliant feat of arms, reenacted every year on Dec 25 by costumed extras, was one of the turning points of the War of Independence. Memorials; museum on Penna. 32 (493-4076). Open daily.

☼☖ **OLD FORT MIFFLIN** (Fort Mifflin Rd., 8 mi./12km SW along Broad St. and Penna. 291) (492-3395): Sometimes called "the Alamo of the War of Independence"; scene of a fierce engagement against the British in the fall of 1777. Rebuilt in 1798. Open Wed–Sun Apr–Nov. Military parades in period uniform on Sun in summer. Should be seen.

☼☖ **POTTSTOWN** (36 mi./57km NW on I-76 and U.S. 422): Here, in 1714, ironmaster John Potts opened Pennsylvania's first industrial foundry. His family home, **Pottsgrove Mansion,** a very fine 1752 example of Colonial architecture on W. King St. (326-4014), is open to visitors Tues–Sun.

Some 13 mi. (20km) SW along Penna. 724 and Penna. 345, look in on the ☼☖ **Hopewell Furnace National Historic Site** (582-8773), a museum-village clustered around an old foundry which was active between 1770 and 1883, and has been restored in the style of the period 1820–40. Interesting museum; demonstrations of blacksmithing in summer. Open daily.

☼☖☖ **PRINCETON** (41 mi./65km NE on I-95 and U.S. 206): Gracious little university town, steeped in history, which was briefly (June–Nov 1783) the capital of the United States. While in session at Princeton, the Congress learned of the signing of the peace treaty ending the Revolutionary War in Sept 1783; from here, too, Washington delivered his famous "Farewell Orders to the Armies."

With its 6,000 students and Anglo-English charm, Ivy League ☼☖☖ **Princeton University,** founded in 1746, is one of the most socially exclusive as well as one of the most distinguished universities on the eastern seaboard. Its faculty has included eight Nobel prize winners (one of them Albert Einstein, who died here in 1955). Interesting tour of the campus, open daily (609/258-3603), with its collection of modern sculptures by Calder, Picasso, Moore, Noguchi, Lipchitz, and others. See, too, the **Woodrow Wilson School of Public and International Affairs,** designed by Minoru Yamasaki, architect of New York's World Trade Center, and **Nassau Hall,** built in 1756, where the Second Continental Congress met in 1783. The **University Art Museum,** open Tues–Sun, has works by such painters as Raphael, Cranach, van Dyke, Rubens, and Monet.

You can visit Princeton along with **New Hope** and **Washington Crossing State Park** (see above).

☼☖ **VALLEY FORGE NATIONAL HISTORICAL PARK** (N. Gulph Rd. and Penna. 23, 20 mi./33km NW on I-76) (783-1077): George Washington's camp from Dec 1777 to June 1778, one of the darkest periods of the Revolutionary War. Some 3,000 soldiers died here of cold, hunger, or disease during that terrible winter. Washington's headquarters, a commemorative chapel, and a museum are open daily; guided tours from the Visitor Center, mid-Apr to Oct. Lovely countryside all around.

☼☖ **WINTERTHUR MUSEUM & GARDENS** (36 mi./57km SW on I-95 and Del. 52) (302/888-4600): Once the 200-bedroom home of chemical tycoon Henry F. DuPont. Sumptuous collection of decorative art and American furniture from the 17th to the 19th century. Resv. a must for conducted tours of the principal collections. Magnificent 200-acre (80ha) English-style park. Open Tues–Sun.

Combine it with a visit to **Longwood Gardens** and the **Brandywine Museum and Battlefield** (see above).

ATLANTIC CITY & CAPE MAY

☼⚂ **ATLANTIC CITY** (215 mi./344km r.t. via N.J. 42S, the Atlantic City Expwy. east, N.J. 585S, the Garden State Pkwy. north, Atlantic City Expwy. west, and N.J. 42N): The trip begins at Atlantic City, Philadelphia's seaside entertainment extension. This seaside resort, flashy and kitsch, was founded as recently as 1852; after the introduction of legalized gaming it was considered Las Vegas's poor relation, but has become the new mecca for American gamblers. In 1976, when the New Jersey legislature legalized roulette wheels and slot machines, Atlantic City awoke from a 25-year sleep; it now accommodates 33 million visitors every year, who leave behind them about $8 billion. Its location—only 3 hr. from New York and 1½ hr. from Philadelphia, by car—has contributed greatly to its prosperity. Two other points of civic pride: the game of *Monopoly* was inspired by Atlantic City street names, and every year since 1921 Miss America has been crowned here.

The city's enormous **Convention Hall** is another curiosity in itself; it seats 41,000 people and has the largest organ in the world, with 32,000 pipes and 1,477 registers.

Along the 5-mi. (8km) **Boardwalk** beside the ocean—the East Coast's answer to the Las Vegas Strip—and at the bay side are the flashy, luxurious casinos, which draw their flocks of conventioneers and package tourists. In an effort to revitalize what has always stood in sharp contrast to the luxury casinos—the surrounding area of shacks, abandoned flophouses, and debris-strewn lots—the city has undergone a $1-billion facelift, building a new convention center and a "corridor" of shops, parks, and entertainment venues linking the convention center to the boardwalk.

Tourist Information

Atlantic City Convention & Visitors Bureau, 2314 Pacific Ave., Atlantic City, NJ 08401 (609/348-7100).

Transportation

Greyhound (bus), Arctic and Arkansas Aves. (609/345-6617): Service to/from New York, Philadelphia, and Washington.

New Jersey Transit (bus), Arctic and Arkansas Aves. (toll free 800/582-5946): Service to/from Cape May, New York, and Philadelphia.

Northwest Airlink (airplane), International Airport (toll free 800/225-2525): Flights to/from Baltimore, Newark, Philadelphia, and Washington.

USAir Express (airplane), International Airport (toll free 800/428-4322): Flights to/from Cape May, Baltimore, Philadelphia, and Washington.

Amtrak (train): Kirkman Blvd. at the foot of the Atlantic City Expwy. (toll free 800/872-7245): Service to/from Philadelphia (five round-trips daily; time, 1 hr.), Washington (one round-trip daily; time, 3 hr.), and New York (one round-trip daily; time, 2 hr. 20 min.).

Guided Tours & Excursions

Gray Line Tours (bus), 9 N. Arkansas Ave. (609/344-0965).

Where to Stay

♟♟♟ **Trump Taj Mahal Hotel & Casino,** 1000 Boardwalk (at Virginia Ave.), Atlantic City, NJ 08401 (609/449-1000; toll free 800/825-8786). 1,250 rms and luxury suites, A/C, cable color TV. AE, CB, DC, MC, V. Free valet parking, pool, health club, sauna, beach, 12 rests. (including Sinbad's) and coffee shops (some open around the clock), 24-hr. bars, rm svce, nightclub, casino, shows, boutiques. *Note:* The latest (Apr 1990) and most extravagant resort of Atlantic City. Pseudo-Indian palace built at a cost of $1.2 billion, this kitschy, 42-story giant complete w. minarets, onion-shaped cupolas, cascading fountains, hanging gardens, and bejeweled 8-ft.-high (2.2m) elephants, has a casino the size of four football fields w. more than 3,000 slot machines and 167 gaming tables. The rms and suites (one of them, the Alexander the Great penthouse suite, costs a mere $10,000 a night) offer incomparable comfort and amenities. Highly professional svce but so-so rests. Direct beach access. Group and convention clientele. **E–VE**

    🛏🛏🛏 **Caesars Hotel Casino,** 2100 Pacific Ave., Atlantic City, NJ 08401 (609/348-4411; toll free 800/443-0104). 646 rms, A/C, color TV, in-rm movies. AE, CB, DC, MC, V. Valet gar. $10, two pools, health club, sauna, three tennis courts, beach, seven rests. (including Le Posh), two 24-hr. coffee shops, 24-hr. bars, rm svce, casino, shows, boutiques. *Note:* This cream of the local hotel crop has undergone a much-needed facelift; the exterior is strident and unconvincing, but the rms are inviting and comfortable. Same management as the famous Caesars Palace establishments at Las Vegas and Lake Tahoe. Rest. (Le Posh) in the highest deluxe category; efficient svce. Direct beach access. **E–VE,** but lower rates off-season.

    🛏🛏🛏 **Harrah's Marina Hotel Casino,** 1725 Brigantine Blvd., Atlantic City, NJ 08401 (609/441-5000; toll free 800/242-7724). 758 rms, A/C, color TV, in-rm movies. AE, CB, DC, MC, V. Valet gar. $10, pool, health club, sauna, three tennis courts, marina, four rests. (including the Meadows), two 24-hr. coffee shops, 24-hr. bars, rm svce, nightclub, casino, shows, hrdrsr, boutiques, free crib. *Note:* The best place to stay in Atlantic City, away from the hubbub of the Boardwalk. Large, ultramodern marina-hotel whose 18 floors overlook the yacht basin and Absecon Bay: a facsimile of the giant Las Vegas casino-hotels with the waterway thrown in. Spacious, very comfortable rms; efficient reception and svce; very complete facilities. Group and convention clientele. **M–E,** but lower rates off-season.

    🛏🛏🛏 **Tropworld Casino Resort** (formerly the Tropicana), Brighton Ave. at the Boardwalk, Atlantic City, NJ 08401 (609/340-4000; toll free 800/257-6227). 1,014 rms, A/C, cable color TV. AE, CB, DC, MC, V. Valet gar., two pools, health club, sauna, two tennis courts, beach, miniature golf, five rests., two 24-hr. coffee shops, 10 24-hr. bars, rm svce, nightclub, casino, Luna Park, boutiques. *Note:* Large casino-hotel on the beach, aimed at the family market (very well-equipped amusement park with roller-coasters, Ferris wheel, dodge-'em cars, clowns, and magicians). Completely renovated interior; very comfortable rms, ultra-professional svce. Two blocks from Convention Center. Package-tour and convention clientele. **M–E,** but lower rates off-season.

    🛏🛏🛏 **Showboat Hotel Casino,** 801 Boardwalk, Atlantic City, NJ 08401 (609/343-4000; toll free 800/621-0200). 516 rms, A/C, cable color TV. AE, CB, DC, MC, V. Valet gar. $10, pool, beach, bowling, 11 rests., coffee shops, and bars (some 24-hr.), rm svce, nightclub, casino, shows, free crib. *Note:* New casino hotel, rather curiously designed with a cut-off corner facade, and direct access to beach. Other than the inevitable casino w. dozens of tables and hundreds of slot machines, the main attraction of the hotel is its 60-lane bowling alley. Flawless comfort and facilities; spacious rms (many w. ocean view); good svce. Group and convention clientele. **M–E,** but lower rates off-season.

    🛏🛏 **Midtown–Bala Motor Inn,** Indiana and Illinois Aves., Atlantic City, NJ 08401 (609/348-3031; toll free 800/932-0534). 300 rms, A/C, cable color TV. AE, CB, DC, MC, V. Free parking, pool, 24-hr. rest. and bar, sun deck. *Note:* Modern, comfortable motel, right in the casino area dwntwn, one block off the beach. Newly renovated rms. Group clientele. Good value on balance. **M,** but lower rates off-season.

    🛏🛏 **Comfort Inn West,** Black Horse Pike at Dover Place, West Atlantic City, NJ 08232 (609/645-1818; toll free, see Choice). 198 rms, A/C, color TV, in-rm movies. AE, CB, DC, MC, V. Free parking, pool, coffee shop, free crib. *Note:* Inviting, modern motel near the international airport. Very comfortable rms; reception and svce w. a smile. Shuttle bus to casino district. Group clientele. **M,** but lower rates off-season.

♀ **Continental Motel,** 137 S. Illinois Ave., Atlantic City, NJ
08404 (609/345-5141). 60 rms, A/C, color TV. AE, MC, V.
Free parking, pool, bar. *Note:* Aging small motel a block or two from the Boardwalk and the casinos. Decently comfortable; ideal for budget travelers. **I–M,** but lower rates off-season.

♀ **HoJo Inn,** Tennessee and Pacific Aves., Atlantic City, NJ 08401
(609/344-4193; toll free, see Howard Johnson's). 72 rms,
A/C, cable color TV. AE, DC, MC, V. Free parking, pool, coffee shop, rm svce.
Note: Modest but well-run motel very nr. the Boardwalk, w. completely renovated decor and facilities. Friendly reception. Good overall value. **I–M,** but lower rates off-season.

Where to Eat

♀♀ **Knife & Fork Inn,** Albany and Atlantic Aves. (344-1133).
A/C. Lunch Mon–Sat, dinner nightly; closed Mon Oct to late
Mar, Dec 25, Yom Kippur. AE. Jkt. *Specialties:* mussels marinière, shellfish, lobster Thermidor, bouillabaisse, crab Newburg, catch of the day; also some meat dishes. *Note:* The best seafood rest., and quite simply the best rest., in the culinary wasteland called Atlantic City. The crabs and scallops are particularly worthwhile. Plush-type decor; uncommonly efficient svce. Resv. strongly advised. A local landmark since 1927. *Seafood.* **M**

♀♀ **Dock's Oyster House,** 2405 Atlantic Ave. (345-0092). A/C.
Dinner only, Tues–Sun; closed Thanksgiving, Dec–Feb. AE,
MC, V. *Specialties:* linguine w. clams, oyster stew, lobster broiled or stuffed w. crabmeat, catch of the day, steak, cheese pie. *Note:* Dock's Oyster House, in the hands of the Dougherty family for four generations, is the oldest (1897) seafood rest. in Atlantic City, notwithstanding its vaguely Scandinavian-contemporary decor. Its success is due to absolutely fresh fish and shellfish. Friendly, relaxed svce; resv. advised. *Steak/Seafood.* **I–M**

♀♀ **Peking Duck House,** 2801 Atlantic Ave., at Iowa Ave. (344-
9090). A/C. Lunch/dinner daily. AE, CB, DC, MC, V. *Specialties:* shrimp lo-mein, shark's-fin soup, Peking duck, chicken w. lotus flour, beef w. tiger-lily flowers, fried ice cream flambé. *Note:* Chinese food at a high level, inventive and refined, from the skillets of the very talented Kenny Poo from Hong Kong. The decor, on the contrary, featuring beige-toned walls and subdued lighting, is not in the least Oriental. The Peking duck is remarkable. A very good place. Resv. advised, particularly on wknds. *Chinese.* **I–M**

☼♀ **Smithville Inn,** on U.S. 9 at Smithville, 10 mi. (16km) north
via U.S. 30 and U.S. 9 (652-7777). A/C. Lunch/dinner daily;
closed Dec 25. AE, CB, DC, MC, V. *Specialties:* chicken pot pie, stuffed pork chops, roast duck. *Note:* Picturesque Colonial-style inn in "The Historic Towne of Smithville," a careful replica of an 18th-century village. The food is acceptable but unimaginative. Much favored by tourists; resv. advised in summer. *American.* **I–M**

♀ **Angelo's Fairmount Tavern,** 2300 Fairmount Ave. (344-
2439). A/C. Lunch/dinner daily. No credit cards. *Specialties:*
fresh homemade soup and pasta, classical Italian dishes, Sicilian specialties. Everyone takes a caffè espresso. *Note:* This former speakeasy, frequented by local politicians and newspaper people, serves the kind of good, tasty food you'd expect from a typical Italian *trattoria.* The menu changes regularly at the whim of owner Angelo "The Meatball" Mancuso. Excellent value. No resv. *Italian/American.* **I**

☼♀ **White House Sub Shop,** 2301 Arctic Ave., at Mississippi Ave.
(345-8599). A/C. Lunch/dinner daily (until midnight). No
credit cards. *Specialties:* submarines, cheese steaks. *Note:* The unchallenged champion of the "submarine" sandwich, the local equivalent of the Philadelphian "hoagie" or the New York "hero": an Italian roll stuffed with salami, ham, turkey, prosciutto, provolone, lettuce, tomatoes, onions, green peppers, etc. The

rest. proudly claims (and has signed photos on the wall to prove it) such famous patrons as Jerry Lewis, Frank Sinatra, Ray Charles, and Joan Rivers. The decor is pure art deco kitsch. A local landmark since 1946. *American.* **B**

SOUTH FROM ATLANTIC CITY: The trip continues along N.J. 585, a scenic route that follows the shoreline for almost 40 mi. (65km), and offers some fine ocean views. At **Margate,** immediately south of Atlantic City, see the amazing ⚓ **Lucy,** a six-story building shaped like an elephant, constructed in 1881; you reach the beast's "stomach" by climbing spiral staircases in its legs. Open daily July–Aug, wknds only in spring and fall; closed the rest of the year. The next stop, 10 mi. (16km) farther south, is **Ocean City,** a beach resort whose resolutely sober family atmosphere is a striking contrast to Atlantic City; the town is "dry," and attracts a number of religious conventions every year.

☀☖♙♙ **CAPE MAY:** Farther along N.J. 585 you come to Cape May, the oldest seaside resort (1631) in the country; its famous visitors have included Presidents Lincoln and Grant, Horace Greeley, and the department-store magnate John Wanamaker. Its Victorian elegance, and its hundreds of pretty old pastel-washed houses with their white porches and lacy carpenter's-Gothic fretwork, seem to have come straight out of a 19th-century picture postcard. The whole town is a designated National Historic Landmark. On its magnificent beach, 4 mi. (7km) long, you can pick up the so-called Cape May diamonds—pebbles of quartz polished by the action of the waves. You can tour the center of the town in a horse-drawn carriage, or in an imitation 19th-century streetcar, leaving from Beach Dr. at Gurney St. (609/884-5404). Paul Volcker, long head of the Federal Reserve Board, comes from Cape May.

Return to Philadelphia by the Garden State Pkwy. and Atlantic City Expwy. An interesting, varied itinerary taking two to three days.

Where to Stay

☀♙♙ **Inn of Cape May,** 601 Beach Dr., Cape May, NJ 08204 (609/884-3500; toll free 800/257-0432). 78 rms (no A/C). Picturesque old hotel (1894) w. antique furnishings. On the ocean. Closed Oct to mid-May. **M–E**

☀♙♙ **The Mainstay Inn & Cottage,** 635 Columbia Ave., Cape May, NJ 08204 (609/884-8690). 13 rms (9 w. private bath), all nosmoking. Charming Victorian structure dating from 1872. At one time a men's gambling club. Minimum stay is three days. Closed Dec–Mar. **M–E**

☀♙♙ **The Queen Victoria,** 102 Ocean St., Cape May, NJ 08204 (609/884-8702). 17 antiques-filled rms (7 w. private bath). Elegantly furnished Victorian villa. Minimum stay on wknds is two to four days. Open year round. **M–E**

Where to Eat

♙♙ **Lobster House,** Fisherman's Wharf (609/884-8296). Lunch/dinner daily. Good seafood rest. on the harbor; very popular locally. **I–M**

☀♙ **Watson's Merion Inn,** 106 Decatur St. (609/884-8363). Dinner only, nightly; in Nov, Fri–Sun only. Hearty dining in an authentic 1885 Victorian setting. **I–M**

GETTYSBURG & PENNSYLVANIA DUTCH COUNTRY

☀☖♙♙ **PENNSYLVANIA DUTCH COUNTRY:** (274 mi./441km r.t. via I-76W, U.S. 222S, U.S. 322W, U.S. 15S, U.S. 30E, U.S. 202N, and I-76E): After visiting **Valley Forge National Historical Park,** site of one of the darker pages of American military history (see "Nearby Excursions," above), you can drive on through Pennsylvania Dutch Country.

Begin your tour at ☀☖ **Ephrata Cloister,** a rural religious community at 632

W. Main St., Ephrata, 6 mi. (9km) south of the Pennsylvania Tpke. and I-76 on U.S. 222S and U.S. 322W (717/733-6600). Founded in 1732 by Conrad Beissel, a Baptist pastor from Germany, this contemplative community of country folk observed an ascetic rule of life: Unmarried people of opposite sexes were segregated, wooden benches and headrests were used instead of beds, and so on. It continued its archaic lifestyle until 1934. You can still visit a dozen buildings from the period 1735–50; open daily.

This stop is a good introduction to a more detailed inspection of Pennsylvania Dutch Country, a region whose people are among the most unusual—and least known—in America. They are often, and wrongly, taken for people of Dutch descent; in fact their ancestors were German ("Deutsch") settlers who came here in the 17th century from the Rhineland and the Palatinate, whose original customs have been preserved almost intact. These austere, devout, hardworking country folk are divided into three main religious denominations: Amish, Brethren, and Mennonite. They agree, however, in rejecting almost everything that smacks of modernity, whether vaccination, chemical fertilizers, automobiles, radios, or quite simply electricity, which the more pious among them regard as an invention of the devil. The "Plain People," as they are called, use only buggies for conveyance and only kerosene lamps for light; they speak the same Low German as their ancestors and wear the same dark-hued, archaic dress vividly portrayed in the movie *Witness*. Some 15,000–20,000 Amish in Pennsylvania Dutch Country live in closed communities observing to the letter the teachings of the Bible. But these Americans from an earlier epoch are progressively disappearing. (There are also Amish communities of some hundreds of souls in Ohio, Indiana, Texas, and Canada. As for the Mennonites, who unlike the Amish have come to terms with some manifestations of progress, such as electricity, there are believed to be some 200,000 of them in the U.S. and Canada.)

For an unforgettable experience, you should visit the ❋⌂ **Amish farms and markets around Lancaster, York, Intercourse, Strasburg, and Bird-in-Hand.** Note, however, that for religious reasons the Amish reject any depiction of the human form, and thus forbid the use of still or video cameras.

Paradoxically, a mere 40 mi. (64km) from this region so firmly rooted in the past you will find the famous nuclear power plant at **Three Mile Island,** where in 1979 the beginning of a meltdown threw the whole of Pennsylvania into a panic. Three Mile Island has played a leading part in alerting mankind to the dangers of nuclear energy.

Some useful addresses for visitors to Pennsylvania Dutch Country:

INFORMATION The **Mennonite Tourist Information Center,** 2209 Millstream Rd., Lancaster, PA 17601 (717/299-0954): Organizes guided tours and house visits with Mennonite families; open Mon–Sat.

Other very active information centers are the **Pennsylvania Dutch Visitors Bureau,** 501 Greenfield Rd., Lancaster, PA 17601 (717/299-8901); and **People's Place,** Main St., Intercourse, PA 17534 (717/768-7171), with an Amish museum, movies, and a library; open Mon–Sat.

⌂ **Farm Visits:** The **Amish Farm and House,** 5 mi. (8km) east of Lancaster on U.S. 30 (717/394-6185), open daily.

⌂ **Market Visits:** The **Central Market,** Pennsylvania Sq., Lancaster, held on Tues, Fri, and Sat; **Meadowbrook Market,** 5 mi. (8km) east of Lancaster at Leola, on Penna. 23, held on Fri and Sat; **Farmer's Market,** 6 mi. (10km) east of Lancaster at Bird-in-Hand on Penna. 340, held on Wed, Fri, and Sat; and the **Farmer's Market,** Market and Penn Sts. in York, held on Tues, Fri, and Sat.

SIGHTS The ⌂ **Landis Valley Museum,** 2451 Kissel Hill Rd., Lancaster, 2 mi. (4km) north on Penna. 272 (717/569-0401): 250,000 authentically old exhibits, from Conestoga wagons to spinning wheels. Interesting. Open Tues–Sun.

🔔 **Strasburg Railroad,** 8 mi. (12km) SE of Lancaster via U.S. 30 and Penna. 896 (717/687-7522): Trip on a steam train through Amish country. Also a spectacular railroad museum. Open daily May–Oct; wknds only, Dec–Mar.

Hershey

After a long look at Lancaster and the surrounding countryside, you go on to 🔔 **Hershey.** Known as "the chocolate capital of the world," this smiling little town of 13,000 people, perpetually pervaded by the aroma of chocolate, is the home of the world's largest chocolate factory. Milton S. Hershey, founder of the Hershey Corporation in 1903, also gave his name to the town. At **Hershey's Chocolate World,** Hersheypark Dr. (open daily), you can see the entire production cycle from the planting of a cocoa tree down to the finished chocolate bar. See also the very interesting **Hershey Museum of American Life,** with scenes from the life and history of the Pennsylvania Dutch and their Native American predecessors.

Hersheypark, on Hersheypark Dr. (toll free 800/437-7439), is a big amusement park with dozens of carousels, roller-coasters, and other attractions; open daily mid-May to Sept; closed the rest of the year. There's a large rose garden, where tulips and chrysanthemums are also grown in season, at **Hershey Gardens,** Hotel Rd., open daily mid-Apr to Oct.

Where to Stay En Route

IN HERSHEY The 🔔🔔🔔 **Hershey Lodge,** Chocolate Ave. at University Dr., Hershey, PA 17033 (717/533-3311; toll free 800/533-3131). 460 rms. Large, modern motel w. adj. tennis courts and golf course. **M**

IN LANCASTER The 🔔🔔🔔 **Willow Valley Resort,** 2416 Willow St. Pike (at U.S. 222), Lancaster, PA 17602 (717/464-2711). 353 rms. Luxurious motel in the heart of the country; does a heavy convention business. **M**

IN MOUNT JOY The ❊ 🔔🔔 **Cameron Estates Inn,** Donegal Springs Rd., Mount Joy, PA 17552 (717/653-1773). 18 rms. Elegant 19th-century manor house surrounded by a beautiful garden. **I–M**

IN STRASBURG The 🔔🔔 **Historic Strasburg Inn,** Penna. 896, Strasburg, PA 17579 (717/687-7691). 103 rms. Charming Colonial-style inn. **M**

Where to Eat En Route

IN BIRD-IN-HAND The 🍽 **Plain and Fancy Farm Restaurant,** on Penna. 340 (717/768-8281). Breakfast/lunch/dinner (until 8pm) Mon–Sat. Tasty family cooking in an authentic Amish farm. **B**

IN MOUNT JOY ❊🍽🍽 **Groff's Farm,** 650 Pinkerton Rd. (717/653-2048). Lunch/dinner (until 7:30pm) Tues–Sat. Typical, rather elaborate Pennsylvania Dutch cooking, in a pleasantly restored 1756 building. Resv. advised, particularly at dinner. **I–M**

☼🔔🔔 **GETTYSBURG NATIONAL MILITARY PARK:** After another 50 mi. (80km) of driving south, you arrive at the Gettysburg National Military Park. The **Visitor Center** is on Penna. 134 (717/334-1124), open daily. Here, on July 1–3, 1863, was fought the bloodiest battle of the Civil War. The Confederate troops of Gen. Robert E. Lee sustained 28,000 casualties, and the Union forces under Gen. George Meade, 23,000. It was this welter of kindred blood that moved Lincoln to compose the famous *Gettysburg Address,* appealing for peace and reconciliation between North and South.

To visit the battlefield thoroughly you must make a circuit of more than 35 mi. (56km). There are hundreds of commemorative objects, including 400 cannons and more than 1,600 monuments, engraved tablets, and markers. The **Battlefield Tower** observation tower is 305 ft. (92m) high, and nearby is a cyclorama with movies depicting the course of the battle.

Not far from the battlefield is the ※▲ **Eisenhower National Historic Site,** reached only by bus from the Visitor Center (717/334-1124). No more than 1,100 people may be admitted on any day; open daily Apr–Oct, Wed–Sun the rest of the year. Many personal items associated with "Ike" and his wife, Mamie.

Then back to Philadelphia via York and Lancaster, so that if need be you can catch anything you missed earlier in Pennsylvania Dutch Country. Fascinating three- to four-day trip; a must for all lovers of history—or of the unusual.

Where to Stay

🔑🔑 **Ramada Inn Gettysburg,** 2634 Emmitsburg Rd., Gettysburg, PA 17325 (717/334-8121). 203 rms. Comfortable, inviting motel next to the Battlefield Visitor Center. Cheerful svce. Good value. **I–M**

CHAPTER 7

PITTSBURGH

□ □ □

Long known as "Smoky City," this once gloomy and polluted industrial center has been transformed in less than two decades into a modern, sparkling metropolis. The glass-and-steel high-rises of "Steel City"—another of Pittsburgh's nicknames—its luxury hotels, and its ultramodern office buildings now reach skyward around the "Golden Triangle," once a slum, now the heart of the business district.

Steel (almost 25% of U.S. output), glass, nuclear engineering (the first American nuclear power plant was built near Pittsburgh), aluminum, data processing, chemicals, robotics, and pharmaceuticals all contribute to the wealth of this dedicated, hardworking city—to say nothing of its busy river port, which handles more than 60 million tons of freight a year. For more than a century Pittsburgh was synonymous with steel and coal, and so renowned for its ugliness that after World War II, when the great architect Frank Lloyd Wright was asked how to go about modernizing the city, he replied that it would make more sense to tear it down and start over. Fortunately this pessimism was ignored when a gigantic urban-renewal plan was put into effect toward the end of the 1960s; it has already borne much fruit, and is still being carried forward through such reconstruction projects as **Renaissance II** (total cost, $6 billion) and the **Pittsburgh Technology Center,** on the site of an old steel mill on the banks of the Monongahela River.

The first settlement was French: Fort Duquesne, built in 1754 at the confluence of the Monongahela, Allegheny, and Ohio Rivers. The British captured it in 1758 and renamed it in honor of their prime minister, William Pitt the Elder; later the fort passed its name on to the city. Pittsburgh was the arsenal of the Union during the War Between the States; three-quarters of a century later it played the same role during World War II. Today "Renaissance City" is the third-largest corporate headquarters after New York and Chicago, home base for 13 Fortune 500 U.S. industries, among which are Alcoa, Heinz Foods, Rockwell International, USX Corporation (formerly U.S. Steel), and Westinghouse. From the summit of **Mount Washington,** reached by cable car, the visitor can again enjoy the view of the city and the three rivers that run through it, now that stringently enforced antipollution laws have almost abolished the obscuring smog once spewed forth by its factories.

Thanks to the lavish donations of such local captains of industry and finance as Carnegie, Frick, and Mellon, Pittsburgh boasts some of the country's wealthiest institutions and most beautiful museums, including the famous **Carnegie Institute** and a justly renowned symphony orchestra, as well as no fewer than seven universities and colleges of great quality such as Carnegie-Mellon University (8,000 students) and the University of Pittsburgh (35,000 students).

Famous people born in Pittsburgh include painter Andy Warhol; choreographer Martha Graham; dancer Gene Kelly; jazz musicians Art Blakey, Billy Eckstine, Roy Eldridge, Errol Garner, Earl Hines, Ahmad Jamal, and Kenny Clarke; conductor Billy May; and Stephen Foster, composer of "Swannee River," "My Old Kentucky Home," and other treasures of American folk song.

BASIC FACTS: State of Pennsylvania. Area code: 412. Time zone: eastern. ZIP Code: 15230. Founded: 1758. Approximate population: city, 370,000; metropolitan area, 2,280,000. 19th-largest U.S. metropolitan area.

CLIMATE: With 200 days of rain a year, bring your umbrella in any season. Winter is moderately cold (Jan mean, 31°F/−1°C). In summer the thermometer rarely goes above 77°F (25°C); the July mean is 75°F (24°C). Spring and autumn are brisk.

DISTANCES: Buffalo, 219 mi. (350km); Cincinnati, 290 mi. (465km); Cleveland, 129 mi. (206km); New York, 368 mi. (590km); Philadelphia, 308 mi. (498km); Washington, 247 mi. (396km).

ARRIVAL & TRANSIT INFORMATION

AIRPORT: Greater Pittsburgh International Airport, 17 mi. (27km) west. Call 472-3525 for information. A brand-new terminal opened in Oct 1992.

DOMESTIC AIRLINES: American (toll free 800/433-7300), Continental (toll free 800/525-0280), Delta (toll free 800/221-1212), Northwest (toll free 800/225-2525), TWA (toll free 800/221-2000), United (toll free 800/241-6522), and USAir (toll free 800/428-4322).

FOREIGN CARRIERS: British Airways (toll free 800/247-9297).

CITY LINK: The **cab** fare from the airport to downtown is about $28; time, 35 min. Bus: **Airlines Transportation Co.** (471-8900), leaves about every 30 min. Mon–Fri and every 60 min. Sat and Sun, serving principal downtown hotels; fare, $12; time, about 40–50 min.

The **bus, streetcar, and subway public transportation** provided by Port Authority Transit/PAT (442-2000) is relatively efficient.

The downtown area isn't big enough to require renting a car.

CAR RENTAL (at the airport unless otherwise indicated): Avis (toll free 800/331-1212); Budget (toll free 800/527-0700); Dollar (toll free 800/800-4000); Hertz (toll free 800/654-3131); National (toll free 800/227-7368); Thrifty (toll free 800/367-2277). For dwntwn locations, consult the local telephone book.

LIMOUSINE SERVICES: Carey Limousine (731-8671), Limo Center (931-1800), and Pittsburgh Limousine (toll free 800/777-3133).

TAXIS: Cabs are few and expensive. Theoretically they can be hailed on the street, but it's better to phone, at least 15–30 min. ahead of time: **People's Cab** (681-3131) or **Yellow Cab** (665-8100).

TRAIN: Amtrak Station, Liberty Ave. and Grant St. (toll free 800/872-7245).

INTERCITY BUSES: Greyhound, 11th St. and Liberty Ave. (392-6513; toll free 800/231-2222).

RIVER CRUISES: 3- to 10-day cruises on the Mississippi and Ohio Rivers aboard the *Delta Queen* or the *Mississippi Queen,* sternwheelers dating from the 1920s. Luxurious kitsch. See Chapter 15 on New Orleans.

INFORMATION & TOURS

TOURIST INFORMATION: The **Greater Pittsburgh Convention and Visitors Bureau,** 4 Gateway Center, PA 15222 (412/281-7711; toll free 800/366-0093).
    Visitor Information Center, 444 Liberty Ave. (412/281-9222).
    For a **telephone recording** with an up-to-date listing of cultural events and shows, call 412/391-6840.

GUIDED TOURS: The **Gateway Clipper Fleet** (boat), Monongahela Wharf, Station Sq. Dock (355-7980): Paddlewheeler trips on the three rivers. Apr–Nov.
    Gray Line Tours (bus) (761-7000): Guided tours of the city and surroundings; serves principal downtown hotels. Apr–Oct.

SIGHTS, ATTRACTIONS & ACTIVITIES

ARCHITECTURAL HIGHLIGHTS: ☼🔔 **Alcoa Building,** 425 Sixth Ave.: The 30-story aluminum-clad building is 410 ft. (125m) high and of revolutionary design; it was one of the first skyscrapers in the world with an aluminum frame. Not open to visitors.
    ☼🔔 **Cathedral of Learning,** University of Pittsburgh campus, Fifth Ave. and Bigelow Blvd. (624-6000): The only university skyscraper in the country, 520 ft. (160m) high, with 42 floors. The Gothic Revival design, now redolent of kitsch, dates from 1935. The 21 lecture rooms grouped around the entrance hall are each decorated in a different idiom: Byzantine, Roman, Renaissance, Tudor, Empire, and so on. Observation platform on the 36th floor. Guided tours. Open daily.
    ☼🔔 **Civic Arena,** Washington Place at Centre and Bedford Aves. (642-1800): Huge 20,000-seat arena with a roof that opens. The shiny stainless-steel dome, three times larger than that of St. Peter's in Rome, can be folded back in 2½ min. Concerts, sports events, and conventions.
    🔔 **CNG Tower,** Liberty Ave. and 7th St.: A 30-story postmodern tower in brown-and-buff granite, capped with a steel arch of unusual design. A 1987 work of architects Bob Evans and William Pedersen.
    🔔 **Heinz Hall,** 600 Penn Ave. (392-4843). A beautiful rococo 1920s movie house converted into a concert hall and now home to the famous Pittsburgh Symphony. Guided tours by appointment.
    ☼🔔🔭 **P. P. G. Place,** Stanwix St. at Fourth Ave. (434-3131): Symbol of the new Pittsburgh designed by the well-known architectural team of Philip Johnson and John Burgee: a group of six ultramodern Neo-Gothic buildings, with facades all in glass, grouped around a huge plaza with a winter garden, shops, restaurants, and stores. The 40-story central tower, PPG Tower, stands 635 ft. (193m) high; its pinnacled silhouette recalls the Houses of Parliament in London. Open-air concerts on the plaza in summer.
    🔔 **Stephen Collins Foster Memorial Hall,** University of Pittsburgh campus, Forbes Ave. at Bigelow Blvd. (624-4100): Imposing monument commemorating Pittsburgh's native son Stephen Collins Foster, who wrote many well-loved songs. Library with personal memorabilia of the composer, and an auditorium where the Three Rivers Shakespeare Festival is held every year, as well as many concerts. For lovers of music history. Open Mon–Fri.
    🔔 **University of Pittsburgh,** Fifth Ave. and Bigelow Blvd. (624-4141): One of the oldest (1787) and most famous of American universities, with 35,000 students. Of the 70 or so buildings scattered across its 132-acre (53ha) campus, several are worth going to see: the **Cathedral of Learning,** the **Heinz Chapel,** and the **Stephen Collins Foster Memorial,** in particular. Campus open daily.

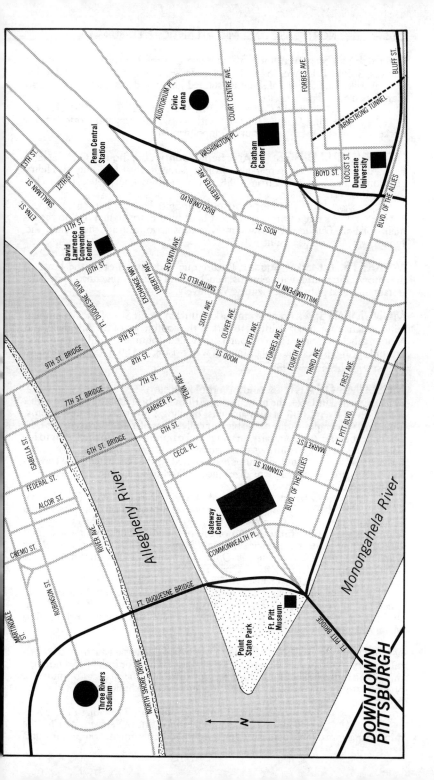

CHURCHES/SYNAGOGUES: ※▲ **Heinz Chapel,** University of Pittsburgh campus, S. Bellefield Ave. (624-4157): Modern building in the French Gothic Revival style, with a series of splendid stained-glass windows, each 73 ft. (22m) high. Open Sun–Fri.

▲ **St. Paul's Cathedral,** Fifth Ave. and Craig (621-4951): Imposing Gothic landmark with its twin towers and world-famous Beckerath organ. Open daily. Tours by appointment.

HISTORIC BUILDINGS: ※▲ **Allegheny County Courthouse,** Grant St. and Fifth Ave. (355-5859): Remarkable Romanesque Revival building by Henry Hobson Richardson dating from 1888; one of the finest courthouses in the U.S. Open Mon–Fri.

※▲ **Fort Pitt Blockhouse,** Point State Park (471-0235): Last vestige of the original fort built by the British in 1764 on the remains of Fort Duquesne; it saw some vigorous action during the French and Indian War. Open Tues–Sun.

MARKETS: ▲ **Market Square:** Picturesque shopping area in the heart of downtown Pittsburgh with gardens, benches, and friendly pigeons; many bars, restaurants, and pubs in the vicinity. Very lively.

MONUMENTS: ※▲ **Point State Park Fountain,** Point State Park: Monumental fountain at the tip of Point State Park at the confluence of the Allegheny and Monongahela Rivers. The computer-controlled fountain, fed by an underground spring, issues colorful plumes of water rising to 150 ft. (45m); Easter to mid-Nov. A spectacular sight.

MUSEUMS OF ART: ▲▲ **Andy Warhol Museum,** 117 Sandusky St. (622-3131): Opened in 1994, the museum pays tribute to this Pittsburgh native with a collection of over 1,000 of his paintings, drawings, prints, sculptures, photos, films, and videotapes—one of the biggest collections of a single artist in the U.S. The collection ranges from early drawings and paintings done in the 1950s to his classic pop silk-screen paintings of consumer goods to the much later *Last Suppers* of 1986. This seven-floor museum, designed by the renowned New York architect Richard Gluckman, is as diversified as Warhol's art, containing a theater, archives, reading room, and café.

※▲▲ **Carnegie Museum of Art,** 4400 Forbes Ave. (622-3313): Lovely museum with an important collection of impressionists and post-impressionists (Sarah Scaife Gallery) alongside classical paintings and sculptures and antique furniture. Among its best-known works: *Virgin and Child with Angel* by Francesco Francia, *Toilette of Venus* by Simon Vouet, *Reefs Near Dieppe* by Monet, *The Something-or-Other Circus* by Jean Dewasne, and George Segal's amazing *Tightrope Walker.* Open Tues–Sun.

※▲▲ **Frick Art Museum,** 7227 Reynolds St. (371-0600): European old masters (Tintoretto, Rubens, Fragonard, Boucher, and others) in an elegant Renaissance-style mansion once the home of the coal-and-steel magnate Henry Clay Frick; also many pieces of furniture that belonged to Marie Antoinette. Open Tues–Sun.

MUSEUMS OF SCIENCE & HISTORY: ※▲▲ **Carnegie Museum of Natural History,** 4400 Forbes Ave. (622-3313): Best known for its hall of dinosaurs, this very handsome natural history museum also has fine displays of minerals, precious stones, and zoology, as well as a fascinating exhibition devoted to the Arctic world. Open Tues–Sun.

▲▲ **Carnegie Science Center,** 1 Allegheny Ave., adj. to Three Rivers Stadium (237-3300): Dubbed "an amusement park for the mind," this remarkably conceived learning and entertainment complex features hands-on exhibits on science, technology, astronomy, etc.; plus the Henry Buhl, Jr., Planetarium, a 350-seat Omnimax theater, and the U.S.S. *Requin,* a World War II submarine. Open daily.

☼☖ **Fort Pitt Museum,** 101 Commonwealth Place, Point State Park (281-9284): Interesting military museum on the French and Indian War. This facsimile of a fort occupies the site of the original (1764) Fort Pitt. Open Tues–Sun.

☖ **Historical Society of Western Pennsylvania,** 4338 Bigelow Blvd. (681-5533): A journey back into 19th-century Pennsylvania, through collections of old furniture, unusual glass bottles, paintings, documents, and other historical items. For lovers of bygone days. Open Tues–Sat.

☖ **Soldiers and Sailors Memorial Hall and Museum,** Fifth Ave. and Bigelow Blvd. (621-4253): Weapons, uniforms, military mementoes, and flags from the country's wars. Open daily.

PANORAMAS: ☼☖☖ **Mount Washington:** There are two cable cars to the top of Mount Washington: the **Monongahela Incline** from W. Carson St. nr. Station Sq. (231-5707) and the **Duquesne Incline** from W. Carson St. near Fort Pitt Bridge (381-1665). Fine view of the city and the Golden Triangle with its three rivers.

☖ **U.S.X. Tower,** 600 Grant St. (471-4100): Fine view of the city from the Top of the Triangle restaurant on the 62nd floor (admission fee). So-so food but congenial bar. Open daily.

PARKS & GARDENS: ☖ **Phipps Conservatory,** Schenley Park, Schenley Dr. (622-6915): Lovely tropical greenhouses and flower shows; splendid cactus and orchid gardens. Open daily.

☼☖ **National Aviary,** Ridge Ave. and Arch St. (323-7234): Wonderful collection of the world's birds, more than 220 species in all, in reconstructions of their natural habitats. Open daily.

☼☖☖ **Point State Park,** at the west end of Fort Duquesne and Fort Pitt Blvds.: A 36-acre (15ha) park on the site of the first settlement, at the confluence of the Monongahela and Allegheny Rivers; panoramic view of the city and Mount Washington. Monumental fountain and traces of old Fort Pitt.

☖ **Schenley Park,** Schenley Dr.: A stone's throw from the University of Pittsburgh, this 456-acre (185ha) park is popular at all times of year; there are several picnic areas, a public golf course, a small lake, several miles of trails, and a skating rink. Cross-country skiing in winter.

PERFORMING ARTS: For daily listings of all shows and cultural events, consult the entertainment pages of the daily paper *Pittsburgh Post-Gazette* (morning), as well as the monthly *Pittsburgh* magazine. **Choice Seats** (333-7328) sells tickets to most productions. They have three downtown ticket booths: Kaufmann's Department Store (400 Fifth Ave.), National Record Mart (230 Forbes Ave.), and Horn's (501 Penn Ave.).

Benedum Theater for the Performing Arts, 719 Liberty Ave. (456-6666): The old Stanley Theater, entirely renovated in 1987. Home of the Pittsburgh Opera (director: Tito Capobianco), the Civic Light Opera, and the Pittsburgh Ballet Theater. Also Broadway hits.

Fulton Theater, 101 6th St. (456-1360): Musicals, plays, and films.

Heinz Hall, 600 Penn Ave. (392-4900): Home of the Pittsburgh Symphony, under principal conductor Lorin Maazel (Sept–May). Concerts and recitals by distinguished soloists. Broadway hits.

Kresge Theater, Carnegie-Mellon University campus, Schenley Park (268-2407): Contemporary theater, musicals.

New City Theatre, Bouquet and Sennott Sts. (431-4400): Modern American theater; home of the City Theatre Company (Sept–May).

Pittsburgh Playhouse Theater Center, 222 Craft Ave. (621-4445): Contemporary and classic theater; children's shows.

Pittsburgh Public Theater, Allegheny Sq. (323-8200): Comedy, drama; the best of Pittsburgh's many theaters.

Stephen C. Foster Memorial Theater, U. of Pittsburgh campus, Forbes Ave. and Bigelow Blvd. (624-4100): Contemporary and classic theater, concerts; the Three Rivers Shakespeare Festival takes place here every year.

SPECIAL EVENTS: For the exact schedule of events below, consult the **Greater Pittsburgh Convention and Visitors Bureau** (see "Tourist Information," above).

Folk Festival (end of May): The food, dance, music, and crafts of the many countries that have contributed to the great ethnic melting pot of Pittsburgh: Ireland, Scotland, Germany, the Czech Republic, Slovakia, Hungary, Russia, and many more. Held at the David L. Lawrence Convention Center.

Three Rivers Shakespeare Festival (late May to mid-Aug): Presents three new plays every year at the Stephen C. Foster Memorial Theater.

Mellon Jazz Festival (mid-June): With the biggest names.

Three Rivers Art Festival (three weeks in June): Open-air art exhibitions, public concerts, movie festival, plays, etc.

Vintage Grand Prix (late July): Vintage car race. One of the few of its kind.

Shadyside Art Festival (early Aug): Draws artists, craftspeople, and spectators from the whole region.

Three Rivers Regatta (first wknd in Aug): Very popular boat races (Formula I and rowing).

SPORTS: Pittsburgh has professional teams in three major sports:
Baseball (Apr–Oct): Pirates, Three Rivers Stadium (321-2827).
Football (Aug–Dec): Steelers, Three Rivers Stadium (323-1200).
Ice Hockey (Oct–Apr): Penguins, Civic Arena (333-7328).

Horse Racing
The Meadows, **Meadowlands,** at Exit 8 from I-79 (563-1224), year round.

STROLLS: ⚓ **Bank Center Mall,** Fourth Ave. and Wood St. (288-9553): Turn-of-the-century houses, charmingly restored, in what was once the heart of Pittsburgh's downtown business district. Fashion shops, stores, movie houses, restaurants. A pleasant place.

☀⚓⚓ **Station Square,** on the south bank of the Monongahela River at the foot of the Smithfield St. Bridge (471-5808). Terminal of the Pittsburgh & Lake Erie Railroad, no longer in use, now the favorite place for strolling, window-shopping, and distractions. Dozens of stalls, bars, and restaurants; lively and colorful day and night.

THEME PARKS: ⚓ **Kennywood Park,** 4800 Kennywood Blvd., in West Mifflin, 8 mi./12km SE along Penna. 837 (461-0500): Typical theme park with many attractions and five different roller coasters. Open Tues–Sun mid-May to Sept.

WINTER SPORTS RESORTS: ⚓ **Boyce Park Ski Area,** 18 mi. (28km) east via I-376 and Penna. 286 (733-4656): Four lifts; open Dec–Mar.

ZOOS: ⚓ **Pittsburgh Zoo,** Highland Ave., Highland Park (665-3640): More than 2,000 animals in reconstructions of their natural habitats, and a very modern aquarium, in a 65-acre (26ha) park. Open daily.

ACCOMMODATIONS

Personal Favorites (in order of preference)

👤👤👤 **Pittsburgh Vista Hotel** (dwntwn), 1000 Penn Ave., PA 15222 (412/281-3700). 614 rms, A/C, color TV, in-rm movies. AE, CB, DC, MC, V. Valet parking $12, pool, health club, sauna, two rests. (including Liberty Grill), coffee shop, bar, 24-hr. rm svce, disco, boutiques, free dwntwn limo, free crib. *Note:* Newest of the big dwntwn hotels; large, massive 26-story tower across from the David L. Lawrence Convention Center w. direct access to it by an enclosed walkway. Ultra-comfortable facilities and furnishings; spacious, inviting rms w. minibars; efficient svce. Good rest. serving American food; three VIP floors; business clientele. **E–VE**

👤👤👤 **Hyatt Regency** (dwntwn), 112 Washington Place at Chatham Center, PA 15219 (412/471-1234; toll free, see Hyatt). 400 rms, A/C, color TV, in-rm movies. AE, CB, DC, MC, V. Valet gar. $10, pool, health club, sauna, rest. (P. H. Rose Chop House), coffee shop, bars, rm svce, disco, free crib. *Note:* Occupies the top 11 floors of a modern, architecturally unattractive, 20-story office building. The hotel is very comfortable and well equipped, but rms are on the small side. Diligent svce; praiseworthy rest.; VIP suites on the top floor. Business clientele; in the heart of the business district. **E–VE**

👤👤 **Sheraton Hotel at Station Square** (nr. dwntwn), 7 Station Sq. Dr., PA 15219 (412/261-2000; toll free, see Sheraton). 293 rms, A/C, in-rm movies. AE, CB, DC, MC, V. Free parking, pool, sauna, rest. (Waterfall Terrace), coffee shop, bar, rm svce, boutiques, free crib. *Note:* Very modern 15-story hotel across the Monongahela River. Impeccable comfort and facilities; futurist seven-story lobby; spacious rms, the best overlooking the river and city. Reasonably efficient svce. In the center of Station Sq. w. its dozens of trendy shops and rests. Group and convention clientele. **E**

☀👤👤 **The Priory** (nr. dwntwn), 614 Pressley St., PA 15212 (412/231-3338). 24 rms, A/C, cable color TV. AE, CB, DC, MC, V. Free parking; no bar or rest., but free breakfast and cocktails. *Note:* Delightful small hotel, charming in a European way, on the quiet North Side across the Allegheny River; the turn-of-the-century structure was originally a Benedictine priory, whence the name. Comfortable, elegant rms; inviting flower-planted patio w. fountain. Polished reception and svce. About as far as you can get from the typical mass-market convention hotel, 5 min. from dwntwn. A very good place to stay. **M**

👤👤 **Hampton Inn Greentree** (nr. dwntwn), 555 Trumbull Dr., PA 15205 (412/922-0100; toll free 800/426-7866). 133 rms, A/C, cable color TV. AE, CB, DC, MC, V. Free parking, rest. nearby, free continental breakfast, free airport shuttle. *Note:* A six-story motel, functionally comfortable. Spacious rms w. a modern flair. Efficient svce. Good value overall. 5 min. from dwntwn via I-279W at Greentree, Exit 4. **I**

Other Accommodations (from top bracket to budget)

👤👤👤 **Hilton Pittsburgh and Towers** (dwntwn), Commonwealth Place in Gateway Center, PA 15222 (412/391-4600; toll free, see Hilton). 718 rms, A/C, color TV, in-rm movies. AE, CB, DC, MC, V. Valet gar. $14, health club, two rests. (including Sterling's), two bars, rm svce, hrdrsr, drugstore, free crib, concierge. *Note:* Recently renovated massive modern building w. the best view in Pittsburgh, from the point where the three rivers come together; ask for a room overlooking Point State Park. Comfortable but rather cramped rms; VIP suites on three top floors; efficient svce. Business and convention clientele. **E–VE**

☀👤👤👤 **Westin William Penn** (dwntwn), 530 William Penn Place, PA 15219 (412/281-7100; toll free, see Westin). 595 rms, A/C, color TV, in-rm movies. AE, CB, DC, MC, V. Gar. $16, two rests. (including the Terrace Room), bar, rm svce, free crib, concierge. *Note:* Since 1906 many distinguished American personalities, including presidents, have seen the crystal chandeliers, the gilt, and the wood paneling in this revered local institution. The plush Edwardian decor is currently undergoing renovation. Huge, luxuriously comfortable rms; very good svce; big business and VIP clientele. The building is a designated historic landmark. **E–VE**

🏨🏨🏨 **Marriott Greentree** (nr. dwntwn), 101 Marriott Dr., PA 15205 (412/922-8400; toll free, see Marriott). 480 rms, A/C, color TV, in-rm movies. AE, CB, DC, MC, V. Free parking, three pools, health club, sauna, two tennis courts, rest. (Prime House), two bars, rm svce, disco, hrdrsr, free airport limo, free crib. *Note:* Large, modern, functional convention hotel 10 min. from dwntwn on I-279. Spacious, well-soundproofed rms (many w. minibars). Agreeable decor and setting. Rest. satisfactory but no more; efficient svce. Group and business clientele. 15 min. from airport. **M–E**

🏨🏨 **Ramada Suites Hotel** (formerly the Bigelow Hotel; dwntwn), 1 Bigelow Sq., PA 15219 (412/281-5800; toll free, see Ramada Inns). 341 suites, A/C, cable color TV. AE, CB, DC, MC, V. Valet parking $8, health club, pool, rest. (Ruddy Duck), bar, rm svce. *Note:* Modern suites-only hotel; comfortable, spacious accommodations w. kitchenette and refrigerator; convenient location at the heart of the business district. Good svce; well-equipped business center; acceptable rest. Business clientele. Good value. **M–E**

🏨🏨 **Holiday Inn–Allegheny Valley** (vic.), 180 Gamma Dr., PA 15238 (412/963-0600; toll free, see Holiday Inns). 184 rms, A/C, color TV, in-rm movies. AE, CB, DC, MC, V. Free parking, pool, coffee shop, bar, rm svce, free crib. *Note:* Typical functional motel, 20 min. from dwntwn on Penna. 28. Spacious rms (some w. refrigerators). The Holiday Inn style. Group clientele. Ideal if you're driving. **M**

🏨🏨 **Best Western–Parkway Center Inn** (nr. dwntwn), 875 Greentree Rd., PA 15220 (412/922-7070; toll free, see Best Western). 151 rms, A/C, color TV, in-rm movies. AE, CB, DC, MC, V. Free parking, pool, health club, sauna, rest., bar, rm svce, hrdrsr, free airport limo, free breakfast (Mon–Fri), free crib. *Note:* Excellently run motel; agreeable rms, some w. kitchenettes and refrigerators. For a motel, very comprehensive facilities. 10 min. from dwntwn on I-279 and 15 min. from the airport; ideal if you're driving. **I–M**

🏨🏨 **Howard Johnson Lodge–South** (vic.), 5300 Clairton Blvd., PA 15236 (412/884-6000; toll free, see Howard Johnson's). 94 rms, A/C, color TV. AE, CB, DC, MC, V. Free parking, pool, adj. coffee shop and bar, rm svce, free breakfast, free crib. *Note:* Older but comfortable motel nr. Allegheny County Airport. Spacious, inviting rms; cheerful svce; good value. 15 min. from dwntwn on Penna. 51; ideal if you're driving. **I–M**

🏨 **Redwood Inn** (vic.), 2898 Banksville Rd., PA 15216 (412/343-3000). 95 rms, A/C, color TV, in-rm movies. AE, CB, DC, MC, V. Free parking, pool, coffee shop, bar, rm svce, free crib. *Note:* Conventional motel but w. huge, comfortable rms and friendly reception and svce. Very good overall value. 10 min. from dwntwn on I-279 and U.S. 19; ideal if you have a car. **I**

🏨 **Econolodge West** (vic.), 4800 Steubenville Pike, PA 15205 (412/922-6900). 110 rms, A/C, color TV, in-rm movies. AE, CB, DC, MC, V. Free parking, pool, adj. 24-hr. coffee shop, crib $3. *Note:* Good value 15 min. from dwntwn on Penna. 60. Very acceptable standards of comfort; some rms w. kitchenettes and refrigerators. Worthwhile reductions for long-term stays. Ideal if you're driving. **B**

Airport Accommodations

🏨🏨 **Ramada Inn Airport** (vic.), 1412 Beers School Rd., Coraopolis, PA 15108 (412/264-8950; toll free, see Ramada Inns). 135 rms, A/C, cable color TV. AE, CB, DC, MC, V. Free parking, pool, rest. (Myron's), bar, rm svce, disco, free crib. *Note:* Inviting, comfortable six-floor motel a quarter mile (400m) from the airport (free shuttle). Spacious, well-soundproofed rms; efficient svce. Business clientele. Perfect for a stopover between flights. **I–M**

YMCA/Youth Hostels
Point Park College Dormitory (dwntwn), 201 Wood St., PA 15222 (412/392-3824 or 391-4100). Clean rms. for rent from June to mid-Aug. Cafeteria. Very central.

RESTAURANTS

Personal Favorites (in order of preference)
Jake's Above the Square (dwntwn), 430 Market St. (338-0900). A/C. Lunch/dinner daily. AE, CB, MC, V. *Specialties:* goat cheese puff w. shiitake mushrooms, capellini Fra Diavolo, blackened shrimp, double veal chop wrapped in prosciutto w. balsamic sauce and homemade fettuccine. Very fine wine list. *Note:* Light regional American and northern Italian cuisine in a bright, multitiered dining rm. Central dwntwn location w. outstanding view. A good choice for a casual lunch or dinner. Entertainment nightly. *American.* **M–E**

The Common Plea (dwntwn), 308 Ross St. (281-5140). A/C. Lunch Mon–Fri, dinner nightly; closed hols. and Sun mid-May to mid-Sept. AE, CB, DC, MC, V. Jkt. *Specialties:* scallops and shrimp Norfolk, bouillabaisse, roulade of veal w. crabmeat, broiled seafood platter, good homemade desserts. Menu changes regularly. *Note:* For more than 15 years this little rest., a stone's throw from the City Council Building and the Court House, has been the lunchtime favorite of local politicians and lawyers. The food is generally excellent, and emphasizes seafood. Heavy wood tables and rococo decor. Very good svce; resv. advised, a must at lunch. Ask to be seated upstairs. *Continental.* **I–M**

Café Allegro (nr. dwntwn), 51 S. 12th St. (481-7788). A/C. Lunch Mon–Fri, dinner Tues–Sun; closed hols. MC, V. *Specialties:* pasta del sole, grilled peppered shrimp, chicken stuffed w. hazelnuts, grilled loin of lamb w. eggplant and roasted peppers, salmon allegro. *Note:* Pleasant South Side rest. in the style of the Riviera coastal cafés. The menu embraces the cuisine of southern France and northern Italy. Relaxed atmosphere and svce. Resv. advised. *Continental.* **I–M**

River Café (nr dwntwn), The Shops at Station Sq. (765-2795). A/C. Lunch/dinner daily. AE, CB, DC, MC, V. *Specialties:* homemade pasta, interesting sandwiches and salads, fresh and smoked seafood. *Note:* New York–style café specializing in fresh smoked items. Turkey and seafood smoked on the premises are the River Café's signature dishes. Overlooks the mall at Station Sq. Locally popular. *American.* **B–I**

Other Restaurants (from top bracket to budget)
Carlton Restaurant (dwntwn), 1 Mellon Bank Center at Grant St. (391-4099). A/C. Lunch Mon–Fri, dinner Mon–Sat; closed hols. AE, CB, DC, MC, V. Jkt. *Specialties:* charcoal-grilled prime meats and fresh seafood, lamb chops, prime rib, roasted quail, Cajun dishes, own pastries. *Note:* A favorite with businesspeople. Voted best steaks in Pittsburgh by readers of *Pittsburgh* magazine. Tables are somewhat close together and the place can get noisy. Service attentive and discreet. Always crowded. Resv. strongly suggested. *American/Continental.* **M–E**

Grand Concourse (nr. dwntwn), 1 Station Sq. (261-1717). A/C. Lunch Mon–Fri, dinner nightly, brunch Sun; closed Thanksgiving, Dec 25. AE, CB, DC, MC, V. *Specialties:* oysters on the half shell, Charley's chowder, linguini primavera, catch of the day, New York strip steak, paella, rack of lamb. *Note:* One of the most unusual rest. settings in the country, in a turn-of-the-century railroad station. The enormous rest., in its wonderful rococo space with soaring vaults and stained-glass windows, specializes in the freshest possible seafood. Lively, congenial atmosphere; ask to be seated in the River Room, at a table w. a river view. Efficient, diligent svce. Locally popular, and a must for the visitor. In spite of its size, you'd be well advised to reserve ahead. *Seafood/American.* **M**

🍷🍷 **Le Pommier** (nr. dwntwn), 2104 E. Carson St. (431-1901).
🍴♨ A/C. Dinner Mon–Sat. AE, CB, DC, MC, V. Jkt. *Specialties:* salmon poached in parchment, pagliatella pasta w. a variety of seafood in saffron sauce, sautéed duck w. black-current sauce, sautéed pork loin w. shiitake, chocolate mousse, apple tatin. Menu changes regularly. *Note:* Remarkable food, inspired by modern French originals, in a prettily converted shop more than a century old. Elegant countrified decor w. unadorned brick walls and candlelit tables; attentive, efficient svce; an excellent place to eat. Resv. a must; 15 min. from dwntwn. *French/American.* **I–M**

🍷🍷 **Louis Tambellini's** (nr. dwntwn), 860 Saw Mill Run Blvd.
🍴♨ (481-1118). A/C. Lunch/dinner Mon–Sat (until midnight); closed hols. AE, DC, MC, V. Jkt. *Specialties:* baked scampi, shrimp Louie, linguini w. mussels, redfish Cajun style, poached salmon w. vegetables, rack of lamb, Italian dishes, caffè espresso. *Note:* In spite of its strong Italian overtones, the cuisine of the Tambellini family gives precedence to seafood—broiled, poached, or baked. Remarkable fish and shellfish. Very elegant modern decor; diligent, unfussy svce. Big enough that resv. are not needed. Valet parking; 15 min. from dwntwn. *Italian/Seafood.* **I–M**

🍷🍷 **Le Mont** (nr. dwntwn), 1114 Grandview Ave. (431-3100).
🍴♨ A/C. Dinner nightly; closed hols. AE, CB, DC, MC, V. Jkt. *Specialties:* escargot, portobello mushrooms stuffed w. crab, homemade pastas, roast raspberry duck, rack of lamb, fruit flambé. *Note:* Perched on top of Mt. Washington, the window-encased dining room grants a great view of Pittsburgh's dwntwn. Food and decor are predictable from a rest. that calls itself "fine dining." High standards in svce. *Continental.* **I–M**

🍷🍷 **Piccolo Piccolo Ristorante** (dwntwn), 1 Wood St. (261-
🍴♨ 7234). A/C. Lunch Mon–Fri, dinner Mon–Sat; closed hols. AE, CB, DC, MC, V. Jkt. *Specialties:* roasted cabanella peppers, fried eggplant, "strudel of pasta" (spinach, ricotta, and Romano cheese wrapped in cheesecloth), ravioli stuffed w. pesto in portobello mushroom cream sauce. *Note:* Roman cuisine for the traditionalist. Interesting antipasto spread. Unimaginative dishes, but solid, authentic cooking. Great list of Italian wines. Attracts mostly those from out of town, especially New Yorkers. *Italian.* **I–M**

🍷🍷 **Chinese on Carson** (nr. dwntwn), 1506 Carson St. (431-
🍴♨ 1717). A/C. Lunch Mon–Sat, dinner daily; closed hols. AE, DC, MC, V. *Specialties:* lobster egg rolls, chicken Kung Pao, Peking duck, ching chioa beef, long-life noodles (w. seafood), braised duck w. crabmeat and scallops. *Note:* Connoisseurs judge this luxurious venture by Richard Lee (also owner of the Oriental Balcony and Mr. Lee's North Garden) to be by a wide margin the finest Far Eastern rest. in Pittsburgh—one of the few major U.S. cities without a Chinatown. Impeccable Cantonese and Szechuan cooking in an attractive lavender-toned Oriental setting. Resv. strongly advised. *Chinese.* **I**

🔆🍷 **Froggy's** (dwntwn), 100 Market St. at First Ave. (471-3764).
🔆♨ A/C. Lunch Mon–Fri, dinner Mon–Sat; closed hols. AE, DC, MC, V. *Specialties:* sandwiches, salads, hamburgers, steaks. *Note:* In the Firstside, the old warehouse district along the Monongahela, this granddaddy of local singles bars is alleged to serve the best drinks in all of dwntwn, as well as excellent steaks and hamburgers. Draws journalists and sports fans, particularly when there's a game at the nearby Three Rivers Stadium. A likable, relaxed place. Resv. suggested. *American.* **B–I**

🔆🍷 **Max's Allegheny Tavern** (nr. dwntwn), 537 Suismon St. at
🔆♨ Middle St. (231-1899). A/C. Lunch/dinner daily. AE, CB,

DC, MC, V. *Specialties:* sauerbraten, wurst platte (sausage plate), wienerschnitzel, weisswurst, apfelstrudel. Draft beer. *Note:* This picturesque turn-of-the-century tavern is one of the oldest on the Northside, a neighborhood across the Allegheny. Authentically German food and atmosphere at very attractive prices. Pretty turn-of-the-century–type decor with Tiffany-style lamps, ceiling fans, tile floors, and superb bar in massive walnut. Noisy but congenial; locally popular. Resv. for parties of five or more only, so you'll have to wait. *German.* **B–I**

　　♀ **Tequila Junction** (nr. dwntwn), 31 Station Sq. (261-3265).
　　🍸 A/C. Lunch/dinner daily. AE, CB, DC, MC, V. *Specialties:* crabmeat enchiladas, chimichangas, tamales, burritos. *Note:* Charming Mexican-inn decor in brick and adobe; good, unpretentious food; svce more friendly than efficient. Locally popular; no resv. *Mexican.* **B–I**

Restaurants in the Vicinity

　　🍽🍽🍽 **The Colony** (vic.), Greentree and Cochran Rds. (561-2060).
　　🍷⊗🍴 A/C. Dinner only, nightly; closed hols. AE, CB, DC, MC, V. Jkt. *Specialties:* lump crabmeat, scampi in garlic sauce, charcoal-broiled steak, filet mignon, veal chop, broiled swordfish. Good desserts; rather weak wine list. *Note:* Fine example of a rest. seriously devoted to American food. The menu is limited to a dozen (remarkable) meat and (impeccably fresh) fish dishes. The decor and atmosphere are those of a luxurious country club, w. an open brick grill in the center of the rm; the svce is in all respects flawless. Business and local VIP clientele. A Pittsburgh landmark since 1960; resv. advisable during the week, indispensable on wknds. Valet parking. 20 min. from dwntwn. *Steak/American.* **M–E**

Cafeterias/Fast Food

　　Primanti Brothers (nr. dwntwn), 46 18th St. (263-2142). Open 24 hr. daily. No credit cards. Sandwich shop elevated to cult status by its huge subs and its notoriously impatient svce staff. Top sellers are the cheese steak and the cappicola ham sandwich.

　　Original Hot Dogs Shop (nr. dwntwn), 3901 Forbes Ave. (621-7388). Lunch/dinner daily (until 4:30am); no credit cards. The "Big O," as the students at the nearby University of Pittsburgh fondly call it, is generally held to serve the best hot dogs in town.

BARS & NIGHTCLUBS

　　Cardillo's Club Café (dwntwn), 56-58 S. 12th St. (381-3777). Thought to host the best modern jazz in town. Open nightly.

　　Chauncey's (nr. dwntwn), Station Sq. (232-0604). Favored by the local yuppies; has an acceptable rest. A preppy place. Open daily.

　　Froggy's (dwntwn), 100 Market St. (471-3764). The granddaddy of local singles bars; excellent drinks in a warm atmosphere; also a rest. serving laudable meat dishes (see "Restaurants," above). Open Mon–Sat.

　　Funny Bone (nr. dwntwn), The Shops at Station Sq. (281-3130). Popular comedy club featuring live cabaret acts. Open Wed–Sat.

　　Gandy Dancer Saloon (nr. dwntwn), 1 Station Sq. (261-1717). Congenial piano bar adjoining the Grand Concourse (see "Restaurants," above). Live music; oyster bar. Open nightly.

　　Graffiti (nr. dwntwn), 4615 Baum Blvd. (682-4210). This nightclub presents a wide-ranging variety of music: jazz, folk, rock, classical. Youthful clientele and atmosphere. Open Tues–Sat.

　　Peter's Pub (nr. dwntwn), 116 Oakland Ave. (681-7465). Raucous hangout near the university, frequented by U. Pitt's athletic teams. Usually jammed. Open Mon–Sat.

　　Shadyside Balcony (nr. dwntwn), 5520 Walnut St. (687-0110). Live modern jazz; praiseworthy rest. Locally popular. Open Mon–Sat.

NEARBY EXCURSIONS

☀☖ **AMBRIDGE** (18 mi./28km NW on Penna. 65) (266-4500): **Old Economy Village** is the former community of the Utopian Christian "Harmony Society," founded around 1825 by a pastor of German origin, George Rapp. Many buildings of the period: communal kitchens, festival hall, workshops, church, granary, cellar, etc., with their original furniture. The community, which practiced celibacy and community property, survived until its dissolution in 1905. A fascinating visit. Open Tues–Sun.

☀☖ **FALLINGWATER** (at Mill Run, 70 mi./112km SE via Penna. 51S, U.S. 40E, and Penna. 381N) (329-8501): With its terraces cantilevered out over Bear Run, this "house over the waterfall," dating from 1936, is one of the most celebrated achievements of Frank Lloyd Wright, the man who can almost be said to have invented the contemporary private house. Open Tues–Sun mid-Apr to mid-Nov, wknds only in winter; resv. advised. Well worth the detour; best combined with a visit to Fort Necessity (see below).

☀☖ **FORT NECESSITY NATIONAL BATTLEFIELD** (58 mi./93km SE via Penna. 51S and U.S. 40E) (329-5512): Site of the first major battle fought by George Washington, at the time a colonel in the British army, against the French and their Native American allies on July 3, 1754. The engagement, which resulted in a British defeat, marked the official beginning of the French and Indian War. Replica of the fort originally built by Washington, museum, early 19th-century tavern. Open daily; best visited in combination with Fallingwater (see above).

☖ **HARTWOOD ACRES** (215 Saxonburg Blvd., 12 mi./19km north via Penna. 8 and Saxonburg Blvd.) (767-9200): Faithful reproduction of a great English country house, with Gothic Tudor buildings, antique furniture, formal gardens, stud farm, etc. Open Tues–Sun; closed Jan–Mar.

☀☖ **PRABHUPADA'S PALACE OF GOLD** (near Wheeling, W. Va., 72 mi./115km SW via I-79S, I-70W, W. Va. 88, U.S. 250S, and Limestone Hill Rd.) (304/843-1600): Sumptuous palace in the Indian style built by Hare Krishna devotees as a sanctuary dedicated to their spiritual director Srila Prabhupada. More than 8,000 sq. ft. (740m²) of 22-karat gold leaf was used in its construction, as well as 52 different kinds of marble, carved teakwood furniture, and crystal chandeliers imported from Austria. Fine gardens with rose gardens, fountains, and original sculptures. Very good rest. (Nathaji's). Open daily.

☖ **PITHOLE CITY** (102 mi./163km north via I-79, U.S. 62E, and Penna. 227N) (814/589-7912): The drilling, on August 27, 1859, of the first U.S. oil well on the banks of Oil Creek, 4 mi. (6km) west, made the fortune of Pithole—for a short while. In five months of the year 1865 its population rose from 15 to 10,000, but in 1867 its prosperity vanished as abruptly as it had come. The first boom town created by "black gold" is now totally abandoned, and only a few vestiges remain of its extraordinary past. Visitor Center open Tues–Sun, Memorial Day–Labor Day.

☀☖ **TOUR-ED MINE** (Red Belt West at Tarentum, 20 mi./32km NW on Penna. 28) (224-4720): Former underground coal mine, first worked in the 1780s. Visit the original plant and buildings. Interesting mining museum. Open daily May–Labor Day.

CHAPTER 8

BALTIMORE

□ □ □

Hub of the 17th-century tobacco trade, Baltimore, like Boston and New York, is one of the continent's oldest metropolises. It is also one of the birthplaces of religious tolerance in America: the Royal Charter of 1649 expressly granted freedom of worship to the colony of Maryland, created 17 years earlier by a decree of King Charles I. Tucked away at the head of the huge Chesapeake Bay (187 mi./300km long), Baltimore, named in honor of the first British "proprietor" of the colony, Cecilius Calvert, 2nd Baron Baltimore, has always been a bustling commercial crossroads between the East Coast and the South. Point of origin of the country's first railroad line (1827)—the legendary Baltimore & Ohio—Maryland's biggest city is still the principal Atlantic outlet for midwestern grain and Appalachian coal.

Port city and home to industry and business (like Black & Decker Corp., the tool and appliance giant), Baltimore is also a bastion of culture: Some of the people associated with the city are Edgar Allan Poe, who died here in 1849; Francis Scott Key, who wrote "The Star-Spangled Banner" here (1814); critic Henry L. Mencken, the "Sage of Baltimore"; author Leon Uris, born here in 1924; and John Dos Passos, who died here in 1970. Baltimore is home to the world famous **Johns Hopkins University,** an internationally known **symphony orchestra,** and an architectural blend of tradition and vitality: the glass-and-steel skyscrapers of **Charles Center** and the patrician homes of **Mount Vernon Place** rubbing shoulders with the picturesque rowhouses, the shot-and-a-beer joints and cobblestone alleyways of **Fell's Point** and **Otterbein Homesteading;** the imposing Victorian architecture of **City Hall;** the delicate grace of the **Walters Art Gallery;** and the United States' oldest Catholic cathedral, the **Basilica of the Assumption** (1821), miraculously spared by the 1904 fire that destroyed much of the historic section. **Fort McHenry,** built in 1794–1805 with star-shaped fortifications characteristic of the period, and tenaciously held against the British during the War of 1812, attracts close to a million visitors each year. The new port area, the **Inner Harbor,** is one of the finest examples of urban renewal in the United States, with many lively and colorful boutiques, stores, and crowded seafood restaurants (Chesapeake Bay blue crabs and oysters are justly famous). This area alone is worth the trip to Baltimore. Other areas worth a look are the old ethnic neighborhoods: **Little Italy** (around High and Pratt Sts., Central and Eastern Aves.); **Greektown** (Eastern Ave. from no. 3500 to no. 4800); **Little Lithuania** (Hollins and Carrollton Sts.); the Polish and Ukrainian neighborhoods of **Highlandtown** (around Patterson Park); and the old Jewish quarter, nicknamed **Corned Beef Row** because of a multitude of deli restaurants (Lombard St. around Lloyd St. and Central Ave.).

Some of Baltimore's famous sons and residents are: Billie Holiday, the great blues singer; drummer Chick Webb; jazz musician Eubie Blake; Wallis Warfield Simpson, who married Edward VIII of England (1937) and became the Duchess of Windsor; composer Philip Glass; and the legendary Babe Ruth, known to baseball fans as the "Sultan of Swat."

BASIC FACTS: State of Maryland. Area code: 410. Time zone: eastern. ZIP Code (of central post office): 21233. Settled: 1661. Founded: 1729. Approximate population: city, 736,000; metropolitan area, 2,400,000. 18th-largest U.S. metropolitan area.

CLIMATE: As in all the Northeast Corridor cities, the winter is cold (mean Jan temperature, 37°F/3°C), but with less snow than in Boston or New York. Summer is hot and humid with sudden downpours due to the proximity of Chesapeake Bay (mean July temperature, 79°F/26°C). Autumn is rainy, and an umbrella is a must Sept–Oct. The best season to visit Baltimore is spring which, although windy, is almost always pleasant.

DISTANCES: New York, 200 mi. (320km); Philadelphia, 93 mi. (150km); Pittsburgh, 218 mi. (350km); Washington, 40 mi. (65km).

ARRIVAL & TRANSIT INFORMATION

AIRPORT: Baltimore-Washington International Airport (BWI): 10 mi. (16km) south of Baltimore, 32 mi. (51km) north of Washington. Call 859-7100 for information.

U.S. AIRLINES: American (toll free 800/433-7300), Delta (toll free 800/221-1212), Northwest (toll free 800/225-2525), TWA (toll free 800/221-2000), United (toll free 800/241-6522), and USAir (toll free 800/428-4322).

FOREIGN CARRIERS: British Airways (toll free 800/247-9297) and Icelandair (toll free 800/223-5500).

CITY LINK: Cab fare to city center, about $15; time, 20 min. Cab fare to dwntwn Washington from BWI, about $40; time, 45 min. Bus: **Airport Van Shuttle** (859-7545); leaves every 30 min.; stops at the major dwntwn hotels; fare, $8; time, 25 min. **Peter Pan** (toll free 800/343-9999) leaves every 90 min. for dwntwn Washington; fare $5; time, 50 min. The proximity of the airport and the compact layout of downtown Baltimore may make car rental superfluous. Good public transportation system by subway and bus (MTA: 539-5000).

CAR RENTAL (at the airport unless otherwise indicated): Avis (toll free 800/331-1212); Budget (toll free 800/527-0700); Dollar (toll free 800/800-4000); Hertz (toll free 800/654-3131); National (toll free 800/227-7368); and Thrifty (toll free 800/367-2277). For dwntwn locations, consult the local telephone book.

LIMOUSINE SERVICES: Ambassador Limousine (686-1234), Carey Limousine (837-1234).

TAXIS: Taxis can be hailed on the street or summoned by telephone. The major companies are **Royal Cab** (327-0330), **Yellow Cab** (685-1212) and **G.T.P.** (to/from the airport only) (859-1103). Baltimore cab fares are among the lowest in the nation.

TRAIN: Amtrak, Pennsylvania Station, 1515 N. Charles St. (toll free 800/872-7245). The MARC commuter train (toll free 800/325-7245) runs every weekday between Baltimore's Camden or Penn stations and Washington's Union Station.

INTERCITY BUSES: Greyhound, 210 W. Fayette St. (752-0868). Open 24 hr.

INFORMATION & TOURS

TOURIST INFORMATION: The **Baltimore Area Convention & Visitors Association,** 100 Light St. (plaza level), MD 21202 (410/837-4636).
   Visitor Center, in the Marsh-Maclennan Building, Pratt and Howard Sts. (410/837-4636; toll free 800/282-6632).

GUIDED TOURS: *Baltimore Patriot* (boat), Inner Harbor (685-4288). Harbor cruise, mid-Apr to mid-Oct.
   Baltimore Trolley Tours (bus) (752-2015). Two-hour guided tour of Baltimore's principal attractions in a replica of an oldtime trolley. Unlimited boarding pass valid all day. 17 boarding locations. Daily May–Sept, weekends rest of the year.
   Clipper Cruise Line (boat): Information: 7711 Bonhomme Ave., St. Louis, MO 63105 (toll free 800/325-0010). Has 7-, 10-, and 14-day luxury yacht cruises (100 berths) along the Atlantic coast from Boston or Baltimore to Jacksonville, Florida, and the Virgin Islands.
   Insomniac Tours (bus), 3414 Philips Dr. (653-2998): An original and highly successful idea, this guided tour of Baltimore for night owls leaves at 1:30am and returns at dawn, with dinner included. Resv. a must.
   Lady Baltimore (boat), W. Bulkhead at Light St. (727-3113): Cruises along Chesapeake Bay and to Annapolis (end of May to Sept).
   Water Taxi (boat) (547-0090). A water shuttle w. landings all around Baltimore's harbor. Unlimited boarding pass valid all day, 11am–11pm daily.

SIGHTS, ATTRACTIONS & ACTIVITIES

ARCHITECTURAL HIGHLIGHTS: ※🔔 **Charles Center,** bounded by Charles, Lombard, and Liberty Sts.: New business district begun in the early 1960s. Among the 15 commercial and residential skyscrapers are the very handsome **One Charles Center,** 24 floors of bronze-colored glass, by Mies van der Rohe; and the 13,000-seat **Baltimore Arena.** This ultramodern architectural ensemble boasts numerous fountains, esplanades (among them, Center Plaza, which recalls Siena's famous piazza del Campo), and sculptures (notably a 32-ft./10m bronze flame by Francesco Somaini). Open-air concerts in summer. Linked by Skywalk to Harborplace and the Convention Center.
   🔔 **World Trade Center,** Pratt St. at Inner Harbor (837-4515): I.M. Pei's innovative pentagonal 30-story building. The observation platform on the 27th floor offers an unobstructed view of the city and the port (see "Panoramas," below).

CHURCHES/SYNAGOGUES: ※🔔 **Basilica of the Assumption,** Cathedral and Mulberry Sts. (727-3564): Be sure to see the United States' oldest Catholic cathedral (1821) with its interesting classical revival architecture. Visits by appointment.

HISTORIC BUILDINGS: 🔔 **Asbury House,** 10 E. Mt. Vernon Place (685-5290): Luxurious private residence dating from the 1850s, with decorative balconies and wrought-iron fences. Very lovely interior decor with a startling three-story spiral staircase. See it. Open Mon–Fri.
   🔔 **City Hall,** 100 N. Holiday St. (396-3190): Baltimore's City Hall is one of the finest examples of Victorian architecture in the United States (1875) and was entirely restored in 1975. Imposing dome, 252 ft. (77m) high. Visits by appointment Mon–Sat.
   ※🔔 **Edgar Allan Poe House,** 203 N. Amity St. (396-7932): The last residence of the famous writer who died in 1849 in still-

mysterious circumstances. Open Wed–Sat. His grave is close by, at **Westminster Presbyterian Church Yard,** Fayette and Greene Sts. (706-2072). A group of admirers leads a graveside ceremony each Jan 19 to commemorate his birthday.

※ 🐚 **Fort McHenry National Monument and Historic Shrine,** at the east end of Fort Ave. (962-4290): Splendidly restored early 19th-century fortress at the entrance to the harbor. When, on the morning of September 14, 1814, from the English warship on which he was held prisoner, Francis Scott Key, a lawyer and sometime poet, saw the tattered flag still streaming above the fort after a night of intense bombardment, he was inspired to write the words to what has become the national anthem. Fort McHenry is one of five public buildings authorized to fly the flag year round. You will also find a museum, a very fine panorama, and military parades in summer; the fort attracts more than 800,000 visitors each year. Open daily.

🐚 **Johns Hopkins University,** Charles and 34th Sts. (516-8000): Founded in 1876 through the generosity of Johns Hopkins, a wealthy local businessman, this is one of the country's most respected universities (3,600 students) and a highly prestigious medical center. The campus has many Georgian-style buildings such as **Gilman Hall,** the elegant **Homewood House,** the interesting **Archeological Museum** (Egyptian and Roman antiquities; open Mon–Fri), and the very original **Bufano Sculpture Garden,** with amusing topiary sculptures by Italian artist Beniamino Bufano. Open daily.

🐚 **Shot Tower,** Fayette and Front Sts. (837-5424): From the top of this slim, 227-ft. (70m) brick tower which dates from 1828, molten lead was poured into a vat of water below to make cannon balls. Open daily.

🐚 **Star-Spangled Banner Flag House,** 844 E. Pratt St. (837-1793): Picturesque small house dating from 1773 and home to an interesting collection of Revolutionary War relics. Here Mary Pickersgill and her teenage daughter sewed the flag that inspired Francis Scott Key's poem, which became the national anthem; at the time it had 15 stars and 15 stripes. (They were paid $405.90 for parts and labor.) The flag on display is a replica; the original is in the National Museum of American History in Washington. Period souvenirs and documents. Open Mon–Sat.

🐚 **U.S. Frigate *Constellation*,** Pier 1, Pratt St., Inner Harbor (539-1797): The oldest U.S. warship (1797) still afloat. Laid up in 1945 after 148 years of continuous faithful service, she is now a floating museum. Open daily.

MARKETS: ※🐚 **Lexington Market,** Lexington and Eutaw Sts. (685-6169): One of the United States' oldest indoor markets (1782). Destroyed by fire in 1949, it was reconstructed in its original form in 1952 and houses more than 160 different food businesses. The city's gastronomic pride, with its extremely colorful decor. Open Mon–Sat.

MONUMENTS: 🐚 **Washington Monument,** Charles and Monument Sts. (396-7939): The oldest monument dedicated to our first president (1842). This massive white column offers a very fine view of the city from 172 ft. (54m) up (no elevator). Open Fri–Tues.

MUSEUMS OF ART: 🐚 **Baltimore Museum of Art,** Art Museum Dr. at 31st St. (396-7100): This interesting museum is just 20 min. from dwntwn and houses many beautiful paintings and sculptures. Among the most famous are Titian's *Man with a Fur;* Rembrandt's *Portrait of Titus;* Renoir's *The Washerwomen;* 43 Matisses, including *Blue Nude* and *Seated Odalisque;* and 16 Picassos, including *Portrait of Allan Stein.* Open Wed–Sun.

※ 🐚 **Peabody Institute,** 1 E. Mt. Vernon Place (659-8100): Home of a renowned music conservatory, it offers free concerts Wed

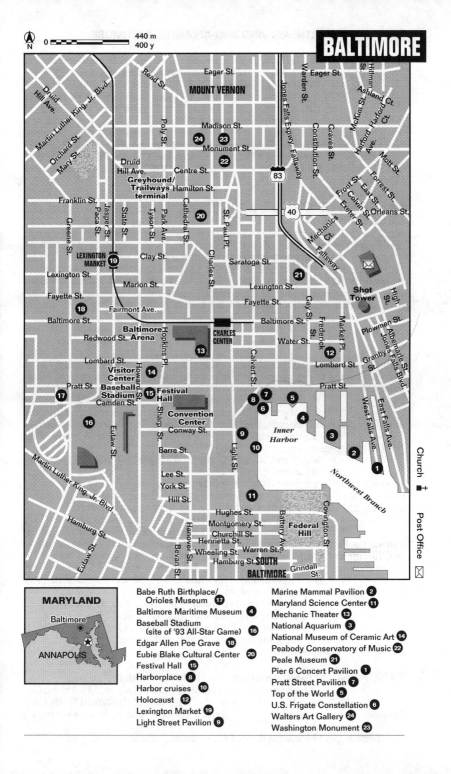

BALTIMORE

0 — 440 m / 400 y

MOUNT VERNON

SOUTH BALTIMORE

Inner Harbor

Northwest Branch

Federal Hill

Shot Tower

Greyhound/Trailways terminal

LEXINGTON MARKET 19

Baltimore Arena

CHARLES CENTER

Visitor Center

Baseball Stadium

Festival Hall 15

Convention Center

Church ■✝

Post Office ⊠

MARYLAND

Baltimore

ANNAPOLIS

Babe Ruth Birthplace/ Orioles Museum 17
Baltimore Maritime Museum 4
Baseball Stadium (site of '93 All-Star Game) 16
Edgar Allen Poe Grave 18
Eubie Blake Cultural Center 20
Festival Hall 15
Harborplace 8
Harbor cruises 10
Holocaust 12
Lexington Market 19
Light Street Pavilion 9

Marine Mammal Pavilion 2
Maryland Science Center 11
Mechanic Theater 13
National Aquarium 3
National Museum of Ceramic Art 14
Peabody Conservatory of Music 22
Peale Museum 21
Pier 6 Concert Pavilion 1
Pratt Street Pavilion 7
Top of the World 5
U.S. Frigate Constellation 6
Walters Art Gallery 24
Washington Monument 23

at noon. Open Mon–Fri. With a six-story atrium, interior balconies, and forged-iron pillars, the library (300,000 volumes) is worth a visit for its design alone.

☀️ 🔔🔔 **Walters Art Gallery,** 600 N. Charles St. (547-9000): Archeology, old masters, jewelry, weapons from antiquity to modern times, and a very rich collection of Armenian manuscripts in the elegant Italian Renaissance–style home of philanthropist William T. Walters, and in the new wing opened in 1974. One of the country's best art museums. Some of its most famous exhibits including Giovanni di Paolo's *Carrying of the Cross,* Raphael's *Madonna of the Candelabra,* Orcagna's *Crucifixion,* Corot's *Very Early Spring,* and Manet's *At the Café-Concert.* Reopened in 1989 after radical renovation. Open Tues–Sun.

MUSEUMS OF SCIENCE & HISTORY: ☀️🔔🔔 Babe Ruth Birthplace and Baseball Center, 216 Emory St. (727-1539): The house in which the most famous baseball player of all time was born (1895) is now a museum devoted to the man known as the "Sultan of Swat." Open daily.

🔔 **Baltimore Museum of Industry,** 1415 Key Hwy., south of Inner Harbor (727-4808): This new museum features exhibits of Baltimore's past and present industries, such as a re-created antique machine shop, print shop, clothing factory, and a "hands-on" cannery factory for children. Live demonstrations and films. For history buffs. Open Tues–Sun in summer, Thurs–Sun the rest of the year.

🔔🔔 **B & O Railroad Museum,** Mount Clare Station, Pratt and Poppleton Sts. (752-2490): The world's biggest collection of old locomotives in a Baltimore & Ohio Railroad station that's the oldest in the United States (1830). Open daily. (In this same station, in 1844 Samuel Morse inaugurated the telegraph system that bears his name, transmitting from Washington the famous message: "What hath God wrought.")

🔔 **H. L. Mencken House,** 1524 Hollins St. (396-7997): Home for more than 68 years of the celebrated journalist, author, and critic Henry Louis Mencken, the "Sage of Baltimore," this stately 19th-century rowhouse is fully restored with Mencken's original furniture and many of his personal belongings. Interesting. Open Wed–Sun.

🔔 **Maryland Science Center,** 601 Light St. (685-2370): Unusual assembly of octagonal structures housing an ultra-sophisticated planetarium **(Davis Planetarium)** that reproduces a space voyage as well as various exhibits on the evolution of science and a giant model of a human cell. IMAX movie theater with a giant five-story screen. Open daily.

☀️🔔🔔 **National Aquarium,** Pier 3, Pratt St., Inner Harbor (576-3800): One of the East Coast's most modern and spectacular aquariums. Futurist architecture in the form of a glass pyramid. 8,000 specimens of 600 different species. Also, a shark tank and facsimiles of natural habitats. A new pavilion, opened in 1990, includes a 1.2-million-gallon (4.5-million-liter) pool with bottlenose dolphins and beluga whales, a 1,300-seat amphitheater, and a 40-ft. (12m) model of a humpback whale suspended in the pavilion's three-story atrium. Attracts more than 1½ million visitors each year. Open daily.

🔔 **Peale Museum,** 225 Holliday St. (396-1149): One of the United States' oldest museums (1814). Once the City Hall, it covers the history of Baltimore from the earliest settlement to the present. Interesting. Open Tues–Sun.

PANORAMAS: Federal Hill Park: See "Parks and Gardens," below.

🔔🔔 **Top of the World,** Pratt St. at Inner Harbor (837-4515): Observation platform on the 27th floor of the **World Trade Center** (see "Architectural Highlights," above). The best panoramic view of the city and the harbor. Open daily.

Washington Monument: See "Monuments," above.

PARKS & GARDENS: ⛲ **Cylburn Arboretum,** 4915 Greenspring Ave. (396-0180): 168-acre (70ha) landscaped park, 20 min. from dwntwn via the Jones Falls Expwy. A favorite of nature lovers, with its numerous trails and its countless varieties of plants. Open daily. The botanical museum **(Cylburn Mansion)** is open Mon–Fri.

⛲ **Druid Hill Park,** Druid Park Lake Dr. (366-5466): Opened in the 1850s, a lovely urban park that's home to the **Baltimore Zoo** (more than 1,000 animals), flower displays **(Conservatory),** lakes, groves, playing fields, and picnic grounds, all 10 min. from dwntwn via Jones Falls Expwy.

Federal Hill Park, Warren and Battery Aves.: Gardens at the southern end of the Inner Harbor affording a very fine view of the city and the harbor.

PERFORMING ARTS: For daily listings of all shows and cultural events, consult the entertainment pages of the daily papers: *Baltimore Sun* (morning) and *Baltimore Evening Sun* (evening); and of the monthly magazine *Baltimore.*

Arena Players, 801 McCulloh St. (728-6500): Modern theater, drama, comedy.

Center Stage, 700 N. Calvert St. (332-0033): Classical and modern theater.

Lyric Opera House, 140 W. Mt. Royal Ave. (727-6000): Baltimore Opera Company in residence, Oct, Mar–Apr (director: Michael Harrison).

Meyerhoff Symphony Hall, 1212 Cathedral St. (783-8000): Home of the Baltimore Symphony Orchestra (principal conductor: David Zinman). Oct–May.

Morris A. Mechanic Theatre, Hopkins Place (625-1400): Broadway hits.

Peabody Institute and Conservatory of Music, 1 E. Mt. Vernon Place (659-8124): Very popular chamber-music recitals.

Pier 6 Concert Pavilion, Pier 6, Inner Harbor (625-1400): Big-name concerts and shows, May–Sept.

Theatre Project, 45 W. Preston St. (752-8558): Experimental theater.

Vagabond Players, 806 S. Broadway (563-9135): One of the oldest "little theaters" in the United States. Drama, comedy, modern theater, Broadway shows.

SHOPPING: **Harborplace,** Light and Pratt Sts. (332-4191): Some 150 food stores, stalls, fashionable boutiques, and restaurants (including City Lights and Phillips) in two huge glass pavilions on the basin of the Inner Harbor. Lively, picturesque ambience. Open daily.

SPECIAL EVENTS: For the exact schedule of the events below, consult the **Baltimore Area Convention & Visitors Association** (see "Tourist Information," above).

Preakness Festival Week (mid-May): Public concerts, exhibits, ballooning exhibitions, and shows the entire week preceding the Preakness Stakes, a famous horse race since 1873 and one of the three events that make up thoroughbred racing's Triple Crown.

Pier 6 Concerts (June–Sept): Open-air concerts on the water's edge. Jazz, classical, pop. Locally very popular.

Showcase of Nations Festival (every wknd, June–Sept): Festival dedicated to the folk music, crafts, and foods of the different ethnic groups living in Baltimore.

I Am an American Day (early Sept): The United States' biggest patriotic parade, with more than 10,000 flags and 25 marching bands. A truly spectacular tradition for more than 50 years. Patterson Park.

Charm City Fair (mid-Sept): Open-air shows, parades, food festival. Memorial Stadium.

New Year's Eve Extravaganza (Dec 31): Concerts, fireworks, parades. Inner Harbor.

SPORTS: Baltimore has two professional teams:
Baseball (Apr–Oct): Orioles, Oriole Park at Camden Yards (685-9800).
Ice Hockey (Oct–Apr): Skipjacks, Baltimore Arena (347-2010).

Horse Racing
Laurel Race Track, U.S. 1, in Laurel (301/725-0400), thoroughbred racing year round; **Pimlico Race Course,** 5201 Park Heights Ave. (542-9400), racing year round and site of the world-famous Preakness Stakes, third Sat in May.

STROLLS: ☼🔍 **Fells Point,** Broadway south of Eastern Ave.: These once-seedy, run-down docks are today undergoing complete renovation, a unique group of more than 300 rowhouses, 2½ centuries old, lining narrow, picturesque cobblestone alleyways. With many restaurants and pubs, the area is lively and bustling after dark.

🔍 **Inner Harbor,** Pratt and Calvert Sts.: The old harbor, now undergoing renovation, is lively and colorful with boutiques, restaurants, yacht marinas, ultramodern aquarium, and museums. It's worth coming to Baltimore just to see it.

☼🔍 **Mount Vernon,** Charles and Monument Sts.: A very handsome ensemble of opulent 19th-century patrician homes, including **Asbury House** (see "Historic Buildings," above), bordered by public gardens. Museums, elegant boutiques. The ideal place for a stroll.

🔍 **Otterbein Homesteading,** around Sharp, Conway, and Hanover Sts.: A group of houses dating from 1780–1800, originally inhabited by German immigrants, still with original gas lamps and cobblestones. Present-day residents were able to buy the houses for a symbolic $1 each, on condition that they would renovate them at their own expense and preserve their original character. See especially the **Old Otterbein United Methodist Church,** at Sharp and Conway Sts., Baltimore's oldest church in continuous use (1786).

ACCOMMODATIONS

Personal Favorites (in order of preference)
☼🕯🕯🕯🕯 **The Latham Hotel** (formerly Peabody Court) (dwntwn), 612 Cathedral St., MD 21201 (410/727-7101; toll free 800/528-4261). 104 rms, A/C, color TV, in-rm movies. AE, CB, DC, MC, V. Valet gar. $10, two rests. (including Citronelle), two bars, rm svce, concierge, free crib. *Note:* "The" grand hotel of Baltimore, facing the very aristocratic Mount Vernon Sq. Rather massive 1930s building, but w. an interior decor that's both intimate and elegant. Very comfortable rms w. Empire-style furniture, marble bathrooms, and minibars. Svce and reception are of rare quality, and the rest. (Citronelle) is top-notch. VIP and big business clientele; the favorite hotel of connoisseurs. Just off the business district. **E–VE**

🕯🕯🕯 **Hyatt Regency** (dwntwn), 300 Light St., MD 21202 (410/528-1234; toll free, see Hyatt). 490 rms, A/C, color TV, in-rm movies. AE, CB, DC, MC, V. Valet gar. $8, pool, tennis, health club, sauna, two rests. (Bistro 300 is one), coffee shop, three bars, rm svce, free crib. *Note:* Built in 1981, this modern high-rise boasts a striking mirrored exterior. Its unique location offers direct access by Skywalk to the Harborplace and the Convention Center. Large, very comfortable rms—the best have a view of the port. Very complete facilities. Efficient svce. Big business clientele. Interesting wknd packages. VIP floor. **E–VE**

☼♚♟♟ **Clarion Hotel Inner Harbor** (dwntwn), 711 Eastern Ave., MD
♟♟ 21202 (410/783-5553; toll free, see Choice). 71 rms, A/C,
color TV, in-rm movies. AE, CB, DC, MC, V. Parking $8, exercise room,
Jacuzzi, rest. (Harrison's Pier 5) bar, rm svce. *Note:* Innovative modern building
w. enormous glassed-in atrium and rest. overlooking the harbor. Opened in
1989, the hotel boasts every modern comfort and facility. Spacious rms w. balconies (the best overlooking the water); efficient, courteous svce. Adjoins the National Aquarium, and neighbors the Convention Center, whence a largely
business clientele. The best location in Baltimore, at the tip of Pier 5; atmosphere
and setting offer the kind of change that is really as good as a rest. **M–VE**

♟♟ **Admiral Fell Inn** (nr. dwntwn), 888 S. Broadway, MD 21231
♟♟ (410/522-7377; toll free 800/292-4667). 40 rms, A/C, col-
or TV. AE, MC, V. Free parking, rest., bar, rm svce, free breakfast, concierge.
Note: Charming little hotel in the heart of the picturesque Fells Point section (see
"Strolls," above). Was once a vinegar factory and long a sailor's lodging house. It
offers luxury without ostentation in spacious, comfortable rms w. canopy beds,
private patios, and ultraprofessional svce. Very creditable rest. An excellent location, 8 min. from dwntwn. Free Inner Harbor shuttle. **M–E**

♟ **Mt. Vernon Hotel** (dwntwn), 24 W. Franklin St., MD 21201
♟ (410/576-8400; toll free, see Choice). 194 rms, A/C, color
TV, in-rm movies. AE, CB, DC, MC, V. Parking $5, rest., coffee shop, bar, free
crib. *Note:* Old but comfortable motel just off the business district. Spacious rms.
Business clientele. Good value. No-smoking rms. **I–M**

Other Accommodations (from top bracket to budget)

♟♟♟♟ **Stouffer Harborplace** (dwntwn), 202 E. Pratt St., MD 21202
♟♟♟♟ (410/547-1200; toll free, see Stouffer). 622 rms, A/C, color
TV, in-rm movies. AE, CB, DC, MC, V. Valet parking $12, pool, health club,
sauna, rest. (Windows), two bars, 24-hr. rm svce, boutiques, concierge. *Note:* Big
new convention hotel, facing the Inner Harbor as its name implies. The modern
design is pleasing, but for a greenish facade in doubtful taste. Comfortable, very
well equipped rms w. minibar, computer-phone hookups, and bathroom phone.
The rest. has a fine view over the harbor. Two blocks from the Convention Center; business clientele; VIP floor. Interesting wknd packages. **E–VE**, but lower
rates off-season.

♟♟♟ **Harbor Court** (dwntwn), 550 Light St., MD 21202 (410/
♟♟♟ 234-0550; toll free, see Preferred). 204 rms, A/C, color TV,
in-rm movies. AE, DC, MC, V. Gar. $12, pool, tennis, health club, sauna, bar,
rm svce, hrdrsr, concierge, free crib. *Note:* Elegant European-style hotel located
on the waterfront of the Inner Harbor. Rms are ultra-comfortable and well-
equipped mini-suites (the best have a view of the port). Attentive, personalized
svce and a very good rest. (Hampton's). An excellent location, 5 min. from
dwntwn. First-grade sports facilities. **E–VE**

♟♟♟ **Sheraton Inner Harbor** (dwntwn), 300 S. Charles St., MD
♟♟♟ 21201 (410/962-8300; toll free, see Sheraton). 334 rms,
A/C, color TV, in-rm movies. AE, CB, DC, MC, V. Gar. $10, pool, health club,
sauna, rest., two bars, 24-hr. rm svce, free crib. *Note:* 15-story hotel of rather char-
acterless modern architecture. Spacious, comfortable rms w. minibars and good
sports facilities. Svce sometimes overburdened. Group and convention clientele.
Very convenient to the Inner Harbor and the business district, w. direct access to
the Convention Center. No-smoking rms. **E–VE**

♟♟ **Society Hill-Hopkins Inn** (nr. dwntwn), 3404 Saint Paul St.,
♟♟ MD 21218 (235-8600). 26 rms, A/C, color TV. AE, CB, DC,
MC, V. Free parking, free breakfast, free crib, nearby rests. *Note:* Located in a
1920s Spanish-revival apartment building, 5 min. from the business district.
Pleasing rms and suites that are individually furnished in a variety of styles. Svce
varies. **M**

    🏨🏨 **Holiday Inn Inner Harbor** (dwntwn), 301 W. Lombard St., MD 21201 (410/685-3500; toll free, see Holiday Inns). 370 rms, A/C, color TV, in-rm movies. AE, CB, DC, MC, V. Parking $6, pool, health club, sauna, rest., bar, rm svce, free crib. *Note:* Classic Holiday Inn style, w. functional comfort and less-than-perfect svce. Group and convention clientele. Across from the Civic Center. Interesting wknd packages. **M**

    🏨🏨 **Days Inn Inner Harbor** (dwntwn), 100 Hopkins Place, MD 21201 (410/576-1000; toll free, see Days Inns). 250 rms, A/C, color TV, in-rm movies. AE, CB, DC, MC, V. Parking $4, pool, coffee shop, bar, rm svce, concierge, free crib. *Note:* Modern, nine-story motel in the middle of dwntwn. Functional comfort and facilities. Well-conceived, spacious rms (some w. minibar) and relatively friendly reception. Business clientele. **I–M**

    🏨 **Ramada Inner Harbor** (dwntwn), 8 N. Howard St., MD 21201 (410/539-1188; toll free, see Ramada). 93 rms, A/C, color TV. AE, CB, DC, MC, V. Parking $6, rest. (Annabelle's), bar, free crib. *Note:* Small and aging, but well placed in the heart of the business district; welcoming and intimate. Entirely modernized rms. A very good value. Regular clientele. **I–M**

    🏨 **Howard Johnson's** (vic.), 5701 Baltimore National Pike, Catonsville, MD 21228 (410/747-8900; toll free, see Howard Johnson's). 147 rms, A/C, color TV, in-rm movies. AE, CB, DC, MC, V. Free parking, pool, coffee shop, valet svce, free breakfast Mon–Fri, free crib. *Note:* Classic motel w. direct access to the Baltimore Beltway, Exit 15. Modern comfort. Some rms have balconies. Ideal if you're driving—25 min. from dwntwn. Good value. **B–I**

    🏨 **Schaefer Hotel** (formerly the Abbey Hotel; nr. dwntwn), 723 St. Paul St. (at Madison), MD 21202 (410/332-0405). 35 rms, A/C, color TV. AE, MC, V. *Note:* Small, antiquated hotel but nicely located quite close to Mount Vernon Place. Big, high-ceilinged rms (some recently renovated). Cheerful svce. Good value. **I**

Airport Accommodations

    🏨🏨🏨 **Guest Quarters Airport** (vic.), 1300 Concourse Dr., Linthicum, MD 21090 (410/850-0747; toll free 800/424-2900). 251 suites, A/C, color TV, in-rm movies. AE, CB, DC, MC, V. Free parking, pool, health club, sauna, rest., bar, rm svce, free crib. *Note:* Modern, functional airport hotel 5 min. from the terminal; suites only, spacious and well laid-out, w. refrigerator; some w. microwave. Elegant atrium; very good svce. The perfect place for a rest between flights. **E–VE**

YMCA/Youth Hostels

    Baltimore Hostel (youth hostel, dwntwn), 17 W. Mulberry St., MD 21201 (410/576-8880). 48 beds in an elegant town house.

RESTAURANTS

Personal Favorites (in order of preference)

    🍴🍴🍴 **Polo Grill** (nr. dwntwn), in the Inn at the Colonnade, 4 W. University Pkwy. (235-8200). A/C. Breakfast/lunch/dinner daily, brunch Sun. AE, CB, DC, MC, V. Jkt. *Specialties:* fried lobster tail, wild-mushroom tart, loin of elk w. woodland mushrooms and black-currant sauce, grilled salmon w. shiitake and soy-seasoned butter sauce, crème brûlée. Well-selected wine list. *Note:* A chic newcomer to the local gastronomic scene. Subtle and inventive upscale American regional cooking. Clubby, stylish setting. Efficient, knowledgeable svce. Resv. advised. Valet parking. *American.* **M**

    🍴🍴 **Pierpoint** (nr dwntwn), 1822 Aliceanna St. (675-2080). A/C. Lunch Tues–Sat, dinner Tues–Sun. AE, DC, MC, V. Jkt. *Specialties:* Smoked crab cakes, lamb and polenta ravioli w. pecan sauce, rabbit sausage w. wilted greens and cider vinaigrette, roasted baby chicken w. mashed-potato fritters, lavish ice cream desserts. *Note:* Deliciously innovative Maryland-style cuisine by Baltimore's wunderkind chef Nancy Longo. Small (the dining room seats only 50), unappealing bistro decor, off the beaten Broadway track in the historic Fells Point district. Resv. a must. The "in" place in Baltimore. *American.* **M–E**

☖☖ **Brass Elephant** (nr. dwntwn), 924 N. Charles St. (547-8480). A/C. Lunch Mon–Fri, dinner nightly; closed hols. AE, CB, DC, MC, V. J&T. *Specialties:* fresh homemade pasta, northern Italian cuisine (the menu changes regularly). Very good desserts. Extensive wine list. *Note:* In an elegant Victorian residence that once belonged to a rich 19th-century businessman, this rest. of great quality is a favorite of local society people. Light, inspired Italian cuisine. Very effective decor of woodwork, marble, and crystal. Excellent svce. The only good Italian rest. outside Baltimore's Little Italy. *Italian.* **M–E**

☖☖ **Paolo's** (dwntwn), first level, Light St. Pavilion, Harborplace (539-7060). A/C. Lunch/dinner daily (until 2am), brunch Sat–Sun. AE, CB, DC, MC, V. *Specialties:* woodburning-oven pizza, fried calamari, tortellini, catch of the day. Menu changes seasonally. Skimpy wine list. *Note:* "The" new Italian spot dwntwn. Praiseworthy food at no-frills prices; panoramic view of the Inner Harbor and the most stylish crowd in town. Noisy and usually overcrowded. No resv. taken, unfortunately. *Italian.* **I–M**

☖ **Louie's Bookstore Café** (dwntwn), 518 N. Charles St. (962-1224). A/C. Lunch/dinner (till 2am) daily; closed hols. MC, V. *Specialties:* soft-shelled crabs, crab chowder, crabcakes, broiled catch of the day, good homemade desserts. *Note:* Artsy blend of seafood bistro and bookstore (enter through the bookstore—the rest. is in back), w. chamber music in the background. Excellent, very inexpensive fish and shellfish; agreeably bohemian atmosphere. Locally popular. *Seafood.* **B–I**

☖ **John W. Faidley Seafood** (dwntwn), Lexington Market, 400 W. Lexington St. (727-4898). Mon–Sat (8am–6pm). AE, MC, V. *Specialties:* fresh Maryland oysters and crabs, clams, crab cakes. *Note:* Superb seafood bar in the picturesque enclosed Lexington Market. Baltimore's most authentic bistro, serving seafood that couldn't be fresher. Fabulous crab cakes. Casual atmosphere. No resv. A local favorite for close to a century. *Seafood.* **B–I**

Other Restaurants (from top bracket to budget)

☖☖☖ **Citronelle** (dwntwn), in the Latham Hotel (see "Accommodations," above) (837-3150). A/C. Lunch Mon–Fri, dinner Mon–Sat, brunch Sun. AE, CB, DC, MC, V. Jkt. *Specialties:* Yellowtail carpaccio w. fresh ginger vinaigrette, tuna tournedos w. green peppercorns in soy shallot sauce, shrimp or scallops wrapped in kaitifi (a Greek pastry), grilled swordfish in al dente flageolets, red snapper in saffron sauce, chocolate crème brûlée. *Note:* Chef and restaurateur Michel Richard's cuisine is becoming an institution in fine dining in America. Perched above Baltimore in the airy penthouse dining room of the Latham Hotel, this third incarnation of the California-based rest. chain lives up to the status of its highly accredited name. *French.* **E–VE**

☖☖☖ **Hampton's** (dwntwn), in the Harbor Court Hotel (see "Accommodations," above) (234-0550). A/C. Dinner Tues–Sun, brunch Sun. AE, DC, MC, V. Jkt. *Specialties:* smoked crab cake, creamed crab bisque w. sweet-potato flan, blackened buffalo, macadamia nut tart. Menu changes regularly; large but pricey wine list. *Note:* The scenic view of the Inner Harbor is great (ask for a seat nr. the window), as are the new American cuisine of chef Michael Rork and the Edwardian surroundings. Extremely professional svce. Big business clientele. Resv. a must. *American.* **E–VE**

☖☖☖ **Tio Pepe** (dwntwn), 10 E. Franklin St. (539-4675). A/C. Lunch Mon–Fri, dinner nightly; closed hols. AE, MC, V. J&T. *Specialties:* gazpacho, gambas al ajillo, paella valenciana, roast suckling pig, baked snapper in brown sauce, rack of lamb Segovia style, brazo gitano. Excellent house sangría and a good Spanish wine list. *Note:* One of the most famous rests. of Baltimore. Remarkable variations on Iberian cuisine in a sober but elegant Castilian cave setting. Impeccable svce. Resv. a must, but barely respected. *Spanish.* **M–E**

Sabatino's (nr. dwntwn), 901 Fawn St., Little Italy (727-9414). A/C. Lunch/dinner daily (until 3am); closed Thanksgiving, Dec 25. Jkt. AE, MC, V. *Specialties:* fresh homemade pasta, shrimp napoletana, veal Bryan. *Note:* A favorite of Baltimore's Italian community, serving serious, unpretentious cuisine in generous portions. Diligent svce and a pleasant ambience. Open very late. *Italian.* **I–M**

Olde Obrycki's Crab House (nr. dwntwn), 1729 E. Pratt St. (732-6399). A/C. Lunch Mon–Fri, dinner nightly; closed mid-Dec to Mar. AE, CB, DC, MC, V. *Specialties:* crab soup, fried clams, blue crabs, crab cakes, seafood, fish of the day. *Note:* One of the best spots in Baltimore for sampling the famous Maryland crabs and washing them down with draft beer (the rest. is only open during crab season, Apr to mid-Dec). Charming, Colonial decor and a pleasant, if noisy, ambience. The adj. annex is rather claustrophobic. An excellent spot. Rest. established in 1865. *Seafood.* **I–M**

Thai Landing (nr. dwntwn), 1207 N. Charles St. (727-1234). A/C. Dinner only, Mon–Sat. AE, MC, V. *Specialties:* traditional Thai curry dishes. *Note:* The Thai fare served at this charming newcomer goes from the fiery hot—the spiciest dishes, made w. the hottest chilies should be ordered "w. beer and tissues," warns the menu—to milder poultry, seafood, and vegetarian dishes. Exotic setting and friendly svce. A very good value. *Thai.* **I**

Bertha's (nr. dwntwn), 734 S. Broadway (327-5795). A/C. Lunch/dinner daily (bar open until 2am). AE, CB, DC, MC, V. *Specialties:* mussels marinière, fish of the day, omelets, steaks, daily pasta specials. *Note:* A truer-than-life old English pub in the picturesque Fells Point section. Daily specials are written on a blackboard. Honest, unpretentious cuisine. Diligent svce. English-style tea in the afternoon (resv. necessary). Locally very popular. *Continental/American.* **B–I**

Ikaros (nr. dwntwn), 4805 Eastern Ave. (633-3750). A/C. Lunch/dinner Wed–Mon; closed Thanksgiving, Dec 25. AE, CB, DC, MC, V. *Specialties:* stuffed grape leaves, lemon soup, calamari, moussaka kapama (lamb and tomatoes), spanakotiropita (cheese-and-spinach pie), catch of the day, baklava. *Note:* The oldest and best Greek rest. in the city. The decor is nothing special, but the cuisine is 100% authentic. Locally very popular. Inevitable waits on wknds. Resv. advised. *Greek.* **B–I**

Cafeteria/Fast Food

Woman's Industrial Exchange (dwntwn), 333 N. Charles St. (752-8926). Breakfast/lunch only, Mon–Fri. No credit cards. *Specialties:* crab cakes, chicken croquettes, sandwiches, salads, dishes of the day, homemade pies, floating island. *Note:* A real local institution, nearly a century old. *Cuisine bourgeoise,* not of the lightest, served in 1920s cafeteria-style decor that's nicely old-fashioned. Motherly svce. Locally very popular.

BARS & NIGHTCLUBS

Balls (dwntwn), 200 W. Pratt St. (659-5844). A sports bar on three levels featuring Top 40 tunes. Casual. Overstuffed sandwiches. Open nightly.

The Cat's Eye (nr. dwntwn), Thames St. (276-9085). Popular Irish bar of the Fell's Point district, bedecked w. harpoons and oars. Features traditional Irish music, blues, or rock 'n' roll nightly.

Hammerjacks (nr. dwntwn), 1101 S. Howard St. (659-7625). High-energy rock in a spacious multilevel setting. Young crowd. Open nightly.

Max's (dwntwn), 735 S. Broadway (675-6297). Live rock and reggae bands. Dark, low-ceilinged, and spacious. Mixed crowd. Open nightly.

Wharf Rat Inn (dwntwn), 801 South Ann St. (276-9034). A colorful bar with 27 varieties of beer on draft. Favored by college students. Open Mon–Sat.

NEARBY EXCURSIONS

ELLICOTT CITY (11 mi./18km west on Md. 144): Former iron-working center, founded in 1774 on the banks of the Patapsco River. It was also the temporary terminus of the United States' first railroad, the Baltimore & Ohio (interesting museum in the old station, which dates from 1830). The city has conserved a good number of its early 19th-century stone and log houses on the hills overlooking the river and an interesting Historic District downtown. For further information, call toll free 800/288-8747.

ANNAPOLIS (28 mi./45km south on Md. 2): Charming colonial town more than 300 years old. Capital of Maryland and home of the U.S. Naval Academy (interesting naval museum). Very picturesque port quarter with beautiful old houses. See Chapter 9 on Washington.

CARROLL COUNTY FARM MUSEUM (in Westminster, 28 mi./45km NW on Md. 140) (410/848-7775): Large agricultural estate dating from 1852, transformed into a living museum of the 19th century, with a Victorian-style dwelling house, forge, stables, craft shops, etc. Interesting slice of history. Open Tues–Fri in summer, wknds only spring and autumn; closed the rest of the year.

FARTHER AFIELD

GETTYSBURG (110 mi./180km r.t. on Md. 140N, Md. 97N, and return): The Civil War's bloodiest battlefield. See Chapter 6 on Philadelphia.

PENNSYLVANIA DUTCH COUNTRY (130 mi./210km r.t. on I-83N/S): Here, the 17th century has left a clear imprint in modern America. See Chapter 6 on Philadelphia.

CHESAPEAKE BAY & WYE MILLS (165 mi./264km r.t. on Md. 2S, U.S. 50E, and Md. 33W): See **Wye Mills,** a picturesque little village that has kept its authentic 18th-century look; **Easton,** famous for its antique shops; **St. Michaels,** with its marvelous maritime museum **(Chesapeake Bay Museum);** and the gorgeous **St. Mary's Square,** with its old houses. Return via **Oxford,** capital of pleasure boating and point of origin for the 300-year-old Oxford–Bellevue ferry, oldest in the country. A very pleasant trip. See also Chapter 9 on Washington.

Where to Stay En Route

IN OXFORD   **Robert Morris Inn,** on Md. 333, Oxford, MD 21654 (410/226-5111). 33 rms. Charming little colonial-style inn with a view of the water. Good rest. Open only on Sat and Sun, Jan–Mar. **M–E**

IN EASTON   **Tidewater Inn,** Dover and Harrison Sts., Easton, MD 21601 (410/822-1300). 120 rms. Elegant 200-year-old, historic landmarked building. Rest. renowned for its seafood. **I–M**

ATLANTIC BEACHES (274 mi./438km r.t. on Md. 2S, U.S. 50E, Md. 528N, Del. 1N, U.S. 9S, Del. 18W, Del. 404W, U.S. 50W, and Md. 2N): Lots of beaches and fashionable seaside resorts between **Ocean City** (to the south) and **Rehoboth Beach** (to the north). See Chapter 9 on Washington. On the way, you can see **Annapolis** (see above).

WASHINGTON, D.C. 🏛🏛🏛

□ □ □

The federal capital, that "city of heroes and monuments," the first city ever planned for a specific purpose, was brought into being by George Washington through an act of political will—and through the visionary genius of Maj. Pierre-Charles l'Enfant. This French architect, who served as a volunteer during the War of Independence, drew up an urban plan of majestic simplicity for a concentric city pierced by wide avenues—a plan that imparts to the city its ordered charm, at once graceful and austere. Even so, the capital of the young Republic almost failed to survive its rough handling in 1814 by the British, who sacked it and burned its principal buildings.

Here and there along the great green carpet of the **Mall** stand some of the most historic (and most visited) landmarks in the country. America's most famous address is 1600 Pennsylvania Avenue, better known as **The White House,** official residence of America's presidents since John Adams in 1800. Not far away, on a little hill, the imposing **Capitol** with its majestic dome, modeled on that of St. Peter's in Rome, dominates the city's skyline, as the architectural embodiment of American democracy properly should. A mile and a half to the west, interrupting the otherwise unbroken prospect down the Mall and across the **Potomac River** to **Arlington Cemetery,** the giant obelisk of the **Washington Monument** leaps skyward to honor the Father of his Country.

City of government offices and museums, embassies, gardens, and statues. City of officials, reporters, and diplomats (some 20,000 in all, from heads of mission to clerical staff). City of monuments ranging from the extraordinary (the **Lincoln Memorial,** the **Jefferson Memorial,** the **National Gallery of Art East Wing**) to the downright disgraceful (the **Pentagon,** the **J. Edgar Hoover Building**). City of Learning, with its five universities and 20 colleges—and strategic heart of the formidable power of the U.S.A. Washington is all these things and more, an elegant, cosmopolitan city like none other in the world.

Nevertheless, unlike their fellow Americans, the inhabitants of Washington are not fully enfranchised. The Founding Fathers, apparently concerned that the local population might loom too large in the eyes of the legislature, constitutionally denied it the right to vote. In 1961 the Congress finally acknowledged the anachronism and gave Washingtonians a vote in presidential elections. Since 1975 they have also been allowed to elect their own mayor—but they still have no vote in Congress.

Sadly, this great city has one of the highest unemployment rates in the country. Side by side with the army of white-collar workers who cluster around the centers of power is an economically distressed population with a high incidence of drug addiction. As a direct consequence of this, FBI statistics credit the nation's capital with a crime rate three times the national average—something of a paradox for a city that's the seat of the Supreme Court, and thus of the Law.

But even so, Washington—with its classical revival buildings, its cluster of museums (including the renowned **Smithsonian Institution** and the **National**

Gallery of Art) unmatched anywhere in the world, its wide tree-lined avenues, its reflecting pools fringed with Japanese cherries (try to be there when they're in flower, in late May or early Apr), and its appealing and historic **Georgetown** district—lacks nothing that the visitor could ask for. Some 20 million pilgrim-tourists, including a million foreigners, visit the capital every year, making travel and tourism the second-largest industry in the city. (However, people are still hesitant to visit the nation's capital because of its image of violence.)

Long considered a cultural desert, with the construction in 1971 of the **John F. Kennedy Center,** Washington acquired a world-class artistic and theatrical complex. Nevertheless, it remains after dark one of the dullest, starchiest places in the country. The only interest offered by Washington's nightlife is the extraordinary profusion of restaurants—French, Caribbean, Ethiopian, Créole, Thai, Arabic, Japanese, Spanish, Italian, Chinese, East European, Vietnamese, Latin American, you name it—which have made the city a sort of gastronomic Tower of Babel.

Washington's famous children include Duke Ellington and his son, Mercer Ellington; the late FBI director J. Edgar Hoover; the late Secretary of State John Foster Dulles; playwright Edward Albee; author Frank Slaughter; comedian and actress Goldie Hawn; actor William Hurt; and singer-dancer Chita Rivera.

A Note on Orientation: The spider-web layout of Washington is divided into four geographic quadrants with the Capitol as their center: Northwest (NW), Northeast (NE), Southwest (SW), and Southeast (SE). Streets running north and south are designated by numbers; those running east and west, by letters of the alphabet. The grid system of numbered and lettered streets is slashed diagonally by wide avenues bearing the names of states of the Union: Massachusetts, Wisconsin, Pennsylvania, Connecticut, etc.

A Note on Telephone Area Codes: Unless otherwise indicated, all phone numbers in this chapter are in area code 202.

BASIC FACTS: District of Columbia. Area codes: 202 (District of Columbia), 301 (Maryland), 703 (Virginia). Time zone: eastern. ZIP Code (of the central post office): 20013. Founded: 1790. Approximate population: city 598,000; metropolitan area, 3,930,000. Eighth-largest metropolitan area in the country.

CLIMATE: The last word you'd think of to describe the Washington climate is "agreeable." It's a hot, sticky steambath in summer (July average temperature, 79°F/26°C), cold and very humid in winter with snowfalls and icy roads (Jan average, 37°F/3°C). That leaves spring and fall, usually sunny and pleasant (especially May and Oct), as the best times of year to visit Washington.

DISTANCES: Atlanta, 608 mi. (975km); Baltimore, 40 mi. (65km); Chicago, 668 mi. (1,070km); New York, 234 mi. (375km); Niagara Falls, 425 mi. (680km); Philadelphia, 134 mi. (215km); Pittsburgh, 247 mi. (395km); Savannah, 633 mi. (1,012km).

ARRIVAL & TRANSIT INFORMATION

AIRPORTS: The **Baltimore-Washington International Airport** (BWI), 32 mi. (51km) NE, for medium- and long-haul flights. Hard to reach from dwntwn Washington; for information, call 410/859-7100.

Dulles International Airport (IAD), 26 mi. (42km) west, for medium- and long-haul flights; for information, call 703/661-2700.

Washington National Airport (DCA), 4 mi. (7km) south, for medium-haul flights; for information, call 703/685-8000.

U.S. AIRLINES: American (toll free 800/433-7300), Continental (toll free 800/525-0280), Delta (toll free 800/221-1212), Northwest (toll free 800/

225-2525), United (toll free 800/241-6522), USAir (toll free 800/428-4322) and USAir Shuttle (toll free 800/428-4322).

FOREIGN CARRIERS: Aeroflot (202/429-4922), Air France (toll free 800/237-2747), All Nippon Airways (toll free 800/235-9262), British Airways (toll free 800/247-9297), Japan Airlines (toll free 800/525-3663), Lufthansa (toll free 800/645-3880).

CITY LINK: The **cab** fare from Baltimore-Washington Airport to dwntwn is about $40–$45; time, 55 min. Cab fare from Dulles International to dwntwn, about $35–$40; time, 45 min. (60 min. or more during rush hours). Cab fare from National Airport to dwntwn, about $12–$14; time, 15–20 min.

   Bus: The **Washington Flyer** (703/685-1400); serves the Air Terminal at 1517 K St. NW and the major dwntwn hotels; leaves National Airport every 30 min. Mon–Fri, every 60 min. Sat–Sun (fare, $8; time, 25 min.); leaves Dulles International every 30 min. (fare, $16; time, 45–60 min.). The Washington Flyer also connects National Airport and Dulles International, leaving every 60 min Mon–Fri, every 120 min. Sat–Sun; fare, $16; time, 45 min. **Airport Shuttle** (410/859-7545) connects Baltimore-Washington Airport and the Air Terminal at 1517 K St. NW, leaving every 90 min.; fare, $14; time, about 60 min.

   A **subway** (Metrorail Blue and Yellow Lines) connects National Airport to dwntwn Washington; fare, $1.05 or more, depending on destination; time, 18 min.

   Public transportation by bus and subway (ultramodern and comfortable) covers the city effectively, but is complicated for visitors; for information on **Metrobus and Metrorail,** call 202/637-7000. With 11,000 cabs on the street there is no shortage, but not all of them are trustworthy.

   The city is not so large that you'll need to rent a car, unless you plan to drive out into the country or along the eastern seaboard; rental rates with unlimited mileage are noticeably lower than in New York.

CAR RENTAL (all at both Dulles and National airports): Avis (toll free 800/331-1212); Budget (toll free 800/527-0700); Dollar (toll free 800/800-4000); Hertz (toll free 800/654-3131); National (toll free 800/227-7368); and Thrifty (toll free 800/367-2277).

   For dwntwn locations, consult the local telephone book.

LIMOUSINE SERVICES: Capital City Limousine (202/396-1500), Carey Limousine (703/892-2000), Dial-A-Limousine (301/983-9557), Evans Limousine (301/350-1722).

TAXIS: Washington cabs are not metered; they charge according to the number of "zones" they must pass through between starting point and destination (there should be a legible city map, with the zones marked, in the passenger compartment). Fares tend to be lower than in many U.S. cities. Drivers can pick up additional passengers as long as they're going the same way; each passenger or party may be charged a separate fare. Many of the drivers are recent immigrants, only superficially acquainted with the English language (and the city).

   Cabs may be hailed on the street, taken from the waiting lines outside major hotels, or called by phone. The principal companies are (all area code 202): **Capitol Cab** (546-2400), **Diamond Cab** (387-6200), **Liberty Cab** (636-1616), **Red Top Cab** (328-3333), and **Yellow Cab** (544-1212).

TRAIN: The Amtrak terminal is at Union Station, 50 Massachusetts Ave. NE (toll free 800/872-7245); the city ticket office, 1721 K St. NW (202/484-7540). For reservations and information for the Metroliner, call toll free 800/523-8720.

INTERCITY BUSES: Greyhound, 1005 1st St. at L St. NE (202/289-5155).

INFORMATION & TOURS

TOURIST INFORMATION: The **Washington Convention and Visitors Association,** 1212 New York Ave. NW, DC 20005 (202/789-7000).
   International Visitors Information Service, 1630 Crescent St. NW, DC 20009 (202/939-5538): Orientation for visitors from abroad.
   Visitor Information Center, 1455 Pennsylvania Ave. NW (202/789-7038). Open 9am–5pm Mon–Sat.
   A **recorded message** giving a list of current shows and cultural events may be reached at 202/737-8866.

GUIDED TOURS: **Charley Horse** (carriage) (202/488-1155): Horse-and-carriage tours of the Mall and surroundings. Leave from the Museum of Natural History. Daily, weather permitting.
   The Georgetown (boat), Lock 3, Georgetown Canal between 30th and Thomas Jefferson Sts. NW (202/653-5844): Trips in a mule-drawn barge along the C.&O. Canal, Wed–Sun mid-Apr through Sept. A picturesque rustic treat that lasts 90 min.
   Gray Line Tours (bus) (202/289-1995): Guided tours of the city and surroundings; departs from its terminal in Union Station.
   Old Town Trolley Tours (bus): Two-hour shuttle tour across the city in a replica of a turn-of-the-century streetcar. A ticket gives unlimited boarding rights. The best sightseeing tours in town. Daily year round, serving major hotels. Fare: $16. For information, call 301/985-3020.
   Spirit Cruises (boat), 6th and Water Sts. SW (202/554-8000): Mini-cruises along the Potomac as far as Mount Vernon; daily Apr–Oct.
   Tourmobile Sightseeing (bus): A very practical shuttle system that allows you to visit Washington's principal monuments, with a couple of dozen stops along the route. Get off and on again as often as you like. Runs daily year round. Fare is $9, payable on the bus. Also serves Arlington National Cemetery and Mount Vernon. For information, call 202/554-5100.
   The Washington Post, 1150 15th St. NW (202/334-7969): Guided tour around one of the largest daily papers in the country—the paper that blew the whistle on Watergate. Fascinating. By appointment only, Mon. Children must be at least age 11.

SIGHTS, ATTRACTIONS & ACTIVITIES

ADVENTURE TOURS: **Adventures Aloft** (balloon), 1938 Lewis Ave., Rockville, Md. (301/881-6262): Balloon rides over the Washington countryside from any of several different launch sites in Maryland or Virginia. Spectacular. Year round.
   Balloons Unlimited (balloon): 2946 Chainbridge Rd., Oakton, Va. (703/281-2300): Balloon rides over the Washington countryside from any of several different launch sites in Virginia. Fare: $150 per person. Spectacular. Year round.

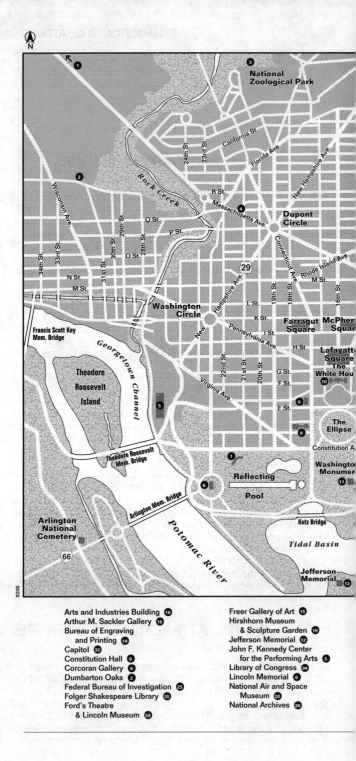

Arts and Industries Building 18
Arthur M. Sackler Gallery 16
Bureau of Engraving
    and Printing 14
Capitol 32
Constitution Hall 0
Corcoran Gallery 9
Dumbarton Oaks 2
Federal Bureau of Investigation 25
Folger Shakespeare Library 35
Ford's Theatre
    & Lincoln Museum 24

Freer Gallery of Art 15
Hirshhorn Museum
    & Sculpture Garden 19
Jefferson Memorial 12
John F. Kennedy Center
    for the Performing Arts 5
Library of Congress 34
Lincoln Memorial 6
National Air and Space
    Museum 20
National Archives 26

WASHINGTON, D.C.

National Gallery of Art ㉓
National Museum
  of African Art ⑰
National Museum
  of American Art ㉗
National Museum
  of American History ㉑
National Museum
  of Natural History ㉒
National Portrait Gallery ㉘
National Postal Museum ㉖

National Zoological Park ③
Phillips Collection ④
Supreme Court ㉝
Union Station ㉚
U.S. Botanic Garden ㉛
U.S. Holocaust Memorial
  Museum ⑬
Vietnam Veterans Memorial ⑦
Washington National Cathedral ①
Washington Monument ⑪
White House ⑩

Blue Ridge Outfitters (boat), W.Va. 340, Harpers Ferry, W. Va. (304/725-3444): White-water raft trips down the rapids of the Shenandoah River or the gorges of the Potomac. Daily Apr–Oct. Canoe rentals.

ARCHITECTURAL HIGHLIGHTS: ※🛍 Bureau of Engraving and Printing,
14th and C Sts. SW (622-2000): Tens of billions of dollars in banknotes, Treasury notes, and stamps are printed here every year. From glassed-in galleries you can watch banknotes being printed and packaged (about $50 million are produced daily). Coins are struck at Philadelphia, Denver, and San Francisco. Not surprisingly, very strict security is imposed here; photography is forbidden. Open Mon–Fri. An encouragement to daydreams.

🛍 **FBI Headquarters–J. Edgar Hoover Building,** E St. between 9th and 10th Sts. NW (324-3447): Headquarters of the war on crime—and one of the ugliest buildings in Washington. Conducted tours Mon–Fri. Marksmanship demonstrations by G-men. Memorabilia of crime in the 1920s and '30s, and an armory with 5,000 weapons on display. For lovers of detective fiction.

※🛍 **John F. Kennedy Center for the Performing Arts,** New Hampshire Ave. and F St. NW (467-4600): Huge cultural complex on the banks of the Potomac, opened in 1971; opera house, theater, cinema, concert hall, and art gallery. The very successful modern design is the work of architect Edward Durrell Stone. The heart of Washington's cultural (and social) life, drawing four million visitors a year. Open daily. Call 416-8341 for tour information.

※🛍 **Old Executive Office Building,** Pennsylvania Ave. and 17th St. NW (395-5895): Adjoining the White House, this interesting example of French classical revival architecture dating from 1871–88 originally housed the Departments of State, the Navy, and War. It now accommodates the vice-president of the U.S. and members of the White House staff. Open Sat by appointment.

※🛍 **Old Post Office,** 1100 Pennsylvania Ave. NW (289-4224): Imposing Victorian building designed by Daniel Burnham and dating from 1899, surmounted by a Big Ben–style tower 315 ft. (96m) high with an observation deck. Once the central post office, it now houses government offices as well as many boutiques and restaurants under an enormous glass roof, The Pavilion. An appealing place. Open daily.

🛍 **Panamerican Union Building,** 17th St. and Constitution Ave. NW (458-3000): A strange compromise between Spanish Colonial and French Renaissance idioms, this graceful 1910 building, designed by Paul Cret and Albert Kelsey, is the headquarters of the Organization of American States (OAS). Lovely interior courtyard; Aztec garden; interesting museum of modern Latin American art adjoining. Open Mon–Fri.

※🛍 **Pentagon Building,** bounded by Jefferson Davis Hwy., Washington Blvd., and Shirley Hwy., Arlington, Va. (703/695-1776): The heart and head of U.S. defense, with five floors on a groundplan of 32 acres (13ha), 17.5 mi. (28km) of corridors, 32,000 employees, and a parking lot for 10,000 cars. Constructed in 1941–43, it's still the biggest office building in the world. Imposing, but without architectural distinction. Guided tours Mon–Fri. Best ways to get there: Bus 16 from dwntwn Washington or the Blue or Yellow subway line.

※🛍 **Supreme Court Building,** Maryland Ave. and 1st St. NE (479-3499): Cass Gilbert's fine exercise in the classical revival style dates from 1935. The white Vermont marble and Corinthian columns are reminiscent of the days of ancient Greece. Majestic interior decoration. When the Court is in session the public is admitted to hearing cases (Mon–Wed Oct–Apr). Guided tours Mon–Fri when the court is not in session.

※🛍 **Union Station,** 40 Massachusetts Ave. NE (298-1908): In sheer size, this marble-and-granite 1907 railroad station is the largest in the country; its majestic design was inspired by the Baths of Diocletian in Rome. Reopened in the fall of 1988 after decades of neglect and decay. Daniel H. Burnham's building, splendidly restored at a cost of $140 million, now houses around 100 boutiques, stores, restaurants, and movie houses on three levels, as well as the station itself. Lively, colorful atmosphere, particularly at lunchtime.

🏛 **Voice of America,** 330 Independence Ave. SW (619-3919): Transmits around the clock to five continents in 42 languages. Guided tours Mon–Fri (resv. advised). For radio hams.

☼🏛 **Watergate Complex,** New Hampshire and Virginia Aves. NW: Luxury complex beside the Potomac; scene of the political scandal that cost Richard M. Nixon the presidency in 1974. Smart shops, restaurants, luxury hotel. The elegant architecture is worth a look.

CHURCHES/SYNAGOGUES: 🏛 Franciscan Monastery, 1400 Quincy St.

NE (526-6800): This Romanesque monastery with its graceful cloister, standing in its own beautiful garden, houses the curious "Holy Land of America"—a faithful facsimile of some of the most sacred places in the Holy Land such as the crib at Bethlehem, the Garden of Gethsemane, and so on, as well as of the Roman catacombs and the grotto at Lourdes. Tours conducted daily by the friars.

🏛 **Islamic Center,** 2251 Massachusetts Ave. NW (332-8343): America's largest mosque, and largest Islamic cultural center, built with funds contributed by all the Muslim countries that have diplomatic relations with the U.S. The center, an elegant building with fine surface carving and a 160-ft. (48m) minaret, oriented toward Mecca, is open to visitors every day except during the Fri prayers.

☼🏛 **National Shrine of the Immaculate Conception,** 620 Michigan Ave. NE (526-8300): The largest Roman Catholic church in the U.S., on the campus of Catholic University; its Romanesque-Byzantine nave is 459 ft. (140m) long and surmounted by a 331-ft. (101m) bell tower. The huge dome is blue, with touches of gold. Organ and carillon concerts on Sun. Open daily.

☼🏛 **St. John's Episcopal Church,** 16th and H Sts. NW (347-8766): On Lafayette Sq. across from the White House, St. John's Episcopal Church was built in 1816 to the design of Benjamin H. Latrobe, the city's first public architect. It has become known as "the Church of the Presidents," because more than a dozen have worshipped there, beginning with James Madison in the year after the church was built. Since then, Pew 54 has traditionally been reserved for the president of the U.S. Open daily.

🏛 **St. Matthew's Cathedral,** 1725 Rhode Island Ave. NW (347-3215): Familiar to many Americans as the scene of funeral services for Pres. John F. Kennedy on November 25, 1963. The cathedral is located a few blocks from the White House.

☼🏛 **Scottish Rite Supreme Council,** 1733 16th St. NW (232-3579): Dating from 1915, this former Masonic temple designed by J. Russell Pope is modeled on the famous tomb of King Mausolus of Halicarnassus, one of the seven wonders of antiquity. Its interior, embellished with purple ceilings, polished black marble columns and doors, and light fixtures in bronze, is sumptuous. Open daily by appointment.

☼🏛🏛 **Washington National Cathedral,** Wisconsin and Massachusetts Aves. NW (537-6200): Very fine cathedral in the Gothic Revival style, Episcopalian but open to all denominations; one of the largest in the country. The interior, particularly the stained glass, is sumptuous. Designed by British architect George Bodley, the cathedral was finally completed in Sept 1990, 83 years from the day when Pres. Theodore Roosevelt presided at the laying of the cornerstone. It stands atop Mount St. Alban, the capital's highest hill

(419 ft./128m). Within is the tomb of Pres. Woodrow Wilson. Library of rare books. Tours daily.

⚖ **Washington Temple,** 9900 Stoneybrook Dr., Kensington, Md., at Beltway Exit 33 (301/587-0144): One of 40 Mormon temples around the world built on the model of the temple at Salt Lake City, to an unusual design executed in 1976. Non-Mormons may not enter the temple, but the Visitor Center is open daily. Particularly impressive when floodlit after dark.

HISTORIC BUILDINGS: ☀⚖ **Blair House,** 1651-1653 Pennsylvania Ave. NW: Blair House and the adjoining **Blair-Lee House,** opposite the White House, have since 1942 served as the official residence of foreign heads of state when visiting the U.S. The two buildings, which have been extensively restored, are not open to the public. The 1824 Blair House has played an important part in American history. It was here, on April 18, 1861, that President Lincoln offered the command of the Union army to Gen. Robert E. Lee; Lee refused, and later became commander-in-chief of the Confederacy. President Truman lived at Blair House from 1948 to 1952 while the White House was being restored.

☀⚖ **The Capitol,** 1st St. between Constitution and Independence Aves. (224-3121): This imposing structure, home of the 435-member House of Representatives and the 100-member Senate, is capped by a dome 258 ft. (79m) high designed by Charles Bulfinch after the dome of St. Peter's in Rome. A 19-ft. (6m) bronze statue of *Liberty,* by Thomas Crawford, crowns the whole. Originally erected in 1793-1812, burned by the British in 1814, and built anew in 1816-29, the building has been enlarged several times, most recently in 1962. Very rich interior decoration with colossal statues and wall paintings, especially in the main **Rotunda,** from which 40-min. conducted tours leave, allowing access to the Visitors' Galleries of the House and the Senate. The **Senate Dining Room,** renowned for its bean soup, is also open to the public. See also, beneath the Rotunda, the crypt originally intended for the tomb of George Washington; here is the catafalque used for the funerary vigil of Abraham Lincoln, and of the unknown soldiers of World War II and the Korean War. From the west front you have a fine view along the Mall to the Washington Monument and the Lincoln Memorial in the distance. Don't miss the Capitol; it's worth the trip to Washington all by itself. Guided tours daily, every 15 min.; call 225-6827 for information.

⚖ **Christian Heurich Mansion,** 1307 New Hampshire Ave. NW (785-2068): Home of the Columbia Historical Society, this luxurious 1892 private house, built of brown sandstone in the Renaissance Revival style, boasts no fewer than 43 rooms. Very fine Victorian furniture; library devoted to the history of the capital. Open Wed-Sat.

☀⚖ **Decatur House,** 748 Jackson Place NW (842-0920): This red-brick town house a stone's throw from the White House, and rich in historical associations, was built in 1818 by Benjamin H. Latrobe for Commodore Stephen Decatur, hero of the war against the Barbary pirates. It has been home to a succession of distinguished men, including one future president (Martin Van Buren), three secretaries of state, and several other prominent politicians. For almost a century and a half it was a center of Washington social life. Splendid period furniture and decoration. Open Tues-Sun.

☀⚖ **Dumbarton Oaks,** 1703 32nd St. NW (338-8278): Elegant small early 19th-century manor house in the heart of historic Georgetown. Since 1940 the house and its lovely landscaped gardens have belonged to Harvard University. It has important collections of Byzantine and pre-Columbian art, and a library of 80,000 books on art. The new wing of the museum was designed in 1963 by Philip Johnson. In 1944 a conference of the four Great Powers (the U.S., Great Britain, China, and the Soviet Union) on international security was held here; this conference worked out the framework for the U.N. Open Tues-Sun. The gardens are open daily.

Ford's Theater, 511 10th St. NW (426-6924): Here Abraham Lincoln was assassinated, on April 14, 1865, by John Wilkes Booth during the performance of a play. The oldest theater in Washington still in use. There is a small Lincoln museum in the basement. Open daily.

Georgetown University, 37th and O Sts. NW (687-5055): Founded in 1789 and still run by the Society of Jesus (the Jesuit order), this is the oldest Roman Catholic university in the U.S.; it has 12,000 students. On a bluff overlooking the Potomac, the campus has a number of interesting buildings in the Gothic style, including the Healy Building, which houses the administrative offices and Information Center. Open daily.

Library of Congress, 10 1st St. SE (707-5458): The world's largest library, in an impressive Italian Renaissance granite building modeled on the Opéra in Paris. The interior is sumptuously decorated. The catalog lists 85 million books and other items in 470 languages, from a Gutenberg Bible to the original draft of the Declaration of Independence, not to mention Pierre-Charles l'Enfant's preliminary plan of Washington. Built around the 6,847 volumes from Thomas Jefferson's personal collection, which he sold to Congress for $23,950 after the original Library had been burned by the British in 1814, the Library of Congress today possesses more than 20 million books; it is a depositary library, and since 1870 has received two free copies of every book published in the United States. Don't fail to see the Library, and particularly the marble staircase of the Grand Hall and the dome of the main Reading Room. Open Mon–Fri. Call 702-8000 for information on tours and exhibits.

Octagon House, 1799 New York Ave. at 18th St. NW (638-3105): Unusual octagonal structure dating from 1798, which served as a temporary home for President Madison after the British burned the White House in 1814; now the headquarters of the American Institute of Architects. Temporary exhibitions; interesting period furniture. Open Tues–Sun.

Old Stone House, 3051 M St. NW (426-6851): Believed to be the oldest surviving building in Washington from the pre-Revolutionary period (about 1765). The charming little two-story house with massive stone walls located in the heart of Georgetown was both a private home and a place of business. Magnificently restored in the original manner and decor of the 18th century. Open Wed–Sun.

Petersen House, 516 10th St. NW (426-6830): The house where President Lincoln was taken after Booth's fatal shot at Ford's Theater across the street (see above); he died here the next morning, April 15, 1865, at 7:22am. Memorabilia of the affair that horrified America. Open daily.

Tudor Place, 1644 31st St. NW (965-0400): Opulent 1810 mansion in the heart of charming old Georgetown; the Greek Revival building designed by William Thornton is one of the finest in Washington. Built for Martha Parke Custis Peter, granddaughter-in-law of George Washington, Tudor Place remained in the hands of the Peter family for eight generations, until 1983. Splendid period furniture and decor. May be seen Tues –Sat.

The White House, 1600 Pennsylvania Ave. NE (456-7041): The most famous building in the U.S., home to every American president since John Adams in 1800. Designed by architect James Hoban following the style of the Irish mansion of the Duke of Leinster, the White House owes its name to the whitewash with which its blackened frontage was hastily covered after the British burned it in 1814. Rebuilt in 1817, the original structure has been often enlarged and altered, particularly by the 1824 addition of a graceful elliptical portico along the side of the house facing the Mall. More than a million and a half visitors pass through the White House each year; tickets are free, and may be obtained from the kiosk in the Ellipse in front of the south front, but only five reception rooms, of the total of 32 rooms in the Executive Mansion, are open to the public; there is no admission either to the president's private quarters on the second floor, or to his office and the offices of his staff in the West Wing. On a busy day, particularly in summer, you may have to wait as long as two hours for your guided tour, but they are given from 10am until noon Tues–Sat; closed Jan 1 and Dec 25. Visitors' entrance is the east gate on E. Executive Ave. If you write far ahead to your senator or congress person, you may be able to obtain a ticket for a "personalized" VIP visit to the White House, which will allow you to avoid the long waiting lines in summer; specify a choice of dates. Requests, in writing, should be addressed to a senator at the United States Senate, Washington, DC 20510, or a congressperson at the United States House of Representatives, Washington, DC 20515.

※※△ **Woodrow Wilson House,** 2340 S St. NW (387-4062): Home of former President Wilson from the end of his second term until his death in 1924, then of his widow until she died in 1961, this elegant red-brick Georgian-style town house is now a museum. Many personal memorabilia of the 28th president and its original furnishings; reconstructs the atmosphere and the way of life of the upper middle class in the 20s. Open Tues–Sun; closed hols.

MARKETS: ※△ **Eastern Market,** 7th St. and North Carolina Ave. SE: The last of the many European-style covered markets once to be found in Washington, dating from 1873. Dozens of open stalls selling meat, poultry, vegetables, fish, cheese, etc. Lively and colorful; open Tues–Sat. Worth a look, especially Sat morning when strolling musicians add to the local color. You can have breakfast or lunch at the △ **Market Lunch,** open 7:30am–2:30pm Tues–Sat; it's at 225 7th St. at C St. SE (547-8444).

MONUMENTS: ※△△ **Arlington National Cemetery,** opposite Memorial Bridge, Arlington, VA (703/692-0931): Overlooking the Potomac, this largest and most famous of America's national cemeteries shelters 213,000 of the dead, both illustrious like Presidents William Howard Taft and John F. Kennedy (before whose tomb burns an eternal flame), Adm. Richard Byrd, Sen. Robert F. Kennedy, Gen. George Marshall, and Pierre-Charles l'Enfant, or nameless, like the Unknown Soldier, whose tomb commemorates the dead of the two World Wars and the Korean and Vietnam Wars. A guard of honor of the Third Infantry ("The Old Guard") watches over the tomb 24 hr. a day; the changing of the guard, every 30 min. Apr–Sept, every hour Oct–Mar, year round, is a spectacular sight. Lovely countryside, and a unique view of Washington from **Arlington House** (see "Panoramas," below). Every year more than four million people visit Arlington; bus trips daily, though the vehicles are not allowed to enter the cemetery itself.

※△△ **Jefferson Memorial,** Tidal Basin, Potomac Park SW (426-6841): A graceful circular building by John Russell Pope (1943) in white marble, surrounded by an Ionic colonnade reminiscent of the Pantheon in Rome. Commemorates the author of the Declaration of Independence and third president of the U.S. A masterpiece of classical architecture which you have to see (try to be there in early Apr when the Japanese cherry trees are in bloom). Remains open daily while undergoing repairs.

※△△ **Lincoln Memorial,** 23rd St. south of Constitution Ave. NW (426-6841): Washington's finest monument, the work of Henry Bacon (1922). Majestic white marble building inspired by the Parthenon in Athens, and setting off the Capitol at the other end of the Mall. A colossal statue of Lincoln by Daniel Chester French looks down on the visiting throngs. The memorial's 36 Doric columns correspond to the states of the Union at the time of Lincoln's death. Engraved on the walls of the two side rooms are the salient sentences from his second Inaugural Address and his famous Gettysburg Address of 1863. Particularly impressive at sunset and when floodlit after dark. Remains open daily while undergoing repairs.

☼☒ **Theodore Roosevelt Memorial,** north end of Theodore Roosevelt Island, reached by footbridge from George Washington Memorial Pkwy. (703/285-2598): Erected in 1965 in memory of the 26th president of the U.S., this austere monument in its wooded setting is an allusion to Theodore Roosevelt's interest in nature conservation; the island is itself a wildlife reserve. Open daily.

☼☒ **U.S. Marine Corps War Memorial,** Rte. 50, Arlington, Va. (703/433-4173): Impressive group in bronze, 64 ft. (23m) high, by Felix de Weldon. Inspired by Joe Rosenthal's photograph of marines raising Old Glory on the island of Iwo Jima in 1945. Fine view over Washington. Military parades on Tues at 7pm June–Aug.

☼☒ **Vietnam Veterans Memorial,** Constitution Ave. at 21st St. NW (634-1568): A 492-ft.-long (150m) monument of polished black granite in the shape of a large letter "V," bearing the names of some 58,000 GIs reported dead or missing during the Vietnam War. The design, by Maya Ying Lin, then a 21-year-old architecture student at Yale, is both tragic and moving in its simplicity. At the same location don't miss the **Vietnam Women's Memorial.** Unveiled in 1993, this 2,000-pound (900kg) bronze statue of three women aiding a wounded man commemorates the nurses who served in the war.

☼☒☒ **Washington Monument,** the Mall near 15th St. NW (426-6841): A majestic 555-ft (169m) obelisk in white Maryland marble designed by architect Robert Mills in 1885, in memory of the first president (see "Panoramas," below).

MUSEUMS OF ART:
☼☒ **Corcoran Gallery of Art,** 17th St. and New York Ave. NW (638-3211): The most important collection of American art after New York's Metropolitan Museum, with works by many artists including Mary Cassatt, Childe Hassam, John Singleton Copley, and Rembrandt Peale; also paintings by such European masters as Rembrandt, Corot, Daumier, and Degas from the Clark Collection. Highly regarded school of fine arts. Very popular temporary exhibitions. Open Wed–Mon.

☒ **Fondo del Sol Art Center,** 2112 R St. NW (483-2777): Unusual museum conceived as a way of presenting and promoting the work of contemporary Caribbean and Latin American artists and artisans. Also has a fine collection of pre-Columbian art and *santos* (religious statues carved in wood). Interesting temporary exhibitions. Open Wed–Sat.

☼☒ **Museum of Modern Art of Latin America,** 201 18th St. at Constitution Ave. NW (458-6016): Part of the Panamerican Union Building (see "Architectural Highlights," above), this enchanting little museum displays a remarkable range of works by contemporary Caribbean and Latin American painters and sculptors; the exhibits are changed every six months. Lovely Aztec garden with giant statue of the god Xochipilli, the "Flower Prince." Open Tues–Sat.

☼☒☒☒ **National Gallery of Art,** Constitution Ave. between 3rd and 7th Sts. NW (737-4215): The cultural jewel of Washington, in a handsome 1941 classical revival setting by John Russell Pope. Along with New York's Metropolitan, this is one of the outstanding museums in the country, and the world. Fabulous collection of paintings from Leonardo da Vinci (his only canvas in the U.S.) to Kandinsky, from Botticelli to Salvador Dalí. The new (east) wing of the museum, designed by I. M. Pei and linked to the main building by an underground passage, is a masterpiece of modern architecture (1978) and houses contemporary works of art by Robert Motherwell, Picasso, Henry Moore, Alexander Calder, and others. Among the gallery's most famous works are Fra Angelico's *Adoration of the Magi,* Titian's *Portrait of Doge Andrea Gritti,* El Greco's *St. Martin and the Beggar,* Rogier van der Weyden's *Portrait of a Woman,* Vermeer's *Woman Weighing Pearls,* a *Self-Portrait* by Rembrandt, *Family of Acrobats* by Picasso, and *Box in a Bag* by Marcel Duchamp. The eight million visitors who come here every year are the largest number for any art gallery in the world; allow at least one full day. Top-class temporary exhibitions (O'Keeffe, Gauguin, etc.). Excellent cafeteria. The National Gallery justifies a trip to Washington all by itself.

    🏛 **National Museum of Women in the Arts,** 1250 New York Ave. NW (783-5000): Founded as recently as 1987, this museum is entirely devoted to women artists. There are some 500 paintings, sculptures, and ceramics, from the Renaissance (Lavinia Fontana) through the impressionists (Mary Cassatt) to the moderns (Georgia O'Keeffe, Helen Frankenthaler, and so on). The impressive Renaissance Revival building dates from 1908 and was originally intended as a Masonic temple with a superb Grand Hall. Open daily.

    ☀🏛 **Phillips Collection,** 1600 21st St. NW (387-2151): The country's oldest (1921) museum of modern art, with very fine European impressionists (Monet, Renoir, Cézanne, van Gogh) and American abstractionists (Mark Rothko, Hans Hofmann, Jackson Pollock) in the Phillips family's elegant mansion. A new $8-million annex was opened to the public in 1989. Open daily.

The Smithsonian Institution

The world's largest complex of museums and research centers for the arts, science, and history. Created in 1846, the foundation has 5,000 members and its 14 establishments are visited by 25 million people annually. They include:

    🏛 **Freer Gallery,** 12th St. and Jefferson Dr. SW (357-2104): Wonderful collection of Far Eastern art (Chinese bronzes, Hindu sculptures, Japanese screens), and some important American paintings by James McNeill Whistler, John Singer Sargent, Winslow Homer, and others, in an elegant "palazzo" in the Florentine tradition. Whistler's *Peacock Room* is worth a visit all to itself. Open daily.

    ☀🏛🏛 **Hirshhorn Museum,** Independence Ave. and 8th St. SW (357-3235): Wonderful modern sculptures and paintings, from Rodin and Miró to Dalí and Henry Moore, in a futurist circular museum designed by Gordon Bunshaft in 1974 and irreverently nicknamed "the doughnut." More than 4,000 paintings and 2,000 sculptures collected over a half century by Joseph H. Hirshhorn, a financier of Latvian origin, and donated by him to the Smithsonian in 1966. Among the most famous works on exhibition: Rodin's *Burghers of Calais,* Snelson's *Needle Tower,* Oldenburg's *Geometric Mouse,* Henry Moore's *Seated Woman,* Brancusi's *Sleeping Muse,* Jackson Pollock's *Aquatic Silhouette,* and *Heads of Jeanette* by Matisse. Open daily.

    ☀🏛🏛 **National Museum of African Art,** 950 Independence Ave. SW (357-4860): This wonderful underground museum designed by Junzo Yoshimura, along with the adjoining Sackler Gallery (see below), cost $73 million and opened in 1987. It houses the nation's largest collection of African art comprising some 6,000 objects in all, from Angolan ceremonial masks by way of Benin metal sculptures and wood figures from Zaire to copper vessels from the Lower Niger. Unusual and fascinating. Open daily.

    ☀🏛 **National Museum of American Art,** 8th and G Sts. NW (357-3111): Paintings, sculptures, and graphics by American artists from Colonial times to the present day, including works by Sargent, Homer, Wyeth, Prendergast, Whistler, and George Catlin, the greatest painter of Native Americans. In the south wing of the building is the 🏛 **National Portrait Gallery,** 8th and F Sts. NW (357-1300), with busts and portraits of famous figures in American history, including Gilbert Stuart's well-known *George Washington* and a portrait of Mary Cassatt by Degas. Open daily.

    🏛 **National Postal Museum,** Massachusetts Ave. and N St. (357-2700): Opened in 1993, it is the first major U.S. museum devoted to postal history and philately. Exhibit includes an 1851 mail-delivery stagecoach, an 1840 British stamp, and other rarities among its collection of 12 million stamps. Open daily.

☼♨ **Arthur M. Sackler Gallery,** 1050 Independence Ave. SW
(357-2104): Another very fine underground museum opened
in 1987, adjoining the National Museum of African Art, a flawless achievement
aesthetically and architecturally. More than 1,000 objects are displayed here from
China, Southeast Asia, India, and the Middle East; the Chinese jades and Persian
manuscripts are particularly beautiful. Open daily.

MUSEUMS OF SCIENCE & HISTORY: ☼♨ Anderson House Museum,
2118 Massachusetts Ave. NW: Home of the respected Society of the Cincinnati
(785-2040), a patriotic organization founded in 1783, this luxurious Beaux Arts
mansion from 1906 displays a rich collection of historical items bearing on the
War of Independence. Portraits, books, period weapons. Many antique art objects. For history buffs. Open Tues–Sat.

♨ **Capital Children's Museum,** 800 3rd St. NE (543-8600):
Kids are allowed—even encouraged—to play with the grown-
up stuff, including the computers. Open daily.

☼♨ **Daughters of the American Revolution/DAR Museum,**
1776 D St. NW (628-1776): A complex of turn-of-the-century
buildings occupied by the DAR, a patriotic organization now numbering some
200,000 members, which was founded in 1890 for descendants of those who
fought in the War of Independence. Includes a museum of decorative art with 33
"State Rooms" decorated in the style of the Revolutionary period; one of the
country's most important genealogical libraries, tracing the family trees of the
earliest immigrants and their descendants; and **Constitution Hall,** a 3,800-seat
auditorium. A must for history buffs. Tours Sun–Fri.

☼♨ **Folger Shakespeare Library,** 201 E. Capitol St. SE (544-
7077): The world's largest collection of Shakespeariana, with
180,000 works; also possesses an Elizabethan-style theater and a scaled-down
replica of London's famous Globe Theatre. Open daily Apr–Aug, Mon–Sat the
rest of the year.

☼♨ **Frederick Douglass Memorial Home,** 1411 W St. SE (426-
5961): The founder of the Black Liberation movement in
America, the African American activist Frederick Douglass, who was himself
born a slave, lived here from 1877 until his death in 1895. Famous orator, journalist, lawyer, and for a time, U.S. ambassador to Haiti, he is looked on as the
father of the civil rights movement—a forerunner of Martin Luther King, Jr.
Interesting personal museum and well-stocked library. Open daily.

☼♨ **Marine Corps Museum,** Bldg. 58, Washington Navy Yard, M
and 9th Sts. SE (433-3840): 200 years of the United States Ma-
rine Corps' history, illustrated by its weapons, its uniforms, and other soldierly
souvenirs, arranged in chronological order from the foundation of this elite unit
in 1775. The museum is hard to reach without a car. Open daily.

♨ **Martin Luther King Library,** 901 G St. NW (727-1111): In
this austerely beautiful black building by Mies van der Rohe is a
library devoted to the winner of the Nobel peace prize, with many works relating
to the struggle for civil rights. Also books, movies, and photographs on the history of the city of Washington, and the archives of the now-defunct daily *Washington Star.*

☼♨♨ **National Archives,** Constitution Ave. between 7th and 9th
Sts. NW (501-5000): Imposing Greek Revival building de-
signed by John Russell Pope, containing the country's most prized historical
documents, from the originals of the Constitution, the Bill of Rights, and the
Declaration of Independence, to the 1783 Treaty of Paris bearing the signature of
Benjamin Franklin and the seal of King George III of England, the 1945 instru-
ments of surrender of Germany and Japan, and the notorious Watergate tapes.
Among innumerable other documents and curiosities is the photo album of
Hitler's mistress, Eva Braun. Fascinating. Open daily.

☀️⚒️⚒️ **National Building Museum,** 401 F St. NW (272-2448): Designed by Montgomery C. Meigs, this remarkable edifice, originally built to house the proliferating offices of the Civil War veterans pension administration, now displays temporary exhibitions. Splendid interior hall with 75-ft. (22m) Corinthian columns. Open daily.

⚒️ **National Geographic Society,** 17th and M Sts. NW (857-7588): Home of the world-famous *National Geographic* magazine. In Explorers Hall you'll find brilliantly conceived exhibitions devoted to the exploration of land, sea, and outer space, and a terrestrial globe 11 ft. (3m) in diameter. Open daily.

☀️⚒️ **National Library of Medicine,** 8600 Rockville Pike, Bethesda, Md. (301/496-6308): The world's largest medical library in an ultramodern building belonging to the National Institutes of Health, with four million books, professional periodicals, manuscripts, and other works in 70 languages, accumulated in the course of 150 years. Visitor Center and guided tours. If you're a disciple of Hippocrates, this is for you. Open Mon–Sat.

⚒️ **Naval Observatory,** 34th St. and Massachusetts Ave. NW (653-1507): Standing amid spacious gardens adjoining the official home of the vice-president of the U.S., this observatory administered by the U.S. Navy is responsible for determining standard American time. Interesting astronomical museum (admission at 8pm Mon). Every Mon budding astronomers may scan the heavens through a 26-in. (65cm) telescope.

☀️⚒️ **Navy Museum,** Bldg. 76, Washington Navy Yard, 9th and M Sts. SE (433-2651): From the mizzenmast of the famed frigate *Constitution* to a replica of the command station of a submarine, complete with periscope, and including a destroyer moored in front of the museum and open to visitors, you'll find here a complete history of the U.S. Navy, from the engagements of the War of Independence to the age of nuclear missiles. Fascinating. Museum hard to reach except by car. Open daily.

☀️⚒️⚒️⚒️ **The U.S. Holocaust Memorial Museum,** 100 Raoul Wallenberg Pl. SW (488-0400): Mandated by the U.S. Congress in 1980, this living memorial to the six million Jews and millions of other victims of Nazi fanaticism who perished in the Holocaust opened in 1993. Using artifacts, oral histories, documentary film, and photographs, the three-floor permanent exhibition tells the story of Jews targeted for annihilation in systematic, state-sponsored genocide, and describes the fate of others who perished such as Gypsies, Poles, homosexuals, Jehovah's Witnesses, and Soviet POWs. Also told are the stories of resistance and rescue that enabled many to survive. The building evokes the stark industrialism of a concentration camp. The Hall of Remembrance, open and free to the public, serves as the national memorial to the victims of the Holocaust. Open daily. Advanced ticket resv. are advised (call 432-7328).

The Smithsonian Institution

As well as the various art museums listed above, the Smithsonian Institution also comprises:

⚒️ **Anacostia Museum,** 1901 Fort Place SE (287-3369): Situated in a largely African American neighborhood in the south of Washington, this museum reopened in 1987 at a new location. It presents temporary exhibitions dealing with the role of minorities, ethnic and other, in American society. Open daily.

☀️⚒️⚒️⚒️ **National Air and Space Museum,** Independence Ave. and 7th St. SW (357-1400): Possibly the most remarkable aeronautical museum in the world, designed by Gyo Obata and opened in 1976. Here, under an enormous vaulted roof, are displayed the most memorable machines in the history of flying and space exploration: the *Kitty Hawk Flyer,* the Wright Brothers' first plane; the *Spirit of St. Louis,* first aircraft to be flown solo across the Atlantic (in 1927); the *Bell X-1,* the first aircraft to exceed the speed of sound; the fastest aircraft in the world, the *X-15,* which has reached Mach 6; a copy of *Sput-*

nik 1, the Soviet satellite which was the first to be placed in orbit around the earth; the *Apollo 11* module, which made the first lunar landing in 1969. There are extraordinary audiovisual shows and an ultramodern planetarium **(Albert Einstein Spacearium).** Washington's most popular attraction—eight million people come here every year. Very good new restaurant (the Wright Place) and cafeteria (Flight Line). Open daily.

National Museum of American History, Constitution Ave. and 14th St. NW (357-1481): Immense museum of science and technology. On the ground floor is a 280-ton (255,000kg) locomotive which had to be moved into place before the museum was built! Comprehensive collection of historic objects, from George Washington's false teeth and the ceremonial dresses of First Ladies to "Old Glory," the original star-spangled banner which inspired Francis Scott Key to write the words of the national anthem, and from Alexander Graham Bell's first telephone to a wooden gunboat that lay for 200 years beneath the waters of Lake Champlain. Open daily.

National Museum of Natural History, Constitution Ave. and 10th St. NW (357-2700): A comprehensive Museum of Man. A spectacular 92-ft. (28m) blue whale; the largest stuffed elephant in the world, weighing 8 tons (7,275kg); a life-size diplodocus. Anthropological material from the Western Hemisphere, Africa, and Asia. Extensive collection of minerals, including the world-famous Hope Diamond of 44 carats. Archeology, biology, fascinating insect "zoo" (the children's favorite), etc. Open daily.

PANORAMAS: **Arlington House/Custis-Lee Mansion,** Arlington National Cemetery, Arlington, Va. (703/557-0613): On a hill above Arlington National Cemetery (see "Monuments," above), this very fine Greek Revival house, once the home of Gen. Robert E. Lee, the Confederate commander-in-chief during the Civil War, has a splendid view of the Potomac River and downtown Washington. Lee abandoned Arlington House in 1861, at the beginning of the war, and never set foot there again. Overlooks the tomb of Pres. John F. Kennedy. Beautiful view. Open daily.

Bell Tower of the Old Post Office, 1100 Pennsylvania Ave. at 12th St. NW (289-4224): This 315-ft. (96m) Gothic Revival clock tower crowns the former central post office and has a spectacular view of downtown Washington. Glass enclosed elevator. Open daily 10am–6pm (to 10pm June–Sept).

Washington Monument, The Mall, nr. 15th St. NW (426-6839): The world's tallest masonry structure, dedicated to the first president of the U.S. A masterpiece of simple grandeur, this monument, which has become the city's symbol, was unveiled in 1885 and opened to the public three years later. From an observation platform 502 ft. (153m) up, there is a truly spectacular panoramic view; on a clear day you can see the Blue Ridge Mountains 50 mi. (80km) away. Elevator. Since more than two million tourists come here every year, you may have a long wait in line, particularly in summer. Open daily: 8am–midnight in summer, 9am–5pm the rest of the year.

Washington National Cathedral, Wisconsin and Massachusetts Aves. NW (537-6200): The Pilgrim Observation Gallery at the top of the cathedral's tower, 300 ft. (91m) above the ground, has a fine view of the northern part of the city as far as the banks of the Potomac. Open daily 10am–5pm (until 9pm in summer).

PARKS & GARDENS: For information about National Park Service monuments and parks in the Washington, D.C., area, call 619-7222. For a recorded message listing daily activities in the parks, call 619-7275.

Botanic Garden Conservatory, Maryland Ave. between 1st and 2nd Sts. SW (225-8333): A tropical jungle under glass, an incredible display of orchids, and some beautiful gardens at the foot of the Capitol: a botanic cross-section of all five continents. Remains open while undergoing renovation.

🔔 **Kenilworth Aquatic Gardens,** Kenilworth Ave. and Douglas St. NE (426-6905): On the bank of the Anacostia River, a wonderful aquatic garden with lotus, water hyacinth, bamboo, and water lilies by the thousand (flowering spectacularly June–Aug). Open daily.

☼🔔 **Lafayette Square,** Pennsylvania Ave., between Jackson Place and Madison Place NW: This charming tree-shaded little square in front of the main facade of the White House is a godsend to footsore tourists (and demonstrators who want to express dissatisfaction outside the White House railings). Besides an equestrian statue (1853) of Andrew Jackson, seventh president, the square is embellished with statues of four foreign-born heroes of the War of Independence: the German Friedrich Wilhelm von Steuben, the Pole Tadeusz Kosciuszko, and two Frenchmen, the Comte de Rochambeau and the Marquis de Lafayette. On the north side of the square is St. John's Episcopal Church, attended by many presidents of the U.S. In the corner of the square, Blair House, at 1651 Pennsylvania Ave. NW, is the official residence of foreign heads of state visiting Washington (not open to the public). If you want to take souvenir snapshots in front of the White House, this is the place to do it.

☼🔔 **The Mall,** between the Capitol and the Potomac River. This broad green carpet runs through the center of Washington on either side of the 655-yard (600m) **Reflecting Pool.** On the **Ellipse,** a great oval of lawn behind the White House, stands the Zero Milestone, placed there in 1923 to mark the zero mile of the great U.S. highways. One of the loveliest views in Washington, and a squirrels' paradise.

☼🔔 **Meridian Hill Park,** 16th St. between Euclid St. and Florida Ave. NW (426-6826): Hidden from public view behind high walls, this 12-acre (5ha) terraced park, though little known to Washingtonians, is perhaps the most beautiful landscaped complex in the capital. Completed in 1936, the park, sometimes known as **Malcolm X Park,** comprises a garden in the French style with clumps of trees, stone benches, and a statue of Joan of Arc on horseback, as well as a baroque Italian garden with a magnificent 13-step waterfall reminiscent of the famous fountains of the Villa d'Este near Rome. A sight you shouldn't miss, but the neighborhood is unsafe after nightfall. Open daily.

🔔 **National Arboretum,** 3501 New York Ave. NE (475-4815): Floral displays throughout the year, particularly impressive in spring when the azaleas are in flower. Pretty Japanese garden and delightful collection of bonsai (dwarf trees). On the banks of the Anacostia River. Worth a detour. Open daily.

☼🔔 **Potomac Park,** along Ohio Dr. SW (619-7222): Extensive tree-lined walk along the Potomac and Washington Channel on either side of the Jefferson Memorial. The beautiful cherry trees given by the Japanese government in 1912 are in flower in late Mar and early Apr around the Tidal Basin and East Potomac Park. Two golf courses; fishing; skating in winter; boat rental. A lovely sight in season. Much favored by joggers. Open daily.

🔔 **Rock Creek Park,** along Rock Creek Pkwy. and Beach Dr. NW (426-6829): 1,754 acres (710ha) of winding, rolling parkland on either side of Rock Creek, a tributary of the Potomac. Golf, tennis, horseback riding, open-air concerts in summer in the **Carter Barron Amphitheater.** A joggers' favorite, but don't go there after dark.

☼🔔 **Roosevelt Island,** Potomac River, reached by a footbridge from the George Washington Pkwy. at Arlington, Va. (703/285-2598): Unspoiled nature 10 min. from downtown, with a memorial dedicated to Pres. Theodore Roosevelt. Open from sunrise to sunset daily.

PERFORMING ARTS: For a daily listing of all shows and cultural events, consult the entertainment pages of the daily papers *Washington Post* (morning) and *Washington Times* (morning), of the weekly magazine *City Paper,* and of the monthly magazine *The Washingtonian.* **Ticket Place,** in the Lisner Auditorium (see below) (842-5387), sells tickets at half price for all same-day performances: shows, ballet, concerts, plays, etc. Open Tues–Fri 12–4, Sat 11–5; cash only.

American Film Institute, Kennedy Center, New Hampshire Ave. NW at Rock Creek Pkwy. (785-4600): The depositary library of the American cinema, with all the great classics.

Arena Stage, 6th St. and Maine Ave. SW (488-3300): Three contiguous theaters; musicals, contemporary and classical theater.

USAir Arena, 1 Harry Truman Dr., Landover, Md. (301/350-3400): Concerts by leading pop and rock stars.

Carter Barron Amphitheater, Rock Creek Park, 4850 Colorado Ave. NW (619-7222): Open-air concerts in a 4,000-seat auditorium in the woods; folk, pop, and jazz. Mid-June to Aug.

Ford's Theater, 511 10th St. NW (347-4833): The theater where Abraham Lincoln was assassinated, now a designated historic monument with the original decor restored. Musicals, modern theater.

John F. Kennedy Center for the Performing Arts, New Hampshire Ave. NW at Rock Creek Pkwy. (467-4600): Major, ultramodern entertainment complex with five different halls and auditoriums: the **Concert Hall,** home of the National Symphony (principal conductor: Mstislav Rostropovich), concerts and recitals of classical music; the **Eisenhower Theater,** modern and classic plays and Broadway hits; the **Opera House,** home of the Washington Opera (director: Martin Feinstein); ballet; the **Terrace Theater,** chamber music; **Theater Lab,** Off Broadway and experimental theater.

Lisner Auditorium, George Washington University, 21st and H Sts. NW (994-6800): Opera, classical concerts, jazz, rock; recitals.

National Theater, 1321 Pennsylvania Ave. NW (628-6161): Musicals, Broadway hits.

Shakespeare Theatre, 450 7th St. NW (393-2700): New 447-seat theater in the venerable Lansburgh Building. Classical theater.

Source Theater, 1835 14th St. NW (462-1073): Modern and experimental theater.

Trinity Theater, 36th and O Sts. NW (965-4680): Musicals, Off-Broadway plays.

Warner Theater, 513 13th St. NW (783-4000): Modern theater, Broadway hits.

Wolf Trap Farm Park for the Performing Arts, 1624 Trap Rd. at Va. 676, Vienna, Va. (703/255-1868): Big open-air auditorium used in summer for shows and concerts—jazz, classical, pop, opera, folk, ballet. Enormously popular. **The Barns at Wolf Trap** (703/938-2404) holds performances indoors in winter.

SHOPPING: In the **Watergate** building, **Les Champs** (338-0700) is an upscale shopping arcade with some 30 luxury boutiques and shops such as Guy Laroche and Yves St. Laurent.

The Shops (1331 Pennsylvania Ave. NW), **International Square** (1850 K St. NW), **The Pavilion at the Old Post Office** (1100 Pennsylvania Ave. NW), and **Esplanade Mall** (1990 K St. NW) are four ultramodern downtown shopping malls, each with dozens of trendy boutiques and shops as well as plenty of bars and restaurants.

Another successfully designed, modern-style shopping center is **Georgetown Park Mall,** 3222 M St. NW, with around 100 establishments doing business in a pretty Victorian-rococo setting.

The traditional department stores have for the most part fled to the huge shopping plazas on the outskirts of the city, the smartest and most accessible of which is **Mazza Gallerie** at 5300 Wisconsin Ave. NW, in Chevy Chase, Md.; there's a subway stop right outside.

Highly recommended for the transient visitor are the gift shops of the various **museums on the Mall** and the **Indian Craft Shop** in the Dept. of the Interior Bldg., 1800 C St. NW; their gifts are original and usually affordable as well. If food is important to you, visit **Dean and Deluca,** 3276 M St. NW, or at 1299 Pennsylvania Ave. NW, Washington's long-awaited imported-food store and café from New York and the city's answer to Fauchon's in Paris.

SPECIAL EVENTS: For the exact schedule of events below, consult the **Washington Convention and Visitors Association** (see "Tourist Information," above).

    Cherry Blossom Festival (late Mar to early Apr): Parade with floats, marathon, fireworks, famous lantern-lighting ceremony, and concerts, when the Japanese cherries are in flower.

    Flying Circus (May–Oct): Displays of aerobatics in old propeller-driven craft of the barnstorming era, every Sunday at 2pm. Picturesque and entertaining. You'll find it at the end of a 40-min. drive from downtown Washington along I-66W, U.S. 211W, and U.S. 17S, on U.S. 17 at Bealeton, Va. (703/439-8661). If you're nostalgic about goggles and leather helmets, this is for you.

    Friday Evening Parade (mid-May to mid-Sept): Unusually spectacular; the marines on parade Fri at 8:45pm, U.S. Marines Barracks, 8th and I Sts. SE. You have to reserve several days ahead (433-6060).

    Sunset Salute (late May to late Aug): The Marine Corps Silent Drill Platoon, the Marine Band and Drum and Bugle Corps offer a Sunset Salute to their slain fellows at the foot of the Iwo Jima Memorial in Arlington, starting at 7:30pm every Tues (433-4173).

    Memorial Day Ceremony (Memorial Day): The president lays a wreath at the tomb of the Unknown Soldier in Arlington National Cemetery. In the evening, the National Symphony gives an open-air concert on the lawn in front of the Capitol.

    Kemper Open PGA Golf Tournament (late May): Great annual tournament on the Avenel Golf Course.

    Kool Jazz Festival (early June): The world's biggest names in jazz come to the Kennedy Center for 48 hrs.

    Outdoor Concerts on the Mall (June–Aug): Places and times vary from day to day; consult the newspapers or call 619-7222.

    Hispanic Festival (July): The city's largest community-run festival. Features parades, ethnic foods, plays, music. More than 350,000 revellers. On the Mall.

    July 4th Celebration (July 4): Concerts and fireworks on the Mall.

    Wolf Trap Festival (June–Sept): Open-air concerts of classical music, jazz, ballet, opera, etc.; draws 600,000 spectators yearly. At Wolf Trap Farm, Vienna, Va. (703/255-1868), 14 mi. (22km) west on George Washington Memorial Pkwy., I-495S, and Dulles Airport Rd.

    Adams-Morgan Day Festival (Sept): A truly international celebration with ethnic food, music, crafts, and wares representing more than 50 countries. The city's biggest block party. At 18th St. and Columbia Rd. NW.

SPORTS: Washington has three professional teams:

    Basketball (Oct–Apr): Bullets, USAir Arena, Landover, Md. (301/622-3865).

    Football (Aug–Dec): Redskins, RFK Stadium (546-2222).

    Ice Hockey (Oct–Apr): Capitals, USAir Arena, Landover, Md. (301/350-3400).

Horse Racing

    Laurel Race Track, Baltimore-Washington Pkwy. exit to Md. 198, 18 mi. (28km) NW in Laurel, Md. (301/725-0400; toll free 800/638-1859), for thoroughbred racing, year round.

    Rosecroft Raceway, 6336 Rosecroft Dr., 8 mi. (13km) SE, in Oxon Hill, Md. (301/567-4000), has harness racing year round.

STROLLS: ⚲ **Adams Morgan,** bounded by Columbia Rd., Florida Ave., and 18th St. NW: A sort of local melting pot, it remains lively and bustling until 2am, unlike the rest of Washington. The neighborhood restaurants reflect the cosmopolitan crowd: Ethiopian, Créole, Chinese, Japanese, French, Mexican, Caribbean, Brazilian, and more. Worth a visit.

⚲ **Potomac Banks** (see the Potomac Park and Roosevelt Island in "Parks and Gardens," above): Very pleasant in fine weather.

⚲ **Embassy Row,** Massachusetts Ave. between Sheridan Circle and Observatory Circle NW: The world's largest diplomatic quarter, with some 80 embassies, consulates, and legations in a span of less than a mile (1.6km). You should see this display of national flags and coats-of-arms.

☀⚲ **Georgetown,** around Wisconsin Ave. and M St. NW: In Colonial days, Georgetown was a leading port for the export of tobacco; today it's a charming residential district. While some of its former elitist glitter has worn off, it's still—with its old houses, little narrow streets, boutiques, nightclubs, and variety of restaurants—both the Greenwich Village and the Soho of the nation's capital. But avoid Georgetown on weekend nights because heavy-drinking crowds often become rowdy and abusive. You should make a point of seeing the **Old Stone House** at 3051 M St. NW, the city's oldest house (1765), and **Dumbarton Oaks,** 1703 32nd St. NW, with its fine collections of Byzantine and pre-Columbian art. You might like to do as many tourists do every summer—take a barge ride on the **C. & O. Canal.** The house where John F. Kennedy lived before his election to the presidency is at 3307 N St. NW; no visitors. **Washington Harbor,** 3030 K St. NW, is a vast terraced esplanade on the Potomac—an imaginative piece of postmodern design by Arthur Cotton Moore. And there are many other things to see; don't miss this stroll.

THEME PARKS: ☀⚲ **Kings Dominion,** I-95 and Va. 30 at Doswell, Va., 78 mi. (124km) SW on I-95 (804/876-5000): Comprehensive theme park on 800 acres (324ha), with a picturesque reconstruction of Old Europe, including a miniature Eiffel Tower. There are 44 rides, featuring four roller coasters (including Shock Wave) and a Log Flume. Big-name shows; safari zoo. Open daily June to Labor Day, wknds only from late Mar to June and Labor Day to late Oct; closed the rest of the year.

⚲ **Wild World,** 13710 Central Ave. at Md. 214, in Mitchellville, Md., 15 mi. (24km) east on E. Capitol St. and Central Ave. (301/249-1500): Giant roller-coaster (Wild One); inner-tube ride; milliongallon (3.8-million-liter) wave pool for surfers, the biggest of its kind in the world; and dozens of other family attractions. 20 min. from downtown Washington. Open daily, early May through Sept.

WINTER SPORTS RESORTS: ⚲ **Blue Knob,** nr. Bedford, Pa., 150 mi. (240km) NW on I-270N and I-70N, Pennsylvania Tpke. west, U.S. 200N, and Penna. 869W (814/239-5111): 4 lifts. Open Dec–Mar.

☀⚲ **Canaan Valley,** nr. Davis, W. Va., 180 mi. (288km) west on I-66W, Va. 55W, and W. Va. 32N (304/866-4121): 3 lifts; one of the best resorts in the region. Open Dec–Mar.

⚲ **Massanutten,** nr. Elkton, Va., 125 mi. (200km) SW on I-66W, I-81S, U.S. 33E, and Va. 644N (703/289-9441): 4 lifts. Open Dec–Mar.

⚲ **Ski Liberty,** nr. Gettysburg, Pa., 65 mi. (104km) NW on I-270N, U.S. 15N, Md. 140W, Penna. 16W, and Penna. 116E (717/642-8282): 7 lifts. Open Dec–Mar.

⚲⚲ **Ski Roundtop,** nr. York, Pa., 121 mi. (194km) north on I-95N, I-695N, I-83N, Penna. 382W, and Penna. 177N (717/432-9631): 10 lifts. Open Dec to mid-Mar.

☼ 🗚🗚 **Wintergreen,** nr. Greenfield, Va., 168 mi. (268km) SW on I-66W, U.S. 29S, I-64W, Va. 6E, and Va. 151S (804/325-2200): 5 lifts. Open Dec–Mar.

ZOOS: ☼🗚🗚 **National Zoological Park,** 3001 Connecticut Ave. NW (673-4800): One of the finest and best-known zoos in the country; almost 3,000 animals representing 600 species, some of them very rare, such as the Indian white tiger, one of the few pairs of Komodo dragons in the western hemisphere, and pandas donated by the People's Republic of China, in facsimiles of their natural environment. Belongs to the Smithsonian Institution. Open daily.

ACCOMMODATIONS

Personal Favorites (in order of preference)

🗚🗚🗚🗚 **Four Seasons** (nr. dwntwn), 2800 Pennsylvania Ave. NW, DC 20007 (202/342-0444; toll free, see Four Seasons). 198 rms, A/C, color TV, in-rm movies. AE, CB, DC, MC, V. Valet parking $16, rest. (Seasons), bar, 24-hr. rm svce, free crib, concierge. *Note:* The luxury hotel w. the highest occupancy rate in Washington. Its ocher brick intended to harmonize w. Georgetown's old houses. Elegantly comfortable; refined interior; polished, personalized svce. Spacious rms w. period furniture, some w. balconies, the best overlooking Rock Creek Park. Excellent rest. Free limo to dwntwn. The VIP's favorite. **VE**

☼🗚🗚🗚🗚 **Sheraton Carlton** (dwntwn), 923 16th St. NW, DC 20006 (202/638-2626; toll free, see Sheraton). 200 rms, A/C, color TV, in-rm movies. AE, CB, DC, MC, V. Valet parking $22, health club, rest. (Allegro), bar, 24-hr. rm svce, hrdrsr, concierge, free crib. *Note:* The great lady among Washington hotels since 1926; reopened in Oct 1988 after 10 months (and $16 million) of renovation, this Italian-Renaissance palace has recaptured its original luster. Only two blocks from the White House, the Sheraton Carlton has accommodated many U.S. presidents. Unusually spacious rms, mahogany-furnished, w. marble bathrooms, refrigerators, and three phones apiece. Personalized svce. Admirable but very expensive Italian rest. Excellent location; attracts many VIPs and foreign dignitaries. **VE**

🗚🗚🗚 **Madison** (dwntwn), 15th and M Sts. NW, DC 20005 (202/862-1600; toll free 800/424-8577). 353 rms, A/C, color TV. AE, CB, DC, MC, V. Gar. $14, two rests. (including the Montpelier Room), two bars, rm svce, crib $25, concierge. *Note:* Ungraceful modern building elegantly and tastefully decorated within, w. period furniture, master paintings, and rich Oriental rugs. Big businesspeople, foreign dignitaries, prominent politicians, and entertainers (including Henry Kissinger, Frank Sinatra, Bob Hope, and David Rockefeller) have been coming here for a quarter of a century. Spacious, comfortable rms w. minibars. Thoroughly professional staff; overpriced, pretentious rest. Opposite the *Washington Post* building. Boasts one of Washington's most expensive suites, at $2,500 a night, plus tax. **VE**

🗚🗚🗚 **Watergate Hotel** (nr. dwntwn), 2650 Virginia Ave. NW, DC 20037 (202/965-2300; toll free 800/225-5843). 238 rms, A/C, color TV, in-rm movies. AE, CB, DC, MC, V. Valet gar. $15, pool, health club, sauna, 2 rests., bars, rm svce, hrdrsr, boutiques, concierge, free crib. *Note:* Relatively modern luxury hotel of original design, part of the celebrated Watergate development on the Potomac, a stone's throw from the Kennedy Center. Inviting, comfortable rms, the best w. river view; elegant decor w. Far Eastern works of art. Remarkable rest. (Jean Louis); flawless svce. Attracts many well-heeled foreigners. 10 min. from dwntwn. **VE**

🗚🗚🗚 **Hilton-Capital** (nr. dwntwn), 1001 16th St. NW, DC 20036 (202/393-1000; toll free, see Hilton). 549 rms, A/C, color TV, in-rm movies. AE, CB, DC, MC, V. Gar. $22, health club, sauna, two rests.

(including Trader Vic's), coffee shop, bar, 24-hr. rm svce, hrdrsr, boutiques, concierge, free crib. *Note:* After many years of neglect and decay, this wonderfully located convention hotel, in the heart of the business district and only three blocks from the White House, recently underwent a $55-million facelift. Rms are now larger, redecorated, and w. minibars; facilities have been completely renovated. Four VIP floors w. their own elevator and concierge. New, fully equipped business center. Svce (at last) efficient and hustling. The airport buses have their terminal here. Business and convention clientele. **VE**

    🔑🔑 **Embassy Row** (nr. dwntwn), 2015 Massachusetts Ave. NW, DC 20036 (202/265-1600; toll free 800/424-2400). 196 rms, A/C, color TV, in-rm movies. AE, CB, DC, MC, V. Valet gar. $12, pool, rest., bar, 24-hr. rm svce, concierge. *Note:* Elegant little hotel in the heart of the embassy district. Built in 1970 and entirely renovated in 1984. Comfortable rms and suites, w. minibars. Foreign and diplomatic clientele. The help speaks a number of languages but the svce is undependable. Acceptable rest. Interesting wknd discounts. **E**

    🔑🔑 **Channel Inn** (nr. dwntwn), 650 Water St. SW, DC 20024 (202/554-2400; toll free 800/368-5668). 100 rms, A/C, color TV. AE, CB, DC, MC, V. Free parking, pool, rest, coffee shop, bar, rm svce, disco, free crib. *Note:* Agreeable motel right on the water; comfortable, more-than-usually spacious rms w. balconies, the best overlooking Washington Channel and the marina. Efficient svce. 5 min. from the Mall and its museums. Tourist clientele. Good value on balance. Interesting wknd discounts. **M–E**

    🔑🔑 **Howard Johnson at Kennedy Center** (nr. dwntwn), 2601 Virginia Ave. NW, DC 20037 (202/965-2700; toll free, see Howard Johnson's). 192 rms, A/C, color TV. AE, CB, DC, MC, V. Free gar., rooftop pool, rest., free crib. *Note:* Traditional eight-floor motel a block or two from the Kennedy Center, opposite the Watergate complex and 10 min. from dwntwn. Functionally comfortable rms w. refrigerators, some w. balconies. Efficient reception and svce. Favored by show-business people. Good overall value. **I–M**

    🔑 **Days Inn Downtown** (dwntwn), 1201 K St. NW, DC 20005 (202/842-1020; toll free, see Days Inns). 220 rms, A/C, color TV, in-rm movies. AE, CB, DC, MC, V. Pay parking adj., pool, rest, bar, rm svce, crib $10. *Note:* Newly renovated motel two blocks from the Convention Center. Functional comfort. Many rms w. view of the U.S. Capitol (some w. kitchenettes). Group and convention clientele. Good value overall. **I–M**

    🔑 **Braxton Hotel** (dwntwn), 1440 Rhode Island Ave. NW, DC 20037 (202/232-7800). 62 rms, A/C, color TV, in-rm movies. AE, MC, V. On-street parking; no bar or rest. *Note:* Small dwntwn budget hotel, offering a respectable level of comfort and a warm welcome. Ideal for shoestring travelers. **B–I**

Other Accommodations (from top bracket to budget)

    🔑🔑🔑 **Ana Hotel** (dwntwn), 2401 M St. NW, DC 20037 (202/429-2400; toll free 800/228-3000). 416 rms, A/C, color TV, in-rm movies. AE, CB, DC, MC, V. Valet gar. $15, pool, health club, sauna, 2 rests. (Colonnade), coffee shop, bars, 24-hr. rm svce, concierge, free crib. *Note:* Opened in 1986 as the Westin, this top-flight hotel, located in the heart of the West End business district, is the flagship of the All Nippon Airways (ANA) hotel group. Elegant art nouveau setting w. many antiques, old Italian statuary, and a glass loggia creating an indoor garden in the lobby. Rms spacious and luxuriously appointed. Exemplary svce. Caters to top businesspeople (most of them Japanese). **VE**

    ☀🔑🔑🔑 **Willard Inter-Continental** (dwntwn), 1401 Pennsylvania Ave. NW, DC 20004 (202/628-9100; toll free, see Inter-Continental). 365 rms, A/C, color TV, in-rm movies. AE, CB, DC, MC, V. Valet parking $16, rest. (Willard Room), coffee shop, bar, 24-hr. rm svce, boutiques, concierge, free crib. *Note:* This venerable Beaux Arts building dates from 1901, is a designated historic monument, and has long been known as "the hotel of presidents." It was long allowed to deteriorate, and indeed threatened with demolition, but a $75-million restoration program completed in 1986 has restored all its old splendor as well as its sumptuous interior. All the world's greats have stayed here, from Mark Twain to Richard Nixon. The standard rms are comfy but cramped; the suites and studios, on the contrary, are unusually elegant and spacious. The lobby promenade known as Peacock Alley was, at the turn of the century, a favorite meeting place for politicians and the representatives of special-interest groups—whence the term *lobbyist.* Highly regarded but overpriced rest. The Round Robin Bar is famous. Svce somewhat erratic. Boasts one of Washington's most expensive suites—$2,800 a night, plus tax. One of the great names among American hotels. **VE**

Grand Hyatt (dwntwn), 1000 H St. NW, DC 20001 (202/ 582-1234; toll free, see Hyatt). 889 rms, A/C, color TV, in-rm movies. AE, CB, DC, MC, V. Parking $14, rest., two bars, rm svce, concierge, free crib. *Note:* Big new brick, stone, and concrete cube, well located across from the Convention Center, but completely lacking in architectural originality. Its 12-story lobby w. skylight, giant waterfall, pool, and indoor grdns is, on the other hand, an altogether praiseworthy piece of design. Huge, well-designed rms; unexpectedly efficient svce given the sheer size of the place. VIP floor; group and convention clientele. **VE**

Hay-Adams Hotel (dwntwn), 1 Lafayette Sq. NW, DC 20006 (202/638-6600; toll free, see Preferred). 138 rms, A/C, color TV. AE, CB, DC, MC, V. Valet gar. $18, rest. (Lafayette), coffee shop, bar, 24-hr. rm svce, concierge. *Note:* The best location in town, right across from the White House. Charming old hotel in the European fashion, a favorite of visiting foreign statesmen and dignitaries for more than half a century. Spacious, elegant rms w. balconies and minibars, some w. fireplaces, the best looking out on Lafayette Sq. Period furniture. Excellent svce, discreet and attentive. Good rests. Quality and style. **VE**

Hilton Washington and Towers (nr. dwntwn), 1919 Connecticut Ave. NW, DC 20009 (202/483-3000; toll free, see Hilton). 1,150 rms, A/C, color TV, in-rm movies. AE, CB, DC, MC, V. Gar. $12, pool, tennis courts, health club, sauna, two rests., coffee shop, two bars, rm svce, drugstore, free crib. *Note:* Massive white tourist barracks in the shape of two arcs of a circle, standing in 7 acres (2.87ha) of grdn. Up-to-date comfort after a $42-million renovation in 1993. Spacious rms w. refrigerators and minibars, some w. balconies. Very complete facilities; rather distracted svce and average rests. Crowded year round by groups and conventions. Two top floors reserved for VIPs (Hilton Towers). It was in front of this hotel that an attempt was made to assassinate President Reagan on March 30, 1981. 10 min. from dwntwn. **VE**

Jefferson Hotel (dwntwn), 1200 16th St. NW (at M St.), DC 20036 (202/347-2200; toll free 800/368-5966). 100 rms, A/C, color TV, in-rm movies. AE, CB, DC, MC, V. Valet parking $20, rest. (the Jefferson), bar, 24-hr. rm svce, concierge, free crib. *Note:* Charming little '20s hotel, tastefully renovated. Each spacious, comfortable rm is decorated in a different style; most have four-poster beds. Flawless personalized svce. The Hunt Club is one of Washington's fashionable rests. Distinction and elegance nr. the embassy district and four blocks from the White House. The politicians' favorite. **VE**

J. W. Marriott (dwntwn), 1331 Pennsylvania Ave. NW, DC 20004 (202/393-2000; toll free, see Marriott). 774 rms, A/C, color TV, in-rm movies. AE, CB, DC, MC, V. Valet parking $16, pool, health club, sauna, three rests. (including Celadon), coffee shop, bars, 24-hr. rm svce, parking, concierge, free crib. *Note:* The flagship hotel of the Marriott chain, an ultramodern palace whose design earns no plaudits, strategically placed a stone's throw from the Mall and the White House. Luckily, the interior decoration and equipment are more successful. Enormous, boastful lobby w. marble floors and huge crystal chandeliers; spacious, well-designed rms; efficient though impersonal svce. As in all Marriotts, so-so rests. Business and convention clientele. VIP floor ("Concierge Floor"); direct access to "The Shops" at National Place, a shopping mall with 110 shops and 20 rests. The movie *Broadcast News* was in part shot here. **VE**

🏨🏨🏨 **Loews L'Enfant Plaza** (nr. dwntwn), 480 L'Enfant Plaza SW, DC 20024 (202/484-1000; toll free, see Loews). 372 rms, A/C, color TV, in-rm movies. AE, CB, DC, MC, V. Valet parking $13, pool, rest. (Cafe Pierre), bar, rm svce, boutiques, concierge, free crib. *Note:* Successful essay in futurist architecture, occupying the top four floors of an ultramodern office complex w. underground shopping mall and direct subway access. Luxurious, comfortable rms w. minibars, most w. balconies. Inviting open-air pool on the 12th floor. Very good svce. A few blocks from the Mall and its museums. Business and group clientele. A good place to stay. **E–VE**

🏨🏨🏨 **One Washington Circle** (dwntwn), 1 Washington Circle NW, DC 20037 (202/872-1680; toll free 800/468-3532). 152 suites, A/C, color TV, in-rm movies. AE, CB, DC, MC, V. Valet parking $12, pool, rest., bar, rm svce, concierge. *Note:* Modern, very comfortable hotel halfway between the White House and Georgetown. Suites only, spacious and w. kitchenettes and refrigerators (most w. balconies). Elegantly decorated and furnished. Irreproachable svce. Business clientele. Inviting little grdn. An excellent place to stay. **E–VE**

🏨🏨🏨 **Ritz-Carlton** (formerly the Fairfax; nr. dwntwn), 2100 Massachusetts Ave. NW, DC 20008 (202/293-2100; toll free 800/424-8008). 206 rms, A/C, color TV, in-rm movies. AE, CB, DC, MC, V. Valet parking $20, rest. (Jockey Club), bar, 24-hr. rm svce, nightclub, concierge, crib $20. *Note:* This elegant, classy old hotel in the heart of the embassy district has undergone a much-needed facelift, and is now smart and distinguished, achieving a harmonious combination of elegance and comfort. There are, however, still shortcomings in maintenance and svce. Spacious rms w. minibars; good hotel rest. (a favorite of President Kennedy and Nancy Reagan). Big business and diplomatic clientele. A Washington landmark. **E–VE**

🏨🏨🏨 **Washington Vista** (dwntwn), 1400 M St. NW, DC 20005 (202/429-1700; toll free, see Hilton). 398 rms, A/C, color TV, in-rm movies. AE, CB, DC, MC, V. Valet parking $14, health club, sauna, two rests. (including Verandah Harvest), two bars, 24-hr. rm svce, concierge, free crib. *Note:* Inviting luxury hotel on the edge of the business district. Fine 14-story glass atrium with café and winter grdn. Very comfortable, well-equipped rms, the best looking out on the atrium. Good rest. serving modern American cuisine. Ultra-professional svce. Group and business clientele; two VIP floors. A very good place to stay. **E–VE**

🏨🏨🏨 **Washington Court** (formerly the Sheraton Grand; dwntwn), 525 New Jersey Ave. NW, DC 20001 (202/628-2100; toll free 800/321-3010). 264 rms, A/C, color TV, in-rm movies. AE, CB, DC, MC, V. Valet parking $15, rest. (Signature Room), bar, 24-hr. rm svce, concierge, free crib. *Note:* The newest of Capitol Hill's luxury hotels: an elegant, modern 15-story building w. a vast pink-marble atrium complete w. waterfall and indoor grdn. Comfortable rms w. refrigerators, some w. picturesque views. Very acceptable rest. serving American cuisine. Efficient svce. Business clientele. A block or two from the Capitol and Union Station. **E–VE**

🏨🏨 **Holiday Inn Capitol** (dwntwn), 550 C St. SW, DC 20024 (202/479-4000; toll free, see Holiday Inns). 529 rms, A/C, color TV, in-rm movies, exercise rm. AE, CB, DC, MC, V. Parking $8, pool, rest. (Smithson's), bar, rm svce, hrdrsr, boutiques, free crib. *Note:* Huge modern nine-floor motel a stone's throw from the Mall and the Capitol. A typical Holiday Inn, w. comfortable rms, efficient reception and svce. Group and convention clientele; interesting wknd discounts. Ideal base for visits to the Mall museums. **E–VE**

🛏🛏 **Hotel Washington** (dwntwn), 515 15th St. (at Pennsylvania Ave.), NW DC 20004 (202/638-5900; toll free 800/424-9540). 344 rms, A/C, color TV, in-rm movies. AE, CB, DC, MC, V. Gar. $16, two rests. (Two Continents), bar, rm svce, free crib. *Note:* Massive, aging luxury hotel now entirely renovated. Very well located 3 min. from the White House and 5 min. from the Mall and its museums. Spacious, comfortable rms; efficient svce. The top-floor bar has one of the finest views of the city. Interesting wknd discounts. A Washington landmark since 1918. **E–VE**

🛏🛏 **Quality Hotel–Capitol Hill** (dwntwn), 415 New Jersey Ave. NW, DC 20001 (202/638-1616; toll free, see Choice). 340 rms, A/C, color TV, in-rm movies. AE, CB, DC, MC, V. Free parking, pool, rest. (The Senators), bar, rm svce. *Note:* Comfortable 10-floor motel 5 min. from the Capitol and Union Station. Functional rms; efficient reception and svce; so-so rest. Caters to groups and conventions. Rooftop pool open in summer w. view of the city. **M–E,** but lower rates off-season.

🛏 **Comfort Inn** (dwntwn), 500 H St. NW, DC 20001 (202/289-5959; toll free, see Choice). 197 rms, A/C, color TV, in-rm movies. AE, CB, DC, MC, V. Parking $10, exercise rm., sauna, rest., bar, valet svce, free crib. *Note:* New hotel very nr. the Convention Center. Comfortable, well-designed rms; efficient reception and svce. Business and group clientele. Interesting wknd discounts. **M–E**

🛏 **Hotel Bellevue** (dwntwn), 15 E St. NW, DC 20001 (202/638-0900). 140 rms, A/C, color TV. AE, DC, MC, V. Free parking, rest. (Tiber Creek), bar, rm svce. *Note:* One of Washington's oldest hotels, but comfort and facilities are maintained at a very acceptable level. Entirely renovated rms, some w. refrigerators; inviting rest. and pub. Friendly svce. A stone's throw from the Capitol and Union Station. Good overall value; interesting wknd discounts. **M**

🛏 **Kalorama Guest House** (2 locations nr. dwntwn), 1854 Mintwood Pl. NW, DC 20009 (667-6369) (30 rms) and 2700 Cathedral Ave. NW, DC 20008 (328-0860) (20 rms). A/C. AE, DC, MC, V. Guest and street parking, free continental breakfast, shared and private baths. *Note:* Very pleasant European-style pensions w. cozy, old-fashioned rms. Friendly innkeepers that make you feel much at home. Quiet locations in great neighborhoods. Complimentary coffee, tea, and afternoon sherry. **I–M**

🛏 **Embassy Inn** (dwntwn), 1627 16th St. NW, DC 20009 (202/234-7800; toll free 800/423-9111). 38 rms, A/C, color TV. AE, MC, V. Street parking, no rest. but free continental breakfast, valet svce. *Note:* Originally a 1920s boarding house, this charming little inn decorated w. antiques is located smack in the heart of dwntwn, four blocks from the White House. Comfortable, homey atmosphere. Complimentary sherry, tea, coffee, fruit. Courteous reception and svce. Very good value. **I–M**

🛏 **Harrington Hotel** (dwntwn), 11th and E Sts. NW, DC 20004 (202/628-8410; toll free 800/424-8532). 308 rms, A/C, color TV. AE, CB, DC, MC, V. Gar. $5, rest. adj. *Note:* Elderly but acceptable grand hotel in a fast-improving neighborhood nr. the Mall and the White House, a few blocks from Pennsylvania Ave. Very commendable standard of comfort. Group clientele. Good value overall. **I**

🛏 **Windsor Park** (nr. dwntwn), 2116 Kalorama Rd. NW, DC 20008 (202/483-7700). 43 rms, A/C, color TV. MC, V. On-street parking. *Note:* A good deal for the budget traveler in the Embassy Row area. Spare, clean rms, all w. private bath and small refrigerator. Short walk to zoo and metro. Very good value. **I**

Airport Accommodations

🛏🛏🛏 **Stouffer Concourse** (vic.), 2399 Jefferson Davis Hwy., Arlington, VA 22202 (703/418-6800; toll free, see Stouffer). 388 rms, A/C, color TV, in-rm movies. AE, CB, DC, MC, V. Parking $9, pool, health club, sauna, rest. (Ondine), two bars, 24-hr. rm svce, nightclub, concierge, free crib. *Note:* Uninspired modern 12-floor tower overwhelmed in a sea of glass and concrete by the office buildings of Crystal City. Fortunately the interior is more attractive, w. spacious, very comfortable rms. Efficient multilingual svce. Group and business clientele; two VIP floors; free shuttle to the National Airport terminal 5 min. away; 15 min. from dwntwn. **E–VE**

♀♀♀ **Renaissance Dulles Airport** (vic.), 13869 Park Center Rd., Herndon, VA 22071 (703/478-2900). 301 rms, A/C, color TV. AE, CB, DC, MC, V. Free parking, two pools, tennis court, health club, sauna, rest., coffee shop, bar, rm svce, hrdrsr, free crib. *Note:* Luxurious, modern airport hotel 2 min. from the terminal (free shuttle). Spacious, well-equipped rms w. refrigerators. Comprehensive facilities. Efficient reception and svce. Ideal for a stopover between flights. Business clientele; two VIP floors. 40 min. from dwntwn. **M–E**

♀ **Econo Lodge Arlington** (vic.), 2485 S. Glebe Rd., Arlington, VA 22206 (703/979-4100; toll free, see Choice). 163 rms, A/C, color TV, in-rm movies. AE, MC, V. Free parking, pool, rest., bar, valet svce, free crib. *Note:* Typical suburban motel 5 min. from National Airport. Rms very large; functional comforts; reception w. a smile. Free shuttle to National Airport, the Pentagon, and nearby subway station. Good value overall. Group clientele. **B–I**

YMCAs/Youth Hostels

International Guest House (nr. dwntwn), 1441 Kennedy St. NW, DC 20011 (202/726-5808). Priority given to visitors from abroad. Operated by the Mennonite church, w. the lowest rates in Washington. Very acceptable comfort.

International Hostel (dwntwn), 1009 11th St. NW, DC 20001 (202/737-2333). 250 rms. Youth hostel open to members and nonmembers. Very central.

RESTAURANTS

Personal Favorites (in order of preference)

♀♀♀♀ **Jean-Louis** (nr. dwntwn), in the Watergate Hotel (see "Accommodations," above) (298-4488). A/C. Dinner only, Tues –Sat; closed hols. AE, CB, DC, MC, V. J&T. *Specialties:* ragoût of cèpes (mushrooms), corn soup, magret of duck w. honey and dates, venison w. artichokes and basil in Chartreuse sauce, oyster fritters w. truffle butter, fresh foie gras w. seasonal fruit, saddle of rabbit w. wild mushrooms. Remarkable desserts. Well-stocked but overpriced wine list. The menu is changed periodically. *Note:* French-style nouvelle cuisine triumphant, under the command of one of the great chefs of his generation, Jean-Louis Palladin, whose prestigious La Table des Cordeliers in Le Gers, France, rated two stars in Michelin. Sauces light as air, refined but simple preparation, the choicest (American) raw materials, perfect cooking, and elegant preparation combine to make his cuisine a genuine masterpiece. Recently renovated decor in pastel tones, but surroundings somewhat claustrophobic. Service exemplary in all respects. A much cheaper pretheater menu of the same items is offered before 6pm. Since there are only 42 seats, you should reserve a number of days ahead. President Reagan had his 70th birthday dinner here. One of the dozen best rests. in the country, but prices to match. *French.* **VE**

♀♀♀ **Vidalia** (dwntwn), 1990 M St. NW (659-1990). A/C. Lunch Mon–Fri, dinner Mon–Sat; closed hols. AE, DC, MC, V. *Specialties:* wild-mushroom ragoût w. Virginia ham and cream gravy served over a rosemary biscuit; roasted onion soup w. spoon bread and farmer cheese; roast monkfish w. lima beans, bacon, fresh corn, and smoked tomato oil; Shenandoah trout w. horseradish; barbecued spiced pork shoulder w. pepper slaw and hush puppies; butter-crusted lemon chess pie w. strawberry sauce. *Note:* Named after the Georgia town famous for its onions, this newcomer invigorates American Southern cooking. Jeffrey Buben's twists on traditional recipes will enhance your vision of what's possible in American cuisine. Decked w. smart pieces of folk art and encased in earth-tone walls and wood floors, the downstairs setting couples well w. food that looks as if it could also be folk art. Wine list is well endowed. This rest. has quickly established itself as a notable rest. in the U.S. Resv. advised. *American.* **M–E**

    I Ricchi (dwntwn), 1220 19th St. NW (835-0459). A/C. Lunch Mon–Fri, dinner Mon–Sat; closed hols. AE, CB, DC, MC, V. Jkt. *Specialties:* ribollita; pasta w. wild mushrooms; risotti; grilled skewer of quail, veal, and sausage; venison w. chianti sauce; fritto misto of seafood; fabulous wood grilled meats. The menu changes regularly. *Note:* Upscale Tuscan *trattoria* offering the simple but wonderful cuisine of chef-owner Francesco Ricchi. Rustic setting w. frescoed walls. Resv. suggested. The Italian choice for many Washingtonians. *Italian.* **M–E**

    Red Sage (dwntwn), 605 14th St. NW (638-4444). A/C. Lunch Mon–Fri, dinner nightly. AE, CB, MC, V. *Specialties:* butternut painted soup; fresh oysters w. serrano mignonette; steak tartar w. chipotle and cactus toast; grilled squab w. black pepper, pear, and wild rice; cowboy ribeye steak w. barbecued black beans and chili onion rings. The menu changes regularly. Ordinary desserts and skimpy wine list. *Note:* Opened in January 1992, this upscale western outpost has been an instant hit. An anthropologist by training, chef-owner Mark Miller, whose cooking at famous Coyote Café in Santa Fe helped popularize southwestern cuisine, is a master of chilies, flavors, and exotic combinations. Despite the lavishness of this multilevel rest.—a fantasy on southwestern themes complete w. sterling-silver horseshoes, 12- by 16-ft. (4 by 5.5m) mural, buffalo suede and custom-made clouds suspended from a dramatic sky—the check remains more than reasonable. Svce friendly and efficient. A very good place. Resv. highly recommended. *American.* **B** (chile bar), **M** (rest.).

    Kinkead's (dwntwn), 2000 Pennsylvania Ave. NW (296-7700). A/C. Lunch/dinner daily, brunch Sun; closed hols. AE, CB, DC, MC, V. Jkt. *Specialties:* grilled squid w. creamy polenta; shrimp pupusa w. pickled cabbage; pepita-crusted salmon w. shrimp, corn, and chilies; grilled swordfish catalan; Brazilian-style pork feijoada w. black beans; chocolate dacquoise w. cappuccino sauce. *Note:* Owner of the once-great Twenty-One Federal, Bob Kinkead has scaled down in price without jeopardizing the excellence in cuisine. You can observe Kinkead himself cooking in the kitchen, which is open to full view of the rest. Exotic and superb entrées. The bar-café downstairs serves a cheaper fare of American tapas, sandwiches, and light meals. *Seafood/American.* **I–M**

    Old Ebbitt Grill (dwntwn), 675 15th St. NW (347-4800). A/C. Breakfast/lunch/dinner daily (until 1am). AE, DC, MC, V. *Specialties:* spaghetti w. four cheeses, cannelloni w. spinach, crab cake, hamburgers, baked scrod, broiled fish of the day, calves' liver w. onions, roast pork w. applesauce, chicken pot pie. Good homemade desserts. *Note:* Founded in 1856, the Old Ebbitt Grill is Washington's oldest saloon, though the present building, once a vaudeville theater, dates only from the turn of the century. The menu includes all the great American classics and some specialties as well. Pretty Victorian setting w. marble floors, Persian rugs, oak beams, and gas lamps; fine bar. Locally popular. Resv. a must. Favored by White House staffers at lunchtime. Same management as Clyde's (see below). *American.* **I–M**

    Crisfield (vic.), 8012 Georgia Ave., Silver Spring, Md. (301/ 589-1306). A/C. Lunch/dinner Tues–Sun; closed Dec 25. No credit cards. *Specialties:* clam chowder, oysters on the half shell, crab cake, crab Imperial, catch of the day sautéed or stuffed with crabmeat. *Note:* Seafood rest. w. no mannerisms or affectations; the decor is period Formica, but the seafood is absolutely fresh and cooked to perfection. You can eat standing at the counter. Quick, efficient svce. Very popular locally; unfortunately no resv., so you'll have to wait. 25 min. from dwntwn. *Seafood.* **I–M**

🍸🍸 **Austin Grill** (nr. dwntwn), 2404 Wisconsin Ave. NW (337-8080). A/C. Lunch/dinner daily. AE, MC, V. *Specialties:* quesadillas, superb chile, beef-and-bean burritos, grilled pork chops, carnitas, steak studded w. chipotle peppers. *Note:* Top-notch Tex-Mex rest.—the favorite of former President Bush. The bar makes the definitive margarita and the kitchen turns out some of the best chile outside Texas. Constantly noisy and overcrowded. A good-time place. No resv., unfortunately. *American.* **I**

🍸🍸 **Enriqueta's** (nr. dwntwn), 2811 M St. NW, Georgetown (338-7772). A/C. Lunch Mon–Fri, dinner nightly; closed hols. AE, CB, DC, MC, V. *Specialties:* tacos, enchiladas verdes, tamales, mussels w. chili, stuffed green pepper, mole poblano (turkey in chocolate sauce), shrimp w. coriander, chicken w. tomatillo sauce, cremitas. *Note:* Enriqueta's dishes have the true Mexican flavor; the setting, too, is as lively, noisy, and colorfully decorated as you could hope for south of the Rio Grande. Diligent svce. Resv. are advised; dinner only. *Mexican.* **I**

🍸 **Sushi Ko** (nr. dwntwn), 2309 Wisconsin Ave. NW, Georgetown (333-4187). A/C. Lunch Tues–Fri, dinner nightly. AE, MC, V. *Specialties:* sushi, miso soup, shrimp tempura, teriyaki, yakitori. *Note:* Many of the patrons of this small, unimaginatively decorated Japanese bistro come from the nearby Japanese Embassy; in spite of the downbeat setting it's the best sushi bar in Washington; opened in 1979. Poker-faced svce; resv. advised. *Japanese.* **I–M**

Other Restaurants (from top bracket to budget)

🍸🍸🍸 **Le Lion d'Or** (dwntwn), 1150 Connecticut Ave. NW, w. entrance on 18th St. (296-7972). A/C. Lunch Mon–Fri, dinner Mon–Sat; closed hols. AE, CB, DC, MC, V. J&T. *Specialties:* lobster meat in whisky sauce, sautéed morels w. fresh pasta (in season), ravioli of foie gras, soufflé of lobster, pompano baked in rock salt, roast filet of lamb w. herbs, rockfish in pastry shell, game (in season), veal kidneys w. shallots. Very good desserts and soufflés; large wine list at reasonable prices. Menu changes regularly. *Note:* The owner, Jean Pierre Goyenvalle, is one of the most talented French chefs now working in the U.S.; his splendid, very elaborate cuisine is a happy marriage of the traditional w. nouvelle tendencies (such as shorter cooking times). The decor is elegantly old-fashioned; the svce is courteous and polished. Can be noisy. Resv. a must, since this is the favorite rest. of local VIPs. One of the best places to eat on the East Coast. Free parking at dinner. *French.* **VE**

🍸🍸 **Seasons** (dwntwn), in the Four Seasons Hotel (see "Accommodations," above) (342-0810). A/C. Breakfast daily, lunch Mon–Fri, dinner nightly. AE, CB, DC, MC, V. Jkt. *Specialties:* smoked haddock cream soup w. malt whisky, tataki of tuna w. spicy salmon tartar, rack of lamb w. Indian spices, venison in bramble-berry sauce, seared rosemary salmon w. citrus vinaigrette, lemon tart in custard. *Note:* The dining room overlooks Rock Creek Park and allows full pleasure of the surroundings. Meals are refreshing in the summer and hearty in the winter, although inconsistent year round. Adroit svce. *American.* **E**

🍸🍸 **Galileo** (dwntwn), 1110 21st St. NW (293-7191). A/C. Lunch Mon–Fri, dinner Mon–Sat; closed hols. AE, CB, DC, MC, V. *Specialties:* olive focaccia, fettuccine w. pistachio and Gorgonzola cheese, risotto w. lobster and tomato sauce, pumpkin ravioli w. black truffles, grilled sweetbreads w. pancetta and wild mushrooms, veal chop w. rosemary, filets of venison w. green-peppercorn sauce and polenta, grilled grouper w. herbs and timbale of endive, braised beef w. Barolo sauce. Undistinguished desserts. Menu changes daily. Reasonable wine list. *Note:* Washington's best Italian *nuova cucina;*

young chef Roberto Donna is a maestro of airy sauces and innovative taste combinations. Light Mediterranean decor w. a large terrace for good-weather outdoor dining. Svce usually efficient but can lapse into chaos. Resv. must be made one or more days ahead, since this place is favored by those in-the-know. Valet parking at dinner. *Italian.* **E**

🍷🍷🍷 **Morton's** (nr. dwntwn), 3251 Prospect St. NW, Georgetown (342-6258). A/C. Dinner only, nightly; closed hols. AE, CB, DC, MC, V. Jkt. *Specialties:* wonderful aged beef, veal or lamb chops, catch of the day, Maine lobster, so-so desserts. *Note:* This pillar of the local dining scene has been acclaimed for a decade as Washington's best steakhouse. Steak, porterhouse, and ribs of beef that are quite exceptional, but also fine fish and gigantic lobsters, broiled to perfection. Comfortable, elegant London club-style interior, w. an interesting collection of paintings by LeRoy Neiman. Excellent svce, quick and efficient. Resv. a must. A successful sibling of the well-known Morton's in Chicago. Rather noisy; a favorite w. local politicians and lobbyists. Valet parking. *Steak/Seafood.* **E**

🍷🍷🍷 **Vincenzo** (dwntwn), 1606 20th St. NW (667-0047). A/C. Lunch Mon–Fri, dinner Mon–Sat; closed hols. AE, CB, DC, MC, V. Jkt. *Specialties:* linguine w. clams, fritto misto di mare (seafood mixed grill), classic regional pasta dishes, risotto w. shellfish, veal saltimbocca, seafood stew, catch of the day. Desserts and wine list both underwhelming. *Note:* The talented Lino Lombardo, who long restricted himself to seafood, has now broadened his menu to include classic dishes from Tuscany—with no less happy results. The decor, involving whitewashed walls and tiled floor, is on the austere side, but the svce is ultra-professional; business clientele and many regulars. The best place in Washington for seafood Italian style. Resv. a must. *Italian/Seafood.* **M–E**

☼ 🍷🍷🍷 **Occidental Grill** (dwntwn), 1475 Pennsylvania Ave. NW (783-1475) A/C. Lunch/dinner daily, closed hols. AE, CB, DC, MC, V. Jkt. *Specialties:* fresh scallops, marinated salmon, rack of pork chop, grilled filet of rockfish, hamburgers, steak, salmon w. roasted eggplant, tuna, blueberry bread pudding, daily flavors of ice cream. Fine list of American wines. *Note:* Once known as "the restaurant where statesmen dine," as witness the 2,500-odd photographs of leading politicians on the walls, this turn-of-the-century rest., now splendidly restored, is a true Washington classic. In the Grill Room on the ground floor, as in the elegant dining room upstairs, the new menu offers American regional cuisine skillfully crafted. Efficient, smiling svce. Resv. a must. An excellent place a stone's throw from the White House. *American.* **M**

🍷🍷🍷 **Palladin By Jean-Louis** (nr. dwntwn), in the Watergate Hotel (see "Accommodations," above) (298-4455). A/C. Breakfast/lunch/dinner daily. AE, CB, DC, MC, V. Jkt. *Specialties:* crayfish salad, Vidalia onion tart w. pancetta and turmeric sauce, ragoût of shrimp and rice beans, sturgeon w. caviar, veal en cocotte, rum-soaked savarin. *Note:* A rest. practicing a modified version of the excellence found at Jean-Louis. The cooking is very French provincial, using less common parts of the animal in the pot-au-feu. Jean-Louis Palladin of Jean-Louis rest. splits his time between both kitchens. But at one-third the price of Jean-Louis, one is tempted to forego the first name and head for the last. *French.* **I–M**

🍷🍷 **Bombay Palace** (dwntwn), 2020 K St. NW (331-4200). A/C. Lunch/dinner daily. AE, CB, DC, MC, V. *Specialties:* samosas, chicken tikka, tandoori prawns, chicken tandoori, curries, ghosh vindaloo (lamb stew). So-so desserts and wine list. *Note:* When the rest. changed locations in 1993 it forsook its exotic elegance for a more generic decor. But the refined cuisine of this first-class Indian rest. hasn't lost its elegance, and will particularly delight those who prefer their exoticism subdued to American tastes. Remarkably attentive svce; business crowd at lunch, tourists at dinner. Resv. advisable; a fine place to eat. *Indian.* **I–M**

🍸🍸 **La Colline** (dwntwn), 400 N. Capitol St. NW (737-0400).
A/C. Breakfast/lunch Mon–Fri, dinner Mon–Sat; closed hols. AE, CB, DC, MC, V. Jkt. *Specialties:* smoked salmon house style, fresh foie gras, gratin of crayfish, salmon w. beurre blanc and baby turnips, braised sweetbreads w. zucchini, parsleyed ham, bouillabaisse, breast of duck w. black currant; skip the desserts. Good wine list at reasonable prices. *Note:* The likable, bearded, 40-ish chef Robert Greault has worked a miracle: He serves excellent, elegant, varied bistro food at half the prices charged by other French rests. of the same caliber. Huge, modern, comfortable dining rm; ultra-professional svce, but a bit overtaxed. Very popular w. the locals, so resv. advised. At the foot of Capitol Hill near Union Station. *French.* **I–M**

🍸🍸 **Mr. Yung's** (dwntwn), 740 6th St. NW, Chinatown (628-1098). A/C. Lunch/dinner daily (till midnight). AE, MC, V. *Specialties:* dim sum (at lunch), noodle soup w. shredded roast duck, crab w. three kinds of mushrooms, stir-fried spareribs in black-bean sauce, frogs steamed w. ham in lotus leaf. *Note:* Unusually long menu of seasonally changing dishes very well done and served. Bright, attractive, clean-lined dining room. Resv. suggested for parties of four or more. One of the best addresses in Chinatown. *Chinese.* **I–M**

🍸 **Nora** (nr. dwntwn), 2132 Florida Ave. NW (462-5143). A/C. Dinner only, Mon–Sat; closed hols. MC, V. *Specialties:* gravlax (pickled salmon w. dill), roast sweet peppers w. goat cheese, grilled pork chop w. tarragon, soft-shelled crabs w. basil, roast chicken w. mustard-cream sauce, smoked trout w. horseradish sauce. Very good homemade desserts. Menu changes regularly. Good wine list at reasonable prices. *Note:* Charming little bistro serving American nouvelle cuisine; only the highest-grade meat, poultry, and fish and the freshest of farm vegetables are used, and these are simply but skillfully prepared. Cool, pleasant rustic setting w. antique furniture and quilts worthy of a museum of American folk art. Ultra-professional svce. Locally popular and a favorite of President Clinton's. A good place to go. Resv. advised. *American.* **I–M**

🍸🍸 **Jean-Michel** (vic.), 10223 Old Georgetown Rd., Bethesda, MD (301/564-4910). A/C. Lunch Mon–Fri, dinner nightly; closed hols. *Specialties:* calamari tempura w. aioli sauce, filet of salmon w. saffron sauce, lamb loin chops w. cumin and coriander, roasted duckling w. raspberry sauce, warm apple tart. Very affordable wine list. *Note:* Comfortable and casual setting to match the homey cooking. Under the guidance of proprietor Jean-Michel Farret the staff is congenial and professional. A fine place to spend an evening. *French.* **I–M**

🍸🍸 **Primi Piatti** (dwntwn), 2013 I St. NW (223-3600). A/C. Lunch Mon–Fri, dinner nightly; closed hols. AE, CB, DC, MC, V. *Specialties:* mixed antipasti, inventive pizzas cooked over a wood fire, fresh homemade pasta, fritto misto, cacciuco di carne (meat stew), fish, chicken and meat broiled with polenta, chocolate terrine with strawberry coulis. Good list of Italian wines. *Note:* Here you will find no sophisticated fare or trendy sauces; the emphasis is rather on basic Italian dishes such as mixed hors d'oeuvres, various kinds of homemade pasta, broiled foods, and pizza, all of them nonetheless pleasing and tasty. Hence the name of this huge, modern, likable *trattoria* in the heart of dwntwn. Noisy, relaxed atmosphere; yuppie patrons; fashionable place. Resv. not honored so you'll have to wait, especially at lunchtime. *Italian.* **I–M**

🍸 **Bacchus** (dwntwn), 1827 Jefferson Place NW (785-0734). A/C. Lunch Mon–Fri, dinner Mon–Sat; closed hols. AE, MC, V. *Specialties:* mezze (hors d'oeuvres), bel lahm (lamb stew w. yogurt), stuffed eggplant w. pomegranate sauce, chicken or lamb or fish kebab, chicken rice pilaf, kafta mechwi (broiled chopped beef w. pine-nut rice), malfouf mahchi (cabbage stuffed w. meat), Oriental pastry. Modest wine list. *Note:* The best place in Washington for authentic Lebanese and Middle Eastern cuisine. Conventional modern setting; considerate svce. Resv. advised. Excellent value; another branch is at 7945 Norfolk Ave., Bethesda, Md. (301/657-1722). *Middle Eastern.* **I**

♀ **Cafe Atlantico** (dwntwn), 1819 Columbia Rd. NW (328-5844). A/C. Dinner only, nightly. AE, CB, DC, MC, V. *Specialties:* shrimp wrapped in yucca root, jerk chicken, grilled pilapia in tequila-and-orange sauce, lamb shank in red-wine sauce w. yucca purée, crepes filled w. caramel squash. *Note:* Creative Caribbean cuisine served in a splashy, modern decor w. large windows, and a skylight offering a wonderful view of Adams-Morgan street life. Efficient, personable svce. Good exotic drinks (don't miss the Brazilian *caipirinha*). No resv. *Caribbean.* **I**

♀ **China Inn** (dwntwn), 631 H St. NW, Chinatown (842-0909). A/C. Lunch/dinner Mon–Sat (until 1am). AE, MC, V. *Specialties:* spiced shrimps, clams w. black-bean sauce, Cantonese roast duck, "fish dipped in boiling water w. spices," roast pork Chow Mai Fun, lemon chicken, steamed sea bass w. ginger. So-so desserts. *Note:* A Chinatown classic for more than half a century, serving above-average Cantonese food at prices very easy on the wallet. Recently modernized and enlarged. Friendly svce (unusual for a Chinese rest.). Locally popular; very good value. *Chinese.* **I**

♀ **Meskerem** (dwntwn), 2434 18th St. NW (462-4100). A/C. Lunch/dinner daily (until midnight). AE, DC, MC, V. *Specialties:* kebabs, sambusas, shrimp wat (stew), kifto (highly seasoned steak tartare), tibbs (beef or lamb sautéed w. onion and sweet pepper), vegetarian dishes. Ho-hum desserts; skimpy wine list. *Note:* Delicious stews wrapped in spicy, flavorful pancakes (injera) and eaten without knives or forks are the staple at this unusual and exotic Ethiopian rest. Beef, lamb, or chicken stews—highly seasoned (*wats*) or somewhat less explosive (*alechas*)—should be washed down w. pitchers of beer. The setting, in contrast to Washington's other Ethiopian rests., is elegant and almost luxurious, particularly on the third (top) floor with its stained-glass skylight. Uncommonly courteous svce. Locally popular; resv. advisable. *Ethiopian.* **I**

♀ **Tony Cheng's Mongolian Restaurant** (dwntwn), 619 H St. NW, Chinatown (842-8669). A/C. Lunch/dinner daily. AE, MC, V. *Specialties:* pickled Chinese cabbage, Mongolian barbecue, Mongolian hot pot. *Note:* One of the best bargains in town. Diners load their bowl w. all-they-can-eat beef, chicken, vegetables, or seafood, then watch while a cook makes it sizzle on a cast-iron grill. Two or more people can also cook their own meal in the boiling stock of charcoal hot pots placed at the center of the table. Oriental decor. Helpful, efficient svce. *Chinese.* **I** (prix fixe).

♀ **Clyde's** (nr. dwntwn), 3236 M St. NW (333-9180). A/C. Lunch/dinner daily (until 1am), brunch Sat–Sun. AE, CB, DC, MC, V. *Specialties:* sandwiches, hamburgers, omelets, steak tartare, specialty salads, broiled foods, barbecued spareribs. *Note:* Once favored by Washington's gilded youth, this likable New York–style saloon still has a devoted following, especially among visitors. Good hamburgers (except when they're overcooked). Lovely greenhouse setting in the back dining rm. Often crowded and noisy; relaxed atmosphere; svce disorganized but good-humored. A landmark in Washington for more than 20 years. *American.* **B–I**

Restaurants in the Vicinity

☀♀♀♀ **L'Auberge Chez François** (vic.), 332 Springvale Rd. (Va. 674), Great Falls, Va. (703/759-3800). A/C. Dinner only, Tues–Sun; closed hols. AE, MC, V. Jkt. *Specialties:* quiche, salmon soufflé, Alsatian choucroute, sautéed kidneys, filet of lamb w. tarragon, red snapper in pastry shell, truffled sweetbreads, duckling bigarade, navarin of seafood, coq au riesling. Very good homemade ice cream and tarts. Fine list of Alsatian wines. Menu changes regularly. *Note:* The food and the atmosphere are those of a deluxe inn in France. Some country dishes (tripe, homemade pâté de campagne), and some more sophisticated (salmon soufflé). Charming rustic decor w. open-air dining in summer; irreproachable svce; resv. a must. 35 min. from dwntwn. A fine place. *French.* **M–E**

🍸 **Old Angler's Inn** (vic.), 10801 MacArthur Blvd., Potomac, MD (301/299-9097). A/C. Lunch/dinner Tues–Sat, brunch Sun. Jkt. *Specialties:* grilled curry sausage w. raisins and couscous, napoleon of house-smoked salmon, muscovy duck w. wild cherries and bacon, red snapper filet w. spicy carrot broth, beef tenderloin w. chilies and Maui onions, blueberry custard tart. *Note:* A cozy setting inside near the fire in the winter and a refreshing one outside on the patio in the summer. The inn, which has been around since 1860, has been the romantic getaway in several Washington romance novels. A great location w. great food to boot. Jeffrey Tomchek's cooking is ambitious, not to mention inventive. *American.* **M–E**

Cafeterias/Specialty Spots

National Gallery Terrace Café (dwntwn), Constitution Ave. and 4th St. NW (347-9401). A/C. Lunch only, daily (till 4:30pm). No credit cards. *Specialties:* sandwiches, soup, quiches. *Note:* Ultramodern, inviting museum cafeteria overlooking the east wing atrium; very acceptable food.

Rocklands (nr. dwntwn), 2418 Wisconsin Ave. NW (333-2558). A/C. Lunch/dinner daily (until 10pm). No credit cards. *Specialties:* barbecued pork, chicken, beef, lamb; grilled vegetables, hefty sandwiches. *Note:* A bright, friendly, popular carry-out and dining countertop. Serves some of the best barbecued meat north of the Carolinas and east of Texas. No alcohol.

Sholl's Colonial Cafeteria (dwntwn), 1990 K St. NW, in Esplanade Mall (296-3065). A/C. Lunch/dinner Mon–Sat (until 8pm); closed Jan 1, Dec 25. No credit cards. *Specialties:* calves' liver w. onions, spaghetti, roast chicken, daily specials, homemade pastry. *Note:* A popular cafeteria, much appreciated by Washingtonians. Offers excellent value; usually crowded at lunch. No alcoholic beverages. A Washington landmark since 1928.

Where to Eat What in Washington

American: Austin Grill (p. 267), Clyde's (p. 270), Kinkead's (p. 266). Nora (p. 269), Occidental Grill (p. 268), Old Angler's Inn (p. 271), Old Ebbitt Grill (p. 266), Red Sage (p. 266), Seasons (p. 267), Vidalia (p. 265)

Cafeterias/Specialty Spots: National Gallery Terrace Café (p. 270), Rocklands (p. 270), Sholl's Colonial Cafeteria (p. 270)

Caribbean: Cafe Atlantico (p. 270)

Chinese: China Inn (p. 270), Mr. Yung's (p. 269), Tony Cheng's Mongolian Restaurant (p. 270)

Ethiopian: Meskerem (p. 270)

French: L'Auberge Chez François (p. 270), La Colline (p. 269), Jean-Louis (p. 265), Jean-Michel (p. 269), Le Lion d'Or (p. 267), Palladin (p. 268)

Indian: Bombay Palace (p. 268)

Italian: Galileo (p. 267), Primi Piatti (p. 269), I Ricchi (p. 266), Vincenzo (p. 268)

Japanese: Sushi Ko (p. 267)

Mexican: Enriqueta's (p. 267)

Middle Eastern: Bacchus (p. 269)

Seafood: Crisfield (p. 266), Morton's (p. 268), Vincenzo (p. 268)

Steak: Morton's (p. 268)

BARS & NIGHTCLUBS

Bayou (nr. dwntwn), 3135 K St. at Wisconsin Ave. NW, Georgetown (333-2897): Love rock and new wave; rough 'n' ready crowd. Open nightly.

The Birchmere (vic.), 3901 Mt. Vernon Ave., Alexandria, Va. (703/549-5919): One of the best clubs in the country for folk and bluegrass; the biggest names appear here. Open Tues–Sat.

Blues Alley (nr. dwntwn), on the alley behind 1073 Wisconsin Ave. NW,

Georgetown (337-4141): The oldest jazz club in Washington, and still the best. All the big names have played here, from Chick Corea to McCoy Tyner. Also acceptable Créole rest. Open nightly; two or three shows an evening.

Brickskeller (nr. dwntwn), 1523 22nd St. NW (293-1885). Very popular bar serving 500 brands of domestic and imported beer; also rest. (so-so). Usually crowded. Open nightly until 2am.

Capital City Brewing Company (dwntwn), 1100 New York Ave. NW (628-2222): Microbrewery serving pale ale, nut brown ale, bitter, and porter. A lively, rustic place in the old Greyhound bus station. Decent food. Open nightly.

Cities (dwntwn), 2424 18th St. NW (328-7194). A hip but noisy watering hole/nightclub/rest., in the heart of the lively Adams-Morgan district. The food is very commendable; funky atmosphere. Open nightly.

Comedy Café (dwntwn), 1520 K St. NW (638-5653). Oldest and best-known comedy club in Washington, presenting all the big names and young local talent as well. Open Wed–Sun; resv. advised.

Fifth Column (dwntwn), 915 F St. NW (393-3632): Luxurious disco in a former branch bank. Marble dance floor, video music, and spectacular laser shows. Also acceptable rest. and art gallery. Open Tues–Sat.

Hard Rock Café (dwntwn), 999 E St. NW (737-7625). Local offspring of the famed London rock joint. The main downstairs bar is shaped like a gigantic piano. Congenial but very noisy atmosphere. Also rest. Directly across the street from FBI headquarters.

Kilimanjaro (dwntwn), 1724 California St. NW (328-3838). Washington's hottest "world music" club, in the Adams Morgan area, with live African, reggae, and calypso music. One of the few clubs in town popular with both Caucasians and African Americans. Open nightly.

9:30 Club (dwntwn), 930 F St. NW (393-0930). Hot new "alternative/progressive" rock bands. Open Mon–Sat.

Tracks (nr. dwntwn), 1111 1st St. SE (488-3320). The fashionable gay club, drawing a very mixed crowd. Disco w. live music. Lots of action. Open nightly (until 6am Fri–Sat).

NEARBY EXCURSIONS

ALEXANDRIA, VA. (7 mi./11km south on George Washington Memorial Pkwy. and Washington St.; area code 703): Founded in the mid-18th century by Scottish merchants, this appealing little Colonial town on the Potomac has not kept pace with its mighty neighbor, Washington. With its cobbled streets, traditional streetlamps, and enchanting old houses, ☼▲ **Old Town Alexandria,** around King and Fairfax Sts., looks like a print from an old British book. No visit to Washington is complete without a pilgrimage to Mount Vernon (see below) and the other historic spots in Alexandria which are associated with the life of George Washington: **Gadsby's Tavern,** 134 N. Royal St. (838-4242), open Tues–Sun; **Carlyle House,** 121 N. Fairfax St. (549-2997), open Tues–Sun; the **Stabler-Leadbeater Apothecary Shop,** 105 S. Fairfax St. (836-3713), open Mon–Sat; the **Lee-Fendall House,** 614 Oronoco St. (548-1789), open Tues–Sun; **Old Presbyterian Meeting House,** with the tomb of the Unknown Soldier of the War of Independence, 321 S. Fairfax St. (549-6670), open Mon–Sat; and **Christ Church,** 118 N. Washington St. (549-1450), open daily.

For other historic buildings in Alexandria, inquire at the **Alexandria Convention and Visitors Bureau,** itself quartered in the oldest house in town, **Ramsay House** (ca. 1724), 221 King St. (838-4200), open daily. Also see **Robert E. Lee's boyhood home,** 607 Oronoco St. (548-8454), open daily.

See also the ☼▲ **George Washington Masonic National Memorial,** an unusual Masonic temple with a 333-ft. (102m) tower copied from the famous Pharos (lighthouse) of Alexandria, one of the seven wonders of antiquity, with an observation platform at the top. The memorial displays a large collection of Washington artifacts, including the family Bible and the clock that was stopped at the time of Washington's death. It's at Shooter's Hill, 101 Callahan Dr. (683-2007), open daily, and well worth the side trip. If you like handcrafts shops you should stop at the **Torpedo Factory Arts Center,** 105 N. Union St. (838-4565). Now a complex for more than 200 professional artists—painters, potters, weavers, sculptors, jewelers, and stained-glass artists—this factory was a munitions-manufacturing center during both World Wars. Open daily.

Where to Eat

Le Gaulois, 1106 King St. (739-9494). Lunch/dinner Mon–Sat. AE, CB, DC, MC, V. Hearty country food in a charming French provincial decor. Very good value. **I–M**

Taverna Cretekou, 818 King St. (548-8688). Lunch/dinner Tues–Sun. AE, CB, DC, MC, V. The best Greek rest. in the Washington, D.C., area. **I–M**

ANNAPOLIS, MD. (31 mi./50km east on U.S. 50; area code 410): Briefly the capital of the U.S. (Congress met here from November 26, 1783, to August 13, 1784), and capital of Maryland since 1695, this lovely 300-year-old harbor town is best known today as the home of the U.S. Naval Academy. It offers a wide range of diversions to the visitor.

You can **cruise the harbor** and the Severn River aboard the *Harbor Queen,* boarding at City Dock at the foot of Main St. (268-7600), daily Memorial Day–Labor Day.

You can visit the **State House** (1772–79), the oldest legislative building still in use in the country, at State Circle (974-3400), open daily. Here, in 1783, George Washington laid down his office as commander-in-chief of the Continental Army. Here, too, in 1784, the Treaty of Paris, which had been signed at Versailles the previous year, was ratified, ending the War of Independence.

Stroll among the beautifully restored old houses of Cornhill St., Maryland Ave., and Prince George St.: the **Hammond-Harwood House, Chase Lloyd House, William Paca House,** and so on.

Watch a noon parade of uniformed midshipmen, admire the model sailing ships at the maritime museum, or meditate before the ※ **tomb of John Paul Jones** in the chapel of the ⌀ **U.S. Naval Academy** at the foot of King George St. (263-6933). There are conducted tours daily Mar–Thanksgiving; more than a million visitors come here annually. Rediscover the 18th century in an old tavern near the docks.

For further information, contact the **State House Visitor Center,** State Circle (974-3400), open daily. Don't fail to visit Annapolis.

Where to Eat

Harbor House, 97 Prince George St. (268-0771). Lunch/dinner daily. AE, MC, V. Successful conversion of an old warehouse looking out over the harbor, w. terrace for fine days. Very good fish and seafood. **I**

Treaty of Paris (Maryland Inn), Church Circle at Main St. (263-2641). Lunch/dinner daily. AE, CB, DC, MC, V. Historic (1776) inn serving excellent traditional food. **I**

DULLES INTERNATIONAL AIRPORT (in Chantilly, Va., 26 mi./42km west via the George Washington Memorial Pkwy., I-495, and Dulles Airport Rd.) (703/661-2700): Lovers of architecture will appreciate the pure lines of the terminal designed in 1962 by the great Finnish-American architect Eero Saarinen. This was the first U.S. airport specifically intended for the jet age, and its roof, in-curved like a hammock and secured by cables, has served as a model for many other buildings around the world. The airport is named after John Foster Dulles, President Eisenhower's much-traveled secretary of state.

Not far from Saarinen's building, on the road leading to the airport, take a look at the astonishing inverted pyramid, in three-colored glass, of the ⚐⚐ **Center for Innovative Technology,** designed by the well-known Miami team of Bernardo Fort-Brescia and Laurinda Spear. The CIT tower is beyond a doubt the most original contemporary building in Washington—a city not greatly endowed with innovative architecture.

☀⚐⚐ **FREDERICKSBURG, VA.** (50 mi./80km south on I-95; area code 703): Halfway between Washington and Richmond, the capital of Virginia, this charming vestige of the past occupies a proud place in American history. Capt. John Smith, founder of Jamestown, the first permanent British settlement on the continent, visited the site in 1608. George Washington spent his childhood here, James Madison practiced law here before going on to become the fifth president of the U.S., and some of the bloodiest battles of the Civil War were fought here, as the town changed hands seven times between 1862 and 1864.

Houses that have seen the passage of one or two centuries line Charles St. and Caroline St. in the heart of the historic district. Among them are: the **Rising Sun Tavern,** 1306 Caroline St. (371-1494), open daily, which was built in 1760 by George Washington's youngest brother, Charles; the **Mary Washington House,** 1200 Charles St. (373-1569), open daily, which George Washington presented to his mother in 1772 and where she lived until her death; the **James Monroe Museum,** 908 Charles St. (899-4559), open daily, where the future president lived; the **Hugh Mercer Apothecary Shop,** 1020 Caroline St. (373-3362), open daily, with its authentic 18th-century interior; and **Kenmore,** 1201 Washington Ave. (373-3381), open daily, one of Virginia's loveliest historic homes, built in 1752 by Col. Fielding Lewis, George Washington's brother-in-law.

☀⚐⚐ **MOUNT VERNON** (15 mi./25km south on the George Washington Memorial Pkwy. and Mount Vernon Memorial Hwy.) (703/780-2000): This splendid Colonial mansion following a design by Washington overlooks the Potomac, and is where George Washington died on December 14, 1799. The main building, with its white, colonnaded Georgian facade turned to the river, was begun in 1754 on land that had been in the family since 1674. Washington lived here as a planter with his wife, the former Martha Custis, for 15 years, from 1759 until 1775 when he became commander-in-chief of the Continental Army. Returning in 1783, he continued to enlarge the house and its gardens. After eight years as president he retired here finally in 1797 and remained until his death two years later. After the death of Martha in 1802, Mount Vernon remained in the Washington family until 1858, when it was purchased, along with 198 acres (80ha), by the Mount Vernon Ladies Association, carefully restored, and operated as a national memorial.

In part built by Washington himself, the main block has 19 rooms, of which the most interesting are the president's library and the room where he died. Very beautiful original furniture. A feature of the main reception room is the key to the Bastille, a gift from Lafayette. A little apart are the kitchen, the workers' and slaves' quarters, and the Washington family vault with the caskets of George and Martha Washington.

Drawing a million people a year, this is one of the most-visited places in the U.S.; long waiting lines on weekends and in summer. The access road is a scenic highway along the river. Open daily.

☀⚐⚐ **NATIONAL AIR & SPACE MUSEUM—PAUL E. GARBER FACILITY** (Old Silver Hill Rd., Suitland, Md.): The restoration workshop and annex of the famous museum in dwntwn Washington. A hundred craft, old (the 1914 Blériot Type XI) and new (the cruise missile) are displayed side by side with machines in process of restoration like the *Enola Gay,* from which the atom bomb was dropped on Hiroshima.

An absolute must for aviation buffs, 30 min. from dwntwn along Independence Ave., Pennsylvania Ave. SE, and Old Silver Hill Rd. Guided tours by appointment only; resv. should be made at least two weeks ahead with the Tour Scheduler at the dwntwn museum (202/357-1400).

WOODLAWN PLANTATION (18 mi./29km south via George Washington Memorial Pkwy. and Mount Vernon Memorial Hwy.) (703/780-4000): Splendid home adjoining Mount Vernon, built between 1800 and 1805 by William Thornton, one of the architects of the Capitol, on land given by George Washington to his adopted daughter as a wedding present. The mansion is a typical Virginia plantation house.

Also on the grounds is the **Pope-Leighey House,** designed by the great Frank Lloyd Wright; this cypress wood, brick, and glass structure was originally erected at Falls Church, Va., in 1940 and was moved to its present location in 1964. It's worth going out of your way to visit these two very dissimilar houses. Woodlawn Plantation is open daily; Pope-Leighey House, daily Mar–Dec, Sat–Sun Jan–Feb.

FARTHER AFIELD

SHENANDOAH NATIONAL PARK: (76 mi./122km west on I-66 to Front Royal at the north entrance to the park): This magnificent wooded park covering 300 sq. mi. (777km²) is 80 mi. (129km) long but only 2–13 mi. (3–21km) wide; encompassing the crests of the **Blue Ridge Mountains,** it is traversed from end to end by one of the most spectacular scenic highways in the country, ❄ **Skyline Drive.** The Blue Ridge Mountains, the easternmost ridge of the Appalachians, owe their name to the veil of bluish mist that usually clings to most of the peaks. Shenandoah Park (it means "daughter of the stars" in the local Native American tongue), which averages about 2,000 ft. (610m) above sea level, is almost entirely covered in a thick forest of conifers, oaks, and birches, which shelter a numerous and varied wildlife including brown bears, deer, foxes, lynx, and more than 200 species of birds. Along the Skyline Drive more than 75 overlooks have been constructed, allowing you views all the way west to the Shenandoah Valley or east to the Piedmont plateau.

Skyline Drive is continued to the south by an equally spectacular mountain road, the **Blue Ridge Parkway,** which is the best route to **Great Smoky Mountains National Park,** 750 mi. (1,200km) to the south (see Chapter 13 on Nashville).

Shenandoah Park and the neighboring **George Washington Forest** are at their best in spring, and even more at the peak of the fall foliage display. They also boast some of the finest caves on the East Coast: **Skyline Caverns,** near Front Royal; ❄ **Luray Caverns** and **Endless Caverns,** near Luray; and **Grand Caverns,** near Grottoes.

The ❄ **natural bridge,** south of Lexington, is also worth a detour. A limestone arch 215 ft. (66m) high and 65 million years old, it has been termed "one of the Seven Wonders of the New World."

The park is open year round. For information, contact the Superintendent, Rte. 4, Box 348, Luray, VA 22835 (703/999-2229). A must for nature lovers.

Some 25 mi. (40km) east of Shenandoah Park, don't fail to visit ❄ **Monticello,** on Va. 53 near Charlottesville (804/984-9822). The luxurious estate of Thomas Jefferson, third president of the U.S., is one of the finest surviving examples of 18th-century American architecture, spectacularly situated on a height of land. Designed and built by Jefferson over a period of 40 years. Period furniture and decoration. The tomb of Thomas Jefferson is in the nearby family graveyard. Open daily.

If you're enticed by Jefferson's skill as an architect, then don't miss the ※🔭 **University of Virginia,** west end of Main St. in Charlottesville (924-1019). Take a guided tour of the tree-lined "Lawn," pavilion gardens, serpentine walls, and the Rotunda—all of which make up Jefferson's "academical village." The facades of the pavilions are replicates of actual Greek temples. You can peek into the room that Edgar Allan Poe occupied as a student of the university. This is one of the most celebrated state university campuses in the country. Open daily

Where to Stay and Eat En Route

IN CHARLOTTESVILLE ※🍴🍴🍴 **Boar's Head Inn,** Ivy Rd. (U.S. 250), Charlottes-ville, VA 22905 (804/296-2181). 175 rms. Delightful country inn built around an 1834 grain-mill. Remarkable comfort and facilities. **M–E**

IN NEW MARKET 🍴 **Shenvalee,** U.S. 11, New Market, VA 22844 (703/740-3181), half a mile south of town. 42 rms. Inviting, comfortable motel on 200 acres (80ha) of park and grdn. Tennis and golf. Excellent value. **B–I**

IN WASHINGTON, VA. ※🍴🍴🍴🍴 **Inn at Little Washington,** Middle and Main Sts., Washington, VA 22747 (703/675-3800). Dinner only, Wed–Mon. Superb new American cooking by highly talented chef Patrick O'Connell and flawless svce in a plush English-inn setting. Also 10 luxuriously comfortable rms. One of the dozen best rests. in the country. Resv. a must, well in advance. **VE** (prix fixe).

🔭🔭 **EASTERN SHORE** (395 mi./632km r.t. via U.S. 50E, U.S. 113S, U.S. 13S, Va. 175E and 175W, U.S. 13N, and U.S. 50W—about 500 mi./800km if you go and return via the Chesapeake Bay Bridge-Tunnel): Leaving Washington on New York Ave. and U.S. 50 (John Hansen Hwy.), you'll soon come to your first stop, **Annapolis** (see "Nearby Excursions," above). The road then follows the shoreline of the **Chesapeake Bay,** a great arm of the sea 185 mi. (300km) long and parallel to the Atlantic Ocean, famous for its seafood. After passing through 🏛 **Wye Mills,** a picturesque little village whose authentic 18th-century character has been preserved, you come to **Easton,** capital of the Eastern Shore. There are many old houses to see, as well as the superb Courthouse Sq. The Third Haven Friends Meeting House, 405 S. Washington St. (410/822-0293), open daily, was built by Quaker settlers in 1682 and is one of the oldest religious buildings in the country.

Before continuing toward Cambridge and Ocean City, go out of your way to the charming little fishing port of ※🏛 **St. Michaels,** where you'll find the fasci-nating 🏛 **Chesapeake Bay Maritime Museum** on Waterside (410/745-2916), open daily Apr–Dec (wknds only the rest of the year), as well as the enchanting St. Mary's Sq. with its old houses.

Another worthwhile side trip is to **Oxford,** a pleasure-sailing center and ter-minus of the oldest ferry in the U.S., the **Oxford–Bellevue Ferry,** which has been in operation for three centuries.

Southwest of **Cambridge,** another little Colonial port, take Md. 16 as far as 🏛 **Church Creek,** where you will come upon Old Trinity Church (1675), one of the oldest in the country. Back on U.S. 50, when you're 5 mi. (8km) west of Mardela Springs, look out for the **Mason-Dixon Line Marker,** the first stone placed in 1763 on the historic line marking the traditional boundary between the northern and southern U.S. (The Mason-Dixon Line owes its name to Charles Mason and Jeremiah Dixon, two British surveyors who in 1763 were instructed to determine the boundaries of the land given 130 years earlier by the Crown to

Cecilius Calvert, 2nd Baron Baltimore, and to William Penn. Following the line of latitude 39 degrees 42 minutes 26.3 seconds from the sea to the Alleghenies, the Mason-Dixon Line forever divides the Yankee North from the Dixie South.)

Then on to ⌂ **Ocean City,** Maryland's only Atlantic coast resort, with a beautiful fine-sand beach 3 mi. (5km) long, and dozens of hotels and motels in all price ranges—but also huge crowds in summer.

Your last stop will be at ⌂⌂ **Assateague Island National Seashore,** a long chain of sand dunes alternating with marshes and pinewoods which are home to myriads of birds and to many wild ponies, said to be descended from those brought here by the first Spanish explorers in their galleons. On the last Wed–Fri of July the ponies are swum across the arm of the sea that separates **Assateague Island** from **Chincoteague Island** to be sold at auction; in the week before this yearly ritual of "pony penning," the whole region devotes itself to carnival—and pony races. A visit to this nature reserve, famous also for its oysters and shellfish, is worth the trip all by itself. For information, contact the Superintendent, Assateague Island National Seashore, Rte. 2, Box 294, Berlin, MD 21811 (410/641-1441), or the Refuge Manager, Chincoteague National Wildlife Refuge, P.O. Box 62, Chincoteague, VA 23336 (804/336-6122).

You can return to Washington either the same way you came, along U.S. 13 and U.S. 50, or by going farther south to the very spectacular 17-mi. (28km) **Chesapeake Bay Bridge-Tunnel** and then jogging back north along I-64 and I-95. This will enable you to visit Williamsburg, Yorktown, and Richmond (see below). Allow at least three or four days for this very comprehensive trip, which you shouldn't miss.

Where to Stay En Route

IN EASTON, MD. ☀☎☎ **Tidewater Inn,** Dover and Harrison Sts., Easton, MD 21601 (410/822-1300). 120 rms. Elegant two-century-old building, now a designated historic monument. Rest. highly regarded for its seafood. **M–E**

IN BERLIN, MD. ☀☎☎ **Atlantic Hotel,** 2 N. Main St., Berlin, MD 21811 (410/641-3589). 16 rms. Romantic 1895 Victorian hotel elegantly restored. Critically acclaimed rest. and wine list. **I–M**

IN OXFORD, MD. ☎☎ **Robert Morris Inn,** Md. 333, Oxford, MD 21654 (410/226-5111). 33 rms. Charming little Colonial-style inn overlooking the water. Praiseworthy rest. **I–M**

IN OCEAN CITY, MD. ☎☎☎ **Sheraton Resort** 10100 Ocean Hwy., Ocean City, MD 21842 (410/524-3535; toll free, see Sheraton). 250 rms. Big, ultramodern 16-story tower on the beach. **E–VE**

☎☎ **Plim Plaza Hotel,** Boardwalk and 2nd St., Ocean City, MD 21842 (410/289-6181). 181 rms. Standard motel. **I–M**

IN CHINCOTEAGUE, VA. ☀☎☎ **Driftwood,** Beach Rd. at Assateague Bridge, Chincoteague, VA 23336 (804/336-6557). 52 rms. Congenial little motel at the entrance to the park. For lovers of the sea. **I–M**

Where to Eat En Route

IN ST. MICHAELS, MD. ☎☎ **Inn at Perry Cabin,** 308 Watkins Lane, St. Michaels, Md. (410/745-2200). Lunch/dinner daily. Ambitious new American cooking —remarkable seafood dishes—in a charming English country-house setting. Lovely view of the bay; resv. advised. **M–E**

IN OXFORD, MD. ♟ **The Masthead Club,** Mill St. at the Strand (410/226-5303). Lunch/dinner Tues–Sun, brunch Sat–Sun. Excellent local seafood. **I–M**

☀☖ **GETTYSBURG & PENNSYLVANIA DUTCH COUN-TRY** (265 mi./424km r.t. via I-270N, U.S. 15N, U.S. 30E and 30W, I-83S, and I-95S): The greatest and most glorious battlefield of the Civil War, and in Amish country, a 17th-century survival (for details, see Chapter 6 on Philadelphia). On the way, stop in **Catoctin Mountain Park** on Md. 77 west of Thurmont. In this lovely rolling, wooded landscape is hidden **Camp David,** country retreat of the presidents and scene of many famous diplomatic meetings. No visitors. A two-day trip interesting on account of its variety. (For recommended accommodations and restaurants, see Chapter 6 on Philadelphia.)

Washingtonians will find a foretaste of Amish country at the **Dutch Country Farmers Market** in Burtonsville, Md., at the intersection of U.S. 29 and Md. 198 (301/421-4046). A score of stands kept by Amish countryfolk wearing traditional garments and head coverings sell farm products from vegetables to meat and from cheese to home-baked pastry—all guaranteed to contain no chemical additives or pesticides. Locally popular; open Thurs–Sat. 30 min from dwntwn Washington.

☖ **POTOMAC VALLEY** (165 mi./264km r.t. via the George Washington Memorial Pkwy., River Rd. West, Whites Ferry, U.S. 15S, Va. 7W, Va. 9W, Va. 671N, Md. 65N, Md. 34E, Alt. U.S. 40E, and I-270S): Picturesque drive running for much of its length along the Potomac River. It begins with a visit to the ☀☖ **Chesapeake & Ohio Canal National Historical Park and Great Falls.** Begun in 1828, the canal was intended to link Georgetown, now a suburb of Washington, with the Ohio Valley, but work was abandoned in the 1870s because of competition from the railroads. There survives to this day, on the stretch near the Great Falls of the Potomac, an entire system of bridges and locks, now surrounded by a pretty wooded park that is maintained jointly by the states of Maryland and Virginia. Interesting little museum; open daily (301/739-4200).

Cross the Potomac at **Whites Ferry** (toll ferryboat) and continue on into ☖ **Leesburg,** a charming little Colonial town founded in 1758 and in great part restored to its original appearance. Be sure to see the **Loudoun County Historical Museum** at 16 W. Loudoun St. (703/777-7427), open daily. Today Leesburg is an important thoroughbred center.

Now on to ☀☖ **Harpers Ferry,** proudly standing at the confluence of the Shenandoah and Potomac Rivers. In this Civil War landmark town, the old U.S. Army arsenal has been completely restored; there are also many historic houses in the Old Town. It's best known as the scene of John Brown's rebellion against slavery in 1859, which later became a symbol to the northern states. It ended in his execution by hanging at **Charles Town,** 8 mi. (13km) south, where the ambience of the 18th century has also been scrupulously preserved. Don't fail to visit John Brown's Fort, rebuilt on the exact site of the drama, on Old Arsenal Sq., open daily.

Continuing northward, you'll come to ☀☖ **Antietam National Battlefield Site and Cemetery,** where the defeat of the Confederate troops of General Lee ended the South's first invasion of the North. This, September 17, 1862, was the single bloodiest day of the entire Civil War, with 23,000 killed and wounded in a matter of a few hours. The battlefield may be visited. Visitor Center and museum on Md. 65 (301/432-5124), open daily.

The last stop is at ☀ **Frederick,** a place of strategic importance during the Civil War and an architectural trove of ante-bellum mansions and museums around Market and Patrick Sts. Be sure to see the **Francis Scott Key Museum,** 123 S. Bentz St. (301/663-8687), open Sat–Sun Apr–Dec, birthplace of the author of the words of the national anthem. His tomb, marked by the U.S. flag, may be seen at Mount Olivet Cemetery at the south end of Market St., open daily. Then back to Washington on I-270. A one-day trip particularly worthwhile in warm weather.

Where to Eat En Route

IN LEESBURG ☀💰 **Green Tree,** 15 S. King St. (703/777-7246). Lunch/dinner daily; authentic 18th-century recipes in a very lovely antique setting. An unusual experience. I

👓 **WILLIAMSBURG & COLONIAL VIRGINIA** (320 mi./ 512km r.t. via I-95S and I-64E, and the reverse route returning): Your first stop will be at ☀💰 **Richmond,** capital of Virginia since 1780 and capital of the Confederacy 1861–65. Founded in 1607 as a trading post for the first settlers and the local Native American tribes, Richmond soon flourished thanks to its tobacco business; on the eve of the Civil War it had some 40 curing plants.

While skyscrapers and modern buildings now cluster along the banks of the James River, bearing witness to the economic and industrial vigor of present-day Richmond, the older neighborhoods of the center city are still a living museum of Virginia's great Colonial epoch. The warehouses of **Shockoe Slip,** at Main, Canal, and Cary Sts., the oldest part of the city, are now home to artists, boutiques, and fashionable restaurants. The respectable middle classes live in the **Fan District,** in the shade of the trees in **Monroe Park. Church Hill** is the district around the wooden church of the Revolutionary patriots, **St. John's Church,** at 25th and Broad Sts. (804/648-5015), open daily; here Patrick Henry made his immortal pronouncement: "As for me, give me Liberty, or give me Death." Somehow the neighborhood has preserved a subtle aura of the 19th century. A more solemn note is struck by ☀ **Monument Avenue,** Richmond's processional boulevard, lined with trees, mansions, and monuments in honor of its most illustrious citizens, particularly Jefferson Davis and Gen. Robert E. Lee.

Try not to miss the **State Capitol** (1788), on Capitol Sq. (804/786-4344), open daily, whose design closely follows that of the Maison Carrée in Nîmes; also the three-story neoclassical ☀ **White House of the Confederacy** and the adjoining museum, rich in historical material, at 1201 E. Clay St. (804/649-1861), open daily; here Jefferson Davis made his home during the Civil War.

You should see the lovely 💰 **Virginia Museum of Fine Arts,** at Boulevard and Grove Ave. (804/367-0844), open Tues–Sun, with fine art nouveau and art deco material, jewelry by Fabergé, and paintings by great European masters.

Driving east from Richmond you will come next to ☀💰 **Williamsburg,** capital of Virginia 1698–1780, and the most famous museum town in the U.S., looking just as it did in the 18th century. Thanks to funding from John D. Rockefeller, Jr., Williamsburg was able to launch, in 1926, a gigantic salvage operation involving almost 150 old buildings. The many craftsmen's workshops, booths, taverns, and displays with people in 18th-century attire attract more than a million visitors to Williamsburg every year. The evidences of the past lie all around you here: the 1705 **State Capitol** (east end of Duke of Gloucester St.); the (British) **Governor's Palace and Gardens** (on Palace Green); the **Raleigh Tavern** (Duke of Gloucester St.), frequented by Jefferson, Henry, and other Revolutionary leaders; and the old **Public Gaol** (Nicholson St.), completed in 1704, where debtors, criminals, and pirates were imprisoned. Most of these historic buildings are open to visitors daily throughout the year. The **Visitor Center,** on Colonial Pkwy. at Va. 132 (804/220-7645), provides useful information, leaflets, and museum tickets, and will make hotel reservations for you.

Williamsburg is worth the trip all by itself, but there are three places nearby that justify a detour. ☀ **Jamestown,** 9 mi. (14km) SW on Colonial Pkwy., was the first permanent British settlement in North America (1607), and has many ruins and historic buildings (including the 1639 💰 **Old Church Tower**) as well as re-created Native American and English villages. Visitor Center (804/229-1733) open daily.

☼Å **Yorktown,** 13 mi. (20km) SE on Colonial Pkwy., was the scene of the last engagement of the War of Independence, where the American and French troops of Washington and Rochambeau, on October 19, 1781, accepted the surrender of General Cornwallis, putting an end to British rule over the Thirteen Colonies. The battlefield may be visited; Visitor Center (804/898-3400) open daily.

Finally, ☼Å **Busch Gardens – The Old Country,** 3 mi. (5km) east on U.S. 60 (804/253-3350), is a 360-acre (121ha) theme park with quaint European villages; open daily mid-May to Labor Day, wknds only in spring and fall; closed the rest of the year. Topped two million guests last year.

On your way back to Washington along I-64W and I-95N, be sure to see **Fredericksburg** and **Alexandria** (see "Nearby Excursions," above).

This is a trip that will appeal to lovers of History with a capital H; allow at least three days.

Where to Stay En Route

IN RICHMOND ☼ÅÅÅ **Jefferson Hotel,** Franklin and Adams Sts., Richmond, VA 23220 (804/788-8000). 276 rms. One of the finest old hotels (1895) in the country. Sumptuous interior superbly restored; the Rotunda and its grand staircase are worth a visit in themselves. **E–VE**

ÅÅ **Embassy Suites,** 2925 Emerywood Pkwy, Commerce Center, Richmond, VA 23294 (804/672-8585). 225 suites. Comfortable hotel 10 minutes from dwntwn. **I–M**

IN WILLIAMSBURG ☼ÅÅÅ **Williamsburg Inn,** Francis St., Williamsburg, VA 23185 (804/229-1000). 102 rms. Elegant Colonial building in the heart of the Historic District, with remarkably good facilities and standards of comfort. Regency decor and furnishings. **VE**

ÅÅÅ **Williamsburg Hospitality House,** 415 Richmond Rd., Williamsburg, VA 23185 (804/229-4020). 313 rms. Modern, very comfortable hotel whose appearance and decor harmonize wonderfully with the Historic District a block or two away. **M**

ÅÅ **Best Western Patrick Henry Inn,** York and Page Sts., Williamsburg, VA 23185 (804/229-9540). 301 rms. Inviting, friendly motel a 2-min. walk from the State Capitol. Very good value. **I–M**

Å **Days Inn Downtown,** 902 Richmond Rd., Williamsburg, VA 23185 (804/229-5060). 100 rms. Small, conventional, but well-run motel near the center of town. Very good value. **I**

Where to Eat En Route

IN RICHMOND ☶☶ **The Frog and the Redneck,** 1423 E. Carey St. (804/648-3764). Dinner only, Mon–Sat; closed hols. Glitzy urban decor w. cartoons on the walls. Simple regional cuisine that tastes great. A truly great place. **I–M**

IN WILLIAMSBURG ☼☶ **Trellis,** Duke of Gloucester St., Merchants Sq. (804/229-8610). Lunch/dinner daily, brunch Sun. Imaginative, delicate American nouvelle cuisine from the hand of the talented chef Marcel Desaulniers; some of the best food in Virginia at extremely reasonable prices. Inviting shady terrace. A fine place. **I–M**

☼☶ **King's Arms Tavern,** Duke of Gloucester St. (804/229-1000). Lunch/dinner daily. Authentic 18th-century tavern with its original Colonial decor attractively restored. Traditional American food. **I**

PART TWO

THE SOUTH

CHAPTER 10

CHARLESTON♛

□ □ □

Called "The Holy City" because of its many churches and dozens of bell towers, Charleston—formerly spelled "Charles Towne," for King Charles II—is one of the most gracious cities in the United States, and one of the most popular among tourists. Under British rule Charleston was the largest Atlantic port south of Philadelphia, enjoying a strategic position at the junction of the Ashley and Cooper Rivers. Elegant and cosmopolitan, Charleston attracted a large Huguenot (French Protestant) colony in the 18th century (until 1928 there were still religious services conducted in French), as well as strong currents of Irish, German, Scottish, and even West Indian immigration.

Charleston surrendered to General Sherman in Feb 1865 after a two-year siege. Despite the wounds of war, a terrible earthquake in 1886, and many devastating fires and hurricanes—among which was the terrifying hurricane Hugo in Sept 1989, one of the 10 worst hurricanes to reach the U.S. mainland in this century (24 people dead and $3.5 billion in property damage in the Carolinas)—this charming, aristocratic city of the Old South, bypassed by time, has conserved a number of interesting traces of the past: **Fort Sumter,** whence came the spark that ignited the Civil War; the **Dock Street Theatre,** the country's oldest (1736); **Cabbage Row,** immortalized as "Catfish Row" in the opera *Porgy and Bess;* the **Charleston Museum,** founded in 1773 (the country's first); the venerable houses of **Old Charleston,** with their Doric columns and wrought-iron balconies; and dozens of plantations with lush tropical gardens. Each spring since 1977 Charleston has played host to the American version of Italy's famous **Spoleto Festival,** offering ballet, theater, and classical and contemporary music to enthusiasts from all over the country.

Center of the rice and indigo trades in Colonial times, then a prosperous slave market before the Civil War, Charleston is presently an active port at the heart of a highly mechanized agricultural region, with a booming tourist trade (more than two million visitors each year), but a hotel capacity that is still relatively limited. Charleston is 14th on the list of the 20 American cities experiencing the most rapid economic growth.

BASIC FACTS: State of South Carolina. Area code: 803. Time zone: eastern. ZIP Code: 29401. Founded: 1670. Approximate population: city, 69,000; metropolitan area, 510,000.

CLIMATE: Almost any season is a good one to discover Charleston. Winter is generally mild (average Jan temperature, 50°F/10°C) and summer hot (average July temperature, 80°F/27°C), although raincoats and umbrellas are in order because of tropical storms. Spring (gardens bloom in Mar and Apr) and autumn, Oct and Nov especially, are the ideal seasons to visit this popular tourist destination.

DISTANCES: Atlanta, 289 mi. (462km); Miami, 455 mi. (728km); Savannah, 106 mi. (170km); Washington, 527 mi. (844km).

ARRIVAL & TRANSIT INFORMATION

AIRPORT: International Airport (CHS): 12 mi. (20km) NW. Information: 767-1100. New contemporary terminal.

AIRLINES: American (toll free 800/433-7300), British Airways (toll free 800/247-9297), Delta (toll free 800/221-1212), and United (toll free 800/241-6522).

CITY LINK: Cab fare to city center, about $16; time, about 20 min. Bus: **Airport Shuttle** (767-7111); fare, $9; time, about 30 min. Although cab fares are reasonable, renting a car with unlimited mileage is advisable for visiting the numerous parks and plantations surrounding the city. Rather inadequate public transportation (bus) system (SCE&G), but fast, convenient dwntwn shuttle (DASH) Mon–Sat only. Call 747-0922 for information.

CAR RENTAL (at the airport unless otherwise indicated): Avis (toll free 800/331-1212); Budget (toll free 800/527-0700); Hertz (toll free 800/654-3131); National (toll free 800/227-7368); Thrifty, 3565 W. Montague (toll free 800/367-2277). For dwntwn locations, consult the local telephone book.

LIMOUSINE SERVICES: Jenning's Limousine Service (853-9726), Lowcountry Limousine (767-7117).

TAXIS: Taxis cannot be hailed on the street but must be summoned by phone: **North Area Cab** (554-7575) or **Yellow Cab** (577-6565). Rates rather low.

TRAIN: Amtrak, 4565 Gaynor Ave. (toll free 800/872-7245), 8 mi. (12km) W of dwntwn.

INTERCITY BUSES: Greyhound, 3610 Dorchester Rd. (744-4247).

INFORMATION & TOURS

TOURIST INFORMATION: Charleston Convention & Visitors Bureau, 81 Mary St., SC 29402 (803/577-2510; toll free 800/868-8118). **Historic Charleston Foundation,** 51 Meeting St., SC 29401 (803/722-3405).
    Visitor Information Center, 375 Meeting St., SC 29402 (803/853-8000). Offers the best printed material.

GUIDED TOURS: Adventure Sightseeing (bus), 1090 Ft. Sumter Dr. (762-0088). Guided tour of the city and environs; serves the major hotels.
    Charleston Carriage Co. (city tour in horse-drawn carriage), 96 N. Market St. (577-0042). Daily year round. Resv. suggested.
    Gray Line Tours (bus) (722-4444). Guided tour of the city and environs. Leaves from major dwntwn hotels.
    Gray Line Water Tours (harbor cruise), Municipal Marina, Lockwood Blvd. (722-1112). Offers a view of the U.S. Navy's famous Polaris submarines. Daily year round.
    Fort Sumter Tour, Municipal Marina, Lockwood Blvd. (722-1691). Worth going out of your way for. Daily except Dec 25.

SIGHTS, ATTRACTIONS & ACTIVITIES

ARCHITECTURAL HIGHLIGHTS: ⚓ **The Citadel,** Moultrie St. and Elm-wood Ave. (953-5006): Also known as "the West Point of the South," this cele-brated military academy, founded in 1842 (1,900 students), occupies the site of an early 19th-century fort built to quell slave revolts. Commanding fortress-style architecture with battlements and turrets, a military museum, and archives of Gen. Mark Clark, World War II hero. Cadet parades on Fri at 3:30pm during the academic year. Open daily.

☀⚓ **U.S.S. _Yorktown,_** Patriots Point, left bank of the Cooper River (884-2727): This World War II aircraft carrier, which has been transformed into a floating museum with planes, helicopters, and weapons, also affords a very lovely view of the city, the harbor, and Fort Sumter. Anchored not far from here is the **_Savannah,_** the first nuclear-powered freighter, and other U.S. Navy ships. Open daily.

BEACHES: ⚓ **Bulls Island,** 3 mi. (5km) off the South Carolina coast: Long stretches of underdeveloped beach and hiking trails. Access by ferry: Cape Ro-maine Charters, Moore's Landing (18 mi./29km N. on SC17) (803/928-3411).

CHURCHES/SYNAGOGUES: ⚓ **Huguenot Church,** 110 Church St. (722-4385): Consecrated in 1687, rebuilt in 1796 and again in 1845 after two fires, this is the only church in the country that has retained the Calvinist liturgy of the Huguenots. Until 1928 services were conducted in French. Open daily, mid-March to mid-June and mid-Sept to mid-Nov.

☀⚓ **Kahal Kadosh Beth Elohim,** 90 Hasell St. (723-1090): The country's second-oldest synagogue, founded in 1749 (the old-est is in Newport, R.I.). The present building, which dates from 1840, is consid-ered one of the most beautiful examples of the Greek Revival style in the country. Open Mon–Fri.

⚓ **St. Michael's Church,** Meeting and Broad Sts. (723-0603): With its 186-ft.-tall (57m) bell tower, this unusual church is Charleston's oldest (1761) and was attended by George Washington. Its distinc-tive portico was painted black in the Revolution to spoil the aim of gunners. The organ dates from 1768. Open daily.

☀⚓ **St. Philip's Church,** 142 Church St. (722-7734): On this site the first Anglican church south of Virginia was built in 1670, the year Charleston was founded. The present building dates from 1838; its soar-ing steeple was an aiming point for Northern gunners during the Civil War. Was severely damaged by hurricane Hugo in 1989, but was completely restored in 1993. The adjacent cemetery is the resting place of many notables, including Edward Rutledge, one of the signers of the Declaration of Independence. Open daily.

HISTORIC BUILDINGS: ☀⚓ **Dock Street Theatre,** Church and Queen Sts. (720-3968): This hall opened in 1936 on the site of the country's oldest theater (1736). The architecture, inspired by the Georgian theaters of the 19th century, includes a carefully restored section of the former Planter's Hotel (1809). Open Mon–Fri.

⚓ **Fort Moultrie,** W. Middle St., Sullivan's Island (883-3123): Col. William Moultrie dealt the English one of their first and gravest defeats of the Revolutionary War here in 1776. The present fort, rebuilt in 1809, served as a prison, in the last year of his life, for the captured Osceola, who led the revolt of the Seminoles in Florida, the bloodiest of the Native Ameri-can Wars. Across the channel from Fort Sumter. Open daily.

♟♟ **Fort Sumter,** Fort Sumter Island (883-3123): One of the hallowed places of American history. Built on an artificial island in the middle of Charleston's harbor, Fort Sumter was the target both of the South's surprise attack that touched off the Civil War (4:30am, April 12, 1861), and of a bloody northern siege 1863–65. Can be reached only by boat from the Municipal Marina (see "Guided Tours," above). Interesting military museum and a very lovely view of the old city's skyline. Open daily.

☀♟♟ **Old Charleston,** around Meeting, George, and Church Sts.: Very lovely vignette of the past—pastel houses with wrought-iron railings and small, narrow cobbled streets. There are many historic homes to see, such as the **Nathaniel Russell House,** 51 Meeting St., a fine example of the Adam style with its splendid staircase (1808); the imposing Greek Revival **Edmondston-Alston House,** 21 E. Battery St., built in 1828 by a wealthy merchant on a choice piece of land with a stunning view of Charleston harbor; the **Heyward-Washington House,** 87 Church St., once home to George Washington (1772); the **Joseph Manigault House,** 350 Meeting St., another magnificent example of the Adam style (1803); the **Thomas Elfe Workshop,** 54 Queen St., former studio of the famous cabinetmaker Thomas Elfe (1760); and the **Calhoun Mansion,** 16 Meeting St., noted for its sumptuous Victorian interiors (1870). All these buildings are open daily to visitors. With more than 2,000 landmarked 18th- and 19th-century buildings, Old Charleston constitutes one of the nation's most spectacular collections of historic architecture. For detailed information, consult the **Visitor Information Center,** 375 Meeting St. (853-8000).

♟ **Provost Dungeon,** 122 E. Bay St. (792-5020): The **Old Exchange Building** (1771), originally used as a customshouse, was a small British fort where American patriots were imprisoned during the Revolutionary War (Provost Dungeon). Interesting exhibition dedicated to this period, plus films about Charleston's artistic heritage. Open daily.

MARKETS: ☀♟ **City Market,** Meeting and Market Sts.: A mixture of flea market and yard sale with merchandise of all kinds. Lively and colorful, it has been the center of local commerce for two centuries.

MUSEUMS OF ART: ☀♟ **City Hall Art Gallery,** 80 Broad St. (724-3799): A very fine collection of famous portraits, including John Trumbull's rendering of George Washington, in an interesting 1801 building. It originally served as the regional office of the Bank of the United States. Open Mon–Fri.

♟ **Gibbes Art Gallery,** 135 Meeting St. (722-2706): An interesting collection of 18th- and 19th-century American paintings, miniatures, and Japanese prints. Temporary exhibitions, as well. Open daily.

MUSEUMS OF SCIENCE & HISTORY: ♟ **Charleston Museum,** 360 Meeting St. (722-2996): The country's oldest museum (1773), in a modern, well-designed building since 1980. Natural history, anthropology, fine arts, relics of colonial times. Contains notably the life-size replica of the first submarine used during the Civil War, the *Hunley.* Open daily.

☀♟ **Old Powder Magazine,** 79 Cumberland St. (722-1623): This former Revolutionary War gun-powder factory was part of the original city fortifications and is Charleston's oldest public building (1713). It undergoes renovation in 1995, but is still open to the public on certain days. Contact the Historic Charleston Foundation at the above number for information.

PARKS & GARDENS: ♟ **Hampton Park,** Rutledge Ave. and Cleveland St.: A splendid array of blooming camellias and azaleas in spring and roses in summer. Open daily.

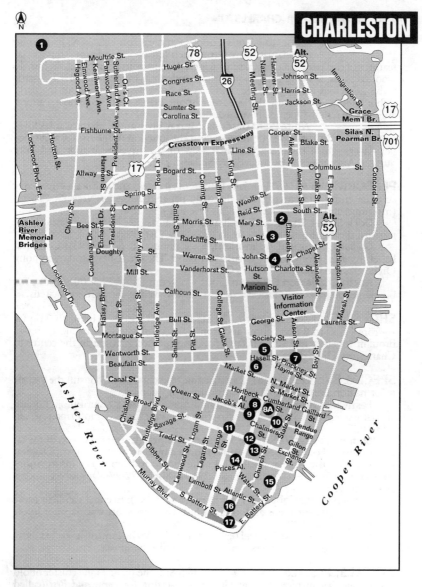

CHARLESTON

SOUTH CAROLINA
★ Columbia
• Charleston

Aiken-Rhett Mansion ❷
American Military Museum ❼
Calhoun Mansion ⓰
Charleston Museum ❸
The Citadel ❶
Congregation Beth Elohim ❺
Dock Street Theatre ❾
Edmondston-Alston House ⓯
French Huguenot Church ❿
Gibbes Museum of Art ❽

Heyward-Washington House ⓭
Joseph Manigault House ❹
Nathaniel Russell House ⓮
Rutledge House ⓫
St. Mary's Roman
    Catholic Church ❻
St. Michael's
    Episcopal Church ⓬
Thomas Elfe Workshop ⓐ
White Point Gardens ⓱

    🛶 **Palmetto Islands County Park,** east on U.S. 17N, half a mile (.8km) past Snee Farm, then left on Long Point Rd.: Special features of this park in a tropical setting include a spacious open meadow, heavily wooded areas, a 2-acre (1ha) pond, and a mile-long canoe trail. Marsh boardwalks as well as jogging, hiking, and bicycle paths wind throughout the park. Public fishing and boating docks border Boone Hall Creek. Pedal boat, canoes, and bicycle rental. Open daily year round.

    🛶 **White Point Gardens,** Murray Blvd. and E. Battery St.: A lovely flowered promenade at the junction of the Ashley and Cooper Rivers which offers a spectacular view of the city, the harbor, and Fort Sumter. A scene not to be missed. Open daily.

PERFORMING ARTS: For daily listings of all shows and cultural events, consult the entertainment pages of the daily papers *Charleston News & Courier* (morning) and *Charleston Evening Post* (evening).

    Dock Street Theatre, Church and Queen Sts. (723-5648): Classical and modern theater, from Shakespeare to Broadway, Oct–May.

    Gaillard Municipal Auditorium, 77 Calhoun St. (723-9693): Concerts, ballet, recitals. Home of the Charleston Ballet Theatre, Charleston Symphony Orchestra, and Charleston Opera Company.

    North Charleston Coliseum, 5001 Coliseum Dr. (529-5000): Venue for big-name, out-of-town musical acts. Also hosts traveling shows like the circus.

SHOPPING: Charleston Place, 130 Market St.: Three dozen luxury boutiques —from Gucci to Ralph Lauren and from Laura Ashley to Godiva chocolates— brought together in a very effective faux antique decor. Right in the center of Charleston. Open daily.

SPECIAL EVENTS: For the exact schedule of events below, consult the **Visitor Information Center** (see "Tourist Information," above).

    Festival of Houses (mid-Mar to mid-Apr): The most beautiful old homes, specially opened to the public. Try to time your visit for it. For information, call 723-1623.

    Spoleto Festival/USA (late May to early June): American version of the famous Italian "Festival of Two Worlds" founded by Gian Carlo Menotti. Classical music, ballet, jazz, opera, theater, art exhibitions, and more. For information, contact P.O. Box 157, Charleston, SC 29402 (803/722-2764); the box office is at 14 George St.

    Garden Candlelight Tours (mid-Sept to mid-Oct): Evening candlelit tours through the city's gardens and loveliest historic homes. Spectacular. For information, call 722-4630.

    International Film Festival (late Oct to early Nov): Annually presents more than 500 works of filmmakers worldwide, plus film symposia.

STROLLS: 🏚 **Cabbage Row,** 89-91 Church St.: The picturesque cluster of old rowhouses that inspired George Gershwin's setting for *Porgy and Bess* (called "Catfish Row" in the opera).

    🔭 **Old Charleston:** See "Historic Buildings," above.

ACCOMMODATIONS

Personal Favorites (in order of preference)

    🏛🏛🏛🏛 **Omni at Charleston Place** (dwntwn), 130 Market St., SC 29401 (803/722-4900; toll free, see Omni). 450 rms, A/C, color TV, in-rm movies. AE, CB, DC, MC, V. Valet gar. $11, pool, health club, sauna, two rests. (including Louis' Charleston Grill), two bars, 24-hr. rm svce, disco, boutiques, concierge, free crib. *Note:* Classy new hotel inaugurated in 1986, w. architecture that blends with the Old Charleston setting. Elegant, refined decor and vast, well-conceived rms w. stylish furniture. Impeccable svce and reception. VIP and big business clientele. At the very heart of historic Charleston, w. direct access to Charleston Place Mall and its luxury boutiques. An excellent location. **VE**

Hawthorn Suites (dwntwn), 181 Church St., SC 29401 (803/577-2644; toll free 800/527-1133). 182 suites, A/C, color TV, in-rm movies. AE, CB, DC, MC, V. Valet parking $9, health club, rest. adj., free breakfast, free crib. *Note:* Brand-new (1991) luxury courtyard hotel featuring oversize suites w. antique reproductions and complete kitchens. Beautiful landscaped grdns. Complimentary breakfast buffet and evening reception daily. Attentive svce. Smack in the heart of Historic Charleston. An excellent place to stay. **M–E**

Lodge Alley Inn (dwntwn), 195 E. Bay St., SC 29401 (803/722-1611; toll free 800/845-1004). 98 rms, A/C, cable color TV. AE, MC, V. Free parking, rest., bar, rm svce, free crib. *Note:* Elegant hotel in a prettily renovated 1773 mansion. Comfortable, tastefully decorated rms and suites w. period furniture, refrigerator, and balcony (some w. kitchenette and fireplace). Distinguished reception and svce. Rest. of quality (French Quarter). Attractive location in the heart of the historic district. **E**, but lower rates off-season.

Quality Inn Heart of Charleston (nr. dwntwn), 200 Meeting St., SC 29401 (803/722-3391; toll free, see Choice). 126 rms, A/C, cable color TV. AE, CB, DC, MC, V. Free parking, pool, rest., bar, valet svce. *Note:* This comfortable, well-maintained motel w. excellent svce is a very good value. A few minutes' walk from Charleston's principal tourist attractions. **I–M**

Two Meeting Street Inn (formerly Carr's Guest House; nr. dwntwn), 2 Meeting St., SC 29401 (803/723-7322). 9 rms, A/C (no single rms). No credit cards. Street parking. *Note:* The charm of an old family-run European pension in a small 1890s villa shaded by live oaks and palmettos. Spacious, inviting rms (some without private bathroom). View of the bay. Good value overall. Resv. a must. **I–M**

Days Inn Historic District (dwntwn), 155 Meeting St., SC 29401 (803/722-8411; toll free, see Days Inns). 124 rms, A/C, cable color TV. AE, DC, MC, V. Free parking, pool, rest., free crib. *Note:* Classic motel particularly well situated for a visit to Old Charleston. Comfortable rms. Good value. **I**

Other Accommodations (from top bracket to budget)

Holiday Inn Mills House (formerly the Hyatt House; dwntwn), 115 Meeting St., SC 29401 (803/577-2400; toll free, see Holiday Inns). 210 rms, A/C, color TV, in-rm movies. AE, CB, DC, MC, V. Gar. $8, pool, rest. (Barbadoes Room), two bars, rm svce, concierge, free crib. *Note:* Comfort and svce above the norm for a Holiday Inn. Elegant decor, stylish furniture, and a deftly reconstructed colonial atmosphere. In the heart of Old Charleston. **E**, but lower rates off-season.

Planters Inn (dwntwn), 112 N. Market St., SC 29401 (803/722-2345; toll free 800/845-7082). 45 rms, A/C, cable color TV. AE, CB, DC, MC, V. No private parking; rest. (Robert's), free crib. *Note:* Charming little luxury hotel that has become a favorite of connoisseurs. Elegant, carefully restored 19th-century building. Spacious rms w. antique furniture (some have fireplaces). Personalized service in an elegant, cushy atmosphere. Renowned rest. Class and style. **M–E**

Sheraton Charleston Hotel (nr. dwntwn), 170 Lockwood Dr., SC 29403 (803/723-3000; toll free, see Sheraton). 338 rms, A/C, color TV, in-rm movies. AE, CB, DC, MC, V. Free parking, pool, rest., bar, rm svce, free crib. *Note:* One of the most recent additions to the local hotel scene, w. spacious, very comfortable rms w. balconies (the best have a view of the Ashley River) and good svce. Very complete facilities. Adequate rest. (Ashley's). 3 min. from the center of historic Charleston (free shuttle bus). **M–E**

☼♀♀ **Vendue Inn** (dwntwn), 19 Vendue Range, SC 29401 (803/ 577-7970; toll free 800/845-7900). 33 rms, A/C, color TV. AE, MC, V. Free parking, rest. (The Library), rm svce, free breakfast. *Note:* Charming little luxury hotel in a lovely three-story residence dating from 1824. Period decor as romantic as can be. Exceptionally polished reception and svce. Well-regarded rest. A very classy place. **M–E**

♀♀ **Holiday Inn Riverview** (nr. dwntwn), 301 Savannah Hwy., SC 29407 (803/556-7100; toll free, see Holiday Inns). 178 rms, A/C, cable color TV. AE, CB, DC, MC, V. Free parking, pool, rest., bar, rm svce, free crib. *Note:* This 14-story tower w. a view of the Ashley River offers functional, balconied rms and a scenic rest.-bar at the top. Holiday Inn style. Good value. 10 min. from dwntwn. **I–M,** but lower rates off-season.

♀ **Dorchester Motor Lodge** (vic.), 3668 Dorchester Ave. (at I-26), SC 29405 (803/747-0961). 200 rms, A/C, color TV. AE, CB, DC, MC, V. Free parking, pool, rest., bar, rm svce. *Note:* Typical but comfortable motel in the northern end of Charleston. Cheerful reception. Its location, just 10 min. from dwntwn, makes it ideal if you're driving. **I**

♀ **Hampton Inn Mt. Pleasant** (nr. dwntwn), 255 U.S. 17N Bypass, SC 29464 (803/881-3300; toll free 800/426-7866). 121 rms, A/C, cable color TV. AE, CB, DC, MC, V. Free parking, pool, rest. adj., free crib, free breakfast. *Note:* New, inviting motel just across Historic Charleston by the Cooper River bridges. Comfortable, functional rms; friendly reception. Good value overall. **B–I**

♀ **Motel 6 South** (vic.), 2058 Savannah Hwy., SC 29407 (803/ 556-5144). 111 rms, A/C, cable color TV. AE, DC, MC, V. Free parking, pool, free crib. *Note:* Ultra-economical, modern, and functional motel that's an excellent value and ideal if you're driving—15 min. from dwntwn (at the intersection of S.C. 7 and U.S. 17). **B**

Accommodations in the Vicinity

☼♀♀♀ **Kiawah Island Inn & Villas** (vic.), Kiawah Island (P.O. Box 12910), SC 29412 (803/768-2121; toll free 800/845-2471). 150 rms, A/C, cable color TV. AE, DC, MC, V. Free parking, four pools, tennis, four golf courses, health club, two rests. (including Jasmine Porch), bar, rm svce, disco, crib $15. *Note:* Luxurious vacation complex that's ideal for water sports offering a 9½-mi. (15km) beach, boat and windsurfer rentals, and waterskiing. Comfortable rms w. balconies and patios. Also available are 350 cottages and villas w. kitchenettes. Svce leaves a bit to be desired. Interesting wknd packages. 20 mi. (32km) south of Charleston on U.S. 17, S.C. 171, and S.C. 700. **E–VE,** but lower rates off-season.

Airport Accommodations

♀♀ **La Quinta** (vic.), 2499 La Quinta Lane, SC 29418 (803/797-8181; toll free, see La Quinta). 122 rms, A/C, color TV, in-rm movies. AE, CB, DC, MC, V. Free parking, pool, rest. adj., rm svce, free breakfast, free crib. *Note:* New motel 5 min. from the airport. Comfortable, spacious rms plus cheerful reception and svce make this a very good value. 20 min. from dwntwn. **I**

RESTAURANTS

Personal Favorites (in order of preference)

♀♀♀ **82 Queen** (dwntwn), 82 Queen St. (723-7591). A/C. Lunch/dinner daily; closed Thanksgiving, Dec 25. AE, MC, V. Jkt. *Specialties:* broiled tuna steak w. marinated shrimp and sun-dried tomatoes, regional dishes. The menu changes regularly. *Note:* An "in" place in a charming early 19th-century residence w. a grdn courtyard for alfresco dining.

Carefully prepared cuisine centering on seafood. First-rate svce. Locally very popular. Resv. highly recommended. The adjacent Wine Bar is the ideal spot for a before- or after-dinner drink. *Seafood.* **M–E**

☼☼♈♈♈ **Poogan's Porch** (dwntwn), 72 Queen St. (577-2337). A/C. Lunch/dinner daily. AE, MC, V. *Specialties:* she-crab soup, gumbo, Cajun shrimp, broiled steak or catch of the day, peanut-butter pie. *Note:* The new fashionable place, in a lovely old house in the historic district. Food of Créole antecedents, elegantly prepared and served. Rather noisy; excellent svce. A very good place to eat—and a popular one, so make resv. even for lunch (ask for a table on the veranda). *American.* **I–M**

♈♈ **Anson's** (dwntwn), 12 Anson St. (577-0551). A/C. Dinner only, nightly; closed Dec 25. AE, CB, DC, MC, V. Jkt. *Specialties:* individual pizza w. Gorgonzola and pistachios, crispy flounder w. apricot and shallot sauce, cashew-crusted grouper w. champagne sauce, chocolate "oblivion" torte. *Note:* An asset to the local gastronomic scene, offering Carolina Low-Country cuisine. Decked out in antique plantation columns and doors and located in the warehouse district of Charleston. Pleasant outdoor balcony seating available. Resv. advised. *American.* **I–M**

♈♈ **Marianne's** (dwntwn), 235 Meeting St. (722-7196). A/C. Dinner only, nightly; closed Jan 1, Thanksgiving, Dec 25. AE, MC, V. Jkt. *Specialties:* house pâtés, rack of lamb, baron of beef, paupiettes of red snapper, excellent homemade pastries. The menu changes regularly. *Note:* French bistro-style cuisine and decor. Good wine list. Friendly svce. Resv. advised. *French.* **I–M**

☼☼♈ **A. W. Shuck's** (dwntwn), 70 State St. (723-1151). A/C. Lunch/dinner daily; closed hols. AE, DC, MC, V. *Specialties:* oysters, clams, scampi, fish of the day, stuffed shrimp, seafood casserole. *Note:* Seafood bistro which serves first-rate fish year round. Generous portions at the bar. Pleasant ambience. Resv. not necessary. *Seafood.* **B–I**

Other Restaurants (from top bracket to budget)

♈♈♈ **Carolina's** (dwntwn), 10 Exchange St. (724-3800). A/C. Dinner only, nightly; closed Dec 24–25. AE, MC, V. *Specialties:* mixed seafood grill, smoked baby back ribs, pasta dishes, swordfish. *Note:* Charleston's upbeat bistro serving modern Carolina cuisine w. an emphasis on grilled seafood to patrons in tuxedos and blue jeans. Black-and-white tile decor. Noisy late at night. Very popular locally. Resv. suggested. *American.* **I–M**

♈♈ **Barbadoes Room** (dwntwn), in the Holiday Inn Mills House Hotel (see "Accommodations," above) (577-2400). Lunch Mon–Sat, dinner nightly, brunch Sun. AE, CB, DC, MC, V. Jkt. *Specialties:* she-crab soup, fried artichokes, lobster bisque, grilled grouper w. sautéed shiitake mushrooms and garlic, mud pie w. Kahlúa ice cream. *Note:* Longstanding favorite for formal dining in the Charleston area. Typical Low-Country cuisine. Professional but stiff svce. Resv. a must. *American.* **I–M**

♈♈ **Slightly North Abroad** (dwntwn), 192 E. Bay St. (723-3424). A/C. Lunch Mon–Fri, dinner Mon–Sat; closed hols. AE, DC, MC, V. Jkt. *Specialties:* grilled chicken breast w. eggplant and goat cheese croutons, caviar, shrimp and grits, crab cakes, key lime pie. *Note:* Owner and chef of the now defunct Colony House have together changed locations, but not much else. Kitchen is open to customer viewing, and the chef will wander out to the dining room to answer questions regarding the preparation of your food. Locally popular. Unfortunately, resv. are not taken. *Seafood/American.* **I–M**

☼☼♈♈ **East Bay Trading Co.** (dwntwn), East Bay and Queen Sts. (722-0722). A/C. Dinner only, nightly; closed hols. AE, DC, MC, V. *Specialties:* scallops in ginger sauce, prime rib, catch of the day, good homemade desserts. *Note:* In an old harbor warehouse w. picturesque, if overelaborate, decor, this pleasant rest. offers good European-inspired cuisine. Cheerful svce. Locally popular. Resv. not taken. *Continental/American.* **I**

     Garibaldi's (dwntwn), 49 S. Market St. (723-7153). A/C. Dinner only, nightly; closed hols. AE, MC, V. *Specialties:* homemade pasta, traditional Italian dishes, seafood. *Note:* Pleasant small *trattoria* in the center of Historic Charleston Market, offering some of the best Italian food in town. Outdoor dining. An excellent locale. *Italian.* **I**

     Charleston Ice House (dwntwn), 188 Meeting St. (723-6123). A/C. Breakfast/lunch/dinner daily (until midnight); closed Thanksgiving, Dec 25. AE, MC, V. *Specialties:* fish of the day, Greek dishes, sandwiches, excellent desserts. *Note:* Picturesque, lively atmosphere in the heart of the Old City Market. Honest, unpretentious cuisine. Excellent value. Locally popular. *Greek/American.* **B–I**

     Salty Mike's (nr. dwntwn), Municipal Marina, Lockwood Blvd. (723-6325). A/C. Breakfast/lunch/dinner Tues–Sat. AE, MC, V. *Specialties:* seafood chowder, seafood, shellfish, salads, fried chicken, hamburgers. *Note:* Generally jam-packed at lunchtime, this bistro on the banks of the Ashley River offers decent cuisine at very reasonable prices. Efficient svce. Pleasant view of the yacht basin. Locally very popular. *Seafood/American.* **B–I**

Cafeterias/Specialty Spots

     Gaulart & Maliclet (dwntwn), 98 Broad St. (577-9797). Breakfast/lunch/dinner Mon–Sat. AE, DC, MC, V. *Specialties:* gazpacho, homemade soups, pâtes, sandwiches, and daily specials that can be eaten at the counter. Fine wine list. *Note:* Small, pleasant bistro especially popular among lawyers and bankers at lunch hour. An excellent spot.

     Reuben's Downtown Delicatessen (dwntwn), 251 Meeting St. (722-6883). Breakfast/lunch daily (until 4pm). No credit cards. *Specialties:* New York–style deli offering hearty sandwiches, homemade soups, and salads. *Note:* Usually packed with locals. Located in old building (1880s). No resv.

BARS & NIGHTCLUBS

     A. W. Shuck's (dwntwn), 70 State St. (723-1151). Inviting oyster bar (see "Restaurants," above). Open Mon–Sat.

     Café 99 (dwntwn), 99 S. Meeting St. (577-4499). Singles bar locally popular. Live music nightly.

     Fannigan's (dwntwn), 159 E. Bay St. (722-6916). High-energy dance club w. a business crowd. Live music on the weekends. Open Mon–Sat.

     Henry's (dwntwn), 54 N. Market St. (723-4363). Congenial bar w. live jazz on the weekends. Open nightly.

NEARBY EXCURSIONS

     BOONE HALL PLANTATION (8 mi./13km NE on U.S. 17) (803/884-4371): Former cotton plantation dating from 1681. Only the slave quarters and the outbuildings are original. The classic Georgian-style house is more than 150 years old and served as the setting for *Gone with the Wind.* Very lovely avenue of century-old oaks. Open daily.

     CHARLES TOWNE LANDING (1500 Old Towne Rd.) (803/852-4200): This colonial village, rebuilt at the spot where the English landed in 1670, faithfully reconstructs the life and atmosphere of the first British colonists. The grounds include 660 acres (267ha) of parks, plantations, and gardens, plus a replica of the 17th-century merchant ship *Adventure.* Open daily.

     CYPRESS GARDENS (23 mi./37km north on U.S. 52) (803/553-0515): Superb camellia and azalea gardens and giant cypresses amid pools, once a part of the Dean Hall Plantation (1725). Boat rides. Open daily.

FRANCIS MARION NATIONAL FOREST (18 mi./ 29km NE on U.S. 17 or S.C. 41): Dotted with lakes and swamps, this 250,000+-acre (100,000+ha) forest contains subtropical vegetation and many remains of Native American and colonial plantings. Camping, boating, fishing, hunting, and a hiker's paradise. For information, contact District Ranger, Rte. 3, Box 630, Moncks Corner, SC 29461 (803/887-3311).

MAGNOLIA PLANTATION (10 mi./16km NW on S.C. 61) (803/571-1266): One of the country's most beautiful gardens, it dates from the late 1670s and boasts 900 varieties of camellias (some more than two centuries old), 250 varieties of azaleas and magnolias, and a majestic avenue of moss-covered, century-old oaks. Open daily.

On the way, visit **Drayton Hall,** 2 mi. (3km) north on S.C. 61 (803/766-0188), one of the oldest plantations of the Southeast (1738), inhabited until 1974 by seven successive generations of the Drayton family. Beautiful Palladian architecture. Open daily.

MIDDLETON PLACE GARDENS (14 mi./22km NW on S.C. 61) (803/556-6020): The oldest and one of the most beautiful landscaped gardens in the country, with cypress groves and thousands of azaleas (1741). The flower beds and plantations were severely damaged by hurricane Hugo in 1989. The gardens and the Tudor-style wing, miraculously spared by Civil War battles, house the Spoleto Festival/USA each year (see "Special Events," above). Open daily.

OLD DORCHESTER STATE PARK (20 mi./32km NW on S.C. 642) (803/873-1740): Archeological reserve close to the source of the Ashley River on the site of a village founded by Massachusetts colonists (1696). The British occupied it during the Revolutionary War and then razed it in 1781. Traces of Fort Dorchester and the church remain. Archeological digs in process. Interesting museum. Open Thurs–Mon.

FARTHER AFIELD

ATLANTIC ISLANDS (318 mi./509km r.t. on U.S. 17S, S.C. 700, S.C. 174, U.S. 21, S.C. 281, S.C. 170, U.S. 278, and U.S. 17N): Vacation excursion for three or more days for lovers of beaches, water sports, and semitropical wildlife more or less untamed. The suggested circuit includes visits (in the following order) to:

Kiawah Island: 9,600 acres (4,000ha) of lush, subtropical vegetation plus 10 mi. (16km) of superb beaches, woods, and ponds haunted by alligators, deer, sea turtles, and 140 different species of birds. Accessible by road. The **Kiawah Island Inn & Villas,** a very comfortable three-star hotel, organizes island tours by Jeep and by boat (803/768-2121; see "Accommodations in the Vicinity," above).

Edisto Island: The best public beach in South Carolina (**Edisto Beach State Park**)—1.8 mi. (3km) of immaculate sand and a real treasure trove for seashell collectors.

Hunting Island: 4,800 acres (2,000ha) of semi-wild nature, deserted beaches, subtropical forests, and swamps. Campgrounds and hiking trails. Island accessible by U.S. 21. Park open year round.

Parris Island: Settled in 1562 by the French Huguenot Jean Ribaut (there's a monument to him here), Parris Island is today home to a well-known U.S. Marines training camp. Military museum, War Memorial Building (803/525-3650). Open daily.

☼ 🛏🛏 **Hilton Head Island:** The largest island on the Atlantic coast between New Jersey and Florida, a fashionable summer getaway since the early 1960s, offers 12 mi. (19km) of beach, 18 golf courses, more than 200 tennis courts, and six marinas, plus a marvelous climate year round and an unpolluted sea. A vacation paradise. There are a dozen luxury hotels and motels, including the ♜♜♜♜ **Westin,** 2 Grasslawn Ave., Hilton Head, SC 29928 (803/681-4000), 415 rms, **VE;** and the ♜♜ **Fairfield Inn,** 9 Marina Side Dr., Hilton Head, SC 29928 (803/842-4800), 120 rms, **I.** Hilton Head is accessible by U.S. 278. Well worth going out of your way.

On the trip back to Charleston, see ☼🛏🛏 **Beaufort:** Built on the island of Port Royal, this pretty little town of 8,600 with charming old houses was home to the first Protestant colony in America (1562), the French Huguenots. Numerous antebellum structures, including St. Helena Episcopal Church (1724), the Arsenal (1795), and the John Mark Verdier House Museum (1790). Visitor Center, 1006 Bay St. (803/524-3163).

CHAPTER 11

SAVANNAH 🎭🎭

□ □ □

Once a major cotton- and tobacco-trading center, today the headquarters of the paper industry, Savannah, like its neighbor and rival, Charleston, is a living page from the history books. It's also one of the most beautiful cities in the U.S. The 13th—and last—of the colonies founded by the British on American shores, Savannah was conceived in 1733 as the continent's first "modern" city. Its founder, Gen. James Oglethorpe, an ecologist ahead of his time, created a checkerboard urban plan of harmonious alternation between gardens, houses, and squares—green oases planted with mossy oaks, pines, and azaleas. Its cover of trees gives Savannah some shelter from the heat of a climate that can be truly oppressive in summer.

Since no house here is like its neighbor, the city displays the whole gamut of southern architectural styles—more than Atlanta, Charleston, or New Orleans, Savannah is *the* city of the Deep South. The colonnaded verandas, ornate facades, and flowered gardens along **Bull Street,** the wrought-iron balconies and pastel-washed houses with their stoops on **Abercorn Street,** come together in a living picture of peaceful, romantic charm straight out of *Gone with the Wind.*

The urban-restoration project in the **Savannah Historic District,** begun more than three decades ago, has been energetically implemented. But though Savannah boasts a complex of old buildings unequalled in America, it is no drowsy, languishing museum city. Miraculously spared during the Civil War by General Sherman because its inhabitants gave him a kindly reception at the end of his famous "March to the Sea" in 1864, Savannah is today a city on the move; you have only to walk along the docks on the **Savannah River,** or around the new **City Market** or **Riverfront Plaza,** the old cotton-mill district, to satisfy yourself of that.

Actor Stacy Keach, poet Conrad Aiken, and songwriter Johnny Mercer were born in Savannah.

BASIC FACTS: State of Georgia. Area code: 912. Time zone: eastern. ZIP Code (of the central post office): 31402. Founded: 1733. Approximate population: city, 151,000; metropolitan area, 250,000.

CLIMATE: A winter almost as mild as Florida's (Jan average, 52°F/11°C) is succeeded by an early, riotous spring (don't miss the azaleas in bloom in mid-Apr). After the hot, sticky summer (81°F/27°C average in July) comes the sunny fall, both typically subtropical with sudden late-afternoon downpours from mid-June to Sept. Every season has something to offer to the visitor.

DISTANCES: Atlanta, 251 mi. (401km); Charleston, 106 mi. (170km); Miami, 496 mi. (794km); Orlando, 292 mi. (467km); Washington, 633 mi. (1,012km).

ARRIVAL & TRANSIT INFORMATION

AIRPORT: Savannah International Airport (Travis Field) (SAV), 8 mi. (13km) NW; for information, call 964-0528.

AIRLINES: American (toll free 800/433-7300), Delta (toll free 800/221-1212), United (toll free 800/241-6522), USAir (toll free 800/428-4322).

CITY LINK: The **cab** fare from the airport to dwntwn is about $15–$17; time, about 20 min. Bus: **McCall's Limos** (966-5364) serves major dwntwn hotels; leaves according to published schedule; fare, $12; time, 25 min.

Since the airport is close in and the city compact, you won't need to rent a car unless you plan excursions into the country around.

Cabs are relatively inexpensive, and public (bus) transportation by **Chatham Area Transit/CAT** (233-5767) is reasonably efficient.

CAR RENTAL (at the airport unless otherwise indicated): Avis (toll free 800/331-1212); Budget (toll free 800/527-0700); Hertz (toll free 800/654-3131); National (toll free 800/227-7368); Thrifty (toll free 800/367-2277). For dwntwn locations, consult the local telephone directory.

LIMOUSINE SERVICES: McCall's Limos (966-5364), Passmore Limousine Service (232-0750).

TAXIS: Cabs may be hailed on the street, taken from the waiting lines outside the major hotels, or—most conveniently—called by phone: **Adam Cab** (927-7466) or **Yellow Cab** (236-1133).

TRAIN: Amtrak Station, 2611 Seaboard Coast Line Dr. (toll free 800/872-7245), 4 mi. (6.5km) outside the city.

INTERCITY BUSES: Greyhound, 610 W. Oglethorpe Ave. (232-2135).

INFORMATION & TOURS

TOURIST INFORMATION: The **Savannah Convention and Visitors Bureau,** 222 W. Oglethorpe Ave., GA 31499 (912/944-0456; toll free 800/444-2427).

Savannah Visitors Center, 301 Martin Luther King, Jr., Blvd. (912/944-0455), open daily.

For a **recorded message** giving a current list of shows and cultural events, call 233-2787.

GUIDED TOURS: Carriage Tours (horse-drawn carriage), Madison Sq. (236-6756): Around Savannah in a horse-drawn carriage. Daily, weather permitting.

Gray Line Tours (bus), 215 W. Boundary St. (234-8687): Two-hour guided tour of the Historic District, serving major hotels and the Visitors Center.

Old Town Trolley Tours (trolley), 601 Cohen St. (233-0083): Narrated tours of dwntwn. Pass allows you to get on and off as often as you want before the end of the loop. Trolley leaves every 30 minutes.

Savannah River Queen Cruises (boat), River St. dock behind City Hall (232-6404): One-hour cruises in the harbor and on the Savannah River; daily March–Nov and Sat Dec–Feb. Dinner and brunch tours offered March–Nov.

Tours by BJ (walking), 219 W. Bryan St. (233-2335): Two-hour private and group tours of the city, especially of places that are said to be haunted and with which a good ghost story is associated. A must.

SIGHTS, ATTRACTIONS & ACTIVITIES

ARCHITECTURAL HIGHLIGHTS: ⚖ **City Hall,** Bull and W. Bay Sts. (651-6790): Fine turn-of-the-century classical revival building capped by a gilded copper dome. Note the two British cannon in bronze, captured at the Battle of Yorktown and given to the city of Savannah by George Washington in 1791. Open daily.

⚖ **U.S. Customs House,** Bull and E. Bay Sts.: Erected in 1850 on the site where the city's founder, Englishman James Oglethorpe, built his first home in 1733. The capitals of its imposing granite columns are carved into the shape of tobacco leaves, as a tribute to this important local source of wealth. Closed to the public.

BEACHES: ⚖ **Savannah Beach,** 18 mi. (28km) east on U.S. 80: Lovely fine-sand beach, some 6 mi. (9.5km) long, on **Tybee Island.** Historic lighthouse (1736) and interesting museum. Many hotels, motels, and restaurants; try the **Sundowner Inn,** Ocean Front at 1609 Strand Ave. (912/786-4532): 20 rms. The beaches are very popular in the warm weather.

CHURCHES/SYNAGOGUES: ⚖ **Christ Episcopal Church,** Johnson Sq. between E. St. Julian and E. Congress Sts. (232-4131): The first church in the colony (1733); among its famous rectors were John Wesley and George Whitefield, founders of the Methodist church. The present church with its immaculate white columns, dating from 1838, is the third to occupy the site. Open Tues and Fri.

⚖ **Congregation Mikve Israel,** 20 E. Gordon St. (233-1547): The only Gothic Revival synagogue in the country, built in 1878 for a congregation of German and Portuguese Jews that had been founded in 1733. Museum with many ancient manuscripts, historical documents, letters from Presidents Washington, Jefferson, and Madison, etc. Guided tours Mon–Fri.

☼⚖ **First African Baptist Church,** 23 Montgomery St. (233-6597): Home of the oldest African American congregation in the country, founded in 1777 at Brampton Plantation. The present church dates from 1861. Open daily.

☼⚖ **Independent Presbyterian Church,** Bull St. and W. Oglethorpe Ave. (236-3346): Founded in 1755 by members of the Church of Scotland; the design recalls the famous London church St. Martin-in-the-Fields on Trafalgar Sq. Georgian interior. Open Tues and Fri.

HISTORIC BUILDINGS: ⚖ **King-Tisdell Cottage,** 514 E. Huntington St. (234-8000): Charming 1896 cottage with intricate gingerbread ornamentation. Dedicated to preserving the African American history and culture of Savannah and the Sea Islands, the exhibit rooms contain art objects, documents, and furniture typical of the turn-of-the-century black middle class. Open daily.

☼⚖⚖ **Savannah's Historic District,** a 2.2-sq.-mi. (5.9km²) area bounded by the Savannah River, Gaston St., and E. and W. Broad Sts.: More than 1,000 19th-century buildings scrupulously restored—the country's largest group of historic houses. Among the most interesting and elegant are:

The **Andrew Low House,** 329 Abercorn St. (233-6854), open Fri–Wed, a charming home dating from 1848. Among its illustrious guests are numbered Gen. Robert E. Lee and British writer William Makepeace Thackeray. Was later the residence of Juliette Gordon Low, founder of the Girl Scouts of America.

Davenport House, 324 E. State St. (236-8097), open daily, is a fine example of the Georgian "Federal" style dating from 1820, with superb old furniture and original elliptical staircase.

The **Green-Meldrim House,** Madison Sq. (233-3845), open Tues and

Thurs–Sat, an interesting Gothic Revival building with a characteristic wrought-iron portico, was General Sherman's headquarters at the end of the Civil War.

The **Juliette Gordon Low Birthplace,** Oglethorpe Ave. and Bull St. (233-4501), open Thurs–Tues, is an elegant 1821 house in Regency style, birthplace of the woman who founded the Girl Scouts of America in 1912.

The **Owens-Thomas House,** 124 Abercorn St. (233-9743), open daily (closed in Jan), is one of the loveliest examples of the Regency idiom in the U.S., built in 1816 to the design of the British architect William Jay. Lafayette stayed here.

The **William Scarbrough House,** 41 W. Broad St. (233-0129), open Mon–Fri, another remarkable example of the Regency style, dates from 1819. The house will be undergoing renovation in 1995. Call for information.

MARKETS: ※♨ **City Market,** W. St. Julian at Jefferson St. (234-2327): Opened in 1986 on the site of the first City Market, which dates back more than a century and a half, this new commercial center boasts hundreds of food, fashion, and handcraft shops, a flea market, and a dozen art galleries, as well as inviting bars and taverns in little Colonial-style brick buildings. Open daily. (The destruction of the original City Market in the 1950s, to make room for a sleazy parking lot, touched off a flood of indignant local patriotism and the creation of the Historic Savannah Foundation, which now protects the city's architectural heritage.)

MUSEUMS OF ART: ※♨ **Telfair Mansion and Art Museum,** 121 Barnard St. (232-1177): Fine old porcelain, silverware, and traditional 18th- and 19th-century painting and sculpture from Europe and America, displayed in an elegant upper-class mansion in the Regency style, the work of William Jay. Be sure to see the splendid Octagon Room. This was the residence of the British governor from 1760 until the end of the War of Independence. Open Tues–Sun.

MUSEUMS OF SCIENCE & HISTORY: ※♨ **Savannah History Museum,** 303 Martin Luther King, Jr., Blvd. (238-1779): Temporary exhibitions and remarkable audiovisual shows illustrating the history of Savannah and the state of Georgia, in a 19th-century locomotive barn cunningly restored. In the **Spirit of the South Theater,** Disney-invented theatronic figures explain the city's 1733 beginnings. Open daily.

♨ **Savannah Science Museum,** 4405 Paulsen St. (355-6705): Botany, zoology (interesting collection of reptiles and amphibians), aquarium. Exhibitions on medicine and physics. Well-designed planetarium. Open Tues–Sun.

♨ **Ships of the Sea Museum,** 503 E. River St. (232-1511): Interesting maritime museum on the banks of the Savannah River, with ship models, old figureheads, and a fine scrimshaw collection. Reconstructions of a ship's carpenter's shop and a chandlery. Open daily.

PANORAMAS: ♨ **Talmadge Memorial Bridge,** north of W. Boundary St.: From this bridge across the Savannah River you'll get a very good view of the city and of Riverfront Plaza along a line from north to south. Worth a look.

PARKS & GARDENS: ※♨ **Bonaventure Cemetery,** Bonaventure Rd., 10 min. east of dwntwn along the Wilmington River: Beautiful scenery. Hurricane-scrubbed boulders rear up from the damp earth and live oaks grieve in veils of Spanish moss. Look for the graves of composer Johnny Mercer and poet Conrad Aiken. Open daily.

※♨♨ **City's Squares,** along Abercorn, Barnard, Bull, Habersham, and Houston Sts.: Wonderful public gardens, planted with azaleas, palm trees, pines, and moss oaks, in the heart of the Historic District. The

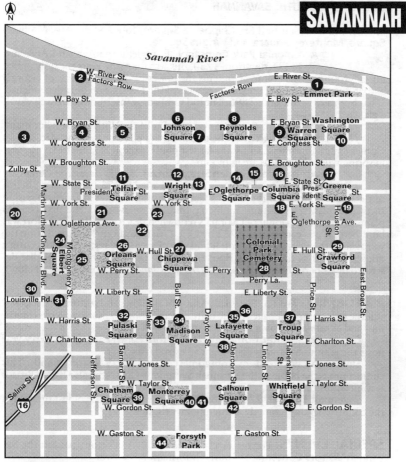

SAVANNAH

Savannah River

W. River St.
Factors' Row
Factors' Row
E. River St.
Emmet Park

W. Bay St.
E. Bay St.

W. Bryan St.
E. Bryan St. Washington Square
W. Congress St.
Johnson Square
Reynolds Square
Warren Square
E. Congress St.

W. Broughton St.
E. Broughton St.

Zulby St.
W. State St.
President St. Telfair Square
Wright Square
Oglethorpe Square
Columbia Square
Greene Square
W. York St.
E. State St.
President St.
E. York St.

W. Oglethorpe Ave.
E. Oglethorpe Ave.

Colonial Park Cemetery

Orleans Square
W. Hull St. Chippewa Square
E. Perry
E. Hull St. Crawford Square
W. Perry St.
Perry La.

Montgomery St.
Elbert Square
Martin Luther King, Jr., Blvd

W. Liberty St.
E. Liberty St.

Louisville Rd.
Visitors Center

W. Harris St.
Pulaski Square
Madison Square
Lafayette Square
Troup Square
E. Harris St.
W. Charlton St.
E. Charlton St.

W. Jones St.
E. Jones St.

Selma St.
W. Taylor St.
E. Taylor St.
Chatham Square
Monterrey Square
Calhoun Square
Whitfield Square
16
W. Gordon St.
E. Gordon St.

W. Gaston St.
E. Gaston St.

Forsyth Park

GEORGIA

Atlanta

Savannah

Andrew Low Home **38**
Calhoun Square **42**
Chamber of Commerce **21**
Chatham Square **39**
Chippewa Square **27**
Christ Episcopal Church **7**
Columbia Square **18**
Colonial Dames House **35**
Colonial Park Cemetery **28**
Crawford Square **29**
Davenport House **16**

Elbert Square **24**
Ellis Square **5**
Evangelical Lutheran Church **13**
Factors' Row **2**
Forsyth Park **44**
Franklin Square **4**
Greene Square **19**
Green-Meldrim Home **33**
Greyhound Terminal **20**
Independent Presbyterian Church **22**
J.G. Low Birthplace **23**
Johnson Square **6**
Lafayette Square **36**
Madison Square **34**
Monterrey Square **40**
Municipal Auditorium **25**
Museum of Antique Dolls **17**
Oglethorpe Square **14**

Orleans Square **26**
Owens-Thomas House & Museum **15**
Pulaski Square **32**
Reynolds Square **8**
Savannah History Museum **30**
Ships of the Sea Maritime Museum **1**
Telfair Mansion & Art Museum **11**
Temple Mikve Israel **41**
Troup Square **37**
Visitors Center **31**
Warren Square **9**
Washington Square **10**
Whitfield Square **43**
William Scarborough House **3**
Wright Square **12**

finest are those along Bull St.: **Chippewa Square, Johnson Square, Madison Square, Monterey Square,** and **Wright Square.**

 Colonial Park Cemetery, E. Oglethorpe Ave. and Abercorn St.: Dating from 1750, this was for many years the only public burial ground in the colony. Contains the graves of many founders of Georgia and of Button Gwinnett, one of the signers of the Declaration of Independence. It has been a city park since 1896. The old tombstone inscriptions are well worth a glance.

 Forsyth Park, Gaston and Bull Sts.: With its great fountain, reminiscent of the one in Paris's place de la Concorde, and its Confederate Monument, this is the largest public park in Savannah. Try to see it in spring when the azaleas are in bloom.

 Trustee's Garden Site, E. Broad St. at E. Bryan St.: Originally the site of a botanic garden planted in 1733 by the first English settlers on the model of the Chelsea Gardens in London, with a view to raising medicinal plants, vines, and mulberry trees for silkworms. The first peaches planted here are the origin of Georgia's renowned peach crop. In 1762 a fort was built here; it was captured in 1782 by Gen. "Mad Anthony" Wayne during the war against the British. Today you'll find several elegantly restored 19th-century houses, as well as the **Pirate's House,** a sailors' tavern reminiscent of that described by Robert Louis Stevenson in *Treasure Island* (see "Restaurants," below).

PERFORMING ARTS: For a daily listing of all shows and cultural events, consult the entertainment pages of the daily papers *Savannah Morning News* (morning) and *Savannah Evening Press* (evening).

 City Lights Theater Company, 15 W. York Lane (234-9860): Every year hosts the famous Savannah Playwright's Festival (Aug).

 Savannah Civic Center, Montgomery St. at Liberty St. (651-6550): This auditorium is the home of the Savannah Symphony Orchestra; also ballet, Broadway hits, musicals.

 Savannah Theater, 222 Bull St. (233-7764): One of the oldest theaters in the country. Drama, comedy, contemporary theater.

SPECIAL EVENTS: For the exact schedule of events below, consult the **Savannah Visitors Center** (see "Tourist Information," above).

 Georgia Heritage Celebration (Feb): Parades, concerts, exhibitions; a 12-day commemoration of the founding of Georgia.

 Savannah Onstage (late Feb): Annual international music festival featuring the brightest young stars in classical music and jazz.

 St. Patrick's Day (mid-Mar): One of the biggest popular parades on the East Coast (250,000 participants every year). Second only to New York's.

 Savannah Tour of Homes and Gardens (late Mar to early Apr): Guided tours, by daylight or by candlelight, of some 30 historic private houses and their gardens.

 Night in Old Savannah (third wknd in Apr): Folklore and food festival; jazz concerts.

 Christmas in Savannah (Dec): A month of festivities in the Historic District, with parades, concerts, house tours, cultural events, etc.

SPORTS: Savannah has a minor-league team in **baseball** (Apr–Oct), the Savannah Cardinals (farm team of the St. Louis Cardinals), Grayson Stadium (351-9150).

Deep-Sea Fishing

 The Georgia coast rivals that of Florida in its abundance of fish, and attracts many sport-fishermen in season. Some recommended charter-boat operators are

Bottom Line Charters, 1412-B Walthour Rd. (897-6503); **Chimney Creek Charters,** 40 Estill Hammock, Tybee Island (786-9857); and **Salt Water Charters,** 111 Wickersham Dr. (598-1814).

STROLLS: ☀⚓ **Bull Street,** between Bay St. and Forsyth Park: Savannah's elegant main street, with many old houses, historic churches, and superb flower-planted squares.

⚓ **Factors Walk,** between Bull and E. Broad Sts.: Running between old buildings formerly used in the cotton business, these narrow cobbled ramps, reached by a network of wrought-iron footbridges, have retained all the flavor of the 19th century. Their cobblestones were once ballast in ships coming here from Europe. There, cotton merchants, called factors in the early 1800s, inspected bales of Sea Island fibers before closing a deal.

☀⚓ **Waterfront Area,** along John P. Rousakis Riverfront Plaza: Old brick warehouses along the Savannah River, now converted into boutiques, restaurants, pubs, art galleries, nightclubs. Lively and colorful by day and night alike. At sunrise and sunset the view from the quays is magnificent. One of the finest examples of urban renovation in the U.S.

ACCOMMODATIONS

Personal Favorites (in order of preference)

♟♟♟ **Radisson Hotel** (dwntwn), 100 General McIntosh Blvd., GA 31401 (912/236-6344; toll free, see Radisson). 385 rms, A/C, color TV, in-rm movies. AE, CB, DC, MC, V. Gar. $8, pool, health club, rest., coffee shop, bar, rm svce, boutiques, concierge, free crib. *Note:* Large, luxury hotel opened in Jan 1992 smack in the middle of Savannah's vibrant riverfront. Spacious, inviting rms and suites (the best w. views on the river); exemplary comfort and facilities. Ultra-professional svce. VIP floor. The "in" place to stay. **M–E**

☀♟♟♟ **The Mulberry** (dwntwn), 601 E. Bay St., GA 31401 (912/238-1200). 125 rms, A/C, color TV, in-rm movies. AE, DC, MC, V. Parking $5, pool, rest. (The Mulberry Room), bar, rm svce, free crib. *Note:* Small, gracious, unusually designed luxury hotel. The main building began life as a livery stable in the 1860s, was converted into a Coca-Cola bottling plant, and has now been tastefully restored, w. an elegant classical revival decor. Period furniture, many art objects; pretty interior grdn. Spacious rms, some w. minibars; impeccable svce; rest. so-so. Distinction and charm in the heart of Old Savannah. **M–E**, but lower rates off-season.

☀♟♟♟ **Foley House Inn** (dwntwn), 14 W. Hull St., GA 31401 (912/232-6622; toll free 800/647-3708). 20 rms, A/C, color TV, in-rm movies. AE, MC, V. Street parking, hot tub, free breakfast, free crib. *Note:* Charming, luxuriously restored 19th-century mansion looking out on Chippewa Sq. in the heart of the Historic District. Original Victorian setting and period furniture. Each rm is decorated in its own style, five having private patios, Jacuzzis, VCRs, and fireplaces. Ultra-polished reception and svce. Since there is no elevator, avoid the rms on the third and fourth floors. For those who love glimpses of the past. Resv. advisable, a good while ahead. **M–E**, but lower rates off-season.

☀♟♟ **Ballastone Inn** (dwntwn), 14 E. Oglethorpe Ave, GA 31401 (912/236-1484). 17 rms, A/C, color TV, in-rm movies. AE, MC, V. Street parking, café nearby, rm svce, concierge, free continental breakfast. *Note:* Charming guesthouse built in 1835. Period furnishings and gracious svce including turn-down w. brandy and pralines. Courtyard grdn w. fountain. **M–E**

♟ **Best Western Riverfront Inn** (dwntwn), 412 W. Bay St., GA 31401 (912/233-1011; toll free, see Best Western). 142 rms, A/C, cable color TV, AE, CB, DC, MC, V. Free parking, pool, rest. (Bottle

Works), bar, free crib. *Note:* Conventional but well-run motel standing, as its name implies, almost on the bank of the Savannah River and very nr. the Historic District. Huge, comfortable, recently renovated rms, friendly reception and svce. Ideal if you're driving. Excellent value. **B–I**, but lower rates off-season.

Economy Inn (dwntwn), 512 W. Oglethorpe Ave., GA 31401 (912/233-9251). 56 rms, A/C, cable color TV. AE, CB, DC, MC, V. Free parking, pool, free coffee. *Note:* Typical small motel very nr. the Visitor Center and the Historic District. Functionally comfortable rms, efficient reception and svce. Good value overall; ideal for the budget traveler. **B–I**

Other Accommodations (from top bracket to budget)

Hyatt Regency (dwntwn), 2 W. Bay St., GA 31401 (912/238-1234; toll free, see Hyatt). 346 rms, A/C, color TV, in-rm movies. AE, CB, DC, MC, V. Valet gar. $9, pool, health club, bike rental, marina, rest. (Windows), coffee shop, bar, rm svce, disco, boutiques, concierge, free crib. *Note:* Upscale convention hotel. Modern, uninspired architecture but large, comfortable rms w. balconies, the best overlooking the Savannah River. Moorings, for a fee. Efficient svce; business and group clientele. Very well located on the river, a couple of blocks from City Hall. Recently renovated. **M–E**

Planters Inn (formerly the Royal Colony; dwntwn), 29 Abercorn St., GA 31401 (912/232-5678; toll free 800/554-1187). 57 rms, A/C, cable color TV. AE, CB, DC, MC, V. Valet gar. $5, rest. adj. bar, rm svce, free breakfast, crib $10. *Note:* Urbane, intimate small hotel looking onto Reynolds Sq. in the center of the Historic District. Elegant, comfortable layouts w. four-poster beds, period furniture, and private balconies. Exceptionally attentive svce. An excellent place to stay. **M–E**

Magnolia Place Inn (dwntwn), 503 Whitaker St., GA 31401 (912/236-7674; toll free 800/238-7674). 13 rms, A/C, color TV, in-rm movies. AE, MC, V. Limited-parking lot, concierge, free continental breakfast. *Note:* Artfully restored Victorian mansion built in 1878 w. landscaped courtyard. Overlooks Forsyth Park. Antique-filled rms w. private patios or balconies (some w. Jacuzzi). Cheerful reception and svce. **M–E**

Hilton–De Soto (dwntwn), Liberty and Bull Sts., GA 31402 (912/232-9000; toll free, see Hilton). 250 rms, A/C, color TV, in-rm movies. AE, CB, DC, MC, V. Parking $5, pool, rest. (Pavilion), coffee shop, bar, rm svce, nightclub, free crib. *Note:* The most famous hotel in Savannah, on the site of the old, and now legendary, De Soto Hotel. The modern building agrees well enough w. its surroundings. Comfortable rms, some w. private balconies or patios. Attentive svce. A favorite w. those in-the-know. Very centrally located. **I–M**

Days Inn Historic District (dwntwn), 201 W. Bay St., GA 31401 (912/236-4440; toll free, see Days Inns). 252 rms, A/C, color TV, in-rm movies. AE, DC, MC, V. Free parking, pool, rest., free crib. *Note:* Modern motel in the heart of Savannah; the dark-red brick facade melds perfectly w. its Historic District setting. Spacious, comfortable rms, some w. kitchenettes, the best overlooking the Savannah River. Efficient svce. Group clientele. Good value. **I**

La Quinta (nr. dwntwn), 6805 Abercorn St., GA 31405 (912/355-3004; toll free, see La Quinta). 154 rms, A/C, color TV, in-rm movies. AE, DC, MC, V. Free parking, pool, free breakfast, free crib. *Note:* Warm, inviting motel nr. Oglethorpe Mall w. its dozens of shops, stores, and rests. Comfortable, well-designed rms. Business clientele. 8 min. from dwntwn. Good value. **B–I**

Airport Accommodations

Quality Inn Airport (vic.), Rte. 5 (at the airport), GA 31408 (912/964-1421; toll free, see Choice). 171 rms, A/C, cable color TV. AE, CB, DC, MC, V. Free parking, pool, rest., bar, rm svce, free crib.

Note: Savannah's only airport hotel. Spacious, functionally comfortable rms w. private patios. Efficient svce. Free airport shuttle. **I**

In the Vicinity

❀❦♔♔♔ **Sheraton Savannah Resort and Country Club** (vic.), 612 Wilmington Island Rd., GA 31410 (912/897-1612; toll free, see Sheraton). 202 rms (in the hotel) or cottages, A/C, color TV, in-rm movies. AE, CB, DC, MC, V. Free parking, pool, sauna, health club, golf course, putting green, five tennis courts, private beach, boats, fishing, water sports, two rests., two bars, rm svce, disco, free crib. *Note:* Very lovely resort hotel on the Wilmington River less than 15 min. by car from Savannah. Tastefully decorated cottages and villas clustering around a charming old 1920s hotel. Acceptable rests.; attentive svce. Ideal for open-air sports, w. one of the finest golf courses in the country. The American Plan is very good value. Planning a multi-million-dollar renovation. **M–E** (hotel) **and VE** (cottages), but lower rates Nov–Mar.

RESTAURANTS

Personal Favorites (in order of preference)

❀❦♟♟♟ **Elizabeth on 37th** (nr. dwntwn), 105 E. 37th St. (236-5547). A/C. Dinner only, Mon–Sat; closed hols and two weeks in Aug. AE, MC, V. Jkt. *Specialties:* wild-mushroom pies, rack of lamb w. eggplant, spiced southern quail, shrimp Savannah, sea bass filets w. vegetables wrapped in parchment, oysters and country ham w. leeks in cream sauce, green onion pancake; superb desserts. Good wine list at reasonable prices. *Note:* Since it opened in 1981 Savannah's top-rated rest. has won plaudits from all the food critics. Imagination, lightness, and top-quality materials (especially seafood) are the three golden rules of Elizabeth Terry, the extraordinary self-taught chef. Her husband, Michael, a former Atlanta lawyer and a wine lover, makes a wonderful sommelier. The rest. occupies a beautifully restored old house just south of Forsyth Park. Praiseworthy svce. A wonderful place to eat, 10 min. from dwntwn. Resv. advised. *American.* **M–E**

♟♟ **River's End** (vic.), 3122 River Rd., in Thunderbolt (354-2973). A/C. Lunch/dinner Mon–Sat; closed hols. AE, CB, DC, MC, V. *Specialties:* scampi, catch of the day, sautéed flounder w. grape sauce, steak, Maine lobsters, homemade pies. *Note:* Elegant, polished cuisine whose billing—"direct from fishing boat to cooking stove"—is fully justified. Fine view of the Intracoastal Waterway and the fleet of shrimp boats (customers can moor their own boats in front of the rest.). Preppy crowd; resv. advised. *Seafood.* **I–M**

♟♟ **Johnny Harris** (nr. dwntwn), 1651 E. Victory Dr. (354-7810). A/C. Lunch/dinner Mon–Sat; closed Jan 1, Dec 25. AE, CB, DC, MC, V. Jkt. (Fri–Sat evenings). *Specialties:* crabmeat au gratin, steak, barbecued pork, southern fried chicken, prime rib, catch of the day. *Note:* A three-generation-old institution for lovers of good, solid food. The beef and the barbecued spareribs, served w. fresh vegetables (something uncommon enough to deserve mention), are highly recommended. Diligent svce. Uninspiring rustic decor. A 10-min. drive from dwntwn. Locally very popular; resv. recommended. *American.* **I–M**

♟♟♟ **Bistro Savannah** (dwntwn), 309 W. Congress St. (233-6266). A/C. Dinner only, nightly. AE, MC, V. *Specialties:* roasted sweet garlic w. herbs, goat cheese, and Vidalia onion relish; angel-hair pasta w. a four-tomato sauce and shaved Parmesan; crispy flounder w. apricot-shallot sauce; jumble-berry cobbler. Great wine list. *Note:* Dining amidst local art and exposed brick walls in a Beaux Art gallery. Very elegant decor and entrées to match. Savannah's most welcomed new rest. Locally popular. *American.* **I–M**

♟ **Mrs. Wilke's Boarding House** (dwntwn), basement of 107 W. Jones St. (232-5997). A/C. Breakfast/lunch Mon–Fri. No credit cards. *Specialties:* barbecued spareribs, southern fried chicken, collard greens, ham and gravy, swordfish steak, homemade cakes, banana pudding. *Note:* Colorful boarding house, serving authentic regional food—all you can eat—in a somewhat minimal setting. Visitors and businesspeople sit side by side, family style. The best value in Savannah. No resv. Locally popular. *American.* **B**

Other Restaurants (from top bracket to budget)

♈♈♈ **45 South** (nr. dwntwn), 20 E. Broad St. (233-1881). A/C. Dinner only, Mon–Sat; closed hols. AE, DC, MC, V. Jkt. *Specialties:* mussels and artichokes w. ginger, roulade of salmon w. leeks, broiled grouper w. burgundy-butter sauce, peppered breast of duck w. polenta and spinach, strawberry puff pastry. *Note:* Inspired, delicate American nouvelle cuisine, particularly noteworthy for its light-as-air sauces. Charming 1832 historic building featuring working fireplaces and lovely antiques. Very good svce. Over the past couple of years has established a strong local following; resv. advised. *American.* **M–E**

☼♈♈ **Olde Pinke House** (dwntwn), 23 Abercorn St. (232-4286). A/C. Dinner only, nightly. AE, MC, V. *Specialties:* she-crab soup, crab cakes, shrimp and country ham in tarragon cream sauce, seared roasted sirloin over caramelized bourbon onions, pecan-roasted chicken w. wild-berry sauce. *Note:* A designated historic monument, this attractive pink mansion (whence the name) serves innovative Southern cuisine and seafood dishes as well. Charming 18th-century decor. Resv. recommended. Congenial tavern (Planters Tavern) in the cellar. *Seafood/American.* **I–M**

☼♈♈ **Pirate's House** (dwntwn), 20 E. Broad St. (233-5757). A/C. Lunch/dinner daily, brunch Sun. AE, CB, DC, MC, V. Jkt. *Specialties:* seafood bisque, "shrab" (combination of shrimp and crabmeat), gumbo, oysters Savannah, jambalaya, seafood w. red rice, flounder Florentine, roast duckling, catch of the day, steak; 40-item dessert menu. *Note:* This huge, picturesque museum-tavern, 2½ centuries old, serves many regional specialties such as "red rice" Savannah style (w. tomatoes and spices). Legend has it that Captain Flint, of Stevenson's classic adventure story *Treasure Island,* drew his last breath here. Amusing maritime decor; splendid bar. Touristy atmosphere. Take care not to lose yourself; the place boasts no fewer than 23 rooms, each decorated differently! Resv. advised. *Seafood/American.* **I–M**

♈ **Garibaldi's Café** (dwntwn), 315 W. Congress St. (232-7118). A/C. Dinner only, nightly. AE, MC, V. *Specialties:* fresh homemade pasta, northern Italian dishes, roast duck, catch of the day. *Note:* Charming old café in a converted 1870s firehouse in the heart of the Historic District. Praiseworthy Italian food; excellent espresso; youthful, trendy atmosphere; resv. advised. *Italian.* **I–M**

☼♈ **Crystal Beer Parlor** (dwntwn), 301 W. Jones St., at Jefferson St. (232-1153). A/C. Lunch/dinner Mon–Sat. AE, MC, V. *Specialties:* hamburgers, crab stew, gumbo, fried-oyster sandwich. *Note:* Congenial, very popular pub w. pleasantly faded decor—yellowed photos on the walls, ceiling fans, worn wood floor. Excellent draft beer and overstuffed sandwiches. A Savannah landmark since 1933. Relaxed atmosphere; no resv. *American.* **B–I**

☼♈ **Wall's Bar-B-Que** (dwntwn), 515 E. York Lane (232-9754). Lunch/dinner Wed–Sat. No credit cards. *Specialties:* sandwiches, southern fried chicken, deviled crab cakes, barbecued spareribs. *Note:* This modest, almost grungy place on an unpaved alley between Houston St. and Price St. is credited by the experts w. the best barbecued ribs and crab cakes in town. The experience should not be missed, in spite of the depressing atmosphere and setting. No resv. *American.* **B**

Cafeterias/Fast Food

Morrisson's (dwntwn), Bull and Bryan Sts. (232-5264). Lunch/dinner daily (until 8:30pm). MC, V. Roast beef, daily specials, salads, sandwiches. Good cafeteria food in an old Savannah setting. Locally popular. Other location: 7804 Abercorn St. at Oglethorpe Mall (352-3521).

BARS & NIGHTCLUBS

Bottom Line (dwntwn), 206 W. St. Julian St. (232-0812). Cozy nightclub w. live music. Open Tues–Sat.

Comedy House (nr. dwntwn), 317 Eisenhower Dr. (356-1045). Typical comedy club presenting comedians from across the U.S. Shows Tues–Sat.

Hard-Hearted Hannah's (dwntwn), in the Hilton–De Soto (see "Accommodations," above) (232-9000). Live jazz Tues–Sat. A mixed crowd of vacationers and locals.

Kevin Barry's Irish Pub (dwntwn), 117 W. River St. (233-9626). Friendly pub overlooking the river. Popular happy hour. Live Irish folk music Wed–Sun. Open nightly until 3am.

Spanky's (dwntwn), 317 E. River St. (236-3009). Congenial saloon on the banks of the Savannah River; an amusing contrast between the historic setting and the youthful atmosphere. Pizzas and sandwiches. Locally popular. Open nightly.

NEARBY EXCURSIONS

FORT JACKSON (3 mi./5km east via President St. and Woodcock Dr.) (232-3945): Situated on the banks of the Savannah River and surrounded by moats, this is one of the oldest (1809) forts in Georgia to survive intact. Its moments of glory were in the War of 1812 and the War Between the States. Now it houses many 19th-century military accessories and devices illustrating the history of its construction and its battles. Interesting. Open daily.

FORT McALLISTER HISTORIC PARK (25 mi./40km south on U.S. 17 and Ga. 144) (727-2339): Carefully restored Civil War fort, originally built by the Confederates for the defense of Savannah. Its capture by Union forces on December 13, 1864, spelled the downfall of the city and marked the end of Sherman's "March to the Sea." Military museum. Open daily.

FORT PULASKI NATIONAL MONUMENT (15 mi./24km east on U.S. 80) (786-5787): One of the largest and best-known defense works on the eastern seaboard, named after the Revolutionary War hero who was killed at the Battle of Savannah in 1779. Witnessed fierce artillery exchanges between North and South during the Civil War. Completely restored before World War II. Museum. Open daily.

HILTON HEAD ISLAND (38 mi./60km NW on U.S. Alt. 17, S.C. 170, S.C. 46, and U.S. 278): Discovered by the Spaniards in 1526, this inviting island has become one of the most sought-after summer resorts in the country, by virtue of its superb beaches, piney woods, and old plantation houses. Dozens of hotels, motels, vacation cottages, art galleries, and elegant boutiques; 200 tennis courts, 18 golf courses, six marinas, etc. For details, see Chapter 10 on Charleston.

FARTHER AFIELD

CUMBERLAND ISLAND NATIONAL SEASHORE (145 mi./232km SW on I-95, Ga. 40, and a ferry): Along the entire Atlantic coast, this is the island most nearly in an unspoiled, natural state. Long uninhabited, this island 16 mi. (26km) long by 1½–3 mi. (2–5km) wide, covered in moss oaks and dwarf palmettos, with its marshes and empty beaches, teems with ibis, duck, alligators, and wild ponies. Reached by boat from **St. Mary's,** daily in summer, Thurs–Mon Sept–June; resv. necessary (for information, call 912/882-4335). Limited number of camping sites available. The tiny (nine-rm) ☼ ▯ **Greyfield Inn,** P.O. Drawer B, Fernandina Beach, FL 32034 (904/261-6408), occupies an old Colonial-style villa built by millionaire Thomas Carnegie, who once owned the island (rates: **VE**). A memorable experience for lovers of nature-in-the-raw. Should be combined with the trip to the **Golden Isles** (see below).

OKEFENOKEE NATIONAL WILDLIFE REFUGE (122 mi./195km SW on U.S. 17, Ga. 196, U.S. 82, and U.S. 1):
The largest wetlands park in the country after Florida's Everglades, with an area of 700 sq. mi. (2,080km²). Enormous variety of flora and fauna: black bear, deer, lynx, alligators, water birds, etc. Canoe trips through the swamp. No overnight facilities. Park open daily year round. For information, ask the refuge manager, Rte. 2, P.O. Box 330, Folkston, GA 31537 (912/496-3331). Combine it with the excursion to the **Golden Isles** (see below).

GOLDEN ISLES (about 180 mi./288km r.t. via I-95S and U.S. 17N):
According to legend, the isles owe their name to the many hoards of treasure buried in their sands by the famous pirate Edward Teach, better known as Blackbeard. Another version attributes it to the wonderfully warm and sunny climate of the Georgia coast. Either way, you'll find some of the lushest, most gracious islands on the Atlantic coast. The Golden Isles offer a whole gamut of vacation activities: fishing, golf, sailing, horseback riding, etc.

First you come to **Jekyll Island,** the smallest but also the most chic of the Golden Isles, originally named Ile de la Somme by the French Huguenots who landed here in 1562; the last shipload of African slaves to enter the U.S. was unloaded here in 1858. Jekyll became an exclusive winter resort for industry and finance moguls from 1885 to the end of World War II: Rockefeller, Gould, J. P. Morgan, Vanderbilt, Joseph Pulitzer, and Goodyear were among those who built sumptuous villas here, which are now open to visitors, daily year round.

On **St. Simons Island,** where until the Civil War there were rich plantations, the English General Oglethorpe, the founder of Savannah, built Fort Frederica, now **Fort Frederica National Monument** (638-3639), in 1736. Burned down in 1758, the fort and the little town it protected were abandoned. Open daily. Wonderful beaches lined with forests of oak, pine, and palm trees. The ▯▯▯ **Sea Palms Golf & Tennis Resort,** 5445 Frederica Rd., St. Simons Island, GA (912/638-3351; toll free 800/841-6268), with 500 rooms and individual villas (rates: **M–VE**), a luxury seaside hotel, offers very interesting packages off-season.

Sea Island boasts many beautiful seaside homes as well as dozens of oceanfront hotels and motels. ▯▯▯▯ **The Cloister,** 100 First St., Sea Island, GA 31561 (912/638-3611; toll free 800/732-4752), is one of the grandest grand hotels on the Georgia coast. Luxurious accommodations (264 rms or cottages. Rates: **VE**).

CHAPTER 12

ATLANTA 🔥

□ □ □

Atlanta, known and loved by generations of movie-goers through *Gone with the Wind,* was the paragon of southern cities at the time of the Civil War: brilliant, lavish, and cultured. After one of the most ferocious battles of that war—117 days of siege by General Sherman (1864)—90% of the city lay in ruins. The only traces that remain from this tragic period are the recently restored **Underground Atlanta** and its famous **Zero Mile Post** marking the terminus of the first Western & Atlantic Railroad line (1837). Not far from here is **Peachtree Street,** dear to the heart of Scarlett O'Hara and today Atlanta's most elegant and lively downtown thoroughfare. Founded as Terminus in 1837 and incorporated as Marthasville in 1843, the city received its present name in 1845, perhaps reflecting a feminine form of Atlantic in the railroad's name.

Like a phoenix, Atlanta rose from the ashes of the Civil War to become the economic and cultural capital of the Deep South. Today it is a modern, ever-expanding metropolis, and ranks first among the American cities in terms of employment growth rate. Testifying to Atlanta's extraordinary financial and industrial vitality are more than 1,800 factories (automobile, aviation, chemical, paper, steel, food), the CNN television empire, 130 banks, and dozens of big corporations (including Georgia Pacific, Nabisco, Delta Airlines, UPS, the package delivery giant, and Coca-Cola, maker of the universally famous beverage, which Doc Pemberton invented here in 1886).

A bustling road, rail, and air transportation hub, Atlanta possesses the second-busiest airport in the world, Hartsfield International Airport. Georgia's capital also boasts some of the most spectacular modern structures in the U.S., including the country's tallest hotel (the **Westin Peachtree Plaza,** an immense glass-and-steel, 73-story tower), the **IBM Building** by Philip Johnson and John Burgee, the **Carter Presidential Center,** and the **World of Coca-Cola,** a high-tech tribute to Atlanta's leading corporate name.

In 1973 Atlanta became the third major American city to elect a black mayor (after Cleveland and Los Angeles). Atlanta was the birthplace of Nobel peace prize winner Martin Luther King, Jr.—don't miss the **Martin Luther King, Jr., Historic District** in the heart of downtown; its children also include historian Daniel Boorstin, novelist Margaret Mitchell, cable TV magnate Ted Turner, and John Portman, creator of the modern hotel architecture.

Atlanta has been chosen as host city for the 1996 Olympic Games.

BASIC FACTS: Capital of the state of Georgia. Area code: 404 (city) and 706 (suburbs). Time zone: eastern. ZIP Code (of central post office): 30301. Founded: 1837. Approximate population: city, 395,000; metropolitan area, 2,830,000. 12th-largest metropolitan area in the country.

CLIMATE: Spring is rather brief but pleasant, especially May. Summer is hot and sticky (mean July temperature, 80°F/27°C, but with 70% humidity). Winter is relatively mild but rainy (mean Jan temperature, 45°F/5°C). The best season to visit Atlanta is autumn; Sept, Oct, and Nov are the sunniest months.

DISTANCES: Miami, 659 mi. (1,055km); Nashville, 242 mi. (387km); New Orleans, 481 mi. (770km); Savannah, 251 mi. (401km); Washington, 608 mi. (975km).

ARRIVAL & TRANSIT INFORMATION

AIRPORT: Hartsfield Atlanta International Airport (ATL): 9 mi. (14km) SW. Its new terminal is the largest in the world. It is, with nearly 50 million passengers each year, the world's second-busiest airport. Information: 530-6600.

DOMESTIC AIRLINES: American (toll free 800/433-7300), Continental (toll free 800/525-0280), Delta (toll free 800/221-1212), Northwest (toll free 800/225-2525), TWA (toll free 800/221-2000), United (toll free 800/241-6522), and USAir (toll free 800/428-4322).

FOREIGN CARRIERS: British Airways (toll free 800/247-9297), Japan Air Lines (toll free 800/525-3663), KLM (toll free 800/556-7777), Lufthansa (toll free 800/645-3880), Sabena (toll free 800/645-3790), Swissair (toll free 800/221-4750).

CITY LINK: Cab fare to city center, about $18; time, 30 min. Bus: **Atlanta Airport Shuttle** (524-3400); leaves every 20 min.; serves major dwntwn hotels; fare, $8–$12; time, 40 min. Direct **subway (MARTA)** connection to dwntwn; leaves every 5 min.; fare, $1.25. The proximity of the airport and the compactness of dwntwn Atlanta may mean that you don't need to rent a car. Atlanta also has an efficient public transportation system (bus, subway), currently being expanded (MARTA) (848-4711).

CAR RENTAL (at the airport unless otherwise indicated): Avis (toll free 800/331-1212); Budget (toll free 800/527-0700); Dollar (toll free 800/800-4000); Hertz (toll free 800/654-3131); National (toll free 800/227-7368); Thrifty, 4708 Riverdale Rd. (toll free 800/367-2277). For dwntwn locations, consult the phone directory.

LIMOUSINE SERVICES: Carey Limousine (681-3366), Dav El Limousine (toll free 800/922-0343), Manhattan Limo (toll free 800/621-5466).

TAXIS: Expensive and undependable, taxis may not be hailed on the street but must be summoned by phone. The best are **Checker Cab** (351-1111), **Style Taxi** (455-8294), and **Yellow Cab** (521-0200).

TRAIN: Amtrak, 1688 Peachtree St. NW (toll free 800/872-7245), 3 mi. (5km) N of dwntwn.

INTERCITY BUSES: Greyhound, 81 International Blvd. (522-6300).

INFORMATION & TOURS

TOURIST INFORMATION: Convention & Visitors Bureau, 231 Peachtree St. NE, Suite 200, GA 30342 (404/521-6600).

Visitor Information Center, Peachtree Center Mall (404/521-6688). Also in Lennox Square (3393 Peachtree Rd. NE in Buckhead) and Underground Atlanta (65 Upper Alabama St.).

GUIDED TOURS: Atlanta Preservation Center Tours, 84 Peachtree St. NW (876-2041): Walking tours of Atlanta dwntwn offered daily Feb–Nov.
Gray Line Tours (bus) (767-0594): Guided tour of the city and environs, serving principal dwntwn hotels.

SIGHTS, ATTRACTIONS & ACTIVITIES

ARCHITECTURAL HIGHLIGHTS: ☀⚖ **Federal Reserve Bank,** 104 Marietta St. NW (521-8747): Imposing Greek Revival building on the site of the Jacobs Pharmacy where, in May 1886, John Pemberton created the famous Coca-Cola formula. Today it houses immense, rigorously guarded workshops where many millions of banknotes are printed each day. Interesting currency museum. Open for groups Mon–Fri by appointment only.
☀⚖⚖ **IBM Building,** 1207 W. Peachtree St. NW (238-2000): Atlanta's most dramatic building (1987). Beautiful postmodern skyscraper, crowned by a 100-ft. (30m) copper pyramid topped by a lantern. Philip Johnson/John Burgee–designed, 50 stories and 825-ft. (251m) high, the building detailing is "American Gothic" and inspired by the famous Tribune Tower in Chicago.
☀⚖⚖ **Peachtree Center,** bounded by Baker, Ellis, Williams, and Courtland Sts. NE: Futurist complex of office skyscrapers, an ultramodern 73-story hotel, and a giant shopping mall with luxury boutiques, restaurants, bars, and interior gardens linked by walkways and footbridges. One of the country's most spectacular architectural assemblies.

BROADCASTING & MOVIE STUDIOS: ⚖ **CNN** (formerly Omni) **Center,** Marietta St. and Techwood Dr. NW (827-2300): One of dwntwn Atlanta's most recent additions. Its ultramodern, sometimes assertive buildings include the **Cable News Network** studios, office buildings, restaurants, movie theaters, hotels, and sports and convention centers. 45-min. guided tour around the studios, editorial offices, and technical equipment of CNN leaves daily every 15 minutes from 10am; call 827-2300 for information.

HISTORIC BUILDINGS & STRUCTURES: ⚖ **A. G. Rhodes Memorial Hall,** 1516 Peachtree St. NW (881-9980): Victorian Romanesque Revival building built in 1903 in the style of a Bavarian castle. Headquarters of the Georgia Trust for Historic Preservation. Interesting changing exhibits. Tours Mon–Fri.
☀⚖ **Alonzo F. Herndon House,** 587 University Place NW (581-9813): Born a slave, Alonzo F. Herndon rose to become the city's wealthiest black citizen as founder of Atlanta Life Insurance Co. The luxurious 15-room mansion he built in 1910 offers a glimpse of a remarkable life. Original furniture and turn-of-the-century memorabilia. Tours Tues–Sat.
☀⚖ **Fox Theatre,** 660 Peachtree St. NE (881-2100): Once a Masonic temple dating from 1929 with an onion dome and minarets, and then a movie theater with rather dizzying Hollywood-Moorish architecture, the Fox, a historical landmark, is now a 4,500-seat concert hall. Guided tours Mon, Thurs, and Sat.

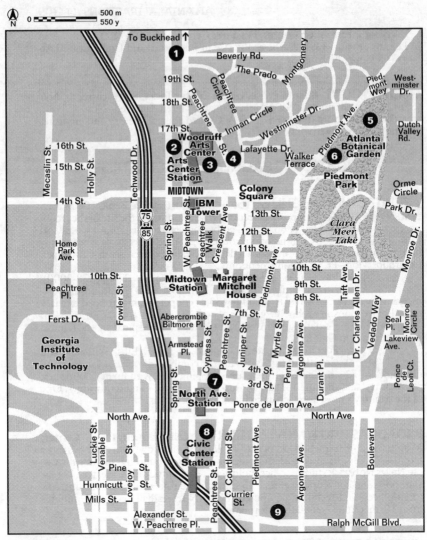

GEORGIA

Atlanta

CENTRAL ATLANTA

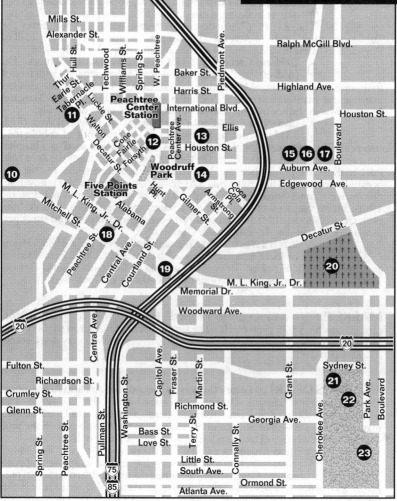

Mills St.
Alexander St.
Hull St.
Thur
Earle St.
Tabernacle
Pl.
Techwood
Williams St.
Spring St.
W. Peachtree
Piedmont Ave.
Ralph McGill Blvd.
Baker St.
Harris St.
Highland Ave.
Peachtree
Center
Station
Luckie St.
Walton
International Blvd.
Houston St.
11
Cone
Fairlie
Peachtree
Center Ave.
Ellis
Forsyth
13
Boulevard
Decatur St.
12
Houston St.
15 **16** **17**
10
Woodruff
Park
14
Auburn Ave.
Five Points
Station
Edgewood Ave.
M. L. King, Jr. Dr.
Hunt
Pl.
Coca
Cola
Pl.
Mitchell St.
Alabama
Gilmer St.
Armstrong
St.
Decatur St.
Peachtree St.
Central Ave.
Courtland St.
18
20
19
M. L. King, Jr., Dr.
Memorial Dr.
Woodward Ave.
20
Central Ave.
20
Fulton St.
Richardson St.
Crumley St.
Glenn St.
Washington St.
Pullman St.
Capitol Ave.
Fraser St.
Martin St.
Richmond St.
Grant St.
Sydney St.
21
Park Ave.
Boulevard
22
Bass St.
Love St.
Terry St.
Connally St.
Georgia Ave.
Cherokee Ave.
Spring St.
Peachtree St.
75
85
Little St.
South Ave.
Atlanta Ave.
Ormond St.
23

Alonzo F. Herndon Home **10**
Atlanta Historical Society–
  Downtown Branch **12**
Atlanta Museum **14**
Birth Home of Martin
  Luther King, Jr. **17**
CNN Center **11**
Cyclorama **22**
Ebenezer Baptist Church **16**
Georgia State Capitol **19**

Grant Park **21**
High Museum at Georgia-
  Pacific Center **13**
Martin Luther King, Jr.,
  Center for Non-Violent
  Social Change **15**
Oakland Cemetery **20**
Underground Atlanta **18**
Zoo Atlanta **23**

     △ **Georgia State Capitol,** Capitol Sq. (656-2350): Georgia's leg-
     △ islative building, dating from 1889, is a replica of the Washing-
ton Capitol. The 237-ft. (72m) dome is covered with gold leaf from the
Dahlonega mines north of Atlanta. The complex includes a very lovely Hall of
Flags and an interesting museum of science and industry. Open Mon–Sat.
     △ **Oakland Cemetery,** 248 Oakland Ave. SE at Memorial Dr.
     △ (658-6019): Landscaped, 84-acre (34ha) cemetery with tens of
thousands of graves, the oldest dating back to the Civil War. The site also has
many grand mausoleums in the Victorian style, including that of Margaret
Mitchell Marsh, author of *Gone with the Wind.* Visitor Center open daily.
     ☼△ **Underground Atlanta,** Alabama St. and Central Ave. (523-
     ☼△ 2311): Beneath the modern city, a labyrinth of cobblestone
streets and houses spared by the fire of 1864. This area was used as a hospital
during the Battle of Atlanta. Under the Central Ave. bridge stands the **Zero Mile
Post,** marking the point where the Western & Atlantic Railroad line, and the city,
began. Reopened in 1989 following a $142-million expansion and renovation,
this festive "Times Square of the South," as much above ground as below the
19th-century viaducts, bustles with restaurants and nightclubs, upscale boutiques, crafts shops, old-fashioned pushcart vendors, and impromptu street performances. A visit you shouldn't miss. Open daily.
     △ **Wren's Nest,** 1050 Abernathy Blvd. NW (753-8535): Home
     △ of Joel Chandler Harris, who created the Uncle Remus stories
and characters: Br'er Rabbit, Br'er Fox, and others. Contains original furnishings, personal papers, and first editions of his works. Open Tues–Sun.

MARKETS: ☼△ **Atlanta State Farmers' Market,** in Forest Park, 10 mi.
(16km) south on I-75 (366-6910): The largest open-air market in the Southeast
(144 acres/60ha). Hundreds of farmers display their produce every day. Grocery
Market open daily.

MUSEUMS OF ART: △ **Emory University Museum of Art and Archeology,**
Emory University Campus, Decatur and Oxford Rds. NE (727-4282): This
small but well-rounded fine-arts museum contains a collection of Greek and Roman antiquities as well as prints and drawings from the Renaissance to the present (including works by Dalí, Kandinsky, and Matisse). Open daily.
     ☼△△△ **High Museum of Art,** 1280 Peachtree St. NE (892-4444):
     Rich collection of European paintings and sculptures, especial-
ly from the Renaissance. Richard Meier designed the ultramodern setting of pure
geometric forms, and won the Pritzker prize (in comparable terms, the Nobel
prize of architecture) for the beauty and originality of his work. The museum is
part of the vast **Robert W. Woodruff Arts Center,** built in 1968 in memory of
the 122 members of the Atlanta Arts Association who died in an air disaster in
Paris (1962). (The French government gave Rodin's *L'Ombre* to the association.)
Among the museum's most famous works: Bellini's *Virgin and Child,* Veronese's
Rest on the Flight into Egypt, Annibale Carracci's *Crucifixion,* and many Picasso
etchings. The Robert Woodruff Arts Center also includes a concert hall **(Symphony Hall),** home of the Atlanta Symphony Orchestra; two theaters (including
the **Alliance Theater**); and the **Atlanta College of Art.** Open Tues–Sun.

MUSEUMS OF SCIENCE & HISTORY: △ **APEX (African-American Panoramic Experience),** 135 Auburn Ave. NE (521-2739): African art, exhibits on
local African American history and rotating exhibits by local and national African American artists in a museum situated a minute away from Dr. King's grave
(see below). Open Tues–Sun.

🔔 **Atlanta Historical Society,** 3101 Andrews Dr. NW (814-4000): Interesting architectural models of Georgian houses, à la *Gone with the Wind.* You can see everything from an 1840s plantation farm **(Tullie Smith House)** to aristocratic Palladian homes **(Swan House)** and slave quarters **(Coach House).** Very lovely old furniture. Open daily.

🔔 **Jimmy Carter Library and Museum,** 1 Copenhill Ave. NE (331-0296): Built on the wooded hill where, according to legend, General Sherman watched Atlanta burn, this group of ultramodern circular buildings includes an international conference center, a museum, and a library with 27 million written and on-film documents concerning the 39th president of the United States. It contains, notably, a faithful replica of the White House's Oval Office. More than 600,000 visitors each year. The complex includes a very beautiful Japanese garden and a lovely view of the Atlanta skyline. Open daily.

🔔 **Cyclorama,** in Grant Park, Cherokee and Georgia Aves. SE (658-7625): This huge fresco of the Battle of Atlanta is the largest circular wall mural in the world (390 by 48 ft./22 by 15m). Painted in 1885–86 by a group of 12 Polish and German artists, it has recently been restored. Sound-and-light show. Open daily.

🔔 **Fernbank Museum of Natural History,** 767 Clifton Rd. NE (378-0127): Open in Oct. 92 this brand new museum is the largest of its kind to be built in the U.S. since the 1930s. It includes a number of hands-on children's exhibits. Spectacular. Open daily.

🔔🔔 **Martin Luther King, Jr., Historic District,** 407 Auburn Ave. NE (524-1956): The life of the Nobel peace prize winner, assassinated in a Memphis hotel in 1968, is retraced in the **King Library and Archives.** His grave is in the middle of a reflecting pool behind the **Ebenezer Baptist Church,** where Martin Luther King, Jr., pursued his pastoral mission from 1960 until his death. In front of the grave burns an eternal flame in memory of the famed civil rights leader. The **King Birthplace** is close by at 501 Auburn Ave. There's an **Information Center** at 413 Auburn Ave. A moving visit. Open daily.

🔔🔔 **SciTrek–The Science of Technology Museum of Atlanta,** 395 Piedmont Ave. NE (522-5500): Ranked as one of the top 10 science and high-technology museums in the U.S., SciTrek houses more than 100 hands-on exhibits. Also live demonstrations, films, etc. Fascinating. Open Tues–Sun.

🔔 **The World of Coca-Cola,** 55 Martin Luther King, Jr., Dr., at Central Ave. (676-5151): A blatantly commercial museum dedicated to the more than 100-year-old history of the famous soft drink. Inaugurated in Aug 1990, this hi-tech structure contains more than 1,000 Coke-related artifacts and memorabilia, including a replica of a 1930s soda fountain, a hi-tech "bottling fantasy," and a 4,500-sq.-ft. (410m^2) company store. Adjacent to the Underground Atlanta complex. Entertaining. Open daily.

PANORAMAS: The ☼🔭 **Sun Dial** bar and revolving restaurant, on the 73rd floor of the Westin Peachtree Hotel (589-7506): Offers the most spectacular view of Atlanta; on a clear day you can see more than 25 mi. (40km).

PARKS & GARDENS: 🔔 **Grant Park,** Cherokee Ave. SE: Vast landscaped park housing a very modern zoo and Civil War fortifications **(Fort Walker),** in addition to the Cyclorama (see "Museums of Science and History," above).

🔔 **Piedmont Park,** Piedmont Ave. at 14th St. NE: This very fine park with lake and swimming area accommodates the annual **Arts Festival** (see "Special Events," below).

Woodruff Park, Peachtree and Pryor Sts. at Auburn Ave.: Gift of Coca-Cola magnate Robert W. Woodruff, this spot in the heart of Atlanta is very popular with lunch-hour picnickers.

Think twice before taking a nighttime stroll in any of Atlanta's parks. The city has one of the higher crime rates among large U.S. cities.

PERFORMING ARTS: For a daily listing of all shows and cultural events, consult the entertainment pages of the daily papers *Atlanta Constitution* (morning) and *Atlanta Journal* (evening), as well as the monthly magazine *Atlanta*.

Academy Theater, 173 14th St. NE (525-4111): Modern comedies and experimental theater.

Atlanta Civic Center, 395 Piedmont Ave. NE (523-6275): Concerts, recitals. Home of the Atlanta Ballet. Hosts each May a series of performances by New York's Metropolitan Opera.

Chastain Memorial Park, between Powers Ferry Rd. and Lake Forrest Dr.: Open-air concerts by the Atlanta Symphony Orchestra, June–Aug.

Fox Theatre, 660 Peachtree St. NE (881-2000): Ballet, concerts, musicals, and a summer film festival. Home of the Theater of the Stars (Broadway shows). Year round.

Seven Stages, 1105 Euclid Ave. (523-7647): Experimental theater, Off-Broadway–style plays.

Symphony Hall, 1280 Peachtree St. NE (892-2414): Home of the Atlanta Symphony Orchestra (principal conductor: Yoel Levi), Sept–May.

Robert W. Woodruff Arts Center, 1280 Peachtree St. NE (892-2414): Home of the Alliance Theater (classical theater, comedy, drama) and the Atlanta Children's Theater.

SHOPPING: Lennox Square/Phipps Plaza, Peachtree and Lenox Rds., Buckhead: Two of the country's largest upscale shopping malls. A tourist attraction and shoppers' paradise with specialty shops galore and top-name department stores (Neiman-Marcus, Saks, Gucci, Tiffany, etc.).

SPECIAL EVENTS: For the exact schedule of events below, consult the **Atlanta Convention & Visitors Bureau** (see "Tourist Information," above).

Dogwood Festival (Apr): Concerts, parades, shows, hot-air balloon rides, tours of old houses. International Flower show to celebrate spring.

Atlanta Hunt and Steeplechase (first Sat in Apr): "The" outdoor social event of the spring. An afternoon of glorious food, fashion, drink, and incidentally, a horse race. At Seven Branches Farm in Cumming.

Bell South Golf Classic (first week in May): PGA tour event. Atlanta Country Club, Paper Mill Rd., Marietta.

Atlanta Jazz Series (late June): Concerts with the biggest stars.

1996 Summer Olympic Games (July 20–Aug 4): For ticket information, contact the Atlanta Committee for the Olympic Games, P.O. Box 1996, GA 30301 (224-1996).

Arts Festival (Sept): Concerts, ballets, art exhibitions in Piedmont Park; the festival attracts 2,000,000 spectators each year.

SPORTS: Atlanta has three professional teams:

Baseball (Apr–Oct): Braves, Atlanta Stadium (577-9100).
Basketball (Oct–Apr): Hawks, Omni Coliseum (827-3800).
Football (Sept–Dec): Falcons, Atlanta Stadium (261-5400).

STROLLS: ⚑ West Paces Ferry Road, between Peachtree Rd. and Northside Pkwy.: One of the most beautiful residential districts in the Southeast. Plenty of winding driveways leading to hidden estates, including the white-columned **Governor's Mansion,** 391 W. Paces Ferry Rd. (261-1776); tours Tues–Thurs.

THEME PARKS: ⚑ Six Flags over Georgia, 7561 Six Flags Rd. (12 mi./19km west on I-20) (948-9290): This giant theme park dedicated to the history of

Georgia boasts more than 100 attractions, including a triple-loop roller coaster (the Mind Bender). Open daily June–Sept, wknds only in spring and autumn; closed the rest of the year. The park attracts more than two million visitors a year.

&& **Stone Mountain,** 16 mi (26km) NE on U.S. 78 (296-8058): Large, 3,200-acre (1,295ha) theme park including a Civil War memorial, an authentic 19th-century plantation, a car museum, a cable car, a paddle-boat lake ride, and an Old West–style steam engine. In addition, there's the impressive, 825-ft.-high (250m) granite monolith (the largest in the world) with giant sculptures resembling those of Mount Rushmore. The 165- by 72-ft. (55- by 24m) bas-relief represents three southern heroes: Confederate Pres. Jefferson Davis, Gen. Robert E. Lee, and Gen. "Stonewall" Jackson. Open daily year round.

ACCOMMODATIONS

Personal Favorites (in order of preference)

♀♀♀♀ **Ritz-Carlton Buckhead** (nr. dwntwn), 3434 Peachtree Rd. NE, GA 30326 (404/237-2700; toll free 800/241-3333). 550 rms, A/C, color TV, in-rm movies. AE, CB, DC, MC, V. Valet parking $10, pool, health club, sauna, two rests. (including The Dining Room), coffee shop, two bars, 24-hr. rm svce, boutiques, concierge, free crib. *Note:* In the heart of the new business and entertainment district of Buckhead, this modern, 22-story structure is one of the most recent additions to the local luxury-hotel scene. Its decor and amenities are in the grand tradition, and its svce is impeccable. The period-furnished rms are spacious and elegant, and colored in pastel tones, w. in-rm safes and bathroom phones. The hotel also boasts Atlanta's best rest. and adjacent luxury shopping areas. Two VIP floors. Big business clientele. Interesting wknd packages. Highly recommended. **E–VE**

♀♀♀♀ **Nikko Hotel–Atlanta** (nr. dwntwn), 3300 Peachtree Rd. NE, GA 30305 (404/365-8100; toll free 800/645-5687). 440 rms, A/C, color TV, in-rm movies. AE, CB, DC, MC, V. Valet parking $10, pool, health club, sauna, two rests. (including Kamogawa), bar, 24-hr. rm svce, concierge. *Note:* Spectacular brand-new luxury hotel in the Buckhead district. Beautiful Japanese garden w. a 35-ft. (10.6m) cascading waterfall. Spacious rms handsomely appointed, all w. marble bath, minibar, and bathroom phone. Courteous, exemplary svce "à la Japanese." Executive business center. Three VIP floors. Asian elegance and effectiveness. **E–VE**

☼♀♀♀ **Westin Peachtree Plaza** (dwntwn), 210 Peachtree St. (at International Blvd.), GA 30343 (404/659-1400; toll free, see Westin). 1,080 rms, A/C, color TV, in-rm movies. AE, CB, DC, MC. V. Valet gar. $13, pool, health club, three rests. (including the Sun Dial), four bars, 24-hr. rm svce, nightclub, boutiques, free crib. *Note:* This futurist, glass-and-steel tower by John Portman is America's tallest hotel—73 stories high—w. waterfalls and interior grdns on eight floors. It offers total comfort, despite rather cramped rms, and efficient svce, despite the hotel's immense size. One of the country's most spectacular buildings, and the most eye-catching spot in Atlanta. Business and group clientele. Recently underwent a $30-million renovation. **E–VE**

♀♀ **Ansley Inn** (nr. dwntwn), 253 15th St. NE, GA 30309 (404/872-9000; toll free 800/446-5416). 15 rms, A/C, cable color TV. Café nearby, valet svce, concierge. *Note:* Beautifully restored 1907 yellow-brick Tudor mansion in the fashionable Ansley Park neighborhood. Elegant, comfortable rms w. period furnishings, working fireplaces, and wet bars. Gracious reception and svce. An excellent alternative to Atlanta's high-rise hotels (it has three stories, but no elevator). **M–E**

♀♀ **Comfort Inn** (formerly the Ibis Hotel; nr. dwntwn), 101 International Blvd., GA 30303 (404/524-5555; toll free, see Choice). 260 rms, A/C, cable color TV, in-rm movies. AE, CB, DC, MC, V. Gar. $5, pool, rest., bar, free crib. *Note:* Ultramodern motel next to the Georgia

World Congress Center. Inviting interior decor and comfortable, well-conceived rms. Cheerful reception and a very adequate rest. w. buffet. Excellent value. Business clientele. **I–M**

    Courtyard Marriott Midtown (nr. dwntwn), 1132 Techwood Dr. NW, GA 30318 (404/607-1112; toll free 800/321-2211). 168 rms, A/C, cable color TV. AE, CB, DC, MC, V. Free parking, pool, health club, rest., valet svce, free crib. *Note:* New, attractive mid-priced hotel located in midtown, nr. the IBM Building and Georgia Tech. Spacious, comfortable rms w. large desks and separate dressing areas. Efficient svce. Good value overall. **I–M**

    Quality Inn-Northeast (nr. dwntwn), 2960 NE Expressway (I-85) at Shallowford Rd., GA 30341 (404/451-5231). 157 rms, A/C, cable color TV. AE, CB, DC, MC, V. Free parking, pool, free continental breakfast, free crib. *Note:* Decent rooms, all with balconies. Great value. Ideal if you're driving. **B–I**

Other Accommodations (from top bracket to budget)

    Marriott Marquis (dwntwn), 265 Peachtree Center Ave., GA 30303 (404/521-0000; toll free, see Marriott). 1,675 rms, A/C, color TV, in-rm movies. AE, CB, DC, MC, V. Valet gar. $12, pool, tennis, health club, sauna, five rests., coffee shop, four bars, 24-hr. rm svce, boutiques, hrdrsr, free crib. *Note:* This new hotel is one of the most spectacular and tallest in the South—50 stories of glass and concrete in the heart of Atlanta, designed by John Portman. The 520-ft.-high (160m) atrium houses interior grdns and glass elevators. Spacious, ultra-comfortable rms and very complete amenities. Two VIP floors. Efficient svce, but very average rest. (like all Marriotts). Interesting wknd packages. **E–VE**

    Swissotel-Atlanta (nr. dwntwn), 3391 Peachtree Rd. NE (at Lenox Sq.), GA 30326 (404/365-0065; toll free 800/637-9477). 365 rms, A/C, color TV, in-rm movies. AE, CB, DC, MC, V. Valet gar. $10, pool, health club, sauna, rests. (Opus), bar, 24-hr. rm svce, hrdrsr, concierge. *Note:* Bauhaus-style luxury hotel in the heart of Buckhead, the city's shopping mecca. Opened in Jan 1991, this soaring, elegant 22-story tower houses unrivaled comfort and facilities. Spacious, well-laid-out rms; very fine hotel rest. Svce worthy of the Swiss tradition. Very comprehensive physical-fitness facilities. A fine place to stay. **E–VE**

    Occidental Grand Hotel (nr. dwntwn), 75 14th St. (in the GLG Grand Bldg), GA 30309 (404/881-9898; toll free 800/952-0702). 246 rms, A/C, cable color TV. AE, CB, DC, MC, V. Valet parking $11, pool, health club, sauna, rests. (including Florencia), 24-hr. rm svce, bar, boutiques, concierge, hrdrsr, free crib. *Note:* Atlanta's newest posh hotel occupying the first 20 floors of the GLG Grand building. Sweeping staircase in the three-story lavish entry is just the first indication of the hotel's gentrified attitude that combines European traditions with Southern hospitality. A grand ballroom on the third floor augments this sentiment. Fifth-floor terrace offers great view of the city's skyline. Boasts Atlanta's most expensive suite at $1,500 a night. **E–VE**

    Hyatt Regency (dwntwn), 265 Peachtree St. NE, GA 30303 (404/577-1234; toll free, see Hyatt). 1,285 rms, A/C, color TV, in-rm movies. AE, CB, DC, MC, V. Valet gar. $13, pool, health club, three rests., bars, rm svce, free crib. *Note:* A hotel classic dating from 1967, w. a 23-story atrium, interior grdns, and glass elevators. Vast rms w. balconies offer lavish comfort. The svce is rather uncertain but the panoramic view of Atlanta from the revolving rest. at the top, Polaris, is spectacular. No-smoking rms. The first of the grand hotels designed by John Portman. Group clientele. Recently renovated. **E–VE**

    Atlanta Renaissance Hotel (formerly Penta; dwntwn), 590 W. Peachtree St. NW, GA 30308 (404/881-6000; toll free 800/225-3456). 505 rms, A/C, color TV, in-rm movies. AE, CB, DC, MC, V.

Valet parking $9, pool, rest., bar, rm svce, free crib. *Note:* Modern, serviceable hotel close to the business district. The rms are spacious and comfortable (some w. refrigerators); personalized svce. Two VIP floors. Business clientele. An excellent place. **E**

Terrace Garden Inn (vic.), 3405 Lenox Rd., GA 30326 (404/261-9250; toll free 800/241-8260). 372 rms, A/C, cable color TV. AE, CB, DC, MC, V. Gar. $8, two pools, health club, sauna, rest. bar, rm svce, free crib. *Note:* Very comfortable luxury hotel w. lovely grdns and spacious balconied rms. Good svce. An excellent location in Buckhead, 20 min. from dwntwn. Ideal for the car traveler. Good recreational facilities. Business clientele. **M–E**

Days Hotel–Atlanta at Lenox (nr. dwntwn), 3377 Peachtree Rd. NE, GA 30326 (404/264-1111; toll free, see Days Inns). 300 rms, A/C, color TV, in-rm movies. AE, CB, DC, MC, V. Free parking, health club, sauna, rest. (Brentwood Café), bar, rm svce, free crib. *Note:* Flagship of the big Atlanta-based hotel chain. Modern, functional 11-story tower in the heart of Buckhead. Comfortable, inviting rms; good svce. Free shuttle to any point within 3 mi. (5km). Right next to the subway (8 min. from dwntwn). Business clientele. Good value. **I–M**

Holiday Inn–Central (formerly Lanier Plaza; nr. dwntwn), 418 Armour Dr. NE, GA 30324 (404/873-4661; toll free, see Holiday Inn). 250 rms, A/C, color TV, in-rm movies. AE, CB, DC, MC, V. Free parking, pool, rest., bar, rm svce, hrdsrs, free crib. *Note:* Undistinguished but inviting hotel away from the bustling city center. Comfortable rms w. balcony and refrigerator; ultra-professional svce. Lovely grdn courtyard. Business clientele. 8 min. from dwntwn. **I–M**

Best Western American (dwntwn), 160 Spring St., GA 30303 (404/688-8600; toll free, see Best Western). 325 rms, A/C, cable color TV. AE, CB, DC, MC, V. Gar. $5, pool, rest. (Gatsby's), bar, rm svce, free crib. *Note:* Modern, functional, eight-story motel. Rms have patios or balconies. The svce is good, as is the value. Business clientele. Next to the Georgia World Congress Center. VIP floor. **I–M**

Comfort Inn–Buckhead (formerly La Quinta; nr. dwntwn), 2115 Piedmont Rd. NE, GA 30376 (404/876-4365; toll free, see La Quinta). 182 rms, cable color TV. AE, CB, DC, MC, V. Free parking, pool, rest., free crib. *Note:* Inviting motel halfway between dwntwn and the new Buckhead business district. Comfortable; friendly, smiling reception. Good value. 10 min. from dwntwn. **I**

Motel 6 West (vic.), 4100 Wendell Dr. SW, GA 30336 (404/696-0757). 175 rms, A/C, color TV, free in-rm movies. AE, DC, MC, V. Free parking, pool, free crib. *Note:* Modern comfort at ultra-economical prices. Located 25 min. from dwntwn and 6 min. from the Six Flags Over Georgia theme park. One of the best values in the area. Ideal for the motorist. **B**

Airport Accommodations

Sheraton Gateway Hotel Atlanta Airport (formerly the Hyatt; vic.), 1900 Sullivan Rd., College Park, GA 30337 (404/997-1100; toll free, see Sheraton). 399 rms, A/C, color TV, in-rm movies. AE, CB, DC, MC, V. Free parking, two pools, health club, rest., bar, rm svce, free crib. *Note:* Modern, comfortable, 12-story hotel affording direct access to the Convention Center (nr. the airport). Spacious, well-soundproofed rms and efficient svce. VIP floor. Group and business clientele. Free airport shuttle. Has undergone a $5-million remodeling and renovation. **M–E**

YMCA/Youth Hostels

Atlanta Dream Hostel (nr. dwntwn), 222 E. Howard Ave. (404/370-0380). 35 beds. Transportation in '69 Cadillac to and from bus and train station. Biergarten/barbecue area. Young people's part of town.

Woodruf AYH-Hostel (nr. dwntwn), 223 Ponce de Leon Ave. (404/872-8844). 50 beds. Clean, safe, and friendly hotel near the North Ave. subway station.

RESTAURANTS

Personal Favorites (in order of preference)

♈♈♈♈ **The Dining Room** (nr. dwntwn), in the Ritz-Carlton Buckhead (see "Accommodations," above) (237-2700). A/C. Dinner only, Mon–Sat; closed hols. AE, CB, DC, MC, V. J&T. *Specialties:* tuna tartar w. seaweed salad on sesame strudel; sautéed foie gras w. glazed plums and onion marmalade; muscovy duck breast w. mushroom polenta; rack of lamb w. sweet-pepper sauce; Black-Angus tenderloin w. spaghetti squash; apricot flan w. cardamon ice cream. The menu changes daily. Splendid wine list w. great vintages sold by the glass (cruvinet). *Note:* Once the owner of the renowned Boheneck restaurant in the Black Forest of Germany (two stars in Michelin), the very talented chef Guenter Seeger has made this classic, elegant palace rest. into one of the finest in the South. Inspired nouvelle cuisine happily unites innovation w. a meticulous attention to detail. Vast marble-and-mahogany dining rm w. stylish furniture and hunting pictures. Exemplary white-gloved svce. One of the dozen best rests. in the country. Resv. a must. Valet parking. 15 min. from dwntwn. *French/Continental.* **E–VE**

♈♈♈ **Resto des Amis** (nr. dwntwn), 3060 Peachtree Rd., in Buckhead (364-2170). A/C. Lunch/dinner daily, brunch Sun; closed hols. AE, CB, DC, MC, V. *Specialties:* oysters on ice, country terrine, marinated salmon gravlax, grilled sausage w. cannellini beans, free-range chicken, beef entrecôte, upside-down apple tart. Expertly chosen wine list. *Note:* The joint venture between two of the very best chefs in America, Guenter Seeger of The Dining Room (see above) and Jean-Louis Palladin of Jean-Louis and Palladin (see "Restaurants," in the chapter on Washington, D.C.). Rest. upholds the flare of both chefs while making sure not to alienate those out for a casual evening. Plump organic chickens (perhaps the best you'll ever taste) slow-roasted over an open hearth. A scrumptious sight. Resv. advised. Valet parking. *Continental.* **M**

♈♈♈ **Pano's & Paul's** (nr. dwntwn), 1232 W. Paces Ferry Rd. (261-3662). A/C. Dinner only, Mon–Sat; closed hols. AE, CB, DC, MC, V. Jkt. *Specialties:* crab cakes, red snapper w. hazelnut butter, quail w. wild mushrooms, roast veal chop w. basil butter, crème brûlée, Mississippi mud pie. Very fine wine list. *Note:* An Atlanta institution. Classic, French-inspired cuisine impeccably presented. Ideally romantic Victorian decor. Distinguished music in the background. Discreet but ultra-professional svce. Trendy clientele. Resv. recommended. 25 min. from dwntwn on I-75 and Northside Pkwy. *Continental.* **M–E**

♈♈ **Azalea** (nr. dwntwn), 3167 Peachtree Rd., in Buckhead (237-9939). A/C. Dinner only, nightly; closed Dec 25. MC, V. *Specialties:* crabmeat, feta, and fresh spinach wrapped in filo dough; sizzling catfish w. black-bean chile sauce; hot smoked salmon in potato crust; grilled shrimp wrapped in prosciutto; Thai red-curry stir fry; fabulous desserts. Good wine list (American). *Note:* Ultra-trendy new hi-tech rest. offering innovative East-West cuisine in a pleasantly casual but noisy atmosphere. Friendly svce. No resv. Valet parking. *American/Oriental.* **I–M**

♈♈ **Bone's** (nr. dwntwn), 3130 Piedmont Rd. NE (237-2663). A/C. Lunch Mon–Fri, dinner nightly; closed hols. AE, CB, DC, MC, V. *Specialties:* excellent meats, Maine lobster, fresh seafood. Average desserts and wine list. *Note:* A local red-meat shrine, this New York–style steakhouse is famous for the high quality of its meat (corn-fed Iowa cattle) and for its generous servings. Rather brusque but efficient svce. Amusing caricatures on the walls as well as old photographs of Atlanta. Business clientele. The tab can climb quickly if you choose lobster over T-bone steak. Resv. advised. Valet parking. *Steakhouse.* **M–E**

♈♈ **Pricci** (nr. dwntwn), 500 Pharr Rd. (237-2941). A/C. Lunch
♈♈ Mon–Thurs, dinner nightly. AE, MC, V. *Specialties:* fried Gorgonzola risotto w. tomato coulis, unique pizzas, homemade pasta (specially pappardelle bolognese), red snapper in parchment w. olives and sun-dried tomatoes, quails and baby veal sausages w. polenta. Menu changes regularly. *Note:* The hottest Italian rest. in Atlanta. As w. the other ventures of Pano Karatassos (see 103 West, below), the decor is ostentatiously opulent yet outrageous, the cuisine outstanding, and the atmosphere casually chic. Svce is of the best. Resv. advised. *Italian.* **I–M**

☼♈ **Mary Mac's Tea Room** (nr. dwntwn), 224 Ponce de Leon Ave.
☼♈ NE (876-1800). A/C. Lunch/dinner Mon–Fri (until 10pm); closed hols. No credit cards. *Specialties:* fried chicken, southern-style shrimp, peanut-butter pie. *Note:* Only the name suggests a tea rm. Rustic, flavorful southern cooking in a relaxed, if generally noisy and overcrowded, atmosphere. An excellent spot w. unbeatable prices. Nr. Georgia Tech. Inevitable waits (sometimes fairly long). *American.* **B**

Other Restaurants (from top bracket to budget)

♈♈♈ **Opus** (nr. dwntwn), in the Swissotel Atlanta (see "Accommo-
♈♈♈ dations." above) (365-0065). A/C. Lunch/dinner daily. AE, CB, DC, MC, V. Jkt. *Specialties:* crab cakes w. fried pasta, apple-cured hot smoked salmon, peppered tuna medallions, seared beef tenderloin w. asparagus and Reggiano cheese, risotto of rock shrimp and calamari in shellfish-and-herb broth, spectacular desserts. *Note:* Though it achieved a place of honor when it first opened, this rest. had had to downscale. But under the guidance of chef Ken Vedrinski, it has done so admirably. Very fine wine list. *Note:* This relative newcomer to the Atlanta gastronomic scene won a place of honor in just a few months under the guidance of its inventive chef Martin Gagne. The setting is sober, warm, and comfortable. Somewhat whimsical svce. Resv. advised. *American.* **M–E**

♈♈♈ **103 West** (nr. dwntwn), 103 W. Paces Ferry Rd. (233-5993).
♈♈♈ A/C. Dinner only, Mon–Sat. AE, CB, DC, MC, V. Jkt. *Specialties:* lump-crabmeat cakes, profiteroles filled w. foie gras, veal chop w. morels, pot-au-feu w. tarragon-scented chicken, broiled noisettes of lamb w. pommes soufflées, roast breast of duck, crème brûlée. Menu changes regularly. Remarkable but pricey wine list. *Note:* Despite its appallingly kitsch decor—fake-marble columns, Aubusson tapestries, trompe-l'oeil wall paintings—crowds have flocked to this successful venture by the inventive Pano Karatassos, who already owns Pano's & Paul's, Pricci, and the Fish Market. Impeccably prepared and served international upscale food, w. prices to match. Resv. a must. *French/ American.* **M–E**

♈♈♈ **Bacchanalia** (nr. dwntwn), 3125 Piedmont Rd. in Buckhead
♈♈♈ (365-0410). A/C. Dinner only, Tues–Sat; closed last two weeks in August and hols. AE, DC, MC, V. *Specialties:* Dungeness crab cakes w. red-pepper relish, roast butternut squash soup w. seared foie gras, sautéed Gulf red snapper olivette, short ribs over whipped potatoes w. red-wine sauce, warm vahlrona chocolate cake w. vanilla-bean ice cream. *Note:* A relative newcomer to Atlanta that quickly gained a reputation as being among the best in the area. Anne Quatro and Clifford Harrison—owners, chefs, and husband and wife— vie for elegant simplicity and originality. With a 60-person capacity the rest. can concentrate on having a daily, fresh menu. Resv. a must. *American.* **M** (prix fixe)

♈♈ **Buckhead Diner** (nr. dwntwn), 3073 Piedmont Rd. (262-
♈♈ 3336). A/C. Lunch/dinner daily (until midnight); closed hols. AE, CB, DC, MC, V. *Specialties:* warm Louisiana oysters, calamari marinara, shrimp pot stickers in gingered soy sauce, pecan-breaded trout, double-smoked pork chops, white-chocolate banana cream pie. Menu changes regularly.

Note: Hip and casual version of yesterday's classic diner complete w. chrome, marble floors, and mahogany wood. Gourmet/nouvelle cuisine. Excellent svce. Trendy clientele. Be prepared to wait since no resv. are taken. *American.* **M**

    La Grotta (nr. dwntwn), 2637 Peachtree Rd. NE (231-1368). A/C. Dinner only, Mon–Sat; closed hols. AE, CB, DC, MC, V. Jkt. *Specialties:* tortellini verdi, carpaccio, scaloppine al grata, antipasto al Italiano. Very good list of Italian wines at reasonable prices. *Note:* Authentic Italian cuisine—especially the remarkable fresh pasta—in a pretty, rustic setting w. terraced grdn offering open-air dining in nice weather. Very good svce. Resv. advised. Valet parking. 20 min. from dwntwn. *Italian.* **M**

    City Grill (dwntwn), 50 Hurt Plaza (524-2489). A/C. Lunch Mon–Fri, dinner Mon–Sat. AE, CB, DC, MC, V. *Specialties:* wild mushrooms in Jack Daniel's custard w. asparagus, blue crab cakes on corn chowder, pan-seared salmon w. Great Lakes–caviar sauce, mustard-crusted New York strip, chocolate-vanilla anglaise. *Note:* Housed in the old Federal Reserve Bank of Atlanta, this rest. has received a boost from its chef Roger Kaplin and his bold approach to cooking, which draws on an impressive variety of American cuisine. Excellent svce; striking setting. Business clientele; resv. strongly advised. A fine place in the heart of dwntwn. *American.* **M**

    Fish Market (nr. dwntwn), 3393 Peachtree Rd. NE (262-3165). A/C. Lunch/dinner Mon–Sat; closed hols. AE, CB, DC, MC, V. Jkt. *Specialties:* lobster tails in mustard sauce, seafood pastas, sautéed Dover sole, Florida stone crabs, fish of the day, chocolate-pecan cake. Fine wine list. *Note:* Elegant rest. w. Mediterranean decor offering Atlanta's largest choice of seafood. Everything is truly fresh, and grilled, fried, or poached to perfection. Excellent svce. Dinner resv. necessary. Locally very popular. Valet parking. *Seafood.* **M**

    Indigo Coastal Grill (nr. dwntwn), 1397 N. Highland Ave. NE (876-0676). A/C. Dinner nightly, brunch Sun; closed hols. AE, MC, V. *Specialties:* lobster corn chowder, bouillabaisse, catfish in sesame crust, key lime pie. *Note:* The best local source for the sunny, savory food of the Caribbean. Decorated like a fisherman's cottage in the South Seas, w. an open kitchen and a view of the chefs bustling around the stove. Relaxed funky atmosphere and svce. Locally popular; unfortunately no resv. accepted. *Caribbean/American.* **M**

    1848 House (vic.), 780 S. Cobb, Marietta (404/428-1848). A/C. Dinner Tues–Sun, brunch Sun. AE, CB, DC, MC, V. Jkt. *Specialties:* Charleston she-crab soup, grilled Georgia shrimp, Vidalia-onion tart w. tomato-thyme cream, slow-cooked peppered duck, bourbon-marinated smoked pork tenderloin, sweet-potato pecan pie. *Note:* Billed as "contemporary southern" cuisine, the food is a fond reminder of where it is served—in a beautiful Greek Revival plantation house that manages not to be a tourist trap. Once an owner of 18 drugstores in Atlanta, proprietor William Dunaway has found a great alternative to retirement. Live jazz during Sunday brunch. I-75 N to exit 111. *American.* **I–M**

    Chopstix (nr. dwntwn), 4279 Roswell Rd. in Chastain Sq. Shopping Center (255-4868). A/C. Lunch Mon–Fri, dinner nightly; closed hols. AE, DC, MC, V. *Specialties:* steamed whole orange roughy, mango roast-duck salad, scallops sautéed in lemon butter. Menu changes regularly. *Note:* Gourmet Chinese cuisine in a casual, elegant setting in muted colors of gray and pink. Intimate atmosphere. Haphazard svce. Resv. advised. *Chinese.* **I–M**

    Nakato (nr. dwntwn), 1893 Piedmont Rd. NE (873-6582). A/C. Dinner only, nightly; closed Jan 1, Dec 25. AE, CB, DC, MC, V. *Specialties:* sushi, sukiyaki, sashimi, teppanyaki, tempura. *Note:* Truly authentic Japanese cuisine. Very handsome Oriental decor w. separate dining rms. Efficient, if slightly abrupt, svce. Locally popular. Resv. advised on wknds. *Japanese.* **I–M**

℧ **The Colonnade** (nr. dwntwn), 1879 Cheshire Bridge Rd. (874-5642). A/C. Lunch/dinner daily. No credit cards. *Specialties:* fried chicken, southern-style vegetables, chicken pot pie, lamb shank, country-fried steak, key lime pie. *Note:* An Atlanta institution since 1927. Nondescript decor and atmosphere but remarkable home-style food cooked just like grandma used to do it. Delicious homemade pastries. Friendly waitresses. Very good value. Locally popular. 20 min. dwntwn. *American.* **B–I**

℧ **Aleck's Barbecue Heaven** (dwntwn), 783 Martin Luther King, Jr., Dr. NW (525-2062). A/C. Lunch/dinner daily (until 11pm). No credit cards. *Specialties:* beef, chicken, and pork barbecue; chopped pork, baby ribs. *Note:* Voted best barbecue in town by *Atlanta* magazine readers. Devilishly hot sauce and incredibly tender meats. Very popular locally, especially at lunchtime. No-frills decor and svce. *American.* **B**

℧ **The Varsity** (nr. dwntwn), 61 North Ave. (881-1706). Lunch/dinner daily (until 12:30am). No credit cards. *Specialties:* hamburgers, chile dogs, sandwiches, orange freezes, apple pie. *Note:* By general consensus, the best hamburgers in Atlanta for close to 50 years. Also prides itself on being the largest drive-in rest. in the world, w. two floors for parking. Every day it serves 15,000 hot dogs, 10,000 burgers, 2,500 lb. (1,135kg) of fries, a ton (910kg) of onion rings, and 300 gal. (1,135l) of homemade chile sauce to top it all. An absolute must-see. Right next to Georgia Tech. An authentic local institution. *American.* **B**

BARS & NIGHTCLUBS

Blind Willie's (nr. dwntwn), 828 N. Highland Ave. (873-2583). Dim club drawing a young crowd for local and occasional big-name rock acts. Serves decent Cajun food. Open nightly.

Blues Harbor (nr. downtown), 229 Peachtree St. (605-0661). Chicago-style blues and jump-swing live. The cover varies with the act. Open nightly.

Dante's Down the Hatch (dwntwn), 86 Alabama St., in Underground Atlanta (577-1800). Jazz and folk music in an old galleon setting that is both picturesque and pleasant. Fondue supper served until 10:30pm. Open nightly.

Good Old Days (nr. dwntwn), 3013 Peachtree Rd. (266-2597). Casual bar serving a light fare of bar food and a good array of beers. Open Tues–Sun.

Manuel's Tavern (nr. dwntwn), 602 N. Highland Ave. (525-3449). Convivial singles bar with English-pub decor and a clientele of journalists and politicians. A classic of its kind for 20 years.

The Masquerade (nr. dwntwn), 695 North Ave. (577-8178). Hard rock to progressive dance music in an original turn-of-the-century mill, Wed–Sun.

The Point (nr. dwntwn), 420 Moreland Ave. (577-6468). Rock, jazz, blues, country, or Cajun by regional or national touring artists. Open nightly.

Punch Line (dwntwn), Pryor and Alabama Sts., in Underground Atlanta (252-5233). Comedy club featuring the best in standup comics. Open nightly.

Velvet (dwntwn), 89 Park Place (681-9936). The favorite meeting place for upscale Atlantans, located in the historic York's Pool Hall building. Open Mon and Wed–Sat.

Waverly Hotel (nr. dwntwn), 2450 Galleria Pkwy. (953-4500). Very crowded tea dances every Fri evening with orchestras à la Glenn Miller and Woody Herman. Attracts hundreds of devotees each wknd.

NEARBY EXCURSIONS

CALLAWAY GARDENS (70 mi./112km SW on I-85S and U.S. 27S in Pine Mountain): One of the most beautiful botanic gardens in the country, with 2,400 acres (1,000ha) of splendid gardens and woods, 13 lakes (fishing, boating, waterskiing), four golf courses, and more than 12½ mi. (20km) of hiking trails. Attracting many thousands of visitors annually, it's well worth the 90-min. car ride from Atlanta. Open daily, year round.

In **Warm Springs,** 15 mi. (24km) farther west, visit the ⚓ **Little White House,** I-85W (706/655-3511), summer home of Pres. Franklin D. Roosevelt, where he died on April 12, 1945.

Where to Stay En Route

IN PINE MOUNTAIN 🍷🍷🍷🍷 **Callaway Gardens Hotel,** Hwy. 27, Pine Mountain, GA 31822-2000 (706/663-2281; toll free 800/282-8181). 800 rms. Four-star hotel, w. three 18-hole and one 9-hole golf courses. **E–VE**

☀⚓ **KENNESAW MOUNTAIN NATIONAL BATTLE-FIELD PARK** (Old U.S. 41 and Stilesboro Rd. in Marietta, 25 mi./40km NW on I-75N) (404/427-4686): Listed as one of the 10 most visited national parks in the U.S., Kennesaw Mountain commemorates a decisive battle of the Civil War (1864). Museum with slide presentation of the battle, hiking trails of original earthworks. Open daily year round.

Also in the vicinity, ⚓ **Big Shanty Museum,** 2829 Cherokee St., Kennesaw (404/427-2117), houses *The General,* one of two vintage locomotives that were the subject of a famous Civil War spy chase re-created in the Walt Disney movie *The Great Locomotive Chase.* Open daily.

⚓ **LAKE LANIER ISLANDS** (42 mi./68km NW on I-85N and U.S. 985 in Buford) (404/932-7200): 1,200-acre (485ha) pine-forested resort surrounding a vast man-made lake with facilities for camping, swimming, sailing, picnicking, tennis, and horseback riding. Open year round.

Accommodations vary from houseboats to the plush 🍷🍷🍷🍷 **Stouffer Pineisle Resort,** Ga. 347, Buford, GA 30518 (404/945-8921); 250 rms with an 18-hole golf course (rates: **E–VE**).

♟♟ **MADISON** (60 mi./96km east on I-20E and U.S. 129N): This truly antebellum southern town just one hour from Atlanta contains Civil War–period houses so beautiful that General Sherman refused to burn them on his devastating march to the sea. Over half of the well-preserved antebellum and Victorian houses are shown during home tours in May and Dec (call 404/342-4454 for information). Has been used from time to time as the setting for movies and TV shows. Worth going out of your way for.

⚓ **ROSWELL** (25 mi./40km north on U.S. 19N): Founded in 1830, this quaint little community in the North Atlanta area features many pre–Civil War houses. Group tours can be arranged through the **Roswell Historical Society,** 98 Bulloch Ave. (404/992-1665). Clustered around Roswell Sq. are a number of boutiques, craft and clothing shops, and restaurants.

CHAPTER 13

NASHVILLE ⍟

□ □ □

And the Great Smoky Mountains

The mecca of country music, deftly portrayed by director Robert Altman in his movie *Nashville,* is today a mixture of southern conservatism and razzle-dazzle prosperity—show business, publishing, banking, insurance, etc. It was founded in 1779 as Fort Nashborough by a group of North Carolina pioneers under the leadership of James Robertson. The little fort of rough-hewn logs named after Revolutionary War hero Gen. Francis Nash may still be seen, scrupulously restored, on the west bank of the Cumberland River.

From its past as a city of the Old South, the capital of Tennessee has retained its gracious, spacious upper-class homes and magnificent gardens, its taste for religion (707 churches), a fondness for education (the city boasts no fewer than 16 colleges and universities) and some venerable traditions. From the explosion of the popularity of country music that began in the 1950s, Nashville derives a multitude of record shops, souvenir stores, and huge billboards; a network of urban highways; the nouveaux riches palaces of the country-music stars, with their year-round congregation of busloads of worshipful fans; and endless suburbs punctuated with screaming neon signs, hamburger joints, and used-car lots. The recording industry contributes to the wealth of "Music City USA" at the rate of $600 million a year. Here, where the famous "Nashville Sound" was born, a hundred recording studios turn out, in good years and bad alike, more than half the country's pop music.

It should, then, come as no surprise that the city's most famous monument is not the life-size replica of the **Parthenon** (whence the name "Athens of the South," bestowed on the city by its inhabitants), not the beautiful **Cheekwood Botanical Garden,** not even the elegant **Hermitage,** where Pres. Andrew Jackson ended his days—but rather that shrine for all lovers of country music, the **Grand Ole Opry.** Into this huge modern auditorium, designed to serve also as a recording studio, thousands of enthusiastic spectators squeeze every weekend to witness the videotaping of TV shows whose popularity, now a full 50 years old, shows no signs of abating. Dreamed up by radio pioneer George D. Hay, the "Grand Ole Opry" (the local pronunciation of "Grand Old Opera") came into the world in Nov 1925 over the airwaves of a little local radio station, 650 WSM; before long it was to be relayed across the country over the NBC network. It was, and remains, the principal instrument of the triumph of country music, and thus of Nashville's prosperity.

From Nashville you can easily reach several interesting tourist destinations: Chattanooga and the Tennessee Valley, the Great Smoky Mountains, and Mammoth Cave National Park, among others. "Music City USA" ranks 15th among U.S. cities in terms of its economic growth rate.

Singer Rita Coolidge was born in Nashville.

BASIC FACTS: Capital of the State of Tennessee. Area code: 615. Time zone: central; ZIP Code: 37202. Founded in: 1779. Approximate population: city, 510,000; metropolitan area, 985,000. Rank among U.S. cities: 23rd.

CLIMATE: The summer in Nashville is a little less humid than in Memphis, but just as hot, averaging 80°F (27°C) in July. From Mar through July the humidity is accentuated by storms, which are sometimes violent. The winters are moderately cold, with Jan temperatures averaging 38°F (3°C). The fall, when the weather is cool but fair, is the best time to visit Tennessee.

DISTANCES: Atlanta, 242 mi. (387km); Cincinnati, 269 mi. (430km); Memphis, 210 mi. (336km); St. Louis, 328 mi. (525km).

ARRIVAL & TRANSIT INFORMATION

AIRPORT: The new Nashville Metropolitan Airport (BNA) is 6 mi. (10km) SE. Information: 275-1675.

AIRLINES: American (toll free 800/433-7300), Delta (toll free 800/221-1212), Northwest (toll free 800/225-2525), Southwest (toll free 800/435-9792), TWA (toll free 800/221-2000), United (toll free 800/241-6522), and USAir (toll free 800/428-4322).

CITY LINK: The **cab** fare to city center is about $14–$18; time, 15–20 min. (30 min. during rush hours). Bus: **Airport Shuttle Service** (275-1180), serving principal hotels; fare, $8; time, 25 min. Also **city bus (MTA)** leaving from the Transit Mall on Deaderick St.: fare, $1.15 time, 30 min.
　　Public transportation is by bus, provided by the Metropolitan Transit Authority/MTA (242-4433); it's inefficient, but unless you plan on excursions out of town (recommended), or a visit to the Grand Ole Opry, the city is small enough that you may not need to rent a car.

CAR RENTAL (at the airport unless otherwise noted): Avis (toll free 800/331-1212); Budget (toll free 800/527-0700); Dollar (toll free 800/800-4000); Hertz (toll free 800/654-3131); National (toll free 800/227-7368); Thrifty, 1315 Vultee Blvd. (toll free 800/367-2277).

LIMOUSINE SERVICE: Carey Limousine (254-9839), Dav El Limousines (toll free 800/922-0343), Capital Limousines (248-6522).

TAXIS: In theory cabs may be hailed on the street, but it's difficult to find one cruising. It's best to telephone: **Checker** (254-5031), **Nashville Cab** (242-7070), or **Yellow Cab** (256-0101).

INTERCITY BUSES: Greyhound, 200 Eighth Ave. S. (255-3556).

MISSISSIPPI CRUISES: 3- to 10-day cruises aboard the 1920s paddlewheeler *Delta Queen* or *Mississippi Queen*. Luxurious kitsch. See Chapter 15 on New Orleans.

INFORMATION & TOURS

TOURIST INFORMATION: The **Nashville Chamber of Commerce– Visitors Division,** 161 Fourth Ave. N., TN 37219 (615/259-4755).

Tourist Information Center, Exit 85 from I-65 at J. Robertson Pkwy. (615/259-4747). Open daily.

GUIDED TOURS: Belle Carol Riverboat Co. (boat), First Ave. N. and Broadway or McGavock Pike Dock (244-3430): Trips on the Cumberland River aboard the heroic-age paddlewheelers *Music City Queen* and *Captain Ann.* Mar–Dec.

General Jackson (boat), 2812 Opryland Dr. (889-6611): Three-hour musical mini-cruises and dinner cruises aboard the giant (1,200-passenger) paddlewheeler *General Jackson.* Year round.

Gray Line Tours (bus), 2416 Music Valley Dr. (227-2270): Guided tour of city and surroundings; serves principal hotels.

Grand Ole Opry Tours, 2810 Opryland Dr. (889-9490), offers a backstage visit to the Grand Ole Opry, as well as a tour of the city's principal attractions, and the homes of country-music stars.

Nashville Trolley (bus) (242-4433): These replicas of old-time trolleys provide excellent tours of the dwntwn area for a low fare (75¢). Runs daily every 10 min April–Oct, Sat only in Nov–March.

SIGHTS, ATTRACTIONS & ACTIVITIES

ARCHITECTURAL HIGHLIGHTS: ⚓ **The Parthenon,** Centennial Park West End and 25th Ave. N. (862-8431); A surprising life-size replica, in marble and reinforced concrete, of the famous Athenian temple of Pericles' time. This version, dating from 1931, houses temporary cultural exhibitions and a giant replica of Phidias's statue of the goddess Athena that once adorned the Parthenon in Athens. Open Tues–Sat.

☼⚓ **Ryman Auditorium,** 116 Fifth Ave. N. (254-1445): This former church in red brick is considered the *real* "Mecca of Country Music" by purists; it was here that the Grand Ole Opry made its home from 1943 until the present auditorium was opened in 1974. Once celebrated for its acoustics, the Ryman Auditorium used to host a very different kind of performer: Sarah Bernhardt, Enrico Caruso, and the like. Today it's a gallery of country-star souvenirs. Open daily.

BROADCASTING STUDIOS: ⚓⚓⚓⚓ **Grand Ole Opry House,** 2804 Opryland Dr., 10 mi. (16km) NE via I-40 and Briley Pkwy. (889-3060): The largest (4,400 seats) recording studio in the world, where the biggest stars of country music perform every Fri and Sat evening (two shows), with additional Tues, Thurs, Sat, and Sun matinee performances in summer. Tickets may be purchased only at the box office, or by mail from 2808 Opryland Dr., TN 37214; in summer, resv. must be made many weeks ahead. Visitors can also view shows being taped for cable TV by the Nashville Network Mon–Fri evenings; for information, call TNN Viewer Services (883-7000).

☼⚓ **Studio B,** Country Music Hall of Fame, 4 Music Sq. E. (256-1639): The historic RCA studio where the likes of Elvis Presley, Chet Atkins, Charley Pride, and Eddy Arnold recorded some of their biggest hits. You can visit it along with the Country Music Hall of Fame (see "Museums of Science and History," below). Open daily.

CHURCHES/SYNAGOGUES: ⚓ **Presbyterian Church,** Church St. and Fifth Ave. N. (254-7584): Remarkable example of the Egyptian Revival architecture so much in vogue at the end of the 19th century; it was used as a hospital for Union casualties during the Civil War. Open daily.

⚓ **Upper Room Chapel,** 1908 Grand Ave. (340-7207): This Georgian-style chapel holds, among its other treasures, a giant reproduction in polychromed wood of Leonardo da Vinci's *Last Supper.* Religious-art kitsch of the highest order. Open Mon–Sat.

HISTORIC BUILDINGS: ☼🏛 **Belle Meade Mansion,** Harding Rd. and Leake Ave., 7 mi. (12km) SW on West End Ave. (356-0501): With its elegant portico and enormous state room, this very lovely 1854 plantation house dubbed "Queen of Tennessee Plantations," was once the home of one of the country's most renowned stud farms (it produced Iroquois, the first American horse to win the English Derby, in 1881). Fine collection of old carriages. Open daily.

🔔 **Belmont Mansion,** 1900 Belmont Blvd. at Acklen Ave. (269-9537): This luxurious 1850s Palladian home was a center of Nashville social life for more than half a century, and has now been magnificently restored to all its former grandeur. On the campus of Belmont College. Open Tues–Sat.

🔔 **Fisk University,** 17th Ave. N. and Jackson St. (329-8500): In the heart of Nashville's historic district, this university, founded in 1866, possesses some interesting old buildings, including **Jubilee Hall** and the **Carl Van Vechten Art Gallery.**

🔔 **Fort Nashborough,** 170 First Ave. N. at Church St. (255-8192): Built on the site of the first white settlement in 1779, this rugged log replica of an 18th-century fort, surrounded by its stockade, admirably reconstructs the daily life of the pioneers, with walk-ons in period clothing. Open daily.

☼🏛🔔 **The Hermitage,** 4580 Rachel's Lane, in Hermitage, 12 mi. (19km) NE via I-40 and Old Hickory Blvd. (889-2941): Andrew Jackson's country house, built in 1819 and enlarged in 1834 after a fire, is one of the finest classical revival buildings in the Deep South. Superb original furniture. The tombs of the seventh president and his wife, Rachel, stand amid lovely gardens. Open daily.

☼🔔 **State Capitol,** Sixth and Charlotte Aves. (741-1621): Built on a hill overlooking the city, this classic of the Greek Revival style is the work of architect William Strickland, who in 1859 was buried within its walls. On the main lawn is the tomb of James Polk, 11th president of the U.S., and statues of local heroes including Pres. Andrew Jackson and Sgt. Alvin York, the most decorated U.S. soldier of World War I. Open daily.

☼🔔 **Travellers' Rest,** 636 Farrell Pkwy., 6 mi. (9km) south on U.S. 31 (832-2962): Plantation house with its original two-story-porch architecture, dating from the early 1800s, standing among groves of giant magnolias and maples. Often visited by Andrew Jackson, Lafayette, and other notables. Open Tues–Sun.

MUSEUMS OF ART: ☼🏛 **Cheekwood Fine Arts Center,** Forrest Park Dr., 7 mi. (11km) SW via U.S. 70S and Tenn. 100 (356-8000): 18th-century English furniture; 19th-century European and American paintings. Temporary exhibitions. Imposing 1932 building in the Georgian style surrounded by an outstandingly lovely botanic garden, with orchids, camellias, rose gardens, Japanese garden, etc. Open daily.

☼🔔 **Van Vechten Gallery,** 17th Ave. N. and Jackson St. (329-8720): This very lovely modern-art museum on the campus of Fisk University has more than 100 works by 20th-century American artists, donated by painter Georgia O'Keeffe after the death of her husband, photographer Alfred Stieglitz. Open Tues–Sun.

MUSEUMS OF SCIENCE & HISTORY: ☼🔔 **Country Music Hall of Fame and Museum,** 4 Music Sq. E. (256-1639): Innumerable memorabilia of all the idols of country music: Chet Atkins's first guitar, the car used by Burt Reynolds in the movie *Smokey and the Bandit,* Dolly Parton's show dresses, Elvis Presley's massive gold Cadillac. Enthralling; an absolute must for all fans. You will also

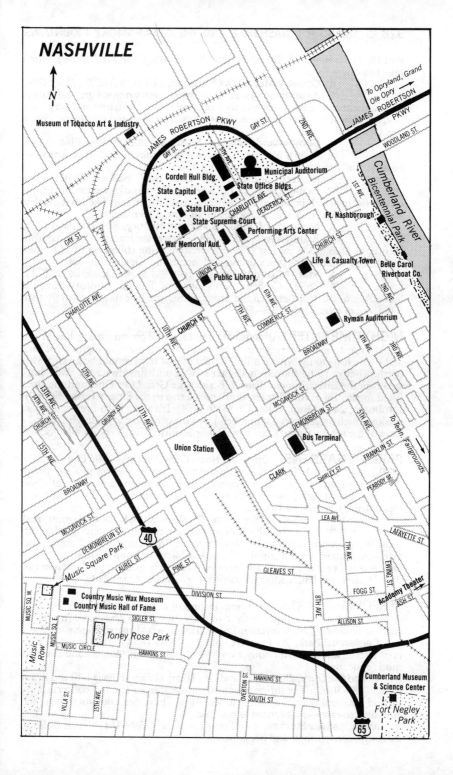

NASHVILLE

N

Museum of Tobacco Art & Industry

JAMES ROBERTSON PKWY

GAY ST.

2ND AVE.

To Opryland, Grand
Ole Opry

JAMES ROBERTSON PKWY

WOODLAND ST.

Cumberland River

Bicentennial Park

Cordell Hull Bldg.

State Office Bldgs.

Municipal Auditorium

State Capitol

1ST AVE.

State Library

CHARLOTTE AVE.

DEADERICK ST.

Ft. Nashborough

State Supreme Court

Performing Arts Center

CHURCH ST.

War Memorial Aud.

Life & Casualty Tower

Belle Carol
Riverboat Co.

UNION ST.

Public Library

2ND AVE.

GAY ST.

CHARLOTTE AVE.

CHURCH ST.

6TH AVE.

7TH AVE.

COMMERCE ST.

Ryman Auditorium

10TH AVE.

12TH AVE.

BROADWAY

4TH AVE.

3RD AVE.

13TH AVE.

14TH AVE. S.

CHURCH ST.

11TH AVE.

GRUNDY ST.

McGAVOCK ST.

DEMONBREUN ST.

5TH AVE.

To Tenn. Fairgrounds

15TH AVE.

Union Station

Bus Terminal

FRANKLIN ST.

BROADWAY

CLARK

SHIRLEY ST.

PEABODY ST.

McGAVOCK ST.

LEA AVE.

LAFAYETTE ST.

DEMONBREUN ST.

40

Music Square Park

7TH AVE.

EWING ST.

Music Square Park

LAUREL ST.

PINE ST.

GLEAVES ST.

FOGG ST.

Academy Theater

MUSIC SQ. W

Country Music Wax Museum
Country Music Hall of Fame

DIVISION ST.

8TH AVE.

ASH ST.

ALLISON ST.

MUSIC SQ. E.

SIGLER ST.

Toney Rose Park

MUSIC CIRCLE

HAWKINS ST.

Music
Row

HAWKINS ST.

Cumberland Museum
& Science Center

VILLA ST.

15TH AVE.

OVERTON ST.

SOUTH ST.

Fort Negley
Park

65

visit the legendary **RCA Studio B** (see "Broadcasting Studios," above). Don't miss this one.

Country Music Wax Museum, 118 16th Ave. S. (256-2490): A pantheon in wax: 60 or so of country music's greatest stars in their authentic stage costumes and their original musical instruments. Very touristy, but a must for all country-music fans. Souvenir shop and restaurant adjoining. Open daily.

Cumberland Science Museum, 800 Ridley Blvd. (862-5160): Interesting material on zoology and Native American history; also a very up-to-date planetarium. Open Tues–Sun.

Howard Brandon Car Collectors' Hall of Fame, 1534 Demonbreun St. (255-6804): Very fine collection of antique cars, most of which belonged to country music or rock stars like Elvis Presley, Roy Orbison, Webb Pierce, and Bobby Goldsboro. Open daily.

Museum of Tobacco Art and History, 800 Harrison St. at Eighth Ave. N. (271-2349): Traces the history of tobacco from its origins among the earliest Native Americans. Fine collection of old pipes, snuffboxes, and tobacco jars. Curious and interesting. Open Mon–Sat.

State Museum, James K. Polk Bldg., 505 Deaderick St. (741-2692): Colorful presentation of Tennessee history from the Stone Age to the War Between the States, illustrated by a display of more than 5,000 old objects. Open Tues–Sun.

NIGHTTIME ENTERTAINMENT: The capital of country music has, as you might expect, one of the country's heaviest concentrations of nightclubs, bars, and dance halls to the square mile. Certain tourist traps should be given a wide berth: They're to be found on Printer's Alley and Broadway, the two "hot" streets in the entertainment district. Besides the Grand Ole Opry and the clubs listed further on in this chapter, don't miss a trip to the **Ernest Tubb Midnight Jamboree,** 2414 Music Valley Dr. (889-2474). It's a sort of country-music jam session which meets every Sat in a well-known record store at midnight, after the show at the nearby Grand Ole Opry. Public admitted free. Very popular locally.

PARKS & GARDENS: **Opryland Hotel Conservatory,** 2800 Opryland Dr. (889-1000): The 10,000 trees and tropical plants arrayed here in a six-story-high greenhouse make this wonderful winter garden, with its streams, waterfalls, and statues—a must for all who visit Opryland, whether or not they stay at the hotel. Open daily; 10 min. from dwntwn.

Tennessee Botanical Gardens–Cheekwood, Forrest Park Dr. (356-8000): Beautiful 30-acre (12ha) botanic garden surrounding the Cheekwood Fine Arts Center (see "Museums of Art," above). Besides greenhouses with a simulated tropical forest and numberless varieties of camellias and orchids, the garden boasts several lovely specialty gardens: rose garden, Japanese garden, wildflower garden, herb garden. Open daily.

PERFORMING ARTS: For current listings of shows and cultural events, consult the entertainment pages of the two daily papers, *The Tennessean* (morning) and *The Nashville Banner* (evening), as well as the weekly paper *Nashville Scene.*

Centennial Park, W. End Ave. and 25th Ave. (862-8400): Open-air concerts by the Nashville Symphony, every wknd June–Aug. Also folk and country-music concerts.

Grand Ole Opry, 2804 Opryland Dr., 10 mi. (16km) NE via I-40 and Briley Pkwy. (889-3060): The shrine of country music. Shows and live concerts every Fri and Sat evening year round; matinees Tues, Thurs, Sat, and Sun in summer. You must reserve—as far ahead as possible.

Municipal Auditorium, 417 Fourth Ave. N. (259-6461): Hosts political meetings, conventions, and live concerts.

Music Village USA, Music Village Blvd. in Hendersonville, 20 mi. (32km) NE via I-65, Two Mile Pkwy., and U.S. 31E (822-1800): Shows and live concerts by the biggest stars in country music. Concerts Mon–Sat year round.

Nashville Academy Theater, 724 Second Ave. S. (254-9103): Specializes in classical theater and children's shows.

Opryland, 2802 Opryland Dr., 10 mi. (16km) NE via I-40 and Briley Pkwy. (889-6611): Live TV shows, live pop, jazz, blues, country, gospel, or rock 'n' roll concerts, Broadway-style revues. Adjoining are the Grand Ole Opry and a giant amusement park. Open daily May–Sept, wknds only Oct. and April; closed the rest of the year.

Tennessee Performing Arts Center, 505 Deaderick St. (741-7975): Ultra-modern complex of three adjoining auditoriums: **Andrew Jackson Hall,** offering concerts (home of the Nashville Symphony, under principal conductor Kenneth Schermerhorn) Sept–May; the **James K. Polk Theater,** for drama, comedy, operetta, chamber-music recitals (home of the Tennessee Repertory Theater); and the **Andrew Johnson Theater,** a theater-in-the-round for modern and avant-garde material (Sept–May; also big-name shows).

War Memorial Auditorium, Memorial Sq., Seventh Ave., and Union St. (262-6129): Pop and classical concerts.

SHOPPING: **The Arcade,** between Fourth and Fifth Aves. N.: Picturesque turn-of-the-century shopping arcade under an elegant glass roof. Dozens of unusual shops and stalls in the heart of dwntwn.

Fountain Square, Metrocenter Blvd. and I-265: Nashville's lakeside shopping center. Boutiques, stores, cafés, restaurants, cinemas, and open-air concerts on the shores of a charming little lake 5 min. from dwntwn.

Record Stores

Many specialized stores around Music Row, including **Conway's Twitty,** 1530 Demonbreun; **Ernest Tubb,** 417 Broadway; **The Great Escape,** 1925 Broadway—offering a huge selection of country-music records at bargain prices; also **Tower Records,** 2400 West End Ave.

Western Wear

Lovers of cowboy boots and western clothing will find an unequaled selection in the innumerable outlets for this kind of merchandise that abound in Nashville. Some of these are: **Boot Country,** 2412 Music Valley Dr.; **Loretta Lynn's Western Wear Stores,** 435 Donaldson Pike; and **Genesco Manufacturing Outlets,** 1415 Murfreesboro Rd. (discount clothing and boots).

SPECIAL EVENTS: For exact dates, consult the **Nashville Chamber of Commerce** (see "Tourist Information," above).

Tennessee Crafts Fair (May): A handcrafts fair which draws more than 150 of the state's best-known craftspeople; very popular locally.

Summer Lights in Music City (early June): Four-day festival of music, dance, theater, and performance art on several stages.

International Country Music Fan Fair (mid-June): Country music's great annual festival, which attracts more than 200,000 fans every year.

Longhorn Rodeo Championships (Nov): One of the most famous professional rodeos east of the Mississippi; local color guaranteed.

SPORTS: Nashville has no major-league teams, but has a minor-league team in —**Baseball** (Apr–Sept.): Sounds, Greer Stadium (242-4371).

THEME PARKS: ☀☗ **Opryland USA,** 2802 Opryland Dr., 10 mi. (16km) NE via I-40 and Briley Pkwy. (889-6611): Adjoining the legendary Grand Ole Opry, this huge, inventive amusement park features popular music of all kinds—country, jazz, blues, folk, rock, musical comedy, etc.—but also offers dozens of carousels, roller-coasters, bars, restaurants, boutiques, and even a mini-zoo for children. Open daily May–Sept, wknds only in Oct and Apr; closed the rest of the year.

ACCOMMODATIONS

Personal Favorites (in order of preference)

Stouffer Hotel (dwntwn), 611 Commerce St., TN 37203 (615/255-8400; toll free, see Stouffer). 673 rms, A/C, color TV, in-rm movies. AE, CB, DC, MC, V. Valet parking $10, pool, health club, sauna, rest., bar, 24-hr. rm svce, concierge, free crib. *Note:* Elegant, ultramodern tower whose 27 stories dominate the Convention Center—an excellent location in the heart of dwntwn. Huge, very comfortable rms; efficient svce; business and convention clientele. Two top floors reserved for VIPs. Direct access to the new Nashville Convention Center. **E–VE**

Loews Vanderbilt Plaza Hotel (nr. dwntwn), 2100 West End Ave., TN 37203 (615/320-1700; toll free 800/235-6397). 340 rms, A/C, cable color TV. AE, CB, DC, MC, V. Valet parking $8, rest. (Plaza Grill), coffee shop, two bars, rm svce, boutiques, hrdrsr, concierge, free crib. *Note:* Modern high-rise hotel located 5 min. from dwntwn, across the street from Vanderbilt University. Luxuriously comfortable rms; attentive personal svce. Two VIP floors. Business clientele. Exercise facility w. pool and tennis courts located one block from the hotel. **M–E**

Union Station Hotel (dwntwn), 1001 Broadway, TN 37206 (615/726-1001). 128 rms, A/C, cable color TV, AE, CB, DC, MC, V. Valet parking $7, three rests. (including Arthur's), bar, rm svce, concierge, free crib. *Note:* The most innovative of the local luxury hotels. Opened in 1987, this elegant, comfortable establishment occupies seven floors of the old Union Station, an imposing turn-of-the-century structure in Railroad Gothic crowned by a tall Big Ben–style tower. Beautifully restored decor w. mosaic floors, stained-glass windows, and hand-carved wood paneling. Very spacious, well-equipped rms; excellent svce. Halfway between dwntwn and Music Row; a fashionable place to stay. **M–E**

Clubhouse Inn Conference Center (dwntwn), 920 Broadway, TN 37203 (615/244-0150). 285 rms, A/C, cable color TV. AE, CB, DC, MC, V. Free parking, pool, rest. bar, free breakfast buffet, complimentary drinks, exercise room, free crib. *Note:* Eight-floor hotel conveniently located nr. the business district. Thoughtful and efficient svce (for a convention hotel). Good value overall. **I–M**

La Quinta (nr. dwntwn), 2001 Metro Center Blvd., TN 37228 (615/259-2130; toll free, see La Quinta). 121 rms, A/C, cable color TV. AE, CB, DC, MC, V. Free parking, pool, 24-hr. coffee shop adj., valet svce, free crib. *Note:* Rustic, but functional and comfortable, motel; friendly reception and svce. Very good value. 8 min. from dwntwn. **I**

Budget Host Inn (nr. dwntwn), 10 Interstate Dr., TN 37213 (615/244-6050; toll free 800/283-4678). 130 rms, A/C, cable color TV. AE, CB, DC, MC, V. Free parking, pool, bar, disco, free crib. *Note:* Comfortable, attractive seven-story motel at the eastern exit from the city on I-65. Modern facilities. Friendly reception; 7 min. from dwntwn. **B**

Other Hotels (from top bracket to budget)

Opryland Hotel (vic.), 2800 Opryland Dr., TN 37214 (615/889-1000). 1,892 rms, A/C, color TV. AE, CB, DC, MC, V. Valet parking $8, three pools, tennis courts, health club, golf, six rests. (including Old Hickory), coffee shop, four bars, 24-hr. rm svce, hrdrsr, boutiques, free crib. *Note:* Enormous vacation complex oriented to mass tourism; ideal for visiting Opryland and the Grand Ole Opry, which it adjoins. Flashy Deep South interior. Spacious, comfortable rms, the best overlooking a lovely indoor botanic grdn ("The Conservatory"); also indoor lagoon w. waterfalls and streams; mediocre rests. Obtrusive package-tour and convention clientele. 20 min. from dwntwn. **E–VE** but lower rates off-season.

🏩🏩🏩 **Holiday Inn Crowne Plaza** (dwntwn), 623 Union St., TN 37219 (615/259-2000; toll free, see Holiday Inns). 478 rms, A/C, color TV, in-rm movies. AE, CB, DC, MC, V. Valet gar. $7, two rests. (including the revolving Pinnacle on the 28th floor), bar, rm svce, concierge, free crib. *Note:* A hefty cube of concrete directly across from the State Capitol, w. a spectacular 28-story glass atrium. Very comfortable rms of agreeably contemporary design; efficient but impersonal svce. Mediocre rests. Large package-tour and convention business (the Convention Center is only two blocks away). Excellent dwntwn location. **M–E**

🏩🏩🏩 **Doubletree Hotel** (formerly the Radisson; dwntwn), 2 Sovran Plaza, TN 37219 (615/244-8200; toll free 800/528-0444). 337 rms, A/C, color TV, in-rm movies. AE, CB, DC, MC, V. Valet gar. $6, pool, health club, sauna, two rests. (including the Hunt Room), bar, rm svce, disco, boutiques, free crib. *Note:* This modern building makes no appeal to the eye, but the rms and interior decoration are elegant and comfortable. Right in the heart of dwntwn Nashville. Efficient svce. The 12th (top) floor is reserved for VIPs. Business clientele. Interesting wknd packages. **M–E**

🌞🏩🏩🏩 **The Hermitage** (dwntwn), 231 Sixth Ave. N., TN 37219 (615/244-3121). 112 suites, A/C, color TV, in-rm movies. AE, CB, DC, MC, V. Valet parking $7, rest. (Hermitage Dining Room), bar, rm svce, free breakfast. *Note:* Elegant small turn-of-the-century hotel of Beaux Arts classic design, splendidly restored; one- and two-bedroom suites, luxuriously decorated, w. minibars and antique furniture. Faultless svce. Good rest. Free breakfast served on a pretty porch. Elegant and charming; the favorite hotel of those in-the-know, in the heart of dwntwn. **M–E**

🏩🏩 **Holiday Inn Vanderbilt** (nr. dwntwn), 2613 West End Ave., TN 37203 (615/327-4707; toll free, see Holiday Inns). 300 rms, A/C, color TV, in-rm movies. AE, CB, DC, MC, V. Free parking, pool, rest. (Commodore), bar, rm svce, disco, free crib. *Note:* Recently renovated 14-floor building very nr. Vanderbilt University. Functionally comfortable in the Holiday Inn manner. Good value. 5 min. from dwntwn. **I–M**

🏩🏩 **Quality Inn Hall of Fame** (nr. dwntwn), 1407 Division St., TN 37203 (615/242-1631; toll free, see Choice). 103 rms, A/C, color TV, in-rm movies. AE, CB, DC, MC, V. Free parking, pool, rest., valet svce, disco, free crib. *Note:* Recently renovated motel, well placed for a visit to the Country Music Hall of Fame and the attractions of Music Row. Comfortable rms; smiling reception. Family and group clientele. Very good value overall. **I**

🏩 **Days Inn Central** (dwntwn), 211 N. 1st St., TN 37213 (615/254-1551; toll free, see Days Inns). 180 rms, A/C, color TV, in-rm movies. AE, DC, MC, V. Free parking, pool, rest., bar, free crib. *Note:* Modern nine-story motel 5 min. from the Capitol and the business district. Serviceably comfortable; friendly reception. Good value; excellent if you're driving since it can be reached from I-24/I-65 via Exit 85. **B–I**, but lower rates off-season.

🏩 **Motel 6** (vic.), 311 W. Trinity Lane, TN 37207 (615/227-9696). 126 rms, A/C, cable color TV, AE, DC, MC, V. Free parking, pool, nearby coffee shop. *Note:* Economy-style but engaging motel 10 min. from dwntwn and 15 min. from the Grand Ole Opry. Up-to-date amenities. Unbeatable value; perfect for the budget traveler. **B**

Airport Accommodations

🏩🏩🏩 **Sheraton Music City** (vic.), 777 McGavock Pike, TN 37214 (615/885-2200; toll free, see Sheraton). 412 rms, A/C, color TV, in-rm movies. AE, CB, DC, MC, V. Free parking, two pools, health club, sauna, two tennis courts, rest. (Belair), two bars, 24-hr. rm svce, disco, concierge.

Note: Crowning a hilltop from which it overlooks its 23 acres (9ha) of park and landscaped grdns, this very handsome convention hotel draws a large business clientele. Luxurious decor; very comfortable rms w. private balcony and refrigerator. Friendly svce and reception. Good rest. serving American cuisine. Free shuttle to the airport terminal 5 min. away; 10 min. from Opryland, 20 min. from dwntwn. **M–E**

⚓ **Courtyard by Marriott** (vic.), 2508 Elm Hill Pike, TN 37214 (615/883-9500; toll free 800/321-2211). 145 rms, A/C, color TV, in-rm movies. AE, DC, MC, V. Free parking, pool, exercise equipment, rest., bar, valet svce. *Note:* Newly built traditional motel w. huge, inviting rms and efficient svce. 5 min. from the airport (free shuttle); great for a stopover between flights. **I–M,** but lower rates on wknds.

RESTAURANTS

Personal Favorites (in order of preference)

🍷🍷🍷 **The Merchants** (dwntwn), 401 Broadway (254-1892). A/C. Lunch Mon–Fri, dinner nightly; closed hols. AE, DC, MC, V. *Specialties:* Long Island duckling w. raspberry glaze, homemade pasta, grilled veal chop w. boursin cheese and prosciutto, seared loin of lamb w. fried spinach and feta cheese, grouper roasted in a corn husk w. poblano chili butter, chocolate pate, appropriate wine list. *Note:* Bright contemporary American cuisine in an 1863 landmark building. Dining on three levels, w. brick walls dividing the upper rms into romantic spaces. Flawless service. Live jazz Fri and Sat. Resv. advised. A very fine place to eat. Valet parking. *American.* **M**

🍷🍷 **Mario's** (nr. dwntwn), 2005 Broadway (327-3232). A/C. Dinner only, Mon–Sat; closed hols. AE, CB, DC, MC, V. Jkt. *Specialties:* fresh homemade pasta, zuppa di pesce, osso bucco, veal marsala, roast duck, broiled fish. Excellent wine list (over 10,000 bottles). *Note:* The jovial Mario Ferrari serves excellent northern Italian food at relatively reasonable prices in his locally popular rest. The svce has too much to do and the place is often noisy. Favored by local celebrities. Resv. strongly advised. *Italian.* **M–E**

☀️🍷 **Texana Grill** (vic.), 847 Bell Rd., in Antioch (731-5610). A/C, Lunch Fri–Sun, dinner nightly. AE, CB, DC, MC, V. *Specialties:* German smoked sausage, mesquite-grilled beef and chicken, pork prime rib, aged western steaks. *Note:* Authentic Tex-Mex cooking, including regional favorites from Texas Hill Country, in one of Nashville's newest and more interesting rests. Colorful, rustic setting complete w. exposed beams and Lone Star State memorabilia. Friendly atmosphere. Good svce. 20 min from dwntwn via I-24S. *American.* **I**

🍷 **Hap Townes** (nr. dwntwn), 493 Humphrey St. (242-7035). A/C. Lunch only, Mon–Fri. No credit cards. *Specialties:* corn bread, fried chicken, potatoes and gravy, roast beef, country-fried steak, chicken 'n' dumplings, blackberry cobbler. *Note:* Honest-to-god Southern cooking that's been true to the heart of Nashville since 1946. "Dips" (piled high) "meat-and-three"-plate lunches (your choice of one meat and three vegetables). Svce is all that you would expect from women who call everyone "hon." No resv. *American.* **B**

☀️🍷 **Elliston Place Soda Shop** (nr. dwntwn), 2111 Elliston Place (327-1090). A/C. Breakfast/lunch/dinner Mon–Sat (until 8pm). No credit cards. *Specialties:* fried chicken, country ham, hamburgers, spaghetti Créole, roast beef au jus, roast turkey, excellent fresh vegetables, banana split. *Note:* An early (1939) precursor of today's fast-food establishments, and a monument of local gastronomy. Nothing in the decor or the atmosphere has changed since it opened, nor has the dependable, tasty family-style cooking. The place is as clean as ever; the waitresses are as motherly as ever; even the original soda fountain is still in action. Most of the patrons are students from nearby Vanderbilt U. A very good place to eat. *American.* **B**

Other Restaurants (from top bracket to budget)

ΥΥΥ **Arthur's** (dwntwn), in the Union Station Hotel (see "Accommodation," above) (255-1494). A/C. Dinner only, nightly; closed hols. AE, CB, DC, MC, V. Jkt. *Specialties:* veal normande, quail stuffed w. foie gras, John Dory in saffron cream, flaming desserts. Menu changes regularly. Good wine list. *Note:* The classical French-inspired haute cuisine and the elegantly luxurious setting under high ceilings w. gold bosses have made this rest. a favorite w. notables, whether local or visiting. The svce is a touch pretentious. Resv. necessary. *Continental.* **E** (prix fixe).

ΥΥ **106 Club** (vic), 106 Harding Place, in Belle Meade (269-5861). A/C. Dinner only, nightly; closed hols. AE, DC, MC, V. Jkt. *Specialties:* house-smoked duck w. mango relish, foie gras w. caramelized apples, Montrachet and herb-crusted rack of lamb w. dijon-and-cilantro sauce, terrine of chocolate chiffon cake, extensive wine list. *Note:* Smart black-and-white photos hang in this art deco dining room. Cuisine is well intentioned, if not a bit trendy. A good place 20 minutes west of dwntwn by taking W. End Ave. Resv. strongly recommended. *Continental.* **M**

ΥΥ **F. Scott's** (nr. dwntwn), 2210 Crestmore Dr. (269-5861). A/C. Lunch/dinner daily, brunch Sun; closed hols. AE, DC, MC, V. Jkt. *Specialties:* duck confit, sea scallops in red-wine sauce, grilled marlin, pan-fried Bucksnort trout w. bourbon-cream sauce, Grand Marnier soufflé, 1,000-wine list. *Note:* A snappy decor w. original Picasso and Degas on the wall. Pleasing seafood dishes w. a French flair. Impressive wine list. Live jazz on Fri and Sat. Resv. strongly advised. *Continental.* **I–M**

ΥΥ **Stock-Yard** (dwntwn), 901 Second Ave. (255-6464). A/C. Lunch Mon–Fri, dinner nightly; closed hols. AE, CB, DC, MC, V. *Specialties:* all kinds of charcoal-grilled steak, pork and lamb chops, broiled chicken. Good desserts. *Note:* Located, as its name suggests, in the old slaughterhouses dwntwn, this picturesque place serves the best broiled steak in Nashville. Country music and dancing every evening in the adj. Bull Pen Lounge. Locally popular; free parking. *Steak.* **I–M**

Υ **Jimmy Kelly's** (nr. dwntwn), 217 Louise Ave. (329-4349). Dinner only, Mon–Sat. (until midnight). AE, DC, MC, V. *Specialties:* steak, Virginia ham, fried chicken, catch of the day. *Note:* A Nashville landmark for more than half a century, popular w. the political crowd. Pleasing Victorian decor, relaxed atmosphere. Very good steaks and authentic southern food. A fine place. Resv. suggested. *American.* **I–M**

Υ **The Iguana** (nr. dwntwn), 1910 Belcourt Ave., Hillsboro Village Mall (383-8920). A/C. Lunch Mon–Sat, dinner nightly. AE, MC, V. *Specialties:* tacos, enchiladas, tamales, chiles relleños, fajitas, fish Veracruzana. *Note:* Nashville's most legitimate Mexican rest., where all the south-of-the-border classics are flawlessly prepared and served. Warm decor and atmosphere; hard-working svce. Locally popular; resv. advisable. *Mexican.* **B–I**

Υ **Satsuma Tea Room** (dwntwn), 417 Union St. (256-5211). A/C. Lunch only, Mon–Fri. No credit cards. *Specialties:* homemade soups and salads, turkey à la king, filet of sole amandine, pork chop w. mashed potato, vegetable luncheon (tomato, zucchini, and leaf vegetables w. fresh pasta), crème caramel, lemon cake, excellent homemade ice cream. Menu changes daily. *Note:* This is the southern home-cooking of your dreams. The Satsuma Tea Room is a local institution, taken over every noon hour by hordes of regulars (ask to be seated upstairs, where the noise level is lower). Good plain decor and svce; no resv. A very fine place. *American.* **B**

Cafeterias/Fast Food

Loveless Motel & Restaurant (vic.), 8400 Tenn. 100 at Rte. 5, 15 mi. (24km) SW (646-9700). Breakfast/lunch/dinner daily (until 9pm). Well worth the 20-min. drive from dwntwn. Despite its dingy appearance, this motel serves some of the best country cooking in all Tennessee.

Remarkable hickory-smoked country ham and fried chicken; excellent home-made biscuits and jam. Friendly waitresses. No alcoholic beverages; no credit cards. In view of its popularity, you should make resv.

Morrison's (nr. dwntwn), 1000 Two Mile Pkwy. at Rivergate Mall (859-1359). A/C. Lunch/dinner daily (till 8pm). MC, V. Cafeteria-buffet offering very good value. The roast beef as well as the desserts are worth your attention.

BARS & NIGHTCLUBS

The capital of country music offers its visitors numberless nightclubs, bars, strip joints, dance halls, and dives where jazz, folk, or country music may be heard. There are, however, tourist traps to be avoided on Printers Alley and Broadway. The list given below includes the best places for lovers of authentic folk and country music.

Ace of Clubs (dwntwn), 114 2nd St. (254-2237). Rowdy rock 'n' roll in an enormous warehouse. Not for the claustrophobic. Open nightly.

Bluebird Café (vic.), 4104 Hillsboro Rd. (383-1461). Live country, folk, and jazz; highly recommended. Also a rest. Open nightly. 20 min. from dwntwn.

Boots Randolph's (dwntwn), 209 Printers Alley (256-5500). The well-known sax player (and owner) Boots Randolph puts on an excellent performance, but the atmosphere is touristy. Open Mon–Sat Apr–Oct; closed the rest of the year.

Bull Pen Lounge (dwntwn), 901 Second Ave. (255-6464). Pleasing bar-disco downstairs in the Stock-Yard rest. (see above). Open nightly.

Captain's Table (dwntwn), 313 Church St. (256-3353). Las Vegas–style supper club; mediocre rest. Open Mon–Sat.

Exit/In (nr. dwntwn), 2208 Elliston Place (321-4400). One of the best rock/country-music joints; Robert Altman filmed *Nashville* here. Also a fair-to-middling rest. Open nightly.

The Merchants (dwntwn), 401 Broadway (254-1892). Live jazz, blues, and pop downstairs in the Merchants rest. (see above) nightly.

Station Inn (dwntwn), 402 12th Ave. (255-3307). Shrine of local bluegrass and "newgrass." Open Tues–Sun.

Tootsie's Orchid Lounge (dwntwn), 422 Broadway (726-0463). Good C&W music and affordable drinks. Many stars got their start from the owner, Tootsie Bess. Open nightly.

Wrangler (vic.), 1204 Murfreesboro Rd. (361-4440). Locally popular disco offering country and western Texas-size dance floor. Nice atmosphere. Nr. the airport and 20 min. from dwntwn. Open nightly.

Zanies Comedy Showplace (nr. dwntwn), 2025 Eighth Ave. S. (269-0221). Very popular comedy club with a star-studded schedule. Also mediocre rest. Open Tues–Sun.

NEARBY EXCURSIONS

CHEATHAM LAKE (30 mi./48km NW on Tenn. 12): Large body of water formed by a dam and locks on the Cumberland River. Water sports, fishing, camping; wildlife reserve. Fine scenic drive along the Cumberland River.

CUMBERLAND CAVERNS PARK (80 mi./128km SE on I-24 and U.S. 70) (668-4396): Impressive patchwork of underground caves, once a saltpeter mine. It includes some of the largest and most impressive caverns in the country, particularly the "Hall of the Mountain King," 600 ft. (183m) wide and 140 ft. (43m) high. The temperature in the caves stays around 56°F (13°C) winter and summer alike. Conducted 90-min. tour daily, May to the end of Oct; by appointment Nov–Apr.

FARTHER AFIELD

☼⚲🔭 **CHATTANOOGA & THE TENNESSEE VALLEY** (515 mi./824km r.t. via I-24S, U.S. 231S, Tenn. 82S, Tenn. 50E, U.S. 64E, I-24S, U.S. 72W, U.S. Alt. 72W, U.S. 45N, Tenn. 22N, U.S. 64E, U.S. 43N, and U.S. 31N): The trip begins with a visit to the famous ⚱ **Jack Daniel's Distillery** at Lynchburg, the country's oldest (1866) registered whisky distillery. The rule here is "look but don't taste"—Lynchburg is in a "dry" county! Open daily; resv. advised (759-4221).

Next stop is **Chattanooga,** a thriving commercial town on the banks of the Tennessee River. Near here, in 1863, was fought one of the decisive engagements of the War Between the States, "the battle above the clouds" on 2,225-ft. (678m) 🔭 **Lookout Mountain,** which dominates the town and offers a fine view over four states. The amazing incline railroad, which rises at an angle of 72°, has its lower terminus at 3917 St. Elmo Ave. (821-4224); operates daily year round. Fine railroad museum, the ⚱ **Tennessee Valley Railroad Museum,** at 4119 Cromwell Rd. (894-8028); open daily Apr to the end of Sept, wknds Oct and Nov.

Nine miles (14km) south of Chattanooga, see ⚱ **Chickamauga and Chattanooga National Military Park,** Georgia, the country's most visited battlefield. Here, on September 19–20 and November 23–25, 1863, Confederates under Gen. Braxton Bragg and Union troops under Gen. George H. Thomas fought two bloody battles, ending in a Northern victory that left 34,000 dead and wounded on both sides. You can drive around the battlefield on a 3-mi. (5km) signposted road. Visitor Center open daily (706/866-9241); worth the detour.

Then on to the ☼🔭 **NASA Space and Rocket Center,** on Governors Dr. in **Huntsville,** Alabama (205/837-3400), with the world's largest space museum. Life-size replica of a lunar crater, simulated test flights into space, simulated launching ramp, museum of rockets and lunar modules, astronaut training center, etc. Fascinating. Open daily.

Before ending this trip with a tour of the battlefield of **Shiloh** (see Chapter 14 on Memphis), turn aside to Florence for a glimpse of the huge ☼⚱ **Wilson Dam,** one of the largest in the world, and its giant lock on the Tennessee River. Visitor Center open daily.

This is a very full three- to four-day trip.

Where to Stay En Route

IN CHATTANOOGA   🍷🍷🍷 **Holiday Inn–Chattanooga Choo-Choo,** 1400 N. Market St., Chattanooga, TN 37402 (615/266-5000; toll free, see Holiday Inns). 327 rms. Built, as you might expect, in the old railroad terminal; original decor. **M**

IN HUNTSVILLE   🍷🍷 **Holiday Inn Space Center,** 3810 University Dr., Huntsville, AL 35816 (205/837-7171). 181 rms. Typical modern Holiday Inn 3 min. from the Space Center. **I**

🍷 **Comfort Inn,** 3788 University Dr., Huntsville, AL 35816 (205/533-3291). 66 rms. Conventional small, well-run hotel 3 min. from the Space Center. **I**

IN FLORENCE   🍷 **Comfort Inn,** 400 S. Court St., Florence, AL 35630 (205/760-8888). 88 rms. Comfortable, inviting motel. **I**

☼⚱ **GREAT SMOKY MOUNTAINS NATIONAL PARK & SURROUNDINGS** (605 mi./968km r.t. along I-40E, Tenn. 441S, U.S. 23N, and I-40W): This vacation trip for nature lovers begins, ironically enough, with a visit to "Atom City"—**Oak Ridge,** where the bomb dropped on Hiroshima was manufactured. Visit the �️🔍 **American Museum of Science and Energy,** largest of its kind in the world, at 300 S. Tulane Ave. (576-3200), open daily. Several atomic facilities are open to the public; for a complete list, check with the Oak Ridge Convention and Visitors Bureau, 300 S. Tulane Ave. (482-7821).

Your second stop will be at 🔍🔍 **Great Smoky Mountain National Park,** which draws more visitors (almost 8.5 million a year) than any other in the country. Within its limited compass—50 mi. (80km) long and 15–19 mi. (25–30km) wide—it contains all the glories of the Appalachians, the oldest mountain range in North America, with more than 20 peaks rising above 6,560 ft. (2,000m), as well as 812 mi. (1,300km) of hiking trails. Its deep forests, home to black bear, deer, and other wildlife, are often wreathed in the mist and tattered clouds that give it its name.

Once the unapproachable realm of the Cherokee Nation, the Great Smoky Mountains park now offers the tourist some magnificent landscapes (particularly from June to mid-July when the rhododendrons are in bloom), and some spectacular scenic drives. Park open daily year round (some park roads may be temporarily closed in winter). You should come to Nashville if only to see it. For information, contact the Superintendent, Great Smoky Mountain National Park, Gatlinburg, TN 37738 (615/436-1200).

At the edge of the park, 🏨 **Gatlinburg,** a popular tourist resort, and its next-door neighbor **Pigeon Forge,** where the singer Dolly Parton operates her theme park **Dollywood,** Dollywood Lane (428-9400), open daily May–Oct, both have many hotels and restaurants. Spectacular ☀️🏨 **aerial tramway** and sightseeing chair lift to the top of **Mount Harrison** at 3,500 ft. (1,065m): 1001 Parkway, Gatlinburg (436-5423), open daily year round. The view from the summit includes Gatlinburg, Pigeon Forge, and the Great Smoky Mountains National Park.

A fitting close to this trip is a visit to the picturesque little hot-springs town of **Asheville,** North Carolina, nestling in the woods east of the park. Birthplace of writer Thomas Wolfe, Asheville boasts some noteworthy buildings including ☀️🔍🔍 **Biltmore House,** once the summer home of millionaire George W. Vanderbilt. Built by architect Richard Hunt, this imposing château in French Renaissance style is said to be the world's largest private house, with 255 rooms, of which barely a quarter are open to the public. The garden was designed by Frederick Law Olmsted, who designed New York's Central Park. You'll find it on U.S. 25 (704/255-1700; toll free 800/543-2961). Open daily. An international exposition of music, folk dancing, food, and crafts is held every Sept.

This four- to five-day trip can be combined with the foregoing itineraries into a feature-packed tour lasting 10 days to two weeks.

Where to Stay En Route

IN GATLINBURG 🍸🍸🍸 **Park Vista Hotel,** Airport Rd., Gatlinburg, TN 37738 (615/436-9211). 315 rms in an 18-story tower w. a scenic view of the mountains. Ultramodern comfort. **I–M**

🍸🍸 **River Terrace,** River Rd., Gatlinburg, TN 37738 (615/436-5161). 206 rms. Comfortable, well-equipped motel. **I**

🍸 **Johnson's Inn,** Baskins Creek Rd., Gatlinburg, TN 37738 (615/436-4881). 78 rms. Inviting small motel located on the bank of a stream. Open year round. **I**

IN GREAT SMOKY MOUNTAINS NATIONAL PARK 🍸 **Wonderland Club Hotel,** P.R. 2, Gatlinburg, TN 37738 (615/436-5490). 27 rms. The only hotel inside the park. Rustic atmosphere. Open May to late Oct. **I**

IN ASHEVILLE ☀️ 🍸🍸🍸🍸 **Grove Park Inn,** 290 Macon Ave., Asheville, NC 28804 (704/252-2711; toll free 800/438-5800). 509 rms. Turn-of-the-century palace built of granite boulders dug from its Blue Ridge Mountain site. Patronized by all the world's notables. Urbane and elegant. **E–VE**

※※♨♨ **Pisgah View Ranch,** N.C. 151S, Candler, NC 28715 (704/ 667-9100). 50 rms. A country inn lost in the forest 13 mi. (20km) from Asheville. Highly recommended. Open May–Oct. **I–M**

※※♨♨♨ MAMMOTH CAVE NATIONAL PARK & KEN-TUCKY COUNTRY (520 mi./832km r.t. via I-65N, Ky. 70,

Ky. 84E, Ky. 61N, U.S. 31W, 31N, and 31S, Blue Grass Pkwy. N, U.S. 68S, U.S. 150N, Blue Grass Pkwy. S, and I-65S): Discovered in 1799 by a bear hunter, the ♨♨ **Mammoth Caves** deserve their name: they are the longest system of underground caves in the world, but only 300 mi. (483km) has been explored so far. They are interspersed with caverns, deep sink-holes, and spectacular underground lakes and rivers. Some chambers are 196 ft. (60m) high. Guided tours (tiring) daily year round. Wear sturdy shoes and warm clothes. Call 502/758-2328 for information on schedules. The recommended approach is via Ky. 70.

Continue to ※♨ **Abraham Lincoln's Birthplace,** a stately marble-and-granite memorial, erected in 1911 by public subscription of more than 100,000 anonymous contributors. Inside is the log cabin where the 16th president was born on February 12, 1809. The museum should not be missed. Open daily year round; for information, call 502/358-3137.

Go a little out of your way to see the legendary ※ **Fort Knox,** on U.S. 31W (502/624-3351), site of the **United States Bullion Depository,** the country's second-largest gold reserve. The treasure is kept in a two-level steel, granite, and concrete cave, proof against bombs and sealed by an armored door weighing 28 tons (25,500kg). Unhappily it's closed to visitors, but on its grounds you may visit the ♨ **Patton Museum** (502/624-3812), with its rich collection of tanks and other weapons of war; open daily year round.

On the way to **Lexington** and the famous **Kentucky Horse Park** (see Chapter 22 on Cincinnati), don't miss **Bardstown,** where you can make a sentimental pilgrimage to ※ **"My Old Kentucky Home"** on U.S. 150 (502/348-3502), open daily year round; this lovely 18th-century Colonial house inspired Stephen Foster to write his immortal ballad. See also the **Oscar Getz Museum of Whiskey,** 5th St. at Xavier Dr. (502/348-2999), open daily (except Mon from Nov to Apr), which traces the history of that popular beverage, and ♨ **St. Joseph's Cathedral,** 310 W. Stephen Foster Ave. (502/348-3126), open daily; built in 1816, this was the first Roman Catholic cathedral west of the Alleghenies. It has a number of paintings presented by King Louis-Philippe of France during his exile.

The last stage of the journey takes you to ※ **Harrodsburg,** the first settlement in Kentucky (1774). ♨ **Old Fort Harrod,** on U.S. 68 (606/734-3314), open daily year round, is an exact replica of the original fort. Two other nearby attractions are: the ※ **Shaker Village at Pleasant Hill,** 3500 Lexington Rd. (606/734-5411), open daily year round, a museum village once inhabited by the Shakers and boasting no fewer than 30 of the original 19th-century buildings; and the ♨ **Perryville Battlefield,** on U.S. 68 (606/332-8631), open daily Apr–Oct, where there's a museum with a diorama of the battle, one of the bloodiest of the War Between the States.

This itinerary is interesting for its variety, and for its beautiful landscapes.

Where to Stay En Route

IN MAMMOTH CAVE NATIONAL PARK   ♬ **Mammoth Cave,** 3 mi. (5km) inside the park on Ky. 70 Park Rd., Mammoth Cave Nat'l. Park, KY 42259 (502/758-2225). 58 rms. Typical functional motel near the entrance to the caves. **B–I**

IN BARDSTOWN   ♬♬ **Parkview,** 418 E. Stephen Foster Ave., Bardstown, KY 40004 (502/348-5983). 32 rms. Small, inviting motel opposite "My Old Kentucky Home." **B**

IN LEXINGTON 🍴🍴 **Master Hosts–Campbell House Inn,** 1375 Harrodsburg Rd., Lexington, KY 40504 (606/255-4281). 365 rms. Luxurious, comfortable motel with golf course. **I–M**

IN HARRODSBURG ※ 🍴🍴 **Inn at Pleasant Hill,** 3501 Lexington Rd., Harrodsburg, KY 40330 (606/734-5411). 80 rms. Comfortable rms built into the original structure of a 19th-century Shaker village. Picturesque old-fashioned charm. Good rest. **I–M**

CHAPTER 14

MEMPHIS

□ □ □

It was in 1541, near the site of modern Memphis, that Hernando de Soto, the first Spanish explorer of the interior, crossed the wide and muddy Mississippi River. His feat was replicated 132 years later by the French explorers Marquette and Joliet; they in turn were followed by Robert Cavelier de LaSalle, who during his 1682 voyage down the Mississippi to the Gulf of Mexico proclaimed French sovereignty over the region.

Memphis occupies a strategic position at a point where the Mississippi bends to welcome the Wolf River. Dominating the Mississippi from a commanding height, much as the ancient Memphis of the Pharaohs towered above the Nile, the city served briefly during the Civil War years as the capital of the Confederacy. This status ended abruptly in 1862, when Memphis was taken by Northern troops in a bloody naval battle in which some 30 ships were engaged.

Memphis owes its prosperity primarily to cotton—often referred to as "white gold"—for which it has long been the major market in the world. Soybeans and hardwood also play important roles in its economy. Its port activity (12 million tons/10.9 billion kg shipped annually) and its dense railroad network have made Memphis one of the busiest shipping centers in the South. Fond of calling itself the "Home of the Blues," Memphis has come to be a comfortable blend of high-rise structures together with traces of a more gracious past, as well as such historic areas as the **Beale Street** section in the old city. It was on Beale St., close by the banks of the Mississippi, that the legendary composer W. C. Handy wrote "Memphis Blues" and "St. Louis Blues," two great classics of traditional jazz. In later years Memphis became the adopted home of Elvis Presley; although the singer died in 1977, idolatrous fans by the tens of thousands still flock to visit his grave and the gardens of **Graceland,** the Presley mansion.

Memphis is the proud birthplace (in 1952) of the first Holiday Inn, now part of one of the largest hotel empires in the world, and boasts the headquarters of the parcel-delivery giant Federal Express as well as 800 other enterprises, concentrated for the most part in the port area of **Presidents Island.** Also acclaimed as the pork barbecue capital of the world, with nearly 100 barbecue restaurants, in four recent national polls Memphis was voted the cleanest, most orderly, and most peaceful city in the United States. It was, however, in a Memphis motel that civil rights leader and Nobel Peace Prize winner Martin Luther King, Jr., was assassinated (April 4, 1968). Among Memphis's celebrated sons and daughters are actor/comedian George Hamilton, actress Cybill Shepherd, author John Grisham, and singers Aretha Franklin and Alberta Hunter.

BASIC FACTS: State of Tennessee. Area code: 901. Time zone: central. ZIP Code: 31801. Founded in 1819. Approximate population: city, 610,000; metropolitan area, 980,000. Ranked 18th in size among the nation's cities and 41st among its metropolitan areas.

CLIMATE: The dominant presence of the Mississippi River guarantees humidity year round, even in winter when the temperature hovers around freezing. In

July and Aug the city resembles a giant sauna, with temperatures around 82° – 86° F (28° –30° C). Spring, and especially autumn, are the only two seasons recommended for your visit.

DISTANCES: Atlanta, 365 mi. (585km); Chicago, 531 mi. (850km); Dallas, 450 mi. (720km); Nashville, 210 mi. (336km); New Orleans, 390 mi. (625km); St. Louis, 284 mi. (455km).

ARRIVAL & TRANSIT INFORMATION

AIRPORT: Memphis International (MEM), 10 mi. (6km) SE (922-8000).

AIRLINES: American (toll free 800/433-7300), Delta (toll free 800/221-1212), Northwest (toll free 800/225-2525), TWA (toll free 800/221-2000), United (toll free 800/241-6522), and USAir (toll free 800/428-4322).

CITY LINK: The **cab** fare from the airport to downtown is about $16; time, 25 min. Bus: **Airport Express** (922-8238) leaves about every hour and serves the principal downtown hotels; fare, $8; time, 30 min.
　　The city itself is not so large that renting a car is essential, but be warned that **public transportation (bus)** is inadequate; for information, call MATA (274-6282).

CAR RENTAL (at the airport unless otherwise noted): Avis (toll free 800/331-1212); Budget (toll free 800/527-0700); Dollar, 2031 E. Brooks Rd. (toll free 800/800-4000); Hertz (toll free 800/654-3131); National (toll free 800/227-7368); Thrifty, 2780 Airways Blvd. (toll free 800/367-2277). Consult the local telephone directory for downtown rental locations.

LIMOUSINE SERVICES: Dav-El Limousines (toll free 800/922-0343), Limousine Service (761-0816).

TAXIS: Taxis may not be hailed in the street but can be summoned by telephone; try **City Wide Cab** (324-4202) or **Yellow Cab** (577-7777).

TRAIN: Amtrak Station, 545 S. Main St. (toll free 800/872-7245). Very unsafe area at night.

INTERCITY BUSES: Greyhound, 203 Union Ave. (523-1184). Unsafe area at night.

MISSISSIPPI CRUISES: 3- to 10-day cruises are available on the **Delta Queen** or the **Mississippi Queen,** paddlewheelers dating from the 1920s. Luxurious kitsch. See Chapter 15 on New Orleans.

INFORMATION & TOURS

TOURIST INFORMATION: The **Memphis Convention and Visitors Bureau,** 47 Union Ave., TN 38103 (901/543-5350).
　　Visitor Information Center, 340 Beale St., TN 38103 (901/543-5333).

GUIDED TOURS: Carriage Tours of Memphis, 393 N. Main St. (527-7542): Offers horse-drawn carriage tours of Old Memphis; daily year round; weather permitting.
　　Center for Southern Folklore, 130 Beale St. (527-6008): Walking tours highlighting the cultural history of the infamous Beale Street. Tour includes a 10-min. multimedia presentation. By appointment only, year round.
　　Main Street Trolley (274-6282): Yesteryear-style trolley linking the major

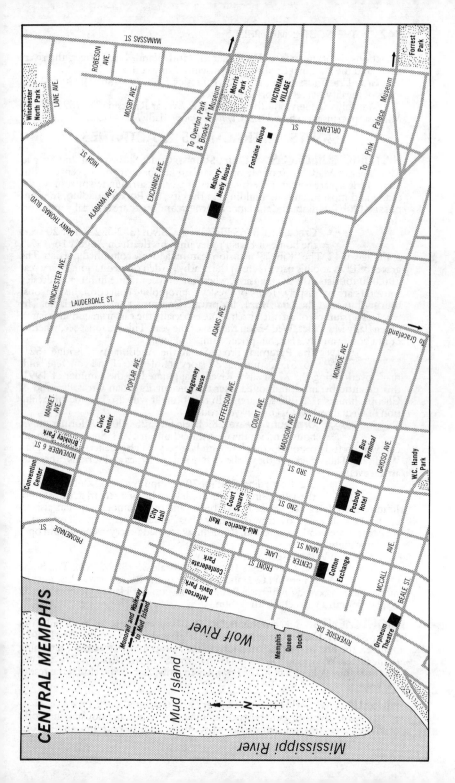

attractions dwntwn such as The Pyramid, Mud Island, Beale Street, the riverfront, and the National Civil Rights Museum. Daily year round.

Gray Line Tours (bus), 2050 Elvis Presley Blvd. (948-8687): Guided bus tours of the city; serves the principal hotels.

Memphis Queen Line (boat), Monroe Ave. at Riverside Dr. (527-5694): Mississippi cruises on board the *Memphis Queen,* daily Mar–Dec.

SIGHTS, ATTRACTIONS & ACTIVITIES

HISTORIC BUILDINGS: ⚓ **Court Square,** Court St. between 2nd St. and Mid America Mall: Heart of Memphis's urban life for more than a century, this pretty little square with its refreshing oases of green is surrounded by some of the oldest and most interesting buildings in the city; the **Porter Building,** the **Tennessee Club Building,** and the **Lincoln American Tower** are especially noteworthy.

☀⚓ **Graceland,** 3765 Elvis Presley Blvd. (332-3322): For 20 years the home of Elvis Presley until his death on August 16, 1977, at the age of 42. The "King's" mansion features a lovely columned portico. The graves of Elvis and his parents are in the nearby garden of meditation. Every year 700,000 tourists visit the mansion, where an almost infinite number of Presley souvenirs are on display. Tours of Presley's automobile collection, his personal touring bus, and the *Lisa Marie,* his private Convair jet are also available. The whole is a triumph of artistic kitsch (note especially the cast-iron entrance gate). Open daily Mar–Oct, Wed–Mon the rest of the year. This is a must-see, whether or not you're an Elvis fan, but pricey admission fees.

☀⚓ **The Pyramid,** Front St. at the Auction Ave. Bridge (521-9675): A stunning 32-story stainless-steel and concrete landmark overlooking the Mississippi River. Inaugurated in the summer of 1991, this gigantic pyramid, fashioned after the ancient Egyptian Great Pyramid of Cheops, houses a 22,000-seat arena. In the future it will also include an exhibition of virtual reality. Open daily year round.

☀⚓ **Orpheum Theater,** 89 Beale St. (525-3000): A former movie house and vaudeville theater built in 1928. Superb rococo decor, wonderfully restored, complete with large crystal chandeliers and a mighty Wurlitzer. These days, the theater hosts musical comedies and various other theatrical events.

☀ **Sun Recording Studio,** 706 Union Ave. (521-0664): Back in the 1950s singer Elvis Presley cut his first record in this studio. Johnny Cash, Jerry Lee Lewis, Roy Orbison, and other famous pop stars also recorded here. The studio is now owned by Elvis Presley Enterprises. Of interest to rock fans. Open daily year round. Recordings are made every evening from 6pm until midnight.

Victorian Village (see "Strolls," below).

⚓ **W. C. Handy's Home,** 352 Beale St. (527-2583): The home where W. C. Handy, "Father of the Blues," wrote his most famous music. Located on historic Beale St. Collection of Handy memorabilia on display. Worth a visit. Open Tues–Sun.

MONUMENTS: ⚓ **Memphis Belle,** Mud Island, access by monorail from Front St. (521-1265): On display under a glass dome, a World War II B-17 bomber, the first to finish 25 missions in the European theater before returning to the States. Was immortalized in David Putman's movie *Memphis Belle* and was also in Sidney Pollock's film *The Firm.* Open daily, Apr–Nov; closed the rest of the year.

MUSEUMS OF ART: ⚓ **Dixon Gallery and Gardens,** 4339 Park Ave. (761-5250): Formerly an elegant upper-class home, now a museum housing the works of French and American impressionist painters, English portraits, and historic furniture and porcelain. Surrounded by 7 acres (2.8ha) of very lovely landscaped gardens featuring outdoor sculpture and generous plantings of azaleas and camellias. Open Tues–Sun.

☀️🏛 **Memphis Brooks Museum of Art,** Overton Park at Poplar Ave. (722-3500): Known especially for its prestigious Samuel H. Kress Collection of valuable Italian Renaissance paintings, this lovely museum also has interesting contemporary American art, and European painting and sculpture from the 17th through the 19th century. Concerts and also films on the history of art. Open Tues–Sun.

☀️🏛 **National Ornamental Metal Museum,** 347 W. California Ave. (774-6380): A museum devoted entirely to the use of metal in art and architecture. The only museum of its kind in the U.S. Demonstrations of iron-working at the forge. Open Tues–Sun.

🏛 **University Gallery,** Norriswood Ave. (678-2224): Interesting collections of African and Egyptian art. Located on the campus of Memphis State University. Open Tues–Sun.

MUSEUMS OF SCIENCE & HISTORY: 🏛 Beale Street Blues Museum,
329 Beale St. (527-6008): Photographs, recordings, musical instruments, sheet music, and other rare memorabilia of famous gospel and blues musicians. See this before moving on to the Memphis Music Hall of Fame (see below).

👓👓 **Memphis Music Hall of Fame,** 97 S. Second St. (525-4007): An exhibition of memorabilia chronicling the development of popular music since the end of WW II. Rare records, photographs, posters, recording and booking contracts, and advertising, as well as instruments owned by Memphis music legends, are shown in this well-fortified museum representing country, jazz, blues, soul, and rock 'n' roll. Open daily.

🏛 **Memphis Pink Palace Museum,** 3050 Central Ave. (320-6320): A venerable museum of local history and natural history in a beautiful building made of pink marble from Georgia (hence its name). Displays of zoological and geological interest; history of the Civil War. Also a planetarium. Open Tues–Sun.

☀️🏛 **Mississippi River Walk,** Mud Island (576-7230): Astonishing giant model of the Mississippi River which reproduces, exactly to scale, the final 1,000 miles (1,600km) of the river's course to the Gulf of Mexico. Also River Museum. Open daily Apr–Nov.

☀️👓👓 **National Civil Rights Museum,** 450 Mulberry St. (521-9699): Symbolically inaugurated on July 4, 1991, this enthralling museum located on the site of the Lorraine Motel, where Dr. Martin Luther King, Jr., was assassinated on April 4, 1968, provides a comprehensive overview of the American Civil Rights Movement of the 1950s and 1960s. Temporary exhibits, displays, and objects such as a Montgomery, Ala., city bus like the one Rosa Parks rode in 1955 trace the history of the movement and its leaders. Open Wed–Mon.

NIGHTTIME ENTERTAINMENT: ☀️🏛 Beale Street, between Riverside Dr.
and 4th St.: The city's principal thoroughfare (Main St.) in the early 1800s became known, a century later, as the "cradle of the Blues." Today, Beale St. is the heart of the old town's pleasure district and its ebullient nightlife. Teems with bars, restaurants, nightclubs, shops (don't miss A. Schwab's Dry Goods store), and theaters. A visit to the street is imperative (see "Strolls," below).

☀️🏛 **Overton Square,** Madison Ave. and Cooper St.: The only place in Memphis that can challenge Beale St. in terms of swinging nightlife. Restaurants, bars, shows. (See "Strolls," below.)

PARKS & GARDENS: Dixon Gallery Gardens (see "Museums of Art,"
above).

    🔔 **Jefferson Davis Park,** Riverside Blvd. at Jefferson Ave.: A
    pleasant little city park offering a lovely view of the Mississippi
and the **Festival Island** amusement park. Faces **Confederate Park,** one of the
battlefields of the Civil War. There are fortifications dating from the war, and also
a statue of Jefferson Davis, president of the Confederacy, who lived in Memphis
after the war.

    🔔 **Memphis Botanic Garden,** 750 Cherry Rd., Audubon Park
    (685-1566): This 87-acre (35ha) landscape contains 12 differ-
ent kinds of gardens, from a rose garden to tropical plants and a Japanese garden.
Spectacular. Open daily.

PERFORMING ARTS: For current listings of shows and cultural events, consult the entertainment pages of the daily newspaper, *Memphis Commercial Appeal* (morning), and the monthly *Memphis.*
    Circuit Playhouse, 1705 Poplar Ave. (726-4656): Contemporary theater,
comedies, and musicals. Sept–June.
    Dixon Meyers Hall, Cook Convention Center, 255 N. Main St. (576-
1200): Big live concerts.
    Mid-South Coliseum, Fairgrounds at E. Parkway South and Southern Ave.
(274-3982): Live rock and country music concerts.
    Opera Memphis, Memphis State University Campus (678-2706): Home
of the city's opera company, directed by Michael Ching.
    Orpheum Theater, 89 Beale St. (525-7800): Comedies, plays, musicals,
opera, ballet. A very lovely art deco vaudeville palace built in 1928, elegantly restored. Open all year.
    Playhouse-on-the-Square, 51 S. Cooper St., at Overton Sq. (726-4656):
The only professional repertory theater in the city. Broadway hits, contemporary
theater. Year round.
    Theater Memphis, 630 Perkins Rd. Ext. (682-8323): Contemporary and
classical theater. Sept–June.
    Vincent de Frank Music Hall, Cook Convention Center, 255 Main St.
(324-3627): Home of the Memphis Symphony Orchestra, under principal conductor Alan Balter. Sept–May.

SPECIAL EVENTS: For exact dates, consult the **Memphis Visitor Information Center** (see "Tourist Information," above).
    Memphis in May International Festival (May): A month-long celebration
honors the culture, art, and music of a different country each year. Also world
championship barbecue cooking contest.
    Carnival Memphis (June): Parades, dances, concerts, regattas. Very color-
ful.
    Elvis Presley International Tribute Week (Aug): A week-long celebration
of the myth and music of Elvis Presley.
    Labor Day Music Festival (early Sept): Jazz, blues, rock, and country music
is performed in legendary Beale St.'s many bars and restaurants during Labor
Day weekend.
    Mid-South Fair (late Sept to early Oct): Renowned agricultural and com-
mercial fair. Features the largest rodeo east of the Mississippi.
    Liberty Bowl Football Classic (Dec): One of the big events of the college
football season.

SPORTS: Memphis has a minor-league team in—**Baseball** (Apr–Oct): Chicks,
Tim McCarver Stadium (272-1687); and **Hockey** (Nov–Mar): River Kings,
Mid-South Coliseum (278-9009).

STROLLS: ☀☖ **Beale Street,** between Riverside Dr. and 4th St.: The "cradle of the Blues." Made world-famous by W. C. Handy, composer of "Memphis Blues" and "St. Louis Blues," who lived on Beale St. in the early 20th century. At Beale St. and 3rd St. you'll find **W. C. Handy Park** and the monument memorializing the composer. A monument to the late "King" of Rock is located nearby in **Elvis Presley Plaza.** This colorful section of the city bustles with activity generated by its old honky-tonks, bars, and pawnshops turned into new nightspots, restaurants, boutiques, and theaters. (See also "Nighttime Entertainment," above.)

☖ **Mid America Mall,** Main St. between the Convention Center and Beale St.: Flanked by stores and skyscrapers, this street in the heart of the business district is reserved for pedestrian traffic. There are gardens and examples of modern sculpture. Very lively by day, deserted at night.

☀☖ **Overton Square,** Madison Ave. and Cooper St.: Charming section of the old town, cleverly restored. You'll find old-time stores, outdoor cafés, restaurants. One of the bastions of Memphis nightlife. (See also "Nighttime Entertainment," above.)

☀☖☖ **Victoria Village,** in the vicinity of 600 Adams Ave.: Delicious 19th-century architectural relic from the days when cotton was still "white gold," and Memphis its capital. The Village contains 20 or so remarkable old buildings, most now classified as historic monuments. Among the more noteworthy are the **Woodruf-Fontaine House,** 680 Adams Ave. (526-1469), open daily, a perfect example of the Second Empire style dating from 1870; **Magevney House,** 198 Adams Ave. (526-4464), open Tues–Sat, Mar–Dec, the oldest building in Memphis, built in 1831 for Irish immigrant Eugene Magevney as recompense for his services as the city's first schoolteacher; and the **Mallory-Neely House,** 652 Adams Ave. (523-1484), open Tues–Sun (closed the rest of the year), a Victorian landmark in the Italian style, dating from 1852. All these buildings have been painstakingly restored with period furniture and decor. A visit to the Victoria Village is a must for those who enjoy beautiful architecture.

THEME PARKS: ☖ **Adventure River Water Park,** 6880 Whitten Bend Cove (382-9283): Huge 25-acre (10ha) park featuring aquatic attractions such as an oversize pool with waves for surf-lovers, giant slides, and swimming pools for children. Open every day from June to the end of Aug, wknds only in May and Sept; closed the rest of the year.

☖ **Libertyland,** Fairgrounds at Central Ave. and East Pkwy. (274-1776): This unusual amusement park salutes our nation's past from the colonial period to the 1900s. Open Wed–Sun mid-June to mid-Aug, wknds only May to June and late Aug to late Sept; closed the rest of the year.

☀☖☖ **Mud Island,** 125 N. Front St. (576-7241): On this island in the middle of the Mississippi are 50 acres (21ha) of gardens, exhibitions, and an immense museum devoted to "Ol' Man River." (See the **Mississippi River Walk** in "Museums of Science and History," above.) Evenings in summer, the Mud Island Amphitheater hosts top-name performers. Accessible by monorail from Front St. Open daily Apr–Nov; closed the rest of the year.

ZOOS: ☖ **Memphis Zoo and Aquarium,** 2000 Galloway, in Overton Park (276-9453): Features more than 2,800 animals from 400 species. Giant aquarium. Outstanding tropical bird house, spectacular reptile facilities, and natural African settings for larger beasts. Spectacular after a recent $30-million renovation. Open daily year round.

ACCOMMODATIONS

Personal Favorites (in order of preference)

☼ ♀♀♀♀ **The Peabody** (dwntwn), 149 Union Ave., TN 38103 (901/ 529-4000; toll free, see Preferred). 468 rms, A/C, color TV, in-rm movies. AE, CB, DC, MC, V. Valet parking $8, pool, sauna, health club, three rests. (including Chez Philippe), three bars, 24-hr. rm svce, hrdrsr, shops, concierge, free crib. *Note:* Fabulous luxury hotel dating from 1869, rebuilt in 1925 and recently restored to its former splendor. Elegant and comfortable. Resplendent entrance hall in Renaissance style w. colonnades and a marble fountain where ducks swim, preen themselves or march in rank across the lobby. Exemplary svce. One of the best in the Deep South. A designated historic monument. **M–E**

♀♀♀ **Adam's Mark Hotel** (formerly the Omni; vic.), 939 Ridge Lake Blvd., TN 38119 (901/684-6664; toll free, see Omni). 380 rms, A/C, color TV, in-rm movies. AE, CB, DC, MC, V. Free parking, pool, rest. (Bravo), bar, rm svce, free crib. *Note:* A 28-story circular tower made of glass and designed by architect John Portman; locals call it "the glass silo." The decor is futuristic and rather chilly. Comfort and facilities are impeccable. Inviting rms w. minibars. Good svce, so-so rest. Caters to businesspeople and groups. 20 min. from dwntwn, 10 min. from the airport (free shuttle). **M–E**

♀♀ **Ramada Inn Convention Center** (nr. dwntwn), 160 Union Ave., TN 38103 (901/525-5491; toll free, see Ramada). 180 rms, A/C, color TV, in-rm movies. AE, CB, DC, MC, V. Free parking, pool, rest. (Seasons), bar, rm svce, free crib. *Note:* Located in the heart of Memphis, this large modern motel is quite comfortable but without any distinctive appeal. Most of the guests are businesspeople, for whom a special VIP floor is reserved. Spacious rms. **I–M**

♀♀ **Holiday Inn Overton Square** (nr. dwntwn), 1837 Union Ave., TN 38104 (901/278-4100; toll free, see Holiday Inns). 143 rms, A/C, color TV, in rm movies. AE, CB, DC, MC, V. Free parking, pool, rest. (Bluff City Diner), bar, rm svce, free crib. *Note:* Modern eight-story motel nr. Overton Sq. and its nightlife. Functional comfort in typical Holiday Inn style. Good value. **I**

♀ **Best Western Riverbluff Inn** (nr. dwntwn), 340 W. Illinois Ave., TN 38106 (901/948-9005; toll free, see Best Western). 99 rms, A/C, cable color TV, AE, CB, DC, MC, V. Free parking, pool, rest. (Riverview), bar, free crib. *Note:* Pleasant six-story motel a minute away from the banks of the Mississippi. The rms are spacious and comfortable; some have refrigerators. Friendly reception and svce. Good value. Lovely view of the Memphis skyline. **B–I**

♀ **Hampton Inn–Medical Center** (nr. dwntwn), 1180 Union Ave., TN 38104 (901/276-1175; toll free 800/426-7866). 126 rms, A/C, color TV, in-rm movies. AE, DC, MC, V. Free parking, pool, café nearby, free continental breakfast, free crib. *Note:* Well-run, comfortable motel 5 min. from dwntwn. Inviting, functional rms, congenial svce. Good overall value. **B–I**

Other Hotels (from top bracket to budget)

♀♀♀ **French Quarter Suites Hotel** (nr. dwntwn), 2144 Madison Ave., TN 38103 (901/728-4000; toll free 800/843-0353). 106 suites, A/C, cable color TV. AE, CB, DC, MC, V. Free parking, health club, rest. (Bourbon Street Café), bar, 24-hr. rm svce, free airport transportation, free breakfast. *Note:* Small luxury hotel w. suites only, spacious and comfortable, w. minibars; some have private balconies. The rest. offers very acceptable Cajun cooking. Personalized svce. Close by is Overton Sq. w. its shops and nightlife. Favored by those in-the-know. **M**

₽₽₽ **Holiday Inn Crowne Plaza** (dwntwn), 250 N. Main St., TN
₺₺₺ 38104 (901/527-7300; toll free, see Holiday Inns). 406 rms,
A/C, color TV, in-rm movies. AE, CB, DC, MC, V. Parking $4, pool, sauna,
health club, rest., coffee shop, bar, rm svce, free crib. *Note:* The local flagship of
the Holiday Inn Corporation. Centrally located 18-story tower w. a view of the
Mississippi. Beautiful contemporary design. Nothing is wanting in comfort and
facilities. Spacious rms w. balconies; most have refrigerators as well. Efficient
svce; good rest. Caters to businesspeople and groups; VIP floor. Direct access to
the Convention Center. **M**

₽₽₽ **Radisson** (dwntwn), 185 Union Ave., TN 38103 (901/528-
₺₺₺ 1800; toll free, see Radisson). 283 rms, A/C, color TV, in-rm
movies. AE, CB, DC, MC, V. Valet parking $4, pool, sauna, bar, rest. (The Ve-
randa), rm svce, free airport transportation, exercise equipment, free crib. *Note:*
Architecturally, a very pleasing blend of an ultramodern 11-story building w. a
lovely old facade of the original historic building. Spectacular six-story lobby w.
trees and fountains. Comfortable, spacious rms; attentive svce. Good rest. offering Créole cuisine. Big business clientele because of the proximity of the financial
district. Good value overall. **M**

₽₽ **Brownstone Hotel** (dwntwn), 300 N. 2nd St., TN 38105
₺₺ (901/525-2511). 243 rms, A/C, color TV, in-rm movies.
AE, CB, DC, MC, V. Free parking, pool, rest., bar, rm svce, free crib. *Note:* Another favorite of business travelers, a few steps from the Convention Center.
Comfortable and functional; recently renovated. Reception and svce no more
than adequate. VIP floor. **I–M**

₽₽ **Days Inn Downtown** (formerly the Benchmark; dwntwn),
₺₺ 164 Union Ave., TN 38103 (901/527-4100; toll free, see
Days Inns). 106 rms, A/C, cable color TV. AE, MC, V. Valet parking $3, rest.
(Cheers), bar, rm svce, free crib. *Note:* Relatively modern hotel in the heart of the
dwntwn area across from the Peabody Hotel. Spacious rms. Newly renovated. An
excellent value. **I**

₽ **La Quinta Medical Center** (nr. dwntwn), 42 S. Camilla St.,
₺ TN 38104 (901/526-1050; toll free, see La Quinta). 130 rms,
A/C, cable color TV. AE, CB, DC, MC, V. Free parking, pool, adj. 24-hr. coffee
shop, valet svce, free crib. *Note:* This is the classic modern motel, comfortable and
functional. Spacious rms, efficient svce. Ideal for those traveling by car. 8 min.
from dwntwn. **B–I**

₽ **Motel 6 Graceland** (vic.), 1360 Springbrook Rd., TN 38116
₺ (901/396-3620). 148 rms, AC, cable color TV. AE, DC, MC,
V. Free parking, pool. *Note:* Functional brand-new motel located near Graceland
and the airport. Unbeatable value 15 min. from dwntwn via I-55 (Exit 5A). Ideal
for a visit to the "King's" mansion (1 mi./0.6km away). **B**

Airport Accommodations

₽₽ **Sheraton Airport Inn** (vic.), 2411 Winchester Rd., TN 38105
₺₺ (901/332-2730; toll free, see Sheraton). 212 rms, A/C, cable
color TV. AE, CB, DC, MC, V. Free parking, pool, two tennis courts, rest., bar,
rm svce, free crib. *Note:* Conventional airport motel 2 min. (by 24-hr. free shuttle) from the terminal. Comfortable, well-soundproofed rms, efficient svce. Business clientele. Interesting wknd packages. 8 min. by car from Graceland. **I–M**

RESTAURANTS

Personal Favorites (in order of preference)

�🍷🍷🍷 **Chez Philippe** (dwntwn), in the Peabody Hotel (see "Accommodations," above) (529-4188). A/C. Dinner only, Mon–
Sat. AE, CB, DC, MC, V. Jkt. *Specialties:* lobster bisque w. scallop quenelles,
lamb tenderloin w. garlic cake, crab mousse w. mustard sauce, sea scallops w. cocoa beans, roast rack of lamb w. Provençal herbs. Excellent wine list. *Note:*

Dubbed "nouvelle Delta" cuisine, the cooking of Chez Philippe's young chef José Gutierrez is a miracle of creativity and balance. Formal, three-tiered dining rm w. painted trompel'oeil murals, crystal chandeliers, and sumptuous tableware. Svce is highly polished, and the total effect is close to perfection. This is the most prestigious rest. in Memphis, as your check will demonstrate. Resv. a must. Free valet parking. *French.* **M–E**

☀☆ ♈♈ **Rendezvous** (dwntwn), 52 S. 2nd St. (General Washburn Alley) (523-2746). A/C. Lunch Fri–Sat, dinner Tues–Sat (until midnight); closed also two weeks in late July and two weeks in late Dec. AE, CB, DC, MC, V. *Specialties:* fantastic barbecued pork ribs. Beer but no wine. *Note:* Picturesque basement rest. that puts you in mind of a country general store; "decorated" w. a profusion of posters, furnishings, and souvenirs of the Old South. The atmosphere is relaxed and the svce diligent. An excellent bet, right in the heart of Memphis. A local institution since 1948, thanks to the Vergos family. *American.* **B–I**

♈♈ **Folk's Folly** (vic.), 551 S. Mendenhall Rd. (762-8200). A/C. Dinner nightly. AE, CB, DC, MC, V. Jkt. *Specialties:* broiled prime beef, Créole-style vegetables. *Note:* The biggest and the best steaks in Memphis. Pleasant decor and atmosphere. Very popular w. locals. Resv. advised. 25 min. by car from dwntwn. *Steak.* **M**

♈♈ **Café Roux** (dwntwn), 94 S. Front St. (525-7689). A/C. Lunch/dinner daily, brunch Sun; closed hols. AE, CB, DC, MC, V. *Specialties:* jambalaya, gumbo, catfish, crawfish étouffée, excellent bread pudding. *Note:* New Orleans's French Quarter look prevails at this rest. serving some of the spiciest Cajun and Créole outside of New Orleans. Quickly becoming an institution in Memphis. Two other locations, one at 7209 Winchester Rd. (755-7689). No resv. *American.* **B–I**

☀☆ ♈ **John Will's Barbecue Pit** (nr. dwntwn), 5101 Sanderland Dr. (761-5101). A/C. Lunch/dinner daily. AE, MC, V. *Specialties:* beef and pork ribs, pork shoulder, beef brisket and sausage barbecued, pork and beef sandwich plates, apple cobbler. *Note:* Significantly named by the readership of *Memphis* magazine the best of the city's 100 or so barbecue rests., Will's has been consistently packed since it opened in 1983, and on Sat evening the wait can be tedious. Modern setting w. natural-wood paneling, inevitably adorned w. photographs of prize hogs and cattle. A fine place with attractive prices. No resv. *American.* **B–I**

Other Restaurants (from top bracket to budget)

♈♈♈ **Justine's** (nr. dwntwn), 919 Coward Place (527-3815). A/C. Dinner only, Tues–Sat (until midnight); closed hols. AE, CB, DC, MC, V. Jkt. *Specialties:* vichyssoise, crabmeat Justine, pompano Claudet, tournedos, béarnaise, trout Marguéry, rum-cream pie. *Note:* Superb classic French cuisine, elegant antebellum decor (the building dates from 1843), surrounded by beautiful grdns. Patrons can dine outdoors in good weather. One of the best rests. in the Deep South. Irreproachable svce. Resv. are indispensable. Valet parking. *French.* **M–E**

♈♈ **Marena's** (dwntwn), 1545 Overton Park (278-9774). A/C. Dinner only, Mon–Sat; closed hols. AE, MC, V. Jkt. *Specialties:* Menu completely changes regularly. *Note:* Every month chef/co-owner Rina Franklin presents a different menu showcasing the cuisines of two Mediterranean countries—one always European. Beautiful interior to suit the exoticism of the food. Friendly svce. Resv. required. *Mediterranean.* **I–M**

♈♈ **Café Society** (nr. dwntwn), 212 N. Evergreen Ave. (722-2177). A/C. Dinner only, Mon–Sat. AE, MC, V. *Specialties:* poppy and sesame seed–crusted salmon w. biscayne sauce, filet of beef stuffed w. blue cheese, oven-roasted free-range chicken. Menu changes regularly. *Note:* Casual but elegant midtown rest. featuring attractively prepared continental cuisine. Warm and attentive svce. Resv. advised. *Continental.* **I–M**

☖☖ **Dux** (dwntwn), in the Peabody Hotel (see "Accommodations," above) (529-4199). A/C. Breakfast/lunch/dinner daily. AE, CB, DC, MC, V. Jkt. *Specialties:* grilled oysters, Black Angus steak, filet of pork in mustard, shrimp scampi, catch of the day, prime beef broiled over a mesquite-wood fire. Delicious desserts. The menu changes frequently. *Note:* A rest. of palatial elegance and cooking of the first order. Lovely rococo decor, exemplary svce. Very "in" for business lunches. Dux's success makes resv. advisable. *American/Seafood.* **I–M**

☖☖ **Grisanti's** (vic.), 1489 Airways Blvd. (458-2648). A/C. Lunch Mon–Fri, dinner Mon–Sat; closed hols. AE, CB, DC, MC, V. Jkt. *Specialties:* fresh homemade pasta, cannelloni alla Gusi, veal cutlet milanese, steaks. Good wine list. *Note:* A Memphis favorite since 1909. The best local Italian rest. Resv. advised. Big John Grisanti, the owner, is a legendary local institution. Casual atmosphere. Valet parking. *Italian.* **I–M**

☖☖ **King Cotton Café** (dwntwn), 50 N. Front St. (576-8150). A/C. Lunch only, Mon–Fri; closed hols. AE, DC, MC, V. *Specialties:* lamb chops, steak, broiled catch of the day. Créole dishes. Good homemade desserts. *Note:* On the mezzanine of the Morgan Keegan Tower in the heart of the cotton-trading district (whence its name), this charming bistro serves tasty and often imaginative "Delta" food. An agreeable atmosphere, perfect for business lunches. Courteous svce. Resv. advised; free parking. *American.* **I–M**

☖ **Landry's Seafood House** (dwntwn), 263 Wagner Place (526-1966). A/C. Lunch/dinner daily. AE, MC, V. *Specialties:* Fish from the Gulf of Mexico, prime cuts of steak, chicken *Note:* Pleasant rest. located in an old warehouse overlooking the Mississippi. *American* **I–M**

☖ **Neely's Interstate BBQ** (nr. dwntwn), 2265 S. 3rd St. (775-2304). A/C. Lunch/dinner daily; closed hols. No credit cards. *Specialties:* barbecue pork ribs and sandwiches. *Note:* Though it has been open since 1980 (a relatively short amount of time for barbecue rests. in Memphis), this rest. has just recently become a local favorite. Meat is smoked over hickory logs for 10 hours, producing a breathtaking flavor. Comfortable dining room serving beer. *American.* **B–I**

☖ **Molly's La Casita** (nr. dwntwn), 2006 Madison Ave. (726-1873). A/C. Lunch/dinner daily. AE, CB, DC, MC, V. *Specialties:* tacos al carbon, burritos, chiles rellenos, enchiladas, tamales verdes. *Note:* One of the best places in town for aficionados of authentic Mexican cuisine. Pleasant atmosphere, typical but pretty decor. Very popular locally. Other location: 4972 Park Ave. (685-1616). *Mexican.* **B–I**

☼☖ **Buntyn** (nr. dwntwn), 3070 Southern Ave. (458-8776). A/C. Lunch/dinner Mon–Fri (until 8pm). No credit cards. *Specialties:* fried chicken, meatloaf, fried catfish, Waldorf salad, special house-style vegetables, banana pudding, cobblers. *Note:* In spite of its unappealing neon-and-Formica decor, this immensely popular rest. has continued to attract faithful followers for over 40 years. Its southern-style fried chicken and platters of house-style vegetables are themselves worth a visit. No resv. accepted. *American.* **B**

Cafeterias/Specialty Spots

Little Tea Shop (dwntwn), 69 Monroe Ave. (525-6000). Lunch only, Mon–Fri. No credit cards. *Specialties:* fried steak, turnip greens w. baked ham, chicken pan pie, pork chop w. broccoli puffs, collard greens, banana cream pie. *Note:* First-rate southern-style home-cooking in a friendly atmosphere. One of Memphis's oldest rests. (since 1918).

BARS & NIGHTCLUBS

Alfred's (dwntwn), 197 Beale St. (525-3711). Popular downtown rock 'n' roll spot. Nightly.

B. B. King's Blues Club (dwntwn), 139–147 Beale St. (524-5464). Newly opened club named after the blues guitar legend B. B. King, who learned his chops on Beale St. decades ago. Open nightly.

Rum Boogie Café (dwntwn), 182 Beale St. (528-0150). Very popular blues-rest. club. Open nightly.

Sleep Out Louie's (dwntwn), 88 Union St. (527-5337). Oyster bar and rest., offering live jazz, rock, or pop to young crowds in their 20s. Open nightly.

NEARBY EXCURSIONS

CHUCALISSA INDIAN VILLAGE (1987 Indian Village Rd., 10 mi./16km SW on U.S. 61) (785-3160): Native American village dating from approximately A.D. 900 and mysteriously abandoned six centuries later (*chucalissa* means "abandoned house"). Numerous dwellings have been re-created based on the findings of ongoing archeological excavations; interesting museum of Choctaw arts and crafts. Open Tues–Sun.

FARTHER AFIELD

SHILOH NATIONAL MILITARY PARK (230 mi./368 km r.t. via U.S. 64 E. and Tenn. 22S and return): Site of the first major land battle of the Civil War, April 6–7, 1862. Northern troops under Gen. Ulysses S. Grant won out after confused and unusually bloody combat—24,000 men were reported dead, wounded, or missing. Films are shown at the military museum, and visitors can take a self-guided 10-mi. (16km) automobile tour of the battlefield. The surrounding countryside is lovely; of particular interest are the numerous tumuli from the pre-Columbian era. For history buffs. The Visitor Center is open daily (901/689-5275).

HOT SPRINGS NATIONAL PARK (396 mi./634km r.t. on I-40W, I-30W, and U.S. 70W and return): One of the most famous and popular in the United States. Well before Spanish explorer Hernando de Soto "discovered" the springs in 1541, Native Americans recognized their healing powers and revered the place as holy. Proclaimed a federal reservation in 1832 by the U.S. Congress and promoted in 1921 to the status of a national park, the springs and the picturesque charm of their locale annually attract hundreds of thousands of visitors seeking treatment for rheumatic and nervous conditions. Every day about a million gallons (4 million liters) of water gush forth, at a temperature of 143°F (62°C), from the 47 separate hot springs within the park. The surrounding countryside with its lakes and wooded mountains is very lovely. The Visitor Center, 600 Central St. at the corner of Court St. (toll free 800/543-2284), is open daily.

Where to Stay Near the Park

Arlington Resort, P.O. Box 5652, Central Ave. at Fountain St., Hot Springs, AR 71901 (501/623-7771; toll free 800/643-1502). 490 rms. A luxury hotel dating from the '20s, pleasingly renovated. **I–M**

Buena Vista, 201 Aberina St., Hot Springs, AR 71913 (501/525-1321; toll free 800/255-9030), 4 mi. (6.5km) south on Ark. 7S. 40 rms w. kitchenettes. Very pleasant cottages on the shores of Lake Hamilton. **I–M**

Where to Eat

Hamilton House, 130 Van Lyell Dr. (501/525-2727), 6 mi. (10km) south on Ark. 7S. Dinner only, nightly. Elegant antique decor, on the shores of Lake Hamilton. *Continental.* **I–M**

NASHVILLE (420 mi./672km r.t. on I-40E and return): The capital of Country Music. Worth a visit. For details, see Chapter 13 on Nashville. Might well be combined with a visit to Shiloh National Military Park (see above).

CHAPTER 15

NEW ORLEANS⚜️

□ □ □

And the Mississippi Delta

Birthplace of Louis Armstrong and Sidney Bechet, this most French of U.S. cities was founded in 1718 by Jean Baptiste Le Moyne, sieur de Bienville, governor of Louisiana. Named in honor of Philippe, Duke of Orléans, Regent of France at the time, the city presents a fascinating fusion of races and cultures.

By turns, French, Spanish, then French again, and finally sold to the U.S. in 1803 by Napoléon I under the terms of the Louisiana Purchase, the city has harmoniously blended its "Créole" inheritance from the first French and Spanish settlers with the "Cajun" influence of Acadian refugees from Canada in 1755, and has subsequently added dashes of Italian, Caribbean, German, Irish, and African American. As a result, what was 250 years ago a village of trappers and gold prospectors is now a cosmopolitan city that has retained its liking for the open sea (its port is second in the U.S. only to New York City's) and for good food (New Orleans, New York, and San Francisco are the country's gastronomic capitals), as well as an inimitably attractive lifestyle. Beloved by European tourists, the "Gateway of the Mississippi" can claim, among its other distinctions, to have invented jazz. (Originally spelled "jass," the word had an indelicate significance in Créole, having to do with sexual intercourse; later it came to denote a kind of African dance.) As for its famous **Mardi Gras,** a festival of 19th-century origin lasting several weeks, its only rival anywhere in the world is the Carnival in Rio. Tourism, with 10 million visitors a year, is already established as the most important source of revenue, ousting both the oil industry (which has been in deep depression since the early '80s) and port traffic. A Rand-McNally poll showed that New Orleans was among the most popular destinations in the country for vacationers. With the recent legalization of gambling in New Orleans, the city has seen an even greater rise in tourism.

With its colorful streets, balustraded old houses, flower-filled courtyards, and wrought-iron balconies, the **French Quarter (Vieux Carré,** literally "Old Square") is an architectural unity of a kind rare in North America. The strolling visitor will chance, unexpectedly but delightfully, on Mississippi docks that haven't changed since the days of the showboats; on the friendly crowds of **Jackson Square,** historic heart of the French Quarter, with its painters and street musicians; on 150-year-old bars still haunted by the memory of pirate Jean Lafitte; on the authentic tradition of Dixieland in venerable **Preservation Hall;** on the impressive 1795 **Cabildo,** once the Spanish governor's palace, now a museum; on the slightly motheaten strip joints of Bourbon St., New Orleans's hot strip. To say nothing of those landmarks of local gastronomy, like Antoine's or Galatoire's, where the finest traditions of Créole cooking are still very much alive: oysters Rockefeller (baked and seasoned with Pernod), gumbo (a thick soup of shrimp, shellfish, crabmeat, and rice), jambalaya (an exotic melange of rice, tomatoes, shrimps, oysters, and sausages or chicken), shrimp with sauce remoulade, bananas Foster (in liqueur, with ice cream), or pompano (a basslike fish) en papillote, to name but a few.

Not far from the French Quarter, the delightful **Garden District,** with its old houses and aura of aristocracy, rubs shoulders with the new city created by black gold, with its inescapable high-rises including the prestigious 53-story **Place St. Charles Building** and the colossal **Superdome,** which with its 90,000 seats is the world's largest indoor stadium. This huge 27-story concrete cathedral of football is entirely air-conditioned. Lovers of the picturesque will not feel that it compensates them for the disappearance of the fabled **Storyville,** a district of saloons, gaming houses, and brothels around Basin St., which was demolished in 1917 at the request of the military, who wished to protect soldiers on leave from its temptations; its destruction was a heavy loss for "The Big Easy," as jazz musicians have nicknamed the city.

The lower Mississippi Valley, and its immense delta opening onto the Gulf of Mexico, represents one of New Orleans's principal tourist attractions. Its lush vegetation of live oaks draped in Spanish moss, of creepers and water lilies; its endless network of bayous (creeks); its elegant 19th-century plantations— these make up the "Cajun country," where live 300,000 descendants of the French-speaking Acadians. There are no terms too strong for recommending a visit to this fascinating, little-known region.

Writer Truman Capote and actress Dorothy Lamour were born here; among the great musicians who first saw daylight in "the cradle of jazz" are Red Allen, Barney Bigard, Lee Collins, Fats Domino, Baby and Johnny Dodds, Bunk Johnson, Nick Larocca, Albert Nicholas, Jelly Roll Morton—and of course, Louis Armstrong and Sidney Bechet.

FBI statistics put New Orleans near the top of the list of U.S. cities in terms of crime. It pays to be careful if you're walking alone, after dark, outside the central streets of the French Quarter. Badly lit streets should always be avoided at night, especially in the area of the Bienville Housing Project, north of the French Quarter. Be sure to take taxis where advised to do so.

BASIC FACTS: State of Louisiana. Area code: 504. Time zone: central. ZIP Code: 70140. Founded in: 1718. Approximate population: city, 495,000; metropolitan area, 1,240,000. Rank among U.S. metropolitan areas: 32nd.

CLIMATE: From its proximity to the Gulf of Mexico, New Orleans derives a subtropical climate. The best time for a visit is between Oct and Mar, since the winters are unusually mild (Jan average, 53°F/12°C), as is the autumn, with temperatures usually above 68°F (20°C) in Oct. Summer is disagreeably hot and sticky (July average, 82°F/28°C). Between Mar and Sept don't forget your raincoat and umbrella; it rains copiously and almost daily. The average annual rainfall of 60.88 in. (1,522mm) is one of the highest in the country.

DISTANCES: Atlanta, 481 mi. (770km); Dallas, 493 mi. (790km); Houston, 356 mi. (570km); Memphis, 390 mi. (625km); Tampa, 633 mi. (1,012km).

ARRIVAL & TRANSIT INFORMATION

AIRPORT: New Orleans International Airport (MSY), 12 mi. (19km) NW. Information: 464-0831.

AIRLINES: American (toll free 800/433-7300), Continental (toll free 800/525-0280), Delta (toll free 800/221-1212), Northwest (toll free 800/225-

2525), Southwest (toll free 800/531-5601), TWA (toll free 800/221-2000), United (toll free 800/241-6522), and USAir (toll free 800/428-4322).

CITY LINK: The **cab** fare to city center is about $23; time, about 25–30 min. Bus: **Airport Shuttle** (522-3500) leaves every 10 min., serving principal downtown hotels; fare, $10; time, 45–60 min.

The public transportation system by bus and streetcar is efficient and cheap; particularly useful is the **Vieux Carré Shuttle,** which operates daily. For information, call the Regional Transit Authority (569-2700). Convenient VisiTour passes.

If your visit is to be confined to the French Quarter and the Central Business District, you won't need to rent a car; on the other hand, if you follow my emphatic advice and travel to the "bayou" and plantation country, to Lake Pontchartrain, or to the shores of the Gulf of Mexico, you will.

CAR RENTAL (at the airport unless otherwise noted): Avis (toll free 800/331-1212); Budget (toll free 800/527-0700); Dollar (toll free 800/800-4000); Hertz (toll free 800/654-3131); National (toll free 800/227-7368); Thrifty, 1415 Airline Hwy., in Kenner (toll free 800/367-2277). For dwntwn locations, consult the local telephone directory.

LIMOUSINE SERVICES: Cappel Limo Service (288-4696), Carey Limousines (523-5466), Dav El Limousines (toll free 800/922-0343).

TAXIS: Taxis may be hailed on the street, taken from the waiting lines in front of the major hotels, or summoned by telephone. Cabs are numerous and their fares are relatively low within the city limits. Recommended companies: **Checker-Yellow Cabs** (525-3311), **Classic Cabs** (835-2227), and **United Cabs** (522-9771).

TRAIN: Amtrak, Union Station, 1001 Loyola Ave. (528-1610; toll free 800/872-7245).

INTERCITY BUSES: Greyhound, 1001 Loyola Ave. (525-6075).

MISSISSIPPI CRUISES: 3- to 10-day cruises on the Mississippi, Ohio, and Cumberland Rivers aboard the *Delta Queen* or the *Mississippi Queen,* paddlesteamers built in the 1920s. Luxurious kitsch. For information, contact the **Delta Queen Steamboat Co.,** 30 Robin St. Wharf, New Orleans, LA 70130 (504/586-0631; toll free 800/543-1949).

INFORMATION & TOURS

TOURIST INFORMATION: The **Greater New Orleans Tourist and Convention Commission,** 1520 Sugar Bowl Dr., LA 70112 (504/566-5011).

Jean Lafitte National Historical Park Visitor Center, French Quarter, 916 N. Peters St. (504/589-2636): Organizes a series of different daily walking tours of the French Quarter and Garden District. Art exhibitions, concerts, audiovisual shows, etc.

Welcome Visitor Center, 529 St. Ann St. (504/566-5031): Also information on Louisiana and the Cajun country.

GUIDED TOURS: The **Canal Street Ferry** (boat), at the foot of Canal St.: Free Mississippi crossing; fine view of river and city. Last ferry leaves from the Canal St. terminal at 9pm.

Aquarium/Zoo Cruise (boat), Canal St. Dock (504/586-8777): A one-hour trip along the Mississippi from the Aquarium of the Americas to the Audubon Park and Zoological Garden. Four round-trips daily year round.

Cajun Queen Cruises (boat), Poydras St. Wharf at Riverwalk (504/529-4567; toll free 800/445-4109): 1½-hr. trips down the Mississippi past the French Quarter, historic plantations, and the site of the battle of New Orleans.

Créole Queen Cruises (boat), Poydras St. Wharf (504/529-4567; toll free 800/445-4109): Trips along the Mississippi to the battlefield of Chalmette; nightly jazz dinners aboard the *Créole Queen,* newest of the Mississippi paddlewheelers. Daily.

Gay '90s Carriages (carriage), 1824 N. Rampart St. (504/943-8820): Carriage tour of the French Quarter leaving from Jackson Sq. Picturesque. Daily year round, weather permitting.

Gray Line Tours (bus), Toulouse St. at the river (504/587-0861): Guided tours of city and surroundings; serves principal dwntwn hotels.

New Orleans Steamboat Co. (boat), Toulouse St. Wharf at Jackson Sq. (504/586-8777; toll free 800/233-2628): Daily 2-hr. tours of the New Orleans harbor with additional nightly dinner and jazz cruises aboard the paddlewheeler *Natchez.*

Southern Seaplane (seaplane), 1 Coquille Dr., Belle Chasse (394-5633): Discover the city, Lake Pontchartrain, and the bayous as seen from above. Spectacular.

Saint Charles Avenue Streetcar (streetcar), Canal St. and Carondelet St.: Follows the route of Tennessee Williams's famous *Streetcar Named Desire;* you can visit the charming Garden District with its lovely old houses. Opened in 1835, this 13-mi.-long (21km) streetcar line is one of the oldest in the world. It's wiser not to ride it at night. Fare: $1 (exact change required). Has recently undergone a $47-million renovation. For information, call 569-2700.

SIGHTS, ATTRACTIONS & ACTIVITIES

ADVENTURES: Honey Island Swamp Tours (boat), 106 Holly Ridge Dr., in Slidell, 24 mi. (38km) NE on I-10 (641-1769): Two-hour guided tour into the heart of one of the country's wildest, remotest wetlands. Fascinating. Daily.

ARCHITECTURAL HIGHLIGHTS: 🏛 **Civic Center,** bounded by La Salle and Poydras Sts. and Loyola and Tulane Aves.: Heart of the **Central Business District,** with interesting high-rise buildings. The imposing 11-story **City Hall** faces the **State Office Building,** the **State Supreme Court Building,** and the **New Orleans Public Library.**

🏛 **Loyola University,** 6363 St. Charles Ave. (865-3240): This highly regarded Catholic university dates from 1912, and has some fine Tudor Gothic buildings. Campus visits by appointment.

🏛 **Superdome,** Sugar Bowl Dr. (587-3810): Largest enclosed stadium in the world, with 90,000 seats; air-conditioned throughout. Scene every year of the famous Sugar Bowl. The dome is 262 ft. (80m) high and 678 ft. (207m) across. Absolutely riveting. Tours daily.

🏛 **World Trade Center,** 2 Canal St. (525-2185): A 33-story high-rise overlooking the harbor, with the offices of many international corporations as well as foreign consulates. The observation platform on the 31st floor and the revolving bar on the 33rd floor have a wonderful view of the French Quarter and the river.

CHURCHES/SYNAGOGUES: 🏛 **Old Ursuline Convent,** Chartres and Ursuline Sts. (529-3040): This Ursuline convent, dating from 1745, once housed an orphanage as well as the city's first school for African American children. Today it's the presbytery and record house of the adjoining Italian church of St. Mary's. It has been recently restored. Open to visitors Tues–Sun.

☼🔔 **St. Louis Cathedral,** Jackson Sq. (525-9585): Built in 1794 on the site of two earlier churches, both destroyed, this is one of the oldest Catholic cathedrals in the country. A fine classical building in the French style. Open daily.

HISTORIC BUILDINGS: ☼🔔🔔 **Beauregard-Keyes House,** 1113 Chartres St. (523-7257): Beautiful Greek Revival house built around 1826, now a designated historic monument. After the War Between the States it was the home of Confederate Gen. Pierre G. T. Beauregard, and later of novelist Frances Parkinson Keyes. Elegant patio and garden; period furniture. Open Mon–Sat.

☼🔔🔔 **Cabildo,** 709 Chartres St., at Jackson Sq. (568-6968): Built in 1795 as the Spanish Governor's Palace. The sale of Louisiana to the U.S. by Napoléon I (the Louisiana Purchase) was ratified here in 1803. After a 1988 fire that damaged much of the building, an $8-million complete restoration ensued. It reopened in 1993 w. exhibits exploring New Orleans' multicultural past. Open Tues–Sun.

☼🔔🔔 **Gallier House,** 1118–1132 Royal St. (523-6722): Luxurious private house built in 1857 by architect James Gallier, with one of New Orleans's finest Victorian interiors. Open daily.

☼🔔 **Hermann-Grima Historic House,** 820 St. Louis St. (525-5661): Plush home typical of New Orleans's "golden age" (1830–60), with flower-planted patios, kitchens (demonstrations of Créole cooking Sat and Sun Oct–May), slave quarters, and stables. Very fine old furniture; a beautiful vignette from the past. Open daily.

🔔 **Longue Vue House and Gardens,** 7 Bamboo Rd. (488-5488): Faithful 1942 replica of a great 19th-century Louisiana plantation, with lovely furniture of the period. 8 acres (3.2ha) of magnificent garden, inspired in part by the famous Generalife at Granada in Spain. Open daily.

🔔 **Madame John's Legacy,** 632 Dumaine St. (568-6968): One of the oldest houses in New Orleans; erected in 1727 and rebuilt after a fire in 1788, it was completely restored in 1981. Part of the Louisiana State Museum, it's closed to the public for the time being.

🔔 **Napoleon House,** 500 Chartres St. (524-9752): Intended for Napoléon I by the mayor of New Orleans, Nicholas Girod, who had dreams of rescuing the fallen emperor from his imprisonment on St. Helena. Picturesque café on the ground floor. Open daily.

☼🔔 **Old Absinthe House,** 240 Bourbon St. (523-3181): The oldest and most famous bar in the Vieux Carré; here Gen. (later Pres.) Andrew Jackson and pirate Jean Lafitte drew up their plan for the Battle of New Orleans against the invading British. (See "Bars and Nightclubs," below.)

🔔 **Pitot House,** 1440 Moss St. (482-0312): On the bank of Bayou St. John, this old plantation house once belonged to James Pitot, first elected mayor of New Orleans; dating from 1799, it's one of the last remaining examples of the Antillean style. Open Wed–Sat.

☼🔔🔔 **Pontalba Apartments,** Jackson Sq.: Built in 1846–49 by Baroness Pontalba, daughter of the last Spanish governor, these were the first apartments constructed in the U.S., in a lovely southern idiom with characteristic grace notes in wrought iron. Writer William Faulkner was among the illustrious tenants. **"The 1850s House,"** 523 St. Ann St. (568-6968), with original furniture and decoration of the period, may be visited Tues–Sun. Another unusual museum is the **Pontalba Historical Puppetorium,** 514 St. Peter St. (522-0344), where the deeds-at-arms of pirate Jean Lafitte, and other pages from the city's history, are portrayed by means of animated puppets. Open daily.

☼🔔🔔 **The Presbytère,** 751 Chartres St. at Jackson Sq. (568-6968): Abutting on St. Louis Cathedral, this 1791 building, in the same style as, but older than, the Cabildo, housed the Supreme Court under Spanish colonial administration. Holds part of the collection of the **Louisiana State Museum,** including many articles and costumes relating to Mardi Gras, as well as fine ceramics in the Newcomb style and engravings of birds by naturalist John James Audubon. Open Tues–Sun.

☀️🔔 **Preservation Hall,** 726 St. Peter St. (522-2841): Grandfather of jazz halls, dating from 1846. The decor is on its last legs but the ambience is incomparable. Open nightly.

🔔 **U.S. Customs House,** Decatur and Canal Sts. (589-2976): Imposing edifice strangely blending the Greek Revival and Egyptian Revival styles, built between 1849 and 1881. The famous marble lobby and scrupulously restored interior decoration should definitely be seen. Open Mon–Fri.

MARKETS: ☀️🔔 **French Market,** bounded by N. Peters, Decatur, St. Ann, and Barracks Sts. (522-2621): A covered market dating from 1836 (the oldest portions from 1791) built on the site of an old Native American market. One of the most interesting sights of the French Quarter, with its picturesque displays of fruit and vegetables, its flea market, trinket merchants, strolling musicians, and terrace cafés, of which the legendary **Café du Monde** is open day and night. Amusing and colorful.

MONUMENTS: 🔔 **Andrew Jackson Statue,** Jackson Sq.: This equestrian statue of Gen. Andrew Jackson, who defeated the British here in 1815, is the work of sculptor Clark Mills. It sits in the middle of the old "Place d'Armes" (Parade Ground), renamed Jackson Sq. when the city's best-known statue was placed here in 1856.

🔔 **Streetcar Named Desire,** Esplanade Ave., in front of the Old U.S. Mint: This streetcar, which once ran along Royal St. and St. Charles Ave., was made famous in Tennessee Williams's play *A Streetcar Named Desire.* The car displayed here dates from 1906.

MUSEUMS OF ART: 🔔 **Contemporary Arts Center,** 900 Camp St. (523-1216): Large cultural complex comprising two auditoriums and three art galleries, in a renovated former warehouse. Interesting temporary exhibitions, music recitals, shows, etc. Open daily.

☀️🔔 **New Orleans Museum of Art/NOMA,** Lelong Dr., City Park (488-2631): Fine Greek Revival building, inside which you'll find a remarkable microcosm of the history of art, from the primitive cultures of Asia, Africa, and the pre-Columbian Americas right down to cubism, via the great masters of the Renaissance (Samuel Kress Endowment) and a fabulous collection of Fabergé eggs. Among the best known of the works on display are Veronese's *Holy Conversation, Snows of Giverney,* by Monet, *Portrait of Estelle Musson* by Degas, and Max Ernst's *Everyone Here Speaks Latin.* A wealth of American art: Georgia O'Keeffe, Andy Warhol, Jacques Lipchitz, etc. Ceramic miniatures. Open Tues–Sun.

MUSEUMS OF SCIENCE & HISTORY: ☀️🔔 **Chalmette National Historical Park,** on Bernard Hwy. in Arabi, 6 mi. (10km) east along St. Claude Ave. (589-4430): The spot where Gen. Andrew Jackson won his victory in 1815 in the last great battle of the War of 1812 against the British. Military museum and 98-ft. (30m) memorial obelisk on the bank of the Mississippi. In the great National Cemetery adjoining lie 12,000 Union soldiers who fell during the Civil War. For history buffs. Open daily.

☀️🔔 **Confederate Museum,** 929 Camp St. (523-4522): The oldest Civil War museum in Louisiana, with a memorial to Jefferson Davis, president of the Confederacy. Interesting. Open Mon–Sat.

☀☖ **Historic New Orleans Collection,** 533 Royal St. (523-4662): The history of Louisiana and New Orleans narrated by means of an interesting collection of maps, pictures, photographs, and historic documents displayed in two lovely old houses, **Merieult House** (1792) and the **Williams Residence** (about 1880). Temporary exhibitions. Open Tues–Sat.

☖ **Louisiana Nature & Science Center,** 11000 Lake Forest Blvd., New Orleans East (246-9381): Science museum featuring up-to-date exhibits, a planetarium with an IMAX theater, and an 86-acre (35ha) wildlife park with nature trails through forest and wetlands. 20 min. from dwntwn via I-10E. Open Tues–Sun.

☀☖☖ **Louisiana State Museum,** in several different buildings (568-6968): Priceless historical collections going back to French and Spanish colonial times, housed in the **Cabildo, The Presbytère, Madame John's Legacy** (currently closed to the public), **"The 1850s House"** (see above), or the **Old U.S. Mint** (see below). For details, see the individual museums.

☀☖ **Old Pharmacy Museum,** 514 Chartres St. (565-8027): An apothecary's store dating from 1823, "La Pharmacie Française," founded by Louis Dufilho, America's first licensed pharmacist. Very picturesque. Open Tues–Sun.

☀☖☖ **Old U.S. Mint,** 400 Esplanade Ave. (568-8213): This fascinating museum, opened in 1982, is housed in an Ionic temple which was once a mint. Displays souvenirs of the early jazz age (instruments that belonged to Louis Armstrong, Bix Beiderbecke, and the Original Dixieland Jazz Band are of special interest), and traces the evolution of the art form from its Afro-American origins to the present day. A must for all jazz fans. Also a museum of Carnival. Open Tues–Sun. Part of the Louisiana State Museum.

☀ **Voodoo Museum,** 724 Dumaine St. (523-7685): Interesting small museum devoted to the cult of Voodoo, which commanded a large following among 19th-century slaves, and its high priestess, the famous Marie Laveau. Occult displays and artifacts. The museum also presents ritual shows and offers walking tours. Open daily.

NIGHTTIME ENTERTAINMENT: The city that, at the beginning of the 20th century gave birth to jazz, still proudly upholds its musical heritage, particularly in the Vieux Carré. After nightfall the quiet, slightly countrified streets of the **French Quarter** come briskly back to life. A throng of idlers moves along the brilliantly lit streets, some of which are closed to wheeled traffic, and which teem with bars, jazz clubs, and other more or less wholesome pleasure resorts. Typical is the famous **Bourbon Street:** you mustn't leave New Orleans without seeing it. For details, see "Bars and Nightclubs," below.

OUTDOOR ART & PLAZAS: ☖ **K & B Plaza,** Lee Circle on St. Charles Ave. (586-1234): Very fine collection of more than 50 modern sculptures in stainless steel, bronze, granite, aluminum, and other materials by U.S. and foreign artists. The outdoor exhibits may be seen daily; those in the hall, only Mon–Fri.

PANORAMAS: ☖ **Greater New Orleans Bridges,** Pontchartrain Expwy.: Spanning the river from New Orleans to Algiers, this great work of art, constructed in 1958, is the second-largest metallic nonsuspension twin bridge in the country; looking north from it you have a nice view of the harbor and the Vieux Carré.

☀☖ **World Trade Center,** 2 Canal St. (525-2185): Observation platform on the 31st floor **(Viewpoint)** and revolving bar on the 33rd floor **(Top of the Mart)** reached by outside glass-walled elevator. Fine view over the city, the Mississippi, and the harbor. Open daily until 1am.

PARKS & GARDENS: ☖ **Audubon Park and Zoological Garden,** St. Charles Ave. opposite Tulane University (861-2537): Beautiful 400-acre (162ha) park ringed with century-old oak trees, on the site of an old sugar plantation on the banks of the Mississippi. Well-known zoological garden (see "Zoos," below); lagoons, golf courses; picnic areas.

☼ ⚱ **City Park,** City Park Ave. at Marconi Dr. (north of the city, almost at the edge of the great Lake Pontchartrain): In a bygone age this was where duelists liked to settle their disputes, and on some Sundays a dozen duels were fought on the favorite ground of **Dueling Oaks.** Fine rose gardens, four public golf courses, many lagoons and lakes for canoeing. The park is almost 2½ mi. (4km) long, and in the southern part is located the New Orleans Museum of Art (see above). You shouldn't fail to visit it.

⚱ **Greenwood Cemetery and Metairie Cemetery,** Metairie Rd. and City Park Ave.: Famous for their sumptuous tombs, particularly those of Gen. Stonewall Jackson and of Josie Arlington, a well-known madam who died in 1914—all standing amid magnolias and tropical trees. Open daily.

⚱ **Louis Armstrong Park,** bounded by N. Rampart, St. Peter, St. Philip, and N. Villere Sts.: Originally known as Congo Sq. and later renamed after the city's most famous jazz musician, this was once a meeting place for African American slaves who came here on Sun to dance, sing spirituals, and generally let off steam. Tradition has it that jazz was born here—where today, appropriately, stand the Municipal Auditorium and the Theater for the Performing Arts.

⚱ **St. Louis Cemetery No. 1,** 400 Basin St.: One of the oldest cemeteries (1788) in the country. Among its splendid mausoleums, raised well above the ground because of the high water table, are those of the chessmaster Paul Morphy and the voodoo queen Marie Laveau. Part of the movie *Easy Rider* was shot here. Don't fail to visit it—but don't venture alone into this unsafe neighborhood. Open daily.

☼ ⚱ **Woldenberg Riverfront Park,** between Toulouse and Canal Sts.: 13 acres (5.3ha) of landscaped green space at a bend of the Mississippi River. A brick promenade along the river features many local artists' work. Ships and paddlewheelers often dock along the park.

PERFORMING ARTS: For current listings of shows and cultural events, consult the entertainment pages of the daily *Times-Picayune/States-Item* (morning and evening), and the monthly *New Orleans* magazine.

Contemporary Arts Center, 900 Camp St. (523-1216): Concerts, ballet, modern and avant-garde theater.

Municipal Auditorium, 1201 St. Peter St. (565-7470): Concerts, opera, touring companies, ballet, etc. Year round.

New Orleans Music Hall, 907 S. Peters St. (522-1979): Music venue with the largest floor in town. Presenting concerts by local and national acts.

Orpheum Theater, 129 University Place (525-0500): Home of the Louisiana Philharmonic Orchestra (Sept–May).

Petit Théâtre du Vieux Carré/The Little Theater, 616 St. Peter St. (522-2081): The city's oldest theater (1797), with a magnificent antique interior. Drama, comedy, classical theater.

Saenger Performing Arts Center, 143 N. Rampart St. (524-2490): A 1920s movie house, an extravagant essay in the Renaissance style, now beautifully restored. Broadway hits, concerts.

State Palace Theatre, 1108 Canal St. (522-4435): Historic theater opened in 1926. Concerts, performing arts, film.

Theater of the Performing Arts, 801 N. Rampart (565-7470): Home of the New Orleans City Ballet and the New Orleans Opera House Association. Also theater in the round.

Tulane University–Dixon Hall, Audubon Place (865-5269): Concerts, recitals, ballet.

SHOPPING: Canal Place, 365 Canal St. (522-9200): The city's most upscale shopping center, with about 50 fashion boutiques and exclusive stores such as Gucci, Bally, Saks Fifth Avenue, and Brooks Brothers. Open daily.

Jax Brewery, Decatur and St. Peter Sts. (587-0749): A 19th-century brewery transformed into a picturesque food bazaar, with more than 75 cafés, restaurants, and stores selling food and amusing gifts. Lively, likable atmosphere. Open daily.

Magazine Street, between Canal St. and Napoleon Ave.: Charming 19th-century commercial thoroughfare with many antique shops.

Riverwalk, Riverside between Canal and Poydras Sts. (522-1555): The newest of the great downtown shopping centers, on the site of the 1984 World's Fair along the Mississippi. Nearly 200 fashion boutiques, elegant stores, cafés, and restaurants. Has drawn crowds ever since its 1987 opening.

Royal Street, between Iberville and Dumaine Sts.: These seven blocks of Royal St. in the French Quarter are chockablock with antiques. Probably concentrate more quality antique jewelry and furnishings than any comparably sized area in the U.S. Becomes a pedestrian mall during shopping hours.

SPECIAL EVENTS: For exact dates, consult the **Greater New Orleans Tourist and Convention Commission** (see "Tourist Information," above).

Sugar Bowl (Jan 1): Three days of popular celebration before the Sugar Bowl football game.

Mardi Gras (Feb–Mar): The only carnival of its kind in the world, and for 150 years New Orleans's most popular annual event. It celebrates Mardi Gras (literally "Fat Tuesday," but more commonly known in English as "Shrove Tuesday"), the eve of Ash Wednesday, the first day of Lent. Carnival was raised to its present level of splendor in 1857 by a secret society known as "The Mystic Krewe of Comus," and although often threatened with prohibition because of the fistfights and public disorders it occasioned, has survived in the teeth of all opposition thanks to the goodwill of 60 or so colorful associations, the "Krewes." It is these Krewes that sweep through the streets on the day of the great final parade, with their gaudy banners and frenzied bands going on before them, each following a different route. The Rex Parade, led by the King ("Rex") and followed by the mostly white Krewes, goes down St. Charles Ave. to Canal St., where the mayor of New Orleans is waiting to drink a toast with the Rex to the glory of the city. The Zulu Parade, with its "Zulu King," and the Indian Parade, both made up of African American Krewes, twist and turn through the downtown streets and the suburbs, never mixing with the parade of the Rex and his subjects, the Mystic Krewe of Comus, Knights of Momus, Krewe of Proteus, Krewe of Bacchus, Knights of Hermes, Krewe of Babylon, and the rest. But in any of the parades the costumes, masks, and floats will be magnificent, the Krewes setting no limit to their imagination and sense of humor. The Carnival season really begins in early Jan with an unbroken series of masked balls, parades, and torchlit processions, culminating on Shrove Tuesday in the country's greatest popular celebration. It's worth going to New Orleans just to see it.

Freeport-McMoRan Golf Classic (late Mar to early Apr): Prestigious PGA tournament with the world's best professional golfers. At English Turn.

French Quarter Festival (Apr): Free open-air concerts, dancing in the streets, boat races on the Mississippi, food sampling; the Vieux Carré's own festival.

Spring Fiesta (four days long, one week after Easter): Costume parades, public balls, art exhibitions. The city's oldest houses and the plantations in the vicinity are open to the public especially for the festival.

New Orleans Jazz and Heritage Festival (Jazzfest) (late Apr to early May): One of the most famous of all jazz festivals, drawing the greatest performers throughout the city; also rock, gospel, rhythm and blues, country and western, blues, Cajun, folk, Latin American, and African concerts. Riverboat concerts. Draws about 350,000 listeners. The great annual music festival.

African Heritage Festival (early Sept): Music, food, dance, arts and crafts. Celebrating local African heritage.

SPORTS: New Orleans boasts a professional football team: **Football** (Aug– Dec): Saints, Superdome (522-2600).

Horseracing

The Fairgrounds, 1751 Gentilly Blvd. (944-5515); racing Wed–Sun Nov– Mar. One of the oldest tracks (1872) in the country.

STROLLS: ☼⚱ **Bourbon Street,** between Canal St. and Ursulines Ave.: On these 10 blocks, New Orleans has turned sin into a pedestrian mall, with innumerable bars, nightclubs, jazz dives, strip joints, and (sometimes slightly sordid) peep shows. Noisy and colorful by night, silent and depressing by day. This is the place Pigalle or Barbary Coast of the Old South.

☼ **Garden District,** around St. Charles Ave. between Jackson and Louisiana Aves.: 19th-century upper-class homes standing in delightful gardens; don't miss this page from the past. Take the picturesque St. Charles Ave. streetcar (it used to be the streetcar named Desire) from Canal St.— but don't come here after dark.

☼⚱⚱ **Jackson Square,** bounded by Decatur, Chartres, St. Peter, and St. Ann Sts.: The oldest public garden in New Orleans, and its historic center; in French Colonial times it was called "The Parade Ground." On it stand some of the city's most notable buildings: the Cabildo, St. Louis Cathedral, the Pontalba Apartments, the old Jackson Brewery, and others, overlooking the equestrian statue of the seventh president of the U.S., which reigns unchallenged over the square. Lively, appealing atmosphere thanks to the crowds of strollers, painters, and street musicians.

⚱ **Moon Walk,** along the quays across Jackson Sq.: Elevated walkway along the bank of the Mississippi, with a scenic view of the heart of the French Quarter and the shipping on Ol' Man River. Owes its name not to its suitability for moonlight walks, but to a former mayor of the city, Moon Landrieu.

⚱ **Pirate's Alley,** between Chartres and Royal Sts.: Once a place of assembly for pirates and smugglers, this narrow alleyway in the shadow of the cathedral now belongs to painters and artists.

☼⚱⚱ **Royal Street,** between Esplanade Ave. and Canal St.: The Vieux Carré's smart street; almost every building on it is worth your attention: the **Gallier House** (no. 118), **Miro House** (no. 529), **Merieult House** (no. 533), **Court of Two Sisters** (no. 613), **Maison Le Monnier** (no. 640). Many boutiques, art galleries, antiques shops, restaurants, etc. The first Carnival ball was held at no. 127 in 1857, thus inaugurating the Mardi Gras festival.

ZOOS: ⚱⚱ **Aquarium of the Americas,** 1 Canal St. (861-2537): Opened in Sept 1990, this hi-tech structure features more than 10,000 specimens and 60 exhibits ranging from the Mississippi Delta to the Amazon rain forest. Open daily.

☼⚱⚱ **Audubon Zoo,** 6500 Magazine St. (861-2537): One of the 10 best in the U.S., with more than 1,500 creatures displayed in reconstructions of their natural habitats, including very rare white tigers and white alligators. Also a fine collection of Australian fauna. Open daily.

ACCOMMODATIONS

Note: Hotel rates take a sharp upturn during the Sugar Bowl Game weekend and Mardi Gras; you can generally only book for three or more nights at these times, and you should make reservations as far ahead as possible.

Personal Favorites (in order of preference)

Windsor Court (dwntwn), 300 Gravier St., LA 70140 (504/523-6000; toll free 800/223-6800). 310 rms and suites, A/C, cable color TV, movies. AE, CB, DC, MC, V. Valet gar. $15, pool, health club, rest. (including the Grill Room), bar, 24-hr. rm svce, concierge, free crib. *Note:* Luxurious, English-style palace very nr. the French Quarter, its facade elegantly clad in pink granite, w. balconies and bay windows. Newly redecorated interior w. fine collection of old English pictures. Ultra-comfortable rms and suites with minibars (some w. kitchenettes) and marble bathrooms. Excellent luxury hotel rest.; thoughtful, polished svce; fashionable clientele. An establishment of the highest class. The favorite of those in-the-know. **VE**

Westin Canal Place (dwntwn), 100 Rue Iberville, LA 70130 (504/566-7006; toll free, see Westin). 438 rms, A/C, color TV, in-rm movies. AE, CB, DC, MC, V. Valet gar. $12, pool, rest. (Le Jardin), two bars, 24-hr. rm svce, boutiques, concierge, free crib. *Note:* One of the newest luxury hotels in the city, located above the elegant Canal Place shopping center. Overlooks the Mississippi from the eminence of its 29 stories. Exceptionally huge, comfortable rms, w. marble bathrooms, minibars, and clear views over the river or the French Quarter. Ultra-professional svce. Very well situated a stone's throw from the Vieux Carré and the World Trade Center. Big business clientele. **E–VE**

Pontchartrain Hotel (nr. dwntwn), 2031 St. Charles Ave., LA 70140 (504/524-0581; toll free 800/777-6193). 100 rms, A/C, cable color TV. AE, CB, DC, MC, V. Valet parking $10, rest. (Caribbean Room), coffee shop, bar, 24-hr. rm svce, concierge, free crib. *Note:* Set amid glorious old mansions of the Uptown district, this *grande dame* of local hotels has been in the hands of its founding family, the Aschaffenburgs, for three generations. Its small size, and the high quality of its svce, make it a haven of peace, much frequented by VIPs and visiting celebrities. Elegant rms w. period furniture; rest. of high quality that appeals to businesspeople for breakfast or lunch. 10 min. from dwntwn. **E–VE**

Soniat House (dwntwn), 1133 Chartres St., LA 70116 (504/522-0570; toll free 800/544-8808). 24 rms, A/C, cable color TV, AE, MC, V. Valet parking $12, valet svce, concierge, free crib. *Note:* Very lovely old 1830s dwelling house w. carriage entrance and majestic staircase. The rms or suites are huge and tastefully decorated, w. beds of hand-carved wood and period furniture. Inviting patio w. fountain and tropical plants. Personalized reception and svce. An excellent place to stay, partaking fully of the charm of the Vieux Carré. Unfortunately, children under 12 are not accepted as guests. **M–E**

Maison Dupuy (dwntwn), 1001 Toulouse St., LA 70112 (504/586-8000; toll free 800/535-9177). 196 rms, A/C, color TV, in-rm movies. AE, CB, DC, MC, V. Valet gar. $9, pool, health club, rest. (Le Bon Créole), bar, rm svce, free crib. *Note:* A large hotel, modern and elegant, on the edge of the French Quarter, built around a delightful flower-planted patio w. a fountain and a heated pool. Very successful imitation-antique decor. Huge, comfortable rms w. balconies, the best overlooking the patio. Efficient svce; acceptable rest. Good value; recommended. **M–E**

Le Richelieu (dwntwn), 1234 Chartres St., LA 70116 (504/529-2492; toll free 800/535-9653). 86 rms, A/C, color TV. AE, CB, DC, MC, V. Free parking, pool, rest., bar, rm svce, concierge, free crib. *Note:* One of the best values in the French Quarter, the Richelieu occupies what used to be a luxurious private house belonging to an old macaroni factory. Like most hotels in the Vieux Carré it's built around an inviting interior courtyard, w. big, welcoming rms tastefully decorated, and all the engaging charm of the slightly outdated. Friendly reception and svce. **M**

☀☇℞ **Château Motor Hotel** (dwntwn), 1001 Chartres St., LA 70116 (504/524-9636). 45 rms, A/C, cable color TV. AE, CB, DC, MC, V. Free garage, pool, bar, rm svce. *Note:* With its red-brick walls, its shutters, its cast-iron balconies, and its creeper-covered facade, this winsome little hotel in the heart of the Vieux Carré offers excellent value. Largish, comfortable rms, the best overlooking the courtyard with its banana palms, azaleas, and fountain. Pleasing terrace for coffee. A good place to stay. **I–M**

℞ **La Salle Hotel** (dwntwn), 1113 Canal St., LA 70112 (504/523-5831; toll free 800/521-9450). 60 rms, A/C, color TV, in-rm movies. AE, CB, DC, MC, V. Parking free next door. *Note:* Small economy hotel, now 60 years old, on the edge of the French Quarter. A commendable standard of comfort is maintained, though some rms lack private baths. Friendly reception; youthful clientele. Ideal for budget travelers. Unsafe area at night. **B–I**

Other Hotels (from top bracket to budget)

☀℞℞℞℞ **Omni Royal Orleans** (dwntwn), 621 St. Louis St., LA 70140 (504/529-5333; toll free, see Omni). 350 rms, A/C, color TV, in-rm movies. AE, CB, DC, MC, V. Valet parking $12, pool, health club, three rests. (including the Rib Room); three bars, 24-hr. rm svce, hrdrsr, concierge, free crib. *Note:* Splendidly situated on the site of the old St. Louis Exchange Hotel in the heart of the Vieux Carré, a stone's throw from Antoine's, Brennan's, and other landmarks of local gastronomy, as well as from the antiques shops of Royal St. Luxuriously elegant 1920s-style decor and atmosphere, w. Italian marble lobby, lavish flower arrangements, and crystal chandeliers. Rms very comfortable, though a little on the small side. Excellent svce; good rests.; fabulous rooftop pool. **E–VE**

℞℞℞ **Hilton Riverside and Towers** (dwntwn), 2 Poydras St., LA 70140 (504/561-0500; toll free, see Hilton). 1,600 rms, A/C, color TV, in-rm movies. AE, CB, DC, MC, V. Valet parking $11, two pools, health club, sauna, nine tennis courts, squash, three rests. (including Kabby's), coffee shop, four bars, 24-hr. rm svce, nightclub, hrdrsr, concierge, free crib. *Note:* Enormous tourist barracks on the river, its massive silhouette by no means improving the view from Riverwalk. All rms overlook the city, the harbor, or both. Irreproachably comfortable; efficient svce; mediocre rests. Well-regarded jazz club (Pete Fountain's Night Club). The top three floors are reserved for VIPs; on one is a Presidential Suite at $1,470 a night. Group and convention clientele of an obtrusive kind; the Convention Center and the French Quarter are nearby. **E–VE**

℞℞℞ **Inter-Continental** (dwntwn), 444 St. Charles Ave., LA 70130 (504/525-5566; toll free, see Inter-Continental). 483 rms, A/C, color TV, in-rm movies. AE, CB, DC, MC, V. Valet parking $12, pool, two rests. (including the Veranda), two bars, 24-hr. rm svce, hrdrsr, concierges. *Note:* Ultramodern luxury hotel in the heart of the Central Business District and 5 min. from the French Quarter, of ungraceful exterior but elegant and urbane within, boasting many contemporary sculptures and other works of art. Spacious and remarkably comfortable rms w. minibars, some w. balconies. Very complete facilities; flawless svce; rest. of quality. Big business clientele. Interesting wknd discounts. **E–VE**

☀℞℞℞ **Maison de Ville** (dwntwn), 727 Toulouse St., LA 70130 (504/561-5858; toll free 800/345-3457). 23 rms, suites, or cottages, A/C, cable color TV. AE, DC, MC, V. Valet parking $14, pool, rest. (Bistro at Maison de Ville), rm svce, concierge. *Note:* The most luxurious and exclusive small hotel in the French Quarter, its main building dates from the mid-19th century, while the adjoining cottages (200-year-old former slave quar-

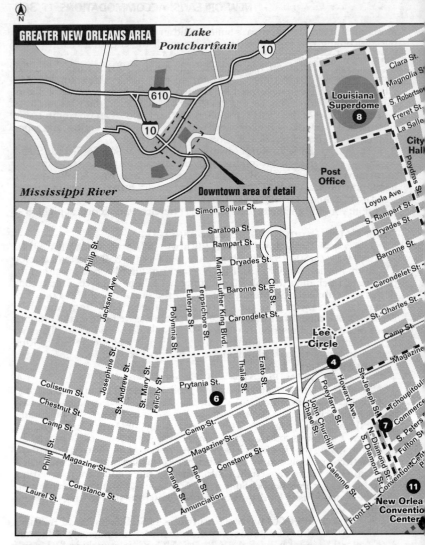

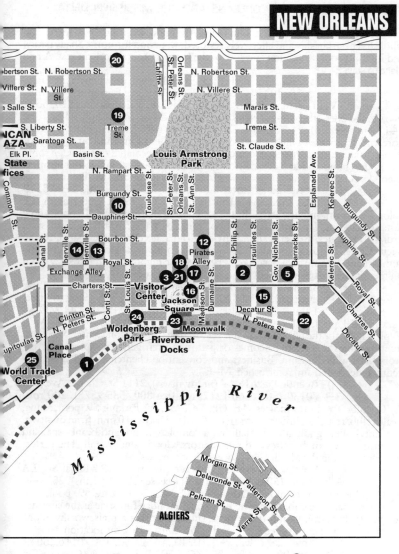

NEW ORLEANS

ters) bear the name of naturalist John James Audubon, who once lived there. The whole has been lavishly and effectively restored, w. period furniture. Shady patios and inviting pool. Reception and svce of the highest order. Excellent rest. A fine place to stay. **E–VE**

    ♙♙ **Fairmont** (formerly the Roosevelt; dwntwn), University Place, ♙♙ LA 70140 (504/529-7111; toll free, see Fairmont). 730 rms, A/C, color TV, in-rm movies. AE, CB, DC, MC, V. Valet parking $10, pool, two tennis courts, three rests. (including Sazerac), 24-hr. coffee shop, 24-hr. bars, 24-hr. rm svce, hrdrsr, drugstore, concierge, free crib. *Note:* An elderly luxury hotel of Victorian elegance, a few steps from the Vieux Carré and on the edge of the Central Business District. Comfortable, lavishly decorated rms, though some are on the cramped side. Lackadaisical svce. Rest. popular at lunch. Big business clientele. A landmark among local hotels. Recently renovated. **M–E**

    ☼♙♙ **Monteleone Hotel** (dwntwn), 214 Royal St., LA 70140 ♙♙ (504/523-3341; toll free 800/535-9595). 600 rms, A/C, color TV, in-rm. movies. AE, CB, DC, MC, V. Valet parking $10, pool, three rests. (including Le Café), coffee shop, three bars (one revolving), rm svce, hrdrsr, boutiques, free crib. *Note:* Inviting older hotel at the entrance to the Vieux Carré. The package-tour and convention guests make a lot of noise, but the comfort and svce are above average; very agreeable nightclub and terrace w. pool on the top floor. A New Orleans landmark for the past century. **M–E**

    ♙♙ **Radisson Suite Hotel** (formerly the Sugar House Park; dwntwn), 315 Julia St., LA 70130 (504/525-1993; toll free, see Radisson). 251 suites, A/C, color TV, in-rm movies. AE, CB, DC, MC, V. Parking $10, pool, rest. (Sugar House), bar, rm svce, concierge, free crib. *Note:* Typical hotel for the business traveler, very nr. the Convention Center. Spacious, inviting suites w. private balconies or patios and refrigerators. Spectacular six-story glass-walled atrium. Business and convention clientele. Good value. Recently redecorated and refurnished. **M–E**

    ♙♙ **Avenue Plaza Hotel** (nr. dwntwn), 2111 St. Charles Ave., LA 70130 (504/566-1212; toll free 800/535-9575). 200 rms. A/C, color TV, in-rm movies. AE, CB, DC, MC, V. Parking $9, pool, sauna, health club, rest., bar, hrdrsr. *Note:* In the Garden District 10 min. from dwntwn, this hotel offers good athletic facilities, a complete health and beauty spa, and inviting rms w. kitchenettes and refrigerators. Good value overall. The perfect place for viewing the Mardi Gras procession as it passes. **M**

    ♙♙ **Holiday Inn French Quarter** (dwntwn), 124 Royal St., LA 70130 (504/529-7211; toll free, see Holiday Inns). 252 rms, A/C, color TV, in-rm movies. AE, CB, DC, MC, V. Parking $9, pool, rest. (Jambo's), bar, free crib. *Note:* The functional Holiday Inn style at the entrance to the Vieux Carré. Comfortable rms. The rest. makes a praiseworthy effort. Package-tour and group clientele. Good value, considering the location. **M**

    ☼♙♙ **Provincial** (dwntwn), 1024 Chartres St., LA 70116 (504/ ♙♙ 581-4995; toll free 800/535-7922). 97 rms, A/C, color TV, in-rm movies. AE, CB, DC, MC, V. Free parking, pool, rest. (Honfleur), bar, rm svce, free crib. *Note:* Delightful older hotel, as quiet and discreet as its name implies, in the Vieux Carré very nr. the French Market. Inviting, comfortable rms w. period furnishings and private balconies. Pretty inner courtyards. The clients are mostly regulars, because they know this is a good place to stay. **M**

    ☼♙♙ **The Columns** (nr. dwntwn), 3811 St. Charles Ave., LA 70115 ♙♙ (504/899-9308). 19 rms, A/C. AE, DC, MC, V. Street parking, rest., bar, free breakfast. *Note:* A prosperous Victorian's elegant home built in 1833 and now a designated historic monument. Enormous rms furnished in period, but some lacking private baths. The movies *Tightrope* and *Pretty Baby* were shot here. Romantic ambience; reception and svce of the friendliest. In the heart of the Garden District, 15 min. from dwntwn by the St. Charles Ave. streetcar. **I–M**

♞♞ **Days Inn Canal Street** (nr. dwntwn), 1630 Canal St., LA 70112 (504/586-0110; toll free, see Days Inns). 216 rms, A/C, cable color TV. AE, CB, DC, MC, V. Free parking, pool, rest., bar, free crib. *Note:* Typical functional motel, recently renovated; 5 min. by car from the Superdome or the French Quarter. Comfortable rms, some w. balconies; efficient reception and svce. Good value overall. **I**

♞♞ **Quality Inn Midtown** (nr. dwntwn), 3900 Tulane Ave., LA 70119 (504/486-5541; toll free, see Choice). 100 rms, A/C, cable color TV. AE, CB, DC, MC, V. Free parking, pool, rest., bar, rm svce, free crib. *Note:* Comfortable, attractive motel a little away from the center. Spacious rms w. balconies. Friendly reception and svce. Great if you're driving; easily accessible from the Pontchartrain Expwy. Free shuttle to Amtrak and Greyhound stations, the airport, and the French Quarter. Good value 10 min. from dwntwn. **I**

♞ **Best Western Patio Motel** (nr. dwntwn), 2820 Tulane Ave., LA 70119 (504/822-0200; toll free, see Best Western). 76 rms, A/C, cable color TV. AE, DC, MC, V. Free parking, pool, adj. coffee shop. *Note:* Congenial small motel 8 min. from dwntwn. Serviceably comfortable rms, the best overlooking the patio w. a pool. Smiling reception and svce. Free shuttle connection w. Amtrak station and bus terminal. Good value. **I**

☼♞ **French Quarter Maisonnettes** (dwntwn), 1130 Chartres St., LA 70116 (504/524-9918). 7 rms, A/C, color TV. No credit cards. Parking $6; nearby coffee shop. *Note:* Gracious little Vieux Carré home built in 1825. The rms, each w. kitchenette and tastefully decorated, open on a pretty shaded courtyard. Reception w. a smile. Excellent value. You'll need to book a number of weeks ahead. Closed in July. A very good place. **I**

♞ **La Quinta Gretna** (nr. dwntwn), 50 Terry Pkwy., in Gretna, LA 70056 (504/368-5600; toll free, see La Quinta). 154 rms, A/C, color TV, in-rm movies. AE, CB, DC, MC, V. Free parking, pool, adj. 24-hr. coffee shop, valet service, free crib. *Note:* Excellent value 10 min. from dwntwn across the Mississippi. Modern comforts; reception and svce w. a smile. Ideal if you're driving. **I**

♞ **St. Charles Inn** (nr. dwntwn), 3636 St. Charles Ave., LA 70115 (504/899-8888). 40 rms, A/C, color TV. AE, CB, DC, MC, V. Parking $3, rest., bar, free breakfast. *Note:* Well-run small budget motel 10 min. from dwntwn on the St. Charles Ave. streetcar. Pleasantly decorated rms; friendly reception. Excellent value. **I**

Airport Accommodations

♞♞♞ **Hilton Airport Hotel & Conference Center** (vic.), 901 Airline Hwy., in Kenner, LA 70062 (504/469-5000; toll free, see Hilton). 312 rms, A/C, color TV, in-rm movies. AE, CB, DC, MC, V. Free parking, pool, two tennis courts, putting green, health club, rest. (Café LaSalle), bar, rm svce, free airport limo. *Note:* Modern luxury hotel right across from the airport. Spacious, well-soundproofed rms overlooking pool or garden. Efficient svce. Business clientele. Great if you're stopping over between flights. 25 min. from dwntwn. **M–E**

YMCA/Youth Hostels

Marquette House International Hostel (nr. dwntwn), 2253 Carondelet St. (504/523-3014). 162 beds. Youth hostel in an antebellum house nr. the Garden District. Only minutes by streetcar to the French Quarter.

YMCA International Center (nr. dwntwn), 936 St. Charles Ave. (504/568-9622). 40 rms. Pool, health club, rest. Men and women.

RESTAURANTS

A Note on New Orleans Food: For more than 150 years New Orleans rightly prided itself on its gastronomic skills. During this period, half a dozen great restaurants have in turn enjoyed their days of glory: Antoine's, which created

Créole cuisine in the 19th century; Galatoire's, at the beginning of the 20th century; Arnaud's, in the 1920s and '30s; Brennan's, in the years following World War II; Le Ruth's, Mosca's, and Commander's Palace, for the past 15 years. These seven "greats" have had their ups and downs over the years, but they are still counted among the best restaurants in the city.

The two great cuisines of New Orleans, ranked by many among the country's greatest gastronomic resources, are "Créole" (the more delicate) and "Cajun" (the earthier). They have one thing in common: Both, in the words of Paul Prudhomme, the truculent figure who is the best-known chef in New Orleans today, are "Louisiana-born with French roots." But if Créole and Cajun food still acknowledge a predominantly French inheritance, they also pay tribute to other cuisines that immigration has brought to the city: Spanish, African, Italian, Caribbean, Native American. However—still quoting Prudhomme—the most compelling influence on Créole cuisine was undoubtedly that of the cooks who had charge of the kitchens in Louisiana plantation homes.

Personal Favorites (in order of preference)

♟♟♟♟ **Emeril's** (vic.), 800 Tchoupitoulas St. (528-9393). A/C. Lunch Mon–Fri, dinner Mon–Sat; closed hols. AE, CB, DC, MC, V. Jkt. *Specialties:* Fried oysters w. roasted-garlic sauce and corn-and-tomato relish, wild-mushroom tart, roast quail Milton, rack of lamb w. mustard crust, pan-roasted salmon w. fresh herbs and wilted greens, Créole cream cheesecake. The menu changes regularly. Small but adequate wine list. *Note:* Former chef of the Commander's Palace, the young and talented Emeril Lagasse performs at the burners and broilers before the diner's eyes. His adventurous and delicate fare must be defined as Créole/Southwestern/New American, or "Haute Créole" as dubbed by some food critics. Carved out of a former factory in the warehouse district, the rest. is decorated in a modernistic style w. brick walls, high ceilings, and exposed pipes. Friendly but professional svce. The best rest. to open recently in New Orleans (1990) and one of the 12 best in the U.S. Resv. a must. *American.* **M–E**

⚡♟♟♟ **Commander's Palace** (nr. dwntwn), 1403 Washington Ave. (899-8221) A/C. Lunch Mon–Fri, dinner nightly, brunch Sat–Sun; closed Shrove Tuesday, Dec 24–25. AE, CB, DC, MC, V. Jkt. *Specialties:* turtle soup, corn-fried oysters, fresh fish w. roasted pecans, roast quail w. shrimp, veal chop Tchoupitoulas, roast rack of lamb for two, bread pudding soufflé. Fine wine list. *Note:* In the heart of the charming old Garden District, a stately Victorian house accommodates New Orleans's most elegant rest., belonging to the senior branch of the well-known Brennan family. While the cuisine has its passing moments of weakness, it remains a font of creative Créole cooking. Exquisite flower-planted courtyard in summer; Dixieland at brunch (very crowded) Sat–Sun. Courteous and efficient svce; resv. a must. 10 min. from dwntwn; valet parking. *Créole.* **M–E**

♟♟♟ **Bayona** (dwntwn), 430 Dauphine St. (525-4455). A/C. Lunch Mon–Fri, dinner Mon–Sat; closed hols. AE, CB, DC, MC, V. *Specialties:* tapenade, garlic soup, sautéed sweetbreads in sherry-mustard butter, pan-roasted salmon w. sauerkraut, grilled duck breast w. pepper jelly, chocolate-espresso layered cake. Small but fine wine list. *Note:* A brilliant newcomer housed in a romantic Créole cottage w. leafy courtyard in the French Quarter. The creative and stylish cuisine of chef-owner Susan Spicer (formerly at the Bistro at Maison de Ville) is equal parts Mediterranean, Créole, and American. Its menu changes daily. Charming patio w. fountain for outdoor dining. Knowledgeable svce. Prices are surprisingly modest considering the quality and inventiveness of Spicer's fare. Resv. a must. *American.* **M**

⚡♟♟ **Galatoire's** (dwntwn), 209 Bourbon St. (525-2021). A/C. Lunch/dinner Tues–Sun; closed Shrove Tuesday and hols. No credit cards. J&T (at dinner). *Specialties:* shrimp remoulade, eggs Sardou, crabmeat ravigote, trout Marguéry, sweetbreads financière, chicken Clemenceau, seafood-stuffed eggplant, oysters Bienville. *Note:* Another landmark since the beginning of the 20th century; the attractive 1900 decor, w. its mirrors and ceiling fans, is guaranteed authentic. The menu is pure Créole, and the svce is exemplary. This is a noisy place, and—another black mark—Galatoire's accepts no resv., inexcusable in a rest. of this quality. The wine list is poor. New Orleans's quintessential bistro. *Créole.* **I–M**

        Crozier's (vic.), 3126 W. Esplanade Ave., Metairie (833-8108). A/C. Lunch Tues–Fri, dinner Tues–Sat; closed hols. AE, CB, DC, MC, V. Jkt. *Specialties:* pâté of duck, coq au vin, tournedos Gérard (w. foie gras), trout w. fennel, steak au poivre, sweetbreads meunière. Weakish wine list. *Note:* Lyon native Gérard Crozier's food is—most unusually for New Orleans—100% French, without any Créole tinge. Charming reception and intimate quarters in the suburb of Metairie, almost on the shores of Lake Pontchartrain. Efficient svce; resv. advised. Very well worth the 20-min. drive from the French Quarter. *French.* **M–E**

        Mike's on the Avenue (nr. dwntwn), 628 St. Charles Ave. in the Lafayette Hotel (523-1709). A/C. Lunch Mon–Fri, dinner nightly; closed hols. AE, DC, MC, V. *Specialties:* dumplings filled w. shrimp, spinach, and ginger; barbecue oysters; grilled lamb chops marinated in a pomegranate and rosemary sauce w. a jalapeño mint glaze; grilled filet mignon stuffed w. roasted garlic and topped w. Fresno chili lime butter; seasonal berry strudel cobbler. Seasonal menu. *Note:* Mike Fennely, who earned prestige as chef at the Santacafé in Santa Fe, has created a venue not only for his skill of mingling different cuisines but also for his abstract paintings. Minimalist decor of stark-white walls allows little disturbance when experiencing the complexity of taste in each bite. Its local popularity warrants a resv. *Southwestern/Asian/Créole.* **I–M**

        NOLA (dwntwn), 543 St. Louis St. (522-6652). A/C. Lunch/dinner daily; closed hols. AE, DC, MC, V. *Specialties:* flaky crab cake w. jalapeño tartar sauce; Lafayette boudin (Cajun sausage) stewed in beer, onions, and cane syrup; cedar-plank-roasted trout w. citrus horseradish crust; deep-dish apple pie. *Note:* Emeril Lagasse of Emeril's (see first entry under "Personal Favorites," above) has downscaled in price, but not in vitality, bringing the same taste and texture that exist at Emeril's to NOLA (shortened form of New Orleans, Louisiana). Very lively, party atmosphere. With the bar and its full food service, it's a great place to come if you are dining alone. *American/Créole.* **I–M**

        Bacco (dwntwn), 310 Chartres St. (522-2426). A/C. Lunch Mon–Sat, dinner nightly, brunch Sun; closed Shrove Tuesday, December 24 and 25. AE, CB, DC, MC, V. *Specialties:* grilled eggplant w. ricotta and goat cheese; fried calamari; homemade pastas; pizzas baked in wood-fired oven; homemade cinnamon ice cream sandwiched between praline cookie. Expertly chosen wine list. *Note:* Another Brennan family (of Commander's, see above) success story. Gothic archways, Venetian chandeliers, and baroque ceiling paintings adorn this glorious space. Chef Fernando Saracchi tempers the Italian cuisine w. a dash of Créole. Very exciting place. Resv. recommended. *Italian.* **I–M**

        Bon Ton Café (dwntwn), 401 Magazine St. (524-3386). A/C. Lunch/dinner Mon–Fri; closed hols. AE, MC, V. Jkt. *Specialties:* turtle soup, crayfish étouffée, jambalaya, crabmeat au gratin, fried catfish, redfish Bon Ton, bread pudding with whisky. *Note:* This old rest., a New Orleans classic for three decades, w. its countrified atmosphere and charming checked red gingham tablecloths, serves some of the most authentic Cajun food going. Generally crowded and noisy at lunch, quieter in the evening. Very near the Vieux Carré. Resv. advised. *Cajun.* **I–M**

        Felix's (dwntwn), 739 Iberville St. (522-4440). A/C. Breakfast Mon–Thurs, lunch/dinner daily (until midnight); closed hols. AE, MC, V. *Specialties:* oysters Rockefeller, steak, gumbo, fish of the day. *Note:* Oyster bar and rest. that is crowded midday and evening by hungry customers. Regulars usually sit at the counter to avoid the long wait for a table. Absolutely fresh oysters on the half shell and seafood, very attractively priced. Noisy, genial atmosphere. No resv. *Seafood.* **B–I**

Other Restaurants (from top bracket to budget)

Veranda (dwntwn), in Inter-Continental Hotel (see "Accommodations," above) (525-5566). A/C. Breakfast/lunch/dinner daily, brunch Sun. AE, CB, DC, MC, V. Jkt. *Specialties:* smoked duck terrine, Tuscan seafood pasta, red snapper w. julienne vegetables, rabbit in cream sauce, steak au poivre, andouille-and-seafood gumbo. Fine desserts and wine list. *Note:* The cuisine of German-born chef Willy Coln is a masterful blend of Deep South classics and continental expertise. Handsome surroundings w. both formal dining rm and courtyard. Polished svce. Resv. suggested. A fashionable place. *Continental.* **M–E**

Christian's (nr. dwntwn), 3835 Iberville St. (482-4924). A/C. Dinner only, Mon–Sat; closed Thanksgiving, Dec. 25. AE, CB, DC, MC, V. Jkt. (tie preferred but not obligatory). *Specialties:* oysters Roland, smoked soft-shell crabs, shrimp remoulade, fish filet w. green-peppercorn sauce, veal Christian, sautéed chicken w. blackberry vinegar, bouillabaisse Marseillaise, good homemade sherbets, chocolate mousse. *Note:* Christian Ansel, a legitimate successor to the Galatoire dynasty, has housed his rest. in a pastel-washed old chapel, where he serves excellent French-inspired Créole food. Original setting, flawless svce; a very good place to eat. Resv. advised. 15 min. from dwntwn. *Créole.* **M–E**

Versailles (nr. dwntwn), 2100 St. Charles Ave. (524-2535). A/C. Dinner only, Mon–Sat; closed Shrove Tuesday and two weeks in July. AE, CB, DC, MC, V. Jkt. *Specialties:* snails in pastry shell, crabmeat Florentine, Madras shrimp curry, bouillabaisse, duck w. port wine, trout sautéed w. capers and artichokes, veal escalope Fleury, filet mignon Helder, orange mousse. Good wine list (especially the German section). *Note:* Like a great wine, this rest. belonging to Günter Preuss continues to improve w. the years. Classic French-Créole food flawlessly prepared and served. Elegant paneling-and-mirror decor. Very popular locally, so resv. highly advisable. Valet parking. 10 min. from dwntwn. *Créole/French.* **M–E**

Antoine's (dwntwn), 713 St. Louis St. (581-4422). A/C. Lunch/dinner Mon–Sat; closed Shrove Tuesday and hols. AE, CB, DC, MC, V. Jkt. *Specialties:* oysters Rockefeller, oysters Foch, pompano en papillote, étouffée of crayfish, filet of beef Robespierre, tournedos marchand de vin, chicken Rochambeau, souffléed potatoes, baked Alaska. Vast wine list backed by 35,000 bottles in the cellar. *Note:* The oldest rest. in the Vieux Carré is by now a sort of living legend. It was here that, in the 19th century, Antoine Alciatore created some of the most renowned Créole dishes, such as oysters Rockefeller and pompano en papillote. The decor has not changed since it was new (in 1840), and the present proprietor, Bernard Guste, is a fifth-generation descendant of the legendary Antoine. The waiters, some of whom have worked here for more than three decades, can be abrupt and the food is somewhat dated. But in spite of its slightly touristy atmosphere this is still one of the three or four best places to eat in the city. Ask to be seated in the big dining rm at the back, w. its dark paneling. Resv. strongly advised. *Créole.* **M–E**

Gautreau's (nr. dwntwn), 1728 Soniat St. (899-7397). A/C. Dinner only, Mon–Sat; closed hols. CB, DC, MC, V. *Specialties:* duck confit w. red-onion marmalade, mustard, and sage; crab cakes w. black beans and tomato-corn salsa; cumin braised lamb shank w. ratatouille; seared rare tuna medallions w. pepper purée; marinated roasted chicken w. wild mushrooms and garlic mashed potatoes; orange crème brûlée. *Note:* Housed in an old pharmacy, the rest. uses the original apothecary cases to display their wine and liquor. Elegance and peacefulness prevail. Larkin Selman's cooking is innovative and pleasing, uniting French and Créole cuisine. Thoughtful svce. This is a tough seat to get, so resv. are strongly suggested. *Créole/French.* **M–E**

♈♈ **Bistro at Maison de Ville** (dwntwn), in the Maison de Ville
⚓⚓ (see "Accommodations," above) (528-9206). A/C. Lunch/
dinner Mon–Sat. AE, DC, MC, V. Jkt. *Specialties:* mushroom cheesecake w. truffle cream anglaise; shrimp and clams in saffron and risotto broth; pan-roasted
tenderloin of pork w. a five-spice apple glaze; grilled quail w. dijon mustard, bacon, and Roquefort cheese; sweetbreads w. mushrooms and eggplant; excellent
crème brûlée. *Note:* Charming, romantic little hotel rest. w. dark paneling, intimate bar, and red upholstery. The cuisine is a happy marriage of classical Créole
tradition w. modern Mediterranean cooking. Since the rest. seats only 40, resv.
are a must. *Créole/French.* **M**

♈♈ **Alex Patout's Louisiana Restaurant** (dwntwn), 221 Royal St.
⚓⚓ (525-7788). A/C. Lunch Mon–Fri, dinner nightly. AE, CB,
DC, MC, V. Jkt. *Specialties:* chicken-and-sausage gumbo, grilled baby beef tenderloin w. crawfish and wild mushroom cream sauce, grilled fresh fish topped w.
shrimp and crabmeat, duck w. oyster dressing, red snapper stuffed w. eggplant
and shrimp, pecan pie. *Note:* Longtime chef-owner of the famous Patout's restaurant in New Iberia, LA., transferred in 1988 to the heart of the French Quarter,
Alex Patout blends his Cajun cooking heritage w. Créole touches from his new
surroundings. The result is "Haute Louisiana" cuisine at its best. Elegant atmosphere. Excellent svce. A local favorite. Resv. strongly suggested. *Cajun/Créole.* **M**

♈♈ **Pelican Club** (dwntwn), 615 Bienville St., entrance on Ex-
⚓⚓ change Alley (523-1504). A/C. Lunch Mon–Fri, dinner
nightly; closed hols. AE, CB, MC, V. *Specialties:* sherry-scented alligator-and-
turtle soup, seared and smoked peppered Atlantic salmon, clay-pot seafood, jambalaya paella style, profiteroles filled w. coffee ice cream. *Note:* New, huge multi-
rm rest. in the handsomely restored antique Exchange Alley. The cuisine of chef
Richard Hugues marries Louisiana's earthy cooking w. sophistication. Soberly
elegant setting w. contemporary paintings. Professional svce. Trendy clientele.
Resv. advised. *American.* **M**

☼♈♈ **K. Paul's Louisiana Kitchen** (dwntwn), 416 Chartres St. (524-
⚓⚓ 7394). A/C. Lunch/dinner Mon–Sat; closed hols. AE. *Specialties:* Cajun popcorn (fried crayfish), jambalaya, shrimp Bayou Têche, duckling
à l'étouffée, blackened redfish, sweet-potato/pecan pie. Menu changes regularly.
Note: This bistro began the revolution in local gastronomy. The chef, Paul
Prudhomme, is a man of weight, both literally and figuratively, who came here
from the Commander's Palace; he is the moving cause of the fashion for Louisiana food throughout the U.S. The food here is authentically Cajun, and the ambience relaxed, casual, and fun-loving, w. Formica decor and paper napkins. The
svce does not aim to please. Food quality uneven due to repeated absences of chef
Prudhomme. Resv. strongly advised. *Cajun.* **I–M**

♈♈ **Peristyle** (dwntwn), 1041 Dumaine St. (593-9535). A/C.
⚓⚓ Lunch Fri, dinner Tues–Sat; closed hols. MC, V. *Specialties:*
shrimp cakes w. sweet-and-sour relish; pan-seared sea scallops w. blood oranges,
leeks, and Pernod; marinated loin of lamb w. thyme and garlic vinegar; sweet-
ened goat cheese w. Armagnac and berries. *Note:* Voted best new chef of 1993 by
other local chefs, John Neal upholds a noble modesty and simplicity in his cooking and proves taste need not be secondary to presentation. An elegant dining
rm. w. turn-of-the-century pastel murals on the walls. Diligent svce. *Continental.*
I–M

☼♈♈ **Pascal's Manale** (nr. dwntwn), 1838 Napoleon Ave. (895-
⚓⚓ 4877). A/C. Lunch Mon–Fri, dinner nightly; closed Dec 25.
AE, CB, DC, MC, V. *Specialties:* barbecued shrimp, gumbo, spaghetti Collins,
veal au marsala, snapper Catherine (w. hollandaise sauce). Skimpy wine list. *Note:*
Another old (1913) landmark of local good food, which harmoniously blends
the Créole influence into a basically Italian repertory. What matters here is the
food, not the setting or the svce. Generally crowded and noisy; resv. rarely honored, so long waits are inevitable, especially on wknds. Not a good neighborhood
at night; take a cab. *Créole/Italian.* **I–M**

Bozo's (vic.), 3117 21st St., Metairie (831-8666). A/C. Lunch/dinner Tues–Sat. CB, MC, V. *Specialties:* fried oysters, catfish and stuffed crab, chicken and andouille gumbo, hot sausage "poor boy." *Note:* Big, casual seafood rest. 15 min. from dwntwn in the suburb of Metairie. Impeccable fish or shellfish deftly boiled or fried. Luncheonette atmosphere and decor. Svce a little slow. Very popular locally. A highly commendable place. *Seafood.* **I**

Acme Oyster House (dwntwn), 724 Iberville St. (522-5973). A/C. Lunch/dinner daily; closed hols. AE, MC, V. *Specialties:* oysters, "poor boys" (Créole sandwiches), fried catfish, gumbo, jambalaya. Draft beer. *Note:* The most representative of the Vieux Carré's oyster bars; the belons, Blue Points, Whitstables, Plaquemines, and so forth are fresh from the sea, and opened under your very eyes. Connoisseurs eat them standing, leaning an elbow on the old counter, and wash them down w. a draft beer. Relaxed atmosphere, full of local color. Excellent value. *Seafood/Créole.* **B–I**

Gumbo Shop (nr. dwntwn), 630 St. Peter St. (525-1486). A/C. Lunch/dinner daily; closed hols. AE, CB, DC, MC, V. *Specialties:* seafood and chicken gumbo, red beans w. rice, shrimp remoulade, good ice cream (try the praline sundae). *Note:* Delightful little Créole bistro serving some of the best seafood gumbo in town. The fresh-fruit daiquiris are outstanding, too. Relaxed, inviting atmosphere, a hop, skip, and jump from Jackson Sq. in the heart of the Old Quarter. Lots of tourists. *Créole.* **B**

Mandina's (nr. dwntwn), 3800 Canal St. (482-9179). A/C. Lunch/dinner daily. No credit cards. *Specialties:* poor boy sandwiches, shrimp remoulade, spaghetti w. meatballs, gumbo, jambalaya, fried soft-shell crabs, Dobergé cake. *Note:* The king of the "poor boy" (a roast beef or sausage sandwich), also serving other commendable Créole dishes. Crowded at lunchtime, this likable neighborhood rest. nonetheless represents one of the best values in the entire city. The atmosphere and the svce are casual and friendly. *Créole.* **B**

Mother's (dwntwn), 401 Poydras St. (523-9656). A/C. Breakfast/lunch/dinner daily; closed hols. No credit cards. *Specialties:* Ferdi (a roast-beef and ham "poor boy" sandwich with "débris" sauce), crayfish étouffée, red beans and rice w. sausage, sandwiches, seafood gumbo, sweet-potato pie. Beer on draft. *Note:* For almost half a century this has been a local landmark for its wonderful "poor boys" and tasty Créole food. Distinctive bistro atmosphere, often w. long waiting lines at lunch. The servings (particularly the "poor boys") are generous. A fine place right in the business district. *Créole.* **B**

Restaurants in the Vicinity

La Provence (vic.), on U.S. 190 in Lacombe (626-7662). A/C. Dinner only, Wed–Sun; closed Dec 25 and the month of Sept. AE, MC, V. Jkt. *Specialties:* salmon mousse, quail gumbo, sweetbreads w. port wine and mushrooms, duck w. Madagascar green peppercorns, steak au poivre Robert Aymes, rack of lamb w. herbs from Provence. Handsome wine list at decent prices. *Note:* In spite of his name, Chris Kerageorgiou is from France, and what's more, from Provence. His remarkable and wholly French cuisine can accommodate itself to influences of Greek and Créole origin. Agreeable country setting, romantic atmosphere and dedicated svce. Successful enough that you'll need resv. 40 min. from dwntwn along the spectacular Pontchartrain Causeway. A fine place. *French.* **M**

Mosca's (vic.), 4137 U.S. 90W in Avondale, 5 mi. (8km) west of the Huey Long Bridge (436-9942). A/C. Dinner only, Tues–Sat; closed hols. No credit cards. *Specialties:* baked oysters Mosca, marinated crabmeat salad, spaghetti bordelaise, shrimp à l'Italienne, chicken cacciatore, game (in season). Unimpressive wine list. *Note:* The unpretentious white building, w. its rather shabby decor, is a full 20 min. by car from dwntwn and hard to find after nightfall. But the marriage of Italian and Créole cuisines achieved by the Mosca family reaches a perfection unequaled anywhere else, particularly in the fresh homemade pastas. The servings are generous, the svce efficient and casual. Often crowded and noisy, so resv. are definitely advised (but none are accepted on Sat). *Créole/Italian.* **M**

Cafeterias/Fast Food/Specialty Spots

※ **Café du Monde** (dwntwn), 800 Decatur St., at St. Anne St. (581-2914). Old café inside the French Market, open round the clock seven days a week, and immensely popular. The beignets (French doughnuts) are renowned. There's an inviting terrace. A New Orleans classic since the 1860s. No credit cards.

※ **Camellia Grill** (nr. dwntwn), 626 S. Carrolton Ave. (866-9573). Breakfast/lunch/dinner daily (till 1am). No credit cards. Noteworthy for all kinds of omelets (try the cheese or the chile). Also very good sandwiches, cheeseburgers, and homemade pastries; the pecan pie is not to be missed. Engaging atmosphere, locally popular far into the night. Take the St. Charles Ave. streetcar to Carrollton Ave., a 25-min. ride.

※ **Central Grocery** (dwntwn), 923 Decatur St. (523-1620). Authentic turn-of-the-century grocery carrying foods of all nations. It prides itself on having originated the famous "muffuletta sandwich" — ham, mozzarella, salami, provolone, and mortadella on a hard roll. Local color (and aroma) guaranteed. Open 8am–5pm daily. No credit cards.

BARS & NIGHTCLUBS

Checkpoint Charlie's (nr. dwntwn), 501 Esplanade (947-0979). Listen to live alternative rock while you do your laundry. Open daily, 24 hrs.

City Lights (nr. dwntwn), 310 Howard Ave. at St. Peter St. (568-1700). The fashionable disco joint in the old warehouse district. Elegantly modern setting; trendy crowd. Valet parking. Open Tues–Sat.

Club Second Line (dwntwn), 216 Bourbon St. (523-2020). Upscale new music club w. live jazz, blues, R&B, and danceable Big Band swing. Open nightly.

Maple Leaf Bar (vic.), 8316 Oak St. (866-9359). The local shrine of Cajun music, rhythm and blues. Exciting ambience. Open nightly.

Michaul's (nr. dwntwn), 701 Magazine St. (522-5517). Cajun dancing on a large dance floor. If you don't know how, they'll teach you. Open nightly (closes at midnight on the weekends).

The Mint (dwntwn), 504 Esplanade Ave. (525-2000). Club featuring a variety of live music and comedy, often combined. An interesting place.

Molly's Irish Pub (dwntwn), 732 Toulouse St. (568-1915). Friendly local hangout w. good Irish beers. Open nightly.

Muddy Waters (dwntwn), 8301 Oak Ave. (866-7174). Excellent live music (mostly blues) in a relaxed, youthful atmosphere; open nightly.

Mulate's (dwntwn), 201 Julia St. (522-1492). Authentic Cajun music and dancing nightly. Also commendable rest. Fiery food and boisterous atmosphere.

Napoleon House (dwntwn), 500 Chartres St. (524-9752). Comfortable, intimate bar serving very good cocktails and fast meals (muffuletta sandwiches). The period decor is of guaranteed authenticity (see "Historic Buildings," above). Open nightly.

Old Absinthe Bar (dwntwn), 400 Bourbon St. (525-8108). In the 1920s it was a speakeasy; now it's an excellent club offering rhythm and blues; the biggest stars appear here regularly. Very popular locally. Open nightly.

Old Absinthe House (dwntwn), 240 Bourbon St. (523-3181). The oldest (1806) and best-known bar in the Vieux Carré, its walls papered with thousands of visiting cards from patrons around the world. Always crowded, but don't fail to pay your respects (see "Historic Buildings," above). Open nightly.

Palm Court Jazz Café (dwntwn), 1204 Decatur St. (525-0200). Popular jazz club–rest. offering live jazz and R&B Wed–Sun. Very decent Créole food. Pleasant atmosphere. Open nightly.

Pat O'Brien's (dwntwn), 718 St. Peter St. (525-4823). The piano bar is noisy, but there's a pretty, shaded courtyard. The cocktails are good (try a "Hurricane"). Open nightly until 4am. The busiest bar in the French Quarter.

Pete Fountain's (nr. dwntwn), in the Hilton Hotel (see "Accommodations," above) (523-4374). New Orleans jazz by the renowned clarinettist Pete Fountain. Open Tues–Sat.

Preservation Hall (dwntwn), 726 St. Peter St. (523-8939). The principal shrine of New Orleans jazz. No refreshments. Concerts nightly. (See "Historic Buildings," above).

Snug Harbor (dwntwn), 626 Frenchmen St. (949-0696). Very good modern-jazz club just outside the French Quarter. Also rest. Open nightly.

Tipitina's (nr. dwntwn), 501 Napoleon Ave. (897-3943). Rhythm and blues, jazz, Cajun music; very far from smart, but definitely amusing. Very popular locally. 15 min. from dwntwn. Open nightly. Also rest.

NEARBY EXCURSIONS

☀☖ **LAKE PONTCHARTRAIN** (north of the city, reached via Pontchartrain Expwy. and West End Blvd. or by Elysian Fields Ave.): A saltwater lake 40 by 25 mi. (64 by 40km) in extent, and nowhere more than 20 ft. (6m) deep. Ideal for fishing, water sports, and swimming, with many inviting beaches. Scenic drive along Lake Shore Dr. and Hayne Blvd. And don't miss the ☀🔍 **Lake Pontchartrain Causeway,** a spectacular over-water toll road opened in 1969, whose two separate but parallel highways run 24 mi. (39km) from one shore of the lake to the other. This is the longest highway bridge in the world, and a riveting sight.

FARTHER AFIELD

🔍 **CAJUN COUNTRY** (420 mi./672km r.t. via U.S. 90W, U.S. 167N, U.S. 190E, La. 1S, and U.S. 90E): After two centuries, the Cajun country still has some 400,000 French-speaking inhabitants, descendants of the Acadian colonists expelled from Canada by the British in 1755. (The word *Cajun* was originally written "Acadian," and referred to the people of the former French territories in Canada; local pronunciation modified it first to "Cadian," then to "Cagian," and finally to the present "Cajun.")

You begin your tour at **Houma,** capital of Terrebonne Parish (a parish is the Louisiana equivalent of a county), an old fishing port specializing in shellfish and dubbed "the Venice of America." Visit the ☖ **Southdown Plantation,** a hybrid of Greek Revival and Victorian traditions built in the latter part of the 19th century and now a museum of Cajun history; it's on La. 311W (504/851-0154), and open daily. Then on to **Morgan City,** an important shrimping harbor, and headquarters for offshore oil exploration. Here you should see the **Swamp Gardens,** a strange marshy botanic garden with foot trails (Heritage Park). On your way to **New Iberia,** founded, as its name indicates, during the Spanish supremacy in Louisiana, stop off at ☀🔍 **Oaklawn Manor Plantation** in Franklin, a sumptuous 1830s dwelling in lovely gardens on Bayou Têche; you'll find it on U.S. 90 (318/828-0434); open daily. There are several other attractions worth stopping for at New Iberia: the pretty Bouligny Plaza at the town's center; **Shadows-on-the-Têche,** 317 E. Main St. (318/369-6446), open daily, a fine 1834 classical revival plantation house; **Avery Island,** birthplace of Tabasco, a big salty island where you should look for ☀🔍 **Jungle Gardens,** a riot of azaleas, camellias, and tropical plants as well as a wildlife refuge for migratory birds, on La. 329; open daily. Another extraordinary garden nearby is **Live Oak Gardens** on La. 14 in Jefferson Island, open daily; the moss-overgrown trees for which it is named are more than a century old.

Your next stop will be at ※ **St. Martinville,** the most French of Cajun towns, renowned for its "butcher's festival" the Sun before Mardi Gras. Founded in 1760 by those Acadian immigrants whose tribulations inspired Longfellow to write his *Evangeline,* this charming little town straight out of old France was once known as "little Paris" because of its splendidly worldly way of life. There is a fine ⚲ **Church of St. Martin of Tours** at 103 Main St., with memorabilia of Louis XVI and Marie Antoinette.

Nine miles (14km) north is ※ **Lafayette,** capital of the new Acadia, a busy commercial center almost half of whose inhabitants are French-speaking. Visit the **Lafayette Museum** at 1122 Lafayette St. (318/234-2208), open Tues–Sun, in what used to be the home of Alexandre Mouton, the first governor of Louisiana (1836); also the interesting **Acadian Village** on U.S. 167 (318/981-2364), open daily, with its scrupulously restored 19th-century buildings. A local festival you should try to catch is the ⚖⚖ **Acadian Festival** in mid-Sept: two days of music and culinary delights. For further information, contact the LaFayette Convention & Visitors Commission, Willow at Evangeline Thrwy. (318/232-3808).

Now you proceed to ⚲ **Opelousas,** another center of the Acadian influence in Louisiana, with its charming antebellum houses and its museum dedicated to Jim Bowie, a hero of the Battle of the Alamo, who lived for a time in this area: **Jim Bowie Museum,** U.S. 190W and Academy St. (318/948-6263), open Mon–Fri.

On your way back to New Orleans, visit **Baton Rouge,** the state capital (see "Plantation Country," below), making a detour to take in ※⚖⚖ **Madewood Plantation House** on La. 308 near Napoleonville (504/369-7151), an 1846 plantation that is one of the best preserved in the entire South, open daily.

Allow four or five days for this trip, which will give you a good idea of this little "France in the Southland," little known but extremely picturesque. If you'd like to learn more about the defense of the French language in Cajun country, and cultural activities in the area, contact **Codofil,** 217 W. Main St., Lafayette, LA 70501 (318/262-5810).

Where to Stay En Route

IN LAFAYETTE 💰💰 **Best Western Acadiana,** 1801 W. Pinhook Rd., Lafayette, LA 70508 (318/233-8120; toll free, see Best Western). 300 rms. Modern, friendly hotel. **I**

💰💰 **Lafayette Hilton and Towers,** 1521 Pinhook Rd., Lafayette, LA 70508 (318/235-6111). 328 rms. Big, modern 15-story glass tower. **I–M**

💰 **La Quinta Motor Inn,** 2100 NE Evangeline Thrwy., Lafayette, LA 70501 (318/233-5610). 139 rms. Conventional but comfortable motel. **I**

💰 **Motel 6,** 2724 NE Evangeline Thrwy., Lafayette, LA 70501 (318/233-2055). 101 rms. New budget motel. **B**

IN NEW IBERIA 💰💰 **Holiday Inn,** 2915 Abbedille St., New Iberia, LA 70560 (318/367-1201). 180 rms. A Holiday Inn modern style. **B–I**

💰 **Best Western,** 2714 Highway 14, New Iberia, LA 70560 (318/364-3030). 103 rms. Well-run classical motel. **B**

Where to Eat En Route

IN BREAUX BRIDGE 🍴🍴 **Mulate's,** 325 Mills Ave. (La. 94) (318/332-4648). Breakfast/lunch/dinner daily. AE, MC, V. Excellent Cajun food. Dancing. Truly a local institution. **I–M**

IN HENDERSON 🍴🍴 **Robin's,** La. 352 (318/228-7594). Lunch/dinner daily. AE, CB, DC, MC, V. One of the best places to eat in Cajun country. **I**

IN LAFAYETTE 🍴🍴 **Café Vermilionville,** 1304 Pinhook Rd. (318/237-0100). Lunch/dinner Mon–Fri, jazz brunch Sun. AE, MC, V. The oldest (1800) rest. in Lafayette, w. excellent Cajun food. **I–M**

🍷🍷 **Don's Seafood,** 301 E. Vermilion St. (318/235-3551). Lunch/dinner daily. AE, CB, DC, MC, V. Very good Cajun-style fish and broiled steak. **I**

🍷 **Randol's,** 2320 Kaliste Saloom Rd. (318/981-7080). Lunch/dinner daily. MC, V. The place is famous for crab. **I**

🔭🔭 GULF COAST, FROM NEW ORLEANS TO MOBILE, ALABAMA (330 mi./528km r.t. via I-10E, Miss. 607S,

U.S. 90E, Miss. 163S, Miss. 188N, and I-10W): Fine shorescapes and historic seafaring towns make this trip a natural extension of your visit to New Orleans.

You begin with a dive into the future at the ☀🔭 **J. C. Stennis National Space Technology Laboratories** (601/688-2370), NASA's second-largest research center, where all space-vehicle engines are tested. It's near Pearlington at Exit 2 from I-10; open daily. Then take a scenic ocean drive along I-90 through the beach resorts of **Bay St. Louis, Pass Christian,** and **Long Beach,** with their luxurious seaside homes once thronged by rich southern families, and on to **Gulfport** and its celebrated **Marine Life Aquarium,** in the Small Craft Harbor (601/864-2511), open daily.

Don't miss the excursion to ☀ **Gulf Islands National Seashore** and a visit to ☀🔭 **Old Fort Massachusetts,** an imposing defense work constructed 1859–66. It was on these islands, the cradle of French-speaking civilization in the southern U.S. from 1699 to 1753, that in 1721 there disembarked 80 "casket girls," who came from France with their dowries and their trousseaux to ensure that Louisiana should not remain unpopulated. Fort Massachusetts was used for a while as a prisoner-of-war camp for Confederate soldiers during the War Between the States. You reach it from Gulfport on the *Pan American Clipper,* Small Craft Harbor (601/864-1014); it's open daily mid-May through Aug.

Drive on to the lovely 🔭 **home of Jefferson Davis,** president of the Confederacy, on W. Beach Blvd. in Beauvoir (601/388-1313), now a museum, open daily. Nearby, at 🔭 **Biloxi,** a very busy shrimp-and-oyster port founded by the French in 1699, there are many lovely old houses standing in stunning tropical gardens. The town also has beaches so magnificent that in summer it becomes a much-sought-after resort.

Farther east, at 🔭 **Pascagoula** with its "singing river" (the Pascagoula River gives off a strange sound, something like a swarm of bees, particularly on summer and fall evenings), visit the Old Spanish Fort (1718), which in spite of its name was built by the French, and is splendidly preserved; it's at 4602 Fort St. (601/769-1505), and is open daily.

At the end of your journey you'll have enough time for a detailed inspection of ☀🔭🔭 **Mobile,** with its old neighborhoods full of fine colonial houses in the French style, and gardens where the azaleas bloom Feb–Apr; look for these around Church St., de Tonti Sq., and Old Dauphinway. See Fort Condé, built by the French in 1724, at 150 S. Royal St., open daily; the Cathedral of the Immaculate Conception at Dauphin St. at Clairborne St., an imposing Greek Revival basilica dating from 1835, open daily; Oakleigh, a magnificent antebellum mansion which derives its name from the centuries-old oaks in its very lovely gardens, 350 Oakleigh Place at Savannah St. (205/432-1281), open daily; and the majestic battleship ☀ **U.S.S. Alabama,** covered with glory from World War II and the Korean War, which lies at anchor opposite the harbor, on Battleship Pkwy. via the George C. Wallace Tunnels (205/433-2703), open daily. For further information, contact the **Mobile Tourism & Travel Dept.,** 150 S. Royal St. (205/434-7304).

On the way back to New Orleans, make a detour via ☀ **Bellingrath Gardens**

and Home, 20 mi. (32km) south of Mobile, to see its sumptuous gardens planted with hundreds of different varieties of flowers, including 250,000 azaleas, some of which were brought from France in 1754; it's on Bellingrath Hwy. at Mon Louis (205/973-2217), open daily. Near ⚓ **Dauphin Island,** a well-known resort town, on August 5, 1864, was fought the sea battle that led to the blockade of Mobile Bay by a Union fleet under the command of Adm. David G. Farragut. Visit Fort Gaines, captured by Union troops on August 23, 1864. Wonderful fine-sand beaches and a bird sanctuary.

This is a very full four- to five-day trip.

Where to Stay En Route

IN BILOXI 🍽🍽**Treasure Bay,** 1980 W. Beach Blvd., Biloxi, MS 39531 (601/388-6610). 264 rms. Comfortable luxury hotel on the ocean. **I–M**

IN MOBILE 🍽🍽🍽 **Adam's Mark Hotel,** 64 Water St., Mobile, AL 36602 (205/438-4000; toll free 800/444-2326). 375 rms. Ultramodern 28-floor tower. **M–E**

☼🍽🍽 **Malaga Inn,** 359 Church St., Mobile, AL 36602 (205/438-4701). 40 rms. Charming 1862 home designated as a historic monument. **I**

Where to Eat En Route

IN BILOXI ☼🍽🍽 **Mary Mahoney's Old French House,** Rue Magnolia and Rue Water (601/374-0163). Lunch/dinner Mon–Sat. Créole and Cajun specialties in a charming upper-class home dating from 1737. **I–M**

🔭 **PLANTATION COUNTRY** (285 mi./456km r.t. via U.S. 90W, La. 18W, La. 1N, U.S. 61N, La. 66N, La. 10E, La. 68S, U.S. 61S, La. 30S, La. 75E, La. 44S, U.S. 61S, and La. 48S): Settled from the beginning of the 18th century by planters, wealthy Créole gentry of French or Spanish origin who exported to Europe the cotton, tobacco, rice, and indigo raised by armies of slaves, the lower Mississippi Valley still displays its garland of luxurious plantations as silent witness of an urbane, elegant past. Your three-day journey through some of the finest plantations in Louisiana begins with a visit to ☼🔭 **Oak Alley Plantation,** on La. 18 at Vacherie (504/523-4351), open daily. Built in 1839 by a rich French sugar planter, Jacques Telesphore Roman, it has been called "the queen of Louisiana plantations" because of its elegant Doric design and the extraordinary span of 300-year-old oak trees that overshadow its main driveway.

Then on to ☼🔭 **Nottoway Plantation,** on La. 1 at White Castle (504/545-2730), open daily. With 64 rooms, this is the largest plantation home in the Southland, built in a gracious blend of Italianate and Greek Revival styles, with a double staircase in the hallway, an impressive ballroom, and a columned front (c. 1859).

As you pass, admire the **Plaquemine Locks** on Main St. at Plaquemine, huge locks built at the beginning of the 20th century with a lookout tower rising above the Mississippi (504/687-3560), open Tues–Sun. Then La. 1 takes you on to ☼ **Baton Rouge,** the capital of Louisiana. Take a look at "Catfish Town," a huge, picturesque covered market in what were once warehouses along the Mississippi, now with dozens of shops and restaurants; it's on Government St. on the River Front (504/346-8888), open daily. You should also see the ⚓ **State Capitol,** dominated by its massive 450-ft. (135m) tower built in 1932 with stone and marble from many countries; from its summit there's an all-around view of the city. It's at Riverside Mall and Spanish Town Rd. (504/342-7317), open daily. Two museums you should see are the ⚓ **Louisiana Arts and Science Center,** occupying a splendid old railroad station no longer in use, at 100 S. River Rd. (504/344-5272), open Tues–Sun; and the ⚓ **Louisiana State University Rural**

Life Museum, where you'll find a score of buildings and craftsmen's workshops from the 19th century, at 6200 Burden Lane at the junction of I-10 (504/765-2437), open Mon–Fri.

Drive on to ※⚓ **Port Hudson Battlefield,** on U.S. 61, 14 mi. (22km) north of Baton Rouge, scene of the longest (and one of the bloodiest) sieges of the Civil War, where 6,800 Confederate troops held off 30,000–40,000 Union soldiers from May 23 to July 9, 1863. Observation towers, museum (504/654-3775). Open daily.

A little farther north, stop at ※ **St. Francisville,** with its charming old houses dating from the day when this little town, built on a ridge overlooking the river, was an important staging point for traffic traveling the Mississippi between New Orleans and Natchez. In the countryside around are many very beautiful plantations, including the 1830 ※▵▵ **Greenwood Plantation,** regarded as the most perfect example of the southern colonial style of architecture; many movies have been made here. It's on Highland Rd. (504/655-4475), open daily. Also ⚓ **Myrtles Plantation,** dubbed "America's Most Haunted House," with its fine wrought-iron balustrade running the whole length of the veranda, on U.S. 61 (504/635-6277), open daily; ※▵▵ **Rosedown Plantation,** built in 1835, one of Louisiana's most sumptuous antebellum homes, standing in superb formal gardens in the French style, on La. 10 (504/635-3332), open daily; and ⚓ **Asphodel Plantation,** built 1820–33, the setting for the Paul Newman/Joanne Woodward movie *The Long Hot Summer,* on La. 68 (504/654-6868), open Mon–Fri.

After returning to Baton Rouge, your route follows the curves of the Mississippi and brings your journey to a close with visits to five of Louisiana's most famous plantations. These are, in order:

※▵▵ **Houmas House Plantation,** on La. 942 at Burnside (504/473-7841), open daily, a sugar plantation built in 1840 in splendid Greek Revival style, with beautiful antique furniture.

▵ **Tezcuco Plantation,** on La. 44 in Darrow (504/562-3929), open daily, a lovely building with wrought-iron-trimmed galleries, ornate friezes, and medallions, now designated as a historic monument.

※▵▵ **San Francisco Plantation,** La. 44 at Garyville (504/535-2341), open daily, an elegant 1856 Gothic Revival plantation house with a magnificent grand staircase and ornate interior decoration.

Finally we come to ※⚓ **Destrehan Plantation,** on La. 48 at Destrehan (504/764-9315), open daily, the oldest intact plantation in the Mississippi Delta.

This itinerary is expressly designed for those who love vivid glimpses of the past; don't miss it.

Where to Stay En Route

IN BATON ROUGE ♟♟♟ **Crown Sterling Suites,** 4914 Constitution Ave., Baton Rouge, LA 70808 (504/924-6566). 224 suites. Very modern suites-only hotel. **M**

※♟♟ **Mt. Hope Plantation,** 8151 Highland Rd., Baton Rouge, LA 70802 (504/766-8600). 2 rms. Authentic Old South–style plantation house built in 1817. **M**

IN JACKSON ※♟♟ **Asphodel Plantation,** La. 68, Jackson, LA 70748 (504/654-6868). 18 rms. A luxurious 1830s antebellum home. **I–M**

♟ **Glencoe,** La. 68, Jackson, LA 70748 (504/629-5387). 12 rms. Fine example of late Victorian Gothic. **M**

IN ST. FRANCISVILLE ※♟♟ **Cottage Plantation,** U.S. 61, St. Francisville, LA 70775 (504/635-3674). 5 rms. Typical Louisiana plantation house dating from 1795. **M**

℗ **St. Francisville Inn,** 118 N. Commerce St., St. Francisville, LA
70775 (504/635-6502). 8 rms. Big Victorian home in a very
handsome park. **I**

IN WHITE CASTLE ☼⚘⚘ **Nottoway Plantation,** La. 1, White Castle, LA 70788
(504/545-2730). 13 rms. Louisiana's largest plantation house, and one of its
most beautiful. Also very good rest. **E–VE**

Where to Eat En Route

IN BATON ROUGE 🍷🍷🍷 **Chalet Brandt,** 7655 Old Hammond Hwy. (504/927-
6040). Lunch Thurs, dinner Mon–Sat. The fish soup and the veal w. chanterelle
and morel mushrooms are among the successful achievements of this excellent
Continental/Créole rest. and its Swiss chef-owner Charles Brandt. Pretty interi-
or. **M–E**

IN BURNSIDE 🍷 **The Cabin,** La. 44 and La. 22 (504/473-3007). Lunch daily,
dinner Thurs–Sat. Excellent fish and Créole dishes in former slave quarters a century and a half old. **I**

IN DONALDSONVILLE ☼🍷 **Lafitte's Landing,** Sunshine Bridge Service Rd. (504/
473-1232). Lunch/dinner Tues–Sun. Remarkable Créole and Cajun food by
chef John Folse. The building on the bank of the Mississippi, dating from 1797,
may once have belonged to pirate Jean Lafitte. **I–M**

CHAPTER 16

FLORIDA'S EAST COAST♊

□ □ □

Florida's Atlantic coast, where swimsuits and suntan oil hold undisputed sway, unrolls its hundreds of miles of white sand beaches and coconut trees from **Amelia Island** on the Georgia border in the north to **Miami** in the south. It has remarkably comprehensive facilities to offer vacationers, often at very attractive prices—as witness the arrival every year of some 25 million U.S. tourists (mostly from the big cities of the Northeast), more than a million Canadians, and some hundreds of thousands of visitors from Europe and Latin America. In reality, the great beach resorts of **Daytona Beach** (famous for its auto races), the elegant and upscale **Palm Beach,** the more easy-going **Fort Lauderdale** and **Pompano Beach, Boca Raton,** and **Miami** (see Chapter 19 on Miami) form a single conglutination of hotels—one of the largest in the world.

But Florida (discovered by Juan Ponce de León on Easter Sunday 1513, it owes its name to this accident of the calendar—the Spanish for "Easter Sunday" is *Pascua Florida*) is more than a string of immaculate beaches, wild mangrove swamps, or a network of fish-filled lakes and rivers. It boasts some of America's most popular tourist attractions. **St. Augustine,** the oldest city in the United States, was founded by the Spanish conquistador Don Pedro Menéndez de Áviles in 1565—just 19 years after Sir Walter Raleigh's short-lived attempt to settle Roanoke Island, "the lost colony," and 55 years before the British colonists disembarked from the *Mayflower* at Plymouth. **Marineland** is the oldest marine zoo in the world and one of the most popular. The **Kennedy Space Center,** headquarters of the astronauts, has been internationally famous since the moon landing and the first shuttle launches. **Lake Okeechobee,** one of the largest freshwater lakes in the country (30 by 40 mi./60 by 48km), is a paradise for bass and catfish fishermen. **Daytona Beach** is a popular resort, invaded every year by tens of thousands of car-racing enthusiasts come to watch the Daytona 24 Hours, the Daytona 500, and other famous races.

Finally, less than two hours by car from the Atlantic coast, three of the world's greatest theme parks await the tourist: the Magic Kingdom of **Walt Disney World;** its twin attraction, **Epcot,** whose 18-story steel-and-concrete sphere has become the new symbol of the state of Florida; and **Disney–MGM Studios,** and **Universal Studios Florida,** two movie theme parks which blend filmmaking with backstage studio tours and ride-through, walk-through attractions. And let's not forget **Sea World,** an enormous marine zoo where sharks, killer whales, and dolphins frolic in the public gaze (see Chapter 18 on Orlando).

BASIC FACTS: State of Florida. Area codes: 904 (St. Augustine and Daytona Beach), 305 or 407 (all others). Time zone: eastern. Founded in: 1565 (St. Augustine), 1567 (first Spanish garrison at Miami). Distance from Amelia Island to Miami Beach: approx. 400 mi. (640km).

CLIMATE: Florida is well known for its sunshine. Winter is the ideal time for a visit—also the most crowded and expensive. The sun shines continually and the mercury swings between 60° and 68°F (16° and 20°C)—perfect for walking, even if too cool for swimming. Summer is hot and humid, with short but frequent tropical downpours, not to speak of prowling hurricanes. Spring and autumn are consistently sunny and pleasant, justifying the legend on Florida auto registration plates which reads "The Sunshine State."

ARRIVAL & TRANSIT INFORMATION

AIRPORTS: There are seven major airports that act as gateways to the Florida east coast:
Daytona Beach Regional Airport (DAB), 5 mi. (8km) west of Daytona.
Fort Lauderdale–Hollywood International Airport (FLL), 6 mi. (9.5km) south of Fort Lauderdale.
Jacksonville International Airport (JAX), 15 mi. (24km) north of Jacksonville.
Melbourne Regional Airport (MLB), 1 mi. (2km) NW of Melbourne.
Miami International Airport (MIA) (see Chapter 19 on Miami).
Orlando International Airport (MCO) (see Chapter 18 on Orlando).
West Palm Beach International Airport (PBI), 3 mi. (5km) west of West Palm Beach.

AIRLINES: Fort Lauderdale—American (toll free 800/433-7300), Continental (toll free 800/525-0280), Delta (toll free 800/221-1212), KLM (toll free 800/374-7747), Northwest (toll free 800/225-2525), TWA (toll free 800/221-2000), United (toll free 800/241-6522), and USAir (toll free 800/428-4322).
Jacksonville—American (toll free 800/433-7300), Continental (toll free 800/525-0280), Delta (toll free 800/221-1212), TWA (toll free 800/221-2000), United (toll free 800/241-6522), and USAir (toll free 800/428-4322).
Miami—See Chapter 19 on Miami.
Orlando—See Chapter 18 on Orlando.

CAR RENTAL: To cover this large area adequately you'll need a car, and besides, rental rates are comparatively reasonable. In addition to the many car-rental agencies in **Miami** and **Orlando** (see those chapters for details), rentals are available at the following gateway cities (at airport locations unless otherwise noted):
Fort Lauderdale—Avis (toll free 800/331-1212); Budget, 1501 N. Federal Hwy. (toll free 800/527-0700); Dollar (toll free 800/800-4000); Hertz (toll free 800/654-3131); and National (toll free 800/227-7368).
Jacksonville—Avis (toll free 800/331-1212); Budget (toll free 800/527-0700); Hertz (toll free 800/654-3131); National (toll free 800/227-7368); and Thrifty (toll free 800/367-2277).

TRAIN: In addition to the Amtrak stations in Miami and Orlando (see those chapters for details), there are stations/stops along the Florida east coast at 200 SW 21st Terrace, Fort Lauderdale; 3570 Clifford Lane, Jacksonville; and Tamarind Ave. and Datura St., West Palm Beach (all toll free 800/872-7245).

INTERCITY BUSES: In addition to the Greyhound offices in Miami and Orlando (see those chapters for details), there are Florida east coast offices at 138 S. Ridgewood Ave., Daytona Beach; 513 NE 3rd St., Fort Lauderdale; 10 N. Pearl

St., Jacksonville; 100 Malaga St. at King St., Saint Augustine; and 100 Banyan St., West Palm Beach (all toll free 800/231-2222).

INFORMATION, TOURS & SPECIAL EVENTS

TOURIST INFORMATION: For general information on the region, write or call the **Florida Division of Tourism,** 126 W. Van Buren St., Tallahassee, FL 32399 (904/487-1462). For more specific information, when in the area, contact:

Boca Raton Chamber of Commerce, 1800 N. Dixie Hwy., Boca Raton, FL 33432 (407/395-4433).

Cocoa Beach Tourism & Convention Council, 400 Fortenberry Rd., Cocoa Beach, FL 32952 (407/459-2200).

Daytona Beach Convention & Visitors Bureau, P.O. Box 910, Daytona Beach, FL 32115 (904/255-0415; toll free 800/854-1234).

Fort Lauderdale Convention & Visitors Bureau, 200 E. Las Olas Blvd., Suite 1500, Fort Lauderdale, FL 33301 (305/765-4466).

Grant (see the Melbourne Chamber of Commerce).

Hallandale Chamber of Commerce, P.O. Box 249, Hallandale, FL 33008 (305/454-0541).

Jacksonville Convention & Visitors Bureau, 3 Independent Dr., Jacksonville, FL 32202 (904/798-9148; toll free 800/733-2668).

Jensen Beach Chamber of Commerce, 1910 SE Jensen Beach Blvd., Jensen Beach, FL 33457 (407/334-3444).

Kissimmee Convention & Visitors Bureau, 1925 E. Irlo Bronson Memorial Hwy. (P.O. Box 422-007), Kissimmee, FL 32742 (407/847-5000).

Melbourne Chamber of Commerce, 1005 E. Strawbridge Ave., Melbourne, FL 32901 (407/724-5400).

Miami Department of Tourism & Conventions (see Chapter 19 on Miami).

Orlando Area Chamber of Commerce (see Chapter 18 on Orlando).

Palm Beach Chamber of Commerce, 45 Coconut Row, Palm Beach, FL 33480 (407/655-3282).

Pompano Beach Chamber of Commerce, 2200 E. Atlantic Blvd., Pompano Beach, FL 33062 (305/941-2940).

St. Augustine Chamber of Commerce, One Riberia, St. Augustine, FL 32084 (904/829-5681).

Titusville Chamber of Commerce, 2000 S. Washington Ave. (P.O. Box 2767), Titusville, FL 32780 (407/267-3036).

West Palm Beach Chamber of Commerce, 401 N. Flagler Dr., West Palm Beach, FL 33401 (407/833-3711).

GUIDED TOURS: For the Miami and Orlando areas, see the chapters on those cities. In other localities on the Florida east coast, consult the local *Yellow Pages* under "Sightseeing."

SPECIAL EVENTS: For exact dates of the events listed below, check with the chambers of commerce and visitors bureaus listed above under "Tourist Information."

Boca Raton
    High Goal Polo (every Sun Jan to early Apr): A popular polo championship event.

Cocoa Beach
National Surfing Tourneys (Easter wknd).

Daytona Beach
Auto Races: Daytona 24 Hours (early Feb); Daytona 500 (mid-Feb), the nation's big stock-car race. Call 904/253-7223 for schedule.
AMA Motorcycle Races (Mar).
Stock-car Races: Pepsi 400 (July 4).
Florida International Festival (late July): Orchestral and chamber concerts, recitals.

Fort Lauderdale
Winterfest and Boat Parade (Dec): Three weeks of cultural, artistic, and sporting events culminating in a spectacular parade on the water.

Grant
Seafood Festival (Feb): A gigantic fish, shellfish, and seafood blowout, attracting 50,000 participants to a glutton's festival that lasts 48 hr.

Hallandale
Seminole Indian Tribal Fair (Feb): A Native American cultural event in which every tribe in North America participates. Dance displays, handcraft exhibition, ethnic cooking. For information, call 305/584-0400.

Jacksonville
Florida National Jazz Festival (Oct): One of the country's best-known modern-jazz events.

Jensen Beach
Turtle Watch (June–July, every evening): Visitors may see enormous (220 –440 lb./100–200kg and up) sea turtles crossing the sand to lay their eggs at the water's edge.

Kissimmee
Silver Spurs Rodeo (third wknd in Feb, and July): For lovers of the real Old West.
Florida State Air Fair (early Oct): Complete with parachute jumps, aerobatics, etc.

Melbourne Beach
Turtle Crawl (June–Aug): Thousands of newly hatched baby turtles struggling to reach the sea. Spectacular.

Pompano Beach
Boat Parade (Dec): The boats are decorated and illuminated.

St. Augustine
Cross & Sword (Mon–Sat mid-June to Aug): A musical celebration of the founding of the city.
Days in Spain (first wknd in Sept): Processions, shows, and fiesta in honor of the first Spanish conquistadors.

Titusville
Valiant Air Command Air Show (early Apr): The world's greatest air show, featuring exclusively World War II combat planes. Aerobatics, ground displays, etc. Call 407/268-1941 for information.

West Palm Beach
Silver Sailfish Derby (mid-Jan to early Feb): Big-game fishing championship events.

SPORTS: The east coast of Florida plays host to five major-league **baseball** teams at their spring training camps (Feb–Mar):

Atlanta Braves, Municipal Stadium, West Palm Beach (407/683-6100).

Los Angeles Dodgers, Holman Stadium, Vero Beach (407/569-4900).

Montréal Expos, Municipal Stadium, West Palm Beach (407/684-6801).

New York Mets, Thomas J. White Stadium, Port St. Lucie (407/871-2115).

New York Yankees, Fort Lauderdale Stadium, Fort Lauderdale (305/776-1921).

DEEP-SEA FISHING: Almost three million visitors go deep-sea fishing in Florida every year, from Fernandina Beach to Key West on the Atlantic coast (sea bream, mackerel, barracuda, swordfish), and from Naples to Pensacola along the Gulf of Mexico (blue marlin, tarpon). Rates for fully equipped big-game fishing boats are around $350 for a half day (6 hr.) or $450 for a full day (10 hr.). For names and phone numbers of charter fishing boats, check with chambers of commerce or visitors' bureaus listed above under "Tourist Information."

Recommendations

Jacksonville: Mike Hargrove (904/225-2789)

Fort Lauderdale: Bahiamar Charter Boats (305/525-9180)

A NORTH TO SOUTH ITINERARY

The section of this guide devoted to the east coast of Florida has been organized as an itinerary, starting at Amelia Island and ending in Miami Beach, a distance of almost 400 miles (640km). Key towns such as Jacksonville, Daytona, Orlando, Palm Beach, Fort Lauderdale, and Miami are linked by air, bus, and train, and car rentals are available everywhere (at reasonable rates, particularly off-season).

Distances Down the Florida East Coast

From	To	Distance
Amelia Island	Fort Caroline	30 mi. (48km)
Fort Caroline	Jacksonville	14 mi. (22km)
Jacksonville	St. Augustine	40 mi. (64km)
St. Augustine	Fort Matanzas	15 mi. (24km)
Fort Matanzas	Marineland of Florida	5 mi. (7km)
Marineland of Florida	Daytona Beach	32 mi. (51km)
Daytona Beach	Kennedy Space Center	52 mi. (83km)
Kennedy Space Center	Orlando	46 mi. (75km)
Orlando	Sea World	13 mi. (21km)
Sea World	Walt Disney World	7 mi. (11km)
Epcot	Cypress Gardens	34 mi. (54km)
Cypress Gardens	Cocoa Beach	97 mi. (155km)
Cocoa Beach	Patrick AFB	5 mi. (8km)
Patrick AFB	Vero Beach	48 mi. (74km)
Vero Beach	Fort Pierce	14 mi. (22km)
Fort Pierce	Jensen Beach	19 mi. (31km)
Jensen Beach	Lake Okeechobee	39 mi. (62km)
Lake Okeechobee	Jupiter Beach	33 mi. (52km)
Jupiter Beach	Palm Beach	18 mi. (28km)
Palm Beach	Boca Raton	28 mi. (45km)
Boca Raton	Pompano Beach	8 mi. (12km)
Pompano Beach	Fort Lauderdale	7 mi. (11km)
Fort Lauderdale	Hollywood	8 mi. (12km)
Hollywood	Miami Beach	17 mi. (26km)

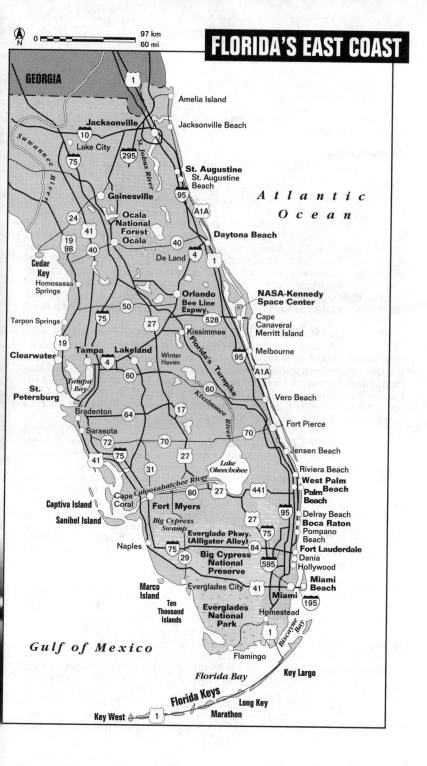

FLORIDA'S EAST COAST

0   97 km
N   60 mi

GEORGIA

1

Amelia Island

Jacksonville
10
Lake City
295
Jacksonville Beach

75

St. Augustine
St. Augustine
Beach
95

Gainesville
A1A

Ocala
National
Forest
Ocala
40

24
41
19
98
40
De Land
4
1

Daytona Beach

Cedar
Key
Homosassa
Springs

A t l a n t i c
O c e a n

Orlando
Bee Line
Expwy.
528
Kissimmee

NASA-Kennedy
Space Center
Cape
Canaveral
Merritt Island

Tarpon Springs
75
50
27

19
Tampa **Lakeland**
4
Winter
Haven
95
Melbourne
A1A

Tampa
Bay
60

St.
Petersburg
Bradenton
64
60

Kissimmee River

Vero Beach

Sarasota
72
70
70

Fort Pierce

41
75
17
27

Jensen Beach

31
Lake
Okeechobee

Riviera Beach
West Palm
Palm **Beach**
Beach

Cape
Coral
Caloosahatchee River
80
27
441
95
Delray Beach
Boca Raton
Pompano
Beach

Captiva Island
Fort Myers
Big Cypress
Swamp
27
75

Sanibel Island
Everglade Pkwy.
(Alligator Alley)
84
Fort Lauderdale
Dania
595
Hollywood

Naples
75
29
Big Cypress
National
Preserve
41
Miami
Beach

Marco
Island
Everglades City
Miami
195

Ten
Thousand
Islands
Everglades
National
Park
Homestead

1

Gulf of Mexico

Biscayne
Bay

Flamingo

Florida Bay
Key Largo

Florida Keys
1
Long Key
Key West
1
Marathon

AMELIA ISLAND: By turns French (a group of Huguenots, or French Protestants, led by Jean Ribaut landed here in 1562), Spanish, British, Mexican, and American—and often a stronghold for pirates and other adventurers—this small island is not on the beaten track, but it offers 14 mi. (20km) of magnificent beaches, and is a fisherman's dream. For further information, contact the **Fernandina Beach Chamber of Commerce**, 102 Centre St. (P.O. Box 472), Fernandina Beach, FL 32035 (904/261-3248).

Where to Stay

Amelia Island Plantation, 3000 First Coast Hwy. (on Fla. A1A, 6 mi./10km south of Fernandina Beach), Amelia Island, FL 32034 (904/261-6161; toll free 800/874-6878). 513 rms or studios. A/C, cable color TV, in-rm movies. Mini-apartments for two to eight people. AE, CB, DC, MC, V. Free parking, 18 pools, 27 tennis courts, three golf courses, putting green, health club, private beach, horseback riding, fishing, bicycles, sauna, six rests. (including Amelia Inn), coffee shop, bars, rm svce, hrdrsr, beauty parlor, grocery, crib $20. *Note:* Luxurious resort complex in a rustic setting on the ocean, with 4 mi. (6km) of magnificent beaches and more than 1,300 acres (526ha) of dunes and woods. A paradise for lovers of sports and fresh air. Spacious rms or mini-apartments w. kitchenettes and private patios. Reception and svce on the impersonal side—but still one of the best hotels in the Southeast. Interesting vacation packages. **E–VE** (apartments), but lower rates off-season.

FORT CAROLINE: Fort Caroline was erected in 1564 at the mouth of the St. John's River by a party of 300 French colonists under the leadership of René de Laudonnière. A few months later the fort was taken by the Spaniards and its entire garrison (except for 70 women and children) put to the sword. In 1568 the French launched a reprisal raid against the Spaniards and burned the fort to the ground. It was partially rebuilt by the British, and achieved its moment of glory during the Civil War. It's located at 12713 Fort Caroline Rd., Jacksonville (904/641-7155); open daily.

JACKSONVILLE: With its 650,000 inhabitants and cluster of ultramodern skyscrapers along the banks of the St. John's River, Jacksonville is one of the Southeast's busiest ports, handling large shipments of automobiles from Japan and Korea. Very busy airport. In terms of economic growth it ranks 16th among major American cities. The **Mayport Naval Base**, at the mouth of the river, is one of the navy's most important, and the home port of the aircraft carriers U.S.S. *Forrestal* and U.S.S. *Saratoga*. With an area of 840 sq. mi. (2,180km²), Jacksonville is the largest city in area in the U.S. The **Cummer Gallery of Art**, 829 Riverside Ave. (904/356-6857), is an interesting art museum with a collection of 700 pieces of Meissen (Dresden) china; open Tues–Sun.

Where to Stay

Omni Hotel, 245 Water St., Jacksonville, FL 32202 (904/355-6664; toll free, see Omni). 354 rms, A/C, color TV, in-rm movies. AE, CB, DC, MC, V. Valet parking $8, pool, health club, rest., bar, rm svce, free crib. *Note:* Latest of the area's luxury palaces—16 stories of austerely postmodern glass and steel at the edge of the St. John's River. Forms part of the new Enterprise Center, a huge complex of office buildings, stores, and rests. Spacious, well-equipped rms w. refrigerators; elegant interior, ultra-professional svce. Strategically located in the heart of dwntwn Jacksonville. Business clientele. Two VIP floors. **I–M**

Marina Hotel at St. John's Place, 1515 Prudential Dr., Jacksonville, FL 32207 (904/396-5100). 321 rms, A/C, color TV, in-rm movies. AE, CB, DC, MC, V. Free parking, pool, tennis courts, rest., bar, rm svce, boutiques. *Note:* five-story hotel located on the banks of the St. John's River. Comfortable rms w. private balconies, the best overlooking the river. Efficient reception and svce. Well located. Group and conventioneer clientele. **I–M**

🍸 **EconoLodge,** 5221 University Blvd. W., Jacksonville, FL 32216 (904/737-1690). 183 rms, A/C, color TV, in-rm movies. AE, CB, DC, MC, V. Free parking, pool, tennis court, rest., free crib. *Note:* Typical up-to-date motel 10 min. from dwntwn along I-95. Comfortable, homelike rms, friendly svce, inviting grdn. Ideal if you're driving. **B–I**

🍸 **Motel 6,** 6107 Youngerman Circle, Jacksonville, FL 32244 (904/777-6100). 126 rms, A/C, cable color TV. AE, DC, MC, V. Free parking, pool, free crib. *Note:* Ideal for motorists; a good value. **B**

IN NEARBY JACKSONVILLE BEACH 🍸🍸 **Jacksonville Beach Ocean Front Hotel,** 1617 N. 1st St., Jacksonville Beach, FL 32250 (904/249-9071; toll free, see Holiday Inns). 150 rms, A/C, color TV, in-rm movies. AE, CB, DC, MC, V. Free parking, pool, sauna, health club, two tennis courts, coffee shop, bar, free crib. *Note:* Standard vacation hotel w. direct access to beach. Functional rms w. balconies and refrigerators; impersonal reception and svce. Typical Holiday Inn style. Tourist clientele. **B–I**

Where to Eat

🍷🍷 **Café on the Square,** 1974 San Marco Blvd. (904/399-4848). A/C. Dinner only, Mon–Sat; closed hols. AE, CB, DC, MC, V. *Specialties:* pasta dishes, catch of the day, steak. *Note:* Popular dwntwn rest. housed in the oldest building in San Marco Sq. (1926). Very decent fare, moderately priced. Entertainment Tues–Sat. Outdoor dining. *American.* **I**

🍷🍷 **Crawdaddy's,** 1643 Prudential Dr. (904/396-3546). A/C. Lunch/dinner daily, brunch Sun. AE, CB, DC, MC, V. *Specialties:* chicken Cajun, jambalaya, seafood gumbo. *Note:* This fisherman's-hut setting will fulfill your wildest dreams of the exotic; the New Orleans cooking is excellent, and the svce attentive. There's dancing too, and the place has a big local following, so resv. are advisable. *Créole.* **I**

🍷 **Patti's,** 7300 Beach Blvd. (904/725-1662). A/C. Lunch Tues–Fri and Sun, dinner nightly; closed Thanksgiving, Dec 25. AE, DC, MC, V. *Specialties:* fresh pasta, lasagna, chicken parmigiana. *Note:* Completely authentic little *trattoria;* food ditto, if a little unimaginative. Locally popular. *Italian.* **I**

🔭 **ST. AUGUSTINE:** The oldest city in the U.S., founded in 1565 by Don Pedro Menéndez de Áviles, this bastion of Spanish colonialism retains a few interesting monuments (scrupulously restored) from its troubled past.

The Sights

🔆 **Castillo de San Marcos National Monument,** Castillo Dr. and Menendez Ave. (904/829-6506): Impressive fortress built in 1672—the oldest masonry fortification in the country—which commands Matanzas Bay. Its 13-ft.-thick (4m) walls make it a weighty symbol of the Spanish military presence in Florida. Splendidly restored. Open daily.

Casa del Hidalgo, St. George and Hypolita Sts. (904/824-2062): Preserves for us the atmosphere of 17th-century St. Augustine. Open daily.

Fountain of Youth, 155 Magnolia Ave. and William St. (904/829-3168): Supposed site of the "Fountain of Youth" discovered by the sailors of Ponce de León in 1513, when they first landed in Florida—making it the first place in North America on which Western Europeans set foot. A $4.50 admission charge entitles you to a cup of water from the original spring. Open daily.

☼ **Lightner Museum,** Cordova and King Sts. (904/824-2874):
Occupying the 300 rooms of the former Alcazar Hotel built in 1888, this museum, bequest of a wealthy Chicago publisher, displays a collection of 19th-century art objects. Open daily.

Oldest House, 14 St. Francis St.: The oldest house (1703) still standing in the city. Open daily.

Oldest Store Museum, 4 Artillery Lane: Amusing 19th-century bazaar, with more than 100,000 period objects on display. Open daily.

☼ **Nombre de Dios Mission,** San Marco Ave.: Site of the country's oldest mission, where the first mass was celebrated in 1565; its huge stainless-steel cross, the highest in the U.S., rises 192 ft. (60m).

Zorayda Castle, 83 King St. (904/824-3097): A replica, constructed in 1833, of the Alhambra of Granada in Spain. Open daily.

And, especially, don't forget **San Augustin Antiguo** (Old St. Augustine), around St. George St., with its picturesque cobbled alleyways and balconied houses made of the local building material, "coquina," a conglomerate of seashells and sand.

A visit to this city is a must. The **Visitor Information Center** is at 12 Castillo Dr. (904/825-1000).

Where to Stay

☼ ♀ 👍 👍 **Ponce de Leon Resort,** 4000 Ponce de Leon Blvd. (U.S. 1), St.
Augustine, FL 32085 (904/824-2821; toll free 800/228-2821). 200 rms, A/C, cable color TV. AE, CB, DC, MC, V. Free parking, pool, 11 tennis courts, golf course, rest., bar, free airport limo, free crib. *Note:* Excellent value 5 min. by car from the beach or the Old City. Enormous, attractive rms w. balconies. Svce efficient and w. a smile. Interesting American Plan and vacation packages. The golfer's or tennis-player's dream. **I–M**

👍 **Comfort Inn,** 1111 Ponce de Leon Blvd., St. Augustine, FL
32084 (904/824-5554; toll free, see Choice). 84 rms, A/C, color TV, in-rm movies. AE, CB, DC, MC, V. Free parking, pool, crib $5. *Note:* A new motel near St. Augustine's Old City. Comfort and facilities up to snuff; cordial reception and svce. Very good value. **I–M,** but lower rates off-season.

♀ **Monterey,** 16 Avenida Menendez, St. Augustine, FL 32084
(904/824-4482). 59 rms, A/C, cable color TV. AE, CB, DC, MC, V. Free parking, pool, adj. coffee shop, free airport limo, crib $7. *Note:* Modest but well-run little motel opposite the Castillo San Marcos. The best rms overlook the bay. Interesting vacation packages. **B–I,** but lower rates off-season.

Where to Eat

🍴 **Raintree,** 102 San Marco Ave. (904/824-7211). A/C. Din-
ner only, nightly; closed Dec 25. AE, CB, DC, MC, V. *Specialties:* broiled fresh tuna w. mango butter, scampi Raintree, brandy peppered steak, broiled Maine lobster, catch of the day. Good homemade desserts (try the chocolate terrine). *Note:* St. Augustine's best rest., in a charming old Victorian-style house, offering simple but tasty food prepared with the finest ingredients. On fine days it's pleasant to eat out in the grdn. Flawless svce, elegant atmosphere; resv. advisable. *Continental.* **M**

🍸 **Columbia,** 98 St. George St. (904/824-3341). A/C Lunch/
dinner daily, brunch Sun. AE, CB, DC, MC, V. *Specialties:* black-bean soup, paella, red snapper Alicante. *Note:* Charming early 20th-century *mesón* in the Castilian style; Spanish- and Cuban-inspired food at very refreshing prices. Agreeable background music, friendly svce. In the heart of St. Augustine's historic quarter. A local favorite since 1905. *Spanish/Latin American.* **I**

🔔 **FORT MATANZAS:** The Spanish name means "Fort of the
Massacres," and on the site of this fortified bastion built in 1740 (restored in 1924), more than 250 French Huguenots were indeed massa-

cred by the Spaniards in 1565. Reached by boat from the Visitor Center; open daily. For information, call 904/471-0116.

    📛 **MARINELAND OF FLORIDA** (on Fla. A1A) (904/471-1111): The world's oldest marine zoo, opened in 1938, where hundreds of sharks, barracuda, porpoises, dolphins, moray eels, and the like may be watched through portholes in two enormous pools. Florida's other great sea zoo, Sea World at Orlando (see below), is more up-to-date and definitely more spectacular. Nevertheless, this one is worth going out of your way for. Open daily.

    📛 **DAYTONA BEACH:** A very popular beach resort (particularly among surfers), with 23 mi. (38km) of sand along which cars may drive freely (though slowly) at low tide; there are also dune buggies for hire.

    The town is also famous for its auto and stock-car races: the Daytona Sunbank 24 Hours and Daytona 500 in Feb, the Pepsi 400 on July 4, etc. The 📛 **Daytona International Speedway,** 1801 Volusia Ave. (904/254-2700), where these events are held, can accommodate 125,000 spectators, and has parking for 35,000 cars! Open to visitors year round.

    You should also see the 📛 **Museum of Arts & Sciences,** 1040 Museum Blvd. (904/255-0285), where a fine collection of Latin American and Caribbean art is displayed in a building of ultramodern design. Open Tues–Sun.

    And take in the 📛 **Ponce de Leon Inlet Lighthouse,** south of the town. Dating from 1884, the 175-ft. (53m) tower has been converted into an original kind of maritime museum (904/761-1821); open daily.

Where to Stay

    🏩🏩🏩 **Hilton Daytona,** 2637 S. Atlantic Ave., Daytona Beach, FL 32018 (904/767-7350; toll free, see Hilton). 215 rms, A/C, color TV, in-rm movies. AE, CB, DC, MC, V. Free parking, pool, two tennis courts, rest. (The Islander), coffee shop, bars, rm svce, free crib. *Note:* Rather ponderous modernist structure, but very spacious, comfortable rms w. refrigerators and their own balconies. Every facility of a great resort hotel. Efficient svce. Caters to groups and conventions. There is a laudable rest. on the top floor. **M–E,** but lower rates off-season.

    🏩🏩 **Ramada Resort,** 2700 N. Atlantic Ave., Daytona Beach, FL 32018 (904/672-3770; toll free, see Ramada). 383 rms, A/C, cable color TV. Free parking, two pools, rest., bar, rm svce, free crib. *Note:* Modern 12-story tower on the beach; the Holiday Inn style at its friendliest and most comfortable. Group clientele. Interesting vacation packages. **I–M,** but lower rates off-season.

    🏩 **Days Inn Oceanfront Central,** 1909 S. Atlantic Ave., Daytona Beach, FL 32018 (904/255-4492; toll free, see Days Inns). 196 rms, A/C, cable color TV. AE, DC, MC, V. Free parking, pool, rest., bar, free crib. *Note:* Comfortable, unpretentious family motel directly on the beach. Rms w. private patios, the best overlooking the ocean. No alcoholic beverages in the rest. **I,** but lower rates off-season.

    YMCA/YOUTH HOSTEL The **Daytona Beach International Hostel,** 140 S. Atlantic Ave., Daytona Beach (904/258-6937). Comfortable youth hostel (100 beds), almost on the beach.

Where to Eat

    🍸 **Aunt Catfish's,** 4009 Halifax Dr. at the west end of Port Orange Bridge (904/767-4768). A/C. Lunch/dinner daily, brunch Sun; closed Thanksgiving, Dec. 25. AE, CB, DC, MC, V. *Specialties:* shell-fish, catch of the day, steak, roast beef au jus, good homemade desserts.

Note: Extra-fresh seafood and honest red meat at reasonable prices. Conventional seafaring decor; relaxed atmosphere. Locally popular. *Steak/Seafood.* **B–I**

CAFETERIA/FAST FOOD Morrison's, 200 N. Ridgewood (904/258-6396). Lunch/dinner daily (till 8:30pm). AE, MC, V. *Specialties:* fried shrimp, fish of the day, roast beef. *Note:* Honest cafeteria food.

☼☼ ♠♠♠ **KENNEDY SPACE CENTER:** Originally known as Cape Canaveral, the **John F. Kennedy Space Center** is America's largest interplanetary target range. Since the first rocket (a converted German V2) was launched in 1950, and including the most recent space shuttles, more than 2,300 devices have been launched into space from this NASA facility, which employs more than 25,000 technicians on its narrow seaside peninsula. It was from here that, on July 16, 1969, *Apollo XI* carried Neil Armstrong, Michael Collins, and Edward Aldrin on their historic mission—Armstrong and Aldrin were the first men to set foot on the moon.

Double-decker buses take guided tours to the giant hangar where space shuttles and space vehicles are assembled; this **Vehicle Assembly Building,** 512 ft. (160m) high, is the largest of its kind in the world. Other highlights of the tour are the astronaut training center and several launching zones. Interesting space museum (**Spaceport USA**) with a five-story-screen, 42- by 50-ft. (13- by 15m) IMAX theater. **Astronauts Memorial,** with the names of the 14 astronauts who have died on duty.

Open daily except Dec 25 and certain launch days. For information on timetables, call 407/452-2121. Don't miss this one. Inside Florida there's a toll-free number (800/432-2153) that will give you advance information on launchings.

Where to Stay in the Area

♠♠♠ **Hilton,** 1550 N. Atlantic Ave., in Cocoa Beach, FL 32931 (407/799-0003; toll free, see Hilton). 300 rms, color TV, in-rm movies. AE, CB, DC, MC, V. Free valet parking, pool, rest., bar, rm svce, free crib. *Note:* Ultramodern six-story hotel on the ocean, w. huge, comfortable rms. VIP floor. Efficient svce. 15 min. by road from Kennedy Space Center. Caters mostly to tourists. **M–E**

♠♠ **Holiday Inn,** 260 E. Merritt Island Causeway, in Merritt Island, FL 32952 (407/452-7711; toll free, see Holiday Inns). 128 rms, A/C, cable color TV, in-rm movies. AE, CB, DC, MC, V. Free parking, pool, tennis court, rest. (Island Oasis), bar, rm svce, nightclub, free crib. *Note:* Modern, functional Holiday Inn–style motel on the banks of the Indian River; ideal for visitors to Cape Kennedy, which is 15 min. away by car. **I–M,** but lower rates off-season.

♠ **Travelodge Apollo,** 3810 S. Washington Ave. (U.S. A1A), in Titusville, FL 32780 (407/267-9111; toll free, see Travelodge). 104 rms, A/C, cable color TV. AE, CB, DC, MC, V. Free parking, pool, rest., bar, crib $5. *Note:* On the Indian River only 15 min. by car from Cape Kennedy; offers very acceptable standards of comfort, a cordial reception, and a good view of the launch pads. Very good value overall. **B–I**

♠ **Motel 6,** 3701 N. Atlantic Ave., in Cocoa Beach, FL 32931 (407/783-3103). 104 rms, A/C, cable color TV. AE, DC, MC, V. Free parking, pool, free crib. *Note:* Unsurpassed value a quarter of an hour from Cape Kennedy; ideal for motorists. Facing beach; no rest. or bar. **B**

IN NEARBY MELBOURNE (25 mi./40km south) ♠♠♠ **Radisson Suite Oceanfront,** 3101 N. Fla. A1A, Indialantic, FL 32903 (407/773-9260; toll free, see Radisson). 166 suites, A/C, color TV, in-rm movies. AE, CB, DC, MC, V. Free parking, pool, health club, sauna, rest., two bars, rm svce. *Note:* Luxury hotel of original postmodern design at the water's edge. Spacious and remarkably comfortable suites w. their own balconies overlooking the ocean. New facilities; excellent svce; 30 min. by car from Kennedy Space Center. Very acceptable rest. Clientele of well-to-do vacationers. **M–E,** but lower rates off-season.

Days Inn, 4455 New Haven Ave., Melbourne, FL 32904 (407/724-5840; toll free, see Days Inns). 161 rms, A/C, cable color TV. AE, DC, MC, V. Free parking, pool, free breakfast, free crib. *Note:* A great place at very reasonable prices. Inviting rms w. balconies; grdn w. small artificial lake. 45 min. by car from the Kennedy Space Center. Very good value. No alcoholic beverages permitted in rest. **B–I,** but lower rates off-season.

Where to Eat in the Area

Mango Tree, 118 N. Atlantic Ave. (407/799-0513). A/C. Dinner only, Tues–Sun; closed hols. AE, MC, V. *Specialties:* grouper Margarette, veal Française, filet mignon béarnaise, chocolate macadamia-nut cake. *Note:* Housed in one of the first cottages in Cocoa Beach. An indoor fish pond, orchid greenhouse, and butterfly collection make this an attractive place to eat well-prepared meats and seafood. Resv advised. *Continental.* **I–M**

Bernard's Surf, 2 S. Atlantic Ave., Cocoa Beach (407/783-2401). A/C. Lunch/dinner daily; closed Dec 25. AE, CB, DC, MC, V. *Specialties:* red snapper, steak, shrimp Louie, catch of the day. *Note:* A very large menu and a softly romantic atmosphere of an evening are the two main attractions of this rest.; the food is commendable but unimaginative. Resv. advised. *Steak/Seafood.* **I**

IN NEARBY MELBOURNE BEACH **Nick's Steakhouse,** 903 Oak St. (407/723-6659). A/C. Dinner only, nightly. AE, CB, DC, MC, V. *Specialties:* clams on the half shell, crab, pompano en papillote, pilapia, roast beef, steak Delmonico broiled over a wood fire. Praiseworthy wine list. *Note:* Inviting, congenial steakhouse. Excellent broiled dishes; intimate atmosphere; good svce. Resv. advisable. *Steak/Seafood.* **I**

ORLANDO (46 mi./74km west of the Kennedy Space Center): The tourist capital of Florida, with a thronged airport and a multitude of hotels, motels, and restaurants. Very near Walt Disney World and other major attractions. For detailed tourist information, see Chapter 18.

SEA WORLD (61mi./95km SW of the Kennedy Space Center): Enormous, ultramodern sea zoo. Shark aquarium with glass tunnel for sightseers; trained orcas (killer whales) and dolphins, sea lions, giant turtles, etc. Waterskiing displays. A spectacle that beggars description— and attracts almost three million tourists yearly. Open daily. For detailed information, see Chapter 18 on Orlando.

WALT DISNEY WORLD (71 mi./115km SW of the Kennedy Space Center): The largest, and most famous, theme park in the world, visited by more than 300 million people since it opened in 1971. With an area of 28,000 acres (11,335ha)—twice the size of Manhattan Island— this is an amusement park on a planetary scale. It's open every day, 12 months a year. For detailed tourist information, see Chapter 18 on Orlando.

EPCOT (71 mi./115km SW of the Kennedy Space Center): This other child of the Walt Disney family, opened in 1982, is a 21st-century theme park with many of the attractions of a World's Fair. Designed to accommodate 25 million visitors a year, it cost $1 billion to build—2½ times more than Walt Disney World and four times more than Disneyland. Connected by monorail to Walt Disney World, this futuristic amusement park, overshadowed by its 18-story steel-and-concrete sphere, is also worth the trip to Florida all by itself. For detailed tourist information, see Chapter 18 on Orlando.

DISNEY-MGM STUDIOS (71 mi./115km SW of the Kennedy Space Center): This newest (1989) member of the Walt Disney family offers you a guided tour through the studios, where you'll be shown workshops, sets, and all kinds of special effects, including earthquakes and tidal waves. You can also watch work in progress on movies, TV series, and cartoons. Fascinating. For detailed tourist information, see Chapter 18 on Orlando.

UNIVERSAL STUDIOS FLORIDA (56 mi./89km SW of the Kennedy Space Center): Open in 1990, this giant movie theme park is the direct rival of its next-door neighbor Disney-MGM Studios. Containing more than 40 amazing rides, like "Back to the Future" or "E.T.," it's also a working studio making films and TV or cartoon movies. For detailed tourist information, see Chapter 18 on Orlando. Don't miss it.

CYPRESS GARDENS (101 mi./164km SW of the Kennedy Space Center): For more than a quarter of a century these magnificent tropical gardens on the shores of Lake Eloise have been one of Florida's principal tourist attractions. Underwater displays; waterskiing ballets in wonderful Esther Williams–style kitsch. Definitely worth the side trip. Open daily. For detailed tourist information, see Chapter 18 on Orlando.

COCOA BEACH: Several miles of fine beaches, celebrated for the beauty of their sunrises. A great place for surfing, big-game fishing—or picnicking while you watch the launches from the nearby Kennedy Space Center.

PATRICK AIR FORCE BASE: Display of the larger spacecraft launched from the Kennedy Space Center in front of the base's Technical Laboratory, reached on Fla. A1A. Impressive. Open daily.

VERO BEACH: Enormous, uncrowded beach, much appreciated by those in-the-know. The charming little town is liberally adorned with flowerbeds.

Where to Stay

Holiday Inn Oceanside, 3384 Ocean Dr., Vero Beach, FL 32963 (407/231-2300; toll free, see Holiday Inns). 104 rms, A/C, cable color TV, in-rm movies. AE, CB, DC, MC, V. Free parking, pool, rest., bar, rm svce, nightclub, free crib. *Note:* Holiday Inn style right on the beach. Serviceably comfortable; rms w. balconies overlooking the ocean. Good value in summer. **M,** but lower rates off-season.

Where to Eat

The Patio, 1103 Miracle Mile (Fla. 60) (407/567-7215). A/C. Lunch/dinner daily (open till 1am), brunch Sun. AE, MC, V. *Specialties:* crab au gratin, scampi, chicken marsala, filet mignon. *Note:* Some of the continental dishes are successful. The decor, as the name suggests, is Spanish inspired, and the two together make for an agreeable stop. *Continental.* **I–M**

FORT PIERCE: Between the ocean and the Indian River lies a 332-acre (135ha) nature reserve, open to the public. There are 21 mi. (30km) of beaches, surfing, swimming, saltwater fishing, and freshwater fishing in the St. Lucie River. The **St. Lucie County Museum,** at 414 Seaway Dr. (407/468-1795), is interesting; it has a reproduction of a Seminole village. Open Tues–Sun year round.

⚓ **JENSEN BEACH:** Once the pineapple capital of Florida, this popular beach resort now specializes in big-game and freshwater fishing. Every evening during June and July, huge sea turtles up to 500 lb. (227kg) crawl onto the beaches of **Hutchinson Island** to lay their eggs. Tourists and residents come at night with flashlights to watch the sight.

Where to Stay

🛏🛏 **Courtyard Marriot** (formerly Sheraton Inn), 10978 S. Ocean Dr., Hutchinson Island, FL 34957 (407/229-1000; toll free, see Marriot). 100 rms, color TV, in-rm movies. AE, CB, DC, MC, V. Free parking, pool, beach, concierge, free crib. *Note:* Modern eight-story building on the beach w. exterior glass elevator. Comfortable rms (some w. balconies). Good value overall. **M–E,** but lower rates off-season.

Where to Eat

🍷 **Conchy Joe's Seafood,** 3945 NE Indian River Rd. (407/334-1130). A/C. Lunch/dinner daily; closed Thanksgiving, Dec 25. AE, MC, V. *Specialties:* local seafood, conch fritters, steak. *Note:* Very popular water-view rest. built by the Seminoles. Unpretentious nautical setting w. outdoor dining and some open fire cooking. *Seafood.* **B–I**

☀⚓ **LAKE OKEECHOBEE** (38 mi./62km SW of Jensen Beach on Fla. 76): The largest freshwater lake in Florida, with an area of 730 sq. mi. (1,890km^2). A fisherman's heaven, with perch, bream, and largemouth bass, of which 1,500 tons (1.36 million kg) are caught annually. You'll find a choice of boat rentals, motels, and campsites at **Belle Glade** and **Okeechobee.**

⚓ **JUPITER BEACH:** Several very beautiful nature reserves dedicated to birds and marine animals (**Joseph Verner Reed Wilderness Sanctuary, Hobe Sound National Wildlife Refuge,** etc.), some of which can be reached only by boat, are well worth visiting. Also the usual beach diversions. Very nearby, **Jonathan Dickinson State Park** marks the spot where the *Reformation,* carrying a group of Quaker settlers, was shipwrecked in 1696; the survivors, captured by Seminoles, succeeded in making their way back to St. Augustine, 225 mi. (360km) to the north, on foot. Perched on a bluff overlooking Jupiter Inlet, the **Jupiter Lighthouse,** first lighted in 1860, still guides ships approaching the Florida Coast. Museum (407/747-6639), open Sun only.

Where to Stay

🛏🛏🛏 **Jupiter Beach Resort,** 5 N FL A1A at Indiantown Rd., FL 33477 (407/746-2511). 193 rms, A/C, cable color TV. AE, CB, DC, MC, V. Free valet parking, pool, beach, rest., bar, nightclub, concierge, spa, tennis, bicycles, snorkeling, free crib. *Note:* A sportsman's paradise that also happens to be a luxurious resort hotel. The rooms have balconies, and the service is courteous and thoughtful. **M–E,** but lower rates off-season.

Where to Eat

🍷 **Harpoon Louie's,** 1065 Fla. A1A (407/744-1300). A/C. Breakfast Sat–Sun, lunch/dinner daily; closed Thanksgiving, Dec 25. AE, MC, V. *Specialties:* catch of the day, broiled meats. *Note:* Agreeable little rest. at the water's edge, overlooking the Jupiter Lighthouse. Simple but good food; svce w. a smile; locally popular. *American/Seafood.* **B–I**

☀︎🜄 **PALM BEACH (& WEST PALM BEACH):** This beach resort is celebrated for its royal palms, its high fashion, and its social exclusiveness; in the eyes of rich Florida vacationers it easily outshines Miami Beach. Worth Ave. and Royal Poinciana Plaza are lined with luxury boutiques. With no fewer than nine polo grounds, the town is considered the world capital for this sport—but with 110 championship courses, it's no less a paradise for golfers.

It still boasts many magnificent mansions built by 19th-century giants of finance, including that of Henry Flagler, the co-founder of Standard Oil and the builder of Florida's first trunk railroad between Daytona Beach and Key West: his 🏛🏛 **Whitehall,** a marble palace dating from 1901 with 55 opulently decorated rooms, must certainly be seen. It's at Coconut Row at Whitehall Way (407/655-2833), and is open Tues–Sun.

The richest private art collection in Florida is to be found at the 🏛🏛 **Norton Gallery of Art,** at 1451 S. Olive Ave. in West Palm Beach (407/832-5194). Included in the 4,000-piece display of Impressionist and Modernist art are works by Gauguin, Picasso, Cézanne, O'Keeffe, Hopper, Pollock, and others. The gallery also has a very impressive collection of Oriental art. Don't miss this. Open Tues–Sun.

At West Palm Beach, don't miss the 🏛 **Union Congregational Church,** at 2727 Georgia Ave. (407/832-0581), with its enormous (75- by 27-ft./23- by 8m) stained-glass window, assembled like a mosaic from 10,000 pieces of colored glass. Designed by Conrad Pick.

Going west 18 mi. (28km) along U.S. 98, you will come to 🏛 **Lion Country Safari,** on Southern Blvd. W. (407/793-1084). This modern wild-animal park covers 640 acres (260ha), and has more than 1,000 wild animals roaming free. It's open daily; visits by car only.

Where to Stay

☀︎🏛🏛🏛🏛 **The Breakers,** S. County Rd., Palm Beach, FL 33480 (407/655-6611; toll free, see Preferred). 562 rms, A/C, cable color TV. Modified American Plan in winter. AE, CB, DC, MC, V. Free parking (valet parking $7), pool, 14 tennis courts, two golf courses, beach, masseur, six rests. (including the Circle), bars, 24-hr. rm svce, nightclub, hrdrsr, boutiques, concierge. *Note:* A jewel among U.S. hotels since 1926. Imposing Italianate palace w. white marble colonnades, Flemish tapestries, and crystal chandeliers. Roomy, comfortable (though slightly somber) rms w. minibars, superb English-style grdns, and direct access to beach. Reception and svce of the highest quality (in season, the hotel has about 1,100 on staff). The Circle is an excellent rest. Comprehensive sports facilities. Interesting wknd packages. Very upscale clientele. One of the 12 best hotels in the country. **VE,** but lower rates off-season.

☀︎🏛🏛🏛 **P.G.A. National Resort,** 400 Ave. of the Champions, Palm Beach Gardens, FL 33410 (407/627-2000; toll free 800/633-9150). 333 rms and mini-suites, A/C, cable color TV. AE, CB, DC, MC, V. Valet parking $5, three pools, 19 tennis courts, five golf courses, private beach, boats, bicycling, health club, sauna, racketball, croquet, putting green, five rests. (including Explorers), three bars, rm svce, hrdrsr, concierge, free crib. *Note:* Paradise for tennis players and golfers at the edge of a large lake, set in 2,360 acres (955ha) of park and grdn. Modern and very comfortable. Spacious minisuites w. refrigerators and private balconies; also fully equipped villas. Attentive svce. 15 min. from the sea by car. Trendy group clientele. **E–VE,** but lower rates off-season.

🏛🏛 **Best Western Palm Beach Lakes** (formerly the Ramada Inn), 1800 Palm Beach Lakes Blvd., West Palm Beach, FL 33401 (407/683-8810; toll free, see Best Western). 200 rms, A/C, color TV. AE, CB,

DC, MC, V. Free parking, pool, golf course, rest., valet svce, free crib. *Note:* Relatively modern, functional motel w. large rms and refrigerators. Group clientele. Good overall value. **I–M,** but lower rates off-season.

℗ **Days Inn,** 2300 W. 45th St., West Palm Beach, FL 33407 (407/689-0450; toll free, see Days Inns). 238 rms, A/C, cable color TV. AE, CB, DC, MC, V. Free parking, pool, putting green, rest., free airport limo, free crib. *Note:* Representative motel, 10 min. from dwntwn Palm Beach. Comfortable rms; quite friendly reception and svce. Rms for nonsmokers. Good value. **I–M,** but lower rates off-season.

Where to Eat

🍷🍷🍷 **Café l'Europe,** 150 Worth Ave., on the Esplanade (407/655-4020). A/C. Lunch Mon–Sat, dinner nightly; closed hols. AE, CB, DC, MC, V. Jkt. (at dinner). *Specialties:* scallops St-Jacques au Noilly, roast duck w. cabbage confit, capon breast sautéed w. leeks and chanterelles, Florida snapper in potato crust w. garlic sauce, roast lamb en croûte. Very good desserts; remarkable wine list. *Note:* A trendy Palm Beach favorite in a warm and romantic setting of paneling, mirrors, and brasswork. Contemporary elegant cuisine; svce (in tuxedos) impeccable. Pleasant classical background music. On its way to becoming one of the greatest rests. on the East Coast. Resv. necessary. *Continental.* **E–VE**

🍷🍷 **Charley's Crab,** 456 S. Ocean Blvd. (407/659-1500). A/C. Lunch/dinner Mon–Sat, brunch Sun. AE, CB, DC, MC, V. Jkt. *Specialties:* Mediterranean fish chowder; mussels à la Muer; pasta pagliara; catch of the day broiled, poached, sautéed, or Cajun style; red snapper; pompano en papillote; luscious homemade desserts. Excellent wine list. *Note:* Florida branch of Detroit's famous Joe Muer's Seafood; no lover of fish or shellfish should miss it. Absolutely fresh produce cooked to perfection; beautifully situated looking out on the ocean, but unimaginatively decorated. Attentive, courteous svce. Reserve ahead, especially at dinner. Valet parking. *Seafood.* **M–E**

🔆🍷 **Testa's Restaurant,** 221 Royal Poinciana Way (407/832-0992). A/C. Breakfast/lunch/dinner daily (until 12am); closed Dec–May 15. AE, CB, DC, MC, V. *Specialties:* stone crabs (in season), steak, seafood, Italian dishes, strawberry pie. *Note:* Family owned since 1921, Testa's has become a landmark. Basically Italian, the cuisine does well also w. native seafoods. Beautiful glass-roofed tropical grdn patio or sidewalk café. Good svce. Resv. advised. *Italian/Seafood.* **I–M**

IN NEARBY MANALAPAN (8 mi./12km) 🍷🍷🍷 **The Dining Room,** in the Ritz-Carlton Palm Beach, 100 S. Ocean Blvd., Manalapan (407/533-6000). A/C. Breakfast/lunch/dinner daily, brunch Sun. AE, CB, DC, MC, V. Jkt. *Specialties:* escargot empañada; duck confit; Wisconsin duck cooked two ways w. orange glaze and wild-berry coulis; roasted veal tenderloin w. caramelized chestnuts, walnuts, and apples; cumin seed–crusted North Atlantic salmon w. eggplant marmalade; white chocolate cheesecake. Large wine list fairly priced. *Note:* One of the newest and most remarkable hotel dining rooms of Florida. Superbly inventive, French-inspired modern cuisine and impeccable svce. Elegant 18th-century decor. Overlooks the ocean. Truly a great place. Resv. preferred. *Continental.* **E–VE**

🏮 **DELRAY BEACH:** A popular resort community as well as a commercial flower-growing center, Delray Beach boasts one of the state's most beautiful and unusual museums, the 🔷🔷 **Morikami Museum of Japanese Art,** 4000 Morikami Park Rd. (407/495-0233), open Tues–Sun. Standing in a 56-acre (23ha) park complete with lakes, waterfalls, Japanese gardens, and a bonsai collection, the enchanting museum offers a comprehensive overview of Japanese culture and folk art, from dolls to painting and traditional furniture.

☀☖ **BOCA RATON:** Charming, and rapidly growing, beachfront city. Seat of **Florida Atlantic University,** with 13,000 students, and the research laboratories of IBM. The **Boca Raton Resort & Club** (see "Where to Stay," below), a magnificent 1930s luxury hotel, is worth the side trip by itself.

Where to Stay

☀♟♟♟♟ **Boca Raton Resort & Club,** 501 E. Camino Real, Boca Raton, FL 33432 (407/395-3000; toll free 800/327-0101). 963 rms, A/C, color TV, in-rm movies. Modified American Plan. AE, CB, DC, MC, V. Valet parking $8, four pools, 29 tennis courts, two golf courses, putting green, marina, waterskiing, health club, sauna, seven rests., eight bars, 24-hr rm svce, hrdrsr, boutiques, free crib. Free jitney to the beach. *Note:* A Spanish baroque luxury hotel from the 1930s is here surprisingly wedded to a modern 27-floor tower overlooking Lake Boca Raton. The best rms (those in the older section) look out on 540 acres (220ha) of lush tropical grdns; the tower rms, w. balconies, face the lake. Exemplary svce, but the group clientele is often quite obtrusive. Remarkable sports facilities and interesting golf/tennis packages. VIP floor. One of the great hotels of the East Coast. **VE,** but lower rates off-season.

♟ **Best Western University Inn,** 2700 N. U.S. 1, Boca Raton, FL 33431 (407/395-5225; toll free, see Best Western). 90 rms, A/C, cable color TV. AE, CB, DC, MC, V. Free parking, pool, adj. rest., bar, free breakfast, free crib. *Note:* A classic small motel, a few steps from the campus of Florida Atlantic University and IBM's Research Laboratory. Huge, comfortable rms; agreeable svce. Good value off-season. **I–M,** but lower rates off-season.

IN NEARBY DEERFIELD BEACH (2 mi./3.2km south) ♟ **La Quinta,** 351 W. Hillsboro Blvd., Deerfield Beach, FL 33441 (305/421-1004). 130 rms, A/C, color TV, in-rm movies. AE, CB, DC, MC, V. Free parking, pool, rest. adj., free crib. *Note:* New motel nr. the Deerfield Beach Country Club, pleasantly designed in Spanish Colonial style. Comfortable, well-laid-out rms, svce w. a smile. 5 min. from the beach; good value. If you're driving, there's direct access to I-95. **I–M**

Where to Eat

♟♟♟♟ **La Vieille Maison,** 770 E. Palmetto Park Rd. (407/391-6701). A/C. Dinner only, nightly (two sittings, at 6:30 and 9:30pm); closed hols. AE, CB, DC, MC, V. Jkt. *Specialties:* Maine lobster bisque, escargot gratin, crevettes au Pernod, filet of pompano w. pecans, grilled venison chops, tarte tatin, lemon crêpe soufflé. Superb wine list. *Note:* Almost perfect modern French cuisine by talented chef Richard Ruize. Sumptuous Mediterranean-style 1920s villa w. a patio; very beautiful cut flowers and antique furniture. Refined atmosphere. Valet parking. Resv. required. *French/Continental.* **E** (prix fixe).

♟♟ **Maxaluna,** Crocker Center, 21150 Military Trail (407/391-7177). A/C. Lunch Mon–Fri, dinner daily; closed Thanksgiving, Dec 25. AE, CB, DC, MC, V. *Specialties:* linguine w. steamed clams, spinach fettuccine w. squab breast and wild mushrooms, stuffed veal chop, prawns wrapped in zucchini, roast squab w. pine nuts, yellowfin tuna w. caramelized onions. Menu changes regularly. Fine, reasonably priced wine list. *Note:* Maxaluna, which likes to describe itself as a "Tuscan rôtisserie," is one of the most interesting new rests. in Florida, serving light, imaginative California-Italian food and using only the finest local produce (particularly seafood). Pretty contemporary decor, but atmosphere rather noisy. Hardworking svce. Yuppie clientele. Resv. highly advisable. *Italian/American.* **I–M**

IN NEARBY LIGHTHOUSE POINT (6 mi./9km) ♟♟ **Cafe Arugula,** 3150 N. Federal Hwy., Lighthouse Point (305/785-7732). A/C. Dinner only, nightly. AE, CB, DC, MC, V. *Specialties:* jumbo lump crab cakes, spicy shrimp taco, pecan-crusted yellowtail snapper, rack of lamb, raspberry crème brûlée. *Note:* Good fresh seafood dishes w. a hint of Latin and Caribbean cuisine. Outstanding desserts. Quiet setting and obliging svce. Resv. strongly advised. *American.* **I–M**

POMPANO BEACH: Perhaps because of its 7 mi. (11km) of beach, this resort has for some time been experiencing the fastest growth in tourism on Florida's Gold Coast. At the **Goodyear Blimp Visitor Center,** 1500 NE Fifth Ave. (305/946-8300), you may pay your respects close up to the famous Goodyear blimp, which is based here every year Nov–May. Open daily.

Where to Stay

Palm Aire Resort & Spa, 2501 Palm Aire Dr., Pompano Beach, FL 33069 (305/972-3300; toll free 800/327-4960). 195 rms, A/C, color TV, in-rm movies. AE, CB, DC, MC, V. Free parking, six pools, three golf courses, six tennis courts, squash, health club, sauna, three rests., bars, rm svce, hrdrsr, crib free. *Note:* Luxurious, comfortable convention hotel standing in 1,800 acres (730ha) of parkland and blooming grdns right on the beach; commodious rms w. private patios (some w. kitchenettes). Hot springs. Family and Modified American Plan (MAP) packages worth looking into. Very good svce and some of the most comprehensive sports facilities in Florida. A wonderful place for lovers of sports and stressed businesspeople. **E–VE,** but lower rates off-season.

Motel 6, 1201 NW 31st Ave., Pompano Beach, FL 33069 (305/977-8011). 127 rms, A/C, cable color TV. AE, DC, MC, V. Free parking, pool, free crib. *Note:* Up-to-date comfort at a modest price, 20 min. from dwntwn. One of the best values in the region. Ideal if you're driving. **B**

Where to Eat

Café Max, 2601 E. Atlantic Blvd. (305/782-0606). A/C. Dinner only, nightly. AE, CB, MC, V. *Specialties:* caviar pie, grilled wahoo w. chilled mango relish and honey-roasted bananas, onion-crusted snapper, mesquite-grilled veal chop, luscious desserts. The menu changes regularly. Excellent wine list. *Note:* The setting has a "California casual" look, w. an open kitchen where chef Oliver Saucy prepares South Florida nouvelle cuisine at his best. First-rate svce. Locally popular. Resv. advised. *American.* **M**

FORT LAUDERDALE: Nicknamed "The Venice of America" because of its 300 mi. (480km) of canals and the 35,000 boats moored there year round, Fort Lauderdale is indeed a tourist attraction of Venetian caliber. Its 23 mi. (36km) of beaches, hundreds of hotels, motels, and rooming houses with a total of 25,000 rooms, 2,500 restaurants of all kinds and in all price ranges, the fashionable boutiques of Las Olas Blvd., one of the world's biggest pleasure-boat harbors (the Bahia Mar Yacht Basin, to which every pleasure sailor would like to make a pilgrimage)—all these attractions have made this busy, friendly city one of the leading tourist resorts in Florida. It doesn't hurt, either, that with 3,000 hours of sunshine annually, Fort Lauderdale holds the U.S. record.

For boat trips down the New River and around the Intracoastal Waterway, try **Jungle Queen Cruises,** Bahia Mar Yacht Basin, Fla. A1A (305/462-5596), which also offers dinner cruises daily, year round.

You should also see ☀️☖ **Butterfly World,** 3600 W. Sample Rd., Coconut Creek (305/977-4400). This theme park opened in 1988 contains thousands of live butterflies from around the world in its giant screened aviaries with tropical gardens and waterfalls. Open daily.

Don't miss the splendid, new **Museum of Art,** a masterpiece by architect Edward Larrabee Barnes, at 1 E. Las Olas Blvd. (305/525-5500), open Tues–

Sun; as well as the $50-million **Broward Center for the Performing Arts,** 624 SW 2nd St. (305/522-5334); or **Ocean World,** 1701 SE 17th St. Causeway (305/525-6611), the classic marine zoo with dozens of sea creatures, from sharks to performing dolphins, from sea lions to giant turtles. Open daily.

Where to Stay

Bonaventure Resort & Spa, 250 Racquet Club Rd., Fort Lauderdale, FL 33326 (305/389-3300; toll free 800/448-8355). 493 rms, A/C, color TV, in-rm movies. AE, CB, DC, MC, V. Valet parking, five pools, two golf courses, 23 tennis courts, health club, horseback riding, six rests. (including Renaissance), coffee shop, bars, rm svce, nightclub, hrdrsr, boutiques, concierge, free crib. *Note:* One of the best-known luxury hotels on the east coast of Florida. Its superb tropical setting, hot springs, and unrivaled sports facilities have made it a favorite of VIPs. Lavish decor and ultra-comfortable layout. Excellent svce. If you're a physical-fitness buff, this is the place for you. **E–VE,** but lower rates off-season.

Pier 66 Resort & Marina, 2301 SE 17th St. Causeway, Fort Lauderdale, FL 33316 (305/525-6666; toll free, see Preferred). 388 rms, A/C, cable color TV. AE, CB, DC, MC, V. Valet parking $6, two pools, two tennis courts, health club, sauna, marina, boats, four rests., four bars (one a revolving bar on the top floor), 24-hr. rm svce, disco, hrdrsr, free shuttle to beach, free crib. *Note:* This is Fort Lauderdale's most famous building, a great white 17-story tower overlooking the Intracoastal Waterway, topped by a revolving bar in the shape of a flying saucer; it recently underwent a $21-million facelift. Capacious rms w. refrigerators, most w. balconies or patios, and a view of the ocean or the marina. Outside glass elevator. Group clientele; efficient svce. Very comprehensive sports facilities. All in all, a very good place to stay. **E–VE,** but lower rates off-season.

Holiday Inn–Fort Lauderdale Beach, 999 N. Atlantic Blvd., Fort Lauderdale, FL 33304 (305/563-5961; toll free, see Holiday Inns). 240 rms, A/C, color TV, in-rm movies. AE, CB, DC, MC, V. Free parking, pool, rest., bar, rm svce, free crib. *Note:* A great, modern 12-story pile, Holiday Inn style, right on the ocean and very near the famous Galeria Mall w. its 150 stores and boutiques. Most rms (some w. balconies, all w. refrigerators) overlook the beach. Svce on the impersonal side. **M–E,** but lower rates off-season.

Beach Plaza Hotel, 625 N. Atlantic Blvd., Fort Lauderdale, FL 33304 (305/566-7631; toll free 800/451-4711). 43 rms, A/C, cable color TV. AE, DC, MC, V. Free parking, pool, adj. 24-hr. coffee shop, free crib. *Note:* Charming little motel right on the beach. Comfortable rms w. private patio or balcony and refrigerator, the best overlooking the pool-grdn. Friendly svce; interesting vacation packages. Good value overall. **I–M,** but lower rates off-season.

Merrimac, 551 N. Atlantic Blvd., Fort Lauderdale, FL 33304 (305/564-2345). 55 rms and suites, A/C, cable color TV. AE, CB, DC, MC, V. Free parking, pool, adj. rest. and bar. *Note:* Modest but well-maintained cluster of mini-apartments (most w. kitchenettes), w. balconies and ocean view; ideal for families. Direct access to the beach. **I–M,** but lower rates off-season.

Motel 6, 1801 Fla. 84, Fort Lauderdale, FL 33315 (305/760-7999). 108 rms, A/C, color TV, in-rm movies. AE, DC, MC, V. Free parking, pool, free crib. *Note:* Good value at an unbeatable price. **B**

IN NEARBY DANIA (5 mi./8km south) **Motel 6,** 825 E. Dania Beach Blvd. (at NE Seventh Ave.), Dania, FL 33004 (305/921-5505). 163 rms, A/C, color TV. AE, DC, MC, V. Free parking, pool, free crib. *Note:* Ideal for motorists. **B**

YMCA/YOUTH HOSTEL **Sol Y Mar/AYH,** 2839 Vistamar St., Fort Lauderdale, FL 33304 (305/566-1023). Youth hostel w. 80 beds, nr. the beach.

Where to Eat

🍷🍷🍷 **Down Under,** 3000 E. Oakland Park Blvd. (305/563-4123). A/C. Lunch Tues–Sun; dinner nightly; closed hols. AE, CB, DC, MC, V. Jkt. *Specialties:* duck confit, chicken Madagascar, red snapper, oysters Rockefeller, trout w. lump crabmeat and hollandaise sauce, Bengal chicken curry. Great Californian and French wine list. *Note:* From the amusing Victorian-rococo interior you will have a fine view of the Intracoastal Waterway and its traffic. Innovative, delicate French-inspired food w. a touch of the exotic. California wines recommended. Sometimes very noisy. Same management as La Vieille Maison in Boca Raton. Valet parking. Resv. advised. One of Florida's great rests. *Continental.* **M–E**

☼🍷🍷 **Mai Kai,** 3599 N. Federal Hwy. (305/563-3272). A/C. Dinner only, nightly (served until midnight); closed hols. AE, CB, DC, MC, V. Jkt. *Specialties:* shrimp Szechuan, lemon chicken, Peking duck, lobster pango-pango, lobster Tahiti. *Note:* The Mai Kai offers you an original selection of food, w. Cantonese and Szechuan dishes predominating, but also including excellent steaks and fabulous Polynesian cocktails (try the "Mystery Drink"). No one could ask for a more exotic decor than this Hollywood-style corner of the South Seas w. its pool, waterfall, and Siamese temple. Impeccable svce. Very popular locally. Valet parking. *Chinese/Polynesian.* **M**

🍷🍷 **Left Bank,** 214 SE Sixth Ave. (305/462-5376). A/C. Dinner only, nightly; closed Super Bowl Sunday. AE, DC, MC, V. Jkt. *Specialties:* filet of paper-thin carpaccio; seafood-stuffed philo strudel w. champagne mustard sauce; almond and macadamia nut–crusted dolphin fish w. orange coconut beurre blanc; Long Island duckling w. a black cherry, pearl onion, and Kirsch sauce; white Godiva chocolate cheesecake. *Note:* Jean-Pierre Brehier has impeccable taste as proprietor and chef, serving sophisticated and time-proven meals in a romantic, candlelit setting filled w. French furniture and antiques. Locally, one of the most popular rests., so be sure to make a resv. *French.* **M**

🍷🍷 **Il Tartufo,** 2980 N. Federal Hwy. (305/564-0607). A/C. Dinner only, nightly. AE, MC, V. *Specialties: nuova cucina* dishes. The menu changes regularly. *Note:* Chef Rino Balzano is the mastermind behind this inviting small *trattoria.* Good seafood and veal dishes, excellent risotti, and lots of creativity w. truffles have made this newcomer a winner. Svce good-natured and efficient. Resv. advised. *Italian.* **M**

🍷 **Nathan's Famous,** in the Sawgrass Mills Mall, 12801 W. Sunrise Blvd. (305/846-1394). A/C. Lunch/dinner daily (8:30am–9:30pm). No credit cards. *Specialties:* fried clams, corned beef, hot dogs, very good homemade french fries. *Note:* The sandwiches and daily specials here are praiseworthy, but no match for those at Miami Beach's Wolfie's Rascal House. Very popular, especially at lunchtime. *American.* **B**

IN NEARBY DAVIE 🍷🍷 **Armadillo Café,** 4630 SW 64th Ave. (305/791-4866). A/C. Dinner only, nightly. AE, CB, DC, MC, V. *Specialties:* corn-and-jalapeño fritters; chiles relleños stuffed w. roast corn, mushrooms, and Monterey jack; blue crab nachos; Texas tenderloin tacos; cedar-planked salmon; boneless marinated leg of lamb w. sun-dried-tomato sauce and wild-rice pancakes; mocha crème brûlée. *Note:* A local pioneer of southwestern cuisine, the Armadillo Café attracts an enthusiastic clientele from all parts of southern Florida. Casual but elegant setting w. Indian motifs and southwestern murals. Svce friendly and professional. A highly commendable place. *American.* **I–M**

IN NEARBY PORT EVERGLADES 🍷🍷 **Burt & Jack's,** Berth 23 (305/522-5225). A/C. Dinner only, nightly; closed Dec 25. AE, CB, DC, MC, V. Jkt. *Specialties:* red meats, broiled fish. *Note:* An old Spanish mission on the ocean, surrounded on three sides by water; one of the owners is actor Burt Reynolds. Wonderful broiled dishes; huge fireplaces; romantic decor w. many art objects. Resv. a must. *Steak/Seafood.* **I–M**

HOLLYWOOD: Founded in the 1920s by a California real-estate promoter (whence the name), this beach resort has always been a great commercial success. With more than 20 public courses, it's the golfer's favorite beach. See the **Seminole Indian Reservation** at 3551 N. Fla. 7 (305/583-7112), one of the last inhabited Native American villages in Florida. Handcrafts, mini-zoo, bingo hall for 1,400 people at 4150 N. Fla. 7 (305/961-4519). Open daily.

Where to Stay

Hilton–Hollywood Beach, 4000 S. Ocean Dr., Hollywood, FL 33019 (305/458-1900; toll free, see Hilton). 304 rms, A/C, cable color TV. AE, CB, DC, MC, V. Valet parking $6, pool, two tennis courts, health club, sauna, three rests. (including Silks), bar, rm svce, hrdrsr, boutiques, free crib. *Note:* Modern 10-story hotel w. direct access to the beach. Spacious, inviting rms w. balconies overlooking the ocean. Efficient, considerate svce. Group/convention clientele. VIP floor. 8 mi. (13km) from Fort Lauderdale airport. **M–E**

MIAMI BEACH: "The Pearl of Florida"! See Chapter 19 on Miami.

CHAPTER 17

TAMPA AND ST. PETERSBURG

□ □ □

This urban agglomeration of about two million people, Florida's largest after Miami, comprises two distinct cities located along the same bay. One, **St. Petersburg,** is an outward-looking vacation community. The more businesslike **Tampa,** with its glittering skyscrapers, and flourishing industries, prides itself on being the site (in 1539) of the first Spanish encampment on U.S. soil. It was from this base camp, at the mouth of the Little Manatee River, just south of Tampa, that Hernándo de Soto and his 600 companions set out on their expedition across the southeastern U.S. in an extraordinary odyssey that took them 4,800 mi. (7,700km), from Florida to Texas and Mississippi. Tampa also boasts one of the highest growth rates in the country: 53% in the last decade.

But it is not the tourist industry, buoyant though it may be, that has brought all this prosperity to Tampa. A youthful population, including many workers who have moved here from the North and a large concentration of refugees from Cuba (Tampa's **Ybor City** district is a kind of Little Havana), has contributed much. St. Petersburg, on the other hand, along with such neighboring resort towns as **Clearwater, Madeira Beach, Indian Shores,** and **Treasure Island,** is best known for its immense beaches and the beauty of its offshore islands, which draw more than a million visitors a year. Tampa, a modern, dynamic port city, puts its major industries on parade along the bay: phosphates, uranium processing, breweries, tobacco. With so large a Cuban population, Tampa could scarcely escape becoming the cigar capital of the U.S.: it turns out more than three million of them every day.

Besides the splendid deep-water bay, Tampa and St. Petersburg have two principal tourist attractions: the numberless excursions that can be made from here either into central Florida (**Walt Disney World, EPCOT, Disney–MGM Studios, Cypress Gardens, Sea World,** etc.) or along the shores of the Gulf of Mexico (Sarasota, Sanibel and Captiva Islands, etc.).

BASIC FACTS: State of Florida. Area code: 813. ZIP Codes (of the central post offices): 33733 (St. Petersburg), 33602 (Tampa). Founded: 1876 (St. Petersburg), 1823 (Tampa). Approximate population: city, 240,000 (St. Petersburg), 280,000 (Tampa); metropolitan area, 2,060,000. 21st-largest metropolitan area in the country.

CLIMATE: St. Petersburg earns its nickname of "Sunshine City"; the sun shines almost all the time, and the Tampa Bay area has one of the most agreeable climates in the U.S. Almost never does the mercury dip below 59°F (15°C) even in the depth of winter; the Jan mean temperature is 61°F (16°C). In summer, the July mean is 82°F (28°C), and the high rarely exceeds 86°F (30°C). To put it succinctly: It's always spring here, and you'll have a pleasant stay any time of year.

DISTANCES: Atlanta, 455 mi. (728km); Miami, 268 mi. (428km); New Orleans, 633 mi. (1,012km); Orlando, 83 mi. (132km).

ARRIVAL & TRANSIT INFORMATION

AIRPORTS: The **St. Petersburg–Clearwater International Airport** (PIE), 9 mi. (14km) north of St. Petersburg, 17 mi. (27km) SW of Tampa. For information, call 813/535-7600.
    Tampa International Airport (TPA), 16 mi. (26km) NE of St. Petersburg, 5 mi. (8km) NW of Tampa. An airport of revolutionary design, one of the most modern in the country. For information, call 813/870-8700.

U.S. AIRLINES: American (toll free 800/433-7300), Continental (toll free 800/525-0280), Delta (toll free 800/221-1212), Northwest (toll free 800/225-2525), TWA (toll free 800/221-2000), United (toll free 800/241-6522), and USAir (toll free 800/428-4322).

FOREIGN CARRIERS: Air Canada (toll free 800/422-6232), Condor (toll free 800/782-2424), and Martinair (toll free 800/336-4655).

CITY LINK: From the two airports to the two cities there is a variety of transportation available.
    To Downtown St. Petersburg: The **cab** fare from St. Petersburg–Clearwater Airport is about $20; time, 20 min. From Tampa Airport: fare, about $35; time, about 40 min. Bus between Tampa Airport and St. Petersburg: **The Limo** (toll free 800/282-6817), serving principal hotels. Fare to St. Petersburg, $10; to St. Petersburg Beach, $10; time, about 40–60 min.
    To Downtown Tampa: The **cab** fare from Tampa Airport is about $14; time, about 15 min. Bus between Tampa Airport and downtown Tampa: **Central Florida Limo Service** (396-3730), serving principal hotels; fare, $11; time, 20 min. **City bus:** Line 30 serves downtown Tampa; fare, $1.
    Public transportation (bus) is inefficient: in Tampa, HART (254-4278); in St. Petersburg, PSTA (530-9911).
    Given the many interesting destinations for excursions around the area, and the very low rates prevailing in Florida, it makes a lot of sense to rent a car with unlimited mileage.

CAR RENTAL (at Tampa International Airport unless otherwise indicated): Avis (toll free 800/331-1212); Budget (toll free 800/527-0700); Dollar (toll free 800/800-4000); Hertz (toll free 800/654-3131); National (toll free 800/227-7368); Thrifty, 1965 NW Shore St. (toll free 800/367-2277). For downtown locations in Tampa and St. Petersburg, consult the appropriate local telephone directory.

LIMOUSINE SERVICES: Carey Limousine (228-7927), Dav El Limousines (toll free 800/922-0343).

TAXIS: In theory cabs may not be hailed on the street, but may be taken from the waiting lines outside the major hotels, or more conveniently, summoned by phone. Recommended companies **in St. Petersburg** are Blue Star Cab (327-4104) and Yellow Cab (821-7777); **in Tampa,** United Cab (253-2424) and Yellow Cab (253-0121). Cab fares are on the high side.

TRAIN: Amtrak has stations at 3101 37th Ave. N. in St. Petersburg and at Nebraska Ave. and Twiggs St. in Tampa (toll free 800/872-7254).

INTERCITY BUSES: Greyhound has terminals at 180 9th St. in St. Petersburg and 610 E. Polk St. in Tampa (both toll free 800/231-2222).

INFORMATION & TOURS

TOURIST INFORMATION: The **St. Petersburg Chamber of Commerce,** 100 Second Ave. N., St. Petersburg, FL 33731 (813/821-4715).
   Suncoast Welcome Center, Junction of Fla. 688 and I-275 (exit 218), St. Petersburg (813/573-1449).
   Tampa Chamber of Commerce, 801 E. John F. Kennedy Blvd., Tampa, FL 33601 (813/228-7777).
   Tampa/Hillsborough Convention and Visitors Association, 111 Madison St., Suite 1010, Tampa, FL 33601 (813/223-1111; toll free 800/826-8358).

GUIDED TOURS: Both St. Petersburg and Tampa have several options for guided tours.

St. Petersburg
   Captain Anderson (boat), 3400 Pasadena Ave. S. (367-7804; toll free 800/533-2288): Scenic luncheon and dinner-dance cruises. Oct–May.
   Gray Line Tours (bus) (535-0208): Guided bus tours of the city and surroundings; year round.

Tampa
   Gray Line Tours (bus) (535-0208): Guided bus tours of the city and surroundings, serving principal hotels; year round.
   Sea Trader Cruises (sailboat), 4005 W. Cleveland St. (286-8512): Half- or full-day sailboat tours of Hillsborough Bay. Sunset or night cruises available. Captain sometimes allows passengers to steer. By reservation year round.
   Tampa Tours (van) (621-6667): Guided 2-hr. tours of historical Tampa; Tues–Sun, year round. Call for appointment.

TAMPA

SIGHTS, ATTRACTIONS & ACTIVITIES

ARCHITECTURAL HIGHLIGHTS: ☼▲ **Performing Arts Center,** 1010 N. MacInnes Place (222-1000): Opened in 1987 at a cost of $55 million, this ultra-modern performing-arts complex comprises three adjacent auditoriums: **Festival Hall,** with 2,400 seats, home of the Florida Symphony Orchestra and the

Tampa Ballet; the 900-seat **Playhouse;** and the 300-seat **Robert and Lorena Jaeb Theater.** Beautifully sited on the Hillsborough River. Worth seeing. Guided tours by appointment.

University of Tampa, 401 John F. Kennedy Blvd. at the Hillsborough River (253-3333): The main building of this university, founded in the 1930s, used to be the Tampa Bay Hotel, a turn-of-the-century palace whose Hispano-Moorish architecture and 13 minarets are imitative of the Alhambra in Granada (Spain). The **Henry B. Plant Museum,** a triumph of rococo styling, is worth a visit all to itself. Open Tues–Sat.

BEACHES: ⚓ **Davis Municipal Beach,** Courtney Campbell Pkwy.: Huge, very popular beach near the airport; noisy.

There are dozens of miles of beaches less than an hour's drive away, at **Bradenton Beach, Clearwater Beach, Crystal Beach, Sarasota,** etc.

MUSEUMS OF ART: ⚓ **Museum of African American Art,** 1308 N. Marion St. (272-2466). Brand-new museum, the first of this kind in Florida, houses the famous Barnett-Aden collection—more than 150 works by African American artists: paintings, sculptures, prints, and traditional handmade items. Captivating. Open Tues–Sun.

Tampa Museum of Art, 601 Doyle Carlton Dr. (223-8130): Greek, Roman, and Egyptian antiquities; paintings by European masters and moderns. Interesting temporary exhibitions. Imposing Greek Revival architecture. Open Tues–Sun.

MUSEUMS OF SCIENCE & HISTORY: ⚓ **Museum of Science and Industry,** 4801 E. Fowler Ave. (987-6300): One of the country's few open-air museums. Many displays and demonstrations relating to the environment, agriculture, geology, electricity, etc. Simulation of a hurricane; observation of sunspots with the aid of a heliostat. Open daily.

PARKS & GARDENS: ⚓ **Lowry Park,** North Blvd. and W. Sligh Ave. (223-8230): 105-acre (42ha) park with recently opened zoo (935-8552) where animals roam freely in specially designed habitats, including a three-flight aviary and a unique manatee aquatic center. Also Fairyland, a theme park based on fable and nursery-rhyme characters. Open daily.

PERFORMING ARTS: For a daily listing of all shows and cultural events, consult the entertainment pages of the daily paper *Tampa Tribune* (morning).

Falk Theater, University of Tampa campus, 401 W. John F. Kennedy Blvd. (253-6212): Ballet, recitals.

Tampa Bay Performing Arts Center, 1010 N. MacInnes Place (222-1000): Ultramodern complex comprising three adjoining performance halls. Concerts, ballet, opera, classic and contemporary theater, Broadway shows. Home of the Florida Orchestra, the Bay Ballet Theatre (season Oct–Mar), and the Tampa Oratorio Society. For the box office, call 221-1045.

Tampa Theater, 711 N. Franklin St. (223-8981): A 1926 movie theater, plushly decorated in the rococo style. Concerts, contemporary theater, movies.

SHOPPING: **The Market on Harbour Island,** 601 S. Harbour Island Blvd. (223-9898): Ultramodern shopping mall which combines the atmosphere of a European open-air market with cobbled streets, fountains, plazas, arcades, and an enormous carousel. More than 50 varied boutiques and stores as well as a score of restaurants, bars, and cafés. Lovely view of the waterfront. Connected to Tampa City by monorail. Very spectacular.

☀ **Ybor Square,** 13th St. and Eighth Ave. (247-4497): Complex of boutiques and stores in a 19th-century cigar factory, now a designated historic monument. Imaginative decor.

SPECIAL EVENTS: For the exact schedule of events below, consult the **Tampa/Hillsborough Convention and Visitors Association** (see "Tourist Information," above).

Florida State Fair (Feb): Very popular agricultural and business fair, with cattle show, handcraft market, flower shows (especially orchids), rodeos, pop concerts. At the Fairgrounds, I-4 and U.S. 301. One of the largest fairs in the Southeast.

GTE Suncoast Classic (mid-Feb): Brings the top stars of the PGA Tour to Tournament Players' Club of Tampa Bay.

Gasparilla Pirate Invasion (Feb): Boat parade, carnival, folklore parades; colorful. Commemorates the taking of Tampa by pirate José Gaspar.

Spring Arts and Crafts Fiesta (Mar): Festival of South American art and folklore. Balls. Held in Ybor City.

SPORTS: Tampa boasts professional teams in three sports (one for spring training only):

Baseball (spring training, Feb–Mar): Cincinnati Reds, Reds Spring Training Field, Plant City (752-7337): New York Yankees, Yankee Complex (875-7753).

Football (Aug–Dec): Buccaneers, Tampa Stadium (879-2827).

Ice Hockey (Sept–Apr): Lightning, Tampa Arena (229-8800).

Horse Racing

Tampa Bay Downs, Race Track Rd., Oldsmar (855-4401), 11 mi. (17km) NW of Tampa on Fla. 580. Thoroughbred racing Tues–Sat Dec–Apr.

Jai Alai

Tampa Fronton, S. Dale Mabry Hwy. and Gandy Blvd. (831-1411), 5 mi. (8km) SW of Tampa on I-275. Matches Mon–Sat, year round.

STROLLS: ☀⚓ **Waterfront,** Harbor St., Shrimp Docks, and 13th St.: The port district, always busy with the unloading of cargoes—fish, bananas, tropical fruit, or whatever. You'll have a good view of the impressive trawler fleet from the 22nd St. Causeway.

☀⚓ **Ybor City,** bounded by Columbus Dr., Fifth Ave., 22nd St., and Nebraska Ave.: A Cuban enclave in the heart of Tampa, complete with cigar factories, shops, and typical restaurants. The first Cuban immigrants to settle here were the cigar-manufacturing workers brought from Key West by Vincente Martinez Ybor in 1886. The scent of tobacco (no longer imported from Cuba, but from Puerto Rico, Honduras, and the Dominican Republic) perfumes a warm, colorful atmosphere embracing the descendants of Cuban and other Spanish-speaking immigrants, and many Italians as well. The **Ybor City State Museum,** 1818 Ninth Ave. (247-6323), traces the history of Cuban cigar manufacturing from its inception in the mid-19th century to the current industry in Florida. Open Tues–Sat. Lively and picturesque, especially at night.

THEME PARKS NEARBY: ⚓ **Adventure Island,** 4545 Bougainvillea Ave. (987-5660): A 19-acre (7ha) park entirely devoted to the pursuit of surfing, div-

Tampa Area

Adventure Island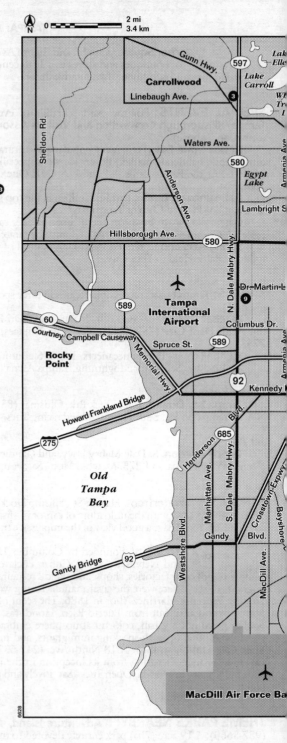
Busch Gardens ⑤
Florida Aquarium ⑫
Garrison Seaport Center ⑬
Henry B. Plant
  Museum ⑯
Lowry Park Zoo ⑦
Museum of African-
  American Art ⑭
Museum of Science
  and Industry ②
Seminole Indian
  Village ⑧
Tampa Bay Downs ③
Tampa Convention
  Center ⑰
Tampa Greyhound
  Track ⑥
Tampa Museum
  of Art ⑮
Tampa Stadium ⑨
University of Tampa ⑪
USF Art Museum ①
Ybor City State
  Museum ⑩

TAMPA AREA ATTRACTIONS

① University of South Florida
②
Fowler Ave.
582
⑤ ④
Busch Gardens
56th St.
Temple Terrace
Busch Blvd.
580
41
⑥
301
75
Sligh Ave.
Sligh Ave.
275
⑧
92
Hillsborough Ave.
4
Tampa
East Lake
Dr. Martin Luther King Jr. Blvd.
574
585
Columbus Dr.
⑩
Ybor City
Adamo Dr.
wntown
⑫
60
Crosstown Expwy.
60
⑬
BUS 41
Harbour Island
McKay Bay
Davis Blvd.
Davis Islands
Causeway Blvd.
676
Peter O. Knight Airport
Bayshore Rd.
676A
allast oint
41
Hills-borough Bay
Nebraska Ave.
Florida Ave.
22nd St.
Nebraska Ave.
Florida Ave.
Malcolm McKinley Dr.
50th St.
baugh
BUS 41
Jr. Blvd.

DOWNTOWN

⑭
Tyler St.
⑮
Cass St.
Polk St.
Zack St.
Florida Ave.
Marion St.
Morgan St.
Twiggs St.
Tampa St.
Franklin St.
Madison St.
Kennedy Blvd.
⑯
Jackson St.
Washington St.
Whiting St.
Hillsborough River
Crosstown Expwy.
⑰
Ashley St.

Airport ✈

ing, and swimming. You can splash in an enormous pool with artificial waves and waterfalls, or float down artificial rapids. Entertaining. Open daily in summer, weekends only in spring and fall; closed in winter. Adjacent to Busch Gardens.

☼ 👓 **Busch Gardens–"The Dark Continent,"** 3000 Busch Blvd. (987-5082): One of the most famous theme parks in Florida, with a vast zoo (3,500 animals), trained animal shows, and reconstructed African villages. Gigantic, thrilling roller-coaster; rides by monorail, boat, or miniature train. Broadway-style shows. Tour of the Anheuser-Busch brewery. Open daily year round. Admission is $25.

☼ 👓 **Silver Springs,** 95 mi. (152km) NE of Tampa on I-75N and Fla. 40E (904/236-2121): The springs of the Silver River, the largest of which attains a record flow rate of half a billion gallons (2 billion liters) a day, from a magnificent lake of remarkably clear water, where many TV movies and documentaries have been made. Glass-bottom-boat rides over the 100,000-year-old underwater grottoes—a truly spectacular sight. Impressive reptile zoo. Jeep jungle safari through a 35-acre (14ha) rain forest. The park attracts more than 1.5 million visitors a year. Open daily year round.

ACCOMMODATIONS

Personal Favorites (in order of preference)

☼ 🛏🛏🛏 **Saddlebrook** (vic.), 100 Saddlebrook Way, Wesley Chapel, FL 34249 (813/973-1111; toll free 800/729-8383). 543 rms and suites, A/C, color TV, in-rm movies. AE, CB, DC, MC, V. Valet parking $4, two pools, two golf courses, putting green, 44 tennis courts, sauna, health club, bike rentals, fishing, three rests. (including the Cypress Room), three bars, rm svce, disco, hrdrsr. *Note:* If you enjoy golf or tennis you'll be in paradise here, 30 min. north of Tampa on I-75 (take Exit 58). Luxurious vacation village standing amid 480 acres (194ha) of gardens, wooded hills, and lakes. Spacious, comfortable suites w. private balconies and refrigerators, many w. kitchenettes. Very acceptable rests. Extravagant outsize pool; as for the golf courses, they were designed by Arnold Palmer himself. For exhausted businesspeople and lovers of outdoor sports. Worthwhile vacation discounts. One of the best places to stay in Florida. **VE,** but lower rates off-season.

🛏🛏🛏 **Wyndham Harbour Island Hotel** (nr. dwntwn), 725 S. Harbour Island Blvd., Harbour Island, FL 33602 (813/229-5000; toll free 800/822-4200). 300 rms, A/C, color TV, in-rm movies. AE, CB, DC, MC, V. Valet gar. $6, pool, health club, 23 tennis courts, marina, boats, rest. (Harbour View), bar, rm svce, boutiques, concierge, crib $20. *Note:* Beautiful grand hotel on the water, w. splendid view of the bay and the Tampa skyline. Luxurious, comfortable rms w. refrigerators and period furniture. Discreet, attentive svce; excellent rest. Adjoining the Market in Harbour Island w. its dozens of shops and rests. Business clientele. 5 min. from dwntwn by Franklin St. Bridge, or 90 seconds by people mover. **E–VE**

🛏🛏 **Embassy Suites** (nr. dwntwn), 555 N. Westshore Blvd., FL 33609 (813/875-1555; toll free 800/362-2779). 221 suites, A/C, color TV, in-rm movies. AE, CB, DC, MC, V. Free valet parking, pool, health club, sauna, rest. (Bay Café), bar, rm svce, free buffet breakfast, free crib. *Note:* Hulking white 16-story tower of conventional design, offering only spacious, very well equipped suites w. kitchenette, minibar, and two remote-control TVs. All have private balcony. Ultra-professional reception and svce. Free shuttle bus to airport (5 min.). Large business clientele; 10 min. from dwntwn. Good value. **M–E**

🛏🛏 **Radisson Bay Harbor Inn** (nr. dwntwn), 7700 Courtney Campbell Causeway, FL 33607 (813/281-8900; toll free, see Radisson). 260 rms, A/C, color TV, in-rm movies. AE, CB, DC, MC, V. Free parking, pool, tennis court, rest. (Damon's), bar, rm svce, hrdrsr, free crib. *Note:* Big six-story hotel on the bay w. private beach. Faultless comfort; very complete facilities; attentive svce. Pretty tropical decor. Business and vacation clientele. Good value. 15 min. from dwntwn, 5 min. from the airport (free shuttle). **M–E**

🍴🍴 **Holiday Inn Downtown** (dwntwn), 111 W. Fortune St., FL 🛏🛏 33602 (813/223-1351; toll free, see Holiday Inns). 313 rms, A/C, color TV, in-rm movies. AE, CB, DC, MC, V. Free parking, pool, health club, rest., bar, rm svce, free airport limo, free crib. *Note:* Modern 14-story building adj. the Performing Arts Center; comfort and facilities above the Holiday Inn average. Spacious rms, some w. minibars. VIP floor. Well located in dwntwn Tampa, and a favorite w. business travelers. Very good value. **I–M**

🍴 **Howard Johnson** (formerly Rodeway Inn Safari; nr. dwntwn), 🛏 4139 Busch Blvd., FL 33617 (813/988-9191; toll free, see Choice). 99 rms, A/C, cable color TV. AE, CB, DC, MC, V. Free parking, pool, sauna, rest., bar, crib $5. *Note:* The perfect base for a visit to nearby Busch Gardens. Comfortable rms w. patio or balcony, some w. refrigerator. Cordial reception; family clientele. Good value. **I**

🍴 **Motel 6** (nr. dwntwn), 333 E. Fowler Ave., FL 33612 (813/ 🛏 932-4948). 150 rms, A/C, cable color TV. AE, DC, MC, V. Free parking, pool. *Note:* Unbeatable value right nr. the famous Busch Gardens. Modern and comfortable; 15 min. from dwntwn by I-275. Ideal for motorists and family parties. **B**

Other Accommodations (from top bracket to budget)

🍴🍴🍴 **Sheraton Grand Hotel** (nr. dwntwn), 4860 W. John F. Ken-🛏🛏🛏 nedy Blvd., FL 33609 (813/286-4400; toll free, see Sheraton). 325 rms, A/C, color TV, in-rm movies. AE, CB, DC, MC, V. Valet gar. $7, pool, three rests. (including J. Fitzgerald's), two bars, 24-hr. rm svce, concierge, free airport limo, free crib. *Note:* 11 floors of spectacular glass-and-steel futurist design; beautiful glass-walled lobby w. indoor grdn. Elegant, refined decor; spacious, ultra-comfortable rms w. refrigerators. Rest. of a high order; personalized svce. One VIP floor. A favorite place w. big-businesspeople; 10 min. from dwntwn and 5 min. from the airport. **M–E**

🍴🍴🍴 **Hyatt Regency** (dwntwn), 2 Tampa City Center, FL 33602 🛏🛏🛏 (813/225-1234; toll free, see Hyatt). 517 rms, A/C, color TV, in-rm movies. Valet gar. $7, pool, sauna, health club, two rests., bars, 24-hr. rm svce, concierge, free crib. *Note:* Rather massive tower a stone's throw from the Hillsborough River; spectacular lobby w. two-story waterfall and grdns. Ultramodern comfort and facilities; well-designed, spacious rms; efficient svce. Centrally located in the heart of the business district; attracts business travelers and groups. Four VIP floors. The largest of the dwntwn hotels. Interesting wknd discounts. Recently renovated. **M–E**

🍴🍴 **Days Inn Downtown** (formerly the Sheraton; dwntwn), 515 🛏🛏 E. Cass St., FL 33602 (813/229-6431; toll free, see Days Inns). 180 rms, A/C, color TV. AE, CB, DC, MC, V. Free gar., pool, rest., free crib. *Note:* Typical motel in dwntwn Tampa; spacious, comfortable rms; entirely redecorated. Business clientele. Efficient svce; very good value; next to the Convention Center. **B–I**

🍴 **Tahitian Inn** (nr. dwntwn), 601 S. Dale Mabry Hwy., FL 🛏 33609 (813/877-6721). 80 rms, A/C, cable color TV. AE, DC, MC, V. Free parking, pool, coffee shop (breakfast and lunch only), rm svce, crib $5. *Note:* Very acceptable small motel; relatively spacious, comfortable rms; friendly svce. Good value. 10 min. from dwntwn and 8 min. from the airport. **B–I**

Airport Accommodations

🍴🍴🍴 **Marriott Airport** (vic.), International Airport, Tampa, FL 🛏🛏🛏 33607 (813/879-5151; toll free, see Marriott). 300 rms, A/C, color TV, in-rm movies. AE, CB, DC, MC, V. Valet parking $6, pool, health club, two rests. (including C.K.'s), bar, rm svce, free crib. *Note:* Modern hotel in the airport terminal. Agreeable, well-soundproofed rms; very complete facilities; efficient svce. C.K.'s, a revolving rest. at the top, is praiseworthy. VIP floor. Business clientele; ideal for a stopover between flights. **M–E**

RESTAURANTS

Personal Favorites (in order of preference)

☼ ♀♀♀ **Bern's Steak House** (nr. dwntwn), 1208 S. Howard Ave. (251-2421). A/C. Dinner only, nightly; closed Dec 25. AE, CB, DC, MC, V. *Specialties:* onion soup, red meats, lamb chops, sautéed chicken w. sesame, "wild fried steak," homemade pastry and sherbet. The enormous wine list weighs 7 lb. (3kg) and offers no fewer than 7,000 different labels. *Note:* Bern's likes to call itself "The World's Best and Most Famous Steak House," but joking apart, the charcoal-broiled steaks are truly remarkable, the vegetables are organically grown—and the prices are highly seasoned. To choose the degree of aging, weight, and cooking time for your steak, you almost need a slide rule. Gaudy opulent decor and a rather high noise level. Gigantic wine cellar (500,000 bottles). Excellent svce. Resv. strongly advised; valet parking. *Steak/American.* **M–E**

♀♀♀ **Mise en Place** (dwntwn), 442 Kennedy Blvd. (254-5373). A/C. Lunch Mon–Fri, dinner Tues–Sat; closed hols. AE, CB, DC, MC, V. *Specialties:* grilled foie gras w. blood-orange vinaigrette; Brie quesadilla w. crab, asparagus, and wild mushrooms; roasted Thai barbecue free-range chicken w. purple jasmine rice and red curry coconut sauce; Brazil nut-crusted rack of lamb. Menu changes daily. Excellent domestic wine list, many by the glass. *Note:* Latest star in the otherwise unimpressive culinary Tampa scene. Marty Blitz's cooking is as tasty as it is innovative. A great palatal experience amidst the din of satisfied customers. Unfortunately, resvs. are not accepted, so the wait can be up to two hours on the weekend. *American.* **I–M**

☼ ♀♀ **Columbia** (dwntwn), 2117 E. Seventh Ave. (248-4961). A/C. Lunch/dinner daily. AE, CB, DC, MC, V. *Specialties:* white-bean soup, red snapper Alicante, filet mignon Columbia, chicken valenciana, paella. *Note:* Huge Spanish baroque-style house in the heart of Ybor City, Tampa's Cuban district. Lovely decor of *azulejos* (blue tiles) and houseplants. Tasty, Spanish-inspired food; flamenco music and show Mon–Sat evenings. Diligent svce; a Tampa landmark since 1905. Resolutely tourist atmosphere; resv. advised. Valet parking. Other location: The Market on Harbour Island (229-2992). *Spanish/Latin American.* **I–M**

♀ **Cepha's** (dwntwn), 1701 E. Fourth Ave. (247-9022). Lunch/dinner Tues–Sat; closed hols. No credit cards. *Specialties:* curry chicken, catch of the day, Jamaican specialties. *Note:* Interesting Caribbean cuisine and a nice patio in the back. Reggae shows throughout the summer. *Caribbean.* **B–I**

Other Restaurants (from top bracket to budget)

♀♀♀ **Harbour View Room** (dwntwn), in the Wyndham Harbour Island Hotel (see "Accommodations," above) (229-5001). A/C. Breakfast/lunch/dinner daily, brunch Sun. AE, CB, DC, MC, V. Jkt. *Specialties:* filet mignon wrapped in smoked bacon, blackened grouper w. yellow-tomato salsa and raspberry vinaigrette, shrimp over fresh linguini w. roasted red pepper coulis, fine desserts. Good wine list. *Note:* This is nouvelle cuisine Florida style, delicate and imaginative, served in a gracious contemporary setting. As its name implies, this luxurious hotel rest. offers wraparound harbor and marina views, and svce as polished as it comes. At lunchtime there's a crowd of businessmen. Resv. strongly advised. Valet parking. *American/Seafood.* **M–E**

♀♀♀ **Donatello** (nr. dwntwn), 232 N. Dale Mabry Hwy. (875-6660). A/C. Lunch Mon–Fri, dinner nightly; closed hols. AE, DC, MC, V. Jkt. *Specialties:* three-pastas sampler, calamari salad, osso bucco milanese w. saffron rice, salmon Stromboli, rack of lamb w. rosemary, Neapolitan cake. Extensive Italian wine list. *Note:* The best, and most expensive, Italian rest. in Tampa. Northern Italian market-sensitive cuisine w. many daily specials. Elegant Mediterranean setting w. stucco archways and rustic floor tiles. Attentive, polished svce. Upscale business clientele. Resv. necessary. Valet parking. Very popular locally. *Italian.* **M**

ṾṾṾ **J. Fitzgerald's** (nr. dwntwn), in the Sheraton Grand Hotel (see "Accommodations," above) (286-4444). A/C. Lunch Mon–Fri, dinner nightly. AE, CB, DC, V. Jkt. *Specialties:* grilled alligator sausage w. cilantro tomatillo sauce, corn meal–breaded soft-shell crabs, grouper au poivre w. tequila flambé, roast rack of spring lamb w. bouquetière of fresh vegetables and sweet garlic in rosemary sauce, elegant desserts. Extensive but pricey wine list. *Note:* Superb palace-style rest. w. dark cherry-wood framing, mauve walls, and luxurious china. Delicate, airy, French-inspired cuisine. Svce exemplary on all counts. Big business clientele. One of Tampa's most contemporary upscale rests. Resv. advised. *Continental.* **M–E**

Ṿ **Café Pepe** (nr. dwntwn), 2006 W. John F. Kennedy Blvd. (253-6501). A/C. Lunch Mon–Fri, dinner Mon–Sat. AE, DC, MC, V. *Specialties:* paella, shrimp suprema, Spanish rice and black beans, chicken w. rice, coconut sherbet. *Note:* With its whitewashed walls, flagons of sangría, and noisy, colorful atmosphere, Café Pepe is a little bit of Old Castile transplanted to Tampa. Locally very popular; resv. advised. *Spanish/Latin American.* **I**

Cafeterias/Fast Food

☀ **Silver Ring Café** (dwntwn), 1831 E. Seventh Ave. (248-2549). Lunch/dinner Mon–Sat. The unchallenged king of the "Cuban sandwich" (ham, salami, pork, Swiss cheese on a toasted bun). A real local landmark.

BARS & NIGHTCLUBS

Cha Cha Coconuts (dwntwn), The Shops on Harbour Island (223-3101). Not your typical tropical bar. Live entertainment nightly.

Side-Splitter's Comedy Club (vic.), 12938 N. Dale Mabry Hwy. (960-1197). Tampa's first all-comedy nightclub. Brings the best of standup comics.

Selena's (nr. dwntwn), 1623 Snow Ave. (251-2116). The fashionable Cajun rock and jazz joint, with live music; also very acceptable rest. Very popular with the locals. Open nightly.

Skipper's Smokehouse (vic.), 910 Skipper Rd. (971-0666). Casual seafood and oyster-bar rest. featuring live blues, rock, zydeco, or reggae. Locally popular. Open nightly.

ST. PETERSBURG

SIGHTS, ATTRACTIONS & ACTIVITIES

ARCHITECTURAL HIGHLIGHTS: ⚓ **Municipal Marina,** 300 Second Ave. SE (893-7329): Lovely pleasure-boat basin on Tampa Bay, with 610 moorings.

☀⚓ **The Pier,** 800 Second Ave. NE (821-6164): Curious five-story inverted pyramid of a building, overlooking the port's 2,400-ft. (730m) jetty. Many boutiques and restaurants. Fine view of the bay from the top-floor Observation Deck. Open daily.

Stetson University College of Law, 15th Ave. at 61st St. (345-1300): Fine exercise in Spanish-colonial architecture set among beautiful courtyards and tropical gardens; one of the loveliest campuses in the country.

Sunshine Skyway Bridge on I-275 linking St. Petersburg and Bradenton: Double road bridge, 12 mi. (19km) long, consisting of one highway on piles dating from 1954, and an ultramodern structure opened in 1987 whose twin 426-ft (130m) towers dominate the entrance to Tampa Bay. This is one of the most spectacular pieces of engineering in the U.S.; from it there's a wonderful view of the bay and the Gulf of Mexico, but don't try it if you suffer from dizzy spells. The approach works best from the south.

BEACHES: **Bay Beach,** N. Shore Dr. and 13th Ave. NE: Fine beach on Tampa Bay.

Municipal Beach, Gulf Blvd. at Treasure Island: The most popular of the public beaches, directly on the ocean; huge and well maintained.

North Shore Beach, N. Shore Dr. and Eighth Ave.: Popular beach on the bay; many sports facilities.

Pass-a-Grille Beach, Gulf Way from 1st to 22nd Aves., St. Petersburgh Beach: The most beautiful, and one of the least crowded, beaches in St. Petersburg.

Spa Beach, Second Ave. NE, The Pier: Most accessible of the St. Petersburg beaches, and often crowded. Many boutiques and restaurants nearby.

MUSEUMS OF ART: **Museum of Fine Arts,** 255 Beach Dr. NE (896-2667): Small but comprehensive museum of painting, sculpture, and decorative arts, from Far Eastern and pre-Columbian art to contemporary American painters and photographers. Open Tues–Sun.

Salvador Dalí Museum, 1000 3rd St. S. (823-3767): The Reynolds Morse Collection makes this one of the world's largest museums entirely devoted to Salvador Dalí. Comprises 93 oils, including *The Discovery of America by Christopher Columbus* and *The Hallucinogenic Toreador;* 200 original watercolors and drawings; and hundreds of sketches, lithographs, sculptures, and pop-art works by the famous surrealist painter. Initially opened in Cleveland, Ohio, the museum was moved to St. Petersburg in 1982 in a new state-of-the-art museum complex. Open daily.

MUSEUMS OF SCIENCE & HISTORY: **St. Petersburg Historical and Flight One Museum,** 335 Second Ave. NE (894-1052): Thousands of artifacts chronicling the history of St. Petersburg, spanning from pre-Columbian and early Spanish times to recent decades. Also on hand is a full-scale replica of the Benoist aircraft that started commercial aviation in 1914. With the closing of the Haas Museum, much of its collection went to the Historical Museum. Open daily.

Science Center of Pinellas County, 7701 22nd Ave. N. (384-0027): Very educational science museum; visitors are asked to take part in all kinds of experiments in computer technology, botany, and natural science. Very modern planetarium. Fascinating for children and adults alike. Open Mon–Fri.

PARKS & GARDENS: **Fort De Soto Park,** Pinellas Bayway at Fla. 679 (866-2484): Covering five little islands at the entrance to Tampa Bay, this 880-acre (356ha) park looking out on the ocean has facilities for every kind of water sport as well as for camping. Fort dating from the Spanish-American War (1898). Access by a long highway toll bridge. Open daily sunrise–sunset.

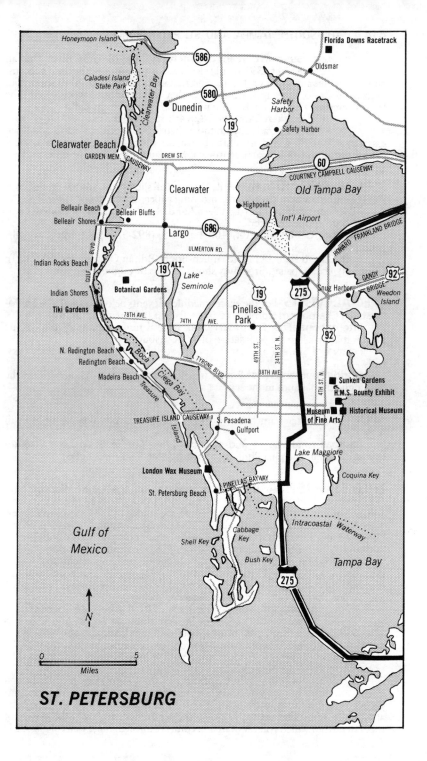

ST. PETERSBURG

Suncoast Seabird Sanctuary, 18328 Gulf Blvd., Indian Shores (391-6211): Refuge for wounded seabirds—pelicans, herons, egrets, and ospreys. In all, representatives of more than 40 species, in huge open-air holding cages, from which they will be released when cured. The largest veterinary hospital of its kind in the U.S. Guided tours daily.

Sunken Gardens, 1825 4th St. N. (896-3186): A kind of tropical paradise, with more than 7,000 species of plants and flowers from around the world, inhabited by parrots, monkeys, and exotic birds. A St. Petersburg landmark for half a century. Open daily.

PERFORMING ARTS: For a daily listing of all shows and cultural events, consult the entertainment pages of the morning paper, *St. Petersburg Times.*
American Stage, 211 3rd St. S. (822-8814): St. Petersburg's resident company. Contemporary theater.
Bayfront Center Theater, 400 1st St. S. (892-5767): Concerts, recitals, ballet, opera.
Ruth Eckerd Hall, 1111 McMullen-Booth Rd., in Clearwater (791-7400): Concerts, recitals, ballet, Broadway shows, operas throughout the year.

SPECIAL EVENTS: For the exact schedule of events below, consult the **St. Petersburg Chamber of Commerce** (see "Tourist Information," above).
International Folk Fair (Mar): Folk festival honoring the diverse ethnic groups that make up the population of St. Petersburg.
Festival of States (late Mar to Apr): Art exhibitions, processions, fireworks, balls.
Florida Tournament of Bands (Apr): Brings together in competition the best high-school bands in the state.

SPORTS: St. Petersburg hosts spring training for two major-league baseball teams:
Baseball (mid-Mar to mid-Apr): St. Louis Cardinals, Al Lang Stadium (894-4773); Philadelphia Phillies, Jack Russell Stadium (442-8496).

THEME PARKS NEARBY: ☀️🐚 **Homosassa Springs Nature World,** 77 mi. (123km) north of St. Petersburg on U.S. 19N (904/628-2311): A beautiful aquatic garden around the springs that are the source of the Homosassa River. They flow at a rate of 100,000 gal. (378,000 liters) a minute; the water is crystal clear, and at 72°F (22°C). For some reason that zoologists don't understand, saltwater as well as freshwater fish are attracted to the springs. Boat rides; underwater observation gallery. This is the only theme park in the country with a group of manatees in captivity, not to mention hippopotamuses as well as alligators and other saurians. Combine with visit to Weeki Wachee Springs (see below) and Tarpon Springs (see "Nearby Excursions," below).
Sarasota Jungle Gardens, 3701 Bayshore Rd., Sarasota, 38 mi. (60km) south of St. Petersburg on I-275S and U.S. 41S (355-5305): More than 5,000 plant species, and hundreds of exotic birds flying free in a spectacular tropical jungle. Also very lovely landscaped gardens with flamingos, swans, and peacocks. Combine it with visits to Sarasota and De Soto National Memorial (see "Nearby Excursions," below).
Weeki Wachee Springs, 57 mi. (91km) north of St. Petersburg on U.S. 19N (904/596-2062): Aquatic displays and Esther Williams–style water nymphs make this one of Florida's most popular attractions. You'll find the world's only theater 16 ft. (4m) below the surface of the water, from which you can watch in comfort through huge walls of glass, 27/8

in. (4cm) thick, while the nymphs go through their revolutions—an amazing sight. Boat rides on the Weeki Wachee River. Very lovely orchid gardens. Open daily year round.

ACCOMODATIONS

Personal Favorites (in order of preference)

🌞 🏠🏠🏠🏠 **Don Cesar Beach Resort** (vic.), 3400 Gulf Blvd., St. Petersburg, FL 33706 (813/360-1881; toll free 800/247-9810). 276 rms, A/C, cable color TV. AE, CB, DC, MC, V. Valet parking $6, pool, health club, sauna, two tennis courts, boating, fishing, waterskiing, beach, three rests. (including Maritana Grille), three bars, 24-hr. rm svce, hrdrsr, boutiques, art gallery, concierge, free crib. *Note:* A 1930s luxury hotel—the light-hearted Spanish baroque building is painted a lovely pink, whence the hotel's nickname, "The Pink Lady." The best rooms, overlooking the Gulf of Mexico, are splendid, but those overlooking the parking lot are much less so. Excellent svce and very good rest. Clientele of upscale groups and trendy vacationers. Beautiful landscaped grdns; direct beach access. A landmark among Florida hotels. **VE,** but lower rates off-season.

🌞 🏠🏠 **The Heritage** (dwntwn), 234 Third Ave. N., St. Petersburg, FL 33701 (813/822-4814). 71 rms, A/C, color TV. AE, CB, DC, MC, V. Free parking, pool, rest., bar, rm svce. *Note:* Gracious small hotel from the 1920s, agreeably restored to its pristine elegance, w. a charming atrium –winter grdn. Very comfortable period-furnished rms; attentive svce; very centrally located. A favorite of those in-the-know. **M–E,** but lower rates off-season.

🏠🏠 **Days Inn Marina** (formerly the Sheraton; nr. dwntwn), 6800 34th St., St. Petersburg, FL 33711 (813/867-1151; toll free, see Days Inns). 158 rms, A/C, cable color TV. AE, CB, DC, MC, V. Free parking, two pools, seven tennis courts, marina, boating, sailboat instruction, private beach, fishing, rest., bar, rm svce, nightclub, free crib. *Note:* Elderly but congenial motel on the bay. The redecorated rms are spacious and comfortable; some have kitchenettes and refrigerators, and all have private balconies or patios. Also 10 rustic bungalows. Efficient svce; pretty tropical grdns. The ideal vacation motel. Near the Sunshine Skyway, 10 min. from dwntwn. **I–M,** but lower rates off-season.

🏠 **Trails End** (vic.), 11500 Gulf Blvd., Treasure Island, FL 33706 (813/360-5541). 54 rms, A/C, cable color TV. AE, CB, DC, MC, V. Free parking, pool, beach, adj. rest. and bar, free crib. *Note:* Small, undistinguished, but inviting motel w. direct beach access. Relatively large rms (two-thirds of them w. kitchenette), the best overlooking pool and grdn. Interesting vacation packages. Good overall value. **I–M,** but lower rates off-season.

🏠 **Treasure Island Motel** (dwntwn), 10315 Gulf Blvd., St. Petersburg, FL 33731 (813/367-3055). 24 rms, A/C, cable color TV. MC, V. Free parking, pool, free crib. *Note:* Family-run motel w. big, comfortable rooms, some with refrigerators. Across the street from the beach. Svce. is friendly and helpful. A very good value considering the location. **B–I**

Other Accommodations (from top bracket to budget)

🏠🏠🏠🏠 **Stouffer Vinoy Resort** (dwntwn), 501 Fifth Ave. NE, St. Petersburg, FL 33701 (813/894-1000; toll free, see Stouffer). 360 rms, A/C, color TV, in-rm movies. AE, CB, DC, MC, V. Valet gar. $9, two pools, 14 tennis courts, golf, health club, marina, four rests., three bars, concierge, free crib. *Note:* Superb Mediterranean Revival–style resort built in 1925 and restored to its former grandeur in 1992 after standing empty for 18 years. The decor combines the elegance and style of an earlier era w. luxurious, contemporary facilities. Huge, comfortable rms (the best looking out on the marina and the bay). Flawless svce. A fine place to stay. **E–VE**

🛏🛏🛏 **Hilton and Towers** (dwntwn), 333 1st St., St. Petersburg, FL 33701 (813/894-5000; toll free, see Hilton). 333 rms, A/C, color TV, in-rm movies. AE, CB, DC, MC, V. Free parking, pool, two rests., deli, bar, rm svce, concierge, free crib. *Note:* Large modern 15-story building in dwntwn St. Petersburg, facing the bay and yacht basin. Spacious, comfortable rms w. offshore view, some w. refrigerators. Efficient svce. Two VIP floors. Group clientele. **M–E,** but lower rates off-season.

🛏🛏 **Alden** (vic.), 5900 Gulf Blvd., St. Petersburg Beach, FL 33706 (813/360-7081; toll free 800/237-2530). 140 mini-suites and studios, A/C, color TV, in-rm movies. AE, CB, DC, MC, V. Free parking, two pools, tennis, boating, windsurfing, café nearby, valet svce. *Note:* Modern, comfortable motel on the beach. One- to three-rm suites w. private balconies or patios and kitchenettes. Agreeable grdns, ideal for vacationers w. children. Good value on balance. Friendly reception. 20 min. from dwntwn St. Petersburg. **M–E,** but lower rates off-season.

🛏🛏 **Dolphin Beach Resort** (vic.), 4900 Gulf Blvd., St. Petersburg Beach, FL 33706. (813/360-7011; toll free 800/237-8916). 174 rms, A/C, color TV, in-rm movies. AE, CB, DC, MC, V. Free parking, pool, boating, waterskiing, rest., bar, rm svce, disco, free crib. *Note:* Attractive vacation motel on the beach; rms w. balconies and gulf view, half w. kitchenettes. Comprehensive facilities. Perfect for sailors. Good value; 20 min. from dwntwn St. Petersburg. **M,** but lower rates off-season.

☼🛏🛏 **La Quinta** (formerly Las Casas; nr. dwntwn), 4999 34th St. N., St. Petersburg, FL 33714 (813/527-8421; toll free, see La Quinta). 120 rms, A/C, cable color TV. AE, CB, DC, MC, V. Free parking, pool, health club, adj. 24-hr. rest., valet svce, free breakfast. *Note:* Charming Castilian-style hacienda in a splendid tropical grdn w. fountain, palm trees, and gardenia bushes. Inviting, comfortable rms; excellent svce. Very good value; a fine place to stay. 10 min. from dwntwn. **I**

🛏 **Comfort Inn** (nr. dwntwn), 1400 34th St. N., St. Petersburg, FL 33713 (813/228-5050; toll free 800/228-5050). 76 rms, A/C, cable color TV. AE, CB, DC, MC, V. Free parking, pool, sauna, free breakfast, free crib. *Note:* Relatively new, comfortable, three-floor motel. Functional rms and facilities; amiable reception. Good overall value. 10 minutes from dwntwn and the beach. **B–I**

🛏 **Beach Park Motor Inn** (dwntwn), 300 Beach Dr. NE, St. Petersburg, FL 33701 (813/898-6325). 26 rms, color TV. AE, MC, V. Free parking, adjacent to public beach, nearby coffee shop, crib $5. *Note:* Small, modern, functional economy motel. Inviting rms w. refrigerator (some w. kitchenette). Well located overlooking Tampa Bay and City Park, and a hop, skip, and a jump from the Pier with its cluster of shops and rests. Friendly svce; good value; interesting vacation packages. **B–I,** but lower rates off-season.

RESTAURANTS

Personal Favorites (in order of preference)

🍷🍷🍷 **Maritana Grille** (vic.), in the Don Cesar Resort (see "Accommodations," above) (360-1881). A/C. Dinner Mon–Sat, brunch Sun. AE, CB, DC, MC, V. Jkt. *Specialties:* fire-roasted portobello mushrooms w. vegetable strudel, whole wood-grilled Gulf fish w. flaming herbs, filet mignon w. wild-mushroom flan and foie gras, soufflés. *Note:* Luxurious grand-hotel dining room w. four fish tanks that have a total of 1,500 gallons of water containing Moorish idols and predatory Gulf fish. Rest. also has a view of the Gulf of Mexico. First-class svce. Resv. a must. *Continental.* **M–E**

ŸŸ **Basta's** (nr. dwntwn), 1625 4th St. S. (894-7880). A/C. Dinner only, nightly; closed hols. AE, MC, V. Jkt. *Specialties:*
homemade pasta dishes, veal Vesuvio, seafood Portofino, flambé desserts. Short
but fine wine list, reasonably priced. *Note:* Here New York's talented chef Frank
Basta now prepares some of the finest northern Italian cuisine on the Sun Coast.
Elegant Mediterranean setting w. etched-glass panels. Efficient, cheerful svce.
Resv. required. *Italian.* **I–M**

ŸŸ **Pepin's** (nr. dwntwn), 4125 4th St. (821-3773). A/C. Lunch
Mon–Fri, dinner nightly; closed hols. AE, MC, V. *Specialties:*
salad Sevillana, shrimp w. almonds, chicken w. yellow rice, red snapper orio,
baked pompano, steak. *Note:* Congenial Spanish-style tavern serving excellent
fish and choice red meats. Friendly, efficient svce; locally very popular (especially
for business lunches), so resv. strongly advised. A fine place to eat. *Spanish/Latin
American.* **I–M**

Ÿ **Blind Pass Grille** (vic.), 9555 Blind Pass Rd., St. Petersburg
Beach (363-1800). A/C. Lunch/dinner daily, brunch Sun.
AE, MC, V. *Specialties:* spicy crayfish, charcoal-grilled grouper and catch of the
day, baby back ribs, steak. *Note:* Located right on the dock on the Intracoastal
Waterway, this casual and inviting rest. serves up the freshest of seafood and meat
at sensible prices. Live entertainment Wed–Sun. Family-style atmosphere. Locally popular. *Seafood/Steak.* **B–I**

Other Restaurants (from top bracket to budget)

ŸŸ **Leverock's Steak House** (vic.), 8800 Bay Pines Blvd. N. (345-
5335). A/C. Lunch/dinner daily. AE, CB, DC, MC, V. *Spe-
cialties:* excellent steak and prime ribs, seafood dishes. *Note:* Waterfront steakhouse spectacularly situated on Boca Ciega Bay in northwest St. Pete w. walls of
glass to frame the magnificent view. Prices are reasonable and the prime-cuts
quality very good. Excellent svce. A local favorite. *Steak.* **I–M**

☀ŸŸ **Heilman's Beachcomber** (vic.), 447 Mandalay Ave., Clearwater Beach (442-4144). A/C. Lunch/dinner daily (until midnight). AE, CB, DC, MC, V. *Specialties:* stone crab (in season), shrimp
Rockefeller, calves' liver w. onions, roast lamb, steak, fried chicken, broiled fish of
the day (snapper, grouper, swordfish, etc.), good homemade desserts. *Note:* The
classic all-American rest., straight out of the 1940s w. decor, food, and waiters to
match. Generous servings. Locally popular since 1948; a very fine place to eat,
right on the beach. Resv. advised. *Steak/Seafood.* **I–M**

Ÿ **Kinjo** (vic.), 4615 Gulf Blvd., St. Petersburg Beach (367-
6762). A/C. Dinner only, nightly; closed hols. AE, CB, DC,
MC, V. *Specialties:* sushi, teriyaki, sukiyaki, teppanyaki. *Note:* Japanese steakhouse in the classical tradition. Popular sushi bar where three sushi chefs create
their culinary magic. The flashing knife-work of the teppanyaki chefs is worthwhile entertainment in itself. Attractive Japanese setting. Unfortunately, resvs.
are not taken. Very good value. 25 min. from dwntwn. *Japanese.* **I–M**

Ÿ **The Kingfish** (vic.), 12789 Kingfish Dr., Treasure Island (360-
0881). A/C. Lunch/dinner daily; closed Thanksgiving, Dec
25. MC, V. *Specialties:* catch of the day, broiled or baked shellfish at bargain
prices. *Note:* Traditional oyster bar and seafood rest. Looks out over the Treasure
Island yacht basin. Absolutely fresh seafood. Unpretentious nautical setting. Locally popular; very good value. *Seafood.* **B–I**

☀Ÿ **Scandia** (vic.), 19829 Gulf Blvd., Indian Shores (595-4928).
A/C. Lunch/dinner Tues–Sun. MC, V. *Specialties:* kolde
bord (hors d'oeuvres), frikadeller (meatballs), roast loin of pork w. braised red
cabbage, remarkable homemade desserts and pastries. *Note:* Nice little inn, con-
vincingly traditional Danish in decor and otherwise, w. small, intimate dining
rms. The tasty food will convince you you're in Denmark—particularly the
house-specialty desserts. Smiling svce. Locally very popular, so resv. advisable.
Very good value. 30 min. from dwntwn St. Petersburg. *Scandinavian.* **B–I**

Cafeterias/Fast Food

Café Croissant (vic.), 3993 Tyrone Blvd. at Park St., northwest St. Petersburg (347-7389). A small, authentic French café and bakery offering mouthwatering croissants, breads, and pastries. Delicious soups, quiches, and sandwiches are also served. Open daily until 7pm.

BARS & NIGHTCLUBS

Coaster's (vic.), 19325 Gulf Blvd., Indian Shores (596-7333). Congenial lounge with live music. Also very praiseworthy rest. Fine location on the water. Open nightly.

Gallery Lounge (vic.), 7500 Blind Pass Rd., St. Petersburg Beach (360-0549). Fashionable disco with live music as well. Open daily.

Shellman's Oyster Bar (vic.), 5501 Gulf Blvd., St. Petersburg Beach (360-6961). Live reggae, rock, blues or jazz nightly. Picturesque shabby decor and eclectic Florida foods.

Zelda's (vic.), in the Don Cesar Beach Resort (see "Accommodations," above, St. Petersburg Beach) (360-1881). Snug, intimate bar with a view of the Gulf of Mexico; preppy clientele. Open nightly.

EXCURSIONS

NEARBY EXCURSIONS

DE SOTO NATIONAL MEMORIAL (on Fla. 64 in Bradenton, 30 mi./48km south of St. Petersburg along I-275 and U.S. 41) (792-0458): Museum of the Spanish Conquest built at the mouth of Tampa Bay, where Hernándo de Soto first dropped anchor on May 30, 1539. Recaptures the 4,000-mi. (6,400km), four-year expedition of the famous conquistador and his 600 companions to explore the Southeast, from Florida to Mississippi. His party included Francisca Hintestrosa, wife of one of his soldiers, who is thought to be the first woman colonist in the United States. Their journey is retraced in detail by a movie shown at the Visitor Center. Small military museum. Open daily.

SARASOTA (39 mi./62km south of St. Petersburg via I-275 and U.S. 41): Sarasota is the birthplace of American golf (the first course in the country was laid out here in 1886 by Scotsman John Hamilton Gillespie), but it has been better known as the world capital of the circus since 1927, when "the King of the Circus," John Ringling himself, chose the town as the winter quarters of the Ringling Bros. & Barnum and Bailey Circus. Today it's the home of the great **Ringling Museum of Art** complex on U.S. 41 (355-5101), comprising four architecturally remarkable buildings. First is John Ringling's own home, **Ca'd'Zan,** a lavish replica of a 32-room Venetian Gothic palace complete with antique furniture and a 4,000-pipe organ. Then comes the superb art gallery with its collection of European masters: El Greco, Frans Hals, Rembrandt, Gainsborough, Poussin, and above all, Rubens. A new wing, recently built, displays contemporary works of art and revolving exhibitions. The **Asolo Museum Theater** is an authentic 18th-century Italian baroque theater, taken down and transported stone by stone to Florida in 1949 from the castle of Asolo, near Venice. Finally, there are a richly stocked **circus museum,** illustrating circus history from Roman times on, and some splendid gardens. Open daily year round.

In early June of every year since 1964 Sarasota has played host to the **Music Festival of Florida,** with its well-attended classical symphony concerts and chamber-music recitals. For information, call 953-4252.

⚓ **TARPON SPRINGS** (35 mi./56km north of St. Petersburg on U.S. 19N): Picturesque little sponge-fishing port with an important Greek community. Pretty view of the docks from Dodecanese Blvd. Fine Greek Orthodox **Cathedral of St. Nicholas,** built in 1943 in the Neo-Byzantine style, at 36 N. Pinellas Ave. (937-3540), open daily. Boat rides from the waterfront to the sponge-fishing grounds and demonstrations of sponge fishing. And don't fail to see the **Spongeorama** at Sponge Docks (942-3771), open daily, a museum entirely devoted to this unusual industry.

Where to Eat

🍷 **Louis Pappas Riverside,** 10 W. Dodecanese Blvd. (937-5101). Lunch/dinner daily. AE, DC, MC, V. Commendable Greek fare and a nice view of the harbor. Local color guaranteed. *Greek.* **B–I**

FARTHER AFIELD

☼⚓⚓ **WALT DISNEY WORLD & CENTRAL FLORIDA** (160 mi./256km r.t. via I-4E, U.S. 17S, U.S. 27S, and Fla. 60W): A very crowded itinerary taking you to the fabulous ⚓⚓⚓ **Walt Disney World,** ⚓⚓⚓ **EPCOT,** ⚓⚓⚓ **Disney–MGM Studios,** ⚓⚓ **Sea World,** ⚓⚓⚓ **Universal Studios–Florida,** and ⚓⚓ **Cypress Gardens** (for these famous theme parks, see Chapter 18 on Orlando). On the way you'll see ⚓ **Bok Tower Gardens** at Lake Wales on U.S. 27A (676-1408), a bird sanctuary surrounded by splendid landscaped gardens. Unusual carillon concerts, with 53 bells weighing from 17 lb. (7kg) to 11 tons (10,000kg), daily at 3pm. Also *Mystery of the Passion,* with 250 performers, on Tues, Thurs, Sat, and Sun from mid-Feb to mid-Apr. For hotels, motels, and restaurants, see Chapter 18 on Orlando.

☼⚓⚓ **EVERGLADES NATIONAL PARK** (313 mi./500km SE of Tampa on I-75S, U.S. 41E, U.S. 1S, and Fla. 997S): The only subtropical national park in the U.S. Its flora and fauna are of exceptional richness. For details, see Chapter 19 on Miami.

☼⚓ **GULF OF MEXICO** (256 mi./409km r.t. from St. Petersburg via I-275S and U.S. 41S, returning on I-75N and U.S. 41N): Dozens of superb, uncrowded beaches: **Longboat Key, Lido Key, Siesta Key,** and **Venice** near Sarasota; **Fort Myers Beach, La Costa,** and **Sanibel** (the best beach in Florida for finding seashells) **and Captiva Islands** near Fort Myers.

On the way, visit the **De Soto National Memorial** and the **Ringling museums** at Sarasota (see "Nearby Excursions," above). At **Fort Myers,** see the ⚓ **Thomas Edison Winter Home,** 2350 McGregor Blvd. (334-3614), where the famous inventor spent his winters for almost half a century. Open daily.

For boat rides on the rivers and swamps of Florida, **Everglades Jungle Cruise,** City Yacht Basin, Fort Myers (334-7474), daily year round.

This one-day trip is perfect for nature lovers.

CHAPTER 18

ORLANDO

□ □ □

With Walt Disney World, EPCOT, and Central Florida

"The City Beautiful," as Orlando residents like to call their town, had modest beginnings as a simple military encampment during the war against the Seminole tribe (1835–42). Today its purpose and chief claim to fame are to host the millions of American and foreign tourists who have made this central Florida area an enormous year-round vacation spot. **Walt Disney World, Cape Kennedy, Sea World, Daytona Beach, Cypress Gardens, St. Augustine, EPCOT, Silver Springs** . . . all are less than two hours by car from the Orlando airport, an ultramodern facility amply served by regular and charter flights coming from the northern states, Europe, and Canada.

An important distribution center for citrus fruits and other Florida fruits and vegetables, this modern, dynamic commercial metropolis, whose population has more than doubled since the Cape Canaveral Space Center (now the **Kennedy Space Center**) was created in 1950, has one of the largest concentrations of hotel accommodations in America (78,000 rooms), more than Los Angeles or Chicago. Orlando's economy is the second fastest growing among major U.S. cities. This garden city, studded with parks and lagoons, is a winter resort favored by many northern residents, and a favorite honeymoon destination for young newlyweds. In addition, the surrounding countryside with its dozens of lakes makes the area a summer paradise for campers and caravaners.

Instead of impressive historical monuments, Orlando and its region offer some of the most famous tourist attractions in the world, beginning with Walt Disney World and its sister facility, the sprawling futuristic EPCOT (25 million visitors annually), the **Disney–MGM Studios,** the **Universal Studios Florida,** and the fabulous Cypress Gardens featuring Esther Williams–style water ballet. In a more traditional vein but also worth visiting is the residential suburb of **Winter Park,** just north of Orlando, with its lovely European-style homes, music and art festivals, and canals reminiscent of Venice.

As a finishing touch, the inauguration in 1983 of the immense **Orange County Convention Center** has made the city one of the most important convention cities in the country.

BASIC FACTS: State of Florida. Area codes: 407 (Orlando/Walt Disney World), 813 or 904 (other zones). ZIP Code: 32802 (city of Orlando). Founded: 1837. Approximate population: city, 165,000; metropolitan area, 1,170,000.

CLIMATE: As in all of Florida, winters in Orlando are mild and sunny (mean Jan temperature, 62°F/17°C). The summer is oppressive, with frequent showers, but somewhat less humid than at the Florida shore (average temperature in July is 82°F/28°C). With the thermometer hovering around 71°–77°F (22°–25°C), spring and fall are uniformly pleasant.

DISTANCES: Atlanta, 436 mi. (698km); Miami, 236 mi. (378km); New Orleans, 644 mi. (1,030km); New York, 1,160 mi. (1,856km); Savannah, 292 mi. (467km); Washington, 925 mi. (1,480km).

ARRIVAL & TRANSIT INFORMATION

AIRPORT: Orlando International Airport (MCO): 8 mi. (13km) SE. For information, call 407/825-2352. The fastest-growing major airport in the country (21.5 million passengers in 1993).

U.S. AIRLINES: American (toll free 800/433-7300), Continental (toll free 800/525-0280), Delta (toll free 800/221-1212), Northwest (toll free 800/225-2525), TWA (toll free 800/221-2000), United (toll free 800/241-6522), and USAir (toll free 800/428-4322).

FOREIGN CARRIERS: British Airways (toll free 800/247-9297), KLM (toll free 800/374-7747), and Icelandair (toll free 800/223-5500).

CITY LINK: The **cab** fare from the airport to dwntwn Orlando is about $22–$24; from the airport to Lake Buena Vista hotels, about $28; from the airport to Walt Disney World, about $35. Bus: **Mears Motor Shuttle** (407/423-5566); serves major hotels in Orlando and the area; fare, $10–$15, according to destination.

Although Orlando and all central Florida are amply served by regular long-distance and excursion bus lines, you should seriously consider renting a car with unlimited mileage for trips to Walt Disney World and other area attractions. Car-rental rates in Florida are among the most reasonable in the entire U.S., while municipal public bus service is woefully lacking; for bus information, call Tri-County Transit (407/841-8240).

CAR RENTAL (at the Orlando International Airport unless otherwise indicated): Avis (toll free 800/331-1212); Budget (toll free 800/527-0700); Dollar (toll free 800/800-4000); Hertz (toll free 800/654-3131); National (toll free 800/227-7368); Thrifty, 5757 S. Semoran Rd. (toll free 800/367-2277). For dwntwn locations, consult the local telephone directory.

LIMOUSINE SERVICES: Associated Limousine (toll free 800/392-7759), Carey Limousine (855-0442), Dav El Limousines (toll free 800/922-0343).

TAXIS: Cabs can be hailed on the street or from waiting lines at designated taxi stations; you can also phone for taxi service, in which case try **Mears** (423-5566) or **Yellow Cab** (699-9999).

TRAIN: Amtrak Station, 1400 Sligh Blvd. (toll free 800/872-7245).

INTERCITY BUSES: Greyhound, 555 N. Magruder Blvd. (toll free 800/231-2222).

INFORMATION & TOURS

TOURIST INFORMATION: The **Orlando/Orange County Convention & Visitors Bureau,** 7208 Sand Lake Rd., FL 32819 (407/363-5800).

Orlando Visitor Information Center, 8445 International Dr., Suite 152, FL 32819 (407/363-5871). Open daily year round.

GUIDED TOURS: Falcon Helicopter Service (helicopter), 8990 International-al Dr., Orlando (407/352-1753): Helicopter flights over Walt Disney World and central Florida area. Spectacular. Daily.

Gray Line Tours (bus), 4950 L. B. McLeod Rd., Orlando (407/422-0744): Guided tour of area attractions, serving major hotels.

SIGHTS, ATTRACTIONS & ACTIVITIES

ADVENTURE TOURS: Rosie O'Grady's Hot Air Balloon Company (balloon tours/ballooning), Church St. Station, Orlando (407/841-8787): Dawn departure on clear days. Champagne brunch flight. Spectacular.

ARCHITECTURAL HIGHLIGHTS: ☼⌂ **Team Disney Building,** Buena Vista Blvd., Lake Buena Vista (407/828-3661): The most original corporate head-quarters ever built, this multicolored cubic structure looks like a nuclear reactor that has been remade into a giant child's toy. Designed by the Japanese architect Arata Isozaki, this building is well worth a glance.

MUSEUMS OF ART: ⌂ **Charles Hosmer Morse Museum of American Art,** 133 E. Welbourne Ave., Winter Park (407/644-3686): Very lovely art deco collection including lamps, blown glass, chandeliers, and stained-glass windows by Louis Comfort Tiffany. Also ceramics, paintings, and furniture. Open Tues–Sun.

⌂ **Orlando Museum of Art,** 2416 N. Mills Ave., Orlando (407/896-4231): Pre-Columbian and primitive African art; also 20th-century American painting and graphics. Interesting temporary exhibits. Open Tues–Sun.

MUSEUMS OF SCIENCE & HISTORY: ⌂ **Flying Tigers Warbird Air Museum,** 231 N. Hoagland Blvd., Kissimmee (407/933-1942): Museum and restoration shop featuring the great warplanes of yesteryear, including B25 Mitchells, Flying Fortress, Chinese-built MiG, etc. A must for aviation buffs. Open daily.

⌂ **Orange County Historical Museum,** 812 E. Rollins St. (897-6350): Traces the history of Florida from prehistory to pioneer times to the 20th century. On display is a 1926 firehouse with antique fire trucks. Worth a look. Open daily.

☼⌂ **Orlando Science Center,** 810 E. Rollins St., Orlando (407/896-7151): Comprehensive museum of science and technology. Plenty of hands-on exhibits and animal "touch times" for the children. Ultra-modern planetarium. Open daily.

PARKS & GARDENS: ⌂ **Bok Tower Singing Gardens,** at Lake Wales, 61 mi. (97km) SW on I-4 and U.S. 27 (813/676-1408): 128-acre (52ha) botanical gardens with a bird sanctuary (**Mountain Lake Sanctuary**) and dominated by a 205-ft. (62m) bell tower, whose 53 bells weigh from 17 lb. (7kg) to 11 tons (10,000kg). Marvelous carillon concerts daily at 3pm. In the nearby **Lake Wales Amphitheater,** on U.S. 27A (813/676-1495), visitors can enjoy performances of the Passion Play with 250 participants (Tues, Wed, Thurs, Sat, and Sun Feb to mid-Apr). Spectacular. (The same troupe presents the Passion Play at Spearfish, June–Aug; see Chapter 34 on Mount Rushmore.)

⌂ **Eola Park,** Rosalind and Robinson Sts., Orlando: Charming little public park located in the middle of the downtown area on the shore of Lake Eola. Flowerbeds; fountains illuminated after dark. Particularly dazzling when the azaleas are in flower, Feb–Mar.

Leu Gardens, 1730 N. Forest Ave., Orlando (407/246-2620): Lovely tropical gardens in the center of Orlando. 56 acres (22ha) of camellias, orchids, roses, and azaleas. Open daily.

Loch Haven Park, Princeton Blvd. and Mills Ave., Orlando: City park that's the site of the principal museums in Orlando: the Orlando Museum of Art, the Orange County Historical Museum, and the Orlando Science Center (see "Museums of Art" and "Museums of Science and History," above).

PERFORMING ARTS: For a daily listing of all shows and cultural events, consult the entertainment pages of the daily paper *Orlando Sentinel* (morning and evening) and *Orlando* magazine.

Annie Russell Theater, Rollins College Campus, Park and Holt Aves., Winter Park (407/646-2145): Modern theater, musical comedies. Year round.

Bob Carr Performing Arts Center, 401 W. Livingston Ave., Orlando (407/849-2577): Ballet, theater, concerts. Home of the Southern Ballet and Orlando Opera Company.

Central Florida Civic Theatre, 1010 E. Princeton, Orlando (407/896-7365): Classical and contemporary theater, musical comedies. Year round.

Tupperware Auditorium, U.S. 441S, Orlando (407/847-1802): Concerts, recitals, big-name entertainers.

SHOPPING: Flea World, U.S. 17/92 in Sanford (14 mi./22.5km NE) (407/647-3976): The largest flea market in the world. More than 1,500 booths and mountains of varied merchandise. Open Fri–Sun 8am–5pm. Worth the trip.

SPECIAL EVENTS: For the exact schedule of events below, consult the **Orlando Convention and Visitors Bureau** (see "Tourist Information," above).

Scottish Highland Games (end of Jan): Festival of dance, music, and athletic events in the grand Scottish tradition.

Central Florida Fair (Feb–Mar): Horse shows, entertainment, parades.

Bach Festival (end of Feb): Concerts of classical music in Winter Park.

Autumn Art Festival (Oct): Art exhibits, concerts; Winter Park.

Florida State Air Fair (end of Oct): Festival of parachuting and aerobatics at Kissimmee. Many aircraft on display. Spectacular.

Citrus Sports Holiday (Dec): Three weeks of sports and competitions culminating in the Citrus Bowl football game on Jan 1.

Christmas Parade (Christmastime): All the famous Walt Disney characters parade daily down Walt Disney World's "Main Street USA."

SPORTS: Orlando has one professional team and one minor-league team, and three major-league teams have spring-training facilities here:

Baseball (spring training Feb–Mar): Cleveland Indians, Chain O'Lakes Park, Winter Haven (813/293-3900); Houston Astros, Osceola Stadium, Kissimmee (407/933-2520); Kansas City Royals, Baseball City Stadium, Davenport (813/424-2424).

Baseball (June–Sept): Orlando Cubs, Tinker Field, Orlando (407/872-7593).

Basketball (Oct–Apr): Orlando Magic, Orlando Arena, Orlando (407/896-2442).

Horse Racing

Ben White Raceway, 1905 Lee Rd., Orlando (407/293-8721), harness training Mon–Sat Oct–May.

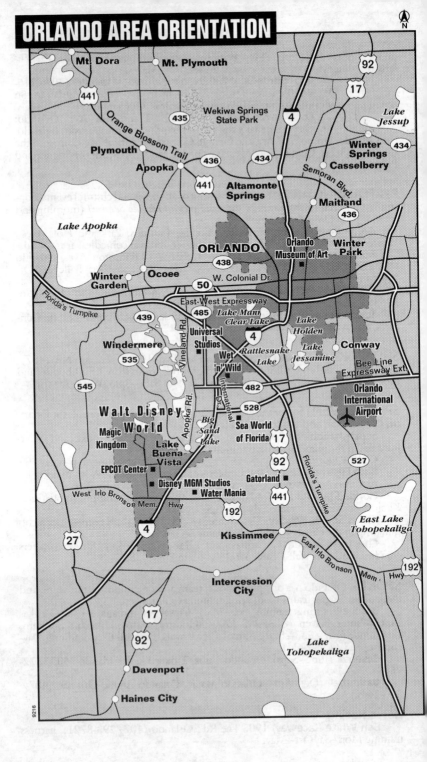

ORLANDO AREA ORIENTATION

N

Mt. Dora

Mt. Plymouth

441

435

Wekiwa Springs
State Park

4

92

17

Lake
Jessup

Orange Blossom Trail

Plymouth

Apopka

436

434

434

Winter
Springs

Casselberry

434

Semoran Blvd

441

Altamonte
Springs

Maitland

436

Lake Apopka

ORLANDO

438

Orlando
Museum of Art

Winter
Park

Winter
Garden

Ocoee

W. Colonial Dr.

50

East-West Expressway

485

Lake Mann
Clear Lake

Lake
Holden

Florida's Turnpike

439

4

Universal
Studios

Rattlesnake
Lake

Lake
Jessamine

Conway

Windermere

535

Wet
'n Wild

Lake

Bee Line
Expressway Ext

Vineland Rd.

545

482

Orlando
International
Airport

International Dr.

528

Walt Disney
World

Magic
Kingdom

Apopka Rd.

Big
Sand
Lake

Sea World
of Florida

17

527

Lake
Buena
Vista

92

EPCOT Center

Gatorland

West Irlo Bronson Mem. Hwy

Disney MGM Studios

Water Mania

441

Florida's Turnpike

East Lake
Tobopekaliga

192

4

192

Kissimmee

East Irlo Bronson Mem. Hwy

192

27

Intercession
City

17

Lake
Tobopekaliga

92

Davenport

Haines City

9216

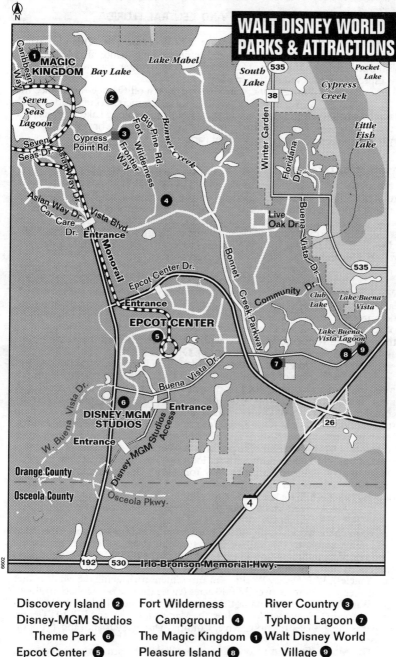

WALT DISNEY WORLD PARKS & ATTRACTIONS

Discovery Island ❷   Fort Wilderness   River Country ❸
Disney-MGM Studios   Campground ❹   Typhoon Lagoon ❼
   Theme Park ❻   The Magic Kingdom ❶ Walt Disney World
Epcot Center ❺   Pleasure Island ❽   Village ❾

STROLLS: ☀⚓ **Church Street Station,** 129 W. Church St., Orlando (407/422-2434): Quaint shops, saloons, restaurants, and nightclubs in a pleasing old-fashioned setting in the heart of Orlando's historical center. Picturesque and lively, especially in the evening. Open daily.

☀⚓ **Winter Park,** 4 mi. (6.4km) north off Orange Ave.: Once the winter home of wealthy northeasterners, Winter Park has retained a small-town atmosphere with its graceful estates along Lake Virginia Park Ave. A four-block shopping district lined with palm trees, has boutiques, specialty stores, and cafés across from Central Park.

THEME PARKS NEARBY: ☀⚓⚓ **Cypress Gardens,** at Winter Haven, 55 mi. (89km) SW by I-4, U.S. 27, and Fla. 540 (813/324-2111): For a good half century these fabulous tropical gardens on the shores of Lake Eloise have been among Florida's principal tourist attractions. There are tours via electric boat of flowers and foliage from five continents (more than 8,000 species from 70 countries). Exotic birds swoop and chatter in the immense aviary. Exhibitions of synchronized waterskiing, Esther Williams–style, are given four times a day year round. One million people come here every year.

☀⚓ **Silver Springs,** near Ocala, 86 mi. (138km) NW by the Florida Tpke., U.S. 27, Fla. 35, and Fla. 40 (904/236-2121): Every year 1.5 million people visit the springs that feed the Silver River and the superb lake whose incredibly clear waters frequently attract moviemakers shooting underwater sequences. The springs produce 500 million gal. (2,000 million liters) of water per day. Tours in glass-bottom boats reveal underwater grottos more than 100,000 years old. Truly spectacular. Also a very beautiful park with deer, and a famous vivarium (Reptile Institute). Open daily.

☀⚓⚓ **Universal Studios Florida,** 10 mi. (16km) SW, at the intersection of I-4 and the Florida Tpke. (407/363-8000): Florida's most recent theme park opened its doors in 1990 at a cost of $600 million. A must for movie buffs, this working motion-picture and television-studio complex—direct rival of Disney–MGM Studios—features thrill rides based on such motion pictures as *King Kong, Jaws, E.T.,* and *Back to the Future.* Among other attractions is the Screen Test Theater where audience volunteers receive costumes, scripts, and a chance to perform in scenes to be edited into TV productions; a walk-through backlot with set locations ranging from a New England village to a San Francisco street to New York City's Upper East Side; and more than 40 restaurants and shops, including Mel's Diner from *American Graffiti.* A one-day ticket is $35 for adults, $28 for children 3–11. Open daily.

☀⚓⚓⚓ **Walt Disney World,** 22 mi. (35km) SW on I-4 at Lake Buena Vista (407/824-4321): The largest and most famous amusement park in the world, rising miraculously from Florida swampland. Opened in 1971—five years after the death of its creator, Walt Disney—the park has already been visited by millions—on a busy day there can be 80,000 people in the park. Conceived along the lines of its older sister park, Disneyland (see Chapter 54 on Los Angeles), Walt Disney World—an amusement park taking the whole planet for its theme—stretches over 27,000 acres (twice the size of Manhattan). In effect, Walt Disney World contains three distinct amusement parks linked by road and monorail: Disney–MGM Studios, the Magic Kingdom, and EPCOT Center as well as the special attractions, River Country, Discovery Island, and Typhoon Lagoon.

The Magic Kingdom: Computer-controlled with chronometric precision, spectacular rides such as Cinderella's Castle, Mission to Mars, Twenty Thousand Leagues Under the Sea, and Pirates of the Caribbean dazzle young and old alike. For convenience, the park is organized as six miniature villages, each with its own style: **Adventureland,** with its boat tour through the jungle; **Fantasyland,** inhabited by the loveable Disney characters; **Frontierland,** in traditional Far West style; **Liberty Square,** with its gallery of 41 U.S. presidents and a house haunted by 999 ghosts; **Main Street USA,** in the style of a turn-of-the-century small town; and **Tomorrowland,** with a space adventure theme.

EPCOT: This theme park of the 21st century, with overtones of a World's Fair, opened its doors in 1982. Drawing up to 25 million visitors each year, EPCOT (acronym for "Experimental Prototype Community of Tomorrow") has only a tenuous thematic link with the fictional world of Mickey Mouse or Donald Duck. Several theme pavilions (Earth, Energy, Transportation, etc.), sponsored by such industrial giants as Exxon, IBM, General Motors, Kodak, and Bell Telephone, adjoin a "window on the world" where scrupulously re-created Japanese temples jostle the Eiffel Tower, Québec's Château Frontenac, St. Mark's Square in Venice, a Bavarian village, Mayan pyramids, a London street, Beijing's Temple of Heaven, etc. The whole ensemble is dominated by a giant 18-story sphere made of reinforced concrete and steel, reminiscent of a huge golf ball, which has become EPCOT's symbol. And there's the largest aquarium in the world, Living Seas, and its 7,500 sea creatures that visitors can observe from an underwater train moving through glass tunnels at the bottom of the gigantic 6-million-gallon (22.6-million-liter) aquarium basin. The futuristic EPCOT, whose construction consumed five years and $1 billion (twice the cost of Walt Disney World and four times that of Disneyland), has turned out the favorite among the Disney parks.

Disney–MGM Studios: This $500-million theme park, opened in 1989 at a site just south of EPCOT, is a dazzling 135-acre (54ha) high-tech playground that blends filmmaking with backstage studio tours and ride-through attractions. Movie and TV productions are shot on its three sprawling film studios and backlot street scenes, while in the animation building, Disney cartoonists churn out shorts for theatrical release. Housed in a copy of Hollywood Boulevard Mann's Chinese Theater, the Great Movie Ride, one of its focal points, transports visitors through classic films such as *The Wizard of Oz, Raiders of the Lost Ark, Alien,* and *Singin' in the Rain.* Superstar Television allows audience volunteers to join the actors in famous television scenes as well as other simulation exhibits. Another highlight is Catastrophe Canyon, where large-scale special effects such as earthquakes and floods are created and cleaned up every 3.5 minutes. Disney–MGM Studios hopes to attract three to five million visitors a year.

Typhoon Lagoon: Disney's new water park for the wet set. Guests are able to snorkel among thousands of tropical fish, plummet down eight different flumes to the 2½-acre (1ha) pool and ride the waves, up to 7 ft. (2m), artificially produced by a giant surf-making machine.

In addition to these innumerable attractions, Walt Disney World offers visitors an immense 7,500-acre (3,000ha) forest reserve of cypress, pine, and laurel trees, two artificial lakes with 4.5 mi. (7km) of sandy beaches, three golf courses, fully equipped camping facilities, and every imaginable sport, including tennis, swimming, waterskiing, sailing, fishing, horseback riding, etc.

There are a dozen or so hotels ideally located for Walt Disney World visitors, among which are the astounding **Contemporary Resort** (served by monorail), the new **Caribbean Beach Resort, Grand Floridian Beach Resort, Disney's Village Resort, Walt Disney World Dolphin and Swan Resorts,** and the more intimate, highly successful **Polynesian Resort.**

Open daily all year, Walt Disney World is in itself worth the trip to Florida. Plan to spend at least two or three full days here, and avoid weekends and holidays. Admission fees: $38 per day for adults, $142 for four days; $30 per day for children, $113 for four days. Albeit fatiguing, this is an experience that should not be missed by children, or by adults who don't want to grow up. Call 407/824-4321 for price and schedule information.

     Wet 'N Wild, in Orlando, 6 mi. (10km) SW on I-4, Exit 435S (407/351-1800): Aquatic fun park with some outstanding attractions: a giant six-story slide, a white-water course, a giant water roller-coaster, and a lagoon with enormous artificial waves for would-be surfers. Spectacular. Open daily mid-Feb to Dec.

ZOOS: ⚲ **Gatorland Zoo,** at Kissimmee, 7 mi. (11km) south on U.S. 17 (407/ 855-5496): Florida's largest alligator farm featuring 6,000 alligators, crocodiles, and giant turtles, as well as pink flamingos and zebras, in a 35-acre (14ha) tropical park. Tour by miniature train. Open daily year round.

    ⚲ **Reptile World Serpentarium,** 5705 E. Irlo Bronson Memorial Hwy., St. Cloud (20 mi./35km south on U.S. 92 and U.S. 192) (407/892-6905): More than 1,500 snakes and other reptiles, including some of the world's most dangerous specimens. Snake venom is collected here for distribution, and visitors have several chances a day to witness the "milking" of cobras, rattlesnakes, and other venomous creatures. If you like horror stories, you'll love this! Open Tues–Sun; closed Sept.

    ☀⚲⚲ **Sea World of Florida,** 7007 Sea World Dr., Orlando (407/ 351-3600): One of the largest marine zoos in the world, surrounded by 150 acres (61ha) of gardens. On display are a giant shark aquarium with walk-through glass tunnel, killer whales, sea lions, sea turtles, and trained dolphins performing on cue. Splendid view from the top of the 450-ft. (140m) revolving tower. There are also waterski shows, a Polynesian show, and a buffet luau every evening. Sea World has almost three million visitors annually. Open daily year round.

ACCOMMODATIONS

Personal Favorites (in order of preference)

    ☀⚲⚲⚲⚲ **Hyatt Regency Grand Cypress,** 1 Grand Cypress Blvd., Orlando, FL 32819 (407/239-1234; toll free, see Hyatt). 750 rms, A/C, color TV, in-rm movies. AE, CB, DC, MC, V. Valet parking $8, two pools, 12 tennis courts, three golf courses, private beach, marina, health club, sauna, boating, three rests. (including Hemingway's), seven bars, 24-hr. rm svce, boutiques, concierge, free crib. *Note:* One of the most spectacular hotels in the U.S., built around a superb lagoon–swimming pool (the largest in the world) w. waterfalls and a giant slide. There's a magnificent 18-story atrium w. extensive plantings of flowers, waterfalls, and glass-walled elevators. Spacious rms w. private patios or balconies. Ultramodern comfort. The decor is elegant, w. master paintings and other works of art. Efficient svce. 1,500 acres (600ha) of grdns and groves; private lake with sandy beach. Home of the famous Jack Nicklaus Academy of Golf. 10 min. from dwntwn, 10 min. from Walt Disney World. The new paragon of Florida luxury hotelkeeping. Two VIP floors. **VE,** but lower rates off-season.

    ⚲⚲⚲⚲ **Walt Disney World Swan,** 1200 Epcot Resort Blvd., Lake Buena Vista, FL 32830 (407/934-3000; toll free, see Westin). 758 rms, A/C, color TV, in-rm movies. AE, CB, DC, MC, V. Valet parking $7, two pools, tennis court, health club, sauna, two rests., coffee shop, bar, 24-hr. rm svce, nightclub, concierge, free crib. *Note:* A new and spectacular achievement of architect Michael Graves; the building, washed in hot pastel tones, has a gigantic sculpture of a swan brooding over each of its four wings (whence the name). Spacious, ultra-comfortable rms; very elegant interiors. Enormous heated lagoon-pool. Flawless reception and svce. Connected to EPCOT Center by tram, and by ferryboat to Disney–MGM Studios. **VE**

    ⚲⚲⚲ **Peabody Orlando,** 9801 International Dr., Orlando, FL 32819 (407/352-4000; toll free 800/732-2639). 891 rms, A/C, color TV, in-rm movies. AE, CB, MC, V. Valet parking $7, pool, tennis court, health club, sauna, three rests. (including Dux), 24-hr. coffee shop, two bars, 24-hr rm svce, nightclub, concierge, free crib. *Note:* Palatial, contemporary 27-story hotel among extensive grounds. Luxurious public facilities and spacious and well-appointed rms. In the fountain of the exquisite marble lobby swim tame ducks, symbol of the Peabody hotel chain. Very good rests. Three VIP floors. Business center well equipped. Unusually polished svce. Located directly across from the Orlando Convention Center and Sea World. A splendid place to stay. **VE**

Twin Towers Hotel, 5780 Major Blvd., Orlando, FL 32819 (407/351-1000; toll free 800/843-8693). 760 rms, A/C, color TV, in-rm movies. AE, CB, DC, MC, V. Free parking, pool, health club, sauna, rest., 24-hr. deli, 24-hr. rm svce, three bars, disco, shops, free crib. *Note:* High-rise twin towers w. extensive convention facilities, situated directly across from the entrance to Universal Studios Florida. Has recently undergone a $29-million renovation. Oversize, comfortable rms. Efficient svce. Business clientele. Good value overall. **M–E,** but lower rates off-season.

Disney's Caribbean Beach Resort, Lake Buena Vista, FL 32830 (407/934-3400; for resv. 407/934-7639). 2,112 rms, A/C, color TV. AE, MC, V. Free parking, seven pools, private beach, marina, boating, coffee shops, bars, boutiques, free crib. *Note:* The perfect base for taking in EPCOT Center, Disney–MGM Studios, and Typhoon Lagoon, this new hotel complex south of the park also offers the lowest rates ($89–$120 a rm). Colorfully decorated in a style w. Caribbean overtones, the hotel comprises dozens of small two-story buildings grouped around a 42-acre (17ha) man-made lake whose shores have been turned into a tropical grdn. Inviting, well-designed rms; pleasant lakeside strolls; amusing bazaar with many cafés and all kinds of fast food. Good value. **M,** but lower rates off-season.

Chalet Suzanne, U.S. 27, Lake Wales, FL 33859 (813/676-6011). 30 rms, A/C, cable color TV. AE, CB, DC, MC, V. Free parking, pool, fishing, boating, rest., bar, crib $10. *Note:* Charming lakeside inn, seemingly right out of a Hans Christian Andersen fairy tale. The decor leans rather heavily toward bric-a-brack, but the rms are comfortable and inviting. Very good rest.; excellent svce. 10 min. by car from Cypress Gardens and Bok Tower Gardens. Private airfield. A very good place to stay. **M–E**

Days Inn–Universal Studios East, 5827 Caravan Court, Orlando, FL 32819 (407/351-3800; toll free, see Days Inns). 261 rms, A/C, color TV, in-rm movies. AE, MC, V. Free parking, pool, 24-hr. rest., free crib. *Note:* Large, standard-style motel. Functional comfort 12 min. by car from Walt Disney World. Totally renovated in 1988. Good value. **I–M**

Motel 6, 5731 W. Irlo Bronson Hwy. (U.S. 192), Kissimmee, FL 32741 (407/396-6333). 347 rms, A/C, cable color TV. AE, DC, MC, V. Free parking, pool, free crib. *Note:* Budget motel 5 min. by car from Walt Disney World. Ideal for families. One of the best values in the entire Orlando area. **B**

Other Accommodations (from top bracket to budget)

Disney's Contemporary Resort, Lake Buena Vista, FL 32830 (407/824-1000; for resv. 407/934-7639). 1,052 rms, A/C, cable color TV. AE, MC, V. Free valet parking, two pools, health club, sauna, tennis courts, beach, waterskiing, two rests., bars, 24-hr rm svce, hrdrsr, boutiques, free crib. *Note:* Original, modern design. This enormous white truncated pyramid, 15 stories high, envelopes the monorail beam, which links it directly to Walt Disney World. Spacious, comfortable rms, all w. balconies or patios, overlooking the surrounding lagoons. The lobby is worth the visit all by itself. Svce a bit vague but courteous. The rest. at the top is good and offers a panoramic view. VIP floor. Among the most spectacular accommodations in the Disney empire. Resv. far in advance are a must. **VE,** but lower rates off-season.

Grenelefe Golf and Tennis Resort, 3200 Fla. 546, Winter Haven, FL 33844 (813/422-7511; toll free 800/237-9549). 950 suites or villas, A/C, color TV, in-rm movies. AE, CB, DC, MC, V. Free parking, four pools, three golf courses, 20 tennis courts, waterskiing, marina, sauna, three rests. (including Grene Heron), bar, disco, crib $15. *Note:* Huge, luxurious vacation complex w. a lovely tropical lagoon. Comfortable suites w.

balconies in two-story bungalows (most w. kitchenette) on the shores of Lake Marion. Svce beyond reproach. Exceptional sports facilities. 8 min. by car from Cypress Gardens, 35 min. from Walt Disney World. **E–VE,** but lower rates off-season.

🍴🍴🍴 **Radisson Plaza Hotel,** 60 Ivanhoe Blvd., Orlando, FL 32804
🛏🛏🛏 (407/425-4455; toll free, see Radisson). 336 rms, A/C, color TV, in-rm movies. AE, CB, DC, MC, V. Valet parking $6, pool, two tennis courts, sauna, health club, rest., bar, rm svce, concierge. *Note:* Large modern 15-story hotel located in the heart of dwntwn. Functional but elegant design. Rms are vast and well laid out, w. minibars. Faultless facilities and comfort; very good svce. Rests. are average. Business travelers and convention-goers are the staple clientele. Two VIP floors. **E**

🍴🍴🍴 **Sheraton Orlando North Hotel and Towers,** Maitland Blvd.
🛏🛏🛏 and I-4, Orlando, FL 32853 (407/660-9000; toll free, see Sheraton). 400 rms, A/C, color TV, in-rm movies. AE, CB, DC, MC, V. Valet parking $2, pool, tennis court, sauna, health club, rest., bar, deli, rm svce, hrdrsr, boutiques, free crib. *Note:* Ultramodern hotel w. an immense glass lobby housing a winter grdn. Very comfortable, elegant rms w. balconies and refrigerators. Comprehensive facilities; attentive svce; rests. no more than adequate. Business and group clientele. VIP floor. 15 min. from Orlando's business section. **M–E**

🍴🍴🍴 **Marriott Orlando,** 8001 International Dr., Orlando, FL
🛏🛏🛏 32809 (407/351-2420; toll free, see Marriott). 1,076 rms, A/C, color TV, in-rm movies. AE, CB, DC, MC, V. Free parking, three pools, four tennis courts, three rests. (including Grove Restaurant), bars, rm svce, disco, free crib. *Note:* Enormous tourist complex composed of two-story cottages surrounded by grdns and exotic lagoons. Spacious, comfortable rms, some w. kitchenettes and refrigerators. Ultra-professional svce and reception. Rests. are so-so. Frequented by convention and other groups. Good value. 10 min. from Walt Disney World, 15 min. from dwntwn. **M**

🍴🍴 **Sheraton Lakeside Inn,** 7711 W. Irlo Bronson Memorial
🛏🛏 Hwy. (U.S. 192), Kissimmee, FL 32741 (407/828-8250; toll free, see Sheraton). 650 rms, A/C, color TV, in-rm movies. AE, CB, DC, MC, V. Free parking, two pools, four tennis courts, pedalboats, miniature golf, three rests., coffee shop, bars, rm svce, crib $5. *Note:* Huge, comfortable motel. Large, inviting rms. Pleasant setting on a lagoon. Good svce overall. 10 min. from Walt Disney World. **M–E,** but lower rates off-season.

🍴🍴 **Delta Orlando Resort** (formerly the Ramada), 5715 Major
🛏🛏 Blvd., Orlando, FL 32819 (407/351-3340; toll free 800/877-1133). 800 rms, A/C, color TV, in-rm movies. AE, CB, DC, MC, V. Free parking, three pools, two tennis courts, sauna, three rests., three bars, rm svce, free crib. *Note:* Vacation and conference motel located halfway between dwntwn Orlando and Walt Disney World. The spacious rms w. balconies (some w. refrigerators) are in small four-story buildings surrounded by grdns. Reasonably complete facilities. Frequented by families and groups. Good value. 10 min. from dwntwn, 15 min. from Walt Disney World. **M–E**

🍴🍴 **Disney's Dixie Landings Resort,** Lake Buena Vista, FL 32830
🛏🛏 (407/934-6000; for resv. 407/934-7639). 1,100 rms, A/C, color TV. AE, MC, V. Free parking, six pools, boating, rest. (Boatwright's), café, bars, boutiques, free crib. *Note:* Brand-new moderately priced resort reminiscent of the Mississippi Delta architecture. Offers a choice between stately plantation manors or more rustic bayou dwellings surrounding a lake shaded by cypress and Spanish moss. Free shuttle to Disney World attractions. Good value. **M**

🍴🍴 **Howard Johnson's Universal Hotel** (formerly Quality Inn),
🛏🛏 5905 International Dr., Orlando, FL 32819 (407/351-2100; toll free 800/446-4656). 300 rms, A/C, color TV, in-rm movies. AE, CB, DC, MC, V. Free parking, pool, rest., bar, rm svce, disco, hrdrsr, free crib. *Note:* Large, round modern 21-story tower. Inviting rms. Functional facilities and

comfort level; efficient svce. Very good value. 20 min. from Walt Disney World, 10 min. from dwntwn. **I–M**, but lower rates off-season.

ፕ ፕ **Days Inn South of Magic Kingdom,** intersection of I-4 and U.S. 27, Lake Buena Vista, FL 32830 (813/424-2596; toll free, see Days Inns). 121 rms, A/C, cable color TV. AE, CB, DC, MC, V. Free parking, pool, adj. rest., free crib. *Note:* Comfortable, appealing rms, the best directly overlooking the pool and grdn. Svce and reception w. a smile. 10 min. from Walt Disney World, 20 min. from Cypress Gardens. Good value. **I**, but lower rates off-season.

ፕ ፕ **Holiday Inn Orlando West,** Fla. 50W at the Florida Tpke., Ocoee, FL 32761 (407/656-5050; toll free, see Holiday Inns). 170 rms, A/C, cable color TV. AE, CB, DC, MC, V. Free parking, pool, rest. (C.W. Dandy's), bar, rm svce, free crib. *Note:* Typical Holiday Inn, w. pool and enticing grdns, comfortable rms, friendly reception and svce. Good value overall, and away from the hurly-burly of holiday trippers. 20 min. from Walt Disney World, 20 min. from the airport. **I**

ፕ ፕ **Admiral's Inn** (formerly USA Inn), 5651 Cypress Gardens Blvd., Cypress Gardens, FL 33884 (813/324-5950). 158 rms, A/C, cable color TV. AE, CB, DC, MC, V. Free parking, pool, rest., bar, crib $10. *Note:* Standard but comfortable motel. Functional rms w. balconies. Adequate rest. Good value. Efficient svce. 5 min. by car from Cypress Gardens, 40 min. from Walt Disney World. **I**, but lower rates off-season.

ፕ **Budget Host Driftwood,** 970 Cypress Gardens Blvd., Winter Haven, FL 33880 (813/294-4229; toll free 800/283-4678). 24 rms, A/C, cable color TV. AE, CB, DC, MC, V. Free parking, pool, adj. rest., crib $6. *Note:* Standard small motel 5 min. from Cypress Gardens. Comfortable rms, some w. kitchenette and refrigerator. Friendly reception and svce. 30 min. from Disney World. **I**, but lower rates off-season.

ፕ **King's Motel,** 4836 W. Irlo Bronson Memorial Hwy. (U.S. 192), Kissimmee, FL 32741 (407/396-4762; toll free 800/ 327-9071). 122 rms, A/C, cable color TV. AE, MC, V. Free parking, pool, fishing, nearby rest. *Note:* Modern, well-maintained motel on attractive Lake Cecil. Comfortable, appealing rms, some w. kitchenette. Friendly, smiling svce. 10 min. from Walt Disney World and Sea World. Good value. **B–I**, but lower rates off-season.

ፕ **Bucket's Bermuda Bay Hideaway** (formerly Orlando Motor Lodge), 1825 N. Mills Ave., Orlando, FL 32803 (407/896-4111). 45 rms, A/C, cable color TV. AE, MC, V. Free parking, pool, fishing, coffee shop. *Note:* Modest but very acceptable bed-and-breakfast inn on Lake Rowena (boats available). Rms w. balconies, some w. kitchenettes. Good value. 30 min. drive to Walt Disney World. **B–I**

ፕ **Motel 6 West,** 7455 W. Irlo Bronson Memorial Hwy. (U.S. 192), Kissimmee, FL 32741 (407/396-6422). 148 rms, A/C, cable color TV. AE, DC, MC, V. Free parking, pool. *Note:* New motel w. unbeatable rates. Functional comfort. 5 min. from Walt Disney World and EPCOT. Excellent value. Ideal for budget travelers. **B**

Airport Accommodations

ፕ ፕ ፕ **Renaissance Hotel–Orlando** (formerly Penta), 5445 Forbes Place, Orlando, FL 32812 (407/240-1000). 300 rms, A/C, color TV, in-rm movies, AE, CB, DC, MC, V. Free valet parking, pool, health club, sauna, two rests., bars, concierge, free airport shuttle, free crib. *Note:* Ultramodern and elegant airport hotel. Luxurious, oversize guest rms w. bathroom phones and minibars. Highly professional svce. European-style atmosphere. VIP floor. Business clientele. 10 min. from dwntwn. **M–E**

ፕ ፕ **Roadway Inn** (formerly Florida Mall Motel), 8601 S. Orange Blossom Trail, Orlando, FL 32809 (407/859-4100). 131 rms, A/C, cable color TV. AE, CB, DC, MC, V. Free parking, pool, adj. 24-hr.

coffee shop, valet svce, free crib. *Note:* Inviting motel 10 min. from the airport and 20 min. from Walt Disney World. Very large, comfortable rms. Good value.

YMCA/Youth Hostels

Orlando International Hostel, 227 N. Eola Dr., Orlando, FL 32801 (407/843-8888). Appealing youth hostel on Lake Eola.

RESTAURANTS

Personal Favorites (in order of preference)

    🍷🍷🍷 **Hemingway's,** Hyatt Regency Grand Cypress (see "Accommodations," above) (407/239-1234). A/C. Lunch/dinner Tues–Sat. AE, CB, DC, MC, V. Jkt. *Specialties:* Cajun shrimp cocktail, steamed clam and mussel pot, paella, Alaskan king crab, mahimahi en papillote. Fine wine list. *Note:* Impressive two-story glass-walled rest. w. food ranging from fine to exceptional. Overlooks a lagoonlike pool and waterfalls. Elegant leafy decor w. palm trees and other greenery. Flawless svce. Resv. highly advised. Orlando's finest address. *French/American.* **E**

    🍷🍷🍷 **Christini's,** 7600 Dr. Phillips Blvd., Orlando (407/345-8770). A/C. Dinner only, Mon–Sat (until midnight). AE, DC, MC, V. *Specialties:* broiled portobello mushrooms w. vinaigrette, spaghetti alla carbonara, braciole alla pizzaiola, Tuscan breast of chicken stuffed w. prosciutto and Bel Paese cheese, sautéed jumbo shrimp w. white wine in saffron-cream sauce, ricotta cheesecake w. raspberry sauce. Very fine list of Italian wines. *Note:* Classic Italian dishes w. a special touch makes Christini's one of the best rests. in town. Elegant, comfortable setting w. discreet alcoves, light woods, and beamed ceilings. Polished svce. Big business clientele. Resv. recommended. *Italian.* **M–E**

    🍷🍷🍷 **Maison et Jardin,** 430 S. Wymore Rd., Altamonte Springs (407/862-4410). A/C. Dinner nightly, brunch Sun; closed hols. AE, CB, DC, MC, V. Jkt. *Specialties:* rack of lamb, scallops saffron, beef Wellington, roast chateaubriand, sweetbreads, sautéed medallions of veal forestière. Fine wine list (over 800 selections). *Note:* Framed by trees and shrubberies of jasmine and azalea, this lovely arcaded Mediterranean-style villa boasts one of the most flower-filled settings in Florida. Antique furniture and Oriental rugs contribute to the opulent decor. Excellent classic French cuisine, though a tad pretentious. Svce excellent. Resv. advised. 45 min. from Walt Disney World. *French/Continental.* **M–E**

    🍷🍷 **Chatham's Place,** 7575 Dr. Phillips Blvd., Orlando (407/345-2992). A/C. Dinner only, nightly. AE, CB, DC, MC, V. *Specialties:* snails w. angel-hair pasta, rack of lamb w. rosemary, grilled yellowfin tuna w. grilled-pineapple salsa, breast of duck w. port-wine sauce, Black Velvet cake. Menu changes regularly. Wine and beer but no hard liquor. *Note:* If you love fish—grilled, steamed, or sautéed—this is some of Orlando's best. The seafood is impeccably fresh, the decor casual w. its blue-tiled open kitchen, the svce friendly and efficient. Note that the rest. is totally no-smoking. A very good place; resv. advisable. *American.* **M**

    🍷🍷 **Barney's Steak House,** 1615 E. Colonial Dr., Orlando (407/896-6864). A/C. Lunch Mon–Fri, dinner nightly; closed Thanksgiving, Dec 25. AE, CB, DC, MC, V. *Specialties:* broiled meats and fish, ribs of beef, giant salad bar. *Note:* The favorite steakhouse of Orlando residents, according to an *Orlando Sentinel* poll. Top cuts of meat, cooked to perfection. Modern decor, pleasant background music. Relaxed atmosphere, very good svce. Resv. advised. *Steak.* **I–M**

    🍷 **Maison des Crêpes,** 348 N. Park Ave., Winter Park (407/647-4469). A/C. Lunch Mon–Sat, dinner Tues–Sat; closed hols. and early July. AE, CB, DC, MC, V. *Specialties:* pancakes (30 varieties), soups, fish of the day, filet Royal. *Note:* As the name indicates, pancakes of various types are the house specialty here, but the daily specials and the chef's soups are equally worth recommending. Rustic, flowery setting. 40 min. from Walt Disney World. *French/Seafood.* **I–M**

Other Restaurants (from top bracket to budget)

☀☆☆☆ **Empress Room,** aboard the *Empress Lilly* riverboat, Disney World Village, Lake Buena Vista (407/828-3900). A/C. Dinner only, nightly. AE, MC, V. Jkt. *Specialties:* oyster soup w. spinach, artichoke bottoms w. salmon mousse, Dover sole w. wild mushrooms, free-range chicken w. tarragon and shallots, roast pheasant w. truffles, soufflé Grand Marnier, cloche au chocolat. Very fine wine list. *Note:* This life-size replica of a paddlewheeler is a fixture in the Disney empire. The dining room's Louis XV decor and the formal svce are impressive. The cuisine is rather pretentious, but dishes such as the sole stuffed w. salmon mousse are truly inspired. Be prepared for a hefty bill. Resv. indispensable (the rest. seats only 52). *Continental.* **E–VE**

☀☆☆☆ **Chalet Suzanne,** U.S. 27N, Lake Wales (813/676-6011). A/C. Breakfast/lunch/dinner daily; closed Mon May–Nov. AE, CB, DC, MC, V. Jkt. *Specialties:* romaine soup, lobster Newburg, curried shrimp, chicken Suzanne, lamb chops English style, rum cream pie, crêpes Suzette. *Note:* One of the best rests. in Florida, in the middle of an orange grove. Picturesquely miscellaneous decor. The cuisine in general and the sauces in particular are meticulously worked out. Even the soups merit an award of excellence; some of them accompanied the *Apollo* astronauts to the moon. Cheerful, conscientious svce. Resv. advised. An excellent establishment that has already celebrated its 50th anniversary. *Continental.* **M–E** (**VE** for prix-fixe dinner).

☆☆ **Dux,** in the Peabody Hotel (see "Accommodations," above) (407/352-4000). A/C. Lunch Mon–Fri, dinner Mon–Sat. AE, DC, MC, V. *Specialties:* portobello pot stickers w. goat cheese and beef jam; wild mushroom cheesecake w. juniper anglaise; evil jungle sea bass w. Thai vegetable stew; lamb w. cardamom masala, fresh chickpeas, and pear chutney; white chocolate macadamia-nut brownie. *Note:* Chef Michael McSweeny goes for a global combination of tastes and succeeds in creating original and inspiring dishes. As the cutesy name indicates, ducks are the motif for decor. Still, a romantic atmosphere. Resv. strongly advised. *American/International.* **E**

☆☆ **Jordan's Grove,** 1300 S. Orlando Ave., Maitland (407/628-0020). A/C. Lunch Tues–Fri, dinner Tues–Sun, brunch Sun. *Specialties:* black-bean soup w. acorn squash; rock shrimp hash; shrimp skewer w. pink-peppercorn sauce; mixed grill of venison and lamb w. berry, apricot, and pepper glaze; blackberry-apple crisp. Menu changes daily. *Note:* Modern American regional cooking at its best in a charming turn-of-the-century restored home. Meats and fish are cured and smoked on the premises, as well as the delicious homemade breads and muffins. Resv. advised. *American.* **M–E**

☆☆ **Le Coq au Vin,** 4800 S. Orange Ave. (407/851-6980). A/C. Lunch Tues–Fri, dinner Tues–Sun; closed hols. AE, CB, DC, MC, V. Jkt. *Specialties:* shrimp André w. beurre blanc, capers, tomatoes, and garlic; chicken liver pâté; grilled eggplant w. crabmeat, shrimp, and Cajun hollandaise; coq au vin; crème brûlée. Menu changes regularly. *Note:* French country-house atmosphere. A favorite among the locals and a nice escape from the tourist commotion. Excellent svce. and a great value. *French/American.* **I–M**

☆☆ **Caruso's Palace,** 8986 International Dr. (407/363-7110). A/C. Dinner nightly, brunch Sun. AE, CB, DC, MC, V. Jkt. *Specialties:* oysters Florentine; carpaccio w. asparagus tips, artichoke hearts, and capers; grilled tuna w. basil pesto; six-course Italian tasting dinners; tiramisù (Italian layered cake). *Note:* The interior is a replica of an Italian opera house complete w. frescoes, marble furnishings, and fountain. Continuous entertainment. Substantial, classic Italian cooking w. a trace of provincial French inspiration. Resv. advised. *Italian.* **M**

♔♔ **Christy's Sundown,** Ave. K and 3rd St. S. (U.S. 17), Winter Haven (813/293-0069). A/C. Lunch/dinner Mon–Sat; closed hols. AE, MC, V. *Specialties:* broiled red snapper, lobster, steak, shish kebab, Greek-style chicken. *Note:* Rest. in rustic Mediterranean decor, very popular w. vacationers in the Cypress Gardens and surrounding areas. Solid, carefully prepared cuisine. Good desserts. Svce rather dour but efficient. Resv. advised. 40 min. from Walt Disney World. Dancing. *Steak/Continental.* **I–M**

☼♔♔ **Lili Marlene's Aviators Pub,** 129 Church St., Orlando (407/422-2434). A/C. Lunch/dinner daily (until midnight), brunch Sun. AE, CB, DC, MC, V. *Specialties:* roast beef, steak aviateur, veal Cordon Bleu, catch of the day. *Note:* Located in the heart of Church Street Station with its yesteryear shops and turn-of-the-century saloon, this pleasant, amusing pub offers a number of serviceable, adequately prepared dishes. Especially lively in the evening. 25 min. from Walt Disney World. *Steak/Continental.* **I–M**

☼♔♔ **Papeete Bay Verandah,** in Disney's Polynesian Village Resort (407/824-1391). A/C. Breakfast/dinner daily, brunch Sun. AE, MC. *Specialties:* teriyaki chicken, beef Bora Bora, ribs of beef, broiled lobster. *Note:* The Tahitian setting is one of the most successful of the Walt Disney World creations. The decor and the Polynesian dancing provide an exotic dining experience, even though the cooking is tempered for mainstream American tastes. The character breakfast buffet is less convincing. Lovely view of the lagoon. Evenings, there's a Polynesian show. Dinner resv. advised. No lunch served. *Polynesian.* **I–M**

♔ **Ran-Getsu of Tokyo,** 8400 International Dr., Orlando (407/345-0044). A/C. Dinner only, nightly. AE, CB, DC, MC, V. *Specialties:* sushi, sukiyaki, shabu-shabu, tempura, yosenabe. *Note:* One of the largest Japanese rest. in the U.S., with the longest sushi bar in Florida. The chefs, trained in the mother house in Tokyo, practice their demonic skills before your eyes. Open, comfortable dining areas on two levels. Locally very popular; resv. advised. *Japanese.* **I–M**

♔ **Townsend's Fish House & Tavern,** 35 W. Michigan, Orlando (407/422-5560). A/C. Lunch Mon–Fri, dinner daily. AE, DC, MC, V. *Specialties:* raw oysters, Cajun alligator tail, mixed grill (alligator, duck breast, venison, andouille sausage), grilled Norwegian salmon, stone crabs (in season), key lime pie. *Note:* Excellent values and impeccably fresh seafood make Townsend's a favorite rest. among residents. Agreeable, relaxed atmosphere w. very popular predinner "happy hour" and live music Wed–Sat evenings. Marble bars and lots of brightwork; efficient though somewhat flustered svce. *Seafood.* **I**

♔ **Linda's La Cantina,** 4721 E. Colonial Dr., Orlando (407/894-4491). A/C. Dinner only, Tues–Sat; closed late July to mid-Aug, Thanksgiving, Dec 25. AE, MC, V. *Specialties:* lasagna, veal parmigiana, Italian dishes, broiled steak. *Note:* Classic steakhouse w. nondescript decor offering decent Italian cooking and choice meats at very affordable prices. Popular w. the locals for over 40 years. No resv. accepted; be prepared to wait. 25 min. from Walt Disney World. *Italian/Steak.* **I**

♔ **Ronnie's,** 2702 E. Colonial Dr., Orlando (407/894-2943). A/C. Breakfast/lunch/dinner daily (7am–11pm). No credit cards. *Specialties:* Jewish deli delights, corned beef, pastrami, homemade desserts (excellent cheesecake). *Note:* New York–style delicatessen, w. gigantic sandwiches and waistline-destroying desserts. Often crowded at lunch. 25 min. from Walt Disney World. *American.* **B**

Cafeterias/Fast Food

Hard Rock Café, 5800 Kirkman Rd., at Universal Studios Florida, Orlando (407/351-7625). Open daily 11am–2am. AE, MC, V. *Specialties:* Burgers, "pig sandwich," barbecue dishes. *Note:* Orlando version of the well-known rockburger joint chain. The building is shaped like a giant electric guitar, w. Elvis

Presley and Chuck Berry stained-glass windows. Rock 'n' roll memorabilia. Very popular among tourist crowds.

Morrison's, 1840 E. Colonial Dr., Orlando (407/896-2091). Open daily (until 8:30pm). MC, V. *Specialties:* roast beef, sandwiches, soups, salads, home-made pastry. *Note:* Cafeteria cooking, honest and well prepared. Other locations: 140 Winter Haven Mall, Winter Haven (813/293-1003), and 700 N. Orlando Ave., Winter Park (407/644-7853).

BARS & NIGHTCLUBS

Bonkerz, 4315 N. Orange Blossom Trail, Winter Park (407/629-2665). The best comedy club in the area, featuring the very top comedians.

Cricketers Arms, 8445 International Dr. (354-0686). Congenial English pub w. a range of musical entertainment. Also rest. Open nightly.

Dekko's, 46 N. Orange Ave. (648-8727). Multilevel dance club and con-cert hall featuring pyrotechnics and light shows. Open Tues–Sun.

J. J. Whispers, 904 Lee Rd., Orlando (407/629-4779). Disco music, live orchestras, five dance floors. A hot spot for several years. Also rest. Open nightly.

Laughing Kookaburra, in the Buena Vista Palace, Walt Disney World Vil-lage, Lake Buena Vista (407/827-2727). Top-40 dance bands nightly. The bar counts 99 brands of domestic and imported beers.

Phineas Phogg's Balloon Works, Church St. Station, 129 W. Church St., Orlando (407/422-2434). Locally popular disco. Amusing ambience. Open nightly.

Rosie O'Grady's Goodtime Emporium, Church St. Station, 129 W. Church St., Orlando (407/422-2434). Dixieland jazz in a turn-of-the-century saloon setting. Very touristy atmosphere. Open nightly.

Sullivan's Trailway Lounge, 1108 S. Orange Blossom Trail, Orlando (407/843-2934). Trendy western club, featuring country music stars.

NEARBY EXCURSIONS

KENNEDY SPACE CENTER/SPACEPORT USA (46 mi./75km east on Fla. 50) (407/452-2121): The primary American space-vehicle launch site. Since 1950 more than 2,200 spacecraft, in-cluding the famous shuttle, have been launched from this narrow finger of land at the tip of Cape Canaveral. Participants on the two-hour guided bus tour visit the rocket- and shuttle-assembly areas, the astronaut training center, and the various launch sites. Interesting space museum. Open daily; closed Dec 25. Call the toll-free number for information on scheduled launchings. (For information on nearby hotels and restaurants, see Chapter 16 on Florida's East Coast.)

DAYTONA BEACH (55 mi./89km NE on I-4): Immense beach, 25 mi. (40km) long, accessible by car and dune buggy. Famous also for automobile racing—the Daytona Sunbank 24 and Daytona 500 in Feb, the Daytona 400 in July, etc. (See Chapter 16 on Florida's East Coast.)

ST. AUGUSTINE (115 mi./185km NE on I-4 and I-95): The oldest city in the U.S., founded in 1565 by Don Pedro Me-néndez de Áviles. Charming Spanish colonial city, cleverly restored (Castillo de San Marcos, Mission Nombre de Dios, Zorayda Castle, etc.). A visit here can readily be combined with a trip to Daytona Beach. (See Chapter 16 on Florida's East Coast.)

FARTHER AFIELD

THE ATLANTIC COAST FROM CAPE CANAVERAL TO MIAMI (390 mi./625km r.t. on Fla. A1A, U.S. 1, and I-95): Very satisfying vacation tour for devotees of sea and shore. Can also include visits to the Kennedy Space Center, Palm Beach, Fort Lauderdale, and Miami. See Chapter 16 on Florida's East Coast and Chapter 19 on Miami.

☀️🔭 **TAMPA/ST. PETERSBURG & THE GULF OF MEXICO** (166 mi./265km r.t. on I-4): Many inviting beaches along the Gulf of Mexico: Treasure Island, St. Petersburg Beach, Longboat Key, Venice. Can also include the cities of Sarasota, Tarpon Springs, etc. See Chapter 17 on Tampa/St. Petersburg.

MIAMI AND MIAMI BEACH🔥🔥

□ □ □

With the Everglades and Key West

Originally known as Fort Dallas, a small military post established in 1835 at the mouth of the Miami River, the youngest of America's great cities officially saw the light in 1870 as a simple post office and trading post. It didn't begin to grow until 1896, when Henry M. Flagler, an enterprising railroad tycoon, decided to extend the East Coast Railroad south from Palm Beach and to build the Royal Palm Hotel at Miami. Today the city (whose name, from the Seminole *Mayami,* means a broad stretch of water) has become synonymous with vacations and lavish hotels, but it has higher aspirations.

First of all this enormous, complex metropolis, growing demographically at an explosive rate (35% in 10 years), would like to outgrow its reputation, disseminated by the TV series "Miami Vice," as a drug dealers' paradise and a racial melting-pot where Cubans, Haitians, Jamaicans, Salvadorans, and other Hispanics engage in confrontation with whites and African Americans rather than assimilation. It is indeed the case that in this tropical, cosmopolitan version of New York City, which in a comparatively few years has become the main financial clearinghouse for trade between the U.S. and Latin America, these different ethnic groups live beside one another or even on top of one another.

There are vacationers drawn to the beaches of **Miami Beach, Key Biscayne,** and **Surfside,** or to a dream cruise in the Caribbean (Miami is the world's cruise-ship capital). There are millionaires who, finding **Coconut Grove** and **Coral Gables** no longer exclusive enough for their tastes, are withdrawing from Miami in favor of **Palm Beach** and **Naples.** There are retirees from New York and Chicago who have come to live out their lives in the Florida sun. There are businesspeople and bankers of all nationalities—at last count there were 144 banks in Miami, 44 of them foreign. There are well-heeled South Americans doing their shopping in the smart stores of **Bal Harbor** and the **Miracle Mile.** There are big-game fishermen and boating buffs who can indulge their passion here—43,000 pleasure boats claim Miami or Miami Beach as their port of registration, from little outboards to 120-ft. (40m) yachts; as to the fishing, biologists can point to no fewer than 600 species in the waters of southern Florida. There are Latin American exiles, anti-Castro Cubans for the most part, who have come to try their luck in the U.S., making Miami the largest bilingual city in the country. Store signs on the picturesque **Calle Ocho** (8th St.), the Main Street of **Little Havana,** bear witness to this in a kind of American-flavored Spanish: "perros calientes," for example, for "hot dogs." In 1960 the "Port of the Americas," as Miami has been termed, was still 75% Anglo; today, only 45%.

The kindly climate brings down every year to Miami and other resort cities as far as **Fort Lauderdale** or even **Boca Raton** (see Chapter 16 on Florida's East Coast) hordes of shivering citizens nicknamed "snowbirds," in flight from the snows and blizzards of the North. Even the hot, humid summer weather has its devotees thanks to lower off-season prices. In all, almost 9 million visitors annually descend on the 650 hotels and motels and the 4,500 restaurants, cafeterias, and snack bars of Miami and Miami Beach, making mass tourism the leading local industry (for the state of Florida as a whole it brings in $10 billion a year).

Despite the devastation wrought by Hurricane Andrew in August 1992, the costliest disaster in American history—35 deaths, more than 130,000 homes and buildings destroyed or damaged, $20 billion worth of damage—tourism, the leading local industry, has bounced back quickly. Most of the parks, museums, and attractions that did experience damage, which are located in South Dade County (near the path taken by the hurricane), have recovered and are back in service.

The second industry is still the trade in early fruits and vegetables and in citrus crops, of which Florida is the country's largest producer. The third is believed to be the drug trade—over the past decade Miami, with Los Angeles, has become the main market and principal drug clearinghouse in North America. In the light of this fact, it will not surprise you to learn that, according to FBI figures, Miami is one of the country's most dangerous cities. Once night has fallen in the downtown business district of Miami, only the rash go out alone on foot.

After the first attacks on visitors in 1993, which included the murders of first a German and then a British tourist, Miami suffered a wave of cancellations from those planning to visit, especially those from foreign countries. In all, 10 foreigners were murdered that year. Those arriving at the Miami International Airport should take heed of the safety information provided on police-assisted telephones installed in the airport terminals. A tourist-oriented police force has been created to patrol the surroundings of the airport, the place targeted by criminals because of the many car-rental agencies based there.

With its innumerable theme parks and its many theaters and museums, the superb, ultramodern **Metro-Dade Cultural Center,** its symphony orchestra, and its internationally famous Miami City ballet, the Floridian metropolis is in no sense a cultural desert. As well as its own attractions, Miami offers the visitor a whole range of interesting excursions: for example, to the famous **Everglades National Park,** severely damaged by Hurricane Andrew. Not to forget the **Florida Keys,** a chain of 43 small coral islands protruding like a huge comma into the Gulf of Mexico as far as **Key West,** barely 90 miles (144km) from the coast of Cuba. Once the lair of pirates and smugglers, the Keys escaped Andrew's wrath and are today a paradise for deep-sea fishermen, and a sort of tourist annex of Miami.

Actor Sidney Poitier is perhaps the best known of Miami's famous children.

BASIC FACTS: State of Florida. Area code: 305. Time zone: eastern. ZIP Codes: 33101 (Miami), 33139 (Miami Beach). Founded: 1870. Approximate population: city, 370,000; metropolitan area, about 3,190,000 (of whom 1,650,000 are Hispanics). 11th in size of U.S. metropolitan areas.

CLIMATE: There is no need to dwell on Miami's benign winters, averaging 69°F (20°C) Dec–Feb; it is this that draws the crowds of lucky vacationers. With its heavy heat (average in July, 82°F/28°C), summer is much less pleasant. For the rest of the year the thermometer rarely goes above 77°F (25°C), ideal for ocean bathing or just doing nothing. But watch out for tropical hurricanes in the fall—in 1992 Hurricane Andrew caused massive destruction.

DISTANCES: Atlanta, 659 mi. (1,055km); Key West, 161 mi. (258km); New Orleans, 856 mi. (1,370km); Orlando, 240 mi. (385km); Savannah, 496 mi. (794km); Washington, D.C., 1,075 mi. (1,720km).

ARRIVAL & TRANSIT INFORMATION

Note: In view of the sheer size of the Miami metropolitan area, which includes 27 different communities and stretches 40 mi. (64km) from north to south, the different places, museums, and monuments referred to below are identified according to district: Miami, Miami Beach, Coral Gables, etc.

AIRPORT: Miami International Airport (MIA), 7 mi. (11km) NW, 9th-busiest U.S. airport, with 25 million passengers each year. There'll be a long wait at Arrivals on international flights. Call 876-7000 for information.

U.S. AIRLINES: American (toll free 800/433-7300), Chalk's (toll free 800/424-2557), Continental (toll free 800/525-0280), Delta (toll free 800/221-1212), Northwest (toll free 800/225-2525), TWA (toll free 800/221-2000), United (toll free 800/241-6522), and USAir (toll free 800/428-4322).

FOREIGN CARRIERS: Air Canada (toll free 800/776-3000), Air France (toll free 800/237-2747), and British Airways (toll free 800/247-9297).

CITY LINK: The **cab** fare to city center is about $15; time, 20 min. Cab fare to Miami Beach, Coral Gables, or Key Biscayne is $18–$22, according to destination.
Airport bus: **Super Shuttle** (871-2000) provides door-to-door service to any Miami or Miami Beach destination; operates at 15-min. intervals, 24-hr. daily (resv. a must when you're traveling *to* the airport); fare, $8–$19, according to destination; time, 30–45 min., according to destination.
Municipal bus: **METROBUS** (638-6700), Lines 3 and 20 to dwntwn; fare, $1; time, 45–50 min.
Cabs are costly because of the distances involved. City public bus transportation is complex and unsafe; the elevated rail system (**METRORAIL** and **METROMOVER**) is modern but still incomplete. The sensible solution is to rent a car with unlimited mileage; Florida rates are very low, and you may be able to leave the car in another city, such as Orlando, Fort Lauderdale, or Tampa, without surcharge.

CAR RENTAL (at Miami International Airport unless otherwise noted): Avis (toll free 800/331-1212); Budget (toll free 800/527-0700); Dollar (toll free 800/800-4000); Hertz (toll free 800/654-3131); National (toll free 800/227-7368); and Thrifty, 2701 W. LeJeune Rd. (toll free 800/367-2277). For dwntwn locations, consult the city telephone directory. *Foreign visitors note:* See "Safety" under "Fast Facts" in Chapter 2.

LIMOUSINE SERVICES: American Limo Service (688-7700), Carey Limousine (764-0615), Executive Limo (947-6144).

TAXIS: In theory cabs may be hailed on the street; in practice it's advisable to take them at the stands outside the major hotels, or simply to phone. The principal cab companies are **Central Cab** (532-5555), **Metro Taxi** (888-8888), and **Yellow Cab** (444-4444).

TRAIN: Amtrak station, 8303 NW 37th Ave., Miami (toll free 800/872-7245).

INTERCITY BUSES: Greyhound, 700 Biscayne Blvd., Miami and 7101 Harding Ave., Miami Beach (both toll free, 800/231-2222).

INFORMATION & TOURS

TOURIST INFORMATION: The **Greater Miami Convention and Visitors Bureau,** 701 Brickell Ave., Suite 2700, Miami, FL 33131 (305/539-3000; toll free 800/283-2707). Call for information about hurricane damage and for safety tips.
   Miami Beach Visitor Information Center, 1920 Meridian Ave., Miami Beach (305/672-1270): Information on Miami Beach.

GUIDED TOURS: **American Sightseeing** (bus), 11077 NW 36th Ave., Miami (688-7700): Guided tour of the city and surroundings; serves the principal hotels.
   Biscayne Helicopter, 12760 SW 137th Ave., Miami (252-3883): Impressive. Daily year-round service.
   Island Queen (boat), Miamarina, 400 SE Second Ave., Miami (379-5119): Trips on the bay; daily year-round service.
   Miami Nice Excursions (bus), 19250 Collins Ave., Miami Beach (949-9180): Guided tours of the city and surroundings. Call for resv.
   Old Town Trolley (bus), Bayside Marketplace (374-8687): 90-min. guided tour of Miami's principal attractions in a replica of an old-time trolley. You may get off and on as often as you please along the route. Daily year round.
   Sea Escape (shipboard cruise), Port Everglades, Fort Lauderdale (379-0000; toll free 800/327-7400): One-day mini cruises to the Bahamas or Freeport and back, with excursions on shore. On board are rests., bars, pool, casino. Fare runs around $100 per person, including meals, plus a hefty $45 port charge.

SIGHTS, ATTRACTIONS & ACTIVITIES

ADVENTURES: **Wilderness Experiences, Inc.** (Land Rover and boat), Loop and Dill Rd., in Big Cypress National Preserve (813/695-3143): Airboat trip lasting one or more days across the swamps of Big Cypress National Preserve, north of Everglades National Park (see "National Parks Nearby," below). This 100-mi. (160km) tour will reveal to you the fauna and flora unique to the Everglades. Year round, by resv. only. For more information, write Everglades Institute, SR1 Box 52, Loop Rd., Ochopee, FL 33943.
   Windjammer Cruises (boat), P.O. Box 120, Miami Beach, FL 33119 (305/672-6453; toll free 800/327-2600): 6-, 13-, and 26-day cruises through the Antilles and the islands of the Caribbean, aboard wonderful old-time sailing ships. Reckon on $825 for six days. A real change.

ARCHITECTURAL HIGHLIGHTS: ☼🏛 **Art Deco District,** around Collins Ave. between 6th and 23rd Sts., and Ocean Dr. between 9th and 15th Sts., Miami Beach: More than 800 fine 1920s and 1930s buildings in pastel hues; the fine flower of art deco. The whole neighborhood is undergoing extensive rehabilitation. Guided walking tours available; call 672-2014 for information.
   ☼🏛 **Atlantis Condominium,** 2025 Brickell Ave., Miami (285-1269): This ultramodern azure-blue building with its giant skylight open to the heavens, by the celebrated architectural team of Bernardo Fort-Brescia and Laurinda Spear, is one of the symbols of the New Miami and has appeared in stock footage for the TV series "Miami Vice."
   🏛 **Bacardi Building,** 2100 Biscayne Blvd., Miami: Modern structures with mosaic murals that recall the famous facade of the University of Mexico in Mexico City.

☼ 🔔♨ **Metro Dade Cultural Center,** 101 W. Flagler St., Miami (375-1125): Ultramodern complex, very Mediterranean in flavor, designed by the architect Philip Johnson. Around a large plaza stand several remarkable buildings: the **Center for the Fine Arts** (see below), the **Historical Museum of Southern Florida** (see below), and the **Miami Public Library,** with 1.5 million volumes. The artistic and cultural heart of Miami.

☼ ♨ **Miamarina,** 401 Biscayne Blvd., Miami (579-6955): Well-known, crowded boat basin for pleasure craft, with more than 200 berths. Boats may be rented for deep-sea fishing or boat trips on Biscayne Bay. A spectacular sight.

☼ ♨ **Miami Beach Hotel Row,** Collins Ave. and Indian Creek between 21st and 71st Sts., Miami Beach: Grand hotels and other sumptuous buildings huddled on the narrow strip of land between the ocean and Indian Creek Canal. A remarkable sight.

♨ **Miami Herald Building,** 1 NE Herald Plaza, Miami (376-2911): A superbly successful piece of modern architectural design; one of the loveliest buildings of its kind. Guided tour of the newspaper on Tues and Wed.; resv. required at least one week in advance.

☼ ♨ **Port of Miami,** American Way, Miami (371-7678): The busiest passenger-ship terminal in the world. Many liners, including the huge *Norway* (formerly the *France*), have their home port here; more than three million passengers pass through yearly. Note to photographers: The liners usually sail Fri–Mon toward the end of the afternoon.

High-Rise Buildings

☼ ♨ **Centrust Tower,** 101 E. Flagler St., Miami (539-5700): Giant 35-story building, 562 ft. (175m) high, looking like a pop-art wedding cake, by the distinguished architect I. M. Pei. Miami's finest skyscraper.

♨ **Southeast Financial Center,** 1 SE Financial Center, Miami: Florida's tallest high-rise, at 764 ft. (238m), 55 floors.

BEACHES: ☼♨♨ **Bill Baggs Cape Florida State Park,** at the southern end of Crandon Blvd., Key Biscayne: The local favorite. Pretty natural setting; badly damaged by Hurricane Andrew.

♨ **Haulover Beach,** 16 mi. (25km) on Fla. 1A, North Miami Beach: Much favored by families; good for surfing and fishing.

♨♨ **Miami Beach,** along Collins Ave.: The private beaches of the great hotels, side by side with several public beaches. The beach has recently been widened for a stretch of many miles. Access via 21st, 35th, 46th, 53rd, 64th, and 73rd Sts.

♨ **South Beach,** 5th St. and Ocean Dr., Miami Beach: For surfers. Trendy bistros.

Surfside, Collins Ave. from 88th to 96th Sts., North Miami: As its name implies, a great beach for surfers.

♨♨ **Venetian Pool,** 2701 De Soto Blvd., Coral Gables: Wonderful Venetian-style lagoon in the heart of town.

♨♨ **Virginia Beach,** 6 mi. (9km) SE along Rickenbacker Causeway, Virginia Key (next to Planet Ocean and Miami Seaquarium): Ideal for scuba-diving.

CHURCHES/SYNAGOGUES: ♨ King Solomon Temple, 910 Lincoln Rd.,

Miami Beach: Built in 1976 exactly according to the plan of King Solomon's temple in Jerusalem as described in the Old Testament.

☼ ♨♨ **Spanish Monastery of St. Bernard,** 16711 W. Dixie Hwy., North Miami Beach (11 mi./18km north) (945-1462): Cloister of the monastery of St. Bernard of Clairvaux, built in 1141 at Segovia in Spain. It was bought and transported, stone by stone, to the U.S. by press baron William Randolph Hearst, and re-erected on its present site in 1952. It houses a number of medieval works of art. Now the property of the Episcopal church. Lovely gardens; well worth going out of your way for.

HISTORIC BUILDINGS: ⌂ **The Barnacle State Historic Site,** 3485 Main Hwy., Coconut Grove (448-9445): One of the most beautiful examples of the local Caribbean-style architecture of the last century. Owned originally by Commodore Ralph Munroe, this luxurious private home, dating from the 1880s, was built in the midst of tropical gardens that are alone worth the visit. A lovely breath of the past. Tours are given Thurs–Mon.

　　☀ ⌂⌂ **Villa Vizcaya,** 3251 S. Miami Ave., Miami (579-2708): Former residence of International Harvester magnate James Deering dating from 1912. This Venetian-style 72-room palace, which stands on the shore of the Atlantic, has fine collections of European art—paintings, furniture, sculpture, and antique rugs—in styles ranging from Renaissance to baroque, rococo, etc. The villa, which served as the meeting place in Sept 1987 for Pope John Paul II and President Reagan, is surrounded by 9.6 acres (4ha) of superb gardens. Badly damaged by Hurricane Andrew. Open daily.

MONUMENTS: ⌂ **Kennedy Memorial Torch of Friendship,** Bayfront Park, Biscayne Blvd. at NE 5th St., Miami: Fountain crowned by a "torch of friendship" with its eternal flame, and a plaque to the memory of the assassinated president. The torch symbolizes friendship among all the nations of the Western Hemisphere.

　　⌂ **Pepper Fountain,** Bayfront Park, Biscayne Blvd. and NE 5th St., Miami: A spectacular fountain honoring the late Claude Pepper, who represented Florida in Congress for almost 60 years. Designed by California sculptor Isamu Noguchi, its jets and lights are computer controlled.

MUSEUMS OF ART: ⌂ **The Art Museum at Florida International University,** SW 8th St. and 107th Ave., University Park (348-2890): Permanent collection of works by North and South American artists. Home to the Cintas Foundation Collection of Contemporary Hispanic Art. Call for current exhibit schedule. Open Mon–Sat.

　　☀ ⌂⌂ **Bass Museum,** 2121 Park Ave., Miami Beach (673-7533): Recently reopened after major alterations, this very comprehensive art museum has a rich collection of European old masters (notably Rubens's *Holy Family*) and moderns, impressionists, and contemporary American painters, as well as a gallery of Far Eastern art. Open Tues–Sun.

　　⌂ **Center for the Fine Arts,** 101 W. Flagler St., Metro-Dade Cultural Center, Miami (375-1700): Interesting modern works and temporary exhibitions in a very beautiful, austere building by Philip Johnson. Open Tues–Sun.

　　⌂ **Cuban Museum of Arts,** 1300 SW 12th Ave., Miami (858-8006): The museum is devoted to the cultural heritage of Miami's important Cuban community. Temporary exhibitions. Open Tues–Sun.

　　⌂ **Lowe Art Museum,** 1301 Stanford Dr., Coral Gables (284-3536): Standing on the University of Miami campus, this ambitious art museum houses part of the famous Samuel H. Kress Collection of Renaissance and baroque art, the Alfred I. Barton Collection of primitive art, and interesting temporary exhibitions. Open Tues–Sun.

MUSEUMS OF SCIENCE & HISTORY: ⌂ **Gold Coast Railroad Museum,** 12400 SW 152nd St. at Coral Reef Dr., South Dade (253-0063): Railroad museum with more than 200 steam locomotives and passenger cars, including the legendary *Ferdinand Magellan* armored car which Presidents Franklin D. Roosevelt, Harry S. Truman, Dwight D. Eisenhower, and Ronald Reagan used as a "rolling White House." Open daily.

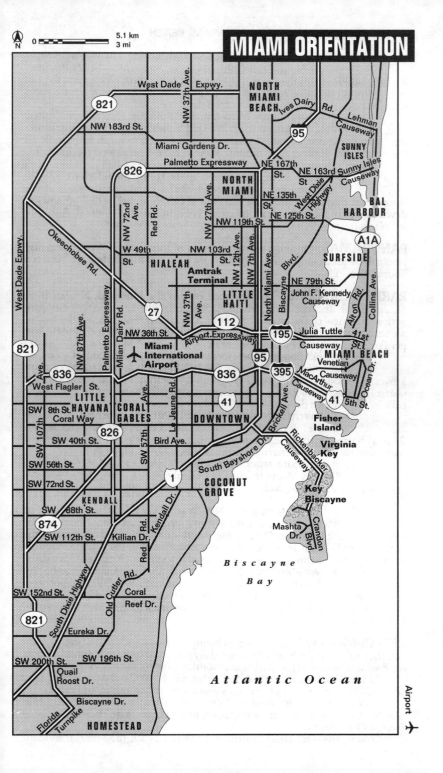

    Ⓐ **Historical Museum of Southern Florida,** 101 W. Flagler St. in the Metro-Dade Cultural Center, Miami (375-1492): Fascinating historical museum that traces the evolution of southern Florida and the Caribbean from the Stone Age to modern times. Native American art; treasures salvaged by divers from shipwrecks. Open daily.

    Ⓐ **Miami Youth Museum,** 5701 Sunset Dr., Bakery Center, South Miami (661-2787): This is definitely a teaching museum; young (and not-so-young) visitors are encouraged to touch and handle all the objects on display. Also mounts very interesting temporary exhibitions. Open daily.

    ☼ⒶⒶ **Museum of Science and Space Transit Planetarium,** 3280 S. Miami Ave., Miami (854-4247): Impressive museum of anthropology, devoted to the fauna and flora of Florida as well as biology and the development of modern science (chemistry, physics, energy sources). Also a giant planetarium with movies of journeys into space. Open daily.

PANORAMAS: The most spectacular view of Miami and its skyscrapers may be obtained for a comparatively modest fare from a ☼ **helicopter** (see "Guided Tours," above).

PARKS & GARDENS: ☼ⒶⒶ **Bayfront Park of the Americas,** NE 5th St. to SE 2nd St. at Biscayne Blvd., Miami (358-7550): Lovely waterfront city park with a clear view of the city and the port. Contains several noteworthy monuments, including the **Kennedy Memorial Torch of Friendship** and the new Pepper Fountain designed by sculptor Isamu Noguchi (see "Monuments," above).

    Ⓐ **Bill Baggs Cape Florida State Park,** south end of Crandon Blvd., Key Biscayne (361-5811): 400 acres (162ha) of mangroves, woods, and inviting beaches 20 min. by car from Miami. You can see the oldest lighthouse in Florida, where there was a bitter battle with the Seminole tribe in 1836. Open daily.

    ⒶⒶ **Fairchild Tropical Gardens,** 10901 Old Cutler Rd., Coral Gables (667-1651): One of the country's largest (83 acres/33.6ha) botanic gardens. Extraordinarily beautiful jungle and tropical gardens with more than 5,000 different varieties of exotic plants. Open daily.

    Ⓐ **Ichimura Japanese Garden,** Watson Park, McArthur Causeway, Miami (538-2121): Lovely little Japanese garden with pagoda, tea house, statues, lake, and waterfalls; romantically exotic. Open Tues–Sun.

    Ⓐ **Lummus Park,** 404 NW North River Dr., Miami (358-8784): On the banks of the Miami River, this park is now the site of the **Fort Dallas** camp, built in 1835 at the mouth of the river and once under the command of William Tecumseh Sherman. Abandoned in 1838, this unique example of pioneer architecture was later moved to its present location. Open daily.

    ☼ⒶⒶ **Venetian Pool,** 2701 De Soto Blvd., Coral Gables (460-5356): Lovely Italian garden with palm trees, waterfalls, and porticos. The wonderful swimming-pool lagoon, in the pit of an old coral-limestone quarry, is enough to justify the trip. Recently underwent a $2.3-million restoration. Open Tues–Sun.

PERFORMING ARTS: For current listings of shows and cultural events, consult the entertainment pages of the two daily papers, *Miami Herald* and *Diário de las Américas* (morning), as well as the monthly *Miami/South Florida* magazine.

    African Heritage Cultural Arts Center, 6161 NW 22nd Ave., Liberty City (638-6771): A training academy and showcase for dance, music, and drama.

    Coconut Grove Playhouse, 3500 Main Hwy., Coconut Grove (442-4000): Modern and classical theater; home of the Players State Theater Company (season Oct–May).

    Colony Theater, 1040 Lincoln Rd., Miami Beach (532-3491): Modern and avant-garde theater; performances by the Miami City Ballet (directors: Tony Catanzaro and Lizette Piedra).

Dade County Auditorium, 2901 W. Flagler St., Miami (547-5414): Ballet, opera, concerts. Home of the Greater Miami Opera (manager: Robert Heuer).

Gusman Center for the Performing Arts, 174 E. Flagler St., Miami (372-0925): Classical concerts, musical comedy, performances by the Miami City Ballet. Former movie theater with flamboyant art deco architecture.

Jackie Gleason Theater of the Performing Arts (TOPA), 1700 Washington Ave., Miami Beach (673-7300): Symphony concerts, recitals by leading artists, Broadway hits. Completely refurbished w. an art deco motif.

Lincoln Theatre, 555 Lincoln Rd., Miami Beach (673-3330): Original streamline modern architecture w. classical music and performances by the Miami City Ballet. Home of the New World Symphony Orchestra (director: Michael Tilson Thomas).

Ring Theater, University of Miami, 1380 Miller Dr., Coral Gables (284-3355): Modern theater, drama, comedy; performs six plays a year.

SHOPPING: **Bal Harbour Shops,** 9700 Collins Ave., Bal Harbour (866-0311): Dozens of luxury boutiques and stores from Saint Laurent and Gucci to Cartier and Neiman-Marcus.

Bayside Marketplace, 401 Biscayne Blvd., Miami (577-3344): Shopping center inaugurated in 1987 running alongside Bayfront Park and its marina. The two great pavilions house 165 unusual boutiques, cafés, and restaurants. Very lively atmosphere.

Lincoln Road Mall, Lincoln Rd. between Alton Rd. and Washington Ave., Miami Beach: More than 175 very reasonably priced boutiques, stores, and art galleries along a pedestrian mall lined with plantings and fountains.

Mayfair Shops in the Grove, Grand Ave. and Mary St., Coconut Grove (448-1700): One of the country's most elegant shopping centers; spectacular architecture with tropical gardens, waterfalls, and lagoons; fashion boutiques (Balmain, Charles Jourdan), antique dealers, restaurants, nightclubs, etc.

Miracle Mile, Coral Way between Douglas and Le Jeune Rds., Coral Gables: The Miami area's most popular shopping street, drawing a very cosmopolitan crowd.

Omni International Mall, 1601 Biscayne Blvd., Miami (374-6664): 185 fashion boutiques and stores of all kinds, six movie houses, and 13 restaurants in a slightly chilly glass-and-steel setting.

SPECIAL EVENTS: For exact dates, consult the **Greater Miami Convention and Visitors Bureau** and the **Miami Beach Visitor and Convention Authority** (see "Tourist Information," above).

Orange Bowl Festival (Jan 1): Eight days of festivities and parades culminating in the Orange Bowl football game.

Coconut Grove Arts Festival (Feb): Hundreds of artists exhibit their work in the streets of Coconut Grove; there's also a food festival. Draws more than half a million visitors every year.

Miami Beach Festival of the Arts (Feb): Concerts, art exhibitions, theater; a very popular festival.

International Boat Show (late Feb): One of the biggest of its kind, at the Miami Beach Convention Center.

Grand Prix of Miami (late Feb or early Mar): GT Grand Prix held in the streets of downtown Miami transformed into a raceway. Spectacular.

Calle Ocho Festival/Carnaval Miami (Mar): Nine days of dancing, parades, and celebration along the famous Calle Ocho in Little Havana. The biggest Hispanic festival in the U.S., drawing more than a million revelers.

Miami Unlimited Hydroplane Regatta (early June): Some of the world's fastest and most powerful boats compete in these outboard races on Biscayne Bay, starting from the Marine Stadium.

Festival of the Americas (late Oct): All Miami's Hispanic communities, headed by the Cubans, meet in Tropical Park for this colorful, exuberant folklore festival.

SPORTS: Miami boasts one of the two newest major-league baseball teams, as well as professional football and basketball franchises, three thoroughbred racetracks, and a major sport uniquely its own—jai alai.
Baseball: Florida Marlins (Apr–Oct), Joe Robbie Stadium (620-5000).
Basketball: Heat (Oct–Apr), Miami Arena (577-4328).
Football (Sept–Dec): Dolphins, Joe Robbie Stadium (620-5000).

Horse Racing
Calder Race Course, 21001 NW 27th Ave., North Dade (625-1311), with racing every weekend May–June.
Gulfstream Park, U.S. 1, Hallandale (944-1242), open Tues–Sun Jan–Mar.
Hialeah Park Race Course, E. 4th Ave. at 22nd St., Hialeah (885-8000), with races Tues–Sun Mar–May.

Jai Alai
Jai Alai Fronton, 3500 NW 37th Ave., Miami (633-6400), has games Mon and Wed–Sat, year round.

Deep-sea Fishing
Lovers of sports fishing may have trouble deciding among the dozens of boat-rental facilities in Miami and Miami Beach. Rates for fully equipped deep-sea fishing boats are around $350 for a half day of 6 hr., or $550 for a full day of 10 hr. For a list of rentals, contact:
Crandon Park Marina, 4000 Crandon Blvd., Key Biscayne (361-1281).
Dinner Key Marina, 3400 Pan American Dr., Coconut Grove (579-6980).
Haulover Beach Park Marina, 10800 Collins Ave., Sunny Isles (947-3525).
Miamarina, 401 Biscayne Blvd., Bay Front Park, Miami (579-6955).

STROLLS: ☀⚐ **Coconut Grove,** around S. Bayshore Dr. and SW 27th Ave.: The "Greenwich Village" of Miami, parts of which date back to 1870, owes its name to its many coconut palms. Many artists live here; there are also smart stores. A lively neighborhood by day or night.

⚐ **Coral Gables,** around Coral Way and LeJeune Rd.: Elegant residential district with parks, Venetian-style canals, and broad, shady avenues. Beautiful homes in Neo-Moorish and Mediterranean idioms. A well-known university.

⚐ **Key Biscayne,** around Crandon Blvd.: Luxury hotels, dream homes, and beautiful Crandon Park with its immense beaches combine to make this island, linked to Miami by a spectacular toll road, one of the favorite retreats of the famous, including ex-President Richard Nixon.

☀⚐ **Little Havana,** SW 8th St. (the famous "Calle Ocho") between SW 12th and 27th Aves.: Havana in the U.S., with Cuban restaurants, fruit stalls, craftshops (including some where cigars are still handmade after the Cuban manner), and Spanish signs. Lots of local color; don't miss a stroll here, especially in the evening. For information, call 324-8127.

☀⚐⚐ **Miami Beach,** along Collins Ave.: Once a marshy, impenetrable, mosquito-ridden mangrove swamp, this narrow 8-mi. (13km) peninsula has become synonymous with vacationing and with flashy luxury. Each year more than eight million tourists come here, summer and winter, to stay in the thousands of hotels, motels, rental apartments, and second homes. Principal attractions are the beaches, recently enlarged and renovated at a cost of $60 million, and the magnificent Art Deco District (see "Architectural Highlights," above). Linked to Miami by five causeways crossing Biscayne Bay.

THEME PARKS: ⬧ **Everglades Alligator Farm,** 40351 SW 192nd Ave., Homestead (247-2628): Offers Everglades airboat tours through the premises that are home to over 3,000 alligators. Don't miss the reptile show while there. Open daily year round.

⬧ **Everglades Holiday Park,** 21940 Griffin Rd. and U.S. 27, Fort Lauderdale (434-8111): Airboat trip through the swamps of the Everglades among the alligators and other wildlife. Organized camping, fishing, and hunting. Well worth the 40 min. by car from Miami. Open daily year round.

⬧⬧ **Fruit and Spice Park,** 24801 SW 187th St. at Coconut Palm Dr., Homestead (247-5727): A botanical garden unique of its kind in the U.S. In a 20-acre (8ha) garden, 200 species of trees and 500 different kinds of shrubs and plants offer a representative selection of the world's exotic fruits and spices, from the black sapodilla to the rosy papaya, the Brazilian jaboticaba, 40 kinds of mango, and 60 kinds of banana. Open daily. 40 min. from dwntwn along U.S. 1S.

⬧ **Monkey Jungle,** 14805 SW 216th St., South Dade (235-1611): Hundreds of primates, from baboons to gorillas, roaming free in a reproduction of an Amazon Basin forest. It's the visitors who are caged, on roads protected by chain-link fences. Open daily. 30 min. from dwntwn on U.S. 1S.

⬧ **Parrot Jungle,** 11000 SW 57th Ave., South Miami (666-7834): Many species of parrots, pelicans, marabou storks, and pink flamingos in a lush tropical garden. Shows by trained birds at set times. Open daily. 20 min. from dwntwn on U.S. 1S.

⬧ **Seaquarium,** 4400 Rickenbacker Causeway, Virginia Key (361-5705): One of the world's biggest marine zoos, with 12,000 fish and sea creatures. Home of the celebrated dolphin Flipper and the killer whale Lolita. Don't miss the fine tropical aquarium. Monorail tour. Open daily. 5 min. from dwntwn.

ZOOS: ⬧⬧ **Metrozoo,** 12400 SW 152nd St. at Coral Reef Dr., South Dade (251-0400): Big zoo of ultramodern design; the animals are semi-free with no bars or cages, on 280 acres (113ha) of gardens and wilderness, reminiscent of the natural habitats of the 240 or so species on display, including the very rare white tigers from Bengal and Australian koalas. You go around on a monorail. Wonderful and fascinating. Open daily.

ACCOMMODATIONS

Note: Many hotels in Miami and Miami Beach require a checkout notice of 24 or 48 hr. Ask about the checkout policy when you register.

Personal Favorites (in order of preference)

⬧⬧⬧⬧ **Grand Bay,** 2669 S. Bayshore Dr., Coconut Grove, FL 33133 (305/858-9600; toll free, see Preferred). 180 suites and minisuites, A/C, cable color TV. AE, CB, DC, MC, V. Valet gar. $10, pool, health club, sauna, two rests. (including the Grand Café), bar, 24-hr. rm svce, hrdrsr, concierge, crib $20. *Note:* With its modern truncated-pyramid design and unobstructed view over Biscayne Bay, this epitome of opulence, opened in 1984, has quickly become *the* place to stay in Miami. Elegant, very comfortable suites w. private balconies; the decor is a harmonious blend of modern art, crystal chandeliers, Oriental rugs, and period furniture. Remarkable svce. Good luxury hotel rest. In front of the hotel stands a fine modern sculpture by Alexander Liberman called *Windward*. The Grand Bay belongs to the Italian hotel chain Ciga. One of the 12 best hotels in the United States, and rates accordingly. **VE**

🏛🏛🏛 **Grand Prix Hotel,** 1717 N. Bayshore Dr., Miami, FL 33132 (305/372-0313; toll free 800/872-7749). 152 rms, A/C, cable color TV. AE, DC, MC, V. Valet parking $9, pool, marina, boating, health club, sauna, rest., bar, rm svce, concierge, crib $10. *Note:* One of Miami's most distinguished new luxury bayfront hotels. Striking modern design and architecture. Spacious guest rms w. first-class amenities. Attentive, multilingual staff. Turn-down svce. Big business clientele. Gourmet Chinese rest. (Tony Chan's Water Club). Direct access through a skywalk to the Omni Mall and its 160 shops and rests. **E–VE,** but lower rates off-season.

🏛🏛🏛 **Inter-Continental,** 100 Chopin Plaza, Miami, FL 33131 (305/577-1000; toll free, see Inter-Continental). 646 rms, A/C, color TV, in-rm movies. AE, CB, DC, MC, V. Valet gar. $10, pool, three rests. (including Le Pavillon), deli, two bars, 24-hr. rm svce, concierge, free crib. *Note:* A big, massive, ultramodern 34-floor tower, groaning under its burden of marble, Flemish tapestries, and other ornaments in flamboyant style. Spacious, very comfortable rms w. refrigerators; very complete facilities; first-grade svce; first-class rest. Spectacular five-story lobby with a 70-ton (63,600kg) monumental sculpture by Henry Moore. In dwntwn Miami, set against sparkling Biscayne Bay; the business traveler's favorite. **E–VE**

🏛🏛🏛 **Don Shula Hotel** (formerly the Miami Lakes Inn), Main St., Miami Lakes, FL 33014 (305/821-1150). 305 rms, A/C, color TV, in-rm movies. AE, CB, DC, MC, V. Free valet parking, two pools, nine tennis courts, squash courts, two golf courses, health club, sauna, putting green, two rests., coffee shop, two bars, rm svce, boutiques, crib $10. *Note:* The resort hotel par excellence, far from the crowds of Miami and Miami Beach, in an elegant country club–like building surrounded by grdns. Spacious, inviting rms w. private balconies or patios; some w. refrigerators. Comprehensive sports facilities. Svce w. a smile and aiming to please. Wknd discounts. Good value. 15 min. from airport, 40 min. from dwntwn. **E,** but lower rates off-season.

☼🏛🏛 **Hotel Place St. Michel,** 162 Alcazar Ave., Coral Gables, FL 33134 (305/444-1666). 27 rms, A/C, color TV. AE, CB, DC, MC, V. Free parking, rest. (Restaurant St. Michel), piano bar, rm svce, free breakfast, no cribs. *Note:* Delightful small hotel of great charm, built in the 1920s and elegantly restored. Every rm is individually decorated w. period furniture and old paintings. Excellent French rest. Polished reception and svce; everything in the old European style. The favorite of those in-the-know, who keep coming back. 10 min. from dwntwn. **M–E**

🏛 **Century,** 140 Ocean Dr., Miami Beach, FL 33139 (305/674-8855). 24 rms and 7 suites, A/C, color TV. AE, MC, V. Street parking, rest. valet svce. *Note:* Alluring little art deco hotel recently renovated. Situated on the quiet, southerly stretch of Ocean Dr. Low-key charm from the roses in the bedroom to the morning coffee, imported from Balducci's and drunk on a sunny veranda. Amicable svce. A popular spot w. artists and photographers from Europe and the United States. **M–E**

☼🏛🏛 **Park Central Hotel,** 640 Ocean Dr., Miami Beach, FL 33139 (305/538-1611). 120 rms, A/C, cable color TV. AE, MC, V. Parking $7, two rests. (including La Zèbre), two bars, rm svce. *Note:* Beautiful 1937 beachfront hotel completely restored, in the heart of the Art Deco District. Stucco rms w. mahogany ceiling fans and period decor. Most have ocean views; all have refrigerators. Earnest, courteous svce. Good French rest. **M,** but lower rates off-season.

♀ **Mardi Gras,** 3400 Biscayne Blvd., Miami, FL 33137 (305/
♀ 573-7700). 50 rms, A/C, cable color TV. AE, CB, DC, MC,
V. Free parking, pool, rest., bar. *Note:* A modest but well-run small motel 5 min.
from dwntwn. Some rms w. kitchenettes. Convenient location; friendly reception. Good value overall. **B–I**

Other Accommodations (from top bracket to budget)

♀♀♀♀ **The Colonnade Hotel,** Ponce de Leon at Miracle Mile, Coral
♀♀♀♀ Gables, FL 33134 (305/441-2600; toll free, see Preferred).
157 rms, A/C, color TV, in-room movies. AE, CB, DC, MC, V. Valet parking
$8, pool, health club, sauna, two rests. (including the Aragon Café), bar, 24-hr.
rm svce, concierge, free crib. *Note:* New luxury hotel located atop a 15-story office building in the fashionable Coral Gables district. Elegant European decor w.
mahogany furnishings. Spacious, comfortable rms w. minibars (some w. balconies). Personalized svce. Excellent rest. A favorite w. those in-the-know. **VE,** but
lower rates off-season.

♀♀♀♀ **Doral Ocean Beach Resort,** 4833 Collins Ave., Miami Beach,
♀♀♀♀ FL 33140 (305/532-3600; toll free 800/327-6334). 420
rms, A/C, color TV, in-rm movies. AE, CB, DC, MC, V. Valet gar. $9, pool,
two tennis courts, health club, sauna, beach, boating, panoramic rest. (Alfredo,
L'originale di Roma), coffee shop, bar, 24-hr. rm svce, drugstore, boutiques, free
crib. *Note:* Built of tinted glass, at the same time modern and baroque, the Doral
Ocean Beach is one of Miami's most luxurious hotels, its spacious, comfortable
rms offering a very fine view of the ocean or of Indian Creek. Direct access to the
beach. Excellent svce. Free limo connection with the five golf courses of the
Doral Resort Country Club. 15 min. from dwntwn. Interesting vacation packages. **VE,** but lower rates off-season.

♀♀♀ **Mayfair House,** 3000 Florida Ave., Coconut Grove, FL 33133
♀♀♀ (305/441-0000; toll free 800/345-3457). 181 rms, A/C,
color TV, in-rm movies. AE, CB, DC, MC, V. Valet parking $10, roof pool, two
rests. (including the Mayfair Grill), bars, 24-hr. rm svce, boutiques, free crib.
Note: An integral part of the super-smart, super-snob Mayfair Mall, w. its dozens
of luxury shops, this charming little European-style hotel combines comfort and
elegance. Tastefully decorated, w. interior courts and fountains; spacious rms w.
private balcony and refrigerator. Personalized svce. Free limousine svce (reserve
ahead). An urbane, stylish place favored by those in-the-know. **VE,** but lower rates
off-season.

♀♀♀ **Fountainebleau Hilton,** 4441 Collins Ave., Miami Beach, FL
♀♀♀ 33140 (305/538-2000; toll free, see Hilton). 1,204 rms,
A/C, color TV, in-rm movies. AE, CB, DC, MC, V. Valet gar. $9, two pools,
health club, sauna, seven tennis courts, boating, beach, bicycles, three rests. (including the Dining Galleries), two coffee shops, four bars, rm svce, disco, hrdrsr,
drugstore, concierge, boutiques, free crib. *Note:* The mammoth of local hotels.
Since 1954 this giant vacation complex, whose extravagant architecture is signed
by Morris Lapidus, now entirely renovated, has been Miami Beach's best-known
address. Spacious, comfortable rms w. balconies (some w. refrigerators). The
overburdened svce at times leaves something to be desired. The lagoon/
swimming pool w. waterfalls and the tropical grdn justify a visit in themselves.
Direct beach access. Group and convention clientele. 20 min. from dwntwn. **E–
VE,** but lower rates off-season.

♀♀♀ **Marriott Hotel & Marina–Biscayne Bay,** 1633 N. Bayshore
♀♀♀ Dr., Miami, FL 33132 (305/374-3900; toll free, see
Marriott). 631 rms, A/C, color TV, in-rm movies. AE, CB, DC, MC, V. Valet
parking $9, two pools, boating, marina, two rests. (including Véronique's), two
bars, rm svce, hrdrsr, boutiques. *Note:* Big convention motel whose twin 31-sto-
ry towers rise straight from the water's edge; marina for 180 boats. Spacious rms
w. balcony and bay view. Every possible comfort; praiseworthy rest. serving Continental cuisine. In spite of all those floors, the svce is efficient—but physical-

fitness facilities are deficient. Direct access to the Plaza Venetia and Omni shopping malls via glassed-in skywalk. Group clientele. **E–VE,** but lower rates off-season.

ℒℒℒ **Omni International Hotel,** 1601 Biscayne Blvd., Miami, FL 33132 (305/374-0000; toll free, see Omni). 535 rms, A/C, color TV, in-rm movies. AE, CB, DC, MC, V. Valet gar. $10, pool, two rests. (including the Fish Market), coffee shop, two bars, rm svce, free crib. *Note:* Truly a city within a city, this 30-story glass-and-concrete tower forms part of the immense Omni/Plaza Venetia Shopping Mall, w. its 160 stores and boutiques, six cinemas, and 13 rests. The interior is done in a rather chilly hi-tech, but the rms are very comfortable, the best overlooking Biscayne Bay. Efficient svce. No physical-fitness facilities on the spot. The favorite of visiting Latin American businessmen. **E–VE,** but lower rates off-season.

ℒℒℒ **Sheraton–Bal Harbour** (formerly the Americana), 9701 Collins Ave., Bal Harbour, FL 33154 (305/865-7511; toll free, see Sheraton). 675 rms, A/C, color TV, in-rm movies. AE, CB, DC, MC, V. Valet parking $9, two pools, two tennis courts, health club, sauna, boating, three rests. (including the Bal Harbour Grille), coffee shop, bars, rm svce, boutiques, free crib. *Note:* All the comfort you might expect from a modern, well-equipped luxury hotel (a $22-million renovation was completed in 1991); spacious rms w. minibars, most w. balconies too. Direct beach access; fine tropical grdn on the ocean. Efficient svce. Attracts groups and conventions. Good value off-season. 25 min. from dwntwn. **E–VE,** but lower rates off-season.

ℒℒ **Doubletree Hotel** (formerly the Coconut Grove), 2649 S. Bayshore Dr., Coconut Grove, FL 33133 (305/858-2500; toll free 800/528-0444). 190 rms. A/C, color TV, in-rm movies. AE, CB, DC, MC, V. Valet parking $8, pool, two tennis courts, fishing, boating, rest. (Café Brasserie), bar, rm svce, crib $10. *Note:* Refined and distinguished—particularly the recently renovated interior. Spacious rms, most w. balcony and ocean view. Exemplary svce. Pleasant all-around view (but uneven food) in the top-floor rest. Opposite Coconut Grove Convention Center and Dinner Key Marina. 15 min. from dwntwn. **E**

ℒℒ **Sheraton–Brickell Point,** 495 Brickell Ave., Miami, FL 33131 (305/373-6000; toll free, see Sheraton). 598 rms, A/C, color TV, in-rm movies. AE, CB, DC, MC, V. Valet parking $10, pool, rest., bar, rm svce, free crib. *Note:* Ultramodern 18-story tower overhanging Biscayne Bay. Comfortable rms w. a view. Rather comprehensive facilities. Lovely tropical decor w. a flower-planted terrace. Acceptable rest. overlooking the bay. Well situated very nr. the financial district. **E,** but lower rates off-season.

ℒℒ **Dupont Plaza,** 300 Biscayne Blvd., Miami, FL 33131 (305/358-2541; toll free 800/327-3480). 433 rms, A/C, color TV. AE, CB, DC, MC, V. Valet gar. $6, two pools, marina, rest., coffee shop, bar, rm svce, free crib. *Note:* Modern, functional hotel right on Biscayne Bay; the best rms have a fine view. Svce not always dependable. Group and convention clientele. In the heart of dwntwn Miami. Good value. **M,** but lower rates off-season.

ℒℒ **Best Western PLM Marina Park Hotel,** 340 Biscayne Blvd., Miami, FL 33132 (305/371-4400; toll free, see Best Western). 199 rms, A/C, cable color TV. AE, CB, DC, MC, V. Free parking, coffee shop, bar, rm svce. *Note:* Comfortable, completely renovated hotel at the edge of Bay Front Park. Inviting rms, the best overlooking the harbor and the bay. Courteous svce. Clientele of groups and package tours. Good value. Next to the Bayside Marketplace. **I–M,** but lower rates off-season.

ℒℒ **Miami River Inn,** 118 SW South River Dr., Miami, FL 33130 (305/325-0045). 40 rms, A/C, color cable TV. AE, MC, V. Free parking, pool, sauna, café nearby, free breakfast. *Note:* Charming bed-and-breakfast recently renovated, on the edge of dwntwn. Consists of four restored 1906 buildings, some of which offer commanding views of the city and river. Comfortable rms w. antiques. Pleasant reception and svce. Good value. **I–M**

♀ **Days Inn Medical Center,** 1050 NW 14th St., Miami, FL
33136 (305/324-0200; toll free, see Days Inns). 214 rms,
A/C, cable color TV. AE, CB, DC, MC, V. Free parking, pool, 24-hr. coffee
shop. *Note:* Typical functional motel 5 min. by car from dwntwn and nr. the Civic Center. Spacious, inviting rms. Good value. Ideal if you're driving. **I–M,** but
lower rates off-season.

♀ **Monaco Resort,** 17501 Collins Ave., Sunny Isles, FL 33160
(305/932-2100). 110 rms, A/C, cable color TV. AE, CB,
DC, MC, V. Free parking, pool, health club, sauna, coffee shop (breakfast/
lunch), bar, free crib. *Note:* Aging but comfortable motel right on the ocean;
pleasing, well-laid-out rms w. refrigerator (some w. kitchenette). Direct beach access. Friendly svce; good value; 35 min. from dwntwn. **I–M,** but lower rates off-
season.

♀ **The Ramada Limited** (formerly Hampton Inn), 5125 NW
36th St., Miami Springs, FL 33166 (305/887-2153; toll free,
see Ramada Inns). 110 rms, A/C, cable color TV. AE, CB, DC, MC, V. Free
parking, valet svce, free Continental breakfast, free crib. *Note:* Well-run conventional six-story motel opposite the airport. Functionally comfortable rms. Efficient svce. 20 min. from dwntwn. Good value overall. **I**

♀ **Ocean Roc,** 19505 Collins Ave, Sunny Isles, FL 33160 (305/
931-7600). 95 rms, A/C, color TV, in-rm movies. AE, CB,
DC, MC, V. Free parking, pool, coffee shop, rm svce. *Note:* Elderly but very well
run small hotel on the beach; nice rms w. balconies and refrigerators (some w.
kitchenettes), the best overlooking the ocean. Friendly reception. In summer,
one of Miami Beach's best bargains. 35 min. from dwntwn. **I,** but lower rates
off-season.

♀ **Royalton Hotel,** 131 SE 1st St., Miami, FL 33132 (305/374-
7451). 130 rms, A/C. AE, CB, DC, MC, V. Parking (for a fee)
adj., coffee shop, bar. *Note:* Older hotel w. small but functional rms in the middle
of the dwntwn Cuban district. While reception and comfort are not of the best,
the prices can't be beat. **I,** but lower rates off-season.

♀ **Bel Aire Hotel,** 6515 Collins Ave., Miami Beach, FL 33141
(305/866-6511). 111 rms, color TV. AE, CB, DC, MC, V.
Free parking, pool, coffee shop, bar. *Note:* Small vacation hotel, economical but
well run, ideal for restricted budgets. Quiet family atmosphere. 20 min. from
dwntwn, and a few steps from a public beach. Very good value. **I,** but lower rates
off-season.

Airport Accommodations
☼♀♀♀ **Hilton Miami Airport and Marina,** 5101 Blue Lagoon Dr.,
Miami, FL 33126 (305/262-1000; toll free, see Hilton). 500
rms, A/C, color TV, in-rm movies. AE, CB, DC, MC, V. Valet parking $7, pool,
three tennis courts, health club, sauna, marina, boating, two rests. (including the
Cove), bars, 24-hr. rm svce, disco, free airport limos, concierge, free crib. *Note:*
Immaculate 14-story tower on a peninsula in the middle of a lagoon; first-grade
comfort and facilities. Elegant, spacious rms w. private balconies or patios. VIP
suites on the three top floors. Efficient svce. Business and convention clientele.
E–VE, but lower rates off-season.

YMCA/Youth Hostel
Clay Hotel/AYH, 1438 Washington Ave., Miami Beach, FL 33139 (305/
534-2988). Very central. 120 beds. Two blocks from a public beach.

RESTAURANTS
Personal Favorites (in order of preference)
♧♧♧♧ **Mark's Place,** 2286 NE 123rd St., North Miami (893-6888).
A/C. Lunch Mon–Fri, dinner nightly. AE, CB, DC, MC, V.

Specialties: crab cakes w. tasso sausage and smoked-pepper butter, deep-fried curried oysters w. banana-tamarind salsa and orange sour cream, pistachio-crusted black grouper in citrus vinaigrette, pork tenderloin w. black beans, grilled swordfish w. mango-Scotch barbecue sauce. Well-chosen and extensive wine list. *Note:* A stylishly casual bistro w. an open kitchen where South Florida's most acclaimed chef-owner, Mark Militello, combines the freshest of ingredients w. creative imagination. Breezy and unpretentious setting w. white walls, multicolored glass, and contemporary artwork. The svce is knowledgeable and efficient. An unforgettable dining experience. Resv. highly recommended. Well worth the 25-min. drive (via Biscayne Blvd.) from dwntwn. *American.* **E**

A Mano, in the Betsy Ross Hotel, 1440 Ocean Dr., Miami Beach (531-6266). A/C. Dinner only, Tues–Sun. AE, DC, MC, V. *Specialties:* pan-seared foie gras w. caramelized onions and papaya vinaigrette, plantain-crusted crab cakes w. pineapple salsa, soy- and honey-marinated grilled tuna, West Indian glazed rack of lamb, "chocolate lovers' fantasy where dreams have no end." *Note:* The most sophisticated and dazzling rest. in the Art Deco District. Renowned chef Norman Van Aken is the creative force in the kitchen. The handsome dining room is filled w. giant mirrors, greenery, and artistic fabrics. Friendly, well-trained service. Resv. a must. *American.* **E**

Brasserie Le Coze, 2901 Florida Ave., Coconut Grove (444-9697). A/C. Dinner only, Tues–Sun. AE, CB, DC, MC, V. Jkt. *Specialties:* fresh Maine crabmeat in artichoke, onion tart, salad of duck magret w. foie gras, pepper-cured salmon w. tabbouleh, coq au vin w. noodles, crème brûlée. Well-chosen wine list fairly priced. *Note:* Coconut Grove's sibling of the famous Le Bernardin, a trendy bastion of superb seafood located on the Big Apple's west side. The French turn-of-the-century bistro setting is more informal than its New York counterpart. Attentive, friendly staff. A very fine place. Resv. a must. *French/Seafood.* **M–E**

Yuca, 177 Giralda Ave., Coral Gables (444-4448). A/C. Lunch Mon–Sat, dinner nightly, brunch Sun. AE, CB, DC, MC, V. Jkt. *Specialties:* smoked ham croquettes w. Brie, citrus plank salmon w. mango-mustard glaze, barbecued ribs w. guava sauce, plantain-coated filet dolphin fish w. tamarind sauce, rice pudding. Skimpy wine list at shocking prices. *Note:* Upscale Cuban cuisine combining nouvelle cuisine techniques and Cuban ingredients. Florid, festive setting w. a floor-to-ceiling mural of hip young diners. This is definitely not an "arroz con pollo" place. Young and congenial staff. Resv. advised. Valet parking. *Latin American.* **M–E**

Joe's Stone Crab, 227 Biscayne St., Miami Beach (673-0365). A/C. Lunch Tues–Sat, dinner nightly; closed May 15–Oct 15. AE, CB, DC, MC, V. Jkt. *Specialties:* oysters on the half shell or fried; everything that swims in the Atlantic or any other ocean, broiled or poached; extraordinary stone crabs w. mustard sauce; key lime pie. *Note:* A Miami landmark since 1913; its black-and-yellow stone crabs are famous coast to coast. Their high season runs Oct–Feb; their claws are removed and they're thrown back into the sea, where the claws grow again. The rest. is often noisy and crowded. Excellent svce; unfortunately no resv., so waits (sometimes rather long) are inevitable. Valet parking. *Seafood.* **M–E**

Le Festival, 2120 Salzedo St., Coral Gables (442-8545). A/C. Lunch Mon–Fri, dinner Mon–Sat; closed hols. and Sept–Oct. AE, MC, V. Jkt. *Specialties:* salmon mousse, cheese soufflé, chicken normande, duck à l'orange, snapper Dugléré, tarte tatin. *Note:* Small French bistro of the refined and elegant sort; chef Jacques Baudeau offers a flawless cuisine. Attentive svce. Well-chosen wine list. A fine place. *French.* **I–M**

Café Tu Tu Tango, 3015 Grand Ave., Coconut Grove (529-2222). A/C. Lunch/dinner daily (until midnight). AE, MC, V. *Specialties:* shrimp ceviche, croquetas of ham and crab w. chive sauce, sesame-ginger snapper, gourmet pizzas, six-flavored chocolate cake. *Note:* A bohemian decor, a dance floor w. tango or flamenco dancers and an inventive tapas-style cuisine (no fullcourse entrées are served) create an eclectic and funny dining experience. No resv. accepted, unfortunately. *Latin American.* **I**

♀ **La Esquina de Tejas,** 101 SW 12th Ave., Miami (545-5341). A/C. Breakfast/lunch/dinner daily (until midnight). AE, MC, V. *Specialties:* fish soup, chicken w. rice, picadillo, pig's-trotter stew, roast pork w. rice and black beans, flan, Cuban coffee. *Note:* One of the small, traditional Cuban rests. of which there are so many in Little Havana, offering absolutely authentic food at very attractive prices. This one has some claim to celebrity in that President Reagan stopped here once on a visit to Miami and tried the chicken w. rice, w. side orders of black beans and fried plantain. Guaranteed atmosphere and local color. No resv. *Latin American.* **B–I**

Other Restaurants (from top bracket to budget)

♀♀♀ **Chef Allen's,** 19088 NE 29th Ave., North Miami Beach (935-2900). A/C. Dinner only, nightly. AE, MC, V. Jkt. *Specialties:* Caribbean antipasto, blackened red snapper w. orange sauce and key lime pasta, veal chop w. double mustard sauce and wild mushrooms, excellent soufflés. Menu changes daily. *Note:* One of Miami's most fashionable rests.; its innovative, imaginative cuisine from the hand of the talented Allen Susser, a rising star among younger American chefs. Elegant setting w. kitchen visible to diners in its enclosure of glass. Friendly, attentive svce; successful enough that you should reserve several days ahead. Valet parking. *American.* **M–E**

♀♀♀ **Giacosa,** 394 Giralda Ave., Coral Gables (445-5858). A/C. Lunch/dinner daily; closed hols. AE, DC, MC, V. *Specialties:* buffalo mozzarella w. steak tomato, pasta filled w. lobster in lobster sauce, risotto w. fresh asparagus tips, roasted rack of baby lamb w. essence of truffles, good desserts. *Note:* Named "Best New Restaurant" in 1992 and "Best Restaurant" in 1993 by *South Florida* magazine, this rest. has quickly established itself in Miami under the expertise of chef Alfredo Alvarez, South American–born and European-trained. Some of the best Italian food you'll find in the region. Resv. required. *Italian.* **M–E**

♀♀♀ **La Bussola,** 270 Giralda Ave., Coral Gables (445-8783). A/C. Lunch Mon–Fri, dinner nightly. AE, DC, MC, V. *Specialties:* pumpkin ravioli, salmon carpaccio, risotto w. squid, baby shrimp, clams and mussels, gnocchi quattro formagi, grilled veal T-bone w. roasted red-pepper sauce, white-chocolate ravioli w. chocolate sauce. Extensive Italian wine list. *Note:* Light and often inventive *nuova cucina* cooking. Refined Renaissance setting recently completely renovated. Excellent svce. Resv. advised. *Italian.* **M–E**

♀♀ **Casa Juancho,** 2436 SW Eighth St., Miami (642-2452). A/C. Lunch/dinner daily. AE, DC, MC, V. *Specialties:* excellent tapas, baked baby goat, grouper steak w. clams, roast lamb, paella, crema catalana. *Note:* The dark, wood-trimmed walls, the multicolored tablecloths, and the mounted animal heads suggest a German bierstube, but the fare is 100% authentic Spanish-Cuban. Most of the game and seafood served here is even imported from Spain. Live entertainment nightly. Casual but efficient svce. Very popular locally. Valet parking. *Spanish/Latin American.* **M–E**

♀♀♀ **Pacific Time,** 915 Lincoln Rd., Miami Beach (534-5979). A/C. Dinner only, nightly; closed hols. AE, DC, MC, V. *Specialties:* seaweed salad; sliced Mongolian lamb salad w. red curry oil; wok-sautéed tuna w. mango, tomato, and green onion vinaigrette; crisp honey-roasted Chinese duck; "the bomb" (melted chocolate in a chocolate crust). *Note:* One of the most interesting menus to appear in Miami in the last few years. Chef Jonathan Eismann gives Floridian staples an Asian twist and turns out delectable dishes. Moody, high-ceiling dining room w. a marble counter facing the open kitchen. Resv. highly advised. *American/Asian.* **M**

♀♀ **Janjo's,** 3131 Commodore Plaza, Coconut Grove (445-5030). A/C. Lunch/dinner Tues–Sun; closed hols. AE, DC,

MC, V. *Specialties:* seared tuna w. Mexican vanilla vinaigrette; grilled sea scallops w. fennel-orange salad; filet mignon w. garlicky buttered spinach, mashed potatoes, and pancetta cracklings; roast monkfish w. mango ragoût and seafood-remoulade sauce; nougat-filled chocolate cookies. Menu changes regularly. *Note:* Chef and owner Jan Jorgensen creates tropical dishes, suiting the island-house feeling of this rest. adorned w. Haitian art and green awnings. Rest. opens up to the sidewalk, where there is additional seating. Resv. recommended. *American/ Caribbean.* **I–M**

♟♟ **Malaga,** 740 SW 8th St., Miami (858-4224). A/C. Lunch/ dinner daily. AE, CB, DC, MC, V. *Specialties:* black-bean soup, carne asada mechada (pot-au-feu), picadillo, hamhocks w. rice, pompano or red snapper w. sauce Créole, arroz con pollo, paella, rice pudding. *Note:* Malaga is an exception to the Miami rule that Cuban rests. have depressing interiors; w. its charming shady patio and domestic Castilian decor, it almost qualifies as a luxury rest. Tasty food served in huge portions; svce with a smile. Very popular locally, so resv. advised. Latin dance shows at dinner. *Latin American.* **I**

♟♟ **Mandarin Garden,** 3268 Grand Ave., Coconut Grove (446-9999). A/C. Lunch Mon–Fri, dinner nightly. AE, DC, MC, V. *Specialties:* hot-and-sour soup, mu shu pork, Yu-Hsiang eggplant, sesame chicken, crispy shrimp w. red sauce and steamed broccoli. *Note:* Most gourmets call this the best Chinese rest. in Miami, a city where Far Eastern food worthy of the name is not easily found. Nondescript Oriental decor and friendly staff. *Chinese.* **I**

♟ **Lulu's,** 1053 Washington Ave., Miami Beach (532-6147). A/C. Lunch/dinner daily. MC, V. *Specialties:* corn and okra fritters, fried catfish sandwich, hush puppies, fried chicken w. mashed potatoes and collard greens. *Note:* Funky roadhouse-style spot complete w. Elvis Presley memorabilia, turquoise banquettes, and an antique Seeburg jukebox. Down-home southern cooking. The portions are cheap and plentiful. *American.* **B–I**

☀♟ **Versailles,** 3555 SW 8th St., Miami (444-0240). A/C. Lunch/dinner daily (until 4am). AE, CB, DC, MC, V. *Specialties:* Cuban sandwiches, homemade soups, rice w. black beans, chicken w. rice, picadillo, Palomilla steak, cheesecake. *Note:* One of the most authentic Cuban rests. on the famous Calle Ocho, the main drag of Little Havana. Straightforward, savory food. In spite of the mirrored ceilings, the name Versailles is not reflected in the decor. Usually crowded and noisy, but a pleasant place. No resv. *Latin American.* **B–I**

☀♟ **Wolfie's Rascal House,** 17190 Collins Ave., Sunny Isles (947-4581). A/C. Breakfast/lunch/dinner daily (until 2am). No credit cards. *Kosher specialties:* soup, corned beef, pastrami, brisket; excellent (and enormously popular) deli items, homemade pastries. *Note:* Ideal for breakfast or a late supper. At lunch customers come in droves. 35 min. from dwntwn. A local landmark since 1947. *American.* **B**

Cafeteria/Fast Food

☀ **Latin American Cafeteria,** 2940 Coral Way, Coral Gables (448-6809). Typical cafeteria, open around the clock and serving enormous sandwiches and tasty, unpretentious Cuban food (fried pork w. rice and beans, pan-fried steak, etc.). 1950s-style decor. Open daily. No credit cards. Several other locations in Miami (see the local telephone book).

BARS & NIGHTCLUBS

The **Jazz Hotline** (382-3938) will give you details of current programming by local jazz clubs.

Baja Beach Club, 3015 Grand Ave., Coconut Grove (445-5499). A favorite of University of Miami students in the mood for hard rock and metal or Top-40 music. Casual but tasteful attire. Open Tues–Sun.

Bang, 1516 Washington Ave., Miami Beach (531-2361). Primarily a great rest., which turns into a fashionable late-night hangout after dinner time.

Improv, Coco Walk, 3015 Grand Ave., Coconut Grove (441-8200). Comedy showcase and rest. featuring nationally known comedians. Open Tues–Sun.

Les Violins, 1751 Biscayne Blvd., Miami (371-8668). Havana-style nightclub which puts on some far-out Latin American floor shows. Also a so-so rest.

Monty Trainer's, 2550 S. Bayshore Dr., Coconut Grove (858-1431). Amusing open-air bar-rest. serving very acceptable seafood. Live jazz and reggae; dancing. Youthful, congenial atmosphere. Open nightly.

Stuart's Bar and Lounge, in the Hotel Place St. Michel (see "Accommodations," above) (444-1666). Intimate bar w. mahogany decor and Happy Hour hors d'oeuvres. Open Mon–Sat.

Swiss Château, 2471 SW 32nd Ave., Miami (445-6103). Popular Latino dance club. A shrine of salsa, merengue, and cumbia.

Tobacco Road, 626 S. Miami Ave., Miami (374-1198). Miami's oldest bar, where the blues play until 5 in the morning and where it never, never seems late.

Warsaw, 1450 Collins Ave., Miami Beach (531-4555). The "in" spot in the Art Deco District. A favorite of local gays and models shooting fashion spreads. DJ disco. Open nightly.

NEARBY EXCURSIONS

🔔 **MICCOSUKEE INDIAN VILLAGE** (27 mi./43km west on U.S. 41) (223-8380): Authentic Native American village of the Miccosukee tribe. Handcraft exhibitions, alligator wrestling, airboat trips into the swamps, restaurant with authentic tribal food. Open daily. Every year an 🔔 **exhibition of Native American art and dance** is held here (late Dec to early Jan), with representatives from more than 40 tribes. Worth going out of your way for, especially if you can combine it with the **Shark Valley Tram Tours** (see "Everglades National Park," below).

NATIONAL PARKS NEARBY

🔔 **BISCAYNE NATIONAL PARK** (30 mi./48km SW on U.S. 1, on the Florida Tpke. at N. Canal Dr., in Homestead): The latest of Florida's national parks, Biscayne, standing on the shore, comprises mostly a considerable stretch of water with a string of inhabited islands and some coral reefs teeming with fish (180,000 acres/73,000ha). A paradise for scuba diving, underwater fishing (snapper, mackerel, dorado), and birdwatching (blue herons, egrets, pelicans). Numerous facilities, including an $8-million visitor center, were destroyed in the hurricane. For information, contact P.O. Box 1369, Homestead, FL 33030 (305/247-2044).

☼🔔 **EVERGLADES NATIONAL PARK** (45 mi./72km SW on U.S. 1 and Fla. 27): Opened in 1947, this is the country's only tropical national park. Alligators, barracudas, sea turtles, pumas, lynxes, pelicans, egrets, pink flamingos, migratory birds, and at least a thousand varieties of fish abound in this enormous (2,100-sq.-mi./5,440km²) stretch of marshes, cypress stands, and mangrove swamps which the Seminoles knew by the beautiful name of Pay-Hay-Okee ("River of Grass"). A 50-mi. (80km) asphalt road, the **Flamingo Road,** makes its way through the park; there are many observation platforms and elevated walkways from which you can admire the landscape. From May to Nov visits are rendered unpleasant by clouds of mosquitos and other bloodthirsty insects, to say nothing of persistent rain during the summer; nevertheless, the rich wildlife and exotic vegetation are certainly worth seeing. **Visitor Center** at Flamingo.

It was in the Everglades that the local Native Americans made their last stand in the terrible Seminole Wars of 1835–42. After 2,000 warriors had successfully held off 20,000 soldiers for three years, they were wiped out or deported to Oklahoma. Although defeated, the Seminoles never signed a peace treaty with the U.S. government, and are thus—theoretically—still in a state of war.

Part of the park was devastated in August 1992 by Hurricane Andrew, and will remain closed indefinitely. Boating and tour concessions outside the park are operating. For further information, contact the Superintendent, Everglades National Park, 40001 State Rd. 9336, Homestead, FL 33034 (305/242-7700).

Guided Tours

Backcountry Cruises (boat) and **Wilderness Tram Tours** (bus) (305/253-2241) leave from Flamingo Area at the south of the park. Resv. advised.

Everglades Boat Tours (boat) (813/695-2591) leave from Park Docks in Everglades City, at the NW corner of the park.

Shark Valley Tram Tours (bus) (305/221-8455) leave from the Shark Valley parking facility on U.S. 41 north of the park. You'll encounter abundant wildlife, especially in winter. Resv. a must.

Where to Stay in the National Park

Flamingo Lodge, at the end of Fla. 27, Everglades National Park, FL 33030 (305/253-2241). 102 rms and 24 bungalows; also houseboats for rent. AE, MC, V. Relatively modern and comfortable. **M**

Everglades Rod & Gun Club, P.O. Box G, Everglades City, FL 33929 (813/695-2101). 17 rms. No credit cards. Comfortable in a rustic way. **I**

JOHN PENNEKAMP CORAL REEF PARK (60 mi./ 96km SW on U.S. 1, in Key Largo): The country's first underwater national park, dating from 1960, is 21.5 mi. (34km) long by 6.5 mi. (10km) wide; the water is nowhere deeper than 45 ft. (15m). There is a superb display of sea flora and fauna, with more than 650 varieties of tropical fish as well as many shipwrecks. Wonderful for scuba-divers; also trips in glass-bottom boats. Spectacular. Open daily year round; for information, phone 305/451-1202.

Where to Stay in the Park

Jules' Undersea Lodge, P.O. Box 3330, Key Largo, FL 33037 (305/451-2353). The only hotel of its kind in the world, with two fully equipped suites (bunks, kitchenette, closed-circuit TV) in a steel capsule anchored 30 ft. (10m) below the surface. Patrons can reach it only by diving and passing through an airlock. Unobstructed view of the underwater life through huge portholes. Rates: $300 per person per day, including meals and unlimited diving. Resv. required, a long time ahead.

FARTHER AFIELD

FLORIDA EAST COAST (640 mi./1,024km r.t. to St. Augustine on U.S. 1N, returning on I-95S): The great vacation artery of the Southeast. At least a week's trip with optional extensions to Orlando and Walt Disney World. For details, see Chapter 16 on Florida's East Coast and Chapter 18 on Orlando.

KEY WEST & THE KEYS HIGHWAY (330 mi./528km on U.S. 1, r.t.): Nicknamed Cayo Hueso (Bone Island) by the Spaniards and later anglicized as Key West, this old pirates' lair is the southernmost city in the continental U.S. Literary and bohemian, the picturesque town of Key West, now a little more than a century and a half old, is an important naval

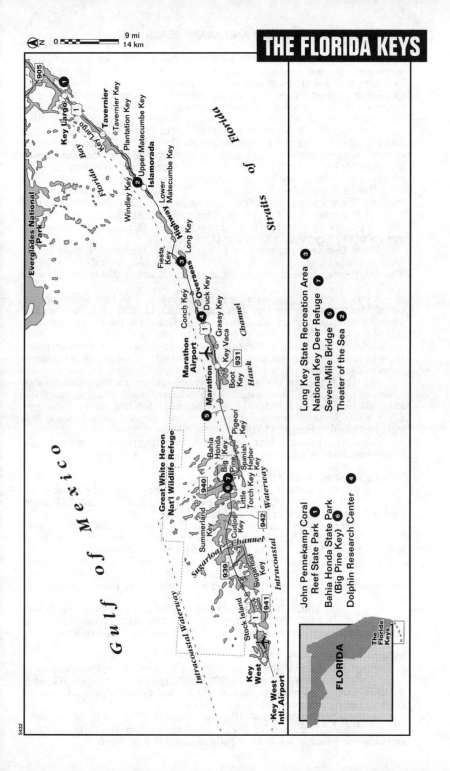

THE FLORIDA KEYS

0 | 9 mi
| 14 km

N

Gulf of Mexico

Everglades National Park

Florida Bay

Key Largo
Key Largo
Tavernier
Tavernier Key
Plantation Key
Upper Matecumbe Key
Windley Key
Islamorada
Lower Matecumbe Key
Fiesta Key
Long Key
Conch Key
Duck Key
Grassy Key
Key Vaca
Marathon Airport
Marathon
Boot Key
Pigeon Key
Bahia Honda Key
Big Pine Key
Spanish Harbor Key
Little Torch Key
Summerland Key
Cudjoe Key
Sugarloaf Key
Sugarloaf Key
Stock Island
Key West
Key West Intl. Airport

Overseas Highway

Great White Heron Nat'l Wildlife Refuge

Intracoastal Waterway

Sugarloaf Channel

Intracoastal Waterway

905
1
931
940
942
939
941
1

Straits of Florida

Hawk Channel

John Pennekamp Coral Reef State Park ①
Bahia Honda State Park (Big Pine Key) ⑥
Dolphin Research Center ④

Long Key State Recreation Area ③
National Key Deer Refuge ⑦
Seven-Mile Bridge ⑤
Theater of the Sea ②

FLORIDA

The Florida Keys

5432

base, a fashionable vacation resort—it was for a while President Truman's summer residence—and the favored retreat of such writers as playwright Tennessee Williams, poet Robert Frost, and novelists John Dos Passos and James Herlihy (*Midnight Cowboy*). Ernest Hemingway lived here and wrote some of his most successful works, including *The Snows of Kilimanjaro* and *For Whom the Bell Tolls*. His house, at 907 Whitehead St. (294-1575), is open daily to visitors. Another well-known resident was naturalist John James Audubon, whose former house at 205 Whitehead St. is today a small ⏶ **museum** (294-2116) devoted to the works of the distinguished artist-ornithologist; open daily. The **Key West Lighthouse Museum,** 938 Whitehead St. (294-0012), open daily, displays some interesting military memorabilia, including a miniature Japanese submarine captured at Pearl Harbor. Splendid view from the top. The famous ⏶ **Key West Aquarium,** Wall and Whitehead Sts. (296-2051), open daily, has a comprehensive collection of the rich marine life of the Gulf of Mexico and the Atlantic Ocean, from the brightly tinted creatures of the tropical reefs to sharks. Pleasant strolls along the ⏶ **streets of old Key West,** particularly Duval St.

The ☀ **Overseas Highway,** by which Key West is reached, is built for the most part on a causeway over the water; the route involves a total of 40 bridges. There are spectacular seascapes, particularly from ⏶⏶ **Seven Mile Bridge** between Marathon and Key West.

A very worthwhile excursion is to the impressive ☀⏶⏶ **Fort Jefferson National Monument** on the Dry Tortugas, 70 mi. (112km) offshore from Key West. The fort, nicknamed "the Gibraltar of the Gulf," was used as a prison at the end of the Civil War; Dr. Samuel Mudd, who gave medical assistance to John Wilkes Booth, the assassin of Abraham Lincoln, was among those detained there. It can be reached by seaplane from Stock Island in 40 min. on Key West Seaplanes Service (294-6978).

Key West is also one of the country's greatest centers for **big-game fishing.** Lovers of the sport will find dozens of places to rent boats. Prices are markedly lower than in Miami; a half-day charter averages $150–$200, and a full day runs $250–$300. Some recommended captains include Admiral Busby & Sons (294-0011) and Yankee Fleet (294-7009).

Allow at least three or four days for this fascinating trip; it can conveniently be combined with a visit to Everglades National Park (see above).

Where to Stay in Key West

     Marriott's Casa Marina, 1500 Reynolds St., Key West, FL 33040 (305/296-3535). 310 rms. AE, CB, DC, MC, V. *Note:* Facing the ocean; luxurious hotel of the 1920s. **VE**

     Pier House, 1 Duval St., Key West, FL 33040 (305/296-4600). 142 rms. AE, CB, DC, MC, V. *Note:* In the center of town; comfortable in a baroque way. **VE,** but lower rates off-season.

     Santa Maria, 1401 Simonton St., Key West, FL 33040 (305/296-5678). 51 rms. AE, CB, DC, MC, V. *Note:* Rather modern, comfortable hotel with a commendable rest. **M–E,** but lower rates off-season.

     South Beach Motel, 508 South St., Key West, FL 33040 (305/296-5611). 47 rms. AE, DC, MC, V. *Note:* Congenial hotel on the water; functional rms w. view. **M–E,** but lower rates off-season.

Where to Eat in Key West

     Pier House, in the Pier House Hotel (see "Where to Stay in Key West," above) (296-4600). Lunch/dinner daily. AE, MC, V. Remarkable Caribbean-inspired cuisine by chef Phillip Heimer. Indoor or outdoor seating and spectacular sunsets. **M–E**

     The Palm Grill, 1029 Southhard St. (296-1744). Dinner only, Mon–Sat. AE, MC, V. Excellent international cuisine w. Asian and Hispanic influences. Indoor or patio dining at its best. **M–E**

Louie's Backyard, 700 Waddell Ave. (294-1061). Lunch/ dinner daily. AE, MC, V. The fashionable place for eating at the water's edge; nouvelle cuisine seafood, served outside in fine weather. **M–E**

Square One, 1075 Duval St. (296-4300). Dinner only, nightly. AE, MC, V. The new fine-dining place in Key West. Innovative American food. Modern and comfortable setting. A very fine place. **M–E**

A & B Lobster House, 700 Front St. (294-2536). Lunch/ dinner Mon–Sat. MC, V. Broiled fish and shellfish; harbor view. **I–M**

Very near here, stop off for a drink at **Sloppy Joe's,** Greene and Duval Sts. (294-5717), Hemingway's favorite bar.

Kyushu, 921 Truman Ave. (294-2995). Lunch/dinner Mon– Sat. AE, DC, MC, V. Very commendable Japanese food; pretty setting, locally popular. **I–M**

Half Shell Raw Bar, 231 Margaret St., Land's End Village (294-7496). Lunch/dinner daily. Good seafood rest. w. very attractive prices; noisy and colorful. No credit cards. **B–I**

PART THREE

THE MIDWEST

CHAPTER 20

DETROIT

□ □ □

"The automobile capital of the world," Detroit is America's most important industrial city after Chicago, accounting for 70% of domestic automobile production and more than half the country's output of weaponry (during World War II the city was known as "the arsenal of the democracies"). It would be more poetic to speak of it as the capital of soul music, the place where Diana Ross and Stevie Wonder began their careers.

The city's site, on a strait (in French, a *détroit*, hence the name) linking Lake Huron and Lake Erie, was first explored by the French in 1610. The city itself was founded 91 years later by an enterprising fur trader, Antoine de la Mothe Cadillac (whose name became world-famous a couple of centuries later when it was attached to a luxury automobile). This garrison town, originally called Fort Pontchartrain, was captured by the British in 1760 and renamed Detroit. The British successfully fended off attacks by a consolidated group of Native Americans led by the Ottawa chief Pontiac (another name destined for a famous automobile), but lost the city with the rest of the Northwest Territory to the Americans in the Revolutionary War. The British stirred up the local tribes to attack the Americans in hopes of regaining the city, but Gen. ("Mad") Anthony Wayne defeated them decisively at the Battle of Fallen Timbers (1794). The opening of steam navigation on the Great Lakes in 1818 touched off Detroit's rocket-trip to prosperity, and when Henry Ford's first mass-produced automobile rolled off the production line in 1901 the rest became inevitable. The city's population rose from 20,000 in 1850 to 280,000 in 1900, 950,000 in 1920, and (suburbs included) over 4.6 million today.

Home to the three giants of the auto industry—General Motors, Ford, and Chrysler—Detroit is also the nation's largest used-car market, as witness the hundreds of billboards cheek by jowl along **Livernois Avenue,** an important petrochemical and space-industry complex. In addition it's the fifth-ranking freshwater port in the U.S., which can accommodate seagoing vessels of up to 25,000 tons coming through the St. Lawrence Seaway. In spite of all these advantages, "the city that put the world on wheels" bore the brunt of the world economic slump, with 200,000 layoffs between 1970 and 1992. The unemployment rate is one of the highest in the country, with peaks of 30% (and up to 60% among young African American workers). The crime rate has followed a similar curve; according to the FBI, Detroit is one of the nation's more violent cities (58 murders per 100,000 people), well ahead of Miami, New York, or Chicago.

After the race riots of July 1967, which left 43 dead and 2,000 wounded, the face of "Motown," as Detroit is often called, changed radically; an exodus caused the population of the city proper to fall by more than 800,000. Stores, hotels, restaurants, offices, and movie houses have forsaken "downtown" for outlying residential suburbs, leaving behind them a kind of no-man's-land, dark tumbledown ghettos, and urban throughways subject to asphyxiating pollution during rush hours. But since 1975 a successful program of urban renewal, pivoting on the **Civic Center,** has spread to the banks of the Detroit River facing the Canadian border. The heart of the program is the **Renaissance Center,** or RenCen, an impressive $750-million architectural complex comprising six glass-clad futurist structures—four of them 39 floors high and two of them 21 stories—and the enormous 73-floor Westin Hotel tower, designed by celebrated architect John Portman and opened in 1977. Another architectural landmark is the new **Millender Center,** a huge modern cluster of offices, a hotel, stores, and restaurants linked to the RenCen by the **Skywalk,** a glass-enclosed walkway.

Famous children of Detroit include the father of the modern automobile industry, Henry Ford, born in the nearby town (now suburb) of Dearborn; director Francis Ford Coppola; actors George Peppard and Tom Selleck; legendary heavyweight champion Joe Louis; singing stars Diana Ross and Aretha Franklin; actresses Gilda Radner and Lily Tomlin; rock musician Alice Cooper; and aviator Charles Lindbergh.

BASIC FACTS: State of Michigan. Area code: 313. Time zone: eastern. ZIP Code: 48226. Founded in: 1701. Approximate population: city, 970,000; metropolitan area, 4,660,000. Sixth-largest metropolitan area in the U.S.

CLIMATE: Because of its unique geographical location, Detroit labors under a humid climate and extremes of temperature—chilling in winter (average Jan temperature: 26°F/−3°C), warm and sticky in summer (average July temperature: 73°F/23°C). Spring is rainy and uncomfortably cool. Only the fall, particularly Oct, offers attractive weather for the tourist.

DISTANCES: Chicago, 268 mi. (430km); Cincinnati, 259 mi. (415km); New York, 634 mi. (1,015km); Niagara Falls, 392 mi. (628km); Washington, 506 mi. (810km).

ARRIVAL & TRANSIT INFORMATION

AIRPORTS: Detroit Metropolitan Airport (DTW), 21 mi. (34km) SW. Call 942-3550 for information.

U.S. AIRLINES: American (toll free 800/433-7300), Continental (toll free 800/525-0280), Delta (toll free 800/221-1212), Midwest Express (toll free 800/452-2022), Northwest (toll free 800/225-2525), TWA (toll free 800/221-2000), United (toll free 800/241-6522), and USAir (toll free 800/428-4322).

FOREIGN CARRIERS: British Airways (toll free 800/247-9297), KLM (toll free 800/374-7747), Lufthansa (toll free 800/645-3880), and Swissair (800/221-4750).

CITY LINK: Cab fare from Detroit Metropolitan Airport to city center is about $36, and time, about 30–40 min.; from Detroit City Airport, about $14, and time, about 15 min. Bus: **Commuter Transportation** (toll free 800/351-5466), serving principal dwntwn hotels and the Renaissance Center, departs Detroit Metropolitan Airport every hour for the 45-min. trip for a fare of $13.

Inadequate public bus transportation system, **DOT** (Department of Transportation; 933-1300), but spectacular automated "People Mover" (224-2160) operating through the entire dwntwn district. Since the metropolitan area is large and the Metropolitan Airport a long way out, it's a good idea to rent a car with unlimited mileage, unless you plan to stay in the heart of dwntwn.

CAR RENTAL (at the airports unless otherwise indicated): Avis (toll free 800/331-1212); Budget (toll free 800/527-0700); Dollar (toll free 800/800-4000); Hertz (toll free 800/654-3131); National (toll free 800/227-7368); Thrifty,

29111 Wick Rd., Romulus (toll free 800/367-2277). For dwntwn locations, consult the local phone directory.

LIMOUSINE SERVICES: Carey Limousine (946-5466), Michigan Limo Service (546-6112).

TAXIS: An abundance of cabs at reasonable rates. You can hail them on the street, take them from the waiting lines outside the big hotels, or summon them by phone. The leading companies are **Checker** (963-7000) and **Lorraine Cab** (582-6900).

TRAIN: Amtrak Station, 2601 Rose St. at Vernor Hwy. (toll free 800/872-7245). Area unsafe, especially at night.

INTERCITY BUSES: Greyhound, 1001 Howard St. at 6th St. (toll free 800/231-2222).

INFORMATION & TOURS

TOURIST INFORMATION: The **Detroit Convention & Visitors Bureau,** 100 Renaissance Center (Suite 1950), MI 48243 (313/259-4333; toll free 800/338-7648).
    24-hour Visitors Hotline giving Detroit's events schedule: 800/338-7648.

GUIDED TOURS: Gray Line Tours (bus), 1301 E. Warren Ave. (313/935-3808). Guided tours of the city, May–Aug.
    Great Water Yachts Charters (boat), 24400 E. Jefferson St. (778-7030). Excursions on the Great Lakes, May–Oct.

SIGHTS, ATTRACTIONS & ACTIVITIES

ARCHITECTURAL HIGHLIGHTS: ※▲ **Civic Center,** Woodward and Jefferson Aves. (224-1010): Ultramodern architectural complex on the banks of the Detroit River in the heart of downtown. Its constituent parts include the 20-story white marble tower of the **City-County Building,** protected by *The Spirit of Detroit,* Marshall Fredericks's massive bronze statue; **Cobo Hall,** one of the country's largest convention and exhibition halls, with 11,000 seats and roof parking for 1,700 vehicles; **Hart Plaza,** a wide esplanade near the spot where Cadillac and his French companions first came ashore in 1701, in the center of which is **Dodge Fountain,** a strange metallic construction with computer-controlled water jets and lights, designed by Isamo Noguchi; **Veterans' Memorial Building,** flanked by picturesque pylons; **Joe Louis Arena,** an indoor stadium with 15,000 seats; **Mariner's Church,** the city's oldest (1848), with a modern belfry and carillon, which was moved 780 ft. (244m) to its present site when the Civic Center was built; **Michigan Consolidated Gas Co. Building,** a 40-story glass skyscraper designed by Minoru Yamasaki.
    ※▲ **Detroit People Mover,** 150 Michigan Ave. (224-2160): Elevated, automated rail system that encircles Detroit's central business district. The 3-mi.-long (5km) concrete ribbon, with 13 artfully decorated stations, links the Renaissance Center, Cobo Hall, Greektown, and the major attractions downtown for just 50¢.
    ▲ **Millender Center,** Randolph St. and Jefferson Ave. (222-1500): Latest of the new downtown architectural complexes, with office buildings, luxury hotel, stores, and restaurants, all linked by a glass Skywalk to the impressive Renaissance Center across Jefferson Ave.
    ※▲▲ **Renaissance Center,** Jefferson Ave. at Randolph St. (568-5600): A spectacular grove of seven skyscrapers inaugurated in 1977, ranging from 20 to 73 floors in height, at the edge of the Detroit River.

The exceptional modern design bears the stamp of John Portman. Giant hotel, stores, restaurants, indoor gardens; symbol of the new Detroit has recently completed a $27-million renovation program.

☼ ☖ **Wayne State University,** 5050 Cass Ave. (577-2424): Founded in 1868, the university is highly regarded for its medical school—one of the finest in the country—and its architecturally distinguished campus, whose 100 buildings house 30,000 students. Among the most noteworthy: **McGregor Memorial Center,** the **College of Education Building,** and the **De Roy Auditorium,** all by Minoru Yamasaki, architect of New York's World Trade Center. Campus open to visitors daily.

HISTORIC BUILDINGS: ☖ **Fisher Building,** 3011 W. Grand Blvd. (874-4444): A 28-story masterpiece of 1930s art deco by Albert Kahn, with restaurants, boutiques, theaters, and art galleries. Sumptuous interior.

☼ ☖ **Fox Theater,** 2211 Woodward Ave. (961-5450): One of the country's largest (5,000 seats) and gaudiest remaining movie palaces (built 1928). Restored in 1988 to its pre-Depression glory as part of a $35-million renovation of downtown Detroit. Looks like the Buddhist temples that inspired it, with its 10-ft. (3m) Chinese dragons and 2-ton (1,800kg) chandelier.

☖ **Orchestra Hall,** 3700 Parsons at Woodward Ave. (833-3700): A 2,000-seat concert hall dating from 1920, "an acoustic miracle" according to the great cellist Pablo Casals. Recently renovated, it is once again the home of the Detroit Symphony Orchestra.

MARKETS: ☖ **Eastern Market,** Russell St. at Fisher Fwy. (833-1560): Picturesque European-style open-air market dating from 1892. The largest flower bedding market in the U.S. Open mornings only, Mon–Sat.

MUSEUMS OF ART: ☼ ☖☖ **Detroit Institute of Arts (DIA),** 5200 Woodward Ave. (833-7900): One of the country's finest, with great masters of European painting, Far Eastern art, superb murals by the Mexican Diego Rivera (*Detroit Industry*), and a fine collection of medieval armor. Among the most famous exhibits: Caravaggio's *Conversion of Mary Magdalene,* Titian's *Man with a Flute,* van Eyck's *St. Jerome,* Pieter Breughel the Elder's *A Village Wedding,* Frans Hals's *Portrait of Hendrick Swalmius,* Cézanne's *Mme Cézanne,* and a self-portrait by Gauguin. There are also works by contemporary American painters including Stuart Davis, Mark Rothko, and Andy Warhol. Open Wed–Sun.

MUSEUMS OF SCIENCE & HISTORY: ☖ **Children's Museum,** 67 E. Kirby Ave. (494-1210): A fascinating place for children and adults alike, with collections relating to the history of Native Americans and exhibits on different cultures (African, Inuit, etc.). Fauna and flora of Michigan; planetarium next door. Amazing sculpture in the shape of a horse, made entirely of automobile bumpers (and what could be more appropriate to Detroit?). Open Mon–Sat.

☖ **Detroit Science Center,** 5020 John R St. (577-8400): This museum houses a wide-ranging cross section of pushbutton exhibits on diverse scientific subjects; the visitor is invited to participate in hands-on fashion. Spherical cinema with 360° projection of science films. Interesting. Open daily.

☼ ☖ **Historical Museum,** 5401 Woodward Ave. (833-1805): Reconstructs the appearance and atmosphere of mid-19th-century Detroit: cobbled streets, stores, restored domestic interiors, models, and temporary exhibitions. For those who love glimpses of the past. Open Wed–Sun.

☼ ⚸ **Motown Museum,** 2468 W. Grand Blvd. (875-2264): Not far from the Wayne State campus, this unpretentious little museum is devoted to the performers who made their name on the Motown record label. See the rough-and-ready sound studio where the Jackson Five, Smokey Robinson, and other Diana Ross discoveries made their first recordings and the "Michael Jackson Room." Open daily. A must for soul-music fans.

⚸ **Public Library,** 5201 Woodward Ave. (833-1000): There are 2.5 million books housed in this 1921 Italian Renaissance building made of Vermont marble and decorated with enormous frescoes. The books include very rare old volumes as well as many works on the history of the auto industry and of the trade-union movement. Open Mon–Sat.

OUTDOOR ART & PLAZAS: Other than the above-mentioned *Spirit of Detroit* by Marshall Fredericks and Dodge Fountain (see "Architectural Highlights," above), the visitor to the Civic Center may take pleasure in Giacomo Manzù's beautiful *Passo di Danza;* the *Joe Louis Monument,* a gigantic black arm with clenched fist hanging from cables by sculptor Robert Graham; and Isamo Noguchi's spiraled *Pylon.* On Cass St. in front of the Michigan Bell Telephone Building, you should take a look at a stabile by Alexander Calder known as *Young Lady and Her Suite.*

PANORAMAS: ☼⚸⚸ **The Summit** is an enclosed observation deck, with an adjacent bar and restaurant on the 73rd floor of the Westin Hotel in Renaissance Center (568-8000). You have to pay for the view—but it's the most spectacular in Detroit.

PARKS & GARDENS: ⚸ **Belle Isle,** MacArthur Bridge (267-7115): On a 3-mi.-long (5km) island in the Detroit River stands this 1,000-acre (400ha) park: swimming, public golf course, jogging, aquarium, naval museum, mini-zoo. Free concerts in summer. Fine view of the city's skyline.

⚸ **Grosse Pointe Shore,** Lake Shore Dr.: An elegant residential neighborhood, with woods and lovely gardens, along Lake St. Clair; it boasts many affluent private houses.

PERFORMING ARTS: For current listings of shows and cultural events, consult the entertainment pages of the two daily papers, *Detroit Free Press* (morning) and *Detroit News* (morning and evening); also the monthly magazines *Detroit Monthly* and *Metropolitan Detroit.*

Art Institute Auditorium, 5200 Woodward Ave. (833-7900): Concerts.

Attic Theater, 7339 Third Ave. (875-8284): Drama and comedy.

Fisher Theater, Second Ave. at Grand Blvd. (872-1000): Broadway hits. Year round.

Fox Theater, 2211 Woodward Ave. (396-7600): Top-notch variety, drama, comedy, and musical events.

Hilberry Theater, 4743 Cass Ave. (577-2972): Classical theater.

Music Hall Center for the Performing Arts, 350 Madison Ave. (963-7680): Dance, concerts.

Orchestra Hall, 3700 Parsons at Woodward Ave. (833-3700): Home of the Detroit Symphony (music director: Neeme Jarvi). Classical and jazz concerts.

Theater Company–University of Detroit, 4001 W. McNichols Rd. (993-1130): Drama and comedy; Sept–May.

SPECIAL EVENTS: For exact dates, consult the **Detroit Convention & Visitors Bureau** (see "Tourist Information," above).

International Auto Show (Jan): Hundreds of foreign and domestic cars on display.

International Grand Prix (early June): A spectacular Formula 1 Grand Prix race, run in downtown Detroit.

International Freedom Festival (late June to early July): Celebrates U.S.– Canadian friendship with parades, shows, food festivals, concerts, and fireworks on either side of the international border.

Meadow Brook Music Festival (late June to Aug): In Rochester, Minn. Open-air concerts of classical music, pop, and jazz.

Montreux-Detroit Jazz Festival (late Aug to early Sept): The biggest stars in the jazz firmament; draws big crowds from the area.

SPORTS: Detroit boasts four professional teams:

Baseball (Apr–Oct): Tigers, Tiger Stadium (962-4000).

Basketball (Oct–May): Pistons, Palace, in Auburn Hills (313/377-0100).

Football (Sept–Jan): Lions, Pontiac Silverdome (the world's largest inflatable dome), in Pontiac (313/335-4151).

Ice Hockey (Oct–May): Red Wings, Joe Louis Arena (396-7600).

Horse Racing

Hazel Park Race Track (harness racing), 1650 E. 10 Mile Rd., in Hazel Park (313/398-1000). Racing Apr to mid-Oct.

Ladbroke-DRC, 28001 Schoolcraft Rd., in Livonia (313/525-7300). Racing Apr–Nov.

Northville Downs (harness racing), 301 S. Center St., in Northville (313/349-1000). Racing Oct–Mar.

STROLLS: ⚅ **Greektown,** Monroe St. at Beaubien St.: The area's most popular nighttime district and the heart of Detroit's important Greek community; lively covered market (Trappers Alley), boutiques, and restaurants.

TROLLEY: ⚅ **Washington Blvd. Trolley Car:** A picturesque old streetcar line whose ramshackle trams were once the pride of Lisbon, Portugal. It runs from the RenCen to Grand Circus Park, and boasts the world's last remaining open-top double-decker (933-1300).

WINTER SPORTS RESORTS: ⚅ **Alpine Valley,** 6775 E. Highland Rd., in White Lake Township (44 mi./70km NW on I-75 and Mich. 59W) (313/887-2180): 10 lifts. Operates Dec–Mar.

ZOOS: ⚅ **Detroit Zoo,** Woodward Ave. and 10 Mile Rd. (10 mi./16km north) (398-3900): One of the best known in the U.S., with 400 species living in careful reconstructions of their natural habitat. The reptiles, penguins, and marine mammals are of particular interest. Miniature-railroad tour. Open daily May–Nov, Wed–Sun the rest of the year.

ACCOMMODATIONS

Personal Favorites (in order of preference)

⚅⚅⚅⚅ **River Place Inn** (nr. dwntwn), 1000 Stroh River Place, MI 48207 (313/259-2500; toll free, see Preferred). 109 rms, A/C, color TV, in-rm movies. AE, CB, DC, MC, V. Free valet parking, pool, tennis court, squash, health club, sauna, bicycling, croquet, rest. (River Room), bar, 24-hr. rm svce, concierge. *Note:* Standing on the Detroit River, this ultra-luxurious hotel, opened in 1989, commands a sweeping view of the downtown high-rises and the Canadian shore. The handsome turn-of-the-century brick building w. its pinnacle roof has been marvelously restored. Unrivaled comfort and amenities; spacious rms w. period furniture, high ceilings, minibar, and private safe. Attentive, personalized svce; acceptable rest.; comprehensive physical-fitness facilities; well-equipped business center. Interesting wknd discounts. By far the best hotel in Detroit; 5 min. from dwntwn. **E–VE**

Radisson Pontchartrain Hotel (dwntwn), 2 Washington Blvd., MI 48226 (313/965-0200; toll free, see Radisson). 420 rms, A/C, color TV, in-rm movies. AE, CB, DC, MC, V. Valet parking $10, pool, health club, sauna, two rests. (including Count's), bar, 24-hr. rm svce, concierge, free crib. *Note:* A modern and comfortable 23-story hotel built on the site of old Fort Pontchartrain. Elegant, well-designed rms, the best looking out over the Detroit River. Very good svce, acceptable rest. The business traveler's favorite. Central location opposite Cobo Hall. No-smoking rms. Interesting wknd packages. Recently underwent a $15-million facelift. **E**

Dearborn Inn Marriott (vic.), 20301 Oakwood Blvd., in Dearborn, MI 48124 (313/271-2700; toll free, see Marriott). 222 rms and cottages, A/C, color TV. AE, CB, DC, MC, V. Free parking, pool, two tennis courts, health club, two rests. (including the Early American Room), bar, rm svce, nightclub, free crib. *Note:* Built in 1931 by Henry Ford I, this big Georgian manor house sits in an enormous grdn halfway between the airport and dwntwn, and very nr. the Ford Museum. Friendly colonial-style rms, as well as very comfortable individual cottages. Attentive reception and svce. Recently renovated and full of charm; ideal if you're driving. **E**

Hotel St. Regis (nr. dwntwn), 3071 W. Grand Blvd., MI 48202 (313/873-3000). 224 rms, A/C, color TV, in-rm movies. AE, CB, DC, MC, V. Valet parking $7, rest. (Restaurant St. Regis), bar, rm svce, entertainment. *Note:* Charming older hotel, opposite the General Motors headquarters building, w. huge, inviting rms, polished svce, and an acceptable rest. Guests are mostly businesspeople and regulars. Recently renovated. 10 min. from dwntwn. **M–E**

Heaven on Earth Inn (formerly Days Inn; dwntwn), 231 Michigan Ave., MI 48226 (313/965-0318). 287 rms, A/C, color TV, in-rm movies. AE, CB, DC, MC, V. Valet parking $5, pool, health club, free continental breakfast, free crib. *Note:* Modern concrete high-rise very nr. the Civic Center and Cobo Hall; rather large functional rms (some no-smoking). Business clientele. **I–M**

Balmar Motel (nr. dwntwn), 3250 E. Jefferson Ave., MI 48207 (313/568-2000). 60 rms, A/C, cable color TV. AE, DC, MC, V. Free parking, pool, rest. adjacent, private grdn, free crib. *Note:* Modest but well-run small motel 15 min. from dwntwn; friendly reception and svce. Good value overall. **B**

Other Accommodations (from top bracket to budget)

Hyatt Regency Dearborn (vic.), Michigan Ave. at Fairlane Town Center, in Dearborn, MI 48126 (313/593-1234; toll free, see Hyatt). 771 rms, A/C, color TV, in-rm movies. AE, CB, DC, MC, V. Free parking (valet parking $7), pool, health club, sauna, three rests., coffee shop, two bars, rm svce, disco, free crib. *Note:* Ultramodern steel-and-glass edifice w. a spectacular 16-story lobby and glass elevator shafts. Revolving bar on top floor. All the usual Hyatt comfort, very good svce, spacious rms. Business clientele. Very near Ford's manufacturing headquarters, 20 min. from dwntwn, 5 min. from the airport—and has its own helicopter pad! Monorail link to a nearby shopping center. VIP floor. **E–VE**

Omni International (dwntwn), 333 E. Jefferson, MI 48226 (313/222-7700; toll free, see Omni). 254 rms, A/C, color TV, in-rm movies. AE, CB, DC, MC, V. Valet indoor parking $9, pool, two tennis courts, sauna, racquetball, rest. (333 East), coffee shop, bar, rm svce, boutiques, free crib. *Note:* 20-story hotel in the recently constructed Millender Center; an elegant modern building w. commodious, comfortable rms (most w.

balconies). Very comprehensive sports facilities. Efficient svce; group and business clientele. A good place to stay in the heart of dwntwn. Connected to RenCen by the Skywalk. **E–VE**

🏨🏨🏨 **Westin Hotel** (dwntwn), Renaissance Center, MI 48243 (313/568-8000; toll free, see Westin). 1,404 rms, A/C, color TV, in-rm movies. AE, CB, DC, MC, V. Gar. $9, pool, health club, sauna, three rests. (one of which, The Summit, is a revolving rest. on the top floor), coffee shop, three bars, 24-hr. rm svce, hrdrsr, boutiques, free crib. *Note:* Futuristic 73-story cylindrical tower which bears the clear imprint of the famous architect John Portman. Eight-story-high lobby, w. indoor grdns and fountains. All rms are cramped but comfortable, and enjoy a panorama of the city or the Detroit River. River Bistro is an acceptable rest. Efficient svce. Convention or business clientele. Has its own heliport. Detroit's most dazzling address. **E–VE**

🏨🏨🏨 **Embassy Suites Hotel** (vic.), 28100 Franklin Rd., in Southfield, MI 48034 (313/350-2000; toll free 800/362-2779). 240 suites, A/C, color TV, in-rm movies. AE, CB, DC, MC, V. Free parking, pool, health club, sauna, whirlpool, rest. (Jacques Demers' Restaurant), bar, disco, free full breakfast and evening cocktails, free crib. *Note:* Luxury all-suites hotel located 30 min. from Detroit Metro Airport and 20 min. from dwntwn. Large, comfortable two-rm suites, each w. refrigerator, three telephones, and two color TVs. Spectacular nine-story landscaped atrium. Flawless svce. **M–E**

🏨🏨 **Holiday Inn Dearborn** (vic.), 22900 Michigan Ave., in Dearborn, MI 48124 (313/278-4800; toll free, see Holiday Inns). 333 rms, A/C, color TV, in-rm movies. AE, CB, DC, MC, V. Free parking, three pools, sauna, three rests. (including Chambertin), bar, rm svce, free crib. *Note:* Archetypal Holiday Inn on the banks of the Rouge River; comfortable balconied rms, some w. kitchenettes. Very creditable rest. Good value. Near the Ford Museum; 20 min. from dwntwn. **I–M**

🏨 **Shorecrest Motor Inn** (dwntwn), 1316 E. Jefferson Ave., MI 48207 (313/568-3000; toll free 800/992-9616). 54 rms, A/C, cable color TV. AE, CB, DC, MC, V. Free parking; rest. (The Clique), rm svce, free crib. *Note:* Aging but decent, comfortable motel; utilitarian rms w. refrigerators. Next to Renaissance Center. Good value. **B–I**

🏨 **Knight's Inn** (formerly Travelodge; vic.), 23730 Michigan Ave., in Dearborn, MI 48124 (313/565-7250). 78 rms, A/C, cable color TV. AE, CB, DC, MC, V. Free parking, pool, coffee shop, no cribs. *Note:* Typical well-run motel; comfortable rms, some w. balconies. Free morning coffee. 5 min. from the Ford Museum and Greenfield Village, 20 min. from dwntwn. Good value. **B–I**

🏨 **Motel 6 North** (vic.), 8300 Chicago Rd., in Warren, MI 48093 (313/826-9300). 118 rms, A/C, cable color TV. AE, DC, MC, V. Free parking, café nearby. *Note:* Unbeatable value, 5 min. from GM Technical Center and 20 min. from dwntwn (via Mich. 53). Good basic accommodations. Ideal if you're driving. **B**

🏨 **Red Roof Inn** (vic.), 26300 Dequindre Dr. (at I-696), in Warren, MI 48091 (313/573-4300; toll free 800/843-7663). 137 rms, A/C, cable color TV. AE, CB, DC, MC, V. Free parking, nearby coffee shop, free crib. *Note:* Inexpensive motel w. little to recommend it but its low rates. Functional comfort but nothing more. Free morning coffee. 20 min. from dwntwn. Ideal if you're driving (direct access to highways). **B**

Airport Accommodations

🏨🏨 **Hilton Suites** (vic.), 8600 Wickham Rd., in Romulus, MI 48174 (313/728-9200; toll free, see Hilton). 151 suites, A/C, color TV, in-rm movies. AE, CB, DC, MC, V. Free parking, pool, health club, whirlpool, rest., bar, rm svce, free crib. *Note:* New all-suites airport motel. Attractive decor; well-soundproofed suites w. refrigerators and balconies; efficient svce. Business clientele. Free airport limo. **M–E**

YMCA/Youth Hostel

YMCA (dwntwn), 2020 Witherell St., MI 48226 (313/962-6126). Men only; also functions as a youth hostel. 220 rms, pool, sauna, health club. Unsafe area, especially at night.

RESTAURANTS

Personal Favorites (in order of preference)

♙♙♙ **Rattlesnake Club** (dwntwn), 300 River Place (567-4400). ♙♙♙ A/C. Lunch Mon–Fri, dinner Mon–Sat; closed Jan 1, Memorial Day, Labor Day, Dec 25. AE, MC, V. Jkt. *Specialties:* salmon cakes w. mustard sauce and chives, soft-shell crabs tempura style w. ginger-pepper butter, roast rack of lamb w. artichokes and peppers, grilled swordfish w. Szechuan peppercorns, three-flavor polenta, white-chocolate ravioli. Fine list of wines at reasonable prices. *Note:* The young, talented chef Jimmy Schmidt (former chef of the now-defunct London Chop House) has successfully established his rest. as one of the finest in Detroit. The modern decor admirably sets off the elegant, imaginative food. Smiling, congenial svce. Resv. strongly advised at this fashionable spot. *American.* **M–E**

※♙♙♙ **The Whitney** (nr. dwntwn), 4421 Woodward Ave. at Canfield ♙♙♙ Ave. (832-5700). A/C. Dinner nightly, brunch Sun; closed hols. AE, MC, V. Jkt. *Specialties:* sautéed foie gras, roast rack of lamb w. rosemary, grilled Maine lobster, game and venison (in season), chocolate ugly cake w. mousse frosting. Menu changes regularly. Long wine list. *Note:* "Hollywood magnificence" would be the best thumbnail description of this opulent setting: a luxurious Victorian mansion filled to bursting w. Flemish tapestries, precious crystal, marble, old paneling, and Tiffany stained-glass windows. Chef Grosz's kitchen dishes up a pretty blend of elegance and simplicity. Polished, attentive svce; distinctive background music. Resv. advised. Valet parking. In spite of the unattractive neighborhood, an excellent place to eat. *American.* **M–E**

♙♙♙ **Joe Muer's Seafood** (nr. dwntwn), 2000 Gratiot Ave. (567-♙♙♙ 1088). A/C. Lunch/dinner Mon–Sat; closed hols. AE, DC, MC, V. J&T. *Specialties:* top-quality fish and shellfish; good list of California wines. *Note:* A local institution since 1929. This immense rest., w. its comfortable wood-paneled and exposed-brick rms, is host every day to crowds of fish- and seafood-lovers, who are attracted by one of the broadest selections in the country. Two black marks: svce rather perfunctory; resv. not accepted. Private valet parking. 15 min. from dwntwn. *Seafood.* **M**

♙♙ **Van Dyke Place** (nr. dwntwn), 649 Van Dyke St. (821-2620). ♙♙ A/C. Dinner only, Tues–Sat, brunch Sun. AE, MC, V. J&T. *Specialties:* asparagus-and-wild-mushroom gratin, roast rack of lamb, broiled North Atlantic salmon, roast half-duckling. Menu changes regularly. Very fine wine list. *Note:* Super-chic rest. housed in the mansion of a 19th-century captain of industry, elegantly decorated in Louis XVI style w. crystal chandeliers, gilt-framed pictures, and period furniture. The cuisine, while praiseworthy, doesn't quite measure up to the decor. Svce is attentive. Resv., in advance, a must. 10 min. from dwntwn. Valet parking. *French/Continental.* **M–E**

♙ **Cocina del Sol** (nr. dwntwn), 28565 Northwestern Hwy., Southfield (350-0055). A/C. Lunch Mon–Sat, dinner nightly; closed hols. AE, MC, V. *Specialties:* four types of quesadillas, black-bean-layered dip, pecan oven-roasted chicken, Western strip fajitas, Cancun platter (rock shrimp enchilada and tostada w. skewered tiger shrimp), brujo (frozen chocolate mousse in tequila anglaise sauce). *Note:* The finest Mexican food to be found in Detroit. Very colorful and breezy environment w. an open wood-burning fireplace and interesting Aztec masks peering from the walls. Though billed as a Mexican rest., this fashionable rest. is serving more and more South-western dishes that are just as delightful. Resvs. are not accepted, but you can enjoy a margarita at the bar while waiting. *Mexican/Southwestern.* **I**

☀☿ **Jacoby's** (dwntwn), 624 Brush St. (962-7067). A/C. Lunch daily, dinner Mon–Fri. AE, DC, MC, V. *Specialties:* schnitzel, sauerbraten, bratwurst, lake perch, sandwiches, German beer on draft. *Note:* The lawyers' and politicians' favorite since 1904. Looks and feels like a picturesque old brewhouse. Solid, honest food somewhat lacking in imagination. Svce w. a smile. Next to RenCen. *German/American.* **B–I**

Other Restaurants (from top bracket to budget)

☿☿☿ **Opus One** (dwntwn), 565 E. Larned St. (961-7766). A/C. Lunch Mon–Fri, dinner Mon–Sat; closed hols. AE, CB, DC, MC, V. Jkt. *Specialties:* lobster bisque, sautéed escalope of veal and lobster tail w. béarnaise sauce, game bird strudel, roast duck in Grand Marnier sauce, apple flan. Wonderful wine list appropriately including the famous California wine Opus One, from which the rest. takes its name. *Note:* A successful newcomer on the local scene; light, imaginative modern food served in a pretty turn-of-the-century setting w. original artwork. Uncommonly efficient svce; resv. a must. Pianist. Valet parking. *French/American.* **M–E**

☿☿☿ **The Golden Mushroom** (vic.) 1800 W. 10 Mile Rd., Southfield (559-4230). A/C. Lunch Mon–Fri, dinner Mon–Sat; closed hols. AE, DC, MC, V. J&T. *Specialties:* foie gras terrine, beluga caviar, fettuccine w. truffles and cream, jumbo Dover sole, venison medallion sautéed w. cognac and chanterelles, chocolate Mozart gâteau. Menu changes seasonally. *Note:* Elegance is the mainstay at this rest. where care goes into the tiniest of details. Under the supervision of chef Milos Cihelka, each dish is created with precision, starting with the smoking of fish and the aging of meat (a smokehouse and aging room are on the premises). Impressive list of over 750 wines. Mushroom specials are shown at the table. Attentive and adroit svce. Well worth the 20-min drive from dwntwn. *French.* **M–E**

☿☿ **Pike Street Restaurant** (vic.), 18 W. Pike St., Pontiac (334-7878). A/C. Lunch Mon–Fri, dinner Mon–Sat; closed hols. AE, MC, V. Jkt. *Specialties:* white-bean soup, sautéed wild mushrooms in puff pastry, pork loin stuffed w. cherries, braised pickerel w. baby white asparagus. The menu changes regularly. *Note:* Located in dwntwn Pontiac, a 40-min. drive from dwntwn Detroit, this favorite of GM executives offers innovative American cuisine by Brian Polcyn, an engaging young chef w. a growing reputation. Comfortable, classy setting in an 1893 historic building. Efficient, knowledgeable svce. Resv. advised. Valet parking. *American.* **M**

☿☿ **Carl's Chop House** (nr. dwntwn), 3020 Grand River Ave. (833-0700). A/C. Lunch Mon–Sat, dinner nightly, brunch Sun; closed hols. AE, CB, DC, MC, V. *Specialties:* the city's best prime ribs, steaks, and lamb chops for more than half a century; also excellent Great Lakes fish and pickled herring. *Note:* All the warmth of an Amtrak waiting room and a strictly flea-market decor, but efficient svce. Not far from Tiger Stadium, Carl's attracts many fans on game days. Resv. advised. Valet parking. *Steak/Seafood.* **I–M**

☿ **Très Vite** (nr. dwntwn), 2203 Woodward Ave., in the Fox Theater Building (964-4144). A/C. Lunch Mon–Fri, dinner Tues–Sat. AE, MC, V. *Specialties:* Italian pasta, pizza w. four cheeses, grilled meats and seafood. *Note:* Hot, new rest., owned by chef Jimmy Schmidt, the cooking genius behind the famous Rattlesnake Club (see "Personal Favorites," above). Light, contemporary American cuisine in a bright, modern urban setting. Popular after a show. Resv. advised. *American.* **I–M**

☿ **Fishbone's Rythm Kitchen Café** (dwntwn), 400 Monroe St. (965-4600). A/C. Lunch Mon–Sat, dinner nightly (until midnight), brunch Sun. AE, MC, V. *Specialties:* whisky ribs, jambalaya, crayfish étouffée, alligator voodoo. *Note:* Spicy and flavorful Cajun and Créole fare in a typical Bourbon St. atmosphere w. tin ceilings and antique lamps. Friendly, efficient svce. Locally popular. In the heart of Greektown. *Créole.* **I–M**

☖ **New Hellas** (dwntwn), 583 Monroe St. (961-5544). A/C.
Lunch/dinner Tues–Sun. (until 2am). AE, MC, V. *Specialties:*
moussaka, broiled lamb, squid, shish kebab, spanakopita (spinach-and-cheese
pie), baklava. *Note:* An absolutely authentic Greek rest. in the heart of
Greektown. Generally noisy and crowded. Open very late. No resv., so inevitable
waits (usually). *Greek.* **B–I**

☖ **Xochimilco** (nr. dwntwn), 3409 Bagley, in Mexican town
(843-0179). A/C. Lunch/dinner daily (until 4am); closed
Thanksgiving, Dec 25. AE, MC, V. *Specialties:* botanas, chimichangas, chiles
relleños, quesadillas, enchiladas. *Note:* Noisy and usually crowded *cantina* offering huge servings of authentic Mexican cooking at very reasonable prices. Very
popular, so plan to wait 20–30 min. while sipping a margarita or sangría. *Mexican.* **B–I**

Restaurants in the Vicinity

☖☖ **La Cuisine** (vic.), 417 Pelissier St., in Windsor, Canada (519/
253-6432). A/C. Lunch/dinner Tues–Sat. DC, MC, V. Jkt.
Specialties: boeuf gros sel, kidneys w. three mustards, bouillabaisse. Good desserts. *Note:* A real French rest., well worth the jaunt into Canada (10 min. by car
through the Windsor Tunnel; non–U.S. citizens should bring their passports).
Congenial bistro atmosphere. Wine but no hard liquor. Resv. advised for dinner.
French. **I–M**

Cafeterias/Specialty Spots

American Coney Island (dwntwn), 114 W. LaFayette St. (961-7758).
A/C. Breakfast/lunch/dinner daily (open around the clock). No credit cards.
By general consent the best hot dogs in town. Locally popular since 1914.

BARS & NIGHTCLUBS

Alvin's Finer Detroit Bar (nr. dwntwn), 5756 Cass Ave. (832-2355). A hip
student bar near Wayne State University. Live classic rock, to reggae, to hardcore,
to jazz. Good deli fare.

Galligan's (dwntwn), 519 E. Jefferson Ave. (963-2098). Detroit's most
popular Irish pub. Plenty of action. Bar food. Noisy and likable. Open Mon–Sat.

The Rhinoceros (nr. dwntwn), 265 Riopelle (259-2208). Fashionable piano bar and soothing atmosphere. Open nightly.

Soup Kitchen (dwntwn), 1585 Franklin St. (259-2643). Blues and jazz in a
nice saloon setting; also a decent rest. Open nightly.

Shelter (dwntwn), 431 E. Congress (961-6358). Enormous three-level
disco in a deconsecrated church two blocks from RenCen. Locally very popular;
open Wed, Fri, Sat.

The State Theater (nr. dwntwn), 2115 Woodward Ave. (961-5450). The
city's biggest dance floor and a lascivious clientele. Located in the cavernous Fox
Theater.

NEARBY EXCURSIONS

⚓ **ANN ARBOR** (46 mi./74km west on I-94): University
town with a happy, youthful personality; seat of the **University
of Michigan,** S. State St. and S. University Ave. (313/763-4636). One of the
largest (35,000 students) and oldest (1817) universities in the Midwest, which
moved here in 1837, 20 years after its founding in Detroit. Many buildings in the
Gothic style; libraries; museums of art, archeology, and natural history. Also
home to the **Gerald R. Ford Presidential Library,** 1000 Beal Ave. (313/741-
2218), housing the personal archives of the 38th president. Campus open to visitors Mon–Fri.

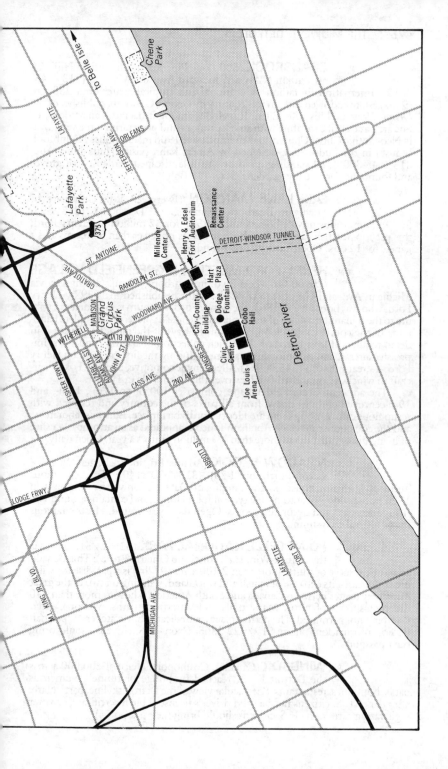

CRANBROOK (500 Lone Pine Rd. in Bloomfield Hills, 25 mi./40km NW via Woodward Ave. and Mich. 1) (313/645-3312): Internationally famous educational and cultural center on a 288-acre (92ha) estate endowed early in this century by George G. Booth, publisher of the *Detroit News*, and his wife, Ellen. It includes among its facilities an academy of fine arts, a scientific institute with an observatory and planetarium, the very lovely Neo-Gothic Christ Church, and an impressive 1908 manor house (Cranbrook House) in the Tudor style designed by Albert Kahn (visits Thurs June–Aug, 313/645-3000), all standing amid beautiful landscaped gardens with groves and fountains. Open daily (gardens, May–Oct only).

FAIR LANE MANSION (Evergreen Rd., University of Michigan–Dearborn Campus, in Dearborn) (313/593-5590): Sumptuous private home built in 1915 for $2 million by Henry Ford; this pseudo-Scottish castle in rough stone boasts no fewer than 56 rooms and a garage for 12 cars! Open Sun–Fri year round.

HENRY FORD MUSEUM & GREENFIELD VILLAGE (20900 Oakwood Blvd. in Dearborn, 10 mi./16km west via Michigan Ave. and U.S. 12) (313/271-1620): Established in 1929 by Henry Ford, who was born here in 1863, the **Henry Ford Museum** is intended as a tribute to the dynamic qualities of the American people. It presents a complete panorama of the country's development from the days of the pioneers. To see it in detail requires at least two days. Very rich collection of art and handcrafts; impressive aircraft and automobile museum, including the first car built by Henry Ford, a great 600-ton (545,000kg) Allegheny locomotive, and the Fokker aircraft in which Admiral Byrd first flew over the North Pole in 1926.

The adjacent **Greenfield Village** comprises 100 or so 17th-, 18th-, and 19th-century buildings drawn from all parts of the country and restored with scrupulous care. Among them are Henry Ford's birthplace, Edison's laboratory, and the courthouse in which Abraham Lincoln appeared as an attorney—a slice of living history that draws more than 1½ million visitors a year. Open daily.

MEADOW BROOK (Adams Rd. in Rochester, 25 mi./40km north on I-75) (313/370-3140): This enormous Tudor-style manor house on the campus of Oakland University was built in 1926 by the widow of automobile tycoon John Dodge, and contains around 100 richly furnished and decorated rooms. Open daily year round. Hosts a famous music festival each summer.

POINT PELEE NATIONAL PARK (32 mi./51km SE via the Detroit-Windsor Tunnel and Ontario Rte. 3): This Canadian nature reserve of a little more than 2,400 acres (972ha) is a paradise for wildlife enthusiasts; its expanse of marsh and woodland, standing on two of the great migratory routes between Canada and South America, is host to more than 340 different species of birds. Many trails and waterfront paths. Visitor Center. Camping not permitted. The perfect place for dedicated birdwatchers. Open daily. For information, phone 519/322-2365. (Non–U.S. citizens should bring their passports.)

WINDSOR (Canada): Cosmopolitan city of 200,000 across the Detroit River, reached by bridge or tunnel. Numerous parks, boutiques, restaurants. Spectacular view of the Detroit skyline, particularly after dark. (U.S. citizens need a valid driver's license, a birth certificate, or voter registration card; non–U.S. citizens should bring their passports.)

CHAPTER 21

CLEVELAND 🔥

□ □ □

This, now the second-largest, city in Ohio (after Columbus) was founded on Lake Erie at the mouth of the **Cuyahoga River** by Gen. Moses Cleaveland. The spelling was later modified by the editor of a local newspaper who found the name too long for his taste. Sprawling over more than 50 mi. (80km), Cleveland's metropolitan area is a riveting microcosm of America's industrial evolution over the last century. Interminable gray, polluted suburbs—home to steel mills, oil refineries, automobile factories, plus electronics and machine-tool plants—lie cheek by jowl with a few luxurious residential areas (**Shaker Heights, Beachwood**) around a downtown which now consists of no more than a couple of dozen blocks surrounding the **Mall** and the completely renovated **Public Square.** The city's tallest building, the 57-story **Society Center,** the 52-story **Terminal Tower,** and the **B. P. America tower** (45 stories) dominate the square. The seventh most populous city in the country in 1950, Cleveland lost nearly a quarter of its population in the 1970s as a result of upheavals in the oil and steel industries; in 1978 Cleveland even became the first major city since the Depression era to go into default. Today the city is in the midst of a building boom— **Tower City Center, Nautica Complex** at the Flats, **North Coast Harbor**—sleek new skyscrapers rise among neoclassic and Gothic structures downtown. The first ground has also been broken for the **Rock-and-Roll Hall of Fame,** a $50-million flashy glass-and-metal museum designed by architect I. M. Pei, scheduled to open in 1995. But despite newfound economy activity, the unemployment rate is still well above 10%, and more than a third of Cleveland's inhabitants live below the poverty line.

Among its other claims to fame, Cleveland can boast the first modern striptease, in the person of an obscure tapdancer named Carrie Findel. Tired of the audience's boos, she declared one night, "I've a surprise for you. Each week, I'll take off one more part of my costume." The show lasted 52 weeks.

Two other truly American legends are associated with Cleveland: Superman, the famous comic-strip hero, who made his first appearance in 1934; and John Davison Rockefeller, the incarnation of capitalism triumphant, who, beginning in 1870, laid the foundations of the immense Standard Oil empire. Cleveland is also headquarters for 35 of the most important U.S. industrial corporations. Medicine is another flourishing aspect of the local economy. Besides schools and research institutes of renown like **Case Western Reserve University** and the **Cleveland State University Hospitals,** the city also has the **Cleveland Clinic,** known worldwide for the organ transplants and cardiac surgery performed here.

Ohio's industrial capital is a veritable mosaic of nationalities, with the second-largest concentration of Hungarians after Budapest, as well as Italian, Irish, Polish, German, Chinese, Greek, Serb, Czech, and Ukrainian communities —overall, a good 60 or so different nationalities are represented. With such a mix of ethnic groups, it's no wonder that Cleveland was the first major U.S. metropolis (1967) to elect an African American mayor, Carl B. Stokes. Cleveland is also rich in first-rate cultural and theatrical institutions: its orchestra is internationally renowned, and its **Museum of Art** is one of the best in the country.

Among Cleveland's famous natives are actors Paul Newman, Burgess Meredith, and Dorothy Dandridge; TV personality Phil Donahue; and composer and band leader Henry Mancini.

BASIC FACTS: State of Ohio. Area code: 216. Time zone: eastern. ZIP Code: 44101. Founded: 1796. Approximate population: city, 500,000; metropolitan area, 2,760,000. 13th-largest metropolitan area in the United States.

CLIMATE: As in all the Great Lakes region, winter is very cold and snowy (average Jan temperature: $27°F/3°C$) and summer hot and humid (average July temperature: $70°F/22°C$). Spring is normally very brief, and autumn mild and sunny; these are the two ideal seasons for visiting Cleveland.

DISTANCES: Chicago, 343 mi. (549km); Cincinnati, 247 mi. (395km); Detroit, 170 mi. (272km); New York, 485 mi. (776km); Washington, 350 mi. (560km).

ARRIVAL & TRANSIT INFORMATION

AIRPORTS: Cleveland Hopkins International Airport (CLE): 10 mi. (16km) SW. Information: 265-6000.

U.S. AIRLINES: American (toll free 800/433-7300), Continental (toll free 800/525-0280), Delta (toll free 800/221-1212), Northwest (toll free 800/225-2525), TWA (toll free 800/221-2000), United (toll free 800/241-6522), and USAir (toll free 800/428-4322).

FOREIGN CARRIERS: Air Canada (toll free 800/776-3000).

CITY LINK: Cab fare to city center from Hopkins International, about $16–$18; time, 25–30 min. (up to 45 min. during rush hr.). An airport–city center **train** leaves every 10–20 min. from the R.T.A. Terminal, Public Sq.; fare, $1.50; time, 25 min. Bus: **Hopkins Airport Limousine** (267-8282): by resv. only, 48 hrs. in advance; serves major dwntwn hotels; fare, $25; time, 35–40 min. Unless your touring will be limited to the dwntwn area, you may wish to rent a car to cope with the sprawling metropolitan area and the difficulty of getting a taxi in the suburbs (the wait sometimes approaches an hour). A rather efficient public transportation system (bus and train); for R.T.A. information, call 621-9500.

CAR RENTAL (at Hopkins International Airport): Avis (toll free 800/331-1212); Budget (toll free 800/527-0700); Dollar (toll free 800/800-4000); Hertz (toll free 800/654-3131); National (toll free 800/227-7368); Thrifty (toll free 800/367-2277). For dwntwn agencies, consult the phone directory.

LIMOUSINE SERVICES: American Limousines Service (221-9330), Elegant Limousine Service (234-0011).

TAXIS: The fares are relatively reasonable. Taxis may be hailed on the street dwntwn, but it's advisable to phone for them: **Americab** (881-1111) or **Yellow Cab** (623-1500).

TRAIN: Amtrak, Lakefront Station, 200 E. Cleveland Memorial Shoreway Dr. (toll free 800/872-7245).

INTERCITY BUSES: Greyhound, 1465 Chester Ave. at E. 14th St. (toll free 800/231-2222).

INFORMATION & TOURS

TOURIST INFORMATION: The **Cleveland Convention & Visitors Bureau,** 3100 Tower City Center, OH 44113 (216/621-4110; toll free 800/321-1001).
  Visitor Center: The Powerhouse, 2000 Sycamore St. (216/623-4494).
  Recorded telephone message giving an up-to-date listing of cultural events and shows: toll free 800/321-1004.

GUIDED TOURS: Goodtime Cruises (boat): Lake Erie and Cuyahoga River cruises. Depart from the E. 9th St. Pier (216/861-5110), May–Oct.
  Trolley Tours (bus), Burke Lakefront Airport (216/771-4484). Narrated two-hour tour aboard a fleet of replica trolley cars. Resv. requested.

SIGHTS, ATTRACTIONS & ACTIVITIES

ARCHITECTURAL HIGHLIGHTS: ⚶ **City Hall,** Lakeside Ave. and E. 6th St. (664-2000): Cleveland's city hall, overlooking Lake Erie. Be sure to see the famous Archibald Willard painting, *Spirit of '76*, in the rotunda. Open Mon–Fri.
  ⚶ **Cleveland Clinic,** 9500 Euclid Ave. (444-2273): Second-largest private hospital in the country after the Mayo Clinic in Rochester, Minn. Employs 8,900 doctors, researchers, and staff. A pioneer in cardiac surgery since 1967, the clinic performs more than 3,000 open-heart operations each year. The world-renowned Cleveland Clinic has treated the likes of ex-King Khaled of Arabia, King Hussein of Jordan, and the former president of Brazil, General Figueiredo. The most recent addition to the complex is the Cesar Pelli–designed clinic building, an enormous white-granite ziggurat.
  ⚶ **Federal Reserve Bank,** 1455 E. 6th St. (579-2284): Built with pink Sienna marble in 1923, this bank features the world's largest vault door and a spectacular interior lobby. Open Mon–Fri.
  ⚶ **Playhouse Square,** Euclid Ave. between E. 13th and E. 17th Sts.: Symbol of Cleveland's cultural renaissance, this urban-renewal project cost $20 million and endowed the city with one of the largest performance and concert hall complexes in the country. The three theaters and the cabaret, elegantly restored, present theatrical performances, ballet, opera, and classical and pop concerts. Open daily. For information on current performances, call 241-6000.
  ⚶ **Public Square,** Ontario St. and Superior Ave.: The heart of the business district, where all the major dwntwn thoroughfares converge: Euclid Ave., Ontario St., and Superior Ave. Towering above the square are the city's tallest buildings: the **Society Center** (57 stories), the **Terminal Tower** (52 stories), and the **B. P. America Tower** (45 stories). Quite lively by day, but not very engaging after dark. Imposing memorial: **Soldiers and Sailors Monument.** The appealing public park is adorned with statues.
  ☀⚶ **Society Center,** Ontario St. at Public Sq.: One of the newer additions to the downtown skyline, this 57-story skyscraper was inaugurated in 1991. At 788 ft. (240m) w. its needle, it's the city's and

Ohio's tallest building. The structure, which occupies a full city block, also includes a 25-story Marriott Hotel.

MARKETS: ☼⚑ **West Side Market,** Lorain Ave. at W. 25th St. (664-3386): Picturesque old European-style covered market with more than 170 food stalls offering products from all over the world. A colorful Cleveland classic dating from 1912. Open Mon, Wed, Fri, and Sat.

MUSEUMS OF ART: ⚑⚑⚑ **Center for Contemporary Art,** 8501 Carnegie Ave. (421-8671): Always on the cutting edge of contemporary art, this 25-year-old gallery has four changing sets of exhibitions a year, each set showcasing four artists of a different medium pursuing a common theme. A very worthwhile experience. Closed Mon and the month of August.

☼⚑⚑⚑ **Museum of Art,** 11150 East Blvd. at University Circle (421-7340): One of the top American art museums. From "The Treasure of the Guelphs" to Rauschenberg, the museum houses a sumptuous panorama of Oriental, European, and American art. Some of the best-known works: El Greco's *Christ on the Cross,* Velázquez's *The Clown Calabazas,* Rembrandt's *The Jewish Student,* Cézanne's *Mont Sainte-Victoire,* and two famous Picassos, *Life* and *Harlequin with Violin.* The handsome, marble Greek Revival building faces the **Cultural Gardens** and its sculptures. Itself worth a trip to Cleveland. Open Tues–Sun.

MUSEUMS OF SCIENCE & HISTORY: ⚑ **Dunham Tavern Museum,** 6709 Euclid Ave. (431-1060): Former coaching inn (1824) along the Buffalo–Detroit route, now a historical museum with interesting temporary exhibitions. Open Wed and Sun only.

☼⚑⚑ **Health Education Museum,** 8911 Euclid Ave. (231-5010): The oldest (and one of the best) medical museums in the country, with Juno, the transparent Plexiglass woman. In all, more than 150 giant anatomical models. Open daily.

⚑ **Howard Dittrick Museum of Medical History,** 11000 Euclid Ave. (368-3648): A natural complement to the Health Education Museum, this museum documents a complete panorama of the evolution of medicine, surgery, and pharmacology through a collection of more than 10,000 old and new medical objects. A must for all disciples of Hippocrates. On the third floor of the Allen Library. Open Mon–Sat.

⚑ **Museum of Natural History,** Wade Oval Dr. at University Circle (231-4600): Very interesting museum displaying rich collections covering animals (dinosaurs, mammoths, giant insects), prehistoric times (including the three-million-year-old "Lucy" skeleton), Native American culture, geology, and more. Open daily.

⚑ **NASA Lewis Research Center,** 21000 Brookpark Rd. (433-2001): This NASA research center adjacent to Hopkins International Airport offers guided tours of research laboratories with a supersonic wind tunnel plus an exhibition and films on space exploration. Open daily.

⚑ **Ralph Mueller Planetarium,** Wade Oval Dr. at University Circle (231-4600): The renowned observatory and planetarium are an integral part of the Museum of Natural History (see above). Astronomy shows and other presentations. Open daily June–Aug, wknds only the rest of the year.

⚑⚑⚑ **Rock and Roll Hall of Fame and Museum,** 545 Terminal Tower (781-7625): This magnificent seven-story glass tent, designed by world-renowned architect I. M. Pei, houses a chronicle of rock 'n' roll to be experienced through interactive exhibits, archives, and memorabilia of the artists, songwriters, producers, and radio disc jockeys who created this art form. And of course there is the music itself, captured on state-of-the-art sound and

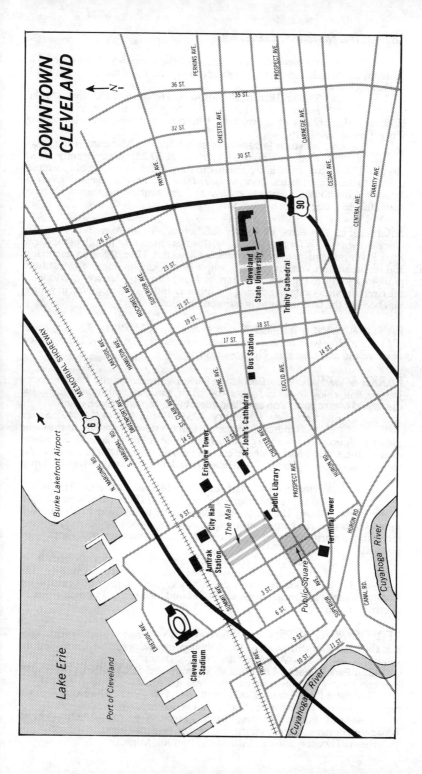

video systems and presented in the context of the sociology of the times. The museum is scheduled to open in 1995 and is expected to draw around 800,000 visitors each year.

Shaker Historical Museum, 16740 S. Park Blvd., Shaker Heights (921-1201): This tiny museum houses furniture, clothing, and artifacts of Cleveland's 19th-century Shaker sect. Interesting. Open Tues–Fri and Sun.

Western Reserve Historical Society Museum, 10825 East Blvd. at University Circle (721-5722): Magnificently reconstructed U.S. history from independence to the present, including old costumes unique to the United States. Contains one of the world's largest genealogical collections. Also houses a vast automotive and aeronautical museum with more than 200 old models. Open Tues–Sun.

NIGHTLIFE: The Flats, Old River Rd. between Front Ave. and Center St.: Once known strictly for heavy industry, this area around the mouth of the Cuyahoga River is the place to be after dark in Cleveland. Here, 20 or so restaurants and nightclubs are crammed into a couple of blocks, running the gamut from punk-rock joints to big-band dance spots. Many have large terraces overlooking the river for outdoor dining during the summer and river-view dining in winter. Has become the favorite haunt of swinging singles.

PANORAMAS: Terminal Tower, Public Sq. (621-7981): 52-story tower (761 ft./238m) with an observation platform on the 42nd floor. The best view of Cleveland and Lake Erie. Open wknds only.

PARKS & GARDENS: Brookside Park, Denison Ave. and Fulton Pkwy.: Joggers will enjoy these 153 acres (64ha) of gardens, which encompass the **Cleveland Metroparks Zoo and Rain Forest** (see "Zoos"). Open daily.

Lake View Cemetery, 12316 Euclid Ave. (421-2665): Splendid landscaped cemetery that overlooks Lake Erie, as the name indicates. Among noteworthy graves here are those of James Garfield, 20th president of the United States, whose enormous mausoleum affords a spectacular view of the city, and John D. Rockefeller, founder of the famous dynasty. Open daily.

North Coast Harbor, E. 9th St. and Lake Erie: This multimillion-dollar harbor, completed in 1989, is the latest addition to the 13-mi. (21km) Lakefront State Park system lining Lake Erie's southern shore. On top of the harbor promenade and park areas, new developments—including a maritime museum, historic shipyard, aquarium, and shops—are planned.

Rockefeller Park, along Liberty Blvd.: A calm, green oasis between Lake Erie and Case Western Reserve University. The park's 296 acres (120ha) offer very fine Japanese gardens, greenhouses, and the **Cultural Gardens,** adorned with sculptures and architectural designs from 24 different countries.

PERFORMING ARTS: For daily listings of all shows and cultural events, consult the entertainment pages of the daily paper *Cleveland Plain Dealer* and the monthly *Cleveland* and *Northern Ohio Live* magazines.

Cain Park Theatre, Lee Rd. and Superior Ave. at Cain Park (291-2828): Summer theater presenting drama, concerts, and dance.

Cleveland Play House, 8500 Euclid Ave. (795-7000): The oldest regional repertory theater in the nation. Classical and contemporary theater.

Cleveland Public Theatre, 6415 Detroit Ave. (631-2727): Off-Off-Broadway theater sometimes featuring big names (Sept–June).

Hanna Theater, 2067 E. 14th St. (621-5000): Musicals.

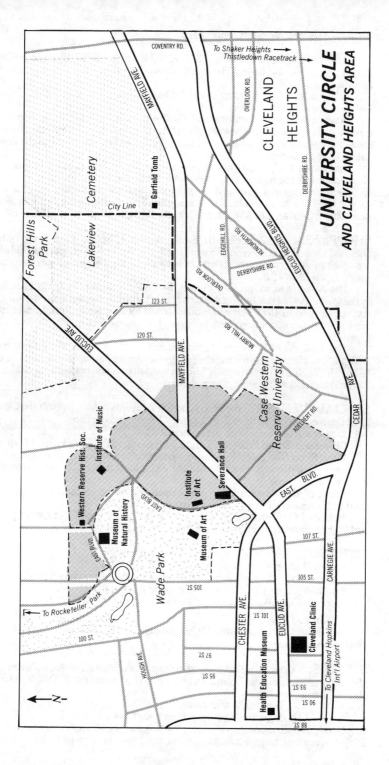

UNIVERSITY CIRCLE
AND CLEVELAND HEIGHTS AREA

COVENTRY RD.

To Shaker Heights →
Thistledown Racetrack →

MAYFIELD AVE.

OVERLOOK RD.

CLEVELAND
HEIGHTS

DERBYSHIRE RD.

Forest Hills Park

Lakeview Cemetery

Garfield Tomb

City Line

EUCLID HEIGHTS BLVD.

KENILWORTH RD.

EDGEHILL RD.

DERBYSHIRE RD.

OVERLOOK RD.

123 ST.

120 ST.

MAYFIELD AVE.

EUCLID AVE.

MURRAY HILL RD.

Case Western Reserve University

ADELBERT RD.

CEDAR AVE.

Institute of Music

Western Reserve Hist. Soc.

Institute of Art

Severance Hall

EAST BLVD.

Museum of Natural History

EAST BLVD.

Museum of Art

EAST BLVD.

107 ST.

← To Rockefeller Park

Wade Park

105 ST.

105 ST.

CHESTER AVE.

EUCLID AVE.

101 ST.

Cleveland Clinic

CARNEGIE AVE.

100 ST.

HOUGH AVE.

97 ST.

95 ST.

Health Education Museum

93 ST.

90 ST.

To Cleveland Hopkins
Int'l Airport

88 ST.

← N

Karamu House & Theatre, 2355 E. 89th St. (795-7070): Experimental theater, concerts, and ballet. The first professional African American theater established outside New York.

Lakewood Little Theater, 17801 Detroit Ave., Lakewood (521-2540): Home of the Kenneth C. Beck Center for Cultural Arts. Sept–June.

Playhouse Square Center, 1501 Euclid Ave. (241-6000): These three contiguous halls—the **Ohio Theater,** the **State Theater,** and the **Palace Theater** offer classical and modern theater, concerts, ballet, and opera, as well as the **Great Lakes Theatre Series.**

Severance Hall, 11001 Euclid Ave. at East Blvd. (231-1111): This pseudo-Greek temple is the home of the Cleveland Orchestra, one of the country's "big six" orchestras, under principal conductor Christoph von Dohnányi (season Aug–May). The orchestra can be heard June–Sept at the superb outdoor **Blossom Music Center,** 1145 W. Steels Corners Rd., Cuyahoga Falls (231-7300).

SHOPPING: ⌂ **The Arcade,** 401 Euclid Ave. (621-8500): One of the oldest enclosed shopping centers in the world (1890), this five-level, glass-skylighted, art nouveau wonder features 80 bars, boutiques, and restaurants. Free concerts at noon. Open Mon–Sat.

The Avenue at Tower City Center, 50 Public Square (771-0033): Located in the lower level of the Terminal Tower and in an old renovated train station, the Avenue opened in 1989 and now houses over 189 shopping, dining, and entertainment venues including Liz Claiborne, J. Crew, and Barney's of New York. Open daily.

The Galleria at Erieview, E. 9th St. and St. Clair Ave. (861-4343): New $43-million glitzy, glass-roofed shopping-and-dining showplace opened in the fall of 1987. Nearly 60 nationally known specialty stores, from Laura Ashley to Eddie Bauer and Ann Taylor. Open daily.

SPECIAL EVENTS: For the exact schedule of events below, consult the **Cleveland Convention & Visitors Bureau** (see "Tourist Information," above).

Jazz Festival (Apr): With the biggest stars.

Cleveland Grand Prix (July): Indie 500 racing at Burke Lakefront Airport.

River Expo (late July): Procession of decorated boats on the Cuyahoga River, waterskiing displays, free open-air concerts, food festival. Draws a crowd of more than half a million.

Feast of the Assumption (Aug): Four-day festival of parades, crafts, and food in Cleveland's Little Italy (see "Strolls," below).

National Air Show (Labor Day wknd): An exhibition of all types of planes and flight demonstrations over Lake Erie. A classic since 1929.

SPORTS: Cleveland boasts four professional teams:

Baseball (Apr–Oct): Indians, Gateway Park (861-1200).
Basketball (Oct to late Apr): Cavaliers, Gateway Arena (659-9100).
Football (Sept–Dec): Browns, Cleveland Stadium (891-5000).
Hockey (Oct–May): Lumberjacks, Gateway Arena (696-0909).

Horse Racing
Northfield Park Raceway, 10705 Northfield Rd., Northfield (467-4101): Harness races year round.

STROLLS: ⌂ **Coventry Road,** enter from Chester Ave.: The local Greenwich Village, with fashionable boutiques and numerous restaurants. Don't miss the annual festival here in July.

⌂ **Historic Warehouse District,** W. 3rd to W. 10th Sts. between Superior Ave. and Front St. (344-3937): The city's former warehouse and garment district downtown features a cluster of newly restored 19th-century buildings, boutiques, restaurants, and antiques galleries.

　🔔 **Little Italy,** around Mayfield and Murray Hill Rds.: This traditional Italian neighborhood has become home to artists' studios, fine-arts galleries, restaurants, cafés, and bakeries. Check out the Murray Hill Market, 2188 Murray Hill Rd. (231-2012), for crafts; and the 2026 Galleries Building, 2026 Murray Hill Rd. (421-9000), a school-turned-gallery space.

　🔔 **Ohio City,** around Lorain Ave. and W. 25th St.: Cleveland's old middle-class neighborhood, with fine Victorian houses, many antiques shops, and restaurants.

　☀🔔 **Shaker Heights,** around N. Park Blvd. and Eaton Rd.: One of the country's plushest residential areas, with splendid, tree-shaded Tudor and Georgian turn-of-the-century homes.

THEME PARKS: ☀🔔 **Cedar Point Amusement Park,** near Sandusky (50 mi./80km west on U.S. 90/250) (419/626-0830): On Lake Erie, this huge amusement park offers among its 55 rides, nine roller coasters, including the world's highest (201 ft./61m) and fastest (70 m.p.h./113kmph), the Magnum XL-200, plus a zoo, aquarium, beach, restaurants, and marina. Open daily mid-May to Labor Day; Sept, wkends only.

　　On the way back, see the 🔔 **Birthplace-Museum of Thomas Edison,** 9 Edison Dr., in Milan (17 mi./27km farther south) (419/499-2135): Residence-turned-museum in memory of the great inventor. Open Tues–Sun Feb–Nov.

　🔔 **Geauga Lake Park,** Ohio 43 near Aurora (26 mi./42km SE) (216/562-7131): A 120-acre (29ha) amusement park featuring a wave pool, water slides, 85 rides, and four roller coasters including the Raging Wolf Bobs, a wooden coaster offering a thrilling 2-min. ride. Spectacular. Open daily Memorial Day–Labor Day, wkends only in May.

　🔔 **Sea World,** 11000 Sea World Dr., in Aurora (23 mi./37km SE on Ohio 43) (216/562-8101): An enormous marine-life zoo in the middle of an 80-acre (32ha) park, with sea lions, elephant seals, dolphins, sharks, and killer whales. Spectacular animal shows. Open daily May–Oct.

WINTER SPORTS RESORTS: 🔔 **Alpine Valley,** 10620 Mayfield Rd., in Chesterland (30 mi./48km east on U.S. 322): Five chair lifts. For information, call 216/285-2211.

ZOOS: 🔔🔔🔔 **Cleveland Metroparks Zoo,** 3900 Brookside Park Dr. (661-6500): One of the oldest and best zoos in the U.S. with over 3,300 animals. A recent $30-million addition, **The RainForest** is a simulated biosphere that includes over 600 animals and insects from seven continents, a huge water curtain, and thunderstorms complete with thunder, lightning, and rain. Open daily.

ACCOMMODATIONS

Personal Favorites (in order of preference)

　🛎🛎🛎 **Ritz Carlton** (dwntwn), Tower City Center, W. 3rd St., OH 44113 (216/623-1300; toll free, see Ritz Carlton). 207 rms, A/C, color TV, in-rm movies. AE, CB, DC, MC, V. Valet parking $14, pool, health club, rest. (The Restaurant), café, bar, 24-hr. rm svce, concierge. *Note:* This new palace hotel, occupying the top nine floors of an ultramodern office building towering over the Cuyahoga River, is Cleveland's most luxurious hotel, and offers panoramic views of the city. Remarkably comfortable rms w. marble bathrooms and minibars; personalized svce; upscale rest. Conveniently located in the heart of the business district. VIP floor; big business clientele. **E–VE**

　🛎🛎🛎 **Omni International Hotel** (nr. dwntwn), 2065 E. 96th St., OH 44106 (216/791-1900; toll free, see Omni). 293 rms, A/C, color TV, in-rm movies. AE, CB, DC, MC, V. Valet parking $6, pool, rest. (Classics), coffee shop, bar, rm svce, concierge, free crib. *Note:* This modern hotel is 10 min. from dwntwn and adjacent to the Cleveland Clinic. It offers spacious, inviting rms and a very satisfactory Olde English tavern–style rest. Two VIP floors. Currently undergoing a complete renovation. Especially attentive svce. **M–E**

♙♙ **Sheraton City Center** (formerly the Bond Court; dwntwn), 777 St. Clair Ave., OH 44114 (216/771-7600; toll free, see Sheraton). 480 rms, A/C, color TV, in-rm movies. AE, CB, DC, MC, V. Gar. $9 rest., bar, rm svce, free crib. *Note:* Relatively modern, 22-story tower offering comfortable rms (the best have a view of Lake Erie) and good svce. Business clientele. Adjacent to the Convention Center in the heart of the business district. Three VIP floors. No-smoking rms. Recently renovated. **E**

☼♙♙ **Glidden House** (nr. dwntwn), 1901 Ford Dr., OH 44106 (216/231-8900). 60 rms, A/C, cable color TV. AE, CB, DC, MC, V. Free parking; no bar or rest.; valet svce, free continental breakfast, free crib. *Note:* Once the private house of the famous Glidden paint-making family, this vaguely French-Gothic turn-of-the-century mansion was made over into a comfortable inn in 1989. Eight inviting suites and 52 rms in a new wing. Soothing, discreet atmosphere, but svce still a trifle undependable. Conveniently located in the heart of the University Circle district, 10 min. from dwntwn. **M–E**

♙ **Budget Inns of America** (formerly Howard Johnson's; vic.), 14043 Brookpark Rd., OH 44142 (216/267-2350). 115 rms, A/C, cable color TV. AE, CB, DC, MC, V. Free parking, rest., bar, rm svce, free crib. *Note:* A very good value, this relatively modern motel is quite convenient to the international airport and offers vast rms w. private patios or balconies and efficient, if hardly cheerful, svce. 8 min. from the airport and 20 min. from dwntwn. Free airport shuttle. Ideal for the motorist. **I**

Other Accommodations (from top bracket to budget)

☼♙♙♙ **Stouffer Tower City Plaza** (dwntwn), 24 Public Sq., OH 44113 (216/696-5600; toll free, see Stouffers). 491 rms, A/C, color TV, in-rm movies. AE, CB, DC, MC, V. Gar. $12, pool, health club, two rests. (including Sans Souci), coffee shop, two bars, rm svce, concierge, free crib. *Note:* Located in the heart of Cleveland, this 1918 Beaux Arts luxury hotel has completed a $37-million renovation. It offers generally comfortable, spacious rms (some very elegant, others merely adequate) w. private patios; impersonal reception and svce; well-regarded rest.; superb art deco pool and a spectacular 10-story atrium. Group and convention clientele; three VIP floors. **E–VE**

♙♙♙ **Radisson Plaza Hotel** (dwntwn), 1701 E. 12th St., OH 44114 (216/523-8000; toll free, see Radisson). 252 suites, A/C, color TV, in-rm movies. AE, CB, DC, MC, V. Valet gar. $10, pool, health club, two tennis courts, sauna, rest., bar, rm svce, free crib. *Note:* Opened in 1990 as a component of the new Reserve Square Center, a 23-floor complex occupying an entire dwntwn block, this hotel comprises spacious, well-designed suites, each w. microwave oven, refrigerator, and marble bathroom. Impeccable comfort; ultraprofessional svce. With its very central location it attracts mainly business travelers, and has a VIP floor. **E**

♙♙ **Holiday Inn Lakeside** (dwntwn), 1111 Lakeside Ave. (at E. 12th St.), OH 44114 (216/241-5100; toll free, see Holiday Inns). 370 rms, A/C, color TV, in-rm movies. AE, CB, DC, MC, V. Parking $5, pool, health club, sauna, rest., coffee shop, bar, rm svce, free crib. *Note:* Modern 18-story building w. an unobstructed view of the city and of Lake Erie. Very satisfying comfort, Holiday Inn style. Groups and business clientele. Two blocks from the Convention Center. **M–E**

♙♙ **Radisson Hotel Beachwood** (formerly Quality Hotel; vic.), 26300 Chagrin Blvd., Beachwood, OH 44122 (216/831-5150; toll free, see Radisson). 199 rms, A/C, color TV, in-rm movies. AE, CB, DC, MC, V. Free parking, pool, health club, rest., bar, rm svce, hrdrsr, free crib.

Note: Appealing, comfortable hotel on the outskirts of the smart residential suburb of Shaker Heights. Good facilities; pleasant, recently renovated rms; efficient svce. Located nr. a number of corporate head offices, it attracts business travelers and (since it offers direct access to the highway system) those traveling by car. 25 min. from dwntwn. **M–E**

Hampton Inn Westlake (vic.), 29690 Detroit Rd., Westlake, OH 44145 (216/892-0333; toll free 800/426-7866). 123 rms, A/C, color TV, in-rm movies. AE, DC, MC, V. Free parking, rest. adjacent, free continental breakfast served in the lobby. *Note:* A good value just off I-90, 15 min. from downtown. Clean, comfortable rms. Ideal for the car traveler. **I**

Travelodge Beachwood (vic.), 3795 Orange Place, Beachwood, OH 44122 (216/831-7200; toll free, see Travelodge). 128 rms, A/C, cable color TV. AE, CB, DC, MC, V. Free parking, adjacent coffee shop, free breakfast, crib $6. *Note:* A convenient, well-kept motel not far from chic Shaker Heights. 25 min. from dwntwn. Ideal for motorists. **I**

Motel 6 (vic.), 7219 Eagle Rd., Middleburg Heights, OH 44130 (216/234-0990). 95 rms, A/C, cable color TV. AE, DC, MC, V. Free parking. *Note:* Small economy motel 5 min. by car from Hopkins International Airport. Unpretentious but up-to-date; friendly reception. Ideal if you're on a budget. **B**

Airport Accommodations

Sheraton Hopkins Airport (vic.), 5300 Riverside Dr., OH 44135 (216/267-1500; toll free, see Sheraton). 243 rms, A/C, color TV, in-rm movies. AE, CB, DC, MC, V. Free parking, pool, health club, sauna, rest. (Amelia's), bar, rm svce, concierge, free crib. *Note:* A grand hotel w. immediate access to the airport terminal. Spacious, comfortable rms w. private patios or balconies. The facilities are very complete, the svce efficient. Free airport shuttle. Very adequate rest. Business clientele. VIP floor. **M–E**

Holiday Inn Cleveland Airport (vic.), 4181 W. 150th St., OH 44135 (216/252-7700; toll free, see Holiday Inns). 144 rms, A/C, cable color TV. AE, CB, DC, MC, V. Free parking, pool, rest., bar, free crib. *Note:* Classic but comfortable five-story motel w. relatively spacious rms and agreeable reception and svce. 5 min. from the airport (free shuttle) and 20 min. from dwntwn. A good overall value. **I**

RESTAURANTS

Personal Favorites (in order of preference)

The Restaurant (dwntwn), in the Ritz Carlton Hotel (see "Accommodations," above) (623-1300). A/C. Breakfast/lunch/dinner daily, brunch Sun. AE, CB, DC, MC, V. Jkt. *Specialties:* Continental cuisine featuring the finest seafood and choice meats; the menu changes daily. Extensive wine list. *Note:* Far and away the most distinguished rest. in Cleveland. Superb, French-inspired cuisine is complimented by warm, attentive svce and a spectacular view of the Cuyahoga River. The menu stresses fresh local fish and game. The decor is of a sober elegance w. period furniture and crystal chandeliers. Big business clientele. Resv. highly recommended for lunch, brunch, and dinner. Valet parking. *Continental.* **M–E**

Ristorante Giovanni (vic.), 25550 Chagrin Blvd., Beachwood (831-8625). A/C. Lunch Mon–Fri, dinner Mon–Sat; closed hols. AE, CB, DC, MC, V. Jkt. *Specialties:* figs and prosciutto; fresh homemade pasta; linguine w. clam sauce; veal chop milanese; swordfish sautéed w. pine nuts, mussels, and white wine; sweetbreads alla Toscana. Fine list of Italian and California wines. *Note:* Nobody would dispute that this is the best of Cleveland's many Italian rests.; the totally authentic menu emphasizes seafood. Elegant setting; flawless svce. At a place so successful resv. are a must. *Italian.* **I–M**

☼♈♈ **That Place on Bellflower** (nr. dwntwn), 11401 Bellflower Rd. (231-4469). A/C. Lunch Tues–Sat, dinner Tues–Sun; closed hols. AE, DC, MC, V. Jkt. *Specialties:* mussels Provençal, roast duck, veal Oscar, Renaissance salmon, beef Wellington w. béarnaise sauce, good desserts. Fine wine list. *Note:* Eclectic, French-inspired cuisine (as its fleur-de-lys, or bellflower, requires) in a former coaching inn that has been elegantly restored. The menu changes periodically. Very good svce. Open-air dinner in summer. Romantic atmosphere. Resv. advised. *French/Continental.* **I—M**

♈♈ **Sans Souci** (dwntwn), in the Stouffer Tower City Plaza Hotel (see "Accommodations," above) (696-5600). Lunch Mon–Fri, dinner nightly. AE, CB, DC, MC, V. *Specialties:* goat cheese, eggplant, and roasted-pepper terrine; empañadillas (ground veal and olives in pastry turnover); fresh fish bouillabaisse; lemon-pepper angel-hair pasta w. lobster-basil cream sauce; lemon-raspberry custard. Seasonal menu. *Note:* French villa decor— hardwood floors, marble furnishings, open hearth, photos of French countryside. Food, like the atmosphere, is inspiring and pleasing. Locally popular, so resv. are highly recommended, especially on Sat. *Mediterranean.* **I—M**

♈ **Great Lakes Brewing Co.** (nr. dwntwn), 2516 Market St. (771-4404). A/C. Lunch/dinner daily (until midnight). AE, DC, MC, V. *Specialties:* homemade soup, salads, sandwiches, meat and cheese pies, daily specials, draft beer. *Note:* Ohio's first (and so far only) microbrewery, occupying a 19th-century warehouse, serves both its widely respected draft beers —Heisman (light) and Elliott's Amber (dark)—in this English-style pub. Good sandwiches and daily specials in a congenial setting which allows for open-air meals during the summer. Patrons are a mixed bag from yuppies to blue-collar workers. Resv. accepted but often unnecessary. One block from the West Side Market. *American.* **B—I**

♈ **The Mad Greek** (nr. dwntwn), 2466 Fairmount Blvd., Cleveland Heights (421-3333). A/C. Lunch Mon–Sat, dinner nightly (until midnight); closed hols. AE, DC, MC, V. *Specialties:* moussaka, stuffed grape leaves, mezedakia, pita, kebabs, and everything in between—the food and Greek wine here are truly authentic. Limited but interesting wine list. *Note:* An enjoyable ambience in a rustic patio setting enveloped by whitewashed walls and a profusion of greenery. It offers agreeable Greek cuisine at low prices as well as some very good Indian dishes: tikka chicken, curries (the owner is Indian and his wife Greek). Friendly, cheerful svce. Locally popular. *Greek.* **B—I**

Other Restaurants (from top bracket to budget)

♈♈♈ **Baricelli Inn** (nr. dwntwn), 2203 Cornell Rd., in the University Circle area (791-6500). A/C. Dinner only, Mon–Sat; closed hols. AE, MC, V. Jkt. *Specialties:* French lentil soup w. duck confit ravioli, red snapper in black-currant butter w. macadamia nuts. The menu changes regularly. *Note:* Highly imaginative midwestern fare by chef-owner Paul Minnillo in a turn-of-the-century renovated brownstone filled w. antiques and stained glass. The cuisine features only the highest-quality products. Elegant atmosphere and svce. Resv. required. Well worth the 10-min. drive from dwntwn. Also seven individually decorated rms and suites. *American.* **M**

♈♈♈ **Sammy's** (dwntwn), 1400 W. 10th St. (523-5560). A/C. Lunch/dinner Mon–Sat; closed hols. AE, CB, DC, MC, V. *Specialties:* lobster bisque w. roasted red peppers and grilled sweet corn; marinated asparagus tips, tomatoes, and fresh mozzarella on bed of lentils; roasted rack of lamb w. pistachio-nut coating w. black-currant sauce. The menu changes regularly. Remarkable desserts (particularly the boule de neige). Outstanding wine list. *Note:* In an old warehouse on the Cuyahoga River, this fashionable rest. offers elegant, inventive cuisine and modern decor of exposed brick and large bay windows w. a view of the river. The svce is exemplary, the ambience rather noisy, and the clientele hip. Resv. a must, given its success. Valet parking. *American/Continental.* **M**

ŶŶ **Top of the Town** (dwntwn), 100 Erieview Plaza (771-1600). A/C. Lunch Mon–Fri, dinner Mon–Sat. AE, CB, DC, MC, V. Jkt. *Specialties:* trio of wild mushrooms in tart shells w. veal glaze, creamy baked polenta, tableside-cooked entrées such as steak Diane and lobster filet, strawberry flambé. The menu changes periodically. *Note:* Very upscale rest. located on the 38th floor of the Galleria Tower. A fine view indeed. White tablecloth svce. and crystal chandeliers add to the elegance. Chosen best rest. by critics and readers alike in *Cleveland* magazine. Resv. highly recommended. *Continental.* **I–M**

ŶŶ **Guarino's** (nr. dwntwn), 12309 Mayfield Rd. (231-3100). A/C. Lunch/dinner Mon–Sat; closed hols. AE, CB, DC, MC, V. Jkt. *Specialties:* fettuccine Alfredo, cannelloni, snails marinara, veal marsala, very good grilled fish. Good list of Italian wines. *Note:* Since 1918 this *trattoria* in the heart of Little Italy has been a local institution. A favorite of musicians and fans of the Cleveland Symphony Orchestra (Severance Hall is nearby), the rest. offers al fresco dining in the patio in summer. Prompt, friendly svce. 10 min. from dwntwn. *Italian.* **I**

Ŷ **Pearl of the Orient** (nr. dwntwn), 20121 Van Aken Blvd., Shaker Heights (751-8181). A/C. Lunch Mon–Fri, dinner nightly; closed Thanksgiving, Dec 25. AE, CB, DC, MC, V. *Specialties:* mu shu pork, hot-and-sour soup, Mongolian duck, steamed fish, beef Szechuan. *Note:* Entirely authentic Chinese cuisine in a rather cold modern decor w. Far Eastern artwork. Attentive svce. Locally popular. Resv. advised. 15 min. from dwntwn. *Chinese.* **I**

ŶŶ **James Tavern** (vic.), 28699 Chagrin Blvd., Woodmere Village (464-4660). A/C. Lunch/dinner daily, brunch Sun. AE, CB, DC, MC, V. *Specialties:* roast beef, roast pork Savannah, chicken Parmesan, fish of the day. *Note:* Warm, pleasant atmosphere of an old colonial tavern w. large fireplaces and old furniture. The very reasonably priced food is more substantial than refined. Friendly, efficient svce; hearty portions. Locally popular. Resv. advised. 25 min. from dwntwn. *American.* **I**

Ŷ **Balaton** (vic.), 12523 Buckeye Rd. (921-9691). A/C. Lunch/dinner Tues–Sat (until 9pm). No credit cards. *Specialties:* goulash, paprika chicken, wienerschnitzel, stuffed cabbage, palacsinta, dobos torte. Hungarian wine and beer, but no hard liquor. *Note:* Exceptionally tasty Hungarian and German cuisine served in a Formica-and-paper-napkins setting. More than generous portions at very modest prices. A favorite rest. of Cleveland's large Hungarian community. *Continental/German.* **B–I**

Ŷ **Hofbrau Haus** (nr. dwntwn), 1400 E. 55th St. (881-7773). A/C. Lunch Mon–Fri, dinner Tues–Sun. AE, DC, MC, V. *Specialties:* bratwurst, Wiener schnitzel, pork hocks. Good wine list. *Note:* The best German rest. in all of Cleveland. Authentic Germanic cuisine and ambience in a fairly noisy atmosphere, w. dancing on wknds. Offers buffet or à la carte dishes. Locally popular. Resv. advised. *German.* **B–I**

Ŷ **Miller's Dining Room** (nr. dwntwn), 16707 Detroit Ave., Lakewood (221-5811). A/C. Lunch Mon–Sat, dinner nightly (until 8pm); closed Memorial Day, July 4, Labor Day. No credit cards. *Specialties:* chicken à la king, veal chop Créole, roast pork, braised leg of lamb, excellent homemade tarts and desserts. *Note:* The most authentic home-cooking in Cleveland at prices you won't believe. The decor is 1930s-retro, and the servers seem to be of that era as well. Generous portions and a relaxed atmosphere. A remarkable value. Regular clientele. 10 min. from dwntwn. **B–I**

Cafeterias/Fast Food/Specialty Spots

Corky & Lenny's (vic.), 13937 Cedar Rd., University Heights (321-3310). Breakfast/lunch/dinner daily (until midnight). No credit cards. *Specialties:* superb sandwiches, homemade soup, smoked fish, and salads. *Note:* There is no decor to speak of in this very popular, rather noisy local hangout. 20 min. from dwntwn. Other location: 27091 Chagrin Blvd. (U.S. 422) in Woodmere (464-3838). Open daily.

BARS & NIGHTCLUBS

Club Isabella (nr. dwntwn), 2025 Abington Rd. (229-1177). Open nightly. Very popular nightclub a few steps from the university. The decor is a pleasing blend of art deco and contemporary styles. Excellent live jazz.

Euclid Tavern (nr. dwntwn), 11629 Euclid Ave. (229-7788). This neighborhood-style bar in the University Circle area is the place to go for serious rock and blues. Open nightly.

Improv Comedy Club (dwntwn), 2000 Sycamore St. (696-4677). Located in the renovated Powerhouse, this new comedy club features top comedians on national tours. Also rest. Resv. recommended. Open nightly.

Metropolis Night Club (dwntwn), 2325 Elm St. (241-1444). Techno two-level dance club that has four bars. Open Thurs–Sun.

Mirage on the Water (nr. dwntwn), 2510 Elm St. (348-1135). The hot new spot. Dancers view the stars through a 20-ft. (6m) retractable roof. Open Wed–Sun.

N.R.G. (dwntwn), 1148 Main Ave. (341-7223). Dance club with a $4-million, high-tech computer-operated light and sound effects. Open Thurs–Sat.

Peabody's Down Under (dwntwn), 1059 Old River Rd. (241-0792). Features local and nationally famous rock bands nightly.

NEARBY EXCURSIONS

⌂ **CANTON** (55 mi./88km south on I-77): Home of former President William McKinley (the 25th president is entombed at 7th St. NW), this major industrial center on the edge of "Steel Valley" houses the ✻⌂ **Pro Football Hall of Fame,** 2121 George Halas Dr. NW (456-8207). There, the gridiron devotee can trace the history of the national sport, from early pro teams like the Canton Bulldogs (led by the legendary Jim Thorpe) to the current Super Bowl champs. Under the football-shaped dome, a 350-seat theater runs a different action movie every hour highlighting great teams and great games. Museum store. Open daily.

On your way back, don't miss a visit to the ✻⌂⌂ **Stan Hywet Hall and Gardens,** 714 N. Portage in **Akron** (836-5533). Listed in the National Register of Historic Places, this 65-room manor house built in 1911–15 by Frank A. Seiberling, founder of the Goodyear Rubber Co., is considered one of the finest examples of Tudor Revival architecture in the United States. Many antiques and art treasures dating from the 14th century. Magnificent gardens with flower displays in spring and fall. Open Tues–Sun.

⌂ **CUYAHOGA VALLEY RAILROAD** (departure from 6311 Granger, at the intersection of Ohio 17 and 21 in Independence, south of Cleveland): An amusing, pleasing trip in a little steam-engine train along the picturesque Cuyahoga Valley to **Hale Farm** (see below) and **Akron** (see above). Runs on Sat and Sun in May, Wed–Sun June–Sept and daily in Oct. For information, call 216/657-2000.

⌂ **HALE FARM & WESTERN RESERVE VILLAGE** (in Bath, 24 mi./38km south on I-77, Bath Rd. exit) (216/575-9137): Small, carefully restored pioneer town from the early 19th century offers pottery making and other period craft demonstrations. Open Wed–Sun June–Oct.

⌂ **KELLEYS ISLAND** (50 mi./80km west on U.S. 6, then by ferry): This charming little vacation island on Lake Erie gets very crowded in summer. Fishing, sailing, camping, beaches, etc. Accessible by ferry from Sandusky (runs daily Apr–Nov; call 419/626-5557 for schedule information). This makes a good joint excursion with Cedar Point (see "Theme Parks," above).

    KIRTLAND (22 mi./35km NE on I-90): Site of the oldest Mormon temple in the country (1836), Kirtland was the place where the westward-bound Mormons made their first stop (see Chapter 31 on Salt Lake City). The temple, at 9020 Chillicothe Rd. in Kirtland Village, is open daily.

CHAPTER 22

CINCINNATI

□ □ □

Following the Roman example, Cincinnati is built around the terraced slopes of seven hills, on the northern bank of the Ohio River where it borders Kentucky and Indiana. Founded in 1788 as Losantiville, it was renamed Cincinnati in 1790 by Gov. Arthur St. Clair in honor of the Order of Cincinnati, a brotherhood founded in 1783 by Revolutionary War army officers who admired the famous Roman hero Lucius Quinctius Cincinnatus.

A Native American way-station before the region was settled, Cincinnati became an important hub of rail, river, and road communication in the 19th century. Despite seven cholera epidemics in less than a century and many catastrophic floods and disastrous harvests, tens of thousands of German and Irish immigrants, as well as a host of notable visitors—Charles Dickens, Harriet Beecher Stowe, John Audubon, Henry Clay, and John Quincy Adams—have helped to make Cincinnati the third-largest city in Ohio and the "queen city of the West," in the words of the poet Longfellow.

The home of many large multinational corporations, including Procter & Gamble, Cincinnati is today one of the most dynamic commercial and industrial urban centers in the Midwest. The friendliness of its inhabitants and their taste for good food, music, and the arts make it one of the five or six most pleasant U.S. cities in which to live, according to polls. Once described by Winston Churchill as the most beautiful city of the American heartland, Cincinnati boasts a symphony orchestra of acknowledged reputation and two well-respected universities, but few praiseworthy monuments. In contrast to many other midwestern cities, Cincinnati has made it a point of honor to preserve the original character of the downtown district and the **Riverfront** area along the Ohio, investing many millions of dollars in architectural renovation and in the construction of a vast, enclosed pedestrian walkway network, the **Skywalk System,** which connects old buildings with new downtown skyscrapers.

On a more prosaic note, Cincinnati was known as "Porkopolis" and the "pork capital of the U.S.A." because of its important meatpacking industry. It now prefers to proclaim itself "the world capital of baseball," having produced the country's first professional baseball team, the Red Stockings in 1869, now called the Red Sox. Food-lovers won't want to miss another local specialty, the famous five-way chile, pride of Cincinnati since 1922: spaghetti smothered in ground beef, onions, beans, and cheese.

Some native children of Cincinnati are William Howard Taft, 27th U.S. president; actors Tyrone Power and Doris Day; ballerina Suzanne Farrell; orchestra conductor James Levine; and director/producer Steven Spielberg.

BASIC FACTS: State of Ohio. Area code: 513. Time zone: eastern. ZIP Code: 45202. Settled: 1788. Approximate population: city, 385,000; metropolitan area, 1,750,000. 23rd-largest metropolitan area in the country.

CLIMATE: A raincoat and umbrella are *de rigueur* in any season in Cincinnati. Winter is cold (around 32°F/0°C, in Jan) and damp; summer is hot and sticky (average July temperature: 76°F/24°C). Spring and autumn are the less soggy seasons and the most pleasant for visitors.

DISTANCES: Chicago, 290 mi. (465km); Cleveland, 247 mi. (395km); Detroit, 259 mi. (415km); Nashville, 269 mi. (430km); Philadelphia, 565 mi. (905km).

ARRIVAL & TRANSIT INFORMATION

AIRPORT: Greater Cincinnati International Airport (CVG): 13 mi. (21km) SW. Information: 606/283-3151.

AIRLINES: American (toll free 800/433-7300), Continental (toll free 800/525-0280), Delta (toll free 800/221-1212), Northwest (toll free 800/225-2525), TWA (toll free 800/221-2000), United (toll free 800/241-6522), and USAir (toll free 800/428-4322).

CITY LINK: Cab fare to city center, about $22; time, around 25 min. Bus: **Jetport Express** (606/767-3702); leaves about every 30 min.; serves principal dwntwn hotels; fare, $10; time, about 35 min. Because corporate offices are dispersed throughout the Cincinnati suburbs, businesspeople may want to rent a car, but because of the compact layout of the city itself, tourists can easily do without. Good public transportation system (bus), **Queen City Metro** (621-4455).

CAR RENTAL (at the airport unless otherwise indicated): Avis (toll free 800/331-1212), Budget (toll free 800/527-0700), Dollar (toll free 800/800-4000), Hertz (toll free 800/654-3131), National (toll free 800/227-7368), Thrifty (toll free 800/367-2277). For dwntwn locations, consult the phone directory.

LIMOUSINE SERVICES: Carey Limousine (531-7321), Dav El Limousines (toll free 800/922-0343).

TAXIS: Taxis may not be hailed on the street but can be gotten by waiting on line in front of the major hotels or can be summoned by phone: **Yellow Cab** (241-2100).

TRAIN: Amtrak station, 1901 River Rd. (toll free 800/872-7245).

INTERCITY BUSES: Greyhound, 1005 Gilbert Ave. (352-6012; toll free 800/231-2222).

INFORMATION & TOURS

TOURIST INFORMATION: The **Cincinnati Convention & Visitors Bureau,** 300 W. 6th St., OH 45202 (513/621-2142; toll free 800/344-3445).

For a **recorded message** with an up-to-date listing of cultural events and shows, call 513/528-9400.

GUIDED TOURS: B. B. Riverboats (boat), at the end of Greenup St., Covington, Ky. (across the river by suspension bridge) (606/261-8500): Ohio River cruises, year round.

Cincinnati Heritage Tours (bus), The Museum Center, 1301 Western Ave. (513/287-7031): Guided tours of the city; call for information and schedule.

STERNWHEELER RIVER CRUISES: 3- and 10-day cruises along the Mississippi and Ohio Rivers on the *Delta Queen* or the *Mississippi Queen* paddlesteamers dating from the 1920s. Luxurious kitsch. (See Chapter 15 on New Orleans.)

SIGHTS, ATTRACTIONS & ACTIVITIES

ARCHITECTURAL HIGHLIGHTS: ▵ **City Hall,** 801 Plum St. at 8th St. (352-3000): Imposing Romanesque city hall in pink granite. Its large marble staircase, stained-glass windows, and ceiling decoration are worth a look. Open Mon–Fri.

▵ **Hamilton County Courthouse,** 1000 Main St. (632-8331): One of the largest law libraries in the country housed in a fine example of Ionic-style architecture. Open Mon–Fri.

▵ **Procter & Gamble Headquarters,** Procter & Gamble Plaza: Twin 24-story postmodernist towers designed by the renowned architecture firm of Kohn, Pedersen, Fox (1985). Dominates two-block-long stretches of beautiful gardens. No visits allowed.

▵ **Riverfront Stadium,** 201 E. Pete Roseway (352-6333): The local shrine for baseball and football fans (60,000 seats). Superb location on the Ohio River. Open Apr–Jan.

☼▵ **Union Terminal,** 1301 Western Ave. (287-7000): No longer in use, this splendid art deco train station by Roland Wank (1931) has some very lovely mosaic murals, Verona marble walls, terrazzo floors, and a huge rotunda. The terminal houses the Museum of Natural History, an Omnimax theater, a café, museum shops, and the Cincinnati Historical Society.

CHURCHES/SYNAGOGUES: ☼▵ **Basilica of the Assumption,** Madison Ave. and 12th St., Covington, Ky. (606/431-2060): A kind of small-scale pastiche of Notre-Dame in Paris (or the nearby Cathedral of St. Denis), with flying buttresses and gargoyles in the purest French Gothic style. Dating from 1901, this basilica has one of the largest stained-glass windows in the world. On the other side of the Ohio River. Open daily.

☼▵ **Isaac M. Wise Temple,** 8th and Plum Sts. (793-2556): Built in 1865, this synagogue, in startling Byzantine-Moorish style topped with two minarets, is named for the founder of the Hebrew Union College (see "Historic Buildings," below). Visits by appointment.

☼▵ **St. Peter in Chains Cathedral,** 8th and Plum Sts. (421-5354): Seat of the archdiocese of Cincinnati, this 1845 cathedral, renovated in the late 1950s, has interesting Greek Revival architecture and a portico supported by 12 Corinthian columns. Striking interior decor and a gold crucifix by the famous Renaissance sculptor Benvenuto Cellini. Open daily.

HISTORIC BUILDINGS: ▵ **Hebrew Union College,** 3101 Clifton Ave. (221-1875): The oldest rabbinical school in the country (1875). Historical library and an interesting museum of archeology and religious art. Call for information.

     ⚲ **John Hauck House,** 812 Dayton St. (721-3570). Ornate 19th-century Italianate town house, once the home of a prominent Cincinnati brewer. An interpretive tour is available through this elegant house-museum, carefully restored and furnished to represent the life of a wealthy family of the late Victorian era. Interesting. Open Thurs, Fri, Sun.

     ☀⚲ **Music Hall,** 1241 Elm St. (621-1919): One of the most famous concert halls in the country, renowned for its exceptional acoustics, it's home to the Cincinnati Symphony Orchestra and the May Festival. Rich interior decoration and very lovely Victorian architecture from 1878.

     ⚲ **Showboat *Majestic,*** Public Landing on the Ohio River at the foot of Broadway: The last floating theater in the country, this authentic showboat is a historic landmark. For information on current shows, call 241-6550; May–Sept.

     ⚲ **Roebling Suspension Bridge,** joining Cincinnati and Covington, Ky., across the Ohio River: Designed by John Roebling, this work of art was, at the time of its construction (opened 1876), the longest suspension bridge in the world. It also served as the model for the famous Brooklyn Bridge in New York, opened 16 years later. Presents a pretty view of the Cincinnati skyline.

     ⚲ **William H. Taft National Historic Site,** 2038 Auburn Ave. (684-3262): Birthplace of the 27th president, this elegantly restored building dates from 1840. Open daily.

MARKETS: ⚲ **Findlay Market,** 18th and Elm Sts.: Picturesque open-air market dating from 1852. A bastion of local gastronomy. Open first two Mons of every month and Wed, Fri, and Sat.

MONUMENTS: ⚲ **Tyler Davidson Fountain,** Fountain Sq.: This bronze fountain was cast in Munich in 1871 and is now the city's emblem. Especially worth a look at night when it's illuminated.

MUSEUMS OF ART: ☀⚲ **Art Museum,** Art Museum Dr. in Eden Park (721-5204): Greek Revival building dating from 1887 housing very rich collections of European paintings, especially impressionists and abstract painters. Among the best-known works: El Greco's *Christ on the Cross,* Gainsborough's *Portrait of Mrs. Thicknesse,* Cézanne's *Blue Still Life,* Gris's *Violin and Score,* Sargent's *Italian Girl,* Matisse's *The Gray Hat,* and Chagall's *The Red Chicken.* Large collection of Persian and medieval art as well. Open Tues–Sun.

     ⚲ **Contemporary Arts Center,** 115 E. 5th St. (721-0390): On the second floor of the **Mercantile Center Building** with its very lovely arcade, this wonderful museum offers temporary exhibitions and events dedicated to modern art in every form (among others, the nationally publicized Mapplethorpe exhibit in 1991). Open daily.

     ⚲ **Taft Museum,** 316 Pike St. (241-0343): European masters (Turner, Goya, Rembrandt, van Dyck, Corot) and Chinese and Limoges porcelain in a beautiful Federal-style upper-class residence, dating from 1820, once owned by President Taft's half-brother. Open daily.

MUSEUMS OF SCIENCE & HISTORY: ⚲ **Cincinnati Fire Museum,** 315 W. Court St. (621-5553): Portrays the history of firefighting since 1808. "Hands-on" displays, firefighting artifacts. Housed in a restored firehouse (1907). Interesting. Open Tues–Sun.

     ☀⚲ **Museum of Natural History,** 1301 Western Ave. (287-7091): An astonishing artificial cavern with waterfalls. Exhibits of local fauna and flora as well as a planetarium. One of the best natural history museums in the country. Open daily. The museum and an Omnimax movie theater are housed in the newly refurbished Union Terminal (see "Architectural Highlights," above).

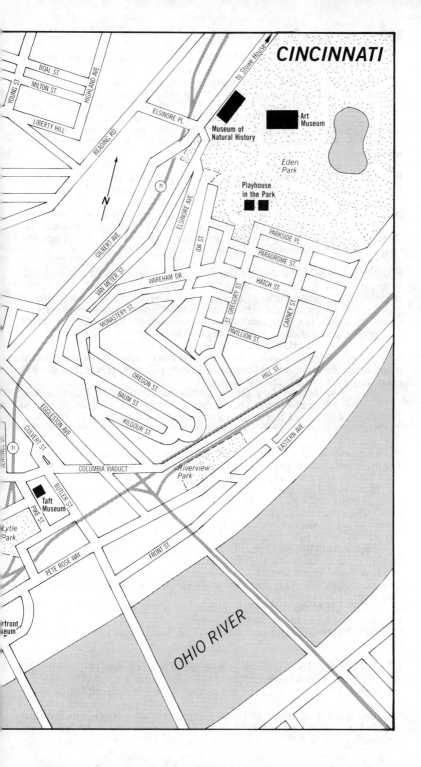

CINCINNATI

to Stowe House

Art
Museum

Museum of
Natural History

Eden
Park

Playhouse
in the Park

BOAL ST.

MILTON ST.

YOUNG ST.

HIGHLAND AVE.

LIBERTY HILL

ELSINORE PL.

READING RD.

PARKSIDE PL.

PARADROME ST.

ELSINORE AVE.

IDA ST.

WAREHAM DR.

ST GREGORY ST.

HATCH ST.

CARNEY ST.

GILBERT AVE.

VAN METER ST.

MONASTERY ST.

PAVILLION ST.

HILL ST.

OREGON ST.

BAUM ST.

KILGOUR ST.

EGGLESTON AVE.

CULVERT ST.

EASTERN AVE.

COLUMBIA VIADUCT

Riverview
Park

Taft
Museum

BUTLER ST.

PINE ST.

Lytle
Park

PETE ROSE WAY

FRONT ST.

rfront
seum

OHIO RIVER

N

  ⚱ **Stowe House,** 2950 Gilbert Ave. (632-5120): Harriet Beecher
  ⚱ Stowe, author of *Uncle Tom's Cabin,* lived here in 1832–36
while she was doing the documentary research for her famous novel. Interesting
exhibition of African American history. Open Mon–Thurs.
  ☀⚱ **Vent Haven Museum,** 33 W. Maple Ave., Fort Mitchell, Ky.
  ☀⚱ (606/341-0461): Marvelous museum entirely dedicated to
the arts of puppetry and ventriloquism. Nearly 600 marionettes on display and a
very rich specialized library. Unusual and wonderful. Visit by appointment year
round.

PANORAMAS: ⚱ **Carew Tower Observatory,** 5th and Vine Sts. (241-3888):
Fine panorama of the city from the top of this 48-story (560-ft./175m) art deco
tower, Cincinnati's tallest building. Open daily.
  ⚱ **Skywalk System,** covers 20 blocks around the Convention
  ⚱ Center and Fountain Sq.: Network of elevated enclosed and
climate-controlled walkways connecting major dwntwn hotels, buildings, and
stores. Affords fine views of the skyline.

PARKS & GARDENS: ⚱ **Ault Park,** east end of Observatory Ave.: Very handsome park offering a panorama along the Ohio River and the city.
  ☀⚱ **Eden Park,** Eden Park Dr. (421-4086): 180 acres (73ha) of
  ☀⚱ park, floral exhibitions, and specialized botanic gardens with
one of the largest tropical greenhouses in the world, the **Krohn Conservatory**
(352-4086), plus museums, overlooking the Ohio.
  ⚱ **Fountain Square,** on 5th St. between Walnut and Vine Sts.: A
  ⚱ bucolic oasis in the heart of the city with agreeable gardens and
monumental fountain (see "Monuments," above). A popular spot for a stroll in
good weather (especially at lunch hour).
  ⚱ **Mount Airy Forest and Arboretum,** 5080 Colerain Ave.
  ⚱ (541-8176): The verdant getaway of Cincinnati. Close to
1,440 acres (583ha) of forest and meadowland less than 9 mi. (15km) from
dwntwn, with picnic grounds and hiking trails.

PERFORMING ARTS: For daily listings of all shows and cultural events, consult the entertainment pages of the daily papers *Cincinnati Enquirer* (morning)
and *Cincinnati Post* (evening), and the monthly *Cincinnati* magazine.
  Music Hall, 1241 Elm St. (621-1919): Home of the Cincinnati Opera, with
director James de Blasis (Feb–July); the Cincinnati Symphony Orchestra, with
principal conductor Jesús López Cobos (Sept–May); and the Cincinnati Ballet
Company, with artistic director Nigel Durgoine (Sept–May). Also houses the fa-
mous May Festival (see "Special Events," below).
  Playhouse in the Park, 962 Mt. Adams Circle (421-3888): Modern theater
in winter and musical comedies in summer.
  Riverbend Music Center, 6295 Kellogg Ave. (232-6220): Concerts by the
Cincinnati Symphony, big-name shows including stars of jazz, rock, and pop.
May–Sept.
  Showboat *Majestic,* Public Landing, foot of Broadway (241-6550): Con-
temporary theater in spring, summer, and fall.
  Taft Theatre, 5th and Sycamore Sts. (721-0411): Road shows, Broadway
musicals.

SPECIAL EVENTS: For the exact schedule of events below, consult the **Cincinnati Convention & Visitors Bureau** (see "Tourist Information," above).
  May Festival (May): The oldest annual choral and operatic festival in the
country (established 1873) features some of the world's finest soloists.
  Riverfront Stadium Festival (late July): One of the most famous and most
attended jazz, rock, soul, and rhythm-and-blues festivals in the country. For information, call 871-3900. At Riverfront Stadium.

ATP Tournament (mid-Aug): Professional tennis tournament held annually at the Jack Nicklaus Sports Center.

Riverfest (Labor Day wknd): 48 hr. of festivities based on themes from Cincinnati's historical heritage. Spectacular fireworks, Ohio River cruises, sports events. Draws 750,000 people every year.

Oktoberfest (last week of Sept): The local version of the renowned Munich beer festival with food, music, games, and ongoing entertainment in the six-block area surrounding Fountain Sq. Cheerful and colorful. 500,000 celebrants.

Winter Festival (mid-Nov to early Jan): Music, crafts, carriage rides, and 19th-century dress in celebration of the Christmas season held at Sharon Woods Village (see "Nearby Excursions," below).

SPORTS: Cincinnati has two professional teams:
Baseball (Apr–Oct): Reds, Riverfront Stadium (421-7337).
Football (Sept–Jan): Bengals, Riverfront Stadium (621-3550).

Horse Racing
River Downs Racetrack, 6301 Kellogg Ave. (10 mi./16km east on U.S. 52) (232-8000). Thoroughbred racing Fri–Wed Apr–Nov.
Turfway Park Race Course, 7500 Turfway Pike, Florence, Ky. (10 mi./16km SW on I-75) (606/371-0200). Thoroughbred racing Wed–Sun Dec–Apr.

STROLLS: ☼⚖ **Covington Landing,** 1 Madison Ave., Covington, Ky. (606/291-9992): The nations's largest floating entertainment complex, offering a spectacular view of the Ohio River and Cincinnati skyline. The $100-million project features a football-size wharf replete with restaurants, bars, shops, and nightclubs.

⚖ **Dayton Street,** between Baymiller and Linn Sts.: This was once known as "Millionaires' Street" because of its magnificent Italianate mansions built 1860–90 by Cincinnati's richest families. One of these luxurious residences is now the **John Hauck House Museum** (see "Historic Buildings" above).

☼⚖ **Main Strasse,** 6th and Philadelphia Sts., Covington, Ky. (606/491-0458): Dozens of different boutiques and stalls constitute this very lively shopping district, once inhabited exclusively by German immigrants. Overlooking it all is a pretty bell tower 105 ft. (33m) high with a 43-bell carillon that plays at scheduled hours.

☼⚖ **Mount Adams,** Eden Park Dr.: The Greenwich Village or the Montmartre of Cincinnati, with narrow streets, museums, art galleries, boutiques, and numerous restaurants in a bohemian-chic setting. This historic area presents a spectacular view of the Ohio River Valley, downtown Cincinnati, and northern Kentucky.

THEME PARKS: ⚖ **The Beach,** 2590 Waterpark Dr., Mason (26 mi./42km NE on I-75) (398-7946): One of the top five water parks in the country, off I-71 across from Kings Island (see below). 25,000-sq. ft. (2,300m²) wave pool with water slides, innertube rides, sand beach, liquid fireworks, etc. Picnic area, restaurants. Open daily Memorial Day–Labor Day.

⚖ **Kings Island,** Kings Mill Rd., Kings Island (26 mi./42km NE on I-71) (398-5600): Ultramodern amusement park on 1,600 acres (650ha). Some 40 attractions, five thrill rides (including the terrifying "Beast" roller-coaster and two log flumes), mini-zoo, reconstructions of old villages, and a miniature Eiffel Tower. Open daily Memorial Day–Labor Day, wknds only in spring and autumn. 25 min. from dwntwn.

Sports fans shouldn't miss the **Jack Nicklaus Golf Center** (398-5200), next door to Kings Island, with two superb golf courses designed and built by Jack Nicklaus himself, and an 8,500-seat tennis stadium. Films, exhibitions. Open daily Apr–Nov, Tues–Sun the rest of the year. A must for sports-lovers.

ZOOS: 🐾 **Cincinnati Zoo,** 3400 Vine St. (281-4700): One of the top 10, and the second oldest, of U.S. zoos. Houses 6,000 animals of 800 species in a variety of realistic habitats, including a feline collection unmatched in the world. Note particularly the white tigers and an impressive band of gorillas. Attracts a million visitors a year. Open daily.

ACCOMMODATIONS

Personal Favorites (in order of preference)

☼ 🏰🏰🏰🏰 **Cincinnatian Hotel** (dwntwn), 601 Vine St., OH 45202 (513/381-3000; toll free, see Preferred). 147 rms, A/C, cable color TV. AE, CB, DC, MC, V. Valet gar. $12, health club, rest. (The Palace), bar, 24-hr. rm svce, concierge, free crib. *Note:* This Victorian palace w. a mansard roof is a historical landmark. Built in 1882, it reopened its doors in 1987 after a $23-million refurbishing that restored its old-world charm and former splendor. Spectacular eight-story atrium w. a large marble staircase. Exceptionally vast and comfortable rms w. period furniture and pastel walls, some w. private balconies overlooking the atrium. Impeccable, personalized svce and a first-rate rest. A fine address in the heart of Cincinnati. **VE**

🏰🏰🏰 **Westin** (dwntwn), Fountain Sq., OH 45202 (513/621-7700; toll free, see Westin). 450 rms, A/C, color TV, in-rm movies. AE, CB, DC, MC, V. Valet gar. $13, pool, health club, sauna, two rests. (including 5th Street Market), two bars, 24-hr. rm svce, drugstore, boutiques, free crib. *Note:* The paragon of luxury hotels in Cincinnati. Ultramodern, comfortable 17-story building of rather cold concrete-and-glass design, but the rms are spacious and have minibars. Good svce and an excellent rest. In the heart of the business district, affording direct access to the Convention Center via the Skywalk. No-smoking floors. **E–VE**

🏰🏰🏰 **Garfield House** (dwntwn), 2 Garfield Place, OH 45202 (513/421-3355; toll free 800/447-9559). 138 suites, A/C, cable color TV. AE, DC, MC, V. Gar. (fee), health club, deli, adj. bar, rm svce. *Note:* Cincinnati's only all-suite dwntwn hotel. Newly renovated, spacious one- or two-bedroom suites w. fully equipped kitchens and in-rm work areas. Elegantly comfortable. Flawless reception and svce. Three blocks from the Convention Center and Fountain Sq. Business and convention clientele. **E–VE**

🏰🏰 **Quality Hotel Riverview** (nr. dwntwn), 666 W. 5th St., Covington, KY 41011 (606/491-1200; toll free, see Choice). 236 rms, A/C, cable color TV. AE, CB, DC, MC, V. Free parking, pool, tennis, health club, sauna, revolving rest. on the top floor (Riverview Room), coffee shop, two bars, rm svce, nightclub, hrdrsr, free crib. *Note:* Modern round 18-story tower w. comfortable, spacious rms. Offers a fine panorama of dwntwn Cincinnati from the other side of the Ohio (ask for a rm w. a river view). Business clientele. Very good value. A favorite of connoisseurs. Free Cincinnati and airport shuttles. **I–M**

🏰 **Best Western Mariemont Inn** (nr. dwntwn), 6880 Wooster Pike, OH 45277 (513/271-2100; toll free, see Best Western). 60 rms, A/C, cable color TV. AE, CB, DC, MC, V. Free parking, rest. (National Exemplar), bar, rm. svce, free crib. *Note:* Quaint little inn built in 1926 w. English manor charm, a few steps from Ault Park. Inviting atmosphere, comfortable rms, and friendly, cheerful svce. Adequate rest. and a very good overall value. 10 min. from dwntwn on Columbia Pkwy. (U.S. 50E). An ideal spot for motorists. **I**

Travelodge Newport (nr. dwntwn), 222 York St., Newport, KY 41071 (606/291-4434; toll free, see Travelodge). 104 rms, A/C, cable color TV. AE, DC, MC, V. Free parking, pool, nearby rest., free coffee, free crib. *Note:* Well-run economy motel 5 min. from dwntwn Cincinnati across the Ohio River. Utilitarian comforts; some rms w. refrigerator and microwave. Good value, particularly for the budget traveler. **B–I**

Other Accommodations (from top bracket to budget)

Hyatt Regency (dwntwn), 151 W. 5th St., OH 45202 (513/579-1234; toll free, see Hyatt). 485 rms, A/C, color TV, in-rm movies. AE, CB, DC, MC, V. Valet parking $12, pool, health club, sauna, two rests. (including Champs), bar, rm svce, boutiques, concierge, free crib. *Note:* Opened in 1984, this large, modern 22-story building has a spectacular, three-story lobby. Excellent facilities and comfort. Vast, well-laid-out rms and ultra-professional svce. VIP floor. Mediocre rests. Business and group clientele. Faces the Convention Center. Direct access to Skywalk. **E–VE**

Omni Netherland Plaza (dwntwn), 35 W. 5th St., OH 45202 (513/421-9100; toll free, see Omni). 621 rms, A/C, color TV. AE, CB, DC, MC, V. Valet gar. $13, three rests. (including Orchids), bars, 24-hr rm svce, hrdrsr, boutiques, concierge. *Note:* Lovely 1920s palace magnificently renovated in 1991 to the tune of $25 million. The splendid art deco lobby is a historical landmark. Spacious, very comfortable rms and efficient, attentive svce. Very central location, steps away from the Convention Center. Excellent rest. Big business clientele. Direct access to the Skywalk. **E–VE**

Clarion Cincinnati (formerly Stouffer's; dwntwn), 141 W. 6th St., OH 45202 (513/352-2100; toll free, see Choice). 887 rms, A/C, color TV, in-rm movies. AE, CB, DC, MC, V. Valet gar. $11, pool, health club, sauna, racquetball, three rests. (including Top of the Crown), bars, rm svce, hrdrsr, concierge, free crib. *Note:* Relatively modern hotel in two adj. towers of 21 and 32 stories. Comfortable rms but rather mediocre svce and rests. Very centrally located. Group clientele (the hotel is directly across from the Convention Center). Three VIP floors. **M–E**

Vernon Manor (nr. dwntwn), 400 Oak St., OH 45219 (513/281-3300; toll free 800/543-3999). 173 rms, A/C, color TV. AE, CB, DC, MC, V. Free valet parking, rest. (The Forum), coffee shop, bar, rm svce, hrdrsr, free crib. *Note:* An old Cincinnati classic tastefully renovated. Spacious rms w. elegant decor (a third w. kitchenettes) and excellent svce. Quiet surroundings. VCR rentals. Regular clientele. 5 min. from dwntwn. **M**

Imperial House West (nr. dwntwn), 5510 Rybolt Rd., OH 45248 (513/574-6000; toll free 800/543-3018). 200 rms, A/C, cable color TV. AE, CB, DC, MC, V. Free parking, pool, sauna, rest. (Dante's), bar, rm svce, disco, free crib. *Note:* Comfortable, well-designed five-story motel w. spacious, inviting rms, some w. kitchenette and refrigerator. Friendly reception and svce. Business and package-tour clientele. Very good value. 20 min. from dwntwn along I-74. **I**

Days Inn Downtown (nr. dwntwn), 2880 Central Pkwy., OH 45225 (513/599-0400; toll free, see Days Inns). 103 rms, A/C, cable color TV. AE, DC, MC, V. Free parking, pool; no bar or rest.; free crib. *Note:* Unassuming little motel nr. the university, completely renovated in 1988. Good overall value; 5 min. from dwntwn. **I**

Accommodations in the Vicinity

Carrousel Inn (formerly Best Western; nr. dwntwn), 8001 Reading Rd., OH 45237 (513/821-5110; toll free 800/543-4970). 261 rms, A/C, cable color TV. AE, DC, MC, V. Free parking, three pools, health club, two tennis courts, sauna, miniature golf, two rests. (including the Brass Ring), bar, rm svce, crib $10. *Note:* Very comfortable country club-style motel on almost 15 acres (6ha) of lovely grdns. Spacious rms w. private balconies or patios (some w. kitchenettes). Comprehensive recreational facilities;

rather efficient svce. Group and convention clientele. Good value overall, 15 min. from dwntwn. **I–M**

Airport Accommodations

☀ ⓟⓟ **Cincinnati Drawbridge Estate Inn** (vic.), I-75 at Buttermilk
ₗₗ ₗₗ Pike, Fort Mitchell, KY 41017 (606/341-2800; toll free 800/354-9793). 505 rms, A/C, color TV, in-rm movies. AE, CB, DC, MC, V. Free parking, three pools, two tennis courts, health club, sauna, four rests. (including the Gatehouse Tavern), 24-hr. coffeeshop, four bars, rm svce, disco, free crib. *Note:* Vast motel w. Tudor decor. Very appealing rms w. balconies, good recreational facilities, and agreeable reception and svce. Business clientele. Excellent value. Very adequate rest. (Gatehouse Tavern). VIP floor. Bavarian brewery adjacent. 8 min. from the airport (free shuttle); 10 min. from dwntwn. **I–M**

YMCA/Youth Hostels

Cincinnati Home Hostel (nr. dwntwn), 2200 Maplewood Ave., OH 45219 (651-2329). Dormitories, 8 min. from dwntwn in a slightly run-down neighborhood.

RESTAURANTS

Personal Favorites (in order of preference)

ⓨⓨⓨⓨ **Maisonette** (dwntwn), 114 E. 6th St. (721-2260). A/C.
Lunch Tues–Fri, dinner Mon–Sat; closed hols. and early Sept. AE, CB, DC, MC, V. J&T. *Specialties:* breast of duck w. honey-lemon sauce, Belgian endives; duck liver terrine; fresh English sole sautéed in lemon butter; Scottish smoked salmon w. onion cream and asparagus tips; rack of lamb; filet of brill and lobster in pastry shell, white-chocolate mousse w. chocolate sauce. Low-fat and low-salt entrées. Long list of French and California wines. *Note:* One of the 12 best rests. in the country. The svce is as polished as it is attentive; the rose-toned decor is luxurious without being ostentatious, and the classic cuisine is altogether remarkable. Resv. a must well in advance. Itself worth the trip to Cincinnati. Valet parking in the evening. A local institution for more than 30 years. *French.* **M–E**

ⓨⓨ **Pigall's Café** (dwntwn), 127 W. 4th St. (651-2233). A/C.
Lunch Mon–Sat, dinner Mon–Sat; closed hols. AE, CB, DC, MC, V. *Specialties:* calypso coconut shrimp, fresh salmon croquettes, pasta dishes, fresh seafood. The menu changes regularly. *Note:* Once an elegant, upscale French rest., Pigall's Café now offers an innovative American menu and very reasonable prices. Bistro-style setting w. murals of Paris. Pleasant atmosphere. Valet parking. *American.* **I**

ⓨⓨ **Chester's Road House** (vic.), 9678 Montgomery Rd. (793-8700). A/C. Lunch Mon–Fri, dinner nightly; closed Jan 1, Superbowl Sunday, Dec 25. AE, CB, DC, MC, V. Jkt. *Specialties:* rack of lamb, prime rib, fish of the day, liqueured cappuccino. Good wine list. *Note:* The bucolic, less refined version of the same owner's Maisonette in a converted 1900 farmhouse. Simple but tasty cuisine in a pretty, rustic setting w. abundant greenery. A local favorite. An excellent locale. No resv. on Sat. 25 min. from dwntwn. *Continental/American.* **I–M**

☀ⓨⓨ **Lenhardt's** (nr. dwntwn), 151 W. McMillan (281-3600).
A/C. Lunch/dinner Tues–Fri; closed first 15 days of Aug, Christmas hols. AE, CB, DC, MC, V. *Specialties:* Wiener schnitzel, sauerbraten, jägerschnitzel, Kassler rippchen, chicken paprikash, goulash, Viennese pastries. Fine list of German wines. *Note:* One of the best German rests. in all Ohio, in the former residence of a wealthy 19th-century brewer a stone's throw from the university. Diligent svce. Resv. advised for evenings and wknds. A classic of its kind for more than 80 years. Very popular locally. Very good value. 10 min. from dwntwn. *German.* **I**

Other Restaurants (from top bracket to budget)

ɛɛɛ **The Phoenix** (dwntwn), 812 Race St. at 9th St. (721-2255). A/C. Dinner Tues–Sat; closed hols. AE, CB, DC, MC, V. Jkt. *Specialties:* Ohio quail stuffed w. smoked duck and walnut dressing, langoustines and smoked scallops in phyllo pastry, lamb chop in tomato-rosemary beurre blanc w. shoestring sweet potatoes, salmon in champagne-cream sauce w. leeks, strawberry milkshake in chocolate bag. Choice wine list. *Note:* As though a phoenix were rising from its own ashes, this luxury rest. was opened in 1988 in the former premises of a men's club, luxuriously renovated at a cost of $5 million. Contemporary American cuisine w. a faint southwestern accent, served in an elegant Victorian setting w. period paneling and stained glass. Smart, opulent surroundings, flawless svce. A good place to eat; be sure to reserve ahead. Valet parking. *American.* I–M

ɛɛ **The Palace** (dwntwn), in the Cincinnatian Hotel (see "Accommodations," above) (381-6006). A/C. Lunch/dinner daily; closed Dec. 25. AE, CB, DC, MC, V. Jkt. *Specialties:* oysters stuffed w. tomatoes, crab, bacon, and smoked cheese; duck breast on winter greens w. plum vinaigrette; swordfish w. linguini, artichokes, and olive-feta butter; crème brûlée. Large wine list, mostly domestic. *Note:* Elegance is at the heart of the success achieved by this locally popular rest. Efficient svce. Resv. advised. *American.* I–M

ɛɛ **Charley's Oyster Bar & Grill** (vic.), 9769 Montgomery Rd. (891-7000). A/C. Dinner only, nightly; closed Jan 1, Thanksgiving, Dec 25. AE, CB, DC, MC, V. Jkt. *Specialties:* clam bake, fish of the day, shellfish. *Note:* The best seafood rest. in Cincinnati (but also very decent steak, veal, and lamb), highly laudable despite often-faltering svce. The marine decor is somewhat incongruous in this 1850s manor house. Resv. advised. Valet parking. 25 min. from dwntwn. *Seafood.* I–M

ɛɛ **The Precinct** (nr. dwntwn), 311 Delta Ave. at Columbia Pkwy. (321-5454). A/C. Dinner only, nightly, closed hols. AE, CB, DC, MC, V. Jkt. *Specialties:* broiled steak, steak au poivre, steak Collinsworth (w. king crab, asparagus, mushrooms, and béarnaise sauce), lobster, catch of the day. The slender wine list nonetheless offers some interesting selections. *Note:* The very best beef in Cincinnati (so say devotees), aged and broiled over a wood fire according to the best principles, from the modest 8-oz. (226gm) filet mignon to the gigantic 22-oz. (622gm) Porterhouse. The setting is a former police precinct looking like a little red-brick castle. Lots of noise from the disco on the second floor; hardworking svce. A businessperson's favorite, so resv. advised. 10 min. from dwntwn. *Steak/Seafood.* I–M

ɛ **Mike Fink's Restaurant** (nr. dwntwn), at the foot of Greenup St. on the Ohio River, Covington, Ky. (606/261-4212). A/C. Lunch/dinner daily; closed Dec 25. AE, CB, DC, MC, V. *Specialties:* raw seafood bar; fried catfish; grilled halibut; filet of sole topped w. shrimp, crabmeat, and scallops; fish of the day. *Note:* Very popular seafood rest. in an old riverboat from the good ol' days. Fine, authentic cuisine and a pleasant ambience. Lovely view of Cincinnati from the other side of the river, especially after dark. Resv. advised. *Seafood.* I–M

ɛ **China Gourmet** (nr. dwntwn), 3340 Erie Ave., East Hyde Park Mall (871-6612). A/C. Lunch/dinner Mon–Sat; closed hols. AE, CB, DC, MC, V. *Specialties:* Chinatown shrimp, Cantonese lobster, Szechuan kung po, pike w. ginger. *Note:* Excellent Chinese cuisine—mostly Cantonese but Hunan and Szechuan dishes are served as well. Modern jungle-style Oriental decor. Friendly ambience. Locally popular. 15 min. from dwntwn. *Chinese.* I

ɛ **Forest View Gardens** (nr. dwntwn), 4508 N. Bend Rd. (661-6434). A/C. Lunch Mon–Fri, dinner Tues–Sun; closed Dec 24 and 25, Jan 1. AE, DC, MC, V. *Specialties:* Bavarian sampler (sauerkraut balls, various cheeses, homemade pâté), Weiner schnitzel, prime rib. *Note:* Traditional

German rest. where all the servers are either students or graduates of opera at Cincinnati's College Conservatory of Music. They give performances of Broadway and opera hits at the rest. in special dinner shows held Thurs–Sun. Resv. required for dinner shows. *German/American.* **B–I**

Restaurants in the Vicinity

☼ ♈ **Golden Lamb** (vic.), 27 S. Broadway, Lebanon (932-5065). A/C. Lunch/dinner daily; closed Dec 25. AE, CB, DC, MC, V. Jkt. *Specialties:* roast leg of spring lamb, duck à l'orange, filet of pork w. sage, Shaker sugar pie. Somewhat pedestrian wine list. *Note:* This charming inn, once a stagecoach rest stop, dates from 1803 and has played host to 10 presidents and countless celebrities. The cuisine is as simple and flavorful as the day it opened. Lovely antique decor. Pleasant ambience and svce. Well worth the 50-min. car ride from Cincinnati. Resv. advised. Also 18 spare, basic rms. *American.* **B–I**

Cafeterias/Specialty Spots

Camp Washington Chili Inc. (nr. dwntwn), Colerain Ave. and Hopple St. (541-0061). In business since 1946, C. W. is considered by purists the best of the countless chile places in Cincinnati. Formica decor but friendly reception and svce. Nr. the university. Unlike many chile chain rests. this one never multiplied. There is only one Camp Washington. Open 24 hr. Mon–Sat and 10am–6pm Sun. No credit cards.

Izzy's (dwntwn), 819 Elm St. (721-4241). The best-known deli in Cincinnati since 1901. Overstuffed kosher sandwiches w. potato pancakes, homemade soup, corned beef, legendary Reubens; the desserts could endanger your figure. Breakfast/lunch/dinner Mon–Sat (until 7pm). Other location: 610 Main St. (241-6246). No credit cards.

Skyline Chili (dwntwn), 643 Vine St. (241-2020). Lunch/dinner Mon–Sat (until 7pm). No credit cards. A must for all visitors. Chile—as the name indicates—is the big house specialty, and is served in many variations. More than 40 other branches in Cincinnati and the suburbs (consult the local phone directory). A Cincinnati institution since 1949.

BARS & NIGHTCLUBS

Arnold's Bar & Grill (dwntwn), 210 E. 8th St. (421-6234). The oldest (1861) tavern in Cincinnati, with live traditional jazz, ragtime, and swing. Acceptable sandwiches and snacks. Locally popular; mixed crowd of yuppies and students. Open Mon–Sat.

Blind Lemon (nr. dwntwn), 936 Hatch St. (241-3885). Acoustic music and easy-listening tunes are performed here nightly.

Caddy's (dwntwn), 230 W. Pete Rose Way (721-3636). Popular nightspot featuring the old goodies of the '50s to the '70s. *American Graffiti* style. Open Wed–Sun.

City View (nr. dwntwn), 403 Oregon St. (241-8439). Cheap beer and great view of the city skyline at this place known as the best dive in town. Open nightly.

Flanagan's Landing (dwntwn), 212 W. Pete Rose Way (421-4055). Engaging Irish pub very nr. Riverside Stadium. Noisy and crowded, especially when the Bengals or the Reds are playing. Pleasant open-air beer grdn on fine days. Live entertainment nightly.

J. D. Brews at Oldenberg (vic.), I-75 at Buttermilk Pike (606/341-2802). Congenial pub and rest. serving beer from next door at the Oldenberg brewery. 15 min. from dwntwn. Open nightly.

The Precinct (nr. dwntwn), 311 Delta Ave. (321-5454). Open nightly. A very popular rest./bar/disco in a former police station. Youthful, relaxed ambience. Very decent steakhouse 10 min. from dwntwn (see "Restaurants," above).

Rookwood Pottery (nr. dwntwn), 1077 Celestial St. (721-5456). Open nightly. This pleasant bar/disco in the quaint original kilns of an old pottery factory at the top of Mt. Adams is very popular with the locals. Also an average rest.

NEARBY EXCURSIONS

DAYTON (60 mi./80km NE on I-75): See the aviation museum at the **Wright-Patterson Air Force Base,** on Ohio 444 (513/255-3284), the largest museum of military aviation in the world: more than 200 aircraft on display, from the Wright Brothers' glider to the huge B-52 bomber and space rockets. Open daily. The graves of Orville and Wilbur Wright are in neighboring **Woodland Cemetery,** at the east end of Woodland Ave.

FORT ANCIENT STATE MEMORIAL (nr. Lebanon, 36 mi./58km NE on I-71 and Ohio 350E) (513/932-4421): Impressive fortified city constructed between 400 B.C. and A.D. 600 by Hopewell Indians (a tribe of the Mound Builders culture who lived at the beginning of our era in Ohio and Wisconsin and about whom historians know almost nothing). The still-visible earthen walls rise to 22 ft. (7m) in some places. Many burial mounds and other relics. Interesting archeological museum. Open Wed–Sun June–Aug, wknds only in Apr–May and Sept–Oct.

KENTUCKY HORSE PARK (in Lexington, 72 mi./115km south on I-75 and Iron Works Pike) (606/233-4303): In the heart of Bluegrass Land and its famous stud farms, this 960-acre (365ha) equestrian museum attracts hundreds of thousands of visitors devoted to the cult of the thoroughbred. Visits to the stable (more than 600 stalls) and training field. Museum dedicated to horse-racing greats. Seasonal parade of stallions and a number of races Apr–Oct. A must for all admirers of "man's most noble conquest." Open daily Apr–Oct, Wed–Sun the rest of the year.

MOUND CITY GROUP NATIONAL MONUMENT (in Chillicothe, 95 mi./152km NE on U.S. 50E and Ohio 104N) (614/774-1125): 23 burial mounds of the Hopewell Indians (500 B.C.–A.D. 600). The largest concentration of prehistoric monuments of this kind in the country. Exhibition of religious relics. Open daily.

Not far from here is the **Sugarloaf Mountain Amphitheater** (enter on U.S. 23N and Ohio 159), offering an interesting theatrical presentation of the heroic life and the death of Tecumseh, leader of the Shawnee tribe and last Native American warrior leader to resist the advance of the "palefaces" east of the Mississippi (1813). Mon–Sat at 8:30pm June to early Sept. For information, call 614/775-0700.

SERPENT MOUNT STATE MEMORIAL (75 mi./120km east on Ohio 32E, 41N, and 73W) (513/587-2796): Native American totem 1,302 ft. (407m) long in the form of a stylized serpent, made of stone and yellow clay between 800 B.C. and A.D. 1400. The largest mound of this type in the U.S. If the grass were clipped around the monument, this unusual work would look even more impressive. Well worth going out of your way for, nevertheless. Open daily. A good joint excursion with Mound City Group National Monument (see above) and with **Fort Hill State Memorial** (15 mi./24km NE of Serpent Mound State Memorial on Ohio 73S and 41N), former fortified camp of the Hopewell people built at the top of a hill. Museum of archeological finds. Open daily.

SHARON WOODS VILLAGE (14 mi./22km NE on U.S. 42) (513/563-9484): A very realistic portrayal of small-town life in Ohio in the mid-19th century. The authentic old houses were transported to Sharon Woods from their original locations. Open Wed–Sun May–Oct, and from mid-Nov to early Jan for Winter Festival (see "Special Events," above).

CHAPTER 23

CHICAGO ♙♙♙

□   □   □

An immense metropolis, with suburbs extending more than 62 miles (100km) along the southwest bank of Lake Michigan, Chicago was the second-largest city in the U.S. until 1984, when it was ousted by Los Angeles. Two French explorers helped found Chicago, a name deriving from the Native American word *checagou* (wild onion), a plant that once grew abundantly on the banks of the Chicago River. The Jesuit Fr. Jacques Marquette and the trapper Louis Joliet were the first Europeans to visit the site, in 1673. Jean Baptiste Point du Sable, an African American businessman native to Haiti, in 1796 created the first fur-trading post on the banks of Lake Michigan, a Native American name meaning "Great Lake." (This founding father is himself a symbol of the ethnic mix that has given the city its uniquely cosmopolitan character: His father was a Frenchman from Québec, his mother was a black slave from Santo Domingo, and his wife was a Potawatomi.) In 1803 a military encampment named Fort Dearborn was built at the mouth of the Checagou River. Its garrison was massacred by local Native American tribes nine years later and the fort was abandoned until 1816. With the mass settlement of homesteaders from the east around 1833, this crossroads city between the Great Lakes and the plains of the Midwest entered a period of prodigious economic growth. Even the virtual destruction of the city by fire in 1871, when it had 300,000 inhabitants, could not check its burgeoning vigor. In 1900 its population had risen to 1.7 million and surpassed 3.5 million in 1960. Though its numbers have since fallen to just under 2,800,000 inhabitants, the third American city after New York and Los Angeles remains the capital of the American heartland.

A city of drive and superlatives—"the city that works," "the city of big shoulders," "second city"—Chicago claims one of the busiest airports in the world (**O'Hare International Airport,** with more than 62 million passengers per year), the largest railroad station, the largest inland port, the tallest skyscraper in the world (the **Sears Tower,** 110 stories and 1,454 ft./443m, 90 ft./30m higher than New York's World Trade Center), the tallest church (the Chicago Temple, 568 ft./173m), the largest water-treatment plant in the world, the world's largest commercial building (**Merchandise Mart**), the world's most important grain exchange, and the largest convention center in the world (**McCormick Place**).

Chicago is the world capital of grain, chewing gum, agricultural machinery, mail order, frivolous magazines (the *Playboy* empire started here), electrical equipment, meat packing, the telephone, and the hamburger (the first McDonald's opened in 1955 in Des Plaines, near O'Hare Airport, and today enjoys the status of a relic). The second financial and industrial center of the U.S. after New York, Chicago also prides itself on possessing the world's first skyscraper, the **Manhattan Building** (1884), designed by William Le Baron Jenney. Today, three of the five tallest buildings in the world are in Chicago.

The merest glance at Chicago's impressive skyline will disclose a greater wealth of architectural theory and practice than you are likely to find in any other U.S. city. By the end of the last century, architects of the famous "Chicago School" (such as William Le Baron Jenney, Daniel Burnham, Dankmar Adler, and Louis Sullivan) had realized some of the masterpieces that anticipated by 20

–30 years the birth of art deco in Europe: **Burnham's** with its 16 stories, at the time the tallest office building in the world; the **Auditorium Building;** the **Carson, Pirie, Scott & Co.** and **Marshall Field** department stores; and **The Rookery,** the world's oldest steel-frame skyscraper (1886), just to cite a few. Frank Lloyd Wright, Sullivan's favorite pupil and the greatest American architect of all time, created in the 1890s his revolutionary "Prairie Style" for individual houses, with low, uncluttered lines married harmoniously to the surrounding foliage and gardens. In the suburb of **Oak Park** you can admire a series of such houses, which, though constructed 90 years ago, still appear remarkably modern. With Wright's example to follow, a succession of architects both American (Root, Holabird and Roche, Raymond Hood, James Gamble Rogers) and foreign (the Germans Ludwig Mies van der Rohe and Walter Gropius, one-time members of the Bauhaus, and Finland's Eero Saarinen) has over the past century made Chicago into a shining light of urban architecture. Witness such classic structures as the **Chicago Tribune Tower,** the **Wrigley Building,** and especially Mies van der Rohe's **Lake Shore Drive Apartment Towers,** where in 1948 the "curtain wall" technique was first used in the United States. There is also Skidmore, Owings and Merrill's superb **John Hancock Center** (affectionately nicknamed "Big John" by Chicagoans) and Helmut Jahn's audacious **State of Illinois Center,** opened in 1986.

Many of us know Chicago as the brutal, opportunistic city seen in classic screen portrayals of the St. Valentine's Day Massacre, Al Capone, Dillinger, and Prohibition. The reality is far more complex: This city is home to one of the most extraordinary ethnic mixtures on the planet. Poles (with 800,000 people of Polish extraction, Chicago is the largest Polish city in the world after Warsaw), Greeks, Italians, Slavs, African Americans, Chinese, Mexicans, Irish, Swedes, Puerto Ricans, and Germans all have their neighborhoods, their lifestyles, their folklore, their museums, and their cuisine (the city has more than 5,000 restaurants of all kinds). Almost a third of current Chicagoans were born outside the United States, and a remarkable racial mix (42% white, 40% African American, 14% Hispanic, 4% Asian) has enhanced the Homeric political contests that have become traditional at municipal elections.

A sprawling city full of contrasts—the chic galleries and stores of the **Magnificent Mile;** the African American areas of the **South Side, Cabrini-Green,** and **Bronzeville;** the frenetic activity of the **Loop,** the financial district constrained within the clangorous tracks of the Elevated; the luxury homes along **North Lake Shore Drive,** the chic restaurants and boutiques of **Printer's Row** and **River North**—Chicago has some of the most fascinating museums, public gardens (574 in all), and urban landscapes in America. Its seven universities include the **University of Illinois, Loyola** (Catholic), and the **University of Chicago,** where in 1942 Enrico Fermi achieved the world's first controlled atomic chain reaction. These plus the nuclear research center, **Argonne National Laboratory** in Darien, are among the most prestigious breeding grounds for American Nobel prize winners (53 to date). Chicago is the birthplace of Walt Disney, Jason Robards, Kim Novak, Johnny Weissmuller (the legendary Tarzan), John Dos Passos, Edgar Rice Burroughs (the creator of Tarzan), and Ernest Hemingway (born, as was Burroughs, in the suburb of Oak Park), and is today one of the three great American art capitals (with New York and Los Angeles), offering a wealth of opportunity to lovers of theater, opera, jazz, and other cultural events. The **Chicago Symphony Orchestra,** directed by such legendary figures as Fritz Reiner and Georg Solti, is considered by experts one of the two or three best instrumental ensembles in the world. A jazz capital since the 1920s and undisputed bastion of the blues, Chicago has also given birth to talents as varied as Benny Goodman, Gene Krupa, Mezz Mezzrow, Bud Freeman, Jo Jones, Lennie Tristano, Quincy Jones, Muggsy Spanier, and Herbie Hancock.

BASIC FACTS: State of Illinois. Area codes: 312 (dwntwn and O'Hare Airport), 708 (suburbs). Time zone: central. ZIP Code: 60607. Settled: 1803. Approximate population: city, 2,780,000; metropolitan area, 8,060,000. Third-largest American city.

CLIMATE: The climate is very rigorous, with glacial winters (sometimes −22°F/−30°C) and lots of snow; spring and autumn are brief. Chicago owes its "Windy City" nickname to the terrible blizzards that blow in from northern Canada across the flat expanse of the Great Lakes. Summer, sometimes quite hot (average temperature: 78°F/26°C) but always breezy, is by far the best season to visit Chicago.

DISTANCES: Detroit, 268 mi. (430km); Indianapolis, 181 mi. (290km); Milwaukee, 87 mi. (139km); Minneapolis, 406 mi. (650km); New York, 806 mi. (1,290km); St. Louis, 290 mi. (465km); Washington, 668 mi. (1,070km).

ARRIVAL & TRANSIT INFORMATION

AIRPORTS: Two major airports: **Midway Airport** (MDW), 11 mi. (17km) SW, with aging facilities. Information: 767-0500.
    O'Hare International Airport (ORD), 18 mi. (29km) NW, the busiest airport in the world (more than 62 million passengers per year), with a takeoff or landing every 20 seconds and served by 50 airlines. Information: 686-2200.

U.S. AIRLINES: American (toll free 800/433-7300), America West (toll free 800/247-5692), Continental (toll free 800/525-0280), Delta (toll free 800/221-1212), Northwest (toll free 800/225-2525), TWA (toll free 800/221-2000), United (toll free 800/241-6522), and USAir (toll free 800/428-4322).

FOREIGN CARRIERS: Air Canada (toll free 800/776-3000), Air France (toll free 800/237-2747), British Airways (toll free 800/247-9297), Lufthansa (toll free 800/645-3880), Sabena (toll free 800/955-2000), and Swissair (toll free 800/221-4750).

CITY LINK: Cab fare to city center **from O'Hare,** about $25–$28; time, about 45 min. Bus: Continental Air Transport (454-7800); leaves every 5–10 min.; stops at the major dwntwn hotels; time, about 60 min.; fare, $15.
    Cab fare to city center **from Midway,** about $20; time, about 20 min. Bus: Continental Air Transport (454-7800); leaves every 15 min.; time, about 35 min.; fare $11.
    Between high cab fares and O'Hare's distance from downtown, renting a car may be advisable if you're planning a prolonged stay. Chicago has a very efficient public transportation system (subway and bus), including notably an express subway connection between the Loop and O'Hare (CTA). Fare, $1.50; time, about 45 min. (call 836-7000 for information). CTA station is located under Terminal 4.

CAR RENTAL (at O'Hare International Airport unless otherwise indicated): Avis (toll free 800/331-1212); Budget (toll free 800/527-0700); Dollar (toll free 800/800-4000); Hertz (toll free 800/654-3131); National (toll free 800/227-7368); and Thrifty (toll free 800/367-2277). For dwntwn agencies, consult the local telephone book.

LIMOUSINE SERVICES: Carey Limousines (763-0009), Dav El Limousine (toll free 800/922-0343), Lake Shore Limousine (334-2343).

TAXIS: Cabs may be hailed on the street, gotten in waiting lines at the entrances to the major hotels, or summoned by phone. The major cab companies are: **American United** (248-7600), **Flash Cab** (561-1444), and **Yellow Cab** (829-4222).

TRAIN: Amtrak, Union Station, 225 S. Canal St., ticket office, 203 N. LaSalle St. (toll free 800/872-7245).

INTERCITY BUSES: Greyhound, 630 W. Harrison St. (toll free 800/231-2222).

INFORMATION & TOURS

TOURIST INFORMATION: Chicago Office of Tourism, 78 E. Washington St. (in the Chicago Cultural Center), IL 60602 (312/744-2400; toll free 800/487-2446). Open Mon–Fri. Information counter located in the lobby of the same building is open daily.
    Information Bureau, Water Tower-in-the-Park, 806 N. Michigan Ave. (312/744-2400). Open daily.
    Cultural Information Hotline giving a recorded listing of cultural events (312/346-3278) and shows (312/977-1755).

GUIDED TOURS: American Sightseeing (bus), 530 S. Michigan Ave. (427-3100): Guided tour of the city. Serves major hotels.
    Chicago Architectural Foundation, 224 S. Michigan Ave. (Santa Fe Building) (922-3431): Wonderful walking, boat, and bus tours around the major architectural achievements of Chicago and its suburbs. Also, photo exhibits, lectures, a well-stocked library, etc. Resv. advised. Daily.
    Chicago Motor Coach Co. (bus), 750 S. Clinton (922-8919): Narrated one-, two-, and three-hour tours of the Loop, Lakefront, Grant Park, West and North Sides aboard a double-decker bus, London style. Departures every 15 min. from Sears Tower. Courtesy hotel pickup available. Daily.
    Gray Line Tours (bus), Palmer House Hilton, 33 E. Monroe St. (346-9506): Guided city tours.
    Mercury Skyline Cruiseline (boat), Wacker Dr. and Michigan Ave. (332-1368): Lake and Chicago River rides May–Sept.
    Oak Park Tour Center (walking tours), 158 N. Forest Ave. and Lake St., Oak Park (708/848-1978): Guided tours of this residential area, cradle of the "Prairie House" style created by Frank Lloyd Wright. Visitor center open daily.
    Untouchable Tours (bus) (881-1195): Chicago's only bus tour of gangland sites, from Al Capone's headquarters to the site of the St. Valentine's Day Massacre. The driver and tour guide dress as gangsters, pack plastic pistols in shoulder holsters, and spice up the commentary with hoodlum argot and their own sound effects. Highly unusual. Departs from Michigan Ave. and Pearson, and from Capone Chicago at Clark and Ohio. Tours daily Apr–Oct, Fri–Sun the rest of the year. Call for resv.

SIGHTS, ATTRACTIONS & ACTIVITIES

ARCHITECTURAL HIGHLIGHTS: ⚓ **Board of Trade,** 141 W. Jackson Blvd. (435-3590): The most important commodity exchange in the world, a huge art deco building with 44 stories (588 ft./184m high) crowned by a giant statue of Ceres, goddess of the harvest. Visitors gallery is on the fifth floor. Open Mon–Fri.

    ☀⚓ **Chicago Mercantile Exchange,** 30 S. Wacker Dr. (930-8249): The world's second-largest grain exchange, as well as one of the most important international currency-futures markets, housed in twin modern towers on the Chicago River. The Visitors' Gallery, open Mon–Fri, offers a spectacular view of the frantic activity on the Exchange floor.

    City Hall, 121 N. La Salle St. (744-7300): Chicago's city hall and county administration building. Imposing neoclassical structure which dates from 1910. Open Mon–Fri.

    Harold Washington Library, 400 S. State St. (747-4300): A $195-million Beaux Arts–style palace of brick and carved granite with five-story arched windows and metal gargoyles. Designed by Thomas Beeby, the dean of the Yale architecture school, this imposing library, inaugurated in 1991, is named after the late Chicago mayor. Open Mon–Sat.

    Illinois Institute of Technology, 3300 S. Federal St.: Technical university (6,000 students) whose campus, remarkable for the purity and simplicity of its lines, was designed by Mies van der Rohe (see especially Crown Hall). For architecture buffs.

    Merchandise Mart, Wells and Kinzie Sts.: The largest commercial building in the world, it was erected in 1928 and has more than 900 furniture showrooms. An astonishing sight to see. Guided tours Mon–Fri (call 644-4664 for resv.).

    Richard J. Daley Center, Richard Daley Plaza (346-3278): Elegant, modern skyscraper in bronze and steel tones (648 ft./ 198m, 31 stories) named for the former mayor of Chicago, it houses the city's administrative services. Be sure to see this building with its giant abstract sculptures by Picasso (48 ft./15m tall) and Miró (34 ft./11m tall) on the plaza.

    State of Illinois Center, 100 W. Randolph St. at La Salle St. (814-6660): Be sure to see this, the most surprising and innovative building in all Chicago. A 1985 "hi-tech" masterpiece, this hemispherical tower of blue and pink tinted glass is built around a gigantic windowed atrium 17 stories tall. This building by German-born architect Helmut Jahn houses administrative offices of the State of Illinois. Unusual fiberglass sculpture by Jean Dubuffet, *Monument with Standing Animal,* in front of the building.

    United States Post Office, 433 W. Van Buren St. (765-3035): The largest post office in the world, it handles more than 40 million letters and 500,000 parcels each day. Interesting tours Mon–Fri Jan–Nov; you must make resv. several days in advance.

    University of Chicago, 5801 S. Ellis Ave. (702-0200): Founded in 1890 by John D. Rockefeller, this is one of the most respected of American universities (8,000 students). There are a number of interesting buildings here by Frank Lloyd Wright, Mies van der Rohe, and Eero Saarinen, among others. On **Stagg Field** (S. Ellis Ave. between E. 56th and E. 57th Sts.) a bronze composition by British sculptor Henry Moore marks the exact spot where on December 2, 1942, history's first controlled nuclear chain reaction was set off by a team of researchers under the direction of Enrico Fermi, Italian Nobel prize winner for physics. Not far from there is the **Oriental Institute** (1155 E. 58th St.) offering very rich collections of Assyrian and Egyptian art (open Tues–Sun), and the Neo-Gothic **Rockefeller Memorial Chapel** (1156 E. 59th St.) with its 72-bell carillon (1910). Guided tour of the campus Mon–Sat Apr–Nov at 10am (call 702-8374 for information).

    University of Illinois, Circle Campus, Dan Ryan Expwy. and Eisenhower Expwy. (996-7000): The most modern university in the United States (1965). Note the futurist architecture, especially the administration building with its 28 stories which get larger toward the top. On the campus is **Hull House** (800 S. Halsted), pioneering center for social work founded in 1889 by Jane Addams, Nobel peace prize winner. Interesting tours Sun–Fri; call 413-5353 for information.

    Water Tower Place, 845 N. Michigan Ave. (440-3165): The most luxurious multi-level shopping center in the United States (see "Shopping," below). The **Water Tower** (opposite), in the form of a

Gothic Revival fortress, is one of the few buildings spared by the great fire of 1871.

Skyscrapers

Amoco Building, 200 E. Randolph Dr.: The second-tallest skyscraper in Chicago and the fourth tallest in the world, 1,107 ft./80 stories (346m) high. Dating from 1973, its facade, initially covered in marble, has been replaced by sturdier granite. No guided tours. Interesting Harry Bertoia "sonic" sculpture on the ornamental pool in front of the tower (see "Outdoor Art and Plazas," below).

Chicago Tribune Tower, 435 N. Michigan Ave. (222-3994): Raymond Hood's amazing octagonal Neo-Gothic skyscraper, 36 stories high, dating from 1925. Home of the *Chicago Tribune,* the city's largest newspaper. (Tours of the paper's printing press at the Freedom Center are given Mon–Fri; call 222-2116 for information.)

First National Bank Building, 1 First National Plaza at Monroe and Dearborn Sts.: Built in 1969 by architects Murphy, Perkins and Will, it's the tallest bank in the world (60 stories).

John Hancock Center, 875 N. Michigan Ave.: Superb derrick-shaped skyscraper with a facade of smoked glass and black and bronze aluminum, 100 stories (1,127 ft./343m) high. The sixth-tallest skyscraper in the world, it combines shops, offices, and apartments in one building. This work by Skidmore, Owings and Merrill is topped with two gigantic telecommunication antennas 336 ft. (100m) tall. Since its construction in 1969, it has become the symbol of Chicago. The observation platform on the 94th floor should not be missed (see "Panoramas," below).

Marina City, 300 N. State St.: The twin artichoke-leaf-shaped towers by architect Bertrand Goldberg date from 1964. The first floors constitute a parking garage with a spiral ramp. These, the most famous apartment buildings in the United States dominate the Chicago River from the top of their 60 stories.

Sears Tower, 233 S. Wacker Dr. (875-9696): The tallest skyscraper in the world, 1,454 ft. (443m) and 110 stories. 17,000 employees work in this huge, vertical ant's nest serviced by 102 elevators. Designed by the same team of architects that did the John Hancock Center, it's the property of Sears Roebuck & Co. Opened in 1974; construction took four years. The installation of two TV antennas brought the tower to a total height of 1,706 ft. (520m). The lobby has a giant Calder mobile called *Universe.* (For more details, see "Panoramas," below.)

333 West Wacker Dr.: This very handsome 36-story glass tower, its frontage delicately curved to follow the bank of the Chicago River, is by New York architect William Pedersen; it won an award from the American Institute of Architects in 1984.

Wrigley Building, 400 N. Michigan Ave.: One of the most famous monuments in Chicago and the headquarters of the Wrigley's chewing gum empire, this architecturally startling 35-story skyscraper (complete with Renaissance campanile) dates from 1924. The four huge clocks at the top of the tower are each two stories tall. Beautifully illuminated in the evening.

BEACHES: North Ave. Beach and Oak St. Beach are the most popular

Chicago beaches, just north of the city. The pollution level of Lake Michigan stays relatively low thanks to seven giant water-purification plants.

CHURCHES/SYNAGOGUES: Chicago Temple, also known as the **First United Methodist Church,** 77 W. Washington St. (236-4548): Built in 1924,

the tallest church in the world—568 ft. (173m) including the cross on top of the Gothic tower—offers the interesting "Chapel in the Sky" on its roof. Open daily.

HISTORIC BUILDINGS: ☼⚑ **Auditorium Building,** 430 S. Michigan Ave. (922-4046): Built in 1887–89 by Louis Sullivan and Dankmar Adler, this is one of the masterpieces of the Chicago School. Extraordinary interior decor. Both concert hall and headquarters of **Roosevelt University** (6,500 students).

☼⚑ **Manhattan Building,** 431 S. Dearborn St.: The first real skyscraper in history (1884) though a mere eight stories, this William Le Baron Jenney building anticipated modern construction techniques.

⚑ **Monadnock Building,** 53 W. Jackson Blvd. (922-1890): When completed in 1893, this was the tallest office skyscraper in the world; designed by Burnham and Root. For art history lovers.

⚑ **Orchestra Hall,** 220 S. Michigan Ave. (435-6666): Dating from 1904, this acoustically perfect auditorium is home to the renowned Chicago Symphony Orchestra, whose music director for many years was Sir Georg Solti. The building figures on the national inventory of historic landmarks. The hall can only be seen by the public during performances.

☼⚑ **Robie House,** 5757 S. Woodlawn Ave. (702-8374): On the University of Chicago campus (see above), this brick building dating from 1909 is the forerunner of Frank Lloyd Wright's "Prairie House" style. Today it is home to the Institute of International Affairs. Open Mon–Sat.

⚑ **The Rookery,** 209 S. La Salle St.: The oldest steel-frame skyscraper in the world (1886); by Burnham and Root. The white-and-gold hall of this historic landmark was redesigned by Frank Lloyd Wright at the turn of the century.

MONUMENTS: ⚑ **Buckingham Fountain,** Grant Park at the end of Congress St.: A colossal public fountain in pink Georgia marble, with a jet rising to more than 131 ft. (41m). Dramatic illuminations and enchanting water shows in the evenings May–Sept. (See also "Outdoor Art and Plazas," below.)

MUSEUMS OF ART: ☼⚑⚑⚑ **Art Institute,** Michigan Ave. and Adams St. (443-3600): Elegant Italian Renaissance–style palazzo, constructed for the World's Fair of 1893 and splendidly renovated. More than a thousand paintings by European and American masters, from Rembrandt to Matisse and from Ben Shahn to Mark Rothko. Among the most famous: Caravaggio's *Resurrection,* El Greco's *Assumption of the Virgin,* Delacroix's *Lion Hunt,* Seurat's *Sunday on the Isle of Grande-Jatte,* van Gogh's *The Bedroom,* Picasso's *The Old Guitarist,* Juan Gris's *Cubist Portrait of Picasso,* Reginald Marsh's *Tattoo and Haircut,* Edward Hopper's *Nighthawks,* and Grant Wood's *American Gothic.* Also, wonderful stained glass by Chagall, and fine collections of Chinese sculpture and pre-Columbian art. Plays host to many prestigious traveling exhibitions. One of the most beautiful art museums in the United States and in the world, with a pleasant cafeteria and open-air restaurant in summer. The Art Institute alone is worth the trip to Chicago. Open daily.

☼⚑⚑ **Chicago Cultural Center,** 78 E. Washington St. (346-3278): In the former **Public Library,** this sumptuous, Renaissance-style building from the end of the 19th century houses distinguished temporary exhibitions. The interior is richly adorned with Carrara marble, mosaics, and Tiffany-style windows. It houses the local office of tourism. Open Mon–Sat.

⚑ **Du Sable Museum of African-American History,** 740 E. 56th Place (947-0600): Very rich, interesting collections of African and African American art. Symbolically bears the name of one of the founders of Chicago, a black businessman from Haiti (see the introduction to this chapter). Open daily.

Mexican Fine Arts Museum, 1852 W. 19th St. (738-1503): The city's newest ethnic museum. Art exhibits and performances from Mexico and Mexican artists in the United States. The only museum of its kind in the Midwest. Open Tues–Sun.

Museum of Contemporary Art, 237 E. Ontario St. (280-5161): A truly marvelous little museum founded in 1967 housing modern and avant-garde art in all forms: painting, sculpture, poetry, film, music, dance, video, photography. Temporary exhibitions. Open Tues–Sun. A new building is due to be completed in 1995.

Newberry Library, 60 W. Walton St. (943-9090): Dating from 1887 and boasting more than 1.4 million volumes as well as several million manuscripts, this library is famous for its works on the Renaissance, Native Americans, and music history. Open Tues–Sat.

Terra Museum of American Art, 664 N. Michigan Ave. (664-3939): Rather small in size but big in content, the Terra Museum, which opened in 1987, is one of the newest museums of American art in the country. A strange blend of modern architectural idioms (large bay windows, white marble from Vermont) adapted to older structures. 800 major works of classical and contemporary American artists: Bingham, Cassatt, Demuth, Homer, Hopper, Morse, Peale, Prendergast, Sargent, Sheeler, Whistler, Wyeth, etc. A must for all art-lovers. Right in the middle of the Magnificent Mile. Open Tues–Sun.

MUSEUMS OF SCIENCE & HISTORY: Academy of Sciences, 2001 N. Clark St. (871-2668): Museum wholly devoted to the natural history and ecology of the Great Lakes region, notably a reconstruction of a 350-million-year-old forest with wildlife displays, as well as a "walk-through" cave and canyon. Open daily.

Adler Planetarium, 1300 S. Lake Shore Dr. (322-0300): This world-renowned institution covers the history of astronomy from the ancients to our time. Space shows and telescope observation in summer. Exhibits on space explorations (*Voyager* and *Apollo II* flights). Fine art deco architecture. Open daily.

Balzekas Museum, 6500 S. Pulaski Rd. (582-6500): Permanent exhibits of antique weapons, armor, dolls, fine and folk art, rare maps and prints spanning more than 1,000 years of Lithuanian history. Interesting. Open daily.

Bicycle Museum of America, 435 E. Illinois St. (on the North Pier) (222-0500): A collection of over 600 bicycles and over 50,000 items related to the bicycle, it is considered one of the top three of its kind in the world. Interesting revolving exhibits. A must for the bicycle enthusiast.

Chicago Fire Academy, 558 W. De Koven St. (747-8151): The famous fire-brigade school built on the site of Patrick O'Leary's stable, where legend puts the origin of the fire that totally ravaged Chicago on October 8, 1871, and left more than 90,000 people homeless. Tours of the training center Mon–Fri.

Chicago Historical Society, Clark St. at North Ave. (642-4600): A wonderful museum dedicated to American history, the Civil War and the life of Abraham Lincoln in particular, as well as to the evolution of Chicago from its founding to the present. Temporary exhibitions, demonstrations of old trades. Fully renovated in 1988. Open daily.

Field Museum of Natural History, Roosevelt Rd. at Lake Shore Dr. (922-9410): One of largest museums of natural history and ethnology in the world, with 200,000 exhibits ranging from reproductions of plants around the world to Egyptian tombs and meteorites. Section devoted to the history of Native Americans not to be missed. Open daily.

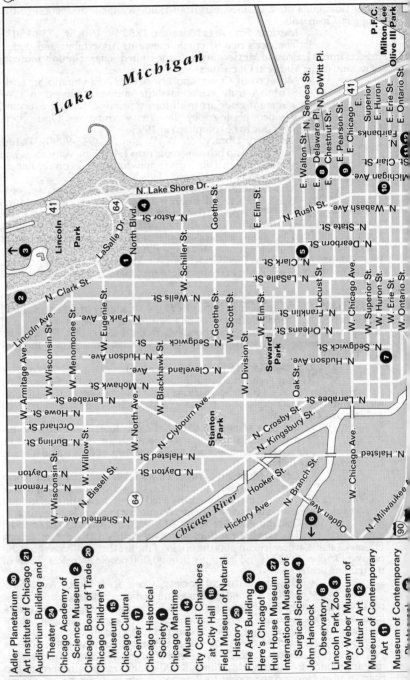

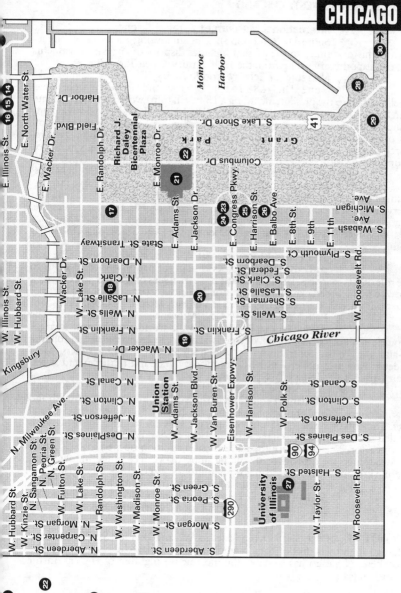

CHICAGO

Newberry Library **5**
North Pier **16**
Peace Museum **7**
Petrillo Music Shell **22**
Polish Museum of America **6**
Sears Tower **19**
Shedd Aquarium **28**
Spertus Museum of Judaica **26**
Terra Museum of American Art **10**

⚑ **International Museum of Surgical Sciences,** 1524 N. Lake Shore Dr. (642-3555): This interesting museum of surgery from prehistoric times to the present includes displays of ancient instruments and of an apothecary's shop from the 19th century. Open Tues–Sun.

☀ ⚑⚑⚑ **Museum of Science and Industry,** E. 57th St. and S. Lake Shore Dr. (684-1414): Science and industry from cave-dwelling days to the present, including a 15-ft.-tall (5m) working model of a human heart. Authentic German U-boat from World War II. Old locomotives, cars, planes by the dozen, plus a re-creation of a working coal mine. There are a number of robots that can be operated by visitors, plus a wing devoted to space research (**Crown Space Center**) with a 360° film-projection system, Omnimax. Four million visitors per year. The world's biggest science museum. Open daily.

⚑⚑ **Oriental Institute Museum,** 1155 E. 58th St. (702-9520): Established in 1894 as part of the University of Chicago, this museum of the ancient Near East displays artifacts of architecture, art, religion, and everyday life of ancient Egypt, Assyria, Mesopotamia, Persia, Syria, and Palestine. Among the important objects on view, a monumental statue of Tutankhamen, a 40-ton winged Assyrian bull, and a fragment of the Dead Sea Scrolls. Open Tues –Sun.

⚑ **The Peace Museum,** 430 W. Erie St. (440-1860): The first and only museum of its kind in the nation dedicated solely to the role of arts, sciences, labor, minorities . . . on issues of war and peace. Recent shows have included exhibits of art by South African artists, the life and times of Martin Luther King, Jr., and the Vietnam Veterans Memorial. Open Tues–Sat.

⚑ **Polish Museum,** 984 N. Milwaukee Ave. (384-3352): The second-largest Polish city in the world after Warsaw by right should and does have a museum devoted to Poland, its art, its culture, its folklore —and the Polish contribution to American history (among others, Gen. Tadeusz Kosciuszko, hero of the Revolutionary War, and musician and statesman Ignace Jan Paderewski). Open daily.

⚑⚑ **J. G. Shedd Aquarium,** 1200 S. Lake Shore Dr. (939-2426): The largest aquarium in the world—more than 8,000 fish and marine animals from the dolphin to the piranha—with its own artificial coral reef. The 460,000 gals. (1.75 million liters) of seawater required for the tanks is hauled by truck and rail from the Atlantic. Since 1929 this has been a must-see for every visitor. The **Oceanarium**, a $43-million addition opened in 1990, gives midwesterners the experience of walking along an ocean coastline and shows off marine life rarely seen outside major aquariums on either coast. Open daily.

⚑ **Spertus Museum of Judaica,** 618 S. Michigan Ave. (922-9012): Rich collection of Jewish manuscripts and religious objects. Paintings, sculptures, temporary exhibitions. Open Sun–Fri.

NIGHTLIFE: ⚑ **Rush St.,** between Chicago Ave. and Division St.: The mecca of Chicago nightowls, full of bars, nightclubs, discos, jazz clubs. Guaranteed atmosphere. (Chicago has some of the most active nightlife of any city in the United States.)

OUTDOOR ART & PLAZAS: In addition to the previously mentioned giant sculptures by Picasso, Miró, and Dubuffet (see "Architectural Highlights," above), Chicago's streets and plazas offer numerous noteworthy works of art: a 3,000-sq.-ft. (280m²) Chagall mosaic, *The Four Seasons* (First National Plaza); *Batcolumn,* a kind of giant steel baseball bat 100 ft. (31m) tall by Claes Oldenburg (600 W. Madison); a 53-ft.-high (16m) Calder sculpture, *Flamingo,* which weighs 50 tons (45,500kg; Federal Center Plaza); a giant bronze sundial by Henry Moore in front of the entrance to the Adler Planetarium (1300 S. Lake Shore Dr.); and a startling "sonic" sculpture by Harry Bertoia that sits above an ornamental pool in front of the Amoco Building (200 E. Randolph Dr.).

PANORAMAS: ※🔔🔔 **John Hancock Center Observatory,** 875 N. Michigan Ave. (751-3681): At 1,127 ft. (343m), the sixth-tallest skyscraper in the world. The observation platform located on the 94th floor offers a unique, impressive view of the city and lake in clear weather. Platform open daily 9am–midnight.

🔔 **Navy Pier,** 600 E. Grand Ave.: This mile-long jetty extending into Lake Michigan dates from the beginning of the century and was once a berth for ocean-going vessels. Its unobstructed view of the Chicago skyline is fabulous. Recently renovated, the pier now hosts several shops, restaurants, and entertainment venues.

※🔔🔔 **Sears Tower Skydeck,** 233 S. Wacker Dr. (875-9696): The tallest skyscraper in the world at 1,454 ft. (443m) and equipped with the fastest elevator in the world (1,753 ft./548m per min.—it takes exactly 70 seconds to reach the 103rd floor), it's the head office of Sears Roebuck & Co. Its asymmetrical cubist structure was designed to offer maximum structural resistance to Chicago's windy weather. Observation platform on the 103rd floor open daily 9am–10pm. In clear weather, you can see for 37 mi. (60km). What a sight! Motorized giant Calder mobile, *Universe,* in the lobby. Not to be missed.

PARKS & GARDENS: 🔔🔔 **Garfield Park,** 300 N. Central Park Blvd. (533-1281): Splendid tropical greenhouses (the largest in the world) with palm trees, luxurious vegetation, 400 kinds of cactus, ornamental lakes, and water lilies. Beautiful floral exhibitions. Quite spectacular. Open daily.

🔔 **Graceland Cemetery,** 4001 N. Clark St. (525-1105): A lovely landscaped cemetery among hills and ornamental ponds. Sumptuous mausoleums housing the mortal remains of rich Chicago families, bankers, industrial magnates, as well as famous architects Louis Sullivan and Daniel Burnham, the founders of the Chicago School. It also offers a panoramic view of Lake Michigan and the city. Open daily.

🔔 **Grant Park,** along Lake Michigan between E. Randolph Dr. and McCormick Place: An enormous public park in the middle of the city with numerous museums and a fine view of the lake and the skyscrapers.

※🔔 **Lincoln Park,** along Lake Shore Dr. between La Salle Dr. and Hollywood Ave.: A sprawling park and lovely botanical garden extending close to 5 mi. (8km) along the shore of Lake Michigan, it is home to the famous zoo (one of the oldest in the United States) plus public beaches and marinas. A nice perspective on the city from a distance. During the tense days of the anti–Vietnam War demonstrations in 1968, it was the meeting spot of the "Yippies" (Youth International Party).

(Just off Lincoln Park, in a garage that once stood at 2122 N. Clark St., the famous Saint Valentine's Day Massacre occurred on February 14, 1929: Seven gangsters were gunned down on the orders of Al Capone. He died in Miami in 1947, after spending eight years in Alcatraz. He is buried in lot 48 of Chicago's Mount Olivet Cemetery.)

PERFORMING ARTS: For a listing of all shows and cultural events, consult the entertainment pages of the daily papers, the *Chicago Sun Times* (morning) and the *Chicago Tribune* (morning), of the weekly *The Reader,* and the monthly magazine *Chicago.* **Hot Tix** sells tickets at significantly reduced prices for all shows on the day of the performance. There are several locations in Chicago; one is at 108 N. State St. Call 977-1755 for a listing of Hot Tix locations and events to which tickets are currently available. Major credit cards accepted. Open Mon–Sat.

Apollo Theater Center, 2540 N. Lincoln Ave. (935-6100): Drama, comedy.

Arie Crown, McCormick Place (791-6000): Modern theater.
Auditorium Theatre, 50 E. Congress Pkwy. (922-2110): Concerts, recitals, ballet performances. Open year round.
Body Politic Theatre, 2261 N. Lincoln Ave. (871-3000): Drama, comedy, musicals, etc.
Chicago Theatre, 175 N. State St. (443-1130): Big-name concerts, Broadway hits.
Civic Opera House, 20 N. Wacker Dr. (346-4744): Home of the Lyric Opera of Chicago. Open Feb–June.
Goodman Theatre, 200 S. Columbus Dr. (443-3800): The oldest theater in Chicago, offering everything from Shakespeare to contemporary theater.
Merle Reskin Theatre, 60605 E. Balbo Ave. (362-8455): Broadway hits.
Orchestra Hall, 220 S. Michigan Ave. (435-6666): Home of the Chicago Civic Orchestra and of the Chicago Symphony Orchestra, one of the five best orchestras in the world (music director: Daniel Barenboim). Open Sept–May.
Petrillo Music Shell, Columbus Dr. and Jackson Blvd., in Grant Park (294-2420): Free outdoor concerts, late June to Aug.
Royal George Theatre, 1641 N. Halsted St. (988-9000): Broadway hits, modern theater.
Shubert Theatre, 22 W. Monroe St. (977-1710): Broadway hits and shows with big-name stars.
Steppenwolf North, 2851 N. Halsted St. (335-1650): Drama, classical theater. One of the best theater buildings of the Chicago School.
Victory Gardens Theatre, 2257 N. Lincoln Ave. (871-3000): Specializing in plays by local playwrights.

SHOPPING: ※ **Marshall Field & Co.,** 111 N. State St.: The most beautiful and most famous department store in Chicago. This almost 100-year-old classic of the consumer society has a superb Tiffany-windowed dome comprising 1.6 million pieces of colored glass. Wonderful ice-cream sundaes for lovers of giant desserts can be found on the third floor (in the Crystal Palace).

※ **Carson, Pirie, Scott & Co.,** 1 S. State St.: Another venerable representative of the local breed of department store and a sample of Chicago School architecture from the end of the 19th century, designed by Louis Sullivan. Splendid rococo entrance hall of ornamental cast metal.

※ **Magnificent Mile,** N. Michigan Ave. between Illinois and Oak Sts.: Chicago's swankiest thoroughfare, with fashion boutiques, art galleries, and such tony stores as Gucci, Burberry's, Saks Fifth Avenue, Neiman Marcus, Charles Jourdan, Louis Vuitton, Chanel, Armani, Bally, and more. This is the local counterpart of New York's Fifth Avenue or Rodeo Drive in Beverly Hills.

State Street, between Wacker Dr. and Congress Pkwy.: The main pedestrian and commercial street at the heart of the Loop. Boutiques and department stores by the dozen offer many a bargain.

※ **Water Tower Place,** 845 N. Michigan Ave.: The country's first "vertical" shopping center covering 2,140,000 sq. ft. (200,000m²), with more than 125 stores, boutiques, 11 restaurants, and seven movie theaters. The shopping area is on the first eight floors of this 74-story tower which houses the Ritz Carlton Hotel. Luxurious, very stylish interior with fountains, gardens, and glass elevators.

SPECIAL EVENTS: For the exact schedule of events below, consult the **Chicago Convention and Tourism Bureau** (see "Tourist Information," above).
Chicago Auto Show (Feb): The most popular auto show in the United States, with an attendance of nearly a million people.
St. Patrick's Day Parade (Mar 17): Pompoms, marching bands, and drum majorettes.

Ravinia Festival (June–Sept): One of the most popular music festivals in the United States, with open-air symphonic concerts, ballet, jazz, and folk music. Highland Park. Call 728-4642 for information.

Grant Park Music Festival (late June to Aug): Free open-air classical concerts, plus a very famous blues festival. For information, call 294-2200.

Taste of Chicago (June/July; date varies): The world's largest culinary festival: 3,000,000 participants. All kinds of food are available for a whole week in Grant Park (744-0573).

Chicago Mackinack Island Yacht Race (July): Boat races on Lake Michigan.

Venetian Night Festival (mid-Aug): Shows and concerts on the lakeshore.

Jazz Festival (Sept): With the greats—the world's largest free jazz festival.

International Film Festival (two weeks in late Oct or early Nov): A tribute to foreign cinema (644-3400).

SPORTS: Chicago has five professional teams:

Baseball (Apr–Oct): Cubs, Wrigley Field (404-2827); White Sox, Comiskey Park (924-1000).

Basketball (Oct–Apr): Bulls, Chicago Stadium (733-5300).

Football (Sept–Dec): Bears, Soldier Field/Grant Park (663-5100).

Ice Hockey (Sept–Apr): Black Hawks, Chicago Stadium (733-5300).

Horse Racing

Arlington International Racecourse, Euclid and Wilke, in Arlington Heights (708/255-4300): Dubbed the "Taj Mahal" of horse racing, this $200-million structure opened in 1989 features sky boxes, marble stairways, and 15 restaurants. Racing daily May–Sept.

Balmoral Park, Dixie Hwy. and Elmscourt Lane, in Crete (312/568-5700).

Hawthorne Park, 3501 S. Laramie Ave., in Cicero (708/780-3700).

Maywood Park, 8600 W. North Ave., in Maywood (708/343-4800): Racing Mon–Sat Feb–May and Oct–Dec.

Sportsman's Park, 3301 S. Laramie Ave., in Cicero (708/652-2812): Racing Feb–Oct.

STROLLS: ⚱ Chinatown, around S. Wentworth Ave. and W. Cermak Rd.: Picturesque Chinese quarter with numerous characteristic stores, restaurants, and guaranteed local color. See especially the ornamental gate built in 1975 at S. Wentworth Ave. at W. Cermak Rd., **City Hall,** the Buddhist temple, and the **Ling Long Museum.**

Gold Coast, Lake Shore Dr. between North Ave. and E. Ontario St.: The spectacular, luxurious face that Chicago presents to Lake Michigan, where skyscrapers about opulent 19th-century palaces and estates.

River North, north of the river and west of Michigan Ave.: Chicago's latest "in" neighborhood replete with trendy rests., galleries, and boutiques. Chicago's answer to New York's Soho.

The Loop, west of Michigan Ave. around State and Madison Sts.: Chicago's business district, complete with department stores, hotels, and restaurants, surrounded by the famous, clanking elevated train (the "El"). The heart of the Loop—the intersection of State and Madison Sts.—is nicknamed "the busiest corner in the world." City streets are oriented from this intersection: north-south in relation to Madison, east-west in relation to State. Animated and colorful by day, to be avoided at night if you're on foot.

Magnificent Mile, N. Michigan Ave. from the Chicago River to E. Oak St.: Lined with chic stores (see "Shopping," above), hotels, boutiques, art galleries, and prestigious buildings, it's one of the most elegant—and snooty—thoroughfares in the United States.

       ▲ **Old Town,** around N. Wells and Division Sts.: The "Latin
       ▲ Quarter" or the "Greenwich Village" of Chicago, with its brick
houses from the 19th century plus restaurants, nightclubs, antiques stores, and
fashionable boutiques. Very lively by night.

       ☼▲▲ **Prairie Ave. Historic District,** Prairie Ave. between 18th and
       ☼▲▲ Cullerton Sts.: The 19th-century millionaire's neighborhood,
currently undergoing renovation. Sumptuous private houses, cobblestone
streets, gas lamps.

       Glessner House, 1800 S. Prairie Ave, by Henry Hobson Richardson
(1886), and neighboring **Clark House,** the oldest house in Chicago (1837). The
Chicago Architectural Foundation organizes guided tours of these homes Fri–
Sun; call 922-3421 for information. Other homes that are not open to the public,
but should be noted: **Kimball House,** 1801 S. Prairie Ave., dates from 1890;
Coleman House, 1811 S. Prairie Ave., from 1886; **Keith House,** 1900 S. Prairie
Ave., from 1871.

THEME PARKS: ▲ **Six Flags Great America,** in Gurnee, 40 mi. (65km) north
on I-94 (708/249-1776): Enormous (200-acre/80ha) amusement park offering hundreds of attractions, with giant roller coasters. Facsimiles of pioneer villages plus shows and special events. Open daily from the end of May to early Sept,
wknds only in spring and autumn; closed the rest of the year.

WINTER SPORTS RESORTS: ▲ **Pines Ski Area** (64 mi./102km SE on I-90
and Ind. 49) (219/477-5993): 5 lifts. Open Dec–Mar.
       ▲ **Ski Valley** (66 mi./106km SE on I-90, U.S. 421, and Ind. 2)
       ▲ (219/326-0123): 5 rope tows. Open Dec–Feb.
       ▲ **Wilmot Ski Area** (54 mi./87km NW on U.S. 12, Ill. 59 and
       ▲ 83, and WI Country C) (414/862-2301): 14 lifts. Open daily
Nov–Mar.

ZOOS: ☼▲▲ **Brookfield Zoo,** entrances at 31st St. and First Ave. (15 mi./24km
SW on W. Cermak Rd., and 22nd St. and First Ave. (708/485-0263): One of
the top 10 zoos in the United States (192 acres/80ha). Natural habitats from the
Sahara Desert to tropical forests and from South America to the Pacific Islands.
Mini-train tour (Mar–Nov). Open daily year round.

ACCOMMODATIONS

Personal Favorites (in order of preference)
       ♟♟♟♟ **The Drake** (nr. dwntwn), 140 E. Walton Place, IL 60611
       ♟♟♟♟ (312/787-2200; toll free, see Hilton). 535 rms, A/C, color
TV in-rm movies. AE, CB, DC, MC, V. Valet gar. $22, two rests. (including the
Cape Cod Room), two bars, 24-hr. rm svce, hrdrsr, boutiques, concierge, free
crib. *Note:* A local institution in the shadow of the John Hancock Center. Here,
all is tranquility, luxury, and pleasure. Spacious rms (the best have a view of the
lake) and an elegant, refined interior w. an imposing marble lobby, grand staircase, and ultra-fashionable tea rm. The flawless svce and reception includes attention to such details as shoeshine and turn-down svce. Its class and style make this
the best hotel in Chicago and one of the 12 best in the United States; its Cape
Cod Room is also one of the city's finest rests. A business clientele and traveling
VIPs enjoy its exceptional location, facing Lake Michigan and a few steps from
the Magnificent Mile (see "Strolls," above). VIP floor. One of the gems of the
Vista International group. Interesting wknd packages. The Drake recently underwent renovation down to the last detail. The best address in Chicago since
1920. **VE**

       ♟♟♟♟ **Four Seasons** (nr. dwntwn), 120 E. Delaware Place, IL 60611
       ♟♟♟♟ (312/280-8800; toll free, see Four Seasons). 343 rms, A/C,
color TV, in-rm movies. AE, CB, DC, MC, V. Valet gar. $20, pool, health club,

sauna, rest. (Seasons), bar, 24-hr. rm svce, boutiques, concierge, free crib. *Note:* Opened in 1989, the Four Seasons is one of the newest of Chicago's luxury palace hotels, occupying Floors 30–46 of a flamboyant 66-floor Neo-Gothic highrise right on the Magnificent Mile. Spacious, elegant rms w. fine view of lake or city; unmatched comfort and facilities; absolutely top-flight svce. Direct access to the Avenue Atrium, a vertical shopping mall with dozens of boutiques and smart shops. A prestige address. **VE**

    🛎🛎🛎 **Swissotel Chicago** (nr. dwntwn), 323 E. Wacker Dr., IL 60601 (312/565-0565; toll free 800/637-9477). 645 rms, A/C, color TV, in-rm movies. AE, CB, DC, MC, V. Garage $18, pool, health club, sauna, rest. (Café Swiss), coffee shop, bar, 24-hr. rm svce, concierge. *Note:* This shimmering triangular building, its 45 floors looking out over Lake Michigan, was opened in 1988—the first hotel built in the U.S. by Swissotel, a subsidiary of Swissair. Very comfortable rms, each w. minibar and two phone lines. Unusually thoughtful facilities for the business traveler, including a TV studio! Svce in the best tradition of Swiss hotels; high-class rest. A favorite w. those in-the-know. **VE**

    🛎🛎🛎 **Embassy Suites Hotel** (nr. dwntwn), 600 N. State St., IL 60610 (312/943-3800; toll free 800/362-2779). 358 suites, A/C, color TV, in-rm movies. AE, CB, DC, MC, V. Gar. $18, pool, health club, sauna, rest., bar, rm svce, concierge, free newspaper, free breakfast, free evening cocktails, free crib. *Note:* Brand-new all-suite hotel three blocks from the Magnificent Mile. The property provides guests w. the chain's standard perks, along w. numerous business amenities such as in-rm modems, meeting rms, photocopy svce, etc. Up-to-date comfort and equipment. Highly professional svce. Executive and Presidential Suites available. Big business clientele. Excellent location nr. the business and financial center. **E–VE**

    ☀🛎🛎 **Raphael** (nr. dwntwn), 201 E. Delaware Place, IL 60611 (312/943-5000; toll free 800/821-5343). 172 rms, A/C, color TV. AE, CB, DC, MC, V. Valet gar. $19, rest., bar, 24-hr. rm svce, nightclub, free crib. *Note:* Small, calm, elegant hotel very close to the Magnificent Mile. Large, comfortable rms w. minibars offer lovely views of the Gold Coast. Polished svce. Interesting wknd packages. Good value overall. **M–E**

    🛎🛎 **Courtyard Hotel** (nr. dwntwn), 30 E. Hubbard St., IL 60611 (312/329-2500; toll free 800/321-2211). 336 rms, A/C, color TV, in-rm movies. AE, CB, DC, MC, V. Parking $9, pool, health club, rest. (30 East Bistro), bar, free crib. *Note:* Brand-new 15-story hotel in the River North District, within walking distance of the Magnificent Mile. Large, comfortable guest rms w. separate sitting area, working desk, and in-rm coffee and tea svce. Efficient staff and reception. Business clientele. A good overall value. **M–E**

    🛎🛎 **Best Western Inn of Chicago** (formerly the St. Clair Hotel; nr. dwntwn), 162 E. Ohio St., IL 60611 (312/787-3100; toll free, see Best Western). 357 rms, A/C, color TV, in-rm movies. AE, CB, DC, MC, V. Parking $11, coffee shop, bar, rm svce. *Note:* Old luxury hotel entirely modernized w. marble lobby and very comfortable rms. Good svce and a very central location close to the Magnificent Mile. A favorite of businesspeople. Interesting wknd packages. **M–E**

    🛎 **Comfort Inn** (nr. dwntwn), 601 W. Diversey Pkwy., IL 60614 (312/348-2810; toll free, see Choice). 73 rms, A/C, cable color TV. AE, CB, DC, MC, V. Street parking; no bar or rest., but free breakfast. *Note:* Small, modern, and comfortable motel very nr. the Lincoln Park Zoo w. spacious rms and friendly, pleasant reception. Good value. **I–M**

Other Accommodations (from top bracket to budget)

    🛎🛎🛎🛎 **Inter-Continental** (nr. dwntwn), 505 N. Michigan Ave., IL 60611 (312/944-4100; toll free, see Inter-Continental). 840 rms, A/C, color TV, in-rm movies. AE, CB, DC, MC, V. Parking $20, pool, health club, sauna, two rests. (including The Boulevard), bar, 24-hr. rm svce, concierge, free crib. *Note:* Originally built in 1929 as the Medinah Athletic Club, this authentic architectural jewel, 42 stories tall, was transformed in 1990 into a luxury hotel w. a museumlike quality setting, notably the fabulous Roman-spa-style pool and the palatial hall of the lions. Spacious rms decorated in European idiom, some w. spectacular views. Ultra-polished svce. Rest. so-so. **VE**

♙♙♙♙ **Nikko Hotel** (nr. dwntwn), 320 N. Dearborn St., IL 60610 (312/744-1900; toll free 800/645-5687). 425 rms, A/C, color TV, in-rm movies. AE, CB, DC, MC, V. Valet gar. $21, health club, two rests. (including Celebrity Café), coffee shop, bars, 24-hr. rm svce, concierge, free crib. *Note:* Big, ultramodern 20-floor tower overlooking the Chicago River, and affording great daytime and romantic nighttime views of both the river and the Loop. Spacious, comfortable Western-style rms w. marble bathroom and minibar, or Japanese rms with tatami mats. Uncommonly effective soundproofing; efficient, smiling svce. Delightful Japanese grdn, and the well-regarded Japanese rest. (Benkay) looks out on the river. American and Japanese business clientele. Four floors ("Nikko floors") reserved for VIPs. **VE**

♙♙♙ **Hyatt Regency** (nr. dwntwn), 151 E. Wacker Dr., IL 60601 (312/565-1234; toll free, see Hyatt). 2,020 rms, A/C, color TV, in-rm movies. AE, CB, DC, MC, V. V. Gar. $19, health club, sauna, two rests. (including Stetson's), coffee shop, bar, 24-hr. rm svce, hrdrsr, boutiques, free crib. *Note:* Luxurious and comfortable rms in two adj. towers of 34 and 36 stories, of modern design. The spectacular glass atrium w. pool and interior grdns on four floors is worth a look. Efficient, if impersonal, svce. One of the best locations in Chicago, on the Chicago River. Business clientele. VIP floor. Interesting wknd packages. Recently renovated decor. **VE**

♙♙♙ **Tremont** (nr. dwntwn), 100 E. Chestnut, IL 60611 (312/751-1900; toll free 800/223-5560). 127 rms, A/C, cable color TV. AE, CB, DC, MC, V. Valet gar. $20, rest. (Cricket's), bar, rm svce, concierge, free crib. *Note:* A hotel known for its excellence for more than half a century. Period furnishings and chandeliers; spacious, comfortable rms. Very British in style; notably good svce. The highly praised rest. is a pale copy of New York's 21 Club. Clientele of well-heeled regulars. **VE**

♙♙♙ **Chicago Hilton & Towers** (formerly the Conrad Hilton; dwntwn), 720 S. Michigan Ave., IL 60605 (312/922-4400; toll free, see Hilton). 1,543 rms, A/C, color TV, in-rm movies. AE, CB, DC, MC, V. Gar. $16, pool, health club, sauna, three rests. (including Buckingham's), coffee shop, two bars, rm svce, hrdrsr, boutiques, concierge, free crib. *Note:* Sturdy pioneer of the production-line hotel, restored to all its original splendor at a cost of $180 million. Heavy, forbidding architecture but a luxurious interior, especially the great lobby w. its imposing staircase and the Versailles-style ballroom. Spacious, comfortable rms, the most pleasant of which have a view of Grant Park. Slightly overburdened svce. Convention and other groups. Three VIP floors and the most expensive suite in Chicago, at $4,000 a night. Good rest. w. modern American cuisine (Buckingham's). Well-equipped business center. Fine location next to the Loop. **E–VE**

♙♙ **Knickerbocker** (nr. dwntwn), 163 E. Walton Place, IL 60611 (312/751-8100; toll free 800/621-8140). 256 rms, A/C, color TV, in-rm movies. AE, CB, DC, MC, V. Valet gar. $20, rest. (Prince of Wales), coffee shop, bar, rm svce, concierge, free crib. *Note:* A landmark among Chicago's hotels since 1927, entirely renovated in 1983. Exceptionally spacious rms, half w. two bathrooms. The lobby, public rms, and rest. have been restored to their original splendor. Very good svce. Well located halfway between the lake and the Magnificent Mile. **E–VE**

♙♙ **Omni Ambassador East** (nr. dwntwn), 1301 N. State Pkwy., IL 60610 (312/787-7200; toll free, see Omni). 274 rms, A/C, color TV, in-rm movies. AE, CB, DC, MC, V. Gar. $17, rest. (The Pump Room), bar, 24-hr. rm svce, boutiques, concierge, free crib. *Note:* Old-world charm, elegance, and comfort in a historic landmark building. Frequented by celebrities since 1926 (Humphrey Bogart and Lauren Bacall spent their honeymoon here). Very fine svce. Mediocre and overpriced rest. Total absence of exercise facilities. Recently renovated. Very close to Old Town and its nightlife. **E–VE**

    The Midland Hotel (dwntwn), 172 W. Adams St., IL 60603 (312/332-1200; toll free 800/621-2360). 260 rms, A/C, color TV, in-rm movies. AE, CB, DC, MC, V. Gar. $13, health club, two rests. (including The Exchange), bar, rm svce, concierge, hrdrsr, complimentary buffet breakfast and cocktails, free taxi svce, free crib. *Note:* Once an exclusive men's club, the building dates back to 1929. Designed in the Beaux Arts style, the lobby features a gold-leaf ceiling and vaulted arches. Thoughtful svce (down to the chocolate cookie left at bedside each night) in a carefully restored setting. Bar nicely fashioned in an art deco style recalling 1920s Paris. Two VIP floors. Convenient location. Interesting wknd packages. **E–VE**

    Claridge Hotel (nr. dwntwn), 1244 N. Dearborn St., IL 60610 (312/787-4980; toll free 800/245-1258). 175 rms, A/C, color TV, in-rm movies. AE, CB, DC, MC, V. Gar. $15, rest., bar, rm svce, free breakfast and daily paper, free crib. *Note:* Engaging older hotel, entirely renovated. Comfortable, intimate setting; inviting, well-laid-out rms w. minibar; efficient svce. A good value overall; many guests are regulars. Very nr. the Old Town and the Magnificent Mile. **M–E**

    Holiday Inn Mart Plaza (nr. dwntwn), 350 N. Orleans St., IL 60654 (312/836-5000; toll free, see Holiday Inns). 525 rms, A/C, color TV, in-rm movies. AE, CB, DC, MC, V. Parking $12, pool, health club, rest., bar, rm svce, hrdrsr, boutiques, free crib. *Note:* This modern and comfortable convention hotel occupies the top eight floors of the Apparel Center Building and faces the Merchandise Mart. Comfort and amenities above the norm for a Holiday Inn. Excellent location quite close to the Loop. Business clientele. Very nice view of the city from most rms. Unsafe neighborhood at night; take a cab. **M–E**

    Blackstone (dwntwn), 636 S. Michigan Ave., IL 60605 (312/427-4300). 307 rms, A/C, color TV. AE, CB, DC, MC, V. Adj. parking lot $16, rest., bar, nightclub, free crib. *Note:* A turn-of-the-century hotel facing Grant Park and Buckingham Fountain. Comfortable, but could use a facelift. Mediocre svce. Interesting family rates. Marble lobby landmark. **M–E**

    Allerton Hotel (nr. dwntwn), 701 N. Michigan Ave., IL 60611 (312/440-1500; toll free 800/621-8311). 450 rms, A/C, color TV. AE, CB, DC, MC, V. Adjacent valet parking lot, rest. (Avenue Café), bar, rm svce, hrdrsr. *Note:* A veteran of the 1920s in the heart of the Magnificent Mile, w. renovated rms and amenities. Still has lots of charm, even if the svce doesn't always measure up. Highly recommendable rest. Interesting wknd packages. Overall, a good value. **M**

    Bismarck Hotel (dwntwn), 171 W. Randolph St., IL 60601 (312/236-0123; toll free 800/643-1500). 515 rms, A/C, color TV. AE, CB, DC, MC, V. Valet parking $17, two rests. (including the Chalet Room), coffee shop, bar, rm svce, hrdrsr, free crib. *Note:* Located right in the heart of the Loop, this Chicago classic still retains much of its beauty. Entirely renovated decor and rm amenities. The svce leaves something to be desired but the rest. is still a favorite of local politicians. Rather obtrusive convention and other groups. Neighborhood unsafe at night; take a taxi. **M**

    Essex Inn (nr. dwntwn), 800 S. Michigan Ave., IL 60605 (312/939-2800; toll free 800/621-6909). 255 rms, A/C, cable color TV. AE, CB, DC, MC, V. Valet parking $9, pool, sauna, rest., bar, rm svce, free crib, free shuttle to and from the Loop. *Note:* Pleasant, recently restored hotel nr. dwntwn. Comfortable rms w. minibars. Efficient svce. Good value. Ideal location for museum visits. **M**

Ramada on-the-Lake (formerly HoJo Inn; nr. dwntwn), 4900 S. Lake Shore Dr., IL (312/288-5800; toll free, see Ramada). 300 rms, A/C, color TV, in-rm movies. AE, CB, DC, MC, V. Free parking, pool, rest., bar, rm svce, free crib, free shuttle to and from dwntwn. *Note:* Relatively modern and functional motel 10 min. from the Loop. Efficient reception and svce. Ideal for drivers. **I–M**

Oxford House (dwntwn), 225 N. Wabash Ave., IL 60601 (312/346-6585; toll free 800/344-4111). 175 rms, A/C, color TV. AE, MC, V. Parking $8, rest. (Café Angelo), bar, rm svce. *Note:* Oldish but newly renovated hotel, conveniently located just steps away from the Loop and the Magnificent Mile. Inviting rms w. wet bars. Good value overall. Friendly svce. **I–M**

Quality Inn Downtown (formerly the Holiday Inn; nr. dwntwn), 1 Mid City Place, IL 60606 (312/829-5000; toll free, see Choice). 405 rms, A/C, color TV, in-rm movies. AE, CB, DC, MC, V. Parking $7, pool, rest., bar, rm svce. *Note:* Modern 17-story motel nr. Union Station. Comfortable rms w. balconies. Uneven svce. Direct access to the highway network makes it an ideal location if you're driving. Interesting wknd packages. **I–M**

Avenue Motel (nr. dwntwn), 1154 S. Michigan Ave., IL 60605 (312/427-8200; toll free 800/621-4196). 78 rms, A/C, color TV. AE, CB, DC, MC, V. Free parking, rest., bar. *Note:* Conventional but well-maintained motel located close to the Field Museum. Overall, a good value. **I**

Ohio House (nr. dwntwn), 600 N. La Salle St., IL 60610 (312/943-6000). 50 rms, A/C, color TV. AE, CB, DC, MC, V. Free parking, adj. coffee shop. *Note:* Small, convenient motel close to the Merchandise Mart. No-frills comfort and a good value for those on a budget. Neighborhood unsafe at night; take a taxi. **I**

Surf Hotel (nr. dwntwn), 555 W. Surf St., IL 60657 (312/528-8400). 60 rms, A/C, color TV. AE, CB, DC, MC, V. Pay parking available, health-club privileges, bars and rest. nearby. *Note:* No-frills small hotel in the heart of Lincoln Park, two blocks from the lakefront. Clean, well-maintained rms at very reasonable prices. Quaint atmosphere. Ideal for shoe-string travelers. **I**

Airport Accommodations

Hyatt Regency O'Hare (vic.), 9300 Bryn Mawr Rd., Rosemont, IL 60018 (708/696-1234; toll free, see Hyatt). 1,100 rms, A/C, color TV, in-rm movies. AE, CB, DC, MC, V. Valet parking $15, pool, health club, sauna, four rests. (including Ventanas), bar, 24-hr. rm svce, disco, hrdrsr, free crib. *Note:* Huge, modern 12-story airport hotel, 8 min. from O'Hare (free shuttle). Comfortable, well-soundproofed rms and efficient svce. Business and group clientele. So-so rests. **E–VE**

Holiday Inn Midway (vic., 15 min. from dwntwn), 7353 S. Cicero Ave., IL 60629 (312/581-5300; toll free, see Holiday Inns). 161 rms, A/C, cable color TV. AE, CB, DC, MC, V. Free parking, pool, rest., bar, rm svce, disco, free crib, free shuttle to and from Midway Airport. *Note:* Classic airport motel in the Holiday Inn style, offering no-frills comfort and facilities. **I–M**

YMCAs/Youth Hostels

International House–AYH (nr. dwntwn), 1414 E. 59th St., IL 60637 (312/753-2270). Youth hostel. 500 rms. Generally packed during the school year; easier to get into in the summer.

YMCA (nr. dwntwn), 30 W. Chicago Ave., IL 60610 (312/944-6211). 500 rms, pool, health club. For men and women.

RESTAURANTS

Personal Favorites (in order of preference)

☀️�♈♈♈♈ **Everest Room** (dwntwn), 440 S. La Salle St. (663-8920). A/C. Dinner only, Tues–Sat; closed hols. AE, DC, MC, V. *Specialties:* green-almond soup w. beluga caviar, lobster lasagne, hog jowl w. green lentils and foie gras, filet of halibut in potato crust, venison w. tiny dumplings, seafood sausage, wild salmon w. prosciutto and cabbage, poppy-seed crêpe w. sweet cheese soufflé, chocolate fantasy. Broad and intelligently chosen wine list. *Note:* As the name implies, the Everest Room commands a breathtaking view of the city from the 40th floor of the Midwest Stock Exchange skyscraper. The fancy and delicate cuisine of Alsatian master chef Jean Joho is up to the setting. Two-level art deco dining rm w. crystal chandeliers, marble stairs, and expanses of mirrors. Efficient and knowledgeable svce. Resv. mandatory. One of the dozen best rests. in the country. Free valet parking. *French.* **E–VE**

♈♈♈ **Charlie Trotter's** (nr. dwntwn), 816 W. Armitage Ave. (248-6228). A/C. Dinner only, Tues–Sat; closed hols. AE, CB, DC, MC, V. Jkt. *Specialties:* foie gras and mango ravioli, soft-shell crabs w. curry cream, roast saddle of lamb w. turnips and foie gras, sweetbreads w. pancetta and coriander butter, venison médaillons w. hazelnut flan and truffled mascarpone, liquid-center bittersweet chocolate cake. Menu changes daily. Judiciously selected wine list at decent prices. *Note:* The "most innovative and imaginative" modern-cuisine rest. in town serving vegetarian or regular degustation menus. Expect the unexpected from the creations of chef-owner Charles Trotter, who came down w. a serious attack of "nouvelle cuisine-itis" after taking his degree in political science at the U. of Wisconsin. The rest. is in an agreeably restored turn-of-the-century house; reception and svce are somewhat on the haughty side. Since this is an "in" place, make resv. several days ahead. Valet parking $5. *American.* **VE** (prix fixe).

♈♈♈ **Spiaggia** (nr. dwntwn), 980 N. Michigan Ave. (280-2750). A/C. Lunch Mon–Sat, dinner nightly; closed hols. AE, CB, DC, MC, V. Jkt. *Specialties:* pizza w. duck sausage and goat cheese, steamed mussels w. garlic-tomato broth, grilled sea scallops w. Belgian endives and lemon dressing, red snapper in crazy water, wood-roasted veal chop in smoked pancetta w. vodka-cream sauce, mascarpone cheese torte w. espresso sauce. Fine Italian wine list. *Note:* Located in the mezzanine of the sparkling One Magnificent Mile Building over Lake Michigan, Spiaggia has rapidly become the best Italian rest. in Chicago. Northern Italian cuisine, modern and sophisticated, by chef Paul Bartolotta. The svce is very able and the postmodern décor a model of elegance. Resv. necessary. *Italian.* **M–E**

♈♈♈ **Carlos'** (vic.) 429 Temple Ave., Highland Park (708/432-0770). A/C. Dinner only, Wed–Mon; closed hols. AE, CB, DC, MC, V. Jkt. *Specialties:* roasted sea scallops w. balsamic vinegar, ravioli of squab meat w. mild garlic sauce, grilled duckling w. braised cabbage, sautéed Atlantic salmon w. miso jus, fresh fruit tart w. two sauces. The wine list is vast and costly. *Note:* Carlos and Deborah Nieto's restaurant is as gracious and welcoming as ever. Small, changing menu of nouvelle cuisine dishes and elaborate desserts. Book ahead, since there are only 60 seats—ask for an upstairs table. Svce prompt and efficient. Resv. recommended. *French.* **E–VE**

♈♈♈ **Jackie's** (nr. dwntwn), 2478 N. Lincoln Ave. (880-0003). A/C. Lunch/dinner Tues–Sat; closed hols. AE, CB, DC, MC, V. Jkt. *Specialties:* sautéed wontons of snails w. ginger-butter sauce, fish trilogy (fish of the day over a crab cake w. avocado and a Szechuan pepper and lemon butter sauce), loin of venison w. kielbasa sausage and buffalo steak in a truffle sauce, chocolate sack w. white-chocolate mousse and fresh fruit. Reasonable wine list. *Note:* The French training and Chinese roots of chef Jackie Shen make her cooking an exciting and complex feast for the palate and eyes. Intimate (17 tables) and elegant atmosphere. Well-trained and informed svce. Resv. required. A very fine place. *Continental.* **M–E**

☖☖☖ **Topolobampo** (nr. dwntwn), 445 N. Clark St. (661-1434). A/C. Lunch Tues–Fri, dinner Tues–Sat. AE, CB, DC, MC, V. *Specialties:* game tamales, sopa Azteca, roast pork loin w. red-chili apricot sauce and pumpkin purée, Oaxacan-style capon breast steamed in banana leaves, tart of pine nuts w. brandied chocolate sauce. The menu changes every other week. *Note:* This stylish dining rm, highlighted by Mexican art, is the new and successful venture of Rick and Deann Bayless (of Frontera Grill fame). The fare is somewhat more refined and expensive, the atmosphere a bit more formal and gracious. Svce may be slow. Due to its success, you must wait even w. a resv. *Mexican.* **M–E**

☖☖ **Prairie** (dwntwn), in the Hyatt on Printers Row, 500 S. Dearborn St. (663-1143). A/C. Breakfast/lunch/dinner daily. AE, CB, DC, MC, V. *Specialties:* smoked waterfish terrine w. horseradish mayonnaise, baked walleye pike stuffed w. wild rice, buffalo steak w. roasted-shallot sauce, hot-fudge sundae. Seasonal menu. *Note:* Amid a setting inspired by Frank Lloyd Wright's "Prairie" designs, chef Stephen Langlois turns out a lightened version of hearty midwestern fare w. family-style vegetables—good mashed potatoes—and homespun desserts. Interesting five-course tasting menu. Svce can be slow. Resv. advised. An original experience. *American.* **M**

☼☖☖ **Berghoff** (dwntwn), 17 W. Adams St. (427-3170). A/C. Lunch/dinner Mon–Sat (until 9:30pm); closed hols. AE, DC, MC, V. *Specialties:* Bismarck herring, wienerschnitzel, ragoût à la Deutsch, Kassler rippchen (smoked pork), sauerbraten, roast goose, whitefish, lavish desserts. Draft beer from Munich plus a good wine list. *Note:* A Chicago classic since 1898, when it opened as a simple saloon. Authentic German paneling, decor, and cuisine offering efficient svce and generous portions. Often packed and noisy. Resv. for parties of six or more. Svce somewhat abrupt. Excellent value. *German.* **I**

☖☖ **Bossa Nova** (nr. dwntwn), 1960 N. Clybourn St. (248-4800). A/C. Dinner only, nightly; closed hols. AE, CB, DC, MC, V. *Specialties:* sesame-crusted tuna medallion, "ribs from hell" w. honey-barbecue, grilled Jamaican jerk chicken, roast chicken breast w. rosemary and garlic, steamed Chinese dumplings w. hot chili oil and sweet/sour sauce; chocolate fettuccine. *Note:* Tapas (more than 60) are the mainstay at this snappy new rest. featuring potent Latin and Caribbean cocktails that go down well w. the live world beat music. Very lively crowd in an ultra-casual atmosphere. A great time to be had here. Resv. highly advised. *Spanish/American.* **B–I**

☼☖ **Carson's, The Place for Ribs** (nr. dwntwn), 612 N. Wells St. (280-9200). A/C. Lunch/dinner daily (until 11:30pm). AE, CB, DC, MC, V. *Specialties:* spareribs, New York sirloin steak, barbecued chicken, potatoes au gratin, ice-cream sundaes. *Note:* A true local institution, which expert opinion credits w. the Midwest's best ribs. The barbecued pork in its sweet but pungent sauce literally melts in the mouth. Also excellent beef. Generous servings in a comfortable, masculine setting; good svce; no resv., so you may have a long wait. Other location: 8617 Niles Center Rd., Skokie (708/675-6800). *American.* **B–I**

Other Restaurants (from top bracket to budget)

☖☖☖ **Ambria** (nr. dwntwn), 2300 N. Lincoln Park W. (472-5959). A/C. Dinner only, Mon–Sat; closed hols. AE, DC, MC, V. Jkt. *Specialties:* lobster gazpacho w. basil, foie gras sauté vinaigrette, salmon tartar w. caviar, pistachio sweetbreads, gâteau d'escargots in beurre blanc, turbot in Oriental sauce, sautéed duck w. wild rice, hare filet w. pears. Apple and crème-caramel cake. *Note:* A must for all lovers of remarkable eating experiences. The "tasting/sampling" menu (must be ordered 24 hr. in advance) is a festival of modern culinary elegance, signed by Gabino Satelino, the excellent Basque chef. Rather depressing paneled decor, insufficiently relieved by touches of art nouveau. Diligent if sometimes disorganized svce. Resv. should be made several days in advance. Valet parking ($4). *French.* **E–VE** (prix fixe).

♔♔♔ **Benkay** (nr. dwntwn), in the Nikko Hotel (see "Accommodations," above) (836-5490). A/C. Breakfast/lunch/dinner Tues–Sat. AE, CB, DC, MC, V. Jkt. *Specialties:* miso soup, sushi, tempura, teppanyaki, kaiseki (multicourse gourmet dinner). *Note:* Stunning Japanese palace complete w. tatami rms, lovely grdns, giant living bamboo stalks, and spectacular river views. The refined Japanese fare, the exquisite table settings and ceremonious svce justify the tab. American and Japanese big business clientele. Resv. advised (at least a day ahead for the kaiseki dinner). Valet parking. *Japanese.* **M–E** (**VE** kaiseki dinner).

♔♔♔ **Jimmy's Place** (nr. dwntwn), 3420 N. Elston St. (539-2999). A/C. Lunch Mon–Fri, dinner Mon–Sat; closed hols. CB, DC, MC, V. Jkt. *Specialties:* tuna tartar, fried snails w. sliced plantain and lemon-mango salsa, catch of the day, sautéed sweetbread w. lentil purée and truffle oil, veal medallions w. wild mushrooms and sweet-pea risotto, coconut-banana crème brûlée. Menu changes every six months. List of expensive French and Californian wines. *Note:* Here, the commanding theme is owner Jimmy Rohr's first love: opera. Posters and photos of operatic scenes hang from the walls and arias lilt from the sound system in the wide-open dining space, from where you can observe chef Kevin Shikami at work in the glass-encased kitchen. Dishes executed w. finesse and skill. A favorite among locals. Best value is the $45 prix-fixe menu. Resv. highly recommended. Ample free parking. *French.* **M–E**

♔♔♔ **Yoshi's Café** (nr. dwntwn), 3257 N. Halsted St. (248-6160). A/C. Dinner only, Tues–Sun. AE, CB, DC, MC, V. Jkt. *Specialties:* tuna tartar w. guacamole; portobello mushroom pizza; veal medallion in caramelized ginger; mixed grill of tuna, salmon, and bass w. three sauces; roulade of lamb and artichokes. The menu changes regularly. Remarkable desserts (notably the green-tea ice cream). *Note:* Japanese variations on the nouvelle cuisine theme by a culinary virtuoso, Yoshi Katsumura. Inventive, refined cuisine at reasonable prices. Charming modern-art decor. Resv. highly advised, given the limited seating (48 places) and the success of this fashionable bistro. *Continental.* **M–E**

♔♔♔ **Arun's** (nr. dwntwn), 4156 N. Kedzie Ave. (539-1909). A/C. Dinner only, Mon–Sat; closed hols. AE, CB, DC, MC, V. *Specialties:* soft crêpes w. shrimp, daikon, and peanuts; fried fish dumplings; larb moo yang (salad of diced grilled pork); "seafood pyramid" (split prawns, seared whitefish, and sea scallops w. saffron and sawleaf-jalapeño sauces); veal medallions w. a ginger, miso, and lemongrass sauce; Thai custards. *Note:* Endowed w. ornate Thai artwork, this Thai rest. is one of Chicago's most enchanting. Very much inspired by French cuisine, the dishes are decorative and finely textured. Huge selection of wonderful appetizers. Impeccable svce. Resv. a must. *Thai.* **M–E**

♔♔ **Nick's Fishmarket** (nr. dwntwn), Dearborn and Monroe Sts. (621-0200). A/C. Lunch Mon–Fri, dinner Mon–Sat; closed hols. AE, CB, DC, MC, V. Jkt. *Specialties:* raw shellfish, fried calamari, ungaretti stew (seafood stew), fresh salmon, abalone, mahimahi (dolphin à la Hawaiian), crab legs, sautéed scallops, all kinds of fish and shellfish. High-priced wine list, long on whites. *Note:* Excellent seafood rest. in an elegant, intimate setting, complete w. private booths. Sister rest. of the famous Nick's Fishmarket in Honolulu. Impeccable svce. Resv. advised. Valet parking ($5). *Seafood.* **M–E**

☼♔ **Eli's, The Place for Steak** (nr. dwntwn), 215 E. Chicago Ave. (642-1393). A/C. Lunch/dinner daily; closed hols. and mid-Dec to Jan. AE, CB, DC, MC, V. Jkt. *Specialties:* very fine meats (as the name indicates), calves' liver w. onions, and the best cheesecake in Chicago. *Note:* A favorite of local journalists and politicians as well as visiting celebrities. Rather cramped and noisy but comfortable; highest-quality svce. Resv. advised. Very popular piano bar. Valet parking ($5). *Steak.* **M**

♈ **Vivere** (dwntwn), 71 W. Monroe St., in the Italian Village complex (332-4040). A/C. Lunch Mon–Fri, dinner Mon–Sat; closed hols. AE, CB, DC, MC, V. *Specialties:* tortelli di ricotta, sea scallops w. arugula, fish "ai Ferri," grilled veal tenderloin w. porcini mushrooms, bistecca fiorentina w. Tuscan white beans, panna cotta w. caramel sauce. Fabulous wine list. *Note:* Funny, baroque, postmodern *trattoria* inside the venerable old Italian Village. Innovative regional Italian fare by talented chef Peter Schonman. Noisy atmosphere. Good-natured service. *Italian.* **M**

☼♈ **Frontera Grill** (nr. dwntwn), 445 N. Clark St. (661-1434). A/C. Lunch/dinner Tues–Sat. AE, CB, DC, MC, V. Jkt. *Specialties:* shrimp-stuffed avocados w. garlic and lime, tacos al carbón, grilled guinea hen w. garlic, ceviche, stuffed green peppers with chili-and-tomato sauce, roast turkey w. red mole, grilled lamb chop, fried plantains w. homemade sour cream. *Note:* The young and talented Rick Bayless is an American chef who's crazy about Mexican food, having lived and traveled south of the Rio Grande for many years. His rather elaborate cuisine is totally authentic and delicious. The decor is pleasantly rustic and the svce friendly. Has enjoyed much success since its 1987 opening. No resv. taken. Expect a long wait after 7pm. *Mexican.* **I–M**

♈ **Hatsuhana** (nr. dwntwn), 160 E. Ontario St. (280-8287). A/C. Lunch Mon–Fri, dinner Mon–Sat; closed hols. AE, CB, DC, MC, V. Jkt. *Specialties:* sushi, sashimi, tempura, teriyaki. *Note:* Excellent authentic Japanese rest. in a modern, immaculate setting. Svce sometimes disorganized. American and Japanese business clientele. The dexterity w. which the chefs handle their knives is a sight in itself. *Japanese.* **I–M**

☼♈ **Shaw's Crab House** (nr. dwntwn), 21 E. Hubbard St. (527-2722). A/C. Lunch Mon–Fri, dinner nightly; closed Thanksgiving, Dec 25. AE, CB, DC, MC, V. *Specialties:* stone crabs and soft-shell crabs (in season), crab cakes, Dungeness crabmeat, sautéed frog legs, garlic chicken, broiled fish, key lime pie, crème brûlée. Skimpy but fairly priced wine list. *Note:* Enormously popular seafood rest. in a redecorated former newspaper warehouse. Mildly nostalgic setting and atmosphere right out of the 1930s. The impeccably fresh fish and seafood are attractively priced, the svce efficient, the value very good. *Seafood.* **I–M**

♈ **Tuttaposto** (nr. dwntwn), 646 N. Franklin St. (943-6262). A/C. Lunch Mon–Fri, dinner nightly. AE, CB, DC, MC, V. *Specialties:* black-olive and goat-cheese pizza, corzetti w. pesto sauce, carpaccio, Moroccan-style grilled fish, cataplana, sherbets. *Note:* A convivial Mediterranean place bringing French, Italian, Greek, and Moroccan cooking into happy coexistence. The fare is earthy, honest, tasty, and reasonably priced. Industrial beam-and-brick look w. some colorful touches. Quick and enthusiastic svce. A fine place. *Mediterranean.* **I–M**

♈ **The Marc** (nr. dwntwn), 311 W. Superior St. (642-3810). A/C. Lunch/dinner Mon–Sat; closed hols. AE, DC, MC, V. *Specialties:* goat-cheese ravioli w. tomato water, roasted garlic risotto w. langoustines and white truffle oil, Napoleon of striped bass w. champagne vinaigrette, roasted rack of lamb w. pommery mustard jus, warm flourless chocolate cake. *Note:* Wood-strewn space allowing no pretension to get in the way of enjoying your meal and having a good time. Andrew Marc Rothschild serves up deftly done constructions. Features a five-course tasting menu. Live jazz on the weekends, a time when the place gets hopping. Resv. advised. *Continental.* **I–M**

☼♈ **Café Ba-Ba-Reeba** (nr. dwntwn), 2024 N. Halsted St. (935-5000). A/C. Lunch Tues–Sat, dinner nightly; closed hols. AE, CB, DC, MC, V. *Specialties:* tapas (Spanish hot and cold hors d'oeuvres), paella, broiled calamari w. lemon and garlic, peppercorn-wrapped beef brochette w. garlic-potato salad and baked goat cheese. Huge selection of sherries. *Note:* Chalk up another triumph for Rich Melman, owner of the successful Lettuce Entertain You restaurant chain. The best tapas in Chicago, and very praiseworthy Spanish regional cooking. As noisy and relaxed as a typical rest. in Madrid, w. droll, festive decor and bemuraled grdn. Helpful, smiling svce. Very popular locally; an excellent place. *Spanish.* I

 ♈ **Casbah** (nr. dwntwn), 514 W. Diversey Pkwy. (935-7570). A/C. Dinner only, Mon–Sat; closed hols. AE, CB, DC, MC, V. Jkt. *Specialties:* stuffed grape leaves, Tangier couscous w. lamb, trout broiled w. herbs, veal w. olives, kibbeh, Armenian dishes, baklava. *Note:* This warm, distinguished Middle Eastern rest. has become a local favorite over the years. The decor is right out of a Chicago version of *1,001 Nights,* music and ambience included. Attentive svce. Resv. advised. Excellent value. *Middle Eastern.* I

 ♈ **Emperor's Choice** (nr. dwntwn), 2238 S. Wentworth Ave. (225-8800). A/C. Lunch/dinner daily (until midnight). AE, MC, V. *Specialties:* steamed oysters w. black-bean sauce and coriander, Hunan shrimp, kwo teh, Peking duck, mu shu pork, sole w. black beans and coriander, inconsequential desserts. *Note:* The best place in Chicago's small Chinatown, serving authentic and often imaginative Hong Kong food. The friendly waiters seem to speak little English. The tiny dining rm is hung w. portraits of Chinese emperors. Resv. advisable; very good value. *Chinese/Seafood.* I

 ♈ **Mare** (nr. dwntwn), 400 N. Clark St. (245-9933). A/C. Lunch Mon–Fri, dinner nightly; closed hols. AE, MC, V. *Specialties:* grilled calamari; crespella w. spinach, cheese, and prosciutto; mussels w. soft polenta; seafood stew; whole fish w. crazy water; tavolozza antipasto; grilled bass w. sautéed escarole; baba Amaretto. *Note:* The mosaics, murals, and frescoed ceilings establish the Venetian setting, in which you'll find food achieving the same authenticity. The menu is inspired by owners Paul and Kathy LoDuca's tasting experiences along the Italian coastline. The newest compliment to a city known for its great Italian cuisine. Resv. recommended. *Seafood/Italian.* I

 ♈ **Yugo Inn** (nr. dwntwn), 2824 N. Ashland Ave. (348-6444). A/C. Dinner only, Thurs–Sun. MC, V. *Specialties:* ajvar, pjeskavica (Serbian hamburgers), moussaka, muckalica, grilled fish. *Note:* From moussaka to goulash, all the authentic flavors of the Balkans. Very good value. Resv. advised. *Balkan.* I

 ♈ **Greek Islands** (nr. dwntwn), 200 S. Halsted St. (782-9855). A/C. Lunch/dinner daily (until midnight); closed Thanksgiving, Dec 25. AE, CB, DC, MC, V. *Specialties:* pastitsio, gyros, moussaka, souvlaki, braised lamb, excellent grilled fish, baklava. *Note:* The best Greek rest., and one of the largest, in Chicago, a city full of Greeks. A modern setting and excellent, authentic cuisine at very good prices. Greek hospitality and a friendly, if noisy, ambience. Free valet parking. *Greek.* **B–I**

 ♈ **Billy Goat's Tavern** (nr. dwntwn), 430 N. Michigan Ave. (222-1525). A/C. Breakfast/lunch/dinner daily (until 2am). No credit cards. *Specialties:* hamburger, cheeseburger, sandwiches, ribs. *Note:* One of Chicago's most famous and colorful hamburger-and-beer joints, tucked beneath Michigan Ave. in front of the Tribune building. This funky, no-frills hangout favored by journalists and construction workers is said to have been the inspiration for John Belushi's legendary "Saturday Night Live" "cheezborger, cheezborger—no Coke, Pepsi" bit. *American.* **B**

 ♈ **Ed Debevic's** (nr. dwntwn), 640 N. Wells St. (664-1707). A/C. Lunch/dinner daily (until midnight); closed Thanksgiving, Dec 25. AE, CB, DC, MC, V. *Specialties:* chile, hamburgers, fried chicken, meatloaf, chocolate milkshakes. *Note:* An amusing replica of a 1950s-style diner that seems to have come right out of *American Graffiti.* Even the background music is from that era. If there's nothing unforgettable about the food, the atmosphere is fun, the prices more than modest, and the crowd particularly diverse. Relaxed svce. Another success from the "Lettuce Entertain You" restaurant chain. No resv. *American.* **B**

 ♈ **Pizzeria Uno** (nr. dwntwn), 29 E. Ohio St. (321-1000). A/C. Lunch/dinner daily (until 1am); closed Thanksgiving, Dec 25. AE, CB, DC, MC, V. *Specialties:* Chicago-style pizza (thick yet light crust), salads, sandwiches, homemade soup (excellent minestrone). *Note:* The best pizza in Chicago and perhaps in America. Noisy atmosphere. Walls decorated w. amusing graffiti. Generous portions (a "medium" pizza is plenty for two). Efficient svce. A local favorite since 1943. Other location: Pizzeria Due, 619 N. Wabash Ave. (943-2400). *Italian.* **B**

Restaurants in the Vicinity

☖☖☖ **Carlos'** (see "Personal Favorites," above).

☀☖☖☖ **The Cottage** (vic.), 525 Torrence Ave., in Calumet City (708/891-3900). A/C. Lunch Tues–Fri, dinner Tues–Sun; closed hols. MC, V. Jkt. *Specialties:* Louisiana crab cakes and bay scallops w. roasted red pepper coulis, mushroom consommé, grilled breast of Wisconsin pheasant w. port wine and cherry sauce, pan-seared rabbit loin and leg confit w. braised leeks, trio of chocolate mousses. The menu changes seasonally. Nice wine list. *Note:* Delightful little old-world inn that has become a shrine for cuisine-lovers. Chef Gregg Flisiak deftly blends American and French influences. Rustic-cozy ambience. Very good svce. Worth the 30-min. car ride from dwntwn on I-94S and Sibley Blvd. Free parking. Resv. advised. *American/French.* **M**

☖☖☖ **Tallgrass** (vic.), 1006 S. State St., in Lockport (815/838-5566). A/C. Dinner only, Thurs–Sun; closed hols. DC, MC, V. Jkt. *Specialties:* shrimp lasagna, grilled tuna w. pesto, cherry chutney–chèvre canapé, seared ahi tuna w. grilled foie gras and black truffles, roasted rack of lamb w. walnut-sorrel pesto and Gorgonzola hollandaise, great desserts. Menu changes periodically. *Note:* Lovely Victorian home in the Illinois prairie is the setting for Robert Burcenski's contemporary twists on European classics. Lavish and innovative creations amidst crystal, silver, and antiques. Expert svce. Worth the 45-min drive on I-55S. Resv. necessary. *Continental.* **M–E.**

Cafeterias/Specialty Spots

D. B. Kaplan's (nr. dwntwn), Water Tower Place (7th floor), 845 N. Michigan Ave. (280-2700). Lunch/dinner daily (until 9pm). No credit cards. *Specialties:* salads, omelets, and giant sandwiches (more than 160 different kinds). *Note:* The best deli in Chicago. Ideal for a light meal before or after a show. **B**

Hard Rock Café (nr. dwntwn), 63 W. Ontario St. (943-2252). Lunch/dinner daily. AE, MC, V. *Specialties:* Very good chile and grilled burgers, ribs, salads, sandwiches. *Note:* Noisy rock-music shrine. Often overcrowded. **B**

Mr. Beef (nr. dwntwn), 666 N. Orleans St. (337-8500). Breakfast/lunch Mon–Sat. No credit cards. *Specialties:* remarkable Italian beef sandwiches (roast beef and roast peppers)—a Chicago specialty. *Note:* The rather depressing decor does not seem to discourage the crowd. **B**

Mrs. Levy's Delicatessen (dwntwn), in the Sears Tower (ground floor), 233 S. Wacker Dr. (993-0530). Breakfast/lunch Mon–Fri (until 3pm). No credit cards. *Specialties:* cabbage soup, corned beef, excellent sandwiches and hot dishes. *Note:* A very popular deli at lunchtime. **B**

Where to Eat What in Chicago

American: Billy Goat's Tavern (p. 529), Bossa Nova (p. 526), The Cottage (p. 530), Carson's The Place for Ribs (p. 526), Charlie Trotter's (p. 525), Ed Debevic's (p. 529), Prairie (p. 526)

Balkan: Yugo Inn (p. 529)

Cafeterias/Specialty Spots: D. B. Kaplan's (p. 530), Hard Rock Café (p. 530), Mr. Beef (p. 530), Mrs. Levy's Delicatessen (p. 530)

Chinese: Emperor's Choice (p. 529)

Continental: Jackie's (p. 526), The Marc (p. 528), Tallgrass (p. 530), Yoshi's Café (p. 527)

French: Ambria (p. 526), Carlos' (p. 525), The Cottage (p. 530), Everest Room (p. 525), Jimmy's Place (p. 527)

German: Berghoff (p. 526)
Greek: Greek Islands (p. 529)
Italian: Mare (p. 529), Pizzeria Uno (p. 530), Spiaggia (p. 525), Vivere (p. 528)
Japanese: Benkay (p. 527), Hatsuhana (p. 528)
Mediterranean: Tuttaposto (p. 528)
Mexican: Frontera Grill (p. 528), Topolobampo (p. 526)
Middle Eastern: Casbah (p. 528)
Seafood: Emperor's Choice (p. 529), Mare (p. 529), Nick's Fishmarket (p. 527), Shaw's Crab House (p. 528)
Spanish: Bossa Nova (p. 526), Café Ba-Ba-Reeba (p. 529)
Steak: Eli's, The Place for Steak (p. 527)
Thai: Arun's (p. 527)

BARS & NIGHTCLUBS

As in New York, there is a magic telephone number in Chicago—**Jazz Institute Hot Line** (427-3300)—with a daily listing of all jazz club programs.

Andy's (nr. dwntwn), 11 E. Hubbard St. (642-6805). The best jazz club in Chicago, according to the experts. Lively, 1920s-style ambience. Rest. as well (jkt. required). Open nightly.

B.L.U.E.S. (nr. dwntwn), 2519 N. Halsted St. (528-1012). A great blues place in a great blues city. Open nightly.

☀ **Butch McGuire's** (nr. dwntwn), 20 W. Division St. (337-9080). Chicago's most famous singles bar. A relaxed, pleasant atmosphere. Original decor. A quite good rest., too. A must for all visitors. Open nightly.

☀ **Buddy Guy's Legends** (dwntwn), 754 S. Wabash St. (427-0333). A down-home comfortable haunt behind the Hilton Hotel owned by blues guitarist Buddy Guy. Blues, rock, and R&B live, nightly.

☀ **Checkerboard Lounge** (nr. dwntwn), 423 E. 43rd St. (624-3240). Another famous locale for lovers of authentic blues. Rough neighborhood at night—take a cab. Open nightly.

Chicago Improv (nr. dwntwn), 504 N. Wells St. (782-6387). Comedy club similar in atmosphere to Improvisations in New York and Los Angeles. Wannabe comics mix with visiting celebs and top-name acts. Open nightly.

☀ **Excalibur** (formerly the Limelight; nr. dwntwn), 632 N. Dearborn St. (266-1944). Enormous disco with multilevel dance floors, game rooms, bars, and rest. in a Romanesque castlelike building. Crazy and hip. Open nightly.

Joe Segal's Jazz Showcase (dwntwn), in the Blackstone Hotel, 636 S. Michigan Ave. (427-4846). Renowned jazz club offering everything from bebop to avant-garde jazz. Classy atmosphere. Open Tues–Sun.

☀ **John Barleycorn Memorial Pub** (nr. dwntwn), 658 W. Belden Ave. (348-8899). Very popular, intimate pub with classical background music and paintings projected on the walls. Open nightly (until 2am).

Kingston Mines (nr. dwntwn), 2548 N. Halsted St. (477-4646). The epitome of the Chicago blues club in the heart of the North Side, a fashionable upperclass neighborhood. Chicago's oldest blues club. Locally popular. Open nightly.

Old Town School of Folk Music (nr. dwntwn), 909 W. Armitage Ave. (525-7793). A temple of Chicago folk music, as the name indicates.

Park West (nr. dwntwn), 322 W. Armitage Ave. (929-5959). Big pop and jazz stars performing almost every night. Rather snobby ambience.

☀ **Second City Theater** (nr. dwntwn), 1616 N. Wells St. (337-3992). A stronghold of improvisation, where comedians like Mike Nichols, Elaine May, John Candy, Dan Ackroyd, John Belushi, and a good many of the "Saturday Night Live" troupe were discovered.

NEARBY EXCURSIONS

🔔🔔 **BATAVIA** (36 mi./56km west on Eisenhower Expwy. and East-West Tollway): Built on 6,800 acres (2,700ha) where peaceful herds of bison graze, the **Fermilab Particle Accelerator,** Kirk Rd. at Pine St., is the largest synchrotron particle accelerator in the world. Its annular tunnel, 4 mi. (6.4km) in circumference, accelerates atomic particles to nearly the speed of light. The Visitors Center is located in **Wilson Hall,** a 16-story building in the center of the synchrotron. Guided tours are given Wed–Fri by appointment only (708/840-3351). A must for physics buffs.

🔔 **ELMHURST** (17 mi./27km west on I-90): The **Lizzadro Museum of Lapidary Art,** 220 Cottage Hill Ave. in Wilder Park (708/833-1616), offers one of the world's largest collections of minerals and worked precious stones, notable jade figurines from the Far East. Open Tues –Sun.

🔔 **EVANSTON** (12 mi./19km north on Lake Shore Dr. and U.S. 41): Site of **Northwestern University** (10,000 students), this pretty residential area on the banks of Lake Michigan houses the headquarters of Rotary International and the United Methodist church. On the university campus, be sure to see the **Dearborn Observatory** (2131 Sheridan Rd.), the **Shakespeare Garden,** and the **Pick-Staiger Concert Hall.**
North of the campus is the **Grosse Point lighthouse,** Sheridan Rd. and Central St., erected after a shipwreck on Lake Michigan off Evanston took 300 lives (tours of the lighthouse Sat–Sun in summer).

☀️🔔🔔 **OAK PARK** (9 mi./14km west on the Eisenhower Expwy.): The suburban cradle of the famous "Prairie School," which greatly influenced American architecture from the beginning of the century. There are at least a score of interesting buildings to see here, work of the famous Frank Lloyd Wright (see "Guided Tours," above). Among the most noteworthy are **Wright's house-studio,** at Forest and Chicago Aves. (open daily year round), in which he lived for more than 20 years; the **Harry Adams House,** 710 Augusta St. (dates from 1913); the **Unity Temple,** 875 Lake St. (dates from 1906); and the **River Forest Tennis Club,** 615 Lathrop Ave. There's a **Visitors Center** at 158 N. Forest Ave. (708/848-1978), open daily.
Authors Ernest Hemingway and Edgar Rice Burroughs, the prolific creator of Tarzan (27 volumes from 1912 to 1964), also hail from Oak Park.

🔔 **PULLMAN COMMUNITY** (I-94 between 104th and 115th Sts.): This model company town, built in 1880 by railroad magnate George Pullman for his employees, is an interesting sample of American social history. The **Visitors Center** is at 614 E. 113th St. (312/785-8181). Don't miss the Sunday brunch at the historic **Hotel Florence,** 11111 S. Forrestville Ave. (312/785-8900).

☀️🔔 **WILMETTE** (16 mi./26km north on Lake Shore Dr. and U.S. 41): Luxurious suburb on the shores of Lake Michigan complete with a fine sand beach. The startling **Baha'i House of Worship,** Sheridan Rd. and Linden Ave. (708/256-4400), is the religious center for the Baha'i faith. Founded in Iran in the last century, the faith has been flourishing in the United States for some 50 years. Innovative design and beautiful gardens overlooking Lake Michigan. Open daily.

FARTHER AFIELD

INDIANA DUNES NATIONAL LAKESHORE (92 mi./ 148km r.t. on I-90E and U.S. 12E, returning the same way): A captivating landscape composed of giant sand dunes—some as high as 192 ft. (60m)—of pine forests, immense beaches with room for many thousands of bathers, and marshes along the shores of Lake Michigan. Unique fauna and flora (notably carnivorous plants, cacti, oaks, and sumacs) flourish on the 14,227 acres (5,760ha) of the park, giving the whole an appearance of tropical vegetation in summer, the best season for a visit. There are also dozens of miles of rambling trails, picnic areas, and fully equipped campsites for nature-lovers. (Four-wheel-drive vehicles and dune buggies are prohibited.) **Visitor Center** at the intersection of Kenil Rd. and U.S. 12. For further information, contact Superintendent, 1100 N. Mineral Springs Rd., Porter, IN 46304 (219/926-4520).

LAKE COUNTRY (124 mi./199km r.t. on I-90N, U.S. 12N, Ill. 120E, and U.S. 14S): A string of rural lakes (**Long Lake, Fox Lake, Pistakee Lake, Grass Lake, Chain O'Lakes State Park**), this favorite fine-weather rural retreat for Chicagoans is a paradise for fishing, sailing, and strolling.

On the way back, go out of your way to pass through **Woodstock,** a peaceful little town of Victorian charm where Orson Welles spent his childhood and made his earliest appearances as a Shakespearean actor in the **Opera House,** 121 Van Buren St. See also the **Old Courthouse Inn & Jail,** 101 N. Johnston St.; **Town Square;** etc.

GALENA & THE BANKS OF THE MISSISSIPPI (406 mi./650km west, r.t. on I-90N, U.S. 20W, Ill. 84S, and I-80 and I-55E): The charming little town of **Galena,** on the banks of the river of the same name, is a former mining town that made its fortune in the last century from lead. A visit here is a pleasant voyage back into history: 85% of its buildings are designated as landmarks, like the **Ulysses S. Grant Home,** 500 Bouthillier St. (815/777-0248), open daily, the former home of the 18th U.S. president. Photographers, and lovers of old buildings, will find here a wonderful glimpse of the past.

This two- or three-day trip leads next along the banks of the Mississippi (a beautiful scenic route) to **Rock Island,** former capital of the Saul and Fox tribes under Chief Black Hawk. The army defeated them in a decisive battle in 1832. **Black Hawk State Park,** with an observation tower overlooking the valley, as well as a Native American museum, commemorates the event. For information, call 309/788-9536. Also see the **Arsenal,** the **John M. Browning Museum** with a rich collection of arms (open daily), and the reconstruction of old **Fort Armstrong.** Return to Chicago on I-80 and I-55, an ideal route for history lovers.

Where to Stay En Route

IN GALENA **DeSoto House,** 230 S. Main St., Galena, IL 61036 (815/777-0090). 55 rms. A more-than-100-year-old hotel, nicely restored. **M**

IN ROCK ISLAND **Plaza,** 17th St. at Third Ave., Rock Island, IL 61201 (309/794-1212). 177 rms. Modern and comfortable. **I**

CHAPTER 24

MILWAUKEE

□ □ □

From its Germanic antecedents the world's brewing capital has inherited a taste for order, work, classical music (its symphony orchestra is justly renowned), and solid food. A city in transition, from a quiet, conservative factory town to a lively, cosmopolitan metropolis, the new Milwaukee is known for its clean streets, relatively low crime rate, and minimal traffic congestion. In a strategic position on Lake Michigan at the confluence of three rivers—the Milwaukee, the Menominee, and the Kinnickinnic—the site of the city, whose original Native American name, Millioki, signifies "gathering-place by the waters," was visited in 1674 by French missionary Jacques Marquette and trapper Louis Joliet. The present economic capital of Wisconsin was founded in 1818 as a trading post by French fur trader Salomon Juneau; it attained stature as a major city in 1889, when the first modern brewery was opened.

Today Milwaukee produces more beer than any other city in the world, and two of the country's largest breweries, Pabst and Miller (both of German origin) have their headquarters here. Other well-known names in the roster of local industry include Harley-Davidson motorcycles, Allis-Chalmers heavy equipment, and Evinrude outboard motors; these and others have contributed to the economic growth of "the machine-shop of America," as Milwaukee has been called, taking advantage of the city's access to the ocean via the Great Lakes and the St. Lawrence Seaway.

"The German Athens"—another of Milwaukee's sobriquets—an austere but by no means charmless city, with its churches, its mixture of historic and ultramodern buildings, its museum, and its lovely lakeside promenade, is known for its *gemütlichkeit,* a warm combination of hospitality and joie de vivre. Moreover, Milwaukee plays host every year to a well-known beer festival, the Oktoberfest, reminiscent of the Munich event of the same name.

It is German immigration that has left the clearest stamp on Milwaukee, from the impressive **City Hall** to the **Pabst Theater,** not to mention the many cafés and "bier gartens," but the influence of other immigrant strains—Irish, Greek, and above all Polish—is also clearly evident. Witness America's first Polish cathedral, **St. Josaphat's Basilica,** built at the beginning of the 20th century, and the **Annunciation Greek Orthodox Church,** last major work of the great architect Frank Lloyd Wright.

Born here were entertainer Liberace, clarinetist Woody Herman, actors Spencer Tracy and Gene Wilder, and singer Al Jarreau.

BASIC FACTS: State of Wisconsin. Area code: 414. Time zone: central. ZIP Code: 53201. Founded in: 1818. Approximate population: city, 630,000; metropolitan area, 1,600,000. Ranks 24th in size among U.S. metropolitan areas.

CLIMATE: Summer and fall are the best seasons for visiting Milwaukee. Temperatures are generally pleasant, though there can be sudden changes; mean temperature in July is 71°F (22°C). Winter is glacial and very windy; the mercury stays well under freezing, with a Jan average temperature of 22°F (−6°C). Spring is brief and brisk (41°–50°F/5°–10°C).

DISTANCES: Chicago, 87 mi. (139km); Duluth, 424 mi. (678km); Minneapolis, 365 mi. (584km); Omaha, 495 mi. (792km); St. Louis, 376 mi. (602km).

ARRIVAL & TRANSIT INFORMATION

AIRPORT: General Mitchell International Airport (MKE), 6 mi. (10km) south. Information: 747-5300.

AIRLINES: American (toll free 800/433-7300), Continental (toll free 800/525-0280), Delta (toll free 800/221-1212), Midwest (toll free 800/452-2022), Northwest (toll free 800/225-2525), TWA (toll free 800/221-2000), United (toll free 800/241-6522), and USAir (toll free 800/428-4322).

CITY LINK: The **cab** fare to city center is about $16; time, 20–25 min. Bus: **A.A.A. Airport Shuttle** (272-1955) leaves every 20 min., serving principal dwntwn and outlying hotels; fare, $7.50–$10 according to destination; time, about 35 min.

Since the airport is near the city, which is not large, it may be unnecessary to rent a car unless you intend to take trips outside the city. Good public transportation system (bus): **Milwaukee County Transit System** (344-6711 for information).

CAR RENTAL (at the airport unless otherwise indicated): Avis (toll free 800/331-1212); Budget (toll free 800/527-0700); Dollar (toll free 800/800-4000); Hertz (toll free 800/654-3131); National (toll free 800/227-7368). For dwntwn locations, consult the local telephone directory.

LIMOUSINE SERVICES: Carey Limousine (271-5466), Dav El Limousines (toll free 800/922-0343).

TAXIS: Cabs may not be hailed on the street; they must be taken from the waiting lines outside the major hotels or summoned by phone. Principal companies are **City Veterans Taxicab** (291-8080) and **Yellow Cab** (271-1800).

TRAIN: Amtrak Station, 433 W. St. Paul Ave. (toll free 800/872-7245).

INTERCITY BUSES: Greyhound, 606 N. 7th St. (toll free 800/231-2222).

INFORMATION & TOURS

TOURIST INFORMATION: The **Milwaukee Convention & Visitors Bureau,** 510 W. Kilbourn Ave., WI 53203 (414/273-3950; toll free 800/231-0903).

For a **recorded message** giving a list of current shows and cultural events, call 799-1177.

GUIDED TOURS: Edelweiss Boat Tours (boat), 1110 Old World 3rd St. Dock (272-3625): Lunch, brunch, and dinner cruises Apr–Oct along the Milwaukee River and into Lake Michigan, aboard the *Edelweiss* or the *Edelweiss II*.

Historic Milwaukee (walking tours) (277-7795): Guided tours of Milwaukee's historic neighborhoods. Call for schedule.

Iroquois Boat Line Tours (boat), Clybourn St. Bridge Dock (332-4194): Trips on Lake Michigan and the Milwaukee River (late June to Sept 1).
Milwaukee County Transit System (bus), 1492 N. 17th St. (937-3253): Conducted tours of city and surroundings (June 1 to Sept 1).

SIGHTS, ATTRACTIONS & ACTIVITIES

ARCHITECTURAL HIGHLIGHTS: 🏛 **Civic Center Plaza,** between N. 7th and N. 9th Sts., north of W. Wells St.: Wide esplanade with fountain, statuary, and monumental bell tower, bordered by the **County Courthouse,** Police Headquarters, the huge **Convention Center (MECCA),** and the **Public Museum.** The heart of the city's government.

🏛 **McKinley Marina,** 1750 N. Lincoln Memorial Dr. (273-5224): Lovely pleasure harbor with 650 moorings on Lake Michigan. Along the breakwaters, devotees of rod and reel pursue their favorite quarry—Coho salmon, trout, and lake perch. Boats may be rented May–Oct.

🏛 **Milwaukee Center,** E. Wells and Water Sts.: This ultramodern $100-million complex, symbol of the new Milwaukee, stands across from City Hall and comprises a 28-floor office tower, the new Wyndham Hotel, two theaters, many stores and boutiques, etc.

🏛 **Oriental Theater,** 2230 N. Farwell Ave. (276-8711): Built in 1927 and recently restored to all its old splendor, the Oriental is worth seeing just for its remarkable East Indian–style decor complete with onion-shaped domes and terra-cotta lions. Movie buffs flock to the foreign and hard-to-find films shown at this landmark movie theater. Open daily.

🏛 **Performing Arts Center/PAC,** 929 N. Water St. (273-7206): This modern (1969), austerely geometric complex comprises four theaters and concert halls as well as an open-air auditorium. Home of the world-famous Milwaukee Symphony Orchestra, the First Stage Milwaukee Theater, the Milwaukee Ballet, and the Florentine Opera Company. Pretty gardens on the Milwaukee River. Visits by appointment only; call 273-7121.

🏛 **Skywalk System,** connecting 10 city blocks around MECCA and the Grand Avenue Mall: Following in the footsteps of the Twin Cities and Cincinnati, Milwaukee has become the third midwestern metropolis to treat itself to a "skywalk," the network of glassed-in, air-conditioned pedestrian walkways that links major downtown buildings. This one, especially the stretch overlooking the river, offers some fine views.

🏛 **War Memorial Complex,** 750 N. Lincoln Memorial Dr. (273-5533): This modern building by the great architect Eero Saarinen, splendidly situated on the shore of Lake Michigan, commemorates the dead of all wars. It houses the **Milwaukee Art Museum** (see "Museums of Art," below), and offers a fine view of lake and city.

BEACHES: 🏛 **Bradford Beach,** 2400 N. Lincoln Memorial Dr. at E. Bradford Ave. (961-9799): The best of the seven public beaches along the lakefront. Even in summer Lake Michigan's water temperature doesn't get much above the low 60s; for dedicated swimmers only.

CHURCHES/SYNAGOGUES: 🏛 **Annunciation Greek Orthodox Church,** 9400 W. Congress St. (461-9400): Last major work of Frank Lloyd Wright (1962), the imaginative Byzantine structure is crowned by a magnificent blue dome in the shape of a flying saucer. Visit by appointment only, Mon–Fri.

🏛 **Central United Methodist Church,** 639 N. 25th St. (344-1600): A triumph of contemporary energy-saving design. Built partially underground, this unusual church, whose roof is also its garden, has a large bell tower which captures and stores solar energy.

☀& **St. Joan of Arc Chapel,** 601 N. 14th St. (224-6873): Authentic medieval French chapel from the 15th century, transported and reerected in 1965, stone by stone, on the campus of **Marquette University** (see "Historic Buildings," below). According to legend, Joan of Arc prayed here before going to the stake. Remarkable example of Gothic architecture. Open daily.

& **St. Josaphat's Basilica,** 2336 S. 6th St. (645-5623): This is the oldest Polish basilica in North America: It was built at the turn of the century by Slavic immigrants with material salvaged from the demolition of the Federal Building in Chicago. Its majestic dome is reminiscent of St. Peter's in Rome; ornate interior with many pictures and relics of Polish saints. Visits by appointment only.

HISTORIC BUILDINGS: ☀& **Capt. Frederick Pabst Mansion,** 2000 W. Wisconsin Ave. (931-0808): Luxurious 37-room home of 19th-century brewer Frederick Pabst (1893); splendid upper-middle-class interior from the turn of the century with period furniture and decoration scrupulously restored. Open daily.

☀& **City Hall,** 200 E. Wells St. (278-2221): Impressive in the purest Flemish Renaissance style, with monumental eight-story lobby surrounded by wrought-iron balconies, and a 393-ft. (122m) belfry. Open Mon–Fri.

☀& **Grain Exchange Room,** 225 E. Michigan Ave. (272-6230): Situated in the Mackie Building, the beautiful Grain Exchange Room, whose gold-leaf trim and giant wall murals have been renovated to their 1879 Victorian Renaissance splendor, depicts the growth and development of Milwaukee during the Gilded Age. Visits by appointment only, Mon–Fri.

& **Kilbourntown House,** 4400 W. Estabrook St., Estabrook Park (5 mi./8km north on I-43) (273-8288): Beautiful Greek Revival house from 1844 with an interesting collection of furniture and art objects from the second half of the 19th century. Open Tues, Thurs, Sat, and Sun July to early Sept.

& **Marquette University,** Wisconsin Ave. between N. 11th and N. 17th Sts. (288-7700): Well-known university (13,000 students) founded in 1881; the campus has many interesting buildings, including the **Joan of Arc Chapel** (see above), the **Marquette Hall Carillon,** which with 48 bells of different sizes is one of the largest in the country (frequent recitals), and the **Haggerty Museum of Art,** with a permanent collection of 5,000 works of art, open daily.

☀& **Pabst Theater,** 144 E. Wells St. (278-3663): Famous for its acoustics and its richly baroque interior, this fine theater, built in 1895, has been restored to all its original splendor. Classical concerts, chamber-music recitals, and theatrical entertainment.

INDUSTRIAL TOURS: Your visit to Milwaukee wouldn't be complete without a visit to the breweries on which its fame and fortune are founded.
Miller, 4251 W. State St. (931-2337): Second-largest brewery in the world. Visits to the plant and museum, with free beer tasting, Mon–Sat mid-May to mid-Sept, Tues–Sat the rest of the year.
Pabst, 915 W. Juneau Ave. (223-3709): One of the city's oldest; plant tours and tasting Mon–Sat June to the end of Aug, Mon–Fri the rest of the year.

MUSEUMS OF ART: & **Charles Allis Art Museum,** 1801 N. Prospect Ave. at 1630 E. Royall Place (278-8295): Huge collection of Asian art from China, Korea, Japan, and Persia, as well as French and contemporary American paintings—property of the late "king of farm machinery," Charles Allis—housed in a very beautiful Tudor-style home built in 1909. Open Wed–Sun.

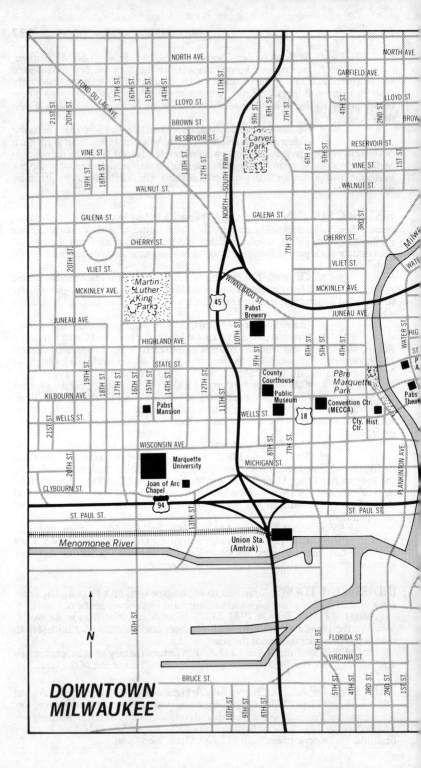

DOWNTOWN MILWAUKEE

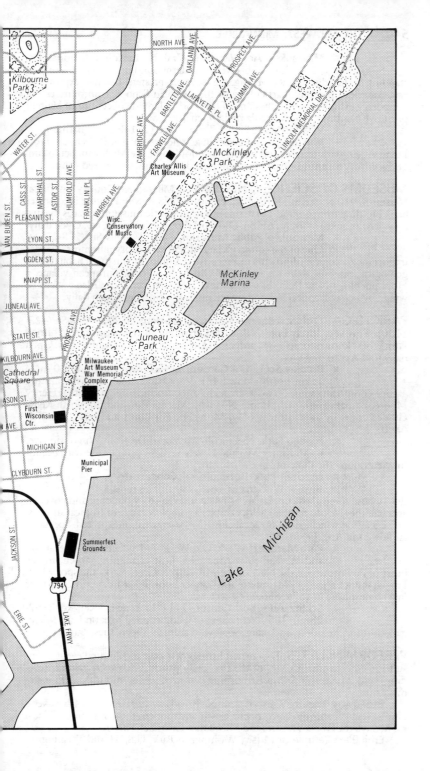

🔍🔍 **Milwaukee Art Museum,** 750 N. Lincoln Memorial Dr. (224-3220): This very modern building by Eero Saarinen standing at the edge of Lake Michigan houses old masters, German expressionists, American painters (particularly of the "Ashcan School"), and interesting temporary exhibitions. Also has one of the world's largest collections of Haitian primitive paintings. Recently enlarged. Open Tues–Sun.

🔍 **Villa Terrace,** 2220 N. Terrace Ave. (271-3656): Charming villa in the Italian Renaissance style designed in 1923 by architect David Adler, with terraces and gardens overlooking Lake Michigan. Sculpture, 18th-century furniture, Shaker handcrafts, old porcelain. Open Wed–Sun.

MUSEUMS OF SCIENCE & HISTORY: 🔍 Milwaukee County Historical Museum, 910 N. 3rd St., Père Marquette Park (273-8288): Housed in a former bank building from around 1910, this interesting little museum retraces the history of Milwaukee in lively fashion. Old workshops, exhibitions, etc. Open daily.

☀️🔍🔍 **Milwaukee Public Museum,** 800 W. Wells St. (278-2751): One of the country's largest natural-history museums. Besides important zoological (dinosaurs in a reconstruction of their natural habitat) and geological exhibits, there's a replica of Old Milwaukee, a European village, a Hopi pueblo, a New Delhi bazaar, a Mexican street scene, etc. Also a "wizard wing," which will appeal to budding scientists. Fascinating. Open daily.

PARKS & GARDENS: 🔍 Boerner Botanical Gardens, 5879 S. 92nd St. (425-1130): This very lovely botanical garden standing in the enormous **Whitnall Park** is best known for its rose gardens and its seasonal flower exhibitions. Open daily mid-Apr to mid-Oct.

🔍 **Bradley Sculpture Garden,** 2145 Brown Deer Rd. (10 mi./ 16km north along I-43): Very handsome modern-sculpture garden comprising some 60 works by such American and foreign artists as Henry Moore, Barbara Hepworth, Isamu Noguchi, Martha Pan, and Ellsworth Kelly. Guided tours by appointment only, Mon–Fri. For hours and resv., call 276-6840.

🔍 **Juneau Park,** N. Lincoln Memorial Dr. from Wisconsin Ave. to McKinley Marina: Lovely verdant promenade with beautiful views along the shore of Lake Michigan.

☀️🔍🔍 **Mitchell Park Horticultural Conservatory,** 524 S. Layton Blvd. at W. Pierce St. (649-9800): This remarkable botanic garden, whose three glass cupolas are as tall as a seven-story building and cover an area half the size of a football field, exhibits a complete range of tropical and desert vegetation which, given the local climate, is somewhat unexpected. Spectacular flowers in Aug. Open daily.

🔍 **Père Marquette Park,** Old World 3rd St. between W. State St. and W. Kilbourn Ave.: This little triangular garden, in the heart of downtown on the bank of the Milwaukee River, marks the spot where French Jesuit Fr. Jacques Marquette and trapper Louis Joliet are supposed to have first come ashore in 1674. Should be seen.

🔍 **Schlitz Audubon Center,** 1111 E. Brown Deer Rd. (352-2880): 185 acres (75ha) of wild, wooded park on Lake Michigan, host to foxes, deer, and many other wild animals. Open Tues–Sun.

PERFORMING ARTS: For current listings of shows and cultural events, consult the entertainment pages of the two daily papers, *Milwaukee Journal* (evening) and *Milwaukee Sentinel* (morning), as well as the monthly *Milwaukee* magazine.

Broadway Theatre Center, 158 N. Broadway (291-7800): Milwaukee's newest venue featuring dance, opera, classic and modern theater. Home of Theatre X, Skylight Opera Theatre, and Milwaukee Chamber Theatre.

Emil Blatz Temple of Music, Washington Park, U.S. 41 and Washington

Blvd. (278-4389): Open-air concerts of classical and pop music: "Music Under the Stars" (July–Aug).

Helfaer Theater, on the campus of Marquette University, 13th and Clybourn Sts. (288-7505): Modern and classical theater; concerts.

Milwaukee Repertory Theater, 108 E. Wells St. (224-1761): Traditional and contemporary theater in a new performing-arts complex with three adjacent auditoriums: the Mainstage Theater, the Stienke Theater, and the Stackner Cabaret. Open Sept–July.

Pabst Theater, 144 E. Wells St. (278-3663): Musical comedy, concerts, and contemporary theater in a lovely turn-of-the-century baroque setting, superbly restored.

Performing Arts Center/PAC, 929 N. Water St. (273-7206): This ultra-modern group of buildings houses the Milwaukee Symphony Orchestra, under principal conductor Zdenek Macal (Sept–June); the Pennsylvania-Milwaukee Ballet (Sept–May); the First Stage Milwaukee Theater (a children's theater); and the Florentine Opera Company and Bel Canto Chorus, under music director Richard Hinson (Nov–May).

Riverside Theater, 116 W. Wisconsin Ave. (276-3300): Broadway hits, touring companies, big-star shows.

UWM Fine Arts Theater, 2200 E. Kenwood Blvd. (229-4947): Concerts of classical music and jazz.

SHOPPING: Grand Avenue Mall, W. Wisconsin Ave. and 3rd St. (224-9720): Enormous shopping mall on three levels, radiating out from a spectacular glassed-in rotunda. More than 180 stores, boutiques, restaurants, and cafés of all kinds. The heart of Milwaukee shopping. Directly connected to the Skywalk system. Open daily.

Old World Third Street, 3rd St. between W. Wells St. and W. Highland Ave.: Well-known food shops such as Usinger's Famous Sausage (founded in the 1870s), the Spice House, and Wisconsin Cheese Mart, Inc., restaurants, antique dealers. A lively, colorful neighborhood, reminiscent of an old European city. Most shops open Mon–Sat.

W.K. Walthers, Inc., N. 60th St. and Florist Ave. (527-0770): The world's largest store entirely devoted to model-railroad equipment; a 50-year-old tradition. A must for all buffs. Open Mon–Sat year round.

SPECIAL EVENTS: For exact dates on the events listed below, consult the **Milwaukee Convention & Visitors Bureau** (see "Tourist Information," above).

Lakefront Festival of the Arts (June): Open-air concerts, art and craft exhibitions.

Summerfest (late June to early July): Top-name entertainers perform on 10 separate stages along Milwaukee's lakefront. Ethnic and American foods festival, sports events, circus, boating displays on the lake. Colorful and crowded.

Great Circus Parade (mid-July): The big annual circus festival, with a very spectacular street parade; it draws more than 800,000 spectators.

Wisconsin State Fair (10 days in Aug): Very popular agricultural fair, also with big-name shows, auto races, fireworks, etc.

Greater Milwaukee Open Golf Tournament (late Aug to early Sept): Annual PGA tournament with top touring golf pros at the beautiful Tuckaway Country Club in Franklin.

Oktoberfest (Sept–Oct): Oceans of beer and music, tons of food; lots of warmth. The country's biggest beer festival.

Holiday Folk Fair (Nov): Folklore shows, food festival, and arts from around the world.

SPORTS: Milwaukee boasts professional teams in four major spectator sports:
Baseball (Apr–Oct): Brewers, County Stadium (933-1818).

Basketball (Oct–Apr): Bucks, Bradley Center (227-0500).
Football (Sept–Dec): Green Bay Packers, County Stadium (342-2717).
Ice Hockey (Sept–Apr): Admirals, Bradley Center (227-0550).

STROLLS: ☀☖ **Lakefront,** along Lincoln Memorial Dr.: One of the country's finest urban landscapes; beautiful gardens and opulent private homes along Lake Michigan.

☀☖ **Old World Third Street,** 3rd St. between W. Wells St. and W. Highland Ave.: The shopping district of Old Milwaukee (see "Shopping," above).

THEME PARKS: ☀☖☖ **Old World Wisconsin,** Wisc. 59 in Eagle (35 mi./ 56km SW) (594-2116): Picturesque museum-village, comprising 50 or so 19th-century buildings, scrupulously restored, with authentic furniture and equipment, and walk-ons in period dress. A pleasant glimpse of the past. Open daily May–Oct.

☖ **Six Flags Great America,** on Grand Ave. in Gurnee, Ill. (32 mi./51km south on I-94) (708/249-1776): 200-acre (80ha) theme park with giant roller coasters, waterfalls with giant slides, and more than 100 other attractions. Facsimile of a pioneer village. Shows. Open daily in summer, wknds only in spring and fall; closed the rest of the year.

WINTER SPORTS RESORTS: ☖ **Alpine Valley,** 36 mi. (57km) SW on Wisc. 15 and County D Rd. (642-7374): 11 lifts. Open Dec to mid-Mar.

☖ **Little Switzerland,** 30 mi. (48km) NW on U.S. 41 and Wisc. AA Rd. (644-5020): 8 lifts. Open Nov–Mar.

ZOOS: ☖☖ **Milwaukee County Zoo,** 10001 W. Bluemound Rd. (7 mi./11km west on U.S. 18) (771-3040): One of the best-designed and most comprehensive zoos in the country, with more than 3,000 animals from giant gorillas to white tigers. See it from the mini-train. Open daily year round. 10 min. from dwntwn.

ACCOMMODATIONS

Personal Favorites (in order of preference)

☀☖☖☖ **Pfister Hotel** (dwntwn), 424 E. Wisconsin Ave., WI 53202 (414/273-8222; toll free, see Preferred). 306 rms, A/C, color TV, in-rm movies. AE, CB, DC, MC, V. Valet parking $8, pool, health club, 2 rests. (including The English Room), coffee shop, two bars, 24-hr. rm svce, nightclub, hrdrsr, concierge, free child's cot. *Note:* Much admired by Enrico Caruso, this luxury hotel from the 1890s was recently expanded w. the addition of an ultramodern tower. Elegant decor w. many works of art. The rms in the old building, w. lake views, are charming; in the tower, they're simply functional. Polished svce; very good rest.; the "grande dame" of local hotels. **E**

☖☖☖ **Hyatt Regency** (dwntwn), 333 W. Kilbourn Ave., WI 53203 (414/276-1234; toll free, see Hyatt). 484 rms, A/C, color TV, in-rm movies. AE, CB, DC, MC, V. Adj. gar. $7, two rests. (one revolving on the top floor), coffee shop, two bars, rm svce, concierge. *Note:* Huge ultramodern glass-and-concrete cube w. spectacular 18-story lobby and glass-walled elevators. Typical Hyatt comfort, bus svce leaves a little to be desired. Group and convention clientele; direct access to the Skywalk system. VIP floor. "333" is a commendable rest. Recently completed a $4-million renovation program. **M–E**

☖☖ **Marc Plaza** (dwntwn), 509 W. Wisconsin Ave., WI 53203 (414/271-7250; toll free 800/558-7708). 500 rms, A/C, color TV, in-rm movies. AE, CB, DC, MC, V. Parking $6, pool, health club, sauna, rest. (including Benson's), coffee shop, bar, rm svce, hrdrsr, free crib. *Note:* The largest and one of the oldest of the hotels in Milwaukee, several times renovated and now w. heated indoor pool and sauna. A favorite of business travelers; a VIP section is reserved for them on the 20th–24th floors. Very central. Excellent svce. Same management as the Pfister Hotel. No-smoking floors. **M–E**

Park East Hotel (dwntwn), 916 E. State St., WI 53202 (414/ 276-8800). 169 rms, A/C, color TV, in-rm movies. AE, CB, DC, MC, V. Free parking, health club, rest. (Signatures), bar, rm svce. *Note:* A modern, functionally designed building within a stone's throw of the lake. Spacious, comfortable rms, some w. lake views. Friendly reception. Very good value. **I–M**

Knickerbocker (dwntwn), 1028 E. Juneau Ave., WI 53202 (414/276-8500). 60 rms, A/C, cable color TV. AE, MC, V. Parking $3, rest. (Café Knickerbocker), coffee shop, bar. *Note:* Elderly but well-maintained hotel; also apts by the week or month. A very acceptable standard of comfort. Some rms have a view of nearby Lake Michigan. An old Milwaukee landmark. **I**

Other Hotels (from top bracket to budget)

Wyndham Milwaukee Center (dwntwn), 139 E. Kilbourn Ave., WI 53202 (414/276-8686; toll free 800/822-4200). 221 rms, A/C, color TV, in-rm movies. AE, CB, DC, MC, V. Gar. $8, health club, sauna, rest. (Kilbourn Café), two bars, rm svce, nightclub, free crib. *Note:* Part of the Milwaukee Center complex, this elegant hotel became the VIP's favorite almost as soon as it opened in 1988. Mahogany paneling, velvet, and a profusion of artworks combine to make the setting both intimate and elegant. Spacious, very comfortable rms; impeccable svce; acceptable rest. Right in the theater district and across from City Hall. **E–VE**

Hilton Inn Milwaukee River (nr. dwntwn), 4700 N. Port Washington Rd., Glendale, WI 53212 (414/962-6040; toll free, see Hilton). 164 rms, A/C, cable color TV. AE, CB, DC, MC, V. Free parking, pool, rest. (Anchorage), bar, rm svce. *Note:* Typical modern luxury motel on the bank of the Milwaukee River. Very good seafood rest. Efficient svce. Comfortable rms, the best w. views across the river. 10 min. from dwntwn. **M**

Astor Hotel (dwntwn), 924 E. Juneau Ave., WI 53202 (414/ 271-4220; toll free 800/558-0200). 96 rms, A/C, cable color TV. AE, CB, DC, MC, V. Parking $2, rest., bar, valet svce, free crib. *Note:* Venerable but charming hotel in a quiet residential neighborhood nr. the lake. Friendly reception and svce. Many antiques and period reproductions. Some rooms w. kitchenettes. Satisfactory rest. (Nantucket Shores). Good value overall. 5 min. from dwntwn (free shuttle). **I–M**

Holiday Inn City Centre (dwntwn), 611 W. Wisconsin Ave., WI 53203 (414/273-2950; toll free, see Holiday Inns). 248 rms, A/C, cable color TV. AE, CB, DC, MC, V. Free valet parking, pool, rest., bar, rm svce, free crib. *Note:* Functional 10-story motel adj. the Convention Center (MECCA). Modern comforts; huge well-designed rms; efficient svce. Group and convention clientele. **I–M**

Ramada Inn Downtown (dwntwn), 633 W. Michigan Ave., WI 53203 (414/272-8410; toll free, see Ramada). 152 rms, A/C, color TV, in-rm movies. AE, CB, DC, MC, V. Free parking, pool, rest., bar, rm svce, free child's cot. *Note:* Conventional motel nr. the business district; spacious, comfortable rms, some w. refrigerators. Good svce. Business clientele. Good value. **I–M**

Continental Motor Inn (nr. dwntwn), 3001 W. Wisconsin Ave., WI 53208 (414/344-7500). 54 rms, A/C, color TV, in-rm movies. AE, CB, DC, MC, V. Free parking, rest. *Note:* Well-run small motel nr. the County Stadium. Functionally comfortable; friendly reception; very good value. 10 min. from dwntwn. **I**

꽃 **Hotel Wisconsin** (dwntwn), 720 N. 3rd St., WI 53203 (414/
271-4900). 110 rms, A/C, cable color TV. AE, CB, DC, MC,
V. Free parking, rest., coffee shop, bar. *Note:* Elderly hotel a little worn at the
edges but clean and well kept. Comfortable though by no means luxurious rms;
friendly reception and svce. Very centrally located a block from Grand Avenue
Mall. Good value for the budget traveler. **B–I**

In the Vicinity

꽃 **The American Club** (vic.), Highland Dr., Kohler, WI 53044
(414/457-8000; toll free 800/344-2838), 50 mi. (80km)
north on I-43 and Wisc. 23. 234 rms, A/C, color TV, in-rm movies. AE, CB,
DC, MC, V. Free gar., pool, health club, 12 tennis courts, two golf courses, sauna, spa, cross-country skiing in season, trap shooting, carriage rides, four rests.
(including Immigrant and Winery), coffee shop, bar, 24-hr. rm svce, concierge,
free crib. *Note:* Splendid British-style country inn standing in a beautiful private
park, an authentic wildlife reserve. Spacious, lavishly comfortable rms in two
small three-story buildings that are designated historic monuments. Impeccable
reception and svce. Very good sports facilities; rests. of real quality. A haven of
peace and elegance one hour from Milwaukee. **E–VE**

Airport Accommodations

꽃 **The Grand Hotel** (formerly the Red Carpet Hotel; vic.) 4747
S. Howell Ave., WI 53207 (414/481-8000; toll free 800/
558-3862). 510 rms, A/C, color TV, in-rm movies. AE, CB, DC, MC, V. Free
parking, two pools, health club, sauna, eight tennis courts, squash, two rests. (including Harold's), bars, rm svce, nightclub, hrdrsr, cinema, free airport limo,
free crib. *Note:* Huge, massive modern six-floor motel opposite the airport. Comfortable, well-soundproofed rms, all recently remodeled. Comprehensive sports
facilities. Business clientele. Good value. 20 min. from dwntwn. **I–M**

꽃 **Motel 6** (vic.), 5037 S. Howell Ave., WI 53207 (414/482-
4414). 119 rms, A/C, cable color TV. AE, DC, MC, V. Free
parking, pool, free crib. *Note:* Unbeatable value, across from the airport and 20
min. from dwntwn. Ideal if you're passing through by car, w. immediate access
to I-94. Resv. suggested. **B**

YMCA/Youth Hostels

Red Barn Hostel (vic.), 6750 Loomis Rd. (414/529-3299). 36 beds.
Country youth hostel open May–Oct; 12 mi. (19km) from dwntwn.

RESTAURANTS

Personal Favorites (in order of preference)

꽃 **Sanford** (nr. dwntwn), 1547 N. Jackson St. (276-9608).
A/C. Dinner only, Mon–Sat; closed hols. AE, CB, DC, MC,
V. Jkt. *Specialties:* gravlax tartar w. fennel and wine gel, charcoal-grilled quail w.
pear-peppercorn sauce, napoleon of foie gras w. glazed turnips, cumin wafers w.
grilled marinated tuna, bittersweet-chocolate tart w. coffee ice cream. Extensive
wine list. Menu changes regularly. *Note:* Since its opening in 1990, Sanford has
set the standard for fine dining at its best in Milwaukee. Strikingly brilliant
nouvelle American cuisine by chef-owner Sandy d'Amato. The storefront location, on a street corner, is far from glamorous. Small, minimally adorned dining
rm. Flawless svce. Resv. a must. A remarkable address. Valet parking. *American.* **E**

꽃 **Karl Ratzsch's** (dwntwn), 320 E. Mason St. (276-2720).
A/C. Lunch/dinner daily; closed hols. AE, CB, DC, MC, V.
Jkt. *Specialties:* rouladen, planked whitefish, sauerbraten, Wiener schnitzel, pork
shank w. sauerkraut, duckling w. red cabbage, schaum torte. Superb 25-page list
of German wines at reasonable prices. *Note:* A landmark of local gastronomy. Atmosphere and decor haven't changed since 1903; classical-music trio at dinner.
Antique paneling, hand-painted murals, and chandeliers. Exemplary svce. Resv.
advisable. Still in the hands of the Ratzsch family. *German/Continental.* **M–E**

 Steven Wade's Café (vic.), 17001 W. Greenfield Ave. (784-0774). A/C. Lunch Mon–Fri, dinner Mon–Sat; closed hols. AE, CB, DC, MC, V. *Specialties:* tortellini w. crabmeat in sherry sauce; raspberry-cured salmon; roasted monkfish w. oriental vegetable stir-fry, langoustines, and jasmine rice; Colorado steer tenderloin w. foie-gras sauce and sun-dried tomato and garlic ravioli; fresh berry Napoleon w. basil-custard sauce. The menu changes daily. *Note:* Inventive contemporary cuisine by the excellent chef Steven Wade Klindt. Intimate, comfortable setting. Efficient, attentive svce. Well worth the 25-min. drive from dwntwn (via I-94). Resv. advised. *American.* **M**

 John Ernst (dwntwn), 600 E. Ogden Ave. (273-1878). A/C. Lunch/dinner Tues–Sun. AE, CB, DC, MC, V. Jkt. *Specialties:* sauerbraten w. potato pancakes, Kassler rippchen, Wiener schnitzel, jägerschnitzel, goulash, Black Forest torte. *Note:* Mock–old-world German tavern, favored by local socialites since 1878. Authentic Bavarian decor w. huge open fireplace. Assiduous svce. Resv. advised. Milwaukee's oldest rest. *German.* **M**

 Toy's Chinatown (dwntwn), 830 N. 3rd St. (271-5166). A/C. Lunch/dinner daily; closed hols. AE, DC, MC, V. Jkt. *Specialties:* Cantonese food: chow mein, sweet-and-sour shrimp, spareribs. *Note:* The food, and the elaborate Far Eastern decor, have made this one of Milwaukee's favorite Chinese rests. for three generations. Svce on the abrupt side. Very good value. Opposite the Hyatt Regency Hotel. *Chinese.* **I**

 The Tamarack (dwntwn), 322 W. State St. (225-2552). A/C. Lunch/dinner daily. AE, CB, DC, MC, V. *Specialties:* sandwiches, salads, barbecued ribs. *Note:* Built as a Schlitz Company tavern in 1889, this casual, fun bar serves the finest barbecued ribs in town. Congenial, comfortable atmosphere. Live blues wknd nights. Resv. accepted. *American.* **B–I**

Other Restaurants (from top bracket to budget)

 Grenadiers (dwntwn), 747 N. Broadway (276-0747). A/C. Lunch Mon–Fri, dinner Mon–Sat; closed hols. AE, CB, DC, MC, V. Jkt. *Specialties:* blue-corn crêpe w. goat cheese, loin of lamb w. spinach-garlic flan, grilled yellowfin tuna in curry sauce, scrumptious desserts. The menu changes regularly; the wine list is good. *Note:* The young German chef, Knut Apitz, is indubitably producing some of the most inventive, delicate food around. Elegant Empire-style classical decor and a delightful glassed-in Garden Room. Very polished svce. One of the best places to eat in Milwaukee, in the heart of dwntwn. Valet parking; resv. suggested. *Continental.* **M–E**

 Mimma's Café (nr. dwntwn), 1307 E. Brandy St. (271-7337). A/C. Lunch Tues–Fri, dinner nightly; closed hols. AE, CB, DC, MC, V. *Specialties:* antipasto misto; cozze zingarella (sea mussels in tomato sauce); fresh pappardelle pasta w. lamb, eggplant, and fresh mozzarella; ravioli di aragosta (black lobster ravioli in Asti sauce); good desserts. *Note:* A locally favorite Italian rest. that continues year after year to capture the title for best Italian rest. in *Milwaukee* magazine. Black-and-white is the motif at this spunky rest. that often reaches a high-decibel range. Unfortunately, resv. are only taken for a party of five or more for dinner, so the wait can be an hour on the weekends. *Italian.* **I–M**

 Boulevard Inn (dwntwn), 925 E. Wells St. (765-1166). A/C. Lunch/dinner daily, brunch Sun; closed hols. AE, CB, DC, MC, V. Jkt. *Specialties:* sauerbraten, sweetbreads w. shallots and champagne, New York steak, sautéed scallops, duckling w. red cabbage, fish of the day, cheesecake. *Note:* All the great standbys of German and continental cuisine, admirably prepared and served, in a new, more attractive setting in the heart of dwntwn. Locally popular; resv. advised. *German/Continental.* **I–M**

 Jack Pandl's Whitefish Bay Inn (vic.), 1319 E. Henry Clay St. (964-3800). A/C. Lunch/dinner daily, brunch Sun; closed hols. AE, CB, DC, MC, V. *Specialties:* fish from Lake Michigan, German dishes, roast duck, schaum torte. *Note:* A favorite of Milwaukee's German colony since 1915. Excellent broiled whitefish. Comfortable atmosphere; fine old decor. Efficient svce; generous servings. German beer on draft. Resv. advised. 20 min. from dwntwn. *German/Seafood.* **I–M**

Maniaci's Café Siciliano (nr. dwntwn), 6904 N. Santa Monica Blvd. (352-5757). A/C. Dinner only, Mon–Sat; closed hols. AE, CB, DC, MC, V. *Specialties:* fresh homemade pasta, chicken cacciatore, piccata of whitefish, shrimp Michelle, veal Grand Prix, cannoli. *Note:* A more authentic Italian *trattoria* you couldn't find in Italy. The food is from the southern part of the country, absolutely authentic and very reasonably priced. Reception and svce w. a smile. Romantic courtyard w. white stucco walls and tile floor. Well worth the 20-min. trip from dwntwn. Resv. advised. *Italian.* **I–M**

Café Knickerbocker, in the Knickerbocker Hotel (see "Accommodations," above) (272-0011). A/C. Breakfast/lunch/dinner daily; closed Thanksgiving and Dec 25. MC, V. *Specialties:* pizza, fish of the day, lamb-and-black-bean quesadilla, ceviche w. scallops, seared ahi tuna, grilled Norwegian salmon, chocolate cake w. vanilla mousse filling. Menu changes periodically. *Note:* A favorite among the locals mainly because it provides the best view of Lake Michigan. Nicely executed meals. Local art decorates the walls in this comfortable, open setting. Be sure to sit on the patio when the weather permits. Svce is friendly but not entirely well versed. Live jazz Fri and Sun. Resv. recommended. *Continental.* **B–I**

Dos Bandidos (nr. dwntwn), 5932 N. Green Bay Ave. (228-1911). A/C. Lunch Mon–Sat, dinner nightly; closed hols. AE, MC, V. *Specialties:* tacos, fajitas, spinach and crabmeat enchiladas, chiles rell"nos, steak ranchero, excellent margaritas. *Note:* Typical Mexican cantina w. an abundance of greenery and an inviting open patio. The food is absolutely authentic and far above average. No resv. 15 min. from dwntwn. *Mexican.* **B–I**

Old Town (nr. dwntwn), 522 W. Lincoln Ave. (672-0206). A/C. Lunch Tues–Fri, dinner Tues–Sun. AE, DC, MC, V. Jkt. *Specialties:* böreck, moussaka, baked lamb, paprika chicken, roast duckling, homemade pies and strudels. *Note:* One of Milwaukee's favorite ethnic rests. Spicy but well-prepared Balkan food in a pretty setting. Hearty portions. Efficient svce. Noisy background music. Resv. advised. *Continental.* **B–I**

Jake's Delicatessen (nr. dwntwn), 1634 W. North Ave. (562-1272). A/C. Open Mon–Sat (10am–4pm). No credit cards. *Specialties:* corned beef, short ribs, giant sausage, pastrami, kosher specialties. *Note:* Likable New York–style deli w. wonderful sandwiches to go. Often crowded at noontime. *American.* **B–I**

Cafeterias/Fast Food/Specialty Spots

Water Street Brewery (dwntwn), 1101 N. Water St. (272-1195). Open daily until 11:30pm. AE, MC, V. Engaging old-time brewery serving a wide choice of its own beers, as well as national and imported labels. Hors d'oeuvres, lavish sandwiches and daily specials are also available.

Watts Tea Shop (dwntwn), 761 N. Jefferson St. (291-5121). AE, MC, V. A century-old Milwaukee tradition; excellent daily specials, sandwiches, and house salads. Breakfast Mon–Fri, lunch Mon–Sat.

BARS & NIGHTCLUBS

Bombay Bicycle Club (dwntwn), in the Marc Plaza (see "Accommodations," above) (271-7250). Excellent piano bar; live jazz. Open Mon–Sat.

Celebrity Club (nr. dwntwn), 2203 N. Prospect Ave. (277-0481). Live alternative rock. Popular hangout for college students. Open nightly.

The Estate (nr. dwntwn), 2423 N. Murray Ave. (964-9923). The best, and best-known, of the city's jazz clubs, featuring live jazz Tues–Sun.

The Globe (dwntwn), 2028 E. North Ave. (276-2233). Venue for local and national rock names. Open nightly.

John Hawk's Pub (dwntwn), 607 N. Broadway at E. Michigan Ave. (272-3199). Model British pub with 40 different brands of beer; a nice place. Live jazz Sat; open daily.

La Playa (dwntwn), in the Pfister Hotel (see "Accommodations," above) (273-8222). Tropical-style nightclub. Superb view from the 23rd floor of the Pfister Hotel. Trendy crowd. Open Mon–Sat.

Major Goolsby's (dwntwn), 340 W. Kilbourn Ave. at N. 4th St. (271-3414). This popular bar across from the MECCA Arena attracts mostly local sports stars and their fans. Sports memorabilia abounds on every wall. Good burgers. Open Mon–Sat.

Safe House (dwntwn), 779 N. Front St. (271-2007). An amusing rest. and nightclub in the James Bond tradition. *Note:* Only an ordinary brass plaque labeled "International Exports Ltd." marks the entrance. The fashionable spot. Open nightly.

NEARBY EXCURSIONS

BROOKS STEVENS AUTOMOTIVE MUSEUM (10325 N. Port Washington, in Mequon, 10 mi./16km north on I-43N) (241-4185): Amazing collection of racing cars and production-line models from 1905 to the present day. One of the country's finest auto museums; a must for car buffs. Open daily.

LIZARD MOUND STATE PARK (County A Rd. at West Bend, 38 mi./60km NW on U.S. 45N and Wisc. 144) (335-4445): Comprises 30 or so mounds of earth in the shape of beasts, birds, or geometric forms, the work of Native Americans dating from A.D. 500–1000. Open daily.

OSHKOSH (83 mi./132km NW on U.S. 41N): On the banks of big Lake Winnebago, this friendly town of 50,000 people plays host for a week every year (late July to early Aug) to the world's largest air show, the E.A.A. International Fly-in Convention, which attracts more than 300,000 spectators and participants. Thousands of early aircraft, from Mustangs to Spitfires and B-26s to World War I biplanes. Aerial acrobatics festival; flight demonstrations. For prop-plane enthusiasts. Interesting aeronautical museum, the **E.E.A. Air Museum,** 3000 Poberezny Rd. (426-4800), open daily. It can be combined with the excursion to Lizard Mound State Park (see above).

RACINE (29 mi./46km SE on I-94S and Wisc. 20E): This pleasant little industrial town on Lake Michigan, most of whose inhabitants are of Danish descent, is the home of Johnson's Wax. The company's head office, built in 1939–50 to the design of the great architect Frank Lloyd Wright, is an outright masterpiece of the modernist style. Guided tour of the buildings at 1525 Howe St. Tues–Fri; resv. a must (631-2154).

FARTHER AFIELD

SPRING GREEN & WISCONSIN DELLS (315 mi./504km r.t. via I-94N, U.S. 12S, Wisc. 60W, U.S. 14E, and I-94S): Three- to four-day trip beginning with a visit to 🔔🔔 **Wisconsin Dells,** where the Wisconsin River has cut beautiful, wild gorges that can be reached only by boat. Guided sightseeing tours daily mid-Apr to late Oct, 11 Broadway (608/254-8555). There is a Winnebago tribal village, Wisc. 13 and River Rd. (608/254-2268), with a museum; tribal dances daily in summer. Many other tourist attractions.

Then on to ☀ **Baraboo,** 12 mi. (19km) south of Wisconsin Dells, with the interesting **Circus World Museum** at 426 Water St. (608/356-0800), open daily mid-May to Sept, once the winter quarters of the famous Ringling Bros. circus. Parades, shows, menagerie, and more than 150 circus caravans of all ages. Also a very fine railroad museum at ⛺ **North Freedom,** 8 mi. (12km) west on Wisc. 136 and County PF (608/522-4261), open daily mid-May to early Sept and weekends through Oct., with a trip in a turn-of-the-century steam train. Amusing.

The next stop is at ☀⛺ **Spring Green,** the town where the well-known architect Frank Lloyd Wright grew up, and where he built one of his houses, **Taliesin East,** 4 mi. (6km) south on Wisc. 23 (608/588-7800). Open daily mid-Apr to mid-Oct. Another worthwhile sight is the extraordinary ⚿⚿ **"House on the Rock,"** by architect Alexander J. Jordan, hanging 450 ft. (137m) above the Wisconsin River, with its waterfalls, pools, and trees integrated spectacularly into the design of the building. It stands 9 mi. (14km) south on Wisc. 23. Open daily Apr–Oct (608/935-3639). Many other attractions nearby, including the world's largest carousel. A fascinating expedition.

Where to Stay in Wisconsin Dells

🏨 **Shamrock Motel,** 1321 Wisconsin Dells Pkwy., Wisconsin Dells, WI 53965 (608/254-8054). 62 rms. An inviting motel standing in its own grdns. Open mid-May to the end of Oct. **B–I**

🏨 **Aloha Beach Resort** (formerly Tiki Motel), 1370 E. Hiawatha Dr., Wisconsin Dells, WI 53965 (608/253-4741). 32 rms. Small, congenial hotel on a lake. Open early late Apr to mid-Oct. **B–I**

Where to Stay in Spring Green

🏨 **The Prairie House,** at the intersection of U.S. 14 and Wisc. 23, Spring Green, WI 53588 (608/588-2088). 51 rms. Classic but well-run motel open year round. **B–I**

Where to Eat in Spring Green

🍸 **Post House Dutch Kitchen,** 127 E. Jefferson St. (588-2595). Lunch Tues–Sun, dinner nightly (except Mon and Tues in the winter). MC, V. Very commendable meats, seafood, and freshwater fish at decent prices. **B–I**

CHAPTER 25

MINNEAPOLIS AND ST. PAUL

□ □ □

Lying on opposite sides of the Mississippi River, the Twin Cities comple-ment each other harmoniously, while each retains its own distinct style and char-acter. Minneapolis is dynamic, active, and mostly Scandinavian and Lutheran. St. Paul, the state capital, is more traditional; its people are mostly Irish or German, and Catholic. Minneapolis has its modern high-rises, its network of Skyways, its bustling nightlife, and the **Minnehaha Falls** of which Longfellow sang. St. Paul has fine classical buildings such as the **State Capitol,** designed by Cass Gilbert, the imposing **City Hall,** and **St. Paul's Cathedral,** one of the country's largest. Minneapolis is politically progressive and tolerant; Hubert Humphrey, the pop-ulist leader who was once vice-president of the U.S., was for many years first may-or of the city and then a senator from Minnesota. St. Paul may be more starchy and conservative, but the liberal Democrat Eugene McCarthy began his career here as a teacher at St. Thomas College. St. Paul is also the birthplace of F. Scott Fitzgerald, the chronicler of the "lost generation." Minneapolis, more prosaical-ly, can lay claim to Charles M. Schulz, the creator of *Peanuts;* the late oil tycoon J. Paul Getty; movie director George Roy Hill; and rock singer Prince.

The site of the Twin Cities was explored in 1680 by the French missionary Fr. Louis Hennepin; their present prosperity began with the construction of the first flour mills in the 1850s. Successive waves of immigration—German, Irish, Polish, and above all, Scandinavian—did the rest. Minneapolis stands where the grain-growing prairies of the Dakotas and Minnesota (a name derived from two Sioux words: *minne,* meaning "water," and *sota,* meaning "sky-colored") meet the waters of the Mississippi River where they are still—but only just—navigable; today it's still one of the country's principal agricultural markets. Along with St. Paul, it has also become the home of important electronic, chemi-cal, forest-product, and food companies such as Honeywell, Control Data, Gen-eral Mills, Pillsbury, and 3M Corporation; and the hub for Northwest Airlines as well as one of the country's capitals of rock music. Following on Prince's reputa-tion, practitioners of the "Minneapolis sound," an aggressive style of rhythm and blues, have gained international acclaim. While the winters are very harsh, Min-neapolis and St. Paul rank among the greenest cities in the country, with 936 lakes and 513 parks or public gardens between them.

The Twin Cities pride themselves on being the intellectual capital of the Midwest, with the University of Minnesota, well-known symphony and cham-ber orchestras, an opera, many museums of high quality, and the famous **Guthrie Theater.** They are also the heart of a fabulous vacationland of deep forests, swift-running rivers teeming with fish, and numberless lakes, including **Lake Superi-or,** at 32,480 sq. mi. (84,130km^2) the world's largest body of fresh water. Such a wealth of tourist attractions has earned for Minneapolis/St. Paul the title of "Gateway to the Land of 10,000 Lakes," and for Minnesota the reputation of a hikers' and campers' paradise, at least during the summer months.

Last but not least, the Twin Cities represent in one sense a haven of peace and safety; by comparison with other great metropolitan areas their crime rate is among the lowest in the country.

BASIC FACTS: State of Minnesota (St. Paul is the state capital). Area code: 612. Time zone: central. ZIP Codes: 55401 (Minneapolis); 55101 (St. Paul). Founded: 1840 (St. Paul); 1847 (Minneapolis). Approximate population: Minneapolis, 370,000; St. Paul, 270,000; metropolitan area, 2,460,000. Rank among U.S. metropolitan areas: 16th.

CLIMATE: With temperatures in July averaging 77°F (22°C), the summer is the only good time for a visit. The first snows of fall appear in mid-Oct. As to the winters, the only adjective that does them justice is "polar." Jan temperatures average 13°F (−10°C), with the mercury sometimes plunging to −22°F to −38°F (−30°C to −40°C), and demonstrating the value of the cities' "Skyways"—two networks of glassed-in, heated pedestrian walkways that link together the principal buildings of downtown Minneapolis and downtown St. Paul, respectively.

DISTANCES: Chicago, 406 mi. (650km); Kansas City, 443 mi. (710km); Milwaukee, 365 mi. (584km); Rapid City, 633 mi. (1,012km); St. Louis, 567 mi. (908km); Winnipeg, 460 mi. (736km).

ARRIVAL & TRANSIT INFORMATION

AIRPORT: Minneapolis/St. Paul International Airport (MSP), 10 mi. (16km) SE of Minneapolis, 9 mi. (15km) SW of St. Paul. Call 726-5555 for information.

U.S. AIRLINES: American (toll free 800/433-7300), Continental (toll free 800/525-0280), Delta (toll free 800/221-1212), TWA (toll free 800/221-2000), United (toll free 800/241-6522), and USAir (toll free 800/428-4322).

FOREIGN CARRIERS: KLM (toll free 800/374-7747).

CITY LINK: The **cab** fare to dwntwn Minneapolis is about $20 for the 25-min. trip; to dwntwn St. Paul, about $18 for the 40-min. trip. Bus: to Minneapolis and St. Paul, **MSP Airport Express** (726-6400), departs every 15–20 min. serving principal dwntwn hotels, at a fare of $10 for the 35-min. trip.

Unless you intend to confine yourself to the two dwntwn districts with their covered walkways, the size of the metropolitan area and its profusion of green space make it advisable to rent a car with unlimited mileage.

The **public bus system, MTC** (349-7000), is trustworthy and practical for trips around dwntwn or between the Twin Cities.

CAR RENTAL (at the airport unless otherwise indicated): Avis (toll free 800/331-1212); Budget (toll free 800/527-0700); Dollar (toll free 800/800-4000); Hertz (toll free 800/654-3131); National (toll free 800/227-7368); and Thrifty (toll free 800/367-2277). For dwntwn locations, consult the local telephone directory.

LIMOUSINE SERVICES: Carey Limousine (623-0565), Dav El Limousines (toll free 800/922-0343), Network Limousine (toll free 800/638-5466).

TAXIS: Cabs may be hailed on the street or taken from the waiting lines outside the big hotels, but are best summoned by phone. Recommended companies: **in Minneapolis,** Blue & White (333-3331), and Yellow Cab (824-4444); in **St. Paul,** Town Taxi (331-8294) and Yellow Cab (222-4433).

TRAIN: Amtrak Station, 730 Transfer Rd., Minneapolis (toll free 800/872-7245).

INTERCITY BUSES: Greyhound, at 29 N. 9th St., Minneapolis and St. Peter at 7th Sts., St. Paul (both toll free 800/231-2222).

MISSISSIPPI CRUISES: 3- to 10-day cruises aboard the *Delta Queen* or the *Mississippi Queen,* paddlewheel steamers built in the 1920s. Luxurious kitsch. See Chapter 15 on New Orleans for details.

MINNEAPOLIS

INFORMATION & TOURS

TOURIST INFORMATION: The **Minneapolis Convention and Visitor Association** (612/661-4700; toll free 800/445-7412).
   The Connection: For information on current shows and cultural events in the Twin Cities, call 922-9000.

GUIDED TOURS: Gray Line Tours (bus), 21160 Holyoke Ave., Lakeville (469-5020): Conducted tours of the city and surroundings. Also serves St. Paul. Wed–Sun June–Aug, weekends Sept, Oct, and May.

SIGHTS, ATTRACTIONS & ACTIVITIES

ARCHITECTURAL HIGHLIGHTS: ✵⚅ **Guthrie Theater,** 725 Vineland Place (377-2224): This hall of ultramodern design is home to one of the country's best-known theatrical companies, founded in 1963 by the late Sir Tyrone Guthrie. The 1,400-seat hall occupies a 200° arc of a circle around an open stage. Year-round concerts and plays.
   ⚅ **Hennepin County Government Center,** Third Ave. S. and 5th St. (348-3848): Twin towers of pink granite, each 339 ft. (106m) high, rise on either side of a huge lobby lit by picture windows, designed by architect John Carl Warnecke.
   ✵⚅ **IDS Tower,** 80 S. 8th St.: At 57 floors, 775 ft. (236m), this flat-topped multifaceted glass tower is one of the tallest high-rises in the Midwest. Designed by architects Philip Johnson and John Burgee.
   ✵⚅⚅ **Mall of America,** I-494 and Cedar Ave., Bloomington (888-8810): At once mega-shopping center and theme park, this 4.2-million-sq.-ft. (392,600m²) $625-million complex opened in Oct 1992 near the airport is the largest shopping mall in the U.S. Besides four depatment stores

and 400 specialty stores, it includes a 7-acre (2.85ha) enclosed theme park complete with a water-flume ride, a giant walk-through aquarium, 18 movie theaters, and dozens of restaurants, bars, and nightclubs. A truly stunning tourist destination. Open daily.

    Minneapolis Grain Exchange, 400 S. 4th St. (338-6212): The world's second-largest grain exchange, noisy and frenetic. The Visitors' Gallery may be visited by appointment only Tues–Thurs.

    Norwest Center, Marquette Ave. at S. 7th St.: New (1989) 57-story building of yellowish-tan stone and glass that evokes the skyscrapers of the 1930s, the General Electric (formerly RCA) Building at Rockefeller Center in New York in particular. This Cesar Pelli–designed tower joins its next-door neighbor, the IDS Center, to give Minneapolis a truly notable skyline.

    Orchestra Hall, 1111 Nicollet Ave. (371-5656): Home of the world-famous Minnesota Orchestra (formerly the Minneapolis Symphony Orchestra, Music Director: Edo de Waart). The austere building has some of the finest acoustics ever achieved. (See "Performing Arts," below.)

    Skyway, around Marquette Ave. and Nicollet Mall: Ingenious system of heated walkways and footbridges connecting downtown's principal hotels, stores, and office buildings. This network—the world's largest—connects some 25 blocks downtown. Very useful in winter, when temperatures drop to −6°F to −22°F (−20°C to −30°C). Take a walk here.

    Upper Locks, Portland Ave. (333-5336): These giant locks, with a rise and fall of 49 ft. (15m), mark the upper limit of the navigable waters of the Mississippi. An observation platform is open daily Apr–Oct. Spectacular.

CHURCHES/SYNAGOGUES: **Basilica of St. Mary,** Hennepin Ave. and 16th St. (333-1381): Renaissance-style building inspired by the basilica of St. John Lateran in Rome. Open daily.

HISTORIC BUILDINGS: **City Hall,** 5th St. and Third Ave. S. (673-2491): The imposing 1891 City Hall, with its Big Ben clock tower, is a surprising contrast to its next-door neighbor, the ultramodern Hennepin County Government Center. Here you will find the *The Father of Waters,* the largest statue ever carved from a single block of Italian Carrara marble. Open Mon–Fri.

    University of Minnesota, Washington Ave. on either side of the Mississippi River (624-6868): One of the Midwest's oldest (1851) and most important universities, with 41,000 students. On its campus, one of the largest in the country, are two museums worth seeing: the **Bell Museum of Natural History,** open Tues–Sun, and the **University Art Gallery,** open daily.

MUSEUMS OF ART: **Minneapolis Institute of Arts,** 2400 Third Ave. S. (870-3000): This very lovely museum of classical design is home to more than 70,000 art objects of all periods and places. Rich collection of great European masters from El Greco to Matisse; also Egyptian and Far Eastern art. Temporary exhibitions. Among the best-known works on display are *Temptation of Christ* by Titian, *Portrait of Cardinal Borghese* by Pietro da Cortona, Rembrandt's *Lucretia,* and van Gogh's *Olive Grove,* as well as *Composition in Red* by Piet Mondrian, *White Plumes* by Matisse, and *Flayed Steer* by Chaim Soutine. Excellent cafeteria. An absolute must. Open Tues–Sun.

    Minneapolis Sculpture Garden, Vineland Place (375-7622): Opened in 1988 across from the Walker Art Center, this sculpture garden, designed by architect Edward Larrabee Barnes, has become one of the country's most important sites of its kind. Many of the 40 works displayed have been commissioned for this specific site, notably Claes Oldenburg's 52-ft.-long (15m) eye-catching sculpture called *Spoonbridge and Cherry* and Frank

Gehry's 22-ft.-high (6m) glass carp poised on its tail. Other works by Roy Lichtenstein, Henry Moore, Siah Armajani, Jacques Lipchitz, Richard Serra, Isamu Noguchi. . . . Open daily.

☀☸△△ **Walker Art Center,** Vineland Place (375-7622): Contemporary art of all kinds—painting, sculpture, photography—as well as concerts, movies, and temporary exhibitions, in an interesting modern building whose new wing was designed by the distinguished Japanese architect Kenze Tangé. Twentieth-century American art is particularly well represented, with works by Edward Hopper, Roy Lichtenstein, Andy Warhol, Robert Rauschenberg, Barnet Newman, Louise Nevelson, George Segal, and others. Fascinating. Open Tues–Sun. Pleasant cafeteria.

MUSEUMS OF SCIENCE & HISTORY: △ American Swedish Institute,
2600 Park Ave. S. (871-4907): This museum of Swedish art and folk tradition is housed in an amusing turn-of-the-century Roman Revival mansion. Also temporary exhibitions devoted to Swedish-American culture. Open Tues–Sun in the afternoon.

△ **Hennepin County Historical Society Museum,** 2303 Third Ave. S. (870-1329): Illustrates in lively fashion the history of the settlement of Minnesota from pioneer days to the turn of the century, with old workshops and reconstructions of domestic interiors. Open Tues–Sun.

△ **Minneapolis Planetarium,** Public Library, 300 Nicollet Mall (372-6644): Relatively small but well-designed planetarium, with a dome 40 ft. (12.5m) high. For star-gazers. Open daily in summer; on Thurs, Sat, and Sun the rest of the year.

PANORAMAS: △ Foshay Tower, 821 Marquette Ave. (341-2522): First local skyscraper, built in 1929. Has a museum and observation deck on the 32nd floor with a 360° panorama of the city. Open Mon–Sat Apr–Oct.

PARKS & GARDENS: ☸△ Minnehaha Park, Minnehaha Pkwy. and
Hiawatha Ave. S. (661-4806): This magnificent park on the banks of the Mississippi, famous for its 54-ft. (17m) waterfall, was immortalized by Longfellow in *The Song of Hiawatha,* where he writes of its "laughing waters."

△ **Wirth Park,** Wayzata Blvd. and Wirth Pkwy.: Starting point of a panoramic drive through parks **(Eloise Butler Wild Flower Gardens)** and past lakes **(Lake Calhoun, Lake Harriet, Lake Hiawatha)** along the Minnehaha Pkwy.

PERFORMING ARTS: For current listings of shows and cultural events, consult the entertainment pages of the daily *Minneapolis Star & Tribune* (morning) and the monthly *Minneapolis–St. Paul.*
Children's Theatre Company, 2400 Third Ave. S. (874-0400): Classics and innovative productions for all ages. Sept–June.
Guthrie Theater, 725 Vineland Place (377-2224): Classical and contemporary theater; one of the country's finest stock companies. Performances Tues–Sun June–Feb. Also concerts.
Hennepin Center for the Arts, 6th St. and Hennepin Ave. (332-4478): Home of the Minnesota Dance Theater.
Uptown Art Fair (early Aug): Nationally acclaimed arts and crafts fair. Lots of food and drinking on a sectioned-off street in the artsy Uptown neighborhood. Call 827-8757 for information.
Loring Playhouse, 1633 Hennepin Ave. (332-1617): Experimental dance and theater. Home of Ballet of the Dolls and Eye of the Storm Theatre Company. Also a rest. and bar (see "Restaurants" and "Bars & Nightclubs," below).
Met Center, 7901 Cedar Ave. S., in South Bloomington (854-1589): Big-name shows, musical comedies, circus shows.
Orchestra Hall, 1111 Nicollet Ave. (371-5656): Recitals, classical concerts.

Home of the Minnesota Orchestra (principal conductor: Edo de Waart). Oct–May.

Showboat, University of Minnesota campus (625-4001): Melodrama, comedy, operetta on board an authentic "showboat" moored on the Mississippi in front of the university campus. June–Aug.

SHOPPING: The Conservatory, 800 Nicollet Mall: Downtown's newest shopping complex. Beautiful pink marble structure featuring 50 upscale shops, from Ann Taylor to F.A.O. Schwarz.

Mall of America, I-94 and Cedar Ave., Bloomington: The largest shopping mall ever built in the U.S. (see "Architectural Highlights," above). Four major department stores (including Bloomingdale's and Nordstrom) plus 400 specialty shops. A world-class shopping experience.

Nicollet Mall, on Nicollet Ave. between Washington Ave. and Grant St.: One of the country's best-known pedestrian malls; 12 blocks of stores, boutiques, and restaurants in the heart of downtown. Pleasant promenade lined with trees and fountains.

Warehouse District, bounded by First and Third Aves. N., and 2nd and 6th Sts. N.: Art galleries, antiques shops, boutiques, restaurants, and bars in beautifully renovated turn-of-the-century buildings. A local landmark.

SPECIAL EVENTS: For exact dates, consult the **Minneapolis Convention and Visitors Commission** (see "Tourist Information," above).

Midsummer (10 days in June): International biennial music festival held in the Hyland Lake Park Reserve in Bloomington. A joyous celebration of music for every taste—pop, classical, jazz, folk, etc.

Aquatennial Festival (late July): Colorful celebration of the many lakes and rivers of the Twin Cities. Parades on the Mississippi, boat races, sporting events, giant torchlight procession, open-air shows.

Viennese Sommerfest (end of July to Aug): Much appreciated by music-lovers. Series of theme concerts by the Minnesota Orchestra, shows, opera.

Renaissance Festival (wknds mid-Aug to late Sept): Re-creation of a 16th-century English village complete with foods, crafts, jugglers, magicians, and music. Takes place in nearby Shakopee; call 445-7361 for more information.

SPORTS: Minneapolis is home to three major-league professional teams and a minor-league basketball team:

Baseball (Apr–Oct): Twins, Hubert Humphrey Metrodome (375-7444).

Basketball (Oct–Apr): Timberwolves, Target Center (673-1313).

Football (Sept–Dec): Vikings, Hubert Humphrey Metrodome (333-8828).

Ice Hockey (Sept–Apr): North Stars, Metro Center (989-5151).

Horse Racing

Canterbury Downs, Minn. 101 and County Rd. 83 in Shakopee (445-0511), 20 mi. (32km) SW on I-35W and Minn. 13 and Minn. 101. Racing Apr–Nov.

STROLLS: Nicollet Mall (see "Shopping," above).

St. Anthony Falls, Main St. SE and Central Ave.: These 45-ft. (15m) falls mark the upper limit of navigation on the Mississippi. Spectacular walk along the dam and the locks. There are many cafés, stores, and restaurants on the riverbanks (River Place, St. Anthony Main, etc.).

THEME PARKS: Murphy's Landing, 2187 E. Minn. 101, in Shakopee, 22 mi. (35km) SW of Minneapolis on I-35W and Minn. 13 and Minn. 101 (445-6900): Replica of an 1850s pioneer village with church, school, blacksmith, grocer's, etc. Extras in period costume; craft demonstrations. The old buildings, all authentic, were moved here from their original sites elsewhere in Minnesota. Open Sun in May and daily June–Sept.

    🛐 **Valleyfair Amusement Park,** Minn. 101 in Shakopee, 20 mi. (32km) SW of Minneapolis on I-35W and Minn. 13 and Minn. 101 (445-6500): Unusual amusement park laid out in turn-of-the-century style. Old carousels, water rides, IMAX theater, and four roller-coasters. Can conveniently be visited along with Murphy's Landing, above.

WINTER SPORTS RESORTS: The **Cross-Country Ski Hotline** (612/559-6778) has information on the 90 mi. (145km) of ski trails around the Twin Cities.

    🛐 **Afton Alps Ski Area,** 19 mi. (30km) SE of St. Paul on U.S. 61 and Minn. 20 (436-5245): 36 ski lifts; open Nov–Mar.

    🛐 **Buck Hill,** 18 mi. (29km) south of Minneapolis on I-35W (435-7174): 7 ski lifts; open Nov–Mar.

    🛐 **Hyland Hills,** 15 mi. (24km) SW of Minneapolis on I-35W and 494 (835-4604): 7 ski lifts; open Nov–Mar.

ZOOS: ❄🛐 **Minnesota Zoo,** 20 mi. (32km) via Cedar Ave. and Minn. 77 to Apple Valley (432-9000): Highly regarded ultramodern zoo covering 495 acres (200ha). From the monorail which takes you around, you can see more than 450 species in their natural habitats. Open daily year round.

ACCOMMODATIONS

Personal Favorites (in order of preference)

    🔔🔔🔔🔔 **The Whitney** (dwntwn), 150 Portland Ave., MN 55401 (612/339-9300; toll free, see Preferred). 97 rms, A/C, cable color TV. AE, CB, DC, MC, V. Valet parking $6, rest. (Whitney Grille), piano bar, 24-hr. rm svce, concierge, free crib. *Note:* Overlooking the Mississippi and the St. Anthony Falls, this former flour mill, luxuriously renovated, has quickly gained acceptance as the best place to stay in Minneapolis. Huge, comfortable, high-ceilinged rms w. mahogany furniture and refrigerator (the best looking out on the river); first-class rest.; flawless svce. Boasts the most expensive ($1,600 a night) suite in town. VIP and celebrity guest list including Prince, Bruce Willis, and Michael Jackson. Free limo to dwntwn. **E–VE**

    🔔🔔🔔 **Radisson Plaza** (dwntwn), 35 S. 7th St., MN 55402 (612/339-4900; toll free, see Radisson). 355 rms, A/C, color TV, in-rm movies. AE, CB, DC, MC, V. Parking $12, health club, sauna, rest. (Festival), coffee shop, two bars, rm svce, boutiques, free crib. *Note:* A tall tower of blue glass in the purest postmodern style, w. an impressive 18-story glass lobby. Huge, luxuriously comfortable rms; attentive, personal svce. Three VIP floors. Well-outfitted health club on the 17th floor. Direct access to the Skyway. Business clientele; this is now *the* place to stay in dwntwn Minneapolis (Soviet leader Mikhail Gorbachev stopped here during his visit to the U.S. in 1990). **E**

    🔔🔔 **Hotel Luxeford** (dwntwn), 1101 La Salle Ave., MN 55403 (612/332-6800; toll free 800/662-3232). 230 suites, A/C, color TV, in-rm movies. AE, CB, DC, MC, V. Parking $7, health club, sauna, rest., bar, rm svce, free crib. *Note:* Nothing but suites, comfortable and spacious, w. kitchenettes and refrigerators; this new 12-story hotel is a favorite w. many business travelers. Very centrally located. Flawless reception and svce. A fine place to stay. **M–E**

    🔔🔔 **Holiday Inn Metrodome** (formerly the Radisson Inn; dwntwn), 1500 Washington Ave. S., MN 55454 (612/333-4646; toll free, see Holiday Inns). 265 rms, A/C, color TV, in-rm movies. AE, CB, DC, MC, V. Parking $7, pool, health club, sauna, rest., bar, rm svce, free

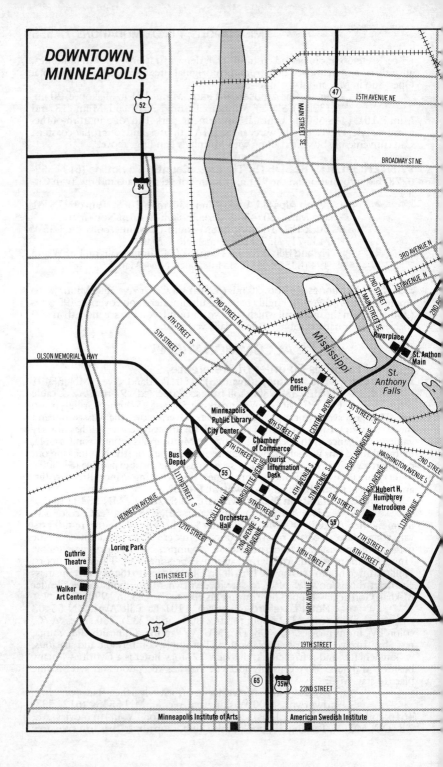

crib. *Note:* Very handsome, comfortable modern hotel right across from the Metrodome and the university campus. Spacious, inviting rms; facilities and svce above the Holiday Inn norm. Good value overall. **M–E**

    🅿🅿 **Regency Plaza** (formerly Best Western; dwntwn), 41 N. 10th St., MN 55403 (612/339-9311; toll free 800/423-4100). 192 rms, A/C, cable color TV. AE, CB, DC, MC, V. Free parking, pool, rest. (Harrigan's), coffee shop, bar, rm svce, free crib. *Note:* Relatively modern but very comfortable hotel almost at the center of town, next to the Greyhound bus terminal. Large, well-designed rms; decor and facilities recently renovated. Friendly reception and svce. Business clientele. Very good value. **I–M**

    🅿 **Econo Lodge** (nr. dwntwn), 2500 University Ave. SE, MN 55414 (612/331-6000; toll free, see Choice). 80 rms, A/C, color TV. AE, CB, DC, MC, V. Free parking, pool, adj. 24-hr. coffee shop, free crib. *Note:* Functional, well-kept motel nr. the university; inviting rms, some w. kitchenettes. Good value; 8 min. from dwntwn. **B–I**

Other Accommodations (from top bracket to budget)

    🅿🅿🅿 **Hyatt Regency Hotel** (dwntwn), 1300 Nicollet Mall, MN 55403 (612/370-1234; toll free, see Hyatt). 534 rms, A/C, color TV, in-rm movies. AE, CB, DC, MC, V. Parking $9, pool, health club, four tennis courts, two rests. (including Taxxi), two bars, 24-hr. rm svce, concierge, free crib. *Note:* An imposing white 20-story mammoth, a 5-min. walk from the Convention Center. All the comfort and facilities you'd expect of a Hyatt. Fine interior lobby with fountain. Two VIP floors, no-smoking floor. Ultraprofessional svce. Group and convention clientele somewhat intrusive. **E–VE**

    🅿🅿🅿 **Marquette Hotel** (dwntwn), 710 Marquette Ave., MN 55402 (612/332-2351; toll free, see Hilton). 280 rms, A/C, color TV, in-rm movies. AE, CB, DC, MC, V. Gar. $12, two rests. (including Windows on Minnesota), bar, rm svce, concierge, free crib. *Note:* This elegant, modern hotel, much favored by business travelers and former President Ford, occupies 19 of the 57 floors of the immense IDS Tower. Remarkably spacious, inviting rms; exemplary comfort and facilities. Very good svce. Access via Skyway to principal dwntwn buildings. Two VIP floors. Windows on Minnesota is a highly regarded rest. w. a panoramic view at the top of the IDS Tower. A good place to stay. **E–VE**

    🅿🅿🅿 **Marriott City Center** (formerly the Amfac; dwntwn), 30 S. 7th St., MN 55402 (612/349-4000; toll free, see Marriott). 582 rms, A/C, color TV, in-rm movies. AE, CB, DC, MC, V. Valet parking $15, sauna, two rests. (including Guscino), coffee shop, two bars, rm svce, health club, hrdrsr, drugstore, boutiques, free crib. *Note:* Here are 32 stories of glass and steel in the heart of dwntwn Minneapolis. Spacious, extremely comfortable rms (23 at the top of the tower are duplex rms), all w. spectacular view. Efficient svce. Two VIP floors. As in all Marriotts, the rests. are mediocre. Big business clientele. Direct access to the Skyway. **E–VE**

    🅿🅿 **Park Inn International** (dwntwn), 1313 Nicollet Mall, MN 55403 (612/332-0371; toll free 800/437-7275). 324 rms, A/C, color TV, in-rm movies. AE, CB, DC, MC, V. Parking $7, pool, sauna, rest., bar, free crib. *Note:* Modern structure right in dwntwn Minneapolis. Functional comfort; acceptable rest. Rather intrusive group and convention clientele. Interesting wknd packages. Very nr. the Convention Center. **M**

    🅿🅿 **Burnsville Fantasuite Hotel** (vic.), 250 N. River Ridge Circle, Burnsville, MN 55337 (612/890-9550; toll free 800/666-7829). 98 rms, A/C, color TV, in-rm movies. AE, MC, V. Free parking, pool, rest., bar, rm svce. *Note:* Guests at this unusual motel, 20 min. from dwntwn and 10 min. from the airport, have a choice: on the one hand, standard, reasonably priced rms; on the other, some 20 suites decorated in a Disneyland-fantasy style and ranging from an Arctic igloo with bearskin on the ceiling via Pharaoh's tomb to the "Moby Dick" suite enclosed in an artificial whale. Kitsch at its purest. For the most popular suites, resv. should be made well ahead. An amusing alternative for the overworked business traveler. **B-I** (rooms); **I-M** (suites).

♀♀ **Days Inn-University** (formerly the Cricket Inn; nr. dwntwn), 2407 University Ave. SE, MN 55119 (612/623-3999; toll free, see Days Inn). 130 rms, A/C, color TV, in-rm movies. AE, CB, DC, MC, V. Free parking, nearby coffee shop, free breakfast, free crib. *Note:* Functional six-floor motel nr. the U. of Minnesota campus. Huge, comfortable rms, some w. refrigerators. Good value. 8 min. from dwntwn. **B-I**

♀♀ **Fair Oaks** (nr. dwntwn), 2335 Third Ave. S., MN 55404 (612/871-2000). 97 rms, A/C, cable color TV. AE, CB, DC, MC, V. Free parking, rest. *Note:* Small, unpretentious, but acceptable hotel only 5 min. from dwntwn. Functional comfort; friendly reception. Ideal for budget travelers. **B-I**

RESTAURANTS

Personal Favorites (in order of preference)

♀♀♀ **Tour Café** (nr. dwntwn), 4924 France Ave. S., Edina (929-1010). A/C. *Specialties:* basil salad w. marinated beets and goat-cheese croquettes, corn-meal-crusted pizzas, curried-shrimp egg rolls w. roasted pineapple chunks and red-pepper coconut dip, portobello tempura w. pickled ginger and wasabe-spiced mayonnaise, pistachio-crusted Szechuan salmon, Jamaican jerked chicken breast, red-pepper meatloaf, fabulous nightly desserts. Seasonal menu. List of mostly Californian wines reasonably priced and a nice array of micro-brewed beers. *Note:* Eclectic, inspiring cuisine by the talented Scott Kee, who treats his customers to a global tour of tastes. Set in a three-story turn-of-the-century house in the wealthy Edina neighborhood, the café also has a multi-terraced patio, making it *the* rest. of choice during the summer. Hanging in the reception is Tour de France winner and co-owner Greg LeMond's yellow jersey. Well-versed svce. Unbeatable prices. Resv. highly recommended. *Continental/American.* **I-M**

♀♀♀ **Kincaid's** (nr. dwntwn), 8400 Normandale Lake Blvd., West Bloomington (921-2255). A/C. Lunch Mon-Sat, dinner nightly, brunch Sun; closed hols. *Specialties:* fresh oysters, roasted veal chop, Maryland-style crab cakes, mesquite-grilled King Salmon, chicken Dijon, rock salt prime rib. Desserts somewhat ordinary. Very good wine list. *Note:* Rated best rest. by *Minneapolis-St. Paul* magazine readers since 1988, this lush yet cozy rest. has a greenery-graced five-story atrium overlooking Lake Normandale. Nebraska corn-fed beef and old standard recipes faultlessly prepared and served. Friendly staff. Resv. a must. Well worth the 20-min drive from dwntwn. The businessmen's favorite for lunch. *American.* **M-E**

♀♀♀ **Goodfellow's** (dwntwn), at the Conservatory, 800 Nicollet Mall (332-4800). A/C. Lunch/dinner Mon-Sat; closed hols. AE, MC, V. Jkt. *Specialties:* chilled red gazpacho, shrimp and scallop stew w. artichoke and caviar cream, Wisconsin veal chop w. polenta lasagna, roast Minnesota pheasant w. sweet corn/goat cheese pudding and apple-shiitake mushroom sauce, sautéed walleye pike w. horseradish cream and tomato-basil sauce, white chocolate fudge strudel. Menu changes seasonally. Remarkable wine list, one of the finest in the Midwest. *Note:* A brainchild of the inventive team of John Dayton and Wayne Kostroski, proprietors of Goodfellows and its younger sibling Tejas (see below). They have since 1988 brought Minneapolis a new style of American cuisine: light, imaginative, and exciting. Spacious, elegant peach-colored space w. modern art on the walls. Excellent svce; resv. a must. Don't miss this gastronomic experience. *American.* **M-E**

♀♀ **New French Café** (dwntwn), 128 N. 4th St. (338-3790). A/C. Breakfast/lunch Mon-Fri, dinner nightly, brunch Sat-Sun. AE, CB, DC, MC, V. *Specialties:* homemade terrines and pâtés, lamb chops

w. green peppercorns, filet of salmon w. white wine and cream of shallots, rack of lamb w. zinfandel, poached halibut w. vermouth and lime, Queen of Sheba (blackberry-and-cream cake), mango sherbet. The menu changes regularly. *Note:* Worthy representative of French-Californian nouvelle cuisine, serving food that's usually inventive and elegant. The white-brick decor, under the high ceiling of this renovated warehouse, is somewhat silly. Trendy clientele; favored by visiting celebs. Resv. strongly advised. Also has a bakery w. excellent take-out. *French/American.* **M**

�♦ **Murray's** (dwntwn), 26 S. 6th St. (339-0909). A/C. Lunch Mon–Fri, dinner nightly. AE, CB, DC, MC, V. *Specialties:* barbecued shrimp, all kinds of meat including an excellent "Butter Knife Steak," catch of the day. *Note:* The steak lover's favorite for more than 40 years. Antiquated decor in dull beige tones and rather intrusive background music at dinner, but the meat is remarkable. Assiduous svce. A local institution. *Steak.* **M**

�♦ **Figlio** (nr. dwntwn), 3001 Hennepin Ave. S., Calhoun Sq. (822-1688). A/C. Lunch/dinner daily (until 1:30am). AE, MC, V. *Specialties:* focaccia sandwiches, gourmet pizzas, pasta dishes, wood-fired grilled fish and meats. *Note:* Lively uptown bistro offering nice Californian-Italian cuisine amid art deco and neon lighting. Active bar and great people-watching. Young, well-trained svce. A yuppie hangout usually crowded till the wee hours. Resv. advised. *Italian.* **I**

♦ **Tejas** (dwntwn), in the Conservatory, 800 Nicollet Mall (375-0800). A/C. Lunch/dinner Mon–Sat. AE, MC, V. *Specialties:* duck empanada w. black-bean sauce and green-chili salsa, tortilla soup w. smoked tomatoes, chicken and avocado, chili-crusted chicken-fried steak, smoked shrimp enchilada, venison chile w. black beans and goat cheese. Menu changes periodically. *Note:* Casual, friendly place offering innovative southwestern cuisine. In the basement of the new Conservatory Shopping Mall. Arrive early or late or expect to wait. *American.* **I**

Other Restaurants (from top bracket to budget)

♦♦♦ **510 Restaurant** (nr. dwntwn), 510 Groveland Ave. (874-6440). A/C. Dinner only, Mon–Sat; closed hols. AE, CB, DC, MC, V. *Specialties:* terrine of seafood, filet of pork w. avocado and red-peppered sour cream, salmon stuffed w. scallop mousse, rack of lamb w. zucchini custard, lamb T-bone w. herbed goat cheese and red bell pepper glaze, macadamia-nut tart. Excellent list of French and California wines. *Note:* The epitome of French cooking in the grand manner in the Twin Cities. Luxurious gray-and-peach decorative scheme, thick carpets, crystal chandeliers, and Chippendale furniture. Flawless svce. Much in favor with local society and visiting celebrities. Resv. indispensable. Valet parking. *French.* **M–E**

♦♦ **D'Amico Cucina** (dwntwn), Butler Sq., 100 N. 6th St. (338-2401). A/C. Dinner only, nightly. AE, CB, MC, V. *Specialties:* sautéed polenta squares w. porcini sauce, tagliatelle w. truffle butter, pan-fried pork chops w. garlicky white-bean timbale, tuna carpaccio, snapper wrapped in eggplant, sautéed lamb w. garlicky mashed potatoes, cannoli w. mascarpone cheese and vanilla. Interesting but pricey list of Italian wines. Menu changes regularly. *Note:* This modern, sophisticated *trattoria* w. its exposed beams and marble floors has established itself as the finest Italian rest. in the Twin Cities (since 1988). Sunlit, imaginative food from Larry D'Amico and Jay Sparks, served in an elegant peach-and-gray setting. Locally very popular; resv. a must. Valet parking. *Italian.* **M–E**

♦♦ **Azur** (dwntwn), 651 Nicollet Mall in the Gaviidae Common (342-2500). A/C. Lunch Mon–Fri, dinner Mon–Sat; closed hols. AE, CB, DC, MC, V. *Specialties:* grilled tomato bread, steak Diane w. porcini mushrooms and truffled asparagus, sautéed grouper w. stewed artichokes and potato purée, sautéed free-range chicken breast w. wild mushrooms and port wine sauce, Catalan burnt cream custard. Seasonal menu. List of southern French regional wines. *Note:* A stylized setting where art deco is given a contemporary twist. The dishes, French in inspiration and Mediterranean in color, evoke a similar response as the decor. The bar, which serves food from the menu, makes this a good place to dine if alone. Live jazz Fri and Sat. Friendly, helpful svce. *French/Mediterranean.* **I−M**

    Loring Café (dwntwn), 1624 Harmon Place (332-1617). A/C. Lunch Mon−Fri, dinner nightly. AE, MC, V. *Specialties:* excellent pizzas and pasta dishes, ribeye steak w. Gorgonzola, manicotti w. lamb and cheese, good pastries. *Note:* Funky American bistro popular w. the Guthrie and its own Loring theater crowd. Eclectic Italian-American food and comfortable bohemian atmosphere. Artsy clientele. Friendly, prompt svce. The "in" place. *American/Italian.* **I−M**

    Royal Orchid (nr. dwntwn), 1835 Nicollet Ave. (872-1938). A/C. Lunch/dinner Tues−Sun; closed hols. MC, V. *Specialties: gaeng* (Thai curry), spring rolls, pineapple rice, satay, *pahd Thai* (vegetables or meat tossed w. rice noodles). *Note:* Truly authentic Thai cooking in modest Far Eastern decor. One of the best ethnic rests. in Minneapolis. Excellent value. *Thai.* **I**

    Black Forest Inn (nr. dwntwn), 1 E. 26th St. (872-0812). A/C. Lunch/dinner daily (till 1am); closed hols. AE, CB, DC, MC, V. *Specialties:* sauerbraten, wienerschnitzel, bratwurst, smoked pork chops w. sauerkraut, hot apfelstrudel, German beer. *Note:* A true-to-life German inn; inviting arbored patio w. pretty fountain for fine days. The clientele of artists and students (the College of Art and Design is nearby) makes for a generally colorful, noisy atmosphere. Very efficient svce. Locally popular. *German.* **B−I**

    Pracna on Main (nr. dwntwn), 117 Main St. (379-3200). A/C. Lunch/dinner daily (until 1am). AE, CB, DC, MC, V. *Specialties:* sandwiches, homemade soups, barbecued spareribs, steak, daily specials. *Note:* A likable imitation of an oldtime saloon on the banks of the Mississippi. Simple but very acceptable food. Open-air terrace for fine weather. Youthful, relaxed atmosphere. Locally popular. *American.* **B−I**

Cafeteria/Fast Food

    The Ediner (nr. dwntwn), 3669 W. 69th St., Edina (925-4008). Open daily. AE, MC, V. Diner amusingly decorated in pastel shades, 1950s style. Hamburgers, daily specials. Good cafeteria food.

BARS & NIGHTCLUBS

Jazzline (633-0329) gives detailed information on current programming at Twin Cities jazz clubs.

    Brave New Workshop (nr. dwntwn), 2605 Hennepin Ave. (332-6620). Highly regarded club staging good comedy shows in an intimate atmosphere. Wed−Sun.

    Fine Line Music Café (dwntwn), 318 First Ave. N. (338-8100). Excellent live blues and jazz in a sophisticated setting. Also rest. Open nightly.

    First Ave. and 7th St. Entry (dwntwn), 701 First Ave. N. (338-8388). Rock and funky jazz in the converted former Greyhound bus depot; lots of warmth. Setting for rock singer Prince's movie *Purple Rain.* Open nightly.

    Grand Slam (dwntwn), 110 N. 5th St. (338-3383). One of the hottest places in town; owned by local rock star Prince. Would-be hipsters clientele. Open Tues−Sat.

    Loring Bar (nr. dwntwn), 1624 Harmon Place (332-1617). Nightly live entertainment of all musical varieties in bohemian atmosphere. No cover charge. Good rest. also (see Loring Café, above).

    New French Bar (dwntwn), 128 N. 4th St. (338-3790). Very "in" singles bar frequented by artists and foundation people. Open nightly.

    Uptown Bar and Grill (nr. dwntwn). 3018 Hennepin Ave. (823-4719).

Local/national alternative rock, roots, or acoustic music nightly. Decent dining as well. Open nightly.

ST. PAUL

INFORMATION & TOURS

TOURIST INFORMATION: The **St. Paul Convention and Visitors Bureau,** 101 Norwest Center, 55 E. 5th St., MN 55101 (612/297-6985; toll free 800/627-6101).

The Connection: For information on current shows and cultural events in the Twin Cities, call 922-9000.

GUIDED TOURS: Gray Line Tours (bus): See "Minneapolis, Guided Tours," above.

Padelford Packet Boat Co. (boat), Harriet Island Park, St. Paul (227-1100): 90-min mini-cruises on the Mississippi aboard four elderly paddlewheelers, the *Jonathan Padelford,* the *Anson Northrup,* the *Betsey Northrup,* and the *Josiah Snelling.* Early May to late Sept.

SIGHTS, ATTRACTIONS & ACTIVITIES

ADVENTURES: Inner Tube Rides, intersection of Wisc. 35 and Wisc. 64 at Somerset, Wisc., 27 mi. (43km) NE of St. Paul on Minn. 5 and Wisc. 64 (715/247-3728): Shooting the rapids of the Apple River on inflated inner tubes. Time: 45 min. to 3 hr., according to distance. The favorite local sport; entertaining and low risk. Open daily mid-May to mid-Sept.

ARCHITECTURAL HIGHLIGHTS: ☀☚ **Ordway Music Theater,** 345 Washington St. (224-4222): Opened in 1985, this splendid auditorium with its glass-and-brick, accordion-fronted facade is now the home of the famous St. Paul Chamber Orchestra and the Minnesota Opera; many other concerts are also given here.

☚ **Minnesota World Trade Center,** 30 E. 7th St. between Wabasha and Cedar Sts. (297-1580): Completed in 1987, this 40-story building is St. Paul's tallest and the hub of international business in the region. Its retail area, with dozens of shops, eateries, and restaurants, has brought additional vigor to the dwntwn revival.

☚ **Skyway,** around 6th and Cedar Sts.: Same network of heated walkways as in Minneapolis, connecting the main dwntwn buildings and department stores.

CHURCHES/SYNAGOGUES: ☚ **Old Muskego Church,** on the campus of Luther Seminary, 2481 Como Ave. (641-3456): The first (1844) church in the country built by Norse immigrants; moved to its present site in 1904. Go to the campus library for the key to the church.

☀☚ **Cathedral of St. Paul,** 239 Selby Ave. (228-1766): Built in 1915, this is a reasonably exact replica of St. Peter's in Rome, with its dome 175 ft. (53m) high, its great west rose window, and its massive granite-and-travertine construction. Open daily.

HISTORIC BUILDINGS: ☚ **Alexander Ramsey House,** 265 S. Exchange St., at Walnut St. (296-8681): Fine Victorian house which was the home of the first governor of the Minnesota Territory (1872). Period furniture and decoration. Open Tues–Sat Apr–Dec.

☀☚ **City Hall and Court House,** 15 W. Kellogg Blvd., at Wabasha St. (298-4012): This 1932 building displays 19 floors of marble and rare woods from around the world. Impressive 60-ton statue, 44 ft. (13m) high, in white onyx by the Swedish sculptor Carl Milles, of *The Indian God of Peace.* Open Mon–Fri.

Fort Snelling, Minn. 5 and Post Rd., 6 mi. (10km) SW on Minn. 5 (726-1171): Former stone fortress from the 1820s, scrupulously restored; attained its greatest importance in the wars against the Sioux and Chippewa. Picturesque site where the Mississippi and Minnesota Rivers meet. Has retained all the flavor of the adventurous 19th-century frontier. Military parades in period uniform, daily May–Oct.

Landmark Center, 75 W. 5th St. (292-3225): This fine 1892 example of the Roman Revival style, once known as the Old Federal Courts Building, is capped by a tall belfry reminiscent of Trinity Church in Boston. Today it's an active cultural center with an auditorium, exhibition galleries, and the **Schubert Piano Museum.** Open daily.

State Capitol, Aurora Ave. between Cedar Park and Park Ave. (296-2881): The Minnesota legislature building, designed by the great Cass Gilbert, has one of the world's largest self-supporting domes, inspired by the work of Michelangelo in Rome. No fewer than 21 kinds of marble and 25 different types of stone are employed in this important building, whose foundation stone was laid in 1896. Open daily.

MUSEUMS OF ART: Minnesota Museum of Art, 305 St. Peter St. (292-4355):

This modest museum, settled here in its new permanent home since 1989, has an interesting collection of American art from the end of the 19th century to the present day, as well as African and Asian art. Open Tues–Sun.

MUSEUMS OF SCIENCE & HISTORY: Children's Museum, 1217 Bandana Blvd. N. (644-5305):

Although this is a teaching museum, it's very popular with children. Among other attractions it has careful replicas of a TV studio, a grocery store, and a doctor's office, as well as computers and dozens of machines of all kinds that visitors can operate themselves. Open daily in summer, Tues–Sun the rest of the year.

Minnesota History Center, 345 Kellogg Blvd. W. (296-6126): Spectacular brand new museum opened in Oct. 92. Features interesting exhibits about early Scandinavian settlers and Native Americans. Open Tues.–Sun.

Science Museum of Minnesota, 30 E. 10th St. (221-9400): Group of ultramodern buildings housing interesting natural-science collections in paleontology, biology, anthropology, geology, etc., as well as an auditorium and an innovative cinema with a giant hemispherical screen, the **William L. McKnight 3M Omnitheater.** Very dramatic. Open daily in summer, Tues–Sun the rest of the year.

PARKS & GARDENS: Cherokee Park, Cherokee Blvd. and Ohio St.:

Lovely view from the heights of the park overlooking the Mississippi.

Como Park, Lexington Pkwy. and W. Como Ave. (292-7400): A 445-acre (180ha) park 15 mi. (24km) by car from dwntwn. Flower shows, zoo, 70-acre (28ha) lake.

Indian Mounds Park, Earl St. and Mounds Blvd.: Funerary mounds of Sioux chiefs on the banks of the Mississippi.

Phalen Park, Arcade St. and Larpenteur Ave.: Huge public garden around a lake, which draws many visitors winter and summer alike. Golf course.

PERFORMING ARTS: For current listings of shows and cultural events, consult the entertainment pages of the daily paper, the *St. Paul Pioneer Press-Dispatch* (morning and evening), as well as the monthly *Minneapolis–St. Paul* magazine.

Civic Center, 143 W. 4th St. (224-7361): Live pop and rock concerts.
Great American History Theatre, Science Museum of Minnesota, 30 E. 10th St. (292-4323): Contemporary plays with American and midwestern themes. Sept–May.
Ordway Music Theater, 345 Washington St. (224-4222): Opera, recitals, pop and classical concerts, dance. Home of the St. Paul Chamber Orchestra— the only full-time chamber orchestra in the U.S.—(principal conductor: Hugh Wolff); and of the Minnesota Opera (general director: Kevin Smith).
O'Shaughnessy Auditorium, 2004 Randolph Ave. (690-6700): Classical concerts, opera.
World Theater, 10 E. Exchange St. (290-1221): Fine old theater beautifully restored. Shows and concerts. This was the original setting for the taping of the popular radio program "Prairie Home Companion," hosted by Garrison Keillor.

SHOPPING: St. Paul Center, 7th and Cedar Sts.: Located at the World Trade Plaza, this elegant shopping mall includes the 100 shops, eateries, and restaurants of Town Court and Town Square (see below), as well as Dayton's and Carson Pirie Scott department stores. Open daily.
Town Square, 7th and Minnesota Sts.: More than 70 boutiques, stores, and cafés in a glass-enclosed public garden where waterfalls, pools, and tropical plants combine to create a beautiful setting. Spectacular.

SPECIAL EVENTS: For exact dates, consult the **St. Paul Convention and Visitors Bureau** (see "Tourist Information," above).
Winter Carnival (late Jan to early Feb): Processions, ice-carving contests, sporting events (marathon), professional car racing (on ice), parades through the city. Very popular since its inception in 1885; draws hundreds of thousands of outdoors enthusiasts every year.
Minnesota State Fair (late Aug to early Sept): This very popular fair-exhibition draws more than a million visitors yearly. Horse shows. Plenty of atmosphere.

SPORTS: Same as Minneapolis (see above).

STROLLS: ☀☖ **Summit Avenue,** around Lexington Ave.: Smart, elegant main drag with opulent churches and upper-class homes from the second half of the 19th century. These include the **James J. Hill House,** 240 Summit Ave. (297-2555), open Wed–Sat, by appointment, built by the railroad magnate in 1891; the house of author **F. Scott Fitzgerald** at 599 Summit Terrace (no visitors); the very lovely 1862 **Burbank-Livingston-Griggs House** at 432 Summit Ave. (no visitors); and the English Tudor **Governor's Mansion** at 1006 Summit Ave. (297-2161), with visits by appointment on Thurs May–Oct.

ACCOMMODATIONS

Hotels (from top bracket to budget)

☀♟♟♟ **St. Paul Hotel** (dwntwn), 350 Market St., MN 55102 (612/292-9292; toll free 800/223-1588). 254 rms, A/C, color TV, in-rm movies. AE, CB, DC, MC, V. Gar. $10, rest. (St. Paul Grill), café, bar, rm svce, concierge, free crib. *Note:* Venerable turn-of-the-century luxury hotel in the European style, decor and facilities elegantly renovated. Quality and style; large, luxuriously comfortable rms; flawless svce. Excellent hotel rest. Centrally located with direct Skyway access; favored by those in-the-know. **M–E**

♟♟♟ **Radisson Hotel St. Paul** (dwntwn), 11 E. Kellogg Blvd., MN 55101 (612/292-1900; toll free, see Radisson). 475 rums, A/C, color TV, in-rm movies. AE, CB, DC, MC, V. Gar. $6, pool, health club, rest (Le Carrousel), bar, rm svce, free crib. *Note:* Modern luxury hotel of conventional type intended for groups and conventions. Comfortable rms, the best overlooking the attractive winter grdn/pool. Revolving rest. on the 22nd floor w. a clear view of the city and the Mississippi River. Efficient svce. VIP floor. In the heart of dwntwn, w. direct access to Skywalk. Completed an $8-million renovation in 1989. **M**

    ♔♔ **Crown Sterling Suites** (dwntwn), 175 E. 10 St., MN 55101 (612/224-5400; toll free 800/433-4600). 210 suites. A/C, color TV, in-rm movies. AE, CB, DC, MC, V. Free parking, pool, sauna, rest. (Woolley's), bar, rm svce, free breakfast and cocktails, free crib. *Note:* Upscale modern hotel built around a glassed-in eight-story atrium w. winter grdns, waterfalls, fountains—and ducks! Suites only: spacious and comfortable, w. kitchenette and refrigerator. Efficient svce; very central. Business clientele. **M**

    ♔♔ **Holiday Inn Express** (formerly the Sunwood Inn; nr. dwntwn), 1010 Bandana Blvd., MN 55108 (612/647-1637; toll free, see Holiday Inn). 108 rms, A/C, color TV, in-rm movies. AE, CB, DC, MC, V. Free parking, pool, sauna, nearby rest., free continental breakfast, free crib. *Note:* One-of-a-kind motel built in a converted turn-of-the-century train depot; old tracks run through the lobby. Comfortable, attractive rms. Efficient reception and svce. Connected by Skywalk to the adjacent Bandana Square shopping mall. Free airport shuttle. Good value overall. In business area, 15 min. from dwntwn via I-94 (Lexington Ave. exit). **I–M**

    ♔ **Best Western Kelly Inn** (dwntwn), 161 St. Anthony St., MN 55103 (612/227-8711; toll free, see Best Western). 127 rms, A/C, color TV. AE, CB, DC, MC, V. Free parking, pool, sauna, rest. (Benjamin's), bar, free crib. *Note:* Modest, unpretentious motel very nr. the State Capitol. Completely remodeled. Functionally comfortable. Ideal for budget travelers. **I**

    ♔ **Days Inn–Civic Center** (dwntwn), 175 W. 7th St., MN 55102 (612/292-8929; toll free, see Days Inn). 203 rms, A/C, color TV, in-rm movies. AE, CB, DC, MC, V. Free parking, 24-hr. rest, bar, rm svce, free crib. *Note:* Huge high-rise motel standing (as you'd expect from its name) across from the Civic Center in the heart of dwntwn. Functionally comfortable; efficient svce. Group and convention traffic. Good value on balance. **I**

Airport Accommodations

    ♔♔♔ **Hotel Sofitel** (vic.), 5601 W. 78th St., in Bloomington, MN 55435 (612/835-1900; toll free 800/876-6303). 288 rms, A/C, color TV, in-rm movies. AE, CB, DC, MC, V. Free valet parking, pool, health club, sauna, three rests. (including Le Café Royal), coffee shop, bar, rm svce, concierge, free crib. *Note:* This modern hotel, part of the French-owned Sofitel chain, strongly upholds the gastronomic standards of its native country w. three good rests. and cafés, one of which (La Terrasse) is open late. Pleasant six-story lobby-grdn. Very comfortable rms; smiling reception. Business clientele. 15 min. from dwntwn Minneapolis, 10 min. from the airport. Interesting wknd discounts. **M–E**

YMCA/Youth Hostel

    Cæcilian Hall (vic.), 2004 Randolph Ave., MN 55104 (612/690-6604). 103 beds. Youth hostel on the campus of St. Catherine's College, halfway between Minneapolis and St. Paul. Open June to late Aug.

RESTAURANTS

Restaurants (from top bracket to budget)

    ♙♙♙ **St. Paul Grill** (dwntwn), in the St. Paul Hotel (see "Accommodations," above) (224-7455). A/C. Lunch Mon–Sat, dinner nightly, brunch Sun. AE, DC, MC, V. Jkt. *Specialties:* fresh seafood, chicken pot pie. The menu changes regularly. Imposing wine list. *Note:* Fairly new, elegant place overlooking Rice Park. St. Paul's hottest spot for a power lunch. Extensive and appealing menu. Fashionable and distinguished atmosphere. Very polished svce. Resv. highly advised. 25 min. from Minneapolis. Valet parking. *Continental.* **M**

🍸 **Forepaugh's** (dwntwn), 276 S. Exchange St. (224-5606). A/C. Lunch Mon–Fri, dinner nightly, brunch Sun. AE, MC, V. Jkt. *Specialties:* sautéed scampi, scallops in beurre blanc, veal Calvados, tournedos béarnaise, filet of beef Wellington. Very good desserts; large wine list. *Note:* Successful union of classical and modern French cuisine under the skilled hand of chef Eric Schlenker, in a big, elegant Victorian house (1870), tastefully restored. Svce of the highest order; romantic atmosphere; very popular locally. Resv. a must. Valet parking. *French.* **M**

🍸 **Lexington** (nr. dwntwn), 1096 Grand Ave. (222-5878). A/C. Lunch Mon–Sat, dinner nightly; closed Dec 24–25. AE, DC, MC, V. Jkt. *Specialties:* steak, prime rib, fresh salmon, roast pheasant, catch of the day. *Note:* This well-established family rest. has enjoyed a solid reputation since 1934. The cooking is professional, but unimaginative despite the 35 dishes on the menu. The cocktails are generously poured. Very popular locally; resv. advised. 8 min. from dwntwn. *Steak/Seafood.* **M**

🍸 **Ristorante Luci** (nr. dwntwn), 470 Cleveland Ave. S. (699-8258). A/C. Dinner only, nightly; closed hols. MC, V. *Specialties:* made-in-house mozzarella and pasta, fusilli alla Luci (spiral pasta w. diced chicken breast, garlic, and broccoli), fettucini w. oyster porcini mushrooms, veal saltimbocca w. fontina cheese and prosciutto, fresh fruit tart. Seasonal menu. Extensive wine list w. over 200 entries. *Note:* Up-and-coming Italian rest. run by the Smith family, all of whom were born in Italy. Spartan, white-interior rest. that packs locals in. Recently listed as one of the favorite rests. in the area by readers of *Minneapolis–St. Paul* magazine. Due to the small size of the rest. (40 seats), resvs. are highly recommended. Friendly, helpful svce. A very good value. *Italian.* **I–M**

🍸 **Sakura** (dwntwn), Galtier Plaza, 175 E. 5th St. (224-0185). A/C. Lunch Mon–Sat, dinner nightly. AE, CB, DC, MC, V. *Specialties:* gyoza, sukiyaki, teriyaki, tempura, sushi, sashimi. Skimpy wine and beer list. *Note:* Small, traditional Japanese rest. w. blond-wood tables and minimalist decor. Congenial, smiling svce. A favorite of connoisseurs. Resv. accepted. *Japanese.* **I**

🍸 **Leann Chin's** (dwntwn), 214 E. 4th St. (224-8814). A/C. Lunch/dinner daily; closed hols. AE, MC, V. *Specialties:* funki soup, cream-cheese wontons, lemon chicken, sweet-and-sour pork, beef Szechuan, Cantonese shrimp, almond cookie ice cream. *Note:* This enormous Far Eastern rest. occupies the former Union Pacific Railroad station. The Cantonese and Szechuan buffet at lunch and dinner is the real thing. Elegantly decorated in pink and beige w. many Chinese vases, jades, and ivory carvings. Efficient svce; locally popular so resv. advised. Other location: 900 Second Ave., Minneapolis (338-8488). *Chinese.* **B–I**

🍸 **Venetian Inn** (nr. dwntwn), 2814 Rice St. at Little Canada (484-7215). A/C. Lunch/dinner Mon–Sat; closed hols. AE, CB, DC, MC, V. *Specialties:* fresh homemade pasta, lasagne, barbecued spareribs, steak, catch of the day. *Note:* The food is mostly Italian but the prime beef is also excellent and very reasonably priced. In the hands of the Vitale family for more than half a century. Friendly, smiling svce. Locally popular; this place can be confidently recommended. Resv. advised. 15 min. from dwntwn. *Italian.* **B–I**

🍸 **Mickey's Diner** (dwntwn), 36 W. 7th St. (222-5633). A/C. Lunch/dinner daily 24 hr. No credit cards. *Specialties:* buckwheat pancakes, homemade soups, sandwiches, hamburgers, fried liver and onions, steak, baked pinto beans, broiled chicken, milkshakes, good desserts. *Note:* Wonderful diner of the traditional kind, gleaming w. chrome and Formica; built in 1937, this is a designated historic structure. Food and prices have changed little in half a century. If you enjoyed *American Graffiti,* you'll love this one. No resv. *American.* **B**

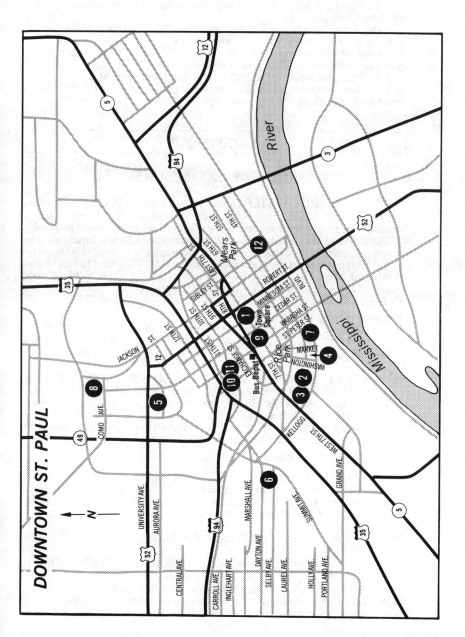

DOWNTOWN ST. PAUL

1. Minnesota Office of Tourism
2. Ordway Music Hall
3. Civic Center
4. St. Paul Public Library
5. State Capitol
6. St. Paul Cathedral
7. Minnesota Museum of Art
8. Minnesota State Fairgrounds
9. Minnesota World Trade Center
10. Science Museum of Minnesota
11. 3M William L. McKnight Omnitheatre
12. Union Depot Place

Cafeteria/Fast Food

Café Latte (nr. dwntwn), 850 Grand Ave. (224-5687). Lunch/dinner daily. AE, MC, V. Interesting soups and daily specials as well as excellent desserts, in a modern neon-and-chrome setting. Very popular locally.

BARS & NIGHTCLUBS

Jazzline (633-0329) gives detailed information on current programming in the Twin Cities jazz clubs.

Dixie (nr. dwntwn), 695 Grand Ave. (222-7345). Fashionable bar; trendy patrons. Also Cajun-Tex-Mex rest. Open nightly.

Gallivan's (dwntwn), 354 Wabasha St. (227-6688). Friendly, jam-packed piano bar with dancing. Also a rest. Open Mon–Sat.

St. Paul's Heartthrob Café and Nightclub (dwntwn), 30 E. 7th St. (224-2783). Noisy, throbbing roller disco; the setting is from the '50s but the crowd is much younger. Also a rest. Open nightly.

EXCURSIONS

NEARBY EXCURSIONS

ROCHESTER (88 mi./140km SE on U.S. 52): One of the capital cities of U.S. medicine. With its 1,000 doctors and hundreds of researchers and technicians, the **Mayo Clinic,** founded in 1898 by Dr. William Worrall Mayo and his sons, William James and Charles Horace, is world-renowned, particularly in the field of cardiac surgery and treats 300,000 patients a year. Walking tours of the general clinic, 200 1st St. SW (507/284-5040), are conducted Mon–Fri. Also the lavish home of the Mayo family, **Mayowood** (507/282-9447), conducted tour Tues–Sun Apr–Oct and Tues, Sat, and Sun Dec–Mar. (Tours leave from the corner of County Roads 22 and 25.)

Where to Stay in Rochester

Radisson Hotel Centerplace, 150 S. Broadway, Rochester, MN 55904 (507/281-8000; toll free, see Radisson). 213 rms. Ultramodern grand hotel w. private entrance to the Mayo Clinic. **M–E**

ST. CROIX VALLEY (32 mi./51km NE on I-35W and Minn. 36): Wonderful panoramic drive on Minn. 95 from **Stillwater** to **Taylors Falls,** 30 mi. (48km) north, along "America's River Rhine," as the St. Croix River has been called.

From **Somerset,** on the right bank of the St. Croix, you can go down the Apple River on an inner tube (see St. Paul "Adventures," above).

Where to Stay En Route

IN STILLWATER **Lowell Inn,** 102 N. 2nd St., Stillwater, MN 55082 (612/439-1100). 21 (very comfortable) rms. AE, CB, DC, MC, V. The elegant colonial setting is more than a century old; the rest. is excellent. Boat trips are available on the St. Croix River. **M–E**

FARTHER AFIELD

GRAND PORTAGE NATIONAL MONUMENT (318 mi./508km NE of Minneapolis via I-35 and U.S. 61): Owes its name to the "portage road" along Lake Superior, where the first French trappers, at the end of the 17th century, carried their canoes on their backs. The original 9-mi. (15km) Native American trail is still there, but muddy and mosquito-infested. At Grand Portage, terminus of the ferry for Isle Royale National Park (see below), which operates from May to mid-Oct (call 715/392-2100 for information), the 1788 fur-trading post has been partially reconstructed to its original form and is worth a visit (open daily, mid-May to mid-Oct). U.S. 61 offers you a panoramic drive along Lake Superior.

ISLE ROYALE NATIONAL PARK (343 mi./548km NE of Minneapolis via I-35 and U.S. 61 and ferry from Grand Portage): America's most unspoiled national park. This magnificent island, 45 by 8 mi. (72 by 13km) in size, was so named by French trappers; it's a kind of open-air zoo, with dozens of animal species from the red fox to the elk and from the wolf to the fish-eagle. The only ways you can get around are by outboard boat (you can rent one there), by canoe, or on foot since no vehicles are allowed on the island. There are 155 mi. (250km) of footpaths through the beautiful, unspoiled landscape, but beware of fog and mosquitos in summer.

Isle Royale is also the scene of many 19th-century shipwrecks, and has been designated a **national underwater museum,** with scuba-diving facilities and guided tours of underwater attractions provided by the National Park Service. Note that scuba diving should be attempted only by experts because of the low water temperature in Lake Superior (60°F/16°C).

The park is open May–Oct. For lovers of nature and/or fishing, a visit (and a stay) here should on no account be missed. For further information, contact the Superintendent, Isle Royale National Park, 87 N. Ripley St., Houghton, MI 49931 (906/482-0984).

Where to Stay in the Park

There are 30 or so camping areas. In addition, **Rock Harbor Lodge,** on the east end of the island, has 60 comfortable rooms and 20 bungalows for rent June –Sept, but reservations must be made very far ahead. In summer apply to National Park Concessions, P.O. Box 405, Houghton, MI 49931 (906/337-4993); off-season, National Park Concessions, Mammoth Cave, KY 42259 (502/773-2191).

VOYAGEURS NATIONAL PARK (294 mi./470km north of Minneapolis via I-35 and U.S. 53): Another miraculously preserved wildlife sanctuary, covering 217,000 scenic acres (88,000ha) of lakes, islands, forests, and watercourses on the Canadian border, with a hundred camping areas but no hotels. Wear warm clothes, even in summer; not for nothing is the nearest city, **International Falls,** known as "America's Icebox," routinely reporting winter temperatures of −30° to −40° F (−34° to −40° C). A fisherman's paradise, with boats available for rent on the spot. For information, contact the Superintendent, Voyageurs National Park, 3131 Hwy. 53, International Falls, MN 56649 (218/283-9821).

LAKE DISTRICT & SUPERIOR NATIONAL FOREST (845 mi./1,352km r.t. via U.S. 10N, Minn. 27E, U.S. 169N, Minn. 18W, Minn. 371N, U.S. 2E, U.S. 169N, Minn. 1E, U.S. 61N, U.S. 615, and I-35S): An enthralling trip for devotees of nature in the raw, through the myriad lakes and endless forests of northern Minnesota.

The trip begins along a smooth-flowing stretch of the Mississippi, taking you to the **boyhood home of Charles A. Lindbergh,** the first man to make a nonstop solo flight across the Atlantic, with many personal mementoes of the famous flyer. At Lindbergh Dr. at Little Falls (612/632-3154), it's open daily May to mid-Sept, and weekends late Sept and Oct; closed the rest of the year.

Then on along **Mille Lacs Lake** and **Leech Lake,** which between them boast 750 mi. (1,200km) of shoreline (there are dozens of friendly inns and motels around **Brainerd, Walker,** and **Grand Rapids,** birthplace of actress and singer Judy Garland). Next, drive to **Chippewa National Forest,** 3,400 sq. mi.

(880,000ha) of dense standing timber with 2,000 lakes of all sizes—a paradise for hunters, fishermen, and canoeists. Superior National Forest is one of the last places in the country where wolves may be found in the wild.

On your way, stop at ⚓ **Hibbing,** "the iron-ore capital of the world," with the world's largest open-pit iron-ore mine, the Hull-Rust Mine, on Third Ave. (218/262-4900). You can inspect the enormous hole, 3 mi. (5km) long and 535 ft. (163m) deep, from an observation platform open daily mid-May through Sept. More than a billion tons of material have been removed from the mine since it opened in 1918. Hibbing has two famous children of whom it is equally proud: the Greyhound Bus Company and singer Bob Dylan.

Just 45 mi. (72km) NE of Hibbing is another well-known iron-ore mine, the ☀⚓ **Soudan Iron Mine,** on Minn. 169 in Soudan (218/753-2245). This, the first underground mine in Minnesota, which closed down in 1962 after 80 years of commercial production, is well worth going out of your way for. Make a point of going the 2,400 ft. (730m) under the surface (in 3 min.) to the now-disused workings, which you can tour in a little electric train; remember to dress for the 52°F (11°C) temperature down there. Fascinating. Open daily Memorial Day–Labor Day.

The excursion ends with a visit to **Grand Portage National Monument** and **Isle Royale National Park** (see above).

On the way back, **Duluth,** a busy commercial port with its astonishing Aerial Lift Bridge, is a stop you should make.

You should allow at least a week for this spectacular drive—but you're not advised to make it in any season except summer!

Where to Stay En Route

As noted above, there are dozens of friendly inns and motels around Brainerd, Walker, and Grand Rapids.

IN DULUTH 🍷🍷🍷 **Fitger's Inn,** 600 E. Superior St., Duluth, MN 55802 (218/722-8826). This converted brewery now boasts 48 rms, most overlooking Lake Michigan. **I–M**

🛏🛏 **Best Western Edgewater East,** 2400 London Rd., Duluth, MN 55812 (218/728-3601). 283 rms. A functionally comfortable roadside motel. **I–M**

Where to Eat En Route

As noted above, there are dozens of friendly inns around Brainerd, Walker, and Grand Rapids.

IN DULUTH 🍷 **Grandma's Saloon and Deli,** 522 Lake Ave. S., near the lift bridge (218/727-4192). Lunch/dinner daily. Honest, down-home food in a quaint early-1900s building. **B–I**

CHAPTER 26

INDIANAPOLIS

□ □ □

Today a flourishing metropolitan area of more than a million inhabitants, Indianapolis was not initially a pioneer encampment like so many other midwestern cities. Its site was determined by simple logic, rather than by some caprice of history or nature: Indianapolis is at the dead center of Indiana. The city's layout was inspired by that of Washington, D.C., and follows a rigorous geometry. Wide diagonal avenues converge on **Monument Circle** like the spokes of a wheel, and a right-angled grid of streets connects the city's principal monuments: the imposing **State Capitol,** the **World War Memorial Hall,** the **Soldiers and Sailors Monument,** the **Scottish Rite Cathedral,** and the national headquarters of the **American Legion.**

Indianapolis was long considered provincial, politically conservative (the John Birch Society originated here), and boring (it was once known as "Naptown"). But over the last 15 years the capital of Indiana has come to be perceived as a modern, lively, and safe city (the crime rate is one of the lowest in the country). Witness the renovation around picturesque **City Market and Union Station,** the construction of the **Hoosier Dome Complex** (an impressive enclosed stadium that seats 63,000), the new $64-million zoo, and the **Eiteljorg Museum,** a remarkable museum of western art that opened in 1989, as well as the brand new **White River State Park** in downtown Indianapolis.

Neither Robert Cavelier, sieur de La Salle, the Frenchman who explored Indiana along the St. Joseph River (1679), nor Gen. William Henry Harrison, who defeated the great Shawnee chief Tecumseh in the battle of Tippecanoe (1811), could have dreamed that Indiana's capital would one day be famous for the world's oldest auto race (since 1911), held on Memorial Day weekend, the thrilling and perilous "Indianapolis 500." At the heart of the famed corn belt, Indianapolis is one of the largest grain and cattle markets in the country. It's also the headquarters of the giant pharmaceutical company Eli Lilly (29,000 employees) and a mecca for amateur sports, as well as one of the most important hubs of rail and road communication in North America, where no fewer than four major Interstate highways converge. The state of Indiana is rightly called "the crossroads of America."

Some of the city's notable native children are guitarist Wes Montgomery, author Kurt Vonnegut, Jr., comedian and talk-show host David Letterman, the late actor Steve McQueen, and the famous bandit John Dillinger.

BASIC FACTS: Capital of Indiana. Area code: 317. Time zone: eastern. ZIP Code: 46204. Founded: 1820. Approximate population: city, 790,000; metropolitan area, 1,250,000. 13th largest city in the U.S.; 31st largest metropolitan area in the U.S.

CLIMATE: Indianapolis weather is typical of the midwestern Great Plains: radiant springs; oppressive, humid summers (mean July temperature 76° F/24° C); mild, pleasant autumns; and rather harsh winters (mean Jan temperature 28°F/ −2°C). Spring is the ideal season to visit the area.

DISTANCES: Chicago, 181 mi. (290km); Cincinnati, 106 mi. (170km); Nashville, 297 mi. (446km); St. Louis, 235 mi. (376km).

ARRIVAL & TRANSIT INFORMATION

AIRPORT Indianapolis International Airport (IND): 7 mi (11km) SW. For information, call 487-7243).

AIRLINES: American (toll free 800/433-7300), Continental (toll free 800/525-0280), Delta (toll free 800/221-1212), Northwest (toll free 800/225-2525), TWA (toll free 800/221-2000), United (toll free 800/241-6522), and USAir (toll free 800/428-4322).

CITY LINK: The **cab** fare from the airport to dwntwn is about $14–$16; time, about 15 min. Bus: **Indy Connection** (241-7100; toll free 800/888-4639), serving major dwntwn hotels, leaves upon request at the airport counter; fare $7; time, about 20 min. Unless you intend to make excursions outside the city, the relatively small dwntwn area makes renting a car unnecessary. The **public bus** transportation system is good, and runs around the clock on some routes. **Metro Trolleys,** a shuttle service using minibuses got up like old streetcars, runs dwntwn Mon–Sat on north-south and east-west routes. For information, call **Metro Transit** (635-3344).

CAR RENTAL: Avis (toll free 800/331-1212), Budget (toll free 800/527-0700), Dollar (toll free 800/800-4000), Hertz (toll free 800/654-3131), National (toll free 800/227-7368), and Thrifty (toll free 800/367-2277).

LIMOUSINE SERVICES: Dynasty Limousine (241-9900), Indy Connection Limousine (241-6700; toll free 800/888-4639).

TAXIS: Taxis are few and relatively expensive; they may be found outside the major hotels or simply summoned by phone: **Yellow Cab** (487-7777).

TRAIN: Amtrak station, 350 S. Illinois St. (toll free 800/872-7245).

INTERCITY BUSES: Greyhound, 127 N. Capitol Ave. (toll free 800/231-2222).

INFORMATION & TOURS

TOURIST INFORMATION: The **Indianapolis City Center,** Pan American Plaza, 201 S. Capitol Ave., IN 46225 (317/237-5206; toll free 800/323-4639). Well-qualified facility for public information.

For a **telephone recording** with an up-to-date listing of cultural events and shows, call 317/237-5210.

GUIDED TOURS: Gray Line Tours (bus), 9075 N. Meridian St. (317/844-1658). Guided tours of the city, serving the major hotels.

Yellow Rose Carriages (horse-drawn carriages), 1327 N. Capitol Ave. (317/634-3400). Nightly rides throughout the downtown area, year round (weather permitting). Resv. recommended.

SIGHTS, ATTRACTIONS & ACTIVITIES

ARCHITECTURAL HIGHLIGHTS: ❊ⵣ **Hoosier Dome,** 100 S. Capitol Ave. (262-3452): This 63,000-seat stadium with a 19-story-high fiberglass roof opened in 1984 and is one of the largest in the country. Built at a cost of $65 million, it can accommodate conventions, auto shows, and trade fairs, as well as the Colts' home football games. The stadium is part of the enormous **Indiana Convention Center** (262-3410), with five exposition halls, two large ballrooms, and 55 meeting rooms. Impressive. Guided tours Mon–Sat.

ⵣ **Indiana University–Purdue University at Indianapolis (IUPUI),** W. Michigan St. (274-5555): These two universities, with 26,000 students in all, were merged in 1969 into the present first-rate educational complex. With six hospitals and 90 clinics, faculties, and specialty schools, the **University Medical Center** enjoys a worldwide reputation in the areas of cancer, heart surgery, and organ transplants. IUPUI is also famous for its high-caliber sports teams. Interesting modern architecture. Campus visits daily.

ⵣⵣ **Indianapolis Motor Speedway,** 4790 W. 16th St. (481-8500): Some 6 mi. (9km) NW, this is the most celebrated auto raceway in the world. Nearly 400,000 spectators come here each May for the spectacular and sometimes deadly "Indy 500," staged on the 2.5-mi. (4km) oval course. Arie Luyendyk holds the track speed record set in 1990—an average of 185.984 m.p.h. (297.574kmph). Interesting racing museum, **Indy Hall of Fame Museum.** Guided tour of the raceway (sorry—the bus goes no faster than 37 mph/60kmph). Open daily. For speed demons. (Seats for the Indianapolis 500 range from $18 to $90 and are scooped up weeks and months in advance. For reservations, call 317/248-6700, or write: P.O. Box 24152, Speedway, IN 46224.)

❊ⵣ **Madame Walker Urban Life Center and Theatre,** 617 Indiana Ave. (236-2099): Built in the late '20s as a tribute to Madame C. J. Walker, the country's first African American female self-made millionaire, this legendary theater with stunning African and Egyptian decor reopened in 1988 after a $3.2-million renovation. Hosts a variety of arts and cultural events including a week-long African American film festival in late Oct. Its splendid interior is worth a visit by itself. Tours by appointment Mon–Fri.

CHURCHES/SYNAGOGUES: ⵣ **Carmelite Monastery,** 2500 Cold Spring Rd. (926-5654): The chapel and entranceway of this medieval castlelike monastery are open to the public. Open daily.

❊ⵣ **Scottish Rite Cathedral,** 650 N. Meridian St. (262-3100): This stunning Gothic-Tudor–style cathedral dates from 1929, and has a 212-ft. (65m) tower with a 54-bell carillon. The baroque interior, wood carvings, and two organs with 5,500 pipes are worth seeing. Open for tours Mon–Fri.

HISTORIC BUILDINGS: ⵣ **Benjamin Harrison Memorial Home,** 1230 N. Delaware St. (631-1898): The former residence of the 23rd president houses interesting furniture, paintings, and period decoration (dates from 1874). Open daily.

ⵣ **State Capitol,** between Washington and Ohio Sts. and Capitol and Senate Aves. (232-8860): The home of the state legislature is a Corinthian-style building from 1888, constructed of Indiana limestone and topped with a large brass dome. Visit by appointment Mon–Fri.

❊ⵣ **Union Station,** 39 Jackson Place (267-0701): A perfect example of urban renewal, this once-abandoned station dating from 1888 is now a vast shopping area with more than 70 stores and boutiques, 40 restaurants, three movie theaters, five nightclubs, and a hotel with unusual decor.

Very lively ambience. Since reopening in 1986, it has attracted more than 25 million visitors. Open daily.

MARKETS: ❋⚖ **City Market,** 222 E. Market St. (634-9266): Picturesque enclosed market dating from 1886 in an original cast-iron structure. Dozens of food stalls, boutiques, little restaurants. Lively and colorful. Open Mon–Sat.

MONUMENTS: ❋⚖ **Soldiers and Sailors Monument,** Monument Circle (237-2222): This imposing monument rising 278 ft. (87m) in the heart of the city was erected in memory of those who died in the Revolutionary War. There is elevator access to the observation platform at the top. Open daily.

   ⚖ **World War Memorial,** 431 N. Meridian St. (232-7615): Monument and commemorative exhibition room dedicated to the dead of the two World Wars, Korea, and Vietnam. Interesting military museum as well as gardens. Open daily. In the northeast corner of the square is a four-story building that is the **American Legion national headquarters.**

MUSEUMS OF ART: ❋⚖⚖ **Eiteljorg Museum of American Indian and Western Art,** 500 W. Washington St., White River State Park (636-9378): This magnificent museum houses, in its single $14-million building opened in 1989, one of the country's most beautiful collections of Native American and western art, including works by Frederic Remington and Georgia O'Keeffe. In all there are 240 paintings, 150 bronzes, and more than a thousand examples of old Native American handcrafts such as wickerwork, pottery, and masks. Open daily July–Aug, Tues–Sun the rest of the year.

   ⚖ **Morris-Butler House Museum,** 1204 N. Park Ave. (636-5409): Interesting museum of Victorian decorative arts (the Helena Rubinstein collection) in a building that dates from 1862. Open Tues–Sun.

   ❋⚖⚖ **Museum of Art,** 1200 W. 38th St. (923-1331): On a hill overlooking the White River, this remarkable art museum comprises three theme pavilions: Clowes Pavilion, medieval and Renaissance art; Krannert Pavilion, Oriental and primitive art; Lily Pavilion of Decorative Arts, European and American paintings (including Turner watercolors, works by El Greco, Claude Lorrain, Rembrandt, van Dyck). Pretty gardens with modern sculptures, including Robert Indiana's pop masterpiece, *LOVE.* Open Tues–Sun.

MUSEUMS OF SCIENCE & HISTORY: ⚖⚖ **Children's Museum,** 3000 N. Meridian St. (924-5431): This very instructional children's museum is the world's largest. It presents very lifelike collections and displays from the earliest times (an Indiana cave, a giant dinosaur, an Egyptian tomb complete with mummies) through the present (a huge miniature railroad network, computers, new planetarium, etc.). Wonderful for children of all ages. Open daily in summer, Tues–Sun the rest of the year.

   ⚖ **Indiana State Museum,** 202 N. Alabama St. (232-1637): This interesting museum, in the former city hall, documents the natural and cultural history of Indiana, especially since the pioneer era. Giant Foucault pendulum in the entranceway. Open daily.

   ⚖ **James Whitcomb Riley Home,** 528 Lockerbie St. (631-5885): Very lovely Victorian house dating from 1872, between 1892 and 1916 the home of James Whitcomb Riley, the "Hoosier poet." Period decor and layout. Open Tues–Sun.

   ⚖ **National Track and Field Hall of Fame,** 200 S. Capitol Ave. (261-0483): Located in the Hoosier Dome, this museum honors American track and field greats like Jim Thorpe and Bruce Jenner. The history of track and field since 1904 is chronicled through the display of photos, uniforms, trophies, and early track equipment. Interesting. Open daily.

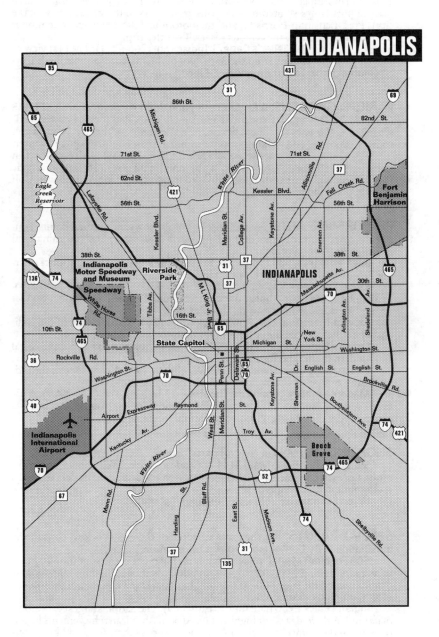

PANORAMAS: ⚱ **Crown Hill Cemetery,** 3402 Boulevard Place (925-8231): This vast landscaped cemetery—one of the largest in the country—is the burial place of poet James Whitcomb Riley (his grave offers an unimpeded view of the city), Pres. Benjamin Harrison, and the notorious John Dillinger. The monumental entranceway to the cemetery is itself worth a trip.

⚱ **The Teller's Cage,** 1 Indiana Sq. (266-5211): The best view of the city from the 35th floor of the Indiana National Bank Tower. Choose the bar over the restaurant. Open Mon–Fri.

PARKS & GARDENS: ⚱ **Eagle Creek Park,** 7840 W. 56th St., west of I-465 (293-4827): This much-frequented and largely unspoiled (deer running wild) setting of 4,400 acres (1,780ha) lies on the western edge of the city. It offers golf courses, canoeing, and walking areas for summer; cross-country skiing in winter.

⚱ **Riverside Regional Park,** 2420 E. Riverside Dr.: Smaller than Eagle Creek Park, with "only" 902 acres (365ha), Riverside Park, steps away from downtown, is divided lengthwise by the White River. Golf courses, pool, and an inviting picnic area.

PERFORMING ARTS: For daily listings of all shows and cultural events, consult the entertainment pages of the daily papers *Indianapolis Star* (morning) and *Indianapolis News* (evening).

Beef 'n Boards, 9301 Michigan Rd. NW (872-9664): Dinner theater offering Broadway shows and recitals with big-name stars.

Circle Theater, 45 Monument Circle (639-4300): Home of the Indianapolis Symphony Orchestra (music director: Raymond Leppard); performances Oct–May. Offers many other musical shows as well.

Clowes Memorial Hall, 4600 Sunset Ave. (283-9696): Home of the Indianapolis Ballet and the Indianapolis Opera; season Oct–Apr.

Indiana Repertory Theatre, 140 W. Washington St. (635-5252): Classical and modern theater; performances Oct–Apr.

Indianapolis Civic Theater, 1200 W. 38th St. (923-4597): One of the oldest theater troupes in the country, performing drama and comedy.

Madame Walker Urban Life Theatre, 617 Indiana Ave. (236-2099): A national historic landmark featuring drama, dance, and jazz on the Avenue—a concert every Fri evening w. local and national musicians.

SHOPPING: **City Market** (see "Markets," above).

Shadeland Antique Mall, 3444 N. Shadeland Ave.: Well-known, and enormous, flea market—mecca for antiques buffs. Nearly a hundred dealers and stalls selling antiques and works of art.

Union Station (see "Historic Buildings," above).

SPECIAL EVENTS: For the exact schedule of the events below, consult the **Indianapolis City Center** (see "Tourist Information," above).

500 Festival (May): Unquestionably *the* big event of the year, the 500 Festival is a month-long city celebration—parades, costume balls, mini-marathon—that leads up to the Indy 500 car race on Memorial Day wknd, one of the world's most prestigious sports events.

Indiana Black Expo (late June to early July): The nation's largest exposition of its kind. A three-day event highlighting African American achievements in culture, art, and commerce. The expo's picnic provides ethnic food and live entertainment.

RCA/U.S. Men's Hardcourt Championships (early Aug): World-class players compete in a week-long event held in a modern 10,000-seat tennis stadium.

Indiana State Fair (Aug.): One of the largest and most colorful agricultural fairs in the country, with horse racing, cattle shows, and more.

MacAllister Awards (late Aug): Semifinals of the National Opera Singers Competition. Some of the most talented young singers in the U.S.

NHRA U.S. Nationals (a week in early Sept): The spectacular U.S. championship of drag racing at Indianapolis Raceway Park. For velocity lovers.

SPORTS: Indianapolis has four professional teams:

Baseball (Apr–Sept): Indians, Bush Stadium (269-3545).
Basketball (Oct–Apr): Pacers, Market Sq. Arena (263-2100).
Football (Sept–Dec): Colts, Hoosier Dome (297-7000).
Ice Hockey (Oct–Apr): Ice, Pepsi Coliseum (924-1234).

STROLLS: ⚑ **Lockerbie Square,** bounded by N. York, College, Michigan, and East Sts.: Narrow, cobblestone streets, brick sidewalks, and pretty, brightly colored 19th-century houses make this a fine area for a stroll.

WINTER SPORTS RESORTS: ⚑ **Nashville Alps Ski World Resort,** 59 mi. (94km) south on Ind. 37 and Ind. 46 (812/988-6638): Two chair lifts. Open mid-Dec to early Mar.

ZOO: ❋⚑ **Indianapolis Zoo,** 1200 W. Washington St. (630-2001): $64-million, 64-acre (26ha) facility, very complete and well conceived with 2,000 animals roaming simulated environments. The nation's first major zoo in decades to be built from the ground up. Rare birds and the world's largest totally enclosed Whale and Dolphin Pavilion. Miniature train rides. Open daily.

ACCOMMODATIONS

Personal Favorites (in order of preference)

🛎🛎🛎 **Westin** (dwntwn), 50 S. Capitol Ave., IN 46204 (317/262-8100; toll free, see Westin). 570 rms, A/C, color TV, in-rm movies. AE, CB, DC, MC, V. Valet parking $8, pool, health club, rest. (Graffitis), pub, 24-hr. rm svce, concierge, crib $10. *Note:* Since opening in 1989 this has supplanted the Hyatt Regency as Indianapolis's most luxurious hotel. A successful venture in postmodern architecture w. a gigantic 15-floor atrium; elegant decor and furnishings. Spacious, well-designed rms, some reserved for nonsmokers. Very good svce. Very well located across from the Capitol and the Convention Center, which can be reached directly by Skywalk. VIP floor; big business clientele. In both size and comfort the city's foremost hotel. **E–VE**

❋🛎🛎🛎 **Canterbury** (dwntwn), 123 S. Illinois St., IN 46225 (317/634-3000; toll free, see Preferred). 99 rms, A/C, cable color TV. AE, CB, DC, MC, V. Valet gar. $8, rest. (Beaulieu), bar, 24-hr. rm svce, concierge, free breakfast, free crib. *Note:* This small, elegant European-style luxury hotel has been sumptuously renovated, 1920s style. Very comfortable rms, w. Chippendale furniture and refrigerators, though some are somewhat cramped. Intimate atmosphere; ultra-correct svce; first-rate rest. Complimentary limousine transportation dwntwn. A favorite of connoisseurs, in the heart of the city. **E–VE**

❋🛎🛎 **Holiday Inn Union Station** (dwntwn), 123 W. Louisiana St., IN 46225 (317/631-2221; toll free, see Holiday Inns). 276 rms, color TV, in-rm movies. AE, CB, DC, MC, V. Free parking, pool, health club, rest. (Louisiana Street), bar, rm svce, boutiques, concierge, free airport shuttle, free crib. *Note:* The most innovative hotel in town stands in the enormous urban-renewal project around the former train station, amid dozens of bars, rests., and fashionable boutiques. Very lively ambience. The customer may choose between classic, comfortable hotel rms and the luxurious Pullman cars of yesteryear. Good overall svce. A delightful experiment by the Holiday Inns chain. Group and convention clientele. **M**

☼☽ **Indianapolis Motor Speedway Motel** (vic.), 4400 W. 16th St., IN 46222 (317/241-2500). 108 rms, A/C, cable color TV, rm movies. AE, DC, MC, V. Free parking, pool, golf, coffee shop, bar, rm svce, Indianapolis 500 museum, free crib. *Note:* Pleasant motel on the grounds of the famous auto raceway. Modern comfort. No resv. during Indy 500 time in May. Very good value. **I**

♟ **Days Inn East** (nr. dwntwn), 7314 E. 21st St., IN 46219 (317/359-5500; toll free, see Days Inn). 120 rms, A/C, cable color TV. AE, DC, MC, V. Free parking, pool, adjacent 24-hr. rest., free crib. *Note:* Conventional motel nr. the new industrial area on the city's eastern periphery and convenient to the beltway (I-465). Functional comfort. Ideal for the motorist. 10 min. from dwntwn. Good value. **B–I**

Other Accommodations (from top bracket to budget)

♟♟♟ **Hyatt Regency** (dwntwn), 1 S. Capitol Ave., IN 46204 (317/632-1234; toll free, see Hyatt). 496 rms, A/C, color TV, in-rm movies. AE, CB, DC, MC, V. Valet gar. $9, pool, health club, three rests. (including a revolving one at the top), bar, 24-hr rm svce, hrdrsr, free crib. *Note:* Luxurious hotel, modern and comfortable. The red-brick construction is rather massive but the 20-story glass-walled atrium is spectacular. Across from the Capitol and the Convention Center. Good overall svce. Very acceptable rest. (Eagle's Nest). VIP floor. Convention facilities. One among the favorites of businesspeople. **E–VE**

♟♟♟ **Omni Severin** (dwntwn), 40 W. Jackson Place, IN 46225 (317/634-6664; toll free, see Omni). 423 rms, A/C, color TV, in-rm movies. AE, CB, DC, MC, V. Gar. $5, pool, health club, rest. (The Severin), bar, rm svce, concierge, free crib. *Note:* Built as the Hotel Severin in 1913, this historic building across from Union Station reopened in 1990 following an extensive renovation. Plush, spacious guest rms w. minibars. Excellent svce. So-so rest. One block from the Hoosier Dome complex and the Convention Center. Business clientele. **M–E**

♟♟♟ **Marriott** (nr. dwntwn), 7202 E. 21st St., IN 46219 (317/352-1231; toll free, see Marriott). 250 rms, A/C, color TV, in-rm movies. AE, CB, DC, MC, V. Free parking, pool, health club, putting green, rest. (Durbin's), bar, rm svce, free crib. *Note:* This large, modern motel on the eastern periphery of Indianapolis is close to the new industrial area. Unusual architecture. Comfortable, spacious rms and efficient svce. Group and business clientele. VIP floor. Interesting wknd packages. 10 min. from dwntwn on I-70. **M**

♟♟ **Embassy Suites North** (vic.), 3912 Vincennes Rd., IN 46268 (317/872-7700; toll free 800/362-2779). 222 suites, A/C, cable color TV. AE, CB, DC, MC, V. Free parking, pool, sauna, rest. (Ellington's), bar, valet svce, free crib. *Note:* Lushly landscaped, eight-story Mediterranean-style all-suites hotel, located in Fortune Park Executive Center, 15 min. from dwntwn. Comfortable one-bedroom suites w. kitchenettes and refrigerators. Ultra-professional svce. Business clientele. **M**

♟♟ **Courtyard by Marriott** (dwntwn), 501 W. Washington St., IN 46204 (317/635-4443; toll free 800/321-2211). 232 rms, A/C, color TV, in-rm movies. AE, CB, DC, MC, V. Free parking, pool, health club, rest. (T. G. I. Friday's), bar, rm svce, free crib. *Note:* Chain motel w. no exceptional attraction or advantage apart from its very central location. Modern comfort. Standard rms w. balconies and refrigerators. Completed a multi-million-dollar renovation in 1989. **I–M**

♀ **La Quinta East** (nr. dwntwn), 7304 E. 21st St., IN 46219
⚎ (317/359-1021; toll free, see La Quinta). 122 rms, A/C, color TV, in-rm movies. AE, CB, DC, MC, V. Free parking, pool, adjacent 24-hr. coffee shop, free crib. *Note:* This classic highway motel is modern and comfortable and 10 min. from dwntwn on I-70. Spacious, inviting rms (some no-smoking). Cheerful svce. Good value. **B–I**

♀ **Red Roof Inn South** (nr. dwntwn), 5221 Victory Dr., IN
⚎ 46203 (317/788-9551; toll free 800/843-7663). 106 rms, A/C, color TV, in-rm movies. AE, DC, MC, V. Free parking, adjacent coffee shop, free crib. *Note:* This modest, unassuming little motel on the southeastern edge of the city offers functional comfort and is ideal for the motorist passing through (direct access to the city beltway, I-465). Good overall value. **B–I**

♀ **Motel 6** (nr. dwntwn), 2851 Shadeland Ave., IN 46219
⚎ (317/546-5864). 285 rms, A/C, cable color TV. AE, DC, MC, V. Free parking, pool, nearby rest. *Note:* An unbeatable value, 10 min. from dwntwn. Functional comfort. Ideal for the motorist. **B**

Airport Accommodations

♀♀ **Holiday Inn Airport** (vic.), 2501 S. High School Rd., IN
⚎⚎ 46241 (317/244-6861; toll free, see Holiday Inn). 274 rms, A/C, color TV, in-rm movies. AE, CB, DC, MC, V. Free parking, pool, sauna, health club, rest. (Chanteclair), coffee shop, bar, rm svce, disco, free airport shuttle, free crib. *Note:* This typical Holiday Inn w. a stunning atrium design has also, strangely enough, one of the most famous rests. in town. Comfortable rms w. balconies. Efficient svce. **M**

RESTAURANTS

Personal Favorites (in order of preference)

♈♈♈ **Beaulieu** (dwntwn), in the Canterbury Hotel (see "Accommodations," above) (634-3000). A/C. Breakfast/lunch/dinner daily, Sun brunch. AE, CB, DC, MC, V. Jkt. *Specialties:* lobster Tivoli, rack of lamb, sole meunière. The menu changes regularly. Interesting wine list. *Note:* Elegantly old-fashioned dining rm w. mahogany paneling and Indiana landscape paintings. The food lives up to the hotel's high reputation. Formal atmosphere (jacket and tie required for dinner). Attentive, polished svce. Late supper until midnight. Resv. strongly advised. Valet parking. A highly commendable place. *Continental.* **M–E**

♈♈♈ **Peter's** (vic.), 8505 Keystone Crossing (465-1155). A/C. Dinner only, Mon–Sat; closed hols. AE, CB, DC, MC, V. Jkt. *Specialties:* cold chicken salad w. peanut-butter sauce and crisp julienne of vegetables, gourmet pizzas, cast-iron-seared breast of Indiana duckling w. fresh berry relish, pan-seared crab cakes w. spicy Créole mustard sauce, beef Angus steak. Menu changes regularly. Good wine list. *Note:* Small, intimate rest. seating only 52, its chaste white walls enlivened by modern paintings. Delicate and often innovative midwestern food. Well worth the 25 min. by car from dwntwn. Resv. essential; a highly recommended spot. *American.* **I–M**

♈♈ **Jonathan's Restaurant and Pub** (vic.), 96th St. and Keystone Crossing (844-1155). A/C, Lunch/dinner daily, brunch Sun; closed hols. AE, DC, MC, V. Jkt. *Specialties:* very fine red meat and fish broiled over a wood fire, spareribs, veal Oscar, roast pork, loin. *Note:* A delightful British-style inn on the northern edge of Indianapolis. Well worth the 25 min. by car from dwntwn. Diligent svce. An excellent locale. Resv. advised. Pub open until 2am. *Steak/Seafood.* **I–M**

♈♈ **Pesto** (dwntwn), 303 N. Alabama St., in the Lockerbie Marketplace (269-0715). A/C. Lunch Mon–Fri, dinner Mon–Sat; closed hols. AE, CB, DC, MC, V. *Specialties:* fried calamari w. smelt and fried spinach; goat-cheese pie; veal Napoleon layered w. spinach, sun-dried tomatoes, prosciutto, and mozzarella; tuna mignon w. peppered pasta and balsamic-tomato sauce; tirami su. Decent wine list. *Note:* Casual *trattoria*-style Italian rest. Friendly, helpful svce. Locally popular, so resv. are highly recommended. *Italian.* I

🍷 **Dodd's Town House** (nr. dwntwn), 5694 N. Meridian St. (257-1872). A/C. Dinner only, Tues–Sun. AE, MC, V. *Specialties:* steak, fried chicken, grilled fish of the day, wonderful homemade cakes and pies. No alcoholic beverages. *Note:* The most popular rest. in town for more than a quarter century. The decor may be as modest as the prices, but Betty Dodd's cooking is very tasty and the portions copious. Efficient svce. Clientele of regulars. Resv. recommended. *American.* B

Other Restaurants (from top bracket to budget)

🍷🍷🍷 **Benvenuti** (dwntwn), 36 S. Pennsylvania St. (633-4915). A/C. Lunch Mon–Fri, dinner Mon–Sat; closed hols. AE, CB, DC, MC, V. Jkt. *Specialties:* lobster ravioli, stuffed quail on peppered polenta, penne w. rabbit and mushrooms, grilled veal chop w. wild mushrooms and marsala wine sauce. The menu changes regularly. Good Italian wine cellar. *Note:* Contemporary Italian cuisine in an elegant European decor w. cherry-wood paneling and tapestry seats. Knowledgeable and congenial svce. Resv. suggested. Big business clientele. *Italian.* M–E

🍷🍷 **King Cole** (dwntwn), 7 N. Meridian St. (638-5588). A/C. Lunch Mon–Fri, dinner Mon–Sat; closed hols. AE, CB, DC, MC, V. Jkt. *Specialties:* roast duckling, baked clams, rack of lamb, pompano en papillote, fish of the day, lemon soufflé. Good wine list. *Note:* A favorite of local businesspeople for more than 50 years. Rich, cozy atmosphere w. old paintings, woodwork, and sumptuous table linens. Irreproachable cuisine and svce. Resv. highly recommended. *Continental.* I–M

�{ 🍷🍷 **St. Elmo Steak House** (dwntwn), 127 S. Illinois St. (635-0636). A/C. Dinner only, nightly; closed hols. and the first 15 days of July. AE, DC, MC, V. Jkt. *Specialties:* aged prime cuts, lamb chops, lobster, seafood. *Note:* A local institution since 1902 and "the" steakhouse par excellence. Pleasant old-fashioned decor. Excellent svce. Resv. advised. Generous cocktails. Free parking. *Steak/Seafood.* I–M

🍷🍷 **Iron Skillet** (nr. dwntwn), 2489 W. 30th St. (923-6353). A/C. Dinner Wed–Sun, brunch Sun; closed Dec 24–25. AE, CB, DC, MC, V. *Specialties:* fried chicken, steak, oven-baked pike. *Note:* In a 19th-century building, this pleasant rest. on the edge of a golf course presents the daily menu on a blackboard and offers honest, tasty regional fare. Attentive, friendly svce. Locally very popular. Resv. recommended. Free parking. *American.* B–I

🍷 **Essential Edibles** (dwntwn), 429 E. Vermont St. (266-8797). A/C. Lunch Tues–Sat, dinner Fri and Sat; closed hols. No credit cards. *Specialties:* roasted-pepper sandwich, vegetable burger, goat-cheese ravioli w. spring pesto sauce, Thai tofu satay, maple walnut pie. Seasonal menu. Well-chosen wine list. *Note:* A fine vegetarian rest. featuring the freshest of vegetables. Bright, open setting. Locally popular. Resv. recommended. Other location, 115 E. 49th St. (931-1080), has take-out only. *Vegetarian.* B–I

🍷 **Shapiro's Delicatessen** (dwntwn), 808 S. Meridian St. (631-4041). A/C. Breakfast/lunch/dinner daily. No credit cards. *Specialties:* giant sandwiches, pastrami, corned beef, stuffed cabbage, brisket, chopped liver, cheesecake. *Note:* The experts agree that this is the best deli around; it's been a classic since 1905. Usually packed at lunchtime (inevitable waits). Other location: 2370 W. 86th St. (872-7255). *American.* B

Restaurants in the Vicinity

🍷🍷 **The Glass Chimney** (vic.), 12901 N. Meridian St., Carmel (844-0921). A/C. Dinner only, Mon–Sat; closed hols. AE, MC, V. Jkt. *Specialties:* lobster bisque w. cognac, pheasant chasseur, wild boar and game (in season), duckling bigarade, rack of lamb, veal kidneys w. mustard sauce, salmon. *Note:* A few remarkable dishes but also some weaknesses in the cooking and svce; the place could do better. Charming old decor and a pleasant patio-grdn. Resv. advised. Locally popular. 35 min. from dwntwn. *Continental.* **I–M**

Cafeterias/Fast Food

L. S. Ayres Tea Room (dwntwn), 1 W. Washington Ave. (899-4411). Lunch only, Mon–Sat. No credit cards. *Note:* Cafeteria in the department store of the same name. Dependable soups and daily specials. Good svce.

Laughner's Cafeteria (nr. dwntwn), 4030 S. East St. (787-3745). Lunch/dinner daily (until 8pm). *Specialties:* fried chicken, roast beef, fish of the day, homemade desserts. *Note:* Very popular cafeteria with charming nostalgic decor. Many more locations (check the local phone book).

BARS & NIGHTCLUBS

The Chatterbox (dwntwn), 435 Massachusetts Ave. (636-0584). A friendly bar w. a wide variety of customers—from politicians to artists. Live jazz. Open Mon–Sat.

Crackers Comedy Club (vic.), 8702 Keystone Crossing (846-2500). Much-frequented comedy club with big-name stars. Open Tues–Sun. Resv. required.

Ike & Jonesy's (dwntwn), 17 W. Jackson Place (632-4553). A disco with a big local following, for fans of the "golden oldies" of the '50s and '60s. Open Mon–Sat.

The Patio Lounge (vic.), 6308 Guilford Ave. (253-0799). Hard rock live. Sponsors underground bands. Locally popular among young crowds. Open Mon–Sat.

Quincy's (vic.) in the Adam's Mark Hotel, 2544 Executive Dr. (248-2481). "In" disco with an elegant atmosphere. Open Mon–Sat.

Rick's Café (dwntwn), Union Station, Track Side (634-6666). The decor comes straight from the movie *Casablanca.* Bastion of "Naptown sound."

NEARBY EXCURSIONS

COLUMBUS (40 mi./64km south on I-65): In the late 1930s this obscure prairie town launched an energetic construction program of buildings both public and private, commissioned from world-famous architects like Eliel and Eero Saarinen, Cesar Pelli, Kevin Roche, Richard Meier, I. M. Pei, and Harry Weese, and enriched with works by artists of the caliber of sculptor Henry Moore. To date some 50 outstanding examples have been completed. Guided tours from the Visitors Center, 506 5th St. (812/372-1954). Open daily Apr–Oct, Mon–Sat the rest of the year.

CONNER PRAIRIE PIONEER SETTLEMENT (13400 Allisonville Rd., Noblesville; 18 mi./28km NE on Ind. 19) (776-6000): This authentic village-museum dating from the 19th century faithfully reproduces pioneer life between 1820 and 1840 with the help of 36 minutely restored old buildings, including the blacksmith's forge and the cobbler's workshop, as well as a plush, patrician residence in the Federal style. Handcraft demonstrations offered in period costume. For history lovers. Open Tues–Sun Apr to late Nov.

MOUNDS STATE PARK (in Anderson, 48 mi./76km NE on I-69 and Ind. 32) (642-6627): A number of prehistoric tumuli including an earthwork 9 ft. (2.7m) tall and 1,280 ft. (400m) in circumference, built by Native American civilizations which remain an enigma to archeologists. Handsome, 247-acre (100ha) park with campgrounds and picnic areas. Open daily.

☼❄⚲ **NASHVILLE** (43 mi./68km south on Ind. 135): This charming authentic pioneer town is now a haven for artists with numerous antique shops, art galleries, etc. A noteworthy point of interest, the ⚲ **John Dillinger Historical Museum,** at 104 S. Van Buren St. (812/988-1933), traces the career of the well-known gangster. Housed in a rambling Victorian mansion, the museum has wax effigies of historical figures from both sides of the law, including J. Edgar Hoover, Melvin Purvis, and Baby Face Nelson, as well as Dillinger himself. There are also displays of Dillinger-related artifacts, among them the pants he wore when he was gunned down by FBI agents in 1934, and his lucky rabbit's foot. Open daily from Mar to mid-Dec.

A few miles south, see the **Brown County State Park:** 15,500 acres (6,275ha) of wooded hills with splendid, glowing bronze tones in autumn; and enormous **Lake Monroe,** both of which offer ideal excursion destinations for nature lovers. (A good joint excursion with a visit to Columbus; see above).

⚲ **ZIONSVILLE** (12 mi./19km north on U.S. 421): Charming little 19th-century town on the outskirts of Indianapolis with many elegant boutiques and an interesting pioneer museum, the **Patrick Henry Sullivan Museum,** 225 W. Hawthorne St. (873-4900). Open Tues–Sat.

CHAPTER 27

ST. LOUIS

□ □ □

Founded in 1764 by Pierre Laclède, a French fur trader and devotee of the sainted King Louis IX of France, then sold to the U.S. in 1803 by Napoleon as part of the Louisiana Purchase, the "Gateway to the West" stands at the confluence of the Illinois River with two greater rivers, the Mississippi and the Missouri. A crossroads for rail, road, and river traffic, its strategic position inevitably made it the starting point for the Westward Expansion in the 19th century. It was from St. Louis that Meriwether Lewis and William Clark started out on their famous expedition, 7,689 mi. (12,302km) to the shores of Oregon and back again in 1804–06. It was from St. Louis, too, that the covered wagons of the pioneers, the heavily laden Conestogas or "prairie schooners," lumbered off on their mission to open up the Middle West to the Pacific.

Once the city of jazz, of former African American slaves, and of great paddlewheelers stemming the current of "Ol' Man River," St. Louis has also been, for a century or more, a thriving industrial center, the home of Monsanto, McDonnell Douglas, General Dynamics, Ralston Purina, and more. Second only to Detroit as a producer of automobiles in the U.S., the "Gateway to the West" prides itself most of all on its leading part in the history of flight. It was the *Spirit of St. Louis* in which Charles Lindbergh made the first solo flight across the Atlantic from west to east in 1927; its descendants include the F-4 *Phantom,* F-15 *Eagle,* F-16 *Fighting Falcon,* and F-18 *Hornet* warplanes, as well as the first *Mercury* and *Gemini* spacecraft.

As a legacy of the heavy inflow of German and Italian immigrants at the turn of the century, St. Louis still possesses the world's largest brewery (Anheuser-Busch) and the best Italian restaurants between New York and the West Coast. Two great culinary inventions, which have attained the status of national icons, first saw the light of day here at the Louisiana Purchase Exposition (St. Louis World's Fair) of 1904: the hot dog and the ice-cream cone. But the finest contemporary symbol of this midwestern city, with its touch of southern charm, is the **Gateway Arch.** The shining 630-ft. (192m) archway of stainless steel, designed by Finnish-American architect Eero Saarinen, rises beside the Mississippi River. Dedicated to the memory of those durable pioneers who won the West, this gigantic double-downstroke has attracted two million visitors a year since it was unveiled in 1965.

Long considered the archetypical provincial town, graceless and boring, in the 1980s St. Louis underwent an artistic, architectural, and cultural boom—witness the success of the St. Louis Symphony, which has become one of the best orchestras in the country. In the past decade the city has undertaken a tremendous program of urban renewal, but rather than mar the glorious view through the Gateway Arch with a jumble of high-rises, St. Louis made an inspired choice: it would make an old city over into a new one. Among the triumphs of renovation are **Compton Heights, Washington Heights (Benton Park),** and mainly **Laclède's Landing,** on the river, with its narrow cobblestone streets, cast-iron lamp standards, and dozens of boutiques, bars, and restaurants. Another resounding success is the former **Union Station,** now a shopping mall delightfully disguised as a medieval castle.

On the darker side, St. Louis has a crime rate that makes solitary walks at night inadvisable.

During the Great Flood of 1993, one of the biggest natural disasters to hit the U.S. in the 20th century, the Mississippi River crept up the St. Louis riverbanks, flooding some residential areas that were built over floodplains. With the exception of some landscape damage around Gateway Arch, no part of the downtown area was severely harmed by the flood. The tourist industry suffered little during this time and is now back to normal.

Famous St. Louis natives include poet and critic T.S. Eliot; actresses Virginia Mayo, Betty Grable, Shelley Winters, and Marsha Mason; actors Vincent Price and Kevin Kline; and singer Josephine Baker.

BASIC FACTS: State of Missouri. Area code: 314. Time zone: central. ZIP Code: 63166. Founded: 1764. Approximate population: city, 396,000; metropolitan area, 2,440,000. 17th-largest metropolitan area in the U.S.

CLIMATE: Unavoidably, given the proximity of the Father of Waters, the climate is disagreeably hot and sticky from June to Sept, with a July mean temperature of 81°F (27°C). Winter is harsh (Jan mean, 33°F/1°C), but snowfall is light. The spring is unusually rainy and windy, with tornados occurring in May and early June. There remains only the fall, by far the best season for a visit, with its cool, sunny days.

DISTANCES: Chicago, 290 mi. (465km); Indianapolis, 235 mi. (376km); Kansas City, 259 mi. (415km); Memphis, 284 mi. (455km); Nashville, 328 mi. (525km).

ARRIVAL & TRANSIT INFORMATION

AIRPORT: Lambert–St. Louis International Airport (STL), 10 mi. (16km) NW. For information, call 314/426-8000.

AIRLINES: American (toll free 800/433-7300), Continental (toll free 800/525-0280), Delta (toll free 800/221-1212), Northwest (toll free 800/225-2525), TWA (toll free 800/221-2000), United (toll free 800/241-6522), and USAir (toll free 800/428-4322).

CITY LINK: The **cab** fare from the airport to downtown is about $18–$20; time, about 35 min. (1 hr. during rush hr.). Bus: **Airport Express** (429-4950), serving major dwntwn hotels, leaves every 20 min.; fare, $6; time, about 40–50 min. **Light Rail: Metro Link,** St. Louis's new system that opened in 1993, has a direct line from the airport to dwntwn, leaving every hour; fare, $1; for more information, call 231-2345. **City bus:** Bi-State has an express service between the airport and dwntwn, leaving every 40 min.; price, $1; time, 1 hr.

The size of the metropolitan area, and its distance from the airport, may make it advisable to rent a car unless you intend to confine yourself to seeing downtown St. Louis. The public transportation system (light rail and bus) is quite extensive. Metro Link serves most major tourist attractions in the dwntwn area: for information, call **Bi-State Transit System** (231-2345).

CAR RENTAL (at Lambert International Airport unless otherwise indicated): Avis (toll free 800/331-1212); Budget (toll free 800/527-0700); Dollar (toll free 800/800-4000); Hertz (toll free 800/654-3131); National (toll free 800/227-7368); and Thrifty, 4140 Cypress Rd., St. Ann (toll free 800/367-2277). For dwntwn locations, consult the local telephone directory.

LIMOUSINE SERVICES: Carey Limousine (946-4114), Dav-El Limousines (toll free 800/922-0343), and Show Me Limo Service (522-0888).

TAXIS: Cabs may, at your pleasure, be hailed on the street, taken from the waiting lines in front of the major hotels, or summoned by phone. Recommended companies: **County Cab** (991-5300), **Laclede Cab** (652-3456), and **Yellow Cab** (361-2345).

TRAIN: Amtrak, 550 S. 16th St. (toll free 800/872-7245).

INTERCITY BUSES: Greyhound, 1450 N. 13th St. (toll free 800/231-2222).

MISSISSIPPI RIVER CRUISES: Sternwheeler river cruises, 3–10 days on the Mississippi aboard the *Delta Queen* or the *Mississippi Queen,* 1920s paddlewheelers. Luxurious kitsch. See Chapter 15 on New Orleans for details.

INFORMATION & TOURS

TOURIST INFORMATION: The **St. Louis Convention and Visitors Commission, 10** S. Broadway, Suite 1000, MO 63102 (314/421-1023; toll free 800/325-7962).
　　Visitors Center, 803 Washington Ave. (314/241-1764).
　　For a **telephone recording** with an up-to-date listing of cultural events and shows, call 421-2100.

GUIDED TOURS: Fostaire Helicopter Ride (helicopter), St. Louis Downtown Airport (421-5440): Helicopter flights over the city; year round, weather permitting.
　　Gateway Riverboat Cruises (boat), St. Louis Levee, beneath the Gateway Arch (621-4040): One-hour trips on the Mississippi aboard the paddlesteamer *Huck Finn, Tom Sawyer,* or *Becky Thatcher,* replicas of 19th-century steamboats. Daily Apr–Oct.
　　Gray Line Tours (bus) (618/271-3056): Conducted tours of the city and surroundings; serves principal downtown and midtown hotels. Daily year round.
　　St. Louis Carriage Co. (carriage) (621-3334): Rides in a horse-drawn carriage, serving downtown and the Riverfront. Year round, weather permitting. Reservations a must.
　　St. Louis Tram Tours (bus), 516 Cerre St. (241-1400): Two-hour conducted tour across the city, in a replica of a turn-of-the-century open streetcar. Serves major hotels. Daily.

SIGHTS, ATTRACTIONS & ACTIVITIES

ARCHITECTURAL HIGHLIGHTS: ⚱ **Busch Stadium,** Walnut St., Broadway, Spruce St., and 7th St. (241-3900): Ultramodern circular stadium, seating 53,000, where Cardinals fans congregate for home games. Also home of the St. Louis Sports Hall of Fame (see "Museums of Science and History," below). Conducted tours of the stadium daily Apr–Dec, Mon–Fri Jan–Mar. No tours on days of games.
　　　　City Hall, Memorial Plaza: Huge building in the Renaissance style, an exact copy of the Hôtel de Ville in Paris.
　　　　Fox Theater, 527 N. Grand Blvd. (534-1678): Originally considered to be one of the two or three finest movie theaters in the country, this 1929 architectural gem has been restored to all its glittering Neo-

ST. LOUIS
Downtown

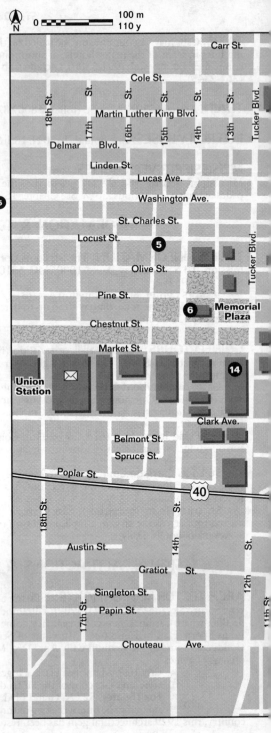

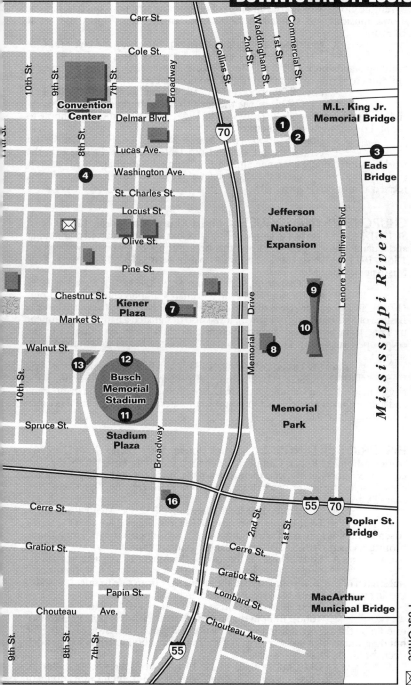

DOWNTOWN ST. LOUIS

Carr St.

Cole St.

Convention
Center

Delmar Blvd.

Lucas Ave.

Washington Ave.

St. Charles St.

Locust St.

Olive St.

Pine St.

Chestnut St.

Kiener
Plaza

Market St.

Walnut St.

Busch
Memorial
Stadium

Spruce St.

Stadium
Plaza

Cerre St.

Gratiot St.

Papin St.

Chouteau Ave.

Carr St.

Cole St.

Broadway

Collins St.

Waddingham St.
2nd St.
1st St.
Commercial St.

M.L. King Jr.
Memorial Bridge

Eads
Bridge

Jefferson
National
Expansion

Lenore K. Sullivan Blvd.

Mississippi River

Memorial Drive

Memorial
Park

Broadway

Cerre St.

2nd St.

1st St.

Gratiot St.

Lombard St.

Chouteau Ave.

Poplar St.
Bridge

MacArthur
Municipal Bridge

Post Office

10th St.
9th St.
7th St.
8th St.

9th St.
8th St.
7th St.

10th St.

Byzantine glory. Now houses all kinds of performing arts: pop concerts, big-star shows, musicals, etc. Guided tours by appointment Tues, Thurs, and Sat at 10:30am.

    🏛 **Metropolitan Square Building,** Broadway at Olive St. (436-1212): The city's first real skyscraper. This modern 42-story building stands only 618 ft. (188m) because a strict city ordinance bans new buildings towering over the 630-ft. (192m) Gateway Arch.

    🏛 **Powell Symphony Hall,** 718 N. Grand Blvd. (533-2500): This old (1925) movie theater also has a sumptuously kitsch ivory-and-gold interior. Splendidly renovated in 1967, it has since then been home to the St. Louis Symphony Orchestra.

    ☀🏛🏛 **Union Station,** 1820 Market St. (421-6655): St. Louis's old central station, dating from 1894 and once the largest in the world, architecturally a strange amalgam of railroad station and medieval fortress. This gloriously successful urban-renewal project cost $135 million. Happy, relaxed atmosphere. Open daily.

CHURCHES/SYNAGOGUES: 🏛 Christ Church Cathedral, 1210 Locust

St. (231-3454): A perfect example of English Gothic, with its carved marble altar and Tiffany stained-glass windows, this beautiful place of worship was erected 1867–1911 on the site of the first Episcopalian parish (1819) built west of the Mississippi. Open Mon–Fri.

    🏛 **Old Cathedral,** 209 Walnut St. (231-3250): Erected in 1831 on the site of the first Roman Catholic church in St. Louis (1770), and given the status of a basilica by Pope John XXIII (its official title is Basilica of St. Louis King of France), it was also designated a national monument by Pres. John F. Kennedy shortly before his death. Religious museum in the crypt, open Tues–Sun. The oldest Roman Catholic cathedral west of the Mississippi.

    ☀🏛🏛 **St. Louis Cathedral,** 4431 Lindell Blvd. at Newstead Ave. (533-2824): This imposing Roman-Byzantine building, the city's "new" Roman Catholic cathedral, dates from 1907; it boasts a giant dome and a nave almost entirely clad in beautiful mosaics. The whole interior is richly decorated. Open daily.

HISTORIC BUILDINGS: 🏛 Campbell House, 1508 Locust St. (421-0325):

Museum-home of Robert Campbell, a rich fur trader in the latter part of the 19th century. Visitors can immerse themselves in the history of the local upper middle class. Original furniture, decorations, and clothing. Interesting. Open Tues–Sun Mar–Dec, closed in Jan–Feb.

    ☀🏛 **Chatillon–de Menil Mansion,** 3352 De Menil Place (771-5828): This handsome 1848 Greek Revival house at the top of Arsenal Hill was long used as a landmark by Mississippi riverboats. Fine antique furniture. Open Wed–Sat. Also a laudable restaurant (lunch only).

    ☀🏛 **Eads Bridge,** at the foot of Washington Ave.: The work of architect James Eads, this was the first bridge (1874) on the central stretch of the Mississippi to span the entire river from side to side. It was also the first to be built with two decks and steel arches.

    🏛 **John B. Myers House,** 180 Dunn Rd., in Florissant (921-4606): Built in the late 1860s, this Palladian-style mansion located near the airport is listed on the National Register of Historic Places. The building and its barn house a variety of craft shops and boutiques, as well as a deli open for lunch. Open Mon–Sat.

    ☀🏛 **Old Courthouse,** 11 N. 14th St. at Market St. (425-4465): This imposing building, with its 173-ft.-high (53m) dome of cast iron decorated with interesting historical frescoes, was completed in 1859.

Here, from 1846 to 1857, was tried the famous case of Dred Scott, the first African American man to contend that slavery could not be enforced outside the states where it was legal. Many memorabilia of this historic case. Open daily.

INDUSTRIAL TOURS: ※ **Anheuser-Busch Brewery,** 13th and Lynch Sts. (577-2626): The largest brewery in the world, whose two major brands, Budweiser and Michelob, sell at the rate of more than five million bottles and cans daily. Free tasting. Don't miss the stables of the famous Clydesdale draft horses, the symbol of Anheuser-Busch. Open Mon–Sat.

MARKETS: ﹩ **Soulard Market,** 7th St. and Lafayette Ave. (622-4180): From meat to vegetables and from homemade preserves to live animals, all the produce of the soil is found in this colorful covered market. A St. Louis landmark since 1847. Open Wed–Sat in the winter and Tues–Sat in the summer.

MONUMENTS: ※﹩ **Gateway Arch,** 2nd St. at the foot of Chestnut St. (425-4465): Colossal arch of stainless steel, 630 ft. (192m) high, designed by the famous Finnish-American architect Eero Saarinen. Completed in 1965, it symbolizes the Winning of the West by the 19th-century pioneers. An elevator composed of small capsules moving at an oblique angle takes you to the top, where the view is splendid. At the base is the interesting Museum of Westward Expansion (see "Museums of Science and History," below) and beneath is the new Arch Odyssey I-Max Theatre. The nation's tallest and most imaginative monument; worth the trip to St. Louis all by itself. Visited by 2.5 million people a year. Open daily.

※﹩ **Wedding of the Waters,** Aloe Plaza at Market St.: Monumental fountain comprising 14 figures in bronze, symbolizing the confluence of the Mississippi and the Missouri, by Swedish sculptor Carl Milles.

MUSEUMS OF ART: ※﹩ **Cupples Art Gallery,** 3673 W. Pine Blvd. (658-3025): This curious 1890s mansion in the Roman style stands on the campus of St. Louis University; its facade is abundantly ornamented with sculpture, while its 32 rooms are luxuriously decorated with wood paneling, Tiffany windows, and wrought iron. Houses a fine collection of modern engravings by Miró, Kandinsky, Chagall, Braque, and others, as well as interesting temporary exhibitions. Open Tues–Fri and Sun.

﹩ **Dog Museum,** 1721 S. Mason Rd. (821-3647): Housed in the historic Jarville House, this museum, which moved from New York City in 1987, presents an extraordinary array of items depicting the dog throughout history. Also a reference library. Open Tues–Sun.

※﹩﹩ **St. Louis Art Museum,** Forest Park, Art Hill (721-0067): Housed in Cass Gilbert's Fine Arts Palace, designed for the 1904 World's Fair, this great museum has recently been enlarged and houses a remarkable collection of art from prehistoric times to the present day. It's particularly strong in European and American painting and sculpture; also Chinese bronzes and African and pre-Columbian art. Among its best-known treasures: Hans Holbein's *Lady Guldeford,* Titian's *Ecce Homo,* Matisse's *Bathers with a Tortoise,* Maurice Prendergast's *Seashore,* John McCrady's *Swing Low, Sweet Chariot,* and Mark Rothko's *Red, Orange, Orange on Red.* Open Tues–Sun.

MUSEUMS OF SCIENCE & HISTORY: ﹩ **Eugene Field House and Toy Museum,** 634 S. Broadway (421-4689): Birthplace of Eugene Field, with many exhibits associated with the author of *Little Boy Blue.* Interesting collection of old toys and dolls. Open Wed–Sun.

﹩ **Magic House Children's Museum,** 516 S. Kirkwood Rd., Kirkwood, 8 mi. (12km) west on U.S. 44 (822-8900): A museum of the extraordinary intended specifically for children. Dozens of attractions including microcomputer games, an electrostatic generator that will literally make your hair stand on end, a three-story-high giant slide, a maze, and so on. An absolute must for kids. Open Tues–Sun. 15 min. from dwntwn.

☖ **McDonnell Douglas Prologue Room,** McDonnell Blvd. and Airport Rd. (232-5421): Small aeronautical and space museum in the company's head-office building. Many preliminary designs, photographs, and scale models of planes and rockets illustrating the company's achievements since it was founded in 1920. Be sure to see the facsimiles of the *Mercury* and *Gemini* space capsules. For aviation buffs. Open Tues–Sat June–Aug; 30 min. from dwntwn.

☀☖ **Missouri Historical Society,** Forest Park, Lindell Blvd. and De Baliviere Ave. (746-4599): Much material on the history of St. Louis, Missouri, and the West: weapons, clothing, models of boats, posters, etc. One section is devoted to the 1904 World's Fair. The Lindbergh Room displays material relating to the 1927 transatlantic flight of the *Spirit of St. Louis.* Fascinating. Open Tues–Sun.

☀☖ **Museum of Westward Expansion,** at the base of Gateway Arch, 2nd St. at the foot of Chestnut St. (425-4465): Remarkable audiovisual display tracing the history of the settlement of the West, and of the construction of the arch. Dioramas, historical films, etc. Open daily.

☖ **National Bowling Hall of Fame and Museum,** 111 Stadium Plaza (231-6340): Traces the history of bowling from Ancient Egypt to the present day. Exhibits associated with the great names in bowling. Open daily.

☀☖☖ **National Museum of Transport,** 3015 Barrett Station Rd., Barretts, 16 mi. (25km) SW on I-44W and I-270N (965-7998): From mule-drawn streetcars to electric locomotives, two centuries of transportation in the U.S. Hundreds of antique locomotives, railroad cars, buses, trucks, streetcars, horse-drawn vehicles, etc. Open daily. 25 min. from dwntwn.

☀☖ **St. Louis Science Center,** Forest Park, 5100 Clayton Ave. (289-4400): Huge educational complex comprising the **McDonnell Planetarium** with its ultramodern equipment (laserium, Star Theater, etc.), the **Medical Museum,** and the **Museum of Science and Natural History.** Among them they offer a complete panorama of the natural sciences and the evolution of man, from a life-size dinosaur to a simulated earthquake. A $34-million expansion has recently quintupled its size. Fascinating. Open daily.

☀☖ **St. Louis Sports Hall of Fame,** Busch Stadium, 100 Stadium Plaza (421-3263): A must for all fans, particularly lovers of football and baseball. Many sports memorabilia, trophies, World Series movies, etc. Open daily year round.

PANORAMAS: ☀☖☖ **Gateway Arch,** 2nd St. at the foot of Chestnut St. (425-4465): From the top of Eero Saarinen's 630-ft. (192m) stainless-steel arch there's a spectacular view of the city and the Mississippi River. On a clear day you can see 30 mi. (48km) in all directions. Access to the Observation Room is by an unusual elevator whose passenger capsules move on an inclined plane (see also "Monuments," above). Open daily.

PARKS & GARDENS: ☀☖ **Forest Park,** bounded by Lindell Blvd., Skinker Blvd., Kingshighway Blvd., and Oakland Ave. (535-0106): 2,000 acres (820ha) of gardens, lakes, and groves less than 15 min. from dwntwn; the 1904 World's Fair was held here. Many museums and a well-known zoo; skating rink; two public golf courses. Open daily.

☀☖ **Grant's Farm,** 10501 Gravois Rd., in Grantwood Village (843-1700): Deer and buffalo roam free on 281 acres (114ha) of park and woodland belonging to the Anheuser-Busch brewery. See the log cabin where, in 1856, lived Ulysses S. Grant, who went on to become Northern commander-in-chief during the Civil War and 18th president of the U.S.; plus the stables of the famous Clydesdales and a very fine collection of horse-drawn vehicles. A mini-train takes you around the exhibits. Open Tues–Sun May–Sept, Thurs–Sun in spring and fall; closed the rest of the year. 25 min. from dwntwn on Mo. 30SW.

※♌♌ **Laumeier Sculpture Park,** Geyer and Rott Rds. (821-1209): One of the country's finest modern-sculpture gardens, with works of such American and foreign artists as Donald Judd, Dennis Oppenheim, Michael Steiner, Giacomo Manzù, David von Schlegell, Lynn Chadwick, Jackie Ferrara, Ernest Trova, etc. Be sure to see *The Way,* a monumental sculpture by Jack Zehrt. Also a gallery offering contemporary art exhibitions, plus a museum shop. Park open daily; gallery Tues–Sun. 20 min from dwntwn on I-44.

♌ **Lone Elk Park,** Mo. 141 and N. Outer Rd. (889-2863): Small wildland park with free-roaming animals—bison, Barbados sheep, elk, deer, etc., which you can see from your car along a scenic drive. Walking trails and picnic area. 25 min. from dwntwn on I-44W. Open daily.

※♌♌ **Missouri Botanical Garden,** 4344 Shaw Blvd. (577-5100): Named Shaw Garden after the businessman and amateur botanist who laid it out in 1859, this magnificent 79-acre (32ha) botanic garden has a superb rose garden, waterfalls, a "scented garden" for the blind, and Seiwa En, the largest Japanese garden in North America. Tropical domed greenhouse w. a true rain forest, the Climatron. You tour the garden in a mini-tram. Open daily.

PERFORMING ARTS: For daily listings of all shows and cultural events, consult the entertainment pages of the daily *St. Louis Post-Dispatch* (morning), the weekly *Riverfront Times,* and the monthly *St. Louis* magazine.

American Theater, 416 N. 9th St. (231-7000): The biggest Broadway hits. The building dates from 1917.

Black Repertory Company, 3016 Grandel Sq. (534-3807): Contemporary theater, dance performances. At the Grandel Square Theater.

CASA/Conservatory and School for the Arts, 560 Trinity Ave. at Delmar (863-3033): Concerts, classical-music recitals, opera.

Edison Theater, Forsyth Blvd. and Hoyt Dr. (955-6543): Contemporary and avant-garde theater; ballet performances by the St. Louis Dancers. On the campus of Washington University.

Fox Theater, 527 N. Grand Blvd. (534-1111): Pop concerts, big-name shows, musicals, etc. Wonderful 1920s rococo interior. Sept–May.

Loretto–Hilton Center, 130 Edgar Rd. (968-4925): Classical and contemporary theater; home of the Repertory Theater of St. Louis and the Opera Theater of St. Louis. Sept–Apr.

Municipal Theater/MUNY, Forest Park (361-1900): 12,000-seat open-air ampitheater presenting musicals, ballet, operettas, Broadway hits. Mid-June to Aug.

Powell Symphony Hall, 718 N. Grand Blvd. (534-1700): Classical concerts and recitals in a richly decorated auditorium. Home of the renowned St. Louis Symphony, founded in 1880, the second oldest in the country (principal conductor: Leonard Slatkin). Mid-May to mid-Sept.

Sheldon Memorial Auditorium, 3648 Washington Blvd. (533-9900): Concerts, recitals of classical music. A prim little chamber-music hall famous for acoustics that rival those of Carnegie Hall in New York.

West Port Playhouse, 600 Westport Place (878-3322): St. Louis's only theater-in-the-round. Contemporary theater, big-name shows, musicals.

SHOPPING: **Maryland Plaza,** between Kingshighway Blvd. and Euclid Ave.: Dozens of luxury stores, bars, restaurants, and unusual boutiques; style and quality both.

Plaza Frontenac, Clayton Rd. at Lindbergh Blvd. (432-5800): Two floors of department stores (Saks Fifth Avenue, Neiman-Marcus), boutiques, and trendy restaurants in an ultramodern setting.

☼ **St. Louis Centre,** bounded by Washington Ave. and 6th, 7th, and Locust Sts. (231-5522): One of the largest urban shopping malls in the country. Opened in 1985, this enormous four-floor complex stretches across two full blocks in the heart of dwntwn, with more than 200 stores, shops, and restaurants.

☼ **Union Station,** 1820 Market St. (421-6655): The old St. Louis Central Railroad Station, built at the turn of the century and now converted, at a cost of $135 million, into a vast shopping mall with more than 120 boutiques, stores, restaurants, and cafés, as well as fountains, a lagoon, and a luxury hotel.

SPECIAL EVENTS: For the exact schedule of events below, consult the **St. Louis Convention and Visitors Commission** (see "Tourist Information," above).

Soulard Mardi Gras (late Feb to Mar): Popular Mardi Gras parade and celebration in the historic neighborhood of Soulard, south of dwntwn, which brings St. Louis's French heritage to life each year.

Gypsy Caravan (Memorial Day): One of the largest flea markets in the Midwest with more than 600 vendors. St. Louis Arena. Also entertainment, arts and crafts exhibits.

Veiled Prophet Fair (four days around July 4): St. Louis's great popular festivity. Parades, fireworks, open-air concerts, marathon, art exhibitions, etc. Draws hundreds of thousands of participants. Riverfront.

Strassenfest (late July to early Aug): The festival of the local German community; music, overeating, and beer flowing—in a manner of speaking—like water.

Jour de Fête à Ste. Geneviève (second wknd in Aug): Parades, art exhibitions, old-house tours (see "Nearby Excursions," below). For information, call 883-7097.

St. Louis Blues Heritage Festival (Labor Day weekend): Live blues and all its relatives—gospel, R&B, jazz, and rock 'n' roll. Downtown area.

Forest Park Balloon Race (Sept): Annual hot-air-balloon race, drawing contestants from all over the country. Forest Park.

SPORTS: St. Louis has two professional teams:
Baseball (Apr–Oct): Cardinals, Busch Memorial Stadium (421-3060).
Ice Hockey (Oct–Apr): Blues, Sports Arena (781-5300).

Horse Racing
Fairmount Park, U.S. 40 at Collinsville, Ill. (618/345-4300): Thoroughbred racing Apr–Oct; harness racing Nov–Mar.

STROLLS: ☖ **The Hill,** around S. Kingshighway and Shaw Blvds.: The local "Little Italy," with food stores and *trattorie* more Italian than in Rome; even the fire hydrants are painted in the Italian national colors. Lively and colorful.

☼☖ **Laclede's Landing,** Riverfront north of Eads Bridge: The heart of historic St. Louis, come to life right out of the 1870s, bears witness to the city's prosperity right after the War Between the States. A nine-block cobblestone area at the river's edge, with cast-iron lamps, old shops, boutiques, nightclubs, and restaurants.

☼☖☖ **The Levee,** N. L. K. Sullivan Blvd., between the Poplar St. Bridge and Eads Bridge: Beside this quay on the Mississippi are moored a number of craft: the giant paddlewheelers *Delta Queen* and *Mississippi Queen*; U.S.S. *Inaugural,* a World War II minesweeper, now a naval museum; and the river cruisers now used for short trips on the Mississippi, *Huck Finn, Belle of St. Louis, Tom Sawyer,* and *Becky Thatcher.*

THEME PARKS: ⚓ **Six Flags over Mid-America,** Allentown Rd., in Eureka, 30 mi. (48km) SW on I-44 (938-4800): Enormous theme park with around 100 rides, roller-coasters, and other attractions, including a huge Ferris wheel known as "Colossus." Open daily from the end of May to Aug, wknds only in spring and fall; closed the rest of the year.

ZOOS: ☼⚓ **St. Louis Zoological Park,** Forest Park (781-0900): One of the top 10 zoos in the country, with 3,400 animals in reconstructions of their natural habitat; be sure to see "Big Cat Country," where lions, tigers, and other big cats live in semi-freedom. Impressive "Jungle of the Apes," with gorillas, chimpanzees, and orangutans. Visit in its mini-train. Open daily.

ACCOMMODATIONS

Personal Favorites (in order of preference)

🛏🛏🛏🛏 **The Ritz Carlton** (nr. dwntwn), 100 Carondelet Plaza, MO 63105 (314/863-6300; toll free 800/241-3333). 301 rms, A/C, cable color TV. AE, CB, DC, MC, V. Valet parking $8, pool, health club, sauna, 2 rests. (including the Restaurant), bar, 24-hr. rm svce, entertainment, concierge, free crib. *Note:* The top St. Louis hotel in the fashionable suburb of Clayton, 15 min. from dwntwn. The setting features marble floors, rich wood paneling, and a $5-million collection of 18th- and 19th-century antiques and fine art. Oversize, elegantly furnished rms w. balconies, marble bathrooms, and minibars. Well-trained and courteous staff. Plush fitness center. Two VIP floors. A haven from the suburb's corporate hubbub. **E–VE**

☼🛏🛏🛏 **Hyatt Regency at Union Station** (formerly the Omni International; dwntwn), 1 Union Station, MO 63103 (314/231-1234; toll free, see Hyatt). 542 rms, A/C, color TV in-rm movies. AE, CB, DC, MC, V. Valet parking $12, rest., coffee shop, bar, rm svce, boutiques, free crib. *Note:* This gem of the local hotel scene occupies a whole lavishly restored wing of the former Union Station, and boasts high vaulting, marble floors, stained glass, and magnificent turn-of-the-century decor (see "Architectural Highlights," above). Huge, elegant rms; ultramodern comfort; excellent svce. Direct access to Union Station Shopping Mall w. its 120 boutiques, cafés, and rests. An unusual, unusually successful, hotel w. a unique atmosphere. Three VIP floors. **E**

☼🛏🛏🛏 **Hotel Majestic** (dwntwn), 1019 Pine St., MO 63101 (314/436-2355; toll free 800/451-2355). 91 rms, A/C, cable color TV. AE, CB, DC, MC, V. Valet gar. $8, rest., bar, 24-hr. rm svce, entertainment, concierge, free crib. *Note:* Elegant small European-style hotel in an old dwntwn building luxuriously rehabilitated. Classy interior w. marble floors and Oriental rugs. All rms are spacious, comfortable mini-suites w. period furniture. Personalized reception and svce. So-so rest. VIP and big business clientele. Style and distinction. **E**

🛏🛏 **Days Inn at the Arch** (formerly the Hilton Bel Air; dwntwn), 333 Washington Ave., MO 63102 (314/621-7900; toll free, see Days Inns). 182 rms, A/C, color TV, in-rm movies. AE, CB, DC, MC, V. Parking $5, pool, sauna, rest., bar, valet svce, free crib. *Note:* Large, modern 17-story tower halfway between the Gateway Arch and the Cervantes Convention Center. Functional but inviting. Spacious rms w. balconies, the best looking out on the arch. Business clientele. Good value on balance. **I–M**

🛏🛏 **Radisson Hotel Clayton** (formerly the Clayton Inn; nr. dwntwn), 7750 Carondelet Ave., Clayton, MO 63105 (314/726-5400; toll free, see Radisson). 191 rms, A/C, color TV, in-rm movies. AE, CB, DC, MC, V. Free valet gar., two pools, health club, sauna, rest., bar, rm svce, nightclub, free breakfast, free crib. *Note:* Modern hotel in a residential neighborhood on the western edge of the city. Spacious contemporary rms w. minibars. Good physical-fitness facilities; diligent svce; acceptable rest. (Max's Bar and Grill offers a fine view of the city). Business and group clientele. Very good value. 15 min. from dwntwn by car. **I–M**

🏠🏠 **Super Inn** (formerly Thrifty Inn; dwntwn), 1100 N. 3rd St., MO 63102 (314/421-6556; toll free 800/325-8300). 48 rms, A/C, color TV. AE, CB, DC, MC, V. Street parking; adj. rest. *Note:* New small motel a hop, skip, and a jump from the nightlife of bohemian Laclede's Landing. Comfortable, functional rms; friendly reception. Very good value 5 min. from the Convention Center. **B**

Other Accommodations (from top bracket to budget)

🏠🏠🏠 **Adam's Mark** (dwntwn), 4th and Chestnut Sts., MO 63102 (314/241-7400; toll free 800/444-2326). 910 rms, A/C, color TV, in-rm movies. AE, CB, DC, MC, V. Valet gar. $12, two pools, health club, sauna, squash, rest. (Faust's), coffee shop, three bars, 24-hr. rm svce, nightclub, hrdrsr, concierge, free crib. *Note:* The best location in St. Louis, at the foot of the Gateway Arch. Ultramodern 18-story building w. unobstructed view of city, arch, or river. Richly decorated interior w. Flemish tapestries, Italian marble, French crystal chandeliers, two Ludovico De Luigi bronze horses in the lobby. Very spacious, comfortable rms, some w. refrigerators. Flawless reception and svce. Noisy, busy atmosphere. Very good rest. Two VIP floors; big business clientele; in the heart of dwntwn. **E–VE**

🏠🏠🏠🏠 **Doubletree Mayfair Suites** (dwntwn), St. Charles St. at 8th St., MO 63101 (314/421-2500; toll free 800/528-0444). 184 suites, A/C, color TV, in-rm movies. AE, CB, DC, MC, V. Gar. $9, pool, health club, rest. (Mayfair Room), bar, rm svce, concierge. *Note:* Originally built in 1925, this luxurious small hotel in the European manner reopened in 1990 after a complete renovation which has magnificently restored its pristine appearance. Suites only, spacious and sinfully comfortable, w. minibar. Polished, considerate svce; rest. of high quality. VIP clients. Very well located near the Cervantes Convention Center. The new *grande dame* of St. Louis's hotels. **E**

🏠🏠 **Embassy Suites** (dwntwn), 901 N. 1st St., MO 63102 (314/241-4200; toll free 800/362-2779). 300 suites, A/C, color TV, in-rm movies. AE, CB, DC, MC, V. Parking $6, pool, health club, sauna, rest. (Dirtwater Fox), bar, rm svce, free breakfast, free crib. *Note:* Modern hotel for the business traveler, suites only, spacious and comfortable w. balconies, minibars, and refrigerators. Spectacular eight-floor-high lobby w. interior grdn. Right in the Laclede's Landing neighborhood, w. its rests., boutiques, and lively nightlife. **M–E**

🏠🏠 **Regal Riverfront Hotel** (formerly Clarion Hotel; dwntwn), 200 S. 4th St., MO 63102 (314/241-9500; toll free, see Choice). 853 rms, A/C, color TV, in-rm movies. AE, CB, DC, MC, V. Gar. $10, two pools, health club, rest. (Top of the Riverfront), coffee shop, bars, rm svce, hrdrsr, concierge, free crib. *Note:* Modern 28-floor circular towers on the Mississippi. Spacious, agreeable rms, some w. refrigerators. Svce functional, but no more. Acceptable revolving rest. on the top floor; unobstructed view of the Gateway Arch (ask for a rm overlooking the river). Rather obtrusive group and convention clientele. Three VIP floors. Recently redecorated and refurnished. **M**

🏠🏠 **Holiday Inn Riverfront** (dwntwn), 200 N. 4th St., MO 63102 (314/621-8200; toll free, see Holiday Inns). 458 rms, A/C, color TV, in-rm movies. AE, CB, DC, MC, V. Gar. $7, pool, rest., deli, bar, rm svce, free crib. *Note:* Huge 30-story tower looking out on the Mississippi. Holiday Inn style, completely modernized. The better rms, w. balconies (a third w. kitchenettes), overlook the river and the Gateway Arch. Efficient svce. Excellent location; business clientele. **I–M**

🏠🏠 **Drury Inn** (dwntwn), Union Station, 201 S. 20th St., MO 63103 (314/231-3900; toll free 800/325-8300). 168 rms, A/C, color TV, in-rm movies. AE, CB, DC, MC, V. Free parking, pool, rest., bar, valet svce, free breakfast, free crib. *Note:* Unusual red-brick structure adj. Union Station—a skillfully renovated turn-of-the-century YMCA! Captivating interior as well; very comfortable rms, some w. refrigerator. Good svce; good value overall. Business clientele. **I–M**

　　　♀ **Red Roof Inn–Hampton** (nr. dwntwn), 5823 Wilson Ave.,
　　　🛏 MO 63110 (314/645-0101; toll free 800/843-7663). 110 rms, A/C, cable color TV. AE, DC, MC, V. Free parking, rest. adjacent. *Note:* Well-run budget motel 10 min. from dwntwn via I-44 (Hampton Ave. exit). Clean, comfortable rms; friendly reception. Excellent value. Ideal if you're driving. **B–I**

　　　♀ **Motel 6 Northeast** (vic.), 1405 Dunn Rd., MO 63138 (314/
　　　🛏 869-9400). 81 rms, A/C, cable color TV. AE, DC, MC, V. Free parking, pool. *Note:* Unbeatable value if you're traveling by car, 20 min. from dwntwn via I-70 and Mo. 367. Functionally comfortable. **B**

Airport Accommodations

　　♀♀♀ **Holiday Inn Airport** (vic.), 4505 Woodson Rd., MO 63134
　　🛏🛏🛏 (314/427-4700; toll free, see Holiday Inns). 155 rms. A/C, color TV, in-rm movies. AE, DC, MC, V. Free parking, pool, health club, sauna, rest. (Oak Room), bar, rm svce. *Note:* Luxurious, cozy airport hotel, recently enlarged. Spacious, very comfortable rms; flawless svce; very acceptable rest. 5 min. from airport (free shuttle). Business clientele. **M–E**

YMCA/Youth Hostel

　　Huckleberry Finn (nr. dwntwn), 1904 S. 12th St., MO 63104 (314/241-0076). 40 beds. Typical youth hostel. Set-up somewhat seedy.

RESTAURANTS

Personal Favorites (in order of preference)

　　♀♀♀♀ **Tony's** (dwntwn), 410 Market St. (231-7007). A/C. Dinner
　　🍷🍷🍷🍷 only, Mon–Sat; closed hols. and the first week in July. AE, CB, DC, MC, V. J&T. *Specialties:* fresh homemade pasta, lobster albanello, veal piemontese, fish of the day, first-class red meats, zabaglione. Superb desserts. Menu changes regularly. Very fine list of European and American wines. *Note:* Since 1949 Vincent Bommarito has presided, diplomatically but firmly, over this shrine of Italian-American gastronomy. Recently reopened in new space in the elegant Equitable Building. Reception and svce of the highest order. Resv. advisable. One of the best Italian rests. in the U.S., w. prices to match. Valet parking. *Italian/Continental.* **M–E**

　　♀♀♀ **Fio's La Fourchette** (nr. dwntwn), 1153 St. Louis Galleria,
　　🍷🍷🍷 Brentwood Blvd. and Clayton Rd. (863-6866). A/C. Dinner only, Tues–Sat; closed hols. AE, DC, MC, V. Jkt. *Specialties:* mousse of veal and Brie cheese in puff pastry, broiled sweetbreads w. leeks, roast duck w. green Madagascar-peppercorn sauce, medallions of veal w. mushroom-and-brandy cream, seafood (flown in daily), very good homemade desserts (particularly the Grand Marnier soufflé). Menu changes regularly. *Note:* With its modern, light-filled decor, luxuriant plants, and pastel-colored walls, this charming rest., hidden away in an outlying shopping center, quickly established itself as the best local exponent of French nouvelle cuisine. Every dish bears witness to the imaginative elegance and refinement of the very talented young Swiss chef Fio Antognini, while the prices are surprisingly moderate. Very good svce. An excellent place to eat; resv. strongly advised. 25 min. from dwntwn. *French.* **M** (prix fixe).

　　♀♀ **Balaban's** (nr. dwntwn), 405 N. Euclid Ave. (361-8085).
　　🍷🍷 A/C. Breakfast Sat, lunch Mon–Sat, dinner nightly, brunch Sun. AE, DC, MC, V. *Specialties:* soft-shell crabs (in season), chilled cucumber bisque, sautéed veal and sweetbreads, smoked fish, fresh lobster, beef Wellington, roast duck. Extensive but pricey wine list. *Note:* Casual, yet trendy eclectic dining spot. Fine American contemporary cuisine w. touches of St. Louis's French heri-

tage. Art deco interior setting w. antique posters; glassed-in sidewalk café plus a noisy and crowded bar. Excellent but relaxed svce. The "in" place in the stylish Central West End district. Resv. not required. *American.* **M**

Nantucket Cove (nr. dwntwn), 40 N. Kingshighway Blvd. (361-0625). A/C. Dinner only, nightly; closed hols. AE, CB, DC, MC, V. *Specialties:* oysters on the half shell, live Maine lobster, grilled swordfish, red snapper, catch of the day. Good selection of French and California wines. *Note:* Expensive seafood rest. housed in a fashionable Central West End building. Cozy New England seafaring decor. Well-prepared and nicely presented fish and seafood flown in daily. Competent svce. Resv. recommended. Big business clientele. Valet parking. 10 min. from dwntwn. *Seafood.* **M–E**

Busch's Grove (nr. dwntwn), 9160 Clayton Rd. (993-0011). A/C. Lunch/dinner Tues–Sat. AE, DC, MC, V. *Specialties:* toasted ravioli (a St. Louis specialty), "Russ's salad," calves' liver w. onions, prime rib, barbecued ribs, steak, fish of the day, berry-berry pie. *Note:* A local tradition for almost a century; if you can eat only one meal in St. Louis, eat it here—particularly in fine weather, when the regulars crowd into the grdn w. its romantic arbors. The food is as serious, and flawless, as the svce. A very fine place. 20 min. from dwntwn. *American.* **I–M**

Café Zoe (nr. dwntwn), 12 N. Meramec (725-5554). A/C. Lunch Mon–Fri, dinner Mon–Sat only. AE, MC, V. *Specialties:* grilled Norwegian salmon w. mango-chutney butter, sandwiches, shrimp w. pesto sauce, broiled chicken w. rosemary, Thai marinated beef, very good desserts. Menu changes regularly. *Note:* Crowded daily at lunch by white-collar workers, Zoe's is the fashionable place for a quick meal. Imaginative dishes w. a touch of American nouvelle cuisine (particularly the specialty salads and the broiled foods) at very attractive prices. Relaxed atmosphere. Resv. advised for dinner. 15 min. by car in Clayton. *American.* **B–I**

Other Restaurants (from top bracket to budget)

Faust's (dwntwn), in the Adam's Mark (see "Accommodations," above) (342-4690). A/C. Lunch Mon–Fri, dinner nightly. AE, CB, DC, MC, V. Jkt. *Specialties:* Mediterranean pasta w. shrimp and tomatoes infused in olive oil, phyllo-wrapped wild mushrooms, rack of lamb w. minted béarnaise, roast breast of duck and confit of leg quarter, sautéed Norwegian salmon w. vegetable-chive vinaigrette, Oreo-crusted white-chocolate cheesecake w. raspberry sauce. Pricey wine list. *Note:* Tasteful and innovative nouvelle American cuisine served in a Bavarian-castle setting that borders on Disneyland kitsch. The dining rm—w. a dance floor—is nevertheless comfortably spacious, and provides a good view of the Arch. Svce is ultra-professional. Resv. suggested. *American.* **M–E**

Giovanni's (nr. dwntwn), 5201 Shaw Ave. (772-5958). A/C. Dinner only, Mon–Sat; closed hols. AE, DC, MC, V. Jkt. *Specialties:* "presidential bow tie" (smoked salmon pasta as served to President Reagan at his inaugural banquet), fettuccine w. lobster and brandy sauce, vitello con porcini, breast of chicken alla piemontese, broiled scampi. Very good desserts; large wine list. *Note:* All the gastronomic classics of northern Italy in an elegant peach-colored setting w. old paintings and crystal chandeliers. Warm, intimate atmosphere. Excellent svce. One of St. Louis's great rests.; resv. necessary. Valet parking. 10 min. from dwntwn. *Italian.* **M–E**

Cardwell's (nr. dwntwn), 8100 Maryland Ave. (726-5055). A/C. Lunch/dinner Mon–Sat; closed hols. AE, CB, DC, MC, V. Jkt. *Specialties:* grilled scallops w. spicy Thai peanut sauce; seafood cassoulet w. jumbo shrimp, clams, fresh fish filet, squid, and saffron-tomato sauce; sautéed catfish w. roasted pecans, fresh fennel, and bacon; broiled pompano filet w. lime butter and papaya jelly; first-class grilled meats cooked over a pecan-wood fire; remarkable souffles. Good wine list. Menu changes regularly. *Note:* St. Louis's most imaginative rest. serving American nouvelle cuisine. The young chef, Bill Cardwell, whose creative talents are becoming more and more evident, never ceases to surprise and to charm. Wood-paneled back rm, open kitchen, and noisy atmosphere. Svce a trifle helter-skelter. Resv. advised. Valet parking. *American.* **M**

🍸🍸 **Ruth's Chris Steak House** (dwntwn), 101 S. 11th St. (241-7711). A/C. Dinner only, nightly; closed hols. AE, CB, DC, MC, V. *Specialties:* absolutely prime meats (try the porterhouse steak for two), Maine lobster, lamb chops, broiled chicken, eight kinds of potato. Ho-hum desserts. *Note:* This well-known chain of rests., headquartered in New Orleans, styles itself "the home of serious steaks," and deserves the title. Corn-fed beef, richly marbled and broiled to a turn. Typical steakhouse setting, conventional but comfortable; efficient svce; business clientele. The best place for meat in St. Louis. Resv. advised. *Steak.* **M**

🍸🍸 **LoRusso's Cucina** (nr. dwntwn), 3121 Watson Rd. (647-6222). A/C. Lunch Mon–Fri, dinner Mon–Sat; closed hols. AE, CB, DC, MC, V. *Specialties:* minestrone soup, capellini LoRusso, calamari in marinara sauce, chicken Teresa, tenderloin mudega, grilled fish, cassata pie. Mainly Italian wine list. *Note:* Solid Italian fare and quick, efficient svce. Recently moved to these more spacious and attractive quarters. The place is favored by those in-the-know. Resv. advised. Well worth the 20-min. drive from dwntwn (via I-44). *Italian.* **I–M**

🍸🍸 **Riddles Penultimate Café** (nr. dwntwn), 6307 Delmar St., University City (725-1777). A/C. Lunch Tues–Sat, dinner Tues–Sun; closed hols. *Specialties:* in-house smoked rainbow trout, mushroom caps stuffed w. crawfish, shrimp rémoulade, sautéed chicken breast w. mango chutney, shrimp Sarah (jumbo shrimp w. garlic, mushrooms, and a port-artichoke-heart cream sauce), homemade ice cream. Extensive wine list including many Missouri wines. *Note:* Eclectic cuisine w. an "anything-goes" ambience. Serving a clientele that ranges from pretheater diners to college students to retirees. Live music five nights a week. Resv. advised, especially on the weekends. 25 min. from dwntwn. *American.* **I–M**

🍸 **La Sala** (dwntwn), 513 Olive St. (231-5620). A/C. Lunch/dinner Mon–Sat (until 10:30pm); closed hols. AE, CB, DC, MC, V. *Specialties:* tacos, chiles rellenos, botana mexicana, enchiladas. Good margaritas. *Note:* Very popular Mexican rest. a stone's throw from Busch Stadium. Agreeable folk-type setting; good, unpretentious food. Crowded on days of games and evenings after shows. The buffet at lunch is good value. Pleasant background music. No resv. *Mexican.* **B–I**

🍸 **Yen Ching** (nr. dwntwn), 1012 S. Brentwood Blvd. (721-7507). A/C. Lunch Mon–Fri, dinner nightly. AE, MC, V. *Specialties:* sizzling-rice soup, Szechuan chicken, princess prawns, spicy crispy beef, sweet-and-sour fish, Mongolian beef, Peking and Szechuan dishes. *Note:* One of the few acceptable Far Eastern rests. in St. Louis. The food is authentic and tasty, the decor totally uninteresting, and the svce friendly. Locally very popular, resv. not taken. *Chinese.* **B–I**

🍸 **Pho Grand** (nr. dwntwn), 3191 S. Grand Blvd. (664-7435). A/C. Lunch/dinner Wed–Mon; closed hols. No credit cards. *Specialties:* egg-noodle soup, rice noodles (especially w. chocolate-broiled pork and lemon sauce), chicken w. hot peppers and lemongrass, sautéed curry scallops w. garlic and coconut milk, French ice coffee. *Note:* Traditional Vietnamese rest. Considered the best Asian food in St. Louis. Very friendly, fast svce. Resv. not taken, so expect to wait up to 20 min. on the weekend. *Vietnamese.* **B**

Cafeterias/Fast Food

Culpeppers (nr. dwntwn), 300 N. Euclid Ave. (361-2828). Lunch/dinner daily (until midnight). AE, MC, V. Remarkably good homemade soups, chicken wings, and substantial sandwiches have made the reputation of this nice, noisy bar.

Miss Hulling's (dwntwn), 11th and Locust Sts. (436-0840). Open Mon–Sat (7am–5pm). AE, DC, MC, V. Very respectable cafeteria food in a pleasant garden setting. A St. Louis tradition for 60 years. Other location: 725 Olive St. (436-0404), same hours.

O'Connell's Pub (nr. dwntwn), 4652 Shaw Ave. at Kingshighway Blvd. (773-6600). Lunch/dinner Mon–Sat (until midnight). MC, V. By general consent the best hamburgers in town. Also excellent roast-beef sandwiches and several kinds of beer. Typical Irish-pub atmosphere.

Ted Drewes Frozen Custard (nr. dwntwn), 4224 S. Grand Blvd. (352-7376). Open daily, summer only. Practically a St. Louis institution. Try the tiramisù sundae or the pistachio concrete. Fabulous stuff. Another location is at 6726 Chippewa St. (481-2652) and is open daily Mar–Dec.

BARS & NIGHTCLUBS

Blueberry Hill (nr. dwntwn), 6504 Delmar St., University City (727-0880). Lots of rock 'n' roll and pop-culture memorabilia in this bar that's extremely popular w. students. Also serves decent bar food. Live bands Fri–Sat.

Funny Bone Comedy Club (dwntwn), 940 W. Port Plaza (469-6398). National and local headliners for a modest price and a two-drink minimum.

Houlihan's (dwntwn), 147 St. Louis Union Station (436-0844). Popular, inviting singles bar with an acceptable rest. Open nightly.

Just Jazz Room (dwntwn), in the Hotel Majestic (see "Accommodations," above (436-2355). Nationally known jazz entertainers featured nightly.

Lucius Boomer's (dwntwn), 707 Claymorgan Alley (621-8155). Local pop and rock bands in the heart of Laclede's Landing. Lively, casual setting. Open nightly with a late-night menu.

Mississippi Nights (dwntwn), 914 N. 1st St. (421-3853). Fashionable nightclub in the heart of Laclede's Landing. Live music schedule varies.

Muddy Waters Saloon (dwntwn), 724 N. 1st St. (421-5335). The best pop-rock club in town. Live music. Trendy clientele. Open nightly.

NEARBY EXCURSIONS

BONNE TERRE (62 mi./99km SW via I-55 and U.S. 67): In this small town, where mining was actively pursued from 1870 to 1962, there still remain enormous excavations under its streets which are open to visitors; inquire at Park and Allen Sts. (358-2148); open daily year round. Don't fail to see the amazing **Billion Gallon Underground Lake,** with its 17 mi. (27km) of navigable channels, visited every year by more than 7,000 scuba divers. North of the town, **Washington State Park,** on Mo. 47 (586-2995), open daily year round, possesses hundreds of Native American petroglyphs. Combine this with the trip to Sainte Geneviève (see below).

Where to Stay

Mansion Hill Country Inn, Mansion Hill Dr., Bonne Terre, MO 63628 (358-5311). 10 rms. Charming, elegantly restored Victorian home. Rest. closed Sun–Mon. **I–M**

CAHOKIA MOUNDS STATE HISTORIC SITE (in Collinsville, Ill., 9 mi./15km east via I-70) (618/346-5160): One of the richest archeological sites in the country—a primitive community extending over 885 acres (380ha), inhabited between A.D. 700 and 1400 and with a population in the tens of thousands. There remain today only two score huge earthen mounds, of the 100 or so originally built, whose size and shape are reminiscent of Mayan pyramids. Particularly impressive is **Monks Mound,** a huge terraced earthwork rising 98 ft. (30m), which owes its name to the Trappist monastery built at its foot in 1809. Interesting archeological museum. Open daily.

FORT KASKASKIA STATE HISTORIC SITE (in Ellis Grove, Ill., 52 mi./83km SE over the Poplar Street Bridge along Ill. 3) (618/859-3741): Built by the French in 1736, and destroyed by them in 1763 to prevent its passing into the hands of the British under the terms of the Treaty of Paris, this fort, of which only traces remain today, occupied a strategic position in a bend of the Mississippi. The nearby **Pierre Menard Mansion,** built in 1802 in the style of a Louisiana plantation house, at the foot of a bluff overlooking the river, is worth a visit. Nicknamed the "Mount Vernon of the West" because of its elegant design, and today superbly restored, the house was visited by Lafayette in 1824. Open daily year round. Combine this with the visit to Cahokia Mounds State Historic Site (above).

HANNIBAL (108 mi./172km NW via I-70 and Mo. 79): Little Mississippi River port where Samuel Langhorne Clemens, better known as Mark Twain, passed much of his youth. Now entirely devoted to the cult of the famous author of *Tom Sawyer* and *Huckleberry Finn,* the city abounds in all kinds of museums. Make a point of seeing the ⚱ **Mark Twain Museum,** with numerous family souvenirs, in the house where he spent his childhood at 208 Hill St. (221-9010), open daily. Also the ⚱ **Mark Twain Cave,** 2 mi. (3km) south on Mo. 79 (221-1656), open daily, which inspired some of the adventures of *Tom Sawyer.*

Mississippi trips aboard the paddlesteamer *Mark Twain,* Center St. Dock (221-3222), daily May–Oct.

JEFFERSON BARRACKS HISTORICAL PARK (Broadway at Kingston Rd., 10 mi./16km south on I-55) (544-5714): Military barracks built in 1826; many of the original buildings have been restored. Interesting military museum. The future Gens. Robert E. Lee and Ulysses S. Grant served here as young officers. Open Wed–Sun.

MERAMEC CAVERNS (at Stanton, 65 mi./104km SW on I-44) (468-3166): Vast limestone caves on five levels, used to store gunpowder during the Civil War, and as a hiding place by Jesse James and his gang in the 1870s. The temperature remains constant at 60°F (16°C). Open daily year round.

SAINTE GENEVIEVE (64 mi./102km south on I-55 and U.S. 61): One of the oldest (1720) French settlements in the Midwest. The town, which once rivaled St. Louis, still has 40 or so buildings dating from the late 18th and early 19th centuries, giving it something of the flavor of Old France. Among them are the 1770 **Bolduc House** at 123 S. Main St., the 1770 **Amoureaux House** on St. Mary's Rd., the 1785 **Guibourd-Valle House** at N. 4th St., and the 1818 **Felix Valle Home** at 198 Merchant St.—all open daily Apr–Nov. Interesting **historical museum** at Merchant St. and Dubourg Sq. (883-3461), open daily year round.

Very popular festival in Aug (see "Special Events," above). The **Tourist Information Office** is at 66 S. Main St., Sainte Geneviève, MO 63670 (314/883-7097).

Where to Stay

St. Gemme Beauvais Inn, 78 N. Main St., Sainte Geneviève, MO 63670 (314/883-5744). 12 rms (10 with bath). Elegant 1847 mansion. **B–I**

☀ **Sainte Geneviève,** Main and Merchant Sts., Sainte Geneviève, MO 63670 (314/883-3562). 14 rms. Charming little late 19th-century inn. **B–I**

⚓ **BRANSON** (250 mi./400km SW via I-44 and U.S. 65): A country-music mecca in the heart of the Ozarks, Branson, a dead-and-alive hole of about 4,000 near the Arkansas border, boasts two outdoor ampitheaters and 26 music theaters owned by such nationally known entertainers as Willie Nelson, Mel Tillis, Andy Williams, Johnny Cash, etc. They offer nearly 40 live country-music and variety shows daily, attracting some four million visitors a year. The 5-mi.-long (8km) jam-packed stretch of Mo. 76 known as the "Strip" glitters with the lights of dozens of theater marquees, motels, restaurants, and tourist attractions. In brief, an odd mixture of Las Vegas glitz, Disneyland excitement, and small-town innocence. With nearly 10,000 motel rooms and 6,000 camping places available, the Branson area does not suffer from a lack of accommodations.

Where to Stay

🛏🛏 **Melody Lane Inn,** Mo. 76, Branson, MO 65516 (417/334-8598; toll free 800/338-8598). 140 rms. Well-kept motel right on the Strip. Closed Jan–Feb. **B–I**

🛏 **Briarwood,** Lakeshore Dr., Branson, MO 65516 (417/334-3929). 16 comfortable cottages on Lake Taneycomo. Open Mar–Thanksgiving. **B–I**

Where to Eat

🍷 **Koi Garden,** 827 W. Main (417/334-0687). Lunch/dinner daily. Good Chinese-American menu. Exotic decor. **B–I**

🍷 **Outback,** 1914 W. Mo. 76 (417/334-6306). Lunch/dinner daily. Australian-style steakhouse. Hefty portions and good value. **B–I**

☀ **STEELVILLE** (92 mi./147km SW on U.S. 44 and Mo. 19): A wooded spot in Crawford County, just southeast of this little country town, has been identified by the U.S. Census Bureau (1990) as the "nation's population center."

CHAPTER 28

KANSAS CITY☉

◻ ◻ ◻

Famous for its slaughterhouses (the country's largest) and the size of its steaks, Kansas City, which has been called "the heart of America," is yet much more than the simple "cow town" it was known as in the days of the Old West. First explored by French trappers, the region around Kansas City is unquestionably one of the richest agricultural areas of America, as well as the world's second-largest cattle market. Its strategic position midway between Chicago and the Rockies made it an obligatory stagecoach stop on both of the two great westward routes of the 19th century: the Santa Fe Trail to Albuquerque and the Mexican frontier, and the Oregon Trail to Portland and the Pacific Northwest. From its double historic role, as a center of communications and cattle raising, Kansas City has retained a tradition of hospitality, some first-class hotels, and some of the nation's finest steakhouses, beginning with the renowned Golden Ox in the very precincts of the famous **Stockyards.**

The city's political past is murky; under the Pendergast brothers, corruption and influence-peddling were elevated to a system of government. In the 1920s Kansas City boasted almost 300 speakeasies, brothels, gaming houses, and jazz clubs. Between the two World Wars these dozens of nightclubs, some respectable and some less so, along Vine and 18th Sts. in a district then known as "Little New York," produced musicians of the caliber of "Fats" Waller, Count Basie, Lester Young, and Charlie Parker, making Kansas City one of the great capitals of jazz. Missouri's second city still hosts, every September, a very popular jazz festival. Other remembrances of things past are the picturesque neighborhoods of **Westport Square** and the **City Market,** an open-air market more than a century and a half old, not far from the Missouri River. Kansas City is noted, too, as America's greeting-card and writing-paper capital, since it is headquarters of the vast Hallmark operation.

The broad avenues with their dozens of statues and fountains (many of European origin), the friendliness of the citizens and their taste for good, solid food, and the beauty of the surrounding countryside, particularly the **Lake of the Ozarks,** make Kansas City an attractive and often-overlooked destination, as well as a thriving metropolis. As early as 1946, French biographer and novelist André Maurois wrote in his *Journal de voyages,* "Who in Europe, or even in America, knows that Kansas City is one of the loveliest cities on earth?"

In 1989 *Fortune* magazine named Kansas City one of the three best metropolitan areas in the U.S. for business (after Dallas–Fort Worth and Atlanta).

Famous people born in Kansas City include the jazz musicians Charlie Parker and Ben Webster, movie director Robert Altman, and actor Ed Asner. Neighboring **Independence** is the birthplace of movie star Ginger Rogers, but is perhaps best known as the beloved hometown of Pres. Harry S Truman.

BASIC FACTS: State of Missouri; its twin city is Kansas City, Kansas, across the state border. Area code: 816. Time zone: central. ZIP Code: 64108. Founded: 1821. Approximate population: city, 425,000; metropolitan area, 1,560,000. Ranks 25th in size among U.S. metropolitan areas.

CLIMATE: The climate of the Midwest plains is the most pleasant in the spring, apart from frequent showers, and in the fall, which is the ideal season for a visit. Summer is hot and humid, with average temperatures in July of 82°F (28°C). Winter is very harsh and often below freezing, especially in Jan with a mean temperature of 30°F (−1°C). *Warning:* There are often tornadoes in late spring.

DISTANCES: Chicago, 500 mi. (800km); Dallas, 490 mi. (785km); Denver, 600 mi. (960km); Memphis, 450 mi. (720km); Minneapolis, 443 mi. (710km); St. Louis, 259 mi. (415km).

ARRIVAL & TRANSIT INFORMATION

AIRPORT: Mid-Continent International Airport (MCI), 18 mi. (29km) NW, one of the most up-to-date in the country. For information, call 243-5237.

AIRLINES: American (toll free 800/433-7300), America West (toll free 800/247-5692), Continental (toll free 800/525-0280), Delta (toll free 800/221-1212), Northwest (toll free 800/225-2525), Southwest (toll free 800/531-5601), TWA (toll free 800/221-2000), United (toll free 800/241-6522), and USAir (toll free 800/428-4322).

CITY LINK: The **cab** fare to city center is about $25–$30; time, 30–40 min. Bus: **KCI Shuttle** (243-5950), serving the principal hotels, leaves every 30 min.; fare, about $10–$15; time, 45 min.

Since the dwntwn district is compact, you may not need to rent a car, unless you intend to make the (very worthwhile) excursions available in the area. Public transportation (bus) is overall efficient; call the Area Transit Authority (**The Metro**) (221-0660) for information. Bright-red open-air **trolleys** run a continuous circuit through Kansas City dwntwn, Westport, Crown Center, and Country Club Plaza with several stops along the route, daily Mar–Dec; fare, $4 with unlimited reboarding passes; call 221-3399 for information.

CAR RENTAL (at Mid-Continent International Airport unless otherwise indicated): Avis (toll free 800/331-1212); Budget (toll free 800/527-0700); Dollar (toll free 800/800-4000); Hertz (toll free 800/654-3131); National (toll free 800/227-7368); and Thrifty, 11530 NW Prairie View Rd. (toll free 800/367-2277). For dwntwn locations, consult the local telephone directory.

LIMOUSINE SERVICES: Carey Limousine (587-4077), Mid-America Limousine (346-4848).

TAXIS: Cabs may not be hailed on the street, but they can be taken at the stands in front of the major hotels, or summoned by telephone: **Checker Cab** (474-8294) or **Yellow Cab** (471-5000).

Warning: Cabs in Kansas City operate on a deregulated meter system and each cab company is free to set its own rates. Consequently, fares can vary widely.

TRAIN: Amtrak station, 2200 Main St. (toll free 800/872-7245).

INTERCITY BUSES: Greyhound, 1101 Troost Ave. (toll free 800/231-2222).

INFORMATION & TOURS

TOURIST INFORMATION: The **Kansas City Convention and Visitors Bureau,** City Center Sq. Building (Suite 2550), 1100 Main St., MO 64105 (816/221-5242; toll free 800/767-7700).
Visitor Information Center, 20 E. 5th St. in the River Market (816/842-4386); open daily.

GUIDED TOURS: Kansas City Riverboat (boat), Westport Landing, at the foot of Grand Ave. (913/281-5300): Trips along the Missouri on board the *Missouri River Queen.* Daily May–Aug, wknds Mar–Apr and Sept–Dec.
Kansas City Sightseeing (bus) (833-4083): Guided tours of the city, serving principal dwntwn hotels.

SIGHTS, ATTRACTIONS & ACTIVITIES

ARCHITECTURAL HIGHLIGHTS: ⚖ **Board of Trade,** 4800 Main St. (753-7500): World's largest winter-wheat market. From the visitors' gallery on the third floor you can watch the frenzied brokers. Open Mon–Fri.
⚖ **City Hall,** 414 E. 12th St. (274-2000): A building from the early '30s in the purest art deco style. From the 30th floor there's a fine view of the city (see "Panoramas," below). Open Mon–Fri.
⚖ **Crown Center,** Pershing St. and Grand Ave. (274-8444): Ultramodern commercial and office complex built on a rise overlooking the city at a cost of $500 million. Includes two luxury hotels; some 60 stores and boutiques; 18 restaurants; six movie houses; a theater, the **Hallmark Visitors Center,** focusing on the history of the greeting card industry; and a huge plaza with free concerts in summer and ice skating in winter. Lively, animated scene. Open daily.

MARKETS: ※⚖ **City Market,** Walnut and 3rd Sts. (842-1271): Picturesque open-air market in existence for more than a century and a half. Dozens of stalls and food stands. Justifies Kansas City's reputation for good food. Open daily. Indoor farmers' market open on changing days during any particular harvest time.

MONUMENTS: ⚖ **Liberty Memorial,** 100 W. 26th St. (221-1918): This 217-ft. (66m) tower (elevator) offers a very fine view of the city. Museum dedicated to those who fought in World War I. Open Wed–Sun.

MUSEUMS OF ART: ⚖ **T. H. Benton Home,** 3616 Belleview Ave. (931-5722): Victorian house and studio which the famous regionalist painter Thomas Hart Benton (nicknamed "the Michelangelo of Neosho, Mo.") occupied from 1937 until his death in 1975. Open daily.
⚖⚖ **Henry Moore Sculpture Garden,** 4525 Oak St. (561-4000): Installed in 17 acres (6.9ha) in front of the Nelson-Atkins Museum of Art (see below), this new sculpture garden opened on June 4, 1989. Contains the most extensive collection of Henry Moore's bronzes outside England. Twelve larger-than-life works in a landscaped setting. Open daily.
⚖ **Kemper Museum of Contemporary Art and Design,** Warwick Blvd. at 45th St. (561-3737): Kansas City's latest cultural enhancement opened in 1994, built with a $6-million donation to the Kansas

City Art Institute. Rotating exhibits and a permanent collection including works by O'Keeffe, Rauschenberg, and Christo. Open Tues–Sun.

☀️🏛️🏛️ **Nelson-Atkins Museum,** 4525 Oak St. (561-4000): Art from ancient civilizations (Sumerian, Greek, and Egyptian). Many paintings by European masters from Titian to van Gogh. Remarkable collection of Far Eastern (particularly Chinese) art. Among the best-known works on display are Caravaggio's *St. John the Baptist,* a *Virgin and Child* by Petrus Christus, Nicolas Poussin's *Triumph of Bacchus,* and Thomas Hart Benton's *Persephone.* Unusually good museum cafeteria. Open Tues–Sun.

MUSEUMS OF SCIENCE & HISTORY: 🏛️ Kansas City Museum, 3218

Gladstone Blvd. (483-8300): Interesting museum of anthropology, housed in the sumptuous 72-room mansion of a 19th-century millionaire. Many Native American art objects. Plays up the importance of Kansas City in the westward expansion. Also a planetarium. Open Tues–Sun.

🏛️ **Linda Hall Library,** 5100 Rockhill Rd. on the University of Missouri campus (363-4600): One of the country's richest libraries, entirely given over to science and technology, with works from as early as the 17th century. Interesting. Open Mon–Sat.

☀️🏛️ **Toy & Miniature Museum,** 5235 Oak St. (333-2055): In a very beautiful, and carefully restored, 1911 building, this fascinating museum displays splendid collections of old toys, miniatures, and dollhouses. Open Wed–Sun.

PANORAMAS: 🏛️ City Hall, 414 E. 12th St. (274-2000): Observation roof on

the 30th floor. Open Mon–Fri.

PARKS & GARDENS: 🏛️ Barney Allis Plaza, 12th St. between Central and

Wyandotte Aves.: Municipal park in the heart of dwntwn, opened in 1986, which has become very popular in fine weather for its shaded benches, hot-dog vendors, and enormous fountain (illuminated at night).

🏛️ **Penn Valley Park,** 31st and Main Sts.: On the site of a former slum area once known as "Vinegar Hill," this beautiful 176-acre (71ha) landscaped park designed by the architect George Kessler offers scenic footpaths among lawns and trees, as well as a small artificial lake.

🏛️ **Swope Park,** Meyer Blvd. and Swope Pkwy.: A very large (1,730-acre/700ha) park at the southern edge of the city. Golf, tennis, boating, and a distinguished zoo (see "Zoos," below). Open daily.

PERFORMING ARTS: For current listings of shows and cultural events, con-

sult the entertainment pages of the daily *Kansas City Star* (morning).

American Heartland Theatre, Crown Center, 2450 Grand Ave. (842-9999): New professional theater company performing well-known Broadway plays and musicals.

Coterie Theater, Crown Center, 2450 Grand Ave. (474-6552): Children's shows; very popular locally. Season is Feb to mid-Dec.

Folly Theater, 12th St. and Central Ave. (474-4444): Modern drama and comedy; concerts, jazz series. Designated historic monument.

Lyric Theater, 1029 Central Ave. (471-7344): Home of the Kansas City Symphony Orchestra (principal conductor: William McGlaughlin), with performances Nov–May; and of the Lyric Opera, with performances Apr and mid-Sept to mid-Oct.

Midland Center for the Performing Arts, 1228 Main St. (421-7500): Home of the Theater League and the renowned State Ballet of Missouri (performances Oct–Mar). Also Broadway hits and theater tours.

Missouri Repertory Theater, 4949 Cherry St. (235-2700): Classical and modern theater on the U. of Missouri campus, with seasons July–Sept and Jan–Apr.

Municipal Auditorium, 1310 Wyandotte St. (871-3706): Musicals, concerts. Striking example of art deco design.

Starlight Theater, in Swope Park, 63rd St. and Swope Pkwy. (333-9481): Open-air concerts and big-star shows, May–Sept. A summer-season classic for the last 30 years.

SHOPPING: The **Town Pavilion,** 1111 Main St. (472-9600): In the heart of the Petticoat Lane business district, this huge complex occupies three of the 38 floors of the new AT&T tower. Comprises more than 45 boutiques, stores, and restaurants, and a satellite facility of the Kansas City Museum.

Country Club Plaza, 47th and Main Sts. (753-0100): Locally known as "The Plaza," this is the country's oldest (1922) shopping center, a monument to the consumer society. More than 185 boutiques, stores, restaurants, and nightclubs in a very successful Spanish-Moorish setting with fountains, statues, murals, and tree-lined walks.

Crown Center, 2400 Pershing Rd. (274-8444): Luxurious avant-garde shopping center with 80 or so boutiques and stores (see "Architectural Highlights," above).

SPECIAL EVENTS: For exact dates, consult the **Kansas City Convention and Visitors Bureau** (see "Tourist Information," above).

Kansas City Rodeo (late June to early July): For rodeo fans.

Blues and Jazz Festival (late July): Very popular, featuring the biggest names in jazz.

American Royal Livestock, Horse Show, and Rodeo (Nov): A triumph of the cowboy idiom; one of the most renowned festivals in the Midwest, and a classic of its kind since 1899.

Dickens Holiday Fair (Dec): The Municipal Auditorium (see "Performing Arts," above) is transformed into a 19th-century Victorian village complete w. musicians, puppeteers, storytellers, and characters out of Dickens's books.

SPORTS: Kansas City has professional teams in two major sports:

Baseball (Apr–Oct): Royals, Royals Stadium at the Harry S Truman Sports Complex (921-8800).

Football (Sept–Dec): Chiefs, Arrowhead Stadium at the Harry S Truman Sports Complex (924-9400).

STROLLS: ⚘ **Antiques and Art Center,** 45th St. and State Line: A score of antiques shops and art galleries in the heart of one of Kansas City's oldest districts.

Southwest Blvd., west off of Broadway: Newly redeveloped Latino section of town featuring several Mexican rests. and Latino bookstores and craft shops on a cobblestone street.

Westport Square, Broadway at Westport Rd. (931-3440): This charming old district has managed to retain the full flavor of the past. Old shops, nicely restored 19th-century buildings, and inviting restaurants. One of the centers of the city's nightlife.

THEME PARKS: ⚘ **Benjamin Ranch on the Santa Fe Trail,** I-435S and E. 87th St. (761-5055): Re-creation of an Old West town, with riding, shows, rodeos in summer, and cowboy food. A pleasant place. Open daily year round.

⚘ **Oceans of Fun,** 12 mi. (19km) NE along I-435 to Exit 54 (454-4545): Enormous lagoon-pool holding a million gallons (3.7 million liters) of water, with giant slides, artificial surf, and dozens of aquatic attractions. Adjoins the Worlds of Fun complex (see below). Open daily Memorial Day–Labor Day.

⚘ **Worlds of Fun,** 10 mi. (16km) NE along I-435 to Exit 54 (454-4545): A 163-acre (66ha) amusement park with more than 135 different attractions, including a thrilling giant roller-coaster, the Timber Wolf. Shows, public concerts. Open daily May–Sept, wknds only in spring and fall; closed the rest of the year.

ZOOS: ♨ **Kansas City Zoo,** Swope Park, I-435 and Gregory Blvd. (333-7405): Fine collection of animals, many in native habitats—African veldt, tropical habitat, ape house, and waterfowl exhibit. Narrow-gauge railroad rides. Open daily.

ACCOMMODATIONS

Personal Favorites (in order of preference)

♛♛♛♛ **Ritz Carlton** (formerly the Alameda Plaza; nr. dwntwn), Wornall Rd. at Ward Pkwy., MO 64112 (816/756-1500; toll free 800/241-3333). 374 rms, A/C, cable color TV. AE, CB, DC, MC, V. Free gar., pool, health club, sauna, two rests. (including Rooftop Restaurant), two bars, 24-hr. rm svce, nightclub, concierge, free crib. *Note:* Luxurious landmark hotel w. an elegant and unusual Spanish interior, graciously renovated. Comfortable rms w. minibars and private balconies. Excellent svce. Very good rest. w. panoramic view and glass-walled elevator. Inviting grdns w. waterfalls and statuary. Elegance w. quality. Served as headquarters for Ronald Reagan during the 1976 Republican National Convention. 15 min. from dwntwn. **E–VE**

♛♛♛ **Hyatt Regency** (nr. dwntwn), 2345 McGee St., MO 64108 (816/421-1234; toll free, see Hyatt). 732 rms, A/C, color TV, in-rm movies. AE, CB, DC, MC, V. Valet gar. $8, pool, health club, sauna, two tennis courts, three rests. (including Peppercorn Duck Club), coffee shop, three bars (Skies is a revolving rest. and bar on the top floor), rm svce, concierge, free crib. *Note:* A 40-story building, more imposing than elegant, this crown jewel among the city's deluxe hotels possesses, like most of the new Hyatts, a spectacular glass-walled foyer six floors high. Spacious, comfortable rms w. refrigerators. Efficient svce. Entirely renovated after the 1981 collapse of two skywalks in the lobby left 111 dead. Group and convention clientele. Two VIP floors; no-smoking rms. **E–VE**

♛♛♛ **Adam's Mark** (nr. dwntwn), 9103 E. 39th St., MO 64133 (816/737-0200; toll free 800/444-2326). 372 rms, A/C, color TV, in-rm movies. AE, CB, DC, MC, V. Free parking, two pools, health club, sauna, two tennis courts, two rests. (including Remington's), coffee shop, two bars, rm svce, nightclub, free crib. *Note:* Adjacent to the Harry S Truman Sports Complex, this modern luxury hotel is typical of its genre, and draws a large number of groups and conventions. Huge well-laid-out rms; very good svce. Remington's is a well-regarded steakhouse. 15 min. from dwntwn on I-70. **M–E**

☼♛♛ **Raphael** (nr. dwntwn), 325 Ward Pkwy., Country Club Plaza, MO 64112 (816/756-3800; toll free 800/821-5343). 124 rms, A/C, cable color TV. AE, CB, DC, MC, V. Free valet gar., rest. (Raphael), bar, rm svce, free breakfast, free crib. *Note:* This is a small, elegant hotel in the European tradition, worlds away from the crowds of organized groups and conventions. Spacious rms w. minibars; discreet svce which anticipates your needs. A good place to stay. Interesting wknd discounts. 15 min. from dwntwn. **M–E**

♛♛ **Radisson Suite Hotel** (formerly the Radisson Muehlbach; dwntwn), 106 W. 12th St. (at Baltimore Ave.), MO 64105 (816/221-7000; toll free, see Radisson). 214 rms and suites, A/C, cable color TV. AE, CB, DC, MC, V. Valet parking $6, health club, rest. (Walt Bodine's Steakhouse), bar, rm svce, free breakfast, free crib. *Note:* Long considered the city's smartest and most elegant hostelry, the Radisson has welcomed every U.S. president from Theodore Roosevelt on. Now restored to its pristine magnificence, it offers rms and suites, spacious and very comfortable, w. a desk, two phones, computer hookup, and minibar. Efficient, careful svce; fully equipped business center. Conveniently located in the heart of the business district. Business and VIP clientele. **M**

    Best Western Country Inn (nr. dwntwn), 7100 NE Parvin Rd, MO 64117 (816/453-3355; toll free, see Best Western). 86 rms, A/C, cable color TV. AE, CB, DC, MC, V. Free parking, nearby rest., pool, free breakfast, free crib. *Note:* Conventional and well-run motel w. functional rms and thoughtful svce. Friendly reception. Very good value w. off-season rates. Ten min. from dwntwn. **B–I**

    Budgetel Inn (nr. dwntwn), 2214 Taney St., North Kansas City, MO 64116 (816/221-1200; toll free 800/428-3438). 100 rms, A/C, cable color TV. AE, CB, DC, MC, V. Free parking, adj. coffee shop, valet svce. *Note:* Modest, unpretentious motel on the north bank of the river. Functionally comfortable; free breakfast. Good value overall. 6 min. from dwntwn. **B**

Other Accommodations (from top bracket to budget)

    Westin Crown Center (nr. dwntwn), 1 Pershing Rd., MO 64108 (816/474-4400; toll free, see Westin). 724 rms, A/C, color TV, in-rm movies. AE, CB, DC, MC, V. Valet gar. $10, pool, health club, sauna, putting green, two tennis courts, three rests. (including Trader Vic's), coffee shop, two bars, 24-hr. rm svce, hrdrsr, boutiques, cinemas, free crib. *Note:* Regarded simply as architecture the massive building doesn't quite come off, but the elegant interior boasts tropical grdns and a five-story waterfall. Comfortable rms w. balconies; friendly reception, good svce. No-smoking floor. Favored by business travelers. Interesting wknd discounts. 8 min. from dwntwn, adj. the Crown Center w. its dozens of stores and boutiques. **E–VE**

    Kansas City Marriot Downtown (formerly Allis Plaza Hotel; dwntwn), 200 W. 12th St., MO 64105 (816/421-6800; toll free, see Marriott). 572 rms, A/C, cable color TV. AE, CB, DC, MC, V. Valet gar. $6, pool, tennis courts, health club, sauna, rest. (Lilly's), bar, rm svce, concierge, free crib. *Note:* An ungraceful ultramodern 22-story tower—but w. lavish interior and furnishings, and a spectacular indoor waterfall. Spacious, very comfortable rms, some w. refrigerators. VIP floor and one no-smoking floor. Efficient reception and svce. Conveniently located across the street from the Convention Center. Business and convention clientele. **M–E**

    Embassy Suites (nr. dwntwn), 220 W. 43rd St., MO 64111 (816/756-1720; toll free 800/362-2779). 266 suites, A/C, color TV, in-rm movies. AE, CB, DC, MC, V. Free parking, pool, sauna, rest., bar, rm svce, free breakfast, free crib. *Note:* New all-suite 12-story hotel located in the business area surrounding Country Club Plaza. Huge bedroom and parlor suites w. refrigerators and in-room work areas. Amenities include fax, photocopy svces, meeting rms, and express checkout. Business clientele. **E**

    Howard Johnson's Central (dwntwn), 610 Washington St., MO 64105 (816/421-1800; toll free, see Howard Johnson's). 185 rms, A/C, cable color TV. AE, CB, DC, MC, V. Free parking, pool, rest., bar, rm svce, free crib. *Note:* Conventional seven-story motel, recently renovated and comfortably up-to-date. Well located very nr. the Convention Center. Favored by business travelers; good value. **I–M**

    Quarterage (nr. dwntwn), 560 Westport Rd., MO 64111 (816/931-0001; toll free 800/942-4233). 123 rms, A/C, cable color TV. AE, DC, MC, V. Free parking, health club, sauna, rest. adj., free breakfast, free crib. *Note:* Aging but well-kept hotel in the lively Westport area. Contemporary theme decor. Pleasant comfortable rms, some on the narrow side. Friendly reception. Good value overall. **I–M**

    Best Western Inn Central (vic.), 501 Southwest Blvd. (at 7th St.), Kansas City, KS 66103 (913/677-3060; toll free, see Best Western). 115 rms, A/C, cable color TV. AE, CB, DC, MC, V. Free parking, pool, adj. coffee shop, bar, valet svce, free continental breakfast, free crib. *Note:*

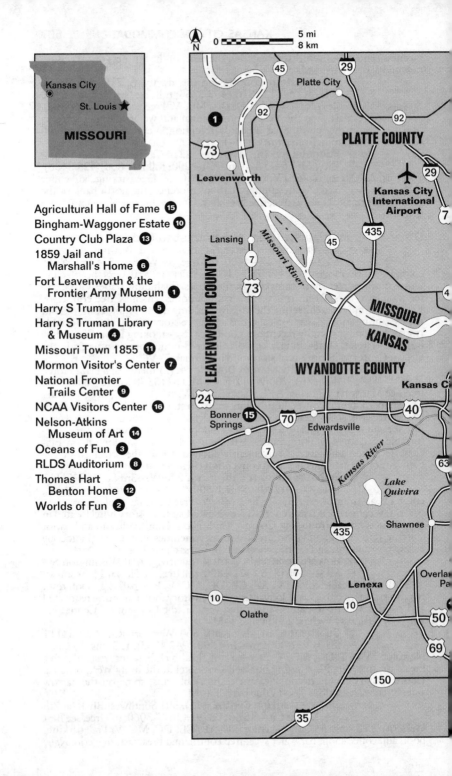

Agricultural Hall of Fame 15
Bingham-Waggoner Estate 10
Country Club Plaza 13
1859 Jail and
   Marshall's Home 6
Fort Leavenworth & the
   Frontier Army Museum 1
Harry S Truman Home 5
Harry S Truman Library
   & Museum 4
Missouri Town 1855 11
Mormon Visitor's Center 7
National Frontier
   Trails Center 9
NCAA Visitors Center 16
Nelson-Atkins
   Museum of Art 14
Oceans of Fun 3
RLDS Auditorium 8
Thomas Hart
   Benton Home 12
Worlds of Fun 2

KANSAS CITY AREA

Inviting and comfortable small motel just across the Kansas border 10 min. from dwntwn. Excellent reception; very good value. **B–I**

🍸 **Travel Inn** (formerly Travelodge; nr. dwntwn), 3240 Broadway, MO 64111 (816/531-9250). 52 rms, A/C, color TV. AE, CB, DC, MC, V. Free parking, adj. coffee shop, free morning coffee, free crib. *Note:* Low-priced but comfortable motel 5 min. from Crown Center and 10 min. from dwntwn. Good overall value. **I**

🍸 **Motel 6 North** (vic.), 8230 NW Prairie View Rd., MO 64152 (816/741-6400). 85 rms, A/C, cable color TV. AE, DC, MC, V. Free parking, pool, free crib. *Note:* Unbeatable value 20 min. from dwntwn along I-29. No bar or rest. Ideal for motorists. **B**

Airport Accommodations

🍸🍸 **Airport Doubletree** (formerly Hilton; vic.), 112th St. NW and I-29, MO 64195 (816/891-8900; toll free 800/222-8733). 350 rms, A/C, color TV, in-rm movies. AE, CB, DC, MC, V. Free parking, two pools, health club, sauna, two tennis courts, two rests., bar, rm svce, free airport limo, free crib. *Note:* Modern, comfortable motel 3 min. from the airport. Good sports facilities; good svce. Spacious, well-soundproofed rms, some w. refrigerators. **M–E**

RESTAURANTS

Personal Favorites (in order of preference)

🍷🍷🍷 **The American Restaurant** (nr. dwntwn), 25th St. and Grand Ave. (426-1133). A/C. Lunch Mon–Fri, dinner Mon–Sat; closed hols. AE, CB, DC, MC, V. Jkt. *Specialties:* grilled shrimp w. basmati rice, beluga caviar, coriander-crusted rack of lamb w. squash linguini and oven-roasted bell peppers, crispy Atlantic salmon w. celery cream, seared Angus beef tenderloin, broiled Maine lobster w. Thai coconut-flavored broth. Delicious desserts, especially the chocolate torte w. roasted banana ice cream. Daily menu. Fine list of California wines. *Note:* Delicate, inventive food; along w. the rustic Golden Ox, this is the place to go in Kansas City. This multilevel rest. atop the Crown Center, elegantly decorated w. mirrors and paneling, affords a clear view over the city. Innovative cuisine, w. pride of place given to local produce. Exemplary svce. Resv. a must; valet parking. *American/Continental.* **E**

🍷🍷🍷 **Bristol Bar and Grill** (nr. dwntwn), 4740 Jefferson St. (756-0606). A/C. Lunch Mon–Sat, dinner nightly, brunch Sun; closed Dec. 25. AE, CB, DC, MC, V. Jkt. *Specialties:* clam chowder, gumbo, scampi sauté; extensive choice of absolutely fresh fish and shellfish, broiled, poached, or baked. Menu changes daily. Fine wine list. *Note:* One of the best fish rests. in all the Midwest; superb seafood flown in daily. Elegant Victorian decor, w. a Tiffany-style glass dome in the back rm. Exemplary svce. The bar is the favorite watering hole for the local yuppies; live jazz. Resv. a must. *Seafood.* **M**

🍷🍷 **Golden Ox** (nr. dwntwn), 1600 Genessee St. (842-2866). A/C. Lunch Mon–Fri, dinner nightly; closed Dec 24–25. AE, CB, DC, MC, V. *Specialties:* wonderful broiled red meats. *Note:* A landmark of local cuisine, in the precincts of the Kansas City stockyards, 15 min. from dwntwn. Even the somber, unoriginal western decor can't detract from the exceptional quality of the meats or the perfection w. which they are prepared (the chefs do their work around enormous broilers in the middle of the dining rm, under the eyes of the diners). Diligent svce. If you love to eat meat, this place belongs in your address book; it's the best steakhouse in Kansas City. Resv. advised. *Steak.* **I–M**

🍷🍷 **Savoy Grill** (dwntwn), 9th and Central (842-3890). A/C. Lunch Mon–Sat, dinner nightly. AE, CB, DC, MC, V. Jkt. *Specialties:* world-famous Kansas City steaks, fresh fish, oysters on the half shell, shrimp de Jonghe, Maine lobster, gumbo. T-bone steak. *Note:* A Kansas City landmark since 1903; urbane old London club atmosphere, w. period svce and decor guaranteed. Resv. advised. *Steak/Seafood.* **I–M**

♥ **Arthur Bryant's Barbecue** (nr. dwntwn), 1727 Brooklyn Ave. (231-1123). A/C. Lunch/dinner daily; closed Thanksgiving, Dec 25. No credit cards. *Specialties:* barbecued short ribs and beef brisket, smoked ham, sandwiches. *Note:* Both the neighborhood and the decor could reasonably be described as shabby-looking, but lovers of barbecue will find it here in generous portions, of remarkable quality. Neon-and-Formica–style setting. The clientele is numerous, and comes back often. No resv. *American.* **B**

♥ **Stroud's** (vic.), 1015 E. 85th St. (333-2132). A/C. Lunch Fri –Sun, dinner nightly; closed Thanksgiving, Dec 24–25. AE, MC, V. *Specialties:* fried chicken, fried catfish, chicken-fried steak. *Note:* This unassuming, discreetly decorated old roadhouse is a shrine to fried chicken Kansas style, and draws a crowd of regulars every day. Atmosphere relaxed and noisy; no resv. (sometimes you'll have a long wait at the bar). Other location: 5410 NE Oak Ridge Rd. (454-9600). *American.* **B–I**

Other Restaurants (from top bracket to budget)

♥♥♥ **La Méditerranée** (nr. dwntwn), 4742 Pennsylvania Ave. (561-2916). A/C. Lunch Mon–Fri, dinner Mon–Sat; closed hols. AE, CB, DC, MC, V. J&T. *Specialties:* bouillabaisse (must be ordered in advance), lobster w. vanilla sauce, sole belle meunière, lamb à la niçoise, salmon en millefeuille, tournedos Gilbert, amaretto soufflé. Magnificent wine list. *Note:* Even if the sauces are a little rich, chef Gérard Jahier's French food is excellent, as is the svce; the rest. has been agreeably redecorated. Free parking; resv. a must. *French/Seafood.* **M**

♥♥ **Café Allegro** (nr. dwntwn), 1815 W. 39th St. (561-3663). A/C. Lunch Mon–Fri, dinner Mon–Sat; closed hols. AE, CB, DC, MC, V. Jkt. *Specialties:* homemade fresh pasta, veal loin stuffed w. wild mushrooms, peppered filet mignon w. Maytag bleu-cheese sauce, grilled salmon w. Chinese mustard glaze, Asian tuna tartar. Good, reasonably priced wine list w. cruvinet storage for wines to be served by the glass. *Note:* Charming bistro serving an eclectic modern cuisine that changes w. the seasons; the general appearance is that of a French country inn. Ultra-professional svce. Very popular locally, so resv. a must at lunch as well as dinner. *American.* **I–M**

♥♥ **Hereford House** (dwntwn), 2 E. 20th St. (842-1080). A/C. Lunch Mon–Fri, dinner nightly; closed hols. AE, CB, DC, MC, V. Jkt. *Specialties:* the finest meats perfectly broiled over an open fire; also excellent hamburgers. *Note:* One of the steakhouses that endears Kansas City to meatlovers. Typical western decor; casual atmosphere; resv. advised. A very fine place to eat. *Steak.* **I–M**

♥♥ **Jasper's** (vic.), 405 W. 75th St. (363-3003). A/C. Dinner only, Mon–Sat; closed hols. and first week of July. Jkt. *Specialties:* scampi Livornese, baby quail w. Sicilian fennel sausage and wild rice, lobster ravioli w. lobster sauce, vitello don Salvatore. List of over 150 Italian wines. *Note:* Baroque Italian design w. plush velvet seating and crystal chandeliers. Classic Italian cuisine. Ultra-professional tuxedoed svce. 20 min. south of dwntwn. Resv. highly advised. *Italian.* **I–M**

♥♥ **Venue** (nr. dwntwn), 4550 Main St. (561-3311). A/C. Breakfast/lunch Mon–Fri, dinner nightly, brunch Sat–Sun; closed hols. AE, DC, MC, V. *Specialties:* lasagna of lamb and wonton wrappers, mushroom-stuffed cabbage, homemade gnocchi, marinated salmon on a bed of sticky rice. *Note:* One of Kansas City's newest and trendiest eateries, serving naturally grown foods such as fresh vegetables. Elegantly casual setting and artsy atmosphere. Earnest and cheerful svce. Valet parking. Resv. accepted but unnecessary. *American.* **I–M**

☟ **Italian Gardens** (dwntwn), 1110 Baltimore Ave. (221-9311).
⛾ A/C. Lunch/dinner Mon–Sat; closed hols. AE, CB, DC, MC, V. *Specialties:* cannelloni, lasagna, fettuccine Lipari, calves' liver alla Veneziana, veal scaloppine w. lemon sauce, steak. *Note:* Nice, unassuming small family rest. Diligent svce. Popular in the community for more than 60 years, especially for lunch. The only attempt at interior decoration is provided by photos of show-business stars. *Italian/American.* **B–I**

☟ **Jerusalem Café** (nr. dwntwn), 431 Westport Rd. (756-2770).
⛾ Lunch/dinner daily; closed hols. AE, DC, MC, V. *Specialties:* tabbouleh salad, Greek salad, falafel, hummus, gyros, kebabs (shrimp, lamb, chicken). *Note:* Fine Middle Eastern cuisine in a bohemian atmosphere. The best place in Kansas City for vegetarians to go. Extremely popular w. locals. Considerate but slow svce. Another location that's open for lunch only: 1012 Locust St. (dwntwn) (472-6767). *Middle Eastern.* **B–I**

☟ **Le Picnique** (nr. dwntwn), Sebree Galleries, 301 E. 55th St.
⛾ (333-3387). A/C. Lunch only Mon–Sat; closed hols. AE, MC, V. *Specialties:* French herb-garden sandwich, grilled fish and chicken, daily specials, tarte au citron, gâteau au chocolat. *Note:* Charming little bistro housed in a European antiques shop w. brick floors. Pleasant country French menu. Unique courtyard and fountain atmosphere. Friendly svce. An excellent place for lunch south of dwntwn. *French.* **B–I**

In the Vicinity

☀️☟☟ **Stephenson's Old Apple Farm** (vic.), 16401 E. U.S. 40 at
☀️⛾⛾ Lee's Summit Rd. (373-5400). A/C. Lunch/dinner daily, brunch Sun; closed Dec 24–25. AE, CB, DC, MC, V. *Specialties:* meat, ham, and chicken smoked over a wood fire; steaks, homemade pies, apple fritters, cider. *Note:* Picturesque country inn occupying an old farmhouse 25 min. from dwntwn. Pleasant countrified setting; very crowded, so resv. advised at this successful rest. *American.* **I–M**

Cafeteria/Fast Food/Specialty Spots

Gates & Sons (nr. dwntwn), 4707 Paseo at Swope Pkwy. (921-0409): A solid contender w. Arthur Bryant's for the title of best barbecued food in Kansas City. Short ribs of beef, smoked ham, sliced beef, barbecued beans—all excellent. There are five other Gates & Sons places in town (consult the city telephone directory). Open daily for lunch and dinner.

Winstead's (nr. dwntwn), 101 Brush Creek Blvd. (753-2244). Drive-in and eat-in hamburger emporium. The hamburgers are made from fresh ground meat. Terrific ice cream and giant sundaes. Seven locations, including the original one at Brush Creek Blvd. Open daily for lunch and dinner.

BARS & NIGHTCLUBS

As you'd expect from the former jazz capital of the world, Kansas City, too, has a magic phone number—the **Jazz Hotline** (763-1052)—which will give you the programs at all the city's jazz concerts and jazz clubs.

Blayneys (nr. dwntwn), 415 Westport Rd. (561-3747). Hosts live bands playing reggae, rock, or jazz in a small basement. Open Mon–Sat.

City Light (nr. dwntwn), 4749 Pennsylvania Ave. (444-6969). Nightly live jazz. Dependable and cozy.

Grand Emporium (nr. dwntwn), 3832 Main St. (531-1504). Rock, blues, and reggae bands weekdays, jazz bands Fri–Sat. Also a rest. Casual atmosphere. Open Mon–Sat.

Houlihan's Old Place (nr. dwntwn), 4743 Pennsylvania Ave. (561-3141). Deservedly popular singles bar, and very acceptable rest. Open nightly.

Kiki's Bon-Ton Maison (nr. dwntwn), 1515 Westport Rd. (931-9417). Live zydeco music and good Cajun food to go along with it. Open nightly.

The Phoenix (dwntwn), 302 W. 8th St. (472-0001). Small, sophisticated jazz piano bar featuring live music Mon–Sat. Also rest.

75th Street Brewery (vic.), 520 W. 75th St. (523-4677). Congenial pub serving its own beer, as well as featuring other local brews. 20-min. drive from dwntwn.

NEARBY EXCURSIONS

FORT OSAGE (21 mi./34km east on U.S. 24 and Sibley Rd., Sibley) (881-4431): The first fort built (1808) west of the Mississippi by the famous expedition of Lewis and Clark (see the Fort Clatsop National Memorial in Chapter 46 on the Pacific Coast), now carefully restored. Officers' cantonments, barracks for other ranks, museum, and trading post all look as though they had been lifted bodily from a period western. It's a good idea to combine this trip with a visit to Independence (see below). Open wknds only from mid-Nov to mid-Apr, daily the rest of the year.

INDEPENDENCE (7 mi./12km east via Independence Ave.): Starting point of the Santa Fe Trail and Oregon Trail, and once the provisional capital of the Mormons.

The **Harry S Truman Library and Museum,** U.S. 24 at Delaware St. (833-1225), open daily, contains among other memorabilia an exact facsimile of the Oval Office at the White House. Also, don't miss the **Harry S Truman National Historic Site,** 219 N. Delaware St. (254-9929), a fine example of Victorian architecture where President Truman lived for more than half a century. Original furniture; open daily in summer, Tues–Sun the rest of the year.

On the way, stop at the **Mormon Visitors Center,** 937 W. Walnut St., which offers a complete history of the Church of Jesus Christ of the Latter-Day Saints. Open daily. Close by, the **World Headquarters Auditorium,** 1001 W. Walnut St., has one of the largest church organs in the U.S.: 6,300 pipes (daily recitals in summer).

Also take a look at the very picturesque **1859 Marshal's Home and Jail Museum** at 217 N. Main St. (252-1892), a genuine 19th-century prison and sheriff's office scrupulously restored. Open daily Apr–Sept, Tues–Sun the rest of the year.

KANSAS CITY, KANSAS (5 mi./8km west on U.S. 24): The twin city across the Kansas River. There is a group of 400 interesting **Native American tombs** in Huron Park, at Center City Plaza between 6th and 7th Sts., in the heart of the business district.

The **Agricultural Hall of Fame,** 630 N. 126th St. (913/721-1075), offers a fascinating course in the development of midwestern farming by means of extensive collections of old agricultural equipment and period buildings. Open daily Mar–Dec.

LIBERTY (15 mi./24km NE on I-35 and Mo. 152): Visit the **Jesse James Bank Museum,** Old Town Sq. (781-4458), where in 1866 Jesse James, the legendary bandit of the Old West, committed the first bank holdup in the country's history. Open daily.

See also the **Historic Liberty Jail,** 216 N. Main St. (781-3188), open daily, where Joseph Smith, founder of the Mormons, was imprisoned with a number of his followers, and where he was vouchsafed many revelations about Mormon doctrine.

OLD SHAWNEE TOWN (in Shawnee, Kans., 18 mi/29km SW along I-35 and Johnson Dr.) (913/268-8772 for information): Detailed reconstruction of a pioneer village in the period 1850–1900, with a dozen original buildings including the school and the jail, plus a score of facsimiles of structures from the time of the westward expansion. Picturesque and amusing. Open daily.

☼☀♨ **ST. JOSEPH** (50 mi./80km north on I-29): Founded in 1826 by a French fur trader, Joseph Robidoux, this little market town, birthplace of the great saxophonist Coleman Hawkins and TV newscaster Walter Cronkite, still offers a whiff of adventure. It was the terminus of the Pony Express, which from Apr 1860 to Oct 1861 was the only link between Missouri and California thanks to its dauntless riders (the record time to Sacramento was 7 days, 17 hr.).

The riders of the Pony Express, the most famous being the young Buffalo Bill, were, according to a contemporary newspaper advertisement, "young, slim, energetic and under 18. They must be consummate horsemen, ready to risk their lives every day. Orphans preferred. Pay: $25 a week." Every rider covered about 90 mi. (145km), with three changes of mount, before being relieved by another. Time allowed for change of mount: 2 min.—and the fastest did it in 15 seconds. At the time it cost $5 (later reduced to $1) to send a half-ounce letter from Missouri to California. A mere four days after the opening of the first transcontinental telegraph line on October 24, 1861, the Pony Express went out of business.

St. Joseph still displays some interesting links with the past: see the **Pony Express Stables Museum,** the company's birthplace, at 914 Penn St. (279-5059), open daily; the **Patee House Museum,** a former 1850s hotel at 12th and Penn Sts. (232-8206), open daily Mar–Dec, wknds only the rest of the year; and the **St. Joseph Museum,** 11th and Charles Sts. (232-8471), with many memorabilia of the westward expansion, open daily year round.

Finally, visit the **Jesse James House,** 12th and Penn Sts. (232-8206), where the famous outlaw was killed in 1882 by a member of his own band for a $10,000 reward. Open daily Apr–Oct, Mon–Sat the rest of the year.

On the way, visit the little pioneer city of ☼♨ **Weston,** on the banks of the Missouri, with its dozens of interesting old houses. Particularly interesting is the **McCormick Distilling Co.,** 1 mi. (1.6km) SE on County Rd. JJ, one of the oldest (1856) distilleries in the U.S.; call 640-2276 for visiting hours.

FARTHER AFIELD

☼♨♨ **LAKE OF THE OZARKS** (100 mi./160km SE on U.S. 71 and Mo. 7): This superb artificial body of water, more than 93 mi. (150km) long and surrounded by dense woods of oak and sassafras, was created in 1931 by the construction of the Bagnell Dam on the Osage River. Famous for its waterskiing, sailing, and fishing, this hilly region is attractive for the friendliness of its inhabitants, and for its wide range of all-season diversions: woodland walks in spring, water sports (more than 1,150 mi./1,840km of waterfront) in summer, cross-country skiing and skating in winter, and in fall the dazzling sight of the turning leaves. Lake excursions on the paddlewheel steamer *Tom Sawyer* from Bagnell Dam, near Lake Ozark (314/365-3300), daily Apr–Oct. There are hotels, motels, and restaurants at Camdenton, Clinton, Lake Ozark, and Osage Beach; three recommended hotels are:

Where to Stay En Route
☼♨♨♨♨ **Marriott's Tan-Tar-A Resort,** State Rd. KK, Osage Beach, MO 65065 (314/348-3131). 1,000 rms. Luxurious resort complex right on the lake. Private marina. **M–E**

♨♨♨ **Lodge of the Four Seasons,** Bus. U.S. 54, Lake Ozark, MO 65049 (314/365-3000). 317 rms. Elegant Spanish-style hotel standing amid 200 acres (80ha) of woods and grdns. Private marina. **E–VE**

♨♨ **Marina Bay Resort,** Lake Rd. 54–30 A., Osage Beach, MO 65065 (314/348-2200). 276 rms. Comfortable, friendly motel on the lake. **I–M**

PART FOUR

THE MOUNTAIN STATES

CHAPTER 29

DENVER

□ □ □

Midway between the Pacific coast and Missouri, Denver lies at the foot of the Rockies against the magnificent natural backdrop of the mountains. The "mile-high city"—to use the name conferred on it by its inhabitants—was dear to the heart of Buffalo Bill, whose grave overlooks the city from atop **Lookout Mountain.** More recently, Jack Kerouac eulogized it in his famous novel and bible of the beat generation, *On the Road.* A former gold and silver prospectors' camp, Denver served as a bridgehead for the westward expansion. Signs of the city's heroic past can be seen in structures like the **Capitol** dome, 243 ft. (76m) high, covered in pure gold leaf from Colorado mines. The neoclassical architecture of the imposing Capitol forms a striking contrast with the ultra-futurist **Denver Art Museum,** on the other side of the **Civic Center** and its gardens. Not far from here, the picturesque **Larimer Square** marks the heart of historic Old Denver with art galleries, cafés, restaurants, and 19th-century gas lamps.

Like all the mushrooming cities of the West, the capital of Colorado experienced an economic boom after World War II. Specializing in growth industries such as oil and mineral exploration, aeronautics, defense, graphics, and electronics, it is one of the energy capitals of the country with its oil, gas, coal, uranium, solar energy, and synthetic fuels. Not surprisingly, Denver, like Dallas and Houston, was severely affected by the oil crisis of the 1980s, and also by the recent events in the Mideast.

The proximity of the Rockies has also made Denver "queen city of the Plains," and one of the great capitals of American tourism.

Opened eight months late in 1994 and $1 billion over initial cost estimates, the $3.2-billion **Denver International Airport** is the first airport to be built from scratch since Dallas–Ft. Worth 20 years ago. Constructed to alleviate the bottleneck situation at the old Stapleton Airport, DIA serves as a veritable timetable between the East and West with its ability to handle three simultaneous landings, or 99 arrivals an hour.

An effective mix of modern skyscrapers, wide tree-lined thoroughfares, and wealthy suburbs, Denver, Colorado's capital, and its satellite, **Boulder,** located less than half an hour by car from downtown Denver, have more than 200 public parks and gardens between them. The one drawback is that the walls of the Rockies form an impassable barrier for automobile emissions and industrial fumes, smothering Denver each winter in a thick cloud of atmospheric pollution whenever the winds blow westward or a temperature inversion occurs. Famous children of Denver include actor Douglas Fairbanks and band leader Paul Whiteman.

BASIC FACTS: Capital of Colorado. Area code: 303. Time zone: mountain. ZIP Code: 80201. Settled: 1858. Approximate population: city, 465,000; metropolitan area, 1,850,000. 22nd-largest metropolitan area in the U.S.

CLIMATE: With close to 300 clear days per year, Denver is one of the sunniest cities in the country. The high altitude and the brisk, dry air make summer very agreeable (average temperature: 68°F/20°C). In spring and autumn the air gets chilly even when the sun is shining. Winter brings blizzards from the Rockies and the temperature plunges to 5°F (−15°C), which can make outings danger-ous (not to mention the frequent smog from mid-Nov to mid-Jan).

DISTANCES: Albuquerque, 421 mi. (675km); Kansas City, 600 mi. (960km); Los Angeles, 1,059 mi. (1,695km); Salt Lake City, 506 mi. (810km); Yellow-stone, 638 mi. (1,022km).

ARRIVAL & TRANSIT INFORMATION

AIRPORT: Denver International Airport (DIA): 23 mi. (37km) NE. Projected to become the second busiest airport in the U.S., after Chicago's O'Hare, trans-porting 32 million people annually. Spread over 53 sq. mi. (85 sq. km), it is the largest airport in the U.S. For information, call toll free 800/247-2336.

AIRLINES: American (toll free 800/433-7300), Continental (toll free 800/525-0280), Delta (toll free 800/221-1212), Northwest (toll free 800/225-2525), United (toll free 800/241-6522), and USAir (toll free 800/428-4322).

CITY LINK: The **cab** fare to city center is about $28–$30, time, 40 min. Bus: **Airporter** (321-3222); leaves approximately every hour; fare, $13. Many local bus lines (A, AS, and Skyride) also serve the airport; fare, about $6. Relatively efficient public transportation system (bus: R.T.D.) with a free **shuttle** in the dwntwn area (16th St. Mall Shuttle) (299-6000). The proximity of the Rocky Mountains and the numerous excursion possibilities make it advisable to rent a car with unlimited mileage.

CAR RENTAL: Avis (toll free 800/331-1212); Budget (toll free 800/527-0700); Dollar (toll free 800/800-4000); Hertz (toll free 800/654-3131); Na-tional (toll free 800/227-7368); Thrifty (toll free 800/367-2277). For dwntwn locations, consult the telephone directory.

LIMOUSINE SERVICES: Carey Limousine (toll free 800/336-4646), Dav El Limousines (toll free 800/922-0343).

TAXIS: Taxis are few and may not be hailed on the street. There are taxi stations in front of all the major hotels, at the bus station, and at the Amtrak station. They may also be summoned by phone. One of the least expensive cities in the country for cab riders. Major companies: **Metro Taxi** (333-3333), **Yellow Cab** (777-7777), and **Zone Cab** (444-8888).

TRAIN: Amtrak, Union Station, 17th and Wynkoop Sts. (toll free 800/872-7245).

INTERCITY BUSES: Greyhound, 1055 19th St. (toll free 800/231-2222).

INFORMATION & TOURS

TOURIST INFORMATION: The **Denver Convention & Visitors Bureau,** 225 W. Colfax Ave., CO 80202 (303/892-1112 or 303/892-1505).

GUIDED TOURS: **Cultural Connection Trolley** (trolley) (299-6000). With stops at most major attractions throughout the dwntwn area. $1 gives you on-and-off privileges. Running daily from Memorial Day to Labor Day.

Gray Line Tours (bus) (303/289-2841). Guided tours of the city and around the Rockies. Serves principal hotels.

SIGHTS, ATTRACTIONS & ACTIVITIES

ADVENTURES: Life Cycle Balloon School (balloon), 2540 S. Steele St. (759-3907): Daily flights over the Rockies, year round weather permitting. Spectacular.

Timberline Bicycle Tours (bicycle), 3261 S. Oneida Way, CO 80244 (759-3804): Leisurely excursions of a week or more into the Colorado Rockies, the Grand Canyon, the national parks of Utah and Wyoming, etc. Board and lodging provided.

For a list of commercial river runners, see Chapter 30 on the Rocky Mountains.

ARCHITECTURAL HIGHLIGHTS: ⚜️ **Boettcher Concert Hall,** 13th and Curtis Sts. (640-2862): Home of the Denver Symphony Orchestra, this building has remarkable architecture and acoustics; the orchestra is positioned in the center of the hall, totally surrounded by the audience.

⚜️ **Denver Center for the Performing Arts,** 14th and Curtis Sts. (893-3272): Artistic and cultural heart of Denver, this ultramodern architectural complex includes six theaters **(Helen Bonfils Theater Complex),** a movie theater for art and experimental film, the Boettcher Concert Hall (see above), and a large shopping arcade under an 80-ft.-high (24m) skylight. Open daily.

⚜️ **Public Library,** 1357 Broadway (640-8800): The largest library in the Mountain States, with 1.5 million volumes including an unrivaled collection of books, photographs, and documents on the history of the Old West. Open daily.

HISTORIC BUILDINGS: ⚜️ **Daniels & Fisher Tower,** Arapahoe St. and 16th St. Mall: This 328-ft. (100m) brick tower was inspired by the renowned campanile in the piazza San Marco in Venice. At the time of its construction (1910) it was the tallest building in Denver. Not open to the public, unfortunately.

⚜️ **Molly Brown House,** 1340 Pennsylvania St. (832-4092): Nouveau-riche Victorian house that belonged to Molly Brown, wife of a gold-mining magnate and famous as "Unsinkable Molly" because she survived the sinking of the *Titanic* in 1912. Lovely old furniture and interesting collections of clothing, tapestries, and turn-of-the-century memorabilia. Open daily in summer, Tues–Sun off-season.

⚜️ **State Capitol,** E. Colfax Ave. at Sherman St. (866-2604): The seat of the state legislature, a formidable granite structure 243 ft. (76m) tall modeled on the Washington Capitol. The dome is covered in pure gold leaf from Colorado mines. Superb panorama from the gallery at the top (elevator and rather steep stairs). Open Mon–Fri.

⚜️ **U.S. Mint,** 320 W. Colfax Ave. (844-3582): In business since 1862; turns out some 20 million coins each day. One of the three gold reserves in the country (Fort Knox and West Point, N.Y., are the other two), with heaps of ingots high enough to set you dreaming. No picture-taking allowed. Open Mon–Fri.

INDUSTRIAL TOURS: Coors Brewery, 13th and Ford Sts., in Golden (277-2337), 15 mi. (24km) west on W. Colfax Ave. and U.S. 40: Tour of the brewery and beer tasting. Open Mon–Sat year round.

MUSEUMS OF ART: ⚜️ **Denver Art Museum,** 100 W. 14th Ave. (640-2793): One of the best collections of Native American and pre-Columbian art, including a unique group of reredos and sculpted religious figures (*santos*).

Among its major works: Van der Weyden's *Portrait of Isabella of Portugal,* Arcimboldo's *Summer,* and Monet's *Waterloo Bridge,* as well as remarkable Oriental art. Surprising architecture in the form of a modern fortified castle covered in shining ceramic, by Gio Ponti and James Sudler. Open Tues–Sun.

    Museum of Western Art, 1727 Tremont Place at 17th St. (296-1880): In the venerable **Old Navarre Building** (1880), which has successively housed a girls' school, restaurants, and a brothel, this wonderful art museum dedicated solely to the heroic age of the Far West offers works by Frederic Remington, Charles Russell, Georgia O'Keeffe, and Albert Bierstadt, notably. Open Tues–Sat.

MUSEUMS OF SCIENCE & HISTORY: **Colorado History Museum,** 1300 Broadway (866-3681): For western history lovers, this museum retraces the life of the early pioneers and the Native Americans. Superb Anasazi pottery and interesting temporary exhibitions. Open daily.

    Forney Transportation Museum, 1416 Platte St. (433-3643): One of the most important transportation museums in the country, with more than 300 cars, various vehicles, and old locomotives, some of which are unique in the world. Open daily.

    Museum of Natural History, City Park, 2001 Colorado Blvd. (322-7009): Very complete museum w. many dioramas of natural habitats, displaying the wildlife of five continents and prehistoric ways of life in America and Europe. Also includes a hall of dinosaurs, the ultramodern Gates planetarium, and a projection room with a four-story screen **(Phipps Imax Theater).** Open daily.

PANORAMAS: **State Capitol,** E. Colfax Ave. at Sherman St. (866-2604): Spectacular panorama of the city and the mountains from the visitors' gallery at the top. Open Mon–Fri.

PARKS & GARDENS: **Cheesman Park,** Franklin St. and E. Eighth Ave.: Vast grass-covered park with a botanic garden and tropical greenhouses (see below). Superb view of the Rockies from Cheesman Memorial.

    City Park, between 17th and 26th Aves., York St., and Colorado Blvd.: Splendid 600-acre (243ha) park in the center of town with a golf course, many lakes and fountains, and a renowned zoo. Open daily.

    Denver Botanic Gardens, 1005 York St. (331-4000): Incredibly beautiful floral park that includes a rose garden, tropical greenhouses displaying more than 850 kinds of plants, a gorgeous Japanese garden, and an unusual alpine garden with its own chalet. Part of Cheesman Park (see above). Open daily.

PERFORMING ARTS: For daily listings of all shows and cultural events, consult the entertainment pages of the daily papers *Denver Post* (morning) and *Rocky Mountain News* (morning), the free weekly magazine *Westword,* and the monthly magazines *Colorado* and *Denver.* **Ticket Bus,** a discount-ticket booth on the 16th St. Mall at Curtis St. (623-1905), sells half-price tickets for all shows on the day of performance only. Accepts MC, V. Open Mon–Sat.

    Arvada Center for the Arts & Humanities, 6901 Wadsworth Blvd. (431-3080): Concerts, drama, comedy. Year round.

    Auditorium Theater, 14th and Curtis Sts. (640-2600): Broadway hits. Year round.

Boettcher Concert Hall, 14th and Curtis Sts. (640-2862): Home of the Denver Symphony Orchestra, with principal conductor Philippe Entremont. Sept–June.

Fiddler's Green Amphitheater, 6350 S. Greenwood Place (220-7000): Big-name shows. Summer only.

Helen Bonfils Theater, 14th and Curtis Sts. (893-4100): Home of the Denver Center Theater Company. Classical theater.

Paramount Theater, 1621 Glenarm Place (534-8336): Shows, concerts.

Red Rocks Amphitheater, Red Rocks Park, Colo. 26 (572-4704): Rock and pop open-air concerts. Summer only.

The Theatre on Broadway, 135 S. Broadway (777-3292): Contemporary theater; Off-Broadway acts.

SHOPPING: Gart Brothers, Tenth Ave. and Broadway: The biggest sporting-goods store in the world. Unbelievable.

Kohleberg's, 1720 Champa St.: The best place in Denver for authentic Native American crafts.

Miller Stockman, 1600 California St.: From Stetson hats to cowboy boots and saddles, one of the best-stocked stores in the West. Seven other Miller Stockman stores throughout Denver.

The Tattered Cover, 2955 E. First Ave.: Stocks over 400,000 titles on four floors of comfortable book-browsing space.

SPECIAL EVENTS: For the exact schedule of events below, consult the **Denver Convention & Visitors Bureau** (see "Tourist Information," above).

National Western Stock Show & Rodeo (10 days in mid-Jan): The largest livestock fair and the biggest rodeo in the country. Celebrates the Old West with special exhibits and events. Cowboy gear is *de rigueur*. This classic has been around since 1906 and should not be missed.

Colorado Indian Market (mid-Mar): Craft exhibits, Native American dances, and traditional cuisines of more than 90 tribes. A wonderfully colorful spectacle.

Red Rocks Park Summer Concerts (throughout the summer): Classical concerts, ballets, musical comedies in an open-air amphitheater that seats 10,000. The amphitheater is in the middle of a very handsome rocky arena 15 mi. (24km) SW of Denver.

Colorado Shakespeare Festival (July–Aug): Mary Rippon Outdoor Theater (University of Colorado at Boulder) presents three Shakespeare works each summer.

Taste of Colorado (Labor Day weekend): Live entertainment, food from local rests., arts, and crafts. Attracts over 40,000 people a year.

SPORTS: There are three major-league professional teams in the Denver area:

Baseball (Apr–Oct): Colorado Rockies, Coors Field (762-5437).

Basketball (Oct to late Apr): Nuggets, McNichols Sports Arena (893-3865).

Football (Sept–Dec): Broncos, Mile High Stadium (433-7466).

STROLLS: **The Financial District,** 17th St. between Broadway and Arapahoe: Known as "Wall Street West," this financial district brings together some of the most spectacular skyscrapers in the Mountain States, including the **Anaconda Tower,** 40 stories of smoked glass; the **First National Bank Building;** and the 30-story **Security Life Building.** For modern-architecture lovers.

Larimer Square, Larimer St. between 14th and 15th Sts. (534-2367): The heart of Old Denver, with art galleries, cafés, boutiques, and restaurants, is especially lively by night. Charming turn-of-the-century Victorian town houses and gas lamps. Quite touristy but pleasant.

    Sakura Square, 19th and Lawrence Sts.: A little piece of Japan in the middle of Colorado, "Cherry Blossom" Sq. has Japanese restaurants, boutiques, grdns, and a Buddhist temple. A welcome change of scenery.

    16th Street Mall, 16th St. between Market St. and Cleveland Place: The business heart of Denver, with dozens of specialized boutiques and department stores, numerous bars, restaurants, theaters. A free shuttle bus runs along the mall. Fountains and public benches make this tree-lined pedestrian street an agreeable place for a stroll.

THEME PARKS: ⚿ **Elitch Gardens,** 4620 W. 38th Ave. at Tennyson St. (455-4771): Very complete theme park with giant roller coasters amid 28 acres (11.3ha) of very lovely gardens. Also offers open-air concerts. Open wknds only in May, daily June–Sept; closed the rest of the year.

WINTER SPORTS RESORTS: With dozens of winter sports resorts, the Colorado Rockies are a skier's paradise. The season runs from mid-Nov to mid-Apr. The most popular are:

    Aspen Mountain and Aspen Highlands, 202 mi. (323km) SW on I-70 and Colo. 82 (toll free 800/525-6200): 19 lifts. This is the luxury resort of the Rockies.

    Copper Mountain, 86 mi. (137km) west on I-70 (303/968-2882): 20 lifts.

    Keystone Resort Ski Area, 78 mi. (124km) west on I-70 (303/468-2316): 19 lifts.

    Snowmass, 199 mi. (313km) west on I-70 and Colo. 82 (303/923-2000; toll free 800/598-2005): 16 lifts.

    Telluride, plane from Denver to Durango, then 123 mi. (196km) north of Durango (303/728-4424): 12 lifts.

    Vail, 105 mi. (168km) west on I-70 (303/476-5601; toll free 800/525-2257): 22 lifts. The poshest of the Colorado resorts.

    Winter Park, 71 mi. (113km) NW on I-70 and U.S. 40 (303/726-5514): 18 lifts.

ACCOMMODATIONS

Personal Favorites (in order of preference)
    Loews–Giorgio Hotel (nr. dwntwn), 4150 Mississippi Ave., CO (303/782-9300; toll free 800/223-0888). 198 rms, A/C, color TV, in-rm movies. AE, CB, DC, MC, V. Free valet parking, rest. (Tuscany), bar, rm svce, concierge, free breakfast. *Note:* This relatively new (1987) luxury hotel located in Denver's exclusive Cherry Creek area has become a favorite roost for passing VIPs. Splendid and refined Italian decor complete w. imported Italian marble and magnificent Renaissance-style frescoes. Spacious and remarkably comfortable rms w. minibars. Top-notch reception and svce. Free access to nearby health club. The best address in town. **E**

    Hyatt Regency (dwntwn), 1750 Welton St., CO 80202 (303/295-1234; toll free, see Hyatt). 511 rms, A/C, color TV, in-rm movies. AE, CB, DC, MC, V. Valet parking $12, pool, tennis, rest., coffee shop, bar, rm svce, concierge, free crib. *Note:* This elegant glass-and-steel tower (26 floors) is the last word in hotel comfort. Spacious, luxuriously arranged rms, each in its own style (most have refrigerators). Excellent svce. VIP and big business clientele. **E**

    Oxford (dwntwn), 1600 17th St., CO 80202 (303/628-5400; toll free 800/228-5838). 80 rms, A/C, color TV. AE, CB, DC, MC, V. Valet gar. $10, health club, sauna, rest., bar, 24-hr. rm svce, concierge, free crib. *Note:* Denver's first luxury hotel (built in 1891) is a delightful little place nicely redone in 1983. The atmosphere is elegant and discreet, the rms comfortable and tastefully decorated, the rm svce excellent. Good rest. and a splendid art deco bar. Clientele of regulars. **M–E**

🔑🔑 **Ramada Sports Center** (formerly Holiday Inn; nr. dwntwn), 🛏🛏 1975 Bryant St. (at 19th Ave.), CO 80204 (303/433-8331; toll free, see Ramada Inns). 168 rms, A/C, color TV, in-rm movies. AE, CB, DC, MC, V. Free parking, pool, rest. (Fans), bar, rm svce, free crib. *Note:* Large, round 13-story tower a few steps from Mile High Stadium offering the functional style and comfort of a Holiday Inn. Lovely view of the skyline and the mountains from the rest. at the top. A very good value. **I**

🔑🔑 **Comfort Inn–Downtown** (dwntwn), 401 17th St., CO 🛏🛏 80202 (303/296-0400; toll free, see Choice). 229 rms, A/C, color TV, in-rm movies. AE, CB, DC, MC, V. Valet parking $8, café opposite, bar, hrdrsr, shops. *Note:* Excellent budget choice in the heart of dwntwn. Originally part of the Brown Palace Hotel (see below), this high-rise motel offers comfortable, clean accommodations at a good-value price. Svce w. a smile. **B–I**

🔑 **La Quinta Central** (nr. dwntwn), 3500 Fox St., CO 80216 🛏 (303/458-1222; toll free, see La Quinta). 106 rms, A/C, cable color TV. AE, CB, DC, MC, V. Free parking, pool, adj. 24-hr. coffee shop, bar, valet svce, free breakfast, free crib. *Note:* Modern, comfortable motel 6 min. from dwntwn. spacious rms and efficient reception and svce. Good value. **B–I**

🔑 **Motel 6 East** (nr. dwntwn), 12020 E. 39th Ave., CO 80239 🛏 (303/371-1980). 137 rms, A/C, cable color TV. AE, DC, MC, V. Free parking, pool. *Note:* An unbeatable value in modern comfort nr. the airport. Ideal for the motorist (direct access to the highways). **B**

Other Accommodations (from top bracket to budget)

☀🔑🔑🔑 **Brown Palace Hotel** (dwntwn), 321 17th St., CO 80202 🛏🛏 (303/297-3111; toll free, see Preferred). 230 rms, A/C, color TV, in-rm movies. AE, CB, DC, MC, V. Valet gar. $12, three rests. (including the Palace Arms), two bars, 24-hr. rm svce, entertainment, hrdrsr, concierge, free crib. *Note:* The *grande dame* of Denver hotels has been frequented by every American president since Theodore Roosevelt. A slightly incongruous modern tower overhangs this Victorian building (1890). Elegant, six-story atrium w. cast-iron balconies, and fairly spacious, entirely renovated rms enhance the hotel's urbane character. Personalized svce and a reputable rest. Interesting wknd packages. **E–VE**

🔑🔑🔑 **Westin Tabor Center** (dwntwn), 1672 Lawrence St., CO 🛏🛏🛏 80202 (303/572-9100; toll free, see Westin). 420 rms, A/C, color TV, in-rm movies. AE, CB, DC, MC, V. Valet gar. $12, pool, health club, sauna, racquetball, two rests. (including Augusta), bar, 24-hr. rm svce, boutiques, free crib. *Note:* This large 19-story building w. rather ungraceful modern architecture offers direct access to the 16th Street Mall and its dozens of boutiques and stores. Luxurious, comfortable rms w. minibars (some w. balconies) and very complete facilities. Very good svce and an exclusive, grand-hotel rest. Business clientele (the financial district is nearby). **E–VE**

🔑🔑🔑 **Burnsley Hotel** (dwntwn), 1000 Grant St., CO 80203 (303/ 🛏🛏🛏 830-1000; toll free 800/345-3457). 82 suites, A/C, cable color TV. AE, CB, DC, MC, V. Free parking, pool, rest. (The Burnsley), bar, rm svce, concierge. *Note:* Small, intimate hotel composed exclusively of suites. Luxurious, ultra-comfortable facilities including vast bedrooms w. period furniture, refrigerators, private balconies, and a lovely view of the Rockies in the distance. Personalized svce, a very good rest. A favorite of connoisseurs. **M–VE**

🔑🔑🔑 **Marriott City Center** (dwntwn), 1701 California St., CO 🛏🛏🛏 80202 (303/297-1300; toll free, see Marriott). 610 rms, A/C, color TV, in-rm movies. AE, CB, DC, MC, V. Valet gar. $15, pool, health club, sauna, two rests. (including Marjolaine's), coffee shop, bar, rm svce, bou-

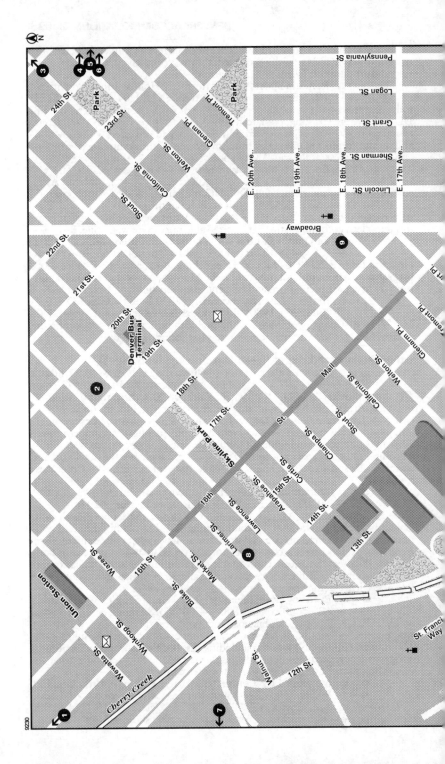

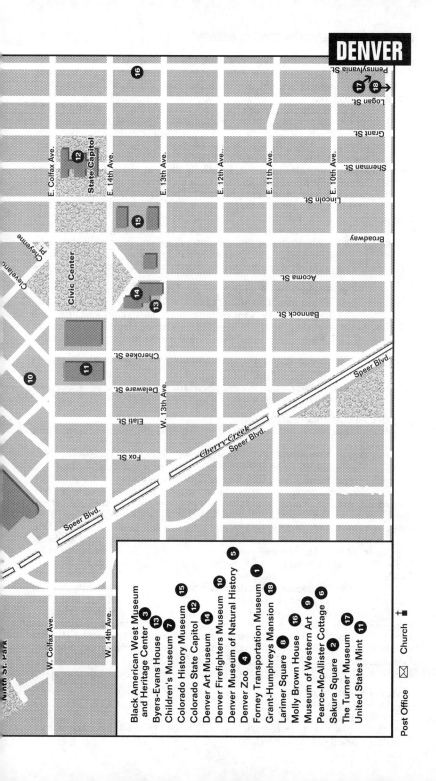

DENVER

Black American West Museum and Heritage Center **3**
Byers-Evans House **13**
Children's Museum **7**
Colorado History Museum **15**
Colorado State Capitol **12**
Denver Art Museum **14**
Denver Firefighters Museum **10**
Denver Museum of Natural History **5**
Denver Zoo **4**
Forney Transportation Museum **1**
Grant-Humphreys Mansion **18**
Larimer Square **8**
Molly Brown House **16**
Museum of Western Art **9**
Pearce-McAllister Cottage **6**
Sakura Square **2**
The Turner Museum **17**
United States Mint **11**

Post Office ■   Church ⊠ ✝

tiques, nightclub, concierge, free crib. *Note:* On the first 20 floors of the Arco Tower (42 floors). Spacious rms w. refrigerators. Ultramodern architecture; irreproachable comfort and facilities; unreliable svce. Two VIP floors. Business clientele. A very good location at the heart of the business district. **M–E**

☎ ☎ **Radisson** (dwntwn), 1550 Court Place, CO 80202 (303/ 893-3333; toll free, see Radisson). 750 rms, A/C, color TV, in-rm movies. AE, CB, DC, MC, V. Gar. $8, pool, health club, sauna, two rests. (including Windows), bar, rm svce, hrdrsr, boutiques, free crib. *Note:* This massive building is something of a tourist barracks. Entirely renovated facilities afford functional comfort and decor. Relatively efficient svce. VIP floor. Very central location, close to the 16th St. Mall. Group and convention clientele. **M–E**

☼ ☎ ☎ **Queen Anne Inn** (dwntwn), 2147 Tremont Place, CO 80205 (303/296-6666). 14 rms, A/C, cable color TV. AE, MC, V. Free parking; no bar or rest., but free breakfast and wine tasting. *Note:* A happily restored gem of Victorian architecture, this little villa stands in the heart of the historic Clements District, 5 min. from dwntwn. Elegant, comfortable rms overlooking city or grdn; many collectibles and period furniture. You must reserve well ahead; if you're allergic to the conveyor-belt style of big hotel, this is for you. **I–M**

☎ **Rockies Inn** (formerly Econo-Lodge; nr. dwntwn), 4760 E. Evans Ave., CO 80222 (303/757-7601). 78 rms, A/C, cable color TV. AE, CB, DC, MC, V. Free parking, pool, health club, rest., bar, crib $5. *Note:* Small, appealing motel 15 min. from dwntwn. Depressing surroundings, just off I-25, but a good overall value. Ideal for the motorist. No-smoking rms. **B**

☎ **Motel 6 West** (nr. dwntwn), 480 Wadsworth Blvd., CO 80226 (303/232-4924). 120 rms, A/C, cable color TV. AE, DC, MC, V. Free parking, pool, free crib. *Note:* An unbeatable value in functional comfort that's ideal for the motorist, 15 min. from dwntwn. **B**

Airport Accommodations

Note: These hotels are near Stapleton Airport—there are no hotels near DIA.

☼ ☎ ☎ ☎ **Stouffer Concourse** (nr. dwntwn), 3801 Quebec St., CO 80207 (303/399-7500; toll free, see Stouffer). 400 rms, A/C, color TV, in-rm movies. AE, CB, DC, MC, V. Indoor valet parking $6, two pools, health club, sauna, rest., bars, 24-hr. rm svce, concierge, free crib. *Note:* Remarkable futurist architecture in the shape of a trapezoid. All the comfort and luxury of a first-rate hotel in a splendid 12-story glass atrium. Vast, well-conceived rms w. refrigerators and private balconies (the best have a view of the mountains). Extremely well soundproofed. Very efficient svce and a mediocre rest., as in all Stouffers. Free airport shuttle. Three top floors are reserved for VIPs. One of the country's most spectacular hotels. 20 min. from dwntwn. **E–VE**

☎ ☎ **Stapleton Plaza Hotel & Athletic Center** (nr. dwntwn), 3333 Quebec St., CO 80207 (303/321-3500; toll free 800/950-6070). 300 rms, A/C, color TV, in-rm movies. AE, CB, DC, MC, V. Free parking, pool, health club, sauna, squash, rest. (Caper's Bistro), rm svce, hrdrsr, boutiques, free crib. *Note:* Modern motel w. futurist decor and a spectacular 10-story atrium w. glass elevators. Comfortable rms w. interior balconies and minibars. Good recreational facilities. Business clientele. Efficient svce. Free airport shuttle. **M–E**

YMCA/Youth Hostels

Denver Youth Hostel (nr. dwntwn), 630 E. 16th Ave., CO 80203 (303/ 832-9996). Dormitories. Clean and inviting.

YMCA (dwntwn), 25 E. 16th Ave., CO 80202 (303/861-8300). 60 rms. Men and women. Pool, health club.

RESTAURANTS

Personal Favorites (in order of preference)

� **The Augusta** (dwntwn), in the Westin Tabor Center (see "Accommodations," above) (572-9100). A/C. Lunch Tues–Fri, dinner Tues–Sat. AE, CB, DC, MC, V. Jkt. *Specialties:* lobster bisque w. citrus-infused croutons, carpaccio of home-smoked swordfish, potato-and-dill-crusted Atlantic salmon w. clam-and-pink-peppercorn sauce, grilled veal chop w. cream of morel sauce and Brie, double chocolate ganache cake. Short but excellent wine list. *Note:* The deluxe rest. of your dreams. With its huge picture windows looking out over the skyline, and its sleek black walls, Augusta is a model of contemporary elegance and provides an appropriate background for the subtle, delicate dishes of youthful chef Odran Campbell. Polished, attentive svce; resv. highly recommended. A splendid place. *American.* **M–E**

♟♟♟ **Zenith American Grill** (dwntwn), 1735 Arapahoe St. (820-2800). A/C. Lunch Mon–Fri, dinner nightly; closed hols. AE, MC, V. Specialties: lemon focaccia, smoked-corn soup w. barbecued shrimp and red-pepper sauce, goat-cheese chile relleno, venison w. serrano huckleberry sauce, ahi tuna w. tomatillo chutney and Scotch-bonnet pepper catsup, jerked pork loin w. spiced black beans and grilled bananas, raspberry crème brûlée. Seasonal menu. Extensive list of American wines moderately priced. *Note:* The latest culinary landmark in Denver. Extremely respectable and eclectic American cuisine by Denver native and self-taught chef Kevin Taylor. His fastidious care in the elements he selects appears in the astounding complexity of taste that's in every morsel. Very lively atmosphere and friendly svce. A good value to boot. Due to its popularity, resv. highly recommended. *American.* **I–M**

♟♟♟ **Cliff Young's** (dwntwn), 700 E. 17th Ave. (831-8900). A/C. Lunch Mon–Fri, dinner nightly. AE, CB, DC, MC, V. Jkt. *Specialties:* rack of lamb encrusted in herbs, filet of tuna charred rare, filet mignon w. lobster-basil sauce, roasted oysters w. sun-dried tomatoes and lemon butter, seared Texas antelope medallions w. black-currant sauce, scrumptious desserts. Extensive wine list. *Note:* Most innovative address of Restaurant Row (17th Ave.), this elegant small rest. serves creative American cuisine w. southwestern flair. The menu is varied, its presentation unsurpassed. Attentive svce; pleasant background music; resv. essential. *American.* **M–E**

♟♟ **La Coupole** (dwntwn), 2191 Arapahoe St. (297-2288). A/C. Lunch/dinner daily; closed hols. AE, CB, DC, MC, V. *Specialties:* escargot, fish mousseline and vegetables in pastry, choucroute, bouillabaisse, canard à l'orange, beef sirloin w. three peppers, entrecôte béarnaise. Menu changes periodically. Short but reasonably priced wine list. *Note:* Lively French bistro w. polished brass and (faux) Tiffany ceilings, appropriately lodged in the beautifully renovated Paris Hotel building in lower dwntwn. Like its Parisian namesake, La Coupole is busy at lunchtime, after theater, and late at night. Pleasant, fair-priced bistro fare; amiable svce. Congenial courtyard in summer. *French.* **I–M**

♟ **Juanita's Uptown** (nr. dwntwn), 1700 Vine St. (333-9595). A/C. Lunch/dinner daily (till 12:30am). AE, MC, V. *Specialties:* burritos, shrimp enchiladas, tacos, Tequila-cured salmon snapper Vera Cruz, chicken mole, flan. *Note:* The nicest of Denver's innumerable Mexican rests. The jukebox, Formica, and neon decor looks like a set out of *American Graffiti,* but the food is for real and the prices attractive. Youthful, relaxed ambience where double-breasted suits and jeans coexist comfortably. Very popular locally; resv. advisable. Other location: 1043 Pearl St., Boulder (449-5273). *Mexican.* **B–I**

♟ **Wynkoop Brewing Company** (dwntwn), 1634 18th St. (297-2700). A/C. Lunch/dinner daily (until 2am). AE, MC, V. *Specialties:* Shepherd's pie, fish and chips, award-winning sausages. *Note:* English-style brewpub located in the historic J. S. Brown Mercantile Building (1899) in lower dwntwn. Hearty pub fare and eight beers on tap brewed fresh on premises. Jazz pianist at dinner. Kindly, relaxed atmosphere and svce. *American.* **B**

Other Restaurants (from top bracket to budget)

♈♈♈ **The Palace Arms** (dwntwn), in the Brown Palace Hotel (297-3111) (see "Accommodations," above). A/C. Lunch Mon–Fri, dinner nightly. J&T. AE, CB, DC, MC, V. *Specialties:* smoked duck, Rocky Mountains trout meunière, Colorado prime rib, rack of lamb dijonnaise, fresh seafood. One of the best—and priciest—wine lists in town. *Note:* By far the most luxurious dining rm in Denver, rich w. Napoleonic-era antiques, fine crystal, and silver. The consistent quality of the excellent—if not particularly innovative—American regional cuisine served here has earned the Palace Arms many awards. The svce is flawless and the atmosphere very chic. Patronized by local executives. Resv. required. Valet parking. *American.* **M–E**

♈♈♈ **Strings** (nr. dwntwn), 1700 Humboldt (831-7310). A/C. Lunch Mon–Sat, dinner nightly. AE, CB, DC, MC, V. Jkt. *Specialties:* grilled eggplant w. mozzarella, pasta dishes, duck breast rosé, swordfish Tamara w. sautéed shrimp and scallops, garlic chicken in tomatillo sauce, remarkable desserts. *Note:* Excellent variations on the California cuisine moderne theme by Noel Cunningham. Hi-tech ocean-liner decor w. an open grill and a pleasant patio for al fresco meals. Friendly, cheerful svce. Hip clientele. Resv. a must in light of its success. *American.* **M**

♈♈ **Tante Louise** (nr. dwntwn), 4900 E. Colfax Ave. (355-4488). A/C. Lunch Fri, dinner Mon–Sat; closed hols. AE, CB, DC, MC, V. Jkt. *Specialties:* grilled free-range veal chop, Colorado rack of lamb, Peking duck, sweetbreads w. wild mushrooms. The menu changes regularly. Fine wine list. *Note:* This turn-of-the-century–style inn is elegant and intimate and offers lovingly prepared, delicate, imaginative cuisine. Agreeable svce. Distinguished musical background. Resv. advised. An excellent spot. 10 min. from dwntwn. *Continental.* **M**

☼♈♈ **Buckhorn Exchange** (nr. dwntwn), 1000 Osage St. (534-9505). A/C. Lunch/dinner daily; closed hols. AE, CB, DC, MC, V. *Specialties:* navy-bean soup, all kinds of meat cuts, T-bone steak, Rocky Mountain oysters, moose and bison steak, venison (in season), roast quail, homemade apple pie. *Note:* Patronized by Buffalo Bill in his day, the oldest rest. in Denver (1893) proudly displays the "No. 1" on its liquor license. First-rate prime cuts generously served. Authentic western decor including a vast collection of guns and hunting trophies. Absolutely worth a visit. Locally very popular. Resv. advised. *Steak.* **I–M**

♈♈ **Imperial Chinese Seafood** (nr. dwntwn), 1 Broadway (698-2800). A/C. Lunch Mon–Sat, dinner nightly. AE, MC, V. *Specialties:* cold noodles w. chili-sesame sauce, steamed whole sea bass in Hunan sauce, sesame chicken, eggplant in garlic sauce, steamed chicken dumplings, toffee fruit fritter. *Note:* Stylish Chinese establishment whose menu offers a cross-country tour of the provinces: Hunan, Szechuan, Canton, Peking. . . . The atmosphere is as quietly elegant as the food served. Efficient svce. Resv. advised. *Chinese.* **I**

☼♈ **Baby Doe's Matchless Mine** (nr. dwntwn), 2520 W. 23rd Ave. (433-3386). A/C. Lunch Sun–Fri, dinner nightly; closed Dec 25. AE, CB, DC, MC, V. *Specialties:* bison steak, beef chops, chicken w. Calvados, duck à l'orange, catch of the day. *Note:* Reproduces the atmosphere of a famous Leadville (Colorado) gold mine from the 1880s. Amusing bric-a-brac decor. Honest, if not terribly original, cuisine. Rather touristy ambience. Dancing nightly as well. *Steak/American.* **I**

♈ **Gasho** (dwntwn), 5071 S. Syracuse St. (773-3277). A/C. Lunch Mon–Sat, dinner nightly. AE, CB, DC, MC, V. *Specialties:* hibachi steak, teriyaki, sashimi, sukiyaki. *Note:* Denver's best Japanese rest. offers classic knife-wielding performances by the cooks under the admiring gaze of the customers. Lovely Japanese decor w. original furniture. Business clientele. Locally popular. Nr. Denver Tech Center. *Japanese.* **I**

 ☘ **Beau Jo's** (nr. dwntwn), 2700 S. Colorado Blvd. (758-1519). ♻ A/C. Lunch/dinner daily; closed hols. AE, MC, V. *Specialties:* pizzas of all varieties. *Note:* The best pizza to be found in the Rockies. Diners design own pies, choosing everything from the thickness and type of crust to the type of cheese to the toppings, some of which you can't believe anyone would actually put on a pizza. Rustic setting w. a lot of old-time western memorabilia. An enjoyable place. Other location: 7805 Wadsworth Blvd. (420-8376). *Italian.* **B–I**

 ☀☘ **Casa Bonita** (vic.), 6715 W. Colfax Ave., Lakewood (232-5115). A/C. Lunch/dinner daily; closed hols. AE, MC, V. *Specialties:* enchiladas, tacos, chile con queso, tamales. *Note:* Huge rest. (seating for 1,100) that's so wild, it's cool. Classic Mexican dishes served in a vibrant, carnival atmosphere: palm trees, a 30-ft. (10m) waterfall, mariachi music, staged shootouts, and puppet shows. Locally popular. *Mexican.* **B**

 ☘ **Daddy Bruce's Bar-B-Que** (nr. dwntwn), 1629 E. Bruce Randolph Ave. (295-9115). A/C. Lunch/dinner Tues–Sat (until 10pm). No credit cards. *Specialties:* spareribs, chicken, barbecued pork and beef, smoked turkey, sweet-potato pie. *Note:* A real institution; Denver's temple of soul food. The neighborhood is less than inviting and the decor is neo-Formica, but the barbecue is remarkable. A must for those in search of the best barbecue in town. No resv. *American.* **B**

Cafeteria/Fast Food

Furr's (nr. dwntwn), 4900 Kipling (423-4602). Open daily (until 8pm). Honest, well-prepared cafeteria food, particularly the roast beef. No credit cards.

BARS & NIGHTCLUBS

Dead Beat Club (dwntwn), 4040 E. Evans at Colorado Blvd. (758-6853). Multilevel dance club w. occasional live rock acts.

 ☀ **El Chapultepec** (dwntwn), 1962 Market St. (295-9126). Since 1980, the best modern jazz in town. A Mexican rest. as well (praiseworthy). Open nightly.

Comedy Works (dwntwn), 1226 15th St. (595-3637). Colorado's premier stand-up comedy nightclub. Open Tues–Sun.

Corner Room (dwntwn), in the Oxford Alexis Hotel, 1600 17th St. (628-5400). Open Mon–Sat. Inviting, elegant art deco piano bar.

Grizzly Rose Saloon (vic.), 5450 N. Valley Hwy. (295-1330). The ultimate country-western dance-saloon experience. Can hold up to 1,500 people. Live music and entertainment nightly. Also rest.

Mercury Cafe (dwntwn), 2199 California St. (294-9258). Everything from acoustic to hip hop to big band appears on the several stages at this café that serves very commendable food as well.

NEARBY EXCURSIONS

 ☀🥛 **BOULDER** (30 mi./48km NW on U.S. 36): This beautiful university town nestled at the edge of the Rocky Mountains has a young, upwardly mobile population keen on sports and the environment. Boulder is home to the **University of Colorado** (24,000 students), which includes a world-renowned medical school and many leading scientific institutes, among them the laboratories of the National Bureau of Standards and the National Center for Atmospheric Research, housed in a futurist building by I. M. Pei at 1850 Table Mesa Dr. (497-8720), open Mon–Fri.

An interesting pioneer museum is the **Boulder Historical Museum,** 1206 Euclid Ave. (449-3464), open Tues–Sat. Don't miss a glance at the charming **Downtown Mall,** Pearl St. between 11th and 15th Sts., with its pedestrians-only street, boutiques, restaurants, and old town houses. (For accommodations and restaurants, see Chapter 30 on the Rockies.)

☀☖ **BUFFALO BILL GRAVE** (in Lookout Mountain Park, 18 mi./28km west on I-70 and U.S. 6) (526-0747): A magnificent view over the city from the mountaintop where lies the tomb of the famous scout. Small museum dedicated to his adventurous career. Open daily in summer, Tues–Sun the rest of the year. On the way, visit the **Colorado Railroad Museum** in Golden (see below).

☀☖☖ **CENTRAL CITY** (34 mi./54km west on I-70 and Colo. 279): Spectacular little mining town from the days of the Gold Rush. The abundance of gold mined here earned it the nickname "the richest square mile on earth." Counting as many as 5,000 inhabitants in the 1870s, the town has barely 350 today. A walking tour of the town is fun but tiring (it was built on the side of a mountain at 8,496 ft./2,590m; start at the top and work downward). See the very handsome **Opera House** from 1878, Eureka St. (582-5202), open June–Aug. The **Lost Gold Mine**, 231 Eureka St. (642-7533), is open daily May–Sept. The **Gold Coin Saloon** on Main St. has been in operation since 1878. The **Teller House,** Eureka St. (279-3200), is a charming little Victorian hotel built in 1872 with a famous bar and a new casino. There is also a picturesque narrow-gauge railroad.

☖ **COMANCHE CROSSING MUSEUM** (in Strasburg, 30 mi./48km east on I-70) (622-4322): Open-air museum devoted to the builders of the 19th-century transcontinental railroad. Original buildings and historic memorabilia of all kinds. Open daily June–Aug only.

☖☖ **DENVER INTERNATIONAL AIRPORT** (27 mi./37km east on I-70): The main terminal at Denver's new airport is also a major architectural feat: 15 acres of Teflon-coated fiberglass stretched and anchored over 35 masts and 10 mi. (16km) of cables. The billowing teepee-like main terminal, designed by Denver local Jim Bradburn, rises and separates into several domes, appearing like a downscaled version of the airport's backdrop— the front range of the Rocky Mountains. Inside the terminal, which has enough huge windows to need no artificial lighting during the day, is $7.5 million worth of artwork, a museum unto itself.

☀☖ **GOLDEN** (15 mi./24km west on W. Colfax Ave. and U.S. 40): The Colorado capital 1862–67. See the **Colorado Railroad Museum,** 17155 W. 44th Ave. (279-4591), with its interesting collection of old locomotives, one of the most important in the nation. Open daily. A recommended joint excursion with the nearby **Buffalo Bill Grave** (see above).

☖ **IDAHO SPRINGS** (34 mi./54km west on I-70): Old gold diggers' town in the midst of a still very active mining zone, now producing uranium, molybdenum, zinc, lead, and tungsten. Today it's also a renowned tourist attraction with radioactive hot springs. The longest mine tunnel in the world (5 mi./7km) once joined Idaho Springs and Central City. Part of the tunnel still exists but is not open to the public. See the **Argo Gold Mill,** 23rd Ave. and Riverside Dr. (567-2421), a gold mine dating from 1913, open daily June–Sept. A recommended joint excursion with **Central City** (see above) and **Mount Evans Scenic Road** (see "Farther Afield," below).

☖ **RED ROCKS PARK** (12 mi./19km SW on W. Colfax Ave. and Colo. 26) (572-4704): A natural, 10,000-seat amphitheater carved out in the middle of reddish rocks more than 300 ft. (100m) high. Offers a spectacular view of the city plus public concerts, big-name performances, and open-air shows in summer. It's also the stage for an open-air mass on Easter Sunday attended by thousands (Easter sunrise service).

NATIONAL PARKS NEARBY: 🔔🔔 **Rocky Mountain National Park,** 70 mi. (112km) NW on U.S. 36 and 34. The most mountainous national park in America boasts 113 peaks of more than 10,000 ft. (3,050m), including **Longs Peak** (14,255 ft./4,345m). Torrents, glaciers, eternal snows, fish-filled lakes, very dense forests, and more than 300 mi. (480km) of hiking trails. Unspoiled nature and a paradise for mountain climbing, camping, and fishing. **Trail Ridge Road** crosses right through the park and offers splendid panoramas, as well as spectacular views of the mountain peaks. The road is closed mid-Oct to mid-June. There are numerous hotels and motels open year round in **Estes Park, Grand Lake,** and **Granby.** The **Moraine Park Visitor Center and Museum** is 1 mi. (1.6km) from the east entrance of the park on U.S. 36 (open daily June–Sept). Note that part of U.S. 34, between Deer Ridge and Timber Creek, is closed in winter. For information, contact the Superintendent, Estes Park, CO 80517-8397 (303/586-2371; toll free 800/443-7837). (For accommodations, see Chapter 30 on the Rockies.)

FARTHER AFIELD

🔔🔔 **MOUNT EVANS SCENIC ROAD** (120 mi./190km 5-hr. r.t. on I-70W, Colo. 103, and Colo. 5): The highest asphalt road in the country: elevation 14,260 ft. (4,346m). Fabulous landscapes can be seen all along the road, which is open in summer only (check in Idaho City before departure). A real trial for people and vehicles, but well worth the trip (not recommended to people with a heart condition or susceptible to vertigo). On the way, visit **Georgetown** and **Central City** (see "Nearby Excursions," above), two picturesque mining towns from the days of the Gold Rush.

🔅🔔🔔 **COLORADO SPRINGS** (134 mi./214km r.t. on I-25S): Quaint garden city at 6,000 ft. (1,800m) frequented year round by tourists and vacationers. Home of the Air Force Academy, NORAD (headquarters for U.S. air defense), and various computer manufacturers; the U.S. Olympic Training Complex represents the city's third major activity, after defense and data processing: sport. The U.S. Olympic Committee has settled in neighboring Colorado Springs, cheek-by-jowl with a couple of dozen sports organizations. These are the city's major tourist attractions.

The 🔔 **U.S. Air Force Academy** lies 10 mi. (16km) north of the city at Exit 156B from I-25 (719/472-2555); its Visitor Center, with a small museum and movie shows, is open year round. On the very handsome campus, don't miss the 17-spired Cadet Chapel, a major landmark of futurist architecture.

Its nerve center buried under the rocky shield of Cheyenne Mountain, southwest of the city, 🔅🔔🔔 **NORAD,** offers guided tours of its underground installations Mon, Thurs, and Sat; applications must be made six months ahead, in writing, giving the intended visitors' names, Social Security numbers, date of visit, and home telephone. Children under 2 years old are not admitted. Write: HQ AF Space COM/PAC, Attn. Tour Program, Peterson AFB, CO 80914-5001. NORAD's Command Center was faithfully reproduced in the movie *War Games.*

A guided tour of the 🔅🔔🔔 **U.S. Olympic Training Complex,** 1750 E. Boulder St. at Union Blvd. (719/578-4644), allows sports fans to watch their favorite athletes in training for boxing, track, basketball, gymnastics, or the like. Open daily.

Lovers of the Old West must also take in the 🔔 **Pro Rodeo Hall of Fame of the American Cowboy,** 101 Pro Rodeo Dr. at Exit 147 from I-25 (719/593-8847), with its museum, films, rodeo trophies, and western memorabilia. Open daily year round. Along the same lines try to see 🔅🔔 **Pike's Peak Ghost Town,**

400 S. 21st St. at U.S. 24 (719/634-0696), open daily mid-May to mid-Oct. This is a real 19th-century pioneer settlement with a strong far western flavor, complete with saloon, prison, hotel, smithy, drugstore, and so on—all certified authentic and of the period.

Numerous and very spectacular excursions in the area, including:

Broadmoor-Cheyenne Mountain Hwy. (access by S. Nevada Ave.): A superb panoramic route and "shrine of the sun" dedicated to the noted entertainer Will Rogers.

Garden of the Gods (access by U.S. 24 and 30th St. NW): Splendid reddish sandstone monoliths, particularly spectacular at sunrise and sunset.

Manitou Springs: A charming mountain spa at 515 Ruxton Ave. in Manitou Springs (719/685-5401) is the terminus of the **Cog Railway,** picturesque route leading to Pike's Peak (daily May–Oct). The **Scenic Incline Railway,** 518 Ruxton Ave. (719/685-9086), is a cable car that goes to the summit of Mount Manitou, offering an impressive view (daily May–Sept).

Pikes Peak (14,110 ft./4,301m): Accessible only in summer by a steep toll road or by the Cog Railway (see above). An excursion not to be missed.

Seven Falls (access by Cheyenne Blvd.): A very beautiful rocky canyon with waterfalls which are illuminated at dusk. Open daily year round. A wonderfully spectacular drive. (For accommodations, see Chapter 30 on the Rockies.)

CHEYENNE (200 mi./320km r.t. on I-25): Founded in the 19th century by the army in an effort to protect Union Pacific Railroad builders against Sioux attacks, the capital of Wyoming has retained its frontier-town flavor. Witness the **State Museum and Art Gallery,** Central Ave. and 24th St. (307/777-7519), open daily in summer, Mon–Sat the rest of the year; the **Frontier Days Old West Museum,** Carey Ave. (307/778-7290), open daily in summer, Tues–Sun the rest of the year; and the superb wall murals of the **State Capitol,** Capitol Ave., open Mon–Fri. Annually since 1897, Cheyenne, named for the Native American tribe, has sponsored the **Cheyenne Frontier Days,** the most fabulous rodeo festival in the country, the world's biggest outdoor rodeo celebration, the "Daddy of 'Em All," with 1,100 entrants and 400,000 cowboy fans. Late July; for information, call 307/778-7200 or toll free 800/227-6336. Itself worth the trip.

Where to Stay in Cheyenne

Best Western Hitching Post Inn, 1700 W. Lincolnway, Cheyenne, WY 82001 (307/638-3301; toll free, see Best Western). 210 rms. First-rate comfort. **I**

La Quinta Inn, 2410 W. Lincolnway, Cheyenne, WY 82001 (307/632-7117; toll free, see La Quinta). 108 rms. Modern comfort. **B–I**

Motel 6, 1735 Westland Rd., Cheyenne, WY 82001 (307/635-6806). 108 rms. A very good, economical value. **B**

CHAPTER 30

THE ROCKY MOUNTAINS 🎿🎿🎿

□ □ □

Comprising several parallel mountain chains, the Rocky Mountains form an impressive system more than 1,875 mi. (3,000km) long, extending from New Mexico to Canada. This granite barrier of almost Himalayan proportions, with 53 peaks reaching more than 14,000 ft. (4,260m), marks the Continental Divide: east of the Rockies, the Missouri and its tributaries flow toward the Gulf of Mexico; to the west, the Colorado ("mother of all rivers" in the evocative phrase of writer James Michener) and its tributaries flow toward the Pacific. The central section of the Rocky Mountain chain, its peaks sculpted into fantastic shapes by erosion, makes Colorado one of the most beautiful states in America.

Some 70 million years old, the Rockies long remained uninhabited—the earliest traces of Native American settlement go back barely 2,000 years. It's as though the reverential awe that the sight of these wild, magnificent mountains must have inspired kept the local tribes away. Although the first white settlers arrived only in 1820, the westward expansion of the succeeding decades made the Rockies an obligatory way station for the famed riders of the Pony Express (eight days from Kansas to California) and for the heavy stagecoaches of the Wells Fargo and Overland companies. The gold rush of 1859–60 caused a further influx of settlers into the mountains.

Today the Colorado Rockies have become one of the nation's great tourist attractions, favored equally by sun worshippers and skiers, with **Aspen, Vail, Steamboat Springs, Keystone, Telluride, Snowmass,** and **Copper Mountain** ranking among the most popular winter sports centers in the U.S. With Denver as their point of departure, motorists may enjoy numerous 2- to 10-day touring itineraries, allowing them to discover such gorgeous landscapes as the peaks and alpine lakes of **Rocky Mountain National Park** to the north, the wild gorges of the **Colorado National Monument** to the east, the desert solitude of the **Great Sand Dunes** and the fabulous Native American archeological sites of **Mesa Verde National Park** to the south. Dozens of **ghost towns** from the gold-rush days, such as Georgetown, Central City, or Cripple Creek, as well as roads affording breathtaking panoramic views, such as those that wind up **Pikes Peak** and **Mount Evans** (at 14,260 ft./4,346m, the highest road in the U.S.), further enhance the unique appeal of the Colorado Rockies. All in all, this is a region not to be missed, as much for the incomparable beauty of its landscapes as for its aura of adventure (see also Chapter 29 on Denver).

BASIC FACTS: State of Colorado. Area code: 303 or 719. Time zone: mountain. Population of Colorado: approx. 2.9 million.

CLIMATE: Very cold and snowy in winter (30°F/−1°C, on average), wonderfully sunny but cool in summer (70°F/21°C, on average), the climate of the Colorado Rockies is a delight for tourists. Spring (47°F/8°C, on average) and above all autumn (51°F/11°C, on average) are the ideal seasons for avoiding the crowds of summer vacationers and winter sports enthusiasts. Sweaters and sunglasses are advisable in all seasons.

ARRIVAL & TRANSIT INFORMATION

NEAREST AIRPORT: Denver International Airport (DIA), 81 mi. (144km) SE of Rocky Mountain National Park; for information call toll free 800/272-2336. The newest and biggest airport in the U.S.

Other airports giving access to the region are at Aspen, Colorado Springs, Durango, Grand Junction, Gunnison, Steamboat Springs, Telluride, and Vail.

AIRLINES: See Chapter 29 on Denver. **Aspen Airways/United Express** (toll free 800/241-6522), **Mesa** (toll free 800/637-2247), and **Rocky Mountain Airways/Continental Express** (toll free 800/525-0280) serve the main regional airports, with departures from Denver.

BUS OR CAR RENTAL? Numerous bus companies, including Greyhound, link Denver with most of the cities in the Rockies. But considering the distances involved and the range of possible touring routes, a rental car with unlimited mileage is strongly recommended.

CAR RENTAL: See Chapter 29 on Denver. For all other cities, consult the local telephone directory.

LIMOUSINE SERVICES: See Chapter 29 on Denver. For all other cities, consult the local telephone directory.

TRAIN: Amtrak (toll free 800/872-7245) has stations at 413 7th St., **Glenwood Springs;** Agate Ave., **Granby;** 2nd and Pitkin Sts., **Grand Junction;** and 420 Railroad Ave. at Fraser, **Winter Park.**

INTERCITY BUSES: Several companies offer service from Denver: **Airport Transportation Service** (toll free 800/247-7074), to Aspen, Beaver Creek, and Vail; **Aspen Limousine** (toll free 800/222-2112), to Aspen, Snowmass, and Vail; **Greyhound** (see Chapter 29 on Denver); **People's Choice Transportation** (toll free 800/777-2388), to the Colorado Front Range; **Resort Express** (toll free 800/334-7433), to Breckenridge, Copper Mountain, and Keystone; and **Steamboat Express Bus** (toll free 800/545-6050) to Steamboat Springs.

INFORMATION & TOURS

TOURIST INFORMATION: Colorado Ski Country USA, 1560 Broadway, Suite 1440, Denver, CO 80202 (303/837-0793): Information on ski resorts throughout the Colorado Rockies. (*Note:* Colorado Tourism Board lost funding in 1993. The state no longer has a general tourist board.)

Other sources of local information include:

Aspen Resort Association, 425 Rio Grande Place, Aspen, CO 81611 (303/925-9000; toll free 800/262-7736).

Boulder Chamber of Commerce, 2440 Pearl St., Boulder, CO 80306 (303/442-1044).

Colorado Springs Convention and Visitors Bureau, 104 S. Cascade, Colorado Springs, CO 80902 (719/635-7506; toll free 800/368-4748).

Denver (see Chapter 29 on Denver).

Durango Chamber Resort Association, 111 S. Camino del Rio, Durango, CO 81302 (303/247-0312; toll free 800/525-8855).

Estes Park Chamber of Commerce, 500 Big Thompson Ave., Estes Park, CO 80517 (303/586-4431; toll free 800/443-7837).

Grand Junction Convention and Visitors Bureau, 360 Grand Ave., Grand Junction, CO 81501 (303/242-3214; toll free 800/962-2547).

Gunnison Chamber of Commerce, 500 E. Tomichi Ave., Gunnison, CO 81230 (303/641-1501; toll free 800/274-7580).

Leadville Chamber of Commerce, 809 Harrison Ave., Leadville, CO 80461 (719/486-3900; toll free 800/933-3901).

Rocky Mountain National Park: Contact the Superintendent, Rocky Mountain National Park, Estes Park, CO 80517 (303/586-2371).

Salida Chamber of Commerce, 406 W. Rainbow Blvd., Salida, CO 81201 (719/539-2068).

Steamboat Springs Chamber Resort Association, 625 S. Lincoln, Steamboat Springs, CO 80477 (303/879-0880; toll free 800/922-2722).

Telluride Chamber Resort Association, 666 W. Colorado Ave., Telluride, CO 81435 (303/728-3041).

Vail Resort Association, 100 E. Meadow Dr., Vail, CO 81657 (303/476-1000; toll free 800/824-5737).

GUIDED TOURS: Gray Line Tours (bus): Tours of one day or longer through the Colorado Rockies (see Chapter 29 on Denver). For all other cities, consult the local telephone directory.

SIGHTS, ATTRACTIONS & ACTIVITIES

ADVENTURES: Adrift Adventures (boat), P.O. Box 606, Fort Collins, CO 80522 (toll free 800/824-0150): One- to five-day trips, by raft or rowboat, down the Green, Dolores, Colorado, Arkansas, and/or Yampa River (May–Sept.).

Adventure Bound (boat), 2392 H Rd., Grand Junction, CO 81505 (303/241-5633; toll free 800/423-4668): One- to five-day rafting trips down the Colorado, Green, and Yampa Rivers (May–Sept.).

Blazing Paddles (boat), Mill and Hyman Sts., Aspen River, CO 81611 (303/925-5651): Half-day to four-day rafting trips down the Roaring Fork, Arkansas, and Colorado Rivers (May–Sept.).

Brown's Rafting (boat), Brown's Fort, on U.S. 50, 7 mi. (11km) west of Cañon City, CO 81212 (719/275-5161): Half- or full-day rafting trips through the canyon of the Arkansas River (May to mid-Oct).

Four Corners Rafting (boat), P.O. Box 1032, Buena Vista, CO 81211 (719/395-4137; toll free 800/332-7238): Half-day to three-day raft trips on the Arkansas, Gunnison, or Dolores River (May–Sept).

Ghost Town Scenic Jeep Tour (all-terrain vehicles), 11150 U.S. 50, Salida, CO 81201 (719/539-2144; toll free 800/525-2081): Jeep tours through the many ghost towns of the region.

River Rats, Inc. (boat), P.O. Box 3231, Aspen, CO 81611 (303/925-7648): Rafting trips down the Roaring Fork, Arkansas, Colorado, Dolores, and Green Rivers (mid-May to mid-Sept).

River Runners Ltd. (boat), 11150 U.S. 50, Salida, CO 81201 (719/539-2144; toll free 800/332-9100 in state; 800/525-2081 out of state): Half- to three-day rafting trips down the Arkansas River (mid-May to mid-Sept).

San Juan Scenic Jeep Tours (all-terrain vehicles), 480 Main St., Ouray, CO 81427 (303/325-4444): Jeep tours in the mountains, with visits to abandoned mines, ghost towns, etc. Also Jeep rentals (June–Oct).

Snowmass Whitewater (boat), 50 Village Sq., Snowmass Village, CO 81615 (303/923-4544): Half- to four-day rafting trips down the Arkansas, Colorado, and Roaring Fork Rivers (May–Sept).

Two Wheel Tours (bike), P.O. Box 2655, Littleton, CO 80161-2655 (toll free 800/343-8940): Mountain biking in the Colorado backcountry. Day hikes or extended trips available.

ATTRACTIONS: ⚓ **Estes Park Aerial Tramway,** 420 Riverside Dr., Estes Park, 65 mi. (105km) NW of Denver on U.S. 36 (303/586-3675): Cable car to the summit of Prospect Mountain (8,896 ft./2,712m). Spectacular view. Bar with picnic area at the summit. Open daily, mid-May to mid-Sept.

☀☂🔔 **Georgetown Loop Railroad,** in Georgetown, 57 mi. (91km) west of Denver on I-70 to Exit 226 or 228 (303/670-1686): Over a 7-mi. (11km), one-hour route, this picturesque narrow-gauge railway makes three complete loops as it runs over four dizzyingly high bridges, culminating at 638 ft. (270m) above the Georgetown Valley. In operation 1884–1939, the "Loop" was put back into service in 1973. The views are spectacular. Six round-trips daily from the end of May to early Sept.

☀🔔 **Mount Manitou Incline,** 518 Ruxton Ave., Manitou Springs, 68 mi. (108km) south of Denver on I-25 and U.S. 24 (719/685-9086): Funicular railway to the summit of Mount Manitou (8,856 ft./2,700m). Impressive. Open daily May–Sept.

☀🔔 **Pikes Peak Cog Railway,** 515 Ruxton Ave., Manitou Springs, 68 mi. (108km) south of Denver on I-25 and U.S. 24 (719/685-5401): One of the highest cog railways in the world (14,110 ft./4,301m). Tremendous view, not to be missed. Open May–Oct 30; round trip takes three hours. Pikes Peak owes its name to Lt. Zebulon Pike, the first American to explore the Rockies, in 1806, on orders from Pres. Thomas Jefferson.

☀🔔 **Royal Gorge,** 11 mi. (19km) west of Cañon City on U.S. 50: Magnificent landscape of gorges along the Arkansas River. The suspension bridge over the canyon is the world's highest (1,053 ft./321m above the river). The funicular railway (303/275-5485) that goes to the bottom is the steepest in the world (slope: 45°). A cable car offers a superb view of the gorges. You may combine all three.

☀🔔 **The Silverton,** Durango, 38 mi. (60km) east of Mesa Verde National Park on U.S. 160, and 379 mi. (606km) SW of Denver on I-25 and U.S. 160 (303/247-2733): In operation since 1882, the Silverton is the last regularly scheduled narrow-gauge railroad in the U.S. Four seven-hour round trips between Durango and Silverton (90 mi./140km) daily May–Oct and Thanksgiving–Jan 1. Splendid scenery along the Animas Canyon. A must for Old West train buffs. Adults pay $38; children, $19. Resv. essential.

CITIES, SIGHTS & EXCURSIONS: ☀🔔 **Aspen,** 202 mi. (323km) SW of Denver on I-70 and Colo. 82: Once a very active mining town, today the most elegant resort in the Rockies (it's nicknamed "Hollywood on Ice"), and the favorite vacation spot of stars, movie moguls, princes, and billionaires. Superb powder skiing. Very popular summer festival of classical music. The largest single mountain resort in North America.

🔔 **Beaver Creek,** 10 mi. (16km) west of Vail on I-70 and U.S. 24: Colorado's most luxurious winter resort. With its immaculate slopes, it could be mistaken for a '50s postcard of a Swiss or Tyrolean village. A real haven of peace and solitude compared to the crowds and commotion of its famous neighbor, Vail. The favorite resort of movie stars and former Pres. Gerald Ford.

☀🔔 **Black Canyon of the Gunnison National Monument,** 70 mi. (112km) west of Gunnison on U.S. 50: Gorges 2,600 ft. (800m) deep cut into the granite. Magnificent landscape, wild and beautiful. Mule rides available. Access to the gorges is controlled. Open year round. Gunnison is one of the nation's coldest cities in winter. For further information, contact the Superintendent, 2233 E. Main St. (P.O. Box 1648), Montrose, CO 81402 (303/249-7036).

※※逸 **Boulder,** 30 mi. (48km) NW of Denver on U.S. 36: A residential community in the mountains near Denver. Famous for its university and scientific research institutes (meteorology, etc.). Interesting museum of the pioneers (see "Nearby Excursions" in Chapter 29 on Denver).

逸 **Cañon City,** 115 mi. (184km) SW of Denver on I-25, Colo. 155, and U.S. 50W: Hemmed in by a close ring of mountains, this picturesque little town settled during the early gold-mining days has always attracted filmmakers, earning the nickname "Colorado's Hollywood." Tom Mix, cowboy star of numerous silent films, made his camera debut here in 1910. The surrounding countryside has been the locale for many films (*Cat Ballou* and *True Grit* are just two examples), as well as several TV series. Cañon City is also the ideal departure point for rafting trips down the canyon of the Arkansas River.

※※逸逸 **Colorado Springs,** 67 mi. (107km) south of Denver on I-25: There is a very nice touring route about 62 mi. (100km) long around Colorado Springs, passing by **Cheyenne Mountain Highway** (superb views from the road and a "Shrine of the Sun" dedicated to the famous cowboy humorist Will Rogers); the **Garden of the Gods** (amazing reddish rock formations, especially impressive at sunrise or sunset); **Manitou Springs,** a beautiful mountain hot spring, and nearby, the **Manitou Cliff Dwellings Museum** on U.S. 24 Bypass (719/685-5242), open daily May–Oct, devoted to ancient Native American cave dwellings; **Pikes Peak** (14,110 ft./4,301m), with its dizzingly steep toll road; and finally **Seven Falls,** a lovely rocky canyon whose waterfalls are illuminated by the setting sun. For more details on these and other attractions (NORAD, the U.S. Air Force Academy, the U.S. Olympic Training Complex, etc.), see Chapter 29 on Denver.

※※逸 **Glenwood Springs,** 202 mi. (270km) SW of Denver on I-70: A vacation resort renowned for its hot thermal pools. Open-air bathing summer and winter. Rafting trips on the Colorado and Roaring Fork Rivers. The famous gunman "Doc" Holliday died here in 1887; his tombstone bears the simple epitaph "He Died in His Bed" (of tuberculosis, actually, at age 35).

※※逸 **Grand Lake,** 115 mi. (184km) NW of Denver on I-70 and U.S. 40: One of the highest yachting harbors in the world (8,380 ft./2,554m). Many other lakes nearby. Splendid alpine scenery.

逸 **Grand Mesa National Forest,** 52 mi. (83km) east of Grand Junction on I-70 and Colo. 65: An abundance of lakes and forests—a paradise for campers, and for fishing and hunting enthusiasts, at an average altitude of 9,840 ft. (3,000m).

逸 **Idaho Springs,** 38 mi. (60km) west of Denver on I-70: Renowned hot-springs resort in the middle of an area rich in minerals. The history of the gold rush is told at the **Argo Gold Mill,** 2350 Riverside Dr. (303/567-2421), open daily May to early Sept. Many excursions in the vicinity, such as Mount Evans, Central City, Georgetown (see Chapter 29 on Denver).

※※逸 **Redstone,** 29 mi. (45km) south of Glenwood Springs via Colo. 82 and Colo. 133: Old mining town, built from scratch by 19th-century magnate John Cleveland Osgood to house his coal miners. Splendidly restored, colorfully painted Victorian buildings. A mile from the town is Cleveholm, an imposing 42-room manor house where Osgood himself lived; its interior decoration and fittings are of unequaled luxury. Visits by appointment Mon–Fri (303/963-3463).

逸 **Steamboat Springs,** 177 mi. (283km) NW of Denver on I-70 and U.S. 40: Very popular hot springs and winter-sports resort (nicknamed "Ski Town U.S.A."). **Tread of Pioneer Museum,** 5th and Oak Sts. (303/879-2214), open daily, late May to mid-Sept.

※※逸逸 **Telluride,** 123 mi. (196km) north of Durango on U.S. 550, Colo. 62, and Colo. 145: Dominated by the sharp peaks and ridges of the San Juan Mountains, this picturesque little mining town, just over a century old, has scarcely aged since the gold-rush days. Its Main St., which could come straight out of an old western, is a designated historic monument. Spared so far from the tourist invasion, Telluride offers superb ski slopes in winter and exciting music and film festivals every summer.

Vail, 105 mi. (168km) west of Denver on I-70: The best-known winter sports resort of the Rockies. Fabulous slopes, and a well-deserved reputation for fine accommodations and dining. Rich and famous clientele.

PANORAMAS: **Glenwood Canyon,** 15 mi. (24km) east of Glenwood Springs on I-70: Very beautiful landscape of gorges along the Colorado River.

Gold Camp Road, 5 mi. (8km) west of Colorado Springs on Cheyenne Blvd.: A tortuous 35-mi. (56km) unpaved road following the track of an abandoned gold-rush railroad. Visit the ghost towns of **Goldfield** and **Cripple Creek** en route. Splendid views. Road open late May to Sept 30. Superb.

Independence Passroad, 24 mi. (38km) SE of Aspen on Colo. 82: Fabulous landscapes high in the mountains, but a difficult road. Summit (12,095 ft./3,686m) closed in winter.

Million Dollar Highway, 23 mi. (36km) along U.S. 550 from Ouray to Silverton: So named because of the large quantity of gold-bearing ore in the land over which it was built, this road offers some of the most beautiful scenery in the whole of Colorado.

Mount Evans, 64 mi. (102km) west of Denver on I-70, Colo. 103, and Colo. 5: The highest road in the U.S. climbs up this mountain, reaching 14,260 ft. (4,346m). A tough ride for both car and driver, but fabulous views. Road open in summer only.

Mount Pisgah Scenic Drive, 1 mi. (1.6km) NW of Cripple Creek on Teller County Rd. 1: Scenic toll highway climbing to the 10,400-ft. (3,170m) peak of Mount Pisgah. Magnificent view of the Continental Divide and Pikes Peak. Open Memorial Day–Oct.

Phantom Canyon, 35 mi. (56km) NE of Cañon City: One of the most spectacular panoramic routes in the U.S., with 25 mi. (40km) of unpaved road between Cañon City and Cripple Creek. Wild and imposing. Road open only May to late Oct. Not recommended for mobile homes.

Pikes Peak, 7 mi. (11km) west of Manitou Springs on U.S. 24 and Pikes Peak Rd.: The most famous mountain road in the U.S., with 18 mi. (28km) of sharp bends and steep climbs ending at 14,110 ft. (4,301m). In clear weather you can see Kansas, 165 mi. (264km) east. It was the splendor of this scenery that inspired Katherine Lee Bates to write "America the Beautiful" in 1893. Toll road open May to mid-Oct. Enough in itself to make your trip to the Rockies worthwhile.

Skyline Drive, 4 mi. (6km) west of Cañon City on U.S. 50: This 3-mi.-long (5km) scenic drive offers a superb view of Cañon City 800 ft. (244m) below, and the surrounding mountains. Closed in bad weather.

Trail Ridge Road, 70 mi. (112km) NW of Denver on U.S. 36: Following an old trail used by the Ute and Arapaho peoples, this section of U.S. 34 between Estes Park and Grand Lake peaks at over 12,168 ft. (3,710m)—a 4-mi. (6km) stretch of the road is above 11,808 ft. (3,600m). Fantastic views of the mountains and the midwestern prairies in the distance. Open early June to mid-Oct.

SPECIAL EVENTS: For detailed information on the festivals listed below, consult the chambers of commerce and visitors' bureaus listed under "Tourist Information," above.

Aspen

Music Festival and School (June–Aug): A renowned festival of classical music and a much-sought-after music school, one of the best in the U.S. A must for music lovers since 1949.

Boulder

Colorado Shakespeare Festival (July–Aug): Outdoor performances. Very popular locally.

Cripple Creek

Cripple Creek Western Theater (mid-June to mid-Sept): Home of Colorado's oldest and most famous melodrama company, the theater in the Imperial Hotel, 123 N. 3rd St. (719/689-2922), is the place to go to watch the hero (hurray!) triumph over the villain (hiss!).

Durango

Fiesta Days (end of July): Rodeo, parades, horse races, square dances. Lively and colorful.

Estes Park

Scottish-Irish Highland Festival (Sept): A week-long competition in bagpipe music, Irish music, Scottish and Irish dancing, and Celtic games. Gathering of clans from throughout the nation.

Leadville

Boom Days (first wknd in Aug): Reconstructs the saga of the gold rush. Local color guaranteed.

Manitou Springs

Pikes Peak Marathon (Aug): A 28-mi. (45km) foot race up Pikes Peak. One of the most demanding sports events in the world.

Salida

Arkansas River Boat Race (end of June): International kayak race, 26 mi. (42km) long, on the tumultuous waters of the Arkansas River. Spectacular.

Telluride

Summer Festival: A series of festivals beginning with films (late May) and bluegrass (June), followed by jazz (early Aug), and ending with chamber music (mid-Aug).

WINTER SPORTS RESORTS: With dozens of winter sports resorts, the Colorado Rockies are a skier's paradise. The most popular resorts are:

Aspen Mountain and Aspen Highlands, 42 mi. (67km) south of Glenwood Springs on Colo. 82 (toll free 800/262-7736 for Aspen Mountain; 303/925-5300 for Aspen Highlands): 19 lifts. Open Nov–Apr.

Beaver Creek, 10 mi. (16km) west of Vail on I-70 and U.S. 24 (303/476-5601): 10 lifts. Open mid-Nov to mid-Apr.

Breckenridge, 92 mi. (147km) west of Denver on I-70 and Colo. 9 (303/453-5000): 15 lifts. Open mid-Nov to mid-Apr.

Copper Mountain, 86 mi. (137km) west of Denver on I-70 and Colo. 9 (303/968-2882): 20 lifts. Open Nov–Apr.

Crested Butte, 30 mi. (48km) north of Gunnison on Colo. 135 (toll free 800/544-8448): 12 lifts. Open from the end of Nov until early Apr.

    Keystone, 78 mi. (124km) west of Denver on I-70 (toll free 800/222-0188): 19 lifts. Open Nov–June.

    Purgatory, 25 mi. (40km) north of Durango on U.S. 550 (303/247-9000; toll free 800/525-0892): 9 lifts. Open from the end of Nov until mid-Apr.

    Snowmass, 30 mi. (48km) south of Glenwood Springs on Colo. 82 (toll free 800/598-2005): 14 lifts. Open Nov–Apr.

    Steamboat Springs, 177 mi. (283km) NW of Denver on I-70, Colo. 90, and U.S. 40 (303/879-6111; toll free 800/922-2722): 19 lifts. Open Nov to mid-Apr.

    Telluride, 105 mi. (168km) north of Durango on I-70 (303/728-4424): 12 lifts. Open from the end of Nov to Apr.

    Vail, 105 mi. (168km) from Denver on I-70 (303/476-5601; toll free 800/525-3875): 22 lifts. Open Nov to mid-Apr.

    Winter Park, 71 mi. (113km) NW of Denver on I-70 and U.S. 40 (303/726-5514): 18 lifts. Open mid-Nov to Apr.

GHOST & MINING TOWNS: The gold rush of 1859–60 and the rich deposits of other minerals in the Rockies (silver, uranium, coal, tin, molybdenum) gave birth to dozens of mining camps, most of which have become ghost towns. Some, such as St. Elmo, are completely abandoned today, while others, such as Leadville, still survive, though yesteryear's luster has long since faded.

    Ashcroft, 15 mi. (24km) south of Aspen on Ashcroft Rd.: A well-preserved ghost town. Many of the buildings date from the 1880s.

    Central City, 44 mi. (70km) west of Denver on I-70, Colo. 119, and Colo. 279: Site of the first discovery of gold in 1859. Spectacular mountainside location. Many museums, hotels, and gold mines. A well-known opera house. (For more details, see "Nearby Excursions" in Chapter 29 on Denver.)

    Creede, 22 mi. (35km) NW of South Fork on Colo. 149: Frequented in its heyday by such legendary figures as Butch Cassidy and Calamity Jane, this mining town hemmed in on all sides by the mountains is today half-deserted.

    Cripple Creek, 40 mi. (64km) west of Colorado Springs on Gold Camp Rd.: Nicknamed "the $300-million cow pasture." Its mines have yielded more than $500 million worth of gold and silver. In 1900 it boasted as many as 500 mines and a population of 25,000 (barely 600 today). Sumptuous 1890s bordello, the **Old Homestead,** 353 E. Myers Ave.; open daily, late May to Oct. Museum and visit to an underground gold mine at the **Mollie Kathleen Gold Mine** on Colo. 67, open daily late May to Oct. In passing, look over the famous ghost towns of **Goldfield** and **Victor.** The road can be treacherous in bad weather.

    Fairplay, 85 mi. (136km) SW of Denver on U.S. 285: More than 30 carefully restored buildings from the gold-rush era. The **South Park City Museum,** 4th and Front Sts. (719/836-2387), open daily mid-May to mid-Oct, is worth looking over.

    Georgetown, 57 mi. (91km) west of Denver on I-70: One of the most famous mining towns in Colorado. Many museums and buildings classified as historic monuments, including the legendary **Hotel de Paris,** 409 Sixth Ave., open daily, built in 1875 by Frenchman Louis Dupuy. Equally interesting is the **Georgetown Loop Railroad,** a spectacular train ride (see "Attractions," above).

    Leadville, 103 mi. (164km) SW of Denver on I-70 and Colo. 91: Boasting up to 40,000 inhabitants in its glory days, this picturesque town perched at 10,150 ft. (3,100m)—which makes it the highest town in the U.S.—today has a mere 3,800 (most of them employees of the Climax mine, from which 90% of the world's production of molybdenum is extracted). It was in one of "Cloud City's" (a nickname given to Leadville) saloons in the 1880s that the famous sign "Don't shoot the pianist. He's doing his best." first appeared. Many museums and original buildings, among them the **Tabor Opera House,** at 308 Harrison Ave. (719/486-1147), open Sun–Fri from the end of May to Oct, and the **Healy House,** built in 1878, 912 Harrison Ave., open daily June–Aug. A must-see. **Mount Elbert,** Colorado's highest summit, 14,433 ft. (4,400m) is 12 miles (18km) south via U.S. 24.

     St. Elmo, 58 mi. (92km) south of Leadville on U.S. 24 and Colo. 162: A spectacular, authentic ghost town from the goldrush era, today completely abandoned. *Caution:* The last part of the road to the town is unpaved and passable only in dry weather.

NATIONAL PARKS NEARBY: **Colorado National Monument,** 4 mi. (6km) west of Grand Junction on Colo. 340 (303/858-3617): Enormous red sandstone monoliths and deep gorges make for a sort of Monument Valley in miniature. Rim Rock Dr., a 22-mi. (35km) scenic drive, crosses the park. Open daily year round.

    Florissant Fossil Beds National Monument, 34 mi. (54km) west of Colorado Springs on U.S. 24 (719/748-3253): About 35 million years ago volcanic lava flows fossilized all the life forms in this prehistoric lake. Exceptionally fine examples of fossilized animals and plants are displayed in the visitor center. Open daily year round.

    Great Sand Dunes National Monument, 234 mi. (374km) south of Denver on I-25, U.S. 160, and Colo. 150 (719/378-2312): Stunning sand dunes, some 700 ft. (210m) or more high, in a mountain setting. Spectacular at sunrise and sunset. Park open daily year round. For more information, contact the Superintendent, Great Sand Dunes National Monument, Mosca, CO 81146; or call the number above.

    Mesa Verde National Park, 430 mi. (688km) SW of Denver on I-25 and U.S. 160 (303/529-4461): The most impressive Native American historic monument in the U.S. (see Chapter 39 on Santa Fe). Worth the trip all by itself. En route, visit Colorado Springs, the Great Sand Dunes National Monument, and The Silverton (see above).

    Rocky Mountain National Park, 70 mi. (112km) NW of Denver on U.S. 36 and U.S. 34 (303/586-2371): The most mountainous of all American wilderness parks, with 113 peaks over 10,000 ft. (3,050m) high, including Longs Peak (14,255 ft./4,345m). Rushing rivers, glaciers, snows that never melt, lakes teeming with fish, dense forests (deer, moose, big-horn sheep, etc.), and over 300 mi. (480km) of hiking trails. Untouched wilderness. A paradise for climbers, campers, fishing enthusiasts, the park is visited by 2.5 million nature lovers annually. The **Trail Ridge Road** (U.S. 34), which follows the route of an ancient Native American trail, cuts right through the park and offers splendid views, as well as spectacular glimpses of the mountaintops (closed mid-Oct to mid-June between Deer Ridge and Timber Creek). Many hotels and motels are open year round in Estes Park, Grand Lake, and Granby (see "Accommodations," below). **Moraine Park Visitor Center** and museum are located 1 mi. (1.6km) from the east entrance to the park on U.S. 36 (open daily June–Sept). For more information, contact the Superintendent, Rocky Mountain National Park, Estes Park, CO 80517-8397. For road and snow conditions in winter, call 303/586-4000.

ACCOMMODATIONS

Personal Favorites (by city)

ASPEN   **Hotel Jerome,** 330 E. Main St., Aspen, CO 81611 (303/920-1000; toll free 800/331-7213). 94 rms, A/C, color TV, in-rm movies. AE, CB, DC, MC, V. Free valet parking, pool, health club, sauna, three rests. (including

Century Room), bar, rm svce, concierge. *Note:* One of the oldest hotels in the Rockies (1889), and a designated historic monument. Exquisitely restored to its original elegance in 1985. Period furniture, many art objects. Spacious rms, tastefully decorated (all w. refrigerators and phones in the bathrooms). Considerate and polished svce. A great deal of distinction and charm, and you pay accordingly. Resv. essential well in advance. **VE,** but lower rates off-season.

     Inn at Aspen, 38750 Colo. 82, Aspen, CO 81611 (303/925-1500; toll free 800/952-1515). 124 studios, A/C, cable color TV. AE, DC, MC, V. Free parking, pool, health club, sauna, skiing, rest., bar, rm svce, concierge. *Note:* Comfortable, inviting motel w. studios only, each having kitchenette, refrigerator, and private balcony or patio. Ideal for long vacations. Pleasant setting at the foot of the slopes; friendly ambience and reception. Good value overall. **E–VE,** but lower rates off-season.

     Grand Aspen, 515 S. Galena St., Aspen, CO 81612 (303/925-1150; toll free 800/242-7736). 175 rms (no A/C), cable color TV. AE, CB, DC, MC, V. Free parking, pool, rest., two bars, rm svce. *Note:* The biggest hotel in this resort town, in the heart of Aspen. Pretty mountain view. Comfortable and well run. Caters to families and groups. Favored by those in-the-know. Recently renovated. **E–VE,** but lower rates off-season.

     Limelite Lodge, 228 E. Cooper Ave., Aspen, CO 81611 (303/925-3025). 63 rms (some w. A/C), color TV, in-rm movies. AE, CB, DC, MC, V. Free parking, two pools, sauna, nearby coffee shop, free breakfast. *Note:* Charming little mountainside hotel nr. Wagner Park. Spacious, comfortable rms w. refrigerators. Family atmosphere. Enticing ski packages. **M–E,** but lower rates off-season.

BASALT **Best Western,** 157 Basalt Center Circle, Basalt, CO 81621 (303/927-3191; toll free, see Best Western). 36 rms (no A/C), color TV, in-rm movies. AE, CB, DC, MC, V. Free parking, fishing, adj. coffee shop–bar, free breakfast. *Note:* Stylish little motel in a pleasant setting on the banks of the Frying Pan River. Comfortable rms (some w. river view). Friendly reception. Good value. 20 min. from Aspen's ski slopes. **I–M,** but lower rates off-season.

BEAVER CREEK **Charter at Beaver Creek,** 120 Offerson Rd., Avon, CO 81620 (303/949-6660; toll free 800/525-6660). 59 rms in the hotel, 104 condos and apts., A/C, color TV. AE, CB, DC, MC, V. Free parking, two pools, health club, sauna, tennis court and golf course nearby, skiing, snowmobiles, rest., bar, rm svce, concierge, free crib. *Note:* Luxurious vacation complex of original alpine-village-style design, in a splendid setting. Ultramodern equipment. Spacious, comfortable rms w. refrigerators. Fully equipped condos and apts. w. kitchenettes and fireplaces. Excellent svce. Affluent tourist clientele. Free airport shuttle. **E–VE,** but lower rates off-season.

BOULDER **Alps Boulder Canyon Inn,** 38619 Boulder Canyon Dr., Boulder, CO 80302 (303/444-5445). 12 rms, no TV or telephone in the rms. AE, CB, DC, MC, V. Free parking, bar, hiking and cross-country skiing trails, fireplace in all of the rms, free breakfast. *Note:* Once a stagecoach stop and bordello, this is one of Colorado's oldest inns. After a two-year renovation, each rm has its own distinct character. Nicely situated 5 min. out of Boulder and next to a forest reserve. **E**

     Boulderado Hotel, 2115 13th St., Boulder, CO 80302 (303/442-4344; toll free 800/433-4344). 160 rms, A/C, color TV, in-rm movies. AE, CB, DC, MC, V. Free valet parking, two rests. (including Teddy Roosevelt's), three bars, rm svce, nightclub, free crib. *Note:* Beautiful turn-of-the-century Victorian palace. Sumptuous rococo decor w. an abundance of marble and paneling. Comfortable rms w. balconies, some w. refrigerators. Polished svce. A wonderful place to stay, in a central dwntwn location. Adequate rest. Good value. **M–E**

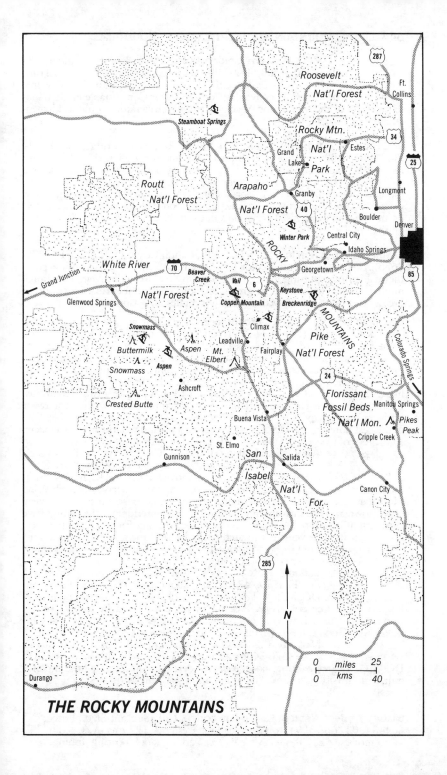

THE ROCKY MOUNTAINS

Best Western Golden Buff, 1725 28th St., Boulder, CO 80302 (303/442-7450; toll free, see Best Western). 112 rms, A/C, color TV, in-rm movies. AE, CB, DC, MC, V. Free parking, pool, sauna, health club, putting green, coffee shop, crib $5. *Note:* Comfortable modern motel w. views of the mountains. Spacious rms w. refrigerators, some w. kitchenettes. Good svce. **I**

BRECKENRIDGE 🛎🛎 **Hilton Hotel,** 550 Village Rd., Breckenridge, CO 80424 (303/453-4500; toll free, see Hilton). 208 rms (no A/C), color TV, in-rm movies. AE, CB, DC, MC, V. Free indoor parking, pool, health club, sauna, rest., coffee shop, bar, nightclub (in winter only). *Note:* Charming mountain hotel, modern and comfortable. Ski slopes a stone's throw away. Huge, inviting rms w. private balconies or patios and refrigerators. Good svce. Caters to groups. Interesting vacation packages. Very good value out of season. **M–E,** but lower rates off-season.

CAÑON CITY 🛎 **Cañon Inn,** 3075 U.S. 50E, Cañon City, CO 81212 (719/275-8676). 104 rms, A/C, cable color TV. AE, CB, DC, MC, V. Free parking, pool, thermal springs, putting green, rest., bar, rm svce, free crib. *Note:* Functional modern motel surrounded by grdns. Spacious comfortable rms. Hot springs. Free airport shuttle. Good value. **I,** but lower rates off-season.

COLORADO SPRINGS ☀🛎🛎🛎🛎 **Broadmoor,** Lake Circle at Lake Ave., Colorado Springs, CO 80906 (719/634-7711; toll free 800/634-7711). 560 rms, A/C, color TV. AE, DC, MC, V. Free parking, three pools, three golf courses, 16 tennis courts, squash, health club, sauna, putting green, skiing, trapshooting, skating, boats, seven rests. (including the Penrose Room), three bars, rm svce, disco, movie theater, concierge, free crib. *Note:* Superb 1920s-style grand hotel built like a castle amid 3,000 acres (1,210ha) of park and private grdns. Luxurious, urbane interior; elegant, comfortable rms w. balconies (some w. kitchenettes or refrigerators). Exemplary svce. Ideal for devotees of every sport imaginable. One of the best hotels in the U.S. Caters to conventions and wealthy holiday-makers. At the foot of Cheyenne Mountain. **VE,** but lower rates off-season.

☀🛎🛎🛎 **Antlers Doubletree Hotel,** 4 S. Cascade Ave. (at Pikes Peak), Colorado Springs, CO 80903 (719/473-5600; toll free 800/528-0444). 275 rms, A/C, color TV, in-rm movies. AE, CB, DC, MC, V. Parking $5, pool, rest. (Palmer's), coffee shop, bar, rm svce, concierge, free crib. *Note:* More than a century old, this charming, elegant hotel boasts a magnificent view of the town and the surrounding mountains. The interior and the fittings have been tastefully restored. Spacious, very comfortable rms; friendly, attentive svce; rest. of quality. Conveniently located in the heart of the dwntwn district. Free shuttles to airport and to Broadmoor Hotel and golf courses. A very good place to stay. **M–E,** but lower rates off-season.

🛎🛎 **LeBaron Hotel,** 314 W. Bijou St., Colorado Springs, CO 80905 (719/471-8680). 206 rms, A/C, color TV, in-rm movies. AE, CB, DC, MC, V. Free parking, pool, rest., bar, rm svce, nightclub, free breakfast, free crib. *Note:* Pleasant motel surrounded by lovely grdns a stone's throw from dwntwn. Comfortable rms w. private balconies or patios. Efficient svce. Good value. **I–M,** but lower rates off-season.

🛎 **Motel 6,** 3228 N. Chestnut St., Colorado Springs, CO 80907 (719/520-5400). 84 rms, A/C, color TV, in-rm movies. AE, DC, MC, V. Free parking, pool. *Note:* Modest but comfortable little motel 5 min. from dwntwn. Rms w. fine mountain views. One of the best values in the area. **B**

DILLON 🛎🛎 **Best Western Lake Dillon Lodge,** 1202 Summit Blvd., Frisco, CO 80443 (303/668-5094; toll free, see Best Western). 127 rms, A/C, color TV, in-rm movies. AE, CB, DC, MC, V. Free parking, pool, boating, fishing, rest., bar, valet svce, free crib. *Note:* Comfortable motel w. a view over the lake and the surrounding mountains. Modern decor and rather comprehensive amenities. Very good svce. Free transport to nearby ski resorts (in winter). Excellent value. **I–M,** but lower rates off-season.

DURANGO ☀ ♟♟♟♟ **Tamarron Resort,** 18 mi. (28km) north on U.S. 550, Durango, CO 81302 (303/259-2000; toll free 800/678-1000). 350 rms and condos, A/C, cable color TV. AE, CB, DC, MC, V. Free parking, pool, health club, saunas, three tennis courts, golf, putting green, skiing, skating rink, snowmobiles, horseback riding, two rests., bars, rm svce, disco, hrdrsr, concierge, free crib. *Note:* One of the most beautiful resort hotels in the U.S., in the heart of the San Juan National Forest. Spacious, extremely comfortable rms w. balconies and refrigerators. Condos w. fully equipped kitchenettes (some w. two bedrooms). Very efficient, friendly svce. Superb location. Hotel organizes rafting trips on the river and Jeep tours. Hunting and fishing guides available. Paradise for lovers of sports and the outdoors. A great place to stay. **E,** but lower rates off-season.

☀ ♟ ♟ **General Palmer House,** 567 Main Ave., Durango, CO 81301 ⌂ ⌂ (303/247-4747; toll free 800/523-3358). 39 rms, A/C, cable color TV. AE, CB, DC, MC, V. Nearby bar and rest., valet svce, free crib. *Note:* Elegant Victorian building dating from the 1890s, marvelously restored. Comfortable rms furnished w. antiques. Library. Friendly svce and reception. Minutes away from the Silverton train stations. **I–M,** but lower rates off-season.

☀ ♟ **Strater,** 699 Main Ave., Durango, CO 81301 (303/247-⌂ 4431). 93 rms, A/C, cable color TV. AE, CB, DC, MC, V. Free valet parking, rest. (Henry's), saloon, valet svce, boutiques. *Note:* Small Victorian-style hotel built in 1887. Enormous rms, comfortable though not elegant. Woeful svce and reception, which denies the Strater a better rating. The Old West–style saloon (Diamond Belle), w. a ragtime pianist and costumed waitresses, deserves a visit all by itself, however. Entertaining parody-melodramas performed in summer in the adj. Diamond Circle Theater (Mon–Sat June–Sept). A fine spot for lovers of the Old West. **I–M,** but lower rates off-season.

ESTES PARK ♟ ♟ **Best Western Lake Estes Resort,** 1650 Big Thompson Ave., Estes Park, CO 80517 (303/586-3386; toll free, see Best Western). 69 rms (no A/C), cable color TV. AE, CB, DC, MC, V. Free parking, pool, health club, sauna, rest., crib $6. *Note:* Rustic alpine lodge w. unobstructed view of the mountains and Lake Estes. Inviting accommodations w. in-rm whirlpool; some rms w. refrigerators and fireplaces. Efficient, helpful staff. Located 4 mi. (6.5km) east of the Rocky Mountain National Park entrance. Good value overall. Open year round. **I–M,** but lower rates off-season.

♟ **Alpine Trail Ridge Inn** (formerly the Friendship Inn), 927 Mo-⌂ raine Ave., Estes Park, CO 80517 (303/586-4585). 48 rms (no A/C), cable color TV. AE, CB, DC, MC, V. Free parking, pool, rest., bar, rm svce, crib $3. *Note:* Friendly small motel w. a superb view of the mountains. Comfortable rms, some w. balconies and refrigerators. Friendly, cheerful reception. Good value. Open early May to mid-Oct. **B–I,** but lower rates off-season.

GLENWOOD SPRINGS ♟ ♟ **Hot Springs Lodge,** 415 6th St., Glenwood Springs, CO 81601 (303/945-6571). 107 rms, A/C, cable color TV. AE, CB, DC, MC, V. Free parking, pool, health club, sauna, miniature golf, rest., bar. *Note:* Congenial modern hotel for those who come to take the waters. Comfortable rms (some w. refrigerators). Excellent location on the banks of the Colorado River and just moments from the hot springs. Has one of the largest naturally heated pools in the world. Good value. **I,** but lower rates off-season.

GRANBY ☀ ♟ ♟ ♟ **C Lazy U Ranch,** Colo. 125, Granby, CO 80446 (303/887-3344). 6 rms in the inn, 33 one- to five-rm bungalows (no A/C), color TV in bar. No credit cards. Free parking, pool, two tennis courts, health club, horseback riding, skiing, skating rink, fishing, hunting, skeet range, rest., bar, open-air barbecue-buffets, valet svce, disco. *Note:* Authentic western ranch some 8,200 ft. (2,500m) up on the shores of a mountain lake. Heaven for riding enthusiasts in summer and cross-country skiers in winter. The bungalow rms are prettily decorated, pleasant, and comfortable. Robust and abundant food. Friendly reception and atmosphere. The best vacation spot in the Colorado Rockies. Rodeos in summer. Closed late Sept to mid-Dec and in Apr and May. $1,200 and up per week in summer (American Plan); $180 and up per day in winter (American Plan).

※ 🕯🕯🕯 **Colorado Guest Ranch,** Colo. 125, Granby, CO 80446 (303/887-2511). 60 rms (no A/C), color TV, in-rm movies. AE, CB, DC, MC, V. Free parking, pool, two tennis courts, health club, sauna, horseback riding, skiing, skating, snowmobile, boating, fishing, bowling alley, trap shooting, rest., bar, rm svce, free crib. *Note:* Luxurious vacation ranch hidden away in the Arapaho National Forest. Comprehensive recreational facilities. Very comfortable rms, some w. balconies; praiseworthy rest. Efficient svce. The hotel boasts its own landing strip as well as 36 acres (14ha) of lake, teeming w. fish. Hunting guides available. Nature-lovers who prefer not to forgo every modern convenience will find this the resort of their dreams. **E–VE** (American Plan).

GRAND JUNCTION 🕯🕯 **Hilton Inn,** 743 Horizon Dr., Grand Junction, CO 81506 (303/241-8888; toll free, see Hilton). 264 rms, A/C, color TV, in-rm movies. AE, CB, DC, MC, V. Free parking, pool, health club, three tennis courts, two rests. (including The Red Cliff), two bars, rm svce, disco, free crib. *Note:* Vast eight-story motel of rather gloomy design; spacious, comfortable rms. Efficient svce and reception. Adequate rest. Free airport shuttle. VIP floor. A highly recommended stopover. **I–M,** but lower rates off-season.

🕯 **Motel 6,** 776 Horizon Dr., Grand Junction, CO 81501 (303/243-2628). 100 rms, A/C, color TV, in-rm movies. AE, DC, MC, V. Free parking, pool. *Note:* The best deal in town if you're passing through by car. Serviceable amenities at unbeatable prices. Airport nearby. **B**

GRAND LAKE 🕯 **Western Riviera,** 419 Garnet St., Grand Lake, CO 80447 (303/627-3580). 17 rms (no A/C), cable color TV. MC, V. Free parking, snowmobiles, coffee shop next door, free crib. *Note:* Charming little motel by the lake. Warm, comfortable rms. Beautiful natural surroundings. Closed Apr to mid-May and mid-Oct to mid-Dec. **I,** but lower rates off-season.

GUNNISON 🕯 **Friendship Inn Colorado West,** 400 E. Tomichi Ave., Gunnison, CO 81230 (303/641-1288; toll free, see Choice). 50 rms, A/C, color TV, in-rm movies. AE, CB, DC, MC, V. Free parking, pool, coffee shop next door, crib $2. *Note:* Pleasant, well-run little motel. Spacious rms. Friendly reception. Free airport shuttle. Good value. **B–I,** but lower rates off-season.

KEYSTONE 🕯🕯 **Keystone Lodge,** 22010 U.S. 6, Keystone, CO 80435 (303/468-2316; toll free, see Preferred). 152 rms, 775 condos and apts. (no A/C), color TV, in-rm movies. AE, CB, DC, MC, V. Free parking, 10 pools, golf, putting green, 14 tennis courts, sauna, skiing, boating, horseback riding, four rests. (including the Ranch), two coffee shops, bars, rm svce, disco, boutiques, concierge, free crib. *Note:* Huge ultramodern vacation complex on the banks of Lake

Keystone in the heart of the Arapaho National Forest. Comfortable rms w. private balconies or patios. One- to four-bedroom condos and apts. Very good sports facilities. Splendid panoramic views over lake and mountains. Caters to conventions and groups. Rather average svce. Ordinary rests. Organizes rafting trips and Jeep tours. Attractive family and vacation packages. **E–VE,** but lower rates off-season.

LEADVILLE 🛎 **Silver King Motor Inn,** 2020 N. Poplar St., Leadville, CO 80461 (719/486-2610). 56 rms (no A/C), color TV, in-rm movies. AE, CB, DC, MC, V. Free parking, skiing, sauna, rest., bar, disco, crib $5. *Note:* Modern motel-chalet in the heart of this legendary gold-rush town. Spacious rms w. balconies. Decent rest. Friendly reception. Attractive vacation packages. (Take note of Leadville's high altitude—10,150 ft./3,100m—and its possible effects on your physical condition.) **I,** but lower rates off-season.

SNOWMASS VILLAGE 🛎🛎🛎 **Snowmass Club,** 239 Snowmass Club Circle, Snowmass Village, CO 81615 (303/923-5600; toll free 800/525-0710). 76 rms in the hotel, 62 separate villas. A/C, color TV, in-rm movies. AE, CB, DC, MC, V. Free parking, two pools, health club, sauna, 13 tennis courts, golf, squash, putting green, skiing, snowmobiles, rest. (Four Corners), bar, rm svce, nightclub, concierge. *Note:* Paradise for sporting enthusiasts. Refined, elegant setting of modern design. Large rms, nicely decorated, w. private balconies or patios and refrigerators (some w. kitchenettes). Luxurious two- and three-bedroom villas. Worthwhile rest. Excellent svce. Free airport connection w. Aspen. Caters to wealthy holiday makers. Closed mid-Apr to late May and mid-Oct to mid-Nov. **E–VE,** but lower rates off-season.

STEAMBOAT SPRINGS 🛎🛎🛎 **Sheraton Steamboat Resort,** 2200 Village Inn Court, Steamboat Springs, CO 80477 (303/879-2220; toll free, see Sheraton). 303 rms, A/C, color TV, in-rm movies. AE, CB, DC, MC, V. Free parking, two pools, four tennis courts, golf course, sauna, skiing, snowmobiles, rest., coffee shop, bars, rm svce, disco, boutiques, concierge. *Note:* A vacation complex at the foot of Mount Werner, comprising a modern hotel and eight stories of comfortable condos w. kitchenettes. Ideal for families. Good vacation and ski packages; good value overall. Closed mid-Apr to May and the end of Sept to mid-Nov. Free airport shuttle. **M–E,** but lower rates off-season.

🛎 **Inn at Steamboat** (formerly the Quality Inn Subalpine), 3070 Columbine Dr., Steamboat Springs, CO 80477 (303/879-2600; toll free 800/872-2601). 31 rms (no A/C), color TV, in-rm movies. AE, CB, DC, MC, V. Free parking, pool, sauna, miniature golf, coffee shop (breakfast only in summer), free crib. *Note:* Quiet, friendly motel. Spacious rms w. balconies. Appealing winter sports packages. Good value. **I–M,** but lower rates off-season.

TELLURIDE 🛎🛎🛎 **Doral Telluride Resort and Spa,** 134 Country Club Dr., Telluride, CO 81435 (303/728-6800; toll free 800/223-6725). 177 rms, 32 suites (no A/C), cable color TV. AE, CB, DC, MC, V. Free valet parking, three pools, saunas, health club, tennis, golf course, putting green, skiing, snowmobiles, bicycles, horseback riding, hiking, climbing wall, rest., bar, rm svce, concierge. *Note:* Perched above the town of Telluride, the Doral offers incredible views, direct access to outdoor activities, and a huge measure of solitude—all while sitting in the lap of luxury. Cozy rms w. refrigerators and minibars, some w. balconies. All have spectacular views. Free airport shuttle. **VE,** but lower rates off-season.

🛎 **Tomboy Inn,** 619 Columbia St., Telluride, CO 81435 (303/728-6621; toll free 800/446-3192). 49 rms (no A/C), cable color TV. AE, CB, DC, MC, V. Free parking, sauna, skiing, nearby coffee shop, crib $4. *Note:* Comfortable, very well run small hotel. Spacious, inviting rms w. refrigerator, some w. kitchenette, most w. balcony and fireplace. Svce w. a smile. Good value. **I–M,** but lower rates off-season.

VAIL ※ 🛏🛏🛏 **Radisson Resort** (formerly Marriott), 715 W. Lionshead Circle, Vail, CO 81657 (303/476-4444; toll free, see Radisson). 350 rms (some w. A/C), color TV, in rm movies. AE, CB, DC, MC, V. Parking $8, two pools, saunas, health club, four tennis courts, skiing, two rests. (including Windows), coffee shop, two bars, rm svce, concierge, free crib. *Note:* Old luxury hotel, entirely renovated. Elegant, comfortable rms w. balconies, some w. kitchenettes. Thoughtful svce. Decent rest. The largest and best hotel in the resort, two steps from the slopes. Caters to groups and conventions. **VE,** but lower rates off-season.

🛏🛏🛏 **Westin Hotel,** 1300 Westhaven Dr., Vail, CO 81657 (303/476-7111; toll free, see Westin). 323 rms (no A/C), color TV, in-rm movies. AE, CB, DC, MC, V. Valet parking $11, pool, four tennis courts, health club, sauna, squash, outdoor thermal spa, rest. (Alfredo's), coffee shop, bars, 24-hr. rm svce, boutiques, concierge, free crib. *Note:* Very beautiful alpine-style hotel. Elegant atmosphere. Spacious, comfortable rms w. minibars and private patios. Excellent svce. Decent rest. Nestled on the banks of Gore Creek. One of the best hotels in the Rockies. Free airport shuttle. The plushest place in town. **VE,** but lower rates off-season.

※ 🛏🛏 **The Lodge at Vail,** 174 E. Gore Creek Dr., Vail, CO 81657 (303/476-5011; toll free 800/331-5634). 175 rms (no A/C), color TV, in-rm movies. AE, CB, DC, MC, V. Free valet parking, pool, sauna, skiing, two rests. (including the Wildflower Inn), bar, rm svce, nightclub, boutiques. *Note:* Huge mountain hotel, quaint and charming. Many rms w. balconies and kitchenettes. Good communal facilities. Outstanding rest. Good svce. Caters to groups. **E–VE,** but lower rates off-season.

※ 🛏🛏 **Sitzmark Lodge,** 183 Gore Creek Dr., Vail, CO 81657 (303/476-5001). 35 rms (no A/C), color TV, in-rm movies. AE, MC, V. Free parking, pool, sauna, skiing, rest. (Left Bank), bar, valet svce, crib $5. *Note:* Delightful mountain chalet in the heart of Vail Village. Lovely mountain view. Huge, comfortable rms w. balcony and refrigerator, some w. fireplace. The very acceptable rest. is unfortunately closed in fall and spring. Winning reception and svce in a friendly, inviting atmosphere. Very good value; you should reserve well ahead. **I–M**

🛏 **Comfort Inn Vail,** 0161 W. Beaver Creek Blvd., Avon, CO 81620 (303/949-5511; toll free, see Choice). 147 rms, A/C, color TV, in-rm movies. AE, CB, DC, MC, V. Free parking, pool, bicycles, coffee shop nearby, free breakfast. *Note:* Modern motel in the classic style. Pleasant, comfortable rms, some w. refrigerators. Friendly svce. 15 min. from dwntwn. Good value. **I–E,** but lower rates off-season.

WINTER PARK 🛏🛏 **Iron Horse Resort,** 257 Winter Park Dr., Winter Park, CO 80482 (303/726-8851; toll free 800/621-8190). 118 studios (no A/C), cable color TV. AE, DC, MC, V. Free parking, pool, health club, sauna, skiing, squash, rest., bar, valet svce. *Note:* A mountain resort for either winter or summer sports. Comfortable studios w. kitchenette, refrigerator, fireplace, and balcony. Efficient svce; family atmosphere. Good value. **E,** but lower rates off-season.

YMCAs/Youth Hostels

COLORADO SPRINGS **Garden of the Gods,** 3704 W. Colorado Ave., Colorado Springs, CO 80904 (719/475-9450; toll free 800/248-9451). 48 beds. Youth hostel. Open mid-Apr to mid-Oct.

ESTES PARK **H-Bar-G Ranch,** 3500 H-Bar-G Rd., Estes Park, CO 80517 (303/586-3688). 130 beds. Youth hostel. Open late May to early Sept.

GRAND LAKE **Shadowcliff Youth Hostel,** Tunnel Rd., Grand Lake, CO 80447 (303/627-9220). 32 beds. Youth hostel. Open June–Sept.

TELLURIDE **Oak Street Inn,** 134 N. Oak St., Telluride, CO 81435 (303/728-3383). 83 beds. Youth hostel. Open year round.

WINTER PARK **Winter Park Hostel,** U.S. 40 at Vasquez Rd., Winter Park, CO 80482 (303/726-5356). 28 beds. Youth hostel. Closed from mid-April to mid-June.

RESTAURANTS
Personal Favorites (by city)

ASPEN ♈♈♈ **The Restaurant at the Little Nell,** 675 E. Durant Rd., in the Little Nell Hotel (303/920-6300). A/C. Breakfast/lunch/dinner daily. AE, CB, DC, MC, V. *Specialties:* grilled crab cakes w. sweet corn purée and fried pasta; salad of blue cheese baked in phyllo, sautéed pears, and grilled portobello mushrooms; charred tuna steak w. wasabi potatoes and lime-cilantro sauce; grilled elk. Splendid wine list, w. prices to match. *Note:* Aspen's power rest., a place where local and Hollywood VIPs indulge in chef Richard Chamberlain's remarkable "American-Alpine" cuisine. Cozy country setting. Gracious svce. Resv. a must. *American.* **E**

♈♈ **Wienerstube,** 633 E. Hyman (303/925-3357). A/C. Breakfast/lunch/dinner Tues–Sun; closed Jan 1, Dec 25. AE, DC, MC, V. *Specialties:* broiled bratwurst, sauerbraten, Wiener schnitzel, veal Stroganoff; desserts on the weighty side. *Note:* Charming, locally popular Austrian-style inn where both food and atmosphere are thoroughly true to the original. Delightful patio-terrace for fine days. Friendly, smiling svce. Resv. advisable. *German/Continental.* **I–M**

♈♈ **Farfalla,** 415 E. Main St. (925-8222). Lunch Mon–Fri, dinner nightly. AE, MC, V. *Specialties:* rollino (rolled pizza bread w. smoked mozzarella and radicchio), thin-crusted pizzas, veal scaloppine stuffed w. mozzarella and eggplant. *Note:* Casual brick-walled *trattoria* setting attracting an extremely lively crowd, especially during ski season. Unfortunately, resv. are not accepted, which means the wait can be up to two hours during peak season. *Italian.* **I–M**

♈ **La Cocina,** 308 E. Hopkins (303/925-9714). No A/C. Dinner nightly; closed Oct–Apr. *Specialties:* tacos, enchiladas, steak. *Note:* Small Mexican-style rest., modest and unpretentious. Popular locally *Mexican/American.* **B**

BEAVER CREEK ☀♈♈♈ **Mirabelle,** 55 Village Rd. (303/949-7728). A/C. Dinner only, Tues–Sun; closed May and mid-Oct to mid-Nov. AE, MC, V. Jkt. *Specialties:* homemade pâté, elk w. poivrade sauce, rack of lamb w. mixed beans and light juice. Exceptional desserts. Fine wine list. *Note:* Light, inventive cooking by the very talented chef, Daniel Goly. Charming, old-fashioned, rustic decor (the building dates from 1898, which makes it one of the oldest ranches in the Vail area). Discreet, attentive svce. An outstanding rest. Many VIPs and wealthy people on vacation among the customers. Resv. highly recommended. *French.* **M–E**

BOULDER ♈♈♈ **Flagstaff House,** Flagstaff Rd. (303/442-4640). A/C. Dinner only, nightly; closed Jan 1, Dec 24–25. AE, CB, DC, MC, V. Jkt. *Specialties:* oysters Rockefeller, angel-hair pasta w. prosciutto and wild mushrooms, crab Lausanne, elk steak, Colorado beef, roast quail. Very good wine list (16,000-bottle cellar). *Note:* An elegant rest. w. a spectacular view of the mountains through huge bay windows. Romantic atmosphere. Terrace open in summer. Attentive svce. Some of the best fare in the region. Resv. advised. *Continental.* **M–E**

John's, 2338 Pearl St. (303/444-5232). A/C. Dinner only, nightly; closed hols. AE, CB, DC, MC, V. *Specialties:* lobster ravioli; steak au poivre; Cajun oysters w. tasso; shrimp, salmon, and mussels in saffron-shellfish stock; chocolate torte w. rasberry sauce and crème anglaise. Mostly Californian wine list. *Note:* A culinary landmark in Boulder for 19 years. Chef/owner John Bizzaro is year after year voted best chef in Boulder, a well-deserved title. Efficient svce in a pleasantly small setting. Resv. recommended. *Continental/American.* **I–M**

BRECKENRIDGE ♀ **Briar Rose,** 109 E. Lincoln St. (303/453-9948). No A/C. Dinner only, nightly; closed the first two weeks of June. AE, DC, MC, V. *Specialties:* game, roast beef, quail, Alaska king crab. Good, homemade desserts. *Note:* Authentic 19th-century guesthouse. Charming old-fashioned decor. The game dishes (in season) are all to be recommended. Excellent svce. *Continental/American.* **I–M**

CENTRAL CITY ☀♀ **Black Forest Inn,** Colo. 279 in Black Hawk (303/279-2333). A/C. Lunch/dinner daily. No credit cards. *Specialties:* game (in season), roast pheasant, wild duck, elk steak. *Note:* One of the most famous rests. in the Rockies. The accent is definitely on wild game. Many German dishes too. Highly colorful German music and decor. Outdoor dining in good weather. Popular locally. Very good value. *German/American.* **I–M**

COLORADO SPRINGS ♀♀ **Edelweiss,** 34 E. Ramona Ave. (719/633-2220). A/C. Lunch Mon–Fri, dinner nightly; closed Dec 24. AE, CB, DC, MC, V. *Specialties:* Wiener schnitzel, sauerbraten, veal Oscar. *Note:* Traditional Bavarian-chalet decor and praiseworthy German food. Dinner outdoors in summer. Efficient svce. Popular locally. Resv. recommended. *German/Continental.* **I**

La Petite Maison, 1015 W. Colorado Ave. (719/632-4887). A/C. Lunch Tues–Fri, dinner Tues–Sat; closed July 4, Dec 25. AE, DC, MC, V. *Specialties:* Anaheim chile stuffed w. goat cheese on black-bean purée, sautéed veal w. Amontillado sherry and fresh herbs, white-chocolate and almond tart w. apricot sauce. Menu changes regularly. *Note:* A charming little rest. housed in a nicely renovated former private residence. Honest, tasty food. Friendly reception and svce. Very good value. Resv. recommended. 5 min. from dwntwn. *French/American.* **I**

CRIPPLE CREEK ☀♀ **Imperial Dining Room,** 123 N. 3rd St. (719/689-2922). No A/C. Breakfast/lunch/dinner daily; closed mid-Oct to mid-May. AE, DC, MC, V. *Specialties:* steak, baron of beef, gourmet buffet. *Note:* Magnificent Victorian dining rm in the Imperial Hotel, a registered historic monument dating from the gold-rush era of the last century. The decor alone makes a visit worthwhile. The food is worthy, but nothing more. Dinner-theater Tues–Sun, for which resv. highly advisable. *American.* **B–I**

DURANGO ☀♀♀ **Palace Grill,** 1 Depot Place (303/247-2018). A/C. Breakfast/lunch (summer only)/dinner daily; closed Thanksgiving, Dec 25. AE, DC, MC, V. *Specialties:* honey duck, sautéed trout Palace, mesquite-grilled steak, house salads and desserts. Good list of Californian wines. *Note:* One of the most agreeable and picturesque rests. in southern Colorado. Authentic Victorian decor w. Tiffany lamps and copper objets d'art (the building itself dates from 1881). Patio dining in summer. Excellent traditional American cooking. Relaxed atmosphere and svce. Very popular locally. Very good value. Resv. highly advisable in summer. Located near the famous Silverton Railroad terminal. *American.* **I–M**

☀♀ **Henry's,** in the Strater Hotel (see "Accommodations," above) (303/247-4431). A/C. Breakfast/lunch/dinner daily. AE, CB, DC, MC, V. *Specialties:* scampi, fresh salmon, roast beef, red meats. *Note:* Housed in the Strater Hotel, a picturesque Victorian building. Classic hotel cuisine. Rather inefficient svce. Pretty, old-fashioned decor. *Continental/American.* **B–I**

EDWARDS 𝕏𝕏𝕏 **Picasso,** in the Lodge at Cordillera (303/926-2200). A/C. Breakfast/lunch/dinner daily. AE, DC, MC, V. *Specialties:* warm snail salad w. almonds, coquilles St-Jacques au beurre blanc, seared duck breast w. chanterelles, lamb medallions w. fava beans, roast grouper w. celery and truffles, fondant of chocolate w. coffee sauce. Menu changes seasonally. *Note:* The best rest. of the Rockies, about 20 min. from Vail. Splendid scenery w. glorious mountain vistas and deliciously inventive cuisine by Farbest Beaudoin. Attentive, knowledgeable svce. Resv. a must. *Continental.* **E**

ESTES PARK 𝕏𝕏 **La Chaumière,** 3211 Pinewood Springs in Lyons, 12 mi. (19km) south (303/823-6521). A/C. Dinner only, Wed–Sun; closed Feb. AE, MC, V. *Specialties:* veal sweetbreads, roast duck, fish of the day, veal cutlet à la normande, rack of lamb, filet mignon. Menu changes regularly. *Note:* Romantic country inn w. a central hearth. Very pleasant French-style cooking. Fixed-price menu. Unrestricted view of the mountains. Friendly svce. Excellent value. Resv. recommended. *French/Continental.* **I–M**

    𝒴 **La Casa,** 222 E. Elkhorn Ave. (303/586-2807). A/C. Lunch/dinner daily; closed Thanksgiving, Dec 25. AE, CB, DC, MC, V. *Specialties:* roast beef, tacos, enchiladas, tamales, Cajun dishes, excellent house margaritas. *Note:* This otherwise typical Mexican rest. also serves some fine Cajun dishes. Patio-terrace overlooking the Big Thomson River. Noisy but agreeable. Resv. advisable at dinner. *Mexican/American.* **I**

GEORGETOWN ☀𝒴 **The Ram,** 606 6th St. (303/569-2300). A/C. Lunch/ dinner daily. AE, MC, V. *Specialties:* roast beef, steaks, good desserts. Good wine list. *Note:* Located in the heart of Georgetown, an old gold-rush town, this 19th-century saloon offers very good red-meat dishes at reasonable prices. Popular locally. *Steak.* **B–I**

GRAND JUNCTION 𝕏𝕏 **Far East,** 1530 North Ave. (303/242-8131). A/C. Lunch/dinner daily; closed hols. AE, CB, DC, MC, V. *Specialties:* Cantonese and Mandarin dishes, beef teriyaki, broiled steak. Also American selections. *Note:* One of the few "exotic" rests. in the Rockies. The Chinese-Polynesian decor is a success, as is the food. Popular locally. *Chinese/American.* **B–I**

LEADVILLE 𝒴 **Silver King,** in the Silver King Motor Inn (see "Accommodations," above) (303/486-2610). No A/C. Breakfast/lunch/dinner daily; closed Nov–Jan. AE, CB, DC, MC, V. *Specialties:* steak, mountain lake trout. *Note:* A modest, unpretentious motel rest. Good red meats and broiled dishes; friendly svce. Dancing in summer. *Steak/American.* **B–I**

LYONS 𝕏𝕏 **Black Bear Inn,** 42 Main St. (303/823-6812). A/C. Lunch/dinner Tues–Sun; closed hols. and mid-Jan to mid-Feb. AE, CB, DC, MC, V. Jkt. *Specialties:* chateaubriand, veal casserole, fish of the day, apple strudel. *Note:* Elegant alpine-style inn w. a big fireplace and hunting trophies. Classical European cooking, w. delicacy. Diligent svce. Resv. recommended. A recommended stop midway between Denver and Rocky Mountain National Park. *Continental.* **I–M**

STEAMBOAT SPRINGS 𝕏𝕏𝕏 **Hazie's,** at the top of Thunderhead Mountain (303/ 879-6111). A/C. Lunch/dinner daily; closed mid-Apr to mid-June and Labor Day to Thanksgiving. AE, MC, V. *Specialties:* escargot w. Brie, chateaubriand w. béarnaise sauce, rack of lamb w. roasted garlic, lace cookie w. berries. Good wine list. *Note:* Hazie's offers you not only an incomparable view of the Rockies from its huge picture windows but—uncommon for a rest. in the "splendid view" category—praiseworthy food from the hand of chef Morten Höj. Lunch is light, dinner more elaborate. Relaxed but efficient svce. The rest. is reached by cable car, and is well worth the trip—it's one of the best places to eat in the Rockies. Reserve ahead. *American.* **I–M**

♀ **Ore House at the Pine Grove,** U.S. 40 (303/879-1190). A/C. Dinner only, nightly; closed Thanksgiving. AE, DC, MC, V. *Specialties:* roast beef, broiled trout, barbecued pork chops, fish of the day, game (in season). *Note:* Pleasant ranch-style decor in a converted turn-of-the-century barn. Honest, tasty cooking. Friendly svce. *American.* **I**

VAIL ☂☂☂ **Wildflower Inn,** in the Lodge at Vail (see "Accommodations," above) (303/476-5011). No A/C. Breakfast/lunch/dinner daily in summer; dinner only in winter, Wed–Mon. AE, CB, DC, MC, V. Jkt. *Specialties:* celeriac tart, fresh pasta w. herbs and pine nuts, confit of poultry w. radicchio, filet of lamb w. green peppercorns, lamb cutlet w. vermouth sauce, braised breast of pheasant, hot plum tart. Very good wine list. Menu changes regularly. *Note:* The dining rm at the Lodge at Vail is a model of elegance and good taste w. its abundant flower decoration and its pastel tones (it won a Design of the Year Award). The cuisine, of French inspiration, is equally elegant. The svce is laudable and the whole amply deserves its three glasses. By far the best in Vail. *Continental.* **M–E**

♀♀ **Sweeet Basil,** 193 E. Gore Creek Dr. (303/476-0125). No A/C. Lunch/dinner daily. AE, MC, V. *Specialties:* saffron angel-hair pasta, lasagna w. chicken confit and chanterelles, grilled pork loin w. horseradish potatoes, fresh fish, chocolate-caramel macadamia-nut tart. Seasonal menu. *Note:* Cherrywood decorated rest. that has quickly become very popular. Inventive contemporary cuisine nicely prepared and served. Many tables w. a view of the creek. Resv. advised. *American.* **M**

♀♀ **Terra Bistro,** 352 E. Meadow Dr. (303/476-6836). No A/C. Dinner only, nightly; closed hols. AE, DC, MC, V. *Specialties:* seared tuna rolls w. wasabi aioli and avocado, lobster w. lemon-thyme vinaigrette, sesame-encrusted salmon w. red curry sauce, roasted lamb w. Indian spices and chickpea tamales. *Note:* Light, inventive cuisine by Cynthia Walt, who nicely encorporates Asian and Indian influences in her cooking. Pleasing atmosphere and friendly svce. Fair prices make it even more worthwhile. *American/ Continental.* **M**

♀♀ **Alpen Rose Tea Room,** 100 E. Meadow Dr. (303/476-3194). No A/C. Breakfast/lunch/dinner Tues–Sun (until 2am); closed Memorial Day, late Apr through June, and mid-Oct to mid-Nov. AE, MC, V. *Specialties:* hausplatte, chicken cordon bleu, Mozart schnitte, roulade of beef w. red wine sauce. *Note:* This bakery-rest. is especially good at breakfast for its hot chocolate and cakes. More substantial fare at lunch, w. a strong emphasis on German dishes. Splendid view, and open-air terraces in fine weather. Popular locally. Resv. advised. *German/Continental.* **I–M**

CHAPTER 31

SALT LAKE CITY

□ □ □

The capital of Utah and the holy city of the Church of Jesus Christ of the Latter-Day Saints, more commonly known as the Mormon church, is situated about 15 mi. (24km) south of the **Great Salt Lake,** for which it is named. The distant, usually snow-covered, peaks of the **Wasatch Range,** more than 9,840 ft. (3,000m) high, enhance the beauty of the setting. In 1825 an adventurous fur trader named Jim Bridger discovered the Great Salt Lake, the largest body of water in the entire western United States. Some 22 years later, in July 1847, the Mormon preacher Brigham Young and 150 of his followers, fleeing religious persecution and open hostility in various East Coast and midwestern cities, founded Salt Lake City after a 1½-year forced march westward. Legend holds that Brigham Young, on seeing the Great Salt Lake and the site of the new Zion, exclaimed, "This is the place!" Today an imposing monument marks the spot where Young first came upon this superb view. Baptized "Deseret" ("honeybee" in Mormon nomenclature), the early encampment soon became Great Salt Lake City, but was called simply Salt Lake City once Utah was admitted to the Union in 1896.

An industrious and prosperous city (electronics, missiles, food processing, medicine, chemicals), the Mormon capital is today a modern metropolis, clean and inviting, carved out of the surrounding desert. Only the Mormons' extraordinary spirit of sacrifice and devotion to work can explain this astonishing transformation in less than a century and a half.

An ideal point of departure for magnificent trips to such national parks as **Zion, Bryce Canyon, Grand Teton, Yellowstone,** and **Canyonlands**—not to mention numerous nearby winter vacation spots—Salt Lake City boasts two monuments directly inspired by the Mormon religion: the **Temple,** a massive granite edifice in the Gothic Revival style (only Mormons are admitted), and the **Tabernacle,** shaped like an immense inverted ship's hull, which has become one of the world's most famous concert halls. The imposing **State Capitol,** built on a hill overlooking the town, is also a symbol of the city. In deference to the Mormon way of life, many Salt Lake City restaurants do not serve any alcoholic beverages, but diners can bring their own (purchased from state package stores). It's best to confirm this arrangement by an advance phone call to the restaurant of your choice. Among Salt Lake City's native children are actresses Maude Adams and Loretta Young.

THE MORMONS: Founded in 1830 in New York State by the visionary Joseph Smith, the Church of Jesus Christ of the Latter-Day Saints (LDS), the church's formal name, imposes a strict behavior code. Mormons, who comprise 70% of Utah's population, eschew drugs, tobacco, alcohol, tea, coffee, and even Coca-Cola. They practice tithing, returning to their rich and powerful church approximately 10% of their personal income.

Most young Mormons of both sexes dedicate two years of their lives to missionary work; they may be sent at their own expense anywhere in the world to proselytize. There are 7.8 million Mormons today throughout the world, half of them in the United States. Their 40 or so temples are all modeled on the one in Salt Lake City. The Mormon practice of polygamy, which caused much of the anti-Mormon persecution during the last century (the church's founder, Joseph Smith, was lynched in 1844) and long delayed Utah's admission to the Union, was officially abolished in 1890. Highly moral, the Mormons are known for their religious zeal, their political conservatism, and their strong family ties.

BASIC FACTS: Capital of the State of Utah. Area code: 801. Time zone: mountain. ZIP Code: 84101. Founded: 1847. Approximate population: city, 168,000; metropolitan area, 1,100,000. 38th largest metropolitan area in the country.

CLIMATE: With its magnificently sunny days and its colorful foliage, autumn is the ideal season for a visit to Salt Lake City and its nearby woodlands. Summers are quite hot but dry (average July temperature, 78°F/26°C). Spring brings a disconcerting alternation of sun and sudden showers (sometimes with snow). Winter is pure pleasure for ski buffs, with the thermometer hovering consistently around 32°F (0°C) Nov–Feb.

DISTANCES: Denver, 506 mi. (810km); Las Vegas, 439 mi. (702km); Portland, 768 mi. (1,230km); San Francisco, 750 mi. (1,200km); Yellowstone, 325 mi. (520km).

ARRIVAL & TRANSIT INFORMATION

AIRPORT: Salt Lake City International Airport (SLC), 3 mi(5km) west. For information, call 539-2400.

AIRLINES: America West (toll free 800/247-5692), American (toll free 800/433-7300), Continental (toll free 800/525-0280), Delta (toll free 800/221-1212), Morris Air (toll free 800/444-5660), Northwest (toll free 800/225-2525), and United (toll free 800/241-6522).

CITY LINK: The **cab** fare from Salt Lake City Airport to dwntwn Salt Lake City is about $12; time, 15 min. **Bus:** The major hotels have their own free limousine service; time, about 20 min. **City bus (UTA** line 50): Serves the dwntwn area; leaves every hour; fare, 65¢; time, 30 min.
  Unless you plan on excursions, the size of the city makes car rental unnecessary. The public bus transportation system is not extensive (Utah Transit Authority, 801/287-4636).

CAR RENTAL (at Salt Lake City Airport unless otherwise indicated): Avis (toll free 800/331-1212); Budget (toll free 800/527-0700); Dollar (toll free 800/800-4000); Hertz (toll free 800/654-3131); National (toll free 800/227-7368); and Thrifty, 2400 W. North Temple St. (toll free 800/367-2277). For dwntwn locations, consult the local telephone directory.

LIMOUSINE SERVICES: Bonneville Limo (364-6520), Dav El Limousines (toll free 800/922-0343).

TAXIS: You'll find taxis in waiting lines at the major hotels; they cannot be hailed on the street. Your best bet is to phone **City Cab** (363-5014) or **Yellow Cab** (521-2100).

TRAIN: Amtrak station, 320 S. Rio Grande (toll free 800/872-7245).

INTERCITY BUSES: Greyhound, 160 W. South Temple St. (toll free 800/231-2222).

INFORMATION & TOURS

TOURIST INFORMATION: The **Salt Lake City Convention and Visitors Bureau,** 180 S. West Temple St., UT 84101 (801/521-2822): Open Mon–Fri.
   Utah Travel Council, Council Hall, Capitol Hill, UT 84114 (801/538-1030): Information on Utah's national parks and tourist attractions. The office is open daily in the summer, Mon–Fri the rest of the year.
   Visitor Information Center, Temple Sq. at S. Temple St. (801/240-2534): Information about the Mormon church. Open daily.

GUIDED TOURS: Gray Line Tours (bus), 553 W. 100 South (521-7060): Guided tours of the city and its outskirts, serving the major hotels.
   Innsbrook Tours (bus), 57 W. Temple, Suite 400 (534-1001): City tour includes hearing the Tabernacle organ. Serves major hotels. Mon–Sat.
   Western Leisure (bus), 1172 E. Brickyard Rd. (467-6100): Week-long tours to filming locations of well-known movies such as *Butch Cassidy and the Sundance Kid, Jeremiah Johnson,* etc. A must for movie buffs. Resv. essential.

SIGHTS, ATTRACTIONS & ACTIVITIES

ADVENTURES: Adrift Adventures (boat), P.O. Box 577, Moab, UT 84532 (259-8594; toll free 800/874-4483): Down the Colorado and Green Rivers in rubber rafts or rowboats. One- to seven-day trips (early Apr through Oct).
   Holiday River Expeditions (boat), 544 E. 3900 South (266-2087; toll free 800/624-6323): Raft trips on the Colorado, Green, and San Juan Rivers (May–Sept).
   Moki Mac River Expeditions (boat), P.O. Box 21242, Salt Lake City, UT 84121 (268-6667; toll free 800/284-7280): Raft trips on the Colorado and Green Rivers, lasting 1–14 days (May–Sept).
   Off the Beaten Path, 109 E. Main St., Bozeman MT 59715 (tel. 406/586-1311 or toll free 800/445-2995) will work with clients to create tours to special or little known places.
   Western River Expeditions (boat), 7258 Racquet Club Dr. (942-6669; toll free 800/453-7450): Raft trips on the Green and Colorado Rivers (May–Sept).
   For other raft trips, see "Adventures" under "Sights, Attractions, and Activities" in Chapter 32 on Utah National Parks.

ARCHITECTURAL HIGHLIGHTS: ⚓ **City and County Building,** Washington Sq. (535-7611): Built in 1894 along the lines of the Mansion House in London, this vast Romanesque edifice in dark sandstone served for 19 years as the State Capitol. Today it houses the city hall and the county's administrative offices. The building is set in a very lovely garden with 45 varieties of trees from around the world. Open Mon–Fri.
   ☼⚓ **LDS Church Office Building,** 50 E. North Temple St. (240-2452): The old Ionic-style building, inaugurated in 1917 (LDS Church Administration Bldg.), contains the offices of the president and

the 12 "apostles" of the Mormon church. The new 30-story building, constructed in 1972, houses the largest genealogical library in the world. Tens of millions of computerized microfiches are said to make possible the reconstruction of genealogical trees for all U.S. citizens and many Europeans. Visitors can use the library Mon–Sat. (Duplicate microfilm is stored in an underground vault dug out of a mountain in Little Cottonwood Canyon, 17 mi./28km south of Salt Lake City.) An observation platform on the 26th floor offers a fine view of the city. Open Mon–Sat.

State Capitol, N. State St. and Capitol Hill (538-3000): One of the most imposing edifices of its type in the U.S., dating from 1916. Inspired by the Capitol in Washington, D.C., its 285-ft. (87m) copper dome dominates the city. Constructed of Georgia marble and Utah state granite. The building houses the State Senate and the House of Representatives as well as Utah's Supreme Court. It has very rich interior decoration (note especially the **Gold Room**). From Capitol Hill you'll have a grand view of the city and of the distant mountains. Open Mon–Fri all year, daily in summer.

Symphony Hall, 123 W. South Temple St. (533-6407): Spectacular modern building with an unusual chamfered design and an immense glass facade. The hall is well known for its fine acoustics, and is the home of the Utah Symphony Orchestra. Part of the Salt Palace Center Complex. Open Mon–Fri in summer, Tues and Thurs the rest of the year.

CHURCHES/SYNAGOGUES: Cathedral of the Madeleine, 331 E.
South Temple St. (328-8941): Topped by two 220-ft. (67m) towers, this Spanish Gothic-style cathedral dating from 1909 features a richly decorated interior: varieties of Tennessee marble, Venetian mosaics, stained-glass windows from Germany, carved oak statues, etc. Open daily.

Mormon Temple: See Temple Square under "Historic Buildings," below.

HISTORIC BUILDINGS: Beehive House, 67 E. South Temple St. (240-
2671): Former residence of Brigham Young, founder of the city and the second president of the Mormon church. Built in 1854, the house was the official residence of Mormon presidents until 1918. On its small tower is the figure of a beehive—betokening the zeal of the Mormons—which is also incorporated in the Utah state seal. Interesting period furniture. Open daily. **(Lion House,** next door, dating from 1856, was Brigham Young's office until his death in 1877, and also the scene of family gatherings for Young's 19 wives and 56 children. Closed to the public).

Council Hall, State and 300 North Sts., Capitol Hill (538-1030): The former city hall and seat of government for the Territory of Utah (1866). Initially erected at 1 E. South St., the hall was moved, stone by stone, to its present location and rebuilt in 1962. Today it houses the Utah Travel Council and its Visitor Information Center (see "Tourist Information," above). Open daily in summer, Mon–Fri the rest of the year.

Deseret Pioneer Village, 2601 Sunnyside Ave. (584-8391): Museum village re-creating the life of the valley's early Mormon pioneers, circa 1850–70. Some of the buildings are facsimiles, while others are the authentic original buildings, moved to their present place. Among them is **Brigham Young's country home,** painstakingly restored (**Brigham Young's Forest Farmhouse**). An interesting slice of history. Nearby you'll find the "This Is the Place" Monument (see "Monuments," below).

☼⚖️ **Fort Douglas,** Wasatch Dr. (588-5188): Constructed in 1862 by order of President Lincoln to protect transcontinental telegraph installations from tribal attacks, the fort has preserved several imposing buildings and fortifications of reddish sandstone. An interesting museum traces Utah's military history after the arrival of the Mormons. Open Tues–Sat.

⚖️ **Hotel Utah,** S. Temple and Main Sts. (531-1000): After 76 years of welcoming famous visitors, this legendary palace of Italian Renaissance design, a designated historic monument, closed its doors in 1987. It has since reopened as an office building and meeting place for the Mormon church (to which it belongs), thus closing a chapter in Salt Lake City history. No visitors.

☼⚖️⚖️ **Temple Square,** bounded by N. Temple, S. Temple, W. Temple, and Main Sts. (240-2534): The historic heart and holy place of Joseph Smith's church. Enclosed within a 13-ft. (4m) wall of unbaked brick, the square contains those buildings that most symbolize the Mormon religion. First and foremost is the **Temple,** an imposing granite edifice in Mormon style, inaugurated in 1893 after 40 years in construction. At each of its two extremities are three pointed towers; the tallest, part of the main facade, measures 209 ft. (64m) in height and is crowned by Cyrus D. Dallin's gold statue of the angel Moroni. Reserved for baptism and marriage celebrations, sermons, and ordinations, the richly decorated Temple is off-limits to non-Mormons. The second noteworthy building, the **Tabernacle,** a vast 6,500-seat concert hall dating from 1867, has a wooden roof shaped like a turtle's carapace. Its exceptional acoustics are demonstrated daily via recitals on the 12,000-pipe organ. Recital times are noon Mon–Fri and 4pm Sat–Sun. Concerts of the famous Mormon Tabernacle Choir are given Thurs at 8pm and Sun at 9:30am. The **Museum of Church History and Art,** 45 N. West Temple St. (240-3310), chronicles the history of Mormonism from 1830 to the present. Contains fine art sculptures and paintings and religious artifacts from all over the world. Interesting; open daily. The last of the major buildings, the **Assembly Hall** (1882), can accommodate as many as 3,000 people for religious observances, concerts, meetings, funerals, etc. Concerts Mon–Sat in summer, Fri–Sat the rest of the year. There are also **visitor centers** with information on Mormon history and religion. Nearly four million visitors come to Temple Sq. each year.

MONUMENTS: ⚖️ Brigham Young Monument, S. Temple and Main Sts.:
Bronze statue of Salt Lake City's founder; note the figures of a Native American and a trapper at the base of the pedestal (1897). On the monument's north side is a plaque bearing the names of those Mormon pioneers who arrived with Brigham Young on July 24, 1847.

☼⚖️ **Eagle Gate,** S. Temple and State Sts.: Originally constructed in 1859 to mark the entrance to Brigham Young's private property, this monumental sculpture, composed of the emblems of the United States (the eagle) and the State of Utah (the beehive) supported by four massive arches, overlooks one of the city's principal intersections.

⚖️ **Grave of Brigham Young,** First Ave. between State and A Sts.: Tomb of the Mormon leader, three of his wives, and several of their children, in a modest garden surrounded by a wrought-iron railing. Lovely view of the city.

⚖️ **Seagull Monument,** Temple Sq.: The figure of a seagull perches atop this bronze column (1913) in commemoration of the sea birds that in 1848 miraculously intervened to eat the grasshoppers threatening the harvest of the first settlers.

☼⚖️ **"This Is the Place" Monument,** Sunnyside Ave. at the entrance to Emigration Canyon: Erected in 1947 for the centennial celebration of the founding of Salt Lake City, the monument, designed by

Brigham Young's grandson, Mahonry Young, marks the place from which the Mormon leader first discerned the site of the future capital of Utah (July 24, 1847). Lovely view of the valley. Visitor center open daily.

MUSEUMS OF ART: ⚱ **Salt Lake Art Center,** 20 S. West Temple St. (328-4201): Temporary art exhibitions (paintings, photos, crafts). Sculpture garden. Concerts, ballet, conferences, films on art, etc. Open daily.

⚱ **Utah Museum of Fine Arts,** University of Utah campus, 300 S. University St. (581-7332): Installed in the building of the Art and Architecture Center, this relatively small but well-rounded museum offers a complete overview of the history of art, from Egyptian antiquities to contemporary American painting. Also a lovely collection of Louis XIV furniture and 17th-century tapestries.

MUSEUMS OF SCIENCE & HISTORY: ☀⚱ **Hansen Planetarium,** 15 S. State St. (538-2098): Well-known planetarium housed in a former turn-of-the-century public library building. A spectacular **Star Chamber** takes visitors on a vicarious tour of the planets. Space museum and specialty library. A must for astronomy buffs. Open daily.

☀⚱ **Pioneer Memorial Museum,** 300 N. Main St. (538-1050): Interesting museum focused on the Mormon era, just a few steps from the State Capitol. Created in 1950, the museum contains numerous and often-touching souvenirs from the time of the early Mormon pioneers (dolls, clothing, manuscripts, furniture, etc.). In the **Carriage House** next door, be sure to see the wagon used by Brigham Young in his 1847 trek to Salt Lake City. Open daily Jun–Aug, Mon–Sat the rest of the year.

⚱ **Utah Museum of Natural History,** University of Utah campus, Wasatch Dr. (581-4303): Rich geological, paleontological, and zoological collections. Outstanding display of five almost-complete dinosaur skeletons uncovered in earlier Utah excavations. Remarkable Hall of Minerals. Open daily.

PANORAMAS: ☀⚱ **LDS Church Office Bldg.,** 50 E. North Temple St. (240-2452): The observation deck on the 26th floor offers (free) the best view of the city and surrounding mountains. Open Mon–Sat.

PARKS & GARDENS: ⚱ **Jordan Park,** 1060 S. 9th West St.: Located on the shores of the Jordan River, this park and the adjacent **International Peace Gardens** features flowers and statues from 22 countries. Also a picnic area and a public swimming pool. Open daily May–Sept; closed the rest of the year.

☀⚱ **Liberty Park,** 1000 South and 600 East Sts. (972-7800): Very lovely 100-acre (41ha) park close to the center of the city. Notable features include a vast pond (boat rides), a children's amusement park, and the **Tracy Aviary.** Open daily.

⚱ **State Arboretum,** University of Utah campus (581-5322): Spread over the university campus are more than 7,000 trees from 350 different species.

PERFORMING ARTS: For a daily listing of all shows and cultural events, consult the entertainment pages of the daily papers the *Salt Lake City Tribune* (morning) and the *Desert News* (evening), and of the bimonthly magazine *Salt Lake City.*

Capitol Theatre, 50 W. 200 South St. (355-2787): Built in 1913, this very lovely rococo theater, sumptuously renovated, offers ballet, opera, top entertainers, and Broadway shows. Home of the Utah Opera Company, the Ballet West, and the Repertory Dance Theatre.

Huntsman Center, Hempstead Rd., University of Utah campus (581-8314):

Circular dome-covered arena seating 15,000. Hosts the "Runnin' Utes" basketball team; also concerts and performances of top entertainers.

Mormon Tabernacle, Temple Sq. (240-3318): Daily organ recitals (free), concerts of sacred music, and performances by the Mormon Tabernacle Choir Thurs and Sun (see "Historic Buildings," above).

Pioneer Memorial Theatre, 300 South and University sts. (581-6961): Classic and contemporary theater, musical comedies (Sept–May). On the University of Utah campus.

Promised Valley Playhouse, 132 S. State St. (364-5696): Elegantly restored building dating from the end of the 19th century. Contemporary theater, drama, musical productions (Sept–May). Musical comedy with the Mormon epic as theme, Tues–Sat all summer (free tickets at the Temple Sq. Visitor Center).

Salt Lake Acting Co., 168 W. 500 North St. (363-7522): Drama, comedy, contemporary theater.

Symphony Hall, Salt Palace Center, 123 W. South Temple St. (533-6407): Very beautiful architecture and peerless acoustics. Concerts, classical-music recitals. Home of the Utah Symphony Orchestra (principal conductor: Joseph Silverstein).

SHOPPING: **REI,** 3285 E. 3300 S. (486-2100): Gigantic sports apparel store that carries outdoor equipment ranging from skis to tents to rock-climbing ropes. Everything you need if you're going to the mountains.

☀ **Trolley Square,** bounded by 5th South and 6th South Sts. and 6th East and 7th East Sts. (521-9877): Former turn-of-the-century trolley depot, intelligently transformed into a business and entertainment center with 100 or so shops, booths, restaurants, and movie theaters. Strolling musicians and sidewalk artists. Lively, colorful atmosphere, lovely Victorian decor. Open daily.

☀ **ZCMI,** Main and S. Temple Sts. (579-6000): Founded by Brigham Young himself in 1868, the Zion's Cooperative Mercantile Institution (ZCMI) is the oldest department store in the United States. Its ornamental cast-iron facade is a designated historic monument. Next door is the **ZCMI Center,** an enormous four-story modern shopping mall containing many shops, specialty stores, and restaurants.

SPECIAL EVENTS: For the exact schedule of events below, consult the **Salt Lake City Convention and Visitors Bureau** (see "Tourist Information," above).

Utah Arts Festival (end of June): Art exhibits, shows, concerts, international food festival, etc.

"Days of 47" Celebration (mid-July): Commemorates the founding of Salt Lake City by the first Mormons. Parades, rodeo. Very colorful spectacle.

Promised Valley (July–Aug): Musical show portraying the saga of Brigham Young and the early pioneers. Promised Valley Playhouse.

Utah State Fair (11 days in mid-Sept): The biggest fair in the state of Utah.

SPORTS: Salt Lake City has three professional teams:

Baseball (mid-June to Sept): Trappers, Derks Field (484-9900); minor-league team.

Basketball (Oct–Apr): Utah Jazz, Delta Center (355-3865).

Ice Hockey (Oct–Apr): Golden Eagles, Delta Center (523-4653).

STROLLS: ⚜ **Arrow Press Square,** West Temple St. across from Salt Palace Center: The old printers' and bookbinders' quarter, with beautifully restored early 19th-century buildings, boutiques, and trendy restaurants.

☀⚜ **South Temple Street,** between Temple Sq. and 7th East St.: The most fashionable and historic street in Salt Lake City, featuring the elegant residences of 19th-century silver and copper magnates.

Among these is the **Kearns Mansion** (see the Governor's Mansion under "Historic Buildings," above). Note also the **Cathedral of the Madeleine** (see "Churches/Synagogues," above) and the **Masonic Temple**, 650 E. South Temple St.

☼⚷☖ **Trolley Square:** See "Shopping," above.

THEME PARKS: ☼☖ **Lagoon Amusement Park and Pioneer Village,** in Farmington, 17 mi. (27km) north on I-15 (801/451-8000): Large amusement park with cleverly re-created 19th-century pioneer village. Stagecoach rides, vast lagoon/swimming pool. Rodeos in the summer, also musical shows. Open daily Memorial Day–Labor Day, wknds only mid-Apr to Memorial Day and Labor Day to mid-Oct.

☖ **Raging Waters,** 1700 S. 1200 West (973-9900): Aquatic amusement park with at least a dozen pools, with 17 giant water slides, waterfalls, artificial surf, etc. Open daily May–Sept.

WINTER SPORTS RESORTS: ☖☖ **Alta,** 28 mi. (45km) SE on Utah 152 and Utah 210 (801/742-3333): 10 lifts. Open mid-Nov to mid-Apr.

☖☖ **Brighton Bowl,** 31 mi. (49km) SE on Utah 152 (801/943-8309): 5 lifts. Open mid-Nov to May.

☖ **Deer Valley,** 30 mi. (48km) SE on I-80 and Utah 224 (801/649-1000): 11 lifts. Open early Dec to mid-Apr.

☖ **Park City,** 27 mi. (43km) east on I-80 (801/649-8111): 14 lifts. Open mid-Nov. to the end of Apr.

☖ **Park West,** 26 mi. (41km) east on I-80 and Utah 224 (801/649-5400): 7 lifts. Open Nov to early April.

☼☖☖ **Snowbird,** 29 mi. (46km) SE on U.S. 83, Colo. 209, and Colo. 210 (801/742-2222): Cable car and 7 lifts. Open mid-Nov to June.

☖ **Solitude Ski Resort,** 23 mi. (36km) SE on Utah 152 (801/534-1400): 5 lifts. Open from the end of Nov through Apr.

☼☖☖ **Sundance Resort,** 63 mi. (100km) SE on I-15, U.S. 189, and Utah 92 (801/225-4107): 4 lifts. Managed by actor Robert Redford, who lives here. Far from the crowds and commotion of the typical ski resort.

ACCOMMODATIONS

Personal Favorites (in order of preference)

♖♖♖ **Red Lion Salt Lake** (dwntwn), 255 S. West Temple St., UT 84101 (801/328-2000; toll free, see Red Lion Inns). 496 rms, A/C, color TV, in-rm movies. AE, CB, DC, MC, V. Parking $3, pool, health club, sauna, rest. (Maxi's), coffee shop, bar, rm svce, nightclub, concierge, free crib. *Note:* Large, very modern 18-story hotel next to the huge Triad Center architectural complex. Peerless comfort and facilities. Spacious, inviting rms, some w. refrigerators. Very good svce, acceptable rest. Frequented by businesspeople and convention-goers (the Salt Palace is across the street). VIP floor. Free airport shuttle. **M–E**

♖♖♖ **Marriott Hotel** (dwntwn), 75 S. West Temple St., UT 84101 (801/531-0800; toll free, see Marriott). 516 rms, A/C, color TV, in-rm movies. AE, CB, DC, MC, V. Valet parking $8, pool, sauna, two rests. (including L'Abeille), two bars, rm svce, nightclub, boutiques, free crib. *Note:* Modern 15-story tower across from the Salt Palace Convention Center. Facilities and comfort are beyond reproach. Spacious rms w. balconies; attentive reception and svce. Rests. are so-so, as elsewhere in the Marriott chain. Business and group clientele. Interesting wknd packages. Free airport shuttle. Direct access to the adj. shopping center. VIP floor. The best location in Salt Lake City. **M–E**

☼ 🛎 🍴 🛏 **Brigham Street Inn** (nr. dwntwn), 1135 E. South Temple St., UT 84102 (801/364-4461). 9 rms, A/C, color TV. AE, MC, V. Free parking, valet svce, free breakfast, free crib. *Note:* Small luxury hotel, intimate and refined, in a charming Victorian residence dating from 1898 (no elevator). Rms are elegantly fitted out, each in its own style (some have fireplaces). Stylish reception and svce. Charm and distinction; 10 min. from dwntwn. **M–E**

🍴 🛏 **Howard Johnson Hotel** (dwntwn), 122 W. South Temple St., UT 84101 (801/521-0130; toll free, see Howard Johnson). 224 rms, A/C, cable color TV. AE, CB, DC, MC, V. Free parking, pool, health club, rest. (J.B.'s), rm svce, free crib. *Note:* Enormous 13-story motel in the center of dwntwn. Comfort up to contemporary standards, and a complete range of facilities. Inviting rms (some w. refrigerator); efficient svce. Free airport shuttle. Good value in a fine location across from the Salt Palace and Temple Sq. **I–M**

🍴 **Travelodge Downtown** (dwntwn), 524 S. West Temple St., UT 84101 (801/531-7100; toll free, see Travelodge). 60 rms, A/C, cable color TV. AE, CB, DC, MC, V. Free parking; pool and rest. adj. *Note:* Small, unassuming but well-run motel w. functional comforts and a friendly reception. Centrally located three blocks from the Salt Palace. Good value. **B–I**

Other Accommodations (from top bracket to budget)

🍴🍴🛏 **Hilton Salt Lake** (nr. dwntwn), 150 W. 500 South St., UT 84101 (801/532-3344; toll free, see Hilton). 351 rms, A/C, color TV, in-rm movies. AE, CB, DC, MC, V. Free parking, pool, sauna, two rests. (including Room at the Top), coffee shop, bar, rm svce, disco, hrdrsr, free crib. *Note:* Large, modern, functional hotel. Rms are comfortable and spacious and have balconies and refrigerators. Svce somewhat lacking. A favorite of business travelers. Good rests. Two VIP floors. 5 min. from dwntwn. **M–E**

🍴🍴🛏 **Little America** (nr. dwntwn), 500 S. Main St., UT 84101 (801/363-6781; toll free 800/453-9450). 850 rms, A/C, cable color TV. AE, CB, DC, MC, V. Free parking, two pools, health club, sauna, two rests. (including Little America), coffee shop, bar, rm svce, hrdrsr, shops, free crib. *Note:* A 17-story hotel, modern and comfortable, surrounded by lovely grdns. Spacious rms, some w. refrigerators. Comprehensive facilities. Efficient reception and svce. Good value. Frequented by convention-goers and other groups. Free airport shuttle. 5 min. from Temple Sq. and the Convention Center. **I–M**

☼ 🍴 🛏 **Peery** (dwntwn), 110 W. 300 South St., UT 84101 (801/521-4300; toll free 800/331-0073). 77 rms, A/C, color TV, in-rm movies. AE, CB, DC, MC, V. Free parking, health club, sauna, two rests. (including the Peery Pub and Café), bar, rm svce, free breakfast, free crib. *Note:* Constructed in 1910, this elegant small hotel, a designated historic monument, was completely renovated in 1985. Rms are huge and very comfortable. Svce is personalized. Free airport shuttle. Only a stone's throw from the Convention Center. Secretarial svces and business equipment. A favorite of those in-the-know. **I–M**

🍴 🛏 **Comfort Inn** (nr. dwntwn), 200 N. Admiral Byrd Rd., UT 84116 (801/537-7444; toll free, see Choice). 154 rms, A/C, color TV, in-rm movies. AE, CB, DC, MC, V. Free parking, pool, rest., rm svce, free crib. *Note:* Up-to-date, comfortable motel in the Salt Lake International Center, less than 5 min. from the airport (free shuttle). Spacious, inviting rms w. balcony and some w. refrigerator. Wholly professional svce; business clientele. **I–M**

🍴 🛏 **Shilo Inn** (dwntwn), 206 S. West Temple St., UT 84101 (801/521-9500; toll free 800/222-2244). 200 rms, A/C, color TV, in-rm movies. AE, CB, DC, MC, V. Free parking, pool, sauna, rest.,

SALT LAKE CITY
Downtown

DOWNTOWN SALT LAKE SIGHTS

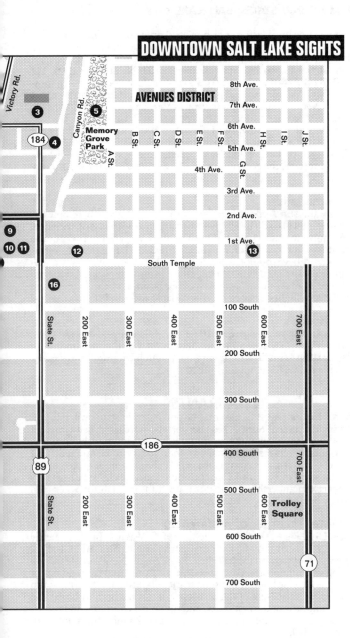

bar, rm svce, shops, free breakfast, free crib. *Note:* Large hotel, comfortable and functional, in the center of town. Pleasant rms. w. balconies and minibars. Good value. Great location across from the Salt Palace. Free airport shuttle. **I**

   🍷 **Royal Executive Inn** (dwntwn), 121 N. 300 West St., UT 84103 (801/521-3450). 94 rms, A/C, color TV, in-rm movies. AE, CB, DC, MC, V. Free parking, pool, coffee shop next door, rm svce, free breakfast, crib $1. *Note:* Modest, unpretentious motel in the heart of dwntwn. Good reception, very decent comfort. Free airport shuttle. Good value. **B**

   🍷 **Motel 6** (nr. dwntwn), 176 W. 600 South St., UT 84101 (801/531-1252). 110 rms, A/C, color TV, free in-rm movies. AE, DC, MC, V. Free parking, pool. *Note:* Small, super-economical but well-maintained motel, very nr. the center of town. An excellent value. Ideal for motorists. **B**

Airport Accommodations

   🍷🍷🍷 **Radisson Airport** (nr. dwntwn), 2177 W. North Temple St., UT 84116 (801/364-5800; toll free, see Radisson). 127 rms, A/C, color TV, in-rm movies. AE, CB, DC, MC, V. Free parking, pool, health club, rest. (Executive Clubroom), bar, rm svce, free breakfast, free airport shuttle, free crib. *Note:* Brand-new top-notch hotel adjacent to the airport and a golf course. Very spacious and comfortable rms, all w. bathroom phones, refrigerators, balconies, and in-rm coffee. Flawless svce. Big business clientele. Excellent for a stopover between flights. A highly commendable address. **I–E**

YMCA/Youth Hostels

   Avenues Youth Hostel (dwntwn), 107 F St. (801/363-8137). 30 beds. Comfortable youth hostel eight blocks from Temple Sq. Open year round.

   University of Utah–Austin Hall (dwntwn), Wasatch Dr. (801/581-6331). Quiet, comfortable rooms for rent mid-June to Aug.

RESTAURANTS

A Note on Utah's Liquor Laws: Liquor may be purchased in state-owned liquor stores, open every day except Sun; 3.2% beer may be purchased daily in most grocery stores. Many fine restaurants have liquor licenses. However, by state law, to be served alcoholic beverages in a restaurant, food must also be ordered. That does not apply in beer taverns or private clubs, where the minimum age to enter is 21. Most bars that serve mixed drinks are considered private clubs; visitors may purchase a two-week membership to most private clubs in Utah for $5 or gain free admittance by being sponsored by a member.

Personal Favorites (in order of preference)

   ☀️ 🍷🍷🍷 **La Caille at Quail Run** (vic.), 9565 S. Wasatch Blvd., in Sandy (942-1751). A/C. Dinner nightly, brunch Sun. AE, CB, DC, MC, V. Jkt. *Specialties:* oysters on the half shell, Black Angus New York steak, rack of lamb, duckling w. fruit, lobster. Basque-style dining on Sun. Wine and liquor available. *Note:* This elegant Louis XVI–style manor about 12 mi. (20km) south of Salt Lake City is the site of one of the best rests. (if not the best) in Utah. The French-inspired cooking is of the first order, and the svce is courteous and distinguished. Lovely grdns. Resv. are a must. Valet parking. 25 min. from dwntwn. *Continental/French.* **M–E**

   🍷🍷🍷 **Mikado** (dwntwn), 67 W. 100 South St. (328-0929). A/C. Dinner only, Mon–Sat; closed hols. AE, CB, DC, MC, V. *Specialties:* sushi, sukiyaki, shrimp tempura, chicken teriyaki, shabu-shabu. Wine and liquor. *Note:* Under the reigns of "Dancin' Gene" Kwon, Mikado has added a vibrant sushi bar to go along w. the western- and tatami-style dining rms that serve the most genuine Japanese food in Salt Lake. Smiling, discreet svce (in kimono). Resv. highly advised. *Japanese.* **I**

♉♉♉ **Peery Café** (dwntwn), in the Peery Hotel (see "Accommodations," above) (521-8919). A/C. Dinner only, Mon–Sat. *Specialties:* grilled potato flatbread w. sun-dried-tomato-and-roasted-garlic jam and saffron-tomato sauce, grilled marinated salmon w. Asian butter sauce, pork tenderloin w. hazelnut-mint crust and orange-ginger sauce. Rather small but well-priced wine list. Seasonal menu. *Note:* Wildly original cuisine using unbelievable but successful combinations. Open-faced booths and brass rails create a bistro atmosphere suitable for intimate or large-party dining. Expert svce. A very good value. The Peery also has a pub menu including a lighter fare of soups, salads, and sandwiches. The pub is open for lunch and dinner. Resv. not taken. *Continental/ American.* **I**

♉♉ **Santa Fe Restaurant** (nr. dwntwn), 2100 Emigration Canyon (582-5888). A/C. Lunch Mon–Fri, dinner Mon–Sat, brunch Sun. MC, V. *Specialties:* enchiladas, fajitas, Mexican dishes, charcoal-broiled steak, seafood. Wine and liquor available. *Note:* The "in" place in Salt Lake City, up historic Emigration Canyon near the university. Warm and inviting southwestern decor complete w. adobe walls, exposed beams, mountain views, and fireplaces. Excellent Mexican-American fare. Friendly svce. Intimate private club also. Resv. advised. Well worth the 10-min. drive from dwntwn. *Mexican/ American.* **I**

☼♉ **Archibald's Restaurant** (vic.), 1095 W. 7800 South, West Jordan (566-6940). No A/C. Breakfast/lunch/dinner daily; closed Dec 25. MC, V. *Specialties:* sandwiches, salads, broiled steak and seafood, roast chicken. *Note:* Built in 1853, this historic mill offers a very unique setting to enjoy good, honest rural American cuisine. Patio dining, weather permitting. Good value. 15 min. from dwntwn. Popular w. the locals. *American.* **B–I**

Other Restaurants (from top bracket to budget)

♉♉♉ **New Yorker** (dwntwn), 48 W. Market St. (363-0166). A/C. Lunch Mon–Fri, dinner Mon–Sat; closed hols. *Specialties:* 21-day dry-aged New York strip sirloin, crab-stuffed breast of chicken, California abalone, fresh pasta, fresh seafood flown in daily. Seasonal menu. *Note:* Posh dining in a discreet, subterranean setting. A favorite of the local elites. Café menu of lighter, less expensive fare is also available. The flagship of the successful Gastronomy chain of restaurants, which includes the Market Street Broiler and Market Street Grill (see below). The New Yorker is a private club, but you can buy a two-week membership for $5. Resv. highly recommended. *Continental.* **M–E**

♉♉ **Fresco Italian Café** (nr. dwntwn), 1513 S. 1500 E. (486-1300). A/C. Lunch Mon–Fri, dinner nightly; closed Thanksgiving and Christmas. AE, MC, V. *Specialties:* baked polenta w. mushroom duxelle; tutti mari (linguine w. prawns, crab, mussels, clams, and fresh fish w. herbed seafood butter sauce); breast of chicken rolled and stuffed w. goat cheese, pine nuts, spinach, and sun-dried tomatoes. Great desserts. *Note:* Sophisticated, delicate decor very much in tune w. the food. Pleasant patio seating in the summer. The best Italian food in Salt Lake. Due to the small size of the rest., resv. are highly advised. Well worth the 20-min drive from dwntwn. *Italian.* **I–M**

♉♉ **Market Street Broiler** (nr. dwntwn), 260 S. 1300 East St. (583-8808). A/C. Breakfast/lunch Mon–Sat, dinner nightly. AE, MC, V. *Specialties:* clam chowder, sautéed scallops, red snapper w. citrus, poached salmon, barbecued ribs, steak, roast chicken, lamb chops. Good homemade desserts. Wine and liquor available. *Note:* Agreeable grill rm in contemporary style, housed in a former fire station. Sister rest. of the Market Street Grill (see below). First-class fish and seafood flown in daily; svce flawless in all particulars. A fine place. No resv. 15 min. from dwntwn. *American/Seafood.* **I–M**

♉♉ **Market Street Grill** (dwntwn), 48 Post Office Place (322-4668). A/C. Breakfast/lunch Mon–Sat, dinner nightly, brunch Sun; closed hols. AE, MC, V. *Specialties:* excellent meats and seafood cooked over a mesquite fire, roast chicken, lamb chops, prime rib. Good desserts.

Wine and liquor. *Note:* Oldtime steakhouse, very popular locally, in a building dating from the early 1900s. The ambience is pleasant, the svce rapid and efficient. Just a few steps from Temple Sq. Very good value. No resv. *American/Steak.* **I–M**

🍸🍸 **Ristorante Della Fontana** (dwntwn), 336 S. 400 East St. (328-4243). A/C. Lunch/dinner Mon–Sat; closed Memorial Day, July 4, Dec 25. AE, DC, MC, V. Jkt. *Specialties:* lasagna, homemade pasta, Italian dishes. Wine and liquor. *Note:* Multicolored stained-glass windows and an indoor waterfall give this rest., converted from an old church, one of the most original settings ever. Very decent Italian cuisine, very good svce. Popular locally; resv. advised. *Italian.* **I–M**

🍸 **The Old Salt City Jail** (nr. dwntwn), 460 S. 1000 East St. (355-2422). A/C. Dinner only, nightly; closed July 4, July 24, Dec 25. AE, DC, MC, V. *Specialties:* roast beef, steaks, barbecued meats, catch of the day. Beer and wine. *Note:* As its name indicates, this rest. is in a converted 19th-century jail. The quality of the meats is excellent, and the decor is amusing even if not authentic. The atmosphere and svce are congenial. Good value. *American/Steak.* **I**

☀🍸 **Lamb's Restaurant** (dwntwn), 169 S. Main St. (364-7166). A/C. Breakfast/lunch/dinner Mon–Sat; closed hols. AE, CB, DC, MC, V. *Specialties:* omelets, excellent, homemade soups, fried trout, broiled snapper, corned beef and cabbage, braised lamb shank, rice pudding. Beer and wine. *Note:* The oldest rest. in Utah (1919). Local businesspeople prefer it for working breakfasts and lunches. Honest, serious family cooking. The pleasantly dated decor is charming and helps create a peaceful atmosphere. Excellent svce. This is a true Salt Lake City landmark. No resv. Very good value. *American.* **B–I**

🍸 **Squatter's Pub Brewery** (dwntwn), 147 W. Broadway (363-2739). A/C. Lunch/dinner daily; closed hols. AE, DC, MC, V. *Specialties:* pizzas, pasta, varied cuisine. Beer brewed on premises. *Note:* A rest. that has soared in popularity since the day it opened its doors. Go for the patio in the summer, when the beer goes extra well with the arid gusts of wind that sweep down from the Wasatch canyons—for which the good selection of house-brewed beers are named. Resv. highly advised. Must be 21 or older to enter. *American.* **B–I**

Cafeterias/Fast Food
Marianne's Delicatessen (dwntwn), 149 W. 200 South St. (364-0486). Open 11am–3pm Tues–Sat. AE, MC, V. Excellent sandwiches, many German specialties (rouladen, sauerbraten, and bratwurst), good daily specials, and memorable desserts explain this deli's popularity. Beer only. No resv.

BARS & NIGHTCLUBS

D. B. Cooper's (dwntwn), 19 E. 200 South St. (532-2948). Very popular disco. One of the oldest private clubs in Salt Lake City. Open Mon–Sat.

Junior's Tavern (dwntwn), 202 E. 500 South St. (322-0318). The favorite local hangout for jazz and blues aficionados. Open Mon–Sat.

Port O'Call (dwntwn), 78 W. 400 South St. (521-0589). Fashionable singles bar, popular locally. There's an entrance fee. Open Mon–Sat.

Zephyr (dwntwn), 79 W. 300 South St. (355-2582). Live rock and reggae at this private club. Open nightly.

NEARBY EXCURSIONS

☀🏛 **BINGHAM CANYON COPPER MINE** (27 mi./43km SW on I-15 and Utah 48) (569-6000): The largest open-pit copper mine in the world, owned by the Kennecott Co. The crater (2½ mi./4km wide and 3,148 ft./960m deep) is the largest man-made excavation in the world.

Five billion tons of rock and minerals have been mined since 1904. An impressive sight. Observation platform. Open daily Apr–Oct.

BONNEVILLE SALT FLAT (125 mi./200km west on I-80): An immense desert of salt 200 mi. (322km) long, as hard as concrete. Used as an automobile test track since 1911. In 1970 the rocket vehicle *Blue Flame* set a then-world speed record of 622.4 mph (1,001.4kmph). Present record: 633.6mph (1,019.7kmph) attained by *Thrust 2*, driven by Richard Noble on Nevada's Black Rock Desert track on October 3, 1983. Races are held each year at the end of Sept, attracting a large crowd.

GREAT SALT LAKE (31 mi./49km NW on I-15): At 72 mi. (115km) long and 30 mi. (48km) wide, but with a maximum depth of barely 28 ft. (8.5m). Great Salt Lake, the remains of Lake Bonneville, a prehistoric sea 13 times greater in size, is the largest natural body of water in the western United States. With ongoing evaporation, the salt content of the lake now averages 25% (seven times that of the oceans); this makes it unlivable for any form of animal life except shrimp. The lake's surface area continues to shrink: from 2,393 sq. mi. (6,200km^2) in 1873 to 1,437 sq. mi. (3,724km^2) today. The salt content is so high that even nonswimmers float with ease. (It's wise to protect your eyes from the salty water.) Because of repeated flooding, **Antelope Island** and **Saltair Beach,** formerly very popular, are no longer accessible.

TIMPANOGOS CAVE NATIONAL MONUMENT (36 mi./58km SE via I-15 and Utah 92) (801/756-5238): Underground limestone caves at a constant temperature of 43° F (6° C). Splendid multicolored, crystalline formations. Visiting the caves can be rather trying. Open daily, spring through fall; closed in winter.

SNOWBIRD SKI & SUMMER RESORT (29 mi./46km SE along State St. and 9400 South St.) (742-2222): A 125-passenger aerial tramway links the floor of Little Cottonwood Canyon, 8,100 ft. (2,470m) above sea level, to the crest of Hidden Peak, 11,000 ft. (3,353m) in elevation. Unobstructed panorama of the Uinta Mountains and the Great Salt Lake Valley. The tramway operates daily year round except in May and late Oct to late Nov. A marvelous sight.

WASATCH-CACHE NATIONAL FOREST: 1,235,000 acres (500,000ha) of forests, lakes, canyons, and mountains to the north, east, and southeast of Salt Lake City. Includes several ski areas, among them Alta, Park West, and Snowbird (see "Winter Sports Resorts," above). The U.S. Ski Team has set up its year-round training site in the Wasatch Mountains. There are numerous camping and picnic areas. Hunting and fishing too. For **information,** contact the Supervisor, 8226 Federal Bldg., 125 S. State St., Salt Lake City, UT 84138 (801/524-5030). Nature unspoiled.

WHEELER HISTORIC FARM (6351 S. 900 East, 21 mi./33km SE on I-15, Exit I-215) (801/264-2212): Authentic farm from the end of the 19th century, magnificently restored. Re-creates to perfection the 1890s lifestyle of the Mormon farmers. Costumed guides conduct the tour; if they wish, visitors can help milk cows, gather eggs, or feed and water the farm animals. An original, historical slice-of-life. Open daily.

FARTHER AFIELD

NORTH OF GREAT SALT LAKE (209 mi./334km r.t. via I-15N, Utah 83, and I-15S): Visit **Bear River Migratory Bird Refuge** near **Brigham City,** the largest migratory bird preserve in the U.S. Photo safaris encouraged. Open daily. Continue on to ⚓ **Golden Spike National Historic Site,** the place where, in 1869, the Central Pacific Railroad line coming from the west met the Union Pacific line from the east, creating the first transcontinental railroad. The anniversary of this event is celebrated each year on May 10 at 12:47pm, the exact day and hour of the original event. There's also a museum (801/471-2209) with exhibits and movies, open daily.

On your return, stop at the **Lagoon Amusement Park** (see "Theme Parks," above).

☀️⚓ SOUTH OF GREAT SALT LAKE (155 mi./248km r.t. via
I-15S, Utah 48, Utah 68, Utah 73, Utah 36, and I-80E): Visit **Bingham Canyon Copper Mine** (see "Nearby Excursions," above), then the **Stagecoach Inn,** former relay station of the legendary Overland Stage Coach Company and the Pony Express. Go on to **Camp Floyd** (801/768-8932), the largest military outpost in the United States during the wars against the local native tribes. Its visitor center is open daily mid-March to mid-Nov. Next stop, **Ophir,** a famous ghost town of early pioneer days. Finally, of course, there is the **Great Salt Lake** itself (see "Nearby Excursions," above). A spectacular circuit.

For complete information on the three following parks, see Chapter 32 on Utah National Parks.

☀️⚓ CANYONLANDS (248 mi./396km SE via I-15, U.S. 6,
U.S. 191, and Utah 313): Magnificent ocher-colored rocky cliffs tower over the Colorado River. Along the way, visit ⚓ **Arches National Park,** where amid the reddish desert you'll find superb peaks and arches carved by erosion.

⚓ DINOSAUR NATIONAL MONUMENT (200 mi./
320km east via I-80 and U.S. 40): The quarries bear many footprints of prehistoric animals. The visitor center displays a remarkable fossil collection. Open daily.

On the way, visit ⚓ **Flaming Gorge** and its exquisite scenery along the Green River, once the hideout of Butch Cassidy and the Sundance Kid.

☀️⚓ GLEN CANYON (319 mi./510km south on I-15 and Utah
28, U.S. 89, Utah 24, and Utah 95): Multicolored cliffs bathed by the blue waters of **Lake Powell.**

En route, be sure to see the unspoiled natural beauty of ⚓ **Capitol Reef National Park,** with its impressive but hard-to-reach canyons.

⚓ **Natural Bridges National Monument,** 45 mi. (72km) south of Glen Canyon, features gigantic rocky arches carved out by erosion.

⚓ PIONEER TRAIL (90 mi./144km r.t. via I-15N, U.S. 89, I-
84E, Utah 66, Utah 65, and Emigration Canyon Rd.): You'll go through **Farmington, Uintah, Weber Canyon, Morgan, East Canyon Lake,** and **Emigration Canyon.** A good third of this trip through gorgeous mountain scenery follows the old trail made by 19th-century Mormon pioneers.

☀️⚓ UINTA NATIONAL FOREST (138 mi./220km r.t. via
I-15S, Utah 92, U.S. 189, Utah 52, and I-15N): You'll visit **Timpanogos Cave National Monument** (see "Nearby Excursions," above) aboard a quaint little steam-powered train, the *Heber Creeper,* which leaves daily, mid-May to mid-Oct, from 6th West and Center Sts. in **Heber City** (801/654-5601).

There are splendid views along **Deer Creek Lake** and the gorges of the **Provo River,** one of the most beautiful spots in the Uinta forest. Don't fail to admire the waterfalls at **Bridal Veil Falls;** there's a funicular railway (801/225-4461) on U.S. 189 between **Wildwood** and **Olmstead,** open daily Apr–Nov. To return to Salt Lake City, take I-15N. A trip packed with things to see.

YELLOWSTONE & GRAND TETON (325 mi./520km north via I-15, U.S. 26, and U.S. 89): The crown jewels among America's national parks (see Chapter 33 on Yellowstone), enough to justify the whole trip west.

On your way, I suggest stopping by the ▲ **Craters of the Moon National Monument** to see the astonishing lunar landscapes sculpted by volcanic eruptions. Closed in winter. For information, contact P.O. Box 29, Arco, ID 83213 (208/527-3257).

ZION NATIONAL PARK (305 mi./488km SW via I-15, Utah 17, and Utah 9): The only canyon in the United States whose floor is accessible by automobile. Lovely landscapes. See Chapter 32 on Utah National Parks.

En route, visit ▲ **Cedar Breaks** and its rocky plateaus pocked with strikingly colored amphitheater-shaped depressions. Be sure also to see ▲▲▲ **Bryce Canyon** with its breathtaking gorges and ravines, almost as awesome as those of the Grand Canyon.

UTAH NATIONAL PARKS ♛

□ □ □

With its 10 great national parks for a population of less than 1.5 million inhabitants, the Mormon State is incontestably the most richly endowed from the point of view of the tourist or the ecologist. Mostly lying in the southern part of the state, these 10 national parks or monuments boast some of the most breathtaking scenery in America. This is particularly true of **Zion National Park,** the only canyon in the country that can be entirely explored by car or on foot. Its many-colored gorges, several hundred feet high, bridling the headlong course of the Virgin River, are a sight not easily forgotten. Nearby **Bryce Canyon National Park** has, according to geologists, some of the most astonishing rock formations in the country, as well as a view almost as enthralling as the Grand Canyon of the Colorado. **Arches National Park** displays ranks of wonderful arches and windows carved by erosion out of the rusty rock of the desert. Its neighbor **Canyonlands National Park** is equally spectacular, with its great ocher-colored cliffs of rock looming above the serpentine curves of the Colorado River, an unforgettable sight at sunrise or sunset. More difficult of access, the wild canyons and rocky spurs of **Capitol Reef National Park** along the Fremont River are a perfect example of nature in the raw. Utah's other great national parks—**Natural Bridges National Monument, Glen Canyon National Recreation Area, Cedar Breaks, Dinosaur National Monument,** and **Rainbow Bridge** (one of the world's largest natural arches, 275 ft./85m across)—rank, each in its degree, among the natural wonders of the United States. Allow at least a week to 10 days just for the highlights.

BASIC FACTS: State of Utah. Area code: 801. Time zone: mountain. Founded: Zion, 1909; Bryce Canyon, 1923; Arches National Park, 1929; Capitol Reef, 1937. Approximate combined area of the parks: 3,196 sq. mi. (8,280km²).

CLIMATE: Utah's climate is like its scenery: beautiful but rugged. Summers are very hot, and winters icy. While in summer the mercury can climb to 95°F (35°C) by day, it can skid precipitously below 68°F (20°C) at night. There are frequent violent storms from July to Sept; watch out, because the heavy rains can convert an unsurfaced road into a mudslide. The best times to escape both climatic extremes and crowds of tourists are May–June and Sept–Oct. In any case, bring woolens for evening wear.

ARRIVAL & TRANSIT INFORMATION

NEAREST AIRPORTS: See Chapter 47 on Las Vegas or Chapter 31 on Salt Lake City.

AIRLINES: See Chapter 47 on Las Vegas and Chapter 31 on Salt Lake City.

BUS OR CAR RENTAL? Greyhound buses serve many communities near Utah's national parks, but offer no direct access to them. Given the distances and the number of places you may wish to visit, it makes sense to rent a car with unlimited mileage. Rates in Nevada (Las Vegas) are more favorable than in Utah (Salt Lake City).

CAR RENTALS: See Chapter 47 on Las Vegas and Chapter 31 on Salt Lake City.

TRAIN: For Amtrak, see Chapter 47 on Las Vegas and Chapter 31 on Salt Lake City. The nearest station to Arches and Canyonlands National Parks: Thompson D.R.G.&W. Station (toll free 800/872-7245). Nearest station to Bryce Canyon and Zion National Parks: Milford Amtrak Station, East and South Sts. (toll free 800/872-7245).

INTERCITY BUSES: The nearest long-distance Greyhound terminals are in Las Vegas (see Chapter 47) and Salt Lake City (see Chapter 31). The nearest local Greyhound stations are at 1355 S. Main St. in Cedar City and 525 E. Main St. in Green River (both toll free 800/231-2222).

INFORMATION & ADVENTURE TOURS

TOURIST INFORMATION: The **Utah Travel Council,** Council Hall, Capitol Hill, Salt Lake City, UT 84114 (801/538-1030). Information on Utah's national parks and other great tourist attractions. For snow conditions, call 801/521-8102.

Visitor Centers
There are visitor centers in all the major parks:
    Arches National Park, at the park entrance (801/259-8161).
    Bryce Canyon National Park, 4 mi. (6km) from Bryce Canyon Airport (801/834-5322).
    Canyonlands National Park, at Island in the Sky Point (801/259-7164).
    Capitol Reef National Park, 6 mi. (9km) from the western entrance (801/425-3791).
    Cedar Breaks National Monument, open from the end of May to mid-Sept only (801/586-9451).
    Dinosaur National Monument, at the park entrance on the Colorado side and 7 mi. (11km) north of Jensen on the Utah side (303/374-2216).
    Glen Canyon National Recreation Area, Glen Canyon Bridge at Page (602/645-2471).
    Natural Bridges National Monument, at the park entrance (801/259-5174).
    Zion National Park, at the south entrance (801/772-3256).

ADVENTURE TOURS: Adrift Adventures (Jeep and boat), 378 N. Main St., Moab (259-8594; toll free 800/874-4483): One- to seven-day trips by raft or rowboat down the Colorado or Green River, operated early Apr to late Oct; also Jeep trips (Apr–Oct) in Canyonlands National Park.
    Adventure River Expeditions (boat), 185 S. Broadway, Green River (801/564-3648; toll free 800/331-3324): Rafting down the Colorado, Green, San Juan, and Dolores Rivers. May–Sept.
    ARA Leisure (boat), Wahweap Lodge, Page (602/278-8888): Boat cruises on Lake Powell and trips to Rainbow Bridge.

Bryce Zion Trail Rides, Inc. (horseback): Rides on horseback or muleback in Bryce Canyon or Zion National Park; daily Apr–Sept. For information, call 801/834-5219 (for Bryce Canyon) or 801/772-3967 (for Zion).

Cedar City Air Service (airplane), 2281 W. Kittyhawk Dr., Cedar City (801/586-3881): Unforgettable flights over Cedar Breaks, Bryce Canyon, and Zion National Parks.

Don Hatch River Expeditions (boat), 411 E. 2nd North (P.O. Box 1150), Vernal, UT 84078 (801/789-4316; toll free 800/342-8243): One- to five-day air-rafting trips on the Green River and the Yampa River in Dinosaur National Park; May–Sept.

Lake Powell Air Service (airplane), Municipal Airport, Page (602/645-2494): Unforgettable flights, lasting 30 min. to 2½ hr., over Lake Powell, Rainbow Bridge, Monument Valley, Bryce Canyon, etc.

Lin Ottinger's Scenic Tours (all-terrain vehicles), 600 N. Main St., Moab (801/259-7312): One-day trips in Arches and Canyonlands National Parks; Apr–Nov.

North American River/Canyonland Tours (Jeep and boat), 534 N. Main St., Moab (801/259-5865): Down the Green and Colorado Rivers by air raft or jetboat; Apr–Oct. Jeep trips into the backcountry of Arches and Canyonlands.

Red Tail Aviation (airplane), Canyonlands Field, on U.S. 191, 18 mi. (28km) north of Moab (801/259-7421): Spectacular flights over Arches and Canyonlands National Parks, Lake Powell, or Monument Valley.

Tag-A-Long Tours (boat), 452 N. Main St., Moab (toll free 800/453-3292): Boat trips down the Green and Colorado Rivers and around Canyonlands National Park; Apr–Oct.

MUSEUMS: ☀⌂ **Anasazi State Park Museum,** Utah 12, Boulder (335-7308): Archeologists' dig on the site of a 100-room Native American dwelling dating from about A.D. 1050. A life-size replica of a six-room Anasazi dwelling reconstructs the life of its inhabitants eight or nine centuries back. At the nearby museum are exhibited many of the objects unearthed at the dig. Fascinating. Open daily.

⌂ **Dan O'Laurie Museum,** 118 E. Center St., Moab (259-7985): Has displays of prehistoric Native American artifacts and exhibits on geology, mineralogy, and pioneer history. Open Mon–Sat.

☀⌂ **Hollywood Stuntmen's Hall of Fame,** 111 E. 100 North St., Moab (259-6100): Houses an extensive collection of movie and stunt-oriented memorabilia, including costumes, weapons, action photographs, as well as a theater where movie stunt footage is shown and live performances are held. Unusual. Open Tues–Sun Mar–Oct.

⌂ **Iron Mission State Historical Museum,** 585 N. Main St., Cedar City (586-9290): Site of the first iron foundry west of the Mississippi (1851). Contains an interesting array of wagons, stagecoaches, and other horse-drawn vehicles from Utah pioneer days. Also displayed are numerous Native American artifacts. Open daily.

☀⌂⌂ **Utah Field House of Natural History Museum,** 235 E. Main St., Vernal (789-3799): Here, 14 life-size artificial dinosaurs welcome the visitor to this handsome garden with its waterfall, artificial lake, and marshy area reproducing their natural habitat. The adjoining museum has a number of (genuine) fossils including an articulated dinosaur skeleton, as well as mineral and archeological collections. Open daily.

NATIONAL PARKS & MONUMENTS

☀⌂⌂ **ARCHES NATIONAL PARK** (236 mi./378km SE of Salt Lake City via I-15, U.S. 6, and U.S. 191): Dozens of stone arches and superb red sandstone spurs, carved over 150 million years by erosion, water, wind, sun, and frost in a dun-colored rocky wasteland. Among them are

Landscape Arch, biggest natural arch in the world (288 ft./88m across); **Park Avenue,** a spectacular rocky corridor between high vertical walls reminiscent of the famous street in New York; the sculptural group called the **Three Gossips;** the huge, precariously poised **Balanced Rock;** the unbelievably elegant **Delicate Arch,** spanning the sheer gorge of the Colorado, which can be reached by a footpath; and the fantastically shaped arches of the beautiful **Devil's Garden.**

There are 21 mi. (34km) of surfaced roads and scores of miles of additional tracks for all-terrain vehicles, along which you can explore this open-air museum of natural architecture. The park is open year round, but beware extremes of temperature, winter and summer both. There are 53 authorized campsites.

For **information,** contact the Superintendent, Arches National Park, 125 W. 200 South, Moab, UT 84532 (801/259-8161 or 259-7164).

BRYCE CANYON NATIONAL PARK (241 mi./385km NE of Las Vegas via I-15, Utah 9, U.S. 89, and Utah 12): One of the most beautiful national parks in America; its huge rock formations are almost as astonishing as those of the Grand Canyon of the Colorado. Lying along the east side of the **Paunsaugunt Plateau** ("Country of the Beavers," in the local tribal tongue), a limestone mesa 8,200 ft. (2,500m) above sea level which, geologically speaking, is the bed of a 60-million-year-old sea, Bryce Canyon displays fairyland scenery of glittering rocks, cliff faces sculpted into gigantic organ pipes, and a dozen stepped amphitheaters in striking colors varying from yellow through orange to deep red (the famous **Pink Cliffs**). The scenic 17-mi. (27km) **Rim Drive,** as well as a number of hiking trails leading to the bottom of the canyon, will take you to dozens of rock formations with strange shapes and poetic names—Cathedral, Queen's Castle, Wall of Windows, Mormon Temple, Tower Bridge, The Alligator—which have won for the park the nickname "Silent City." Particularly in summer you'll also see plentiful and varied wildlife: cougars, gray foxes, coyote, mule deer, prairie dogs, chipmunks, and more than 160 species of birds. There are unforgettable views from **Sunset Point, Inspiration Point,** and **Bryce Point.** Rim Dr. is partly closed in winter. Camping permitted (218 sites).

For **information,** contact the Superintendent, Bryce Canyon National Park, Bryce Canyon, UT 84717 (801/834-5322).

CANYONLANDS NATIONAL PARK (248 mi./396km SE of Salt Lake City via I-15, U.S. 6, U.S. 191, and Utah 313): Huge, ocher-orange-colored rocky cliffs frowning down on the sinuous windings of the Green and Colorado Rivers, a fantasy world when seen at sunrise or sunset. Fabulous views from **Dead Horse Point, Grand View Point,** and **Needles Overlook.** Canyonlands National Park is a rocky maze cut out by 300 million years of erosion. The Colorado River, swollen with the waters of its Green River tributary, turns into a runaway bulldozer as it charges through **Cataract Canyon,** cutting gorges deep into the rock and carving out arches, columns, and needles which stand several hundred feet above the floor of the valley.

The park has only 25 mi. (40km) of surfaced roads, in the **Island in the Sky** sector; the rest, in the **Needles** and **Maze** sectors, can be reached only by Jeep, on foot, or on horseback. Many hiking trails; 80 authorized tentsites. Park open year round.

For **information,** contact the Superintendent, Canyonlands National Park, 125 W. 2nd St., Moab, UT 84532 (801/259-7164).

CAPITOL REEF NATIONAL PARK (209 mi./334km SE of Salt Lake City via I-15, Utah 28, U.S. 89, and Utah 24): Wild canyons, beetling cliffs, and rounded rocky domes reminiscent of the Capitol in Washington, whence the name. The interior of the park is difficult of access (the famous bandit Butch Cassidy once took refuge here). Along this enormous mountain wall runs a spectacular unsurfaced scenic highway, the **Scenic Drive,** following the rim of a 25-mi. (40km) chain of gorges channeled by the Fremont River. Many rock paintings bear witness to Native American cultures from the 9th to the 13th century. The north of the park, reachable only by Jeep, displays the most beautiful rock formations, particularly **Cathedral Valley.** Authorized camping (40 sites). Park open year round.

For **information,** contact the Superintendent, Capitol Reef National Park, Torrey, UT 84775 (801/425-3791).

CEDAR BREAKS NATIONAL MONUMENT (215 mi./ 344km NE of Las Vegas via I-15, Utah 14, and Utah 148): An enormous natural amphitheater created by erosion in the **Markagunt Plateau,** which rises to 9,840 ft. (3,000m). Natural rock carvings in beautiful hues of red, orange, violet, and yellow make a vivid contrast with the deep greens of the conifers of Dixie National Forest and the alpine meadows on the mountain peaks, covered with wildflowers from mid-June to mid-Aug. Scenic drive (Rim Dr.), 6 mi. (11km) long. Camping permitted. Park open mid-May to mid-Oct.

For **information,** contact the Superintendent, Cedar Breaks National Monument, P.O. Box 749, Cedar City, UT 84720 (801/586-9451).

DINOSAUR NATIONAL MONUMENT (200 mi./ 320km east of Salt Lake City along I-80 and U.S. 40): Quarries with many vestiges of prehistoric animals. The **Dinosaur Quarry Visitor Center** has remarkable animal fossils, including an extremely rare 140-million-year-old stegosaurus. Excavations in progress.

The Colorado sector of the park, an area of rugged desert and canyons sometimes as much as 2,625 ft. (800m) deep, offers unobstructed views of the Green and Yampa Rivers running below; access via U.S. 40, 2 mi. (3km) east of Dinosaur, Colo., and a 32-mi. (51km) unsurfaced road (Harpers Corner Rd.). Camping permitted. Visitor center and excavation area open year round; rest of the park closed mid-Nov to mid-Apr as dictated by snowfall.

For **information,** contact the Superintendent, Dinosaur National Monument, Harpers Corner Rd. and U.S. 40 (P.O. Box 210), Dinosaur, CO 81610 (303/374-2216); or the Quarry Visitor Center (801/789-2115).

On your way, take a side trip through the ᐃ **Flaming Gorge National Recreation Area,** 55 mi. (88km) NW of Dinosaur National Monument via U.S. 40 and U.S. 191, a huge recreation area brought into existence by the 502-ft.-high (153m) Flaming Gorge Dam on the Green River. The artificial lake, 91 mi. (146km) long, offers fishing, sailing, water sports, and marinas. Lovely scenery. For information, contact the Ranger District Office, P.O. Box 278, Manila, UT 84076 (801/784-3445).

It was in **Brown's Hole,** an inaccessible valley downstream from the dam and almost on the Colorado border, that Butch Cassidy, the Sundance Kid, and their "Wild Bunch" used to take refuge after their raids.

GLEN CANYON NATIONAL RECREATION AREA (286 mi./457km NE of Las Vegas via I-15, Utah 9, and U.S. 89): The park covers about a million acres (more than 4,000km²), off the beaten tourist track. Its multicolored cliffs are washed by the blue waters of **Lake Powell,** 196 mi. (315km) long and with 1,900 mi. (3,058km) of desert shoreline, the second-largest artificial lake (after Lake Mead) in the country. All water sports and wonderful fishing for perch, rainbow trout, moonfish, etc. Superb sunsets. A paradise for hikers and campers. Boat trips from Page to **Rainbow Bridge,** one of the biggest natural rock arches in the world, 278 ft. (85m) across by 290 ft. (88m) high. Camping permitted. Park open year round.

For **information,** contact the Superintendent, Glen Canyon National Recreation Area, P.O. Box 1507, Page, AZ 86040 (602/645-2471). (Also see Chapter 40 on Navajoland.)

☼🔔 NATURAL BRIDGES NATIONAL MONUMENT (350

mi./560km SE of Salt Lake City via I-15, Utah 28, U.S. 89, Utah 24, and Utah 95): In the comparatively small compass of 7,770 acres (3,150ha), this very beautiful, wild, colorful park, inaugurated in 1908, offers the visitor three great rock arches carved by two tributaries of the Colorado: **Kachina Bridge** (206 ft./63m across), **Owachomo Bridge** (180 ft./55m across), and **Sipapu Bridge** (258 ft./82m across). The site, once settled by the legendary Anasazi peoples, has more than 200 interesting architectural ruins, easily reached by the visitor. **Bridge View Drive** is a splendid 8-mi. (13km) scenic route winding across the canyons from the visitor center. Park open year round, but be careful in bad weather since the area is subject to violent storms.

For **information,** contact the Superintendent, Natural Bridges National Monument, P.O. Box 1, Lake Powell, UT 84533 (801/259-5174). The monument is administered from Canyonlands National Park (see above).

☼🔔🔔 ZION NATIONAL PARK (169 mi./270km NE of Las

Vegas along I-15 and Utah 9): For 225 million years the headlong Virgin River and its tributaries have carved their courses into the sandstone, limestone, and schists of the mighty **Markagunt Plateau,** creating an extraordinary triangle of precipitous gorges as deep as 2,950 ft. (900m). The river's erosion has produced a landscape of pillars, domes, and rock needles assuming the shapes of cathedrals, statues, and monuments—all under a play of colors that vary, according to the time of day and season of the year, from grayish-white through orange and bright red to the deepest violet. **Zion Canyon,** largest of these gorges, splashed with pink, red, and white, follows the windings of the Virgin River North Fork, and is fringed with woods of poplar, oak, and maple. **Zion Canyon Scenic Drive,** 7 mi. (10km) long, offers views of some of the most spectacular peaks—**The Sentinel** (7,157 ft./2,181m), **Mountain of the Sun** (6,723 ft./2,049m), **Lady Mountain** (6,940 ft./2,115m), **The Great White Throne** (6,744 ft./2,056m)—on its way to the end of the gorge and the **Temple of Sinawava,** a natural amphitheater which is at the same time a lush oasis.

Along the many hiking trails you'll encounter some surprises. One of the most popular leads from the Temple of Sinawava to **The Narrows,** an amazing rocky defile through a canyon whose walls seem almost to touch overhead, and to **Weeping Rock Trail,** where the spring welling out from the cliff face appears to be weeping (whence the name). For the more adventurous, there's the **Hidden Canyon Trail** leading to the almost inaccessible canyon, **Zion Shangri La.**

The **Mukuntuweap Valley** (the Native American name for Zion Canyon), has been inhabited by several Native American cultures, particularly the Anasazi, Pueblo, and Paiute, since about the 6th century A.D. The present names, often biblical in origin, were bestowed by the Mormon missionaries who explored the area from 1861 on. The only canyon in the country that can be seen by car "from the inside," Zion National Park is open year round, and is visited by 1.8 million people annually. Camping permitted (376 sites).

For **information,** contact the Superintendent, Zion National Park, Springdale, UT 84767 (801/772-3256).

SUGGESTED TOURING ITINERARIES

☼🔔🔔 EAST UTAH PARKS (707 mi./1,131km r.t. from/to Salt

Lake City via I-15S, U.S. 6, U.S. 191, Utah 95, Utah 24, U.S. 89, Utah 28, and I-15N): Comprehensive itinerary taking in Arches National Park, Canyonlands National Park, Natural Bridges National Monument, Glen

Canyon National Recreation Area, and Capitol Reef National Park (for details on all these, see above).

☼☖☖☖ **SOUTH UTAH PARKS** (712 mi./1,139km r.t. from/to Las Vegas via I-15N, Utah 14, Utah 148, Utah 14, U.S. 89, Utah 12, U.S. 89, Utah 9, and I-15S): One of the most beautiful trips the U.S. can offer, allowing you to see Cedar Breaks National Monument, Bryce Canyon National Park, Glen Canyon National Recreation Area, and Zion National Park (for details on all these, see above).

ACCOMMODATIONS & RESTAURANTS

PERSONAL FAVORITES: The following hotels and restaurants are grouped by location near or in individual parks.

Arches National Park and Canyonlands National Park

Best Western Green Well, 105 S. Main St., Moab, UT 84532 (801/259-6151; toll free, see Best Western). 71 rms, A/C, color TV, in-rm movies. AE, CB, DC, MC, V. Free parking, pool, rest. (beer served), coffee shop, crib $4. *Note:* Typical functional motel; huge, comfortable rms; friendly reception. In the center of town. **I,** but lower rates off-season.

Travelodge Moab, 550 S. Main St., Moab, UT 84532 (801/259-6171; toll free, see Travelodge). 56 rms, A/C, color TV, in-rm movies. AE, CB, DC, MC, V. Free parking, pool, rest., free crib. *Note:* Relatively old, but well-kept motel. Large rms. Friendly reception. Attractive family packages. **B–I,** but lower rates off-season.

Apache Motel, 166 S. 4th St., Moab, UT 84532 (801/259-5727; toll free 800/228-6882). 33 rms, A/C, color TV, in-rm movies. AE, CB, DC, MC, V. Free parking, pool, free morning coffee. *Note:* A small, inexpensive motel. Attentive svce. Some rms w. kitchenettes. Organizes river-rafting trips. Good value. **B–I,** but lower rates off-season.

☼♉ **Grand Old Ranch House,** 1266 U.S. 191 N, Moab, UT (801/259-5753). A/C. Dinner only, nightly. AE, CB, DC, MC, V. *Note:* The decor is a melange of Old West and Victorian styles (the building dates from 1896). Friendly, efficient svce. Good, German-inspired cuisine. Wine, beer, and liquor. A fine place. *Continental/American.* **I–M**

Bryce Canyon National Park

Best Western Ruby's Inn, Utah 63 (1 mi./0.6km north of the park entrance), UT 84764 (801/834-5341; toll free, see Best Western). 216 rms, A/C, color TV, in-rm movies. AE, CB, DC, MC, V. Free parking, pool, skiing and snowmobiles in winter, rodeos in summer, riding, rest., bar, boutiques, free crib. *Note:* A nice, efficient, modern motel w. a small private lake. Comfortable rms w. balconies and fireplaces (some w. kitchenettes). Very good location (5 min. from the park by car). Friendly reception and svce. Organizes helicopter tours of Bryce Canyon. An excellent place to stay. **I–M**

Bryce Canyon Pines, Utah 12 (6 mi./10km from the NW park entrance) Bryce, UT 84759 (801/834-5441). 50 rms, most w. A/C, color TV. DC, MC, V. Free parking, pool, horseback riding, rest. (beer served), crib $3. *Note:* Small, inviting motel w. huge, prettily decorated rms, some w. fireplaces. Free airport shuttle. Horseback excursions into the canyon in summer. Good value. **B–I,** but lower rates Nov–June.

☼♉ **Bryce Canyon Lodge,** Utah 12, Bryce Canyon National Park, UT 84717 (801/834-5361). 110 rms (cottages), a third w. A/C. AE, CB, DC, MC, V. Free parking, pool, horseback riding, rest., coffee shop, grocery store, crib $4. *Note:* Wonderful location in the heart of the park. Some rms modern and comfortable, others aging a little. Acceptable rest. Open mid-May to Oct; closed the rest of the year. Horseback or muleback trips into the canyon. For reservations, contact T. W. Services, 451 N. Main St. (P.O. Box 400), Cedar City, UT 84720 (801/586-7686). **I–M**

Capitol Reef National Park

Capitol Reef Inn, 300 W. Main St., Torrey, UT 84775 (801/425-3271). 10 rms, A/C, color TV. MC, V. Free parking, coffee shop. *Note:* Tiny, well-maintained, serviceable hotel. Friendly reception. Open Mar to late-Nov. **B**

Cedar Breaks National Monument

Best Western El Rey Inn, 80 S. Main St., Cedar City, UT 84720 (801/586-6518; toll free, see Best Western); 26 mi. (41km) from the park entrance. 75 rms, A/C, color TV, in-rm movies. AE, CB, DC, MC, V. Free parking, pool, sauna, rest. (beer served), rm svce, crib $4. *Note:* Comfortable, functional rms. Reception w. a smile; acceptable rest. (Sullivan's). Free airport shuttle. **B–I,** but lower rates off-season.

The Lodge at Brianhead, 314 Hunter Ridge Dr., Brianhead, UT 84719 (801/677-3222); 10 mi. (16km) north of the park entrance on Utah 143. 93 rms. A/C, color TV, in-rm movies. AE, CB, DC, MC, V. Free parking, sauna, health club, skiing in winter, coffee shop. *Note:* Engaging little resort motel 9,800 ft. (2,900m) above sea level in the heart of Dixie National Forest. Comfortable, inviting rms w. refrigerator. Friendly reception and svce. Free shuttle connection w. Cedar City airport. **I**

Dinosaur National Monument

Weston Plaza, 1684 W. U.S. 40, Vernal, UT 84078 (801/789-9550), 19 mi. (30km) west of the park entrance. 102 rms, A/C, color TV, in-rm movies. AE, CB, DC, MC, V. Free parking, pool, putting green, rest., bar, valet svce, disco, free breakfast, crib $10. *Note:* Modern, comfortable motel; spacious rms; efficient reception and svce. The best place to stay in the region. **B–I**

Weston Lamplighter Inn, 120 E. Main St., Vernal, UT 84078 (801/789-0312), 19 mi. (30km) west of the park entrance. 200 rms, A/C, color TV, in-rm movies. AE, CB, DC, MC, V. Free parking, pool, coffee shop, valet svce, crib $5. *Note:* Inviting, well-run small motel; functionally comfortable. Good value. **B–I,** but lower rates off-season.

Glen Canyon & Rainbow Bridge

Wahweap Lodge and Marina, on U.S. 89, Page, AZ 86040 (602/645-2433; toll free 800/528-6154), 5 mi. (8km) NW of Glen Canyon Bridge. 267 rms, A/C, color TV, in-rm movies. AE, CB, DC, MC, V. Free parking, two pools, beach, boating, fishing, rest., coffee shop, bar, rm svce, disco, crib $6. *Note:* Modern building, splendidly located on Lake Powell. Spacious, comfortable rms w. balconies or patios, some w. refrigerators. Reception and svce on the chilly side. Free airport shuttle. One- or several-day excursions arranged on Lake Powell and to Rainbow Bridge. Resv. advised, well ahead. **I–M,** but lower rates off-season.

Holiday Inn Page, 287 N. Lake Powell Blvd., Page, AZ 86040 (602/645-8851; toll free, see Holiday Inns), 1 mi. (1.6km) from Glen Canyon Bridge. 129 rms, A/C, color TV, in-rm movies. AE, CB, DC, MC, V. Free parking, pool, rest., bar, rm svce, hrdrsr, free crib. *Note:* Typical Holiday Inn; huge, comfortable rms w. balconies or patios, the best overlooking Lake Powell. Good svce. Free airport shuttle. **I–M,** but lower rates off-season.

Lake Powell Motel, on U.S. 89, Page, AZ 86040 (602/645-2477; toll free 800/528-6154), 5 mi. (8km) northwest of Glen Canyon Bridge. 24 rms, A/C, color TV. AE, CB, DC, MC, V. Free parking, free morning coffee, crib $5. *Note:* Unpretentious little motel w. a fine view of Glen Canyon and Lake Powell. Boats for rent; free airport shuttle. Same management as the Wahweap Lodge and Marina. **B–I,** but lower rates off-season.

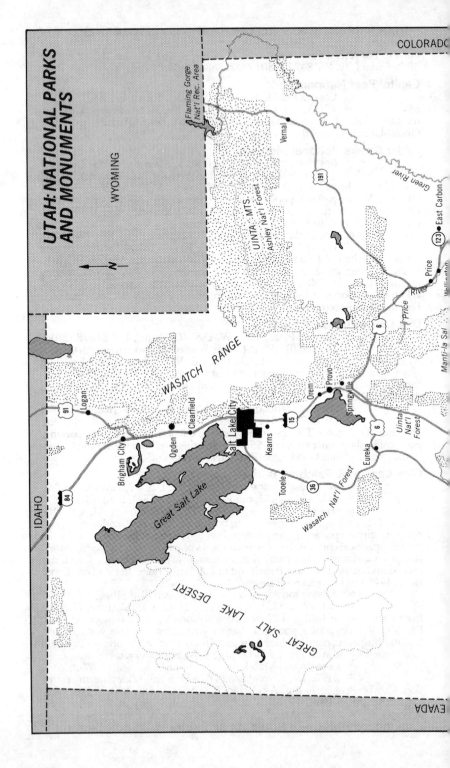

UTAH: NATIONAL PARKS
AND MONUMENTS

N

WYOMING

COLORADO

Flaming Gorge
Nat'l Rec. Area

Vernal

191

Green River

East Carbon

123

Price

Price River

Wellington

6

UINTA MTS.

Ashley Nat'l Forest

Manti-La Sal

WASATCH RANGE

Provo

Orem

Springville

6

Uinta Nat'l Forest

IDAHO

Logan

91

Brigham City

Ogden

Clearfield

Salt Lake City

15

Kearns

84

Great Salt Lake

Tooele

36

Eureka

Wasatch Nat'l Forest

GREAT SALT LAKE DESERT

NEVADA

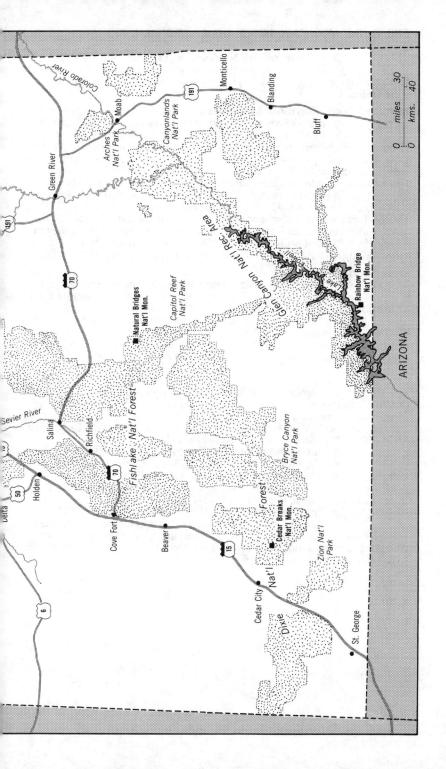

♀ **Bella Napoli,** 810 N. Navajo Dr., Page (602/645-2706). A/C.
♈ Dinner only, nightly; closed Nov to early Mar. MC, V. *Note:*
Small *trattoria* serving grilled scampi, pizza, and honest Italian entrees. Beer and wine. *Italian.* **I**

Natural Bridges National Monument

♀ **Best Western Gateway,** 88 E. Center St., Blanding, UT
⫣ 84511 (801/678-2278; toll free, see Best Western), 46 mi.
(74km) east of the park entrance. 57 rms, A/C, color TV, in-rm movies. AE, CB, DC, MC, V. Free parking, pool, nearby coffee shop. *Note:* Comfortable, very well-run small motel a 45-min. drive from Natural Bridges National Monument. Spacious rms; friendly reception. Free airport shuttle. A very good address. **B–I**

♀ **San Juan Inn,** on U.S. 163 at the San Juan River, Mexican Hat,
⫣ UT 84531 (801/683-2220). 22 rms, A/C, color TV. AE,
MC, V. Free parking, coffee shop (beer served), crib $4. *Note:* Modest but serviceable motel on the San Juan River, 15-min. drive from Monument Valley and 45 min. from Natural Bridges National Monument. Good value on balance. Arranges rafting trips down the river and conducted tours of Monument Valley. **B**

Zion National Park

☼⫣♀ **Best Western Driftwood Lodge,** on Utah 9, Springdale, UT
84767 (801/772-3262; toll free, see Best Western), 2 mi.
(3.5km) south of the park entrance. 47 rms, A/C, color TV. AE, CB, DC, MC, V. Free parking, pool, rest. (beer and wine served), rm svce, crib $2. *Note:* Charming little motel surrounded by grdns and trees. Comfortable rms w. balconies, overlooking the park; friendly reception and svce. Very acceptable rest. An excellent place to stay. **B–I,** but lower rates off-season.

☼♀ **Zion Lodge,** Scenic Dr., Zion National Park, UT 84767 (801/
772-3213). 121 rms, A/C. AE, CB, DC, MC, V. Free parking,
rest. (beer served), coffee shop, crib $4. *Note:* The only motel inside the park itself, in a superb natural setting. Friendly reception and svce; rustic comforts. Horseback excursions and conducted bus tours through the canyon arranged. For resv., contact T.W. Services, 451 N. Main St. (P.O. Box 400), Cedar City, UT 84720 (801/586-7686). Open Apr–Nov. **I–M**

♀ **Bumbleberry Inn,** 897 Zion Park Blvd. (Utah 9), Springdale,
⫣ UT 84767 (801/772-3224), 1 mi. (1.6km) south of the park
entrance. 24 rms, A/C, color TV. CB, DC, MC, V. Free parking, pool, rest. *Note:* Well-run, functional small motel. Spacious rms, some w. balconies. Inviting grdn. Good value. **B,** but lower rates off-season.

♀ **Zion Park Motel,** Utah 9, Springdale, UT 84767 (801/772-
⫣ 3251), 1 mi. (1.6km) south of the park entrance. 24 rms, A/C,
color TV, in-rm movies. AE, MC, V. Free parking, pool, adjacent coffee shop. *Note:* Unpretentious motel offering decent standards of comfort; caters mostly to families. **B–I,** but lower rates off-season.

CHAPTER 33

YELLOWSTONE NATIONAL PARK🍦🍦🍦🍦

□ □ □

And Grand Teton National Park

A masterpiece of unspoiled nature, **Yellowstone National Park** is the most beautiful in the U.S., and probably in the world; nowhere else on the surface of the planet will you find such an astonishing variety of scenery gathered together in one place. With its boiling geysers, hot springs, steep canyons, mud volcanoes, frozen lakes, deep pine forests, dizzying waterfalls, and fossilized trees, Yellowstone is a glorious, untamed cross section of the North American continent—and one which, geologists tell us, has been three billion years in the making.

The wildlife is the entire animal kingdom in a nutshell: bison, elk, deer, pronghorn, black bear, grizzly, wild sheep, coyote, cougar, beaver, muskrat, and countless species of birds and fish. The whole great volcanic plateau, 60 mi. (100km) long and 56 mi. (90km) wide, lying some 7,870 ft. (2,400m) above sea level, is stitched together by 250 mi. (400km) of impeccably surfaced roads and more than 1,000 mi. (1,600km) of marked trails. The park is open, weather permitting, May–Oct, but its northern and northeastern entrances remain open year round (for snowmobiles only in winter). In all, nearly 2.8 million people every summer, and almost 100,000 every winter, visit the park, its six hotels and 12 campgrounds. Needless to say, reservations are a must for the peak months of July and Aug.

The uncanny alliance of the two normally hostile elements of fire and water constitute Yellowstone's principal tourist attractions. The park possesses no fewer than 10,000 hot springs and almost 200 geysers bubbling up from the bowels of the earth. To the amazement of many visitors, some geysers like the famous **Old Faithful** spew their columns of steam and boiling water dozens of feet into the air with clockwork regularity; others lie dormant for weeks, or years, before bursting forth again. All around lies an ominous landscape of evil-smelling fumaroles, multicolored pools, and boiling cauldrons of bubbling, sulfurous mud. Yet only a few miles away, the golden splendor of the **Grand Canyon of the Yellowstone** with its falls higher than Niagara's, or the azure depths of **Yellowstone Lake,** the largest mountain lake in the country at an elevation of 7,731 ft. (2,357m), await to take your mind off the nightmare spectacle of **Mud Volcano** or **Dragon Mouth.** The catastrophic 1988 fires consumed 780,000 of the 2.2 million acres of the park (315,800ha of the park's 890,000ha). The recovery process has added a new dimension to this wonder of nature, larger than the state of Rhode Island—fire-blackened trees now stand in fields of lush grass, shrubs, and wildflowers. Yellowstone Park's major attractions, including the Grand Canyon of the Yellowstone River, were unaffected by the fires of '88; most of the fire damage was in the park's backcountry areas.

Yellowstone is too large, and too varied, for a quick visit; many of its slopes are still untrodden, and can be reached only on foot or horseback.

Grand Teton National Park, one-seventh the size of Yellowstone and more mountainous in its contours, is open year round. Its impressive mountain range numbers 31 peaks rising above 10,825 ft. (3,300m); the highest, **Grand Teton** itself, soars to 13,770 ft. (4,197m). This is a "young" granite range, little more than 10 million years old. It owes its name to the romantic imagination of 19th-century French-Canadian trappers, who saw in these sparkling, pointed snow-capped peaks rising above the valley of **Jackson Hole,** some fancied likeness to a woman's breast. More than 187 mi. (300km) of marked trails offer an unlimited choice of hiking or skiing excursions, according to the season. With the torrential **Snake River,** deep forests, lakes full of fish, and inaccessible mountain peaks, Grand Teton National Park encompasses some of the most beautiful natural landscapes in the U.S.

Wildlife Warning! While Yellowstone is a paradise for campers and mobile-home owners, camping is subject to very strict rules enforced by watchful rangers. As in all national parks, camping in the wild is strictly forbidden. There are also some simple precautions that must be taken regarding animals. Living free as they do, with no reason to fear human beings, animals will allow themselves to be photographed from quite close, especially around dawn and sunset. However, prudence is mandatory if you suddenly come face to face with a bear (there are about 500 black and grizzly bears inside the park), an elk (about 30,000), or a buffalo (about 2,500). Never feed or hold food within reach of an animal.

BASIC FACTS: State of Wyoming (with slight enroachments into the neighboring states of Idaho and Montana). Area code: 307. Time zone: mountain. ZIP Codes: Yellowstone, 82190; Grand Teton, 83013. Inaugurated: 1872 (Yellowstone is the oldest nature reserve in the world); 1929 (Grand Teton). Area: Yellowstone, 3,472 sq. mi. (8,993km²); Grand Teton, 486 sq. mi. (1,260km²).

CLIMATE: At these altitudes, winter is long and icy at Yellowstone and Grand Teton; mean temperatures are 5°F (−15°C). Heavy snowfalls, sometimes 16 ft. (5m) or more, make it very difficult to get around, even by snowmobile, from late Oct through Apr. Summer is short, sunny, and cool; everyone wears a sweater in the evening. You should take a raincoat or poncho too, because of occasional heavy rain in the afternoon. Fall is the perfect time for the color photographer. Whatever the season, don't try a swim in the lakes; even in summer the water temperature never goes above 40°F (5°C), and if you were to fall in you wouldn't survive as long as half an hour.

DISTANCES: Denver, 638 mi. (1,022km); Mount Rushmore, 549 mi. (875km); Salt Lake City, 325 mi. (520km); Seattle, 762 mi. (1,219km).

ARRIVAL & TRANSIT INFORMATION

NEAREST AIRPORTS: Bozeman Gallatin Field (BZN), 131 mi. (210km) NW of Yellowstone National Park; open year round.

Jackson Hole (JAC), 13 mi. (21km) south of Grand Teton National Park and 79 mi. (128km) south of Yellowstone National Park; open year round.

West Yellowstone (WYS), 30 mi. (48km) west of Yellowstone National Park; open in summer only.

AIRLINES: Several airlines fly into the area's three airports:
At Bozeman Gallatin Field: Continental (toll free 800/525-0280), Delta (toll free 800/221-1212), and Northwest (toll free 800/225-2525).
At Jackson Hole: American (toll free 800/433-7300), Continental (toll free 800/525-0280), and Delta (toll free 800/221-1212).

At West Yellowstone: Delta Connection (toll free 800/221-1212), in summer only.

BUS OR CAR RENTAL? Greyhound serves neither Yellowstone nor Grand Teton National Park.

Gray Line Tours provides a shuttle bus from Jackson (307/733-4325) and **West Yellowstone** (404/646-9374) (one departure daily Memorial Day–Labor Day). **4×4 Stage** (toll free 800/517-8243) provides a shuttle bus from **Bozeman** (five departures daily from mid-Dec to late March and two daily from mid-June to mid-Sept). The same companies operate bus tours inside Yellowstone and Grand Teton Parks.

Given the distances, it makes sense to rent a car, but rates are relatively high and the choice of models is restricted.

CAR RENTAL: Rental cars are available at all three area airports.

At Bozeman Gallatin Field: Avis (toll free 800/331-1212), Budget (toll free 800/527-0700), Hertz (toll free 800/654-3131), and National (toll free 800/227-7368).

At Jackson Hole: Avis (toll free 800/331-1212), Budget (toll free 800/527-0700), Hertz (toll free 800/654-3131), and National (toll free 800/227-7368).

At West Yellowstone Airport (summer only): Avis (toll free 800/331-1212), Budget (toll free 800/527-0700), Hertz (toll free 800/654-3131), and National (toll free 800/227-7368).

TRAIN: The nearest Amtrak station is 135 mi. (215km) SW of Grand Teton National Park at 300 S. Harrison Ave., Pocatello, Idaho (toll free 800/872-7245).

INTERCITY BUSES: Greyhound has stations at 625 N. 7th St., Bozeman (406/587-3110), open year round; and at 127 Yellowstone Ave., West Yellowstone (406/646-7666), open in summer only.

INFORMATION & TOURS

TOURIST INFORMATION: The **Cody County Chamber of Commerce,** 836 Sheridan Ave. (P.O. Box 2777), Cody, WY 82414 (307/587-2297).

Grand Teton National Park: Superintendent, P.O. Drawer 170, Moose, WY 83012 (307/733-2880). There are visitors centers at Colter Bay, Jenny Lake, and Moose.

Jackson Hole Area Chamber of Commerce, 532 N. Cache St. (P.O. Box E), Jackson, WY 83001 (307/733-3316; toll free 800/782-0011).

Yellowstone National Park Headquarters: P.O. Box 168, Yellowstone, WY 82190 (307/344-2107). There are visitors centers at Canyon Village, Fishing Bridge, Grant Village, Mammoth Hot Springs, Norris, and Old Faithful.

GUIDED TOURS: Gray Line Tours (bus): Conducted bus tours of Grand Teton and Yellowstone National Park. Serves principal hotels in Jackson from 140 N. Cache St. (307/733-4325) and West Yellowstone (406/646-9374).

TW Recreational Services, Inc. (307/344-7901): Offering a score of all-season recreational excursions including bus tours, horseback riding, hiking, and boating; serves the park's principal hotels at Canyon Village, Fishing Bridge, Mammoth Hot Springs, and Old Faithful.

SIGHTS, ATTRACTIONS & ACTIVITIES

ADVENTURES: Backcountry Bicycle Tours (bicycle), P.O. Box 4029, Bozeman, MT 59772 (406/586-3556): Six-day bicycle tours of Yellowstone National Park. $1,079 per head, including lodging in hotels, all meals, and van support. June–Sept. Offering paddling trips also.

Exum School of Mountaineering (climbing), P.O. Box 56, Moose, WY 83012 (307/733-2297): One- or two-day climbs, with guides, in Grand Teton National Park (year round). Also climbing school.

Wagons West (covered wagons), P.O. Box 1156, Afton, WY 83110 (toll free 800/447-4711): Back to the days of the pioneers with two-, four-, or six-day covered-wagon trips. Serves the principal Jackson hotels; resv. a must. Mon–Sat late May to early Sept. Spectacular.

Jackson Hole Climbing School (climbing), 165 N. Glenwood (P.O. Box 547), Teton Village, WY 83205 (307/733-4979): Climbing school and guided climbs in summer. For the dedicated.

Jackson Hole Llamas (llama), P.O. Box 7375, Jackson, WY 83001 (307/739-1437): Five-day llama treks through Yellowstone and the Tetons. Weekly from June to mid-Sept. About $170 a day per head, including van service, meals, and any pertinent equipment.

Lewis & Clark Expeditions (boat), 145 W. Gill St., Jackson, WY 83001 (307/733-4022; toll free 800/648-2602): White-water float trips down the Grand Canyon of the Snake River, a three- to six-hour trip. June to mid-Sept. Amusing.

National Park Float Trips (boat), P.O. Box 120, Moose, WY 83012 (307/733-6445): Boat or raft trips in Grand Teton National Park; bus connection from Jackson. Late May to mid-Sept.

Teton Country Prairie Schooner Holiday (covered wagons), Bar-T-Five Ranch, P.O. Box 2140, Jackson, WY 83001 (307/733-5386): Four-day covered-wagon trip between Yellowstone National Park and Grand Teton National Park; a guaranteed whiff of adventure. $545 per head, including meals. Mid-June to Aug.

Wild West Jeep Tours (four-wheel-drive), P.O. Box 7506, Jackson, WY 83001 (307/733-9036 or 602/941-8355): Half-day tours of the Grand Tetons and other areas. Daily June–Sept.

Wyoming River Trips (boat), 1701 Sheridan Ave., Cody, WY 82414 (307/587-6661): Float trips through Red Rock Shoshone Canyon; spectacular. May to early Oct.

☀🐚🏔 **GRAND TETON NATIONAL PARK:** The entrance is 13 mi. (21km) north of Jackson via U.S. 89.

☀🏔 **Jackson Hole,** 8 mi. (13km) north from Jackson on U.S. 89: A huge basin ("hole" was the vernacular term for basin, or valley, among the *coureurs de bois*) of glacial origin, 50 mi. (80km) long and 14 mi. (23km) wide at its widest, traversed by the turbulent **Snake River** and dotted by clear lakes teeming with fish: **Jackson Lake, Jenny Lake, Phelps Lake, Emma Matilda Lake,** etc. This high alpine valley, moist and fertile, with an abundance of elk, deer, buffalo, white pelicans, duck, and wild geese, has some magnificent views across to the granite crests of the **Grand Teton Range.** Many **campsites,** particularly at Colter Bay, Jenny Lake, Lizard Creek, Gros Ventre, and Signal Mountain. **Boat rental** at Jackson and Jenny Lakes. The **John D. Rockefeller**

Parkway (U.S. 89), crossing the park from north to south, is usable year round. For information on road conditions, weather, and park activities, call 307/733-2880.

☀☖☖ **Rendezvous Peak,** 12 mi. (19km) NW of Jackson via Wyo. 22 and Wyo. 390: Aerial tramway from **Teton Village** to the top of Rendezvous Peak, 10,450 ft. (3,185m) high. Wonderful view of Jackson Hole Valley and the Grand Tetons. Late May to late Sept. For information, call 307/733-2291.

Scenic Drives

☖ **Bridger-Teton National Forest,** 56 mi. (89km) between Dubois and Moran Junction along U.S. 26: Splendid forest scenery.

☀☖☖ **John D. Rockefeller Parkway,** 58 mi. (92km) between Jackson and Yellowstone National Park along U.S. 89: Follows the Snake River and the shore of Jackson Lake through very fine mountain scenery. Spectacular.

☀☖ **Signal Mountain Rd.,** 13 mi. (20km) NE of Moose Junction via Teton Park Rd.: Scenic drive 5 mi. (8km) long; from the top you'll have an unequalled view of Jackson Lake and the surrounding peaks.

☀☖☖☖ **YELLOWSTONE NATIONAL PARK:** The main entrance is 59 mi. (95km) north of Jackson via U.S. 89; east entrance, 53 mi. (85km) west of Cody via U.S. 20; north entrance, 85 mi. (136km) SE of Bozeman via I-90 and U.S. 89.

☖ **Gibbon Falls,** 29 mi. (47km) south of Mammoth Hot Springs on Grand Loop Rd.: Broad falls, with a drop of 84 ft. (26m) along the river of the same name.

☀☖☖ **Grand Canyon of the Yellowstone,** 37 mi. (60km) SE of Mammoth Hot Springs on Grand Loop Rd.: The most glorious scenery in the park. Two dizzying falls, the 308-ft. (94m) **Lower Falls** (1½ times the height of Niagara) and the 109-ft. (33m) **Upper Falls.** Wild gorges, up to 1,200 ft. (366m) deep in places, with a perpetual play of yellow-to-orange color over their walls (whence the name of the Yellowstone River). A scenic drive links the main observation points, of which those at **Inspiration Point** and **Artist Point** are the most interesting.

☖ **Obsidian Cliff,** 15 mi. (24km) south of Mammoth Hot Springs on Grand Loop Rd.: A great cliff, 246 ft. (75m) high and 885 ft. (270m) wide, composed of volcanic glass (obsidian), from which the Native Americans used to quarry material for their arrowheads.

☖ **Shoshone Lake,** 8 mi. (13km) east of Old Faithful on Grand Loop Rd., then 2½ mi. (4km) south by footpath: Beautiful wild isolated lake, reachable only on foot or on horseback. For lovers of unspoiled nature.

☀☖ **Tower Falls,** 21 mi. (33km) east of Mammoth Hot Springs on Grand Loop Rd.: Spectacular 132-ft. (40m) falls on the Yellowstone River; its name comes from its rock formations in the shape of towers or broken columns.

☖ **Virginia Cascades,** 24 mi. (38km) SE of Mammoth Hot Springs on Grand Loop Rd.: Beautiful waterfalls and rapids in the depths of the forest; one-way scenic drive.

☀☖☖ **Yellowstone Lake,** 22 mi. (36km) north of the southern entrance to the park on U.S. 89: The highest (7,731 ft./2,357m), and, with its azure-blue waters, perhaps the most beautiful mountain lake in the U.S. It covers 138 sq. mi. (360km²) and is 308 ft. (94m) deep at its deepest. The water is icy-cold even in summer. View clear over to the distant **Absaroka Range,** with a dozen peaks rising above 9,840 ft. (3,000m). Boat trips from **Bridge Bay Marina** and **Grant Village Marina.**

Geysers and Thermal Springs

Yellowstone National Park has almost 200 geysers, more than any other place in the world except Iceland and New Zealand, and some 10,000 hot springs. Among the most impressive are:

Artist Paint Pots, between Norris Junction and Madison Junction along Grand Loop Rd.: A little footpath leads from Gibbon Meadows to these multicolored hot springs.

Beryl Spring, between Norris Junction and Madison Junction along Grand Loop Rd.: One of the most beautiful springs in the park.

Lower Geyser Basin, between Madison Junction and Old Faithful along Grand Loop Rd.: Comprises 25 geysers and 700 hot springs, among them **Fountain Paint Pot,** a flamboyant yellow-and-red cauldron, and two reliable geysers: **Great Fountain Geyser** erupts every 6–10 hr. to a height of 98–196 ft. (30–60m), and **White Dome Geyser** erupts every 17–90 min. to a height of 19–29 ft. (6–9m), with a fine concretion dome.

Mammoth Hot Springs, 5 mi. (8km) south of the northern entrance to the park on U.S. 89: Fantastic limestone terraces formed from suspended material deposited by some 60 hot springs issuing at temperatures of 64°–165°F (18°–74°C). The steps, in a variety of shades of white, bright yellow, ocher, and green, have been built up since prehistoric times to heights of as much as 196 ft. (60m) in places. A wonder of natural beauty. Scenic drive to the top.

Midway Geyser Basin, between Madison Junction and Old Faithful along Grand Loop Rd.: Famous for its colorful hot springs, particularly the **Excelsior Geyser,** a deep-blue lake 393 ft. (120m) long on the site of a huge geyser which has been dormant since 1888, and the **Grand Prismatic Spring,** a great smoking pool whose waters refract all the colors of the rainbow (elevated observation road).

Monument Geyser, between Norris Junction and Madison Junction along Grand Loop Rd.: Along a little footpath from the bridge across the Gibbon River, you'll have a two-hour walk to this continually active geyser with a throw of 5–10 ft. (1.5–3m).

Mud Volcano and Black Dragon's Cauldron, between Yellowstone Lake and Canyon Village along Grand Loop Dr.: Huge witches' cauldron, grumbling and boiling, whose super-heated mud wells up and bursts in great evil-smelling bubbles. A fascinating sight.

Norris Geyser Basin, 1 mi. (1.6km) west of Norris Junction along Grand Loop Dr.: Has some of the park's most spectacular hot springs, including the lovely emerald-colored **Emerald Springs** and the astonishing rainbow-colored **Porcelain Basin** (elevated observation road), as well as such impressive geysers as **Constant Geyser** (erupts several times an hour to a height of 30–40 ft./9–12m), and **Steamboat Geyser,** the highest in the park, with a throw of 20–380 ft. (6–116m) every 30–60 sec. Visitor center at **Norris.**

Old Faithful, in front of the Old Faithful Inn at Old Faithful: The park's most famous, and most photographed, attraction. For more than a century Old Faithful has erupted with clockwork regularity for 2–5 min., to a mean height of 130 ft. (40m), once an hour. Since 1986, however, it has shown signs of flagging, and now erupts on the average every 72 min. A boon to devotees of souvenir snapshots.

Sulphur Cauldron, between Yellowstone Lake and Canyon Village along Grand Loop Rd.: Boiling springs emitting sulfurous steam along the steep banks of the Yellowstone River.

Upper Geyser Basin, between Madison Junction and Old Faithful along Grand Loop Rd.: Nearly 70 geysers clustered around Old Faithful; among the most spectacular are **Castle Geyser** (every 3–10 hr.; 65–100 ft./20–30m), **Daisy Geyser** (irregular; 75 ft./23m), **Grand Geyser** (every 18–90 hr.; 200 ft./60m), and **River Side Geyser** (every 6–9 hr.; 75 ft./23m). Across Grand Loop Rd. in **Black Sand Basin** are countless petrified trees and a splendid emerald-green hot spring, **Emerald Pool,** issuing at 158°F (70°C). The most impressive group of geological phenomena in the park.

🔔 **West Thumb Geyser Basin,** on the western shore of Yellowstone Lake by Grand Loop Rd.: Miniature geysers and an array of hot springs beside the lake; beautiful scenery.

Scenic Drives

☀🔔 **Buffalo Bill Highway,** 80 mi. (128km) between Fishing Bridge, Yellowstone Lake, and Cody along U.S. 20: A two-hour drive of rare scenic splendor passing **Shoshone Canyon, Sylvan Pass,** and the **Absaroka Mountains.** Wonderful view of **Yellowstone Lake** from **Lake Butte** (8,344 ft./2,544m).

☀🔔🔔 **Canyon Rim Scenic Road,** 1 mi. (1.6km) east or 2½ mi. (4km) south of Canyon Village on Grand Loop Rd.: A scenic drive of some 5 mi. (8km), partly on a one-way highway, along both rims of the Grand Canyon of the Yellowstone. Wonderful views of gorges and falls from **Inspiration Point, Lookout Point, Artist Point,** and **Grandview Point.**

☀🔔🔔 **Grand Loop Road,** 22 mi. (35km) north of the southern entrance to the park: Yellowstone Park's busiest road, a 142-mi. (227km) "figure 8," linking all the park's scenic sights and tourist attractions.

☀🔔🔔 **Mount Washburn Trail,** 10 mi. (17km) NE of Canyon Village along Grand Loop Rd.: If you make an 8-mi. (13km) hike to the 10,243-ft. (3,122m) top of **Mount Washburn** (6½-hr. r.t.), you'll find the most beautiful view in the entire park, from the distant Grand Tetons to Jackson Lake. Only for seasoned walkers.

SPECIAL EVENTS: For the exact schedule of events below, consult the **Cody County Chamber of Commerce** and **Jackson Hole Area Chamber of Commerce** (see "Tourist Information," above).

Cody

Frontier Festival (June): Music, dancing, craft shows, open-air meals, horse shows, games . . . the Old West come to life again.

Plains Indian Powwow (late June): Festival of traditional Native American music and dance; many tribes from the U.S. and Canada take part. Colorful.

Jackson

Shriner's Cutter Race (Feb): Dog-sled championship.

"The Shootout" (Memorial Day–Labor Day): Amusing parody of a western melodrama performed nightly evenings in the Town Sq.

Jackson Hole Rodeo (Memorial Day–Labor Day): Real cowboy atmosphere; Wed and Sat. For information, call 307/733-2805.

Jackson Hole Fall Arts Festival (three weeks from mid-Sept to early Oct): Art shows, performances, dance, theater, film festival, etc.

Teton Village

Grand Teton Music Festival (June–Aug): Symphony concerts, chamber music, classical recitals—more than 40 different programs. At Teton Village, a very popular festival; for information, call toll free 800/959-4863.

WINTER SPORTS RESORTS: 🔔🔔 **Alta-Grand Targhee Resort,** 42 mi. (67km) NW of Jackson via Wyo. 22, Idaho 31, and Idaho 33 (307/353-2304; toll free 800/827-4433): Three lifts; open mid-Nov to mid-Apr.

🔔 **Old Faithful,** 30 mi. (48km) SE of West Yellowstone via U.S. 20 and Grand Loop Rd. (307/344-7381): No lifts; cross-country skiing only. Open mid-Dec to mid-Mar.

🎿 **Snow King Mountain,** 0.6 mi. (1km) south of Jackson on U.S.
⛷ 26 (307/733-5200): Three lifts. Open Dec–Apr.
🎿🎿 **Teton Village,** 13 mi. (20km) NW of Jackson via Wyo. 22 and
⛷⛷ Wyo. 390 (703/733-2292; toll free 800/443-6931): One
aerial tram, eight lifts. Also cross-country skiing, climbing. Open Dec to mid-
Apr.

ACCOMMODATIONS

Personal Favorites Inside the Parks (in order of preference)

GRAND TETON For reservations for the three hotels listed, contact **Grand Teton
Lodge Co.,** P.O. Box 250, Moran, WY 83013 (307/543-2855).
☼🛏🛏 **Jackson Lake Lodge,** U.S. 89, Moran, WY 83013 (307/543-
2855). 385 rms (42 in the hotel, others in cottages), A/C.
AE, MC, V. Free parking, pool, horseback riding, fishing, bicycles, rest.
(Mural Room), coffee shop, bar, rm svce (until 10pm), nightclub, hrdrsr, airport
shuttle, boutiques, free crib. *Note:* Large, modern, comfortable chalet-hotel
overlooking Jackson Lake. The best rms (w. patios or balconies) are in the
main building; the cottages are more rustic. Magnificent view of the Grand
Tetons; beautiful glass-walled dining rm overlooking the lake. Very acceptable
food and svce. Organizes downstream rafting trips. The best place to stay in
Grand Teton National Park; hosted the American-Soviet discussions between
James Baker and Edward Shevardnadze in 1989. Open June to mid-Sept
only. **M**
☼🛏🛏 **Jenny Lake Lodge,** Jenny Lake Rd., Moran, WY 83013 (307/
733-4647). 30 bungalows (no A/C). AE, MC, V. Free park-
ing, fishing, horseback riding, bicycles, rest., airport shuttle, free crib. *Note:* Log-
cabin bungalows in the woods, w. private patios. Rustic comfort; for nature lovers. Has the best rest. in the park (resv. a must). Cheerful reception. Open June to
mid-Sept. **VE** (Modified American Plan).
🛏 **Colter Bay Village,** U.S. 89, Moran, WY 83013 (307/543-
2855). 209 rms in bungalows (no A/C). AE, MC, V. Free
parking, fishing, marina, horseback riding, rest., coffee shop, bar, boutiques, free
crib. *Note:* Bungalows among pine trees on Jackson Lake; pleasing rustic decor.
Very good value. Open May–Sept. **I–M**

YELLOWSTONE For reservations for the six hotels listed, contact **TW Recreational Services,** Yellowstone National Park, WY 82190 (307/344-7311). Unless
otherwise indicated none of the hotels listed below is air-conditioned.
☼🛏🛏 **Lake Yellowstone Hotel,** Grand Loop Rd., Yellowstone National Park, WY 82190 (307/344-7311). 292 rms (half w.
bath). AE, MC, V. Free parking, fishing, boating, rest., bar, hrdrsr, free crib.
Note: Aging but still-elegant hotel beautifully situated on the shores of Yellowstone Lake. Huge, relatively comfortable rms (ask for a lake view); agreeable
glass-walled dining rm; food and svce acceptable but no better. Open from the
end of May through Sept. Also 110 bungalows offering rudimentary comforts.
I–M
☼🛏 **Old Faithful Inn,** Grand Loop Rd., Yellowstone National Park,
WY 82190 (307/344-7311). 320 rms (half w. bath). AE, MC,
V. Free parking, coffee shop, bar, nightclub, free crib. *Note:* A 1902 hotel in a
diverting baroque-chalet style; wonderful entrance lobby, all in wood and four
stories high. Rms are spacious but stark (ask for one overlooking the Old Faithful
geyser). The plumbing could use some improvements, as could the food and the
reception. The place is pleasant on balance, however—and its situation is like no
other in the world. Open May to mid-Oct only; the neighboring **Old Faithful
Snow Lodge** (65 rms) is open Dec–Mar. **B–I**

♀ **Canyon Village Lodge & Cabins,** Grand Loop Rd., Yellowstone National Park, WY 82190 (307/344-7311). 588 rms (chalets). AE, MC, V. Free parking, horseback riding, rest., coffee shop, bar, hrdrsr, boutiques, free crib. *Note:* Rustic group of comfortable little cottages. Mediocre food, as everywhere in the park. Open June–Aug. **B–I**

♀ **Grant Village,** on U.S. 89, Yellowstone National Park, WY 82190 (307/344-7311), 2 mi. (3.25km) south of Grand Loop Rd. 296 rms. AE, DC, MC, V. Free parking, coffee shop, bar. *Note:* The newest (1984) and most up-to-date motel in the park, on Yellowstone Lake. Functionally comfortable. Open June–Sept. **I**

♀ **Mammoth Hot Springs Hotel & Cabins,** Grand Loop Rd. and U.S. 89, Yellowstone National Park, WY 82190 (307/344-7311). 94 rms (two-thirds w. bath) and 132 bungalows (half w. bath). AE, MC, V. Free parking, adj. coffee shop, bar, free crib. *Note:* Run-down old hotel 5 mi. (8km) south of the northern park entrance. Ask for a bungalow overlooking the petrified hot springs. Dour reception; resolutely mediocre coffee shop. Closed Apr and Oct–Nov; open all the rest of the year. **B–I**

☼♀ **Roosevelt Lodge & Cabins,** Grand Loop Rd. at Tower Junction, Yellowstone National Park, WY 82190 (307/344-7311). 80 rms and cottages (a third w. bath). AE, MC, V. Free parking, horseback riding, coffee shop. *Note:* The most primitive, but also the most inviting, of the park's motels; it stands on a favorite campsite of Pres. Theodore Roosevelt, whence its name. Rather austere but pleasantly homelike log cabins in the woods. Stagecoach rides and evening steak cookouts cowboy style. For western fans. Open June to mid-Sept. **B–I**

Personal Favorites Outside the Parks (in order of preference)

♀♀♀ **Jackson Hole Racquet Club,** Star Rte. 3647, Jackson, WY 83001 (307/733-3990; toll free 800/443-8616). 120 suites and apts., cable color TV. AE, MC, V. Free parking, two pools, tennis court, squash, health club, sauna, skiing, rest., bar, grocery store, free crib. *Note:* The most luxurious resort hotel in the area. Elegantly countrified decor. Spacious, comfortable suites w. kitchenettes, refrigerators, fireplaces, and balconies or private patios; also two- or three-bedroom apts. Flawless reception and svce; clientele of groups and racquets buffs. Open year round; reserve a long time ahead. Free shuttle to ski slopes. **E–VE,** but lower rates off-season.

♀♀ **Alpenhof Lodge,** on Wyo. 390, Teton Village, WY 83025 (307/733-3242). 40 rms, cable color TV. AE, CB, DC, MC, V. Free parking, pool, sauna, skiing, horseback riding, rest. (Alpenhof), rm svce, crib $6. *Note:* Charming little alpine chalet; inviting rms, most w. balconies. Attentive svce; excellent rest. (one of the best in the area). Ideal for winter sports or for visiting Grand Teton Park. A fine place to stay. Owner Dietrich Oberreit and his family run it in the best tradition of Tyrolean innkeeping. Closed Apr to mid-May and Oct–Nov. **M–E**

♀♀ **Snow King Resort,** 400 E. Snow King Dr. (U.S. 89), Jackson, WY 83001 (307/733-5200; toll free 800/522-5464). 204 rms, A/C, cable color TV. AE, CB, DC, MC, V. Free parking, pool sauna, skiing, rest., coffee shop, bar, rm svce, disco, hrdrsr. *Note:* Large, modern, comfortable hotel at the base of the Snow King slopes. Huge, inviting rms, some w. balcony and views of the mountains. Ideal for winter sports. Good svce; acceptable rest. (Rafferty's); free airport shuttle. Open year round; group and convention clientele. **E,** but lower rates off-season.

☼♀♀ **Shoshone Lodge,** U.S. 20 (P.O. Box 790WT), Cody, WY 82414 (307/587-4044), 4 mi. (6km) east of the eastern entrance to Yellowstone National Park. 16 cottages (3 w. kitchenette). MC, V. Free parking, fishing, skiing, horseback riding, coffee shop, crib $2. *Note:* Small, inviting rustic motel on Grinnell Creek. Comfortable, individual log cabins. The kind of relaxed western atmosphere you associate w. campfires and square

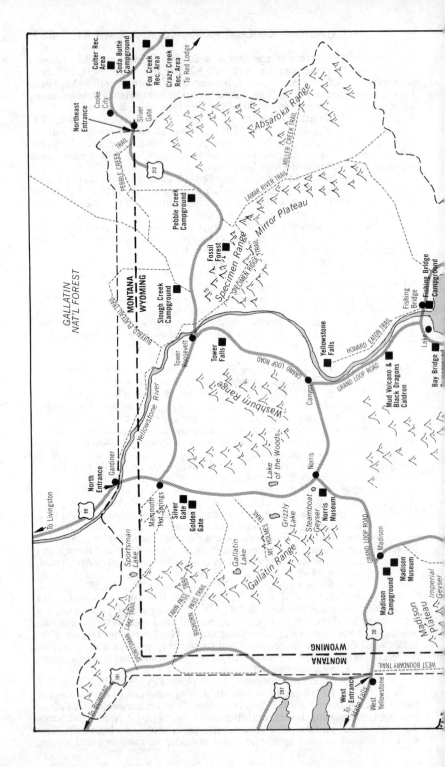

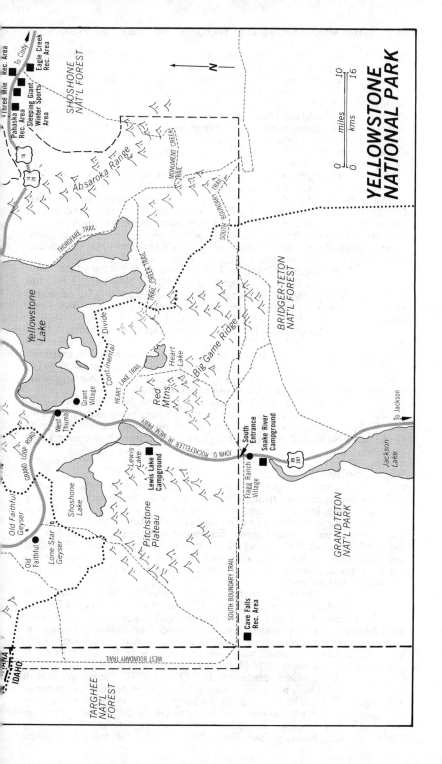

dances. The perfect place for nature lovers; run by the same family for three generations. Excellent value. Closed Nov–May. **B–I**

☀�%♀♀ **Wort Hotel,** 50 N. Glenwood, Jackson, WY 83001 (307/733-2190; toll free 800/322-2727). 45 rms, A/C, color TV, in-rm movies. AE, CB, DC, MC, V. Free parking, nearby pool and tennis court (free shuttle), rest. (Goldpiece Dining Room), bar, rm svce, disco. *Note:* A hotel straight out of a western movie, w. Old West atmosphere, fieldstone lobby fireplaces, and mounted animal heads. Huge, very comfortable rms; efficient, attentive svce; acceptable rest. The Silver Dollar Bar is very popular w. the locals. **M–E,** but lower rates off-season.

♀ **Signal Mountain Lodge,** Interpark Rd. (U.S. 89), Moran, WY 83013 (307/543-2831). 78 rms. AE, MC, V. Free parking, marina w. boating, bicycles, rest. (Aspens), bar, grocery store, free crib. *Note:* Comfortable motel on Jackson Lake w. unimpeded view of the Grand Tetons; friendly reception and svce. Pleasant rms w. private patios or balconies (some w. kitchenette and refrigerator). Many open-air activities available: fishing, swimming, boating, downstream rafting. Campsites adj. Open mid-May to mid-Oct. Very good value. **I–M,** but lower rates off-season.

☀%♀ **Hatchet Motel,** on U.S. 26, Moran, WY 83013 (307/543-2413), 8 mi. (13km) east of Moran Junction. 23 rms (no A/C). MC, V. Free parking, coffee shop. *Note:* Rustic elegance: a log-cabin chalet w. a view clear out over the mountains. Snugly comfortable rms; friendly reception w. a smile. Offers raft trips downriver. Good value. **I**

♀ **Stagecoach Inn,** Madison and Dunraven Sts., West Yellowstone, MT 59758 (406/646-7381). 96 rms, cable color TV. AE, CB, DC, MC, V. Free parking, sauna, snowmobiling, rest., bar, entertainment. *Note:* Classic, well-run motel. Agreeable reception; acceptable rest. Located three blocks from the western entrance to Yellowstone National Park. Open year round; good value. **I,** but lower rates off-season.

♀ **Motel 6,** 1370 W. Broadway, Jackson, WY 83001 (307/733-1620). 155 rms, A/C, color TV, free in-rm movies. AE, DC, MC, V. Free parking, pool, nearby rest. *Note:* Unbeatable value for visitors to Grand Teton National Park. Functionally comfortable; friendly reception. Open year round. **B**

Guest Ranches

Guest ranches are legion around Grand Teton and Yellowstone National Parks. Some of them make their livelihood from the tourist business, organizing horseback riding, Jeep excursions, and rafting, hunting, or fishing parties. Others are authentic cattle ranches, where (paying) guests can follow the lifestyle of the last cowboys. Most of these ranches offer American Plan rates that include lodging, full board, and all the horseback riding you can handle. Since this kind of open-air vacation is becoming more and more popular, you should reserve a good way ahead. None of the ranches listed below is air-conditioned. Some recommended establishments:

♀♀ **Absaroka Ranch,** Star Rte., Dubois, WY 82513 (307/455-2275), 45 mi. (72km) SE of Grand Teton National Park via U.S. 26. 4 cabins w. one or two bedrooms and bath (caters to 18 guests); one-week minimum stay. Free parking, sauna, horseback riding, hiking, fishing, café, overnight pack trips. *Note:* Small, comfortable ranch at the headwaters of the Wind River. Provides solitude and beauty on a grand scale. Relaxed, inviting atmosphere. Very decent food. **M** (American Plan).

♀ **Crossed Sabres Ranch,** P.O. Box WTC, Wapiti, WY 82450 (307/587-3750), 9 mi. (14km) east of the eastern entrance to Yellowstone National Park on U.S. 20. 18 bungalows w. bath (accommodating 50 guests); one-week minimum stay. Free parking, horseback riding, fishing, rest., bar, square dancing, free crib. *Note:* The oldest guest ranch in Wyoming (1898; the main building dates from 1906). Comfortable log cabins in the woods. Smiling reception; family atmosphere. A wealth of open-air activities (rafting, cookouts, fishing, rodeos, horseback trips from one to several days). Closed Oct–Jun. **M** (American Plan).

$ $ $ **Lost Creek Ranch,** P.O. Box 95, Moose, WY 83012 (307/ 733-3435), 20 mi. (32km) north of Jackson along U.S. 26 and an unnumbered gravel-surfaced road 8 mi. (13km) north of Moose. 10 cottages w. private bath (accommodating 40–60 guests); one-week minimum stay. Free parking, heated pool, tennis court, horseback riding, fishing, skeet shooting, trap range, rest., bar, nightclub, free crib. *Note:* The most luxurious, and most expensive, guest ranch in the entire valley, running about $3,500 per person per week. Very comfortable countrified cottages w. private veranda, refrigerator, and fireplace. Spectacular view of the Grand Tetons. Comprehensive fitness facilities. Efficient svce and reception. Rafting and horseback trips through the Grand Tetons are available. Free airport shuttle. Clientele of yuppies looking for the Old West. Closed Oct–May. **VE** (American Plan).

Moose Head Ranch, on U.S. 89 (P.O. Box 214), Moose, WY 83012 (307/877-3141), 26 mi. (42km) north of Jackson. 14 bungalows; 5-day minimum stay. Free parking, horseback riding, fishing, rest., free crib. *Note:* Functionally comfortable bungalows w. verandas and fireplaces. Organizes mountain trips and rafting. For open-air lovers. Private lake on 123 acres (50ha) of woodland and pasture. Closed Oct to mid-June. **VE** (American Plan).

Red Rock Ranch, U.S. 89 and Gros Ventre River Rd. (P.O. Box 38), Kelly, WY 83011 (307/733-6288), 30 mi. (48km) NE of Jackson. 15 cottages (caters to 30 guests); one-week minimum stay. Free parking, heated pool, sauna, horseback riding, fishing, rest. *Note:* A real working stock-rearing ranch on the banks of Crystal Creek, whose very comfortable cottages stand in deep woods. Certified western atmosphere. Guests may join in the fall stock roundups. Free airport shuttle. Closed mid-Oct to June. **E** (American Plan).

$ $ **R Lazy S Ranch,** P.O. Box 308, Teton Village, WY 83025 (307/733-2655), 13 mi. (20km) NW of Jackson along Wyo. 22 and Wyo. 390. 14 bungalows w. bath (accommodating 45); one-week minimum stay. Free parking, horseback riding, fishing, cookouts, evening programs. *Note:* Comfortable ranch at the foot of the Grand Tetons looking out across the mountains. Inviting log cabins, some w. living rm and fireplace. A nice place, w. tasty home-cooking, run since 1948 by the McConaghy family. Closed Oct to mid-June. **E** (American Plan).

Triangle X Ranch, P.O. Box 120, Moose, WY 83012 (307/ 733-2183), 26 mi. (41km) north of Jackson on U.S. 26. 23 bungalows w. shower (accommodating 60); one-week minimum stay. Free parking, horseback riding, skiing, snowmobiling, fishing, square dancing, free crib. *Note:* One of the best places to stay in the Tetons if you enjoy horseback riding and a western flavor. This is a real breeding ranch on 1,200 acres (480ha) of woodland and meadow. Countrified comfort; spectacular views. Rafting and horseback trips offered in summer, big-game hunting parties in fall. Free airport shuttle. Closed Apr and Nov–Dec. **E** (American Plan).

YMCA/Youth Hostels

Teton Village Hostel, McCollister Dr., Teton Village, WY 83025 (307/ 733-3415). 240 beds. Comfortable youth hostel, open also to nonmembers both summer and winter. Nr. the snowfields. Resv. essential long in advance.

RESTAURANTS

Personal Favorites (in order of preference)

Y Y Y **Strutting Grouse,** Jackson Hole Golf and Tennis Estates, 7 mi. (11 km) north of Jackson Hole on U.S. 89 (733-7788). A/C.

Lunch/dinner Tues–Sun; closed Oct to mid-May. AE, MC, V. Jkt. *Specialties:* snails Florentine, poached salmon steak, veal w. lemon and mushrooms, remarkable chocolate mousse. *Note:* The view of the Grand Tetons is so spectacularly beautiful that there's a danger of overlooking the really excellent European-inspired food at this elegant country club. Modern decor w. beautiful hand-woven tapestries. Excellent svce. Resv. strongly advised, especially at dinner. A very good place. *Continental.* **I–M**

🍸🥂 **Jenny Lake Lodge,** in the Jenny Lake Lodge (see "Accommodations," above) (733-4647). No A/C. Breakfast/lunch/dinner daily; closed mid-Sept to early June. AE, MC, V. *Specialties:* poached salmon w. capers in hollandaise sauce, roast leg of lamb boulangère, broiled rainbow trout, steak Delmonico w. bordelaise sauce. Menu changes regularly. Very fine wine list. *Note:* Excellent food in an unassuming log-cabin setting. Relaxed, cheerful atmosphere. Small enough that resv. are a must. A very good place to eat. *American/Continental.* **I–M**

🍸🥂 **Cadillac Grille,** 55 N. Cache St., Jackson (733-3279). A/C. Lunch/dinner daily. AE, MC, V. *Specialties:* mixed salads, Cajun dishes, tuna or swordfish grilled over mesquite, tournedos w. Roquefort cheese, medallions of elk Cumberland, excellent desserts. Menu changes regularly. *Note:* The contemporary California cuisine of this engaging rest. perfectly matches its art deco pink-and-turquoise decorative scheme. Pleasant terrace in fine weather. Painstaking svce in a rather elegant setting. Locally popular; resv. a must. *American.* **I–M**

🍸 **Aspens,** in the Signal Mountain Lodge (see "Accommodations," above), in Moran (543-2831). No A/C. Breakfast/lunch/dinner daily; closed mid-Oct to mid-May. AE, MC, V. *Specialties:* prime rib, sautéed trout, steak, burgers, catch of the day. *Note:* Honest, unimaginative home-cooking served in large portions against an unforgettable backdrop of Jackson Lake and the Grand Tetons. Deft svce w. a smile; relaxed atmosphere; good value on balance. *American.* **B–I**

🍸 **Vista Grande,** Teton Village Rd., 7½ mi. (12km) NW of Jackson via Wyo. 22 and Teton Village Rd. (733-6964). A/C. Dinner only, nightly; closed hols. MC, V. *Specialties:* chimichangas, fajitas, enchiladas, tacos al carbón. Excellent margaritas. *Note:* The Mexican food is as authentic and colorful as the decor, w. a fine view of the mountains thrown in. Cheerful svce. Locally popular, so resv. advised. Very good value. *Mexican.* **B–I**

NEARBY EXCURSIONS

☼🏛🏛 **CODY** (80 mi./128km east of Fishing Bridge on Yellowstone Lake on U.S. 20): Founded in 1901 by the legendary "Buffalo Bill" (William Cody was his real name), and birthplace of the famous abstract painter Jackson Pollock, this picturesque pioneer settlement has retained its authentic far western flavor. Saloons, western boutiques, rodeos nightly June–Aug (587-5155 for information).

The 🏛🏛 **Buffalo Bill Historical Center,** dedicated to the famous scout and buffalo-hunter, is at 720 Sheridan Ave. (307/587-4771), open daily May–Oct, Tues–Sun Mar–Apr and Nov; closed Dec–Feb. Under one roof it houses four different collections, which make it one of the richest museums in the country on the Far West and its period. There are the **Buffalo Bill Museum** (personal memorabilia of William Cody), the **Winchester Arms Museum** (more than 5,000 firearms, including many specimens from the days of the Winning of the West), the **Whitney Gallery of Western Art** (fine paintings and sculptures by Bierstadt, Catlin, Miller, Moran, Remington, Russell, Wyeth, etc.), and the **Plains Indian Museum,** with an interesting collection of Native American ethnology; weapons, clothing, handcrafts, etc.

Nearby are the ⚓ **Old Trail Town** and the **Museum of the Old West,** 1 mi. (1.6km) west on Yellowstone Hwy. (587-5302), open daily mid-May to late Sept, with authentic turn-of-the-century houses, which once stood beside the old stagecoach trail, now re-erected on the original site of Cody. Among the buildings in this open-air museum that re-create the authentic flavor of a frontier town are the inevitable saloon, the general store, school, forge, and so on.

Lovers of the colossal won't overlook Gertrude Vanderbilt Whitney's **Buffalo Bill Monument,** at the west end of Sheridan Ave., believed to be the world's largest equestrian statue in bronze.

Where to Stay in Cody

♟♟ **Holiday Inn,** 1701 Sheridan Ave., Cody, WY 82414 (307/ 587-5555). 184 rms. Very comfortable. **I–M**

☀♟♟ **The Irma Hotel,** 1192 Sheridan Ave., Cody, WY 82414 (307/ 587-4221). 37 rms. Built (and named) by Buffalo Bill in 1902 for his daughter, Irma, and still has its period furniture and decor. A must for lovers of the Old West. **I**

Where to Eat in Cody

☀♟ **Irma Grill,** 1192 Sheridan Ave. (587-4221). Breakfast/lunch/ dinner daily. In Buffalo Bill's old hotel (see above), a superb rm of the period. *American.* **B–I**

⚓ **JACKSON** (57 mi./92km south of the southern entrance to Yellowstone National Park): The ultimate cowboy town; relaxed, comfortable atmosphere. Many western boutiques. Don't miss seeing the ☀ **"Million Dollar Cowboy Bar,"** 25 N. Cache St. (733-2207); the bar itself is 87 ft. (25m) long, and the stools are shaped like western saddles.

⚓ **Dirty Jack's Wild West Theater and Opera House,** 140 N. Cache St. (733-4775), presents western-style musicals in an idiom much appreciated by fans, nightly June–Sept.

GHOST TOWNS: ⚓⚓ **Virginia City,** 85 mi. (136km) NW of West Yellowstone

via U.S. 191, U.S. 287, and Mont. 287: One of the most picturesque and best-preserved ghost towns in the Northwest. Founded in 1863 by prospectors, this former capital of the Montana territory, along with its sister town of **Nevada City,** once boasted 10,000 inhabitants—today barely 200 remain. There are many original buildings scrupulously restored: workshops, schools, brewery (Gilbert Brewery), Wells Fargo Express office, general store, offices of the *Montana Post* newspaper, opera house, Chinatown, and so on. So authentic is the setting that many westerns have been filmed here, notably *Little Big Man* and *The Missouri Breaks.* Interesting historical museum (Wallace St. in Virginia City) and railroad museum (Nevada City depot). The recommended accommodation (below) dates from gold-rush days.

The ghost towns of Virginia City and Nevada City, connected by a narrow-gauge railroad, are open to visitors June–Aug. Don't miss them—they're worth the side trip.

For **information,** contact Historic Virginia City, P.O. Box 338, Virginia City, MT 59755 (406/843-5377).

Where to Stay in Virginia City

☀ **Fairweather Inn,** on Mont. 287, Virginia City, MT 59755 (406/843-5377). 15 hotel rms (6 w. bath) and 17 rms in cabins. MC, V. Adj. coffee shop. Restored gold-camp hotel. Quaint rms decorated in the style of the 1880s. Closed Sept–June. **B**

CHAPTER 34

THE BLACK HILLS AND MOUNT RUSHMORE⚜⚜

□ □ □

Several of the country's most renowned tourist attractions lie within a two-hour drive of **Rapid City,** the second-largest town in South Dakota. The **Black Hills,** a huge, wooded outcrop of rock, 93 mi. (150km) long by 62 mi. (100km) wide and rising in places to 6,400 ft. (2,000m), frown across the great cereal-growing plains of the Dakotas (a Sioux word meaning "alliance of friends"). The Black Hills, rich in seams of ore, were the scene in 1874 of the country's penultimate gold rush, before that of Alaska's Klondike. Several ghost towns or almost-deserted mining camps remain to bear witness to those wild times, when fame alighted on adventurers like Wild Bill Hickok, Calamity Jane, and Preacher Smith, all three of whom lie buried in the Mount Moriah Cemetery at **Deadwood.** Southeast of the Black Hills, **Wind Cave National Park** has underground limestone caverns considered among the finest in the world.

Some 60 mi. (100km) to the east, the glorious national park of the **Badlands** rears its contorted sandstone cliffs, whose savage beauty brings to mind the Grand Canyon of the Colorado; the colorful gorges are best seen at sunrise or sunset.

Finally, **Mount Rushmore National Memorial,** visited every year by more than 2½ million tourists, is one of the most extraordinary monuments in America. Here the features of Presidents George Washington, Thomas Jefferson, Abraham Lincoln, and Theodore Roosevelt, each some 60 ft. (20m) high, have been carved from the living rock. These colossal portraits, the work of visionary artist Gutzon Borglum (and after his death, his son, Lincoln) required 14 years (1927–41) of stubborn effort, and the removal of 450,000 tons of rock. After darkness falls, the sight of these enormous granite faces illuminated by floodlights is enthralling indeed. Not far from Mount Rushmore, another solitary sculptor, Borglum's pupil, Korczak Ziolkowski, began work in 1948, with explosives, pneumatic drills, and bulldozers, on another huge mountainside statue: an equestrian figure, 564 ft. (172m) high and 640 ft. (195m) long of the renowned Sioux chief Crazy Horse, who defeated Lt.-Col. George A. Custer at the battle of the Little Big Horn. Here, too, the sculptor's work was continued after his death (in 1982) by his sons. When finished, sometime around the year 2000, the **Crazy Horse Memorial** will be by far the largest statue in the world.

BASIC FACTS: State of South Dakota. Area code: 605. Time zone: mountain. Zip Code: 57751.

CLIMATE: Summer, with mean July temperatures of 74°F (23°C) and occasional peaks of 95°F (35°C), or autumn, still sunny but cooler, are the best times to visit the Black Hills. Winter, too, has its own savage beauty, though the mercury rarely climbs above 14°F (−10°C) and the snow falls abundantly.

DISTANCES: Chicago, 896 mi. (1,434km); Denver, 375 mi. (600km); Minneapolis, 635 mi. (1,045km); Salt Lake City, 680 mi. (1,088km); Yellowstone, 549 mi. (878km).

ARRIVAL & TRANSIT INFORMATION

NEAREST AIRPORT: Rapid City Regional Airport (RAP), 9 mi. (15km) SE of the town. For information, call 393-9924.

AIRLINES: Continental (toll free 800/525-0280), Delta (toll free 800/221-1212), Northwest (toll free 800/225-2525), and United (toll free 800/241-6522).

CITY LINK: An airport bus, **Airport Limo** (343-5358), serves the principal Rapid City hotels: fare, $7; time, 20 min.

CAR RENTAL (at the airport unless otherwise noted): Avis (toll free 800/331-1212); Budget (toll free 800/527-0700); Dollar, 410 N. Campbell, Rapid City (toll free 800/800-4000); Hertz (toll free 800/654-3131); National (toll free 800/227-7368); and Thrifty (toll free 800/367-2277).

Car-rental rates are high, and the choice of models is limited—but even so, you can't do better than rent a car with unlimited mileage, given the distances to be covered and the many interesting places to see.

INTERCITY BUSES: Jack Rabbit Lines and Powder River Transportation, 333 6th St., Rapid City (348-3300). Both honor the Greyhound Ameripass.

INFORMATION & TOURS

TOURIST INFORMATION: The **Black Hills, Badlands, and Lakes Association,** 900 Jackson Blvd., Rapid City, SD 57702 (605/341-1462).

Rapid City Visitors and Conventions Bureau, 444 Mt. Rushmore Rd., Rapid City, SD 57709 (605/343-1744).

Custer County Chamber of Commerce, 447 Crook St., Custer, SD 57730 (605/673-2244).

Deadwood–Lead Chamber of Commerce, 735 Historic Main St., Deadwood, SD 57732 (605/578-1876).

Mount Rushmore National Memorial Visitor Center, U.S. 16A, Keystone, SD 57751 (605/574-2523).

GUIDED TOURS: Golden Circle Tours (bus), 40 N. 5th St., Custer (605/673-4349): 80-mi. (130km) minibus tour of Custer, Mount Rushmore, and the Black Hills. Daily May–Sept.

Gray Line of the Black Hills (bus), 1600 E. St. Patrick St., Rapid City (605/342-4461): Guided tours around the whole region; serves principal Rapid City hotels.

Jeep to the Buffalo (Jeep), State Game Lodge, U.S. 16A, Custer (605/255-4541): Jeep trips through the buffalo herds of Custer State Park—for wildlife photographers.

Original Deadwood Tour (bus), P.O. Box 363, Deadwood, SD 57732 (605/578-1546): Guided 1-hr. tours of Deadwood and Boot Hill. Daily mid-May to early Oct.

Rushmore Helicopters (helicopter), Keystone Helipad, Keystone (605/666-4461): Trips lasting 4–20 min. over Mount Rushmore and the Black Hills. Spectacular. Mid-May to mid-Sept.

Stagecoach West (bus), P.O. Box 264, Rapid City, SD 57709 (605/343-3113): A 9-hr. guided tour of the whole region; serves principal Rapid City hotels. Daily June–Sept.

THE MAJOR SIGHTS & ATTRACTIONS

☀☍ **BADLANDS NATIONAL PARK** (83 mi./132km east of Rapid City on I-90 and S.D. 240): Spectacular canyons carved by erosion in the multicolored hills of clay and sandstone—a spectacle whose singular beauty has fascinated travelers through the ages. Several herds of buffalo roam free here. Badlands National Park was set up in 1939. **Visitor Center** open daily year round at Cedar Pass, east of the park. For information, call 605/433-5361.

☍ **BLACK HILLS** (10 mi./16km west of Rapid City on U.S. 16): Glorious wooded mountains overlooking the vast Dakota plains, whose mineral wealth touched off a gold rush in 1874; several ghost towns still stand as witness. Once this land was held sacred by the Dakota.

☀☍ **CRAZY HORSE MEMORIAL** (41 mi./65km SW of Rapid City on U.S. 16) (605/673-4681): The world's largest statue, 640 by 564 ft. (195 by 172m), is being created here. The work, begun in 1948, has already required the removal of eight million tons of rock—18 times more than at Mount Rushmore. Boston sculptor Korczak Ziolkowski, a pupil of Borglum's who at one time worked with him on the nearby Mount Rushmore Memorial, conceived and began this gigantic equestrian figure, carved with bulldozers and explosives from the granite of Thunderhead Mountain. The memorial pays tribute to the pride and greatness of Native Americans, in the person of the famous Crazy Horse, chief of the Oglala Sioux, and one of those who defeated Lt.-Col. George Armstrong Custer at the battle of the Little Big Horn. A model in the Visitor Center will give you an idea of the size and shape envisaged for the finished work: the horse's head will be as high as a 22-story building. After the sculptor died in 1982, his wife, Ruth, and his 10 sons took over the work and expect to complete it around the end of the century. An impressive sight; open daily year round.

☀☍ **MOUNT RUSHMORE NATIONAL MEMORIAL** (24 mi./38km SW of Rapid City on U.S. 16) (605/574-2523): Unique colossal sculptures, twice as big as the Sphinx in Egypt, cut into a granite cliff 6,000 ft. (1,830m) high. One of the most extraordinary memorials that history can record, the work of a single man (though completed by the hand of his son), John Gutzon de La Mothe Borglum, a sculptor of Danish descent from Idaho. Begun in 1927 when the sculptor was well over 50, these four gigantic portraits, each about 60 ft. (20m) high and carved from the rock with explosives and pneumatic drills, were not completed until 1941, some months after his death. They symbolize the contribution made to U.S. history by four great presidents: George Washington, the struggle for independence; Thomas Jefferson, the foundation of a democratic state; Abraham Lincoln, the equality of all citizens and the preservation of the Union; Theodore Roosevelt, the influence of America on the world and the conservation of natural resources. Among others, Alfred Hitchcock's famous movie *North by Northwest* was shot here. Almost 2½ million people come here every year; the spectacular (in the most literal sense) sight is enough to make the trip worthwhile. Open daily year round.

☀☖☖ **WIND CAVE NATIONAL PARK** (nr. Hot Springs, 53 mi./84km south of Rapid City on U.S. 16) (605/745-4600): One of the country's most beautiful natural caverns, lying at a depth of 196–328 ft. (60–100m) beneath the slopes of the Black Hills. There's a pedestrian walkway running 1.2–8 mi. (2–12km) through the colorful chambers of the cavern. Wear warm clothing and sturdy shoes—and don't try the walk unless you're in good shape physically. Discovered in 1881, the Wind Cave owes its name to the violent winds that blow between the cavern and the outer world according to changes in atmospheric pressure. Open for (exhausting) visits daily year round.

OTHER SIGHTS, ATTRACTIONS & ACTIVITIES

MUSEUMS OF SCIENCE & HISTORY: ☖ **Dahl Fine Arts Center,** 713 7th St., Rapid City (394-4101): Rotating exhibits of local and Native American art. Also houses an enormous 200-ft. (60m) circular mural by Bernard Thomas, depicting 200 years of American history. Open daily.

☖ **Museum of Geology,** 500 E. St. Joseph St., Rapid City (394-2467): A rich collection of animal fossils (dinosaurs, *Tyrannosaurus*) and minerals; gold nuggets. Open daily.

☖ **Rushmore-Borglum Story and Gallery,** Main St., Keystone (666-4449): An entire museum devoted to the sculptor of Mount Rushmore and his work. Photographs, paintings, models; history of the work. Interesting. Open daily mid-Apr to Oct.

☖ **Sioux Indian Museum,** 515 West Blvd., Rapid City (348-0557): One of the country's finest Native American museums. Interesting old utensils, Sioux handcrafts. The adjoining **Minnilusa Pioneer Museum** is devoted to the period of the westward expansion. Open daily June–Sept, Tues–Sun the rest of the year.

☖ **South Dakota Air & Space Museum,** at Ellsworth Air Force Base, 11 mi. (17km) east of Rapid City off I-90 at Exit 66 (385-5188): Military museum whose special distinction is a score of different aircraft from the old reliable DC-3 to the giant B-52. Open daily year round. Also guided tours of the base, daily mid-May to mid-Sept.

SPECIAL EVENTS: Passion Play at Spearfish (June–Aug): Performance by a 250-ensemble of 22 scenes depicting the life of Christ. For information call the Passion Play Box (605/642-2646).

Black Hills Roundup at Belle Fourche (July 4 wknd): One of the best-known rodeos in the Midwest; not to be missed.

Central States Fair at Rapid City (Aug): Agricultural fair, rodeo, Native American dances, auto races, parades. Colorful.

Days of '76 at Deadwood (first wknd in Aug): Big historical parade in honor of the gold-rush days; rodeo; lively and colorful.

Black Hills Motorcycle Classic at Sturgis (first week in Aug): Each Aug over 100,000 "bikers" and spectators celebrate this week-long, internationally famous motorcycle-racing extravaganza.

Custer State Park Buffalo Roundup (early Oct): One of the largest bison roundups in the country. Spectacular.

WINTER SPORTS RESORTS: ☖ **Deer Mountain,** at Lead, 49 mi. (78km) NW of Rapid City on I-90 and U.S. Alt 14 (584-3230): Five lifts. Open Nov–Mar.

Terry Peak, at Lead, 49 mi. (78km) NW of Rapid City on I-90 and U.S. Alt 14 (584-2165): Five lifts. Open Nov–Mar.

ACCOMMODATIONS IN THE AREA

Personal Favorites (in order of preference)

🍷🍷🍷 **Holiday Inn–Rushmore Plaza,** 505 N. 5th St., Rapid City, SD 57701 (605/348-4000; toll free, see Holiday Inns). 205 rms, A/C, cable color TV. AE, CB, DC, MC, V. Free parking, pool, health club, sauna, rest., bar, rm svce, disco, concierge, free crib. *Note:* Brand-new luxury hotel w. a spectacular eight-story atrium complete w. indoor grdn and a 60-ft. (18m) waterfall. Spacious, inviting rms (some w. wet bars). Very decent rest. (Tiffany Grille). Facilities and svce above the Holiday Inn norm. Business clientele. By far the best hotel of the Black Hills region. **I–M**

🍷🍷 **Hilton Inn,** 445 Mt. Rushmore (at Main St.), Rapid City, SD 57701 (605/348-8300; toll free, see Hilton). 177 rms, A/C, cable color TV. AE, CB, DC, MC, V. Free parking, pool, health club, rest. (Sylvan Room), coffee shop, bar, rm svce, boutiques, free crib. *Note:* Modern grand hotel in the center of Rapid City. Comfortable, spacious rms, most w. views of the Black Hills. Efficient svce; acceptable rest. The best place to stay in town. Open year round. **I–M,** but lower rates off-season.

🔆🍷🍷 **State Game Lodge,** on U.S. 16A, Custer, SD 57730 (605/255-4541; toll free 800/658-3530). 67 rms (no A/C), color TV in public area. AE, MC, V. Free parking, fishing, horseback riding, rest. (Pheasant Dining Room), bar. *Note:* Elegant 1920s country hotel in the heart of Custer State Park; Presidents Calvin Coolidge (1927) and Dwight Eisenhower (1953) took a summer vacation here. Comfortable rms or bungalows w. kitchenette; very satisfactory rest.; friendly svce. Jeep trips arranged to the park's herds of buffalo. A fine place for nature lovers. Closed Oct–Apr. **I–M**

🍷🍷 **Bavarian Inn,** U.S. 16, Custer, SD 57730 (605/673-2802). 64 rms, A/C, cable color TV. AE, CB, DC, MC, V. Free parking, pool, sauna, tennis court, rest., bar, free crib. *Note:* An agreeable small motel w. distinction. Friendly reception; comfortable rms w. private balconies; very commendable food. Nr. the Crazy Horse Memorial. One of the best places to stay in the region. Open year round. **I,** but lower rates off-season.

🍷🍷 **Best Western Golden Hills,** 900 Miners Ave., Lead, SD 57754 (605/584-1800; toll free, see Best Western). 100 rms, A/C, cable color TV. AE, CB, DC, MC, V. Free parking, pool, health club, racquetball, skiing and snowmobiling in winter, rest. (Mountain Rose), bar, rm svce. *Note:* Large, inviting, up-to-date convention hotel opened in 1989. Spacious, comfortable rms; very fine physical-fitness facilities; efficient svce. Free shuttle link w. the casinos in Deadwood. Package-tour and business clientele. **I–M,** but lower rates off-season.

🔆🍷🍷 **Franklin Hotel,** 700 Main St., Deadwood, SD 57732 (605/578-2241). 70 rms, cable color TV. AE, CB, DC, MC, V. Free parking, rest. (1903 Dining Room), two bars. *Note:* One of the oldest hotels (1903) in the Black Hills region. Elegant old decor, prettily restored. Nice rms, but avoid the annex on the other side of the street. Gambling hall and poker rm. Acceptable rest. Open year round. **B–I,** but lower rates off-season.

🍷 **Best Western Town and Country,** 2505 Mt. Rushmore Rd., Rapid City, SD 57701 (605/343-5383; toll free, see Best Western). 100 rms, A/C, cable color TV. AE, CB, DC, MC, V. Free parking, two pools, rest., bar, crib $5. *Note:* Comfortable, well-run motel on the road to Mount Rushmore. Friendly reception. Most rms have private balconies or patios. Open year round. **I,** but lower rates off-season.

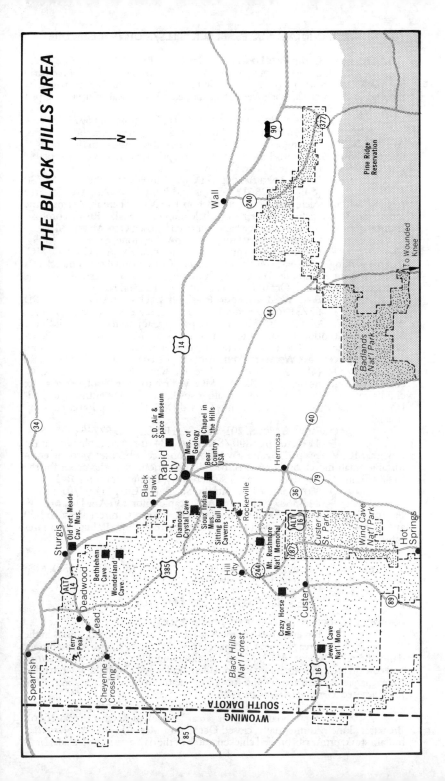

☼ ℘ **Cedar Pass Lodge,** U.S. 16, Cedar Pass, SD 57750 (605/433-
⌂ 5460). 24 bungalows, A/C. AE, CB, DC, MC, V. Free park-
ing, rest. *Note:* Spruce rustic cabins inside Badlands National Park, managed by
the Oglala Sioux tribe. For lovers of unspoiled nature. Beautiful view. Open
April–Oct 15. **B**

℘ **Powder House Lodge,** U.S. 16, Keystone, SD 57751 (605/
⌂ 666-4646 or 605/343-0611 during the off-season). 35 rms.
AE, MC, V. Free parking, rest., bar. *Note:* Comfortable cottages in the woods, 4
mi. (6km) from Mount Rushmore. Friendly reception and svce. Very acceptable
rest. Open May to the end of Sept. Good value. **B–I.**

☼ ℘ **Sylvan Lake Resort,** S.D. 89, Custer State Park, SD 57730
⌂ (605/574-2561). 65 rms and bungalows. AE, MC, V. Free
parking, fishing, beach, boats, rest., coffee shop, bar. *Note:* There are 29 rms in the
motel and 36 bungalows, some rms w. balconies on the lake. Rustic comfort;
country atmosphere. Rates somewhat overpriced. Closed Oct–May. **I–M**

℘ **Rushmore View Inn,** U.S. 16A, Keystone, SD 57751 (605/
⌂ 666-4466). 31 rms, A/C, cable color TV. AE, CB, DC, MC,
V. Free parking, rest., bar, child's cot $4. *Note:* Conventional small motel w. a
view of Mount Rushmore. The Copper Room is an acceptable rest. Good value
on balance. Closed mid-Oct to May. **B–I,** but lower rates off-season.

℘ **Best Western Four Presidents,** U.S. 16A, Keystone, SD
⌂ 57751 (605/666-4472; toll free, see Best Western). 30 rms,
A/C, color TV. AE, CB, DC, MC, V. Free parking, adj. coffee shop, child's cot
$3. *Note:* Conventional small motel 3 mi. (5km) from Mount Rushmore. Func-
tionally comfortable. Closed Dec to the end of Mar. **I,** but lower rates off-season.

℘ **Best Western Plains Motel,** 712 Glenn St., Wall, SD 57790
⌂ (605/279-2145; toll free, see Best Western). 74 rms, A/C,
color TV, in-rm movies. AE, CB, DC, MC, V. Free parking, pool, coffee shop,
child's cot $3. *Note:* Typical but appealing small motel at the entrance to Bad-
lands National Park. Comfortable rms. Closed Dec–Mar. **I,** but lower rates off-
season.

℘ **Super 8 Motel,** 201 Main St., Hill City, SD 57745 (605/574-
⌂ 4141; toll free 800/843-1991). 34 rms, A/C, color TV, in-rm
movies. MC, V. Free parking, nearby coffee shop, free crib. *Note:* Modern, comfortable small motel. Spacious rms; friendly reception. Near the depot for the
"1880 Train" (see the Hill City excursion, below). Open year round. **B–I**

℘ **Motel 6,** 620 E. Latrobe St., Rapid City, SD 57701 (605/
⌂ 343-3687). 150 rms, A/C, cable color TV. AE, DC, MC, V.
Free parking, pool. *Note:* Economy motel north of town w. direct access to I-90
at Exit 59. Serviceable and well run; great if you're driving. **B,** but lower rates
off-season.

YMCA/Youth Hostels
    YMCA, 815 Kansas City St., Rapid City, SD 57701 (605/342-8538). Men
and women; also youth hostel. 16 cots. Pool.

RESTAURANTS IN THE AREA
Personal Favorites (in order of preference)
� **Bavarian Inn** (see the Bavarian Inn in "Accommodations in the
⌂ Area," above), in Custer (673-4412). A/C. Breakfast/dinner
daily (dinner only Sept–May); closed Thanksgiving, Dec 25. MC, V. *Specialties:*
veal cordon bleu, Wiener schnitzel, rouladen, walleye pike, spätzle, apfel strudel.
Note: Classic German setting and food; likable atmosphere. Dancing in season.
Resv. advised. *German/American.* **I–M**

℘ **Powder House Lodge** (see the Powder House Lodge in "Ac-
⌂ commodations in the Area," above), in Keystone (666-4646).
Breakfast/lunch/dinner daily; closed Oct to mid-May. AE, MC, V. *Specialties:*
buffalo steak, prime rib, broiled chicken, catch of the day, a variety of salads. *Note:*

A rustic dining rm in the heart of the woods. Very praiseworthy food. Good value. *American.* **B–I**

☼♀ **Pheasant Dining Room,** in the State Game Lodge (see "Accommodations in the Area," above), in Custer (255-4541). A/C. Breakfast/lunch/dinner daily; closed Nov–Apr. AE, MC, V. *Specialties:* buffalo steak, prime rib, broiled trout, roast pheasant, good homemade desserts. *Note:* Huge western-style dining rm more than half a century old; flavorful country cooking flawlessly prepared and served. Relaxed atmosphere. Locally popular; resv. advised. *Steak/American.* **I–M**

♀ **Ruby House,** U.S. 16A, in Keystone (666-4404). A/C. Lunch Mon–Fri, dinner nightly; closed Dec–Feb. AE, CB, DC, MC, V. *Specialties:* meats broiled over wood fire, Italian dishes. *Note:* Picturesque Far West–style saloon rest., the dining rm attractively decorated as a turn-of-the-century bawdy house. Attentive svce; laudable food. Worth a visit. *Steak.* **I**

♀ **Firehouse Brewing Co.,** 610 Main St., in Rapid City (348-1915). A/C. Lunch/dinner daily; closed hols. AE, CB, DC, MC. *Specialties:* buffalo sausage, marinated buffalo steak, shepherd's pie, good beer. *Note:* Housed in the old 1915 firehouse, this is South Dakota's first brewpub. A good selection of beers from lager to stout brewed on the premises. Locally very popular. Proficient svce. *American.* **B–I**

☼♀ **Faro's Dining Room,** in the Franklin Hotel (see "Accommodations in the Area," above), in Deadwood (578-1465). A/C. Breakfast/lunch/dinner daily; closed Dec 25. AE, DC, MC, V. *Specialties:* hamburger, steak, fish of the day, Cajun dishes. *Note:* The Victorian dining rm of the venerable Franklin Hotel dates from the turn of the century; so do the decor and atmosphere. The food, though acceptable, is unimaginative, the svce efficient. Resv. suggested in tourist season. Pleasant patio dining in summer. *American.* **B–I**

☼♀ **Flying T Chuckwagon Suppers,** on U.S. 16, 6 mi. (10km) south of Rapid City (342-1905). No A/C. Dinner only, nightly at 7:30pm sharp; closed mid-Sept through May. MC, V. *Specialties:* barbecued beef, baked potatoes, beans, biscuits. Beer, but no wine or liquor. *Note:* Real cowboy chuckwagon suppers served as they used to be in tin plates and cups; live country and western music. An old barn and pioneers' covered wagons add to the local color. Resv. advisable; very popular w. the tourist trade. *American.* **B**

♀ **Railhead,** Swanzey St., in Keystone (666-4561). Breakfast/lunch/dinner daily; closed Nov–Apr. MC, V. *Specialties:* hamburgers, Black Hills trout, buffalo buffet. *Note:* Pleasant eating spot w. country decor and antiques. Serves the cheapest (but good) food in town. *American.* **B**

☼♀ **Chute Rooster,** U.S. 385, in Hill City (574-2122). Dinner only, nightly, closed Mon–Tues in winter, Memorial Day, Dec 24–25. MC, V. *Specialties:* steak, prime rib, barbecued meats, catch of the day, beef stew. *Note:* A 19th-century barn turned into a western-style rest. Plentiful portions of solid food. Far West atmosphere, w. square dances in summer. Locally popular. *American.* **B–I**

☼♀ **Buffalo Room,** on S.D. 244, Keystone (574-2515). A/C. Breakfast/lunch/dinner daily (until 8pm; until 5pm from early Oct to the end of May). AE, MC, V. *Specialties:* fried chicken, prime rib, good desserts. *Note:* A rustic cafeteria, w. its western decor and fine art by South Dakota artists; magnificent bay window overlooking Mount Rushmore and its sculptures. Very acceptable food; swift, efficient svce. *American.* **B**

☼♀ **World Famous Roadkill Cafe,** 1333 Main St., in Sturgis (347-4502). Breakfast Mon–Fri, lunch daily, dinner Sat–Sun (seasonal hours of operation, call ahead); closed hols. No credit cards. *Specialties:* tuna melt, hamburgers, buffalo, and kill of the day ("Guess That Mess"). *Note:* As the name indicates, the café offers specialties that are "from your grill to ours" such as "Smidgen of Pigeon" and "The Chicken That Didn't Quite Cross the Road." Obviously, good local color. *American.* **B**

☼♈♉ **Wall Drug Store,** 510 Main St., Wall (279-2175). A/C. Breakfast/lunch/dinner daily (until 10pm in summer, 8pm in spring and fall, 5pm in winter); closed hols. and Sun in winter. AE, MC, V. *Specialties:* steak, fried chicken, soups, sandwiches. *Note:* Self-service cafeteria in the middle of a huge, jumbled country store reminiscent of gold-rush days. The sight is worth your time—the food, less so. Kitsch and overpriced. *American.* **B**

NEARBY EXCURSIONS

☼♉ **BEAR COUNTRY USA** (8 mi./12km south of Rapid City on U.S. 16) (343-2290): Wildlife reserve with bears, wolves, cougar, buffalo, elk, and other animals roaming free; you stay in your car. Guaranteed excitement. Open daily late May to mid-Oct.

♉ **CHAPEL IN THE HILLS** (5 mi./8km west of Rapid City on S.D. 44 and Chapel Lane) (342-8281): Exact replica of the famous 12th-century "Borgund Stavkirke" in Laerdal, Norway; a magnificent building in carved wood. Open daily May–Oct, by request the rest of the year.

☼♉♉ **DEADWOOD** (40 mi./64km NW of Rapid City on I-90 and U.S. Alt. 14): Picturesque gold-prospectors' town, still haunted by the redoubtable shades of such as Wild Bill Hickok, Calamity Jane, Preacher Smith, and Potato Creek Johnny. Its gold-rush population of 25,000 has fallen to barely 2,000 today, but its **Main Street** is on the National Register of Historic Monuments. Visit the famous **Saloon #10,** where Wild Bill Hickok was killed, at 657 Main St. (578-3346); open daily. At the **Old Town Hall,** on Lee St. (578-3583), you can see an amusing skit on his murderer's trial, Mon–Sat June–Aug. Other popular attractions: a gold mine, the **Broken Boot Mine,** on U.S. Alt. 14 (578-9997), open daily mid-May to mid-Oct; and the **Mount Moriah Cemetery,** with tombs of famous Wild West characters, at **Boot Hill,** open daily.

A gaming law enacted in 1989 has made Deadwood the only city in the state with gambling since the practice was outlawed in the 1960s. In the 80 saloons of the town that Wild Bill Hickok helped put on the map, the only games allowed today are at poker and blackjack tables and in slot machines; the maximum bet on card games is $5.

☼♉♉ **DEVILS TOWER NATIONAL MONUMENT** (126 mi./ 201km NW of Rapid City via I-90 and Wy. 24): Enormous (1,280-ft./390m) tower of streaked basalt, like the trunk of a giant tree, towering over the lovely Fourche River which washes its feet. The colors of this impressive volcanic bastion, which has inspired many legends and was used by Steven Spielberg as a setting for *Close Encounters of the Third Kind,* change with the time of day. Some thousand brave souls climb it every year. A truly riveting sight. Site of the nation's first National Monument, dedicated by Pres. Theodore Roosevelt in 1906. Visitor Center open daily May–Oct. For information, contact the Superintendent, P.O. Box 8, Devils Tower, WY 82714 (307/283-2501).

☼♉ **HILL CITY** (28 mi./44km SW of Rapid City on U.S. 16): This charming little mountain village at the foot of **Harney Peak,** South Dakota's highest at 7,242 ft. (2,207m), boasts one of the Black Hills' best tourist draws: the **1880 Train.** Here you can travel to Keystone and back, a two-hour round-trip, aboard an authentic steam train, Far Western style—a picturesque journey through lovely countryside. Open daily mid-June to the end of Aug. For information, call 574-2222; resv. advised.

HOT SPRINGS (74 mi./118km SW of Rapid City on U.S. 16 and U.S. 385): Highly regarded thermal springs, with the world's largest indoor pool of naturally heated water, the **Evans Plunge,** 1145 N. River St. (745-5165). Open daily year round.

You might also want to visit the ❋ **Mammoth Site,** on U.S. 18 bypass (745-6017), a huge 26,000-year-old mammoth graveyard under active excavation by paleontologists; it's believed to have a larger store of bones of this type than any other deposit in the Western Hemisphere. A fascinating place to visit. Open daily year round.

JEWEL CAVE NATIONAL MONUMENT (59 mi./ 94km SW of Rapid City on U.S. 16) (673-2288): One of the most beautiful caverns in the country; superb formations of crystalline calcite produce unique visual effects. You should be in good physical condition, wearing warm clothes and sturdy walking shoes—it's a tiring visit. Open daily in the summer, Mon–Fri the rest of the year.

LEAD (49 mi./78km NW of Rapid City via I-90 and U.S. Alt. 114): Clinging to its mountainside, this old pioneer village, now a very popular winter-sports resort, boasts the country's largest gold mine. Opened in 1876 and still in production, the **Homestake Gold Mine,** Main and Mill Sts. (584-3110), is also the country's deepest at 8,000 ft. (2,440m); it takes 45 min. just to ride to the bottom in the elevator cage, and the temperature when you get there can be as high as 132°F (56°C). The surface installations of the mine are open to visitors daily in the summer, Mon–Fri spring and fall; closed Oct–Apr.

From the nearby 7,076-ft. (2,157m) **Terry Peak,** accessible either by road or by chair lift (584-2165), there's a clear view of the Black Hills and the neighboring states of Wyoming, Montana, North Dakota, and Nebraska.

SPEARFISH (47 mi./75km NW of Rapid City on I-90): Famous for its trout hatcheries. Spearfish has also presented, June –Aug of every year since 1939, the **Black Hills Passion Play,** with 250 characters; it may be seen every Tues, Thurs, and Sun evening at 400 St. Joe St. (642-2646).

The **Matthews Opera House,** 614 Main St. (642-7973), a fine baroque structure from 1906, stages amusing melodramas from the gold-rush era on Mon, Wed, and Fri mid-June to mid-Aug.

STURGIS (29 mi./46km NW of Rapid City on I-90): The **Old Fort Meade Cavalry Museum,** 1 mi. (1.6km) east on S.D. 34 (347-2818), may be visited daily from mid-May to the end of Sept. It was here that the 140 survivors of Lt.-Col. George Armstrong Custer's Seventh Cavalry regiment took refuge after their unit had been cut to pieces by 4,000 Sioux and Cheyenne under Sitting Bull and Crazy Horse at the battle of the Little Big Horn on June 25, 1876. The museum has many memorabilia from those historic times; all western-history buffs should see it. It was at Fort Meade that "The Star-Spangled Banner" was first played in 1892 at official functions, a custom that led to its becoming the national anthem in 1931.

WALL (54 mi./86km SE of Rapid City on I-90): Gateway to **Badlands National Park** (see "The Major Sights and Attractions" above), this tiny town founded in 1907 as a station on the Chicago & Northwestern Railroad is the home of the unusual and well-known **Wall Drug Store.** The legend is that the Wall Drug Store began booming in the 1930s, when the owners posted signs on the highway advertising free ice water. From a little storefront pharmacy, Wall Drug has grown into a sprawling museum of Americana selling mostly overpriced souvenirs and other kitsch. Western art decorates the wall, buffalo burgers are a specialty, and ice water is still free. Roadside signs won't let you miss the place, on U.S. 14 and I-90 (279-2175). Open daily Apr–Dec, Mon–Sat the rest of the year.

    🛏 **WOUNDED KNEE** (89 mi./142km SE of Rapid City via S.D. 44 and Indian Rd. 27): Here, on December 29, 1890, the U.S. Army finally broke the resistance of the Sioux, killing 256 unarmed Native Americans including women and children. Some commentators have discerned in this sorry episode a sort of revenge exacted for Little Big Horn (see "Sturgis," above). Wounded Knee was also the scene of a symbolic Native American revolt in 1973. A monument marks the place of the massacre. For western-history fans. The visit can conveniently be combined with the trip to Badlands National Park (see "The Major Sights and Attractions," above).

GHOST TOWNS: 🛏 **Rockerville,** 12 mi. (19km) SW of Rapid City on U.S. 16 (343-6667): An authentic 1878 prospectors' village with old workshops, restaurant, saloon, and theater all carefully restored. Guaranteed local color. Open daily mid-May to Oct.

    🛏 **CUSTER STATE PARK** (42 mi./67km SW of Rapid City on U.S. 16): Some 73,000 acres (180,000ha) of dense forests, lakes, and unspoiled natural beauty, with one of the country's largest buffalo herds (about 1,500) as well as many deer, elk, mountain goats, and other creatures. The **Needles Highway Scenic Drive** (closed in winter) is a 14-mi. (22km) panoramic road well worth the detour. The park, open all year, hosts more than a million visitors annually. For further information, contact Park Director, HCR 83, P.O. Box 70, Custer, SD 57730 (605/255-4515).

PART FIVE

THE SOUTHWEST

CHAPTER 35

DALLAS AND FORT WORTH 🔥

□ □ □

A city for the 21st century, "Big D" to its admirers, Dallas somehow captures the myth of modern America. Its futurist buildings and grand hotels worthy of Ancient Egypt rival in their brashness the New York and Chicago skylines: witness **City Hall,** with its unadorned, geometric lines; the **Dallas Theater Center;** the startling **Allied Bank Tower,** with its beveled architecture; the immense blue-tinted facade of the **Hyatt Regency Hotel;** and next door, the **Reunion Tower** and its geodesic dome, resembling an enormous crown when illuminated at night. With a more diversified economy than its great rival Houston (oil, textiles, aeronautics, banking, insurance, publishing, chemicals, electronics), Dallas continues to sustain an enviable economic growth rate, despite the depression that has gripped Texas since the early '80s. It is a town of pioneers, founded less than 150 years ago by John Neely Bryan, a Tennessee lawyer who came seeking trade with the Caddo and Cherokee tribes. Named after then–Vice-President George Mifflin Dallas, the city entered its great boom period after World War II. Known as "the New York of the South," Texas's largest city is also one of the country's three great fashion capitals; its designer houses and shops are particularly famous for their luxury and elegance. In addition, Dallas has more retail shopping space per capita than any other U.S. city. While it has been disparagingly identified with the evil-doer "J.R." in its namesake TV series, Dallas rightly prides itself on its millionaire district—**Highland Park**—more like a city within a city, with private police, exclusive schools and clubs, dream houses, and its very own moral code. It is an indicator of its wealth that, outside Saudi Arabia, Dallas boasts more Cadillacs per capita than any other city in the world.

Dallas first built its fortune on cotton, then oil in the 1930s, and continues to be one of the country's most artistically and culturally active cities despite the current economic slump. This is in keeping with the spiritual tradition of the city's early settlers, a group of 200 Utopian scientists, painters, writers, and naturalists from France, Switzerland, and Belgium who came here in the 1850s. The Dallas of today boasts a nationally famous orchestra and opera—the **Dallas Symphony Orchestra** and the **Dallas Opera**—and one of the most prestigious schools in the South, **Southern Methodist University** (9,000 students). The recently opened **Museum of Art,** furthermore, is a remarkable achievement, and modern architecture rises proudly over the city, with works by I. M. Pei, Richard Keating, Frank Lloyd Wright, Philip Johnson, Martin Growald, and Edward Larrabee Barnes gracing the urban landscape.

John F. Kennedy was assassinated on November 22, 1963, from the **Texas School Book Depository,** an undistinguished yellow-brick building now partly transformed into a museum, which continues to draw tens of thousands of the 35th president's admirers each year.

Although the police force is regarded as quick on the draw, the Dallas–Fort

Worth metropolitan area ranks fifth among the most dangerous cities in the country.

With more than 40,000 hotel rooms in town, 20% of them built in the last 10 years, there's rarely a problem finding somewhere to stay.

BASIC FACTS: State of Texas. Area codes: 214 (Dallas), 817 (Fort Worth). Time Zone: central. ZIP Codes: 75221 (Dallas), 76101 (Fort Worth). Founded: 1841 (Dallas), 1849 (Fort Worth). Approximate population: city 1,010,000 (Dallas), 450,000 (Fort Worth); metropolitan area (Dallas and Fort Worth), 3,880,000. Ninth-largest metropolitan area in the country.

CLIMATE: The Dallas climate fits the popular image of Texas: harsh and extreme. Brutal downpours punctuate the exceptionally hot, even torrid, summer (mean July temperature: 86°F/30°C, with peaks of 104°F/40°C and higher), but air conditioning reigns supreme. Winter is generally mild but punctuated by unpredictable temperature plunges (sometimes from 60°F/15°C to freezing in 24 hr.). Spring and autumn are interspersed with often-violent thunderstorms and rather spectacular dust storms.

DISTANCES: Albuquerque, 637 mi. (1,020km); Houston, 243 mi. (390km); Memphis, 450 mi. (720km); New Orleans, 493 mi. (790km); San Antonio, 270 mi. (432km).

ARRIVAL & TRANSIT INFORMATION

AIRPORTS: The **Dallas–Fort Worth International Airport** (DFW) is 13 mi. (21km) west of Dallas, 17 mi. (28km) east of Fort Worth. Ultramodern in conception, the Dallas–Fort Worth airport is the world's second largest in surface area (16,800 acres/6,800ha)—as big as Manhattan. Fourth-busiest airport in the world with 42 million passengers a year. For information, call 214/574-8888.

Dallas's **Love Field** (DAL) is 7 mi. (12km) north, for commuter flights. For information, call 214/670-6080.

U.S. AIRLINES: American (toll free 800/433-7300), Continental (toll free 800/525-0280), Delta (toll free 800/221-1212), Northwest (toll free 800/225-2525), Southwest (toll free 800/422-1616), TWA (toll free 800/221-2000), and United (toll free 800/241-6522).

FOREIGN CARRIERS: British Airways (toll free 800/247-9297), El Al Airlines (toll free 800/223-6700), and Lufthansa (toll free 800/645-3880).

CITY LINK: Cab fare **from Dallas–Fort Worth Airport to downtown Dallas,** about $35; time, 40 min. Bus for the same route: Super-Shuttle (817/329-2000); provides door-to-door service to any Dallas destination; leaves by request; fare $10; time, about 45 min.

Cab fare from Dallas–Fort Worth Airport **to downtown Fort Worth,** about $33; time, 40 min. Bus for the same route: Airporter Bus Service (817/334-0092); runs on the half hour from the Airporter Terminal at 1000

Weatherford St. and dwntwn Fort Worth hotels to DFW Airport; fare, $8. Super-Shuttle (817/329-2000); provides door-to-door service to any Fort Worth destination, leaving by request; fare, $12; time, about 40 min.

Service is by Super-Shuttle **from Love Field:** fare to dwntwn Dallas, $8.50; cab fare, $12.

The **bus system** is thoroughly deficient (in Dallas, DART, 214/979-1111; in Fort Worth, T.A.F.W., 817/871-6200), the taxis few and expensive. This plus the enormous size of the metropolitan area makes renting a car with unlimited mileage a good idea. The **McKinney Avenue trolley** (214/855-0006) runs a 2.8-mi. (4.5km) route through dwntwn, the Arts District, and the McKinney Strip (McKinney Ave.); fare is $1.50.

CAR RENTAL (at Dallas–Fort Worth Airport unless otherwise indicated): Avis (toll free 800/331-1212), Budget (toll free 800/527-0700), Dollar (toll free 800/800-4000), Hertz (toll free 800/654-3131), National (toll free 800/227-7368), and Thrifty (toll free 800/367-2277). For dwntwn locations, consult the local telephone directory.

LIMOUSINE SERVICES: Carey Limousine (214/638-4828), Scripps Edward Limousine (toll free 800/223-6710), and Sunset Limousine (214/827-1425).

TAXIS: You'll find taxis in waiting lines at the major hotels; they may not be hailed on the street. The best arrangement, however, is to phone: **Republic Taxi** (214/631-5544 in Dallas) or **Yellow Cab** (214/426-6262 in Dallas, 817/534-5555 in Fort Worth).

TRAIN: Amtrak (toll free 800/872-7245) has stations **in Dallas** (Union Station) at 400 S. Houston St. and **in Fort Worth** at 1501 Jones St.

INTERCITY BUSES: Greyhound (toll free 800/231-2222), 205 S. Lamar St., Dallas, or 901 Commerce St., Fort Worth (817/332-4564).

DALLAS

INFORMATION & TOURS

TOURIST INFORMATION: The **Dallas Convention & Visitors Bureau,** 1200 Elm St., TX 75270 (214/746-6679; toll free 800/752-9222).

There's also an **information office** open daily at Union Station, 400 S. Houston St. (214/746-6600), and a **Special Events Info Line** (214/746-6679).

GUIDED TOURS: **Gray Line Tours Dallas** (bus) (214/824-2424): Guided tour of the city, serving major hotels.

SIGHTS, ATTRACTIONS & ACTIVITIES

ARCHITECTURAL HIGHLIGHTS: ⚱⚱ **City Hall,** City Hall Plaza (670-3957): Impressive, futurist building in the shape of an inverted pyramid, a work of I. M. Pei. There's a lovely Henry Moore sculpture on the entrance plaza. Open Mon–Fri.

☀⚱ **Dallas Market Center,** 2100 Stemmons Fwy. (655-6151): This group of ultramodern buildings (**Apparelmart, Dallas Trade Mart, Decorative Center District, Infomart, World Trade Center,** etc.) makes up the world's biggest wholesale market. Interesting modern sculptures dot the surrounding grdns (**Sculpture Garden**). Guided tours by appointment.

☀⚱ **Dallas Theater Center,** 3636 Turtle Creek Blvd. (526-8857): Two 460-seat halls and one of the country's most important theatrical companies. Daring cantilevered architecture by Frank Lloyd Wright.

☀⚱⚱ **First Interstate Bank Tower,** Fountain Place: Designed by Henry Cobb, a pupil of I. M. Pei, this huge, beveled-glass prism stands 60 stories high and commands the 200 fountains and the cypresses of Fountain Place, a recently opened business center in downtown's north end.

☀⚱ **Infomart,** 1950 Stemmons Fwy. (746-3500): This modern replica by Martin Growald of London's famous 1851 Crystal Palace houses the country's most important permanent marketing exhibition for the data-processing industry. Part of the Dallas Market Center complex.

⚱⚱ **Morton H. Meyerson Symphony Center,** 2301 Flora St. (692-0203): The only concert hall designed by I. M. Pei, this shoebox-shaped limestone building with audacious glass curves, soaring lobbies, and unusually high ceilings was inaugurated in 1989 at a cost of $106 million. Dubbed "The Mort" by local residents, the 2,066-seat hall is acoustically perfect. A huge canopy of wood and onyx above the stage moves up and down to adjust the sound to the performers.

☀⚱⚱ **Texas Commerce Tower,** 2200 Ross Ave. (922-2300): The most spectacular building in Dallas. Designed by Richard Keating, of Skidmore, Owings & Merrill, this 55-story skyscraper of glass and granite is among the most compelling towers to rise in this decade in the U.S. Crowned by a great arch bringing the building to a dramatic conclusion, the Texas Commerce Tower presents a vast "sky window"—75 ft. (22m) high, 27 ft. (8.25m) wide—that slices out the center of the 41st through the 49th floors.

⚱ **Texas Stadium,** Tex. 183 at Loop 12, in Irving (214/554-1804): One of the country's football shrines (holds 65,000) and home to the famous Cowboys. Guided tours daily (except on game days).

HISTORIC BUILDINGS: ⚱ **Hall of State,** in State Fair Park, Parry and Second Aves. (421-4500): A handsome art deco ensemble of huge wall murals, temporary exhibitions on the history of Texas, and memorabilia of famous Texas heroes. For those who enjoy the gigantic. Open Tues–Sun.

⚱ **John Neely Bryan Cabin,** Main, Elm, and Market Sts.: Log cabin built in 1841 by the city's founder, it was later used as a post office and then a courthouse. Standing in a stark downtown plaza, the cabin is supposed to mark the spot where the city was founded. It's not open to the public, but have a look at it anyway.

⚱ **Southern Methodist University,** Hillcrest Ave. at University Park (692-2000): Founded in 1915, this is one of the Southwest's most famous universities (9,000 students). On the 164-acre (66ha) campus there are nearly 100 Georgian-style buildings, plus the **Owen Arts Center** (see "Museums of Art," below).

⚱ **J. F. K. Historical Exhibit,** 411 Elm St. (653-6666): According to the official version, Lee Harvey Oswald shot President Kennedy from the Texas School Book Depository Building, now the Dallas County

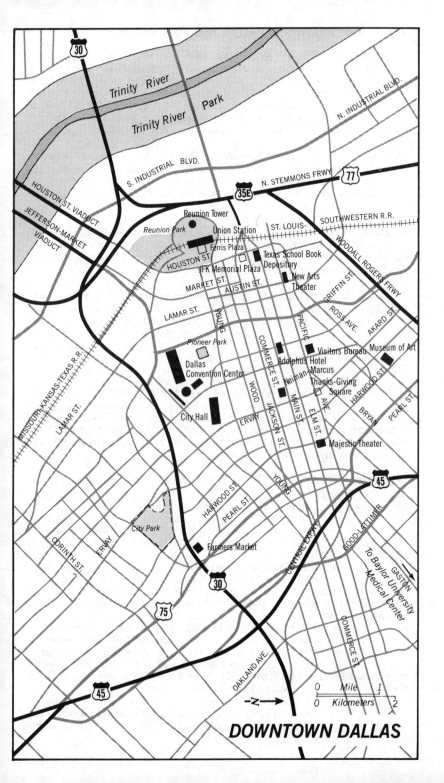

DOWNTOWN DALLAS

Administration Building. The sixth floor of the building has been transformed into a $3.5-million exhibit pertinently named "The Sixth Floor" and featuring films, 400 photographs, artifacts, and interpretive displays on the cultural context of John F. Kennedy's death. The window area from which Oswald allegedly fired the fatal shots has been re-created as it was that day, but it's behind a wall of glass. Visitors can look out through immediately adjacent windows with almost the same view of the motorcade route and Dealy Plaza. Open daily.

MARKETS: ☖ **Farmers Produce Market,** 1010 S. Pearl Expwy. (748-2082): Located in the southeast corner of downtown Dallas, the striped sheds of the Dallas Farmers' Market offers all the season's fresh fruits, vegetables, flowers, and plants from the surrounding area. Open sunrise to sunset daily. Noisy and colorful.

MONUMENTS: ☀☖ **John F. Kennedy Memorial,** J. F. K. (formerly Dealy) Plaza, at Main, Commerce, and Market Sts.: Granite cenotaph by Philip Johnson, sober and austere, near the place where President Kennedy was assassinated. Kind of an open-air cube with 30-ft.-high (9m) walls.

MUSEUMS OF ART: ☀☖☖☖ **Dallas Museum of Art,** 1717 N. Harwood St. (922-1200): The most recent (1984) of the large Texas museums houses pre-Columbian art, great European masters (Cézanne, Gauguin, Monet, Pissarro, van Gogh), modern American painting (notably Jackson Pollock), as well as rich collections of African art. Don't miss the extraordinary giant sculpture by Claes Oldenburg, *Stake Hitch.* All this is housed in a splendid modern building by Edward Larrabee Barnes. Lovely gardens with waterfalls, shaded groves, and an uninterrupted view of the Dallas skyline. Open Tues–Sun.
   ☖ **Owen Arts Center,** Hillcrest Ave. (768-2787): This huge arts complex on the Southern Methodist University campus includes the **Bob Hope Theatre** (built with a donation from the famous comedian, but Shakespeare is the playwright of choice here); the **Meadows Museum,** dedicated to classical Spanish painting and also offering temporary exhibitions; and a very fine modern-sculpture garden. Open Thurs–Sun.

MUSEUMS OF SCIENCE & HISTORY: ☖ **Age of Steam Railroad Museum,** 7226 Wentwood Dr., Fair Park (428-0101): Superb collection of old steam locomotives. Open Thurs–Sun, daily during the State Fair.
   ☖ **Biblical Arts Center,** 7500 Park Lane (691-4661): A surprising spectacle which includes a 124- by 20-ft. (38- by 6m) painting of the miracle of Pentecost with a sound-and-light show plus a replica of Christ's tomb. Open Tues–Sun.
   ☖ **Dallas Museum of Natural History,** Second and Grand Aves., Fair Park (421-3466): This neoclassical building is a museum of southwestern and Texas natural history. More than 50 facsimiles of natural habitats plus rich zoological and botanical collections, including a 90-million-year-old fossil fish. Open daily.
   ☖ **Kennedy Historical Exhibit,** "The Sixth Floor": In the Texas School Book Depository (see "Historic Buildings," above).
   ☀☖ **Old City Park,** Gano and Harwood Sts. (421-5141): Authentic 19th-century Texas town restored in minutest detail, with a train station, booths, church, bank, school, etc. There are 40-some original buildings in all, from all over Texas. Open Tues–Sun.
   ☖ **The Science Place,** First Ave. and Martin Luther King, Jr. Blvd., Fair Park (428-5555): Remarkably conceived exhibits on science, energy, and ecology. History of anatomy depicted on transparent human bodies; a planetarium too. Open daily.

OUTDOOR ART & PLAZAS: Apart from the **Sculpture Garden** in the middle of Dallas Market Center (see "Architectural Highlights," above), **City Hall** offers two interesting modern sculptures: Henry Moore's *The Dallas Piece,* three bronze blocks weighing 13 tons; and two "floating" sculptures by Marta Pan on an ornamental lake.

PANORAMAS: ⛰ **Reunion Tower,** 300 Reunion Blvd. (651-1234): This 50-story tower capped with a geodesic dome where computer-operated lights dance at night is the new symbol of Dallas. Observation deck at the top. Open daily until 10pm on weekdays and midnight on weekends.

PARKS & GARDENS: ⛲ **Civic Garden Center,** First Ave. and Martin Luther King, Jr. Blvd., in State Fair Park: Lovely botanic garden with rose gardens and a tropical hothouse. Open daily.

⛲ **Dallas Aquarium,** First Ave. and Martin Luther King, Jr. Blvd., in State Fair Park (670-8441): This modest-sized (and hence, perhaps, un-Texan) aquarium is one of the most modern and complete in the Southwest, with 350 species of fish, reptiles, and amphibians. Open daily.

⛲ **Dallas Arboretum and Botanical Gardens,** 8525 Garland Rd. (327-8263): 66 acres (27ha) of beautiful gardens on the eastern shore of White Rock Lake, just minutes from dwntwn. Features acres of fragrant azaleas and wildflowers, tall shade trees, and a fern garden. Open daily.

☀⛲ **State Fair Park,** Parry and Second Aves. (670-8400): Immense, 240-acre (97ha) fairground with fountains, ponds, floral exhibitions, an aquarium, and numerous museums (see above), as well as the famous **Cotton Bowl Stadium,** where the Cotton Bowl is played each Jan. 1. In Oct it's the site of the **Texas State Fair,** which attracts three million visitors annually.

⛲ **Thanks-Giving Square,** bounded by Bryan St., Ervay St., and Pacific Ave.: A green oasis built below street level in the heart of the city with an unusual spiral chapel and meditation garden designed by Philip Johnson, a striking contrast to neighboring skyscrapers.

PERFORMING ARTS: For a daily listing of all shows and cultural events, consult the entertainment pages of the daily paper, the *Dallas Morning News* (morning), and of the monthly magazine *D.*

Bob Hope Theatre, Owen Arts Center, Hillcrest Ave. (768-2787): Modern and classical theater on the Southern Methodist University campus.

Dallas Repertory Theatre, 1030 N. Park Center (369-8966): Classical theater, drama, comedy.

Dallas Theater Center, 3636 Turtle Creek Blvd. (526-8857): From Shakespeare to contemporary theater, Sept–May. Daring Frank Lloyd Wright architecture.

Majestic Theatre, 1925 Elm St. (880-0137): Theater, recitals, and a variety of performances in a splendid, recently restored building.

McFarlin Auditorium, on the campus of Southern Methodist University (768-3129): The university's largest performance hall featuring concerts, plays, and film screenings.

Morton H. Meyerson Symphony Center, 2301 Flora St. (692-0203): The Dallas Symphony Orchestra, with music director Eduardo Mata, in its spectacular home (Sept–May). Also big-name recitals of both classic and pop music.

Music Hall, First and Parry Aves., in State Fair Park (565-1116): Home of the Dallas Opera (director: Plato Karayanis) (Nov–Dec) and the Dallas Ballet. Also offers Broadway hits (June–Aug).

Theatre Three, 2800 Routh St. (871-3300): Drama, comedy.

RODEOS: ⚲ **Kow Bell Indoor Rodeo,** U.S. 287 in Mansfield (15 mi./24km SW on I-20 and Tex. 157) (817/477-3092): The only rodeo in the country open year round, with events each Mon, Fri, Sat–Sun at 8pm. In an authentic breeding ranch that offers horseback riding daily.

    ⚲⚲ **Mesquite Rodeo,** I-635 at Military Pkwy. in Mesquite (13 mi./21km west on Tex. 352) (214/285-8777): Rodeos 8pm Fri–Sat Apr–Sept. Experts consider this the most demanding, most violent rodeo challenge in all Texas. Guaranteed local color. 15 min. from dwntwn.

SHOPPING: The Galleria, L. B. J. Fwy. and Dallas Pkwy.: A monument of modern shopping that has been often copied, never matched. More than 200 luxury boutiques (Cartier, Tiffany, Charles Jourdan, etc.), stores, theaters, restaurants, and even a skating rink, all in air-conditioned comfort (*de rigueur* in Texas) under an enormous glass dome. 15 min. from dwntwn.

Luskey's, Forest Lane and Webb Chapel Rd.: Texas riding boots and all the necessary equipment for a real (or pretend) cowboy.

Neiman-Marcus, Main and Ervay Sts.: The most chic, most expensive department store in the country. You can find anything at Neiman-Marcus, even the most imagination-defying gift ideas. Those with thin billfolds are advised to stay away.

Resistol Hat Shop, 721 Marion Dr., Garland: One of the largest assortments of cowboy hats in all Texas (no small claim, that).

Wild Bill's, 603 Munger St.: The "Official Dallas Western Store" where you can get Wrangler jeans, cowboy boots, and Stetson hats.

SPECIAL EVENTS: For the exact schedule of events below, consult the **Dallas Convention & Visitors Bureau** (see "Tourist Information," above).

Cotton Bowl Festival (Jan 1): Eight days of festivities culminating in the famous football game. A classic since 1956.

Texas State Fair (Oct): Shows, rodeos, sporting and special events—this animated fair attracts three million visitors each year.

Texas–O.U. Weekend (Oct): Spectacular annual confrontation between the University of Texas and Oklahoma University football teams. An autumn ritual for the last 60 years.

SPORTS: Dallas has three professional teams:

Baseball (Apr–Oct): Texas Rangers, The Ballpark in Arlington (817/273-5100).

Basketball (Oct–Apr): Dallas Mavericks, Reunion Arena (214/658-7068).

Football (Sept–Dec): Dallas Cowboys, Texas Stadium (214/556-2500).

THEME PARKS: ⚲ **International Wildlife Park,** I-30 at Wild Life Pkwy., Grand Prairie (214/263-2201): Drive your car through this vast zoo-safari and see wild animals (including African wildlife) in their natural habitat. Open daily year round.

    ☼⚲ **Six Flags Over Texas,** I-30 and Tex. 360, Arlington (817/640-8900): Huge, "Texas style" amusement park (192 acres/78ha) with more than 100 different attractions including a giant roller-coaster. Events, performances, etc. Open daily from the end of May to early Sept, wknds only in spring and autumn; closed the rest of the year.

ZOOS: The ☖ **Dallas Zoo,** 621 E. Clarendon Dr. (946-5154): One of the most comprehensive zoos in the United States, with 2,000 animals on 48 acres (19.5ha). Open daily.

ACCOMMODATIONS

Personal Favorites (in order of preference)

☀☖☖☖☖☖ **The Mansion on Turtle Creek** (nr. dwntwn), 2821 Turtle Creek Blvd., TX 75219 (214/559-2100; toll free, see Preferred). 145 rms, A/C, cable color TV. AE, CB, DC, MC, V. Valet parking $10, pool, two rests. (including Mansion on Turtle Creek Restaurant), bar, 24-hr. rm svce, nightclub, concierge, free crib. *Note:* Elegant Moorish-style manor house dating from the 1920s built on the grounds of a former oilman's 5-acre (2ha) terraced estate. Refined period furniture w. pastel decor and flowers everywhere. Spacious, ultra-comfortable rms w. balconies or private patios. Highly skilled, attentive svce. First-rate rest. A big favorite of businesspeople and celebrities. One of the dozen best hotels in the country. Owned by the wealthy Hunt family of Texas. **VE**

☀☖☖☖☖ **Hyatt Regency** (dwntwn), 300 Reunion Blvd., TX 75207 (214/651-1234; toll free, see Hyatt). 940 rms, A/C, color TV, in-rm movies. AE, CB, DC, MC, V. Valet gar. $10, pool, two tennis courts, health club, sauna, two rests. (including Fausto's), coffee shop, three bars, rm svce, disco, free crib. *Note:* This illustrious grand hotel displays a 27-story, blue-tinted glass facade that reflects neighboring skyscrapers. Waterfall and interior grdns in the 19-story lobby. Unparalleled facilities and comfort plus an extraordinary view from the revolving rest. at the top (Atrium), although the cuisine is mediocre. Very efficient svce. Quite close to the business district. Interesting wknd packages. VIP floor. Has undergone a $25-million facelift. **E–VE**

☖☖☖ **Plaza of the Americas** (dwntwn), 650 N. Pearl Blvd., TX 75201 (214/979-9000; toll free 800/225-5843). 442 rms, A/C, cable color TV. AE, CB, DC, MC, V. Valet gar. $10, health club, sauna, rest. (650 North), bar, rm svce, hrdrsr, boutiques, concierge, free crib. *Note:* Some of the most spectacular luxury-hotel architecture in Texas, w. an immense 15-story plant-filled atrium w. glass elevators overlooking a skating rink. Vast, luxurious rms w. balconies and modern, elegant decor. Very good svce and a renowned rest. Big business clientele. Part of the British group Forte Hotels, which owns the Travelodge chain. Very central location. **E–VE**

☖☖☖ **Stouffer** (nr. dwntwn), 2222 Stemmons Frwy., TX 75207 (214/631-2222; toll free, see Stouffer). 542 rms, A/C, color TV, in-rm movies. AE, CB, DC, MC, V. Free parking, pool, health club, sauna, two rests. (including Bay Tree), bar, rm svce, free crib. *Note:* Right in the famous Dallas Market Center, this huge elliptical 30-story tower of pink granite makes up in originality for what it lacks in elegance. Up-to-the-minute comfort and facilities; spacious, well-planned rms. Many works of art and enormous three-story-high light fixture in lobby. Efficient reception and svce. Business clientele. Well located 5 min. from dwntwn and 20 min. from Dallas–Fort Worth Airport. Worthwhile wknd packages. **E–VE**

☖☖ **Stoneleigh Hotel** (nr. dwntwn), 2927 Maple Ave., TX 75201 (214/871-7111; toll free 800/447-9559). 142 rms, A/C, color TV. AE, CB, DC, MC, V. Free parking, pool, tennis, rest. (Ewald's), 24 hr. rm svce, concierge, free crib. *Note:* Oldish but comfortable hotel surrounded by 10 acres (4ha) of grdns, close to dwntwn. A favorite of show-business people. Spacious rms, some w. kitchenettes. Attentive svce. Good value overall. **M–E**

☖☖ **Best Western Market Center** (nr. dwntwn), 2023 Market Center Blvd., TX 75207 (214/741-9000; toll free, see Best Western). 96 rms, A/C, cable color TV. AE, CB, DC, MC, V. Free parking, pool, rest., bar, free crib. *Note:* Conventional but comfortable motel quite close to the Market Center. Direct access to the highway network. Good-natured reception and svce. This very good value is ideal for the car traveler—8 min. from dwntwn and 10 min. from Love Field. **I**

♀ **Days Inn Texas Stadium** (vic.), 2200 E. Airport Fwy., TX 75062 (214/438-6666; toll free, see Days Inns). 178 rms, A/C, cable color TV. AE, CB, DC, MC, V. Free parking, pool, coffee shop adj., free crib. *Note:* Typical highway motel across from Texas Stadium. Serviceable comforts; ideal if you're driving through. 15 min. from dwntwn. **B–I**

♀ **Motel 6 North** (nr. dwntwn), 2753 Forest Lane, TX 75234 (214/620-2828). 100 rms, A/C, cable color TV. AE, DC, MC, V. Parking, pool, free crib. *Note:* Modern, ultra-economical motel located 15 min. from dwntwn and 5 min. from the Galleria Shopping Mall. One of the best values in the area. Easy access to the highways makes it ideal for the car traveler. **B**

Other Accommodations (from top bracket to budget)

☼♀♀♀♀ **The Adolphus** (dwntwn), 1321 Commerce St., TX 75202 (214/742-8200; toll free 800/221-9083). 430 rms, A/C, color TV, in-rm movies. AE, CB, DC, MC, V. Valet parking $10, health club, sauna, three rests. (including the French Room), bar, piano bar, 24-hr. rm svce, hrdrsr, boutiques, concierge, free crib. *Note:* A venerable palace, engagingly sumptuous, built in 1912 by beer magnate Adolphus Busch, and a historical landmark for its original rococo architecture. Inside are lovely 17th-century Flemish tapestries and spacious, elegant rms w. Chippendale furniture and minibars (some have a private patio). Good svce and a very good rest. (The French Room). This celebrated locale in the heart of dwntwn Dallas hosts luminaries from all over the world. A favorite of connoisseurs. **VE**

♀♀♀ **Crescent Court Hotel** (nr. dwntwn), 400 Crescent Court, TX 75201 (214/871-3200; toll free, see Preferred). 218 rms, A/C, cable color TV. AE, CB, DC, MC, V. Valet gar. $10, pool, health club, sauna, rest. (Beau Nash), bar, 24-hr. rm svce, boutiques, concierge, free crib. *Note:* This palace hotel designed by Philip Johnson is part Versailles, part Walt Disney World. But if the exterior provokes a bit of a giggle, the interior decoration is a masterpiece of classic elegance, w. numerous works of art and stylish furnishings. Vast, luxurious rms w. marble bathrooms, and each suite decorated in a different style. Exemplary svce and a rest. that's full of businesspeople at lunchtime. Same management as the Mansion on Turtle Creek (see above). **VE**

♀♀♀ **Fairmont** (dwntwn), 1717 N. Akard St., TX 75201 (214/720-2020; toll free, see Fairmont). 543 rms, A/C, color TV, in-rm movies. AE, CB, DC, MC, V. Valet gar. $15, pool, health club, two rests. (including the Pyramid Room), bars, 24-hr. rm svce, boutiques, free crib. *Note:* Long "the" chic palace of Dallas (the most expensive suite costs more than $1,500 a night). Two modern towers w. elegant, luxurious interior decoration and spacious, very comfortable rms. Svce is of the highest caliber in an opulent, tasteful atmosphere. Excellent rest. Wealthy Texan and big business clientele. No-smoking floor. In the heart of dwntwn. Recently renovated. **E–VE**

♀♀♀ **Loews Anatole** (nr. dwntwn), 2201 Stemmons Fwy., TX 75207 (214/748-1200; toll free, see Loews). 1,765 rms, A/C, color TV, in-rm movies. AE, CB, DC, MC, V. Valet parking $8, three pools, six tennis courts, putting green, health club, sauna, eight rests. (including L'Entrecôte), 24-hr. coffee shop, eight bars, disco, rm svce, hrdrsr, boutiques, concierge. *Note:* A veritable city-within-a-city, the Anatole is the largest hotel in Dallas. The ultramodern interior (the exterior of this 27-floor reddish monolith is somewhat reminiscent of a prison) includes a superb 14-story grdn-lobby and very comfortable rms. Specializing in groups and convention clientele, this enormous futurist hotel is also a favorite of businesspeople. Good svce and very complete recreational facilities w. a hot spring. Three VIP floors. 7 acres (3ha) of grdns w. ponds, fountains, and groves, all facing the Dallas Market Center. Interesting wknd deals. **E–VE**

♗♗♗ **Westin Galleria** (vic.), 13340 Dallas Pkwy., TX 75240 (214/ 934-9494; toll free, see Westin). 440 rms, A/C, cable color TV. AE, CB, DC, MC, V. Valet parking $10, pool, four rests. (including the Huntington Grill), coffee shop, two bars, 24-hr. rm svce, free crib. *Note:* Modern, 21-story grand hotel in the famous Galleria Mall Shopping Center and its 200 stores and shops. The architecture lacks imagination, but the comfort and facilities are remarkable. All rms have balconies and refrigerators. Very efficient svce. Business and group clientele. No-smoking floors. 20 min. from dwntwn. **E–VE**

☀♗♗ **Melrose Hotel** (formerly Omni; nr. dwntwn), 3015 Oak Lawn, TX 75219 (214/521-5151). 185 rms, A/C, color TV, in-rm movies. AE, CB, DC, MC, V. Free parking, rest. (Landmark Café), bar, rm svce, library, concierge, free crib. *Note:* Charming 1920s hotel, entirely renovated to the tune of $12 million. Elegant art deco decor; rms on the small side, but comfortable (some w. refrigerators). Attentive svce. Business clientele. VIP floor. Offering a free shuttle to and from Love Field, it's also close to the Dallas Theater Center. **E**

♗♗ **Holiday Inn Aristocrat** (formerly Clarion; dwntwn), 1933 Main St., TX 75201 (214/741-7700; toll free, see Holiday Inn). 172 suites, A/C, color TV, in-rm movies. AE, CB, DC, MC, V. Parking $3, rest., bar, rm svce, free crib. *Note:* A venerable Conrad Hilton palace built in 1925, now a historical landmark. It was carefully restored in 1985 in all its antique splendor. Offers only spacious, comfortable mini-suites (w. refrigerators). Attentive, personalized svce. A good overall value in the heart of the business district. Very adequate rest. **M–E**

♗♗ **Southland Center Hotel** (dwntwn), 400 N. Olive St., TX 75201 (214/922-8000; toll free 800/272-8007). 498 rms, A/C, color TV, in-rm movies. AE, CB, DC, MC, V. Valet gar. $8, health club, rest., coffee shop, two bars, rm svce, concierge. *Note:* Modern, 30-story tower w. three VIP floors. Spacious, comfortable rms and relatively efficient svce. Entirely renovated decor and facilities. Obtrusive group clientele. No recreational facilities. In the heart of Dallas. **M–E**

♗♗♗ **Holiday Inn-North** (formerly Summi Hotel) (vic.), 2645 LBJ Fwy., TX 75234 (214/243-3363; toll free see Holiday Inn), at Josey Lake. 376 rms, A/C, color TV, in-rm movies. AE, CB, DC, MC, V. Free parking, pool, sauna, rest. (Gabriel's), coffee shop, bar, rm svce, disco, concierge, free crib. *Note:* Large convention and package-tour motel on the northern outskirts of Dallas, housed in a drably functional modern building. Inviting, comfortable rms w. balcony (some w. refrigerator). Flawless svce. 15 min. from Dallas–Fort Worth Airport and 20 min. from Dallas's Love Field (free shuttle service to both). Interesting wknd packages. Good value. **I–M**

♗♗ **Howard Johnson's Downtown** (dwntwn), 1015 Elm St., TX 75202 (214/748-9951; toll free, see Howard Johnson's). 306 rms, A/C, color TV, in-rm movies. AE, CB, DC, MC, V. Parking $7, pool, rest., bar, rm svce, free crib. *Note:* Functional Holiday Inn accommodations in a modern 19-story tower in the heart of Dallas. Rather spacious rms w. balconies and very mediocre svce. Business and group clientele. Close to the Medical Center. **I–M**

♗♗ **Quality Hotel Market Center** (nr. dwntwn), 2015 N. Market Center Blvd., TX 75207 (214/741-7481; toll free, see Choice). 280 rms, A/C, color TV, in-rm movies. AE, CB, DC, MC, V. Free parking, pool, health club, free breakfast, coffee shop, bar, free crib. *Note:* Modern 11-story motel offering easy access to the Market Center, comfortable rms w. balconies or private patios, and friendly reception and svce. Business clientele.

VIP floor. Very good value. 8 min. from dwntwn and 10 min. from Love Field (free shuttle). **I–M**

🏩 **La Quinta Inn–Central** (nr. dwntwn), 4440 N. Central Expwy., TX 75206 (214/821-4220; toll free, see La Quinta). 101 rms, A/C, color TV, in-rm movies. AE, CB, DC, MC, V. Free parking, adjacent 24-hr. coffee shop, free crib. *Note:* A good value, 15 min. from dwntwn and close to Love Field. Spacious, comfortable (but rather dark) rms w. balconies; friendly reception and svce. Ideal for the car traveler. **I**

🏩 **Classic Motor Inn** (nr. dwntwn), 9229 Carpenter Fwy., TX 75247 (214/631-6633). 135 rms, A/C, color TV, free in-rm movies. AE, MC, V. Free parking, pool, sauna, health club, café adj., valet svce, free breakfast, free crib. *Note:* Well-maintained motel 15 min. from dwntwn on Carpenter Frwy. (Tex. 183). Inviting rms; some w. refrigerators. Close to the Texas Stadium. Very good value. **B–I**

🏩 **Park Cities Inn** (nr. dwntwn), 6101 Hillcrest Ave., TX 75205 (214/521-0330). 53 rms, A/C, color TV, in-rm movies. AE, CB, DC, MC, V. Crib $3. Free parking, nearby coffee shop, free breakfast, crib. *Note:* Small, modest motel across from Southern Methodist University. Satisfactory comfort and facilities. Some rms w. refrigerators. 10 min. from dwntwn. **B–I**

Accommodations in the Vicinity

🏩🏩🏩🏩 **Omni Mandalay** (vic.), 221 E. Las Colinas Blvd., Irving, TX 75039 (214/556-0800; toll free, see Omni). 424 rms, A/C, color TV, in-rm movies. AE, CB, DC, MC, V. Valet parking $5, pool, tennis, health club, sauna, two rests. (including Enjolie), coffee shop, three bars, rm svce, free crib. *Note:* An impressive 27-story white tower on the lake at Las Colinas, an enormous apartment complex known as Little Venice because of its canals and water taxis. Ultramodern facilities and comfort. Luxurious rms w. balconies and a spectacular view (the best overlook the lake). Efficient svce and a first-rate rest. Group and wealthy conventioneer clientele. Three VIP floors. 10 min. from dwntwn and 10 min. from Dallas–Fort Worth Airport. **E**

Airport Accommodations

🏩🏩🏩 **Hyatt Regency Airport** (vic.), Dallas–Fort Worth Airport, TX 75261 (214/453-1234; toll free, see Hyatt). 1,388 rms, A/C, color TV, in-rm movies. AE, CB, DC, MC, V. Free parking, pool, eight tennis courts, two golf courses, putting green, health club, sauna, four rests., coffee shop, three bars, rm svce, disco, boutiques, free 24-hr. airport shuttle. *Note:* Ultramodern twin-tower hotel located inside DFW Airport; the largest airport hotel in the world. Irreproachable comfort and efficient svce. Well-soundproofed rms, most w. refrigerators. Rather intrusive business, group, and convention clientele. Interesting wknd packages. Good recreational equipment. Three VIP floors. Recently totally renovated. **E**

🏩 **La Quinta Inn–DFW Airport East** (vic.), 4105 W. Airport Fwy., Irving, TX 75062 (214/252-6546; toll free, see La Quinta). 168 rms, A/C, color TV, in-rm movies. AE, CB, DC, MC, V. Parking, pool, adj. 24-hr. coffee shop, free crib. *Note:* Modern, functional motel w. huge, comfortable rms and efficient svce. A very good value, 5 min. from the Dallas–Fort Worth Airport (free shuttle). **B–I**

RESTAURANTS

Personal Favorites (in order of preference)

🍴🍴🍴🍴 **The French Room** (dwntwn), in the Adolphus (see "Accommodations," above) (742-8200). A/C. Dinner only, Mon–Sat. AE, CB, DC, MC, V. J&T. *Specialties:* red snapper w. watercress sauce, smoked-salmon salad, roast rack of lamb, goose liver in aspic and brioche, braised turbot w. morels, oysters and asparagus en croûte w. citrus sauce, sherbet plate, praline mousse. The menu changes regularly. *Note:* Dallas's most romantic dining rm. The cuisine—a remarkable updating of classic French recipes—is supervised by Jean Banchet, longtime owner of the illustrious Le Français rest. in Wheeling, Ill. Opulent baroque decor w. crystal chandeliers, cherubim on the ceiling, and Louis XVI furniture. The svce is of rare distinction. Resv. a definite must. Valet parking. *French.* **E–VE**

    🍷🍷 **Café Pacific** (nr. dwntwn), 24 Highland Park Village, Preston Rd. and Mockingbird Lane (526-1170). A/C. Lunch/dinner Mon–Sat; closed hols. AE, DC, MC, V. Jkt. *Specialties:* clam chowder, fried clams, fresh grilled salmon, sautéed seafood, catch of the day. Complete wine list at appropriate prices. *Note:* Irreproachably fresh seafood makes this elegant rest. a favorite of connoisseurs. Modern, inviting decor of woodwork, polished brass, mirrors, and a wealth of plants. Attentive svce. Resv. advised, but the waits are sometimes long. An excellent place. *Seafood/American.* **I–M**

    🍷🍷 **Chamberlain's Prime Chop House** (nr. dwntwn), Town Hall Sq., 5330 Belt Line Rd., Addison (934-2467). A/C. Dinner only, Mon–Sat; closed hols. *Specialties:* tomato-and-onion salad, Brazilian black-bean soup, grilled beef-steak mushrooms, prime rib, New York strip, grilled veal chop, melted dark chocolate cake w. vanilla-bean ice cream. *Note:* Former chef at the Little Nell hotel in Aspen, Richard Chamberlain has opened this fine rest. in his home town. Excellent meats in huge portions. Southwestern art deco lends flair and sophistication to this latest addition to the Texan tradition of chophouses. Well worth the 20-min. drive from dwntwn. Resv. highly recommended. *Steak/American.* **I–M**

    🍷🍷 **Pomodoro** (dwntwn), 2550 Cedar Springs Rd. (871-1924). A/C. Lunch Mon–Fri, dinner nightly. AE, CB, DC, MC, V. *Specialties:* bresaola w. pine nuts, orange, and raisins; swordfish carpaccio w. tomato-basil vinaigrette; Gorgonzola and radicchio; gnocchetti w. sausage; osso buco. Rather short wine list but extensive grappa collection. *Note:* Brightly cacophonous rest. offering some of the city's most memorable Italian cuisine. Pleasant outdoor patio dining on cool evenings. Noisy, lively atmosphere. Friendly and efficient svce. Resv. advised in light of its success. *Italian.* **I–M**

    🔆🍷 **Mario's Chiquita** (nr. dwntwn), 4514 Travis St. (521-0721). A/C. Lunch/dinner daily; closed Jan 1, Thanksgiving, Dec 25. AE, MC, V. *Specialties:* tacos al carbón, chile relleño, carne asada, mole poblano. *Note:* The most authentic of the countless Mexican rests. in Dallas, w. a pleasant atmosphere and vibrant, colorful decor. Efficient svce. Locally very popular. No resv. Other location: 221 W. Parker Rd., Plano (423-2977). *Mexican.* **B–I**

    🔆🍷 **Sonny Bryan's** (nr. dwntwn), 2202 Inwood Rd. (357-7120). A/C. Breakfast/lunch daily (until 4pm). No credit cards. *Specialties:* barbecue, ham, pork chops, and beef. Beer but no wine. *Note:* A contender, w. Dickey's Barbecue (see below), for the "Best Barbecue in Dallas" award. Cooked over hickory-wood fires and smothered in an inimitable sauce, Sonny's barbecue has inspired a cult following. Shabby decor and nonexistent svce. Close to the Medical Center. An authentic local legend for nearly 30 years. No resv. Other location: 302 N. Market, in dwntwn (744-1610); open daily 11am–10pm. *American.* **B**

    🍷 **Aw Shucks** (nr. dwntwn), 3601 Greenville Ave. (821-9449). A/C. Lunch/dinner daily. AE, CB, DC, MC, V. *Specialties:* oysters on the half shell or fried, cornmeal-fried shrimp, crab cakes, fried catfish. *Note:* A casual, tiny seafood bar w. an outdoor patio and picnic-style tables. Impeccably fresh oysters and other seafood creatures. No-frills, convivial atmosphere, but loud music background. Locally popular. No resv. *Seafood.* **B**

Other Restaurants (from top bracket to budget)

    🔆🍷🍷🍷🍷 **Mansion on Turtle Creek** (nr. dwntwn), in the Mansion on Turtle Creek (see "Accommodations," above) (526-2121).

A/C. Breakfast daily, lunch Mon–Fri, dinner nightly, brunch Sat–Sun; closed Dec 25. AE, CB, DC, MC, V. J&T. *Specialties:* smoked shrimp w. pinto beans, Texas lentil and lamb-sausage soup, sirloin steak w. pesto and smoked bacon, lobster tacos, quail quesadillas. The menu changes regularly. Extensive wine list. *Note:* Chef Dean Fearing's ultra-sophisticated cuisine combines French culinary finesse w. southwestern flavors. Super-chic, Hispanic-Texan decor. Very correct svce. A favorite of local celebrities and high-rolling businesspeople. Resv. required. Valet parking. *American.* **E–VE**

The Riviera (nr. dwntwn), 7709 Inwood Rd. (351-0094). A/C. Dinner only, nightly; closed hols. AE, CB, DC, MC, V. J&T. *Specialties:* snails and spinach tortellini, fettuccine w. smoked chicken and wild mushrooms, rack of lamb, rosemary-stuffed quail w. Gorgonzola-cheese polenta, grilled steak w. herbs Provençal, duck breast w. orange-brandy sauce, crème brûlée Grand Marnier. Good wine list, mostly Californian. *Note:* David Holben, a young chef who came here from the Café Royal in the Plaza of the Americas Hotel, deftly applies a blend of French and Italian techniques to prime Texas produce—particularly fresh vegetables, game, and fish. Pretty, flower-filled country-Provençal decor appropriate to the name; warm, attentive svce. Locally very popular; resv. a must. Valet parking. *Italian/Continental.* **E–VE**

Baby Routh (nr. dwntwn), 2708 Routh St. (871-2345). A/C. Lunch Mon–Fri, dinner nightly, brunch Sun; closed hols. AE, CB, DC, MC, V. *Specialties:* sesame-seared scallops, smoked corn chowder, barbecue, grilled chicken w. honey and spices, beef tenderloin, ultimate banana split, crème brûlée w. pumpkin and ginger. *Note:* The more relaxed, less snobby offshoot of the once-famous Routh Street Café offers inventive modern cuisine from the talented Kevin Rathbun. Spotlessly white, elegant decor w. a lovely patio. An "in" place. Resv. advised. *American.* **M–E**

Old Warsaw (nr. dwntwn), 2610 Maple (528-0032). A/C. Dinner only, nightly; closed Christmas and Jan 1. AE, DC, MC, V. Jkt. *Specialties:* steak tartar, foie gras, fresh Dover sole, steak au poivre, pheasant w. game sauce, rack of lamb w. garlic sauce and eggplant purée, soufflés. Extensive wine list of over 350 wines. *Note:* Ultra-romantic atmosphere augmented by the dark exposed wood and the piano and violin duet. Astute preparation and heavy, richly textured sauces define the strengths of the cooking. Resv. required. Valet parking. *French/Continental.* **M–E**

Calluaud's (nr. dwntwn), 5405 W. Lover's Ln. (352-1997). A/C. Lunch Mon–Fri, dinner Mon–Sat; closed hols. AE, CB, DC, MC, V. Jkt. *Specialties:* mesclun salad greens w. goat cheese and lemon–olive oil dressing, Dover sole, rack of lamb, grilled chicken breast. w. herbs de Provence, Grand Marnier soufflé. *Note:* French Provençal-style decor, crystal chandeliers, smart flower arrangements, and French classics prepared in their traditional manner make this a favorite of the Dallas elite. Friendly but somewhat slack svce. Resv. recommended, especially wknds. *French.* **M**

Dakota's (dwntwn), 600 N. Akard St. (740-4001). A/C. Lunch Mon–Fri, dinner nightly; closed hols. AE, CB, DC, MC, V. *Specialties:* homemade pasta, blackened red snapper, mesquite-grilled steaks, game dishes. *Note:* With its marble walls, its cascading waterfall, and its elegant patio, all below ground level, this rest. draws Dallas's own VIPs as well as visiting celebrities. Good selection of grills, mainly steaks, chops, and seafood. Svce is first-rate. Resv. advised. Valet parking. *American.* **M**

Cafe Panda (nr. dwntwn), 7979 Inwood Rd., no. 121 (902-9500). A/C. Lunch/dinner daily. AE, DC, MC, V. *Specialties:* shar char prawns, pineapple chicken, shrimp w. black-bean sauce, tangerine beef. *Note:* Tony Chinese bistro on the edge of the Park Cities, close to Love Field airport. Unusual and standard dishes from different regions of China attractively presented. Quietly intimate atmosphere. Courteous svce. A very good place. Resv. accepted. *Chinese.* **I–M**

 Newport's (dwntwn), 703 McKinney (954-0220). A/C. Lunch Mon–Fri, dinner nightly; closed hols. AE, MC, V. *Specialties:* raw oysters, ceviche, mesquite-grilled seafood, fresh salmon and swordfish, toothsome cheesecake. *Note:* Another well-established favorite for business lunches and dinners. Located in a converted turn-of-the-century brewery, Newport's is one of the neatest rustic rests. in town. The atmosphere is relaxing, the fish superb. Pleasant svce. Resv. recommended. *Seafood.* **I–M**

 Royal Tokyo (vic.), 7525 Greenville Ave. (368-3304). A/C. Lunch/dinner daily, brunch Sun; closed hols. AE, CB, DC, MC, V. Jkt. *Specialties:* sushi, tempura, sukiyaki, teppanyaki, shabu shabu. *Note:* The experts agree that this is the best Japanese rest. in Dallas. Elegant Japanese decor w. a lovely water grdn. Very good svce. An excellent locale, 20 min. from dwntwn. *Japanese.* **I–M**

 Mia's (nr. dwntwn), 4322 Lemmon Ave. (526-1020). A/C. Lunch/dinner Mon–Sat. MC, V. *Specialties:* bean-and-bacon soup, queso flameado w. chorizo, chicken burritos, chimichangas, chiles rellenos. *Note:* Roomy Mexican rest. w. sunny terra-cotta setting. The excellent Tex-Mex cuisine attracts hordes of patrons, so you have to wait in line. Attentive, prompt svce. *Mexican.* **I**

 S. & D. Oyster Company (nr. dwntwn), 2701 McKinney Ave. (880-0111). A/C. Lunch/dinner Mon–Sat. AE, MC, V. *Specialties:* gumbo, oysters, Mexican Gulf shrimp, fish of the day. *Note:* Irreproachably fresh seafood served in a usually packed house, w. very effective New Orleans decor and a noisy, friendly ambience. No resv. unfortunately. *Seafood.* **I**

 Allen Street Bar & Grill (nr. dwntwn), 2900 McKinney Ave. (871-0256). A/C. Lunch/dinner daily. AE, CB, MC, V. *Specialties:* gazpacho, nachos, hamburgers, grilled three-cheese sandwich, quesadillas, grilled tuna steak, broiled chicken, scrumptious desserts. *Note:* Friendly, hospitable hangout w. dark-wood setting. Good, eclectic food and generous portions at pygmy prices. *American.* **B–I**

 Tolbert's Texas Chili Parlor (dwntwn), One Dallas Center, 350 N. St. Paul (953-1353). A/C. Lunch/dinner daily (until 8pm). AE, CB, DC, MC, V. *Specialties:* "donkey tails" (hot-dog tortillas), chile con carne. *Note:* The state's most celebrated chili parlor, a must for all visitors. Relaxed atmosphere. In case you're allergic to chile, try the Sonofabitch Stew. Other location: 1800 N. Market (871-2062). *American.* **B**

Restaurants in the Vicinity

 Clark's Outpost Barbecue Restaurant (vic.), U.S. 377 at Gene Autry Dr., Tioga (817/437-2414). A/C. Lunch/dinner Wed–Sun. AE, MC, V. *Specialties:* calf fries; chile; fried zucchini w. horseradish; smoked sausage w. barbecue sauce; chicken-fried steak; barbecued spareribs, beef, ham, and turkey; homemade apple pie. *Note:* Way out in the country a full hour's drive north of Dallas, this tiny (nine tables) rest. of undistinguished but authentic appearance will serve you the best barbecues anywhere in Texas, lovingly prepared by Warren Clark. Ranchers flock here from all the surrounding country; in the parking lot their Jeeps and four-by-fours stand shoulder-to-shoulder with the Mercedeses and Rolls-Royces of the wealthy burghers from Dallas. A classic of its kind for almost 20 years; don't miss it. To get here, take I-35 north from Dallas, then the 288 loop as far as U.S. 380, east to U.S. 377, and then north again. *American.* **B–I**

Cafeterias/Fast Food

 Luby's (vic.), 10425 N. Central Expwy. at Meadow Central Mall (361-9024). A/C. Lunch/dinner daily (until 8pm). No credit cards. Respectable fast-food cuisine. Other location: 5954 Alpha Rd. (233-3275).

 Highland Park (nr. dwntwn), 4611 Cole St. (526-3801). A/C. Lunch/dinner Mon–Sat (until 8pm). No credit cards. Excellent cafeteria w. low prices.

BARS & NIGHTCLUBS

Borrowed Money (nr. dwntwn), 9100 N. Central Expwy. (361-9996). A saloon of typically Texan atmosphere w. dancing and the requisite country music.

Club Dada (nr. dwntwn), 2720 Elm St. (744-3232). Jazz, rockabilly, and New Wave in the heart of the artists' quarter of Deep Ellum in East Dallas. Draws a young crowd that would be at home in New York's Soho.

Dick's Last Resort (dwntwn), 101 N. Market (747-0001). Popular joint w. a good beer selection and raucous crowds. Open Mon–Sat.

Fish Dance (nr. dwntwn), 3606 Greenville Ave. (828-2277). New top dance club w. a funny "Captain Nemo and Little Mermaid" atmosphere.

Hard Rock Café (nr. dwntwn), 2601 McKinney Ave. (855-0007). A replica of the rock clubs operating under the same name in New York, Los Angeles, San Francisco, etc. Youthful crowd; noisy; the tourists' favorite. Open daily.

☀ **Longhorn Ballroom** (nr. dwntwn), 216 Corinth (421-6262). Open Wed–Sat. A country-music fixture for more than 20 years.

Poor David's Pub (nr. dwntwn), 1924 Greenville Ave. (821-9891). A Dallas classic featuring every style of music from live reggae to jazz or blues. Open Mon–Sat.

Tree's (nr. dwntwn), 2709 Elm St. (748-5009). A diverse range of local and national acts in a huge warehouse w. pool tables in the loft. Open daily.

FORT WORTH

Once a true cowboy town on the Trinity River, Fort Worth was known in the 19th century as "the town where the West begins," where the huge herds of Texas cattle were watered on the way to the railhead in Kansas. Established in 1849 to defend the pioneers against the Comanches, this former garrison town attracted some of the most famous and formidable characters of the West, from Doc Holliday to Wyatt Earp, as well as Butch Cassidy and the Sundance Kid. Inseparable neighbors, Dallas and Fort Worth constitute a gigantic metroplex almost 50 mi. (80km) long, crisscrossed with four-lane highways and nicknamed "Silicon Prairie" because of the area's high concentration of leading electronics companies. Despite its boots and Stetsons, the most Texan of Texas cities makes good use of its aeronautical, oil, and computer resources. Fort Worth nevertheless remains one of the biggest livestock (see the famous **Stockyards**) and grain markets in the country. Its famous rodeos continue to draw huge crowds, as do the very popular **Amon Carter Museum**, dedicated to the era of the Far West, and the splendid and futurist **Kimbell Art Museum**. The infamous "J.R." of "Dallas," Larry Hagman, is a celebrated son of Fort Worth.

Note: The area code for Fort Worth is 817. For arrival and transit information, see p. 710.

INFORMATION & TOURS

TOURIST INFORMATION: The **Fort Worth Convention & Visitors Bureau**, 100 E. 15th St., TX 76102 (817/336-8791; toll free 800/433-5747).
Visitor Information Center, 130 E. Exchange Ave. (817/624-4741).

GUIDED TOURS: **Gray Line Tours Fort Worth** (bus) (817/625-5887): Guided tour of the city, serving major hotels.
Tarantula Steam Train (625-7245): Daily 1½-hr. trips through the center

of Fort Worth and to the Stockyards aboard luxury cars pulled by an 1856 Baldwin steam engine. Board at the Eight Avenue Train Yard (2318 S. Eight Ave.).

SIGHTS, ATTRACTIONS & ACTIVITIES

ARCHITECTURAL HIGHLIGHTS: ☼▲ **Water Garden,** Houston and 14th Sts.: Superb landscape gardens in the middle of the city with concrete terraces, plantings, and futurist waterfalls. The water flows at a rate of 19,000 gallons (72,000 liters) per min. Designed by Philip Johnson; dates from 1974.

▲ **Will Rogers Memorial Center,** 3400 W. Lancaster St. (871-8150): Dedicated to the famous cinema cowboy and humorist, this vast exhibition center includes the **Memorial Coliseum** and the **Will Rogers Auditorium,** where the big concerts, rodeos, auto shows, and other Fort Worth events take place, as well as several major museums of Fort Worth (see the Amon Carter Museum, Kimbell Art Museum, and Museum of Science & History, below).

HISTORIC BUILDINGS: ▲ **Log Cabin Village,** 2100 Log Cabin Village Lane (926-5881): A group of authentic pioneer homes dating from the mid-19th century. For lovers of western history. Open daily.

☼▲ **The Stockyards National Historic District,** Exchange Ave. and W. Main St. (625-9715): Fort Worth's original claim to fame. Retains some of the flavor of the old cattle drives and contains a variety of shops, art galleries, saloons, western boutiques, and restaurants. The atmosphere is amusing although rather touristy. Try to visit on a weekend.

☼▲ **Sundance Square,** bounded by Commerce, Houston, 2nd, and 3rd Sts.: The historic heart of Fort Worth, with old houses, brick sidewalks, and period gas lamps. Lots of restaurants, boutiques, and art galleries as well. Good for a stroll.

▲ **Thistle Hill,** 1509 Pennsylvania, at Summit (336-1212): The last of the luxurious manors (1903) belonging to the surpassingly rich "cattle barons" of the 19th century. Magnificently restored in all its Texan opulence. Open Sun–Fri.

MUSEUMS OF ART: ☼▲▲ **Amon Carter Museum of Western Art,** 3501 Camp Bowie Blvd. (738-1933): American painting and sculpture, with special attention to western lore (notably paintings by Frederic Remington and Charles Russell). The marvelous triangular Philip Johnson building, dedicated to the founder of the *Fort Worth Star-Telegram,* Amon Carter, also houses works by such contemporary artists as Georgia O'Keeffe, Ben Shahn, Grant Wood, and Stuart Davis. Open Tues–Sun.

▲ **Fort Worth Museum of Modern Art,** 1309 Montgomery St., at Camp Bowie Blvd. (738-9215): Interesting temporary and permanent exhibits of 20th-century art including works by Pablo Picasso, Jackson Pollock, Mark Rothko, Clyfford Still, Frank Stella, and Andy Warhol. Among the best known of the works on display are *Manhattan II* by Lyonel Feininger, Ellsworth Kelly's *Curved Red on Blue,* Roy Lichtenstein's *Atom Burst,* and *En haut, à gauche* by Vassily Kandinsky. Open Tues–Sun.

☼▲▲▲ **Kimbell Art Museum,** 3333 Camp Bowie Blvd. (332-8451): A Louis Kahn masterpiece from 1973, this building houses all forms of art from prehistoric times to Picasso and includes one of the finest private collections of European masters in the country. Among its most famous holdings: Giovanni Bellini's *Christ in Benediction,* Caravaggio's *The Cheaters,*

Goya's *Matador Pedro Romero*, Rembrandt's *Portrait of a Young Jew*, and Picasso's *Man with a Pipe*. Open Tues–Sun. The patio restaurant is agreeable in good weather.

    ⚱ **Sid Richardson Collection of Western Art**, 309 Main St. (332-6554): Very fine collection of "western art" formed by the late oil tycoon Sid Richardson. The two most famous artists of this 19th-century romantic movement—Frederic Remington and Charles M. Russell—are represented by some 50 paintings. Open Tues–Sun.

MUSEUMS OF SCIENCE & HISTORY: ⚱ **Museum of Science & History,** 1501 Montgomery St. (732-1631): A very educational museum of humankind with a section on medical sciences and on anthropology, as well as a hemispherical dome for 70mm film among the most modern in the world **(Omni Theater).** Open daily.

PARKS & GARDENS: ⚱ **Botanic Gardens,** 3200 Botanic Garden Dr. (871-7686): Very lovely botanic garden displaying more than 2,000 plant varieties as well as an enchanting Japanese garden with authentically Japanese tea houses. Open daily.

PERFORMING ARTS: For a daily listing of all shows and cultural events, consult the entertainment pages of the daily paper *Fort Worth Star Telegram* (morning and evening), and of the monthly magazine *Texas Monthly.*
    Casa Mañana, 3101 W. Lancaster Ave. (332-2272): Broadway hits, concerts, modern theater. Texas's most famous theater-in-the-round.
    Circle Theater, 230 W. Fourth St. (877-3040): Drama, comedy.
    Hip Pocket Theatre, 1620 Las Vegas Trail N. (927-2833): Open-air theater.
    Tarrant County Convention Center Theatre, 1111 Houston St. (884-2222): Home of the Fort Worth Opera, the Fort Worth Ballet, and the Fort Worth Symphony Orchestra (music director: John Giordano) (Sept–May).
    Will Rogers Auditorium, 3301 W. Lancaster Ave. (332-0909): Concerts, recitals, shows with top stars.
    William Edrington Scott Theater, 3505 W. Lancaster Ave. (738-6509): Modern and classic theater.

RODEOS: ⚱ **Cowtown Coliseum,** 123 E. Exchange Ave., at the Stockyards (625-1025): Rodeos 3 and 8pm on Fri and Sat Apr–Nov, in a spirited atmosphere. Call for winter schedule.

SHOPPING: Justin Boot Co., 717 W. Vickery: Factory outlet with prices 30%–50% below list. A good bet.
    N. L. Leddy's Boots & Saddles, 2455 N. Main St.: Custom boots. Among the best.

SPECIAL EVENTS: For the exact schedule of events below, consult the **Fort Worth Convention & Visitors Bureau** (see "Tourist Information," above).
    Southwestern Exposition and Livestock Show (late Jan to Feb): One of the country's best-known rodeos, for fans of real flesh-and-blood cowboys. A nearly 100-year-old tradition.
    Chisholm Trail Round-up (second wknd in June): Lively and colorful cowboy parades, square dances, and barbecues.
    Shakespeare in the Park (June and July): Open-air, free performances in Trinity Park Playhouse, West Fort Worth.
    Pioneer Days Celebration (late Sept): A lively celebration of the cult of the cowboy with carnivals, parades, and public dances.

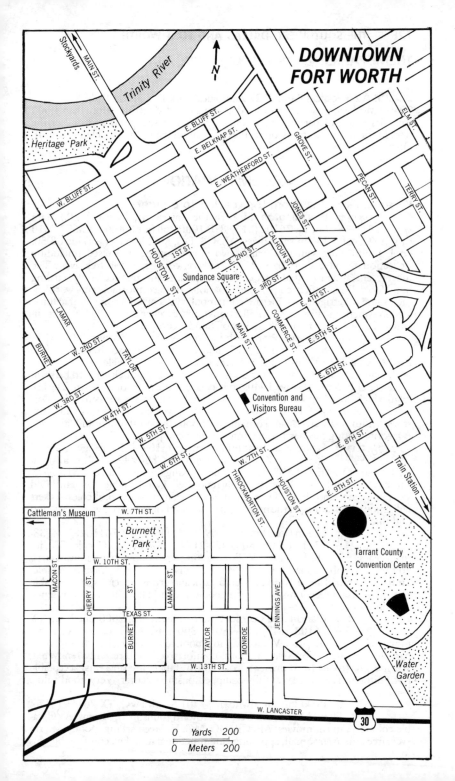

THEME PARKS: See "Theme Parks" in Dallas, above.

ZOOS: ⚓ **Zoological Park,** 2727 Zoological Park Dr., Forest Park (817/871-7050): Modern, very well-conceived zoo in a wooded setting. More than 4,500 animal species; of particular interest, a spectacular seal pond and one of the world's richest collections of reptiles and amphibians (in the Herpetarium). Open daily.

ACCOMMODATIONS

Personal Favorites (from top bracket to budget)

🏨🏨🏨🏨 **Worthington** (formerly the Americana; dwntwn), 200 Main St., TX 76102 (817/870-1000; toll free 800/433-5677). 510 rms, A/C, color TV, in-rm movies. AE, CB, DC, MC, V. Valet parking $8.50, pool, health club, sauna, ice rink, two tennis courts, two rests. (including Reflections), coffee shop, bars, 24-hr. rm svce, concierge, crib free. *Note:* The most recent, and most luxurious, of the local palaces, this architecturally startling hotel looks like a truncated pyramid. Spacious, ultra-comfortable rms w. balconies, some w. refrigerators. Elegant contemporary decor, very complete facilities, a good American-cuisine rest. (Reflections), and excellent svce. Big business clientele. In the heart of Fort Worth just off Sundance Sq. **E**

🏨🏨🏨 **Radisson Plaza Hotel** (formerly Hyatt; dwntwn), 815 Main St., TX 76102 (817/870-2100; toll free, see Radisson). 515 rms, A/C, color TV, in-rm movies. AE, CB, DC, MC, V. Valet gar. $8, pool, health club, sauna, two rests. (including the Cactus Bar and Grill), two bars, rm svce, free crib. *Note:* Massive 1940s-style palace in the heart of dwntwn. The hotel in which President Kennedy spent the night before he was assassinated in Dallas. Luxurious, comfortable layout w. spacious, well-conceived rms and a six-story atrium w. a waterfall and ornamental pools. Impeccable svce and fair rests. A favorite among businesspeople. Interesting wknd packages. **E**

☀🏨🏨🏨 **Stockyards Hotel** (nr. dwntwn), 109 E. Exchange Ave., TX 76106 (817/625-6427; toll free 800/423-8471). 52 rms, A/C, color TV. AE, CB, DC, MC, V. Valet parking $5, rest., bar, crib $10. *Note:* The city's oldest (1902) hotel, carefully renovated. Comfortable, congenial Old West ambience and decor. Decent rest. and excellent svce. Local color seekers will enjoy the location, in the heart of the slaughterhouse district w. its rests. and nightlife. **M**

🏨🏨 **Green Oaks Inn** (vic.), 6901 West Fwy., TX 76116 (817/738-7311; toll free 800/433-2174). 282 rms, A/C, color TV, in-rm movies. AE, CB, DC, MC, V. Free parking, two pools, two tennis courts, golf, health club, sauna, rest., bars, rm svce, disco, free crib. *Note:* Agreeable, Tudor-style motel amid 10 acres (4ha) of park and grdns. Spacious, comfortable rms and pleasant reception and svce. A good value and a favorite of connoisseurs; 15 min. from dwntwn. **I–M**

🏨🏨 **Clarion and Comfort Inn** (nr. dwntwn), 2000 Beach St., TX 76103 (817/534-4801). 300 rms, A/C, color TV, in-rm movies. AE, CB, DC, MC, V. Free parking, pool, tennis court, health club, rest., bar, rm svce, free crib. *Note:* Spacious, comfortable hotel, recently renovated, about 3 mi. (5km) from dwntwn Fort Worth. Huge, inviting rms; acceptable rest.; ultra-professional svce; fully equipped business center. Very good value. **I–M**

🏨 **HoJo Inn** (nr. dwntwn), 4201 South Fwy., TX 76115 (817/923-8281; toll free, see Howard Johnson's). 98 rms, A/C, cable color TV, in-rm movies. AE, CB, DC, MC, V. Free parking, pool, rest., rm svce, free crib. *Note:* Small, appealing, and functional motel w. comfortable rms and affable reception and svce. A very good value that's ideal for the car traveler, 10 min. from dwntwn. **B–I**

🍷 **Motel 6 North** (nr. dwntwn), 3271 I-35W, TX 76106 (817/
625-4359). 106 rms, A/C, cable color TV. AE, DC, MC, V.
Free parking, pool, free crib. *Note:* An unbeatable value 10 min. from dwntwn, offering functional comfort and a warm welcome. **B**

RESTAURANTS

Personal Favorites (from top bracket to budget)

🍷🍷🍷 **La Piazza** (nr. dwntwn), 3431 W. 7th St. (334-0000). A/C.
Lunch/dinner Mon–Sat; closed hols. AE, CB, DC, MC, V.
Specialties: penne w. walnuts and Gorgonzola sauce, veal chop w. porcini mushrooms, red snapper Livornese, scampi Pernod w. linguine, zabaglione Grand Marnier, tiramisù. Good Italian and Californian wine list. *Note:* The "in" place in Fort Worth's uptown. The menu is a plainly stated listing of familiar Italian dishes brilliantly executed by chef Salvo Pampallona. Warm, sunny setting. Flawless svce. Resv. a must. *Italian.* **M–E**

🍷🍷 **Saint Emilion** (nr. dwntwn), 3617 W. 7th St. (737-2781).
A/C. Lunch Tues–Fri (except in summer when closed for lunch) dinner nightly; closed hols. AE, MC, V. *Specialties:* crayfish and crabmeat ravioli, pan-fried mountain trout w. fried parsley, roast duck w. currant sauce, pecan chocolate-chip cake w. coffee ice cream. Seasonal wine list. Well chosen wine list. *Note:* Fort Worth's best French rest. Blackboard specials change daily. Pleasant country-grdn atmosphere. Polite, amiable staff. Resv. *French.* **M–E**

🍷🍷 **Juanita's** (dwntwn), 115 W. 2nd St. (335-1777). A/C.
Lunch/dinner daily; closed Dec 25. AE, MC, V. *Specialties:* nachos, fajitas, broiled chicken w. chili butter, quail braised in tequila, flan. *Note:* The most attractive of the town's innumerable Tex-Mex eating places. The slightly fussy food is more Mex than Tex. The setting is delightfully period, and on fine days you can eat outdoors. Svce w. a smile. Resv. advisable. Valet parking. The "in" place on Sundance Sq. *Mexican.* **I–M**

🍷🍷 **Michael's** (nr. dwntwn), 3413 W. Seventh St. (877-3413).
A/C. Lunch Mon–Fri, dinner Mon–Sat; closed Christmas.
AE, DC, MC, V. *Specialties:* goat-cheese tart, jalapeño shrimp, Gulf crab cakes w. ancho chili cream sauce, pan-seared Montana pheasant w. raspberry-chipotle sauce, jalapeño–apple pie w. basil ice cream. All-American wine list. *Note:* Excellent Southwestern cuisine that stretches the use of chilies and jalapeños (see the dessert, above). Ranch atmosphere w. cement floors and contemporary artwork. Everything from tuxes to cowboy boots (often worn together) has a place here. Friendly, well-versed svce. *American.* **I–M**

☀️🍷🍷 **Winfield's 08** (dwntwn), 301 Main St. (870-1908). A/C.
Lunch Mon–Fri, dinner Mon–Sat; closed hols. AE, CB, DC, MC, V. *Specialties:* wonderful hickory-broiled meat and fish. *Note:* A charming little American rest. in a turn-of-the-century house on Sundance Sq. w. etched-glass windows and Victorian decor. Attentive, efficient svce. Resv. advisable. Valet parking. A very good place. *American.* **I**

☀️🍷 **Joe T. Garcia's** (nr. dwntwn), 2201 N. Commerce St. (626-
4356). A/C. Lunch/dinner daily; closed hols. No credit cards. *Specialties:* nachos, chile relleño, tacos, enchiladas, quesadillas, chimichangas, excellent margaritas. *Note:* A Tex-Mex family favorite for more than half a century, w. an agreeable patio and guaranteed local color. No resv. Locally very popular. Inevitable waits on the wknds. *American/Mexican.* **B–I**

🍷 **Szechuan** (nr. dwntwn), 5712 Locke Ave. at Camp Bowie
Blvd. (738-7300). A/C. Lunch/dinner daily. AE, DC, MC, V. *Specialties:* Szechuan chicken, Peking duck, sweet-and-sour shrimp. *Note:* The

only Chinese rest. in Fort Worth that's worthy of the title, w. an extensive menu and generous portions. Classic Oriental decor and pleasant svce. *Chinese.* **B–I**

Cafeterias/Fast Food

Kincaid's (nr. dwntwn), 4901 Camp Bowie Blvd. (732-2881). A/C. Lunch Mon–Sat 10am–6pm. No credit cards. The best burgers in town in a one-time neighborhood grocery. Also excellent banana pudding.

☼ **Paris Coffee Shop** (nr. dwntwn), 704 W. Magnolia St. (335-2041). Breakfast Mon–Sat, lunch Mon–Fri. No credit cards. A local institution. Whether you're a cowboy, a trucker, a Texas millionaire, or a society lady, sooner or later you'll come to the Paris Coffee Shop. Very good chicken-fried steak, enchiladas, and chile.

BARS & NIGHTCLUBS

Billy Bob's Texas (nr. dwntwn), 2520 Rodeo Plaza (624-7117). Claims to be the world's largest honkytonk. Located a stone's throw away from the Stockyards' Cowtown Coliseum. Open for music and dancing nightly.

Caravan of Dreams (dwntwn), 312 Houston St. (877-3000). Fashionable nightclub with excellent jazz and live blues.

J & J Blues Bar (dwntwn), 937 Woodward (870-2337). Offers the best in live blues entertainment Tues–Sun.

Stagecoach Ballroom (nr. dwntwn), 2516 E. Belknap (831-2261). Huge, locally popular western dance hall with a guaranteed cowboy atmosphere.

☼ **The White Elephant Saloon** (nr. dwntwn), 106 E. Exchange Ave. (624-1887). Open daily. Country-and-western music just around the corner from the famous Stockyards. A classic for more than a century, with relaxed decor and ambience, plus decent barbecue.

NEARBY EXCURSIONS

☼🔍 **GRANBURY** (38 mi./60km SW of Fort Worth on U.S. 377): Charming little Texas town that has conserved and restored many of its buildings from the days of the great westward migration. Start with the picturesque **Opera House,** dating from 1886 and reopened to the public in 1975 after 50 years of slumber. Performances Thurs–Sun Mar–Dec; for information, call 817/573-9191.

On the way, see the 🚌 **Pate Museum of Transportation,** U.S. 377 between Fort Worth and Cresson (14 mi./22km south of Fort Worth) (817/332-1161): Small transportation museum, from the double-decker bus to the DC-3 and from the minesweeper to the venerable Model T. Rather jumbled but amusing. Open Tues–Sun.

Where to Eat in Granbury

🍽 **The Cuckoo's Nest,** 110 E. Pearl St. (817/573-9722): Lunch/dinner Tues–Sun. AE, DC, MC, V. Original decor in a remodeled 19th-century theater. **B–I**

🍽 **Nutt House,** Town Sq. (817/573-9362): Delightful Victorian decor from the 1890s. Lunch only, Tues–Sun. MC, V. The Nutt House also has a dozen rms to rent, with old-fashioned but comfortable furniture. **I**

☼🏛 **WAXAHACHIE** (30 mi./48km south of Dallas on I-35E): Called "Gingerbread City," Waxahachie boasts nearly 200 gingerbread-style and Victorian buildings, all historical landmarks and magnificently restored. Many movies were shot here, including *Tender Mercies* and *Place in the Sun.* Waxahachie was selected to be home to the giant atom smasher—the

Super-Conducting Super-Collider. However, construction, after being well under way, ended in 1993 when Congress voted to halt funding for the supercollider, which was expected to be the most expensive scientific instrument in the world.

Where to Eat in Waxahachie

 ♟ **Kirkpatrick's,** 207 S. College (214/937-0010): Lunch only, Mon–Fri. AE, MC, V. Light New American fare in a tiny, softly lit, high-ceilinged setting. The svce is as charming as the atmosphere. No beer or wine (BYOB). ▮

CHAPTER 36

HOUSTON☿

□ □ □

Where 150 years ago there was nothing but a muddy, mosquito-infested tent town, there stands today the Sunbelt's second-greatest city. Houston, once the capital of the Republic of Texas, owes its name to the first elected president of that short-lived nation—Sam Houston. One of the first Spanish explorers of the North American continent, Alvar Nuñez Cabeza de Vaca, remarked as early as 1528 on Houston's strategic position on the shore of Buffalo Bayou, and "The Bayou City," as Houston is sometimes called, is now the country's third-largest port (after New York and New Orleans). Its access to the sea is via the Ship Channel, a canal 50 mi. (80km) long, 400 ft. (122m) wide, and 40 ft. (12m) deep, passable by the largest deep-water vessels and each year carrying more than 70 million tons of goods.

Like its neighbor and rival, Dallas, Houston is a boom town—a mushrooming city with congested freeways and a spectacular skyline where more than 200 giant corporations have chosen to build their headquarters. Houston continued to flourish into the early 1980s, with annual economic and population growth averaging 15%. After the devastating oil bust of the mid-1980s and the slump in farm-product prices, the local economy (refining, petrochemicals, steel-making, electronic components, cotton, rice, etc.) is showing signs of recovery—almost 80% of the 220,000 lost jobs have been regained.

Houston negatives include: no coherent city planning, almost nonexistent public transportation, snarled auto traffic, a disturbing pollution level, a rising crime rate, and a police force generally regarded as quick on the draw.

World capital of the oil industry, Houston is also a city of science, culture, and sport. The **Lyndon B. Johnson Space Center,** headquarters for America's conquest of space, guided the first steps on the moon as well as every space flight launched from the Kennedy Space Center or California. The first word spoken by the first man to set foot on the moon, on July 20, 1969, was "Houston." The **Texas Medical Center,** the world's largest hospital complex with its 6,000 beds, two million patients a year, and 52,000 doctors, nurses, and employees, is known internationally for heart surgery and cancer research. Houston's six universities, its opera, and its symphony orchestra enjoy—and deserve—a high reputation. The **Astrodome,** an amazing covered stadium with 76,000 seats, 18 stories high, and air-conditioned throughout, is one of the most striking examples of contemporary American architecture.

Typically Texan, Houston is on the way to becoming a great cosmopolitan city as well; more than 52 consulates and 64 foreign banks have offices here.

Houston is the birthplace of singer Kenny Rogers, actors Dennis and Randy Quaid, actress Shelley Duvall, cardiac-transplant pioneer Prof. Denton Cooley, and the late billionaire businessman and movie producer Howard Hughes.

BASIC FACTS: State of Texas. Area code: 713. Time zone: central. ZIP Code: 77052. Founded: 1836. Approximate population: city, 1,690,000; metropolitan area, 3,700,000. Fourth-largest city and 10th-largest metropolitan area in the country.

CLIMATE: Due to the proximity of the Gulf of Mexico, Houston's winters are agreeably mild (average 51°F/11°C in Jan), while spring and fall are relatively hot. In summer the temperature is high (average 86°F/30°C in July) and so is the humidity, but since everything is fiercely air-conditioned, you may need something warm to wear in hotels, restaurants, and office buildings. There are tornadoes, often violent, in the fall.

DISTANCES: Dallas, 243 mi. (390km); Mexican border, 360 mi. (576km); New Orleans, 356 mi. (570km); San Antonio, 197 mi. (315km).

ARRIVAL & TRANSIT INFORMATION

AIRPORTS: The **Houston Intercontinental Airport** (IAH), 20 mi. (32km) north, handles 15 million passengers a year. For information, call 230-3000.

W. P. Hobby Airport (HOU), 10 mi. (16km) SE, has 7.5 million passengers a year. For information, call 643-4597.

U.S. AIRLINES: American (toll free 800/433-7300), Continental (toll free 800/525-0280), Delta (toll free 800/221-1212), Northwest (toll free 800/225-2525), Southwest (toll free 800/422-1616), TWA (toll free 800/221-2000), United (toll free 800/241-6522), and USAir (toll free 800/428-4322).

FOREIGN CARRIERS: Air Canada (toll free 800/776-3000), Air France (toll free 800/237-2747), British Airways (toll free 800/247-9297), KLM (toll free 800/374-7747), and Lufthansa (toll free 800/645-3880).

CITY LINK: Cab fare **from Houston Intercontinental Airport to city center,** is about $30; time, about 40 min. Bus: Airport Express (523-8888), every 30 min.; makes five stops dwntwn; fare, $13; time, about 60 min.

Cab fare **from Hobby Airport to city center,** is about $20; time, 25 min. Airport Express connects Hobby Airport to the city center; fare, $8; time, about 50–60 min.

This is one of the country's most sprawling cities, and cab fares are high, so renting a car is probably the best solution, although for this, too, rates are among the highest in the country. Public (bus) transportation is extensive and reaches far out into the suburbs, and there is rather efficient minibus service downtown (**Metropolitan Transit Authority/METRO;** call 635-4000 for information).

CAR RENTAL: (all at Houston Intercontinental Airport) Avis (toll free 800/331-1212), Budget (toll free 800/527-0700), Dollar (toll free 800/800-4000), Hertz (toll free 800/654-3131), National (toll free 800/227-7368), and Thrifty (toll free 800/367-2277). For dwntwn offices, consult the local telephone directory.

LIMOUSINE SERVICES: Carey Limousine Service (367-4759), Nico's Luxury Limousine (880-5466), and Southwest Carriage (toll free 800/322-8007).

TAXIS: Theoretically cabs can't be hailed on the street, but it's easy to find one outside any of the large hotels, or to call one by phone: **Fiesta Cab** (225-2666), **United Cab** (699-0000), or **Yellow Cab** (236-1111).

TRAIN: Amtrak station, 902 Washington Ave. (toll free 800/872-7245).

INTERCITY BUSES: Greyhound, 2121 S. Main St. (toll free 800/231-2222). Area unsafe.

INFORMATION & TOURS

TOURIST INFORMATION: The **Houston Chamber of Commerce,** 1200 Smith, Suite 700, TX 77002 (713/651-2197).
The **Houston Convention and Visitors Bureau,** 801 Congress St., TX 77002 (713/227-3100; toll free 800/365-7575).

GUIDED TOURS: Gray Line Tours (bus), 602 Sampson St. (223-8800): Guided tours of the city with departures from principal dwntwn hotels.

SIGHTS, ATTRACTIONS & ACTIVITIES

ARCHITECTURAL HIGHLIGHTS: ☼🔔 **Astrodome,** Kirby Dr. and Loop 610 (799-9595): Second-largest (in height) covered stadium in the world, after that in New Orleans, with 76,000 seats. The plastic roof rises 18 stories. Used not only for sports events but also for concerts, exhibitions, and political meetings. Impressive; the most-visited building in Texas. Guided tours daily.

☼🔔 **George R. Brown Convention Center,** 1001 Convention Center Blvd. (853-8000): New convention center opened in 1987. The brightly colored steamboat-shaped building has overtones of Paris's Centre Pompidou; its unbuttressed dome spans six city blocks and can accommodate a crowd of 35,000.

☼🔔🔔 **Houston Civic Center,** I-45 at Milam St., between Texas and Dallas Aves.: A huge quadrilateral of ultramodern high-rises and municipal buildings in the heart of Houston, featuring the **Sam Houston Coliseum;** the **George R. Brown Convention Center** (see above); **Tranquility Park,** on 32 levels with its oversize fountain (see below); **City Hall;** the **Public Library,** with an amusing sculpture (*Geometric Mouse*) by Claes Oldenburg; and an auditorium, **Jesse H. Jones Hall** (see below). Very eye-catching.

🔔 **Jesse H. Jones Hall for the Performing Arts,** 615 Louisiana St. (227-3974): A concert hall with remarkable acoustics, home of the Houston Symphony Orchestra. A daring design by the architect Caudill Rowlett Scott, with a movable ceiling that can be arranged to seat 1,800–3,000 people.

☼🔔🔔 **Nina Vance Alley Theatre,** 615 Texas Ave., at Louisiana St. (228-8421): This futurist structure, comprising two auditoriums divided by a party wall, is one of Houston's most innovative buildings—a sort of 21st-century fortress designed by Ulrich Fransen.

☼🔔🔔 **Pennzoil Towers,** Pennzoil Place: Twin towers shaped like oblique prisms, with slanted roofs, interior gardens at ground level, and a gigantic glass curtain wall rising 36 floors; a spectacular achievement of architects Philip Johnson and John Burgee (1976).

🔔 **Republic Bank Bldg.,** Republic Bank Center: A strange 56-story postmodern skyscraper with a Neo-Gothic gabled roof suggesting the banking houses of early Antwerp, another exciting building by the Johnson-Burgee team. The 105-ft.-high (35m) entrance hall is reminiscent of Piranesi's drawings of the palaces of ancient Rome.

🔔 **Texas Commerce Tower,** Texas Ave. at Travis St.: Fine modern building, five-sided and 75 floors high. The tallest building in the U.S. west of the Mississippi (1,002 ft./300.6m).

Texas Medical Center, bounded by Fannin St., Outer Belt, and Holcombe Blvd. (797-0100): Huge hospital complex covering 600 acres (243ha), considered the most up-to-date in the world. Its 14 hospitals and nine medical facilities attract researchers, students, and patients from all over the world. An acknowledged leader in cardiology, cancer care, rehabilitation, biomathematics, and space medicine. See, among others, the new and spectacular St. Luke's Medical Tower by architect Cesar Pelli. The Visitor Information Center (790-1136) arranges individual or guided-tour visits Mon–Fri.

Wortham Theater Center, 500 Texas Ave. (237-1439): Imposing $72-million performing arts complex dating from 1987. Home of the Houston Ballet and Houston Grand Opera. The gigantic lobby is well worth a glance.

CHURCHES/SYNAGOGUES: Rothko Chapel, 3900 Yupon St., at Sul Ross (524-9839): This octagonal chapel in an out-of-the-way district was designed by Philip Johnson in austere reinforced concrete. It houses 14 dark, brooding paintings created by Mark Rothko in 1965 and 1966. Barnett Newman's very beautiful *Broken Obelisk*, a sculpture dedicated to Martin Luther King, Jr., sits in a reflection pool in front of the chapel. Don't miss this wonderful setting for meditation and contemplation. Open daily.

HISTORIC BUILDINGS: Rice University, 6100 S. Main St. (527-4929): Small in size with only 3,500 students, but greatly renowned for its faculties of science and engineering, this university founded in 1912 boasts dozens of very beautiful neoclassical and Mediterranean-style buildings, including **Lovett Hall,** the **Sewall Art Gallery,** and the ultramodern and original **Herring Hall** by architect Cesar Pelli.

MUSEUMS OF ART: Bayou Bend Collection, 1 Westcott St. (529-8773): Beautiful collection of American furniture from the 17th through the 19th century, housed in 28 rooms of the vast Renaissance-style home of Ima Hogg, daughter of a former governor of Texas. Can be seen Tues–Sat by appointment.

Contemporary Arts Museum, 5216 Montrose Blvd. (526-3129): This strange silvered-aluminum parallelogram presents movies and temporary exhibitions of modern art and industrial design. Focuses on post-1945 American art. Open Tues–Sun.

Cullen Sculpture Garden, 1001 Bissonnet (639-7300): This outdoor extension of the Museum of Fine Arts, designed by Isamu Noguchi, contains selected pieces from the museum's permanent collection, traveling exhibitions, and loans, positioned on landscaped levels with corresponding backdrops. On display are works by Bourdelle, Maillol, Matisse, Giacometti, Alexander Calder (*Crab*), Frank Stella (*Decanter*), and others.

Menil Collection, 1515 Sul Ross (525-9400): The personal collection of Dominique de Menil, which drew large crowds when it was exhibited a few years ago at the Petit Palais in Paris, is now housed in a building worthy of it. It comprises more than 10,000 works of art covering 5,000 years of history, from Etruscan and Anatolian sculpture to the works of such avant-garde painters as Pollock, Rothko, Rauschenberg, and Warhol, and surrealists like de Chirico and Magritte. The remarkable, light-filled modern building was designed by Renzo Piano, the architect of many distinguished buildings, including Paris's famous Centre Pompidou. This is among the world's most highly regarded private museums. Open Wed–Sun.

Museum of Fine Arts, 1001 Bissonnet (639-7300): A mixture of neoclassical and modern architecture (the interior of one of its modern wings, designed by Mies van der Rohe, presents an unusual theme of broken concrete shafts), this wonderful museum houses a splendid collection of European masters and well-known American painters (particularly

Frederic Remington) and is rich in Native American pottery and pre-Columbian art. Some of the remarkable works on display are Fra Angelico's *Temptation of St. Anthony*, a *Virgin and Child* by Rogier van der Weyden, *Waterlilies* by Claude Monet, and van Gogh's *The Rocks*. Open Tues–Sun.

MUSEUMS OF SCIENCE & HISTORY: ☼▲▲ Museum of Natural Science, 1 Hermann Circle, Dr. Hermann Park (639-4600):

From the diplodocus to the space rocket and from oil wells to artificial earthquakes, this is one of the biggest and best natural-science museums in the country. Here, too, are the **Hall of Medical Science,** with its giant models of the human body, and the **Burke Baker Planetarium,** where visitors can follow the transit of comets and the motion of the planets against the star-studded dome. Open daily.

PANORAMAS: The finest ▲▲ overall view of this city of skyscrapers is to be had at ground level from the Buffalo Bayou Sesquicentennial Park (see below).

    🔔 **Transco Tower,** 2800 Post Oak Blvd. (439-2000): From the 51st floor of this new skyscraper next to the Galleria Center you can have a wonderful view of the skyline. Lovely fountain with a waterfall at the foot of the tower. Open Mon–Fri.

PARKS & GARDENS: 🔔 Allen's Landing, Main and Commerce Sts.:

A tiny park overshadowed by skyscrapers, on the spot where the city's founders (two New York promoters named Augustus and John Allen) first moored their boat in 1836. For a long time this was Houston's commercial harbor. Particularly fine view.

    🔔 **Buffalo Bayou Sesquicentennial Park,** Smith St. and Texas Ave.: New $5-million downtown park on the banks of the historic bayou where the city was founded in 1836. Features an overlook and water cascades with stairs. Offers a stunning view of the skyscrapers downtown.

    🔔 **Memorial Park,** Woodway and Loop 610 (861-3765): A 155-acre (63ha) public park near downtown Houston. Paths for strollers; botanic garden. Houston's "lung."

    🔔 **Sam Houston Historical Park,** 1100 Bagby St. (655-1912): Seven historic buildings (from a village church to a Texas-style plantation house) and stores dating from the 19th century, meticulously restored. Interesting journey into the past of the city and its inhabitants. Open daily.

    ☼🔔 **Tranquility Park,** bounded by Rusk, Bagby, Smith, and Walker Sts.: This very unusual park in the heart of downtown commemorates the historic *Apollo 11* mission of 1969—first landing by a manned space vehicle on the moon, in the Sea of Tranquility. The park has a 32-level fountain covering two city blocks, and five rocket-shaped towers. At every entrance, bronze tablets commemorate the Apollo mission in 15 languages.

PERFORMING ARTS: For current listings of shows and cultural events, con-

sult the entertainment pages of the two daily papers, *Houston Post* (morning) and *Houston Chronicle* (morning and evening), and the *Texas Monthly* magazine.

    Alley Theatre, 615 Texas Ave. (228-8421): One of the country's most renowned stock companies; from classical to experimental theater. Performances Tues–Sun Oct–May.

    Jesse H. Jones Hall for the Performing Arts, 615 Louisiana St. (227-2787): Home of the Houston Symphony Orchestra (principal conductor: Christoph Eschenbach). Season Sept–May and July.

    Miller Outdoor Theater, 100 Concert, Dr. Hermann Park (520-3290):

Free open-air performances in summer. Shakespeare Festival, Houston Symphony Orchestra concerts, musical comedies, opera, pop concerts, etc.
Music Hall, 810 Bagby St. (247-1048): Home of the Theater Under the Stars (musical comedy, Broadway hits). Season Feb–May and Oct–Dec.
Stages Repertory Theatre, 3201 Allen Pkwy. (527-8243): Modern and experimental theater. One of the best repertory companies in the Southwest.
Tower Theater, 1201 Westheimer Rd. (529-5966): Drama, comedy, contemporary theater.
Wortham Theater Center, 501 Texas Ave. (237-1439): Lyric theater opened in 1987. Home of the Houston Grand Opera (under director David Gockley), which performs Sept–Mar; also of the Houston Ballet, the only permanent dance company in the Southwest.

RODEOS: ※ **Round Up Coliseum,** on Tex. 1093, in Simonton, 35 mi. (56km) west along Westheimer Rd. (346-1534): Rodeo, western dancing, barbecue dinner every Sat from 6pm on. Open year round except Sept. Guaranteed local color. 45 min. from dwntwn.

SHOPPING: ※ **Galeria Mall,** 5015 Westheimer Rd. (621-1907): Houston's ultimate shopping extravaganza, with more than 250 luxury boutiques from Neiman-Marcus to Tiffany's, restaurants, stores, bars, and even a public ice-skating rink, all air-conditioned under an enormous dome. Gigantism Texas style, elegant and spectacular.
　　※ **Stelzig's,** 3123 Post Oak Blvd. (629-7779): Western wear at its best. Has everything from elaborate saddles to steer-skull string ties. Various other locations.

SPECIAL EVENTS: For exact dates, consult the **Houston Convention and Visitors Bureau** (see "Tourist Information," above).
Houston Livestock Show and Rodeo (late Feb to early Mar): Rodeos, concerts, parades; one of the world's largest, with 25,000 entries and a million visitors yearly; guaranteed western atmosphere.
Houston International Festival (Apr): Dance, theater, art exhibitions, concerts.
Westheimer Colony Art Festival (Apr and Oct): Art exhibitions, public concerts on the "Strip." Worth seeing (see "Strolls," below).
Offshore Technology Conference (late Apr to early May): The world's biggest annual petroleum-industry exhibition.

SPORTS: Houston boasts professional teams in three major sports:
Baseball (Apr–Oct): Astros, the Astrodome (799-9555).
Basketball (Dec–Apr): Rockets, the Summit (627-0600).
Football (Sept–Dec): Oilers, the Astrodome (797-1000).

STROLLS: ⚓ **Old Market Square,** bounded by Congress, Milam, Preston, and Travis: Boutiques, pubs, and saloons in the style of the Old West's frontier days, all in attractively restored 19th-century rowhouses.
　　※⚓ **River Oaks,** River Oaks Blvd. between Westheimer Rd. and the River Oaks Country Club: Dream homes and sumptuous oil barons' mansions.
　　※⚓ **The "Strip,"** Westheimer Rd. from about no. 100 to no. 1600: Terraced cafés, exotic restaurants, art galleries, antique shops, bookstores, nightclubs, flea market. Houston's liveliest district. Art festivals in Apr and Oct.

THEME PARKS: ⚓ **AstroWorld,** S. Loop 610 at Kirby Dr. (799-1234): Enormous (75-acre/30ha) amusement park with more than 100 attractions including the giant "Texas Cyclone" roller coaster. Shows; concerts. Open daily June–Sept, wknds only in spring and fall; closed the rest of the year.

🅰 **WaterWorld,** Kirby Dr. and S. Loop 610 (799-1234): Very popular aquatic amusement park adjoining AstroWorld. Enormous pool with artificial waves for surfers; giant slides; lagoon swimming pool with waterfalls. Spectacular. Open daily June–Aug, wknds only in May and Sept; closed the rest of the year.

ZOOS: 🅰 **Zoological Gardens,** Zoo Circle Dr. in Hermann Park (525-3300): Very fine zoo, known for its tropical jungle and its gorillas. The vampire bats eat lunch every day at 2:30pm. Huge aquarium.

ACCOMMODATIONS

Personal Favorites (in order of preference)

♟♟♟♟ **Ritz Carlton** (nr. dwntwn), 1919 Briar Oaks Lane, TX 77027 (713/840-7600; toll free 800/241-3333). 232 rms, A/C, color TV, in-rm movies. AE, CB, DC, MC, V. Valet parking $13.50, pool, three rests. (including the Restaurant and the Grill), bar, nightclub, 24-hr. rm svce, concierge, free crib. *Note:* The most elegant, and one of the newest of Houston's luxury hotels, in the smart River Oaks section near Memorial Park. A beautiful melding of American efficiency and European charm. Furnishings include many works of art and old pictures. Spacious, very comfortable rms; personalized reception and svce. Rest. of great quality. Discreet and stylish atmosphere. Rich business clientele. Boasts the city's most expensive suite at $1,900 a night. 20 min. from dwntwn. **E–VE**

♟♟♟♟ **Hyatt Regency Downtown** (dwntwn), 1200 Louisiana St., TX 77002 (713/654-1234; toll free, see Hyatt). 958 rms, A/C, color TV, in-rm movies. AE, CB, DC, MC, V. Valet gar. $11, pool, three rests., revolving rest.-bar (Spindletop) on the 33rd floor, entertainment, rm svce, free crib. *Note:* Typical Hyatt "smack in the eye" design; 30-floor foyer w. balconies, indoor grdns, and glass-caged elevators. Well-designed, friendly rms; irreproachable svce. Big business clientele. In the heart of Houston next to the Convention Center. VIP floor. Linked by "Skywalk" and air-conditioned tunnel to other dwntwn buildings. **E–VE**

☼♟♟♟ **Lancaster Hotel** (dwntwn), 701 Texas Ave., TX 77002 (713/228-9500; toll free 800/345-3457). 93 rms, A/C, color TV. AE, CB, DC, MC, V. Valet parking $6, health club, rest. (Bistro Lancaster), bar, rm svce, concierge, free crib. *Note:* A luxurious little 1920s palace built in 1926 and completely refurbished in 1982. Somewhat cramped but welcoming rms furnished w. antiques. Very British atmosphere. Professional and good-natured staff. The rest. is a favorite w. audiences from the Jesse H. Jones Concert Hall and the Alley Theater, right across from the hotel. Charm and quality. Limousine svce to dwntwn. **E–VE**

♟♟♟ **Houstonian Hotel & Conference Center** (nr. dwntwn), 111 N. Post Oak Lane, TX 77024 (713/680-2626; toll free 800/231-2759). 297 rms, A/C, color TV, in-rm movies. AE, CB, DC, MC, V. Free gar. (valet parking $9), two pools, health club, five tennis courts, squash, sauna, coffee shop, bar, rm svce, boutiques, concierge, free crib. *Note:* Inviting modern hotel in a very handsome wooded setting across from Memorial Park. Former President Bush claims Suite 271 in the Houstonian Hotel as his legal residence. Comfortable, spacious rms w. minibars. Has one of the swankiest (and best-equipped) health clubs in town; hotel guests have full use of the health-spa facilities. Excellent svce; VIP floor ("Presidential Wing"). 5 min. from Galleria Center, 20 min. from dwntwn. A very good place to stay. **E**

♟♟ **Allen Park Inn** (nr. dwntwn), 2121 Allen Pkwy., TX 77019 (713/521-9321; toll free 800/231-6310). 250 rms, A/C, color TV, in-rm movies. AE, CB, DC, MC, V. Free parking, pool, health club,

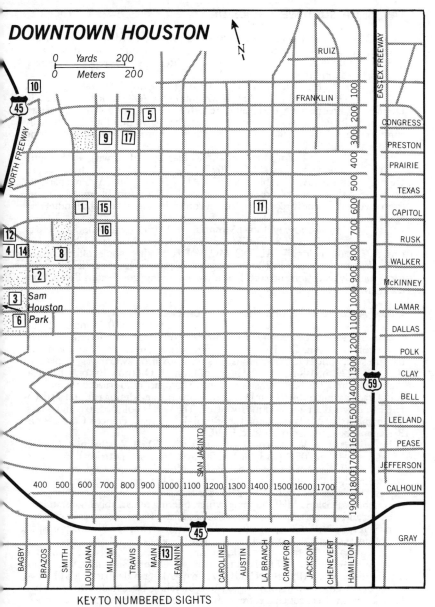

DOWNTOWN HOUSTON

0 Yards 200
0 Meters 200

KEY TO NUMBERED SIGHTS

1. Alley Theater
2. City Hall
3. Sam Houston Park
4. Sam Houston Coliseum
5. Pillot House
6. The Long Row
7. Old Cotton Exchange
8. Tranquility Park
9. Convention and Visitors Center
10. Amtrak Station
11. Greyhound Terminal
12. Music Hall
13. Trailways Terminal
14. Albert Thomas Space Hall of Fame
15. Jones Hall for Performing Arts
16. Pennzoil Towers
17. Old Market Square Park

sauna, 24-hr. coffee shop (Nashville Rm), bar, rm svce, hrdrsr, free crib. *Note:* Friendly, modern hotel of traditional type. Spacious, comfortable rms w. balconies. Reception w. a smile. Very laudable rest. Caters largely to repeat customers; good value. 8 min. from dwntwn. **I–M**

    Heaven on Earth Plaza Hotel (dwntwn), 801 Calhoun St., TX 77002 (713/659-2222). 600 rms, A/C, color TV. AE, CB, DC, MC, V. Free parking, pool, sauna, rest., free breakfast, crib $10. *Note:* Huge, modern, well-laid-out 30-story hotel, very nr. the Exxon Building. Functionally comfortable; relatively efficient svce; business and group clientele. Interesting wknd discounts. **B–I**

    La Quinta Inn–Greenway Plaza (nr. dwntwn), 4015 Southwest Fwy., TX 77027 (713/623-4750; toll free, see La Quinta). 128 rms, A/C, cable color TV. AE, CB, DC, MC, V. Free parking, pool, coffee shop, rm svce, free crib. *Note:* Modern, comfortable motel 20 min. from dwntwn. Friendly reception. Ideal if you're driving. Like all La Quinta motels, a good value. **I**

    Rodeway Inn–Memorial Park (nr. dwntwn), 5820 Katy Fwy., TX 77007 (713/869-9211; toll free, see Choice). 108 rms, A/C, cable color TV. AE, DC, MC, V. Free parking, pool, coffee shop adj. *Note:* Well-run conventional motel very nr. Memorial Park; serviceable comforts; friendly reception and svce. Fine if you're driving; good value. 8 min. from dwntwn. **B**

Other Accommodations (from top bracket to budget)

    La Colombe d'Or Inn (nr. dwntwn), 3410 Montrose Blvd., TX 77006 (713/524-7999; toll free, see Preferred). 6 suites, A/C, color TV. AE, CB, DC, MC, V. Free parking, rest. (La Colombe d'Or), bar, rm svce, concierge. *Note:* Houston's most luxuriously extravagant place to stay, this 1923 mansion, once the home of Humble Oil (now Exxon) chairman Walter Fondren, has been transformed into a compact mini-palace w. a mere six suites, each having its own huge bedroom, living rm, and dining rm, and all decorated w. objets d'art and antique furniture. The svce is polished to a high gloss. The name is that of a famous hotel at St-Paul-de-Vence on France's Côte d'Azur. Resv. must be made far in advance. **E–VE**

    J. W. Marriott (nr. dwntwn), 5150 Westheimer Rd., TX 77056 (713/961-1500; toll free, see Marriott). 518 rms, A/C, color TV, in-rm movies. AE, CB, DC, MC, V. Free parking, pool, tennis court, health club, sauna, racquetball, rest. (the Brasserie), bar, rm svce, boutiques, concierge, free crib. *Note:* Ultramodern 23-story luxury hotel opposite the celebrated Galeria Mall shopping center, offering remarkably high standards of layout and comfort. Spacious rms; luxurious foyer featuring works by contemporary Texas artists. Comprehensive sports facilities; impeccable svce; prosperous business clientele. 20 min. from dwntwn. **E–VE**

    Omni Houston Hotel (nr. dwntwn), 4 Riverway, TX 77056 (713/871-8181; toll free, see Omni). 383 rms, A/C, color TV, in-rm movies. AE, CB, DC, MC, V. Free parking (valet parking $11), two pools, health club, two tennis courts, sauna, bicycling, basketball, two rests., two bars, 24-hr. rm svce, concierge, free crib. *Note:* A modern hotel of real quality in Houston's most elegant neighborhood; lavishly comfortable rms w. balconies and views of Memorial Park (the best ones), but the older standard rms are small. Comprehensive facilities; La Reserve is an excellent rest. Personalized svce; caters to top businesspeople and rich Texans. No-smoking floor. Inviting grdn w. sculptures, fountains, a waterfall, and a little lake w. black swans. **E–VE**

    The Wyndham Warwick (nr. dwntwn), 5701 S. Main St., TX 77251 (713/526-1991; toll free 800/822-4200). 298 rms, A/C, color TV, in-rm movies. AE, CB, DC, MC, V. Valet gar. $10, pool, sauna, health club, two rests. (including the Hunt Rm), bar, 24-hr rm svce, concierge, free crib. *Note:* Venerable 1920s luxury hotel in the European tradition, slightly disfigured by a new wing. A wealth of marbles, Aubusson tapestry, and wood paneling. Large, comfortable rms, some w. two bathrooms. Exemplary svce; view of Hermann Park. A place of elegance and charm; the favorite of politicians and visiting celebrities. **E–VE**

🍷🍷🍷 **Doubletree–Allen Center** (dwntwn), 400 Dallas St. (at Bagby), TX 77002 (713/759-0202; toll free 800/528-0444). 355 rms, A/C, color TV, in-rm movies. AE, CB, DC, MC, V. Valet gar. $10, two rests. (including Dover's), bar, rm svce, concierge, free crib. *Note:* This modern 20-floor tower of original design stands right in the Civic Center, one of the best locations in Houston. Comfortable, elegantly decorated rms; courteous, efficient svce. Very acceptable rests. Business clientele. Five blocks from the George R. Brown Convention Center. Interesting wknd packages. **M–E**

🍷🍷🍷 **Hilton Houston Plaza** (nr. dwntwn), 6633 Travis St., TX 77030 (713/524-6633; toll free, see Hilton). 185 suites, color TV, in-rm movies. AE, CB, DC, MC, V. Indoor parking $6, pool, health club, sauna, rest., bar, piano bar, rm svce, free crib. *Note:* Very comfortable hotel offering only mini-suites, very well laid out, w. refrigerators. Near Hermann Park and the museum district. Courteous reception and svce. Business clientele. Good overall value. **M–E**

🍷🍷🍷 **Hilton Nassau Bay** (vic.), 3000 NASA Rd. One, Clear Lake City, TX 77058 (713/333-9300; toll free, see Hilton). 244 rms, A/C, color TV, in-rm movies. AE, CB, DC, MC, V. Free parking, pool, fishing, water sports, marina, rest. (Marina Bar & Grill), bar, rm svce, disco, boutiques, hrdrsr, free limo to Hobby Airport, free crib. *Note:* This 14-floor hotel-marina on Clear Lake is ideal for visiting NASA's Lyndon B. Johnson Space Center. Comfortable, ultramodern facilities; spacious rms, w. balconies and lake view; efficient svce. Very good value; a fine place to stay, 35 min. from dwntwn. **M**

🍷🍷 **Ramada–Galleria West** (nr. dwntwn), 7787 Katy Fwy., TX 77024 (713/681-5000; toll free, see Ramada). 287 rms, A/C, color TV, in-rm movies. AE, CB, DC, MC, V. Free parking, pool, rest., coffee shop, bar, rm svce, disco, free breakfast, crib $10. *Note:* Comfortable, up-to-date 11-story motel at the western exit from the city on I-10. Comfortable and functional. Friendly rms w. balconies. Ideal if you're driving. Good value. Interesting wknd packages. **I–M**

🍷 **Best Western–Greenspoint Inn** (nr. dwntwn), 11211 North Fwy., TX 77037 (713/447-6311; toll free, see Best Western). 144 rms, A/C, cable color TV. AE, CB, DC, MC, V. Free parking, pool, rest., bar, crib $10. *Note:* Typical motel at the northern exit from Houston on I-45. Functional comfort; cheerful svce. Ideal if you're traveling by car. 20 min. from dwntwn, 10 min. from Houston Intercontinental Airport (free airport limo). Good value. **B–I**

🍷 **Days Inn Wayside** (nr. dwntwn), 2200 S. Wayside Dr., TX 77023 (713/928-2800; toll free, see Days Inn). 100 rms, A/C, cable color TV. AE, DC, MC, V. Free parking, pool, free breakfast, free crib. *Note:* Comfortable, functional hotel, halfway between Hobby Airport and dwntwn; 15 min. from dwntwn. Good value. **B–I**

🍷 **Motel 6** (nr. dwntwn), 9638 Plainfield Rd., TX 77036 (713/778-0008). 205 rms, A/C, cable color TV. AE, DC, MC, V. Free parking, pool. *Note:* Modern, appealing motel w. very low rates. Close to Houston Baptist University; 25 min. from dwntwn by car via the Southwest Pkwy. Ideal if you're driving. One of the best values in the area. **B**

Airport Accommodations

🍷🍷🍷 **Marriott Houston Airport Hotel** (vic.), 18700 John F. Kennedy Blvd., TX 77032 (713/443-2310; toll free, see Marriott). 569 rms, A/C, color TV, in-rm movies. AE, CB, DC, MC, V. Free parking, pool, health club, two rests. (one, C.K.'s, on the top floor, revolves), two bars, rm svce, hrdrsr, free crib. *Note:* The architecture of this hotel, the only one in the airport complex, is original; the rms are comfortable and well soundproofed, w. refrigerators (some have private patios). Efficient svce; average rests. Business clientele. Free subway train to the terminal. VIP floor. Interesting wknd packages. **E**

Roadway Inn–Hobby Airport (vic.), 1505 College Ave., TX 77587 (713/946-5900; toll free, see Choice). 124 rms, A/C, color TV, in-rm movies. AE, CB, DC, MC, V. Free parking, pool. *Note:* Relatively up-to-date and comfortable airport motel. Friendly reception and svce. Free airport shuttle. 5 min. from the terminal. **B–I**

YMCA/Youth Hostels

Houston International Hostel (nr. dwntwn), 5302 Crawford St., TX 77004 (713/523-1009). 30 beds. Nr. the museums. Friendly staff; good neighborhood.

YMCA (dwntwn), 1600 Louisiana St., TX 77002 (713/659-8501). Men and women's rms. 147 rms, rest.

RESTAURANTS

Personal Favorites (in order of preference)

Tony's (nr. dwntwn), 1801 Post Oak Blvd. (622-6778). A/C. Lunch Mon–Fri, dinner Mon–Sat; closed hols. AE, CB, DC, MC, V. J&T. *Specialties:* crab gazpacho, linguine pescatore, grilled salmon Foulard (w. artichokes and truffles), cappellini al bianco, veal chop in cabernet sauce w. wild mushrooms, fruit soufflés. *Note:* Remarkable French-inspired cuisine, deftly and delicately prepared. Exemplary svce from waiters in tuxedos; plush, flowery setting worthy of the rest.'s reputation. One of the Southwest's finest wine cellars, w. 60,000 bottles. Resv. a must; the city's top power rest. for 20 years. Valet parking; 20 min. from dwntwn. *Continental.* **E–VE**

Café Annie (nr. dwntwn), 1728 Post Oak Blvd. (840-1111). A/C. Lunch Mon–Fri, dinner Mon–Sat; closed hols. AE, CB, DC, MC, V. Jkt. *Specialties:* mussel soup w. serrano chiles, grilled sea scallops w. roasted tomato sauce and garlic cream, cinnamon-roasted pheasant w. green-chili vinaigrette, grilled quail and potato taco, rabbit in red jalapeño, caramel custard. Very good wine list, fairly priced. *Note:* Few young Texan chefs of Robert Del Grande's generation offer so inventive and sophisticated a cuisine, in particular his remarkably light sauces. Trimly smart two-tiered setting w. high ceilings and wood accents. Disorganized but friendly staff. Noisy atmosphere. Resv. indispensable well ahead. Valet parking. *American.* **E**

Américas (nr. dwntwn), 1800 Post Oak Blvd. (961-1492). A/C. Lunch Mon–Fri, dinner Mon–Sat. AE, CB, DC, MC, V. *Specialties:* seafood gazpacho, taquitos of bacon-wrapped quail stuffed w. mushrooms and chilies, tiritas (potato-crusted filets of squid), grilled chicken w. pineapple and coconut, sautéed jumbo shrimp w. cachaça-butter and roasted leeks, coconut ice cream in a caramel pastry cup. *Note:* Named "Restaurant of the Year" for 1993 by *Esquire* magazine, this relative newcomer has gained as much attention for its interior as its food, which together reach a happy symmetry. The interior, inspired by Incan myths and motifs, defies the American penchant for straight lines, recalling the organic, cavernous architecture of Gaudi. Excellent cuisine by Michael and Glenn Cordua of Churrascos (see below) that draws from and superbly represents the cuisine of all the Americas. Due to its popularity, resv. are highly advised. *Continental.* **M–E**

Churrascos (vic.), 9788 Bissonnet (541-2100). A/C. Lunch Mon–Fri, dinner nightly. AE, CB, DC, MC, V. *Specialties:* arepa (cheese tortilla), calamares rellenos (stuffed squid), cerdo (broiled pork filet), meat and vegetable empanada, corvina (South American fish), churrasco (broiled beef) w. chimichurri sauce. Good list of wines at reasonable prices. *Note:* Since it was opened in 1988 by two self-taught brothers from Nicaragua (one has a doctorate in medicine and the other in economics) this rest. has been consistently crowded. In a city full to overflowing w. Mexican rests., the food at Churrascos comes as an agreeable surprise. Colorful, comfortable setting; friendly svce. 25 min. out along the Southwest Fwy. Other location: 2055 Westheimer Rd. (527-8300). Resv. advisable. *Latin American.* **I–M**

    ♀♀ **Ninfa's** (nr. dwntwn), 2704 Navigation (228-1175). A/C. Lunch/dinner daily; closed July 4, Thanksgiving, Dec 25. AE, CB, DC, MC, V. *Specialties:* tacos al carbón, flautas, carnitas, chalupas, chilpanzingas, queso a la parrilla, sopaipillas. *Note:* The most popular of the (numberless) Mexican rests. in Houston; a local institution, usually crowded and noisy. No resv. are accepted over the wknd, and a wait is unavoidable. Other location: 6154 Westheimer Rd. (781-2740). Check the *Yellow Pages* for other locations. *Mexican.* **B–I**

    ♀ **Café Express** (nr. dwntwn), 1800 Post Oak Blvd. (963-9222). A/C. Lunch/dinner daily. AE, DC, MC, V. *Specialties:* chilled pasta w. pesto peppers and olives, black-bean soup, roast-beef sandwich, chicken salad, pizzas, daily specials. *Note:* Good, modestly priced food in a stylishly bright, pleasant setting. Café Express benefits from the tutelage of Robert Del Grande, the famed chef-owner of Café Annie (see above). No resv. Other location: 3200 Kirby (522-3994). *American.* **B–I**

    ☼♀ **Goode Company Barbecue** (nr. dwntwn), 5109 Kirby Dr. (522-2530). A/C. Lunch/dinner daily. AE, MC, V. *Specialties:* barbecued beef, ham, and pork; chicken, sausages, and duck grilled over mesquite. *Note:* A real local landmark. Wonderful barbecued meats attractively priced: from $3 for a sandwich to $10 for a full meal w. three kinds of meat and two vegetables. Amusing funky decor and Texas atmosphere, right down to the picnic tables. Rather obtrusive background country music. Generally crowded. Other location: 8911 Katy Fwy (464-1901). *American.* **B**

Other Restaurants (from top bracket to budget)

    ♀♀♀ **De Ville** (dwntwn), in the Four Seasons Hotel, 1300 Lamar Ave. (650-1300, ext. 4184). A/C. Breakfast Sun–Fri, lunch Mon–Fri, dinner Mon–Sat, brunch Sun. AE, CB, DC, MC, V. Jkt. *Specialties:* gulf shrimp and snapper broth w. tomato, fennel, and saffron; tossed chicory salad w. walnuts in Gorgonzola dressing; roast guinea hen; juniper-marinated elk w. caramelized laurel jus; veal chop w. balsamic sauce; chocolate parfait. Very nice wine list. *Note:* The archetype of a luxury rest. Innovative, refined cooking. Contemporary decor, crystal, and Murano chandeliers reminiscent of the Edwardian era. Impeccable svce. Everything in the grand style, including prices. The realm of expense-account dining. Resv. strongly advised. *French/American.* **M–E**

    ♀♀♀ **Charley's 517** (dwntwn), 517 Louisiana St. (224-4438). A/C. Lunch Mon–Fri, dinner Mon–Sat; closed hols. AE, CB, DC, MC, V. *Specialties:* grilled gulf oysters w. pasta, grilled quail w. black-eyed-pea relish, buffalo tenderloin w. tomato-basil coulis, roast rack of lamb w. rosemary-mint sauce, sautéed gulf snapper w. jumbo lump crabmeat and lime-butter sauce. Seasonal menu. Splendid wine list. *Note:* One of Houston's top rests. The always-inspired and often-innovative cuisine of chef Clive Berkman features game and local produce. Elegant decor w. stained glass and a profusion of flowers. Business clientele at lunch, theater-goers at dinner—the rest. is across from Jesse H. Jones Hall and the Alley Theater. Resv. highly recommended. Valet parking. *American/Continental.* **M–E**

    ♀♀ **River Oaks Grill** (nr. dwntwn), 2630 Westheimer at Kirby (520-1738). A/C. Lunch Mon–Fri, dinner nightly; closed hols. AE, DC, MC, V. *Specialties:* crab pancakes, wild-mushroom strudel, ribeye steak, grilled Norwegian salmon w. lemon-butter sauce, fresh Maine lobster, excellent cheesecakes. *Note:* Straightforward, hearty cooking in a dimly lit, clublike atmosphere. Simple, white-tableclothed elegance replete w. piano player. Exceptional svce. *American.* **M–E**

☼ ♟♟♟ **Rotisserie for Beef and Bird** (vic.), 2200 Wilcrest Dr. (977-
♟ ♟♟♟ 9524). A/C. Lunch Mon–Fri, dinner Mon–Sat; closed hols.
AE, MC, V. Jkt. *Specialties:* cream of pheasant soup, sautéed quail, grilled lobster,
roast goose, pheasant and game, aged prime steak and venison, snapper sautéed
in brown butter, very good homemade desserts. Fine wine list. *Note:* Lovers of
unexpected delicacies will find here, year round, Asian venison, antelope, or Russian wild boar, but the more conventional dishes of game, venison, or ordinary
red meat are equally recommended. The ovens and broilers are in full view of the
patrons, enhancing the elegant country-club layout. Very good svce; yuppie clientele. Valet parking. *American/Steak.* **M**

♟♟♟ **Brennan's** (nr. dwntwn), 3300 Smith St. (522-9711). A/C.
♟♟♟ Lunch/dinner daily, jazz brunch Sat–Sun; closed Dec 25. AE,
CB, DC, MC, V. Jkt. *Specialties:* turtle soup, shrimp rémoulade, oysters Bienville,
veal cutlet Tchoupitoulas, sautéed redfish w. crabmeat, bread pudding soufflé,
bananas Foster. Good wine list. *Note:* Affiliated w. the famous Commander's Palace in New Orleans. Excellent Créole cuisine; pleasant setting in an old brick
house w. a shady patio. Efficient svce; valet parking. Locally popular, especially
for brunch, so resv. advised. *Créole.* **I–M**

♟♟ **La Mora Cucina Toscana** (nr. dwntwn), 912 Lovett (522-
♟♟ 7412). A/C. Lunch Tues–Fri, dinner nightly; closed hols. AE,
MC, V. *Specialties:* tortelli al burro e salvia; tagliatelle in cream sauce; quail w.
polenta; veal pillows stuffed w. mozzarella, prosciutto, and tomato; daily fish
specials; tiramisù. Excellent Italian wine list. *Note:* This relative newcomer has
quickly become a local favorite for Tuscan cuisine aficionados. Reasonable prices
add to its appeal. Handsome setting w. a cozy little front rm and an airy atrium at
the rear. Friendly svce. Resv. recommended. *Italian.* **I–M**

♟♟ **Cadillac Bar** (nr. dwntwn), 1802 Shepherd Dr. at Katy Fwy.
♟♟ (862-2020). A/C. Lunch/dinner daily; closed Thanksgiving,
Dec 25. AE, CB, DC, MC, V. *Specialties:* fajitas, garrito, cabrito grilled over a
mesquite-wood fire, barbecues, roast quail, chorizo and melted cheese. *Note:* Authentic northern Mexican cooking, tasty and highly spiced. Guaranteed local
color from the shoeshine boy through the guitar player. Locally popular; resv.
advised. *Mexican.* **B–I**

♟♟ **Kim Son** (nr. dwntwn), 2001 Jefferson at Charter (222-2461).
♟♟ A/C. Lunch Mon–Fri, dinner nightly; closed hols. AE, DC,
MC, V. *Specialties:* hot-and-sour shrimp soup, charcoal-broiled beef w.
lemongrass and mint, black-pepper crabs, clay-pot duck, Vietnam pork-filled
crêpes, Vietnamese iced coffee. *Note:* This latest Houston culinary landmark has
been transformed from what started as a storefront operation into what is now a
300-seat rest. and the rage of the town. The rest. is part of the success tale of the
Tri La family, owners and operators of the rest., who came to the U.S. from Vietnam w. hardly anything in their pockets. Incredible menu of over 200 dishes.
Excellent, inviting svce. Other location: 8200 Wilcrest at Beechnut (498-7841).
Vietnamese. **B–I**

♟ **Tony Mandola's Blue Oyster Bar** (nr. dwntwn), 8105 Gulf
♟ Fwy. (640-1117). A/C. Lunch/dinner Mon–Sat. No credit
cards. *Specialties:* gulf oysters, gumbo, red beans and rice, crayfish à l'étouffée,
spaghetti w. shrimp and crab. *Note:* Wonderful Créole bistro whose flavorful, colorful food is worthy of the finest rests. in New Orleans. No pretensions to elegance, but friendly svce. Very popular locally; no resv.; 20 min. from dwntwn.
Other location: 1962 W. Gray (528-3474). *Créole/Seafood.* **B–I**

☼♟ **Captain Benny's Half Shell** (nr. dwntwn), 8018 Katy Fwy.
♟ (683-1042). A/C. Lunch/dinner Mon–Sat. No credit cards.
Specialties: oysters and shrimp from the gulf, stuffed crab, crayfish (in season),
fried catfish, gumbo. *Note:* Absolutely fresh seafood efficiently served—and the
prices are a pleasant surprise. A favorite of connoisseurs and usually packed, so
you'll have to wait. Unusual nautical decor. One of the best places to eat in Houston. Other location: 8506 S. Main (666-5469). *Seafood.* **B–I**

♈ **Otto's Barbecue** (nr. dwntwn), 5502 Memorial Dr. (864-2573). A/C. Lunch/dinner Mon–Sat; closed hols. AE, MC, V. *Specialties:* barbecued brisket, ham, and sausages; hamburgers. *Note:* Generally agreed to offer Houston's best barbecued beef; Otto serves more than 1,400 lb. (600kg) daily—a reference in itself! Hamburger reigns supreme at the burger bar nr. the entrance. Unpretentious western setting and svce. Locally very popular since 1950. The favorite of President Bush. *American.* **B**

A Restaurant in the Vicinity

☼ ♈ **Frank's Café** (vic.), 603 E. U.S. 90, 37 mi. (60km) east of Houston in Dayton (409/258-2598). A/C. Lunch/dinner Wed–Sun. AE, MC, V. *Specialties:* oysters, crabs, shrimp, and red snapper from the gulf; fried catfish; filet mignon; club steak; ribs of beef Delmonico; homemade pies. *Note:* One of the most famous roadhouses in Texas, on the old U.S. 90 from Houston to New Orleans. Remarkably fresh seafood; superb meats stored in a glass-enclosed aging refrigerator w. steaks on view, from which you can make your own choice—and all this at very reasonable prices. Cheerful, friendly svce. Frequented by people in-the-know since 1948 and well worth the 45-min. drive from the city. Resv. suggested. *American/Steak.* **I**

Cafeterias/Fast Food

Butera's (nr. dwntwn), 4621 Montrose Blvd. (523-0722). Lunch/dinner daily. AE, CB, DC, MC, V. *Note:* Fine cafeteria-style deli on the grounds of the Chelsea Market. Generous sandwiches, flavorful salads.

Luby's (nr. dwntwn), 5215 Buffalo Speedway (664-4852). Open until 8pm daily. *Specialties:* Mexican dishes, fish of the day, steak, roast beef. *Note:* Decent food at very decent prices. There are 20 other locations in Houston; consult the city telephone directory.

BARS & NIGHTCLUBS

Al Mark's Melody Lane Ballroom (nr. dwntwn), 3027 Crossview (785-5301). Giant dance hall with live music; very popular locally, so local color guaranteed. 25 min. from dwntwn.

The Ale House (nr. dwntwn), 2425 W. Alabama at Kirby (521-2333). More than 100 different beers are on offer at this well-patronized bar; disco with new wave music upstairs. Open daily.

La Carafe (dwntwn), 813 Congress Ave. (229-9399). Stark, brick-laden bar in the oldest commercial building in Houston. A lively place.

Cody's (nr. dwntwn), 3400 Montrose Blvd. (522-9747). A singles bar that is much frequented by yuppies after the day's toil; also very acceptable rest. and live jazz. Beautiful view of the city. Open Tues–Sat.

Fitzgerald's (nr. dwntwn), 2706 White Oaks Dr. (862-7625). Featuring a score of local and national pop performers in this most popular of Houston clubs.

☼ **The Great Caruso** (vic.), 10001 Westheimer Rd. at Briar Park (780-4900). Original rest.-nightclub for lovers of opera and bel canto; even the waiters contribute to the illusion. Wonderful 1900s rococo opera-house decor. An entertaining place, well worth the 30-min. drive from dwntwn. Very acceptable food. Valet parking. Open nightly.

The Red Lion (nr. dwntwn), 7315 S. Main St. (795-5000). Congenial pub atmosphere w. nightly entertainment ranging from folk to heavy rock 'n' roll.

NEARBY EXCURSIONS

⚓ **PORT OF HOUSTON** (5 mi./8km east along Clinton Dr.): You'll get a fine view of the port, which handles more than 6,000 vessels a year, from the observation platform at Wharf No. 9; open daily. Free boat tours of the harbor Tues–Sun year round (670-2416 for resv.).

SAN JACINTO BATTLEGROUND (21 mi./34km SE on I-45S, I-610N, Tex. 225, and Tex. 134) (479-2421): Battlefield on which Gen. Sam Houston's Texas volunteers won a decisive engagement against the Mexican dictator Santa Anna, only two months after the latter's victory at the Alamo (see Chapter 37 on San Antonio). A gigantic memorial column (elevator), capped with the Lone Star of Texas, was erected in 1939; at 570 ft. (174m), it's the tallest monument in the world, 15 ft. (5m) higher than the Washington Monument. The view from the observation deck at 489 ft. (150m) is spectacular. Made of concrete clad in polished limestone, it weighs a total of 32,000 tons. Nearby is the battleship *Texas,* veteran of two World Wars, which served as General Eisenhower's headquarters during the Normandy landings of 1944. At the foot of the monument is a Museum of the History of Texas. Open daily.

LYNDON B. JOHNSON SPACE CENTER (25 mi./ 40km SE along I-45 and NASA Rd. 1 in Clear Lake City) (483-4321): The nerve center of NASA, from which guidance has been provided for all manned space flights since 1962 (including the *Gemini, Apollo,* and *Mercury* missions and the space-shuttle flights), with live TV coverage for viewers around the world. There are 40,000 technicians on the payroll. The wonderful **Space Museum** has several models of spacecraft, including the gigantic *Saturn V,* genuine moon rocks, and a replica of the lunar landing module *Apollo 17,* which holds the record for the longest human stay: 75 hr. Guided tours of the **Control Center** and the astronaut training areas. A brand-new 50-acre (20ha) $70-million **visitor's complex,** designed by Walt Disney Imagineering and opened in Oct 1992, features full-scale mockups of space vehicles, hands-on training simulators, a movie theater with a five-story-tall screen and up-to-the-minute live-camera eavesdropping on Mission Control, the launchpad in Florida, and crews in orbit. Open daily.

GALVESTON (51 mi./82km south on I-45): This beach resort and busy port was almost totally destroyed in 1900 by a tidal wave which left 6,000 dead. There are many fine examples of upper-class 19th-century homes along the Strand, between 20th and 25th Sts., and on Broadway, among them the **Bishop's Palace,** 1402 Broadway, open daily, and **Ashton Villa,** 2328 Broadway, open daily, which belongs to former Texas Gov. Ross Sterling. Very popular beaches. **Railroad Museum** in the former Santa Fe Union station, 123 Rosenberg (409/765-5700): the largest collection of restored railroad equipment in the Southwest. Open daily. On-the-way stop for a visit to the LBJ Space Center (see above).

Where to Stay in Galveston

Tremont House, 2300 Ship's Mechanic Row, Galveston, TX 77550 (409/763-0300). 117 rms. AE, CB, DC, MC, V. *Note:* An elegantly renovated 1880s hotel retaining its gracious Victorian atmosphere. **M–E**

HUNTSVILLE (71 mi./113km north on I-45): Native city of Texas's founder and first elected president, Sam Houston. His birthplace, home, and tomb at 1836 Sam Houston Ave. (409/295-7824) may be seen Tues–Sun.

NATIONAL PARKS NEARBY

PADRE ISLAND NATIONAL SEASHORE (236 mi./ 378km SW on U.S. 59, U.S. 77 and 37, and Tex. 358): A 113-mi.-long (182km) peninsula with an average width of 3 mi. (5km). Almost entirely uninhabited, this long sweep of sand, with dunes rising to 45 ft. (15m) in places, has once again become a paradise for campers (fully equipped camping grounds), fishermen, and sailors after sustaining severe damage from a disastrous oil slick in 1979. The spine of the peninsula, less contaminated by civilization, has been made into a nature reserve for some 350 species of birds. The park is connected to Corpus Christi by the John F. Kennedy Causeway and to Port Isabel by the South Padre Causeway. For lovers of unspoiled nature. For **information,** contact the Superintendent, Padre Island National Seashore, 9405 S. Padre Island Dr., Corpus Christi, TX 78418 (512/937-2621).

On the way, stop off at the ⚓ **King Ranch,** on Tex. 141 at Kingsville (37 mi./ 59km SW of Corpus Christi via Tex. 44 and U.S. 77). Symbolic of Texan wealth and power, this ranch of about 820,000 acres (332,000ha), the size of the state of Rhode Island, is the largest privately held agricultural property in the world. Founded in 1853 by Richard King, an enterprising sea captain, the property is still owned by descendants of the King family. A 12-mi. (19km) loop road (impassable in bad weather) will allow you to gain a good impression of life on the ranch. Open daily; for information, call 512/592-8055. A must for lovers of wide-open spaces.

Where to Stay

There are hotels, motels, and restaurants at Corpus Christi (north of Padre Island) and at Port Isabel, to the south, almost at the Mexican border.

Radisson South Padre Resort, 500 Padre Blvd., at the Causeway, South Padre Island, TX 78597 (210/761-6511; toll free, see Radisson). 188 rms. Large modern hotel on the ocean. **M–E**

Best Western Sandy Shores, 3200 Surfside, Corpus Christi, TX 78403 (512/883-7456; toll free, see Best Western). 254 rms. Comfortable, functional motel right on the beach. **I–M**

Yacht Club Hotel, 700 Yturria St. (two blocks north of Tex. 100), Port Isabel, TX 78578 (210/943-1301). 30 units. Small and modest but well-run motel across from the boat harbor. **B–I**

CHAPTER 37

SAN ANTONIO ☗

☐ ☐ ☐

The first of America's great cities to elect a mayor of Mexican origin (Henry Cisneros in 1981), San Antonio is a living symbol of the Hispanic influence north of the Rio Grande; every year it attracts 11 million visitors.

Founded in 1718 as the Spanish military outpost of San Antonio de Bexar, with an accompanying Franciscan mission of San Antonio de Valero (both on the site of what is now the fort of the **Alamo**), the city was the capital of the Spanish province of Texas when, a century later, Mexico achieved independence. It shortened its name, changing its flag and its allegiance. But the restless settlers of Texas soon achieved confrontation with the Mexican authorities. On February 23, 1836, the redoubtable Gen. Antonio López de Santa Anna, at the head of 5,000 Mexican soldiers, arrived to lay siege to the fort and mission of the Alamo, in the heart of San Antonio. After 13 days of furious fighting, the assault was mounted on Mar 6. The Mexicans lost 1,600 men in the battle, but they took the town and killed every last man of the heroic garrison: 187 American and foreign volunteers, including Col. William Travis and the two legendary scouts Davy Crockett and Jim Bowie. "Remember the Alamo" became the Texans' battle cry, until their final victory over the Mexicans a month later at San Jacinto (see Chapter 36 on Houston). The famous Rough Riders, those volunteers who won so much renown in Cuba during the Spanish-American War, came into being in San Antonio in 1898. Among the recruiters of this army of firebrands was the future president Theodore Roosevelt, who signed up many of his Rough Riders at the bar of the famous **Menger Hotel,** still one of the city's greatest tourist attractions.

San Antonio has preserved many interesting architectural relics of its eventful past, perhaps the most important being the church of the Alamo, at once museum and historic shrine; a half dozen Franciscan missions, including the superb **San José Mission;** and the **Spanish Governor's Palace.** If you take into account the picturesque Mexican district with its colorful market, the **Mercado;** the German enclave of the **King William District** with its opulent 1870s homes; the **Paseo del Rio,** a pretty flower-planted promenade along the river with water buses, restaurants, cafés, and shops; or the charming **Villita,** a little bit of 18th-century Spain in the heart of the city, you'll see that San Antonio is unquestionably the most firmly rooted in history of all the great cities of Texas, though one of the most vigorous as well, with its food, garment, cement, and above all aircraft-maintenance industries (the huge **Kelly Air Force Base** is nicknamed "The Home of the Air Force," and the adjoining **Lackland Air Force Base** is the country's largest air force training base). San Antonio's growth rate ranks sixth among the country's major cities.

Famous San Antonians include Conrad Hilton, founder of the hotel chain that bears his name, and actresses Carol Burnett and Joan Crawford.

BASIC FACTS: State of Texas. Area code: 210. Time zone: central. ZIP Code: 78205. Founded: 1718. Approximate population: city, 935,000; metropolitan area, 1,320,000. The nation's 10th-largest city, 30th-largest metropolitan area.

CLIMATE: Renowned for its year-round sunshine, San Antonio proudly proclaims itself "The City Where Sunshine Spends the Winter"; if you love fine weather, this is the place for you. While winter is pleasantly mild (rarely below 51°F/10°C in Jan), summer is on the sultry side (July average, 84°F/29°C), only partly relieved by the occasional tropical storm coming up from the Gulf of Mexico.

DISTANCES: Albuquerque, 861 mi. (1,378km); Dallas, 270 mi. (432km); Houston, 197 mi. (315km); Mexican border, 157 mi. (252km); New Orleans, 548 mi. (877km); Tucson, 883 mi. (1,412km).

ARRIVAL & TRANSIT INFORMATION

AIRPORT: San Antonio International Airport (SAT), 8 mi. (12km) north. For further information, call 821-3411.

AIRLINES: American (toll free 800/433-7300), Continental (toll free 800/525-0280), Delta (toll free 800/221-1212), Southwest (toll free 800/422-1616), United (toll free 800/241-6522), and USAir (toll free 800/428-4322).

CITY LINK: The **cab** fare from the airport to downtown is about $12–$14; time, 15 min. Bus: **Star Shuttle** (366-3183), leaves every 20 min.; serves major dwntwn hotels; fare, $5; time, about 20 min.

Good public transportation system by bus and streetcar via **Metropolitan Transit** (227-2020). Cabs are quite numerous and affordable. Unless you intend to visit the Franciscan missions around the city, you won't need to rent a car.

CAR RENTAL (at the airport): Avis (toll free 800/331-1212); Budget (toll free 800/527-0700); Dollar (toll free 800/800-4000); Hertz (toll free 800/654-3131); National (toll free 800/227-7368); and Thrifty (toll free 800/367-2277). For dwntwn locations, consult the local telephone directory.

LIMOUSINE SERVICES: Carey Limousine (525-0007) and Dav El Limousine (toll free 800/922-0343).

TAXIS: Theoretically, cabs can be hailed on the street, but it's more usual to take one from the waiting lines outside the major hotels, or from one of the stands along Paseo del Rio—or to phone. Major companies: **Checker Cab** (222-2151) and **Yellow Cab** (226-4242). There are also **taxi-boats** operating along Paseo del Rio (222-1701).

TRAIN: Amtrak station, 1174 E. Commerce St. off I-37 at the Montana St. exit (toll free 800/872-7245).

INTERCITY BUSES: Greyhound, 500 N. St. Mary's St. (toll free 800/231-2222).

INFORMATION & TOURS

TOURIST INFORMATION: The **San Antonio Convention and Visitors Bureau,** 121 Alamo Place (P.O. Box 2277), TX 78298 (210/270-8700; toll free 800/447-3372).

San Antonio Conservation Society, 107 King William St. (210/224-6163): Information on the King William Historic District.

Visitor Information Center, 317 Alamo Place (210/225-4636).

GUIDED TOURS: Gray Line Tours (bus), 1430 E. Houston St. (226-1706): Guided tours of the city and surroundings; serves principal hotels.

River Boat Tours (boat), 430 E. Commerce St. (222-1701): Barge trips along Paseo del Rio (seven landing stages); also dinner cruises. Daily year round.

San Antonio City Tours (bus), Alamo Place (520-8687): Half-day guided tours of the missions around the city.

SIGHTS, ATTRACTIONS & ACTIVITIES

ARCHITECTURAL HIGHLIGHTS: ⚜ **Alamodome,** just east of HemisFair Plaza (see below), across I-35/37 (223-3663): New sports, concert, and convention center is covered by a cable-suspended roof, which is anchored from four concrete towers, and seats a maximum of 73,200 for its football, basketball, and hockey games. Guided tours daily, except on days of events.

☼⚜ **Arneson River Theater,** 503 Villita St. (299-8610): Open-air theater of original design: The river flows between the spectators and the stage. Should be seen, preferably during a performance.

⚜ **HemisFair Plaza,** bounded by Commerce, Market, Durango, and Alamo Sts. (299-8570): A huge esplanade, once the site of the HemisFair '68 World's Fair. There's an ultramodern **Convention Center** whose frontage displays a giant mosaic by the Mexican artist Juan O'Gorman, and several other interesting buildings: the **Tower of the Americas,** the city's tallest high-rise (see "Panoramas," below), the **Theater for the Performing Arts,** the **Mexican Cultural Institute** (see "Museums of Art," below), and the **Institute of Texan Cultures** (see "Museums of Science and History," below). Open daily.

CHURCHES/SYNAGOGUES: ☼⚜ **San Antonio Missions National Historical Park:** Four Franciscan missions built between 1720 and 1731, and offering an interesting glimpse of Spanish Colonial culture in the 18th century. For information, call 229-5701. The ⚜ **Mission San José de Aguayo,** 6539 San José Dr., 5 mi. (9km) south on Roosevelt Ave. (922-0543), is the most elegantly beautiful of all; superb chapel with richly carved sacristy window, and Native American encampment. Open daily. ⚜ **Mission San Francisco de la Espada,** 10040 Espada Rd., 6 mi. (10km) south on Roosevelt Ave. (627-2064), has been completely restored; note also, halfway between Mission San José and Mission San Juan Capistrano, the Espada Dam and aqueduct built by the friars (1731–45) to supply the missions. Open daily. ⚜ **Mission San Juan Capistrano,** 9101 Graf Rd., 6 mi. (10km) south on Roosevelt Ave. (229-5734), is very near San Francisco de la Espada; the well-preserved church is still in use. Open daily. ⚜ **Mission de la Purisima Concepción de Acuña,** 807 Mission Rd. via Roosevelt Ave. (229-5732), is near downtown; it's the oldest unrestored Spanish mission in the country, and one of the best preserved. The chapel's wall paintings, and its acoustics, are famous. Open daily.

⚜ **San Fernando Cathedral,** 114 Military Plaza (227-1297): Fine example of 19th-century (1873) Gothic, on the site of an earlier (1758) church built by settlers from the Canary Islands. The remains of the defenders of the Alamo are supposed to have been buried in its foundations. Open daily.

HISTORIC BUILDINGS: ☼⚜ **The Alamo,** Alamo Plaza (225-1391): Makes every Texan heart beat faster. Of the fort of the Alamo (the Spanish word for "poplar"), dating from 1744 and once so gallantly defended by Davy Crockett, Jim Bowie, Colonel Travis, and their 186 comrades-in-arms, there remain only the chapel, now a memorial of the battle, and the "Long Barrack," once the Franciscan convent of San Antonio de Valero, where the last defenders were killed on March 6, 1836. Today it houses a museum of Texas history. Open daily.

☼⚜ **Cos House,** 416 La Villita (299-8610): The most famous building in the La Villita Historic District. It was here that Gen. Perfecto de Cos, on December 10, 1835 (three months before the siege of the Alamo), signed the instrument whereby the Mexicans surrendered the town to the patriots of Texas. Open daily.

☼ 🏛 **Menger Hotel,** 204 Alamo Plaza (223-4361): A local landmark since 1859. Historical figures of the caliber of Gens. Robert E. Lee and Ulysses S. Grant, not to mention Sam Houston, a founding father of the state of Texas, have frequented the place. At the bar here, in 1898, Theodore Roosevelt, the future president, recruited volunteers for his famous Rough Riders to serve in the Spanish-American War.

☼ 🏛 **Navarro House State Historic Site,** 228 S. Laredo St. (226-4801): Interesting buildings of adobe (native-style unbaked bricks made in this instance of *caliche,* a mixture of gravel, clay, and limestone) and whitewashed stone, and blending a number of unrelated architectural styles: Spanish Colonial, German, French, Victorian. Built in the 1850s, these three houses, still with their original furniture and decoration, were the home of José Antonio Navarro, a rich Texan rancher and politician, born at San Antonio in 1795. Open Wed–Sat.

☼ 🏛 **Spanish Governor's Palace,** 105 Military Plaza (224-0601): Official residence of the Spanish governors, built in 1749—witness the date and the coats-of-arms of the Habsburgs and of King Philip V engraved on the keystone. A fine colonial building with 2-ft.-thick (61cm) walls and carved doors, still with its original furniture; the only one of its kind surviving in Texas. Open daily.

🏛 **Steves Homestead,** 509 King William St. (225-5924): This fine Gothic Revival home on the banks of the San Antonio River dates from 1876; it's a mute witness to the wealth and urbanity of the German merchants who in the 19th century lived in the King William Historic District (see "Strolls," below). Splendid old furniture; huge landscaped garden with an indoor pool (River Haus). Open daily.

INDUSTRIAL TOURS: ☼🏛 **Lone Star Brewing Co.–Buckhorn Hall of Horns,** 600 Lone Star Blvd. (270-9400): This unusual museum, inside the brewery, displays an astonishing variety of 3,500 hunting trophies from around the world—polar bears to African antelope—as well as the Hall of Fins (marine life) and the Hall of Feathers (mounted birds). Reconstruction of the 1887 Buckhorn Saloon; free beer tasting. The adjoining **Hall of Texas History** has exhibits dealing with the history of the state from the time of the first Spanish explorers. Open daily.

MARKETS: ☼🏛 **Market Square,** bounded by Dolorosa, San Saba, W. Commerce, and Santa Rosa Sts. (299-8600): The local retailing center for more than a century, it includes the **Farmers' Market,** dealing in fruit and vegetables; the Mexican market **El Mercado,** where you may haggle in a colorful, authentically Mexican environment; and the **Centro de Artes del Mercado,** an arts-and-crafts market in a restored 1922 building. All are open daily year round; some businesses are open around the clock. Very lively.

MUSEUMS OF ART: ☼🏛 **Marion Koogler McNay Art Museum,** 6000 N. New Braunfels Ave. at U.S. 81 (824-5368): Some old master paintings, but mostly moderns (Picasso, Chagall, Cézanne, Gauguin, van Gogh), pre-Columbian art, and 19th- and 20th-century bronzes, in a lovely Mediterranean-style villa overlooking San Antonio. Also temporary exhibitions. Open Tues–Sun.

🏛 **Mexican Cultural Institute,** HemisFair Plaza (227-0123): Mexican art, crafts, and archeology; revolving exhibits of work by contemporary Mexican artists. Interesting museum administered by the National University of Mexico; open Tues–Sun.

☼🏛🏛 **San Antonio Museum of Art,** 200 W. Jones Ave. (829-7262): This new museum, housed in the former Lone Star Brewery (an 1880s building, magnificently restored and converted to its new use with interior overhead walkways and glass-walled elevators), is a complete success both artistically and architecturally. The important Robert W. Kinn and Nelson A. Rockefeller collections of pre-Columbian and Mexican art are on display here, as are Roman antiquities, Far Eastern and Spanish Colonial art, and 20th-century American painting and photography. Lovely modern-sculpture garden. All this is an inviting setting on the banks of the San Antonio River. Open daily.

MUSEUMS OF SCIENCE & HISTORY: The **Buckhorn Hall of Horns and Hall of Texas History** (see the Lone Star Brewing Co. under "Industrial Tours," above.)

☼ ⚓ **Fort Sam Houston Museum,** on I-35 at New Braunfels Ave., Bldg. 123 (221-1211): Headquarters of the Fifth U.S. Army, Fort Sam Houston is one of the oldest (1879) and most famous military posts in the southern U.S. It was here that the Apache chief Geronimo was imprisoned; here, too, U.S. military aviation was born in 1910. The museum contains thousands of objects from the 19th century (uniforms, weapons, documents, etc.). For military history buffs. Open daily.

☼ ⚓ **Hertzberg Circus Collection,** 210 W. Market St. (299-7810): More than 20,000 items illustrating the history of the circus: posters, photographs, models of the Big Top, miniature circuses, souvenirs of Tom Thumb and the legendary Phineas T. Barnum. One of the most important collections of its kind in the world. Open daily May–Oct, Mon–Sat the rest of the year.

⚓ **Institute of Texan Cultures,** HemisFair Plaza (558-2300): An entity of the University of Texas, this museum illustrates in lively visual fashion the historical and cultural contributions made by various nations and ethnic groups to the foundation and expansion of Texas. Spectacular. Open Tues–Sun.

☼ **Texas Ranger Museum Memorial Hall,** 3805 Broadway (822-9011): The history of the legendary Texas Rangers from their foundation in 1828 onward, illustrated by hundreds of drawings, photographs, old weapons, saddles, badges, souvenirs of pioneer days, etc. Interesting. Open Tues–Sun May–Aug, Wed–Sun the rest of the year.

☼ ⚓ **Witte Museum,** 3801 Broadway at Tuleta St. (829-7262): Fine museum of history, anthropology, and natural science entirely devoted to Texas. From dinosaurs and prehistoric Native American artifacts to houses of 19th-century pioneers, brought from different places across the state and rebuilt here. Open daily.

PANORAMAS: ☼⚓ **Tower of the Americas,** HemisFair Plaza (299-8615): Soaring concrete tower 750 ft. (229m) high including its crowning TV antenna, the tallest building in the city. The observation platform 622 ft. (189m) up offers a unique view, for a radius of 100 mi. (160km) in fine weather. Revolving restaurant (mediocre) at the top. Open daily until 11pm.

PARKS & GARDENS: ⚓ **Brackenridge Park,** N. Broadway, 2 mi. (3.5km) north of the city: Lovely park on 340 acres (138ha) of rolling country a 5-min. drive from downtown. Celebrated zoo; miniature train and cable-car rides. Water gardens in the pit of an abandoned quarry (**Sunken Oriental Gardens**). **Texas Ranger Memorial Hall** and **Witte Museum** (see above). Many picnic areas.

☼ ⚓⚓ **San Antonio Botanical Gardens,** 555 Funston Place at N. New Braunfels Ave. (821-5115): On a height of land above the city (fine view from the Gazebo Observatory), this 33-acre (13ha) botanic garden includes a lovely rose garden, a little lake, a sunken courtyard surrounded by ab-

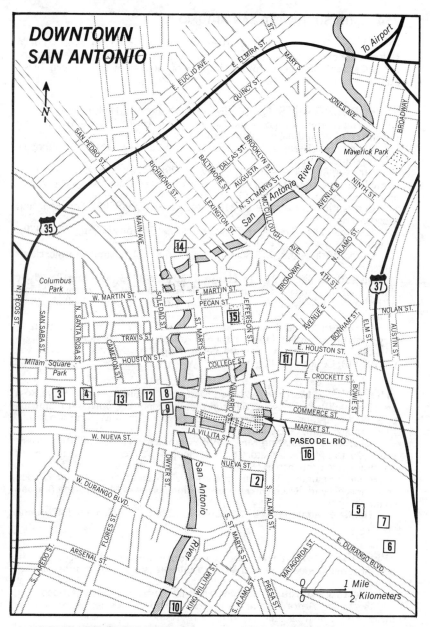

DOWNTOWN SAN ANTONIO

KEY TO NUMBERED SIGHTS
1. The Alamo
2. La Villita
3. Market Square
4. Fiesta Plaza
5. Tower of the Americas
6. The Institute of Texan Cultures
7. San Antonio Museum of Transportation
8. Main Plaza
9. Military Plaza
10. King William Historical Area
11. The Heart of Texas
12. San Fernando Cathedral
13. Spanish Governor's Palace
14. Southwest Craft Center
15. Travis Park
16. Convention and Visitors Bureau

stract glass structures designed by Argentine architect Emilio Ambasz (the **Lucile Halsell Conservatory**), a garden for the blind labeled in Braille (the **Touch-and-Smell Garden**), and an enormous sampling of the flora of Texas. Open Tues–Sun.

PERFORMING ARTS: For daily listings of all shows and cultural events, consult the entertainment pages of the daily paper *San Antonio Express-News* (morning and evening) and the magazine *Texas Monthly.*
    Alamo City Theater, 339 W. Josephine St. (734-4646): Contemporary theater, comedy, drama.
    Arneson River Theater, 503 Villita St. (299-8610): A theater of unprecedented design—the spectators are on one bank of Paseo del Rio while the stage and the actors are on the other. Open-air music and theater (June–Aug).
    Convention Center Arena, 210 E. Market St. (299-8500): Pop, rock, and jazz concerts.
    Joe and Harry Freeman Coliseum, 3201 E. Houston St. (224-6080): Country-and-western concerts.
    Laurie Auditorium, 715 Stadium Dr. (736-8117): Chamber music, classical recitals.
    Majestic Theatre, 212 E. Houston St. (226-3333): Visiting Broadway shows, touring companies. Beautiful 1920s interior splendidly restored. Home of the San Antonio Symphony (principal conductor: Christopher Wilkins) (Sept –June).
    San Antonio Little Theater, 800 W. Ashby (733-7258): Shows, contemporary theater (Sept–May). Home of the San Antonio Little Theater.
    Lila Cockrell Theater for the Performing Arts, Market St. and Bowie (299-8500): Concerts, ballet, opera.

SHOPPING: **El Mercado/Mexican Market,** W. Commerce and Santa Rosa Sts. (299-8600): Bargains for collectors of folk art: pottery, piñatas (ornamental pots filled with candies), handcrafts, silver jewelry, typical Mexican foodstuffs. Lively and colorful. Open daily.
    Rivercenter Shopping Mall, 849 E. Commerce St. (225-0000): A classy, glassy, 10-acre (4ha), three-story dining, shopping, and entertainment complex on Paseo del Rio, opened in 1988 at a total cost of $200 million, with 135 shops, stores, and restaurants. With its little bridges across the river, all-glass facades, and mariachi band, Rivercenter is an astonishing blend of Mexico, America, and Venice.
    Tienda Guadalupe, 1001 S. Alamo St. (226-5873): Genuine folk art and crafts.

SPECIAL EVENTS: For the exact schedule of events listed below, consult the **San Antonio Convention and Visitors Bureau** (see "Tourist Information," above).
    Livestock Exposition and Rodeo (Feb): Popular stock fair and rodeo.
    Fiesta San Antonio (mid-Apr): Parades, battle of flowers, processions on the river. One of Texas's most colorful festivals since 1891.
    Cinco de Mayo (May 5): When the city celebrates Mexico's national holiday.
    Fiesta Flamenco, Fiesta Fandango, Fiesta Noche del Rio (June–Aug): Open-air dance and theater at Arneson River Theater. Held respectively Sun–Tues, Wed, and Thurs–Sat.
    Texas Folklife Festival (early Aug): Some 6,000 representatives from more than 30 ethnic groups who settled and built Texas join to share their traditions, crafts, skills, music, folk dances, and authentic cuisine at the Institute of Texan Cultures.

Las Posadas (mid-Dec): Nighttime candlelight procession along Paseo del Rio; a tradition for more than 250 years.

SPORTS: San Antonio has one NBA and one minor-league professional baseball team:

Baseball (Apr–Aug): Dodgers, Municipal Stadium (434-9311).
Basketball (Oct–Mar): Spurs, Alamodome (554-7787).

STROLLS: ☼⚖ **El Mercado/Mexican Market,** W. Commerce and Santa Rosa Sts.: The heart of the Mexican quarter; food stalls, craft shops. Lively and colorful; open daily (see "Shopping," above).

☼⚖ **King William Historic District,** around King William and S. St. Mary's Sts.: The 19th-century German district, now a residential neighborhood. King William St. (so named in honor of William I of Germany) is the main drag, lined with fine homes dating from 1870–90. Among them, no. 107, built in 1873, now houses the **San Antonio Conservatory Society** (free descriptive leaflets on the King William Historic District). Don't miss the **Steves Homestead** (see "Historic Buildings," above) at no. 509.

☼⚖⚖ **Paseo del Rio,** along the San Antonio River: Pretty riverwalk, shaded with palm trees and cypresses, along the San Antonio River. Lined with cafés, restaurants, hotels, shops, and art galleries. The river (which meanders for 2½ mi./4km through downtown), its narrow bridges, and its water buses have won for San Antonio the nickname "Venice of the West."

☼⚖ **La Villita,** S. Presa, Alamo, and Nueva Sts. (299-8610): A corner of 18th-century Spain in the middle of San Antonio. The old adobe houses, deftly restored, now shelter galleries and craft shops surrounded by flower-planted patios, bougainvilleas, and banana palms. Don't overlook **Cos House,** where in 1835 was signed the first Mexican surrender to the Texans (see "Historic Buildings," above).

THEME PARKS: ☼⚖⚖ **Sea World of Texas,** 10500 Sea World Dr. (523-3611): The world's largest marine-life theme park, with dozens of attractions on its 250 acres (101ha): "Shamu" the killer whale, sea lions, walrus, trained-dolphin shows, waterski ballets. Ultramodern facilities opened in 1988. Attracts more than three million visitors each year. Open daily June–Sept; call for schedule during other times of the year.

☼⚖ **Fiesta Texas,** I-10 at Loop 1604 (697-5050): Brand-new Texas-style amusement park with dozens of spectacular attractions, including "The Rattler," the world's tallest, steepest, and fastest wooden coaster. Open daily late May to early Sept, wknds only in spring and autumn.

ACCOMMODATIONS

Personal Favorites (in order of preference)

☼♟♟♟ **St. Anthony Hotel** (dwntwn), 300 E. Travis St., TX 78205 (210/227-4392; toll free 800/338-1338). 350 rms, A/C, color TV, in-rm movies. AE, CB, DC, MC, V. Valet gar. $9, pool, health club, rest. (the Café), bars, rm svce, disco, concierge, free crib. *Note:* A major San Antonio landmark since 1909. Elegant and urbane, w. Oriental rugs and a profusion of marble and crystal. Spacious, completely renovated rms. Period furnishings. Personalized svce. The best rms overlook Travis Park. Big business clientele; the best place to stay in the city. Good rest. serving American cuisine. **M–E**

☼♟♟♟ **La Mansión del Rio** (dwntwn), 112 College St., TX 78205 (210/225-2581; toll free, see Preferred). 337 rms, A/C, cable color TV. AE, CB, DC, MC, V. Valet gar. $7, pool, rest. (Las Canarias), coffee shop, bar, 24-hr. rm svce, concierge, free crib. *Note:* Opened in 1968, the Spanish Colonial hotel includes a part of the old building of St. Mary's University, skillfully restored. Pretty courtyard w. pool and bougainvilleas. Inviting but slightly constricting rms w. balconies and minibars. Efficient svce; elegant but expensive rest. Ask for a rm overlooking Paseo del Rio. Business and group clientele. Excellent location. **M–VE**

🛏🛏🛏 **Marriott Rivercenter** (dwntwn), 101 Bowie St., TX 78205 (210/223-1000; toll free, see Marriott). 1,004 rms, A/C, color TV, in-rm movies. AE, CB, DC, MC, V. Gar. $7, pool, health club, sauna, two rests., bar, 24-hr. rm svce, concierge, free crib. *Note:* This giant among local hotels looks down from its 38-story glass-and-concrete tower over Hemisfair Plaza and the Alamo; the effect of this unabashed postmodernity, in so historic a place, is almost ludicrous. Huge, inviting comfortable rms; ultra-professional svce. Direct access to Rivercenter Shopping Mall w. its dozens of shops, boutiques, and rests. Business and convention clientele (the hotel is right across from the Convention Center). Two VIP floors. **E**

🔆🛏🛏 **Menger Hotel** (dwntwn), 204 Alamo Plaza, TX 78205 (210/223-4361; toll free 800/345-9285). 350 rms, A/C, color TV, in-rm movies. AE, CB, DC, MC, V. Valet garage $9, pool, health club, sauna, rest., bar, 24-hr rm svce, boutiques, free crib. *Note:* An old hotel (1859) fraught w. history (see "Historic Buildings," above, for some of its illustrious guests). Has retained all its period flavor. Comfort and renovated facilities, but the svce leaves something to be desired. Pleasant indoor grdn. Unusually good location across from the Alamo. Good value. **I–M**

🛏🛏 **Travelodge on the River** (dwntwn), 100 Villita St., TX 78205 (210/226-2271; toll free, see Travelodge). 132 rms, A/C, color TV, in-rm movies. AE, CB, DC, MC, V. Parking $5, pool, rest., bar, rm svce. *Note:* Newish motel overlooking the San Antonio River. Comfortable rms w. private balconies; charming Spanish-style interior. Efficient svce; good value. **I,** but lower rates off-season.

🛏 **Rodeway Inn Downtown** (dwntwn), 900 N. Main Ave., TX 78204 (210/223-2951; toll free, see Choice). 128 rms, A/C, color TV, in-rm movies. AE, CB, DC, MC, V. Free parking, pool, rest. adj., free crib. *Note:* Conventional but well-run motel 5 min. by car from Paseo del Rio and the Alamo compound. Functional comforts. Svce a little flaky. Good overall value; fine if you're on a budget. **B–I**

Other Accommodations (from top bracket to budget)

🛏🛏🛏🛏 **Plaza San Antonio** (dwntwn), 555 S. Alamo St., TX 78205 (210/229-1000; toll free 800/421-1172). 252 rms, A/C, color TV, in-rm movies. AE, CB, DC, MC, V. Valet parking $7, pool, two tennis courts, health club, sauna, rest. (the Anaqua Grill), bar, 24-hr. rm svce, concierge, free crib. *Note:* Lovely modern hotel a stone's throw from La Villita and the Convention Center. Elegant and comfortable w. exotic touches. Luxurious rms w. private balconies overlooking a beautiful tropical grdn. Very good svce; excellent rest. Upscale business clientele. A very fine place. **E–VE**

🔆🛏🛏🛏 **Fairmount Hotel** (dwntwn), 401 S. Alamo St., TX 78205 (210/224-8800; toll free 800/345-3457). 37 rms and suites, A/C, color TV, in-rm movies. AE, CB, DC, MC, V. Parking $6, rest. (Fairmount), bar, rm svce, concierge, free crib. *Note:* This luxurious three-story Victorian-style home, built in 1906, was transported some 550 yards (500m) to its present location on a wheeled platform—a world's record in all respects. Refined interior w. old paneling and Italian marble; the suites, the most luxurious and best equipped of any San Antonio hotel, have three phones, four-poster beds, and VCR. Polished svce; rest. of a high order. The favorite of those in-the-know. Opposite the Convention Center. **E–VE**

🛏🛏🛏 **Hyatt Regency Hill Country Resort** (vic.), 9800 Hyatt Resort Dr., TX 78251 (210/647-1234; toll free, see Hyatt). 500 units, A/C, cable color TV. AE, CB, DC, MC, V. Valet parking $7, tennis, health club, golf, two pools, beach, two rests., three bars, rm svce, entertainment, concierge, free crib. *Note:* $100-million hotel and resort developed over a 2,700-acre cattle and agricultural ranch. The hotel's limestone facade and wood-trimmed porches reflect the region's architecture and cohabit well with the surrounding rolling hills and thick patches of oak trees. Artificial, 1,000-ft. (305m) river for inner tubing. Comfortable, inviting rms with refrigerators and minibars. Professional svce. Convention clientele. VIP level. 20 min. from dwntwn. **E–VE**

Hyatt Regency (dwntwn), 123 Losoya St., TX 78205 (210/222-1234; toll free, see Hyatt). 632 rms, A/C, color TV, in-rm movies. AE, CB, DC, MC, V. Valet parking $8, pool, two rests. (including Chaps), bars, rm svce, disco, boutiques, concierge. *Note:* Futuristic 16-story building w. indoor grdns, waterfalls, and spectacular glass lobby. Ultra-comfortable rms w. private balconies, the best overlooking the San Antonio River. Very good svce. Group and business clientele; VIP floor; interesting wknd discounts. Very near the Alamo and the Convention Center. **E**

Sheraton Gunter (dwntwn), 205 E. Houston St., TX 78205 (210/227-3241; toll free, see Sheraton). 325 rms, A/C, color TV, in-rm movies. AE, CB, DC, MC, V. Valet gar. $9, pool, health club, rest. (Houston Street Café), coffee shop, bar, rm svce, concierge, free crib. *Note:* This venerable institution dates from 1909, but furnishings and facilities have been completely renovated. Vast, inviting rms, some w. refrigerators; svce w. a smile. Wonderful location very nr. Paseo del Rio and the Alamo. Group and convention clientele. A San Antonio landmark. **M–E**

Best Western Crockett Hotel (dwntwn), 320 Bonham St., TX 78205 (210/225-6500; toll free, see Best Western). 202 rms, A/C, color TV, in-rm movies. AE, CB, DC, MC, V. Valet parking $10, pool, rest. (Lela B's), coffee shop, bar, rm svce, free crib. *Note:* Reopened in 1983 after a rejuvenation costing over $15 million, this elderly grand hotel from the 1910s has recaptured all the elegance and charm of its distinguished past. Many works of art and period furniture. Rms a little cramped but comfortable and pleasantly decorated. Perfunctory svce; charming patio–coffee shop. VIP floor. Wonderfully located across from the Alamo. **I–M**

La Quinta Convention Center (dwntwn), 1001 E. Commerce St., TX 78205 (210/222-9181; toll free, see La Quinta). 140 rms, A/C, color TV, in-rm movies. AE, CB, DC, MC, V. Free parking, pool, rest. nearby, valet svce, free crib. *Note:* Comfortable, serviceable motel a block or two from the Convention Center. Cheerful reception and svce. Group and convention clientele. **I–M**

Holiday Inn Market Square (nr. dwntwn), 318 W. Durango St., TX 78207 (210/225-3211; toll free, see Holiday Inns). 317 rms, A/C, color TV, in-rm movies. AE, CB, DC, MC, V. Free parking, pool, rest., bar, rm svce. *Note:* A typical Holiday Inn a 5-min. drive from the Alamo and the Convention Center. Functional rms w. balconies; efficient svce; recently renovated. Interesting wknd discounts. Good value on balance. **I**

Days Inn Northeast (nr. dwntwn), 3443 N. Pan Am Expwy., TX 78219 (210/225-4521; toll free, see Days Inns). 122 rms, A/C, cable color TV. AE, DC, MC, V. Free parking, pool, free breakfast. *Note:* Motel in the traditional manner, across from Water Park USA and 5 min. from dwntwn along I-35. Serviceably comfortable rms; friendly reception and svce. Good overall value; w. direct access to the freeways, it's particularly so if you're driving. **B–I**

Motel 6 East (nr. dwntwn), 138 NW White Rd., TX 78219 (210/333-1850). 100 rms, A/C, cable color TV. AE, DC, MC, V. Free parking, pool. *Note:* Unbeatable value 10 min. from dwntwn. Comfortable, serviceable rms. Direct access to the San Antonio bypass motorway. Ideal if you're driving through. **B**

Airport Accommodations

♀ **La Quinta Airport East** (vic.), 333 NE Loop I-410, TX 78216
(210/828-0781; toll free, see La Quinta). 198 rms, A/C, color TV, in-rm movies. AE, CB, DC, MC, V. Free parking, pool, free breakfast, rm svce. *Note:* Modern, comfortable motel; free airport limo. Also great if you're driving. **I**

YMCA/Youth Hostels

Bullis House Inn International Hostel (nr. dwntwn), 621 Pierce St., TX 78208 (210/223-9426). 60 beds. Comfortable youth hostel in a fine old house. Open year round.

RESTAURANTS

Personal Favorites (in order of preference)

♀♀♀ **Anaqua Grill** (dwntwn), in the Plaza San Antonio (see "Accommodations," above) (229-1000). A/C. Breakfast/lunch/dinner daily, brunch Sun. AE, CB, DC, MC, V. Jkt. *Specialties:* tapas, toasted ravioli, masa-battered shrimp w. orange-jicama salad, lamb en brochette w. ginger-soy sauce, game hen marinated in yogurt, very good desserts. Menu changes regularly. Fine wine list. *Note:* The luxury-hotel rest. at its best; creative New World cuisine by chef Michael Bomberg, superbly prepared and served. Elegant, intimate decor and a prospect of grdns, patios, and fountains. Open-air dining on fine days. Exemplary svce; resv. a must. Big business clientele. *American.* **M–E**

♀♀♀ **Biga** (nr. dwntwn), 206 E. Locust St. at McCullough Ave. (225-0722). A/C. Lunch Tues–Fri, dinner Mon–Sat. AE, CB, DC, MC, V. *Specialties:* beer-battered onion rings w. habañero ketchup, Texas nilgai antelope w. rosemary and agarita-berry sauce, potato pancakes w. duck confit, grilled sweetbreads on spinach and crunchy noodles, outstanding desserts and homemade breads. Daily menu. Over 50 wines by the glass. *Note:* Modern southwestern cuisine at its best by Bruce Auden, a local culinary superstar. Stylish-casual setting in a 100-year-old mansion. Informal but efficient svce. Resv. a must. By far the best new place in town. *American.* **M**

♀♀ **L'Etoile** (nr. dwntwn), 6106 Broadway at Albany (826-4551). A/C. Lunch Mon–Sat, dinner nightly. AE, CB, DC, MC, V. *Specialties:* shrimp Toulouse-Lautrec (sautéed w. creamy basil sauce), lamb in herbal croûte, sea scallops provençale, salmon in pastry shell, linguine w. lamb sausage. The menu changes daily. Good wine list fairly priced. *Note:* Lively French café w. typical bistro atmosphere; the managers and most of the staff are French. Outdoor dining. Locally popular. Resv. advised. *French.* **I–M**

♀♀ **Liberty Bar** (nr. dwntwn), 328 E. Josephine (227-1187). Lunch/dinner daily, brunch Sun; closed hols. AE, DC, MC, V. *Specialties:* goat cheese and piloncillo sauce, chile relleño w. nogada salsa, grilled quail w. green mole, grilled snapper w. cilantro sauce, crab cakes, coconut custard. Texas beer, Shiner Bock, on tap. *Note:* Old cowboy cooking in what was originally built as a saloon in 1890. At the rest. is the original bar and the same wooden floors that slant from the structural damage done in the great flood of 1922. A favorite of local Tommy Lee Jones. Friendly, competent svce. Resv. accepted. *American.* **I–M**

♀ **Casa Rio** (dwntwn), 430 E. Commerce St. on Riverwalk (225-6718). A/C. Lunch/dinner daily; closed hols. AE, CB, DC, MC, V. *Specialties:* carne asada, tacos, enchiladas, steak ranchero, chile relleño, menudo (tripe). *Note:* The almost aggressively tourist decor and atmosphere should not spoil your pleasure in the very acceptable Mexican food at extremely reasonable prices. Pleasant terrace along Paseo del Rio. Svce friendly enough, but short on efficiency. Riverboat dinners organized for groups of eight or more; mariachi music at dinner. Picturesque. Resv. advisable. *Mexican.* **B–I**

♀ **Earl Abel's** (nr. dwntwn), 4200 Broadway (822-3358). A/C.
⚲ Breakfast/lunch/dinner daily (around the clock); closed Dec
25. AE, MC, V. *Specialties:* fried chicken, hamburgers, T-bone steak, fried catfish,
broiled trout, pecan pie. *Note:* For more than half a century this worthy exponent
of large-scale food svce (more than a million meals a year) has been a family favorite. Decent, unpretentious food in generous portions; rather gloomy decor. Svce
generally rushed. No resv.; 10 min. from dwntwn. *American/Steak.* **B–I**

Other Restaurants (from top bracket to budget)

♀♀♀ **Chez Ardid** (nr. dwntwn), 1919 San Pedro Ave. (732-3203).
⚲⚲⚲ A/C. Lunch Mon–Fri, dinner Mon–Sat; closed hols. AE,
MC, V. Jkt. *Specialties:* seafood sausage, hot crabmeat Ardid, escalope of veal
normande, tournedos périgourdine, rack of lamb w. herbs, mussels in cream
sauce, braid red snapper and Norwegian salmon w. three peppers, floating island
dessert. Menu changes regularly. Good wine list. *Note:* San Antonio's worthy exponent of true French cuisine. Intimate atmosphere in a 19th-century mansion.
Flawless svce; resv. recommended. 15 min. from dwntwn, 10 min. from airport.
Valet parking. *French.* **M–E**

☼♀♀ **Little Rhein Steak House** (dwntwn), 231 S. Alamo Plaza
⚲⚲ (225-2111). A/C. Dinner only, nightly. AE, CB, DC, MC, V.
Specialties: top-quality prime cuts, pepper steak, lamb chops, chicken, seafood.
Extensive American wine list. *Note:* The best (and the priciest) steaks in town in a
lovely 150-year-old stone house overlooking the river at its most scenic spot. Superb outdoor dining w. table-filled landscaped terraces. Professional svce. Resv.
advised. *Steak.* **M–E**

♀♀♀ **Crumpet's** (nr. dwntwn), 5800 Broadway (821-5454). A/C.
⚲⚲ Lunch/dinner daily; closed Dec 25, Jan 1. AE, MC, V. Jkt.
Specialties: fettuccine w. scallops, beef tenderloin w. green-peppercorn sauce, loin
of veal w. morels, veal piccata w. lemon sauce, scrumptious homemade desserts.
Average wine list. *Note:* The flawless European-derived food, the elegant setting,
and the classical music in the background make this one of the best places to eat in
town, much favored by the local Establishment. Warm and attentive svce. Resv.
strongly advised. *Continental.* **I–M**

♀♀ **Boudro's** (dwntwn), 421 E. Commerce St. (224-8484). A/C.
⚲⚲ Lunch/dinner daily. AE, MC, V. *Specialties:* gumbo (duck and
sausage), smoked shrimp enchiladas, blackened prime rib w. aromatic herb butter, bread pudding w. whisky sauce. *Note:* This charming rest. on Paseo del Rio,
w. its massive stone walls, which serves the best Créole food in San Antonio, is
also strong on steaks and seafood. Pleasant little shady patio. Good svce; very
relaxed atmosphere. Resv. strongly advised. *Créole.* **I–M**

♀♀ **Luna Notte** (nr. dwntwn), 6402 N. New Braunfels (822-
⚲⚲ 4242). A/C. Lunch Mon–Fri, dinner daily; closed hols. AE,
CB, DC, MC, V. *Specialties:* pizzas, lobster ravioli w. ginger-orange sauce, potato
gnocchi w. sun-dried tomatoes and artichokes, hazelnut-roasted chicken breast
stuffed w. goat cheese, chocolate mousse cake. Extensive wine list. *Note:* The excess of steel within the high-tech, industrial-inspired dining room makes it an
unusual spot in San Antonio. High-decibel clientele at the bar, especially on the
weekends. Excellent Italian fare. Resv. recommended. *Italian.* **I**

♀♀ **Paesano's** (nr. dwntwn), 1715 McCullough Ave. (226-
⚲⚲ 9541). A/C. Lunch Tues–Fri, dinner Tues–Sun; closed hols.
AE, DC, MC, V. *Specialties:* shrimp Paesano, steak pizzaiola, filet of red snapper
w. mushrooms, scaloppine Francesca, spumone. *Note:* Charming small *trattoria,*
intimate and inviting. Genuine Italian cuisine; good svce. Popular among local
politicians and sports fans; resv. advised. *Italian.* **I**

☼♀ **La Fogata** (nr. dwntwn), 2427 Vance Jackson Rd. (340-
⚲ 1337). A/C. Breakfast Fri–Sun, lunch/dinner daily; closed
Dec 25, Jan 1. AE, CB, DC, MC, V. *Specialties:* queso flameado, enchiladas
verdes, chimichangas, fajitas. All food is charcoal-broiled. *Note:* In spite (or per-

haps because) of its spare, unassuming setting, La Fogata is held by purists to be the best of San Antonio's countless Mexican rests.; it's worth visiting the city just to try the homemade tortillas! Pleasant patio dining. Generous helpings; marvelously obliging and engaging svce. A favorite of those in-the-know. 15 min. from dwntwn. No resv. *Mexican.* **B–I**

♀ **Hunan River Garden** (dwntwn), 506 Riverwalk (222-0808). A/C. Lunch/dinner daily. AE, MC, V. *Specialties:* classic Hunan and Szechuan dishes; highly seasoned sauces. *Note:* San Antonio's most picturesque Chinese rest., and its best, right on Paseo del Rio. Generous portions; efficient svce; often crowded. Excellent value. *Chinese.* **B–I**

♀ **La Calesa** (nr. dwntwn), 2103 E. Hildebrand St. (822-4475). A/C. Breakfast Sat–Sun, lunch/dinner daily; closed hols. AE, CB, DC, MC, V. *Specialties:* enchiladas, quesadillas, cochinita pibil (barbecued pig), pollo en escabeche, carne poblana (marinated beef), Kahlúa–ice-cream pie. *Note:* Small, family-style rest. serving earthy, true Mexican (not Tex-Mex) food, including specialties from the Yucatán region. Casual, friendly atmosphere; the dining rms are decorated w. Diego Rivera posters and folk art. Consistently good and crowded. *Mexican.* **B–I**

Cafeterias/Fast Food

☼ **Mi Tierra** (dwntwn), 218 Produce Row (225-1262). Breakfast/lunch/dinner daily around the clock. AE, MC, V. Popular and colorful Mexican rest. across from the famous Mercado. A favorite w. the Mexican community as well as local gringos and tourists.

BARS & NIGHTCLUBS

Dick's Last Resort (dwntwn), 406 Navarro, on the Paseo del Rio (224-0026). Live dixieland jazz performed here nightly until 2am.

Farmer's Daughter (vic.), 542 NW White Rd. (333-7391). Big, colorful western-style dance hall, open Wed–Sun. 15 min. from dwntwn.

Herman's Roaring 20s (vic.), 13445 Blanco Rd. (492-1353). The local shrine of the Big Band sound. For nostalgics of the '20s.

Jim Cullum's Landing, in the Hyatt Regency (see "Accommodations," above) (223-7266). Live New Orleans jazz Tues–Sat. Locally popular.

Menger Hotel Bar, in the Menger Hotel (see "Accommodations," above) (223-4361). Famous (see "Historical Buildings," above) and congenial bar attracting a good share of the city's tourists.

NEARBY EXCURSIONS

☼🏛 **AQUARENA SPRINGS** (32 mi./51km NE on I-35) (512/396-8900): The springs of the San Marcos River, with splendid aquatic gardens; the crystal-clear water gives you a wonderful view of the rich vegetation and underwater life. Glass-bottom-boat rides; underwater shows in summer. Open daily year round.

☼🏛 **AUSTIN** (78 mi./124km NE on I-35): Founded as Waterloo in 1839 and later renamed in honor of Stephen F. Austin, one of the founders of Texas, the state capital is built on hills rising above the Colorado River (not to be confused with the river of the same name in the state of Colorado). **Old Pecan Street** is a charming historic district, with old houses, shops, and restaurants (6th St.). The imposing **State Capitol** in pink granite, north end of Congress Ave. (512/463-0063), is open daily. The **Lyndon B. Johnson Library and Museum,** on the University of Texas campus (512/482-

5137), open daily, honors the 36th president of the U.S. The **French Legation Museum,** at 802 San Marcos St. (512/472-8180), open Tues–Sun, is the only foreign mission to the U.S. ever built outside Washington, D.C. (in 1840, when Texas was still an independent republic). The capital of Texas has also become the capital of "New Country Music" in the style of Willie Nelson and Waylon Jennings. Note the unusual downtown street-lighting system intended to produce "artificial moonlight."

CASCADE CAVERNS PARK (16 mi./26km NW on I-10) (755-8080):
Very fine limestone caves with illuminated 88-ft. (27m) waterfall. Many marine fossils in the walls. Guided tours. Open daily.

☀☖ **NATURAL BRIDGE CAVERNS** (17 mi./27km NE via I-35 and FM 3009) (651-6101): Immense underground caves once inhabited by primitive peoples; among the finest in Texas. Many chambers with strange shapes and evocative names: "Sherwood Forest," with its columns shaped like totem poles; "The Castle of the White Giants," with its 40-ft.-high (12m) "King's Throne," etc. The temperature inside the caves varies little, year round, from 70°F (21°C). Guided tours lasting about an hour. Open daily.

FARTHER AFIELD

☀☖☖ **BIG BEND NATIONAL PARK** (394 mi./630km west via U.S. 90 and U.S. 385): One of the wildest and most beautiful of America's national parks. Impressive canyons along the Rio Grande, the river marking the Mexican border, whose right-angled "Big Bend" S of the **Chisos Mountains** gives the park its name. The rocky walls rise perpendicularly from the river to heights of 1,300 ft. (400m) at places such as **Santa Elena Canyon, Mariscal Canyon,** and **Boquillas Canyon.** The steep crests, once a refuge of the Comanche peoples, with their forests of oak, pine, and juniper and their great variety of wildlife (deer, coyote, peccary, mountain lion, and 400 species of birds), lie next to the Chihuahuan Desert, bristling with giant cactus and home to snakes, kangaroo rats, and roadrunners. There are also many dinosaur fossils in the park.

At its western edge are the ghost town of **Terlingua** and the little frontier town of **Lajitas,** whose Main St. comes straight out of a John Ford movie.

For air-rafting down the Rio Grande, contact **Big Bend River Tours,** P.O. Box 317, Lajitas, TX 79852 (915/424-3219); or **Far Flung Adventures,** P.O. Box 377, Terlingua, TX 79852 (915/371-2489); or **Outback Expeditions,** P.O. Box 229, Terlingua, TX 79852 (915/371-2490; toll free 800/343-1640).

Warning! There are no gas stations between the Marathon on U.S. 90 and the park headquarters at **Chisos Basin,** 68 mi. (110km) to the south.

For **information,** contact the Superintendent, Big Bend National Park, TX 79834 (915/477-2251).

Sights En Route
On the way, don't fail to see **Alamo Village** at **Brackettville,** 122 mi. (195km) west on U.S. 90 (210/563-2580), a faithful reconstruction of San Antonio in the 1830s, built in 1959 for the shooting of John Wayne's famous movie *The Alamo.* From a classic saloon to an attack on a stagecoach, complete with enough musketry to make you laugh, every horse-opera cliché gets its turn. Native American museum. Open daily year round; amusing.

Also see the ☖☀ **Judge Roy Bean Courtroom** at **Langtry,** 213 mi. (340km) west on U.S. 90 (915/291-3340). The legendary Roy Bean was, at the time of the Wild West, in his own person "the law west of Pecos." He did justice, after his fashion, in his saloon-court, "The Jersey Lily" (named, like the town, after Lillie Langtry, "The Jersey Lily," a famous British beauty of the day), now a designated historic monument. A picturesque page of living history. Open daily.

Where to Stay En Route

IN THE PARK   The 🍸 **Chisos Mountain Lodge,** Chisos Basin, Big Bend National Park, TX 79834 (915/477-2291). 72 rms and bungalows, the park's only accommodations. Rustic comforts; cafeteria. **I–M**

AT LAJITAS   The 🍸 **Lajitas Hotel on the Rio Grande,** Star Rte. 70, Box 400, Lajitas, TX 79852 (915/424-3471). 81 rms. Picturesque replica of an original Far West hotel. Comfortable rms; rest., tennis, golf. **B–I**

🔭 HILL COUNTRY & LYNDON B. JOHNSON RANCH

(328 mi./525km r.t. via I-10W, Tex. 46W, Tex. 16N, Tex. 27N, Tex. 41W, I-10E, Tex. 16N, U.S. 290E, and I-35S): You come first to ⌂ **Boerne,** founded by German settlers in 1849; its old stone houses with narrow windows and gabled roofs still bear witness to their Germanic origins. Note the Kendall Inn, an old coaching inn built in 1859.

You now take Tex. 46 to ☼⌂ **Bandera,** a picturesque little western town nicknamed "the cowboy capital of the world" (rodeos and open-air festivals). Interesting **Frontier Times Museum,** 506 13th St. (210/796-3864), open daily.

Near **Mountain Home,** 60 mi. (96km) north, visit the ☼⌂ **Y.O. Ranch,** on Tex. 41W (210/640-3222), one of the largest stock ranches in Texas (100 sq. mi./259km²). As well as a herd of more than 1,500 longhorns, the ranch has antelope, zebra, ostrich, and giraffe roaming free. Photo safaris arranged daily.

On to ☼⌂ **Fredericksburg,** the main destination of German immigrants to Texas in the 1850s, which has retained many of its original buildings and an unusual "Old European" flavor. Be sure to see the **Vereins Kirche,** a replica of the first church built in 1847, on Market Sq., open Mon–Fri; and the **Admiral Nimitz State Historical Park** at 340 E. Main St. (210/997-4379), open daily, a monument to the hero of World War II in the Pacific, who was a native of the town.

Continuing eastward, you come to **Lyndon B. Johnson State Historical Park,** 15 mi. (24km) west of Johnson City on U.S. 290, dedicated to the 36th president of the U.S.; free bus connection from the visitor center (210/644-2252), open daily, to the ☼ **LBJ Ranch House** and his birthplace; his tomb is in the family cemetery. Many memorabilia of the man who succeeded John F. Kennedy in the White House. At ⌂ **Johnson City** you can visit the Victorian **Boyhood Home,** one block south of Main St. (210/868-7128), open daily, where Lyndon B. Johnson lived 1913–34.

Now on to ☼⌂ **Austin,** capital of the state of Texas (see "Nearby Excursions," above).

Return to San Antonio via ☼⌂ **New Braunfels,** an engaging little German town founded in the 19th century by 5,000 German immigrants whose descendants have preserved unspoiled many of their inherited traditions: there's a very popular Wurstfest or sausage festival lasting for 10 days at the beginning of Nov. On the way, stop to admire ☼⌂ **Aquarena Springs** near **San Marcos** (see "Nearby Excursions," above).

Your last stop on the return leg should be at ☼⌂ **Natural Bridge Caverns** (see "Nearby Excursions," above).

This picturesque trip, with lots to see, should take you three or four days.

Where to Stay En Route

IN AUSTIN   The 🍸🍸🍸 **Driskill Hotel,** 604 Brazos St., Austin, TX 78701 (512/474-5911). 175 rms. Luxury hotel of great quality dating from 1886. **M–E**

♀ **La Quinta Inn,** 300 E. 11th St., Austin, TX 78701 (512/476-
1166). 145 rms. Typical motel, one block to state capitol. Recently renovated. **B–I**

IN FREDERICKSBURG The ⚎ **Ad Dietzel Motel,** on U.S. 87, Fredericksburg, TX
78624 (210/997-3330), 1 mi. (1.6km) west of town. 20 rms. A small and modest but very well run motel. Rest. adjacent. **B**

IN KERRVILLE The ⚎⚎ **Inn of the Hills River Resort,** 1001 Junction Hwy.,
Kerrville, TX 78028 (210/895-5000). 217 rms. Large, modern, comfortable
resort motel. **I–M**

Where to Eat En Route

IN AUSTIN ⚎⚎⚎ **Zoot,** 509 Hearn St. (512/477-6535). Contemporary continental cuisine from veal w. juniper-berry reduction to bouillabaisse. Served in a
cozy, recently restored cottage. Open for dinner only, nightly. Resv. highly recommended.

IN FREDERICKSBURG The ⚎ **Hill Top Café,** 10 mi. (16km) north on U.S. 87 (210/
997-8922). Superb country fare w. Cajun-Greek overtones. The decor is
jalapeño-kitsch and the clientele ranges from Austin politicians to local cowboys. Resv. advised on wknds. Lunch Wed–Sat, dinner Wed–Sun, brunch Sun.
B–I

☀⚒ **PADRE ISLAND NATIONAL SEASHORE** (165 mi./
264km SE via I-37 and Tex. 358): Wildlife sanctuary for sea
creatures and birds on a deserted sandspit 113 mi. (182km) long; see Chapter 36
on Houston.

CHAPTER 38

ALBUQUERQUE♨♨

□ □ □

And the Rio Grande Valley

Standing 5,300 ft. (1,600m) above sea level, in a ring of desolate mountains which define the valley of the **Rio Grande,** Albuquerque was founded in 1706 by Don Francisco Cuervo y Valdés, then governor of New Mexico. Named in honor of the Duke of Alburquerque (the first "r" has dropped out over the years), viceroy of New Spain, the city retains few traces of the colonial period. Only the **Old Town** with its fine **Plaza** bears witness to the past ascendancy of Spain, and here the atmosphere is distinctly touristy. Not far away are the ranks of impersonal office buildings and inevitable neon signs of the modern city.

Albuquerque was a staging post on the Spanish colonial "Camino Real" between Mexico City and Santa Fe and, during the frontier days of the Far West, on the Santa Fe Trail. When the first transcontinental railroads were built in the last century, it was an important stop on the Santa Fe Railroad. Today it's the largest city in New Mexico, and its population, which quintupled between 1950 and 1980, is still growing. The city's industries—lasers, data processing, pharmaceuticals, solar energy, and nuclear weapons—face resolutely toward the future. In terms of industry and commerce Albuquerque ranks 12th among the 20 fastest-growing cities in the country. **Sandia Laboratories,** where in the years after 1942 the famous Manhattan Project resulted in history's first atomic bomb, employs 6,000 researchers and technicians and still dominates the city's industry. Noted for a very dry climate and an unusually cloudless sky (sunshine for 76% of the year), Albuquerque has become the world capital for ballooning, with a spectacular rally every Oct. The city is also an ideal point of departure for numerous excursions: toward **Santa Fe** (see Chapter 39); the cable car to the magnificent views at **Sandia Peak** (10,378 ft./3,163m); and the **Rio Grande Valley** (White Sands Desert, Valley of Fires, Mescalero Indian Reserve). Then there are the Native American **pueblos** of the fabled kingdom of Cibola, such as **Acoma** and **Zuñi,** and the **El Morro National Monument.**

Famous people born in Albuquerque include jazzman John Lewis of Modern Jazz Quartet fame.

BASIC FACTS: State of New Mexico. Area code: 505. Time zone: mountain. ZIP Code: 87101. Founded: 1706. Approximate population: city, 388,000; metropolitan area, 480,000. 38th-largest city in the country.

CLIMATE: Perpetual sunshine and low humidity make the climate of Albuquerque special. In summer the thermometer can run quickly up to 95°F (35°C) or higher. In winter, brisk but sunny weather and plentiful snowfall above 8,000 ft. permit skiing on nearby Sandia Peak. Spring and, even better, fall are the ideal seasons for a trip.

DISTANCES: Dallas, 637 mi. (1,020km); Denver, 421 mi. (675km); El Paso, 267 mi. (427km); Kansas City, 790 mi. (1,265km); Phoenix, 453 mi. (725km); Salt Lake City, 609 mi. (975km); Santa Fe, 61 mi. (98km).

ARRIVAL & TRANSIT INFORMATION

AIRPORT: Albuquerque International Airport (ABQ), 5 mi. (8km) SE. For information, call 842-4366.

AIRLINES: American West (toll free 800/247-5692), American (toll free 800/433-7300), Continental (toll free 800/525-0280), Northwest (toll free 800/225-2525), Southwest (toll free 800/531-5601), United (toll free 800/241-6522), and USAir (toll free 800/428-4322).

CITY LINK: The **cab** fare to city center is about $10; time, 15 min. **City bus:** SUNTRAN (no. 50) until 6pm; fare, 75¢; time, 25 min. **Airport bus** to dwntwn Santa Fe (seven times a day): Shuttlejack (243-3244); fare, $20; time, 1 hr. 10 min.

Since public transportation within the city by SUNTRAN bus is not very efficient (call 843-9200 for information), and excursions around the city are many and fascinating, it's highly advisable to rent a car with unlimited mileage.

CAR RENTAL (at the airport): Avis (toll free 800/331-1212); Budget (toll free 800/527-0700); Dollar (toll free 800/800-4000); Hertz (toll free 800/654-3131); National (toll free 800/227-7368). For dwntwn locations, consult the phone directory.

LIMOUSINE SERVICES: Dav El Limo (toll free 800/922-0343).

TAXIS: Cabs must be summoned by phone; they may not be hailed on the street. Try **Albuquerque Cab** (883-4888) or **Yellow Cab** (247-8888).

TRAIN: Amtrak station, 314 1st St. SW (toll free 800/872-7245).

INTERCITY BUSES: Greyhound, 300 2nd St. SW (243-4435).

INFORMATION & TOURS

TOURIST INFORMATION: The **Albuquerque Convention and Visitors Bureau,** 121 Tijeras NE, NM 87102 (505/842-9918; toll free 800/733-9918). **Old Town Visitors Center,** 301 Romero St. NW at N. Plaza (505/243-3215).

GUIDED TOURS: Gray Line Tours (bus) (265-8311): Guided tours of city and surroundings. Depart from principal hotels.

SIGHTS, ATTRACTIONS & ACTIVITIES

ADVENTURES: Rainbow Ryders (ballooning), 430 Monclaire SE (505/268-3401; toll free 800/725-2477): Champagne balloon flights, weddings. Year round. Groups from two to eight. Resv. required.
    Wolf Whitewater Kayaking and Canoeing School (boat), P.O. Box 666,

Sandia Park, NM 87407 (505/281-5042): Rafting down the Rio Grande rapids. May–July.

World Balloon Corp. (ballooning), 4800 Eubank Blvd. NE (505/293-6800): Leaves at dawn only when skies are clear. Best time of year: autumn or winter. About $135 per hour of flying time. Resv. required.

CHURCHES/SYNAGOGUES: ☀⚓ **Church of San Felipe de Neri,** on Old Town Plaza: The most representative building from the Spanish period. Built in 1793 on the site of a church of 1706 destroyed in 1790, this colonial-style church and the adjacent convent are still in use for religious purposes. See the spiral staircase in the choir, wrapped around the trunk of a spruce. Open daily.

HISTORIC BUILDINGS: ☀⚓ **University of New Mexico,** E. Central Ave. and University Blvd. (277-4001): One of the oldest (1889) and most respected universities in the Southwest (24,000 students). Remarkable example of Pueblo Native American architecture, standing amid 672 acres (280ha) of gardens. Several museums (see below). Visitors Bureau in the Fine Arts Center (277-0111).

MUSEUMS OF ART: ⚓ **Albuquerque Museum,** 2000 Mountain Rd. NW (242-4600): Interesting exhibits on the history of New Mexico; exhibitions of contemporary work by local artists. Features the largest collection of Spanish Colonial artifacts in the U.S. Open Tues–Sun.

⚓ **Fine Arts Center,** Central and Cornell Aves. (277-4001): Large cultural complex including a fine-arts museum (**Art Museum**) mainly used for contemporary exhibitions, the **Fine Arts Library,** and several theaters and concert halls (**Keller Hall, Rodey Theatre, Popejoy Hall,** etc.). On the university campus. Closed Mon and Sat.

☀⚓⚓ **Indian Pueblo Cultural Center,** 2401 12th St. NW (843-7270): This cultural institute, operated by the Association of the 19 Pueblos of New Mexico, offers a complete overview of Native American art and customs. Original design derived from the architecture of Pueblo Bonito (see "Farther Afield," below). Traditional dances performed on weekends in summer. Craft shop. Authentic Native American restaurant. Guided tours of the pueblos. Open daily.

MUSEUMS OF SCIENCE & HISTORY: ☀⚓⚓ **Maxwell Museum of Anthropology,** Redondo Rd. at Ash St. NE (277-4404): One of the finest museums in the country devoted to the culture of the Native American. Everything about the "civilization of the Pueblos," particularly the mysterious Anasazi. Very fine Mimbres pottery. Equally rich in prehistoric material. On the university campus. Open daily.

⚓ **Museum of Geology and Meteoritics,** 200 Yale Blvd. (277-4204): Unique collection of more than 200 meteorites from around the world. For students of astronomy. On the university campus. Open Mon–Fri.

☀⚓⚓ **Museum of Natural History,** 1801 Mountain Rd. NW (841-8837): The first such museum to be opened in the U.S. in 50 years. This hi-tech masterpiece, opened in 1986, offers a fascinating panorama of the land of the Rio Grande Valley, its plants and its animals, from prehistoric reptiles to a startling model of a volcano in eruption. Open daily.

⚓ **National Atomic Museum,** Kirtland Air Force Base, Bldg. 20358, on Wyoming Blvd., 7 mi. (11km) from dwntwn (845-6670): Unusual museum devoted to nuclear weapons, with movies showing their effects, from the first A-bomb to the Minuteman missile. Pacifists should stay away. Open daily.

    ⚓ **Rio Grande Nature Center,** 2901 Candelaria Rd. NW (344-7240): Standing on the east bank of the Rio Grande amid 7.2 acres (3ha) of park and woods, this all-glass structure houses rich collections of local geology, zoology, and history. Open daily.

PANORAMAS: ☀ **Sandia Crest,** 36 mi./58km NE along I-40E and N.M.
14, N.M. 165, and N.M. 536: Wonderful scenic drive (highest in the Southwest) through dense forests of oak, spruce, Ponderosa pine, and other conifers up to Sandia Crest (10,678 ft./3,255m) at the top of the Sandia Mountains. You can see 100 mi. (160km) in every direction, including the foothills of the Rockies and the valley of the Rio Grande. Highway open year round; Sandia Crest House, a restaurant with a panoramic view (243-0605), open daily.

    ☼ **Sandia Peak,** Tramway Blvd. (5 mi./8km NE along I-25): With its summit 10,378 ft. (3,163m) above sea level, the impressive Sandia Peak towers over Albuquerque and the Rio Grande Valley. On clear days (as they usually are) you can see the foothills of the Colorado Rockies 125 mi. (200km) to the north, and as far as the Mexican border 187 mi. (300km) south. Access is by the world's longest single-span tramway (it rises 3,728 ft./1,165m over a journey of 2.5 mi./4km). For information on timetables, call 298-8518. The High Finance restaurant offers a panoramic view.

PARKS & GARDENS: ☀⚓ **Petroglyph National Monument** 6900 Unser
Blvd., 9 mi. (14km) west on I-40 (897-8814): Some 15,000 petroglyphs (figures carved from rock)—in this case, from lava by the ancestors of the Pueblo tribes between A.D. 1100 and 1600. Open daily.

PERFORMING ARTS: For current listings of shows and cultural events, con-
sult the entertainment pages of the two daily papers, *Albuquerque Journal* (morning) and *Albuquerque Tribune* (evening), and the monthly *Albuquerque* magazine.

    Albuquerque Little Theatre, 244 San Pasquale SW (242-4750): Broadway hits, star-studded shows. Sept–June.

    Keller Hall, U. of N.M. campus (277-4402): Concerts and recitals.

    KiMo Theatre, 423 Central Ave. NW (764-1700): Home of the Albuquerque Opera Theater (Sept–May) and the New Mexico Repertory Theater (drama, comedy, classic theater).

    Popejoy Hall, U. of N.M. campus (277-3121): Home of the Albuquerque Civic Light Opera (musical comedy, operetta) and of the New Mexico Symphony Orchestra. Sept–May. For information, call 842-8565. Also concerts, classic and modern dance theater.

    Rodey Theatre, U. of N.M. campus (277-4402): Modern theater.

    The Vortex Theatre, 2004 W. Central Ave. (247-8600): Modern and classical theater; also experimental productions.

SPECIAL EVENTS: For exact dates, consult the **Albuquerque Convention &**
Visitors Bureau (see "Tourist Information," above).

    Gathering of Nations Powwow (mid-Apr): The largest and most spectacular of the 300 powwows held across the country each year. 30,000 Native Americans from all over North America, among them more than 1,300 dancers and singers competing in traditional costumes and styles. University Arena.

    New Mexico Arts and Crafts Fair (late June): Over 200 artists show their work at this four-day festival that includes food, music, and children's exhibits. At the New Mexico Fairgrounds.

New Mexico State Fair (Sept): Rodeo, horse races, country-music concerts. Local color guaranteed!

International Balloon Fiesta (early Oct): World's greatest dirigible-balloon rally, attracting more than 500 participants from the U.S. and abroad since 1972. Features mass ascensions at sunrise. A splendid spectacle.

Fiesta Encantada (Dec): Public concerts, folklore festivals, exhibitions; the Old Town is beautifully lit with candles.

SPORTS: Albuquerque is home to a minor-league professional team:

Baseball (Apr–Sept): Albuquerque Dukes (Triple-A farm team of the L.A. Dodgers), Albuquerque Sports Stadium (243-1791).

Horse Racing

The Downs, State Fairgrounds, 201 California St. (262-1188): Thoroughbred and quarter-horse racing Wed and Fri–Sun Jan–June.

STROLLS: ※🏛 **Old Town,** around Old Town Plaza: The heart of historic Albuquerque, with its beautiful tree-shaded Plaza, brick sidewalks, and bandstand. Several old buildings in Spanish Colonial idiom including the above-mentioned Church of San Felipe de Neri. More than 100 boutiques, art galleries, souvenir shops, and restaurants. It flaunts its pitch for the tourist trade, but it's certainly picturesque.

WINTER SPORTS RESORTS: 🏛 **Sandia Peak Ski Area** (30 mi./48km NE on I-40, N.M. 14, and N.M. 536): Four ski lifts. Operates Dec to mid-Mar. Can also be reached by cable car from Tramway Rd. north of Albuquerque. For information on snow conditions, call 242-9052.

ZOOS: 🏛 **Rio Grande Zoo,** 903 10th St. SW (843-7413): More than 1,300 animals of all kinds in beautifully designed "natural" habitats, including a rain forest; picnic area and swimming pools nearby. Open daily.

ACCOMMODATIONS

Personal Favorites (in order of preference)

🏨🏨🏨 **Hyatt Regency** (dwntwn), 330 Tijeras NW, NM 87102 (505/842-1234; toll free, see Hyatt). 396 rms, A/C, color TV, in-rm movies. AE, CB, DC, MC, V. Valet gar. $11, pool, health club, saunas, rest. (McGrath's), bar, rm svce, boutiques, free crib. *Note:* The newest (1990) and most luxurious hotel in town. Built beneath an unmistakable red pyramid cap, the 20-story neoclassic building provides panoramic views of the mountains and the city. Spectacular atrium graced by 28-ft. (8.5m) palm trees. Spacious, elegant rms w. two telephones and computer access. Very efficient svce. In the heart of dwntwn business and government districts. **M–E**

🏨🏨🏨 **Sheraton Old Town Inn** (dwntwn), 800 Rio Grande Blvd., NM 87104 (505/843-6300; toll free, see Sheraton). 190 rms, A/C, color TV, in-rm movies. AE, CB, DC, MC, V. Free parking, pool, Jacuzzi, rest. (Rio Grande Customs House), coffee shop, bar, rm svce, hrdrsr, boutiques, free airport limo, free crib. *Note:* Albuquerque's only hotel, near Old Town Plaza. Elegant modern architecture. Spacious and comfortable rms, some w. terraces and minibars. Svce and welcome impeccable. Decor warm and colorful. Rest. very acceptable. Caters mostly to tourists. Recently renovated. **M**

☼♀♀ **La Posada de Albuquerque** (dwntwn), 125 2nd St. NW, NM 87102 (505/242-9090; toll free, see Choice). 114 rms, A/C, color TV, in-rm movies. AE, CB, DC, MC, V. Free valet parking, rest. (Conrad's), bar, rm svce, hrdrsr, free airport shuttle, free crib. *Note:* Charming old hotel from the late '30s. A recent facelift has retained its appealing period flavor—a pretty fountain in the lobby, heavy overhanging eaves, and murals. Rms are more comfortable than elegant. Welcome and svce w. a smile. Very well located, not 5 min. from the Plaza. Good quality-to-price ratio. An excellent place to stay. **I–M**

♀♀ **Barcelona Court** (nr. dwntwn), 900 Louisiana Ave. NE, NM 87110 (505/255-5566). 164 suites w. kitchenettes, A/C, cable color TV, AE, CB, DC, MC, V. Free parking, two pools, sauna. Coffee shop next door, rm svce, free airport limo, free breakfast, free crib. *Note:* This motel, 6 min. from the airport, has only spacious and welcoming suites, w. kitchenettes and refrigerators. Private balconies or patios. Decor is elegant and airy. Attentive svce. Business clientele, since the new business district is a few steps away. **I–M**

♀ **Friendship Inn** (dwntwn), 717 Central Ave. NW, NM 87102 (505/247-1501; toll free, see Choice). 144 rms, A/C, cable color TV. AE, CB, DC, MC, V. Free parking, pool, rest., bar, free airport limo, crib $6. *Note:* Functional six-floor motel, completely modernized. Rms are attractive; the best have a park view. Agreeable svce, very good price-to-quality ratio. **B**

♀ **Motel 6 Midtown** (nr. dwntwn), 1701 University Blvd., NM 87102 (505/843-9228). 118 rms, A/C, cable color TV. AE, DC, MC, V. Free parking, nearby coffee shop, free crib. *Note:* This motel, 5 min. from the city center, offers an unbeatable price-to-quality ratio. Down-to-earth comfort. Ideal for motorists. Nr. the university campus. **B**

Other Accommodations (from top bracket to budget)

♀♀♀ **Hilton Inn** (nr. dwntwn), 1901 University Blvd. NE, NM 87102 (505/884-2500; toll free, see Hilton). 264 rms, A/C, color TV, in-rm movies. AE, CB, DC, MC, V. Free parking, two pools, two tennis courts, sauna, rest. (The Rancher's Club), coffee shop, bar, rm svce, free airport limo, free crib. *Note:* Grand hotel, large and comfortable, w. 12 floors, largest in Albuquerque. Efficient svce and welcome. Spacious rms w. refrigerators (some w. balconies). Rest. renowned for its grill. Good recreational facilities. 5 min. from dwntwn by car. Guests mostly groups and conventions. Worthwhile wknd discounts. Two floors reserved for VIPs. **M**

♀♀ **Doubletree** (dwntwn), 201 Marquette Ave. NW (at 2nd St.), NM 87102 (505/247-3344; toll free 800/528-0444). 292 rms, A/C, color TV, in-rm movies. AE, CB, DC, MC, V. Valet parking $3, rest. (La Cascada), bar, rm svce, free airport limo, free crib. *Note:* Massive 15-story tower w. roof-grdn overlooking the Convention Center. Utilitarian comfort and svce. Recently underwent major modernization. Very centrally located. Caters mostly to groups and conventions. **M**

♀♀ **Holiday Inn Midtown** (nr. dwntwn), 2020 Menaul Blvd. NE, NM 87107 (505/884-2511; toll free, see Holiday Inns). 360 rms, A/C, color TV, in rm movies. AE, CB, DC, MC, V. Free parking, pool, health club, sauna, rest., bar, rm svce, disco, free airport limo, free crib. *Note:* A typical Holiday Inn, 5 min. by car from dwntwn. Comfortable rms w. balconies. Svce and welcome impersonal. Good overall price-to-quality ratio. **I–M**

♀ **La Quinta North** (nr. dwntwn), 5241 San Antonio Dr. NE, NM 87109 (505/821-9000; toll free, see La Quinta). 130 rms, A/C, cable color TV. AE, CB, DC, MC, V. Free parking, pool, 24-hr. coffee shop, valet svce, free crib. *Note:* Comfortable, enticing country-style motel w. unusually large and well-designed rms. Friendly reception and svce. If you're driving through this should suit you fine, w. its direct access to I-25. 8 min. from dwntwn. **I**

♀ **De Anza Motor Lodge** (nr. dwntwn), 4301 Central Ave. NE,
♭ NM 87108 (505/255-1654). 84 rms, A/C, cable color TV.
AE, CB, DC, MC, V. Free parking, coffee shop, crib $4. *Note:* Small, unassuming but very well run motel w. an engaging Native American layout. Serviceably comfortable rms; smiling reception. Great if you're on a budget. 5 min. from dwntwn. Very good value. **B**

An Airport Hotel

♀♀♀ **Best Western Fred Harvey** (nr. dwntwn), 2910 Yale Blvd. SE,
♭♭♭ NM 87106 (505/843-7000; toll free 800/227-1117). 269 rms, A/C, color TV, in-rm movies. AE, CB, DC, MC, V. Free parking, pool, two tennis courts, health club, sauna, rest. ("Lil's"), coffee shop, bar, rm svce, free airport shuttle, free crib. *Note:* Large, modern hotel 3 min. from the terminal. Ultra-professional svce; huge, comfortable rms w. balcony (some w. refrigerator). Fine for a stopover between planes. 12 min. from dwntwn. **I–M**

YMCA/Youth Hostels

Route 66 Hostel (dwntwn), 1012 Central Ave. W., NM 87102 (505/247-1813). Youth hostel w. 45 rms, very centrally located.

RESTAURANTS

Personal Favorites (in order of preference)

♀♀♀ **Monte Vista Firestation** (nr. dwntwn), 3201 Central Ave. NE
♭♭♭ (255-2424). A/C. Lunch Mon–Fri, dinner nightly; closed hols. AE, DC, MC, V. *Specialties:* fresh homemade pasta dishes, grilled seafood; the menu changes daily. Good wine list. *Note:* New American cuisine irreproachably prepared and served in an authentic old fire station complete w. brass fire pole and an inviting bar upstairs in former sleeping quarters. Outdoor dining in good weather. Flawless svce. Resv. advised. *American.* **I–M**

♀♀ **Conrad's,** in La Posada de Albuquerque (see "Accommodations," above) (242-9090). A/C. Breakfast/lunch/dinner daily. AE, DC, MC, V. *Specialties:* marinated cactus leaves w. lemon juice and cilantro dressing, shrimp w. garlic-wine sauce, blackened quail w. chipotle-cilantro butter sauce, paella w. saffron rice, chocolate mousse w. piñon nuts. *Note:* Black-and-white checkerboard motif creates an upbeat, unpretentious setting for chef Dan Well's Spanish Yucatán cuisine. Voted "Best Restaurant" for its class in 1993 by *Albuquerque* magazine. Very good value. Friendly svce. Resv. highly recommended. *Spanish/Mexican.* **B–I**

♀♀ **Stephens** (dwntwn), 1311 Tijeras NW (842-1773). A/C. Lunch Mon–Fri, dinner nightly. AE, MC, V. Jkt. *Specialties:* chicken w. tequila-and-lime sauce, rack of lamb, catch of the day, broiled prime beef cuts. *Note:* One of Albuquerque's most elegant rests., Stephens serves excellent contemporary American food drawing heavily on local produce and recipes. Efficient svce; locally very popular, so resv. strongly advised. *American.* **I–M**

♀ **M. & J. Sanitary Tortilla Factory** (dwntwn), 403 2nd St. SW
(242-4890). A/C. Breakfast/lunch/dinner Mon–Sat; closed hols. No credit cards. *Specialties:* burritos de carne adovada, tacos, menudos, enchiladas. *Note:* Considered by purists one of the most authentic Mexican rests. in the area. Decor Formica and neon style; continuous Mexican music; relaxed atmosphere. Locally popular. No resv. *Mexican.* **B**

Other Restaurants (from top bracket to budget)

♀♀♀ **Prairie Star** (vic.), 1000 Jemez Dam Rd. in Bernalillo, 17 mi./
♭♭♭ 27km north at I-25 Exit 242 (867-3327). A/C. Dinner nightly, brunch Sun; closed hols. AE, DC, MC, V. *Specialties:* shrimp Margarita, chateaubriand, charcoal-broiled prime cuts and seafood. The menu changes regularly. *Note:* Creative southwestern and continental cuisine served in the

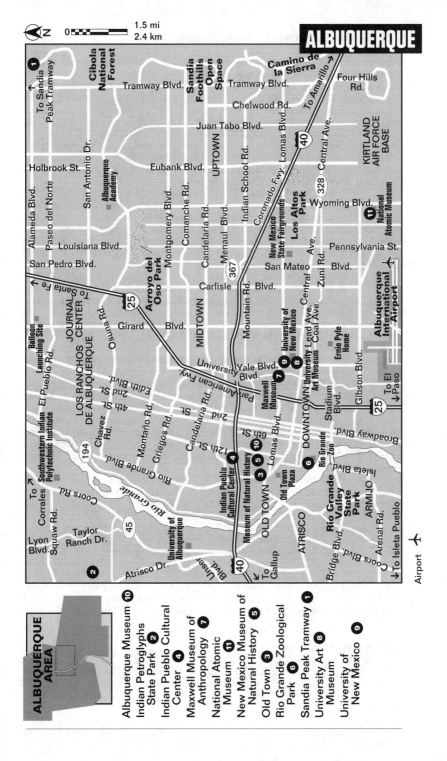

ALBUQUERQUE

ALBUQUERQUE AREA

Albuquerque Museum **10**
Indian Petroglyphs State Park **2**
Indian Pueblo Cultural Center **4**
Maxwell Museum of Anthropology **7**
National Atomic Museum **11**
New Mexico Museum of Natural History **5**
Old Town **3**
Rio Grande Zoological Park **6**
Sandia Peak Tramway **1**
University Art Museum **8**
University of New Mexico **9**

comfort of a rambling adobe mansion featuring a stunning view of the Rio Grande Valley and the mountains. Attentive and efficient svce. Well worth the 20-min. drive from dwntwn. Resv. recommended. *American/Continental.* **I–M**

☀ 🍸 **Casa Vieja** (vic.), 4541 Corrales Rd. in Corrales (via Rio Grande Blvd. and N.M. 46N) (505/898-7489). A/C. Dinner only, Tues–Sun; closed Jan 1, Thanksgiving, Dec 25. AE, CB, DC, MC, V. Jkt. *Specialties:* osso bucco w. risotto alla milanese, homemade pasta, veal scaloppine, saltimbocca, veal marsala, lime pie. *Note:* Charming adobe hacienda, more than a century and a half old, 12 mi. (19km) north of Albuquerque. Nice colonial decor w. open fires. Pleasant Italian-inspired cuisine. Efficient svce; resv. advised. 25 min. from dwntwn. *Italian/Continental.* **I–M**

🍸 **The Artichoke Cafe** (dwntwn), 424 Central Ave. SE (243-0200). A/C. Lunch Mon–Fri, dinner Mon–Sat., closed hols. AE, MC, V. *Specialties:* Salade nicoise, duck breast w. currant and cassis sauce, pork tenderloin w. orange-rosemary relish; well-rounded wine list. *Note:* Upbeat New American bistro w. exciting and innovative food moderately priced. Pleasant, modern setting. Cheerful svce. Totally nonsmoking. Resv. advised. *American* **I–M**

☀ 🍸 **Maria Teresa** (dwntwn), 618 Rio Grande Blvd. NW (242-3900). A/C. Lunch/dinner daily; closed Thanksgiving, Dec 25. AE, CB, DC, MC, V. Jkt. *Specialties:* steak, lobster, quail, truite amandine. Good wine list. *Note:* Beautiful hacienda (1840) standing in its own grdns, and designated as a historic monument. Very convincing decor. Meticulous presentation; svce on the slow side. Resv. advised. A few steps from Old Town Plaza. *Continental.* **I–M**

🍸 **Assets Grille Brewing Company** (nr. dwntwn), 6910 Montgomery NE (889-6400). A/C. Lunch Mon–Sat, dinner nightly; closed Thanksgiving and Dec 25. DC, MC, V. *Specialties:* wood oven–baked pizzas and calzones, chicken-and-green-chili quesadilla, fresh grilled ahi tuna w. shiitake mushroom sauce, grilled beef filet. Beer brewed on premises. *Note:* Bright, rustic atmosphere where the excellent food goes down smoothly w. an extensive range of beers. A good place for a long evening of food and drink. Upstanding svce. Due to its local popularity, resv. are highly recommended. Worth the 7-min. drive from dwntwn to its location in Northeast Heights. *American.* **B–I**

🍸 **New Chinatown** (nr. dwntwn), 5001 Central Ave. NE (265-8859). A/C. Lunch/dinner daily, brunch Sun; closed Thanksgiving, Dec 25. AE, CB, DC, MC, V. *Specialties:* Cantonese-Szechuan. *Note:* The best Chinese rest. in Albuquerque. Modern Oriental decor; good food and exotic drinks. Svce leaves something to be desired. Very good price-to-quality ratio at the buffet lunch. 10 min. from dwntwn. *Chinese.* **B–I**

🍸 **La Hacienda** (dwntwn), 302 San Felipe NW (243-3131). A/C. Lunch/dinner daily; closed Jan 1, Thanksgiving, Dec 25. CB, DC, MC, V. *Specialties:* enchiladas, burritos, sopaipillas. *Note:* Pleasing, original Mexican-hacienda interior, w. three great trees at the center of the dining rm, but resolutely tourist atmosphere. Mexican-American cuisine no better than acceptable. Svce and welcome so-so. High noise level, agreeable music. Right on Old Town Plaza. Resv. advised. *Mexican.* **B–I**

Cafeterias/Fast Food

Furr's (nr. dwntwn), 2272 Wyoming Blvd. NE (298-6886). Lunch/dinner daily (until 8pm). AE, MC, V. *Specialties:* roast beef, daily specials, sandwiches, baked fish. *Note:* Pleasant surroundings and atmosphere. Well regarded locally. Other locations: 6100 Central Ave. SE (265-1022) and 109 Montgomery Plaza NE (881-3373).

66 Diner (nr. dwntwn), 1405 Central Ave. NE (U.S. 66) (247-1421). Breakfast/lunch/dinner daily; closed hols. AE, MC, V. *Specialties:* burgers, blue plates, chicken fried steak; beer and wine. *Note:* Nostalgic roadside diner on historic Rte. 66 complete w. soda fountain, photographs, and music hits of the '40s. Locally popular.

BARS & NIGHTCLUBS

Caravan East (nr. dwntwn), 7605 Central Ave. NE (265-7877). The local shrine of country music; a jumping joint. Open daily.

The Cooperage (nr. dwntwn), 7220 Lomas Blvd. NE (255-1657). Live jazz; dancing Wed–Sat. Also an acceptable rest.

El-Rey (dwntwn), 624 Central St. (242-9300). Old movie theater that now features an eclectic bag of live music ranging from bluegrass to punk. Local and national acts.

Golden West Saloon, the same location and telephone number as El-Rey (see above). Local bands perform just inside the front windows of the bar. Open nightly.

NEARBY EXCURSIONS

CIBOLA NATIONAL FOREST: 1,536,000 forested acres (640,000ha) surrounding Albuquerque, Mountainair, Grants, and Magdalena. Roads offering fine views, camping, hunting, fishing, skiing in midwinter, etc. For information: 2113 Osuna Rd. NE, Albuquerque, NM 87113 (505/761-4650).

CORONADO STATE PARK & MONUMENT (22 mi./ 35km north via I-25 and N.M. 44N) (867-5351): Kuava ruins, Native American pueblo dating from A.D. 1300. The Spanish conquistador Francisco Vásquez de Coronado pitched his camp here during his fruitless search for a mythical Eldorado known to historians under the name of "the seven golden cities of Cibola." Interesting Native American museum. Visit to a restored *kiva* (place of worship). Open daily.

NATIVE AMERICAN PUEBLOS: There are 19 pueblos (villages) inhabited by 40,000 Native Americans as well as another dozen abandoned or in ruins, in central New Mexico, all antedating the arrival of the Spanish colonists about 3½ centuries ago. The Anasazi peoples, close relatives of the Aztecs and great builders, built these too, between A.D. 700 and 1100. **Bandelier National Monument** (see "Nearby Excursions" in Chapter 39 on Santa Fe), and especially **Chaco Canyon** (see "Farther Afield" in Chapter 39 on Santa Fe), both now in ruins, are among the most important archeological monuments of Native American culture. The Pueblo or Zuñi peoples who live there today are the descendants of the legendary Anasazi. The most isolated of minorities, the Pueblo or Zuñi tribes of New Mexico, and their Hopi cousins in Arizona, have always been settlers, as distinct from such nomadic peoples as the Apaches and Navajos, who formed a large majority of the Native American population in the Southwest.

Half a dozen of their pueblos near Albuquerque are open to tourists between sunrise and sunset, generally for a fee of around $3–$4 per car. The best time for a visit is during the yearly festival or on days of religious ceremony; calendar from Albuquerque Convention & Visitors Bureau, 121 Tijeras NE (505/ 842-9918). *Note:* For religious reasons, some villages do not allow cameras (movie, still, or video) or tape recorders. In others, photographers must pay a fee of $3–$6.

The most picturesque of these pueblos are:

&& **Acoma Pueblo,** 65 mi. (104km) west by I-40W and N.M. 23
(505/252-1139): The oldest continuously inhabited site in
the U.S., believed to have been settled around A.D. 600. Perched 6,400 ft.
(1,955m) up on a rocky mesa, "Sky City," as historians have dubbed it, is by far
the loveliest Native American pueblo in the country, and the least corrupted by
Western civilization. Fine Spanish mission of San Esteban Rey (1629). Photography permitted; fee, $6.

& **Isleta Pueblo,** 14 mi. (22km) south on U.S. 85 (505/869-
3111): Busy handcraft center. The original church of 1620 was
destroyed during the Indian Rebellion of 1680 and rebuilt 13 years later. Photographs permitted.

& **Jémez Pueblo,** 48 mi. (76km) north by I-25, N.M. 44, and
N.M. 4 (505/834-7359): Renowned for its embroidery and
basket-making; no photographs. Not far away, at Jémez Springs, is a beautiful
Spanish mission dating from 1621.

& **Zía Pueblo,** 34 mi. (54km) north by I-25 and N.M. 44 (505/
867-3304): Another pueblo well known for its pottery. Spanish mission dating from 1692. No photographs.

&& **Zuñi Pueblo,** 179 mi. (286km) west via I-40, N.M. 32, and
N.M. 53 (505/782-4481): One of the "seven golden cities of
Cibola." The Zuñi, a separate branch of the Pueblo people, are excellent potters
and jewelers. Photography permitted; fee, $2 for still and $4 for movie. Late Nov
or early Dec is the season of the Zuñi "shalako" (council of the gods), the most
beautiful, and spectacular, Native American ceremony in the U.S. By all means
go—but movie/still cameras are not allowed during "shalako."

GHOST TOWNS: In New Mexico there are a round dozen old mining towns
dating from last century's gold and silver rushes; some of them are now completely abandoned. Examples are **White Oaks** (15 mi./24km NE of Valley of
Fires State Park along U.S. 54 and N.M. 349) and & **Shakespeare** (46 mi./73km
SW of Silver City by N.M. 90 and U.S. 70), where most of the ornate exteriors are
still standing.

Others are still more or less intact, but drained of their former vitality: **Chloride** (38 mi./60km NW of Truth or Consequences along I-25, N.M. 142, and
N.M. 52), and **Hillsboro, Kingston,** and **Piños Altos** (see "Farther Afield," below).

Among the ghost towns closer to Albuquerque, the most picturesque are &
Cerrillos (48 mi./76km NE via I-40 and N.M. 14) and & **Madrid** (45 mi./72km
NE via I-40 and N.M. 14); for these two villages, see Chapter 39 on Santa Fe.

FARTHER AFIELD

& **SANDIA LOOP DRIVE** (80 mi./128km r.t. via I-40E,
N.M. 14N, N.M. 536W, N.M. 165W, and I-25S): A panoramic route leading to the peak of **Sandia Crest** (10,678 ft./3,260m). Wonderful
view over the Rio Grande Valley and surrounding countryside. The **Sandia Peak
Ski Area** can also be reached by cable car (see "Panoramas," above). An unpaved
portion of N.M. 165 is open to regular traffic May 15–Oct 15 only.

&& **SANTA FE & THE NATIVE AMERICAN PUEBLOS**
(240 mi./384km r.t. via I-25N, N.M. 44N and 4E, U.S. 285S,
and I-25S): Exhilarating two-day drive (longer if a visit is made to **Coronado
State Park;** see "Nearby Excursions," above). The route continues through two
typical Native American villages (see "Nearby Excursions," above), **Zía Pueblo**
and **Jémez Pueblo,** best known for pottery and basketwork, respectively. Stop
for a look at & **Valle Grande,** ranked by geologists as the world's largest volcanic
crater (area, 175 sq. mi./453km², mean depth, 486 ft./152m). Then on to the
beautiful **Bandelier National Monument** (see "Nearby Excursions" in Chapter

39 on Santa Fe); **Los Alamos,** the historic birthplace of the atom bomb; and the pueblo of **San Ildefonso** with its beautiful plaza (see "The Pueblos," in Chapter 39 on Santa Fe), before reaching the capital of New Mexico with its monuments and its museums (for places to stay, see Chapter 39 on Santa Fe). Return to Albuquerque by I-25S. Set aside at least 48 hr. for the trip.

🔭🔭 **SKY CITY & CHACO CANYON** (473 mi./758km r.t. via I-25N, N.M. 44N and 57S; I-40W; N.M. 32S, 53W, and 53E; I-40E; N.M. 38S and 23N; and I-40E): A full three- or four-day trip for devotees of archeology and Native American culture, it takes you first to **Coronado State Park** (see "Nearby Excursions," above), then on to the astonishing ☀🔭🔭 **Chaco Culture National Historical Park,** an archeological gem from our Amerindian past. Deserted by the Anasazi peoples around the end of the 13th century, this cluster of 75 ruined pueblos, one of which, Pueblo Bonito, boasted in its glory days no fewer than 800 rooms and 37 *kivas* (places of worship), well deserves a special trip. *Warning:* The road to Chaco Canyon is unsurfaced; dry weather only. A visitor center is located 2 mi. (3km) from the south entrance on N.M. 57; open daily (988-6727).

The third stage of the journey leads you to **Gallup,** "the Indian capital of the world." Every Aug some 50 tribes from all over the U.S. and Canada meet for the 🔭 **Intertribal Indian Ceremonial,** a very lively four-day festival with dances, parades, rodeos, and handcraft displays. Then on to **Zuñi Pueblo,** home of the famous "shalako" ritual (see "Native American Pueblos," above), and 🔭 **El Morro National Monument,** a shaft of rock 211 ft. (64km) high with many Native American rock carvings as well as inscriptions by Spanish conquistadors and early settlers in the Old West—an interesting sight. Visitor center open daily (783-4226).

The trip ends with a leisurely visit to the beautiful **Acoma Pueblo,** or "Sky City" (see "Native American Pueblos," above), before returning to Albuquerque via I-40E. This exciting trip is strongly recommended; it can be prolonged to take in **Mesa Verde National Park,** an important center of Native American culture (see Chapter 39 on Santa Fe), **Monument Valley,** or **Canyon de Chelly** (see Chapter 40 on Navajoland).

Where to Stay En Route

IN GALLUP Three motels are recommended:

🛎 **Best Western–The Inn,** 3009 W. U.S. 66, Gallup, NM 87301 (505/722-2221). 124 rms. **I–M**

🛎 **Motel 6,** 3306 W. U.S. 66, Gallup, NM 87301 (505/863-4492). 80 rms. **B**

🛎 **Travelodge,** 1709 W. U.S. 66, Gallup, NM 87301 (505/863-9301). 50 rms. **B**

☀🔭🔭 **WHITE SANDS & THE RIO GRANDE VALLEY** (582 mi./932km r.t. via I-25S, U.S. 82E, N.M. 24N, U.S. 70E, U.S. 380W, and I-25N): After driving along the Rio Grande Valley for almost 225 mi. (360km), you'll come to 🔭🔭 **White Sands National Monument,** an extraordinary desert of gypsum whose dazzling-white sand dunes, as much as 45 ft. (15m) high, create an ever-changing landscape of otherworldly beauty. For information, contact the Superintendent, White Sands National Monument, P.O. Box 1086, Holloman A.F.B., NM 88330 (505/479-6124). Also not to be missed: the 🔭🔭 **Alamogordo Space Center** on U.S. 54N (505/437-2840; toll free 800/545-4021). The Space Center Museum, an all-glass cube overlooking the White Sands Proving Ground, has a fine collection of U.S. and Soviet satellites and space capsules, moon rocks, models of old and new rockets, etc., as well as a very up-to-date planetarium. Open daily.

Then on to 🔭 **Cloudcroft,** an agreeable little winter-sports resort with a flourishing artists' colony and the highest golf course (8,700 ft./2,650m above sea level) in the U.S. If you can, go on to visit **Mescalero,** capital of the lovely Apache reservation of the same name; museum, exhibition of Native American handcrafts.

The fourth stage takes you to **Ruidoso,** a ski resort in the middle of a forest, and to **Lincoln,** famous in the days of the Old West and now a museum town. The legendary Pat Garrett, the man who killed Billy the Kid, was long its sheriff. Billy the Kid is buried at **Fort Sumner,** also famous during the winning of the West, about 125 mi. (200km) north. Be sure to see the museum and the ⚑ **old courthouse** on U.S. 380 at Lincoln (505/653-4372).

Finish the journey by crossing the ⚑⚑ **Valley of Fires,** a desert of gray-and-black lava from an old volcano. At ⚑ **Trinity Site** near Alamogordo, 30 mi. (50km) west, on July 16, 1945, the first atomic bomb was tested as a trial run for Hiroshima and Nagasaki. Area open to the public the first Sat of Apr and Oct. For information, call 505/678-1134. This beautiful three- or four-day trip can be combined with the visit to the ⚑⚑ **Gila Cliff Dwellings** (see below).

Where to Stay En Route

IN CLOUDCROFT 🍸🍸 **The Lodge,** U.S. 82, Cloudcroft, NM 88317 (505/682-2566). 47 rms. Designated historic building. **I–M**

IN MESCALERO ☼🍸🍸🍸 **Inn of the Mountain Gods,** Carrizo Canyon, Mescalero, NM 88340 (505/257-5141). 250 rms. This luxurious resort complex, w. its private golf course, tennis courts, and lake, is on the Apache reservation of Mescalero. Spectacular. **M**

IN RUIDOSO 🍸 **Best Western Swiss Chalet Inn,** on N.M. 37, Ruidoso, NM 88345 (505/258-3333). 82 rms. **I–M**

🍸 **Super 8,** 100 Cliff Dr. (U.S. 70), Ruidoso, NM 88345 (505/378-8180). 63 rms. **I**

☼⚑⚑ GILA CLIFF DWELLINGS & SILVER CITY (635 mi./1,016km r.t. via I-25S; N.M. 90W, 35N, 15N, 15S; U.S. 180N; N.M. 12N; U.S. 60E; and I-25N):

A journey of three to four days across the vast **Gila National Forest,** beginning with a visit to **Isleta Pueblo** and its lovely church built in 1693 (see "Native American Pueblos," above). At **Socorro,** 50 mi. (80km) farther south, you can admire the fine fortified mission of ⚑ **San Miguel,** 403 Camino Real (open Mon–Fri), built in 1615. Then on to ⚑ **Truth or Consequences** and its hot springs, and to **Hillsboro** and ⚑ **Kingston,** almost-deserted ghost towns from gold-rush days. Kingston once had 22 saloons for its 1,800 inhabitants. Go on to see the ⚑ **Gila Cliff Dwellings National Monument,** N.M. 15 (505/536-9461), in ⚑ **Gila National Forest;** for information, contact Ranger District, 3005 E. Camino del Bosque, Silver City, NM 88061 (505/388-8201).

Then drive to the old stagecoach stop of ⚑ **Silver City,** once thronged with gold and silver miners, scene of the early exploits of the famous outlaw Butch Cassidy. As you pass it, stop for a look at ⚑ **Piños Altos,** a picturesque ghost town built by gold miners in the 19th century, and often under attack by the Apaches under Cochise and Geronimo. Its most famous inhabitant was Judge Roy Bean, known as the "hanging judge."

On the road back to Albuquerque, make a detour through **Mogollon** (74 mi./118km north of Silver City via U.S. 80 and N.M. 78), another famous ghost town from the 19th century. One last sight you shouldn't miss, to your left as you follow U.S. 60E 14 mi. (22km) beyond Datil, is the forest of antenna dishes that make up the ☼⚑⚑⚑ **Very Large Array Telescope,** one of the largest radiotelescopes in the world with 27 giant parabolic dishes each weighing more than 200 tons. Visitor center open daily. For information, call 505/835-7000.

Where to Stay En Route

IN SILVER CITY ⚷ **Drifter Motel,** 711 Silver Heights Blvd., Silver City, NM 88061 (505/538-2916). 69 rms. **B**

⚷ **Holiday Motor Hotel,** U.S. 180E, Silver City, NM 88061 (505/538-3711). 80 rms. **B**

CHAPTER 39

SANTA FE🕯🕯

☐ ☐ ☐

And the Pueblos

A state capital of truly human dimension, "La Villa Real de la Santa Fe de San Francisco" (the Royal City of the Holy Faith of St. Francis), now called simply Santa Fe, is the offspring of an unusual amalgam of Native American, Hispanic, and Anglo-Saxon traditions. Instead of urban motorways or great avenues intersecting at right angles, you'll find shady streets, most of them narrow and winding. Neon signs are banned from downtown. No glass or concrete skyscrapers—just low-rise ocher or beige houses of adobe (sun-dried brick), typically in traditional Native American design. The lovely **Plaza,** standing at the historic heart of the city, where the legendary **Santa Fe Trail** ends; the 1610 **Mission de San Miguel,** one of the oldest churches in the country; the **Palace of the Governors,** also dating from 1610; even the modern **State Capitol,** whose massive rounded shape recalls the old *kivas* (Native American places of worship)—all evoke a sense of the past. And the city's museums house many treasures from the Native American civilizations. Indeed, Santa Fe is the only state capital in the country that won't permit commercial jets to land at its airport, lest its authenticity be impaired!

Vigilantly protecting its colonial heritage, more than 3½ centuries old (the city was founded in 1609—11 years before the Pilgrims landed at Plymouth—by Don Pedro de Peralta, governor of the Spanish province of New Mexico), this oldest of the country's state capitals has never lacked for painters, sculptors, musicians, and writers. From D. H. Lawrence to Max Weber and Georgia O'Keeffe, from Ezra Pound to Aaron Copland, they came, attracted by the region's unique charm, the extraordinary luminosity of its skies, the majestic backdrop of the **Sierra Sangre de Cristo,** the southernmost spur of the Rocky Mountains. About 5,000 artists today live in Santa Fe.

Apart from the picturesque and colorful beauty of its own narrow streets and flower-filled patios, Santa Fe is the ideal starting point for many fascinating excursions to **Mesa Verde National Park** or to the surrounding **Hopi pueblos.** Some of these "pueblos" (villages) are already tainted by the "civilization" of electrical appliances and mass tourism. Others, such as **Taos Pueblo, San Ildefonso,** and **Santo Domingo,** have at least preserved their original appearance, if not their authentic character.

Note that, at an elevation of 7,000 ft. (2,134m), Santa Fe may give you a problem for your first few days, until you're accustomed to the altitude.

BASIC FACTS: Capital of the State of New Mexico. Area code: 505. Time zone: mountain. ZIP Code: 87501. Founded: 1609. Approximate population, 62,500; metropolitan area, 99,650.

CLIMATE: With more than 300 days of sunshine annually, you could say that the sun is a year-round fixture in Santa Fe but, thanks to the altitude, it's never unpleasantly hot; the July average temperature is 71°F (22°C). The evenings are cool even in summer. There is heavy snow in winter, for the delectation of skiers, on the slopes of the Sierra Sangre de Cristo; Jan average temperature, 35°F (2°C). In a word, it's always a good time of year to visit Santa Fe.

DISTANCES: Albuquerque, 61 mi. (98km); Denver, 386 mi. (618km); El Paso, 266 mi. (425km); Grand Canyon National Park, 465 mi. (744km); Phoenix, 521 mi. (834km); Salt Lake City, 610 mi. (976km).

ARRIVAL & TRANSIT INFORMATION

NEAREST MAJOR AIRPORT: Albuquerque International Airport (ABQ), 61 mi. (98km) SW (505/842-4366).

AIRLINES (at the Albuquerque airport): America West (toll free 800/247-5692), American (toll free 800/433-7300), Delta (toll free 800/221-1212), Southwest (toll free 800/531-5601), and United (toll free 800/241-6522).

CITY LINK: Daily flights on **Mesa Airlines** operate up to four times a day between Albuquerque International Airport and Santa Fe Municipal Airport; flight time, 25 min. For information and reservations, call toll free 800/637-2247.

From **Albuquerque International Airport,** a minibus operated by Shuttlejack (505/982-4311) runs eight times a day to/from the principal Santa Fe hotels; fare $20; time, about 75 min. Resv. advised.

However, given the distance from Albuquerque to Santa Fe and the countless tempting excursions in the surrounding countryside, it makes a lot of sense to rent a car with unlimited mileage. Moreover, there is no real public transportation system in Santa Fe and cabs are hard to come by.

CAR RENTAL (at Albuquerque International Airport): Avis (toll free 800/331-1212), Budget (toll free 800/527-0700), Dollar (toll free 800/800-4000), Hertz (toll free 800/654-3131), and National (toll free 800/227-7368).

LIMOUSINE SERVICES: Limotion VIP Limo Service (471-1265).

TAXIS: Cabs may not be hailed on the street but may be summoned by phone. Recommended company: **Capital City Cab** (989-1211 or 989-8888).

TRAIN: The nearest Amtrak station is on N.M. 41 at Lamy, 19 mi. (30km) south on U.S. 285 (toll free 800/872-7245).

A shuttle runs daily between downtown Santa Fe and the station; contact Lamy Shuttle Service, 1476 Miracerros Loop N. (982-8829). Resv. advised.

INTERCITY BUSES: Greyhound, 858 St. Michaels Dr. (toll free 800/231-2222).

INFORMATION & TOURS

TOURIST INFORMATION: The **Santa Fe Chamber of Commerce,** 510 N. Guadalupe St., NM 87501 (505/983-7317).

Santa Fe Convention and Visitors Bureau, Sweeney Center, 200 W. Marcy St. (P.O. Box 909), NM 87504 (505/984-6760; toll free 800/777-2489).
New Mexico State Department of Tourism, P.O. Box 20003, NM 87503 (505/827-7400; toll free 800/545-2040 outside New Mexico): Information on all New Mexico's treasures of tourism.
Northern Indian Pueblos Council, P.O. Box 969, San Juan Pueblo, NM 87566 (505/852-4265). Information on the eight principal Native American pueblos around Santa Fe, activity schedule, etc.

GUIDED TOURS: Gray Line Tours (bus), 220 N. Guadalupe St. (983-9491): Guided bus tours of the city and environs. Serves the main hotels.
Native American Tours, P.O. Box 22658, NM 87502 (986-0804; toll free 800/578-3256). A variety of trips including a two-hour walking tour of Santa Fe, a half-day visit to studios of Indian artisans, and a two-week camping expedition. All guides are Native Americans.
Santa Fe Detours, in the La Fonda Hotel, 100 E. San Francisco St. (983-6565; toll free 800/338-6877): Two-hour walking tours of Santa Fe. Daily.

SIGHTS, ATTRACTIONS & ACTIVITIES

ADVENTURES: Kokopelli River Tours (boat), 100 E. San Francisco St. (505/983-6556; toll free 800/338-6877): Half-day, full-day, and overnight trips down the Rio Grande and Rio Chama. Pictograph tours also offered. Traditional Native American meals provided.
New Wave Rafting Co. (boat), Rte. 5, Box 302A, NM 87501 (505/984-1444): White-water rafting down the Rio Grande, Rio Chama, and Arkansas River. Summer only.
Santa Fe Detours (see "Guided Tours," above): Offers a wide range of excursions: river rafting (see Kokopelli River Tours, above), airplane tours (see Southwest Safaris, below), ballooning, horseback riding, hiking, cross-country skiing, and more.
Southwest Safaris (airplane), P.O. Box 945, Santa Fe, NM 87504 (toll free 800/338-6877): One-day trips by plane to Grand Canyon National Park, Mesa Verde, Canyon de Chelly, Monument Valley, and Carlsbad Caverns. Spectacular. Departures year round from Santa Fe Municipal Airport.

ARCHITECTURAL HIGHLIGHTS: ※⚜ **La Fonda,** 100 E. San Francisco St. (982-5511): One of the most history-laden hotels in the U.S., going back to the opening of the Santa Fe Trail in the 1870s. A favorite stopping place for trappers, pioneers, and early traders. Billy the Kid was a dishwasher here at the beginning of his career of adventure. Long known as "The Inn at the End of the Trail," and often rebuilt (the last time was in 1919), La Fonda (literally "The Inn") is still one of the best hotels in the city.
 ※⚜ **Santa Fe Opera,** on U.S. 84, 7 mi. (11km) north (986-5900): Splendid conch-shaped open-air auditorium built on a mesa at the foot of the Jemez Mountains; a very successful piece of modern design. Every summer it hosts a highly regarded opera festival (see "Special Events," below). Open afternoons Mon–Sat during the opera season (June–Aug); it's advisable to make reservations.
 ⚜ **State Capitol,** Old Santa Fe Trail and Paseo de Peralta: One of the newest (1966) state capitols in the country; an unusual circular building reminiscent of a traditional Native American *kiva* (place of worship). The New Mexico legislature meets here. Open Mon–Fri.

CHURCHES/SYNAGOGUES: ⚜ **Cathedral of St. Francis of Assisi,** Cathedral Plaza (982-5619): Built between 1869 and 1884 by Archbishop Jean Baptiste Lamy on the site of an older church destroyed by natives in 1680, said to be the country's oldest Marian shrine. Its *La Conquistadora*, brought here by the Spaniards in 1692, is the oldest statue of the Virgin still in existence in the U.S. A classic piece of architecture in the French Romanesque Revival style. Open daily.

☀️👤🔔 **Cristo Rey Church,** Canyon Rd. and Camino Cabra: The largest Native American–style church in the country; its adobe walls are 7 ft. (2m) thick. Valuable stone reredos (altar screens) dating from 1760. Open daily.

☀️👤🔔 **Loreto Chapel,** 219 Old Santa Fe Trail (984-7971): Gothic Revival chapel modeled on the Sainte-Chapelle in Paris, with an amazing spiral staircase, "The Famous Staircase," the work of an unknown cabinetmaker in 1878. Its 33 treads rise to a height of 22 ft. (7m), and are held together without nails or any visible support. Loreto Chapel is sometimes called Our Lady of Light Chapel. Open daily.

☀️👤👤🔔 **Mission of San Miguel,** 401 Old Santa Fe Trail, at E. De Vargas St. (983-3974): This, the oldest church in the country still used for worship, was originally built around 1610 for residents of the Barrio. Its often-restored walls of thick adobe hide a wonderful interior, with the famous San José Bell which was cast in 1356 in Spain, a superb reredos (1798), and several old paintings. Open daily.

☀️👤🔔 **Santuário de Guadalupe,** 100 Guadalupe St. (988-2027): One of the oldest shrines of the Virgin in the country, dating from about 1776–95. Dedicated to Our Lady of Guadalupe, the patron saint of Mexico, it houses some interesting handcrafts and religious art from the Spanish Colonial period. Open Mon–Sat.

🔔 **Scottish Rite Temple,** Washington Ave. (982-4414): Enormous Masonic temple whose baroque design harks back to the Alhambra of Granada, Spain. No visitors.

HISTORIC BUILDINGS: ☀️🔔 **Oldest House,** 215 E. De Vargas St.: Believed to be the oldest building in the country still in use, this Native American house built of clay and straw was part of the original pueblo that stood on the site of Santa Fe in the 13th century. A fine example of early domestic adobe construction, the building has been converted into a souvenir shop. A stone's throw from the Mission of San Miguel. Open daily.

☀️👤👤 **Palace of the Governors,** The Plaza (827-6483): Both palace and fortress, this massive, elegant building has been the home, successively, of Spanish, Mexican, and U.S. governors; it's the oldest (1610) public building in continuous use in the U.S. Constructed of mud and partly destroyed in the Indian Rebellion of 1680, the original building with its patios, storehouses, and outbuildings has been restored many times. The author Lew Wallace, at the time governor of New Mexico, used his idle moments here to write the major part of his famous novel *Ben Hur* in 1880. Interesting museum, Native American craft shop, and impromptu market under the Portal, a long covered porch. Open daily Mar–Dec, Tues–Sun the rest of the year.

MUSEUMS OF ART & HISTORY: 🔔 **Institute of American Indian Arts Museum,** 108 Cathedral Place (988-6281): A comprehensive panorama of modern Native American (including Inuit) arts and handcrafts: sculpture, pottery, textiles, jewelry, painting, etc. Fascinating. Temporary exhibitions. Open daily.

☀️👤🔔 **Laboratory of Anthropology/Museum of Indian Arts and Culture,** 708-710 Camino Lejo (827-6344): Rich collection of Native American (particularly Navajo and Pueblo) art, from pottery to kachina dolls. Excellent specialized library. Open daily Mar–Dec, Tues–Sun the rest of the year.

☀️👤👤 **Museum of Fine Arts,** 107 W. Palace Ave. at Lincoln (827-4455): More than 8,000 works of southwestern artists from 1898 to the present, including several works by Georgia O'Keeffe. Handsome traditional adobe building dating from the turn of the century. Open daily Mar–Dec, Tues–Sun the rest of the year.

    Museum of International Folk Art, 706 Camino Lejo (827-6350): One of the best American museums of popular art and tradition, displaying dolls, masks, toys, religious objects, clothing—more than 125,000 different objects. Open daily Mar–Dec, Tues–Sun the rest of the year.

    Museum of New Mexico System (827-6463): Important grouping of four museums of art and culture, it comprises the **Museum of Fine Arts,** the **Palace of the Governors,** the **Museum of International Folk Art,** and the **Museum of Indian Arts and Culture** (see above); a fifth, the **Laboratory of Anthropology,** is open only to scholars and researchers.

    Wheelwright Museum, 704 Camino Lejo (982-4636): All kinds of Native American art—jewelry, pottery, textiles, and wickerwork. The design of this 1937 museum is based on traditional Navajo hogans or earthen huts. Interesting Native American craft shop. Open daily.

PANORAMAS: ⚐ **Cross of the Martyrs** is a great white cross on the crest of a hill with a fine view over the city. Erected in 1920, the monument commemorates the Franciscans who were killed in the Indian Rebellion of 1680. A brick walkway leading here from the intersection of Paseo de Peralta and Otero St. was opened in 1986.

PARKS & GARDENS: ⚐ **River Park,** along the Santa Fe River between Old Santa Fe Trail and Don Gaspar Ave.: Pretty flower-planted, tree-shaded walk along the Santa Fe River (which is usually dry as a bone), marking the boundary of the Analco barrio ("the other side of the river" in the local tribal language), the old (11th- to 15th-century) Native American pueblo before the arrival of the Spanish settlers.

PERFORMING ARTS: For daily listings of all shows and cultural events, consult the entertainment pages of the daily papers, the *Albuquerque Journal* (morning) and *The New Mexican* (morning), particularly the latter's Friday supplement, *Pasatiempo,* or the "Day by Day" column of the weekly *Santa Fe Reporter.*

    Center for Contemporary Arts, 291 E. Barcelona Rd. (982-1338): Ballet, poetry recitals, big-name shows, theater.

    Greer Garson Theater, College of Santa Fe campus, St. Michael's Dr. (473-6511): Contemporary and classic theater.

    Lensic Theater, 211 W. San Francisco (988-4640): Home of the Orchestra of Santa Fe (music director: William Kirschke). Bach and Mozart festivals in alternate years. Sept–May.

    New Mexico Repertory Theater, 1050 Old Pecos Trail (983-2382): Drama, comedy, contemporary theater.

    Paolo Soleri Outdoor Amphitheatre, Santa Fe's Indian School campus (256-1777): Big-name shows, rock concerts (summer only).

    Railyard Performance Center, 430 W. Manhattan Ave. at Guadalupe (982-8309): Theater, dance, and music; year round.

    St. Francis Auditorium, 107 W. Palace Ave. (983-2075): Home of the renowned Santa Fe Chamber Music Festival (July–Aug). Classical concerts, recitals.

    Santa Fe Opera, on U.S. 84, 7 mi. (11km) north (982-3855): Open-air theater; cycle of five operas every summer (June–Aug). Nationally acclaimed.

SHOPPING: Deriving most of its income from tourism, Santa Fe abounds in Native American crafts shops, art galleries (almost 500), and all kinds of stalls that put unseemly prices on their goods and generate an unpleasantly rapacious

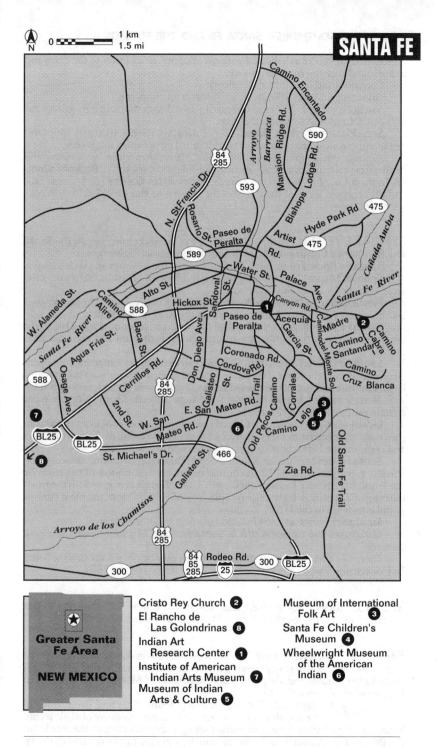

0 | 1 km
0 | 1.5 mi

N

Greater Santa
Fe Area

NEW MEXICO

Cristo Rey Church **2**

El Rancho de
Las Golondrinas **8**

Indian Art
Research Center **1**

Institute of American
Indian Arts Museum **7**

Museum of Indian
Arts & Culture **5**

Museum of International
Folk Art **3**

Santa Fe Children's
Museum **4**

Wheelwright Museum
of the American
Indian **6**

atmosphere. If you're a dedicated window-shopper, in addition to the Plaza and its surroundings you may want to see:

Canyon Road (see "Strolls," below).

Guadalupe Street: The new "in" address for shopping.

Santa Fe Village, 227 Don Gaspar St.: Two dozen shops and art galleries in a fake pueblo setting very near the Plaza.

Sena Plaza and Prince Plaza, 115 E. Palace Ave.: Some 40 luxury shops and restaurants around pretty patios in two elegant 19th-century mansions.

Among the shops offering authentic Native American art objects and handcrafts (and not Taiwanese, Mexican, or Filipino knockoffs): **Packard's Indian Trading Co.** (61 Old Santa Fe Trail), **Bellas Artes Gallery** (301 García St.), and the museum shops at the Palace of the Governors and the Wheelwright Museum (see above).

SPECIAL EVENTS: For the exact schedule of events below, consult the **Santa Fe Chamber of Commerce** (see "Tourist Information," above).

Santa Fe Rodeo (mid-July): The great event for cowboys and rodeo lovers.

Spanish Market (last wknd of July): Exhibition of Hispanic crafts under the arcades of the Palace of the Governors.

Fiesta at Santo Domingo Pueblo (late July to early Aug): The best-known and most colorful Native American fiesta in the Rio Grande Valley.

Santa Fe Chamber Music Festival (six weeks in July and Aug): One of the best classical-music festivals in the country; for information and resv. call 983-2075.

Santa Fe Opera (July–Aug): Summer mecca for opera amateurs in an open-air auditorium in the sierra. Few big names, but a nursery for young talent with a large, faithful audience of opera lovers. Resv. a must, well ahead (call 986-5900).

Taos Summer Music Festival (mid-June to early Aug): Very popular chamber-music festival (776-2388).

Indian Market (mid-Aug): One of the biggest Native American markets in the country; tribes from every quarter of the compass come to display their arts and crafts on the Plaza. Folk dances. 100,000 visitors each year.

Santa Fe Fiesta (three days in mid-Sept): Parades, processions, dancing; celebrated every year since 1712 to commemorate the reconquest of the town by the Spaniards after the Indian Rebellion of 1680. The fiesta begins with the ritual burning of Zozobra, a 40-ft. (12m) papier-mâché effigy. One of the most famous popular festivals in the U.S.

Sundown Dance at Taos Pueblo (late Sept): Colorful festival.

Christmas Eve Celebrations in Santa Fe (Dec 24): Lights, dancing, processions.

Dates of other **Native American festivals** may be obtained from the Santa Fe Convention and Visitors Bureau, 200 W. Marcy St. (984-6760).

SPORTS: Horse Racing (Wed and wknds, early May to Labor Day): **The Downs,** 5 mi. (8km) south on I-25 (471-3311). Thoroughbred racing.

STROLLS: ☀⚐ **Canyon Road:** The old road to Pecos in the days of the Santa Fe Trail, now an arts-and-crafts street. More than 50 galleries, shops, and restaurants. Other studios and shops on nearby **Camino del Monte Sol.** Commercial but picturesque atmosphere.

☀⚐⚐ **The Plaza:** The historic heart of Santa Fe, a fine, lively, colorful sight with its gardens, its 1862 commemorative obelisk, its old houses, and its Native American market set up every morning in the arcades of the Palace of the Governors. In the SE corner, a plaque marks the end of the fabled Santa Fe Trail, linking Independence, Mo., with the Rio Grande Valley. It was opened in 1822 by William Becknell, a particularly enterprising Kansas City businessman.

WINTER SPORTS RESORTS: ⚓ Santa Fe Basin, 17 mi. (27km) NE on
N.M. 475 (505/982-4429): Seven lifts; open Nov–Apr.

⚓ **Sipapu Ski Area,** 60 mi. (96km) NE via U.S. 84, N.M. 503, N.M. 76, and N.M. 518 (505/587-2240): Three lifts; open Dec–Mar.

☼⚓⚓ **Taos Ski Valley,** 89 mi. (142km) NE via U.S. 84, N.M. 68, U.S. 64, and N.M. 150 (505/776-2291): Nine lifts; open Nov–Apr.

For a recording giving **snow conditions** at different resorts, call 984-0606.

ACCOMMODATIONS

Personal Favorites (in order of preference)

☼👜👜👜 **The Bishop's Lodge** (vic.), Bishop's Lodge Rd. (3 mi./5km north on N.M. 22), NM 87501 (505/983-6377). 74 rms, A/C, color TV. AE, MC, V. Free parking, pool, sauna, four tennis courts, trap shooting, horseback riding, rest. (Bishop's Lodge Restaurant), bar, rm svce, free crib. *Note:* Luxurious vacation ranch on the outskirts of Santa Fe. Very comfortable rms w. private patios, some w. fireplaces; very complete facilities. Superb setting and surroundings on 1,000 acres (400ha) at the foot of the Sangre de Cristo Mountains. Attentive svce; rest. of quality. Once the home of Archbishop Jean Lamy, on whom Willa Cather based her famous novel *Death Comes for the Archbishop.* Closed early Jan through the end of Mar. A classic of Santa Fe since 1918. 5 min. from dwntwn. **E–VE** (Modified American Plan June–Aug).

👜👜👜 **Eldorado Hotel** (dwntwn), 309 W. San Francisco St. NM 87501 (505/988-4455; toll free 800/955-4455). 218 rms, A/C, color TV, in-rm movies. AE, CB, DC, MC, V. Valet gar. $6, pool, saunas, rest. (The Old House), coffee shop, bar, rm svce, nightclub, boutiques, concierge. *Note:* Imposing, new dwntwn luxury hotel. A very successful design, deftly combining the imperatives of modern hostelry with the traditional esthetics of Santa Fe: adobe walls, exposed beams, and colorful decor w. Native American motifs. Luxurious, well-designed rms w. private balconies or patios and minibars (some w. fireplaces). Rooftop pool w. views clear across the city. Exemplary svce; very acceptable rest. Well-heeled tourist clientele. A stone's throw from the Plaza; an excellent place to stay. **E–VE,** but lower rates off-season.

☼👜👜 **La Fonda** (dwntwn), 100 E. San Francisco St., NM 87501 (505/982-5511; toll free 800/523-5002). 153 rms, A/C, cable color TV. AE, CB, DC, MC, V. Parking $2, pool, rest. (La Plazuela), bars, rm svce, nightclub, art gallery, free crib. *Note:* Charming old Spanish Colonial–style hotel right on the Plaza. A genuine landmark (see "Architectural Highlights," above); the present building dates from 1919. Fine accommodations w. comfortable, tastefully decorated rms, some w. balconies and fireplaces. Pretty covered patio; acceptable rest.; pleasant rooftop bar; romantic atmosphere. Very good value in spite of the utterly inefficient svce. The best location in Santa Fe. **M,** but lower rates off-season.

☼👜👜 **La Posada de Santa Fe** (dwntwn), 330 E. Palace Ave., NM 87501 (505/986-0000; toll free 800/727-5276). 116 rms, A/C, color TV, in-rm movies. AE, CB, DC, MC, V. Free parking, pool, rest. (Staab House), bar, rm svce, hrdrsr, crib $5. *Note:* Very pretty little older hotel in a lovely grdn; elegant Spanish Colonial decor. Huge, comfortable rms (some w. kitchenette and fireplace) and adobe casitas w. private patios. A stone's throw from the Plaza and the Palace of the Governors. Diligent svce; good rest. located in a luxury old 19th-century house. One of the best values in town. **M—E,** but lower rates off-season.

♀ **El Rey Inn** (nr. dwntwn), 1862 Cerrillos Rd., NM 87504 (505/982-1931). 56 rms, A/C, cable color TV. AE, DC, MC, V. Free parking, pool, free breakfast, free crib. *Note:* Engaging, well-run small motel in a verdant oasis 8 min. from dwntwn. Inviting rms w. exposed beams, some w. kitchenettes, refrigerators, and fireplaces. Attractive grdn w. fountain. Good value. **I—M**

Other Accommodations (from top bracket to budget)

♀♀♀ **Inn of the Anasazi** (dwntwn), 113 Washington Ave., NM 87501 (505/988-3030; toll free 800/688-8100). 60 rms, A/C, color TV, in-rm movies. AE, CB, DC, MC, V. Valet parking $10, rest. (Anasazi Restaurant), rm svce, concierge, free crib. *Note:* The newest (June 1991) and the city's most luxurious intimate hotel, one block from the Plaza. Indian pueblo architecture w. *kiva* fireplaces, stonework, handcrafted art and furnishings. Personalized svce. Excellent New American rest. Only black mark: the total lack of physical-fitness facilities. **VE**

☼♀♀♀ **St. Francis** (dwntwn), 210 Don Gaspar Ave., NM 87501 (505/983-5700; toll free 800/666-5700). 82 rms, A/C, cable color TV. AE, MC, V. Free parking, rest. (On Water), bar, pub, rm svce, concierge, free crib. *Note:* This elegant little survivor from the '20s has preserved all its intimate, romantic flavor. Beautifully redecorated and reequipped at a cost of $6 million, it boasts comfortable, although small, rms w. period furniture and paintings. Thoughtful, personalized svce; good rest. Afternoon tea served daily in lobby. Excellent value only two blocks from the Plaza; the favorite of those in-the-know. **M—E**

♀♀ **Hilton of Santa Fe** (dwntwn), 100 Sandoval St., NM 87501 (505/988-2811; toll free, see Hilton). 150 rms, A/C, color TV, in-rm movies. AE, CB, DC, MC, V. Free parking, pool, rest. (Tinon Grill), coffee shop, bar, rm svce, nightclub, free crib. *Note:* Relatively modern motel whose adobe design fits reasonably well into the colonial setting around it; 2-min. walk from the Plaza. Comfortable, well-equipped rms; efficient svce; so-so rest. Group and convention clientele. **M—E,** but lower rates off-season.

♀♀ **Garrett's Desert Inn** (dwntwn), 311 Old Santa Fe Trail, NM 87501 (505/982-1851). 82 rms, A/C, cable color TV. AE, MC, V. Free parking, pool, rest. (Le Café on the Trail), free crib. *Note:* Classic motel a few blocks from dwntwn. Very convincing colonial decor; vast, comfortable rms; attentive svce. A fine place to stay. **I—M,** but lower rates off-season.

♀ **Park Inn** (nr. dwntwn), 2900 Cerrillos Rd., NM 87501 (505/472-2481; toll free 800/279-0894). 83 rms, A/C, cable color TV. AE, MC, V. Free parking, pool, rest. nearby, free coffee in-rm, crib $4. *Note:* Classic but well-run motel 10 min. from the Plaza. Functional, comfortable rms. Friendly reception and svce. A good place for budget travelers. **B—I**

♀ **Motel 6** (nr. dwntwn), 3007 Cerrillos Rd., NM 87501 (505/473-1380). 104 rms, A/C, cable color TV. AE, DC, MC, V. Free parking, pool. *Note:* Unbeatable value 8 min. from dwntwn in a rather depressing neighborhood. Inviting, functional rms; 24-hr. coffee shop across the street. Perfect if you're driving. **B**

Accommodations in the Vicinity

☼♀♀♀ **Rancho Encantado** (vic.), N.M. 4 (P.O. Box 57C), Tesuque, NM 87501 (505/982-3537), 8 mi. (13.5km) north on U.S. 285. 78 rms (22 in the hotel, 56 in cottages or mini-apts.), A/C, color TV. AE, CB, DC, MC, V. Free parking, two pools, tennis court, horseback riding, rest., bar, crib $15. *Note:* Luxurious resort complex w. traditional adobe architecture, nestled in the mountains north of Santa Fe. Comfortable cottages and apts in a beautiful grdn. Private patios. Valuable Native American furnishings and artifacts. Upscale clientele. Library. Very good svce. Resv. should be made a number of weeks ahead, given the limited number of rms. One of the most famous hotels in the country; its guestbook has been signed by John Wayne, Maria Callas, Henry Fonda, and Gregory Peck. 15 min. from dwntwn. Open year round. **E–VE,** but lower rates off-season.

YMCA/Youth Hostels
Santa Fe International Hostel (nr. dwntwn), 1412 Cerrillos Rd., NM 87501 (505/988-1153). Beautiful adobe hostel. Dormitories; rms for couples and families. Open year round.

RESTAURANTS
Personal Favorites (in order of preference)
♟♟♟ **Santacafe** (dwntwn), 231 Washington Ave. (984-1788). A/C. Lunch Mon–Sat, dinner nightly. MC, V. *Specialties:* smoked-pheasant spring rolls w. four-chili sauce, spinach and green-chili ravioli w. shrimp and asparagus, cassoulet, crispy duck breast w. ginger-honey glaze, grilled filet mignon w. roasted garlic and serrano-chile butter, stuffed chile, bread pudding w. honeyed whipped cream, tiramisù. Menu changes regularly. *Note:* The ultimate southwestern restaurant w. a subdued elegance. A great place for impressing visitors. Airy, imaginative dishes by chef Tracy Pikhart Ritter. The adobe Padre Gallegos House, where the rest. is housed, is a two-century-old designated historic monument. Flowery courtyard dining in good weather. Flawless svce; resv. a must; a first-rate place. *American/Mexican.* **I–M**

☼ ♟♟ **Pink Adobe** (dwntwn), 406 Old Santa Fe Trail (983-7712). A/C. Lunch Mon–Fri, dinner nightly; closed Jan 1, Labor Day, Thanksgiving, Dec 25. AE, CB, DC, MC, V. *Specialties:* chicken in brandy sauce, tournedos w. bordelaise sauce, steak Dunigan (w. green chili), pork Napoleon w. madeira sauce, Mexican dishes. Fine wine list. *Note:* One of the prettiest and most popular rests. in Santa Fe, in a three-century-old building. Charming setting in a number of small rms, w. a profusion of greenery and an open patio in summer. The food is very good on the whole, but New Mexican dishes are only average. Diligent svce. Often crowded and noisy; resv. a must. A Santa Fe classic. *Continental/Mexican.* **I–M**

♟♟♟ **Coyote Café** (dwntwn), 132 W. Water St. (983-1615). A/C. Lunch Sat–Sun, dinner nightly. AE, DC, MC, V. *Specialties:* enchiladas w. green-chile sauce, griddled buttermilk pancakes w. chipotle shrimp, "cowboy-cut" ribeye steak w. red chilled onion rings, pan-seared Pacific salmon w. avocado crema, marinated chicken on red chard and black-bean salsa. Menu changes regularly. *Note:* The rest., in what was once the Greyhound bus terminal, has high ceilings, bare walls enlivened by modern paintings, papier-mâché sculptures, and rustic tapestries which just accentuate the austerity of the decor. Ten years after its opening, the setting is as dramatic and funny as ever. But the quality of the cuisine has taken a nose dive due to the numerous absences of chef-owner and chili guru Mark Miller. Friendly, smiling svce; successful enough that resv. are strongly advised. You'll have a memorable meal here. *American.* **I–M**

♟♟♟ **Cafe Escalera** (dwntwn), 130 Lincoln St. (989-8188). A/C. Lunch Mon–Sat, dinner nightly; closed Dec 25. MC, V. *Specialties:* organic tomato salad, steamed clams, polenta torta, bouillabaisse, grilled chicken paillard, catch of the day, couscous, roast pork Tuscan-style, frozen lemon soufflé. Daily menu. Changing list of up to 30 wines by the glass. *Note:* Breezy, bright dining room and refined, simple cuisine leave a feeling of refreshment in this warmly welcomed addition to Santa Fe. Local produce swung into a Mediterranean mode. Skillful, adroit svce. A fine place. Resv. highly recommended. *Mediterranean.* **I–M**

♟♟♟ **Cafe Pasqual's** (dwntwn), 121 Don Gaspar St. (983-9340). Breakfast/lunch Mon–Sat, dinner nightly, brunch Sun; closed Dec. 24 and 25. AE, MC, V. *Specialties:* breakfast quesadilla w. guacamole and chorizo, warm French Brie w. whole roasted garlic and tomatillo salsa, arugula and mizuna salad w. parmigiana reggiano and Asian pears, Yucatán-spiced breast of free-range chicken, blackberry-lime tart. Seasonal menu. *Note:* Wildly original global cooking by Katharine Kagel, who ought to put a patent on each of her creations. Conspicuous corner location w. an exotic, tiled interior. A very popular rest. w. the locals, so reserve for dinner. Expect a wait for brunch. *Continental.* **B–I**

☼♥ **Maria's New Mexican Kitchen** (nr. dwntwn), 565 W. Cordo-
♨☙ va Rd. (983-7929). A/C. Lunch/dinner daily. AE, CB, DC, MC, V. *Specialties:* fajitas, enchiladas, tamales, alas picosas de pollo (spicy chicken wings), natillas. Excellent margaritas and a wide choice of beers. *Note:* Engaging, typically Mexican cantina, which the experts credit w. the best fajitas in Santa Fe. Its blue-corn enchiladas and its chili salsa are also worth the trip. Old adobe setting w. open fireplaces. Relaxed atmosphere and svce; a local favorite for more than 40 years. *Mexican.* **B**

Other Restaurants (from top bracket to budget)

♥♥♥ **Compound** (nr. dwntwn), 653 Canyon Rd. (982-4353).
☙☙☙ A/C. Dinner only, Tues–Sun; closed hols. and Jan. AE. Jkt. *Specialties:* tomato bisque, roast rack of lamb au jus, baked filet of salmon, fresh foie gras w. braised endive, chocolate-walnut torte w. raspberry sauce. *Note:* A happy marriage of Spanish Colonial setting and modern atmosphere 5 min. from the Plaza. Elegantly intimate decor; polished French-inspired cuisine. Pretty, open patio; uneven, stuffy svce. Resv. required. The chicest place in Santa Fe. *Continental.* **M–E**

♥♥ **La Traviata** (dwntwn), 95 W. Marcy St. (984-1091). A/C.
Lunch Mon–Fri, dinner nightly. AE, MC, V. *Specialties:* daily lasagna special, lombata di vitello alla saltimbocca, tiramisu. Fairly priced Italian wine list. *Note:* Lively *trattoria* featuring first-rate Italian food. Usually crowded and noisy, although it has recently doubled in size. Inevitable opera music background. Amiable, efficient svce. The "in" place in dwntwn Santa Fe. Resv. necessary. *Italian.* **M**

♥ **The Steaksmith at El Gancho** (nr. dwntwn), Old Las Vegas
Hwy. (988-3333). A/C. Dinner only, nightly; closed hols. AE, MC, V. *Specialties:* tapas, steak, broiled catch of the day, good homemade desserts. *Note:* Generally crowded, this congenial, rustic steakhouse serves excellent beef cuts and remarkably fresh fish at sensible prices. Relaxed atmosphere; locally popular. A fine place, 8 min. from dwntwn. *Steak/Seafood.* **M**

☼♥♥ **La Casa Sena** (dwntwn), 20 Sena Plaza, 125 E. Palace Ave.
♨☙ (988-9232). A/C. Lunch/dinner daily, brunch Sun; closed Dec 25. AE, CB, DC, MC, V. *Specialties:* black-bean soup, trout stuffed w. smoked salmon, chile dishes. Award-winning wine list (600 selections). *Note:* Excellent southwestern food in a charming adobe *mesón* dating from the 1860s in Old Santa Fe. It's near enough to the Plaza to attract a big tourist business. A nice place. *Continental/Mexican.* **I–M**

♥ **Shohko Café** (dwntwn), 321 Johnson St. at Guadalupe St.
(983-7288). A/C. Lunch Mon–Fri, dinner Mon–Sat; closed hols. AE, MC, V. *Specialties:* Imperial rolls, tempura, sushi, teriyaki, sukiyaki. *Note:* This little Chinese-Japanese rest. behind the Hilton Hotel serves the best Far Eastern food in town. Simple and unpretentious. Resv. advised. *Chinese/Japanese.* **B–I**

☼♥ **Tomasita's** (dwntwn), 500 S. Guadalupe St. (983-5721).
♨☙ A/C. Lunch/dinner Mon–Sat; closed hols. MC, V. *Specialties:* hot red and green chiles enchiladas and burritos, sopaipillas w. honey butter. Mexican beer and potent margaritas. *Note:* A longtime favorite, in the old Santa Fe train station dating from 1894. Locals and tourists line up for their blue-corn tortillas and fiery chili dishes. Fast, friendly svce. Outdoor dining. *Mexican/American.* **B–I**

⚜☿ **The Shed** (dwntwn), 113½ E. Palace Ave. (982-9030). A/C. Lunch only, Mon–Sat; closed hols. No credit cards. *Specialties:* enchiladas, burritos, hamburgers, posolé, tacos, good homemade desserts (mocha cake). *Note:* Delightful little rest. in the shadow of the cathedral, open for lunch only. Excellent Mexican-inspired food in a very picturesque colonial setting w. colorful murals (the building dates from 1692). Pleasant open courtyard. Locally popular. Wine and beer. Unfortunately, no resv. *American/Mexican.* B

Cafeterias/Fast Food

Furr's (nr. dwntwn), Coronado Center, 522 W. Cordova Rd. (982-3816). Lunch/dinner daily (until 8pm). MC, V. Praiseworthy cafeteria food at very low prices: chicken-fried steak, baked fish, etc.

Swiss Bakery (dwntwn), 320 Guadalupe St. (988-3737). Open Mon–Sat 7am–6pm. As you'd expect from the name, the house specialties are croissants and pastry—but the pizzas, quiches, sandwiches, and soups of the day are fine too. Agreeable open-air patio.

BARS & NIGHTCLUBS

Bull Ring Lounge (dwntwn), 414 Old Santa Fe Trail (983-3328). Congenial bar, disco. Also honorable rest. Open Mon–Sat.

El Farol (nr. dwntwn), 808 Canyon Rd. (983-9912). Live rock and R&B nightly starting at 9:30.

NEARBY EXCURSIONS

⚜🏛 **BANDELIER NATIONAL MONUMENT** (45 mi./72km NW via U.S. 84 and N.M. 4) (672-3861): Ruins of Native American cave dwellings and cliff houses dating from the 13th century, in a lovely wild setting on Frijoles Canyon ("Canyon of Beans"). The monument is named after Swiss ethnologist and writer Adolph Bandelier, who explored the area thoroughly in the 1880s. Along 70 mi. (113km) of footpaths you, too, can explore the caves and ruins of the different pueblos in the park. Among them are **Tyuonyi,** a three-story circular ruin which once had 400 rooms and three *kivas* (places of worship); **Long House,** which had more than 300 rooms; and the **Ceremonial Cave** *kiva,* in a cave 150 ft. (46km) above the valley floor that can be reached only by ladders. Visitor center with archeological museum. Open daily; quite a tiring visit. Combine it, if possible, with a trip to Los Alamos (see below).

⚜🏛 **CORONADO STATE PARK & MONUMENT** (45 mi./72km south via I-25 and N.M. 44N) (867-5351): Ruins of a Kuava pueblo going back to A.D. 1300. The Spanish conquistador Francisco Vásquez de Coronado camped here in 1540 during his fruitless search for the mythical Eldorado known to historians as "the seven gold cities of Cibola." Interesting Native American museum. Visit to a restored *kiva.* Open daily.

⚜🏛 **LOS ALAMOS** (40 mi./65km NW on U.S. 84 and N.M. 4): Once the secret city of atomic research ("Atomic City"), this is where Robert Oppenheimer and his team devised the first A-bomb in 1942–43 as part of the so-called Manhattan Project. The **Bradbury Science Museum** on Diamond Dr. (667-4444), open daily, is an interesting museum of nuclear science and nuclear energy, with full-size models of "Little Boy" and "Fat Man," respectively the Hiroshima and Nagasaki bombs.

On the way, visit **San Ildefonso** (see "The Pueblos," below) and 🏛 **Puye**

Cliff Ruins on N.M. 5 (753-7326), with a number of prehistoric dwellings and the ruins of a very large pueblo seven to eight centuries old. Guided tours daily.

🔔 OLD CIENEGA VILLAGE MUSEUM (15 mi./24km SW on U.S. 85): Authentic museum-village tucked into the mountainside, depicting the life of the Spanish settlers between 1660 and the 19th century. Interesting; visits Wed–Sun June–Sept, Apr–May by appointment only. Folklore festivals some weekends. For schedules, call 471-2261.

☀🔔 PECOS NATIONAL MONUMENT (25 mi./40km SE on I-25) (757-6032): Remains of a 14th-century pueblo which once had some 2,500 inhabitants; two magnificent *kivas* have been completely restored. The principal dwelling house was five stories high. Nearby are ruins of the first Spanish mission built in New Mexico (1542), destroyed during the Indian Rebellion of 1680. Church rebuilt in 1701 and finally abandoned at the end of the 18th century. Open daily.

☀🏠🏠 TAOS (70 mi./112km NE via U.S. 285 and N.M. 68): Picturesque little Spanish-Mexican-American community nestled in the foothills of the Sierra Sangre de Cristo ("Christ's Blood Mountains"), so called by the Spaniards because at twilight in winter the snow appears to take on a purplish cast. An artists' colony for more than a century, Taos now deploys dozens of art galleries and an unfortunate abundance of souvenir shops, but its museums and its pretty **Plaza** are enough to justify the trip. Among the more interesting museums: the **Ernest L. Blumenschein Home**, with its many works by local painters, at 222 Ledoux St., open daily; and the **Bent House Museum**, 18 Bent St., open daily Mar–Dec, residence of the first American governor of New Mexico, Charles Bent, who was killed and scalped there by native tribes in 1847. You should also see the house, and tomb, of the famous frontiersman Kit Carson, nicknamed "The Crack Shot of the West," who lived here for 24 years, at the **Kit Carson Home**, E. Kit Carson Rd. (758-0505), open daily; the beautiful Spanish mission of **San Francisco de Asis**, rebuilt in 1772, at Ranchos de Taos, 4 mi. (6.5km) south on N.M. 68 (758-2754), and the great 🏠🏠 **Rio Grande Bridge** looking down on the river from its height of 650 ft. (198m), 10 mi. (16km) NW on U.S. 64.

You'll find it a good idea to combine this with a trip to **Taos Pueblo** (see "The Pueblos," below).

On your way back to Santa Fe, take the "High Road to Taos" along N.M. 3 and N.M. 76, dotted with delightful little Spanish Colonial villages like **Chimayo** (beautiful old church with a legend of healing powers, weavers' workshops), **Truchas** (where the movie *The Milagro Beanfield War* was shot), and **Cordova**. A trip full of worthwhile sights.

Where to Eat En Route

IN TAOS ☀🍷 **Apple Tree at Taos,** 123 Bent St. (758-1900). Breakfast/lunch/dinner daily. Attractive adobe house w. shady patio; the food is typically southwestern. *Mexican/American.* **B–I**

🍷 **Ogelvie's,** The Plaza (758-8866). Lunch/dinner daily. *Mexican/American.* **B–I**

IN CHIMAYO The 🍷🍷 **Rancho de Chimayo,** on N.M. 520 (984-2100). Lunch/dinner daily in summer, Tues–Sun the rest of the year; closed Jan. One of the best regional rests. in the state. Don't miss it. *Mexican.* **B–I**

IN TRUCHAS ♈ **Truchas Mountain Café,** N.M. 76 (689-2444). Breakfast/ lunch/dinner daily. Family-run café offering good Mexican-style dishes. Every meal comes w. homemade tortillas or remarkable sopaipillas. *Mexican/ American.* **B-I**

GHOST TOWNS: ▲ **Cerrillos,** 28 mi. (44km) SW via I-25 and N.M. 14: This old prospectors' town had 2,500 inhabitants, eight hotels, and 20 saloons in the 1880s; today its population is barely 200, but it still has many vestiges of its golden age. Sometimes used as a film set.

▲ **Madrid,** 30 mi. (48km) SW via I-25 and N.M. 14: Once an important coal-mining center, now down to 200 inhabitants. Interesting mining museum and dozens of abandoned houses. Open-air jazz and bluegrass concerts in summer. For information, call 473-0743.

THE PUEBLOS

There are more than a dozen still-inhabited Native American pueblos (the Spanish word for villages) within a 125-mi. (200km) radius of Santa Fe, almost all going back beyond the arrival of the colonizing Spaniards 3½ centuries ago. Heirs of the famous Anasazi people of the Middle Ages, the Pueblo peoples fall into four major families: the Hopi (see Chapter 40 on Navajoland), the Zuñi and the Acoma in west-central New Mexico, and the Rio Grande tribes, who live around the valley of the same name. Their numbers, perhaps 20,000 when the Spaniards came, declined to 5,000–6,000 in the 19th century, but have now reached almost 40,000.

The pueblos of the Rio Grande peoples may be visited between sunrise and sunset on payment of a fee of $3–$4 per vehicle; try to make your visit coincide with the annual festival or a religious ceremony (Jan 1, 22, 23; Feb 2; Easter; May 3; June 13, 24; Aug 10; Sept 29, 30; Nov 12; Dec 12, 25, 31). *Warning:* You must not photograph the village or its people unless authorized to do so (usually for a fee) by the chief of the pueblo. Discreet and respectful behavior is appropriate at all times.

The **Santa Fe Convention and Visitors Bureau,** 200 W. Marcy St. (984-6760), will give you the dates of festivities; information may also be obtained from the **Eight Northern Pueblos Council,** P.O. Box 969, San Juan Pueblo, NM 87566 (852-4265). The most picturesque pueblos are:

☼▲ **Acoma Pueblo,** 127 mi. (204km) SW via I-25S, I-40W, and N.M. 23 (252-1139): The oldest community in the U.S., believed to have been first settled around A.D. 600. Perched 6,560 ft. (2,000m) up on a rocky mesa, "Sky City," as the historians have dubbed it, is by far the country's most beautiful pueblo, and the least tainted by Western "civilization." Spanish Mission of San Estebán Rey (1629). Photography permitted for a $6 fee.

▲ **Cochití Pueblo,** 30 mi. (48km) SW via U.S. 85S and U.S. 22N (465-2244): Antedates the Spaniards; a center for the crafting of silver-and-precious-stone jewelry, ceramics, and drums, on the banks of the Rio Grande. No photographs.

☼▲ **Jémez Pueblo,** 75 mi. (120km) south via I-25S, N.M. 44N, and N.M. 4N (834-7359): Famous for its embroidery, weaving, and wickerwork. No photographs. Not far away, at **Jemez Springs,** is a pretty Spanish Franciscan mission dating from 1621, near a prehistoric village.

☼▲ **San Ildefonso Pueblo,** 28 mi. (44km) NW via U.S. 84 and N.M. 4 (455-2274): Lovely plaza with open-air market; best known for its Native American pottery and ceramics. One of the best-known Rio Grande pueblos. Photography permitted ($5).

▲ **San Juan Pueblo,** 28 mi. (44km) north on U.S. 285 (852-4400): Chosen by the Spaniards as the site of their first capital in 1598. The great rebellion of 1680 originated in San Juan; it culminated with the taking of Santa Fe and the massacre of all the Spanish garrisons. It took the forces of Don Diego de Vargas 12 years to put the rebellion down. There's a restaurant with typical Native American food. Photography permitted ($5).

🅰 **Santa Clara Pueblo,** 27 mi. (43km) NW on U.S. 84 (753-7326): A typical example of pueblo architecture; fine pottery. Photography permitted ($5).

🅰 **Santo Domingo Pueblo,** 32 mi. (51km) SW via U.S. 85 and N.M. 22 (465-2214): The most authentic and traditional of the pueblos; turquoise jewelry and blankets. No photographs.

🅰 **Taos Pueblo,** 72 mi. (115km) NE via U.S. 285 and N.M. 68 (758-9593): The cultural capital of the Pueblo Nation, with the 13,000-ft. (3,970m) peaks of the Sangre de Cristo as a distant backdrop. It retains the traditional 13th-century ground-plan of terraces in dark-yellow or brown adobe, with construction on four or five levels linked by rudimentary flights of steps. Ruins of Mission San Gerónimo (1598) are adjacent to the central plaza. A firmly tourist atmosphere but a splendid setting. Photography permitted ($5).

🅰 **Tesuque Pueblo,** 8 mi. (13km) NW on U.S. 285 (983-2667): The site has been continuously inhabited since about A.D. 1250. A mission, now ruined, was built here at the beginning of the 18th century. Crafts (pottery, jewelry, embroidery) and remarkable dancing at different times of year. Photography permitted ($5).

🅰 **Zía Pueblo,** 65 mi. (104km) SW via I-25S and N.M. 44N (867-3304): Also famous for its pottery. Fine natural site. Spanish Mission of Nuestra Señora de la Asunción (1692). No photographs.

For more details on this and other New Mexico pueblos, see Chapter 38 on Albuquerque.

FARTHER AFIELD

🅰 **CUMBRES & TOLTEC SCENIC RAILROAD** (220 mi./ 352km r.t. on U.S. 84N and 84S): One of the highest and most spectacular railroads in the country, crossing the Cumbres Pass elevation 10,015 ft. (3,054m). The little Far Western train makes a 64-mi. (102km) trip to link **Chama,** N.M., and **Antonito,** Colo., through splendid mountain and forest scenery and along wild gorges. Time: Seven hours round-trip; operates daily from the end of May to mid-Oct. Round-trip fare: $32 for adults, $16 for children. Resv. a must 2–3 weeks in advance, obtainable from P.O. Box 789, Chama, NM 87520 (756-2151). A must for steam-train buffs; can be combined with a visit to Taos (see "Nearby Excursions," above).

🅰 **MESA VERDE NATIONAL PARK** (580 mi./930km r.t. via U.S. 84N, N.M. 96E, N.M. 44W, U.S. 550N, U.S. 160W, and the reverse route to return): America's greatest monument from its Native American civilizations (8th through 13th centuries). Dozens of multilevel houses, towers, terraces, streets miraculously clinging to the cliff face, in a glorious setting of desert canyons. Every year 600,000 visitors confront the astonishing sight of these ghost villages, silent now for centuries. The sudden disappearance of their inhabitants, the Anasazi peoples, six centuries ago is still a riddle to historians: Was it an epidemic? a persistent drought? an invasion by wandering tribes? a slow leaching-out of the soil? A visit to these cliffs and their ruins, of which the most impressive are **Cliff Palace** (217 rooms and *kivas*) and **Spruce Tree House** (114 rooms, 8 *kivas*), is permitted only when accompanied by a ranger; it calls for stout shoes and good physical condition. Remarkable **Native American museum** near the visitor center, open daily. Unique view of the states of Colorado, Utah, Arizona, and New Mexico from **Park Point Fire Lookout** at 8,572 ft. (2,613m), halfway between the park entrance and the visitor center. Park open to vehicles daily year round.

For **information,** contact the Superintendent, P.O. Box 8, Mesa Verde National Park, CO 81330 (303/529-4465).

Along the way, visit the ☀️♙♙ **Chaco Culture National Historical Park,** with ruins of 16 Anasazi pueblos abandoned around the end of the 13th century, another Amerindian gem. Some of these pueblos, like Pueblo Bonito, have no fewer than 800 rooms and 37 *kivas.* Unsurfaced access road, passable only in dry weather. Visitor center 2 mi. (3.2km) from the southern entrance on N.M. 57 (988-6716), open daily.

It's also well worth making the side trip to ♙ **Aztec Ruins National Monument,** at Aztec (334-6174), one of the best-preserved primitive pueblos in the Southwest. Large 13th-century *kiva,* splendidly restored. Open daily.

And don't miss taking a ride on the ♙♙ **Silverton,** a little Far Western train dating from 1882, which takes seven hours to cover the 50 mi. (80km) from **Durango** to **Silverton,** and the return leg, through glorious mountain scenery; one of the most popular tourist attractions in the West. Operates daily mid-May to Oct. For resv. (a must), contact the railroad at 479 Main Ave., Durango, CO 81301 (303/247-2733). Round-trip fare: $43 for adults, $22 for children.

This 580-mi. (930km) round-trip from Santa Fe and back again is enough in itself to warrant visiting the city.

Where to Stay En Route

IN THE PARK ♙♙ **Far View,** P.O. Box 277, Mancos, CO 81328 (303/529-4421). 150 rms w. mountain views. A comfortable motel inside the park. Open from mid-Apr to the end of Oct. **I–M**

IN CORTEZ The ♙ **Anasazi,** 666 S. Broadway, Cortez, CO 81321 (303/565-3773). 87 rms. Open year round. **B–I**

♙ **Best Western Sands,** 1120 E. Main St., Cortez, CO 81321 (303/565-3761). 81 rms. Open year round. **I**

IN DURANGO The ☀️ ♙ **Strater Hotel,** 699 Main Ave., Durango, CO 81301 (303/247-4431). 94 rms. **I–M**

☀️♙♙ **General Palmer House,** 567 Main Ave., Durango, CO 81301 (303/247-4747). 39 rms. **I–M**

☀️♙♙ **NAVAJOLAND** (about 560 mi./900km r.t. via I-25S, I-40W, N.M. 264W, Ariz. 264W, and the reverse on the return trip): Spectacular scenery **(Monument Valley, Canyon de Chelly),** and the largest reservation in the U.S. See Chapter 40 on Navajoland.

On the way, visit the picturesque **Zuñi and Acoma Pueblos** (see Chapter 38 on Albuquerque). A spectacular itinerary.

NAVAJOLAND 👙

□ □ □

With Monument Valley and Canyon de Chelly

Covering an area larger than Massachusetts, New Hampshire, and Vermont combined, the territory of Navajoland offers its visitors some of the most fantastic natural wonders of the North American continent: a spectacularly scenic expanse of red, pink, orange, and khaki-brown desert, pueblos perched on arid plateaus (the mesas), and the immense **Lake Powell.** Ironically nicknamed "The 51st State," Navajoland, or Navajo Country, is indeed the largest Native American reserve in the U.S. The land takes up much of northeastern Arizona and spills over into Utah and New Mexico. The Navajo, whose numbers at the end of the Indian Wars in 1864 had been reduced to a mere 8,000 by the depredations of Kit Carson and his soldiery, now administer the territory themselves from their capital at **Window Rock,** 112 mi. (180km) west of Albuquerque.

Nearly half the tribespeople on the reservation live below the official poverty line, and about a third are out of work. The enormous mineral wealth underlying Navajo territory—estimated at 2.5 million tons of coal, 80 million tons of uranium ore, 100 million barrels of oil, and 26 billion cubic yards of natural gas— have been leased to corporations by the auction method, and now bring in only $50 million a year in royalties to the Navajo.

The Navajo are generally tolerant of the tourists who visit them, but they impose some rules which must be respected. Native Americans and their homes may not be photographed without advance permission. Some sacred areas or monuments—for example, the Navajo Fortress in the Canyon de Chelly—are forbidden except to Native Americans. Additional information may be obtained on the spot.

The best known of the wonders of Navajoland is **Monument Valley,** not far from the Utah border; the setting of countless Hollywood Westerns (such as *Stagecoach*), its twisted canyons and pillars of red rock 980 ft. (300m) high (called the "cathedrals of the desert") have been seen by millions of Americans in TV commercials featuring a car perched atop an impossibly steep spire of rock. A tour of Monument Valley by car takes two to three hours in dry weather and is an unforgettable experience. In winter you'll need a Jeep (see "Guided Tours," below).

The **Canyon de Chelly** (pronounced "de Shay"), 93 mi. (150km) to the south, is another fascinating place that can be reached by car, but explored only in an all-terrain vehicle (see "Guided Tours," below); its Native American settlements, dating from the 4th century, are worth the visit by themselves.

The **Navajo National Monument,** not far from Monument Valley, can be

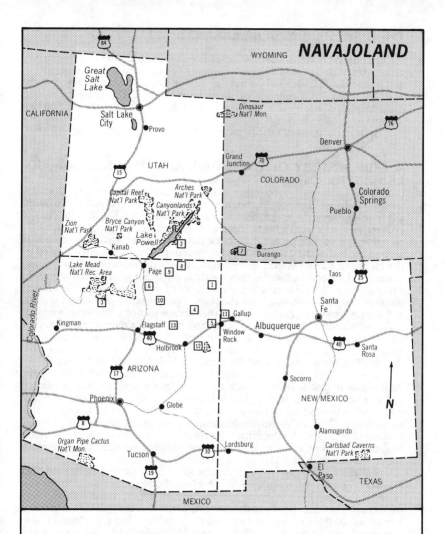

KEY TO NUMBERED SIGHTS:

1. **Canyon de Chelly National Monument**
2. **Glen Canyon National Rec. Area**
3. **Grand Canyon National Park**
4. **Hopi Mesas/Reservation**
5. **Hubbell Trading Post**
6. **John Wesley Powell Memorial Museum**
7. **Mesa Verde National Park**
8. **Monument Valley**
9. **Navajo National Monument**
10. **Navajo Reservation**
11. **Navajo Tribal Museum**
12. **Petrified Forest National Park**
13. **Wupatki National Monument**

reached only on horseback or on foot; it has well-preserved ruins of 13th-century Native American pueblos. Nearer the center of Navajoland are the mesas inhabited by the Hopi, traditional enemies of the Navajo, which frown down on the Arizona desert from a height of many hundred feet. The Hopi are skilled craftspeople, producing silver jewelry, pottery, Kachina dolls, and beautiful basketwork.

As in all the country's tribal reservations, the sale of beer or liquor is forbidden in Navajoland.

A BRIEF HISTORY OF THE NATIVE AMERICANS OF NAVAJO-LAND: When Christopher Columbus first set foot on American soil, he thought he had arrived at the Indies; under this misapprehension, he dubbed the natives "Indians." The peoples thus misnamed had always comprised two mutually hostile groups: the settler tribes and the nomadic tribes. The **Navajo** (Navajo, or Navaho, comes from a Native American word meaning "people of the soil") are settlers; a warrior people, they came down from the northwest of Canada around the end of the 15th century and overran the lands hitherto occupied by the Hopi and Pueblo in northern Arizona. Under the influence of the Spanish colonists, this nomadic hunting tribe—whose physical appearance is captured in a Navajo poem: "My skin as brown as the face of Mother Earth, my hair as black as the sky of night"—became, over the years, a people of shepherds and grazers, and learned from the Pueblo peoples their techniques of cultivation, weaving, and sandpainting. The Navajo, who in 1864 had been almost exterminated by the famous scout Kit Carson and his white volunteers, are now America's largest Native American tribe. The 1990 census shows 1,450,000 Native Americans living on 285 reservations in about 30 states, of which 200,000 are Navajo.

The Navajo speak an extraordinarily complex language belonging to the Athapaskan linguistic family, which also includes the Apaches of New Mexico and southern Arizona. A strongly spiritual people with a rich religious heritage and mystical bonds to their land and animals, the Navajo live in modest villages of traditional "hogans"—windowless wooden homes and huts of earth and clay supported by logs, with a door that must always face east. More open to outsiders than the Pueblo or the Hopi, the Navajo generally allow strangers to be present at the sacred rites and colorful religious ceremonies.

The **Hopi** (which means "peaceable people" in the native tongue) and their **Pueblo** neighbors belong to the great Shoshone family, which includes the Comanche, Ute, and Paiute tribes as well as others, all distant cousins of the Aztecs of Mexico. The Hopi are direct descendants of the Anasazi ("the Old Ones"), a race of remarkable builders, as witnessed in the ruins of Mesa Verde and Chaco Canyon. Driven from their villages, probably during the 15th century, by drought and famine, the Hopi, who today number around 6,000, were thrown back onto the mesas by the conquering thrust of the Navajo. Like their blood-brothers the Pueblo of New Mexico, the Hopi are a sedentary tribe, given to farming and stock breeding. For more than 1,000 years they have cultivated strains of corn that can survive in arid country, and a number of indigenous plants and vegetables, such as beans, pumpkin, tobacco, squash, potatoes, and tomatoes. In their isolated villages of stone-and-mortar houses, which cling like eagles' aeries to the high plateaus of the mesas, the Hopi practice the talent inherited from their Anasazi ancestors for the working of silver and for basket weaving (the Anasazi are known to archeologists as the "Basket Maker Pueblo"). They have also kept alive a religious tradition of ritual dances to invoke rain and avert bad luck: fire dances, eagle dances, serpent dances, and the like.

Their elaborate mythology is visibly manifested in the Kachina masks, which embody the spirits of ancestors, animals, or plants. Kachina dolls, much prized by visitors for their startling forms and colors, are a sort of miniature pantheon of the Hopi deities. Unlike the Navajo, the Hopi are intensely suspicious of strangers, and try to keep outsiders away from their religious ceremonies. Even to visit a

Hopi village you must have advance authorization, which may be obtained from the Hopi Cultural Center at Second Mesa. For the schedule of Navajo and Hopi festivals, see "Special Events," below.

Those interested in the way of life, arts, and history of Native Americans should contact the **Bureau of Indian Affairs,** Office of Public Information, 18th and E Sts. NW, Washington, DC 20240 (202/208-3710).

BASIC FACTS: States of Arizona, New Mexico, and Utah. Area code: 602. Time zone: mountain. Approximate area: 25,100 sq. mi. (65,000km²). Reservation founded in: 1868. Nonmigrant tribal population: 200,000 Navajo and 6,000 Hopi.

CLIMATE: As in all semi-desert regions, summer (the season that draws most tourists) can be burning hot (95°–104°F/35°–40°C) by day, but is much cooler at night. In spring and fall you'll need a sweater even in the daytime. Aug and Sept are the rainy season. In winter, the first snow falls on the mesas in Nov, and the mercury sometimes drops to 13°F(−10°C).

ARRIVAL & TRANSIT INFORMATION

NEAREST AIRPORTS: The **Albuquerque International Airport** (ABQ), 112 mi. (180km) east of Window Rock.
   Flagstaff Pulliam Field (FLG), 180 mi. (290km) SW of Monument Valley.
   Phoenix Sky Harbor International (PHX), 210 mi. (340km) SW of the mesas.

AIRLINES AT ALBUQUERQUE AIRPORT: American (toll free 800/433-7300), America West (toll free 800/247-5692), Delta (toll free 800/221-1212), Southwest (toll free 800/531-5601), TWA (toll free 800/221-2000), and United (toll free 800/241-6522).

BUS OR CAR RENTAL? Given the distances to be covered, the sensible thing is to rent a car with unlimited mileage. There is no intercity bus service to Navajoland.

CAR RENTAL IN ALBUQUERQUE (at the Albuquerque International Airport unless otherwise noted): Avis (toll free 800/331-1212); Budget (toll free 800/527-0700); Dollar (toll free 800/800-4000); Hertz (toll free 800/654-3131); and National (toll free 800/227-7368). See also Chapter 41 on the Grand Canyon and Chapter 42 on Phoenix.

NEAREST TRAIN STATIONS: Amtrak (toll free 800/872-7245) has stations at 201 E. U.S. 66, in **Gallup,** New Mexico, and E. 2nd St., in **Winslow,** Arizona.

NEAREST BUS STATIONS: Greyhound (toll free 800/231-2222) has terminals at 300 2nd St. SW, **Albuquerque,** New Mexico; 399 S. Malpais Lane, **Flagstaff,** Arizona; and 105 S. Dean St., **Gallup,** New Mexico.

INFORMATION & TOURS

TOURIST INFORMATION: Canyon de Chelly National Monument: Superintendent, P.O. Box 588, Chinle, AZ 86503 (602/674-5436). Visitor center.
   Hopi Reservation: Cultural Center, P.O. Box 67, Second Mesa, AZ 86043 (602/734-2401); Tribal Office (602/734-2441, ext. 360).
   Hubbell Trading Post: Ariz. 264 (P.O. Box 150), Ganado, AZ 86505 (602/755-3475). Visitor center.
   NACA (Native Americans for Community Action): 2717 N. Steves Blvd., Suite 11, Flagstaff, AZ 86004 (602/526-2968). Information on cultural activities, art festivals, and powwows scheduled for the Hopi, Navajo, and Apache reservations in Arizona.
   Navajo Nation: P.O. Box 663, Window Rock, AZ 86515 (602/871-6436 or 871-6659). Visitor center.
   There are other visitor centers at **Monument Valley** and **Navajo National Monument.**

GUIDED TOURS: You can visit the major sights of Navajoland on guided tours by car, bus, and airplane.

All-Terrain-Vehicle Excursions in Monument Valley
   Goulding's Lodge Valley Tour, U.S. 163, Gouldings (801/727-3231). Full- and half-day trips. Daily year round.
   Crawley's Monument Valley Tours, U.S. 163, Kayenta (602/697-3463). Full- and half-day trips. Daily year round.

All-Terrain-Vehicle Excursions in Canyon de Chelly
   Thunderbird Lodge Tours, Chinle (602/674-5841). Full- and half-day trips. Daily year round.

Bus Trips to the Hopi and Navajo Reservations
   Nava-Hopi Tours (Gray Line), 114 W. Santa Fe, Flagstaff (602/774-5003; toll free 800/892-8687). Tours run Mon, Wed, and Fri Apr–Oct.

Flights Over Navajoland and Lake Powell
   Lake Powell Air Service, Page Airport (602/645-2494).
   Monument Valley Flying Service, Chinle (602/674-5657).

ADVENTURES: Ara Leisure Services (boat), P.O. Box 56909, Phoenix, AZ 85079 (602/278-8888; toll free 800/528-6154). Cruises of three days and up on Lake Powell aboard fully equipped rented houseboats—a sort of floating motor home for 6–10 people, which will take you everywhere in the lake and into its dozens of splendid desert canyons. Rates begin at $1,240 a week in summer, $930 in spring or fall, and $745 in winter; three- and four-day rentals also available. You should reserve very far in advance.

MONUMENTS & SIGHTS IN NAVAJOLAND

☼ ☖☖☖ **CANYON DE CHELLY NATIONAL MONUMENT** (225 mi./360km NW of Albuquerque along I-40, U.S. 666, Ariz. 264, and U.S. 191): Spectacular landscapes which can be seen only from a Jeep (Apr–Oct). Native American cave dwellings from the 4th to the 14th century, including the **White House, Mummy Cave,** and **Antelope House.** In 1864 in this savagely beautiful canyon there took place one of the last engagements between the troops of Kit Carson and the native tribespeople who had taken refuge at the top of the **Navajo Fortress,** a huge rocky spur which is now sacred ground, forbidden to strangers. This is one of the few canyons in the country whose interior can be explored from an all-terrain vehicle. As well as the **Canyon de Chelly** itself, with its steep red sandstone walls, and **Spider Rock,** the 800-ft. (262m) needle of rock which is its most remarkable feature, the monument also includes the lateral canyons, **Canyon del Muerto** ("Dead Man's Canyon"), **Black Rock Canyon,** and **Monument Canyon.** At the visitor center, open year round, there is an interesting small archeological museum.

For **information,** contact the Superintendent, Canyon de Chelly National Monument, P.O. Box 588, Chinle, AZ 86503 (602/674-5436). (See, also, the Thunderbird Lodge, in "Motels and Restaurants," below.)

GLEN CANYON & LAKE POWELL (122 mi./195km west of Monument Valley along U.S. 163, U.S. 160, and Ariz. 98): **Lake Powell,** 196 mi. (315km) long with 1,900 mi. (3,058km) of shoreline, was created in 1963 by the construction of the **Page Dam** on the Colorado River; it has turned the **Glen Canyon National Recreation Area** into a tourist mecca for lovers of water sports, with its beautiful landscapes where the red-brown-ocher cliffs are mirrored in the clear blue lake, and its wonderful fishing for oversize trout, carp, and pike. Glen Canyon is no less rich in its variety of land animals: Rocky Mountain sheep, deer, coyote, puma, and even the occasional, extremely rare, golden eagle. At **Page** you can hire a comfortable houseboat to visit Lake Powell (see "Adventures," above).

For **information,** contact the Superintendent, Glen Canyon National Recreation Area, P.O. Box 1507, Page, AZ 86040 (602/645-2471).

HOPI MESAS (134 mi./214km NE of Flagstaff along U.S. 89, U.S. 160, and Ariz. 264): Primitive Native American villages, some as much as eight centuries old, clinging like eagles' nests to the rocky plateaus (mesas). Spectacular views. Authorization for visits must be obtained from the Hopi Cultural Center at Kykotsmovi (see "Tourist Information," above).

MONUMENT VALLEY (170 mi./272km NE of Flagstaff along U.S. 89, U.S. 160, and U.S. 163): This is the country's best-known picture postcard, in glorious Technicolor: one of the most amazing landscapes in creation, more than 25 million years old. The "desert cathedrals," the red sandstone monoliths almost 2,000 ft. (more than 600m) high, with their evocative names—Camel Butte, Sentinel Mesa, Three Sisters, Big Chief, Elephant Butte—have provided the backdrop for countless westerns like *Stagecoach, Fort Apache, My Darling Clementine, The Searchers,* and *Billy the Kid,* as well as for Walt Disney's famous *The Living Desert.*

The recent history of Monument Valley is closely linked with that of Harry Goulding, an enterprising businessman who in 1923 opened a trading post and coaching inn on the site of the motel that now bears his name (see "Motels and Restaurants," below). It was Goulding who, in 1938, persuaded John Ford to shoot his first major western, *Stagecoach,* in this magnificent natural setting, thus making Monument Valley a symbol of the Wild West in dozens of movies still to come.

Private cars are admitted during the summer for the 14-mi. (23km) circuit, beginning at the visitor center; off-season, Jeeps only. For **information,** contact Park Headquarters, Monument Valley Navajo Tribal Park, P.O. Box 93, UT 84536 (801/727-3287).

🔔 **NAVAJO NATIONAL MONUMENT** (135 mi./216km NE of Flagstaff on U.S. 89 and U.S. 160): Very well preserved 13th-century Native American cave dwellings, reachable on foot or horseback only. The most beautiful of the ruins, "Keet Seel," is 8 mi. (12km) from the visitor center. For **information,** contact Navajo National Monument, HC 71, Box 3, Tonalea, AZ 86044-9704 (602/672-2366).

MONUMENTS & SCENERY
OUTSIDE THE NAVAJO RESERVE

☀️🔔🔔🔔 **GRAND CANYON OF THE COLORADO** (181 mi./288km SW of Monument Valley via U.S. 163, U.S. 160, U.S. 89, and Ariz. 64): See Chapter 41 on the Grand Canyon.

☀️🔔🔔🔔 **MESA VERDE NATIONAL PARK** (159 mi./254km NE of Monument Valley via U.S. 163 and U.S. 160): See Chapter 39 on Santa Fe.

☀️🔔 **METEOR CRATER** (46 mi./74km east of Flagstaff on I-40) (602/774-8350): Some 22,000 years ago a two-million-ton meteorite crashed to earth here at a record speed of 33,000 mph (52,800 kmph), forming the world's largest nonvolcanic crater, 4,160 ft. (1.2km) across (3 mi./4.8km in circumference) and 557 ft. (170m) deep. It was used by NASA to train astronauts before their moon shots. Impressive. Open daily.

☀️🔔 **PETRIFIED FOREST NATIONAL PARK** (102 mi./163km SW of Canyon de Chelly on U.S. 191 and I-40): This petrified forest, the largest in the world, is 200 million years old. Countless animals and plants have been fossilized by the lakebed sediments or by volcanic ash. It's best to enter from the south at **Rainbow Forest,** with its interesting museum illustrating the petrification of wood. Visitor center open daily. The **Painted Desert,** north of the visitor center, displays a blinding pattern of shimmering colors —blues, reds, and tawnies—particularly at sunrise and sunset. Scenic drive. *Warning:* It is strictly prohibited to take petrified woods or fossils as souvenirs.

For **information,** contact the Superintendent, Petrified Forest National Park, AZ 86028 (602/524-6228).

☀️🔔 **RAINBOW BRIDGE** (reached by boat from Page, on Lake Powell): One of the largest natural spans in the world, 278 ft. (85m) across and 290 ft. (88m) high. It was a filming location for *2001: A Space Odyssey.* A Navajo legend holds that the bridge is a rainbow turned to stone.

🔔 **SUNSET CRATER NATIONAL MONUMENT** (17 mi./27km NE of Flagstaff on U.S. 89): Crater of a volcano that has been dormant for nine centuries; spectacular formations of reddish-orange lava. Open daily. For information, call 602/556-7042.

🔔 **WUPATKI NATIONAL MONUMENT** (35 mi./56km north of Flagstaff on U.S. 89): Ruins of a Native American village which was inhabited around A.D. 1100; the largest dwelling had some 100 bedrooms. Archeological museum. Open daily. For information, call 602/556-7040.

OTHER SIGHTS, ATTRACTIONS & ACTIVITIES

MUSEUMS: ⚓ **Hubbell Trading Post National Historic Site,** 42 mi. (67km) south of Canyon de Chelly on Ariz. 264 at Ganado (602/755-3475): Picturesque trading post opened in 1876 by John Lorenzo Hubbell, an idealistic businessman who became a friend and protector to the Navajo. The present structure, with its unusual layout, dates from 1885; it houses an interesting ethnological collection, and is still a trading post for the local tribespeople. Open daily year round.

⚓ **John Wesley Powell Memorial Museum,** 6 N. Lake Powell Blvd. in Page, 130 mi. (208km) north of Flagstaff (602/645-9496): This little-known small museum pays tribute to the intrepid 19th-century geologist John Wesley Powell, the first to shoot the Grand Canyon rapids in a canoe. Fascinating. Also an astonishing collection of fluorescent minerals. Open daily Apr–Oct; closed the rest of the year.

⚓ **Navajo Tribal Museum,** 159 mi. (254km) NW of Albuquerque at the junction of Ariz. 264 and Indian Rte. 12, at Window Rock (602/871-6673): Remarkable Navajo jewelry, pottery, wickerwork, and weaving. Library, temporary exhibitions. Open Mon–Sat in summer, Mon–Fri the rest of the year.

SPECIAL EVENTS: *Warning:* The Hopi people limit the number of visitors to what are regarded as sacred religious events. Cameras (still, movie, and video) and tape recorders are not permitted at any Hopi or Navajo festivals.

Hopi Festivals
For information and exact dates, call the **Hopi Cultural Center** (602/734-2401) or the **Hopi Tribal Office** (602/734-2441, ext. 360).
Niman or summer solstice festival (about June 21).
Hopi Home Dances (late July).
Snake or **Flute Dance** (Aug): Tourists allowed, but subject to restrictions.
Basket Dance (end of Oct to early Nov).
Soyal or winter solstice festival (about Dec 31).

Navajo Festivals
For information and exact dates, call the **Navajo Nation** (602/871-6436).
All Indian Days (early July): Powwow and rodeo at Window Rock.
Squaw Dances (throughout the summer).
Navajo Nation Fair (early Sept): One of the most important Native American occasions in the country; dancing, horse racing, rodeo, art exhibition. At Window Rock. For information call 602/871-6478.
Northern Navajo Fair (Oct): More than 2,000 Native Americans from various southwestern tribes attend this giant powwow at Shiprock.
Western Navajo Fair (mid-Oct): Parades, rodeos, handcrafts show, dance festival. At Tuba City.
Yei-bi-chi, or **Navajo Fire Dance** (throughout the winter).

Intertribal Festivals
Annual Gallup Indian Ceremonial (five days in mid-Aug): Brings together representatives of a dozen tribes from all over the country for a festival of traditional dance like the Gaan Dance of the Apache, the Basket and Butterfly Dances

of the Hopi, the Ribbon Dance of the Navajo, and so on. A great spectacle. For information: P.O. Box 1, Church Rock, NM 87311 (505/863-3896; toll free 800/233-4528).

MOTELS & RESTAURANTS

Personal Favorites (in order of preference)

IN MONUMENT VALLEY 🍴 **Goulding's Monument Valley Lodge,** 2 mi. (3.2km) west of U.S. 163, Monument Valley, UT 84536 (801/727-3231). 62 rms, A/C, color TV, in-rm movies (John Wayne classics). AE, MC, V. Resv. required. Free parking, coffee shop. *Note:* A rustic motel at the foot of a towering cliff, this famous landmark was specially built for the filming of John Wayne's *She Wore a Yellow Ribbon.* Decently comfortable and w. an unforgettable view. Functional rms w. patios or balconies; Boy Scout summer-camp atmosphere. If the reception and svce were friendlier, it would be a good place to stay. The coffee shop is only just acceptable—but it's the only one within 19 mi. (30km). No alcoholic beverages. An ideal starting point for Jeep trips across Monument Valley ($62 for a full day). Don't miss stopping here. Hotel and coffee shop open year round. **M,** but lower rates off-season.

🍴 **Holiday Inn,** junction of U.S. 160 and U.S. 163, Kayenta, AZ 86033 (602/697-3221); toll free, see Holiday Inns). 160 rms, A/C, cable color TV. AE, CB, DC, MC, V. Free parking, pool, rest., rm svce, free crib. *Note:* Typical motel, in the middle of the desert. Functionally comfortable. Open year round. 30 min. by road from Monument Valley (conducted tours by Jeep). **M,** but lower rates off-season.

🍴 **Wetherill Inn,** U.S. 163, Kayenta, AZ 86033 (602/697-3231). 54 rms, A/C, cable color TV. AE, MC, V. Free parking, adj. coffee shop, free crib. *Note:* Rustic motel w. limited comforts. Open year round. Organizes Jeep tours of Monument Valley. **I,** but lower rates Nov–Apr.

🍴 **Recapture Lodge,** U.S. 191, Bluff, UT 84512 (801/672-2281). 28 rms, color TV. AE, MC, V. Free parking, pool, adj. coffee shop, free crib. *Note:* Pioneer-house-style rustic motel w. no air conditioning, but friendly reception and atmosphere; some rms have kitchenettes and refrigerators. Starting point for guided tours of the desert and rafting down the Colorado River. Also accommodations for groups and families. Open year round. 45 min. by car from Monument Valley. **B**

🍴 **San Juan Inn,** U.S. 163, Mexican Hat, UT 84531 (801/683-2220). 22 rms, A/C, color TV. AE, MC, V. Free parking, coffee shop, crib $4. *Note:* Small, unpretentious hotel; limited comforts. Along the San Juan River. 15 min. by car from Monument Valley. **I**

IN CANYON DE CHELLY ☀🍴 **Thunderbird Lodge,** 3 mi. (5km) SE of U.S. 191, Chinle, AZ 86503 (602/674-5841). 72 rms, A/C, cable color TV. AE, MC, V. Free parking, coffee shop, crib $6. *Note:* Rustic but comfortable hotel at the entrance to Canyon de Chelly. Reception w. a smile. Very acceptable coffee shop open until 8:30pm. No alcoholic beverages. Organizes Jeep trips into the canyons; fare, $31–$50 according to duration. Resv. advisable in summer. Don't miss staying here; it's an excellent value. Open year round. **I–M,** but lower rates off-season.

🍴 **Canyon de Chelly Motel,** Navajo Rte. 7 (nr. U.S. 191), Chinle, AZ 86503 (602/674-5875). 51 rms, A/C, cable color TV, in-rm movies. AE, DC, MC, V. Free parking, pool, free crib. *Note:* Typical motel nr. the canyon entrance; adj. coffee shop open 7am–9pm. Designed and furnished in the Navajo style. Open year round. **I–M,** but lower rates off-season.

ON THE HOPI RESERVATION ☀🍴 **Hopi Cultural Center,** Ariz. 264 at Piñon Rd., Second Mesa, AZ 86043 (602/734-2401). 33 rms, A/C, cable color TV. AE, DC, MC, V. Free parking, rest. *Note:* Motel of unusual Pueblo design, functionally comfortable. Very acceptable rest. serving Hopi or American food, open until 8pm (to 10pm in summer). No alcoholic beverages. Among the typical Hopi dishes are nok qui ve (stew of hominy and mutton) and ba duf su ki (stew of pinto beans and hominy). Adj. museum and craft shop. Don't miss staying here, but you'll need to reserve way ahead. Motel and rest. open year round. **I**

ON THE NAVAJO RESERVATION ✵**Navajo Nation Inn,** Ariz. 264, Window Rock, AZ 86515 (602/871-4108). 52 rms, A/C, color TV. AE, MC, V. Free parking, rest. *Note:* Typical small motel next to the Navajo Museum. Rest. open until 9pm. No alcoholic beverages. **I**

IN RAINBOW BRIDGE The **Wahweap Lodge and Marina** and **Holiday Inn Page** (see Chapter 32 on Utah National Parks).

CHAPTER 41

GRAND CANYON NATIONAL PARK ♦♦♦♦

□ □ □

Discovered in 1540 by the Spaniard Garcia Lopez de Cárdenas, a member of Vásquez de Coronado's famous gold-seeking expedition, the Grand Canyon is one of the seven natural wonders of the world. It has taken more than 16 million years for the surging current of the Colorado River to carve its way down through the gray-white limestone, red sandstone, and green clay schist of the Kaibab Plateau; wind, heat, snow, and frost have done the rest. A true force of nature, the Colorado River in flood can run 224 ft. (70m) deep and 288 ft. (90m) wide. The river's intense yellow-brown color comes from the huge quantities of silt and alluvium that are continuously carried along. The gorges reach a height of 5,120 ft. (1,600m) in some places, and comprise an open book of terrestrial evolution: from the hard pre-Cambrian rocks (2 *billion* years old, the oldest on the planet), to the soft, fossil-rich tertiary rocks. Separated by 18 mi. (30km) at their widest points, the canyon's two rims offer extraordinary vistas over the 277-mi. (445km) stretch of canyon, and are accessible by car as well as on foot. The glorious views, notably at sunrise and sunset, make this masterpiece of creation one of the most astounding natural settings in the United States, and an ideal place for watching the wildlife, which includes 250 species of birds, 70 of mammals, 27 of reptiles, and 5 of amphibians.

The Grand Canyon of the Colorado (situated in Arizona; it's named for the river, not the state) became a national park in 1919. The **South Rim**—the more accessible—is open year round; the **North Rim** is open in summer only. Near **Grand Canyon Village,** the two rims are connected by a steep footpath of 21 mi. (34km); the road distance is closer to 218 mi. (350km).

Given the profusion of summer tourists and the relatively limited accommodations of the park, it's strongly advised that reservations be made weeks—if not months—in advance. This is true also for those who plan to go rafting down the Colorado or descend into the canyon on mule-back (see "Adventure Tours," below). About four million people visit the Grand Canyon each year.

BASIC FACTS: State of Arizona. Area code: 602. Time zone: mountain. ZIP Codes: 86023 (South Rim), 86052 (North Rim). First discovered by Europeans: 1540. Park dimensions: 1,875 sq. mi. (4,856km²). A national park since 1919.

CLIMATE: In summer, the tourist season par excellence, the high country of Arizona is very hot. Brief but violent downpours are a feature of virtually every July and Aug noontime. *Warning:* If the ground-level temperature is 95° – 104° F (35° – 40° C), it can easily reach 122° F (50° C) in the depths of the canyon. Winter is bitterly cold, with regular snowfalls which create a new and splendid landscape. The two ideal seasons for a visit to the Grand Canyon are autumn and especially spring, when the wildflowers are in bloom.

DISTANCES (from Grand Canyon Village): Albuquerque, 404 mi. (647km); Las Vegas, 291 mi. (465km); Los Angeles, 533 mi. (852km); Phoenix, 218 mi. (350km); Salt Lake City, 518 mi. (828km); San Francisco, 819 mi. (1,310km).

ARRIVAL & TRANSIT INFORMATION

NEAREST AIRPORTS: There is one local airport, and two others nearby.

SOUTH RIM   **Grand Canyon Airport** (GCN): 6 mi. (10km) south. Daily connections with Las Vegas and Phoenix.
Flagstaff Pulliam Field (FLG): 80 mi. (129km) SE. Daily connections with Phoenix.

NORTH RIM   **Page Municipal Airport** (PGA): 120 mi. (198km) NE. Daily connections with Las Vegas and Salt Lake City.

AIRLINES: At **Grand Canyon Airport:** Air Nevada (toll free 800/634-6377) and Scenic Airlines (toll free 800/634-6801).
In **Flagstaff:** America West (toll free 800/235-9292) and Delta Connection (toll free 800/221-1212).

CAR RENTAL (at Pulliam Airport in Flagstaff unless indicated): Avis (toll free 800/331-1212); Budget (toll free 800/527-0700); Dollar (toll free 800/800-4000); Hertz (toll free 800/654-3131); and National, 2320 Lucky Lane, Flagstaff (toll free 800/227-7368).

BUS OR CAR RENTAL? Given the distances and the advantageous rental fees in Arizona as well as in neighboring California, renting a car with unlimited mileage is particularly recommended. Hitchhiking is prohibited inside Grand Canyon National Park.

TRAIN: The closest Amtrak station is at 1 E. Santa Fe Ave., Flagstaff (toll free 800/872-7245).

INTERCITY BUSES: Greyhound buses are not permitted in Grand Canyon National Park. The closest Greyhound station is at 399 S. Malpais Lane, Flagstaff (toll free 800/231-2222). Connections between Flagstaff and the Grand Canyon via **Gray Line/Nava-Hopi** (774-5003); twice a day.

SEEING THE GRAND CANYON

TOURIST INFORMATION: Write or phone the **Arizona Office of Tourism,** 1100 W. Washington St., Phoenix, AZ 85007 (602/542-8687); **Kaibab National Forest,** Forest Supervisor, 800 S. 6th St., Williams, AZ 86046 (602/635-2681); or **Grand Canyon Chamber of Commerce,** P.O. Box 3007, AZ 86023 (602/638-2901).
On site, go to the **Visitor Center,** Grand Canyon Village (eastern area). Open daily.
For a **recorded telephone message** with weather conditions, tourist advice, and road conditions 24 hr. a day, call 602/638-7888.

GUIDED TOURS: Bus Tours: Grand Canyon National Park Lodges, Grand Canyon Village (638-2401).

Grand Canyon Railway (train) (toll free 800/843-8724): After a gap of 21 years steam trains again run along the 64-mi. (103km) route from Williams to the South Rim of the Grand Canyon, daily Apr–Oct (call for days of operation during Feb, Mar, Nov, and Dec); time, 2 hr. 15 min. each way; fares $48 round-trip for adults, $15 for children 12 and under. Spectacular.

Plane rides over the Grand Canyon: Grand Canyon Airlines, Grand Canyon Airport (10 mi./16km south) (638-2407). Impressive.

Helicopter rides over the Grand Canyon: Papillon Helicopters, Tusayan Heliport (8mi./13km south) (638-2419). From $80. Unforgettable.

ADVENTURE TOURS: Rafting down the Colorado (3–18 days): 22 authorized operators. For locations and rates, contact River Unit, Grand Canyon National Park, AZ 86023 (602/638-2401). Resv. must be made weeks (or months) in advance. The cost is about $150–$200 per day.

Walking excursions between the two rims (Kaibab Trail and Bright Angel Trail): 12 hr. minimum (it takes 3–4 hr. to hike to the bottom on the popular Bright Angel Trail and twice as long to trek back up to the rim). This trek is physically trying, even for seasoned hikers, especially in summer when the temperature can reach 122°F (50°C) at the bottom of the canyon. Be sure to bring reserves of water and food, and don't stray from the trails under any circumstances. For information, call 638-7888 Mon–Fri.

Mule-back excursions between the two rims (resv. mandatory): Grand Canyon National Park Lodges, Grand Canyon Village (638-2401). People weighing more than 200 lb. (91kg), pregnant women, children under age 12, those who don't speak fluent English, and those susceptible to vertigo are prohibited. In winter the descent ends at Phantom Ranch (5-hr. trip). Guided mule trips cost from $25 (half day) to $52 (full day) per person; reserve six months ahead.

SIGHTS, ATTRACTIONS & ACTIVITIES

SOUTH RIM: ☼♙♙ **West Rim Drive,** 18 mi. (13km) west of Grand Canyon Village: Splendid views over the canyon at **Maricopa Point, Hopi Point, Mohave Point, Pima Point** (the most beautiful view of the South Rim), and **Hermit's Rest,** a large, rustic building that dates from 1914. Private cars are prohibited on this road between May and mid-Sept. (there's a free shuttle bus).

☼♙♙♙ **East Rim Drive,** 23 mi. (37km) east of Grand Canyon Village: Comprises, with West Rim Dr., one of the most beautiful spectacles in creation. Superb panoramas of the canyon at **Yavapai Point** (with an interesting museum), **Yaki Point, Grandview Point** (one of the loveliest views of the canyon), **Moran Point, Tusayan Ruins** (with an interesting museum), and **Desert View.** Enjoy an incomparable view of the **Painted Desert** and the neighboring forest from atop the restored **Indian Watchtower.** Private cars are permitted on this road year round.

NORTH RIM (open summer only): ♙ **Bright Angel Point:** This spot offers a wonderful view of the canyon and is the point of departure for trips to the bottom of the gorge and toward the South Rim.

☼♙♙♙ **Cape Royal:** At an elevation of 8,576 ft. (2,614m), this is the most magnificent view of the canyon and the Painted Desert. On the way, don't miss the view from Point Imperial, the highest point of either rim (8,803 ft./2,683m).

☼♙♙ **Point Sublime:** Worthy of its name, this point is reachable only in dry weather via a 17-mi. (27km) unpaved road.

☼♙♙ **EXCURSIONS BETWEEN THE TWO RIMS** (218 mi./350km via Ariz. 64E, U.S. 89N, Alt. U.S. 89W, and Ariz.

67S): Besides the rigorous Kaibab Trail and Bright Angel Trail, mentioned previously (see "Adventure Tours," above), there is a magnificent car route along the South Rim—the barren reaches of **Echo Cliffs** and **Vermilion Cliffs** and the dense conifer forest of the **Kaibab Plateau.** On the way you'll get a unique perspective on the Colorado River from **Navajo Bridge,** one of the most spectacular spots in Arizona, which overlooks the riverbed from a height of more than 467 ft. (140m). This is a two-day trip, with recommended lodging at the Grand Canyon Lodge or the Kaibab Lodge (see "Accommodations and Restaurants, North Rim," below).

MUSEUMS: ⚶ **Tusayan Ruins,** 20 mi. (32km) west of Grand Canyon Village: Traces of an Anasazi community from the 12th century and an archeological museum. Open daily.

　　　　⚶ **Yavapai Museum,** Grand Canyon Village: An interesting geological history of the Grand Canyon. Open daily.

OTHER ATTRACTIONS: ⚶⚶ **Grand Canyon Imax Theater,** Ariz. 64 and U.S. 180 at the south entrance to the park (638-2203): Discover the "hidden secrets" of the Grand Canyon on this original Imax motion picture shown on a seven-story-high, 82-in.-wide (2m) screen in 34 min. Spectacular.

WINTER SPORTS RESORTS: ⚶ **Fairfield Snow Bowl,** 73 mi. (117km) SE of the Grand Canyon on U.S. 180: Cross-country and downhill (2,300-ft./690m slope) skiing. Eight chair lifts. Open mid-Nov to mid-Apr. For information, call 779-6126 (or 779-4577 for snow conditions).

ACCOMMODATIONS & RESTAURANTS

Reservations Inside the National Park

The National Park Service has contracted out all the food and lodging places inside Grand Canyon National Park to concessionaires, one for the North Rim and another for the South Rim. For reservations anywhere inside the park, contact the concessionaires directly:

South Rim: Contact Grand Canyon National Park Lodges, P.O. Box 699, Grand Canyon, AZ 86203 (602/638-2401).

North Rim: Contact T. W. Services, 451 N. Main St. (P.O. Box 400), Cedar City, UT 84720 (801/586-7686).

Inside the Park (South Rim)

Note: In general, thanks to the Fred Harvey Co., in all food and lodging places on the South Rim the service is not up to par, the reception is barely civil, with unprofessional personnel who are perpetually snowed under, waits at the restaurants (where the cuisine is mediocre and expensive) can be two hours long and reservations are not always honored.

　　　☀⚶ **El Tovar Hotel,** Village Loop Dr., AZ 86203 (602/638-2631). 76 rms, A/C, cable color TV. AE, CB, DC, MC, V. Free parking, rest., bar, rm svce, night club, boutique, free airport shuttle, free crib. *Note:* Exceptional location on the edge of the canyon. The rustic 1905 architecture—squared-off tree trunks and boulders—may lack sophistication, but it has a certain charm. Functional rm comfort (some rms are cramped); there are a few suites w. balconies and a splendid view of the Grand Canyon. **M–E**

　　　⚶ **Maswik North,** U.S. 180W, AZ 86023 (602/638-2631). 160 rms, A/C, cable color TV. AE, CB, DC, MC, V. Free parking, coffee shop, bar, free crib. *Note:* The latest addition to Grand Canyon motels offers functional rms, some w. private balconies. **M**

Kachina Lodge, Village Loop Dr., AZ 86023 (602/638-2631). 48 rms, cable color TV. AE, CB, DC, MC, V. Free parking, check-in at the El Tovar Hotel, adj. coffee shop, free crib. *Note:* Relatively modern motel w. functional rms, the best of which afford a view of the canyon. **M**

Thunderbird Lodge, Village Loop Dr., AZ 86023 (602/638-2631). 55 rms, cable color TV. AE, CB, DC, MC, V. Free parking, check-in at the Bright Angel Lodge, adj. coffee shop, free crib. *Note:* Relatively modern motel that adjoins the Bright Angel Lodge. Functional rms, the best of which afford a view of the canyon. **M**

Bright Angel Lodge, W. Rim Dr., AZ 86023 (602/638-2631). 37 rms (15 w. bath), 50 bungalows, cable color TV. AE, CB, DC, MC, V. Free parking, coffee shop, bar, nightclub, organized raft trips down the Colorado and mule-back excursions down into the canyon, free crib. *Note:* Old, rustic building surrounded by bungalows. Average comfort. A few rms w. views of the canyon. **I–M**

Yavapai Lodge, Mather Center, AZ 86023 (602/638-2631). 351 rms, cable color TV. AE, CB, DC, MC, V. Free parking, coffee shop, bar, disco, grocery store, free crib. *Note:* Functional motel in a pine grove across from the Visitors Center. **I**

Maswik Lodge, U.S. 180W, AZ 86023 (602/638-2631). 90 rms, 38 bungalows. AE, CB, DC, MC, V. Free parking, coffee shop, bar. *Note:* A tree-shaded rustic motel and individual bungalows. Rudimentary comfort. Closed Nov–Apr. **I–M**

Phantom Ranch, on the canyon floor, Grand Canyon Village, AZ 86023 (602/638-2631). 40 beds in the dormitory and 10 bunk-bedded cabins. AE, CB, DC, MC, V. Pool, fishing, coffee shop. *Note:* The Grand Canyon's most spectacular and most authentic hotel. At the foot of the gorge, accessible only on foot or mule-back (at least a five-hour trip). Interesting mule-rental/lodging/meals package. Resv. necessary six months in advance for summer visits, as authorized descents into the canyon are limited to 90 people per day. **B–I**

Inside the Park (North Rim)

Grand Canyon Lodge, Bright Angel Point, AZ 86052 (602/638-2611; resv. through T. W. Services). 40 rms and 160 individual cottages, A/C. AE, CB, DC, MC, V. Free parking, rest., coffee shop, bar, movie theater, crib $5. *Note:* The relatively modern, functional motel and the rustic cottages for two to five people (the "western cabins" are the best choice) afford a magnificent view of the canyon. Adequate rest. Organizes raft trips down the Colorado and mule-back trips along the rim. Closed Oct–May. **B–I**

Outside the Park (South Rim)

Best Western Grand Canyon Squire Inn, Ariz. 64, AZ 86023 (602/638-2681; toll free, see Best Western), 2 mi. (3km) south of the park entrance. 250 rms, A/C, cable color TV. AE, CB, DC, MC, V. Free parking, pool, hot tub, tennis, bowling, sauna, rest., coffee shop, bar, crib available. *Note:* This relatively modern motel is one of the most appealing and comfortable in the entire Grand Canyon area. Rustic, Native American–style decor. No-smoking rms. A 15-min. car ride from Grand Canyon Village. **M,** but lower rates off-season.

Moqui Lodge, Ariz. 64, AZ 86023 (602/638-2424), at the park entrance. 135 rms, cable color TV. AE, CB, DC, MC, V. Free parking, horseback riding, coffee shop, bar. *Note:* This convenient and basic motel offers reasonable comfort in 10 min. from the canyon. Closed Dec–Jan. **I–M,** but lower rates off-season.

Quality Inn Grand Canyon, Ariz. 64, AZ 86023 (602/638-2673; toll free, see Choice), 1 mi. (1.6km) south of the park entrance. 176 rms, A/C, color TV. AE, DC, MC, V. Free parking, pool, rest.,

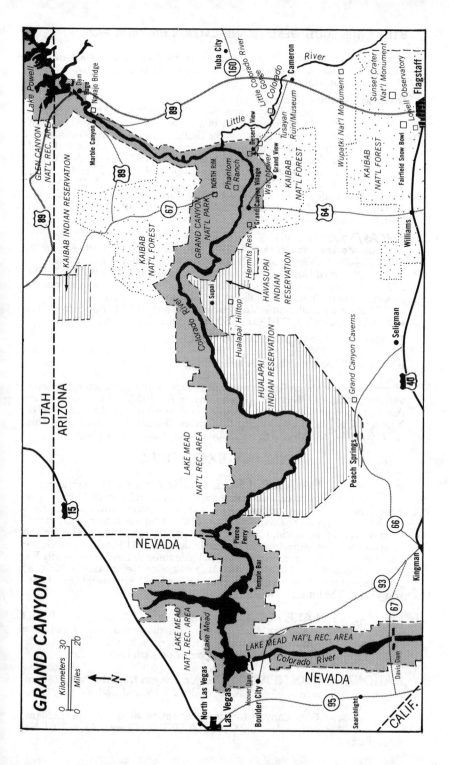

crib $10. *Note:* Modern, comfortable motel w. spacious, balconied rms and cheerful reception; some rms w. minibar. 10 min. from Grand Canyon Village. **M,** but lower rates off-season.

Outside the Park (North Rim)

Kaibab Lodge, Ariz. 67, AZ 86022 (602/638-2389; toll free 800/525-0924). 24 bungalows. MC, V. Free parking, rest. *Note:* Small, pleasant motel away from the Grand Canyon crowds, 30 min. north of the North Rim. Ideal for the motorist. Fine location in the heart of Kaibab National Forest. Excellent value. Open mid-May to mid-Oct and Dec–Mar. **I–M**

Jacob Lake Inn, at the junction of Alt. U.S. 89 and Ariz. 67, AZ 86051 (602/643-7232). 36 rms. AE, CB, DC, MC, V. Free parking, coffee shop, grocery store. *Note:* Rustic motel in Kaibab National Forest, 44 mi. (70km) north of the North Rim. Modest but functional comfort. Motel units and cabins. **B–I**

YMCAs/Youth Hostels

Downtowner Youth Hostel, 19 S. San Francisco, Flagstaff, AZ 86001 (602/774-8461). Very clean, well-run hostel. Open mid-May to late Aug.

Weatherford Hostel, 23 N. Leroux St., Flagstaff, AZ 86001 (602/774-2731). 60 beds. Individual rms or dormitory accommodations in a beautiful almost-100-year-old hotel w. coffee shop. Close to the train station.

An alternative solution is **Motel 6** (nr. dwntwn), 2010 E. Butler Ave., Flagstaff, AZ 86001 (602/774-1801). 150 rms. Pool. AE, DC, MC, V. **B**

Backpacking Campgrounds and Campsites

Permits are required for overnight hikes (but not for day hikes) in the national park. Permits are issued for three campgrounds, including Bright Angel at the bottom of the canyon near Phantom Ranch, and for 10 campsites, including Hermit Rapids at the end of Hermit Trail. For reservations, **Backcountry Reservations Office,** P.O. Box 129, Grand Canyon, AZ 86023. Hikers may also appear in person at a reservation office (on both rims) on the day of their hike. Names will be placed on a waiting list for cancellations. For information only, call 602/638-7888 Mon–Fri; reservations are not accepted by phone.

NEARBY EXCURSIONS

HAVASUPAI RESERVATION (62 mi./100km along an unpaved road from Ariz, 66 after Grand Canyon Caverns, plus 8 mi./13km on foot or horseback to the bottom of Grand Canyon): This primitive Native American reservation with its 300 inhabitants is completely cut off from the rest of the world. Camping is $10 per day per person, and there's an inexpensive 24-rm bungalow, **Havasupai Lodge;** add a $12 registration fee, but resv. are a must. Accommodations are available through Havasupai Tourist Enterprise, Supai, AZ 86435 (602/448-2121). **Papillon Helicopters** (638-2419) provides exclusive air service to the remote Havasupai Village from Grand Canyon Village. The ultimate change of scene.

LAKE POWELL (138 mi./220km NE on Ariz. 64W and U.S. 89N): Water sports and magnificent landscapes, including the celebrated **Rainbow Bridge,** the largest natural arch in the world (span of 272 ft./85m). For more details, see Chapter 32 on Utah National Parks.

NATIONAL PARKS NEARBY: **Bryce Canyon National Park,** 285 mi. (456km) north via Ariz. 64W, U.S. 89N, Alt. U.S. 89, and Utah 9W: See Chapter 32 on Utah National Parks.

Glen Canyon National Recreation Area, 138 mi. (220km) NE via Ariz. 64W and U.S. 89N: See Chapter 32 on Utah National Parks.

👓 **Zion National Park,** 253 mi. (405km) NW via Ariz. 64W, U.S. 89N, Alt. U.S. 89, and Utah 12: See Chapter 32 on Utah National Parks.

FARTHER AFIELD

☀️👓 **HOPI & NAVAJO PUEBLOS** (280 mi./450km r.t. from the Grand Canyon on Ariz. 64E, U.S. 89N, U.S. 160N, Ariz. 264E): See Chapter 40 on Navajoland.

FLAGSTAFF & VICINITY (395 mi./632km r.t. on Ariz. 64S, U.S. 180W, I-17S, U.S. 89N, and Ariz. 64N): You'll need at least two days to enjoy the wonderful variety this trip offers, including the interesting sights below. **Sedona** is a suggested stopover town (for more details, see "Farther Afield" in Chapter 42 on Phoenix).

☀️👓 **Lowell Observatory,** Mars Hill Rd., Flagstaff (602/774-2096): The country's oldest observatory (1894), where the planet Pluto was discovered in 1930. Open daily Apr–Nov, Mon–Sat the rest of the year. For astronomy lovers.

☀️👓 **Meteor Crater,** 46 mi. (74km) east of Flagstaff: A meteor hit the earth 22,000 years ago on this site at a speed of 33,000 m.p.h. (52,800kmph) and left the world's best-preserved crater—4,160 ft. (1.2km) in diameter, 3 mi. (4.8km) in circumference, and 557 ft. (170m) deep. NASA uses it for astronaut training. Impressive. For information, call 602/774-8350.

☀️👓 **Montezuma Castle National Monument,** 50 mi. (80km) south of Flagstaff: Extraordinary, five-tier cave dwelling perched 64 ft. (20m) above the ground in a cliff shelter. Built by the Sinagua tribes in the 13th century, it's in remarkable condition. Open daily. For information, call 602/567-3322.

☀️👓 **Oak Creek Canyon,** 15 mi. (24km) south of Flagstaff: Splendid rocky gorge landscapes that are almost as spectacular as the Grand Canyon; they've been used as the setting for many a western film. On the way, see **Sedona,** a picturesque little pioneer town that is today dedicated to modern painting and Native American crafts.

👓 **Sunset Crater National Monument,** 17 mi. (27km) north of Flagstaff: Volcanic crater that has been dormant for nine centuries. Spectacular red-orange lava formations. Open daily. For information, call 602/556-7042.

👓 **Wupatki National Monument,** 35 mi. (56km) north of Flagstaff: Ruins of a Sinagua village from circa A.D. 1100. The main dwelling contains around 100 rooms. Archeological museum. Open daily. For information, call 602/556-7040.

LAS VEGAS (611 mi./978km r.t. from the Grand Canyon on Ariz. 64S, U.S. 40W, U.S. 93, and U.S. 95N): The world capital of gambling, in the heart of the desert (see Chapter 47 on Las Vegas). On the way, see:

👓 **Grand Canyon Caverns,** 124 mi. (198km) SW of the Grand Canyon on Ariz. 64S, U.S. 40W, and Ariz. 66 (602/422-3223): Spectacular caverns 210 ft. (64m) underground (access by elevator) with a ¾-mi. (1km) trail. Open year round. Interior temperature is 56°F (13°C).

👓 **Oatman,** 193 mi. (308km) SW of the Grand Canyon on Ariz. 64S, U.S. 40W, and old U.S. 66 SW off Kingman: Superb, remarkably preserved ghost town from the days of the gold rush. It had as many as

10,000 inhabitants around 1910, but has barely 100 today. Regularly used as the backdrop of western movies. For information, call 602/768-3839.

Lake Mead and Hoover Dam, 259 mi. (415km) west of the Grand Canyon on Ariz. 64S, U.S. 40W, and U.S. 93N: See Chapter 47 on Las Vegas.

CHAPTER 42

PHOENIX ⊖

□ □ □

Standing foursquare in the center of the **Valley of the Sun,** Arizona's capital, from the air, looks like a verdant oasis in the midst of a sandy, mountainous desert. The Hohokam, a people who mysteriously disappeared without a trace around the year A.D. 1400, appear to have devised a sophisticated irrigation system for the area, but around the turn of our century more up-to-date methods were initiated, and now Phoenix is the center of a green belt with market gardens, fields of cotton and alfalfa, citrus and olive groves, and even date palms. The city owes its name, too, to its Native American antecedents. As with the mythical bird reborn from its own ashes, the inhabitants of Phoenix have given new life to an arid plain that had been long left empty to the scorching sun.

Less than a century old, Phoenix is a successful blend of the romantic West and 20th-century America vigor. A perfect base for excursions to such vacation wonderlands as the Grand Canyon of the Colorado, Navajoland, Tucson and southern Arizona, or the Apache Trail (in the 19th century the region witnessed savage battles with the Apache under Cochise and Geronimo), Phoenix itself has become one of the principal tourist attractions of the West, especially in winter. Witness its 25,000 hotel rooms, its 80 golf courses, the **Heard Museum,** finest Native American museum in the country, and its dozen luxury grand hotels, including the famous **Arizona Biltmore** designed by the great Frank Lloyd Wright. With 300 days of sunshine a year and low humidity, **Sun City,** as Phoenix calls itself, is also a dream come true for tens of thousands of well-to-do retirees.

Covering an enormous area 25 mi. (40km) long by 40 mi. (65km) wide with its low ranch or Spanish Colonial houses, and lacking any conspicuous buildings (or even a downtown, properly so called), Phoenix may be showing us the shape of cities to come—a sort of Los Angeles in the desert, with a dizzying rate of population growth. Between 1950 and 1990 the number of people living in the city and its inner suburbs (the super-smart **Scottsdale** and **Paradise Valley,** and the less exclusive **Glendale, Mesa,** and **Tempe**) rose from 200,000 to 2,120,000—more than 900% in less than a third of a century. It comes as no surprise, then, that Phoenix enjoys the third-fastest economic growth among America's major cities, right behind Austin and Orlando.

Besides its many high-tech industries, such as electronics, telecommunications, and aerospace, Phoenix is headquarters of financial-services giant Greyhound, and of two of the largest hotel chains, Ramada Inns and Best Western.

BASIC FACTS: Capital of the state of Arizona. Area code: 602. Time zone: mountain. ZIP Code: 85026. Founded: 1864. Approximate population: city, 980,000; metropolitan area, 2,120,000. 20th-largest metropolitan area in the U.S.

CLIMATE: With one of the largest amounts of sunshine (86% sunny days) in the U.S., the inhabitants of Phoenix are the spoiled children of nature. Winter is brilliantly sunny by day (Jan average, 54°F/12°C) and cool at night. In summer the thermometer can easily rise above 95°F (35°C), but the dry desert air and the omnipresent air conditioning make the heat easy to take. Spring and fall are very pleasant, especially Apr and Oct. The rainy season is July–Aug, with only an occasional downpour in winter.

DISTANCES: Albuquerque, 453 mi. (725km); Denver, 805 mi. (1,288km); Grand Canyon National Park, 218 mi. (350km); Las Vegas, 285 mi. (456km); Los Angeles, 390 mi. (625km); Mexican border, 183 mi. (293km); Salt Lake City, 650 mi. (1,040km); San Diego, 355 mi. (568km); Tucson, 118 mi. (189km).

ARRIVAL & TRANSIT INFORMATION

AIRPORT: Phoenix Sky Harbor International (PHX), 4 mi. (6.5km) SE (273-3300).

AIRLINES: America West (toll free 800/253-9292), American (toll free 800/433-7300), Continental (toll free 800/525-0280), Delta (toll free 800/221-1212), Northwest (toll free 800/225-2525), Southwest (toll free 800/435-9792), United (toll free 800/241-6522), and USAir (toll free 800/428-4322).

CITY LINK: The **cab** fare from the airport to downtown is $7–$9 (rates vary widely among different cab companies, so inquire in advance); time, 10–15 min. Bus: **Supershuttle** (244-9000; toll free 800/331-3565); serves any address in Phoenix or the metropolitan area on request; fare, $6–$16; time, 15–20 min. Cab fares are very high, and the public bus transportation theoretically provided by **Phoenix Transit Systems/PTS** (253-5000) is almost useless in practice. There's also a free downtown shuttle **(DASH)** Mon–Fri to 6pm.

Given the size of the metropolitan area and the numerous excursion destinations around about, it makes a great deal of sense to rent a car with unlimited mileage, particularly at the low rates prevailing in Arizona.

CAR RENTAL (at the airport unless otherwise noted): Avis (toll free 800/331-1212); Budget (toll free 800/527-0700); Dollar (toll free 800/800-4000); Hertz (toll free 800/654-3131); National (toll free 800/227-7368); and Thrifty, 4114 E. Washington St. (toll free 800/367-2277). For dwntwn locations, consult the local telephone directory.

LIMOUSINE SERVICES: Arizona Limousines/Dav El (267-7097), Carey Limousine (996-1955), and Coachman Limousine (265-4667).

TAXIS: Taxis cannot be hailed on the street. Your best bet is to call **Ace Taxi** (254-1999), **Checker Cab** (257-1818), or **Yellow Cab** (252-5071). Be sure to negotiate the fare in advance.

TRAIN: Amtrak, Union Station, 401 W. Harrison St. (toll free 800/872-7245).

INTERCITY BUSES: Greyhound, 525 E. Washington St. (248-4040).

INFORMATION & TOURS

TOURIST INFORMATION: The **Arizona Office of Tourism,** 1100 W. Washington St., Phoenix, AZ 85007 (602/542-8687; toll free 800/842-8245). Information covering the whole state of Arizona. Open Mon–Fri.

Phoenix and Valley of the Sun Convention and Visitors Bureau, 400 E. Van Buren St., Phoenix, AZ 85004 (602/254-6500).
For a **telephone recording** with an up-to-date list of cultural events and shows, call 602/252-5588.

GUIDED TOURS: Gray Line (bus), (495-9100): Guided tours of Phoenix and surroundings; serves principal hotels.
Scenic Airlines (airplane), 15000 N. Airport Dr., Scottsdale (991-8252): One-day air trips over the Grand Canyon and Monument Valley.
Sky Cab (airplane), 14700 N. Airport Dr., Scottsdale (998-1778): Half- and full-day flights over the Grand Canyon, Lake Powell, Monument Valley, etc. Spectacular.

SIGHTS, ATTRACTIONS & ACTIVITIES

ADVENTURES: A Balloon Experience (balloon), 7119 E. Shea Blvd., Suite 363, Scottsdale (820-3866): Spectacular balloon overflights of Phoenix and environs.
Arizona River Runners (boat), P.O. Box 47788, Phoenix AZ 85068 (867-4866): Rafting down the Colorado River through the Grand Canyon; three-, six-, and eight-day round-trips. Apr–Sept.
Salt River Recreation (boat), P.O. Box 6568, Mesa, AZ (984-3305): Rafting near Phoenix; one-day or longer trips.
Unicorn Balloon Company (balloon), 15001 N. 74th St., Scottsdale (991-3666): Dawn or afternoon balloon rides over Phoenix and the area; spectacular.
Wilderness Adventures, P.O. Box 63282, Phoenix, AZ 85082 (220-1414): Training in backpacking, rock climbing, mountaineering, etc., with excursions to Superstition Mountains, Sonoran Desert, Grand Canyon, and so on. Great adventures year round.
Wild West Jeep Tours, Inc. (Jeep), 7127 E. Becker Lane, Suite 74, Scottsdale (941-8355): One-day excursions into the mountain and desert country around Phoenix.

ARCHITECTURAL HIGHLIGHTS: ☀☖ **A.S.U. Nelson Fine Arts Center,** the campus of Arizona State University, Tempe (965-2787): Spectacular grayish-purple stucco structure looking like a futuristic version of a Mayan sculpture. Designed by Antoine Predock, this sprawling architectural complex full of balconies, steps, loges, and arcades contains the A.S.U. Art Museum (see below), a 500-seat theater, a dance laboratory, and rehearsal halls.
☀☖ **Gammage Center for the Performing Arts,** the campus of Arizona State University, Apache Blvd. at Mill Ave., Tempe (965-3434): The last major work of Frank Lloyd Wright, opened in 1964 after his death. The huge auditorium, a great architect's celebration of the curved line, has astonishing acoustics. Guided tours Mon–Fri.
☖ **Mystery Castle,** 7 mi. (11km) south on Central Ave. at 800 E. Mineral Rd., Phoenix (268-1581): A huge, bizarre structure at the foot of South Mountain Park, built by hand between 1927 and 1945 by the solitary eccentric Boyce Luther Gulley from a wide assortment of scavenged materials. It boasts no fewer than 18 rooms and 13 fireplaces, not to mention a chapel and a strange cantilevered staircase. Open Tues–Sun Oct–July 4.
☖ **State Capitol,** W. Washington St. and 17th Ave., Phoenix (542-4581): The home of the Arizona legislature is an imposing turn-of-the-century structure in limestone and Arizona granite, capped with

a copper-plated dome. Interesting museum of western history, open Mon–Fri. The beautiful gardens display a comprehensive selection of the local flora.

☀� **Symphony Hall,** Civic Plaza, 225 E. Adams St., Phoenix (264-4754): Ultramodern auditorium where the Phoenix Symphony makes its home, across from the famous **Convention Center.** The huge central court, embellished with fountains and statues, lies above an underground parking lot with more than 1,000 spaces.

CHURCHES/SYNAGOGUES: 🏛 Mormon Temple, 14 mi. (22km) east on

U.S. 60 at 525 E. Main St., Mesa (964-7164): Mormon Temple of unusual design in a lovely garden. Non-Mormons not admitted to the temple, but visitor center open daily, with audiovisual program on the history of the Mormon religion.

🏛 **St. Francis Xavier Church,** 4715 N. Central Ave., Phoenix (279-9547): Beautiful Jesuit church dating from 1959. On the facade, the statues of the Jesuit Fr. Eusebio Kino, the great missionary to Arizona, and of the famous Franciscan Fr. Junípero Serra, who evangelized California, stand on either side of St. Francis Xavier, one of the most illustrious members of the Society of Jesus. Inside, splendid stained-glass windows by Gabriel Loire. Open daily.

MUSEUMS OF ART: ☀🏛 A.S.U. Art Museum, on the campus of Arizona

State University, Tempe (965-2787): Historical survey of American painting and sculpture, Native American and Latin American art, plus a comprehensive print collection. American crockery and contemporary ceramics. Spectacular architecture. Open Tues–Sun.

☀🏛 **Phoenix Art Museum,** 1625 N. Central Ave., Phoenix (257-1222): This interesting, relatively young (1969) museum displays 18th- to 20th-century French painting (Boucher, Greuze, Courbet, Fantin-Latour, Watteau, Dufy, Picasso), Oriental miniatures, and a fine collection of western art including works by Frederic Remington, Robert Henri, Charles Marion Russell, and the like. Open Tues–Sun.

MUSEUMS OF SCIENCE & HISTORY: 🏛 Arizona Historical Society

Museum, 1300 N. College Ave., Tempe (929-0292): Photographs and artifacts illustrating the 20th-century history of Central Arizona. Topics include tourism, retirement, World War II, and the building of the Roosevelt Dam. Open Tues–Sat. (The museum is planned to open sometime in 1995. Call ahead.)

🏛 **Arizona Mineral Museum,** 1502 W. Washington St., Phoenix (255-3791): From gold nuggets to copper ore, by way of precious stones and slices of petrified wood, a complete selection of the geological riches of Arizona. Interesting. Mon–Fri.

🏛 **Center for Meteorite Studies,** Arizona State University campus, University Dr., Tempe (965-3576): Distinguished center for meteorite studies, with one of the world's largest collections (1,400 items) of extraterrestrial objects. For ardent astronomers. Open Mon–Fri.

🏛 **Hall of Flame Museum,** 6101 E. Van Buren St., Phoenix (275-3473): A large museum entirely devoted to fire-fighting paraphernalia. Interesting collection of old fire engines, the oldest going back to 1725. Amusing. Open daily.

☀🏛🏛🏛 **Heard Museum,** 22 E. Monte Vista Rd., Phoenix (252-8840): The finest and one of the largest museums of anthropology and primitive art in the U.S., housed in an elegant Spanish Mission–style building. Although it has some African, Asian, and Oceanic pieces of quality, the museum has specialized since its foundation in 1929 in the Amerindian cultures, particularly those of the Southwest, and especially the Hohokam, Mogollon, Anasazi, and Pueblo. Fine hall of prehistoric arts and a splendid group of Kachina dolls given by former Sen. Barry Goldwater; also exhibitions of contemporary Native American art. Spanish Colonial room evidencing the Spanish cultural influence on the southwestern U.S. and Mexico. Open daily.

Phoenix Museum of History, 1002 W. Van Buren St., Phoenix (253-2734): 2,000 years of Arizona history from prehistoric times through the civilization of the Hohokam peoples and the first European settlements to the present day. Fascinating. Open Wed–Sun.

Pueblo Grande Museum, 4619 E. Washington St., Phoenix (495-0900): Site of excavations that have unearthed a Native American village more than 2,000 years old. An observation platform allows you to follow the diggings under way, particularly on irrigation canals cut between the 6th and 8th centuries A.D. Remarkable archeological museum. Pueblo Grande was inhabited between 300 B.C. and A.D. 1450 by the mysterious Hohokam people. Open daily.

PANORAMAS: Arizona Club, 241 N. Central Ave., Phoenix (253-1121): Restaurant on the 37th floor of the Bank One Building with the best view of the city and the mountains (admission fee). The food is unimpressive but the bar is congenial. Open Mon–Sat (until midnight).

South Mountain Park, 10919 S. Central Ave., Phoenix (495-0222): Fine view of the city and the Valley of the Sun from **Dobbins Lookout** at 2,330 ft. (710m).

PARKS & GARDENS: **Desert Botanical Garden,** 1201 N. Galvin Pkwy. at Papago Park, Phoenix (941-1225): All kinds of desert vegetation, including 1,400 different species of cactus, growing in a beautiful 150-acre (60ha) mountainside park. An energetic 45-min. walk, but well worth it. Spectacular cactus exhibition in Mar. Open daily.

Encanto Park, N. 15th Ave. and W. Encanto Blvd., Phoenix: Golf, tennis, and canoeing in the heart of town; the inviting lake is a wildlife reserve for waterfowl.

South Mountain Park, 10919 S. Central Ave., Phoenix (495-0222): Large mountainous park covering 16,000 acres (6,475ha), with scenic drives, unspoiled canyons, weird rock formations, and dozens of miles of hiking trails—nature in the raw, 15 min. from downtown. Fine view of the city and valley.

Squaw Peak Recreation Area, 2701 E. Squaw Peak Dr., Phoenix (262-7901): Northeast of town in the foothills of the Phoenix Mountains, this steeply contoured park has a 1.2-mi. (2km) trail with a panoramic view of the city.

PERFORMING ARTS: For daily listings of all shows and cultural events, consult the entertainment pages of the daily papers *Arizona Republic* (morning) and *Phoenix Gazette* (evening), as well as of the monthly *Phoenix* magazine.

Celebrity Theater, 440 N. 32nd St., Phoenix (244-0404): Comedy, drama, concerts, Broadway hits.

Gammage Center for the Performing Arts, on the campus of Arizona State University, Apache Blvd. at Mill Ave., Tempe (965-3434): Contemporary theater, ballet, classical concerts in a Frank Lloyd Wright auditorium (see "Architectural Highlights," above).

Herberger Theater Center, 222 E. Monroe St., Phoenix (252-8497): New cultural complex with two adjoining theaters. There are more than 600 performances (Broadway shows, contemporary theater) a year.

Kerr Cultural Center, 6110 N. Scottsdale Rd., Scottsdale (965-5377): Concerts of classical music, recitals, stage plays.

Phoenix Little Theater, Civic Center, 25 E. Coronado Rd., Phoenix (254-2151): Contemporary theater (highly eclectic programs).

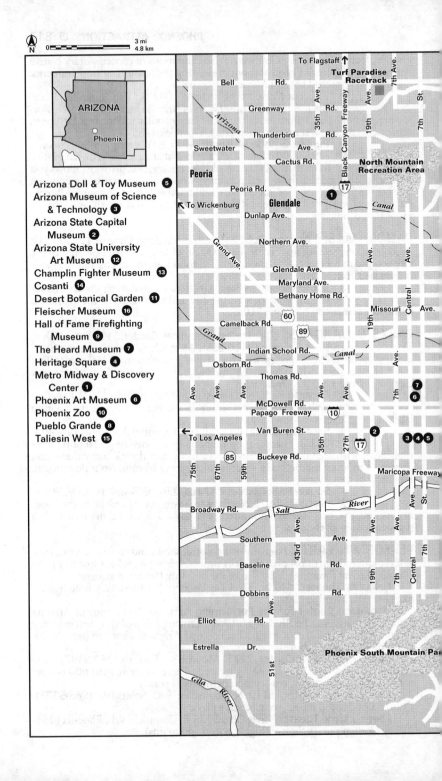

PHOENIX ATTRACTIONS

Arizona Doll & Toy Museum **5**

Arizona Museum of Science & Technology **3**

Arizona State Capital Museum **2**

Arizona State University Art Museum **12**

Champlin Fighter Museum **13**

Cosanti **14**

Desert Botanical Garden **11**

Fleischer Museum **16**

Hall of Fame Firefighting Museum **9**

The Heard Museum **7**

Heritage Square **4**

Metro Midway & Discovery Center **1**

Phoenix Art Museum **6**

Phoenix Zoo **10**

Pueblo Grande **8**

Taliesin West **15**

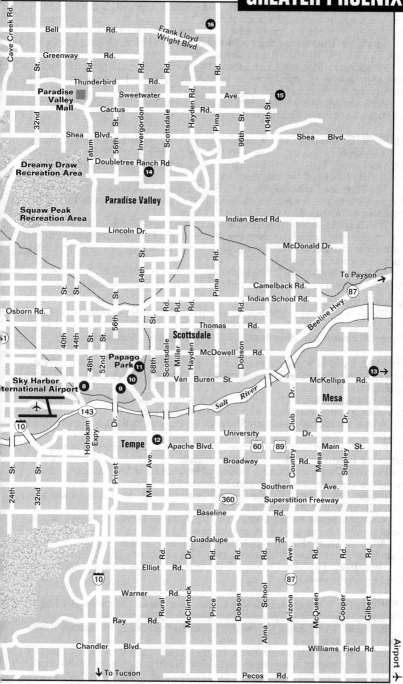

GREATER PHOENIX

Scottsdale Center for the Arts, 7383 Scottsdale Mall, Scottsdale (994-2787): Contemporary and classic theater, dance, chamber music, concerts. Home of the Arizona Theatre Company. Annual Shakespeare Festival.
Sundome Theater for the Performing Arts, 19403 R. H. Johnson Blvd., Sun City West (975-1900): Big-name recitals.
Symphony Hall, Civic Center Plaza, 2nd and Monroe Sts. (264-6363): Ultramodern home of the Phoenix Symphony (principal conductor: James Sedares) and the Arizona Opera Company.
Veterans Memorial Coliseum, 1826 W. McDowell Rd., Phoenix (258-6711): Rock concerts; leading pop stars.

SHOPPING: Arizona Center, on Van Buren between 3rd and 5th Sts., Phoenix (271-4000): Phoenix's answer to the Big Apple's South Street Seaport or Boston's Faneuil Hall. An oasis of bars, restaurants, and shops opened in 1990 on eight city blocks of dwntwn Phoenix.
The **Biltmore Fashion Park,** 2470 E. Camelback Rd., Phoenix (955-8400): 50 luxury stores and restaurants, including Saks Fifth Avenue, Gucci, and Ralph Lauren, in an ultramodern setting. High fashion.
The Borgata, 6166 N. Scottsdale Rd., Scottsdale (998-1822): One of the most imaginative, luxurious shopping centers in the U.S., its architecture modeled on that of a medieval Italian village (whence the name). Some 50 stores and shops of surpassing elegance.
Fifth Avenue Shops, 7120 Fifth Ave., Scottsdale (949-7997): 150 shops, art galleries, luxury ready-to-wear, and restaurants. Very elegant atmosphere.

Native American Art
For lovers of authentic Native American art, visit the **Heard Museum Shop,** 22 E. Monte Vista Rd., Phoenix: **Godber's,** Metrocenter, 9653A Metro Pkwy. W.; and **Atkinson's Trading Post,** 3597 N. Brown Ave., Scottsdale.

SPECIAL EVENTS: For the exact schedule of events below, consult the **Phoenix and Valley of the Sun Convention and Visitors Bureau** (see "Tourist Information," above).
Fiesta Bowl Classic (Jan 1): Three days of festivities, parades, and concerts, culminating in the renowned Fiesta Bowl football game.
Arizona National Livestock Show (Jan): Popular cattle show; guaranteed local color.
Phoenix Open Golf Tournament (Jan): The world's greatest players compete at the Tournament Players Club, Scottsdale.
World's Championship JCs Rodeo of Rodeos (mid-Mar): Rodeo championships, horseback parades; everyone's a cowboy on this day.
Indian Fair (Mar): Exhibitions of Native American crafts; traditional dances; food festival. At the Heard Museum.
Wrangler Jeans Rodeo Showdown (Oct): One of the Southwest's largest, complete with country-and-western concerts.
Arizona State Fair (mid-Oct): One of the Southwest's biggest fair-exhibitions; cattle show, public concerts, games, etc. Plenty of atmosphere.
Thunderbird Balloon Classic (Nov): Air-balloon races drawing competitors from around the world.

SPORTS: The Phoenix area is home to one major-league and two minor-league professional teams:
Baseball (Apr–Aug): Firebirds, Scottsdale Stadium, Scottsdale (275-0500); minor league.
In addition, seven major-league baseball teams have their spring-training camps in the Phoenix area (Feb–Mar): California Angels, Tempe Diablo Stadium, Tempe (438-9300); Chicago Cubs, Ho Ho Kam Park, Mesa (964-4467); Milwaukee Brewers, Compadre Stadium, Chandler (895-1200); Oakland Ath-

letics, Phoenix Stadium, Phoenix (397-0217); San Diego Padres, Peoria Stadium, Peoria (412-4213); San Francisco Giants, Scottsdale Stadium, Scottsdale (990-7972); and Seattle Mariners, Peoria Stadium, Peoria (412-4213).

Basketball (Oct–May): Suns, America West Arena, Phoenix (379-7900).

Football (Sept–Dec): Cardinals, Sun Devil Stadium, Tempe (379-0101).

Dog Racing
Greyhound Park, 3801 E. Washington St., Phoenix (273-7181): Daily year round.

Horse Racing
Turf Paradise, 1501 W. Bell Rd., Phoenix (942-1101): Sept–May.

Tubing
Arizona's most popular summer sport: floating down the rapids of the Salt River or the Verde River on well-inflated inner tubes; helmets must be worn because of the rocks. Spectacular and not really risky. More than 20,000 enthusiasts meet every weekend (mid-Apr to mid-Oct) at **Salt River Recreation, Inc.,** 33 mi. (54km) east via U.S. 60 (Apache Blvd.) and Bush Hwy. Mesa; for information, call 984-3305.

STROLLS: ☀️⛺ **Heritage Square,** E. Monroe and 7th Sts., Phoenix (262-5071): A group of perfectly restored 19th-century houses, including the very typical **Rosson House,** open Wed–Sun, once the luxurious home of Dr. Roland Rosson who was mayor around 1895; and the **Silva House Museum,** open Tues –Sun. The historic heart of Phoenix; shops and restaurants.

☀️⛺ **Scottsdale,** around Scottsdale and Osborn Rds., Scottsdale: The smart suburb of Phoenix, with luxury hotels, fashionable restaurants, elegant shops, art galleries (around Fifth Ave. and Main St.), and the amazing **Borgata** at 6166 N. Scottsdale Rd. (see "Shopping," above), the last word in shopping centers.

THEME PARKS: ☀️⛺ **Big Surf,** 1500 N. Hayden Rd., Tempe (947-7873): 5-ft. (2m) artificial waves for surfers, in a huge lagoon-pool. Spectacular; open daily Memorial Day–Labor Day.

☀️⛺ **Rawhide,** 23023 N. Scottsdale Rd., Scottsdale (563-1880): Re-created 1880s Far West village; shops, restaurants, rodeos, stagecoach rides, mock gunfire. Entertaining; if you love western movies, this is for you. Open daily.

ZOOS: ⛺ **Phoenix Zoo,** 5810 E. Van Buren St., Papago Park, Phoenix (273-7771): Modern, comprehensive zoo with some 1,300 animals in reconstructions of their natural habitats, including a herd of very rare Arabian oryx. Pretty scenery; mini-train for visitors. Open daily.

ACCOMMODATIONS

Personal Favorites (in order of preference)
☀️♟♟♟♟ **Hyatt Regency Scottsdale at Gainey Ranch** (vic.), 7500 E. Doubletree Ranch Rd., Scottsdale, AZ 85258 (602/991-3388; toll free, see Hyatt). 475 rms or suites and 13 individual villas, A/C, color TV, in-rm movies. AE, CB, DC, MC, V. Free valet parking, 10 pools, health club, sauna, three golf courses, eight tennis courts, putting green, boating, bicycling, two rests. (including the Golden Swan), coffee shop, three bars, 24-hr. rm svce, nightclub, concierge, free crib. *Note:* New ultra-luxurious resort complex on a little lake w. private beach, three-story water slide, and Venetian gondolas.

Elegant Mediterranean-style buildings and spectacular lobby w. three-story-high modern sculpture. Spacious suites w. minibars and private balconies; individual villas w. two or four bedrooms. Very comprehensive sports facilities; excellent svce. 640 acres (256ha) of lawns and lush tropical grdns w. dozens of fountains, waterfalls, and 300 palm trees. The epitome of Arizona's luxury resorts. **VE**, but lower rates off-season.

☀ ♈♈♈♈ **Scottsdale Princess** (vic.), 7575 E. Princess Dr., Scottsdale, AZ 85255 (602/585-4848; toll free 800/223-1818). 600 rms, A/C, color TV, in-rm movies. AE, CB, DC, MC, V. Free valet parking, three pools, health club, sauna, massage, two golf courses, nine tennis courts, racquetball, putting green, bicycles, five rests. (including The Hacienda), seven bars, 24-hr. rm svce, disco, boutiques, hrdrsr, concierge, free crib. *Note:* Scottsdale's premier luxury resort among 450 acres (185ha) of elaborate landscaping w. desert views that often include wildlife. Gracious flamingo-pink architecture. Elegant, spacious accommodations w. balconies or terraces and refrigerators. Outstanding recreational facilities (three heated pools, two golf courses, nine tennis courts, including the 10,000-seat stadium court). Excellent rests. Polished, professional staff. Provides the best of the Southwest. **VE**, but lower rates off-season.

☀ ♈♈♈♈ **The Pointe Hilton at Squaw Peak** (vic.), 7677 N. 16th St., Phoenix, AZ 85020 (602/997-2626; toll free, see Hilton). 563 suites and villas, A/C, color TV, in-rm movies. AE, CB, DC, MC, V. Free parking, seven pools, health club, sauna, eight tennis courts, racquetball, putting green, four rests. (including Beside the Pointe), two bars, rm svce, hrdrsr, concierge, crib $10. *Note:* Luxury hotel-village in a lovely natural setting. The Spanish Colonial design, w. shaded patios and fountains, comes off beautifully. Spacious suites or individual cottages w. minibars and private balconies. Unusually high level of comfort and physical-fitness facilities. Praiseworthy panoramic rest. Very good svce. Tourist and convention clientele. A hotel of great quality surrounded by 280 acres (113ha) of unspoiled land and beautiful grdns. 20 min. from dwntwn. **VE**, but lower rates off-season.

♈♈♈ **Ritz Carlton Phoenix** (nr. dwntwn), 2401 E. Camelback Rd., Phoenix, AZ 85016 (602/468-0700; toll free 800/241-3333). 281 rms, A/C, cable color TV. AE, CB, DC, MC, V. Valet parking $10, pool, health club, sauna, two tennis courts, two rests. (including The Restaurant), bar, 24-hr. rm svce, concierge, free crib. *Note:* Luxury hotel in the grand tradition across the street from the Biltmore Fashion Park mall. Elegant setting w. museum-quality art. Beautiful guest rms lavishly decorated. Exemplary svce. Very comprehensive physical-fitness facilities. Big business clientele. VIP floor. A highly commendable address. **E–VE**, but lower rates off-season.

♈♈♈ **Crescent Hotel** (nr. dwntwn), 2620 W. Dunlap Ave., Phoenix, AZ 85021 (602/943-8200; toll free 800/423-4126). 344 rms, A/C, color TV, in-rm movies. AE, CB, DC, MC, V. Free parking, pool, health club, sauna, two tennis courts, racquetball, rest. (Charlie's), bar, rm svce, concierge, free crib. *Note:* Corporate-oriented brand-new hotel w. resort amenities. Elegant guest rms and suites w. in-rm computer hookups, speakerphones, and fully equipped business center. Attentive, personal svce. Two VIP floors. **M–E**, but lower rates off-season.

♈♈ **Fountain Suites Hotel** (vic.), 2577 W. Greenway Rd., Phoenix, AZ 85023 (602/375-1777; toll free 800/338-1338). 316 rms, A/C, color TV, in-rm movies. AE, CB, DC, MC, V. Free parking, pool, health club, sauna, two tennis courts, racquetball, rest. (Fountain's Café), bar, rm svce, disco. *Note:* Modern, very attractive hotel in the heart of "High Tech Corridor" (Black Canyon Fwy.). Spectacular lobby w. elegant colonnade, fountains, and octagonal vault. Spacious suites w. minibar, TV w. remote control, and electronic door locks. Efficient svce; very comprehensive facilities. Business clientele. 20 min. from dwntwn along I-17. Good value. **M–E**, but lower rates off-season.

Ⓠ **Quality Inn Desert Sky** (nr. dwntwn), 3541 E. Van Buren St.,
Phoenix, AZ 85008 (602/273-7121; toll free, see Choice) 90
rms, A/C, color TV, in-rm movies. AE, CB, DC, MC, V. Free parking, pool,
rest., bar, rm svce, free crib. *Note:* Comfortable, well-run small motel very nr. the
airport; inviting grdn and pool. Friendly svce; very good overall value. Package-
tour and group clientele. 5 min. from dwntwn. **I,** but lower rates off-season.

Ⓠ **Motel 6 Central** (nr. dwntwn), 2323 E. Van Buren St., Phoenix, AZ 85006 (602/267-7511). 245 rms, A/C, cable color
TV. AE, DC, MC, V. Free parking, pool, rest. nearby. *Note:* Unbeatable value
halfway between dwntwn and the airport. Functionally comfortable rms; excellent location 5 min. from dwntwn. Ideal if you're driving. **B**

Other Accommodations (from top bracket to budget)

☀Ⓠ Ⓠ Ⓠ **The Phoenician** (vic.), 6000 E. Camelback Rd. (at 60th St.),
Scottsdale, AZ 85251 (602/941-8200; toll free 800/888-
8234). 580 rms, A/C, color TV, in-rm movies. AE, CB, DC, MC, V. Free parking, seven pools, health club, sauna, massage, golf course, 11 tennis courts, hiking, bicycles, four rests. (including Mary Elaine's), bars, 24-hr. rm svce,
boutiques, hrdrsr, concierge, free crib. *Note:* Extravagant, nouveau-riche $300-
million hostelry built by developer Charles Keating of Lincoln Savings fame.
Now owned jointly by the U.S. government and the Kuwaiti Investment Corp.,
this flashy mini-city of 580 rms and individual casitas on Camelback Mountain
features seven pools in a three-tiered single area, an 18-hole championship golf
course, 11 tennis courts, and a health spa. Luxurious accommodations w. hand-
crafted furnishings. Impeccable svce. Fashionable rests. A world-class resort. **VE,**
but lower rates off-season.

☀Ⓠ Ⓠ Ⓠ **Marriott's Camelback Inn** (vic.), 5402 E. Lincoln Dr.,
Scottsdale, AZ 85252 (602/948-1700; toll free, see
Marriott). 423 rms, A/C, color TV, in-rm movies. AE, CB, DC, MC, V. Free
parking, three pools, health club, health spa, two golf courses, 10 tennis courts,
horseback riding, putting green, three rests. (including Chaparral), three bars, rm
svce, nightclub, hrdrsr, concierge, free crib. *Note:* A vacationers' paradise: little
two-story cottages scattered through 125 acres (50ha) of splendid grdns w. the
mountains as a backdrop. Almost as luxurious as the Phoenician, but less smart
and—even more important—less stuffy. Spacious rms w. minibars and private
patios or balconies (some w. kitchenettes and fireplaces); polished svce; food as
indifferent as all Marriotts. Worthwhile vacation packages. Comprehensive
physical-fitness facilities. Clientele of rich tourists. A real oasis in the desert, 20
min. from dwntwn. **VE,** but lower rates off-season.

☀Ⓠ Ⓠ Ⓠ **Arizona Biltmore** (nr. dwntwn), 24th and Missouri Sts., Phoenix, AZ 85016 (602/955-6600; toll free, see Westin). 502
rms, A/C, color TV, in-rm movies. AE, CB, DC, MC, V. Free parking, five
pools, health club, sauna, two golf courses, 8 tennis courts, putting green, bicycles, two rests. (including L'Orangerie), two bars, open-air buffet, rm svce, boutiques, hrdrsr, concierge, free crib. *Note:* This luxurious grand hotel designed by
Frank Lloyd Wright in a blend of art deco and traditional regional styles has been
one of the glories of American hotelkeeping for more than half a century. Long
favored by Hollywood stars and famous politicians, the Biltmore is among the
city's finest hotels. Its superb grdns blazing w. flowers and planted w. palm trees
and cactus, pools, tennis courts, and two golf courses are all a fitting complement
to the spacious, elegant rms (some w. private balconies or patios), faultless svce,
and excellent food. VIP and big business clientele. Rates are more affordable in
summer. 15 min. from dwntwn. Has recently undergone a $20-million renova-
tion. **VE,** but lower rates off-season.

☀Ⓠ Ⓠ Ⓠ **Regal McCormick Ranch** (vic.), 7401 N. Scottsdale Rd.,
Scottsdale, AZ 85253 (602/948-5050; toll free 800/222-
8888). 125 rms and 51 villas, A/C, color TV, in-rm movies. AE, CB, DC, MC,
V. Free parking, pool, golf course, four tennis courts, boats, windsurfing, rest.

(Piñon Grill), bar, rm svce, disco, concierge, crib $10. *Note:* Luxury motel on Camelback Lake. Very comfortable rms or individual villas w. private balconies and refrigerators. Decorated Castilian style. Splendid mountain view; attentive svce; comprehensive physical-fitness facilities and many outdoor activities, including hikes into the surrounding desert. Regular clientele. Very interesting summer discounts; a fine place to stay. **E–VE,** but lower rates off-season.

Holiday Inn Crown Plaza (formerly Omni Adams; dwntwn), 111 N. Central Ave. (at Adams St.), Phoenix, AZ 85001 (602/257-1525; toll free, see Holiday Inn). 534 rms, A/C, color TV, in-rm movies. AE, CB, DC, MC, V. Parking $6, pool, health club, rest. (Sandpainter), coffee shop, bar, rm svce, hrdrsr, free crib. *Note:* Modern, clean-lined 19-story tower in the heart of dwntwn, a stone's throw from the Convention Center; light, spacious rms w. refrigerators, some w. private patios. Faultless standards of comfort; good svce; ongoing renovations. Group and business clientele. **M–E,** but lower rates off-season.

Ramada Valley Ho Resort (vic.), 6850 Main St., Scottsdale, AZ 85251 (602/945-6321; toll free, see Ramada Inns). 289 rms, A/C, color TV, in-rm movies. AE, CB, DC, MC, V. Free parking, three pools, three tennis courts, rest. (Summerfield's), bar, rm svce, hrdrsr, free crib. *Note:* Large, pleasant, comfortable motel nr. the smart Fifth Ave. stores in a huge tropical grdn. Comfortable, spacious rms w. private patios or balconies and refrigerators. Efficient svce; good value off-season. Group and convention clientele. 15 min. from dwntwn. **M–E,** but lower rates off-season.

Best Western Grace Inn at Ahwatukee (nr. dwntwn), 10831 S. 51st St., Phoenix, AZ 85044 (602/893-3000; toll free, see Best Western). 160 rms, A/C, color TV, in-rm movies. AE, CB, DC, MC, V. Free parking, pool, health club, sauna, tennis court, rest. (Matthew's), bar, rm svce, hrdrsr, free crib. *Note:* Inviting hotel in an elegant modern building near South Mountain Park. Faultless comfort and facilities; spacious rms w. refrigerator and private balcony. With direct access to I-10, it's very convenient if you're driving. VIP floor. 10 min. from the airport (free shuttle) and from the Arizona State U. campus. **M,** but lower rates off-season.

Best Western Executive Park Hotel (formerly Westcoast; nr. dwntwn), 1100 N. Central Ave., Phoenix, AZ 85004 (602/252-2100; toll free, see Best Western). 105 rms, A/C, color TV, in-rm movies. AE, CB, DC, MC, V. Free parking, pool, health club, sauna, rest. (Rose's), bar, rm svce, free crib. *Note:* Ideal for the business traveler, in the heart of dwntwn Phoenix. A very successful venture in modern architecture, w. glassed-in exterior elevators. Huge, inviting rms w. refrigerator and private balcony (some w. panoramic view of the mountains). Highly professional svce. Good value. **I–M,** but lower rates off-season.

Quality Hotel (formerly Holiday Inn; nr. dwntwn), 3600 N. Second Ave., Phoenix, AZ 85013 (602/248-0222). 280 rms, A/C, color TV, in-rm movies. AE, CB, DC, MC, V. Free parking, two pools, rest. (Sazzoni's), bar, rm svce, free crib. *Note:* Modern 10-floor motel adj. Park Central Mall w. its 75 shops and rests. Acceptable rest.; impersonal svce. Business clientele (the financial district is a block or two away). Free airport limo. **I–M,** but lower rates off-season.

Best Western Innsuites at Squaw Peak (nr. dwntwn), 1615 E. Northern Ave., Phoenix, AZ 85020 (602/997-6285; toll free, see Best Western). 125 rms, A/C, color TV, in-rm movies. AE, CB, DC, MC, V. Free parking, pool, adj. rest., free breakfast, free crib. *Note:* Inviting, serviceable motel on the foothills of Squaw Peak. All rms come w. microwave and refrigerator. Good value overall. 10 min. from dwntwn. **I–M,** but lower rates off-season.

Desert Rose (nr. dwntwn), 3424 E. Van Buren St., Phoenix, AZ 85008 (602/275-4421). 56 rms, A/C, color TV. AE, CB, DC, MC, V. Free parking, pool, coffee shop, rm svce, crib $4. *Note:* One of the best buys in Phoenix, 5 min. from dwntwn. Comfortable rms w. private balconies. Ideal if you're driving. **B,** but lower rates off-season.

Airport Accommodations

🍷🍷 **Fiesta Inn** (nr. dwntwn), 2100 S. Priest Dr., Tempe, AZ 85282
ᘒ ᘒ (602/967-1441; toll free 800/528-6481). 270 rms, A/C, color TV, in-rm movies. AE, CB, DC, MC, V. Free parking, pool, health club, sauna, three tennis courts, driving range, putting green, rest., bar, rm svce, concierge, free crib. *Note:* The ideal motel for a stopover between flights. Spacious, comfortable rms w. refrigerators. Good physical-fitness facilities; good rest. (The Other Place); excellent svce. Pretty, countrified decor w. original works of art. 8 min. from airport (free shuttle). Good value. **M,** but lower rates off-season.

Accommodations in the Vicinity

☀️🍷🍷🍷🍷 **The Boulders Resort and Club** (vic.), 34631 N. Tom Darling-
ᘒ ᘒ ᘒ ᘒ ton Rd., Carefree, AZ 85377 (602/488-9009; toll free 800/
553-1717). 160 casitas, A/C, color TV, in-rm movies. AE, CB, DC, MC, V. Free parking, two pools, health club, two golf courses, six tennis courts, putting green, horseback riding, four rests. (including Latilla Dining Rm), bar, rm svce, free crib. *Note:* The ultimate desert resort, set in Arizona's dramatic Sonoran Wilderness. The adobe-style casitas (individual villas) blend into the dun-and-ocher landscape behind them. Spacious rms decorated w. Native American motifs, all w. refrigerators, fireplaces, and private patios. Exemplary svce; rest. of quality. Jeep trips organized into the desert. Clientele of well-heeled tourists; this is the perfect vacationers' grand hotel. Closed July to early Sept. 40 min. from dwntwn by Scottsdale Rd. **VE** (Modified American Plan), but lower rates off-season.

Guest Ranch

☀️🍷🍷🍷 **Rancho de los Caballeros** (vic.), 1551 S. Vulture Mine Rd.,
ᘒ ᘒ ᘒ Wickenburg, AZ 85390 (602/684-5484). 73 rms, A/C, color TV. No credit cards. Free parking, pool, golf course, four tennis courts, horseback riding, trapshooting, rest., bar. *Note:* At once a luxury hotel and a true stock ranch w. cattle and real cowboys. Rustic but comfortable ambience. More than 20,000 acres (8,000ha) of desert lie open to riders, in groups or alone. Friendly reception and svce. Interesting American Plan packages. Open Oct to mid-May. Resv. must be made very far in advance at this successful place. One-hour drive from Phoenix by U.S. 89N. A highly recommended spot. **E–VE** (American Plan), but lower rates off-season.

YMCA/Youth Hostels

Metcalf House International Hostel (nr. dwntwn), 1026 N. 9th St., Phoenix, AZ 85006 (602/254-9803). 35 beds. Conventional youth hostel, 5 min. from dwntwn.
YMCA–Phoenix (dwntwn), 350 N. First Ave., Phoenix, AZ 85003 (602/253-6181). Men and women. Pool, health club. Very central location.

RESTAURANTS

Personal Favorites (in order of preference)

🍷🍷🍷🍷 **Vincent on Camelback** (nr. dwntwn), 3930 E. Camelback Rd., Phoenix (224-0225). A/C. Lunch Mon–Fri, dinner Mon–Sat; closed hols. AE, DC, MC, V. Jkt. *Specialties:* blue crab cake w. corn salsa and orange sauce, grilled Maine lobster w. chipotle pasta, grilled beef tenderloin w. potato-leek pancakes and green chili sauce, duck tamale w. green chilies and raisins, fresh berries crème brûlée served in a sweet taco shell, lemon tart, sorbet. Splendid wine list. *Note:* Unquestionably the finest food in Phoenix and one of the dozen best rests. in the U.S. The young, talented Vincent Guerithault, who learned his trade in France at the prestigious Oustau de Baumanière at Les Baux de Provence, serves a felicitous mix of recipes culled from his native France combined w. the ingredients and style of the American Southwest: Mexican ingredients and mesquite broiling at relatively bargain prices. Also offers low-calorie dishes. Warm, rustic decor, w. exposed beams, furniture of country charm, and flowers everywhere. Excellent svce; atmosphere at once elegant and relaxing. Resv. a must. A very fine place. Valet parking. *French/American.* **M–E**

   🍷🍷🍷 **Mary Elaine's** (vic.), in The Phoenician (see "Accommodations," above), Scottsdale (423-2530). A/C. Dinner only, Mon–Sat. AE, CB, DC, MC, V. Jkt. *Specialties:* garlic- and herb-crusted rack of lamb, gratin of herbed cannelloni, roasted sea scallops w. curry-carrot sauce and mango chutney. Impressive wine list. *Note:* Rated one of Arizona's best, this sumptuous rooftop rest. features elegant Mediterranean cuisine and spectacular views of the valley. Refined atmosphere and ultra-correct svce. Unobtrusive live music. Resv. essential. *Seafood/Mediterranean.* **E**

   🍷🍷 **Tapas Papa Frita** (nr. dwntwn), 3213 E. Camelback Rd., Phoenix (381-0474). A/C. Lunch Mon–Fri, dinner nightly (until midnight); closed hols. AE, DC, MC, V. *Specialties:* tapas, grouper w. clams, stuffed partridge, oxtail stew, paella, roast suckling pig; good sangría. *Note:* The house's specialty is—what else?—tapas, those terrific small Spanish snacks. But the other dishes are also worth high praise. Lively, bustling atmosphere. Friendly svce. *Spanish.* **I–M**

   🍷🍷 **Jean Claude's Petit Café** (vic.), 7340 E. Shoeman Lane, Scottsdale (947-5288). A/C. Lunch Mon–Fri, dinner Mon–Sat; closed hols. AE, CB, DC, MC, V. Jkt. *Specialties:* duck w. raspberry-vinegar sauce, salmon w. tarragon sauce, chocolate soufflé. Menu changes regularly. Wine list limited but well balanced. *Note:* If you love modern, imaginative French cuisine, the excellent chef Jean Claude Poncet has made this the place for you. Charming Parisian-bistro decor; cheerful svce; congenial, romantic atmosphere. Resv. strongly advised. *French.* **I–M**

   🌣🍷🍷 **The Stockyards** (nr. dwntwn), 5001 E. Washington St., Phoenix (273-7378). A/C. Lunch Mon–Fri, dinner nightly; closed Dec 25 and Sun June–Oct. AE, DC, MC, V. *Specialties:* oysters on the half shell, "Rocky Mountain oysters," excellent meats of all kinds, steak, T-bone, prime ribs. Unimpressive desserts and wine list. *Note:* For almost 50 years this steak-house has been serving prime beef cuts, broiled to perfection, at reasonable prices. Wonderful turn-of-the-century–style decor. The bar is worth a visit all by itself. Efficient svce. *Steak.* **I–M**

   🍷🍷 **Romano's Macaroni Grill** (vic.), 7245 E. Gold Dust, Scottsdale (596-6676). A/C. Lunch/dinner daily; closed hols. AE, CB, DC, MC, V. *Specialties:* Nachos Napoli (fried wontons w. mozzarella and Parmesan cheeses and Italian sausage), osso bucco, pollo arrosto con rosmarino, mesquite-grilled salmon w. teriyaki glaze, farfalle pasta w. grilled chicken, apple custard cake w. caramel sauce. Decent wine list. *Note:* Quirky, fast-paced rest. that often reaches a crescendo in satisfied voices. Delicate preparations and innovative creations (like the Italian nachos) that don't fail to please. Italian lessons are pumped out the speakers in the restrooms. A great place that unfortunately doesn't take resv., so be prepared to wait. *Italian.* **I**

   🍷🍷 **Shogun** (vic), 12615 N. Tatum Blvd., Scottsdale (953-3264). A/C. Lunch Mon–Sat, dinner nightly; closed hols. AE, MC, V. *Specialties:* sushi, tempura, sukiyaki, karage chicken. *Note:* The best Japanese rest. in the valley. Modern and elegant interior. Terrific sushi bar w. its two skilled craftsmen carving raw fish. Portions tend to be small, Japanese style. Speedy service. Resv. suggested. *Japanese.* **I**

   🍷 **Garcia's Del Este Restaurant** (nr. dwntwn), 3301 W. Peoria Ave., Phoenix (866-1850). A/C. Lunch/dinner daily; closed Easter, Thanksgiving, Dec. 25. AE, MC, V. *Specialties:* soup w. meatballs, pollo fundido, chimichangas, quesadillas, fajitas. Excellent margaritas. *Note:* One of the lowest-priced and most authentic Mexican rests. in the region. Colorful setting and atmosphere; mariachi band evenings. Friendly, relaxed svce. Locally popular; generally crowded. Check the *Yellow Pages* for their several other locations. *Mexican/American.* **B-I**

Other Restaurants (from top bracket to budget)

♈♈♈ **Christopher's** (vic.), 2398 E. Camelback Rd., Phoenix (957-3214). A/C. Dinner only, nightly; closed hols. AE, CB, DC, MC, V. Jkt. *Specialties:* smoked squab salad w. tarragon and quinoa, crêpe of foie gras, confit of duck w. turnips and lavender honey, gratin of veal w. walnut sauce. Excellent wine list. *Note:* Former chef de cuisine of Vincent on Camelback (see above), Cris Gross was recently named one of the 10 best chefs in the U.S.; his cuisine is a miracle of contemporary delicacy and imagination. Small but elegant setting, rich w. brocade and Limoges china. Ultra-polished svce; formal atmosphere. Resv. essential. *French/American.* **E-VE**

♈♈ **Etienne's Different Pointe of View** (nr. dwntwn), in the Pointe at Tapatio Cliffs Hotel, 11111 N. 7th St., Phoenix (866-7500). A/C. Dinner nightly, brunch Sun; closed Sun-Mon June-Aug. AE, CB, DC, MC, V. Jkt. *Specialties:* gnocchi verdi, filet mignon capella, rack of lamb w. herbs, game (in season), salmon en papillard, duck cakes w. wine sauce. Wholly remarkable wine list. *Note:* Formal classic French-inspired cuisine, executed w. great success. Very handsome hi-tech setting and fabulous panoramic view of Phoenix and the Valley of the Sun at sunset (ask for a table nr. the picture window). Svce of a high order. Free shuttle from the hotel's parking lot at the foot of the hill. One of the best rests. in Phoenix. Resv. a must. Valet parking. *French/Continental.* **E-VE**

♈♈ **8700 at the Citadel** (vic.), 8700 E. Pinnacle Peak Rd., Scottsdale (994-8700). A/C. Dinner only, daily; closed hols. AE, CB, DC, MC, V. Jkt. *Specialties:* pumpkin soup, smoked duck w. jalapeño pasta, ribeye steak w. horseradish-mustard sauce, salmon fajitas, rack of lamb w. Mendocino mustard and roasted pistachios, mesquite-grilled cabrito (baby goat) w. adobo and smoke-chile chipotle, sumptuous homemade desserts. Large list of European and American wines. *Note:* The area's finest southwestern rest., where the standbys are green chile, blue corn, pine nuts, and dishes broiled over mesquite wood. Charming Santa Fe-rustic decor and a wonderful view out over the valley at sunset from the second-floor bar. Open-air dining in a pleasant patio. Courteous, efficient svce. Resv. highly advisable. Well worth the 25-min. drive from dwntwn. Valet parking. *American.* **M-E**

※♈♈ **El Chorro Lodge** (vic.), 5550 E. Lincoln Dr., Scottsdale (948-5170). A/C. Lunch/dinner daily; brunch Sat-Sun; closed hols. AE, CB, DC, MC, V. Jkt. *Specialties:* chicken livers, chateaubriand, rack of lamb, deep-fried lobster, good desserts (cinnamon "sticky buns"). *Note:* One of the handsomest western settings in Arizona, w. an enchanting patio for open-air dining. The cuisine is particularly polished, the svce impeccable, and the decor countrified elegant w. wood beams and fireplaces. A Phoenix landmark since 1937. Resv. a must; valet parking. *Continental/American.* **M**

♈♈ **Mancuso's** (vic.), in the Borgata, 6166 N. Scottsdale Rd., Scottsdale (948-9988). A/C. Dinner only, nightly; closed Thanksgiving, Dec 25. AE, CB, DC, MC, V. *Specialties:* fresh homemade pasta, cannelloni Alfredo, chicken Agnesi, sautéed frogs' legs, duck à l'orange, sole Oscar, tournedos béarnaise. Good list of European and domestic wines. *Note:* Slightly theatrical decor in the style of a Renaissance château, but the mostly French and Italian food is of great quality, if not up-to-date. Exemplary svce. In the heart of the Borgata shopping center; heavily patronized by locals. Resv. advised; valet parking. *Italian/Continental.* **M**

♈♈ **Café Terra Cotta** (vic.), 6166 Scottsdale Rd., Scottsdale (948-8100). A/C. Lunch/dinner daily; closed Thanksgiving, Dec. 25. AE, DC, MC, V. *Specialties:* corn risotto w. jalapeños, havarti cheese, and salsa fresca; large prawns stuffed w. herbed goat cheese; pork tenderloin w. black beans; lamb chops w. cranberry cascabel sauce; chocolate mousse pie. Extensive, all-Californian wine list. *Note:* An incarnation of the wildly popular Café Terra Cotta in Tucson (see "Restaurants," under the chapter on Tucson). Chef/owner Donna Nordin continues her success with her contemporary, innovative Southwestern cuisine. Local artists featured in the bright, "deserty" dining room. Resv. recommended. *American.* **I–M**

🍷🍷 **Rox Sand** (vic.), 2594 E. Camelback Rd., Scottsdale (381-0444). Lunch/dinner daily; closed hols. AE, CB, DC, MC, V. *Specialties:* curried lamb wrapped in rice tamale w. Thai peanut sauce; horseradish-crusted chili and sea bass w. romescu sauce; roast rack of lamb w. dijon mustard, roasted garlic, and polenta cake; air-dried duck w. Szechuan black-bean sauce. Choice of 15–35 exquisite desserts each day. *Note:* Globally inspired cooking (in every dish!) at this glitzy, gallery-like rest. that would seem more at home in New York City than at its Phoenix location. Too many remarkable desserts to choose from. A very good value to boot. *American/International.* **I–M**

🍷🍷 **Tomaso's** (nr. dwntwn), 3225 E. Camelback Rd., Phoenix (956-0836). A/C. Lunch Mon–Fri, dinner nightly; closed hols. AE, CB, DC, MC, V. *Specialties:* pasta w. beans, caponata (marinated eggplant w. capers), insalata caprese, seafood pasta, chicken cacciatore, veal scaloppine milanese, braciolone (Sicilian rolled beef), bouillabaisse, tiramisù. Good list of Italian wines. *Note:* Tomaso Maggiore, already the energetic proprietor of the rest. Chianti, opened Tomaso's in 1981, and since then it has established itself as one of the best places in Phoenix for lovers of true Italian food. There is no praise too high for the fresh homemade pasta. Warm Mediterranean setting; friendly, attentive svce. Resv. strongly advised. *Italian.* **I–M**

🍷🍷 **Havana Café** (nr. dwntwn), 4225 E. Camelback Rd., Phoenix (952-1991). A/C. Lunch Mon–Sat, dinner nightly; closed hols. AE, MC, V. *Specialties:* black-bean soup, shrimp pancakes, bacalão, arroz con pollo, ropa vieja, roast leg of pork, rice pudding. *Note:* Small, cozy café w. tropical-print tablecloths offering flavorful Spanish and Cuban specialties. Often crowded and noisy. No resv. accepted. *Spanish/Cuban.* **I**

🌄🍷 **Depot Cantina** (vic.), 300 S. Ash Ave., Tempe (966-6677). A/C. Lunch/dinner daily. AE, DC, MC, V. *Specialties:* fajitas, carnitas, menudo (tripe), tamales, chile relleño, steak ranchero. *Note:* This colorful establishment in Tempe's historic Old Town train depot offers generous helpings of all the standard Mexican dishes, flawlessly prepared. Considerate svce in a kitsch setting. Resv. advised. An excellent place, 15 min. from dwntwn and almost on the Arizona State U. campus. *Mexican.* **I**

🍷🍷 **Rancho Pinot Grill** (nr. dwntwn), 4709 N. 20th St. (468-9463). A/C. Dinner only, Mon–Sat; closed hols. MC, V. *Specialties:* goat-cheese phyllo w. caramelized onions; grilled shrimp w. Thai-style slaw and mango relish; grilled ahi tuna w. black olive and tomato relish; grilled Yucatán-marinated pork chop; grilled trio of chicken, sausage, and polenta; great desserts. No beer or wine (BYOB). *Note:* A place where elegance in symmetry seems to be the top item in decor and cooking. This relative newcomer presents a strange hybrid of Italian *cucina* and western cookin' by chef Chrysa Kaufman. Relaxed atmosphere. Resv. a must. *American/Italian.* **I**

🌄🍷 **Pinnacle's Peak Patio** (vic.), 10426 E. Jomax Rd., Scottsdale (967-8082). A/C. Dinner nightly, brunch Sun; closed Thanksgiving, Dec 24–25. AE, MC, V. *Specialties:* charcoal-broiled T-bone steak (1 lb./450g) and porterhouse steak (2lb./900g), chateaubriand, hamburger, broiled chicken. *Note:* Enormous (seats 2,000) western-style steakhouse w. the McDowell Mountains in the background. The view of the valley at sunset is worth the trip all by itself, but so are the enormous servings of prime beef. Relaxed svce; country music and dancing. Mock gunfights. Very touristic atmosphere; no resv.; don't wear a tie! *Steak.* **B–I**

♀ **The Quilted Bear** (vic.), 6316 N. Scottsdale Rd., Scottsdale (948-7760). A/C. Breakfast/lunch/dinner daily; closed Dec 25. AE, CB, DC, MC, V. *Specialties:* homemade soups, gazpacho, salads, sandwiches, steak, roast beef, catch of the day, fried chicken. *Note:* Rest.-cafeteria w. comfortable, picturesque atmosphere. Colorful decor w. stained glass and a profusion of greenery. Excellent family-style cuisine and the best salad bar in the valley. Locally popular. *American.* **B–I**

Cafeterias/Fast Food

☼ **Ed Debevic's Short Orders Deluxe** (nr. dwntwn), 2102 E. Highland, Phoenix (956-2760). 1950s-style diner complete w. gum-chewing, wisecracking servers and tableside jukeboxes: homemade meatloaf, burgers, chili, turkey dinner, salads, grilled chicken, sundaes, and shakes. Lunch/dinner daily. AE, MC, V.

Miracle Mile Deli (dwntwn), Park Central Mall, 3121 N. Third Ave., Phoenix (277-4783). Breakfast/lunch/dinner daily. Outstanding New York–style deli: overstuffed sandwiches, homemade soups and desserts, and an impressive salad bar. The best corned beef in town.

BARS & NIGHTCLUBS

Like other major cities, Phoenix has a magic phone number, the **Jazz Hotline** (254-4545), giving programs for all the jazz clubs.

Char's Has the Blues (nr. dwntwn), 4631 N. 7th Ave., Phoenix (230-0205). Locally popular blues joint w. nightly live local and national acts.

Chuckwalla's (vic.), 2000 Westcourt Way, Tempe (225-9000). Classy nightspot featuring live West Coast bands. State-of-the-art video system. Open nightly.

Denim & Diamonds (nr. dwntwn), 3905 E. Thomas Rd. at Tower Plaza, Phoenix (225-0182). Popular honky tonk w. DJ country and rock music. Open nightly.

Oscar Taylor (nr. dwntwn), 2420 E. Camelback Rd., Phoenix (956-5705). Singles bar got up like a Chicago speakeasy during Prohibition. Lots of action. Also an acceptable rest. Open nightly.

Phoenix Live (dwntwn), 455 N. 3rd St., Phoenix (252-2112). Mega-entertainment complex featuring three nightclubs under one roof.

Rustler's Rooste (nr. dwntwn), in the Pointe at South Mountain, 7777 S. Pointe Pkwy., Phoenix (431-6474). Very good live country music; dancing. Also an acceptable western rest. with a wonderful view of the city. Open nightly.

Timothy's (nr. dwntwn), 6335 N. 16th St., Phoenix (277-7634). Excellent live modern jazz; also praiseworthy rest. Locally popular. Open nightly.

Toolie's Country (nr. dwntwn), 43rd Ave. and Thomas Rd., Phoenix (272-3100). Western saloon and dance hall featuring live country music nightly, with an array of top-name entertainers. Voted the "Friendliest Club in Arizona."

NEARBY EXCURSIONS

☼ **ARCOSANTI** (65 mi./104km north on I-17 to the Cordes Junction exit) (632-7135): A prototype of the city of the future, under construction since 1970; this first attempt at a synthesis of architecture and ecology has been dubbed "arcology." It's the work of visionary Italian architect Paolo Soleri, with the help of many students and young volunteers; the desert megalopolis, still largely in embryo, displays strange, rounded shapes which are worth going out to see. Workshop open to visitors daily. See also the Cosanti Foundation, below.

☼ **CASA GRANDE RUINS NATIONAL MONUMENT** (52 mi./84km SE via U.S. 60E and Ariz. 87S) (723-3172): One of the most amazing monuments of Native American civilization in the

U.S. Built around 1350 by the Hohokam peoples (the word means "those who have disappeared"), the imposing structure, four stories high and with walls 4 ft. 11 in. (1.5m) thick at the base, bears obvious resemblances to the ruins at Zacatecas in Mexico; it still constitutes a riddle for archeologists. Was it an official residence, a temple, an astronomical observatory, or a watchtower looking out over the valley? No one knows. The Hohokam, a race of remarkable builders and near relatives of the Anasazi and Pueblo peoples, left their mark on the valleys of the Gila and Salt Rivers from 300 B.C. to A.D. 1400, when they mysteriously disappeared; in particular, they built dozens of miles of irrigation canals, 6 ft. 6 in. (2m) wide and 3 ft. 3 in. (1m) deep, to water their crops of beans, corn, squash, and cotton. The **Casa Grande** ("Big House," in Spanish) was so named by Fr. Eusebio Kino, the Jesuit missionary who explored southern Arizona in the 1690s. Built of caliche, a composition of clay gravel and calcium carbonate, Casa Grande has been protected since 1932 by a metal roof, not aesthetically appropriate but essential because caliche crumbles easily. Archeological museum. Open daily.

COSANTI FOUNDATION (6433 Doubletree Rd., Scottsdale) (948-6145): Workshop of the famous Italian architect Paolo Soleri, a pupil of Frank Lloyd Wright and the creator of Arcosanti (see above), the "city of the future" rising north of Phoenix. Exhibition of futurist urban projects, including a model of Arcosanti, and windbells by Paolo Soleri. Fascinating. Open daily.

FOUNTAIN HILLS (26 mi./42km NE via Scottsdale Rd. and E. Shea Blvd.) (837-1654): The world's largest fountain, leaping 560 ft. (170m) from the middle of a little lake. The column of water weighs 8 tons.

GILA RIVER INDIAN ARTS & CRAFTS CENTER (30 mi./48km south along I-10 to Exit 175 at Casablanca Rd.) (963-3981): Replicas of Native American villages tracing the history of the Hohokam, Pima, Maricopa, and Apache tribes. Museum; handcrafts center (open daily). Should be combined with the trip to Casa Grande Ruins National Monument (see above).

SUN CITY (14 mi./22km NW on Grand Ave., U.S. 60): Model community for well-to-do retirees, opened in the early 60s. It now has approximately 46,000 residents. **Sun City West,** another equally luxurious residential development, is under construction 2½ mi. (4km) west.

TALIESIN WEST (108th St. at Cactus Rd., Scottsdale) (860-2700): Winter home and studio of the most famous American architect of the 20th century, Frank Lloyd Wright. The stone, glass, and steel buildings, modern and austere, contrast vividly with the surrounding desert; they house Wright's school of architecture, operated since his death in 1959 by the Taliesin Foundation. The buildings are a designated historic monument. Guided tours daily except holidays.

FARTHER AFIELD

APACHE TRAIL (168 mi./268km r.t. via Ariz. 88E and U.S. 60W): The old trail of Cochise and Geronimo, through wonderful desert-mountain scenery in violently contrasting colors. Your first stop is at **Tortilla Flat,** an old gold-prospectors' camp (population: 6) in the heart of the **Superstition Mountains,** complete with saloon, hotel, restaurant, and post office; open daily year round (984-1776). Then drive along picturesque **Apache Lake,** a perch-fisherman's paradise, as far as the imposing ☀️🔔 **Roosevelt**

Lake, formed by the construction in 1910 of **Roosevelt Dam,** one of the largest dams in the world made entirely of hand-cut stone. Fishing, boat rentals. Very close is ☀☖ **Tonto National Monument,** in the midst of a 1,100-acre (450ha) park covered in giant cactus. Clinging to the rock vault above the visitor center (467-2241; open daily) are two very fine Native American cave dwellings, each with a score of rooms, which can be reached with relative ease; dating from the 14th century, they are the work of the Salado people, cousins of the famous Anasazi.

Then on to ☀☖ **Globe,** once famous for its silver and copper mines. See the ☀ **Besh-Ba-Gowah Indian Ruins** on Jesse Hayes Rd., site of a huge cave dwelling inhabited by the Salado peoples between A.D. 1225 and 1400, with more than 200 rooms. Archeological excavations under way.

At **Inspiration, 3** mi. (5km) west of Globe on U.S. 60, see also the immense open-pit copper mine of the **Consolidated Copper Co.,** open Mon–Fri.

At **Superior,** 17 mi. (27km) farther west, don't fail to visit the ☀☖ **Boyce Thompson Southwestern Arboretum** on U.S. 60 (689-2811), open daily, a beautiful 39-acre (16ha) botanic garden with more than 10,000 species of desert plants from around the world, meticulously labeled.

On the return trip, make a small detour between Florence Junction and Apache Junction, turning left off U.S. 60 to ☖ **Kings Ranch,** an authentic 19th-century Far Western village where movies are often made.

In **Mesa** is our last stop, the ☖ **Champlin Fighter Museum,** Falcon Field, 4636 Fighter Aces Dr., Mesa (830-4540), open daily. Here you'll find some 30 pursuit planes from World Wars I and II, splendidly restored, as well as souvenirs of U.S. fighter aces. A must for aviation buffs.

The trip is ideal for nature lovers, but take note that part of the road from Tortilla Flat to Roosevelt Lake is unsurfaced, and treacherous in wet weather. Allow one or two days.

Where to Stay En Route

NEAR GLOBE ☖ **Best Western Copper Hills Inn,** U.S. 60, Miami, AZ 85539 (602/425-7151). 68 rms. Conventional but very well run motel. **I–M**

☀☖☖☖☖ **GRAND CANYON NATIONAL PARK** (218 mi./350km NW via I-17 and U.S. 180): One of the seven wonders of the world; see Chapter 41 on the Grand Canyon. 4½-hr. drive from Phoenix.

☖☖ **MOGOLLON RIM** (239 mi./382km r.t. via Ariz. 87N, Ariz. 260E, Old Rim Rd. West, and Ariz. 87S): Leave Phoenix by McDowell Rd. and Ariz. 87N. Wonderful scenery of wooded mountains, stretches of desert, lakes, and wild canyons as you cross ☀ **Tonto National Forest.**

Your first stop will be at ☀☖ **Payson,** an old gold-prospectors' town now known for its rustic cowtown heritage and its many festivals: the Festival of Country Music at the end of June; the Sawdust Festival, a national lumbermen's contest, at the end of July; a giant rodeo in mid-Aug; and the Old-Time Fiddlers Festival of folk music at the end of Sept. For schedules, call 602/474-4515. Local color guaranteed. Surrounded by the lakes and dense woodlands of Tonto National Forest and the nearby Mogollon Rim, dear to the heart of Zane Grey, the famous author of westerns, Payson has become a convenient getaway for motorists, with Phoenix only two hours away.

Leaving Payson, after 30 mi. (48km) on Ariz. 260, turn left on Old Rim Rd. toward the enchanting ☀ **Woods Canyon Lake, Bear Canyon Lake,** and **Knoll Lake.** This picturesque little mountain road (to be avoided in winter or bad weather) snakes along the ridges of Tonto National Forest before rejoining Ariz. 87 a little north of **Strawberry,** a hill resort much appreciated by inhabitants of Phoenix seeking relief from the city's midsummer heat. Following Ariz. 87

about 5 mi. (8km) south of the Mormon village of **Pine,** take a look at the ☀☀⌂ **Tonto Natural Bridge,** the world's largest natural arch of travertine limestone; 400 ft. (121m) across, it rises 183 ft. (55m) above the waters of Pine Creek, a tributary of the Verde River.

Return to Phoenix, 100 mi. (163km) south, on Ariz. 87. This two- or three-day trip is particularly recommended for lovers of wide-open spaces and woodland hikes.

Where to Stay En Route

IN PAYSON 🍴 **Best Western Paysonglo Lodge,** 1005 S. Beeline Hwy., Payson, AZ 85541 (602/474-2382). 28 rms. Small, very comfortable motel, the ideal base for a number of excursions into Tonto National Forest. **I–M**

☀☀🔔🔔 **NAVAJOLAND** (Canyon de Chelly, Monument Valley, etc.; about 250 mi./400km NE via I-17, U.S. 89, and U.S. 160): The land of the Hopi and Navajo; see Chapter 40 on Navajoland.

🔔🔔 **OAK CREEK CANYON** (322 mi./515km r.t. via I-17N, Ariz. 69N, U.S. Alt. 89N, Ariz. 179S, and I-17S): First stop is **Arcosanti,** the futurist city of architect Paolo Soleri (see "Nearby Excursions," above). Then follow Ariz. 69 to ☀🔔🔔 **Prescott,** founded in 1864 and once capital of the Arizona Territory, which to this day retains something of a frontier-town flavor. Witness the interesting Native American material in the **Smoki Museum,** 147 N. Arizona Ave. (602/445-1230), open Thurs–Tues May–Oct (by appointment the rest of the year); also the group of buildings from 1860–80 that constitutes the **Sharlot Hall Museum,** 415 W. Gurley St. (602/445-3122), open daily (except Mon in the winter), including the **Governor's Mansion, Old Fort Misery,** and the **John C. Frémont House.** Prescott is also the scene every July 4 of a rodeo famous throughout the West. Lovely pinewoods around the town.

Some 30 mi. (48km) farther north, you'll come to the remarkable little mining town of ☀🔔🔔 **Jerome,** now a kind of ghost town, with little wooden houses clinging to the mountainside; its population has fallen from 15,000 in 1929 to fewer than 500 today. Many craft shops, art galleries, and restaurants; mining museum on Main St., open daily. **Jerome State Historic Park** on U.S. 89A (602/634-5381), open daily, traces the history of Jimmy "Rawhide" Douglas, the picturesque founder of the United Verde Mine.

Continue north on U.S. Alt. 89 to **Cottonwood,** a tourist resort in the Verde Valley, where you'll be near ☀ **Tuzigoot National Monument,** the ruins of a 12th-century Native American pueblo with no fewer than 92 enormous rooms. Archeological museum, on Broadway (602/634-5564). Open daily.

Your next stop, the charming ☀⌂ **Sedona,** once a pioneer town, is now a renowned resort with a flourishing artists' colony; painter Max Ernst lived here from 1945 to 1953. Stroll through the streets of **Tlaquepaque,** the art-gallery district with its original Mexican houses.

From Sedona you can conveniently visit ☀🔔🔔 **Oak Creek Canyon,** just north of the town: a splendid rocky gorge 16 mi. (26km) long, whose walls display a range of ocher, yellow, and white hues; it's almost as spectacular as the Grand Canyon of the Colorado, and many westerns have been shot here.

Leaving Sedona along Ariz. 179 and I-17S, you'll come to ☀🔔🔔 **Montezuma Castle National Monument,** an extraordinary cave dwelling five floors high, perched 70 ft. (21m) above the ground in a cleft of the cliff. Built by the Sinagua peoples, it dates from the 13th century, and is so remarkably preserved that it's one of the finest monuments of primitive culture in the U.S. Unfortunately, you're not allowed inside. Visitor center open daily; for information, call 602/567-3322.

On the way back to Phoenix, stop at the ☀⌂ **Fort Verde State Historic Park,**

2 mi. (3km) east of Camp Verde. This 1870s cavalry fort on U.S. 279 (602/567-3275), open daily, was the U.S. Army's principal base for its many operations against the Apache tribe; it has now been splendidly restored.

This very full three- to four-day journey would be worth the trip to Arizona all by itself, but you can combine it conveniently with a visit to the Grand Canyon (see Chapter 41) or to Navajoland (see Chapter 40).

Where to Stay En Route

IN PRESCOTT   The ☼ ⁛⁛ **Hassayampa Inn,** 122 E. Gurley St., Prescott, AZ 86301 (602/778-9434). 67 rms. Charming old hotel going back to the 1920s; pleasant and comfortable. Highly thought-of rest. **I–M**

⁛ **Comfort Inn,** 1290 White Spar Rd., Prescott, AZ 86301 (602/778-5770). 61 rms. Inviting, comfortable motel, open year round. **B–I**

⁛ **Motel 6,** 1111 E. Sheldon St., Prescott, AZ 86301 (602/776-0160). Small, well-run low-priced motel; this place is ideal for budget travelers. **B**

IN SEDONA   ☼⁛⁛ **Los Abrigados,** 160 Portal Lane, Sedona, AZ 86336 (602/282-1777). 172 suites. Luxurious Spanish Colonial–style tourist complex; lovely gardens. **VE,** but lower rates off-season.

☼⁛⁛ **Poco Diablo Resort,** Ariz. 179, Sedona, AZ 86336 (602/282-7333). 200 rms. Charming little vacation hotel w. very comfortable individual villas standing in a grdn. **M–E**

⁛ **Sky Ranch Lodge,** Airport Rd., Sedona, AZ 86336 (602/282-6400). 94 rms. Conventional but inviting motel overlooking Oak Creek Canyon. Good value. **I–M**

Where to Eat En Route

IN JEROME   ⁒ **Jerome Palace,** 410 Clark St. (634-0554). Lunch/dinner Fri–Sun only. Picturesque little Victorian-style rest. **B–I**

IN SEDONA   ⁒⁒ **L'Auberge de Sedona,** 301 L'Auberge Lane (602/282-1667). Breakfast/lunch/dinner daily. Elegant, imaginative French cuisine in a romantic setting. **M–E**

⁒ **Shugrue's,** 2250 W. Ariz. 89A (602/282-2943). Breakfast Tues–Sun, lunch/dinner daily. Attractive, contemporary decor and cuisine. **B–I**

☼⛏ **PETRIFIED FOREST NATIONAL PARK** (225 mi./360km NE via Ariz. 87 and I-40): The world's largest petrified forest, with innumerable animal and vegetable fossils. At the southern entry to the park, on U.S. 180, you can visit an interesting museum explaining the process of fossilization. The nearby **Painted Desert** displays canyons, mesas, and pillars of stratified rock in a striking palette of colors. See Chapter 40 on Navajoland.

TUCSON & SOUTHERN ARIZONA (370 mi./592km r.t. via Ariz. 87, I-10S, U.S. 80S, Ariz. 82W, Ariz. 83N, I-10N, and U.S. 89N):

This spectacular tour, requiring four or five days, begins with a visit to ☼🏛 **Casa Grande Ruins National Monument** (see "Nearby Excursions," above). Continuing south on I-10 you'll come to ☼🏛 **Saguaro National Monument** (602/883-6366), open daily year round, a fine wildland park full of giant cactus (saguaro) growing to 50 ft. (15m), such as you might find in the Sonora Desert. Spectacular flowering in May and June.

Next stop 🏛 **Tucson.** A favorite stopping place for tourists as well as a vigorous commercial metropolis. Tucson has an interesting museum of Native

American culture, the ☀️⚓ **Arizona State Museum,** Park Ave. and University Blvd. (602/621-6302), open daily; the splendid ☀️⚓⚓ **Mission San Xavier del Bac,** San Xavier Rd. (602/294-2624), open daily, a masterpiece of Spanish Colonial baroque; one of the most beautiful zoological/botanical gardens in the country, the ⚓⚓ **Arizona-Sonora Desert Museum,** Kinney Rd. (602/883-1380), open daily; a remarkable museum of aviation displaying more than 130 aircraft of all periods, the ⚓⚓ **Pima Air Museum,** 6000 E. Valencia Rd. (602/574-9658); and ⚓ **Old Tucson,** a Far West village replica built in 1939 as a location for western movies, at 201 S. Kinney Rd. (602/883-6457), open daily.

Between Tucson and Tombstone, 70 mi. (113km) south, you can make a detour to **Colossal Cave,** Colossal Cave Rd. (602/647-7275), open daily, a spectacular cavern with many marine fossils, proving that in a prehistoric era the Arizona desert was covered by the ocean.

Last stop, ☀️⚓⚓ **Tombstone,** the Far West's most famous ghost town, scene of the bloody "Gunfight at the O.K. Corral." Immortalized in many westerns, Tombstone still has many buildings dating from its glory days; if you're nostalgic about the Winning of the West, here's the place to daydream.

Back to Phoenix via U.S. 89, which runs from the Mexican to the Canadian border; also known as the ⚓⚓ **Pinal Pioneer Trail,** it's one of the most spectacular highways in the West.

For more details on the places, towns, and monuments mentioned in this itinerary, as well as for recommended accommodations and dining, see Chapter 43 on Tucson.

CHAPTER 43

TUCSON ♙♙

□ □ □

And Southern Arizona

Rearing up like a mirage from the surrounding mountains and desert, this former capital (1867–77) of the Arizona Territory has lived through more exciting times in its two-century life span than almost any other city in the Far West. First Native American, then Spanish (who built the first fort in 1776 to fend off the Apaches), then Mexican, and finally American, Tucson (pronounced *"Too-sahn"*) was described in the 19th century as "the kingdom of crime, vice, and debauchery." With its dozens of dangerous saloons, dubious gaming houses, and ill-famed brothels, it was dubbed by contemporary newspapers "The Worst Hellhole in the West."

As in too many cities where the bulldozer has been allowed to run riot, Tucson has in the last three decades razed to the ground its old residential downtown, replacing it with graceless air-conditioned office buildings. But there are still interesting fragments of the city's heritage, such as the enchanting **Mission San Xavier del Bac,** called "the white dove of the desert," or **Frémont House.** And there are always wonderful things to see in southern Arizona: the giant cactus of **Saguaro National Park;** the wild landscapes of the **Chiricahua National Monument,** once the stronghold of the tribal chiefs Cochise and Geronimo; the Spanish mission at **Tumacacori;** the living museum of the **Arizona-Sonora Desert;** and the epic town of **Tombstone,** made notorious by the famous "Gunfight at the O.K. Corral."

A favorite stopping place for tourists, Tucson is also a lively business metropolis, ranking fifth among major American cities in its economic growth rate. Because of its exceptionally low humidity, it performed an odd service for the airline industry during the great world oil crisis of 1973–74; many American and European airlines lacking fuel to fly their jets parked them at Tucson airport, where they could be left without fear of rust.

Singer Linda Rondstadt was born in Tucson.

BASIC FACTS: State of Arizona. Area code: 602. Time zone: mountain. ZIP Code: 85702. Founded: 1775. Approximate population: city, 405,000; metropolitan area, 700,000.

CLIMATE: Tucson averages 318 days of clear skies every year, one of the highest figures in the U.S. The persistent sunshine results in oppressive temperatures in summer (July average, 89°F/32°C), and scarcely less so in spring and fall. However, the exceptionally dry air and the cool of the desert evening make the heat bearable. With a Dec–Jan average of 53°F (12°C), winter is a joy if you like your days brisk and sunny.

DISTANCES: Albuquerque, 441 mi. (705km); Mexican border, 65 mi. (104km); Los Angeles, 512 mi. (819km); Phoenix, 118 mi. (189km); San Antonio, 883 mi. (1,412km); San Diego, 415 mi. (664km).

ARRIVAL & TRANSIT INFORMATION

AIRPORT: Tucson International Airport (TUS), 7 mi. (11km) south (573-8000). First municipal airport opened in U.S. (1919).

AIRLINES: American (toll free 800/433-7300), America West (toll free 800/253-9292), Continental (toll free 800/525-0280), Northwest (toll free 800/225-2525), United (toll free 800/241-6522), and USAir (toll free 800/428-4322).

CITY LINK: The **cab** fare from the airport to downtown is about $14–$20; time, 20 min. Bus: **Arizona Stagecoach** (889-1000), serves principal dwntwn hotels on request; fare, $8–$14; time, 25–35 min., depending on destination. Municipal bus: Sun Tran Line No. 11, until 7pm; fare 75¢.
  The rudimentary public transportation (bus) system provided by **Sun Tran** (792-9222), the very high cab fares given the size of the city, and the many fascinating excursions into the surrounding country combine to suggest the wisdom of renting a car with unlimited mileage.

CAR RENTALS: Avis (toll free 800/331-1212); Budget (toll free 800/527-0700); Dollar (toll free 800/800-4000); Hertz (toll free 800/654-3131); National (toll free 800/227-7368); Practical Rent-a-Car, 5756 E. Speedway Blvd. (571-0099), a local renter with favorable rates; and Thrifty, 6610 S. Tucson Blvd. (toll free 800/367-2277). For dwntwn locations, consult the local telephone directory.

LIMOUSINES: Carey Limousine (toll free 800/336-4646) and Dav El/All-State Limousines (toll free 800/922-0343).

TAXIS: Cabs may not be hailed on the street, but may be summoned by phone: **ABC Cab** (623-7979), **Checker Taxi** (623-1133), and **Yellow Cab** (624-6611).

TRAIN: Amtrak station, 400 E. Toole St. (toll free 800/872-7245).

INTERCITY BUSES: Greyhound, 2 S. Fourth Ave. (toll free 800/231-2222).

INFORMATION & TOURS

TOURIST INFORMATION: The **Tucson Convention and Visitors Bureau,** 130 S. Scott Ave., AZ 85701 (602/624-1817).

GUIDED TOURS: **Gray Line Tours** (bus) (622-8811): Guided bus tours of the city and surroundings; serves principal hotels.

Tucson Tour Company (bus), 180 E. Tangerine Rd. (297-2911): Guided van tours of Tucson, the Arizona-Sonora Desert Museum, and Old Tucson. Operates daily by appointment.

SIGHTS, ATTRACTIONS & ACTIVITIES

ADVENTURES: Balloon America (balloon), P.O. Box 64600, AZ 85740 (299-7744): Hot-air balloon trips over Tucson and the surrounding desert; spectacular. Free shuttle. Daily Oct–June.

Outdoor Adventures, 9402 El Cajon (296-9437): Hiking, bird watching, and nature walks conducted by an experienced naturalist guide.

Southern Arizona Balloon Excursion (balloon), 530 W. Sahuaro (624-3599): Hot-air-balloon trips over Tucson and the surrounding desert; spectacular. Daily weather permitting.

Sunshine Jeep Tours (Jeep), 9040 N. Oracle, Suite D (742-1943): Half-day or longer Jeep trips into the desert around Tucson.

ARCHITECTURAL HIGHLIGHTS: ⚖ **Pima County Courthouse,** 115 N. Church Ave. (740-3200): An old baroque building whose dome is covered with colored tiles in geometric patterns. A mixture of Spanish Colonial style, with columns, arches, and carved facade, and typical southwestern architecture. Pretty interior courtyard with fountain. Open Mon–Fri.

⚖ **University of Arizona,** Park Ave. and University Blvd. (621-2211): Founded in 1885, this is now one of the most important universities in the Southwest, with 37,000 students. The huge campus, covering 345 acres (140ha), is embellished with lovely gardens and flowerbeds and several remarkable buildings: the **McKale Memorial Center,** the **College of Law,** the **Library,** and the **College of Medicine,** as well as several interesting museums described below.

CHURCHES/SYNAGOGUES: ☀⚖ **Mission San Xavier del Bac,** San Xavier Rd., 9 mi. (14km) SW of Tucson on I-19 (294-2624): Nicknamed "the white dove of the desert" on account of its elegant silhouette and immaculate white walls, the mission was originally founded in 1700 by Jesuit Fr. Eusebio Kino in his attempt to convert the Pima tribespeople to Christianity. The present buildings were erected by the Franciscans between 1783 and 1797; with asymmetrical bell towers and ocher-colored facade, it's the finest surviving example of Spanish Colonial architecture in the U.S. Splendid baroque interior with Native American wall paintings. Open daily.

⚖ **St. Augustine Cathedral,** 192 S. Stone Ave. (623-6351): Another perfect example of Spanish religious architecture, this one dating from 1896. Wonderful carved sandstone facade, modeled after the cathedral at Querétaro in Mexico, surmounted by a statue of St. Augustine and three symbols of the desert: the yucca, the saguaro, and the horned toad. Open daily. (Don't miss the vibrant and colorful mariachi mass, Sun at 8am.)

HISTORIC BUILDINGS: ☀⚖ **John C. Frémont House,** 151 S. Granada Ave. (622-0956): Dating from the 1880s and furnished in period, this modest adobe house of typically Mexican appearance was the home of the explorer Gen. John C. Frémont, then governor of the Arizona Territory. Interesting temporary exhibitions. Open Wed–Sat.

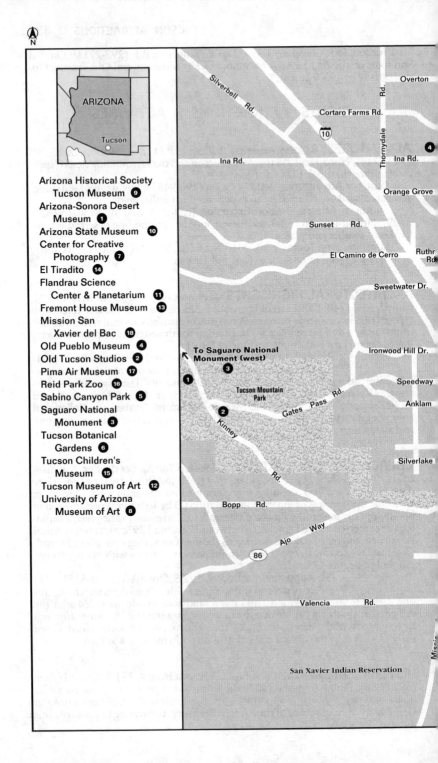

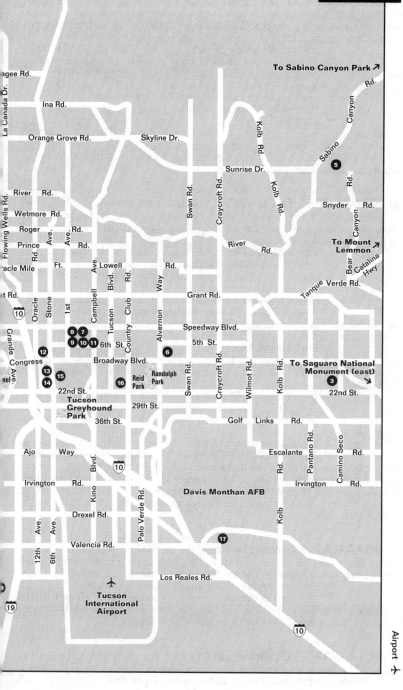

TUCSON

MUSEUMS OF ART: ☀☖ **Center for Creative Photography,** 1030 Olive Rd. (621-7968): One of the country's finest photography museums. A remarkable collection, with more than 100 of the most famous photographers represented; also changing exhibits. A must for camera buffs. Open Sun–Fri.

☖ **Tucson Museum of Art,** 140 N. Main Ave. (624-2333): Housed in six meticulously restored 19th-century adobe buildings that were once part of the Tucson Presidio, this museum offers a very impressive selection of pre-Columbian and Mexican art, as well as Spanish Colonial and contemporary art in the southwestern U.S. Open daily.

☀☖ **University Museum of Art,** Olive Rd. and Speedway Blvd. (621-7567): Splendid art museum on the university campus, whose contents include a part of the famous Kress collection of Renaissance paintings, and an impressive group of modern paintings and sculptures from the Leonard Pfeiffer and E. J. Gallagher collections: Picasso, Rodin, Moore, N. C. Wyeth, etc. Open Sun–Fri.

MUSEUMS OF SCIENCE & HISTORY: ☖ **Arizona Historical Society,** 949 E. 2nd St. at Park Ave. (628-5774): History of Arizona from the Spanish settlers to the present day; geological specimens; costume museum; well-stocked library on the history of the West. Open daily.

☖ **Arizona State Museum,** Park Ave. and University Blvd. (621-6302): Fascinating panorama of prehistoric (as far as 10,000 years back) and contemporary Native American culture; one of the best archeological collections in the Southwest. Open daily.

☀☖ **Grace H. Flandrau Planetarium,** Cherry Ave. and University Blvd. (621-7827): Very modern space museum and planetarium of innovative spherical design. Observations through the telescope every evening. For budding astronomers; open Wed–Sun.

☀☖ **Fort Lowell Museum,** 2900 N. Craycroft Rd. (885-3832): Partly rebuilt military post, which was important in the Indian Wars at the end of the 19th century. Interesting Apache Wars Museum. Open Wed–Sat.

☖ **Mineralogical Museum,** E. North Campus Dr., Geology Bldg. (621-4227): 10,000 different mineral specimens; large collection of precious stones from around the world and Arizona fossils. Open Mon–Sat.

☀☖☖ **Pima Air Museum,** 6000 E. Valencia Rd., 9 mi. (14km) east to Exit 269 on I-10 (574-9658): More than 200 civil and military aircraft, from the end of the '30s to the present day, collected in one place. One of the country's finest private aircraft collections; a spectacular history of American aviation from the venerable *Liberator* to the gigantic B-52 *Stratofortress*. More than a million visitors have passed through its gates since the museum opened in 1976. Open daily.

PANORAMAS: ☀☖ **Mount Lemmon,** 35 mi. (56km) NE on the Catalina Hwy.: Fine view over Tucson Valley and the surrounding mountains; reached over a lovely scenic highway. The southernmost ski area in the nation.

☖ **Sentinel Peak Park,** Sentinel Peak Rd. at Congress St.: Spectacular view of the city, particularly at nightfall when the lights of Tucson are twinkling at your feet. The giant "A" on the mountainside is the symbol of the University of Arizona. Open daily 7am–10pm.

PARKS & GARDENS: ☖ **Randolph City Park,** Broadway and Alvernon Way (325-2811): Huge, shady park in the center of town; two public golf courses, pool, 24 tennis courts, rose garden, and mini-zoo. Open daily.

    Reid Park, 22nd St. and Country Club Rd. (791-4873): Pleasant oasis of greenery in the heart of Tucson. Pretty rose garden; small but well-designed zoo; picnic area; sizable lake (fishing permitted). Open daily.

    Tohono Chul Park, 7366 N. Paseo del Norte (742-6455): Glorious 35-acre (14ha) garden displaying more than 400 species of arid-zone and desert plants, grouped by genus. Paths for strolling. Also a bird sanctuary: from roadrunners to hummingbirds and from cactus wrens to woodpeckers. A must for nature lovers. Open daily.

    Tucson Mountain Park, 12 mi. (19km) west via Ariz. 86 and Kinney Rd. (883-4200): The "green lung" of Tucson—16,000 acres (6,500ha) of sun-scorched ocher rocks, succulents, and giant cactus. This is the park most visited by tourists, the western part of the Saguaro National Monument (see "Nearby Excursions," below), including Old Tucson (see "Theme Parks," below) and the extraordinary zoological/botanic garden of the Arizona-Sonora Desert Museum (see "Zoos," below). Open daily.

PERFORMING ARTS: For daily listings of all shows and cultural events, consult the entertainment pages of the daily papers *Arizona Daily Star* (morning) and *Tucson Citizen* (evening).

    Centennial Hall, University of Arizona Campus, University Blvd. (621-3341): Classical and jazz concerts, Broadway hits, ballet, top-performer recitals.

    Convention Center Music Hall, 260 S. Church Ave.: Concerts, recitals, opera. Home of the Arizona Opera (293-4336) and the Arizona Light Opera Company (Oct–Mar), and of the Tucson Symphony (principal conductor: Robert Bernhardt) (882-8585) (Oct–May).

    Gaslight Theatre, 7010 E. Broadway (886-9428): Musical comedies, melodrama, family shows. Year round.

    Invisible Theater, 1400 N. First Ave. (882-9721): Experimental and Off-Broadway theater (Sept–June).

    Reid Park Bandshell, 22nd St. and Country Club Rd. (791-4873): Open-air classical concerts by the Tucson Pops Orchestra (May–July).

    Temple of Music and Art, 330 S. Scott Ave. (622-2823). Contemporary and classic theater. Home of the Arizona Theatre Company. Oct–May.

SHOPPING: Old Town Artisans, 186 N. Meyer Ave. (623-6024): Some 150 local artists and craftspeople exhibit their work in a picturesque 19th-century adobe building in the heart of old Tucson. Lovers of authentic Native American crafts will go to the **Adobe Trading Post,** 4042 E. Grant Rd.; **Desert Son,** 4759 E. Sunrise Dr.; and **Kaibab Shop,** 2841 N. Campbell Ave. Anywhere else, you may often find that your prized Native American artifact is stamped "Made in Hong Kong."

SPECIAL EVENTS: For the exact schedule of events below, consult the **Tucson Convention and Visitors Bureau** (see "Tourist Information," above).

    Fiesta de los Vaqueros (Feb): Tucson's big annual event since 1928. History parade, concerts, dances, rodeos.

    Tucson Gem and Mineral Show (Feb): The largest of its kind in the world.

    International Mariachi Conference (Apr): An international gathering of performers of this Mexican folk music.

    Yaqui Indian Easter Celebration (Easter): Very colorful Native American festival.

    Pima County Fair (Apr): Big agricultural fair; horse show, Native American art exhibition. Guaranteed local color.

    San Xavier Fiesta (Apr): Religious procession, Native American dances, fireworks commemorating the founding of the San Xavier del Bac Mission.

SPORTS: Tucson is home to one professional major-league baseball team for spring training, and a minor-league team:
Baseball: Colorado Rockies, Hi Corbett Field (327-9467), spring-training camp, Feb–Mar; Tucson Toros, Hi Corbett Field (325-2621), Apr–Aug.

THEME PARKS: ☀⚓ **Old Tucson,** 201 S. Kinney Rd. in Tucson Mountain Park (883-6457): Built in 1939 as a setting for the movie *Arizona,* this replica of Tucson in the 1860s has 100 houses and saloons, a prison, a gold mine, and a steam railroad. Has been and still is used from time to time for movies and TV series (*Rio Bravo, Gunfight at the OK Corral, High Chaparral,* and so on). Mock gunfights, stunt shows, stagecoach rides. Entertaining. Open daily.

WINTER SPORTS RESORTS: ☀⚓ **Mount Lemmon Ski Valley,** 35 mi. (56km) on Lemmon Hwy. (576-1400): Three lifts; open late Dec to mid-Apr. The southernmost ski resort in the U.S.

ZOOS: ☀⚓⚓ **Arizona-Sonora Desert Museum,** Tucson Mountain Park, 14 mi. (22km) west via Ariz. 86 and N. Kinney Rd. (883-1380): One of the country's most interesting zoological/botanical gardens, devoted to plants and animals of the southwestern deserts. Hundreds of desert animals, from mountain lions and jaguars to prairie dogs, from tarantulas to rattlesnakes, living in their natural habitat. An underground gallery allows you to watch the behavior of creatures that live below the surface. Splendid wild scenery. Open daily.

ACCOMMODATIONS

Personal Favorites (in order of preference)

☀⚓⚓⚓ **Westin La Paloma** (vic.), 3800 E. Sunrise Dr., AZ 85718 (602/742-6000; toll free, see Westin). 486 rms, A/C, color TV, in-rm movies. AE, CB, DC, MC, V. Free valet parking, pool, 12 tennis courts, three golf courses, sauna, health club, three rests. (including La Villa), bar, 24-hr. rm svce, boutiques, hrdrsr, concierge, free crib. *Note:* Ultramodern luxury vacation and convention hotel a 15-min. drive from dwntwn, at the foot of the Santa Catalina Mountains on 650 acres (263ha) of beautiful untamed scenery. Very successful Spanish-mission architecture, w. pastel-washed arcades and flower-filled grdns. Spacious, well-designed rms w. minibars; excellent svce; comprehensive sports facilities. Caters to upscale business clients and well-heeled tourists. The golf courses were designed by former U.S. champion Jack Nicklaus. Airport shuttle. Lots of quality and style. **VE,** but lower rates off-season.

⚓⚓⚓ **Sheraton El Conquistador** (vic.), 10000 N. Oracle Rd., AZ 85737 (602/742-7000; toll free, see Sheraton). 440 rms, A/C, color TV, in-rm movies. AE, CB, DC, MC, V. Free parking, two pools, 16 tennis courts, three golf courses, putting green, health club, sauna, horseback riding, four rests. (including the White Dove), coffee shop, bars, 24-hr. rm svce, nightclub, boutiques, concierge, free crib. *Note:* One of the most modern and luxurious resort hotels in the Southwest; a sort of oasis in the desert a 30-min. drive north of Tucson. Intimate, inviting little three-story buildings surrounded by grdns and palm trees in the shadow of the Santa Catalina Mountains. Elegant, comfortable rms w. minibars and private balconies or patios, the best overlooking the huge pool in the middle of the grdns. Exemplary reception and svce; very comprehensive sports facilities. If you want a complete change of scene, this is it. **VE,** but lower rates off-season.

⚓⚓⚓ **Doubletree Hotel** (nr. dwntwn), 445 S. Alvernon Way, AZ 85711 (602/881-4200; toll free 800/528-0444). 296 rms, A/C, color TV, in-rm movies. AE, CB, DC, MC, V. Free parking, pool, health club, three tennis courts, golf, two rests. (including Cactus Rose), coffee shop, bar, rm svce, disco, free crib. *Note:* Right opposite Randolph Park, this large, modern nine-story hotel is a favorite w. business travelers. Spacious rms w. refrigerators and private patios. Efficient, attentive svce. Group clientele; interesting wknd discounts. **M–E,** but lower rates off-season.

♔♔ **Holiday Inn Broadway** (dwntwn), 181 W. Broadway, AZ
🔑🔑 85701 (602/624-8711; toll free, see Holiday Inns). 310 rms, A/C, color TV, in-rm movies. AE, CB, DC, MC, V. Free gar., pool, rest., bar, rm svce, free crib. *Note:* Typical modern hotel a stone's throw from La Placita and its shopping. Serviceable comfort and facilities; so-so rest. Group and business clientele. A Holiday Inn at its best; very central location adjacent to the Convention Center; good value on balance. **I–M,** but lower rates off-season.

♔ **Motel 6 Central** (nr. dwntwn), 960 S. Freeway, AZ 85745
🔑 (602/628-1339). 112 rms, A/C, cable color TV. AE, DC, MC, V. Free parking, pool, adj. coffee shop. *Note:* The best buy in Tucson if you're driving through; functional comfort at unbeatable prices. 5 min. from dwntwn. **B**

Other Accommodations (from top bracket to budget)

☼♔♔♔♔ **Loews Ventana Canyon Resort** (vic.), 7000 N. Resort Dr.,
🔑🔑🔑 AZ 85715 (602/299-2020; toll free, see Loews). 398 rms, A/C, color TV, in-rm movies. AE, CB, DC, MC, V. Free valet parking, two pools, 10 tennis courts, golf, putting green, health club, sauna, three rests. (including the Ventana Room), bar, 24-hr. rm svce, disco, boutiques, concierge, free crib. *Note:* On a mesa w. a splendid view of Tucson Valley 3,000 ft. (900m) below and the surrounding mountains, this luxury hotel boasts a superb wild setting. The typically southwestern building overlooks an 80-ft. (24m) waterfall which feeds a little lake lying below the hotel. Spacious, inviting rms w. balconies and refrigerators; attentive svce; quality rest. Wonderful golf course in the open desert. A very good place to stay, 20 min. from dwntwn. **VE,** but lower rates off-season.

☼♔♔♔ **Westward Look** (vic.), 245 E. Ina Rd., AZ 85704 (602/297-
🔑🔑🔑 1151; toll free 800/722-2500). 245 rms, A/C, color TV, in-rm movies. AE, CB, DC, MC, V. Free parking, three pools, eight tennis courts, health club, horseback riding, rest. (Gold Room), bar, rm svce, disco, free crib. *Note:* Luxury hotel in 78 acres (31ha) of grdn and woodland in the foothills of the Santa Catalina Mountains, w. spectacular view over Tucson and the valley. Pretty one- or two-floor cottages around the pool, w. very comfortable rms (minibars and private patios). Worthwhile AP and MAP packages; the rest. is highly regarded. Cheerful, friendly svce. A Tucson landmark for 40 years. **E–VE,** but lower rates off-season.

♔♔ **Radisson Suite** (nr. dwntwn), 6555 E. Speedway Blvd., AZ
🔑🔑 85710 (602/721-7100; toll free, see Radisson). 304 suites, A/C, color TV, in-rm movies. AE, CB, DC, MC, V. Free parking, pool, health club, 17 tennis courts adjoining, putting green, rest. (Café Dorado), bar, rm svce, free breakfast and cocktails, free crib. *Note:* Modern, inviting hotel w. suites only, spacious, w. balcony, refrigerator, and microwave; the best look out on the pool-patio. Efficient svce. Business and convention clientele. 12 min. from dwntwn. **M–E,** but lower rates off-season.

♔♔ **Aztec Inn** (nr. dwntwn), 102 N. Alvernon Way, AZ 85711
🔑🔑 (602/795-0330). 156 rms, A/C, color TV. AE, CB, DC, MC, V. Free parking, pool, adj. rest., rm svce, hrdrsr, free crib. *Note:* Very engaging Spanish Colonial architecture and interior; comfortable rms w. refrigerators, the best overlooking the charming patio w. pool. Rms w. kitchenettes and no-smoking rms available. Efficient reception and svce; good value. 10 min. from dwntwn. **I–M,** but lower rates off-season.

♔ **La Quinta Inn** (nr. dwntwn), 665 N. Freeway, AZ 85705
🔑 (602/622-6491; toll free, see La Quinta Motor Inns). 132 rms, A/C, color TV, in-rm movies. AE, CB, DC, MC, V. Free parking, pool, adj. 24-hr. coffee shop, valet svce. *Note:* Elegant Mexican-style building; huge, intelli-

gently designed rms w. separate sleeping alcoves. Friendly reception; very good value. **I**

      Discovery Inn (nr. dwntwn), 1010 S. Freeway, AZ 85745 (602/622-5871). 146 rms, A/C, cable color TV. MC, V. Free parking, pool, rest., bar, valet svce, crib $5. *Note:* Classic motel w. basic conveniences at an attractive price, 5 min. from dwntwn and 12 min. from the airport (free shuttle). Laundrette. Reception and svce w. a smile. **B**, but lower rates off-season.

Guest Ranches

    Guest ranches, commonly known as "dude ranches," are the ideal solution if you like open-air vacations and horseback riding; they offer luxury comforts and svce while you play cowboy.

      Tanque Verde Guest Ranch (vic.), 14301 E. Speedway Blvd., AZ 85710 (602/296-6275). 67 rms, A/C, color TV available. AE, MC, V. Free parking, two pools, five tennis courts, horseback riding, outdoor sports, rest., bar, valet svce, free crib. *Note:* Old stock ranch and stagecoach station dating from 1868; picturesque rustic decor. Spacious rms (in *casitas*) w. refrigerators and private patios, some w. fireplaces. Open-air barbecues; excursions in the area. Informal but elegant atmosphere; a very good place. Free airport limo. Open year round. **VE** (American Plan), but lower rates off-season.

      White Stallion Ranch (vic.), 9251 Twin Peaks Rd., AZ 85743 (602/297-0252). 30 rms (no A/C). No credit cards. Free parking, pool, two tennis courts, horseback riding, outdoor sports, rest., bar, free crib. *Note:* Authentic ranch, straight out of a western movie, w. herds and real cowboys, on 3,000 acres (1,230ha) of untamed land. Comforts of rather a rustic nature, but engaging family atmosphere. Open-air barbecues, rodeos, horse-and-cart rides. Airport limo. Open Oct–Apr only. **E–VE** (American Plan).

      Lazy K Bar Guest Ranch (vic.), 8401 N. Scenic Dr., AZ 85743 (602/744-3050; toll free 800/321-7018). 23 rms, A/C, no TVs in the rms. AE, DC, MC, V. Free parking, pool, tennis courts, horseback riding, trap shooting, outdoor sports, rest., bar, library, crib $20. *Note:* 50-year old ranch spread over 160 acres (65ha) of beautiful mountainous desert complete w. hiking trails. Inviting rms., some w. private patios. A good family experience; picnic tables, cookouts, rodeos, and hayrides. Open year round. Free airport limo. **E–VE**

Airport Accommodations

      Clarion Hotel Airport (vic.) 6801 S. Tucson Blvd., AZ 85706 (602/746-3932; toll free, see Choice). 194 rms, A/C, color TV, in-rm movies. AE, CB, DC, MC, V. Free parking; pool; rest.; bar; rm svce; free breakfast, evening cocktails, and late-night snacks; crib $10. *Note:* Modern airport hotel a quarter mile north from the terminal (free shuttle). Agreeable shaded courtyard w. picnic tables and grills. Comfortable rms. w. private patios and refrigerators. Attentive, efficient svce. Very good value. Ideal for a stopover between flights. **I–M**, but lower rates off-season.

RESTAURANTS

Personal Favorites (in order of preference)

      Janos (dwntwn), 150 N. Main Ave. (884-9426). A/C. Dinner only, Mon–Sat; closed hols. and Mon mid-May to Sept. AE, MC, V. Jkt. *Specialties:* trilogy of blue corn fritters w. nantua; exotic mushroom-and-brie relleño w. smoky tomato coulis and jicama salad; short stack of beef tenderloin, bull's-eye of two sauces, and eggplant taco; veal-venison chop w. wild game sauce; warm chocolate soufflé tort and mint sorbet. Seasonal menu. Average wine list. *Note:* The young chef Janos Wilder broke new ground when (in 1985) he opened the first rest. serving French-inspired southwestern cuisine in Tucson. Since then his success has never faltered. The rest. occupies a picturesque 19th-century adobe building w. exposed beams, a designated historic landmark adobe home. Open-air dining on fine days. Excellent svce. Tucson's most inspired and imaginative food; resv. are a must. *American.* **M–E**

🍷🍷 **Café Terra Cotta** (nr. dwntwn), 4310 N. Campbell Ave. (577-
♣♣♣ 8100). A/C. Lunch/dinner daily; closed hols. AE, DC, MC, V. *Specialties:* pizzas nouvelle cuisine, garlic custard w. warm salsa vinaigrette and herbed hazelnuts, roast chili pepper stuffed w. chicken and corn, prawns stuffed w. goat cheese, black-bean and beef chili. Engaging homemade desserts. Menu changes regularly. *Note:* Inventive, praiseworthy contemporary southwestern cuisine from chef-owner Donna Nordin, who has gained enough success to branch out to Phoenix. Airy and comfortable decor; cheerful svce. Resv. requested. Excellent value. *American.* **I–M**

🍷🍷 **Scordato's** (nr. dwntwn), 4405 Speedway Blvd. (624-8946). A/C. Dinner only, Tues–Sun; closed July 4, Thanksgiving, Dec 25. AE, CB, DC, MC, V. Jkt. *Specialties:* classic Italian food: veal Stresa, fresh homemade pasta, catch of the day, broiled prime cuts. Good wine list. *Note:* On a height overlooking the city, this charming little house w. its tile roof has been for 20 years one of Tucson's best Italian rests., and one of the most popular. Elegant, romantic atmosphere. The veal, represented by no fewer than 13 different recipes on the menu, is the choicest reared in Wisconsin. Attentive svce; resv. requested. *Italian/Continental.* **I–M**

🍷🍷 **El Adobe** (dwntwn), 40 W. Broadway at Church St. (791-
♣♣ 7458). A/C. Lunch/dinner Mon–Sat; closed hols. AE, MC, V. *Specialties:* flautas, tamales, enchiladas, carne seca (sun-dried beef), Sonoran-style dishes. Excellent homemade margaritas. *Note:* In this pretty adobe hacienda dating from 1868 the food is authentically Mexican; there's also a romantic shady patio-grdn. Prompt, efficient svce. Locally very popular; right in the historic district. *Mexican.* **B–I**

🍷 **Pinnacle Peak** (vic.), 6541 E. Tanque Verde Rd. (296-0911).
♣ A/C. Dinner only, nightly; closed Thanksgiving, Dec 25. MC, V. *Specialties:* cowboy steak, ribs, and other meats; barbecued chicken; broiled fish. *Note:* Same successful formula as its sister spot in Phoenix: excellent beef cuts broiled over a mesquite fire. Pleasant western decor; locally popular. Well worth the 20-min. drive from dwntwn. No resv. *Steak.* **I**

🔆🍷 **Cup Café** (dwntwn), 311 E. Congress St. (798-1618). A/C.
🔆♣ Breakfast/lunch/dinner daily. AE, MC, V. *Specialties:* quesadillas w. fresh salsa and black-bean relish, sandwiches, salads, Mexican dishes. *Note:* Hip little café located in the historic Hotel Congress (1919). Features fresh baked goods and light entrées w. a southwestern flair. Sidewalk dining w. a view of the old Southern Pacific depot. Relaxed atmosphere. In the heart of dwntwn Tucson. *American/Mexican.* **B–I**

Other Restaurants (from top bracket to budget)

🔆🍷🍷 **Charles** (vic.), 6400 E. El Dorado Circle (296-7173). A/C.
🔆♣♣ Dinner only, Mon–Sat; closed Memorial Day, July 4. AE, DC, MC, V. Jkt. *Specialties:* crêpes El Dorado, steak Diane, veal El Dorado, game (in season), shrimp dijon. Menu changes regularly. Fine wine list. *Note:* In an elegant freestone manor house which once belonged to the Pond cosmetics family, this luxury rest. serves some of the most refined traditional cuisine in Tucson. Very polished reception and svce; stately grdn w. fountain; prices to match. A lovely cypress avenue leads up to the rest. 20 min. from dwntwn; valet parking; resv. strongly advised. *Continental.* **M–E**

🍷🍷🍷 **Daniel's** (nr. dwntwn), 4340 N. Campbell at River Rd. (742-
♣♣♣ 3200). A/C. Dinner only, nightly; closed hols. AE, CB, DC, MC, V. *Specialties:* zuppa di pesce, spinach and smoked salmon pasta, seafood vermicelli, veal cutlet stuffed w. ham and cheese, filet of beef w. green peppercorns, molten truffle cake. Seasonal menu. Fine list of American wines. *Note:* The rest., opened in 1986 by Daniel Scordato, heir of a dynasty of local restaurateurs,

is attempting to produce a contemporary version of classic Italian cuisine. Elegant setting; overlooks St. Phillip's Plaza. Proper and attentive svce. A fashionable place; resv. advised. *Italian.* **M**

Jerome's (vic.), 6958 E. Tanque Verde Rd. (721-0311). A/C. Dinner nightly, brunch Sun; closed Dec 25. AE, MC, V. Jkt. *Specialties:* chilled oysters, sweetwater barbecued duck, blackened redfish, Créole and Cajun dishes, broiled fish. *Note:* With its paneled walls, exposed beams, and big brick fireplace, the decor is more Boston than Louisiana, but Jerome's food is authentic New Orleans. Swift, efficient svce; successful, so resv. advised. 25 min. from dwntwn. *Créole.* **I–M**

Le Rendez Vous (nr. dwntwn), 3844 E. Fort Lowell Rd. (323-7373). A/C. Lunch Tues–Fri, dinner Tues–Sun; closed Jan 1, Dec 25. AE, CB, DC, MC, V. *Specialties:* scallops au gratin, salmon jalousie, bouillabaisse, pepper steak, sweetbreads w. mushrooms and Dijon-mustard sauce, rack of lamb provençal, soufflé Grand Marnier. Good wine list. *Note:* Inviting, intimate little bistro w. lots of charm serving the first-rate classical cuisine of chef Jean-Claude Berger. Elegant enclosed patio. Flawless svce. For those who value real French food at reasonable prices, this is the best place to eat in Tucson. Resv. advisable. *French.* **I–M**

Olive Tree (nr. dwntwn), 7000 E. Tanque Verde Rd. (298-1845). A/C. Lunch Mon–Sat, dinner nightly; closed hols. AE, MC, V. *Specialties:* lamb chops, shish kebabs, dolmathes, Greek dishes, broiled fish. *Note:* Enormously popular rest. 20 min. from dwntwn. Mainly Greek food, straightforward and tasty. Intimate indoor or outdoor dining. Efficient svce; very good value; an excellent place. *Greek/Continental.* **I**

Dakota Café (nr. dwntwn), 6541 E. Tanque Verde Rd. (298-7188). A/C. Lunch/dinner Mon–Sat; closed Thanksgiving, Dec. 25. AE, CB, DC, MC, V. *Specialties:* tempura coconut shrimp w. chutney marmalade, barbecued Southwestern meatloaf, beef tenderloin w. brandy-pepper-cream sauce, catch of the day. *Note:* Locally popular café w. a nicely balanced menu that doesn't forget vegetarians. Full bar svce., means it's a good place to dine if you are alone. Somewhat curt svce. Resv. not accepted for less than five. *American.* **B–I**

El Charro (dwntwn), 311 N. Court Ave. (622-5465). A/C. Lunch/dinner daily, brunch Sun; closed hols. AE, CB, DC, MC, V. *Specialties:* tostada con carne seca, stuffed chile, chimichangas, topopo salad (chicken and avocado), burritos, pastelito de fruta, almendrado. *Note:* Typical rest., serving authentic Mexican food since 1922. In an 1887 building in the heart of old Tucson. Inviting patio for outdoor dining; diligent, friendly svce. Locally popular; excellent value. *Mexican.* **B–I**

Oven's Restaurant (nr. dwntwn), 4280 N. Campbell Ave. (577-9001). A/C. Lunch/dinner daily; closed July 4, Dec. 25, Jan 1. AE, MC, V. *Specialties:* rotisserie pork and chicken, pizzas baked in wood-burning oven, Thai pasta, crème brûlée. *Note:* Pleasant bistro setting w. patio dining. Eclectic dishes priced very reasonably. Efficient svce. *American.* **B–I**

Cafeterias/Fast Food

Bowen & Bailey (dwntwn), 135 S. Sixth Ave. (792-2623). Breakfast/lunch/dinner Mon–Sat. AE, MC, V. European-style café serving a variety of cold meats, pâtés, cheeses, and salads. Full bar; espresso.

El Minuto (dwntwn), 354 S. Main Ave. (882-4145). Open daily 11am–1am. AE, MC, V. Excellent homemade Mexican food in a charming southwestern atmosphere. A classic for more than 50 years. Usually packed w. locals.

BARS & NIGHTCLUBS

The Baron's (nr. dwntwn), 2401 S. Wilmot Rd. (747-3503). Trendy disco; locally popular. Open nightly. Also rest.

Hotel Congress Historic Tap Room (dwntwn), 311 E. Congress St. (622-8848). A throwback in time to the year of this bar's birth—1938. Friendly crowd. Nightclub across the hall featuring progressive, alternative music that's sometimes live. Open nightly.

Javelina Cantina (nr. dwntwn), in the Doubletree Hotel (see "Accommodations," above) (881-4200). Singles bar-disco much favored by the young professional crowd and the students of the nearby university. Open nightly.

Laffs Comedy Café (nr. dwntwn), 2900 E. Broadway (323-8669). The best comedy club in town. Open Tues–Sun.

The Maverick (nr. dwntwn), 4700 22nd St. (748-0456). Live country-and-western music; very cowboy atmosphere. Open Mon–Sat.

Terry & Zeke's (nr. dwntwn), 4376 E. Speedway Blvd. (325-3555). Hole-in-the-wall spot turned out a local institution. Live Texas blues and R&B nightly. Great beer selection.

NEARBY EXCURSIONS

BIOSPHERE 2 (35 mi./56km north via U.S. 89 and Ariz. 77 in Oracle) (602/825-6200): Much debated ecological experiment started in Sept 1991 in the Santa Catalina Mountains north of Tucson. A giant greenhouse (7.2-million-cu.-ft, 204,000m³) is sealed under 4 acres (1.6ha) of glass. It contains some 3,800 species of plants, insects, and animals that are supposed to feed each other. The Biosphere is arrayed in seven different climatic zones or "biomes," and is designed to be totally independent of the outside world. Has become a major tourist attraction complete with plans for a conference center, hotel, golf course, and space camp. Outside tours are conducted daily ($12.95).

CASA GRANDE RUINS NATIONAL MONUMENT (69 mi./110km NW via I-10 and Ariz. 87) (602/723-3172): See Chapter 42 on Phoenix.

COLOSSAL CAVE (25 mi./40km SE via I-10 and Colossal Cave Rd.) (602/647-7275): Unique natural caves, only partially explored, with astonishing crystal formations. Many marine fossils bear witness that Arizona was once the bed of a prehistoric sea. The temperature in the caves stays at 72°F (22°C) year round. Open daily.

CORONADO NATIONAL FOREST: 1,790,000 acres (720,000ha) of forest and desert around Tucson, Nogales, Patagonia, Benson, and Wilcox. Scenic drives, camping, fishing, horseback riding, skiing in winter, etc. For information, contact the Supervisor, Federal Bldg., 300 W. Congress St., Tucson, AZ 85701 (670-4552). There's a **visitor center** at Sabino Canyon (see below).

DAVIS-MONTHAN AIR FORCE BASE (Craycroft Rd. at GolfLinks Rd., 7 mi./11km SE) (602/750-4717): More than 20,000 warplanes, from World War II relics to Vietnam War jets, parked in endless rows. You can view the 2-mi.-long (3km) graveyard through the airfield fence when you travel west on Irvington Rd. to Wilmot Rd. Visits Mon and Wed by resv. An absolute must for aviation buffs.

KITT PEAK NATIONAL OBSERVATORY (56 mi./ 90km SW via Ariz. 86 and Ariz. 386) (602/325-9200): Considered by scholars one of the world's greatest astronomical observatories. At an elevation of 6,882 ft. (2,098m) up in the Sonora desert, it boasts the largest solar telescope in the world and the third-largest stellar telescope in the U.S., 158 in. (4m) in diameter and weighing 375 tons, housed in a 19-story building. Open daily; fascinating. Splendid surrounding scenery.

SABINO CANYON (16 mi./25km east via Tanque Verde and Sabino Canyon Rds.) (602/749-2327): A kind of green oasis in the desert of the Santa Catalina Mountains; forms part of the immense Coronado National Forest. No private cars are permitted in Sabino Canyon, but there are guided bus tours every half-hour. A must for nature lovers.

SAGUARO NATIONAL MONUMENT (17 mi./27km east via Broadway and Old Spanish Trail; or 16 mi./25km west via W. Speedway Blvd. and Saguaro Rd.): America's most spectacular giant-cactus forest; some saguaros grow 52 ft. (16m) tall and live for two centuries. Wide variety of flora and fauna, including coyote, peccary, and various kinds of deer. The park is divided into two sections: the **Rincon Mountain Unit** (east of Tucson), the more spectacular, and the **Tucson Mountain Unit** (west of Tucson). Try to go in May and June, when the saguaros are in flower. Visitor centers open year round; hiking trails, camping permitted. For information, contact the Superintendent, 3693 S. Old Spanish Trail, Tucson, AZ 85730 (602/670-6680).

Where to Eat

Saguaro Corners, 3750 S. Old Spanish Trail (886-5424). Opposite Saguaro National Monument East. Open for lunch/ dinner Tues–Sun; closed Aug. I

TITAN MISSILE MUSEUM (Duval Mine Rd. in Green Valley, 26 mi./41km south on I-19 to Exit 69) (602/791-2929): World's only ballistic-missile museum. Guided tour (exhausting) of the silo containing the huge nuclear missile, 110 ft. (33m) high, deactivated in 1983 after standing on 24-hr. alert for 19 years. Impressive. Open daily Nov–Apr, Wed–Sun the rest of the year.

GHOST TOWNS: There are a good 20 ghost towns dating from the gold rush days in the area around Tombstone, Nogales, and Chiricahua National Monument. Some, such as Ruby (near Nogales), are closed to the public; others, such as Hilltop or Paradise (near Chiricahua National Monument) are quite hard to reach. In addition to Tombstone—the liveliest, least ghostly ghost town in the West—(see "Tombstone," below), two others are well worth seeing: Gleeson (16 mi./26km east of Tombstone) and Pearce (28 mi./45km NE of Tombstone).

FARTHER AFIELD

CHIRICAHUA NATIONAL MONUMENT (121 mi./ 194km SE via I-10E and Ariz. 186E): Picturesque rock formations of volcanic origin in a former Apache hunting ground (see "Tombstone," below).

☼☾🅰 **NOGALES** (145 mi./232km r.t. via I-19S, Ariz. 82, Ariz. 83N, and I-10W): Picturesque excursion toward the Mexican border, beginning with a visit to the ☼🛆🛆 **Mission San Xavier del Bac** (see "Churches/Synagogues," above). Drive on to 🛆 **Tubac Presidio State Historic Park,** on U.S. 89 (602/398-2252), open daily, the first Spanish settlement in Arizona. The remains of the fort, now a museum, date from 1752.

Then 5 mi. (8km) south, at ☼🛆 **Tumacacori National Monument,** see the uncompleted Franciscan mission of San José (about 1800), with a lovely courtyard garden. The Native American village of Tumacacori (602/398-2341) was first visited in 1691 by Jesuit Fr. Eusebio Kino, the great Spanish missionary to Arizona. Open daily.

At the end of I-19, ☼ **Nogales,** a very touristy border town bisected by high fences, is worth a look. No documents are required for U.S. citizens if you're just going to cross the border for a few hours of shopping (pottery, leather goods, baskets, glass, and tin items) or sightseeing. Some shops worth visiting are El Changarro (93 Calle Elías), El Continental (98 Obregón Ave.), and El Zarape (161 Obregón Ave.).

Continue east along the 200 acre (80ha) **Patagonia Lake,** complete with beach, marina, etc., and the picturesque little town of 🛆 **Patagonia.** Visit the unusual **Stradling Museum of the Horse** at 350 McKeown Ave. (602/394-2264), open Tues–Sun, containing everything that has to do with "man's noblest conquest," from classical Greece to the age of the cowboy. Not far from Patagonia, on Ariz. 82, is the wonderful 🛆 **Patagonia-Sonoita Creek Sanctuary,** where willows, ash, and sycamores along the banks of the Sonoita brook shelter more than 250 different species of birds. Many western movies were shot in the neighboring **Empire Valley** (around **Sonoita** and **Elgin**) in the late 1940s and 1950s: *Duel in the Sun, Red River,* and *Winchester 73* among others.

On the way back, visit the 🛆 **Colossal Cave** (see "Nearby Excursions," above) and the ☼🛆🛆 **Pima Air Museum** (see "Museums of Science and History," above). A wonderful expedition for nature lovers.

Where to Eat in Nogales

🍸 **La Rocca,** 91 Calle Elías (52-631/20-760), is a typical restaurant on the Mexican side. Open daily 11am–midnight.

☼☾🅰 **ORGAN PIPE CACTUS NATIONAL MONUMENT** (139 mi./222km west via Ariz. 86W and Ariz. 85S): One of the country's wildest and loveliest desert-land parks, on the Mexican border. The cactuses for which the park is named reach 20 ft. (6m) in height, with as many as 30 vertical arms stacked like organ pipes; they flower in May and June. Two scenic highways traverse this seldom-visited park. Visitor center open year round; camping permitted. For information, contact the Superintendent, Rte. 1, Ajo, AZ 85321 (602/387-6849).

☼☾🅰🅰 **TOMBSTONE** (355 mi./568km r.t. via I-10E, U.S. 80E, an unsurfaced road between Rodeo–Portal and Chiricahua National Monument in summer only or U.S. 666N and Ariz. 181E in winter, Ariz. 186W, Apache Pass Rd., and I-10W): This spectacular trip, full of sights for the lover of frontier history, begins with a visit to ☼🛆🛆 **Tombstone,** "The Town Too Tough to Die," so called both because of its innumerable shoot-outs (such as the famous "Gunfight at the O.K. Corral" between the Earp brothers and the Clanton brothers, and for the series of catastrophes that overtook its gold and silver mines). Today it's a museum town, with many picturesque buildings from the 1880s: the **Boothill Graveyard,** on U.S. 80 (602/457-9344), with its unusual epitaphs; a **courthouse** dating from 1882 with many remembrances of the town's eventful past, at Toughnut and 3rd Sts. (602/457-3311), open daily; the **Bird Cage Theater,** Allen and 6th Sts. (602/457-3421), open daily, which was once dubbed "the wildest and wickedest spot between Basin St. and the Barbary Coast," and numbered the beautiful Lola Montez among its attractions; the **Crystal Palace Saloon,** 5th and Allen Sts., open daily, another house of ill-repute famous in the 1880s; the office of the *Tombstone Epitaph,* 5th and Allen Sts. (457-2211), the local daily paper founded in 1880 and published continuously since then; the **O.K. Corral** on Allen between 3rd and 4th Sts. (602/457-3456), scene of the famous gunfight; and more. No horse-opera buff can afford to miss Tombstone. For information, contact the **Tombstone Tourism Association,** 9 S. 5th St. (602/457-2211).

Next stop is ✻ **Bisbee,** a real pioneer town sprawled along the sides of Mule Pass Gulch with turn-of-the-century houses. Luckier than Tombstone, it remained prosperous for a full century, its last open-pit copper mines closing only in 1975. Visit the underground ⚓ **Queen Mine** copper mine, where the temperature in the bowels of the earth never rises above 49° F (9° C)—but take a sweater or a jacket even in summer—and its open-pit neighbor the **Lavender Pit,** on U.S. 80 (602/432-2071 for both mines), open daily; resv. suggested. At the ⚓ **Bisbee Mining Historical Museum,** 5 Copper Queen Plaza (602/432-7071), open daily, are interesting souvenirs from Bisbee's mining days.

Continue south on U.S. 80 to **Douglas,** an engaging stagecoach-stop town on the Mexican border; take a look at the extravagant ⚐⚐ **Gadsden Hotel,** originally built in 1907 and rebuilt after a fire in 1929; the sumptuously rococo interior has been used as a set for many westerns.

Your next stop is at ⚓ **Chiricahua National Monument,** whose spectacular landscape of volcanic rocks and deep gorges once gave sanctuary to the Apache chiefs Cochise and Geronimo. Wonderful scenic drive (Bonita Canyon Rd.) and dozens of miles of trails. Camping permitted. Visitor center at the park entrance on U.S. 181 (602/824-3560). Not far away, at ⚓ **Fort Bowie National Historic Site** (602/847-2500), you'll see the ruins of two military posts built to protect the coaches of the legendary Butterfield Stage Coach line from Native American attacks. The site can only be reached by walking 1 mi. (1.6km) on a foot trail; beware of flash floods and rattlesnakes. Open daily.

Drive back to Tucson along the Texas Canyon, by way of ⚓ **Willcox;** see the **Cochise Visitor Center** on Fort Grant Rd. (602/384-2272), open daily, the best museum of the Apache days.

For this itinerary you should set aside two or three days. If you're a western-history buff, this is the trip for you.

Where to Stay En Route

IN BISBEE ✻🛎🛎 **Copper Queen Hotel,** 11 Howell Ave., Bisbee, AZ 85603 (602/432-2216). 43 rms. Charming turn-of-the-century hotel, now elegantly restored. **I–M**

✻🛎🛎 **Bisbee Grand Hotel,** 61 Main St., Bisbee, AZ 85603 (602/432-5900; toll free 800/421-1909). 11 rms. Delightfully restored 1900s hotel. Elegant Victorian atmosphere; numerous antiques. Totally nonsmoking. **I–M**

IN DOUGLAS ✻🛎🛎 **Gadsden Hotel,** 1046 G. Ave., Douglas, AZ 85607 (602/364-4481). 145 rms. Beautiful rococo 1907 hotel, a designated historic monument. **I–M**

IN TOMBSTONE 🛎 **Best Western Lookout Lodge,** on U.S. 80, Tombstone, AZ 85638 (602/457-2223). 40 rms. Inviting motel w. a view of the Dragoon Mountains. **I–M**

IN WILLCOX 🍽 **Best Western Plaza Inn,** 1100 W. Rex Allen Dr., Willcox, AZ 85643 (602/384-3556). 93 rms. Comfortable motel of the usual type. **I–M**

PART SIX

THE NORTHWEST

CHAPTER 44

PORTLAND ⚡

□ □ □

Dominated by the imposing, snow-crowned **Mount Hood** (11,235 ft./ 3,424m) in the distance, Portland figures consistently at the head of America's 243 major cities in various surveys having to do with the "quality of life." Downtown, where high-rises are few and all vehicular traffic is forbidden with the exception of (free) buses and cabs, the pedestrian zone of the **Mall,** with its stores, restaurants, fountains, and statues, is proof of the concern of Portland's inhabitants for their environment.

If you want to gather an overall impression of the "City of Roses," the best way is to drive around the 50-mi. (80km) **Scenic Drive,** which encircles the city, from the heights above it through its innumerable parks and its botanic garden. Famous for its rose gardens (whence its nickname), its humidity, and its mountain scenery, Oregon's largest city is a vigorous commercial and industrial metropolis, important in lumber, electronics, food, clothing, and aluminum. Stern legislation has banished smog and pollution; salmon are once again being taken from the **Willamette River,** which divides the city in two, and the drinking water drawn from it is rated among the purest in the western U.S.

Although 112 mi. (108km) from the ocean, Portland is one of the most active seaports on the Pacific coast, handling more than 26 million tons of cargo annually. It boasts the largest floating drydock in the western U.S.

Many excursions can be made, using Portland as a base, into the mountains of the **Cascade Range** and the **Coast Range,** or up the splendid **Columbia River Gorge.** The region is famous for its seafood: salmon and sturgeon from the **Columbia River,** trout and crayfish from the **Sun River,** oysters and crabs from the Pacific. So make a point of visiting some of the multitude of (excellent) seafood restaurants in town. Among Portland's famous native sons are Linus Pauling, the Nobel Laureate in chemistry; famous journalist and radical activist John Reed; and food critic James Beard.

BASIC FACTS: State of Oregon. Area code: 503. Time zone: Pacific. ZIP Code: 97208. Founded: 1842. Approximate population: city, **440,000;** metropolitan area, **1,480,000.** 27th-largest metropolitan area in the U.S.

CLIMATE: With more than 150 days of rainfall a year, Portland is one of the wettest cities in the country, but it is precisely this fine, persistent, London-style drizzle that has made it a garden city. Winter (Jan mean, 40°F/4°C) is relatively mild, with little snow; spring is cool, but it rains, on average, every other day from Oct to May. The best time to visit the city is between June and Sept, when the thermometer hovers around 68°F (20°C) and it sometimes doesn't rain for two weeks on end (whereupon the locals become anxious and talk about drought).

DISTANCES: Reno, 574 mi. (918km); Salt Lake City, 768 mi. (1,230km); San Francisco, 634 mi. (1,015km); Seattle, 175 mi. (280km).

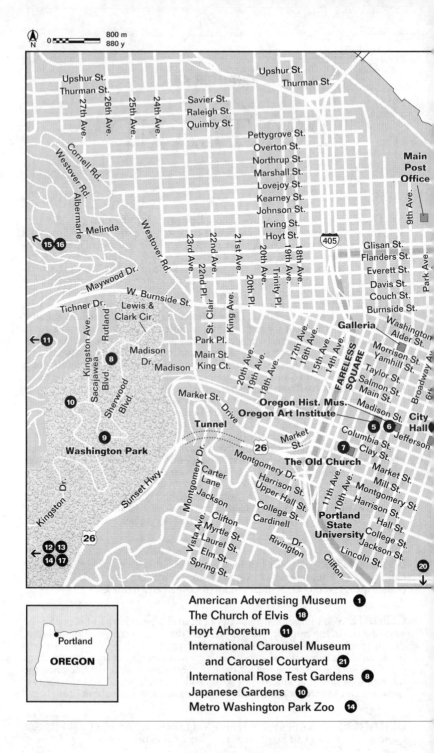

American Advertising Museum **1**
The Church of Elvis **18**
Hoyt Arboretum **11**
International Carousel Museum
    and Carousel Courtyard **21**
International Rose Test Gardens **8**
Japanese Gardens **10**
Metro Washington Park Zoo **14**

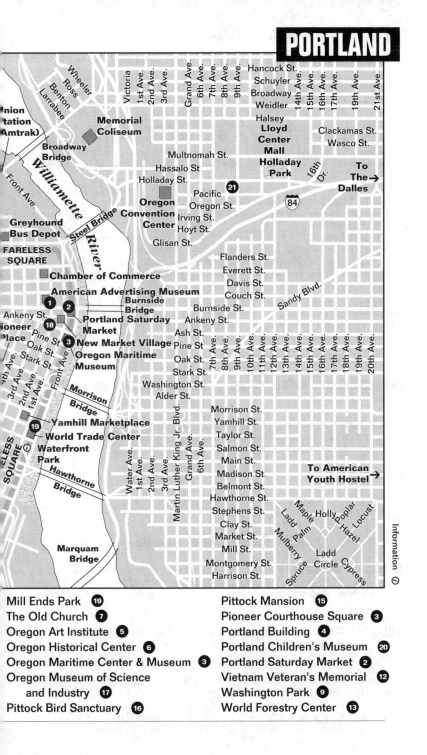

PORTLAND

Wheeler
Ross
Benton
Larrabee

Victoria
1st Ave.
2nd Ave.
3rd Ave.

Grand Ave.
6th Ave.
7th Ave.
8th Ave.
9th Ave.

Hancock St.
Schuyler
Broadway
Weidler

14th Ave.
15th Ave.
16th Ave.
17th Ave.
19th Ave.
21st Ave.

Union
Station
(Amtrak)

Memorial
Coliseum

Halsey
Lloyd
Center
Mall

Clackamas St.
Wasco St.

Broadway
Bridge

Williamette River

Front Ave.

Multnomah St.
Hassalo St
Holladay St.

Holladay
Park

16th
Dr.

To
The →
Dalles

Greyhound
Bus Depot

Steel Bridge

Oregon
Convention
Center

Pacific ㉑
Oregon St.
Irving St.
Hoyt St.

84

FARELESS
SQUARE

Glisan St.

Chamber of Commerce

Flanders St.
Everett St.
Davis St.
Couch St.

Sandy Blvd.

American Advertising Museum
Burnside
Bridge

❶ ❷

Burnside St.

Ankeny St.

Burnside St.
Ankeny St.

Pioneer
Place

❿

Pine St
Oak St.
Stark St.

Portland Saturday
Market

Ash St.
Pine St
Oak St.
Stark St.

7th Ave.
8th Ave.
9th Ave.
10th Ave.
11th Ave.
12th Ave.
13th Ave.
14th Ave.
15th Ave.
16th Ave.
17th Ave.
18th Ave.
19th Ave.
20th Ave.

❸ New Market Village
Oregon Maritime
Museum

4th Ave.
3rd Ave.
2nd Ave.
1st Ave.
Front Ave.

Washington St.
Alder St.

Morrison
Bridge

Yamhill Marketplace

⓳ World Trade Center

Waterfront
Park

Hawthorne
Bridge

Water Ave.
1st Ave.
2nd Ave.
3rd Ave.

Martin Luther King Jr. Blvd.

Grand Ave.
6th Ave.

Morrison St.
Yamhill St.
Taylor St.
Salmon St.
Main St.
Madison St.
Belmont St.
Hawthorne St.
Stephens St.
Clay St.
Market St.
Mill St.
Montgomery St.
Harrison St.

To American
Youth Hostel →

FARELESS
SQUARE

Marquam
Bridge

Maple Holly Poplar Locust
Ladd Palm Hazel
Mulberry
Spruce Cypress
Ladd
Circle

Information ⓘ

ARRIVAL & TRANSIT INFORMATION

AIRPORT: Portland International Airport (PDX), 9 mi. (14km) NE. For information, call 335-1234.

AIRLINES: Alaska (toll free 800/426-0333), America West (toll free 800/253-9292), American (toll free 800/433-7300), Continental (toll free 800/525-0280), Delta (toll free 800/221-1212), Northwest (toll free 800/225-2525), United (toll free 800/241-6522), and USAir (toll free 800/428-4322).

CITY LINK: The **cab** fare from the airport to dwntwn is about $22; time, about 25 min. Bus: **Raz Trans Airporter** (246-4676) leaves every 30 min., serving principal dwntwn hotels and the Greyhound terminal; fare, $7; time, 30 min. (60 min. during rush hour).
　　Tri-Met Max, 701 SW Sixth Ave. (238-7433), provides remarkable public transportation by bus (free in the dwntwn area) and streetcar. However, since the metropolitan area is extensive and the number of (recommended) excursions into the surrounding country considerable, it's advisable to rent a car with unlimited mileage.

CAR RENTAL (at the airport unless otherwise indicated): Avis (toll free 800/331-1212); Budget (toll free 800/527-0700); Dollar (toll free 800/800-4000); Hertz (toll free 800/654-3131); National (toll free 800/227-7368); and Thrifty, 10800 NE Holman St. (toll free 800/367-2277). For dwntwn locations, consult the local telephone directory.

LIMOUSINE SERVICES: Oregon Limo Service (252-5882) and Prestige Limousine (282-5009).

TAXIS: Taxis are comparatively few and expensive; they may not be hailed on the street, but can be taken from the waiting lines outside the major hotels, or hired by phone: **Broadway Cab** (227-1234) or **Radio Cab** (227-1212).

TRAIN: Amtrak station, 800 NW Sixth Ave. (toll free 800/872-7245).

INTERCITY BUSES: Greyhound, 550 NW Sixth Ave. (toll free 800/231-2222).

INFORMATION & TOURS

TOURIST INFORMATION: The **Portland/Oregon Visitors Association,** 26 SW Salmon St., OR 97204 (503/275-9750; toll free 800/962-3700).
　　For a **recorded message** giving a list of all current cultural events and shows, call 233-3333.

GUIDED TOURS: Eagle Flight Center (airplane), Portland-Hillsboro Airport, Hillsboro (648-7151): Flights over Mount St. Helens, the Columbia Gorge, or the Pacific coast (during the whale migrations). Spectacular. Year round, weather permitting.
　　Evergreen Gray Line Tours (bus), 4320 N. Suttle Rd. (285-9845): Guided bus tours of Portland and surroundings (Mount Hood, Columbia River, Mount St. Helens, etc.). Daily mid-Apr through Oct.
　　Oregon Vineyard Tours (bus), 2926 SW Periander (Suite 100), Portland (786-0732): Guided tours of Oregon's principal wineries; includes lunch and wine-tasting. Resv. required.

Cascade Sternwheeler (boat), SW Front Ave. and Stark St. (223-3928): Sternwheeler trips on the Willamette and Columbia Rivers, Fri–Sun Oct–June 15. The rest of the year the *Columbia Gorge* makes daily excursion trips through the Columbia Gorge, leaving from Cascade Locks.

SIGHTS, ATTRACTIONS & ACTIVITIES

ADVENTURES: River Drifters Whitewater Tours (boat), 13570 NW Lakeview Dr. (224-9625): Rafting down different rivers in the area; Mar–Sept.

ARCHITECTURAL HIGHLIGHTS: ☼☖ Arlene Schnitzer Concert Hall, 1057 SW Broadway (248-4496): Formerly the Paramount, this is a magnificent, flamboyantly rococo movie palace from the 1920s converted at a cost of $9 million into an auditorium, the Arlene Schnitzer Concert Hall (known locally as "The Schnitz"), where you can hear concerts of classical music as well as jazz and pop. Home of the Oregon Symphony Orchestra. With three other contiguous performance facilities, it constitutes the **Portland Center for the Performing Arts.**

☖ **Civic Auditorium,** 222 SW Clay St. (248-4496): Ultramodern concert hall, acoustically one of the finest in the U.S. Home of the Portland Opera Association and the Portland Ballet. In front of the building lies Ira's Fountain (see "Monuments," below) with its spectacular array of terraces, basins, and waterfalls.

☖ **Portland Building,** 1120 SW Fifth Ave. (823-4000): The most defiantly postmodern building in the U.S.; a sort of gigantic concrete birthday cake (others think that "jukebox" or "cookie tin" is more appropriate), in pastel tones of blue, beige, and brown, housing federal government offices, shops, and a restaurant. It's a 1982 work of architect Michael Graves, and you should see it, if only out of curiosity.

☖ **Portland Center for the Performing Arts (PCPA),** SW Broadway and Main St. (248-4496): Opened in 1987, this elegant architectural exercise in red brick and smoked glass comprises two adjoining auditoriums: the 900-seat **Intermediate Theater** and the 370-seat **Dolores Winningstad Theater;** the Arlene Schnitzer Concert Hall (see above) is across the street, and the Civic Auditorium (see above) is five blocks south. In this cultural heart of Portland you'll find the Civic Theater, the New Rose Theater, and the Oregon Shakespeare Festival.

☖ **U.S. Bancorp Tower,** 111 SW Fifth Ave. (275-6111): An unexpected kind of skyscraper: beautiful pink granite and mirror glass, dubbed "Big Pink" by its admirers. One of the major features of the Portland skyline.

CHURCHES/SYNAGOGUES: ☖ First Congregational Church, 1126 SW Park Ave. (228-7219): A fine example of Venetian Gothic from around 1900. Its helical spire and downstairs gallery of contrasting beige and black stone are well worth seeing. Open Sun–Fri.

☼☖ **The Grotto (Sanctuary of Our Sorrowful Mother),** Sandy Blvd. and NE 85th Ave. (254-7371): Open-air cathedral carved out of the foot of a great rock face 10 stories high. At the top of the cliff is a monastery surrounded by beautiful gardens, overlooking the Columbia River. Opened in 1924, this Marian sanctuary is visited each year by half a million of the faithful. Open daily.

HISTORIC BUILDINGS: ☖ Bybee-Howell House, Howell Park Rd., Sauvie Island, 14 mi. (22km) north via U.S. 30 (621-3344): A typical 19th-century farmhouse, originally built in 1856 and scrupulously restored. Illustrates the lifestyle of the first Oregon settlers; interesting little museum of agriculture. Open Sat–Sun June to early Sept.

    🔔 **City Hall,** 1220 SW Fifth Ave. (823-4000): Designed by architect William Whidden to look like an Italian palazzo, this unusual building is rich in rococo ornament and decoration in true 19th-century style (1895).

    🔔 **Pioneer Courthouse,** Fifth Ave. and Morrison St. (326-2107): This elegant Victorian courthouse, the first federal building in the Northwest (1875), has recovered its original luster after long and careful restoration. Its architecture is one of the charms of Pioneer Courthouse Sq., a complex of gardens with fountain, waterfall, and stepped terraces which appeals greatly to strollers.

    🌣🔔 **Pittock Mansion,** 3229 NW Pittock Dr. (823-3623): Built between 1909 and 1914 by the founder of *The Oregonian,* the most important daily paper in the city, this enormous manor house in French Renaissance style still has an abundance of antique furniture as well as 46 acres (19ha) of beautiful gardens. Wonderful view of the city and the distant mountains. Open daily; closed hols. and the first three weeks in Jan.

INDUSTRIAL TOURS: The **Pendleton Woolen Mills,** 10505 SE 17th Ave., Milwaukie (654-0444), 6 mi. (10km) south on Ore. 99E: Some of the finest sweaters and woolens in the U.S. come from the famous Pendleton plant. You can watch every stage in the manufacturing process, from the sorting of raw wool to washing and weaving. Interesting. Visits Mon–Fri by appointment; closed two weeks in July.

MARKETS: 🔔 **Portland Saturday Market,** 108 W. Burnside St., under the Burnside Bridge (222-6072): Every Sat and Sun 10am–5pm more than 300 artists, craftspeople, and farmers display their wares in this picturesque open-air market. Very popular with the locals since 1973. Open from Mar to Christmas.

MONUMENTS: 🌣🔔 **Ira's Fountain,** Third Ave. and SW Clay St.: A spectacular futurist design by Lawrence Halprin comprising basins, waterfalls, and fountains down which flows 13,000 gal. (49,500 liters) of water a minute. In the heart of downtown; lots of splashing around in summer.

    🌣🔔 **Portlandia,** 1120 SW Fifth Ave.: This gigantic figure by Raymond Kaskey, 35 ft. (10m) high, represents a kind of marine Venus, on her knees with a trident in one hand. Its size never fails to surprise visitors. Standing in front of the Portland Building (see "Architectural Highlights," above), this comically pompous work in beaten copper turns out to be nothing but a giant reproduction of the city's official seal.

    🌣🔔 **Weather Machine,** Pioneer Courthouse Sq.: Built by the Omen Design Group, the whimsical *Weather Machine,* dating from 1988, is one of the city's most bizarre public artworks. The 25-ft (7.6m) column gauges the changing environmental conditions with an eccentric collection of lights, figurines, and symbols. The best time to visit the mechanical sculpture is during the daily forecast at noon, a 2-min. festival complete with fanfares, plumes of steam, and flashing lights.

MUSEUMS OF ART: 🌣🔔 **American Advertising Museum,** 9 NW Second Ave. at Couch St. (226-0000): The world's first museum entirely devoted to commercial publicity in all its forms, from 18th-century shop signs and sandwich-man's boards to modern radio and TV spot commercials. More than 7,000 ads, some of which are genuine works of art. Unusual and fascinating. Open Wed–Sun.

    🔔 **Lawrence Gallery,** 842 SW First Ave. (843-3633): Temporary exhibitions of painting, ceramics, sculpture, modern jewelry, etc., with more than 250 different artists represented. Open daily.

※ ♨ Ⓐ **Portland Art Museum,** 1219 SW Park Ave. (226-2811): One of the best art museums in the Northwest, with fine collections of pre-Columbian, Far Eastern, African, and Pacific Northwest Native American material. The museum also features the very productive contemporary art community in the area. The main building, by Pietro Belluschi, dates from 1932. The open-air **Sculpture Mall** with its fountains is worth a visit by itself. Open Tues–Sun.

MUSEUMS OF SCIENCE & HISTORY: Ⓐ **Oregon Historical Center,** 1230

SW Park Ave. (222-1741): A comprehensive panorama of the Native American civilizations of the Pacific Northwest, both before and after the coming of the white man. The history of the Oregon Trail and its pioneers is illustrated by collections of miniature covered wagons and boat models. Well-stocked library on the settlement of the Northwest. Interesting. Open Tues–Sun.

※ ♨ Ⓐ **Oregon Museum of Science and Industry/OMSI,** 1945 SE Water St. (797-4000): A remarkable museum of science, instructive and up-to-date, covering the whole span from prehistory to outer space. Among its principal attractions are a robot with 3-D vision, a model of the space station of the future, and a Navy diesel submarine. Also the home of the **Murdock Sky Theater.** Open daily.

Ⓐ **World Forestry Center,** 4033 SW Canyon Rd. (228-1367): Across from **Washington Park Zoo,** this group of modern all-wood buildings has an information center on one of Oregon's principal natural resources: its forests. Exhibits relating to the forest-products industry; 70-ft. (21m) "talking tree"; very realistic re-creation of a forest fire; model of a paper mill, etc. Interesting. Open daily.

PANORAMAS: ※ **Atwater's:** See "Restaurants," below.

※ ♨ Ⓐ **Council Crest Park,** SW Greenway Ave. (823-1600): This little public park not far from downtown rises to a maximum elevation of 1,073 ft. (327m), the highest point in the city. Belvedere with unobstructed view of the Willamette River, Mount Hood, Mount St. Helens, and the Portland skyline below.

※ ♨ Ⓐ **Pittock Mansion:** See "Historic Buildings," above.

PARKS & GARDENS: ※ Ⓐ **Crystal Springs Rhododendron Garden,** SE

28th Ave. near SE Woodstock Blvd. (771-8386): A must for every visitor; more than 2,500 rhododendron bushes, as well as azaleas, flower here in Apr–May, and a superb sight they are. Open daily.

Ⓐ **Hoyt Arboretum,** 4000 SW Fairview Blvd. (823-3654): Established in 1928, this 180-acre (73ha) garden, part of Washington Park (see below), contains the largest collection of conifers in the country: 650 varieties. 10 miles of gentle trails wind past such special features as the Vietnam Veterans' Memorial and the Winter Garden, while offering spectacular views of the city and Mount Hood. Open daily.

Ⓐ **Mount Tabor Park,** SE 60th Ave. between Yamhill and Division Sts. (823-1600): The only municipal park in the country that occupies the crater of an extinct volcano. Fine view of the city and the mountains; public concerts in summer. Open daily.

Ⓐ **Sauvie Island,** 14 mi. (22km) NW on U.S. 30: This island in the Columbia River is very popular in summer, the ideal place for picnics, fishing, walking, bicycling, or just doing nothing. Among its main attractions is the Bybee-Howell House (see "Historic Buildings," above).

Ⓐ **Tom McCall Waterfront Park,** SW Front Ave. between Steel Bridge and River Place: This pretty, tree-shaded 23-acre (9ha) park, the pride of Portland, occupies land originally intended for a riverfront highway. With its many shops and restaurants along the edge of the park, it's an agreeable place for a walk, a stone's throw from downtown.

☀️🏂🏂 **Washington Park,** reached by West Burnside St. or Canyon
Rd. (823-1600): This 145-acre (60ha) park overlooks Portland from its hilltop emplacement; it features the very beautiful **Japanese Garden** and the magnificent **International Rose Test Garden,** with more than 400 different varieties of roses. The best times for a visit are June and Sept. Splendid view of the city.

PERFORMING ARTS: For daily listings of all shows and cultural events, consult the entertainment pages of the daily paper *The Oregonian* (morning and evening) as well as the weekly *Willamette Week*.

Arlene Schnitzer Concert Hall, 1057 SW Broadway (248-4496): Very fine 1920s building, magnificently restored. Classical concerts and recitals. Home of the Oregon Symphony (principal conductor: James De Preist).

Interstate Firehouse Cultural Center, 5340 N. Interstate Ave. (823-2000): Multicultural, experimental theater.

Memorial Coliseum, 1401 N. Wheeler Ave. (248-4496): Pop and rock concerts; big-name shows.

Portland Center for the Performing Arts, 1111 SW Broadway (248-4496): Very up-to-date entertainment complex offering contemporary and classical theater, ballet, and concerts. The Portland Center Stage, the Oregon Ballet Theater, and the Tygre's Shakespeare Theater make their home here.

Portland Civic Auditorium, 222 SW Clay St. (248-4496): Concerts, Broadway hits, musicals. Home of the Portland Opera Association (performances Sept–May) and the well-known Portland Ballet.

Portland Repertory Theater, 25 SW Salmon St. (224-4491): Contemporary theater; wide-ranging program. The best local repertory company.

Washington Park Amphitheater, Washington Park (823-1600): Open-air public concerts and free recitals (late July to Aug).

SHOPPING: Lloyd Center, NE Ninth Ave. and NE Multnomah St. (282-2511): One of the oldest and largest shopping centers in the country, with more than 100 shops and department stores. Flower-planted walkways. Skating rink in winter. Spectacular. Open daily.

Powell's Books, 1005 W. Burnside St. (228-4651): A Portland institution. With about a million books, this is one of the largest new- and used-book stores in the country. The very pleasant Anne Hughes Coffee Shop is part of the store. Pick up a map of the cavernous one-block-long building as you enter, or you risk getting lost. Open daily.

Water Tower at John's Landing, 5331 SW Macadam Ave. (228-9431): Picturesque shopping center in a renovated turn-of-the-century furniture factory. Congenial shops, pubs, and restaurants around a delightful cobbled courtyard. Open daily.

SPECIAL EVENTS: For the exact schedule of events below, consult the **Portland Convention and Visitors Association** (see "Tourist Information," above).

Rhododendron Show (second wknd in May): Beautiful flower show at the Crystal Springs Rhododendron Garden.

Portland Rose Festival (June): Procession of flowered carnival parades, flower show, auto races, dirigible-balloon rally, etc. Very popular since 1907.

Chamber Music Northwest (late June to late July): A well-known chamber-music festival of 25 recitals; for information, call 294-6400.

Mount Hood Festival of Jazz (early Aug): Two days of open-air jazz concerts, with leading performers, at Gresham, 15 mi. (24km) east on I-84 (666-3810).

Artquake Festival (Labor Day weekend): Concerts, ballets, art shows on the Mall and in Old Town; very popular.

Rheinlander Oktoberfest (late Sept): German folk dancing, music, and beer swilling. A popular event. Call 232-3000 for information.

SPORTS: Portland has teams in two professional sports:
Basketball (Oct–Apr): Trail Blazers, Memorial Coliseum (231-8000).
Ice Hockey (Oct–Apr): Winter Hawks, Memorial Coliseum (238-6366).

Horse Racing
Portland Meadows, 1001 N. Schmeer Rd. (285-9144), with thoroughbred and quarter-horse racing Oct–Apr.

STROLLS: ☼⚱ **The Mall,** SW Fifth and Sixth Aves. around SW Alder St.: A
huge pedestrians-only zone with brick sidewalks and cobbled streets lined with
shops and restaurants, and embellished with gardens and fountains. The only vehicles allowed are the (free) buses, trolleys, and cabs. Very lively.

⠀⠀⠀⠀☼⚱ **Old Town,** SW 1st St. to SW Fifth Ave. on either side of W.
⠀⠀⠀⠀Burnside St.: The historic heart of Portland along the Willamette River, with one of the country's finest remaining groups of 19th-century
cast-iron building fronts. Antique dealers, amusing shops, restaurants, cafés. A
likable place.

WINERIES: Located just west and south of Portland, are more than 35 wineries
that make up Oregon's prime Wine Country. The climate in this area is similar to
that of northern Europe and many of Oregon's wineries have won just acclaim.
Tasting rooms are open to the public year round. Among the best known:
⠀⠀⠀**Amity Vineyards,** 18150 Amity Vineyards Rd. in Amity, 48 mi. (77km)
SW via Ore. 18 and Ore. 99W (835-2362): A small family operation specializing
in pinot noir. Tasting room open daily Mar–Dec, wknds only Jan; closed Feb.
⠀⠀⠀**Chateau Benoit Winery,** 6850 NE Mineral Springs Rd. in Carlton, 36 mi.
(57km) SW via Ore. 18 (864-2991): Located on a scenic hillside near Lafayette,
this winery established in 1972 features premium varietal and sparkling wines.
Tasting room open daily. Visitors are welcomed to picnic and enjoy the view.
⠀⠀⠀**Rex Hill Vineyards,** 23 mi. (36km) SW at 30835 N. Ore. 99W, in Newberg
(538-0666): Specializes in pinot noir and chardonnay. Tasting room open daily
Apr–Dec, Fri–Sun Feb–Mar; closed Jan.
⠀⠀⠀**Sokol Blosser Winery,** 5000 Sokol Blosser Lane, in Dundee, 26 mi. (42km)
SW on Ore. 99W (582-6668): The vineyards have a very fine view over the Wil-
lamette Valley and the mountains. Tasting room open daily year round:
⠀⠀⠀**Tualatin Vineyards,** Clapshaw Hill Rd., in Forest Grove, 30 mi. (48km)
west via U.S. 26 and Ore. 8 (357-5005): One of Oregon's largest wine cellars,
which you may visit. Tasting room open daily Feb–Dec.

WINTER SPORTS RESORTS: ☼⚱⚱ **Mount Bachelor Ski Area,** 180 mi.
(288km) SE via I-5, Ore. 22, U.S. 20, and Century Dr. (382-2442): 12 lifts;
open Nov–May. The best resort in Oregon.
⠀⠀⠀⚱⚱ **Mount Hood Meadows,** 68 mi. (108km) east via I-84, U.S.
⠀⠀⠀⠀26, and Ore. 35 (337-2222): 9 lifts; open Nov–May.
⠀⠀⠀⚱ **Summit Ski Area,** 57 mi. (91km) east via I-84 and U.S. 26
⠀⠀⠀⠀(621-3684): 3 lifts; open Nov–Mar.
⠀⠀⠀⚱⚱ **Timberline Lodge Ski Area,** 60 mi. (96km) east via I-84 and
⠀⠀⠀⠀U.S. 26 (231-7979): 7 lifts; open Nov–May.

ACCOMMODATIONS

Personal Favorites (in order of preference)
⠀⠀☼♟♟♟♟ **The Heathman** (dwntwn), 1009 SW Broadway (at Salmon),
⠀⠀OR 97205 (503/241-4100; toll free, see Preferred). 152 rms,
A/C, color TV, in-rm movies. AE, CB, DC, MC, V. Valet gar. $10, rest.

(Heathman Restaurant), bar, 24-hr. rm svce, entertainment, concierge, crib $7. *Note:* After rejuvenation at a cost of $16 million, this Beaux Arts–style 1920s palace, rife w. wood paneling, Italian marble, and white Spanish granite, has recovered all its old luster. Many works of art, including a collection of Andy Warhols, add something new to its plush elegance. Very spacious, comfortable rms; exemplary svce. Its rest. is the best in town. A stone's throw from the Center for the Performing Arts. By far the best place to stay in Portland. **E–VE**

The Governor (dwntwn), 611 SW 10th St. OR 97205 (503/224-3400; toll free 800/554-3456). 100 rms, A/C, cable color TV. AE, CB, DC, MC, V. Garage $10, rest. (The Celilo), bar, pool, health club, sauna, 24-hr. rm svce, free crib. *Note:* Reopened in 1993 after a $16-million renovation, this hotel, built in 1909, is a standing testament to what preservationists call the last of America's handmade buildings. The 60-ft. (18m)-wide mural in the lobby depicts a scene from the Lewis and Clark expedition. Comfortable rms w. refrigerators and minibars, some w. fireplaces. Ask for a rm w. a balcony view of Mt. Hood or the Willamette River. **E–VE**

Marriott (dwntwn), 1401 SW Front Ave., OR 97201 (503/226-7600; toll free, see Marriott). 506 rms, A/C, color TV, in-rm movies. AE, CB, DC, MC, V. Valet gar. $12, pool, health club, sauna, two rests., two bars, rm svce, hrdrsr, concierge, free crib. *Note:* Big, rather bulky convention hotel pleasantly located on the Willamette River. Ultramodern comforts; spacious rms, some w. balconies and refrigerators, the best w. a view of the river and Mount Hood. Efficient svce; so-so rests. Pretty Japanese garden. Group and business clientele; in the heart of dwntwn. VIP floor. **M–E**

Hilton Portland (dwntwn), 921 SW Sixth Ave., OR 97204 (503/226-1611; toll free, see Hilton). 455 rms, A/C, color TV, in-rm movies. AE, CB, DC, MC, V. Gar. $12, pool, health club, sauna, rest. (Alexander's), coffee shop, bar, rm svce, hrdrsr, concierge, free crib. *Note:* Huge, relatively modern 23-story tower in the heart of the financial district. Completely redecorated. Inviting, comfortable rms; good svce. The rest. doesn't deserve its reputation but has a fine view of distant Mount Hood. Group and convention clientele. **M–E**

Imperial Hotel (dwntwn), 400 SW Broadway (at Stark), OR 97205 (503/228-7221; toll free 800/452-2323). 168 rms, A/C, cable color TV. AE, CB, DC, MC, V. Free parking, rest., bar, rm svce, free crib. *Note:* Older, very well run hotel in the center of Portland. The decor may be a little tired, but there's nothing at all wrong w. the comfort. Friendly reception and svce. Excellent value; regular and business clientele. **I**

Red Lion Coliseum (nr. dwntwn), 1225 N. Thunderbird Way, OR 97227 (503/235-8311; toll free, see Red Lion Inns). 214 rms, A/C, color TV, in-rm movies. AE, CB, DC, MC, V. Free parking, pool, rest., coffee shop, bar, valet svce, free crib. *Note:* Large, conventional motel on the Willamette River, opposite the Memorial Coliseum. Spacious, well-designed rms; cheerful reception and svce; free airport limo. Excellent value; group clientele. **I–M**

Mallory Hotel (nr. dwntwn), 729 SW 15th Ave. (at Yamhill St.), OR 97205 (503/223-6311; toll free 800/228-8657). 144 rms, A/C, color TV, in-rm movies. AE, CB, DC, MC, V. Free parking, rest., bar, rm svce, free crib. *Note:* Aging but inviting hotel, recently modernized, a stone's throw from dwntwn and across from the Portland Civic Theater. Quiet location. Agreeable, pleasantly furnished rms, some w. refrigerators. Perfect for budget travelers; good value. **B–I**

Other Accommodations (from top bracket to budget)

Riverplace Hotel (dwntwn), 1510 SW Harbor Way, OR 97201 (503/228-3233; toll free 800/227-1333). 84 rms, A/C, cable color TV. AE, CB, DC, MC, V. Valet gar. $10, whirlpool, sauna, rest. (The Esplanade), bar, 24-hr. rm svce, boutiques, free breakfast, free crib. *Note:* A newcomer on the local scene, this small luxury hotel is part of an ultra-modern real-estate development w. a marina, residential buildings, rests., etc., on the Willamette River. The interior decoration and furnishing are of unusual elegance. Spacious, comfortable rms in delicate pastel shades of pale yellow and lime green, w. balconies, the best overlooking the river. Reception and svce of a high order. Well-regarded rest. serving American cuisine. VIP and upscale business clientele; a very fine place to stay. **E–VE**

♀♀♀ **The Benson** (dwntwn), 309 S. Broadway, OR 97205 (503/
♀♀♀ 228-2000; toll free 800/426-0670). 287 rms, A/C, color TV,
in-rm movies. AE, CB, DC, MC, V. Valet parking $10, two rests. (including the London Grill), bar, 24-hr. rm svce, concierge, free crib. *Note:* Massive grand hotel in the heart of dwntwn, built around 1910 and long regarded as the *grande dame* on the Portland scene. Comfortable, not to say plush, w. very tastefully decorated guest rms. Exemplary svce. The more famous of the two rests., the London Grill, isn't what it used to be. Business and convention clientele. Interesting wknd packages. **E–VE**

♀♀♀ **Red Lion Inn Columbia River** (vic.), 1401 N. Hayden Island
♀♀♀ Dr., OR 97217 (503/283-2111; toll free, see Red Lion Inns).
350 rms, A/C, color TV, in-rm movies. AE, CB, DC, MC, V. Free parking, pool, putting green, Jacuzzi, rest. (Brickstone's), coffee shop, two bars, rm svce, disco, hrdrsr, free crib. *Note:* Luxury motel on the Columbia River. Inviting, well-designed rms w. private patios and balconies. Good physical-fitness facilities; agreeable grdn and setting. Very good svce. Group and convention clientele; 15 min. from dwntwn, 10 min. from the airport (free shuttle). Interesting wknd packages. A good place for the exhausted executive. **M–E**

☼♀♀ **Vintage Plaza Hotel** (dwntwn), 422 SW Broadway, OR
♀♀ 97205 (503/228-1212; toll free 800/243-0555). 107 rms,
A/C, color TV, in-rm movies. AE, CB, DC, MC, V. Valet parking $12, health club, rest. (Pazzo), bar, 24-hr. rm svce, concierge, free crib. *Note:* Completely rebuilt and refurbished historic brick Romanesque hotel. Dramatic 10-story atrium w. lobby setting inspired by Oregon vineyards. Comfortable, attractive rms decorated in Empire style, but on the small side. Luxurious duplex suites w. mountain views. Pleasant northern Italian rest. Attractive, personalized svce. The "in" place in Portland. **M–E**

♀♀ **Portland Inn** (dwntwn), 1414 SW Sixth Ave., OR 97201
♀♀ (503/221-1611; toll free 800/648-6440). 172 rms, A/C, cable color TV. AE, CB, DC, MC, V. Free parking, pool, rest., bar, rm svce, crib $5. *Note:* Older but completely renovated motel halfway between the Civic Auditorium and the university campus. Comfortable, inviting rms; efficient svce. Business and group clientele. Good value on balance. **I–M**

♀♀ **Travelodge Hotel** (nr. dwntwn), 1441 NE Second Ave., OR
♀♀ 97232 (503/233-2401; toll free, see Travelodge). 240 rms,
A/C, color TV, in-rm movies. AE, CB, DC, MC, V. Free parking, pool, health club, rest., bar, rm svce, free crib. *Note:* Typical 10-story motel nr. the Memorial Coliseum and Lloyd Center shopping mall. Comfortable and well run; efficient svce; free coffee in rm; free airport shuttle. Business clientele. Good value. Part of the British Trusthouse-Forte hotel chain. **I–M**

♀ **Caravan** (nr. dwntwn), 2401 SW Fourth Ave., OR 97201
♀ (503/226-1121). 40 rms, A/C, cable color TV. AE, CB, DC,
MC, V. Free parking, pool, bar, crib $6.50. *Note:* Modest but well-run small motel 8 min. from dwntwn. Spacious, serviceable rms w. free coffee; friendly reception and svce. Good value; ideal if you're driving since it offers direct access to the highway system. **B–I**

♀ **Motel 6** (nr. dwntwn), 3104 SE Powell Blvd., OR 97202
♀ (503/238-0600). 70 rms, A/C, cable color TV. AE, DC, MC,
V. *Note:* Small, unpretentious economy motel 10 min. from dwntwn across the

Ross Island Bridge. Very acceptable level of comfort; one of the best buys in Portland. Ideal for the budget traveler. **B**

Airport Accommodations

🛏🛏 **Sheraton Inn Airport** (vic.), 8235 NE Airport Way, OR 97220 (503/281-2500; toll free, see Sheraton). 216 rms, A/C, color TV, in-rm movies. AE, CB, DC, MC, V. Free parking, pool, health club, sauna, rest. (Première), coffee shop, bar, 24-hr. rm svce, crib $5. *Note:* Classic airport hotel 3 min. from the terminal (free shuttle). Comfortable and serviceable. Acceptable rest.; good svce; interesting wknd packages. Business clientele. **M**

YMCA/Youth Hostels

Portland International Hostel (nr. dwntwn), 3031 SE Hawthorne Blvd., OR 97214 (503/236-3380). 50 beds. Well-run youth hostel; open year round.

RESTAURANTS

Personal Favorites (in order of preference)

🍸🍸🍸 **Heathman Restaurant** (dwntwn), in the Heathman (see "Accommodations," above) (241-4100). A/C. Breakfast/lunch/dinner daily. AE, CB, DC, MC, V. Jkt. *Specialties:* Spanish-style tapas, Chinook salmon w. capers and horseradish sauce, Umpqua oysters w. mignonette of jalapeño pepper, Thai pork on a skewer w. apricots and mandarin sauce. Menu changes regularly. Fine, reasonably priced wine list. *Note:* The cuisine of this elegant, intimate luxury rest. emphasizes local produce, particularly seafood; it's prepared in ways that are often innovative and delicate. Beautiful old-world setting and atmosphere (the hotel dates from 1928). Very polished svce. The preferred dwntwn location for business meals; successful enough that resv. are strongly advised. *American/Seafood.* **M–E**

🍸🍸 **Couch Street Fish House** (dwntwn), 103 NW Third Ave. (223-6173). A/C, Dinner only, Mon–Sat.; closed July 4, Thanksgiving, Dec 24–25. AE, CB, DC, MC, V. Jkt. *Specialties:* anything that swims, served broiled, poached, or in a sauce—Dungeness crab, Chinook salmon, Oregon sturgeon, excellent mahi-mahi (dolphin Hawaiian style). Good list of Northwest wines. *Note:* The best known of Portland's many seafood rests., in the heart of Old Town. Everything is absolutely fresh and impeccably cooked. Pretty Victorian decor on a background of exposed-brick and white walls. Svce a touch pompous. Valet parking. Resv. strongly advised. *Seafood.* **M**

🍸🍸 **Westmoreland Bistro** (vic.), 7015 SE Milwaukie (236-6457). A/C. Lunch/dinner Tues–Sat. AE, MC, V. *Specialties:* calamari pasta, pan-fried ravioli w. red-pepper pesto, hazelnut-encrusted red snapper, roasted chicken w. black-bean sauce, luscious homemade desserts. Menu changes regularly. Skimpy wine list. *Note:* Friendly, tiny (23-seat) bistro in an obscure Portland neighborhood serving sophisticated New American cuisine by Caprial Pence, once the nationally acclaimed chef at Seattle's Fullers rest. Casual svce and atmosphere. Resv. a must. *American.* **I–M**

🍸🍸 **Ringside West** (nr. dwntwn), 2165 W. Burnside St. (223-1513). A/C. Dinner only, nightly; closed hols. AE, MC, V. Jkt. *Specialties:* steak, prime rib, superb onion rings, fresh seafood. Mediocre wine list. *Note:* Long-established steakhouse, three blocks west of the Civic Stadium. Dimly lit roadhouse atmosphere, w. sports decor and prizefight pictures (as the name implies). Excellent beef cuts moderately priced. New York strip is a favorite. Efficient tuxedo-clad waiters. Locally popular. Resv. essential. Other location: The Ringside East, 14021 NE Glisan (255-0750); lunch Mon–Fri, dinner nightly. *Steak/Seafood.* **I–M**

🍸 **Papa Haydn** (nr. dwntwn), 701 NW 23rd Ave. (228-7317). A/C. Lunch/dinner Tues–Sat, brunch Sun; closed hols. AE, MC, V. *Specialties:* tasteful entrées and light dishes w. an emphasis on seafood and chicken, remarkable European-style pastries and desserts. Wine and beer.

Note: Very popular café w. sidewalk seating, weather permitting. There's always a crowd gathered around the pastry counter. Other location: 5829 SE Milwaukie (232-9440). *Continental.* **B–I**

Other Restaurants (from top bracket to budget)

♔♔♔ **Atwater's** (dwntwn), U.S. Bancorp Tower, 111 SW Fifth Ave. (275-3600). A/C. Dinner only, nightly. AE, CB, DC, MC, V. Jkt. *Specialties:* seared sea scallops on cold smoked salmon w. endive salad and caviar vinaigrette, grilled marinated swordfish on spring vegetables w. roasted peppers and marjoram, oven-roasted herb-marinated chicken w. caramelized onion broth. Remarkable wine list, especially for northwestern vineyards. *Note:* Not many of the country's skyscraper rests. deserve three glasses; this one does. On the 30th floor of the U.S. Bancorp Tower in the heart of dwntwn Portland, Atwater's will entice you not only w. its contemporary regional cuisine featuring local seafood, but also w. a panoramic view of city and mountains. Elegant setting; faultless svce; big business clientele. Resv. required. *American/Seafood.* **M–E**

♔♔ **Chen's Dynasty** (dwntwn), 622 SW Washington St. (248-9491). A/C. Lunch/dinner daily. AE, DC, MC, V. *Specialties:* stir-fried pork w. pickled mustard greens and peanuts, Chang Sa chicken, cracked crab w. Hunan black beans. *Note:* One of the best Chinese rests. in the Northwest. Impressive Mandarin-style menu w. 100-plus items. Formal Oriental setting reminiscent of an upscale rest. in Hong Kong. Svce relatively efficient. Resv. advised in light of its success. *Chinese.* **I–M**

♔♔ **Jake's Famous Crawfish** (nr. dwntwn), 401 SW 12th St. at Stark (226-1419). A/C. Lunch Mon–Fri, dinner nightly; closed July 4, Thanksgiving, Dec. 25. AE, CB, DC, MC, V. *Specialties:* salmon, crawfish, halibut, and everything else fresh from the Pacific. Daily menu. *Note:* For over 100 years this rest. has been one of the favorites of locals looking for the freshest of Pacific catch. Clientele come in anything from shorts to tuxes. Resv. recommended. *Seafood.* **I–M**

♔♔ **Zefiro** (nr. dwntwn), 500 NW 21st Ave. (226-3394). A/C. Lunch Mon–Fri, dinner Mon–Sat; closed hols. AE, DC, MC, V. *Specialties:* grilled Alaskan spot prawns and calamari w. romesco sauce, sautéed Pacific salmon w. potato crust and arugula sauce, braised lamb shank, grilled rib-eye steak w. potato-and-wild-mushroom gratin, Braeburn apple cobbler. Menu changes every two weeks. *Note:* The most recent endowment to the local culinary scene. Fresh Northwest ingredients prepared w. a Mediterranean flair. Minimalist decor accented by pumpkin and black colors. Interesting copper bar. A fine place. Valet parking. Resv. advised. *Mediterranean.* **I–M**

♔♔ **Rheinlander** (nr. dwntwn), 5035 NE Sandy Blvd. (288-5503). A/C. Dinner nightly, brunch Sun; closed Thanksgiving, Dec 24–25. AE, MC, V. *Specialties:* Wiener schnitzel, sauerbraten, hassenpfeffer (jugged hare in cream sauce), apfelstrudel. *Note:* Generous portions of authentic German food in an appropriate Bavarian-inn setting. Noisy but cheerful music. Locally popular; very good value. *German.* **I**

♔ **Dan and Louis Oyster Bar** (dwntwn), 208 SW Ankeny St. (227-5906). A/C. Lunch/dinner daily; closed hols. AE, CB, DC, MC, V. *Specialties:* oysters on the half shell, oyster soup, shellfish, crabs, fisherman's stew. Beer and wine. *Note:* A true local institution, this venerable seafood rest. has its own oyster beds on the Pacific coast. Since 1907, four generations of fishermen and restaurant-owners of the Wachsmuth family have succeeded to this establishment; photos, ship models, and personal souvenirs adorn the walls. Often crowded and noisy. A place you shouldn't miss. *Seafood.* **B–I**

♔♔ **Esparaza's Tex Mex Cafe** (nr. dwntwn), 2725 SE Ankeny St. (234-7909). Lunch/dinner Tues–Sat; closed hols. MC, V. *Specialties:* smoked meats, seafood, enchiladas, nightly specials. *Note:* The best

Mexican food in Portland. Rambunctious crowd. Western music pumped out of the jukebox. Unfortunately, no resv, so wait can be up to an hour. *American/ Mexican.* **B–I**

> ♀ **Rose's East** (nr. dwntwn), NE 122nd Ave. at Glisan St. (254-
> ♟ 6545). A/C. Breakfast/lunch/dinner daily; closed hols. DC, MC, V. *Specialties:* kosher dishes, stuffed cabbage, corned beef, blintzes, over-stuffed sandwiches, Viennese pastry. *Note:* A deli in the grand old New York tradition; the desserts are absolutely superb. Open late; locally popular. *American.* **B**

Cafeterias/Fast Food

> ☼ **Original Pancake House** (vic.), 8600 SW Barbur Blvd. at 24th
> ☼ Ave. (246-9007). Breakfast/lunch only, Wed–Sun. No credit cards. Has reigned unchallenged for more than a quarter of a century—pancakes w. apple, w. orange, w. cointreau, w. cream, w. cherries, and on and on. A local landmark, overrun on wknds. Pleasant colonial-style decor. Well worth the 15-min. drive from dwntwn on I-5S to Exit 296B.

> ♀ **Big Dan's West Coast Bento** (dwntwn), 2340 NW Westover
> ♟ Rd. (227-1779). Lunch only, Mon–Fri (9:30 to 2:30). No credit cards. Cheap, traditional Japanese fare to go. The bento (chicken skewers over rice, around $3) has become an appetizing word around the dwntwn area.

BARS & NIGHTCLUBS

Brasserie Montmartre (dwntwn), 626 SW Park Ave. (224-5552). Classy nightspot featuring live jazz seven nights a week. Also appealing rest.

Bridgeport Brewpub (nr. dwntwn), 1313 NW Marshall St. (241-7179). Brewery and pub offering outstanding pizzas and some of the best homemade beers brewed in the Pacific Northwest. Rustic and warm atmosphere. Totally nonsmoking. Open nightly.

Goose Hollow Inn (dwntwn), 1927 SW Jefferson St. (228-7010). Friendly, congenial pub belonging to Portland's colorful former mayor Bud Clark. Locally popular with aspiring progressive politicos.

Key Largo (dwntwn), 31 NW First Ave. (223-9919). Blues, jazz, or rock at its best. Tropical atmosphere with open patio (weather permitting). Open nightly.

La Luna (nr. dwntwn), 215 SE Ninth Ave. (241-5862). Two bars, coffee room, and stage where alternative local and national acts perform on various evenings. Bar open nightly.

Lotus Card Room and Café (dwntwn), 932 SW Third Ave. at Salmon (227-6185). The hippest of Portland's dance clubs offering everything from techno to hip hop. Open nightly.

Red Sea (dwntwn), 318 SW Third Ave. (241-5450). Live reggae and world beat Thurs–Sat. Also an acceptable rest.

NEARBY EXCURSIONS

☼♟♟ **COLUMBIA RIVER GORGE** (65 mi./104km east as far as the Hood River via U.S. 30 or I-84): Some of the grandest scenery in the Northwest. The Columbia River, marking the northern border of the state of Oregon, cuts its channel between the steep rock faces of the mountains of the **Cascade Range.** Two fine roads parallel it: I-84, which follows the river at the foot of the gorges, and the scenic U.S. 30, which zigzags along the heights between forest and precipice, passing 11 great waterfalls from **Troutdale** to Bonneville Dam. Unforgettable view from **Crown Point State Park,** rising 1,968 ft. (600m) above the romantic landscape of fjords delineated by the Columbia River.

About 23 mi. (38km) from Portland you'll come upon **Multnomah Falls,** fourth highest (620 ft./189m in two stages) in the U.S., spanning the basalt cliff like the **Latourell Falls,** a little farther on, where the river suddenly drops 246 ft. (75m). And 9 mi. (14km) east of Multnomah Falls, stop at **Bonneville Dam** to watch the salmon (in springtime) and other kinds of fish (Mar–Nov) ascending the Columbia River; spectacular. An excursion well worth taking is the two-hour cruise aboard the 600-passenger sternwheeler *Columbia Gorge* from **Cascade Locks,** daily year round; for resv. call 374-8427 or 223-3928.

☼ 🔔🔔 **FORT VANCOUVER NATIONAL HISTORIC SITE** (10 mi./16km north across the Columbia River in neighboring Vancouver, Wash.) (206/696-7655): One of the oldest white settlements in the Northwest. Between 1825 and 1849 this was the center of operations for the legendary Hudson's Bay Company and its fur-trading empire; in 1848 the U.S. Army built its first military post here. The fort and the stockaded pioneer village have been reconstructed by the National Park Service as a facsimile of the original. A must for history buffs. Open daily.

☼ 🔔🔔🔔 **WARM SPRINGS RESERVATION** (119 mi./190km SE on U.S. 26): Established by a treaty of 1885, this reserve, inhabited by the Paiute and Wasco tribes, is visited every year by thousands of Americans and foreigners, attracted by the hot springs, authentic Native American dances (every Sun May–Sept), many open-air activities (horseback riding, rafting, golf, fishing, etc.), very comfortable hotel run by the Inter-tribal Council, and the excellence of its food. Resv. must be made as far ahead as possible.

Where to Stay

☼ 🏨 **Kah-Nee-Ta Lodge and Village,** P.O. Box K, Warm Springs, OR 97761 (503/553-1112). Besides the hotel's 140 rms, there are a score of rustic cottages and even tepees for lovers of local color. *Hotels and cottages,* **M;** *tepees,* **I**—but lower rates off-season.

FARTHER AFIELD

☼ 🔔🔔 **COLUMBIA RIVER GORGE & MOUNT HOOD** (190 mi./360km r.t. via U.S. 30E, Wash. 14E, I-84W, Ore. 35S, and U.S. 26W): As far as Bonneville Dam, follow the route described above for a visit to the **Columbia Gorge** (see "Nearby Excursions," above). From Bonneville Dam, take the Wash. 14 scenic route along the north bank of the Columbia River as far as ⚓ **The Dalles,** the western end of the famous Oregon Trail. It was at this once-active little river port that the pioneers from far-off Missouri left their heavy covered wagons for boats, in which they traveled to the mouth of the Columbia River on the last stage of their long odyssey. See mementoes of the period at the **Fort Dalles Museum,** 15th and Garrison Sts. (296-4547), open daily Mar –Oct, Wed–Sun the rest of the year (closed first two weeks in Jan); and at the **Wasco County Courthouse,** 406 W. 2nd St. (296-2207), open Mon–Fri year round.

After a look at the dam and enormous lock on the Columbia River at the **Dalles Dam and Reservoir,** 3 mi. (4.8km) east on I-84, open Wed–Sun Apr– May, daily in summer, closed the rest of the year, return to the Hood River on the Interstate which follows it. The very scenic Ore. 35S will then take you through the wooded mountains of the **Cascade Range** to the winter-sports resort of 🔔🔔 **Mount Hood Meadows,** halfway up 11,235-ft. (3,424m) **Mount Hood,** highest peak in Oregon. Wonderful view of the surrounding crests; however, novices are not advised to try climbing Mount Hood.

Return to Portland on U.S. 26. This trip is a nature lover's delight.

Where to Stay En Route

☼ 🏨🏨🏨 **Columbia Gorge,** 4000 Westcliff Dr., Hood River, OR 97031 (503/386-5566; toll free 800/345-1921). 42 rms. Handsome 1920s hotel overlooking the gorges. Excellent rest. **E–VE**

☀☲☲ **Timberline Lodge,** 6 mi. (10km) NE on U.S. 26 in the Timberline Ski Area, OR 97028 (503/272-3311; toll free 800/547-1406). 59 rms. Imposing ski lodge at the foot of Mount Hood. **I–M**

☀☖☖ **MOUNT ST. HELENS NATIONAL VOLCANIC MONUMENT** (210 mi./336km r.t. via I-5N, Wash. 504E, and the reverse on the way back): This national monument, with an area of about 110,000 acres (44,517ha), was created as recently as 1982; it encompasses Mount St. Helens itself and the whole area devastated by the volcano's sudden eruption on May 18, 1980, after a century of deceptive slumber. The gigantic explosion threw ashes and burning gas 12 mi. (19km) up into the atmosphere, and caused the death of 58 people. Five subsequent eruptions reduced the surrounding countryside to ashes and created some startling lunar landscapes. Having lost 1,300 ft. (396m) of its height in the course of the first eruption, Mount St. Helens now reaches an elevation of only 8,377 ft. (2,554m).

Two scenic roads are open year round: Wash. 503 to **Yale Lake,** south of the volcano, or Wash. 504 to the visitor center on **Silver Lake,** west of Mount St. Helens. The **visitor center** (206/274-2100), open daily, has much movie and still-photo documentation of the 1980 eruption, as well as a giant model of the volcano. The **CineDome Theater** (206/274-8000), on Wash 504 near the junction with I-5, shows the Academy Award–nominated film, *The Eruption of Mount St. Helens,* on its 70-millimeter projection system that captures the experience of being right in the middle of the phenomenon. Near the top of Wash. 504 visit the **Coldwater Ridge Visitor Center** (206/274-2131), a newly constructed panoramic lookout station that has the best views of the destruction wreaked by the volcano and computer simulations showing how the mountain looked before the eruption and how it will probably change in the next 200 years.

The forest roads to the east of Mount St. Helens (FR 25, FR 81, FR 83, and FR 90 in particular), from which you can get the most spectacular views, are generally impassable in bad weather, and closed by snow Oct–May. For highway information in the volcano area, call 206/750-3900. In summer, 100 climbers a day are allowed to climb as far as the crater under the supervision of guides from the U.S. Forest Service. Visitors can also fly over Mount St. Helens in a small plane or helicopter; call Pacific West Aviation (206/705-3469) or Bluebird Helicopters (206/238-5326).

For **general information,** contact Mount St. Helens National Volcanic Monument, 42218 NE Yale Bridge Rd., Amboy, WA 98601 (206/247-5473). It's well worth going out of your way to visit Mount St. Helens and the surrounding countryside.

☀☖☖ **PACIFIC COAST, SALEM & OREGON CITY** (380 mi./608km r.t. via U.S. 30W, U.S. 101S, U.S. 20E, and I-5N): Wonderful seascapes and picturesque fishing villages along the Pacific coast between **Astoria** (particularly fine view from the **Astoria Column** at the mouth of the Columbia River) and **Newport,** 135 mi. (216km) to the south. Take the trip if only for the beauty of the scenery. For a detailed description of this part of the itinerary, see Chapter 46 on the Pacific Coast.

You return to Portland via U.S. 20E and I-5N, stopping at ☖ **Salem,** capital of the state of Oregon. Visit the **State Capitol,** a handsome marble building in Greek Revival style, at Court and Summer Sts. (378-4423), open daily; also ☖ **Mission Mill Village,** 1313 Mill St. SE (585-7012), open daily, an interesting group of carefully restored old houses.

Your last stop will be at ☖ **Oregon City,** at the foot of the falls on the Willamette River; the **McLoughlin House National Historic Site** at 713 Center St. (656-5146), open Tues–Sun (closed Jan), is a perfect example of an 1845 colonial residence. This splendidly restored museum-home was built by the former administrator of the Hudson's Bay Company and of the British territories in the Northwest 1824–46.

Where to Stay En Route

☼ ♟♟♟♟ **Salishan Lodge,** on U.S. 101, Gleneden Beach, OR 97388 (503/764-2371; toll free 800/452-2300). 200 rms. One of the best hotels in the U.S. Contemporary urbanity on Siletz Bay. **E–VE**

♟♟♟ **Embarcadero Resort,** 1000 SE Bay Blvd., Newport, OR 97365 (503/265-8521). 90 rms. Luxurious hotel-marina on the Yaquina River. **M**

♟♟ **Tolovana Inn,** 3400 S. Hemlock St., Tolovana Park, OR 97145 (503/436-2211). 180 rms. Comfortable vacation motel w. views of the ocean and Haystack Rock. **I–M**

CHAPTER 45

SEATTLE

□ □ □

Hidden away at the head of the fjord called **Puget Sound,** almost surrounded by water, crowned from afar by the snowy pyramid of **Mount Rainier,** 14,140 ft. (4,392m) high, and the crests of the **Cascade Mountains,** the "San Francisco of the North" rejoices in some of the country's most magnificent scenery. Like its California equivalent, Seattle is fortunate in having a setting and a climate that are an inseparable part of its identity.

Named after the Native American chief Noah Sealth, who in 1851 gave a friendly reception to the first white settlers, five families from the Midwest, Seattle was originally no more than a village of trappers and loggers. Its prosperity came first with the Klondike gold rush of 1897, and subsequently with its two natural resources, lumber and fish. The millions of ties that went into the construction of the first western railroads came mostly from around Seattle and from the state of Washington. Though the famous 605-ft. (184m) **Space Needle,** left over from the 1962 "Century 21 Exposition," and its attendant downtown high-rises have supplanted what was once a forest of Douglas pines, lumber still accounts for a good deal of the local wealth, as does the sea (one out of every six inhabitants owns a boat) and its products. The leading fishing port in the U.S., Seattle is also the capital of the aerospace industry. Almost one out of every two airliners now in service in the Western world first took off from **King County International Airport,** headquarters of Boeing Corporation. A downtown building boom with many skyscrapers in the 60-story range and the tallest building on the West Coast, the 76-story **Columbia Center,** led in 1989 to a drastic measure sharply limiting the size and quantity of downtown towers.

The largest city in the state of Washington has grown from the ashes of a disastrous fire in 1889 that spared only the picturesque **Pioneer Square** enclave, once the heart of the ill-famed Skid Row district. The soggy climate of the "Emerald City," as Seattle is sometimes called, has made it one of the greenest places in the U.S. Moreover, within easy reach the tourist will find the magnificent forests of **Olympic National Park,** while the superb snowfields of **Snoqualmie National Forest** await the skiing enthusiast. If you enjoy the pleasures of the table, you'll find in the city's restaurants the whole gamut of local seafood which is the gastronomic glory of the Pacific Northwest: oysters from Olympia and Quilcene, Chinook salmon from the Copper River, Columbia River sturgeon, squid from Puget Sound, and Dungeness crabs, to name only the most enticing. The people of Seattle are among the most friendly and hospitable in the U.S.

Author Mary McCarthy, choreographer Robert Joffrey, screen actor Bruce Lee, and guitarist Jimi Hendrix were all born in Seattle.

BASIC FACTS: State of Washington. Area code: 206. Time zone: Pacific. ZIP Code: 98101. Founded: 1851. Approximate population: city, 520,000; metropolitan area, 2,560,000. 14th-largest metropolitan area in the U.S.

CLIMATE: Slickers and umbrellas are appropriate in Seattle at all times of year. With an annual average of 160 days of rainfall, the better part of it between Oct and Apr, it's one of the dampest cities in the country. Warmed on one side by the Japan Current in the Pacific, and protected on the other by the Cascade range,

Seattle enjoys a temperate climate even in winter (Jan average, 41°F/5°C), while in summer the mercury rarely rises above 78°F (25°C); the average for July is 66°F (19°C).

DISTANCES: Portland, 175 mi. (280km); Salt Lake City, 834 mi. (1,335km); San Francisco, 810 mi. (1,295km); Vancouver, 144 mi. (230km); Yellowstone, 762 mi. (1,219km).

ARRIVAL & TRANSIT INFORMATION

AIRPORT: Sea-Tac International Airport (SEA), 14 mi. (23km) south. For information, call 433-5217.

U.S. AIRLINES: Alaska (toll free 800/426-0333), American (toll free 800/433-7300), Continental (toll free 800/525-0280), Delta (toll free 800/221-1212), Hawaiian (toll free 800/367-5320), Northwest (toll free 800/225-2525), TWA (toll free 800/221-2000), United (toll free 800/241-6522), and USAir (toll free 800/428-4322).

FOREIGN CARRIERS: Air Canada (toll free 800/663-8868), British Airways (toll free 800/247-9297), and SAS (toll free 800/221-2350).

CITY LINK: The **cab** fare from the airport to downtown is about $30–$35; time, 25 min. Bus: **Gray Line Airport Express** (626-6088); leaves approx. every 30 min., serving principal dwntwn hotels; fare, $7; time, about 25 min. The **Metro Transit System** (bus no. 194) also provides service from Sea-Tac International Airport to dwntwn Seattle every 20–30 min.; fare, $1.10.

Excellent **public transportation** by bus, trolley car, and streetcar (free in dwntwn). Spectacular **monorail** link between Seattle Center and Westlake Mall at Fourth Ave. and Pine St., leaving every 15 min. 10am–midnight; fare, 50¢; time, 95 seconds. Don't miss it. For information on public transportation, call the Metro Transit System (553-3000).

Cabs are expensive and their drivers not always honest.

You won't need to rent a car unless you're planning excursions (recommended) around Puget Sound or into the surrounding mountains.

CAR RENTALS: Avis (toll free 800/331-1212); Budget (toll free 800/527-0700); Dollar (toll free 800/800-4000); Hertz (toll free 800/654-3131); National (toll free 800/227-7368); Thrifty (toll free 800/367-2277). For dwntwn locations, consult the local telephone directory.

LIMOUSINE SERVICES: Carey Limousine (285-5505), De's Connection (722-4805), and Network Limousine (toll free 800/638-5466).

TAXIS: May be hailed on the street, taken from the waiting lines outside major hotels, or summoned by phone. Recommended companies are **Farwest Cabs** (622-1717) and **Yellow Cab** (622-6500).

TRAIN: Amtrak, King St. Station, 3035 S. Jackson St. (toll free 800/872-7245).

INTERCITY BUSES: Greyhound, Eighth Ave. and Stewart St. (toll free 800/231-2222).

FERRIES: Clipper Navigation, Pier 69, 2701 Alaskan Way (206/448-5000; toll free 800/888-2535). Service between Seattle and Victoria aboard the catamaran *Victoria Clipper.* Daily year round. Time: 2½ hr. each way.

Washington State Ferry System, Pier 52 (Colman Dock), Alaskan Way S. at Marion St. (206/464-6400; toll free 800/843-3779). Passenger and vehicle service to Bremerton and Winslow daily throughout the year. Splendid views; low fares.

INFORMATION & TOURS

TOURIST INFORMATION: The **Seattle–King County Convention and Visitors Bureau,** 520 Pike St., Suite 1300, WA 98101 (206/461-5800).
Visitor Center, 800 Convention Place (206/461-5840).

GUIDED TOURS: ※ **Bill Speidel Underground Tours** (walking tours), 610 First Ave. (682-4646): Guided tours of the original houses and shops on Pioneer Sq. spared by the great fire of 1889 and now 10 ft. (3m) below the surface. Unusual and entertaining. Resv. a must; tours daily.
Chinatown Discovery Tours (on foot), P.O. Box 3406 (236-0657): Guided tours of the International District, Seattle's bustling Asian quarter. Tours include a stop for lunch, tea-time, or dinner. Resv. required.
Gray Line Tours (bus or boat), 720 S. Forest St. (624-5077): Conducted tours of the city and surroundings, serving principal hotels.
Seattle Harbor Tours (boat), Pier 55, Waterfront (623-1445): Boat trips in the harbor and on Elliott Bay; daily year round.

SIGHTS, ATTRACTIONS & ACTIVITIES

ADVENTURES: Downstream River Runners, Inc., 12112 NE 195th St., Bothell (206/483-0335): Rafting down the rivers of the Pacific Northwest, Apr–Oct.
Orion River Expeditions, 1516 11th Ave. NW (322-9130): Air-rafting down the rivers of Washington State, of the Cascade Range, or of British Columbia; trips last one to five days. Apr–Oct.

ARCHITECTURAL HIGHLIGHTS: ※⚐ **Evergreen Point Floating Bridge,** on Wash. 520E between Seattle and the suburb of Bellevue: The longest (7,514-ft./2,291m) floating bridge in the world, with 33 pontoons. Very fine view of Lake Washington.
⚐ **The Kingdome,** 201 S. King St. (296-3100): Impressive 60,000-seat covered stadium in the heart of downtown. The Seattle Mariners and Seattle Seahawks play their home games here; also rock concerts and trade shows. Adjoining is the **Royal Brougham Sports Museum.** Guided tours Mon–Sat, except on days of events.
※⚐⚐ **Lake Washington Canal,** linking Puget Sound to Lake Union: After those of the Panama Canal, the largest locks in the Western Hemisphere. An impressive sight. An unobstructed view of the seagoing traffic moving through the **Hiram M. Chittenden Locks** may be had from NW Seaview Ave. or NW 54th St. Visitor center (783-7059) open daily June–Sept, Thurs–Mon the rest of the year.
※⚐ **Pier 59,** Alaskan Way at the foot of Pike St.: The jewel of Seattle's waterfront rejuvenation program, with two of the city's most popular tourist attractions: the **Omnidome Theater** (622-1868), open daily, with its giant circular screen for 70mm movies; and the remarkable **Seattle Aquarium** (see "Museums of Science and History," below).
※⚐⚐ **Seattle Center,** Fifth Ave. and Harrison St. (684-7200): A 73-acre (30ha) tourist and arts complex on the site of the 1962 World's Fair. Comprises several museums, an opera house, theater, convention hall, covered stadium, dozens of shops and restaurants, and the Space Needle, a spectacular 605-ft. (184m) tower (see "Panoramas," below). A monorail takes

you from Westlake Mall, at Fourth Ave. and Pine St., to the Seattle Center in 95 seconds. Open daily.

☼☖ **University of Washington,** NE 17th Ave. and NE 45th St. (543-9198): Founded in 1861, this is one of the oldest universities in the western U.S., as well as one of the largest, with 35,000 students. Noteworthy buildings on the enormous campus are the **Henry Art Gallery** with 19th- and 20th-century material, the **Burke Museum** (see "Museums of Science and History," below), and the enchanting **Henry Suzzallo Library,** based on an Italian Renaissance model. On Red Sq. is *Broken Obelisk,* an interesting sculpture by Barnett Newman. On University Way, known to the student body as "The Ave.," are bars, boutiques, bookstores, taverns, and record stores. Visitor center at 4014 University Way, open Mon–Fri.

DEEP-SEA FISHING: If you dream of catching salmon (chum, Coho, or blackmouth), Seattle is where your dream can come true. Many charter boats go daily into Puget Sound from Piers 54 and 56. Some recommended operators are **Ballard Salmon Charters** (789-6202), **Ledger Marine Charters** (283-6160), and **Sport Fishing of Seattle** (623-6364).

Also recommended, at Edmonds, just north of Seattle, are **Captain Coley's Charters** (778-4110) and **Reel Fun Charters** (775-7133).

INDUSTRIAL TOURS: ☼ **Boeing 747 Plant,** on Wash. 526 in Everett, 29 mi. (47km) north on I-5 to Exit 189 (342-4801): The assembly plant for the jumbo jets and the 767s; largest covered space in the world. Bus tours (90 min.) Mon–Fri year round. Impressive. Resv. required.

Château Sainte Michelle, 14111 NE 145th St. in Woodinville, 15 mi. (24km) NE via I-90 and Wash. 405 (488-1133): Fine 87-acre (35ha) estate of vineyards with a pretty château modeled on those in the bordeaux country of France. Tour of the cellars and tasting daily.

MARKETS ☼☖ **Pike Place Public Market,** First Ave. and Pike St. (682-7453): Since 1907 this colorful covered market has been displaying its stalls of fish, fruit, or vegetables side by side with jewelers' booths, fabric shops, junk dealers, little restaurants, etc. Picturesque, noisy, and enjoyable. Open daily; closed major hols.

MUSEUMS OF ART: ☖ **Frye Art Museum,** 704 Terry Ave. (622-9250): Very rich private collection of European paintings, emphasizing Munich and Vienna schools, as well as 19th- and 20th-century American works; interesting temporary exhibitions. One wing houses an Alaskan art collection. Open daily.

☼☖☖ **Seattle Art Museum,** 100 University St. (625-8900): The beautiful Fuller Collection of Far Eastern (Chinese jade, Haniwa pottery figures) and Inuit art, the White Collection of African art, and the Kress Collection of works from the Italian Renaissance and the golden age of Dutch painting in a brand-new $62-million postmodern building designed by Robert Venturi; also interesting temporary shows, particularly of Native American art from the Pacific Northwest. Open Tues–Sun.

MUSEUMS OF SCIENCE & HISTORY: ☼☖ **Burke Museum,** University of Washington campus, NE 45th St. at NE 17th Ave. (543-5590): Fine museum devoted to the natural history and ethnology of the Pacific Rim; one of the finest U.S. collections of Native American art (particularly some superb masks) from the Pacific Northwest. Open daily.

☖ **Klondike Gold Rush National Historical Park,** 117 S. Main St. (442-7220): Recapitulates the epic of the gold rush to Alaska in 1897–98; many photographs from the period, as well as original tools and possessions of the Klondike miners. Picturesque and instructive. Open daily.

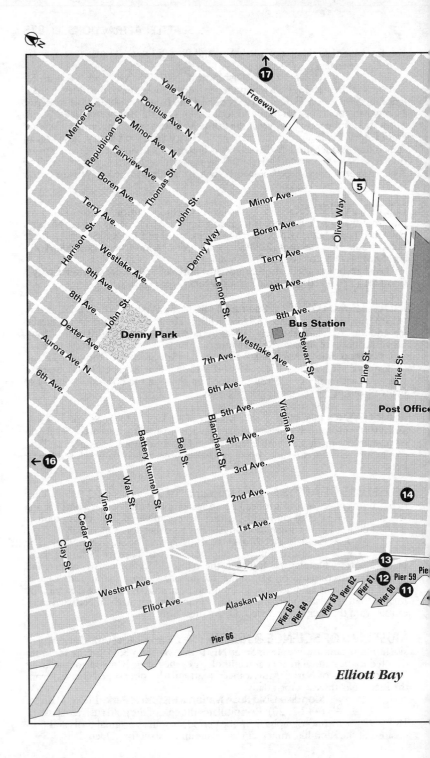

SEATTLE

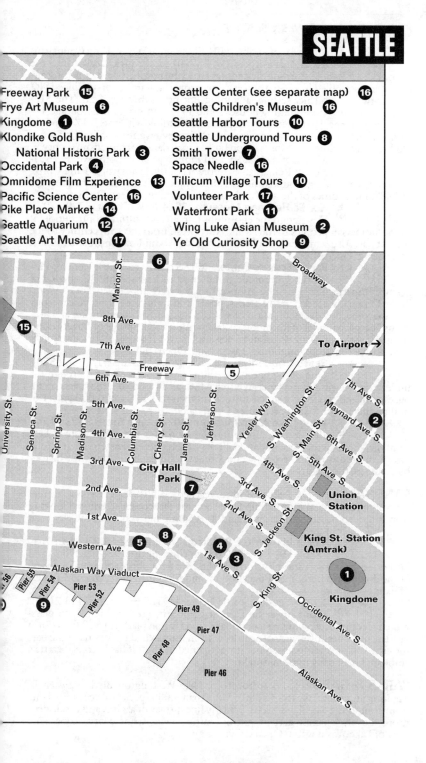

Freeway Park **15**
Frye Art Museum **6**
Kingdome **1**
Klondike Gold Rush
    National Historic Park **3**
Occidental Park **4**
Omnidome Film Experience **13**
Pacific Science Center **16**
Pike Place Market **14**
Seattle Aquarium **12**
Seattle Art Museum **17**

Seattle Center (see separate map) **16**
Seattle Children's Museum **16**
Seattle Harbor Tours **10**
Seattle Underground Tours **8**
Smith Tower **7**
Space Needle **16**
Tillicum Village Tours **10**
Volunteer Park **17**
Waterfront Park **11**
Wing Luke Asian Museum **2**
Ye Old Curiosity Shop **9**

Broadway

Marion St.

8th Ave.

7th Ave.

To Airport →

Freeway

6th Ave.

5

7th Ave. S.

Maynard Ave. S.

2

5th Ave.

Jefferson St.

Yesler Way

S. Washington St.

S. Main St.

6th Ave. S.

University St.

Seneca St.

Spring St.

Madison St.

Columbia St.

Cherry St.

James St.

4th Ave.

3rd Ave.

City Hall Park

7

4th Ave. S.

3rd Ave. S.

5th Ave. S.

Union Station

2nd Ave.

2nd Ave. S.

1st Ave.

8

S. Jackson St.

King St. Station (Amtrak)

Western Ave.

5

4 **3**

1st Ave. S.

Alaskan Way Viaduct

Pier 56

Pier 55

Pier 54

Pier 53

Pier 52

9

S. King St.

1

Kingdome

Pier 49

Occidental Ave. S.

Pier 47

Pier 48

Pier 46

Alaskan Ave. S.

※⚓ **Museum of Flight,** 9404 E. Marginal Way S., King County International Airport (764-5720): Long tucked away into the historic "Red Barn," a turn-of-the-century structure in which the first Boeing aircraft were assembled in 1916, this very fine aeronautical museum has since 1987 had a new and worthier setting, adjoining Boeing Corp.'s test field. The $15-million glass-and-steel building houses some 30 aircraft from the heroic age, beginning with the 1916 B&W hydroplane and ending with the B-17 bomber. Also a gallery devoted to space exploration: "Twenty-Five Years of Manned Space Flight." An absolute must for aviation buffs. Open daily; 10 min. from dwntwn.

⚓ **Museum of History and Industry,** 2700 24th Ave. E. (324-1125): Remarkable panorama of the history of Boeing Corp., and of the city since its foundation in 1851. Objects salvaged from the great fire of 1889, mementoes of the gold rush, maritime exhibition, etc. Open daily.

⚓ **Nordic Heritage Museum,** 3014 NW 67th St. (789-5707): Devoted to the enormous human and cultural contribution of the Scandinavian peoples to the Pacific Northwest, from the 18th century to the present day. Also temporary exhibitions of modern Scandinavian art and folk art. Interesting. Open Tues–Sun.

※⚓⚓ **Pacific Science Center,** 200 Second Ave., Seattle Center (443-2001): Ultramodern museum, nicknamed the "Cathedral of Science." Spectacular design by Minoru Yamasaki (creator of New York's World Trade Center), with decorative arches, pools, and fountains. From volcanology to astronomy and the exploration of space; particularly interesting are an enormous fiberglass model of the moon, a planetarium, a scale model of Puget Sound complete with miniature waves and tides, and a reconstruction of a Pacific Northwest Native American longhouse. Fascinating. Open daily.

※⚓⚓ **Seattle Aquarium,** Pier 59, 1483 Alaskan Way (386-4320): One of the finest aquariums on the West Coast. Through the underwater viewing dome you can watch while, all around you, the sharks, octopuses, fish, and all kinds of sea creatures strut their stuff in the 400,000-gal. (1.5-million-liter) pool. Truly spectacular. Open daily.

⚓ **Wing Luke Asian Museum,** 407 Seventh Ave. S. (623-5124): Illustrates Chinese immigration into the northwestern U.S. from the 1860s to the present day. Galleries devoted to Far Eastern art and folklore. Exhibitions of photography and Chinese calligraphy. A must for history buffs. Open Tues–Sun.

PANORAMAS: ※⚓ **Ballard Bridge,** reached via NW 15th Ave: Spectacular view of the Lake Washington Ship Canal and the Fishermen's Terminal looking from south to north; turn around and look south and you'll see the city with Mount Rainier in the distance.

※⚓ **Columbia Center Building,** Columbia St. and Fourth Ave. (386-5151): The tallest high-rise in Seattle: 954 ft. (290m) and 76 stories. The Observation Platform on the 73rd floor offers a breathtaking view of the downtown buildings, Puget Sound, and Mount Rainier. Open Mon–Fri 8:30am–4:30pm.

※⚓⚓ **Space Needle,** Seattle Center, 203 Sixth Ave. N. (443-2100): Giant tower on three legs, 605 ft. (184m) high, with glass-walled elevators, revolving restaurant, and observation platform 520 ft. (160m) up. The most beautiful view of Seattle, with an unmatched panorama of the bay, the city, and the mountains. Since it was opened in 1962 it has become Seattle's emblem. Open daily until midnight.

PARKS & GARDENS: ⚓ **Arboretum,** Lake Washington Blvd. between E. Madison and Montlake (543-8800): More than 5,000 species of trees and plants from around the world, with a particularly fine display of azaleas and rhododendrons. Lovely Japanese garden, gift of Seattle's twin Japanese city, Kobe. Fine view of Lake Washington. Open daily.

☀☂ **Carkeek Park** (NW 110th St.) and **Golden Garden Park** (NW Seaview Ave.): Two big parks on the shore of Puget Sound; splendid view of the fjord and the distant mountains. Great for picnics; swimming, too, for the foolhardy (water temperature in summer, 54°F/12°C).

☀☂ **Discovery Park,** 3801 W. Government Way (386-4236): On a headland overlooking the entrance to the Washington Ship Canal, this large (more than 500 acres/200ha) public park, with its undulating meadows and woodlands, gives you a superb view over Puget Sound from Magnolia Bluff. 2-mi. (3.2km) beach, but no swimming. Picnic areas, hiking trails. The **Daybreak Star Indian Cultural Center** (285-4425), with its exhibitions of Native American arts and crafts, is open Wed–Sun; the park itself is open daily dawn–11pm.

☀☂ **Freeway Park,** in the heart of downtown Seattle: Represents a successful attempt by the city government to "cover the ditch" created by sunken motorways in the center city. Part of it sits atop I-5 and part above an underground municipal parking garage. It boasts an engaging artificial stream and cascade (with a window behind it through which you can watch the traffic passing below), trails for urban hill-climbers, and pleasingly varied plantings. An elegant, urbane oasis above the traffic.

☀☂ **Gas Works Park,** N. Northlake Way and Meridian Ave. (684-4075): Pretty 20-acre (8ha) park around an old gas works, deftly converted into a modern sculpture; fine view of the city, Union Lake, and the passing ships. Open daily.

☀☂ **Seward Park,** Lake Washington Blvd. and S. Juneau St.: Popular park and beach, with swimming from June to early Sept, on Lake Washington, with the snowy peak of Mount Rainier as a backdrop. Wonderful view. Open daily.

☀☂ **Volunteer Park,** 15th Ave. E. and E. Prospect St. (684-4743): At the top of Capitol Hill, this beautiful public park around the Seattle Art Museum offers a clear view of the Olympic Mountains, the Space Needle, and Puget Sound. Observation platform on a Gothic Revival water tower, 520 ft. (159m) high (no elevator).

☀☂ **Waterfront Drive,** Alaskan Way: Picturesque walk along the dockside. At Pier 59 there's the last word in great aquariums (see the Seattle Aquarium, under "Museums of Science and History," above); there are gardens at the water's edge from Pier 57 to Pier 61 and Pier 71 to Pier 89. Wonderful view of Puget Sound and its shipping.

☂ **Woodland Park,** 50th St. and Phinney Ave. N. (684-4026): Huge park on Green Lake, whose western section is a zoo of modern design with over 1,000 animals. Splendid rose garden. Open daily.

PERFORMING ARTS: For daily listings of all shows and cultural events, consult the entertainment pages of the daily papers *Post Intelligencer* (morning) and *Seattle Times* (evening) and the monthly *Pacific Northwest* magazine.

Bagley Wright Theater, 225 W. Mercer St., Seattle Center (443-2222): Interesting postmodern design crossed with art nouveau. Classic and contemporary theater. Home of the famous Seattle Repertory Theater (director: Daniel Sullivan) (Oct–May).

Bathhouse Theatre, 7312 W. Green Lake Dr. N. (524-9108): Experimental theater.

Coliseum, Seattle Center (684-7200): Rock concerts, big-name shows.

A Contemporary Theatre/ACT, 100 W. Roy St. (285-5110): Modern theater, comedy, drama. One of the major resident theaters in the country.

Empty Space Theater, 107 Occidental Ave. (547-7633): Experimental theater.

5th Avenue Theater, 1308 Fifth Ave. (625-1418): Broadway shows, pop concerts.

Opera House, Seattle Center (443-4711): Concerts, ballet. Home of the

Seattle Opera Association (July–May; director: Speight Jenkins), the Pacific Northwest Ballet, and the Seattle Symphony Orchestra (Sept–May; principal conductor: Gerard Schwarz); call (443-4747 for symphony tickets).

Paramount Theater, 907 Pine St. (682-1414): Elegantly restored old theater; big-name shows.

Pioneer Square Theater, 512 Second Ave. (622-2016): Modern and Off-Broadway theater.

Seattle Center Playhouse, 155 W. Mercer St., Seattle Center (626-0782): Modern and experimental theater; home of the Intiman Theatre Co.

SHOPPING: **Food Circus Court,** Center House, 305 Harrison St., Seattle Center (684-7200): Cooking and food products from around the world (26 shops), set in an indoor garden with fountains. Perfect for a meal on the run.

Nordstrom, 1501 Fifth Ave. (628-2111): The flagship of the well-known clothing-store chain.

Pier 70, 2815 Alaskan Way (448-0708): Souvenir and clothing shops, exotic boutiques, and restaurants in a huge warehouse building by the old harbor. Amusing and picturesque. Open daily.

Uwajimaya, Sixth Ave. S. and King St. (624-6248): The largest Asian retail store in the U.S., established in 1928; foods, giftware, cookware. Open daily.

Westlake Center, 400 Pine St. (467-1600): Shopping center of ultramodern design in the heart of downtown, with 75 luxury boutiques, shops, cafés, and restaurants around a four-story glass atrium. Handsome plaza paved in contrasting colors of granite. The terminus of the monorail line between the Seattle Center and downtown is here.

Ye Olde Curiosity Shop, Pier 54, 1001 Alaskan Way, Waterfront (682-5844): Wonderfully kitschy bazaar, almost a century old—museum and souvenir shop at the same time. Many Far Eastern goods. Open daily.

SPECIAL EVENTS: For the exact schedule of events below, consult the **Seattle Visitors and Convention Bureau** (see "Tourist Information," above).

International Film Festival (May): A flourishing tradition since 1974.

Asian Week (early May): Colorful parades; shows. The big celebration for Seattle's Oriental communities.

Pacific Northwest Arts and Crafts Fair (end of July): Very popular arts-and-crafts show, held at Bellevue, 4 mi. (6.5km) east on I-90.

Wagner Festival (end of July to Aug): Complete "Ring" cycle, alternately in German and English.

Seattle Seafair (to early Aug): Processions, regattas, marathon, ship review.

SPORTS: Seattle has three professional teams:

Baseball (Apr–Oct): Mariners, Kingdome (628-3555).

Basketball (Oct–Apr): Supersonics, Coliseum (281-5800).

Football (Aug–Dec): Seahawks, Kingdome (827-9777).

Horse Racing

Off-Track Racetrack, 1621 SW 16th St., at Renton (226-3131), 11 mi. (17km) SE on I-5 and I-405: Racing Wed–Sun, year round.

STROLLS: ☀⚓ **Fishermen's Terminal,** W. Emerson St. at 15th Ave. W.: The largest fishing harbor in the U.S., and winter quarters of the Alaska fishing fleet. Hundreds of boats of all sizes are moored along the Washington Ship Canal. Many seafood restaurants. Fine view from Ballard Bridge.

🏛 **International District,** bounded by Fifth Ave. S., Eighth Ave. S., S. Yesler Way, and S. Lane St.: Seattle's Chinatown and Japantown. Many Far Eastern shops and restaurants, Japanese theater, Chinese opera house, Buddhist temple. At the intersection of King and Maynard Sts. is a fine gateway presented by the city of Taipeh. Lively and picturesque.

☀🏛 **Pioneer Square District,** bounded by First Ave., James St., and Yesler Way: This is where Seattle began in 1851. Yesler Way, called "Skid Row" in the days of the 19th-century gold rush, was the "hottest" street in this pleasure district. The street was named "Skid Row" because, in the earliest days of Seattle, logs were "skidded" (dragged by teams of horses) down here from the surrounding hills for the construction of the first houses. These once built, the street was almost abandoned and became the preferred resort of drunks and bums. Today it's lined with shops, art galleries, and congenial restaurants. On Pioneer Sq. itself there's a 59-ft. (18m) totem pole carved by the Tlingit peoples. Very lively, especially after dark.

☀🏛 **Waterfront Drive,** Alaskan Way along Elliott Bay: Souvenir shops, Native American Inuit, and Far Eastern craft shops, bars, and seafood restaurants are arrayed in dozens along the piers. The elevated highway (Alaskan Way Viaduct) offers a fine view of harbor and bay.

THEME PARKS: 🏛 **Enchanted Village,** 36201 Enchanted Pkwy., Federal Way (661-8000), 27 mi./47km south along I-5 to Exit 142b and Enchanted Pkwy.: A sort of miniature Disneyland. Enchanted Village itself is a family amusement park with carousels, roller coasters, children's museums, musical shows, etc. Adjoining it is **Wild Waves Water Park,** with giant water slides, artificial surf, heated lagoon-pool, and rafting down the rapids. Locally very popular. Both parks are open daily Memorial Day–Labor Day; Enchanted Village is also open wknds May–Memorial Day and in Sept.

☀🏛 **North West Trek,** 11610 Trek Dr. E., Eatonville (832-6116 or 847-1901), 55 mi./88km south along I-5 and Wash. 161: Very handsome safari-zoo covering 600 acres (240ha) where a comprehensive selection of animals of the Northwest—elk, caribou, bison, various kinds of deer, eagles, lynx, cougar, mountain goat, and bighorn sheep—roams a romantic mountain-and-moorland landscape. You can choose between a one-hour guided tour by mini-train or an independent visit on foot. Open daily mid-Mar through Oct, Fri–Sun the rest of the year.

WINTER SPORTS RESORTS: ☀🏛 **Alpental,** 54 mi. (86km) SE on I-90 and Alpental Rd. (236-1600): 8 lifts. Open mid-Nov to Apr.

☀🏛 **Crystal Mountain,** 80 mi. (128km) SE via I-5, Wash. 169, Wash. 410, and Crystal Mountain Rd. (663-2265): 10 lifts; lovely resort on the slopes of Mount Rainier. Open Nov–Apr.

🏛 **Ski Acres,** 58 mi. (92km) SE on I-90 (236-1600): 13 lifts. Open mid-Nov to Apr.

🏛 **Snoqualmie Summit,** 56 mi. (89km) SE on I-90 (236-1600): 12 lifts. Open mid-Nov to Apr.

ACCOMMODATIONS

Personal Favorites (in order of preference)

♙♙♙♙ **Four Seasons Olympic** (dwntwn), 411 University St., WA 98101 (206/621-1700; toll free, see Four Seasons). 450 rms, A/C, in-rm movies. AE, CB, DC, MC, V. Valet gar. $15, pool, health club, sauna, three rests. (including the Georgian Room), bars, 24-hr. rm svce, disco, hrdrsr, boutiques, concierge, free crib. *Note:* For decades regarded as the great lady of the Seattle hotel scene, the Olympic has recaptured its former grandeur after a complete remodeling in 1982. The Italian Renaissance–style structure, in the heart of Seattle, is a designated historic monument. Very spacious, comfortable rms w. minibars; urbanely elegant interior. Well-regarded rest.; exemplary svce. Big business and VIP clientele. A very fine place to stay. **VE**

☼ ♀♀♀♀ **The Sorrento** (dwntwn), 900 Madison St., WA 98101 (206/ 622-6400; toll free, see Preferred). 76 rms, A/C, cable color TV. AE, MC, V. Valet parking $10, rest. (Hunt Club), bar, rm svce, concierge, free crib. *Note:* Luxurious small palace hotel in the European style, three-quarters of a century old and now restored to its pristine glory. Period furniture; spacious, comfortable rms w. minibars; personalized svce. The Hunt Club is a highly regarded rest. The VIP's favorite; a good place to stay. **E–VE**

♀♀♀ **Stouffer Madison** (dwntwn), 515 Madison St., WA 98104 (206/583-0300; toll free, see Stouffer). 554 rms, A/C, color TV, in-rm movies. AE, CB, DC, MC, V. Garage $12, pool, health club, rest. (Prego), coffee shop, 24-hr. rm svce, hrdrsr, concierge, free crib. *Note:* Modern 28-story tower in the heart of the business district. Exceptionally comfortable, well-designed rms w. minibar, most w. a fine view of Puget Sound or the mountains. Acceptable panoramic rest. Highly professional svce. Business clientele; three VIP floors. **E–VE**

☼♀♀ **Edgewater Inn** (nr. dwntwn), 2411 Alaskan Way, Pier 67, WA 98121 (206/728-7000; toll free 800/624-0670). 240 rms, A/C, color TV, in-rm movies. AE, CB, DC, MC, V. Valet parking $16, rest. (Ernie's), bar, rm svce, nightclub, drugstore, free crib. *Note:* Modern, comfortable hotel right on the water. If your room overlooks the bay, you can rent a rod at the desk, fish from your balcony, and take your catch down to the rest. to be cooked (but if you want such a rm, you must reserve it well ahead!). Decor and facilities totally renovated. Good value; 5 min. from dwntwn. **M–E**

♀♀ **Mayflower Park Hotel** (dwntwn), 405 Olive Way, WA 98101 (206/623-8700; toll free 800/426-5100). 173 rms, A/C, color TV, in-rm movies. AE, CB, DC, MC, V. Valet parking, $9, rest., bar, 24-hr. rm svce, free crib. *Note:* Elderly hotel, completely renovated, in the heart of town a stone's throw from the waterfront. Comfortable and well run; spacious rms w. slightly faded charm; friendly svce. Good value; clientele of regulars. **M–E**

♀ **Days Inn Town Center** (dwntwn), 2205 Seventh Ave., WA 98121 (206/448-3434; toll free, see Days Inns). 92 rms, A/C, cable color TV. AE, CB, DC, MC, V. Free parking, rest., bar, free crib. *Note:* Good value right in the business district. Rms adequately large and comfortable; reception and svce with a smile. Group and business clientele. 5 min. from the Seattle Center. **I**

Other Accommodations (from top bracket to budget)

☼ ♀♀♀♀ **Alexis Hotel** (dwntwn), 1007 First Ave., WA 98104 (206/ 624-4844; toll free 800/426-7033). 97 rms and suites, A/C, color TV, in-rm movies. AE, CB, DC, MC, V. Valet parking $13, suana, rest. (Painted Table), bar, 24-hr. rm svce, concierge, free breakfast, free crib. *Note:* All the charm and elegance of a magnificently restored luxurious private home from around 1900. Elegant, tastefully decorated interior; spacious rms w. period furniture and minibars, some w. balconies and fireplaces. Beautiful view. Personalized svce of a high order; excellent rest. Very conveniently located an easy walk from the business district and the Pike Place Public Market. The favorite of those in-the-know. **E–VE**

♀♀♀ **Sheraton Hotel and Towers** (dwntwn), 1400 Sixth Ave., WA 98101 (206/621-9000; toll free, see Sheraton). 840 rms, A/C, color TV, in-rm movies. AE, CB, DC, MC, V. Valet parking $15, pool, health club, sauna, rest. (Fullers), coffee shop, bars, 24-hr. rm svce, disco, hrdrsr, concierge, crib $4. *Note:* Big, modern 35-story tower, right in the business district, whose ineffably insipid exterior is belied by a carefully thoughtout, imaginative scheme of interior decoration involving some 2,000 art objects, paintings, and sculptures by local artists. Spacious, ultra-comfortable rms, most looking out on Puget Sound or the mountains. Four VIP floors. Fullers is the city's best rest. Flawless reception and svce. Group and upscale business clientele. **E–VE**

🔑🔑🔑 **The Westin** (dwntwn), 1900 Fifth Ave. (at Westlake), WA 98101 (206/728-1000; toll free, see Westin). 865 rms, A/C, color TV, in-rm movies. AE, CB, DC, MC, V. Valet gar. $17, pool, health club, sauna, two rests. (including the Palm Court), coffee shop, three bars, 24-hr. rm svce, nightclub, hrdrsr, boutiques, concierge, free crib. *Note:* Flagship of the Westin hotel chain. Two circular towers, 40 and 45 stories high, in the dwntwn business district. The rms, huge and comfortable, w. minibars, all have a spectacular panoramic view of city, mountains, or Puget Sound. Elegantly redecorated interior; efficient svce; good luxury rest. (Palm Court). Big business and group clientele. Seattle's most glittering hotel. Interesting wknd packages. **E–VE**

🔑🔑 **Meany Tower Hotel** (nr. dwntwn), 45th St. and NE Brooklyn Ave., WA 98105 (206/634-2000; toll free 800/648-6440). 155 rms, A/C, cable color TV. AE, CB, DC, MC, V. Free parking, rest., bar, rm svce, free crib. *Note:* Modern 16-story tower nr. the university, 10 min. from dwntwn. Excellent reception; comfortable rms, most w. panoramic view of Lake Washington and the mountains. Good value. Group clientele. **M**

🔑🔑 **Best Western Continental Plaza** (nr. dwntwn), 2500 Aurora Ave. N., WA 98109 (206/284-1900; toll free, see Best Western). 94 rms, A/C, cable color TV. AE, CB, DC, MC, V. Free parking, pool, coffee shop (breakfast only), free breakfast, free crib. *Note:* Very comfortable motel 15 min. from dwntwn. The rms, most w. balconies, some w. kitchenettes, look out on Lake Union and the mountains. Good value; appeals to motorists, since it's 5 min. from the entrance to I-5. **I–M**, but lower rates off-season.

🔑🔑 **University Inn** (nr. dwntwn), 4140 Roosevelt Way NE, WA 98105 (206/632-5055; toll free 800/733-3855). 102 rms, A/C, cable color TV. AE, CB, DC, MC, V. Free parking, pool, health club, free breakfast, nearby rest. *Note:* Recently added wing and renovations to already-existing rms have raised the comfort level of this well-managed motel nr. the university. A favorite of visiting academics and others in-the-know. Spacious, reasonably priced rms; some have kitchenettes. 15 min. from dwntwn. **I–M**

🔑 **West Coast Vance Hotel** (dwntwn), 620 Stewart St., WA 98101 (206/441-4200; toll free 800/426-0670). 164 rms (no A/C), color TV. AE, CB, DC, MC, V. Gar. $9, rest., bar, valet svce, free crib. *Note:* Aging hotel, rather outmoded as to comfort, in the very center of Seattle; principal attractions are the excellent location and the low rates. Friendly reception and svce. **I–M**

Airport Accommodations

🔑🔑🔑 **Red Lion Hotel Sea-Tac** (vic.), 18740 Pacific Hwy. S., WA 98188 (206/246-8600; toll free, see Red Lion Inns). 850 rms, A/C, color TV, in-rm movies. AE, CB, DC, MC, V. Free parking, pool, health club, two rests. (including Maxi's), coffee shop, bars, rm svce, disco, hrdrsr, concierge, crib $15. *Note:* Huge, ultramodern luxury motel in a 28-acre (11ha) grdn, capped by a 14-story tower w. glass-walled elevators. Spacious rms w. balconies and superb views of Lake Washington and the mountains. Comprehensive facilities. Efficient reception and svce; group and business clientele. Opposite the airport (free limo), 20 min. from dwntwn. **M–E**

🔑 **Motel 6** (vic.), 18900 47th Ave. S., WA 98188 (206/241-1648). 147 rms, A/C, cable color TV. AE, DC, MC, V. Free parking, pool. *Note:* Spacious, engaging rms, but rather noisy surroundings; unequaled value 3 min. from the airport, 20 min. from dwntwn. Ideal if you're driving. **B**

YMCA/Youth Hostels

AYH International Hostel (dwntwn), 84 Union St., WA 98122 (206/622-5443). 138 beds. Typical youth hostel, impeccably run.

YMCA (dwntwn), 909 Fourth Ave., WA 98104 (206/382-5000). 212 rms. Men, women, families. Health club, pool.

RESTAURANTS

Personal Favorites (in order of preference)

ΥΥΥ **Fullers** (dwntwn), in the Sheraton Hotel and Towers (see "Accommodations," above) (447-5544). A/C. Lunch Mon–Fri, dinner Mon–Sat. AE, CB, DC, MC, V. Jkt (J&T at dinner). *Specialties:* gravlax of salmon and ahi tuna, spinach salad w. smoked duck, seafood chowder Puget Sound, roast sweetbreads w. caviar, grilled halibut w. pistachio butter, pork tenderloin w. fennel-peach purée and cream of port wine. Menu changes daily. Superb list of French and American wines, emphasizing the finest vintages of the Northwest. *Note:* By far the most elegant rest., serving the most sophisticated food, in Seattle. The light, imaginative New American cuisine emphasizes local seafood prepared w. Asian and French touches. Many works by such northwestern artists as Morris Graves and Mark Tobey and a remarkable collection of glass from the local Pilchuck School embellish the decor by happy coincidence, the rest. bears the name of the late founder of the Seattle Art Museum, Richard Fuller. Svce a touch pretentious. Resv. strongly advised; big business clientele. *American.* **M–E**

ΥΥΥ **Hunt Club** (dwntwn), in the Sorrento (see "Accommodations," above) (622-6400). A/C. Breakfast/lunch/dinner daily, brunch Sat–Sun. AE, CB, DC, MC, V. *Specialties:* king salmon w. young ginger in black-bean sauce; rack of lamb w. tomato-baked eggplant, white vegetable purée, and parsley jus; grilled filet of beef in roasted garlic jus w. stewed cherry tomatoes; pan-roasted medallions of venison w. red-wine-cumin sauce; vanilla crème brûlée. Seasonal menu. Splendid wine list. *Note:* Each dish comes w. an unexpected blend of flavors; results are usually very praiseworthy. Sumptuous English-club decor. Open-air terrace for fine days. Efficient, polished svce. Be sure to reserve ahead. One of the finest rests. in the Northwest. *American.* **M–E**

ΥΥ **Dahlia Lounge** (nr. dwntwn), 1904 Fourth Ave. (682-4142). A/C. Lunch Mon–Fri, dinner nightly; closed hols. AE, CB, DC, MC, V. *Specialties:* crab cakes w. Wild West sauce, bread salad, grilled salmon w. hoisin sauce, dry spiced Bengal duck, pear tart w. caramel sauce. Seasonal menu. Well-rounded wine list. *Note:* Superb, intriguing Pacific Rim cuisine by *wunderkind* chef Tom Douglas. Noisy, bilevel black-and-red dining rm. Busy, efficient svce. Resv. advised. *American.* **M**

ΥΥ **Labuznik** (dwntwn), 1924 First Ave. (441-8899). A/C. Dinner only, Tues–Sat; closed hols and three weeks at the end of July and early Aug. AE, DC, MC, V. *Specialties:* roast duck, smoked pork tenderloin w. sautéed morels, Wiener schnitzel, veal chop, rack of lamb, baked pear. Seasonal menu. *Note:* One of the few Czech rests. in the U.S., and, in all likelihood, the best. Petr Cipra, chef/owner of Labuznik (meaning "lover of food"), has been consistently drawing a crowd for 17 years, mainly for his skillfulness in roasting meats. Clean and simple decor conducive to the serious business at hand —eating. A fine place. *Czech.* **I–M**

ΥΥ **Nikko** (nr. dwntwn), in the Westin (see "Accommodations," above) (322-4641). A/C. Lunch Mon–Fri, dinner Mon–Sat; closed hols. AE, DC, MC, V. *Specialties:* sushi, sashimi, sautéed geoduck (a local variety of clam) w. fried Rex sole filets, sake kasu black cod. *Note:* Experts say that this is the most imaginative, and the best, of Seattle's many Japanese rests. Prodigious culinary and aesthetic skills are particularly well displayed in the preparation of sushi. The setting is truly Japanese. A worthwhile experience; be sure to reserve ahead. *Japanese.* **I–M**

Υ **Emmett Watson's Oyster Bar** (dwntwn), 1916 Pike Pl. (448-7721). Lunch/dinner daily; closed hols. No credit cards. *Specialties:* oysters (Quilcenes, Canterburies, Olympias, Middlebrooks, etc.) on the half shell, chowder, clams, ceviche. More than 50 brands of beer on draft or in bottle. *Note:* The best-known eating place in Pike Place Public Market, offering one of the widest selections of oysters on the West Coast, all of exemplary freshness and quality. No interior decoration to speak of: just a dozen bar stools and a few outside tables in fine weather. Quick, efficient svce. Local color guaranteed. *Seafood.* **B–I**

Other Restaurants (from top bracket to budget)

🍷🍷🍷 **Rover's** (nr. dwntwn), 2808 E. Madison St. (325-7442). No A/C. Dinner only, Tues–Sat; closed hols. AE, DC, MC, V. Jkt. *Specialties:* warm wild mushroom salad w. balsamic vinegar sauce, Columbian River sturgeon w. Olympia oyster flan and sea urchin sauce, venison medallions w. wild mushrooms and green lentils in black-peppercorn sauce, berry clafoutis. *Note:* This cozy, innovative rest., under the master hand of the accomplished French chef Thierry Rautureau, has quickly established itself as one of the city's best. The food is a happy blend of French and Pacific northwestern traditions; gracious countrified decor; w. an inviting grdn for open-air dining on fine days. Friendly svce. Resv. suggested. 20 min. from dwntwn. *French.* **M–E**

🍷🍷 **Adriatica** (nr. dwntwn), 1107 Dexter Ave. (285-5000). A/C. Dinner only, nightly; closed hols. AE, DC, MC, V. *Specialties:* fried calamari, prawns Constantina, pork tenderloin w. port sauce and sun-dried cranberries, petrale sole w. lemon-tarragon butter, Parmesan-encrusted chicken, chocolate espresso soufflé. Excellent wine list (California and northwestern varietals). *Note:* Fresh, delicious eastern Mediterranean fare, w. a Greek and Italian spin, served in a 1920s European-style villa overlooking Lake Union. Friendly, attentive staff. Resv. a must in light of its success. *Mediterranean.* **M**

🍷🍷 **McCormick's Fish House** (dwntwn), 722 Fourth Ave. (682-3900). A/C. Lunch Mon–Fri, dinner nightly; closed hols. AE, DC, MC, V. Jkt. *Specialties:* oysters on the half shell; Dungeness crab; bouillabaisse; more than 40 kinds of fish (salmon, white sturgeon, yellowfin tuna, swordfish, mahi-mahi, scorpion fish, etc.) broiled, poached, or sautéed; steak. Good wine list at reasonable prices. *Note:* On the street level of the Columbia Center Building, this locally popular rest. offers a huge variety of the freshest possible fish and shellfish. The decor is that of an old-time Irish pub. At both lunch and dinner the two oyster bars are overrun by businesspeople. Highly professional svce; resv. advisable. A true local landmark in the heart of the business district. *Seafood.* **M**

🍷🍷 **Metropolitan Grill** (dwntwn), 818 Second Ave. (624-3287). A/C. Lunch Mon–Fri, dinner nightly; closed hols. AE, CB, MC, V. Jkt. *Specialties:* oysters on the half shell, broiled salmon, filet mignon, roast beef. Wine list featuring local vineyards. *Note:* A typical steakhouse, cozy and comfortable. Excellent beef and good broiled fish. 60-ft. (18m) bar; thoughtful, efficient svce. Resv. advisable. A business district landmark. *Steak.* **M**

🍷🍷 **Le Provençal** (vic.), 212 Central Way, in Kirkland, 30 min. from dwntwn via the Evergreen Point Floating Bridge (827-3300). A/C. Dinner only, nightly; closed hols. AE, CB, DC, MC, V. *Specialties:* scallopine of venison w. pepper sauce, salmon in pastry shell, filet Casanova, cassolette of seafood, roast rack of lamb w. garlic and herbs, fish of the day, dessert cart. Menu changes regularly. Good wine list. *Note:* Charming little country inn, typically French. The very Mediterranean cuisine of owner-chef Philippe Gayte justifies the rest.'s name. Cheerful, friendly svce. Business clientele; resv. advised. An excellent place to eat. *French.* **M**

🍷🍷 **Lampreia** (dwntwn), 2400 First Ave. (443-3301). A/C. Dinner only, Tues–Sat; closed hols. AE, MC, V. *Specialties:* venison carpaccio w. Parmesan and pine nuts, garlic risotto w. sun-dried tomato oil, lamb loin w. gratin of turnip, fresh halibut w. artichoke salad, white-chocolate polenta pudding w. vanilla sauce. Seasonal menu. *Note:* Chef/owner Scott Carsberg, who trained under Guenter Seeger at Atlanta's Ritz-Carlton, endows his cooking w. a precise sense of timing and deeply flavorful sauces. Minimalist decor and earth-tone hues engage diners in what is sure to be a pleasurable experience. *American/Italian.* **I–M**

     Pirosmani (nr. dwntwn), 2220 Queen Anne Ave., N. (285-3360). A/C. Dinner only, Tues–Sat; closed hols. MC, V. *Specialties: tabaka* chicken (seared whole poussin w. a saffron-and-walnut sauce), lamb *basturma* (skewered lamb marinated in pomegranate juice and herbs), Lebanese duck (breast of duck w. cognac-and-cinnamon sauce), ricotta cheesecake. Seasonal menu. *Note:* The most interesting rest. to appear in Seattle in the last few years. A menu combined of Georgian (meaning the country, not the state in the American South) and Mediterranean food, two cuisines which are, in fact, not so distant. Co-owner/chef Laura Dewell, who traveled extensively through the countries represented in her menu, performs hat-tricks w. spices. Georgian oil paintings, including a Pirosmani (the most famous Georgian artist, for whom the rest. is named), establish the appropriate ambience inside. Resv. recommended. *Georgian/Mediterranean.* **I–M**

     Ray's Boat House (nr. dwntwn), 6049 Seaview Ave. NW (789-3770). A/C. Lunch/dinner daily; closed Jan 1, Easter, Dec 24–25. AE, CB, DC, MC, V. *Specialties:* chowder, broiled salmon w. sorrel, crab, oysters, sake kasu black cod, calamari in black-bean sauce. Good list of northwestern wines. *Note:* Burned to the ground in 1987, the rest. has risen from its ashes like a phoenix. As with other Seattle seafood rests., fresh salmon is a house specialty at Ray's. Pretty, countrified decor w. lots of paneling and greenery; splendid view of Shilshole Bay and the mountains. Engagingly romantic atmosphere in the evenings. Popular, so resv. advised. 20 min. from dwntwn. *Seafood.* **I–M**

     Wild Ginger (dwntwn), 1400 Western Ave. (623-4450). A/C. Lunch Mon–Sat, dinner nightly; closed hols. AE, DC, MC, V. *Specialties:* satays, curries, fish specials, noodle dishes, sherbets. *Note:* Stylized Asian fare, including Vietnamese, Thai, and Korean dishes, and the city's only satay bar w. skewered foods grilled to order. Gracious, warm setting and atmosphere. Resv. accepted. *Pan-Asian.* **I–M**

     Four Seas (dwntwn), 714 S. King St. (682-4900). A/C. Lunch/dinner daily (until 2am); closed Jan 1, Thanksgiving, Dec 25. AE, MC, V. *Specialties:* Hong Kong dim sum, Cantonese beef, moo goo gai pan, garlic spareribs, hot-and-spicy chicken. *Note:* The best rest. in Chinatown, and one of the most elegant. Modern Far Eastern decor; rather sophisticated Cantonese food; inefficient svce. Locally popular. *Chinese.* **I**

Cafeterias/Fast Food/Specialty Spots

     Café Sport (dwntwn), 2020 Western Ave. (443-6000). Breakfast Sat–Sun, lunch/dinner daily. AE, DC, MC, V. *Specialties:* black-bean soup, Dungeness crabcakes, pan-fried oysters, grilled chicken w. spicy noodles, steamed mussels, broiled catch of the day. *Note:* An engaging art deco bistro; the light menu emphasizes local fish and shellfish at remarkably low prices. Excellent value; a splendid place very nr. Pike Place Public Market.

     Torrefazione Italia (dwntwn), 320 Occidental Ave. S. (624-5773). The first and the best of the countless coffee bars that proliferated in dwntwn Seattle. Serves authentic espresso, cappuccino, and caffè latte w. pastries 7:30am–5:30pm Mon–Sat.

BARS & NIGHTCLUBS

     The Central (dwntwn), 207 First Ave. S. (622-0209). Good beer, live music, and big crowds near Pioneer Sq. Open nightly.

     F. X. McRory's (nr. dwntwn), Occidental Ave. and King St. (623-4800). Oyster bar, very popular with the locals. Huge selection of beer and bourbon. On the noisy side, but entertaining; also an acceptable rest. Open nightly until 2am.

Jazz Alley (dwntwn), Sixth Ave. at Lenora St. (441-9729). The best jazz club in town; intimate and engaging. Also average rest. Open nightly.

Off Ramp (dwntwn), 109 Eastlake Ave. E (628-0232). A good place to sample the now-infamous "Seattle sound." Open nightly. Also a café.

Swannies Comedy Underground (dwntwn), 222 S. Main St. (628-0303). Typical comedy club, presenting the biggest names in the genre.

NEARBY EXCURSIONS

MOUNT RAINIER NATIONAL PARK (95 mi./153km SE via I-5, Wash. 7, and Wash. 706): Mountain scenery in all its grandeur; many glaciers and fields of eternal snow. Wash. 706, open year round, takes you as far as the **Paradise Visitor Center,** 5,398 ft. (1,646m) up. The northern part of the park is generally not accessible in winter. If you intend to climb the rest of the way to the 14,410-ft. (4,392m) summit of this great volcano, now 2,000 years dormant, you'll need wiry legs and some mountaineering experience even in the company of your officially licensed guides.

The most popular of the 300 mi. (483km) of hiking trails in the park is the **Wonderland Trail,** which winds around the slopes of the mountain, crossing in succession deep forests, wildflower-covered alpine meadows, and glaciers. The 140 mi. (224km) of surfaced road that encircles the highest peak in the Cascades will afford you fabulous views of Mount Rainier's three crests and some of its 26 glaciers; Wash. 410 and Wash. 123 are particularly rewarding.

For information, contact the Superintendent, Mount Rainier National Park, Tahoma Woods, Star Rte., Ashford, WA 98304 (206/569-2211).

Where to Stay

Paradise Inn, on Wash. 706 (20 mi./32km east of the Nisqually entrance to the park), Ashford, WA 98304 (206/ 569-2275). 127 rms (95 w. bath). *Note:* Very pretty rustic chalet built in the 1920s in an outstandingly beautiful location. Open mid-May–Sept. **I–M**

MOUNT ST. HELENS NATIONAL VOLCANIC MONUMENT (153 mi./245km south via I-5S and Wash. 504E): One of the most recently active of American volcanoes, recording a major eruption on May 18, 1980. Breathtaking lunar landscapes. Highways are closed for a 20-mi. (32km) radius around the crater, but many hiking trails open to the public. There's a **visitor center** with a giant model of the volcano on Wash. 504 at Silver Lake, 5 mi. (8km) east of I-5 (206/274-2100); open year round. (For details, see the excursion section in Chapter 44.)

OLYMPIC NATIONAL PARK (reached by ferry to Winslow, then 89 mi./142km NW via Wash. 305, Wash. 3, Wash. 104, and U.S. 101): More than 1,430 sq. mi. (3,700km²) of unspoiled wilderness, with astonishing contrasts between the glaciers of **Mount Olympus** (7,965 ft./2,428m), the luxurian forests of the slopes facing the ocean, and the little desert islands along the Pacific. Rains of tropical violence fall daily Oct–Apr on the west face of the park (average annual rainfall, 140 in./356cm), so that the thickly wooded slopes of the region are referred to as "rain forests." Abundant wildlife: black bear, eagles, elk, deer, mountain lion, seal, and sea elephant. More than 600 mi. (966km) of hiking trails crisscross the park, and around it runs a magnificent 330-mi. (531km) circular highway, the **Olympic Peninsula Scenic Drive** (U.S. 101). The park draws about three million visitors a year. For **information,** contact the Superintendent, Olympic National Park, 3002 Mt. Angeles

Rd., Port Angeles, WA 98362 (206/452-0330). Park open year round (winter skiing at the **Hurricane Ridge Ski Area,** with three lifts). You can combine it with a trip to Port Townsend (see below).

Where to Stay in the Park
Kalaloch Lodge, U.S. 101, Kalaloch Beach, WA 98331 (206/962-2271). 58 rms and bungalows. Rustic motel on a cliff overlooking the ocean. Spectacular views; open year round. **I–M**

Lake Crescent Lodge, U.S. 101, Port Angeles, WA 98362 (206/928-3211). 49 rms and cottages. The main chalet dates from 1916 while the cottages are newer; they stand beside a wonderful mountain lake. Praiseworthy rest. Open late May–Nov **I–M**

PORT TOWNSEND (reached by ferry to Winslow, then 49 mi./78km NW via Wash. 305, 3, 104, and 20): Charming little port town on Puget Sound, with fine San Francisco–style pastel-washed Victorian houses and splendid seascapes, and two delightful 19th-century inns. Port Townsend is well worth visiting; you can do so along with Olympic National Park (see above).

Where to Stay
Manresa Castle, 7th and Sheridan Sts., Port Townsend, WA 98368 (206/385-5750). 42 Victorian-style rms, most overlooking the bay. Cozy rest. and bar. AE, MC, V. **I–E**

James House, 1238 Washington St., Port Townsend, WA 98368 (206/385-1238). 12 comfortable rms w. period furniture and pretty views. MC, V. **I–M**

SNOQUALMIE NATIONAL FOREST (about 50 mi./80km east on I-90): 1,220,000 acres (490,000ha) of deep forests, lakes, mountains, waterfalls, superb scenery, and well-equipped winter sports resorts, all less than an hour's drive from Seattle. Many excursions. Stampede Pass (alt. 3,700 ft./1,125m) is the "snowiest" place in the U.S. with average annual snowfall of 432 in. (11m).

Where to Eat
Salish Lodge, on Wash. 202 at North Bend (206/888-2556). Breakfast/lunch/dinner daily. AE, CB, DC, MC, V. *Note:* Very popular locally. Overlooks the famous Snoqualmie Falls. Also a hotel w. 90 comfortable rms. *American.* **I–M**

TILLICUM VILLAGE (on Blake Island, reached by boat from Pier 56) (206/443-1244): At this re-creation of life in a 19th-century Native American village, the tribal-style salmon dinner and the folk-dance exhibition will cost you $45. Daily May to mid-Oct; call for days of operation during the rest of the year.

FARTHER AFIELD

NORTH CASCADES & GLACIER NATIONAL PARKS (1,548 mi./2,476km r.t. via I-5N, Wash. 20E, Wash. 155S, Wash. 174E, U.S. 2E, Wash. 25N, Wash. 20E, U.S. 2E, U.S. 89N, Going-to-the-Sun Rd. W., U.S. 2W, U.S. 93S, and I-90W): An ideal 7- to 10-day trip for lovers of the wide-open spaces, taking in two of the Northwest's loveliest national parks, North Cascades National Park and Glacier National Park, on the Canadian frontier.

North Cascades National Park
You come first to North Cascades National Park, 132 mi. (211km) from Seattle, its 504,000 acres (204,000ha) of magnificent mountain scenery—glaciers

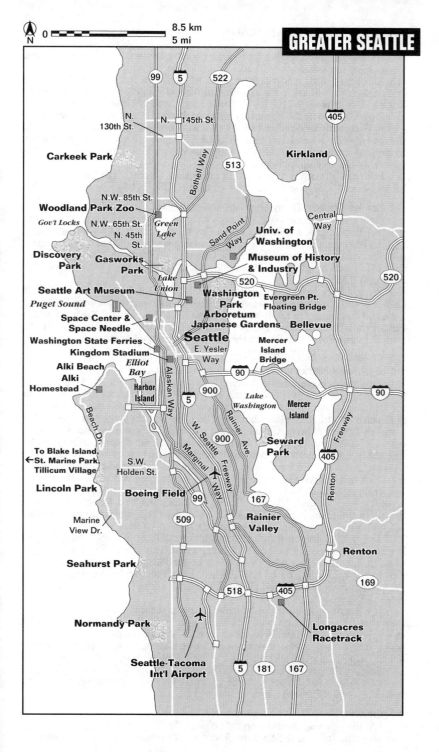

GREATER SEATTLE

0   8.5 km
    5 mi

N

Carkeek Park

N. 130th St.   N. 145th St.

Kirkland

Bothell Way

513

405

N.W. 85th St.

Woodland Park Zoo

Gov't Locks   N.W. 65th St.   Green Lake

N. 45th St.

Sand Point Way

Univ. of Washington

Discovery Park

Gasworks Park

Lake Union

Museum of History & Industry

520

520

Seattle Art Museum

Washington Park Arboretum

Evergreen Pt. Floating Bridge

Puget Sound

Space Center & Space Needle

Japanese Gardens

Bellevue

Washington State Ferries

Seattle

Kingdom Stadium

E. Yesler Way

Mercer Island Bridge

Alki Beach

Alki Homestead

Elliot Bay

Harbor Island

Alaskan Way

90

900

Lake Washington

Mercer Island

90

Beach Dr.

5

W. Seattle Freeway

900

Rainier Ave.

Seward Park

405

To Blake Island, St. Marine Park, Tillicum Village

S.W. Holden St.

Marginal Way

Renton Freeway

Lincoln Park

Boeing Field

99

167

Rainier Valley

Marine View Dr.

509

Renton

Seahurst Park

518

405

169

Normandy Park

Longacres Racetrack

Seattle-Tacoma Int'l Airport

5   181   167

99   5   522

(318 of them), innumerable lakes, and majestic crests covered with bristling forests—sitting astride the Canadian border. Many hiking trails crisscross this expanse of unspoiled wilderness north of the Cascades. It took 15 million years of glacial erosion to carve the granite into narrow valleys and abrupt crests like **Goode Mountain** (9,220 ft./2,810m) and **Mount Shuskan** (9,127 ft./ 2,782m). Watered by the moist breezes from the Pacific, the western slope of the park is luxuriantly wooded and abounds in wild animals (grizzly, black bear, elk, wolves, eagles), whereas its eastern counterscarp is characterized by sparser growths of conifers and brush. Camping, fishing, rock climbing, hiking in summer; cross-country skiing in winter.

Information centers are open in summer at Chelan, Marblemount, Newhalem, Sedro Wooley, and Colonial Creek (206/856-5700).

☼⚓ Grand Coulee Dam and Roosevelt Lake

Continue on scenic Wash. 20, one of the most spectacular highways in the state of Washington, to **Grand Coulee Dam.** At 5,223 ft. (1,592m) wide and 550 ft. (168m) high, this impressive piece of engineering and the generating station that it houses make up one of the largest reinforced-concrete structures in the world (total weight used, 20 million tons). Open daily; for information, call 509/633-9265.

Penned back by the dam is the 151-mi. (243km) **Franklin D. Roosevelt Lake,** a popular vacation and water-sports area. Following the shore of Roosevelt Lake and continuing to the east, you pick up the scenic Wash. 20 again at Kettle Falls. From here, crossing the northern part of Idaho, you come upon the fishfilled **Lake Pend Oreille** and the **Kaniksu National Forest,** before reaching the incomparably lovely wilderness of Glacier National Park.

☼⚓⚓ Glacier National Park

This and Yellowstone are America's two most beautiful national parks. Lying in the northern part of Montana, 611 mi. (978km) northeast of Seattle on the Canadian border (it's the U.S. section of the **Waterton-Glacier International Peace Park,** of which the adjoining Canadian section is the Waterton Lakes National Park in Alberta, Canada), this huge expanse of mountainous territory covers 1,583 sq. mi. (4,100km²) and is bisected from north to south by the Continental Divide. There's a particularly striking contrast between its two faces: The western face is humid, with pines, aspens, and red cedars flourishing below the meadows on the precipitous crests; while the eastern face is drier, windy, and often rendered dangerous by the Chinook. With its 60 glaciers (some of them accessible), its 650 azure lakes of all sizes, its waterfalls, and forests, the park is definitely alpine in character. It shelters a wealth of wildlife: grizzly, black bear, elk, bighorn sheep, and mountain goat, to name only a few.

The ☼⚓⚓ **Going-to-the-Sun Road,** 50 mi. (80km) of unbelievable hairpin bends blasted out of the side of a very steep mountain, crosses the park from side to side, crossing the Continental Divide at **Logan Pass** (closed by snowfalls from mid-Oct to mid-June), 6,664 ft. (2,031m) above sea level, before beginning the long and gripping descent to Lake McDonald, affording you some unforgettable views of the scenery.

It's worth coming to the Northwest just to see this park. There are many campsites (62) and motels inside the park, often full in July and Aug (more than two million people come here every year). The park is open year round, but watch out for avalanches in winter. For **information,** contact the Superintendent, Glacier National Park, West Glacier, MT 59936 (406/888-5441).

Leaving the park via U.S. 2W and U.S. 93S, you follow the shore of the enormous **Flathead Lake** for some 20 mi. (32km) to I-90W, on which you return to Seattle, 472 mi. (755km) west.

⚓ Spokane

On the way you should stop at Spokane, Washington's second-largest city. The very fine **falls** on the Spokane River are illuminated at night. See also the magnificent Gothic **Cathedral of St. John the Evangelist,** 1125 S. Grand Blvd. (509/838-4277), open daily, and **Riverfront Park,** on Spokane Falls Blvd., site of Expo 1974, the first international exhibition for the protection of the environment.

Then it's back to Seattle on I-90W. If you're a nature lover, the glorious scenery you'll encounter on this trip will thrill you.

Where to Stay En Route

COEUR D'ALENE, IDAHO 🛎🛎🛎 **Coeur d'Alene Resort,** 115 S. 2nd St., Coeur d'Alene, ID 83814 (208/765-4000). 340 rms. AE, MC, V. *Note:* Large, modern 18-story hotel on Coeur d'Alene Lake. Spectacular. **M–E**

GLACIER NATIONAL PARK ☼🛎🛎 **Glacier Park Lodge,** on Mont. 49 (near the junction with U.S. 2), East Glacier Park, MT 59434 (406/226-5551). 155 rms. MC, V. *Note:* Large, picturesque hotel dating from 1912 w. splendid views, open mid-June to late Sept. **I–M**

☼🛎🛎 **Lake McDonald Lodge,** Going-to-the-Sun Rd., West Glacier, MT 59936 (406/226-5551). 102 rms. MC, V. *Note:* Rustic hotel and bungalows on Lake McDonald; lovely views. Open June to late Sept. **I–M**

☼🛎🛎 **Many Glacier Hotel,** U.S. 89, East Glacier Park, MT 59434 (406/226-5551). 210 rms. MC, V. *Note:* A four-story structure built of local timber in 1917. Superbly located on Swiftcurrent Lake; open June to late Sept. **I–M**

🛎🛎 **Izaak Walton Inn,** U.S. 2, Essex, MT 59916 (406/888-5700). 30 rms. MC, V. *Note:* Older, historic hotel south of the park; open year round. **I**

🛎🛎 **St. Mary Lodge,** junction of U.S. 89 and Going-to-the-Sun Rd., St. Mary, MT 59434 (406/732-4431). 105 rms. AE, MC, V. *Note:* Very inviting motel on the river. Open mid-May to Oct. **I–M**

GRAND COULEE DAM, WASHINGTON 🛎 **Coulee House,** 110 Roosevelt Way at Birch St., Coulee Dam, WA 99116 (509/633-1101). 61 rms. AE, CB, DC, MC, V. *Note:* Comfortable little motel w. a view of the dam. **B–I**

SPOKANE, WASHINGTON 🛎🛎🛎 **Cavanaugh's Inn at the Park,** W. 303 North River Dr., Spokane, WA 99201 (509/326-8000). 402 rms. AE, CB, DC, MC, V. *Note:* Ultra-comfortable motel across from Riverfront Park. **I–M**

🛎🛎🛎 **Westcoast Ridpath Hotel,** 515 W. Sprague at First Ave., Spokane, WA 99210 (509/838-2711). 350 rms. *Note:* Inviting hotel in the heart of dwntwn. **I–M**

🏛 THE PACIFIC COAST, FROM NEAH BAY TO HOQUIAM-ABERDEEN (408 mi./653km r.t. by ferry to

Winslow, then Wash. 305N, Wash. 3N, Wash. 104N, U.S. 101N, Wash. 12W, Wash. 112E, U.S. 101S, U.S. 12E, Wash. 8E, U.S. 101S, and I-5N): Magnificent coastal route requiring three or four days, and taking in **Port Townsend** (see "Nearby Excursions," above), the ☼ **Makah Reservation, Olympic National Park** (see "Nearby Excursions," above), and the twin towns of **Hoquiam-Aberdeen,** with numerous stretches of scenic highway along the **Straits of San Juan de Fuca** and the Pacific coast.

On the way back, stop at ☼🏛 **Olympia,** the capital of Washington State, an old, delightful, carefully groomed city at the head of Puget Sound. While there, be sure to see the imposing Doric **Legislative Building** on Capitol Way (586-8687), open daily, with its 287-ft.-high (88m) dome; also the **State Capitol Museum,** 211 W. 21st Ave. (753-2580), open Tues–Sun, with interesting works of art and historical material displayed in a gracious Spanish-style building dating from 1920.

Drive back to Seattle on I-5N by way of **Tacoma,** birthplace of Bing Crosby.

☀☖ **VICTORIA & VANCOUVER, BRITISH COLUMBIA** (by catamaran year round to Victoria; 144 mi./230km north on I-5 to Vancouver): Two captivating Canadian cities which attract many tourists. There's a complete contrast between the English Tudor of Victoria and the 20th-century modernism of Vancouver. The catamaran, operated by Clipper Navigation, Pier 69, 2701 Alaskan Way, Seattle (448-5000), takes only 2½ hr., and there are daily trips year round.

For tourist information, contact the **Vancouver Travel Info Center,** 555 Burrard St., Vancouver, BC V6C 2J6 (604/683-2772); or **Victoria Tourism,** 612 View St., Victoria, BC V8W 1T3 (604/382-2127). Both cities amply justify the side trip.

Note: U.S. citizens need no passports to cross into Canada, but are advised to be in possession of proof of citizenship (birth certificate, voter's registration, or the like). Non-U.S. nationals should carry their passports, with a valid U.S. visa, to be sure of being readmitted to the U.S.

CHAPTER 46

THE PACIFIC
COAST⚑⚑

□ □ □

From the Olympic Mountains to
San Francisco Bay

Favored by a springlike climate for eight months of the year, the Pacific coast extends for hundreds of miles, its long, sandy beaches often almost deserted—perhaps because the icy currents sweeping down from the Arctic make bathing hazardous as well as uncomfortable. Nature is usually benign here—with some catastrophic exceptions, such as the eruption of **Mount St. Helens** in 1980, after 123 years of slumber.

While the winters in northern California are relatively dry, the Oregon and the Washington coasts can expect regular heavy showers Nov–Mar; the Olympic Mountains, in the extreme northwest, hold the U.S. record for rainfall with an average 142 in. (3,556mm) annually. As a result, the vegetation is often lush; not for nothing is Washington called "The Evergreen State."

For the 1,060 mi. (1,700km) between the Canadian border and San Francisco Bay, the Pacific coast alternates rocky shores, immense forests of giant conifers, swift-running rivers down which you can raft, and long stretches of white-sand beach punctuated by dozens of picturesque little fishing ports. Between the ocean and the coastal mountains of the **Coast Ranges** and the **Cascade Range** lie several national parks, among the most beautiful in the West and well worth seeing. Outstanding among them are the extraordinary **Olympic National Park** with its impenetrable rain forests; **Redwood National Park** with its thousand-year-old sequoias; **Crater Lake Park,** where one of the world's loveliest lakes (also, at 1,932 ft./589m, the deepest in the U.S.) lies in the crater of an extinct volcano; and **Oregon Caves National Monument** with its superb caverns of marble.

In short, a bounteous landscape, still largely unspoiled, which contrasts with the "civilized," built-up coast of southern California several hundred miles farther south.

BASIC FACTS: States of Washington, Oregon, and California. Area codes: 206 (Washington), 503 (Oregon), 707 (California). Distance from Cape Flattery (Washington) to San Francisco: about 1,060 mi. (1,700km).

CLIMATE: Two parallel mountain ranges running a little inland, the Coast Ranges and the Cascade Range, shelter the Pacific coast against the chill winds from the northeast, so that its climate from the Canadian border to San Francisco is uniformly temperate. In winter the thermometer seldom goes below 42° –

46° F (6° –8° C), while in summer temperatures hover around 68° F (20° C), ideal for a visit. Spring is measurably warmer and dryer than fall; the (very wet) rainy season lasts from Oct to Mar.

ARRIVAL & TRANSIT INFORMATION

AIRPORTS: The **Eureka-Arcata Airport** (ACV), 16 mi. (25km) north.
Portland International Airport (PDX): See Chapter 44 on Portland.
San Francisco International Airport (SFO): See Chapter 50 on San Francisco.
Sea-Tac International Airport (SEA): See Chapter 45 on Seattle.

AIRLINES: At the **Eureka-Arcata** airport: United (toll free 800/241-6522).
At the Portland, Seattle, and San Francisco airports: see Chapters 44, 45, and 50 respectively.

BUS OR CAR RENTAL? The Greyhound Bus Co. has excellent service along the whole Pacific coast. However, the distances are so great, and the attractions so many, that it makes a lot of sense to rent a car with unlimited mileage. Rates are usually lowest in California.

CAR RENTAL: See Chapters 44 on Portland, 45 on Seattle, and 50 on San Francisco.

TRAIN: For the Amtrak stations in Portland, Seattle, and San Francisco, see Chapters 44, 45, and 50 respectively.

INTERCITY BUSES: Greyhound (toll free 800/231-2222) has terminals along the Pacific coast at 956 SW 10th St., Newport, Ore. and 1603 4th St., Eureka, Calif.
For terminals in Portland, Seattle, and San Francisco, see Chapters 44, 45, and 50 respectively.

INFORMATION, TOURS, ADVENTURES & SPECIAL EVENTS

TOURIST INFORMATION: Information on the Pacific coast is available from both state government and local sources.
State Government Sources
California Office of Tourism, 801 K St., Suite 1600, Sacramento, CA 95814 (916/322-2881; toll free 800/862-2543, ext. 100).
Oregon Economic Development Dept.–Tourism Division, 775 Summer St. NE, Salem, OR 97310 (503/373-1270; toll free 800/547-7842).
Washington Tourism Development Division, 101 General Administration Bldg., Olympia, WA 98504 (206/586-2088; toll free 800/544-1800).
Local Sources
Astoria Chamber of Commerce, 111 W. Marine Dr. (P.O. Box 176), Astoria, OR 97103 (503/325-6311).

Coos Bay Chamber of Commerce, 50 E. Central Ave. (P.O. Box 210), Coos Bay, OR 97420 (503/269-0215).

Eureka Chamber of Commerce, 2112 Broadway, Eureka, CA 95501 (707/442-3738; toll free 800/356-6381).

Newport Chamber of Commerce, 555 SW Coast Hwy., Newport, OR 97365 (503/265-8801).

For Portland, Seattle, and San Francisco, see Chapters 44, 45, and 50 respectively.

GUIDED TOURS: For Portland, Seattle, and San Francisco, see Chapters 44, 45, and 50 respectively.

For other localities: consult the local *Yellow Pages* under "Sightseeing."

ADVENTURES: Six- to eight-hour trips down the Rogue River by raft or motorboat:

From Gold Beach, Ore.

Court's White Water Trips, Rogue River Bridge (503/247-6504), May–Oct; Jerry's Rogue Jet Boat Trips, Rogue River Bridge (503/247-4571), May to Oct; and Mail Boat Whitewater Trips, Mail Boat Dock (503/247-7033), May to Oct.

From Grants Pass, Ore.

Hellgate Excursions, 971 S. 6th St. (503/479-7204), May to Sept; and Orange Torpedo Trips (503/479-5061), June–Sept.

SPECIAL EVENTS: For exact dates of the events listed below, check with the chambers of commerce listed under "Tourist Information" (above) as well as with those below.

Crescent City Chamber of Commerce, Cultural Center, 1001 Front St., Crescent City, CA 95531 (707/464-3174).

Depoe Bay Chamber of Commerce, P.O. Box 21, Depoe Bay, OR 97341 (503/765-2889).

Port Orford Chamber of Commerce, Battle Rock Park, U.S. 101S (P.O. Box 637), Port Orford, OR 97465 (503/332-8055).

Astoria, Ore.

Great Astoria Crab Feed & Seafood Festival (Apr): Celebration of Astoria's maritime heritage; food, wine, arts and crafts.

Scandinavian Midsummer Festival (mid-June): Parades, folk dancing, craft shows.

Astoria Regatta (mid-Aug): Carnival, parades, and seafood galore.

Crescent City, Calif.

World Championship Crab Races (end of Feb).

July 4th Celebration (July 4): Parades, marathon, fireworks.

Depoe Bay, Ore.

Fleet of Flowers Ceremony (Memorial Day): Commemoration of victims of the sea, with religious service and chaplets of flowers thrown into the water.

Eureka, Calif.

Rhododendron Festival (late Apr to early May): Parades, races, art shows, etc.

Newport, Ore.
Loyalty Days and Sea Fair Festival (late Apr to early May): Regattas, boat review, art shows, etc.

Port Orford, Ore.
Port Orford Jubilee Celebration (July 4): Commemoration of the Battle of Battle Rock against the Native Americans; giant barbecue, parade, fireworks.

A NORTH TO SOUTH ITINERARY

The section of this guide devoted to the Pacific coast has been organized as an itinerary, starting at Neah Bay and ending at San Francisco, a distance of about 1,060 mi. (1,700km). You may choose not to drive the whole distance; Seattle, Portland, and San Francisco, as well as many points in between, are linked by air, bus, and train. Car rentals are not hard to find; bear in mind, however, that rates are often lower in California than in Washington and Oregon, and that there may be a significant charge if you rent a car in one state and drop it off in another.

Distances Down the Pacific Coast

From	To	Distance
Neah Bay	Quinault	113 mi. (182km)
Quinault	Hoquiam-Aberdeen	40 mi. (64km)
Hoquiam-Aberdeen	Westport	20 mi. (32km)
Westport	Long Beach	75 mi. (120km)
Long Beach	Astoria	23 mi. (36km)
Astoria	Fort Clatsop Nat'l. Memorial	6 mi. (10km)
Fort Clatsop	Seaside	10 mi. (18km)
Seaside	Cannon Beach	8 mi. (13km)
Cannon Beach	Tillamook	39 mi. (62km)
Tillamook	Pacific City	27 mi. (43km)
Pacific City	Lincoln City	15 mi. (24km)
Lincoln City	Depoe Bay	12 mi. (19km)
Depoe Bay	Devil's Punchbowl State Park	5 mi. (9km)
Devil's Punchbowl	Newport	8 mi. (12km)
Newport	Yachats	24 mi. (39km)
Yachats	Sea Lion Caves	15 mi. (24km)
Sea Lion Caves	Florence	12 mi. (19km)
Florence	Reedsport	32 mi. (51km)
Reedsport	Coos Bay	27 mi. (44km)
Coos Bay	Bandon	24 mi. (38km)
Bandon	Port Orford	27 mi. (43km)
Port Orford	Gold Beach	53 mi. (84km)
Gold Beach	Crescent City	59 mi. (95km)
Crescent City	McKinleyville	70 mi. (112km)
McKinleyville	Eureka	10 mi. (16km)
Eureka	Avenue of the Giants	41 mi. (65km)
Avenue of the Giants	Fort Bragg	86 mi. (138km)
Fort Bragg	Noyo	2 mi. (4km)
Noyo	Mendocino	5 mi. (8km)
Mendocino	Point Arena	35 mi. (56km)
Point Arena	Fort Ross	48 mi. (76km)
Fort Ross	Bodega Bay	22 mi. (36km)
Bodega Bay	Point Reyes Nat'l. Seashore	32 mi. (50km)
Point Reyes	San Francisco	35 mi. (56km)

NEAH BAY: At the western tip of the **Olympic Peninsula** the little ports of **Neah Bay** and **Sekiu,** about 12 mi. (19km) apart, are very popular sportfishing resorts (boat rentals). Drive to **Cape Flattery,** the northwesternmost point in the contiguous United States, with a land's end of cliffs, caves, pounding sea, and isolated **Tatoosh Island.** At Neah Bay is the interesting archeological museum of the **Makah Reservation,** on B/A Hwy. 1 (206/645-2711), open daily in summer, Wed–Sun the rest of the year; it houses more than 55,000 works of art or handcrafts, some more than 500 years old.

QUINAULT: Starting point for a visit to **Olympic National Park,** a superb and inviolate nature reserve covering 1,430 sq. mi. (3,700km²), whose treasures include the glaciers of **Mount Olympus,** rain forests, desert isles along the Pacific shore, and a unique population of wildlife. Deep-blue **Lake Quinault** and glacier-fed streams offer some of the finest steelhead trout fishing in the Northwest. Views of wonderful scenery. Be sure to see the rain forest and the Enchanted Valley. Open year round. For details, see "Nearby Excursions" in Chapter 45 on Seattle.

Where to Stay

Lake Quinault Lodge, South Shore Rd., Quinault, WA 98575 (206/288-2571; toll free 800/562-6672). 89 rms (no A/C). AE, MC, V. Free parking, pool, sauna, boating, beach, rest., bar. *Note:* Comfortable historic little country inn on Lake Quinault dating back to the 1920s. Rms w. balconies, some w. fireplaces. Avoid the new lakeside addition (34 rms). Friendly reception; very acceptable rest. For nature lovers. Open year round. **M**

Where to Eat

Lake Quinault Lodge, South Shore Rd. (206/288-2571). No A/C. Breakfast/lunch/dinner daily. AE, DC, MC, V. *Specialties:* fresh salmon, fish of the day, shellfish, steak, prime rib. *Note:* Pretty, rustic decor w. a clear view of Lake Quinault and the mountains. Classic hotel food; cheerful svce. Resv. advised; a good place to eat. *Steak/Seafood.* **I**

HOQUIAM-ABERDEEN: Picturesque harbor town on Grays Harbor Gulf, comprising the twin cities of **Hoquiam,** the commercial and fishing port, and **Aberdeen,** with its woodworking plants and fish canneries.

Where to Stay

Nordic Inn, 1700 S. Boone St., Aberdeen, WA 98520 (206/533-0100). 66 rms (no A/C), cable color TV. AE, CB, DC, MC, V. Free parking, café, bar, free crib. *Note:* Small, inviting motel; spacious rms, some w. refrigerator; acceptable rest. Good value. **B–I**

Red Lion, 521 W. Wishkah St., Aberdeen, WA 98520 (206/532-5210; toll free, see Red Lion Inns). 67 rms (no A/C), cable color TV. AE, CB, DC, MC, V. Free parking, free crib. *Note:* Modern motel not far from dwntwn Aberdeen. Adj. rest. Spacious, serviceable rms; free morning coffee. **B–I**

Westwood Inn, 910 Simpson Ave., Hoquiam, WA 98550 (206/532-8161). 65 rms (no A/C), cable color TV. AE, MC, V. Free parking, nearby coffee shop, crib $5. *Note:* Conventional, unpretentious motel; comfortable rms, some w. kitchenette. Free morning coffee; good value. **B–I**

Where to Eat

Bridge's, 112 N. G St. (206/532-6563). A/C. Lunch/dinner daily; closed hols. AE, DC, MC, V. *Specialties:* seafood, fish, prime rib, prime cuts, oysters. *Note:* Praiseworthy seafood rest. nr. the harbor; everything is absolutely fresh. Attractive modern decor; good svce; no-smoking area. Resv. advised. *Steak/Seafood.* **B–I**

WESTPORT: This little port, with its fleet of 150 charter boats, is a favorite summer resort for sportfishing (salmon, bass, halibut, etc.). Its **Westport Aquarium,** 321 Harbor St. (206/268-0471), open daily Feb–Nov, is justly renowned. The nearby **Twin Harbors State Park** has beautiful beaches, but swimming is hazardous.

Where to Stay

Château Westport (formerly the Canterbury), on Wash. 105 Westport, WA 98595 (206/268-9101). 110 rms (no A/C), cable color TV. AE, CB, DC, MC, V. Free parking, pool, free breakfast, crib $3. *Note:* Inviting motel on the beach. Spacious rms w. balconies and refrigerators, some w. kitchenettes and fireplaces. Pleasant reception and svce; nearby rest. **I**

Where to Eat

Sourdough Lil's, 202 Dock St. (206/268-9700). No A/C. Lunch/dinner Thurs–Tues; closed Thanksgiving and Dec 25. MC, V. *Specialties:* fish of the day, shellfish, prime rib, steak. *Note:* Like a 1900s saloon, w. good fish and meat. Entertaining atmosphere. *Steak/Seafood.* **B–I**

LONG BEACH: Sweeping 28 mi. (45km) in a single stretch, this is one of the world's longest sand beaches. **Wash. 103,** the coast road from Long Beach to **Oysterville,** is a scenic highway; it will take you to **Fort Canby** (206/642-3078), open daily year round. On Wash. 101 you'll find **Fort Columbia** (206/777-8221), open daily May–Nov, closed the rest of the year. From either one of these meticulously restored military posts dating from pioneer days, there's a wonderful view of the mouth of the Columbia River.

Where to Stay

Chautauqua Lodge, 304 14th St. NW, Long Beach, WA 98631 (206/642-4401). 180 rms (no A/C), cable color TV. AE, MC, V. Free parking, pool, sauna, adj. rest., bar, disco, crib $2. *Note:* Large, modern motel w. direct beach access; huge, well-designed rms w. balconies and refrigerators, some w. kitchenettes. Good svce; a fine place to stay. **I–M,** but lower rates off-season.

Shaman Motel, 115 3rd St. S., Long Beach, WA 98631 (206/642-3714). 40 rms (no A/C), cable color TV. AE, MC, V. Free parking, pool, adj. coffee shop. *Note:* Typical motel nr. the beach; huge inviting rms, some w. kitchenette and fireplace. **B–I,** but lower rates Oct–May.

IN NEARBY CHINOOK **Youth Hostel,** Fort Columbia State Park, Chinook, WA 98614 (206/777-8755). 23 beds. Open year round.

Where to Eat

Shoalwater, 1 mi. (1.6km) south on Wash. 103 at 45th St., Seaview (206/642-4142). No A/C. Lunch/dinner daily. AE, DC, MC, V. *Specialties:* oysters, Oregon duck, salmon. Award-winning wine list. *Note:* Widely acclaimed Northwest regional cookery. Romantic setting w. stained glass and antiques. In the historic Shelburne Inn (1896). Resv. advised. *American.* **I–M**

ASTORIA: Dating from 1811, this is one of the oldest American settlement points west of Mississippi. It was originally a trading post for furs, belonging to the wealthy John Jacob Astor, owner of the American Fur Co. Today it's a charming little fishing port with a strong flavor of the 19th century. If you climb the 128 steps of the **Astoria Column** you'll be

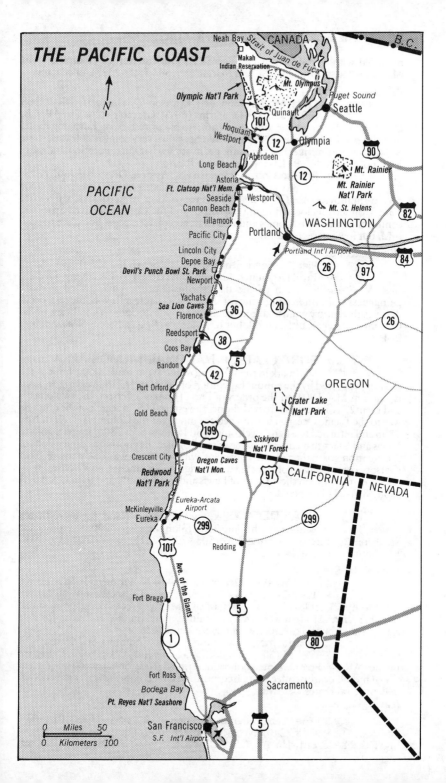

rewarded with a wonderful view. There's also the interesting **Columbia River Maritime Museum** at 17th St. and Marine Dr. (503/325-2323), open daily.

Where to Stay

Crest Motel, 5366 Leif Erickson Dr., Astoria, OR 97103 (503/325-3141). 34 rms (no A/C), cable color TV. AE, CB, DC, MC, V. Free parking, whirlpool bath; no bar or rest. *Note:* Engaging motel on a cliff overlooking the Columbia River. Spacious, very comfortable rms, some w. balcony and refrigerator. Inviting grdn; somewhat curt reception and svce. Free morning coffee. **B–I,** but lower rates off-season.

Red Lion Inn, 400 Industry St. Astoria, OR 97103 (503/325-7373; toll free, see Red Lion Inns). 124 rms (no A/C), color TV, in-rm movies. AE, CB, DC, MC, V. Free parking, rest., bar, disco, free crib. *Note:* Wonderfully located facing the harbor and the Columbia River. Spacious, comfortable rms w. balconies and fine view; acceptable rest. A fine place to stay. **I–M,** but lower rates off-season.

Where to Eat

Pier 11 Feed Store, 77 11th St. (503/325-0279). A/C. Breakfast/lunch/dinner daily; closed Thanksgiving, Dec 25. MC, V. *Specialties:* catch of the day, shellfish, prime cuts, grilled salmon, Dungeness crab. Interesting wine list. *Note:* As its name tells you, the rest. occupies a 19th-century grain and feed warehouse on the docks, w. a good view of the Columbia River. Faultless food, but terrible svce. Resv. advised. *Steak/Seafood.* **B–I**

FORT CLATSOP NATIONAL MEMORIAL: A major landmark in the Winning of the West, marking the limit of the territory explored by the famous expedition of Lewis and Clark. Leaving St. Louis, Mo., in May 1804 on the orders of Pres. Thomas Jefferson, the two officers and their 27 companions crossed the northwestern U.S. in search of the quickest way to the Pacific Ocean. They reached the mouth of the Columbia River in Nov 1805 and returned to a hero's welcome in St. Louis in Sept 1806. It was thanks to Lewis and Clark that Americans began to recognize the enormous dimensions of their nation, or rather of the continent with which it was co-extensive. Fort Clatsop, completely reconstructed using original documents, now houses an interesting museum on the odyssey of Lewis and Clark; you'll find it on U.S. 101A (503/861-2471), open daily.

SEASIDE: A well-known oceanside resort for more than a century, with a fine 2-mi. (3km) beach. At 200 N. Promenade St. there's an interesting **aquarium** (503/738-6211), open daily Mar–Nov, Wed–Sun the rest of the year.

Where to Stay

Best Western Ocean View, 414 N. Promenade St., Seaside, OR 97138 (503/738-3334; toll free, see Best Western). 95 rms (no A/C), cable color TV. AE, CB, DC, MC, V. Free parking, pool, sauna, rest., bar. *Note:* Modern, very well maintained motel on the beach; comfortable rms w. sun deck and ocean view; family packages. **I–M**

Sundowner, 125 Ocean Way at Columbia St., Seaside, OR 97138 (503/738-8301). 22 rms (no A/C), color TV, in-rm movies. MC, V. Free parking, pool, sauna, crib $3. *Note:* Small, well-run conventional motel; nearby coffee shop, free morning coffee; some rms w. kitchenettes. **B–I,** but lower rates Oct–May.

Where to Eat

The Crab Broiler, intersection of U.S. 26 and U.S. 101 (503/738-7240). No A/C. Dinner only, nightly; closed Thanksgiving, Dec 24–25, early Jan. AE, CB, DC, MC, V. *Specialties:* catch of the day, seafood, lobster. *Note:* Agreeable rustic atmosphere (four fireplaces, grdn view) and excellent seafood impeccably broiled or otherwise prepared. Very good svce; resv. advised. *Seafood.* **B–I**

☼☾⚓ **CANNON BEACH:** Very popular resort, with a beach 6.8 mi. (11km) long; another bird and aquatic refuge, its principal feature is a huge solitary rock, 235 ft. (72m) high just offshore from the beach, known as **Haystack Rock.** Flourishing artists' community. From here you have your choice of two interesting excursions: to the 3,820-ft. (1,000m) **Saddle Mountain,** for its views of the coast and the ocean; or to **Ecola Park** on the shoreline, with its seabird and sea lion rookeries on offshore rocks.

Where to Stay

IN NEARBY TOLOVANA PARK The ⚑⚑ **Tolovana Inn,** 3400 S. Hemlock St., Tolovana Park, OR 97145 (503/436-2211; toll free 800/333-8890). 180 rms (no A/C), color TV, in-rm movies. AE, MC, V. Free parking, pool, sauna, rest., bar, free crib. *Note:* Large vacation motel w. direct access to beach. Spacious, comfortable rms w. private patios or balconies and refrigerators, some w. kitchenettes. Ask for a rm looking out on the ocean and Haystack Rock. Interesting family discounts. Two-day minimum stay on wknds and in July–Aug. **I–M**

☼☾⚓ **TILLAMOOK:** Nicknamed "Little Holland" because of its dikes and dairy farms. **Loop Rd.** is a very beautiful scenic highway 19 mi. (31km) long around **Cape Meares** and the Pacific shore. While in town be sure to visit the ⚓ **World War II Blimp Hangar Museum** at the Tillamook Naval Air Station, 4000 Blimp Blvd. (842-3680), a collection of a functioning blimp and 17 restored World War II airplanes including the Spitfire, P-51 Mustang, and F4U Corsair—all housed in an enormous hangar that measures 1,076 ft. (328m) long, 296 ft. (90m) wide, and 192 ft. (59m) tall. A must for aviation buffs.

Where to Stay

⚑ **Mar-Clair Inn,** 11 Main Ave., Tillamook, OR 97141 (503/842-7571). 47 rms (no A/C), cable color TV. AE, CB, DC, MC, V. Free parking, pool, sauna, rest. *Note:* Modern motel in the center of town; comfortable rms, some w. kitchenettes. Solarium **B–I,** but lower rates off-season.

⚓ **PACIFIC CITY:** Famous for its fishermen and their wooden dories which can ride the long Pacific swells (for a small fee you can come along). On your way, stop to look at the ocean from **Cape Lookout,** 18 mi. (30km) north.

⚓ **LINCOLN CITY:** A popular town for summer homes, with five communities grouped around a beach 3.7 mi. (6km) long. Many art galleries and crafts shops.

Where to Stay

☼⚑⚑ **The Inn at Spanish Head,** 4009 S. U.S. 101, Lincoln City, OR 97367 (503/996-2161; toll free 800/547-5235). 120 rms, cable color TV. AE, CB, DC, MC, V. Free valet parking, pool, sauna, rest., bar, free crib. *Note:* A 10-story hotel facing the ocean. Vast, comfortable rms, most w. private balconies or patios and an outstanding ocean view, all w. kitchenettes. Adj. beach. Good svce; a fine place to stay. **M–E,** but lower rates off-season.

♀♀ **Shilo Inn,** 1501 NW 40th St., Lincoln City, OR 97367 (503/
♌♌ 994-3655; toll free 800/222-2244). 186 rms (no A/C), color
TV, in-rm movies. AE, CB, DC, MC, V. Free parking, pool, sauna, rest., bar, rm
svce, nightclub, free crib. *Note:* Three-story motel (no elevator) overlooking the
ocean; spacious, comfortable rms w. refrigerators, the best w. a fine view. Free
airport limo. Very commendable rest. Good value. **I–M**

♀ **Lincoln Shores** (formerly Nidden Hof), 136 NE U.S. 101,
♌ Lincoln City, OR 97367 (503/994-8155; toll free 800/423-
6240). 30 rms (no A/C), cable color TV. AE, DC, MC, V. Free parking, nearby
coffee shop, free crib. *Note:* Engaging little motel across from D River Park. Inviting rms w. balconies. Beach nearby. **B–I,** but lower rates Nov–May.

IN NEARBY GLENEDEN BEACH The ☼ ♌♌♌♌ **Salishan Lodge,** U.S. 101, Gleneden
Beach, OR 97388 (503/764-2371; toll free 800/452-2300). 200 rms, A/C,
color TV, in-rm movies. AE, MC, V. Free covered parking, pool, four tennis
courts, golf course, sauna, health club, rest. (Dining Room), coffee shop, bar, rm
svce, disco, hrdrsr, art gallery, boutiques, concierge, crib $10. *Note:* One of the
best hotels in the country; up-to-date elegance in the middle of 700 acres (283ha)
of woods and grdns. Wonderful setting between the forest and Siletz Bay. Inviting, comfortable two-story buildings overlooking the golf course; spacious rms
w. fireplaces, private balconies and patios, the best w. ocean view. Rest. of a high
order; excellent svce. A memorable place to stay. **E–VE,** but lower rates Nov–
Apr.

Where to Eat

♈♈ **The Bay House,** 5911 SW U.S. 101 (503/996-3222). A/C.
♋♋ Dinner only, nightly; closed hols. and Mon–Tues Nov–May.
MC, V. *Specialties:* fresh oysters and seafood, fowl, duck and lamb dishes. Good
wine list. *Note:* This rest. overlooking Siletz Bay ranks as one of the Oregon
coast's classic eateries. The seafood is impeccably fresh and well prepared. Intimate atmosphere. Resv. advised. *American.* **I–M**

IN NEARBY GLENEDEN BEACH ♈♈♈ **The Dining Room,** in the Salishan Lodge (see
"Where to Stay," above) (503/764-2371). A/C. Dinner only, nightly. AE, CB,
DC, MC, V. Jkt. *Specialties:* Dungeness crab, Chinook salmon, filet of sole, chateaubriand, Oregon lamb chops. Very good wine list, with more than 1,000 labels. *Note:* One of the best rests. on the Pacific coast. Three-level dining rm,
recently renovated, elegantly paneled and w. a pretty view over the bay. Exciting,
innovative cuisine, based on remarkably fine local produce—seafood, lamb,
game, wild mushrooms, etc. Exemplary svce. Resv. required. *Continental/
Seafood.* **M–E**

♈♈ **Chez Jeannette,** 7150 Old U.S. 101 (503/764-3434). No
♋♋ A/C. Dinner only, Tues–Sat (nightly July–Aug); closed Dec.
AE, MC, V. *Specialties:* catch of the day and seafood, rack of lamb, game (in season). *Note:* Elegant, meticulously prepared cuisine of French inspiration, in a
charming 1920s country cottage. Friendly, efficient svce. Resv. advisable. Locally
popular. *French/American.* **I–M**

🛑 **DEPOE BAY:** Tiny, picturesque fishing port; you must stop
in the center of town to look at the **Spouting Horns,** natural
rock tubes that spout like geysers under the violent assault of the waves; don't
miss them. Depoe Bay is a good base for deep-sea fishing.

Where to Stay

♀ **Best Western Surfrider,** U.S. 101, Depoe Bay, OR 97341
♌ (503/764-2311; toll free, see Best Western). 40 rms (no
A/C), cable color TV. AE, CB, DC, MC, V. Free parking, pool, sauna, rest., bar,
crib $5. *Note:* Small, likable, serviceable motel at the water's edge; comfortable

rms w. balconies overlooking the Pacific (some w. kitchenettes and fireplaces). Excellent reception. **I–M,** but lower rates Oct–May.

IN NEARBY OTTER ROCK ₤₤ **The Inn at Otter Crest,** Otter Rock, OR 97369 (503/765-2111; toll free 800/452-2101), a quarter mile west of U.S. 101. 98 rms and studios (no A/C), cable color TV. AE, DC, MC, V. Free parking, pool, sauna, four tennis courts, miniature golf, beach, nearby rest., crib $5. *Note:* Comfortable, inviting motel on a wooded headland overlooking the Pacific. Pretty woodland decor. Spacious rms w. private balcony and refrigerator (some w. kitchenette and fireplace). Studios have two bedrooms. Efficient, smiling svce. Wonderful view of the ocean. **M–E**

☼⚐ **DEVIL'S PUNCH BOWL STATE PARK:** Giant bowl-shaped rock formation which fills at each high tide. Beach; aquatic garden. From **Cape Foulweather,** so named by British navigator Capt. James Cook in 1778, you'll have a fine view of the ocean.

☼⚏ **NEWPORT:** One of the busiest fishing ports on the Pacific coast, with fine Victorian houses and colorful docks. **Hatfield Marine Science Center,** Marine Science Dr. (503/867-0100), open daily, is an excellent museum of oceanography affiliated with Oregon State University. There's also a renowned saltwater aquarium, **Undersea Gardens,** at 267 SW Bay Blvd. (503/265-2206), open daily, which offers views of marine plants and native sealife, including Armstrong the giant octopus, through large underwater windows.

Where to Stay

₤₤₤ **Embarcadero Resort,** 1000 SE Bay Blvd., Newport, OR 97365 (503/265-8521; toll free 800/547-4779). 80 rms (no A/C), color TV, in-rm movies. AE, CB, DC, MC, V. Free parking, pool, sauna, marina, boating, rest. (Embarcadero), bar, crib $5. *Note:* Luxurious vacation hotel on the Yaquina River, w. marina and boat dock. Elegant, comfortable rms, all w. private balconies or patios, some w. kitchenettes. Flawless reception and svce; excellent rest.; beautiful views of the bay. **M–E,** but lower rates Nov–Apr.

☼₤₤ **Sylvia Beach,** 267 NW Cliff St., Newport, OR 97365 (503/265-5428). 20 rms. (no A/C). AE, MC, V. Free parking, rest. (Tables of Content), library, free breakfast. *Note:* A booklover's paradise. Every bedroom in the whole, huge 1912 wooden structure overlooking the ocean is dedicated to a different writer and decorated accordingly. The most original are the Edgar Allan Poe Rm, Colette Rm, and Agatha Christie Rm. Almost all have a fine ocean view. Four floors, no elevator. Commendable rest. You should reserve a long way ahead, especially in summer. **I–M**

₤ **Jolly Knight Motel,** 606 SW Coast Hwy., Newport, OR 97365 (503/265-7723). 43 rms, cable color TV. AE, MC, V. Free parking, adj. 24-hr. rest., free crib. *Note:* Small, unpretentious oceanfront motel; spacious, serviceable rms, the best with a fine view. **B–I,** but lower rates Oct–May.

Where to Eat

♆♆ **Embarcadero,** in the Embarcadero Resort (see "Where to Stay," above) (503/265-8521). A/C. Breakfast/lunch/dinner daily, brunch Sun. AE, CB, DC, MC, V. *Specialties:* catch of the day, shellfish, steak. *Note:* All-purpose seafaring decor but pretty view of the harbor. First-class food; absolutely fresh seafood. *Steak/Seafood.* **B–I**

♆ **Mo's,** 622 SW Bay Blvd. (503/265-2979). No A/C. Lunch/dinner daily. MC, V. *Specialties:* clam chowder, oysters on the half shell or barbecued, crab salad, broiled fish, peanut-butter cake, apple cobbler. *Note:* One of the Oregon coast's long-standing beacons. The parent establishment, as well as the annex across the road and the half dozen other Mo's rests. scattered along the coast from Lincoln City to Coos Bay, serve the best clam chowder in the state as well as impeccably fresh seafood at reasonable prices. Amusing seafaring decor. Noisy but pleasant; a fine place to eat. *Seafood.* **B–I**

YACHATS: Fashionable seaside resort with a beautiful fine-sand beach and a very craggy shoreline. (**Cape Perpetua,** just south of town, is the highest point on the Oregon coast: 800 ft./243m.) The coastal highway here is beautiful beyond description. Good sea fishing.

Where to Stay

Adobe Motel, U.S. 101 (P.O. Box 219), Yachats, OR 97498 (503/547-3141; toll free 800/522-3623). 92 rms (no A/C), cable color TV. AE, CB, DC, MC, V. Free parking, whirlpool, sauna, rest., bar, crib $5. *Note:* Appealing little motel right on the ocean; huge, inviting rms w. refrigerators (most w. balconies and fireplaces), the best overlooking the Pacific. Cheerful reception and svce; free morning coffee. An excellent place to stay. **I,** but lower rates off-season.

Where to Eat

La Serre, 2nd and Beach Sts. (503/547-3420). A/C. Dinner Wed–Mon, brunch Sun; closed Jan. AE, DC, MC, V. *Specialties:* catch of the day, seafood, steak, homemade desserts. *Note:* A nice, attractive rest. serving honest, tasty (but not very imaginative) food in a family atmosphere. Locally popular. *American.* **B–I**

SEA LION CAVES (U.S. 101) (503/547-3111): A basalt grotto 1,500 ft. (450m) long, 208 ft. (63m) below the surface (elevator), inhabited by wild sea lions. The animals can easily be observed in their natural surroundings outside the cave in spring and summer, or inside the cave in fall and winter. Open daily; touristy, but spectacular nonetheless.

FLORENCE: A charming little town with an interesting "Old Town" area and a wealth of flowers on the Siuslaw River, very near a chain of 17 lakes well stocked with fish and the **Siuslaw National Forest.** It marks the northern boundary of the **Oregon Dunes National Recreation Area,** a huge sandspit 50 mi. (80km) long, whose dunes rise as high as 524 ft. (160m). Dunebuggy rides available (503/271-3611).

Where to Stay

Le Château, 1084 Coast Hwy., Florence, OR 97439 (503/ 997-3481). 48 rms (no A/C), cable color TV. AE, DC, MC, V. Free parking, pool, sauna, nearby coffee shop, crib $5. *Note:* Typical vacation motel w. direct beach access. Functionally comfortable rms; cheerful reception; free morning coffee. **B–I**

Where to Eat

Windward Inn, 3757 U.S. 101 (503/997-8243). A/C. Breakfast/lunch/dinner daily; closed Thanksgiving, Dec 24–25. AE, CB, DC, MC, V. *Specialties:* fish and shellfish of the day, very fine prime cuts, fresh fruit and vegetables. *Note:* The two major achievements of this excellent rest., much appreciated by those in-the-know, are the low prices it charges for materials of the highest quality, and its well-stocked wine list. A classic since 1932. Resv. advised. *Steak/Seafood.* **B–I**

🔔 **REEDSPORT:** Both saltwater and freshwater fishing enthusiasts can enjoy themselves here at the head of **Winchester Bay.** The headquarters of the **Oregon Dunes National Recreation Area** (see above) is here, at 855 Highway Ave. (503/271-3611).

🔔 **COOS BAY:** The world's biggest lumber port; also a busy fishing port. At **North Bend,** on the same bay, there's an interesting museum devoted to the settlement of Oregon, the **Coos County Historical Museum,** Simpson Park on U.S. 101 (503/756-6320), open Mon–Sat June –Sept, Tues–Sat the rest of the year.

☀️🏔 Crater Lake National Park

Some 182 mi. (292km) SE of Coos Bay via Ore. 42 and Ore. 38 is one of the loveliest mountain lakes in the U.S., or indeed in the world, in the caldera of the extinct volcano **Mount Mazama.** A violent eruption some 6,600 years ago created this steep-sided, circular basin, 7 mi. (11km) across and, at 1,932 ft. (589m), the deepest lake in the country. The reflection of the surrounding peaks and craters in its clear dark-blue waters delineates a surprisingly beautiful volcanic landscape. **Rim Drive,** a 33-mi. (53km) scenic highway, follows the shoreline; there are many **hiking trails,** including a steep path leading up to Watchman's Peak (8,022 ft./2,457m) with its unparalleled view. There are **observation platforms,** which can be reached by car, at the top of Cloudcap (8,060 ft./ 2,457m) and Pinnacles (5,585 ft./1,672m), strange needles of tufa and pumice carved out by erosion. Many wild animals live around Crater Lake: black bear, elk, red fox, coyote, wildcat, and others; fish, on the other hand, are few and fishing is strictly regulated. Boat rides may be taken on the lake, but be careful if you go swimming: The water is ice-cold even in summer.

Given the status of a national park in 1902, Crater Lake is open year round (except for the northern entrance, which is closed mid-Oct to mid-June because of snowslides). At any time of year take warm clothing—it snows 10 months out of the 12. Campsites and a rustic motel are inside the park.

For **information,** contact the Superintendent, Crater Lake National Park, P.O. Box 7, Crater Lake, OR 97604 (503/594-2211).

Where to Stay

💲💲 **Red Lion Inn,** 1313 N. Bayshore Dr., Coos Bay, OR 97420 (503/267-4141; toll free, see Red Lion Inns). 145 rms, A/C, cable color TV. AE, CB, DC, MC, V. Free parking, pool, rest., bar, rm svce, disco, free crib. *Note:* In a lovely situation w. a view of the bay. Vast, inviting rms; up-to-date, comfortable facilities; good svce; free airport limo. **I–M**

Youth Hostel, 438 Elrod, Coos Bay, OR 97420 (503/267-6114). 20 beds. Open late May to Sept.

🔔 **BANDON:** Little harbor, very popular with tourists, at the mouth of the Coquille River. Lovely beaches famed for the agates and other semiprecious stones you can pick up here.

Where to Stay

💲 **Harbor View Motel,** U.S. 101, Bandon, OR 97411 (503/ 347-4417). 57 rms (no A/C), color TV, in-rm movies. AE, MC, V. Free parking, adj. coffee shop, crib $4. *Note:* Small motel on a cliff overlooking the harbor; decent standard of comfort; some rms w. balconies and refrigerators. **I,** but lower rates Oct–May.

Youth Hostel, 375 2nd St., Bandon, OR 97411 (503/347-9632). 40 beds. Open year round.

Where to Eat

 ⏝ **Bandon Boatworks,** 275 Lincoln Ave. SW (503/347-2111). No A/C. Lunch/dinner Tues–Sun; closed Jan and hols. MC, V. *Specialties:* fish of the day, steak, milk-fed veal, beef dishes. *Note:* Excellent fish, as well as some good prime cuts. Nice view of the jetty and lighthouse. Congenial atmosphere; good svce. *American.* **B–I**

 ☼☀☖ **PORT ORFORD:** Some of the loveliest seascapes on the Oregon coast. In 1851 the little port, which was then the westernmost city in the contiguous U.S., was the scene of a bloody battle between native tribes and white settlers. At ☖ **Cape Blanco,** 7½ mi. (12km) NW on U.S. 101, there's an unusual black-sand beach in spite of its name (*blanco* means "white" in Spanish).

Where to Stay

 ⏝ **Sea Crest,** U.S. 101, Port Orford, OR 97465 (503/332-3040). 18 rms, cable color TV. MC, V. Free parking, nearby coffee shop. *Note:* Mini-motel w. ocean and mountain views. Rms no better than serviceable, but inviting grdn and cheerful reception. **B–I,** but lower rates off-season.

 ☖ **GOLD BEACH:** Owes its name to the gold nuggets that used to be found at the mouth of the **Rogue River** until, in 1861, a disastrous flood swept them all out to sea. Fine excursions into the nearby **Siskiyou National Forest;** also rafting down the Rogue River (see "Adventures," above).

Where to Stay

 ☼☖☖☖ **Tu Tu' Tun Lodge,** 96550 N. Bank Rogue, Gold Beach, OR 97444 (503/247-6664). 19 rms (no A/C). MC, V. Free parking, pool, fishing, putting green, rest., bar, crib $3. *Note:* Charming country cottage on the Rogue River; boat trips available. Spacious, inviting rms w. balconies; well-stocked library for inveterate idlers. An agreeable, relaxing stopover. Open on a limited basis Nov–Apr. **M–E**

 ⏝ **Ireland's Rustic Lodges,** 1120 S. Ellensburg, Gold Beach, OR 97444 (503/247-7718). 40 rms and cottages (no A/C), cable color TV. No credit cards. Free parking, private beach, nearby coffee shop, crib $4. *Note:* Pretty little bungalows in a grdn overlooking the ocean; the best have ocean views. Spacious rms w. balconies, some w. kitchenettes and fireplaces. Good value on balance. **B–I,** but lower rates Oct–May.

 ☖ **CRESCENT CITY:** The first important town across the northern border of California, deriving its name from its crescent-shaped coastline. Picturesque working lighthouse (1856) on Battery Point at the end of A St.; accessible only at low tide (tours Wed–Sun Apr–Sept). From here you can easily venture into Redwood National Park (see below).

☼ **Redwood National Park**

Just 4 mi. (6km) east of Crescent City, this forest of giant sequoias (redwoods), 46 mi. (75km) long by 6 mi. (10km) wide, stands on the shore. Some redwoods, more than 10 centuries old, have grown to 295 ft. (90m); the present record is held by the prosaically nicknamed **Tall Tree,** 368 ft. (112m) high, with a diameter of 14 ft. (4.20m). This is the largest-known living creature in the world. Abundant wildlife: elk, deer, mountain lion, bald eagle, brown pelican, and peregrine falcons. The park is traversed by a splendid scenic highway, U.S. 101. Many hiking trails, campsites, and picnic areas.

There are three other redwood forests nearby: **Jedediah Smith State Park, Del Norte Coast State Park,** and **Prairie Creek State Park;** along with Redwood National Park they make up the **Redwood Empire,** a vast tract of woodlands extending from the northern border of California to the outskirts of San Francisco.

For **information,** contact the Superintendent, Redwood National Park, 1111 2nd St., Crescent City, CA 95531 (707/464-6101).

※ẟ Oregon Caves National Monument

These marble caverns, 85 mi. (136km) NE of Crescent City via U.S. 199 and Ore. 46, comprising a number of evocatively named chambers—Paradise Lost, Ghost Chamber, Joaquin Miller's Chapel—were discovered in 1874 by a hunter in pursuit of a bear; they are among the most unusual and beautiful in the U.S. Their air temperature is a constant 42° F (6° C). Tours (strenuous) daily year round. For **information,** contact Oregon Caves National Monument, P.O. Box 128, Cave Junction, OR 97523 (503/592-3400).

Around the caves is ẟ **Siskiyou National Forest,** whose cedars—200- to 300-year-old pine trees growing as tall as 130 ft. (40m)—conifers, orchids, and rare plants make it a botanist's paradise.

Where to Stay

♀ **Value Lodge,** 353 L St., Crescent City, CA 95531 (707/464-6124). 35 rms (no A/C), cable color TV. AE, MC, V. Free parking, nearby rest., sauna, free crib. *Note:* A fine ocean view is the main attraction of this typical small motel. Comfortable rms; free morning coffee. **B-I,** but lower rates off-season.

IN NEARBY SMITH RIVER The ♀♀ **Best Western Ship Ashore,** U.S. 101, Smith River, CA 95567 (707/487-3141; toll free, see Best Western). 50 rms (no A/C), cable color TV. AE, CB, DC, MC, V. Free parking, whirlpool, boating, fishing, rest., bar, crib $6. *Note:* Small, modern motel overlooking the ocean; comfortable rms w. balconies and Pacific or river views. Boat rentals for sportfishing. Free morning coffee. Parking for motor homes. **I-M,** but lower rates off-season.

Where to Eat

♀ **Harbor View Grotto,** 155 Citizen's Dock (707/464-3815). A/C. Lunch/dinner daily; closed Jan 1, Thanksgiving, Dec 25. MC, V. *Specialties:* clam chowder, seafood, prime rib, steak, catch of the day. *Note:* Classic fish rest. on the docks; absolutely fresh seafood nicely prepared. From the upstairs rm you have a harbor view. *Steak/Seafood.* **B-I**

ẟ **McKINLEYVILLE:** Look over the world's largest totem pole, 162 ft. (50m) high and weighing 26 tons. It was carved from the trunk of a single tree, more than 500 years old.

※ẟẟ **EUREKA:** This very busy port town has a sheltered harbor at the head of **Humboldt Bay,** but is often foggy even in summer. Many beautiful frame houses (wood is the principal local resource). Picturesque **Old Town District** (bounded by 1st, 3rd, C, and G Sts.) with original buildings of early Eureka, plus antiques and specialty shops. See the splendid 1885 ẟ **Carson Mansion** at 143 M St., a perfect specimen of Victorian architecture, unfortunately not open to visitors.

A dozen miles to the south, the little town of ẟ **Ferndale** is a living museum of the Victorian style proclaimed a state historical landmark.

Where to Stay

※♀♀ **Eureka Inn,** 7th and F Sts., Eureka, CA 99501 (707/442-6441; toll free 800/862-4906). 108 rms (no A/C), cable color TV. AE, CB, DC, MC, V. Free parking, pool, sauna, rest. (Rib Room), coffee shop, rm svce, pub, free crib. *Note:* Elegant, comfortable Tudor-style inn dating from 1922; huge, inviting rms w. balconies and minibars. Exemplary svce; very commendable rest.; free airport limo. An excellent place to stay. **M–É**

        Super 8, 1304 4th St., Eureka, CA 99501 (707/443-3193; toll free 800/800-8000). 50 rms, cable color TV. AE, CB, DC, MC, V. Free parking, pool, sauna, adj. coffee shop, bar, crib $5. *Note:* Well-kept conventional motel; inviting rms w. balconies; free morning coffee. **I–M**

IN NEARBY ARCATA   **Motel 6,** 4755 Valley West Blvd., Arcata, CA 95521 (707/ 822-7061). 81 rms, A/C, cable color TV. AE, DC, MC, V. Free parking, pool; nearby bar and rest.; free crib. *Note:* Unbeatable value 10 min. from dwntwn Eureka. Serviceable comfort; friendly reception. Ideal for the budget traveler. **B**

IN NEARBY FERNDALE   **Gingerbread Mansion,** 400 Berding St., Ferndale, CA 95536 (707/786-4000). 9 rms (no A/C), MC, V. Free parking, bicycles, free breakfast. *Note:* Delightful turn-of-the-century Victorian house in a very pretty English-style grdn in the heart of Ferndale's historic district. Elegant rms w. period furniture, some without baths. Impeccable reception and svce. Resv. essential, well ahead. Totally nonsmoking. **M–E**

Where to Eat

      Lazio's Seafood, 327 2nd St. (707/443-9717). A/C. Lunch/dinner daily; closed hols. AE, CB, DC, MC, V. *Specialties:* crab, fresh seafood, sourdough bread. *Note:* Opened in 1946 in an old fish cannery, this rest. is the proud possession of the Lazio family, fishermen from father to son for more than a century. The seafood is superb, as you'd expect. New decor w. trilevel dining; attentive svce. *Seafood.* **B–I**

      Samoa Cookhouse, Samoa Blvd. (707/442-1659). No A/C. Breakfast/lunch/dinner daily; closed Thanksgiving, Dec 25. AE, CB, DC, MC, V. *Specialties:* barbecued meats, western-style food. *Note:* This locally popular place is more like a museum than a rest., w. its many mementoes of pioneer days. Dates from 1885. Specializes in lumber camp–style cooking; excellent value. *American.* **B**

      AVENUE OF THE GIANTS: An extraordinary slash through the middle of the redwoods of **Humboldt National Forest,** the Avenue of the Giants runs parallel to U.S. 101 for 33 mi. (52km), beginning south of Pepperwood, like a sort of giant green tunnel lined with 300-ft.-tall (92m) redwoods.

Where to Stay

IN GARBERVILLE The   **Benbow Inn,** 445 Lake Benbow Dr., Garberville, CA 95440 (707/923-2124). 55 rms, A/C, cable color TV (in half the rms). AE, MC, V. Free parking, private beach, golf course, putting green, boating, rest., bar, nightclub, classic vintage movie nightly. *Note:* An old English manor house on the shore of a wooded lake, for a perfect picture-postcard vacation. Charming decor and reception. Avoid the third and fourth floors—no elevators. Closed Jan 2 to mid-Apr. **M–E**

IN PIERCY The   **Hartsook Country Inn,** 900 U.S. 101, Piercy, CA 95467 (707/247-3305). 62 rms (no A/C), color TV (in lounge). AE, MC, V. Free parking, private beach, rest., crib $3. *Note:* Spacious, comfortable rms in little bungalows along the Eel River in a 30-acre (12ha) park. Very acceptable rest.; friendly reception and svce. Good overall value. **B–I**

Where to Eat

IN GARBERVILLE The ♈ **Benbow Inn,** in the Benbow Inn (see "Where to Stay," above) (707/923-2125). Breakfast/dinner daily; closed Jan to mid-Apr. AE, MC, V. *Specialties:* fresh salmon in season, filet mignon, fish of the day, sweetbreads Marnie, rack of lamb. *Note:* Praiseworthy hotel rest. in a pretty waterside park w. open-air dining in summer. Faultless food; agreeable background music. Totally nonsmoking. Resv. required for dinner. *Continental/Seafood.* **I–M**

FORT BRAGG: This charming little harbor town, originally founded in 1857 and standing in the center of a superb stretch of rocky coast, was rebuilt after the 1906 earthquake that also destroyed San Francisco. The scenery is lovely. Take a ride on the **California Western Railroad** (affectionately known as "The Skunk"), a Far West–style line which follows the Noyo River through some magnificent redwood (sequoia) forests as far as Willits, a 40-mi. (64km) scenic trip; it leaves from Laurel St. (707/964-6371). The round-trip takes seven hours and operates daily year round.

Where to Stay

Harbor Lite Lodge, 120 N. Harbor Dr., Fort Bragg, CA 95437 (707/964-0221). 70 rms (no A/C), cable color TV. AE, CB, DC, MC, V. Free parking, beach, sauna, nearby coffee shop, crib $6. *Note:* Vacation motel a stone's throw from the beach. Inviting rms w. balconies, the best overlooking Noyo harbor. Direct beach access; good value. **I,** but lower rates off-season.

Where to Eat

♈ **The Restaurant,** 418 N. Main St. (707/964-9800). Lunch Thurs–Fri, dinner Thurs–Tues, brunch Sun; closed hols. and three weeks in Mar. MC, V. *Specialties:* fresh salmon in season, pork schnitzel, trout stuffed w. crabmeat, saltimbocca of chicken. *Note:* This little rest. in the heart of dwntwn serves some rather unusual fare at a very reasonable price. Resv. advised. Totally nonsmoking. *Continental.* **B–I**

NOYO: Picturesque little fishing village at the mouth of the Noyo River. The **Mendocino Coast Botanical Gardens,** on Calif. 1 (707/964-4352), open daily, is a magnificent 17-acre (6.8ha) flower garden overlooking the ocean.

MENDOCINO: Very pretty little harbor town perched on a rock, which has retained a carefully cultivated 19th-century flavor with its Victorian houses, artists' colony, art galleries, antique dealers, and tourist restaurants.

Another 3.7 mi. (6km) south, 🐾 **Van Damme State Park** on Calif. 1 is a very unusual pigmy forest. The poverty of the soil has stunted the trees so that some of them, as much as 200 years old, are only 3 ft. (1m) tall and 2 in. (6cm) through the trunk.

Where to Stay

Mendocino Hotel, 45080 Main St., Mendocino, CA 95460 (707/937-0511; toll free 800/548-0513). 51 rms, A/C, cable color TV (in most rms). AE, MC, V. Free parking, rest., bar, rm svce. *Note:* Picturesque hotel from the 1870s, beautifully preserved. The rms (some without bath) are inviting and tastefully decorated; a certain number have balconies and fireplaces. Three stories (no elevator). Laudable rest.; magnificent grdn. Lovely views of the harbor and ocean; attentive reception and svce. A fine place to stay, but you must reserve well ahead of time. **I–VE,** but lower rates off-season.

IN NEARBY LITTLERIVER The ☼ ☙☙ **Heritage House,** 5200 Calif. 1, Littleriver, CA 95456 (707/937-5885; toll free 800/235-5885). 72 units. (no A/C). MC, V. Free parking, rest., bar. *Note:* Delightfully romantic little cottages on a cliff overlooking the ocean. The main building dates from 1878. Elegant old furniture; spacious, attractive rms w. private balconies or patios, the best overlooking the Pacific. Renowned rest. w. an outstanding wine list. In spite of the high rates, this is a very good place to stay; you have to reserve well in advance. Was the setting for the movie *Same Time Next Year.* Closed Jan to mid-Feb. **E–VE** (MAP)

Where to Eat

☼☙ **Café Beaujolais,** 961 E. Ukiah St. (707/937-5614). No A/C. Dinner nightly, brunch Sat–Sun; closed Jan–Feb, Thanksgiving, Dec 25. No credit cards. *Specialties:* white-bean and tomato soup, polenta, fresh salmon (in season), waffles, coffee cake. *Note:* Delightful bistro; decor a faithful Victorian re-creation w. an outdoor patio for fine days. Traditional but pleasing food. Resv. advisable. Totally nonsmoking. *Continental/Seafood.* **B–I**

☼☙ **Mendocino Hotel** (see "Where to Stay," above) (707/937-0511). A/C. Breakfast/lunch/dinner daily. AE, MC, V. *Specialties:* fish of the day, steak, tartar, prime rib, homemade cakes. *Note:* The dining rm of that magnificent designated landmark, the 1878 Mendocino Hotel, w. crystalware, beveled mirrors, and Oriental rugs. Charming and picturesque; the setting deserves better in the way of food. Resv. advised. *Steak/Seafood.* **B–I**

IN NEARBY LITTLERIVER The ☼☙☙ **Ledford House,** Calif. 1 (707/937-0282). No A/C. Dinner only, Wed–Sun; closed Thanksgiving, early Dec, Dec 25. No credit cards. Jkt. *Specialties:* shrimp cannelloni, fish of the day, lamb. *Note:* Beautiful, inviting century-old house overlooking the ocean; inspired cuisine and some fine California wines. Attentive svce; resv. a must. *Continental/Seafood.* **I–M**

IN NEARBY ALBION The ☼☙☙ **Albion River Inn,** 3790 Calif. 1 (707/937-1919). No A/C. Dinner only, nightly. MC, V. Jkt. *Specialties:* pasta primavera, linguine w. clams, bouillabaisse, fish of the day. *Note:* Delightful little inn perched on a cliff overlooking Albion Cove. Simple but careful cuisine; many works by local artists adorn the walls. Romantic atmosphere; resv. advised. A fine place. *Continental/Seafood.* **I–M**

🏛 **POINT ARENA:** Beautiful ocean view from Point Arena, with its famous lighthouse; **Manchester Beach** is nearby.

Where to Stay

IN NEARBY GUALALA The ☼ ☙☙ **St. Orres,** Calif. 1, Gualala, CA 95445 (707/884-3303). 8 rms and 11 cottages (no A/C). MC, V. Free parking, whirlpool, sauna, rest., free breakfast. *Note:* Charming tiny inn, w. architecture reminiscent of a Russian *dacha* and its onion-domed towers, facing the ocean; inviting rms w. balconies (some without bath), or little individual redwood cottages. Unusual interiors w. lovely old paneling. Top-notch rest.; direct beach access. One of the best places to stay on the coast. **I** (rooms), **M–E** (cottages).

☼☙☙ **Gualala Hotel,** on Calif. 1, Gualala, CA 95445 (707/884-3441). 19 rms, A/C, color TV in lounge. AE, MC, V. Free parking, rest. (Gualala), bar. *Note:* Picturesque little turn-of-the-century hotel across from the beach. Small but tastefully decorated rms, of which two-thirds have no private bath. Antique furniture, library, interesting rest. Very good value; you should reserve well ahead. **B–I**

Where to Eat

IN NEARBY GUALALA The ☼☙☙ **St. Orres,** in the St. Orres Hotel (see "Where to Stay," above) (707/884-3335). No A/C. Dinner only, nightly; closed Wed Jan

–May. No credit cards. Jkt. *Specialties:* rack of lamb dijonnaise, roast quail, New York steak, catch of the day. *Note:* Pretty stained-glass window and old paneling; very successful French-inspired cuisine. Charming, romantic atmosphere; resv. a must. Totally nonsmoking. *Continental.* **M** (prix fixe).

FORT ROSS: The main Russian outpost in America, this trading post was founded in 1812 by the Russian-American Co. as a base for seal hunting. It was sold in 1841 to the Swiss John Sutter, founder of Sacramento and an important figure in the early development of California. There remain only the fine Russian Orthodox chapel, dating from about 1820, and a few buildings from the fort. It's on Calif. 1 (707/865-2391), open daily.

BODEGA BAY: Attractive little harbor at the head of a deep bay, the setting for Alfred Hitchcock's movie *The Birds.*

Where to Stay

Best Western Bodega Bay Lodge, Calif. 1, Bodega Bay, CA 94923 (707/875-3525; toll free, see Best Western). 78 rms (no A/C), color TV, in-rm movies. AE, CB, DC, MC, V. Free parking, pool, health club, sauna, rest. *Note:* Functional motel overlooking the bay and Doran Park beach. Spacious rms w. balconies and refrigerators; some w. fireplaces. Adj. golf course; free morning coffee. Rates on the high side for an ordinary motel. **E–VE**

POINT REYES NATIONAL SEASHORE (35 mi./56km NW of San Francisco): 74,000-acre (29,960ha) wildlife reserve on the Pacific; see Chapter 50 on San Francisco.

Where to Stay

Youth Hostel, Limantour Rd., Point Reyes Station, CA 94956 (415/663-8811). 44 beds. Open nightly for groups and individuals. Spectacularly situated.

PART SEVEN

THE WEST

CHAPTER 47

LAS VEGAS ⚜

□ □ □

"**T**he Gambling Capital of the World" bears no relation to any ordinary city. It's a huge, enthralling slot machine that functions around the clock. This brilliant, showy outburst of neon and glass plumb in the middle of the Mojave Desert is well worth going out of your way to see. Arriving by air at night is a whole show in itself.

Las Vegas (a name which in Spanish means "the green meadows") was founded in the mid-19th-century by Mormons on the colonial trail from Santa Fe to California. Thereafter it went into a long decline until the construction of the Union Pacific's first line of track in 1905. The adoption of new gambling laws by the State of Nevada in 1931 made the fortune of Las Vegas, which writer Tom Wolfe has called "the most American of American cities." The population has grown from barely 8,000 in 1940 to 740,000 today. This figure does not include the 20 million tourists who come, year after year, to try their luck at the casino tables, sports and race betting, or the famous slot machines. Las Vegas has some 33,000 slot machines and 1,300 blackjack tables. In this city everything revolves around gambling, an industry with annual revenues of almost $4 billion—there are slot machines even in restrooms. Nevada's largest city cannot show a single monument or museum worthy of its standing; its only gesture in the direction of culture is the big floor show, presenting the brightest stars in the entertainment firmament, from Jerry Lewis or Frank Sinatra to Liza Minnelli, or Donna Summer to Julio Iglesias.

The glittering palaces along the "Strip," Las Vegas's main drag, offer their rooms at bargain-basement prices. Food at the city's 725 restaurants, cafeterias, and snack bars costs half what it would anywhere else in the country. But don't mistake this for philanthropy or hospitality—it reflects a (justified) expectation that visitors or conventioneers, bitten by the gambling fever, will rush to unload precious dollars on the green baize tables or in the slots of the "one-armed bandits" before plane or bus comes to take them away.

If gambling, show business, and conventions are Las Vegas's principal industries, the dozens of "wedding chapels," open until midnight on weekdays and around the clock on weekends, represent the brighter side of the local economy. Las Vegas has more churches, chapels, and other places of worship per thousand inhabitants than any other city in the country. Every year, under the accommodating laws of Nevada, more than 60,000 "marriages on the wing" are performed in Las Vegas by an army of ministers familiarly known as "Marryin' Sams"—between games of poker, blackjack, or baccarat.

Thanks to its low car-rental rates Las Vegas is also a good base for excursions nearby (**Lake Mead, Valley of Fire, Hoover Dam, Red Rock Canyon, Mount Charleston**) or farther afield (the **Grand Canyon** of the Colorado, **Death Valley,** the **Utah national parks**).

BASIC FACTS: State of Nevada, Area code: 702. Time zone: Pacific. ZIP Code: 89114. Founded: 1855. Approximate population: city, 260,000; metropolitan area, 740,000.

CLIMATE: Dry heat and a cloudless sky are the rule here. Summer is a scorcher (as high as 104°F/40°C or even higher in July–Aug). Spring and fall are more temperate (68° –77°F/20° –25°C on the average), but as always, in the desert the nights can be chilly. In winter, although the sun still shines (as it's guaranteed to do for 320 days a year), temperatures vary around a mean of 50°F (10°C).

DISTANCES: Denver, 780 mi. (1,248km); Furnace Creek (Death Valley), 142 mi. (227km); Los Angeles, 282 mi. (451km); Phoenix, 285 mi. (456km); Salt Lake City, 439 mi. (702km); San Francisco, 568 mi. (908km).

ARRIVAL & TRANSIT INFORMATION

AIRPORT: McCarran International Airport (LAS), 10 mi. (6km) south, handles more charter traffic than any other airport in the world. Spectacular futuristic decor.

AIRLINES: Air Nevada (toll free 800/634-6377), America West (toll free 800/235-9292), American (toll free 800/433-7300), Continental (toll free 800/525-0280), Delta (toll free 800/221-1212), Scenic Air Lines (toll free 800/634-6801), TWA (toll free 800/221-2000), and United (toll free 800/241-6522).

CITY LINK: Your cab fare to the Strip will run about $10 (to dwntwn, $15); time, about 15–20 min. Bus: **Gray Line Airport Express** (384-1234) leaves every hour for the Strip and for dwntwn. Serves principal hotels; fare, $4.50; time, about 25–35 min.

Cabs are expensive; **public transporation** (bus, **Citizens Area Transit/ CAT**) is low priced and relatively efficient (but should be avoided at night); for information, call 228-7433. Bus no. 301 runs the whole length of the Strip around the clock (basic fare: $1). The **Trolley Shuttle** runs dwntwn along Fremont St. Walking can be exhausting, particularly in summer; the city's avenues are unending, and without the least patch of shade or the smallest tree; remember that summer temperatures are in the range of 95° –104°F (35° –40°C). Air-conditioned cars can be rented anywhere at attractive prices.

CAR RENTAL (at McCarran International Airport unless otherwise noted): Abbey, 3745 Las Vegas Blvd. (736-4988), a local company with attractive rates; Avis (toll free 800/331-1212); Budget (toll free 800/527-0700); Dollar (toll free 800/800-4000); Hertz (toll free 800/654-3131); National (toll free 800/227-7368); and Thrifty, 5190 S. Paradise Rd. (toll free 800/367-2277). (All except Abbey and Avis offer free pickup/delivery at place of residence.) For dwntwn locations, consult the local telephone directory.

LIMOUSINE SERVICES: Bell Trans (toll free 800/274-7433) and Lucky 7 Luxury Limousine (739-8497).

TAXIS: Cab may be hailed on the street or taken from the lines outside the big hotels, but it's more convenient to use the phone. Recommended companies: **Checker** (873-2227), **Whittlesea Blue Cab** (384-6111), or **Yellow Cab** (873-2227).

TRAIN: Amtrak Station, Union Plaza, 1 Main St. (toll free 800/872-7245).

INTERCITY BUSES: Greyhound, 200 S. Main St. (toll free 800/231-2222).

INFORMATION & TOURS

TOURIST INFORMATION: The **Las Vegas Chamber of Commerce,** 711 E. Desert Inn Rd., NV 89104 (702/735-1616).
  Las Vegas Convention and Visitors Authority, Convention Center, 3150 Paradise Rd., NV 89109 (702/892-0711; toll free 800/332-5333).

GUIDED TOURS: ASI/Ray & Ross Tours (646-4661), and **Gray Line Tours,** 1550 Industrial Rd. (384-1234): Guided (bus) tours of the city, serving the principal hotels.
   Lake Mead Cruises (boat), Nev. 41, Boulder Harbor (293-6180): 1½-hr. excursions on Lake Mead as far as Hoover Dam; daily year round.

SIGHTS, ATTRACTIONS & ACTIVITIES

ADVENTURES: Black Canyon Raft Tours (boat), P.O. Box 96, Boulder City, NV 89005 (293-3776): Rafting down the Colorado River from Boulder City; Feb–Nov.
   National Nuclear Test Site Tours (bus), in Mercury: 10½-hr., 260-mi. (420km) bus tour offered three to four times every week to the Nevada Test Site, the proving ground at which the nation's nuclear weapons are tested. Tours arranged by the Nevada Operations Office of the U.S. Department of Energy, 2753 S. Highland Dr., Las Vegas, NV 89193 (702/295-1000). American citizens must provide their name, address, birth date, and Social Security number. Foreign nationals must give 45 days' notice. ID with photo (such as a driver's license) must be presented at the time of the tour. Visitors must be at least 14 years old. Pregnant women are discouraged from visiting, "because of long bus rides and rough terrain." Highly unusual tour.
   Scenic Airlines (air), 241 E. Reno Ave. (toll free 800/634-6801): Air trips over the Grand Canyon. **Air Nevada** (air), 6005 S. Las Vegas Blvd. (736-8900): One-day excursion, including lunch, $180; daily year round.

ARCHITECTURAL HIGHLIGHTS: ✷⚖ **Circus Circus,** 2880 Las Vegas Blvd. (634-3450): Looking like the Big Top of some gigantic circus, this is the most originally designed hotel-casino in Vegas. While the gamblers are trying their luck at the casino tables, trapeze artists, tightrope walkers, and acrobats are strutting their stuff overhead. Children are permitted in the gallery but not on the casino floor.
   ⚖ **Convention Center,** 3150 Paradise Rd. (892-0711): One million square feet (100,000m²) of covered exhibition space make this modern steel-and-concrete structure the country's largest one-level convention hall. It has room for more than 7,000 participants at meetings or banquets. Las Vegas has developed the convention business (the city averages one a day) into a source of revenue second only to gambling.

CHURCHES/SYNAGOGUES: The **Wedding Chapels:** With some 40 of these institutions at last count, Las Vegas can style itself the country's wedding capital as well as its gaming capital. There's only one requirement under Nevada law: that both prospective spouses be over 18 (or over 16 with parental consent). No blood test is asked for; no time-consuming banns need be read. All you need is a $35 license—obtainable at Clark County Court House, 3rd and Carson Sts. (455-3156), open daily—and the wedding chapel will do the rest! They're open 8am–midnight Mon–Fri, and around the clock on weekends. The cost of solemnizing a marriage, including the minister's fee and the hired witnesses, generally runs $60–$100. An astounding 60,000 people are married each year in churches or chapels here.

HISTORIC BUILDINGS: ⚖ **Old Mormon Fort,** Las Vegas Blvd. N. at Washington Ave. (486-3511): Built in 1855 by a group of 30 Mormon pioneers from Utah, this adobe construction, originally designed to protect the settlers from attack by local Native American tribes, is the oldest building in the entire state. Fine example of architectural restoration. Open Sat–Mon. For lovers of the Old West.

MUSEUM OF ART: ♨ **Art Museum, 3333** W. Washington Ave. (647-4300): Works by local and other American artists; interesting temporary exhibitions. Open daily.

MUSEUMS OF SCIENCE & HISTORY: ♨ **Clark County Heritage Museum,** 1830 S. Boulder Hwy., Henderson (455-7955): Interesting history museum. Depicts southern Nevada historical heritage from dinosaur fossils to the first European settlements. Re-created ghost town and turn-of-the-century railroad. Open daily.

♨ **Imperial Palace Auto Collection,** 3535 Las Vegas Blvd. (731-3311): This collection of more than 300 valuable antique cars is to be found on the fifth floor of the Imperial Palace Hotel parking garage. It includes the King of Siam's 1928 Delage, Howard Hughes's 1954 Chrysler, an armored Mercedes that once belonged to Hitler, and other cars formerly the property of Al Capone, Eleanor Roosevelt, etc. A must for antique-car enthusiasts. Open daily.

♨ **Las Vegas Museum of Natural History,** 3700 Las Vegas Blvd. S. (384-3466): This spectacular new natural-history museum displays one of the country's largest collections of prehistoric animals; life-size animated models of dinosaurs, triceratops, etc. Open daily.

☼♨ **Liberace Museum,** 1775 E. Tropicana Ave. (798-5595): An entire museum devoted to the self-glorification of the late pianist and showman Liberace: from his collection of antique cars and pianos to his glittering million-dollar wardrobe. The triumph of unrestrained Hollywood kitsch. Open daily.

NIGHTTIME ENTERTAINMENT: ☼♨♨ **Casino Center,** around Fremont St. and Casino Center Blvd.: The heart of the city's gaming kingdom; the country's (and perhaps the world's) largest concentration of casinos and gambling houses. Particularly spectacular after dark, when Fremont St., better known to locals as "Glitter Gulch," is illuminated to daytime levels by an extravagance of lights and multicolored neon signs.

☼♨♨ **"The Strip,"** Las Vegas Blvd. between Tropicana Rd. and Sahara Ave.: The name is a pun, with references both to striptease and to neon strip-lighting; it describes the city's 3-mi. (5km) multicolored light show offered by its principal hotels, casinos, and nightclubs. The sight of "the Broadway of Las Vegas" after dark is fascinating indeed.

PANORAMAS: ♨ **Skye Room,** 128 E. Fremont St. (382-1600): A bar-restaurant-dance hall on the 23rd floor of the Binion's Horseshoe Hotel, in the heart of downtown. Offers the most spectacular after-dark view of the city. Glass-walled outside elevator. Open daily.

PERFORMING ARTS: For current listings of shows and cultural events, consult the entertainment pages of the daily papers, *Las Vegas Review-Journal* (morning and evening) and *Las Vegas Sun* (morning), as well as the monthly *Nevada* magazine.

Artemus W. Ham Concert Hall, U. of Nevada campus, 4505 Maryland Pkwy. (895-3801): Opera, ballet, jazz, and concerts; home of the Nevada Dance Theater.

Charleston Heights Art Center, 800 Brush St. (229-6383): Concerts and plays; home of the New West Stage Company.

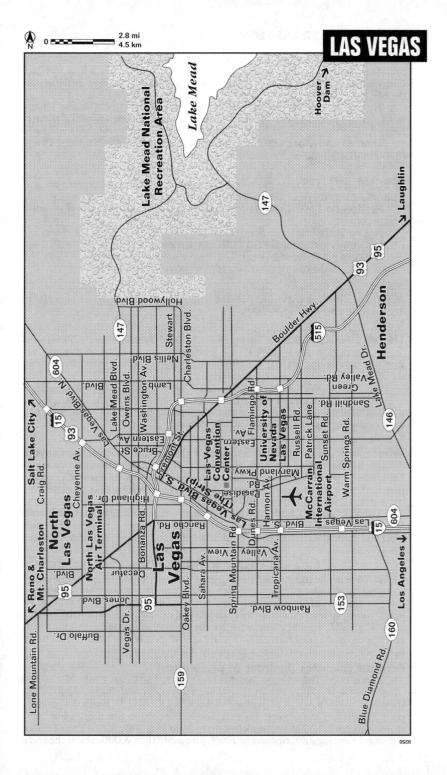

LAS VEGAS

Judy Bayley Theater, U. of Nevada campus, 4505 Maryland Pkwy. (895-3801): In the little plaza adjoining the theater, be sure to take a look at Claes Oldenburg's colossal (39-ft./13m) sculpture *Flashlight.* Modern and classical theater; big-star shows.

Theater Under the Skies, Spring Mountain Ranch (see "Nearby Excursions," below) (875-4141): Open-air shows; modern and experimental theater. June–Aug.

Thomas and Mack Center, U. of Nevada campus, 4505 Maryland Pkwy. (895-3900): Pop and rock concerts.

SPECIAL EVENTS: For exact dates, consult the **Las Vegas Convention and Visitors Authority** (see "Tourist Information," above).

Helldorado Festival (end of May or early June): Rodeos, street parades, beauty contest.

Jaycee State Fair (early Sept): Carnival, big-star shows, livestock shows.

Las Vegas Invitational PGA Golf Tournament (Oct).

National Finals Rodeo (Dec): The "Superbowl" of professional rodeos, the richest rodeo in the country. Attracts top cowboys in every event.

SPORTS: Baseball (Apr–Oct): Stars (Triple-A farm club of the San Diego Padres), Cashman Field (386-7200).

THEME PARKS: ⚓ **Bonnie Springs Ranch/Old Nevada,** 20 mi. (32km) west on W. Charleston Blvd. (875-4191): Pioneer village of 1843, with nicely restored saloons and stores. Far Western railroad; shows; mock gun battles between sheriff and outlaws. Western buffs will enjoy it. Open daily.

⚓ **Wet 'n Wild,** 2600 Las Vegas Blvd. S. (737-7873): Huge aquatic amusement park; the artificial surf has 4-ft. (1.2m) waves. The giant slide is 75 ft. (23m) high; also waterfalls, shooting the rapids, etc. Locally popular. Open daily late Mar to Sept.

WINTER SPORTS RESORTS: ⚓ **Mount Charleston Park** and **Lee Canyon,** 34 mi. (54km) NW on U.S. 95 and Nev. 157: Beautiful pine forest rising to 11,918 ft. (3,623m) on Mount Charleston, and winter-sports resort at Lee Canyon, both very popular at all times of year. For a report on snow conditions during the skiing season, call 646-0008. Three ski lifts.

The ☼ ♨ **Mount Charleston Hotel,** 2 Kyle Canyon Rd., Mount Charleston, NV 89124 (872-5500), is a likable chalet with a rest. serving very acceptable meat and game dishes. Open daily; 63 rms. **I–M**

ACCOMMODATIONS

A Note on Accommodations: Over and above the gamblers and the entertainment fans (some of the top shows in the country are given in Las Vegas), there's a year-round crush of groups and conventions filling the 85,000 available hotel rooms, so reservations are essential. If you call 702/736-1666, or toll free 800/873-5577, you'll be told what rooms are available at any given moment, and you can make your reservation for free on the spot. Note that at certain times of the year some hotels require a minimum stay of three nights.

Personal Favorites (in order of preference)

☼♨♨♨♨ **The Mirage** (nr. dwntwn), 3400 Las Vegas Blvd., NV 89109 (702/791-7111; toll free 800/627-6667; 702/792-7777 for show resv.). 3,049 rms, A/C, color TV. AE, CB, DC, MC, V. Free valet parking, pool, health club, sauna, six rests (including Kokomo's), coffee shop, 24-hr. bars, rm svce, nightclub, shows, casino, boutiques, crib $15. *Note:* Vegas's most elaborate hotel extravaganza, opened in 1989. The more than 3,000 rms in the three

30-floor towers boast their own amusement park, complete with artificial volcano erupting every 15 min., tropical jungle under glass, giant aquarium w. sharks and a clutch of white tigers roaming around. The whole megillah cost $630 million. Spacious, extremely comfortable rms, acceptable rests., lovely indoor grdns bright w. orchids and bougainvilleas among the 80-ft. (25m) palm trees. The casino has a private rm for high rollers where the lowest stake is $1,000. Part of the Mirage Resort hotel chain. **M–E**

Sheraton Desert Inn (nr. dwntwn), 3145 Las Vegas Blvd. S., NV 89109 (702/733-4444; toll free 800/634-6906). 819 rms, A/C, color TV, in-rm movies. AE, CB, DC, MC, V. Free valet parking, two pools, golf course, 10 tennis courts, health club, sauna, putting green, four rests. (including Portofino), 24-hr. bars, 24-hr. rm svce, shows, hrdrsr, boutiques, concierge, free crib. *Note:* The quietest of the local palaces; even the decor has a degree of self-control. Very comfortable rms w. private balconies or patios and refrigerators. Remarkable rm svce. Good rests. This was where the late billionaire Howard Hughes liked to come for a rest. The best location on the Strip, set in 160 acres (62ha) of lawns and grdns. Highly regarded golf course. **M–E**

Alexis Park (nr. dwntwn), 375 E. Harmon Ave., NV 89109 (702/796-3300; toll free 800/582-2228). 500 suites, A/C, color TV, in-rm movies. AE, CB, DC, MC, V. Free parking, three pools, two tennis courts, health club, sauna, putting green, rest. (Pegasus), bar, 24-hr. rm svce, hrdrsr, concierge, crib $10. *Note:* One of the newest, finest flowers in the local bouquet of deluxe hotels and one of the few Las Vegas hotels without a casino. Has only spacious suites, splendidly fitted out, with minibars and refrigerators. Exemplary reception and svce. 10 acres (4ha) of lovely grdns w. waterfalls and fountains, only a few steps away from the Strip. Admirable luxury hotel rest. Caters to VIPs. Quiet and relaxed atmosphere. **M–VE**

MGM Grand Hotel (nr. dwntwn), 3799 Las Vegas Blvd. S., NV 89109 (702/891-1111; toll free 800/929-1111). 5,005 rms and suites, A/C, color TV, in-rm movies. AE, CB, DC, MC, V. Free valet parking, pool, four tennis courts, health club, sauna, seven rests. (including Coyote Cafe), 24-hr. coffee shop, 24-hr. bars, rm svce, shows, arena, theme park, casino, hrdrsr, boutiques, concierge, free crib. *Note:* With over 5,000 rms in four towers, this is the world's largest hotel, topping the Mirage (see above) in expenditure at $1 billion. Inside this dizzying monolith are a 15,200-seat arena for sporting events and concerts, an amusement park (including roller-coaster!) nearing the size of Disneyland, the world's largest casino, and the Emerald City theme park, taken from the fictitious city in *The Wizard of Oz*. Television screens pervade the surroundings, especially in the lobby, where 80 screens are mounted behind the front desk. In the midst of all this frenzied kitsch, believe it or not, are two very good rests. (Wolfgang Puck's and the Coyote Café). Annoyingly friendly svce. Child care available. **I–M** (rms), **I–VE** (suites).

Hacienda (nr. dwntwn), 3950 Las Vegas Blvd. S., NV 89119 (702/739-8911; toll free 800/634-6713). 1,142 rms, A/C, color TV, in-rm movies. AE, CB, DC, MC, V. Free valet parking, pool, tennis court, two rests. (including Charcoal Room), 24-hr. coffee shop, 24-hr. bar, rm svce, nightclub, casino, boutiques, free crib. *Note:* Modern, comfortable hotel-casino right on the Strip; spacious, welcoming rms, some w. refrigerators. Nicely landscaped grounds. Friendly svce. Parking for motor homes. Very good value. **B–I**

Circus Circus Hotel (nr. dwntwn), 2880 Las Vegas Blvd. S., NV 89109 (702/734-0410; toll free 800/634-3450). 2,793 rms, A/C, color TV. AE, CB, DC, MC, V. Free valet parking, three pools, two rests., two 24-hr. coffee shops, 24-hr. bars, casino, circus, hrdrsr, boutiques, crib $6. *Note:* Right on the Strip, w. a newly constructed 29-story tower adj. to the original building. The interior is the most enterprising in all of Las Vegas, w. trapeze artists and tightrope walkers cavorting above the heads of the casino gamblers beneath a pink-and-white make-believe circus marquee. The favorite hotel of parents w. children. Huge, inviting rms; acceptable buffet meals at modest prices. Very good value. Worthwhile discounts on wknds. Enormous parking lot for RVs. **B–I**

    🏨 **Motel 6** (nr. dwntwn), 195 E. Tropicana Ave., NV 89109 (702/798-0728). 880 rms, A/C, cable color TV, in-rm movies. AE, DC, MC, V. Free parking, pool, nearby rest., free crib. *Note:* Vegas's best bargain, offering functional but inviting rms at unbeatable prices. A few steps away from the Strip and the airport. **B**

Other Accommodations (from top bracket to budget)

    ☀️🏨🏨🏨🏨 **Caesars Palace** (nr. dwntwn), 3570 Las Vegas Blvd. S., NV 89109 (702/731-7110; toll free 800/634-6001 for rm resv., 800/634-6661 for show resv.). 1,640 rms, A/C, color TV, in-rm movies. AE, CB, DC, MC, V. Free valet parking, two pools, four tennis courts, squash, health club, sauna, seven rests. (including the Bacchanal Room), coffee shop, 24-hr. bars, rm svce, disco, shows, casino, hrdrsr, boutiques, cinema, concierge, free crib. *Note:* Long the Las Vegas favorite hotel in the heart of the Strip: 22 floors of marble, stucco, crystal, and red velvet. The style—a Hollywood version of ancient Rome—is rather eccentric; the waitresses are dressed straight out of the movie *Ben Hur.* Huge, luxurious, comfortable rms; sumptuous suites. Svce diligent to the point of excess. Several highly acceptable rests. The Las Vegas style at its highest pitch; this place alone is worth the trip. Resv. long in advance. Recently has undergone a complete remodeling and renovation. **E–VE**

    🏨🏨🏨 **Bally's–Las Vegas** (nr. dwntwn), 3645 Las Vegas Blvd. S., NV 89109 (702/739-4111; toll free 800/634-3434). 2,830 rms, A/C, color TV, in-rm movies. AE, CB, DC, MC, V. Free valet parking, pool, 10 tennis courts, health club, sauna, four rests. (including Caruso), three coffee shops, 24-hr. bars, rm svce, nightlife, shows, casino, cinema, hrdrsr, boutiques, free crib. *Note:* Gigantic hotel-casino comprising two modern 26-story towers. Completely renovated since a fire that caused 84 deaths in 1980, and now the masterpiece of Las Vegas kitsch. Spacious, comfortable rms w. balconies, good sports facilities, good svce, but so-so rests. Intrusive group and convention clientele. Puts on some of the best shows in Vegas. Right on the Strip. **M–E**

    🏨🏨🏨 **Emerald Springs Holiday Inn** (nr. dwntwn), 325 E. Flamingo Rd., NV 89109 (702/732-9100; toll free 800/732-7889). 150 rms, A/C, color TV, in-rm movies. AE, DC, MC, V. Free parking, pool, rest. (Veranda Café), bar, rm svce, concierge, crib $10. *Note:* One of the newest and smallest luxury hotels of Las Vegas, just one block from the Strip. Spacious rms and suites tastefully decorated, w. refrigerators and other special amenities. Personalized reception and svce. Quiet, intimate atmosphere. Free airport and casino transportation. Business center. A favorite with those-in-the-know. **M**

    🏨🏨🏨 **Luxor** (nr. dwntwn), 3900 Las Vegas Blvd. S., NV 89119 (702/262-4000; toll free 800/288-1000). 2,500 rms and suites, A/C, color TV, in-rm movies. AE, CB, DC, MC, V. Free valet parking, pool, tennis, health club, sauna, masseuse, seven rests., 24-hr. coffee shop, 24-hr. bars, rm svce, concierge, nightclub, shows, casino, hrdrsr, boutiques, cribs $10. *Note:* $375-million structure recalling an Egyptian pyramid. Replete w. interior waterways and a replica of King Tut's tomb. The "inclinator," an elevator that ascends at a 39-degree angle, takes you up the pyramid. Virtual reality games put you in three different futuristic cities. Laser shows. Ultra-polite svce. **I–VE.**

    ☀️🏨🏨🏨🏨 **Golden Nugget** (dwntwn), 129 E. Fremont St., NV 89125 (702/385-7111; toll free 800/634-3454). 1,800 rms, cable color TV. AE, CB, DC, MC, V. Free parking, pool, health club, sauna, three rests., 24-hr. coffee shop, bars, rm svce, entertainment, casino, hrdrsr, free crib. *Note:* An unlikely marriage between a marble-fronted Victorian house abundantly paneled in mahogany, and an ultramodern 22-story tower (Town House Tower) w. sumptuous duplex suites. The opulent interior in the style of the Roaring '20s is sufficient justification for a visit. Huge, ultra-comfortable rms; excellent svce. Recently rejuvenated at a cost of $75 million. Along with the Mirage, this is the most spectacular hotel and enjoyable casino, in Las Vegas. Right in the middle of Casino Center with its bustling nightlife. I–E

Hilton Las Vegas (nr. dwntwn), 3000 Paradise Rd., NV 89109 (702/732-5111; toll free, see Hilton; 800/732-7117 for show resv.). 3,174 rms, A/C, cable color TV. AE, CB, DC, MC, V. Free valet parking, pool, health club, sauna, six tennis courts, 12 rests. (including Le Montrachet), coffee shop, 24-hr. bars, rm svce, disco, shows, hrdrsr, boutiques, free crib. *Note:* With 30 floors of glass and concrete, this is one of the largest hotels in Vegas. It's taken by assault year round by the throngs of package tourists and conventioneers. Spacious rms w. balconies; lively ambience. In spite of the hotel's size the svce is good. Inside, a "children's hotel" offers childcare for parents trying their luck at the tables. Renovated after a fire in 1981. Very near the Strip and the Convention Center. I–E

Treasure Island (nr. dwntwn), 3300 Las Vegas Blvd., NV 89109 (702/894-7111; toll free 800/944-7444). 2,900 rms and suites, A/C, cable color TV. AE, CB, DC, MC, V. Free valet parking, two pools, health club, sauna, six rests., 24-hr coffee shop, 24-hr. bars, casino, shows, hrdrsr, boutiques, free crib. *Note:* A $475-million attempt to put you in the Robert Louis Stevenson novel. Six times a day a British frigate does battle w. a pirate ship in the hotel lagoon in a show that lasts 15 min. and involves 22 actors. Continuing the theme of pirate looting inside, precious jewels and other treasure are patterned on the walls. Surprisingly comfortable rms that let you relax a little from the hotel's overriding theme; welcoming svce dressed as expected. Decent rests. Belongs to the Mirage Resort chain. I–E

Excalibur (nr. dwntwn), 3850 Las Vegas Blvd. S., NV 89119 (702/597-7777; toll free 800/937-7777). 4,032 rms, A/C, color TV, in-rm movies. AE, DC, MC, V. Valet parking lot, three pools, five rests., 24-hr. coffee shop, 24-hr. bars, rm svce, entertainment, casino, hrdrsr, boutiques, crib $7. *Note:* Elephantine hotel-casino-Camelot theme park w. $290-million worth of medieval towers, drawbridges, battlements, jousting tournaments, knights, and jugglers, plus 100,000 sq. ft. (9,300m^2) of slot machines and blackjack tables. Two dinner shows nightly offer performances based on legend of King Arthur. Functionally comfortable rms. Svce—in colorful costumes right out of the Middle Ages—is often overburdened. Good value overall. Belongs to the Circus-Circus hotel empire. I–M

Harrah's Hotel Casino (nr. dwntwn), 3475 Las Vegas Blvd. S., NV 89109 (702/369-5000; toll free 800/634-6765). 1,725 rms, A/C, color TV, in-rm movies. AE, CB, DC, MC, V. Free valet parking, pool, health club, sauna, four rests. (including Claudine's), 24-hr. coffee shop, 24-hr. bars, rm svce, entertainment, casino, hrdrsr, boutiques, free crib. *Note:* Built to resemble a giant Mississippi paddlewheeler and topped by an ultramodern 23-story tower, it is unusual enough to surprise even those well acquainted w. the Las Vegas style of architectural extravagance. Comfort and facilities are flawless, as well as their svce. Group and convention clientele. In the heart of the Strip. Recently renovated and expanded. I–M

Union Plaza Hotel (dwntwn), 1 Main St., NV 89125 (702/386-2110; toll free 800/634-6575). 1,036 rms, A/C, color TV. AE, CB, DC, MC, V. Free valet parking, pool, four tennis courts, two rests. (including Center Stage), 24-hr. bars, rm svce, shows, casino, boutiques, crib $8. *Note:* Modern comfort and facilities housed in a 22- and a 25-story tower in the heart of dwntwn Vegas, adjoining the Greyhound bus terminal and the Amtrak train station. Inviting rms w. balconies and refrigerators. The rest. has a spectacular view of dwntwn casinos. Free parking for RVs. I

Center Strip Inn (nr. dwntwn), 3688 Las Vegas Blvd. S., NV 89109 (702/739-6066; toll free 800/777-7737). 148 rms, A/C, color TV, in-rm movies, VCR. AE, DC, MC, V. Free parking, pool, 24-hr. coffeeshop, free breakfast, free crib. *Note:* Conventional but well-run motel smack in the middle of the Strip, as the name implies. Commodious, well-laid-out rms w. refrigerators. Cheerful reception and svce. Good value. **B–I**

    📍 **Vegas World** (nr. dwntwn), 2000 Las Vegas Blvd. S., NV
     🛏 89104 (702/382-2000; toll free 800/634-6277). 891 rms, A/C, cable color TV. AE, CB, DC, MC, V. Free valet parking, pool, rest., coffee shop, two 24-hr. bars, casino, entertainment. *Note:* Huge 23-floor motel right on the Strip, decorated in the style of *2001: A Space Odyssey.* Functional and comfortable; recently renovated and expanded; good value. **B–I**

YMCA/Youth Hostel
    Las Vegas Hostel (nr. dwntwn), 1208 Las Vegas Blvd. S., NV 89104 (702/385-9955). 50 beds. Youth hostel.

RESTAURANTS

Personal Favorites (in order of preference)
    🍷🍷🍷 **Pegasus,** in the Alexis Park (see "Accommodations," above)
    🍽🍽🍽 (796-3300). A/C. Dinner only, nightly. AE, CB, DC, MC, V.
Specialties: quail egg and mandarin orange salad w. sweet mustard dressing, Maine lobster sautéed w. black truffles in madeira-bordelaise sauce, daily game special, sautéed tenderloin of rabbit w. chambrot-cream sauce. Handsome wine list. *Note:* Sophisticated French-style cuisine flawlessly prepared and served. Opened in 1984, Pegasus is one of the few rests. in Las Vegas that can be described as both luxurious and discreet. Perfection in every detail—which must, of course, be paid for. Open-air dining on fine days. Resv. required. *French/Continental.* **E–VE**

    🍷🍷🍷 **Coyote Cafe,** in the MGM Grand Hotel (see "Accommoda-
    🍽🍽🍽 tions," above) (891-1111). A/C. Breakfast/lunch/dinner daily (café), dinner nightly (dining room). AE, MC, V. *Specialties:* buttermilk corn cakes w. chipotle shrimp and salsa fresca, cowboy rib chop w. black beans and onion rings, pumpkin-seed-crusted salmon, caramel sundae w. toasted piñon. *Note:* Sister rest. of the Coyote Café in Santa Fe and the Red Sage in Washington, D.C. Papier-mâché sculptures and rustic tapestries continue the tradition of the chain's dramatic, humorous decor. Unfortunately, executive chef/owner Mark Miller makes an appearance only about six times a year. Still, some of the most original food to be found in Las Vegas. Resv. advised for dinner. *American.* **B–I** (café), **M–E** (dining room)

    🍷🍷🍷 **Bacchanal Room** (nr. dwntwn), in Caesars Palace (see "Ac-
    🍽🍽🍽 commodations," above) (734-7110). A/C. Dinner only, Tues –Sat. AE, CB, DC, MC, V. Jkt. *Specialties:* The prix-fixe menus (seven courses from hors d'oeuvres to dessert, accompanied by three different wines) change regularly. French-inspired continental food. *Note:* Local taste apparently requires that every waitress wear a *peplos* while the waiters are tricked out as Roman centurions—but the food generally meets high standards. Prices match the opulent "Pompeian" scheme of decoration. Resv. required. Three seatings nightly, beginning at 6pm. *Continental.* **VE** (prix fixe).

    🍷🍷 **Port Tack** (nr. dwntwn), 3190 W. Sahara Ave. (873-3345).
    🍽🍽 A/C. Lunch/dinner daily (until 5am); closed hols. AE, CB, DC, MC, V. *Specialties:* lamb chops, catch of the day, salmon steak, broiled prime cuts, roast beef, Maine lobster, Alaska king crab. *Note:* Along w. its sister establishment (**Starboard Tack,** 2601 Atlantic Ave.; 457-8794), this is one of the rests. most favored by the locals. The catch of the day is excellent. Charming rustic-seafaring decor; likable relaxed atmosphere and some of the best seafood in town. *Steak-Seafood.* **I–M**

    🍷🍷 **Chin's** (nr. dwntwn), 3200 Las Vegas Blvd. S. (733-8899).
    🍽🍽 A/C. Lunch/dinner daily; closed hols. AE, MC, V. *Specialties:* shark's-fin soup, spring rolls, shrimp puffs, chicken w. strawberries, beef à la Chin's, crystal shrimp, crispy pudding. *Note:* In the unanimous view of the purists this is the best Far Eastern rest. on the Strip. Authentic (if slightly American-

ized) Chinese food; for instance, the chicken w. strawberries is a local variant on the classic Chinese lemon chicken. The result is almost always delicious, and the decor is elegant; accordingly the place has been very successful, and resv. are strongly advised. Valet parking. *Chinese.* **I–M**

🍷🍷 **Wolfgang Puck Café,** in the MGM Grand Hotel (see "Accommodations," above) (891-1111). A/C. Lunch/dinner daily. MC, V. *Specialties:* Chinois chicken salad, calamari w. cilantro sauce, gourmet pizzas, homemade pasta, smoked-salmon pizza, apple tarte tatin. *Note:* Colorful interior design festooned w. pizza-shaped tiles. Light, imaginative California cuisine from the successful restaurateur, Wolfgang Puck (see Spago, below). A good value. Friendly, dedicated svce. Unfortunately, resv. not taken. *American.* **I**

🍷🍷 **Vineyard** (nr. dwntwn), 3630 Maryland Pkwy. (731-1606). A/C. Lunch/dinner daily; closed hols. AE, MC, V. Jkt. *Specialties:* fresh homemade pasta (fettuccine Alfredo, lasagna, cannelloni), pizza, veal parmigiana, scampi sauté. *Note:* Straightforward Italian-inspired food in a Neapolitan-operetta setting (including an accordionist). Friendly, smiling svce. Attracts crowds from the community. No resv. *Italian.* **I**

🍷 **Garcia's** (nr. dwntwn), 1030 E. Flamingo Rd. (731-0628). A/C. Lunch/dinner daily; closed Thanksgiving, Dec 25. AE, CB, DC, MC, V. *Specialties:* chimichangas, fajitas, tacos, enchiladas, fried ice cream. *Note:* Authentic Mexican food and excellent margaritas in a brightly colored hacienda setting. On the hottest days, the profusion of plants creates the pleasant illusion that you're in a green, growing grdn. Attentive svce. Locally popular. *Mexican.* **B**

Other Restaurants (from top bracket to budget)

🍷🍷🍷 **Ah-So Japanese Steak Garden** (nr. dwntwn), in Caesars Palace (see "Accommodations," above) (731-7110). A/C. Dinner only, Tues–Sat. AE, CB, DC, MC, V. Jkt. *Specialties:* sushi, sashimi, teppanyaki (broiled steak, lobster, and vegetables). *Note:* The chefs wield their knives w. devilish dexterity under the eyes of the diners, in a charming plastic reproduction of a Japanese tea house, complete w. grdns, streams, and miniature bridges. Friendly, efficient svce. Resv. advised. *Japanese.* **E** (prix fixe).

🍷🍷🍷 **Spago,** (nr. dwntwn) in Caesars Palace (see "Accommodations," above) (369-6300). A/C. Lunch/dinner daily. AE, CB, DC, MC, V. *Specialties:* home-smoked salmon and sturgeon, Sonoma lamb chops, roasted Chinese duck, spicy chicken pizza, crème brûlée. *Note:* Another creation of Wolfgang Puck (see above), maintaining a respectable height in cuisine and decor. Scrumptious gourmet pizzas to be found on the dining rm and café menus. Professional svce. Resv. requested. *American.* **B** (café) **M–E** (dining room)

🍷🍷 **Golden Steer Steak House** (nr. dwntwn), 308 W. Sahara Ave. (384-4470). A/C. Dinner only, nightly (till midnight); closed Thanksgiving, Dec 25. AE, CB, DC, MC, V. *Specialties:* giant (1½-lb./680g) steaks, prime rib, steak au poivre, rack of lamb, fresh pasta (first-rate ravioli and linguine with clams), game, roast suckling pig. Good wine list. *Note:* Remarkable steakhouse, but often crowded and noisy; a local favorite for 25 years. Western-1900s decor; exemplary svce; resv. advised. Valet parking. *Steak/American.* **M**

🍷🍷 **Tillerman** (nr. dwntwn), 2245 E. Flamingo Rd. (731-4036). A/C. Dinner only, nightly; closed hols. AE, CB, DC, MC, V. Jkt. *Specialties:* broiled steak, scallops in cream sauce, sole meunière, catch of the day. *Note:* In this light-filled space w. its green plants, its giant ficus trees, and its enormous skylights, you have the agreeable feeling that you're dining under the stars. First-quality meat and fish impeccably prepared. Excellent svce; one of Vegas's most highly recommended rests. *Steak/Seafood.* **M**

🍷🍷 **Alpine Village Inn** (nr. dwntwn), 3003 Paradise Rd. (734-6888). A/C. Dinner only, nightly; closed Thanksgiving, Dec 25. AE, CB, DC, MC, V. *Specialties:* sauerbraten, Wiener schnitzel, frikadellen, kohlrouladen, apfelstrudel. German beers. *Note:* Decorated as a Swiss-Bavarian chalet, somewhat incongruous where the mercury goes up to 95° F (35°C) in the shade! Plentiful, decent food; efficient svce (in Tyrolean costume). There's a noisy piano bar/tavern in the cellar. A Las Vegas landmark since 1950, opposite the Las Vegas Hilton. Valet parking. *German/Continental.* I–M

♀ **Battista's Hole in the Wall** (nr. dwntwn), 4041 Audrie St.
🍴 (732-1424). A/C. Dinner only, nightly; closed Thanksgiving and the last two weeks in Dec. AE, CB, DC, MC, V. Jkt. *Specialties:* fresh homemade pasta (spaghetti cacciatore, lasagne, etc.), scampi, eggplant parmigiana. *Note:* The most Italian of Vegas's Italian rests.; the decor and the agreeable atmosphere suggest an old *trattoria,* and the resemblance is enhanced when the owner, Battista Locatelli, belts out a few operatic arias. Unlimited free house wine. Locally popular; resv. advised. *Italian.* I–M

♀ **Pasta Mia** (nr. dwntwn), 2585 E. Flamingo Rd. (733-0091).
🍴 A/C. Lunch/dinner daily; closed hols. No credit cards. *Specialties:* antipasto platter w. calamari; tortellini bolognese; penne w. broccoli, spinach, and garlic; homemade lasagna. Limited Italian wine list. *Note:* Quite recently opened storefront *trattoria* serving light Italian cooking in an informal atmosphere. Entrées are listed on a blackboard. Leisurely, casual svce. *Italian.* I

♀ **Silver Dragon** (nr. dwntwn), 1510 E. Flamingo Rd. (737-
🍴 1234). A/C. Lunch/Dinner daily (till 5am). AE, MC, V. *Specialties:* lemon shrimp, Silver Dragon crab claws, Lover's Delight, Szechuan lobster, other characteristic Cantonese and Szechuan dishes. *Note:* One of the best, and most frequented, Chinese rests. in Vegas. Even if the decor is the usual cliché, the food is really Chinese. Svce on the abrupt side, but hardworking. *Chinese.* I

♀ **Yolie's Brazilian Steakhouse** (nr. dwntwn), 3900 Paradise
🍴 Rd. (794-0700). Lunch Mon–Fri, dinner nightly. AE, CB, DC, MC, V. *Specialties:* steak, chicken, fish specialties, skewered lamb, Brazilian dishes. *Note:* Good selection of charcoal-broiled meat and fish attractively priced. Pleasant atmosphere and svce. Outdoor dining. Locally popular. Resv. accepted. *Steak/Brazilian.* B–I

♀ **Golden Nugget Buffet** (dwntwn), in the Golden Nugget (see
🍴 "Accommodations," above) (385-7111). A/C. Dinner only, daily. AE, DC, MC, V. *Specialties:* barbecued spareribs, roast beef, Chinese dishes, ham hock w. sauerkraut, salads, good desserts (including bread pudding). Unbeatable value in the heart of dwntwn; you can fill your plate as often as you choose. Locally popular. *American/Continental.* B (prix fixe).

Cafeterias/Specialty Spots

Park Deli (nr. dwntwn), 3900 Paradise Rd. (369-3354). Breakfast/lunch (until 6pm) Mon–Sat. MC, V. By far the best-stocked deli in town. Giant sandwiches, pastrami, corned beef, chopped liver. Don't miss the matzoh-ball soup.

BARS & NIGHTCLUBS

HOTEL SHOWS: No city in the world boasts more bars, casinos, discos, shows, or strip joints to the square mile than Las Vegas. All the major hotels offer, besides several bars and discos apiece, very high-quality shows, of which the most popular are those at **Bally's–Las Vegas, Caesars Palace,** the **Desert Inn,** the **Dunes Hotel,** the **Hilton Las Vegas** (Moulin Rouge Revue), the **Mirage, Sahara, Sands, Stardust,** and **Tropicana** (Folies Bergères Revue).

OTHER CHOICES: Gipsy (nr. dwntwn), 4605 Paradise Rd. (731-1919). Disco with a big local following; late at night the life-forms can be very varied. Open daily.

Shark Club (nr. dwntwn), 75 E. Harmon Ave. (795-7525). Crowded piano bar/rest./disco. Open nightly till dawn.

Silver Dollar Saloon (nr. dwntwn), 2501 E. Charleston Blvd. (382-6921). Live country music; certified cowboy setting. Open nightly.

For lovers of the female form divine and of (relatively) daring floor shows:

Crazy Horse Saloon (nr. dwntwn), 4034 Paradise Rd. (732-1116).

Palomino Club (nr. dwntwn), 1848 Las Vegas Blvd. N. (642-2984).

NEARBY EXCURSIONS

LAKE MEAD & HOOVER DAM (27 mi./43km SE on U.S. 93): This beautiful artificial lake, one of the largest in the world, is 116 mi. (180km) long; it was formed by the construction of the Hoover Dam, which holds back the waters of the Colorado River after it passes through the Grand Canyon. The azure waters are as deep as 590 ft. (180m). Fishing, waterskiing, and sailing are on offer along the 550 mi. (880km) of shoreline, and each year more than seven million visitors come here. The 726-ft. (221m) dam and the impressive generating plant date from 1935, and are ranked among the country's greatest architectural achievements. Visitor center open daily (702/293-8367).

OVERTON (65 mi./104km NE on I-15 and Nev. 169): Just 5 mi. (8km) south of this former 19th-century Mormon colony lies a huge Native American settlement, along the banks of the Muddy River, which 1,200 years ago was peopled by the ancestors of the Hopi. Interesting museum at the dig **(Lost City Museum)**, with a rich archeological collection (397-2193): pottery, wickerwork, primitive tools. Open daily.

You can advantageously combine this excursion with a visit to the **Valley of Fire** (see below).

RED ROCK CANYON (15 mi./24km west along W. Charleston Blvd.): Wonderful rocky gorges of white and reddish sandstone, with spectacular views. Gorgeous 13-mi. (21km) panoramic drive. Visitor center (363-1921).

SPRING MOUNTAIN RANCH (18 mi./29km west along W. Charleston Blvd.) (875-4141): This fine 528-acre (214ha) ranch, very near Red Rock Canyon, dates back to the 1870s, and has been the property of Vera Krupp, heiress of the German steel tycoons and then of Howard Hughes. It now belongs to the State of Nevada. Interesting. Self-guided tours daily. Guided tours available on wknds and hols.

VALLEY OF FIRE STATE PARK (58 mi./93km NE on I-15): Very beautiful rock-strewn desert of reddish hue (whence the name), overlooking Lake Mead, formed 150 million years ago. A spectacular sight at sundown, and offers some astonishing landscape panoramas at any time. Many petroglyphs (Native American rock drawings). Camping permitted. Visitor center open daily year round. For information, call 397-2088.

GHOST TOWNS: ⚖ **Calico,** 143 mi. (230km) SW on I-15: The most picturesque and best preserved of California's ghost towns. There were rich silver mines here in the 1880s, and the place had as many as 3,000 inhabitants; today there are a dozen. After the restoration undertaken in 1950, Main Street looks as though it has been taken bodily from a John Ford western. It's on the main highway to Los Angeles. For information, call 619/254-2122.

Goldsprings, 38 mi. (60km) SW by I-15 and Nev. 161: At its height around a century ago this little gold-rush town boasted as many as 2,000 inhabitants; today there are about 100. The **Pioneer Saloon** is a magnificent period piece.

NATIONAL PARKS NEARBY

DEATH VALLEY (142 mi./228km NW on U.S. 95, Nev. 373, and Cal. 190): America's most beautiful desert; see Chapter 48 on Death Valley.

GRAND CANYON OF THE COLORADO (291 mi./ 465km SE on U.S. 93, I-40, and Ariz. 64): One of the seven natural wonders of the world. See Chapter 41 on the Grand Canyon.

ZION NATIONAL PARK (162 mi./260km NE on I-15 and Utah 9) and **Bryce Canyon** (243 mi./389km east on I-15 and Utah 20, U.S. 89, and Utah 12): Two of the country's best-known national parks. See Chapter 32 on Utah's national parks.

CHAPTER 48

DEATH VALLEY NATIONAL MONUMENT 🍦🍦🍦

□ □ □

Long the unchallenged domain of the Panamint tribe, an offshoot of the Shoshone, Death Valley is one of the two or three most enthralling natural wonders in the United States. If you're fortunate enough to set eyes on it for the first time from atop the rocky platform symbolically named **Dante's View,** you may well feel that you're present at the Creation. At the foot of the dizzying sheer drop of 5,120 ft. (1,600m) there sprawls in blinding clarity the vast expanse of the salt flats and the lowest point on the continent, 282 ft. (86m) below sea level. On the other side of **Devil's Golf Course** and its weird salt formations, the eternal snows of distant Mount Whitney rise in striking contrast with sun-colored rocks and sun-blasted dunes. This two-billion-year-old valley, once the bed of an Ice Age sea, is home to a surprisingly diverse animal life. Among its denizens are no fewer than 36 species of mammals, including coyote, porcupine, and kangaroo rat; dozens of insect and reptile species, including the formidable rattlesnake; and birds, notably crows and vultures. Certain kinds of small fish such as the pupfish can be found nowhere on earth except in the scanty waters of this splendid but terrifying blast furnace: **Salt Creek** or the palm groves of **Furnace Creek** in the center of the valley. The region was named when a group of California-bound pioneers died of thirst and fatigue while attempting to cross the valley on Christmas Day 1849. The area experienced short-lived activity in the 1880s when borax was discovered; with its many industrial uses, borax became known as "the white gold of the desert."

Two excellent paved highways span the valley north to south and east to west. This living desert museum is today one of the most popular tourist spots in California. The extraordinary landscapes, veiled during the heat of the day by a soft-hued, ever-changing haze, draw thousands of visitors to the three motels in Death Valley each winter and spring (two stay open in summer). It goes without saying that reservations are recommended, except in summer, when Death Valley is virtually abandoned by tourists because of scorching heat.

HINTS TO MOTORISTS: When visiting Death Valley by car, drive at a moderate speed, especially during the summer, to avoid overheating the engine. Before you set out, make sure that you have a full tank of gas, check your oil, and deflate the tires by a couple of pounds below normal pressure. If you break down between Death Valley Junction and Furnace Creek, or between Stove Pipe Wells and Scotty's Castle, there won't be a living soul within 30 miles! Main roads, however, are regularly patrolled. When driving on unpaved roads, *always* have with you a few gallons of reserve water; in summer, an untrained person will die of dehydration in three hours under the Death Valley sun.

BASIC FACTS: State of California (extending into Nevada). Area code: 619. Time zone: Pacific. Zip Code: 92328. A National Monument since 1933. Area: 3,123 sq. mi. (8,090km²), one-fifth of it below sea level. Approximate dimensions: 140 mi. (225km) long, 4–16 mi. (6–26km) wide. Recommended time for visiting: Oct to late Apr.

CLIMATE: As you might expect from its name, Death Valley is one of the most inhospitable areas on the planet. In summer, temperatures frequently reach 113°F (45°C) in the shade (the record, set in July 1913, is 134°F/56.7°C). From late Oct to Apr, on the other hand, the mercury rarely goes above 86°F (30°C) in the daytime, with very cool nights, especially during the winter months (record low: 15°F/−9°C). Rainfall is practically nonexistent—less than 2 in. (5cm) per year.

DISTANCES: Las Vegas, 142 mi. (228km); Los Angeles, 305 mi. (490km); Reno, 285 mi. (456km); San Francisco, 531 mi. (851km).

ARRIVAL & TRANSIT INFORMATION

NEAREST AIRPORTS: The **Death Valley Municipal Airport** (DTH): 1 mi. (1.6km) west.
   Las Vegas McCarran International Airport (LAS): 142 mi. (228km) SE.
   Los Angeles International Airport (LAX): 305 mi. (490km) SW.

AIRLINES: Air Nevada (toll free 800/634-6377) offers charter flights from Las Vegas to Death Valley Municipal Airport. For other airlines, see Chapter 47 on Las Vegas and Chapter 54 on Los Angeles.

CAR RENTAL: See Chapter 47 on Las Vegas and Chapter 54 on Los Angeles.

TRAIN: For the closest Amtrak station, see Chapter 47 on Las Vegas.

INTERCITY BUSES: For the closest bus stations, see Chapter 47 on Las Vegas.
   Greyhound does not serve Death Valley, but KT Tours, 200 S. Main St., Las Vegas (644-2233), makes daily runs between Beatty (north entrance of Death Valley) and Las Vegas. Given the long distances involved, however, renting a car with unlimited mileage (preferably in California where the rates are lowest) is the best plan.

INFORMATION

TOURIST INFORMATION: Superintendent, Death Valley National Monument, Death Valley, CA 92328 (619/786-2331).
   Visitor center at Furnace Creek, open daily; also a desert museum.

SIGHTS, ATTRACTIONS & ACTIVITIES

ARCHITECTURAL HIGHLIGHTS: ❀▲▲ **Scotty's Castle,** 52 mi. (84km) NW of Furnace Creek on Calif. 190 and Grapevine Rd. (619/786-2392). The valley's only monument worthy of the title, a mirage in the middle of the desert. Wealthy Chicago businessman Albert Johnson and his friend, Walter Scotty, a professional cowboy from the Buffalo Bill troupe, built this sumptuously decorated and improbable castle in Hollywood Hispano-Moorish style between 1922 and 1931. Don't miss it—you may never see anything else like it! Guided tours promptly on the hour. Open daily.

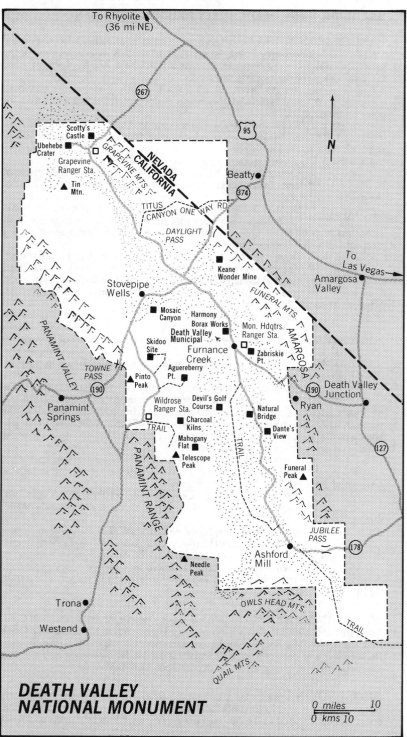

DEATH VALLEY
NATIONAL MONUMENT

PANORAMAS & EXCURSIONS (all distances measured from Furnace Creek): ☼🔆🏕 **Aguereberry Point,** 48 mi. (77km) west. A wonderful view of the valley, especially in the afternoon, from an altitude of 6,275 ft. (1,961m). The last 5 mi. (8km) of the ascent is unpaved.

🏕 **Artists Drive,** 11 mi. (18km) south: Narrow, one-way road amid splendid gorges and multicolored landscapes. A treat for color photographers.

☼🔆🏕🔭 **Badwater,** 16 mi. (26km) south: This spring is the source of undrinkable water, which never dries up even in the middle of summer. Next to the lowest point on the American continent (282 ft./86m below sea level), it's also the hottest place in the valley.

🏕 **Charcoal Kilns,** 61 mi. (98km) SW: Beehive-shaped charcoal kilns from pioneer days. Picturesque. The last 2 mi. (3km) of the road is unpaved.

☼🔆🏕🔭🔭 **Dante's View,** 23 mi. (38km) SE: One of the most breathtaking landscapes in creation, this panoramic platform 5,475 ft. (1,669m) high offers an unforgettable view of the valley. The road up is very steep and quite hard on the transmission.

☼🔆🏕🔭 **Devil's Golf Course,** 8 mi. (12km) south: A vast salt flat studded with 20-in.-high (50cm) salt rocks that lives up to its name.

🏕 **Golden Canyon,** 4 mi. (6km) south: This 0.6-mi. (1km) footpath cuts through splendid rock formations of gold, bright red, ochre, and bronze. A photographer's dream.

🏕 **The Racetrack,** 83 mi. (134km) NW: This long clay valley, the scene of strange geological displacements, is one of the valley's biggest mysteries. Last 27 mi. (44km) is unpaved road. For lovers of legends.

☼🔆🏕🔭 **Sand Dunes,** 21 mi. (35km) NW: Enormous sand dunes perpetually reshaped by the wind. A miniature Sahara in the middle of California.

☼🔆🏕🔭 **Telescope Peak,** 65 mi. (104km) SW: The highest point in the valley, at 11,049 ft. (3,368m). From **Mahogany Flat** (the last 2 mi./4km unpaved), a 6.8-mi. (11km) steep and arduous footpath leads to the summit, where you may enjoy an exceptional view of Death Valley and the neighboring mountains. Don't undertake this trip in summer. In any case, consult the ranger station in neighboring **Wildrose.**

🏕 **Titus Canyon,** 33 mi. (54km) north: The 26 mi. (42km) of the one-way track through this steep gorge are accessible only to four-wheel-drive vehicles. Superb landscapes.

🏕 **Twenty-Mule-Team Canyon,** 6 mi. (10km) SE: A tortuous, unpaved, one-way route zigzags through this splendid rocky setting.

🏕 **Ubehebe Crater,** 55 mi. (88km) NW: The only volcanic crater in the area, 2,560 ft. (800m) across and 390 ft. (122m) deep.

☼🔆🏕🔭 **Zabriskie Point,** 6 mi. (10km) SE: Strange, rocky "dunes" in tawny shades offering a superb view of the valley, Telescope Peak, and the Panamint Mountains, especially at sunrise and sunset. The setting for the Antonioni film of the same name.

ENTERTAINMENT: ☼🔆🏕🔭 **Amargosa Opera House,** at the junction of Calif. 127 and Calif. 190, Death Valley Junction (31 mi./50km SE of Furnace Creek on Calif. 190)(619/852-4441): The smallest opera house in the world. Martha Becket plays and dances solo to Offenbach's *La Vie Parisienne, Swan Lake,* and other classics. Surprising show and decor. Open Oct–mid-May.

GHOST TOWNS (all distances measured from Furnace Creek): 🏕 **Harmony Borax Works,** 1 mi. (1.6km) north: Remains of an old borax mine. From here borax was transported to the Mojave railway, 162 mi. (260km) farther south, on heavy carts which, even in the hottest weather, were drawn by the unbelievably enduring "20-mule teams."

    Panamint City, 77 mi. (124km) SW: Remains of a 19th-century mining town. On the way, visit another ghost town, **Ballarat.** Difficult access road.

    Rhyolite, 36 mi. (59km) NE: Vestiges of one of the most famous 1904 gold-rush towns, boasting as many as 6,000 residents around 1910. See the unusual house made of 50,000 bottles. You can also discover the history of the Stone City at Rhyolite's Desert Museum.

    Skidoo, 46 mi. (74km) west: Former miners' camp that has been periodically revitalized over the course of a century. The last stretch of the access road is difficult. Had as many as 500 inhabitants in its day, circa 1906.

NATIONAL PARKS NEARBY: **Sequoia National Park,** 362 mi. (580km) west on Calif. 190, 178, 65, and 198: This kingdom of the forest giants is barely 87 mi. (140km) away as the crow flies, but almost 375 mi. (600km) by road, a spectacular route through Panamint Valley and Sequoia National Forest. For the park itself, see Chapter 52.

SUGGESTED TOURING ITINERARIES IN THE VALLEY

    NORTH CIRCUIT (150 mi./241km r.t. from Furnace Creek): Visit **Rhyolite** (see "Ghost Towns," above), **Titus Canyon** (four-wheel-drive vehicles only), **Scotty's Castle** (see "Architectural Highlights," above), and **Ubehebe Crater** (see "Panoramas and Excursions," above). Optional excursion to **Racetrack** for four-wheel-drive vehicles only.

    WEST CIRCUIT (126 mi./202km r.t. from Furnace Creek): Visit **Sand Dunes, Aguereberry Point, Charcoal Kilns,** and optional excursions to **Telescope Peak** (for all of which, see "Panoramas and Excursions," above).

    SOUTH CIRCUIT (88 mi./142km r.t. from Furnace Creek): Visit **Zabriskie Point, Twenty-Mule-Team Canyon, Dante's View, Golden Canyon, Artists Drive, Devil's Golf Course,** and **Badwater** (for all of which, see "Panoramas and Excursions," above). The most spectacular circuit through the valley.

ACCOMMODATIONS & RESTAURANTS

Personal Favorites (in order of preference)

    Furnace Creek Inn, Calif. 190, Furnace Creek, CA 92328 (619/786-2361). 68 rms, A/C, cable color TV. AE, CB, DC, MC, V. Free parking, pool, four tennis courts, sauna, health club, horseback riding, two rests. (including L'Ottimos), bar, rm svce, disco, library, concierge, free breakfast. *Note:* Very busy luxury hotel built in 1927 in a vaguely Spanish, massive, and ungraceful idiom. Vast rms that are functional at the expense of elegance; the best open onto a lovely tropical grdn w. palm trees. Antiquated plumbing and other facilities; young, untrained svce, like all the Fred Harvey hotels. The pretentious rest. (jacket required, servers in long dresses) offers mediocre and expensive food. An ideal point of departure for a number of valley excursions (Dante's View, Badwater, and Zabriskie Point are less than 30 min. away by car). The hotel is open mid-Oct to mid-May only. **VE** (American Plan on request).

    Stove Pipe Wells, Calif. 190, Stove Pipe Wells Village, CA 92328 (619/786-2387). 82 rms, A/C. MC, V. Free parking, pool, coffee shop, bar, disco, grocery store, service station, crib $5. *Note:* This small motel offering functional comfort appears to rise out of the desert like a mirage amid a dramatic dune landscape. Mediocre cafeteria but a pleasant bar. Svce less than friendly. Open year round. **I,** but lower rates off-season.

Furnace Creek Ranch, Calif. 190, Furnace Creek, CA 92328 (619/786-2345). 224 rms, A/C, cable color TV. AE, CB, DC, MC, V. Free parking, pool, golf, two tennis courts, horseback riding, coffee shop, two rests. (winter), bar, grocery store, service station. *Note:* Classic motel built in a sort of oasis shaded by palm, date, and other trees. Inviting rms (some w. balconies) plus an adequate cafeteria. Ideal place from which to explore the whole valley. Adjacent motor-home parking. Motel open year round. Organizes guided tours of Death Valley. **I–M,** but lower rates off-season.

Amargosa Hotel, at the junction of Calif. 127 and Calif. 129, Death Valley Junction, CA 92328 (619/852-4441). 15 rms, A/C, color TV. MC, V. Free parking, rest. *Note:* Tiny, historic hotel reopened in 1990. Cleanliness and location make up for the somewhat spartan accommodations. Ideal if you're driving. Opposite the Amargosa Opera House (see "Entertainment," above). Resv. advised Oct–Apr. Open year round. **B–I**

Scotty's Castle, Grapevine Rd., Grapevine Canyon, CA 92328. Cafeteria open 9am–6pm year round. Service station. Across from the astonishing Scotty's Castle. A green oasis in the heart of the desert.

CHAPTER 49

RENO AND LAKE TAHOE

□ □ □

"The biggest little city in the world," coyly announces an enormous arch spanning the main street of this former gold prospectors' town, 120 years old. Long known as the world capital of divorce, Reno today has also become the capital of love at first sight, to judge from the innumerable "Wedding Chapels" where, for the modest sum of $30–$40—credit cards accepted—those aged 18 and over who wish to be married can be lawfully wedded instantly, day or night, seven days a week. This is possible because Nevada law is particularly liberal in matters of marriage and divorce. In the case of divorce, the law requires the petitioner to be a resident of Nevada for six weeks before the granting of the decree; marriage, however, requires but one formality: the purchase of a $25 license from the Marriage Bureau at the Washoe County Courthouse, S. Virginia and Court Sts., Reno, NV 89520 (702/328-3275), open daily 8am–midnight. The ceremony at the Wedding Chapel, which lasts no more than 10 min., requires two witnesses (provided by the chapel if necessary). Flowers (plastic), rice, and the obligatory "Wedding March" cost extra. More than 30,000 such instant weddings are performed annually in Reno.

Though honeymooners constitute a significant part of the local hotel trade (the number of honeymoon suites in the great hotels and even in motels is beyond number), the bulk of business is provided by lovers of roulette, baccarat, and slot machines (total annual earnings: $800 million). Though less flashy and ostentatious, Reno is a sort of replica of Las Vegas, about 400 mi. (700km) away across the desert. As at Las Vegas, slot machines greet the visitor right at the airport, overflow from the casinos onto the sidewalks of **Virginia St.**—the local Broadway or Wilshire Blvd.—and clatter away day and night in the gaming room of one of the largest casino-hotels in the world, **Bally's Reno.**

You should not, however, allow the lure of gambling to distract you altogether from the splendid scenery in the nearby **Sierra Nevada,** beginning with **Lake Tahoe** and **Pyramid Lake,** two of the most beautiful mountain lakes in the U.S. Not far from Lake Tahoe, the ghost town of **Virginia City,** one of the great gold-rush towns of the 19th century, preserves its old houses and saloons almost intact, like something right out of a western.

BASIC FACTS: State of Nevada. Area code: 702 (or 916 in South Lake Tahoe, Tahoe Vista, and Kings Beach, California). Time zone: Pacific. ZIP Code: 89501. Founded: 1868. Approximate population: city, 140,000; metropolitan area, 270,000.

CLIMATE: Reno, in the heart of the desert, enjoys a dry climate, sunny and invigorating. Summers are dazzlingly bright, but only moderately hot (July average, 68°C/20°F). Spring and fall are usually chilly; at night the temperature falls rapidly. Because of the altitude (4,498 ft./1,370m), winter offers a standing invitation to skiers in the area's resorts (Jan average, 34°F/1°C). With more than 300 days of sunshine a year and beautiful surroundings, the Reno–Lake Tahoe area is a nature lover's paradise.

DISTANCES: Las Vegas, 447 mi. (715km); Los Angeles, 470 mi. (752km); Portland, 574 mi. (918km); Salt Lake City, 523 mi. (837km); San Francisco, 229 mi. (366km).

RENO

ARRIVAL & TRANSIT INFORMATION

AIRPORT: Reno-Cannon International Airport (RNO), 4 mi. (6km) SE. For further information, call 328-6400.

AIRLINES: America West (toll free 800/235-9292), American (toll free 800/433-7300), Delta (toll free 800/221-1212), Northwest (toll free 800/225-2525), United (toll free 800/241-6522), and USAir (toll free 800/428-4322).

CITY LINK: The **cab** fare from the airport to dwntwn is about $6; time, about 10 min.
    Bus: **Bell Limousine** (702/323-3727), serves major dwntwn hotels; fare, $3; time, about 15 min.
    Tahoe Casino Express (702/785-2424), serves the Lake Tahoe area.
    Except for nearby excursions (recommended), the small size of the town makes renting a car unnecessary. Public transportation (bus) is not very efficient (**Reno Citifare:** 348-7433).

CAR RENTAL (all at the airport unless otherwise indicated): Avis (toll free 800/331-1212); Budget (toll free 800/527-0700); Dollar (toll free 800/800-4000); Hertz (toll free 800/654-3131); National (toll free 800/227-7368); and Thrifty, 200 E. 6th St. (toll free 800/367-2277). For dwntwn locations, consult the local telephone directory.

LIMOUSINE SERVICES: Bell Limousine (786-3700), Executive Limousine (333-3300) and Sierra West Limousine (329-4310).

TAXIS: Taxis are relatively affordable, but few in number. They can be called by telephone or taken from the waiting lines outside the major hotels. Recommended companies: **Reno-Sparks Cab** (333-3333), **Whittlesea Checker Taxi** (322-2222), and **Yellow Cab** (355-5555).

TRAIN: Amtrak Station, E. Commercial Row and Lake St. (toll free 800/872-7245).

INTERCITY BUSES: Greyhound, 155 Stevenson St. (toll free 800/231-2222).

INFORMATION & TOURS

TOURIST INFORMATION: The **Greater Reno Chamber of Commerce,** 405 Marsh Ave., NV 89505 (702/686-3030).

Reno-Sparks Convention and Visitors Authority, 4590 S. Virginia St. (P.O. Box 837), NV 89504 (702/827-7667; toll free 800/367-7366).

GUIDED TOURS: Gray Line Tours (bus), 2050 Glenndale Ave., Sparks (331-1147): Guided tours of the city and surrounding area.
Zephyr Balloons (balloon), 552 N. McCarran St., Sparks (329-1700): Balloon tours over the Reno and Lake Tahoe region. Truly spectacular.

SIGHTS, ATTRACTIONS & ACTIVITIES

ADVENTURES: River Adventures and More (RAM) (boat), P.O. Box 5283, NV 89513 (toll free 800/466-7238): Air-rafting down the Truckee River (May –Sept).

ARCHITECTURAL HIGHLIGHTS: ☼⚓ **Reno Arch,** Virginia St. at Commercial Row: Reno's arch, spanning Virginia St. with its renowned slogan—"The Biggest Little City in the World"—is one of the most recognized city symbols in America. The new art deco arch with its 1,600 lightbulbs and 800 ft. (245m) of neon is actually the fourth arch since the original was built in 1927 and is dedicated to the millions of tourists who visit Reno each year.

MUSEUMS OF ART: ⚓ **Sierra Nevada Museum of Art,** 549 Court St. (329-3333): Located in the Neo-Georgian Hawkins House, a designated historic monument, this museum displays an interesting collection of works by contemporary artists of the American West, including paintings, sculpture, prints, decorative arts, and Native American art. Also temporary exhibitions. The **E. L. Wiegand Museum** is in the annex at 160 W. Liberty St. Open Tues–Sun.

MUSEUMS OF SCIENCE & HISTORY: ⚓ **Fleischmann Planetarium,** 1650 N. Virginia St. (784-4811): Very modern in conception, this planetarium is located on the University of Nevada–Reno campus. Laser shows, museum of astronomy, telescopes available for stargazing. A treat for lovers of astronomy. Open daily.
⚓ **Harold's Club Gun Collection and Museum,** 250 N. Virginia St. (329-0881): Very fine collection of old firearms, from 16th-century Chinese cannon to the Remingtons, Colts, and Winchesters of the Old West. More than 500 different items. On the second floor of Harold's Club, one of the oldest casinos in Nevada (1935). Open daily.
☼⚓⚓ **Harrah's Foundation National Automobile Museum,** 10 S. Lake St. at Mill St. (333-9300): Billing itself as "one of the great national treasures of America," this automobile museum has a fine collection of more than 200 old vehicles. Many are extremely rare or one of a kind, splendidly restored, such as the 1890 Philion, one of the oldest existing American-built automobiles, or the 1907 Thomas Flyer that won a 25,000-mi. (40,250km) race from New York to Paris through Alaska and Siberia. The museum's new home is a state-of-the-art building conceived as a piece of sculpture. Open daily.
⚓ **Liberty Belle's Slot Machine Collection,** 4250 S. Virginia St. (825-1776): An amusing collection of old player pianos and slot machines (the oldest dating from 1898), maintained by the Liberty Belle Saloon. Open daily.
⚓ **MacKay Mining Museum,** 9th and N. Center Sts. (784-6988): Extensive geological collection (minerals, precious stones, fossils, etc.). Displays on the history of the gold rush. A facility of the MacKay

School of Mines, one of the oldest (1874) and most highly regarded mining schools in the U.S. Interesting. Open Mon–Fri.

    Nevada Historical Society Museum, 1650 N. Virginia St. (688-1190): Displays on the prehistory and modern history of Nevada. Beautiful collection of Native American artifacts. Mementoes of the Winning of the West. Open Mon–Sat.

    Wilbur D. May Museum, 1502 Washington St., in Rancho San Rafael Park (785-5961): This new museum has hundreds of fascinating items collected by the late Wilbur D. May, department-store magnate, pilot, adventurer, world traveler, and big-game hunter during the 1920s and '30s. The relics of May's Indiana Jones–style life include his re-created trophy room with mounted heads of more than 80 animals as well as rare horse sculptures from the Tang Dynasty. Beautiful adjoining arboretum. One of the most interesting small museums in the West. Open Wed–Sun in winter, daily the rest of the year.

NIGHTLIFE: As in Las Vegas, the most important aspect of nightlife in Reno, Sparks, and South Lake Tahoe is to be found in the gaming rooms of the casinos. Most of the big hotels—**Bally's, Harrah's,** the **Hilton, John Ascuaga's Nugget** —also offer frequent floor shows, big-name performers, discos, bars, etc. (see "Accommodations," below).

PERFORMING ARTS: For daily listings of all shows and cultural events, consult the entertainment pages of the daily morning paper *Reno Gazette Journal* and the monthly *Nevada* magazine.

    Church Fine Arts Theater, on the University of Nevada–Reno campus, 9th and N. Virginia Sts. (784-6145): Classical and contemporary plays, and musicals.

    Little Theater, 690 N. Sierra St. (329-0661): Modern theater. Drama and comedy (Sept–June). Also offers children's theater.

    Pioneer Center for the Performing Arts, 100 S. Virginia St. at State St. (786-5105): Classical music concerts, opera, ballet, recitals. Home of the Nevada Festival Ballet (Sept–Jan), the Nevada Opera (Oct–Apr), and the Reno Philharmonic (Oct–Apr), under Ron Daniels, principal conductor.

    Reno-Sparks Convention Center, 4590 S. Virginia St. (827-7600): Pop concerts. Hosts an International Jazz Festival annually (Mar).

    Wingfield Riverside Park, S. Arlington Ave. at Island St. (851-0759): Free outdoor concerts in this park on the banks of the Truckee River. Mon–Fri at noon, June–Sept.

SPECIAL EVENTS: For the exact schedule of events below, consult the **Reno-Sparks Convention and Visitors Authority** (see "Tourist Information," above); the **Carson City Chamber of Commerce,** 1900 S. Carson St., Carson City, NV 89701 (702/882-1565); or the **Lake Tahoe Visitors Authority,** 1156 Ski Run Blvd., South Lake Tahoe, CA 96150 (916/544-5050).

    Silver State Square Dance Festival (Reno; Apr–May): One of the most important square-dance festivals in the U.S. More than 7,000 dancers come from all over the U.S. and Canada to take part. A great spectacle, and a tradition for more than 40 years.

    Reno Rodeo (Reno; eight days in mid-June): A rodeo festival famous throughout the West. Those not wearing western dress are fined. Exciting atmosphere.

    Valhalla Summer Arts and Music Festival (Lake Tahoe, various lake sites; mid-June to Sept): Weekend outdoor classical concerts and midweek chamber-music performances. Also musicals and Broadway revues.

    Shakespeare Festival (Lake Tahoe; Aug): *The* place to be for theater lovers

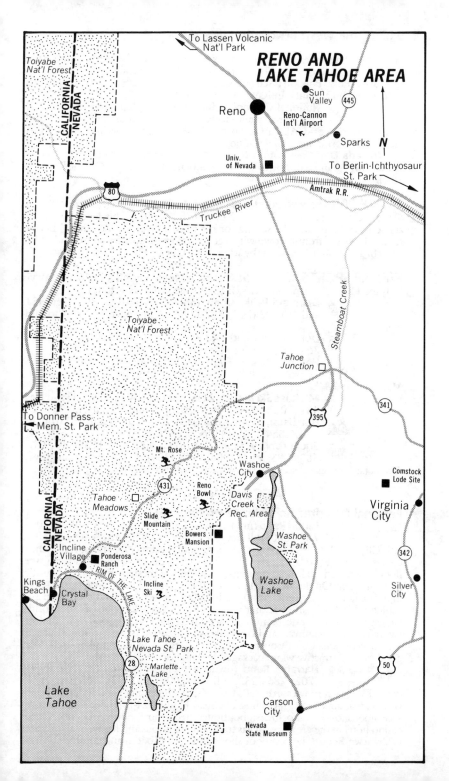

in summer. Shakespearean plays performed outdoors in the lovely natural setting of Sand Harbor State Park. For information, call toll free 800/468-2463.

Great Reno Balloon Race (Reno; Sept): A hot-air-balloon race, usually with more than 100 entrants. In Rancho San Rafael Park.

☼ **National Championship Air Races** (Reno; four days in mid-Sept): Prop-plane races since 1963, the most famous such competition in the world. Also an aerobatics display. Truly spectacular. At Stead Air Field. For information, call 972-6663.

Nevada Day Celebration (Carson City; four days in late Oct): Parades, "powwow," grand costume ball. Commemorates Nevada's joining the Union in 1864.

THEME PARKS: ☼🏠 **Ponderosa Ranch,** at Incline Village, 35 mi. (56km) SW via U.S. 395, Nev. 431, and Nev. 28 (831-0691): This legendary ranch above Lake Tahoe was the setting for the television series "Bonanza." Reconstructed western frontier town with a general store, saloon, firehouse, and a little church. Tours on horseback or by stagecoach. Open daily.

WINTER SPORTS RESORTS: 🏠 **Alpine Meadows,** 48 mi. (76km) SW via I-80 and Calif. 89 (916/583-4232): 13 lifts; open mid-Nov to June.

🔔 **Diamond Peak,** 35 mi. (56km) SW via U.S. 395, Nev. 431, and Nev. 28 (702/832-1177): 7 lifts; open mid-Nov to mid-Apr.

🔔 **Donner Ski Ranch,** 43 mi. (68km) SW on I-80 (916/426-3635): 5 lifts; open Dec–Apr.

☼🔔🔔 **Heavenly Valley,** 59 mi. (94km) south via U.S. 395 and U.S. 50 (toll free 800/243-2836): 24 lifts; open mid-Nov to mid-May.

🔔 **Mt. Rose Ski Resort,** 24 mi. (38km) SW via U.S. 395 and Nev. 431 (702/849-0704): 5 lifts; open mid-Nov. to Apr.

🔔🔔 **Northstar,** 39 mi. (62km) SW via I-80 and Calif. 267 (toll free 800/466-6784): 14 lifts; open Nov–Apr.

☼🔔🔔🔔 **Squaw Valley,** 44 mi. (70km) SW via I-80 and Calif. 89 (916/583-6985; toll free 800/545-4350): 32 lifts; open mid-Nov to Apr. A famous resort, scene of the Winter Olympics in 1960.

ACCOMMODATIONS

Personal Favorites (in order of preference)

☼🕯🕯🕯🕯 **Hilton Reno** (nr. dwntwn), 2500 E. 2nd St., NV 89595 (702/789-2000; toll free, see Hilton). 2,000 rms, A/C, color TV. AE, CB, DC, MC, V. Free valet parking, pool, health club, sauna, eight tennis courts, bowling (50 lanes), six rests. (including Caruso's), 24-hr. bars, rm svce, floor shows, casino, hrdrsr, boutiques, four movie theaters, free airport shuttle, free crib. *Note:* On the ground floor, 163,000 sq. ft. (1.5ha) in area, this 26-story high-rise houses a gigantic casino, with 2,000 slot machines and more than 120 roulette, blackjack, and baccarat tables. The hotel's theater boasts the world's largest stage. Interior decoration is in a nouveau-riche Hollywood style, but rms (w. refrigerators) are vast and comfortable. Extensive sports facilities. Efficient svce; decent rests. Usually overcrowded and noisy. Worth a trip all by itself. Very good value. Attractive wknd packages. Parking for campers. **I–M**

🕯🕯🕯 **Harrah's Reno** (dwntwn), 219 N. Center St., NV 89504 (702/786-3232; toll free 800/648-3773). 565 rms, A/C, color TV, in-rm movies. AE, CB, DC, MC, V. Free valet parking, pool, health club, sauna, three rests. (including The Steak House), 24-hr. coffee shop, bars, rm svce, floor shows, casino, hrdrsr, boutiques, free airport shuttle, free crib. *Note:* A casino-hotel in the great Las Vegas tradition, luxurious and flashy, in a noisy area of dwntwn Reno. The best floor shows in Reno. Modern and comfortable rms (the best are in the new tower). Caters to groups. Good rest. (Steak House). **I–M,** but lower rates off-season.

🔑🔑 **Eldorado Hotel** (dwntwn), 4th and Virginia Sts., NV 89505 (702/786-5700; toll free 800/648-5966). 800 rms, A/C, cable color TV. AE, CB, DC, MC, V. Free valet parking, pool, six rests. (including La Strada), 24-hr. coffee shop, bars, 24-hr. rm svce, floor shows, casino, free crib. *Note:* Big casino-hotel in the middle of dwntwn Reno topped by a new 25-story tower inaugurated in 1989. Spacious, comfortable rms w. refrigerators. Good svce. Rather noisy neighborhood. Caters to groups and conventions. Acceptable rests. Good value. **I–M**

🔑🔑 **Riverboat** (dwntwn), 34 W. 2nd St. (at Sierra St.), NV 89501 (702/323-8877; toll free 800/888-5525). 120 rms, A/C, color TV, in-rm movies. AE, CB, DC, MC, V. Free valet parking, rest., 24-hr. coffee shop, bar, rm svce, nightclub, casino, free crib. *Note:* Relatively new casino-hotel styled after an old-time Mississippi paddlewheeler. Extremely comfortable; efficient svce; rest. acceptable but no more. Very centrally located. Good value. **I–M**

🔑 **Motel 6 Central** (nr. dwntwn), 866 N. Wells Ave., NV 89512 (702/786-9852). 142 rms, A/C, cable color TV. AE, DC, MC, V. Free parking, pool. *Note:* One of the best hotel values in Reno. Comfortable modern rms. 8 min. from dwntwn. **B**

Other Accommodations (from top bracket to budget)

🔑🔑🔑 **Flamingo Hilton Reno** (dwntwn), 225 N. Sierra St., NV 89501 (702/322-1111; toll free, see Hilton). 599 rms, A/C, color TV, in-rm movies. AE, CB, DC, MC, V. Free valet gar., four rests., 24-hr coffee shop, 24-hr. bars, rm svce, casino, floor shows, hrdrsr, free crib. *Note:* Big Las Vegas–style casino-hotel. Pleasant, spacious rms (ask for one w. a view of the Sierra). Vast gaming rms at street level. Rather noisy area. Acceptable rest. (Top of the Hilton). Svce somewhat overburdened. Caters to groups and package tours. In the heart of dwntwn Reno. **I–E**

🔑🔑 **John Ascuaga's Nugget Casino Resort** (nr. dwntwn), 1100 Nugget Ave., Sparks, NV 89431 (702/356-3300; toll free 800/648-1177). 1,000 rms, A/C, cable color TV. AE, CB, DC, MC, V. Free valet parking, pool, health club, six rests. (including Trader Dick's), 24-hr. coffee shop, 24-hr. bars, rm svce, floor shows, disco, casino, free crib. *Note:* Ultramodern 28-story casino-hotel. Comfortable, spacious rms. Efficient reception and svce. Obtrusive group clientele. 15 min. from dwntwn. **M**

🔑🔑 **Clarion** (nr. dwntwn), 3800 S. Virginia St., NV 89502 (702/825-4700; toll free 800/826-7860). 600 rms and suites, A/C, cable color TV. AE, CB, DC, MC, V. Free valet parking, pool, health club, sauna, 24-hr. rest., 24-hr. bar, rm svce, casino, nightclub, free crib. *Note:* A 12-story casino-hotel recently adding a new tower w. modernized facilities. Comfortable rms (especially the new wing). Pleasant buffet setting in a glass aviary. Good value. Situated across the street from Reno-Sparks Convention Center, drawing many business travelers. Free airport shuttle. **I–M** (rms), **I–VE** (suites)

🔑🔑 **Peppermill** (nr. dwntwn), 2707 S. Virginia St., NV 89502 (702/826-2121; toll free 800/648-6992). 629 rms, A/C, color TV, in-rm movies. AE, CB, DC, MC, V. Free valet parking, pool, health club, sauna, two rests. (including Le Moulin), coffee shop, 24-hr. bars, 24-hr. rm svce, casino, cabaret, hrdrsr, free crib. *Note:* A 15-story casino-hotel recently modernized and enlarged. Comfortable rms (especially the new wing). Efficient svce. Caters to groups and conventions. Good value. Situated 5 min. from the airport (free shuttle) and 8 min. from dwntwn. **I–M**

🔑🔑 **Circus Circus** (dwntwn), 500 N. Sierra St., NV 89503 (702/329-0711; toll free 800/648-5010). 1,625 rms, A/C, color TV, in-rm movies. AE, CB, DC, MC, V. Free valet parking, two rests., 24-hr. coffee shop, bars, casino, crib $6. *Note:* Clever decor, like a gigantic, multicolored circus tent. Circus acts and gambling all over the place; worth a look. Serviceably comfortable; attractive rates. A good choice in the center of Reno, much frequented by families. **B–I**, but lower rates off-season.

Motel 6 West (nr. dwntwn), 1400 Stardust St., NV 89503 (702/747-7390). 122 rms, A/C, cable color TV. AE, DC, MC, V. Free parking, pool. *Note:* One of the best values in Reno. Comfortable, modern rms. 5 min. from dwntwn. **B**

RESTAURANTS

Personal Favorites (in order of preference)

La Table Française (nr. dwntwn), 3065 W. 4th St. (323-3200). A/C. Dinner only, Tues–Sat; closed hols. AE, CB, DC, MC, V. Jkt. *Specialties:* Soupe au pistou, sea perch Riviera, crêpes au curry, duckling w. blueberry sauce, scallops w. leeks and ginger, game (in season), hazelnut-chocolate mousse cake. Menu changes regularly. Good wine list. *Note:* Yves Pimparel, head chef and source of inspiration for this excellent French rest., retired in 1984. His daughter, Muriel, who succeeded him, has a master's touch, and this remains the best rest. in Reno. The cooking is a perfect blend of French and Californian nouvelle cuisine. Charmingly got up as both inn and windmill. Well-trained staff; romantic atmosphere. Resv. essential. 8 min. from dwntwn. *French/Continental.* **M–E**

Steak House (dwntwn), in Harrah's Reno (see "Accommodations," above) (786-3232). A/C. Lunch Mon–Fri, dinner nightly. AE, CB, DC, MC, V. Jkt. *Specialties:* beef saty, steak Diane, osso bucco, roast rack of lamb. Very good desserts. *Note:* Despite its name, the specialty of this rest. is not its good, big steaks—which are, nonetheless, excellent—but subtler dishes such as grilled salmon and excellent curries. Elegant decor; good svce. On the ground floor of Harrah's. Valet parking. *Continental.* **M**

Ichiban (dwntwn), 635 N. Sierra St. (323-5550). A/C. Dinner only, nightly; closed Dec 25. AE, CB, DC, MC, V. *Specialties:* sushi, tempura, teppanyaki, chicken teriyaki. *Note:* The best Japanese food in Reno. Rather banal Far Eastern decor. Attentive svce. Popular locally; resv. advised. Tatami-style seating for purists. *Japanese.* **I–M**

Club Cal-Neva (dwntwn), 2nd and Virginia Sts. (323-1046). A/C. Breakfast/lunch/dinner daily around the clock. No credit cards. *Specialties:* steak, roast beef, salads, catch of the day, good desserts. *Note:* A godsend to Reno's hungry visitors any hour of the day or night, seven days a week. This dwntwn casino has three rests.: The Top Deck, The Copper Ledge, and The Hofbrau, which offer an around-the-clock breakfast and a prime rib dinner. *Steak/American.* **B**

Other Restaurants (from top bracket to budget)

Top of the Hilton (dwntwn), in the Flamingo Hilton Reno (see "Accommodations," above) (322-1111). A/C. Dinner nightly, brunch Sun. AE, CB, DC, MC, V. Jkt. *Specialties:* salmon w. three sauces, roast duck w. raspberry sauce, bouillabaisse, rack of lamb. *Note:* From the 21st floor of the Hilton Flamingo Reno, this deluxe rest. offers a spectacular view of the city and surrounding mountains. Flawless traditional hotel cuisine; elegant decor and svce; very high prices by local standards. Resv. advised. Dancing nightly; valet parking. *Continental.* **M–E**

Rapscallion (nr. dwntwn), 1555 S. Wells Ave. (323-1211) A/C. Lunch Mon–Fri, dinner nightly, brunch Sun; closed Thanksgiving, Dec 25. AE, MC, V. *Specialties:* oysters on the half shell; shellfish; Maine lobster; catch of the day broiled, baked, or prepared w. sauce; bouillabaisse. Adequate wine list. *Note:* The best seafood rest. in Reno. Everything is flown in daily for absolute freshness, and more than 20 kinds of fish figure on the menu. Nice 1900 setting with old gaslights and Tiffany-style stained glass. Competent, friendly svce. Resv. advisable. *Seafood.* **I–M**

☿ **Presidential Car at Harolds Club** (dwntwn), 250 N. Virginia St. (329-0881). A/C. Dinner only, nightly. AE, CB, DC, MC, V. *Specialties:* prime rib, steak, catch of the day, cheesecake. *Note:* Clever 19th-century railroad setting; good though unimaginative food; efficient svce. Very good value. *Steak/Seafood.* **I–M**

☼☿ **Louis' Basque Corner** (dwntwn), 301 E. 4th St. (323-7203). A/C. Lunch Mon–Sat, dinner nightly. AE, CB, MC, V. *Specialties:* tripe, chicken basquaise, paella, tongue à la basquaise, braised calves' sweetbreads, mutton stew, oxtail. *Note:* This rest., w. its family atmosphere and walls decorated w. earthenware and pictures from the Pyrenees, features Basque cooking, both French and Spanish (there are many shepherds of Basque origin in Nevada). Chef Louis Erreguible's robust delicious food treats your wallet gently, served in the generous portions you'd expect. Congenial atmosphere; a great place to eat. Very popular locally. Resv. advised. *French/Spanish.* **B–I**

☿ **El Borracho** (nr. dwntwn), 1601 S. Virginia St. (322-0313). A/C. Lunch/dinner Wed–Mon; closed Thanksgiving, Dec 25. AE, CB, DC, MC, V. *Specialties:* chiles rellenos, tacos, enchilada verde, flauta encantada. *Note:* A little Mexican place, popular locally. Authentic, unpretentious food. Good value. Pretty hacienda decor. *Mexican.* **B**

LAKE TAHOE

ACCOMMODATIONS

Personal Favorites (in order of preference)

🍷🍷🍷🍷 **Harrah's Lake Tahoe**, U.S. 50 and Stateline Ave., Stateline, NV 89449 (702/588-6611; toll free 800/648-3773). 540 rms, A/C, color TV, in-rm movies. AE, CB, DC, MC, V. Free valet parking, pool, health club, sauna, six rests. (including the Summit), 24-hr. coffee shop, 24-hr. bars, rm svce, floor shows, casino, disco, hrdrsr, boutiques, concierge, free crib. *Note:* Prestigious casino-hotel with a 393-ft.-long (120m) gaming rm. Its floor shows and amenities rival the best in Las Vegas. Spacious rms, modern and elegant (the best have a view of Lake Tahoe), w. minibars; outstanding svce; good rests. Excellent location between the lake and the mountain. A very fine hotel; you pay accordingly. **E–VE**, but lower rates off-season.

🍷🍷 **Lakeland Village**, 3535 Lake Tahoe Blvd., South Lake Tahoe, CA 95705 (916/544-1685; toll free 800/367-7052). 212 suites and studios, A/C, cable color TV. AE, DC, MC, V. Free parking, two pools, two tennis courts, sauna, boating, private beach, rests. nearby, snack bar, free crib. *Note:* Attractive resort facility right on the beach; comfortable suites and studios w. refrigerator, kitchenette, fireplace, and private balcony, the best w. lake view. Also two-story town houses w. one to four bedrooms. At the water's edge w. 19 acres (7ha) of lawns and grdns. Friendly reception and svce. 5 min. from casinos and ski slopes. Good overall value. **M–E** rms, **E–VE** (town houses), but lower rates off-season.

🍷 **Tahoe West Motor Lodge**, 4107 Pine Blvd., South Lake Tahoe, CA 95729 (916/544-6455; toll free 800/522-1021). 59 rms (no A/C), cable color TV. AE, CB, DC, MC, V. Free parking, pool, sauna, coffee shop nearby, free crib. *Note:* Pleasant little motel a stone's throw from Lake Tahoe and the casinos. Comfortable rms w. private balconies or patios. Private beach privileges. Very good value. Friendly reception and svce. **B–I**, but lower rates off-season.

🍷 **Cedar Glen Lodge**, 6589 N. Lake Blvd., Tahoe Vista, CA 95732 (916/546-4281; toll free 800/341-8000). 31 rms (no A/C), cable color TV. AE, CB, DC, MC, V. Free parking, pool, sauna, adj. beach, coffee shop nearby, free breakfast, free crib. *Note:* Charming little motel beside Lake Tahoe, surrounded by pretty grdns. Cozy rms w. private patios (half w. kitchenettes). Calm, countrified atmosphere. Friendly svce. Very good value overall. **B–I,** but lower rates off-season.

Other Accommodations (from top bracket to budget)

♉♉♉ **Hyatt Regency Lake Tahoe,** Lakeshore Blvd. and Country Club Dr., Incline Village, NV 89450 (702/831-1111; toll free, see Hyatt). 460 rms, A/C, color TV, in-rm movies. AE, CB, DC, MC, V. Free valet parking, pool, health club, sauna, two tennis courts, private beach, bicycles, three rests. (including Hugo's Rôtisserie), 24-hr. coffee shop, bar, 24-hr. rm svce, casino, boutiques, concierge, free crib. *Note:* Luxurious casino-hotel in a lovely wooded setting on the shores of Lake Tahoe. Spacious, ultra-comfortable rms w. balconies (some w. refrigerators and fireplaces), the best overlooking the lake. Efficient svce; very acceptable rest. Ideal for a long vacation stay. Two VIP floors. Recently underwent a $20-million renovation. **VE,** but lower rates off-season.

♉♉♉ **Lake Tahoe Horizon,** U.S. 50, Stateline, NV 89449 (702/588-6211; toll free 800/648-3322). 536 rms, A/C, cable color TV. AE, CB, DC, MC, V. Free valet parking, pool, sauna, two rests. (including Josh's), 24-hr. coffee shop, 24-hr. bars, 24-hr. rm svce, nightclub, casino, hrdrsr, boutiques, free crib. *Note:* Classic Las Vegas–style casino-hotel, w. 1,200 slot machines and dozens of gaming tables. Recently renovated. Pleasant, large rms (some w. balconies and lake views). Good svce. Attractive vacation packages. Caters to groups. **M–E,** but lower rates off-season.

♉♉ **Cal-Neva Lodge,** 2 Stateline Dr., Crystal Bay, NV 89402 (702/832-4000; toll free 800/225-6382). 220 rms, A/C, cable color TV. AE, CB, DC, MC, V. Free parking, pool, health club, sauna, tennis court, bicycles, rest. 24-hr. bars, rm svce, nightclub, casino, hrdrsr, crib $10. *Note:* Modern grand hotel on a headland overlooking the lake that marks the border between California and Nevada (whence the name). Comfortable rms w. mountain and lake views, some w. private balcony. Efficient svce in an agreeable setting. A Lake Tahoe landmark. **M–E,** but lower rates off-season.

♉♉ **Royal Valhalla,** 4104 Lakeshore Blvd., South Lake Tahoe, CA 95729 (916/544-2233). 80 rms (no A/C), cable color TV. AE, CB, DC, MC, V. Free parking, pool, private beach, café nearby, free breakfast. *Note:* Comfortable little motel w. direct access to the beach. Inviting rms w. lake or mountain views (most w. private patios or balconies; one-third w. kitchenettes). Good svce. Just minutes from the casinos of Stateline. Good overall value. **I–M,** but lower rates off-season.

♉ **Motel 6,** 2375 Lake Tahoe Blvd., South Lake Tahoe, CA 95731 (916/542-1400). 140 rms, A/C, cable color TV. AE, DC, MC, V. Free parking, pool. *Note:* Unbeatable value two steps from the lake. Modern and comfortable. Midway between the ski slopes and the casinos. **B**

RESTAURANTS

Personal Favorites (in order of preference)

♟♟♟ **Le Petit Pier,** 7250 N. Lake Tahoe Blvd., Tahoe Vista (916/546-4464). A/C. Dinner only, nightly; closed Tues in winter. AE, CB, DC, MC, V. Jkt. *Specialties:* country pâté, braised pheasant forestière, tournedos w. marrow in marchand de vin sauce, quail w. green peppercorns. Good wine list. *Note:* Some of the best fare in Lake Tahoe, w. a lovely view of the mountains and the lake thrown in. Formal French dining. Elegant, quiet atmosphere. Excellent svce. Resv. advised. *French.* **M–E**

♟♟ **Captain Jon's,** 7252 N. Lake Blvd., Tahoe Vista (916/546-4819). A/C. Lunch Tues–Sun in summer, dinner Tues–Sun; closed the first three weeks in Dec. AE, CB, DC, MC, V. *Specialties:* roast duck w. oyster sauce, sautéed scallops w. shiitake mushrooms and snow peas, grape snails, catch of the day. Very good desserts. *Note:* This inviting inn rises straight from the water; the European-style food is elegantly prepared and served. Agreeable seafaring decor and summer open-air terrace w. spectacular views of Lake Tahoe. Efficient svce; good value; resv. suggested. *Continental.* **I–M**

    Swiss Chalet, Lake Tahoe Blvd. at Sierra Blvd., South Lake Tahoe (916/544-3304). A/C. Dinner only, Tues–Sun; closed Easter, Thanksgiving, Dec 25. AE, MC, V. *Specialties:* schnitzel St. Moritz, sauerbraten, steak, veal cordon bleu, catch of the day. *Note:* Decor and atmosphere of an alpine chalet. French- and German-inspired cooking. Warm and cozy. A landmark since 1957. Resv. recommended. *Continental.* **I–M**

Other Restaurants (from top bracket to budget)

    The Summit, in Harrah's Lake Tahoe (see "Accommodations," above) (702/588-6611). A/C. Dinner only, Wed–Mon. AE, CB, DC, MC, V. Jkt. *Specialties:* California-style dishes. The menu changes daily. Good wine list w. prices to match. *Note:* Superb view of lake and mountains from the 18th floor of Harrah's. The decor is exceedingly elegant. Light, inventive contemporary cuisine by chef Elizabeth Welliver-Gregory, impeccably prepared and served. Stylish and classy. Very high prices by local standards. Resv. strongly advised. *Continental.* **M–E**

    Chart House, Kingsbury Grade (1.5 mi./2.5km off U.S. 50), Stateline (702/588-6276). A/C. Dinner only, nightly; closed Dec 26. AE, MC, V. *Specialties:* filet of beef teriyaki, prime rib, catch of the day. *Note:* Congenial little rest. w. a fine panoramic view of Lake Tahoe from the heights of Stateline. Good food w. no fuss. Friendly svce. A good spot, away from the hustle and bustle of the big casino-hotels along the lake. *American.* **I–M**

    La Playa, 7046 N. Lake Blvd., Tahoe Vista (916/546-5903). No A/C. Dinner nightly; open for lunch daily in summer. AE, DC, MC, V. Jkt. *Specialties:* rack of lamb, sea scallops sautée, grilled salmon, swordfish steak, catch of the day. Skimpy wine list. *Note:* Charming inn on the shores of Lake Tahoe. Conventional cooking, but very well done. Open-air patio for fine-weather dining, w. view of the lake and the mountains. Friendly reception and svce. A fine place to eat. Resv. recommended. *Continental.* **I–M**

    Sierra Restaurant, in Harrah's Lake Tahoe (see "Accommodations," above) (702/588-6611). A/C. Breakfast/lunch/dinner. AE, CB, DC, MC, V. *Note:* Americanized Chinese food, sandwiches, steaks, and hamburgers. 24 hr. a day. A few dishes (chicken pot pie, cashew chicken salad) are very acceptable. Often packed. All-purpose modern decor. *Chinese/American.* **B–I**

EXCURSIONS

NEARBY EXCURSIONS

    BERLIN-ICHTHYOSAUR STATE PARK (175 mi./ 280km SE via I-80, U.S. 50, Nev. 361, and Nev. 844): Unknown to most tourists, this park, lying east of Gabbs in Union Canyon, is nonetheless fascinating for two reasons. First, it includes the ghost town of **Berlin,** a former miners' community that had several hundred inhabitants at the turn of the century, but has been completely abandoned for more than 75 years. The second and more important of the park's attractions is its large number of fossilized ichthyosaur remains. These enormous prehistoric reptiles, up to 65 ft. (20m) long, with characteristics of both fish and lizard, made their appearance on the planet some 225 million years ago and became extinct 155 million years later. A total of 34 fossilized ichthyosaurs has been discovered so far in the Shoshone Mountains, all uncovered by water erosion during the last glacial period. Guided tours (867-3001) of the park and Berlin are offered Sat–Sun at 11am Mar–Sept.

The park is open daily mid-June to Labor Day, Fri–Mon the rest of the year, but is closed during bad weather.

⚜ CARSON CITY (30 mi./48km south on U.S. 395):

Founded in 1858, Carson City—named after the famous scout Kit Carson, who undertook the first explorations of Nevada, in 1843–45 —is one of the smallest state capitals in the U.S. Nonetheless, the city has a beautiful group of Victorian mansions. The **State Capitol,** on N. Carson St. (687-5030), opened in 1871 with its typical silver dome symbolic of Nevada's principal mineral resource, is worth a look; open Mon–Fri. The **Nevada State Museum** deserves a visit, with interesting displays of relics from the days of the pioneers and prospectors; you'll find it on N. Carson and Robinson Sts. (687-4810), open daily. Also see its annex, the **Nevada State Railroad Museum,** S. Carson St. and Fairview Dr. (687-6953), open Wed–Sun, featuring old steam engines, freight cars, and passenger cars.

☼⚜ DONNER PASS MEMORIAL STATE PARK (43 mi./

68km SW on I-80): This mountain pass was the scene of a famous episode in the history of the westward expansion. In Oct 1846, 89 pioneers attempting to cross the Sierra Nevada found their way blocked by the snows of an unusually early winter. With no food left, and unable to go on through the blizzards, 42 of them died from hunger and exhaustion. The other 47 survived only by resorting to cannibalism. The **Emigrant Trail Museum,** on the old U.S. 40 (916/587-3841), open daily, traces the story of the Donner party.

☼⚜ FORT CHURCHILL HISTORIC STATE MONUMENT

(85 mi./136km SE via Nev. 341, U.S. 395, U.S. 50, and Nev. 28): Remains of a small fort used by the U.S. Army in the 1860s in the war against the Paiute tribe. The fort also served as a staging post for the riders of the Pony Express. Visitor center open daily (702/577-2345).
On the way, visit **Virginia City** (see below).

☼⚜⚜ LAKE TAHOE (34 mi./54km SW via U.S. 395 and Nev.

431, or U.S. 395 and U.S. 50): Lying in the heart of the Sierra Nevada at an altitude of 6,230 ft. (1,900m), this superb mountain lake, its azure depths reaching down to 1,600 ft. (490m), is among the country's greatest tourist attractions. The clarity of the lake dazzles visitors who gaze through many fathoms of water at objects far below on the sandy bottom. In fact, Lake Tahoe is reputed to be the purest body of water in the world. Surrounded by granite peaks and coniferous forests, this immense stretch of water (200 sq. mi./520km^2) is bordered by a very beautiful scenic road about 72 mi. (116km) long. At the southwestern end of the lake, be sure to see the enchanting **Emerald Bay** and **Eagle Falls,** which plunges 1,508 ft. (460m) down the mountainside.
There are many hotels and restaurants in South Lake Tahoe, Incline Village, Crystal Bay, Stateline, and other towns on the lake (see Lake Tahoe "Accommodations" and "Restaurants," above).
Ideal for lovers of water sports, the lake has no fewer than 12 public beaches. Paddlewheel-boat trips aboard the M.S. *Dixie* depart from the Zephyr Cove Marina, 4 mi. (6.5km) north of Stateline on U.S. 50 (702/588-3508), open daily mid-May to Oct; or the *Tahoe Queen* departs from the Ski Run Marina, at the foot of Ski Run Blvd., South Lake Tahoe (916/541-3364), open daily year round. Lake Tahoe alone is worth the trip to Reno.

☼⚜ LASSEN VOLCANIC NATIONAL PARK (150 mi./

240km NW via U.S. 395, Calif. 36, and Calif. 89): The southernmost outpost of a long chain of volcanic mountains in the Cascade Range, which stretches from Mt. Baker, Mt. Rainier, and Mt. St. Helens (Washington) in the north, by way of Mt. Hood and Crater Lake (Oregon) in the middle, to

Mt. Shasta (California) in the south, Lassen Peak is one of the only two active volcanos in the continental U.S. (the other is Mt. St. Helens).

Lassen Peak, named after the Danish explorer Peter Lassen, has not erupted since 1921, but it could happen at any time. The landscape is strange and awe-inspiring, with desolate fields of lava, black ash, plumes of smoke and sulfurous vapors, little lakes teeming with fish, thick forests, and muddy hot springs. The 10,457-ft. (3,187m) summit of Lassen Peak, with a superb panoramic view of the area, can be reached by a two- to three-hour walk up a marked trail. There is also a fine scenic drive 30 mi. (48km) long between the park's southern entrance and Manzanita Lake (Lassen Park Rd.).

The park is open year round, but heavy snowslides prevent access to Lassen Park Rd. and certain areas of the park from late Oct through early June. Seven fully equipped campgrounds. For **information,** contact the Superintendent, Lassen Volcanic National Park, Mineral, CA 96063 (916/595-4444). **Visitor center** open in summer on Manzanita Lake.

Where to Stay

Childs Meadow Resort, on Calif. 89 (P.O. Box 3000), Mill Creek, CA 96061 (916/595-3383), 9 mi. (14km) south from the SW entrance of the park. 47 rustic but comfortable motel rms. I

PYRAMID LAKE (36 mi./58km NE via I-80 and Nev. 447; return by Nev. 445): Last vestige of the prehistoric inland sea known as Lake Lahontan, Pyramid Lake, 30 mi. (48km) long by 9 mi. (14km) wide, is strangely beautiful, surrounded by bald and barren mountains whose tawny red hues are reflected in its crystalline blue waters. Gen. John C. Frémont, the first European to explore the region, in 1844 christened it Pyramid Lake because of the conical shape of several islands of porous volcanic rock that rise from its center. The largest, Anahoe Island, serves as a sanctuary for a colony of 10,000 white pelicans. Pyramid Lake is also famous for its rainbow and cutthroat trout, which weigh up to 50 lb. (23kg), as well as for the curious qui-ui fish, a prehistoric survival. Fishing permits are issued at the Pyramid Lake Marina (702/476-1156). The northern part of the lake, with its strange lunar landscapes, is sacred ground to the Paiute people, and off-limits to tourists.

VIRGINIA CITY (25 mi./40km SE on U.S. 395 and Nev. 341): This, the most famous mining town of the Old West, is not, properly speaking, a ghost town—about 700 people still live here today. Founded in 1859 on the site of the richest vein of gold and silver in Nevada, the legendary Comstock Lode—which alone produced more than $1 billion worth of precious metals—Virginia City in its heyday during the 1870s boasted up to 30,000 inhabitants. As evidence of its unabashed wealth at the time, the town could show off four banks, six churches, a luxurious opera house in which the great Caruso once sang, six theaters, and the only elevator between Chicago and San Francisco, not to mention 110 saloons, by official count.

Clinging to the slopes of Mt. Davidson, Virginia City has been in large part restored as it was in its golden age in the 19th century, its principal street (C St.) lined with covered galleries and wooden sidewalks, many small museums (**The Way It Was Museum, The Wild West Museum, Nevada State Fire Museum,** etc.), the offices of the *Territorial Enterprise,* where Mark Twain worked as a reporter, and many saloons with picturesque names (the Bucket of Blood Saloon, the Delta Saloon with its famed Suicide Table, etc.). Also not to be missed are **Piper's Opera House,** B and Union Sts. (702/847-0433), open daily June through Sept, on weekends in May and Oct (by appointment the rest of the year), and **The Castle,** a luxurious Norman-style manor built in 1868 by the superintendent of the Empire Mine, at 70 B St. (702/847-0275), open daily Memorial Day–Oct.

An entertaining little steam train, the **Virginia and Truckee Railroad** (702/

847-0380), operating daily May–Sept, links Virginia City with Gold Hill. Truly spectacular **camel and ostrich races** take place on the second weekend in Sept. Visitor center, on C St. between Taylor and Union Sts. (702/847-0177), open daily.

Where to Stay En Route

☀☉♀♀ **The Gold Hill Hotel,** on Nev. 341 (P.O. Box 304), Virginia City, NV 89440 (702/847-0111). 14 rms. Nevada's oldest hotel (1859). Rooms furnished w. period antiques (some w. fireplaces). Charming and colorful. Very acceptable rest. (Crown Point). **I–M**

☀♠♠♠ **YOSEMITE NATIONAL PARK** (177 mi./283km south on U.S. 395 and Calif. 120): Breathtaking waterfalls and superb granite peaks. One of the two or three most beautiful national parks in the U.S. Note that Calif. 120 is closed in winter, necessitating a detour on Calif. 108. For more information, see Chapter 53 on Yosemite National Park.

FARTHER AFIELD

♠♠ **LAKE TAHOE & VIRGINIA CITY** (145 mi./232km r.t. via U.S. 395S, Nev. 431S, Calif. 28S, Calif. 89S, U.S. 50E, Nev. 341N, and U.S. 395N): Your first stop will be at **Mount Rose Ski Resort,** a very popular winter sports resort in a lovely natural setting. Make a detour to see ☀♠♠**Ponderosa Ranch** at Incline Village, (see "Theme Parks," above).

Then take the successive scenic highways along ☀♠♠ **Lake Tahoe,** with its splendid scenery (Calif. 28, Calif. 89, and U.S. 50; see "Nearby Excursions," above). Along the way, don't miss **Squaw Valley,** the famous resort where the 1960 Winter Olympics were held. At the southern end of the lake, stop off at beautiful ☀♠♠ **Emerald Bay State Park,** where the water is as clear as crystal. At **Stateline,** on the California-Nevada border, there are many luxury hotels and casinos.

Now on to ♠ **Carson City,** the state capital and a city of Victorian charm (see "Nearby Excursions," above).

Your last stop on this two- or three-day journey should be at ☀♠♠ **Virginia City,** the most famous gold-rush town in the West, which looks like something out of a John Ford or Sam Peckinpah movie. Then back to Reno on U.S. 395N.

CHAPTER 50

SAN FRANCISCO 🍦🍦🍦

□ □ □

And the California Wine Country

They say that "If you live in San Francisco, you never have to take a vacation." Where else would you find a more beautiful sight than its bay? Or a more enjoyable climate than the 59° F (15° C) average, winter and summer alike, which makes San Francisco the world's first naturally air-conditioned city? Visitors—about 13 million of them every year—and longtime residents alike share a love at first sight for this charming, colorful city. Generating about $3 billion in revenue annually, tourism is the city's No. 1 industry.

Luxurious mansions jostling little pastel-colored cottages on steep hillsides; the old **cable cars** struggling up, or hurtling down, the precipitous streets; the cutting edge of the **Transamerica Pyramid** towering above the exotic pagodas of Chinatown, one of the largest Far Eastern communities outside Asia; the huge, flamboyant silhouette of the **Golden Gate Bridge** framed against the Pacific; the splendid backdrop of **San Francisco Bay,** with the dark island of Alcatraz anchored amid its icy blue waves, especially at sunset—all these are the details of an amazing urban composition. San Francisco, "the Pearl of the West Coast," tops the list of cities "where every American dreams of going to live."

Although today's San Francisco, standing at the crossroads of East and West, is one of the world's great financial clearinghouses, the city came on the scene comparatively late. The first men to explore the Pacific coast, Portuguese Juan Rodríguez Cabrillo and English Sir Francis Drake, both missed the narrow passage into the bay. It was not until 1776 that the great Franciscan missionary to California, Fray Junípero Serra, built the **Mission Dolores,** dedicated to St. Francis of Assisi, a little south of the site of the present imposing City Hall. At the same time, there arose on what is now **Portsmouth Square,** at the edge of Chinatown, a hamlet which the Spaniards called Yerba Buena ("Good Herbs"). Some 70 years later, on July 19, 1846, when Capt. John B. Montgomery of the U.S.S. *Portsmouth* took possession of the town in the name of the people of the United States, it was still no more than a little settlement of trappers and whalers.

The discovery in 1848 of the first veins of gold in California's rocks touched off the famous "gold rush" in the following year, and the population of the town exploded in the space of two years from 900 inhabitants to 50,000. Since then nothing—not even the terrible earthquake of 1906, which registered 8.2 on the Richter Scale, or the conflagration that followed it—has impaired the magnetic attraction of "Baghdad by the Bay" for generations of immigrants. Chinese, Mexicans, Japanese, Italians, White Russians, South Americans, French Basques, Filipinos, Germans, and Irish have all been drawn hither, and have all contributed to the city's cosmopolitan character. Even now, 43% of its inhabitants are first- or second-generation Americans, and newspapers are published here in 13 languages including English. The beneficent effects of the melting pot have made of this polyglot place the most amusing, the most tolerant, and one of the most sophisticated cities in the U.S. San Francisco has more gay people (100,000) of both sexes in relation to its population (barely 730,000 inhabitants) than any other American city; there are even gay deputy mayors on the city council of America's "spiritual capital" of homosexuality. This same respect for minority rights, reinforced by a tradition of nonconformity, has allowed a number of contemporary ideologies to flourish in San Francisco: the beatniks in the '50s, student protest at **Berkeley** and the hippies in the '60s, the psychedelic movement at the beginning of the '70s, and so on. The flip side of the coin is a disquieting multiplication of sects, "religions," and extremist groups.

Another cloud on the horizon is the proximity of the **San Andreas Fault,** which runs 560 mi. (900km) along the California coast, and keeps San Francisco permanently at risk of another earthquake like that of 1906, or the one of Oct 1989, more vivid in everyone's memory (66 people dead, more than $7 billion in property damage); there's even a telephone number (329-4025) to call for current information on shocks registered by local seismographs.

Continuing a century-old tradition, three renowned universities, the Roman Catholic **University of San Francisco,** founded in 1855, with 7,000 students; the **University of California at Berkeley,** founded in 1868, with 32,000 students; and **Stanford University** at **Palo Alto,** founded in 1891, with 13,000 students, makes San Francisco one of the most important centers of higher education and research in the country.

No trip to California can be called complete without an attentive visit to this joyful, flamboyant city which has inspired so many poets, movie directors, novelists, and songwriters, and which has served as a photogenic backdrop to dozens of movies and television shows from *Bullitt* to *Vertigo* and from *The Maltese Falcon* to *Presidio.* From the gaudy frontages of Chinatown to the sublime panorama of the bay seen from the Golden Gate, by way of the roller-coaster contours of **Telegraph Hill,** the arrogant high-rises of the **Financial District,** where such great corporations as Chevron, Bank of America, Bechtel, Wells Fargo, and Levi Strauss make their headquarters, or the sea scent of **Fisherman's Wharf,** San Francisco is unique. Its immediate, and more distant, surroundings are in themselves worth the visit, beginning with the charming little ports of **Sausalito** and **Tiburon** across the bay, and moving on to the renowned vineyards of the **Napa Valley,** the magnificent **Seventeen-Mile Drive** between Monterey and Carmel —one of the most spectacular highways in the U.S.—and the legendary **Silicon Valley,** headquarters of electronics research and development for the entire country, with one of the heaviest concentrations of high-tech industries in the world. As for longer trips, the motorist's hardest problem is to choose among **Sequoia** and **Yosemite National Parks** (see Chapters 52 and 53), the mountain grandeur of **Lake Tahoe** (see Chapter 49 on Reno), or Calif. 1, the wonderful coast road from San Francisco to Los Angeles, better known as the **Cabrillo Hwy.** (see Chapter 51 on the California Coast).

Food is not the least of San Francisco's attractions. With New York, Los Angeles, and New Orleans, the Golden Gate City is one of the four gastronomic capitals of the U.S. Its Chinese and Japanese restaurants are among the best in the world, and its French and Italian restaurants are as good, not to mention its renowned restaurants serving seafood and a gamut of exotic cuisines: Korean, Filipino, Mexican, Indian, Javanese, Armenian, Caribbean, Vietnamese, and many more. In spite of their boast that their city has more restaurants per capita (more than 3,500) than any other in the country, the favorite sport of San Franciscans seems to be discovering new ones. Note, also, that although the city claims more international-class hotels for its size than any other city in the U.S., they're often completely booked; reservations should be made far in advance.

There is no end to the list of the city's famous children. They include writers Jack London and Irving Stone, poet Robert Frost, movie director Mervin LeRoy, newspaper magnate William Randolph Hearst, dancer Isadora Duncan, banker and statesman Robert S. McNamara, actor Clint Eastwood, musician Carlos Santana, and singer Johnny Mathis.

Warning: Never use the abbreviation "Frisco" for "San Francisco"; the inhabitants consider it insulting.

BASIC FACTS: State of California. Area code: 415 (and 510 for the East Bay). Time zone: Pacific. ZIP Code: 94101. Founded: 1776. Approximate population: city, 730,000; metropolitan area, 6,250,000. Fourth-largest metropolitan area in the U.S.

CLIMATE: "Disconcerting" is the mildest word that can be applied to San Francisco's climate; Mark Twain wrote, "The coldest winter I ever spent was a summer in San Francisco." There are so many micro-climates that meteorologists run out of technical terms for them. In broad terms, late spring, summer, and a good part of the fall are sunny but cool; temperatures average 61°F (16°C) June–Oct. Winter is gloomier, though the mercury rarely drops below 58°F (10°C) in Dec–Jan. Showers are frequent Nov–Mar, as is morning fog over the bay in summer and fall.

DISTANCES: Denver, 1,234 mi. (1,975km); Las Vegas, 568 mi. (908km); Los Angeles, 381 mi. (608km); Portland, 634 mi. (1,015km); Reno, 229 mi. (366km); Salt Lake City, 750 mi. (1,200km).

ARRIVAL & TRANSIT INFORMATION

AIRPORTS: The **Oakland International Airport** (OAK), 18 mi. (28km) SE (510/577-4000).
 San Francisco International Airport (SFO), 16 mi. (26km) south (415/761-0800), one of the most up-to-date in the country, ranking fifth in volume of traffic among U.S. airports (31 million passengers per year), but ranks at the bottom among major airports in terms of on-time arrival of planes.

U.S. AIRLINES: Alaska (toll free 800/426-0333), American (toll free 800/433-7300), Continental (toll free 800/525-0280), Delta (toll free 800/221-1212), Hawaiian (toll free 800/367-5320), Northwest (toll free 800/225-2525), TWA (toll free 800/221-2000), United (toll free 800/241-6522), and USAir (toll free 800/428-4322).

FOREIGN CARRIERS: Air Canada (toll free 800/776-3000), Air France (toll free 800/237-2747), British Airways (toll free 800/247-9297), Canadian Airlines International (toll free 800/426-7000), Japan Air Lines (toll free 800/525-3663), KLM (toll free 800/374-7747), Lufthansa (toll free 800/645-3880), Quantas (toll free 800/227-4500), and Virgin Atlantic (toll free 800/862-8621).

CITY LINK: The **cab** fare from the San Francisco airport to dwntwn is about $30; time, about 35 min. (45 min. during rush hour). Cab fare from the Oakland airport to dwntwn, about $30; time, about 35 min. Bus: **Airporter** (495-8404), leaving the San Francisco airport every 10 min.; serves principal hotels dwntwn, in the financial district, and around Fisherman's Wharf, and the Airlines Terminal at Taylor and Ellis Sts.; fare $8; time, about 40 min. The **Bayporter Express** (467-1800) also links the Oakland airport and the Airlines Terminal; fare, $11; time, 50 min. Van: **Bay Area SuperShuttle** (558-8500) serves all the dwntwn hotels; fare $10.

The **public transportation system,** both surface by bus and streetcar, MUNI (673-6864), and by express subway, BART (788-2278), is excellent throughout the Bay Area. Be sure to pick up a **MUNI Passport,** available at the Visitor Information Center at Hallidie Plaza (see "Information and Tours," below), which entitles you to rides for one day ($6), three days ($10), or one week ($15) on all forms of municipal transport, including the cable car. Cabs are nu merous but very expensive.

Given the attractive rates offered in California and the large number of enticing excursions around San Francisco, it's highly advisable to rent a car with unlimited mileage. *Warning:* When parking on a hill in San Francisco, it's mandatory to turn your front wheels inward toward the curb to prevent the vehicle from slipping.

CAR RENTALS (at the San Francisco International Airport unless otherwise indicated): Avis (toll free 800/331-1212); Budget (toll free 800/527-0700); Dollar (toll free 800/800-4000); Hertz (toll free 800/654-3131); National (toll free 800/227-7368); Bob Leech's Auto Rental, 435 S. Airport Blvd., South San Francisco (583-2727), a local agency with attractive rates; Thrifty, 309 E. Millbrae Ave., Millbrae (toll free 800/367-2277). For dwntwn locations, consult the local telephone directory.

LIMOUSINE SERVICES: Carey Limousine (468-7550), Dav El Limousines (toll free 800/922-0343), and Regency Limousine (922-0123).

TAXIS: Cabs may rarely be hailed on the street, but can be found on the waiting lines outside major hotels, or better still, summoned by phone. Fares are very high. Try **DeSoto Cab** (673-1414), **Luxor Cab** (282-4141), **Veteran's Cab** (552-1300), or **Yellow Cab** (626-2345).

TRAIN: Amtrak, Transbay Terminal, 425 Mission St., at 1st St. (toll free 800/ 872-7245); avoid this neighborhood after dark. There is a regular shuttle-bus link with the station at Oakland, terminus for the major routes to the east and along the Pacific coast.

INTERCITY BUSES: Greyhound, 425 Mission St. (toll free 800/231-2222).

FERRIES: Golden Gate Ferries, Ferry Bldg., Market St. (332-6600): Service to Sausalito.
Red & White Fleet, Pier 41, Fisherman's Wharf (546-2628): Service to Tiburon, Angel Island, and Vallejo.

INFORMATION & TOURS

TOURIST INFORMATION: The **San Francisco Convention and Visitors Bureau,** 201 3rd St., CA 94101 (415/974-6900).
Visitor Information Center, Hallidie Plaza, Powell and Market Sts. (415/ 391-2000).
International Visitors Center, 312 Sutter St., Suite 402 (415/986-1388): Reception facilities for foreign visitors.
San Francisco Chamber of Commerce, 465 California St., CA 94104 (415/392-4511).
For a **telephone recording** with an up-to-date listing of cultural events and shows, call 415/391-2001.

GUIDED TOURS: Alcatraz Tours (boat), Pier 41, The Embarcadero (546-2628): Guided tours of the penitentiary; it's advisable to make resv., one or more days in advance in summer.
Bay cruises (boat), Blue & Gold Fleet, Pier 39, The Embarcadero (705-

5444), and Red & White Fleet, Pier 41, The Embarcadero (546-2628): Boat trips on the bay; wonderful views. Daily year round.

Chinatown Discovery Tours (walking), 812 Clay St. (982-8839): Behind-the-scenes tour includes a visit to a private Buddhist temple, an herb shop, and a fortune-cookie factory. Guided by a native of this bustling neighborhood.

Golden Gate Tours (bus), serving the principal hotels (788-5775): City and Bay Area tours.

Gray Line Tours (bus), 350 8th St. (558-9400): Many tours in the city and surroundings. Departs from Union Sq. (Powell and Geary Sts.).

San Francisco Helicopter Tours (helicopter) (635-4500): Helicopter flights over the bay; unforgettable. Daily.

Tower Tours (minibus), 77 Jefferson St. (434-8687): Visits to the wine cellars of Napa Valley; also one-day trips to Carmel, Monterey, Yosemite National Park, and Muir Woods.

Wine Adventures, Inc. (bus), P.O. Box 3273, Yountville, CA 94599 (707/257-0353): One- or several-day visits to Wine Country cellars; limo transfer from San Francisco.

SIGHTS, ATTRACTIONS & ACTIVITIES

ARCHITECTURAL HIGHLIGHTS: ☼▨▨ **Alcatraz Island,** a rocky island in the bay, reached by boat from Pier 41 (556-0560): Nicknamed "The Rock," this former fort, converted in 1934 to a high-security prison, numbered among its famous inmates Al Capone, Alvin Karpis, Robert Stroud (alias "The Birdman of Alcatraz"), "Doc" Barker, and "Machine Gun" Kelly. Owes its name to the innumerable pelicans (*alcatraces* in Spanish) that used to roost there. Reputed to be "the prison from which no one escapes," the penitentiary was closed in 1963 by order of then–Attorney General Robert Kennedy because of its excessive operating costs; it has been converted into a museum visited by 800,000 people a year. It was occupied by a group of Native Americans 1969–71, by way of a symbolic protest. The visit is worthwhile, because the experience is unique and the island affords you an otherwise-unobtainable view of the bay, but it's a tiring excursion. Open daily (see "Guided Tours," above).

▨ **Castro Theater,** Castro and Market Sts. (621-6120): Extravagant 1930s-style movie house in the heart of the gay district. Shows American and foreign classics, complete with an organist and enthusiastic audiences.

▨ **Center for the Arts at Yerba Buena Gardens,** Third St., between Mission and Howard Sts. (978-2787): The most recent architectural and cultural endowment to San Francisco, a $44-million project, is the showcase for three distinctly designed structures: the visual arts building, designed by Japanese architect Fumihiko Maki; the theater building, designed by James Stewart Polshek; and the new **Museum of Modern Art,** designed by Swiss architect Mario Botta (scheduled to open Jan 1995). Also part of the center is a tree-lined esplanade, replete with an outdoor theater and cafés.

▨ **City Hall,** Civic Center Plaza (554-4000): Imposing 1915 building in the French classical revival idiom, capped by a dome higher than the Capitol's in Washington.

☼▨ **Embarcadero Center,** Clay and Sacramento Sts. between Drumm and Battery Sts.: The new business district, with a group of high-rises by well-known architect John Portman. Pedestrian walkways at several levels, fountains, modern sculpture, open-air concerts on fine days.

▨ **Ferry Building,** Embarcadero and Market St. (332-6600): Once the terminal for the ferries that crisscrossed the bay in all directions before the construction of the Golden Gate and Bay Bridges. Its 236-ft. (72m) tower, erected in 1903, is a copy of the Moorish La Giralda tower in Seville. Today it houses the Port Authority; ferries leave for Sausalito from the southern end of the building.

✳☀⚲⚲⚲ **Golden Gate Bridge,** linking San Francisco to Sausalito, to the north of the bay: Designed by Joseph Strauss, the world's most famous (and most beautiful) bridge was built between 1933 and 1937 at a cost of $35 million. Its construction was a technological masterpiece, involving 200,000 tons of steel, 523,000 cu. yds. (400,000m³) of concrete, and 80 mi. (128km) of high-tension steel cable. It's also the world's "deadliest" bridge; 11 people were killed during construction, and another 700 have committed suicide from it since it was opened on May 28, 1937. The shining Golden Gate Bridge towers 220 ft. (67m) above the waters of the bay, and is used every day by almost 120,000 vehicles. Maintenance for the two 746-ft. (227m) towers and the 8,856-ft. (2.7km) span is provided by a team of 25 painters, who use two tons of red lead every week. Unforgettable view of San Francisco and the bay (overlook parking at the north end of the bridge). There's a toll, for southbound vehicles only. Worth the trip to San Francisco all by itself.

⚲ **Levi Strauss Factory,** 250 Valencia St. (565-9153): This is where, in 1853, a Bavarian immigrant named Levi Strauss created history's first pair of blue jeans—and it's still operating. Adopted first by the miners of the gold rush, then by cowboys, blue jeans still serve as an emblem of American life. Tours Wed. Resv. requested.

✳☀⚲ **Louise M. Davies Symphony Hall,** Van Ness Ave. and Grove St. (431-5400): Home of the San Francisco Symphony Orchestra. Opened in 1980, this ultramodern 3,000-seat concert hall by Skidmore, Owings and Merrill has extremely sophisticated acoustics.

⚲ **Marriott Hotel,** 55 4th St. (896-1600): Nicknamed "The Wurlitzer," this 40-floor tower looking like a jukebox or a giant thermometer is San Francisco's most controversial building. Designed by California architect Tony Lumsden, the 1,500-room hotel opened in 1989. Its two-colored mirror-glass frontage has a certain shock value.

✳☀⚲⚲ **Transamerica Pyramid,** 600 Montgomery St. (983-4000): Designed by architect William L. Pereira, this 48-floor pyramid capped by a knife-edged point cost $34 million to build, and is considered by many to be the most spectacular and original high-rise in the U.S. Since the 853-ft. (260m) building was completed in 1972, it has become one of the emblems of San Francisco. There's an observation deck on the 27th floor.

⚲ **War Memorial Opera House,** Van Ness Ave. and Grove St. (864-3330): Home of the San Francisco Opera since its inauguration (1932). In 1945 the United Nations came into existence in this auditorium, and in 1951 it witnessed the signing of the American-Japanese peace treaty.

BEACHES: ⚲ **Baker Beach,** Lincoln Blvd., Presidio: Wonderful for sunbathing, but no swimming allowed.

⚲ **China Beach,** Sea Cliff and 29th Aves.: Small fine-sand, wind-protected beach near Lincoln Park; swimming permitted in summer.

⚲ **Ocean Beach,** Great Highway: 4 mi. (6km) of beaches and dunes, much frequented by hang-glider enthusiasts. Swimming here is unsafe.

⚲ **Stinson Beach,** 16 mi. (25km) NW on Calif. 1: Pretty beach at the foot of a mountain; swimming permitted in summer.

CABLE CARS: San Francisco's open-air ✳⚲⚲ **cable cars**—drawn by cables as the name implies—the city's most famous tourist attraction since 1873, were suspended from service from Sept 1982 to the spring of 1984 for an overhaul of their traction system. Since this involuntary interruption, the city's engaging streetcars, with standing passengers clustering on the steps like bunches of grapes, are once again scaling the steep streets of Nob Hill and Russian Hill, whose gradient in places reaches 21%. Of the 19th century's eight lines and 112 mi. (180km) of area reached, only three lines remain today, covering 11 mi. (17km): No. 59 (Powell-Mason), No. 60 (Hyde-Powell), and No. 61 (California –Van Ness). There's a flat $2 fare; the most scenic line is No. 60, from Hyde St. to Powell St.

CHURCHES/SYNAGOGUES: ☼⚱ St. Mary's Cathedral, Geary and Gough Sts. (567-2020): San Francisco's new (1970) cathedral, a spectacular modern building designed by Italian architect Pier Luigi Nervi on the site of the old basilica, which burned down in 1962. It comprises four soaring vaults of concrete clad in white Italian travertine, which meet at a height of 196 ft. (60m) in the shape of a cross. See the futuristic sculpture above the altar. Open daily.

HISTORIC BUILDINGS: ☼⚱ Haas-Lilienthal House, 2007 Franklin St. (441-3004): Dating from 1886, this magnificent example of Queen Anne–style Victorian is one of the few private houses that survived the 1906 earthquake. Very fine furniture of the period. Open Wed and Sun afternoons.

☼⚱🔭 **Mission Dolores** (sometimes called **Mission San Francisco de Asis**), 16th and Dolores Sts. (621-8203): Sixth of the 21 missions built in California by the Franciscan Fr. Junípero Serra, this is the historic birthplace of San Francisco (1776). A fine Spanish Colonial building of white-washed adobe brick that survived four major earthquakes. In the little cemetery adjoining are the graves of the first settlers and of the Native Americans who built the mission. Beside it, and in startling contrast to the primitive humility of the mission itself, is the huge Basilica of Mission Dolores (1916), a pompous piece of Spanish-Mexican baroque. Open daily.

MUSEUMS OF ART: ☼🔭 Asian Art Museum, Golden Gate Park (668-8921): The collection of Avery Brundage, once president of the International Olympic Committee, includes more than 10,000 works of art from Japan, China, Korea, etc., some more than 3,000 years old; their value, particularly that of the T'ang ceramics and the Khmer sculptures, is impossible to estimate. Because of the size and importance of the collection, it is exhibited in rotation. One of the most beautiful Far Eastern museums in the world, housed in the west wing of the M. H. De Young Museum (see below). Open Wed–Sun.

☼🔭 **California Palace of the Legion of Honor,** Lincoln Park (750-3600): Master paintings from the 16th to the 20th century: Fragonard, Georges de la Tour, Corot, Monet, Cézanne, etc. Fine Gobelins tapestries and an exceptional graphic-arts collection with more than 100,000 drawings, engravings, and illustrated books. Sculptures by Rodin. Among the best-known works on display are a *Madonna and Child* by Tintoretto, El Greco's *St. John the Baptist,* and Frans Hals's *Cavalier in White.* The Beaux Arts building, dating from 1924, is an exact replica of the Palace of the Legion of Honor in Paris. Fine surrounding park and splendid view of the Golden Gate. (Open Wed–Sun; closed for renovation until Fall 1995.)

⚱ **Mexican Museum,** Fort Mason Center, Bldg. D, Laguna St. and Marina Blvd. S. (441-0404): Temporary exhibitions and permanent collection of Mexican art from the pre-Columbian and colonial periods to the present day. Also works by modern Mexican-American artists. Open Wed–Sun. Scheduled to move to the Center for the Arts at Yerba Buena Gardens in Jan 1995. (See "Architectural Highlights," above.)

☼🔭 **M. H. De Young Museum,** Golden Gate Park (750-3600): The city's most diversified museum boasting 22 galleries of American art ranging from the 17th century to the 20th, from Copley, Homer, and Whistler to Cassatt, Willson Peale, and Demuth. No less impressive are the collec-

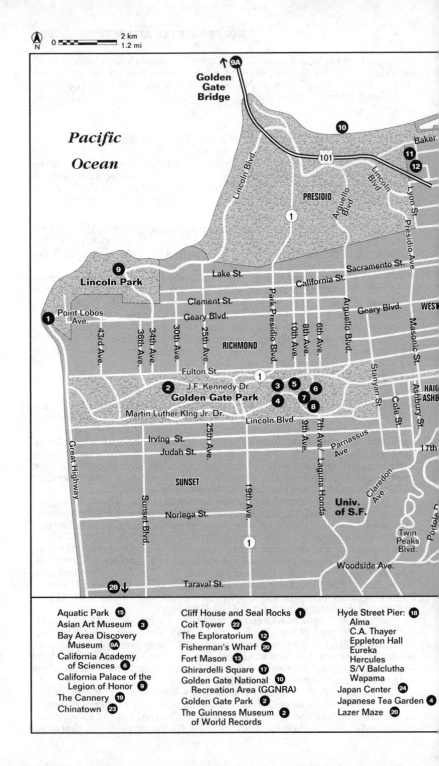

N 0 2 km / 1.2 mi

Pacific Ocean

Golden Gate Bridge

PRESIDIO

Baker

Lincoln Blvd.

101

Arguello Blvd.

Lyon St.

Presidio Ave.

Lincoln Park

Point Lobos Ave.

Lake St.

California St.

Sacramento St.

Clement St.

Geary Blvd.

Geary Blvd.

WEST

43rd Ave.

36th Ave.

34th Ave.

30th Ave.

25th Ave.

Park Presidio Blvd.

10th Ave.

8th Ave.

6th Ave.

Arguello Blvd.

Masonic Ave.

RICHMOND

Fulton St.

J.F. Kennedy Dr.

Golden Gate Park

Martin Luther King Jr. Dr.

Lincoln Blvd.

Stanyan St.

Cole St.

Ashbury St.

HAIG ASHB

Irving St.

Judah St.

25th Ave.

9th Ave.

7th Ave./ Laguna Honda

Parnassus Ave.

Claredon Ave.

17th

Great Highway

Sunset Blvd.

SUNSET

19th Ave.

Noriega St.

Univ. of S.F.

Twin Peaks Blvd.

Portola D

Woodside Ave.

Taraval St.

Aquatic Park **15**
Asian Art Museum **3**
Bay Area Discovery Museum **9A**
California Academy of Sciences **6**
California Palace of the Legion of Honor **9**
The Cannery **19**
Chinatown **23**

Cliff House and Seal Rocks **1**
Coit Tower **22**
The Exploratorium **12**
Fisherman's Wharf **20**
Fort Mason **13**
Ghirardelli Square **17**
Golden Gate National Recreation Area (GGNRA) **10**
Golden Gate Park **2**
The Guinness Museum of World Records **2**

Hyde Street Pier: **18**
Alma
C.A. Thayer
Eppleton Hall
Eureka
Hercules
S/V Balclutha
Wapama
Japan Center **24**
Japanese Tea Garden **4**
Lazer Maze **20**

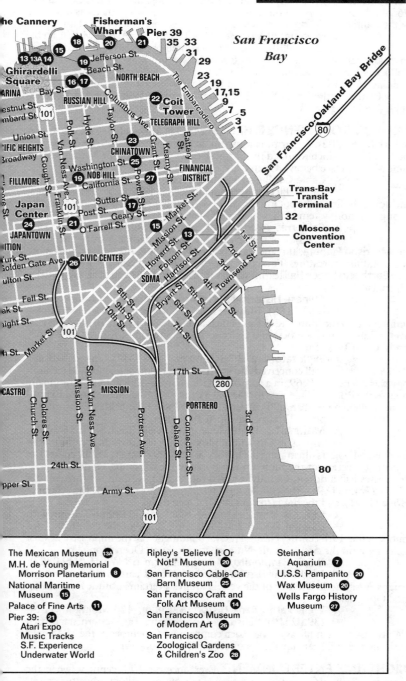

SAN FRANCISCO

The Cannery
Fisherman's Wharf
Pier 39
18
15
20
21
35 33
31
29
San Francisco Bay

13 13A 14
19 Jefferson St.
Beach St.
23
19
17,15
9
7 5
3
1

Ghirardelli Square
16 17
NORTH BEACH
MARINA Bay St.
RUSSIAN HILL Columbus Ave.
22 Coit Tower
TELEGRAPH HILL

estnut St.
mbard St. 101
Union St.
IFIC HEIGHTS
Broadway
Hyde St.
Taylor St.
The Embarcadero
Battery St.

San Francisco-Oakland Bay Bridge

Gough St.
Van Ness Ave.
Polk St.
23
CHINATOWN
25
27
Kearny St.
Grant St.
FINANCIAL DISTRICT
80

FILLMORE
19 NOB HILL
Washington St.
California St.
Powell St.

Japan Center
24
101
Franklin St.
Sutter St.
17 Post St.
Geary St.
15
Market St.
Mission St.
13
Trans-Bay Transit Terminal
32
Moscone Convention Center

JAPANTOWN
ITION
21
O'Farrell St.
Howard St.
Folsom St.
Harrison St.
1st St.
2nd St.

urk St.
Golden Gate Ave.
26 CIVIC CENTER
ulton St.
SOMA
Bryant St.
5th St.
6th St.
3rd St.
Townsend St.
St.

Fell St.
ak St.
hight St.
8th St.
9th St.
10th St.
7th St.

h St. Market St. 101

17th St.
280

CASTRO
MISSION
PORTRERO
South Van Ness Ave.
Mission St.
Dolores St.
Church St.
Pottrero Ave.
Connecticut St.
Deharo St.
3rd St.

80

24th St.
pper St.
Army St.
101

The Mexican Museum 13A
M.H. de Young Memorial Morrison Planetarium 8
National Maritime Museum 15
Palace of Fine Arts 11
Pier 39: 21
    Atari Expo
    Music Tracks
    S.F. Experience
    Underwater World

Ripley's "Believe It Or Not!" Museum 20
San Francisco Cable-Car Barn Museum 25
San Francisco Craft and Folk Art Museum 14
San Francisco Museum of Modern Art 26
San Francisco Zoological Gardens & Children's Zoo 28

Steinhart Aquarium 7
U.S.S. Pampanito 20
Wax Museum 20
Wells Fargo History Museum 27

tions of textiles, African art, and ancient art from Mesoamerica and Central and 963South America. All of this is housed in an 1894 building that was once part of the Californian Midwinter International Exposition. Open Wed–Sun.

    Museum of Modern Art, 401 Van Ness Ave. at McAllister St. (252-4000): The best of contemporary art; hundreds of remarkable paintings and sculptures from Matisse and Mark Rothko to Jackson Pollock. Occupies the third and fourth floors of the War Memorial Veterans Building. Open Tues–Sun. The museum is scheduled to move to a new building at the Center for the Arts at Yerba Buena Gardens in Jan 1995. (See "Architectural Highlights," above.)

MUSEUMS OF SCIENCE & HISTORY: *Balclutha,* Hyde St. Pier, Aquatic Park (556-3002): A maritime museum, in an authentic British Cape Horner, built in 1886, which rounded the Horn 17 times. It's part of the National Maritime Museum (see below). Open daily.

    Cable Car Barn Museum, Washington and Mason Sts. (474-1887): Picturesque museum of San Francisco's own streetcars, including the first to be put into service in 1873. Movies, old photos, etc. See the strange traction system of the cable cars. Open daily.

    California Academy of Sciences, Golden Gate Park (750-7145): Comprehensive museum of natural history, including the **Morrison Planetarium** and the renowned **Steinhart Aquarium,** with more than 14,000 sea creatures. Fine collection of fossils and of North American birds. The **Earth and Space Hall** features a very realistic reproduction of an earthquake. Open daily.

    Chinese Historical Society of America, 650 Commercial St. (391-1188): Illustrates the important part played by Chinese immigrants in the founding of San Francisco and the settlement of the American West. Unusual mementoes; fine collection of photographs. A must for history buffs. Open Tues–Sat.

    Exploratorium, 3601 Lyon St. (563-7337): This remarkably well conceived and instructive museum of science and technology was opened in 1969, in a sort of imitation Greco-Roman temple originally built as the Palace of Fine Arts for the 1915 Panama-Pacific International Exposition. It offers more than 600 participatory exhibits in the fields of science, art, and human perception. Fascinating. Open Tues–Sun.

    National Maritime Museum, Polk and Beach Sts. (556-3002): Interesting maritime museum in an Edwardian casino. Ship models and objects illustrating the history of navigation on the Pacific coast. The "floating" section of the museum is moored at the adjoining Hyde St. Pier: it comprises half a dozen carefully restored old ships, including the three-master *C. A. Thayer* (1895), the paddlewheel ferryboat *Eureka* (1890), the schooner *Alma* (1891), and the tug *Hercules* (1907). Open daily.

    Old U.S. Mint, 5th and Mission Sts. (744-6830): Along with those in Denver and Philadelphia, one of the country's three mints. A fine 19th-century classical revival building. Note the impressive heap of gold ingots in the circular vault. Numismatic museum. Open Mon–Fri.

    U.S.S. *Pampanito,* Pier 45, Fisherman's Wharf (929-0202): World War II submarine which took part in the Pacific campaigns. Visiting the interior of the vessel requires a certain aptitude for gymnastics! Open daily.

    Wells Fargo Bank History Museum, 420 Montgomery St. (396-2619): "History Room" with a Far Western stagecoach (Wells Fargo began life as a stagecoach company). Mementoes of the 1848 gold rush and the 1906 earthquake. Picturesque. Open Mon–Fri.

NIGHTTIME ENTERTAINMENT: Ever since the 19th century, when the legendary Barbary Coast was an irresistible attraction to sailors, adventurers, set-

tlers, and gold prospectors, San Francisco has always been broad-minded about its nightlife. Witness today the porno dives and risqué nightclubs of Broadway and Columbus Ave., the domain of the topless, of dancing nude couples, and of mud-wrestling women. The biggest concentration of nightlife is in the **North Beach** neighborhood, particularly around Washington Sq., but jazz joints, bars, nightclubs, comedy clubs, and discos flourish all over town. As a general rule, nightclubs are not permitted to serve alcoholic beverages after 2am (see "Bars and Nightclubs," below).

OUTDOOR ART & PLAZAS: & Embarcadero Center, Clay and Sacramen-

to Sts. between Drumm and Battery Sts.: The sidewalk galleries and plazas of this ultramodern complex are embellished with monumental sculptures by Willi Gutmann, Louise Nevelson, and Nicholas Schöffer, as well as with many paintings and tapestries. At the eastern end of the center is an astonishing futuristic fountain by Armand Vaillancourt.

    St. Mary's Square, California and Quincy Sts.: Resplendent stainless-steel statue by Benjamino Bufano of Sun Yat-sen, founder and first president (1911–12) of the Republic of China, who lived in San Francisco for a while.

PANORAMAS: & Bank of America, 555 California St. (433-7500): In the

heart of the financial district, the West Coast's answer to Wall Street. Bar-restaurant (so-so), the **Carnelian Room,** on the 52nd floor (admission charge); one of the finest views of the city. Open daily from 3pm.

    Coit Tower, Telegraph Hill Blvd. (362-0808): This 210-ft. (64m) tower, erected in 1933 on the top of Telegraph Hill as a memorial to the city's volunteer firemen, offers as beautiful a panorama of the bay as you're likely to find, especially at dawn or sunset. Beautiful mural frescoes. Open daily (elevator).

    Golden Gate Bridge, north of Presidio Park via U.S. 101: Wonderful panorama of the city and bay, looking south; overlook parking at the northern end of the bridge. Worth the trip all by itself (see "Architectural Highlights," above).

    San Francisco–Oakland Bay Bridge, between San Francisco and Oakland via I-80: Opened six months before the Golden Gate, on November 12, 1936, this enormous two-deck bridge has a particularly spectacular view of the city and bay, looking west (its upper deck was severely damaged by the earthquake of Oct. 1989).

    Sausalito and Tiburon: See "Nearby Excursions," below.

    Twin Peaks, Twin Peaks Blvd.: Nicknamed "los pechos de la Chola" (the Indian woman's breasts) by the first Spanish settlers, these twin peaks, 910 ft. (277m) high, are famous for their breathtaking view of San Francisco and the bay, particularly at twilight.

PARKS & GARDENS: ※& Acres of Orchids, 1450 El Camino Real (Calif.

82), South San Francisco (871-5655): The world's largest display of orchids and gardenias. Splendid tropical gardens. Guided tour of the laboratory where orchids are cloned. Fascinating. Open daily.

    Angel Island, in the bay, reached by boat from Pier 43½: Small garden-island reserved for pedestrians, cyclists, and picnickers, with dozens of free-roaming stags and does. Frequent boat service daily in summer; wknds only the rest of the year. Fine view of the town.

    Golden Gate Park, bounded by Lincoln Way, Great Hwy., Fulton St., and Stanyan St. (556-0560): Lying on the ocean to the west, this magnificent 1,017-acre (412ha) park, one of the most beautiful in the U.S., was reclaimed beginning in 1868 from a tract of bare sand dunes. Contains more than 6,000 different species of trees and plants, including acacia, spruce, and eucalyptus. Several museums (see above). Splendid Japanese garden and tropical hot houses.

☀☜♨ **Golden Gate Promenade,** Marine Dr. between Fort Point and Fort Mason: Landscaped park along the shore of the bay; from Fort Point you have a clear view of the bridge and the city skyline.

♨ **Harding Park,** Lake Merced and Sloat Blvds.: Huge oceanfront park taking in Lake Merced (canoeing, fishing), a modern zoo, and a public golf course. Very popular with San Franciscans in summer.

☀☜♨ **Lincoln Park,** 34th Ave. and Clement St.: On the ocean at the NW extremity of the city; very fine view of the Golden Gate Bridge, the city, and the Pacific.

☀☜♨ **The Presidio,** bounded by Lincoln Blvd., Mason St., W. Pacific Ave., and Lyon St. (561-4115): The headquarters of the U.S. Sixth Army is on the site occupied by the original Spanish garrison fort in 1776, and lies in 1,450 acres (588ha) of park and shady garden. Military museum open Tues–Sun. Enter from Lombard and Lyon Sts. to the east, or 25th Ave. and El Camino del Mar to the west; there's a lovely scenic drive between these two points.

♨ **Seal Rocks,** Point Lobos Ave.: Reefs thronged with elephant seals, sea lions, marine birds, and other ocean life; fine view.

♨ **Sigmund Stern Memorial Grove,** along Sloat Blvd. near 19th Ave. (252-6252): Natural amphitheater sheltered by eucalyptus, redwoods, and fir trees. On summer Sun afternoons hosts free outdoor concerts, Broadway musicals, operas, and ballets. This 63-acre (25.5ha) grove is also the perfect place for barbecues and picnics.

PERFORMING ARTS: For daily listings of all shows and cultural events, consult the entertainment pages of the daily papers *San Francisco Chronicle* (morning) and *San Francisco Examiner* (evening), especially their joint Sunday edition, as well as the monthly *San Francisco Focus* magazine.

Note that **TIX,** a kiosk on Stockton St. at Union Sq. (433-7827), provides half-price, in-person sales of unsold tickets for day-of-performance events. Cash only, Tues–Sat.

Center for the Arts at Yerba Buena Gardens, Third St., between Mission and Howard Sts. (978-2787): New arts complex that includes a proscenium theater, film and video theater, and outdoor theater. Classic and contemporary music, theater, dance, video, and film are all represented here. (See "Architectural Highlights," above.)

Civic Auditorium, Civic Center (431-5400): Recitals; concerts by the San Francisco Pops Orchestra.

Club Fugazzi, 678 Green St. (421-4222): An old North Beach standby; cabaret-style shows.

Curran Theater, 445 Geary St. (474-3800): Musicals, Broadway hits.

Golden Gate Theatre, 25 Taylor St. at Golden Gate and Market Sts. (474-3800): Contemporary theater, Broadway hits.

Herbst Theatre, Civic Center, 401 Van Ness Ave. (392-4400): Ballet, opera, concerts, children's shows.

Louise M. Davies Symphony Hall, Civic Center, 201 Van Ness Ave. (431-5400): Home of the San Francisco Symphony, under principal conductor Michael Tilson Thomas (Sept–May); recitals, concerts.

Magic Theater, Fort Mason Center, Bldg. D, Laguna St. and Marina Blvd. (441-8822): Modern and avant-garde theater.

Mason Street Theater, 340 Mason St. at Geary (982-5463): Off-Broadway theater, comedy.

Masonic Auditorium, 1111 California St. (776-4702): Classical concerts, recitals, ballet.

Orpheum Theatre, 1192 Market St. (474-3800): Drama, comedy, touring companies. Home of the Civic Light Opera (May–Dec).
Palace of Fine Arts Theatre, 3601 Lyon St. (567-6642): Opera, concerts. The International Film Festival is held here annually.
Sigmund Stern Memorial Grove, Sloat Blvd. and 19th Ave. (252-6252): A 25,000-seat open-air auditorium; symphony concerts, opera, jazz, ballet. Free shows every Sun at 2pm June to mid-Aug, a tradition more than 50 years old.
Theatre on the Square, 450 Post St. (433-9500): Contemporary theater, drama, comedy.
Theater Rhinoceros, 2926 16th St. (861-5079): Modern and avant-garde theater of interest to the gay community.
War Memorial Opera House, Civic Center, 301 Van Ness Ave. (864-3330): Home of the San Francisco Ballet (artistic director: Helgi Tomasson), oldest company in the U.S. and, along with American Ballet Theater and New York City Ballet, one of the most highly regarded; also home of the San Francisco Opera Company (musical director: Donald Runnicles). Sept–Dec.

SHOPPING: **The Cannery,** 2801 Leavenworth St. at Jefferson (771-3112): The 19th-century Del Monte fruit-processing factory, now a deluxe shopping center, with 50 boutiques, stores, and restaurants, a stone's throw from Fisherman's Wharf. Open daily.
Cost Plus Imports, 2552 Taylor St. (928-6200): Gadgets and objects from around the world at rock-bottom prices, a stone's throw from Fisherman's Wharf. Open daily.
Cow Hollow, Union St. between Van Ness Ave. and Steiner St.: The district for antiques dealers and smart stores, with many bars and restaurants. Used as a setting for the movie *The Conversation.* Picturesque old houses.
Crocker Galleria, 50 Post St. (393-1505): Opened in 1982, this innovative shopping arcade is arranged on three levels under a spectacular glass canopy 70 ft. (21m) high and 275 ft. (83m) long; it resembles the well-known Galleria Vittorio Emmanuele in Milan. More than 50 shops, stores, and restaurants.
Ghirardelli Square, 900 North Point St. (775-5500): Incorporated into a former chocolate factory near Fisherman's Wharf, this picturesque shopping complex, embellished with patios and fountains, is a textbook example of urban renewal. Around 100 shops and restaurants. Very popular with tourists. Open daily.
Japan Center, bounded by Post, Geary, Laguna, and Fillmore Sts. (922-6776): Designed by famous architect Minoru Yamasaki, this huge commercial development dates from 1986; it houses dozens of boutiques, shops, and art galleries as well as many restaurants, sushi bars, and Japanese baths. Exotic. Open daily.
Pier 39, The Embarcadero (981-7437): Yet another example of the city's talent for converting old industrial buildings (in this instance, a commercial dock not far from Fisherman's Wharf) into lively modern shopping centers. More than 140 different shops and restaurants. Open-air shows. Open daily.
San Francisco Shopping Centre, 865 Market St. (495-5656): The city's newest shopping mall—in a city already legendary for its shopping centers—opened in 1989. Nine-level atrium with a circular escalator designed by Mitsubishi, the first in the country. Four floors are devoted to small shops, while Nordstrom's occupies the top five, earning the title of "store in the sky."

SPECIAL EVENTS: For the exact schedule of events below, consult the **San Francisco Convention and Visitors Bureau** (see "Tourist Information," above).
Chinese New Year (late Jan to Feb): Colorful dragon procession and fireworks through Chinatown's streets.
International Film Festival (Apr–May): The oldest film festival in the U.S., and one of the most distinguished, held at the AMC Kabuki Cinemas.
Cherry Blossom Festival (Apr): Festival of the Japanese community, timed

to coincide with the flowering of the cherry trees in Japantown. Flower show, Japanese art festival.

Bay to Breakers Race (mid-May): World's biggest footrace: 7.5 mi. (12km) through the streets of San Francisco. 100,000 participants every year, some in the most bizarre costumes—a mixture of marathon and Mardi Gras.

Midsummer Music Festival (June–Aug): Open-air classical-music festival in the Sigmund Stern Memorial Grove.

Lesbian-Gay Freedom Day Parade (June): Tumultuous parade of the San Francisco gay community; colorful. Some 200,000 participants.

San Francisco Marathon (end of July): Third in importance (after Boston and New York) in the U.S.; attracts more than 10,000 participants.

San Francisco Fair & Exhibition (Sept): Annual event.

Columbus Day Parade (Oct): Parades, drum majorettes, and oom-pah-pah oom-pah-pah; the Italian community festival at North Beach and Fisherman's Wharf.

Fleet Week (Oct): U.S. Navy regatta in the bay, with the Blue Angels doing their stuff overhead. The great sailors' festival.

Grand National Rodeo and Livestock Exposition (late Oct to early Nov): Horse show, cattle fair, rodeos. Cowboy atmosphere. At the Cow Palace.

SPORTS: San Francisco has four professional teams:

Baseball (Apr–Oct): Oakland A's, Oakland Stadium (510/638-0500); Giants, Candlestick Park (467-8000).

Basketball (Oct–Mar): Golden State Warriors, Oakland Coliseum (762-2277).

Football (Aug–Dec): 49ers, Candlestick Park (562-4949).

Horse Racing

Bay Meadows Racetrack, Bayshore Fwy. (U.S. 101) and Hillsdale Blvd., San Mateo, 20 mi. (35km) south (574-7223): Thoroughbred racing Wed–Sun early Sept through Jan.

Golden Gate Fields, 1100 Eastshore Hwy., Albany, across the San Francisco–Oakland Bay Bridge (510/526-3020): Thoroughbred racing Feb–June and harness racing mid-June to mid-Aug, Wed–Sun.

Deep-Sea Fishing

Sport-fishing enthusiasts will find a charter fleet based year round at Fisherman's Wharf, with boats going out every day at dawn, particularly during salmon season (mid-Feb to mid-Nov). Average cost is $40 per person. Some recommended operators include **New Easy Rider Charters** (285-2000), **Ketchikan Sport Fishing Boat** (965-3474), **Lucky Lady Charter Boat** (826-6815), and **Sea Breeze Sportfishing** (474-7748).

STROLLS: ⚑ **Castro Street,** around Market St.: The heart of San Francisco's most important gay neighborhood. Bars, restaurants, movie houses, and stores all—or almost all—bear the impress of one of the largest and most organized homosexual communities in the U.S., 100,000 strong. Straights are welcome; gawking is not.

☼⚑⚑ **Chinatown,** bounded by Broadway and Bush, Kearny, and Stockton Sts.: With 80,000 inhabitants, one of the largest Chinese cities outside Asia. Pagoda roofs, tea houses, dragon-shaped lamps, and gaudy shopfronts make this the most picturesque neighborhood in the city; its restaurants are among the best in the country, and its foodstalls are justly renowned. You should see the Chinatown Gateway Arch at Grant Ave. and Bush St., the monumental entry to Chinatown, erected in 1970; Old St. Mary's Church, the former cathedral built in 1854, at Grant Ave. and California St.; the Buddha Universal Church on Washington St. across from Portsmouth Sq., the largest Buddhist temple in the U.S.; and the surprising statue of Sun Yat-sen, founder and first president of the Republic of China, on St. Mary's Sq. Tours organized by the Chinese Culture Center, 750 Kearny St. (986-1822).

🔔 **Cow Hollow** (see "Shopping," above).

☀️🔔 **Filbert Street,** between Hyde and Leavenworth Sts.: The steepest street in San Francisco, descends a 31.5° slope. Spectacular.

🔔 **Fisherman's Wharf,** the Embarcadero, between Taylor and Powell Sts: Once the city's fishing port, with more than 400 boats; today excessively commercialized. Cafés, bars, restaurants (mostly mediocre) in a fairground atmosphere. The most popular tourist attraction in the U.S. after Walt Disney World, drawing 13 million visitors a year.

☀️🔔🔔 **49 Mile Drive:** A 49-mi. (78km) circular drive, marked by signs showing a blue-and-white seagull. The trip can be made by car inside a day, and will take you to most of the city's tourist attractions: Chinatown, Nob Hill, Fisherman's Wharf, Golden Gate Park, Mission Dolores, the Civic Center, Golden Gate Bridge, Telegraph Hill, etc. A free map of the route may be obtained from the Visitor Information Center, Hallidie Plaza (lower level), Powell and Market Sts.

☀️🔔 **Japantown/Nihonmachi,** Geary and Post Sts. between Fillmore and Laguna Sts.: A Japanese enclave in the heart of San Francisco. Japan Center, with dozens of stores, tea houses, and Japanese restaurants (see "Shopping," above); kabuki theater; Cultural Center, with interesting temporary exhibitions. Note the handsome Peace Plaza with its monumental gate, Japanese gardens, and Peace Pagoda. Martial-arts demonstrations; Japanese music and dance.

☀️🔔 **Lombard Street,** between Hyde and Leavenworth Sts.: The crookedest (and most blooming) street in San Francisco, with 10 hairpin bends in less than 500 ft. (150m). One of the chase sequences in the movie *Bullitt* was shot here.

🔔 **Nob Hill,** around California and Powell Sts.: "Millionaires' Hill," rising to a height of 376 ft. (115m). Once home to California gold-mining and railroad tycoons ("Nob" is a contraction of "Nabob"); now a neighborhood of luxury hotels and smart apartment buildings. Remains a bastion of the city's old money. Note the Gothic Revival Grace Cathedral at 1051 Taylor St. and the Masonic Temple at California and Taylor Sts. Elegant.

☀️🔔 **North Beach,** around Washington Sq.: The city's Little Italy and Greenwich Village, both. In spite of its name, it has no beach; it's more like a neighborhood in Genoa or Bologna. A multitude of food shops, *trattorie,* cafés, strip joints, nightclubs (this is where the "topless" phenomenon first saw the light, to say nothing of beatniks and hippies). A colorful neighborhood, where at least a third of San Francisco's 150,000 Italians make their homes, as well as Basque and Chinese descendants. You should visit the **City Lights bookstore** at 261 Columbus Ave. (362-8193), a shrine of modern American poetry made famous by Lawrence Ferlinghetti; also the nearby literary bars, **Vesuvio's Café,** 255 Columbus Ave. (362-3370), and **Tosca Café,** 242 Columbus Ave. (391-1244).

🔔 **Russian Hill,** around Green and Leavenworth Sts.: In the 19th century this was the artists' and writers' quarter; now it's one of the city's smartest residential neighborhoods. Dozens of interesting homes and buildings along Green St.

🔔 **SoMa** (South of Market St.), bounded by Mission, 1st, Townsend, and Division Sts.: San Francisco's version of New York's Soho. Once the rough, threatening preserve of butcher-supply houses, winos, struggling artists, and gay men dressed in black-leather motorcycle outfits, SoMa has suddenly become fashionable. Now the streets are lined with hit restaurants, art galleries, nightclubs, and trendy fashion outlets.

☼♨♨ **Telegraph Hill,** around Lombard and Kearny Sts.: The steepest of San Francisco's hills, rising up to the Coit Tower and its famous view. A tangle of steep lanes, flights of steps, tiny gardens, and enchanting old frame houses on Montgomery St., Filbert Steps St., Greenwich Steps, Calhoun Terrace, Alta St., and so on. A demanding walk, but you mustn't miss it.

☼♨ **Union Square,** bounded by Powell, Stockton, Post, and Geary Sts.: The heart of the city's shopping district, with shops, department stores, hotels, restaurants, and fashionable bars. Very lively. On the east side of the square, with its gardens and fountain by Ruth Azawa, is the elegant little Maiden Lane, lined with luxury shops. In the 19th century it was, under the name of Morton Alley, the most ill-famed street on the Barbary Coast, the old red-light district destroyed by the 1906 earthquake.

THEME PARKS: ☼♨ **Marine World Africa USA,** Marine World Pkwy., in Vallejo, 30 mi. (48km) NE on I-80 (707/643-6722): Huge theme park and zoo with over 1,000 animals, from killer whale and dolphin to elephant and tiger. Also such water sports as boating and waterskiing, animal acts. Open Wed–Sun year round; 40 min. from dwntwn. Ferry service from Fisherman's Wharf (50 min.) by Red and White Shuttle Line (546-2700).

♨ **Great America Theme Park,** in Santa Clara, 45 mi. (72km) SE off U.S. 101 (408/988-1800): A 100-acre (40ha) amusement park with more than 100 attractions including four giant roller-coasters and The Edge, a real terrorizer, free-fall ride. Variety shows. Reconstructions of pioneer villages. Open daily in summer, wknds only in spring and fall; closed in winter. 45 min. from dwntwn.

ZOOS: ☼♨ **San Francisco Zoo,** Sloat Blvd. at 45th Ave. (753-7080): Zoo of very modern design on the ocean. More than 1,000 animals from around the world, including such rarities as a white tiger, dwarf hippopotamus, okapis, and koalas. Fine collection of apes and exotic monkeys. Mini-train for visitors. You should see it, if only for the beauty of the setting. Open daily.

ACCOMMODATIONS

Personal Favorites (in order of preference)

☼♙♙♙♙ **Sheraton Palace** (dwntwn), 2 New Montgomery St., CA 94105 (415/392-8600; toll free, see Sheraton). 555 rms, A/C, color TV, in-rm movies. AE, CB, DC, MC, V. Valet parking $20, pool, sauna, health club, three rests. (including the world-famous Garden Court), bar, 24-hr. rm svce, entertainment, boutiques, concierge, free crib. *Note:* A historic landmark, built in 1875 and reopened in 1991 after 27 months of restoration to the stunning tune of $150 million. Blends harmoniously the elegance of yesteryear w. today's modern standards of comfort. Good-sized, quiet guest rms w. antique furnishings, refrigerators, and computer hookups. Sumptuous, glass-domed Garden Court rest. Polished, superior svce. Adj. the financial district. VIP and upscale business clientele. This is one of the best hotels in the U.S. **VE**

♙♙♙♙ **Stanford Court Stouffer** (dwntwn), 905 California St., CA 94108 (415/989-3500; toll free, see Stouffer). 396 rms, A/C, color TV, in-rm movies. AE, CB, DC, MC, V. Valet gar. $22, two rests. (including Fournou's Ovens), bars, 24-hr. rm svce, boutiques, concierge, free crib. *Note:* Cozy European-style grand hotel. From the Tiffany-style glass-domed courtyard to the four-poster beds in the rms or the miniature TV sets in the marble bathrooms, you'll find a happy combination of luxury and elegance in an atmosphere exuding the charm of a gentleman's club. Svce is exemplary, and the rest. one of the best in San Francisco. In the heart of the fashionable Nob Hill district. Complimentary limo svce to the financial district. Big business clientele; no groups, no conventions. A San Francisco landmark since 1912. **VE**

✵ 🄻 🎧 🎧 **Sherman House** (nr. dwntwn), 2160 Green St., CA 94123 (415/563-3600). 14 rms, A/C, cable color TV. AE, MC, V. Gar. $16, rest., 24-hr. rm svce, concierge, butler svce. *Note:* Enchanting four-story Victorian house (no elevator), regarded as the "in" place to stay in San Francisco. Perfection in every detail, from the luxurious Second Empire decor of its rms (w. fireplaces and four-poster beds) to the inspired cuisine of chef Donia Bijan and the faultless svce; you'll have a memorable stay here. Private grdn. Frequented by show-biz personalities (Bill Cosby and Johnny Carson among them) who appreciate its intimacy and elegance. You'll have to reserve a long time in advance. **VE**

✵ 🄻 🎧 🎧 **Mansion Hotel** (nr. dwntwn), 2220 Sacramento St., CA 94115 (415/929-9444). 21 rms (no A/C). AE, CB, DC, MC, V. Limited parking, rest., rm svce, free breakfast. *Note:* Elegant Queen Anne–style home in the heart of Pacific Heights, a designated historic landmark, w. a score of comfortable period-furnished rms. Interesting, unusual ambience and decor; note the sculptures by Benjamino Bufano. Highly recommended rest. Winning reception and svce; concerts every evening; nice little private grdn—in a word, everything you could want if you hate mass tourism. **M–VE**

🎧 🎧 **Harbor Court** (dwntwn), 165 Steuart St., CA 94102 (415/882-1300; toll free 800/346-0555). 132 rms, A/C, cable color TV. AE, CB, DC, MC, V. Parking $15, pool, health club, rest., bar, concierge, free crib. *Note:* Lovely new hotel in a revamped '20s YMCA, right on the waterfront. Victorian decor. Rms are small but elegantly decorated, half of them overlooking the bay. Popular saloon-rest. (Harry Denton's). Cheerful reception and svce. Good value overall. **M**

🎧 **Marina Inn** (nr. dwntwn), 3110 Octavia St., CA 94123 (415/928-1000). 40 rms, A/C, cable color TV. AE, MC, V. Street parking, hrdrsr, free continental breakfast. *Note:* Small, inviting hotel in a restored 1928 building within walking distance of Ghirardelli Sq. Pleasant guest rms w. English country decor. Courteous svce. One of the most reasonably priced inns in San Francisco. Very good value. **I–M**

🎧 **Essex** (dwntwn), 684 Ellis St. (at Larkin), CA 94109 (415/474-4664; toll free 800/453-7739). 100 rms (no A/C), color TV. AE, MC, V. Coffee shop adj., free tea and coffee. *Note:* Elderly but very well kept small hotel near the Civic Center. Serviceably comfortable, meticulously clean rms, some w. balconies but some sharing a bath. Reception w. a smile. An excellent buy for the budget traveler. **B–I**

Other Accommodations (from top bracket to budget)

🎧 🎧 🎧 🎧 **Four Seasons Clift** (dwntwn), 495 Geary St., CA 94102 (415/775-4700; toll free, see Four Seasons). 329 rms, A/C, color TV, in-rm movies. AE, CB, DC, MC, V. Valet parking $22, health club, rest. (the French Room), bar, piano bar, 24-hr. rm svce, concierge, free crib. *Note:* Distinguished old grand hotel, elegantly and tastefully decorated; spacious rms w. minibars. The personalized svce is quite remarkable. Renowned rest. and wine cellar; superb art deco bar (Redwood Room). Upscale business clientele. Old-world charm. Free limo to financial district. One of the best places to stay in San Francisco since 1915. Interesting wknd discounts. **VE**

✵ 🄻 🎧 🎧 🎧 **Mandarin Oriental** (dwntwn), 222 Sansome St., CA 94104 (415/885-0999; toll free 800/526-6566). 160 rms, A/C, color TV, in-rm movies. AE, CB, DC, MC, V. Valet parking $20, rest. (Silks), bar, 24-hr. rm svce, nightclub, boutiques, concierge, free crib. *Note:* A grand hotel in the sky, on the top 11 floors of the First Interstate Center, two twin 48-story towers, linked by "skybridges" w. an unparalleled view of the city and the bay. On each floor there are no more than seven very spacious rms or suites w. private balconies, minibars, and wonderful views. Ultra-luxurious pastel-toned decor and furnishings. Exemplary svce; fine quality rest.; well-equipped business center. Belongs to Hong Kong's Mandarin chain of luxury hotels. **VE**

ℒℒℒℒ **Ritz Carlton** (dwntwn), 600 Stockton St. (at California St.), CA 94108 (415/296-7465; toll free 800/241-3333). 336 rms, A/C, cable color TV. AE, CB, DC, MC, V. Valet garage $23, pool, sauna, health club, two rests. (including the Dining Room), two bars, 24-hr. rm svce, entertainment, concierge, free crib. *Note:* San Francisco's latest luxury grand hotel, built in an elegant but neglected neoclassical building that has been restored to its 1920s look w. Italian marble, handcrafted moldings, silk wall coverings, crystal chandeliers, and Persian carpets. The spacious rms are decorated in quiet tones of blue and green and include every imaginable amenity from minibars and terry bathrobes to disposable cameras. Exemplary staff. Highly praiseworthy rests. Free limo svce to surrounding financial district and Chinatown. Stylishly elegant and urbane. **VE**

☀ℒℒℒ **Campton Place Kempinski** (dwntwn), 340 Stockton St., CA 94108 (415/781-5555; toll free 800/426-3135). 126 rms, A/C, color TV, in-rm movies. AE, CB, DC, MC, V. Valet parking $19, rest. (Campton Place), bar, rm svce, concierge, free crib. *Note:* Chic and intimate hotel just off Union Sq., entirely renovated at a cost of $18 million. All the comfort, elegance, and refinement of a European grand hotel. Soundproofed rms w. period furniture and marble bathrooms. Polished, attentive svce. Rest. of a very high order; roof grdn. The favorite of those in-the-know. **VE**

ℒℒℒ **Nikko** (dwntwn), 222 Mason St. (at O'Farrell St.), CA 94102 (415/394-1111; toll free 800/645-5687). 525 rms, A/C, color TV, in-rm movies. AE, CB, DC, MC, V. Valet parking $23, pool, health club, sauna, rest., coffee shop, bars, 24-hr. rm svce, hrdrsr, concierge, free crib. *Note:* Ultramodern and impressive 25-floor tower; huge elegant rms w. marble bath, minibar, and remote-control TV. Rest. of quality; fully equipped business center; thoughtful, polished svce. Both Japanese and American big business favor this hotel, which has free shuttle svce to the financial district. Interesting wknd packages; very central location. **VE**

ℒℒℒ **The Donatello** (formerly the Pacific Plaza; dwntwn), 501 Post St., CA 94102 (415/441-7100; toll free 800/227-3184). 95 rms, A/C, color TV, in-rm movies. AE, CB, DC, MC, V. Valet gar. $16, health club, sauna, rest., bar, rm svce, concierge, free crib. *Note:* One of the new stars of the local luxury-hotel scene, just off Union Sq. Elegant Italian Renaissance decor; spacious, elegant rms w. balconies, minibars, and a profusion of houseplants. Personalized svce; serene, intimate ambience. Very good Italian rest. Clientele of VIPs and wealthy Europeans. Member of the prestigious Relais et Châteaux hotel chain. **E–VE**

ℒℒℒ **Hyatt Regency San Francisco** (dwntwn), 5 Embarcadero Center, CA 94111 (415/788-1234; toll free, see Hyatt). 803 rms, A/C, color TV, in-rm movies. AE, CB, DC, MC, V. Valet gar. $20, two rests. (including the Equinox), coffee shop, revolving bar at the top, rm svce, concierge, free crib. *Note:* Building of interesting futuristic structure, inspired by the Aztec pyramids, in the Embarcadero Center, within easy reach of the business district; dramatic 17-story lobby w. indoor grdns, fountains, and sculpture. Modern, comfortable rms, but so-so svce. Group and business clientele. Wknd discounts. **E–VE**

ℒℒ **Holiday Inn Financial District** (dwntwn), 750 Kearny St., CA 94108 (415/433-6600; toll free, see Holiday Inns). 566 rms, A/C, color TV, in-rm movies. AE, CB, DC, MC, V. Gar. $7.50, pool, rest., coffee shop, bar, rm svce, boutiques. *Note:* Enormous 27-floor tourist barracks nr. Chinatown. All rms have balconies; many overlook the bay. The essence of Holiday Inns. Group and business clientele; Chinese cultural museum on the third floor. **M–E**

ℒℒ **Miyako** (nr. dwntwn), 1625 Post St., CA 94115 (415/922-3200; toll free 800/533-4567). 218 rms, A/C, color TV, in-rm movies. AE, CB, DC, MC, V. Gar. $15, rest. (Elka), bar, rm svce, boutiques, concierge, free crib. *Note:* Modern, comfortable tower in the Japan Center; spacious lobby overlooking pretty Japanese grdns. Choice of Western or tatami rms. Efficient bilingual svce; excellent rest. Clientele of Japanese tourists and American business travelers. Recently underwent a $10-million renovation. **M–E**

☼ 𝄞 𝄞 **Queen Anne** (nr. dwntwn), 1590 Sutter St., CA 94109 (415/ 441-2828; toll free 800/227-3970). 49 rms (no A/C), color TV. AE, CB, DC, MC, V. Gar. $12; no bar or rest.; valet svce, free breakfast, free sherry, crib $10. *Note:* Beautiful century-old Victorian building, a designated historic landmark, now elegantly restored. Each rm or suite (some w. fireplace) is decorated in a different style. Much period furniture; fine carved staircase. Romantic atmosphere; attentive reception and svce. Excellent place to stay, 10 min. from dwntwn. **M–E**

𝄞 𝄞 **Raphael Hotel** (dwntwn), 386 Geary St. (at Mason), CA 94102 (415/986-2000; toll free 800/821-5343). 152 rms, A/C, color TV, in-rm movies. AE, CB, DC, MC, V. Gar. $16, rest., bar, rm svce, free crib. *Note:* Charming, cozy, comfortable hotel nr. Union Sq. Elegantly decorated rms, some on the skimpy side. Uneven svce. Very centrally located. Good value overall; a fine place to stay. **M**

𝄞 𝄞 **Villa Florence** (dwntwn), 225 Powell St., CA 94102 (415/ 397-7700; toll free 800/553-4411). 180 rms, A/C, color TV, in-rm movies. AE, CB, DC, MC, V. Gar. $17, rest. (Kuleto's), bar, rm svce, concierge, free crib. *Note:* Older European-style hotel, friendly and inviting. The decor of the lobby is a little faded, but rms are comfortable and pleasant, w. refrigerator. Very good rest. serving (as it should) Italian food. Friendly svce. Conveniently located a block from Union Sq. but in a spot with lots of noise, particularly from streetcars. Package-tour and convention clientele. **M**

𝄞 **Cartwright** (dwntwn), 524 Sutter St., CA 94102 (415/421- 2865; toll free 800/227-3844). 114 rms, A/C (in a third of the rms), cable color TV. AE, DC, MC, V. Parking $12, coffee shop (breakfast only), valet svce, free crib. *Note:* Small hotel nr. Union Sq., aging but remarkably well run. Rms relatively small but comfortable and prettily decorated (antiques and fresh flowers in every rm), w. views over the city, most of them w. refrigerators. Rather noisy neighborhood. Good value; clientele of regulars. **M**

𝄞 **Chancellor** (dwntwn), 433 Powell St., CA 94102 (415/362- 2004; toll free 800/428-4748). 140 rms (no A/C), color TV, in-rm movies. AE, CB, DC, MC, V. Adj. parking $16, rest. (Chancellor Café), bar, valet svce, free crib. *Note:* Modernized old hotel centrally located in the heart of San Francisco. Original Edwardian decor w. marble lobby, orchids, and potted palms. Rather skimpy rms. Comfort and svce above average; acceptable rest. Good value. Family owned since 1914. **M**

☼ 𝄞 **Seal Rock Inn** (nr. dwntwn), 545 Point Lobos Ave., CA 94121 (415/752-8000). 27 rms, A/C, cable color TV. AE, CB, DC, MC, V. Free parking, pool, rest. (breakfast and lunch only), valet svce, crib $2. *Note:* Charming little rococo hotel right on the ocean. Fine view of the Pacific and the reefs populated w. sea creatures. Spacious, inviting rms w. refrigerators, some w. kitchenettes and fireplaces. Private grdn and patio. An excellent place to stay if you like to be away from it all; 25 min. from dwntwn. **I–M** but lower rates mid-Sept to mid-May.

𝄞 **Grant Plaza** (dwntwn), 465 Grant St., CA 94108 (415/434- 3883; toll free 800/472-6899). 72 rms, A/C, color TV. AE, MC, V. Parking $8, adj. coffee shop, crib $7. *Note:* Small hotel, economy-class but acceptable, on the edge of Chinatown. Recently redecorated and refurnished. Functionally comfortable rms. Book at least two weeks ahead. Good value. **B–I**

𝄞 **San Remo** (dwntwn), 2237 Mason St., CA 94133 (415/776- 8688; toll free 800/352-7366). 62 rms, A/C. MC, V. Parking $8, rest., bar. *Note:* Nice elderly hotel of Victorian appearance, halfway between Fisherman's Wharf and North Beach. Antique furniture and original works of art. Inviting rms, all w. shared bath. Friendly svce; good value overall. **B–I**

    ♀ **Sheehan Hotel** (dwntwn), 620 Sutter St., CA 94102 (415/
    ♭ 775-6500; toll free 800/848-1529). 68 rms (no A/C), color
TV. AE, DC, MC, V. Parking $12, pool, health club, valet svce, free breakfast.
Note: Clean, comfortable old hotel close to Union Sq. and across the street from
trendy art galleries. Elegant lobby. Friendly management. A very good value. **B–I**

Airport Accommodations

    ♀ ♀ ♀ **Hyatt Regency Airport** (vic.), 1333 Bayshore Hwy., Burlin-
    ♭ ♭ ♭ game, CA 94010 (415/347-1234; toll free, see Hyatt). 790
rms, A/C, color TV, in-rm movies. AE, CB, DC, MC, V. Valet parking $11,
pool, health club, sauna, massage, rest., 24-hr. deli, bars, 24-hr. rm svce, concierge, free crib. *Note:* Large, modern nine-story hotel 5 min. from the terminal
(free shuttle). Dramatic, skylighted atrium w. bamboo trees and waterfalls. Over-
sized, well-soundproofed rms, some w. wet bars or refrigerators. Ultra-
professional svce. 25 min. from dwntwn. **E–VE**

Accommodations in the Vicinity

    ☼♭♭♭♭ **Claremont Resort Hotel** (vic.), Domingo and Ashby Aves.,
    Oakland, CA 94623 (510/843-3000; toll free, see Preferred).
239 rms, A/C, color TV, in-rm movies. AE, CB, DC, MC, V. Valet parking $8,
pool, health club, 10 tennis courts, sauna, massage, rest. (Pavilion Room), coffee
shop, bar, rm svce, disco, hrdrsr, free crib. *Note:* Splendid turn-of-the-century castle on 20 acres (8ha) of park and grdn. Elegant Victorian decor w. period furniture, Oriental rugs, and a fine collection of artwork. The guestbook bears the
signatures of innumerable celebrities, from former Pres. Harry S. Truman to actor Clint Eastwood. Spacious, inviting rms, the best overlooking San Francisco
Bay; excellent rest.; comprehensive health spa w. exercise rms and saunas; unusually polished svce. A tranquil green oasis 35 min. from dwntwn San Francisco.
Free shuttle to/from the Oakland airport. **E–VE**

    ☼♭♭ **Alta Mira Hotel** (vic.), 125 Bulkley Ave., Sausalito, CA 94965
    (415/332-1350). 29 units (no A/C). AE, CB, DC, MC, V.
Free valet parking, rest., bar, rm svce. *Note:* Enchanting little hotel on the heights
of Sausalito, looking out over the bay and the splendid panorama of San Francisco. Elegantly decorated rms, some w. views of the city and the Golden Gate. Individual cottages w. fireplaces. Attentive, personalized svce; acceptable rest. An
elegant, comfortable haven of peace 25 min. from dwntwn across the Golden
Gate Bridge. Resv. advised, well ahead of time. **M–E**

    ☼♭♭ **Casa Madrona** (vic.), 801 Bridgeway, Sausalito, CA 94965
    (415/332-0502). 32 rms and 5 cottages (no A/C). AE, MC,
V. Parking $5, rest., rm svce, concierge, free breakfast, free wine tasting in the
afternoons. *Note:* Italianate mansion dating from 1885. Period furniture in the
rms, most of which have refrigerators, fireplaces, and balconies; those in the new
wing are particularly comfortable. Courteous reception and svce; romantic atmosphere; pretty, country-style decor. Very praiseworthy rest. serving French-
Californian food. You should reserve far in advance. **M–VE** (hotel), **E** (cottages).

YMCA/Youth Hostels

    Fort Mason International Hostel (nr. dwntwn), Bldg. 240, Fort Mason,
San Francisco, CA 94123 (415/771-7277). 165 beds. Clean youth hostel offering limited comfort. Resv. advised. 20 min. from dwntwn.
    Golden Gate Hostel (vic.), 941 Fort Barry Rd., Sausalito, CA 94965
(415/331-2777). 60 beds; resv. a must in summer. Rustic youth hostel set
among trees and grdns. 30 min. from dwntwn, across the Golden Gate Bridge.
    YMCA (dwntwn), 855 Sacramento St., San Francisco, CA 94111 (415/
982-4412). 160 rms. Men only. Very centrally located. Pool, health facilities.
    YMCA (nr. dwntwn), 220 Golden Gate Ave., San Francisco, CA 94102
(415/885-0460). 100 rms. Men and women. Health club, pool. 5 min. from
dwntwn.

RESTAURANTS

Personal Favorites (in order of preference)

☼ ♟♟♟♟ **Lark Creek Inn** (vic.), 234 Magnolia Ave., Larkspur (924-7766). Lunch Mon–Fri, dinner nightly, brunch Sun; closed Dec 25. AE, CB, DC, MC, V. *Specialties:* braised oxtail w. scalloped turnips; roast quail w. homemade egg noodles and wild mushrooms; braised pork shoulder w. white beans, kale, and smoked ham hock; grilled salmon w. shrimp and scallion fritters; Yankee pot roast; butterscotch pudding. Menu changes daily. Magnificent wine list at enticing prices. *Note:* Bradley Ogden, who created a golden age at Campton Place (see below) took over the reins in 1989 at this delightful country house in the heart of the woods complete w. babbling brook. Inspired country cooking: highest quality fresh-grown produce at very reasonable prices served in an elegant Victorian setting. Outdoor dining on fine days. Svce w. a smile. Well worth the 25-min. drive from San Francisco over the Golden Gate Bridge and along U.S. 101N to the Tamalpais-Paradise exit. One of the 12 greatest rests. in the U.S. *American.* **M–E**

♟♟♟ **Campton Place Restaurant** (dwntwn), in the Campton Place Kempinski (see "Accommodations," above) (781-5555). A/C. Breakfast/lunch/dinner daily, brunch Sun. AE, CB, DC, MC, V. Jkt. *Specialties:* sautéed foie gras w. salsify and blood-orange sauce; sweetbreads w. eggplant and preserved lemons; beef shortribs w. potato purée and horseradish; lobster cioppino w. mussels, clams, and red-pepper rouille; banana-red pancakes w. ginger syrup and macadamia nuts. Splendid list of California wines; menu changes regularly. *Note:* Long directed by Bradley Ogden, one of the most talented exponents of American nouvelle cuisine (see the Lark Creek Inn, above), Campton Place makes it a point of honor to use only the finest regional ingredients, drawn from all over the U.S. The result is an imaginative, sophisticated bill of fare by chef Todd Humphries, deserving all manner of high praise. Plush, intimate decorative scheme in tones of taupe and salmon-pink w. some exotic Oriental touches. Flawless svce; resv. several days ahead. One of the best rests. in California. Valet parking. *American.* **M–E**

♟♟♟ **Fleur de Lys** (nr. dwntwn), 777 Sutter St. (673-7779). A/C. Dinner only, Mon–Sat; closed hols. and the last week in June and first week in July. AE, CB, DC, MC, V. J&T. *Specialties:* seared ahi tuna w. sesame oil vinaigrette, filet of squab on cabbage salad braised w. foie vinaigrette, roasted sea bass on leek-flavored mashed potatoes w. lobster-saffron broth, grilled filet mignon w. ratatouille and roasted garlic, roast lamb chops w. mustard seed and sage, tropical sorbets. Menu changes periodically. Large wine list. *Note:* High-flown decor in a sort of campy *Thousand and One Nights* style, but the cuisine of Hubert Keller, a disciple of the famous French chef Roger Vergé, is a miracle of lightness and delicacy. Reception and svce flawless in all respects. The favorite rest. of San Francisco society. Resv. a must; a very fine place to eat. Valet parking ($4). *French.* **E–VE**

♟♟ **Square One** (dwntwn), 190 Pacific Ave. at Front St. (788-1110). A/C. Lunch Mon–Fri, dinner nightly; closed hols. AE, DC, MC, V. Jkt. *Specialties:* tapas, paella, Moroccan mixed grill w. couscous, Provençal duck w. lavender honey and thyme, homemade ice creams. Superb wine list at restrained prices. *Note:* The contemporary decor w. a view of the open kitchen is no great added attraction, but the Mediterranean-inspired cooking of Joyce Goldstein is worth a visit for its own sake. Emphasis is on quality ingredients; the menu changes daily according to season. Exemplary svce; many regular patrons. Resv. strongly advised. *American.* **M**

☼♟ **Tadich Grill** (dwntwn), 240 California St. (391-2373). A/C. Lunch/dinner Mon–Sat (until 9pm); closed hols. MC, V. Jkt. *Specialties:* clam chowder, tortellini Alfredo, sole Rex, hangtown fry, cioppino (California seafood stew), broiled sea bass, shrimp Diablo, steak, lamb chops, catch of the day. Excellent cheesecake. *Note:* The oldest rest. in San Francisco, dating from the gold-rush year 1849, keeps delighting lovers of steak and seafood generation after generation. Choice ingredients; the old-pub decor is original. Lackadaisical svce. Packed at lunch, mostly w. bankers and businesspeople; no resv., but you can have an agreeable wait at the bar nr. the entrance where regulars prefer to have their lunch. *Steak/Seafood.* **M**

🍷🍷 **China Moon Café** (dwntwn), 639 Post St. (775-4789). A/C. closed hols. MC. V. Dinner only, nightly. *Specialties:* crispy spring rolls w. ground chicken, pot-browned noodle pillows, cold poached salmon tiles w. ginger-black bean vinaigrette. Menu changes weekly. Interesting selection of California wines. *Note:* This nontraditional Chinese food reflects the originality of the excellent American chef, Barbara Tropp. The Californian and Chinese blend results in some new and often admirable taste sensations. Funky decor and atmosphere in vaguely art deco style. No smoking; resv. a must. *Chinese/American.* **I–M**

🍷 **Dol Ho** (dwntwn), 808 Pacific Ave. (392-2828). A/C. Breakfast/lunch daily (8am–5pm). No credit cards. *Specialties:* dim sum. *Note:* San Francisco's best dim sum tea house, according to purists. This small, crowded Chinatown café is the perfect place for a relaxing afternoon tea and dim sum dumplings served piping hot from carts continuously replenished. Don't miss the delicate shrimp-filled har gow, the pork-filled shiu mai, the sweet doughy sesame balls, and the pork-filled pot-stickers. A meal w. about six types of dim sum runs around $10–$15 for two—a delicious bargain. No resv. *Chinese.* **B**

Other Restaurants (from top bracket to budget)

🍷🍷🍷🍷 **Ernie's** (dwntwn), 847 Montgomery St. (397-5969). A/C. Dinner only, Mon–Sat; closed hols. and the first two weeks in Jan. AE, CB, DC, MC, V. J&T. *Specialties:* confit of Hudson Valley foie gras, creamy soup of wild and cultivated mushrooms w. essence of black truffles, Caesar salad prepared tableside, roast rack of lamb w. basil oil and natural juices, herb-breaded medallions of monkfish w. verjus of chardonnay, fresh black plum tart w. plum coulis. One of America's great wine lists. *Note:* A haunt of celebrities, local or passing through, this San Francisco landmark has recently updated its menu w. some very nouvelle cuisine dishes by dazzling chef David Kinch. Victorian ambience w. elegant champagne-colored silk walls and crystal chandeliers (served as a backdrop for the Hitchcock movie *Vertigo*). Exemplary svce; resv. essential; valet parking ($5). *Continental.* **E–VE**

🍷🍷🍷 **Masa's** (dwntwn), in the Vintage Court Hotel, 648 Bush St. (989-7154; toll free 800/258-7694). A/C. Dinner only, Tues –Sat; closed July 4, Thanksgiving, and Dec 25 to early Jan. AE, MC, V. Jkt. *Specialties:* poached oysters w. vermouth and caviar, marinated raw lamb, foie gras sautéed w. truffles, boudin of lobster, medallions of New Zealand venison w. caramelized apples. Daily menu. Very good desserts, particularly the frozen praline soufflé. Remarkable, but pricey, wine list. *Note:* The most innovative rest. serving French nouvelle cuisine in San Francisco. After the founder, Masataka Kobayashi, died, lamented by all in 1985, he was succeeded by the talented Bill Galloway, then more recently by the young Julian Serrano, whose cuisine is both delicate and inspired; the appearance of his dishes is in itself a feast for the eye. Modern paneled decor w. superb flower arrangements, but a tiny space (20 tables). Flawless svce. Resv. indispensable, several days ahead. The best rest. in town according to a recent *San Francisco Focus* readers' poll. Valet parking ($5). *French.* **E–VE**

🍷🍷🍷 **Postrio** (dwntwn), 545 Post St. (776-7825). A/C. Breakfast/ lunch Mon–Fri, dinner nightly, brunch Sat–Sun; closed hols. AE, CB, DC, MC, V. *Specialties:* home-smoked sturgeon w. trio of horseradish on potato pancake, grilled quail w. spinach-and-soft-egg ravioli, roasted leg of Sonoma lamb w. garlic-potato purée and niçoise olive sauce, roasted salmon w.

almond-pepper crust, grilled squab w. black-pepper-huckleberry sauce, vanilla bean crème brûlée. Daily menu. Extensive list of mostly Californian wines. *Note:* The most notable rest. to enter this prestigious culinary region in the last five years. Created by Wolfgang Puck, this is probably the finest of his many ventures. Superb Californian cuisine augmented with Mediterranean and Asian influences and maintained by the husband-and-wife team of David and Annie Gingrass. Contemporary decor splashed w. modern art. Flawless svce. Resv. required for lunch and dinner. *American.* **M–E**

⚜ 🍷🍷🍷 **Stars** (nr. dwntwn), 150 Redwood Alley (861-7827). A/C. ☖☖☖ Lunch Mon–Fri, dinner nightly. AE, DC, MC, V. *Specialties:* black-bean cakes w. ancho cream, smoked duck w. turnips and aioli, oysters, spiced lamb sausage, tuna steak w. ginger-and-coriander vinaigrette, the city's best desserts. Daily menu. Enormous list of California wines in all price ranges. *Note:* Jeremiah Tower, who forsook architecture for the stove, is one of the gurus of contemporary American cuisine; he works wonders w. light sauces, unexpected taste combinations, and a mesquite grill. Engaging old-fashioned brasserie setting, w. retro posters for decoration and noisy ambience. Relaxed but efficient svce. Heavily patronized by lawyers and politicians (the Civic Center is in easy reach); resv. strongly advised. *American.* **M–E**

🍷🍷🍷 **Cypress Club** (dwntwn), 500 Jackson St. (296-8555). A/C. Dinner nightly (open for lunch during month of Dec). AE, CB, DC, MC, V. Jkt. *Specialties:* hangtown-fry salad, pork loin chop w. Parmesan polenta, yellow-fin tuna w. shiitake mushrooms, tandoori pork w. cilantro sausage, sweetbreads in red wine, ginger crème brûlée. The menu changes regularly. Great California wine list reasonably priced. *Note:* Named after the eatery in Raymond Chandler's *The Big Sleep.* The Cypress Club's stylishly extravagant decor is as eclectic as the high-style American food by the young and gifted chef Cory Schreiber. The svce is smooth and professional. Resv. a must, as expected for one of the city's top hot spots. *American.* **M–E**

🍷🍷🍷 **Elka** (nr. dwntwn), in the Miyako Hotel (see "Accommoda-☖☖☖ tions," above) (922-7788). A/C. Breakfast/lunch/dinner daily. AE, CB, DC, MC, V. *Specialties:* Japanese box (a sampling of seafood such as ahi tuna tartar, shrimp tempura, abalone), kaso-marinated sturgeon w. grilled rice cakes and pickled plum vinaigrette, grilled salmon w. roasted garlic and green lentils, breakfast pasta (spaghetti w. scrambled eggs and Italian sausage). *Note:* Multitalented Elka Gilmore marries Western and Asian cuisine, crafting delicate and deeply flavorful dishes at this most exciting of recent openings in San Francisco. Rice-paper light fixtures augment the sleek Asian decor. Svce not up to par w. the food. A fine place for breakfast as well. Resv. required for lunch and dinner. *American/Asian.* **M–E**

⚜🍷🍷 **Bix** (dwntwn), 56 Gold St. (433-6300). A/C. Lunch Mon–Fri, dinner nightly. AE, MC, V. Jkt. *Specialties:* double lamb chops w. scalloped potatoes; roasted snapper w. shellfish paella; chicken hash; potato and leek pancake w. smoked salmon, crème fraîche, and caviar; swordfish w. vegetable ragoût; gratin of chocolate. *Note:* This monument to art deco, which looks like a luxury liner from the '30s, has been very successful since it opened in 1988. The kitchen is supervised by the brilliant Cindy Pawlcyn, justly renowned as the former presiding genius at San Francisco's Fog City Diner and of the Mustards Grill in the Wine Country (see below). Magnificent two-level dining rm w. elegant mezzanine and inviting bar decorated with frescos in Cotton Club style. A place for seeing and being seen. Svce still a little uncertain. Live jazz at dinner. Resv. a must. *American.* **M**

🍷🍷 **La Folie** (nr. dwntwn), 2316 Polk St. at Green St. (776-5577). ☖☖ A/C. Dinner only, Mon–Sat; closed hols. AE, MC, V. Jkt. *Specialties:* chilled zucchini and basil soup w. sun-dried tomatoes, flan of foie gras w. potatoes and hazelnut vinaigrette, horseradish and celery-root–crusted salmon w. cucumber and yogurt sauce, cappuccino crème brûlée. The menu changes regularly. Fairly priced wine list. *Note:* Intimate, upscale bistro serving a light, delicate French food w. southwestern touches, all moderately priced. Cheerful decor w. whimsical clouds painted on the sky-blue ceiling. Polite bistro-style svce. Resv. highly advised. *French.* **M**

    ♉♉ **Alain Rondelli** (nr. dwntwn), 126 Clement St. (387-0408). A/C. Dinner only, Tues–Sun; closed Thanksgiving, Dec 25. MC, V. *Specialties:* Dungeness crab w. tomato water and asparagus, lamb pot-au-feu w. oregano and asparagus, crispy skin of salmon w. mashed-potato coulis and tarragon sauce, lobster w. orange-dill broth and fava beans, financier. Affordable wine list. *Note:* Alain Rondelli, the exuberant young chef who achieved glory at Ernie's, has established this minimally decorated bistro that allows his creative stature to shine, such as with his Roquefort cheese over pear tarte tatin w. champagne vinegar. Small menu that lists dishes by their main ingredient, such as "salmon," and forgets the prosey description. Excellent value. Resv. recommended. A fine place. *French.* **l–M**

    ♉♉ **Gaylord India** (nr. dwntwn), Ghirardelli Sq., 900 North Point St. (771-8822). A/C. Lunch/dinner daily, brunch Sun; closed Thanksgiving, Dec 25. AE, CB, DC, MC, V. Jkt. *Specialties:* mulligatawny soup, samosas, chicken tikka masala, chicken tandoori, lamb w. cream and walnuts, curries. *Note:* All the subtle flavors of true Indian cuisine; luxurious decor and splendid views of the bay from every table. Attentive svce; agreeable background music. Resv. advised. One of a worldwide chain originally started in New Delhi. *Indian.* **l–M**

    ♉♉ **Greens** (nr. dwntwn), Bldg. A, Fort Mason (771-6222). A/C. Lunch Tues–Sat, dinner Mon–Sat, brunch Sun. MC, V. *Specialties:* fresh pasta w. vegetables, homemade soups, mixed salads, pizza provençal, vegetable soufflés, quiches, vegetable gratins, good homemade desserts. Daily menu. Award-winning list of French and California wines at reasonable prices. *Note:* Purists look on this as the crowning glory of California vegetarian cuisine; the excellent chef, Annie Sommerville, devises light, sophisticated, innovative dishes. The floor-to-ceiling windows of this former military barracks give you a superb view of the bay and the Golden Gate Bridge. Very popular w. the business community at lunch; 10-min. drive from dwntwn. Resv. a must. *American.* **l–M**

    ♉♉ **Hong Kong Flower Lounge** (nr. dwntwn) 5322 Geary Blvd. (668-8998). A/C. Lunch/dinner daily. AE, MC, V. *Specialties:* dim sum, prawns w. fried milk, fried catfish w. soy-cilantro sauce, cold chicken marinated in wine, Peking duck w. steamed buns, sautéed fresh abalone. *Note:* Huge, elegant Hong Kong–style rest. dressed up w. pink walls, crystal chandeliers, and live-fish tanks crammed w. sea creatures. Svce efficient but somewhat brusque. A local favorite. Resv. recommended. *Chinese.* **l–M**

    ♉♉ **Lulu** (dwntwn), 816 Folsom St. (495-5775). A/C. Lunch Mon–Sat, dinner nightly. AE, MC, V. *Specialties:* iron-skillet-roasted mussels; salt-roasted prawns w. aioli; roasted Dungeness crab w. garlic; grilled sardines w. vinaigrette of parsley, cucumber, and garlic; quail wrapped in pancetta bacon w. bay leaves and polenta; strawberry-rhubarb tart. Extensive list of Californian and European wines. *Note:* Museumesque piazza setting where the din reaches such a level that the chefs must wear headsets and earphones to keep in contact. Pizzas and pastas pale in comparison to main dishes. Located in chic area of SoMa, making it a people-watching experience. A great value. Resv. highly advised. *American.* **l–M**

    ♉♉ **One Market** (dwntwn), 1 Market St. (777-5577). A/C. Lunch Mon–Fri, dinner nightly, brunch Sun; closed Thanksgiving, Dec 25, Jan 1. AE, DC, MC, V. *Specialties:* grilled asparagus w. roasted pepper and calamata olive vinaigrette, steak tartar w. sweet crab and sun-dried tomato rouille, braised lamb w. stewed white beans and gremolada, pan-roasted chicken breast w. creamy polenta, English toffee crunch sundae. Seasonal menu. List of over 500 American wines. *Note:* Voted "Best New Restaurant" in recent survey by *San Francisco Focus.* Opened by Bradley Ogden of Lark Creek Inn fame (see "Personal Favorites," above) in 1993, this sleek new rest. has done gangbusters ever since. Hearty portions and rich flavors come w. every dish. Great location overlooking the bay. Resv. highly recommended. *American.* **I-M**

🍸🍸 **Scott's Seafood** (nr. dwntwn), 2400 Lombard St. (563-
🍸🍸 8988). Lunch/dinner daily; closed Thanksgiving, Dec 25–26. AE, CB, DC, MC, V. *Specialties:* fisherman's stew, grilled sole petrale, fried calamari, sautéed seafood, catch of the day, shellfish. Good desserts. *Note:* In a small, two-story rowhouse typical of San Francisco, this rest. has achieved great local popularity by serving simple food without fuss, and the freshest fish you could ask for. Cheerful svce; often crowded. Resv. advised. Other location: 3 Embarcadero Center (981-0622). Both are excellent places to eat. *Seafood.* **I-M**

🍸🍸 **Pacific Heights** (nr. dwntwn), 2001 Fillmore St. (567-3337).
🍸🍸 A/C. Lunch Wed–Sun, dinner nightly. AE, MC, V. *Specialties:* oysters on the half shell, poached prawn and snow-pea skewers w. red-currant Asian dip, Mediterranean penne pasta. Good list of California wines at reasonable prices. *Note:* San Francisco's best oyster bar; on any given day it serves at least 10 different varieties of the succulent bivalve from both Pacific and Atlantic. The other seafood offered is also impeccably fresh. Charming Victorian decor. A very fine place; excellent value. Resv. advised; valet parking at dinner. *Seafood.* **I-M**

🍸🍸 **Zuni Café** (dwntwn), 1658 Market St. (552-2522). A/C.
🍸🍸 Breakfast/lunch/dinner Tues–Sun; closed hols. AE, MC, V. *Specialties:* pumpkin soup w. chili and escarole, crab-and-shrimp rémoulade w. aioli, squab salad, brick-oven roast chicken, fritto misto, polenta w. mascarpone, caramel "pot de crème." Daily menu. Very fine wine list at very reasonable prices. *Note:* In two or three years Zuni has succeeded in becoming a local landmark; it has been enlarged and spruced up (but avoid the little rms on the second floor). The talented Judy Rogers dishes up a California cuisine which never fails in originality and flavor. The setting is Santa Fe style. Erratic svce. Wildly popular, so resv. a must. *American/Mediterranean.* **I-M**

🍸🍸 **Corona Bar & Grill** (dwntwn), 88 Cyril Magnin St. (392-
🍸🍸 5500). A/C. Lunch/dinner Mon–Sat. AE, CB, DC, MC, V. *Specialties:* clam-and-corn chowder w. cream and cilantro pesto, grilled prawns w. black-bean cake and tomato salsa, empanada of chorizo (spicy sausage) and chili poblano, quesadillas w. shiitake mushrooms and Roquefort and Jack cheese, papaya sorbet, coconut custard. Short but well-thought-out wine list. *Note:* Shimmering blue-and-pink setting w. Mexican masks, and a riot of plants and cactus. Friendly but noisy. Excellent svce. Resv. advised. A very good place. *American/Mexican.* **I**

🍸 **Harry Denton's** (dwntwn), in the Harbor Court (see "Accom-
🍸 modations," above) (882-1333). A/C. Breakfast/lunch/ dinner daily. AE, CB, DC, MC, V. *Specialties:* crab cakes, pasta dishes, hamburgers, pot roast w. buttermilk mashed potatoes, steak. *Note:* An instantly popular saloon which offers American favorites from burgers to crabcakes and great drinks, enhanced by a view of the waterfront and Bay Bridge. Harry Denton is one of the city's most beloved younger characters and this new rest. reflects his sense of fun. Informal, convivial svce and atmosphere. Dancing nightly. *American.* **I**

🍸🍸 **Timo's at the Zanzibar** (dwntwn), 842 Valencia St. (647-
🍸🍸 0558). A/C. Dinner only, nightly; closed Thanksgiving, Dec 24–25. MC, V. *Specialties:* tapas that include prawns sautéed w. sliced garlic, salt cod and potato cake w. cilantro-mint salsa, *pescado tikin xic* (fish filet rubbed w. annatto), salmon filet in puff pastry. Great desserts. *Note:* Upbeat atmosphere w. bright green and purple walls and terracotta-tiled floors. Superb authentic and American-style tapas by chef Carlos Corrador. Tapas start at $2.50—a great value. Resv. highly advised. *Spanish.* **B-I**

🍸 **Wu Kong** (dwntwn), 101 Spear St. (in the Rincon Center)
🍸 (957-9300). A/C. Lunch/dinner daily. AE, MC, V. *Specialties:* dim sum, hot-and-sour fish soup, Shanghai pan-fried noodles w. vegetables,

crispy eels, drunken squab, vegetable goose. *Note:* Some of the best Shanghai-style food this side of the Pacific can be found in this elegant and rather formal dining rm. Dazzling fare at moderate prices. Good natured and generally efficient staff. Resv. advised. *Chinese.* **B–I**

Restaurants in the Vicinity

♟♟♟♟ **Lark Creek Inn** (see "Personal Favorites," above).

♟♟ **Chez Panisse** (vic.), 1517 Shattuck Ave., Berkeley (510/548-5525). A/C. Lunch/dinner Mon–Sat (café), dinner Mon–Sat (rest.) AE, DC, MC, V. *Specialties:* California cuisine w. the freshest and purest ingredients. The menu changes daily. Good but pricey wine list. *Note:* Chez Panisse (the rest. downstairs) is only a shadow of what it was under the guiding hand of its founders Jeremiah Tower and Alice Waters. Prices, especially on the wine list, continue to go up. If food-lovers still come here, it's in reverent pilgrimage to the historic shrine of California cuisine. The café upstairs is a good value overall. *American.* **I–M** (café), **E–VE** (rest.).

Cafeterias/Fast Food

Mama's (dwntwn), 398 Geary St. (788-1004). Breakfast/lunch/dinner daily. AE, DC, MC, V. *Specialties:* roast chicken, sandwiches, daily specials, good homemade desserts. Beer and wine. *Note:* Excellent cafeteria food; inviting atmosphere. Locally popular.

Salmagundi (dwntwn), 442 Geary St. (441-0894). Open daily. AE, MC, V. *Specialties:* homemade soup, quiche, salad, homemade desserts. Beer and wine. *Note:* Quality, no-frills meal; fast and easy on the wallet. Other location: 1236 Market St. (431-7337), open until 9pm.

Where to Eat What

American: Bix (p. 971), Campton Place (p. 969), Chez Panisse (p. 974), Cypress Club (p. 971), Elka (p. 971), Greens (p. 972), Harry Denton's (p. 973), Lark Creek Inn (p. 969), Lulu (p. 972), One Market (p. 972), Postrio (p. 970), Square One (p. 969), Stars (p. 971), Zuni Café (p. 973)

Asian: Elka (p. 971)

Chinese: China Moon Café (p. 970), Dol Ho (p. 970), Hong Kong Flower Lounge (p. 972), Wu Kong (p. 973)

Continental: Ernie's (p. 970)

Cafeterias/Fast Food: Mama's (p. 974), Salmagundi (p. 974)

French: Alain Rondelli (p. 972), Fleur de Lys (p. 969), La Folie (p. 971), Masa's (p. 970)

Indian: Gaylord India (p. 972)

Mexican: Corona Bar & Grill (p. 973)

Seafood: Pacific Heights (p. 973), Scott's Seafood (p. 973), Tadich Grill (p. 969)

Spanish: Timo's at the Zanzibar (p. 973)

Steak: Tadich Grill (p. 969)

BARS & NIGHTCLUBS

☀ **Buena Vista Café** (dwntwn), 2765 Hyde St. (474-5044). One of San Francisco's most renowned cafés, credited with launching the fashion of Irish coffee in the U.S. Fine view of the bay and Alcatraz. Also a commendable rest. Very popular with tourists. Bar open until 2am.

☀ **Caffè Trieste** (dwntwn), 609 Vallejo St. (392-6739). The city's best-known literary café; since it opened in 1956, this longtime haunt of the Beat poets has played host to every prominent literary figure in town. Francis Ford Coppola wrote the script of *The Godfather* here. Italian-bohemian atmosphere. Open daily (7am–midnight).

Cava 555 (dwntwn), 555 Second St. (543-2282). An ideal place to sample the music that put San Francisco on the jazz map. Live music Mon–Sat.

Cesar's Latin Palace (nr. dwntwn), 3140 Mission St. (648-6611). California's biggest Latino nightclub. The huge room can hold 1,000 people. Here merengue and salsa are king.

Club DV8 (dwntwn), 540 Howard St. (777-1419). One of the city's hottest nightspots in the famous SoMa (south of Market) district. Live entertainment and disco. Punk, chic crowds.

Club O (formerly Oasis); (nr. dwntwn), 11th and Folsom Sts. (621-8119). Fashionable disco in what used to be a public swimming pool; outlandish hi-tech decor. Youthful, trendy clientele.

Club 36 (dwntwn), in the Hyatt on Union Square, 345 Stockton St. (398-1234). Posh, aerie jazz club atop the Hyatt. Open nightly.

DNA Lounge (dwntwn), 375 11th St. (626-1409). Hot local bands and DJ. Avant-garde music and atmosphere.

☀ **Eli's Mile High Club** (vic.), 3629 Martin Luther King Way, Oakland (510/655-6661). The best blues joint on the West Coast; worth the trip across the bay. The patrons are a very Berkeley crowd.

El Rio (nr. dwntwn), 3158 Mission St. (282-3325). Another Latin nightclub, very popular locally. The rhythms you'll meet here—samba, merengue, rock, Afro-Cuban, and Caribbean—are almost as varied as the clientele of artists, yuppies, gays, and Latinos. Open nightly.

Finocchio's (dwntwn), 506 Broadway (982-9388). The best-known nightspot featuring female impersonators in the U.S.

Great American Music Hall (dwntwn), 859 O'Farrell St. (885-0750). Live big-name rock, folk, and jazz concerts.

Hard Rock Café (dwntwn), 1699 Van Ness Ave. (885-1699). The Smithsonian of rock 'n' roll. Hard rock; youthful patrons. Good hamburgers; locally very popular. Open nightly.

I-Beam (nr. dwntwn), 1748 Haight St. (668-6023). The favorite of San Francisco's younger set for rock and new wave. Live music and DJs turn and turn about. Very noisy, with laser lights and giant video screens. Mostly students and well-brought-up yuppies.

Paradise Lounge (dwntwn), 1501 Folsom St. (861-6906). A megacomplex of nighttime entertainment w. three stages, five bars, and up to five bands a night. Open nightly until 2am.

☀ **Perry's** (dwntwn), 1944 Union St. (922-9022). Singles bar in the New York tradition; youthful, relaxed atmosphere. Also an unassuming rest. Recommended as a premier pickup spot; open nightly until 1:30am.

Punch Line (dwntwn), 444 Battery St. (397-7573). The best, and best known, of the city's comedy clubs; showcases beginners as well as established stars. Very popular locally. Open nightly.

Rawhide (dwntwn), 280 7th (621-1197). Country-and-western joint, as the name implies. Mixed crowd/gay/lesbian. Open nightly.

☀ **Top of the Mark** (dwntwn), in the Mark Hopkins Inter-Continental, California and Mason Sts. (392-3434). Elegant panoramic bar in a superb art deco setting. Dancing; fine view of the bay. Open nightly until 1:30am.

Tosca Café (dwntwn), 242 Columbus Ave. (391-1244). A popular hangout in the old Italian neighborhood of North Beach. The jukebox plays only opera records.

☀ **Washington Square Bar and Grill** (dwntwn), 1707 Powell St. (982-8123). Lively bar-saloon; also an acceptable Italian rest., but the food is an excuse to talk, celebrate, and rub elbows with the city's most noted characters. Agreeable jazz piano. Open nightly.

Yoshi's (vic.), 60300 Claremont Ave., Oakland (510/652-9200): One of the best jazz spots on the coast; the biggest names perform here. Very good Japanese rest. adj. 25 min. from dwntwn over the Bay Bridge. Open nightly.

NEARBY EXCURSIONS

BERKELEY (12 mi./20km east via the San Francisco–Oakland Bay Bridge and I-80): A cosmopolitan place filled with museums, libraries, theaters, bookstores, and other cultural sites, this city of 105,000 on the east side of San Francisco Bay became a symbol for a generation. The Free Speech Movement—the first campus revolt of the 1960s—began here, capturing the attention of the nation. The University of California's largest campus (32,000 students), Berkeley is one of the oldest (1868) and most famous schools in the country. Among its 1,600 faculty members are no fewer than 12 Nobel Prize winners and 76 members of the prestigious National Academy of Sciences. From its 307-ft. (93m) campanile, a copy of that on the piazza San Marco in Venice, you'll have a wonderful view (there's an elevator). The imposing **Bancroft Library** on University Dr. is one of the nation's richest, with six million volumes. The **visitor center** in University Hall, Oxford St. and University Ave. (510/642-5215), organizes guided tours of the campus Mon, Wed, and Fri. You should also see the university's very beautiful **Art Museum** at 2626 Bancroft Way (510/642-1207), open Wed–Sun.

MUIR WOODS NATIONAL MONUMENT (16 mi./25km north via the Golden Gate Bridge, U.S. 101, and Calif. 1): Splendid redwood forest, with some trees more than 2,000 years old, growing 230 ft. (70m) or more tall and 12 ft. (3.6m) in diameter. From the top of nearby Mt. Tamalpais (2,604 ft./794m) there's a magnificent view over San Francisco Bay and the Pacific. Access is along a panoramic road from Mill Valley. No camping or picnicking permitted. For more information, contact the Site Manager, Mill Valley, CA 94941 (415/388-2595).

OAKLAND (10 mi./16km east across the San Francisco–Oakland Bay Bridge): This busy port and industrial city, founded in 1850, has a large African American community (the Black Panthers originated here), and one of the most beautiful, and original, museums to be found on the West Coast. The **Oakland Museum,** at 1000 Oak St. (510/238-3401), open Wed–Sun, is the work of architect Kevin Roche; its tiered design, with terraced gardens, is quite outstanding. It houses rich material on California art and history, as well as paintings by Hans Hofmann and a splendid film library.

Note also the picturesque **Jack London Square** around the Inner Harbor, bounded by Broadway, Webster St., and the Embarcadero, with restaurants, bars, and shops got up in the turn-of-the-century spirit of Jack London's life and writings. The novelist lived in the vicinity, and wrote a number of his books at Heinold's First and Last Chance Saloon, 56 Jack London Sq. Open daily.

POINT REYES NATIONAL SEASHORE (35 mi./56km north via the Golden Gate Bridge, U.S. 101, and Calif. 1): A 70,000-acre (28,000ha) wildlife reserve on a peninsula jutting out into the Pacific, harboring more than 350 species of birds and mammals. The landscape is beautifully flower-bedecked Feb–July. Beaches; camping; swimming permitted in summer. For lovers of authentic nature. **Visitor centers** at Bear Valley, open daily, and at Drakes Beach, open Sat–Sun and hols. (663-1092).

SAN RAFAEL (19 mi./30km north via the Golden Gate Bridge and U.S. 101): The **Mission San Rafael Arcángel,**

20th and next-to-last of those founded by the Franciscans in California, was built in 1817 and rebuilt in 1949 on the original site at 1104 Fifth Ave. at A St. (456-3016), open daily.

See also the very fine **Marin County Civic Center,** one of the last major works of the great Frank Lloyd Wright, who died in 1959 before it was completed; it's 2 mi. (3.2km) north on San Pedro Rd. (499-7407). Guided and self-guided tours Mon–Fri.

☼🔔🔔 **SAUSALITO** (8 mi./12km north via the Golden Gate Bridge and U.S. 101): The California equivalent of a fashionable European resort like Juan-les-Pins or Portofino, equally attractive to millionaires, artists, and hippies. This gracious pleasure harbor lies across the Golden Gate Bridge from San Francisco, with a wonderful view of the bay. Many shops and art galleries, congenial bars and restaurants. You should see the **San Francisco Bay and Delta Model,** 2100 Bridgeway (332-3870), open Tues–Sat, an enormous (2-acre/0.8ha) hydraulic model which faithfully reproduces the tidal action and marine currents of San Francisco Bay.

SILICON VALLEY: See "South of the Bay and Silicon Valley," under "Farther Afield," below.

🔔 **TIBURON** (18 mi./28km north via the Golden Gate Bridge, U.S. 101, and Calif. 131): Another charming little pleasure harbor near Sausalito, north of the bay. Wonderful view of San Francisco. Many bars, fashionable shops, and fish and seafood restaurants with fine views of the bay. A place that contrives to be both elegant and relaxing.

THE CALIFORNIA WINE COUNTRY

California, which produces more than 70% of all U.S. wines, boasts more than 250 wineries grouped in three main regions. The Central Valley around Fresno produces mass-market table wines. Santa Clara and Monterey, south of San Francisco Bay, produce light, likable wines, particularly whites. Finally, the Napa Valley and Sonoma Valley areas, north of San Francisco Bay, indisputably produce the state's finest wines, beginning with the renowned cabernet sauvignon.

☼🍷🍷 **VISITING THE WINERIES:** Napa Valley and Sonoma Valley, about 50 mi. (80km) NE of San Francisco, are known as "Wine Country." You can arrange for visits and tastings at many of its wineries; for information, contact the **Napa Valley Chamber of Commerce,** 1556 1st St., Napa, CA 94559 (707/226-7455), and the **Sonoma Valley Visitors Bureau,** 453 E. 1st St., Sonoma, CA 95476 (707/996-1090). Among the most interesting wineries are:

Calistoga

Calistoga is 29 mi. (46km) NW of Napa on Calif. 29.

Château Montelena Winery, 1429 Tubbs Lane (707/942-5105), open daily, is a century-old stone castle with a Chinese garden alongside.

Sterling Vineyards, at 1111 Dunaweal Lane (707/942-3300), a lovely estate with the look of an Italian monastery which perches atop a knoll reached by a 300-ft (92m) aerial tramway, is open for (tiring) visits daily.

On the way, see 🔔 **Old Faithful Geyser,** 1299 Tubbs Lane (707/942-6463), which spouts a steamy 60-ft (18m) plume about every 40 min.

Napa

Napa, 44 mi. (70km) north of San Francisco via I-80 and Calif. 29, is one of the centers of wine making in California.

Clos du Val, 5330 Silverado Trail (707/252-6711), is open daily.

Oakville

Oakville is 13 mi. (20km) NW of Napa on Calif. 29.

Robert Mondavi, 7801 St. Helena Hwy. (707/963-9611), is open daily. Arts exhibits and concerts are frequently presented in the graceful building modeled on a Franciscan mission. Resv. recommended.

Rutherford

Rutherford is 15 mi. (24km) NW of Napa on Calif. 29.

Beaulieu Vineyard, 1960 St. Helena Hwy. (707/963-2411), has cellars dating from the turn of the century; open daily.

Inglenook Vineyards, on Calif. 29 (707/967-3300), is in a fine 1883 Gothic Revival cellar house with a half-mile approach avenue leading to the ivy-covered main building, and has an interesting museum of viticulture; open daily.

St. Helena

St. Helena is 19 mi. (30km) NW of Napa on Calif. 29.

Beringer Vineyard, 2000 Main St. (707/963-7115), features the Rhine House built by the founders in 1883 to emulate their ancestral home in Germany; open daily.

Heitz Wine Cellars, 436 St. Helena Hwy. (707/963-3542), has guided tours Mon–Fri.

Charles Krug, 2800 Main St. (707/963-2761), whose handsome decor dates from 1861. Tours Thurs–Tues by appointment.

Louis Martini Winery, 254 St. Helena Hwy. S. (707/963-2736); open daily.

Sonoma

Sonoma, 16 mi. (25km) west of Napa on Calif. 12, along with Napa is the center of the California wine industry. These vineyards, of which Europe is now envious, were started in the 1820s by Spanish Franciscan missionaries, and have been tended since then by German, French, Hungarian, and Italian growers. The vintage is harvested from Sept to early Nov. Some of the more interesting wineries are:

Buena Vista Winery, 18000 Old Winery Rd. (707/938-1266), open daily, is the oldest wine-making estate in California, founded in 1857 by the Hungarian Agoston Haraszthy. Classical concerts in summer.

Sebastiani Vineyards, 389 4th St. E. (707/938-5532), has an interesting museum of viticulture and collection of antique carved vats; open daily.

On the way, take a look at ☼⚓ **Jack London State Historic Park,** on London Ranch Rd. at **Glen Ellen** (707/938-5216), where the author of *Call of the Wild* killed himself in 1916; he's buried here. Beautiful scenery; museum open daily. Also, be sure to see the ⚓ **Mission San Francisco Solano** with its pretty plaza, 21st and last of the missions founded in California by the Spanish Franciscans, in 1823. It's at E. Spain and 1st Sts. E. (707/938-1519); open daily.

Kenwood

Kenwood is 13 mi. (20km) NW of Sonoma.

Château St. Jean, Calif. 12 (707/833-4134), is a very handsome winery in Bavarian peasant style; open daily.

Yountville

Yountville is 10 mi. (16km) NW of Napa on Calif. 29.

Domaine Chandon, 1 California Dr. (707/944-2280), is the U.S. property of the great French champagne house of Moët et Chandon. Cellars open daily May–Oct (Wed–Sun the rest of the year) to visitors who can observe all phases of champagne production.

BALLOON EXCURSIONS: For an unforgettable overview of the Napa Valley take a hot-air-balloon ride. Offered by **Balloon Aviation of Napa Valley,**

6525 Washington St., Yountville (707/252-7067), and **Once in a Lifetime Balloon Co.,** P.O. Box 795, Calistoga, CA 94515 (707/942-6541). Prices range from $120 to $180 per person, including brunch.

FOOD & LODGING IN WINE COUNTRY: As you might imagine, where there's wine, there are restaurants—and places to bed down for the night as well.

Napa

   Budget Inn, 3380 Solano Ave., Napa, CA 94558 (707/257-6111). 58 rms. Ultra-clean accommodations and a small pool. The valley's best deal. **B**

   Bistro Don Giovanni, 4110 St. Helena Hwy. (707/224-3300). Lunch/dinner daily. Excellent gourmet pizzas and other continental dishes reasonably priced in a subdued barn setting. **I–M**

Rutherford

   Auberge du Soleil, 180 Rutherford Hill Rd., Rutherford, CA 94573 (707/963-1211). 50 rms. The most chic and best-known place to stay in the Wine Country. Luxurious Mediterranean-style inn and rest. Member of the prestigious Relais et Châteaux hotel chain. **VE**

Sonoma

   El Dorado Hotel, 405 1st St. W., Sonoma, CA 95476 (707/996-3030; toll free 800/289-3031). 27 rms. Cozy country inn in a renovated 1843 landmark building. Excellent Italian rest. (Piatti). **E**

   Sonoma Mission Inn, 18140 Sonoma Hwy., Boyes Hot Springs, CA 95476 (707/938-9000; toll free, see Preferred). 170 rms. Wonderfully renovated, Spanish-mission–style hotel from the '20s. Unsurpassed svce and facilities; prices to match. **E–VE**

St. Helena

   Meadowood Resort, 900 Meadowood Lane, St. Helena, CA 94574 (707/963-3646; toll free 800/458-8080). 82 rms and suites. Everything that a first-class modern luxury hotel should be: a blend of country elegance and sophistication. Enormous rms or individual cottages surrounded by a great forested park. First-rate rest. **VE**

   Wine Country Inn, 1152 Lodi Lane, St. Helena, CA 94574 (707/963-7077). 25 rms. Charming old country inn. **M–E**

   Catahoula Restaurant and Saloon, 1457 Lincoln Ave. (707/942-2275). Breakfast/lunch/dinner Wed–Mon. Red-hot Southern fare by Louisianan chef/owner Jan Birnbaum, who, before this gig, cooked at the illustrious Campton Place in San Francisco. **I–M**

   Tra Vigne, 1050 Charter Oak Ave. (707/963-4444). Lunch/dinner daily. Refined Italian-Californian cuisine. Outdoor dining in season. **I–M**

   Bordeaux House, 6711 Washington St., Yountville, CA 94599 (707/944-2855). Tiny inn w. only 6 rms; elegantly countrified. Rms recently remodeled. **M**

   Mustards Grill, 7399 St. Helena Hwy. (707/944-2424). Lunch/dinner daily. Excellent entrées grilled over a wood fire; locally popular. **I–M**

   The Diner, 6476 Washington Ave. (707/944-2626). Breakfast/lunch/dinner Tues–Sun. Serving Mexican-American food. **B–I**

FARTHER AFIELD

   CALIF. 1, THE COASTAL HIGHWAY (398 mi./639km r.t. via I-280S, Calif. 17S, and Calif. 1S and 1N): One of the most beautiful drives in the U.S. For a good way it follows the old Camino Real, the 200-year-old highway of the Spanish Franciscan missions. You'll see **Monterey, 17-Mile Drive, Carmel, Big Sur,** and the **Hearst Castle** (see Chapter 51 on the California Coast); then back to San Francisco by the coastal road. Can readily be combined with a visit to areas south of the bay and Silicon Valley (see below). This makes for a fine two- to three-day trip.

LASSEN NATIONAL PARK (246 mi./394km NE via I-5, Calif. 36, and Calif. 89): One of the only two active volcanoes on the U.S. mainland (the other is Mount St. Helens). Rugged scenery. For details, see Chapter 49 on Reno.

REDWOOD EMPIRE (345 mi./552km r.t. via U.S. 101N, Calif. 20W, and Calif. 1S): Magnificent redwood forests inland, and wonderful seascapes along the Pacific coast; can easily be combined with a visit to the vineyards of the **Wine Country** (see above). You'll pass through **Clear Lake,** a huge mountain lake with fishing and sailing; the picturesque fishing ports of **Fort Bragg** and **Mendocino; Noyo,** with its superb 17-acre (6.8ha) botanic garden overlooking the Pacific; and **Fort Ross,** a Russian trading post founded in 1812. It still has many of its original buildings, including its Russian Orthodox chapel; for details, see Chapter 51 on the California Coast. Your last stop might be **Point Reyes National Seashore** (see "Nearby Excursions," above), for a total of a two- to three-day trip.

Where to Stay En Route

Heritage House, 5200 Calif. 1, Littleriver, CA 95456 (707/937-5885), south of Fort Bragg. 72 units. Delightful little cottages on the ocean. Good rest. Closed Jan to mid-Feb. **E–VE** (MAP)

St. Orres, on Calif. 1, Gualala, CA 95445 (707/884-3303), between Mendocino and Fort Ross. Charming tiny (19 rms and cottages) inn; excellent rest. **M–E**

SACRAMENTO & LAKE TAHOE (448 mi./716km r.t. via I-80E, Calif. 89S, U.S. 50W, and I-80W): Lake Tahoe is one of the loveliest mountain lakes in the U.S. (see Chapter 49 on Reno), in an area which offers all kinds of recreational sports in summer and many ski resorts in winter.

On the way you pass through 🔍🔍 **Sacramento,** capital of the state of California, with a history as interesting as any city in the West. Now nicknamed the "Camellia Capital of the World," it first rose to prominence as a center of the 1848–49 gold rush. You should certainly see the 🔍 **State Capitol,** more than a century old and now sumptuously restored, on 10th St. at Capitol Mall (916/324-0333), open daily. Take in **Sutter's Fort State Historic Park,** an adobe fort built in 1839 by the Swiss John Sutter, founder of Sacramento, at 2701 L St. (916/445-4209), open daily. Finally, visit the **Old Sacramento Historic District,** a picturesque old neighborhood along the Sacramento River, restored to its 1850–80 period. Some buildings you shouldn't overlook: the **Old Eagle Theater,** oldest in California (1849), at Front and J Sts., open Tues–Sun; the **California State Railroad Museum,** as fine as any in the country, 2nd and I Sts. (916/448-4466), open daily; and the **Hastings Building,** once the western terminus of the legendary Pony Express, whose hundred dauntless horsemen (one of them the great Buffalo Bill) used to cover in 10 days, at full gallop, the 1,965 mi. (3,145km) between St. Joseph, Missouri (see Chapter 28 on Kansas City), and Sacramento. It was only the coming of the telegraph, in the 1860s, that put an end to their feats. The Hastings Building also at one time housed the California Supreme Court. It's at 2nd and J Sts.; open daily.

Near Sacramento are many ☀ **mining towns** from the gold-rush days; among the most picturesque are **Coloma** (where gold was first discovered in

1848), **Placerville, Fair Play, Rough and Ready, Grass Valley,** and **Nevada City.**
This spectacular trip will take you three or four days.

Where to Stay in Sacramento

♟♟♟ **Hyatt Regency,** 1209 L St., Sacramento, CA 95814 (916/
443-1234). 500 rms. New palace hotel across from the State Capitol, w. all the usual Hyatt comforts. **E–VE**

♟♟♟ **Clarion,** 700 16th St., Sacramento, CA 95814 (916/444-8000). 239 rms. Elegantly renovated old hotel standing in a lovely grdn across from the Governor's Mansion. Commendable rest. **M**

♟♟ **Radisson** (formerly the Woodlake Inn), 500 Leisure Lane, Sacramento, CA 95815 (916/922-2020). 314 rms. Luxurious convention hotel located on a private lake. **M**

♟ **Motel 6,** 1415 30th St., Sacramento, CA 95816 (916/457-0777). 94 rms. Motel, no-frills but acceptable, nr. Sutter's Fort and the State Capitol. **B**

Where to Eat in Sacramento

♟♟♟ **Chanterelle,** in the Sterling Hotel, 1300 H St. (916/442-0451). Breakfast Mon–Fri, dinner nightly. One of the city's best culinary offerings. *American.* **I–M**

♟♟ **Biba,** 2801 Capitol Ave. (916/455-2422). Lunch Mon–Fri, dinner Mon–Sat. All the mainstays of Italian cuisine, impeccably prepared and served. *Italian.* **I–M**

♟♟ **Firehouse,** 1112 2nd St. (916/442-4772). Lunch Mon–Fri, dinner Mon–Sat. A handsome antique setting in an 1853 firehouse. *Continental/American.* **I–M**

♟♟ **Crawdad's River Cantina,** 1375 Garden Hwy. (916/929-2268). Lunch/dinner daily. Fashionable rest. on the banks of the Sacramento River serving inventive, flavorful Tex-Mex food. **I**

SEQUOIA NATIONAL PARK (270 mi./432km SE via I-580, I-5, and Calif. 198): The kingdom of the forest giants. See Chapter 52 on Sequoia National Park.

SOUTH OF THE BAY & SILICON VALLEY (155 mi./ 248km r.t. via U.S. 280, U.S. 101S, and I-280N): Leaving San Francisco along U.S. 280, you should first visit **Filoli** on Canada Rd., Woodside (415/364-2880). This imposing Georgian-style manor house, built in 1919, was the set for the Carrington mansion in the TV series "Dynasty." Also open to the public are the 16 acres (6ha) of splendid landscaped gardens. Open Tues–Sat mid-Feb to mid-Nov (call ahead for information). Continuing along U.S. 280 you come to **Palo Alto,** home of **Stanford University,** on Camino Real (Calif. 82), with no fewer than 10 Nobel laureates on the faculty. With 13,000 students, it's one of the most highly regarded of U.S. universities, particularly in the fields of technology, medicine, and high-tech electronics. Elegant red-tiled Romanesque buildings. You get a good view of the campus from the 285-ft. (87m) Hoover Tower. Campus open daily; for information on tours, check with the information booth at the end of Palm Dr. (415/723-2560).

Heading south, you next come to **Mountain View,** the gateway to Silicon Valley, where space buffs will certainly visit the **Ames Research Center** at the Moffett Field exit from U.S. 101 (415/604-5000). NASA's research laboratory here boasts one of the largest wind-tunnels in the world, powered by six giant turbines. The laboratory can be seen (a 2½-mi./4km trip on foot) by appointment only; you must reserve two weeks in advance. Open Mon–Fri.

Stop off at **Great America,** the huge theme park at **Santa Clara** (see "Theme Parks," above).

Though ❊ **Silicon Valley** (named after the silicon chips on which electronic circuits are based) may not be found on most maps, for two decades a surprising number of very bright people have been working here. For a radius of 30 mi. (50km) around **Sunnyvale, Los Altos, Mountain View,** and **Santa Clara,** yesterday's almond and orange groves have given way to the world's leading hothouse for innovation. Some 3,000 corporations in all, from giants like National Semiconductor and Intel to workshops employing half a dozen people, make Silicon Valley the world capital of electronics. As a living illustration of "neocapitalism," not only are the technicians and researchers employed in Silicon Valley among the best-paid employees in the U.S., but also many participate in the management, and in the profits, of their firms.

Drive 3 mi. (5km) south of Santa Clara to ❊ **San Jose,** the former state capital, to see the ⚱ **Egyptian Museum** and its important collection of antiquities at 1342 Naglee Ave. (408/947-3636), open daily; ⚱ **Alum Rock Park,** 16240 Alum Rock Ave. (408/259-5477), and the curious rock formations that have earned it the name of "Little Yosemite"; the ⚱ **Lick Observatory,** with its 36-in. (91cm) telescope, 25 mi. (40km) SE on Mount Hamilton (408/274-5061), with visits by appointment daily, for astronomy buffs; the **Mirassou** winery, 3000 Aborn Rd. (408/274-4000), open daily; and above all the unbelievable ❊⚱⚱ **Winchester Mystery House,** 525 S. Winchester Blvd. (408/247-2101), open daily, with its 160 bedrooms, 13 baths, 2,000 doors, 10,000 windows, 47 fireplaces, secret corridors, blank walls, trap doors, and false staircases. This was the last home of Sarah Winchester, widow of the famous gunmaker, and during the last 38 years of her life (1884–1922) she never stopped adding to the house—a clairvoyant had told her that she would not die as long as she went on building! It cost her $6 million—a much huger sum then than now.

Your last stop will be in **Saratoga,** where you should visit the elegant ⚱ **Villa Montalvo,** with its art galleries and beautiful gardens, at 15400 Villa Montalvo Rd. (408/741-3421); gardens open daily, galleries open Thurs–Sun. Also the **Paul Masson** winery, 14831 Pierce Rd. (408/741-5183), has classical and jazz concerts June–Sept. (It's no longer a working winery.)

This trip can be made inside a day, but it's best combined with the itinerary along Calif. 1, the Coastal Highway (see above).

Where to Eat in Silicon Valley

♟♟♟ **Eulipia,** 373 S. 1st St., San José (408/280-6161). Lunch Tues –Fri, dinner Tues–Sun. AE, MC, V. The most imaginative California cuisine in the valley. Attractive decor. *American.* **M**

♟♟ **Scott's Seafood Grill,** 2300 E. Bayshore Rd., Palo Alto (415/ 856-1046). Lunch Mon–Fri, dinner nightly. AE, CB, DC, MC, V. Sibling of the famous San Francisco rest. Cape Cod decor. *Seafood.* **I–M**

❊⚱⚱⚱ **YOSEMITE NATIONAL PARK** (210 mi./336km east via I-580, I-205, and Calif. 120): Nature in the raw. See Chapter 53 on Yosemite.

CHAPTER 51

THE CALIFORNIA COAST♛

□ □ □

San Francisco to San Diego

From the extraordinary panorama of San Francisco in the north, for 604 mi. (974km) south to lovely San Diego on the Mexican border, the California coast offers the visitor some of the country's most spectacular landscapes. It's an unexpected patchwork of fertile valleys, great cities, and unspoiled forests of pine or sequoia, of rocky headlands and wonderful beaches (though the currents sweeping in from the north can often chill the water). The California coast, however, is more than a colorful tract of American geography; it embodies a typically Californian way of life compounded of sun, relaxation, and communion with nature.

From the steep cliffs of **Big Sur,** a favorite meeting place for America's literary bohemia, to the fine sand beaches of **Santa Barbara** or **Huntington Beach,** the surfer's paradise, this great "Pacific Riviera" is a standing invitation to travelers, and to lovers of beauty. Thus the motorist who takes the celebrated coastal Hwy. 1 (Calif. 1), the "Cabrillo Highway," will encounter the period charm of the old Spanish colonial settlements like **Monterey,** so beloved by John Steinbeck; the trendy elegance of **Carmel;** the fabled castle of billionaire William Randolph Hearst at **San Simeon;** the rosary of Franciscan missions that runs the length of the coast from **San Juan Bautista** to **San Juan Capistrano;** or the mighty silhouette of **Morro Rock,** the Gibraltar of the West Coast, whose massive 563-ft. (172m) bulk looms over the Pacific. And let's not overlook the untold wealth of the late J. Paul Getty's Roman villa at **Malibu,** or the luxury of **La Jolla,** with its Riviera-like beauty. Along the incredible **"Seventeen-Mile Drive"** (27km) between Carmel and Monterey, are centuries-old cypresses and tidal rocks covered with sea anemones and peopled with sea lions and elephant seals, where every winter and spring you may watch the passing migration of the gray whales. The California coast, goal of any east-west trip across the U.S., will never cease to enchant the visitor.

For detailed information on the larger cities along the California coast, see the chapters on **Los Angeles, San Diego,** and **San Francisco.**

Note: The name "California," used by the first Spanish conquistadors, comes from a tale of medieval chivalry, and denotes a legendary isle lying to the east of Paradise, inhabited by dusky Amazons and by gryphons, with eagles' heads and lions' bodies.

BASIC FACTS: State of California. Area codes: 619 (San Diego), 714 (San Bernardino), 213 and 310 (Los Angeles), 805 (Santa Barbara), 408 (Monterey), 415 and 510 (San Francisco), 818 (Burbank). Time zone: Pacific. Founded:

1769 (San Diego); 1770 (Monterey); 1776 (San Francisco). Approximate distance from San Francisco to San Diego: 604 mi. (974 km).

CLIMATE: The California coast is no less fortunate in its climate than in its scenery. In winter (though this is no name by which to call such a season) the mercury never dips below 46°–50°F (8°–10°C), though there can be heavy rains at times in the northern and central parts of the state. Summer is very hot but dry; spring and autumn are wonderful to behold, and filled with unbelievably vibrant light, especially in the south. Aside from a few short weeks of bad weather in winter, this is a year-round paradise.

ARRIVAL & TRANSIT INFORMATION

AIRPORTS: There are five major airports on the California coast:
Los Angeles International Airport (LAX) (see Chapter 54 on Los Angeles).
Monterey Peninsula Airport (MRY), 4 mi. (6.5km) SE; for information, call 408/648-7000.
San Diego Lindbergh International Airport (SAN) (see Chapter 55 on San Diego).
San Francisco International Airport (SFO) (see Chapter 50 on San Francisco).
Santa Barbara Municipal Airport (SBA), 10 mi. (16km) west; for information, call 805/683-4011.

AIRLINES: See the Los Angeles, San Diego, and San Francisco chapters for listings of domestic and international airlines.

CAR RENTAL: See the Los Angeles, San Diego, and San Francisco chapters.

BUS OR CAR RENTAL? Greyhound buses provide frequent, convenient service for the entire coastal region of California. On the other hand, car-rental rates in the state are very low—and the possibilities for interesting side trips are almost unlimited—so it's a very good idea to rent a car, or mobile home, with unlimited mileage.

TRAIN: The Amtrak (toll free 800/872-7545) stations are: 200 E. 4th St. in **Oxnard,** 40 Railroad Ave. in **Salinas (Monterey),** 1011 Railroad Ave. at Santa Rosa St. in **San Luis Obispo,** 209 State St. in **Santa Barbara;** see the Los Angeles, San Diego, and San Francisco chapters for offices in these cities.

INTERCITY BUSES: In addition to the Greyhound (toll free 800/231-2222) offices in San Francisco, Los Angeles, and San Diego (see these chapters for details), there are California coastal offices at 1042 del Monte Ave., **Monterey;** 150 South St., **San Luis Obispo;** 34 W. Carrillo St., **Santa Barbara;** and 425 Front St., **Santa Cruz.**

INFORMATION & TOURS

TOURIST INFORMATION: For general information on the region, write or call the **California Office of Tourism,** 801 K St., Suite 1600, Sacramento, CA 95814 (916/322-2881; toll free 800/862-2543, ext. 99). For more specific information, contact the following:
Los Angeles Visitors & Convention Bureau (see Chapter 54 on Los Angeles).
Monterey Chamber of Commerce, 380 Alvarado St., CA 93940 (408/649-1770).
San Francisco Visitors Bureau (see Chapter 50 on San Francisco).

San Luis Obispo Chamber of Commerce, 1039 Chorro St., CA 93401 (805/781-2777).
Santa Barbara Conference and Visitors Bureau, 510A State St., CA 93101 (805/966-9222; toll free 800/927-4688).

GUIDED TOURS: See the chapters on San Francisco, Los Angeles, and San Diego; for other cities, look under "Sightseeing" in the local *Yellow Pages.*

SPECIAL EVENTS: For exact dates on the events listed below, consult the local chambers of commerce listed under "Tourist Information" (above), as well as the **Carmel Business Association,** San Carlos and 7th, CA 93921 (408/624-2522); the **Oxnard Tourism Bureau,** 711 S. A St., CA 93030 (805/385-7545); the **San Clemente Chamber of Commerce,** 1100 N. El Camino Real, CA 92672 (714/492-1131); the **Santa Cruz Conference and Visitors Council,** 701 Front St., CA 95061 (408/425-1234); the **Solvang Visitors Bureau,** 1511-A Mission Dr., CA 93463 (toll free 800/468-6765); and the **Ventura Visitor and Convention Bureau,** 89-C California St., CA 93001 (805/648-2075).

Carmel
Carmel Bach Festival (last two weeks in July, beginning of Aug): Concerts, opera, poetry recitations, theater.

Gilroy
Garlic Festival (last full wknd of July): Features a giant open-air kitchen, a Garlic Queen pageant, garlic braiding, arts and crafts.

Monterey
Monterey Jazz Festival (mid-Sept): Attracts the biggest names in jazz today. The oldest continuous jazz festival in the nation.

Oceanside
San Luís Rey Fiesta (third wknd in July): Reenactment of the Padres, an elaborate pageant. Dances, entertainment, Spanish-style pit barbecue.

Oxnard
Strawberry Festival (May): Wine tasting, entertainment, strawberry foods, crafts.

Pebble Beach
Classic Cars Elegance Contest (end of Aug): Almost 200 classic cars, from the Bugatti Royale to the Cord L-29. One of the world's largest rallies of luxury cars.

San Clemente
La Cristianita Pageant (end of July): Commemorates the first baptisms by the Spanish missionaries.

San Luis Obispo
Mozart Festival (end of July to early Aug): Concerts, choirs, recitals.

Santa Barbara
Music Academy of the West Festival (July–Aug): Chamber and orchestral concerts, opera.
Old Spanish Days Fiesta (early Aug): Parades, historic pageants.

Santa Cruz
Cabrillo Music Festival (end of July to early Aug): Classical and contemporary music; one of California's most celebrated festivals.

Solvang
Danish Days Festival (third wknd in Sept): Costume festival celebrating the Danish national holiday.
Theaterfest (June–Oct): Open-air theatricals.

Ventura
   County Fair (Aug): Parades, carnival, rodeo, cattle show. Very colorful.

A NORTH-TO-SOUTH ITINERARY

Down the California Coast from San Francisco

To:	Distance	To:	Distance
Santa Cruz	81 mi. (131km)	Ventura	413 mi. (666km)
Gilroy	104 mi. (166km)	Oxnard	421 mi. (679km)
San Juan Bautista	115 mi. (185km)	Malibu	455 mi. (734km)
Castroville	132 mi. (213km)	Pacific Palisades	463 mi. (747km)
Monterey	143 mi. (231km)	Santa Monica	472 mi. (761km)
17-Mile Drive	145 mi. (234km)	Los Angeles	490 mi. (790km)
Carmel	157 mi. (253km)	Huntington Beach	520 mi. (839km)
Big Sur	184 mi. (297km)	Newport Beach	526 mi. (848km)
San Simeon	248 mi. (400km)	Laguna Beach	535 mi. (863km)
Morro Rock	276 mi. (445km)	San Juan Capistrano	547 mi. (882km)
San Luis Obispo	290 mi. (468km)	San Clemente	554 mi. (894km)
Lompoc	327 mi. (527km)	Oceanside-Carlsbad	580 mi. (935km)
Solvang	339 mi. (547km)	La Jolla	589 mi. (950km)
Santa Barbara	386 mi. (623km)	San Diego	604 mi. (974km)

   SANTA CRUZ (81 mi./131km): Busy fishing port with a long pier and 28 mi. (45km) of public beaches much frequented by swimmers. Last refuge of the hippies. Reproduction, one-half original size, of the Santa Cruz Mission, destroyed by an earthquake in the 19th century and now undergoing restoration. At **Año Nuevo State Reserve** (21 mi./34km north on Calif. 1), the unusual spectacle of hundreds of sea lions, elephant seals, and other marine animals lazily sunning themselves on the rocks. At **Felton** (7 mi./11km north on Calif. 9) is the Roaring Camp and Big Trees Railroad (408/335-4400), where a picturesque little train from the early West will take you through the sequoia forests (daily).

Where to Stay
   Dream Inn, 175 W. Cliff Dr., Santa Cruz, CA 95060 (408/426-4330). 164 rms, A/C, cable color TV. AE, CB, DC, MC, V. Free parking, pool, rest., bar, rm svce, crib $10. *Note:* Modern 10-floor motel, comfortable and attractive; the best rms (w. balconies) overlook the beach. Good svce. Direct access to beach. **M–E**

Where to Eat
   Crow's Nest, 2218 E. Cliff Dr. (408/476-4560). A/C. Lunch/dinner daily, brunch Sun; closed Thanksgiving, Dec 24–25. AE, MC, V. *Specialties:* fresh salmon (in season), fish of the day, steak. *Note:* Likable fish rest. standing on the jetty of the yacht basin; beautifully fresh fish prepared without any imagination. Svce w. a smile. Terrace for fine days, w. a view of the harbor. Dancing. Resv. advised. *Steak/Seafood.* **B–I**
   Taco Moreno, 1053 Watcher (408/429-6095). A/C. Lunch/dinner daily. No credit cards. *Specialties:* tacos, burritos (w. barbecued pork, carnitas, beef asado, beans, tongue, and green chili), quesadillas. *Note:* This hole-in-the-wall joint run by Esteban Moreno and his family offers the best burritos in town. The four tables are squeezed between cases of natural sodas or boxes of tortillas and its jukebox occupies about a quarter of the

dining rm. A favorite of the students at University of California Santa Cruz. No resv. *Mexican.* **B**

IN NEARBY CAPITOLA 🍴🍴**Shadowbrook,** 1750 Wharf Rd. (408/475-1511). No A/C. Dinner nightly, brunch Sun. *Specialties:* fresh salmon (in season), abalone (in season), excellent meat. *Note:* One of the coast's most popular rests., reached by a little funicular from the highway, below which it stands on the edge of a pretty inlet, surrounded by greenery. Good svce; resv. advised. *Steak/Seafood.* **I–M**

🍴 **GILROY** (104 mi./166km): Will Rogers called this self-proclaimed "garlic capital of the world" "the only town in America where you can marinate a steak by hanging it on the clothesline." Gilroy is famous for its Garlic Festival, an annual extravaganza held the last full wknd of July, complete with garlic-recipe cook-off, garlic braiding, and Gourmet Alley's alfresco kitchen with more than 85 food booths.

🌅🏛 **SAN JUAN BAUTISTA** (115 mi./185km): The **Mission of San Juan Bautista,** 2nd and Mariposa Sts. (408/623-4528), open daily. California's largest Franciscan mission (1797), and one of the best preserved. Fine **plaza** with many buildings from the 1850s, including the splendid Plaza Hotel on 2nd St. (408/623-4881), open daily.

Where to Eat

🌅🍸 **Cademartori's,** 1st and San José Sts. (408/623-4511). No A/C. Lunch Tues–Sat, dinner Tues–Sun; Dec 24–25. AE, DC, MC, V. *Specialties:* veal parmigiana, saltimbocca, calamari, homemade pasta. *Note:* This Italian-American rest. occupies a former outbuilding of the San Juan Bautista Mission, standing in a beautiful grdn. It offers honorable, meticulous cuisine and a wonderful view over the San Juan Valley. Open-air patio in summer; a good place. *Italian/American.* **I**

🍴 **CASTROVILLE** (132 mi./213km): In this town, modestly styling itself the "artichoke capital of the world," you may try this delicious vegetable prepared in every conceivable way—fried, boiled, as a cream soup, sautéed, or even in a cake—at the Giant Artichoke Restaurant, 11261 Merritt St. (408/633-3204). Entertaining festival every Sept, with election of an "artichoke queen."

Where to Stay

IN NEARBY SALINAS 🛏 **Motel 6,** 1010 Fairview Ave., Salinas, CA 93901 (408/758-2122). 58 rms, cable color TV. AE, DC, MC, V. Free parking, pool, free crib. *Note:* A small, reasonably priced motel offering serviceable comfort on a shoestring. An unbeatable value. **B**

🌅🏛🏛 **MONTEREY** (143 mi./231km): Lively and colorful, Monterey is the most Spanish of Californian towns, still evidencing many traces of its colonial days: the **Presidio** (1846), seat of the Spanish government, on Pacific St. (408/647-5414), open Mon–Fri; the old **Custom House** (1827), 1 Custom House Plaza; the **Royal Presidio Chapel,** at 550 Church St., founded by Spanish settlers in 1770; **California's First Theater,** the oldest theater in the state, at Pacific and Scott Sts. (408/375-4916), where performances have been given without interruption since 1847; the **Colton Hall Museum,** formerly the City Hall, at 522 Pacific St., whose cellar was used as a prison during the Mexican War. There are some charming **old houses,** one of which, at 530 Houston St., belonged to Robert Louis Stevenson, the author of *Treasure Island.*

You should also see the harbor district and **Cannery Row,** made famous by John Steinbeck; at 886 Cannery Row (408/648-4888) is the splendid, ultramodern **Monterey Bay Aquarium,** inaugurated in 1984, open daily, with more than 5,000 specimens including many sharks and giant octopi; it was used as a setting for the movie *Star Trek IV.*

Where to Stay

Hyatt Regency, 1 Old Golf Course, Monterey, CA 93940 (408/372-1234; toll free, see Hyatt). 579 rms, color TV, in-rm movies. AE, CB, DC, MC, V. Free parking, two pools, six tennis courts, golf course, health club, sauna, putting green, two rests. (including the Peninsula), rm svce, bars, concierge, free crib. *Note:* One of the best hotels along the California coast; modern and elegant, w. almost 15 acres (6ha) of grdns facing the Del Monte golf course. Excellent svce; favored by groups and wealthy sports-lovers. Recently modernized and enlarged. Two VIP floors. **E–VE**

Monterey Plaza, 400 Cannery Row, Monterey, CA 93940 (408/646-1700; toll free 800/631-1339). 290 rms, A/C, color TV, in-rm movies. AE, CB, DC, MC, V. Valet gar. $10, health club, private beach, rest. (Duck Club), bar, rm svce, boutiques, concierge. *Note:* The most recent of Monterey's palaces; three elegant four-story Spanish Colonial buildings on Cannery Row halfway between Fisherman's Wharf and the Aquarium. The interior decoration, featuring Oriental rugs, teak panels, a profusion of marble, objets d'art, and period furniture, comes together in a magnificent triumph of luxury and sophistication. Huge, comfortable rms that come w. minibars and a terrycloth robe, most w. ocean view; impeccable svce. One of the best places on the Pacific coast. **E–VE**

Cypress Tree Inn, 2227 Fremont Rd., Monterey, CA 93940 (408/372-7586). 55 rms, cable color TV. AE, MC, V. Free parking, bakery, crib $6. *Note:* Typical small motel, modest but well run. Spacious rms w. balconies and mini-refrigerators (some w. kitchenettes). Free morning coffee. Located 5 min. from dwntwn and from Monterey State Beach. **I–M,** but lower rates off-season.

Motel 6, 2124 N. Fremont St., Monterey, CA 93940 (408/646-8585). 51 rms, color TV. AE, DC, MC, V. Free parking, pool, free crib. *Note:* Small budget hotel nr. dwntwn, adequately comfortable. Unbeatable value. **B**

Where to Eat

Fresh Cream, 100C Heritage Harbor (408/375-9798). A/C. Lunch Fri, dinner nightly; closed hols. DC, MC, V. Jkt. *Specialties:* lobster ravioli in shrimp butter, rack of lamb dijonnaise, roast duckling w. black currants, stuffed swordfish w. red bell pepper butter and salsa. Well-rounded, selective wine list. *Note:* A mecca for classical French cuisine elegantly prepared w. a California flair. Warm, low-key atmosphere w. Impressionist paintings, beautiful flower arrangements, and muted tapestried upholstery. Impeccable svce. A highly commendable address w. an ocean view. Resv. recommended. *French.* **M–E**

Sardine Factory, 701 Wave St. (408/373-3775). A/C. Dinner only, nightly; closed for one week at Christmas. AE, CB, DC, MC, V. J&T. *Specialties:* abalone bisque, fish of the day, Monterey bay prawns w. shallots, Cannery Row linguini. Fine list of reasonably priced wines. *Note:* This famous rest., though its former glory has perhaps faded a trifle, still overlooks Cannery Row. Exemplary meat and fish prepared in a rather outdated fashion. Splendid Conservatory Room amid a tropical greenhouse. Svce so-so. Comfortable, welcoming bar. Resv. advisable. Valet parking. *Continental/Seafood.* **M–E**

The Fishery, 21 Soledad Dr. (408/373-6200). A/C. Dinner only, Tues–Sat; closed Dec–Jan. MC, V. *Specialties:* fishburgers, broiled filet of Coho salmon, catfish Louisiana style, Thai-style seafood platter, squid. *Note:* The community's favorite fish rest., serving the freshest possible food prepared w. some exotic touches (Malaysian and Thai recipes in

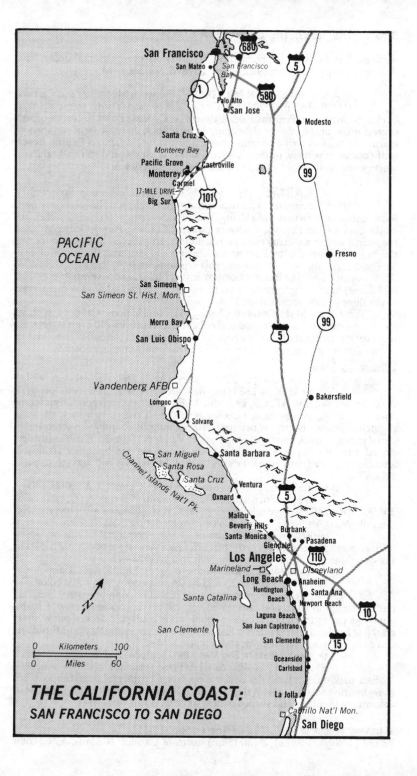

THE CALIFORNIA COAST:
SAN FRANCISCO TO SAN DIEGO

particular) and at very acceptable prices. Rather elaborate Oriental decor. Fast, deft svce. In view of its popularity, resv. advised. *Seafood.* **I–M**

🔆🔍 **"SEVENTEEN-MILE DRIVE"** (between **Monterey** and **Carmel,** 145 mi./234km): One of the country's most scenic roads, it circles the Monterey Peninsula along the shore. **Cypress Point** features a superb cypress grove at the edge of the ocean. At **Seal Rock** there are large numbers of marine animals as well as dream houses and the world-famous **Pebble Beach golf course.** If you saw nothing else in California, this would still make the trip worthwhile, as attested by the 1½ million visitors every year.

🔆🔍 **CARMEL** (157 mi./253km): This charming little artists' community, spruce and covered in flowers, has become a fashionable tourist attraction and a Shangri-La for lucky retirees and personalities (including actor Clint Eastwood, former mayor of Carmel). Along Ocean Ave. and the nearby streets are many open-air restaurants, art galleries, and boutiques. See the beautiful **San Carlos Borromeo Mission** (1770), and the tomb of Fray Junípero Serra, founder of the California missions, at 3080 Rio Rd. (408/624-3600), open daily. The **Biblical Garden** at Lincoln St. and Seventh Ave. (408/624-3550) has a complete collection of the trees, plants, and flowers mentioned in the Bible or originating in the Holy Land.

Point Lobos State Reserve (3 mi./5km south along Calif. 1), with its rocks thronged with sea lions and sea birds, and its centuries-old cypress trees, is a must for nature-lovers. There's a popular Bach Festival at the end of July. Make a point of coming here, but try to avoid the crowds on summer weekends.

Where to Stay

🔆🛏🛏🛏🛏 **Quail Lodge,** 8205 Valley Green Dr., Carmel, CA 93923 (408/624-1581; toll free, see Preferred). 100 rms (cottages), A/C, cable color TV. AE, CB, DC, MC, V. Free parking, two pools, four tennis courts, putting green, sauna, bicycles, rest. (The Covey), two bars, rm svce, nightclub, hrdrsr, library, concierge. *Note:* Delightful country inn set in manicured grdns w. duck ponds, adj. the Carmel Valley golf course. Luxuriously decorated rms w. fireplaces, minibars, patios, and private balconies. Polished, attentive svce; elegantly romantic atmosphere. Interesting golf and tennis packages. **VE**

🛏🛏 **La Playa,** Camino Real at 8th St., Carmel, CA 93921 (408/624-6476; toll free 800/582-8900). 75 rms, A/C, cable color TV. AE, DC, MC, V. Free valet parking, pool, rest. (Terrace Grill), bar, rm svce, free crib. *Note:* Attractive Spanish Colonial hotel dating from the early 20th century, w. an entirely renovated interior. Large, comfortable rms w. minirefrigerators and private patios, the best offering a view of the ocean and the Point Lobos wildlife reserve. Inviting grdns; efficient svce. **M–VE**

🛏🛏 **Cobblestone Inn,** Junipero St. at Eighth Ave., Carmel, CA 93921 (408/625-5222). 24 rms (no A/C), cable color TV. AE, MC, V. Limited parking lot; no bar or rest., but complimentary breakfast buffet, afternoon wine, and hors d'oeuvres; valet svce, concierge. *Note:* Charming two-story inn wrapped around a cobblestone courtyard decked out w. flowers. New England country decor. Each rm has a fireplace, country pine furniture, and a refrigerator. Gracious svce and reception. **M–E**

🛏 **Best Western Bay View Inn,** Junipero and Sixth Sts., Carmel, CA 93921 (408/624-1831). 55 rms, cable color TV. AE, MC, V. Free parking, pool, nearby coffee shop, free Continental breakfast, crib $5. *Note:* Inviting small motel nr. the San Carlos Borromeo Mission; large, comfortable rms w. fireplaces and shaded patios, some w. ocean view. **M–E**

IN NEARBY PEBBLE BEACH 🔆🛏🛏🛏🛏 **The Lodge,** 17-Mile Dr., Pebble Beach, CA 93953 (408/624-3811), 3 mi. (5km) north of Carmel. 163 rms, A/C, color

TV, in-rm movies. AE, CB, DC, MC, V. Free valet parking, private beach, pool, 14 tennis courts, four golf courses, sauna, riding, two rests. (including Club XIX), coffee shop, bar, 24-hr. rm svce, hrdrsr, boutiques, concierge, free crib. *Note:* Pure luxury on the ocean. Serene, subdued, and sublimely comfortable hotel built in 1919; tasteful decor w. period furniture and many artworks. Spacious rms w. fireplaces and minibars, and balconies or patios w. a view of the ocean (in the better ones) or the golf course. Excellent rest. (Club XIX). Remarkable sports facilities. Airport limo. Interesting golf and wknd packages. Resv. should be made well in advance. **VE**

Where to Eat

🍷🍷 **Crème Carmel,** San Carlos St. and Seventh Ave. (408/624-
🍷🍷 0444). A/C. Dinner only, nightly; closed Jan 1, Thanksgiving, Dec 25. MC, V. *Specialties:* lamb w. apple-mint chutney, salmon w. basil-spinach sauce, jumbo sea scallops w. fricassée of wild mushrooms, filet of beef au cabernet, roast duck, soufflés, goat-cheese pie. The menu changes regularly. *Note:* Small (35-seat) rest. w. a warm, vital ambience. Modern Californian cuisine, elegant and imaginative, but feebly supported by the wine list. Svce is the best; an excellent place to eat. Resv. a must. *American/Continental.* **M–E**

🍷🍷 **Rio Grill,** Calif. 1 at Rio Rd. (408/625-5436). A/C. Lunch/
🍷🍷 dinner daily, brunch Sun; closed Thanksgiving, Dec 25. MC, V. *Specialties:* oakwood-grilled chicken, fish, and meat; quesadillas; excellent homemade desserts. Menu changes daily. *Note:* Under the same management as the Fog City Diner in San Francisco and Mustards Grill in Napa Valley, this fashionable rest. offers inventive and elegant California cuisine. Decor recalls the Native American pueblos of New Mexico: adobe walls, heavy exposed beams, and cactus. Svce on the relaxed side, but a very congenial atmosphere. A discovery. *American.* **I–M**

🍷🍷 **Rocky Point,** Calif. 1 at Rocky Point, 12 mi. (19km) south of
🍷🍷 Carmel (408/624-2933). A/C. Lunch/dinner daily; closed Thanksgiving, Dec 25. AE, MC, V. *Specialties:* meat from the broiler, swordfish, barbecued chicken. *Note:* Perched on a cliff, this popular rest. looks right out over the ocean and its wildlife (the rocks below are floodlit at night). Satisfying steaks and irreproachably fresh fish of the day. Resv. advised. *Steak/Seafood.* **I–M**

🍷 **Flying Fish Grill,** Seventh Ave. and Mission St. (408/625-
🍷 1962). A/C. Dinner only, Wed–Mon (nightly in summer); closed hols. MC, V. *Specialties:* paper-wrapped catfish, ying-yang salmon, seafood claypot. *Note:* Quirky papier mâché flying fish decorations. Good Japanese menu serving local ingredients. *Japanese.* **B–I**

🍷 **Hog's Breath Inn,** San Carlos St. and Fifth Ave. (408/625-
🍷 1044). A/C. Lunch/dinner daily. AE, MC, V. *Specialties:* sandwiches, variety of salads, catch of the day, good homemade desserts. *Note:* Country inn w. appealing shady patio, perfect for a pleasant meal on the wing. Honest, unpretentious food; the owner is none other than the famous actor (and former mayor of Carmel) Clint Eastwood. *American.* **B–I**

IN NEARBY PEBBLE BEACH 🍷🍷🍷 **Club XIX,** at the Lodge (see "Where to Stay," above) (408/625-1880). A/C. Lunch/dinner daily. AE, CB, DC, MC, V. Jkt. *Specialties:* lamb Wellington, fresh salmon (in season), grilled pheasant, rack of lamb bouquetière, soufflé Grand Marnier. Good wine list. *Note:* Elegant, sumptuous rest. appropriate to a palatial hotel. Classic but delicate French cooking. Magnificent view of Pebble Beach golf club and the ocean. Exemplary svce. Dining by candlelight. One of the best on the coast. Resv. advised. *French.* **M–E**

☀️🏕 **BIG SUR** (184 mi./297km): In the 1950s this was the haunt of America's literary bohemians. Its splendid rocky cliffs and its pine and redwood forest have served as a backdrop for innumerable movies, TV series, and novels. Henry Miller, who passed his last years here, devoted one of his most famous passages to the place. Very beautiful beach, deserted more often than not.

Where to Stay

♀♀♀ **Post Ranch Inn,** Calif. 1 (P.O. Box 291), Big Sur 93920 (408/
♌♌♌ 667-2200; toll free 800/527-2200). 30 cabins (no TV in rms). AE, MC, V. Free parking, two pools, sauna, rest. (Sierra Mar), bar, rm svce, massage, concierge, free breakfast, free crib. *Note:* The only Big Sur hotel on the ocean's edge, developed w. low environmental impact (only one tree was removed for construction). Cabins dwell in the hillside, offering spectacular views of the ocean or the mountains. All rms have fireplaces, hot tubs, and, Nakamachi stereo gear. One great touch: terry-cloth robes await your arrival. Rest. of a very high order. Prices to match comfort. **VE**

☼♀♀ **Ventana Inn,** Calif. 1 at Ventana Village, CA 93920 (408/
♌♌ 667-2331; toll free 800/628-6500). 60 rms, A/C, color TV, in-rm movies. AE, CB, DC, MC, V. Free parking, two pools, sauna, solarium, rest., bar. *Note:* Romantic country inn alone on a secluded mountaintop 1,000 ft. (305m) above the Pacific. One of the most widely known hotels on the California coast, w. a spectacular ocean view. Very comfortable rms w. fireplaces, balconies, and minibars, but even so, rates are excessive for the quality of the svce and facilities. **E–VE**

♀ **Big Sur Lodge,** Calif. 1, Big Sur, CA 93920 (408/667-2171).
♌ 61 cottages (no TV or telephones in rms). MC, V. Free parking, pool, grocery store, coffee shop. *Note:* Comfortable bungalows (some w. fireplaces and kitchenettes) in the midst of a grove of redwoods, which is part of Pfeiffer–Big Sur State Park. Very rustic atmosphere; ideal for family parties. **M**

Where to Eat

♈♈♈ **Sierra Mar,** in the Post Ranch Inn (see "Where to Stay," above) (667-2200). Lunch Sat–Sun, dinner nightly. AE, MC, V. Jkt. *Specialties:* seared rare ahi tuna w. crispy noodle salad and wasabi, peppered filet of beef w. porcini mushroom gravy, Napoleon of eggplant w. feta cheese and shiitake mushrooms, blood-orange sorbet. Daily four-course menu. Wine list of over 2,500 selections won the *Wine Spectator* grand award. *Note:* Stunning wood-laden dining room and breathtaking ocean-view setting. Chef Wendy Little shows a graceful hand and a creative sense of design in her Californian, Asian-inspired cuisine. Attentive svce. Resv. required for lunch and dinner. *American.* **E–VE**

☼♈♈ **Ventana,** at the Ventana Inn (see "Where to Stay," above) (408/667-2331). A/C. Lunch/dinner daily. AE, DC, MC, V. *Specialties:* homemade pasta, fish and meat from the wood-fire grill, rack of lamb, very good homemade desserts. Fine list of California wines. *Note:* Beautiful greenhouse of a dining rm looking out over the ocean (*ventana* is the Spanish word for window); cedar paneling, warm colors. Overhanging the water is a terrace where you can enjoy your lunch in the open air. Modern California-style cuisine; friendly, relaxed svce. One of the best-known establishments on the coast. Resv. required for dinner. *American.* **I–M**

☼♈ **Nepenthe,** Calif. 1, 3 mi. (5km) south of the entrance to the state park (408/667-2345). No A/C. Lunch/dinner daily. AE, MC, V. *Specialties:* ambrosia burger, quiche, broiled fish, roast chicken. *Note:* From its clifftop, this well-known country inn gives you a splendid view of the sea. Limited menu of food straightforwardly prepared, at reasonable prices. Enjoyable if slightly touristy atmosphere; good svce. *American.* **B–I**

☼⌂⌂⌂ **HEARST–SAN SIMEON STATE HISTORICAL MON-
UMENT** (248 mi./400km): The imposing Spanish-Moorish castle that crowns the hill of **Cuesta Encantada** was designed and built by newspaper magnate William Randolph Hearst, and is without a doubt America's most extravagant and insanely baroque edifice. Hearst's larger-than-life-size ec-

centricities were the inspiration of Orson Welles's masterpiece, *Citizen Kane*. From 1919 until Hearst's death in 1951, armies of workers labored on the enormous mansion standing in its splendid Italianate gardens—but it's still unfinished in spite of the $30 million (in comparatively uninflated money!) spent on it. The interior, a mixture of Etruscan, Roman, Greek, Gothic, and Renaissance styles, holds hundreds of works of art which Hearst's unbridled passion for collecting, and his wealth, led him to acquire in Europe for immense sums. Don't miss the enormous banquet hall, Neptune's swimming pool, the great salon with its priceless tapestries, and the owner's lavish private quarters. Visitors have a choice of four tours, of which tour no. 1, leaving hourly on the half hour, is the most interesting. Resv. advisable through California MISTIX agencies (check for addresses in local telephone books). For information on timetables and prices, call 805/927-2020; for resv., call toll free 800/444-7275. A visit to Hearst Castle is worth the trip all by itself.

Where to Stay

🍷🍷 **San Simeon Pines Resort,** 7200 Moonstone Beach Dr., San Simeon, CA 93452 (805/927-4648), 1½ mi. (2.5km) south of the Hearst Castle. 60 rms, cable color TV. AE, MC, V. Free parking, pool, golf, beach, nearby coffee shop. *Note:* Comfortable little motel in a wood environment nr. the ocean; some rms w. terraces and extensive views. Ideal for visiting the castle. Free morning coffee. Agreeable svce and reception. Good value. **I–M**

🍷 **Best Western Cavalier Inn,** 9415 Hearst Dr., San Simeon, CA 93452 (805/927-4688; toll free, see Best Western), 3 mi. (5km) south of the Hearst Castle. 90 rms, color TV, in-rm movies. AE, CB, DC, MC, V. Free parking, two pools, health club, coffee shop, rm svce, boutiques, free crib. *Note:* Modern, functional beachfront motel; comfortable rms w. private balconies and mini-refrigerators (most w. fireplaces), the best w. ocean view. Good svce; good value. **I–M**

Where to Eat

IN NEARBY CAMBRIA 🍽🍽 **Brambles Dinner House,** 4005 Burton Dr., Cambria (805/927-4716), 9 mi. (15km) south of the Hearst Castle. No A/C. Dinner nightly, brunch Sun. AE, MC, V. *Specialties:* broiled fresh salmon (in season), steak broiled over wood, roast beef w. Yorkshire pudding, roast rack of lamb. *Note:* Fine Victorian house, tastefully decorated. First-rate broiled meat and fish. Thoughtful svce; romantic atmosphere. Resv. advisable in summer. *Steak/Seafood.* **I–M**

🍸 **Ian's,** 2150 Center St. (927-8649). Lunch Sat–Sun (summer only), dinner nightly; closed hols. AE, MC, V. *Specialties:* grilled rack of lamb w. cilantro-mint sauce, seared ahi tuna w. ginger-sesame vinaigrette, salmon w. sweet-mustard butter, Angus beef. Seasonal menu. *Note:* Multilevel rest. serving seafood and meats nicely prepared. Totally nonsmoking. *Steak/Seafood.* **I–M**

🏛 **MORRO ROCK** (276 mi./445km): Called the "Gibraltar of the Pacific," this 563-ft. (172m) monolith of volcanic rock dominates the approach to the pretty fishing port of **Morro Bay.** Beautiful nearby beaches include **Cayucos Beach, Atascadero Beach,** and **Morro Strand Beach.** Very near here, in the marshes at the mouth of **Los Oros Creek,** the largest wetlands on the California coast, live no fewer than 250 varieties of birds.

Where to Stay

☀🍷🍷🍷 **Inn at Morro Bay** (formerly the Best Western Golden Tee), 19 Country Club Dr., Morro Bay, CA 93442 (805/772-5651; toll free 800/321-9566). 97 rms, cable color TV. AE, CB, DC, MC, V. Free parking, pool, bicycling, fishing, rest. (Blue Heron), bar, rm svce, disco, concierge, free crib. *Note:* Pleasant motel almost in the ocean, exactly halfway between San Francisco and Los Angeles. Private marina. Comfortable rms w. balconies; view over the bay and Morro Rock. Amiable, competent svce; very acceptable rest. All in all, good value; recommended. **M–E**

    🍸🍸 **Bay View,** 225 Harbor St., Morro Bay, CA 93442 (805/772-
    🛏🛏 2771; toll free 800/742-8439). 22 rms, color TV, in-rm movies. AE, CB, DC, MC, V. Free parking, whirlpool bath, nearby coffee shop, crib $4. *Note:* Small, rustic motel nr. the water. Comfortable rms w. fireplaces and refrigerators, the best w. ocean view. Coffee in rm. **I**, but lower rates off-season.

    🛏 **Motel 6,** 298 Atascadero Rd., Morro Bay, CA 93442 (805/
    🛏 772-5641). 72 rms, color TV, free in-rm movies. AE, DC, MC, V. Free parking, pool, free crib. *Note:* Small budget hotel, adequately comfortable. Unbeatable value. **B**

Where to Eat

    🍴🍷 **Galley,** 899 Embarcadero (805/772-2806). A/C. Lunch/
    🍴🍷 dinner daily; closed Thanksgiving through Dec 25. MC, V. *Specialties:* clam chowder, raw oysters, calamari, shrimp and crab Louis, salads. Seasonal menu. List of over mostly 200 Californian wines. *Note:* An outstanding place for seafood lovers; providing the absolutely freshest of local catch served in generous portions. Glass-encased dining rm providing ocean view from its waterfront location. Friendly svce; family-run rest. for nearly 30 years. Totally nonsmoking. Resv. a must in summer. *Seafood.* **I–M**

    ☀🔔 **SAN LUIS OBISPO** (290 mi./468km): Founded in 1772 by Fr. Junípero Serra, this commercial town, overlooked by two nearby volcanic peaks, is the site of the magnificent **San Luis Obispo de Tolosa Mission,** now a parish church and museum, at Monterey and Broad Sts. (805/543-6850), open daily. Very near the mission is the interesting **San Luis Obispo County Historical Museum,** 696 Monterey St. (805/543-0638), open Wed–Sun, devoted to the history of the Spanish colonial era. Some 19th-century commercial buildings should not be overlooked: Sinsheimer Bros. at 849 Monterey St. and Ah Louis Store at 800 Palm St. Here was built in 1925 **Motel Inn,** the world's first motel. The Spanish-style building, designed by Alfred Heineman, stands, still quiet and inviting, at 2223 Monterey St. (805/543-4000).

Where to Stay

    ☀🛏🛏 **Madonna Inn,** 100 Madonna Rd., San Luis Obispo, CA
    93401 (805/543-3000). 109 rms, cable color TV. MC, V. Free parking, rest., bar, rm svce, disco, free crib. *Note:* Outrageously campy four-story building (no elevators) where every rm is decorated in a different style or period, from tropical jungle to fake Louis XVI—not to mention the rm w. artificial moonlight or the celestial suite full of cherubs. A triumph of Hollywood kitsch and bad taste. Some of the rms (the Cloud Nine Suite, w. angels, or the Elegance Room, in lavender, blue, and pink) are booked three to six months ahead. The rest. is well worth a glance, not so the fare. Svce doesn't measure up. **M–E**

    🛏 **Motel 6,** 1433 Calle Joaquin, San Luis Obispo, CA 93401
    (805/549-9595). 87 rms, color TV, free in-rm movies. AE, DC, MC, V. Free parking, pool, free crib. *Note:* Small budget hotel, adequately comfortable. Unbeatable value. **B**

IN NEARBY AVILA BEACH The 🛏🛏🛏 **San Luis Bay Inn,** Avila Rd., Avila Beach, CA 93424 (805/595-2333; toll free 800/438-6493). 68 rms, A/C, color TV, in-rm movies. AE, MC, V. Free parking, pool, tennis court, golf, rest. (Cove), bar, rm svce, free crib. *Note:* Beautiful resort hotel a few feet from the beach. The best rms (w. balconies) look out over Avila Beach and the charming little port of San Luis. Excellent svce; one of the best hotels on the Pacific coast. Resv., several weeks ahead, are a must. Lovely grdns. Deep-sea fishing. **E–VE**

IN NEARBY LOS OLIVOS The ☼ ĭ ĭ ĭ **Los Olivos Grand Hotel,** 2860 Grand Ave., Los Olivos, CA 93441 (805/688-7788; toll free 800/446-2455). 21 suites, A/C, cable color TV. AE, MC, V. Free parking, pool, rest., bar, rm svce. *Note:* In the heart of the Santa Ynez Valley, this delightful turn-of-the-century inn boasts some 20 luxurious suites, each decorated in the style of a famous European impressionist painter. Magnificent grdns; svce and reception very polished; rest. offers truly remarkable French cooking. A peaceful, sophisticated retreat a little more than two hours by road from Los Angeles. **VE**

Where to Eat

♉ **Izzy Ortega's,** 1850 Monterey St. (805/543-3333). A/C. ☗ Lunch/dinner daily; closed hols. MC, V. *Specialties:* fajitas, chile rellenos, grilled chicken sandwiches, steak. *Note:* Respectable Mexican fare, though not always authentic. Festive cantina atmosphere popular w. students. Totally nonsmoking. Resv. accepted for lunch only. A good value. *Mexican/American.* **B–I**

🔔 **LOMPOC** (327 mi./527km): Near **Vandenberg Air Force Base** and its missile launchers, this little town of 20,000 people, known as "Valley of the Flowers," accounts for more than half of all the flower seeds sold throughout the world. North 3 mi. (5km) along Calif. 246 is **La Purísima Concepción Mission,** founded in 1787 and rebuilt in 1812, at Purisima and Mission Gate Rds. (805/733-3713), open daily. It's one of the finest, and best restored, in California, with beautiful gardens.

☼⌂ **SOLVANG** (339 mi./547km): A little corner of Scandinavia in the heart of California. Founded by Danish settlers in 1911, this unexpected glimpse of old Europe, with its windmills, bakeries, and dovecotes, attracts many tourists. You'll like the stores and restaurants. The attractive **Santa Inés Mission,** at 1760 Mission Dr. (805/688-4815), is open daily.

Where to Stay

☼ĭ ĭ ĭ **Alisal Guest Ranch,** 1054 Alisal Rd., Solvang, CA 93463 (805/688-6411), 3 mi. (5km) south of Solvang. 74 rms and 3 bungalows, cable color TV in main lounge. AE, MC, V. Free parking, pool, tennis court, golf, riding, boating, rest., bars. *Note:* A real stock ranch carrying more than 2,000 head of cattle on almost 9,900 acres (4,000ha) of rolling land with a large private lake. For lovers of the Far Western way of life there are horseback riding and open-air barbecues. Very comfortable; relaxed svce and reception. Excellent value. **VE** (Modified American Plan).

☼ĭ ĭ **Petersen Village Inn,** 1576 Mission Dr., Solvang, CA 93463 (805/688-3121; toll free 800/468-6765 in California). 42 rms, A/C, cable color TV. AE, CB, DC, MC, V. Free parking, rests., rm svce. *Note:* Gracious old-world-style country inn, part of a re-created Danish village w. shops, galleries, bakery, and sidewalk cafés. Spacious, beautifully decorated rms w. canopy beds (some w. private patios or balconies). Charming atmosphere. Very good svce. A very fine place to stay. **M–E**

ĭ **Best Western King Frederik,** 1617 Copenhagen Dr., Solvang, CA 93463 (805/688-5515; toll free, see Best Western). 46 rms, A/C, cable color TV. AE, CB, DC, MC, V. Free parking, pool, nearby coffee shop, free breakfast, crib $4. *Note:* Charming little Scandinavian-style motel; comfortable rms w. balconies; in the heart of town. Good value. **I**

Where to Eat

☼ ♉♉ **Danish Inn,** 1547 Mission Dr. (805/688-4813). A/C. Breakfast Sat–Sun (daily in summer), lunch/dinner daily. AE, MC, V. *Specialties:* smörgåsbord, beef Lindström, veal Oscar, fresh salmon, rack of lamb, Danish pastries. *Note:* This spruce, comfortable rest. w. its Scandinavian contemporary decor (try to sit in the Windmill Room) is deservedly a favorite w. visitors to Solvang. *Scandinavian/Continental.* **B–I**

☀☆♙♙ **SANTA BARBARA:** (386 mi./623km): Enchanting seaside resort at the foot of the Santa Ynez Mountains that has become a favorite home for movie stars and the California rich. Many Spanish-style adobe houses. The **Santa Barbara Mission** (1786), E. Los Olivos and Upper Laguna Sts. (805/682-4713), with its twin pink-and-white towers, is one of the state's most popular tourist attractions. Nicknamed "the queen of the missions" because of its architectural splendor, it has a wonderful view over the town and the ocean. Open daily.

Other remarkable specimens of the colonial style include the Spanish-Moorish palace of the **County Courthouse**, 1100 Anacapa St., with spacious lawns and panoramic views from the tower, and the **Presidio** (1782), 123 E. Cañon Perdido (805/966-9719), one of the four fortresses built by the Spanish in California. Buildings include a chapel, barracks, residence, and padres' quarters. And don't forget the very beautiful **Museum of Art** at 1130 State St. (805/963-4364), open Tues–Sun, renowned for its collection of Greek and Roman art; or the picturesque **De la Guerra Plaza** and **El Paseo,** a group of courtyards, plazas, and alleys dating from 1827 and now boasting art galleries, boutiques, and sidewalk cafés.

See also the unusual giant fig tree, the **Moreton Bay Fig Tree,** at Chapala and Montecito Sts., more than 120 years old, whose branch spread—160 ft. (49m) —can shade 10,000 people from the sun; and the **Stearns Wharf,** at the foot of State St., a three-block-long wharf built in 1872, featuring restaurants, shops, and marine-life exhibits.

Where to Stay

♙♙♙♙ **Four Seasons Biltmore,** 1260 Channel Dr., Santa Barbara, CA 93108 (805/969-2261; toll free, see Four Seasons). 217 rms and 11 cottages (holding two to eight people each), color TV, in-rm movies. AE, CB, DC, MC, V. Valet parking $12, two pools, sauna, three tennis courts, putting green, beach, rest., coffee shop, bar, 24-hr. rm svce, disco, concierge, free crib. *Note:* Elegant beachfront resort housed in a beautiful Spanish-Moorish building at the edge of the ocean surrounded by 19 acres (7.7ha) of superb tropical grdns. Luxurious rms w. private balconies and an unobstructed view of either the Santa Ynez Mountains or the Pacific. Efficient svce. Has ranked as one of the country's finest hotels since it opened in 1927. **VE**

☀♙♙♙ **El Encanto Hotel & Garden Villas,** 1900 Lasuen Rd., Santa Barbara, CA 93103 (805/687-5000). 84 cottages, color TV, in-rm movies. AE, CB, DC, MC, V. Free valet parking, pool, tennis court, rest. (El Encanto), bar, rm svce, concierge, free airport limo, free crib. *Note:* Captivating adobe cottages nestling in a glorious exotic grdn, thick w. eucalyptus trees, which looks clear over the Pacific and the Santa Barbara heights. Luxurious, comfortable suites w. private balconies or patios. Exemplary svce. Rest. highly recommended. Fresh from a complete refurbishing, this place has the style and atmosphere of a European resort hotel. **E–VE**

♙♙ **Miramar Hotel-Resort,** 1555 S. Jameson Lane, Santa Barbara, CA 93108 (805/969-2203; toll free 800/322-6983). 212 rms, color TV. AE, CB, DC, MC, V. Free parking, two pools, four tennis courts, saunas, health club, private beach, rest., coffee shop, rm svce, hrdrsr, crib $8. *Note:* With its unusual blue roof, this old (and somewhat dated) hotel right on the ocean is the connoisseurs' favorite. Commodious, comfortable rms or individual cottages w. kitchenettes; the best have balconies and ocean views. Caters to groups and conventions. Direct beach access. Svce inconsistent. On balance, good value. **I–M**

☗ **Motel 6 Beach,** 443 Corona del Mar, Santa Barbara, CA
　 93103 (805/564-1392). 52 rms, cable color TV. AE, DC,
MC, V. Free parking, pool, free crib. *Note:* Small, reasonably priced motel, nr.
the beach as its name suggests, and a few steps from the zoo. Unsurpassable
value. **B**

　　　☗ **Motel 6 State St.,** 3505 State St., Santa Barbara, CA 93105
　　　　(805/687-5400). 60 rms, cable color TV. AE, DC, MC, V.
Free parking, pool, free crib. *Note:* Another small, reasonably priced motel 8 min.
from dwntwn. Serviceable comfort on a shoestring; another unbeatable value. **B**

IN NEARBY MONTECITO　The ☼ ☗☗☗ **San Ysidro Ranch,** 900 San Ysidro Lane,
Montecito, CA 93108 (805/969-5046). 21 cottages, cable color TV. MC, V.
Free parking, pool, tennis court, riding, rest., bar, rm svce, nightclub, free crib.
Note: The small hotel of your dreams, in a 494-acre (200ha) grdn surrounded by
mountains. For nearly a century the little white cottages have been home to some
of the greatest names in art and politics, including Sir Winston Churchill, Somerset Maugham, and Sir Laurence Olivier. President and Mrs. Kennedy spent
their honeymoon here. Huge, sumptuous rms, some w. fireplaces. Exemplary
svce. Excellent rest. (Stonehouse). Resv. essential—and well in advance. Member of the very chic Relais et Châteaux hotel chain. **VE**

IN NEARBY REFUGIO PASS　The ☼ ☗☗ **Circle Bar B Guest Ranch,** 1800 Refugio
Rd., Goleta, CA 93017 (805/968-1113), 1¼ mi. (2km) south of Refugio Pass.
14 rms. AE, MC, V. Free parking, pool, riding, meals included in package, dinner theater (Apr–Dec). *Note:* This rustic ranch on 988 unspoiled acres (400ha)
some 20 mi. (32km) north of Santa Barbara is a big attraction: its next-door
neighbor is Rancho del Cielo, the country home of former Pres. Ronald Reagan.
Simple but comfortable rms, agreeable atmosphere. Heavily attended theatrical
shows in summer. Resv. advised a number of weeks ahead. Well worth a stay.
Very fine view of the ocean and the Channel Islands. **M–E** (Modified American
Plan).

Where to Eat

　　☖☖☖ **Citronelle,** in the Santa Barbara Inn, 901 Cabrillo Blvd. (805/
　　　　963-0111). A/C. Breakfast/lunch/dinner daily. AE, DC,
MC, V. Jkt. *Specialties:* tuna-burger on toasted brioche, feuilleté of shiitake mushrooms w. garlic cream, sautéed foie gras, salmon napoleon, chicken in a porcini-
mushroom crust, baby rack of lamb, scrumptious pastries and desserts. *Note:* The
brilliant, trendy fare of this relative newcomer is supervised by French chef
Michel Richard of L.A.'s Citrus fame—that just shows it. The large picture windows feature a wonderful view of the harbor and wharf. Totally unprofessional
svce staff. Resv. a must. *French/Californian.* **M–E**

　　☖☖ **Downey's,** 1305 State St. (805/966-5006). Lunch Tues–Fri,
　　　　dinner Tues–Sun; closed Dec 25 and Jan 1. AE, MC, V. *Specialties:* grilled lamb loin w. wild mushrooms and roasted garlic, king salmon w.
sorrel sauce, grilled squab w. warm spinach salad, local mussels w. chili vinaigrette, fresh raspberries w. white chocolate mousse in puff pastry. Daily menu.
Extensive list of Californian wines. *Note:* Creatively prepared seafood and meats
served in a cheery, peach-colored setting. Dine amidst local artwork. Attentive
svce. Live jazz on Fri. Resv. highly advised. *Seafood/American.* **M–E**

　　☖ **La Super-Rica,** 622 N. Milpas St. (805/963-4940). Lunch/
　　　dinner daily. AE, MC, V. *Specialties:* tacos, frijoles and
chorizos, chiles rellenos, tamales, broiled chicken. *Note:* The tireless Mama
Gonzalez, bustling behind her stoves, keeps a sharp eye on the preparation of her
sauces, marinated meats, and spiced frijoles to ensure that they will be to the taste
of her regular customers. Absolutely authentic cooking; the decor is insignificant
—but so are the prices. Inviting covered patio for lunch or dinner al fresco. Has a
large local following. *Mexican.* **B**

IN NEARBY MONTECITO ☟ **Pronto Piatti,** 516 San Ysidro Rd. at Calif. 192 (805/969-7520). A/C. Lunch/dinner daily; closed Dec 25. AE, MC, V. *Specialties:* pizza from a wood-burning oven, homemade pasta, fritto misto, excellent mesquite-grilled fish and meat, authentic regional Italian dishes. *Note:* Pleasant Californian decor, brightened w. large mural paintings; gracious, congenial svce. Outdoor patio dining. A good spot. *American/Italian.* **I–M**

IN NEARBY OJAI The ✱☟☟☟ **Ranch House,** 102 Besant Rd. (805/646-2360). A/C. Lunch/dinner Wed–Sun; closed hols. and at lunch Oct–Mar. AE, DC, MC, V. *Specialties:* crab voisin, beef Bali Hai, pork au Cointreau, fish of the day, excellent desserts. *Note:* One of the most innovative rests. in California, created by the late chef Alan Hooker, who left a legacy of refined and inventive cuisine. Herbs and vegetables fresh from the grdn; excellent home-baked bread and pastry. You'll enjoy the grdn; background music is classical and agreeable. Two sittings a night, at 6 and 8:30pm. A local institution for more than 30 years. *American/Continental.* **I–M**

🔔 **VENTURA** (413 mi./666km): The **San Buenaventura Mission,** 211 E. Main St. (805/643-4318), was the last (1782) to be founded by the great Franciscan missionary, Fray Junípero Serra. It still has its original wooden bells. Open daily. Interesting **County Museum** at 100 E. Main St. (805/653-0323), open Tues–Sun, and fascinating **archeological excavations** in progress at 113 E. Main St.

An Offshore Side Trip

☀☟☟ **Channel Islands National Park** (about 10 mi./16km offshore): Group of five small uninhabited islands stretching for some 150 mi. (242km) parallel to the coast. The five islands—**Anacapa, San Miguel, Santa Barbara, Santa Cruz,** and **Santa Rosa**—are now marine-life sanctuaries; their flora and fauna are different from those of the mainland, and include 830 species not found anywhere else in California. But it is the animal and marine life that constitutes their principal attraction: sea anemones, sea urchins, abalone, crayfish, dolphins, sponges, foxes, seabirds, and half a dozen varieties of sea lions, for a start.

Camping is allowed, by previous arrangement, on Anacapa and Santa Barbara. For **park information,** contact the Superintendent, Channel Islands National Park, 1901 Spinnaker Dr., Ventura, CA 93001 (805/658-5730).

The islands can be reached only by boat from Oxnard or Ventura on the mainland. The recommended carrier is **Island Packer Company,** 1867 Spinnaker Dr., Ventura (805/642-1393).

Where to Stay

☟☟ **Pierpoint Inn,** 550 San Jon Rd., Ventura, CA 93001 (805/643-6144). 71 rms, color TV. AE, CB, DC, MC, V. Free parking, pool, tennis court, rest., bar, rm svce, free crib. *Note:* Small, charming English-style inn; rms (w. balconies or terraces) are pleasing and almost all offer a view of Pierpoint Bay. Good rest.; interesting wknd packages. Good value. **I**

☟ **Motel 6,** 2145 E. Harbor Blvd., Ventura, CA 93003 (805/643-5100). 200 rms, cable color TV. AE, DC, MC, V. Free parking, pool, free crib. *Note:* Small, reasonably priced motel; serviceable comfort. Unsurpassable value. **B**

Where to Eat

☟ **Sportsman,** 53 S. California St. (805/643-2851). A/C. Breakfast Sat–Sun, lunch/dinner daily; closed hols. MC, V. *Specialties:* broiled meat and fish, roast beef, sandwiches. *Note:* The simple, unpretentious cuisine rates a big hand. Lovers of hunting and fishing will enjoy the decor. Locally popular. *Steak/Seafood.* **B–I**

🏛 **OXNARD** (421 mi./679km): Like Ventura, a departure point for trips to the **Channel Islands,** 10 mi. (16km) offshore, where tens of thousands of birds, sea lions, and other marine animals can be seen in their natural environment. (See "An Offshore Side Trip" under Ventura, above.)

Where to Stay

🔔🔔🔔 **Casa Sirena Marina,** 3605 Peninsula Rd., Oxnard, CA 93030 (805/985-6311; toll free 800/228-6026). 274 rms, color TV. AE, CB, DC, MC, V. Free parking, pool, tennis court, putting green, saunas, bicycles, marina, rest. (Lobster Trap), coffee shop, two bars, rm svce, free airport limo, free crib. *Note:* Vast, well-equipped resort hotel. Rms w. balconies and harbor view. Ideal for visits to the Channel Islands. A little boisterous and overcrowded. Good rest.; worthwhile discount packages. **M**

Where to Eat

🍸 **Lobster Trap,** at Casa Sirena Marina (see "Where to Stay," above) (805/985-6361). A/C. Lunch/dinner daily, brunch Sun. AE, CB, DC, MC, V. *Specialties:* fish of the day, shellfish, prime cuts. *Note:* Good hotel cuisine, well prepared w. few surprises. Fine view over the yacht basin and beyond. Slowish svce. Agreeable oyster bar. *Steak/Seafood.* **B–I**

☀🏛🏛🏛 **MALIBU** (455 mi./734km): Immense fine-sand beach. Home of such movie celebrities as Sylvester Stallone, Barbra Streisand, Larry Hagman, Julie Andrews, Robert Redford, and Steven Spielberg. Don't miss the **J. Paul Getty Museum,** one of the two or three wealthiest in the world. There is an exact replica of the 1st-century A.D. "Villa of the Papyrus" from Herculaneum near Naples. (See "Museums" in Chapter 54 on Los Angeles.)

🏛 **PACIFIC PALISADES** (463 mi./747km): Resort town and, like Malibu, home to many movie and television stars. **Will Rogers State Park,** on Sunset Blvd. between Amalfi Dr. and Brooktree Rd., former ranch home of the famous movie cowboy and humorist, is worth a visit (see Chapter 54 on Los Angeles).

Where to Eat

🍸 **Gladstones 4 Fish,** 17300 W. Pacific Coast Hwy., Pacific Palisades (310/454-3474). A/C. Breakfast/lunch/dinner daily (until midnight). *Specialties:* All kinds of fish and shellfish. Valet parking. *Seafood.* **I**

🏛 **SANTA MONICA** (472 mi./761km): Enormous, busy beach. Picturesque pier with amusements.

Where to Eat

See Chapter 54 on Los Angeles for the following restaurant recommendations: **Bikini, Camelions, DC3, Michael's,** and **Valentino.**

🏛🏛🏛 **LOS ANGELES** (490 mi./790km): See Chapter 54 on Los Angeles for information on the city and its surroundings.

🏛 **HUNTINGTON BEACH** (520 mi./839km): Another vast beach popular with surfers and skin-divers (beware of sharks!).

☀🏛 **NEWPORT BEACH** (526 mi./848km): One of California's smartest and most fashionable beaches, with splendid homes and luxury boutiques and restaurants—but also a very busy fishing port (**New-**

port Pier) for more than a century. The beauty of its coastal scenery has earned it the nickname "The American Riviera." The **Harbor Art Museum** at 850 San Clemente Dr. (714/759-1122), open Tues–Sun, makes this a mecca for lovers of the avant-garde and of American experimental art.

Where to Eat

John Domini's, 2901 W. Coast Hwy. (714/650-5112). A/C. Dinner nightly, brunch Sun. AE, DC, MC, V. *Specialties:* clam chowder; sashimi; cioppino; Chinese chicken salad; opakapaka; lobster and fish, broiled, baked, or sautéed; excellent desserts. Good but pricey wine list. *Note:* A local offspring of the famous John Domini's in Honolulu, this luxurious beachside establishment serves the same remarkable selection of fish and seafood at stiff prices, in the same extravagant setting, complete w. huge picture windows, fountains, and indoor waterfalls. Relaxed, efficient svce. Resv. highly advisable. *Seafood.* **M–E**

Pascal, 1000 N. Bristol St. (714/752-0107). A/C. Lunch Mon–Fri, dinner Mon–Sat; closed two weeks in Sept. AE, DC, MC, V. *Specialties:* steamed mussels in basil-orange sauce, snails beaujolaise, soupe de poissons, chicken provençale, baked sea bass in champagne sauce, lemon tart w. raspberry sauce. Reasonably priced French and California wines. *Note:* Light Provençal cuisine at its best by chef-owner Pascal Olhat, a French native. Rustic setting in a somewhat ordinary shopping mall. Cheerful svce. Convivial atmosphere. Resv. required. Totally nonsmoking. *French.* **M–E**

LAGUNA BEACH (535 mi./863km): Very beautiful, fashionable beach lying at the foot of steep hills. Many boutiques and open-air restaurants. Fire erupted in the foothills of this town in Nov 1993, spreading over 16,684 acres (6800ha) and destroying 318 homes. Estimated damage was $270 million. Beachfront tourist attractions, however, were left relatively unharmed.

Where to Stay

Casa Laguna Inn, 2510 S. Coast Hwy., Laguna Beach, CA 92651 (714/494-2996; toll free 800/233-0449). 20 rms, A/C, cable color TV. AE, CB, DC, MC, V. Free parking, pool; no bar or rest.; concierge, free wine and hors d'oeuvres, crib. *Note:* Enticing little Spanish Colonial–style inn w. panoramic view of the Pacific. As far as you can get from production-line tourism. Elegantly decorated rms, each in a different style. Private, luxuriant patios and grdns. Polished svce and welcome. Interesting vacation packages. **M–E**

Ben Brown's Aliso Creek Inn, 31106 Coast Hwy., South Laguna, CA 92677 (714/499-2271). 62 suites w. kitchenettes, cable color TV. AE, MC, V. Covered parking, pool, golf, Jacuzzi, rest., bar, disco, crib $5. *Note:* Likable little hotel hidden in a peaceful inlet beside the ocean. Huge, comfortable rms w. balconies. Very acceptable rest. Hardworking, congenial svce. A nice place, one hour by car from Los Angeles. **M–E**

IN NEARBY LAGUNA NIGUEL The **Ritz Carlton,** 33533 Ritz Carlton Dr., Laguna Niguel, CA 92677 (714/240-2000; toll free 800/241-3333). 393 rms, A/C, color TV, in-rm movies. AE, CB, DC, MC, V. Valet parking $15, two pools, four tennis courts, golf, health club, sauna, two rests. (including the Dining Room), coffee shop, bars, 24-hr. rm svce, nightclub, hrdrsr, boutiques, concierge, free crib. *Note:* On its clifftop overlooking the Pacific, this four-story palace opened in 1984 is one of the latest blossoms of American luxury hotelkeeping. Mediterranean-style architecture surrounded by magnificent grdns w. fountains and covered patios. Splendid view of the ocean and Catalina Island. No visiting VIP can afford to miss it, which is why resv. must be made many days, or weeks, ahead. Sumptuous rms w. private balconies, minibars, and period furniture; antiques and works of art in the public rms and foyer. Ultra-polished svce and reception. The Dining Room is one of the best rests. on the West Coast. VIP floor. Free bus to the beach. **VE**

Where to Eat

🍷🍷 **Kachina,** 222 Forest Ave. (714/497-5546). A/C. Lunch/
🍴🍴 dinner daily, brunch Sun. AE, MC, V. *Specialties:* blue-corn smoked-chicken taquitos, barbecued duck saddlebags, shrimp and sweet-corn tamale, piñon-pecan pie. *Note:* Dazzling eatery featuring southwestern cuisine w. California touches. The surroundings are very chic and the svce impeccable. An address to remember. Resv. highly advised. *American.* **M**

🍷🍷 **Las Brisas,** 361 Cliff Dr. (714/497-5434). A/C. Breakfast
🍴🍴 Mon–Sat, lunch/dinner daily, brunch Sun; closed hols. AE, CB, DC, MC, V. *Specialties:* fish Mexican style, sopa de frijoles, carne asada, enchiladas, squid. *Note:* Inviting terrace overlooking the ocean, or a comfortable dining rm w. indoor waterfall. Good Mexican cuisine tailored to North American tastebuds. Has had a large following in the community for more than 10 years. Resv. a must. Valet parking. *Mexican/Seafood.* **I**

IN NEARBY LAGUNA NIGUEL 🍷🍷🍷 **The Dining Room,** at the Ritz Carlton Laguna Niguel (see "Where to Stay," above) (714/240-5008). A/C. Dinner only, nightly. AE, CB, DC, MC, V. Jkt. *Specialties:* Maine lobster salad w. fresh mango and raspberry-lime vinaigrette, squab risotto w. sautéed duck liver and sherry jus, sautéed prawns w. parmigiano-reggiano galette and garlic risotto, herb-crusted filet of sautéed beef w. Chartreuse of chanterelle mushrooms and wine sauce, orange-chocolate fondant w. orange sorbet and blood-orange sauce. Menu changes periodically. Very fine wine list. *Note:* This palatial rest., w. its old master paintings and crystal chandeliers, is redolent of luxury and good taste. Quite remarkable contemporary French cuisine (but prices to match). Svce polished to a high gloss. Distinguished background music. Resv., several days ahead, a must. Some of the finest food in southern California. *French/Mediterranean.* **E** (Prices based not on individual items but on the number of courses ordered, with a choice of two to five courses. A fine idea.)

☀🔭 **SAN JUAN CAPISTRANO** (547 mi./882km): Perched between mountain and sea, the **San Juan Capistrano Mission** (714/248-2049), open daily, is the most famous, and probably the most beautiful in California; take I-5, leave it at the Ortega Hwy. exit. Founded in 1776 by Fray Junípero Serra, this lovely mission, laid out in the shape of a Latin cross, was almost entirely destroyed by an earthquake in 1812. There survive the Serra Chapel, the ruins of the cloister, and a little museum surrounded by superb tropical gardens where, every year, the swallows come to nest about Mar 20.

Don't overlook the **Regional Library & Cultural Center,** at 31495 El Camino Real (714/493-1752), open Mon–Thurs and Sat, whose elegant postmodern architecture bears the name, and the stamp, of Michael Graves.

Where to Stay

🍸 **Best Western Capistrano Inn,** 27174 Ortega Hwy., San Juan
🍸 Capistrano, CA 92675 (714/493-5661; toll free, see Best Western). 108 rms, A/C, cable color TV. AE, CB, DC, MC, V. Free parking, pool, 24-hr. rest. adj., bar, valet svce, crib $4. *Note:* Comfortable motel very nr. the famous San Juan Capistrano Mission. Agreeable rms, some w. balconies; a perfect stopover for visiting the mission. Free morning coffee and happy hour. **I**

IN NEARBY DANA POINT ☀🍸🍸🍸 **Blue Lantern Inn,** 34343 Street of the Blue Lantern, Dana Point, CA 92629 (714/661-1304). 29 rms, A/C, cable color TV. AE, MC, V. Free parking, health club, rest adj., concierge, free gourmet breakfast and afternoon tea or wine, free crib. *Note:* Brand-new inn located on a bluff overlooking the yacht harbor. Romantic atmosphere. All rms and suites w. fireplaces, antique furnishings, in-rm whirlpools, refrigerators, and panoramic views of the coast; some w. private sun decks. Attentive, courteous staff. Totally nonsmoking. A wonderfully posh hideaway. **E–VE**

Best Western Marina Inn, 24800 Dana Point Harbor Dr., Dana Point, CA 92629 (714/496-1203; toll free, see Best Western). 135 rms (one-third w. kitchenettes), A/C, color TV, in-rm movies. AE, CB, DC, MC, V. Free parking, pool, rest. adj., free crib. *Note:* Modern, functional motel within the marina of Dana Point, where boats may be rented. Commodious rms w. balconies, the best overlooking the Pacific. **I–M**

Where to Eat

El Adobe, 31891 Camino Capistrano (714/493-1163). A/C. Lunch/dinner daily, brunch Sun; closed Labor Day, Dec 25. AE, MC, V. *Specialties:* prime rib, steak, Mexican dishes. *Note:* Old Spanish courthouse (1776), a designated historical monument, converted into a handsome rest. Menu limited, but first-class meats. Enjoyable atmosphere, w. a roof that opens in summer. Resv. advised. *Steak/American.* **B–I**

SAN CLEMENTE (554 mi./894km): Beach resort made fashionable by former Pres. Richard Nixon, who made his summer home there (Casa Pacifica) during his term of office.

OCEANSIDE-CARLSBAD (580 mi./935km): Miles of beach, almost deserted except for surfers and surf fishers. 4 mi. (6.5km) east along Calif. 76 stands the imposing **San Luis Rey de Francia Mission** (619/757-3651), one of the few in California that was *not* founded by the tireless Fray Junípero Serra, but rather by one of his assistants, Father Lasuén, in 1798. Dedicated to the canonized King Louis IX of France, it once housed 3,000 Native Americans, and still displays many mementoes of Spanish colonial days in its remarkable museum. It continues to serve its original purpose as a parish church and school for the surrounding tribal reservations. Open daily.

A further 48 mi. (77km) east along Calif. 76 is the famous **Mount Palomar Observatory** with its 200-in. (5.1m) reflector telescope, one of the world's largest. The dome may be visited daily; for information, call 619/742-2119. (See Chapter 55 on San Diego).

Where to Stay

La Costa Hotel & Spa, Costa del Mar Rd., Carlsbad, CA 92008 (619/438-9111; toll free 800/854-5000). 485 rms and individual cottages, A/C, cable color TV. AE, CB, DC, MC, V. Free parking, five pools, 21 tennis courts, two golf courses, health club, sauna, steam rm, four rests. (including Figaro's) and bars, 24-hr. rm svce, hrdrsr, boutiques, free crib. *Note:* Resting on almost 5,000 wooded acres (2,025ha) nr. the ocean, this is one of the finest vacation complexes on the West Coast. Comfortable, luxuriously decorated rms or suites. Impeccable svce; excellent facilities. A paradise for sports-lovers or those taking a cure, but priced accordingly (some suites run $2,000 a day). Wknd and American Plan packages are interesting. For those who love going on a (costly) diet. **VE**

Best Western Beach View, 3180 Carlsbad Blvd., Carlsbad, CA 92008 (619/729-1151; toll free, see Best Western). 41 rms, A/C, cable color TV. AE, CB, DC, MC, V. Free parking, pool, Jacuzzi, beach, nearby coffee shop, free crib. *Note:* Friendly small motel facing the beach; comfortable rms w. mini-refrigerators, some also w. balconies or fireplaces, the best overlooking the ocean. Reception w. a smile. **M**

Motel 6, 1403 Mission Ave., Oceanside, CA 92054 (619/721-6662). 79 rms, cable color TV. AE, DC, MC, V. Free parking, pool, free crib. *Note:* Small, reasonably priced motel; serviceable comfort. Unsurpassable value. **B**

IN NEARBY RANCHO SANTA FE   The ※ ቤቤቤ **Inn at Rancho Santa Fe,** 5951 Linea del Cielo, Rancho Santa Fe, CA 92067 (619/756-1131; toll free 800/654-2928). 103 rms, A/C, color TV. AE, CB, DC, MC, V. Free parking, pool, health club, three tennis courts, rest., bar, rm svce, crib $20. *Note:* Deluxe motel and pleasing bungalows set in 19 acres (7.7ha) of beautiful grdns; ideal for lovers of sports and fresh air. Very satisfactory rest. Spacious rms w. private patios, some w. kitchenettes. Good svce, good value. **M–VE**

Where to Eat

IN NEARBY SAN MARCOS   The ൬൬ **Quails Inn,** 1025 La Bonita Dr. (619/744-0120). A/C. Lunch/dinner daily, brunch Sun. AE, MC, V. *Specialties:* seafood salad bar, prime rib, lobster, barbecued chicken. *Note:* The rest. of this beautiful Lake San Marcos resort is festooned in colors of peach, coral, and light blue-green, w. a view of the lake from almost every seat. Good basic American menu and Sun buffet brunch. Friendly svce. Resv. advised. *American.* **I–M**

IN NEARBY RANCHO SANTA FE   ൬൬൬൬ **Mille Fleurs** (see Chapter 55 on San Diego).

IN NEARBY DEL MAR   ൬൬ **When in Rome,** 828 N. U.S. 101 (619/944-1771). No A/C. Lunch Tues–Fri, dinner Tues–Sun; closed hols. AE, MC, V. *Specialties:* fresh homemade pasta, filet of beef w. peppers, scaloppine w. lemon, broiled fish, chicken cacciatore. *Note:* One of southern California's best Italian rests., serving light, delicate food. The colonnaded rm is full of light; the svce comes w. a smile; this is a first-rate place. *Italian.* **I**

※☆ ⚷⚷ **LA JOLLA** (589 mi./950km): California's most sought-after summer resort, a sort of West Coast equivalent of Europe's Amalfi or Juan-les-Pins. Beautiful beaches hidden by little inlets, luxurious oceanfront homes, open-air stores, and restaurants. Important museums, particularly the **Museum of Contemporary Art.** (See "Nearby Excursions" in Chapter 55 on San Diego.)

Where to Eat
See Chapter 55 on San Diego for the following restaurant recommendations: **Cindy Black's, George's at the Cove,** and **Top o' the Cove.**

IN NEARBY PACIFIC BEACH   See Chapter 55 on San Diego for my restaurant recommendation of **El Chalan.**

IN NEARBY CORONADO   See Chapter 55 on San Diego for the following restaurant recommendation: **Marius.**

⚷⚷ **SAN DIEGO** (604 mi./974km): See Chapter 55 on San Diego for information on the city and its surroundings.

CHAPTER 52

SEQUOIA NATIONAL PARK

□ □ □

And Kings Canyon

Domain of the giant trees, Sequoia National Park is, after Yellowstone, the oldest national park in the U.S. Set up in 1890 to safeguard the redwood (sequoia) forests on the slopes of the **Sierra Nevada,** the park's magnificent scenery embraces granite mountain crests, canyons, mountain lakes, and dense forests. Around Sequoia and the adjoining **Kings Canyon National Park,** inaugurated in 1940, lie giant mountain peaks including **Mount Whitney,** highest in the "lower 48" (14,495 ft./4,418m), **Split Mountain** (14,054 ft./4,285m), and **Mount Goethe** (13,274 ft./4,047m). But though the natural setting is incomparable, the main interest of the two parks is their forests of giant conifers.

The redwood, or sequoia, owes its name to the famous Native American leader Sequoyah, inventor of the alphabet in which the Cherokee language is written. The tree has been known to grow as high as 295 ft. (90m), with a circumference at the base of 98 ft. (30m) or more. Its bark, 2 ft. (60cm) thick, is resistant to both fire and insects. The largest redwood now standing in the park, the **General Sherman Tree,** stands more than 275 ft. (84km) tall, and its estimated age of 2,500 years makes it the oldest living creature on earth.

In spite of the huge area they cover, Sequoia and Kings Canyon National Parks have only 75 mi. (120km) of surfaced roads between them; points off these highways can be reached only on horseback or on foot. There are, however, 900 mi. (1,450km) of walking trails. Sequoia National Park, while it remains open year round, can be negotiated only with chains or snowtires Oct–May; Kings Canyon is closed all winter.

The motels in the two parks have a limited capacity of 300 rooms; reservations should therefore be made far in advance.

BASIC FACTS: State of California. Area code: 209. Time zone: Pacific. ZIP Code: 93262. Approximate Area: 1,300 sq. mi. (3,370km²). Founded: 1890 (Sequoia); 1940 (Kings Canyon).

CLIMATE: Icy and snowy in winter (the snowfall can reach 13 ft./4m, and the thermometer sometimes drops to −4°F/−20°C), the climate of Sequoia National Park is brisk and invigorating at all times of the year. Even in midsummer, bring warm clothes for the evenings.

DISTANCES: Las Vegas, 506 mi. (810km); Los Angeles, 220 mi. (354km); Sacramento, 257 mi. (411km); San Francisco, 270 mi. (432km).

ARRIVAL & TRANSIT INFORMATION

AIRPORTS NEARBY: The **Fresno Municipal Airport** (FAT), 70 mi. (112km) west.
Visalia Municipal Airport (VIS), 45 mi. (72km) NE.

AIRLINES: At the Fresno Municipal Airport: American (toll free 800/433-7300), Delta (toll free 800/221-1212), and United (toll free 800/241-6522). At the Visalia airport: United (toll free 800/241-6522).

BUS OR CAR RENTAL? Given the distances and the attractive rates offered in California, the sensible solution is to rent a car with unlimited mileage.

CAR RENTALS (at the Fresno Municipal Airport): Avis (toll free 800/331-1212), Budget (toll free 800/527-0700), Dollar (toll free 800/800-4000), Hertz (toll free 800/654-3131), and National (toll free 800/227-7368).

TRAIN: The nearest Amtrak (toll free 800/872-7245) stations are at 2650 Tulare St., Fresno and 200 Santa Fe Ave., Hanford.

INTERCITY BUSES: There is no regular service to Sequoia or Kings Canyon National Park. (A daily **shuttle bus** links Fresno to Sequoia National Park, Apr–Oct; for information, call Yosemite Grayline at 209/443-5240.
  The nearest regular-service bus stations, both **Greyhound** (toll free 800/231-2222) are at 432 7th W. St., Hanford; 1033 Broadway, Fresno, and 1927 E. Mineral King, Visalia.

INFORMATION & SIGHTSEEING

INFORMATION: Contact the **Superintendent, Sequoia and Kings Canyon National Parks,** Ash Mountain, Three Rivers, CA 93271 (209/565-3341) or the **Sequoia Regional Visitors Council,** 2800 W. Burrel Ave., Visalia, CA 93291 (209/733-6284).
  Visitor centers are located at Lodgepole (565-3782), Ash Mountain (565-3341), and Kings Canyon's Grant Grove (335-2856).
  For information on **road and weather conditions** (and snow conditions in winter), call 565-3351.

MOUNTAINEERING: ☼☖☖ **Mount Whitney,** reached by the High Sierra Trail, east of the Kern Canyon Ranger Station: Mount Whitney, at 14,495 ft. (4,418m), is the highest peak in the contiguous United States. The top can be reached by a number of routes, some requiring technical climbing skills. The easiest and most popular, the 10.7-mi. (17km) **Whitney Trail,** can be followed by hikers. The round-trip can be made in 12–14 hr. by the very fit. **Camping** is by permit only, and only 50 campers may stay on the mountain each night May 20–Oct 15. Requests should come to the Mount Whitney Ranger District, P.O. Box 8, Lone Pine, CA 93545. A ranger (call 619/876-6200) will answer questions about the choice of trails.

SCENERY & SIGHTS: ☀️🏔 **Cedar Grove,** reached on Calif. 180: The village at the dead end of Kings River South Fork. The surrounding peaks look down on the riverbed from a height of more than a mile (1,600m). Road closed in winter. A wonderful sight.

🏔 **Crystal Cave,** 6 mi. (9km) east of Giant Forest Village: Splendid limestone cavern with astonishing mineral growths; the temperature inside holds steady near 50° F (10° C). Vehicle road, then foot trail; mid-June to mid-Sept, daily.

☀️🏔🏔 **Giant Forest,** around Giant Forest Village on Calif. 198: Here you'll find the biggest redwoods in the park, including the **General Sherman Tree,** 275 ft. (84m) high and 103 ft. (32m) in circumference; estimated weight is 2,000 tons. There's enough wood in the tree to build 40 five-room cabins. At about 2,500 years, this is the world's oldest living thing.

☀️🏔 **Grant Grove,** intersection of Calif. 180 and Calif. 198: Stand of giant redwood including the second-tallest in the park, the **General Grant Tree,** 267 ft. (81m) high and 107 ft. (33m) in circumference.

🏔 **High Sierra Trail:** 40-mi. (64km) hiking trail linking Giant Forest Village to the western tip of the park and the John Muir Trail. Splendid scenery. For walkers in good physical shape.

☀️🏔 **John Muir Trail:** A hiking trail about 80 mi. (128km) long, running north-south along the eastern edge of the park. Spectacular landscapes. For seasoned walkers with some mountain experience. Horses and mules may be rented at Wolverton Stables, Grant Grove, and Cedar Grove.

☀️🏔🏔 **Kings Canyon,** reached by Calif. 180: The gorges of the Kings River South Fork display some of the most breathtaking scenery in the park: steep granite cliffs and dizzying drops of up to 8,216 ft. (2,505m), frozen lakes, and giant redwoods. Their beauty is reminiscent of the Yosemite Valley (see Chapter 53). The 36-mi. (58km) route east into the national park (Calif. 180) hangs on the edge of a cliff, 3,000 ft. (915m) above crashing white water before descending to river level inside the park. Road closed in winter.

☀️🏔 **Moro Rock,** 4 mi. (6km) south of Giant Forest Village: One of the most impressive granite monoliths in the Sierra Nevada range, rising 2,080 ft. (1,300m) above the banks of the Kaweah River Middle Fork. There's a path to the top, from which you'll have a fine all-around view of the mountains and the surrounding forest.

🏔 **Muir Grove,** reached by footpath from Lost Grove on Calif. 198: Very fine redwood stand.

🏔 **Zumwalt Meadow,** reached by footpath from Cedar Grove: Huge alpine meadow, particularly beautiful when the summer wildflowers are in bloom.

WINTER SPORTS RESORTS: 🏔 **Giant Forest Village and Lodgepole:** 35 mi. (56km) of cross-country skiing; no lifts.

🏔 **Wolverton Ski Bowl** (565-3381): Three lifts; open mid-Nov to mid-Apr.

ACCOMMODATIONS

Personal Favorites Inside the Parks (in order of preference)

For reservations inside Sequoia and Kings Canyon National Parks, contact the **Reservations Manager,** Sequoia and Kings Canyon Hospitality Service, P.O. Box 789, Three Rivers, CA 93271 (209/561-3314).

🏠 **Giant Forest Lodge,** on Calif. 198, Giant Forest Village, CA 93262 (209/561-3314). 245 rms (half w. bath; no A/C). MC, V. Free parking, skiing, horseback riding, rest., coffee shop, bar, crib $8.

Note: Rustic motel in the heart of the redwood forest; cottages w. basic comforts. So-so cafeteria. Some bungalows have open-air barbecues. Open year round. **B–M**

☼♀ **Cedar Grove Lodge,** at the end of Calif. 180, Kings Canyon ⌐ National Park, CA 93633 (209/561-3314). 18 rms, A/C. MC, V. Free parking, fishing, coffee shop, crib $8. *Note:* The most inviting motel in the park, well located on the banks of the Kings River. Serviceably comfortable; rms w. balcony. Open May–Oct only. **I–M**

♀ **Stony Creek Lodge,** Generals Hwy., Sequoia National Park, ⌐ CA 93262 (209/561-3314). 11 rms (no A/C). MC, V. Free parking, coffee shop (open until 9pm). *Note:* Small, rustic but relatively comfortable hotel deep in the forest. Acceptable cafeteria. Open from the end of May to mid-Sept only. **M**

♀ **Grant Grove Lodge,** Calif. 180, Kings Canyon National Park, ⌐ CA 93633 (209/561-3314). 51 rms (9 w. bath; no A/C). MC, V. Free parking, coffee shop (open until 9pm), bar, groceries, crib $7.50. *Note:* Cottages and bungalows w. primitive comforts (most have fabric roofs and no electricity). Only for open-air enthusiasts. Open year round but fewer facilities in winter. **B–I**

Personal Favorites Outside the Parks (in order of preference)

♀ **Best Western Holiday Lodge,** on Calif. 198, Three Rivers, CA ⌐ 93271 (209/561-4119; toll free, see Best Western). 55 rms, A/C, cable color TV. AE, CB, DC, MC, V. Free parking, pool, free coffee in rms, fishing, rest. half mi. away, crib $4. *Note:* Smart little motel looking out on the Kaweah River. Spacious rms w. balconies, some w. fireplaces and refrigerators. Inviting tree-shaded pool. Serviceable facilities; good value. 10 min. by car from the western entrance to the park. **B–I**

♀ **The River Inn,** 45176 Sierra Dr. (Calif. 198), Three Rivers, CA ⌐ 93271 (209/561-4367). 12 rms, A/C, cable color TV. MC, V. Free parking, adj. grocery store. *Note:* Tiny motel overlooking the Kaweah River in a pretty, natural setting. Comfortble rms w. balconies and refrigerators. 15-min. drive from the western entrance to the park. **B–I**

♀ **Lazy J Ranch,** 39625 Sierra Dr., Three Rivers, CA 93271 ⌐ (209/561-4449). 18 rms, A/C, cable color TV. AE, MC, V. Free parking, pool, fishing, free coffee in rms, adj. cafeteria, free crib. *Note:* Small rustic cottages w. refrigerators, some w. kitchenettes, on the Kaweah River. Only moderately comfortable, but well situated. Pretty tree-shaded grdns. 15-min. drive from the western entrance to the park. **B–I**

NEARBY EXCURSIONS

☼ **HANFORD** (63 mi./100km SW on Calif. 198): Founded in ☼ 1882 to house the immigrant Chinese working on the Southern Pacific Railroad, this was one of the country's largest Chinatowns in the 19th century. From its pioneer past there remain today only a few buildings around China Alley, scrupulously restored, including a Taoist temple and one of the most remarkable restaurants in the U.S.

Where to Eat

☼♀♀♀♀ **Imperial Dynasty,** 2 China Alley, 7th and Green Sts. (209/ ☼ 582-0196). Dinner only, Tues–Sun. AE, MC, V. Run by the Wing family since 1883, this rest., whose food is a strange but successful blend of French and Chinese traditions, is well worth going out of your way for. Be sure to call days ahead for the spectacular $50 nine-course gourmet dinner, for which you must leave $25 deposit upon resv. **I–M**

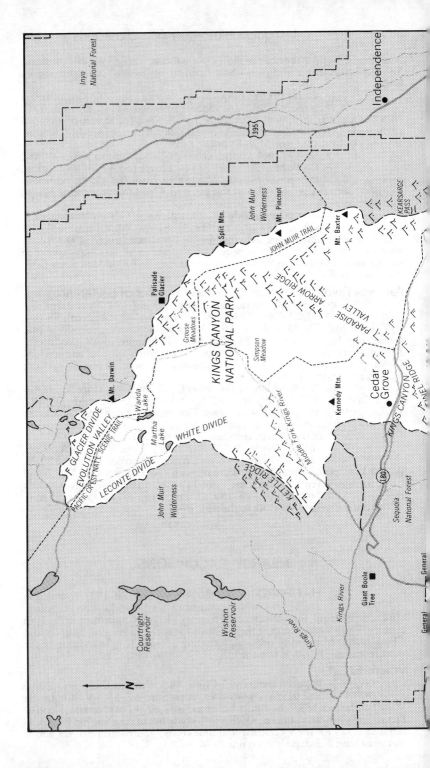

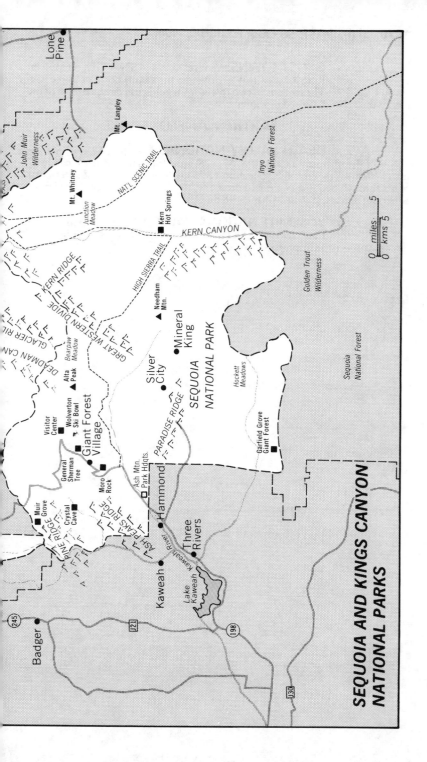

SEQUOIA AND KINGS CANYON NATIONAL PARKS

Lone Pine

John Muir Wilderness

Mt. Langley ▲

Inyo National Forest

Mt. Whitney ▲

NAT'L SCENIC TRAIL

Junction Meadow

Kern Hot Springs ■

KERN CANYON

HIGH SIERRA TRAIL

KERN RIDGE

Golden Trout Wilderness

GREAT WESTERN DIVIDE

Needham Mtn. ▲

GLACIER RIL

Bearpaw Meadow

DEADMAN CAN

Alta Peak ▲

Mineral King ●

Silver City ●

SEQUOIA NATIONAL PARK

Sequoia National Forest

Wolverton Ski Bowl

Visitor Center

Giant Forest Village ■

PARADISE RIDGE

Hockett Meadows

General Sherman Tree

Moro Rock ●

Ash Mtn. □ Park Hdqts.

Garfield Grove Giant Forest ■

Muir Grove ■

Crystal Cave

PINE RIDGE

ASH PEAKS RIDGE

Hammond ●

Three Rivers ●

Kaweah River

Kaweah ●

Lake Kaweah

(245)

Badger ●

(121)

(198)

(130)

0 miles 5
0 kms 5

GHOST TOWNS: Mineral King and **Silver City,** on Mineral King Rd., reached by driving 3 mi. (4km) north of Three Rivers on Calif. 198: The remains of two towns from gold-rush days; a stretch of the road is unsurfaced. Closed in winter.

FARTHER AFIELD

DEATH VALLEY NATIONAL PARK (362 mi./580km east via Calif. 198, 65, 178, and 190): The distance is barely 87 mi. (140km) as the crow flies, but almost 375 mi. (600km) along the spectacular roads through Sequoia National Forest and the Panamint Valley. Loveliest of American deserts. (See also Chapter 48 on Death Valley.)

YOSEMITE NATIONAL PARK (178 mi./284km NW via Calif. 198, 180, and 41): One of the country's most beautiful national parks (see Chapter 53).

YOSEMITE NATIONAL PARK ♛♛♛

□ □ □

The surpassing beauty of Yosemite National Park should be seen for the first time in May or June, when the waterfalls, swollen by snowmelt, plunge dizzily out of the sky for hundreds of feet to the rocks below. Some, like **Yosemite Falls,** the world's second largest after Angel Falls in Venezuela, are as much as 2,425 ft. (739m) from lip to basin—13 times as high as Niagara! In summer and fall the falls dry up, but you can still contemplate the grandeur of the million-year-old glacial **Yosemite Valley,** walled in by steep granite cliffs 5,000 ft. (1,500m) high. On the uplands, stands of giant redwoods and plateaus covered in flowery meadows contribute to a landscape of unspoiled splendor.

This huge (as large as Rhode Island) wildlife reserve deep in the **Sierra Nevada** (naturalists have counted no fewer than 220 species of birds and 75 of mammals—including deer, wild goat, black bear, and coyote) draws about 3½ million visitors each summer. Because it's within relatively easy reach of San Francisco and Los Angeles, it has become one of California's most popular tourist attractions; in July and August traffic jams paralyze its two main access roads. Yet until as late as 1851, when the Yosemite Gap was first discovered by the soldiers of the Mariposa Battalion, this had been for 4½ millennia the secret kingdom of the Miwok people and their forebears. They called it Ahwahnee, "the deep grassy valley."

When you set eyes on Yosemite Valley and the peaks of the **High Sierras** from the lookout at **Glacier Point,** or when you see **El Capitan,** a monolith 2½ times as high as the Rock of Gibraltar, whose lowering granitic mass forms a kind of natural fortress in a bend of the valley, you'll feel that scenery of this magnificence is enough to make the trip worthwhile in spite of the summer crowds.

Yosemite National Park (the name is a corruption of *U-zu-mate,* the Native American word for grizzly bear) is open year round.

BASIC FACTS: State of California. Area code: 209. Time zone: Pacific. ZIP Code: 95389. Founded: 1890. Area: 1,190 sq. mi. (3,082km²).

CLIMATE: As in most of the western national parks, spring and fall, both sunny but cool, are the best times for seeing Yosemite. Runoff from the snowmelt swells the waterfalls to their heaviest rate of flow in spring. Fall paints the forest in a splendor of glowing bronze. Summer is dry and reasonably warm, averaging 71°F (22°C). In winter the snow can lie more than 13 ft. (4m) deep, and daytime temperatures average 34°F (1°C). Cross-country skiers take note: Information on snow conditions can be obtained by calling 209/372-1338.

DISTANCES: Las Vegas, 465 mi. (745km); Los Angeles, 315 mi. (504km); Reno, 177 mi. (283km); San Francisco, 210 mi. (336km).

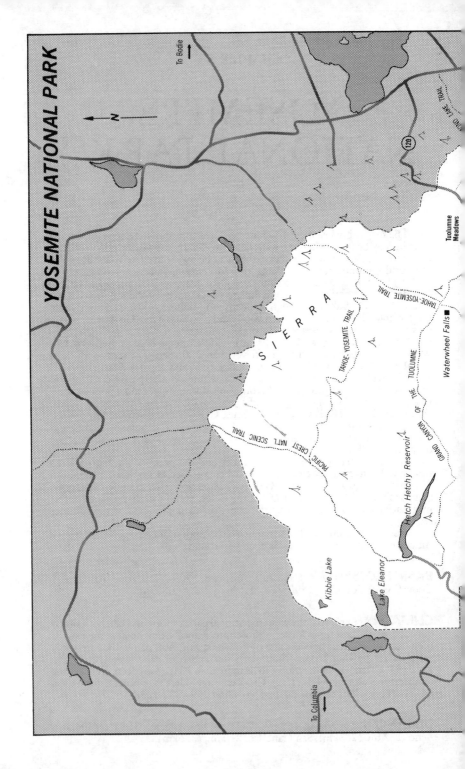

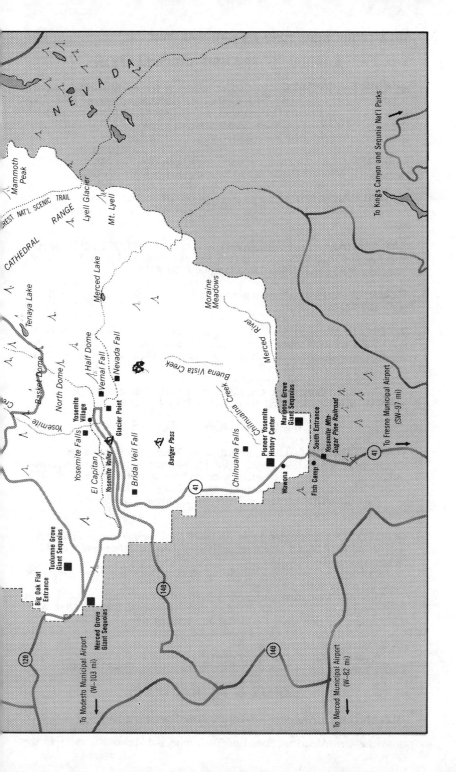

ARRIVAL & TRANSIT INFORMATION

NEAREST AIRPORTS: The largest nearby is **Fresno Municipal Airport** (FAT), 97 mi. (156km) SW. Other local airports include the **Merced Municipal Airport** (MCE), 82 mi. (131km) west; and the **Modesto Municipal Airport** (MOD), 103 mi. (165km) west. Yosemite Gray Line, Merced (383-1563), provides bus service from the Merced airport.

AIRLINES (all at the Fresno airport): American (toll free 800/433-7300), Delta (toll free 800/221-1212), and United (toll free 800/241-6522).

BUS OR CAR RENTAL? Given the distances to be covered, and the attractive rates offered in California, the best solution is to rent a car with unlimited mileage.

CAR RENTAL (at the Fresno airport): Avis (toll free 800/331-1212), Budget (toll free 800/527-0700), Dollar (toll free 800/800-4000), Hertz (toll free 800/654-3131), and National (toll free 800/227-7368).

TRAIN: The nearest Amtrak station is at 324 W. 24th St., Merced (toll free 800/872-7245).

INTERCITY BUSES: There is no regular bus service to Yosemite National Park. There are daily shuttle buses between Fresno, Merced, and Yosemite; for information and/or a timetable, contact **Yosemite Via Bus Lines,** 300 Grogan Ave., Merced, CA 95340 (209/722-0366); or **Yosemite Gray Line,** P.O. Box 2711, Fresno, CA 93708 (209/443-5240).

The nearest **Greyhound bus stations** are at 1033 Broadway in Fresno and at 725 W. Main St. in Merced (both toll free 800/231-2222).

INFORMATION & TOURS

TOURIST INFORMATION: Information Office, Yosemite National Park, P.O. Box 577, CA 95389 (209/372-0265). Information on wilderness permits and activities in the park. For information on **horseback riding,** call 209/372-1248. For **weather and road conditions,** call 209/372-0200.

There are **visitor centers** at Tuolumne Meadows (summer only) and Yosemite Village (open year round).

GUIDED TOURS: Golden Eagle Air Tours (airplane), Fresno Municipal Airport (251-7501): Flights over Yosemite National Park and the peaks of the High Sierras. Spectacular. May–Oct.

Shuttle Bus: There is free shuttle-bus service in the valley, leaving from the visitors center at Yosemite Village.

Yosemite Mountain–Sugar Pine Railroad (steam train), on Calif. 41 in Fish Camp, 4 mi. (6km) south of the southern entrance to the park (209/683-7273): Beautiful ride across the Sierras on a little narrow-gauge railroad; amusing. Open daily Apr–Oct; closed the rest of the year (see The Narrow Gauge Inn under "Accommodations," below).

Yosemite Transportation System (bus): Trips around the park, starting from The Ahwahnee in Yosemite Village or Yosemite Lodge (372-1240).

SIGHTS & ATTRACTIONS

ADVENTURES: Outdoor Adventure River Specialists (OARS) (boat), P.O. Box 67, Angels Camp, CA 95222 (209/736-4677): One- or two-day raft trips down the Kern, American, Stanislaus, Tuolumne, and Merced Rivers. Daily Apr

–Oct. Angels Camp is a two-hour drive from Yosemite Village along Calif. 120W and Calif. 49N. Spectacular.

SCENERY & SIGHTS: ☀️⛰️ **Waterfalls:** Most of these are in Yosemite Valley; they reach their most impressive proportions in the spring, dry up in the summer heat from mid-July to Aug, and revive with the first storms of autumn. The most spectacular are **Yosemite Falls,** with a total height of 2,425 ft. (739m) in three stages; **Ribbon Fall,** 1,612 ft. (491m); **Bridal Veil Fall,** 620 ft. (189m); and **Nevada Fall,** 594 ft. (181m). One of the great beauties of nature.

    ☀️ **Giant Sequoias Stands:** The finest is **Mariposa Grove,** near the southern entrance. It includes the 2,700-year-old Sequoia **Grizzly Giant,** 209 ft. (64m) high and 34 ft. (11m) in diameter.

    ☀️⛰️ **Glacier Point,** 5 mi. (8km) SE of Yosemite Village by (difficult) footpath, or 36 mi. (57km) by road: Splendid panoramic view of the valley 3,254 ft. (992m) below, the waterfalls, and the peaks of the Sierra Nevada: **North Dome, Basket Dome, Mount Watkins, Half Dome,** and others. Hiking trail or vehicle road (open in summer only). The finest view in the park.

    ☀️⛰️ **Tuolumne Meadows,** 55 mi. (89km) NE of Yosemite Village: Wonderful unspoiled grassland in a lovely mountain setting; a paradise for campers and hikers. Abundant wildlife including black bear and deer. Access road closed in winter. Well-known rock-climbing school (372-1335 June–Aug or 372-1244 Sept–May).

    ☀️⛰️⛰️⛰️ **Yosemite Valley,** west of Yosemite Village: Enclosed valley such as you might find in the Alps, about 8 mi. (13km) long, coming to a dead end. Walled in by vertical granite cliffs 3,300 ft. (1,000m) high, over which, when the snow melts, tumble dizzying waterfalls. Most impressive is **El Capitan,** a 3,591-ft. (1,095m) monolith, the dream (or nightmare) of every rock climber. Its southern wall is overlooked by the huge **Sentinel Rock,** 7,035 ft. (2,145m) high, the most characteristic rock of this mountain setting. It's worth coming to the park just to see this spectacular valley.

WINTER SPORTS RESORTS: ⛷️ **Badger Pass Ski Area,** 21 mi. (33km) south of Yosemite Village via Calif. 41 and Glacier Point Rd. (372-1330): Six lifts; cross-country skiing; open late Nov to mid-Apr.

    ⛷️ **Yosemite Valley:** Cross-country skiing only; late Nov to mid-Apr. For a recording giving snow conditions, call 372-1338.

ACCOMMODATIONS

Personal Favorites Inside the Park (in order of preference)

    To make reservations at the four following hotels, contact the **Yosemite Concessions Services Co.,** Yosemite National Park, CA 95389 (209/252-4848).

    Unless the contrary is specifically indicated, none of the following hotels is air-conditioned.

    ☀️♛♛ **The Ahwahnee,** on Calif. 140 in Yosemite Village, Yosemite National Park, CA 95389 (209/252-4848). 121 rms (some w. A/C), color TV. AE, CB, DC, MC, V. Free valet parking, pool, two tennis courts, horseback riding, rest. (resv. required), bar, rm svce, concierge, free crib. *Note:* Luxurious 1920s hotel built like a fortress, w. stone walls and exposed beams. Opened in 1927, the Ahwahnee was conceived to enhance the material grandeur of the towering cliffs of Yosemite; craftspeople incorporated Native American motifs, boulders, and entire logs into the design. Comfortable rms, but furnished without distinction, some w. fireplaces and balconies; also 24 adj. cottages. Quaint plumbing and equipment. Rest. so-so (jkt. required at dinner). Offhand svce. Noisy and crowded in summer. Open year round. Celebrities who have stayed here over the years include Herbert Hoover, John F. Kennedy, Walt Disney, Queen Elizabeth II and the Duke of Edinburgh, Sir Winston Churchill, and Gertrude Stein. Fall and winter are less busy times at the Ahwahnee (in summer, resv. are a must, a year in advance). **VE**

☀��l�l **Wawona Hotel,** on Calif. 41, Yosemite National Park, CA 95389 (209/252-4848). 105 rms (half w. bath), color TV in bar. AE, CB, DC, MC, V. Free parking, pool, golf course, tennis court, horseback riding, rest. (resv. indispensable), bar. *Note:* Charming old hotel in the Victorian style dating from 1856 in a beautiful country setting. Deer roam freely across the lawn. The rms provide only rather primitive comforts; cheerful reception and svce; good rest. Stagecoach rides around the countryside. The favorite hotel of those in-the-know. Open Apr–Nov; a 40-min. drive from Yosemite Village. **I–M**

�l **Yosemite Lodge,** at the intersection of Calif. 140 and Calif. 41, Yosemite National Park, CA 95389 (209/252-4848). 484 rms and cabins (75% w. bath). AE, CB, DC, MC, V. Free parking, pool, bicycling, rest., coffee shop, bar, crib $5. *Note:* Relatively modern motel surrounded by very rustic cabins; comforts are rudimentary but there's a fine view out over the valley. Overrun in summer. Nonexistent svce. Open year round. **I–M** (in lodge), **I** (in bungalows).

�l **Curry Village Motel,** at the intersection of Calif. 140 and Calif. 41, Yosemite National Park, CA 95389 (209/252-4848). 190 rms and cabins (half w. bath), and 420 tents. AE, CB, DC, MC, V. Free parking, pool, skating (in winter), bicycling, horseback riding, coffee shop, bar, camping facilities, crib $5. *Note:* Motel and cabins are functionally comfortable, nothing more. The Yosemite climbing school is located here. Rafting trips organized in summer. Nonexistent svce. For open-air enthusiasts; open Mar–Oct. **I** (in motel or bungalows), **B** (in tents).

Personal Favorites Outside the Park (in order of preference)

�l�l�l **Marriott's Tenaya Lodge,** 1122 Calif. 41, Fish Camp, CA 93623 (209/683-6555; toll free, see Marriott). 242 rms, A/C, color TV, in-rm movies. AE, CB, DC, MC, V. Free parking, two pools, health club, sauna, massage, horseback riding, bicycling, cross-country skiing in winter, rest. (Sierra), deli, bar, rm svce, entertainment, concierge, free crib. *Note:* The first luxury hotel to open in the area in over 50 years. Located 2 mi. (3km) from the southern entrance to the park, this massive construction has an attractive wood-beam lobby w. a three-story fireplace. Elegant Southwest Indian decor. Guest rms are spacious and comfortable but all face the parking lot. Ultraprofessional svce. Rest. as indifferent as at all Marriotts. **VE,** but lower rates off-season.

☀☀☀ **The Narrow Gauge Inn,** on Calif. 41, Fish Camp, CA 93623 (209/683-7720). 27 rms (no A/C), color TV. AE, CB, DC, MC, V. Free parking, pool, rest., bar, crib $7. *Note:* Picturesque little alpine chalet 4 mi. (6km) from the southern entrance to the park; rms w. private balconies or patios and fine mountain view. Very acceptable rest.; friendly reception and svce. Excursions in a little steam train (for information, call 209/683-7273). Closed Nov to mid-Mar. **M**

�l�l **Shilo Inn,** 40644 Calif. 41, Oakhurst, CA 93644 (209/683-3555). 80 mini-suites, A/C, color TV, in-rm movies. AE, CB, DC, MC, V. Free parking, pool, health club, sauna, adj. rest., free continental breakfast, free crib. *Note:* Modern four-story all-suites motel, 25 mi. (40km) from the southern entrance to the park. Very comfortable mini-suites w. microwaves, refrigerators, and wet bars; some w. private patios or balconies. Reception w. a smile. Good value on balance for families. **M,** but lower rates off-season.

�l�l **Boulder Lodge,** on Calif. 158, June Lake, CA 93529 (619/648-7533). 60 rms (no A/C), cable color TV. AE, MC, V. Free parking, pool, sauna, tennis court, fishing, nearby coffee shop. *Note:* Comfortable motel, w. less comfortable bungalows, on June Lake, 22 mi. (35km) SE of the eastern entrance to the park via U.S. 395 and Calif. 120 (the latter closed in winter). Friendly reception. A good base for a visit to Devils Postpile National Monument. Open year round. Very good value. **I,** but lower rates off-season.

☀☿♀♀ **Pines Resort,** North Shore Rd., Bass Lake, CA 93604 (209/642-3121). 84 bungalows w. kitchenettes (no A/C), cable color TV. AE, MC, V. Free parking, beach, tennis court, boating, three rests., bar, disco. *Note:* Engaging frame bungalows w. private patios, some w. fireplaces, an easy walk from the lake. It's 18 mi. (28km) from the southern entrance to the park via Calif. 222 and Calif. 41, far from the hurly-burly of Yosemite's vacationers; ideal for families. Open year round. **M–E,** but lower rates off-season.

♀ **Best Western Yosemite Gateway Inn,** 40530 Calif. 41, Oakhurst, CA 93644 (209/683-2378; toll free, see Best Western). 118 rms, A/C, color TV, in-rm movies. AE, CB, DC, MC, V. Free parking, pool, sauna, health club, adj. rest., bar, crib $2. *Note:* Small, appealing motel deep in the woods, 15 mi. (24km) from the southern entrance to the park on Calif. 41. Very comfortable rms, some w. kitchenettes and refrigerators, most w. mountain views. Cheerful reception and svce; good value. **I,** but lower rates off-season.

♀ **Best Western Lake View,** 30 Main St., Lee Vinning, CA 93541 (619/647-6543; toll free, see Best Western). 45 rms (most w. A/C), cable color TV. AE, CB, DC, MC, V. Free parking, nearby coffee shop, crib $5. *Note:* Typical small motel very nr. Mono Lake, 14 mi. (22km) from the eastern entrance to the park on Calif. 120 (closed in winter), and 21 mi. (33km) south of the ghost town of Bodie on U.S. 395. Functionally comfortable; attractive landscaping; free coffee in rms. **B–I**

RESTAURANTS

Personal Favorites (in order of preference)

☀♀♀♀ **Erna's Elderberry House,** Victoria Lane at Calif. 41, Oakhurst (683-6800). A/C. Lunch Wed–Fri, dinner Wed–Sun, brunch Sun. MC, V. Jkt. *Specialties:* Brie-and-artichoke quiche, roast veal in fennel-Pernod sauce and pear chutney, broiled salmon w. basil butter, remarkable desserts. Menu changes regularly. Very good wine list. *Note:* Some of the best food in California is to be found in this remote little village, nestling in the foothills of the Sierra Nevada some 15 mi. (24km) from the southern entrance to Yosemite National Park. Austrian-born chef Erna Kubin serves up a wonderful, light, creative cuisine at very attractive prices. Its six-course dinners are a feast for the eye as well as the palate. Elegant country-style decor; open-air terrace in good weather. Flawless svce. A very fine place—definitely reserve ahead. *French/Continental.* **E,** ($58 prix-fixe menu)

♀ **Charles Street Dinner House,** Calif. 140 at 7th St., Mariposa (966-2366). A/C. Dinner only, Wed–Sun; closed Dec 25. MC, V. *Specialties:* beef en brochette, steak, catch of the day. *Note:* Nice little rest. in a restored 19th-century house 30 mi. (48km) from the main park entrance. Good flavorful food; good svce; good value. *Steak/Seafood.* **I–M**

♀ **The Narrow Gauge Inn,** in the Narrow Gauge Inn (see "Accommodations," above) (683-6446). A/C. Dinner only, nightly; closed Nov to mid-Mar. AE, CB, DC, MC, V. *Specialties:* broiled steak and fresh seafood, homemade desserts. *Note:* Good mountain views. Acceptable but unimaginative food. Rustic decor w. open-air terrace in summer and inviting fireplace in winter. Friendly reception and svce. Good value; resv. advised in summer. *Seafood/American.* **B–I**

NEARBY EXCURSIONS

☀♨ **BODIE** (96 mi./153km east of Yosemite Village via Calif. 140W, Calif. 120E, U.S. 395N, and Calif. 270E) (619/647-6445): This old gold prospectors' town had 10,000 inhabitants in 1880 and enjoyed an unhappy celebrity for its violence—seven shoot-outs a week on average.

It was destroyed by two great fires, in 1892 and 1932. There remain some several dozen buildings more or less well preserved, including the church, the school, and the prison; there's also a little museum. Spectacular. *Note:* The last 3 mi. (5km), by unsurfaced road, are impassable in winter.

On the way, glance at the large saltwater **Mono Lake** on Calif. 120 (closed in winter), now a refuge for waterfowl.

COLUMBIA (80 mi./128km NW of Yosemite Village via Calif. 140W, 120W, and 49N) (209/532-4301): One of the best-preserved ghost towns in California. Museums, workshops, and many restored buildings including the picturesque **State Driver's Retreat Saloon,** the **What Cheer Saloon,** and the **City Hotel.** It's certifiably in period, just the way it was in the palmy days of the gold rush.

On the way, take a side trip to look at **Sonora,** a place of importance in the westward expansion.

Where to Stay

City Hotel, Main St., Columbia, CA 95310 (209/532-1479). 9 rms. AE, MC, V. An Old West period hotel. Rest. open Tues–Sun for dinner and Sun for brunch. **I–M**

NATIONAL PARKS IN THE VICINITY

DEVIL'S POSTPILE NATIONAL MONUMENT (98 mi./156km SE of Yosemite Village via Calif. 140W, Calif. 120E, U.S. 395S, and Calif. 203W): An unusual sight—hundreds of bluish basalt shafts, 50–60 ft. (16–18m) high and perhaps 100,000 years old, which look like the torn-up pages of a book. All this is set against a luxuriant backdrop of forests, mountain streams, hot springs, and lava flows. Spectacular. Park open mid-June through Oct. *Note:* Calif. 120 is closed in winter.

For **information,** contact the Ranger Station, P.O. Box 501, Mammoth Lakes, CA 93546 (619/934-2289 mid-June through Oct, 619/934-2505 the rest of the year).

SEQUOIA & KINGS CANYON NATIONAL PARKS (178 mi./284km SE of Yosemite Village via Calif. 41 and 180): Forests of giant sequoias and majestic granite crests. See Chapter 52 on Sequoia National Park.

CHAPTER 54

LOS ANGELES ♟♟

□ □ □

With Hollywood, Disneyland, and Palm Springs

The first great U.S. city designed and built in the Automobile Age, Los Angeles has become the prototype of the sprawling megalopolis. It consists of a group of distinct urban areas, often a long way apart, which lie like the rim of a wheel around the center city hub, here reduced to its lowest common denominator. The scale of Los Angeles—90 mi. (145km) long by 50 mi. (80km) wide—defies belief. Around it lie the suburbs, each of which amounts to a miniature city, from **Glendale, Van Nuys,** and the foothills of the **San Gabriel Mountains** on the north to **Anaheim, Costa Mesa,** and **Long Beach** on the south; from **Ontario** and **Pasadena** on the east to **Santa Monica, Redondo Beach,** and the shores of the Pacific on the west. This vibrant, sprawling city is surpassed only by New York in population, and only by Jacksonville, Florida, in area; at 464 sq. mi. (1,202km²) it's about half the size of the state of Rhode Island.

A sign of the times: The TV giants, ABC, CBS, and NBC, have ousted the movie studios from Hollywood. The run-down slum areas of **Watts** lie a short distance from the daring office skyscrapers of **Bunker Hill** and the twin 52-story towers of **ARCO Plaza.** The huge arena of the **Memorial Coliseum,** where the Olympic Games were held in 1932 and 1984, sits cheek-by-jowl with the fairy kingdom of **Disneyland.** The fashionable restaurants of **Sunset Boulevard**—a name dear to all movie addicts—and the plush homes of **Bel Air,** with their azure-blue pools and manicured lawns, rub shoulders with factory buildings or the famous **Stack,** a giant four-level traffic interchange not far from the **Music Center.** Bohemian **Venice,** with its colorful population of roller-skaters, and the charred ruins of **Koreatown** and **South-Central L.A.,** the two major battlefields of the bloody 1992 riots, are hardly a half hour's drive from the millionaires' boutiques of **Beverly Hills** or the new business district of **Century City.**

Los Angeles seasons have jokingly been called earthquake, fire, flood, and drought. But it is a joke that refers to a serious bit of reality concerning its location in the desert and along the San Andreas fault. Indeed, the environment is a hostile one. Angelenos received two powerful reminders of this in 1993 and 1994, when, first, a firestorm erupted in many surrounding residential areas of Los Angeles. Most seriously harmed during the fires was Laguna Beach, where 16,684 acres (6,840ha) and 318 homes burned. The entire community had to be evacuated. Three months later an earthquake struck, measuring 6.6 on the Richter scale, and buckling houses, buildings, and freeways and sending thousands of people out of their homes and onto the streets. The epicenter was in the San Fernando Valley community of North Ridge and the damage was concentrated in the northern residential areas of the city. Though not the expected "Big One," this earthquake caused over $30 billion worth of damage. However, most tourist destinations escaped with slight damage or none at all during both of these catastrophes.

The ever-choked freeways—L.A. is linked by more than 687 mi. (1,100km) of urban highways—and the oilwells in the heart of the city are part of its urban landscape, as are the surf on the beaches, the interminable tracts of small suburban houses, the intrusive areas of wasteland, and the purple-colored smog, the city's tribute to the internal-combustion engine. Because of the city's sheer size, its residents ("Angelenos") spend twice as much time every day in their cars as anyone else on the face of the earth. As a result, there are by now innumerable drive-in banks, drive-in restaurants, drive-in movie theaters, and even drive-in churches.

El Pueblo de Nuestra Señora la Reina de Los Angeles de Porciúncula (The Town of Our Lady of Porciúncula, Queen of the Angels)—Los Angeles for short —was founded in 1781 by Don Felipe de Neve, governor of Spanish California; the site had been explored as early as 1542 by the Portuguese-born navigator, Juan Rodriguez Cabrillo. The California gold rush of 1849 inaugurated a period of rapid growth, further accelerated by the completion of the Southern Pacific's railroad in 1876 and the first oil discoveries in 1892. In half a century the city's population grew 2,600%, from 50,000 in 1890 to 320,000 in 1910 and 1,500,000 in 1940. Today this huge urban nebula numbers, with its outlying communities, more than 14.5 million inhabitants, including at least 3.5 million "Chicanos" of Mexican origin, and is oriented toward the cutting edge of industry—electronics, aviation, petrochemicals, printing, publishing, tourism (more than 40 million visitors a year), television, movies (more than three-quarters of those made in the U.S.)—but also banking and insurance, to the point where Los Angeles has superseded San Francisco, its older sibling to the north, as New York's economic counterpart on the West Coast.

The city, first of all and most of all, is a patchwork of exotic races and nationalities: the Far Eastern neighborhoods of **Chinatown, Little Tokyo,** and **Koreatown,** the Mexican stretch along **Olvera Street,** the African American slums of **Watts** or **South Central L.A.,** epicenter of the tragic riots of April 1992 (52 dead), and the "Latino" ghettos of **East Los Angeles** and **Boyle Heights.** With its hundreds of thousands of Chinese, Japanese, Koreans, Filipinos, Vietnamese, Formosans, Thais, and Laotian immigrants, Los Angeles has already become the most Asian of U.S. metropolises.

Angelenos, more relaxed and approachable than the people of the great eastern seaboard cities, emphatically affirm that Los Angeles is principally a state of mind, the so-called mellow way of life, which is special in being "cooler" and more harmonious. True, one humorist has defined the place as "a bunch of suburbs in search of a city," but in spite of its size Los Angeles is truly a whole, and a unique one. **Sepulveda Boulevard,** for example, stretches unbroken for 45 mi. (72km). In the absence of decent public transportation this city's traffic assumes nightmare proportions every rush hour on the urban highways so misleadingly referred to as "freeways." The interchange between the Harbor Fwy. and Santa Monica Fwy. (I-10 and Cal. 110), in the heart of Los Angeles, holds the world record for traffic density, with peaks of 480,000 vehicles a day. Another, even less enviable record: the country's highest concentration of carbon monoxide pollutants from internal-combustion engines.

After nurturing for many years a cultural inferiority complex toward New York, the U.S. capital of movies and TV has for more than a decade been living through an intellectual boom—artistic (music, ballet, cinema, architecture, graphic arts), scientific, and cultural. Witness its 35 museums, including the new and spectacular **MOCA (Museum of Contemporary Art),** its dozens of art galleries (Los Angeles is the premier American market for contemporary art, after New York), its hundred or so theaters, 29 symphony and chamber orchestras, 17 theater and opera companies, and 36 ballet companies, some of world class. On the scientific side, thanks to its famous universities and research institutes such as

UCLA, Loyola University, CalTech, and the **Jet Propulsion Laboratory,** Los Angeles can pride itself on the world's highest concentration of Nobel laureates.

The economic and cultural capital of the West Coast has been called (not without reason) "dynamic," "fascinating," "inhuman"; it may seduce you or shock you, according to your taste. Only one thing is for sure: The visitor who encounters this enormous and sometimes disturbing city for the first time will not soon forget it. In spite of its TV and film portraits, it's relatively safe: FBI statistics rank it 15th among American cities for crime (but first for rape).

Among the city's famous children are Pres. Richard M. Nixon (born in the nearby suburb of Yorba Linda); Democratic presidential candidate Adlai Stevenson; the late sculptor Isamu Noguchi; former Chief Justice Earl Warren; food expert Julia Child; actresses Marilyn Monroe, Liza Minnelli, Candice Bergen, and Mia Farrow; and actors Robert Redford, Dustin Hoffman, and Ryan O'Neal.

BASIC FACTS: State of California. Area codes: 213 (Los Angeles), 310 (Inglewood, West L.A., Long Beach, Malibu, and Santa Monica), 818 (San Fernando Valley, Burbank, and Glendale), 714 (Anaheim). Time zone: Pacific. ZIP Code: 90053. Founded: 1781. Approximate population: city, 3,500,000 (second largest in the U.S.); metropolitan area, 14,530,000 (also second largest), including 150,000 Chinese, 160,000 Japanese, 300,000 Koreans, 3,520,000 Chicanos of Mexican origin, 350,000 Salvadorans, 200,000 Nicaraguans, and 60,000 Guatemalans.

CLIMATE: Before the coming of the automobile, Los Angeles had one of the most pleasant climates on the West Coast, dry and sunny, with a mild and rainy winter (lows of 50°F/10°C), a very tolerable summer averaging 75°F (24°C), in spite of 95°F (35°C) peaks when the hot Santa Ana wind blows out of the desert, and a glorious spring and fall. The smog has ruined everything. Given windless weather and auto pollution, when smog clamps down on the center city and the San Fernando Valley basin, whole districts disappear in the thick, corrosive murk, which sometimes lingers for a full week, especially in summer.

DISTANCES: Denver, 1,059 mi. (1,695km); Las Vegas, 282 mi. (451km); Phoenix, 390 mi. (625km); San Diego, 125 mi. (200km); San Francisco, 403 mi. (645km).

ARRIVAL & TRANSIT INFORMATION

Note: Given the sheer size of Los Angeles, the concepts of "downtown" and "suburb" lose all meaning. The places, museums, and monuments referred to below are classified by *districts:* downtown, Hollywood, Beverly Hills, Santa Monica, etc. Establishments not found in any particular district are listed under Los Angeles. Unless otherwise indicated, all phone numbers in this chapter are in area code 213.

AIRPORTS: Los Angeles International Airport (LAX), 17 mi. (27km) SW. Fourth-largest airport in the world by volume of traffic, handling 45 million passengers a year, and the country's third-largest international gateway. For information, call 310/646-5252.

Regional airports include: **Hollywood-Burbank Airport** (BUR), 15 mi. (24km) NW (for information, call 818/840-8840); **Long Beach Municipal Airport** (LGB), 21 mi. (33km) SE; **Ontario International Airport** (ONT), 50 mi. (80km) east; and **Orange County–John Wayne Airport** (SNA), 30 mi. (48km) SE. (For information, call 714/252-5200.)

U.S. AIRLINES: Alaska (toll free 800/426-0333), American (toll free 800/433-7300), America West (toll free 800/247-5692), Continental (toll free 800/525-0280), Delta (toll free 800/221-1212), Hawaiian Air (toll free 800/367-5320), MGM Grand Air (toll free 800/933-2646), Northwest (toll free

800/225-2525), TWA (toll free 800/221-2000), United (toll free 800/241-6522), and USAir (toll free 800/428-4322).

FOREIGN CARRIERS: Air Canada (toll free 800/422-6232), Air France (toll free 800/237-2747), Air New Zealand (toll free 800/262-1234), British Airways (toll free 800/247-9297), Japan Air Lines (toll free 800/525-3663), KLM (toll free 800/374-7747), Lufthansa (toll free 800/645-3880), Quantas (toll free 800/227-4500), and Virgin Atlantic (toll free 800/862-8621).

CITY LINK: The **cab** fare from Los Angeles International to dwntwn is about $30; to Beverly Hills, $28; to Hollywood, $35; to Santa Monica, about $18. Time, depending on destination and time of day, 50–75 min.

    Airport Bus: Several shuttle van companies can be summoned through courtesy phones in the baggage-claim area or by calling 310/417-8988. There's no need to make a reservation. The best one, **Super Shuttle** (310/338-1111; toll free 800/554-3146), provides door-to-door service to any address in Los Angeles; fare varies according to destination, $12 (dwntwn) to $35 (Orange County).

    Cabs are very expensive, and often impossible to find away from the big hotels. Public transportation is sadly lacking—a **light-rail system** covering a a 22-mi. (35km), 22-station route between dwntwn and Long Beach, the "Blue Line," began operation in 1990; one-way fare, $1.10. Scheduled for completion in May 1995, the "Green Line" will run from Norwalk to El Segundo/LAX. The "Red Line," a subway line still under construction, now runs 4 mi. (6km) between Union Station and MacArthur Park; fare: 25¢. For information on the **public bus and rail (RTD) service** or the **downtown shuttle** (DASH), call 213/626-4455.

    An easy way to get to popular spots at night is by **After 5** (toll free 800/896-4545), a bus service with stops at major dwntwn hotels, Little Tokyo, Hollywood, Century City, etc. Fare: $10 each way.

    The only solution that makes sense is to rent a car; rates with unlimited mileage in California are among the best in the country.

CAR RENTAL (at Los Angeles International Airport unless otherwise indicated): Avis (toll free 800/331-1212); Budget (toll free 800/527-0700); Dollar (toll free 800/800-4000); Hertz (toll free 800/654-3131); National (toll free 800/227-7368); and Thrifty (toll free 800/367-2277). For in-town locations, consult the local telephone directories.

LIMOUSINE SERVICES: Carey Limousine (310/275-4153), Dav El Limousines (toll free 800/922-0343), Glitter Limousine (toll free 800/726-1837), and Network Limo Service (toll free 800/638-5466).

TAXIS: Cabs may be hailed on the street, taken from the stands outside the major hotels, or summoned by phone. This is one of the more expensive cities in the country for cab rides. Recommended companies include: **Checker** (654-8400), **Independent** (385-8294), **Los Angeles Taxi** (627-7000), and **United** (653-5050).

TRAIN: Amtrak, Union Terminal, 800 N. Alameda St., dwntwn (toll free 800/872-7245). An ill-reputed district, dangerous at night.

INTERCITY BUSES: Greyhound (toll free 800/231-2222) has terminals at 1716 E. 7th St., dwntwn, a rough neighborhood at night, and at 1409 N. Vine St., Hollywood.

INFORMATION & TOURS

TOURIST INFORMATION: The **Automobile Club of Southern California,** dwntwn at 2601 S. Figueroa St., CA 90007 (213/741-3111): Practical information for motorists, maps. Fine Colonial building.

Greater Los Angeles Convention and Visitors Bureau, 633 W. 5th St., Suite 600, CA 90071 (213/624-7300; toll free 800/228-2452): Accepts only written requests for information.

Los Angeles Chamber of Commerce, 404 S. Bixel St., CA 90017 (213/629-0602).

Visitors Information Center, dwntwn at 685 S. Figueroa St., CA 90071 (213/461-4213): Information on Los Angeles and the metropolitan area; multilingual hostesses. Other location: 6541 Hollywood Blvd., Hollywood (213/461-4213).

For a recorded update on upcoming happenings in the L.A. area, call the 24-hr. **events hotline** (213/689-8822), with messages in Spanish, French, Japanese, and German, as well as in English.

GUIDED TOURS: Grave Line Tours (bus), East Wall of Mann's Chinese Theater, on Hollywood Blvd. at Orchid Ave., Hollywood: The name, with overtones of macabre humor, perfectly describes the purpose of the tour—to show you the places where celebrities and movie stars (Rudolf Valentino, Marilyn Monroe, Sharon Tate, and the like) drew their last breath, or now lie awaiting eternity. It lasts two hours and you ride in an old Cadillac hearse. For lovers of the spooky and the unusual. Reserve ahead (469-3127).

Gray Line Tours (bus), 340 N. Camden Dr., Beverly Hills (310/285-1890): Guided tours of the city; pickup at all major hotels.

Hollywood Fantasy Tours (bus), 6773 Hollywood Blvd., Hollywood (469-8184): Guided tour of the neighborhoods where the movie stars live and other attractions; pickup at all major hotels.

Los Angeles Harbor Cruises (boat), Ports O'Call Village, Harbor Blvd., San Pedro (310/831-0996): mini-cruises around the Port of Los Angeles and Long Beach. Year round.

SIGHTS, ATTRACTIONS & ACTIVITIES

ARCHITECTURAL HIGHLIGHTS: ⚖ **Capitol Records,** 1750 Vine St., Hollywood: Amusing structure, shaped like a stack of records, concept of composer Johnny Mercer and his associate Nat King Cole. No visits.

⚖ **City Hall,** 200 N. Spring St., dwntwn (485-2891): 454-ft.-high (138m) landmark dating back to the mid '20s. First tall building constructed in L.A. The hall was cast as the home of the *Daily Planet* in the "Superman" TV series. Observation deck on the 27th floor open Mon–Fri.

⚖ **Coca-Cola Bottling Co.,** 1334 S. Central Ave., dwntwn: 1935 bottling plant disguised as an art deco steamboat; a triumph of California kitsch by architect Robert Derrah. No visits.

☼⚖ **First Interstate World Center,** 633 W. 5th St., dwntwn: Made famous by the TV show "L.A. Law," this brand-new cylindrical skyscraper by I. M. Pei (73 stories, 1,017 ft./310m) is the tallest building west of the Mississippi River.

⚖ **Fox Plaza,** 2121 Ave. of the Stars, Century City (310/282-0047): Two triangular buildings designed by Minoru Yamasaki. These spectacular twin towers are among the city's most photographed, and served as backdrop for the TV show "Remington Steele." Former President Reagan maintains his office on the 34th floor.

☀ **Hollywood Sign,** Durand Dr., North Hollywood: As famous as the Eiffel Tower or the Statue of Liberty, these nine great white letters, each 45 ft. (12m) high, erected on Mt. Wilson, have been the trademark of Los Angeles since 1923. Reached via Beechwood Dr.

🏛 **Los Angeles Memorial Coliseum,** 3939 S. Figueroa St., dwntwn (747-7111): Built for the 1932 Olympics, this magnificent art deco stadium, with a capacity of 102,000, was completely renovated for the 1984 Olympics. Between times, it houses the home football games of the L.A. Raiders, rodeos, pop concerts, motocross races, etc. Open daily.

☀🏛 **Music Center,** 135 N. Grand Ave., dwntwn (972-7483): The Los Angeles equivalent of New York's Lincoln Center. Three futuristic-looking concert halls opened in 1964—the **Dorothy Chandler Pavilion,** the **Ahmanson Theater,** and the **Mark Taper Forum**—frame a marble plaza with a vast pool and an impressive sculpture by Jacques Lipchitz entitled *Peace on Earth.* Every year the Oscar award ceremony is held here. Tours Tues and Thurs–Sat. For information on shows, call 972-7211.

👓 **Pacific Design Center,** 8687 Melrose Ave., West Hollywood (310/657-0800): Nicknamed "The Blue Whale," this amazing 1975 tinted-glass building designed by Cesar Pelli houses showrooms of home-furnishings manufacturers. The adjoining cubic green building, also designed by Cesar Pelli, was opened in 1988.

🏛 **Tail o' the Pup,** 329 N. San Vicente Blvd., West Hollywood (310/652-4517): Bar shaped like a giant hot dog, one of the few surviving relics of California pop architecture. Amusing.

🏛 **Union Station,** 800 N. Alameda St., dwntwn (624-0171): The city's central station is a magnificent 1939 example of the Hollywood-Spanish style; more than 65 movies have been shot here. Avoid the neighborhood after dark.

🏛 **University of California–Los Angeles (UCLA),** 405 Hilgard Ave., Westwood (310/206-8147): Founded in 1919, the local campus of the University of California moved to its present site in 1929. With 34,000 students it's the state's largest. Among the many points of interest on the huge 410-acre (166ha) campus are: a very lovely **botanic garden** with modern sculpture, including works of Matisse and Noguchi; **Schoenberg Hall,** named in memory of the Austrian composer who taught here in the '30s and '40s; and above all the **Wight Art Gallery** and the **Fowler Museum of Cultural History** (see "Museums," below). The **Visitors Center,** 10945 Leconte Ave., offers walking tours of the campus Mon–Fri.

BEACHES: 🏖 **Corona del Mar State Beach,** 42 mi. (67km) SE: One of the most beautiful beaches around Los Angeles, perfect for swimmers.

🏖 **Huntington Beach,** 36 mi. (58km) SE: The surfers' paradise; the sport began here in 1907, and the U.S. Championships are held here every year. On the beach is a monument to the Unknown Surfer.

☀🏖🏖 **Laguna Beach,** 48 mi. (76km) SE: The favorite beach for artists and yuppies, reached by a magnificent coastal road from Newport Beach.

🏖 **Long Beach,** 22 mi. (35km) south: One of the most popular beaches in the Los Angeles area.

☀🏖🏖 **Malibu,** 19 mi. (30km) West: One of the region's most beautiful, particularly **Malibu Surfrider State Beach,** but strong waves. For experienced surfers.

🏖 **Manhattan Beach,** 18 mi. (29km) SW: Agreeable, relatively uncrowded beach, popular with teenagers.

🏖 **Santa Monica,** 15 mi. (24km) west: This popular beach and promenade has been virtually taken over by hundreds of homeless. Picturesque pier and amusement park.

⌂ **Sunset Beach,** 33 mi. (54km) SE: The favorite beach of sea-soned surfers.

⌂ **Venice,** 16 mi. (26km) SW: The kingdom of the roller-skaters. "Pop" and amusing by day; riskier after dark. Also popular with bodybuilders (**"Muscle Beach,"** 1800 Ocean Front Walk).

⌂ **Zuma Beach,** 25 mi. (40km) west: The nudists' beach, with great surf.

BROADCASTING & MOVIE STUDIOS: ABC, 4151 Prospect Ave., Holly-
wood (818/506-0067): Tapings of TV shows, open to the public. Tickets must be applied for one or two days in advance. Open Mon–Fri.

CBS, 7800 Beverly Blvd., Los Angeles (852-2624): Tapings of TV shows, open to the public. Tickets must be applied for one or two days in advance. Open daily.

NBC, 3000 W. Alameda Blvd., Burbank (818/840-3537): The country's largest TV studio. Backstage tours, including a visit to Studio 1 (home of "The Tonight Show"), run every 30 min. Mon–Fri. Taping of TV shows, open to the public. Tickets must be applied for one or two days in advance.

Paramount, Bronson and Melrose Aves., Hollywood: The wrought-iron entrance gates were made famous by the movie *Sunset Boulevard.* No admission to the studio.

Paramount Film and TV Studios, 860 N. Gower St., Hollywood (213/956-1777): Offers a two-hour walking tour of the studios, and tapings of sitcoms and talk shows. Tour admission: $15. Mon–Fri.

☀☆ **Universal Studios Tour,** 3900 Lankershim Blvd., Universal City (818/777-3750): The first theme park dedicated to the Seventh Art; offers two-hour conducted mini-train tours behind the scenes of Hollywood's largest movie studio. From the *Star Wars* style of attack from outer space through the collapsing railroad bridge, the *Ten Commandments* passage of the Red Sea, the devouring Great White shark from *Jaws,* or the exploits of *King Kong* on the streets of New York to the new *E.T.* automated ride created by director Steven Spielberg, nothing, or almost nothing, is spared the sensation-seeking visitor. Kitsch and crowded, but amusing; it draws three million people a year. Open daily except Thanksgiving and Dec. 25. Admission: $30 (adults), $24 (children).

Warner Bros. VIP Tours, 4000 Warner Blvd., Burbank (818/954-1744): Tour on foot and by minibus through the movie and TV studios of Warner Bros. and Columbia Pictures. You can watch the shooting of a movie or a TV show being taped. Resv. must be made well ahead. Highly recommended to movie buffs, but exhausting. No movie or still cameras or tape recorders allowed. Price, $27; open Mon–Sat.

CHURCHES/SYNAGOGUES: ☀☆ Crystal Cathedral, 12141 Lewis St.,
Garden Grove, 28 mi. (45km) SE on I-5 (714/971-4013): Philip Johnson's star-shaped, beveled-glass, 3,000-seat church-auditorium, the most modern in the U.S. A spectacular sight, 10 min. by car from Disneyland. Open daily.

☀⌂ **Los Angeles Mormon Temple,** 10777 Santa Monica Blvd., Los Angeles (310/474-1549): One of the largest Mormon temples in the world standing in 20 acres (8ha) of beautiful landscaped garden. The temple's principal tower, 257 ft. (78m) high, is crowned by a 15-ft. (4m) statue of the Angel Moroni. Non-Mormons are not admitted to the Temple it-self, but the interesting visitor center is open daily.

⌂ **St. Vincent de Paul Church,** 612 W. Adams Blvd. at Figueroa St., Los Angeles (749-8950): Generally admired as one of the city's handsomest churches; the Spanish baroque architecture and Mexican mo-saic ornamental tiling make a stunning impact. Across the intersection at 514 W. Adams is ⌂ **St. John's Church,** a modern replica of the great 11th-century church at Toscanello in Italy.

⚱ **Wayfarer's Chapel,** 5755 W. Palos Verdes Dr., Rancho Palos Verdes (310/377-1650): Designed by Lloyd Wright, architect son of the great Frank Lloyd Wright, this splendid 1949 glass-and-sequoia-wood chapel overlooks the Pacific. Open to all denominations. Open daily.

HISTORIC BUILDINGS: ⚱⚱ **Bradbury Building,** 3rd St. at Broadway, dwntwn (489-1893): A late 19th-century jewel designated as a national historic landmark (1893). Marble staircases and Victorian wrought-iron balconies. Wonderful interior atrium under an elegant skylight. Open Mon–Sat.

⚱ **Casa de Adobe,** 4605 N. Figueroa St., Highland Park (221-2163): An exact replica of an 1850s Mexican hacienda, the building dates from 1918 and is used as an annex to the Southwest Museum (see below). Interesting period decoration and furniture. Open Tues–Sun.

☼⚱⚱ **El Pueblo de Los Angeles State Historic Park** (see "Strolls, Downtown," below).

☼⚱ **Greystone Mansion,** 905 Loma Vista Dr., Beverly Hills (310/550-4654): A modern-day Versailles built in the early 1920s by oil mogul Doheny for his son. The 55-room Tudor-Jacobean mansion on the grounds, is closed to the public, but the glorious gardens, woods, ponds, and walkways are open daily and offer a stunning view of L.A. The triumph of the Beverly Hills' architectural outrageousness.

☼⚱ **Hollyhock House,** 4800 Hollywood Blvd., Hollywood (662-7272): Built in 1919 as the home of oil heiress Aline Barnsdall, Frank Lloyd Wright's first Los Angeles building was inspired by pre-Columbian themes, and is considered one of his greatest achievements. Open Tues–Sun.

⚱ **Lummis Home,** 200 E. Ave. 43, Lincoln Heights (222-0546): Picturesque turn-of-the-century home of rustic character (rough-hewn stones and exposed beams), once the property of the distinguished historian and archeologist Charles Lummis. Now the headquarters of the Historical Society of Southern California. It can conveniently form part of a combined expedition to the Casa de Adobe (see above) and the Southwest Museum (see "Museums of Science and History," below). Open Fri–Sun.

☼⚱ **Mann's Chinese Theater,** 6925 Hollywood Blvd., Hollywood (464-8111): Opened in 1927 and originally known as Grauman's Chinese Theater, this is probably the world's most famous movie house. Cast in concrete on the sidewalk in front of it are the footprints of 160 stars of the silver screen. The architecture is Hollywood Chinese, and the interior is the finest kitsch.

⚱ **Mission San Fernando Rey de España,** 15151 San Fernando Mission Blvd., Mission Hills (818/361-0186): Spanish mission founded in 1797 by the indefatigable Fr. Junípero Serra (the 17th of 21 missions built by Spanish religious between 1769 and 1823). Original adobe architecture with walls 4 ft. (1.20m) thick, and a very lovely arcade. Superbly restored, and surrounded by beautiful gardens. Museum. Open daily.

☼⚱ **Mission San Gabriel Arcangel,** 537 W. Mission Dr., San Gabriel (818/282-5191): The oldest (1771) stone building in California, the work of Fr. Junípero Serra, and one of the most beautiful of the Spanish missions in the U.S. Renowned for its vineyards; interesting museum.

⚱ **Pico House** (see El Pueblo de Los Angeles Historic Monument in "Strolls, Downtown," below).

☼⚱ **Queen Mary,** Pier J, Long Beach (310/435-3511): The largest (81,000 tons) and longest ocean liner still afloat. Launched in 1934, this one-time pride of the British merchant marine is now an art deco monument and floating museum. Open daily.

☼⚱ **Watts Towers,** 1765 E. 107th St., Watts (569-8181): Eight surrealist metal towers, built single-handedly over 33 years with the most incongruous of salvaged material (70,000 shells, bottles, tin cans, tiles, etc.) by Watts resident Simon Rodia, who died in 1956. An astonishing achievement of naïve art; declared a national monument in 1991. Not a good place to be at night.

MARKETS: ⚱ **Farmers Market,** 6333 W. 3rd St. at Fairfax Ave., Los Angeles (933-9211): Picturesque covered market with more than 160 food stalls; also vendors of clothing and handcrafts from around the world. An ideal place to eat on the run, but somewhat touristy. Open daily.

☀⚱ **Grand Central Market,** 315 S. Broadway, dwntwn (624-2378): A little less touristy, but no less colorful, than Farmers Market (see above). You can find anything here, from sheep's heads, fresh chilis, tripe, and fish to costume jewelry, bargains in clothing, and bottles of vitamins. Open daily.

MUSEUMS OF ART: ☀⚱ **Armand Hammer Museum of Art,** 10899 Wilshire Blvd., Los Angeles (310/443-7000): L.A.'s latest temple of culture. An unsightly gray-and-white marble monolith has galleries set around an open courtyard. Among the hundreds of masterpieces that the late Occidental Petroleum mogul collected over decades are works by Goya, Rembrandt, Monet, Cézanne, van Gogh, Daumier, Wyeth and the famous "Codex Hammer," Leonardo da Vinci's drawings notebook. Open Tues–Sun.

☀⚱⚱⚱ **J. Paul Getty Museum,** 17985 Pacific Coast Hwy., Malibu (310/458-2003): Housed in the replica of a Roman villa of the 1st century A.D. (the "Papyrus Villa" at Herculaneum near Naples), the museum displays a fabulous collection of Greek and Roman material, and of European furniture, bronzes, painting, and sculpture from antiquity through the 18th century, as well as such remarkable contemporary masterpieces as *The Entry of Christ into Brussels in 1889* by James Ensor or *Irises* by Vincent van Gogh, acquired in 1990. Splendid gardens and fountains. Parking space must be reserved at least one week in advance. Worth the trip all by itself. Open Tues–Sun.

☀⚱⚱ **Henry Huntington Library,** 1151 Oxford Rd., San Marino (818/405-2100): The very rich collection includes almost three million old manuscripts and 350,000 rare books, as well as English 18th- and 19th-century paintings, housed in an elegant Greek Revival building dating from 1911. Splendid 200-acre (81ha) botanic garden. Among the well-known works on exhibit: Gainsborough's *Blue Boy, Pinkie* by Sir Thomas Lawrence, Turner's *The Grand Canal, Venice,* Constable's *View of the Stower,* the Ellesmere Manuscript of Chaucer's *Canterbury Tales,* a 1455 Gutenberg Bible, and a manuscript autobiography of Benjamin Franklin. Open Tues–Sun.

☀⚱⚱⚱ **Los Angeles County Museum of Art (LACMA),** 5905 Wilshire Blvd., Los Angeles (857-6111): One of the country's most remarkable museums of art, notwithstanding the controversial modern design by architects William Pereira and Norman Pfeiffer, of which the only successful component is the covered-patio entryway. Splendid collection of impressionists and of contemporary painting and sculpture. Among the well-known exhibits: a supposed portrait of Nicolò Barberini by Lorenzo Lotto, Rembrandt's *Raising of Lazarus,* Georges de la Tour's *The Magdalene with the Candle,* Veronese's *Allegory of Navigation,* Copley's *Portrait of Hugh Montgomerie,* Cézanne's *Still Life with Cherries,* van Gogh's *St. Paul's Hospital,* and Picasso's portrait of Sebastian Juñer Vidal. Open Tues–Sun.

☀⚱⚱⚱ **Museum of Contemporary Art (MOCA),** 250 S. Grand Ave., dwntwn (626-6222): Five buildings of red sandstone and glass in pure geometric shapes—a cube, a pyramid, the arc of a circle—a masterpiece by Japanese architect Arata Isozaki, opened in 1986 at a cost of $23 million. Houses a sumptuous collection of modern painting and sculpture by Mark Rothko, Claes Oldenburg, Franz Kline, Robert Rauschenberg, Roy Lichtenstein,

Willem de Kooning, Edward Ruscha, Jackson Pollock, Frank Stella, Louise Nevelson, Richard Serra, etc. Temporary exhibitions. Open Tues–Sun.

    Museum of Neon Art (MONA), 1000 Universal City Dr. 154 (on the CityWalk), Universal City (617-1580): Here you will learn that even neon can be a means of artistic expression. Surprising and entertaining. Open daily.

    Norton Simon Museum, 411 W. Colorado Blvd., Pasadena (818/449-6840): Cultural showcase of the University of California at Los Angeles (UCLA), art in all its forms in a rather disconcerting futurist building. Many modern paintings (Paul Klee, Kandinsky) and sculptures (Rodin's *Burghers of Calais*), but also Far Eastern art (note particularly a group of 10th-century Chola bronzes) and European masters, including Raphael's *Virgin and Child with a Book,* Dierick Bouts' *Resurrection,* Bassano's *The Flight into Egypt, Exotic Landscape* by the douanier Rousseau, Cézanne's *Tulips in a Vase,* Braque's *Still Life with Pipe,* and 88 bronze figurines by Degas. Open Thurs–Sun.

    Pacific Asia Museum, 46 N. Los Robles Ave., Pasadena (818/449-2742): A Chinese-style imperial palace built around a "meditation garden," housing interesting temporary exhibitions of Asian and Pacific art. It is best visited in conjunction with the Huntington Library and Norton Simon Museum (see above). Open Wed–Sun.

    Temporary Contemporary Museum, 152 N. Central Ave., dwntwn (626-6222): This old warehouse in Little Tokyo was used as a temporary shelter for the museum's collection while the new building was under construction; now it serves as an annex, and attracts sizable crowds. Works by Rothko, Rauschenberg, Claes Oldenburg, Roy Lichtenstein, and Jasper Johns, along with many avant-garde American artists. Trendy cultural events in an unexpected setting. Open Tues–Sun. (Closed for renovation until spring 1995.)

    Wight Art Gallery, 405 Hilgard Ave., on the north UCLA campus, Westwood (310/825-9345): An art museum built to house (often very interesting) temporary exhibitions. Also collections of African and Asian art. Adjoining it is a lovely modern-sculpture garden. Open Tues–Sun.

MUSEUMS OF SCIENCE & HISTORY: **Amateur Athletic Foundation,** 2141 W. Adams Blvd., Los Angeles, 5 mi. (8km) SW via the Santa Monica Fwy. (730-9600): A must for all sports fans; the collection contains more than 50,000 items drawn from all kinds of sports, from Jack Dempsey's boxing gloves through the track shoes of sprinter Jesse Owens to the baseball uniforms of Babe Ruth, Lou Gehrig, Stan Musial, and so on. Replicas of medals from the Olympics and other competitions. Also an extensive sports library. Open Mon–Fri.

    Beit HaShoa Museum of Tolerance, 9786 W. Pico Blvd., just outside of Beverly Hills (310/553-9036): Funded by a donation from former Governor Deukmejian, this new $5-million museum uses interactive audiovisual techniques to depict the Holocaust, anti-Semitism, and the genocide of Native Americans. Also explored are ways to gain tolerance in society, using the U.S. civil rights movement as one example. Mandatory tours run Sun–Fri and last 2½ hr.

    Cabrillo Marine Aquarium, 3720 Stephen White Dr., San Pedro (310/548-7562): Fine oceanographic museum, with no fewer than 34 aquariums containing specimens of more than 100 forms of Pacific marine life. Fascinating. In winter, boat trips are organized for closeup observation of whale migrations. Open Tues–Sun.

    California Museum of Science and Industry, 700 State Dr., Exposition Park, Los Angeles (744-7400): Nicknamed "the museum that loves to be touched," it contains dozens of robots and hands-on displays that involve viewer participation. New IMAX theater with a six-story-high screen. Recently added, the Aerospace Hall is a formidably designed structure by Frank Gehry that has a real F-104 Starfighter cantilevering off the front. One of the country's best teaching museums. Open daily.

     🏛 **Dr. Bly's Weird Museum,** 1641 N. Cahuenga Blvd., Hollywood (462-7078): A shrine to the macabre, featuring the remains of the alleged real Prince Dracula, a 3,000-year-old mummy, and the severed hand of a murderer. This unmarked museum is open daily.

     🏛 **Fowler Museum of Cultural History,** 405 Hilgard Ave., on the north UCLA campus, Westwood (310/825-4361). A fine collection of African, Oceanic, and American art and cultural artifacts housed in a new three-story museum. Open Wed–Sun.

     🔆🏛 **Gene Autry Western Heritage Museum,** 4700 Western Heritage Way, Los Angeles (667-2000): This handsome museum in Griffith Park celebrates the tradition of the Far West with more than 16,000 exhibits, ranging from tools, weapons, and clothing of cowboys, Native Americans, and pioneers to old western movies and relics of the Spanish Colonial era. Among its proudest possessions are Buffalo Bill's saddle, Teddy Roosevelt's Winchester, and many works of art by Frederic Remington, Charles Russell, and others. Open Tues–Sun.

     🔆🏛🏛 **George C. Page La Brea Discoveries Museum,** 5801 Wilshire Blvd., Los Angeles (936-2230): More than a million prehistoric fossils (including 9,000 mammals) of creatures engulfed 9,000–40,000 years ago in the nearby "tar pits," dug up and now on exhibit as fragments or reconstructed skeletons, including a 10-ton mammoth and the "La Brea Woman," 9,000 years old. Many stone tools. Dozens of excavations still under way. Fascinating. Open daily.

     🏛 **Hollywood Studio Museum,** 2100 N. Highland Ave., Hollywood (874-2276): The old barn where in 1913 Cecil B. deMille shot the industry's first full-length feature, *The Squaw Man,* now a museum with displays and screenings from the heroic days of silent film. Fascinating. Open Thurs–Sun in summer, Sat–Sun the rest of the year.

     🏛 **Japanese American National Museum,** 369 E. 1st St. (dwntwn) (625-0414): Collection of artifacts and mementos documenting the Japanese American experience. Housed in what was originally a Buddhist temple and what later became a warehouse for the possessions of the Japanese forced into internment camps during World War II. Open Tues–Sun.

     🏛 **Museum of Flying,** 2772 Donald Douglas Loop, Santa Monica (310/392-8822): California's newest aviation museum located at the Santa Monica airport. This modern structure of glass and steel displays up to 20 historic aircraft on a rotating basis, exhibits, and models. A movie theater shows classic aviation films. Open Tues–Sun in summer, Wed–Sun the rest of the year.

     🏛 **Natural History Museum,** 900 Exposition Blvd., Exposition Park, Los Angeles (744-3414): Interesting museum of natural history and ethnology with important collections of archeology (pre-Columbian art), mineralogy (one of the largest in the world), dioramas of animals in their native habitats, and marine ecology. Open Tues–Sun.

     🏛 **Southwest Museum,** 234 Museum Dr., Highland Park (221-2163): Museum of Native American civilization, designed by historian Charles F. Lummis around an exceptional collection of tribal art and handcrafts. Will delight devotees of the history of the Old West. Open Tues–Sun; closed mid-Aug to mid-Sept.

     🏛 **Wells Fargo History Museum,** 333 S. Grand Ave., dwntwn (253-7166): It's like being there in the days of the westward expansion: stagecoaches, a collection of gold nuggets, 19th-century post office, posters, photographs, etc. Amusing. Open Mon–Fri.

OUTDOOR ART & PLAZAS: Boyle Heights and East Los Angeles: These

Chicano neighborhoods have some of the finest street murals in the city—on

Grand Vista Ave., Alcazar St., Olympic Blvd., Lorena St., Ramona Gardens, Estrada Courts, etc. Dangerous after dark, even in a car.

The Mall, Main and Los Angeles Sts., near City Hall, dwntwn: Gardens, fountains, statuary, and the extraordinary glass **Triforium Tower,** which in the evenings offers a computer-generated symphony of sound and color.

Venice (see "Strolls, West and North Los Angeles," below): Wonderful pop-art murals in trompe l'oeil on the fronts of several buildings near the Arcades in the center of Venice and on Windward Ave. on the ocean. Visit not recommended on foot after dark.

PANORAMAS: 🏛 **City Hall,** 200 N. Spring St., dwntwn (485-2121): Was the home of the *Daily Planet* on TV's "Superman" show. Splendid view of the dwntwn high-rises and—on a clear day—of the mountains and the Pacific, from the 27th floor. Open Mon–Fri.

☼🏛 **Mullholland Drive,** North Beverly Hills: A twisting road which winds across the crest of the Santa Monica Mountains, offering a wonderful view of the city and the ocean in clear weather (best after dark). Very popular with lovers at night. Reached by Laurel Canyon Blvd. in Hollywood or by Coldwater Canyon Dr. in Beverly Hills.

🏛 **Griffith Park** (see "Parks and Gardens," below).

PARKS & GARDENS: 🏛 **Descanso Gardens,** 1418 Descanso Dr., La Cañada (818/952-4400): Some 100,000 camellias bloom here Nov–Mar in the middle of a lovely oak grove. Rosebeds; Japanese garden.

🏛 **Elysian Park,** Academy Rd., Los Angeles (485-5027): 552-acre (225ha) crescent-shaped landscaped park very near the Dodger stadium. Its hilly terrain offers some fine views of the dwntwn skyline.

☼🏛 **Forest Lawn Memorial Park,** 1712 S. Glendale Ave., Glendale (818/241-4151): This splendid landscaped cemetery is a sort of funerary theme park, unique in the U.S. Many marble and bronze replicas of famous classical sculptures, and a gigantic (192- by 44-ft./60- by 14m) *Crucifixion* by Jan Styka, the largest devotional painting in the world. Inspired Evelyn Waugh's novel *The Loved One.* Tombs of Clark Gable, Errol Flynn, Humphrey Bogart, Sammy Davis, Jr., and Jean Harlow among others. Open daily.

🏛 **Griffith Park,** Los Feliz Blvd. at Vermont Ave., Los Angeles (665-5188): The country's largest city park (4,107 acres/ 1,663ha), with a planetarium-observatory from which in fine weather there's a wonderful view of the city, especially at night. Located inside the park is **Forrest Ackerman's Sci-Fi and Monster Mansion,** which houses over 300,000 cinematic artifacts ranging from the Dracula cape worn by Bela Lugosi to models used in the 1933 version of King Kong. (Call 666-6326 for resv.; tours given only on Sat.) Also an ultramodern zoo (see "Zoos," below) and **Travel Town,** a transportation museum with an interesting collection of old locomotives, plus lovely rural landscapes, three golf courses, horseback riding, picnic grounds, and 50 mi. (80km) of footpaths.

🏛 **Hollywood Bowl,** 2301 N. Highland Ave., Hollywood (850-2000): A 17,000-seat open-air amphitheater with perfect acoustics; every year since 1922 classical jazz and rock concerts as well as variety shows have been given here. Built on a former Native American campsite.

☼🏛 **Hollywood Memorial Park,** 6000 Santa Monica Blvd., Hollywood (469-1181): The cemetery of the stars: tombs of Rudolf Valentino, Cecil B. deMille, Douglas Fairbanks, Tyrone Power, and dozens of others. Sumptuously kitsch. Open daily. (One great name not to be found here is Marilyn Monroe. Admirers take note: she's buried in a small, bucolic graveyard, **Westwood Memorial Park,** 1218 Glendon Ave., Westwood.)

🏛 **Palisades Park,** Ocean Ave. between Colorado Ave. and San Vicente Blvd., Santa Monica (310/458-8310): This beautiful park has been called "California's French Riviera." Bordered with palm trees, it snakes along a cliff overlooking, and offering a fine view of, the Pacific, from the Palos Verdes peninsula on the south as far as Malibu to the north.

Will Rogers State Park, 14253 Sunset Blvd., Pacific Palisades (310/454-8212): This big public park used to be the ranch of the legendary cowboy-humorist Will Rogers; his personal memorabilia are on display, along with collections of Native American artifacts. Footpaths for strollers, polo matches Sat–Sun, picnics, horseback riding. Open daily.

PERFORMING ARTS:
For current listings of shows and cultural events, consult the entertainment pages of the two daily morning papers, *Los Angeles Times* and *Los Angeles Daily News*, as well as the monthlies *Los Angeles* and *California*. After New York, Los Angeles has more theaters and concert halls (some 200 in all) than any other city in the country.

Ahmanson Theater, 135 N. Grand Ave., in the Music Center, dwntwn (972-7211): Home of the Center Theater Group. Comedy, drama, modern and classical theater; musical comedies and operettas.

Doolittle Theater, 1615 Vine St., Hollywood (462-6666): Musicals, shows, touring companies.

Dorothy Chandler Pavilion, 135 N. Grand Ave., in the Music Center, dwntwn (972-7211): Home of the Los Angeles Philharmonic under principal conductor Esa-Pekka Salonen (Oct–May), the Los Angeles Music Center Opera, Los Angeles Master Chorale, and the Joffrey Ballet.

Embassy Theater, 851 S. Grand Ave., dwntwn (388-5083): Beautiful Beaux Arts building: home of the Los Angeles Chamber Orchestra.

Greek Theater, 2700 N. Vermont Ave., Griffith Park, Los Angeles (665-1927): Open-air concerts with major pop or rock stars (May–Oct).

Henry Fonda Theater, 6126 Hollywood Blvd., Hollywood (634-1300): Broadway hits.

Hollywood Bowl, 2301 N. Highland Ave., Hollywood (850-2000): Vast 17,000-seat natural amphitheater. Classical concerts with the Los Angeles Philharmonic; also jazz, rock, and variety shows (June–Sept).

Los Angeles Theater Center, 514 S. Spring St., dwntwn (627-6500): Ultramodern four-hall complex opened in 1985; home of the Los Angeles Actors' Theater (contemporary and avant-garde theater); also jazz, classical concerts, and ballet. Has a superb skylight and a very fine marble interior.

Mark Taper Forum, 135 N. Grand Ave., in the Music Center, dwntwn (972-7211): Circular theater for chamber-music concerts; the Center Theater Group performs here in its repertory of contemporary plays.

Orange County Performing Arts Center, 600 Town Center Dr., Costa Mesa (714/556-2787): This ultramodern 3,000-seat auditorium was opened in 1986 at a cost of more than $70 million. Now it offers year-round prestige programs: opera, symphony concerts, ballet, etc.

Pantages Theater, 6233 Hollywood Blvd., Hollywood (468-1770): A 1930s art deco movie house, magnificently restored. Musical comedies, Broadway hits, modern plays with famous actors. The Oscar awards were given here 1949–59.

Pasadena Playhouse, 39 S. El Molino Ave., Pasadena (818/356-7529): Opened in 1925, it is regarded as one of the finest repertory houses for modern and contemporary theater.

Shrine Auditorium, 665 W. Jefferson Blvd. Los Angeles (749-5123): This enormous (6,300-seat) 1926 hall offers remarkably fine acoustics for its concerts, operas, and ballets. On occasion, hosts the Oscar awards ceremony.

Shubert Theater, 2020 Ave. of the Stars, ABC Entertainment Center, Century City (310/201-1500): Musical comedies, star vehicles.

Terrace Theater, 300 E. Ocean Blvd., Long Beach (310/436-3661): Home of the Long Beach Symphony Orchestra, and the Long Beach Civic Light Opera and Long Beach Ballet companies. Musicals, musical comedies, etc.

Universal Amphitheatre, 3900 Lankershim Blvd., Universal City (818/

777-3931): In the Universal Studios complex. Big-name recitals, musicals. Year round.

Westwood Playhouse, 10886 Le Conte Ave., Westwood (310/208-5454): Near the UCLA campus; contemporary and avant-garde theater.

Wilshire Theater, 8440 Wilshire Blvd. at La Cienega Blvd., Beverly Hills (468-1716): Comedy, drama, modern theater.

Wiltern Theater, 3790 Wilshire Blvd. at Western Ave., Los Angeles (380-5005): Handsome art deco theater, home of the Los Angeles Opera. Also classical concerts.

SHOPPING: ARCO Plaza, 505 S. Flower St., dwntwn: The country's largest underground shopping center: dozens of stores, boutiques, art galleries, and restaurants occupying several levels under the giant ARCO/Bank of America Towers. If you suffer from claustrophobia, forget it.

Beverly Center, Beverly and La Cienega Blvds., West Hollywood: Elegant, ultramodern shopping center whose hi-tech architecture seems to be modeled on the Musée Beaubourg in Paris. More than 200 boutiques and stores, 13 restaurants, 15 cinemas and theaters; even a disco. Open daily.

Garment District, Los Angeles St. between 7th St. and Washington Blvd., dwntwn: Clothing of all kinds at unbeatable prices for more than half a century, particularly in the **California Mart** or the **Cooper Building.**

Larry Edmund's Bookstore, 6644 Hollywood Blvd., Hollywood (463-3273): The best specialist bookstore in the country for the movie industry; a kind of living history of the silver screen. Open Mon–Sat.

Melrose Avenue between La Cienega Blvd. and La Brea Ave., Los Angeles: Trendy fashion boutiques; the California "in" style.

☼ **Rodeo Drive,** between Santa Monica and Wilshire Blvds., Beverly Hills: The country's, and possibly the world's, smartest street, equivalent to Madison Ave. in New York, Bond St. in London, or the rue Faubourg St-Honoré in Paris. From Giorgio to Hermès, from Tiffany to Gucci, not to mention the unbelievable Bijan, the most outrageous of luxury boutiques are to be found here. The new **Two Rodeo Drive,** at Rodeo Drive and Wilshire Blvd., is even more upscale.

Santa Monica Antique Market, 1607 Lincoln Blvd., Santa Monica (310/314-4899). 232 dealers under one roof. Unusual items dating from the 19th century to the present are for sale, including movie props.

Seventh Market Place, 735 S. Figueroa St., dwntwn: Extraordinary mixture of an underground shopping center, a Japanese garden, and a tropical conservatory, designed by Jon Jerde. Open daily.

Virgin Megastore, 8000 Sunset Blvd., West Hollywood (650-8666). Enormous record store offering a fine collection of international releases. The first American store of this worldwide chain. You can also buy a plane ticket on Virgin Atlantic here.

SPECIAL EVENTS: For exact dates, consult the **Anaheim Visitor and Convention Bureau,** 800 W. Katella Ave., Anaheim, CA 92803 (714/999-8999); the **Laguna Beach Chamber of Commerce,** 357 Glenneyre St. (P.O. Box 396), Laguna Beach, CA 92652 (714/494-1018); the **Long Beach Convention and Visitors Council,** 1 World Trade Center, Long Beach, CA 90802 (310/436-3645); the **Los Angeles Visitors and Convention Bureau,** 633 W. Fifth St., Los Angeles, CA 90071 (213/624-7300); or the **Pasadena Convention and Visitors Bureau,** 171 S. Los Robles Ave., Pasadena, CA 91105 (818/795-9311).

Anaheim
Halloween Festival (end of Oct): Parades; giant masked ball.

Chinatown
Chinese New Year (mid-Jan or early Feb): Dragon Parade and costumed processions in honor of the Chinese New Year. Picturesque.

Downtown Los Angeles
L.A. Marathon (Mar): Third-largest marathon in the country after New York and Boston.

Academy Awards Ceremony (late Mar or early Apr): The world-famous ceremony at which moviedom's prized Oscars are conferred.

El Pueblo de Los Angeles
Cinco de Mayo Procession (May 5): The great annual festival of the Mexican-American community.

Las Posadas (end of Dec): Christmas festivities Mexican style; colorful.

Hollywood
Hollywood Bowl Summer Festival (July–Aug): The Los Angeles Philharmonic offers more than 40 concerts at its summer home. Wknd fireworks spectaculars. Also jazz and pop concerts.

Laguna Beach
Winter Festival (Feb–Mar): Art exhibitions, shows, handcrafts fair.

Little Tokyo
Hanamatsuri (Apr): Festival in honor of Buddha's birth.

Nisei Week (Aug): Annual Japanese cultural festival, very popular locally.

Long Beach
Long Beach Toyota Grand Prix (mid-Apr): Formula I Grand Prix along the streets of dwntwn Long Beach; spectacular, drawing more than 200,000 spectators every year.

International Sea Festival (Aug): Very lively, with boat races, regattas, processions, competitions.

Pasadena
Tournament of Roses (Jan 1): Flower-covered floats, two dozen bands, and 300 equestrians parade along Orange Grove and Colorado Blvds.; a million spectators on the streets and 100 million more watching on television. Timed for a few hours before the Rose Bowl football game. Celebrated its 100th birthday in 1988.

Pomona
Los Angeles County Fair (end of Sept): The country's biggest fair exhibition; 28 mi. (45km) SE of dwntwn.

SPORTS: Los Angeles is blessed with a multitude of professional teams, as well as three racetracks:

Baseball (Apr–Sept): California Angels, Anaheim Stadium (714/634-2000); Dodgers, Dodgers Stadium (224-1500).

Basketball (Oct to late Apr): Clippers, L.A. Sports Arena (748-0500); Lakers, The Forum, Inglewood (310/419-3100).

Football (Sept–Dec): Raiders, L.A. Coliseum (310/322-5901); Rams, Anaheim Stadium (714/937-6767).

Ice Hockey (Sept to late Apr): Kings, The Forum, Inglewood (310/673-1300).

Horse Racing
Del Mar Thoroughbred Club, Jimmy Durante Dr., Del Mar (619/755-1141): Directly on the beach; open late July to mid-Sept.

Hollywood Park, Century Blvd. and Prairie Ave., Inglewood (310/419-1500). Racing from mid-Apr to late July and mid-Nov to the end of Dec.

Santa Anita Park, Huntington Dr. and Baldwin Ave., Arcadia (818/574-7223): Racing from early Oct to early Nov and late Dec to late Apr.

STROLLS: Los Angeles is so big, with so many delightful areas for strolling, that this section is divided into two parts: Downtown, and West and North L.A.

Downtown

Chinatown, bounded by Alpine, Spring, and Yale Sts., and Bambas Lane, dwntwn: Stalls, restaurants, pagoda-shaped buildings; a pungent, gimcrack, lively Chinese district.

El Pueblo de Los Angeles Historic Monument, bounded by Macy, Alameda, Spring, and Arcadia Sts., dwntwn: The historic heart of Los Angeles since its foundation in 1781. From the **Avila Adobe,** the city's oldest (1818) house, now a museum of California history, to the **Old Plaza Firehouse** (1884), and from the **Church of Nuestra Señora Reina de los Angeles** (1822) to the **Merced Theater** (1870) or the **Pico House,** once the city's most luxurious hotel (1870), El Pueblo can show you a dozen or more 19th-century buildings, carefully restored, along **Main Street, Olvera Street,** and **Old Plaza,** a delightful, shady little square in the purest Spanish-Mexican style, with a wrought-iron bandstand. A living picture of the past, not to be missed. The **visitor center** is at 622 N. Main St. (628-1274). Also see, on the south wall of the Italian Hall, the superb giant (16- by 80-ft./5- by 24.5m) **fresco** created in 1932 by the famous Mexican artist David Alfaro Siqueiros. Rather touristy but pleasant atmosphere. Open daily. Guided tours Tues–Sat.

Financial District, bounded by 1st, 6th, Olive, and Figueroa Sts., dwntwn: "The Wall Street of the West Coast." Scarcely 15 years old (until 1957 there was a 13-floor limit on construction because of the earthquake hazard), this new financial district now collects skyscrapers. Among the most striking are the First Interstate World Center, with 73 stories the city's tallest building; the five 35-floor glass cylinders of the Westin Bonaventure Hotel, the 48-story Wells Fargo Building, the Security Pacific Bank (55 stories), and the twin 52-story towers of the ARCO/Bank of America building.

Little Tokyo, bounded by 1st, Alameda, 3rd, and San Pedro Sts., dwntwn: Los Angeles, with 160,000 inhabitants who are Japanese or of Japanese descent, is the largest Japanese city outside Asia. Many stores, Buddhist temples, art galleries, restaurants. Exquisite Japanese garden and very active cultural center.

West and North Los Angeles

Bel Air and Beverly Hills, north of Sunset Blvd.: The two smart neighborhoods of Los Angeles; mansions of millionaires and movie stars hidden behind trees and locked iron gates, including that of former president, Ronald Reagan, at 668 St. Cloud Rd., Bel Air. Super-deluxe boutiques on Beverly Hills' Rodeo Dr. Even the local post office at 312 S. Beverly Dr. offers valet parking to its customers—which says it all. For a little daydreaming.

Hollywood, around Hollywood Blvd. and Vine St.: Once "the movie Mecca," and known as Tinseltown—but the industry, which was officially born in 1910 when the first studio was built, has now only its former glories to live on. The legendary Hollywood is a community of undistinguished stores, gloomy motels, tattered palm trees, sex shops on Hollywood Blvd., and an intimidating local populace after dark (walking at night is definitely not recommended). Among its attractions are Mann's Chinese Theater (see "Historic Buildings," above), the Hollywood Studio Museum (see "Museums of Science and History," above), and the celebrated Walk of Fame (see below). A laudable attempt to clean up the community has recently been set in motion.

Marina del Rey, Admiralty Way: Superb marina on the Pacific, where more than 6,000 boats are moored; a favorite place with prosperous bohemia and trendy night-owls. A bogus but picturesque New England fishing village (Fisherman's Village).

    Pasadena, via the Pasadena Fwy.: One of the country's scientific strongholds; CalTech (California Institute of Technology), 1201 E. California Blvd., is a veritable hotbed of Nobel laureates in physics and chemistry. Its visitor center is at 315 S. Hill Ave. (818/395-6328). The jewel in CalTech's crown is NASA's Jet Propulsion Laboratory, where the *Voyager* space vehicles were assembled, "permitting more astronomical discoveries in two decades than in the preceding two millennia." JPL is open to visitors, by advance resv., twice a month; call 818/354-4321. See also the entries on the Norton Simon Museum and the Pacific Asia Museum (see "Museums of Art," above).

    Ports O'Call Village, Berths 76–79, Harbor Blvd., in San Pedro, 36 mi. (51km) south along the Harbor Fwy. (310/831-0287): Recaptures the atmosphere of a Spanish-colonial port of the 1850s, with its gas-lit cobbled streets, its dozens of stalls and restaurants. Boat trips around the harbor.

    Santa Monica Pier, Ocean Ave. at the foot of Colorado Ave., Santa Monica (310/458-8900): The granddaddy of California's amusement parks, built on the pier in 1909. The giant carousel figured in the setting of the movie *The Sting.* Well-mannered kitsch.

    Sunset Boulevard, from Doheny Dr. to Vine St., Beverly Hills/Hollywood: This legendary "main drag of the movies," blazing at night from all its billboards, is a good part of Los Angeles's nightlife. Restaurants, rock clubs, hotels—but also agents, recording and movie studios. The central section of Sunset Blvd., "The Strip," is the stronghold of show business. Not to be missed (best time, at night).

    Universal CityWalk, next to the Universal Studios (see "Broadcasting and Movie Studios," above) in Universal City: A $100-million street of streets. Scaled-down models of fashionable areas in L.A., such as Melrose Ave., Sunset Strip, and Venice Beach—all within this four-block mini-version of L.A. You'll also find scores of shops, rests., entertainment venues, and nightclubs, as well as a theater that simulates a roller-coaster ride and the **Museum of Neon Art** (see "Museums of Art," above).

    Venice, around Ocean Front Walk and Venice Blvd., Venice: This beach resort was founded in 1904 by Abbot Kinney, an eccentric millionaire who sought to reproduce the city of the doges, canals, and all, on the Pacific coast; he even imported genuine gondolas with singing gondoliers. With its eclectic mix of body-builders, roller-skaters, gays, artists, gigantic pop murals ("murales"), and drug dealers, it is today the most bohemian—and the most entertaining—beach in California.

    "Walk of Fame," along Hollywood Blvd. and Vine St., Hollywood: "The promenade of the stars," where nearly 2,000 bronze stars set in the sidewalk evoke the greats of the silver screen, radio, and television; since 1958 new names are added to the list every month. Worth a snapshot, but don't walk it after dark.

    Westwood Village, around Westwood Plaza, Westwood: Los Angeles's "Latin Quarter" or "Greenwich Village"; stroll on the vast UCLA campus (see "Architectural Highlights," above). Dozens of bookstores, record shops, movie houses, restaurants, etc. Very lively, especially after dark.

THEME PARKS: **Disneyland,** 1313 Harbor Blvd., in Anaheim, 24 mi. (38km) SE on I-5 (714/999-4565): Opened by Walt Disney himself in 1955, this is the archetype of the great American amusement parks. Much smaller than its two Florida siblings, Walt Disney World (opened in 1971) and EPCOT (1982), Disneyland is still one of the country's most popular tourist attractions, visited so far by more than 300 million people, big and little. From "Sleeping Beauty's Castle" to "Fantasyland" and on to "Pirates of the Caribbean" by way of the Far West train that takes you to "Frontierland," not to mention the mysterious jungle of "Adventureland" or "Carnival in New Orleans," 60 different attractions await the visitor. The latest of these is an outer-space Disneyland, in tune with the times, entitled "Star Tours" and created under the supervision of the famous movie director George Lucas. 45 min. by car from dwntwn. Open daily year round. Set aside at least one whole day for your visit. Crowded on wknds. Admission: $31 (adults), $25 (children).

Knott's Berry Farm, 8039 Beach Blvd., in Buena Park, 20 mi. (32km) SE on I-5 and Calif. 39 (714/220-5200): 10 min. by car from Disneyland you'll find a reconstruction of the Far West: attacks on stagecoaches, ghost town, etc.; also an amusement park with 135 attractions and impressive roller-coasters, including Montezuma's Revenge. Big-name shows. The most recent development is a multisensory special-effects show centering on Indian legends and occurring within a replica of an Indian tribal house. This ranks as the country's fourth most popular amusement park, next after the Disney trio. Admission: $27 (adults), $16 (children). Open daily.

Movieland Wax Museum, 7711 Beach Blvd., Buena Park, 20 mi. (32km) SE via I-5 and Calif. 39 (714/522-1154): What the Grévin Museum is to Paris or Mme Tussaud's to London, this is to the movie industry. More than 200 waxwork stars in scenes or settings from the movies that made them famous. Costumes, memorabilia, and old posters recapitulate the history of the "Seventh Art." You can combine the museum with a visit to the nearby Knott's Berry Farm (see above). Open daily.

Six Flags Magic Mountain, 26101 Magic Mountain Pkwy., in Valencia, 32 mi. (52km) NW on I-5 (805/255-4111): A 260-acre (105ha) theme park with 100 attractions including the world's largest wooden roller coaster (1.8 mi./3km long with dizzy drops of 92 ft./30m); if your heart is weak, don't ride it. Less touristy but no less entertaining than Disneyland. Open daily Apr to mid-Sept, wknds and school breaks only the rest of the year.

WINTER SPORTS RESORTS: ⛷ **Angeles National Forest,** about 62 mi. (100km) NE via I-5 and Calif. 2: Mount Waterman, with 3 ski lifts (818/440-1041); Ski Sunrise, with 5 lifts (619/249-6150).

Big Bear Lake, 112 mi. (180km) east via I-10 and Calif. 18: Bear Mountain, 11 lifts (909/585-2519); Snow Summit, 12 lifts (909/866-5766); open mid-Nov to mid-Apr.

Mount Baldy, 51 mi. (82km) east on I-10 and Calif. 83 (909/981-3344): 4 lifts.

Snow Valley, 76 mi. (122km) NE along I-10 and Calif. 30, Calif. 330, and Calif. 18 (909/867-2751): 13 lifts; this most popular of local ski resorts is crowded on wknds. Open mid-Nov to mid-Apr.

ZOOS: ⛲ **Los Angeles Zoo,** Griffith Park, 5333 Zoo Dr. (666-4090): One of the top 10 zoos in the country, with 2,500 animals from all around the world distributed over 113 acres (46ha) of rolling hills. Among the biggest draws is the Ahmanson Koala House and its collection of these engaging Australian mammals. Open daily.

ACCOMMODATIONS

Note: In a city this big, concepts such as "dwntwn" or "vic." don't apply; Wilshire Blvd., the main east-west artery, is 16 mi. (27km) long. The hotels (and restaurants) mentioned below are designated by districts (dwntwn,

Beverly Hills, Hollywood, etc., and Los Angeles for those not in any particular district).

Personal Favorites (in order of preference)

♑♑♑♑ **Four Seasons,** 300 S. Doheny Dr. (at Burton Way), Los Angeles, CA 90048 (310/273-2222; toll free, see the Four Seasons). 285 rms, A/C, color TV, in-rm movies. AE, CB, DC, MC, V. Valet parking $15, pool, health club, three rests. (including Gardens), bar, 24-hr. rm svce, 24-hr. concierge. *Note:* Opened in 1988, this palace hotel (smallish for its kind) is one of the smartest and most luxurious in California. The handsome postmodern 16-story building is surrounded by a splendid tropical grdn w. waterfalls and fountains. Quiet, serene atmosphere. The interior is gracious and in excellent taste: huge, superbly comfortable rms w. private balcony, minibar, and all-around view. Considerate, personalized svce; highly prized rest.; free limousine to Rodeo Dr.'s fashionable boutiques. One of the dozen best hotels in the country. **VE**

♑♑♑♑ **Regent Beverly Wilshire,** 9500 Wilshire Blvd. (at Rodeo Dr.), Beverly Hills, CA 90212 (310/275-5200; toll free 800/545-4000). 300 rms, A/C, color TV, in-rm movies. AE, CB, DC, MC, V. Valet gar. $15 pool, health club, sauna, two rests. (including The Dining Room), coffee shop, bar, 24-hr. rm svce, hrdrsr, florist, concierge, free crib. *Note:* Now part of the Regent luxury-hotel chain of Hong Kong, this aging (1928) palace underwent a complete renovation in 1988 at a cost of $65 million. The Beverly Hills landmark, a stone's throw from the boutiques of Rodeo Dr., is again a symbol of refinement and elegance which attracts diplomats and royalty. Huge, comfortable rms w. period furniture and minibars. Polished, discreet svce; rest. of the highest order. **VE**

☼♑♑♑ **Hotel Bel Air,** 701 Stone Canyon Dr., Bel Air, CA 90077 (310/472-1211; toll free, see Preferred). 92 rms, A/C, color TV, in-rm movies. AE, CB, DC, MC, V. Valet gar. $12.50, pool, rest., bar, 24-hr. rm svce, concierge. *Note:* Hidden in an exclusive L.A. neighborhood, this charming small hotel, in the Spanish mission style, stands among enchanting grdns w. bougainvilleas and a little lake w. swans, breathing a serene intimacy. Elegant rms w. private patios, some w. fireplaces. Honeymooners reserve here months in advance. Fussy rest. (The Restaurant). A favorite w. the Establishment. **VE**

♑♑♑ **Disneyland Hotel,** 1150 W. Cerritos Ave., Anaheim, CA 92802 (714/778-6600). 1,131 rms, A/C, cable color TV. AE, CB, DC, MC, V. Parking $10, three pools, 10 tennis courts, private beach, marina, four rests. (including Granville's), coffee shop, bars, rm svce, boutiques, crib $5. *Note:* Both a resort and a convention hotel, this enormous complex is linked directly to Disneyland by monorail. Its three 14-story towers rise around an enormous lagoon/swimming pool. Very comfortable rms w. private balconies or patios and refrigerators. Efficient svce. Beautiful tropical grdn w. waterfalls and little lakes stocked w. goldfish. Somewhat obtrusive package-tourists and conventioneers predominate here. 5 min. from the Anaheim Convention Center. Good value overall. **M–VE,** but lower rates off-season.

☼♑♑ **Radisson Hollywood Roosevelt Hotel,** 7000 Hollywood Blvd., Hollywood, CA 90028 (213/466-7000; toll free, see Radisson). 310 rms, A/C, color TV, in-rm movies. AE, CB, DC, MC, V. Valet parking $8, pool, rest. (Theodore's), bar, rm svce, boutiques, free crib. *Note:* A hallowed spot in the history of the cinema. The first Oscars were awarded here in 1929; it was here also that Clark Gable and Carole Lombard concealed their love affair from the public eye. All the great stars, from Errol Flynn to Douglas Fairbanks and Maureen O'Hara, came here in its heyday. It reopened its doors in 1986 after a $40-million restoration program, and has now recaptured all its former magnificence. The splendid interior is Neo-Castilian crossed with art deco. The rms, w. minibars, are comfortable and inviting; the Cinegrill bar is famous.

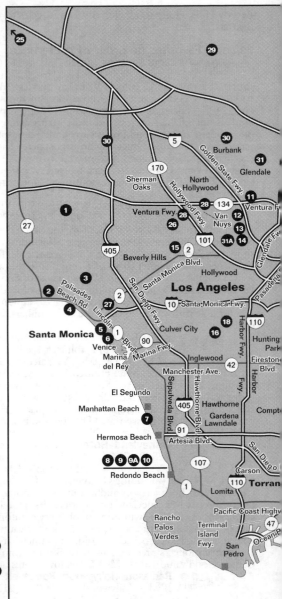

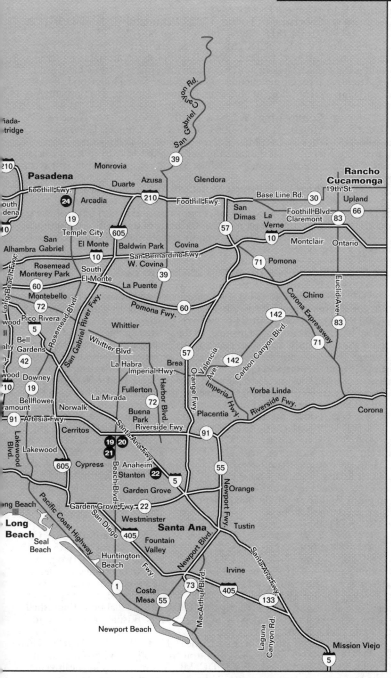

LOS ANGELES

Friendly, smiling svce. The Celebrity Floor is reserved for VIPs. Opposite the renowned Mann's Chinese Theater. **M–E**

♈♈ **Sportsmen's Lodge,** 12825 Ventura Blvd., Studio City, CA 91604 (818/769-4700; toll free 800/821-8511). 196 rms, A/C, cable color TV. AE, CB, DC, MC, V. Free parking, pool, health club, rest., coffee shop, bars, rm svce, free crib. *Note:* Luxuriously comfortable motel in a beautiful grdn w. falls, lagoons, and swans. Inviting rms w. private balconies or patios. Attentive svce. Group clientele. Good value. Near Hollywood, Beverly Hills, and Universal Studios; 20 min. from dwntwn. Limo svce to Burbank Airport. **M**

♈ **Comfort Inn–Wilshire,** 3400 W. 3rd St., Los Angeles, CA 90020 (213/385-0061; toll free, see Choice). 120 rms, A/C, cable color TV. AE, CB, DC, MC, V. Free parking, pool, adj. coffee shop, rm svce, free crib. *Note:* Typical utilitarian motel a 5-min. drive from the financial district. Comfortable rms, some w. kitchenette and refrigerator. Efficient svce. Very good value. **I**

♈ **Royal Host Olympic Motel,** 901 W. Olympic Blvd. (dwntwn), Los Angeles, CA 90015 (213/626-6255). 54 rms, A/C, cable color TV. AE, DC, MC, V. Free parking, nearby rest. and airport bus svce. *Note:* Modest but very well run budget motel in the heart of dwntwn L.A. Comfortable rms, some w. complete kitchens. Friendly reception. Meal coupon for rest. next door. Very good value. **B–I**

Other Accommodations (from top bracket to budget)

♈♈♈♈ **L'Ermitage,** 9291 Burton Way, Beverly Hills, CA 90210 (310/278-3344). 112 suites (each w. one or two bedrooms), A/C, color TV, in-rm movies. AE, CB, DC, MC, V. Free valet gar., pool, private rest. (Café Russe), bar, roof grdn, 24-hr. rm svce, concierge. *Note:* Very luxurious residential hotel in the European manner, in the smartest neighborhood of Beverly Hills. Sumptuously decorated suites w. balconies and minibars, some w. kitchenettes. Elegant, intimate setting w. period furniture and numerous works of art by Chagall, Renoir, van Gogh, and Miró. The svce is of a distinction seldom encountered. The hotel has a presidential super-suite at $1,600 (plus taxes) a night. Setting aside considerations of expense, one of the best addresses in Beverly Hills. Undergoing complete renovation, the hotel reopens in early 1995. **VE**

♈♈♈♈ **Loews Santa Monica,** 1700 Ocean Ave., Santa Monica, CA 90401 (310/458-6700; toll free 800/235-6397). 350 rms, A/C, color TV, in-rm movies. AE, CB, DC, MC, V. Valet parking $15, pool, health club, sauna, steam rm, massages, bicycle rental, rest. (Riva), coffee shop, bar, 24-hr. rm svce, entertainment, hrdrsr, boutiques, concierge, free crib. *Note:* L.A.'s first luxury beachfront hotel built in more than 20 years, this brand-new palace has a spectacular atrium-lobby from which guests can watch the pier and Ocean Front Walk in air-conditioned splendor and Victorian-Californian decor. Gracious accommodations w. balconies. Elegant Italian rest. Snappy, flawless svce. VIP and Hollywood celebrity clientele. **VE**

♈♈♈♈ **J. W. Marriott,** 2151 Ave. of the Stars, Century City, CA 90067 (310/277-2777; toll free, see Marriott). 375 rms, A/C, color TV, in-rm movies. AE, CB, DC, MC, V. Valet gar. $16, two pools, health club, sauna, rest. (J.W.), bars, 24-hr. rm svce, hrdrsr, boutiques, concierge. *Note:* New hotel, entertainingly designed to resemble a Hollywood palace of the '30s. Flawless comforts and facilities. Spacious rms w. minibar, private patio or balcony, and all-around view. Efficient svce. Rests. at the usual undistinguished Marriott level. Free limo to Rodeo Dr. in Beverly Hills. Business clientele; interesting wknd packages. **VE**

♈♈♈♈ **Nikko Hotel,** 465 La Cienega Blvd., West Los Angeles, CA 90035 (310/247-0400; toll free 800/645-5687). 304 rms, A/C, color TV, in-rm movies. AE, CB, DC, MC, V. Free gar., pool, health club, Japanese spa, massage, two rests., bar, 24-hr. rm svce, entertainment, concierge, free crib. *Note:* Owned and operated by Japan Air Lines (JAL), this brand-new hostelry, located in the heart of the westside business district, is geared to the particular needs of the business traveler: each rm is equipped w. its own fax machine, voice-mail svce, and executive desk. The setting blends contemporary American architecture w. elegant Japanese touches. Highly efficient multilingual staff. Two VIP floors. **VE**

Peninsula Beverly Hills, 9882 Santa Monica Blvd, Beverly Hills, CA 90212 (310/273-4888; toll free 800/462-7899). 195 rms and villas, A/C, color TV, in-rm movies. AE, CB, DC, MC, V. Valet gar. $17, pool, health club, sauna, massage, two rests. (including The Belvedere), bar, 24-hr. rm svce, boutiques, concierge, free crib. *Note:* Beverly Hills's newest Asian-style luxury hotel, part of a tradition of excellence established by the legendary Peninsula in Hong Kong. Rms are large, opulent, and filled w. gadgets. Atmosphere of subdued elegance. Top-notch rest. Friendly, gracious svce. Complimentary Rolls-Royce limo svce to Rodeo Dr. Caters to a discriminating corporate clientele. **VE**

Hotel Sofitel Ma Maison, 8555 Beverly Blvd., Century City, CA 90048 (310/278-5444; toll free, see Resinter). 311 rms, A/C, color TV, in-rm movies. AE, CB, DC, MC, V. Valet parking $14, pool, health club, two rests. (including La Cajole), two bars, 24-hr. rm svce, hrdrsr, boutiques, concierge, free crib. *Note:* A newcomer to the city's luxury-hotel scene; an imaginative modern building w. an interior in the Mediterranean (and an atmosphere in the French) manner. Comfortable, well-designed rms; beautiful flower arrangements. Diligent, efficient svce. La Cajole is an engaging brasserie, but the rest., Ma Maison, is affected and overpriced. Very well located in the heart of "Restaurant Row" and across from the Beverly Center. Business and European clientele. **E–VE**

Beverly Pavilion Hotel, 9360 Wilshire Blvd., Beverly Hills, CA 90212 (310/273-1400; toll free 800/441-5050). 110 rms, A/C, cable color TV, AE, CB, DC, MC, V. Valet gar. $9, pool, rest. (Colette), bar, rm svce, free crib. *Note:* Small, inviting boutique-hotel a few minutes walk from the smart shopping of Rodeo Dr. The pool and solarium on the eighth floor have an all-around view of the city. Spacious, pleasant rms w. refrigerator; friendly, smiling svce. Praiseworthy French rest. **E–VE**

Hotel Inter-Continental, 251 S. Olive St. (dwntwn), CA 90012 (213/617-3300; toll free, see Inter-Continental). 469 rms, A/C, color TV, in-rm movies. AE, CB, DC, MC, V. Valet parking $18, pool, health club, sauna, two rests., two bars, 24-hr. rm svce, concierge, free crib. *Note:* The newest hotel in L.A. Plush rms featuring the absolute in modern amenities for the business traveler. Located adjacent to the Museum of Contemporary Art in the heart of dwntwn L.A. **E–VE**

Portofino Hotel, 260 Portofino Way, Redondo Beach, CA 90277 (310/379-8481; toll free 800/338-2993). 105 rms, A/C, color TV, in-rm movies. AE, CB, DC, MC, V. Parking $5, pool, fishing, marina, bicycling, rest. (Marina Café and Grill), bars, rm svce, free crib. *Note:* Most likable hotel-marina in Los Angeles, overlooking the Redondo Beach yacht basin. Comfortable rms w. private patio or balcony and minibar. Friendly, smiling svce. Entirely redecorated and refurnished after a destructive tidal wave. Free airport shuttle. **E–VE**

New Otani Hotel and Garden, 120 S. Los Angeles St. (dwntwn), Los Angeles, CA 90012 (213/629-1200; toll free 800/421-8795). 435 rms, A/C, color TV, in-rm movies. AE, CB, DC, MC, V. Parking $17, Japanese health spa, three rests. (including 1,000 Cranes), two bars, 24-hr. rm svce, hrdrsr, boutiques, free crib. *Note:* Japanese style, geared to American taste; modern and well designed. Rms w. tatami mats or Western style, w. refrigerators. Very pretty Japanese grdn. Courteous, efficient svce. Business clientele. Very nr. the Little Tokyo business district. Recently renovated at a cost of $2 million. **M–E**

♀♀ **Radisson Bel Air Summit,** 11461 Sunset Blvd., Bel Air, CA
♀♀ 90049 (310/476-6571; toll free, see Radisson). 162 rms,
A/C, color TV, in-rm movies. AE, CB, DC, MC, V. Valet parking $5, pool,
tennis court, rest. (Echo), bar, 24-hr. rm svce, free breakfast, free crib. *Note:*
Small, gracious, comfortable hotel set in a lovely grdn and recently renovated.
Spacious, elegant rms w. refrigerators and private balconies or patios. Good svce;
good value; very commendable rest. **M–E**

♀♀ **Carlyle Inn,** 1119 S. Robertson Blvd., just south of Beverly
♀♀ Hills (310/275-4445; toll free 800/322-7595). 32 rms.,
A/C, color TV, in-rm movies. AE, CB, DC, MC, V. Valet parking $6, café,
sundeck, health club, Jacuzzi, free buffet breakfast, crib $10. *Note:* A sleek
European-style hotel within a postmodernist, concave structure. Inviting rms w.
minibars, coffee makers, and bathrobes. Shuttle svce within a 5-mi. (8km) radius.
A fine place w. reasonable rates. **M**

☼♀♀ **Château Marmont,** 8221 Sunset Blvd., Hollywood, CA
♀♀ 90046 (213/656-1010; toll free 800/826-0015). 62 rms and
cottages, A/C, cable color TV. AE, CB, DC, MC, V. Valet gar. $3, pool, rest.,
bar, rm svce. *Note:* A movie monument, in which innumerable stars (Greta
Garbo, Boris Karloff, John Lennon, Robert de Niro, Richard Gere, Sidney
Poitier, John Belushi) once lived, or still live, it looks like a fake château rendered
in Hollywood kitsch. Spacious rms w. private balconies and refrigerators, or
pleasant bungalows around the pool. Small tropical grdn. An oasis of rest and
peace in the heart of the "Strip." Inconsistent svce. Good value on balance. **M**

♀♀ **Holiday Inn Downtown,** 750 Garland Ave. (dwntwn), Los
♀♀ Angeles, CA 90017 (213/628-5242; toll free, see Holiday
Inns). 204 rms, A/C, cable color TV. AE, CB, DC, MC, V. Free gar., pool, rest.
(Garland Café), bar, rm svce, free crib. *Note:* Conventional six-story motel very
nr. the Convention Center; functionally comfortable. Business clientele. Good
value. Newly renovated. **I–M**

♀♀ **Park Sunset Hotel,** 8462 Sunset Blvd., West Hollywood, CA
♀♀ 90069 (213/654-6470; toll free 800/821-3660). 62 rms,
A/C, cable color TV. AE, CB, DC, MC, V. Free parking, pool, rest., rm svce,
hrdrsr, crib $10. *Note:* Small, comfortable motel in the heart of Sunset Strip.
Large, inviting rms and suites, some w. fully equipped kitchens. Pleasant reception and svce. Good location, halfway between Hollywood and Beverly Hills.
Very decent Thai rest. Good value overall. **I–M**

♀ **Best Western Mikado,** 12600 Riverside Dr., North Holly-
♀ wood, CA 91607 (818/763-9141; toll free, see Best Western).
58 rms, A/C, color TV. AE, CB, DC, MC, V. Free parking, pool, rest., bar, rm
svce, free breakfast, crib $5. *Note:* Friendly motel in the hills overlooking Holly-
wood; vaguely exotic decor. Comfortable rms; friendly reception and svce. Very
acceptable Japanese rest. Good value. **I–M**

♀ **Hollywood Metropolitan Hotel,** 5825 Sunset Blvd., Holly-
♀ wood, CA 90028 (213/962-5800). 90 rms, A/C, color TV.
AE, CB, DC, MC, V. Free gar., rest., bar, rm svce, crib $15. *Note:* Modern hotel
w. a rest. on the top floor offering a fine view of Hollywood and its hills. Spectacular outside elevator. Art deco–style interior. Inviting rms; ideal for visiting
Hollywood and Universal Studios. **I–M**

♀ **Days Inn–Hollywood,** 7023 Sunset Blvd., Hollywood, CA
♀ 90028 (213/464-8344). 72 rms, A/C, cable color TV. AE,
CB, DC, MC, V. Free parking, pool; no bar or rest., but breakfast served every
morning. *Note:* Amiable reception; utilitarian rms, some w. kitchenette and
Jacuzzi, most w. balcony overlooking the pool and picnic tables. Good overall
value 5 min. from "the Strip" and the sights of Hollywood. **I**

♀ **Tropicana Inn,** 1540 S. Harbor Blvd., Anaheim, CA 92802
♀ (714/635-4082; toll free 800/828-4898). 195 rms, A/C,
color TV, in-rm movies. AE, CB, DC, MC, V. Limited parking lot, pool, rest.
adj. *Note:* The ideal motel if you're planning to visit Disneyland (located just

across the street). Large, comfortable guest rms, some w. kitchenettes. Good value. **I**, but lower rates off-season.

  ♀ **Vagabond Inn,** 1904 W. Olympic Blvd., Los Angeles, CA
  ♭ 90006 (213/380-9393; toll free, see Vagabond Inns). 54 rms, A/C, color TV. AE, DC, MC, V. Free parking, pool, nearby rest., free breakfast, free crib. *Note:* Small, standard, but well-run motel, located 5 min. from the Convention Center. Functional rms; friendly reception. Good value. **I**

  ♀ **Vagabond Inn,** 3101 S. Figueroa St., Los Angeles, CA 90007
  ♭ (213/746-1531; toll free, see Vagabond Inns). 72 rms, A/C, color TV. AE, DC, MC, V. Free parking, pool, coffee shop, free breakfast, free crib. *Note:* Great value close to Exposition Park and the Memorial Coliseum. Serviceably comfortable rms; reception w. a smile. 8 min. from dwntwn. **I**

  ♀ **Motel 6,** 1001 S. San Gabriel Blvd., Rosemead, CA 91770
  ♭ (818/572-6076). 130 rms, A/C, cable color TV. AE, DC, MC, V. Free parking, pool, café adj. open 24 hrs, free crib. *Note:* Modern, functional motel at ultra-reasonable prices, 20 min. from dwntwn along Calif. 60 and U.S. 101. Ideal if you're driving; excellent value. **B**

  ♀ **Motel 6,** 7450 Katella Ave., Stanton, CA 90680 (714/891-
  ♭ 0717). 207 rms, A/C, cable color TV. AE, DC, MC, V. Free parking, pool. *Note:* Typical motel at ultra-reasonable prices; ideal as a base for visiting Disneyland and Knott's Berry Farm (10 min. by car). Excellent value. **B**

Airport Accommodations

  ♀♭♀ **Sheraton L.A. Airport,** 6101 W. Century Blvd., Los Angeles,
  ♭♭♭ CA 90045 (310/642-1111; toll free, see Sheraton). 789 rms, A/C, color TV, in-rm movies. AE, CB, DC, MC, V. Valet parking $9, pool, health club, Jacuzzi, two rests. (including Landry's), two rests, 24-hr. rm svce, hrdrsr, concierge, free crib. *Note:* Massive and unsightly luxury airport motel. Rms comfortable rather than elegant, w. minibar. Efficient but impersonal svce. Landry's is a very acceptable rest. Business and convention clientele. Good value overall. Free shuttle-bus connection w. airport (3 min.) and beach. **M–E**

  ♀♭ **Travelodge Hotel,** 5547 W. Century Blvd., Los Angeles, CA
  ♭♭ 90045 (310/649-4000; toll free, see Travelodge). 150 rms, A/C, color TV, in-rm movies. AE, CB, DC, MC, V. Free parking, pool, 24-hr. coffee shop, bar, rm svce, free airport limo, crib $4. *Note:* Recently renovated airport motel. Spacious, comfortable rms, the best overlooking the pool. Very efficient svce. A good value, 5 min. from the terminal. **I**

YMCA/Youth Hostel

  YMCA, 1553 N. Hudson Ave., Hollywood, CA 90028 (213/467-4161). 29 beds, pool, health club, coffee shop. For men and women; also a youth hostel.
  AYH–Santa Monica International Hostel, 1436 2nd St., Santa Monica, CA 90401 (310/393-9913). 200 beds. Opened in late 1989. Near the Santa Monica Pier and the beach.

RESTAURANTS

Personal Favorites (in order of preference)

  ♀♀♀♀ **Citrus,** 6703 Melrose Ave., Los Angeles (857-0034). A/C.
  ♭♭♭♭ Lunch Mon–Fri, dinner Mon–Sat. AE, CB, DC, MC, V. Jkt. *Specialties:* shiitake and garlic Napoleon w. mushroom sauce, sautéed scallops w. Maui onion rings, rare peppered tuna steak w. diable sauce, grilled swordfish w. ratatouille of spring vegetables, chicken and mushroom skin w. porcini sauce, roasted veal w. mashed potatoes and horseradish sauce. Remarkable desserts and pastries. Wine list on the weak side. *Note:* The truculent but genial Michel Richard, one of the most original French chefs working in this country, is a virtuoso at combining French and Californian nouvelle cuisine. Immaculate modern decor w. flowery indoor patio (but noisy w. uncomfortable chairs). Courteous, efficient svce. A favorite of movie stars and celebrities. Resv. essential—this is an

"in" place. Valet parking. One of the country's 12 finest rests. *French/American.* **E–VE**

▽▽▽▽ **Patina,** 5955 Melrose Ave., Hollywood (467-1108). A/C.
♨♨♨ Lunch Mon–Fri, dinner nightly. AE, CB, DC, MC, V. Jkt.
Specialties: scallop roll in potato crust w. brown-butter vinaigrette, crabcakes w. red bell-pepper rémoulade, lobster w. puréed potatoes and potato truffle chips, salmon w. Manila clams vinaigrette, gratin of lamb w. garlicky mashed potatoes, baby turnips stuffed w. wild mushrooms in parsley sauce, corn crème brûlée. Good but very pricey wine list. *Note:* Long the *wunderkind* of the L.A. rest. establishment, German-born, French-trained master chef-owner Joachim Splichal has regained Patina's number-one rank. The drab gray exterior and the minimalist and noisy setting totally lack warmth and coziness, but its superb Franco-Californian cuisine is really worth the spending. First-rate staff svce, elegantly attired by Hugo Boss. Studio executive clientele. Resv. a must. Go for the celebrities as much as for the food. Valet parking (fee). *Californian.* **E–VE**

▽▽▽ **Bikini,** 1413 5th St., Santa Monica (310/395-8611). A/C.
♨♨♨ Lunch Mon–Fri, dinner Mon–Sat. AE, MC, V. *Specialties:* egg foo yong w. gingered duck confit, mushrooms, and bamboo shoots; Bombay lamb grilled w. Indian spices, curry sauce, and yogurt raita; Yucatán veal mole; quail salad; grilled sea scallops; hazelnut terrine; chocolate tamale. *Note:* Sophisticated postmodern two-level rest. w. a grand staircase, a waterfall sculpture, and a stylized triptych hanging in the mezzanine. But the house's real artwork is John Sedlar's glorious food, an imaginative combination of disparate ethnic influences: Japan, China, France, Mexico, India. Nice and efficient svce. Chic-fun clientele and atmosphere. Resv. advised. Valet parking. *Californian.* **E**

▽▽▽ **Campanile,** 624 La Brea Ave., Los Angeles (938-1447). A/C.
♨♨♨ Breakfast daily, lunch Mon–Fri, dinner Mon–Sat. AE, MC, V.
Jkt. *Specialties:* ravioli w. potatoes and truffles, cedar-smoked salmon w. fennel, grilled prime rib w. black-olive purée and sautéed bitter greens, fabulous desserts. The menu changes from time to time. *Note:* Charlie Chaplin built this imitation Italian *palazzo* in the '20s; Campanile opened here in 1989 and has been a roaring success. If you want to try Mark Peel's and Nancy Silverton's "country *haute cuisine*" you'd better reserve days, or even weeks, ahead. The trip is worthwhile just for the breads—onion and anchovy, olive, fig, chocolate and cherry, etc.—turned out at their adj. La Brea Bakery. The setting is half Moorish, half medieval; svce is efficient and cheerful. *Italian/American.* **M**

▽▽ **Castel,** 12100 Wilshire Blvd., West Los Angeles (310/207-
♨♨ 4273). A/C. Lunch Mon–Fri, dinner Mon–Sat. Jkt. *Specialties:* smoked-salmon salad, steamed mussels w. apple cider, roast lamb stromboli, grilled mahi-mahi w. lentils, "butcher's cut" steak, baked Chilean sea bass w. fennel and potato purée, candied-chestnut crème brûlée, tarte Tatin w. caramel sauce. Excellent wine selection at relative bargain prices. *Note:* Genuine French-style bistro on the ground floor of a new Wilshire Blvd. high-rise. Bright, heartening decor and atmosphere w. outdoor terrace. The food is surprisingly good and reasonably priced. Flawless svce. Resv. advised. *French.* **M**

▽▽ **Katsu,** 1972 Hillhurst Ave., Los Angeles (665-1891). A/C.
♨♨ Lunch Mon–Fri, dinner nightly. AE, MC, V. *Specialties:* sushi, sashimi, kaiseki dinner (Japanese ceremonial banquet). *Note:* A place of pilgrimage for sushi lovers, very nr. Griffith Park, because of the exceptional freshness of the seafood and the refinement w. which it's prepared and presented. The decor is a rather chilly modern, relieved by a collection of Mineo Mizuno's beautiful ceramics. The sushi is excellent value, but beware of the bill for the kaiseki dinner; resv. recommended. *Japanese.* **I–M** (**M** for kaiseki dinner).

▽▽ **Ca'Brea,** 346 S. La Brea Ave., Hollywood (938-2863). A/C.
♨♨ Lunch Mon–Fri, dinner Mon–Sat. AE, CB, DC, MC, V. *Specialties:* carpaccio w. mushrooms, baby back ribs w. sage-scented white beans, risotto w. ragù of mixed porcini, bigoletti w. lobster, scallops and saffron sauce, osso buco, grilled lamb chops and mustard-mushroom sauce w. truffles, dolce

Ca'Brea w. espresso sauce. Overpriced wine list. *Note:* Very hip, very noisy up-scale *trattoria* serving great Italian food by chef Antonio Tommasi. Sophisticated setting w. peach-colored walls and modern paintings. Very good svce. Resv. a must. *Italian.* **M**

♀ **Korean Gardens,** 950 S. Vermont Ave., Los Angeles (388-3042). A/C. Lunch/dinner daily. AE, MC, V. *Specialties:* juk (rice w. abalone), kunjol pan (vegetable pancake), mandu-kuk (beef bouillon w. dumplings), bul-kogi (marinated beef); tabletop barbecue of beef, pork, and chicken. *Note:* With some 200,000 Koreans living in Los Angeles, the food here has to be authentic. Many delicate flavors, but spicy-hot dishes as well, thanks to the redoubtable Korean kim chee (pickled shredded cabbage w. fermented shell-fish). Vaguely exotic decor; diligent svce. For lovers of the unusual. *Korean.* **I**

☼♀ **R.J.'s, The Rib Joint,** 252 N. Beverly Dr., Beverly Hills (310/274-3474). A/C. Lunch Mon–Sat, dinner nightly, brunch Sun. AE, CB, DC, MC, V. *Specialties:* barbecued spareribs, short ribs, chile, broiled chicken, steak, fresh fish of the day, chocolate cake. *Note:* A real local insti-tution, w. sawdust on the floor and ceiling fans. Straightforward, tasty food in generous portions, w. more than 55 dishes on the menu. Gigantic salad bar. Very popular locally, so resv. advisable. One of the best buys in Los Angeles. *American.* **I**

Other Restaurants (from top bracket to budget)

♀♀♀♀ **Valentino,** 3115 Pico Blvd., Santa Monica (310/829-4313). A/C. Lunch Fri only, dinner Mon–Sat (until midnight); closed hols. AE, CB, DC, MC, V. Jkt. *Specialties:* gnocchi w. seafood, vegetable risotto, carpaccio of tuna, baby lamb w. broccoli and mousse of lima beans, rou-lade of swordfish w. shrimp and lime juice, ragoût of kidneys, venison w. polenta. Seasonal menu. One of California's finest cellars (70,000 bottles, 90,000 before the earthquake) w. the best wines from California, France, and Italy. *Note:* Unlike the legendary Rudolf Valentino, whose name the rest. has borrowed, the propri-etor, Piero Selvaggio, is Sicilian and not Apulian. His brilliant, inventive cook-ing, his elegantly renovated decor, and his polished svce combine to make this one of the best rests. in the country. Very fashionable clientele; resv. a necessity. Valet parking. *Italian.* **E–VE**

♀♀♀ **Aristoff,** 321 N. Robertson Blvd., West Hollywood (310/271-0576). A/C. Lunch/dinner Mon–Sat. AE, DC, MC, V. Jkt. *Specialties:* caviar, Mediterranean fish soup, salad of Russian crab, fresh foie gras w. black truffles, smoked Scottish salmon, potatoes w. salmon caviar, excel-lent sorbets. Champagne by the glass. *Note:* Caviar—sevruga, osetra, and beluga —is the mainstay at this elegant, almost stately setting. One of the few rests. of its kind to gain success in L.A. Discreet, attentive svce. Resv. advised. *Continental.* **M–E**

♀♀♀ **Röx,** 1224 Beverwil Dr. (in the Beverly Prescott Hotel), Bever-ly Hills (310/772-2999). A/C. Breakfast/dinner daily, lunch Mon–Fri. AE, DC, MC, V. *Specialties:* lobster tempura w. warm gnocchi and a trio of sauces, chicken and sun-dried tomato tortellini w. pine nut–goat cheese sauce, ginger-crusted salmon on soba-noodle cake w. plum wine–shiitake sauce, grilled New York sirloin w. country-fried onions and smoked chipotle sauce. Ex-cellent desserts. List of mostly California wines. *Note:* Chef Hans Röckenwager has joined the top tier of L.A. chefs by displaying an astute sensibility for design and texture in his Californian-Asian cuisine. Pacific Rim decor enhanced by the kimono-like uniforms of the servers, who are enthusiastic and well versed about the food. A fine place for breakfast, as well. Resv. advised, especially on the week-ends. *Californian.* **M–E**

♀♀♀ **Spago,** 1114 Horn Ave., West Hollywood (310/652-4025). A/C. Dinner only, nightly. CB, DC, MC, V. Jkt. *Specialties:* variety of California-style pizzas baked in wood-burning brick oven, roasted baby Sonoma lamb, grilled salmon, excellent desserts. Menu changes daily. *Note:* The rest. that launched L.A.'s most famous chef and restaurateur, Wolfgang Puck. A star-studded clientele is a given, but the main reason to go is for the pizzas, which are like no other ones you've had before. Being the most popular of L.A. rests., resv. are needed 2–3 weeks in advance. *Italian/Californian.* **M–E**

Camelions, 246 26th St., Santa Monica (310/395-0746). A/C. Lunch Tues–Sat, dinner Tues–Sun, brunch Sun. *Specialties:* poached oysters and scallops in basil dressing, sautéed whitefish w. ginger sauce, cold eggplant soup w. roast pepper, Peking duck salad w. cucumber, sautéed king salmon in truffle butter, roast squab w. thyme and wild rice, lemon pie, banana cream pie. Rather abbreviated wine list. *Note:* The chef's whim, and availability of ingredients, determine daily changes in the menu, but the outcome is invariably a success. Mediterranean-villa setting w. pretty patio, lots of greenery, pastel-washed walls. Very good svce. Resv. strongly advised. *American.* **M–E**

DC 3, 2800 Donald Douglas Loop N., Santa Monica Airport, Santa Monica (310/399-2323). A/C. Lunch Mon–Fri, dinner Tues–Sat, brunch Sun. AE, MC, V. *Specialties:* grilled round of Norwegian salmon, braised lamb shank w. rosemary-veal glaze, raspberry crème brûlée. *Note:* The only airport rest. in the entire U.S. to rate three glasses. The new fashionable place for Los Angeles's trendsetters to eat, a collaboration among two recognized masters: the innovative architecture is Frank Gehry's and the elegant modern decor Chuck Arnoldi's. The huge, bright, light-filled dining rm offers you a view of aircraft entering and leaving Santa Monica Airport. The simple, light, straightforward food is much to the yuppie taste. Svce w. a smile. Resv. advised. Valet parking. *American.* **M**

The Ivy, 113 N. Robertson Blvd., West Hollywood (310/274-8303). A/C. Lunch/dinner daily, brunch Sun. AE, CB, DC, MC, V. *Specialties:* corn chowder, Louisiana crabcakes, cappellini w. mussels, chicken tostados, blackened prime rib, mesquite-grilled catch of the day, lemon and white-chocolate pie. *Note:* This popular hangout for Hollywood executives attracts stars of stage and screen for its eclectic California cuisine. The decor is pleasing, the atmosphere noisy but relaxed, svce generally efficient. Resv. strongly advised. An "in" place. Valet parking. *American.* **M**

Pacific Dining Car, 1310 W. 6th St., Los Angeles (213/483-3030). A/C. Breakfast/lunch/dinner daily (open around the clock). AE, MC, V. Jkt. *Specialties:* chile, french-fried zucchini, spareribs, excellent steaks broiled to perfection, fish of the day, Caesar salad, cheesecake. Fine wine list (300 labels). *Note:* Since 1921 this authentic railroad diner and its annex have brought joy to Angeleno meat-lovers around the clock. The beef and lamb are of the highest quality. When you order, make it quite clear how you like your meat cooked. Good svce. Resv. advised. Valet parking at dinner. *Steak.* **M**

Water Grill, 523 W. 6th St., dwntwn (891-0900). A/C. Lunch Mon–Fri, dinner nightly. AE, CB, DC, MC, V. *Specialties:* fried calamari, Dungeness crab cakes, oysters on the half shell, sautéed swordfish w. grain-mustard sauce, grilled rare big-eyed tuna w. blue prawns and Chinese pesto, sautéed king salmon w. shiitake mushrooms and port, bluegrass pie. Very creditable wine and beer list. *Note:* Modern, lush, and lively seafood rest. in the old Pacific Mutual Building. The decor features lots of wood, glass, and colorful marine murals. The menu celebrates impeccably fresh seafood from every corner of the American continent. Inviting oyster bar. Earnest and knowledgeable staff. The model of a contemporary seafood house. Resv. recommended. *Seafood.* **M**

Cicada, 8478 Melrose Ave., West Hollywood (655-5559). A/C. Lunch Mon–Fri, dinner Mon–Sat. AE, MC, V. *Specialties:* romaine-endive salad w. Roquefort cheese, crab cakes w. lemon-caper sauce, carpaccio w. fresh artichoke hearts and Parmesan cheese, penne w. porcini mushrooms, veal chops w. fennel and sweet onions, grilled Mediterranean bass w. sautéed spinach, flourless chocolate cake soufflé. Good selections of wine by the glass. *Note:* A hot spot for the recording-industry crowd in a cheerful, attractive setting. Once an eatery for Californian cuisine, the rest. now has an Italian menu that's just as impressive, and much cheaper. Gracious, efficient svce. Resv. advised. Valet parking. *Italian.* **I–M**

🍷🍷 **Horikawa,** 111 S. San Pedro St., dwntwn (680-9355). A/C. Lunch Mon–Fri, dinner Mon–Sat. AE, CB, DC, MC, V. *Specialties:* sushi, shabu-shabu, tempura, seafood nabe, teppanyaki, robata-yaki. *Note:* This huge but elegant food emporium complete w. sushi bar, tempura bar, teppanyaki rm, and other dining facilities, is continually jam-packed, mostly w. Japanese patrons. The cooking is highly professional, even quite brilliant. The svce is occasionally slow. Tatami rms for special dinners. Valet parking. *Japanese.* **I–M**

🍷🍷 **Le Dome,** 8720 Sunset Blvd., Los Angeles (310/659-6919). A/C. Lunch Mon–Fri, dinner Mon–Sat. (until midnight). AE, CB, DC, MC, V. Jkt. *Specialties:* ragoût of veal w. mustard and fresh thyme, cassoulet, rabbit chasseur, osso bucco, choucroute garnie, tempting desserts. Good wine list. *Note:* A few really earthy dishes make this luxurious, trendy brasserie one of the most likable of Los Angeles's fashionable eating places. Elegant modernist decor. Broad, inviting circular bar. Resv. advised. Valet parking. *French.* **I–M**

🍷🍷 **Georgia,** 7250 Melrose Ave., Los Angeles (933-8420). A/C. Lunch Mon–Fri, dinner nightly; closed hols. A, MC, V. *Specialties:* crab cake, black-eyed pea salad, barbecue ribs, smoked catfish, fried chicken, pork chops w. onion gravy, peach cobbler. *Note:* With investors like Eddie Murphy and Denzel Washington, this rest. opened w. as much hoopla as a movie premier. But the down-home Southern cooking served in a simulation of a country house (replete w. Spanish moss and mahogany floors) warrants a visit. A bit pricey for the fare. Resv. recommended. *American.* **I–M**

🍷🍷 **Mon Kee's,** 679 N. Spring St., dwntwn (628-6717). A/C. Lunch/dinner daily. AE, CB, DC, MC, V. *Specialties:* crab w. garlic sauce, twice-cooked scallops, lobster w. black-bean sauce, pan-fried fresh squid w. garlic and black beans, stir-fried rock cod in sweet-and-sour sauce, boiled whole shrimp. Beer and wine. *Note:* A longtime favorite among the 1,200-or-so Chinese rests. of L.A. The decor is rather primitive and the cooking seems to have lost some of its previous luster, but the seafood remains outstanding and Mon Kee's is still a good bet overall. Prepare for a (sometimes long) wait. *Chinese/Seafood.* **I–M**

🍷🍷 **Il Pastaio,** 400 N. Cañon Dr., Beverly Hills (310/205-5444). A/C. Lunch/dinner Mon–Sat; closed hols. AE, DC, MC, V. *Specialties:* Sicilian-style ratatouille, swordfish carpaccio, whole-wheat penne w. fresh ricotta and mint, lobster-and-zucchini ravioli, wild-mushroom risotto, pumpkin-stuffed tortelloni, lemon-meringue torte. *Note:* As indicated by the name, meaning "the macaroni maker," the stock-in-trade is pasta, and lots of it. One of the best Italian eateries to come on the L.A. scene in the recent past, this rest. maintains its zeal thanks to its operators—the four Drago brothers. A good value. Adroit, helpful svce. Due to its popularity, resv. are advised. *Italian.* **I–M**

🍷🍷🍷 **Pinot Bistro,** 12969 Ventura Blvd., Studio City (818/990-0500). A/C. Lunch Mon–Fri, dinner nightly; closed Jan 1, July 4, Dec 25. AE, CB, DC, MC, V. *Specialties:* farinette (bread-and-cheese brittle cake w. chicken and roasted shallots), braised oxtail ragoût w. parsley gnocchi, venison leg w. celery-root gratin and dried cherry and peppercorn sauce, grilled salmon w. creamy potatoes and horseradish sauce, chocolate crème brûlée. Fine selection of wines by the glass or half bottle. *Note:* Stunning interior decorating by Cheryl Brantner transports you to a Paris of the 1920s, where the words of expatriate writers are scribbled on mirrors. Owner Joachim Splichal of Patina (see above) endows the menu w. bistro classics from several European countries. Ask for a table in the Dali-esque rear rm, where the ceiling is shaped like a pair of lips and a huge inoperative clock hangs on the wall. Resv. are a must. *French/Continental.* **I–M**

Rebecca's, 2025 Pacific Ave., Venice (310/306-6266). A/C. Dinner only, nightly. AE, CB, DC, MC, V. *Specialties:* broiled swordfish tostadas w. black beans, ceviche, tamales w. red-chili sauce, duck-stuffed chiles, grilled whitefish w. lime butter, broiled lobster w. pink-grapefruit salsa, leg of lamb adobado, espresso ice cream. Seasonal menu. *Note:* Decor by Frank Gehry, the farthest-out in all Los Angeles, w. a giant mural fresco and crocodiles in Plexiglas or Formica hanging from the ceiling. Add remarkable Mexican food, an interesting wine list at reasonable prices, smiling, helpful svce, and a fashionable clientele, and you have the sure-fire formula for Rebecca's overwhelming success. Resv. a must. Valet parking. *Mexican.* **I–M**

West Beach Café, 60 N. Venice Blvd., Venice (310/823-5396). A/C. Breakfast/lunch Sat–Sun, dinner nightly. AE, CB, DC, MC, V. Jkt. *Specialties:* steak tartar, braised lamb w. baked garlic cloves and roasted potatoes, seafood sausage w. herbs, asparagus risotto, sabayon w. fruit. *Note:* Highly imaginative California-style cuisine and avant-garde setting w. frequently changing modern paintings are the two principal attractions at this stylish rest. just one block from the ocean, while the spectacular bar and fine svce also contribute to its success. The menu changes regularly, and there's a wide selection of wines by the glass or the bottle. Caters to local artists and trendy Angelenos. Resv. highly recommended. Valet parking. *American.* **I–M**

Antonio's, 7472 Melrose Ave., Los Angeles (655-0480). A/C. Lunch Tues–Fri, dinner Tues–Sun; closed July 4 and Labor Day. AE, MC, V. Jkt. *Specialties:* green pepper stuffed w. coriander, chicken pipián, steak w. green sauce, ropa vieja, mole poblano, jicama salad, fruit flan. Good wine list. *Note:* Antonio Gutierrez offers delicious and inventive Mexican fare, keeping well off the beaten track of Mexican rest. clichés. Despite a rather loud color scheme, the decor is much less original than the food. Friendly svce. Mariachi bands at dinner. Popular locally. Resv. recommended. Valet parking at dinner. *Mexican.* **I**

Musso & Frank Grill, 6667 Hollywood Blvd., Hollywood (467-7788). A/C. Lunch/dinner Tues–Sat; closed hols. AE, CB, DC, MC, V. Jkt. *Specialties:* calves' liver w. onions, bouillabaisse, chicken pot pie, lamb chops, sauerbraten, corned beef and cabbage, creamed spinach, fish of the day, flan. *Note:* Of roughly the same age as the movie industry (1919), Musso & Frank is a Hollywood monument. The food is uneven, but generally pleasing and substantial; the svce is surly. Comfortable interior w. dark-wood paneling and red leather. Much frequented by press and movie people. *Continental/American.* **I**

Siamese Princess, 8048 W. 3rd St., West Hollywood (653-2643). A/C. Lunch Thurs–Fri, dinner nightly. AE, CB, DC, MC, V. *Specialties:* nam chim salad, mu wan (calamari w. coriander), duck w. ginger, sea bass and mussel mousse, lamb saté, ma haw (spiced pork), chicken wing kai. *Note:* The best of the multitude of Thai rests. that have grown and flourished in California over the past decade. Tasty but delicate food, and (what's uncommon in a Far Eastern rest.) a very good wine list. Slightly kitsch Victorian interior w. portraits of the Thai royal family and other dignitaries on the walls. Very good svce. Resv. advised. *Thai.* **I**

Sofi, 8030 3/4 W. 3rd St., Los Angeles (651-0346). A/C. Lunch Mon–Sat, dinner daily; closed Jan 1, Dec 25. AE, MC, V. *Specialties:* dolmades, moussaka, keftedes, (meatballs), kreatopita, souvlaki, swordfish kebabs, arni bouti (marinated leg of lamb), baklava, galaktoboureko (cream-filled pastry). Good selection of Greek wines. *Note:* One of Los Angeles's few Greek rests. to emphasize food rather than decor or atmosphere. Talented chef Sofi Lazarides, a former doctor who traded her stethoscope for a skillet when she left her native Greece, prepares fine examples of all the classic Greek dishes, particularly moussaka. Enticing patio-grdn on fine days. Very good svce. A splendid place. Resv. advised; valet parking. *Greek.* **I**

♉ **Broadway Deli,** 1457 3rd St. Promenade, Santa Monica
(310/451-0616). A/C. Breakfast/lunch/dinner daily (until
midnight). AE, MC, V. *Specialties:* smoked fish, salmon w. creamed spinach,
meatloaf, carpaccio, daily soups, chicken pot pie, Caesar salad, wondrous desserts. *Note:* The hi-tech streamlined black-and-silver design bears very little resemblance to a typical New York deli. The food is also more California style than
Jewish, but the final result is very good indeed. First-rate svce. No resv., unfortunately. *American.* **B–I**

♉ **Chin Chin,** 8618 Sunset Blvd., West Hollywood (310/652-
1818). A/C. Lunch/dinner daily. AE, MC, V. *Specialties:* dim
sum, chicken salad, spring rolls, moo shu pork, ginger duck, barbecued spareribs.
Note: The rest. that popularized dim sum (tasty hot or cold hors d'oeuvres Cantonese style) in Los Angeles, and started a fashion. The other specialties of the
house are just as good. Usually crowded and noisy; hard-working svce; regular
customers; very good value. Other location: 12215 Ventura Blvd., Studio City
(818/985-9090). *Chinese.* **B–I**

♉ **El Cholo,** 1121 S. Western Ave., Los Angeles (734-2773).
A/C. Lunch/dinner daily; closed Thanksgiving, Dec 25. AE,
MC, V. *Specialties:* enchiladas, tacos, burritos dorados, chiles relleños, tamales
verdes, tostadas. *Note:* Of the innumerable Mexican rests. in Los Angeles, purists
think this is the best overall value, w. its absolutely authentic food and setting. A
classic of its kind since 1927; resv. advised. *Mexican.* **B**

☼♉ **Nate 'n Al's,** 414 N. Beverly Dr., Beverly Hills (310/274-
0101). A/C. Breakfast/lunch/dinner daily (until 8:30pm).
MC, V. *Specialties:* giant sandwiches, herring in sour cream, roast turkey, pastrami, stuffed cabbage, corned beef, homemade cheesecake. *Note:* A Beverly Hills
classic since 1945, an authentic New York deli serving generous portions at very
modest prices. Unpretentious decor; efficient, smiling svce. Very popular locally,
especially at lunchtime. No resv. *American.* **B**

CAFETERIAS/SPECIALTY SPOTS: ☼ **Cassell's,** 3266 W. 6th St., Los An-
geles (387-5502). Lunch only, Mon–Sat. No credit cards. The best hamburgers
in all Los Angeles; excellent sandwiches.

Jody Maroni's The Sausage Kingdom, 2011 Ocean Front Walk at Venice
Blvd., Venice (310/306-1995). Lunch/dinner daily (until 7pm). No credit
cards. This modest stall fronting the beach serves no fewer than 22 varieties of
delicious homemade sausage, from "Yucatán" (chicken, duck, coriander, and
chile serrano) to "Bombay Bangers" (lamb curry and raisins) and Cajun boudín.

Original Pantry, 877 S. Figueroa St., Los Angeles (972-9279). Open daily
around the clock. No credit cards. Excellent cafeteria food and commendable
steaks at very reasonable prices; popular since the '20s. A favorite of Mayor Richard Riordan, who also happens to own the place.

Philippe's The Original, 1001 N. Alameda St., dwntwn (628-3781).
Breakfast/lunch/dinner daily. No credit cards. A local landmark since 1908.
Overstuffed "French dip sandwiches" (choice of ham, beef, pork, or lamb) for
$4. You'll see truck drivers here alongside bank directors and tourists shoulder-
to-shoulder w. bums. Right next to Union Station.

☼ **Pink's,** 709 N. La Brea Blvd., dwntwn (931-4223). Open daily
(until 2am). No credit cards. By general consent the best hot
dogs in the city (and a dynamite chile sauce); also good hamburgers. A legend in
L.A. since 1939.

Where to Eat What in Los Angeles
American: Broadway Deli (p. 1049), Camelions (p. 1046), Campanile (p.
1044), Citrus (p. 1043), DC 3 (p. 1045), Georgia (p. 1047), The Ivy (p. 1046),
Musso & Frank Grill (p. 1048), Nate 'n Al's (p. 1049), R. J.'s, The Rib Joint (p.
1045), West Beach Café (p. 1048).

Californian: Bikini (p. 1044), Patina (p. 1044), Röx (p. 1045), Spago (p. 1045).

Chinese: Chin Chin (p. 1049), Mon Kee's (p. 1047).

Continental: Aristoff (p. 1045), Musso & Frank Grill (p. 1047), Pinot Bistro (p. 1047).

Cafeterias/Fast Food: Cassell's (p. 1048), Jody Maroni's The Sausage Kingdom (p. 1049), Original Pantry (p. 1049), Philippe's The Original (p. 1049), Pink's (p. 1049), R. J.'s, The Rib Joint (p. 1045).

French: Castel (p. 1044), Citrus (p. 1043), Le Dome (p. 1047), Pinot Bistro (p. 1047).

Greek: Sofi (p. 1048).

Italian: Ca' Brea (p. 1044), Campanile (p. 1044), Cicada (p. 1046), Il Pastaio (p. 1047), Spago (p. 1045), Valentino (p. 1045).

Japanese: Horikawa (p. 1047), Katsu (p. 1044).

Korean: Korean Gardens (p. 1045).

Mexican: Antonio's (p. 1048), El Cholo (p. 1049), Rebecca's (p. 1048).

Seafood: Mon Kee's (p. 1047), Water Grill (p. 1046).

Steak: Pacific Dining Car (p. 1046).

Thai: Siamese Princess (p. 1048).

Late-night Service: Broadway Deli (until midnight), Le Dome (Mon–Sat until midnight), Original Pantry (daily 24 hr.), Pacific Dining Car (daily 24 hr.), Pink's (daily until 2am), Valentino (Mon–Sat until midnight).

BARS & NIGHTCLUBS

The insistent rhythm of Los Angeles by night makes it hard to draw up a list of "in" places; discos, bars, and nightclubs grow, wither, and die here with the leaves on the trees. However, here are some more durable names:

Casey's, 613 S. Grand Ave., dwntwn (629-2353). Pub favored by yuppies from the financial district. Warm paneled interior with sporting posters.

Club Lingerie, 6507 W. Sunset Blvd., Hollywood (466-8557). Cool, comfortable music club popular with the chic set. Bare-bones brick decor. Open Mon –Sat.

The Comedy Store, 8433 W. Sunset Blvd., West Hollywood (656-6225). One of the West Coast's best-known and most popular comedy clubs, where the biggest names in the business appear regularly. Trendy people in a trendy place.

Gengis Cohen, 740 N. Fairfax Ave., Los Angeles (653-0640). A haven for '60s and '70s survivors. Live music, good Chinese food, and a smart music-biz crowd. Open nightly.

Hard Rock Café, 8600 Beverly Blvd., Los Angeles (310/276-7605). Los Angeles version of the well-known chain. Rock 'n' roll theme-park decor complete with a green Cadillac plunging through the roof. Perpetually crowded and noisy, good hamburgers, hard rock, young customers. Open nightly until midnight.

House of Blues, 8430 Sunset Blvd., West Hollywood (650-0247). Nightly blues performances set in a Mississippi Delta–style atmosphere. Also offering Southern cooking.

☼ **The Improv.,** 8162 Melrose Ave., West Hollywood (651-2583). Granddaddy of the local comedy clubs; shows generally of high quality, sometimes with big-name stars.

Largo, 432 N. Fairfax Ave., Los Angeles (852-1073). A venue for the avant-garde in music, comedy, and performance art. Also a lively bar. Open Mon–Sat.

The Mint, 6010 W. Pico Blvd., Los Angeles (937-9630). Blues heads the menu in this intimate place featuring top names and hot up-and-comers. Open Mon–Sat.

The Palace, 1735 N. Vine St., Hollywood (462-3000). 1930s dance hall, wonderfully restored. Thunderous PA system. Laser machines, TV clips, good live music. Open nightly.

Palomino, 6907 Lankershim Blvd., North Hollywood (818/764-4010).

The fashionable country-and-western place; come in boots and cowboy hat. Open nightly.

Redwoods 2nd Street Saloon, 316 W. 2nd St., dwntwn (617-2867). Most of the customers here work at the *Los Angeles Times*. Setting and atmosphere are comfortable.

Roxbury, 8225 Sunset Blvd., West Hollywood (310/656-1750). A high-energy forum for the latest on pop, rock, blues, and jazz. Trilevel funhouse w. separate areas for dancing, dining, and live music. VIP room admits only the wealthy and famous. Open Tues–Sat.

Roxy, 9009 Sunset Blvd., West Hollywood (310/276-2222). The mecca of California rock; music live. Dates vary. Decor in the style of the Roaring '20s.

Vine Street Bar & Grill, 1610 N. Vine St., Hollywood (463-4375). Jazz, blues, and swing nightly in an intimate art deco setting.

Viper Room, 8852 Sunset Blvd., West Hollywood (310/358-1880). The club owned by Johnny Depp where twenty-something film stars can pretend they're slumming. Now legendary due to the attention received when River Phoenix died outside its doors. Famous bands are known to drop in and jam.

NEARBY EXCURSIONS

MISSION SAN JUAN CAPISTRANO (49 mi./78km along I-5 to the Ortega Hwy. exit) (714/248-2048): Perched between the mountains and the sea, this was the most famous, and probably the loveliest, of California's missions. Founded in 1776 by the Spanish Franciscan Fr. Junípero Serra, it was badly damaged by an earthquake in 1812, but retains part of its cloister, Serra's chapel, ruins of the church with arches and pillars, and the priests' dormitory. In its enchanting gardens, thousands of swallows nest Mar–Oct; there's also an interesting little archeological museum. Open daily.

See also the **Regional Library and Cultural Center** at 31495 El Camino Real (714/493-1752), an elegant postmodern building by Michael Graves with temporary art exhibits. Open daily.

MOUNT WILSON OBSERVATORY (25 mi./40km NE on Calif. 2) (818/793-3100): This small astronomy museum and observatory boasts a 100-in. (2.54m) telescope; it is reached by a beautiful access road with a magnificent view of the entire Los Angeles region. Open Sat–Sun.

PLANES OF FAME MUSEUM (7000 Merrill Ave., Chino Airport, 30 mi./48km E via Calif. 10 to Euclid turnoff) (909/597-3722): 80 vintage military planes ranging from World War I to the Vietnam War, and especially from World War II. Besides a wide variety of American planes, the museum also houses Japanese and German ones. A wonderland for the aviation buff. Open daily.

RICHARD NIXON LIBRARY & BIRTHPLACE (18001 Yorba Linda Blvd. at Eureka St., Yorba Linda, 30 mi./48km SE via I-5 and Calif. 91E) (714/993-3393): Inaugurated in 1990, this 9-acre (3.6ha) museum features Nixon's small wooden birth house (the 37th president was born here in 1913), a pink limestone library, and four gardens. It is also where the 37th president and his wife are laid to rest. Included in the museum are a 292-seat theater, a biographical gallery, a re-creation of the Lincoln Sitting Room from the White House, and a Watergate area where visitors can hear excerpts from the sadly famous White House tapes. Open daily.

RONALD REAGAN PRESIDENTIAL LIBRARY (Presidential Dr. off Madera Rd. in Simi Valley, 35 mi./56km NW via I-5 and Calif. 118) (805/522-8444): $60-million Spanish-style library built on 100 acres (40ha) of rocky scrub-covered hills, where western movies were once filmed, as is proper for the 40th president. Dedicated in Nov 1991, the library contains not only 55 million documents, photographs, films, videotapes, and museum objects, but 22,000 sq. ft. (2,050m²) of exhibit area that celebrate the Reagan years—including a jagged, 6,000-lb. (2,700kg) segment of the defunct Berlin Wall. A must for history buffs. Open daily.

SANTA CATALINA ISLAND (or CATALINA ISLAND) (22 mi./35km offshore from San Pedro): A paradise for bicyclists and big-game fishermen, this 22-mi.-long (35km) island, purchased in 1919 by chewing-gum king William Wrigley, Jr., who had dreams of making it into a second Capri, is now entirely given over to tourism. There's a casino, some decorously rococo hotels, and boat trips.

Two good rests. in the port of Avalon are the **Ristorante Villa Portofino,** 111 Crescent Ave. (310/510-0508), open for dinner nightly, with an Italian menu; and **Armstrong's,** 306 Crescent Ave. (310/510-0113), open for lunch/dinner daily, with very good grilled fish.

The island can be reached in 20 min. by the **Island Express** helicopter service, Berth 95, Harbor Blvd., San Pedro (310/510-2525 for resv., required); or in two hours or less by boat, **Catalina Island Cruises,** Berths 95 and 96, Harbor Blvd., San Pedro (310/491-5559), and **Catalina Express** (310/519-1212).

GHOST TOWNS: Rosamond, 75 mi. (120km) north on I-5 and Calif. 14, is the site of the 19th-century **Tropico Gold Mine** (no visits). The little town from the days of the westward expansion has been scrupulously restored.

Nearby ⌂ **Edwards Air Force Base,** where the space shuttle regularly touches down, has an interesting little space museum, part of NASA's **Ames-Dryden Flight Research Center.** Though Edwards AFB is usually off-limits to civilians, visitors are allowed in to watch each shuttle touch-down. For information on dates, timetables, etc., call 805/258-3446.

NATIONAL PARKS NEARBY: ☀︎⌂⌂⌂ **Death Valley,** 305 mi. (490km) NE on I-15, Calif. 127, and Calif. 190: One of the natural wonders of the world (see Chapter 48 on Death Valley). On the way, stop at ⌂⌂ **Calico,** 10 mi. (16km) northeast of **Barstow,** a wonderful ghost town from the days of the gold rush (see "Ghost Towns" in Chapter 47 on Las Vegas).

Sequoia National Park, 220 mi. (354km) north along I-5 and Calif. 198: The home of the giant trees (see Chapter 52). On the way, see ⌂ **Kern County Pioneer Village,** 3801 Chester Ave. (3 mi./5km east of Calif. 99), in Bakersfield (805/861-2132), open daily. Largest and best-preserved pioneer village in the entire state; see the Far West in its natural grandeur.

FARTHER AFIELD

JOSHUA TREE NATIONAL MONUMENT (304 mi./486km r.t. via the Pomona Fwy./Calif. 60, I-10, and Calif. 60E, I-10E, and return): Cactus desert in flower Mar–May: a place of wild beauty. The yuccas, or Joshua trees, which have given the park its name, can grow to 64 ft. (20m). From **Salton View** (altitude 4,972 ft./1,554m), you can see as far as the Mexican frontier, 93 mi. (150km) to the south. Splendid rocky landscapes, but watch for the temperature, especially in summer; it can rise high enough to cause engine overheating—and there are only three places in the whole park where you can get water. The **visitor center** at Twentynine Palms Oasis (619/367-7511) is open daily.

On the road, go a little out of your way through ⌂ **Riverside,** capital of the "Orange Empire," for a look at two of the most unusual buildings on the West Coast: **Heritage House,** 8193 Magnolia Ave., dating from 1891, an incredible mixture of Spanish, Victorian, and Tudor styles; and the **Mission Inn,** 3649 7th St. at Orange, a charming Spanish-Moorish hotel, now almost a century old, where many well-known personalities (including Humphrey Bogart and Richard Nixon) have been married in the adjoining wedding chapel.

In nearby **Perris,** the home of hot-air ballooning, balloon rides can be arranged at about $100 per half hour through **Full of Hot Air Balloon Co.** (714/530-0110), or **Scorpion Balloons, Inc.** (714/657-6930).

PALM SPRINGS (216 mi./344km r.t. by I-10E, Calif. 111S, and return): A millionaires' city built in the middle of a desert at the foot of 10,804-ft. (3,295m) **Mount San Jacinto.** Don't miss the trip to the top by cable car on the ❅ **Palm Springs Aerial Tramway,** Tramway Rd. (619/325-1391); at 2.5 mi. (4km) it's the world's longest single-span aerial tramway, ascending to 8,516 ft. (2,596m) elevation.

Once no more than a stagecoach stop, Palm Springs has become, in less than a century, one of the snootiest resorts in the country; dozens of celebrities from Bob Hope to Frank Sinatra, from President Ford to Dean Martin, have favored it. Palm Springs and neighboring **Rancho Mirage** boast no fewer than 7,000 pools (one for every five inhabitants), 400 tennis courts, and 70 golf courses. The dry climate and continual (350 days a year) sunshine attract almost two million tourists a year. Hotels offer attractive rates in summer. There's a very fine **Desert Museum,** 101 Museum Dr. (619/325-7186), open Tues–Sun mid-Sept to early June.

Where to Stay in the Palm Springs Area

Hyatt Grand Champions Resort, 44-600 Indian Wells Lane, Indian Wells, CA 92210 (619/341-1000; toll free, see Hyatt). Splendid new palace hotel w. 336 very comfortable rms and suites as well as 20 individual villas, standing in 35 acres (14ha) of landscaped grdn. Two golf courses. The acme of luxury. **VE**

Palm Springs Marqui Crown Plaza, 150 S. Indian Ave., Palm Springs, CA 92262 (619/322-2121). 267 rms. Luxurious resort hotel looking clear out across the San Jacinto Mountains. Unsurpassed comfort. **E–VE**

Shadow Mountain Resort, 45-750 San Luis Rey, Palm Desert, CA 92260 (619/346-6123; toll free 800/472-3713). 140 elegant, comfortable suites. Tennis heaven (16 courts). **M–E**

Motel 6, 595 E. Palm Canyon Dr., Palm Springs, CA 92262 (619/325-6129). 124 rms. Strictly functional motel at unbeatable prices. **B**

Where to Eat in the Palm Springs Area

Cuistot, 73-111 El Paseo, Palm Desert (619/340-1000). Lunch Tues–Sat, dinner Tues–Sun. MC, V. *French.* **M–E**

Le Vallauris, 385 W. Tahquitz Canyon Way, Palm Springs (619/325-5059). Lunch/dinner daily; closed Aug. AE, CB, DC, MC, V. *French.* **M–E**

Las Casuelas Nuevas, 70-050 Calif. 111, Rancho Mirage (619/328-8844). Lunch/dinner daily; closed Thanksgiving, Dec 25. *Mexican.* **I–M**

Louise's Pantry, 124 S. Palm Canyon Dr., Palm Springs (619/325-5124). Breakfast/lunch/dinner daily. No credit cards. *American.* **B**

COASTAL ROAD CALIF. 1 TO SAN FRANCISCO OR SAN DIEGO: One of the country's most spectacular panoramic highways; see Chapter 51 on the California Coast.

CHAPTER 55

SAN DIEGO ⚲⚲

□ □ □

Discovered in 1542 by Juan Rodríguez Cabrillo, a Portuguese explorer in the Spanish service, San Diego Bay is one of the most spectacular natural settings on the West Coast. Don Gaspar de Portolá established the first garrison (Presidio) here in 1769 on the site of the present-day **Presidio Park,** thus making San Diego the point of departure for Spanish settlement in California. At the same time, the celebrated Franciscan Fr. Junípero Serra built here the first of his missions. From this storied colonial past, California's second-largest city (after Los Angeles) has retained vestiges of Spanish and Mexican as well as American influence.

San Diego is not only an important market for the produce of the fertile lands around it (for example, two-thirds of the avocados consumed in the U.S. are grown here), but a vigorous port and industrial city with its face turned resolutely toward the future, with its centers of electronics, aerospace (General Dynamics), missile technology, medicine (the Salk Institute), and oceanography (Scripps Institution of Oceanography). This southernmost city in California has the 13th-fastest economic growth rate among U.S. metropolitan areas, and its population is keeping pace, rising 34.2% between 1980 and 1990. Finally, it's the largest naval base in the country after Norfolk, Virginia; in fact, the navy is the largest employer in the San Diego area with 140,000 people on active duty. The movie *Top Gun* was shot at the **Miramar Naval Air Station** north of San Diego.

For a number of years a huge urban-renewal project has been in progress in downtown San Diego, beside the charming **Gaslamp Quarter;** its symbol is the astonishing **Horton Plaza** commercial complex. At the same time, its gentle climate, its relaxed lifestyle, its exotic overtones (the Mexican city of **Tijuana** is half an hour's drive across the border), and its setting among green hills rising from the turquoise waters of its bay, combine to make it a vacation and convention city overrun by visitors year round (36 million last year). Tourism ranks third among San Diego's industries, bringing in $3 billion a year. The crime rate, among the lowest in the country, is not the least of its attractions.

Over and above the vestiges of the Spanish Colonial era—including **Old Town** and **San Diego de Alcala,** the oldest Franciscan mission in California (1769)—San Diego offers dozens of miles of superb beaches, a paradise for surfers and scuba-divers; the tropical luxuriance of **Balboa Park** and its world-famous zoo; **Coronado** island and its legendary 19th-century Hotel del Coronado; and the unequalled view of the Pacific from **Point Loma.** The adjoining community of **La Jolla** (a corruption of the Spanish "La Joya," the jewel) is a charming little beach resort which is establishing itself more and more firmly as the chic, trendy place for a vacation home in southern California.

Famous people born in San Diego and La Jolla include actors Gregory Peck (La Jolla), Robert Duvall, and Cliff Robertson.

BASIC FACTS: State of California. Area code: 619. Time zone: Pacific. ZIP Code: 92101. Founded: 1769. Approximate population: city, 1,110,000; metropolitan area, 2,500,000. Sixth-largest city and 15th-largest metropolitan area in the U.S.

CLIMATE: Sheltered at the head of its bay, San Diego lives in a perpetual spring-time; the yearly average temperature is 64°F (18°C). Mild in winter though with occasional storms (Jan average: 55°F/13°C), deliciously temperate in spring and fall, quite warm during the summer days (up to 86°F/30°C), but cool at night the year round, San Diego's climate approaches perfection. You'll need a swimsuit and sunglasses no matter when you come.

DISTANCES: Las Vegas, 331 mi. (550km); Los Angeles, 125 mi. (200km); Mexican border, 18 mi. (28km); Phoenix, 355 mi. (568km); San Francisco, 540 mi. (865km); Tucson, 414 mi. (662km).

ARRIVAL & TRANSIT INFORMATION

AIRPORT: Lindbergh International Airport (SAN), 3 mi. (5km) NW. Charles Lindbergh's immortal *The Spirit of St. Louis* was built in San Diego, whence the airport's name. For information, call 231-5220.

U.S. AIRLINES: America West (toll free 800/247-5692), American (toll free 800/433-7300), Continental (toll free 800/525-0280), Northwest (toll free 800/225-2525), United (toll free 800/241-6522), and USAir (toll free 800/428-4322).

CITY LINK: The **cab** fare to city center is about $10; time, about 10 min. Bus: **Super Shuttle** (278-8877), serving principal dwntwn hotels; fare, $6. Municipal bus: **San Diego Transit** Line 2 stops on Broadway; fare, $1.50.
    The city bus system, the **MTS,** is extensive, but slow (for information, call 233-3004). There's also a modern express trolley system, still at an early stage of development: **San Diego Trolley** (for information, call 231-8549).
    Taxis are reasonably inexpensive, but renting a car with unlimited mileage is advisable, given the large number of attractions outside the city. California has very favorable car-rental rates.

CAR RENTAL (at the airport unless otherwise indicated): Avis (toll free 800/331-1212); Budget (toll free 800/527-0700); Dollar (toll free 800/800-4000); Hertz (toll free 800/654-3131); Ladki (local renter with very competitive rates), 929 W. Laurel St. (233-9333); National (toll free 800/227-7368); and Thrifty, 1120 W. Laurel St. (toll free 800/367-2277).

LIMOUSINE SERVICES: Carey Limousine (225-9551), Coronado Livery Service (435-6310), and My Chauffeur Limousine (698-7970).

TAXIS: Cabs may be summoned by phone or taken from the waiting lines outside the major hotels. Recommended companies: **American Cab** (292-1111), **Orange Cab** (291-3337), and **Yellow Cab** (234-6161).

TRAIN: Amtrak station, Kettner Blvd. at Broadway (toll free 800/872-7245).

INTERCITY BUS: Greyhound, 120 W. Broadway at First Ave. (toll free 800/231-2222).

INFORMATION & TOURS

TOURIST INFORMATION: The **San Diego Convention and Visitors Bureau,** 401 B. St., Suite 1400, CA 92101 (619/232-3101).
Visitor Information Center, 11 Horton Plaza (619/236-1212).

GUIDED TOURS: Corporate Helicopters (helicopter), 2904 Pacific Hwy. (291-4356). 30-min. chopper trips over San Diego Bay leaving from Lindbergh Airport. A fine spectacle. Resv. required; daily year round.
Gray Line Tours (bus), 1775 Hancock St., Suite 130 (491-0011): Guided tours of the city and surroundings; serves major hotels.
Old Town Trolley (bus) (298-8687): Guided tours of the major tourist attractions in and around San Diego, on a bus got up to look like an old-time trolley car. Board and get off as many times as you like along the route. Daily year round.
San Diego Harbor Excursion (boat), Broadway at Harbor Dr. (619/234-4111): Boat trips around the harbor and bay, daily year round.
San Diego Trolley (231-8549): Fast, ultramodern light railway connecting the Amtrak station in the center of San Diego (Kettner Blvd. at C St.) to the suburb of San Ysidro on the Mexican border across from Tijuana. Leaves every 15 min. 5am–1am; takes about 40 min; fare, $1.75.

SIGHTS, ATTRACTIONS & ACTIVITIES

ADVENTURES: Sky Surfer Balloon Co. (balloon), 1221 Camino del Mar, Del Mar (481-6800): Hot-air-balloon trips over San Diego and the Pacific coast. Spectacular. Daily year round.
Whale-Watching Trips: The **Natural History Museum,** Park Blvd., Balboa Park (232-3821), arranges boat trips to watch whale migrations between mid-Dec and mid-Feb. At least 200 whales are encountered daily off San Diego during this period. Also at **Fisherman's Landing,** 2838 Garrison St. (222-0391), and **H. & M. Landing,** 2803 Emerson St. (222-1144).

ARCHITECTURAL HIGHLIGHTS: ☀☖ **Horton Plaza,** bounded by First Ave., Fourth Ave., Broadway, and G St. (238-1596): The farthest-out shopping center in the U.S., featuring the daring postmodern design and pastel mauve, green, orange, and pink decor of architect Jon Jerde. It's an extravagant hodge-podge of facades, colonnades, and porticos that might remind you of a Venetian palace, an art deco theater, or a Spanish mission, but for the more than 150 retail outlets, restaurants, movie houses, etc. Open daily.
☀☖ **San Diego Convention Center,** 111 W. Harbor Dr. at Fifth Ave. (525-5000): The most imaginative, and the handsomest, convention center in the country. Opened in 1989, the spectacular building, which takes the form of a huge concrete sailboat anchored beside San Diego Bay, is by architect Arthur Erickson. The main Exhibition Hall, covering 250,000 sq. ft. (24,000m²) can accommodate 6,000 people.
☀☖ **Emerald-Shapery Center,** bounded by Broadway and C, State, and Columbia Sts. (239-4500): Eight luminous green hexagonal towers of 25 and 30 stories built in two clusters of four skyscrapers, linked by a 100-ft. (31m) glass atrium. Offering an unsurpassed view of San Diego and the bay, this spectacular, new (1991) addition to the city's skyline was designed by architect C. W. Kim.

University of California at San Diego/USSD, La Jolla Village Dr., I-5, and N. Torrey Pines Rd., La Jolla (534-8273): Founded in 1912 and now numbering more than 17,000 students, this campus specializes in biological and medical research. On the lawns is a fine collection of modern sculpture. Each of the four colleges is built in a different architectural style.

BEACHES: **Black's Beach,** 15 mi. (25km) north along I-5, Genesee Rd., and Torrey Pines Scenic Dr.: Since you must first go down a 300-ft. (92m) cliff (and, of course, eventually go back up again), this beach south of Torrey Pines State Park is not easy of access; perhaps for that reason it draws many nudists.

Border Field Beach, 20 mi. (32km) south via I-5 and Monument Rd.: Right at the Mexican border. Horseback riding authorized on the beach; surfing.

Coronado Municipal Beach, 5 mi. (8km) west on Calif. 75: A family beach, with huge white-sand stretches.

La Jolla Cove, 12 mi. (19km) NW via I-5 and Ardafer Rd.: The prettiest beach, and the most chic. Protected by cliffs on three sides; wonderful scuba-diving and hang-gliding.

Mission Beach, 8 mi. (12km) NW on W. Mission Bay Dr.: Favorite of local younger set; overcrowded in summer.

Ocean Beach, 6 mi. (9km) west on U.S. 8: Dangerous marine streams, so relatively uncrowded.

Torrey Pines State Beach, 20 mi. (32km) north via I-5 and County Rd. 21: Huge unspoiled beach with overhanging cliffs and pine woods. Lovely seascapes.

Windansea Beach, 10 mi. (16km) north along Mission Blvd. and La Jolla Blvd.: One of San Diego's most picturesque beaches. Here the surfboard reigns unchallenged.

CHURCHES/SYNAGOGUES: **San Diego Mormon Temple,** take Nobel Dr. exit along I-5 between La Jolla and San Diego: The most recently built of the 44 Mormon temples in the world, this structure looming above the San Diego skyline serves the 45,000 Mormons living in the San Diego area. The spires are covered with three layers of translucent glass and capped with gold leaf. Like all Mormon temples, the inside of this one is off-limits to non-Mormons.

HISTORIC BUILDINGS: **Hotel del Coronado,** 1500 Orange Ave., Coronado (435-6611): One of the most historic hotels in the U.S. Opened in 1888, the "Del," as San Diegans affectionately call it, was the first hotel in the world to be equipped with electric power (the installation was done under the personal supervision of Thomas Edison) and elevators. The imposing Victorian frame building, with its bright-red pointed roofs, was a setting for the movie *Some Like It Hot.* Legend has it that it was here, in 1920, that the future King Edward VIII of England first met the woman for whom he later gave up the throne, Wallis Simpson, who was to become Duchess of Windsor. Guided tours Thurs–Sat at 10am and 11am.

Mission San Diego de Alcala, 10818 San Diego Mission Rd. (283-7319): Known as "The Mother of Missions," this oldest mission in California was originally built on the site of the present-day **Presidio Park** in 1769 by the Spanish Franciscan Fr. Junípero Serra (beatified in 1988 by papal decree). Destroyed by earthquakes in 1803 and 1812, it was rebuilt following the original plans on the banks of the San Diego River in 1813, and is one of the most beautiful religious edifices on the West Coast. San Diego de Alcala was the first of the 21 missions built by the Franciscans between the Mexican border and Sonoma 540 mi. (860km) to the north, beyond San Francisco Bay, along what later became known as El Camino Real (the Royal Way). Each mission was one day's journey on horseback from its neighbors. Open daily.

☼ 🔍 **Old Town San Diego State Historic Park,** bounded by Congress, Wallace, Twigg, and Juan Sts.: The historic center of San Diego, with its Spanish Colonial adobe houses. Many interesting buildings from the years 1820–70, lining a huge plaza where cockfights and bullfights were once held. Note the **Casa de Estudillo** (1820), residence of the governor of San Diego when it was part of Mexico. The **Casa de Lopez** (1834) houses a quaint candle museum. The **San Diego Union Building** is the office of a newspaper first published in 1868. The **Seeley Stables** (1869) was long the depot for the stagecoaches of the U.S. Mail. Collection of horse-drawn vehicles. The **Old California Museum,** besides a collection of horse-drawn vehicles, has a model of 19th-century San Diego. At the north corner of the plaza, where the **Casa de Pico,** residence of the first governor of California, once stood, is now the **Bazaar del Mundo,** a replica of a typical Spanish-Mexican marketplace, with craft shops, souvenir shops, art galleries, and restaurants set in courtyards and gardens. There's a signposted walk through Old Town for the benefit of visitors. Shouldn't be missed, despite its touristy atmosphere; **visitor center** at 4002 Wallace St. (220-5422). Open daily.

☼ 🔍 **Villa Montezuma,** 1925 K St. (239-2211): Magnificent piece of Victorian architecture contemporary with the Hotel del Coronado (1887). Colorful exterior decoration; very fine rococo interior with superb stained-glass windows. Temporary art exhibitions. Open Sat and Sun.

🔔 **Whaley House,** 2482 San Diego Ave. (298-2482): The oldest (1856) brick building in southern California; until 1871 it housed the local law courts. Believed to be haunted by the ghost of a man who was hanged here in 1852. Original furnishings and decoration. An easy walk from Old Town Plaza. Open daily.

MONUMENTS: ☼ 🔍 **Cabrillo National Monument,** Cabrillo Memorial Dr. at Point Loma, 10 mi. (16km) west on Calif. 209 (557-5450): Dedicated to Juan Rodríguez Cabrillo, discoverer of California, the monument with its lighthouse, dating from 1855, gives you a fine view of San Diego Bay and the Pacific Ocean. It shares with the Statue of Liberty in New York the distinction of being the most-visited monument in the U.S. From here you can watch the offshore migration of the gray whales mid-Dec to mid-Feb. Museum. Open daily. The monument closes at sunset.

MUSEUMS OF ART: ☼ 🔍 **Museum of Art,** 1450 El Prado, Balboa Park (232-7931): A vast panorama of the history of art—European, American, and Far Eastern—in a typical Spanish Colonial building. From Rembrandt and Rubens to Salvador Dalí and the richly wrought frescoes of Mexican artist Diego Rivera. Among the most famous works on display: Zurbarán's *Agnus Dei,* Canaletto's *View of the Mole at Venice,* Frans Hals's *Portrait of Isaac Massa,* El Greco's *The Penitent St. Peter,* and *Still Life* by Juan Sanchez-Cotán. One of the best art museums on the West Coast. Open Tues–Sun.

☼ 🔍 **Museum of Contemporary Art,** 700 Prospect St., La Jolla (454-3541): If it were only for its site, in a garden overlooking the ocean, this superb museum of modern art would be worth visiting—but among 3,000 works on display there are also some signed by Roy Lichtenstein, Andy Warhol, Frank Stella, Ellsworth Kelly, Richard Serra, and many others. Temporary exhibitions of painting, sculpture, photography, design, and architecture. Open Tues–Sun. The building, however, will be closed for renovation until early 1996. Part of the collection, as well as other temporary exhibits, can be viewed at the museum's other, smaller location at 1001 Kettner Blvd. at Broadway (dwntwn) (234-1001).

Museum of Photographic Arts, Casa de Balboa, Balboa Park (239-5262): Display of photographs old and new by photographers foreign and American; a must for shutterbugs. Open daily.

Timken Museum, 1500 El Prado, Balboa Park (239-5548): In a building which is not among the great successes of modern architecture you'll find a fine collection of Russian icons, 19th-century American painting, and European masters—Brueghel, Rembrandt, Cézanne, and others. Among the best-known paintings here: *Death of the Virgin* by Petrus Christus, *The Parable of the Sower* by Brueghel the Elder, Martin Heade's *Magnolia Blossom,* and John Singleton Copley's portrait of *Mrs. Thomas Gage.* Open Tues–Sun; closed the month of Sept.

MUSEUMS OF SCIENCE & HISTORY: Aerospace Museum, 2001 Pan
American Plaza, Balboa Park (234-8291): History of aviation and space flight from 1880 to the present day. Many models of old aircraft and gliders; also a life-size replica of Lindbergh's legendary *The Spirit of St. Louis,* the original of which was built in San Diego in 1927, and a space capsule. Hall devoted to the heroes and heroines of the story of aeronautics. Well-stocked aviation library. Open daily.

Birch Aquarium-Museum, 2300 Expedition Dr., La Jolla (534-3474): Interpretive center for the Scripps Institution of Oceanography at the University of California at San Diego, this handsome museum of oceanography, one of the best known in the country, displays a comprehensive selection of Californian and Mexican marine life. Also offers a spectacular view of the harbor. Open daily.

Mormon Battalion Memorial, 2510 Juan St. (298-3317): Military museum dedicated to the memory of 500 soldiers of a Mormon battalion which, during the Mexican War of 1846–47, made the longest march in the history of the U.S. Army: more than 2,000 miles from Illinois to San Diego. Only 350 of them reached their goal. Also an exhibition on the history of the Mormons. Open daily.

Museum of Man, 1350 El Prado, Balboa Park (239-2001): Superb natural-history museum in an elegant Spanish Colonial building, one of whose notable possessions is the skeleton of Del Mar Man, the oldest humanoid ever found in the U.S. (about 48,000 years old). Giant model of the human body. Fine collection of Hopi and Mayan art. Open daily.

Natural History Museum, 1788 El Prado, Balboa Park (232-3821): Fauna and flora of southern California; the whale skulls are impressive. A seismograph registers all earth tremors, no matter how slight. Open daily.

Reuben H. Fleet Space Theater, 1875 El Prado, Balboa Park (238-1233): The largest planetarium in the U.S., with a wholly remarkable audiovisual program. Giant OMNIMAX hemispheric screen for 70mm projection. Exhibitions on space technology. Hands-on science center. A must for amateur astronomers; open daily.

Serra Museum, 2727 Presidio Dr., Presidio Park (297-3258): The history of California and its missions, with a valuable antiquarian library, in a charming Spanish Colonial–style building dedicated to the Franciscan missionary Junipero Serra and built on the site of the first Presidio erected by the Spaniards in 1769. Fine view of Mission Bay. Open Tues–Sun.

Star of India, 1306 N. Harbor Dr., Embarcadero (234-9153): Launched in Britain in 1863 and taken out of service in 1923, this is one of the last great 19th-century sailing ships still afloat. She sailed around the world 21 times. Belongs to the Maritime Museum. Open daily.

CALIFORNIA

San Diego

Balboa Park **7**
Cabrillo National
 Monument **13**
Convention Center **2**
Coronado Bay Bridge **11**
Cowboy Museum **20**
Firehouse Museum **1**
Gaslamp Quarter **4**
Heritage Park **17**
Horton Plaza **3**
Hotel del Coronado **12**
Junipero Serra Museum **16**
Maritime Museum **9**
Mission Basilica San
 Diego de Alcala **22**
Mormon battalion
 Visitors Center **18**
Old Town State
 Historic Park **21**
Presidio Park **15**
San Diego Zoo **8**
Seaport Village **6**
Sea World **14**
Villa Montezuma **10**
Whaley House **19**
William Heath Davis
 House **5**

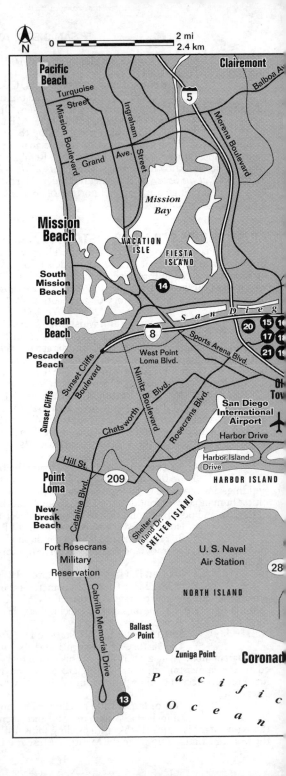

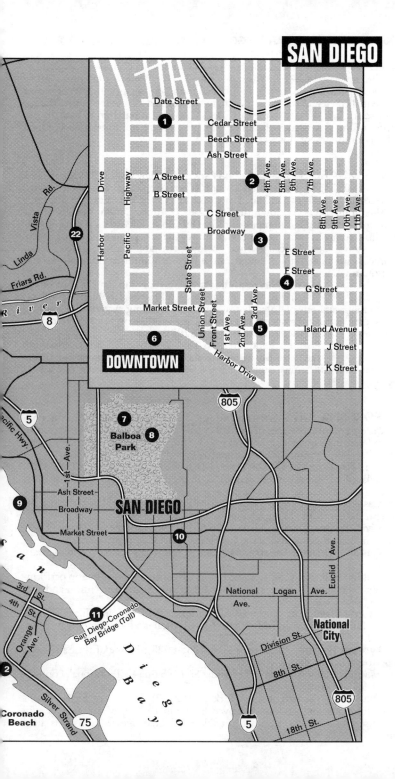

PANORAMAS: ※&& **Cabrillo National Monument,** Cabrillo Memorial Dr. at Point Loma, 10 mi. (16km) west on Calif. 209 (557-5450): On a promontory overlooking San Diego Bay, the lighthouse and adjoining monument command an unequalled view of the Pacific Ocean to the west, La Jolla to the north, Mexico to the south, and the city to the east. Dec–Feb you can watch from here the migration of the gray whales offshore in the bay. A sight not to be missed. Open daily. The monument closes at sunset.

PARKS & GARDENS: ※&& **Balboa Park,** reached by way of El Prado or Park Blvd. (239-0512): This superb 1,158-acre (468ha) tropical park of woods, lawns, and lakes in the heart of San Diego shelters half a dozen museums (see above); a world-famous zoo (see below); the **Spreckels Outdoor Organ,** world's largest open-air organ, with 5,000 pipes; and the **Old Globe Theatre,** a replica of William Shakespeare's theater in London, home to the very popular National Shakespeare Festival (see "Special Events," below); two golf courses; a well-known botanical garden; etc. It was the site of the Panama-California-International Exposition in 1915.

※& **Mission Bay Aquatic Park,** West Mission Bay Dr., Sea World Dr., and E. Mission Bay Dr.: 4,600 acres (1,860ha) of parkland around the great body of water that is Mission Bay; fishing, waterskiing, surfing, beaches, etc. Beautiful scenery. The famous **Sea World** marine zoo is here. Visitor center at 2688 E. Mission Bay Dr. (276-8200).

& **Presidio Park,** Presidio Dr.: This wooded hill overlooking the Serra Museum (see above) marks the original site of the first Spanish fortifications, built in 1769 (the Presidio). Pretty view of Mission Bay.

PERFORMING ARTS: For daily listings of all shows and cultural events, consult the entertainment pages of the daily paper *San Diego Union-Tribune* (morning and evening), as well as the weekly *Del Mar News-Press* and free San Diego *Reader,* and the monthly *San Diego* magazine.

Arts Tix, a kiosk in Horton Plaza, 121 Broadway at First Ave. (238-3810), sells tickets for all shows at reduced prices on the day of performance. Cash only; open Tues–Sat.

Cassius Carter Centre Stage, Balboa Park (239-2255): Drama, musicals, modern theater (Sept–May); adjoins the Old Globe Theatre.

Civic Theatre, Third and B St. (236-6510): Home of the San Diego Opera, Ian Campbell, director; also of the California Ballet Company.

Gaslamp Quarter Theatre, 444 Fourth Ave. (234-9583): Contemporary theater.

Golden Hall, 202 C St. (236-6510): Rock concerts, shows by top performers. With the Civic Theatre, part of the huge San Diego Convention and Performing Arts Center.

La Jolla Playhouse, on the UCSD Campus, 2910 La Jolla Village Dr. and Torrey Pines Rd., La Jolla (550-1070): Classical and contemporary plays; musicals.

Lyceum Theatre, 79 Horton Plaza (235-8025): Home of the San Diego Repertory Theatre; drama, comedy.

Marquis Public Theater, 3717 India St. (295-5654): Traditional, contemporary, and experimental theater.

Old Globe Theatre, Balboa Park (239-2255): Replica of Shakespeare's Globe Playhouse in London; destroyed by fire in 1978, it was rebuilt by public subscription. Every summer the National Shakespeare Festival is held here.

Symphony Hall (Fox Theater), 1245 Seventh Ave. (699-4200): Classical concerts and recitals; home of the San Diego Symphony under principal conductor Yoav Talmi.

Theatre in Old Town, 4040 Twiggs (688-2494): Contemporary theater; musicals.

SHOPPING: ☀ **Bazaar del Mundo,** Juan St., Old Town (296-3161): Picturesque Mexican-style market with restaurants and shops selling clothing, gifts, jewelry, etc. Very aesthetically pleasing decor even through the touristy atmosphere. Open daily.

☀ **Horton Plaza,** bounded by First Ave., Fourth Ave., Broadway, and G St. (238-1596): The country's most spectacular shopping center, in the downtown Gaslamp district. Rather disconcerting postmodern architecture, embellished with original sculpture and galleries at several levels. Four department stores, more than 150 stores, restaurants, movie houses, and a farmers' market. Open daily.

La Jolla, around Girard Ave. and Prospect St.: The two shopping streets of this elegant beach resort. Fashionable shops, chic stores, and art galleries. The luxury shopping center at **Coast Walk,** 1298 Prospect St. (454-3031), designed by architect Robert A. M. Stern, is one of the handsomest in the U.S.—with prices to match.

Seaport Village, Pacific Hwy. and W. Harbor Dr. (235-4014): Unusual shopping center on the ocean, which reconstructs the atmosphere of a 19th-century Victorian village in California: 15 restaurants; 70 stores, shops, and art galleries. Wonderful turn-of-the-century–style carousel. Open daily.

Tijuana: See "Nearby Excursions," below.

SPECIAL EVENTS: For the exact schedule of events below, consult the **San Diego Convention and Visitors Bureau** (see "Tourist Information," above).

New Year's Day Yacht Regatta (Jan 1): Sailboat race in San Diego Bay.

Buick Invitational Open (early Feb): PGA golf tournament at Torrey Pines Golf Course in La Jolla.

Cinco de Mayo Festival (May 5): Mariachi concerts, art shows, banjo competition, buffalo barbecue. In Old Town.

Corpus Christi Fiesta (late May to early June), at the Mission San Antonio de Pala, 50 mi. (80km) north via I-15 and Calif. 76: Open-air mass, folk dancing. A typical Spanish fiesta celebrated every year since 1816; colorful.

Del Mar Fair (late June to early July): Flower and horse show on the Del Mar Fairgrounds, 9 mi. (14km) north; very popular locally.

National Shakespeare Festival (mid-June to Sept): Shakespeare plays in series throughout the summer, at the Old Globe Theatre, Balboa Park. A very well-attended festival.

Festival of Bells (wknd in July): Festival of bells commemorating the foundation of the Mission of San Diego de Alcala on July 17, 1769.

Admission Day (early Sept): Commemorates California's admission to the Union in 1850. Mariachi concerts, folk dancing, food festival.

Cabrillo Festival (late Sept): Celebrates the discovery of California. Dancing, folklore displays, parades; very lively.

Christmas–Light Boat Parade (third Sun in Dec): Procession of illuminated boats in San Diego Harbor.

SPORTS: San Diego has two professional teams:

Baseball (Apr–Oct): Padres, Jack Murphy Stadium (280-4636).

Football (Aug–Dec): Chargers, Jack Murphy Stadium (280-2111).

Horse Racing
Del Mar Racetrack, County Fairgrounds (755-1141). Thoroughbred racing Wed–Mon late July to mid-Sept.

Deep-Sea Fishing
Every year tens of thousands of rod-and-reel enthusiasts go deep-sea fishing in the waters of southern California, to the Mexican border and beyond: Their destined prey include barracuda, sea bass, yellowtail, bonito, and blue marlin. The charter rates for a fully equipped deep-sea-fishing boat are about $400 for a half day of 6 hr. and $500 for a full day of 10 hr. Some recommended charters: **Fisherman's Landing,** 2838 Garrison St. (222-0391); **H. & M. Landing,** 2803 Emerson St. (222-1144); **Lee Palm Sportfishing,** 2801 Emerson St. (224-3857); and **Point Loma Sportfishing,** 1403 Scott St. (223-1627).

STROLLS: ☀⚓ **Embarcadero,** Harbor Dr. between Market and Grape Sts.: San Diego's fishing and commercial harbor; fine view of bay and shipping. The vessels of the U.S. Navy moored at Broadway Pier may be visited Sat–Sun 1–4pm; for information, call 532-1430.

⚓ **Gaslamp Quarter,** Fifth Ave. between Broadway and Market St.: The 16-block Victorian district downtown is jammed with trendy shops, artists' studios, and fashionable restaurants. A lot of work has gone into restoring the old buildings, many of which date to the 1880s. The Gaslamp Quarter Foundation, 410 Island Ave. (233-4692), offers guided tours of the historic buildings and neighborhoods every Sat.

⚓ **Harbor and Shelter Islands,** reached via North Harbor Dr. and Rosecrans St.: Two big artificial islands built at the north of the bay on millions of tons of material dredged from the bay itself. A wonderful place for fishing, or loafing, surrounded by marinas, yachts, restaurants, and luxury hotels.

☀⚓⚓ **Old Town,** around Wallace, Congress, and Juan Sts.: The historic heart of San Diego, with many shops, restaurants, old houses (see "Historic Buildings," above). Lively and colorful.

☀⚓⚓ **Scenic Drive:** A 52-mi. (84km) loop posted with signs in the form of a blue-and-yellow seagull. In about three hours of driving you'll see most of the tourist attractions described above: the Embarcadero, Shelter Island, Cabrillo National Monument, Old Town, Balboa Park, etc. The drive begins at Broadway Pier.

THEME PARKS: ☀⚓⚓ **Sea World,** 1720 S. Shores Rd., Mission Bay Park (226-3901): In a 135-acre (55ha) parkland setting, this huge marine-life theme park boasts more than 5,500 sea creatures, including seals, sea elephants, dolphins, and three killer whales. Giant 26,400-gal. (100,000-liter) aquarium just for the sharks. Japanese fishing village; Skytower, a 321-ft. (98m) observation tower. A must-see for visitors since 1964; open daily.

☀⚓ **Wild Animal Park,** 15500 San Pasqual Valley Rd., Escondido (747-8702): 30 mi. (48km) NE via I-15 and Calif. 78: A 1,800-acre (730ha) wildlife park with more than 2,200 free-ranging animals: lions, zebras, giraffes, rhinoceroses, etc. African village. One of the finest safari zoos in the U.S.; you see it by monorail. Open daily.

ZOOS: ☀⚓⚓ **San Diego Zoo,** Zoo Dr., Balboa Park (234-3153): The richest and most beautiful zoo in the U.S., visited each year by almost four million people, with more than 3,500 wild animals and 3,000 exotic birds drawn from 800 animal species, in 100 acres (40ha) of superb undulating tropical gardens with luxuriant vegetation. Among the rarest creatures are Australian koala bears, Komodo dragons (giant lizards from Indonesia), and the only New Zealand kiwis acclimatized to life in the U.S. Your visit can be made by bus, on a moving sidewalk, or by the Skyfari cable car. Not to be missed; open daily.

ACCOMMODATIONS

Personal Favorites (in order of preference)

Pan Pacific Hotel (dwntwn), 400 W. Broadway, CA 92101 (619/239-4500; toll free 800/327-8585). 436 rms, A/C, color TV, in-rm movies. AE, CB, DC, MC, V. Valet gar. $13, pool, health club, spa, massage, two rests. (including the Grill), bar, rm svce, boutiques, concierge, free crib. *Note:* Lavish, $90-million brand-new showplace in the heart of the business district, part of the spectacular Emerald-Shapery Center (see "Architectural Highlights," above). Features a dazzling array of svces and amenities including bright, huge, comfortable rms and suites w. commanding views of the city skyline and the bay. Superb svce staff. Comprehensive business center w. secretarial svces. Complete fitness facilities. Free airport and convention center transportation. Very good location, a short walk from the Embarcadero and the Gaslamp Quarter. Top corporate clientele. **E–VE**

U.S. Grant (dwntwn), 326 Broadway, CA 92101 (619/232-3121; toll free, see Preferred). 280 rms, A/C, color TV, in-rm movies. AE, CB, DC, MC, V. Valet gar. $7, health club, two rest. (the Grant Grill), bar, 24-hr. rm svce, concierge, crib $20. *Note:* Built around 1910 by Ulysses S. Grant, Jr., son of the 18th president of the U.S., this luxurious grand hotel has been sumptuously restored to its original elegance. Works of art, antique furniture, marble floors, and crystal chandeliers adorn the lobby and public rms. Rms are huge, agreeably furnished in Queen Anne style w. travertine bathrooms. Excellent business rest.; ultra-polished svce; intimacy and distinction. In the heart of dwntwn across from the Horton Plaza Mall. Upscale business clientele. A designated historic monument. **E–VE**

Bed and Breakfast Inn at La Jolla (vic.), 7753 Draper Ave., La Jolla, CA 92037 (619/456-2066). 16 rms, A/C, color TV in sitting rm. MC, V. Free parking, beach nearby, free continental breakfast and afternoon wine and cheese. *Note:* Beautiful cliffside house built in 1913 by cubist architect Irving Gill along an ocean cove. Many of the 16 guest rms have ocean views; some have refrigerators. Intimate atmosphere. Elegant, rustic setting. Polished svce and reception. Resv. must be made far in advance. A favorite of those in-the-know. **M–VE**

Humphrey's Half Moon Inn (nr. dwntwn), 2303 Shelter Island Dr., CA 92106 (619/224-3411; toll free 800/345-9995). 182 rms, A/C, color TV, in-rm movies. AE, CB, DC, MC, V. Free parking, pool, bicycling, putting green, boating, marina, rest. (Humphrey's), bar, rm svce, nightclub, crib $10. *Note:* A charming little hotel in a beautiful grdn, looking out over glorious San Diego Bay. Pretty South Seas decor; comfortable rms w. balconies and views over the bay or the marina (some w. refrigerators and kitchenettes); friendly reception and svce. Agreeable rest.; free airport limo. Great for the budget-minded; an excellent place to stay. **M–E**

Town and Country Hotel (nr. dwntwn), 500 Hotel Circle N., CA 92108 (619/291-7131; toll free 800/854-2608). 960 rms, A/C, color TV, in-rm movies. AE, CB, DC, MC, V. Parking $5, four pools, health club, four rests. (including Le Pavillon), two coffee shops, three bars, rm svce, disco, hrdrsr, free crib. *Note:* Big convention hotel in 32 acres (12ha) of nicely landscaped grdns, in Mission Valley, 10 min. from dwntown. Its dimensions make it a favorite of groups and conventioneers. Huge rms and very comfortable facilities; efficient svce; good value. **M–E**

Catamaran Hotel (nr. dwntwn), 3999 Mission Blvd., Pacific Beach, CA 92109 (619/488-1081; toll free 800/223-0888). 315 rms, A/C, cable color TV. AE, CB, DC, MC, V. Parking $7, pool, health club, boating, beach, rest., bar, rm svce, nightclub, free crib. *Note:* Luxury convention hotel on the ocean. Elegant Polynesian decor; spectacular lobby w. tropical grdns and waterfalls. Supremely comfortable rms w. balcony overlooking Mission Bay or the Pacific, most w. refrigerator. Efficient svce. Group/convention clientele. 20 min. from dwntwn. A very fine place to stay. Recently completed a $25-million renovation. **M–E**

Sands of La Jolla (vic.), 5417 La Jolla Blvd, La Jolla, CA 92037 (619/459-3336). 38 rms, cable color TV. AE, CB, DC, MC, V. Free parking, pool, crib $3. *Note:* Small, inviting motel a stone's throw from the beach, 5 min. from La Jolla's shopping district, and 25 min. from dwntwn San Diego. Comfortable rms w. refrigerators (some w. balconies and views over the ocean). Friendly reception and svce. Good value off-season. Interesting holiday packages. **I–M**, but lower rates off-season.

Grosvenor Inn (nr. dwntwn), 810 Ash St., CA 92101 (619/233-8826). 55 rms, A/C, color TV. AE, MC, V. Free parking, Jacuzzi, pool, nearby 24-hr. coffee shop. *Note:* Modest but well-run motel very nr. dwntwn, a stone's throw from Balboa Park and the business district. Serviceable, completely renovated rms; free coffee in rms; good value. **B–I**

Other Accommodations (from top bracket to budget)

Loews Coronado Bay Resort (nr. dwntwn), 4000 Coronado Bay Rd., Coronado, CA 92118 (619/424-4000; toll free, see Loews). 443 rms, A/C, color TV, in-rm movies. AE, CB, DC, MC, V. Valet gar. $11, three pools, health club, sauna, five tennis courts, marina, boating, two rests. (including Azzura Point), bars, 24-hr. rm svce, boutiques, concierge, free crib. *Note:* Brand-new glittery resort located on a 15-acre (6ha) peninsula in San Diego Bay. Ultra-comfortable rms and four spectacular cottages ($1,500), all w. water views. Guests have a private pedestrian underpass to Silver Strand State Beach. There's also an 80-slip marina and a water taxi to dwntwn San Diego (20 min.). Flawless, personalized svce. The new star in the San Diego luxury hotel scene. **VE**

Hyatt Regency La Jolla (vic.), 3777 La Jolla Village Dr., La Jolla, CA 92122 (619/552-1234; toll free, see Hyatt). 400 rms, A/C, color TV, in-rm movies. AE, CB, DC, MC, V. Valet gar. $11, pool, health club, tennis court, three rests. (including Barcino), two bars, rm svce, concierge, free crib. *Note:* A newcomer on the local luxury-hotel scene. The spectacular neo-modernist structure by Michael Graves is worth seeing for its own sake. Spacious, extremely comfortable rms w. minibar. Flawless svce. Two VIP floors. Direct access to the ultramodern Aventine complex of rests., boutiques, and stores. Convention and business clientele. **E–VE**

Hyatt Regency San Diego (dwntwn), 1 Market Place, CA 92101 (619/232-1234; toll free, see Hyatt). 875 rms, color TV, in-rm movies. AE, CB, DC, MC, V. Valet parking $11, pool, health club, sauna, four tennis courts, two rests. (including Lael's), 24-hr rm svce, two bars, boutiques, concierge, free crib. *Note:* A newcomer on the local luxury hotel scene. This 40-story structure allows each room a panoramic view of the harbor and marina. Its proximity to the Convention Center means that the hotel is business-oriented. Luxurious rms, some w. refrigerators and minibars. Seven VIP floors. Free airport shuttle. **E–VE**

Hotel del Coronado (nr. dwntwn), 1500 Orange Ave., Coronado, CA 92118 (619/435-6611; toll free 800/468-3533). 689 rms (half w. A/C), cable color TV. AE, CB, DC, MC, V. Valet parking $12, two pools, health club, sauna, six tennis courts, beach, boating, bicycling, two rests. (including the Crown Room), coffee shop, bars, rm svce, 24-hr deli:, disco, hrdrsr, boutiques, concierge, free crib. *Note:* The Victorian *grande dame* of local hotels, a 5-min. drive from dwntwn by the San Diego Coronado Bay Bridge; almost every president of the U.S. in the past century, as well as many visiting VIPs, has stayed here. Built in 1888, this was the first hotel in the world to be equipped w. electricity and elevators. Elegant period atmosphere. Direct beach access. Relatively spacious rms w. refrigerators and private patios or balconies, the best w. ocean view. Some shortcomings in comfort and facilities; polished svce; lovely grdns. Part of the movie *Some Like It Hot* was filmed here. **E–VE**

Horton Grand Hotel (dwntwn), 311 Island Ave., CA 92101 (619/544-1886; toll free 800/542-1886). 134 rms, A/C, cable color TV. AE, CB, DC, MC, V. Valet parking $8, rest. (Ida Bailey rest.), bar, rm svce, nightclub, concierge, free crib. *Note:* Charming 19th-century hotel which has retained its Victorian elegance, centrally located in the heart of the Gaslamp district. Superb carved exterior; interior decoration and fittings opulently renovated; impressive grand staircase and picturesque skylight in the lobby. Spacious rms w. fireplaces, some w. balconies and period furniture. Intimate atmosphere; faultless svce. Upscale business clientele. **M–E**

Best Western Inn by the Sea (vic.), 7830 Fay Ave., La Jolla, CA 92037 (619/459-4461; toll free, see Best Western). 132 rms, A/C, color TV, in-rm movies. AE, CB, DC, MC, V. Free parking, pool, health club, adj. coffee shop, rm svce, free crib. *Note:* Inviting, modern motel in the heart of La Jolla. Spacious, comfortable rms w. village or ocean views, some w. balconies, kitchens, and refrigerators. Just footsteps to the shore. Friendly reception; good svce. Good value overall. A nice motel popular w. tourists. **M–E,** but lower rates off-season.

Handlery Hotel and Country Club (nr. dwntwn), 950 Hotel Circle N., CA 92108 (619/298-0511; toll free 800/676-6567). 216 rms, A/C, color TV, in-rm movies. AE, CB, DC, MC, V. Free parking, three pools, eight tennis courts, two golf courses, health club, putting green, rest. (Ironwood), 24-hr. coffee shop, bars, rm svce, hrdrsr, free crib. *Note:* Comfortable, inviting motel 15 min. from dwntwn. Surrounded by pretty grdns. Spacious rms, some w. private balconies or patios. Comprehensive sports facilities. Cheerful svce. Group and convention clientele. **I–M**

Seapoint Hotel (nr. dwntwn), 4875 N. Harbor Dr., CA 92106 (619/224-3621; toll free 800/662-8899). 237 rms, A/C, color TV, in-rm movies. AE, CB, DC, MC, V. Free parking, pool, health club, sauna, rest., rm svce, free crib. *Note:* Large, modern, comfortable hotel across from San Diego's municipal sportfishing pier. Spacious, inviting rms looking out over the bay or marina, some w. private balcony or patio and refrigerator. Efficient, amiable svce. 5 min. from the airport (free shuttle); 10 min. from dwntwn. Good value on balance. **I–M,** but lower rates off-season.

Days Inn (dwntwn), 1919 Pacific Hwy., CA 92101 (619/232-1077). 67 rms, A/C, cable color TV, AE, CB, DC, MC, V. Free parking, pool, adj. coffee shop. *Note:* Congenial, very well run motel well located nr. the Embarcadero. Comfortable rms w. refrigerators, some w. balconies. Friendly reception and svce; free coffee in rms. Totally renovated. **I,** but lower rates off-season.

Comfort Inn (nr. dwntwn), 4610 De Soto St., CA 42109 (619/483-9800). 85 rms, A/C, cable color TV. AE, CB, DC, MC, V. Free parking, pool, 24-hr. coffee shop adj. Breakfast served daily. *Note:* New small motel next to the Mission Bay golf course. Comfortable, serviceable rms, some w. view. Friendly reception; efficient svce. 15 min. from dwntwn on I-5. Ideal if you're driving. **I,** but lower rates off-season.

Motel 6 (nr. dwntwn), 2424 Hotel Circle N., CA 92108 (619/296-1612). 202 rms, A/C, cable color TV. AE, DC, MC, V. Free parking, pool, adj. rest., free crib. *Note:* Unbeatable value a stone's throw from Mission Bay Park and Old Town. Serviceably comfortable. 8 min. from the airport, 10 min. from dwntwn. **B**

Accommodations in the Vicinity

Rancho Bernardo Inn (vic.), 17550 Bernardo Oaks Dr., Rancho Bernardo, CA 92128 (619/487-1611; toll free 800/854-1065). 287 rms, A/C, color TV, in-rm movies. AE, CB, DC, MC, V. Free parking, two pools, health club, sauna, massage, five golf courses, 12 tennis courts, putting green, horseback riding, bicycling, two-rests. (including El Bizcocho), bars, rm svce, disco, concierge, free crib. *Note:* Luxurious sports-lover's paradise w. five golf courses and 12 tennis courts, nr. Wild Animal Park and 30 min. from dwntwn. Charming Spanish Mission decor; spacious, elegant rms w. balconies or private patios among 265 acres (108ha) of courtyards, patios and flowered landscape. Excellent svce; young, upscale crowd. Well-known tennis school; interesting golf and tennis packages. The ideal vacation hotel. **VE,** but lower rates off-season.

Airport Accommodations

♔♔♔ **Sheraton Harbor Island** (nr. dwntwn), 1380 Harbor Island Dr., CA 92101 (619/291-2900; toll free, see Sheraton). 712 rms, A/C, color TV, in-rm movies. AE, CB, DC, MC, V. Valet parking $11, three pools, health club, spa, massage, sauna, four tennis courts, marina, boating, two rests. (including Spencer's), two bars, 24-hr. rm svce, nightclub, boutiques, concierge, free crib. *Note:* Large, luxurious, modern airport hotel w. very comprehensive facilities. Comfortable rms w. balconies, the best overlooking the bay or the marina. Efficient svce. VIP suites on the top three floors; beautiful grdns. Business clientele; 2 min. from the airport (free limo). One of the best places to stay in San Diego. **E–VE**

♔ **Travelodge Airport** (nr. dwntwn), 2353 Pacific Hwy., CA 92101 (619/232-8931; toll free, see Travelodge). 74 rms, A/C, cable color TV. AE, CB, DC, MC, V. Free parking, pool, rest. nearby. *Note:* Conventional but well-run small motel 3 min. from the airport (free shuttle) and 5 min. from dwntwn. Functional comfort; friendly svce. Very good value. **I**

YMCA/Youth Hostels

Elliot–Point Loma Hostel (nr. dwntwn), 3790 Udall St., CA 92107 (619/223-4778). 60 beds. Youth hostel near Mission Bay Park.

YMCA (dwntwn), 500 W. Broadway, CA 92101 (619/232-1133). 265 rms. Pool, health club, rest. Men and women; also youth-hostel members. Very central.

RESTAURANTS

Personal Favorites (in order of preference)

♙♙♙♙ **Mille Fleurs** (vic.), 6009 Paseo Delicias (Country Sq. Courtyard), Rancho Santa Fe (756-3085). A/C. Lunch Mon–Fri, dinner daily; closed Thanksgiving, Dec 25. AE, CB, DC, MC, V. Jkt. *Specialties:* mixed salads, salmon in honey-mustard sauce, fresh homemade foie gras w. red-cabbage salad in sherry vinaigrette, rack of Sonoma baby lamb w. garden vegetables, filet of turbot encrusted w. fresh herbs, rib-eye steak of Angus beef w. Roquefort-and-tarragon sauce, veal chop w. morel mushrooms, excellent desserts (try the Bavarian cream w. chocolate mousse). Menu changes regularly. Large wine list. *Note:* Wizard-chef Martin Woesle, an outstanding sauces creator, was trained at Munich's famous L'Aubergine French rest., which boasts three stars in Michelin. French-inspired nouvelle cuisine, sophisticated and light-handed. Charming, cozy Hispano-Moorish decor w. old mosaics, and pretty patio—as romantic a setting as anyone could wish. Top-notch svce staff. Resv. a must. 25 min. from dwntwn. One of the finest rests. in the country. *French.* **E–VE**

♙♙♙ **Cindy Black's** (vic.), 5721 La Jolla Blvd., La Jolla (456-6299). A/C. Lunch Fri only, dinner nightly. MC, V. Jkt. *Specialties:* grilled portobello mushrooms, Provençal chicken stew, risotto w. chipolata sausage, roast leg of lamb w. basil-and-garlic mousse, grilled duck w. fried ginger shreds on a bed of leeks, seasonal vegetable risotto, steamed garlic clams w. green chili rouille. Seasonal menu. Limited but reasonably priced wine list. *Note:* Talented Cindy Black, who rose to fame as chef at the renowned (but now closed) Sheppard's Restaurant a few years back, has now decided to fly solo. Her new rest., opened early in 1990, has consistently drawn crowds. Attractive flower-adorned setting. Excellent svce; resv. a must. A very fine place. *Continental.* **M**

🍸🍸🍸 **George's at the Cove** (vic.), 1250 Prospect St., La Jolla (454-4244). A/C. Lunch/dinner daily. AE, CB, DC, MC, V. *Specialties:* fettuccine w. rock shrimp, quesadillas w. Jamaican jerk chicken, lamb roast braised in Cabernet Sauvignon, char-broiled swordfish w. capers in a basil-vinaigrette marinade, tiramisù. 150-item wine list. *Note:* Offering creative California cuisine w. an emphasis on fresh seafood, this chic but informal rest. has a sober decor and a postcard view of La Jolla's famous cove. Umbrellaed terrace for outdoor dining. Amateurish but cheerful svce. Trendy clientele. Resv. advised. Valet parking. *Californian/Seafood.* **M–E**

☼🍸🍸 **Dobson's** (dwntwn), 956 Broadway Circle (231-6771). A/C. Lunch Mon–Fri, dinner Mon–Sat. AE, MC, V. Jkt. *Specialties:* mussel bisque, oysters w. white butter and caviar, rack of lamb in bordelaise sauce, broiled salmon w. three kinds of peppercorns, sautéed scallops Provençal, médaillon of veal w. morel mushrooms, gâteau St. Honoré. Daily menu. *Note:* Historic old pub, now a hangout for politicians, yuppies, and local businesspeople, particularly at lunch. Nice turn-of-the-century decor agreeably restored. Ask for a table upstairs w. a view of the bar. Usually a lively place; very good food in the heart of dwntwn. Resv. a must. *Continental.* **M**

🍸🍸 **Il Fornaio** (vic.), 1555 Camino del Mar, Del Mar (755-8876). Lunch Mon–Fri, dinner nightly, brunch Sat–Sun; closed July 4, Dec 25. *Specialties:* baked focaccia w. Parma prosciutto, grana arugula, and truffle oil; roasted duck w. balsamic vinegar and rosemary; osso bucco w. soft polenta; Angus porterhouse steak marinated in olive oil and rosemary; three-layer chocolate terrine. Decently priced list of Californian and Italian wines. *Note:* The frescos trimming the walls and the Carrara marble covering the counters make for an authentically Italian dining experience, only to be augmented by a menu of Northern Italian classics and an astounding view. Locally, a favorite. Patio dining. Courteous, helpful svce. 30-min drive from dwntwn. Resv. recommended. *Italian.* **I–M**

☼🍸 **Casa de Bandini** (nr. dwntwn), 2574 Calhoun St., Old Town (297-8211). A/C. Lunch/dinner daily; closed hols. AE, CB, DC, MC, V. *Specialties:* crabmeat enchiladas, chimichangas, burritos, fish Veracruz style. Giant margaritas. *Note:* Surrounded by grdns, flowers, and fountains, this enchanting house built in 1829 by a rich Mexican businessman, Juan Bandini, belongs in a museum of Spanish Colonial architecture. The food draws on traditional Mexican and California recipes; the fish is unusually good. Svce and atmosphere as colorful as the setting; mariachi bands. A must for every visitor. Reserve ahead. *Mexican.* **I**

☼🍸 **Point Loma Seafoods** (nr. dwntwn), 2805 Emerson St. (223-1109). A/C. Lunch/dinner daily (till 8pm); closed hols. No credit cards. *Specialties:* crabmeat sandwiches, seafood salad, fish taquitos, fried shellfish, broiled or hickory-smoked fish. *Note:* Local seafood-lovers have been coming here for more than 30 years. Point Loma Seafoods, both fishmarket and café, lays claim to "the freshest fish in town"—and you can see them being offloaded from the nearby boats! Inviting patio overlooking harbor and bay. Relaxed setting and svce. No resv.; excellent value. *Seafood.* **B–I**

Other Restaurants (from top bracket to budget)

🍸🍸🍸 **Marius** (nr. dwntwn), in the Meridien Hotel, 2000 2nd St., Coronado (435-3000). A/C. Dinner only, Tues–Sun. AE, CB, DC, MC, V. J&T. *Specialties:* wild-mushroom ravioli w. herbed butter, Napoleon of smoked salmon w. truffle sauce, roasted Maine lobster w. vanilla butter, sautéed foie gras, turban of Dover sole w. leek-salmon sauce, sea scallops w. Cabernet-Sauvignon butter, excellent desserts. Opulent wine list. *Note:* The palace rest. in all its majesty. The Provençal-inspired cooking contrives to be sophisticated and simple at once. Cushy, sophisticated setting w. wonderful flower arrangements. Attentive svce in the French manner. Resv. highly advisable. 15 min. from dwntwn; valet parking. A favorite place w. those in-the-know. *French.* **E**

    ♈♈♈ **Grant Grill & Lounge** (dwntwn), in the U.S. Grant (see "Accommodations," above) (239-6806). A/C. Breakfast/ lunch/dinner daily, brunch Sat–Sun. AE, CB, DC, MC, V. *Specialties:* mock turtle soup, sautéed trout w. Japanese seaweed and melon-liqueur sauce, quail stuffed w. peaches and macadamia nuts, grilled seafood. Superior wine list. *Note:* Venerable (1910), clubby dining rm filled w. mahogany wood, brass fixtures, and English hunting prints. Continental cuisine elegantly prepared and served. Resv. recommended. *Continental.* **M–E**

    ☼♈♈♈ **Top O' the Cove** (vic.), 1216 Prospect St., La Jolla (454-7779). A/C. Lunch/dinner daily, brunch Sun; closed hols. AE, MC, V. Jkt. *Specialties:* rack of lamb w. garlic and rosemary sauce, pan-seared sirloin w. madeira wine, foie gras w. wild mushrooms. Huge wine list w. more than 900 selections. *Note:* Chef Julius Semon's dishes are delicate and inventive; the English country-cottage setting is acceptably luxurious, the ocean view magnificent, and the crowd well-heeled, including many stars of both large and small screen. The check is also gilt-edged. Resv. required. Valet parking. *Seafood/ Continental.* **M–E**

    ♈♈ **Pacifica Grill** (dwntwn), 1202 Kettner Blvd. (696-9226). A/C. Lunch Mon–Fri, dinner nightly; closed hols. AE, CB, DC, MC, V. *Specialties:* shrimp-and-chicken pot stickers w. roasted corn-cream sauce, New Zealand green-lip mussels w. garlic and white wine, takoshimi of peppered Hawaiian ahi w. Chinese salsa, grilled lamb chops w. Cabernet sauce, crème brûlée. *Note:* This elegant rest., on the atrium balcony of a shrewdly restored old warehouse, specializes in original and eclectic, Pacific-southwestern cuisine. Excellent svce; resv. a must. Next to the Amtrak station in the heart of dwntwn. Valet parking $2. *American.* **M**

    ♈♈ **Fio's** (dwntwn), 801 Fifth Ave. (234-3467). A/C. Lunch Mon–Fri, dinner nightly. AE, CB, DC, MC, V. *Specialties:* wood-fired oven pizzas, innovative pasta dishes, fried calamari, osso buco w. risotto milanese, amaretto and hazelnut cheesecake. Moderate wine list. *Note:* The "in" place since it opened in 1990, this lively and noisy Gaslamp Quarter rest. offers solid Italian fare and gourmet pizzas. Stylish setting w. postmodern overtones and theatrical murals. Enthusiastic, though harried, and slow svce. Popular w. San Diego media types and VIPs. Resv. necessary. *Italian.* **M**

    ♈♈ **Jake's Del Mar** (vic.), 1660 Coast Blvd., Del Mar (755-2002). Lunch Tues–Fri, dinner nightly, brunch Sun; closed Thanksgiving, Dec 25. AE, MC, V. *Specialties:* grilled basil prawns w. prosciutto, fresh ahi Szechuan, rack of New Zealand lamb w. mint-mango chutney butter, seafood pasta Provençal, Kimo's hula pie. List of very moderately priced Californian wines. *Note:* The dramatic view is as much a reason to go as is the food. Clever seafood preparations using the freshest of catches. Well worth the 30-min drive from dwntwn. Resv. recommended. Inside is totally nonsmoking. Other location: 570 Marina Pkwy, South Bay (476-0400). *Seafood/Continental.* **I–M**

    ♈ **Liaison** (nr. dwntwn), 2202 Fourth Ave. (234-5540). A/C. Lunch Tues–Fri, dinner nightly. AE, MC, V. *Specialties:* escargots, veal normande w. demi-glace, lamb curry, medallions of beef béarnaise, roast duckling à l'orange, salmon au beurre d'écrevisse, filet mignon au poivre, soufflé Grand Marnier. 5-course prix-fixe menu. The menu changes regularly. *Note:* The menu selection of this cozy bistro w. dark-wood beams and tangles of greenery is posted in chalk on a blackboard in the best French tradition. Hearty, bourgeois fare at bargain-basement prices. Resv. advised. *French.* **I**

    La Gran Tapa (dwntwn), 611 B St. (234-8272). A/C. Lunch Mon–Fri, dinner nightly; closed hols. AE, MC, V. *Specialties:* black-bean soup, spiced lamb skewers, gambas al ajillo (shrimp w. pepper and garlic), deep-fried calamari, Catalan-style snails, empanadas w. ground-beef or wild-mushroom filling, so-so desserts. Good selection of sherries and Spanish wines. *Note:* You could easily believe you were in a real Madrid *tasca* when you visit this congenial bar serving tapas (hot and cold Spanish hors d'oeuvres). Warm, inviting wood-paneled decor; diligent svce. A theater-district rest., crowded before and after the show. Resv. advised. *Spanish.* **I**

    Tom Ham's Lighthouse (nr. dwntwn), 2150 Harbor Island Dr. (291-9110). A/C. Lunch Mon–Fri, dinner nightly, brunch Sun; closed Dec 25. AE, CB, DC, MC, V. *Specialties:* scallops, carne asada, broiled sea bass, steak. *Note:* In a genuine 19th-century lighthouse, this popular tourist rest. has a fine view of the bay and the city. Classical marine decor; very decent if not terribly imaginative food. Good svce; resv. advised. Good value. *Steak/Seafood.* **I**

    La Tour Eiffel (nr. dwntwn), 412 University Ave., Hillcrest (298-5200). A/C. Lunch/dinner daily. AE, CB, DC, MC, V. *Specialties:* magret de canard, roast rack of lamb w. herb-and-Dijon sauce, lamb shank w. bordeaux sauce, veal scaloppine w. calvados sauce, salmon of sea bass w. velouté sauce, tarte tatin. *Note:* Another great bistro in San Diego serving excellent dishes from the Dijon region of France. Small setting w. very simple decor. Five-course prix-fixe menu at $17 is one of the city's best buys. Dignified French svce. Resv. recommended. *French.* **I**

    Alfonso's Hideaway (vic.), 1251 Prospect St., La Jolla (454-2232). A/C. Lunch/dinner daily. AE, MC, V. *Specialties:* carne asada, steak ranchero, burritos, chile colorado, tacos. *Note:* With the Mexican border only 18 mi. (26km) away, the Mexican food at Alfonso's cannot but be authentic. Some sauces are very spicy, but the steak ranchero is tasty. Charming shady patio. Often crowded and noisy; an excellent, colorful place, 25 min. from dwntwn. *Mexican.* **B–I**

    Emerald Chinese Seafood Restaurant (nr. dwntwn), 3709 Convoy St. (565-6888). Lunch/dinner daily. AE, DC, MC, V. *Specialties:* steamed chicken in lotus leaves, scallops w. black-bean sauce, dim sum, fried bean curd w. crabmeat sauce, sautéed dried squid w. yellow leek. *Note:* Endless list of truly exotic Cantonese fare. Pleasantly smart decor that doesn't get carried away in theme. Courteous svce. Some of the best Asian food to be found in the area. Resv. suggested. *Chinese/Seafood.* **B–I**

    Corvette Diner, Bar & Grill (nr. dwntwn), 3946 Fifth Ave. (542-1001). A/C. Lunch/dinner daily (until midnight); closed hols. AE, DC, MC, V. *Specialties:* burgers, meatloaf, chicken-fried steak, blue-plate specials, milkshakes. *Note:* Amusing 1950s-style diner complete w. old-fashioned soda fountain, assorted memorabilia, and a shiny red Corvette displayed nr. the bar. Very good mid-American diner fare. Lively (but noisy) atmosphere. Voted San Diego's favorite informal dining spot. No resv. *American.* **B–I**

    Kansas City Barbeque (dwntwn), 610 W. Market St. (231-9680). A/C. Lunch/dinner daily (till 2am). MC, V. *Specialties:* chicken and ribs combinations w. all the fixin's. Beer and wine. *Note:* Barbecue fans swear by the superb meat and sauces served in this rustic dwntwn eatery, where scenes from the movie *Top Gun* were shot. Resv. for parties of eight or more only. Good value. *American.* **B**

Cafeterias/Fast Food

    Hob Nob Hill (dwntwn), 2271 First Ave. (239-8176). Breakfast/lunch/dinner daily. AE, CB, DC, MC, V. *Specialties:* superb family cooking at very considerate prices: corned beef and cabbage, turkey croquettes, ham and yams, chicken-fried steak, roast pork w. apple sauce, very good homemade desserts. *Note:* A local landmark since 1946. The service is commendable but you may have a long wait; resv. advised.

BARS AND NIGHTCLUBS

Bodie's (dwntwn), 523 F St. (236-8988). Roomy bar w. some of the best local rock, blues, and rockabilly music live. Open nightly. Open jam Sun.

Cafe Lulu (dwntwn), 419 F St. (238-0114). A bohemian hangout featuring wine and beer, as well as good coffee. Open nightly.

Cannibal Bar (nr. dwntwn), in the Catamaran Hotel (see "Accommodations," above) (488-1081). Excellent live jazz and disco. Pleasant outdoor patio. Open Wed–Sun.

The Comedy Store (vic.), 916 Pearl St., La Jolla (454-9176). Comedy seven nights a week. Amateur nights Mon.

Croce's Restaurant & Jazz Bar (dwntwn), 802 Fifth Ave. (233-4355). Fashionably urban rest. and bar w. great live jazz and R&B every night.

Dick's Last Resort (nr. dwntwn), 345 Fourth Ave., in the Gaslamp Quarter (231-9100). Nightly rock, blues, or jazz in this wildly decorated atmosphere. Excellent beer selection from around the world. Also a pretty good rest. serving Southern fare in a bucket.

In Cahoots (vic.), 5373 Mission Center Rd., Mission Valley (291-8635). Very hot nightspot. DJs spin country favorites Mon–Sat; live bands.

Marine Room (vic.), 2000 Spindrift Dr., La Jolla (459-7222). This classy oceanfront lounge on the shore has a splendid view of the Pacific. Likable reception; ditto music. Good rest. adjoining. Open nightly.

Pal Joey's (nr. dwntwn), 5147 Waring Rd., Allied Gardens (286-7873). A rather kitschy big dance hall, 1930s style. Live Dixieland weekends. Near San Diego State University.

Patrick's II (dwntwn), 428 F St. (233-3077). Some of the best blues in San Diego is to be found at this hip-swing bar.

Whaling Bar (vic.), in the La Valencia Hotel in La Jolla (454-0771). Yuppie bar; also a decent rest.; well-heeled, trendy patrons. Open nightly.

NEARBY EXCURSIONS

☀☙ **ANZA BORREGO DESERT STATE PARK** (90 mi./ 144km NE via I-8, Calif. 79, and Calif. 78): 600,000 acres (240,000ha) of largely unexplored desert wilderness adjoining the **Salton Sea**, largest lake in California, 278 ft. (85m) below sea level in the **Colorado Desert** (sailing, water sports, abundant fishing). The contrast between the lake, dotted with holidaymakers, and the nearby desert is particularly striking. Two surfaced roads cross the park from side to side. Among its most remarkable sights are **Font's Point, Borrego Palm Canyon, Split Mountain,** and **Seventeen Palms Oasis.** When the desert plants and shrubs are in flower, late Jan to Apr, they are a sight to be seen. *Note:* Temperatures run very high in summer; be sure to carry drinking water. **Visitor center** open daily year round at Borrego Springs (619/767-5311). On the way, visit the mining town of Julian (see below).

Where to Stay

☀☙☙☙ **La Casa del Zorro,** Yaqui Pass at Borrego Springs Rd., Borrego Springs, CA 92004 (619/767-5323; toll free 800/824-1884). 77 rms. AE, CB, DC, MC, V. Luxurious 1930s oasis hotel in the middle of the desert. Three pools, adj. golf course, highly regarded rest. **M–VE**

☀☙ **LA JOLLA** (pronounced "La Hoya"; 12 mi./19km NW via I-5, Ardath Rd., and Torrey Pines Rd.): The fashionable place for a summer home, the California equivalent of Palm Beach or Saint Tropez.

Lovely beaches, luxurious oceanfront homes, trendy shops, and restaurants. You ought to visit the **Museum of Contemporary Art** with its very fine modern-art collection; and the **Birch Aquarium-Museum,** one of the most famous museums of oceanography in the world (see "Museums of Art" and "Museums of Science and History," above).

MINING TOWNS: ☀☖ **Julian,** 64 mi. (102km) NE via I-8 and Calif. 79: This picturesque prospectors' town, which had several thousand inhabitants in 1885 and barely 1,300 today, still boasts many buildings preserved from its adventurous past, including the very fine **Julian Hotel,** where Ulysses S. signed the register when it was a stop on the Butterfield Stagecoach route. Visit the legendary ☖ **Eagle Mine,** a gold mine dating from 1870, on C St. (765-0036); open daily.

Where to Stay

☀☖ **Julian Hotel,** Julian, CA 92036 (619/765-0201). 18 rms. AE, MC, V. **M–E**

☖ **Julian Lodge,** 2720 C St. (Calif. 78), Julian, CA 92036 (619/765-1420). 23 rms. AE, MC, V. **I–M**

Where to Eat

☖ **Bailey Barbecue,** 2307 Main St. (765-9957). Open daily. MC, V. **B**

☀☖☖ **MOUNT PALOMAR OBSERVATORY** (65 mi./104km NE via I-15 and County Rd. S.6) (742-2119): One of the most famous astronomical observatories in the world; for two decades (until 1976) its 200-in. (508cm) telescope, with a 13-ton lens, was the largest in the world. An impressive sight. Visitors' gallery open daily. The surrounding mountains are very beautiful.

☖ **TIJUANA** (18 mi./28km south on I-5): Mexican border town, fake but colorful, full of pleasure spots intended for the tourist. Bullfights Sun May–Sept, dog track, horse races, casino, jai-alai Fri–Wed. For information, State Tourism Office, plaza Patria on bulevar Agua Caliente, or phone 52-66/81-94-92 or 81-94-93. Many tax-free craft shops and bazaars, including **Sara,** avenida Revolución 635; **Mercado Artesanía,** avenida Negrete and calle 1; **Dorian's Niños,** paseo de los Héroes and calle 2; **Tolan,** avenida Revolución 1111, opposite the jai-alai fronton; **Maxim,** avenida Revolución 717; and **Bazar Las Palomas,** calle 6 between Revolución and Madero. Open daily.

Avenida Revolución, near the main border-crossing point with the United States, is still dotted with noisy honky-tonks, cabarets, tattoo parlors, and strip joints catering, as in decades past, to young American men looking for female company.

Note: Foreign drivers must obtain temporary Mexican insurance, for sale at the border. Tourists may be unpleasantly surprised by Tijuana cab fares (see San Diego Trolley under "Guided Tours," above). No visa is necessary for U.S. citizens visiting Mexico, but they should bring either a passport or birth certificate, which is needed at the border to obtain a tourist permit. Tourists of other nationalities should consult the Mexican Consulate in San Diego, 610 A St. (231-8414).

Where to Eat

☖ **Los Arcos,** bulevar Salinas 210, at calle Escuadrón (86-31-71). Lunch/dinner daily. The best place in town for seafood. **I–M**

☖☖ **Pedrin's,** avenida Revolución 1115 (85-40-67). Lunch/dinner daily. Excellent fish/seafood rest. across from the jai-alai fronton. **I**

☖ **La Espadaña,** bulevar Sánchez Teboada 10813 (34-14-88). Breakfast/lunch/dinner daily. Good Mexican fare in an old hacienda atmosphere. **I**

PART EIGHT

HAWAII AND ALASKA

CHAPTER 56

HONOLULU AND THE HAWAIIAN ISLANDS♊

□ □ □

This mecca for honeymooners and vacationers, the "navel of the Pacific," or as it is also known, the "Aloha State" (*aloha* means "welcome" in Hawaiian), has only three industries: tourism, agriculture—and the armed services! The enormous base at **Pearl Harbor** is America's nerve center for Pacific defense. **Waikiki Beach** in Honolulu boasts the world's greatest concentration of hotels, far ahead of Florida, the Balearics, or Hong Kong: 220 hotels to the square mile (80 to the square kilometer), with a total of 40,000 rooms.

Discovered in 1778 by the famous British explorer Capt. James Cook (who was killed the following year by the Hawaiians), the islands have been endowed by nature with some of the planet's lushest landscapes. With its ideal climate and legendary natural beauty, the Aloha State attracts more than six million visitors every year, and some $7 billion of tourist money. Most of these visitors are Americans, but there are a growing number of Koreans, Japanese, Canadians, and Australians. The usual array of leis and pareos (wrap-around skirts) awaits the battalions of tourists who land every day on charter flights or in tour groups at Honolulu, capital of the state of Hawaii and principal city of the island of Oahu and of the entire archipelago.

Besides swimming and surfing on **Waikiki** and **Makaha Beaches,** the visitor will no doubt want to discover all the other local places of pilgrimage: **Pearl Harbor** (where the sunken U.S.S. *Arizona* impressively commemorates Japan's surprise attack on December 7, 1941, and attracts more than a million visitors a year); **Diamond Head,** a well-mannered volcano overlooking magnificent Honolulu Bay (*honolulu* means "abundance of peace" in Hawaiian); the splendid **State Capitol,** whose architecture contrives to be at once elegant and daring; **Punchbowl Crater,** a great military cemetery with an unforgettable view of the Waikiki skyscrapers and the ocean beyond; or the famous **Iolani Palace,** the only royal palace ever built on (what later became) American soil.

As with other cities that are financially and otherwise dependent on the tourist industry, Honolulu's Shangri-La image has its flip side: architecture is flashy, atmospheric pollution is bad, and local growth industries include prostitution and pickpocketing. Another drawback for the tourist is the high prices of everything from hotel rooms to T-shirts and snack foods.

Alone among the 50 states, Hawaii has a minority (24%) of Caucasian inhabitants. The five main islands of the chain have a population 48% Asian (23% Japanese, 12% Filipino, 5% Chinese), and 20% indigenous (more or less, reflecting many generations of intermarriage), that speaks Hawaiian, a Polynesian-derived language that has only five vowels and seven consonants.

Food is held in high honor in the islands, and some delectable surprises await you, such as pupu (Hawaiian appetizers), opakapaka (steamed fish), lomi-lomi (raw fish marinated with vegetables), laulau (pork and fish wrapped in taro leaves and cooked), mahimahi (slices of Pacific dolphin—the fish, not the mammal—fried or broiled), kalua (roast pork), or poi (a gruel made from taro).

The airlines flying between California and Hawaii offer very attractive excursion fares and discount packages for the various islands: in addition to **Oahu, Hawaii,** the largest, with its two active volcanoes (Mauna Loa and Kilauea); **Maui,** with its famous Haleakala nature reserve; **Molokai,** famous for its Polynesian temples, while **Kauai** offers a landscape devastated in most parts of the island as a result of Hurricane Iniki in September 1992.

The Hawaiian Islands were settled comparatively late: it was not until the 5th century of our era that the first inhabitants arrived from the Marquesas, followed four or five centuries later by Tahitians. For a long time the archipelago was wholly isolated from the rest of the world, developing a culture which, despite its Polynesian roots, was all its own. The first white missionaries and traders came in the 1820s; not far behind were the Chinese and Japanese fieldworkers destined for the pineapple and sugarcane plantations (Hawaii is today the largest sugar-growing state in the Union, and the world's largest producer of pineapples). Meanwhile, the indigenous population was decimated by imported diseases to which it had little natural resistance. Those of pure Hawaiian stock now account for only 1.3% of the population of the islands.

BASIC FACTS: Honolulu is the state capital of Hawaii (a word of Polynesian origin meaning "native country"). Area code: 808. Time zone: Hawaiian (six hours behind New York in spring and summer, five hours otherwise). ZIP Code: 96815. First European contact: 1778. U.S. possession since: 1898. Became the 50th state of the Union in 1959. Approximate population: city of Honolulu, 370,000; island of Oahu, 860,000; total for the state, 1,120,000.

CLIMATE: The subtropical climate of the Hawaiian Islands can best be described in a single word: delightful. The mean temperature in winter is 68°F (20°C) and in summer 77°F (28°C); from year's end to year's end it doesn't move far from these levels. Even in mid-Aug the nights are cool and pleasant, thanks to the trade winds. Hours of sunshine at all seasons reach levels unknown in less fortunate regions. Between Apr and Oct a south wind known as the "kona" often brings with it brief local downpours. The highest temperature recorded in downtown Honolulu was 88°F (31°C); the lowest was 57°F (14°C).

ARRIVAL & TRANSIT INFORMATION

AIRPORT: Honolulu International Airport (HNL), 5 mi. (8km) NW. For information, call 836-6413. The nation's fourth-largest international gateway.

U.S. AIRLINES: Aloha (toll free 800/367-5250), American (toll free 800/433-7300), Continental (toll free 800/525-0280), Hawaiian (toll free 800/367-5320), Northwest (toll free 800/225-2525), and United (toll free 800/241-6522).

FOREIGN CARRIERS: Air New Zealand (toll free 800/262-1234), Canadian International (toll free 800/426-7000), Japan Airlines (toll free 800/525-3663), Qantas (toll free 800/227-4500), and Singapore Airlines (toll free 800/742-3333).

CITY LINK: The **cab** fare to Waikiki is about $16–$18 (to dwntwn, $12); time, 20–25 min. Bus: **Airport Motor Coach Service** (839-0911) leaves approximately every 30 min., serving the principal Waikiki hotels; fare, $6; time, about 40 min. Cab fares are high, but the **public transportation (bus)** network is excellent and cheap. The many excursions around Honolulu, and the attractive car-rental rates available in Hawaii, make it advisable to rent a car with unlimited mileage.

CAR RENTAL (all at the Honolulu International Airport): Avis (toll free 800/331-1212); Budget (toll free 800/527-0700); Dollar (toll free 800/800-4000); Hertz (toll free 800/654-3011); National (toll free 800/227-7368); Tradewinds (834-1465), a local organization with good rates. For dwntwn locations, consult the telephone directory.

LIMOUSINE SERVICES: Aloha Limousines (955-0055), Carey Limousine (593-1422), and First Class Limousine (839-0944).

TAXIS: In theory cabs can't be hailed on the street, though in practice they often stop. You can phone for a cab from **Century Cab** (528-4655), **Charley's** (531-1333), or **Sida** (836-0011).

CITY BUSES: Both in and outside Honolulu, the best and cheapest (60¢) way of getting around is usually the bus service of the **Municipal Transit Lines,** informally called **"TheBUS."** Information is available in all hotels or from MTL, 811 Middle St. (848-5555).

INFORMATION & TOURS

TOURIST INFORMATION: Statewide, try the **Hawaii Visitors Bureau (HVB),** with headquarters in Honolulu at 2270 Kalakaua Ave., Suite 801, HI 96815 (808/923-1811).

GUIDED TOURS: Atlantis Submarine, 500 N. Nimitz Hwy. (973-8811): Explore the seabed of Honolulu Bay off Diamond Head in a 46-seat submarine with big portholes. The 45-min. trip takes place at a mean depth of 100 ft. (30m) so that you have a fine view of the underwater fauna and flora. Fascinating. Daily, year round. Leaves from the Hilton Hawaiian dock; fare, $75.
    E Noa Tours (bus), (599-2561): Guided minibus tour of the island; pickup at principal hotels.
    Gray Line Tours (bus) (833-8000): Guided bus tours of city and island; pickup at principal hotels.
    Pearl Harbor Cruises (boat), Kewalo Basin (536-3641): Three-hour boat tour of Pearl Harbor Bay and the U.S.S. *Arizona* Memorial; one departure daily, at 8:30am aboard the *Pearl Kai I* and *II.*
    Papillon Helicopters, Honolulu International Airport (836-1566): Spectacular helicopter trip over the bay and the island. Tours from 10 to 90 min.
    Waikiki Trolley (526-0112): Guided tour of Waikiki, Chinatown, and dwntwn Honolulu in a mock-up of an old-time streetcar. Board and leave as often as you like along the route. Highly recommended for a quick overview. Daily 8am–4:30pm; fare, $15.
    Windjammer Dinner Sail, Pier 7, Honolulu Harbor (537-1122): Entrancing sunset trip and dinner aboard a sailboat. Leaves at 5:15 every evening; resv. essential.

CRUISES: American Hawaii Cruises, 550 Kearny St., San Francisco, CA 94108 (415/392-9400; toll free 800/765-7000): Seven-night inter-island cruise departing Sat from Honolulu aboard the S.S. *Independence* and S.S. *Constitution,* each of 30,000 tons and a passenger capacity of 790. Year round. Cost, $1,050–$4,000 including transfers.

SIGHTS, ATTRACTIONS & ACTIVITIES

ARCHITECTURAL HIGHLIGHTS: ☀️🏛️ **State Capitol,** 400 S. Beretania St. (548-2211): This futuristic building, elegantly designed in the form of an open crater (a reference to the volcanic origins of the islands) and surrounded by tall columns symbolizing palm trees, houses the State Legislature. Built in 1969. Open Mon–Fri. In front of it, note the very fine statue of Queen Liliuokalani, who while a prisoner for nine months in 1894, after the demise of the monarchy, wrote the words of the famous song "Aloha O'e."

BEACHES: ☼ᴀ **Hanauma Beach,** 10 mi. (16km) east via Hi. 72: In its conspicuously beautiful setting, this beach is situated in the crater of an ancient volcano; scuba-diving. The beach where Burt Lancaster and Deborah Kerr had their romantic encounter in the movie *From Here to Eternity.*

ᴀ **Kahana Bay Beach Park,** 32 mi. (51km) north along Hi. 61 and Hi. 83: Deserted and peaceful, far away from the throngs of Waikiki.

ᴀ **Kailua Beach Park,** 25 mi. (40km) north along Hi. 61: All kinds of sailing; a quiet family beach. Great for windsurfing.

☼ᴀᴀ **Lanikai Beach,** 27 mi. (43km) NE on Hi. 61 and Kalaheo Dr.: A gem of white sand and azure water. Mokulua Island and the offshore reefs shelter the beach from strong currents. Crowded on weekends but often empty during the week.

ᴀ **Makaha Beach,** 38 mi. (60km) west by H-1 and Hi. 93: The champion surfers' beach; only for the seasoned athlete.

ᴀᴀ **Sunset Beach,** 46 mi. (73km) NW on H-1, H-2, Hi. 99, and Hi. 83: The most famous surfing beach in all the Hawaiian islands; safe in summer but dangerous in winter.

☼ᴀᴀ **Waikiki Beach,** Kalakaua Ave.: One of the world's most famous beaches, with 2½ mi. (4km) of sand overlooked by a forest of huge hotels. Often crowded. Good for novice surfers.

ᴀ **Waimanalo Beach Park,** 19 mi. (30km) east along Hi. 72: For hang-gliding enthusiasts. Spectacular views of the Koolau Mountains. Great for learning surfing because of the small, gentle waves.

☼ᴀᴀ **Waimea Beach Park,** 42 mi. (67km) NW by H-1, H-2, Hi. 99, and Hi. 83: Calm and safe in summer; only for experienced surfers in winter. In a magnificent setting.

☼ᴀ **Yokohama Bay Beach,** 43 mi. (69km) NW along H-1 and Hi. 93: Huge sandy beach; the water is sometimes rough but the sunsets are magnificent.

CHURCHES/SYNAGOGUES: ☼ᴀ **Kawaiahao Church,** 957 Punchbowl St. (522-1333): Nicknamed "The Westminster Abbey of the Pacific," this was the church of the kings of Hawaii from 1842 on. The classic ecclesiastical architecture makes use of an unconventional material: 14,000 blocks of coral cut from the local reefs! The tomb of King Lunalilo is in the garden. Services in Hawaiian and English every Sun, open daily.

ᴀ **Royal Mausoleum,** 2261 Nuuanu Ave. (537-1716): Contains the tombs of the former Hawaiian monarchs of the Kamehameha Dynasty; an unexpected cross-shaped Neo-Gothic chapel under the Pacific skies. Open Mon–Fri.

HISTORIC BUILDINGS: ᴀ **Iolani Palace,** King and Richards Sts. (538-1471): The only royal palace ever built on U.S. territory. It was erected by King David Kalakaua in 1882 and served as a prison for the last monarch, Queen Liliuokalani, in 1894. In the Florentine style; notice the throne room and the grand dining room. A historical curiosity set in beautiful gardens. Very popular public concerts on Fri. Guided tours Wed–Sat; resv. advised (522-0832).

ᴀ **Judiciary Building,** 417 South St.: Built in 1874, this neoclassical palace, which once housed the Hawaiian parliament, will look familiar to fans of the TV series "Hawaii Five-O," several episodes of which were filmed here; open Mon–Fri. Enthroned in front of the building is an imposing copy in gilded bronze of a statue of King Kamehameha I, called "The Napoleon of the Pacific" (the original is on the island of Hawaii). The king wears the *malo*, the great royal cape of feathers, and the traditional Hawaiian headdress. For his feast (Kamehameha Day, June 11), the statue is bedecked with a mass of leis, or necklaces of flowers.

Queen Emma's Summer Palace, 2913 Pali Hwy. (Hi. 61) (595-3167): This elegant Victorian (1843) house standing above the luxuriant Nuunau Valley was the summer residence of Queen Emma; after her husband King Kamehameha IV died in 1863, she retired here. Original furniture and decoration; many memorabilia of the Hawaiian monarchy. Handsome tropical gardens. Open daily.

Washington Place, Beretania and Miller Sts.: Washington Place, across from the state capitol, was built in 1846 by John Dominis, a wealthy sea captain and merchant who later became governor of Oahu. Since 1922 it has been the official residence of the governors of Hawaii. Fine Federal design with a colonnaded gallery encircling the building. No visitors.

MARKETS: ※▲ **Tamashiro Market,** 802 N. King St. (841-8047): Colorful Japanese market very close to the Bishop Museum; piles of fish and shellfish; lots of bustle; nice little Japanese restaurants. Open daily.

MONUMENTS: ※▲▲ **U.S.S.** *Arizona* **Memorial,** Halawa Gate Boat Landing, Pearl Harbor (422-0561): Impressive memorial erected in the center of Pearl Harbor Bay over the wreck of the battleship *Arizona*, which was sunk with 1,102 of the crew during the Japanese surprise attack on December 7, 1941. The museum, open Tues–Sun, attracts nearly 1.5 million visitors a year. U.S. Navy boats leave the visitor center for the memorial every 30 min. from 8am to 3pm.

MUSEUMS OF ART: ▲ **Contemporary Museum,** 2411 Makiki Heights Dr. (526-0232): Housed since 1988 in its new quarters here, this interesting museum of modern art displays works by 500 contemporaries from Andy Warhol to David Hockney (his remarkable stage set for *L'enfant et les sortilèges* is well worth seeing). Hawaiian artists such as Isami Doi, Madge Tennet, and Satoru Abe are prominently featured. Traveling exhibitions. Also offers a fine view of the city. Open Wed–Mon.

Honolulu Academy of Arts, 900 S. Beretania St. (532-8701): Graceful modern building with fine collections of Far Eastern (Chinese, Japanese, Korean) as well as European art, including such well-known names as Braque, van Gogh, Matisse, and Picasso. Among the best-known works on exhibition: Segna di Bonaventura's *Madonna and Child* and John Singleton Copley's portrait of Nathaniel Allen. Open Tues–Sun.

MUSEUMS OF SCIENCE & HISTORY: ※▲▲ **Bishop Museum,** 1525 Bernice St. (847-3511): This museum, founded in 1898, houses not only the world's richest collection of Polynesian art, but also a center for anthropological research unique in the Pacific Basin. As well as remarkable exhibits of historic objects and handcrafts, it offers regular performances of Hawaiian music and dance. There is also a planetarium. Open daily.

Fort de Russy Army Museum, Kalia Rd. (438-2821): A comprehensive museum of arms, from the primitive weapons used by the natives of Hawaii to those of World War II and Vietnam. For military-history buffs. Open Tues–Sun.

Hawaii Maritime Center, Pier 7, Honolulu Harbor (536-6373): Spanning centuries of Hawaiian maritime history, the center comprises interesting exhibits both indoor and outdoor, including the

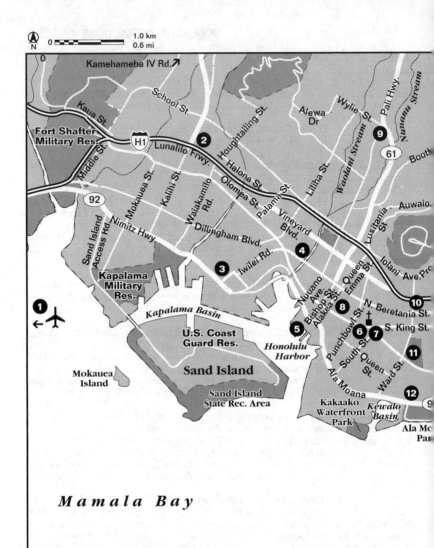

Kamehameha IV Rd. ↗

School St.

Kaua St.

Fort Shafter Military Res.

H1 Lunalilo Frwy.

Middle St.

92

Sand Island Access Rd

Nimitz Hwy.

Mokauea St.

Kalihi St.

Waiakamilo Rd.

Dillingham Blvd.

Halona St.

Olompa St.

Palama St.

Houghtailing St.

Alewa Dr

Wylie St.

Pali Hwy.

Nuuanu Stream

9

61

Booth

Lililha St.

Waolani Stream

Auwaio.

Lusitania St.

Iolani Ave. Pro

Vineyard Blvd.

Iwilei Rd.

❷

❸

❹

Kapalama Military Res.

Kapalama Basin

U.S. Coast Guard Res.

Sand Island

Honolulu Harbor

Nuuanu Ave.

Bishop St.

Alakea

❽

Queen St.

Emma St.

N. Beretania St.

❿

❺

❻ ❼

S. King St.

Punchbowl St.

South Queen St.

Ala Moana

⓫

⓬

Ward St.

9

Mokauea Island

Sand Island State Rec. Area

Kakaako Waterfront Park

Kewalo Basin

Ala Mo Par

Mamala Bay

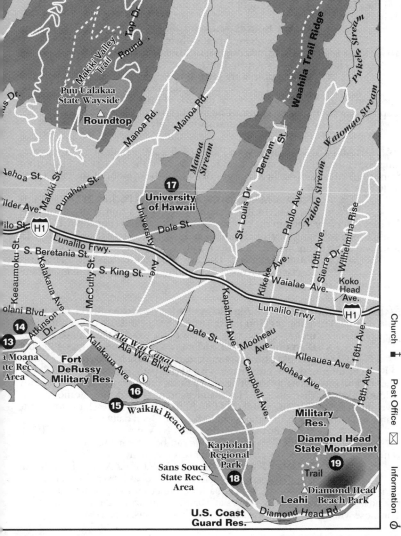

HONOLULU

Falls of Clyde, the world's only four-masted, full-rigged sailing ship still afloat, and the *Hokulea,* a re-created double-hulled traditional Polynesian canoe. Open daily.

    Mission Houses Museum, 553 King St. (531-0481): The three missionaries' houses here are the oldest on the islands, dating from 1821, and have their original furnishings and fittings. An interesting glimpse of Hawaiian history. Open daily.

    Pacific Submarine Museum, Bowfin Park, Kamehameha Bay (423-1341): New museum devoted to the age of the submarine from World War I to the present day. Many historical documents, photographs, and various objects culminating in a survivor of World War II, the U.S.S. *Bowfin,* which may be inspected in detail. Open daily.

PANORAMAS: Aloha Tower, Pier 8 (537-9260): Built in 1925, this was long the tallest building on the island. Fine view of the old city and its harbor from the 10th floor (reached by elevator). Once the symbol of the city. Open daily.

    National Memorial Cemetery of the Pacific, 2177 Puowaina Dr. (541-1430): Hawaii's most visited tourist site. From this military cemetery, lying in the crater of an extinct volcano (Punchbowl Crater), you'll have a sweeping view of Honolulu and the coast. More than 36,000 G.I.s who died in battle are buried here. Open daily.

    Round Top Park, Tantalus and Round Top Drs.: The most spectacular prospect of Honolulu, from a beautiful mountainside tropical park.

PARKS & GARDENS: Ala Moana Park, Ala Moana Blvd.: This lovely 76-acre (30ha) park fringes Honolulu's favorite beach, and also draws numerous joggers. Many picnic areas; unobstructed view of the bay and the Waikiki skyline.

    Diamond Head State Monument, Diamond Rd.: A 400,000-year-old extinct volcano, rearing its 760 ft. (232m) over Waikiki Bay. The interior of the crater may be visited (the path begins at Makalei Place). The volcano owes its name to 19th-century European sailors who mistook shiny volcanic glass for diamonds. A Hawaiian legend has it that the volcano was the dwelling-place of Pele, the goddess of fire. Allow 90 min. to reach the top of the crater and return; for information, call 548-7455. Open daily.

    Foster Botanic Garden, 180 N. Vineyard Blvd. (522-7066): All the flora of the Pacific can be seen at this one spot in the center of Honolulu; spectacular orchid house. Open daily.

    Kapiolani Park, Kalakaua and Montserrat Aves.: Hawaii's oldest public park, dating from 1877, boasts a very lovely rose garden, 38-acre (15ha) zoo, splendid aquarium, public concerts, Hawaiian dances ("Kodak Hula Show," Tues–Thurs at 10am; for information, call 833-1661). For those who like souvenir snapshots of their vacations. Open daily.

PERFORMING ARTS: For current listings of shows and cultural events, consult the entertainment pages of the two daily papers, *Honolulu Advertiser* (morning) and *Honolulu Star Bulletin* (evening), as well as the weekly *Sun Press* and the monthly *Honolulu.*

    Blaisdell Center Arena, Ward Ave. and King St. (521-2911): Rock concerts; star-studded shows.

    Blaisdell Concert Hall, Ward Ave. and King St. (591-2211): Home of the Honolulu Symphony Orchestra (principal conductor: Donald Johanos) Oct–May; also operatic performances Jan–Feb, recitals, etc.

    Diamondhead Theater, 520 Makapuu Ave. (734-0274): Home of the Diamondhead Community Theater, the islands' best stock company. Drama, comedy, and Broadway hits.

John F. Kennedy Theater, University of Hawaii, 1770 East-West Rd. (956-7655): Classical and modern theater, ballet.

Manoa Valley Theater, 2833 E. Manoa Rd. (988-6131): Home of the Hawaii Performing Arts Company. From Shakespeare to avant-garde theater to musical comedy in a delightfully rustic setting.

Waikiki Shell, Kapiolani Park (521-2911): Open-air concerts in summer, including a number by the Honolulu Symphony Orchestra.

SHOPPING: Ala Moana Center, Ala Moana Blvd. at Atkinson Dr.: One of the country's largest and newest shopping centers, with more than 200 stores and exotic restaurants. Open daily.

International Market Place, 2230 Kalakaua Ave.: For a quarter of a century this Polynesian version of a Middle Eastern open-air bazaar, with its lantern-decorated giant banyan tree, has been drawing strollers and shoppers in droves. There's a food court with 17 different types of foods. Open daily.

Royal Hawaiian Shopping Center, 2201 Kalakaua Ave.: Largest in the islands, laid out on three levels along Kalakaua Ave. From luxury fashion boutiques (Vuitton, Cartier, Chanel, etc.) to Hawaiian handcraft stores. Many cafés and restaurants. Street performers (mimes, jugglers, musicians, etc.) and open-air concerts. Open daily. Don't miss the fragrant lei-stringing shops lining Maunakea and Beretania Sts. Maile. Orchid leis cost about $12–$15. **Cindy's,** 115 N. Hotel St., probably has the best prices, selection, and staff.

SPECIAL EVENTS: For exact dates, consult the **Hawaii Visitors Bureau (HVB)** (see "Tourist Information," above).

Hula Bowl (mid-Jan): Annual college all-star game at Aloha Stadium.

Hawaiian Open International Golf Tournament (Jan): $1.1-million PGA golf tournament featuring top professional golfers. Waialae Golf and Country Club.

Chinese New Year (mid-Jan to Feb): Parades, costumed processions. Chinatown in Honolulu, and on the other islands.

King Kamehameha Celebration (June 11): Public holiday in honor of King Kamehameha I (c. 1738–1819), the first to establish his rule over the entire island chain. His statue in Honolulu is draped with many leis. Processions, floats—a very colorful occasion.

Japan Festival (July): The island's Japanese heritage is commemorated in Honolulu and Waikiki. Music, food, arts, etc.

Hula Festival (Aug): Hawaiian dancing (Honolulu).

Aloha Week (late Sept): Parades, concerts, dances, boat races in Honolulu and the other islands. The archipelago's biggest festival.

Ironman World Triathlon Championship (Oct): The most grueling sports event in the world: a 2.4-mi. (3.8km) swim, a 112-mi. (180km) bike ride, and a 26.2-mi. (42km) run at a stretch. For super-athletes only. Kailua Kona on the Big Island.

Surfing Championships (Nov–Dec): Professional and amateur events. Makaha Beach and the beaches on the North Shore of Oahu (Sunset and Waimea beaches, for example).

SPORTS: Deep-Sea Fishing: Thousands of deep-sea fishermen flock to Hawaii every year in (usually successful) pursuit of the local mahimahi (dolphinfish), ono (wahoo), ahi (yellowfin tuna), aku (skipjack tuna) or even, for the most venturesome, the renowned a'u (marlin). Reckon $500 for a full-day charter of eight hours, $400 for a half-day (four-hour) charter. Among the most reliable charter boats:

Honolulu: Island Charters (536-1555), *Coreene C* Charters (226-8421), and Blue Nun (596-2443).

Hawaii: Glen Hodson, Kailua Kona (329-6303); Kona Marina Charters, Kailua Kona (329-1115); and Ihu Nui Sport-fishing (885-4686).

Kauai: Anini Fishing Charters (828-1285), and Sport Fishing Kauai, Koloa (742-7013).

Maui: Ken Takashima, Lahaina (661-0480), and Gent-Lee Charters (245-7504).

STROLLS: 🏛 **Chinatown,** around King and Smith Sts.: Honolulu's picturesque Chinese quarter. Buddhist temple, open-air market, and restaurants by day; rather sleazy nightclubs and sex shops after dark. Visitor Center in Maunakea Marketplace (537-2586).

☀️ 🔭 **Waikiki,** along Kalakaua Ave.: The heart of the tourist's Honolulu, with dozens of skyscrapers, luxury hotels, restaurants, boutiques, and the world-renowned (and partly artificial) **Waikiki Beach,** nirvana of surfing and other water sports.

ACCOMMODATIONS

Personal Favorites (in order of preference)

☀️ 👑👑👑👑 **Halekulani Hotel** (nr. dwntwn), 2199 Kalia Rd., HI 96815 (808/923-2311; toll free, see Preferred). 456 rms, A/C, cable color TV. AE, CB, DC, MC, V. Free valet parking, pool, private beach, health club, three rests. (including La Mer), two bars, 24-hr. rm svce, nightclub, boutiques, hrdrsr, concierge. *Note:* Waikiki Beach's super-luxury hotel, set amid 5 acres (2ha) of flower grdns. This urbane ultramodern structure occupies the site of a 1920s predecessor, and retains a few vestiges of its distinguished past, notably the bar and two of the three rests. Luxuriously comfortable, spacious rms w. private verandas, minibars, and very complete facilities; most have an ocean view. The swimming pool, w. its enormous blue mosaic of an orchid, is worth a look all by itself. Svce and reception of the highest order make this one of the 12 best hotels in the country. Its name (*halekulani* means in Hawaiian "a house worthy of paradise") is well deserved. **VE.**

👑👑👑 **Hawaii Prince Hotel** (nr. dwntwn), 1677 Ala Moana Blvd. (at Holomoana St.), Honolulu, HI 96815 (808/956-1111; toll free 800/321-6248). 521 rms, A/C, color TV, in-rm movies. AE, CB, DC, MC, V. Valet parking $10, pool, health club, four rests. (including the Prince Court), rm svce, bar, boutiques, concierge. *Note:* On an episode of "Magnum P.I.," televiewers around the world watched the dynamiting of the old Kaiser-Permanente Hospital on this site; it was replaced by twin 32-story towers of a luxury hotel that opened early in 1990. The innovative design is by architect Ellerbe Becket. Spacious, very comfortable rms, each overlooking the ocean and Ala Wai Yacht Harbor, with minibar, VCR, and Italian-marble bathroom. Impeccable svce; good location away from the turmoil of Waikiki. Convention and tourist clientele. Free shuttle to/from dwntwn business district. **VE**

☀️ 👑👑👑 **Kahala Hilton** (vic.), 5000 Kahala Ave., HI 96816 (808/734-2211; toll free, see Hilton). 370 rms. A/C, color TV, in-rm movies. AE, CB, DC, MC, V. Valet-parking $5, beach, three rests. (including Maile), bars, 24-hr. rm svce, disco, hrdrsr, boutiques, free crib. *Note:* Plushy 12-story building and a group of charming bungalows, clustered around a tropical lagoon (w. dolphins), far from Waikiki's crowds. Lavish, comfortable rms w. refrigerators and private balconies; commanding views of the ocean or Diamond Head. Exemplary svce, and one of the city's finest rests. A jewel among local hotels since 1964; its guestbook has been signed by former President Reagan and Prince Charles of England, among others. 20 min. from dwntwn. **VE**

☀️ 👑👑 **Colony Surf** (nr. dwntwn), 2895 Kalakaua Ave., HI 96815 (808/923-5751; toll free 800/252-7873). 90 suites, A/C, cable color TV, AE, CB, DC, MC, V. Free parking, beach, two rests. (including Michel's), bar, rm svce, crib $15. *Note:* Charming small hotel opposite Kapiolani Park in the shadow of Diamond Head, offering remarkably spacious and comfortable studios and mini-suites w. kitchenettes, the best w. a splendid view of the ocean. Highly polished reception and svce. Michel's rest. does not wholly deserve its high reputation. The favorite hotel of those in-the-know. **E**

 🏨🏨 **New Otani Kaimana Beach** (nr. dwntwn), 2863 Kalakaua Ave., HI 96815 (808/923-1555; toll free 800/421-8795). 125 rms, A/C, cable color TV. AE, CB, DC, MC, V. Parking $6, beach, two rests. (including Hau Tree Lanai), bar, rm svce. *Note:* Of modest size compared to the giants of Waikiki Beach, this intimate, comfortable hotel is the favorite of Japanese businessmen. Friendly rms, a little on the skimpy side (ask for a double room). Excellent svce; very commendable (but very expensive) Japanese rest. Direct access to Sans Souci Beach. A good place to stay. **M–E**

 🏨 **Outrigger Waikiki Surf** (nr. dwntwn), 2200 Kuhio Ave., HI 96815 (808/923-7671; toll free 800/733-7777). 303 rms, A/C, color TV, in-rm movies. AE, CB, DC, MC, V. Parking $7, pool, nearby coffee shop, bar, free crib. *Note:* Honolulu's big bargain—modern, quiet, and well maintained, 5 min. from Waikiki Beach. Friendly reception. Attractive rms w. balconies, some w. kitchenettes. One of the best values in the city. Family clientele. Entirely renovated in 1988. **I–M**

 🏨 **Pleasant Holiday Isle** (nr. dwntwn), 270 Lewers St. (at Kalakana Ave.), Honolulu, HI 96815 (808/923-0777). 264 rms, A/C, color TV. AE, CB, DC, MC, V. Gar. $6, pool, bar, boutiques. *Note:* Relatively new tower right in the center of Waikiki and one block from the beach. Serviceably comfortable rms w. balcony. On the noisy side. Friendly reception and svce. Good value on balance. **I–M**

Other Accommodations (from top bracket to budget)

 ☼🏨🏨🏨🏨 **Sheraton Moana Surfrider** (nr. dwntwn), 2365 Kalakaua Ave., HI 96815 (808/922-3111; toll free, see Sheraton). 786 rms, A/C, color TV, in-rm movies. AE, CB, DC, MC, V. Valet gar. $13, pool, private beach, boating, three rests. (including Banyan Court), coffee shop, bar, 24-hr. rm svce, free crib. *Note:* The oldest (1901) palace hotel on the island, known as "the first lady of Waikiki." The Victorian decor was magnificently restored in 1989, and the building is a designated historic monument. Rms completely done over in pastel shades w. exotic furnishings and minibars. Lovely roof grdn. Direct beach access. Amelia Earhart and the Prince of Wales are among the celebrities who have stayed here. **VE**

 🏨🏨🏨 **Hilton Hawaiian Village** (nr. dwntwn), 2005 Kalia Rd., HI 96815 (808/949-4321; toll free, see Hilton). 2,524 rms, A/C, color TV, in-rm movies. AE, CB, DC, MC, V. Valet gar. $9, three pools, boating, beach, grdns, six rests. (including Bali-by-the-Sea), two coffee shops, five bars, 24-hr rm svce, Polynesian show, more than 100 boutiques (in the Rainbow Bazaar), hrdrsr, private docking, free crib. *Note:* The largest hotel in the Pacific, raising its four towers and its 38 floors above Waikiki Beach in the midst of 22 acres (9ha) of tropical grdns. Wonderful lagoon-style pool surrounded by palm trees. The rms in the Rainbow and the Tapa towers have a fine ocean view. Commendable comfort; efficient svce. Caters mostly to groups and conventions. Offers sailing trips in a catamaran. Recently underwent a $100-million rejuvenation. **VE**

 🏨🏨🏨 **Hyatt Regency Waikiki** (nr. dwntwn), 2424 Kalakaua Ave., HI 96815 (808/923-1234; toll free, see Hyatt). 1,234 rms, A/C, color TV, in-rm movies. AE, CB, DC, MC, V. Valet parking $10, pool, beach, boats, three rests. (including Ciao Mein), coffee shop, two bars, rm svce, 70 boutiques. *Note:* Twin 40-story towers dominating all of Waikiki Bay and constituting a sort of miniature city within the city. The 10-story lobby comes complete w. tropical forest, lagoon, and waterfalls; sumptuous and spectacular. Spacious, elegantly decorated rms w. private lanais, the best overlooking the beach, others the city. Impeccable comfort; exemplary svce. Two floors reserved for VIPs. **VE**

☀ ♨♨♨ **Sheraton Royal Hawaiian Hotel** (nr. dwntwn), 2259 Kalakaua Ave., HI 96815 (808/923-7311; toll free, see Sheraton). 525 rms, A/C, color TV, in-rm movies. AE, CB, DC, MC, V. Parking $6, pool, beach, two rests. (including the Monarch Room), coffee shop, bars, 24-hr. rm svce, Polynesian show. *Note:* "The hotel of kings and presidents," a 1920s palace known as "the pink lady" because of its pastel-colored Spanish-Moorish facade. Loads of rococo charm. Most rms are huge and comfortable but some are a little cramped (avoid those in the new wings). Efficient svce. Luau on Mon. Beautiful tropical grdns. Caters mostly to vacationers. **VE**

♨♨♨ **Outrigger Waikiki** (nr. dwntwn), 2335 Kalakaua Ave., HI 96815 (808/923-0711; toll free 800/733-7777). 530 rms, A/C, color TV, in-rm movies. AE, CB, DC, MC, V. Gar. $7, pool, beach, health club, spa, boats, seven rests. (including Monterey Bay Canners), coffee shop, bars, rm svce, nightclub, boutiques. *Note:* The flagship property of the Hawaiian's Outrigger chain. This elegant 15-story tower located right on the middle of Waikiki Beach has recently completed a $45-million renovation. Comfortable guest rms in refreshing pastels w. lanai and refrigerators, many w. ocean view. Efficient reception and svce. One of the best-priced beachfront hotels. A vacationer's favorite. **E–VE**

♨♨ **Waikiki Parc Hotel** (nr. dwntwn), 2233 Helumoa St., HI 96815 (808/921-7272; toll free 800/422-0450). 298 rms, A/C, cable color TV. AE, CB, DC, MC, V. Valet gar. $7, pool, two rests., rm svce, free crib. *Note:* The plainer, cheaper younger brother of the renowned Halekulani Hotel next door. New and comfortable; elegant decor and furnishings. Polished Japanese-style svce. A fine place almost on the beach. **E–VE**

♨♨ **Hawaiian Waikiki Beach** (nr. dwntwn), 2570 Kalakaua Ave., HI 96815 (808/922-2511). 715 rms, A/C, color TV, in-rm movies. AE, CB, DC, MC, V. Parking $3, pool, rest., coffee shop, bar, rm svce, nightclub, free crib. *Note:* A typical Holiday Inn right on Waikiki Beach, most w. a splendid view of the ocean and Diamond Head. Modern and functional; group clientele. Captain's Table is a very decent rest. Good value out of season. **M–E,** but lower rates off-season.

♨♨ **Inn on the Park** (nr. dwntwn), 1920 Ala Moana Blvd., HI 96815 (808/946-8355; toll free 800/922-7866). 230 rms, A/C, cable color TV. AE, CB, DC, MC, V. Parking $6, pool, rest., crib $8. *Note:* Modern, comfortable hotel. Rms w. terraces and refrigerators, some overlooking the ocean. Good value overall. **I–M,** but lower rates off-season.

♨♨ **Ocean Resort Hotel** (nr. dwntwn), 175 Paoakalani Ave. (808/922-3861). 451 rms, A/C, color TV, in-rm movies. AE, CB, DC, MC, V. Gar. $5, two pools, rest., bar, rm svce. *Note:* Large resort hotel offering sound value. Inviting, comfortable rms (ask for the newer Pali Tower), most w. kitchenette. Efficient reception and svce. One block from Kapiolani Park and the beach. Fine for families. **I–M**

♨ **Aloha Surf Hotel** (nr. dwntwn), 444 Kanekapolei St., HI 96815 (808/923-0222; toll free 800/367-5205). 204 rms, A/C, color TV. AE, CB, DC, MC, V. Parking $6, rest., crib $5. *Note:* Modest but pleasant, well-run hotel, recently modernized, away from the hurly-burly of Waikiki. Good value 5 min. from the beach. **I–M**

♨ **Outrigger Edgewater** (nr. dwntwn), 2168 Kalia Rd., HI 96815 (808/922-6424; toll free 800/367-5170). 184 rms, A/C, color TV, in-rm movies. AE, CB, DC, MC, V. Parking $7, pool, four rests. (including Trattoria), three bars, rm svce, shops, free crib. *Note:* Serviceable comfort and smiling svce. Enticing Italian rest.; some rms w. kitchenettes. Very good value, a few steps from the beach. **I–M**

♨ **Outrigger Royal Islander** (nr. dwntwn), 2164 Kalia Rd., HI 96815 (808/922-1961; toll free 800/367-5170). 98 rms, A/C, color TV. AE, CB, DC, MC, V. Parking $7, rest. *Note:* Contemporary comfort; somewhat cramped rms w. terraces and a view of Waikiki Beach. Overall good value. **I–M**

♀ **Royal Grove Hotel** (nr. dwntwn), 151 Uluniu Ave., HI 96815 (808/923-7691). 90 studios and mini-apts, A/C, cable color TV. AE, DC, MC, V. On-street parking, pool, two rests. *Note:* Charming rose-colored residential hotel w. only comfortable studios or mini-suites; each has a private balcony and kitchenette. Two blocks from Waikiki Beach. Very good value. **B–I**

Airport Accommodations

♀♀ **Best Western Plaza Hotel** (formerly the Ramada; vic.), 3253 N. Nimitz Hwy., HI 96819 (808/836-3636; toll free, see Best Western). 274 rms, A/C, color TV, in-rm movies. AE, CB, DC, MC, V. Free parking, pool, rest., bar, rm svce, nightclub. *Note:* Modern, friendly eight-story motel 3 min. from the airport and 25 min. from Waikiki. Comfortable rms w. refrigerators; cordial reception and svce. The best place to stay for a stopover between flights, w. free 24-hr. airport limousine svce. 5 min. from Aloha Stadium, 10 min. from Pearl Harbor. **M,** but lower rates off-season.

Accommodations Around the Island of Oahu

☼♀♀♀ **Hilton Turtle Bay,** 57-091 Kamehameha Hwy., Kahuku, HI 96731 (808/293-8811; toll free, see Hilton). 487 rms and cottages, A/C, color TV, in-rm movies. AE, CB, DC, MC, V. Parking $3.50, two pools, two golf courses, 10 tennis courts, horseback riding, water sports, beach, two rests. (including Cove), coffee shop, two bars, rm svce, disco, hrdrsr, boutiques. *Note:* Luxury hotel in the middle of a 5-mi. (8km) beach on the north shore of the island, 1½ hr. by car from Honolulu. Luxury in peace. The huge, comfortable rms overlook the ocean. Excellent svce; very good sports facilities, w. golf course designed by Arnold Palmer. For lovers of tranquility and of nature. **E–VE**

YMCA/Youth Hostel

Hale Aloha Youth Hostel (nr. dwntwn), 2417 Prince Edward St., HI 96815 (808/926-8313). 50 beds. Two blocks off Waikiki Beach. Resv. required.

Manoa Hostel (nr. dwntwn), 2323A Seaview Ave., HI 96822 (808/946-0591). 40 beds. Clean, well-run youth hostel nr. the university.

RESTAURANTS

A Note on Hawaiian Food: Hawaiian cuisine, a blend of Polynesian and Asian (Philippine, Chinese, Japanese, and Korean) strains, draws extensively on local produce simply prepared: pork, fish, taro leaves, sweet potatoes, Maui onions, avocado, pineapple, guava, etc. Typical dishes include the following:

haupia: coconut pudding.
laulau: pork, taro, and fish, steamed, wrapped in the leaves of the ti plant.
lilikoi: passion fruit, a local favorite.
lomi-lomi: strips of raw salmon with tomatoes and green onions.
mahimahi: Pacific dolphin (fish) roast, broiled or fried.
malasadas: sugared doughnuts eaten hot.
manapua: dumplings stuffed with roast suckling pig.
poi: paste of boiled taro flour, the Hawaiian substitute for potatoes.

Personal Favorites (in order of preference)

☼♀♀♀♀ **La Mer** (nr. dwntwn), in the Halekulani Hotel (see "Accommodations," above) (923-2311). A/C. Dinner only, nightly. AE, CB, DC, MC, V. Jkt. *Specialties:* broiled squab, whole red snapper baked in a rock-salt crust, warm duck salad w. papaya and truffles, spinach custard, filet of beef w. sweet peppers, sautéed curried moana, gratin of strawberries; excellent desserts. Menu changes regularly. *Note:* Occupying the original 1920s building of the old Halekulani Hotel, this magnificent rest. looking out to sea is the most elegant, the most polished, and the most costly in Honolulu. Superb, inspired French-Polynesian nouvelle cuisine from chef George Mavrothalassitis; first-class svce. The sound of the surf on the nearby beach underlines the elegance of the decor. One of the best rests. in the country, w. prices to match. Resv. a must. Valet parking. *French/Seafood.* **E–VE**

☀☆♔♔♔ **John Dominis** (dwntwn), 43 Ahui St. (523-0955). A/C. Dinner nightly, brunch Sun. AE, CB, DC, MC, V. Jkt. *Specialties:* every kind of Pacific seafood oven-broiled or cooked in its broth, clam chowder, cioppino fish-and-prawns dish, macadamia-nut cream pie. Good wine list. *Note:* One of the best, and handsomest, rests. in all the islands. Absolutely fresh-caught fish and shellfish. Splendid glass-walled dining rm, from which you can see the sea creatures swimming in their saltwater holding pools carved out of living rock. Splendid view of the harbor, w. Diamond Head in the distance. Cordial, smiling svce; friendly bar; the favorite of the local smart set. Resv. advised. *Seafood/ Polynesian.* **E–VE**

♔♔♔ **Roy's** (vic.), 6600 Kalanianaole Hwy., Hawaii Kai (396-7697). A/C. Dinner only, nightly. AE, MC, V. *Specialties:* dim sum, mesquite-grilled chicken, pizzas, broiled shrimp in curry-chutney sauce, scallops w. ginger-and-basil sauce. Menu changes regularly. *Note:* The young and talented chef Roy Yamaguchi opened this very up-to-date establishment in 1989 in the residential suburb of Hawaii Kai. His cuisine is a happy blend of Oriental ingredients and California style. The second-floor dining rm has a fine view of Maunalua Bay and the mountains. Warm, attentive svce. Well worth the 20-min. drive from Waikiki. The most popular eatery in Honolulu. Resv. a must. *American/Asian.* **M–E**

♔♔ **Uraku** (nr. dwntwn), 1341 Kapiolani Blvd. (951-5111). A/C. Dinner only, nightly; closed hols. AE, CB, DC, MC, V. *Specialties:* bento (assortment of Japanese dishes), ahi (yellowfin tuna) tartar, duck appetizer w. buckwheat crêpes, smoked rack of lamb, fresh seafood, tiramisù. The menu changes regularly. Small, select, but pricey wine list. *Note:* Continental and Oriental nouvelle cuisines elegantly combined by master chef Yoshimi Saito: Both the menu and the presentation are peerless. Serene, refined atmosphere. Very attentive svce. The new "in" place in Honolulu. Resv. highly advised. *Continental/Asian.* **M**

♔♔ **Kyo-Ya** (nr. dwntwn), 2057 Kalakaua Ave. (947-3911). A/C. Lunch Mon–Sat, dinner daily; closed hols. AE, DC, MC, V. *Specialties:* sushi, sukiyaki, shabu shabu, tempura, kaiseki dinner. *Note:* After a $15-million, two-year renovation this Waikiki landmark rest. is again open for business. Chef Shizuo Tsubata expertly prepares some of the best Japanese food this side of the Pacific, w. ingredients that change w. the four seasons. Great care has been taken to provide a relaxed Japanese atmosphere. Flawless svce. Tatami rms available for purists. *Japanese.* **I–M**

☀☆♔ **Fisherman's Wharf** (nr. dwntwn), 1009 Ala Moana Blvd. (538-3808). A/C. Lunch/dinner daily. AE, CB, DC, MC, V. *Specialties:* every variety of Pacific seafood, absolutely fresh and at prices easy on your wallet; shrimp Louie salad, clam chowder, cioppino, scampi sautéed in garlic butter. *Note:* Honolulu's most popular fish rest. for three decades; often crowded and noisy, in spite of which the waitresses contrive to work miracles. Pleasant nautical decor and pretty view of Kewalo yacht basin. Resv. recommended. *Seafood.* **I–M**

♔ **Kim Chee Two** (nr. dwntwn), 3569 Waialae Ave. (737-0006). A/C. Lunch/dinner daily. MC, V. *Specialties:* seaweed soup, bi bim kook soo (noodles w. meat and vegetables), man doo (fried dumplings stuffed w. pork, cabbage, and tofu), barbecued chicken and meat dishes, fried yellowfish w. rice and vegetables. *Note:* The readers of *Honolulu* magazine picked this as Honolulu's best Korean rest. for three years in a row—a noteworthy decision in a city where Korean food has long been respected. Some dynamite condiments, but overall the flavors are subdued, the servings generous, and the prices low. The decor adds nothing, and the place is often noisy. Very popular locally. Other location: 1040 S. King St. (536-1426). *Korean.* **B**

Other Restaurants (from top bracket to budget)

♈♈♈ **Prince Court** (nr. dwntwn), in the Hawaii Prince Hotel (see "Accommodations," above) (956-1111). A/C. Breakfast/ lunch/dinner daily, brunch Sun. AE, CB, DC, MC, V. Jkt. (at dinner). *Specialties:* ahi- (yellowfin tuna) and-salmon tartar, seafood and taro-leaf ministrone, lobster and shrimp in coconut-saffron sauce. The menu changes regularly. Outstanding wine list. *Note:* Sited on the second floor of Waikiki's lush new Prince hotel, and overlooking the Ala Wai yacht harbor, this quietly elegant rest. offers bright, Hawaiian regional cuisine w. an emphasis on seafood. Make sure to request a window seat, especially at sunset. Crisp, knowledgeable svce. Elegant breakfasts served daily. Resv. highly advised. *American.* **E**

☀♈♈♈ **Golden Dragon** (nr. dwntwn), in the Hilton Hawaiian Village (see "Accommodations," above) (946-5336). A/C. Dinner only, Tues–Sun. AE, CB, DC, MC, V. *Specialties:* cold ginger chicken, stir-fried lobster in curry sauce, Peking duck, ginger ice cream, haupia (coconut pudding), delicious homemade desserts. A large wine list, not commonly found in Asian rests. *Note:* The most luxurious and expensive Chinese rest. in Honolulu, featuring impeccably prepared and served Cantonese haute cuisine from the skilled hand of chef Dai Hoy Chang. Some extremely sophisticated dishes such as the Imperial Beggar's Chicken (wrapped in lotus leaves and braised for 6 hr. in a hermetically sealed clay pot) must be ordered 24 hr. ahead. Sumptuous setting w. a view over a dream lagoon. Faultless svce. Resv. strongly advised. *Chinese.* **M–E**

♈♈ **Jameson's by the Sea** (vic.), 62–540 Kamehameha Hwy., Haleiwa (637-4336). Breakfast Sat–Sun, lunch/dinner daily. AE, DC, MC, V. *Specialties:* sashimi, crab-stuffed mushrooms, panko-crusted mahimahi, opakapaka (Hawaiian pink snapper) w. garlic-hollandaise sauce, catch of the day. *Note:* Casual dining downstairs on the patio or formal white-tablecloth dining upstairs. Either way you get the freshest of local catch that at times lacks creativity when it comes to preparation. Efficient svce. Resv. highly advised. *Seafood/Continental.* **M–E**

♈♈♈ **Nick's Fish Market** (nr. dwntwn), in the Waikiki Gateway Hotel, 2070 Kalakaua Ave. (955-6333). A/C. Dinner only, nightly. AE, CB, DC, MC, V. Jkt. *Specialties:* Every imaginable kind of seafood is cooked and served here: Maine lobster, Florida stone crab, and Louisiana softshell crab (delivered by air daily) appear cheek by jowl w. daily. Pacific dolphin (mahimahi), swordfish, and bass (opaka paka). Excellent bouillabaisse and linguine w. clam sauce; also top sirloin steaks. Very good wine list. *Note:* One of the country's outstanding fish rests.; elegant maritime decor; exemplary svce. Resv. a must. Valet parking. *Seafood.* **M–E**

♈♈ **Bon Appetit** (nr. dwntwn), 1778 Ala Moana Blvd. (942-3837). A/C. Dinner only, Tues–Sun. AE, CB, DC, MC, V. *Specialties:* mousse of scallops w. caviar, fish soup w. saffron, snails in puff pastry, sliced breast of duck w. four-peppercorn sauce, tarte tatin. Menu changes regularly. *Note:* Guy Banal rules w. dexterity and finesse over the stove of this charming French-style bistro located unexpectedly in the middle of the Discovery Bay Shopping Center. Walls decorated w. bamboo; pastel-colored tablecloths. Very friendly reception and svce. If you like authentic French cooking and affordable prices, this is one of the best places on the island for you. Resv. advised. *French.* **M**

♈♈ **Hy's Steak House** (nr. dwntwn), 2440 Kuhio Ave. (922-5555). A/C. Dinner only, nightly. AE, CB, DC, MC, V. Jkt. *Specialties:* oysters Rockefeller, Delmonico steak, filet mignon, glazed New York peppercorn steak, barbecued pork chops, beef burgundy, roast rack of lamb, cherries Jubilee. *Note:* If you enjoy filling food, this is your place. Excellent beef broiled to perfection in a glass-enclosed grill at the end of the rm. Elegant Victorian setting; super-professional tuxedoed waiters. Resv. recommended. Valet parking. *Steak.* **M**

    Café Sistina (nr. dwntwn), 1314 S. King St. (526-0071). A/C. Lunch Mon–Fri, dinner nightly; closed hols. MC, V. *Specialties:* shrimp alla vodka, scaloppine w. porcini mushrooms and pine nuts, saffron linguine w. mussels. Good selection of Italian wines. *Note:* Chic, dress-up kind of *trattoria* where Honolulu's trendy yuppies hang out for good Italian food at decent prices. No resv. accepted unfortunately, so expect a wait at the bar. Svce prompt and earnest. *Italian.* **I–M**

    Keo's Thai Cuisine (nr. dwntwn), 625 Kapahulu Ave. (737-8240). A/C. Dinner only, nightly. AE, MC, V. *Specialties:* spicy chicken soup, minted spring rolls, beef w. coconut milk, Penang duck, beef saté w. hot peanut sauce, mango sherbet. *Note:* Given the enormous menu w. its more than 200 dishes ranging from the mildest through the moderately spicy to the volcanic, the lover of exotic foods should not fail to visit this friendly, elegant temple of Thai cooking. Charming tropical-grdn decor w. lots of orchids; attentive, efficient svce; an "in" place to eat. Resv. an absolute must. Other location: 1200 Ala Moana Blvd., Ward Center (533-0533). *Thai.* **I–M**

    Yanagi Sushi (nr. dwntwn), 762 Kapiolani Blvd. (537-1525). A/C. Lunch/dinner daily. AE, DC, MC, V. *Specialties:* sushi, California roll, sashimi, salmon-skin salad, shrimp-vegetable tempura. *Note:* In the opinion of connoisseurs, this cozy little Japanese eatery may have the best sushi in all Oahu. Wide variety and superb quality for quite a reasonable price. Always crowded. Reliable staff. Great for late-night sake and soba. Resv. recommended. *Japanese.* **I**

    Auntie Pasto's (nr. dwntwn), 1099 S. Beretania St. (523-8855). Lunch Mon–Fri, dinner nightly; closed hols. MC, V. *Specialties:* gorgonzola bread, roasted peppers, polenta and mozzarella, chicken cacciatore, veal marsala, eggplant Parmesan, crème brûlée. *Note:* Very straightforward Italian cooking that's a notch above the mainstream. Exposed brick and big windows make for a comfortable setting. Friendly, down-to-earth svce. Resv. not accepted, so there could be a wait. A great value. *Italian.* **B–I**

    California Pizza Kitchen (dwntwn), 1910 Ala Moana (955-5161). Lunch/dinner daily. AE, MC, V. *Specialties:* gourmet pizzas w. unbelievable toppings, such as guacomole and salsa. *Note:* The best pizza to be found on the island. Scrumptious creations that may take some getting used to. Check the *Yellow Pages* for other locations. *American.* **B–I**

    King Tsin (nr. dwntwn), 1110 McCully St. at Young St. (946-3273). A/C. Lunch/dinner daily. AE, CB, DC, MC, V. *Specialties:* Hunan shrimp, Shanghai fried noodles, moo shu pork, pot stickers, Szechuan duck, Mongolian beef, "Beggar's Chicken," Hunan pork w. broccoli. *Note:* The decor of this little rest. is nothing to write home about, but the Szechuan-style food is 100% authentic, and some of the best Chinese cooking to be found on the island. Some dishes are highly spiced. Repeat customers. A fine place to eat; resv. advised. *Chinese.* **B–I**

    Ono Hawaiian Food (nr. dwntwn), 726 Kapahulu Ave. (737-2275). A/C. Lunch/dinner Mon–Sat (until 7:30pm). No credit cards. *Specialties:* rice soup w. chicken, Kalúa pig (roast suckling pig), lomi-lomi, laulau, curried beef, pipikaula (spiced sun-dried beef), haupia. *Note:* In spite of some major flaws (no alcoholic beverages, no resv., no credit cards accepted) Ono Hawaiian food has always drawn crowds. Every afternoon from 4:30 on patrons line up outside the entrance for one of the rare available tables. The reason is the excellent, authentic Hawaiian food. *Ono* means "delicious" in Hawaiian. An absolute must for every visitor to the islands. *Polynesian.* **B**

Cafeteria/Fast Food

    Garden Café (dwntwn), in the Honolulu Academy of Arts, 900 S. Beretania St. (532-8734). Lunch only, Tues–Fri. No credit cards. In the museum's modern setting, excellent sandwiches, salads, and daily specials. Closed June–Sept.

The Patisserie (nr. dwntwn), Kahala Mall Shopping Center, 4211 Waialae Ave. (735-4402). Breakfast/lunch daily, dinner Mon–Sat. MC, V. Good cafeteria food at extremely attractive prices: homemade soups, salads, sandwiches, daily specials, excellent pastry. A good place to eat on the wing. For other locations, see the phone book.

BARS & NIGHTCLUBS

Anna Banana (vic.), 2440 S. Beretania St., Waikiki (946-5190). Two-tiered venue for alternative rock bands. Not for those w. sensitive lungs or ears.

Beach Bar (nr. dwntwn), in the Sheraton Moana Surfrider (see "Accommodations," above) (922-3111). For 80 years this has been Honolulu's most famous bar; the perfect spot for your before-dinner drink. Open nightly.

Hard Rock Café (dwntwn), 1837 Kapiolani Blvd. (955-7383). Honolulu branch of the internationally trendy rest. and bar. Open nightly.

Honolulu Comedy Club (nr. dwntwn), in the Ilikai Hotel, 1777 Ala Moana Blvd. (922-5998). Local young comics as well as the hottest stand-up comedians in the U.S. Shows Tues–Sun.

Monarch Room (nr. dwntwn), in the Sheraton Royal Hawaiian Hotel (see "Accommodations," above) (923-7311). Very popular Polynesian show by the brothers Cazimero.

Polynesian Palace (nr. dwntwn), in the Outrigger Reef Towers Hotel, 227 Lewers St. (923-7469). This is where you see well-known Hawaiian showman Don Ho perform in a dinner show.

Studebaker's (nr. dwntwn), 1 Waterfront Plaza, 500 Ala Moana Blvd. (531-8844). Nonstop bop nightly. Crowds line up to enjoy music of the '50s to '70s. Even waiters and waitresses dance. Dress code.

The Wave (nr. dwntwn), 1877 Kalakaua Ave. (941-0424). Locally popular nightclub with live music; you'll find the best local rock groups. Open nightly.

LUAUS (BUFFET & POLYNESIAN SHOW)

Paradise Cove Luau (vic.), a 40-min. drive from Honolulu (free buses from principal Waikiki hotels) (973-5828). Resv. required. Excellent buffet dinner and Polynesian show in a lovely natural setting. Slanted to tourists and crowded, but recommended nonetheless. Open nightly.

Polynesian Cultural Center (vic.), 1½ hr. from Honolulu by car via Hi. 61 and Hi. 83; transportation (for a fee) available from Waikiki hotels (call 293-3333 for resv.). Open Mon–Sat. The biggest and best Polynesian show in the Pacific. Since the center is run by the Mormons, no alcoholic beverages.

Also at the **Sheraton Royal Hawaiian Hotel** (Mon) and the **Sheraton Waikiki** (Tues).

NEARBY EXCURSIONS

HAIKU GARDENS (46-336 Haiku Rd., Kaneohe, 15 mi./ 24km north on Hi. 61) (247-6671): Tropical jungle with bamboo thickets and giant waterlilies at the foot of the **Koolau Mountains.** An exotic picture-postcard sight.

Valley of the Temples Memorial Park, at 47-200 Kahekili Hwy., Kaneohe (247-6671), adjoining Haiku Gardens, is an exact replica of the famous Byodo-In temple near Kyoto in a wonderful natural setting of Japanese gardens, fountains, and statues. Open daily.

Stop at **Nuuanu Pali Lookout,** offering one of the best views on the island.

In 1795 this was the scene of a bloody battle, after which hundreds of the defeated warriors were hurled over the cliff by the soldiers of King Kamehameha.

☼🐚🐚 **POLYNESIAN CULTURAL CENTER** (at Laie, 38 mi./ 60km north along Hi. 61 and Hi. 83) (293-3333; toll free 800/367-7060): The most popular attraction of the Hawaiian Islands. Seven carefully reconstructed Polynesian villages, representing the whole gamut of Pacific cultures (Hawaii, Tahiti, Samoa, Fiji, Tonga, etc.), standing in 42 acres (17ha) of beautiful gardens. Excellent displays of folk-dancing (resv. recommended for the evening buffet dinner-shows). Not far away is a spectacular Mormon temple (the Mormons manage the Polynesian Cultural Center). Open Mon –Sat. Bus svce from Honolulu; 1½ hr.

🐚 **SEA LIFE PARK** (on Makapuu Point at Waimanalo, 16 mi./ 26km east on Hi. 72) (259-7933): Outstanding marine zoo opposite the very beautiful Makapuu Beach; offers a complete selection of Pacific marine life from sea anemones to sharks and from dolphins to sea lions. Whaling museum. 30 min. from dwntwn. Open daily.

☼🐚 **WAIMEA FALLS PARK** (42 mi./67km NW on H-1, H-2, and Hi. 83) (638-8511): 1,730 acres (700ha) of jungle, tropical gardens, trails, and rock terraces with some very lovely waterfalls in which swimming is permitted. Open daily.

THE ISLANDS: HIGHLIGHTS

GETTING THERE: You can get from island to island by recreational tour boats and luxury cruisers (consult your travel agent), or by air. **Aloha Airlines** (808/ 484-1111) and **Hawaiian Airlines** (808/537-5100) offer inter-island transportation. Passengers holding full-fare round-trip tickets from the mainland may travel to other islands for an additional charge of about $40–$50 per stopover.

THE ISLAND OF HAWAII: "The Volcano Isle," 40 min. from Honolulu by air (also known as "The Big Island" or "Orchid Island"). At 4,038 sq. mi. (10,460km²)—almost the size of Connecticut—Hawaii is the largest island in the chain. Its sources of revenue are tropical produce (particularly orchids), cattle rearing, and tourism. The island's largest city (and capital), **Hilo**, acts as food, lodging, and transportation hub (flights to/from the mainland and other islands) for visitors. Hawaii is a microcosm of the physical geography of the islands, with its luxuriant vegetation, its white, green, and black sand beaches, and its two active volcanoes: **Kilauea**, in perpetual eruption since 1983, and the stately **Mauna Loa**, whose 13,000-ft. (4,000m) crest is crowned with snow in winter— an unusual sight in these tropical latitudes. The **Keck Observatory** with its giant twin 396-in. (10m) telescopes stands atop the extinct volcano Mauna Kea, highest point in the islands at 13,796 ft. (4,206m); it's the world's most powerful, twice as large as the instrument at Mount Palomar in California. It is expected to begin operations in 1996.

It was from this island that the great Kamehameha, seeking to end the internecine quarrels of the archipelago, set out to conquer the neighboring islands and unite their people under his rule. Hawaii's southern extremity, **Ka Lae** or **South Cape**, is the southernmost point of U.S. territory.

Sights and Attractions
Among the island's most interesting tourist attractions are:

☼🐚 **Akaka Falls State Park,** north of Hilo along the beautiful Hamakua coast road: Lovely park with giant 432-ft. (135m) waterfalls.

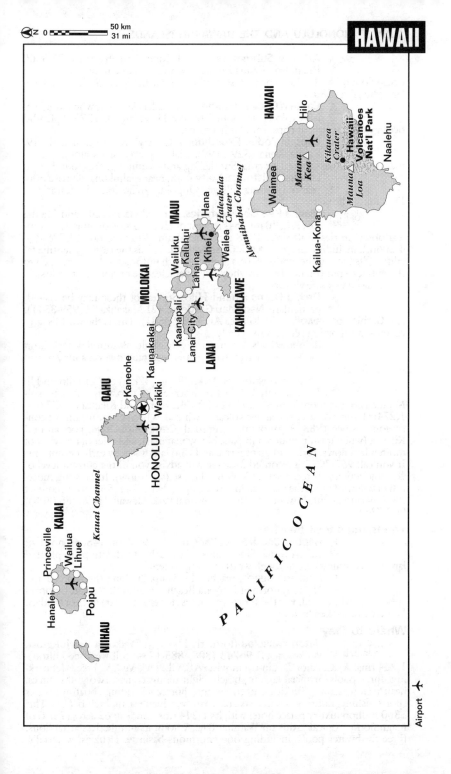

Atlantis Submarine, Hotel King Kamehameha, 75-5660 Palani Rd., Kailua Kona (329-6626): A one-hour voyage to the ocean floor off Kailua Kona on a 46-seat submarine with big portholes. Spectacular sights; fare, $80.

Captain Cook Monument, at Kealakekua Bay, where the British explorer was killed by the Hawaiians in 1779. Splendid ocean view. Daily boat trips from Kailua Kona.

Captain Zodiac Expeditions, Gentry's Kona Marina, Hi. 19, Kailua Kona (329-3199): Half-day excursions along the romantic Kona coast aboard air rafts. Snorkeling and swimming. Year round.

Lapakahi Historical State Park, near Mahukona: Site of a 600-year-old fishing village. Ongoing archeological excavations. Don't miss the view.

Mauna Kea Observatories, reached via Hi. 200 and Mauna Kea Rd., 40 mi. (64km west of Hilo): Group of nine astronomical observatories built since 1968 atop the Mauna Kea volcano (13,796 ft./4,206m), including the giant **Keck Observatory.** This is the largest scientific facility of its kind in the world. Access highway, with unforgettable views, open to the public—but you need a four-wheel-drive vehicle. The notion of altitude sickness may deter some visitors.

Orchid Farms around Hilo: Several of these may be visited, particularly **Nani Mau Gardens,** 421 Makalika St. (959-3541), and **Orchids of Hawaii,** 2801 Kilauea Ave. (959-3581). This is the world's largest orchid-exporting center. Open daily.

Rainbow Falls, Waianuenue Ave., Hilo: Beautiful waterfalls on the Wailuku River, with guaranteed rainbows on sunny mornings. Splendid trails for walkers.

Volcanoes National Park, 29 mi. (47km) SW of Hilo on Hi. 11: The only U.S. nature reserve with two active volcanoes—Mauna Loa, the more impressive (13,680ft./4,275m), and Kilauea (4,077 ft./1,274m), the world's most active volcano, which has been erupting almost continuously since 1983. A panoramic ring road, **Crater Rim Drive,** goes around Kilauea (when it isn't rendered impassable by magma!), and offers a fine view of molten lava flows, forests of giant ferns, and land laid waste by earlier eruptions. If you call 967-7977, a recorded message will advise you of the current level of volcanic activity. You can stay at Volcano House (see below). Interesting museum of volcanology at the park headquarters, open daily. For information, contact the Superintendent, Hawaii Volcanoes National Park, Hawaii, HI 96785 (808/967-7311).

The Island's Best Beaches

Hapuna Beach State Park, on Hi. 19, 30 mi. (48km) north of Kailua Kona: Fine long sandy beach edged with palm-planted lawns. Swimming here in rough weather is imprudent.

Kaunaoa Beach, reached by footpath along the shore, 1 mi. (1.6km) north of Hapuna Beach (see above): A huge, beautiful crescent of white sand. For the very lovely access footpath, wear shoes or sandals. Largely overlooked by tourists.

Where to Stay

Hilton Waikoloa (formerly Hyatt), 1 Waikoloa Beach Resort, Waikoloa, HI 96743 (808/885-1234; toll free, see Hilton). 1,244 rms, A/C, color TV, in-rm movies. AE, CB, DC, MC, V. Free valet parking, three pools, artificial lagoon, beach, eight tennis courts, two golf courses, health club, sauna, Turkish bath, massage, horseback riding, boating, water sports, fishing, hunting, seven rests., bars, rm svce, luau Fri, nightclub. *Note:* This $360-million luxury palace hotel with its 1,244 rms stands in 62 acres (25ha) of magnificent tropical grdns on Waiulua Bay. Among its numberless attractions: three freshwater pools, including one enormous basin w. Jacuzzis, waterfalls, and artificial sea caves; a monorail and fake Venetian canals linking the three principal buildings; an auto racetrack; wild-boar hunts in the nearby mountains; etc. The rms in the three towers are unusually spacious and comfortable; 75% of them overlook the ocean. Ultra-comprehensive physical-fitness facilities. Large as the place is, the svce is efficient. **VE**

Mauna Lani Bay Hotel, Hi. 19, Kohala Coast, Kawaihae, HI 96743 (808/885-6622; toll free 800/367-2323). 351 rms, A/C, color TV, in-rm movies. AE, CB, DC, MC, V. Free valet parking, pool, two golf courses, putting green, 10 tennis courts, sauna, private beach, fishing, boating, horseback riding, four rests. (including the Canoe House), coffee shop, three bars, 24-hr rm svce, disco, boutiques. *Note:* One of the most luxurious hotels in the Pacific basin; a modern building designed like a ship's prow and standing in its own lovely tropical grdns. Splendid lobby w. indoor pool and palm trees. Elegant, richly furnished rms w. ocean or mountain view. Attentive, personalized svce. Caters mostly to groups and a monied clientele. **VE**

Royal Kona Beach & Tennis Resort, 75-5852 Alii Dr., Kailua Kona, HI 96740 (808/329-3111; toll free 800/774-5662). 452 rms, A/C, color TV, in-rm movies. AE, CB, DC, MC, V. Free parking, pool, artificial lagoon, golf course, three tennis courts, rest., bar, coffee shop, rm svce, free crib. *Note:* Futuristic building right on the ocean; beautiful rms w. private patios and spectacular view of the Pacific. Tropical grdns. Good svce. One of the best hotels in the Islands. Group clientele. **E–VE,** but lower rates off-season.

Kona Surf Hotel, 78-128 Ehukai St., Keauhou Kona, HI 96740 (808/322-3411; toll free 800/367-2603). 532 rms, A/C, color TV, in-rm movies. AE, CB, DC, MC, V. Free parking, two pools, golf course, three tennis courts, rest., bars, rm svce, hrdrsr, free crib. *Note:* Very lovely modern hotel on the ocean. Comfortable rms w. refrigerators and private balconies. Excellent svce. Magnificent tropical grdns. Very good value; the favorite of those in-the-know. **E–VE,** but lower rates off-season.

Kanaloa at Kona, 78-261 Manukai St., Kailua Kona, HI 96740 (808/322-9625; toll free 800/777-1700). 118 suites and villas (no A/C), cable color TV. AE, CB, DC, MC, V. Free parking, three pools, two tennis courts, beach, golf, rest., bar. *Note:* Luxurious resort complex on magnificent Keauhu Bay, in 13 acres (5ha) of tropical grdns. Comfortable, spacious suites and villas, all w. kitchenette and private terrace. Elegant layout and decor. Interesting vacation packages. A good place. **E–VE**

Keauhou Beach Hotel, 78-6740 Alii Dr., Keauhou Kona, HI 96740 (808/322-3441; toll free 800/367-6025). 317 rms, A/C, color TV, in-rm movies. AE, CB, DC, MC, V. Free parking, pool, six tennis courts, sauna, health club, private beach, rest. (Kuk), bar, rm svce. *Note:* Modern, comfortable hotel partly overhanging the water. Huge, well-laid-out rms w. private balconies and panoramic views. Good value, but svce a little undependable. **M–E,** but lower rates off-season.

Hilo Bay Hotel (Uncle Billy's), 87 Banyan Dr., Hilo, HI 96740 (808/935-0861; toll free 800/367-5102). 150 rms, A/C, cable color TV. AE, CB, DC, MC, V. Free parking, pool, rest., adj. nightclub. *Note:* Engaging little countrified family hotel standing in pleasant tropical grdns w. a goldfish pool. Serviceably comfortable rms w. terrace, the best overlooking the grdn; some w. kitchenette and refrigerator. Friendly reception and svce. Good value. **I–M**

Parker Ranch Lodge, on Hi. 19 (P.O. Box 458), Kamuela, HI 96743 (808/885-4100). 21 rms (no A/C), cable color TV. AE, MC, V. Free parking, rest. and bar adjoining. *Note:* Small, sound, unpretentious motel. Huge, comfortable rms, half w. kitchenette. Good value on balance. **I–M**

Volcano House, HI. 11, in Volcanoes National Park, HI 96718 (808/967-7321). 42 rms (no A/C). AE, CB, DC, MC, V. Free parking, sauna, rest., bar. *Note:* One of the loveliest sites in the islands, in the heart of Volcanoes National Park. Rustic, somewhat basic comfort; very acceptable rest. (but mobbed by visitors at lunch). You should reserve as far ahead as possible. Some rms have a fine view of the crater. Open year round. A truly unique experience. **I–M**

Country Club Hotel, 121 Banyan Dr., Hilo, HI 96720 (808/935-7171). 149 rms, A/C, color TV. AE, CB, DC, MC, V. Free parking, pool, rest., bar, disco. *Note:* Relatively modern hotel on the ocean, w. palm-tree–lined tropical grdns. Homelike rms w. private balconies, most w. refrigerators. Svce w. a smile. Interesting vacation packages. Nr. the airport. Good value. **I**

Where to Eat

Canoe House, in the Mauna Lani Bay Hotel (see "Where to Stay," above). A/C. Dinner only, nightly. AE, CB, DC, MC, V. Jkt. *Specialties:* pupus (Hawaiian appetizers); barbecued baby back ribs w. fresh corn relish and mirin dressing; taro chips w. Oriental-style avocado salsa; tempura ahi wrapped in nori seaweed w. soy-mustard sauce and tomato-ginger relish. *Note:* Exquisite Pacific Rim cooking by master chef Alan Wong. Romantic terrace setting w. a spotlit view of the ocean and swaying palms. Top-notch svce. Resv. a must. *American/Asian.* **E**

Merriman's, on Hi. 19 at Opelo Plaza, Waimea (885-6822). A/C. Lunch Mon–Fri, dinner nightly. AE, MC, V. *Specialties:* bouillabaisse, penne pasta, vine-ripe tomatoes w. Maui onions, wok-charred ahi, slow-roasted chicken w. chili-pepper-mint sauce, veal tenderloin w. shiitake mushrooms and macadamia nuts, remarkable desserts. *Note:* The young chef Peter Merriman, formerly at the renowned Mauna Lani Bay Hotel, is one of the most original and imaginative in the islands. His cuisine features local produce and local techniques. Interesting contemporary decor. Amiable svce. Resv. a must. A very good place. *American/Polynesian.* **M**

Edelweiss, Kawaii Hae Rd. at Hi. 19, Waimea (885-6800). A/C. Lunch/dinner Tues–Sat; closed Sept. MC, V. *Specialties:* papaya Edelweiss, pasta al fresco, roast pork w. sauerkraut, roast duck Bigarade, Black Velvet cake. *Note:* A misplaced Bavarian chalet under tropical skies, Edelweiss is the brainchild of another refugee from the Mauna Lani Bay Hotel, the accomplished German chef Hans-Peter Hager. His cooking, though predominantly Continental, admits the occasional exotic touch. First-class svce; a local favorite since 1983. Unfortunately no resv. *Continental.* **I–M**

Parker Ranch Broiler, Hi. 19 and Hi. 190, Kamuela (885-7366). A/C. Lunch/dinner daily; closed Dec 25. AE, DC, MC, V. *Specialties:* grilled red meats and fish, panlolo stew. *Note:* The excellent beef is home-reared on the ranch. The chef is one of the best on the island; attractive Victorian bar and lobby. Very popular locally. Resv. advised. *Steak/Seafood.* **I**

Roussel's, 60 Keawe St., Hilo (935-5111). No A/C. Lunch Mon–Fri, dinner nightly; closed hols. AE, MC, V. *Specialties:* soft-shell crab "Rising Sun," boiled shrimp w. zesty Créole sauce, Louisiana-style trout, catch of the day. *Note:* Renovated turn-of-the-century building in historic dwntwn Hilo featuring fine New Orleans cuisine and Hawaiian seafood. A real find. *Créole/Polynesian.* **I**

Kona Inn, Kona Inn Shopping Center, 75-5744 Alii Dr., Kailua Kona (329-4455). A/C. Lunch/dinner daily, brunch Sun. AE, MC, V. *Specialties:* fried oysters, broiled scampi and calamari, catch of the day, steak, roast beef, guava sherbet. *Note:* Congenial rest. on Kailua Bay w. a fine view of the ocean and its magnificent sunsets. Inviting wood-paneled setting. The freshest of local produce prepared honorably but without much imagination. Hardworking svce. Very popular locally; resv. advised. *American.* **I**

Volcano House–Ka Ohelo Dining Room, in the Volcano House (see "Where to Stay," above) (967-7321). A/C. Lunch/dinner daily. AE, CB, DC, MC, V. *Specialties:* teriyaki (broiled marinated meat), mahi-mahi (broiled dolphin), steak, prime rib. *Note:* A superb setting inside Volcanoes National Park itself. Very decent food. Buffet at lunchtime. Friendly svce. Resv. a must. *Japanese/Polynesian.* **I**

Ocean View Inn, 75-5683 Alii Dr., Kailua Kona (329-9998). Breakfast/lunch/dinner Tues–Sun. No credit cards. *Specialties:* broiled catch of the day; hamburgers; Japanese, Chinese, and Polynesian dishes. The huge menu boasts some 200 different dishes and combinations. *Note:* One of the most popular rests. on the Big Island, right across from the harbor. The food is a strange medley from around the Pacific Rim: Hawaiian, Japanese, Chinese, Philippine, and American. Sturdy helpings; low prices. Usually noisy and crowded, but full of local color; a local landmark for more than half a century. Resv. accepted. *American/Polynesian.* **B–I**

MAUI: "The Valley Isle," 25 min. from Honolulu by air. Maui is the second largest of the islands in area: 729 sq. mi. (1,890km²). It's called the "Valley Isle" because of the long, low-lying fertile isthmus that joins the island's two craggy extremities. On the southeast coast stands the astonishing extinct volcano Haleakala, whose enormous arid crater could hold Manhattan Island. In 1802 King Kamehameha I chose Maui as the site of his capital, Lahaina. Now it's a favorite vacation spot for lovers of big-game fishing and scuba-diving.

The Sights

Haleakala National Park, 26 mi. (42km) SE of Kahului on Hi. 37 and Hi. 378: Big nature reserve, over which looms the Haleakala volcano (known as "The House of the Sun"), which has been dormant for 200 years; the huge crater is 6 mi. (10km) long, 3 mi. (5km) wide, and about 2,900 ft. (900m) deep. According to Hawaiian legend it was the home of the god Maui, who was able to make the sun stand still in its course. If you want to visit the crater you should be in good shape, and wear stout shoes and warm clothing. Spectacular view of much of the island chain. Visitor center open daily; for information, call 572-9306, or 572-7749 for recorded information on the weather.

Hana Highway, Hi. 36, 360, and 31 from Lower Paia to Obeo Gulch: In its 50-mi. (80km) length this scenic highway clinging to a mountainside overlooking the ocean has 600 turns and some 50 one-way bridges. All this in a setting of tropical jungles, waterfalls, and precipitous ravines. Tourists, unfortunately, flock here. Try the drive late in the afternoon or early in the morning to avoid the rush.

Iao Valley State Park, near Wailuku: Wonderful green valley, over which towers a spectacular rock needle 1,197 ft. (365m) high, blanketed with vegetation.

Kaanapali Beach, near Lahaina: One of the finest beaches in the entire state—but also the most crowded—on the island's northwest shore.

Lahaina: Picturesque little harbor that was a favorite port of call for whalers in the 19th century. An amusing little train drawn by a steam engine runs a connecting service to Kaanapali (661-0080). Japanese cultural center, the Lahaina Joda Mission on Ala Moana St., with a giant statue of Buddha; open daily.

The Island's Best Beaches

D. T. Fleming Beach County Park, on Hi. 30, 5 mi. (8km) north of Kanapali (take the turnoff to the ocean): Lying between two rocky, wave-beaten headlands is a lovely sand beach, uncrowded on weekdays.

Hamoa Beach, on Hi. 31, 1 mi. (2.5km) south of Hana: One of the loveliest in the islands; a wonderful semicircle of sand beach fringed with palm trees. Glorious swimming.

☼ 🐚🐚🐚 **Kapalua Beach,** Shore Rd., 1.5 mi. (2km) south of Hi. 30 at Honokaua: Rated "America's most lovable beach." A small crescent-shaped beach with soft white sand and year-round warm water in a beautiful shade of green.

Where to Stay

☼ 👑👑👑👑 **Hyatt Regency Maui,** 200 Nohea Kai Dr., Kaanapali Beach, HI 96761 (808/661-1234; toll free, see Hyatt). 815 rms, A/C, color TV, in-rm movies. AE, CB, DC, MC, V. Valet parking $5, two pools, two golf courses, six tennis courts, health club, sauna, boats, four rests. (including the Swan Court), coffee shop, five bars, 24-hr rm svce, hrdrsr, boutiques. *Note:* Three ultramodern buildings on the beach w. splendid tropical grdns, indoor waterfalls, and a giant swimming pool. Spacious, comfortable rms. The interior decoration includes many Asian and Polynesian works of art. Excellent svce; comprehensive sports facilities. Interesting vacation packages. One of Hawaii's best hotels. VIP suites on the top three floors of the main building. **VE**

👑👑👑👑 **Kea Lani Hotel,** 4100 Wailea Alanui Dr., Wailea, HI 96753 (808/875-4100; toll free 800/882-4100). 413 suites and 37 villas, A/C, color TV, in-rm movies. AE, CB, DC, MC, V. Free valet parking, lagoon-pool, beach, golf course, six tennis courts, health club, water sports, three rests., coffee shop, bars, entertainment, free crib. *Note:* Surrounded by white sand beaches, this quintessential Hawaiian paradise is Maui's first all-suite luxury resort. Each suite has a fully stocked kitchenette and a marble bathroom. Beautiful tropical grdns. Impeccable comfort and svce. The favorite of those in-the-know. **VE**

👑👑👑 **Maui Inter-Continental Hotel,** 3700 Alanui Dr., Wailea, HI 96753 (808/879-1922; toll free, see Inter-continental). 516 rms, A/C, color TV, in-rm movies. AE, CB, DC, MC, V. Valet parking $3, three pools, two golf courses, 11 tennis courts, beach, water sports, two rests. (including Hula Moons), three bars, rm svce, nightclub, hrdrsr, boutiques. *Note:* Luxury hotel on the ocean w. 1,450 acres (587ha) of tropical grdns and woodlands. Spacious, completely refurbished rms w. views of the ocean or Mount Haleakala. Comfort and facilities above reproach; very good svce; very commendable rests. One of the finest hotels in the islands. **E–VE**

👑👑 **Maui Lu Resort,** 575 S. Kihei Rd., Kihei, HI 96753 (808/879-5881; toll free 800/922-7866). 182 rms, A/C, cable color TV. AE, CB, DC, MC, V. Free parking, pool, two tennis courts, rest. (Longhouse), bar. *Note:* Hotel decorated in tropical style w. direct beach access; 19 acres (7.7ha) of grdns and palm groves. Comfortable rms w. refrigerators. Less-than-ideal svce, but good overall value. **M**, but lower rates off-season.

👑 **Maui Vista,** 2191 S. Kihei Rd., Kihei HI 96753 (808/879-7966; toll free 800/922-7866). A/C. 53 apts and studios, cable color TV. AE, MC, V. Free parking, no bar or rest., three pools, six tennis courts. *Note:* Pleasant resort hotel across from the beach w. a nice array of sport opportunities. Spacious studios or apts w. kitchenettes, maid svce, and private balconies. Outdoor barbecues. A good value on balance. **I–M**

Where to Eat

🍴🍴🍴 **Kincha,** in the Grand Wailea Hotel, 3859 Wailea Alanui, Wailea (875-1234). A/C. Dinner only, nightly. AE, CB, DC, MC, V. *Specialties:* sushi, tempura, udon noodles, chicken yakitori, kaiseki dinners. *Note:* This $22-million Japanese rest. is set in the midst of an eloquent Japanese-style garden that nicely reflects the delicacy of Tsuyoshi Yoshida's preparations. The kaiseki meals can run you anywhere from $150 to $500, a bargain compared to what it costs in Japan. Resv. are required. *Japanese.* **M–VE**

☼ 🍴🍴🍴 **Gerard's,** in the Plantation Inn, 174 Lahainaluna Rd., Lahaina (661-8939) A/C. Breakfast/lunch/dinner daily. AE, MC, V. *Specialties:* raw fish à la tahitienne, oysters and shiitake mushrooms in puff pastry, rack of lamb persillade, catch of the day, confit of duck fricassée. Desserts are irre-sistible. *Note:* One of the best French rests. in the islands. The cuisine of master chef Gerard Reversade is a delicate blend of French ideas with Maui-grown ingre-dients and produce such enchantments as ahi (tuna) w. béarnaise sauce and bean sprouts. Very good wines to complement the food. Brightly lit decor w. period oak and stained glass. Smooth and informal svce. Resv. essential. *French.* **M–E**

☖☖☖ **David Paul's Lahaina Grill,** 127 Lahainaluna Rd., Lahaina (667-5117). A/C. Dinner only, nightly. AE, MC, V. *Special-ties:* superbly inventive New American cuisine; the menu changes regularly. 1,200-bottle climate-controlled wine cellar. *Note:* The hottest new rest. in Lahaina. Chef David Paul's cooking blends perfectly Californian technique and local produce w. a touch of exotic, as in the "tequila shrimp w. firecracker rice," its signature dish. Elegant modern decor. Resv. highly advised. *American.* **M**

☖☖ **Mama's Fish House,** 799 Poho Place, Paia (579-8488). A/C. Lunch/dinner daily. AE, DC, MC, V. *Specialties:* fried calamari, cold papaya-and-coconut soup, crab cooked in beer, oven-baked fish w. tarragon, ahi (tuna) teriyaki w. ginger, fried sweet potatoes, Hookipa sundae. *Note:* As the name suggests, the house specialty is fish of all kinds; the menu also features chicken and meat. Beautiful location w. wrap-around ocean view through huge picture windows. Efficient svce. Resv. advisable. *Seafood.* **I–M**

☖ **Ming Yuen Chinese Restaurant,** 162 Alamaha St., Kahului (871-7787). A/C. Lunch Mon–Sat, dinner nightly. AE, CB, DC, MC, V. *Specialties:* hot-and-sour soup, sweet-and-sour shrimp, broccoli beef, eggplant Szechuan style. *Note:* Informed opinion rates this Maui's best Chinese rest.; what's more, the prices are very reasonable. Real Chinese food, mostly Can-tonese or Szechuan; one-scheme-fits-all Asian decor. Resv. advised. *Chinese.* **B–I**

KAUAI: "The Garden Isle," 25 min. from Honolulu by air, is rebuilding itself as an island paradise since Hurricane Iniki hit Hawaii (Sept. 1992), the strongest hurricane to hit the island in this century. **Mount Waialeale,** a huge (5,208-ft./ 1,587m high) extinct volcano, holds the world's wet-weather record, with 350 rainy days and 460 in. (11.45m) of rainfall yearly! Kauai was the first Hawaiian island visited by Captain Cook (1778). It was also the last independent kingdom in the archipelago. Its tortuous contours make for difficult traveling. The capital is **Lihue.**

The Sights

Among the more interesting places to visit are:

☀☖ **Hanalei:** A fashionable spa nestling at the head of a sweeping bay.

☀☖☖ **Na Pali Coast:** This rocky shoreline at the NW end of the island was severely damaged in the hurricane. Hi. 56 from Princeville to Kee Beach has a spectacular 10-mi. (16km) drive among rarely crowded beaches and impressive ridges of rock covered with lush vegetation; this sight alone is worth the trip to Kauai.

☀☖ **Wailua Falls,** north of Lihue: Beautiful twin falls, and the spec-tacular **Fern Grotto** carpeted with tropical ferns. This popular attraction can be reached only by boat from Wailua River Marina.

☀☖☖ **Waimea Canyon State Park,** near Waimea: Magnificent gorges with walls of multicolored rock, reminiscent of Colorado's Grand Canyon. The last section of the road to **Kalalau Lookout** of-fers some fine views.

The Island's Best Beaches

☖ **Kauapea Beach,** reached by a steep footpath from Kauapea Rd. near Kilauea Lighthouse: Deserted coral-sand beach.

☖ **Kee Beach,** at western end of Hi. 56, 2 mi. (3km) west of Haena: Fine-sand beach several miles long. The surf here is dangerous in winter.

☀�🅐 **Polihale State Park,** reached via a 5-mi. (8km) unsurfaced but
usable road at the western end of Hi. 50: Huge sandy beach
overlooked by the magnificent inaccessible cliffs of Na Pali.

Where to Stay

🏮🏮🏮🏮 **Westin Kauai,** Hi. 51 at Kalapaki Beach, Lihue, HI 96766
(808/245-5050; toll free, see Westin). 850 rms, A/C, color
TV, in-rm movies. AE, CB, DC, MC, V. Free valet parking, pool (biggest in Hawaii), five Jacuzzis, private beach, Turkish bath, health club, sauna, massage, eight
tennis courts, two golf courses, boating, fishing, water sports, horseback riding,
six rests. (including Inn on the Cliff), coffee shop, five bars, 24-hr. rm svce, nightclub, Polynesian show, boutiques. *Note:* The island's super-palace, an 800-
acre (323ha) tropical oasis on a half-mile (1km) private beach east of Kauai. The
modern architecture surrounded by idyllic grdns is a little overwhelming. Luxurious if slightly flashy interior. Largish rms in pastel colors w. private patio and
refrigerator. Remarkable sports facilities (the two golf courses were designed by Jack Nicklaus). Underwent complete renovation because of hurricane
damage. **VE**

🏮🏮🏮 **Hyatt Regency Kauai,** 1571 Poipu Rd., Koloa, HI 96756
(808/742-1234; toll free, see Hyatt). 600 rms, color TV, in-
rm movies. AE, CB, DC, MC, V. Free valet parking, pool, golf course, tennis,
health club, sauna, water sports, four rests. (including Dondero's), six bars, rm
svce, nightclub, boutiques, Hawaiian arts and crafts demonstrations and classes.
Note: Low-rise hotel set in the midst of 50 acres (21ha) of lavish surroundings.
Prim gardens, open-air courtyards, and a long stretch of ocean-front terrace recall
a 1920s style of luxury. Plush rms w. minibars and private balconies, the best
overlooking the ocean. Score of water-sport opportunities. Formidable rest.
Friendly, pleasant svce. **VE**

☀🏮🏮🏮 **Princeville Hotel,** 5520 Ka Haku Rd., Princeville, HI 96746
(808/826-9644; toll free 800/826-4400). 252 rms, A/C,
color TV, in-rm movies. AE, CB, DC, MC, V. Free valet parking, pool, 21 tennis
courts, two golf courses, health club, spa, water sports, two rests. (including La
Cascate), two bars, 24-hr rm svce, disco, concierge, cinema. *Note:* One of the
most elegant luxury hotels in the islands, built in an original terraced style on a
cliff rising from the magnificent Hanalei Bay. Spacious, ultra-comfortable rms w.
refrigerators and private patios, the best overlooking the ocean. Rest. of great distinction. Very complete sports facilities. Serious hurricane damage; underwent a
$35-million renovation. **VE**

☀🏮🏮🏮 **Coco Palms Resort Hotel,** Hi. 56 and Hi. 580, Wailua Beach,
HI 96766 (808/822-4921; toll free 800/426-2779). 390
rms and private cottages, A/C, cable color TV. AE, CB, DC, MC, V. Free parking, three pools, nine tennis courts, sauna, beach, three rests. (including the Sea
Shell Room), bars, rm svce, nightclub, boutiques. *Note:* Very handsome
Polynesian-style hotel in a palm grove; a favorite w. honeymooners. Has been the
scene of numerous movies, *Blue Hawaii* among them. The palm grove, 45 acres
(18ha) of splendid tropical grdns, and the lagoons were once part of a royal property. Spacious rms w. refrigerators (the cottages by the lovely lagoons are prefera-
ble). Irreproachable standards of comfort and svce. Rest. highly recommended.
Polynesian shows. Good value. For those who love the out-and-out exotic.
Closed for renovation until sometime in 1995. **M–E**

🏮🏮 **Aston Kauai Beach Boy,** 4-484 Kuhio Hwy., Waipouli Beach,
HI 96746 (808/822-3441; toll free 800/922-7866). 243
rms, A/C, cable color TV. AE, CB, DC, MC, V. Free parking, pool, tennis
court, beach, rest., bar. *Note:* Comfortable modern hotel on the site of an old
coconut plantation. Large, friendly rms w. refrigerators and private verandas
overlooking the ocean. Good svce. Underwent renovations because of hurricane
damage. **M**

♟♟ **Outrigger Plantation Hale,** 484 Kuhio Hwy., Kapaa, HI
96746 (808/822-4941; toll free 800/367-5170). 151 suites,
A/C, color TV, in-rm movies. AE, CB, DC, MC, V. Free parking, pools, putting
green, adj. rest. *Note:* Near the Wailua River and almost on the beach, this inviting, well-run residential hotel has congenial suites w. kitchenette and private terrace. Friendly reception. Lovely exotic grdns. Recently renovated. The adj.
Coconut Plantation Market Place has numerous rests. and stores. **M**

Where to Eat

🍷🍷🍷 **Casa di Amici,** 2484 Keneke St. at Lighthouse Rd., Kilauea
(828-1388). Dinner only, nightly. AE, CB, DC, MC, V. *Specialties:* cannelloni, boursin cheese wrapped in phyllo w. red sauce, polenta w.
pesto sauce, porcini-crusted loin of lamb w. rosemary-port sauce, salmon stuffed
w. crab cake poached in saffron-lobster broth, mango-lime cheesecake. *Note:* The
"in place" on Kauai. Classic Italian food mixed w. some rather inventive specials.
Choice of seating in an airy interior or on the patio. Upbeat, friendly svce. Resv. a
must. *Italian/Continental.* **I–M**

🍷🍷 **Pacific Café,** 3148 Kuhio Hwy., Kapaa (822-0013). A/C.
Dinner only, Tues–Sun. DC, MC, V. *Specialties:* Vietnamese
spring rolls, deep-fried sashimi, wok-charred mahimahi w. a sesame crust,
paniolo steak w. crisp Maui onions. *Note:* Outstanding Franco–Pacific Rim cuisine by French chef-owner, Jean-Marie Josselin. Appealing interior. The "in"
dining spot in Kauai since its opening in 1990. Resv. advised. *French/Asian.* **M**

🍷🍷 **Plantation Gardens,** in the Kiahuna Plantation Resort, Poipu
Rd., Koloa (742-1695). Dinner only, nightly. AE, MC, V. Jkt.
Specialties: crab-stuffed mushrooms, sashimi. *Note:* A lovely old house overlook-
ing tropical grdns. Closed at presstime. *American.* **I–M**

🍷 **Kintaro,** 4-370 Kuhio Hwy., Kapaa (822-3341). A/C. Dinner
only, nightly. AE, MC, V. *Specialties:* sushi, sashimi, teriyaki,
tempura. *Note:* Teppan-yaki is the real specialty here, though Kintaro is known
locally as the place to go for sushi and sashimi. Classic Japanese decor w. light
wood and shoji screens. Homey atmosphere. *Japanese.* **I**

🍷 **Barbecue Inn,** 2982 Kress St., Lihue (245-2921). A/C.
Breakfast/lunch/dinner Mon–Sat. AE, MC, V. *Specialties:*
steak teriyaki, shrimp tempura, baked salmon steak, seafood platter, T-bone
steak, corned beef and cabbage. *Note:* Decent, inexpensive local food in a simple,
unadorned setting. Abrupt, almost rude, svce. Very popular locally. Excellent
value; resv. unnecessary. *Japanese/American.* **B–I**

MOLOKAI: "The Friendly Isle," 25 min. from Honolulu by air. This rectan-
gular island, 38 mi. (61km) long by 10 mi. (16km) wide, was long a religious
sanctuary guarded by the Kahuna priesthood from profane intrusion. In the
19th century a Belgian missionary, Joseph de Veuster, known as Father Damien,
established a leper colony here. Even today the island is relatively ignored by
tourists, yet the Kalaupapa Peninsula is—without exaggeration—the most spectacular view in Hawaii. Mossy volcanic cliffs rise up at extraordinary angles from a
lurid ultramarine sea set with dramatic little islands.

The Sights

☼ **Halawa Valley,** at the NE of the island on Hi. 450: A succession of tidal waves has sharply reduced the once-large population of this fertile valley. Spectacular waterfalls and numerous Polynesian
temples (*heiaus*), once the scene of human sacrifices.

☼ **Father Damien's Leprosarium,** at Kalaupapa: Site of the old
leprosarium founded in 1873 by the famous Belgian mission-
ary; he himself contracted, and died of, the dread disease in 1889 at the age of 49,
and his tomb is here. Impressive. More than 100 former sufferers of Hansen's
disease, as leprosy is now known, remain at Kalaupapa. Open daily (but only to

visitors over 16 years old). For the mule ride (seven-hour round-trip) to get there, resv. required at least five days in advance; contact Damien Tours (567-6171).

    Molokai Ranch Wildlife Park Safari, Hi. 460 at Maunaloa (552-2741): Safari zoo on 1,000 acres (400ha) of scrubby, semi-desert savanna, scarcely at all reminiscent of the natural habitat of the African and Asian animals kept here: giraffe, zebra, antelope, nandu, oryx, etc. Two 1½-hr. minibus tours Fri–Mon.

    Umilehi Point: From near here rears the world's highest cliff, towering dizzily 3,296 ft. (1,005m) above the sea.

The Island's Best Beaches

    Kepuhi Beach, reached via Hi. 460 and Kepuhi Rd., 5 mi. (8km) NW of Maunaloa: Fine white-sand beach much frequented by surfers.

    Papohaku Beach Park, adjoining Kepuhi Beach, above: Largest and loveliest on the island. Magnificent white sand, but dangerous for swimming in winter and sometimes even in summer.

    Other uncrowded beaches are **Halava Beach, Moonomi Beach,** and **Kahaiawa Beach.**

Where to Stay

    Kaluakoi Hotel & Golf Club, Kepuhi Beach, HI 96770 (808/552-2555; toll free 800/777-1700). 126 rms, A/C, color TV, in-rm movies. AE, CB, DC, MC, V. Free parking, pool, golf course, four tennis courts, private beach, two rests. (including Ohia Lodge), bar, nightclub, boutiques. *Note:* The 32 charmingly pretty Polynesian cottages stand at the water's edge. Tranquil, elegant setting. Spacious, comfortable rms w. refrigerators. Good svce. A great place to stay to live in isolation. **M–E**

    Wavecrest Resort, Star Rte. 155, Kaunakakai, HI 96748 (808/558-8103). 126 mini-apts, color TV. MC, V. Free parking, pool, two tennis courts, grocery store. *Note:* Modern building, right on the beach, w. mini-apts and studios (w. maid service) for one to six persons, all w. kitchenette and private terrace. Good value for family parties. Minimum stay of three nights. No bar, no rest. **I–M**

    LANAI: "The Pineapple Isle," 30 min. from Honolulu by air. This small island, only 17 mi. (27km) long, is the most authentic—and the least visited—in the Hawaiian chain. It belongs to the food conglomerate, Dole Pineapple Company, and boasts the world's largest pineapple plantation. Tourism is still in its infancy here, so there are superb beaches standing almost empty.

The Best Beach on the Island

    Hulopo'e Beach, at the southern end of Manele Rd.: Wonderful white-sand beach shaded by palm trees; its usually calm water makes it very attractive for swimming and diving.

THE ISLANDS OF NIIHAU & KAHOOLAWE: These two islands, alone in the chain, have escaped the tidal wave of tourism. The former is privately owned by the Robinson family; its 250 or so inhabitants speak only Hawaiian. The latter is an arid military reservation, closed to visitors.

CHAPTER 57

ANCHORAGE AND ALASKA

□ □ □

With its skyscrapers rising against the mountain backdrop, its bustle and its cosmopolitan crowds, Anchorage may at first sight look like the Manhattan of the Far North, but it turns out to have some rustic ways as well. The 20-story hotels and modern office buildings rub shoulders with old frame houses standing in their own little gardens. The new glass-and-steel **William A. Egan Convention Center** faces the **Visitors Information Center,** housed in a log cabin that would have been at home in the gold rush. It's not uncommon for Alaskans to fly 500 mi. (800km) or more out of the bush to Anchorage to see the latest movie or hear a special concert; parked outside a deluxe French restaurant you may well see a four-wheel-drive wagon that would be more at home on a backcountry trail. This pioneer atmosphere is not the least of Alaska's charms.

The city, founded in 1915 as a work camp on the Alaska Railroad, has grown up slowly around the excellent harbor provided by Cook Inlet (the "anchorage" from which it derives its name). In 1940 the future economic capital of Alaska had barely 3,500 inhabitants; its strategic importance only became apparent during World War II. The first oil discoveries in the Kenai Peninsula in 1957, and those at Prudhoe Bay 11 years later, made the city's fortune. Its population rose from 48,000 in 1970 to the present 225,000—two-fifths of the state's population.

Anchorage nestles at the foot of Cook Inlet, the great arm of the sea discovered two centuries ago by British explorer James Cook. Today it's Alaska's financial, communications, and transportation center, as well as an important hub for transpolar air flights, with more than three million passengers passing through its air terminal every year. Even the severe earthquake of 1964, which destroyed part of the city, scarcely checked its growth-oriented civic spirit. Nevertheless, the local economy has had difficulty getting over the substantial drop in raw oil prices during the past 12 years, the real-estate stagnation, and the negative fallouts on tourism of the *Exxon Valdez* oil spill in the area close to Valdez and Prince William Sound (see "Alaska: Highlights," below). Having only recently celebrated its 75th birthday, Anchorage is short on historic buildings, but it offers the visitor its incomparable site. It has two remarkable museums of Native American and Inuit art, the **Museum of History & Art** and the **Heritage Library & Museum,** and the nation's most northerly rose garden. Its location, on the sea and behind the natural barrier of the **Chugach Mountains** to the north and east, gives Anchorage a surprisingly temperate climate. Winter is only a little colder than in Denver or Chicago, and summer is often warmer than in San Francisco.

Anchorage is also an ideal base for exploring the whole of northern Alaska, from **Nome** and **Kotzebue,** in the land of the Midnight Sun and the dogsled, to the **Pribilof Islands** and **Katmai National Park** with their unusual wildlife. Then there is **Denali National Park** where **Mount McKinley** rises with its eternal snows to 20,320 ft. (6,193m), the highest mountain in North America (see "Alaska: Highlights," below).

BASIC FACTS: State of Alaska. Area code: 907. Time zone: Alaska (four hours behind New York) and Aleutian/Hawaiian (five hours behind New York). ZIP Code: 99502. Founded: 1915. Approximate population: 225,000.

CLIMATE: With its relatively mild winters (averaging 13°F/−9°C in Jan), agreeable summers (57°F/15°C in July), and sunlit autumns (though snow can often fall heavily after mid-Oct), the climate of Anchorage is far from being the stereotype of Far Northern severity.

The rest of Alaska, on the other hand, does offer wider swings in temperature, differing from one part of the state to another. The south coast is windy and rainy; average temperatures at **Sitka** are 32°F (0°C) in Jan and 66°F (19°C) in July. The uplands of the interior have a dry, continental climate, with temperatures at **Fairbanks** sometimes rising above 86°F (30°C) in the summer, and falling to −42°F (−40°C) in the winter. The **Arctic North,** or Far North (a quarter of the state's area lies above the Arctic Circle), is very windy and dry, with truly polar winter readings as low as −79°F (−62°C) and more temperate summers averaging 64°F (18°C); the short summer is followed by a mild fall. At **Barrow,** the northernmost city in the country, the harbor is ice-bound Oct–Aug—but the sun never sets from May 10 to Aug 2. Equally, it never rises from mid-Nov to the end of Jan. Unless you're a winter-sports enthusiast, Alaska is best visited between early June and late Sept, when average temperatures should run from 35°F (2°C) at the low end to 86°F (30°C) at the highest.

DISTANCES: Denali National Park, 239 mi. (382km); Fairbanks, 364 mi. (582km); Haines, 775 mi. (1,240km); Seward, 127 mi. (203km); Skagway, 890 mi. (1,424km); Valdez, 317 mi. (507km); Whitehorse (Canada), 715 mi. (1,145km).

ARRIVAL & TRANSIT INFORMATION

AIRPORT: Anchorage International Airport (ANC), 5 mi. (8km) SW.

Other major airports in Alaska are **Fairbanks International Airport** (FAI), 4 mi. (6.5km) SE of Fairbanks; and **Juneau Municipal Airport** (JNU), 8 mi. (13km) north of Juneau.

U.S. AIRLINES: Alaska (toll free 800/426-0333), Delta (toll free 800/221-1212), Markair (toll free 800/627-5247), Northwest (toll free 800/225-2525), Reeve Aleutian (243-4700), and United (toll free 800/241-6522).

FOREIGN CARRIERS: Balair (toll free 800/322-5247), British Airways (toll free 800/247-9297), Korean Airlines (toll free 800/438-5000), and Lufthansa (toll free 800/645-3880).

CITY LINK: The **cab** fare from the airport to dwntwn is about $15; time, 15 min. Bus: **Alaska Backpacker Shuttle** (344-8775) leaves about every hour serving principal hotels; fare, $5; time, 20 min. The local bus line, the **People Mover** (343-6543), provides good service to major dwntwn hotels Mon–Sat. Given the climate, renting a car for excursions is advisable only Apr–Sept.

CAR RENTAL (at Anchorage International Airport unless otherwise indicated): Avis (toll free 800/331-1212); Budget (toll free 800/527-0700); Hertz (toll free 800/654-3131); National (toll free 800/227-7368); and Thrifty,

3730 Spennard Rd. (toll free 800/367-2277). In other cities, check the local telephone book.

LIMOUSINE SERVICES: My Chauffeur (562-5466).

TAXIS: Few and costly; may not be hailed on the street but must be called by phone: **Checker Cab** (276-1234) and **Yellow Cab** (272-2422).

TRAIN: Alaska Railroad, 411 W. First Ave. (P.O. Box 107500), Anchorage, AK 99510 (907/265-2494; toll free 800/544-0552): Serves Anchorage–Fairbanks via Denali National Park and Anchorage–Seward–Whittier. Runs year round, with reduced service Oct–May. Resv. a must—at least two weeks ahead. Spectacular. Call or write for information.

INTERCITY BUSES: Alaska Direct Bus Line, P.O. Box 501, AK 99510 (277-6652): Three weekly trips to Whitehorse, Yukon, with ongoing connection to Skagway.

FERRY: The **Alaska Marine Highway,** 333 W. Fourth Ave. (907/272-7116), is a kind of seagoing bus, carrying cars and passengers on comfortable, modern ships; it gives the ports of southeastern Alaska on the Inside Passage route (Haines, Juneau, Ketchikan, Petersburg, Sitka, Skagway, Wrangell) a year-round connection to Bellingham, Washington, and to Prince Rupert in Canada. Spectacular landscapes. Another service leaves Whittier, Valdez, and Cordova for Kodiak Island and the Kenai Peninsula. For timetables, write P.O. Box 25535, Juneau, AK 99802; or call: 907/272-4482 in Anchorage, 907/766-2111 in Haines, 907/465-3941 in Juneau, 604/627-1744 in Prince Rupert, B.C., 206/676-8445 in Bellingham, 907/983-2941 in Skagway, or toll free 800/642-0066.

INFORMATION & TOURS

TOURIST INFORMATION: Contact the **Alaska Division of Tourism, Information Office,** P.O. Box 110801, Juneau, AK 99811 (907/465-2010), for information on Alaska in general.

    Alaska Public Lands Information Center, 605 W. 4th St., Suite 105, Anchorage, AK 99501 (907/271-2737): Information on Alaska's national parks and wildlife services.

    Anchorage Convention & Visitors Bureau, 1600 A St., Anchorage, AK 99501 (907/276-4118); also a **Visitors Information Center,** Log Cabin, 546 Fourth Ave. (at F St.), Anchorage, AK 99509 (907/274-3531).

    A **recorded message** gives information on current cultural and sporting events at 907/276-3200.

GUIDED TOURS: Alaska Sightseeing Tours (bus and boat), 513 W. Fourth Ave., Anchorage, AK 99501 (907/276-1305; toll free 800/478-7141): Guided tours of the principal cities and regions of Alaska, serving Anchorage, Fairbanks, Haines, Juneau, Ketchikan, and Skagway (for local numbers in these cities, consult the telephone book for the appropriate city).

    Era Helicopters, 6160 S. Airpark Dr., Anchorage, AK 99502 (907/248-4422; toll free 800/843-1947): Helicopter flights over the mountains and glaciers around Anchorage, Fairbanks, Juneau, Prudhoe Bay, or Valdez (for local numbers in these cities, consult the phone book for the appropriate city).

   Gray Line Tours of Alaska (bus), 745 W. Fourth Ave., Anchorage, AK 99510 (907/277-5581; toll free 800/544-2206): Guided tours of the principal cities and regions of Alaska, serving Anchorage, Fairbanks, Juneau, Ketchikan, Skagway, and Valdez (for local numbers in these cities, consult the phone book for the appropriate city).

SIGHTS, ATTRACTIONS & ACTIVITIES

ADVENTURES: Alaska Whitewater (raft) (337-7238): Rafting down the Eagle River in the Chugach Mountains; transportation from Anchorage provided. June 1–Sept 10.
   Chugach Express Dog Sled Rides, P.O. Box 261-T, Girdwood, AK 99587 (907/783-2266): One-hour dogsled rides on the slopes around Anchorage. Nov 15–Apr 15.

CRUISES: The popular Inside Passage cruises visit such ports as Juneau, Ketchikan, Skagway, Sitka, and Glacier Bay. The newer Gulf of Alaska sailings visit ports between Vancouver and Anchorage, including Inside Passage ports. These two cruising areas are not affected by the 1989 *Exxon Valdez* oil spill.
   Among the principal tour operators are:
   Clipper Cruise Line (toll free 800/325-0010): Sails on 7- and 14-day Inside Passage cruises from late May through early Aug.
   Cunard (toll free 800/528-6273): Sails on 11-day Gulf of Alaska itineraries between Vancouver and Anchorage from June to early Aug.
   Holland America Line–Westours (toll free 800/426-0327): Sails on 7-day Inside Passage cruises from Vancouver and 14-day Gulf of Alaska cruises between Vancouver and Seward. Late May to late Sept.
   Princess Cruises (toll free 800/421-0522): Sails on 7-day Inside Passage cruises from Vancouver and 10-day round-trip sailings from San Francisco. Late May to Sept.
   Regency Cruises (toll free 800/388-9090): Offers 7-day Gulf of Alaska sailings from mid-May to mid-Sept.

CHURCHES/SYNAGOGUES: St. Nicholas Church, 6724 E. Fourth Ave. (277-6731): Typical Russian Orthodox Church; interesting view; can be seen by appointment only.

HISTORIC BUILDINGS: Oscar Anderson House, 420 M St. (274-2336). Built by a Swedish immigrant in 1915, this modest frame house is one of the oldest in the city. Carefully restored, the Anderson House with its great cast-iron stove and its period furniture is a living vestige of the past, with a fine view over Cook Inlet. Daily guided tours in summer.

MUSEUMS: Heritage Library & Museum, Northern Lights Blvd. at C St. (265-2834): Native American and Inuit handcrafts and mementos of the gold rush. Large collection of works on the history of Alaska. Open Mon–Fri.
       Museum of History and Art, 121 W. Seventh Ave. (343-4326): Prehistoric tools, art from the Aleutian, Inuit, and Athapascan cultures, works from the 19th century onward inspired by Alaska. Interesting temporary exhibitions. Open Tues–Sun.
       Wildlife Museum, at Fort Richardson, Bldg. 600 (5 mi./8km NE) (384-0431): More than 200 specimens of fish, mammals, and birds, covering the whole range of Alaskan wildlife. Open Mon–Fri.

PANORAMAS: Earthquake Park, at the western end of Northern Lights Blvd.: Overlooking Cook Inlet and its seascapes, this beautiful 135-acre (54ha) park bears eloquent witness to the violence of the 1964 earthquake. Splendid view of **Talkeetna Mountains** to the NE and **Chugach Mountains** to the east.

&&   **Resolution Park,** Third Ave. and L St.: This downtown park offers you not only a statue of Captain Cook (who visited these parts in 1778 in his famous ship *Resolution*), but also a very fine view over Cook Inlet and the legendary **Mt. Susitna,** whose shape suggests a sleeping woman. On a fine day you can see as far as **Mt. McKinley,** 140 mi. (225km) away as the crow flies.

PERFORMING ARTS: For daily listings of all shows and cultural events, consult the entertainment section of the daily newspaper, the *Anchorage Daily News* (morning), or call 276-ARTS (276-2787) for a recorded list of current cultural events.

Performing Arts Center, 621 W. Sixth Ave. (263-2900): Building of very forward-looking design opened in 1988 and comprising three separate auditoriums. Concerts, big-name recitals, modern theater, Broadway shows.

Sydney Laurence Auditorium, Sixth Ave. and F St. (263-2787): The home of the Anchorage Civic Opera (Sept–Mar) and the Anchorage Symphony Orchestra (Nov–Apr).

University of Alaska–Anchorage Theater, 3211-T Providence Dr. (786-1800): Classical and contemporary theater Nov–Mar.

SHOPPING: A few addresses for those interested in authentic Native American and Inuit artifacts in horn, leather, or wood, jewelry, etc.: **Alaska Fur Exchange,** Old Seward Hwy. and Tudor Rd.; **Alaska Native Arts and Crafts Showroom,** 333 W. Fourth Ave.; **Rusty Harpoon,** 411 W. Fourth Ave.; and **Taheta Arts & Cultural Group,** 605 A St.

SPECIAL EVENTS: For a current schedule, inquire at the **Anchorage Visitors & Convention Bureau** (see "Tourist Information," above).

Fur Rendez-Vous (Feb): Dogsled races, shows, costume ball, sports events, etc., held at the time of the great annual fur auction.

Iditarod Trail Sled Dog Race (Mar): World-famous annual dogsled race from Anchorage to Nome, with more than 50 entries for these two weeks of racing. A classic for more than 50 years. Record time for the race: 11 days, 1 hr., 53 min., and 23 sec. (by Susan Butcher, in 1990).

Midnight Sun Marathon (late June or early Aug): A popular local event.

SPORTS: Baseball: The Anchorage Glacier Pilots (274-3627) and the Bucs (272-2827), two semi-pro teams, play at Mulcahy Baseball Stadium from June to early Aug.

The **Sled Dog Race Track** on Tudor Rd. pits local against "foreign" champions, Sat–Sun in winter. For a timetable, call 272-7333.

WINTER SPORTS RESORTS: The popular ▲ **Alyeska Resort,** 40 mi. (64km) SE via Ak. 1 (754-1111), has four ski lifts and a hotel. Season: Nov–Apr; also summer skiing.

ZOOS: The relatively new ▲ **Alaska Zoo,** 9 mi. (14km) SW at 4731 O'Malley Rd. (346-2133), offers a full range of native Alaskan animals: polar bears, brown and black bears, foxes, reindeer, moose, etc. Open daily year round.

ACCOMMODATIONS

Personal Favorites (from top bracket to budget)

♀♀♀   **Captain Cook Hotel** (dwntwn), Fifth Ave. and K St., AK 99150 (907/276-6000; toll free, see Preferred). 584 rms, color TV, in-rm movies. AE, CB, DC, MC, V. Indoor parking $6, pool, health club,

Alaska Pacific University ❾
Alaska Public Lands Information Center ⓴
Anchorage Avation Heritage Museum ❶
Anchorage Museum of History and Art ⓱

Centennial Park ⑪
Earthquake Park ❷
George M. Sullivan Sports Arena ❺
Goose Lake ❽
Heritage Library and Museum ❹

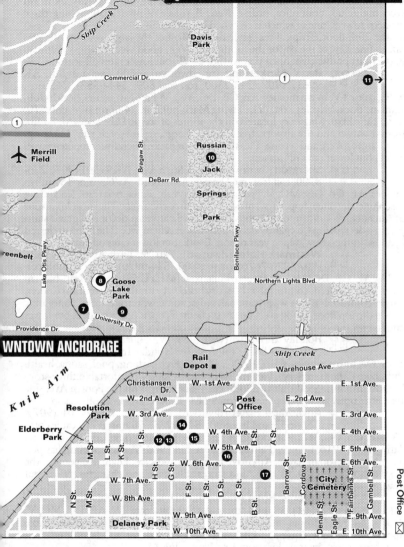

ANCHORAGE ATTRACTIONS

Ship Creek

Davis Park

Commercial Dr.

1

11 →

1

Merrill Field

Bragaw St.

Russian

10

Jack

DeBarr Rd.

Springs

Park

Boniface Pkwy.

Lake Otis Pkwy.

reenbelt

Northern Lights Blvd.

8 Goose Lake Park

7

9

University Dr.

Providence Dr.

WNTOWN ANCHORAGE

Knik Arm

Ship Creek

Rail Depot ■

Warehouse Ave.

Christiansen Dr.

W. 1st Ave.

E. 1st Ave.

W. 2nd Ave.

Post Office

E. 2nd Ave.

Resolution Park

W. 3rd Ave.

E. 3rd Ave.

Elderberry Park

14

W. 4th Ave.

B St.

A St.

E. 4th Ave.

12 13

15

W. 5th Ave.

E. 5th Ave.

M St.

L St.

K St.

H St.

16

E. 6th Ave.

W. 6th Ave.

Barrow St.

Cordova St.

G St.

17

E. 7th Ave.

W. 7th Ave.

F St.

E St.

D St.

C St.

City Cemetery

N St.

M St.

W. 8th Ave.

B St.

Denali St.

Eagle St.

Fairbanks St.

Gambell St.

W. 9th Ave.

E. 9th Ave.

Delaney Park

W. 10th Ave.

E. 10th Ave.

Post Office

Post Office ⊠

Imaginarium 12

Log Cabin Information Center 15

Z. J. Loussac Public Library 6

Reeve Aviation Picture Museum 16

Russian Jack Springs Park 10

University of Alaska— Anchorage 7

Visual Arts Center 13

Westchester Lagoon Waterfowl Sanctuary 3

sauna, three rests. (including the Crow's Nest), coffee shop, four bars, 24-hr rm svce, nightclub, boutiques, hrdrsr. *Note:* A palace of luxury comprising three modern towers, one of which is crowned by a panoramic rest. (the Crow's Nest) on the 20th floor. Tropical sea–style decor. Most of the large, comfortable rms offer a fine view of the bay or the mountains. Very good svce; business clientele; in the heart of dwntwn; open year round. **E–VE,** but lower rates off-season.

Regal Alaskan Inn (nr. dwntwn), 4800 Spenard Rd., AK 99517 (907/243-2300; toll free 800/544-0553). 248 rms, A/C, color TV, in-rm movies. AE, CB, DC, MC, V. Free gar., sauna, health club, seaplane dock, bicycles, rest. (The Flying Machine), bar, 24-hr rm svce, crib $10. *Note:* New luxury hostelry located on the shores of scenic Lake Spenard, 8 min. from dwntwn and the airport (free shuttle). Large, stylish guest rms. Hunting-lodge atmosphere and setting. Pleasant outdoor patio. Friendly, competent svce. **E–VE,** but lower rates off-season.

Sheraton (dwntwn), 401 E. Sixth Ave., AK 99501 (907/276-8700; toll free, see Sheraton). 375 rms, A/C, color TV, in-rm movies. AE, CB, DC, MC, V. Free gar., health club, sauna, two rests. (including Josephine's), coffee shop, bars, rm svce, disco, free crib. *Note:* The most luxurious of Anchorage's large modern hotels. Impressive native art decor and grand stair-case in jade; spacious, elegantly decorated rms, excellent svce. The hotel preferred by those in-the-know. Open year round. **E–VE,** but lower rates off-season.

Westmark Hotel (dwntwn), 720 W. Fifth Ave., AK 99501 (907/276-7676; toll free 800/544-0970). 200 rms, cable color TV. AE, CB, DC, MC, V. Free parking, rest. (Mesa Grill), coffee shop, bar, rm svce. *Note:* Modern, comfortable 14-story hotel very nr. the Convention Center. Large, comfortable rms w. private balconies, some w. refrigerators. Panoramic bar on the top floor. Good svce; business clientele; open year round. **E,** but lower rates off-season.

Holiday Inn (dwntwn), 239 W. Fourth Ave., AK 99501 (907/279-8671; toll free, see Holiday Inns). 252 rms, A/C, color TV, in-rm movies. AE, CB, DC, MC, V. Free parking, pool, sauna, health club, rest. (The Greenery), bar, rm svce. *Note:* Classic, comfortable three-story Holiday Inn w. a good dwntwn location—but the rms on the Fourth Ave. side are a little noisy at night; open year round. **M–E,** but lower rates off-season.

Anchorage Hotel (dwntwn), 330 E St., AK 99501 (907/272-4553; toll free 800/544-0988). 20 rms, A/C, cable color TV. AE, CB, DC, MC, V. Parking $4, rest. adj., bar. *Note:* Small, delightful hotel dating from 1916, reopened after long disuse in 1988. The remodeling has pre-served the Victorian flavor. Attentive reception and svce. Dwntwn, very nr. the Convention Center w. its rests. and stores. Elegance and character. **M–E,** but lower rates off-season.

Voyager Hotel (dwntwn), 501 K St., AK 99501 (907/277-9501). 38 mini-suites, A/C, cable color TV. AE, DC, MC, V. Parking $4, rest. (dinner only), bar. *Note:* Small hotel offering only comfortable mini-suites w. fully equipped kitchenette. Tasteful decor and layout; efficient svce; convenient dwntwn location. Excellent value. **M**

Ramada Inn (nr. dwntwn), 598 W. Northern Lights Blvd., AK 99503 (907/561-5200; toll free, see Ramada). 155 rms, color TV. AE, DC, MC, V. Free parking, rest., bar, rm svce, free airport limo. *Note:* Comfortable modern hotel halfway between dwntwn and the airport. Good svce; caters mostly to business travelers and groups. Good overall value; open year round. **M**

Super 8 Motel (nr. dwntwn), 3501 Minnesota Dr., AK 99503 (907/276-8884; toll free 800/800-8000). 84 rms, color TV, in-rm movies. AE, CB, DC, MC, V. Free parking, nearby rest., free airport limo. *Note:* Modern, functional hotel halfway between dwntwn and the airport. Com-fortable rms, free morning coffee; overall good value; open year round. **I–M**

YMCAs/Youth Hostels

AYH, 700 H St., AK 99503 (907/276-3635). Youth hostel open year round. Clean rms; excellent location.

Airport Accommodations

🍷🍷 **Best Western–Barratt Inn** (nr. dwntwn), 4616 Spenard Rd., AK 99517 (907/243-3131; toll free, see Best Western). 217 rms, color TV, in-rm movies. AE, CB, DC, MC, V. Free parking, rest., bar, free 24-hr. airport limo svce. *Note:* Welcoming country-style motel nr. the seaplane base at Spenard Lake, and 3 min. from the international airport. Very comfortable rms, some w. kitchenettes. Acceptable rest.; efficient svce; open year round. Ideal for a stopover between flights. **M–E,** but lower rates off-season.

RESTAURANTS

Personal Favorites (from top bracket to budget)

🍷🍷🍷 **Crow's Nest** (dwntwn), in the Captain Cook Hotel (see "Accommodations," above) (276-6000). A/C. Dinner Tues–Sun, brunch Sun. AE, CB, DC, MC, V. Jkt. *Specialties:* lobster bisque in pastry shell, salmon stuffed w. shrimp, halibut à la Berval, game and venison (in season), choice meats. Good wine list. *Note:* From the 20th floor of the Captain Cook Hotel, this distinguished rest. offers a fine panorama of the mountains and Cook Inlet. Elegant, contemporary cuisine making full use of local resources in game and seafood. The stylish svce anticipates your needs. Best rest. in all of Alaska; resv. highly advisable. *Continental/Seafood.* **M–E**

�🍷🍷 **Marx Bros. Café** (dwntwn), 627 W. Third Ave. (277-6279). Dinner only, Mon–Sat; closed hols. AE, MC, V. *Specialties:* crab Imperial, catch of the day, seafood mousse napolitano, venison dishes (in season), halibut macadamia, roast duck w. raspberries, rack of lamb. Fine wine list. *Note:* Located in a picturesque little house built in 1916, this American-style rest. is very popular locally. Some original dishes; good svce; resv. advised. *American/Seafood.* **M**

🍷🍷 **Sourdough Mining Co.** (nr. dwntwn), 5200 Juneau St. (563-2272). A/C. Lunch/dinner daily. AE, CB, MC, V. *Specialties:* barbecued baby back ribs, chicken, and pork; corn fritters w. honey butter. *Note:* A fun place in a replica of the Mill House at Independence Mine, complete w. antiques and memorabilia of gold-rush days. Hearty food and great atmosphere. Good svce. Shuttle-bus svce. to/from dwntwn hotels. No resv. necessary. *American.* **I**

🍷🍷 **Simon & Seafort's** (dwntwn), 420 L St. (274-3502). A/C. Lunch Mon–Sat, dinner nightly; closed hols. AE, MC, V. *Specialties:* steak, rock-salt-roasted prime rib, grilled halibut w. lime butter and ginger, catch of the day, Alaska fish and shellfish (in season), brandy ice. Very good wine list. *Note:* Pleasantly decorated as a saloon from the Gay '90s. Good, tasty food at very reasonable prices for Alaska. Remarkably fresh fish, cooked as you wish—grilled, fried, or poached. Relaxed setting and fine view of the mountains and Cook Inlet. Try it. Resv. suggested. *Steak/Seafood.* **I**

🍷 **Kumagoro** (dwntwn), 533 W. Fourth Ave. (272-9905). A/C. Lunch/dinner daily. AE, MC, V. *Specialties:* sushi, miso soup, teriyaki, shabu shabu. *Note:* The preferred rest. of Japan Air Lines crews stopping over at Anchorage—a good reference. All-purpose Oriental decor. Diligent svce; excellent value. *Japanese.* **B–I**

🍷🍷 **Mexico in Alaska** (nr. dwntwn), 7305 Old Seward Hwy. (349-1528). Lunch Mon–Sat, dinner nightly; closed hols. AE, MC, V. *Specialties:* tacos, cold seafood and chicken marinated in lime, cactus fried w. onion and tomatoes, flan. *Note:* As the sign in the restaurants warns, "We do not serve Mexican-American style," the food is wholly authentic, and delicious. By far, some of the best Mexican food to be found in the state. Proprietor Maria Elena Ball serves as a gracious host. Resv. advised. *Mexican.* **B–I**

🍸 **Downtown Deli** (dwntwn), 525 W. Fourth Ave. (276-7116). Breakfast/lunch/dinner daily. MC. *Specialties:* homemade soups, sandwiches, corned beef, kosher specialties, fish, daily specials, homemade desserts. *Note:* An Anchorage institution, much patronized by businesspeople and local dignitaries. Usually crowded at breakfast and lunch. Friendly, smiling svce. Well-located, very nr. the Captain Cook and Hilton hotels. *American.* **B**

NEARBY EXCURSIONS

EKLUTNA (26 mi./42km NE via Ak. 1) (276-5701): A picturesque Athapascan village whose Russian Orthodox church, **St. Nicholas Church** (built in 1870), has an interesting collection of icons. The grave-markers in the cemetery are topped, Native American fashion, with a little house for the departed spirit to live in. Here, you can also visit beautiful **Lake Eklutna** and its waterfalls.

PORTAGE GLACIER (50 mi./80km SE via Ak. 1): Offers an impressive spectacle as it "calves," shedding great pieces of itself which tumble into Portage Lake below. Visitor center open daily in summer; not-to-be-missed boat trip along the glacier on the *Ptarmigan* (277-5581).

AN ALASKA OVERVIEW

At once the largest and the least populous state in the Union, Alaska runs to extremes in everything: climate, geography, natural resources, and, above all, distances. The south shore of **Misty Fjords National Monument** in the southern part of the state is 1,435 mi. (2,300km) away from **Barrow,** the northernmost town in the U.S. From the western tip of the great **Aleutian Islands,** pointed toward Siberia like the tusk of an elephant at bay, to the frontier with Canada's Yukon and British Columbia, Alaska (from an Aleut word meaning "peninsula") sprawls across two time zones. Its area of 586,400 sq. mi. (1,520,000km²) is 2½ times that of Texas, but is home to barely half a million inhabitants, 70,000 of whom are Native Americans, Inuit (Eskimos), and Aleuts.

INTRODUCING ALASKA

The history of Alaska is inseparable from that of *Homo sapiens* in North America. The settlement of the continent was begun in 35,000–25,000 B.C. by invaders from Asia who at that time were able to cross what is now the Bering Strait on foot. And it was from Alaska that the "Amerindians" leapfrogged down the Pacific coast, reaching Tierra del Fuego, the southernmost point of South America, a few thousand years later. The history of the state in modern times goes back no further than 1728, when Vitus Bering, a Danish explorer in the service of Tsar Peter the Great of Russia, discovered the 57-mi. (92km) passage between Siberia and North America that still bears his name. In 1867 Secretary of State William H. Seward purchased Alaska, which had become a Russian colony, for $7.2 million, or around 2¢ per acre—a deal that his political opponents, who knew nothing of the fabulous wealth below Alaska's surface, nicknamed "Seward's Folly," or "Seward's Icebox." But Seward's vision was corroborated by the gold discoveries of 1896 and the large-scale oil discoveries, the first of which was made in 1957.

Today, Alaska (which became the 49th state in 1959) spends considerably more a year on publicity than the $7.2 million that more than a century ago was the purchase price paid to the Russians for their American colony—because, along with crude oil, fisheries, and forest products, tourism (700,000 visitors a year) is one of the mainstays of the local economy. A visit to the "Frontier State," as it is sometimes called, will give you a deeper insight into Alaska's attraction for lovers of nature, solitude, and wide-open spaces. There are no grander landscapes than the snowy peaks of **Mt. McKinley,** highest in North America, or **Denali National Park;** the mysterious depths of **Tongass National Forest** (twice the size of Ireland) and of **Wrangell–St. Elias National Park;** the blue-shadowed expanse of **Glacier Bay National Park;** the picturesque necklace of islands along the **Inside Passage** with its history-laden little harbors at **Sitka, Petersburg, Ketchikan,** and **Wrangell;** the fissured shores of **Kenai Fjords National Park** or **Prince William Sound** (damaged by the 1989 oil spill); the desolate tundra of **Gates of the Arctic National Park;** the scalding mineral springs of **Circle Hot Springs,** or the "Valley of 10,000 Smokes," in **Katmai National Park.** All of these are unforgettable sights, especially at dawn, or when the summer evenings draw out forever in sunsets of glowing bronze. The state is also heaven on earth for fishermen, hunters (who must have permits), or just plain nature photographers, who won't know where to point their lenses in such a wealth of wildlife: black and brown bear, grizzlies, wolves, mountain goats, Sitka deer, elk, lynx, eagles, caribou, beavers, otters, wolverines, seals, walruses, sea lions—and, unfortunately, mosquitos, plague of the Alaskan summer.

ALASKA: HIGHLIGHTS

ADMIRALTY ISLAND NATIONAL MONUMENT
(reachable by seaplane from Juneau and Sitka, or by Alaska Marine Hwy. ferry): Lying at the heart of the Inland Passage, this wild and beautiful island, 100 mi. (160km) long by 25 mi. (40km) wide, is inhabited by more brown bears and Sitka deer than humans. Its rain forests, mountain peaks, dozens of lakes and rushing streams, and rocky coasts make it a small-scale replica of Alaska. Admiralty Island is also home to the largest eagle colony in North America.

Shelter: Log cabins and camping sites only. For lovers of nature in the raw. For **information,** contact the U.S. Forest Service, 101 Egan Dr., Juneau, AK 99801 (907/586-8751).

ALEUTIAN ISLANDS
(reachable by plane from Anchorage): This island chain stretches more than 1,500 mi. (2,400km) southwestward from Alaska toward the shores of Asia. Almost uninhabited, these magnificent windswept islands with their numerous wildlife reserves are a very beautiful destination for the tourist (direct flights between Anchorage and Dutch Harbor/Unalaska). The Aleutians were the scene of a 19-day battle in May 1943 between U.S. and Japanese forces, the only mainland U.S. territory to see combat during World War II. The island of **Attu,** westernmost in the chain, is nearer to Moscow or Tokyo than to Washington, D.C.

Where to Stay
Unisea Inn, Pouch 503-T, Dutch Harbor, AK 99692 (907/581-1325). 46 rms, cable color TV. MC, V. Rest., bar, boutiques. *Note:* Serviceable, pleasant, welcoming small motel facing the Mall. Open year round. The ideal place to stay for a visit to the Aleutians. **M**

BARROW
(reachable by air from Fairbanks or Anchorage): A picturesque Inuit village whose 2,200 people make their living from fishing and handcrafts, particularly bone carving. Lying 340 mi. (544km)

north of the Arctic Circle, this is the northernmost town in the U.S. At the airport is a memorial to cowboy-movie star and humorist Will Rogers and his pilot, Wiley Post, who were killed in an air crash nearby in 1935. The midnight sun shines here for 82 successive days every summer.

Where to Stay

Top of the World, P.O. Box 189-T, Barrow, AK 99723 (907/852-3900; toll free 800/882-8478). 40 rms, color TV, in-rm movies. AE, MC, V. Adj. rest. (Pepe's). *Note:* The farthest-north hotel in the Americas; rustic, even though comfortable. Stuffed polar bears to welcome you in the lobby. Friendly, refrigerator-equipped rms; entirely redecorated in 1986. About as complete a change of scenery as you can get! Free airport shuttle; open year round. **M–E**

CIRCLE HOT SPRINGS (136 mi./218km NE of Fairbanks along Ak. 2 and Ak. 6): Around these hot (139°F/59°C) springs, discovered in 1897 by a gold prospector, has grown up a spa very popular with Alaskans in winter and with tourists the rest of the year. Thanks to a network of hot-water canals, market gardeners of the region produce the finest fresh vegetables in Alaska.

Where to Stay

Circle Hot Springs Resort, P.O. Box 254, Central, AK 99730 (907/520-5113). 75 rms, color TV. MC, V. Spa, rest. *Note:* Delightful 1930s hotel, recently restored. Hostel-type accommodations and cabins. **I–M**

CORDOVA (reachable by air from Anchorage and Juneau, or by Alaska Marine Hwy. ferry from Whittier and Valdez): This old copper-mining town, which flourished from 1908 to 1938, has taken a renewed lease on life as a busy fishing port. Beautiful site to the east of Prince William Sound. There is an interesting historical museum, the **Cordova Historical Museum,** Centennial Building (907/424-6665); open year round.

DENALI NATIONAL PARK (125 mi./201km south of Fairbanks and 240 mi./386km north of Anchorage on Ak. 3; also reachable by train from Anchorage on the Alaska Railroad, a 7¾-hr. trip): This second-largest (9,375 sq. mi./24,280km², 2½ times the size of Yellowstone) of our national parks was established in 1917; it is also one of the wildest and most majestic. Almost at the center of the park, and often hidden in summer by clouds, **Mt. McKinley,** the highest peak in North America, stands 20,320 ft. (6,196m) tall. An 87-mi. (140km) road in the northern part of the park, as well as many trails, allow the visitor to reach the heart of Denali National Park (its name is from a Native American word meaning "the high one"), and to observe its exceptionally rich wildlife—grizzlies, wolves, caribou, elk, and more than 155 species of birds. From both the **Polychrome Overlook** and the **Eielson Visitor Center** (sled-dog demonstrations every day in summer) there are unobstructed views over mountain, forest, and glacier. You'll need warm clothes, a raincoat, and stout shoes. There's a daily guided visit by bus year round from the **Riley Creek Visitor Center** (toll free 800/622-7275).

For **information,** contact the Superintendent, Denali National Park, P.O. Box 9, Denali Park, AK 99755 (907/683-2294). This park alone is worth the trip to Alaska.

Where to Stay

Denali Princess Lodge, Parks Hwy., Milepost 238.5, Denali Park, AK 99755 (907/683-2282). 280 rms. AE, MC, V. Free parking, open-air Jacuzzis, two rests., bar. *Note:* The newest hotel in the park, on the Nana River w. spectacular mountain views. Very comfortable rms decorated

Alaskan style; acceptable rests. Free airport and railroad-station shuttles. A fine place. Open late May to mid-Sept. **E,** but lower rates off-season.

🏩🏩 **McKinley Chalets,** Park Hwy. (Ak. 3, Milepost 238), Denali Park, AK 99755 (907/683-2215). 288 mini-suites. AE, MC, V. *Note:* Rustic but very comfortable chalets, on the bank of the Nenana River, w. a fine view. Excellent rest. Can arrange park excursions, rafting, or light-aircraft trips. Interesting dinner theater. Very nr. park entrance; caters mostly to groups. Open mid-May through Sept; resv. (907/276-7234) must be made well in advance. **E**

☀🏩🏩 **Denali National Park Hotel,** Park Rd., Milepost 240, Denali Park, AK 99755 (907/683-2215). 100 rms. AE, MC, V. Free parking, rest., coffee shop, bar. *Note:* Adjacent to the Alaska Railroad train station and the visitor center, this is the only hotel in the park itself, offering you friendly rms w. bath. The hotel can arrange excursions in the park, rafting on the river, or flights in light aircraft. Open end of May through Sept. Resv. (907/276-7234), far in advance, are a must. **M**

⚓ **FAIRBANKS** (365 mi./588km north of Anchorage by Ak. 3; direct flights from most cities in Alaska; train from Anchorage on the Alaska Railroad, an 11-hr. trip): Alaska's second city (pop. 30,800), almost at the geographical center of the state, is first and foremost a supply base for the towns north of the Arctic Circle and for the oilfields of Prudhoe Bay, and thus a busy commercial hub. The most notable of its attractions include:

⚓ **Alaskaland,** Airport Way and Peger Rd. (907/459-1087): This amusement park (open daily late May to early Sept) has a replica of a gold-rush town, open-air museum, restaurant aboard an old paddlewheel steamer, etc. Entertaining.

⚓ **Ester** (8 mi./12km SW on Ak. 3): An authentic turn-of-the-century gold-prospectors' town. The old Cripple Creek District and the Malemute Saloon are worth going out of your way to see.

University Museum, University Campus, College Rd. (907/474-7505), open daily, has an interesting natural-history collection including a 36,000-year-old buffalo, and Native American and Inuit art and handcrafts. A visit to the university ⚓ **campus** is recommended.

Four-hour ⚓ **cruises** on the Chena River and Tanana River aboard a picturesque paddlewheel steamer: *Riverboat Discovery,* Discovery Rd. (907/479-6673), mid-May to mid-Sept. Unusual.

For more information, check with the **Fairbanks Convention & Visitors Bureau,** 714 Fourth Ave., Fairbanks, AK 99701 (907/456-5774; toll free 800/327-5774).

Where to Stay

🏩🏩 **Westmark Fairbanks,** 813 Noble St., Fairbanks, AK 99701 (907/456-7722; toll free 800/544-0970). 240 rms, A/C, color TV, in-rm movies. AE, DC, MC, V. Free parking, rest. (Bear 'N Seal), coffee shop, bar, rm svce. *Note:* Typical dwntwn business hotel. Comfortable rms; efficient svce. Free airport shuttle. **E,** but lower rates off-season.

☀🏩🏩 **Captain Bartlett Inn,** 1411-T Airport Way, Fairbanks, AK 99701 (907/452-1888; toll free 800/544-7528). 200 rms, color TV. AE, DC, MC, V. Free parking, sauna, health club, rest. (The Captain's Table), bar, rm svce, free airport limo. *Note:* Comfortable hotel decorated in a picturesque "Far North" style (the reception area is floored w. spruce logs), and boasting "the biggest fireplace in Alaska." Comfortable rms; average rest.; winning atmosphere; good svce. Nr. the Alaskaland theme park and the airport; 8 min. from dwntwn. Open year round. **M,** but lower rates off-season.

🏩🏩 **Great Land Hotel** (formerly the Chena View Hotel), 723 First Ave., Fairbanks, AK 99701 (907/452-6661). 90 rms, cable color TV. AE, DC, MC, V. Free parking, rest., bar, rm svce. *Note:* Dwntwn motel

w. panoramic view of the Chena River. Spacious, comfortable rms; friendly welcome and svce; overall good value. Open year round. **I–M**

🛏 **Super 8 Motel,** 1909 Airport Way, Fairbanks, AK 99701 (907/451-8888; toll free 800/800-8000). 77 rms, cable color TV. AE, CB, DC, MC, V. Free parking, adj. rest., free morning coffee, free airport limo. *Note:* Typical motel featuring functional comfort. 8 min. from dwntwn. Open year round. **I–M**

Where to Eat

🍷🍷 **Clinkerdagger, Bickerstaff & Petts** (nr. dwntwn), 24 College Rd. (452-2756). A/C. Lunch Mon–Fri, dinner nightly; closed hols. AE, DC, MC, V. *Specialties:* steak, catch of the day, homemade desserts. *Note:* A local favorite got up like a fake-Tudor English pub. Decent food, generous helpings. Live music at dinner. Resv. advisable. *Steak/Seafood.* **I**

☀🍷🍷 **The Pump House** (nr. dwntwn), 1.3 mile on Chena Pump Rd. (479-8452). A/C. Lunch/dinner daily, brunch Sun. AE, DC, MC, V. *Specialties:* choice meat and fish from the broiler; lavish buffet at Sun brunch. *Note:* A real pump-house (and designated historic monument) on the Chena River, handsomely transformed into a rest. w. magnificent terrace for open-air meals in summer. A local favorite. No resv. needed. *American.* **I**

☀🍷 **Alaska Salmon Bake,** in the Alaskaland theme park, Airport Way and Peger Rd. (452-7274). Lunch/dinner daily mid-May to mid-Sept. No credit cards. *Specialties:* fresh salmon, halibut, king crab, barbecued meats. *Note:* A must for every tourist: the Alaska equivalent of a New England clam bake—delicious open-air cooking at a very reasonable price. A colorful, entertaining experience that you shouldn't miss. Free transportation from dwntwn. *Seafood.* **B–I**

⚓ **FORT YUKON** (reachable by air from Fairbanks): Former Hudson's Bay Co. trading post dating from 1847 and situated astride the Arctic Circle. Attracts many tourists for its authentic Native American handcrafts and its furs. Temperatures as high as 107° F (42° C) in summer and as low as −78° F (−61° C) in winter have been recorded here.

☀⚓ **GATES OF THE ARCTIC NATIONAL PARK** (reachable only by charter plane from Fairbanks): Established in 1980, this enormous park lies wholly north of the Arctic Circle. With the adjoining **Kobuk Valley National Park** (weird sand dunes and traces of glacial deposits) and **Noatak National Preserve** (on the trail of caribou, black bears, and wolves), it's one of the last wholly wild reservations in North America. Wonderful mountain and tundra landscapes, with the Noatak River slashing a 62-mi. (100km) canyon across this wilderness untouched by human hands. Unfortunately, it's difficult of access for the general run of tourists.

Information: Superintendent, Gates of the Arctic National Park, 201 First Ave., Fairbanks, AK 99707 (907/456-0281).

☀⚓ **GLACIER BAY NATIONAL PARK** (reachable by air or boat from Juneau): One of Alaska's noblest and most impressive natural beauties, this glorious bay, 50 mi. (80km) long by 2.5–10mi. (4–16km) broad and reminiscent of the Norwegian fjords, is cradled between two mountainous peninsulas whose many glaciers (including the superb **Muir Glacier**) throw off dazzling blue-white reflections. Rearing above the whole is the majestic outline of 15,320-ft. (4,663m) **Mt. Fairweather.** Great chunks of the glaciers are continually falling into the bay with a deafening roar which enhances the fascinating spectacle. Rich wildlife and marine life.

You can take a three-day boat trip across Glacier Bay—not to be missed—on **Glacier Bay Cruises,** Juneau (907/586-6300; toll free 800/426-7702). Operates from late May to mid-Sept. Also glacier overflights on a seaplane from **L.A.B. Flying Service,** Merchant's Wharf, Juneau (907/766-2222). These two excursions are worth the trip all by themselves.

Park access is limited during tourist season. For **information,** call 907/697-2230.

Where to Stay

☀☙️🛏️ **Glacier Bay Lodge,** Bartlett Cove (P.O. Box 108), Gustavus, AK 99826 (907/697-2225; toll free 800/622-2042). 55 rms. DC, MC, V. Marina, boating, fishing, rest., bar. *Note:* The only hotel in Glacier Bay National Park; the ideal starting point for trips by boat, by plane, or on foot in Glacier Bay. Elegant rustic architecture in the heart of a forest. Comfortable rms; rest. w. a panoramic view. A place that nature-lovers won't forget—but you should book far ahead. Open from the end of May through mid-Sept. Campsite adj. **M–E**

Where to Eat

☀🍷🥂 **Glacier Bay Lodge Dining Room,** in Glacier Bay Lodge (see "Where to Stay," above) (697-2225). Breakfast/lunch/dinner daily; closed from the end of Sept through the end of May. MC, V. *Specialties:* salmon, trout, halibut, king crab, shellfish, meats from the broiler. *Note:* Wonderful hotel dining rm w. a view of Glacier Bay and the mountains that is one of Alaska's finest. Excellent cooking, relying heavily on local seafood. Attentive service; resv. a must. *American/Seafood.* **I–M**

☀🛎️ **HAINES** (775 mi./1,240km SE of Anchorage by the Alaska Hwy. and Haines Hwy.; reachable by air from Juneau, or by the Alaska Marine Hwy. ferry): This little fishing port, tucked between the sea, the Chilkat River, and Mt. Kipinsky at the northern end of the Inside Passage, offers a number of attractions:

🛎️ **Sheldon Museum,** Main St. at the Boat Harbor (907/766-2366): Devoted to the history of the Alaska pioneers and collections of Native American objects; open daily in summer, on Mon, Wed and Sun the rest of the year.

🛎️ **Fort William H. Seward,** Mud Bay Rd. (907/766-2540): A turn-of-the-century army post with a replica of a small Native American village. Not to be missed are the demonstrations of tribal dancing in summer in the Chilkat Center for the Arts. Call 766-2160 for information. Open daily.

☀🛎️ **Chilkat Bald Eagle Preserve,** adjoining the town: Home from late Oct to Dec of every year of 4,000 eagles, the world's largest colony of this species. **Chilkat Guides,** P.O. Box 170, Haines, AK 99827 (907/766-2491) offers four-hour guided trips by boat during May–Sept.

Where to Stay

♀🛏️ **Hotel Hälsingland,** 13 Fort Seward Dr., Haines, AK 99827 (907/766-2000; toll free 800/542-6363). 50 rms (most w. bath). AE, CB, DC, MC, V. Free parking, rest. (Commander's Room), bar. *Note:* This picturesque Victorian-style hotel occupies what used to be the officers' quarters of Fort Seward, offering a fine view of the Lynn Canal and the surrounding mountains. Charming rms w. functional comfort (most w. private bath). Very creditable rest.; welcome w. a smile. Facing Totem Village and adj. a campsite. Very good value. Open mid-April to Sept. **I–M**

Where to Eat

🍷 **Commander's Room** in the Hotel Hälsingland (see "Where to Stay," above) (766-2000). Breakfast/lunch/dinner daily; closed from Sept to mid-Apr. AE, CB, DC, MC, V. *Specialties:* fresh salmon, halibut, scallops, sautéed prawns, steak. *Note:* Very creditable hotel cuisine served in the former officers' mess of Fort Seward. Fine view of the Lynn Canal and the mountains. Cheerful, friendly svce; very good value. *American/Seafood.* **B–I**

    HOMER (225 mi./360km SW of Anchorage by Ak. 1; reachable by air from Anchorage; Alaska Marine Hwy. ferry connection to Kodiak): A deep-water, ice-free port. Boat trips to the beautiful ♦ **Kachemak Bay,** rimmed by the Kenai Mountains. A small, well-laid-out natural-history museum is the ♦ **Pratt Museum,** 3779 Bartlett St. (907/235-8635); open daily May–Sept, Tues–Sun the rest of the year. Lovely city and bay views from **Skyline Drive,** reached via E. Hill Rd.

    For information, go to the **Homer Visitor Center,** 135 Sterling Hwy. (907/235-7740).

Where to Stay

    Best Western Bidarka Inn, 575 Sterling Hwy., Homer, AK 99603 (907/235-8148; toll free, see Best Western). 74 rms, cable color TV. AE, DC, MC, V. Free parking, health club, Jacuzzi, rest., bar, free airport shuttle. *Note:* Comfortable, inviting motel on Kachermak Bay in an agreeable rustic setting. Spacious rms, some w. kitchenette. Friendly reception. Open year round. **I–M**

    Driftwood Inn, 135 W. Bunnell Ave., Homer, AK 99603 (907/235-8019). 20 rms, color TV. AE, MC, V. Free parking; no bar or rest., but free coffee. *Note:* Charming old hotel of family type, one block from the water and nr. dwntwn. Rustic but comfortable. Good-humored svce. Sea-fishing parties organized. Good value; open year round. **I–M**

    JUNEAU (reachable by direct flights from Anchorage or Seattle, or by Alaska Marine Hwy. ferry): Nestling at the feet of the snowcapped **Mt. Juneau** and **Mt. Roberts,** Alaska's picturesque capital is nicknamed "Little San Francisco" because of its narrow streets and the flights of wooden steps hugging the hillsides on which its multicolored houses are built. Besides the ultramodern **State Capitol,** Main and 4th Sts. (admission Mon–Fri in summer only), and the elegant **Governor's Mansion,** Calhoun Ave. at 9th St., with its colonial pillars, you should see the unusual Russian Orthodox ♦ **St. Nicholas Church,** at 5th and Gold Sts., a wooden octagon dating from 1894 (open daily). The ♦ **House of Wickersham,** 213 7th St. (907/586-9001), open Mon–Sat mid-May through Sept, offers you a fine sweeping view, as well as collections of historical memorabilia from the days of the pioneers and the Russian colonists.

    The very fine ♦ **Alaska State Museum,** Whittier St. at Egan Dr. (907/465-2901), open daily, displays an instructive panorama of the history of Alaska's Inuit and Native Americans (Aleuts, Athapascans, Tlingits), as well as mastodon tusks more than 50,000 years old, totem poles, etc.

    The ♦ **Juneau-Douglas City Museum,** 4th and Main Sts. (586-3572), open in the afternoons daily, concentrates on Alaska's 19th-century mining boom. Many memorabilia, photos, tools, and everyday articles from the pioneer period.

    For information, contact the **Juneau Visitors Information Center,** 134 3rd St. (907/586-2201).

    A short trip (13 mi./20km NW via Glacier Hwy.) to ♦♦ **Mendenhall Glacier** should be given high priority. This great river of ice, 12 mi. (19km) long by 1.5 mi. (2.5km) wide, is retreating at about 67 ft. (21m) a year; it has taken more than 10,000 years to move 4.3 mi. (7km) back from the sea, giving birth to a lake at the foot of the dizzying crevasses that fall sheer to the floor of the valley it has carved out. Visitor center with observatory at the foot of the glacier. Bus service to the glacier through **MGT** (907/789-5460).

    On **Douglas Island,** offshore from Juneau, is the **Eagle Crest** winter-sports resort (907/586-5284), open Dec–Apr.

Juneau is also a base for boat trips to the 🏔 **Tracy Arm–Ford's Terror Wilderness,** where the glaciers tumble into fjords 960 ft. (300m) and more deep.

Where to Stay

☀☗♀♀ **Baranof Westmark Hotel,** 127 N. Franklin St., Juneau, AK 99801 (907/586-2660; toll free 800/544-0970). 193 rms, color TV, in-rm movies. AE, DC, MC, V. Free parking, rest. (Gold Room), coffee shop, bar, rm svce. *Note:* The *grande dame* of local hostelries, right on Franklin St., the historic main street of dwntwn. Opulent decor; comfortable rms (some w. kitchenettes); good rest.; attentive svce. Caters mostly to groups; open year round. **M–E**

♀☗ **Breakwater Inn,** 1711 Glacier Ave., Juneau, AK (907/586-6303). 40 rms, cable color TV. AE, CB, DC, MC, V. Free parking, rest., bar. *Note:* Very comfortable motel w. a spectacular view of the harbor and the mountains. Pleasant rms w. private balconies (some w. kitchenettes). Smiling svce; good value; open year round. **I–M**

♀☗ **Driftwood Lodge,** 435 Willoughby Ave. W., Juneau, AK 99801 (907/586-2280; toll free 800/544-2239). 62 rms, cable color TV. AE, MC, V. *Note:* Inviting dwntwn motel not far from the ferry terminal. Modern and comfortable; some rms w. kitchenette. Friendly reception and svce. Free shuttles to the airport and the ferry terminal. Open year round. **I–M**

Where to Eat

♀♀ **Fiddlehead Restaurant & Bakery,** 429 W. Willoughby Ave. ☗☗ (586-3150). Lunch Wed–Fri, dinner daily. AE, MC, V. *Specialties:* pasta Greta Garbo (w. smoked salmon), chicken and eggplant Szechuan, fresh seafood; memorable breads, pastries and desserts. *Note:* One of Juneau's favorite rests. Bright, airy setting w. lots of light woods and hanging plants. Tasty food impeccably presented and served. Resv. advised. *American.* **I**

☀♀♀ **Silverbow Inn** (in hotel of the same name), 120 2nd St. (586-☗☗ 4146). Dinner only, daily; closed hols. AE, DC, MC, V. *Specialties:* regional French dishes, catch of the day; menu changes regularly. *Note:* Charming old (1914) building, pleasingly restored. Ultra-romantic setting (dinner by candlelight) and regional American cooking. Attentive svce; resv. advisable. *American.* **I**

☀♀ **Mike's Fine Food and Spirits,** 1102 2nd St., in nearby Douglas (364-3271). Lunch Tues–Fri, dinner Tues–Sun. AE, DC, MC, V. *Specialties:* king crab, fresh salmon, catch of the day, steak. *Note:* A local landmark across the Juneau-Douglas Bridge, Mike's claims to be one of Alaska's oldest rests. Excellent fish and seafood; spectacular view of Gastineau Channel and the harbor. A very good place; resv. advised. *American/Seafood.* **I**

♀ **Armadillo Tex-Mex Café,** 431 S. Franklin St. (586-1880). ☗ Lunch Mon–Sat, dinner daily. MC, V. *Specialties:* chile, fajitas, barbecued hot link sausages. *Note:* Spicy, flavorful Tex-Mex food at modest prices. A local favorite. Across from the Old Ferry Terminal. *American/Mexican.* **B–I**

☀☗ **KATMAI NATIONAL PARK** (reachable by air from Anchorage, or from Kodiak as far as King Salmon): A beautiful nature preserve of 4.1 million acres (16,600km²) in the NE of the Alaska Peninsula. Deep forests shelter brown bears, which are clever salmon-fishers (don't overlook a visit to the 🏔 **McNeil River Sanctuary** at the east end of the park). Many lakes and active volcanoes. The unusually violent eruption of **Mt. Katmai** in 1912 created the lunar landscape of the 🏔 **Valley of Ten Thousand Smokes,** as well as striking cliffs of white ash 90–300 ft. (30–100m) high.

For **information,** contact the Superintendent, Katmai National Park, P.O. Box 7, King Salmon, AK 99613 (907/246-3305); open early June to Sept.

      🔔 **KENAI** (158 mi./252km SW of Anchorage along Ak. 1; or reachable by air from Anchorage): This is the second-oldest city in the state (founded by Russians in 1791) and, thanks to an active offshore drilling program, one of the oil capitals of Alaska. A fine Russian Orthodox church of 1896, the ⛪ **Assumption of the Virgin Mary Church,** is well worth a look; visit by appointment (907/283-4122). For local information, contact the **Kenai Visitors Center,** 11471 Kenai Spur Hwy. (907/283-1991).

Where to Stay

      🛏 **Kings Inn,** 10352 Spur Hwy., Kenai, AK 99611 (907/283-6060). 50 rms, cable color TV. AE, CB, DC, MC, V. Free parking, rest., bar, nightclub. *Note:* Classic motel 1 mi. (1.6km) east of town on the Kenai Spur Hwy. Modern comforts; great if you're driving through. Good value; open year round. **M,** but lower rates off-season.

KENAI FJORDS NATIONAL PARK: See Seward.

      🔔 **KETCHIKAN** (reachable by air from Seattle, Juneau, or Sitka; or by Alaska Marine Hwy. ferry): Alaska's southernmost city holds the U.S. record for rainfall—160 in. (4m) a year! Nicknamed "the world's salmon capital," this important fishing port is also home to the world's largest collection of Native American totem poles in 🗿🗿 **Saxman Totem Park,** 3 mi. (5km) south on S. Tongass Hwy. (open daily); the **Totem Heritage Center,** 601 Deermount St. (907/225-5900), open daily in summer, Tues–Fri the rest of the year; and the **Totem Bight Historical Site,** 10 mi. (16km) north on N. Tongass Hwy., open daily. There are more than 60 totem poles in these three locations, and they're worth the trip all by themselves. But while you're here, take a look at the charming little frame houses on Creek St., and visit the interesting **Tongass Historical Museum,** 629 Dock St. (907/225-5600), open daily in summer, Wed–Sun the rest of the year, with Native American and gold-rush exhibits. For information, contact the **Ketchikan Visitors Bureau,** 131 Front St. (907/225-6166).

Where to Stay

      ☀🛏 **Ingersoll Hotel,** 303 Mission St., Ketchikan, AK 99901 (907/225-2124). 60 rms, color TV. AE, DC, MC, V. Free parking, bar, free breakfast, rm svce. *Note:* This charming older hotel, at the center of "The Block," the heart of historic Ketchikan, and looming over the harbor, has pleasant but small rms, a locally popular rest., and likable atmosphere. Open year round. **M,** but lower rates off-season.

      First United Methodist Church, Grant and Main Sts., Ketchikan, AK 99901 (907/225-3780). Youth hostel open from the end of May to the end of Aug.

Where to Eat

      🍷🍸 **Salmon Falls Resort,** N. Tongass Hwy. at mile 17 (225-2752). Dinner only, nightly; closed Oct–Apr. AE, MC, V. *Specialties:* steak, fresh halibut, king crab. *Note:* Absolute freshest catch served in attractive log building 17 mi. (27km) north of town. Great view overlooking the ocean. Locally popular, so resv. are advised. *Steak/Seafood.* **M–E**

      ☀🔔 **KODIAK** (reachable by air from Anchorage or by Alaska Marine Hwy. ferry from Homer and Seward): Capital of Russian America (1784–99) and now the home port of the state's most important fishing fleet. For an insight into Alaska's Russian heritage, don't fail to visit the ⛪ **Baranof Museum,** 101 Marine Way (907/486-5920), Alaska's oldest building (1793), a wood-frame structure which the colony's governor, Alexander Baranof, used for fur storage (open daily in the summer, closed Sun and Thurs the rest of the year); or the ⛪ **Holy Resurrection Church** (1794), again the state's oldest, with its typical bulbous domes and some very fine icons and old paintings; visits by appointment (907/486-3854). The **Kodiak Information Center** is at 100 Marine Way (907/486-4782).

The western half of Kodiak Island is a ⛪ **nature reserve,** rich in wildlife—particularly the giant brown Kodiak bear, which can grow up to 1,500 lb. (600kg); a total of 2,400 Kodiak bears live on the island. The reserve can be reached by boat or plane from Kodiak. For information, contact Kodiak Wildlife Refuge, 1390 Buskin River Rd., Kodiak, AK 99615 (907/487-2600).

Where to Stay

Westmark Kodiak (formerly the Sheffield), 236 Rezanof W., Kodiak, AK 99615 (907/486-5712; toll free 800/544-0970). 81 rms, cable color TV. AE, DC, MC, V. Free parking, rest., bar, crib $15. *Note:* Typical contemporary motel. Serviceably comfortable rms, some very small. Well located across from the fishing-boat harbor. A giant Kodiak bear (stuffed) presides over the lobby. Good value on balance. Open year round. **M**

Shelikof Lodge, 211 Thorsheim Ave., Kodiak, AK 99615 (907/486-4141). 39 rms, cable color TV. AE, DC, MC, V. Free parking, rest. (Fox Inn), bar. *Note:* Overlooking the harbor and the city, this modern comfortable two-story motel is not far from the ferry terminal. Rms recently renovated; acceptable rest.; overall good value. Open year round. **I**

Where to Eat

Chartroom Restaurant, in the Westmark Kodiak (see "Where to Stay," above) (486-5712). A/C. Breakfast/lunch/dinner daily. AE, DC, MC, V. *Specialties:* Alaska crab, grilled salmon, steak, catch of the day. *Note:* Faultless but unimaginative hotel food. The rest. has a fine view of the harbor. Good svce. *American.* **I**

KOTZEBUE (reachable only by air, from Anchorage, Fairbanks, and Nome): Just north of the Arctic Circle, this little (pop. 2,000) town is home to one of the oldest Inuit communities in Alaska, which has lived there at least 300–400 years. It owes its name to the Baltic baron Otto von Kotzebue, who explored these parts around 1840. The ice covering its bay melts in spectacular fashion around the beginning of June. The very modern and interesting ⛪ **Nana Museum of the Arctic,** near the airport (907/442-3301), open Mon–Fri, will show you scenes of everyday Inuit life (dances, songs, the blanket game, dogsled races, handcraft demonstrations) and well-designed dioramas of the Arctic environment, particularly the region's wildlife.

Where to Stay

Nullagvik Hotel, P.O. Box 336-T, Kotzebue, AK 99752 (907/442-3331). 80 rms. AE, MC, V. Rest., bar, hrdrsr. *Note:* In spite of its tongue-twisting name, this comfortable motel is a favorite w. visitors to the Far North; in summer, you can sit at your ease and admire the midnight sun as well as the view of the Arctic Ocean and Kotzebue Sound. Unusual decor; excellent buffet; very good svce. Open year round. **M–E**

MALASPINA GLACIER: See Yakutat.

MENDENHALL GLACIER: See Juneau.

MISTY FJORDS NATIONAL MONUMENT (reachable by boat or seaplane from Ketchikan): Lying between two narrow bays, this lovely natural park, encompassing glaciers, granite cliffs falling sheer into the ocean, and many crystal-clear lakes, marks the southern frontier between Alaska and Canada. Rich wildlife, comprising particularly seals, whales (in the **Behm Canal**), and innumerable waterfowl.

For **information,** contact the U.S. Forest Service, Federal Bldg., 3031 Tongass Ave., Ketchikan, AK 99901 (907/225-2148).

MOUNT MCKINLEY: See Denali National Park.

NOME (reachable only by air, from Anchorage or Fairbanks): Standing on the Bering Sea only an hour's flying time from Russia, this busy port city reached its apogee in 1898 with the first gold rush, which attracted 40,000 prospectors; today it has 2,900 inhabitants. The commercial and economic capital of northwestern Alaska, Nome (a contraction of "No Name") has since 1979 witnessed a sharp upturn in exploration for crude oil, and has also become a tourist center for lovers of fishing, hunting, Inuit dances, and Native American handcrafts. An interesting museum of Inuit art, the **Carrie McClain Memorial Museum** on Front St. (907/443-5133), open Mon–Sat Feb–Nov, also has displays on the history of the gold rush on the shores of the Bering Sea. Nome is also the scene of the celebrated annual ☼ **Iditarod Trail Race,** the dogsled marathon that's run every Mar over the 1,049 mi. (1,680km) of virgin country between Nome and Anchorage.

Where to Stay

Nugget Inn, Front St. (P.O. Box 430-T), Nome, AK 99762 (907/443-2323). 47 rms, color TV. AE, DC, MC, V. Rest., bar. *Note:* With its wooden exterior and "Gold Rush" decor, the Nugget Inn might be a set for an adventure movie. Very comfortable rms (the best looking out over the Bering Strait). Likable bar. Svce efficient. Resv. required. Caters mostly to groups and organized tours. Open year round. **M**

PETERSBURG (reachable by air from Juneau or Sitka, or by Alaska Marine Hwy. ferry): Nicknamed "Little Norway" because of its many Scandinavian settlers, this charming little fishing port situated at the center of the Inside Passage is a point of departure for boat or seaplane excursions to the spectacular ⚓ **Le Conte Glacier,** 25 mi. (40km) away; for information, contact Viking Travel, 106 N. Nordic Dr., Petersburg, AK 99833 (907/772-3818). The town's ⚓ **Clausen Memorial Museum,** 2nd and Fram Sts. (907/772-3598), open daily in summer, Wed and Sat the rest of the year, offers a real lure for fishing enthusiasts: the world-record King salmon (126.5 lb./57kg!). For general information, contact the **Petersburg Visitors Center,** 221 Harbor Way (P.O. Box 649-TD), Petersburg, AK 99833 (907/772-3646).

PORTAGE GLACIER: See Anchorage

PRIBILOF ISLANDS (reachable only by air from Anchorage and Cold Bay): Lost in the Bering Sea, 750 mi. (1,200km) from Anchorage as the crow flies, this chaplet of green islands shrouded in fog and mist is heaven on earth for naturalists, with more than 200 species of animals and the world's largest seal colony (over a million between May and Sept); it's the Far North's answer to the Galapagos.

St. **Paul,** the archipelago's largest island, boasts a picturesque Aleut village with a pretty Russian Orthodox church. Season: early June to late Aug.

For **information,** contact Reeve Aleutian Airways, 4700 W. International Rd., Anchorage, AK 99502 (907/243-4700; toll free 800/544-2248).

PRUDHOE BAY (reachable by air from Anchorage and Fairbanks or by car from Fairbanks via the Dalton Hwy., 450 mi./720km): With crude-oil and natural-gas reserves equivalent to 2½ times those of Texas, Alaska's black-gold capital stands amid a flat and desolate landscape on the shores of the Arctic Sea. The terminal of an enormous (800-mi/1,280km) pipeline, which since 1977 has linked it to the harbor of Valdez on the Pacific,

Prudhoe is a living museum of technology. You'll be able to see for yourself the technology involved in tapping a reservoir which lies under the permafrost, with wells that sometimes go to a depth of 1.5 mi. (3,000m)—and you'll see it in a town which in summer is surrounded by herds of wandering caribou and flocks of migrant birds. Visits from late May to Sept.

For **information,** contact the Arctic Caribou Lodge (907/659-2368).

Note: The James W. Dalton Hwy. is open to regular automobile traffic only as far as Disaster Creek, 211 mi. (338km) north of Fairbanks. You'll need a special permit for your car (they're granted very sparingly) for the section of Dalton Hwy. between Disaster Creek and Prudhoe Bay; check with the local authorities at Fairbanks. If you have a breakdown, the Dalton Hwy. has only two gas/ service stations along its entire length: at the Yukon River crossing (Mile 56) and at Coldfoot (Mile 175). For lovers of the great unspoiled outdoors. **Gray Line Tours,** 1980 S. Cushman St., Fairbanks (907/456-7741; toll free 800/544-2206), has regular bus service along the Dalton Hwy. as far as Prudhoe Bay, returning by air to Fairbanks.

Where to Stay

♀ **Prudhoe Bay Hotel,** Pouch 34004, Prudhoe Bay, AK 99734 (907/659-2449). 207 rms. AE, MC, V. Sauna, rest. (no alcoholic beverages since Prudhoe Bay is a "dry" town), TV lounge. *Note:* Large modern hotel adjacent to the airport. Comfortable rms; clientele mostly groups and those w. business in the oilfields. Open year round. A boon to the traveler; the nearest town (Barrow) and hotel are 240 mi. (386km) away as the crow flies. **M–E**

SEWARD (127 mi./203km south of Anchorage via Ak. 1 and Ak. 9; or reachable by air or the Alaska Railroad from Anchorage): Ringed by mountains at the southern tip of the Kenai Peninsula, this little fishing port was badly damaged by the 1964 earthquake. Terminus of the Alaska Railroad, which links it to Fairbanks, the town takes its name from Secretary of State William H. Seward, who negotiated the Alaska Purchase in the 19th century. The tourist office, **Visitor Information Cache,** Third Ave. and Jefferson St. (907/224-3094), is housed in the old dining car that Pres. Warren G. Harding used on his visit to Alaska in 1923. Open daily, summer only. Be sure, too, to visit ⚓ **St. Peter's Episcopal Church,** Second Ave. and Adams St., for the beautiful painting of the Resurrection, done in 1925 by the Dutch artist Jan van Emple, using Alaskans as models and Resurrection Bay as a background.

Aside from its lovely natural setting, Seward is also the starting-point for excursions, by boat, seaplane, or automobile, to ❊▲ **Kenai Fjords National Park.** Embracing several vast icefields on the eastern slope of the Kenai Mountains (one of which is the **Exit Glacier**), this park, set up in 1980, is a tangled network of fjords and jagged shores, where whales, porpoises, seals, and sea birds hold undisputed sway. The southern shore of the park was significantly damaged by the "black tide" resulting from the *Exxon Valdez* episode in 1989, but the accident had only a slight impact on tourist activities: Boat excursions leaving from Seward are confined to nearer and unpolluted coastal zones.

For **information,** contact the Superintendent, Kenai Fjords National Park, P.O. Box 1727, Seward, AK 99664 (907/224-3874 or 224-3175).

Where to Stay

♀♀ **Best Western Hotel Seward,** 221 Fifth Ave., AK 99664 (907/224-2378; toll free, see Best Western). 38 rms, color TV, in-rm movies. AE, CB, DC, MC, V. Free parking, rest. adj., crib $5. *Note:* Comfortable motel centrally located dwntwn, one block from the ferry terminal. Very well equipped and furnished rms. **M–E,** but lower rates off-season.

♀ **Marina Motel,** Mile 1 on Ak. 9, AK 99664 (907/224-5518). 18 rms, cable color TV. AE, CB, DC, MC, V. Free parking. *Note:* Friendly little motel w. a splendid view of bay and harbor. Comfortable rms, inviting grdns w. a picnic area. Free morning coffee; free airport and ferry limo. Open year round. **I–M**

Where to Eat

� **Harbor Dinner Club & Lounge,** Fifth Ave. (907/224-3012). Lunch/dinner daily. MC, V. *Specialties:* fresh salmon, halibut, prime rib. *Note:* Fresh seafood is the specialty of this popular rest. on the harbor. Straightforward, unassuming decor. Friendly svce. Very good value. **I**

SITKA (reachable by plane from Juneau, Ketchikan, or Seattle; or by Alaska Marine Hwy. ferry): The splendid site was discovered in 1741 by the explorer Vitus Bering, and the town, once nicknamed "the Paris of the Pacific," was picked in 1804 as Alaska's capital by Alexander Baranof, first governor of Russian America; it remained so until 1906, when Juneau was chosen to replace it.

Proud of its history, Sitka offers the visitor many evidences of its Russo-American heritage: ▲ **St. Michael's Cathedral,** Lincoln St. (907/747-8120), open Mon–Sat June–Sept (by appointment the rest of the year), with its valuable icons, is an exact replica of the original Russian Orthodox church of 1844, which was destroyed by fire in 1966. The ▲ **Russian Bishop's House,** Lincoln St. (907/747-6281), open daily in summer (by appointment the rest of the year), is Bishop Ivan Veniaminor's log cabin dating from 1842, a designated historic monument.

Among other noteworthy attractions are the ▲ **Sheldon Jackson State Museum,** Sheldon Jackson College Campus, 104 College Dr. (907/747-8981), open daily in summer (Sun and Tues–Fri the rest of the year), which has memorabilia of the Russian period, as well as Native American and Inuit masks; and the ▲ **Sitka National Historic Park,** at the end of Lincoln St. (907/747-6281), open daily year round, site of the "battle for Alaska" between Russians and the Tlingit tribe in 1804, the last stand of the original inhabitants against white domination. Fine collection of 18 Native American totem poles.

For information, contact the **Sitka Visitors Center,** 330 Harbor Dr. (907/747-5940 or 747-3739).

Where to Stay

Westmark Shee Atika Lodge, 330 Seward St., Sitka, AK 99835 (907/747-6241; toll free, 800/544-0970). 98 rms, cable color TV. AE, CB, DC, MC, V. Free parking, fishing, rest., bar, rm svce. *Note:* Modern hotel opposite the Convention Center, of unusual design that draws heavily on local materials, particularly wood. Comfortable, spacious rms looking out either over the harbor or toward the mountains. Good svce. Open year round. **M,** but lower rates off-season.

Potlatch House, 713 Katlian St., Sitka, AK 99835 (907/747-8611). 30 rms, cable color TV. AE, DC, MC, V. Free parking, rest., bar. *Note:* Comfortable motel 5 min. by car from dwntwn (free shuttle). Comfortable rms overlooking the harbor on Mt. Edgecumbe. You'll be a welcome, well-looked-after guest. Good value; open year round. **I–M**

Where to Eat

Channel Club, 2908 Halibut Point Rd., 3½ mi. (6km) north of town (907/747-9916). Dinner only, nightly; closed hols. AE, DC, MC, V. Jkt. *Specialties:* steak, fresh salmon, king crab, fish of the day. *Note:* Highly regarded locally for its excellent food and its magnificent view of the Western Channel and the impressive Mt. Edgecumbe. Choice seafood and prime cuts; extensive salad bar. Resv. highly advisable. *Steak/Seafood.* **M**

SKAGWAY (reachable by air from Haines or Juneau, or by Alaska Marine Hwy. ferry): Formerly the port of entry for the Klondike, Skagway has preserved the appearance and atmosphere of the 1898 gold rush better than any other town in Alaska. At that time it boasted 20,000 inhabitants; today, only about 800. ⚐ **Broadway,** Skagway's main drag, and the **Trail of '98 Museum,** City Hall, Seventh Ave. and Spring St. (907/983-2420), open daily May–Oct (by appointment in winter), perfectly reconstruct the age of the 19th-century gold prospectors. Recommended: ⚐ *In the Days of '98,* tragicomic melodrama about the gold rush, staged in Eagles Hall, 6th St. and Broadway (907/983-2545), presented daily May to mid-Sept.

On the outskirts, be sure to see the "ghost town" of **Dyea** (11 mi./18km NE on the Klondike Hwy.) or **Bennett Lake** (65 mi./106km NE on the Klondike Hwy.), on the edge of which stands the picturesque Canadian village of Carcross.

Reopened in 1988 after an interval of several years, the narrow-gauge railroad of the ⚐⚐ **White Pass & Yukon Route** takes tourists from Skagway to Fraser in the footsteps of the Klondike gold-rush pioneers. The 30 mi. (48km) trip crosses some of the most spectacular country in Alaska, including the famous White Pass (2,900 ft./885m) straddling the Canadian frontier. The White Pass & Yukon Route railway, Second Ave. at Broadway (907/983-2217; toll free 800/343-7373), operates from mid-May to mid-Sept, depending on the incidence of snowslides.

Hardier visitors will brave the rigors of the ⚐ **Chilkoot Trail,** a scenic mountain trail once used by the prospectors (a three- to four-day hike to Lake Bennett).

Skagway is one of the most popular tourist attractions of Alaska. There's a Visitor Center at Second Ave. and Broadway (907/983-2854), open May 15–Sept 30.

Where to Stay

☼⚐⚐ **Golden North Hotel,** 3rd St. and Broadway, Skagway, AK 99840 (907/983-2451). 34 rms. AE, DC, MC, V. Free parking, rest., bar. *Note:* With its singular gilded dome, this agreeable little hotel, a survivor from the gold rush, is one of Skagway's most interesting buildings, as well as being the oldest operating hotel in Alaska (since 1897). Comfortable rms w. period furnishings, each decorated in a different style. Guaranteed local color. Open year round. **I–M**

⚐ **Westmark Inn,** (formerly the Klondike Hotel), 3rd and Spring Sts., Skagway, AK 99840 (907/983-2291; toll free 800/544-0970). 209 rms AE, MC, V. Free parking, rest. (Chilkoot Room), coffee shop, bar. *Note:* Enormous, ungraceful modern motel, whose interior decoration is intended to evoke the great days of the Klondike. Comfortable and functional; favored by rather intrusive tour groups. Free airport and ferry limo. Rates excessive for a motel. Open mid-May to the end of Sept. **M**

Where to Eat

⚐ **Northern Lights Café,** Broadway at 4th St. (907/983-2225). Lunch/dinner daily. MC, V. *Specialties:* fresh salmon, halibut, steak. *Note:* A longtime Skagway classic; decent, unpretentious cooking at very reasonable prices. A boon to the tourist. *American/Seafood.* **B–I**

☼⚐ **TONGASS NATIONAL FOREST** (reached by boat or seaplane from Juneau, Ketchikan, Petersburg, Sitka, etc.): Largest national forest in the U.S.: 17 million acres (69,000km^2). Covers most of the Alaska panhandle from Juneau to Ketchikan. Notable features are **Misty Island National Monument** and **Misty Fjords National Monument** (see above). A verdant paradise of deep fjords, unspoiled islands, rocky mountains more than 10,000 ft. (3,000m) high in places, and trackless rain forests. Camping permits available; also rustic bungalows.

For **information,** contact the U.S. Forest & National Park Service, 101 Egan Dr., Juneau, AK 99801 (907/586-8751), or 3031 TP Tongass Ave., Ketchikan, AK 99901 (907/225-2148).

⚓ **VALDEZ** (317 mi./507km NE of Anchorage via Ak. 1 and Ak. 4; also reachable by air from Anchorage or Fairbanks, and by Alaska Marine Hwy. ferry from Whittier or Seward): Standing north of the Arctic Circle in a grandly mountainous setting at the foot of Prince William Sound, Valdez, once dubbed "the Switzerland of Alaska," is the terminal of the Prudhoe Bay crude-oil pipeline—and the third-busiest port in the U.S. in terms of tonnage. You can arrange a fascinating visit to the ⚓ **Trans-Alaska Pipeline.**

Valdez is also the starting point for an expedition to the great 3.7-mi.-wide (6km) 🏔 **Columbia Glacier** where it falls sheer into the sea. For information, contact Columbia Glacier Cruises (907/835-5141), Era Helicopters (907/835-2595), or Gray Line Tours (907/835-2357).

It was some 50 nautical miles (80km) south of Valdez that on March 24, 1989, the tanker *Exxon Valdez* ran aground, causing the largest "black tide" in U.S. history: 260,000 barrels (34,000 tons) of crude oil spilled into the majestic waters of Prince William Sound, wreaking havoc on marine, bird, and terrestrial wildlife. Some 350,000 birds, more than 3,000 seals and sea otters, and dozens of bears and other large mammals were killed, according to the official count, without reckoning the thousands of tons of fish polluted by the deadly seepage. However, in spite of an oil slick that affected 1,100 mi. (1,760km) of shoreline, less than 1% of the Alaska coast was touched by the black tide—a flea bite on the continent's skin. After two cleanup campaigns involving 11,000 people and 1,400 boats, 80% of the surface of Prince William Sound was restored, more or less, to its original condition—a fact that should reassure the 700,000 visitors who come to Alaska on vacation every year.

For information, contact the **Valdez Visitors Center,** 200 Chenega St. (907/835-2984; toll free 800/770-5954).

Where to Stay

🛏🛏 **Westmark Valdez,** 100 Fidalgo Dr., Valdez, AK 99686 (907/835-4391; toll free 800/544-0970). 100 rms, cable color TV. AE, MC, V. Free parking, marina, boat, fishing, rest. (Captain's Table), bar, rm svce. *Note:* Comfortable motel on the yacht basin. Spacious, comfortable rms (the best overlooking the harbor). Satisfactory rest. Nr. the Ferry Terminal. Guided tours of Columbia Glacier daily in summer. Open year round. **M–E**

🛏 **Village Inn,** Meals Ave. and Richardson Hwy., Valdez, AK 99686 (907/835-4445). 100 rms, color TV. AE, MC, V. Free parking, health club, sauna, rest. (Gay Nineties), bar. *Note:* Modest but well-run motel nr. the Ferry Terminal offering your choice of functionally comfortable rms (some w. private bath) or individual cottages w. kitchenettes. Guided tours of Columbia Glacier daily in summer. Open year round. **M**

⚓ **WRANGELL** (reachable by air from Ketchikan or Juneau, or by Alaska Marine Hwy. ferry): The only city in Alaska to have flown, in succession, the Russian, British, and U.S. flags, Wrangell has also lived through no fewer than three gold rushes, in 1863, 1873, and 1898. Be sure to see the ⚓ **Bear Tribal House,** Chief Shakes Island (907/874-3747), open varying days and times, for its fine carved totem poles, and the mysterious ⚓ **Native American rock carvings** that may be seen at low tide on the beach near the Ferry Dock.

For information, contact the **Wrangell Visitors Center,** Brueger St. and Outer Dr. (907/874-3901), open May–Sept (call 907/874-3770 the rest of the year).

🔆⚓ **WRANGELL–ST. ELIAS NATIONAL PARK** (reachable by the Glenn and Richardson Hwys. to the north of the park, or by boat from Yakutat to the south of the park): With an area of 12,730 sq. mi.

(39,270km²), and created in 1981, this is our largest national park—3½ times the size of Yellowstone. The peaks of **Mt. Blackburn** (16,523 ft./4,995m) in the Wrangell Mountains and **Mt. St. Elias** (18,008 ft./5,489m) in the St. Elias Mountains rear above this great stretch of wildland, which, with the adjoining **Kluane National Park,** to the south across the Canadian border, makes up the world's largest assembly of glaciers, other than those of the polar icecaps. Among them is the enormous **Malaspina Glacier,** the biggest icefield in North America. There are only two roads for vehicles into the park interior: the Nabesha Rd., open year round, and McCarthy Rd., open May–Oct.

For **information,** contact the Superintendent, Wrangell–St. Elias National Park and Preserve, P.O. Box 29-T, Glenallen, AK 99588 (907/822-5234), and at the ranger stations at Chitina, Copper Center, and Slana. For lovers of unspoiled nature-in-the-raw.

YAKUTAT (reachable by air from Anchorage or Juneau): A former Tlingit village, on the sea half way between Cordova and Inside Passage, Yakutat is the ideal jumping-off point for a boat or kayak trip along **Russel Fjord** and the **Hubbard Glacier,** or for a flight over the majestic **Malaspina Glacier,** bigger than the state of Rhode Island.

For **information,** contact Gulf Air Taxi, Yakutat, AK 99689 (907/784-3240).

SPECIAL EVENTS AROUND ALASKA

For exact dates on the following special events, check with the following sources of travel information:

Cordova Chamber of Commerce, P.O. Box 99, Cordova, AK 99574 (907/424-7260).

Fairbanks Convention & Visitors Bureau, 714 Fourth Ave., Fairbanks, AK 99701 (907/456-5774; toll free 800/327-5774).

Haines Visitors Bureau, P.O. Box 518, Haines, AK 99827 (907/766-2234; toll free 800/458-3579).

Juneau Convention & Visitors Bureau, 369 S. Franklin St., Suite 201, Juneau, AK 99801 (907/586-1737).

Kodiak Area Chamber of Commerce, P.O. Box 1485, Kodiak, AK 99615 (907/486-5557).

Nome Convention and Visitors Bureau, P.O. Box 240, Nome, AK 99762 (907/443-5535).

Seward Chamber of Commerce, P.O. Box 749, Seward, AK 99664 (907/224-3046).

Sitka Convention & Visitors Bureau, P.O. Box 1226, Sitka, AK 99835 (907/747-5940).

Skagway Convention & Visitors Bureau, P.O. Box 415, Skagway, AK 99840 (907/983-2854).

Valdez Convention & Visitors Bureau, P.O. Box 1603, Valdez, AK 99686 (907/835-2984; toll free 800/770-5954).

ANCHORAGE: Iditarod Trail Sled Dog Race (early to mid-Mar): The world's most famous and grueling dog race—1,049 mi. (1,690km) from Anchorage to Nome. Information: 907/376-5155.

CORDOVA: Ice Worm Festival (early Feb): Colorful parade through the town's streets led by a 100-ft.-long (30m) "ice worm" supposed to be emerging from hibernation.

FAIRBANKS: North Pole International Sled Dog Races (end of Mar): Hotly contested dogsled championship.

Yukon 800 River Boat Race (mid-June): Outboard-motor boats race 800 mi. (1,280km) along the Yukon River.

Midnight Sun Baseball: A popular local match played between 10pm and midnight every June 20 or 21.

World Eskimo Indian Olympics (July): Sporting and cultural events bringing together representatives of the main Native American, Inuit, and Aleut tribes. Information: 907/452-6646.

HAINES: Chilkat Dancers (June–Sept): Twice-a-week displays of Native American dance at Fort William H. Seward.

JUNEAU: Alaska Folk Festival (early Apr): Shows, dance, music, arts and crafts exhibits. Information: 586-2066.

Golden North Salmon Derby (Aug): Salmon-fishing championship.

KODIAK: King Crab Festival (end of May): Annual festival in honor of the region's most famous crustacean.

Rodeo & State Fair (late Aug): Heavily attended fair-exhibition-rodeo.

SEWARD: Mount Marathon Race (July 4): With 200 runners from all over the world.

SITKA: Summer Music Festival (June): Chamber-music recitals.

New Archangel Dancers (June–Sept): Displays of Russian folk dancing; in the Centennial Building.

Alaska Day (Oct): Annual 3-day reenactment of the transfer of authority from Russia to the U.S. on October 18, 1867; on Castle Hill.

SKAGWAY: *In the Days of '98* (mid-May to mid-Sept): Tragi-comic melodrama about the 1898 gold rush; staged in Eagles Hall, nightly.

VALDEZ: Winter Carnival (mid-Mar): Dogsled races, dance displays, concerts, festival of food.

APPENDIX

□ □ □

STATE TOURIST OFFICES

Alabama: Bureau of Tourism & Travel, 401 Adams Ave., Montgomery, AL 36104 (205/242-4169; toll free 800/252-2262).

Alaska: Division of Tourism, Information Office, P.O. Box 110801, Juneau, AK 99811 (907/465-2010).

Arizona: Office of Tourism, 1100 W. Washington St., Phoenix, AZ 85007 (602/542-8687; toll free 800/842-8257).

Arkansas: Department of Parks & Tourism, 1 Capitol Mall, Little Rock, AR 72201 (501/682-7777; toll free 800/628-8725).

California: Office of Tourism, 801 K St., Suite 1600, Sacramento, CA 95814 (916/322-2881; toll free 800/862-2543).

Colorado: the only state without a tourism board.

Connecticut: Department of Economic Development, 865 Brook St., Rocky Hill, CT 06106 (203/258-4355; toll free 800/282-6863).

Delaware: Travel Service, 99 Kings Hwy. (P.O. Box 1401), Dover, DE 19903 (302/739-4271; toll free 800/441-8846).

District of Columbia: Washington, D.C. Convention & Visitors Association, 1212 New York Ave. NW, Washington, DC 20005 (202/789-7000).

Florida: Division of Tourism, 126 Van Buren St., Tallahassee, FL 32301 (904/487-1462).

Georgia: Tourist Division, 285 Peachtree Center Ave. P.O. Box 1776, Atlanta, GA 30301 (404/656-3590).

Hawaii: Visitors Bureau, 2270 Kalakaua Ave., Suite 801, Honolulu, HI 96815 (808/923-1811).

Idaho: Travel Council, 700 W. State St., Boise, ID 83720 (208/334-2470; toll free 800/635-7820).

Illinois: Bureau of Tourism, P.O. Box 7905, Mt. Prospect, IL 60056 (toll free 800/223-0121).

Indiana: Tourism Division, 101 N. Governor St., Evansville, IN 47711 (812/423-1000; toll free 800/289-6646).

Iowa: Division of Tourism, 200 E. Grand Ave., Des Moines, IA 50309 (515/242-4705; toll free 800/345-4692).

Kansas: Travel & Tourist Division, 700 SW Harrison St., Suite 1300, Topeka, KS 66603 (913/296-2009; toll free 800/252-6727).

Kentucky: Department of Travel Development, 2200 Capitol Plaza Tower, Frankfort, KY 40601 (502/564-4930; toll free 800/225-8747).

Louisiana: Office of Tourism, P.O. Box 94291, 1051 N. Third St., Baton Rouge, LA 70804 (504/342-8119; toll free 800/334-8626).

Maine: Publicity Bureau, P.O. Box 23000, Hallowell, ME 04347 (207/623-0363; toll free 800/533-9595).

Maryland: Office of Tourism Development, 217 E. Redwood St., Baltimore, MD 21202 (301/333-6611; toll free 800/543-1036).

Massachusetts: Division of Tourism, 100 Cambridge St., Leverett Saltonstall Bldg., 13th Floor, Boston, MA 02202 (617/727-3201; toll free 800/447-6277).

Michigan: Travel Bureau, Department of Commerce, P.O. Box 30226, Law Bldg., Lansing, MI 48909 (517/373-0670; toll free 800/543-2937).

Minnesota: Tourism Division, 100 Metro Sq., 121 Seventh Pl. E., St. Paul, MN 55101 (612/296-5029; toll free 800/657-3700).

Mississippi: Department of Tourism Development, P.O. Box 849, Jackson, MS 39205 (601/359-3297; toll free 800/927-6378).

Missouri: Division of Tourism, 301 W. High St. (P.O. Box 1055), Jefferson City, MO 65102 (314/751-4133; toll free 800/877-1234).

Montana: Travel Promotion Bureau, 1424 Ninth Ave., Helena, MT 59620 (406/444-2654; toll free 800/541-1447).

Nebraska: Department of Travel & Tourism, 700 S. 16th St., Lincoln, NE 68509 (402/471-3796; toll free 800/228-4307).

Nevada: Commission on Tourism, Capitol Complex, Carson City, NV 89710 (702/687-4322; toll free 800/638-2328).

New Hampshire: Office of Travel & Tourism, P.O. Box 856, Concord, NH 03302 (603/271-2343).

New Jersey: Division of Travel & Tourism, 20 W. State St., CN 826, Trenton, NJ 08625 (609/292-6335; toll free 800/537-7397).

New Mexico: Department of Tourism, 491 Old Santa Fe Trail, Santa Fe, NM 87503 (505/827-7400; toll free 800/545-2040).

New York: Division of Tourism, State Dept. of Commerce, 99 Washington Ave., Albany, NY 12245 (518/474-4116; toll free 800/225-5697).

North Carolina: Travel & Tourism Division, 430 N. Salisbury St., Raleigh, NC 27611 (919/733-4171; toll free 800/847-4862).

North Dakota: North Dakota Tourism Promotion, Liberty Memorial Bldg., 604 East Blvd., Bismarck, ND 58505 (701/224-2525; toll free 800/435-5663).

Ohio: Office of Travel & Tourism, P.O. Box 1001, Columbus, OH 43266 (614/466-8844; toll free 800/282-5393).

Oklahoma: Tourism Promotion Division, 500 Will Rogers Bldg., Oklahoma City, OK 73105 (405/521-3981; toll free 800/652-6552).

Oregon: Tourism Division, 775 Summer St. NE, Salem, OR 97310 (503/986-0000; toll free 800/547-7842).

Pennsylvania: Office of Travel Marketing, 453 Forum Bldg., Harrisburg, PA 17120 (717/787-5453; toll free 800/847-4872).

Rhode Island: Tourist Promotion Division, 7 Jackson Walkway, Providence, RI 02903 (401/277-2601; toll free 800/556-2484).

South Carolina: Division of Tourism, P.O. Box 71, Columbia, SC 29202 (803/734-0235).

South Dakota: Division of Tourism, 711 E. Wells Ave., Pierre, SD 57501 (605/773-3301; toll free 800/732-5682).

Tennessee: Department of Tourist Development, 601 Broadway (P.O. Box 23170), Nashville, TN 37202 (615/741-2158).

Texas: Travel & Information Division, P.O. Box 5064, Austin, TX 78763 (512/483-3780; toll free 800/888-8839).

Utah: Travel Council, Council Hall, Capitol Hill, Salt Lake City, UT 84114 (801/538-1030).

Vermont: Travel Division, 134 State St., Montpelier, VT 05602 (802/828-3236).

Virginia: Division of Tourism, 1021 E. Cary St., Richmond, VA 23219 (804/786-4484; toll free 800/932-5827).

Washington: Tourism Development Division, 101 General Administration Bldg., Olympia, WA 98504 (206/586-2088; toll free 800/544-1800).

West Virginia: Department of Commerce, Tourism Information Office, Capitol Complex, Charleston, WV 25305 (304/558-2766; toll free 800/225-5982).

Wisconsin: Division of Tourism, P.O. Box 7606, Madison, WI 53707 (608/266-2161; toll free 800/432-8747).

Wyoming: Travel Commission, I-25 at College Dr., Cheyenne, WY 82002 (307/777-7777; toll free 800/225-5996).

PRINCIPAL HOTEL/MOTEL CHAINS
For reservations, see "Toll-Free Numbers," below.

Best Western, Best Western Way (P.O. Box 10203), Phoenix, AZ 85604 (602/957-4200).

Four Seasons, 1165 Leslie St., Toronto, ON M3C 2K8, Canada (416/449-1750).

Friendship Inns, 10750 Columbia Pike, Silver Spring, MD 20901 (301/593-5600).

Hilton, 9336 Civic Center Dr., Beverly Hills, CA 90210 (310/278-4321).

Holiday Inns, 3 Ravinia Dr., Atlanta, GA 30346 (404/604-2000).

Howard Johnson, Inc., 339 Jefferson Rd., Parsippany, NJ 07054 (201/428-9700).

Hyatt, Madison Plaza, 200 W. Madison St., Chicago, IL 60606 (312/750-1234).

La Quinta Motor Inns, 112 E. Pecan St., San Antonio, TX 78275 (210/302-6000).

Marriott, 1 Marriott Dr., Washington, DC 20058 (301/380-9000).

Motel 6, 14651 Dallas Pkwy., Dallas, TX 75240 (214/386-6161).

Quality Inns, 10750 Columbia Pike, Silver Spring, MD 20901 (301/593-5600).

Radisson, Carlson Pkwy. (P.O. Box 59159), Minneapolis, MN 55441 (612/540-5526).

Ramada Inns, 339 Jefferson Rd., Parsippany, NJ 07054 (201/428-9700).

Sheraton, 60 State St., Boston, MA 02109 (617/367-3600).

Travelodge, 1973 Friendship Dr., El Cajon, CA 92090 (619/448-1884).

Westin, 2001 6th Ave., Westin Bldg., Seattle, WA 98121 (206/443-5000).

Toll-free numbers, recognizable by their "800" area code, are available for your convenience from many airlines, car-rental companies, hotel chains, etc. When you call "1-800" plus a normal seven-digit number, your call is paid for by the subscriber, no matter how far away you may be. Here follows a list of useful toll-free numbers (if you need one not listed here, call 800/555-1212 to reach "information" for all 800 numbers):

AIRLINES: See the individual city chapters for airline phone numbers.

BUS: The national toll-free number for Greyhound is 800/231-2222.

HOTELS/MOTELS: The following are the national toll-free reservations numbers for the major hotel chains:

Best Western (800/528-1234)
Choice (800/424-6423)
Days Inns (800/325-2525)
Fairmont (800/527-4727)
Four Seasons (800/332-3442)
Hilton (800/445-8667)
Holiday Inns (800/465-4329)
Howard Johnson's (800/446-4656)
Hyatt (800/233-1234)
Inter-Continental Hotels (800/327-0200)
La Quinta Motor Inns (800/531-5900)
Loews (800/235-6397)
Marriott (800/228-9290)

Meridien (800/543-4300)
Omni (800/843-6664)
Preferred (800/323-7500)
Radisson (800/333-3333)
Ramada Inns (800/272-6232)
Red Lion Inns (800/547-8010)
Resinter (800/221-4542)
Sheraton (800/325-3535)
Stouffer (800/468-3571)
Travelodge (800/255-3050)
Vagabond Hotels (800/522-1555)
Westin (800/228-3000)
Wyndham (800/822-4200)

CAR-RENTAL AGENCIES: The following are the national toll-free reservations numbers for the major car-rental chains:

Alamo (800/327-9633)   **Hertz** (800/654-3131)
Avis (800/331-1212)   **National** (800/227-7368)
Budget (800/527-0700)   **Rent-A-Wreck** (800/535-1391)
Dollar Rent-A-Car (800/800-4000)   **Sears Rent-A-Car** (800/527-0770)
                                          Thrifty (800/367-2277)

The numbers for many local car-rental agencies will be found in the individual city chapters.

TRAINS: Amtrak's 800 numbers vary from state to state; consult local telephone directories. The national toll-free number is 800/872-7245 (800/USA-RAIL).

FOR THE FOREIGN VISITOR: MEASUREMENTS & CONVERSIONS

Length

1 inch (in.)	=	2.54 cm				
1 foot (ft.)	=	12 in.	=	30.48cm	=	.305m
1 yard	=	3 ft.	=	.915m		
1 mile (mi.)	=	5,280 ft.	=	1.609km		

To convert miles to kilometers, multiply the number of miles by 1.61 (for example, 50 mi. × 1.61 = 80.5km). Note that this conversion can be used to convert speeds from miles per hour (m.p.h.) to kilometers per hour (kmph).

To convert kilometers to miles, multiply the number of kilometers by .62 (example, 25km × .62 = 15.5 mi.). Note that this same conversion can be used to convert speeds from kilometers per hour to miles per hour.

Capacity

1 fluid ounce (fl. oz.)	=	.03 liter		
1 pint	=	16 fl. oz.	=	.47 liter
1 quart	=	2 pints	=	.94 liter
1 gallon (gal.)	=	4 quarts	=	3.79 liter = .83 Imperial gal.

To convert U.S. gallons to liters, multiply the number of gallons by 3.79 (example, 12 gal. × 3.79 = 45.48 liters)

To convert U.S. gallons to Imperial gallons, multiply the number of U.S. gallons by .83 (example, 12 U.S. gal. × .83 = 9.95 Imperial gal.)

To convert liters to U.S. gallons, multiply the number of liters by .26 (for example, 50 liters × .26 = 13 U.S. gal.).

To convert Imperial gallons to U.S. gallons, multiply the number of Imperial gallons by 1.2 (example, 8 Imperial gal. × 1.2 = 9.6 U.S. gal.).

Weight

1 ounce (oz.)	=	28.35 grams				
1 pound (lb.)	=	16 oz.	=	453.6 grams	=	.45 kilograms
1 ton	=	2,000 lb.	=	907 kilograms	=	.91 metric ton

To convert pounds to kilograms, multiply the number of pounds by .45 (example, 90 lb. × .45 = 40.5kg).

To convert kilograms to pounds, multiply the number of kilos by 2.2 (example, 75kg × 2.2 = 165 lb.).

Temperature

°C −18°   −10   0   10   20   30   40

°F   0° 10   20   32 40   50   60   70   80   90 100

To convert degrees Fahrenheit to degrees Celsius, subtract 32 from °F, multiply by 5 then divide by 9 (example 85° F − 32 × 5/9 = 29.4°C).
To convert degrees Celsius to degrees Fahrenheit, multiply °C by 9, divide by 5, and add 32 (example, 20°C × 9/5 + 32 = 68°F).

CLOTHING SIZES

Women's Sizes

American	4	6	8	10	12	14	16	18
Continental	36	38	38	40	42	44	46	48
British	6	8	10	12	14	16	18	20

Women's Shoes

American	5	6	7	8	9	10
Continental	36	37	38	39	40	41
British	3½	4½	5½	6½	7½	8½

Note: Foot width should also be taken into account.

Children's Clothing

American	3	4	5	6	6X
Continental	98	104	110	116	122
British	18	20	22	24	26

Men's Suits

American	34	36	38	40	42	44	46	48
Continental	44	46	48	50	52	54	56	58
British	34	36	38	40	42	44	46	48

Men's Shirts

American	14½	15	15½	16	16½	17	17½	18
Continental	37	38	39	41	42	43	44	45
British	14½	15	15½	16	16½	17	17½	18

Note: Shirts are sized on a combination of collar and sleeve length.

Men's Shoes

American	7	8	9	10	11	12	13
Continental	39½	41	42	43	44½	46	47
British	6	7	8	9	10	11	12

Note: Foot width should also be taken into account.

INDEX

Please Send Me the Books Checked Below:

FROMMER'S COMPREHENSIVE GUIDES
(Guides listing facilities from budget to deluxe,
with emphasis on the medium-priced)

	Retail Price	Code		Retail Price	Code
☐ Acapulco/Ixtapa/Taxco 1993–94	$15.00	C120	☐ Japan 1994–95 (Avail. 3/94)	$19.00	C144
☐ Alaska 1994–95	$17.00	C131	☐ Morocco 1992–93	$18.00	C021
☐ Arizona 1993–94	$18.00	C101	☐ Nepal 1994–95	$18.00	C126
☐ Australia 1992–93	$18.00	C002	☐ New England 1994 (Avail. 1/94)	$16.00	C137
☐ Austria 1993–94	$19.00	C119	☐ New Mexico 1993–94	$15.00	C117
☐ Bahamas 1994–95	$17.00	C121	☐ New York State 1994–95	$19.00	C133
☐ Belgium/Holland/ Luxembourg 1993–94	$18.00	C106	☐ Northwest 1994–95 (Avail. 2/94)	$17.00	C140
☐ Bermuda 1994–95	$15.00	C122	☐ Portugal 1994–95 (Avail. 2/94)	$17.00	C141
☐ Brazil 1993–94	$20.00	C111	☐ Puerto Rico 1993–94	$15.00	C103
☐ California 1994	$15.00	C134	☐ Puerto Vallarta/Manzanillo/ Guadalajara 1994–95 (Avail. 1/94)	$14.00	C028
☐ Canada 1994–95 (Avail. 4/94)	$19.00	C145	☐ Scandinavia 1993–94	$19.00	C135
☐ Caribbean 1994	$18.00	C123	☐ Scotland 1994–95 (Avail. 4/94)	$17.00	C146
☐ Carolinas/Georgia 1994–95	$17.00	C128	☐ South Pacific 1994–95 (Avail. 1/94)	$20.00	C138
☐ Colorado 1994–95 (Avail. 3/94)	$16.00	C143	☐ Spain 1993–94	$19.00	C115
☐ Cruises 1993–94	$19.00	C107	☐ Switzerland/Liechtenstein 1994–95 (Avail. 1/94)	$19.00	C139
☐ Delaware/Maryland 1994–95 (Avail. 1/94)	$15.00	C136	☐ Thailand 1992–93	$20.00	C033
☐ England 1994	$18.00	C129	☐ U.S.A. 1993–94	$19.00	C116
☐ Florida 1994	$18.00	C124	☐ Virgin Islands 1994–95	$13.00	C127
☐ France 1994–95	$20.00	C132	☐ Virginia 1994–95 (Avail. 2/94)	$14.00	C142
☐ Germany 1994	$19.00	C125	☐ Yucatán 1993–94	$18.00	C110
☐ Italy 1994	$19.00	C130			
☐ Jamaica/Barbados 1993–94	$15.00	C105			

FROMMER'S $-A-DAY GUIDES
(Guides to low-cost tourist accommodations and facilities)

	Retail Price	Code		Retail Price	Code
☐ Australia on $45 1993–94	$18.00	D102	☐ Israel on $45 1993–94	$18.00	D101
☐ Costa Rica/Guatemala/ Belize on $35 1993–94	$17.00	D108	☐ Mexico on $45 1994	$19.00	D116
☐ Eastern Europe on $30 1993–94	$18.00	D110	☐ New York on $70 1994–95 (Avail. 4/94)	$16.00	D120
☐ England on $60 1994	$18.00	D112	☐ New Zealand on $45 1993–94	$18.00	D103
☐ Europe on $50 1994	$19.00	D115	☐ Scotland/Wales on $50 1992–93	$18.00	D019
☐ Greece on $45 1993–94	$19.00	D100	☐ South America on $40 1993–94	$19.00	D109
☐ Hawaii on $75 1994	$19.00	D113			
☐ India on $40 1992–93	$20.00	D010	☐ Turkey on $40 1992–93	$22.00	D023
☐ Ireland on $45 1994–95 (Avail. 1/94)	$17.00	D117	☐ Washington, D.C. on $40 1994–95 (Avail. 2/94)	$17.00	D119

FROMMER'S CITY $-A-DAY GUIDES
(Pocket-size guides to low-cost tourist accommodations
and facilities)

	Retail Price	Code		Retail Price	Code
☐ Berlin on $40 1994–95	$12.00	D111	☐ Madrid on $50 1994–95 (Avail. 1/94)	$13.00	D118
☐ Copenhagen on $50 1992–93	$12.00	D003	☐ Paris on $50 1994–95	$12.00	D117
☐ London on $45 1994–95	$12.00	D114	☐ Stockholm on $50 1992–93	$13.00	D022

FROMMER'S WALKING TOURS
(With routes and detailed maps, these companion guides point out
the places and pleasures that make a city unique)

	Retail Price	Code		Retail Price	Code
☐ Berlin	$12.00	W100	☐ Paris	$12.00	W103
☐ London	$12.00	W101	☐ San Francisco	$12.00	W104
☐ New York	$12.00	W102	☐ Washington, D.C.	$12.00	W105

FROMMER'S TOURING GUIDES
(Color-illustrated guides that include walking tours, cultural and historic
sights, and practical information)

	Retail Price	Code		Retail Price	Code
☐ Amsterdam	$11.00	T001	☐ New York	$11.00	T008
☐ Barcelona	$14.00	T015	☐ Rome	$11.00	T010
☐ Brazil	$11.00	T003	☐ Scotland	$10.00	T011
☐ Florence	$ 9.00	T005	☐ Sicily	$15.00	T017
☐ Hong Kong/Singapore/			☐ Tokyo	$15.00	T016
Macau	$11.00	T006	☐ Turkey	$11.00	T013
☐ Kenya	$14.00	T018	☐ Venice	$ 9.00	T014
☐ London	$13.00	T007			

FROMMER'S FAMILY GUIDES

	Retail Price	Code		Retail Price	Code
☐ California with Kids	$18.00	F100	☐ San Francisco with Kids		
☐ Los Angeles with Kids			(Avail. 4/94)	$17.00	F104
(Avail. 4/94)	$17.00	F103	☐ Washington, D.C. with Kids		
☐ New York City with Kids			(Avail. 2/94)	$17.00	F102
(Avail. 2/94)	$18.00	F101			

FROMMER'S CITY GUIDES
(Pocket-size guides to sightseeing and tourist accommodations and
facilities in all price ranges)

	Retail Price	Code		Retail Price	Code
☐ Amsterdam 1993–94	$13.00	S110	☐ Montréal/Québec		
☐ Athens 1993–94	$13.00	S114	City 1993–94	$13.00	S125
☐ Atlanta 1993–94	$13.00	S112	☐ Nashville/Memphis		
☐ Atlantic City/Cape			1994–95 (Avail. 4/94)	$13.00	S141
May 1993–94	$13.00	S130	☐ New Orleans 1993–94	$13.00	S103
☐ Bangkok 1992–93	$13.00	S005	☐ New York 1994 (Avail.		
☐ Barcelona/Majorca/Minorca/			1/94)	$13.00	S138
Ibiza 1993–94	$13.00	S115	☐ Orlando 1994	$13.00	S135
☐ Berlin 1993–94	$13.00	S116	☐ Paris 1993–94	$13.00	S109
☐ Boston 1993–94	$13.00	S117	☐ Philadelphia 1993–94	$13.00	S113
☐ Budapest 1994–95 (Avail.			☐ San Diego 1993–94	$13.00	S107
2/94)	$13.00	S139	☐ San Francisco 1994	$13.00	S133
☐ Chicago 1993–94	$13.00	S122	☐ Santa Fe/Taos/		
☐ Denver/Boulder/Colorado			Albuquerque 1993–94	$13.00	S108
Springs 1993–94	$13.00	S131	☐ Seattle/Portland 1994–95	$13.00	S137
☐ Dublin 1993–94	$13.00	S128	☐ St. Louis/Kansas		
☐ Hong Kong 1994–95			City 1993–94	$13.00	S127
(Avail. 4/94)	$13.00	S140	☐ Sydney 1993–94	$13.00	S129
☐ Honolulu/Oahu 1994	$13.00	S134	☐ Tampa/St.		
☐ Las Vegas 1993–94	$13.00	S121	Petersburg 1993–94	$13.00	S105
☐ London 1994	$13.00	S132	☐ Tokyo 1992–93	$13.00	S039
☐ Los Angeles 1993–94	$13.00	S123	☐ Toronto 1993–94	$13.00	S126
☐ Madrid/Costa del			☐ Vancouver/Victoria 1994–		
Sol 1993–94	$13.00	S124	95 (Avail. 1/94)	$13.00	S142
☐ Miami 1993–94	$13.00	S118	☐ Washington, D.C. 1994		
☐ Minneapolis/St.			(Avail. 1/94)	$13.00	S136
Paul 1993–94	$13.00	S119			

SPECIAL EDITIONS

	Retail Price	Code		Retail Price	Code
☐ Bed & Breakfast Southwest	$16.00	P100	☐ Caribbean Hideaways	$16.00	P103
☐ Bed & Breakfast Great American Cities (Avail. 1/94)	$16.00	P104	☐ National Park Guide 1994 (avail. 3/94)	$16.00	P105
			☐ Where to Stay U.S.A.	$15.00	P102

Please note: if the availability of a book is several months away, we may have back issues of guides to that particular destination. Call customer service at (815) 734-1104.